NAME

CHURCH / SCHOOL

ADDRESS

PHONE

My Group Members

Name	Address	Phone

Building Up One Another .

NAME	ADDRESS	PHONE

. IN THE BODY OF CHRIST

SERENDIPITY STUDENT BIBLE

EDITOR-IN-CHIEF:
Lyman Coleman

EDITORS:
Matthew Lockhart, Andrew Sloan, Cathy Tardif,
Steve Sheely, Ben Bussard

DESIGN AND PRODUCTION TEAM:
Erika Tiepel, Sharon Penington, Maurice Lydick,
Chris Werner

SERENDIPITY HOUSE
P.O. Box 1012
Littleton, Colorado 80120

Zondervan Publishing House
5300 Patterson Avenue, SE
Grand Rapids, Michigan 49530

Serendipity Student Bible, New International Version

Serendipity is a publishing house specializing in equipping pastors and church leaders for small group ministry. A list of training events and catalog of resources can be obtained by writing to: SERENDIPITY HOUSE, P.O. Box 1012, Littleton, CO 80160 *or* call: 1-800-525-9563. Please visit our Web site at www.serendipityhouse.com.

Also, the following commentaries were cited in the New Testament study notes:
Brown, Raymond, *The Gospel of John*, The Anchor Bible Series, Doubleday and Co., Garden City, NY, 1970.
Davids, Peter H., *James*, Good News Commentary, Harper and Row, 1973.
France, R.T., *Matthew*, Tyndale New Testament Commentaries, Eerdmans, Grand Rapids, MI, 1985.

Printed in the United States of America.

02 01 00 99 8 7 6 5 4

You will be pleased to know that a portion of the purchase price of your new NIV Bible has been provided to International Bible Society to help spread the gospel of Jesus Christ around the world!

TABLE OF CONTENTS

BOOKS OF THE BIBLE

Abbreviations Key:

v. – verse
vv. – verses
f – verse following
ff – verses following
ch. – chapter(s)
c. – about, approximately
e.g. – for example
i.e. – that is
NT – New Testament
OT – Old Testament

HOW TO USE THE SERENDIPITY STUDENT BIBLE

What is unique about this Bible?

This Bible is designed specifically for youth groups. It is filled with discussion questions and exercises that help young people share every aspect of their lives in the context of God's Word.

How can groups use this Bible?

In lots of ways! For starters, look at the ready-made Lesson Plans on pages 14–24. Here you will find 120 relevant topics, grouped into eight different categories. After choosing a topic, all you have to do is decide whether to use the questionnaire from a story passage or the questionnaire from a teaching passage. Each lesson plan includes an ice-breaker from the center section that you can use to start the meeting.

AWARENESS

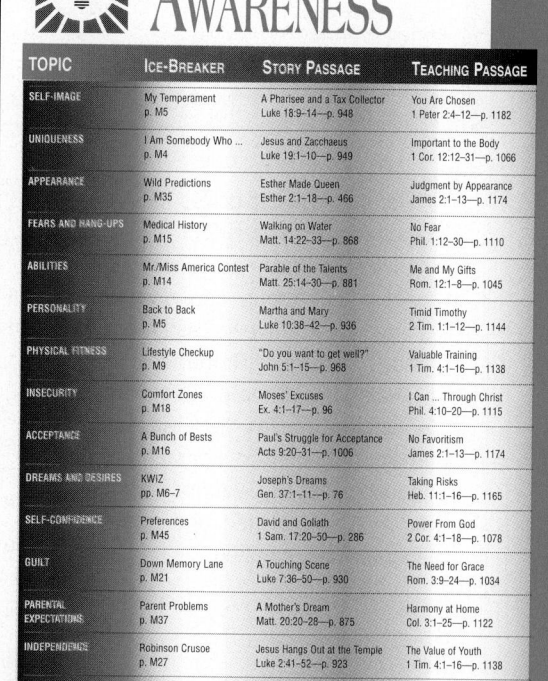

TOPIC	ICE-BREAKER	STORY PASSAGE	TEACHING PASSAGE
SELF-IMAGE	My Temperament p. M5	A Pharisee and a Tax Collector Luke 18:9-14—p. 948	You Are Chosen 1 Peter 2:4-12—p. 1182
UNIQUENESS	I Am Somebody Who ... p. M4	Jesus and Zacchaeus Luke 19:1-10—p. 949	Important to the Body 1 Cor. 12:12-31—p. 1066
APPEARANCE	Wild Predictions p. M35	Esther Made Queen Esther 2:1-18—p. 466	Judgment by Appearance James 2:1-13—p. 1174
FEARS AND HANG-UPS	Medical History p. M15	Walking on Water Matt. 14:22-33—p. 868	No Fear Phil. 1:12-30—p. 1110
ABILITIES	Mr./Miss America Contest p. M14	Parable of the Talents Matt. 25:14-30—p. 881	Me and My Gifts Rom. 12:1-8—p. 1045
PERSONALITY	Back to Back p. M5	Martha and Mary Luke 10:38-42—p. 936	Timid Timothy 2 Tim. 1:1-12—p. 1144
PHYSICAL FITNESS	Lifestyle Checkup p. M9	"Do you want to get well?" John 5:1-15—p. 968	Valuable Training 1 Tim. 4:1-16—p. 1138
INSECURITY	Comfort Zones p. M18	Moses' Excuses Ex. 4:1-17—p. 96	I Can ... Through Christ Phil. 4:10-20—p. 1115
ACCEPTANCE	A Bunch of Bests p. M16	Paul's Struggle for Acceptance Acts 9:20-31—p. 1006	No Favoritism James 2:1-13—p. 1174
DREAMS AND DESIRES	KWIZ pp. M6-7	Joseph's Dreams Gen. 37:1-11—p. 76	Taking Risks Heb. 11:1-16—p. 1165
SELF-CONFIDENCE	Preferences p. M45	David and Goliath 1 Sam. 17:20-50—p. 286	Power From God 2 Cor. 4:1-18—p. 1078
GUILT	Down Memory Lane p. M21	A Touching Scene Luke 7:36-50—p. 930	The Need for Grace Rom. 3:9-24—p. 1034
PARENTAL EXPECTATIONS	Parent Problems p. M37	A Mother's Dream Matt. 20:20-28—p. 875	Harmony at Home Col. 3:1-25—p. 1122
INDEPENDENCE	Robinson Crusoe p. M27	Jesus Hangs Out at the Temple Luke 2:41-52—p. 923	The Value of Youth 1 Tim. 4:1-16—p. 1138
ADOPTED CHILDREN	My Childhood Supper Table p. M22	Moses Goes Back to His Roots Ex. 2:1-25—p. 94	Adopted by God Eph. 1:3-14—p. 1099

17

Is it a good idea to study one category at a time by going down the list in the Lesson Plan?

Sure. That would work well in any of the eight categories—particularly in the Issues, Beliefs and Discipleship categories. Another option which provides more variety would be to use a different category each week (a topic from Awareness the first week, Relationships the next week, etc.).

Are there any studies beyond those found in the Lesson Plans?

Yes. On pages 31–32, you can see how the story questionnaires that don't cover topics in the 120 Lesson Plans can be used for other specific topics. You can also use the index of 150 favorite Bible stories on pages 26–30 to create your own course—for example, stories about David, the miracles or parables of Jesus, or "Jesus' Last Week."

ISRAEL'S GREAT KINGS

The Lord Calls Samuel. . . . . 1 Sam. 3:1–14. . .
Israel Asks for a King. . . . . 1 Sam. 8:1–22. . .
Samuel Rebukes Saul . . . . 1 Sam. 13:1–15. . .
Samuel Anoints David . . . . 1 Sam. 16:1–13. . .
David and Goliath . . . . 1 Sam. 17:20–50. . .
Saul's Jealousy of David . . . . 1 Sam. 18:1–16. . .
David and Jonath
David Spares Sau
Saul Takes His Lif
David and Bathsh
Nathan Rebukes
David Grieves . .
Amnon Rapes Tar
Absalom Kills Amr
Solomon's Wise F
Solomon's Splend
The Kingdom Is D

STORIES FR

Elijah and the Pro
Elisha and the Wi
Naaman Healed of Leprosy. . . . . 2 Kings 5:1–16. . .
Elisha and the Chariots of Fire . . . . 2 Kings 6:8–23. . .
Jonah Flees From the Lord . . . . Jonah 1:1–17. . .
Jonah Goes From the Fish to Nineveh . . . . Jonah 2:1–3:10. . .
Jonah's Anger at God's Compassion . . . . Jonah 4:1–11. . .

Samuel Anoints David . . . . 1 Sam. 16:1–13. . .
David and Goliath . . . . 1 Sam. 17:20–50. . .
Saul's Jealousy of David . . . . 1 Sam. 18:1–16. . .
David and Jonathan . . . . 1 Sam. 20:1–13,18–42. . .
David Spares Saul's Life . . . . 1 Sam. 24:1–22. . .
Saul Takes His Life . . . . 1 Sam. 31:1–13. . .
David and Bathsheba. . . . . 2 Sam. 11:1–27. . .
Nathan Rebukes David . . . . 2 Sam. 12:1–14. . .
David Grieves . . . . 2 Sam. 12:15–25. . .

Can we use this Bible to do a book study?

Absolutely! There are questionnaires your group can use to study all the New Testament books from Romans to Revelation. Simply use the questionnaires as they appear in the Scripture text. For some of the longer books, you may want to cover more than one questionnaire per meeting.

Romans 1:8–17

1. What is one place you have never seen that you would like to visit?
2. What do you learn about Paul in this passage?
3. Reading between the lines, what is the problem in the church in Rome that Paul wants to address in this letter?
4. How would you compare your commitment to the Gospel to Paul's in verse 16?
5. What is God saying to you in this passage?
6. How can this group help you in prayer this week?

What do the icons that are on some of the questionnaires mean?

They show that the questionnaire is used by a lesson plan in a particular category. However, all the questionnaires should be quite relevant to any group of students. The eight categories are listed below:

- AWARENESS
- RELATIONSHIPS
- CHOICES
- STRESS
- ISSUES
- CRISIS
- BELIEFS
- DISCIPLESHIP

ROMANS 12:9–21

1. What is your favorite love song or romantic movie?
2. Who was your first true love? What happened to this relationship?
3. As a child, who was the troublemaker in your family? Who was the peacemaker?
4. When was the last time you were rejected by someone? How did it feel?
5. When you feel you've been wronged, what do you generally do: "Grin and bear it"? "Forgive and forget"? Get even? Or something else?
6. What can you do this week, in a practical way, to "live at peace" with someone who irritates you?
7. This past week, have you felt more "overcome with evil" or have you "overcome evil with good"?
8. How can this group pray for you?

What is the purpose of the notes below some questionnaires?

To help students understand key words and concepts of the Scripture passage covered by the questionnaire. In some cases, the notes also provide background information about what preceded the passage in that book of the Bible. Here is an example from Romans 12:9–21:

Paul focuses first on relationships between Christians (vv. 9–13) and then on relationships with those outside the church (vv. 14–21).

12:9 ***Love.*** *Agape* love is, self-giving action on behalf of others, made possible by God's Spirit. ***sincere.*** Genuine, not counterfeit or showy. It is possible to pretend (even to one's self) to love others.

12:10 ***brotherly love.*** A second word for love, *philadelphia,* denoting family affection.

12:12 What makes it possible to endure affliction is joyful hope in one's inheritance in the age to come, coupled with daily, continuous prayer.

12:13 To be "renewed" is not just a matter of mind and emotions, but involves concrete action such as giving to those in need.

12:17 ***Do not repay anyone evil for evil.*** A common Christian teaching (see 1 Thess. 5:15 and 1 Peter 3:4). Christians are called upon to do not just what the consensus calls "good," but those things that are inherently "good." These deeds will be recognized as such by those of good will.

12:20 ***heap burning coals on his head.*** Providing kindness of every sort to one's enemies may induce the kind of inner shame that leads to repentance, and hence to reconciliation and true friendship.

12:21 People who retaliate have allowed evil to overcome them. They have given in to their evil desires and have become like their enemy.

Is there a particular flow in the questions?

Yes. The questions are arranged to move across the "Disclosure Scale" from NO RISK at the beginning of the questionnaire to HIGH RISK at the end.

Can individuals use this Bible for a reading plan?

There is a Personal Reading Plan at the beginning of the Introduction to each book of the Bible. You can check off the passages as you read them.

Personal Reading Plan

- ☑ Romans 5:12–6:23
- ☑ Romans 7:1–8:17
- ☑ Romans 8:18–9:29
- ❒ Romans 9:30–10:21

Introduction to

ROMANS

Personal Reading Plan

❒ Romans 1:1–32	☑ Romans 5:12–6:23	❒ Romans 11:1–36
❒ Romans 2:1–29	☑ Romans 7:1–8:17	❒ Romans 12:1–13:14
❒ Romans 3:1–31	☑ Romans 8:18–9:29	❒ Romans 14:1–15:13
❒ Romans 4:1–5:11	❒ Romans 9:30–10:21	❒ Romans 15:14–16:27

Author

The writer is the apostle Paul.

Date

Paul wrote his letter during a three-month period spent in Corinth at the home of his friend and convert Gaius (16:23). It was winter. The time was probably A.D. 56–57 (though it was certainly sometime between A.D. 54–59).

Theme

Being right with God through faith in Christ.

Historical Background

For nearly 10 years Paul had been at work evangelizing the Gentile territories ringing the Aegean Sea. Now that there were established churches throughout the region, he turns his eyes to fresh fields. He would go to Spain, the oldest Roman colony in the West. But first there was unfinished business: He had taken up a collection to aid the poor in Jerusalem—a fine gesture on the part of the newer churches—and now he had to take this to Jerusalem, though he did so with some misgiving (15:31).

After Jerusalem, he planned to travel to Spain, stopping enroute to fulfill a long-held dream. He would visit Rome—the capital of the world. In anticipation of that visit, he wrote the letter to the Romans by way of introduction (the Roman Christians did not know him, though—as chapter 16 reveals—he had friends there). He was also eager to assure the Roman Christians, contrary to false rumors they might have heard, that the Gospel he was preaching was, indeed, the gospel of Jesus

What other information is found in the Introduction to each book of the Bible?

After the Personal Reading Plan, you will find helpful summaries about the author, date, theme and characteristics of each book. For the books that contain study questionnaires, there is a chart listing those questionnaires at the end of the Introduction. The passages that are used for the topical Lesson Plans are shown first, followed by the passages that are covered by general questionnaires (those without an icon).

How can our group use the Interactive Exercises section in the middle of the Bible?

The first category—Ice-Breakers—has numerous exercises designed to kick off meetings (as listed in the Lesson Plans on pages 17–24). The next three categories—Biblical Inventories, Case Studies and Scripture Reflections—provide additional resources that groups can take advantage of as they desire. The final category—Affirmation—contains both fun and serious affirmation exercises, which can be used to close a meeting or special event. Lastly, the center section offers an Evaluation for groups to use.

LIFESTYLE CHECKUP

How healthy is your lifestyle? Mark with an **"X"** on the lines below where you would rate yourself for each of the areas. Then, in groups of 2 to 4, take turns sharing the results of your checkup.

DIET / NUTRITION
health food ______________________________ junk food

EXERCISE / PHYSICAL ACTIVITY
marathon runner ______________________________ couch potato

SLEEPING HABITS
"Good morning, Lord!" ______________________________ "O Lord, it's morning!"

TOBACCO
Mr. Clean ______________________________ Joe Camel

STRESS / HYPERACTIVITY
Garfield ______________________________ Tazmanian Devil

MENTAL ALERTNESS
Road Runner ______________________________ Wile E. Coyote

OVERALL FITNESS / VITALITY
Energizer Bunny ______________________________ dead battery

What is the hope and dream for this Bible?

To provide the tools for groups of students to experience "serendipity" ("happy chance discoveries"). That is what happens when a group of people get together to share their lives around the Scripture and, as a result, the Holy Spirit does something special.

PICK A TOPIC

120 LESSON PLANS

IN EIGHT CATEGORIES

3 Steps to Make a Lesson Plan

1: Choose a TOPIC

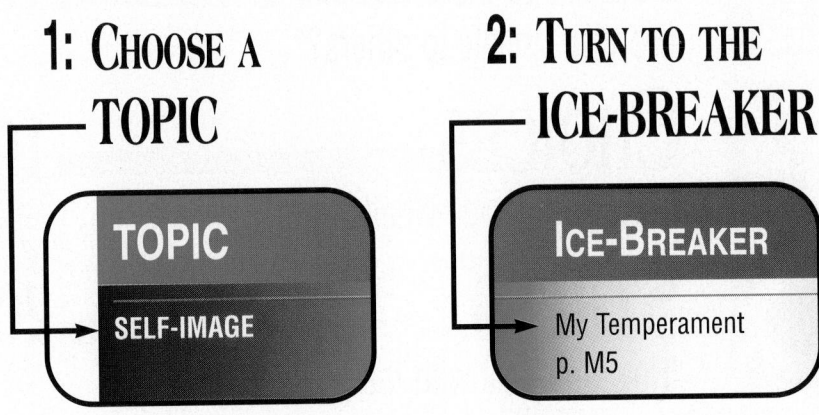

TOPIC

SELF-IMAGE

2: Turn to the ICE-BREAKER

ICE-BREAKER

My Temperament
p. M5

3: Decide Which BIBLE STUDY

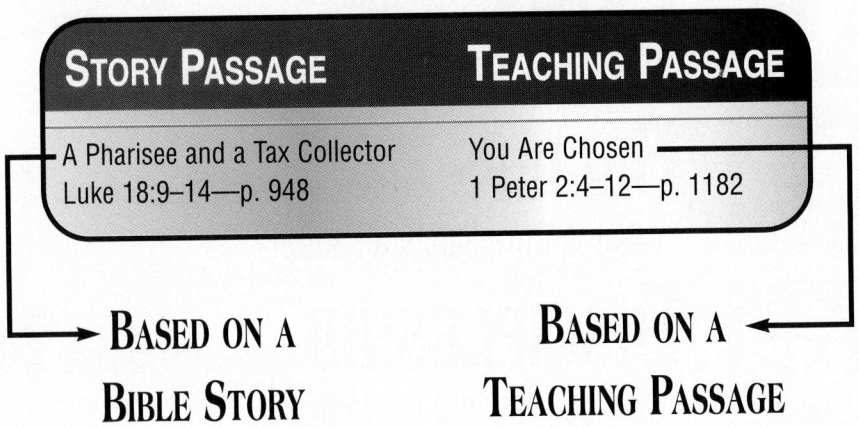

Story Passage	Teaching Passage
A Pharisee and a Tax Collector Luke 18:9–14—p. 948	You Are Chosen 1 Peter 2:4–12—p. 1182

Based on a Bible Story

Based on a Teaching Passage

AWARENESS

TOPIC	ICE-BREAKER	STORY PASSAGE	TEACHING PASSAGE
SELF-IMAGE	My Temperament p. M5	A Pharisee and a Tax Collector Luke 18:9–14 p. 948	You Are Chosen 1 Peter 2:4–12 p. 1182
UNIQUENESS	I Am Somebody Who ... p. M4	Jesus and Zacchaeus Luke 19:1–10 p. 949	Important to the Body 1 Cor. 12:12–31 p. 1066
APPEARANCE	Wild Predictions p. M35	Esther Made Queen Esther 2:1–18 p. 466	Judgment by Appearance James 2:1–13 p. 1174
FEARS AND HANG-UPS	Medical History p. M15	Walking on Water Matt. 14:22–33 p. 868	No Fear Phil. 1:12–30 p. 1110
ABILITIES	Mr./Miss America Contest p. M14	Parable of the Talents Matt. 25:14–30 p. 881	Me and My Gifts Rom. 12:1–8 p. 1045
PERSONALITY	Back to Back p. M5	Martha and Mary Luke 10:38–42 p. 936	Timid Timothy 2 Tim. 1:1–12 p. 1144
PHYSICAL FITNESS	Lifestyle Checkup p. M9	"Do you want to get well?" John 5:1–15 p. 968	Valuable Training 1 Tim. 4:1–16 p. 1138
INSECURITY	Comfort Zones p. M18	Moses' Excuses Ex. 4:1–17 p. 96	I Can ... Through Christ Phil. 4:10–20 p. 1115
ACCEPTANCE	A Bunch of Bests p. M16	Paul's Struggle for Acceptance Acts 9:20–31 p. 1006	No Favoritism James 2:1–13 p. 1174
DREAMS AND DESIRES	KWIZ pp. M6–7	Joseph's Dreams Gen. 37:1–11 p. 76	Taking Risks Heb. 11:1–16 p. 1165
SELF-CONFIDENCE	Preferences p. M45	David and Goliath 1 Sam. 17:20–50 p. 286	Power From God 2 Cor. 4:1–18 p. 1078
GUILT	Down Memory Lane p. M21	A Touching Scene Luke 7:36–50 p. 930	The Need for Grace Rom. 3:9–24 p. 1034
PARENTAL EXPECTATIONS	Parent Problems p. M37	A Mother's Dream Matt. 20:20–28 p. 875	Harmony at Home Col. 3:1–25 p. 1122
INDEPENDENCE	Robinson Crusoe p. M27	Jesus Hangs Out at the Temple Luke 2:41–52 p. 923	The Value of Youth 1 Tim. 4:1–16 p. 1138
ADOPTED CHILDREN	My Childhood Supper Table p. M22	Moses Goes Back to His Roots Ex. 2:1–25 p. 94	Adopted by God Eph. 1:3–14 p. 1099

RELATIONSHIPS

TOPIC	ICE-BREAKER	STORY PASSAGE	TEACHING PASSAGE
FRIENDSHIPS	Friendship Survey p. M19	David and Jonathan—Part 1 1 Sam. 18:1–16 p. 287	Livivng a Life of Love Eph. 5:1–21 p. 1104
TRUST	Four Facts / One Lie p. M12	David and Jonathan—Part 2 1 Sam. 20:1–13,18–42 p. 289	"Love is ... " 1 Cor. 13:1–13 p. 1067
CLIQUES	The Old Neighborhood p. M39	Peter's Stretching Vision Acts 10:1–23 p. 1008	Divisions in the Church 1 Cor. 1:10–17 p. 1054
DATING —THE RIGHT WAY	Living Under the Influence p. M45	Jacob Meets Rachel Gen. 29:1–14 p. 68	God's Standards Eph. 5:22–33 p. 1105
DATING —THE WRONG WAY	Mr./Miss America Contest p. M14	Samson's Dating Disaster Judg. 14:1–20 p. 256	Unequally Yoked 2 Cor. 6:14–7:1 p. 1080
GETTING HURT	911 Phone Numbers p. M14	Jesus Is Betrayed and Deserted Matt. 26:47–56 p. 884	When You're Mistreated Matt. 5:38–48 p. 857
GRUDGES	Ups and Downs p. M27	Absalom's Revenge 2 Sam. 13:23–39 p. 313	Overcome Evil With Good Rom. 12:9–21 p. 1046
FORGIVENESS	Parent Problems p. M37	Parable of the Unmerciful Servant Matt. 18:21–35 p. 872	"Forgive as the Lord forgave you" Col. 3:1–25 p. 1122
REACHING OUT	Precious Time p. M29	Jesus Talks With Samaritan Woman John 4:1–26 p. 967	True Love 1 John 3:11–24 p. 1198
JEALOUSY	Who Influences You? p. M28	Saul's Jealousy of David 1 Sam. 18:1–16 p. 287	Inner Desires James 4:1–12 p. 1176
ACCOUNTABILITY	The Grand Total p. M10	Nathan Rebukes David 2 Sam. 12:1–14 p. 310	Sharing the Load Gal. 6:1–10 p. 1096
FAMILY CONFLICTS	My Coat of Arms p. M12	Parable of the Prodigal Son Luke 15:11–32 p. 944	Quick to Listen, Slow to Anger James 1:19–27 p. 1173
SIBLING RIVALRY	How's the Weather? p. M18	Jacob and Esau Gen. 25:19–34 p. 64	Taming the Tongue James 3:1–18 p. 1175
STEPFAMILIES	My People Tree p. M24	Hagar and Ishmael Sent Away Gen. 21:1–21 p. 59	One in Christ Eph. 2:11–22 p. 1101
PARENTAL DEMANDS	Family Expectations p. M13	Jesus and His Mom at a Wedding John 2:1–11 p. 964	Children and Parents Eph. 6:1–4 p. 1106

CHOICES

TOPIC	ICE-BREAKER	STORY PASSAGE	TEACHING PASSAGE
FRIENDS	Choosing Friends p. M19	Four Friends Who Cared Mark 2:1–12 p. 893	Unequally Yoked 2 Cor. 6:14–7:1 p. 1080
LOVE	Warm Memories p. M33	Jesus Washes His Disciples' Feet John 13:1–17 p. 980	"Love is ... " 1 Cor. 13:1–13 p. 1067
HONESTY / INTEGRITY	Brain Food p. M38	Ananias and Sapphira Acts 5:1–11 p. 1000	Living in the Light Eph. 4:17–32 p. 1103
MONEY	Money and Success p. M31	Parable of the Rich Fool Luke 12:13–21 p. 939	The Love of Money 1 Tim. 6:3–21 p. 1140
POSSESSIONS	Wallet Scavenger Hunt p. M16	The Rich Young Man Mark 10:17–31 p. 905	Where's Your Treasure? Luke 12:22–34 p. 940
TIME / LEISURE	My Favorite Things p. M15	Jesus Feeds the Five Thousand Mark 6:30–44 p. 900	Idle Time 2 Thess. 3:6–15 p. 1132
DECISIONS	Old-Fashioned Auction p. M34	The Wisdom of Solomon 1 Kings 3:16–28 p. 331	God's Wisdom 1 Cor. 1:18–2:5 p. 1055
HEALTHY HABITS	Lifestyle Checkup p. M9	Manna From the Lord Ex. 16:1–35 p. 108	Disciplined Living 1 Tim. 4:1–16 p. 1138
SEXUAL ABSTINENCE	Some of My Feelings p. M25	Joseph and Potiphar's Wife Gen. 39:1–23 p. 79	Control Yourself 1 Thess. 4:1–12 p. 1128
SUCCESS / AMBITION	My Coat of Arms p. M12	James and John Make a Request Mark 10:35–45 p. 906	Nothing Compares to Knowing Christ Phil. 3:1–11 p. 1113
NO COMPROMISE	Lay It on the Line p. M26	Solomon's Wealth and Women 1 Kings 10:23–11:13 p. 339	Live by the Spirit Gal. 5:16–26 p. 1095
MEDIA / ENTERTAINMENT	Take Your Choice p. M13	Dirty Dancing Mark 6:14–29 p. 899	Guard Your Hearts 1 Cor. 10:1–13 p. 1063
FUTURE PLANS	Assessing the Future p. M23	Parable of the Rich Fool Luke 12:13–21 p. 939	Boasting About Tomorrow James 4:13–17 p. 1177
SETTING PRIORITIES	My Daily Routine p. M11	Parable of the Sower Matt. 13:1–23 p. 865	Counting the Cost Luke 14:25–35 p. 943
CHOOSING A CAREER	Our Un-Calling p. M26	Paul Stirs Up the Silversmiths Acts 19:23–41 p. 1020	Living Sacrifices Rom. 12:1–8 p. 1045

STRESS

TOPIC	ICE-BREAKER	STORY PASSAGE	TEACHING PASSAGE
PEER PRESSURE	Who Influences You? p. M28	Jesus Pressured by the Crowd John 8:1–11 p. 973	Imitators of God Eph. 5:1–21 p. 1104
SCHOOL / GRADES	How's the Weather? p. M18	Slaving Away in Egypt Ex. 5:1–21 p. 97	Trials and Temptations James 1:2–18 p. 1172
COMPETITION	Competition vs. Cooperation p. M40	Jockeying for Position Mark 10:35–45 p. 906	The Prize 1 Cor. 9:24–27 p. 1062
POPULARITY	The Dating Game p. M17	Esther Chosen Queen Est. 2:1–18 p. 466	Divisions in the Church 1 Cor. 1:10–17 p. 1054
SHATTERED DREAMS	Stress Test p. M33	On the Road to Emmaus Luke 24:13–35 p. 958	The Pain and the Hope Rom. 8:18–27 p. 1040
THE FUTURE	Assessing the Future p. M23	Parable of the Talents Matt. 25:14–30 p. 881	Not to Worry Matt. 6:25–34 p. 858
WORRY AND ANXIETY	Emotional Dashboard p. M41	The Storm Mark 4:35–41 p. 896	God's Peace Phil. 4:2–9 p. 1115
CHANGE	You Are What You Eat p. M11	Abram and Sarai on the Move Gen. 12:1–9 p. 51	Content in Any Situation Phil. 4:10–20 p. 1115
PRIORITIES	A Slice of Life p. M20	Mary Chooses What's Best Luke 10:38–42 p. 936	Living for God 1 Peter 4:1–11 p. 1185
PATIENCE AND WAITING	My Temperament p. M5	Noah Waits in the Ark Gen. 8:1–22 p. 47	"Be patient and stand firm" James 5:7–20 p. 1178
ANGER	911 Phone Numbers p. M14	Jesus Clears the Temple Mark 11:12–19 p. 907	"In your anger do not sin" Eph. 4:17–32 p. 1103
LONELINESS	My People Tree p. M24	Jesus in Gethsemane Mark 14:32–42 p. 912	Paul's Loneliness 2 Tim. 4:9–18 p. 1147
FAILURE	Medical History p. M15	Peter Disowns Jesus Luke 22:54–62 p. 955	Grace for Paul 1 Tim. 1:12–20 p. 1136
SPIRITUAL STRUGGLES	Things That Drive You Crazy p. M23	Jacob Wrestles With God Gen. 32:22–32 p. 72	Tested by Trials 1 Peter 1:3–12 p. 1181
WORKING ATTITUDES	Our Un-Calling p. M26	Parable of Workers in the Vineyard Matt. 20:1–16 p. 874	Job Stress 2 Cor. 11:16–33 p. 1085

ISSUES

TOPIC	ICE-BREAKER	STORY PASSAGE	TEACHING PASSAGE
DRUGS / ALCOHOL	What Are Your Values? p. M46	Clean Bodies—Keen Minds Dan. 1:1–21 p. 773	Live by the Spirit Gal. 5:16–26 p. 1095
SEXUAL INTIMACY	Living Under the Influence p. M45	Love's Delight Song 1:1–2:7 p. 609	"You are not your own" 1 Cor. 6:12–20 p. 1059
LUST / PORNOGRAPHY	Hallowed Inhibitions p. M39	David and Bathsheba 2 Sam. 11:1–27 p. 309	Lust in the Eye Matt. 5:27–30 p. 856
MUSIC, MOVIES, ETC.	Music in My Life p. M44	Dirty Dancing Mark 6:14–29 p. 899	Good Character 2 Peter 1:1–11 p. 1190
FAMILY INTERFERENCE	My Childhood Supper Table p. M22	Jesus' Family Thinks He's Crazy Mark 3:20–35 p. 895	Children and Parents Eph. 6:1–4 p. 1106
RACISM	The Old Neighborhood p. M39	Peter's Vision Acts 10:1–23 p. 1008	"Love your neighbor as yourself" Rom. 13:8–14 p. 1047
GANGS / VIOLENCE	Headache Survey p. M25	Parable of the Good Samaritan Luke 10:25–37 p. 936	Hate or Love? 1 John 4:7–21 p. 1199
CULTS	Back to Back p. M5	Paul Confronts a Sorcerer Acts 13:1–12 p. 1011	Test the Spirits 1 John 4:1–6 p. 1199
SUICIDE	Some of My Feelings p. M25	Judas Commits Suicide Acts 1:12–26 p. 995	Comfort for Despair 2 Cor. 1:3–11 p. 1075
ASSISTED SUICIDE	Comfort Zones p. M18	Saul's Sad Death 1 Sam. 31:1–13 p. 298	Longing for "Home" 2 Cor. 5:1–10 p. 1079
DIVORCE	Ups and Downs p. M27	Joseph's Tough Decision Matt. 1:18–25 p. 851	One Flesh Matt. 19:1–12 p. 873
WAR	Lay It on the Line p. M26	The Fall of Jericho Josh. 5:13–6:21 p. 226	"God is our refuge and strength" Ps. 46:1–11 p. 522
CAPITAL PUNISHMENT	My Last Will and Testament p. M37	Cain: The First Murderer Gen. 4:1–16 p. 44	An Eye for an Eye Matt. 5:38–48 p. 857
SEXUALITY	Life Signs p. M43	Sodom and Gomorrah Gen. 19:1–29 p. 57	Moral Standards Rom. 1:18–32 p. 1032
AIDS	The Life Raft p. M28	The Golden Calf Ex. 32:1–35 p. 122	These "Earthly Tents" 2 Cor. 5:1–10 p. 1079

CRISES

TOPIC	ICE-BREAKER	STORY PASSAGE	TEACHING PASSAGE
TEEN PREGNANCY	Problem Survey p. M32	Mary's Surprising News Luke 1:26–38 p. 920	Doing Good to All Gal. 6:1–10 p. 1096
ABORTION	Wallet Scavenger Hunt p. M16	David Grieves 2 Sam. 12:15–25 p. 311	"You knit me together ..." Ps. 139:1–24 p. 567
ABUSE	My Roles p. M44	Jesus Beaten and Mocked Matt. 27:26–31 p. 886	Nothing Is Able to Separate Us From God's Love Rom. 8:28–39 p. 1041
DATE RAPE	Choosing Friends p. M19	Amnon Rapes Tamar 2 Sam. 13:1–22 p. 312	Don't Take Advantage 1 Thess. 4:1–12 p. 1128
ADDICTION	You Are What You Eat p. M11	A Possessed Man Set Free Luke 8:26–39 p. 932	Inner Battle Rom. 7:7–25 p. 1039
DEPRESSION	Headache Survey p. M25	Renewal of Hope Luke 24:13–35 p. 958	Don't Lose Heart 2 Cor. 4:1–18 p. 1078
REJECTION	My Risk Quotient p. M20	Jesus Rejected by Hometown Luke 4:14–30 p. 925	When You're Mistreated Rom. 12:9–21 p. 1046
MORAL FAILURE	Life Signs p. M43	A Woman Caught in Adultery John 8:1–11 p. 973	Confession and Forgiveness 1 John 1:5–2:6 p. 1195
CHRONIC ILLNESS / DISABILITY	Things That Drive You Crazy p. M23	Jesus Heals a Man Born Blind John 9:1–15,24–34 p. 975	The Pain and the Hope Rom. 8:18–27 p. 1040
DEATH AND DYING	Last Will and Testament p. M37	Jesus Raises Lazarus John 11:17–44 p. 978	Through the Valley Ps. 23:1–6 p. 510
GRIEF AND LOSS	Stress Test p. M33	Jesus Appears to Mary Magdalene John 20:1–18 p. 988	Nothing Is Able to Separate Us From God's Love Rom. 8:28–39 p. 1041
TRAGEDY AND DISASTER	Emotional Dashboard p. M41	Job Gets Wiped Out Job 1:6–22 p. 473	The God of All Comfort 2 Cor. 1:3–11 p. 1075
FINANCIAL PROBLEMS	Fun Money p. M22	Elisha and the Widow's Oil 2 Kings 4:1–7 p. 358	"In plenty or in want" Phil. 4:10–20 p. 1115
LOSING FRIENDS	Friendship Survey p. M19	Paul and Barnabas Part Company Acts 15:36–41 p. 1015	"The Lord stood at my side" 2 Tim. 4:9–18 p. 1147
WEATHERING LIFE'S STORMS	How Was Your Day? p. M8	The Wise and Foolish Builders Matt. 7:24–29 p. 860	God Cares 1 Peter 5:1–11 p. 1186

BELIEFS

TOPIC	ICE-BREAKER	STORY PASSAGE	TEACHING PASSAGE
GOD THE FATHER	Warm Memories p. M33	God the Father Speaks Matt. 3:1–17 p. 853	Knowing the Father John 8:12–20 p. 973
JESUS CHRIST	Music in My Life p. M44	"Who do you say I am?" Matt. 16:13–28 p. 870	The Supremacy of Christ Col. 1:15–23 p. 1120
THE HOLY SPIRIT	Like Music to My Ears p. M40	The Holy Spirit Comes at Pentecost Acts 2:1–24,36–41 p. 996	Promise of the Spirit John 14:15–27 p. 982
SIN	What Are Your Values? p. M46	The Fall Gen. 3:1–24 p. 43	No One Is Righteous Rom. 3:9–24 p. 1034
ETERNAL LIFE	Brain Food p. M38	Jesus Teaches Nicodemus John 3:1–21 p. 965	Death's Defeat 1 Cor. 15:35–58 p. 1070
CONVERSION	Places in My Life p. M17	Paul's Encounter With Christ Acts 9:1–19 p. 1005	New Creation 2 Cor. 5:11–6:2 p. 1079
GOD'S LOVE	Precious Time p. M29	Parable of the Prodigal Son Luke 15:11–32 p. 944	"God is love" 1 John 4:7–21 p. 1199
GOD'S FORGIVENESS	Hallowed Inhibitions p. M39	"Father, forgive them" Luke 23:26–49 p. 956	God's Grace Eph. 2:1–10 p. 1100
RESURRECTION	Sharing Dreams p. M32	Christ's Resurrection Matt. 28:1–20 p. 888	Resurrection of the Dead 1 Cor. 15:12–34 p. 1069
HEAVEN AND HELL	Living Under the Influence p. M45	The Rich Man and Lazarus Luke 16:19–31 p. 946	Judgment Day Rev. 20:11–21:8 p. 1227
THE SECOND COMING	Final Jeopardy p. M41	Parable of the Ten Virgins Matt. 25:1–13 p. 881	The Coming of the Lord 1 Thess. 4:13–5:11 p. 1128
SATAN / OCCULT	My Roles p. M44	The Temptation of Jesus Luke 4:1–13 p. 925	The Armor of God Eph. 6:10–20 p. 1106
ANGELS	Wild Predictions p. M35	The Christmas Angels Luke 2:1–20—p. 921	God's Son and God's Angels Heb. 1:1–14 p. 1156
THE CHURCH	Power People p. M42	The Fellowship of Believers Acts 2:42–47 p. 997	Unity in the Body of Christ Eph. 4:1–16 p. 1103
THE BIBLE	Christian Basics p. M36	Philip Explains the Scripture Acts 8:26–40 p. 1005	"All Scripture is God-breathed" 2 Tim. 3:10–4:8 p. 1146

DISCIPLESHIP

TOPIC	ICE-BREAKER	STORY PASSAGE	TEACHING PASSAGE
GOD'S CALL	Like Music to My Ears p. M40	First Disciples Called Luke 5:1–11 p. 927	Pressing on Toward the Goal Phil. 3:12–21 p. 1114
FAITH	Christian Basics p. M36	Three Young Men and a Fiery Furnace Dan. 3:1–12,19–27 p. 776	Heroes of Faith Heb. 11:1–16 p. 1165
PRAYER	I Dream of Genie p. M42	A Pharisee and a Tax Collector Luke 18:9–14 p. 948	The Lord's Prayer Matt. 6:5–18 p. 857
SHARING YOUR FAITH	Scouting Report p. M9	Peter Heals a Crippled Beggar Acts 3:1–16 p. 998	Christ's Ambassadors 2 Cor. 5:11–6:2 p. 1079
DEVOTIONAL LIFE	A Slice of Life p. M20	Jesus Takes Time to Pray Mark 1:29–39 p. 892	The Beatitudes Matt. 5:1–12 p. 854
A SERVANT'S HEART	Sharing Dreams p. M32	Jesus Washes His Disciples' Feet John 13:1–17 p. 980	The Attitude of Christ Phil. 2:1–11 p. 1111
TEMPTATION	My Risk Quotient p. M20	The Temptation of Jesus Luke 4:1–13 p. 925	Struggling With Sin Rom. 7:7–25 p. 1039
DOUBTS	Final Jeopardy p. M41	Jesus Appears to "Doubting Thomas" John 20:24–31 p. 989	Confident Faith 1 John 5:1–15 p. 1200
GIVING	Old-Fashioned Auction p. M34	The Widow's Offering Mark 12:41–44 p. 910	"God loves a cheerful giver" 2 Cor. 9:6–15 p.1083
CONTENTMENT	KWIZ pp. M6–7	Paul and Silas in Prison Acts 16:22–40 p. 1016	Content in Every Situation Phil. 4:10–20 p. 1115
COMPASSION	The Grand Total p. M10	The Sheep and the Goats Matt. 25:31–46 p. 882	Loving With Actions 1 John 3:11–24 p. 1198
BLOWING IT	Problem Survey p. M32	Peter Disowns Jesus Luke 22:54–62 p. 955	Confession and Forgiveness 1 John 1:5–2:6 p. 1195
SPIRITUAL GIFTS	Dream Career p. M30	Choosing the First Deacons Acts 6:1–7 p. 1001	Using Your Gifts Rom. 12:1–8 p. 1045
KNOWING GOD'S WILL	Wow, So-So, or Ho-Hum p. M21	Jesus in Gethsemane Mark 14:32–42 p. 912	God Knows What You Need Matt. 6:25–34 p. 858
RELATING TO AUTHORITY	Down Memory Lane p. M21	Paying Taxes to Caesar Mark 12:13–17 p. 909	Submission to Authorities Rom. 13:1–7 p. 1046

Serendipity Is
What Happens When
Two or Three Get
Together and Share
Their Lives and the
Holy Spirit Does
Something Beautiful
When You Least
Expect It.

150 BIBLE STORIES

WITH QUESTIONNAIRES

OLD TESTAMENT

150 BIBLE STORIES
WITH QUESTIONNAIRES *(continued)*

150 BIBLE STORIES

WITH QUESTIONNAIRES *(continued)*

ADDITIONAL TOPICS

The questionnaires for these stories, which are not part of the Lesson Plans on pages 17–24, can be used for the following topics:

ADDITIONAL TOPICS

(continued)

Preface

THE NEW INTERNATIONAL VERSION is a completely new translation of the Holy Bible made by over a hundred scholars working directly from the best available Hebrew, Aramaic and Greek texts. It had its beginning in 1965 when, after several years of exploratory study by committees from the Christian Reformed Church and the National Association of Evangelicals, a group of scholars met at Palos Heights, Illinois, and concurred in the need for a new translation of the Bible in contemporary English. This group, though not made up of official church representatives, was transdenominational. Its conclusion was endorsed by a large number of leaders from many denominations who met in Chicago in 1966.

Responsibility for the new version was delegated by the Palos Heights group to a self-governing body of fifteen, the Committee on Bible Translation, composed for the most part of biblical scholars from colleges, universities and seminaries. In 1967 the New York Bible Society (now the International Bible Society) generously undertook the financial sponsorship of the project—a sponsorship that made it possible to enlist the help of many distinguished scholars. The fact that participants from the United States, Great Britain, Canada, Australia and New Zealand worked together gave the project its international scope. That they were from many denominations—including Anglican, Assemblies of God, Baptist, Brethren, Christian Reformed, Church of Christ, Evangelical Free, Lutheran, Mennonite, Methodist, Nazarene, Presbyterian, Wesleyan and other churches—helped to safeguard the translation from sectarian bias.

How it was made helps to give the New International Version its distinctiveness. The translation of each book was assigned to a team of scholars. Next, one of the Intermediate Editorial Committees revised the initial translation, with constant reference to the Hebrew, Aramaic or Greek. Their work then went to one of the General Editorial Committees, which checked it in detail and made another thorough revision. This revision in turn was carefully reviewed by the Committee on Bible Translation, which made further changes and then released the final version for publication. In this way the entire Bible underwent three revisions, during each of which the translation was examined for its faithfulness to the original languages and for its English style.

All this involved many thousands of hours of research and discussion regarding the meaning of the texts and the precise way of putting them into English. It may well be that no other translation has been made by a more thorough process of review and revision from committee to committee than this one.

From the beginning of the project, the Committee on Bible Translation held to certain goals for the New International Version: that it would be an accurate translation and one that would have clarity and literary quality and so prove suitable for public and private reading, teaching, preaching, memorizing and liturgical use. The Committee also sought to preserve some measure of continuity with the long tradition of translating the Scriptures into English.

In working toward these goals, the translators were united in their commitment to the authority and infallibility of the Bible as God's Word in written form. They believe that it contains the divine answer to the deepest needs of humanity, that it sheds unique light on our path in a dark world, and that it sets forth the way to our eternal well-being.

The first concern of the translators has been the accuracy of the translation and its fidelity to the thought of the biblical writers. They have weighed the significance of the lexical and grammatical details of the Hebrew, Aramaic and Greek texts. At the same time, they have striven for more than a word-for-word translation. Because thought patterns and syntax differ from language to language, faithful communication of the meaning of the writers of the Bible demands frequent modifications in sentence structure and constant regard for the contextual meanings of words.

A sensitive feeling for style does not always accompany scholarship. Accordingly the Committee on Bible Translation submitted the developing version to a number of stylistic consultants. Two of them read every book of both Old and New Testaments twice—once before and once after the last major revision—and made invaluable suggestions. Samples of the translation were tested for clarity and ease of reading by various kinds of people—young and old, highly educated and less well educated, ministers and laymen.

Concern for clear and natural English—that the New International Version should be idiomatic but not idiosyncratic, contemporary but not dated—motivated the translators and consultants. At the same time, they tried to reflect the differing styles of the biblical writers. In view of the international use of English, the translators sought to avoid obvious Americanisms on the one hand and obvious Anglicisms on the other. A British edition reflects the comparatively few differences of significant idiom and of spelling.

As for the traditional pronouns "thou," "thee" and "thine" in reference to the Deity, the translators judged that to use these archaisms (along with the old verb forms such as "doest," "wouldest" and "hadst") would violate accuracy in translation. Neither Hebrew, Aramaic nor Greek uses special pronouns for the persons of the Godhead. A present-day translation is not enhanced by forms that in the time of the King James Version were used in everyday speech, whether referring to God or man.

For the Old Testament the standard Hebrew text, the Masoretic Text as published in the latest editions of *Biblia Hebraica,* was used throughout. The Dead Sea Scrolls contain material bearing on an earlier stage of the Hebrew text. They were consulted, as were the Samaritan Pentateuch and the ancient scribal traditions relating to textual changes. Sometimes a variant Hebrew reading in the margin of the Masoretic Text was followed instead of the text itself. Such instances, being variants within the Masoretic tradition, are not specified by footnotes. In rare cases, words in the consonantal text were divided differently from the way they appear in the Masoretic Text. Footnotes indicate this. The translators also consulted the more important early versions—the Septuagint; Aquila, Symmachus and Theodotion; the Vulgate; the Syriac Peshitta; the Targums; and for the Psalms the *Juxta Hebraica* of Jerome. Readings from these versions were occasionally followed where the Masoretic Text seemed doubtful and where accepted principles of textual criticism showed that one or more of these textual witnesses appeared to provide the correct reading. Such instances are footnoted. Sometimes vowel letters and vowel signs did not, in the judgment of the translators, represent the correct vowels for the original consonantal text. Accordingly some words were read with a different set of vowels. These instances are usually not indicated by footnotes.

The Greek text used in translating the New Testament was an eclectic one. No other piece of ancient literature has such an abundance of manuscript witnesses as does the New Testament. Where existing manuscripts differ, the translators made their choice of readings according to accepted principles of New Testament textual criticism. Footnotes call attention to places where there was uncertainty about what the original text was. The best current printed texts of the Greek New Testament were used.

There is a sense in which the work of translation is never wholly finished. This applies to all great literature and uniquely so to the Bible. In 1973 the New Testament in the New International Version was published. Since then, suggestions for corrections and revisions have been received from various sources. The Committee on Bible Translation carefully considered the suggestions and adopted a number of them. These were incorporated in the first printing of the entire Bible in 1978. Additional revisions were made by the Committee on Bible Translation in 1983 and appear in printings after that date.

As in other ancient documents, the precise meaning of the biblical texts is sometimes uncertain. This is more often the case with the Hebrew and Aramaic texts than with the Greek text. Although archaeological and linguistic discoveries in this century aid in understanding difficult passages, some uncertainties remain. The more significant of these have been called to the reader's attention in the footnotes.

In regard to the divine name *YHWH,* commonly referred to as the *Tetragrammaton,* the translators adopted the device used in most English versions of rendering that name as "LORD" in capital letters to distinguish it from *Adonai,* another Hebrew word rendered "Lord," for which small letters are used. Wherever the two names stand together in the Old Testament as a compound name of God, they are rendered "Sovereign LORD."

Because for most readers today the phrases "the LORD of hosts" and "God of hosts" have little meaning, this version renders them "the LORD Almighty" and "God Almighty." These renderings convey the sense of the Hebrew, namely, "he who is sovereign over all the 'hosts' (powers) in heaven and on earth, especially over the 'hosts' (armies) of Israel." For readers unacquainted with Hebrew this does not make clear the distinction between *Sabaoth* ("hosts" or "Almighty") and *Shaddai* (which can also be translated "Almighty"), but the latter occurs infrequently and is always footnoted. When *Adonai* and *YHWH Sabaoth* occur together, they are rendered "the Lord, the LORD Almighty."

As for other proper nouns, the familiar spellings of the King James Version are generally retained. elled with "ch," except where it is final, are usually spelled in this translation with "k" or "c," since the biblical languages do not have the sound that "ch" frequently indicates in English—for example, in *chant.* For well-known names such as Zechariah, however, the traditional spelling has been retained. Variation in the spelling of names in the original languages has usually not been indicated. Where a person or place has two or more different names in the Hebrew, Aramaic or Greek texts, the more familiar one has generally been used, with footnotes where needed.

To achieve clarity the translators sometimes supplied words not in the original texts but required by the context. If there was uncertainty about such material, it is enclosed in brackets. Also for the sake of clarity or style, nouns, including some proper nouns, are sometimes substituted for pronouns, and vice versa. And though the Hebrew writers often shifted back and forth between first, second and third personal pronouns without change of antecedent, this translation often makes them uniform, in accordance with English style and without the use of footnotes.

Poetical passages are printed as poetry, that is, with indentation of lines with separate stanzas. These are generally designed to reflect the structure of Hebrew poetry. This poetry is normally characterized by parallelism in balanced lines. Most of the poetry in the Bible is in the Old Testament, and scholars differ regarding the scansion of Hebrew lines. The translators determined the stanza divisions for the most part by analysis of the subject matter. The stanzas therefore serve as poetic paragraphs.

As an aid to the reader, italicized sectional headings are inserted in most of the books. They are not to be regarded as part of the NIV text, are not for oral reading, and are not intended to dictate the interpretation of the sections they head.

The footnotes in this version are of several kinds, most of which need no explanation. Those giving alternative translations begin with "Or" and generally introduce the alternative with the last word preceding it in the text, except when it is a single-word alternative; in poetry quoted in a footnote a slant mark indicates a line division. Footnotes introduced by "Or" do not have uniform significance. In some cases two possible translations were considered to have about equal validity. In other cases, though the translators were convinced that the translation in the text was correct, they judged that another interpretation was possible and of sufficient importance to be represented in a footnote.

In the New Testament, footnotes that refer to uncertainty regarding the original text are introduced by "Some manuscripts" or similar expressions. In the Old Testament, evidence for the reading chosen is given first and evidence for the alternative is added after a semicolon (for example: Septuagint; Hebrew *father*). In such notes the term "Hebrew" refers to the Masoretic Text.

It should be noted that minerals, flora and fauna, architectural details, articles of clothing and jewelry, musical instruments and other articles cannot always be identified with precision. Also measures of capacity in the biblical period are particularly uncertain (see the table of weights and measures following the text).

Like all translations of the Bible, made as they are by imperfect man, this one undoubtedly falls short of its goals. Yet we are grateful to God for the extent to which he has enabled us to realize these goals and for the strength he has given us and our colleagues to complete our task. We offer this version of the Bible to him in whose name and for whose glory it has been made. We pray that it will lead many into a better understanding of the Holy Scriptures and a fuller knowledge of Jesus Christ the incarnate Word, of whom the Scriptures so faithfully testify.

The Committee on Bible Translation
June 1978
(Revised August 1983)

Names of the translators and editors may be secured
from the International Bible Society,
translation sponsors of the New International Version,
1820 Jet Stream Drive, Colorado Springs, Colorado
80921-3696 U.S.A.

THE OLD TESTAMENT

Introduction to
GENESIS

Personal Reading Plan

❐ Genesis 1:1–3:24	❐ Genesis 21:22–23:20	❐ Genesis 37:1–38:30
❐ Genesis 4:1–5:32	❐ Genesis 24:1–25:34	❐ Genesis 39:1–41:40
❐ Genesis 6:1–9:17	❐ Genesis 26:1–27:40	❐ Genesis 41:41–42:38
❐ Genesis 9:18–11:32	❐ Genesis 27:41–30:24	❐ Genesis 43:1–44:34
❐ Genesis 12:1–15:21	❐ Genesis 30:25–31:55	❐ Genesis 45:1–47:12
❐ Genesis 16:1–18:33	❐ Genesis 32:1–34:31	❐ Genesis 47:13–48:22
❐ Genesis 19:1–21:21	❐ Genesis 35:1–36:43	❐ Genesis 49:1–50:26

Author

Moses is assumed to be the author and editor of most of the first five books of the OT (the Pentateuch).

Date

It is difficult to set a firm date for the writing of the Pentateuch. Conservative estimates place it in either the fifteenth or thirteenth century B.C., depending on when the Exodus occurred.

Theme

Everything begins with God, who elects a people of his own.

Historical Background and Characteristics

Archaeological findings and ancient history have much in common with certain details of the Genesis narrative. The socio-cultural environment of the patriarchal narratives (Gen. 12–50) fits well within the context of the Middle Bronze Age (c. 1950–1550 B.C.) in Palestine. This "Book of Beginnings" is the origin for many of the major themes discussed in Scripture. Humanity's origin and mission, its fall and predicament, human responsibility and divine sovereignty, God's justice and mercy, his atonement for sin, the obedience of faith, the covenant of grace—all find their roots in Genesis. But Genesis is perhaps most often read for its vivid account of the pioneers of our faith—Abraham, Isaac and Jacob—through whom God is known and can be trusted.

Passages for Topical Group Study

3:1–24	SIN	The Fall
4:1–16	CAPITAL PUNISHMENT	Cain and Abel
8:1–22	PATIENCE AND WAITING	Noah in the Ark
12:1–9	CHANGE	The Call of Abram
19:1–29	SEXUALITY	Sodom and Gomorrah Destroyed
21:1–21	STEPFAMILIES	Isaac Born; Ishmael Sent Away
25:19–34	SIBLING RIVALRY	Jacob and Esau
29:1–14	DATING—THE RIGHT WAY	Jacob and Rachel
32:22–32	SPIRITUAL STRUGGLES	Jacob Wrestles with God
37:1–11	DREAMS and DESIRES	Joseph's Dreams
39:1–23	SEXUAL ABSTINENCE	Joseph and Potiphar's Wife

See the Lesson Plans in the front of this Bible.

Passages for General Group Study

1:1–2:3	The Beginning	13:1–18	Abram and Lot Separate	37:12–36	Joseph Sold by Brothers
2:4–25	Adam and Eve	18:16–33	Abraham's Intercession	41:1–40	Pharaoh's Dreams
6:5–7:12	The Flood	22:1–19	Abraham Tested	45:1–28	Joseph Identifies Himself

The Beginning

1 In the beginning God created the heavens
and the earth. 2Now the earth was[a] formless and empty, darkness was over the surface of the deep, and the Spirit of God was
hovering over the waters.

3And God said, "Let there be light," and there
was light. 4God saw that the light was good,
and he separated the light from the darkness. 5God called the light "day," and the
darkness he called "night." And there was
evening, and there was morning—the first
day.
6And God said, "Let there be an expanse between the waters to separate water from water." 7So God made the expanse and separated the water under the expanse from the
water above it. And it was so. 8God called
the expanse "sky." And there was evening,
and there was morning—the second day.
9And God said, "Let the water under the sky be
gathered to one place, and let dry ground
appear." And it was so. 10God called the dry
ground "land," and the gathered waters he
called "seas." And God saw that it was good.
11Then God said, "Let the land produce
vegetation: seed-bearing plants and trees on
the land that bear fruit with seed in it, according to their various kinds." And it was
so. 12The land produced vegetation: plants
bearing seed according to their kinds and
trees bearing fruit with seed in it according
to their kinds. And God saw that it was
good. 13And there was evening, and there
was morning—the third day.
14And God said, "Let there be lights in the expanse of the sky to separate the day from the
night, and let them serve as signs to mark
seasons and days and years, 15and let them
be lights in the expanse of the sky to give
light on the earth." And it was so. 16God
made two great lights—the greater light to
govern the day and the lesser light to govern
the night. He also made the stars. 17God set
them in the expanse of the sky to give light
on the earth, 18to govern the day and the
night, and to separate light from darkness.
And God saw that it was good. 19And there
was evening, and there was morning—the
fourth day.
20And God said, "Let the water teem with living
creatures, and let birds fly above the earth
across the expanse of the sky." 21So God
created the great creatures of the sea and
every living and moving thing with which
the water teems, according to their kinds,
and every winged bird according to its kind.
And God saw that it was good. 22God

GENESIS 1:1–2:3

1. Did you ever create anything when you were a kid? Mud pies? A treehouse? A wacky invention?
2. When are you more creative: In the morning or at night?
3. What modern "creation" is most important to you? Computer? Stereo? Car?
4. How much of your creative potential are you using in your life right now? 50%, 99%, 1%?
5. What are you doing to take care of the environment that God told the human race to look after?
6. How do you feel when you see all the things God has created?
7. What is God up to in your life right now? If God were to spend a day creating something in your life you are in need of, what would it be?

[a] 2 Or possibly *became*

1:1 A summary statement introducing the six days of creative activity. The Bible always assumes, and never argues, God's existence. Although everything else had a beginning, God has always been (Ps. 90:2).

1:3 ***God said.*** Merely by speaking, God brought all things into being (Heb. 11:3).

1:5 ***God called.*** Both day and night belong to the Lord. ***first day.*** Some say that the creation days were 24-hour periods, others that they were indefinite periods.

1:26 ***image.*** Made in God's image, every human being is worthy of honor and respect. Believers are to be "conformed to the likeness of Christ" (Rom. 8:29) and will someday be "like him" (1 John 3:2).

1:27–28 ***male and female.*** Alike they bear the image of God, and together they share in the divine benediction that follows. The man and woman go forth with God's blessing—flourishing, filling the earth with their kind, and exercising dominion over the other earthly creatures. As God's representative in the creaturely realm, they are stewards of God's creation.

2:2 God rested on the seventh day, not because he was weary, but because nothing formless or empty remained. His creative work was completed—and it was totally effective, perfect, "very good" (1:31). It didn't have to be repeated or revised.

2:3 Although the word "Sabbath" is not used here, the Hebrew verb translated "rested" is the origin of the noun "Sabbath."

blessed them and said, "Be fruitful and increase in number and fill the water in the seas, and let the birds increase on the
earth." 23And there was evening, and there
was morning—the fifth day.
24And God said, "Let the land produce living creatures according to their kinds: livestock, creatures that move along the ground, and wild animals, each according to its kind."
And it was so. 25God made the wild animals
according to their kinds, the livestock according to their kinds, and all the creatures that move along the ground according to their kinds. And God saw that it was good.
26Then God said, "Let us make man in our image, in our likeness, and let them rule over the fish of the sea and the birds of the air, over the livestock, over all the earth,[a] and over all the creatures that move along the ground."

27So God created man in his own image,
in the image of God he created him;
male and female he created them.

28God blessed them and said to them, "Be
fruitful and increase in number; fill the earth and subdue it. Rule over the fish of the sea and the birds of the air and over every living creature that moves on the ground."
29Then God said, "I give you every seed-
bearing plant on the face of the whole earth and every tree that has fruit with seed in it.
They will be yours for food. 30And to all the
beasts of the earth and all the birds of the air and all the creatures that move on the ground—everything that has the breath of life in it—I give every green plant for food."
And it was so.
31God saw all that he had made, and it
was very good. And there was evening, and there was morning—the sixth day.

2 Thus the heavens and the earth were completed in all their vast array.

2By the seventh day God had finished the work
he had been doing; so on the seventh day
he rested[b] from all his work. 3And God
blessed the seventh day and made it holy, because on it he rested from all the work of creating that he had done.

Adam and Eve

4This is the account of the heavens and the earth when they were created.

When the LORD God made the earth and the
heavens— 5and no shrub of the field had yet
appeared on the earth[c] and no plant of the field

> ## GENESIS 2:4–25
>
> 1. What are some of the pets you have had? What were their names?
> 2. If you could live anywhere in the world, where would you like to live?
> 3. Who was the first person you had a crush on? What happened?
> 4. Like Adam, when have you felt all alone? Are you the type of person who enjoys being alone—or the type who hates being alone?
> 5. If you had to call on someone to talk about some heavy stuff, who would you call?
> 6. Which type of relationship do you have the biggest problems with: Your relationship with God? The opposite sex? Your parents? Your school friends?
> 7. Would you describe your life right now more like a "paradise" or "the pits"? How would you like this group to pray for you?

[a]26 Hebrew; Syriac *all the wild animals* [b]2 Or *ceased*; also in verse 3 [c]5 Or *land*; also in verse 6

Genesis 1:1–2:3 is a general account of creation, while Genesis 2:4–4:26 focuses on the beginning of human history.

2:7 *formed.* The Hebrew for this verb commonly referred to the work of a potter (see Isa. 45:9; Jer. 18:6), who fashions vessels from clay (see Job 33:6).

2:9 *tree of life.* Signifying and giving life, without death, to those who eat its fruit (see 3:22; Rev. 2:7). ***tree of the knowledge of good and evil.*** Signifying and giving knowledge of good and evil, leading ultimately to death, to those who eat its fruit (v. 17; 3:3).

2:15 *work ... take care.* See note on 1:28. Man is now charged to govern the earth responsibly under God's sovereignty. His first act of dominion over the creatures around him would be to name them (v. 19).

2:18 *not good ... to be alone.* Without female companionship and a partner in reproduction, the man could not fully realize his humanity.

2:24 *a man will leave his father and mother.* Instead of remaining under the protective custody of his parents, a man leaves them and, with his wife, establishes a new family unit. ***united ... one flesh.*** The divine intention for husband and wife was monogamy. Together they were to form an inseparable union, of which "one flesh" is both a sign and an expression.

2:25 *naked ... no shame.* Freedom from shame, signifying moral innocence, would soon be lost as a result of sin (see 3:7).

had yet sprung up, for the LORD God had not sent
rain on the earth[a] and there was no man to
work the ground, 6but streams[b] came up from
the earth and watered the whole surface of the
ground— 7the LORD God formed the man[c] from
the dust of the ground and breathed into his nostrils the breath of life, and the man became a
living being.
8Now the LORD God had planted a garden in
the east, in Eden; and there he put the man he
had formed. 9And the LORD God made all kinds of
trees grow out of the ground—trees that were
pleasing to the eye and good for food. In the
middle of the garden were the tree of life and the
tree of the knowledge of good and evil.
10A river watering the garden flowed from
Eden; from there it was separated into four head-
waters. 11The name of the first is the Pishon; it
winds through the entire land of Havilah, where
there is gold. 12(The gold of that land is good;
aromatic resin[d] and onyx are also there.) 13The
name of the second river is the Gihon; it winds
through the entire land of Cush.[e] 14The name of
the third river is the Tigris; it runs along the east
side of Asshur. And the fourth river is the Euphrates.
15The LORD God took the man and put him in
the Garden of Eden to work it and take care of it.
16And the LORD God commanded the man, "You
are free to eat from any tree in the garden; 17but
you must not eat from the tree of the knowledge
of good and evil, for when you eat of it you will
surely die."
18The LORD God said, "It is not good for the
man to be alone. I will make a helper suitable for
him."
19Now the LORD God had formed out of the
ground all the beasts of the field and all the birds
of the air. He brought them to the man to see
what he would name them; and whatever the
man called each living creature, that was its
name. 20So the man gave names to all the livestock, the birds of the air and all the beasts of the
field.

But for Adam[f] no suitable helper was found.
21So the LORD God caused the man to fall into a
deep sleep; and while he was sleeping, he took
one of the man's ribs[g] and closed up the place
with flesh. 22Then the LORD God made a woman
from the rib[h] he had taken out of the man, and
he brought her to the man.
23The man said,

"This is now bone of my bones
and flesh of my flesh;
she shall be called 'woman,[i]'
for she was taken out of man."

24For this reason a man will leave his father and
mother and be united to his wife, and they will
become one flesh.
25The man and his wife were both naked, and
they felt no shame.

The Fall of Man

3 Now the serpent was more crafty than any of
the wild animals the LORD God had made.
He said to the woman, "Did God really say, 'You
must not eat from any tree in the garden'?"
2The woman said to the serpent, "We may eat
fruit from the trees in the garden, 3but God did
say, 'You must not eat fruit from the tree that is
in the middle of the garden, and you must not
touch it, or you will die.'"
4"You will not surely die," the serpent said to
the woman. 5"For God knows that when you eat
of it your eyes will be opened, and you will be
like God, knowing good and evil."
6When the woman saw that the fruit of the
tree was good for food and pleasing to the eye,
and also desirable for gaining wisdom, she took
some and ate it. She also gave some to her husband, who was with her, and he ate it. 7Then the
eyes of both of them were opened, and they realized they were naked; so they sewed fig leaves
together and made coverings for themselves.
8Then the man and his wife heard the sound
of the LORD God as he was walking in the garden
in the cool of the day, and they hid from the LORD
God among the trees of the garden. 9But the
LORD God called to the man, "Where are you?"
10He answered, "I heard you in the garden,
and I was afraid because I was naked; so I hid."
11And he said, "Who told you that you were
naked? Have you eaten from the tree that I commanded you not to eat from?"
12The man said, "The woman you put here
with me—she gave me some fruit from the tree,
and I ate it."
13Then the LORD God said to the woman,
"What is this you have done?"

The woman said, "The serpent deceived me,
and I ate."
14So the LORD God said to the serpent, "Because you have done this,

"Cursed are you above all the livestock
and all the wild animals!
You will crawl on your belly
and you will eat dust
all the days of your life.

[a]5 Or *land*; also in verse 6 [b]6 Or *mist* [c]7 The Hebrew for *man (adam)* sounds like and may be related to the Hebrew for *ground (adamah)*; it is also the name *Adam* (see Gen. 2:20). [d]12 Or *good; pearls* [e]13 Possibly southeast Mesopotamia [f]20 Or *the man* [g]21 Or *took part of the man's side* [h]22 Or *part* [i]23 The Hebrew for *woman* sounds like the Hebrew for *man.*

15And I will put enmity
between you and the woman,
and between your offspring[a] and hers;
he will crush[b] your head,
and you will strike his heel."

16To the woman he said,

"I will greatly increase your pains in
childbearing;
with pain you will give birth to children.
Your desire will be for your husband,
and he will rule over you."

17To Adam he said, "Because you listened to
your wife and ate from the tree about which I
commanded you, 'You must not eat of it,'

"Cursed is the ground because of you;
through painful toil you will eat of it
all the days of your life.
18It will produce thorns and thistles for you,
and you will eat the plants of the field.
19By the sweat of your brow
you will eat your food
until you return to the ground,
since from it you were taken;
for dust you are
and to dust you will return."

20Adam[c] named his wife Eve,[d] because she
would become the mother of all the living.
21The LORD God made garments of skin for
Adam and his wife and clothed them. 22And the
LORD God said, "The man has now become like
one of us, knowing good and evil. He must not be
allowed to reach out his hand and take also from
the tree of life and eat, and live forever." 23So the
LORD God banished him from the Garden of Eden
to work the ground from which he had been tak-
en. 24After he drove the man out, he placed on
the east side[e] of the Garden of Eden cherubim
and a flaming sword flashing back and forth to
guard the way to the tree of life.

Cain and Abel

4 Adam[c] lay with his wife Eve, and she became pregnant and gave birth to Cain.[f] She
said, "With the help of the LORD I have brought
forth[g] a man." 2Later she gave birth to his brother Abel.
Now Abel kept flocks, and Cain worked the
soil. 3In the course of time Cain brought some of
the fruits of the soil as an offering to the LORD.
4But Abel brought fat portions from some of the
firstborn of his flock. The LORD looked with favor
on Abel and his offering, 5but on Cain and his
offering he did not look with favor. So Cain was
very angry, and his face was downcast.
6Then the LORD said to Cain, "Why are you

> ***GENESIS 3:1–24***
>
> 1. What is your favorite food? What "junk food" is hardest for you to resist?
> 2. When you were a kid, what was "off limits" to you?
> 3. What are the subtle, day-to-day temptations you face at school?
> 4. If you were to judge Adam, Eve and the serpent for the crime of sin, what percentage of blame would you assign to each?
> 5. How would you describe your relationship with God at the moment: Close? Distant? Somewhere in between?
> 6. What have you found helpful in dealing with temptation?
> 7. Where in your life are you tempted to sin? How can your group pray for you?

[a] *15* Or *seed* [b] *15* Or *strike* [c] *20,1* Or *The man* [d] *20* *Eve* probably means *living.* [e] *24* Or *placed in front*
[f] *1* *Cain* sounds like the Hebrew for *brought forth* or *acquired.* [g] *1* Or *have acquired*

3:1 *serpent.* The great deceiver clothed himself as a serpent, one of God's good creatures. He portrayed rebellion as clever, but essentially innocent, self-interest. Therefore "the devil, or Satan," is later referred to as "that ancient serpent" (Rev. 12:9; 20:2). ***Did God really say ... ?*** The question and the response changed the course of history. By causing the woman to doubt God's word, Satan brought evil into the world and alienated people from God.

3:4–5 *You will not surely die.* The blatant denial of God's specific command (2:17). ***God knows.*** Satan accuses God of having unworthy motives.

3:12–13 *The woman you put here ... gave me.* Adam blames God and the woman—anyone but himself—for his sin. In turn, Eve blames the serpent rather than herself.

3:15 The antagonism between people and snakes is used to symbolize the outcome of the struggle between God and the evil one—played out in the hearts and history of humanity. The woman's offspring will eventually crush the serpent's head, a promise fulfilled in Christ's victory over Satan—a victory in which all believers will share.

3:23–24 Before sinning, man had worked in a beautiful garden. Now he would have to work ground cursed with thorns and thistles (v. 18). The sword of God's judgment stood between fallen man and God's garden. The reason is given in verse 22. Only through God's redemption in Christ does man have access again to the tree of life (Rev. 22:14).

angry? Why is your face downcast? [7]If you do
what is right, will you not be accepted? But if you
do not do what is right, sin is crouching at your
door; it desires to have you, but you must master it."

GENESIS 4:1–16

1. Where are you in the birth order of your family—oldest, youngest or somewhere in the middle? What's the best and worst part about your birth order?
2. What is the closest you have come to wanting to "terminate" your brother or sister?!
3. From the story, what would you have done to Cain if you were God?
4. If you were governor of your state and had to make a decision whether or not to grant a convicted murderer a stay of execution—what would you do? (See note on 4:15.)
5. When have you felt "stabbed in the back" by someone close to you? How did you deal with it?
6. How do you typically react when you are angry? What have you found helpful to control your anger?
7. How can the group pray for you this week?

[8]Now Cain said to his brother Abel, "Let's go
out to the field."[a] And while they were in the
field, Cain attacked his brother Abel and killed
him.

[9]Then the LORD said to Cain, "Where is your
brother Abel?"

"I don't know," he replied. "Am I my brother's keeper?"

[10]The LORD said, "What have you done? Listen! Your brother's blood cries out to me from the
ground. [11]Now you are under a curse and driven
from the ground, which opened its mouth to receive your brother's blood from your hand.
[12]When you work the ground, it will no longer
yield its crops for you. You will be a restless wanderer on the earth."

[13]Cain said to the LORD, "My punishment is
more than I can bear. [14]Today you are driving me
from the land, and I will be hidden from your
presence; I will be a restless wanderer on the
earth, and whoever finds me will kill me."

[15]But the LORD said to him, "Not so[b]; if anyone kills Cain, he will suffer vengeance seven
times over." Then the LORD put a mark on Cain
so that no one who found him would kill him.
[16]So Cain went out from the LORD's presence and
lived in the land of Nod,[c] east of Eden.

[17]Cain lay with his wife, and she became pregnant and gave birth to Enoch. Cain was then
building a city, and he named it after his son
Enoch. [18]To Enoch was born Irad, and Irad was
the father of Mehujael, and Mehujael was the
father of Methushael, and Methushael was the
father of Lamech.

[19]Lamech married two women, one named
Adah and the other Zillah. [20]Adah gave birth to
Jabal; he was the father of those who live in tents
and raise livestock. [21]His brother's name was Ju-
bal; he was the father of all who play the harp and
flute. [22]Zillah also had a son, Tubal-Cain, who
forged all kinds of tools out of[d] bronze and iron.
Tubal-Cain's sister was Naamah.

[23]Lamech said to his wives,

"Adah and Zillah, listen to me;
  wives of Lamech, hear my words.
I have killed[e] a man for wounding me,
  a young man for injuring me.

[a]8 Samaritan Pentateuch, Septuagint, Vulgate and Syriac; Masoretic Text does not have *"Let's go out to the field."* [b]15 Septuagint, Vulgate and Syriac; Hebrew *Very well* [c]16 *Nod* means *wandering* (see verses 12 and 14). [d]22 Or *who instructed all who work in* [e]23 Or *I will kill*

4:3–4 The contrast in offerings is not between an offering of plant life and an offering of animal life, but between a careless, thoughtless offering and a choice, generous offering. Motivation and heart attitude are all-important, and God looked with favor on Abel and his offering because of Abel's faith (Heb. 11:4).

4:8 The first murder was especially monstrous because it was committed with deliberate deceit ("Let's go out to the field"), against a brother, and against a good man.

4:11 ***curse.*** The ground had been cursed because of human sin (3:17), and now Cain himself is cursed. Formerly he had worked the ground, and it had produced life for him (vv. 2–3). However, now the ground, soaked with his brother's blood, would symbolize death and would no longer yield for him its produce (v. 12).

4:13 ***My punishment is more than I can bear.*** Confronted with his crime and its resulting curse, Cain responded not with remorse but with self-pity.

4:15 ***mark.*** A warning sign to protect Cain from an avenger. For now the murderer's life is spared. Later, capital punishment for premeditated murder was decreed (Gen. 9:6; Ex. 21:12–14). Some Christians believe capital punishment is still appropriate and condoned in the NT (Rom. 13:1–4; 1 Peter 2:13–14). Others believe Jesus' teachings and example (Matt. 5:38–48; John 8:7; Luke 23:34) negate capital punishment, and the OT requirement of death for murder is met by Christ's death on the cross.

24If Cain is avenged seven times,
then Lamech seventy-seven times."

25Adam lay with his wife again, and she gave
birth to a son and named him Seth,[a] saying,
"God has granted me another child in place of
Abel, since Cain killed him." 26Seth also had a
son, and he named him Enosh.

At that time men began to call on[b] the name
of the LORD.

From Adam to Noah

5 This is the written account of Adam's line.

When God created man, he made him in the
likeness of God. 2He created them male and female and blessed them. And when they were
created, he called them "man.[c]"
3When Adam had lived 130 years, he had a
son in his own likeness, in his own image; and he
named him Seth. 4After Seth was born, Adam
lived 800 years and had other sons and daughters. 5Altogether, Adam lived 930 years, and then
he died.
6When Seth had lived 105 years, he became
the father[d] of Enosh. 7And after he became the
father of Enosh, Seth lived 807 years and had
other sons and daughters. 8Altogether, Seth lived
912 years, and then he died.
9When Enosh had lived 90 years, he became
the father of Kenan. 10And after he became the
father of Kenan, Enosh lived 815 years and had
other sons and daughters. 11Altogether, Enosh
lived 905 years, and then he died.
12When Kenan had lived 70 years, he became
the father of Mahalalel. 13And after he became
the father of Mahalalel, Kenan lived 840 years
and had other sons and daughters. 14Altogether,
Kenan lived 910 years, and then he died.
15When Mahalalel had lived 65 years, he became the father of Jared. 16And after he became
the father of Jared, Mahalalel lived 830 years and
had other sons and daughters. 17Altogether, Mahalalel lived 895 years, and then he died.
18When Jared had lived 162 years, he became
the father of Enoch. 19And after he became the
father of Enoch, Jared lived 800 years and had
other sons and daughters. 20Altogether, Jared
lived 962 years, and then he died.
21When Enoch had lived 65 years, he became
the father of Methuselah. 22And after he became
the father of Methuselah, Enoch walked with
God 300 years and had other sons and daughters.
23Altogether, Enoch lived 365 years. 24Enoch
walked with God; then he was no more, because
God took him away.
25When Methuselah had lived 187 years, he
became the father of Lamech. 26And after he became the father of Lamech, Methuselah lived
782 years and had other sons and daughters.
27Altogether, Methuselah lived 969 years, and
then he died.
28When Lamech had lived 182 years, he had a
son. 29He named him Noah[e] and said, "He will
comfort us in the labor and painful toil of our
hands caused by the ground the LORD has
cursed." 30After Noah was born, Lamech lived
595 years and had other sons and daughters.
31Altogether, Lamech lived 777 years, and then
he died.
32After Noah was 500 years old, he became
the father of Shem, Ham and Japheth.

The Flood

6 When men began to increase in number on
the earth and daughters were born to them,
2the sons of God saw that the daughters of men
were beautiful, and they married any of them
they chose. 3Then the LORD said, "My Spirit will
not contend with[f] man forever, for he is mortal[g]; his days will be a hundred and twenty
years."
4The Nephilim were on the earth in those
days—and also afterward—when the sons of
God went to the daughters of men and had children by them. They were the heroes of old, men
of renown.
5The LORD saw how great man's wickedness
on the earth had become, and that every inclination of the thoughts of his heart was only evil all
the time. 6The LORD was grieved that he had
made man on the earth, and his heart was filled
with pain. 7So the LORD said, "I will wipe mankind, whom I have created, from the face of the
earth—men and animals, and creatures that
move along the ground, and birds of the air—for
I am grieved that I have made them." 8But Noah
found favor in the eyes of the LORD.

9This is the account of Noah.

Noah was a righteous man, blameless among
the people of his time, and he walked with God.
10Noah had three sons: Shem, Ham and Japheth.
11Now the earth was corrupt in God's sight
and was full of violence. 12God saw how corrupt
the earth had become, for all the people on earth
had corrupted their ways. 13So God said to Noah,
"I am going to put an end to all people, for the
earth is filled with violence because of them. I am
surely going to destroy both them and the earth.
14So make yourself an ark of cypress[h] wood;

[a]25 *Seth* probably means *granted.* [b]26 Or *to proclaim* [c]2 Hebrew *adam* [d]6 *Father* may mean *ancestor;* also in verses 7-26. [e]29 *Noah* sounds like the Hebrew for *comfort.* [f]3 Or *My spirit will not remain in* [g]3 Or *corrupt*
[h]14 The meaning of the Hebrew for this word is uncertain.

make rooms in it and coat it with pitch inside and out. 15This is how you are to build it: The ark is to be 450 feet long, 75 feet wide and 45 feet high.[a] 16Make a roof for it and finish[b] the ark to within 18 inches[c] of the top. Put a door in the side of the ark and make lower, middle and upper decks. 17I am going to bring floodwaters on the earth to destroy all life under the heavens, every creature that has the breath of life in it. Everything on earth will perish. 18But I will establish my covenant with you, and you will enter the ark—you and your sons and your wife and your sons' wives with you. 19You are to bring into the ark two of all living creatures, male and female, to keep them alive with you. 20Two of every kind of bird, of every kind of animal and of every kind of creature that moves along the ground will come to you to be kept alive. 21You are to take every kind of food that is to be eaten and store it away as food for you and for them."

22Noah did everything just as God commanded him.

7 The LORD then said to Noah, "Go into the ark, you and your whole family, because I have found you righteous in this generation. 2Take with you seven[d] of every kind of clean animal, a male and its mate, and two of every kind of unclean animal, a male and its mate, 3and also seven of every kind of bird, male and female, to keep their various kinds alive throughout the earth. 4Seven days from now I will send rain on the earth for forty days and forty nights, and I will wipe from the face of the earth every living creature I have made."

5And Noah did all that the LORD commanded him.

6Noah was six hundred years old when the floodwaters came on the earth. 7And Noah and his sons and his wife and his sons' wives entered the ark to escape the waters of the flood. 8Pairs of clean and unclean animals, of birds and of all creatures that move along the ground, 9male and female, came to Noah and entered the ark, as God had commanded Noah. 10And after the seven days the floodwaters came on the earth.

11In the six hundredth year of Noah's life, on the seventeenth day of the second month—on that day all the springs of the great deep burst forth, and the floodgates of the heavens were opened. 12And rain fell on the earth forty days and forty nights.

13On that very day Noah and his sons, Shem, Ham and Japheth, together with his wife and the wives of his three sons, entered the ark. 14They had with them every wild animal according to its kind, all livestock according to their kinds, every creature that moves along the ground according

Genesis 6:5–7:12

1. If your house was about to be washed away in a flood, what three things would you quickly grab?
2. How would you feel if God told you to build a boat the size of a football field in a landlocked area? What would your friends and neighbors think of your project?
3. How do you feel when someone makes fun of you?
4. Have you ever taken an unpopular stand at school, work or with your family or friends? What happened?
5. If you were in charge of your school, what would you do to improve the moral climate?
6. If you compared your life right now to the weather, what report would you give: Thunderstorms? Cloudy and gray? Warm and sunny?

[a] 15 Hebrew *300 cubits long, 50 cubits wide and 30 cubits high* (about 140 meters long, 23 meters wide and 13.5 meters high)
[b] 16 Or *Make an opening for light by finishing* [c] 16 Hebrew *a cubit* (about 0.5 meter) [d] 2 Or *seven pairs*; also in verse 3

6:5–6 One of the Bible's most vivid descriptions of human depravity. And because human nature remained unchanged, things were no better after the flood (8:21). ***his heart was filled with pain.*** Man's sin is God's sorrow (see Eph. 4:30).

6:17 *floodwaters on the earth to destroy all life under the heavens.* Some believe that the deluge was worldwide, partly because of the apparently universal terms of the text—both here and elsewhere. Others argue that nothing in chapters 6–9 prevents the flood from being understood as regional—destroying everything in its wake, but of relatively limited scope. "All life under the heavens" may mean all life within the range of Noah's perception, or to all the inhabited areas of earth.

6:18 *covenant.* Noah would understand the full implications of God's covenant with him only after the floodwaters had dried up and God sealed his covenant with a rainbow (9:8–17). The story of Noah's salvation from the flood illustrates God's redemption of his children (Heb. 11:7; 2 Peter 2:5) and typifies baptism (1 Peter 3:20–21).

6:19 *two of all living creatures.* Though morally innocent, the animal world, as creatures under man's corrupted rule, shared in his judgment. Most animals were doomed to die in the flood, but at least one pair of each kind was preserved to restock the earth after the waters subsided. According to 7:2, seven ceremonially "clean" animals were taken—to be used for burnt offerings (8:20) and for food (9:3).

to its kind and every bird according to its kind, everything with wings. 15Pairs of all creatures that have the breath of life in them came to Noah and entered the ark. 16The animals going in were male and female of every living thing, as God had commanded Noah. Then the LORD shut him in.

17For forty days the flood kept coming on the earth, and as the waters increased they lifted the ark high above the earth. 18The waters rose and increased greatly on the earth, and the ark floated on the surface of the water. 19They rose greatly on the earth, and all the high mountains under the entire heavens were covered. 20The waters rose and covered the mountains to a depth of more than twenty feet.[a, b] 21Every living thing that moved on the earth perished—birds, livestock, wild animals, all the creatures that swarm over the earth, and all mankind. 22Everything on dry land that had the breath of life in its nostrils died. 23Every living thing on the face of the earth was wiped out; men and animals and the creatures that move along the ground and the birds of the air were wiped from the earth. Only Noah was left, and those with him in the ark.

24The waters flooded the earth for a hundred and fifty days.

8 But God remembered Noah and all the wild animals and the livestock that were with him in the ark, and he sent a wind over the earth, and the waters receded. 2Now the springs of the deep and the floodgates of the heavens had been closed, and the rain had stopped falling from the sky. 3The water receded steadily from the earth. At the end of the hundred and fifty days the water had gone down, 4and on the seventeenth day of the seventh month the ark came to rest on the mountains of Ararat. 5The waters continued to recede until the tenth month, and on the first day of the tenth month the tops of the mountains became visible.

6After forty days Noah opened the window he had made in the ark 7and sent out a raven, and it kept flying back and forth until the water had dried up from the earth. 8Then he sent out a dove to see if the water had receded from the surface of the ground. 9But the dove could find no place to set its feet because there was water over all the surface of the earth; so it returned to Noah in the ark. He reached out his hand and took the dove and brought it back to himself in the ark. 10He waited seven more days and again sent out the dove from the ark. 11When the dove returned to him in the evening, there in its beak was a freshly plucked olive leaf! Then Noah knew that the water had receded from the earth. 12He waited sev-

> ### *GENESIS 8:1–22*
>
> 1. What's the longest you've ever had to wait in line? For what? Was it worth it?
> 2. When you were a kid, what was something you used to do on a rainy day?
> 3. How do you handle impatience when you are waiting for something important? What could help you be more patient?
> 4. How do you think Noah and his family felt cooped up on the ark for nearly a year—waiting for the water to go down?
> 5. How would you complete the sentence: "God isn't through with me yet, because...?
> 6. What is the big thing you are waiting on God to do? What might God be waiting on you to do?
> 7. Immediately after leaving the ark, Noah worshiped God. What has God done recently that you could thank him for?

[a]20 Hebrew *fifteen cubits* (about 6.9 meters) [b]20 Or *rose more than twenty feet, and the mountains were covered*

8:1 So far the flood story has been an account of judgment; from this point on it is a story of deliverance. ***God remembered Noah.*** Though Noah and his family had been in the ark for 150 days, God had not forgotten them. To "remember" in the Bible is not merely to recall to mind; it is to express concern for someone, to act with loving care for them.

8:4 ***mountains of Ararat.*** Refers to a mountain range (not necessarily the 17,000 foot Mt. Ararat) east of modern Turkey.

8:6 ***window.*** Noah's ark probably had a series of small windows encircling the entire vessel 18 inches from the top to admit light and air (see 6:16).

8:11 ***When the dove returned ... in its beak was a freshly plucked olive leaf!*** Olives do not grow at high elevations, so the fresh leaf was a sign to Noah that the water had receded from the earth. The modern symbol of peace represented by a dove carrying an olive branch in its beak has its origin in this story.

8:21 ***smelled the pleasing aroma.*** A figurative way of saying the Lord takes delight in his children's worship. ***even though every inclination of his heart is evil.*** Because of humanity's extreme wickedness, God destroyed them by means of a flood. Although righteous Noah and his family had been saved, he and his offspring were descendants of Adam and carried in their hearts the inheritance of sin. God graciously promises never again to deal with sin by sending a flood (see 9:11,15).

en more days and sent the dove out again, but
this time it did not return to him.
13By the first day of the first month of Noah's
six hundred and first year, the water had dried up
from the earth. Noah then removed the covering
from the ark and saw that the surface of the
ground was dry. 14By the twenty-seventh day of
the second month the earth was completely
dry.
15Then God said to Noah, 16"Come out of the
ark, you and your wife and your sons and their
wives. 17Bring out every kind of living creature
that is with you—the birds, the animals, and all
the creatures that move along the ground—so
they can multiply on the earth and be fruitful and
increase in number upon it."
18So Noah came out, together with his sons
and his wife and his sons' wives. 19All the animals and all the creatures that move along the
ground and all the birds—everything that moves
on the earth—came out of the ark, one kind after
another.
20Then Noah built an altar to the LORD and,
taking some of all the clean animals and clean
birds, he sacrificed burnt offerings on it. 21The
LORD smelled the pleasing aroma and said in his
heart: "Never again will I curse the ground because of man, even though[a] every inclination of
his heart is evil from childhood. And never again
will I destroy all living creatures, as I have done.

22"As long as the earth endures,
seedtime and harvest,
cold and heat,
summer and winter,
day and night
will never cease."

God's Covenant With Noah

9 Then God blessed Noah and his sons, saying
to them, "Be fruitful and increase in number
and fill the earth. 2The fear and dread of you will
fall upon all the beasts of the earth and all the
birds of the air, upon every creature that moves
along the ground, and upon all the fish of the sea;
they are given into your hands. 3Everything that
lives and moves will be food for you. Just as I gave
you the green plants, I now give you everything.
4"But you must not eat meat that has its lifeblood still in it. 5And for your lifeblood I will
surely demand an accounting. I will demand an
accounting from every animal. And from each
man, too, I will demand an accounting for the life
of his fellow man.

6"Whoever sheds the blood of man,
by man shall his blood be shed;
for in the image of God
has God made man.

7As for you, be fruitful and increase in number;
multiply on the earth and increase upon it."
8Then God said to Noah and to his sons with
him: 9"I now establish my covenant with you and
with your descendants after you 10and with every
living creature that was with you—the birds, the
livestock and all the wild animals, all those that
came out of the ark with you—every living creature on earth. 11I establish my covenant with
you: Never again will all life be cut off by the
waters of a flood; never again will there be a flood
to destroy the earth."
12And God said, "This is the sign of the covenant I am making between me and you and every living creature with you, a covenant for all
generations to come: 13I have set my rainbow in
the clouds, and it will be the sign of the covenant
between me and the earth. 14Whenever I bring
clouds over the earth and the rainbow appears in
the clouds, 15I will remember my covenant between me and you and all living creatures of every kind. Never again will the waters become a
flood to destroy all life. 16Whenever the rainbow
appears in the clouds, I will see it and remember
the everlasting covenant between God and all
living creatures of every kind on the earth."
17So God said to Noah, "This is the sign of the
covenant I have established between me and all
life on the earth."

The Sons of Noah

18The sons of Noah who came out of the ark
were Shem, Ham and Japheth. (Ham was the father of Canaan.) 19These were the three sons of
Noah, and from them came the people who were
scattered over the earth.
20Noah, a man of the soil, proceeded[b] to
plant a vineyard. 21When he drank some of its
wine, he became drunk and lay uncovered inside
his tent. 22Ham, the father of Canaan, saw his
father's nakedness and told his two brothers outside. 23But Shem and Japheth took a garment and
laid it across their shoulders; then they walked in
backward and covered their father's nakedness.
Their faces were turned the other way so that
they would not see their father's nakedness.
24When Noah awoke from his wine and found
out what his youngest son had done to him, 25he
said,

"Cursed be Canaan!
The lowest of slaves
will he be to his brothers."

26He also said,

[a] *21* Or *man, for* [b] *20* Or *soil, was the first*

"Blessed be the LORD, the God of Shem!
May Canaan be the slave of Shem.[a]
27May God extend the territory of Japheth[b];
may Japheth live in the tents of Shem,
and may Canaan be his[c] slave."

28After the flood Noah lived 350 years. 29Altogether, Noah lived 950 years, and then he died.

The Table of Nations

10 This is the account of Shem, Ham and Japheth, Noah's sons, who themselves had sons after the flood.

The Japhethites

2The sons[d] of Japheth:
Gomer, Magog, Madai, Javan, Tubal, Meshech and Tiras.
3The sons of Gomer:
Ashkenaz, Riphath and Togarmah.
4The sons of Javan:
Elishah, Tarshish, the Kittim and the Rodanim.[e] 5(From these the maritime
peoples spread out into their territories by their clans within their nations, each with its own language.)

The Hamites

6The sons of Ham:
Cush, Mizraim,[f] Put and Canaan.
7The sons of Cush:
Seba, Havilah, Sabtah, Raamah and Sabteca.
The sons of Raamah:
Sheba and Dedan.

8Cush was the father[g] of Nimrod, who grew
to be a mighty warrior on the earth. 9He was a
mighty hunter before the LORD; that is why it is said, "Like Nimrod, a mighty hunter before the
LORD." 10The first centers of his kingdom were
Babylon, Erech, Akkad and Calneh, in[h] Shinar.[i] 11From that land he went to Assyria,
where he built Nineveh, Rehoboth Ir,[j] Calah
12and Resen, which is between Nineveh and Calah; that is the great city.

13Mizraim was the father of
the Ludites, Anamites, Lehabites, Naphtuhites, 14Pathrusites, Casluhites (from
whom the Philistines came) and Caphtorites.
15Canaan was the father of
Sidon his firstborn,[k] and of the Hittites,
16Jebusites, Amorites, Girgashites, 17Hi-
vites, Arkites, Sinites, 18Arvadites, Zemarites and Hamathites.

Later the Canaanite clans scattered 19and the borders of Canaan reached from Sidon toward Gerar as far as Gaza, and then toward Sodom, Gomorrah, Admah and Zeboiim, as far as Lasha.
20These are the sons of Ham by their clans and languages, in their territories and nations.

The Semites

21Sons were also born to Shem, whose older brother was[l] Japheth; Shem was the ancestor of all the sons of Eber.

22The sons of Shem:
Elam, Asshur, Arphaxad, Lud and Aram.
23The sons of Aram:
Uz, Hul, Gether and Meshech.[m]
24Arphaxad was the father of[n] Shelah,
and Shelah the father of Eber.
25Two sons were born to Eber:
One was named Peleg,[o] because in his time the earth was divided; his brother was named Joktan.
26Joktan was the father of
Almodad, Sheleph, Hazarmaveth, Jerah,
27Hadoram, Uzal, Diklah, 28Obal, Abimael, Sheba, 29Ophir, Havilah and Jobab.
All these were sons of Joktan.

30The region where they lived stretched from Mesha toward Sephar, in the eastern hill country.
31These are the sons of Shem by their clans and languages, in their territories and nations.

32These are the clans of Noah's sons, according to their lines of descent, within their nations. From these the nations spread out over the earth after the flood.

The Tower of Babel

11 Now the whole world had one language
and a common speech. 2As men moved
eastward,[p] they found a plain in Shinar[i] and settled there.

3They said to each other, "Come, let's make bricks and bake them thoroughly." They used
brick instead of stone, and tar for mortar. 4Then
they said, "Come, let us build ourselves a city, with a tower that reaches to the heavens, so that we may make a name for ourselves and not be scattered over the face of the whole earth."

[a]26 Or *be his slave* [b]27 *Japheth* sounds like the Hebrew for *extend.* [c]27 Or *their* [d]2 *Sons* may mean *descendants* or *successors* or *nations*; also in verses 3, 4, 6, 7, 20-23, 29 and 31. [e]4 Some manuscripts of the Masoretic Text and Samaritan Pentateuch (see also Septuagint and 1 Chron. 1:7); most manuscripts of the Masoretic Text *Dodanim* [f]6 That is, Egypt; also in verse 13 [g]8 *Father* may mean *ancestor* or *predecessor* or *founder*; also in verses 13, 15, 24 and 26. [h]10 Or *Erech and Akkad—all of them in* [i]10,2 That is, Babylonia [j]11 Or *Nineveh with its city squares* [k]15 Or *of the Sidonians, the foremost* [l]21 Or *Shem, the older brother of* [m]23 See Septuagint and 1 Chron. 1:17; Hebrew *Mash* [n]24 Hebrew; Septuagint *father of Cainan, and Cainan was the father of* [o]25 *Peleg* means *division.* [p]2 Or *from the east*; or *in the east*

5But the LORD came down to see the city and the tower that the men were building. 6The LORD said, "If as one people speaking the same language they have begun to do this, then nothing they plan to do will be impossible for them. 7Come, let us go down and confuse their language so they will not understand each other."

8So the LORD scattered them from there over all the earth, and they stopped building the city. 9That is why it was called Babel[a]—because there the LORD confused the language of the whole world. From there the LORD scattered them over the face of the whole earth.

From Shem to Abram

10This is the account of Shem.

Two years after the flood, when Shem was 100 years old, he became the father[b] of Arphaxad. 11And after he became the father of Arphaxad, Shem lived 500 years and had other sons and daughters.

12When Arphaxad had lived 35 years, he became the father of Shelah. 13And after he became the father of Shelah, Arphaxad lived 403 years and had other sons and daughters.[c]

14When Shelah had lived 30 years, he became the father of Eber. 15And after he became the father of Eber, Shelah lived 403 years and had other sons and daughters.

16When Eber had lived 34 years, he became the father of Peleg. 17And after he became the father of Peleg, Eber lived 430 years and had other sons and daughters.

18When Peleg had lived 30 years, he became the father of Reu. 19And after he became the father of Reu, Peleg lived 209 years and had other sons and daughters.

20When Reu had lived 32 years, he became the father of Serug. 21And after he became the father of Serug, Reu lived 207 years and had other sons and daughters.

22When Serug had lived 30 years, he became the father of Nahor. 23And after he became the father of Nahor, Serug lived 200 years and had other sons and daughters.

24When Nahor had lived 29 years, he became the father of Terah. 25And after he became the father of Terah, Nahor lived 119 years and had other sons and daughters.

26After Terah had lived 70 years, he became the father of Abram, Nahor and Haran.

27This is the account of Terah.

Terah became the father of Abram, Nahor and Haran. And Haran became the father of Lot. 28While his father Terah was still alive, Haran died in Ur of the Chaldeans, in the land of his birth. 29Abram and Nahor both married. The name of Abram's wife was Sarai, and the name of Nahor's wife was Milcah; she was the daughter of Haran, the father of both Milcah and Iscah. 30Now Sarai was barren; she had no children.

31Terah took his son Abram, his grandson Lot son of Haran, and his daughter-in-law Sarai, the wife of his son Abram, and together they set out from Ur of the Chaldeans to go to Canaan. But when they came to Haran, they settled there.

32Terah lived 205 years, and he died in Haran.

The Call of Abram

12 The LORD had said to Abram, "Leave your country, your people and your father's household and go to the land I will show you.

2"I will make you into a great nation
and I will bless you;
I will make your name great,
and you will be a blessing.
3I will bless those who bless you,
and whoever curses you I will curse;
and all peoples on earth
will be blessed through you."

4So Abram left, as the LORD had told him; and

[a] 9 That is, Babylon; *Babel* sounds like the Hebrew for *confused*. [b] 10 *Father* may mean *ancestor*; also in verses 11-25.
[c] 12,13 Hebrew; Septuagint (see also Luke 3:35, 36 and note at Gen. 10:24) *35 years, he became the father of Cainan. 13And after he became the father of Cainan, Arphaxad lived 430 years and had other sons and daughters, and then he died. When Cainan had lived 130 years, he became the father of Shelah. And after he became the father of Shelah, Cainan lived 330 years and had other sons and daughters*

Abram grew up in a place called Ur. Many years before this, the Lord had called Abram to leave Ur and go to a land that God would show him. Abram's father Terah and Abram's nephew Lot left Ur with him. However, the group settled in Haran. Now that Terah has died, Abram sets out again. This time Abram travels to Canaan, where God would later change his name to Abraham ("father of many"). Eventually Abraham would become the "father of Israel"—the founder of the Jewish people.

12:2–3 God's promise to Abram contains both blessing and responsibility. God's original blessing on all humankind (1:28) would be restored and fulfilled through Abram and his offspring.

12:4 ***Abram left, as the LORD had told him.*** Prompt obedience grounded in faith characterized Abram throughout his life. He is presented in the NT as the outstanding example of those who live "by faith" and as the "father of all who believe" (Heb. 11:8–12; Rom. 4:11,16–17; Gal. 3:6–9).

12:5 ***people they had acquired.*** Wealthy people in that ancient world always had servants to help them with their flocks and herds. Not all servants were slaves; many were voluntarily employed.

12:7 ***The LORD appeared.*** God frequently appeared visibly to Abram and to others, but not in all his glory. ***an altar.*** The first of several that Abram built at places where he had memorable spiritual experiences. He acknowledged that the land of Canaan belonged to the Lord in a special way.

Lot went with him. Abram was seventy-five years old when he set out from Haran. 5He took his wife Sarai, his nephew Lot, all the possessions they had accumulated and the people they had acquired in Haran, and they set out for the land of Canaan, and they arrived there.

6Abram traveled through the land as far as the site of the great tree of Moreh at Shechem. At that time the Canaanites were in the land. 7The LORD appeared to Abram and said, "To your offspring[a] I will give this land." So he built an altar there to the LORD, who had appeared to him.

8From there he went on toward the hills east of Bethel and pitched his tent, with Bethel on the west and Ai on the east. There he built an altar to the LORD and called on the name of the LORD. 9Then Abram set out and continued toward the Negev.

Genesis 12:1–9

1. What is the longest trip you have taken with your family in a car? How many times did you have to stop to go to the bathroom?
2. What is the closest you have come to moving to a new country and starting all over again? Was it hard or easy to make new friends? What did you miss the most?
3. Where do you think you'll be living 10 years from now?
4. Is there a promise from God that keeps you going when times are tough?
5. If God called you to be a missionary to a Third World country, what would you say?
6. What is God calling you to do? How can this group pray for you as you strive to answer that call?

(Study notes on page 50)

Abram in Egypt

10Now there was a famine in the land, and Abram went down to Egypt to live there for a while because the famine was severe. 11As he was about to enter Egypt, he said to his wife Sarai, "I know what a beautiful woman you are. 12When the Egyptians see you, they will say, 'This is his wife.' Then they will kill me but will let you live. 13Say you are my sister, so that I will be treated well for your sake and my life will be spared because of you."

14When Abram came to Egypt, the Egyptians saw that she was a very beautiful woman. 15And when Pharaoh's officials saw her, they praised her to Pharaoh, and she was taken into his palace. 16He treated Abram well for her sake, and Abram acquired sheep and cattle, male and female donkeys, menservants and maidservants, and camels.

17But the LORD inflicted serious diseases on Pharaoh and his household because of Abram's wife Sarai. 18So Pharaoh summoned Abram. "What have you done to me?" he said. "Why didn't you tell me she was your wife? 19Why did you say, 'She is my sister,' so that I took her to be my wife? Now then, here is your wife. Take her and go!" 20Then Pharaoh gave orders about Abram to his men, and they sent him on his way, with his wife and everything he had.

Abram and Lot Separate

13 So Abram went up from Egypt to the Negev, with his wife and everything he had, and Lot went with him. 2Abram had become very wealthy in livestock and in silver and gold.

3From the Negev he went from place to place until he came to Bethel, to the place between Bethel and Ai where his tent had been earlier 4and where he had first built an altar. There Abram called on the name of the LORD.

5Now Lot, who was moving about with Abram, also had flocks and herds and tents. 6But the land could not support them while they stayed together, for their possessions were so great that they were not able to stay together. 7And quarreling arose between Abram's herdsmen and the herdsmen of Lot. The Canaanites and Perizzites were also living in the land at that time.

8So Abram said to Lot, "Let's not have any quarreling between you and me, or between your herdsmen and mine, for we are brothers. 9Is not the whole land before you? Let's part company. If you go to the left, I'll go to the right; if you go to the right, I'll go to the left."

10Lot looked up and saw that the whole plain of the Jordan was well watered, like the garden of the LORD, like the land of Egypt, toward Zoar. (This was before the LORD destroyed Sodom and Gomorrah.) 11So Lot chose for himself the whole plain of the Jordan and set out toward the east. The two men parted company: 12Abram lived in the land of Canaan, while Lot lived among the cities of the plain and pitched his tents near Sod-

[a]7 Or *seed*

om. 13Now the men of Sodom were wicked and were sinning greatly against the LORD.

14The LORD said to Abram after Lot had parted from him, "Lift up your eyes from where you are and look north and south, east and west. 15All the land that you see I will give to you and your offspring[a] forever. 16I will make your offspring like the dust of the earth, so that if anyone could count the dust, then your offspring could be counted. 17Go, walk through the length and breadth of the land, for I am giving it to you."

18So Abram moved his tents and went to live near the great trees of Mamre at Hebron, where he built an altar to the LORD.

GENESIS 13:1–18

1. Who is your favorite aunt, uncle, niece or nephew?
2. On a scale of 1 (clenched fists) to 10 (open palms), how were you at sharing your toys when you were a little kid?
3. When was the last time you gave something away that was valuable to you? How did it feel?
4. Do you see Abram as a generous giver or a weak-willed wimp?
5. When you have a disagreement with someone are you more likely to cave in, or go for the jugular? How, if at all, do you need to change?
6. What was the most difficult "good-bye" you ever had to say to someone?
7. If you could ask God to change one thing about your most difficult relationship, what would it be?

Abram Rescues Lot

14 At this time Amraphel king of Shinar,[b] Arioch king of Ellasar, Kedorlaomer king of Elam and Tidal king of Goiim 2went to war against Bera king of Sodom, Birsha king of Gomorrah, Shinab king of Admah, Shemeber king of Zeboiim, and the king of Bela (that is, Zoar). 3All these latter kings joined forces in the Valley of Siddim (the Salt Sea[c]). 4For twelve years they had been subject to Kedorlaomer, but in the thirteenth year they rebelled.

5In the fourteenth year, Kedorlaomer and the kings allied with him went out and defeated the Rephaites in Ashteroth Karnaim, the Zuzites in Ham, the Emites in Shaveh Kiriathaim 6and the Horites in the hill country of Seir, as far as El Paran near the desert. 7Then they turned back and went to En Mishpat (that is, Kadesh), and they conquered the whole territory of the Amalekites, as well as the Amorites who were living in Hazazon Tamar.

8Then the king of Sodom, the king of Gomorrah, the king of Admah, the king of Zeboiim and the king of Bela (that is, Zoar) marched out and drew up their battle lines in the Valley of Siddim 9against Kedorlaomer king of Elam, Tidal king of Goiim, Amraphel king of Shinar and Arioch king of Ellasar—four kings against five. 10Now the Valley of Siddim was full of tar pits, and when the kings of Sodom and Gomorrah fled, some of the men fell into them and the rest fled to the hills. 11The four kings seized all the goods of Sodom and Gomorrah and all their food; then they went away. 12They also carried off Abram's nephew Lot and his possessions, since he was living in Sodom.

13One who had escaped came and reported this to Abram the Hebrew. Now Abram was living near the great trees of Mamre the Amorite, a brother[d] of Eshcol and Aner, all of whom were allied with Abram. 14When Abram heard that his relative had been taken captive, he called out the 318 trained men born in his household and went

[a] *15* Or *seed*; also in verse 16 [b] *1* That is, Babylonia; also in verse 9 [c] *3* That is, the Dead Sea [d] *13* Or *a relative*; or *an ally*

God called Abram to Canaan, where he promised to make him the founder of a great nation. After a short stay, famine drove Abram, his wife Sarai, and his nephew Lot to Egypt. Now they return to the "promised land."

13:6 ***the land could not support them.*** Livestock made up the greater part of Abram and Lot's possessions, and the region around Bethel and Ai did not have enough water or pasture for such large flocks and herds.

13:8–9 ***brothers.*** Relatives (as often in the Bible). Abram, always generous, gave his young nephew the opportunity to choose the land he wanted. He himself would not obtain wealth except by the Lord's blessing.

13:10 ***This was before the LORD destroyed Sodom and Gomorrah.*** Archaeology has confirmed that, prior to the great catastrophe recorded in Genesis 19, this now dry area east and southeast of the Dead Sea had ample water and was well populated.

13:12 ***Lot ... pitched his tents near Sodom.*** Since the men of Sodom were known to be wicked (see v. 13), Lot was flirting with temptation by choosing to live near them. Compare the actions of Abram in verse 18—moving elsewhere and worshiping the Lord.

13:14 ***Lift up your eyes ... and look.*** Lot and Abram are a study in contrasts. The former looked selfishly and coveted (v. 10); the latter looked as God commanded and was blessed.

in pursuit as far as Dan. 15During the night
Abram divided his men to attack them and he
routed them, pursuing them as far as Hobah,
north of Damascus. 16He recovered all the goods
and brought back his relative Lot and his possessions, together with the women and the other
people.

17After Abram returned from defeating Kedor-
laomer and the kings allied with him, the king of
Sodom came out to meet him in the Valley of
Shaveh (that is, the King's Valley).

18Then Melchizedek king of Salem[a] brought
out bread and wine. He was priest of God Most
High, 19and he blessed Abram, saying,

"Blessed be Abram by God Most High,
  Creator[b] of heaven and earth.
20And blessed be[c] God Most High,
  who delivered your enemies into your
    hand."

Then Abram gave him a tenth of everything.

21The king of Sodom said to Abram, "Give me
the people and keep the goods for yourself."

22But Abram said to the king of Sodom, "I have
raised my hand to the LORD, God Most High,
Creator of heaven and earth, and have taken an
oath 23that I will accept nothing belonging to you,
not even a thread or the thong of a sandal, so that
you will never be able to say, 'I made Abram
rich.' 24I will accept nothing but what my men
have eaten and the share that belongs to the men
who went with me—to Aner, Eshcol and Mamre. Let them have their share."

God's Covenant With Abram

15 After this, the word of the LORD came to
Abram in a vision:

"Do not be afraid, Abram.
  I am your shield,[d]
  your very great reward.[e]"

2But Abram said, "O Sovereign LORD, what
can you give me since I remain childless and the
one who will inherit[f] my estate is Eliezer of
Damascus?" 3And Abram said, "You have given
me no children; so a servant in my household
will be my heir."

4Then the word of the LORD came to him:
"This man will not be your heir, but a son coming
from your own body will be your heir." 5He took
him outside and said, "Look up at the heavens
and count the stars—if indeed you can count
them." Then he said to him, "So shall your offspring be."

6Abram believed the LORD, and he credited it
to him as righteousness.

7He also said to him, "I am the LORD, who
brought you out of Ur of the Chaldeans to give
you this land to take possession of it."

8But Abram said, "O Sovereign LORD, how can
I know that I will gain possession of it?"

9So the LORD said to him, "Bring me a heifer,
a goat and a ram, each three years old, along with
a dove and a young pigeon."

10Abram brought all these to him, cut them in
two and arranged the halves opposite each other;
the birds, however, he did not cut in half. 11Then
birds of prey came down on the carcasses, but
Abram drove them away.

12As the sun was setting, Abram fell into a
deep sleep, and a thick and dreadful darkness
came over him. 13Then the LORD said to him,
"Know for certain that your descendants will be
strangers in a country not their own, and they
will be enslaved and mistreated four hundred
years. 14But I will punish the nation they serve as
slaves, and afterward they will come out with
great possessions. 15You, however, will go to
your fathers in peace and be buried at a good old
age. 16In the fourth generation your descendants
will come back here, for the sin of the Amorites
has not yet reached its full measure."

17When the sun had set and darkness had fall-
en, a smoking firepot with a blazing torch appeared and passed between the pieces. 18On that
day the LORD made a covenant with Abram and
said, "To your descendants I give this land, from
the river[g] of Egypt to the great river, the
Euphrates— 19the land of the Kenites, Keniz-
zites, Kadmonites, 20Hittites, Perizzites, Rephaites, 21Amorites, Canaanites, Girgashites and
Jebusites."

Hagar and Ishmael

16 Now Sarai, Abram's wife, had borne him
no children. But she had an Egyptian
maidservant named Hagar; 2so she said to Abram,
"The LORD has kept me from having children.
Go, sleep with my maidservant; perhaps I can
build a family through her."

Abram agreed to what Sarai said. 3So after
Abram had been living in Canaan ten years, Sarai
his wife took her Egyptian maidservant Hagar and
gave her to her husband to be his wife. 4He slept
with Hagar, and she conceived.

When she knew she was pregnant, she began
to despise her mistress. 5Then Sarai said to
Abram, "You are responsible for the wrong I am
suffering. I put my servant in your arms, and now
that she knows she is pregnant, she despises me.
May the LORD judge between you and me."

6"Your servant is in your hands," Abram said.

[a] 18 That is, Jerusalem [b] 19 Or *Possessor*; also in verse 22 [c] 20 Or *And praise be to* [d] 1 Or *sovereign*
[e] 1 Or *shield; / your reward will be very great* [f] 2 The meaning of the Hebrew for this phrase is uncertain. [g] 18 Or *Wadi*

"Do with her whatever you think best." Then
Sarai mistreated Hagar; so she fled from her.
7The angel of the LORD found Hagar near a
spring in the desert; it was the spring that is
beside the road to Shur. 8And he said, "Hagar,
servant of Sarai, where have you come from, and
where are you going?"
"I'm running away from my mistress Sarai,"
she answered.
9Then the angel of the LORD told her, "Go back
to your mistress and submit to her." 10The angel
added, "I will so increase your descendants that
they will be too numerous to count."
11The angel of the LORD also said to her:

"You are now with child
    and you will have a son.
You shall name him Ishmael,[a]
    for the LORD has heard of your misery.
12He will be a wild donkey of a man;
    his hand will be against everyone
    and everyone's hand against him,
and he will live in hostility
    toward[b] all his brothers."

13She gave this name to the LORD who spoke
to her: "You are the God who sees me," for she
said, "I have now seen[c] the One who sees me."
14That is why the well was called Beer Lahai
Roi[d]; it is still there, between Kadesh and Bered.
15So Hagar bore Abram a son, and Abram gave
the name Ishmael to the son she had borne.
16Abram was eighty-six years old when Hagar
bore him Ishmael.

The Covenant of Circumcision

17 When Abram was ninety-nine years old,
the LORD appeared to him and said, "I am
God Almighty[e]; walk before me and be blameless. 2I will confirm my covenant between me
and you and will greatly increase your numbers."
3Abram fell facedown, and God said to him,
4"As for me, this is my covenant with you: You
will be the father of many nations. 5No longer
will you be called Abram[f]; your name will be
Abraham,[g] for I have made you a father of many
nations. 6I will make you very fruitful; I will make
nations of you, and kings will come from you. 7I
will establish my covenant as an everlasting covenant between me and you and your descendants
after you for the generations to come, to be your
God and the God of your descendants after you.
8The whole land of Canaan, where you are now
an alien, I will give as an everlasting possession
to you and your descendants after you; and I will
be their God."
9Then God said to Abraham, "As for you, you
must keep my covenant, you and your descendants after you for the generations to come.
10This is my covenant with you and your descendants after you, the covenant you are to keep:
Every male among you shall be circumcised.
11You are to undergo circumcision, and it will be
the sign of the covenant between me and you.
12For the generations to come every male among
you who is eight days old must be circumcised,
including those born in your household or bought
with money from a foreigner—those who are not
your offspring. 13Whether born in your household or bought with your money, they must be
circumcised. My covenant in your flesh is to be
an everlasting covenant. 14Any uncircumcised
male, who has not been circumcised in the flesh,
will be cut off from his people; he has broken my
covenant."
15God also said to Abraham, "As for Sarai your
wife, you are no longer to call her Sarai; her name
will be Sarah. 16I will bless her and will surely
give you a son by her. I will bless her so that she
will be the mother of nations; kings of peoples
will come from her."
17Abraham fell facedown; he laughed and said
to himself, "Will a son be born to a man a hundred years old? Will Sarah bear a child at the age
of ninety?" 18And Abraham said to God, "If only
Ishmael might live under your blessing!"
19Then God said, "Yes, but your wife Sarah
will bear you a son, and you will call him Isaac.[h]
I will establish my covenant with him as an everlasting covenant for his descendants after him.
20And as for Ishmael, I have heard you: I will
surely bless him; I will make him fruitful and will
greatly increase his numbers. He will be the father of twelve rulers, and I will make him into a
great nation. 21But my covenant I will establish
with Isaac, whom Sarah will bear to you by this
time next year." 22When he had finished speaking with Abraham, God went up from him.
23On that very day Abraham took his son Ishmael and all those born in his household or
bought with his money, every male in his household, and circumcised them, as God told him.
24Abraham was ninety-nine years old when he
was circumcised, 25and his son Ishmael was thirteen; 26Abraham and his son Ishmael were both
circumcised on that same day. 27And every male
in Abraham's household, including those born in

[a] *11 Ishmael* means *God hears.* [b] *12* Or *live to the east / of* [c] *13* Or *seen the back of* [d] *14 Beer Lahai Roi* means *well of the Living One who sees me.* [e] *1* Hebrew *El-Shaddai* [f] *5 Abram* means *exalted father.* [g] *5 Abraham* means *father of many.* [h] *19 Isaac* means *he laughs.*

his household or bought from a foreigner, was
circumcised with him.

The Three Visitors

18 The LORD appeared to Abraham near the
great trees of Mamre while he was sitting
at the entrance to his tent in the heat of the day.
2Abraham looked up and saw three men standing
nearby. When he saw them, he hurried from the
entrance of his tent to meet them and bowed low
to the ground.
3He said, "If I have found favor in your eyes,
my lord,[a] do not pass your servant by. 4Let a
little water be brought, and then you may all
wash your feet and rest under this tree. 5Let me
get you something to eat, so you can be refreshed
and then go on your way—now that you have
come to your servant."
"Very well," they answered, "do as you say."
6So Abraham hurried into the tent to Sarah.
"Quick," he said, "get three seahs[b] of fine flour
and knead it and bake some bread."
7Then he ran to the herd and selected a
choice, tender calf and gave it to a servant, who
hurried to prepare it. 8He then brought some
curds and milk and the calf that had been prepared, and set these before them. While they ate,
he stood near them under a tree.
9"Where is your wife Sarah?" they asked him.
"There, in the tent," he said.
10Then the LORD[c] said, "I will surely return
to you about this time next year, and Sarah your
wife will have a son."
Now Sarah was listening at the entrance to the
tent, which was behind him. 11Abraham and Sarah were already old and well advanced in years,
and Sarah was past the age of childbearing. 12So
Sarah laughed to herself as she thought, "After I
am worn out and my master[d] is old, will I now
have this pleasure?"
13Then the LORD said to Abraham, "Why did
Sarah laugh and say, 'Will I really have a child,
now that I am old?' 14Is anything too hard for the
LORD? I will return to you at the appointed time
next year and Sarah will have a son."
15Sarah was afraid, so she lied and said, "I did
not laugh."
But he said, "Yes, you did laugh."

Abraham Pleads for Sodom

16When the men got up to leave, they looked
down toward Sodom, and Abraham walked along
with them to see them on their way. 17Then the

GENESIS 18:16–33

1. Who is the most patient person in your family? The least patient?
2. When you want something from your parents, how do you try to persuade them?
3. How do you think a stranger would view the conversation between God and Abraham? Explain.
4. Which of Abraham's qualities would you most like to have: His boldness? Goodness? Compassion? Prayer power?
5. When was the last time you bargained with God to get something you wanted or to get something for someone else?
6. When you pray, what do you expect God to do: Listen carefully? Grant your requests? Talk back? Ignore you? Or what?
7. What is the most pressing or important prayer request you can think of? Close your group meeting by praying for those requests together.

[a]3 Or *O Lord* [b]6 That is, probably about 20 quarts (about 22 liters) [c]10 Hebrew *Then he* [d]12 Or *husband*

18:16 ***the men.*** Abraham and his wife Sarah had just been visited by three "men." At least two of the visitors were angels (see 19:1). The third may have been the Lord himself (see vv. 1,22).

18:17 Because Abraham was the Lord's covenant friend, God convened his heavenly council at Abraham's tent. God gave Abraham opportunity to speak in his court and to intercede for the righteous in Sodom and Gomorrah. This illustrates the privilege of prayer God gives his covenant people.

18:21 ***I will go down.*** Not a denial of God's infinite knowledge but a figurative way of stating that he does not act out of ignorance or on the basis of mere complaints.

18:23 This was the second time Abraham intervened for Sodom and his nephew Lot who lived there (see 14:14–16).

18:25 ***Judge of all the earth.*** Abraham based his plea on the justice and authority (see NIV text note on "Judge") of God, confident that God would do what was right.

18:27 ***dust and ashes.*** In contrast to God, Abraham described himself as insignificant.

18:32 ***just once more.*** Abraham's questioning in verses 23–32 did not arise from a spirit of haggling but of compassion for his relatives and of wanting to know God's ways. ***ten.*** Perhaps Abraham stopped at 10 because he had been counting while praying: Lot, his wife, possibly two sons (see 19:12), at least two married daughters and their husbands (see 19:14), and two unmarried daughters (see 19:8).

LORD said, "Shall I hide from Abraham what I am
about to do? 18Abraham will surely become a
great and powerful nation, and all nations on
earth will be blessed through him. 19For I have
chosen him, so that he will direct his children
and his household after him to keep the way of
the LORD by doing what is right and just, so that
the LORD will bring about for Abraham what he
has promised him."
20Then the LORD said, "The outcry against Sodom and Gomorrah is so great and their sin so
grievous 21that I will go down and see if what
they have done is as bad as the outcry that has
reached me. If not, I will know."
22The men turned away and went toward Sodom, but Abraham remained standing before the
LORD.[a] 23Then Abraham approached him and
said: "Will you sweep away the righteous with
the wicked? 24What if there are fifty righteous
people in the city? Will you really sweep it away
and not spare[b] the place for the sake of the fifty
righteous people in it? 25Far be it from you to do
such a thing—to kill the righteous with the wicked, treating the righteous and the wicked alike.
Far be it from you! Will not the Judge[c] of all the
earth do right?"
26The LORD said, "If I find fifty righteous people in the city of Sodom, I will spare the whole
place for their sake."
27Then Abraham spoke up again: "Now that I
have been so bold as to speak to the Lord, though
I am nothing but dust and ashes, 28what if the
number of the righteous is five less than fifty?
Will you destroy the whole city because of five
people?"
"If I find forty-five there," he said, "I will not
destroy it."
29Once again he spoke to him, "What if only
forty are found there?"
He said, "For the sake of forty, I will not do it."
30Then he said, "May the Lord not be angry,
but let me speak. What if only thirty can be found
there?"
He answered, "I will not do it if I find thirty
there."
31Abraham said, "Now that I have been so
bold as to speak to the Lord, what if only twenty
can be found there?"
He said, "For the sake of twenty, I will not
destroy it."
32Then he said, "May the Lord not be angry,
but let me speak just once more. What if only ten
can be found there?"
He answered, "For the sake of ten, I will not
destroy it."
33When the LORD had finished speaking with
Abraham, he left, and Abraham returned home.

Sodom and Gomorrah Destroyed

19 The two angels arrived at Sodom in the
evening, and Lot was sitting in the gateway of the city. When he saw them, he got up to
meet them and bowed down with his face to the
ground. 2"My lords," he said, "please turn aside
to your servant's house. You can wash your feet
and spend the night and then go on your way
early in the morning."
"No," they answered, "we will spend the
night in the square."
3But he insisted so strongly that they did go
with him and entered his house. He prepared a
meal for them, baking bread without yeast, and
they ate. 4Before they had gone to bed, all the
men from every part of the city of Sodom—both
young and old—surrounded the house. 5They
called to Lot, "Where are the men who came to
you tonight? Bring them out to us so that we can
have sex with them."
6Lot went outside to meet them and shut the
door behind him 7and said, "No, my friends.
Don't do this wicked thing. 8Look, I have two
daughters who have never slept with a man. Let
me bring them out to you, and you can do what
you like with them. But don't do anything to
these men, for they have come under the protection of my roof."
9"Get out of our way," they replied. And they
said, "This fellow came here as an alien, and now
he wants to play the judge! We'll treat you worse
than them." They kept bringing pressure on Lot
and moved forward to break down the door.
10But the men inside reached out and pulled
Lot back into the house and shut the door.
11Then they struck the men who were at the
door of the house, young and old, with blindness
so that they could not find the door.
12The two men said to Lot, "Do you have anyone else here—sons-in-law, sons or daughters,
or anyone else in the city who belongs to you?
Get them out of here, 13because we are going to
destroy this place. The outcry to the LORD against
its people is so great that he has sent us to destroy it."
14So Lot went out and spoke to his sons-in-
law, who were pledged to marry[d] his daughters.
He said, "Hurry and get out of this place, because
the LORD is about to destroy the city!" But his
sons-in-law thought he was joking.
15With the coming of dawn, the angels urged
Lot, saying, "Hurry! Take your wife and your two
daughters who are here, or you will be swept
away when the city is punished."

[a]22 Masoretic Text; an ancient Hebrew scribal tradition *but the LORD remained standing before Abraham* [b]24 Or *forgive*; also in verse 26 [c]25 Or *Ruler* [d]14 Or *were married to*

16When he hesitated, the men grasped his
hand and the hands of his wife and of his two
daughters and led them safely out of the city, for
the LORD was merciful to them. 17As soon as they
had brought them out, one of them said, "Flee for
your lives! Don't look back, and don't stop anywhere in the plain! Flee to the mountains or you
will be swept away!"
18But Lot said to them, "No, my lords,[a]
please! 19Your[b] servant has found favor in
your[b] eyes, and you[b] have shown great kindness to me in sparing my life. But I can't flee to
the mountains; this disaster will overtake me,
and I'll die. 20Look, here is a town near enough
to run to, and it is small. Let me flee to it—it is
very small, isn't it? Then my life will be spared."
21He said to him, "Very well, I will grant this

> ***GENESIS 19:1–29***
>
> 1. What's the closest you've come to rescuing someone or being rescued?
> 2. If this passage were made into a movie, would it be a hit? Would you go see it?
> 3. How would you compare the sexual standards in your school to Sodom?
> 4. Do you think Lot's morals had changed by living in Sodom? In what ways?
> 5. How do you react or treat people who have values that are different from yours?
> 6. What is the moral of this story?
> 7. When it comes to getting out of situations that are dangerous, what have you found helpful?

request too; I will not overthrow the town you
speak of. 22But flee there quickly, because I cannot do anything until you reach it." (That is why
the town was called Zoar.[c])
23By the time Lot reached Zoar, the sun had
risen over the land. 24Then the LORD rained
down burning sulfur on Sodom and Gomorrah—
from the LORD out of the heavens. 25Thus he
overthrew those cities and the entire plain, including all those living in the cities—and also the
vegetation in the land. 26But Lot's wife looked
back, and she became a pillar of salt.
27Early the next morning Abraham got up and
returned to the place where he had stood before
the LORD. 28He looked down toward Sodom and
Gomorrah, toward all the land of the plain, and
he saw dense smoke rising from the land, like
smoke from a furnace.
29So when God destroyed the cities of the
plain, he remembered Abraham, and he brought
Lot out of the catastrophe that overthrew the cities where Lot had lived.

Lot and His Daughters

30Lot and his two daughters left Zoar and settled in the mountains, for he was afraid to stay in
Zoar. He and his two daughters lived in a cave.
31One day the older daughter said to the younger,
"Our father is old, and there is no man around
here to lie with us, as is the custom all over the
earth. 32Let's get our father to drink wine and
then lie with him and preserve our family line
through our father."
33That night they got their father to drink
wine, and the older daughter went in and lay
with him. He was not aware of it when she lay
down or when she got up.
34The next day the older daughter said to the
younger, "Last night I lay with my father. Let's
get him to drink wine again tonight, and you go
in and lie with him so we can preserve our family
line through our father." 35So they got their father to drink wine that night also, and the younger daughter went and lay with him. Again he

[a]18 Or *No, Lord*; or *No, my lord*   [b]19 The Hebrew is singular.   [c]22 *Zoar* means *small.*

19:1 God had just revealed to Abraham that he will destroy the city of Sodom (where Abraham's nephew Lot lived) unless he finds at least 10 righteous people there. ***two angels.*** Called "men" in 18:2. ***Lot was sitting in the gateway.*** Lot had probably become a member of Sodom's ruling council, since a city gateway served as the city's administrative and judicial center where legal matters were discussed and prosecuted.

19:5 ***have sex with them.*** Homosexuality was so characteristic of the men of Sodom (see Jude 7) that it is still often called sodomy. Both the OT (Lev. 18:22) and NT (Rom. 1:26–27) condemn the practice of homosexuality, though some see the real wickedness in this story as rape.

19:16 ***hesitated.*** Perhaps Lot hesitated because of his reluctance to leave his material possessions. ***his hand and the hands of his wife and of his two daughters.*** The 10 righteous people required to save Sodom (see 18:32) had now been reduced to four. ***the LORD was merciful to them.*** Deliverance is due to divine mercy, not to human righteousness (see Titus 3:3–5).

19:24 ***rained down burning sulfur.*** Perhaps from a violent earthquake spewing up asphalt, such as is still found in this region.

19:26 ***Lot's wife looked back, and she became a pillar of salt.*** Her disobedient hesitation (see v. 17) became proverbial in later generations (see Luke 17:32). Even today, grotesque salt formations near the Dead Sea are reminders of her folly.

was not aware of it when she lay down or when
she got up.
36So both of Lot's daughters became pregnant
by their father. 37The older daughter had a son,
and she named him Moab[a]; he is the father of
the Moabites of today. 38The younger daughter
also had a son, and she named him Ben-Ammi[b];
he is the father of the Ammonites of today.

Abraham and Abimelech

20 Now Abraham moved on from there into
the region of the Negev and lived between Kadesh and Shur. For a while he stayed in
Gerar, 2and there Abraham said of his wife Sarah,
"She is my sister." Then Abimelech king of Gerar
sent for Sarah and took her.
3But God came to Abimelech in a dream one
night and said to him, "You are as good as dead
because of the woman you have taken; she is a
married woman."
4Now Abimelech had not gone near her, so he
said, "Lord, will you destroy an innocent nation?
5Did he not say to me, 'She is my sister,' and didn't
she also say, 'He is my brother'? I have done this
with a clear conscience and clean hands."
6Then God said to him in the dream, "Yes, I
know you did this with a clear conscience, and so
I have kept you from sinning against me. That is
why I did not let you touch her. 7Now return the
man's wife, for he is a prophet, and he will pray
for you and you will live. But if you do not return
her, you may be sure that you and all yours will
die."
8Early the next morning Abimelech summoned all his officials, and when he told them all
that had happened, they were very much afraid.
9Then Abimelech called Abraham in and said,
"What have you done to us? How have I wronged
you that you have brought such great guilt upon
me and my kingdom? You have done things to
me that should not be done." 10And Abimelech
asked Abraham, "What was your reason for doing
this?"
11Abraham replied, "I said to myself, 'There is
surely no fear of God in this place, and they will
kill me because of my wife.' 12Besides, she really
is my sister, the daughter of my father though not
of my mother; and she became my wife. 13And
when God had me wander from my father's
household, I said to her, 'This is how you can
show your love to me: Everywhere we go, say of
me, "He is my brother." ' "
14Then Abimelech brought sheep and cattle
and male and female slaves and gave them to
Abraham, and he returned Sarah his wife to him.
15And Abimelech said, "My land is before you;
live wherever you like."
16To Sarah he said, "I am giving your brother
a thousand shekels[c] of silver. This is to cover
the offense against you before all who are with
you; you are completely vindicated."
17Then Abraham prayed to God, and God
healed Abimelech, his wife and his slave girls so
they could have children again, 18for the LORD
had closed up every womb in Abimelech's household because of Abraham's wife Sarah.

The Birth of Isaac

21 Now the LORD was gracious to Sarah as he
had said, and the LORD did for Sarah what
he had promised. 2Sarah became pregnant and
bore a son to Abraham in his old age, at the very
time God had promised him. 3Abraham gave the
name Isaac[d] to the son Sarah bore him. 4When
his son Isaac was eight days old, Abraham circumcised him, as God commanded him. 5Abra-
ham was a hundred years old when his son Isaac
was born to him.
6Sarah said, "God has brought me laughter,
and everyone who hears about this will laugh
with me." 7And she added, "Who would have
said to Abraham that Sarah would nurse children? Yet I have borne him a son in his old age."

Hagar and Ishmael Sent Away

8The child grew and was weaned, and on the
day Isaac was weaned Abraham held a great feast.
9But Sarah saw that the son whom Hagar the
Egyptian had borne to Abraham was mocking,
10and she said to Abraham, "Get rid of that slave
woman and her son, for that slave woman's son
will never share in the inheritance with my son
Isaac."
11The matter distressed Abraham greatly because it concerned his son. 12But God said to
him, "Do not be so distressed about the boy and
your maidservant. Listen to whatever Sarah tells
you, because it is through Isaac that your offspring[e] will be reckoned. 13I will make the son
of the maidservant into a nation also, because he
is your offspring."
14Early the next morning Abraham took some
food and a skin of water and gave them to Hagar.
He set them on her shoulders and then sent her
off with the boy. She went on her way and wandered in the desert of Beersheba.
15When the water in the skin was gone, she
put the boy under one of the bushes. 16Then she
went off and sat down nearby, about a bowshot
away, for she thought, "I cannot watch the boy
die." And as she sat there nearby, she[f] began to
sob.

[a]37 *Moab* sounds like the Hebrew for *from father.* [b]38 *Ben-Ammi* means *son of my people.* [c]16 That is, about 25 pounds (about 11.5 kilograms) [d]3 *Isaac* means *he laughs.* [e]12 Or *seed* [f]16 Hebrew; Septuagint *the child*

17God heard the boy crying, and the angel of
God called to Hagar from heaven and said to her,
"What is the matter, Hagar? Do not be afraid;
God has heard the boy crying as he lies there.
18Lift the boy up and take him by the hand, for I
will make him into a great nation."
19Then God opened her eyes and she saw a
well of water. So she went and filled the skin
with water and gave the boy a drink.
20God was with the boy as he grew up. He
lived in the desert and became an archer.
21While he was living in the Desert of Paran, his
mother got a wife for him from Egypt.

GENESIS 21:1–21

1. When has a new member—a little brother, sister, stepparent, stepbrother or stepsister joined your family? How did you react?
2. What do you think is the ideal family size? How many brothers and sisters would you like to have? Would you rather be the oldest, youngest or in the middle?
3. Do you ever feel as though your parents or stepparents play favorites? How does it make you feel?
4. When have you been jealous of a friend or someone in your family? How did it affect your relationship with that person?
5. What advice would you give a friend who had a stepparent like Sarah?
6. What is the closest you have come to feeling like Ishmael—rejected or abandoned?
7. In your own family right now, what is one relationship that you would like your group to pray for?

The Treaty at Beersheba

22At that time Abimelech and Phicol the commander of his forces said to Abraham, "God is
with you in everything you do. 23Now swear to
me here before God that you will not deal falsely
with me or my children or my descendants. Show
to me and the country where you are living as
an alien the same kindness I have shown to
you."
24Abraham said, "I swear it."
25Then Abraham complained to Abimelech
about a well of water that Abimelech's servants
had seized. 26But Abimelech said, "I don't know
who has done this. You did not tell me, and I
heard about it only today."
27So Abraham brought sheep and cattle and
gave them to Abimelech, and the two men made
a treaty. 28Abraham set apart seven ewe lambs
from the flock, 29and Abimelech asked Abraham,
"What is the meaning of these seven ewe lambs
you have set apart by themselves?"
30He replied, "Accept these seven lambs from
my hand as a witness that I dug this well."
31So that place was called Beersheba,[a] because the two men swore an oath there.
32After the treaty had been made at Beersheba, Abimelech and Phicol the commander of his
forces returned to the land of the Philistines.
33Abraham planted a tamarisk tree in Beersheba,
and there he called upon the name of the LORD,
the Eternal God. 34And Abraham stayed in the
land of the Philistines for a long time.

Abraham Tested

22 Some time later God tested Abraham. He
said to him, "Abraham!"
"Here I am," he replied.
2Then God said, "Take your son, your only
son, Isaac, whom you love, and go to the region
of Moriah. Sacrifice him there as a burnt offering
on one of the mountains I will tell you about."
3Early the next morning Abraham got up and
saddled his donkey. He took with him two of his
servants and his son Isaac. When he had cut
enough wood for the burnt offering, he set out for

a31 *Beersheba* can mean *well of seven* or *well of the oath.*

As promised (see 18:10), the Lord gave Abraham and his wife Sarah a son—though they were past the age of childbearing.

21:9 *the son whom Hagar the Egyptian had borne to Abraham.* Ishmael, who was 14 years old when Isaac was born (16:16, 21:5). As recorded in Genesis 16, Abraham and Sarah had practiced a common custom of their time: Since Sarah was childless, she gave Abraham her maidservant to bear a child in order to continue the family line. ***mocking.*** What was probably Ishmael's typical older-brother behavior toward Isaac was more than Sarah could bear.

21:10 *Get rid of that slave woman and her son.* By doing so, Ishmael would be cut off from the double-portion of the inheritance that normally went to the oldest son.

21:11 *The matter distressed Abraham greatly.* Both love and legal custom played a part in Abraham's anguish. He knew that the customs of his day prohibited the arbitrary expulsion of a servant's son.

21:12–13 While not commending Sarah's action, God assures Abraham that Isaac is indeed the son through whom the promise will be kept. (See Rom. 9:6–8 for spiritual applications of this.) Nevertheless, Ishmael will also father a great nation. Modern day Arabs claim Ishmael as their ancestor.

21:17 *God heard the boy crying.* The name Ishmael means "God hears." Given originally as a sign that God had heard Abraham's plea for a son, it now indicates a special relationship God had with this boy.

the place God had told him about. 4On the third day Abraham looked up and saw the place in the distance. 5He said to his servants, "Stay here with the donkey while I and the boy go over there. We will worship and then we will come back to you."

6Abraham took the wood for the burnt offering and placed it on his son Isaac, and he himself carried the fire and the knife. As the two of them went on together, 7Isaac spoke up and said to his father Abraham, "Father?"

"Yes, my son?" Abraham replied.

"The fire and wood are here," Isaac said, "but where is the lamb for the burnt offering?"

8Abraham answered, "God himself will provide the lamb for the burnt offering, my son." And the two of them went on together.

9When they reached the place God had told him about, Abraham built an altar there and arranged the wood on it. He bound his son Isaac and laid him on the altar, on top of the wood. 10Then he reached out his hand and took the knife to slay his son. 11But the angel of the LORD called out to him from heaven, "Abraham! Abraham!"

"Here I am," he replied.

12"Do not lay a hand on the boy," he said. "Do not do anything to him. Now I know that you fear God, because you have not withheld from me your son, your only son."

13Abraham looked up and there in a thicket he saw a ram[a] caught by its horns. He went over and took the ram and sacrificed it as a burnt offering instead of his son. 14So Abraham called that place The LORD Will Provide. And to this day it is said, "On the mountain of the LORD it will be provided."

15The angel of the LORD called to Abraham from heaven a second time 16and said, "I swear by myself, declares the LORD, that because you have done this and have not withheld your son, your only son, 17I will surely bless you and make your descendants as numerous as the stars in the sky and as the sand on the seashore. Your descendants will take possession of the cities of their enemies, 18and through your offspring[b] all nations on earth will be blessed, because you have obeyed me."

19Then Abraham returned to his servants, and they set off together for Beersheba. And Abraham stayed in Beersheba.

Nahor's Sons

20Some time later Abraham was told, "Milcah is also a mother; she has borne sons to your brother Nahor: 21Uz the firstborn, Buz his brother, Kemuel (the father of Aram), 22Kesed, Hazo, Pildash, Jidlaph and Bethuel." 23Bethuel became the father of Rebekah. Milcah bore these eight sons to Abraham's brother Nahor. 24His concubine, whose name was Reumah, also had sons: Tebah, Gaham, Tahash and Maacah.

GENESIS 22:1–19

1. What is a tough test you've taken lately?
2. What possession would be the hardest for you to give up?
3. What would you do if God asked you to give up a relationship that you really wanted?
4. How does this story remind you of the Gospel of Jesus Christ? (Hint: See last two notes on vv. 8-9 and 13.)
5. How do you sense God is testing or challenging you now? What grade would you give yourself on that test?
6. What area of your life do you need to commit totally to the Lord right now in prayer?

[a] *13* Many manuscripts of the Masoretic Text, Samaritan Pentateuch, Septuagint and Syriac; most manuscripts of the Masoretic Text *a ram behind ⌞him⌟* [b] *18* Or *seed*

22:1 ***tested.*** Not "tempted," for God does not tempt (James 1:13). Satan tempts us in order to make us fall (1 Thess. 3:5), while God tests us to strengthen us (James 1:3).

22:2 ***your only son, Isaac.*** Ishmael was also Abraham's son, but Isaac was the only son of the promise (21:12). ***Moriah.*** Later identified as the temple mount in Jerusalem (2 Chron. 3:1). ***Sacrifice him.*** Abraham had committed himself by covenant to be obedient to the Lord and had consecrated his son Isaac to God by circumcision. The Lord put his servant's faith and loyalty to the supreme test, thereby instructing Abraham, Isaac and their descendants as to the kind of dedication God requires.

22:3 ***Early the next morning.*** Prompt obedience to God, even under such trying circumstances, characterized Abraham's life.

22:5 ***we will come back.*** By faith, Abraham "reasoned that God could raise the dead" (Heb. 11:17–19) if that were necessary to fulfill his promise.

22:8–9 ***God himself will provide the lamb.*** The immediate fulfillment of Abraham's trusting response was the ram of verse 13, but its ultimate fulfillment is the Lamb of God (John 1:29,36). ***bound his son Isaac and laid him on the altar, on top of the wood.*** Isaac is here a type, or prefiguring symbol, of Christ.

22:13 ***instead of.*** Substitutionary sacrifice of one life for another is here mentioned for the first time in Scripture. As the ram died in Isaac's place, so also Jesus gave his life as a ransom for many (Mark 10:45).

The Death of Sarah

23 Sarah lived to be a hundred and twenty-
seven years old. 2She died at Kiriath Arba
(that is, Hebron) in the land of Canaan, and Abraham went to mourn for Sarah and to weep over
her.
3Then Abraham rose from beside his dead wife
and spoke to the Hittites.[a] He said, 4"I am an
alien and a stranger among you. Sell me some
property for a burial site here so I can bury my
dead."
5The Hittites replied to Abraham, 6"Sir, listen
to us. You are a mighty prince among us. Bury
your dead in the choicest of our tombs. None
of us will refuse you his tomb for burying your
dead."
7Then Abraham rose and bowed down before
the people of the land, the Hittites. 8He said to
them, "If you are willing to let me bury my dead,
then listen to me and intercede with Ephron son
of Zohar on my behalf 9so he will sell me the cave
of Machpelah, which belongs to him and is at the
end of his field. Ask him to sell it to me for the
full price as a burial site among you."
10Ephron the Hittite was sitting among his
people and he replied to Abraham in the hearing
of all the Hittites who had come to the gate of his
city. 11"No, my lord," he said. "Listen to me; I
give[b] you the field, and I give[b] you the cave
that is in it. I give[b] it to you in the presence of
my people. Bury your dead."
12Again Abraham bowed down before the people of the land 13and he said to Ephron in their
hearing, "Listen to me, if you will. I will pay the
price of the field. Accept it from me so I can bury
my dead there."
14Ephron answered Abraham, 15"Listen to me,
my lord; the land is worth four hundred shekels[c] of silver, but what is that between me and
you? Bury your dead."
16Abraham agreed to Ephron's terms and
weighed out for him the price he had named in
the hearing of the Hittites: four hundred shekels
of silver, according to the weight current among
the merchants.
17So Ephron's field in Machpelah near
Mamre—both the field and the cave in it, and all
the trees within the borders of the field—was
deeded 18to Abraham as his property in the presence of all the Hittites who had come to the gate
of the city. 19Afterward Abraham buried his wife
Sarah in the cave in the field of Machpelah near
Mamre (which is at Hebron) in the land of Canaan. 20So the field and the cave in it were deeded to Abraham by the Hittites as a burial site.

Isaac and Rebekah

24 Abraham was now old and well advanced
in years, and the LORD had blessed him in
every way. 2He said to the chief[d] servant in his
household, the one in charge of all that he had,
"Put your hand under my thigh. 3I want you to
swear by the LORD, the God of heaven and the
God of earth, that you will not get a wife for my
son from the daughters of the Canaanites, among
whom I am living, 4but will go to my country and
my own relatives and get a wife for my son
Isaac."
5The servant asked him, "What if the woman
is unwilling to come back with me to this land?
Shall I then take your son back to the country you
came from?"
6"Make sure that you do not take my son back
there," Abraham said. 7"The LORD, the God of
heaven, who brought me out of my father's
household and my native land and who spoke to
me and promised me on oath, saying, 'To your
offspring[e] I will give this land'—he will send his
angel before you so that you can get a wife for my
son from there. 8If the woman is unwilling to
come back with you, then you will be released
from this oath of mine. Only do not take my son
back there." 9So the servant put his hand under
the thigh of his master Abraham and swore an
oath to him concerning this matter.
10Then the servant took ten of his master's
camels and left, taking with him all kinds of good
things from his master. He set out for Aram Naharaim[f] and made his way to the town of Nahor.
11He had the camels kneel down near the well
outside the town; it was toward evening, the
time the women go out to draw water.
12Then he prayed, "O LORD, God of my master
Abraham, give me success today, and show kindness to my master Abraham. 13See, I am standing
beside this spring, and the daughters of the
townspeople are coming out to draw water.
14May it be that when I say to a girl, 'Please let
down your jar that I may have a drink,' and she
says, 'Drink, and I'll water your camels too'—let
her be the one you have chosen for your servant
Isaac. By this I will know that you have shown
kindness to my master."
15Before he had finished praying, Rebekah
came out with her jar on her shoulder. She was
the daughter of Bethuel son of Milcah, who was
the wife of Abraham's brother Nahor. 16The girl
was very beautiful, a virgin; no man had ever lain
with her. She went down to the spring, filled her
jar and came up again.
17The servant hurried to meet her and said,
"Please give me a little water from your jar."

[a]3 Or *the sons of Heth*; also in verses 5, 7, 10, 16, 18 and 20 [b]11 Or *sell* [c]15 That is, about 10 pounds (about 4.5 kilograms) [d]2 Or *oldest* [e]7 Or *seed* [f]10 That is, Northwest Mesopotamia

18“Drink, my lord,” she said, and quickly
lowered the jar to her hands and gave him a
drink.
19After she had given him a drink, she said,
“I’ll draw water for your camels too, until they
have finished drinking.” 20So she quickly emptied her jar into the trough, ran back to the well
to draw more water, and drew enough for all
his camels. 21Without saying a word, the man
watched her closely to learn whether or not the
LORD had made his journey successful.
22When the camels had finished drinking, the
man took out a gold nose ring weighing a beka[a]
and two gold bracelets weighing ten shekels.[b]
23Then he asked, “Whose daughter are you?
Please tell me, is there room in your father’s
house for us to spend the night?”
24She answered him, “I am the daughter of
Bethuel, the son that Milcah bore to Nahor.”
25And she added, “We have plenty of straw and
fodder, as well as room for you to spend the
night.”
26Then the man bowed down and worshiped
the LORD, 27saying, “Praise be to the LORD, the
God of my master Abraham, who has not abandoned his kindness and faithfulness to my master. As for me, the LORD has led me on the journey to the house of my master’s relatives.”
28The girl ran and told her mother’s household
about these things. 29Now Rebekah had a brother
named Laban, and he hurried out to the man at
the spring. 30As soon as he had seen the nose
ring, and the bracelets on his sister’s arms, and
had heard Rebekah tell what the man said to her,
he went out to the man and found him standing
by the camels near the spring. 31“Come, you who
are blessed by the LORD,” he said. “Why are you
standing out here? I have prepared the house and
a place for the camels.”
32So the man went to the house, and the camels were unloaded. Straw and fodder were
brought for the camels, and water for him and his
men to wash their feet. 33Then food was set before him, but he said, “I will not eat until I have
told you what I have to say.”
“Then tell us,” ⌞Laban⌟ said.
34So he said, “I am Abraham’s servant. 35The
LORD has blessed my master abundantly, and he
has become wealthy. He has given him sheep and
cattle, silver and gold, menservants and maidservants, and camels and donkeys. 36My master’s
wife Sarah has borne him a son in her[c] old age,
and he has given him everything he owns. 37And
my master made me swear an oath, and said,
‘You must not get a wife for my son from the
daughters of the Canaanites, in whose land I live,
38but go to my father’s family and to my own
clan, and get a wife for my son.’
39“Then I asked my master, ‘What if the woman will not come back with me?’
40“He replied, ‘The LORD, before whom I have
walked, will send his angel with you and make
your journey a success, so that you can get a wife
for my son from my own clan and from my father’s family. 41Then, when you go to my clan,
you will be released from my oath even if they
refuse to give her to you—you will be released
from my oath.’
42“When I came to the spring today, I said,
‘O LORD, God of my master Abraham, if you will,
please grant success to the journey on which I
have come. 43See, I am standing beside this
spring; if a maiden comes out to draw water and
I say to her, “Please let me drink a little water
from your jar,” 44and if she says to me, “Drink,
and I’ll draw water for your camels too,” let her
be the one the LORD has chosen for my master’s
son.’
45“Before I finished praying in my heart, Rebekah came out, with her jar on her shoulder.
She went down to the spring and drew water,
and I said to her, ‘Please give me a drink.’
46“She quickly lowered her jar from her shoulder and said, ‘Drink, and I’ll water your camels
too.’ So I drank, and she watered the camels also.
47“I asked her, ‘Whose daughter are you?’
“She said, ‘The daughter of Bethuel son of Nahor, whom Milcah bore to him.’
“Then I put the ring in her nose and the bracelets on her arms, 48and I bowed down and worshiped the LORD. I praised the LORD, the God of
my master Abraham, who had led me on the
right road to get the granddaughter of my master’s brother for his son. 49Now if you will show
kindness and faithfulness to my master, tell me;
and if not, tell me, so I may know which way to
turn.”
50Laban and Bethuel answered, “This is from
the LORD; we can say nothing to you one way or
the other. 51Here is Rebekah; take her and go,
and let her become the wife of your master’s son,
as the LORD has directed.”
52When Abraham’s servant heard what they
said, he bowed down to the ground before the
LORD. 53Then the servant brought out gold and
silver jewelry and articles of clothing and gave
them to Rebekah; he also gave costly gifts to her
brother and to her mother. 54Then he and the
men who were with him ate and drank and spent
the night there.
When they got up the next morning, he said,
“Send me on my way to my master.”
55But her brother and her mother replied, “Let

[a]22 That is, about 1/5 ounce (about 5.5 grams) [b]22 That is, about 4 ounces (about 110 grams) [c]36 Or *his*

the girl remain with us ten days or so; then you[a]
may go."
56 But he said to them, "Do not detain me, now
that the LORD has granted success to my journey.
Send me on my way so I may go to my master."
57 Then they said, "Let's call the girl and ask
her about it." 58 So they called Rebekah and asked
her, "Will you go with this man?"
"I will go," she said.
59 So they sent their sister Rebekah on her way,
along with her nurse and Abraham's servant and
his men. 60 And they blessed Rebekah and said to
her,

"Our sister, may you increase
to thousands upon thousands;
may your offspring possess
the gates of their enemies."

61 Then Rebekah and her maids got ready and
mounted their camels and went back with the
man. So the servant took Rebekah and left.
62 Now Isaac had come from Beer Lahai Roi, for
he was living in the Negev. 63 He went out to the
field one evening to meditate,[b] and as he looked
up, he saw camels approaching. 64 Rebekah also
looked up and saw Isaac. She got down from her
camel 65 and asked the servant, "Who is that man
in the field coming to meet us?"
"He is my master," the servant answered. So
she took her veil and covered herself.
66 Then the servant told Isaac all he had done.
67 Isaac brought her into the tent of his mother
Sarah, and he married Rebekah. So she became
his wife, and he loved her; and Isaac was comforted after his mother's death.

The Death of Abraham

25 Abraham took[c] another wife, whose
name was Keturah. 2 She bore him Zimran, Jokshan, Medan, Midian, Ishbak and Shuah.
3 Jokshan was the father of Sheba and Dedan; the
descendants of Dedan were the Asshurites, the
Letushites and the Leummites. 4 The sons of Midian were Ephah, Epher, Hanoch, Abida and Eldaah. All these were descendants of Keturah.
5 Abraham left everything he owned to Isaac.
6 But while he was still living, he gave gifts to the
sons of his concubines and sent them away from
his son Isaac to the land of the east.
7 Altogether, Abraham lived a hundred and
seventy-five years. 8 Then Abraham breathed his
last and died at a good old age, an old man and
full of years; and he was gathered to his people.
9 His sons Isaac and Ishmael buried him in the
cave of Machpelah near Mamre, in the field of
Ephron son of Zohar the Hittite, 10 the field Abraham had bought from the Hittites.[d] There Abraham was buried with his wife Sarah. 11 After
Abraham's death, God blessed his son Isaac, who
then lived near Beer Lahai Roi.

Ishmael's Sons

12 This is the account of Abraham's son Ishmael, whom Sarah's maidservant, Hagar the Egyptian, bore to Abraham.
13 These are the names of the sons of Ishmael,
listed in the order of their birth: Nebaioth the
firstborn of Ishmael, Kedar, Adbeel, Mibsam,
14 Mishma, Dumah, Massa, 15 Hadad, Tema, Jetur,
Naphish and Kedemah. 16 These were the sons of
Ishmael, and these are the names of the twelve
tribal rulers according to their settlements and
camps. 17 Altogether, Ishmael lived a hundred
and thirty-seven years. He breathed his last and
died, and he was gathered to his people. 18 His
descendants settled in the area from Havilah to
Shur, near the border of Egypt, as you go toward
Asshur. And they lived in hostility toward[e] all
their brothers.

Jacob and Esau

19 This is the account of Abraham's son Isaac.

Abraham became the father of Isaac, 20 and
Isaac was forty years old when he married Rebekah daughter of Bethuel the Aramean from Paddan
Aram[f] and sister of Laban the Aramean.
21 Isaac prayed to the LORD on behalf of his
wife, because she was barren. The LORD answered his prayer, and his wife Rebekah became
pregnant. 22 The babies jostled each other within
her, and she said, "Why is this happening to
me?" So she went to inquire of the LORD.
23 The LORD said to her,

"Two nations are in your womb,
and two peoples from within you will be
separated;
one people will be stronger than the other,
and the older will serve the younger."

24 When the time came for her to give birth,
there were twin boys in her womb. 25 The first to
come out was red, and his whole body was like a
hairy garment; so they named him Esau.[g] 26 After this, his brother came out, with his hand
grasping Esau's heel; so he was named Jacob.[h]
Isaac was sixty years old when Rebekah gave
birth to them.
27 The boys grew up, and Esau became a skillful hunter, a man of the open country, while Ja-

[a] 55 Or *she* [b] 63 The meaning of the Hebrew for this word is uncertain. [c] 1 Or *had taken* [d] 10 Or *the sons of Heth*
[e] 18 Or *lived to the east of* [f] 20 That is, Northwest Mesopotamia [g] 25 *Esau* may mean *hairy*; he was also called Edom, which means *red.* [h] 26 *Jacob* means *he grasps the heel* (figuratively, *he deceives*).

cob was a quiet man, staying among the tents.
28Isaac, who had a taste for wild game, loved
Esau, but Rebekah loved Jacob.
29Once when Jacob was cooking some stew,

Genesis 25:19–34

1. What is the story behind your name? How did your parents come up with it? What does it mean?
2. Would you like to have a twin? Why or why not?
3. How much of a problem has "sibling rivalry" been in your family?
4. Who are you more disgusted with in this story: Jacob for stealing his brother's birthright or Esau for trading his birthright for a meal?
5. In your family, who gets most of the attention from your mother? From your father?
6. On a scale from 1 (poor) to 10 (great), how's your relationship with your parents going this week?
7. What needs to happen in your relationships with your brothers and sisters for you to get along? How can this group help you in prayer?

Esau came in from the open country, famished.
30He said to Jacob, "Quick, let me have some of
that red stew! I'm famished!" (That is why he
was also called Edom.[a])
31Jacob replied, "First sell me your birthright."
32"Look, I am about to die," Esau said. "What
good is the birthright to me?"
33But Jacob said, "Swear to me first." So he
swore an oath to him, selling his birthright to
Jacob.
34Then Jacob gave Esau some bread and some
lentil stew. He ate and drank, and then got up
and left.

So Esau despised his birthright.

Isaac and Abimelech

26 Now there was a famine in the land—
besides the earlier famine of Abraham's
time—and Isaac went to Abimelech king of the
Philistines in Gerar. 2The LORD appeared to Isaac
and said, "Do not go down to Egypt; live in the
land where I tell you to live. 3Stay in this land for
a while, and I will be with you and will bless you.
For to you and your descendants I will give all
these lands and will confirm the oath I swore to
your father Abraham. 4I will make your descendants as numerous as the stars in the sky and will
give them all these lands, and through your offspring[b] all nations on earth will be blessed, 5be-
cause Abraham obeyed me and kept my requirements, my commands, my decrees and my laws."
6So Isaac stayed in Gerar.
7When the men of that place asked him about
his wife, he said, "She is my sister," because he
was afraid to say, "She is my wife." He thought,
"The men of this place might kill me on account
of Rebekah, because she is beautiful."
8When Isaac had been there a long time,
Abimelech king of the Philistines looked down
from a window and saw Isaac caressing his wife
Rebekah. 9So Abimelech summoned Isaac and
said, "She is really your wife! Why did you say,
'She is my sister'?"

Isaac answered him, "Because I thought I
might lose my life on account of her."
10Then Abimelech said, "What is this you have
done to us? One of the men might well have slept
with your wife, and you would have brought guilt
upon us."
11So Abimelech gave orders to all the people:
"Anyone who molests this man or his wife shall
surely be put to death."
12Isaac planted crops in that land and the same

[a]30 *Edom* means *red.* [b]4 Or *seed*

25:22 *jostled each other.* The intense struggle between Jacob and Esau began in the womb.

25:23 *the older will serve the younger.* In ancient times the younger son would normally be subservient to the older. God's choice of the younger son highlights the fact that God's people are the product not of natural or worldly development but of his intervention. Part of this verse is quoted in Romans 9:10–12 as an example of God's sovereign right to do whatever pleases him.

25:26 *his hand grasping Esau's heel.* Hostility between the Israelites (Jacob's descendants) and Edomites (Esau's descendants) became the rule rather than the exception (e.g. Num. 20:14–21). ***Jacob.*** See NIV footnote (v. 26). The name became synonymous with the quality of deception.

25:31 *sell me your birthright.* Custom provided that at least a double share of the father's property be given to the firstborn son when the father died. Jacob was ever the schemer, seeking by any means to gain advantage over others. But it was by God's appointment and care, not Jacob's wits, that he came into the blessing.

25:33 *Swear to me first.* A verbal oath was all that was required to make the transaction legal.

25:34 *Esau despised his birthright.* In so doing, he proved himself to be "godless" (Heb. 12:16), since at the heart of the birthright were the covenant promises that Isaac inherited from Abraham.

year reaped a hundredfold, because the LORD blessed him. 13The man became rich, and his wealth continued to grow until he became very wealthy. 14He had so many flocks and herds and servants that the Philistines envied him. 15So all the wells that his father's servants had dug in the time of his father Abraham, the Philistines stopped up, filling them with earth.

16Then Abimelech said to Isaac, "Move away from us; you have become too powerful for us."

17So Isaac moved away from there and encamped in the Valley of Gerar and settled there. 18Isaac reopened the wells that had been dug in the time of his father Abraham, which the Philistines had stopped up after Abraham died, and he gave them the same names his father had given them.

19Isaac's servants dug in the valley and discovered a well of fresh water there. 20But the herdsmen of Gerar quarreled with Isaac's herdsmen and said, "The water is ours!" So he named the well Esek,[a] because they disputed with him. 21Then they dug another well, but they quarreled over that one also; so he named it Sitnah.[b] 22He moved on from there and dug another well, and no one quarreled over it. He named it Rehoboth,[c] saying, "Now the LORD has given us room and we will flourish in the land."

23From there he went up to Beersheba. 24That night the LORD appeared to him and said, "I am the God of your father Abraham. Do not be afraid, for I am with you; I will bless you and will increase the number of your descendants for the sake of my servant Abraham."

25Isaac built an altar there and called on the name of the LORD. There he pitched his tent, and there his servants dug a well.

26Meanwhile, Abimelech had come to him from Gerar, with Ahuzzath his personal adviser and Phicol the commander of his forces. 27Isaac asked them, "Why have you come to me, since you were hostile to me and sent me away?"

28They answered, "We saw clearly that the LORD was with you; so we said, 'There ought to be a sworn agreement between us'—between us and you. Let us make a treaty with you 29that you will do us no harm, just as we did not molest you but always treated you well and sent you away in peace. And now you are blessed by the LORD."

30Isaac then made a feast for them, and they ate and drank. 31Early the next morning the men swore an oath to each other. Then Isaac sent them on their way, and they left him in peace.

32That day Isaac's servants came and told him about the well they had dug. They said, "We've found water!" 33He called it Shibah,[d] and to this day the name of the town has been Beersheba.[e]

34When Esau was forty years old, he married Judith daughter of Beeri the Hittite, and also Basemath daughter of Elon the Hittite. 35They were a source of grief to Isaac and Rebekah.

Jacob Gets Isaac's Blessing

27 When Isaac was old and his eyes were so weak that he could no longer see, he called for Esau his older son and said to him, "My son."

"Here I am," he answered.

2Isaac said, "I am now an old man and don't know the day of my death. 3Now then, get your weapons—your quiver and bow—and go out to the open country to hunt some wild game for me. 4Prepare me the kind of tasty food I like and bring it to me to eat, so that I may give you my blessing before I die."

5Now Rebekah was listening as Isaac spoke to his son Esau. When Esau left for the open country to hunt game and bring it back, 6Rebekah said to her son Jacob, "Look, I overheard your father say to your brother Esau, 7'Bring me some game and prepare me some tasty food to eat, so that I may give you my blessing in the presence of the LORD before I die.' 8Now, my son, listen carefully and do what I tell you: 9Go out to the flock and bring me two choice young goats, so I can prepare some tasty food for your father, just the way he likes it. 10Then take it to your father to eat, so that he may give you his blessing before he dies."

11Jacob said to Rebekah his mother, "But my brother Esau is a hairy man, and I'm a man with smooth skin. 12What if my father touches me? I would appear to be tricking him and would bring down a curse on myself rather than a blessing."

13His mother said to him, "My son, let the curse fall on me. Just do what I say; go and get them for me."

14So he went and got them and brought them to his mother, and she prepared some tasty food, just the way his father liked it. 15Then Rebekah took the best clothes of Esau her older son, which she had in the house, and put them on her younger son Jacob. 16She also covered his hands and the smooth part of his neck with the goatskins. 17Then she handed to her son Jacob the tasty food and the bread she had made.

18He went to his father and said, "My father."

"Yes, my son," he answered. "Who is it?"

19Jacob said to his father, "I am Esau your firstborn. I have done as you told me. Please sit up and eat some of my game so that you may give me your blessing."

[a]20 *Esek* means *dispute.* [b]21 *Sitnah* means *opposition.* [c]22 *Rehoboth* means *room.* [d]33 *Shibah* can mean *oath* or *seven.* [e]33 *Beersheba* can mean *well of the oath* or *well of seven.*

20Isaac asked his son, "How did you find it so
quickly, my son?"
"The LORD your God gave me success," he
replied.
21Then Isaac said to Jacob, "Come near so I
can touch you, my son, to know whether you
really are my son Esau or not."
22Jacob went close to his father Isaac, who
touched him and said, "The voice is the voice of
Jacob, but the hands are the hands of Esau." **23**He
did not recognize him, for his hands were hairy
like those of his brother Esau; so he blessed him.
24"Are you really my son Esau?" he asked.
"I am," he replied.
25Then he said, "My son, bring me some of
your game to eat, so that I may give you my
blessing."
Jacob brought it to him and he ate; and he
brought some wine and he drank. **26**Then his father Isaac said to him, "Come here, my son, and
kiss me."
27So he went to him and kissed him. When
Isaac caught the smell of his clothes, he blessed
him and said,

"Ah, the smell of my son
  is like the smell of a field
  that the LORD has blessed.
28May God give you of heaven's dew
  and of earth's richness—
  an abundance of grain and new wine.
29May nations serve you
  and peoples bow down to you.
Be lord over your brothers,
  and may the sons of your mother bow
    down to you.
May those who curse you be cursed
  and those who bless you be blessed."

30After Isaac finished blessing him and Jacob
had scarcely left his father's presence, his brother
Esau came in from hunting. **31**He too prepared
some tasty food and brought it to his father. Then
he said to him, "My father, sit up and eat some
of my game, so that you may give me your blessing."
32His father Isaac asked him, "Who are you?"
"I am your son," he answered, "your firstborn,
Esau."
33Isaac trembled violently and said, "Who was
it, then, that hunted game and brought it to me?
I ate it just before you came and I blessed him—
and indeed he will be blessed!"
34When Esau heard his father's words, he
burst out with a loud and bitter cry and said to his
father, "Bless me—me too, my father!"
35But he said, "Your brother came deceitfully
and took your blessing."
36Esau said, "Isn't he rightly named Jacob[a]?
He has deceived me these two times: He took my
birthright, and now he's taken my blessing!"
Then he asked, "Haven't you reserved any blessing for me?"
37Isaac answered Esau, "I have made him lord
over you and have made all his relatives his servants, and I have sustained him with grain and
new wine. So what can I possibly do for you, my
son?"
38Esau said to his father, "Do you have only
one blessing, my father? Bless me too, my father!" Then Esau wept aloud.
39His father Isaac answered him,

"Your dwelling will be
  away from the earth's richness,
  away from the dew of heaven above.
40You will live by the sword
  and you will serve your brother.
But when you grow restless,
  you will throw his yoke
  from off your neck."

Jacob Flees to Laban

41Esau held a grudge against Jacob because of
the blessing his father had given him. He said to
himself, "The days of mourning for my father are
near; then I will kill my brother Jacob."
42When Rebekah was told what her older son
Esau had said, she sent for her younger son Jacob
and said to him, "Your brother Esau is consoling
himself with the thought of killing you. **43**Now
then, my son, do what I say: Flee at once to my
brother Laban in Haran. **44**Stay with him for a
while until your brother's fury subsides. **45**When
your brother is no longer angry with you and
forgets what you did to him, I'll send word for
you to come back from there. Why should I lose
both of you in one day?"
46Then Rebekah said to Isaac, "I'm disgusted
with living because of these Hittite women. If
Jacob takes a wife from among the women of this
land, from Hittite women like these, my life will
not be worth living."

28 So Isaac called for Jacob and blessed[b]
him and commanded him: "Do not marry
a Canaanite woman. **2**Go at once to Paddan
Aram,[c] to the house of your mother's father
Bethuel. Take a wife for yourself there, from
among the daughters of Laban, your mother's
brother. **3**May God Almighty[d] bless you and
make you fruitful and increase your numbers until you become a community of peoples. **4**May he
give you and your descendants the blessing given

[a]*36 Jacob* means *he grasps the heel* (figuratively, *he deceives*). [b]*1* Or *greeted* [c]*2* That is, Northwest Mesopotamia; also in verses 5, 6 and 7 [d]*3* Hebrew *El-Shaddai*

to Abraham, so that you may take possession of
the land where you now live as an alien, the land
God gave to Abraham." 5Then Isaac sent Jacob on
his way, and he went to Paddan Aram, to Laban
son of Bethuel the Aramean, the brother of Rebekah, who was the mother of Jacob and Esau.
6Now Esau learned that Isaac had blessed Jacob and had sent him to Paddan Aram to take a
wife from there, and that when he blessed him
he commanded him, "Do not marry a Canaanite
woman," 7and that Jacob had obeyed his father
and mother and had gone to Paddan Aram. 8Esau
then realized how displeasing the Canaanite
women were to his father Isaac; 9so he went to
Ishmael and married Mahalath, the sister of Nebaioth and daughter of Ishmael son of Abraham,
in addition to the wives he already had.

Jacob's Dream at Bethel

10Jacob left Beersheba and set out for Haran.
11When he reached a certain place, he stopped
for the night because the sun had set. Taking one
of the stones there, he put it under his head and
lay down to sleep. 12He had a dream in which he
saw a stairway[a] resting on the earth, with its top
reaching to heaven, and the angels of God were
ascending and descending on it. 13There above
it[b] stood the LORD, and he said: "I am the LORD,
the God of your father Abraham and the God of
Isaac. I will give you and your descendants the
land on which you are lying. 14Your descendants
will be like the dust of the earth, and you will
spread out to the west and to the east, to the
north and to the south. All peoples on earth will
be blessed through you and your offspring. 15I am
with you and will watch over you wherever you
go, and I will bring you back to this land. I will
not leave you until I have done what I have promised you."
16When Jacob awoke from his sleep, he
thought, "Surely the LORD is in this place, and I
was not aware of it." 17He was afraid and said,
"How awesome is this place! This is none other
than the house of God; this is the gate of
heaven."
18Early the next morning Jacob took the stone
he had placed under his head and set it up as a
pillar and poured oil on top of it. 19He called that
place Bethel,[c] though the city used to be called
Luz.
20Then Jacob made a vow, saying, "If God will
be with me and will watch over me on this journey I am taking and will give me food to eat and
clothes to wear 21so that I return safely to my
father's house, then the LORD[d] will be my God
22and[e] this stone that I have set up as a pillar
will be God's house, and of all that you give me
I will give you a tenth."

Jacob Arrives in Paddan Aram

29 Then Jacob continued on his journey and
came to the land of the eastern peoples.
2There he saw a well in the field, with three
flocks of sheep lying near it because the flocks
were watered from that well. The stone over the
mouth of the well was large. 3When all the flocks
were gathered there, the shepherds would roll
the stone away from the well's mouth and water
the sheep. Then they would return the stone to
its place over the mouth of the well.
4Jacob asked the shepherds, "My brothers,
where are you from?"
"We're from Haran," they replied.
5He said to them, "Do you know Laban, Nahor's grandson?"
"Yes, we know him," they answered.
6Then Jacob asked them, "Is he well?"
"Yes, he is," they said, "and here comes his
daughter Rachel with the sheep."
7"Look," he said, "the sun is still high; it is not
time for the flocks to be gathered. Water the
sheep and take them back to pasture."
8"We can't," they replied, "until all the flocks
are gathered and the stone has been rolled away
from the mouth of the well. Then we will water
the sheep."

[a]12 Or *ladder* [b]13 Or *There beside him* [c]19 *Bethel* means *house of God.* [d]20,21 Or *Since God . . . father's house, the LORD* [e]21,22 Or *house, and the LORD will be my God, 22then*

29:1 *continued on his journey.* Jacob was on a long journey for two reasons (see 27:42–28:2): (1) After deceiving his father Isaac to get Esau's blessing, Jacob was running away from Esau's wrath; (2) He was complying with his parents' wishes that he go and marry one of his mother's relatives, rather than marrying a local Canaanite woman as his brother Esau had done (26:34–35). The NT also emphasizes the importance of believers not being "yoked together with unbelievers" (2 Cor. 6:14).

29:3 *return the stone to its place.* Either to prevent the water from being polluted or tampered with, or to prevent anyone from falling in.

29:5 *Do you know Laban, Nahor's grandson?* In response to his parents' request, Jacob was looking for his uncle—his mother's brother.

29:9 *shepherdess.* The task of caring for sheep and goats in the Middle East was shared by both men and women.

29:10 *rolled the stone away.* A feat of unusual strength for one man, because the stone was large (see v. 2).

29:11 *kissed.* At this point, this was likely the customary kiss between relatives, as occurred also when Jacob and Laban met (v. 13). ***weep aloud.*** For joy.

29:14 *flesh and blood.* The English equivalent of a Hebrew phrase that means literally "bone and flesh" and that stresses blood kinship.

[9]While he was still talking with them, Rachel came with her father's sheep, for she was a shepherdess. [10]When Jacob saw Rachel daughter of Laban, his mother's brother, and Laban's sheep, he went over and rolled the stone away from the mouth of the well and watered his uncle's sheep. [11]Then Jacob kissed Rachel and began to weep aloud. [12]He had told Rachel that he was a relative of her father and a son of Rebekah. So she ran and told her father.

[13]As soon as Laban heard the news about Jacob, his sister's son, he hurried to meet him. He embraced him and kissed him and brought him to his home, and there Jacob told him all these things. [14]Then Laban said to him, "You are my own flesh and blood."

GENESIS 29:1–14

1. What do you know about how your parents met and fell in love?
2. Where is *the* spot for people your age to hang out and meet the opposite sex?
3. What's the best way to get someone you like to notice you?
4. What do you look for in someone you date?
5. Do you ever feel pressure from your family to date certain types of people?
6. If you loved people you dated the same way God wants you to love everyone, would your dating relationships be different?
7. Do you think you are too anxious to find someone or do you need some encouragement when it comes to taking a risk and dating? How can this group help you in prayer?

(Study notes on page 67)

Jacob Marries Leah and Rachel

After Jacob had stayed with him for a whole month, [15]Laban said to him, "Just because you are a relative of mine, should you work for me for nothing? Tell me what your wages should be."

[16]Now Laban had two daughters; the name of the older was Leah, and the name of the younger was Rachel. [17]Leah had weak[a] eyes, but Rachel was lovely in form, and beautiful. [18]Jacob was in love with Rachel and said, "I'll work for you seven years in return for your younger daughter Rachel."

[19]Laban said, "It's better that I give her to you than to some other man. Stay here with me." [20]So Jacob served seven years to get Rachel, but they seemed like only a few days to him because of his love for her.

[21]Then Jacob said to Laban, "Give me my wife. My time is completed, and I want to lie with her."

[22]So Laban brought together all the people of the place and gave a feast. [23]But when evening came, he took his daughter Leah and gave her to Jacob, and Jacob lay with her. [24]And Laban gave his servant girl Zilpah to his daughter as her maidservant.

[25]When morning came, there was Leah! So Jacob said to Laban, "What is this you have done to me? I served you for Rachel, didn't I? Why have you deceived me?"

[26]Laban replied, "It is not our custom here to give the younger daughter in marriage before the older one. [27]Finish this daughter's bridal week; then we will give you the younger one also, in return for another seven years of work."

[28]And Jacob did so. He finished the week with Leah, and then Laban gave him his daughter Rachel to be his wife. [29]Laban gave his servant girl Bilhah to his daughter Rachel as her maidservant. [30]Jacob lay with Rachel also, and he loved Rachel more than Leah. And he worked for Laban another seven years.

Jacob's Children

[31]When the LORD saw that Leah was not loved, he opened her womb, but Rachel was barren. [32]Leah became pregnant and gave birth to a son. She named him Reuben,[b] for she said, "It is because the LORD has seen my misery. Surely my husband will love me now."

[33]She conceived again, and when she gave birth to a son she said, "Because the LORD heard that I am not loved, he gave me this one too." So she named him Simeon.[c]

[34]Again she conceived, and when she gave birth to a son she said, "Now at last my husband will become attached to me, because I have borne him three sons." So he was named Levi.[d]

[35]She conceived again, and when she gave birth to a son she said, "This time I will praise the LORD." So she named him Judah.[e] Then she stopped having children.

[a]17 Or *delicate* [b]32 *Reuben* sounds like the Hebrew for *he has seen my misery*; the name means *see, a son.* [c]33 *Simeon* probably means *one who hears.* [d]34 *Levi* sounds like and may be derived from the Hebrew for *attached.* [e]35 *Judah* sounds like and may be derived from the Hebrew for *praise.*

30 When Rachel saw that she was not bearing Jacob any children, she became jealous of her sister. So she said to Jacob, "Give me children, or I'll die!"

2Jacob became angry with her and said, "Am I in the place of God, who has kept you from having children?"

3Then she said, "Here is Bilhah, my maidservant. Sleep with her so that she can bear children for me and that through her I too can build a family."

4So she gave him her servant Bilhah as a wife. Jacob slept with her, 5and she became pregnant and bore him a son. 6Then Rachel said, "God has vindicated me; he has listened to my plea and given me a son." Because of this she named him Dan.[a]

7Rachel's servant Bilhah conceived again and bore Jacob a second son. 8Then Rachel said, "I have had a great struggle with my sister, and I have won." So she named him Naphtali.[b]

9When Leah saw that she had stopped having children, she took her maidservant Zilpah and gave her to Jacob as a wife. 10Leah's servant Zilpah bore Jacob a son. 11Then Leah said, "What good fortune!"[c] So she named him Gad.[d]

12Leah's servant Zilpah bore Jacob a second son. 13Then Leah said, "How happy I am! The women will call me happy." So she named him Asher.[e]

14During wheat harvest, Reuben went out into the fields and found some mandrake plants, which he brought to his mother Leah. Rachel said to Leah, "Please give me some of your son's mandrakes."

15But she said to her, "Wasn't it enough that you took away my husband? Will you take my son's mandrakes too?"

"Very well," Rachel said, "he can sleep with you tonight in return for your son's mandrakes."

16So when Jacob came in from the fields that evening, Leah went out to meet him. "You must sleep with me," she said. "I have hired you with my son's mandrakes." So he slept with her that night.

17God listened to Leah, and she became pregnant and bore Jacob a fifth son. 18Then Leah said, "God has rewarded me for giving my maidservant to my husband." So she named him Issachar.[f]

19Leah conceived again and bore Jacob a sixth son. 20Then Leah said, "God has presented me with a precious gift. This time my husband will treat me with honor, because I have borne him six sons." So she named him Zebulun.[g]

21Some time later she gave birth to a daughter and named her Dinah.

22Then God remembered Rachel; he listened to her and opened her womb. 23She became pregnant and gave birth to a son and said, "God has taken away my disgrace." 24She named him Joseph,[h] and said, "May the LORD add to me another son."

Jacob's Flocks Increase

25After Rachel gave birth to Joseph, Jacob said to Laban, "Send me on my way so I can go back to my own homeland. 26Give me my wives and children, for whom I have served you, and I will be on my way. You know how much work I've done for you."

27But Laban said to him, "If I have found favor in your eyes, please stay. I have learned by divination that[i] the LORD has blessed me because of you." 28He added, "Name your wages, and I will pay them."

29Jacob said to him, "You know how I have worked for you and how your livestock has fared under my care. 30The little you had before I came has increased greatly, and the LORD has blessed you wherever I have been. But now, when may I do something for my own household?"

31"What shall I give you?" he asked.

"Don't give me anything," Jacob replied. "But if you will do this one thing for me, I will go on tending your flocks and watching over them: 32Let me go through all your flocks today and remove from them every speckled or spotted sheep, every dark-colored lamb and every spotted or speckled goat. They will be my wages. 33And my honesty will testify for me in the future, whenever you check on the wages you have paid me. Any goat in my possession that is not speckled or spotted, or any lamb that is not dark-colored, will be considered stolen."

34"Agreed," said Laban. "Let it be as you have said." 35That same day he removed all the male goats that were streaked or spotted, and all the speckled or spotted female goats (all that had white on them) and all the dark-colored lambs, and he placed them in the care of his sons. 36Then he put a three-day journey between himself and Jacob, while Jacob continued to tend the rest of Laban's flocks.

37Jacob, however, took fresh-cut branches from poplar, almond and plane trees and made white stripes on them by peeling the bark and exposing the white inner wood of the branches. 38Then he placed the peeled branches in all the watering troughs, so that they would be directly

[a]6 *Dan* here means *he has vindicated.* [b]8 *Naphtali* means *my struggle.* [c]11 Or *"A troop is coming!"* [d]11 *Gad* can mean *good fortune* or *a troop.* [e]13 *Asher* means *happy.* [f]18 *Issachar* sounds like the Hebrew for *reward.* [g]20 *Zebulun* probably means *honor.* [h]24 *Joseph* means *may he add.* [i]27 Or possibly *have become rich and*

in front of the flocks when they came to drink. When the flocks were in heat and came to drink, 39they mated in front of the branches. And they bore young that were streaked or speckled or spotted. 40Jacob set apart the young of the flock by themselves, but made the rest face the streaked and dark-colored animals that belonged to Laban. Thus he made separate flocks for himself and did not put them with Laban's animals. 41Whenever the stronger females were in heat, Jacob would place the branches in the troughs in front of the animals so they would mate near the branches, 42but if the animals were weak, he would not place them there. So the weak animals went to Laban and the strong ones to Jacob. 43In this way the man grew exceedingly prosperous and came to own large flocks, and maidservants and menservants, and camels and donkeys.

Jacob Flees From Laban

31 Jacob heard that Laban's sons were saying, "Jacob has taken everything our father owned and has gained all this wealth from what belonged to our father." 2And Jacob noticed that Laban's attitude toward him was not what it had been.

3Then the LORD said to Jacob, "Go back to the land of your fathers and to your relatives, and I will be with you."

4So Jacob sent word to Rachel and Leah to come out to the fields where his flocks were. 5He said to them, "I see that your father's attitude toward me is not what it was before, but the God of my father has been with me. 6You know that I've worked for your father with all my strength, 7yet your father has cheated me by changing my wages ten times. However, God has not allowed him to harm me. 8If he said, 'The speckled ones will be your wages,' then all the flocks gave birth to speckled young; and if he said, 'The streaked ones will be your wages,' then all the flocks bore streaked young. 9So God has taken away your father's livestock and has given them to me.

10"In breeding season I once had a dream in which I looked up and saw that the male goats mating with the flock were streaked, speckled or spotted. 11The angel of God said to me in the dream, 'Jacob.' I answered, 'Here I am.' 12And he said, 'Look up and see that all the male goats mating with the flock are streaked, speckled or spotted, for I have seen all that Laban has been doing to you. 13I am the God of Bethel, where you anointed a pillar and where you made a vow to me. Now leave this land at once and go back to your native land.' "

14Then Rachel and Leah replied, "Do we still have any share in the inheritance of our father's estate? 15Does he not regard us as foreigners? Not only has he sold us, but he has used up what was paid for us. 16Surely all the wealth that God took away from our father belongs to us and our children. So do whatever God has told you."

17Then Jacob put his children and his wives on camels, 18and he drove all his livestock ahead of him, along with all the goods he had accumulated in Paddan Aram,[a] to go to his father Isaac in the land of Canaan.

19When Laban had gone to shear his sheep, Rachel stole her father's household gods. 20Moreover, Jacob deceived Laban the Aramean by not telling him he was running away. 21So he fled with all he had, and crossing the River,[b] he headed for the hill country of Gilead.

Laban Pursues Jacob

22On the third day Laban was told that Jacob had fled. 23Taking his relatives with him, he pursued Jacob for seven days and caught up with him in the hill country of Gilead. 24Then God came to Laban the Aramean in a dream at night and said to him, "Be careful not to say anything to Jacob, either good or bad."

25Jacob had pitched his tent in the hill country of Gilead when Laban overtook him, and Laban and his relatives camped there too. 26Then Laban said to Jacob, "What have you done? You've deceived me, and you've carried off my daughters like captives in war. 27Why did you run off secretly and deceive me? Why didn't you tell me, so I could send you away with joy and singing to the music of tambourines and harps? 28You didn't even let me kiss my grandchildren and my daughters good-by. You have done a foolish thing. 29I have the power to harm you; but last night the God of your father said to me, 'Be careful not to say anything to Jacob, either good or bad.' 30Now you have gone off because you longed to return to your father's house. But why did you steal my gods?"

31Jacob answered Laban, "I was afraid, because I thought you would take your daughters away from me by force. 32But if you find anyone who has your gods, he shall not live. In the presence of our relatives, see for yourself whether there is anything of yours here with me; and if so, take it." Now Jacob did not know that Rachel had stolen the gods.

33So Laban went into Jacob's tent and into Leah's tent and into the tent of the two maidservants, but he found nothing. After he came out of Leah's tent, he entered Rachel's tent. 34Now Rachel had taken the household gods and put them inside her camel's saddle and was sitting on

[a] *18* That is, Northwest Mesopotamia [b] *21* That is, the Euphrates

them. Laban searched through everything in the tent but found nothing.

35Rachel said to her father, "Don't be angry, my lord, that I cannot stand up in your presence; I'm having my period." So he searched but could not find the household gods.

36Jacob was angry and took Laban to task. "What is my crime?" he asked Laban. "What sin have I committed that you hunt me down? 37Now that you have searched through all my goods, what have you found that belongs to your household? Put it here in front of your relatives and mine, and let them judge between the two of us.

38"I have been with you for twenty years now. Your sheep and goats have not miscarried, nor have I eaten rams from your flocks. 39I did not bring you animals torn by wild beasts; I bore the loss myself. And you demanded payment from me for whatever was stolen by day or night. 40This was my situation: The heat consumed me in the daytime and the cold at night, and sleep fled from my eyes. 41It was like this for the twenty years I was in your household. I worked for you fourteen years for your two daughters and six years for your flocks, and you changed my wages ten times. 42If the God of my father, the God of Abraham and the Fear of Isaac, had not been with me, you would surely have sent me away emptyhanded. But God has seen my hardship and the toil of my hands, and last night he rebuked you."

43Laban answered Jacob, "The women are my daughters, the children are my children, and the flocks are my flocks. All you see is mine. Yet what can I do today about these daughters of mine, or about the children they have borne? 44Come now, let's make a covenant, you and I, and let it serve as a witness between us."

45So Jacob took a stone and set it up as a pillar. 46He said to his relatives, "Gather some stones." So they took stones and piled them in a heap, and they ate there by the heap. 47Laban called it Jegar Sahadutha,[a] and Jacob called it Galeed.[b]

48Laban said, "This heap is a witness between you and me today." That is why it was called Galeed. 49It was also called Mizpah,[c] because he said, "May the LORD keep watch between you and me when we are away from each other. 50If you mistreat my daughters or if you take any wives besides my daughters, even though no one is with us, remember that God is a witness between you and me."

51Laban also said to Jacob, "Here is this heap, and here is this pillar I have set up between you and me. 52This heap is a witness, and this pillar is a witness, that I will not go past this heap to your side to harm you and that you will not go past this heap and pillar to my side to harm me. 53May the God of Abraham and the God of Nahor, the God of their father, judge between us."

So Jacob took an oath in the name of the Fear of his father Isaac. 54He offered a sacrifice there in the hill country and invited his relatives to a meal. After they had eaten, they spent the night there.

55Early the next morning Laban kissed his grandchildren and his daughters and blessed them. Then he left and returned home.

Jacob Prepares to Meet Esau

32 Jacob also went on his way, and the angels of God met him. 2When Jacob saw them, he said, "This is the camp of God!" So he named that place Mahanaim.[d]

3Jacob sent messengers ahead of him to his brother Esau in the land of Seir, the country of Edom. 4He instructed them: "This is what you are to say to my master Esau: 'Your servant Jacob says, I have been staying with Laban and have remained there till now. 5I have cattle and donkeys, sheep and goats, menservants and maidservants. Now I am sending this message to my lord, that I may find favor in your eyes.' "

6When the messengers returned to Jacob, they said, "We went to your brother Esau, and now he is coming to meet you, and four hundred men are with him."

7In great fear and distress Jacob divided the people who were with him into two groups,[e] and the flocks and herds and camels as well. 8He thought, "If Esau comes and attacks one group,[f] the group[f] that is left may escape."

9Then Jacob prayed, "O God of my father Abraham, God of my father Isaac, O LORD, who said to me, 'Go back to your country and your relatives, and I will make you prosper,' 10I am unworthy of all the kindness and faithfulness you have shown your servant. I had only my staff when I crossed this Jordan, but now I have become two groups. 11Save me, I pray, from the hand of my brother Esau, for I am afraid he will come and attack me, and also the mothers with their children. 12But you have said, 'I will surely make you prosper and will make your descendants like the sand of the sea, which cannot be counted.' "

13He spent the night there, and from what he had with him he selected a gift for his brother Esau: 14two hundred female goats and twenty male goats, two hundred ewes and twenty rams, 15thirty female camels with their young, forty cows and ten bulls, and twenty female donkeys and ten male donkeys. 16He put them in the care

[a]47 The Aramaic *Jegar Sahadutha* means *witness heap.* [b]47 The Hebrew *Galeed* means *witness heap.* [c]49 *Mizpah* means *watchtower.* [d]2 *Mahanaim* means *two camps.* [e]7 Or *camps*; also in verse 10 [f]8 Or *camp*

of his servants, each herd by itself, and said to his
servants, "Go ahead of me, and keep some space
between the herds."
17He instructed the one in the lead: "When
my brother Esau meets you and asks, 'To whom
do you belong, and where are you going, and who
owns all these animals in front of you?' 18then
you are to say, 'They belong to your servant Jacob. They are a gift sent to my lord Esau, and he
is coming behind us.'"
19He also instructed the second, the third and
all the others who followed the herds: "You are
to say the same thing to Esau when you meet
him. 20And be sure to say, 'Your servant Jacob is
coming behind us.'" For he thought, "I will paci-
fy him with these gifts I am sending on ahead;
later, when I see him, perhaps he will receive
me." 21So Jacob's gifts went on ahead of him, but
he himself spent the night in the camp.

Jacob Wrestles With God

22That night Jacob got up and took his two
wives, his two maidservants and his eleven sons
and crossed the ford of the Jabbok. 23After he had
sent them across the stream, he sent over all his
possessions. 24So Jacob was left alone, and a man
wrestled with him till daybreak. 25When the man
saw that he could not overpower him, he
touched the socket of Jacob's hip so that his hip
was wrenched as he wrestled with the man.
26Then the man said, "Let me go, for it is daybreak."
But Jacob replied, "I will not let you go unless
you bless me."
27The man asked him, "What is your name?"
"Jacob," he answered.
28Then the man said, "Your name will no longer be Jacob, but Israel,[a] because you have struggled with God and with men and have overcome."
29Jacob said, "Please tell me your name."
But he replied, "Why do you ask my name?"
Then he blessed him there.
30So Jacob called the place Peniel,[b] saying, "It
is because I saw God face to face, and yet my life
was spared."
31The sun rose above him as he passed Peniel,[c] and he was limping because of his hip.
32Therefore to this day the Israelites do not eat
the tendon attached to the socket of the hip, because the socket of Jacob's hip was touched near
the tendon.

GENESIS 32:22–32

1. What is your nickname? How did you get it? Do you like it?
2. When you were a little kid, were you more likely to use your fists, feet or brains to get out of trouble?
3. Name one struggle you have had in the last year that you can see has resulted in some good.
4. With what are you wrestling now: People? Evil powers? Fear? The past? A decision?
5. Are you winning, losing or just "limping along"?
6. Where are you in your "wrestling match" with God? Are you still fighting or fully surrendered?
7. How do you feel about sharing your struggles with this group? How can the group pray for you?

Jacob Meets Esau

33 Jacob looked up and there was Esau, coming with his four hundred men; so he divided the children among Leah, Rachel and the

[a]28 *Israel* means *he struggles with God.* [b]30 *Peniel* means *face of God.* [c]31 Hebrew *Penuel*, a variant of *Peniel*

Twenty years earlier Jacob had deceitfully stolen the firstborn's blessing their father intended for Jacob's brother Esau. Hearing of Esau's threats to kill him, Jacob fled to the land his family had come from. Now, with his wives, children and possessions, he is about to return home. After preparing many gifts for Esau (32:13–15), Jacob spends the night alone.

32:24 *a man.* God himself (as Jacob eventually realized; see v. 30) in the form of an angel. ***wrestled.*** Jacob had struggled all his life to prevail, first with Esau, then with Laban. Now as he was about to reenter Canaan, he was shown that it was with God that he must "wrestle." It was God who held his destiny in his hands.

32:25 *could not overpower him ... touched the socket.* God came to him in such a form that Jacob could wrestle with him successfully, yet he showed Jacob that he could disable him at will.

32:26 *I will not let you go.* Jacob's persistence was rewarded (v. 29). ***unless you bless me.*** Jacob finally acknowledged that the blessing must come from God.

32:28 Now that Jacob had acknowledged God as the source of blessing and was about to reenter the promised land, the Lord acknowledged Jacob as his servant by changing his name to "Israel"—"he struggles with God." Here in Father Jacob/Israel, the nation of Israel got her name and her characterization: the people who struggle with God and with men and overcome.

two maidservants. [2]He put the maidservants and their children in front, Leah and her children next, and Rachel and Joseph in the rear. [3]He himself went on ahead and bowed down to the ground seven times as he approached his brother.

[4]But Esau ran to meet Jacob and embraced him; he threw his arms around his neck and kissed him. And they wept. [5]Then Esau looked up and saw the women and children. "Who are these with you?" he asked.

Jacob answered, "They are the children God has graciously given your servant."

[6]Then the maidservants and their children approached and bowed down. [7]Next, Leah and her children came and bowed down. Last of all came Joseph and Rachel, and they too bowed down.

[8]Esau asked, "What do you mean by all these droves I met?"

"To find favor in your eyes, my lord," he said.

[9]But Esau said, "I already have plenty, my brother. Keep what you have for yourself."

[10]"No, please!" said Jacob. "If I have found favor in your eyes, accept this gift from me. For to see your face is like seeing the face of God, now that you have received me favorably. [11]Please accept the present that was brought to you, for God has been gracious to me and I have all I need." And because Jacob insisted, Esau accepted it.

[12]Then Esau said, "Let us be on our way; I'll accompany you."

[13]But Jacob said to him, "My lord knows that the children are tender and that I must care for the ewes and cows that are nursing their young. If they are driven hard just one day, all the animals will die. [14]So let my lord go on ahead of his servant, while I move along slowly at the pace of the droves before me and that of the children, until I come to my lord in Seir."

[15]Esau said, "Then let me leave some of my men with you."

"But why do that?" Jacob asked. "Just let me find favor in the eyes of my lord."

[16]So that day Esau started on his way back to Seir. [17]Jacob, however, went to Succoth, where he built a place for himself and made shelters for his livestock. That is why the place is called Succoth.[a]

[18]After Jacob came from Paddan Aram,[b] he arrived safely at the[c] city of Shechem in Canaan and camped within sight of the city. [19]For a hundred pieces of silver,[d] he bought from the sons of Hamor, the father of Shechem, the plot of ground where he pitched his tent. [20]There he set up an altar and called it El Elohe Israel.[e]

Dinah and the Shechemites

34 Now Dinah, the daughter Leah had borne to Jacob, went out to visit the women of the land. [2]When Shechem son of Hamor the Hivite, the ruler of that area, saw her, he took her and violated her. [3]His heart was drawn to Dinah daughter of Jacob, and he loved the girl and spoke tenderly to her. [4]And Shechem said to his father Hamor, "Get me this girl as my wife."

[5]When Jacob heard that his daughter Dinah had been defiled, his sons were in the fields with his livestock; so he kept quiet about it until they came home.

[6]Then Shechem's father Hamor went out to talk with Jacob. [7]Now Jacob's sons had come in from the fields as soon as they heard what had happened. They were filled with grief and fury, because Shechem had done a disgraceful thing in[f] Israel by lying with Jacob's daughter—a thing that should not be done.

[8]But Hamor said to them, "My son Shechem has his heart set on your daughter. Please give her to him as his wife. [9]Intermarry with us; give us your daughters and take our daughters for yourselves. [10]You can settle among us; the land is open to you. Live in it, trade[g] in it, and acquire property in it."

[11]Then Shechem said to Dinah's father and brothers, "Let me find favor in your eyes, and I will give you whatever you ask. [12]Make the price for the bride and the gift I am to bring as great as you like, and I'll pay whatever you ask me. Only give me the girl as my wife."

[13]Because their sister Dinah had been defiled, Jacob's sons replied deceitfully as they spoke to Shechem and his father Hamor. [14]They said to them, "We can't do such a thing; we can't give our sister to a man who is not circumcised. That would be a disgrace to us. [15]We will give our consent to you on one condition only: that you become like us by circumcising all your males. [16]Then we will give you our daughters and take your daughters for ourselves. We'll settle among you and become one people with you. [17]But if you will not agree to be circumcised, we'll take our sister[h] and go."

[18]Their proposal seemed good to Hamor and his son Shechem. [19]The young man, who was the most honored of all his father's household, lost no time in doing what they said, because he was delighted with Jacob's daughter. [20]So Hamor and his son Shechem went to the gate of their city to

[a]17 *Succoth* means *shelters.* [b]18 That is, Northwest Mesopotamia [c]18 Or *arrived at Shalem, a* [d]19 Hebrew *hundred kesitahs*; a kesitah was a unit of money of unknown weight and value. [e]20 *El Elohe Israel* can mean *God, the God of Israel* or *mighty is the God of Israel.* [f]7 Or *against* [g]10 Or *move about freely*; also in verse 21 [h]17 Hebrew *daughter*

speak to their fellow townsmen. 21"These men are friendly toward us," they said. "Let them live in our land and trade in it; the land has plenty of room for them. We can marry their daughters and they can marry ours. 22But the men will consent to live with us as one people only on the condition that our males be circumcised, as they themselves are. 23Won't their livestock, their property and all their other animals become ours? So let us give our consent to them, and they will settle among us."

24All the men who went out of the city gate agreed with Hamor and his son Shechem, and every male in the city was circumcised.

25Three days later, while all of them were still in pain, two of Jacob's sons, Simeon and Levi, Dinah's brothers, took their swords and attacked the unsuspecting city, killing every male. 26They put Hamor and his son Shechem to the sword and took Dinah from Shechem's house and left. 27The sons of Jacob came upon the dead bodies and looted the city where[a] their sister had been defiled. 28They seized their flocks and herds and donkeys and everything else of theirs in the city and out in the fields. 29They carried off all their wealth and all their women and children, taking as plunder everything in the houses.

30Then Jacob said to Simeon and Levi, "You have brought trouble on me by making me a stench to the Canaanites and Perizzites, the people living in this land. We are few in number, and if they join forces against me and attack me, I and my household will be destroyed."

31But they replied, "Should he have treated our sister like a prostitute?"

Jacob Returns to Bethel

35 Then God said to Jacob, "Go up to Bethel and settle there, and build an altar there to God, who appeared to you when you were fleeing from your brother Esau."

2So Jacob said to his household and to all who were with him, "Get rid of the foreign gods you have with you, and purify yourselves and change your clothes. 3Then come, let us go up to Bethel, where I will build an altar to God, who answered me in the day of my distress and who has been with me wherever I have gone." 4So they gave Jacob all the foreign gods they had and the rings in their ears, and Jacob buried them under the oak at Shechem. 5Then they set out, and the terror of God fell upon the towns all around them so that no one pursued them.

6Jacob and all the people with him came to Luz (that is, Bethel) in the land of Canaan. 7There he built an altar, and he called the place El Bethel,[b] because it was there that God revealed himself to him when he was fleeing from his brother.

8Now Deborah, Rebekah's nurse, died and was buried under the oak below Bethel. So it was named Allon Bacuth.[c]

9After Jacob returned from Paddan Aram,[d] God appeared to him again and blessed him. 10God said to him, "Your name is Jacob,[e] but you will no longer be called Jacob; your name will be Israel.[f]" So he named him Israel.

11And God said to him, "I am God Almighty[g]; be fruitful and increase in number. A nation and a community of nations will come from you, and kings will come from your body. 12The land I gave to Abraham and Isaac I also give to you, and I will give this land to your descendants after you." 13Then God went up from him at the place where he had talked with him.

14Jacob set up a stone pillar at the place where God had talked with him, and he poured out a drink offering on it; he also poured oil on it. 15Jacob called the place where God had talked with him Bethel.[h]

The Deaths of Rachel and Isaac

16Then they moved on from Bethel. While they were still some distance from Ephrath, Rachel began to give birth and had great difficulty. 17And as she was having great difficulty in childbirth, the midwife said to her, "Don't be afraid, for you have another son." 18As she breathed her last—for she was dying—she named her son Ben-Oni.[i] But his father named him Benjamin.[j]

19So Rachel died and was buried on the way to Ephrath (that is, Bethlehem). 20Over her tomb Jacob set up a pillar, and to this day that pillar marks Rachel's tomb.

21Israel moved on again and pitched his tent beyond Migdal Eder. 22While Israel was living in that region, Reuben went in and slept with his father's concubine Bilhah, and Israel heard of it.

Jacob had twelve sons:

23The sons of Leah:

Reuben the firstborn of Jacob,
Simeon, Levi, Judah, Issachar and Zebulun.

24The sons of Rachel:

Joseph and Benjamin.

25The sons of Rachel's maidservant Bilhah:

Dan and Naphtali.

[a]27 Or *because* [b]7 *El Bethel* means *God of Bethel.* [c]8 *Allon Bacuth* means *oak of weeping.* [d]9 That is, Northwest Mesopotamia; also in verse 26 [e]10 *Jacob* means *he grasps the heel* (figuratively, *he deceives*). [f]10 *Israel* means *he struggles with God.* [g]11 Hebrew *El-Shaddai* [h]15 *Bethel* means *house of God.* [i]18 *Ben-Oni* means *son of my trouble.* [j]18 *Benjamin* means *son of my right hand.*

26The sons of Leah's maidservant Zilpah:
Gad and Asher.

These were the sons of Jacob, who were born to him in Paddan Aram.

27Jacob came home to his father Isaac in Mamre, near Kiriath Arba (that is, Hebron), where Abraham and Isaac had stayed. 28Isaac lived a hundred and eighty years. 29Then he breathed his last and died and was gathered to his people, old and full of years. And his sons Esau and Jacob buried him.

Esau's Descendants

36 This is the account of Esau (that is, Edom).

2Esau took his wives from the women of Canaan: Adah daughter of Elon the Hittite, and Oholibamah daughter of Anah and granddaughter of Zibeon the Hivite— 3also Basemath daughter of Ishmael and sister of Nebaioth.

4Adah bore Eliphaz to Esau, Basemath bore Reuel, 5and Oholibamah bore Jeush, Jalam and Korah. These were the sons of Esau, who were born to him in Canaan.

6Esau took his wives and sons and daughters and all the members of his household, as well as his livestock and all his other animals and all the goods he had acquired in Canaan, and moved to a land some distance from his brother Jacob. 7Their possessions were too great for them to remain together; the land where they were staying could not support them both because of their livestock. 8So Esau (that is, Edom) settled in the hill country of Seir.

9This is the account of Esau the father of the Edomites in the hill country of Seir.

10These are the names of Esau's sons:
Eliphaz, the son of Esau's wife Adah, and Reuel, the son of Esau's wife Basemath.
11The sons of Eliphaz:
Teman, Omar, Zepho, Gatam and Kenaz.
12Esau's son Eliphaz also had a concubine named Timna, who bore him Amalek. These were grandsons of Esau's wife Adah.
13The sons of Reuel:
Nahath, Zerah, Shammah and Mizzah. These were grandsons of Esau's wife Basemath.
14The sons of Esau's wife Oholibamah daughter of Anah and granddaughter of Zibeon, whom she bore to Esau:
Jeush, Jalam and Korah.

15These were the chiefs among Esau's descendants:

The sons of Eliphaz the firstborn of Esau:
Chiefs Teman, Omar, Zepho, Kenaz, 16Korah,[a] Gatam and Amalek. These were the chiefs descended from Eliphaz in Edom; they were grandsons of Adah.
17The sons of Esau's son Reuel:
Chiefs Nahath, Zerah, Shammah and Mizzah. These were the chiefs descended from Reuel in Edom; they were grandsons of Esau's wife Basemath.
18The sons of Esau's wife Oholibamah:
Chiefs Jeush, Jalam and Korah. These were the chiefs descended from Esau's wife Oholibamah daughter of Anah.

19These were the sons of Esau (that is, Edom), and these were their chiefs.

20These were the sons of Seir the Horite, who were living in the region:
Lotan, Shobal, Zibeon, Anah, 21Dishon, Ezer and Dishan. These sons of Seir in Edom were Horite chiefs.
22The sons of Lotan:
Hori and Homam.[b] Timna was Lotan's sister.
23The sons of Shobal:
Alvan, Manahath, Ebal, Shepho and Onam.
24The sons of Zibeon:
Aiah and Anah. This is the Anah who discovered the hot springs[c] in the desert while he was grazing the donkeys of his father Zibeon.
25The children of Anah:
Dishon and Oholibamah daughter of Anah.
26The sons of Dishon[d]:
Hemdan, Eshban, Ithran and Keran.
27The sons of Ezer:
Bilhan, Zaavan and Akan.
28The sons of Dishan:
Uz and Aran.
29These were the Horite chiefs:
Lotan, Shobal, Zibeon, Anah, 30Dishon, Ezer and Dishan. These were the Horite chiefs, according to their divisions, in the land of Seir.

[a]*16* Masoretic Text; Samaritan Pentateuch (see also Gen. 36:11 and 1 Chron. 1:36) does not have *Korah.* [b]*22* Hebrew *Hemam,* a variant of *Homam* (see 1 Chron. 1:39) [c]*24* Vulgate; Syriac *discovered water;* the meaning of the Hebrew for this word is uncertain. [d]*26* Hebrew *Dishan,* a variant of *Dishon*

The Rulers of Edom

31These were the kings who reigned in Edom before any Israelite king reigned[a]:

32Bela son of Beor became king of Edom. His city was named Dinhabah.
33When Bela died, Jobab son of Zerah from Bozrah succeeded him as king.
34When Jobab died, Husham from the land of the Temanites succeeded him as king.
35When Husham died, Hadad son of Bedad, who defeated Midian in the country of Moab, succeeded him as king. His city was named Avith.
36When Hadad died, Samlah from Masrekah succeeded him as king.
37When Samlah died, Shaul from Rehoboth on the river[b] succeeded him as king.
38When Shaul died, Baal-Hanan son of Acbor succeeded him as king.
39When Baal-Hanan son of Acbor died, Hadad[c] succeeded him as king. His city was named Pau, and his wife's name was Mehetabel daughter of Matred, the daughter of Me-Zahab.

40These were the chiefs descended from Esau, by name, according to their clans and regions:

Timna, Alvah, Jetheth, 41Oholibamah, Elah, Pinon, 42Kenaz, Teman, Mibzar, 43Magdiel and Iram. These were the chiefs of Edom, according to their settlements in the land they occupied.

This was Esau the father of the Edomites.

Joseph's Dreams

37 Jacob lived in the land where his father had stayed, the land of Canaan.

2This is the account of Jacob.

Joseph, a young man of seventeen, was tending the flocks with his brothers, the sons of Bilhah and the sons of Zilpah, his father's wives, and he brought their father a bad report about them.

3Now Israel loved Joseph more than any of his

GENESIS 37:1–11

1. As a kid what did you want to be when you grew up?
2. What's the strangest dream you've ever had?
3. What's one dream you now hold for your future?
4. When Joseph shared his dream with his brothers, they hated him (v. 5). How are you at listening to others' dreams?
5. How would you describe your life lately: Sweet dreams? A nightmare? Why?
6. How do you feel about sharing your dreams and desires with this group?
7. What is one of your wildest dreams–one only God could bring about?

other sons, because he had been born to him in his old age; and he made a richly ornamented[d] robe for him. 4When his brothers saw that their father loved him more than any of them, they hated him and could not speak a kind word to him.

5Joseph had a dream, and when he told it to his brothers, they hated him all the more. 6He said to them, "Listen to this dream I had: 7We were binding sheaves of grain out in the field when suddenly my sheaf rose and stood upright,

[a]31 Or *before an Israelite king reigned over them* [b]37 Possibly the Euphrates [c]39 Many manuscripts of the Masoretic Text, Samaritan Pentateuch and Syriac (see also 1 Chron. 1:50); most manuscripts of the Masoretic Text *Hadar* [d]3 The meaning of the Hebrew for *richly ornamented* is uncertain; also in verses 23 and 32.

Jacob (given the new name "Israel" by God) had 12 sons, who would become the founding fathers of the 12 "tribes" of Israel. The mother of the two youngest sons was Rachel, Jacob's favorite wife, who died giving birth to Benjamin. This story, as well as the rest of Genesis, centers around Joseph—Jacob's eleventh son and Rachel's firstborn.

37:2 ***Joseph.*** In his generation, he, more than any other, represented Israel—as a people who struggled with God and with men and overcame and as a source of blessing to the nations (see 12:2–3). Through the life of Joseph, the covenant family in Canaan becomes an emerging nation in Egypt.

37:3 ***richly ornamented robe.*** A mark of Jacob's favoritism.

37:5 ***dream.*** Dreams were a frequent mode of revelation in both the Old and New Testaments (Num. 12:6; 1 Kings 3:5; Dan. 7:1; Matt. 1:20; 2:12–13; 27:19).

37:7 ***bowed down.*** Joseph's dream would later come true (42:6; 43:26; 44:14).

37:8 ***Will you actually rule us?*** Joseph would later receive "the rights of the firstborn" (1 Chron. 5:1–2), including the double portion of the inheritance usually given to the oldest son, since his father Jacob adopted his two sons (48:5).

37:10 ***your mother.*** Jacob possibly refers to Leah, since Rachel has already died.

37:11 ***kept the matter in mind.*** A hint that Jacob later recalled Joseph's dreams when events brought about their fulfillment.

while your sheaves gathered around mine and bowed down to it."

8His brothers said to him, "Do you intend to reign over us? Will you actually rule us?" And they hated him all the more because of his dream and what he had said.

9Then he had another dream, and he told it to his brothers. "Listen," he said, "I had another dream, and this time the sun and moon and eleven stars were bowing down to me."

10When he told his father as well as his brothers, his father rebuked him and said, "What is this dream you had? Will your mother and I and your brothers actually come and bow down to the ground before you?" 11His brothers were jealous of him, but his father kept the matter in mind.

Joseph Sold by His Brothers

12Now his brothers had gone to graze their father's flocks near Shechem, 13and Israel said to Joseph, "As you know, your brothers are grazing the flocks near Shechem. Come, I am going to send you to them."

"Very well," he replied.

14So he said to him, "Go and see if all is well with your brothers and with the flocks, and bring word back to me." Then he sent him off from the Valley of Hebron.

When Joseph arrived at Shechem, 15a man found him wandering around in the fields and asked him, "What are you looking for?"

16He replied, "I'm looking for my brothers. Can you tell me where they are grazing their flocks?"

17"They have moved on from here," the man answered. "I heard them say, 'Let's go to Dothan.'"

So Joseph went after his brothers and found them near Dothan. 18But they saw him in the distance, and before he reached them, they plotted to kill him.

19"Here comes that dreamer!" they said to each other. 20"Come now, let's kill him and throw him into one of these cisterns and say that a ferocious animal devoured him. Then we'll see what comes of his dreams."

21When Reuben heard this, he tried to rescue him from their hands. "Let's not take his life," he said. 22"Don't shed any blood. Throw him into this cistern here in the desert, but don't lay a hand on him." Reuben said this to rescue him from them and take him back to his father.

GENESIS 37:12–36

1. Who in your family picks on you the most? Who stands up for you?
2. What kind of pranks have you pulled? Was there ever a time when your prank went too far? If so, when?
3. Who is someone you've taken under your wing, someone you look out for?
4. On a scale of 1 (no problem) to 10 (big problem), how hard is it for you to refuse to go along with the crowd when they do stupid things?
5. Joseph's brothers wanted to kill him (vv. 18,20) in part because of jealousy. Who or what makes you jealous? How do you deal with it?
6. How can this group pray for you this week?

23So when Joseph came to his brothers, they stripped him of his robe—the richly ornamented robe he was wearing— 24and they took him and threw him into the cistern. Now the cistern was empty; there was no water in it.

25As they sat down to eat their meal, they looked up and saw a caravan of Ishmaelites coming from Gilead. Their camels were loaded with spices, balm and myrrh, and they were on their way to take them down to Egypt.

Jacob's favorite son Joseph was already hated by his brothers (37:4) when he shared about his dreams that elevated him above the rest of the family.

37:19 ***dreamer.*** The Hebrew for this word means "master of dreams" or "dream expert" and is used here with obvious sarcasm.

37:21 ***Reuben ... tried to rescue him.*** As Jacob's firstborn, he felt responsible for Joseph. He would later remind his brothers of this day (42:22).

37:23–24 Similarly, in Egypt Joseph (though innocent of any wrongdoing) would be stripped of his position of privilege and thrown into prison—also as a result of "domestic violence" (ch. 39). Joseph's cloak would also be shown to Potiphar, but he would be rescued.

37:28 ***twenty shekels of silver.*** In later times, this amount was the value of a male of Joseph's age who had been dedicated to the Lord (see Lev. 27:5).

37:34 ***tore his clothes.*** As an act of great remorse (see v. 29). ***put on sackcloth.*** Wearing coarse and uncomfortable sackcloth instead of ordinary clothes was a sign of mourning.

37:36 ***sold.*** As a slave. The peoples of the Arabian Desert were long involved in international slave trade. ***guard.*** The Hebrew for this word can mean "executioners" (the captain of whom was in charge of the royal prisoners) or "butchers" (the captain of whom was the chief cook in the royal court).

26Judah said to his brothers, "What will we gain if we kill our brother and cover up his blood? 27Come, let's sell him to the Ishmaelites and not lay our hands on him; after all, he is our brother, our own flesh and blood." His brothers agreed.

28So when the Midianite merchants came by, his brothers pulled Joseph up out of the cistern and sold him for twenty shekels[a] of silver to the Ishmaelites, who took him to Egypt.

29When Reuben returned to the cistern and saw that Joseph was not there, he tore his clothes. 30He went back to his brothers and said, "The boy isn't there! Where can I turn now?"

31Then they got Joseph's robe, slaughtered a goat and dipped the robe in the blood. 32They took the ornamented robe back to their father and said, "We found this. Examine it to see whether it is your son's robe."

33He recognized it and said, "It is my son's robe! Some ferocious animal has devoured him. Joseph has surely been torn to pieces."

34Then Jacob tore his clothes, put on sackcloth and mourned for his son many days. 35All his sons and daughters came to comfort him, but he refused to be comforted. "No," he said, "in mourning will I go down to the grave[b] to my son." So his father wept for him.

36Meanwhile, the Midianites[c] sold Joseph in Egypt to Potiphar, one of Pharaoh's officials, the captain of the guard.

Judah and Tamar

38 At that time, Judah left his brothers and went down to stay with a man of Adullam named Hirah. 2There Judah met the daughter of a Canaanite man named Shua. He married her and lay with her; 3she became pregnant and gave birth to a son, who was named Er. 4She conceived again and gave birth to a son and named him Onan. 5She gave birth to still another son and named him Shelah. It was at Kezib that she gave birth to him.

6Judah got a wife for Er, his firstborn, and her name was Tamar. 7But Er, Judah's firstborn, was wicked in the LORD's sight; so the LORD put him to death.

8Then Judah said to Onan, "Lie with your brother's wife and fulfill your duty to her as a brother-in-law to produce offspring for your brother." 9But Onan knew that the offspring would not be his; so whenever he lay with his brother's wife, he spilled his semen on the ground to keep from producing offspring for his brother. 10What he did was wicked in the LORD's sight; so he put him to death also.

11Judah then said to his daughter-in-law Tamar, "Live as a widow in your father's house until my son Shelah grows up." For he thought, "He may die too, just like his brothers." So Tamar went to live in her father's house.

12After a long time Judah's wife, the daughter of Shua, died. When Judah had recovered from his grief, he went up to Timnah, to the men who were shearing his sheep, and his friend Hirah the Adullamite went with him.

13When Tamar was told, "Your father-in-law is on his way to Timnah to shear his sheep," 14she took off her widow's clothes, covered herself with a veil to disguise herself, and then sat down at the entrance to Enaim, which is on the road to Timnah. For she saw that, though Shelah had now grown up, she had not been given to him as his wife.

15When Judah saw her, he thought she was a prostitute, for she had covered her face. 16Not realizing that she was his daughter-in-law, he went over to her by the roadside and said, "Come now, let me sleep with you."

"And what will you give me to sleep with you?" she asked.

17"I'll send you a young goat from my flock," he said.

"Will you give me something as a pledge until you send it?" she asked.

18He said, "What pledge should I give you?"

"Your seal and its cord, and the staff in your hand," she answered. So he gave them to her and slept with her, and she became pregnant by him. 19After she left, she took off her veil and put on her widow's clothes again.

20Meanwhile Judah sent the young goat by his friend the Adullamite in order to get his pledge back from the woman, but he did not find her. 21He asked the men who lived there, "Where is the shrine prostitute who was beside the road at Enaim?"

"There hasn't been any shrine prostitute here," they said.

22So he went back to Judah and said, "I didn't find her. Besides, the men who lived there said, 'There hasn't been any shrine prostitute here.' "

23Then Judah said, "Let her keep what she has, or we will become a laughingstock. After all, I did send her this young goat, but you didn't find her."

24About three months later Judah was told, "Your daughter-in-law Tamar is guilty of prostitution, and as a result she is now pregnant."

Judah said, "Bring her out and have her burned to death!"

25As she was being brought out, she sent a message to her father-in-law. "I am pregnant by

[a] *28* That is, about 8 ounces (about 0.2 kilogram) [b] *35* Hebrew *Sheol* [c] *36* Samaritan Pentateuch, Septuagint, Vulgate and Syriac (see also verse 28); Masoretic Text *Medanites*

the man who owns these," she said. And she
added, "See if you recognize whose seal and cord
and staff these are."
26Judah recognized them and said, "She is
more righteous than I, since I wouldn't give her
to my son Shelah." And he did not sleep with her
again.
27When the time came for her to give birth,
there were twin boys in her womb. 28As she was
giving birth, one of them put out his hand; so the
midwife took a scarlet thread and tied it on his
wrist and said, "This one came out first." 29But
when he drew back his hand, his brother came
out, and she said, "So this is how you have broken out!" And he was named Perez.[a] 30Then his
brother, who had the scarlet thread on his wrist,
came out and he was given the name Zerah.[b]

Joseph and Potiphar's Wife

39 Now Joseph had been taken down to
Egypt. Potiphar, an Egyptian who was
one of Pharaoh's officials, the captain of the
guard, bought him from the Ishmaelites who had
taken him there.
2The LORD was with Joseph and he prospered,
and he lived in the house of his Egyptian master.
3When his master saw that the LORD was with
him and that the LORD gave him success in everything he did, 4Joseph found favor in his eyes and
became his attendant. Potiphar put him in charge
of his household, and he entrusted to his care
everything he owned. 5From the time he put him
in charge of his household and of all that he
owned, the LORD blessed the household of the
Egyptian because of Joseph. The blessing of the
LORD was on everything Potiphar had, both in
the house and in the field. 6So he left in Joseph's
care everything he had; with Joseph in charge, he
did not concern himself with anything except the
food he ate.
Now Joseph was well-built and handsome,
7and after a while his master's wife took notice of
Joseph and said, "Come to bed with me!"
8But he refused. "With me in charge," he told
her, "my master does not concern himself with
anything in the house; everything he owns he
has entrusted to my care. 9No one is greater in
this house than I am. My master has withheld
nothing from me except you, because you are his
wife. How then could I do such a wicked thing
and sin against God?" 10And though she spoke to
Joseph day after day, he refused to go to bed with
her or even be with her.
11One day he went into the house to attend to
his duties, and none of the household servants
was inside. 12She caught him by his cloak and

? *GENESIS 39:1–23*

1. What famous person would you like to go on a date with?
2. Have you ever been accused of something you didn't do? What happened?
3. Joseph is described as "well-built and handsome" (v. 6). When you are attracted to someone, how important are their looks?
4. How do you deal with sexual temptation? What lesson can you learn from Joseph?
5. What is the most important reason to save sex for marriage?
6. What is the best way to respond when someone tries to coax you into compromising your sexual standards?
7. In what way can you sense that the Lord is with you, as he was with Joseph, in the midst of the pressures you face?

[a]29 *Perez* means *breaking out.* [b]30 *Zerah* can mean *scarlet* or *brightness.*

39:1 *taken down to Egypt.* Joseph's brothers had sold him to a caravan of merchants passing through Canaan on their way to Egypt. Joseph's experiences in Egypt, as well as those of his youth in Canaan (see note on 37:23–24), are similar to Israel's national experiences in Egypt. Both Joseph and Israel were first received with honor in Egypt; then subjected to cruel bondage; and finally raised up by God in the eyes of the Egyptians as they came to recognize that these people did indeed hold their lives in their hands. The author of Genesis shows how the history of the patriarchs foreshadowed the Exodus.

39:2 *The LORD was with Joseph.* This fact is mentioned several times (vv. 3,21,23). Though Joseph's situation kept changing drastically, God's relationship to him remained the same.

39:5 *the LORD blessed the household of the Egyptian because of Joseph.* The offspring of Abraham are becoming a blessing to the nations (see 12:2–3).

39:6 *left in Joseph's care everything he had.* Joseph had full responsibility for the welfare of Potiphar's house, as later he would have full responsibility in prison (vv. 22–23) and later still in all Egypt (41:41). Always this Israelite came to hold the welfare of his "world" in his hands—but always by the blessing and overruling of God.

39:7 *took notice of.* Looked at with desire.

39:9 *sin against God.* All sin is against God, first and foremost (see Ps. 51:4).

said, "Come to bed with me!" But he left his
cloak in her hand and ran out of the house.
13When she saw that he had left his cloak in
her hand and had run out of the house, 14she
called her household servants. "Look," she said
to them, "this Hebrew has been brought to us to
make sport of us! He came in here to sleep with
me, but I screamed. 15When he heard me scream
for help, he left his cloak beside me and ran out
of the house."
16She kept his cloak beside her until his master came home. 17Then she told him this story:
"That Hebrew slave you brought us came to me
to make sport of me. 18But as soon as I screamed
for help, he left his cloak beside me and ran out
of the house."
19When his master heard the story his wife
told him, saying, "This is how your slave treated
me," he burned with anger. 20Joseph's master
took him and put him in prison, the place where
the king's prisoners were confined.
But while Joseph was there in the prison, 21the
LORD was with him; he showed him kindness and
granted him favor in the eyes of the prison warden. 22So the warden put Joseph in charge of all
those held in the prison, and he was made responsible for all that was done there. 23The warden paid no attention to anything under Joseph's
care, because the LORD was with Joseph and gave
him success in whatever he did.

The Cupbearer and the Baker

40 Some time later, the cupbearer and the
baker of the king of Egypt offended their
master, the king of Egypt. 2Pharaoh was angry
with his two officials, the chief cupbearer and the
chief baker, 3and put them in custody in the
house of the captain of the guard, in the same
prison where Joseph was confined. 4The captain
of the guard assigned them to Joseph, and he
attended them.
After they had been in custody for some time,
5each of the two men—the cupbearer and the
baker of the king of Egypt, who were being held
in prison—had a dream the same night, and each
dream had a meaning of its own.
6When Joseph came to them the next morning, he saw that they were dejected. 7So he asked
Pharaoh's officials who were in custody with him
in his master's house, "Why are your faces so sad
today?"
8"We both had dreams," they answered, "but
there is no one to interpret them."
Then Joseph said to them, "Do not interpretations belong to God? Tell me your dreams."
9So the chief cupbearer told Joseph his dream.
He said to him, "In my dream I saw a vine in
front of me, 10and on the vine were three
branches. As soon as it budded, it blossomed, and
its clusters ripened into grapes. 11Pharaoh's cup
was in my hand, and I took the grapes, squeezed
them into Pharaoh's cup and put the cup in his
hand."
12"This is what it means," Joseph said to him.
"The three branches are three days. 13Within
three days Pharaoh will lift up your head and
restore you to your position, and you will put
Pharaoh's cup in his hand, just as you used to do
when you were his cupbearer. 14But when all
goes well with you, remember me and show me
kindness; mention me to Pharaoh and get me out
of this prison. 15For I was forcibly carried off from
the land of the Hebrews, and even here I have
done nothing to deserve being put in a dungeon."
16When the chief baker saw that Joseph had
given a favorable interpretation, he said to Joseph, "I too had a dream: On my head were three
baskets of bread.[a] 17In the top basket were all
kinds of baked goods for Pharaoh, but the birds
were eating them out of the basket on my head."
18"This is what it means," Joseph said. "The
three baskets are three days. 19Within three days
Pharaoh will lift off your head and hang you on a
tree.[b] And the birds will eat away your flesh."
20Now the third day was Pharaoh's birthday,
and he gave a feast for all his officials. He lifted up
the heads of the chief cupbearer and the chief
baker in the presence of his officials: 21He restored the chief cupbearer to his position, so that
he once again put the cup into Pharaoh's hand,
22but he hanged[c] the chief baker, just as Joseph
had said to them in his interpretation.
23The chief cupbearer, however, did not remember Joseph; he forgot him.

Pharaoh's Dreams

41 When two full years had passed, Pharaoh
had a dream: He was standing by the
Nile, 2when out of the river there came up seven
cows, sleek and fat, and they grazed among the
reeds. 3After them, seven other cows, ugly and
gaunt, came up out of the Nile and stood beside
those on the riverbank. 4And the cows that were
ugly and gaunt ate up the seven sleek, fat cows.
Then Pharaoh woke up.
5He fell asleep again and had a second dream:
Seven heads of grain, healthy and good, were
growing on a single stalk. 6After them, seven other heads of grain sprouted—thin and scorched by
the east wind. 7The thin heads of grain swallowed up the seven healthy, full heads. Then
Pharaoh woke up; it had been a dream.
8In the morning his mind was troubled, so he
sent for all the magicians and wise men of Egypt.

[a]16 Or *three wicker baskets* [b]19 Or *and impale you on a pole* [c]22 Or *impaled*

Pharaoh told them his dreams, but no one could
interpret them for him.
9Then the chief cupbearer said to Pharaoh,
"Today I am reminded of my shortcomings.

> ### *Genesis 41:1–40*
>
> 1. Would you rather play second string on a winning team or first string on a losing team?
> 2. If you were suddenly summoned to the White House to meet with the president of the United States, what would your first thought be?
> 3. How do you typically respond when someone gives you a lot of praise: Blush? Accept it? Deny it?
> 4. Do you think God uses your trials to prepare you for something? If yes, what?
> 5. When was the last time you wondered if God had forgotten about you?
> 6. How does a story like this remind you that God is always there for you?
> 7. Like Joseph did, what strength or ability can you give God credit for? Conclude your group accordingly in prayer.

10Pharaoh was once angry with his servants, and
he imprisoned me and the chief baker in the
house of the captain of the guard. 11Each of us
had a dream the same night, and each dream had
a meaning of its own. 12Now a young Hebrew
was there with us, a servant of the captain of the
guard. We told him our dreams, and he interpreted them for us, giving each man the interpretation of his dream. 13And things turned out exactly as he interpreted them to us: I was restored to
my position, and the other man was hanged.[a]"
14So Pharaoh sent for Joseph, and he was
quickly brought from the dungeon. When he had
shaved and changed his clothes, he came before
Pharaoh.
15Pharaoh said to Joseph, "I had a dream, and
no one can interpret it. But I have heard it said of
you that when you hear a dream you can interpret it."
16"I cannot do it," Joseph replied to Pharaoh,
"but God will give Pharaoh the answer he desires."
17Then Pharaoh said to Joseph, "In my dream
I was standing on the bank of the Nile, 18when
out of the river there came up seven cows, fat
and sleek, and they grazed among the reeds. 19Af-
ter them, seven other cows came up—scrawny
and very ugly and lean. I had never seen such
ugly cows in all the land of Egypt. 20The lean,
ugly cows ate up the seven fat cows that came up
first. 21But even after they ate them, no one could
tell that they had done so; they looked just as ugly
as before. Then I woke up.
22"In my dreams I also saw seven heads of
grain, full and good, growing on a single stalk.
23After them, seven other heads sprouted—
withered and thin and scorched by the east wind.
24The thin heads of grain swallowed up the seven
good heads. I told this to the magicians, but none
could explain it to me."
25Then Joseph said to Pharaoh, "The dreams of
Pharaoh are one and the same. God has revealed
to Pharaoh what he is about to do. 26The seven
good cows are seven years, and the seven good
heads of grain are seven years; it is one and the
same dream. 27The seven lean, ugly cows that
came up afterward are seven years, and so are the
seven worthless heads of grain scorched by the
east wind: They are seven years of famine.
28"It is just as I said to Pharaoh: God has
shown Pharaoh what he is about to do. 29Seven
years of great abundance are coming throughout
the land of Egypt, 30but seven years of famine will

[a]13 Or *impaled*

First, Joseph was sold into slavery by his jealous brothers. He came to be in charge of his master's household in Egypt, until he was falsely accused of assaulting his master's wife—for which he was thrown in prison. While in prison, he accurately interpreted the dreams of two fellow inmates. Joseph asked one of them, Pharaoh's chief cupbearer, to remember him when he was set free (40:14); however, the cupbearer "forgot" Joseph (40:23).

41:2 ***out of the river there came up seven cows.*** Cattle often submerged themselves up to their necks in the Nile to escape sun and insects.

41:6 ***scorched by the east wind.*** Winds from the desert in late spring and early fall often withers vegetation.

41:8 ***magicians.*** Probably Egyptian priests who claimed to possess occult knowledge.

41:13 ***things turned out exactly as he interpreted them.*** Because Joseph's words were from the Lord (see Ps. 105:19).

41:14 ***Pharaoh sent for Joseph.*** Effecting his permanent release from prison.

41:27 ***seven years of famine.*** Long famines were rare in Egypt because of the regularity of the annual overflow of the Nile, but not uncommon elsewhere.

41:32 Repetition of a divine revelation was often used for emphasis (see 37:5–9).

41:40 ***You shall be in charge.*** Pharaoh took Joseph's advice (v. 33) and decided that Joseph himself should be in command.

follow them. Then all the abundance in Egypt will be forgotten, and the famine will ravage the land. **31**The abundance in the land will not be remembered, because the famine that follows it will be so severe. **32**The reason the dream was given to Pharaoh in two forms is that the matter has been firmly decided by God, and God will do it soon.

33"And now let Pharaoh look for a discerning and wise man and put him in charge of the land of Egypt. **34**Let Pharaoh appoint commissioners over the land to take a fifth of the harvest of Egypt during the seven years of abundance. **35**They should collect all the food of these good years that are coming and store up the grain under the authority of Pharaoh, to be kept in the cities for food. **36**This food should be held in reserve for the country, to be used during the seven years of famine that will come upon Egypt, so that the country may not be ruined by the famine."

37The plan seemed good to Pharaoh and to all his officials. **38**So Pharaoh asked them, "Can we find anyone like this man, one in whom is the spirit of God[a]?"

39Then Pharaoh said to Joseph, "Since God has made all this known to you, there is no one so discerning and wise as you. **40**You shall be in charge of my palace, and all my people are to submit to your orders. Only with respect to the throne will I be greater than you."

Joseph in Charge of Egypt

41So Pharaoh said to Joseph, "I hereby put you in charge of the whole land of Egypt." **42**Then Pharaoh took his signet ring from his finger and put it on Joseph's finger. He dressed him in robes of fine linen and put a gold chain around his neck. **43**He had him ride in a chariot as his second-in-command,[b] and men shouted before him, "Make way[c]!" Thus he put him in charge of the whole land of Egypt.

44Then Pharaoh said to Joseph, "I am Pharaoh, but without your word no one will lift hand or foot in all Egypt." **45**Pharaoh gave Joseph the name Zaphenath-Paneah and gave him Asenath daughter of Potiphera, priest of On,[d] to be his wife. And Joseph went throughout the land of Egypt.

46Joseph was thirty years old when he entered the service of Pharaoh king of Egypt. And Joseph went out from Pharaoh's presence and traveled throughout Egypt. **47**During the seven years of abundance the land produced plentifully. **48**Joseph collected all the food produced in those seven years of abundance in Egypt and stored it in the cities. In each city he put the food grown in the fields surrounding it. **49**Joseph stored up huge quantities of grain, like the sand of the sea; it was so much that he stopped keeping records because it was beyond measure.

50Before the years of famine came, two sons were born to Joseph by Asenath daughter of Potiphera, priest of On. **51**Joseph named his firstborn Manasseh[e] and said, "It is because God has made me forget all my trouble and all my father's household." **52**The second son he named Ephraim[f] and said, "It is because God has made me fruitful in the land of my suffering."

53The seven years of abundance in Egypt came to an end, **54**and the seven years of famine began, just as Joseph had said. There was famine in all the other lands, but in the whole land of Egypt there was food. **55**When all Egypt began to feel the famine, the people cried to Pharaoh for food. Then Pharaoh told all the Egyptians, "Go to Joseph and do what he tells you."

56When the famine had spread over the whole country, Joseph opened the storehouses and sold grain to the Egyptians, for the famine was severe throughout Egypt. **57**And all the countries came to Egypt to buy grain from Joseph, because the famine was severe in all the world.

Joseph's Brothers Go to Egypt

42 When Jacob learned that there was grain in Egypt, he said to his sons, "Why do you just keep looking at each other?" **2**He continued, "I have heard that there is grain in Egypt. Go down there and buy some for us, so that we may live and not die."

3Then ten of Joseph's brothers went down to buy grain from Egypt. **4**But Jacob did not send Benjamin, Joseph's brother, with the others, because he was afraid that harm might come to him. **5**So Israel's sons were among those who went to buy grain, for the famine was in the land of Canaan also.

6Now Joseph was the governor of the land, the one who sold grain to all its people. So when Joseph's brothers arrived, they bowed down to him with their faces to the ground. **7**As soon as Joseph saw his brothers, he recognized them, but he pretended to be a stranger and spoke harshly to them. "Where do you come from?" he asked.

"From the land of Canaan," they replied, "to buy food."

8Although Joseph recognized his brothers, they did not recognize him. **9**Then he remembered his dreams about them and said to them,

[a]38 Or *of the gods* [b]43 Or *in the chariot of his second-in-command*; or *in his second chariot* [c]43 Or *Bow down*
[d]45 That is, Heliopolis; also in verse 50 [e]51 *Manasseh* sounds like and may be derived from the Hebrew for *forget.*
[f]52 *Ephraim* sounds like the Hebrew for *twice fruitful.*

“You are spies! You have come to see where our
land is unprotected.”
10“No, my lord,” they answered. “Your servants have come to buy food. 11We are all the
sons of one man. Your servants are honest men,
not spies.”
12“No!” he said to them. “You have come to
see where our land is unprotected.”
13But they replied, “Your servants were twelve
brothers, the sons of one man, who lives in the
land of Canaan. The youngest is now with our
father, and one is no more.”
14Joseph said to them, “It is just as I told you:
You are spies! 15And this is how you will be tested: As surely as Pharaoh lives, you will not leave
this place unless your youngest brother comes
here. 16Send one of your number to get your
brother; the rest of you will be kept in prison, so
that your words may be tested to see if you are
telling the truth. If you are not, then as surely as
Pharaoh lives, you are spies!” 17And he put them
all in custody for three days.
18On the third day, Joseph said to them, “Do
this and you will live, for I fear God: 19If you are
honest men, let one of your brothers stay here in
prison, while the rest of you go and take grain
back for your starving households. 20But you
must bring your youngest brother to me, so that
your words may be verified and that you may not
die.” This they proceeded to do.
21They said to one another, “Surely we are
being punished because of our brother. We saw
how distressed he was when he pleaded with us
for his life, but we would not listen; that’s why
this distress has come upon us.”
22Reuben replied, “Didn’t I tell you not to sin
against the boy? But you wouldn’t listen! Now we
must give an accounting for his blood.” 23They
did not realize that Joseph could understand
them, since he was using an interpreter.
24He turned away from them and began to
weep, but then turned back and spoke to them
again. He had Simeon taken from them and
bound before their eyes.
25Joseph gave orders to fill their bags with
grain, to put each man’s silver back in his sack,
and to give them provisions for their journey.
After this was done for them, 26they loaded their
grain on their donkeys and left.
27At the place where they stopped for the
night one of them opened his sack to get feed for
his donkey, and he saw his silver in the mouth of
his sack. 28“My silver has been returned,” he said
to his brothers. “Here it is in my sack.”
Their hearts sank and they turned to each other trembling and said, “What is this that God has
done to us?”
29When they came to their father Jacob in the
land of Canaan, they told him all that had happened to them. They said, 30“The man who is
lord over the land spoke harshly to us and treated
us as though we were spying on the land. 31But
we said to him, ‘We are honest men; we are not
spies. 32We were twelve brothers, sons of one
father. One is no more, and the youngest is now
with our father in Canaan.’
33“Then the man who is lord over the land
said to us, ‘This is how I will know whether you
are honest men: Leave one of your brothers here
with me, and take food for your starving households and go. 34But bring your youngest brother
to me so I will know that you are not spies but
honest men. Then I will give your brother back to
you, and you can trade[a] in the land.’ ”
35As they were emptying their sacks, there in
each man’s sack was his pouch of silver! When
they and their father saw the money pouches,
they were frightened. 36Their father Jacob said to
them, “You have deprived me of my children.
Joseph is no more and Simeon is no more, and
now you want to take Benjamin. Everything is
against me!”
37Then Reuben said to his father, “You may
put both of my sons to death if I do not bring him
back to you. Entrust him to my care, and I will
bring him back.”
38But Jacob said, “My son will not go down
there with you; his brother is dead and he is the
only one left. If harm comes to him on the journey you are taking, you will bring my gray head
down to the grave[b] in sorrow.”

The Second Journey to Egypt

43 Now the famine was still severe in the
land. 2So when they had eaten all the
grain they had brought from Egypt, their father
said to them, “Go back and buy us a little more
food.”
3But Judah said to him, “The man warned us
solemnly, ‘You will not see my face again unless
your brother is with you.’ 4If you will send our
brother along with us, we will go down and buy
food for you. 5But if you will not send him, we
will not go down, because the man said to us,
‘You will not see my face again unless your brother is with you.’ ”
6Israel asked, “Why did you bring this trouble
on me by telling the man you had another
brother?”
7They replied, “The man questioned us closely
about ourselves and our family. ‘Is your father
still living?’ he asked us. ‘Do you have another
brother?’ We simply answered his questions.

[a]34 Or *move about freely* [b]38 Hebrew *Sheol*

How were we to know he would say, 'Bring your
brother down here'?"
8Then Judah said to Israel his father, "Send the
boy along with me and we will go at once, so that
we and you and our children may live and not
die. 9I myself will guarantee his safety; you can
hold me personally responsible for him. If I do
not bring him back to you and set him here before you, I will bear the blame before you all my
life. 10As it is, if we had not delayed, we could
have gone and returned twice."
11Then their father Israel said to them, "If it
must be, then do this: Put some of the best products of the land in your bags and take them down
to the man as a gift—a little balm and a little
honey, some spices and myrrh, some pistachio
nuts and almonds. 12Take double the amount of
silver with you, for you must return the silver
that was put back into the mouths of your sacks.
Perhaps it was a mistake. 13Take your brother
also and go back to the man at once. 14And may
God Almighty[a] grant you mercy before the man
so that he will let your other brother and Benjamin come back with you. As for me, if I am bereaved, I am bereaved."
15So the men took the gifts and double the
amount of silver, and Benjamin also. They hurried down to Egypt and presented themselves to
Joseph. 16When Joseph saw Benjamin with them,
he said to the steward of his house, "Take these
men to my house, slaughter an animal and prepare dinner; they are to eat with me at noon."
17The man did as Joseph told him and took the
men to Joseph's house. 18Now the men were
frightened when they were taken to his house.
They thought, "We were brought here because of
the silver that was put back into our sacks the
first time. He wants to attack us and overpower
us and seize us as slaves and take our donkeys."
19So they went up to Joseph's steward and
spoke to him at the entrance to the house.
20"Please, sir," they said, "we came down here
the first time to buy food. 21But at the place
where we stopped for the night we opened our
sacks and each of us found his silver—the exact
weight—in the mouth of his sack. So we have
brought it back with us. 22We have also brought
additional silver with us to buy food. We don't
know who put our silver in our sacks."
23"It's all right," he said. "Don't be afraid.
Your God, the God of your father, has given you
treasure in your sacks; I received your silver."
Then he brought Simeon out to them.
24The steward took the men into Joseph's
house, gave them water to wash their feet and
provided fodder for their donkeys. 25They prepared their gifts for Joseph's arrival at noon, because they had heard that they were to eat there.
26When Joseph came home, they presented to
him the gifts they had brought into the house,
and they bowed down before him to the ground.
27He asked them how they were, and then he
said, "How is your aged father you told me about?
Is he still living?"
28They replied, "Your servant our father is still
alive and well." And they bowed low to pay him
honor.
29As he looked about and saw his brother Benjamin, his own mother's son, he asked, "Is this
your youngest brother, the one you told me
about?" And he said, "God be gracious to you, my
son." 30Deeply moved at the sight of his brother,
Joseph hurried out and looked for a place to
weep. He went into his private room and wept
there.
31After he had washed his face, he came out
and, controlling himself, said, "Serve the food."
32They served him by himself, the brothers by
themselves, and the Egyptians who ate with him
by themselves, because Egyptians could not eat
with Hebrews, for that is detestable to Egyptians.
33The men had been seated before him in the
order of their ages, from the firstborn to the
youngest; and they looked at each other in astonishment. 34When portions were served to them
from Joseph's table, Benjamin's portion was five
times as much as anyone else's. So they feasted
and drank freely with him.

A Silver Cup in a Sack

44 Now Joseph gave these instructions to the
steward of his house: "Fill the men's
sacks with as much food as they can carry, and
put each man's silver in the mouth of his sack.
2Then put my cup, the silver one, in the mouth
of the youngest one's sack, along with the silver
for his grain." And he did as Joseph said.
3As morning dawned, the men were sent on
their way with their donkeys. 4They had not gone
far from the city when Joseph said to his steward,
"Go after those men at once, and when you catch
up with them, say to them, 'Why have you repaid
good with evil? 5Isn't this the cup my master
drinks from and also uses for divination? This is
a wicked thing you have done.' "
6When he caught up with them, he repeated
these words to them. 7But they said to him,
"Why does my lord say such things? Far be it
from your servants to do anything like that! 8We
even brought back to you from the land of Canaan the silver we found inside the mouths of our
sacks. So why would we steal silver or gold from
your master's house? 9If any of your servants is

[a]14 Hebrew *El-Shaddai*

found to have it, he will die; and the rest of us
will become my lord's slaves."
10"Very well, then," he said, "let it be as you
say. Whoever is found to have it will become my
slave; the rest of you will be free from blame."
11Each of them quickly lowered his sack to the
ground and opened it. 12Then the steward proceeded to search, beginning with the oldest and
ending with the youngest. And the cup was
found in Benjamin's sack. 13At this, they tore
their clothes. Then they all loaded their donkeys
and returned to the city.
14Joseph was still in the house when Judah and
his brothers came in, and they threw themselves
to the ground before him. 15Joseph said to them,
"What is this you have done? Don't you know
that a man like me can find things out by divination?"
16"What can we say to my lord?" Judah replied. "What can we say? How can we prove our
innocence? God has uncovered your servants'
guilt. We are now my lord's slaves—we ourselves and the one who was found to have the
cup."
17But Joseph said, "Far be it from me to do
such a thing! Only the man who was found to
have the cup will become my slave. The rest of
you, go back to your father in peace."
18Then Judah went up to him and said:
"Please, my lord, let your servant speak a word
to my lord. Do not be angry with your servant,
though you are equal to Pharaoh himself. 19My
lord asked his servants, 'Do you have a father or
a brother?' 20And we answered, 'We have an
aged father, and there is a young son born to him
in his old age. His brother is dead, and he is the
only one of his mother's sons left, and his father
loves him.'
21"Then you said to your servants, 'Bring him
down to me so I can see him for myself.' 22And
we said to my lord, 'The boy cannot leave his
father; if he leaves him, his father will die.' 23But
you told your servants, 'Unless your youngest
brother comes down with you, you will not see
my face again.' 24When we went back to your
servant my father, we told him what my lord had
said.
25"Then our father said, 'Go back and buy a
little more food.' 26But we said, 'We cannot go
down. Only if our youngest brother is with us
will we go. We cannot see the man's face unless
our youngest brother is with us.'
27"Your servant my father said to us, 'You
know that my wife bore me two sons. 28One of
them went away from me, and I said, "He has
surely been torn to pieces." And I have not seen
him since. 29If you take this one from me too and
harm comes to him, you will bring my gray head
down to the grave[a] in misery.'
30"So now, if the boy is not with us when I go
back to your servant my father and if my father,
whose life is closely bound up with the boy's life,
31sees that the boy isn't there, he will die. Your
servants will bring the gray head of our father
down to the grave in sorrow. 32Your servant guaranteed the boy's safety to my father. I said, 'If I do
not bring him back to you, I will bear the blame
before you, my father, all my life!'
33"Now then, please let your servant remain
here as my lord's slave in place of the boy, and let
the boy return with his brothers. 34How can I go
back to my father if the boy is not with me? No!
Do not let me see the misery that would come
upon my father."

Joseph Makes Himself Known

45 Then Joseph could no longer control himself before all his attendants, and he cried
out, "Have everyone leave my presence!" So
there was no one with Joseph when he made
himself known to his brothers. 2And he wept so
loudly that the Egyptians heard him, and Pharaoh's household heard about it.
3Joseph said to his brothers, "I am Joseph! Is
my father still living?" But his brothers were not
able to answer him, because they were terrified
at his presence.
4Then Joseph said to his brothers, "Come
close to me." When they had done so, he said, "I
am your brother Joseph, the one you sold into
Egypt! 5And now, do not be distressed and do not
be angry with yourselves for selling me here, because it was to save lives that God sent me ahead
of you. 6For two years now there has been famine
in the land, and for the next five years there will
not be plowing and reaping. 7But God sent me
ahead of you to preserve for you a remnant on
earth and to save your lives by a great deliverance.[b]
8"So then, it was not you who sent me here,
but God. He made me father to Pharaoh, lord of
his entire household and ruler of all Egypt. 9Now
hurry back to my father and say to him, 'This is
what your son Joseph says: God has made me lord
of all Egypt. Come down to me; don't delay.
10You shall live in the region of Goshen and be
near me—you, your children and grandchildren,
your flocks and herds, and all you have. 11I will
provide for you there, because five years of famine are still to come. Otherwise you and your

[a] *29* Hebrew *Sheol*; also in verse 31
[b] *7* Or *save you as a great band of survivors*

household and all who belong to you will become
destitute.'
12"You can see for yourselves, and so can my
brother Benjamin, that it is really I who am
speaking to you. 13Tell my father about all the
honor accorded me in Egypt and about everything you have seen. And bring my father down
here quickly."
14Then he threw his arms around his brother
Benjamin and wept, and Benjamin embraced
him, weeping. 15And he kissed all his brothers
and wept over them. Afterward his brothers
talked with him.

Genesis 45:1–28

1. Is there anyone you haven't seen in a long time that you would like to see again?
2. When it comes to making up, are you more likely to apologize quickly or wait and let the other person make the first move?
3. How do you think Joseph's brothers felt when they discovered their little brother was so successful?
4. How do you think Joseph was able to forgive his brothers for selling him as a slave (see note on v. 5)? What's the lesson here for you?
5. What do you do when someone close to you really hurts you: Strike back? Keep a silent grudge? Forgive and forget? Withdraw and try not to get hurt again?
6. On the other hand, what do you do when you find out *you* have hurt someone?
7. Joseph saw God's control in every aspect of his life. In what area of your life do you struggle to see God in control?

16When the news reached Pharaoh's palace
that Joseph's brothers had come, Pharaoh and all
his officials were pleased. 17Pharaoh said to Joseph, "Tell your brothers, 'Do this: Load your
animals and return to the land of Canaan, 18and
bring your father and your families back to me. I
will give you the best of the land of Egypt and you
can enjoy the fat of the land.'
19"You are also directed to tell them, 'Do this:
Take some carts from Egypt for your children and
your wives, and get your father and come. 20Nev-
er mind about your belongings, because the best
of all Egypt will be yours.' "
21So the sons of Israel did this. Joseph gave
them carts, as Pharaoh had commanded, and he
also gave them provisions for their journey. 22To
each of them he gave new clothing, but to Benjamin he gave three hundred shekels[a] of silver
and five sets of clothes. 23And this is what he sent
to his father: ten donkeys loaded with the best
things of Egypt, and ten female donkeys loaded
with grain and bread and other provisions for his
journey. 24Then he sent his brothers away, and as
they were leaving he said to them, "Don't quarrel
on the way!"
25So they went up out of Egypt and came to
their father Jacob in the land of Canaan. 26They
told him, "Joseph is still alive! In fact, he is ruler
of all Egypt." Jacob was stunned; he did not believe them. 27But when they told him everything
Joseph had said to them, and when he saw the
carts Joseph had sent to carry him back, the spirit
of their father Jacob revived. 28And Israel said,
"I'm convinced! My son Joseph is still alive. I will
go and see him before I die."

Jacob Goes to Egypt

46 So Israel set out with all that was his, and
when he reached Beersheba, he offered
sacrifices to the God of his father Isaac.
2And God spoke to Israel in a vision at night
and said, "Jacob! Jacob!"
"Here I am," he replied.
3"I am God, the God of your father," he said.
"Do not be afraid to go down to Egypt, for I will
make you into a great nation there. 4I will go

[a] 22 That is, about 7 1/2 pounds (about 3.5 kilograms)

After being sold by his brothers, Joseph went from slave to prisoner to second in command in Egypt. Due to famine, his brothers came to buy grain. Joseph recognized them, but they didn't recognize him. He refused to let them buy more food without returning with his beloved younger brother Benjamin. Later, when Joseph sent them on their way again, he had his own silver cup planted in Benjamin's sack. When Joseph declared Benjamin would become his slave, the others fell down and begged for mercy.

45:2 *wept so loudly.* Both emotional and sensitive, Joseph wept often (vv. 14–15; 42:24; 43:30; 46:29).

45:3 *his brothers ... were terrified.* Either because they thought they were seeing a ghost or because they were afraid of what Joseph would do to them.

45:5 *God sent me.* Instead of being bitter, Joseph realized God had a purpose to work through his brothers' cruel and thoughtless act (see vv. 7–9). Likewise, God had a purpose for Jesus' suffering (Acts 2:22–23).

45:9 *hurry back ... don't delay.* Joseph is anxious to see his father Jacob as soon as possible (see v. 13).

45:15 *his brothers talked with him.* In intimate fellowship and friendship, rather than hostility or fear, for the first time in over 20 years (see 37:4).

45:24 *Don't quarrel.* Joseph wanted nothing to delay their return (see note on v. 9), and he wanted them to avoid accusing each other about the past.

down to Egypt with you, and I will surely bring
you back again. And Joseph's own hand will close
your eyes."
5Then Jacob left Beersheba, and Israel's sons
took their father Jacob and their children and
their wives in the carts that Pharaoh had sent
to transport him. 6They also took with them
their livestock and the possessions they had acquired in Canaan, and Jacob and all his offspring
went to Egypt. 7He took with him to Egypt his
sons and grandsons and his daughters and
granddaughters—all his offspring.

8These are the names of the sons of Israel (Jacob and his descendants) who went to Egypt:

Reuben the firstborn of Jacob.
9The sons of Reuben:
Hanoch, Pallu, Hezron and Carmi.
10The sons of Simeon:
Jemuel, Jamin, Ohad, Jakin, Zohar and
Shaul the son of a Canaanite woman.
11The sons of Levi:
Gershon, Kohath and Merari.
12The sons of Judah:
Er, Onan, Shelah, Perez and Zerah (but
Er and Onan had died in the land of
Canaan).
The sons of Perez:
Hezron and Hamul.
13The sons of Issachar:
Tola, Puah,[a] Jashub[b] and Shimron.
14The sons of Zebulun:
Sered, Elon and Jahleel.
15These were the sons Leah bore to Jacob in
Paddan Aram,[c] besides his daughter Dinah.
These sons and daughters of his were thirty-three
in all.

16The sons of Gad:
Zephon,[d] Haggi, Shuni, Ezbon, Eri, Ar-
odi and Areli.
17The sons of Asher:
Imnah, Ishvah, Ishvi and Beriah.
Their sister was Serah.
The sons of Beriah:
Heber and Malkiel.
18These were the children born to Jacob by
Zilpah, whom Laban had given to his daughter
Leah—sixteen in all.

19The sons of Jacob's wife Rachel:
Joseph and Benjamin. 20In Egypt, Manasseh and Ephraim were born to Joseph by Asenath daughter of Potiphera,
priest of On.[e]
21The sons of Benjamin:
Bela, Beker, Ashbel, Gera, Naaman, Ehi,
Rosh, Muppim, Huppim and Ard.
22These were the sons of Rachel who were
born to Jacob—fourteen in all.

23The son of Dan:
Hushim.
24The sons of Naphtali:
Jahziel, Guni, Jezer and Shillem.
25These were the sons born to Jacob by Bilhah,
whom Laban had given to his daughter Rachel—
seven in all.

26All those who went to Egypt with Jacob—
those who were his direct descendants, not
counting his sons' wives—numbered sixty-six
persons. 27With the two sons[f] who had been
born to Joseph in Egypt, the members of Jacob's
family, which went to Egypt, were seventy[g] in
all.

28Now Jacob sent Judah ahead of him to Joseph
to get directions to Goshen. When they arrived in
the region of Goshen, 29Joseph had his chariot
made ready and went to Goshen to meet his father Israel. As soon as Joseph appeared before
him, he threw his arms around his father[h] and
wept for a long time.
30Israel said to Joseph, "Now I am ready to die,
since I have seen for myself that you are still
alive."
31Then Joseph said to his brothers and to his
father's household, "I will go up and speak to
Pharaoh and will say to him, 'My brothers and
my father's household, who were living in the
land of Canaan, have come to me. 32The men are
shepherds; they tend livestock, and they have
brought along their flocks and herds and everything they own.' 33When Pharaoh calls you in
and asks, 'What is your occupation?' 34you should
answer, 'Your servants have tended livestock
from our boyhood on, just as our fathers did.'
Then you will be allowed to settle in the region
of Goshen, for all shepherds are detestable to the
Egyptians."

47 Joseph went and told Pharaoh, "My father and brothers, with their flocks and
herds and everything they own, have come from
the land of Canaan and are now in Goshen." 2He
chose five of his brothers and presented them
before Pharaoh.
3Pharaoh asked the brothers, "What is your
occupation?"
"Your servants are shepherds," they replied to

[a] 13 Samaritan Pentateuch and Syriac (see also 1 Chron. 7:1); Masoretic Text *Puvah* [b] 13 Samaritan Pentateuch and some Septuagint manuscripts (see also Num. 26:24 and 1 Chron. 7:1); Masoretic Text *Iob* [c] 15 That is, Northwest Mesopotamia [d] 16 Samaritan Pentateuch and Septuagint (see also Num. 26:15); Masoretic Text *Ziphion* [e] 20 That is, Heliopolis [f] 27 Hebrew; Septuagint *the nine children* [g] 27 Hebrew (see also Exodus 1:5 and footnote); Septuagint (see also Acts 7:14) *seventy-five* [h] 29 Hebrew *around him*

Pharaoh, "just as our fathers were." 4They also
said to him, "We have come to live here awhile,
because the famine is severe in Canaan and your
servants' flocks have no pasture. So now, please
let your servants settle in Goshen."
5Pharaoh said to Joseph, "Your father and your
brothers have come to you, 6and the land of
Egypt is before you; settle your father and your
brothers in the best part of the land. Let them
live in Goshen. And if you know of any among
them with special ability, put them in charge of
my own livestock."
7Then Joseph brought his father Jacob in and
presented him before Pharaoh. After Jacob
blessed[a] Pharaoh, 8Pharaoh asked him, "How
old are you?"
9And Jacob said to Pharaoh, "The years of my
pilgrimage are a hundred and thirty. My years
have been few and difficult, and they do not
equal the years of the pilgrimage of my fathers."
10Then Jacob blessed[b] Pharaoh and went out
from his presence.
11So Joseph settled his father and his brothers
in Egypt and gave them property in the best part
of the land, the district of Rameses, as Pharaoh
directed. 12Joseph also provided his father and
his brothers and all his father's household with
food, according to the number of their children.

Joseph and the Famine

13There was no food, however, in the whole
region because the famine was severe; both
Egypt and Canaan wasted away because of the
famine. 14Joseph collected all the money that was
to be found in Egypt and Canaan in payment for
the grain they were buying, and he brought it to
Pharaoh's palace. 15When the money of the people of Egypt and Canaan was gone, all Egypt came
to Joseph and said, "Give us food. Why should we
die before your eyes? Our money is used up."
16"Then bring your livestock," said Joseph. "I
will sell you food in exchange for your livestock,
since your money is gone." 17So they brought
their livestock to Joseph, and he gave them food
in exchange for their horses, their sheep and
goats, their cattle and donkeys. And he brought
them through that year with food in exchange for
all their livestock.
18When that year was over, they came to him
the following year and said, "We cannot hide
from our lord the fact that since our money is
gone and our livestock belongs to you, there is
nothing left for our lord except our bodies and
our land. 19Why should we perish before your
eyes—we and our land as well? Buy us and our
land in exchange for food, and we with our land
will be in bondage to Pharaoh. Give us seed so
that we may live and not die, and that the land
may not become desolate."
20So Joseph bought all the land in Egypt for
Pharaoh. The Egyptians, one and all, sold their
fields, because the famine was too severe for
them. The land became Pharaoh's, 21and Joseph
reduced the people to servitude,[c] from one end
of Egypt to the other. 22However, he did not buy
the land of the priests, because they received a
regular allotment from Pharaoh and had food
enough from the allotment Pharaoh gave them.
That is why they did not sell their land.
23Joseph said to the people, "Now that I have
bought you and your land today for Pharaoh, here
is seed for you so you can plant the ground. 24But
when the crop comes in, give a fifth of it to Pharaoh. The other four-fifths you may keep as seed
for the fields and as food for yourselves and your
households and your children."
25"You have saved our lives," they said. "May
we find favor in the eyes of our lord; we will be
in bondage to Pharaoh."
26So Joseph established it as a law concerning
land in Egypt—still in force today—that a fifth of
the produce belongs to Pharaoh. It was only the
land of the priests that did not become Pharaoh's.
27Now the Israelites settled in Egypt in the
region of Goshen. They acquired property there
and were fruitful and increased greatly in number.
28Jacob lived in Egypt seventeen years, and the
years of his life were a hundred and forty-seven.
29When the time drew near for Israel to die, he
called for his son Joseph and said to him, "If I
have found favor in your eyes, put your hand
under my thigh and promise that you will show
me kindness and faithfulness. Do not bury me in
Egypt, 30but when I rest with my fathers, carry
me out of Egypt and bury me where they are
buried."
"I will do as you say," he said.
31"Swear to me," he said. Then Joseph swore
to him, and Israel worshiped as he leaned on the
top of his staff.[d]

Manasseh and Ephraim

48 Some time later Joseph was told, "Your
father is ill." So he took his two sons Manasseh and Ephraim along with him. 2When Jacob was told, "Your son Joseph has come to you,"
Israel rallied his strength and sat up on the bed.
3Jacob said to Joseph, "God Almighty[e] appeared to me at Luz in the land of Canaan, and
there he blessed me 4and said to me, 'I am going
to make you fruitful and will increase your num-

[a]7 Or *greeted* [b]10 Or *said farewell to* [c]21 Samaritan Pentateuch and Septuagint (see also Vulgate); Masoretic Text *and he moved the people into the cities* [d]31 Or *Israel bowed down at the head of his bed* [e]3 Hebrew *El-Shaddai*

bers. I will make you a community of peoples,
and I will give this land as an everlasting possession to your descendants after you.’
5“Now then, your two sons born to you in
Egypt before I came to you here will be reckoned
as mine; Ephraim and Manasseh will be mine,
just as Reuben and Simeon are mine. 6Any children born to you after them will be yours; in the
territory they inherit they will be reckoned under
the names of their brothers. 7As I was returning
from Paddan,[a] to my sorrow Rachel died in the
land of Canaan while we were still on the way, a
little distance from Ephrath. So I buried her there
beside the road to Ephrath” (that is, Bethlehem).
8When Israel saw the sons of Joseph, he asked,
“Who are these?”
9“They are the sons God has given me here,”
Joseph said to his father.
Then Israel said, “Bring them to me so I may
bless them.”
10Now Israel’s eyes were failing because of old
age, and he could hardly see. So Joseph brought
his sons close to him, and his father kissed them
and embraced them.
11Israel said to Joseph, “I never expected to
see your face again, and now God has allowed me
to see your children too.”
12Then Joseph removed them from Israel’s
knees and bowed down with his face to the
ground. 13And Joseph took both of them, Ephraim on his right toward Israel’s left hand and Manasseh on his left toward Israel’s right hand, and
brought them close to him. 14But Israel reached
out his right hand and put it on Ephraim’s head,
though he was the younger, and crossing his
arms, he put his left hand on Manasseh’s head,
even though Manasseh was the firstborn.
15Then he blessed Joseph and said,

“May the God before whom my fathers
Abraham and Isaac walked,
the God who has been my shepherd
all my life to this day,
16the Angel who has delivered me from all
harm
—may he bless these boys.
May they be called by my name
and the names of my fathers Abraham and
Isaac,
and may they increase greatly
upon the earth.”

17When Joseph saw his father placing his right
hand on Ephraim’s head he was displeased; so he
took hold of his father’s hand to move it from
Ephraim’s head to Manasseh’s head. 18Joseph
said to him, “No, my father, this one is the firstborn; put your right hand on his head.”
19But his father refused and said, “I know, my
son, I know. He too will become a people, and he
too will become great. Nevertheless, his younger
brother will be greater than he, and his descendants will become a group of nations.” 20He
blessed them that day and said,

“In your[b] name will Israel pronounce this
blessing:
‘May God make you like Ephraim and
Manasseh.’ ”

So he put Ephraim ahead of Manasseh.
21Then Israel said to Joseph, “I am about to
die, but God will be with you[c] and take you[c]
back to the land of your[c] fathers. 22And to you,
as one who is over your brothers, I give the ridge
of land[d] I took from the Amorites with my
sword and my bow.”

Jacob Blesses His Sons

49 Then Jacob called for his sons and said:
“Gather around so I can tell you what will
happen to you in days to come.

2“Assemble and listen, sons of Jacob;
listen to your father Israel.

3“Reuben, you are my firstborn,
my might, the first sign of my strength,
excelling in honor, excelling in power.
4Turbulent as the waters, you will no longer
excel,
for you went up onto your father’s bed,
onto my couch and defiled it.

5“Simeon and Levi are brothers—
their swords[e] are weapons of violence.
6Let me not enter their council,
let me not join their assembly,
for they have killed men in their anger
and hamstrung oxen as they pleased.
7Cursed be their anger, so fierce,
and their fury, so cruel!
I will scatter them in Jacob
and disperse them in Israel.

8“Judah,[f] your brothers will praise you;
your hand will be on the neck of your
enemies;
your father’s sons will bow down to you.
9You are a lion’s cub, O Judah;
you return from the prey, my son.
Like a lion he crouches and lies down,
like a lioness—who dares to rouse him?
10The scepter will not depart from Judah,

[a]7 That is, Northwest Mesopotamia [b]20 The Hebrew is singular. [c]21 The Hebrew is plural. [d]22 Or *And to you I give one portion more than to your brothers—the portion* [e]5 The meaning of the Hebrew for this word is uncertain. [f]8 *Judah* sounds like and may be derived from the Hebrew for *praise.*

nor the ruler's staff from between his feet,
until he comes to whom it belongs[a]
and the obedience of the nations is his.
11 He will tether his donkey to a vine,
his colt to the choicest branch;
he will wash his garments in wine,
his robes in the blood of grapes.
12 His eyes will be darker than wine,
his teeth whiter than milk.[b]

13 "Zebulun will live by the seashore
and become a haven for ships;
his border will extend toward Sidon.

14 "Issachar is a rawboned[c] donkey
lying down between two saddlebags.[d]
15 When he sees how good is his resting place
and how pleasant is his land,
he will bend his shoulder to the burden
and submit to forced labor.

16 "Dan[e] will provide justice for his people
as one of the tribes of Israel.
17 Dan will be a serpent by the roadside,
a viper along the path,
that bites the horse's heels
so that its rider tumbles backward.

18 "I look for your deliverance, O LORD.

19 "Gad[f] will be attacked by a band of raiders,
but he will attack them at their heels.

20 "Asher's food will be rich;
he will provide delicacies fit for a king.

21 "Naphtali is a doe set free
that bears beautiful fawns.[g]

22 "Joseph is a fruitful vine,
a fruitful vine near a spring,
whose branches climb over a wall.[h]
23 With bitterness archers attacked him;
they shot at him with hostility.
24 But his bow remained steady,
his strong arms stayed[i] limber,
because of the hand of the Mighty One of
Jacob,
because of the Shepherd, the Rock of
Israel,
25 because of your father's God, who helps you,
because of the Almighty,[j] who blesses
you
with blessings of the heavens above,
blessings of the deep that lies below,
blessings of the breast and womb.
26 Your father's blessings are greater
than the blessings of the ancient
mountains,
than[k] the bounty of the age-old hills.
Let all these rest on the head of Joseph,
on the brow of the prince among[l] his
brothers.

27 "Benjamin is a ravenous wolf;
in the morning he devours the prey,
in the evening he divides the plunder."

28 All these are the twelve tribes of Israel, and
this is what their father said to them when he
blessed them, giving each the blessing appropriate to him.

The Death of Jacob

29 Then he gave them these instructions: "I am
about to be gathered to my people. Bury me with
my fathers in the cave in the field of Ephron the
Hittite,
30 the cave in the field of Machpelah, near
Mamre in Canaan, which Abraham bought as a
burial place from Ephron the Hittite, along with
the field.
31 There Abraham and his wife Sarah
were buried, there Isaac and his wife Rebekah
were buried, and there I buried Leah.
32 The field
and the cave in it were bought from the Hittites.[m]"

33 When Jacob had finished giving instructions
to his sons, he drew his feet up into the bed,
breathed his last and was gathered to his people.

50 Joseph threw himself upon his father and
wept over him and kissed him.
2 Then Jo-
seph directed the physicians in his service to em-
balm his father Israel. So the physicians embalmed him,
3 taking a full forty days, for that was
the time required for embalming. And the Egyptians mourned for him seventy days.

4 When the days of mourning had passed, Joseph said to Pharaoh's court, "If I have found
favor in your eyes, speak to Pharaoh for me. Tell
him,
5 'My father made me swear an oath and
said, "I am about to die; bury me in the tomb I
dug for myself in the land of Canaan." Now let
me go up and bury my father; then I will return.'"

6 Pharaoh said, "Go up and bury your father, as
he made you swear to do."

7 So Joseph went up to bury his father. All Pharaoh's officials accompanied him—the dignitaries
of his court and all the dignitaries of Egypt—
8 besides all the members of Joseph's household
and his brothers and those belonging to his father's household. Only their children and their
flocks and herds were left in Goshen.
9 Chariots

[a] 10 Or *until Shiloh comes*; or *until he comes to whom tribute belongs* [b] 12 Or *will be dull from wine, / his teeth white from milk* [c] 14 Or *strong* [d] 14 Or *campfires* [e] 16 *Dan* here means *he provides justice.* [f] 19 *Gad* can mean *attack* and *band of raiders.* [g] 21 Or *free; / he utters beautiful words* [h] 22 Or *Joseph is a wild colt, / a wild colt near a spring, / a wild donkey on a terraced hill* [i] 23,24 Or *archers will attack . . . will shoot . . . will remain . . . will stay* [j] 25 Hebrew *Shaddai* [k] 26 Or *of my progenitors, / as great as* [l] 26 Or *the one separated from* [m] 32 Or *the sons of Heth*

and horsemen[a] also went up with him. It was a very large company.

10When they reached the threshing floor of Atad, near the Jordan, they lamented loudly and bitterly; and there Joseph observed a seven-day
period of mourning for his father. 11When the Canaanites who lived there saw the mourning at the threshing floor of Atad, they said, "The Egyptians are holding a solemn ceremony of mourning." That is why that place near the Jordan is called Abel Mizraim.[b]

12So Jacob's sons did as he had commanded
them: 13They carried him to the land of Canaan and buried him in the cave in the field of Machpelah, near Mamre, which Abraham had bought as a burial place from Ephron the Hittite, along
with the field. 14After burying his father, Joseph returned to Egypt, together with his brothers and all the others who had gone with him to bury his father.

Joseph Reassures His Brothers

15When Joseph's brothers saw that their father was dead, they said, "What if Joseph holds a grudge against us and pays us back for all the wrongs we did to him?"
16So they sent word to Joseph, saying, "Your father left these instructions before he died:
17'This is what you are to say to Joseph: I ask you to forgive your brothers the sins and the wrongs they committed in treating you so badly.' Now please forgive the sins of the servants of the God of your father." When their message came to him, Joseph wept.

18His brothers then came and threw themselves down before him. "We are your slaves," they said.

19But Joseph said to them, "Don't be afraid.
Am I in the place of God?
20You intended to harm me, but God intended it for good to accomplish what is now being done, the saving of many
lives.
21So then, don't be afraid. I will provide for you and your children." And he reassured them and spoke kindly to them.

The Death of Joseph

22Joseph stayed in Egypt, along with all his father's family. He lived a hundred and ten years
23and saw the third generation of Ephraim's children. Also the children of Makir son of Manasseh were placed at birth on Joseph's knees.[c]

24Then Joseph said to his brothers, "I am about to die. But God will surely come to your aid and take you up out of this land to the land he promised on oath to Abraham, Isaac and Jacob."
25And Joseph made the sons of Israel swear an oath and said, "God will surely come to your aid, and then you must carry my bones up from this place."

26So Joseph died at the age of a hundred and ten. And after they embalmed him, he was placed in a coffin in Egypt.

[a]9 Or *charioteers* [b]11 *Abel Mizraim* means *mourning of the Egyptians.* [c]23 That is, were counted as his

Introduction to
EXODUS

Personal Reading Plan

❐ Exodus 1:1–3:22	❐ Exodus 15:1–16:36	❐ Exodus 28:15–29:46
❐ Exodus 4:1–6:12	❐ Exodus 17:1–18:27	❐ Exodus 30:1–31:18
❐ Exodus 6:13–8:19	❐ Exodus 19:1–21:36	❐ Exodus 32:1–33:23
❐ Exodus 8:20–10:20	❐ Exodus 22:1–23:33	❐ Exodus 34:1–35:29
❐ Exodus 10:21–12:51	❐ Exodus 24:1–25:40	❐ Exodus 35:30–38:20
❐ Exodus 13:1–14:31	❐ Exodus 26:1–28:14	❐ Exodus 38:21–40:38

Author

Moses is assumed to be the author and editor of most of the first five books of the OT (the Pentateuch).

Date

It is difficult to set a firm date for the writing of the Pentateuch. Conservative estimates place it in either the fifteenth or thirteenth century B.C., depending on when the Exodus occurred.

Theme

Deliverance from Egypt; giving the Law; building the Tabernacle.

Historical Background

No direct evidence fixes the events of this book within a specifically dated historical context. The Bible does not provide the name of the pharaoh of the Exodus, and extra-biblical texts and archaeology are silent concerning the Israelites' sojourn in and escape from Egypt. Indirect evidence present throughout the Bible can be used to support a wide range of dates. Certain recent archaeological evidence from Palestine suggests a late thirteenth century date for the appearance of the Israelites in Canaan, by which it would be inferred that Moses and the events of this book may date earlier in this same century, sometime between 1300 and 1250 B.C.

Characteristics

The book of Exodus is dominated by the life and actions of Moses and arranged around two outstanding redemptive acts, the Exodus from Egypt and the establishment of the covenant at Sinai. In fact, Moses and these events are so fundamental to an understanding of God's plan for human redemption that it could be argued that much of the Bible is a dialogue which reacts to, explains, implements, elaborates and completes the redemptive plan of God as it is revealed in this book.

Passages for Topical Group Study

2:1–25	ADOPTED CHILDREN	The Beginning of Moses' Life
4:1–17	INSECURITY	Signs for Moses
5:1–21	SCHOOL / GRADES	Bricks Without Straw
16:1–35	HEALTHY HABITS	Manna and Quail
32:1–35	AIDS	The Golden Calf

See the Lesson Plans in the front of this Bible.

Passages for General Group Study

3:1–22	Moses and the Burning Bush	14:5–31	Crossing the Sea
6:28–7:24	The Plagues Begin	19:10–20:21	Receiving the Ten Commandments
12:1–30	The Passover		

The Israelites Oppressed

1 These are the names of the sons of Israel
who went to Egypt with Jacob, each with his
family: 2Reuben, Simeon, Levi and Judah; 3Issa-
char, Zebulun and Benjamin; 4Dan and Naphtali;
Gad and Asher. 5The descendants of Jacob numbered seventy[a] in all; Joseph was already in
Egypt.
6Now Joseph and all his brothers and all that
generation died, 7but the Israelites were fruitful
and multiplied greatly and became exceedingly
numerous, so that the land was filled with them.
8Then a new king, who did not know about
Joseph, came to power in Egypt. 9"Look," he said
to his people, "the Israelites have become much
too numerous for us. 10Come, we must deal
shrewdly with them or they will become even
more numerous and, if war breaks out, will join
our enemies, fight against us and leave the country."
11So they put slave masters over them to oppress them with forced labor, and they built Pi-
thom and Rameses as store cities for Pharaoh.
12But the more they were oppressed, the more
they multiplied and spread; so the Egyptians
came to dread the Israelites 13and worked them
ruthlessly. 14They made their lives bitter with
hard labor in brick and mortar and with all kinds
of work in the fields; in all their hard labor the
Egyptians used them ruthlessly.
15The king of Egypt said to the Hebrew midwives, whose names were Shiphrah and Puah,
16"When you help the Hebrew women in childbirth and observe them on the delivery stool, if it
is a boy, kill him; but if it is a girl, let her live."
17The midwives, however, feared God and did
not do what the king of Egypt had told them to
do; they let the boys live. 18Then the king of
Egypt summoned the midwives and asked them,
"Why have you done this? Why have you let the
boys live?"
19The midwives answered Pharaoh, "Hebrew
women are not like Egyptian women; they are
vigorous and give birth before the midwives arrive."
20So God was kind to the midwives and the
people increased and became even more numerous. 21And because the midwives feared God, he
gave them families of their own.
22Then Pharaoh gave this order to all his people: "Every boy that is born[b] you must throw
into the Nile, but let every girl live."

The Birth of Moses

2 Now a man of the house of Levi married a
Levite woman, 2and she became pregnant
and gave birth to a son. When she saw that he
was a fine child, she hid him for three months.
3But when she could hide him no longer, she got
a papyrus basket for him and coated it with tar
and pitch. Then she placed the child in it and put
it among the reeds along the bank of the Nile.
4His sister stood at a distance to see what would
happen to him.
5Then Pharaoh's daughter went down to the
Nile to bathe, and her attendants were walking
along the river bank. She saw the basket among
the reeds and sent her slave girl to get it. 6She
opened it and saw the baby. He was crying, and
she felt sorry for him. "This is one of the Hebrew
babies," she said.
7Then his sister asked Pharaoh's daughter,
"Shall I go and get one of the Hebrew women to
nurse the baby for you?"
8"Yes, go," she answered. And the girl went
and got the baby's mother. 9Pharaoh's daughter
said to her, "Take this baby and nurse him for
me, and I will pay you." So the woman took the
baby and nursed him. 10When the child grew
older, she took him to Pharaoh's daughter and he
became her son. She named him Moses,[c] saying, "I drew him out of the water."

Moses Flees to Midian

11One day, after Moses had grown up, he went
out to where his own people were and watched
them at their hard labor. He saw an Egyptian
beating a Hebrew, one of his own people.
12Glancing this way and that and seeing no one,
he killed the Egyptian and hid him in the sand.
13The next day he went out and saw two Hebrews fighting. He asked the one in the wrong,
"Why are you hitting your fellow Hebrew?"
14The man said, "Who made you ruler and
judge over us? Are you thinking of killing me as
you killed the Egyptian?" Then Moses was afraid
and thought, "What I did must have become
known."
15When Pharaoh heard of this, he tried to kill
Moses, but Moses fled from Pharaoh and went to
live in Midian, where he sat down by a well.
16Now a priest of Midian had seven daughters,
and they came to draw water and fill the troughs
to water their father's flock. 17Some shepherds
came along and drove them away, but Moses got
up and came to their rescue and watered their
flock.
18When the girls returned to Reuel their father, he asked them, "Why have you returned so
early today?"
19They answered, "An Egyptian rescued us
from the shepherds. He even drew water for us
and watered the flock."

[a] *5* Masoretic Text (see also Gen. 46:27); Dead Sea Scrolls and Septuagint (see also Acts 7:14 and note at Gen. 46:27) *seventy-five*
[b] *22* Masoretic Text; Samaritan Pentateuch, Septuagint and Targums *born to the Hebrews*
[c] *10* *Moses* sounds like the Hebrew for *draw out.*

20“And where is he?” he asked his daughters.
“Why did you leave him? Invite him to have
something to eat.”
21Moses agreed to stay with the man, who
gave his daughter Zipporah to Moses in marriage.
22Zipporah gave birth to a son, and Moses named
him Gershom,[a] saying, “I have become an alien
in a foreign land.”
23During that long period, the king of Egypt
died. The Israelites groaned in their slavery and
cried out, and their cry for help because of their
slavery went up to God. 24God heard their groaning and he remembered his covenant with
Abraham, with Isaac and with Jacob. 25So God
looked on the Israelites and was concerned about
them.

Exodus 2:1–25

1. How much do you know about your birth: Time? Place? Weight? Anything else?
2. If you were adopted, do you think you would explore your “roots” like Moses did (v. 11)? Why or why not?
3. What would you do if you came across someone beating up your friend?
4. If you were “Chief of Police” what charges would you bring against Moses (vv. 11–12): Murder? A lesser crime? No charges at all?
5. What got into Moses to cause him to give up life in the palace to fight for the oppressed? Do you think he had any regrets?
6. Do you think what happened to Moses as a child was a coincidence or part of God’s plan for his people?
7. Knowing God is “concerned” (v. 25) about people, what is something this group can do to help the oppressed? Pray about this.

Moses and the Burning Bush

3 Now Moses was tending the flock of Jethro
his father-in-law, the priest of Midian, and
he led the flock to the far side of the desert and
came to Horeb, the mountain of God. 2There the
angel of the LORD appeared to him in flames of
fire from within a bush. Moses saw that though
the bush was on fire it did not burn up. 3So Moses thought, “I will go over and see this strange
sight—why the bush does not burn up.”
4When the LORD saw that he had gone over to
look, God called to him from within the bush,
“Moses! Moses!”
And Moses said, “Here I am.”
5“Do not come any closer,” God said. “Take
off your sandals, for the place where you are
standing is holy ground.” 6Then he said, “I am
the God of your father, the God of Abraham, the
God of Isaac and the God of Jacob.” At this, Moses hid his face, because he was afraid to look at
God.
7The LORD said, “I have indeed seen the misery of my people in Egypt. I have heard them
crying out because of their slave drivers, and I am
concerned about their suffering. 8So I have come
down to rescue them from the hand of the Egyptians and to bring them up out of that land into a
good and spacious land, a land flowing with milk
and honey—the home of the Canaanites, Hittites, Amorites, Perizzites, Hivites and Jebusites.
9And now the cry of the Israelites has reached
me, and I have seen the way the Egyptians are
oppressing them. 10So now, go. I am sending you
to Pharaoh to bring my people the Israelites out
of Egypt.”
11But Moses said to God, “Who am I, that I
should go to Pharaoh and bring the Israelites out
of Egypt?”
12And God said, “I will be with you. And this

[a]22 *Gershom* sounds like the Hebrew for *an alien there.*

About 400 years earlier, Jacob (whose name God changed to Israel) and his family moved to Egypt. Since then the Egyptians became so fearful of the rapidly growing population of Israelites that they enslaved them and now even ordered them to drown all their male newborns in the Nile River.

2:2 *a fine child.* Moses was “no ordinary child” (Acts 7:20; Heb. 11:23). The account of Moses’ remarkable deliverance in infancy foreshadows the deliverance from Egypt that God would later perform through him.

2:10 *he became her son.* According to Acts 7:22, “Moses was educated in all the wisdom of the Egyptians and was powerful in speech and action.”

2:11 *Moses had grown up.* He was now 40 years old (see Acts 7:23).

2:14 *Who made you ruler and judge over us?* Unknowingly, the speaker made a prediction that would be fulfilled 40 years later (see Acts 7:30,35). The Hebrew word for “judge” could also refer to a deliverer, as in the book of Judges. According to Acts 7:25, “Moses thought that his own people would realize that God was using him to rescue them, but they did not.”

2:15 *Pharaoh.* Perhaps Thutmose III. The word “pharaoh,” which is Egyptian in origin and means “great house,” is a royal title rather than a personal name. ***Midian.*** Located in southeastern Sinai and west central Arabia. Dry and desolate, it formed a stark contrast to Moses’ former home in the royal court. He lived in Midian 40 years.

will be the sign to you that it is I who have sent
you: When you have brought the people out of
Egypt, you[a] will worship God on this mountain."

EXODUS 3:1–22

1. Have you ever seen anything really strange, or something that defied common sense? What was it?
2. Where is the holiest place you have ever been?
3. What is your favorite excuse for doing nothing?
4. Do you think Moses was more uncertain of himself or God?
5. Have you ever felt God was asking you to do something? How did you react?
6. What has the burning bush (God's attention-getter) been in your life: Good times? Bad times? A personal experience with God?
7. How would you describe your relationship with God right now: A burning bush? A flickering shrub? A few ashes in the wind?

13Moses said to God, "Suppose I go to the Israelites and say to them, 'The God of your fathers
has sent me to you,' and they ask me, 'What is his
name?' Then what shall I tell them?"
14God said to Moses, "I AM WHO I AM.[b] This
is what you are to say to the Israelites: 'I AM has
sent me to you.'"
15God also said to Moses, "Say to the Israelites,
'The LORD,[c] the God of your fathers—the God
of Abraham, the God of Isaac and the God of
Jacob—has sent me to you.' This is my name
forever, the name by which I am to be remembered from generation to generation.
16"Go, assemble the elders of Israel and say to
them, 'The LORD, the God of your fathers—the
God of Abraham, Isaac and Jacob—appeared to
me and said: I have watched over you and have
seen what has been done to you in Egypt. 17And
I have promised to bring you up out of your
misery in Egypt into the land of the Canaanites,
Hittites, Amorites, Perizzites, Hivites and Jebusites—a land flowing with milk and honey.'
18"The elders of Israel will listen to you. Then
you and the elders are to go to the king of Egypt
and say to him, 'The LORD, the God of the Hebrews, has met with us. Let us take a three-day
journey into the desert to offer sacrifices to the
LORD our God.' 19But I know that the king of
Egypt will not let you go unless a mighty hand
compels him. 20So I will stretch out my hand and
strike the Egyptians with all the wonders that I
will perform among them. After that, he will let
you go.
21"And I will make the Egyptians favorably disposed toward this people, so that when you leave
you will not go empty-handed. 22Every woman is
to ask her neighbor and any woman living in her
house for articles of silver and gold and for clothing, which you will put on your sons and daughters. And so you will plunder the Egyptians."

Signs for Moses

4 Moses answered, "What if they do not believe me or listen to me and say, 'The LORD
did not appear to you'?"
2Then the LORD said to him, "What is that in
your hand?"
"A staff," he replied.
3The LORD said, "Throw it on the ground."
Moses threw it on the ground and it became a
snake, and he ran from it. 4Then the LORD said to
him, "Reach out your hand and take it by the
tail." So Moses reached out and took hold of the

[a] *12* The Hebrew is plural. [b] *14* Or *I WILL BE WHAT I WILL BE* [c] *15* The Hebrew for *LORD* sounds like and may be derived from the Hebrew for *I AM* in verse 14.

3:1 Though an Israelite by birth, Moses was adopted by Pharaoh's daughter. After killing an Egyptian slave driver who was beating an Israelite slave, Moses fled to Midian. ***tending the flock.*** Like David, Moses was called from tending sheep to be the shepherd of God's people. ***Horeb.*** Either an alternate name for Mount Sinai or another high mountain in the same vicinity in the southeast region of the Sinai peninsula.

3:2 ***appeared to him in flames of fire.*** God's revelation of himself and his will was often accompanied by fire (see Ex. 13:21; 19:18; 1 Kings 18:24,38).

3:5 ***Take off your sandals.*** A practice still followed by Muslims before entering a mosque. ***holy ground.*** The ground was not holy by nature but was made so by the divine presence. Holiness involves being consecrated to the Lord's service and thus being separated from the commonplace.

3:14 ***I AM WHO I AM.*** The name by which God wished to be known and worshiped by Israel—the name expressing his character as the dependable and faithful God who desires the full trust of his people. ***I AM.*** The shortened form of the name. Jesus applied the phrase to himself; in so doing he claimed to be God and risked being stoned for blasphemy (John 8:58–59).

3:15 ***The LORD.*** The Hebrew is Yahweh (often incorrectly spelled "Jehovah"). It means "He is" or "He will be" and is the third-person form of the verb translated "I will be" in verse 12 and "I AM" in verse 14.

snake and it turned back into a staff in his hand.
5“This,” said the LORD, “is so that they may believe that the LORD, the God of their fathers—the
God of Abraham, the God of Isaac and the God of
Jacob—has appeared to you.”

EXODUS 4:1–17

1. Who does most of the talking when your family sits down for supper?
2. On a scale of 1 (no sweat) to 10 (sweating bullets), how would you feel about speaking in front of your whole school?
3. What is something you “have to do” which you don’t feel qualified to do?
4. If God called you on the phone today and asked you to do something special for him, what would you say?
5. What excuses do you give when it comes to getting closer to God?
6. What helps you overcome your fears: Prayer? Encouragement from a friend? Other?
7. How do you feel about opening up to this group? How can the group pray for you?

6Then the LORD said, “Put your hand inside
your cloak.” So Moses put his hand into his cloak,
and when he took it out, it was leprous,[a] like
snow.
7“Now put it back into your cloak,” he said. So
Moses put his hand back into his cloak, and when
he took it out, it was restored, like the rest of his
flesh.
8Then the LORD said, “If they do not believe
you or pay attention to the first miraculous sign,
they may believe the second. 9But if they do not
believe these two signs or listen to you, take
some water from the Nile and pour it on the dry
ground. The water you take from the river will
become blood on the ground.”
10Moses said to the LORD, “O Lord, I have never been eloquent, neither in the past nor since
you have spoken to your servant. I am slow of
speech and tongue.”
11The LORD said to him, “Who gave man his
mouth? Who makes him deaf or mute? Who gives
him sight or makes him blind? Is it not I, the
LORD? 12Now go; I will help you speak and will
teach you what to say.”
13But Moses said, “O Lord, please send someone else to do it.”
14Then the LORD’s anger burned against Moses
and he said, “What about your brother, Aaron the
Levite? I know he can speak well. He is already
on his way to meet you, and his heart will be glad
when he sees you. 15You shall speak to him and
put words in his mouth; I will help both of you
speak and will teach you what to do. 16He will
speak to the people for you, and it will be as if he
were your mouth and as if you were God to him.
17But take this staff in your hand so you can perform miraculous signs with it.”

Moses Returns to Egypt

18Then Moses went back to Jethro his father-
in-law and said to him, “Let me go back to my
own people in Egypt to see if any of them are still
alive.”
Jethro said, “Go, and I wish you well.”
19Now the LORD had said to Moses in Midian,
“Go back to Egypt, for all the men who wanted to
kill you are dead.” 20So Moses took his wife and
sons, put them on a donkey and started back to
Egypt. And he took the staff of God in his hand.
21The LORD said to Moses, “When you return
to Egypt, see that you perform before Pharaoh all
the wonders I have given you the power to do.
But I will harden his heart so that he will not let
the people go. 22Then say to Pharaoh, ‘This is
what the LORD says: Israel is my firstborn son,

[a]6 The Hebrew word was used for various diseases affecting the skin—not necessarily leprosy.

God has just revealed himself to Moses at the burning bush—telling him to return to Egypt to lead the Israelites out of bondage.

4:1 *What if ... ?* Moses’ third expression of reluctance (see 3:11,13), in spite of God’s assurance in 3:18–20.

4:2–3 *staff.* Probably a shepherd’s crook. ***snake.*** Throughout much of Egypt’s history the pharaoh wore a cobra made of metal on the front of his headdress as a symbol of his sovereignty.

4:8 *miraculous sign.* A supernatural event or phenomenon designed to demonstrate authority, provide assurance, bear testimony, give warning or encourage faith.

4:10 Moses’ fourth expression of reluctance. ***I am slow of speech and tongue.*** Not in the sense of a speech impediment (see Acts 7:22). He complained, instead, of not being eloquent or quick-witted enough to respond to the pharaoh (see 6:12).

4:13 *please send someone else.* Moses’ fifth and final expression of reluctance.

4:14 *the LORD’s anger burned against Moses.* Although the Lord is “slow to anger,” he does not withhold his anger or punishment from his disobedient children forever (see Ex. 34:6–7). ***Levite.*** Under Aaron’s leadership, Israel’s priesthood would come from the tribe of Levi.

4:15–16 As God transmits his word through his prophets to his people, so Moses will transmit God’s message through Aaron.

23 and I told you, “Let my son go, so he may worship me.” But you refused to let him go; so I will
kill your firstborn son.’ ”
24 At a lodging place on the way, the LORD met
⌊Moses⌋[a] and was about to kill him. 25 But Zipporah took a flint knife, cut off her son’s foreskin
and touched ⌊Moses’⌋ feet with it.[b] “Surely you
are a bridegroom of blood to me,” she said. 26 So
the LORD let him alone. (At that time she said
“bridegroom of blood,” referring to circumcision.)
27 The LORD said to Aaron, “Go into the desert
to meet Moses.” So he met Moses at the mountain of God and kissed him. 28 Then Moses told
Aaron everything the LORD had sent him to say,
and also about all the miraculous signs he had
commanded him to perform.
29 Moses and Aaron brought together all the
elders of the Israelites, 30 and Aaron told them
everything the LORD had said to Moses. He also
performed the signs before the people, 31 and
they believed. And when they heard that the
LORD was concerned about them and had seen
their misery, they bowed down and worshiped.

Bricks Without Straw

5 Afterward Moses and Aaron went to Pharaoh
and said, “This is what the LORD, the God of
Israel, says: ‘Let my people go, so that they may
hold a festival to me in the desert.’ ”
2 Pharaoh said, “Who is the LORD, that I should
obey him and let Israel go? I do not know the
LORD and I will not let Israel go.”
3 Then they said, “The God of the Hebrews has
met with us. Now let us take a three-day journey
into the desert to offer sacrifices to the LORD our
God, or he may strike us with plagues or with the
sword.”
4 But the king of Egypt said, “Moses and Aaron,
why are you taking the people away from their
labor? Get back to your work!” 5 Then Pharaoh
said, “Look, the people of the land are now numerous, and you are stopping them from working.”
6 That same day Pharaoh gave this order to the
slave drivers and foremen in charge of the people: 7 “You are no longer to supply the people
with straw for making bricks; let them go and
gather their own straw. 8 But require them to
make the same number of bricks as before; don’t
reduce the quota. They are lazy; that is why they
are crying out, ‘Let us go and sacrifice to our
God.’ 9 Make the work harder for the men so that
they keep working and pay no attention to lies.”
10 Then the slave drivers and the foremen went
out and said to the people, “This is what Pharaoh
says: ‘I will not give you any more straw. 11 Go
and get your own straw wherever you can find it,
but your work will not be reduced at all.’ ” 12 So

Exodus 5:1–21

1. What do you like the most about school? What do you dislike the most?
2. What keeps you from getting better grades?
3. Are the expectations of your parents generally too high, reasonable or too low?
4. Concerning schoolwork, whose expectations cause you the most stress: Your teachers’? Your parents’? Your own?
5. What about the expectations you have for yourself, are you too hard or too easy on yourself?
6. What expectations do you think God has for you?
7. In the past week in your spiritual life, are you encouraged or discouraged? Close in prayer.

[a]24 Or ⌊*Moses’ son*⌋; Hebrew *him* [b]25 Or *and drew near* ⌊*Moses’*⌋ *feet*

Forty years before this, Moses (who had been raised by Pharaoh’s daughter) killed an Egyptian slave driver who was beating one of Moses’ fellow Israelites. After living in exile all those years, Moses was called by God to go back to Egypt and lead his people out of slavery into the promised land. Now Moses and his brother Aaron approach Pharaoh for the first time.

5:1 ***Pharaoh.*** According to traditional dating of the Exodus, the pharaoh (or king) of Egypt at this time was Amunhotep II. He was the son of Thutmose III, who ruled Egypt when Moses fled. According to 4:19, all the men who wanted to kill Moses were now dead.

5:3 ***three-day journey.*** Probably a conventional expression for a short trip rather than a journey of exactly three days. ***desert.*** God had met with Moses there (3:1–2) and would meet with him there again (3:12). ***offer sacrifices.*** Where the Egyptians could not see them, because the offerings would be detestable in their sight (see 8:25–26).

5:6 ***slave drivers.*** Probably the same as the “slave masters” in 1:11. ***foremen.*** Israelite supervisors who were appointed by the Egyptian slave drivers and were responsible to ensure that the Hebrews met their quota of bricks (v. 14).

5:7 ***straw.*** Chopped and mixed with the clay as binder to make the bricks stronger.

5:9 ***lies.*** The pharaoh labels all hopes of a quick release for Israel as presumptuous and false.

the people scattered all over Egypt to gather stubble to use for straw. 13 The slave drivers kept pressing them, saying, "Complete the work required of you for each day, just as when you had straw." 14 The Israelite foremen appointed by Pharaoh's slave drivers were beaten and were asked, "Why didn't you meet your quota of bricks yesterday or today, as before?"

15 Then the Israelite foremen went and appealed to Pharaoh: "Why have you treated your servants this way? 16 Your servants are given no straw, yet we are told, 'Make bricks!' Your servants are being beaten, but the fault is with your own people."

17 Pharaoh said, "Lazy, that's what you are—lazy! That is why you keep saying, 'Let us go and sacrifice to the LORD.' 18 Now get to work. You will not be given any straw, yet you must produce your full quota of bricks."

19 The Israelite foremen realized they were in trouble when they were told, "You are not to reduce the number of bricks required of you for each day." 20 When they left Pharaoh, they found Moses and Aaron waiting to meet them, 21 and they said, "May the LORD look upon you and judge you! You have made us a stench to Pharaoh and his officials and have put a sword in their hand to kill us."

God Promises Deliverance

22 Moses returned to the LORD and said, "O Lord, why have you brought trouble upon this people? Is this why you sent me? 23 Ever since I went to Pharaoh to speak in your name, he has brought trouble upon this people, and you have not rescued your people at all."

6 Then the LORD said to Moses, "Now you will see what I will do to Pharaoh: Because of my mighty hand he will let them go; because of my mighty hand he will drive them out of his country."

2 God also said to Moses, "I am the LORD. 3 I appeared to Abraham, to Isaac and to Jacob as God Almighty,[a] but by my name the LORD[b] I did not make myself known to them.[c] 4 I also established my covenant with them to give them the land of Canaan, where they lived as aliens. 5 Moreover, I have heard the groaning of the Israelites, whom the Egyptians are enslaving, and I have remembered my covenant.

6 "Therefore, say to the Israelites: 'I am the LORD, and I will bring you out from under the yoke of the Egyptians. I will free you from being slaves to them, and I will redeem you with an outstretched arm and with mighty acts of judgment. 7 I will take you as my own people, and I will be your God. Then you will know that I am the LORD your God, who brought you out from under the yoke of the Egyptians. 8 And I will bring you to the land I swore with uplifted hand to give to Abraham, to Isaac and to Jacob. I will give it to you as a possession. I am the LORD.' "

9 Moses reported this to the Israelites, but they did not listen to him because of their discouragement and cruel bondage.

10 Then the LORD said to Moses, 11 "Go, tell Pharaoh king of Egypt to let the Israelites go out of his country."

12 But Moses said to the LORD, "If the Israelites will not listen to me, why would Pharaoh listen to me, since I speak with faltering lips[d]?"

Family Record of Moses and Aaron

13 Now the LORD spoke to Moses and Aaron about the Israelites and Pharaoh king of Egypt, and he commanded them to bring the Israelites out of Egypt.

14 These were the heads of their families[e]:

The sons of Reuben the firstborn son of Israel were Hanoch and Pallu, Hezron and Carmi. These were the clans of Reuben.

15 The sons of Simeon were Jemuel, Jamin, Ohad, Jakin, Zohar and Shaul the son of a Canaanite woman. These were the clans of Simeon.

16 These were the names of the sons of Levi according to their records: Gershon, Kohath and Merari. Levi lived 137 years.

17 The sons of Gershon, by clans, were Libni and Shimei.

18 The sons of Kohath were Amram, Izhar, Hebron and Uzziel. Kohath lived 133 years.

19 The sons of Merari were Mahli and Mushi.

These were the clans of Levi according to their records.

20 Amram married his father's sister Jochebed, who bore him Aaron and Moses. Amram lived 137 years.

21 The sons of Izhar were Korah, Nepheg and Zicri.

22 The sons of Uzziel were Mishael, Elzaphan and Sithri.

23 Aaron married Elisheba, daughter of Amminadab and sister of Nahshon, and she bore him Nadab and Abihu, Eleazar and Ithamar.

24 The sons of Korah were Assir, Elkanah

a3 Hebrew *El-Shaddai* b3 See note at Exodus 3:15. c3 Or *Almighty, and by my name the LORD did I not let myself be known to them?* d12 Hebrew *I am uncircumcised of lips*; also in verse 30 e14 The Hebrew for *families* here and in verse 25 refers to units larger than clans.

and Abiasaph. These were the Korahite clans.

25Eleazar son of Aaron married one of the daughters of Putiel, and she bore him Phinehas.

These were the heads of the Levite families, clan by clan.

26It was this same Aaron and Moses to whom the LORD said, "Bring the Israelites out of Egypt by their divisions." 27They were the ones who spoke to Pharaoh king of Egypt about bringing the Israelites out of Egypt. It was the same Moses and Aaron.

Aaron to Speak for Moses

28Now when the LORD spoke to Moses in Egypt, 29he said to him, "I am the LORD. Tell Pharaoh king of Egypt everything I tell you."

30But Moses said to the LORD, "Since I speak with faltering lips, why would Pharaoh listen to me?"

7 Then the LORD said to Moses, "See, I have made you like God to Pharaoh, and your brother Aaron will be your prophet. 2You are to say everything I command you, and your brother Aaron is to tell Pharaoh to let the Israelites go out of his country. 3But I will harden Pharaoh's heart, and though I multiply my miraculous signs and wonders in Egypt, 4he will not listen to you. Then I will lay my hand on Egypt and with mighty acts of judgment I will bring out my divisions, my people the Israelites. 5And the Egyptians will know that I am the LORD when I stretch out my hand against Egypt and bring the Israelites out of it."

6Moses and Aaron did just as the LORD commanded them. 7Moses was eighty years old and Aaron eighty-three when they spoke to Pharaoh.

Aaron's Staff Becomes a Snake

8The LORD said to Moses and Aaron, 9"When Pharaoh says to you, 'Perform a miracle,' then say to Aaron, 'Take your staff and throw it down before Pharaoh,' and it will become a snake."

10So Moses and Aaron went to Pharaoh and did just as the LORD commanded. Aaron threw his staff down in front of Pharaoh and his officials, and it became a snake. 11Pharaoh then summoned wise men and sorcerers, and the Egyptian magicians also did the same things by their secret arts: 12Each one threw down his staff and it became a snake. But Aaron's staff swallowed up their staffs. 13Yet Pharaoh's heart became hard and he would not listen to them, just as the LORD had said.

The Plague of Blood

14Then the LORD said to Moses, "Pharaoh's heart is unyielding; he refuses to let the people go. 15Go to Pharaoh in the morning as he goes out to the water. Wait on the bank of the Nile to meet him, and take in your hand the staff that was changed into a snake. 16Then say to him,

Exodus 6:28–7:24

1. What did you do the last time you saw a snake or a spider: Scream? Run away? Get a closer look?
2. What do you do at the sight of blood?
3. How do you feel when someone tells you what to do?
4. When are you the most stubborn?
5. Who has been your "Aaron"—the person you have leaned on to get through big challenges or tough times?
6. How long has it been since you thanked that person? How can you best do that soon?
7. How are you and God getting along right now: Getting close? Having problems communicating? Close in prayer.

Pharaoh was not receptive to Moses' and Aaron's first visit. He not only refused to let the Israelites go worship the Lord in the desert, he increased their suffering (ch. 5).

7:3 ***harden.*** Nine times in Exodus the hardening of the pharaoh's heart is ascribed to God, as here. Another nine times, Pharaoh is said to have hardened his own heart. Pharaoh alone was the agent of the hardening in each of the first five plagues. Not until the sixth plague did God confirm the pharaoh's willful action, as he told Moses.

7:11 ***wise men and sorcerers.*** Probably Egyptian priests who claimed to possess occult knowledge. According to tradition, two of the magicians who opposed Moses were named Jannes and Jambres (see 2 Tim. 3:8). ***did the same things by their secret arts.*** Either through sleight of hand or by means of demonic power.

7:12 ***Aaron's staff swallowed up their staffs.*** Demonstrating God's mastery over the pharaoh and the gods of Egypt. The cobra was seen as a symbol of Pharaoh's power.

7:17 ***Nile.*** Egypt's dependence on the Nile led to its deification as the god Hopi. ***changed into blood.*** The first nine plagues may have been a series of miraculous intensifications of natural events taking place in less than a year, and coming at God's bidding. If so, the first plague resulted from the flooding of the Nile as large quantities of red sediment were washed down from Ethiopia, causing the water to become as red as blood. Only by filtering the water through the sandy soil could it be safe for drinking (v. 24).

'The LORD, the God of the Hebrews, has sent me
to say to you: Let my people go, so that they may
worship me in the desert. But until now you have
not listened. 17 This is what the LORD says: By this
you will know that I am the LORD: With the staff
that is in my hand I will strike the water of the
Nile, and it will be changed into blood. 18 The fish
in the Nile will die, and the river will stink; the
Egyptians will not be able to drink its water.' "
19 The LORD said to Moses, "Tell Aaron, 'Take
your staff and stretch out your hand over the
waters of Egypt—over the streams and canals,
over the ponds and all the reservoirs'—and they
will turn to blood. Blood will be everywhere in
Egypt, even in the wooden buckets and stone
jars."
20 Moses and Aaron did just as the LORD had
commanded. He raised his staff in the presence of
Pharaoh and his officials and struck the water
of the Nile, and all the water was changed into
blood. 21 The fish in the Nile died, and the river
smelled so bad that the Egyptians could not drink
its water. Blood was everywhere in Egypt.
22 But the Egyptian magicians did the same
things by their secret arts, and Pharaoh's heart
became hard; he would not listen to Moses and
Aaron, just as the LORD had said. 23 Instead, he
turned and went into his palace, and did not take
even this to heart. 24 And all the Egyptians dug
along the Nile to get drinking water, because
they could not drink the water of the river.

The Plague of Frogs

25 Seven days passed after the LORD struck the
8 Nile. 1 Then the LORD said to Moses, "Go to
Pharaoh and say to him, 'This is what the
LORD says: Let my people go, so that they may
worship me. 2 If you refuse to let them go, I will
plague your whole country with frogs. 3 The Nile
will teem with frogs. They will come up into your
palace and your bedroom and onto your bed, into
the houses of your officials and on your people,
and into your ovens and kneading troughs. 4 The
frogs will go up on you and your people and all
your officials.' "
5 Then the LORD said to Moses, "Tell Aaron,
'Stretch out your hand with your staff over the
streams and canals and ponds, and make frogs
come up on the land of Egypt.' "
6 So Aaron stretched out his hand over the waters of Egypt, and the frogs came up and covered
the land. 7 But the magicians did the same things
by their secret arts; they also made frogs come up
on the land of Egypt.
8 Pharaoh summoned Moses and Aaron and
said, "Pray to the LORD to take the frogs away
from me and my people, and I will let your people
go to offer sacrifices to the LORD."
9 Moses said to Pharaoh, "I leave to you the
honor of setting the time for me to pray for you
and your officials and your people that you and
your houses may be rid of the frogs, except for
those that remain in the Nile."
10 "Tomorrow," Pharaoh said.
Moses replied, "It will be as you say, so that
you may know there is no one like the LORD our
God. 11 The frogs will leave you and your houses,
your officials and your people; they will remain
only in the Nile."
12 After Moses and Aaron left Pharaoh, Moses
cried out to the LORD about the frogs he had
brought on Pharaoh. 13 And the LORD did what
Moses asked. The frogs died in the houses, in the
courtyards and in the fields. 14 They were piled
into heaps, and the land reeked of them. 15 But
when Pharaoh saw that there was relief, he hardened his heart and would not listen to Moses and
Aaron, just as the LORD had said.

The Plague of Gnats

16 Then the LORD said to Moses, "Tell Aaron,
'Stretch out your staff and strike the dust of the
ground,' and throughout the land of Egypt the
dust will become gnats." 17 They did this, and
when Aaron stretched out his hand with the staff
and struck the dust of the ground, gnats came
upon men and animals. All the dust throughout
the land of Egypt became gnats. 18 But when the
magicians tried to produce gnats by their secret
arts, they could not. And the gnats were on men
and animals.
19 The magicians said to Pharaoh, "This is the
finger of God." But Pharaoh's heart was hard and
he would not listen, just as the LORD had said.

The Plague of Flies

20 Then the LORD said to Moses, "Get up early
in the morning and confront Pharaoh as he goes
to the water and say to him, 'This is what the
LORD says: Let my people go, so that they may
worship me. 21 If you do not let my people go, I
will send swarms of flies on you and your officials, on your people and into your houses. The
houses of the Egyptians will be full of flies, and
even the ground where they are.
22 " 'But on that day I will deal differently with
the land of Goshen, where my people live; no
swarms of flies will be there, so that you will
know that I, the LORD, am in this land. 23 I will
make a distinction[a] between my people and
your people. This miraculous sign will occur tomorrow.' "
24 And the LORD did this. Dense swarms of flies

[a]23 Septuagint and Vulgate; Hebrew *will put a deliverance*

poured into Pharaoh's palace and into the houses
of his officials, and throughout Egypt the land was
ruined by the flies.
[25]Then Pharaoh summoned Moses and Aaron
and said, "Go, sacrifice to your God here in the
land."
[26]But Moses said, "That would not be right.
The sacrifices we offer the LORD our God would
be detestable to the Egyptians. And if we offer
sacrifices that are detestable in their eyes, will
they not stone us? [27]We must take a three-day
journey into the desert to offer sacrifices to the
LORD our God, as he commands us."
[28]Pharaoh said, "I will let you go to offer sacrifices to the LORD your God in the desert, but you
must not go very far. Now pray for me."
[29]Moses answered, "As soon as I leave you, I
will pray to the LORD, and tomorrow the flies will
leave Pharaoh and his officials and his people.
Only be sure that Pharaoh does not act deceitfully
again by not letting the people go to offer sacrifices to the LORD."
[30]Then Moses left Pharaoh and prayed to the
LORD, [31]and the LORD did what Moses asked: The
flies left Pharaoh and his officials and his people;
not a fly remained. [32]But this time also Pharaoh
hardened his heart and would not let the people go.

The Plague on Livestock

9 Then the LORD said to Moses, "Go to Pharaoh and say to him, 'This is what the LORD,
the God of the Hebrews, says: "Let my people go,
so that they may worship me." [2]If you refuse to
let them go and continue to hold them back, [3]the
hand of the LORD will bring a terrible plague on
your livestock in the field—on your horses and
donkeys and camels and on your cattle and sheep
and goats. [4]But the LORD will make a distinction
between the livestock of Israel and that of Egypt,
so that no animal belonging to the Israelites will
die.' "
[5]The LORD set a time and said, "Tomorrow the
LORD will do this in the land." [6]And the next day
the LORD did it: All the livestock of the Egyptians
died, but not one animal belonging to the Israelites died. [7]Pharaoh sent men to investigate and
found that not even one of the animals of the
Israelites had died. Yet his heart was unyielding
and he would not let the people go.

The Plague of Boils

[8]Then the LORD said to Moses and Aaron,
"Take handfuls of soot from a furnace and have
Moses toss it into the air in the presence of Pharaoh. [9]It will become fine dust over the whole
land of Egypt, and festering boils will break out
on men and animals throughout the land."
[10]So they took soot from a furnace and stood
before Pharaoh. Moses tossed it into the air, and
festering boils broke out on men and animals.
[11]The magicians could not stand before Moses
because of the boils that were on them and on all
the Egyptians. [12]But the LORD hardened Pharaoh's heart and he would not listen to Moses and
Aaron, just as the LORD had said to Moses.

The Plague of Hail

[13]Then the LORD said to Moses, "Get up early
in the morning, confront Pharaoh and say to him,
'This is what the LORD, the God of the Hebrews,
says: Let my people go, so that they may worship
me, [14]or this time I will send the full force of my
plagues against you and against your officials and
your people, so you may know that there is no
one like me in all the earth. [15]For by now I could
have stretched out my hand and struck you and
your people with a plague that would have wiped
you off the earth. [16]But I have raised you up[a] for
this very purpose, that I might show you my power and that my name might be proclaimed in all
the earth. [17]You still set yourself against my people and will not let them go. [18]Therefore, at this
time tomorrow I will send the worst hailstorm
that has ever fallen on Egypt, from the day it was
founded till now. [19]Give an order now to bring
your livestock and everything you have in the
field to a place of shelter, because the hail will
fall on every man and animal that has not been
brought in and is still out in the field, and they
will die.' "
[20]Those officials of Pharaoh who feared the
word of the LORD hurried to bring their slaves
and their livestock inside. [21]But those who ignored the word of the LORD left their slaves and
livestock in the field.
[22]Then the LORD said to Moses, "Stretch out
your hand toward the sky so that hail will fall all
over Egypt—on men and animals and on everything growing in the fields of Egypt." [23]When
Moses stretched out his staff toward the sky, the
LORD sent thunder and hail, and lightning flashed
down to the ground. So the LORD rained hail on
the land of Egypt; [24]hail fell and lightning flashed
back and forth. It was the worst storm in all
the land of Egypt since it had become a nation.
[25]Throughout Egypt hail struck everything in the
fields—both men and animals; it beat down everything growing in the fields and stripped every
tree. [26]The only place it did not hail was the land
of Goshen, where the Israelites were.
[27]Then Pharaoh summoned Moses and Aaron.
"This time I have sinned," he said to them. "The

[a]16 Or *have spared you*

LORD is in the right, and I and my people are in
the wrong. 28Pray to the LORD, for we have had
enough thunder and hail. I will let you go; you
don't have to stay any longer."
29Moses replied, "When I have gone out of the
city, I will spread out my hands in prayer to the
LORD. The thunder will stop and there will be no
more hail, so you may know that the earth is the
LORD's. 30But I know that you and your officials
still do not fear the LORD God."
31(The flax and barley were destroyed, since
the barley had headed and the flax was in bloom.
32The wheat and spelt, however, were not destroyed, because they ripen later.)
33Then Moses left Pharaoh and went out of the
city. He spread out his hands toward the LORD;
the thunder and hail stopped, and the rain no
longer poured down on the land. 34When Pharaoh saw that the rain and hail and thunder had
stopped, he sinned again: He and his officials
hardened their hearts. 35So Pharaoh's heart was
hard and he would not let the Israelites go, just as
the LORD had said through Moses.

The Plague of Locusts

10 Then the LORD said to Moses, "Go to
Pharaoh, for I have hardened his heart
and the hearts of his officials so that I may perform these miraculous signs of mine among them
2that you may tell your children and grandchildren how I dealt harshly with the Egyptians and
how I performed my signs among them, and that
you may know that I am the LORD."
3So Moses and Aaron went to Pharaoh and
said to him, "This is what the LORD, the God of
the Hebrews, says: 'How long will you refuse to
humble yourself before me? Let my people go, so
that they may worship me. 4If you refuse to let
them go, I will bring locusts into your country
tomorrow. 5They will cover the face of the
ground so that it cannot be seen. They will devour what little you have left after the hail, including every tree that is growing in your fields.
6They will fill your houses and those of all your
officials and all the Egyptians—something neither your fathers nor your forefathers have ever
seen from the day they settled in this land till
now.'" Then Moses turned and left Pharaoh.
7Pharaoh's officials said to him, "How long
will this man be a snare to us? Let the people go,
so that they may worship the LORD their God. Do
you not yet realize that Egypt is ruined?"
8Then Moses and Aaron were brought back to
Pharaoh. "Go, worship the LORD your God," he
said. "But just who will be going?"
9Moses answered, "We will go with our young
and old, with our sons and daughters, and with
our flocks and herds, because we are to celebrate
a festival to the LORD."
10Pharaoh said, "The LORD be with you—if I
let you go, along with your women and children!
Clearly you are bent on evil.[a] 11No! Have only
the men go; and worship the LORD, since that's
what you have been asking for." Then Moses and
Aaron were driven out of Pharaoh's presence.
12And the LORD said to Moses, "Stretch out
your hand over Egypt so that locusts will swarm
over the land and devour everything growing in
the fields, everything left by the hail."
13So Moses stretched out his staff over Egypt,
and the LORD made an east wind blow across the
land all that day and all that night. By morning
the wind had brought the locusts; 14they invaded
all Egypt and settled down in every area of the
country in great numbers. Never before had
there been such a plague of locusts, nor will there
ever be again. 15They covered all the ground until
it was black. They devoured all that was left after
the hail—everything growing in the fields and
the fruit on the trees. Nothing green remained on
tree or plant in all the land of Egypt.
16Pharaoh quickly summoned Moses and Aaron and said, "I have sinned against the LORD your
God and against you. 17Now forgive my sin once
more and pray to the LORD your God to take this
deadly plague away from me."
18Moses then left Pharaoh and prayed to the
LORD. 19And the LORD changed the wind to a very
strong west wind, which caught up the locusts
and carried them into the Red Sea.[b] Not a locust
was left anywhere in Egypt. 20But the LORD hardened Pharaoh's heart, and he would not let the
Israelites go.

The Plague of Darkness

21Then the LORD said to Moses, "Stretch out
your hand toward the sky so that darkness will
spread over Egypt—darkness that can be felt."
22So Moses stretched out his hand toward the
sky, and total darkness covered all Egypt for three
days. 23No one could see anyone else or leave his
place for three days. Yet all the Israelites had light
in the places where they lived.
24Then Pharaoh summoned Moses and said,
"Go, worship the LORD. Even your women and
children may go with you; only leave your flocks
and herds behind."
25But Moses said, "You must allow us to have
sacrifices and burnt offerings to present to the
LORD our God. 26Our livestock too must go with
us; not a hoof is to be left behind. We have to use
some of them in worshiping the LORD our God,
and until we get there we will not know what we
are to use to worship the LORD."

[a]*10* Or *Be careful, trouble is in store for you!*
[b]*19* Hebrew *Yam Suph*; that is, Sea of Reeds

27But the LORD hardened Pharaoh's heart, and
he was not willing to let them go. 28Pharaoh said
to Moses, "Get out of my sight! Make sure you do
not appear before me again! The day you see my
face you will die."
29"Just as you say," Moses replied, "I will never appear before you again."

The Plague on the Firstborn

11 Now the LORD had said to Moses, "I will
bring one more plague on Pharaoh and on
Egypt. After that, he will let you go from here,
and when he does, he will drive you out completely. 2Tell the people that men and women
alike are to ask their neighbors for articles of silver and gold." 3(The LORD made the Egyptians
favorably disposed toward the people, and Moses
himself was highly regarded in Egypt by Pharaoh's officials and by the people.)
4So Moses said, "This is what the LORD says:
'About midnight I will go throughout Egypt. 5Ev-
ery firstborn son in Egypt will die, from the firstborn son of Pharaoh, who sits on the throne, to
the firstborn son of the slave girl, who is at her
hand mill, and all the firstborn of the cattle as
well. 6There will be loud wailing throughout
Egypt—worse than there has ever been or ever
will be again. 7But among the Israelites not a dog
will bark at any man or animal.' Then you will
know that the LORD makes a distinction between
Egypt and Israel. 8All these officials of yours will
come to me, bowing down before me and saying,
'Go, you and all the people who follow you!' After
that I will leave." Then Moses, hot with anger,
left Pharaoh.
9The LORD had said to Moses, "Pharaoh will
refuse to listen to you—so that my wonders may
be multiplied in Egypt." 10Moses and Aaron performed all these wonders before Pharaoh, but the
LORD hardened Pharaoh's heart, and he would
not let the Israelites go out of his country.

The Passover

12 The LORD said to Moses and Aaron in
Egypt, 2"This month is to be for you the
first month, the first month of your year. 3Tell the
whole community of Israel that on the tenth day
of this month each man is to take a lamb[a] for his
family, one for each household. 4If any household
is too small for a whole lamb, they must share
one with their nearest neighbor, having taken
into account the number of people there are. You
are to determine the amount of lamb needed in
accordance with what each person will eat. 5The
animals you choose must be year-old males without defect, and you may take them from the
sheep or the goats. 6Take care of them until the
fourteenth day of the month, when all the people
of the community of Israel must slaughter them
at twilight. 7Then they are to take some of
the blood and put it on the sides and tops of
the doorframes of the houses where they eat

EXODUS 12:1–30

1. What's the most elaborate meal you've ever eaten?
2. What rules or customs does your family have at mealtime?
3. What is a special feast your family observes? What makes it special?
4. What is the difference between the sacrifice of the "lamb" in this story and the "Lamb of God" in the New Testament?
5. If you had been one of the Hebrew children that night, how would you have felt when you walked out of Egypt a "free" person?
6. What is the closest you have come to experiencing this same freedom in your life?
7. How can the group pray for you this week?

a3 The Hebrew word can mean *lamb* or *kid*; also in verse 4.

In spite of nine spectacular plagues, Pharaoh had repeatedly refused to let the Israelite slaves hold a worship festival in the desert. Finally, Moses warned Pharaoh that he would actually beg the Hebrews to leave after the firstborn of Egypt were slain. This event would be so significant it inaugurated the Jewish religious calendar (v. 2).

12:5 *animals ... without defect.* Future sacrifices must likewise be flawless (Lev. 22:17–20). Similarly, Jesus was like "a lamb without blemish or defect" (1 Peter 1:19).

12:7 *blood.* Symbolizes a sacrifice offered as a substitute, one life laid down for another. Thus Israel escapes the judgment about to fall on Egypt (see Heb. 9:22; 1 John 1:7).

12:8 *bitter herbs.* Eating them would recall the bitter years of servitude in Egypt. ***bread made without yeast.*** Reflecting the haste with which the people left Egypt (vv. 11,39).

12:13 *sign.* Just as the plagues were miraculous signs of judgment on Pharaoh and his people, so the Lord's "passing over" the Israelites who placed themselves under the sign of blood was a pledge of God's mercy.

12:14 *celebrate it as ... a lasting ordinance.* Frequent references to Passover observance occur in the rest of Scripture, including the occasion of Jesus' "last supper" (Matt. 26:17–19). The ordinance is still kept by orthodox Jews today.

12:21 *Passover lamb.* Jesus is "our Passover lamb" (1 Cor. 5:7), sacrificed "once for all" (Heb. 7:27) for us.

the lambs. 8That same night they are to eat the meat roasted over the fire, along with bitter herbs, and bread made without yeast. 9Do not eat the meat raw or cooked in water, but roast it over the fire—head, legs and inner parts. 10Do not leave any of it till morning; if some is left till morning, you must burn it. 11This is how you are to eat it: with your cloak tucked into your belt, your sandals on your feet and your staff in your hand. Eat it in haste; it is the LORD's Passover.

12"On that same night I will pass through Egypt and strike down every firstborn—both men and animals—and I will bring judgment on all the gods of Egypt. I am the LORD. 13The blood will be a sign for you on the houses where you are; and when I see the blood, I will pass over you. No destructive plague will touch you when I strike Egypt.

14"This is a day you are to commemorate; for the generations to come you shall celebrate it as a festival to the LORD—a lasting ordinance. 15For seven days you are to eat bread made without yeast. On the first day remove the yeast from your houses, for whoever eats anything with yeast in it from the first day through the seventh must be cut off from Israel. 16On the first day hold a sacred assembly, and another one on the seventh day. Do no work at all on these days, except to prepare food for everyone to eat—that is all you may do.

17"Celebrate the Feast of Unleavened Bread, because it was on this very day that I brought your divisions out of Egypt. Celebrate this day as a lasting ordinance for the generations to come. 18In the first month you are to eat bread made without yeast, from the evening of the fourteenth day until the evening of the twenty-first day. 19For seven days no yeast is to be found in your houses. And whoever eats anything with yeast in it must be cut off from the community of Israel, whether he is an alien or native-born. 20Eat nothing made with yeast. Wherever you live, you must eat unleavened bread."

21Then Moses summoned all the elders of Israel and said to them, "Go at once and select the animals for your families and slaughter the Passover lamb. 22Take a bunch of hyssop, dip it into the blood in the basin and put some of the blood on the top and on both sides of the doorframe. Not one of you shall go out the door of his house until morning. 23When the LORD goes through the land to strike down the Egyptians, he will see the blood on the top and sides of the doorframe and will pass over that doorway, and he will not permit the destroyer to enter your houses and strike you down.

24"Obey these instructions as a lasting ordinance for you and your descendants. 25When you enter the land that the LORD will give you as he promised, observe this ceremony. 26And when your children ask you, 'What does this ceremony mean to you?' 27then tell them, 'It is the Passover sacrifice to the LORD, who passed over the houses of the Israelites in Egypt and spared our homes when he struck down the Egyptians.'" Then the people bowed down and worshiped. 28The Israelites did just what the LORD commanded Moses and Aaron.

29At midnight the LORD struck down all the firstborn in Egypt, from the firstborn of Pharaoh, who sat on the throne, to the firstborn of the prisoner, who was in the dungeon, and the firstborn of all the livestock as well. 30Pharaoh and all his officials and all the Egyptians got up during the night, and there was loud wailing in Egypt, for there was not a house without someone dead.

The Exodus

31During the night Pharaoh summoned Moses and Aaron and said, "Up! Leave my people, you and the Israelites! Go, worship the LORD as you have requested. 32Take your flocks and herds, as you have said, and go. And also bless me."

33The Egyptians urged the people to hurry and leave the country. "For otherwise," they said, "we will all die!" 34So the people took their dough before the yeast was added, and carried it on their shoulders in kneading troughs wrapped in clothing. 35The Israelites did as Moses instructed and asked the Egyptians for articles of silver and gold and for clothing. 36The LORD had made the Egyptians favorably disposed toward the people, and they gave them what they asked for; so they plundered the Egyptians.

37The Israelites journeyed from Rameses to Succoth. There were about six hundred thousand men on foot, besides women and children. 38Many other people went up with them, as well as large droves of livestock, both flocks and herds. 39With the dough they had brought from Egypt, they baked cakes of unleavened bread. The dough was without yeast because they had been driven out of Egypt and did not have time to prepare food for themselves.

40Now the length of time the Israelite people lived in Egypt[a] was 430 years. 41At the end of the 430 years, to the very day, all the LORD's divisions left Egypt. 42Because the LORD kept vigil that night to bring them out of Egypt, on this night all the Israelites are to keep vigil to honor the LORD for the generations to come.

a40 Masoretic Text; Samaritan Pentateuch and Septuagint *Egypt and Canaan*

Passover Restrictions

43The LORD said to Moses and Aaron, "These are the regulations for the Passover:

"No foreigner is to eat of it. 44Any slave you have bought may eat of it after you have circumcised him, 45but a temporary resident and a hired worker may not eat of it.

46"It must be eaten inside one house; take none of the meat outside the house. Do not break any of the bones. 47The whole community of Israel must celebrate it.

48"An alien living among you who wants to celebrate the LORD's Passover must have all the males in his household circumcised; then he may take part like one born in the land. No uncircumcised male may eat of it. 49The same law applies to the native-born and to the alien living among you."

50All the Israelites did just what the LORD had commanded Moses and Aaron. 51And on that very day the LORD brought the Israelites out of Egypt by their divisions.

Consecration of the Firstborn

13 The LORD said to Moses, 2"Consecrate to me every firstborn male. The first offspring of every womb among the Israelites belongs to me, whether man or animal."

3Then Moses said to the people, "Commemorate this day, the day you came out of Egypt, out of the land of slavery, because the LORD brought you out of it with a mighty hand. Eat nothing containing yeast. 4Today, in the month of Abib, you are leaving. 5When the LORD brings you into the land of the Canaanites, Hittites, Amorites, Hivites and Jebusites—the land he swore to your forefathers to give you, a land flowing with milk and honey—you are to observe this ceremony in this month: 6For seven days eat bread made without yeast and on the seventh day hold a festival to the LORD. 7Eat unleavened bread during those seven days; nothing with yeast in it is to be seen among you, nor shall any yeast be seen anywhere within your borders. 8On that day tell your son, 'I do this because of what the LORD did for me when I came out of Egypt.' 9This observance will be for you like a sign on your hand and a reminder on your forehead that the law of the LORD is to be on your lips. For the LORD brought you out of Egypt with his mighty hand. 10You must keep this ordinance at the appointed time year after year.

11"After the LORD brings you into the land of the Canaanites and gives it to you, as he promised on oath to you and your forefathers, 12you are to give over to the LORD the first offspring of every womb. All the firstborn males of your livestock belong to the LORD. 13Redeem with a lamb every firstborn donkey, but if you do not redeem it, break its neck. Redeem every firstborn among your sons.

14"In days to come, when your son asks you, 'What does this mean?' say to him, 'With a mighty hand the LORD brought us out of Egypt, out of the land of slavery. 15When Pharaoh stubbornly refused to let us go, the LORD killed every firstborn in Egypt, both man and animal. This is why I sacrifice to the LORD the first male offspring of every womb and redeem each of my firstborn sons.' 16And it will be like a sign on your hand and a symbol on your forehead that the LORD brought us out of Egypt with his mighty hand."

Crossing the Sea

17When Pharaoh let the people go, God did not lead them on the road through the Philistine country, though that was shorter. For God said, "If they face war, they might change their minds and return to Egypt." 18So God led the people around by the desert road toward the Red Sea.[a] The Israelites went up out of Egypt armed for battle.

19Moses took the bones of Joseph with him because Joseph had made the sons of Israel swear an oath. He had said, "God will surely come to your aid, and then you must carry my bones up with you from this place."[b]

20After leaving Succoth they camped at Etham on the edge of the desert. 21By day the LORD went ahead of them in a pillar of cloud to guide them on their way and by night in a pillar of fire to give them light, so that they could travel by day or night. 22Neither the pillar of cloud by day nor the pillar of fire by night left its place in front of the people.

14 Then the LORD said to Moses, 2"Tell the Israelites to turn back and encamp near Pi Hahiroth, between Migdol and the sea. They are to encamp by the sea, directly opposite Baal Zephon. 3Pharaoh will think, 'The Israelites are wandering around the land in confusion, hemmed in by the desert.' 4And I will harden Pharaoh's heart, and he will pursue them. But I will gain glory for myself through Pharaoh and all his army, and the Egyptians will know that I am the LORD." So the Israelites did this.

5When the king of Egypt was told that the people had fled, Pharaoh and his officials changed their minds about them and said, "What have we done? We have let the Israelites go and have lost their services!" 6So he had his chariot made ready and took his army with him. 7He took six hundred of the best chariots, along with all the other chariots of Egypt, with officers over all of

[a] *18* Hebrew *Yam Suph*; that is, Sea of Reeds [b] *19* See Gen. 50:25.

them. 8The LORD hardened the heart of Pharaoh
king of Egypt, so that he pursued the Israelites,
who were marching out boldly. 9The Egyptians—
all Pharaoh's horses and chariots, horsemen[a]
and troops—pursued the Israelites and overtook
them as they camped by the sea near Pi Hahiroth,
opposite Baal Zephon.

EXODUS 14:5–31

1. If you had to get out of your house in 30 seconds, what one thing would you grab?
2. Have you ever been chased? What happened?
3. When you're caught between a rock and a hard place (like Israel was), do you react more with faith—or fear?
4. What is the closest you have come to seeing God perform a miracle like the one in this story?
5. If you had to compare your spiritual journey to the Hebrews in this story, where would you be: Standing at the edge of the water, scared stiff? Seeing the waters start to part? Starting to step out in faith? Somewhere in the big middle walking by faith?
6. What is the biggest challenge you are facing right now in your life?

10As Pharaoh approached, the Israelites looked
up, and there were the Egyptians, marching after
them. They were terrified and cried out to the
LORD. 11They said to Moses, "Was it because
there were no graves in Egypt that you brought
us to the desert to die? What have you done to us
by bringing us out of Egypt? 12Didn't we say to
you in Egypt, 'Leave us alone; let us serve the
Egyptians'? It would have been better for us to
serve the Egyptians than to die in the desert!"
13Moses answered the people, "Do not be
afraid. Stand firm and you will see the deliverance the LORD will bring you today. The Egyptians you see today you will never see again.
14The LORD will fight for you; you need only to be
still."
15Then the LORD said to Moses, "Why are
you crying out to me? Tell the Israelites to move
on. 16Raise your staff and stretch out your hand
over the sea to divide the water so that the Israelites can go through the sea on dry ground. 17I
will harden the hearts of the Egyptians so that
they will go in after them. And I will gain glory
through Pharaoh and all his army, through his
chariots and his horsemen. 18The Egyptians will
know that I am the LORD when I gain glory
through Pharaoh, his chariots and his horsemen."
19Then the angel of God, who had been traveling in front of Israel's army, withdrew and went
behind them. The pillar of cloud also moved from
in front and stood behind them, 20coming between the armies of Egypt and Israel. Throughout
the night the cloud brought darkness to the one
side and light to the other side; so neither went
near the other all night long.
21Then Moses stretched out his hand over the
sea, and all that night the LORD drove the sea
back with a strong east wind and turned it into
dry land. The waters were divided, 22and the Israelites went through the sea on dry ground, with
a wall of water on their right and on their left.
23The Egyptians pursued them, and all Pharaoh's horses and chariots and horsemen followed
them into the sea. 24During the last watch of the
night the LORD looked down from the pillar of fire
and cloud at the Egyptian army and threw it into
confusion. 25He made the wheels of their chariots come off[b] so that they had difficulty driving.
And the Egyptians said, "Let's get away from the

[a]9 Or *charioteers*; also in verses 17, 18, 23, 26 and 28 [b]25 Or *He jammed the wheels of their chariots* (see Samaritan Pentateuch, Septuagint and Syriac)

As a result of the tenth plague—the death of the Egyptian firstborn on the night of Passover—Pharaoh had finally let the Israelites go.

14:14 ***The LORD will fight for you.*** A necessary reminder that although Israel was "armed for battle" (13:18) and "marching out boldly" (v. 8), the victory would be won by God alone.

14:19 ***pillar of cloud.*** The visible symbol of God's presence among his people. By day the Lord went ahead of the people in a pillar of cloud and by night in a pillar of fire (13:21). The Lord often spoke to them from the pillar (Num. 12:5–6; Deut. 31:15–16).

14:20 The pillar of cloud (signifying the Lord's presence) protected Israel.

14:21 ***strong east wind.*** See 10:13. In 15:8–10 the poet praises the Lord and calls the wind the "blast of your nostrils," affirming (as here) that the miracle occurred in accordance with God's timing and direction.

14:22 ***through the sea on dry ground.*** In later times, psalmists and prophets reminded Israel of what God had done for them (see Ps. 66:6; 136:13–14; Isa. 63:11–13).

14:28 ***Not one of them survived.*** The Lord's victory over Pharaoh's army was complete.

14:31 ***feared the LORD.*** Reverential trust in God that includes commitment to his revealed will. ***put their trust in him and in Moses.*** Faith in God's mighty power and confidence in Moses' leadership.

Israelites! The LORD is fighting for them against
Egypt."
26 Then the LORD said to Moses, "Stretch out
your hand over the sea so that the waters may
flow back over the Egyptians and their chariots
and horsemen." 27 Moses stretched out his hand
over the sea, and at daybreak the sea went back
to its place. The Egyptians were fleeing toward[a]
it, and the LORD swept them into the sea. 28 The
water flowed back and covered the chariots and
horsemen—the entire army of Pharaoh that had
followed the Israelites into the sea. Not one of
them survived.
29 But the Israelites went through the sea on
dry ground, with a wall of water on their right
and on their left. 30 That day the LORD saved Israel
from the hands of the Egyptians, and Israel saw
the Egyptians lying dead on the shore. 31 And
when the Israelites saw the great power the LORD
displayed against the Egyptians, the people feared
the LORD and put their trust in him and in Moses
his servant.

The Song of Moses and Miriam

15 Then Moses and the Israelites sang this song to the LORD:

"I will sing to the LORD,
for he is highly exalted.
The horse and its rider
he has hurled into the sea.
2 The LORD is my strength and my song;
he has become my salvation.
He is my God, and I will praise him,
my father's God, and I will exalt him.
3 The LORD is a warrior;
the LORD is his name.
4 Pharaoh's chariots and his army
he has hurled into the sea.
The best of Pharaoh's officers
are drowned in the Red Sea.[b]
5 The deep waters have covered them;
they sank to the depths like a stone.

6 "Your right hand, O LORD,
was majestic in power.
Your right hand, O LORD,
shattered the enemy.
7 In the greatness of your majesty
you threw down those who opposed you.
You unleashed your burning anger;
it consumed them like stubble.
8 By the blast of your nostrils
the waters piled up.
The surging waters stood firm like a wall;
the deep waters congealed in the heart of
the sea.
9 "The enemy boasted,
'I will pursue, I will overtake them.
I will divide the spoils;
I will gorge myself on them.
I will draw my sword
and my hand will destroy them.'
10 But you blew with your breath,
and the sea covered them.
They sank like lead
in the mighty waters.

11 "Who among the gods is like you, O LORD?
Who is like you—
majestic in holiness,
awesome in glory,
working wonders?
12 You stretched out your right hand
and the earth swallowed them.

13 "In your unfailing love you will lead
the people you have redeemed.
In your strength you will guide them
to your holy dwelling.
14 The nations will hear and tremble;
anguish will grip the people of
Philistia.
15 The chiefs of Edom will be terrified,
the leaders of Moab will be seized with
trembling,
the people[c] of Canaan will melt away;
16 terror and dread will fall upon them.
By the power of your arm
they will be as still as a stone—
until your people pass by, O LORD,
until the people you bought[d] pass by.
17 You will bring them in and plant them
on the mountain of your inheritance—
the place, O LORD, you made for your
dwelling,
the sanctuary, O Lord, your hands
established.
18 The LORD will reign
for ever and ever."

19 When Pharaoh's horses, chariots and horsemen[e] went into the sea, the LORD brought the
waters of the sea back over them, but the Israelites walked through the sea on dry ground.
20 Then Miriam the prophetess, Aaron's sister,
took a tambourine in her hand, and all the wom-
en followed her, with tambourines and dancing.
21 Miriam sang to them:

"Sing to the LORD,
for he is highly exalted.
The horse and its rider
he has hurled into the sea."

[a] 27 Or *from* [b] 4 Hebrew *Yam Suph*; that is, Sea of Reeds; also in verse 22 [c] 15 Or *rulers* [d] 16 Or *created*
[e] 19 Or *charioteers*

The Waters of Marah and Elim

22Then Moses led Israel from the Red Sea and
they went into the Desert of Shur. For three days
they traveled in the desert without finding water.
23When they came to Marah, they could not
drink its water because it was bitter. (That is why
the place is called Marah.[a]) 24So the people
grumbled against Moses, saying, "What are we to
drink?"

25Then Moses cried out to the LORD, and the
LORD showed him a piece of wood. He threw it
into the water, and the water became sweet.

There the LORD made a decree and a law for
them, and there he tested them. 26He said, "If
you listen carefully to the voice of the LORD your
God and do what is right in his eyes, if you pay
attention to his commands and keep all his decrees, I will not bring on you any of the diseases
I brought on the Egyptians, for I am the LORD,
who heals you."

27Then they came to Elim, where there were
twelve springs and seventy palm trees, and they
camped there near the water.

Manna and Quail

16 The whole Israelite community set out
from Elim and came to the Desert of Sin,
which is between Elim and Sinai, on the fifteenth
day of the second month after they had come out
of Egypt. 2In the desert the whole community
grumbled against Moses and Aaron. 3The Israelites said to them, "If only we had died by the
LORD's hand in Egypt! There we sat around pots
of meat and ate all the food we wanted, but you
have brought us out into this desert to starve this
entire assembly to death."

4Then the LORD said to Moses, "I will rain
down bread from heaven for you. The people are
to go out each day and gather enough for that day.
In this way I will test them and see whether they
will follow my instructions. 5On the sixth day
they are to prepare what they bring in, and that
is to be twice as much as they gather on the other
days."

6So Moses and Aaron said to all the Israelites,
"In the evening you will know that it was the
LORD who brought you out of Egypt, 7and in the
morning you will see the glory of the LORD, because he has heard your grumbling against him.
Who are we, that you should grumble against
us?" 8Moses also said, "You will know that it was
the LORD when he gives you meat to eat in the
evening and all the bread you want in the morning, because he has heard your grumbling against
him. Who are we? You are not grumbling against
us, but against the LORD."

? *EXODUS 16:1–35*

1. What is the strangest thing you have ever eaten?
2. What food could you eat every day?
3. Are you more likely to complain or be grateful for the food you eat?
4. Are you more likely to keep yourself fit physically or spiritually?
5. How would you describe your spiritual diet: Fast food? Sunday dinner? Leftovers?
6. If you could receive one thing from the Lord every day, what would you choose?
7. If the others in your group would join you in a spiritual discipline, what would you be willing to commit to for the next seven days?

9Then Moses told Aaron, "Say to the entire
Israelite community, 'Come before the LORD, for
he has heard your grumbling.' "

10While Aaron was speaking to the whole Isra-

[a]23 *Marah* means *bitter.*

16:1 *fifteenth day of the second month.* Exactly one month had passed since Israel's exodus from Egypt (12:2,6,31).

16:2 *grumbled.* During their desert wanderings, the Israelites grumbled against Moses and Aaron whenever they faced a crisis. In reality, however, they were grumbling "against the LORD" (v. 8). Paul warns us not to follow their example (1 Cor. 10:10).

16:4 *bread from heaven.* Jesus referred to this story when he called himself "the true bread from heaven" and "the bread of life" (John 6:32–35). ***gather enough for that day.*** Probably the background for Jesus' model petition in the "Lord's Prayer"—"Give us today our daily bread" (Matt. 6:11).

16:14 *thin flakes like frost.* A description of manna, the bread from heaven. Some researchers have likened manna to a honeydew excretion of a number of desert insects. However, the natural explanation of this miracle cannot account for the quantity and timing of the manna in Israel's camp.

16:15 *What is it?* See verse 31 and NIV text note. Its unknown nature is evidence that the manna was supernatural.

16:23 *Sabbath*. The first occurrence of the word itself, though the principle of the seventh day as a day of rest and holiness is set forth in the account of creation (see note on Gen. 2:3).

16:35 *ate manna forty years.* The manna stopped when the Israelites celebrated their first Passover in Canaan (Josh. 5:10–12).

elite community, they looked toward the desert,
and there was the glory of the LORD appearing in
the cloud.
11The LORD said to Moses, 12"I have heard the
grumbling of the Israelites. Tell them, 'At twilight you will eat meat, and in the morning you
will be filled with bread. Then you will know that
I am the LORD your God.'"
13That evening quail came and covered the
camp, and in the morning there was a layer of
dew around the camp. 14When the dew was
gone, thin flakes like frost on the ground appeared on the desert floor. 15When the Israelites
saw it, they said to each other, "What is it?" For
they did not know what it was.
Moses said to them, "It is the bread the LORD
has given you to eat. 16This is what the LORD has
commanded: 'Each one is to gather as much as he
needs. Take an omer[a] for each person you have
in your tent.'"
17The Israelites did as they were told; some
gathered much, some little. 18And when they
measured it by the omer, he who gathered much
did not have too much, and he who gathered
little did not have too little. Each one gathered as
much as he needed.
19Then Moses said to them, "No one is to keep
any of it until morning."
20However, some of them paid no attention to
Moses; they kept part of it until morning, but it
was full of maggots and began to smell. So Moses
was angry with them.
21Each morning everyone gathered as much as
he needed, and when the sun grew hot, it melted
away. 22On the sixth day, they gathered twice as
much—two omers[b] for each person—and the
leaders of the community came and reported this
to Moses. 23He said to them, "This is what the
LORD commanded: 'Tomorrow is to be a day of
rest, a holy Sabbath to the LORD. So bake what
you want to bake and boil what you want to boil.
Save whatever is left and keep it until morning.'"
24So they saved it until morning, as Moses
commanded, and it did not stink or get maggots
in it. 25"Eat it today," Moses said, "because today
is a Sabbath to the LORD. You will not find any of
it on the ground today. 26Six days you are to
gather it, but on the seventh day, the Sabbath,
there will not be any."
27Nevertheless, some of the people went out
on the seventh day to gather it, but they found
none. 28Then the LORD said to Moses, "How long
will you[c] refuse to keep my commands and my
instructions? 29Bear in mind that the LORD has
given you the Sabbath; that is why on the sixth
day he gives you bread for two days. Everyone is
to stay where he is on the seventh day; no one is
to go out." 30So the people rested on the seventh
day.
31The people of Israel called the bread manna.[d] It was white like coriander seed and tasted
like wafers made with honey. 32Moses said, "This
is what the LORD has commanded: 'Take an omer
of manna and keep it for the generations to come,
so they can see the bread I gave you to eat in the
desert when I brought you out of Egypt.'"
33So Moses said to Aaron, "Take a jar and put
an omer of manna in it. Then place it before the
LORD to be kept for the generations to come."
34As the LORD commanded Moses, Aaron put
the manna in front of the Testimony, that it
might be kept. 35The Israelites ate manna forty
years, until they came to a land that was settled;
they ate manna until they reached the border of
Canaan.
36(An omer is one tenth of an ephah.)

Water From the Rock

17 The whole Israelite community set out
from the Desert of Sin, traveling from
place to place as the LORD commanded. They
camped at Rephidim, but there was no water for
the people to drink. 2So they quarreled with Moses and said, "Give us water to drink."
Moses replied, "Why do you quarrel with me?
Why do you put the LORD to the test?"
3But the people were thirsty for water there,
and they grumbled against Moses. They said,
"Why did you bring us up out of Egypt to make us
and our children and livestock die of thirst?"
4Then Moses cried out to the LORD, "What am
I to do with these people? They are almost ready
to stone me."
5The LORD answered Moses, "Walk on ahead
of the people. Take with you some of the elders
of Israel and take in your hand the staff with
which you struck the Nile, and go. 6I will stand
there before you by the rock at Horeb. Strike the
rock, and water will come out of it for the people
to drink." So Moses did this in the sight of the
elders of Israel. 7And he called the place Massah[e] and Meribah[f] because the Israelites quarreled and because they tested the LORD saying,
"Is the LORD among us or not?"

The Amalekites Defeated

8The Amalekites came and attacked the Israelites at Rephidim. 9Moses said to Joshua, "Choose
some of our men and go out to fight the Amalek-

[a] *16* That is, probably about 2 quarts (about 2 liters); also in verses 18, 32, 33 and 36 [b] *22* That is, probably about 4 quarts (about 4.5 liters) [c] *28* The Hebrew is plural. [d] *31* *Manna* means *What is it?* (see verse 15). [e] *7* *Massah* means *testing.* [f] *7* *Meribah* means *quarreling.*

ites. Tomorrow I will stand on top of the hill with
the staff of God in my hands."
10So Joshua fought the Amalekites as Moses
had ordered, and Moses, Aaron and Hur went to
the top of the hill. 11As long as Moses held up his
hands, the Israelites were winning, but whenever he lowered his hands, the Amalekites were
winning. 12When Moses' hands grew tired, they
took a stone and put it under him and he sat on
it. Aaron and Hur held his hands up—one on one
side, one on the other—so that his hands remained steady till sunset. 13So Joshua overcame
the Amalekite army with the sword.
14Then the LORD said to Moses, "Write this
on a scroll as something to be remembered and
make sure that Joshua hears it, because I will
completely blot out the memory of Amalek from
under heaven."
15Moses built an altar and called it The LORD is
my Banner. 16He said, "For hands were lifted up
to the throne of the LORD. The[a] LORD will be at
war against the Amalekites from generation to
generation."

Jethro Visits Moses

18 Now Jethro, the priest of Midian and
father-in-law of Moses, heard of everything God had done for Moses and for his people
Israel, and how the LORD had brought Israel out
of Egypt.
2After Moses had sent away his wife Zipporah,
his father-in-law Jethro received her 3and her
two sons. One son was named Gershom,[b] for
Moses said, "I have become an alien in a foreign
land"; 4and the other was named Eliezer,[c] for
he said, "My father's God was my helper; he
saved me from the sword of Pharaoh."
5Jethro, Moses' father-in-law, together with
Moses' sons and wife, came to him in the desert,
where he was camped near the mountain of God.
6Jethro had sent word to him, "I, your father-in-
law Jethro, am coming to you with your wife and
her two sons."
7So Moses went out to meet his father-in-law
and bowed down and kissed him. They greeted
each other and then went into the tent. 8Moses
told his father-in-law about everything the LORD
had done to Pharaoh and the Egyptians for Israel's sake and about all the hardships they had met
along the way and how the LORD had saved them.
9Jethro was delighted to hear about all the
good things the LORD had done for Israel in rescuing them from the hand of the Egyptians. 10He
said, "Praise be to the LORD, who rescued you
from the hand of the Egyptians and of Pharaoh,
and who rescued the people from the hand of the
Egyptians. 11Now I know that the LORD is greater
than all other gods, for he did this to those who
had treated Israel arrogantly." 12Then Jethro, Moses' father-in-law, brought a burnt offering and
other sacrifices to God, and Aaron came with
all the elders of Israel to eat bread with Moses'
father-in-law in the presence of God.
13The next day Moses took his seat to serve as
judge for the people, and they stood around him
from morning till evening. 14When his father-in-
law saw all that Moses was doing for the people,
he said, "What is this you are doing for the people? Why do you alone sit as judge, while all
these people stand around you from morning till
evening?"
15Moses answered him, "Because the people
come to me to seek God's will. 16Whenever they
have a dispute, it is brought to me, and I decide
between the parties and inform them of God's
decrees and laws."
17Moses' father-in-law replied, "What you are
doing is not good. 18You and these people who
come to you will only wear yourselves out. The
work is too heavy for you; you cannot handle it
alone. 19Listen now to me and I will give you
some advice, and may God be with you. You must
be the people's representative before God and
bring their disputes to him. 20Teach them the
decrees and laws, and show them the way to live
and the duties they are to perform. 21But select
capable men from all the people—men who
fear God, trustworthy men who hate dishonest
gain—and appoint them as officials over thousands, hundreds, fifties and tens. 22Have them
serve as judges for the people at all times, but
have them bring every difficult case to you; the
simple cases they can decide themselves. That
will make your load lighter, because they will
share it with you. 23If you do this and God so
commands, you will be able to stand the strain,
and all these people will go home satisfied."
24Moses listened to his father-in-law and did
everything he said. 25He chose capable men from
all Israel and made them leaders of the people,
officials over thousands, hundreds, fifties and
tens. 26They served as judges for the people at all
times. The difficult cases they brought to Moses,
but the simple ones they decided themselves.
27Then Moses sent his father-in-law on his
way, and Jethro returned to his own country.

At Mount Sinai

19 In the third month after the Israelites left
Egypt—on the very day—they came to
the Desert of Sinai. 2After they set out from Rephidim, they entered the Desert of Sinai, and Israel

[a] 16 Or *"Because a hand was against the throne of the LORD, the*
[c] 4 *Eliezer* means *my God is helper.*
[b] 3 *Gershom* sounds like the Hebrew for *an alien there.*

camped there in the desert in front of the mountain.
3 Then Moses went up to God, and the LORD
called to him from the mountain and said, "This
is what you are to say to the house of Jacob and
what you are to tell the people of Israel: 4 'You
yourselves have seen what I did to Egypt, and
how I carried you on eagles' wings and brought
you to myself. 5 Now if you obey me fully and
keep my covenant, then out of all nations you will
be my treasured possession. Although the whole
earth is mine, 6 you[a] will be for me a kingdom of
priests and a holy nation.' These are the words
you are to speak to the Israelites."
7 So Moses went back and summoned the elders of the people and set before them all the
words the LORD had commanded him to speak.
8 The people all responded together, "We will do
everything the LORD has said." So Moses brought
their answer back to the LORD.
9 The LORD said to Moses, "I am going to come
to you in a dense cloud, so that the people will
hear me speaking with you and will always put
their trust in you." Then Moses told the LORD
what the people had said.
10 And the LORD said to Moses, "Go to the people and consecrate them today and tomorrow.
Have them wash their clothes 11 and be ready by
the third day, because on that day the LORD will
come down on Mount Sinai in the sight of all the
people. 12 Put limits for the people around the
mountain and tell them, 'Be careful that you do
not go up the mountain or touch the foot of it.
Whoever touches the mountain shall surely be
put to death. 13 He shall surely be stoned or shot
with arrows; not a hand is to be laid on him.
Whether man or animal, he shall not be permitted to live.' Only when the ram's horn sounds a
long blast may they go up to the mountain."
14 After Moses had gone down the mountain
to the people, he consecrated them, and they
washed their clothes. 15 Then he said to the people, "Prepare yourselves for the third day. Abstain from sexual relations."
16 On the morning of the third day there was
thunder and lightning, with a thick cloud over
the mountain, and a very loud trumpet blast. Everyone in the camp trembled. 17 Then Moses led
the people out of the camp to meet with God, and
they stood at the foot of the mountain. 18 Mount
Sinai was covered with smoke, because the LORD
descended on it in fire. The smoke billowed up
from it like smoke from a furnace, the whole
mountain[b] trembled violently, 19 and the sound
of the trumpet grew louder and louder. Then Moses spoke and the voice of God answered him.[c]
20 The LORD descended to the top of Mount

Exodus 19:10–20:21

1. Who lays down the law in your home? How do you try to bend the rules?
2. If you were principal or dean for a year, what new rules would you put into place for your school?
3. If your school had to live by the Ten Commandments, what changes would have to be made?
4. What are some idols or false gods you see today? How do you avoid "bowing down" to them?
5. In what way can the "fear of God" be good for you (see note on 20:20)?
6. How would you describe your first experience with God: A mountaintop experience or more peaceful valley?
7. How satisfied are you with the way you are "meeting" with God now?

[a] 5,6 Or *possession, for the whole earth is mine. 6You* all the people [b] 18 Most Hebrew manuscripts; a few Hebrew manuscripts and Septuagint [c] 19 Or *and God answered him with thunder*

19:10–11 Outward preparation to meet God symbolizes the inward consecration God requires of his people.

19:12–13 Mount Sinai wasn't holy by nature but was made so by God's presence.

19:15 ***Abstain from sexual relations.*** Not because sex is sinful but because it may leave the participants ceremonially unclean (see Lev. 15:18).

20:3–4 No deity, real or imagined, is to rival the one true God. ***idol.*** Because God has no visible form, any idol intended to resemble him would be a sinful misrepresentation of him. Since other gods are not to be worshiped, making idols of them would be equally sinful (see Deut. 4:15–19).

20:12 ***Honor.*** (1) Prize highly (see Prov. 4:8), (2) care for (see Ps. 91:15), (3) show respect for (see Lev. 19:3; 20:9), and (4) obey (see Deut. 21:18–21; Eph. 6:1). ***so that you may live long.*** "The first commandment with a promise" (Eph. 6:2).

20:13 See Jesus' teaching in Matthew 5:21–26. ***murder.*** The Hebrew for this verb refers to a premeditated, deliberate act.

20:14 See Jesus' teaching in Matthew 5:27–30. ***adultery.*** A sin "against God" (Gen. 39:9) as well as the marriage partner.

20:20 ***Do not be afraid.*** Do not think that God's display of his majesty is intended simply to fill you with terror. ***fear of God.*** "Fear" in the sense of reverential trust in God that includes commitment to his will.

Sinai and called Moses to the top of the mountain. So Moses went up 21and the LORD said to
him, "Go down and warn the people so they do
not force their way through to see the LORD and
many of them perish. 22Even the priests, who
approach the LORD, must consecrate themselves,
or the LORD will break out against them."
23Moses said to the LORD, "The people cannot
come up Mount Sinai, because you yourself
warned us, 'Put limits around the mountain and
set it apart as holy.' "
24The LORD replied, "Go down and bring Aaron up with you. But the priests and the people
must not force their way through to come up to
the LORD, or he will break out against them."
25So Moses went down to the people and told
them.

The Ten Commandments

20 And God spoke all these words:
2"I am the LORD your God, who
brought you out of Egypt, out of the
land of slavery.
3"You shall have no other gods before[a] me.
4"You shall not make for yourself an idol in
the form of anything in heaven above
or on the earth beneath or in the waters below. 5You shall not bow down
to them or worship them; for I, the
LORD your God, am a jealous God,
punishing the children for the sin of
the fathers to the third and fourth
generation of those who hate me,
6but showing love to a thousand ⌞gen-
erations⌟ of those who love me and
keep my commandments.
7"You shall not misuse the name of the
LORD your God, for the LORD will not
hold anyone guiltless who misuses
his name.
8"Remember the Sabbath day by keeping it
holy. 9Six days you shall labor and do
all your work, 10but the seventh day
is a Sabbath to the LORD your God.
On it you shall not do any work, neither you, nor your son or daughter,
nor your manservant or maidservant,
nor your animals, nor the alien within your gates. 11For in six days the
LORD made the heavens and the
earth, the sea, and all that is in them,
but he rested on the seventh day.
Therefore the LORD blessed the Sabbath day and made it holy.
12"Honor your father and your mother, so
that you may live long in the land the
LORD your God is giving you.
13"You shall not murder.
14"You shall not commit adultery.
15"You shall not steal.
16"You shall not give false testimony against
your neighbor.
17"You shall not covet your neighbor's
house. You shall not covet your
neighbor's wife, or his manservant or
maidservant, his ox or donkey, or
anything that belongs to your neighbor."

18When the people saw the thunder and lightning and heard the trumpet and saw the mountain in smoke, they trembled with fear. They
stayed at a distance 19and said to Moses, "Speak
to us yourself and we will listen. But do not have
God speak to us or we will die."
20Moses said to the people, "Do not be afraid.
God has come to test you, so that the fear of God
will be with you to keep you from sinning."
21The people remained at a distance, while
Moses approached the thick darkness where God
was.

Idols and Altars

22Then the LORD said to Moses, "Tell the Israelites this: 'You have seen for yourselves that I
have spoken to you from heaven: 23Do not make
any gods to be alongside me; do not make for
yourselves gods of silver or gods of gold.
24" 'Make an altar of earth for me and sacrifice
on it your burnt offerings and fellowship offerings,[b] your sheep and goats and your cattle.
Wherever I cause my name to be honored, I will
come to you and bless you. 25If you make an altar
of stones for me, do not build it with dressed
stones, for you will defile it if you use a tool on it.
26And do not go up to my altar on steps, lest your
nakedness be exposed on it.'

21 "These are the laws you are to set before
them:

Hebrew Servants

2"If you buy a Hebrew servant, he is to serve
you for six years. But in the seventh year, he shall
go free, without paying anything. 3If he comes
alone, he is to go free alone; but if he has a wife
when he comes, she is to go with him. 4If his
master gives him a wife and she bears him sons
or daughters, the woman and her children shall
belong to her master, and only the man shall go
free.
5"But if the servant declares, 'I love my master

[a]3 Or *besides* [b]24 Traditionally *peace offerings*

and my wife and children and do not want to go
free,' 6then his master must take him before the
judges.[a] He shall take him to the door or the
doorpost and pierce his ear with an awl. Then he
will be his servant for life.
7"If a man sells his daughter as a servant, she
is not to go free as menservants do. 8If she does
not please the master who has selected her for
himself,[b] he must let her be redeemed. He has
no right to sell her to foreigners, because he has
broken faith with her. 9If he selects her for his
son, he must grant her the rights of a daughter.
10If he marries another woman, he must not deprive the first one of her food, clothing and marital rights. 11If he does not provide her with these
three things, she is to go free, without any payment of money.

Personal Injuries

12"Anyone who strikes a man and kills him
shall surely be put to death. 13However, if he
does not do it intentionally, but God lets it happen, he is to flee to a place I will designate. 14But
if a man schemes and kills another man deliberately, take him away from my altar and put him
to death.
15"Anyone who attacks[c] his father or his
mother must be put to death.
16"Anyone who kidnaps another and either
sells him or still has him when he is caught must
be put to death.
17"Anyone who curses his father or mother
must be put to death.
18"If men quarrel and one hits the other with
a stone or with his fist[d] and he does not die but
is confined to bed, 19the one who struck the blow
will not be held responsible if the other gets up
and walks around outside with his staff; however,
he must pay the injured man for the loss of his
time and see that he is completely healed.
20"If a man beats his male or female slave with
a rod and the slave dies as a direct result, he must
be punished, 21but he is not to be punished if the
slave gets up after a day or two, since the slave is
his property.
22"If men who are fighting hit a pregnant
woman and she gives birth prematurely[e] but
there is no serious injury, the offender must be
fined whatever the woman's husband demands
and the court allows. 23But if there is serious
injury, you are to take life for life, 24eye for eye,
tooth for tooth, hand for hand, foot for foot,
25burn for burn, wound for wound, bruise for
bruise.
26"If a man hits a manservant or maidservant
in the eye and destroys it, he must let the servant
go free to compensate for the eye. 27And if he
knocks out the tooth of a manservant or maidservant, he must let the servant go free to compensate for the tooth.
28"If a bull gores a man or a woman to death,
the bull must be stoned to death, and its meat
must not be eaten. But the owner of the bull will
not be held responsible. 29If, however, the bull
has had the habit of goring and the owner has
been warned but has not kept it penned up and
it kills a man or woman, the bull must be stoned
and the owner also must be put to death. 30How-
ever, if payment is demanded of him, he may
redeem his life by paying whatever is demanded.
31This law also applies if the bull gores a son or
daughter. 32If the bull gores a male or female
slave, the owner must pay thirty shekels[f] of silver to the master of the slave, and the bull must
be stoned.
33"If a man uncovers a pit or digs one and fails
to cover it and an ox or a donkey falls into it,
34the owner of the pit must pay for the loss; he
must pay its owner, and the dead animal will be
his.
35"If a man's bull injures the bull of another
and it dies, they are to sell the live one and divide
both the money and the dead animal equally.
36However, if it was known that the bull had the
habit of goring, yet the owner did not keep it
penned up, the owner must pay, animal for animal, and the dead animal will be his.

Protection of Property

22 "If a man steals an ox or a sheep and
slaughters it or sells it, he must pay back
five head of cattle for the ox and four sheep for
the sheep.
2"If a thief is caught breaking in and is struck
so that he dies, the defender is not guilty of
bloodshed; 3but if it happens[g] after sunrise, he
is guilty of bloodshed.
"A thief must certainly make restitution, but if
he has nothing, he must be sold to pay for his
theft.
4"If the stolen animal is found alive in his
possession—whether ox or donkey or sheep—
he must pay back double.
5"If a man grazes his livestock in a field or
vineyard and lets them stray and they graze in
another man's field, he must make restitution
from the best of his own field or vineyard.
6"If a fire breaks out and spreads into thornbushes so that it burns shocks of grain or standing
grain or the whole field, the one who started the
fire must make restitution.
7"If a man gives his neighbor silver or goods

a6 Or *before God* b8 Or *master so that he does not choose her* c15 Or *kills* d18 Or *with a tool* e22 Or *she has a miscarriage* f32 That is, about 12 ounces (about 0.3 kilogram) g3 Or *if he strikes him* for safekeeping and they are stolen from the neighbor's house, the thief, if he is caught, must pay back double. [8]But if the thief is not found, the owner of the house must appear before the judges[a] to determine whether he has laid his hands on the other man's property. [9]In all cases of illegal possession of an ox, a donkey, a sheep, a garment, or any other lost property about which somebody says, 'This is mine,' both parties are to bring their cases before the judges. The one whom the judges declare[b] guilty must pay back double to his neighbor.

[10]"If a man gives a donkey, an ox, a sheep or any other animal to his neighbor for safekeeping and it dies or is injured or is taken away while no one is looking, [11]the issue between them will be settled by the taking of an oath before the LORD that the neighbor did not lay hands on the other person's property. The owner is to accept this, and no restitution is required. [12]But if the animal was stolen from the neighbor, he must make restitution to the owner. [13]If it was torn to pieces by a wild animal, he shall bring in the remains as evidence and he will not be required to pay for the torn animal.

[14]"If a man borrows an animal from his neighbor and it is injured or dies while the owner is not present, he must make restitution. [15]But if the owner is with the animal, the borrower will not have to pay. If the animal was hired, the money paid for the hire covers the loss.

Social Responsibility

[16]"If a man seduces a virgin who is not pledged to be married and sleeps with her, he must pay the bride-price, and she shall be his wife. [17]If her father absolutely refuses to give her to him, he must still pay the bride-price for virgins.

[18]"Do not allow a sorceress to live.

[19]"Anyone who has sexual relations with an animal must be put to death.

[20]"Whoever sacrifices to any god other than the LORD must be destroyed.[c]

[21]"Do not mistreat an alien or oppress him, for you were aliens in Egypt.

[22]"Do not take advantage of a widow or an orphan. [23]If you do and they cry out to me, I will certainly hear their cry. [24]My anger will be aroused, and I will kill you with the sword; your wives will become widows and your children fatherless.

[25]"If you lend money to one of my people among you who is needy, do not be like a moneylender; charge him no interest.[d] [26]If you take your neighbor's cloak as a pledge, return it to him by sunset, [27]because his cloak is the only covering he has for his body. What else will he sleep in? When he cries out to me, I will hear, for I am compassionate.

[28]"Do not blaspheme God[e] or curse the ruler of your people.

[29]"Do not hold back offerings from your granaries or your vats.[f]

"You must give me the firstborn of your sons. [30]Do the same with your cattle and your sheep. Let them stay with their mothers for seven days, but give them to me on the eighth day.

[31]"You are to be my holy people. So do not eat the meat of an animal torn by wild beasts; throw it to the dogs.

Laws of Justice and Mercy

23 "Do not spread false reports. Do not help a wicked man by being a malicious witness.

[2]"Do not follow the crowd in doing wrong. When you give testimony in a lawsuit, do not pervert justice by siding with the crowd, [3]and do not show favoritism to a poor man in his lawsuit.

[4]"If you come across your enemy's ox or donkey wandering off, be sure to take it back to him. [5]If you see the donkey of someone who hates you fallen down under its load, do not leave it there; be sure you help him with it.

[6]"Do not deny justice to your poor people in their lawsuits. [7]Have nothing to do with a false charge and do not put an innocent or honest person to death, for I will not acquit the guilty.

[8]"Do not accept a bribe, for a bribe blinds those who see and twists the words of the righteous.

[9]"Do not oppress an alien; you yourselves know how it feels to be aliens, because you were aliens in Egypt.

Sabbath Laws

[10]"For six years you are to sow your fields and harvest the crops, [11]but during the seventh year let the land lie unplowed and unused. Then the poor among your people may get food from it, and the wild animals may eat what they leave. Do the same with your vineyard and your olive grove.

[12]"Six days do your work, but on the seventh day do not work, so that your ox and your donkey may rest and the slave born in your household, and the alien as well, may be refreshed.

[13]"Be careful to do everything I have said to you. Do not invoke the names of other gods; do not let them be heard on your lips.

[a]8 Or *before God*; also in verse 9 [b]9 Or *whom God declares* [c]20 The Hebrew term refers to the irrevocable giving over of things or persons to the LORD, often by totally destroying them. [d]25 Or *excessive interest* [e]28 Or *Do not revile the judges* [f]29 The meaning of the Hebrew for this phrase is uncertain.

The Three Annual Festivals

14"Three times a year you are to celebrate a festival to me.

15"Celebrate the Feast of Unleavened Bread; for seven days eat bread made without yeast, as I commanded you. Do this at the appointed time in the month of Abib, for in that month you came out of Egypt.

"No one is to appear before me empty-handed.

16"Celebrate the Feast of Harvest with the firstfruits of the crops you sow in your field.

"Celebrate the Feast of Ingathering at the end of the year, when you gather in your crops from the field.

17"Three times a year all the men are to appear before the Sovereign LORD.

18"Do not offer the blood of a sacrifice to me along with anything containing yeast.

"The fat of my festival offerings must not be kept until morning.

19"Bring the best of the firstfruits of your soil to the house of the LORD your God.

"Do not cook a young goat in its mother's milk.

God's Angel to Prepare the Way

20"See, I am sending an angel ahead of you to guard you along the way and to bring you to the place I have prepared. 21Pay attention to him and listen to what he says. Do not rebel against him; he will not forgive your rebellion, since my Name is in him. 22If you listen carefully to what he says and do all that I say, I will be an enemy to your enemies and will oppose those who oppose you. 23My angel will go ahead of you and bring you into the land of the Amorites, Hittites, Perizzites, Canaanites, Hivites and Jebusites, and I will wipe them out. 24Do not bow down before their gods or worship them or follow their practices. You must demolish them and break their sacred stones to pieces. 25Worship the LORD your God, and his blessing will be on your food and water. I will take away sickness from among you, 26and none will miscarry or be barren in your land. I will give you a full life span.

27"I will send my terror ahead of you and throw into confusion every nation you encounter. I will make all your enemies turn their backs and run. 28I will send the hornet ahead of you to drive the Hivites, Canaanites and Hittites out of your way. 29But I will not drive them out in a single year, because the land would become desolate and the wild animals too numerous for you. 30Little by little I will drive them out before you, until you have increased enough to take possession of the land.

31"I will establish your borders from the Red Sea[a] to the Sea of the Philistines,[b] and from the desert to the River.[c] I will hand over to you the people who live in the land and you will drive them out before you. 32Do not make a covenant with them or with their gods. 33Do not let them live in your land, or they will cause you to sin against me, because the worship of their gods will certainly be a snare to you."

The Covenant Confirmed

24 Then he said to Moses, "Come up to the LORD, you and Aaron, Nadab and Abihu, and seventy of the elders of Israel. You are to worship at a distance, 2but Moses alone is to approach the LORD; the others must not come near. And the people may not come up with him."

3When Moses went and told the people all the LORD's words and laws, they responded with one voice, "Everything the LORD has said we will do." 4Moses then wrote down everything the LORD had said.

He got up early the next morning and built an altar at the foot of the mountain and set up twelve stone pillars representing the twelve tribes of Israel. 5Then he sent young Israelite men, and they offered burnt offerings and sacrificed young bulls as fellowship offerings[d] to the LORD. 6Moses took half of the blood and put it in bowls, and the other half he sprinkled on the altar. 7Then he took the Book of the Covenant and read it to the people. They responded, "We will do everything the LORD has said; we will obey."

8Moses then took the blood, sprinkled it on the people and said, "This is the blood of the covenant that the LORD has made with you in accordance with all these words."

9Moses and Aaron, Nadab and Abihu, and the seventy elders of Israel went up 10and saw the God of Israel. Under his feet was something like a pavement made of sapphire,[e] clear as the sky itself. 11But God did not raise his hand against these leaders of the Israelites; they saw God, and they ate and drank.

12The LORD said to Moses, "Come up to me on the mountain and stay here, and I will give you the tablets of stone, with the law and commands I have written for their instruction."

13Then Moses set out with Joshua his aide, and Moses went up on the mountain of God. 14He said to the elders, "Wait here for us until we come back to you. Aaron and Hur are with you, and anyone involved in a dispute can go to them."

15When Moses went up on the mountain, the

a31 Hebrew *Yam Suph*; that is, Sea of Reeds b31 That is, the Mediterranean c31 That is, the Euphrates
d5 Traditionally *peace offerings* e10 Or *lapis lazuli*

cloud covered it, 16and the glory of the LORD settled on Mount Sinai. For six days the cloud covered the mountain, and on the seventh day the
LORD called to Moses from within the cloud. 17To
the Israelites the glory of the LORD looked like a
consuming fire on top of the mountain. 18Then
Moses entered the cloud as he went on up the
mountain. And he stayed on the mountain forty
days and forty nights.

Offerings for the Tabernacle

25 The LORD said to Moses, 2"Tell the Israelites to bring me an offering. You are to
receive the offering for me from each man whose
heart prompts him to give. 3These are the offerings you are to receive from them: gold, silver
and bronze; 4blue, purple and scarlet yarn and
fine linen; goat hair; 5ram skins dyed red and
hides of sea cows[a]; acacia wood; 6olive oil for
the light; spices for the anointing oil and for the
fragrant incense; 7and onyx stones and other
gems to be mounted on the ephod and breastpiece.
8"Then have them make a sanctuary for me,
and I will dwell among them. 9Make this tabernacle and all its furnishings exactly like the pattern
I will show you.

The Ark

10"Have them make a chest of acacia wood—
two and a half cubits long, a cubit and a half wide,
and a cubit and a half high.[b] 11Overlay it with
pure gold, both inside and out, and make a gold
molding around it. 12Cast four gold rings for it
and fasten them to its four feet, with two rings on
one side and two rings on the other. 13Then
make poles of acacia wood and overlay them with
gold. 14Insert the poles into the rings on the sides
of the chest to carry it. 15The poles are to remain
in the rings of this ark; they are not to be removed. 16Then put in the ark the Testimony,
which I will give you.
17"Make an atonement cover[c] of pure gold—
two and a half cubits long and a cubit and a half
wide.[d] 18And make two cherubim out of hammered gold at the ends of the cover. 19Make one
cherub on one end and the second cherub on the
other; make the cherubim of one piece with the
cover, at the two ends. 20The cherubim are to
have their wings spread upward, overshadowing
the cover with them. The cherubim are to face
each other, looking toward the cover. 21Place the
cover on top of the ark and put in the ark the
Testimony, which I will give you. 22There, above
the cover between the two cherubim that are
over the ark of the Testimony, I will meet with
you and give you all my commands for the Israelites.

The Table

23"Make a table of acacia wood—two cubits
long, a cubit wide and a cubit and a half high.[e]
24Overlay it with pure gold and make a gold
molding around it. 25Also make around it a rim a
handbreadth[f] wide and put a gold molding on
the rim. 26Make four gold rings for the table and
fasten them to the four corners, where the four
legs are. 27The rings are to be close to the rim to
hold the poles used in carrying the table. 28Make
the poles of acacia wood, overlay them with gold
and carry the table with them. 29And make its
plates and dishes of pure gold, as well as its pitchers and bowls for the pouring out of offerings.
30Put the bread of the Presence on this table to be
before me at all times.

The Lampstand

31"Make a lampstand of pure gold and hammer
it out, base and shaft; its flowerlike cups, buds
and blossoms shall be of one piece with it. 32Six
branches are to extend from the sides of the
lampstand—three on one side and three on the
other. 33Three cups shaped like almond flowers
with buds and blossoms are to be on one branch,
three on the next branch, and the same for all six
branches extending from the lampstand. 34And
on the lampstand there are to be four cups
shaped like almond flowers with buds and blossoms. 35One bud shall be under the first pair of
branches extending from the lampstand, a second bud under the second pair, and a third bud
under the third pair—six branches in all. 36The
buds and branches shall all be of one piece with
the lampstand, hammered out of pure gold.
37"Then make its seven lamps and set them up
on it so that they light the space in front of it.
38Its wick trimmers and trays are to be of pure
gold. 39A talent[g] of pure gold is to be used for
the lampstand and all these accessories. 40See
that you make them according to the pattern
shown you on the mountain.

The Tabernacle

26 "Make the tabernacle with ten curtains of
finely twisted linen and blue, purple and
scarlet yarn, with cherubim worked into them by
a skilled craftsman. 2All the curtains are to be the
same size—twenty-eight cubits long and four cu-

a5 That is, dugongs
b10 That is, about 3 3/4 feet (about 1.1 meters) long and 2 1/4 feet (about 0.7 meter) wide and high
c17 Traditionally *a mercy seat*
d17 That is, about 3 3/4 feet (about 1.1 meters) long and 2 1/4 feet (about 0.7 meter) wide
e23 That is, about 3 feet (about 0.9 meter) long and 1 1/2 feet (about 0.5 meter) wide and 2 1/4 feet (about 0.7 meter) high
f25 That is, about 3 inches (about 8 centimeters)
g39 That is, about 75 pounds (about 34 kilograms)

bits wide.[a] 3Join five of the curtains together,
and do the same with the other five. 4Make loops
of blue material along the edge of the end curtain
in one set, and do the same with the end curtain
in the other set. 5Make fifty loops on one
curtain and fifty loops on the end curtain of the
other set, with the loops opposite each other.
6Then make fifty gold clasps and use them to
fasten the curtains together so that the tabernacle
is a unit.

7"Make curtains of goat hair for the tent over
the tabernacle—eleven altogether. 8All eleven
curtains are to be the same size—thirty cubits
long and four cubits wide.[b] 9Join five of the curtains together into one set and the other six into
another set. Fold the sixth curtain double at the
front of the tent. 10Make fifty loops along the
edge of the end curtain in one set and also along
the edge of the end curtain in the other set.
11Then make fifty bronze clasps and put them in
the loops to fasten the tent together as a unit.
12As for the additional length of the tent curtains,
the half curtain that is left over is to hang down
at the rear of the tabernacle. 13The tent curtains
will be a cubit[c] longer on both sides; what is left
will hang over the sides of the tabernacle so as to
cover it. 14Make for the tent a covering of ram
skins dyed red, and over that a covering of hides
of sea cows.[d]

15"Make upright frames of acacia wood for the
tabernacle. 16Each frame is to be ten cubits long
and a cubit and a half wide,[e] 17with two projections set parallel to each other. Make all the
frames of the tabernacle in this way. 18Make
twenty frames for the south side of the tabernacle
19and make forty silver bases to go under them—
two bases for each frame, one under each projection. 20For the other side, the north side of the
tabernacle, make twenty frames 21and forty silver
bases—two under each frame. 22Make six frames
for the far end, that is, the west end of the tabernacle, 23and make two frames for the corners at
the far end. 24At these two corners they must be
double from the bottom all the way to the top,
and fitted into a single ring; both shall be like
that. 25So there will be eight frames and sixteen
silver bases—two under each frame.

26"Also make crossbars of acacia wood: five for
the frames on one side of the tabernacle, 27five
for those on the other side, and five for the
frames on the west, at the far end of the tabernacle. 28The center crossbar is to extend from end
to end at the middle of the frames. 29Overlay the
frames with gold and make gold rings to hold the
crossbars. Also overlay the crossbars with gold.

30"Set up the tabernacle according to the plan
shown you on the mountain.

31"Make a curtain of blue, purple and scarlet
yarn and finely twisted linen, with cherubim
worked into it by a skilled craftsman. 32Hang it
with gold hooks on four posts of acacia wood
overlaid with gold and standing on four silver
bases. 33Hang the curtain from the clasps and
place the ark of the Testimony behind the curtain. The curtain will separate the Holy Place
from the Most Holy Place. 34Put the atonement
cover on the ark of the Testimony in the Most
Holy Place. 35Place the table outside the curtain
on the north side of the tabernacle and put the
lampstand opposite it on the south side.

36"For the entrance to the tent make a curtain
of blue, purple and scarlet yarn and finely twisted
linen—the work of an embroiderer. 37Make gold
hooks for this curtain and five posts of acacia
wood overlaid with gold. And cast five bronze
bases for them.

The Altar of Burnt Offering

27 "Build an altar of acacia wood, three cubits[f] high; it is to be square, five cubits
long and five cubits wide.[g] 2Make a horn at each
of the four corners, so that the horns and the altar
are of one piece, and overlay the altar with
bronze. 3Make all its utensils of bronze—its pots
to remove the ashes, and its shovels, sprinkling
bowls, meat forks and firepans. 4Make a grating
for it, a bronze network, and make a bronze ring
at each of the four corners of the network. 5Put
it under the ledge of the altar so that it is halfway
up the altar. 6Make poles of acacia wood for the
altar and overlay them with bronze. 7The poles
are to be inserted into the rings so they will be on
two sides of the altar when it is carried. 8Make
the altar hollow, out of boards. It is to be made
just as you were shown on the mountain.

The Courtyard

9"Make a courtyard for the tabernacle. The
south side shall be a hundred cubits[h] long and is
to have curtains of finely twisted linen, 10with
twenty posts and twenty bronze bases and with
silver hooks and bands on the posts. 11The north
side shall also be a hundred cubits long and is
to have curtains, with twenty posts and twenty
bronze bases and with silver hooks and bands on
the posts.

12"The west end of the courtyard shall be fifty

[a] 2 That is, about 42 feet (about 12.5 meters) long and 6 feet (about 1.8 meters) wide
[b] 8 That is, about 45 feet (about 13.5 meters) long and 6 feet (about 1.8 meters) wide
[c] 13 That is, about 1 1/2 feet (about 0.5 meter)
[d] 14 That is, dugongs
[e] 16 That is, about 15 feet (about 4.5 meters) long and 2 1/4 feet (about 0.7 meter) wide
[f] 1 That is, about 4 1/2 feet (about 1.3 meters)
[g] 1 That is, about 7 1/2 feet (about 2.3 meters) long and wide
[h] 9 That is, about 150 feet (about 46 meters); also in verse 11

cubits[a] wide and have curtains, with ten posts and ten bases. 13On the east end, toward the sunrise, the courtyard shall also be fifty cubits wide. 14Curtains fifteen cubits[b] long are to be on one side of the entrance, with three posts and three bases, 15and curtains fifteen cubits long are to be on the other side, with three posts and three bases.

16"For the entrance to the courtyard, provide a curtain twenty cubits[c] long, of blue, purple and scarlet yarn and finely twisted linen—the work of an embroiderer—with four posts and four bases. 17All the posts around the courtyard are to have silver bands and hooks, and bronze bases. 18The courtyard shall be a hundred cubits long and fifty cubits wide,[d] with curtains of finely twisted linen five cubits[e] high, and with bronze bases. 19All the other articles used in the service of the tabernacle, whatever their function, including all the tent pegs for it and those for the courtyard, are to be of bronze.

Oil for the Lampstand

20"Command the Israelites to bring you clear oil of pressed olives for the light so that the lamps may be kept burning. 21In the Tent of Meeting, outside the curtain that is in front of the Testimony, Aaron and his sons are to keep the lamps burning before the LORD from evening till morning. This is to be a lasting ordinance among the Israelites for the generations to come.

The Priestly Garments

28 "Have Aaron your brother brought to you from among the Israelites, along with his sons Nadab and Abihu, Eleazar and Ithamar, so they may serve me as priests. 2Make sacred garments for your brother Aaron, to give him dignity and honor. 3Tell all the skilled men to whom I have given wisdom in such matters that they are to make garments for Aaron, for his consecration, so he may serve me as priest. 4These are the garments they are to make: a breastpiece, an ephod, a robe, a woven tunic, a turban and a sash. They are to make these sacred garments for your brother Aaron and his sons, so they may serve me as priests. 5Have them use gold, and blue, purple and scarlet yarn, and fine linen.

The Ephod

6"Make the ephod of gold, and of blue, purple and scarlet yarn, and of finely twisted linen—the work of a skilled craftsman. 7It is to have two shoulder pieces attached to two of its corners, so it can be fastened. 8Its skillfully woven waistband is to be like it—of one piece with the ephod and made with gold, and with blue, purple and scarlet yarn, and with finely twisted linen.

9"Take two onyx stones and engrave on them the names of the sons of Israel 10in the order of their birth—six names on one stone and the remaining six on the other. 11Engrave the names of the sons of Israel on the two stones the way a gem cutter engraves a seal. Then mount the stones in gold filigree settings 12and fasten them on the shoulder pieces of the ephod as memorial stones for the sons of Israel. Aaron is to bear the names on his shoulders as a memorial before the LORD. 13Make gold filigree settings 14and two braided chains of pure gold, like a rope, and attach the chains to the settings.

The Breastpiece

15"Fashion a breastpiece for making decisions—the work of a skilled craftsman. Make it like the ephod: of gold, and of blue, purple and scarlet yarn, and of finely twisted linen. 16It is to be square—a span[f] long and a span wide—and folded double. 17Then mount four rows of precious stones on it. In the first row there shall be a ruby, a topaz and a beryl; 18in the second row a turquoise, a sapphire[g] and an emerald; 19in the third row a jacinth, an agate and an amethyst; 20in the fourth row a chrysolite, an onyx and a jasper.[h] Mount them in gold filigree settings. 21There are to be twelve stones, one for each of the names of the sons of Israel, each engraved like a seal with the name of one of the twelve tribes.

22"For the breastpiece make braided chains of pure gold, like a rope. 23Make two gold rings for it and fasten them to two corners of the breastpiece. 24Fasten the two gold chains to the rings at the corners of the breastpiece, 25and the other ends of the chains to the two settings, attaching them to the shoulder pieces of the ephod at the front. 26Make two gold rings and attach them to the other two corners of the breastpiece on the inside edge next to the ephod. 27Make two more gold rings and attach them to the bottom of the shoulder pieces on the front of the ephod, close to the seam just above the waistband of the ephod. 28The rings of the breastpiece are to be tied to the rings of the ephod with blue cord, connecting it to the waistband, so that the breastpiece will not swing out from the ephod.

29"Whenever Aaron enters the Holy Place, he will bear the names of the sons of Israel over his heart on the breastpiece of decision as a continuing memorial before the LORD. 30Also put the

[a] *12* That is, about 75 feet (about 23 meters); also in verse 13
[b] *14* That is, about 22 1/2 feet (about 6.9 meters); also in verse 15
[c] *16* That is, about 30 feet (about 9 meters)
[d] *18* That is, about 150 feet (about 46 meters) long and 75 feet (about 23 meters) wide
[e] *18* That is, about 7 1/2 feet (about 2.3 meters)
[f] *16* That is, about 9 inches (about 22 centimeters)
[g] *18* Or *lapis lazuli*
[h] *20* The precise identification of some of these precious stones is uncertain.

Urim and the Thummim in the breastpiece, so
they may be over Aaron's heart whenever he enters the presence of the LORD. Thus Aaron will
always bear the means of making decisions for
the Israelites over his heart before the LORD.

Other Priestly Garments

31“Make the robe of the ephod entirely of blue
cloth, 32with an opening for the head in its center. There shall be a woven edge like a collar[a]
around this opening, so that it will not tear.
33Make pomegranates of blue, purple and scarlet
yarn around the hem of the robe, with gold bells
between them. 34The gold bells and the pomegranates are to alternate around the hem of the
robe. 35Aaron must wear it when he ministers.
The sound of the bells will be heard when he
enters the Holy Place before the LORD and when
he comes out, so that he will not die.

36“Make a plate of pure gold and engrave on it
as on a seal: HOLY TO THE LORD. 37Fasten a blue
cord to it to attach it to the turban; it is to be on
the front of the turban. 38It will be on Aaron's
forehead, and he will bear the guilt involved in
the sacred gifts the Israelites consecrate, whatever their gifts may be. It will be on Aaron's
forehead continually so that they will be acceptable to the LORD.

39“Weave the tunic of fine linen and make the
turban of fine linen. The sash is to be the work of
an embroiderer. 40Make tunics, sashes and headbands for Aaron's sons, to give them dignity and
honor. 41After you put these clothes on your
brother Aaron and his sons, anoint and ordain
them. Consecrate them so they may serve me as
priests.

42“Make linen undergarments as a covering
for the body, reaching from the waist to the
thigh. 43Aaron and his sons must wear them
whenever they enter the Tent of Meeting or approach the altar to minister in the Holy Place, so
that they will not incur guilt and die.

“This is to be a lasting ordinance for Aaron and
his descendants.

Consecration of the Priests

29 “This is what you are to do to consecrate
them, so they may serve me as priests:
Take a young bull and two rams without defect.
2And from fine wheat flour, without yeast, make
bread, and cakes mixed with oil, and wafers
spread with oil. 3Put them in a basket and
present them in it—along with the bull and the
two rams. 4Then bring Aaron and his sons to the
entrance to the Tent of Meeting and wash them
with water. 5Take the garments and dress Aaron
with the tunic, the robe of the ephod, the ephod
itself and the breastpiece. Fasten the ephod on
him by its skillfully woven waistband. 6Put the
turban on his head and attach the sacred diadem
to the turban. 7Take the anointing oil and anoint
him by pouring it on his head. 8Bring his sons
and dress them in tunics 9and put headbands on
them. Then tie sashes on Aaron and his sons.[b]
The priesthood is theirs by a lasting ordinance. In
this way you shall ordain Aaron and his sons.

10“Bring the bull to the front of the Tent of
Meeting, and Aaron and his sons shall lay their
hands on its head. 11Slaughter it in the LORD's
presence at the entrance to the Tent of Meeting.
12Take some of the bull's blood and put it on the
horns of the altar with your finger, and pour out
the rest of it at the base of the altar. 13Then take
all the fat around the inner parts, the covering of
the liver, and both kidneys with the fat on them,
and burn them on the altar. 14But burn the bull's
flesh and its hide and its offal outside the camp.
It is a sin offering.

15“Take one of the rams, and Aaron and his
sons shall lay their hands on its head. 16Slaughter
it and take the blood and sprinkle it against the
altar on all sides. 17Cut the ram into pieces and
wash the inner parts and the legs, putting them
with the head and the other pieces. 18Then burn
the entire ram on the altar. It is a burnt offering
to the LORD, a pleasing aroma, an offering made
to the LORD by fire.

19“Take the other ram, and Aaron and his sons
shall lay their hands on its head. 20Slaughter it,
take some of its blood and put it on the lobes
of the right ears of Aaron and his sons, on the
thumbs of their right hands, and on the big toes
of their right feet. Then sprinkle blood against
the altar on all sides. 21And take some of the
blood on the altar and some of the anointing oil
and sprinkle it on Aaron and his garments and on
his sons and their garments. Then he and his
sons and their garments will be consecrated.

22“Take from this ram the fat, the fat tail, the
fat around the inner parts, the covering of the
liver, both kidneys with the fat on them, and
the right thigh. (This is the ram for the ordination.)
23From the basket of bread made without yeast,
which is before the LORD, take a loaf, and a cake
made with oil, and a wafer. 24Put all these in the
hands of Aaron and his sons and wave them before the LORD as a wave offering. 25Then take
them from their hands and burn them on the
altar along with the burnt offering for a pleasing
aroma to the LORD, an offering made to the LORD
by fire. 26After you take the breast of the ram for
Aaron's ordination, wave it before the LORD as a
wave offering, and it will be your share.

27“Consecrate those parts of the ordination

[a]32 The meaning of the Hebrew for this word is uncertain. [b]9 Hebrew; Septuagint *on them*

ram that belong to Aaron and his sons: the breast that was waved and the thigh that was presented. 28This is always to be the regular share from the Israelites for Aaron and his sons. It is the contribution the Israelites are to make to the LORD from their fellowship offerings.[a]

29“Aaron’s sacred garments will belong to his descendants so that they can be anointed and ordained in them. 30The son who succeeds him as priest and comes to the Tent of Meeting to minister in the Holy Place is to wear them seven days.

31“Take the ram for the ordination and cook the meat in a sacred place. 32At the entrance to the Tent of Meeting, Aaron and his sons are to eat the meat of the ram and the bread that is in the basket. 33They are to eat these offerings by which atonement was made for their ordination and consecration. But no one else may eat them, because they are sacred. 34And if any of the meat of the ordination ram or any bread is left over till morning, burn it up. It must not be eaten, because it is sacred.

35“Do for Aaron and his sons everything I have commanded you, taking seven days to ordain them. 36Sacrifice a bull each day as a sin offering to make atonement. Purify the altar by making atonement for it, and anoint it to consecrate it. 37For seven days make atonement for the altar and consecrate it. Then the altar will be most holy, and whatever touches it will be holy.

38“This is what you are to offer on the altar regularly each day: two lambs a year old. 39Offer one in the morning and the other at twilight. 40With the first lamb offer a tenth of an ephah[b] of fine flour mixed with a quarter of a hin[c] of oil from pressed olives, and a quarter of a hin of wine as a drink offering. 41Sacrifice the other lamb at twilight with the same grain offering and its drink offering as in the morning—a pleasing aroma, an offering made to the LORD by fire.

42“For the generations to come this burnt offering is to be made regularly at the entrance to the Tent of Meeting before the LORD. There I will meet you and speak to you; 43there also I will meet with the Israelites, and the place will be consecrated by my glory.

44“So I will consecrate the Tent of Meeting and the altar and will consecrate Aaron and his sons to serve me as priests. 45Then I will dwell among the Israelites and be their God. 46They will know that I am the LORD their God, who brought them out of Egypt so that I might dwell among them. I am the LORD their God.

The Altar of Incense

30 “Make an altar of acacia wood for burning incense. 2It is to be square, a cubit long and a cubit wide, and two cubits high[d]—its horns of one piece with it. 3Overlay the top and all the sides and the horns with pure gold, and make a gold molding around it. 4Make two gold rings for the altar below the molding—two on opposite sides—to hold the poles used to carry it. 5Make the poles of acacia wood and overlay them with gold. 6Put the altar in front of the curtain that is before the ark of the Testimony—before the atonement cover that is over the Testimony—where I will meet with you.

7“Aaron must burn fragrant incense on the altar every morning when he tends the lamps. 8He must burn incense again when he lights the lamps at twilight so incense will burn regularly before the LORD for the generations to come. 9Do not offer on this altar any other incense or any burnt offering or grain offering, and do not pour a drink offering on it. 10Once a year Aaron shall make atonement on its horns. This annual atonement must be made with the blood of the atoning sin offering for the generations to come. It is most holy to the LORD.”

Atonement Money

11Then the LORD said to Moses, 12“When you take a census of the Israelites to count them, each one must pay the LORD a ransom for his life at the time he is counted. Then no plague will come on them when you number them. 13Each one who crosses over to those already counted is to give a half shekel,[e] according to the sanctuary shekel, which weighs twenty gerahs. This half shekel is an offering to the LORD. 14All who cross over, those twenty years old or more, are to give an offering to the LORD. 15The rich are not to give more than a half shekel and the poor are not to give less when you make the offering to the LORD to atone for your lives. 16Receive the atonement money from the Israelites and use it for the service of the Tent of Meeting. It will be a memorial for the Israelites before the LORD, making atonement for your lives.”

Basin for Washing

17Then the LORD said to Moses, 18“Make a bronze basin, with its bronze stand, for washing. Place it between the Tent of Meeting and the altar, and put water in it. 19Aaron and his sons are to wash their hands and feet with water from it. 20Whenever they enter the Tent of Meeting, they shall wash with water so that they will not

a28 Traditionally *peace offerings* b40 That is, probably about 2 quarts (about 2 liters) c40 That is, probably about 1 quart (about 1 liter) d2 That is, about 1 1/2 feet (about 0.5 meter) long and wide and about 3 feet (about 0.9 meter) high e13 That is, about 1/5 ounce (about 6 grams); also in verse 15 die. Also, when they approach the altar to minister by presenting an offering made to the LORD by fire, 21they shall wash their hands and feet so that they will not die. This is to be a lasting ordinance for Aaron and his descendants for the generations to come."

Anointing Oil

22Then the LORD said to Moses, 23"Take the following fine spices: 500 shekels[a] of liquid myrrh, half as much (that is, 250 shekels) of fragrant cinnamon, 250 shekels of fragrant cane, 24500 shekels of cassia—all according to the sanctuary shekel—and a hin[b] of olive oil. 25Make these into a sacred anointing oil, a fragrant blend, the work of a perfumer. It will be the sacred anointing oil. 26Then use it to anoint the Tent of Meeting, the ark of the Testimony, 27the table and all its articles, the lampstand and its accessories, the altar of incense, 28the altar of burnt offering and all its utensils, and the basin with its stand. 29You shall consecrate them so they will be most holy, and whatever touches them will be holy.

30"Anoint Aaron and his sons and consecrate them so they may serve me as priests. 31Say to the Israelites, 'This is to be my sacred anointing oil for the generations to come. 32Do not pour it on men's bodies and do not make any oil with the same formula. It is sacred, and you are to consider it sacred. 33Whoever makes perfume like it and whoever puts it on anyone other than a priest must be cut off from his people.' "

Incense

34Then the LORD said to Moses, "Take fragrant spices—gum resin, onycha and galbanum—and pure frankincense, all in equal amounts, 35and make a fragrant blend of incense, the work of a perfumer. It is to be salted and pure and sacred. 36Grind some of it to powder and place it in front of the Testimony in the Tent of Meeting, where I will meet with you. It shall be most holy to you. 37Do not make any incense with this formula for yourselves; consider it holy to the LORD. 38Whoever makes any like it to enjoy its fragrance must be cut off from his people."

Bezalel and Oholiab

31 Then the LORD said to Moses, 2"See, I have chosen Bezalel son of Uri, the son of Hur, of the tribe of Judah, 3and I have filled him with the Spirit of God, with skill, ability and knowledge in all kinds of crafts— 4to make artistic designs for work in gold, silver and bronze, 5to cut and set stones, to work in wood, and to engage in all kinds of craftsmanship. 6Moreover, I have appointed Oholiab son of Ahisamach, of the tribe of Dan, to help him. Also I have given skill to all the craftsmen to make everything I have commanded you: 7the Tent of Meeting, the ark of the Testimony with the atonement cover on it, and all the other furnishings of the tent— 8the table and its articles, the pure gold lampstand and all its accessories, the altar of incense, 9the altar of burnt offering and all its utensils, the basin with its stand— 10and also the woven garments, both the sacred garments for Aaron the priest and the garments for his sons when they serve as priests, 11and the anointing oil and fragrant incense for the Holy Place. They are to make them just as I commanded you."

The Sabbath

12Then the LORD said to Moses, 13"Say to the Israelites, 'You must observe my Sabbaths. This will be a sign between me and you for the generations to come, so you may know that I am the LORD, who makes you holy.[c]

14" 'Observe the Sabbath, because it is holy to you. Anyone who desecrates it must be put to death; whoever does any work on that day must be cut off from his people. 15For six days, work is to be done, but the seventh day is a Sabbath of rest, holy to the LORD. Whoever does any work on the Sabbath day must be put to death. 16The Israelites are to observe the Sabbath, celebrating it for the generations to come as a lasting covenant. 17It will be a sign between me and the Israelites forever, for in six days the LORD made the heavens and the earth, and on the seventh day he abstained from work and rested.' "

18When the LORD finished speaking to Moses on Mount Sinai, he gave him the two tablets of the Testimony, the tablets of stone inscribed by the finger of God.

The Golden Calf

32 When the people saw that Moses was so long in coming down from the mountain, they gathered around Aaron and said, "Come, make us gods[d] who will go before us. As for this fellow Moses who brought us up out of Egypt, we don't know what has happened to him."

2Aaron answered them, "Take off the gold earrings that your wives, your sons and your daughters are wearing, and bring them to me." 3So all the people took off their earrings and brought them to Aaron. 4He took what they handed him and made it into an idol cast in the shape of a calf, fashioning it with a tool. Then they said, "These

[a] *23* That is, about 12 1/2 pounds (about 6 kilograms) [b] *24* That is, probably about 4 quarts (about 4 liters) [c] *13* Or *who sanctifies you*; or *who sets you apart as holy* [d] *1* Or *a god*; also in verses 23 and 31

are your gods,[a] O Israel, who brought you up
out of Egypt."
5When Aaron saw this, he built an altar in
front of the calf and announced, "Tomorrow

> ### EXODUS 32:1–35
>
> 1. When was the last time you got angry for good reason?
> 2. Where does the "party crowd" in your school go for a wild party?
> 3. What do you say when you are invited to these "wild parties"?
> 4. Do you think diseases like AIDS are a modern "plague" of God's judgment? Why or why not?
> 5. Why do you think the Hebrews went wild and broke all the rules right after they experienced deliverance from Egypt?
> 6. When you sin and get caught, how do you usually respond?
> 7. What does it mean for you to be "for the Lord" (v. 26) in the way you live your life? How can this group help?

there will be a festival to the LORD." 6So the next
day the people rose early and sacrificed burnt
offerings and presented fellowship offerings.[b]
Afterward they sat down to eat and drink and got
up to indulge in revelry.
7Then the LORD said to Moses, "Go down, because your people, whom you brought up out of
Egypt, have become corrupt. 8They have been
quick to turn away from what I commanded them
and have made themselves an idol cast in the
shape of a calf. They have bowed down to it and
sacrificed to it and have said, 'These are your
gods, O Israel, who brought you up out of Egypt.'
9"I have seen these people," the LORD said
to Moses, "and they are a stiff-necked people.
10Now leave me alone so that my anger may burn
against them and that I may destroy them. Then
I will make you into a great nation."
11But Moses sought the favor of the LORD his
God. "O LORD," he said, "why should your anger
burn against your people, whom you brought out
of Egypt with great power and a mighty hand?
12Why should the Egyptians say, 'It was with evil
intent that he brought them out, to kill them in
the mountains and to wipe them off the face of
the earth'? Turn from your fierce anger; relent
and do not bring disaster on your people. 13Re-
member your servants Abraham, Isaac and Israel,
to whom you swore by your own self: 'I will make
your descendants as numerous as the stars in the
sky and I will give your descendants all this land
I promised them, and it will be their inheritance
forever.'" 14Then the LORD relented and did not
bring on his people the disaster he had threatened.
15Moses turned and went down the mountain
with the two tablets of the Testimony in his
hands. They were inscribed on both sides, front
and back. 16The tablets were the work of God;
the writing was the writing of God, engraved on
the tablets.
17When Joshua heard the noise of the people
shouting, he said to Moses, "There is the sound
of war in the camp."
18Moses replied:

"It is not the sound of victory,
it is not the sound of defeat;
it is the sound of singing that I hear."

19When Moses approached the camp and saw
the calf and the dancing, his anger burned and he
threw the tablets out of his hands, breaking them
to pieces at the foot of the mountain. 20And he
took the calf they had made and burned it in the
fire; then he ground it to powder, scattered it on
the water and made the Israelites drink it.

[a]4 Or *This is your god*; also in verse 8 [b]6 Traditionally *peace offerings*

32:1 *so long.* Moses was gone 40 days.

32:4 *idol cast in the shape of a calf.* Probably modeled after the Egyptian bull-god Apis. Its manufacture was a flagrant violation of the Ten Commandments, which the people had just received (see 20:4–5).

32:6 *indulge in revelry.* A pagan symbol evoked pagan religious practices (1 Cor. 10:6–8). The verb translated "indulge in revelry" often has sexual connotations. Orgies often accompanied pagan worship.

32:19 *breaking them to pieces.* By breaking the stone tablets inscribed with the Ten Commandments, Moses demonstrated that Israel had broken their covenant with God.

32:24 *out came this calf.* Aaron could hardly expect Moses to believe such a story.

32:30 *make atonement for your sin.* By making urgent intercession before God. No sacrifice could atone for this sin, but Moses so identified himself with his people that he made his own death the condition for God's destroying them. Jesus offered himself on the cross as an atonement for his people.

32:33 *Whoever has sinned ... I will blot out.* Moses' offer is refused, because the person who sins is responsible for his own sin.

32:35 *plague.* The exact nature and timing of the plague isn't clear. Additional judgment may have occurred at this point in the story or sometime later, or the "plague" could refer to when 3,000 of the people died at the hands of the Levites (v. 28).

21He said to Aaron, "What did these people do
to you, that you led them into such great sin?"
22"Do not be angry, my lord," Aaron answered. "You know how prone these people are
to evil. 23They said to me, 'Make us gods who
will go before us. As for this fellow Moses who
brought us up out of Egypt, we don't know what
has happened to him.' 24So I told them, 'Whoever has any gold jewelry, take it off.' Then they
gave me the gold, and I threw it into the fire, and
out came this calf!"
25Moses saw that the people were running
wild and that Aaron had let them get out of control and so become a laughingstock to their enemies. 26So he stood at the entrance to the camp
and said, "Whoever is for the LORD, come to me."
And all the Levites rallied to him.
27Then he said to them, "This is what the
LORD, the God of Israel, says: 'Each man strap a
sword to his side. Go back and forth through the
camp from one end to the other, each killing his
brother and friend and neighbor.' " 28The Levites
did as Moses commanded, and that day about
three thousand of the people died. 29Then Moses
said, "You have been set apart to the LORD today,
for you were against your own sons and brothers,
and he has blessed you this day."
30The next day Moses said to the people, "You
have committed a great sin. But now I will go up
to the LORD; perhaps I can make atonement for
your sin."
31So Moses went back to the LORD and said,
"Oh, what a great sin these people have committed! They have made themselves gods of gold.
32But now, please forgive their sin—but if not,
then blot me out of the book you have written."
33The LORD replied to Moses, "Whoever has
sinned against me I will blot out of my book.
34Now go, lead the people to the place I spoke of,
and my angel will go before you. However, when
the time comes for me to punish, I will punish
them for their sin."
35And the LORD struck the people with a
plague because of what they did with the calf
Aaron had made.

33 Then the LORD said to Moses, "Leave this
place, you and the people you brought up
out of Egypt, and go up to the land I promised on
oath to Abraham, Isaac and Jacob, saying, 'I will
give it to your descendants.' 2I will send an angel
before you and drive out the Canaanites, Amorites, Hittites, Perizzites, Hivites and Jebusites.
3Go up to the land flowing with milk and honey.
But I will not go with you, because you are a
stiff-necked people and I might destroy you on
the way."
4When the people heard these distressing
words, they began to mourn and no one put on
any ornaments. 5For the LORD had said to Moses,
"Tell the Israelites, 'You are a stiff-necked people. If I were to go with you even for a moment,
I might destroy you. Now take off your ornaments
and I will decide what to do with you.' " 6So the
Israelites stripped off their ornaments at Mount
Horeb.

The Tent of Meeting

7Now Moses used to take a tent and pitch it
outside the camp some distance away, calling it
the "tent of meeting." Anyone inquiring of the
LORD would go to the tent of meeting outside the
camp. 8And whenever Moses went out to
the tent, all the people rose and stood at the
entrances to their tents, watching Moses until he
entered the tent. 9As Moses went into the tent,
the pillar of cloud would come down and stay at
the entrance, while the LORD spoke with Moses.
10Whenever the people saw the pillar of cloud
standing at the entrance to the tent, they all stood
and worshiped, each at the entrance to his tent.
11The LORD would speak to Moses face to face, as
a man speaks with his friend. Then Moses would
return to the camp, but his young aide Joshua son
of Nun did not leave the tent.

Moses and the Glory of the LORD

12Moses said to the LORD, "You have been telling me, 'Lead these people,' but you have not let
me know whom you will send with me. You have
said, 'I know you by name and you have found
favor with me.' 13If you are pleased with me,
teach me your ways so I may know you and continue to find favor with you. Remember that this
nation is your people."
14The LORD replied, "My Presence will go with
you, and I will give you rest."
15Then Moses said to him, "If your Presence
does not go with us, do not send us up from here.
16How will anyone know that you are pleased
with me and with your people unless you go with
us? What else will distinguish me and your people from all the other people on the face of the
earth?"
17And the LORD said to Moses, "I will do the
very thing you have asked, because I am pleased
with you and I know you by name."
18Then Moses said, "Now show me your
glory."
19And the LORD said, "I will cause all my goodness to pass in front of you, and I will proclaim
my name, the LORD, in your presence. I will have
mercy on whom I will have mercy, and I will
have compassion on whom I will have compassion. 20But," he said, "you cannot see my face, for
no one may see me and live."
21Then the LORD said, "There is a place near
me where you may stand on a rock. 22When my
glory passes by, I will put you in a cleft in the rock

and cover you with my hand until I have passed by. 23Then I will remove my hand and you will see my back; but my face must not be seen."

The New Stone Tablets

34 The LORD said to Moses, "Chisel out two stone tablets like the first ones, and I will write on them the words that were on the first tablets, which you broke. 2Be ready in the morning, and then come up on Mount Sinai. Present yourself to me there on top of the mountain. 3No one is to come with you or be seen anywhere on the mountain; not even the flocks and herds may graze in front of the mountain."

4So Moses chiseled out two stone tablets like the first ones and went up Mount Sinai early in the morning, as the LORD had commanded him; and he carried the two stone tablets in his hands. 5Then the LORD came down in the cloud and stood there with him and proclaimed his name, the LORD. 6And he passed in front of Moses, proclaiming, "The LORD, the LORD, the compassionate and gracious God, slow to anger, abounding in love and faithfulness, 7maintaining love to thousands, and forgiving wickedness, rebellion and sin. Yet he does not leave the guilty unpunished; he punishes the children and their children for the sin of the fathers to the third and fourth generation."

8Moses bowed to the ground at once and worshiped. 9"O Lord, if I have found favor in your eyes," he said, "then let the Lord go with us. Although this is a stiff-necked people, forgive our wickedness and our sin, and take us as your inheritance."

10Then the LORD said: "I am making a covenant with you. Before all your people I will do wonders never before done in any nation in all the world. The people you live among will see how awesome is the work that I, the LORD, will do for you. 11Obey what I command you today. I will drive out before you the Amorites, Canaanites, Hittites, Perizzites, Hivites and Jebusites. 12Be careful not to make a treaty with those who live in the land where you are going, or they will be a snare among you. 13Break down their altars, smash their sacred stones and cut down their Asherah poles.[a] 14Do not worship any other god, for the LORD, whose name is Jealous, is a jealous God.

15"Be careful not to make a treaty with those who live in the land; for when they prostitute themselves to their gods and sacrifice to them, they will invite you and you will eat their sacrifices. 16And when you choose some of their daughters as wives for your sons and those daughters prostitute themselves to their gods, they will lead your sons to do the same.

17"Do not make cast idols.

18"Celebrate the Feast of Unleavened Bread. For seven days eat bread made without yeast, as I commanded you. Do this at the appointed time in the month of Abib, for in that month you came out of Egypt.

19"The first offspring of every womb belongs to me, including all the firstborn males of your livestock, whether from herd or flock. 20Redeem the firstborn donkey with a lamb, but if you do not redeem it, break its neck. Redeem all your firstborn sons.

"No one is to appear before me empty-handed.

21"Six days you shall labor, but on the seventh day you shall rest; even during the plowing season and harvest you must rest.

22"Celebrate the Feast of Weeks with the firstfruits of the wheat harvest, and the Feast of Ingathering at the turn of the year.[b] 23Three times a year all your men are to appear before the Sovereign LORD, the God of Israel. 24I will drive out nations before you and enlarge your territory, and no one will covet your land when you go up three times each year to appear before the LORD your God.

25"Do not offer the blood of a sacrifice to me along with anything containing yeast, and do not let any of the sacrifice from the Passover Feast remain until morning.

26"Bring the best of the firstfruits of your soil to the house of the LORD your God.

"Do not cook a young goat in its mother's milk."

27Then the LORD said to Moses, "Write down these words, for in accordance with these words I have made a covenant with you and with Israel." 28Moses was there with the LORD forty days and forty nights without eating bread or drinking water. And he wrote on the tablets the words of the covenant—the Ten Commandments.

The Radiant Face of Moses

29When Moses came down from Mount Sinai with the two tablets of the Testimony in his hands, he was not aware that his face was radiant because he had spoken with the LORD. 30When Aaron and all the Israelites saw Moses, his face was radiant, and they were afraid to come near him. 31But Moses called to them; so Aaron and all the leaders of the community came back to him, and he spoke to them. 32Afterward all the Israelites came near him, and he gave them all the commands the LORD had given him on Mount Sinai.

33When Moses finished speaking to them, he

[a] *13* That is, symbols of the goddess Asherah
[b] *22* That is, in the fall

put a veil over his face. 34But whenever he entered the LORD's presence to speak with him, he
removed the veil until he came out. And when he
came out and told the Israelites what he had been
commanded, 35they saw that his face was radiant.
Then Moses would put the veil back over his face
until he went in to speak with the LORD.

Sabbath Regulations

35 Moses assembled the whole Israelite
community and said to them, "These are
the things the LORD has commanded you to do:
2For six days, work is to be done, but the seventh
day shall be your holy day, a Sabbath of rest to the
LORD. Whoever does any work on it must be put
to death. 3Do not light a fire in any of your dwellings on the Sabbath day."

Materials for the Tabernacle

4Moses said to the whole Israelite community,
"This is what the LORD has commanded: 5From
what you have, take an offering for the LORD.
Everyone who is willing is to bring to the LORD
an offering of gold, silver and bronze; 6blue, purple and scarlet yarn and fine linen; goat hair;
7ram skins dyed red and hides of sea cows[a];
acacia wood; 8olive oil for the light; spices for the
anointing oil and for the fragrant incense; 9and
onyx stones and other gems to be mounted on
the ephod and breastpiece.

10"All who are skilled among you are to come
and make everything the LORD has commanded:
11the tabernacle with its tent and its covering,
clasps, frames, crossbars, posts and bases; 12the
ark with its poles and the atonement cover and
the curtain that shields it; 13the table with its
poles and all its articles and the bread of the
Presence; 14the lampstand that is for light with its
accessories, lamps and oil for the light; 15the altar
of incense with its poles, the anointing oil and
the fragrant incense; the curtain for the doorway
at the entrance to the tabernacle; 16the altar of
burnt offering with its bronze grating, its poles
and all its utensils; the bronze basin with its
stand; 17the curtains of the courtyard with its
posts and bases, and the curtain for the entrance
to the courtyard; 18the tent pegs for the tabernacle and for the courtyard, and their ropes; 19the
woven garments worn for ministering in the
sanctuary—both the sacred garments for Aaron
the priest and the garments for his sons when
they serve as priests."

20Then the whole Israelite community withdrew from Moses' presence, 21and everyone who
was willing and whose heart moved him came
and brought an offering to the LORD for the work
on the Tent of Meeting, for all its service, and for
the sacred garments. 22All who were willing,
men and women alike, came and brought gold
jewelry of all kinds: brooches, earrings, rings and
ornaments. They all presented their gold as a
wave offering to the LORD. 23Everyone who had
blue, purple or scarlet yarn or fine linen, or goat
hair, ram skins dyed red or hides of sea cows
brought them. 24Those presenting an offering of
silver or bronze brought it as an offering to the
LORD, and everyone who had acacia wood for any
part of the work brought it. 25Every skilled woman spun with her hands and brought what she
had spun—blue, purple or scarlet yarn or fine
linen. 26And all the women who were willing and
had the skill spun the goat hair. 27The leaders
brought onyx stones and other gems to be mounted on the ephod and breastpiece. 28They also
brought spices and olive oil for the light and for
the anointing oil and for the fragrant incense.
29All the Israelite men and women who were
willing brought to the LORD freewill offerings for
all the work the LORD through Moses had commanded them to do.

Bezalel and Oholiab

30Then Moses said to the Israelites, "See, the
LORD has chosen Bezalel son of Uri, the son of
Hur, of the tribe of Judah, 31and he has filled him
with the Spirit of God, with skill, ability and
knowledge in all kinds of crafts— 32to make artistic designs for work in gold, silver and bronze,
33to cut and set stones, to work in wood and to
engage in all kinds of artistic craftsmanship.
34And he has given both him and Oholiab son of
Ahisamach, of the tribe of Dan, the ability to
teach others. 35He has filled them with skill to do
all kinds of work as craftsmen, designers, embroi-
derers in blue, purple and scarlet yarn and fine
linen, and weavers—all of them master crafts-
36 men and designers. 1So Bezalel, Oholiab
and every skilled person to whom the
LORD has given skill and ability to know how to
carry out all the work of constructing the sanctuary are to do the work just as the LORD has commanded."

2Then Moses summoned Bezalel and Oholiab
and every skilled person to whom the LORD had
given ability and who was willing to come and do
the work. 3They received from Moses all the offerings the Israelites had brought to carry out the
work of constructing the sanctuary. And the people continued to bring freewill offerings morning
after morning. 4So all the skilled craftsmen who
were doing all the work on the sanctuary left
their work 5and said to Moses, "The people are
bringing more than enough for doing the work
the LORD commanded to be done."

[a]7 That is, dugongs; also in verse 23

6Then Moses gave an order and they sent this word throughout the camp: "No man or woman is to make anything else as an offering for the sanctuary." And so the people were restrained from bringing more, 7because what they already had was more than enough to do all the work.

The Tabernacle

8All the skilled men among the workmen made the tabernacle with ten curtains of finely twisted linen and blue, purple and scarlet yarn, with cherubim worked into them by a skilled craftsman. 9All the curtains were the same size—twenty-eight cubits long and four cubits wide.[a] 10They joined five of the curtains together and did the same with the other five. 11Then they made loops of blue material along the edge of the end curtain in one set, and the same was done with the end curtain in the other set. 12They also made fifty loops on one curtain and fifty loops on the end curtain of the other set, with the loops opposite each other. 13Then they made fifty gold clasps and used them to fasten the two sets of curtains together so that the tabernacle was a unit.

14They made curtains of goat hair for the tent over the tabernacle—eleven altogether. 15All eleven curtains were the same size—thirty cubits long and four cubits wide.[b] 16They joined five of the curtains into one set and the other six into another set. 17Then they made fifty loops along the edge of the end curtain in one set and also along the edge of the end curtain in the other set. 18They made fifty bronze clasps to fasten the tent together as a unit. 19Then they made for the tent a covering of ram skins dyed red, and over that a covering of hides of sea cows.[c]

20They made upright frames of acacia wood for the tabernacle. 21Each frame was ten cubits long and a cubit and a half wide,[d] 22with two projections set parallel to each other. They made all the frames of the tabernacle in this way. 23They made twenty frames for the south side of the tabernacle 24and made forty silver bases to go under them—two bases for each frame, one under each projection. 25For the other side, the north side of the tabernacle, they made twenty frames 26and forty silver bases—two under each frame. 27They made six frames for the far end, that is, the west end of the tabernacle, 28and two frames were made for the corners of the tabernacle at the far end. 29At these two corners the frames were double from the bottom all the way to the top and fitted into a single ring; both were made alike. 30So there were eight frames and sixteen silver bases—two under each frame.

31They also made crossbars of acacia wood: five for the frames on one side of the tabernacle, 32five for those on the other side, and five for the frames on the west, at the far end of the tabernacle. 33They made the center crossbar so that it extended from end to end at the middle of the frames. 34They overlaid the frames with gold and made gold rings to hold the crossbars. They also overlaid the crossbars with gold.

35They made the curtain of blue, purple and scarlet yarn and finely twisted linen, with cherubim worked into it by a skilled craftsman. 36They made four posts of acacia wood for it and overlaid them with gold. They made gold hooks for them and cast their four silver bases. 37For the entrance to the tent they made a curtain of blue, purple and scarlet yarn and finely twisted linen—the work of an embroiderer; 38and they made five posts with hooks for them. They overlaid the tops of the posts and their bands with gold and made their five bases of bronze.

The Ark

37 Bezalel made the ark of acacia wood—two and a half cubits long, a cubit and a half wide, and a cubit and a half high.[e] 2He overlaid it with pure gold, both inside and out, and made a gold molding around it. 3He cast four gold rings for it and fastened them to its four feet, with two rings on one side and two rings on the other. 4Then he made poles of acacia wood and overlaid them with gold. 5And he inserted the poles into the rings on the sides of the ark to carry it.

6He made the atonement cover of pure gold—two and a half cubits long and a cubit and a half wide.[f] 7Then he made two cherubim out of hammered gold at the ends of the cover. 8He made one cherub on one end and the second cherub on the other; at the two ends he made them of one piece with the cover. 9The cherubim had their wings spread upward, overshadowing the cover with them. The cherubim faced each other, looking toward the cover.

The Table

10They[g] made the table of acacia wood—two cubits long, a cubit wide, and a cubit and a half high.[h] 11Then they overlaid it with pure gold and made a gold molding around it. 12They also

[a] 9 That is, about 42 feet (about 12.5 meters) long and 6 feet (about 1.8 meters) wide
[b] 15 That is, about 45 feet (about 13.5 meters) long and 6 feet (about 1.8 meters) wide
[c] 19 That is, dugongs
[d] 21 That is, about 15 feet (about 4.5 meters) long and 2 1/4 feet (about 0.7 meter) wide
[e] 1 That is, about 3 3/4 feet (about 1.1 meters) long and 2 1/4 feet (about 0.7 meter) wide and high
[f] 6 That is, about 3 3/4 feet (about 1.1 meters) long and 2 1/4 feet (about 0.7 meter) wide
[g] 10 Or *He*; also in verses 11-29
[h] 10 That is, about 3 feet (about 0.9 meter) long, 1 1/2 feet (about 0.5 meter) wide, and 2 1/4 feet (about 0.7 meter) high

made around it a rim a handbreadth[a] wide and put a gold molding on the rim. [13]They cast four gold rings for the table and fastened them to the four corners, where the four legs were. [14]The rings were put close to the rim to hold the poles used in carrying the table. [15]The poles for carrying the table were made of acacia wood and were overlaid with gold. [16]And they made from pure gold the articles for the table—its plates and dishes and bowls and its pitchers for the pouring out of drink offerings.

The Lampstand

[17]They made the lampstand of pure gold and hammered it out, base and shaft; its flowerlike cups, buds and blossoms were of one piece with it. [18]Six branches extended from the sides of the lampstand—three on one side and three on the other. [19]Three cups shaped like almond flowers with buds and blossoms were on one branch, three on the next branch and the same for all six branches extending from the lampstand. [20]And on the lampstand were four cups shaped like almond flowers with buds and blossoms. [21]One bud was under the first pair of branches extending from the lampstand, a second bud under the second pair, and a third bud under the third pair—six branches in all. [22]The buds and the branches were all of one piece with the lampstand, hammered out of pure gold.

[23]They made its seven lamps, as well as its wick trimmers and trays, of pure gold. [24]They made the lampstand and all its accessories from one talent[b] of pure gold.

The Altar of Incense

[25]They made the altar of incense out of acacia wood. It was square, a cubit long and a cubit wide, and two cubits high[c]—its horns of one piece with it. [26]They overlaid the top and all the sides and the horns with pure gold, and made a gold molding around it. [27]They made two gold rings below the molding—two on opposite sides—to hold the poles used to carry it. [28]They made the poles of acacia wood and overlaid them with gold.

[29]They also made the sacred anointing oil and the pure, fragrant incense—the work of a perfumer.

The Altar of Burnt Offering

38 They[d] built the altar of burnt offering of acacia wood, three cubits[e] high; it was square, five cubits long and five cubits wide.[f] [2]They made a horn at each of the four corners, so that the horns and the altar were of one piece, and they overlaid the altar with bronze. [3]They made all its utensils of bronze—its pots, shovels, sprinkling bowls, meat forks and firepans. [4]They made a grating for the altar, a bronze network, to be under its ledge, halfway up the altar. [5]They cast bronze rings to hold the poles for the four corners of the bronze grating. [6]They made the poles of acacia wood and overlaid them with bronze. [7]They inserted the poles into the rings so they would be on the sides of the altar for carrying it. They made it hollow, out of boards.

Basin for Washing

[8]They made the bronze basin and its bronze stand from the mirrors of the women who served at the entrance to the Tent of Meeting.

The Courtyard

[9]Next they made the courtyard. The south side was a hundred cubits[g] long and had curtains of finely twisted linen, [10]with twenty posts and twenty bronze bases, and with silver hooks and bands on the posts. [11]The north side was also a hundred cubits long and had twenty posts and twenty bronze bases, with silver hooks and bands on the posts.

[12]The west end was fifty cubits[h] wide and had curtains, with ten posts and ten bases, with silver hooks and bands on the posts. [13]The east end, toward the sunrise, was also fifty cubits wide. [14]Curtains fifteen cubits[i] long were on one side of the entrance, with three posts and three bases, [15]and curtains fifteen cubits long were on the other side of the entrance to the courtyard, with three posts and three bases. [16]All the curtains around the courtyard were of finely twisted linen. [17]The bases for the posts were bronze. The hooks and bands on the posts were silver, and their tops were overlaid with silver; so all the posts of the courtyard had silver bands.

[18]The curtain for the entrance to the courtyard was of blue, purple and scarlet yarn and finely twisted linen—the work of an embroiderer. It was twenty cubits[j] long and, like the curtains of the courtyard, five cubits[k] high, [19]with four posts and four bronze bases. Their hooks and bands were silver, and their tops were overlaid with silver. [20]All the tent pegs of the tabernacle and of the surrounding courtyard were bronze.

The Materials Used

[21]These are the amounts of the materials used

[a] *12* That is, about 3 inches (about 8 centimeters) [b] *24* That is, about 75 pounds (about 34 kilograms) [c] *25* That is, about 1 1/2 feet (about 0.5 meter) long and wide, and about 3 feet (about 0.9 meter) high [d] *1* Or *He*; also in verses 2-9 [e] *1* That is, about 4 1/2 feet (about 1.3 meters) [f] *1* That is, about 7 1/2 feet (about 2.3 meters) long and wide [g] *9* That is, about 150 feet (about 46 meters) [h] *12* That is, about 75 feet (about 23 meters) [i] *14* That is, about 22 1/2 feet (about 6.9 meters) [j] *18* That is, about 30 feet (about 9 meters) [k] *18* That is, about 7 1/2 feet (about 2.3 meters)

for the tabernacle, the tabernacle of the Testimony, which were recorded at Moses' command by the Levites under the direction of Ithamar son of Aaron, the priest. 22(Bezalel son of Uri, the son of Hur, of the tribe of Judah, made everything the LORD commanded Moses; 23with him was Oholiab son of Ahisamach, of the tribe of Dan—a craftsman and designer, and an embroiderer in blue, purple and scarlet yarn and fine linen.) 24The total amount of the gold from the wave offering used for all the work on the sanctuary was 29 talents and 730 shekels,[a] according to the sanctuary shekel.

25The silver obtained from those of the community who were counted in the census was 100 talents and 1,775 shekels,[b] according to the sanctuary shekel— 26one beka per person, that is, half a shekel,[c] according to the sanctuary shekel, from everyone who had crossed over to those counted, twenty years old or more, a total of 603,550 men. 27The 100 talents[d] of silver were used to cast the bases for the sanctuary and for the curtain—100 bases from the 100 talents, one talent for each base. 28They used the 1,775 shekels[e] to make the hooks for the posts, to overlay the tops of the posts, and to make their bands.

29The bronze from the wave offering was 70 talents and 2,400 shekels.[f] 30They used it to make the bases for the entrance to the Tent of Meeting, the bronze altar with its bronze grating and all its utensils, 31the bases for the surrounding courtyard and those for its entrance and all the tent pegs for the tabernacle and those for the surrounding courtyard.

The Priestly Garments

39 From the blue, purple and scarlet yarn they made woven garments for ministering in the sanctuary. They also made sacred garments for Aaron, as the LORD commanded Moses.

The Ephod

2They[g] made the ephod of gold, and of blue, purple and scarlet yarn, and of finely twisted linen. 3They hammered out thin sheets of gold and cut strands to be worked into the blue, purple and scarlet yarn and fine linen—the work of a skilled craftsman. 4They made shoulder pieces for the ephod, which were attached to two of its corners, so it could be fastened. 5Its skillfully woven waistband was like it—of one piece with the ephod and made with gold, and with blue, purple and scarlet yarn, and with finely twisted linen, as the LORD commanded Moses.

6They mounted the onyx stones in gold filigree settings and engraved them like a seal with the names of the sons of Israel. 7Then they fastened them on the shoulder pieces of the ephod as memorial stones for the sons of Israel, as the LORD commanded Moses.

The Breastpiece

8They fashioned the breastpiece—the work of a skilled craftsman. They made it like the ephod: of gold, and of blue, purple and scarlet yarn, and of finely twisted linen. 9It was square—a span[h] long and a span wide—and folded double. 10Then they mounted four rows of precious stones on it. In the first row there was a ruby, a topaz and a beryl; 11in the second row a turquoise, a sapphire[i] and an emerald; 12in the third row a jacinth, an agate and an amethyst; 13in the fourth row a chrysolite, an onyx and a jasper.[j] They were mounted in gold filigree settings. 14There were twelve stones, one for each of the names of the sons of Israel, each engraved like a seal with the name of one of the twelve tribes.

15For the breastpiece they made braided chains of pure gold, like a rope. 16They made two gold filigree settings and two gold rings, and fastened the rings to two of the corners of the breastpiece. 17They fastened the two gold chains to the rings at the corners of the breastpiece, 18and the other ends of the chains to the two settings, attaching them to the shoulder pieces of the ephod at the front. 19They made two gold rings and attached them to the other two corners of the breastpiece on the inside edge next to the ephod. 20Then they made two more gold rings and attached them to the bottom of the shoulder pieces on the front of the ephod, close to the seam just above the waistband of the ephod. 21They tied the rings of the breastpiece to the rings of the ephod with blue cord, connecting it to the waistband so that the breastpiece would not swing out from the ephod—as the LORD commanded Moses.

Other Priestly Garments

22They made the robe of the ephod entirely of blue cloth—the work of a weaver— 23with an opening in the center of the robe like the opening of a collar,[k] and a band around this opening, so that it would not tear. 24They made pomegran-

[a] *24* The weight of the gold was a little over one ton (about 1 metric ton). [b] *25* The weight of the silver was a little over 3 3/4 tons (about 3.4 metric tons). [c] *26* That is, about 1/5 ounce (about 5.5 grams) [d] *27* That is, about 3 3/4 tons (about 3.4 metric tons) [e] *28* That is, about 45 pounds (about 20 kilograms) [f] *29* The weight of the bronze was about 2 1/2 tons (about 2.4 metric tons). [g] *2* Or *He*; also in verses 7, 8 and 22 [h] *9* That is, about 9 inches (about 22 centimeters) [i] *11* Or *lapis lazuli* [j] *13* The precise identification of some of these precious stones is uncertain. [k] *23* The meaning of the Hebrew for this word is uncertain.

ates of blue, purple and scarlet yarn and finely
twisted linen around the hem of the robe. [25]And
they made bells of pure gold and attached them
around the hem between the pomegranates.
[26]The bells and pomegranates alternated around
the hem of the robe to be worn for ministering,
as the LORD commanded Moses.

[27]For Aaron and his sons, they made tunics of
fine linen—the work of a weaver— [28]and the
turban of fine linen, the linen headbands and the
undergarments of finely twisted linen. [29]The sash
was of finely twisted linen and blue, purple and
scarlet yarn—the work of an embroiderer—as
the LORD commanded Moses.

[30]They made the plate, the sacred diadem, out
of pure gold and engraved on it, like an inscription on a seal: HOLY TO THE LORD. [31]Then they
fastened a blue cord to it to attach it to the turban, as the LORD commanded Moses.

Moses Inspects the Tabernacle

[32]So all the work on the tabernacle, the Tent of
Meeting, was completed. The Israelites did everything just as the LORD commanded Moses.
[33]Then they brought the tabernacle to Moses: the
tent and all its furnishings, its clasps, frames,
crossbars, posts and bases; [34]the covering of ram
skins dyed red, the covering of hides of sea
cows[a] and the shielding curtain; [35]the ark of the
Testimony with its poles and the atonement cover; [36]the table with all its articles and the bread
of the Presence; [37]the pure gold lampstand with
its row of lamps and all its accessories, and the oil
for the light; [38]the gold altar, the anointing oil,
the fragrant incense, and the curtain for the entrance to the tent; [39]the bronze altar with its
bronze grating, its poles and all its utensils; the
basin with its stand; [40]the curtains of the courtyard with its posts and bases, and the curtain for
the entrance to the courtyard; the ropes and tent
pegs for the courtyard; all the furnishings for the
tabernacle, the Tent of Meeting; [41]and the woven
garments worn for ministering in the sanctuary,
both the sacred garments for Aaron the priest
and the garments for his sons when serving as
priests.

[42]The Israelites had done all the work just as
the LORD had commanded Moses. [43]Moses in-
spected the work and saw that they had done
it just as the LORD had commanded. So Moses
blessed them.

Setting Up the Tabernacle

40 Then the LORD said to Moses: [2]"Set up
the tabernacle, the Tent of Meeting, on
the first day of the first month. [3]Place the ark of
the Testimony in it and shield the ark with the
curtain. [4]Bring in the table and set out what belongs on it. Then bring in the lampstand and set
up its lamps. [5]Place the gold altar of incense in
front of the ark of the Testimony and put the
curtain at the entrance to the tabernacle.

[6]"Place the altar of burnt offering in front of
the entrance to the tabernacle, the Tent of Meeting; [7]place the basin between the Tent of Meeting and the altar and put water in it. [8]Set up the
courtyard around it and put the curtain at the
entrance to the courtyard.

[9]"Take the anointing oil and anoint the tabernacle and everything in it; consecrate it and all its
furnishings, and it will be holy. [10]Then anoint the
altar of burnt offering and all its utensils; consecrate the altar, and it will be most holy. [11]Anoint
the basin and its stand and consecrate them.

[12]"Bring Aaron and his sons to the entrance to
the Tent of Meeting and wash them with water.
[13]Then dress Aaron in the sacred garments,
anoint him and consecrate him so he may serve
me as priest. [14]Bring his sons and dress them in
tunics. [15]Anoint them just as you anointed their
father, so they may serve me as priests. Their
anointing will be to a priesthood that will continue for all generations to come." [16]Moses did everything just as the LORD commanded him.

[17]So the tabernacle was set up on the first day
of the first month in the second year. [18]When
Moses set up the tabernacle, he put the bases in
place, erected the frames, inserted the crossbars
and set up the posts. [19]Then he spread the tent
over the tabernacle and put the covering over the
tent, as the LORD commanded him.

[20]He took the Testimony and placed it in the
ark, attached the poles to the ark and put the
atonement cover over it. [21]Then he brought
the ark into the tabernacle and hung the shielding curtain and shielded the ark of the Testimony, as the LORD commanded him.

[22]Moses placed the table in the Tent of Meeting on the north side of the tabernacle outside
the curtain [23]and set out the bread on it before
the LORD, as the LORD commanded him.

[24]He placed the lampstand in the Tent of
Meeting opposite the table on the south side of
the tabernacle [25]and set up the lamps before the
LORD, as the LORD commanded him.

[26]Moses placed the gold altar in the Tent of
Meeting in front of the curtain [27]and burned fragrant incense on it, as the LORD commanded him.
[28]Then he put up the curtain at the entrance to
the tabernacle.

[29]He set the altar of burnt offering near the
entrance to the tabernacle, the Tent of Meeting,

[a] *34* That is, dugongs

and offered on it burnt offerings and grain offerings, as the LORD commanded him.
30He placed the basin between the Tent of
Meeting and the altar and put water in it for
washing, 31and Moses and Aaron and his sons
used it to wash their hands and feet. 32They
washed whenever they entered the Tent of
Meeting or approached the altar, as the LORD commanded Moses.
33Then Moses set up the courtyard around the
tabernacle and altar and put up the curtain at the
entrance to the courtyard. And so Moses finished
the work.

The Glory of the LORD

34Then the cloud covered the Tent of Meeting,
and the glory of the LORD filled the tabernacle.
35Moses could not enter the Tent of Meeting because the cloud had settled upon it, and the glory
of the LORD filled the tabernacle.
36In all the travels of the Israelites, whenever
the cloud lifted from above the tabernacle, they
would set out; 37but if the cloud did not lift, they
did not set out—until the day it lifted. 38So the
cloud of the LORD was over the tabernacle by day,
and fire was in the cloud by night, in the sight of
all the house of Israel during all their travels.

Introduction to
LEVITICUS

Personal Reading Plan

- ❒ Leviticus 1:1–3:17
- ❒ Leviticus 4:1–5:13
- ❒ Leviticus 5:14–7:10
- ❒ Leviticus 7:11–8:36
- ❒ Leviticus 9:1–10:20
- ❒ Leviticus 11:1–47
- ❒ Leviticus 12:1–13:46
- ❒ Leviticus 13:47–14:32
- ❒ Leviticus 14:33–15:33
- ❒ Leviticus 16:1–34
- ❒ Leviticus 17:1–18:30
- ❒ Leviticus 19:1–37
- ❒ Leviticus 20:1–27
- ❒ Leviticus 21:1–23:8
- ❒ Leviticus 23:9–24:23
- ❒ Leviticus 25:1–55
- ❒ Leviticus 26:1–46
- ❒ Leviticus 27:1–34

Author

Moses is assumed to be the author and editor of most of the first five books of the Old Testament (the Pentateuch).

Date

It is difficult to set a firm date for the writing of the Pentateuch. Conservative estimates place it in either the fifteenth or thirteenth century B.C., depending on when the Exodus occurred.

Theme

Reconciliation and sanctification.

Historical Background

The name of this book, from the Greek and Latin versions, comes from its emphasis on the Levitical priesthood. The ministry of the tabernacle was conducted by the sons of Moses' brother Aaron. These newly appointed priests were assisted by many of their relatives from the tribe of Levi. The events of the book of Leviticus take place after the Exodus from Egypt and the giving of the Law at Sinai, and concern the formalizing of Israelite religious practice. In Exodus, instructions were given for the building of the tabernacle; here in Leviticus, regulations are given for how to worship there.

Characteristics

After the covenant at Sinai, Israel was the earthly representation of God's kingdom (the theocracy), and, as her King, the Lord established his administration over all of Israel's life. Her religious, communal and personal life were so regulated as to establish her as God's holy people and to instruct her in holiness. To the modern reader, Leviticus may appear hopelessly outdated with its strange, disturbing economic practices, and the blood and gore of animal sacrifice, yet the questions it seeks to answer are as important for us as they were for the Israelites. How do we remain reconciled to God? What is the proper way to worship a holy God? How are we to act toward each other within the context of God's covenant? Leviticus answers these and other questions faced by the Israelites using symbols familiar to them. For us, then, the key to understanding Leviticus is looking beyond these strange symbols to the underlying principles describing God's way of holiness and reconciliation.

The Burnt Offering

1 The LORD called to Moses and spoke to him
from the Tent of Meeting. He said, 2“Speak
to the Israelites and say to them: ‘When any of
you brings an offering to the LORD, bring as your
offering an animal from either the herd or the
flock.

3“ ‘If the offering is a burnt offering from the
herd, he is to offer a male without defect. He
must present it at the entrance to the Tent of
Meeting so that it[a] will be acceptable to the
LORD. 4He is to lay his hand on the head of the
burnt offering, and it will be accepted on his behalf to make atonement for him. 5He is to slaughter the young bull before the LORD, and then
Aaron’s sons the priests shall bring the blood and
sprinkle it against the altar on all sides at the
entrance to the Tent of Meeting. 6He is to skin
the burnt offering and cut it into pieces. 7The
sons of Aaron the priest are to put fire on the altar
and arrange wood on the fire. 8Then Aaron’s sons
the priests shall arrange the pieces, including the
head and the fat, on the burning wood that is on
the altar. 9He is to wash the inner parts and the
legs with water, and the priest is to burn all of it
on the altar. It is a burnt offering, an offering
made by fire, an aroma pleasing to the LORD.

10“ ‘If the offering is a burnt offering from the
flock, from either the sheep or the goats, he is to
offer a male without defect. 11He is to slaughter
it at the north side of the altar before the LORD,
and Aaron’s sons the priests shall sprinkle its
blood against the altar on all sides. 12He is to cut
it into pieces, and the priest shall arrange them,
including the head and the fat, on the burning
wood that is on the altar. 13He is to wash the
inner parts and the legs with water, and the
priest is to bring all of it and burn it on the altar.
It is a burnt offering, an offering made by fire, an
aroma pleasing to the LORD.

14“ ‘If the offering to the LORD is a burnt offering of birds, he is to offer a dove or a young
pigeon. 15The priest shall bring it to the altar,
wring off the head and burn it on the altar; its
blood shall be drained out on the side of the altar.
16He is to remove the crop with its contents[b]
and throw it to the east side of the altar, where
the ashes are. 17He shall tear it open by the
wings, not severing it completely, and then the
priest shall burn it on the wood that is on the fire
on the altar. It is a burnt offering, an offering
made by fire, an aroma pleasing to the LORD.

The Grain Offering

2 “ ‘When someone brings a grain offering to
the LORD, his offering is to be of fine flour.
He is to pour oil on it, put incense on it 2and take
it to Aaron’s sons the priests. The priest shall take
a handful of the fine flour and oil, together with
all the incense, and burn this as a memorial portion on the altar, an offering made by fire, an
aroma pleasing to the LORD. 3The rest of the grain
offering belongs to Aaron and his sons; it is a
most holy part of the offerings made to the LORD
by fire.

4“ ‘If you bring a grain offering baked in an
oven, it is to consist of fine flour: cakes made
without yeast and mixed with oil, or[c] wafers
made without yeast and spread with oil. 5If your
grain offering is prepared on a griddle, it is to be
made of fine flour mixed with oil, and without
yeast. 6Crumble it and pour oil on it; it is a grain
offering. 7If your grain offering is cooked in a pan,
it is to be made of fine flour and oil. 8Bring the
grain offering made of these things to the LORD;
present it to the priest, who shall take it to the
altar. 9He shall take out the memorial portion
from the grain offering and burn it on the altar as
an offering made by fire, an aroma pleasing to the
LORD. 10The rest of the grain offering belongs to
Aaron and his sons; it is a most holy part of the
offerings made to the LORD by fire.

11“ ‘Every grain offering you bring to the LORD
must be made without yeast, for you are not to
burn any yeast or honey in an offering made to
the LORD by fire. 12You may bring them to the
LORD as an offering of the firstfruits, but they are
not to be offered on the altar as a pleasing aroma.
13Season all your grain offerings with salt. Do not
leave the salt of the covenant of your God out of
your grain offerings; add salt to all your offerings.

14“ ‘If you bring a grain offering of firstfruits to
the LORD, offer crushed heads of new grain roasted in the fire. 15Put oil and incense on it; it is a
grain offering. 16The priest shall burn the memorial portion of the crushed grain and the oil, together with all the incense, as an offering made
to the LORD by fire.

The Fellowship Offering

3 “ ‘If someone’s offering is a fellowship offering,[d] and he offers an animal from the herd,
whether male or female, he is to present before
the LORD an animal without defect. 2He is to lay
his hand on the head of his offering and slaughter
it at the entrance to the Tent of Meeting. Then
Aaron’s sons the priests shall sprinkle the blood
against the altar on all sides. 3From the fellowship offering he is to bring a sacrifice made to the
LORD by fire: all the fat that covers the inner parts
or is connected to them, 4both kidneys with the
fat on them near the loins, and the covering of

[a] 3 Or *he* [b] 16 Or *crop and the feathers*; the meaning of the Hebrew for this word is uncertain. [c] 4 Or *and*
[d] 1 Traditionally *peace offering*; also in verses 3, 6 and 9

the liver, which he will remove with the kidneys.
5Then Aaron's sons are to burn it on the altar on
top of the burnt offering that is on the burning
wood, as an offering made by fire, an aroma
pleasing to the LORD.

6" 'If he offers an animal from the flock as a
fellowship offering to the LORD, he is to offer
a male or female without defect. 7If he offers a
lamb, he is to present it before the LORD. 8He is
to lay his hand on the head of his offering and
slaughter it in front of the Tent of Meeting. Then
Aaron's sons shall sprinkle its blood against the
altar on all sides. 9From the fellowship offering
he is to bring a sacrifice made to the LORD by fire:
its fat, the entire fat tail cut off close to the backbone, all the fat that covers the inner parts or is
connected to them, 10both kidneys with the fat
on them near the loins, and the covering of the
liver, which he will remove with the kidneys.
11The priest shall burn them on the altar as food,
an offering made to the LORD by fire.

12" 'If his offering is a goat, he is to present it
before the LORD. 13He is to lay his hand on its
head and slaughter it in front of the Tent of Meeting. Then Aaron's sons shall sprinkle its blood
against the altar on all sides. 14From what he
offers he is to make this offering to the LORD by
fire: all the fat that covers the inner parts or is
connected to them, 15both kidneys with the fat
on them near the loins, and the covering of the
liver, which he will remove with the kidneys.
16The priest shall burn them on the altar as food,
an offering made by fire, a pleasing aroma. All the
fat is the LORD's.

17" 'This is a lasting ordinance for the generations to come, wherever you live: You must not
eat any fat or any blood.' "

The Sin Offering

4 The LORD said to Moses, 2"Say to the Israelites: 'When anyone sins unintentionally and
does what is forbidden in any of the LORD's
commands—

3" 'If the anointed priest sins, bringing guilt on
the people, he must bring to the LORD a young
bull without defect as a sin offering for the sin he
has committed. 4He is to present the bull at the
entrance to the Tent of Meeting before the LORD.
He is to lay his hand on its head and slaughter it
before the LORD. 5Then the anointed priest shall
take some of the bull's blood and carry it into the
Tent of Meeting. 6He is to dip his finger into the
blood and sprinkle some of it seven times before
the LORD, in front of the curtain of the sanctuary.
7The priest shall then put some of the blood on
the horns of the altar of fragrant incense that is
before the LORD in the Tent of Meeting. The rest
of the bull's blood he shall pour out at the base of
the altar of burnt offering at the entrance to the
Tent of Meeting. 8He shall remove all the fat from
the bull of the sin offering—the fat that covers
the inner parts or is connected to them, 9both
kidneys with the fat on them near the loins, and
the covering of the liver, which he will remove
with the kidneys— 10just as the fat is removed
from the ox[a] sacrificed as a fellowship offering.[b] Then the priest shall burn them on the
altar of burnt offering. 11But the hide of the bull
and all its flesh, as well as the head and legs, the
inner parts and offal— 12that is, all the rest of the
bull—he must take outside the camp to a place
ceremonially clean, where the ashes are thrown,
and burn it in a wood fire on the ash heap.

13" 'If the whole Israelite community sins unintentionally and does what is forbidden in any of
the LORD's commands, even though the community is unaware of the matter, they are guilty.
14When they become aware of the sin they committed, the assembly must bring a young bull as
a sin offering and present it before the Tent of
Meeting. 15The elders of the community are to
lay their hands on the bull's head before the
LORD, and the bull shall be slaughtered before the
LORD. 16Then the anointed priest is to take some
of the bull's blood into the Tent of Meeting. 17He
shall dip his finger into the blood and sprinkle it
before the LORD seven times in front of the curtain. 18He is to put some of the blood on the
horns of the altar that is before the LORD in the
Tent of Meeting. The rest of the blood he shall
pour out at the base of the altar of burnt offering
at the entrance to the Tent of Meeting. 19He shall
remove all the fat from it and burn it on the altar,
20and do with this bull just as he did with the bull
for the sin offering. In this way the priest will
make atonement for them, and they will be forgiven. 21Then he shall take the bull outside the
camp and burn it as he burned the first bull. This
is the sin offering for the community.

22" 'When a leader sins unintentionally and
does what is forbidden in any of the commands of
the LORD his God, he is guilty. 23When he is
made aware of the sin he committed, he must
bring as his offering a male goat without defect.
24He is to lay his hand on the goat's head and
slaughter it at the place where the burnt offering
is slaughtered before the LORD. It is a sin offering.
25Then the priest shall take some of the blood of
the sin offering with his finger and put it on the
horns of the altar of burnt offering and pour out
the rest of the blood at the base of the altar. 26He
shall burn all the fat on the altar as he burned the

[a] *10* The Hebrew word can include both male and female.
[b] *10* Traditionally *peace offering*; also in verses 26, 31 and 35

fat of the fellowship offering. In this way the
priest will make atonement for the man's sin, and
he will be forgiven.

27" 'If a member of the community sins unintentionally and does what is forbidden in any of
the LORD's commands, he is guilty. 28When he is
made aware of the sin he committed, he must
bring as his offering for the sin he committed a
female goat without defect. 29He is to lay his
hand on the head of the sin offering and slaughter
it at the place of the burnt offering. 30Then the
priest is to take some of the blood with his finger
and put it on the horns of the altar of burnt offering and pour out the rest of the blood at the base
of the altar. 31He shall remove all the fat, just as
the fat is removed from the fellowship offering,
and the priest shall burn it on the altar as an
aroma pleasing to the LORD. In this way the priest
will make atonement for him, and he will be
forgiven.

32" 'If he brings a lamb as his sin offering, he
is to bring a female without defect. 33He is to lay
his hand on its head and slaughter it for a sin
offering at the place where the burnt offering is
slaughtered. 34Then the priest shall take some of
the blood of the sin offering with his finger and
put it on the horns of the altar of burnt offering
and pour out the rest of the blood at the base of
the altar. 35He shall remove all the fat, just as the
fat is removed from the lamb of the fellowship
offering, and the priest shall burn it on the altar
on top of the offerings made to the LORD by fire.
In this way the priest will make atonement for
him for the sin he has committed, and he will be
forgiven.

5 " 'If a person sins because he does not speak
up when he hears a public charge to testify
regarding something he has seen or learned
about, he will be held responsible.

2" 'Or if a person touches anything ceremonially unclean—whether the carcasses of unclean
wild animals or of unclean livestock or of unclean
creatures that move along the ground—even
though he is unaware of it, he has become unclean and is guilty.

3" 'Or if he touches human uncleanness—
anything that would make him unclean—even
though he is unaware of it, when he learns of it
he will be guilty.

4" 'Or if a person thoughtlessly takes an oath to
do anything, whether good or evil—in any matter one might carelessly swear about—even
though he is unaware of it, in any case when he
learns of it he will be guilty.

5" 'When anyone is guilty in any of these ways,
he must confess in what way he has sinned 6and,
as a penalty for the sin he has committed, he
must bring to the LORD a female lamb or goat
from the flock as a sin offering; and the priest
shall make atonement for him for his sin.

7" 'If he cannot afford a lamb, he is to bring
two doves or two young pigeons to the LORD as a
penalty for his sin—one for a sin offering and the
other for a burnt offering. 8He is to bring them to
the priest, who shall first offer the one for the sin
offering. He is to wring its head from its neck, not
severing it completely, 9and is to sprinkle some of
the blood of the sin offering against the side of
the altar; the rest of the blood must be drained
out at the base of the altar. It is a sin offering.
10The priest shall then offer the other as a burnt
offering in the prescribed way and make atonement for him for the sin he has committed, and
he will be forgiven.

11" 'If, however, he cannot afford two doves or
two young pigeons, he is to bring as an offering
for his sin a tenth of an ephah[a] of fine flour for
a sin offering. He must not put oil or incense on
it, because it is a sin offering. 12He is to bring it
to the priest, who shall take a handful of it as a
memorial portion and burn it on the altar on top
of the offerings made to the LORD by fire. It is a
sin offering. 13In this way the priest will make
atonement for him for any of these sins he has
committed, and he will be forgiven. The rest of
the offering will belong to the priest, as in the
case of the grain offering.' "

The Guilt Offering

14The LORD said to Moses: 15"When a person
commits a violation and sins unintentionally in
regard to any of the LORD's holy things, he is to
bring to the LORD as a penalty a ram from the
flock, one without defect and of the proper value
in silver, according to the sanctuary shekel.[b] It
is a guilt offering. 16He must make restitution for
what he has failed to do in regard to the holy
things, add a fifth of the value to that and give it
all to the priest, who will make atonement for
him with the ram as a guilt offering, and he will
be forgiven.

17"If a person sins and does what is forbidden
in any of the LORD's commands, even though he
does not know it, he is guilty and will be held
responsible. 18He is to bring to the priest as a
guilt offering a ram from the flock, one without
defect and of the proper value. In this way the
priest will make atonement for him for the wrong
he has committed unintentionally, and he will be
forgiven. 19It is a guilt offering; he has been guilty
of[c] wrongdoing against the LORD."

[a] *11* That is, probably about 2 quarts (about 2 liters) [b] *15* That is, about 2/5 ounce (about 11.5 grams) [c] *19* Or *has made full expiation for his*

6 The LORD said to Moses: 2“If anyone sins and is unfaithful to the LORD by deceiving his neighbor about something entrusted to him or left in his care or stolen, or if he cheats him, 3or if he finds lost property and lies about it, or if he swears falsely, or if he commits any such sin that people may do— 4when he thus sins and becomes guilty, he must return what he has stolen or taken by extortion, or what was entrusted to him, or the lost property he found, 5or whatever it was he swore falsely about. He must make restitution in full, add a fifth of the value to it and give it all to the owner on the day he presents his guilt offering. 6And as a penalty he must bring to the priest, that is, to the LORD, his guilt offering, a ram from the flock, one without defect and of the proper value. 7In this way the priest will make atonement for him before the LORD, and he will be forgiven for any of these things he did that made him guilty.”

The Burnt Offering

8The LORD said to Moses: 9“Give Aaron and his sons this command: ‘These are the regulations for the burnt offering: The burnt offering is to remain on the altar hearth throughout the night, till morning, and the fire must be kept burning on the altar. 10The priest shall then put on his linen clothes, with linen undergarments next to his body, and shall remove the ashes of the burnt offering that the fire has consumed on the altar and place them beside the altar. 11Then he is to take off these clothes and put on others, and carry the ashes outside the camp to a place that is ceremonially clean. 12The fire on the altar must be kept burning; it must not go out. Every morning the priest is to add firewood and arrange the burnt offering on the fire and burn the fat of the fellowship offerings[a] on it. 13The fire must be kept burning on the altar continuously; it must not go out.

The Grain Offering

14“ ‘These are the regulations for the grain offering: Aaron’s sons are to bring it before the LORD, in front of the altar. 15The priest is to take a handful of fine flour and oil, together with all the incense on the grain offering, and burn the memorial portion on the altar as an aroma pleasing to the LORD. 16Aaron and his sons shall eat the rest of it, but it is to be eaten without yeast in a holy place; they are to eat it in the courtyard of the Tent of Meeting. 17It must not be baked with yeast; I have given it as their share of the offerings made to me by fire. Like the sin offering and the guilt offering, it is most holy. 18Any male descendant of Aaron may eat it. It is his regular share of the offerings made to the LORD by fire for the generations to come. Whatever touches them will become holy.[b]’ ”

19The LORD also said to Moses, 20“This is the offering Aaron and his sons are to bring to the LORD on the day he[c] is anointed: a tenth of an ephah[d] of fine flour as a regular grain offering, half of it in the morning and half in the evening. 21Prepare it with oil on a griddle; bring it well-mixed and present the grain offering broken[e] in pieces as an aroma pleasing to the LORD. 22The son who is to succeed him as anointed priest shall prepare it. It is the LORD’s regular share and is to be burned completely. 23Every grain offering of a priest shall be burned completely; it must not be eaten.”

The Sin Offering

24The LORD said to Moses, 25“Say to Aaron and his sons: ‘These are the regulations for the sin offering: The sin offering is to be slaughtered before the LORD in the place the burnt offering is slaughtered; it is most holy. 26The priest who offers it shall eat it; it is to be eaten in a holy place, in the courtyard of the Tent of Meeting. 27Whatever touches any of the flesh will become holy, and if any of the blood is spattered on a garment, you must wash it in a holy place. 28The clay pot the meat is cooked in must be broken; but if it is cooked in a bronze pot, the pot is to be scoured and rinsed with water. 29Any male in a priest’s family may eat it; it is most holy. 30But any sin offering whose blood is brought into the Tent of Meeting to make atonement in the Holy Place must not be eaten; it must be burned.

The Guilt Offering

7 “ ‘These are the regulations for the guilt offering, which is most holy: 2The guilt offering is to be slaughtered in the place where the burnt offering is slaughtered, and its blood is to be sprinkled against the altar on all sides. 3All its fat shall be offered: the fat tail and the fat that covers the inner parts, 4both kidneys with the fat on them near the loins, and the covering of the liver, which is to be removed with the kidneys. 5The priest shall burn them on the altar as an offering made to the LORD by fire. It is a guilt offering. 6Any male in a priest’s family may eat it, but it must be eaten in a holy place; it is most holy.

7“ ‘The same law applies to both the sin offering and the guilt offering: They belong to the priest who makes atonement with them. 8The priest who offers a burnt offering for anyone may

[a] 12 Traditionally *peace offerings* [b] 18 Or *Whoever touches them must be holy*; similarly in verse 27 [c] 20 Or *each*
[d] 20 That is, probably about 2 quarts (about 2 liters) [e] 21 The meaning of the Hebrew for this word is uncertain.

keep its hide for himself. 9Every grain offering
baked in an oven or cooked in a pan or on a
griddle belongs to the priest who offers it, 10and
every grain offering, whether mixed with oil or
dry, belongs equally to all the sons of Aaron.

The Fellowship Offering

11" 'These are the regulations for the fellowship offering[a] a person may present to the LORD:
12" 'If he offers it as an expression of thankfulness, then along with this thank offering he is
to offer cakes of bread made without yeast and
mixed with oil, wafers made without yeast and
spread with oil, and cakes of fine flour well-
kneaded and mixed with oil. 13Along with his
fellowship offering of thanksgiving he is to
present an offering with cakes of bread made
with yeast. 14He is to bring one of each kind as an
offering, a contribution to the LORD; it belongs to
the priest who sprinkles the blood of the fellowship offerings. 15The meat of his fellowship offering of thanksgiving must be eaten on the day it is
offered; he must leave none of it till morning.
16" 'If, however, his offering is the result of a
vow or is a freewill offering, the sacrifice shall be
eaten on the day he offers it, but anything left
over may be eaten on the next day. 17Any meat
of the sacrifice left over till the third day must be
burned up. 18If any meat of the fellowship offering is eaten on the third day, it will not be accepted. It will not be credited to the one who offered
it, for it is impure; the person who eats any of it
will be held responsible.
19" 'Meat that touches anything ceremonially
unclean must not be eaten; it must be burned up.
As for other meat, anyone ceremonially clean
may eat it. 20But if anyone who is unclean eats
any meat of the fellowship offering belonging
to the LORD, that person must be cut off from
his people. 21If anyone touches something unclean—whether human uncleanness or an unclean animal or any unclean, detestable thing—
and then eats any of the meat of the fellowship
offering belonging to the LORD, that person must
be cut off from his people.' "

Eating Fat and Blood Forbidden

22The LORD said to Moses, 23"Say to the Israelites: 'Do not eat any of the fat of cattle, sheep or
goats. 24The fat of an animal found dead or torn
by wild animals may be used for any other purpose, but you must not eat it. 25Anyone who eats
the fat of an animal from which an offering by fire
may be[b] made to the LORD must be cut off from
his people. 26And wherever you live, you must
not eat the blood of any bird or animal. 27If anyone eats blood, that person must be cut off from
his people.' "

The Priests' Share

28The LORD said to Moses, 29"Say to the Israelites: 'Anyone who brings a fellowship offering to
the LORD is to bring part of it as his sacrifice to
the LORD. 30With his own hands he is to bring the
offering made to the LORD by fire; he is to bring
the fat, together with the breast, and wave the
breast before the LORD as a wave offering. 31The
priest shall burn the fat on the altar, but the
breast belongs to Aaron and his sons. 32You are to
give the right thigh of your fellowship offerings to
the priest as a contribution. 33The son of Aaron
who offers the blood and the fat of the fellowship
offering shall have the right thigh as his share.
34From the fellowship offerings of the Israelites,
I have taken the breast that is waved and the
thigh that is presented and have given them to
Aaron the priest and his sons as their regular
share from the Israelites.' "
35This is the portion of the offerings made to
the LORD by fire that were allotted to Aaron and
his sons on the day they were presented to serve
the LORD as priests. 36On the day they were
anointed, the LORD commanded that the Israelites give this to them as their regular share for the
generations to come.

37These, then, are the regulations for the
burnt offering, the grain offering, the sin offering,
the guilt offering, the ordination offering and the
fellowship offering, 38which the LORD gave Moses on Mount Sinai on the day he commanded
the Israelites to bring their offerings to the LORD,
in the Desert of Sinai.

The Ordination of Aaron and His Sons

8 The LORD said to Moses, 2"Bring Aaron and
his sons, their garments, the anointing oil,
the bull for the sin offering, the two rams and the
basket containing bread made without yeast,
3and gather the entire assembly at the entrance
to the Tent of Meeting." 4Moses did as the LORD
commanded him, and the assembly gathered at
the entrance to the Tent of Meeting.
5Moses said to the assembly, "This is what the
LORD has commanded to be done." 6Then Moses
brought Aaron and his sons forward and washed
them with water. 7He put the tunic on Aaron,
tied the sash around him, clothed him with the
robe and put the ephod on him. He also tied the
ephod to him by its skillfully woven waistband;
so it was fastened on him. 8He placed the breastpiece on him and put the Urim and Thummim in
the breastpiece. 9Then he placed the turban on

[a] *11* Traditionally *peace offering*; also in verses 13-37 [b] *25* Or *fire is*

Aaron's head and set the gold plate, the sacred
diadem, on the front of it, as the LORD commanded Moses.
[10]Then Moses took the anointing oil and
anointed the tabernacle and everything in it, and
so consecrated them. [11]He sprinkled some of the
oil on the altar seven times, anointing the altar
and all its utensils and the basin with its stand,
to consecrate them. [12]He poured some of the
anointing oil on Aaron's head and anointed him
to consecrate him. [13]Then he brought Aaron's
sons forward, put tunics on them, tied sashes
around them and put headbands on them, as the
LORD commanded Moses.
[14]He then presented the bull for the sin offering, and Aaron and his sons laid their hands on
its head. [15]Moses slaughtered the bull and took
some of the blood, and with his finger he put it
on all the horns of the altar to purify the altar. He
poured out the rest of the blood at the base of the
altar. So he consecrated it to make atonement for
it. [16]Moses also took all the fat around the inner
parts, the covering of the liver, and both kidneys
and their fat, and burned it on the altar. [17]But the
bull with its hide and its flesh and its offal he
burned up outside the camp, as the LORD commanded Moses.
[18]He then presented the ram for the burnt offering, and Aaron and his sons laid their hands on
its head. [19]Then Moses slaughtered the ram and
sprinkled the blood against the altar on all sides.
[20]He cut the ram into pieces and burned the
head, the pieces and the fat. [21]He washed the
inner parts and the legs with water and burned
the whole ram on the altar as a burnt offering, a
pleasing aroma, an offering made to the LORD by
fire, as the LORD commanded Moses.
[22]He then presented the other ram, the ram
for the ordination, and Aaron and his sons laid
their hands on its head. [23]Moses slaughtered the
ram and took some of its blood and put it on the
lobe of Aaron's right ear, on the thumb of his
right hand and on the big toe of his right foot.
[24]Moses also brought Aaron's sons forward and
put some of the blood on the lobes of their right
ears, on the thumbs of their right hands and on
the big toes of their right feet. Then he sprinkled
blood against the altar on all sides. [25]He took the
fat, the fat tail, all the fat around the inner parts,
the covering of the liver, both kidneys and their
fat and the right thigh. [26]Then from the basket of
bread made without yeast, which was before the
LORD, he took a cake of bread, and one made with
oil, and a wafer; he put these on the fat portions
and on the right thigh. [27]He put all these in the
hands of Aaron and his sons and waved them
before the LORD as a wave offering. [28]Then Moses
took them from their hands and burned them on
the altar on top of the burnt offering as an ordination offering, a pleasing aroma, an offering made
to the LORD by fire. [29]He also took the breast—
Moses' share of the ordination ram—and waved
it before the LORD as a wave offering, as the LORD
commanded Moses.
[30]Then Moses took some of the anointing oil
and some of the blood from the altar and sprinkled them on Aaron and his garments and on his
sons and their garments. So he consecrated Aaron and his garments and his sons and their garments.
[31]Moses then said to Aaron and his sons,
"Cook the meat at the entrance to the Tent of
Meeting and eat it there with the bread from the
basket of ordination offerings, as I commanded,
saying,[a] 'Aaron and his sons are to eat it.'
[32]Then burn up the rest of the meat and the
bread. [33]Do not leave the entrance to the Tent of
Meeting for seven days, until the days of your
ordination are completed, for your ordination
will last seven days. [34]What has been done today
was commanded by the LORD to make atonement
for you. [35]You must stay at the entrance to the
Tent of Meeting day and night for seven days and
do what the LORD requires, so you will not die;
for that is what I have been commanded." [36]So
Aaron and his sons did everything the LORD commanded through Moses.

The Priests Begin Their Ministry

9 On the eighth day Moses summoned Aaron
and his sons and the elders of Israel. [2]He said
to Aaron, "Take a bull calf for your sin offering
and a ram for your burnt offering, both without
defect, and present them before the LORD. [3]Then
say to the Israelites: 'Take a male goat for a sin
offering, a calf and a lamb—both a year old and
without defect—for a burnt offering, [4]and an
ox[b] and a ram for a fellowship offering[c] to sacrifice before the LORD, together with a grain offering mixed with oil. For today the LORD will appear to you.' "
[5]They took the things Moses commanded to
the front of the Tent of Meeting, and the entire
assembly came near and stood before the LORD.
[6]Then Moses said, "This is what the LORD has
commanded you to do, so that the glory of the
LORD may appear to you."
[7]Moses said to Aaron, "Come to the altar and
sacrifice your sin offering and your burnt offering
and make atonement for yourself and the people;
sacrifice the offering that is for the people and

[a]*31* Or *I was commanded:* [b]*4* The Hebrew word can include both male and female; also in verses 18 and 19.
[c]*4* Traditionally *peace offering*; also in verses 18 and 22

make atonement for them, as the LORD has commanded."
8So Aaron came to the altar and slaughtered
the calf as a sin offering for himself. 9His sons
brought the blood to him, and he dipped his finger into the blood and put it on the horns of the
altar; the rest of the blood he poured out at the
base of the altar. 10On the altar he burned the
fat, the kidneys and the covering of the liver from
the sin offering, as the LORD commanded Moses;
11the flesh and the hide he burned up outside the
camp.
12Then he slaughtered the burnt offering. His
sons handed him the blood, and he sprinkled it
against the altar on all sides. 13They handed him
the burnt offering piece by piece, including the
head, and he burned them on the altar. 14He
washed the inner parts and the legs and burned
them on top of the burnt offering on the altar.
15Aaron then brought the offering that was for
the people. He took the goat for the people's sin
offering and slaughtered it and offered it for a sin
offering as he did with the first one.
16He brought the burnt offering and offered
it in the prescribed way. 17He also brought the
grain offering, took a handful of it and burned it
on the altar in addition to the morning's burnt
offering.
18He slaughtered the ox and the ram as the
fellowship offering for the people. His sons handed him the blood, and he sprinkled it against the
altar on all sides. 19But the fat portions of the ox
and the ram—the fat tail, the layer of fat, the
kidneys and the covering of the liver— 20these
they laid on the breasts, and then Aaron burned
the fat on the altar. 21Aaron waved the breasts
and the right thigh before the LORD as a wave
offering, as Moses commanded.
22Then Aaron lifted his hands toward the people and blessed them. And having sacrificed the
sin offering, the burnt offering and the fellowship
offering, he stepped down.
23Moses and Aaron then went into the Tent of
Meeting. When they came out, they blessed the
people; and the glory of the LORD appeared to all
the people. 24Fire came out from the presence
of the LORD and consumed the burnt offering and
the fat portions on the altar. And when all the
people saw it, they shouted for joy and fell facedown.

The Death of Nadab and Abihu

10 Aaron's sons Nadab and Abihu took their
censers, put fire in them and added incense; and they offered unauthorized fire before
the LORD, contrary to his command. 2So fire came
out from the presence of the LORD and consumed
them, and they died before the LORD. 3Moses
then said to Aaron, "This is what the LORD spoke
of when he said:

" 'Among those who approach me
  I will show myself holy;
in the sight of all the people
  I will be honored.' "

Aaron remained silent.
4Moses summoned Mishael and Elzaphan,
sons of Aaron's uncle Uzziel, and said to them,
"Come here; carry your cousins outside the
camp, away from the front of the sanctuary." 5So
they came and carried them, still in their tunics,
outside the camp, as Moses ordered.
6Then Moses said to Aaron and his sons Eleazar and Ithamar, "Do not let your hair become
unkempt,[a] and do not tear your clothes, or you
will die and the LORD will be angry with the
whole community. But your relatives, all the
house of Israel, may mourn for those the LORD
has destroyed by fire. 7Do not leave the entrance
to the Tent of Meeting or you will die, because
the LORD's anointing oil is on you." So they did as
Moses said.
8Then the LORD said to Aaron, 9"You and your
sons are not to drink wine or other fermented
drink whenever you go into the Tent of Meeting,
or you will die. This is a lasting ordinance for the
generations to come. 10You must distinguish between the holy and the common, between the
unclean and the clean, 11and you must teach the
Israelites all the decrees the LORD has given them
through Moses."
12Moses said to Aaron and his remaining sons,
Eleazar and Ithamar, "Take the grain offering left
over from the offerings made to the LORD by fire
and eat it prepared without yeast beside the altar,
for it is most holy. 13Eat it in a holy place, because
it is your share and your sons' share of the offerings made to the LORD by fire; for so I have been
commanded. 14But you and your sons and your
daughters may eat the breast that was waved and
the thigh that was presented. Eat them in a ceremonially clean place; they have been given to you
and your children as your share of the Israelites'
fellowship offerings.[b] 15The thigh that was presented and the breast that was waved must be
brought with the fat portions of the offerings
made by fire, to be waved before the LORD as a
wave offering. This will be the regular share for
you and your children, as the LORD has commanded."
16When Moses inquired about the goat of the
sin offering and found that it had been burned
up, he was angry with Eleazar and Ithamar, Aaron's remaining sons, and asked, 17"Why didn't

[a]6 Or *Do not uncover your heads*
[b]14 Traditionally *peace offerings*

you eat the sin offering in the sanctuary area? It is most holy; it was given to you to take away the guilt of the community by making atonement for them before the LORD. 18Since its blood was not taken into the Holy Place, you should have eaten the goat in the sanctuary area, as I commanded."

19Aaron replied to Moses, "Today they sacrificed their sin offering and their burnt offering before the LORD, but such things as this have happened to me. Would the LORD have been pleased if I had eaten the sin offering today?" 20When Moses heard this, he was satisfied.

Clean and Unclean Food

11 The LORD said to Moses and Aaron, 2"Say to the Israelites: 'Of all the animals that live on land, these are the ones you may eat: 3You may eat any animal that has a split hoof completely divided and that chews the cud.

4" 'There are some that only chew the cud or only have a split hoof, but you must not eat them. The camel, though it chews the cud, does not have a split hoof; it is ceremonially unclean for you. 5The coney,[a] though it chews the cud, does not have a split hoof; it is unclean for you. 6The rabbit, though it chews the cud, does not have a split hoof; it is unclean for you. 7And the pig, though it has a split hoof completely divided, does not chew the cud; it is unclean for you. 8You must not eat their meat or touch their carcasses; they are unclean for you.

9" 'Of all the creatures living in the water of the seas and the streams, you may eat any that have fins and scales. 10But all creatures in the seas or streams that do not have fins and scales—whether among all the swarming things or among all the other living creatures in the water—you are to detest. 11And since you are to detest them, you must not eat their meat and you must detest their carcasses. 12Anything living in the water that does not have fins and scales is to be detestable to you.

13" 'These are the birds you are to detest and not eat because they are detestable: the eagle, the vulture, the black vulture, 14the red kite, any kind of black kite, 15any kind of raven, 16the horned owl, the screech owl, the gull, any kind of hawk, 17the little owl, the cormorant, the great owl, 18the white owl, the desert owl, the osprey, 19the stork, any kind of heron, the hoopoe and the bat.[b]

20" 'All flying insects that walk on all fours are to be detestable to you. 21There are, however, some winged creatures that walk on all fours that you may eat: those that have jointed legs for hopping on the ground. 22Of these you may eat any kind of locust, katydid, cricket or grasshopper. 23But all other winged creatures that have four legs you are to detest.

24" 'You will make yourselves unclean by these; whoever touches their carcasses will be unclean till evening. 25Whoever picks up one of their carcasses must wash his clothes, and he will be unclean till evening.

26" 'Every animal that has a split hoof not completely divided or that does not chew the cud is unclean for you; whoever touches ⌞the carcass of⌟ any of them will be unclean. 27Of all the animals that walk on all fours, those that walk on their paws are unclean for you; whoever touches their carcasses will be unclean till evening. 28Anyone who picks up their carcasses must wash his clothes, and he will be unclean till evening. They are unclean for you.

29" 'Of the animals that move about on the ground, these are unclean for you: the weasel, the rat, any kind of great lizard, 30the gecko, the monitor lizard, the wall lizard, the skink and the chameleon. 31Of all those that move along the ground, these are unclean for you. Whoever touches them when they are dead will be unclean till evening. 32When one of them dies and falls on something, that article, whatever its use, will be unclean, whether it is made of wood, cloth, hide or sackcloth. Put it in water; it will be unclean till evening, and then it will be clean. 33If one of them falls into a clay pot, everything in it will be unclean, and you must break the pot. 34Any food that could be eaten but has water on it from such a pot is unclean, and any liquid that could be drunk from it is unclean. 35Anything that one of their carcasses falls on becomes unclean; an oven or cooking pot must be broken up. They are unclean, and you are to regard them as unclean. 36A spring, however, or a cistern for collecting water remains clean, but anyone who touches one of these carcasses is unclean. 37If a carcass falls on any seeds that are to be planted, they remain clean. 38But if water has been put on the seed and a carcass falls on it, it is unclean for you.

39" 'If an animal that you are allowed to eat dies, anyone who touches the carcass will be unclean till evening. 40Anyone who eats some of the carcass must wash his clothes, and he will be unclean till evening. Anyone who picks up the carcass must wash his clothes, and he will be unclean till evening.

41" 'Every creature that moves about on the ground is detestable; it is not to be eaten. 42You are not to eat any creature that moves about on the ground, whether it moves on its belly or

[a] *5* That is, the hyrax or rock badger   [b] *19* The precise identification of some of the birds, insects and animals in this chapter is uncertain.

walks on all fours or on many feet; it is detestable. 43 Do not defile yourselves by any of these creatures. Do not make yourselves unclean by means of them or be made unclean by them. 44 I am the LORD your God; consecrate yourselves and be holy, because I am holy. Do not make yourselves unclean by any creature that moves about on the ground. 45 I am the LORD who brought you up out of Egypt to be your God; therefore be holy, because I am holy.

46 " 'These are the regulations concerning animals, birds, every living thing that moves in the water and every creature that moves about on the ground. 47 You must distinguish between the unclean and the clean, between living creatures that may be eaten and those that may not be eaten.' "

Purification After Childbirth

12 The LORD said to Moses, 2 "Say to the Israelites: 'A woman who becomes pregnant and gives birth to a son will be ceremonially unclean for seven days, just as she is unclean during her monthly period. 3 On the eighth day the boy is to be circumcised. 4 Then the woman must wait thirty-three days to be purified from her bleeding. She must not touch anything sacred or go to the sanctuary until the days of her purification are over. 5 If she gives birth to a daughter, for two weeks the woman will be unclean, as during her period. Then she must wait sixty-six days to be purified from her bleeding.

6 " 'When the days of her purification for a son or daughter are over, she is to bring to the priest at the entrance to the Tent of Meeting a year-old lamb for a burnt offering and a young pigeon or a dove for a sin offering. 7 He shall offer them before the LORD to make atonement for her, and then she will be ceremonially clean from her flow of blood.

" 'These are the regulations for the woman who gives birth to a boy or a girl. 8 If she cannot afford a lamb, she is to bring two doves or two young pigeons, one for a burnt offering and the other for a sin offering. In this way the priest will make atonement for her, and she will be clean.' "

Regulations About Infectious Skin Diseases

13 The LORD said to Moses and Aaron, 2 "When anyone has a swelling or a rash or a bright spot on his skin that may become an infectious skin disease,[a] he must be brought to Aaron the priest or to one of his sons[b] who is a priest. 3 The priest is to examine the sore on his skin, and if the hair in the sore has turned white and the sore appears to be more than skin deep,[c] it is an infectious skin disease. When the priest examines him, he shall pronounce him ceremonially unclean. 4 If the spot on his skin is white but does not appear to be more than skin deep and the hair in it has not turned white, the priest is to put the infected person in isolation for seven days. 5 On the seventh day the priest is to examine him, and if he sees that the sore is unchanged and has not spread in the skin, he is to keep him in isolation another seven days. 6 On the seventh day the priest is to examine him again, and if the sore has faded and has not spread in the skin, the priest shall pronounce him clean; it is only a rash. The man must wash his clothes, and he will be clean. 7 But if the rash does spread in his skin after he has shown himself to the priest to be pronounced clean, he must appear before the priest again. 8 The priest is to examine him, and if the rash has spread in the skin, he shall pronounce him unclean; it is an infectious disease.

9 "When anyone has an infectious skin disease, he must be brought to the priest. 10 The priest is to examine him, and if there is a white swelling in the skin that has turned the hair white and if there is raw flesh in the swelling, 11 it is a chronic skin disease and the priest shall pronounce him unclean. He is not to put him in isolation, because he is already unclean.

12 "If the disease breaks out all over his skin and, so far as the priest can see, it covers all the skin of the infected person from head to foot, 13 the priest is to examine him, and if the disease has covered his whole body, he shall pronounce that person clean. Since it has all turned white, he is clean. 14 But whenever raw flesh appears on him, he will be unclean. 15 When the priest sees the raw flesh, he shall pronounce him unclean. The raw flesh is unclean; he has an infectious disease. 16 Should the raw flesh change and turn white, he must go to the priest. 17 The priest is to examine him, and if the sores have turned white, the priest shall pronounce the infected person clean; then he will be clean.

18 "When someone has a boil on his skin and it heals, 19 and in the place where the boil was, a white swelling or reddish-white spot appears, he must present himself to the priest. 20 The priest is to examine it, and if it appears to be more than skin deep and the hair in it has turned white, the priest shall pronounce him unclean. It is an infectious skin disease that has broken out where the boil was. 21 But if, when the priest examines it, there is no white hair in it and it is not more than skin deep and has faded, then the priest is to put him in isolation for seven days. 22 If it is spreading

[a] 2 Traditionally *leprosy*; the Hebrew word was used for various diseases affecting the skin—not necessarily leprosy; also elsewhere in this chapter. [b] 2 Or *descendants* [c] 3 Or *be lower than the rest of the skin*; also elsewhere in this chapter

in the skin, the priest shall pronounce him unclean; it is infectious. 23But if the spot is unchanged and has not spread, it is only a scar from
the boil, and the priest shall pronounce him
clean.
24"When someone has a burn on his skin and
a reddish-white or white spot appears in the raw
flesh of the burn, 25the priest is to examine the
spot, and if the hair in it has turned white, and it
appears to be more than skin deep, it is an infectious disease that has broken out in the burn. The
priest shall pronounce him unclean; it is an infectious skin disease. 26But if the priest examines it
and there is no white hair in the spot and if it is
not more than skin deep and has faded, then the
priest is to put him in isolation for seven days.
27On the seventh day the priest is to examine
him, and if it is spreading in the skin, the priest
shall pronounce him unclean; it is an infectious
skin disease. 28If, however, the spot is unchanged
and has not spread in the skin but has faded, it is
a swelling from the burn, and the priest shall
pronounce him clean; it is only a scar from the
burn.
29"If a man or woman has a sore on the head
or on the chin, 30the priest is to examine the
sore, and if it appears to be more than skin deep
and the hair in it is yellow and thin, the priest
shall pronounce that person unclean; it is an itch,
an infectious disease of the head or chin. 31But if,
when the priest examines this kind of sore, it
does not seem to be more than skin deep and
there is no black hair in it, then the priest is to
put the infected person in isolation for seven
days. 32On the seventh day the priest is to examine the sore, and if the itch has not spread and
there is no yellow hair in it and it does not appear
to be more than skin deep, 33he must be shaved
except for the diseased area, and the priest is to
keep him in isolation another seven days. 34On
the seventh day the priest is to examine the itch,
and if it has not spread in the skin and appears to
be no more than skin deep, the priest shall pronounce him clean. He must wash his clothes, and
he will be clean. 35But if the itch does spread in
the skin after he is pronounced clean, 36the priest
is to examine him, and if the itch has spread in
the skin, the priest does not need to look for
yellow hair; the person is unclean. 37If, however,
in his judgment it is unchanged and black hair
has grown in it, the itch is healed. He is clean,
and the priest shall pronounce him clean.
38"When a man or woman has white spots on
the skin, 39the priest is to examine them, and if
the spots are dull white, it is a harmless rash that
has broken out on the skin; that person is clean.
40"When a man has lost his hair and is bald, he
is clean. 41If he has lost his hair from the front of
his scalp and has a bald forehead, he is clean.
42But if he has a reddish-white sore on his bald
head or forehead, it is an infectious disease breaking out on his head or forehead. 43The priest is to
examine him, and if the swollen sore on his head
or forehead is reddish-white like an infectious
skin disease, 44the man is diseased and is unclean. The priest shall pronounce him unclean
because of the sore on his head.
45"The person with such an infectious disease
must wear torn clothes, let his hair be unkempt,[a] cover the lower part of his face and cry
out, 'Unclean! Unclean!' 46As long as he has the
infection he remains unclean. He must live alone;
he must live outside the camp.

Regulations About Mildew

47"If any clothing is contaminated with mildew—any woolen or linen clothing, 48any woven or knitted material of linen or wool, any
leather or anything made of leather— 49and if
the contamination in the clothing, or leather, or
woven or knitted material, or any leather article,
is greenish or reddish, it is a spreading mildew
and must be shown to the priest. 50The priest is
to examine the mildew and isolate the affected
article for seven days. 51On the seventh day he is
to examine it, and if the mildew has spread in the
clothing, or the woven or knitted material, or the
leather, whatever its use, it is a destructive mildew; the article is unclean. 52He must burn up
the clothing, or the woven or knitted material of
wool or linen, or any leather article that has the
contamination in it, because the mildew is destructive; the article must be burned up.
53"But if, when the priest examines it, the mildew has not spread in the clothing, or the woven
or knitted material, or the leather article, 54he
shall order that the contaminated article be
washed. Then he is to isolate it for another seven
days. 55After the affected article has been
washed, the priest is to examine it, and if the
mildew has not changed its appearance, even
though it has not spread, it is unclean. Burn it
with fire, whether the mildew has affected one
side or the other. 56If, when the priest examines
it, the mildew has faded after the article has been
washed, he is to tear the contaminated part out of
the clothing, or the leather, or the woven or knitted material. 57But if it reappears in the clothing,
or in the woven or knitted material, or in the
leather article, it is spreading, and whatever has
the mildew must be burned with fire. 58The
clothing, or the woven or knitted material, or any
leather article that has been washed and is rid of

[a] *45* Or *clothes, uncover his head*

the mildew, must be washed again, and it will be clean."

59These are the regulations concerning contamination by mildew in woolen or linen clothing, woven or knitted material, or any leather article, for pronouncing them clean or unclean.

Cleansing From Infectious Skin Diseases

14 The LORD said to Moses, 2"These are the regulations for the diseased person at the time of his ceremonial cleansing, when he is brought to the priest: 3The priest is to go outside the camp and examine him. If the person has been healed of his infectious skin disease,[a] 4the priest shall order that two live clean birds and some cedar wood, scarlet yarn and hyssop be brought for the one to be cleansed. 5Then the priest shall order that one of the birds be killed over fresh water in a clay pot. 6He is then to take the live bird and dip it, together with the cedar wood, the scarlet yarn and the hyssop, into the blood of the bird that was killed over the fresh water. 7Seven times he shall sprinkle the one to be cleansed of the infectious disease and pronounce him clean. Then he is to release the live bird in the open fields.

8"The person to be cleansed must wash his clothes, shave off all his hair and bathe with water; then he will be ceremonially clean. After this he may come into the camp, but he must stay outside his tent for seven days. 9On the seventh day he must shave off all his hair; he must shave his head, his beard, his eyebrows and the rest of his hair. He must wash his clothes and bathe himself with water, and he will be clean.

10"On the eighth day he must bring two male lambs and one ewe lamb a year old, each without defect, along with three-tenths of an ephah[b] of fine flour mixed with oil for a grain offering, and one log[c] of oil. 11The priest who pronounces him clean shall present both the one to be cleansed and his offerings before the LORD at the entrance to the Tent of Meeting.

12"Then the priest is to take one of the male lambs and offer it as a guilt offering, along with the log of oil; he shall wave them before the LORD as a wave offering. 13He is to slaughter the lamb in the holy place where the sin offering and the burnt offering are slaughtered. Like the sin offering, the guilt offering belongs to the priest; it is most holy. 14The priest is to take some of the blood of the guilt offering and put it on the lobe of the right ear of the one to be cleansed, on the thumb of his right hand and on the big toe of his right foot. 15The priest shall then take some of the log of oil, pour it in the palm of his own left hand, 16dip his right forefinger into the oil in his palm, and with his finger sprinkle some of it before the LORD seven times. 17The priest is to put some of the oil remaining in his palm on the lobe of the right ear of the one to be cleansed, on the thumb of his right hand and on the big toe of his right foot, on top of the blood of the guilt offering. 18The rest of the oil in his palm the priest shall put on the head of the one to be cleansed and make atonement for him before the LORD.

19"Then the priest is to sacrifice the sin offering and make atonement for the one to be cleansed from his uncleanness. After that, the priest shall slaughter the burnt offering 20and offer it on the altar, together with the grain offering, and make atonement for him, and he will be clean.

21"If, however, he is poor and cannot afford these, he must take one male lamb as a guilt offering to be waved to make atonement for him, together with a tenth of an ephah[d] of fine flour mixed with oil for a grain offering, a log of oil, 22and two doves or two young pigeons, which he can afford, one for a sin offering and the other for a burnt offering.

23"On the eighth day he must bring them for his cleansing to the priest at the entrance to the Tent of Meeting, before the LORD. 24The priest is to take the lamb for the guilt offering, together with the log of oil, and wave them before the LORD as a wave offering. 25He shall slaughter the lamb for the guilt offering and take some of its blood and put it on the lobe of the right ear of the one to be cleansed, on the thumb of his right hand and on the big toe of his right foot. 26The priest is to pour some of the oil into the palm of his own left hand, 27and with his right forefinger sprinkle some of the oil from his palm seven times before the LORD. 28Some of the oil in his palm he is to put on the same places he put the blood of the guilt offering—on the lobe of the right ear of the one to be cleansed, on the thumb of his right hand and on the big toe of his right foot. 29The rest of the oil in his palm the priest shall put on the head of the one to be cleansed, to make atonement for him before the LORD. 30Then he shall sacrifice the doves or the young pigeons, which the person can afford, 31one[e] as a sin offering and the other as a burnt offering, together with the grain offering. In this way the priest will make atonement before the LORD on behalf of the one to be cleansed."

32These are the regulations for anyone who

[a] *3* Traditionally *leprosy*; the Hebrew word was used for various diseases affecting the skin—not necessarily leprosy; also elsewhere in this chapter. [b] *10* That is, probably about 6 quarts (about 6.5 liters) [c] *10* That is, probably about 2/3 pint (about 0.3 liter); also in verses 12, 15, 21 and 24 [d] *21* That is, probably about 2 quarts (about 2 liters) [e] *31* Septuagint and Syriac; Hebrew *31such as the person can afford, one*

has an infectious skin disease and who cannot
afford the regular offerings for his cleansing.

Cleansing From Mildew

33The LORD said to Moses and Aaron, 34"When
you enter the land of Canaan, which I am giving
you as your possession, and I put a spreading
mildew in a house in that land, 35the owner of
the house must go and tell the priest, 'I have seen
something that looks like mildew in my house.'
36The priest is to order the house to be emptied
before he goes in to examine the mildew, so that
nothing in the house will be pronounced unclean. After this the priest is to go in and inspect
the house. 37He is to examine the mildew on the
walls, and if it has greenish or reddish depressions that appear to be deeper than the surface of
the wall, 38the priest shall go out the doorway of
the house and close it up for seven days. 39On the
seventh day the priest shall return to inspect the
house. If the mildew has spread on the walls,
40he is to order that the contaminated stones be
torn out and thrown into an unclean place outside the town. 41He must have all the inside walls
of the house scraped and the material that is
scraped off dumped into an unclean place outside
the town. 42Then they are to take other stones to
replace these and take new clay and plaster the
house.

43"If the mildew reappears in the house after
the stones have been torn out and the house
scraped and plastered, 44the priest is to go and
examine it and, if the mildew has spread in the
house, it is a destructive mildew; the house is
unclean. 45It must be torn down—its stones, timbers and all the plaster—and taken out of the
town to an unclean place.

46"Anyone who goes into the house while it is
closed up will be unclean till evening. 47Anyone
who sleeps or eats in the house must wash his
clothes.

48"But if the priest comes to examine it and
the mildew has not spread after the house has
been plastered, he shall pronounce the house
clean, because the mildew is gone. 49To purify
the house he is to take two birds and some cedar
wood, scarlet yarn and hyssop. 50He shall kill one
of the birds over fresh water in a clay pot. 51Then
he is to take the cedar wood, the hyssop, the
scarlet yarn and the live bird, dip them into the
blood of the dead bird and the fresh water, and
sprinkle the house seven times. 52He shall purify
the house with the bird's blood, the fresh water,
the live bird, the cedar wood, the hyssop and the
scarlet yarn. 53Then he is to release the live bird
in the open fields outside the town. In this way
he will make atonement for the house, and it will
be clean."

54These are the regulations for any infectious
skin disease, for an itch, 55for mildew in clothing
or in a house, 56and for a swelling, a rash or a
bright spot, 57to determine when something is
clean or unclean.

These are the regulations for infectious skin
diseases and mildew.

Discharges Causing Uncleanness

15 The LORD said to Moses and Aaron,
2"Speak to the Israelites and say to them:
'When any man has a bodily discharge, the discharge is unclean. 3Whether it continues flowing
from his body or is blocked, it will make him
unclean. This is how his discharge will bring
about uncleanness:

4" 'Any bed the man with a discharge lies on
will be unclean, and anything he sits on will be
unclean. 5Anyone who touches his bed must
wash his clothes and bathe with water, and he
will be unclean till evening. 6Whoever sits on
anything that the man with a discharge sat on
must wash his clothes and bathe with water, and
he will be unclean till evening.

7" 'Whoever touches the man who has a discharge must wash his clothes and bathe with water, and he will be unclean till evening.

8" 'If the man with the discharge spits on
someone who is clean, that person must wash his
clothes and bathe with water, and he will be
unclean till evening.

9" 'Everything the man sits on when riding
will be unclean, 10and whoever touches any of
the things that were under him will be unclean
till evening; whoever picks up those things must
wash his clothes and bathe with water, and he
will be unclean till evening.

11" 'Anyone the man with a discharge touches
without rinsing his hands with water must wash
his clothes and bathe with water, and he will be
unclean till evening.

12" 'A clay pot that the man touches must be
broken, and any wooden article is to be rinsed
with water.

13" 'When a man is cleansed from his discharge, he is to count off seven days for his ceremonial cleansing; he must wash his clothes and
bathe himself with fresh water, and he will be
clean. 14On the eighth day he must take two
doves or two young pigeons and come before the
LORD to the entrance to the Tent of Meeting and
give them to the priest. 15The priest is to sacrifice
them, the one for a sin offering and the other for
a burnt offering. In this way he will make atonement before the LORD for the man because of his
discharge.

16" 'When a man has an emission of semen, he
must bathe his whole body with water, and he
will be unclean till evening. 17Any clothing or
leather that has semen on it must be washed with

water, and it will be unclean till evening. 18When
a man lies with a woman and there is an emission
of semen, both must bathe with water, and they
will be unclean till evening.
19" 'When a woman has her regular flow of
blood, the impurity of her monthly period will
last seven days, and anyone who touches her will
be unclean till evening.
20" 'Anything she lies on during her period will
be unclean, and anything she sits on will be unclean. 21Whoever touches her bed must wash his
clothes and bathe with water, and he will be
unclean till evening. 22Whoever touches anything she sits on must wash his clothes and bathe
with water, and he will be unclean till evening.
23Whether it is the bed or anything she was sitting on, when anyone touches it, he will be unclean till evening.
24" 'If a man lies with her and her monthly
flow touches him, he will be unclean for seven
days; any bed he lies on will be unclean.
25" 'When a woman has a discharge of blood
for many days at a time other than her monthly
period or has a discharge that continues beyond
her period, she will be unclean as long as she has
the discharge, just as in the days of her period.
26Any bed she lies on while her discharge continues will be unclean, as is her bed during her
monthly period, and anything she sits on will
be unclean, as during her period. 27Whoever
touches them will be unclean; he must wash his
clothes and bathe with water, and he will be
unclean till evening.
28" 'When she is cleansed from her discharge,
she must count off seven days, and after that she
will be ceremonially clean. 29On the eighth day
she must take two doves or two young pigeons
and bring them to the priest at the entrance to
the Tent of Meeting. 30The priest is to sacrifice
one for a sin offering and the other for a burnt
offering. In this way he will make atonement for
her before the LORD for the uncleanness of her
discharge.
31" 'You must keep the Israelites separate from
things that make them unclean, so they will not
die in their uncleanness for defiling my dwelling
place,[a] which is among them.' "
32These are the regulations for a man with a
discharge, for anyone made unclean by an emission of semen, 33for a woman in her monthly
period, for a man or a woman with a discharge,
and for a man who lies with a woman who is
ceremonially unclean.

The Day of Atonement

16 The LORD spoke to Moses after the death
of the two sons of Aaron who died when
they approached the LORD. 2The LORD said to
Moses: "Tell your brother Aaron not to come
whenever he chooses into the Most Holy Place
behind the curtain in front of the atonement cover on the ark, or else he will die, because I appear
in the cloud over the atonement cover.
3"This is how Aaron is to enter the sanctuary
area: with a young bull for a sin offering and a
ram for a burnt offering. 4He is to put on the
sacred linen tunic, with linen undergarments
next to his body; he is to tie the linen sash around
him and put on the linen turban. These are sacred garments; so he must bathe himself with
water before he puts them on. 5From the Israelite
community he is to take two male goats for a sin
offering and a ram for a burnt offering.
6"Aaron is to offer the bull for his own sin
offering to make atonement for himself and his
household. 7Then he is to take the two goats and
present them before the LORD at the entrance to
the Tent of Meeting. 8He is to cast lots for the
two goats—one lot for the LORD and the other
for the scapegoat.[b] 9Aaron shall bring the goat
whose lot falls to the LORD and sacrifice it for a
sin offering. 10But the goat chosen by lot as the
scapegoat shall be presented alive before the
LORD to be used for making atonement by sending it into the desert as a scapegoat.
11"Aaron shall bring the bull for his own sin
offering to make atonement for himself and his
household, and he is to slaughter the bull for his
own sin offering. 12He is to take a censer full of
burning coals from the altar before the LORD and
two handfuls of finely ground fragrant incense
and take them behind the curtain. 13He is to put
the incense on the fire before the LORD, and the
smoke of the incense will conceal the atonement
cover above the Testimony, so that he will not
die. 14He is to take some of the bull's blood and
with his finger sprinkle it on the front of the
atonement cover; then he shall sprinkle some of
it with his finger seven times before the atonement cover.
15"He shall then slaughter the goat for the sin
offering for the people and take its blood behind
the curtain and do with it as he did with the
bull's blood: He shall sprinkle it on the atonement cover and in front of it. 16In this way he will
make atonement for the Most Holy Place because
of the uncleanness and rebellion of the Israelites,
whatever their sins have been. He is to do the
same for the Tent of Meeting, which is among
them in the midst of their uncleanness. 17No one
is to be in the Tent of Meeting from the time
Aaron goes in to make atonement in the Most
Holy Place until he comes out, having made

[a] 31 Or *my tabernacle* [b] 8 That is, the goat of removal; Hebrew *azazel*; also in verses 10 and 26

atonement for himself, his household and the
whole community of Israel.
18“Then he shall come out to the altar that is
before the LORD and make atonement for it. He
shall take some of the bull’s blood and some of
the goat’s blood and put it on all the horns of the
altar. 19He shall sprinkle some of the blood on it
with his finger seven times to cleanse it and to
consecrate it from the uncleanness of the Israelites.
20“When Aaron has finished making atonement for the Most Holy Place, the Tent of Meeting and the altar, he shall bring forward the live
goat. 21He is to lay both hands on the head of the
live goat and confess over it all the wickedness
and rebellion of the Israelites—all their sins—
and put them on the goat’s head. He shall send
the goat away into the desert in the care of a man
appointed for the task. 22The goat will carry on
itself all their sins to a solitary place; and the man
shall release it in the desert.
23“Then Aaron is to go into the Tent of Meeting and take off the linen garments he put on
before he entered the Most Holy Place, and he
is to leave them there. 24He shall bathe himself
with water in a holy place and put on his regular
garments. Then he shall come out and sacrifice
the burnt offering for himself and the burnt offering for the people, to make atonement for himself
and for the people. 25He shall also burn the fat of
the sin offering on the altar.
26“The man who releases the goat as a scapegoat must wash his clothes and bathe himself
with water; afterward he may come into the
camp. 27The bull and the goat for the sin offerings, whose blood was brought into the Most
Holy Place to make atonement, must be taken
outside the camp; their hides, flesh and offal are
to be burned up. 28The man who burns them
must wash his clothes and bathe himself with
water; afterward he may come into the camp.
29“This is to be a lasting ordinance for you: On
the tenth day of the seventh month you must
deny yourselves[a] and not do any work—
whether native-born or an alien living among
you— 30because on this day atonement will be
made for you, to cleanse you. Then, before the
LORD, you will be clean from all your sins. 31It is
a sabbath of rest, and you must deny yourselves;
it is a lasting ordinance. 32The priest who is
anointed and ordained to succeed his father as
high priest is to make atonement. He is to put on
the sacred linen garments 33and make atonement
for the Most Holy Place, for the Tent of Meeting
and the altar, and for the priests and all the people of the community.
34“This is to be a lasting ordinance for you:
Atonement is to be made once a year for all the
sins of the Israelites.”
And it was done, as the LORD commanded Moses.

Eating Blood Forbidden

17 The LORD said to Moses, 2“Speak to Aaron and his sons and to all the Israelites
and say to them: ‘This is what the LORD has commanded: 3Any Israelite who sacrifices an ox,[b] a
lamb or a goat in the camp or outside of it 4in-
stead of bringing it to the entrance to the Tent of
Meeting to present it as an offering to the LORD
in front of the tabernacle of the LORD—that man
shall be considered guilty of bloodshed; he has
shed blood and must be cut off from his people.
5This is so the Israelites will bring to the LORD
the sacrifices they are now making in the open
fields. They must bring them to the priest, that is,
to the LORD, at the entrance to the Tent of Meeting and sacrifice them as fellowship offerings.[c]
6The priest is to sprinkle the blood against the
altar of the LORD at the entrance to the Tent of
Meeting and burn the fat as an aroma pleasing to
the LORD. 7They must no longer offer any of their
sacrifices to the goat idols[d] to whom they prostitute themselves. This is to be a lasting ordinance
for them and for the generations to come.’
8“Say to them: ‘Any Israelite or any alien living
among them who offers a burnt offering or sacrifice 9and does not bring it to the entrance to the
Tent of Meeting to sacrifice it to the LORD—that
man must be cut off from his people.
10“ ‘Any Israelite or any alien living among
them who eats any blood—I will set my face
against that person who eats blood and will cut
him off from his people. 11For the life of a creature is in the blood, and I have given it to you to
make atonement for yourselves on the altar; it is
the blood that makes atonement for one’s life.
12Therefore I say to the Israelites, “None of you
may eat blood, nor may an alien living among you
eat blood.”
13“ ‘Any Israelite or any alien living among you
who hunts any animal or bird that may be eaten
must drain out the blood and cover it with earth,
14because the life of every creature is its blood.
That is why I have said to the Israelites, “You
must not eat the blood of any creature, because
the life of every creature is its blood; anyone who
eats it must be cut off.”
15“ ‘Anyone, whether native-born or alien,
who eats anything found dead or torn by wild
animals must wash his clothes and bathe with
water, and he will be ceremonially unclean till

[a]29 Or *must fast*; also in verse 31 [b]3 The Hebrew word can include both male and female. [c]5 Traditionally *peace offerings*
[d]7 Or *demons*

evening; then he will be clean. [16]But if he does not wash his clothes and bathe himself, he will be held responsible.’ ”

Unlawful Sexual Relations

18 The LORD said to Moses, [2]“Speak to the Israelites and say to them: ‘I am the LORD your God. [3]You must not do as they do in Egypt, where you used to live, and you must not do as they do in the land of Canaan, where I am bringing you. Do not follow their practices. [4]You must obey my laws and be careful to follow my decrees. I am the LORD your God. [5]Keep my decrees and laws, for the man who obeys them will live by them. I am the LORD.

[6]“ ‘No one is to approach any close relative to have sexual relations. I am the LORD.

[7]“ ‘Do not dishonor your father by having sexual relations with your mother. She is your mother; do not have relations with her.

[8]“ ‘Do not have sexual relations with your father’s wife; that would dishonor your father.

[9]“ ‘Do not have sexual relations with your sister, either your father’s daughter or your mother’s daughter, whether she was born in the same home or elsewhere.

[10]“ ‘Do not have sexual relations with your son’s daughter or your daughter’s daughter; that would dishonor you.

[11]“ ‘Do not have sexual relations with the daughter of your father’s wife, born to your father; she is your sister.

[12]“ ‘Do not have sexual relations with your father’s sister; she is your father’s close relative.

[13]“ ‘Do not have sexual relations with your mother’s sister, because she is your mother’s close relative.

[14]“ ‘Do not dishonor your father’s brother by approaching his wife to have sexual relations; she is your aunt.

[15]“ ‘Do not have sexual relations with your daughter-in-law. She is your son’s wife; do not have relations with her.

[16]“ ‘Do not have sexual relations with your brother’s wife; that would dishonor your brother.

[17]“ ‘Do not have sexual relations with both a woman and her daughter. Do not have sexual relations with either her son’s daughter or her daughter’s daughter; they are her close relatives. That is wickedness.

[18]“ ‘Do not take your wife’s sister as a rival wife and have sexual relations with her while your wife is living.

[19]“ ‘Do not approach a woman to have sexual relations during the uncleanness of her monthly period.

[20]“ ‘Do not have sexual relations with your neighbor’s wife and defile yourself with her.

[21]“ ‘Do not give any of your children to be sacrificed[a] to Molech, for you must not profane the name of your God. I am the LORD.

[22]“ ‘Do not lie with a man as one lies with a woman; that is detestable.

[23]“ ‘Do not have sexual relations with an animal and defile yourself with it. A woman must not present herself to an animal to have sexual relations with it; that is a perversion.

[24]“ ‘Do not defile yourselves in any of these ways, because this is how the nations that I am going to drive out before you became defiled. [25]Even the land was defiled; so I punished it for its sin, and the land vomited out its inhabitants. [26]But you must keep my decrees and my laws. The native-born and the aliens living among you must not do any of these detestable things, [27]for all these things were done by the people who lived in the land before you, and the land became defiled. [28]And if you defile the land, it will vomit you out as it vomited out the nations that were before you.

[29]“ ‘Everyone who does any of these detestable things—such persons must be cut off from their people. [30]Keep my requirements and do not follow any of the detestable customs that were practiced before you came and do not defile yourselves with them. I am the LORD your God.’ ”

Various Laws

19 The LORD said to Moses, [2]“Speak to the entire assembly of Israel and say to them: ‘Be holy because I, the LORD your God, am holy.

[3]“ ‘Each of you must respect his mother and father, and you must observe my Sabbaths. I am the LORD your God.

[4]“ ‘Do not turn to idols or make gods of cast metal for yourselves. I am the LORD your God.

[5]“ ‘When you sacrifice a fellowship offering[b] to the LORD, sacrifice it in such a way that it will be accepted on your behalf. [6]It shall be eaten on the day you sacrifice it or on the next day; anything left over until the third day must be burned up. [7]If any of it is eaten on the third day, it is impure and will not be accepted. [8]Whoever eats it will be held responsible because he has desecrated what is holy to the LORD; that person must be cut off from his people.

[9]“ ‘When you reap the harvest of your land, do not reap to the very edges of your field or gather the gleanings of your harvest. [10]Do not go over your vineyard a second time or pick up the grapes that have fallen. Leave them for the poor and the alien. I am the LORD your God.

[11]“ ‘Do not steal.

[a]*21* Or *to be passed through* ⌞*the fire*⌟ [b]*5* Traditionally *peace offering*

“ ‘Do not lie.
“ ‘Do not deceive one another.
12“ ‘Do not swear falsely by my name and so
profane the name of your God. I am the LORD.
13“ ‘Do not defraud your neighbor or rob him.
“ ‘Do not hold back the wages of a hired man
overnight.
14“ ‘Do not curse the deaf or put a stumbling
block in front of the blind, but fear your God. I
am the LORD.
15“ ‘Do not pervert justice; do not show partiality to the poor or favoritism to the great, but
judge your neighbor fairly.
16“ ‘Do not go about spreading slander among
your people.
“ ‘Do not do anything that endangers your
neighbor’s life. I am the LORD.
17“ ‘Do not hate your brother in your heart.
Rebuke your neighbor frankly so you will not
share in his guilt.
18“ ‘Do not seek revenge or bear a grudge
against one of your people, but love your neighbor as yourself. I am the LORD.
19“ ‘Keep my decrees.
“ ‘Do not mate different kinds of animals.
“ ‘Do not plant your field with two kinds of
seed.
“ ‘Do not wear clothing woven of two kinds of
material.
20“ ‘If a man sleeps with a woman who is a
slave girl promised to another man but who has
not been ransomed or given her freedom, there
must be due punishment. Yet they are not to be
put to death, because she had not been freed.
21The man, however, must bring a ram to the
entrance to the Tent of Meeting for a guilt offering to the LORD. 22With the ram of the guilt offering the priest is to make atonement for him before the LORD for the sin he has committed, and
his sin will be forgiven.
23“ ‘When you enter the land and plant any
kind of fruit tree, regard its fruit as forbidden.[a]
For three years you are to consider it forbidden[a]; it must not be eaten. 24In the fourth year
all its fruit will be holy, an offering of praise to the
LORD. 25But in the fifth year you may eat its fruit.
In this way your harvest will be increased. I am
the LORD your God.
26“ ‘Do not eat any meat with the blood still
in it.
“ ‘Do not practice divination or sorcery.
27“ ‘Do not cut the hair at the sides of your
head or clip off the edges of your beard.
28“ ‘Do not cut your bodies for the dead or put
tattoo marks on yourselves. I am the LORD.
29“ ‘Do not degrade your daughter by making
her a prostitute, or the land will turn to prostitution and be filled with wickedness.
30“ ‘Observe my Sabbaths and have reverence
for my sanctuary. I am the LORD.
31“ ‘Do not turn to mediums or seek out spiritists, for you will be defiled by them. I am the
LORD your God.
32“ ‘Rise in the presence of the aged, show
respect for the elderly and revere your God. I am
the LORD.
33“ ‘When an alien lives with you in your land,
do not mistreat him. 34The alien living with you
must be treated as one of your native-born. Love
him as yourself, for you were aliens in Egypt. I am
the LORD your God.
35“ ‘Do not use dishonest standards when measuring length, weight or quantity. 36Use honest
scales and honest weights, an honest ephah[b]
and an honest hin.[c] I am the LORD your God,
who brought you out of Egypt.
37“ ‘Keep all my decrees and all my laws and
follow them. I am the LORD.’ ”

Punishments for Sin

20 The LORD said to Moses, 2“Say to the Israelites: ‘Any Israelite or any alien living in
Israel who gives[d] any of his children to Molech
must be put to death. The people of the community are to stone him. 3I will set my face against
that man and I will cut him off from his people;
for by giving his children to Molech, he has defiled my sanctuary and profaned my holy name.
4If the people of the community close their eyes
when that man gives one of his children to Molech and they fail to put him to death, 5I will set
my face against that man and his family and will
cut off from their people both him and all who
follow him in prostituting themselves to Molech.
6“ ‘I will set my face against the person who
turns to mediums and spiritists to prostitute himself by following them, and I will cut him off from
his people.
7“ ‘Consecrate yourselves and be holy, because
I am the LORD your God. 8Keep my decrees and
follow them. I am the LORD, who makes you
holy.[e]
9“ ‘If anyone curses his father or mother, he
must be put to death. He has cursed his father or
his mother, and his blood will be on his own
head.
10“ ‘If a man commits adultery with another
man’s wife—with the wife of his neighbor—
both the adulterer and the adulteress must be put
to death.
11“ ‘If a man sleeps with his father’s wife, he
has dishonored his father. Both the man and the

[a]23 Hebrew *uncircumcised* [b]36 An ephah was a dry measure. [c]36 A hin was a liquid measure. [d]2 Or *sacrifices*; also in verses 3 and 4 [e]8 Or *who sanctifies you*; or *who sets you apart as holy*

woman must be put to death; their blood will be
on their own heads.
12“ ‘If a man sleeps with his daughter-in-law,
both of them must be put to death. What they
have done is a perversion; their blood will be on
their own heads.
13“ ‘If a man lies with a man as one lies with a
woman, both of them have done what is detestable. They must be put to death; their blood will
be on their own heads.
14“ ‘If a man marries both a woman and her
mother, it is wicked. Both he and they must be
burned in the fire, so that no wickedness will be
among you.
15“ ‘If a man has sexual relations with an animal, he must be put to death, and you must kill
the animal.
16“ ‘If a woman approaches an animal to have
sexual relations with it, kill both the woman and
the animal. They must be put to death; their
blood will be on their own heads.
17“ ‘If a man marries his sister, the daughter of
either his father or his mother, and they have
sexual relations, it is a disgrace. They must be cut
off before the eyes of their people. He has dishonored his sister and will be held responsible.
18“ ‘If a man lies with a woman during her
monthly period and has sexual relations with her,
he has exposed the source of her flow, and she
has also uncovered it. Both of them must be cut
off from their people.
19“ ‘Do not have sexual relations with the sister of either your mother or your father, for that
would dishonor a close relative; both of you
would be held responsible.
20“ ‘If a man sleeps with his aunt, he has dishonored his uncle. They will be held responsible;
they will die childless.
21“ ‘If a man marries his brother’s wife, it is an
act of impurity; he has dishonored his brother.
They will be childless.
22“ ‘Keep all my decrees and laws and follow
them, so that the land where I am bringing you
to live may not vomit you out. 23You must not
live according to the customs of the nations I am
going to drive out before you. Because they did all
these things, I abhorred them. 24But I said to you,
“You will possess their land; I will give it to you
as an inheritance, a land flowing with milk and
honey.” I am the LORD your God, who has set you
apart from the nations.
25“ ‘You must therefore make a distinction between clean and unclean animals and between
unclean and clean birds. Do not defile yourselves
by any animal or bird or anything that moves
along the ground—those which I have set apart
as unclean for you. 26You are to be holy to me[a]
because I, the LORD, am holy, and I have set you
apart from the nations to be my own.
27“ ‘A man or woman who is a medium or
spiritist among you must be put to death. You are
to stone them; their blood will be on their own
heads.’ ”

Rules for Priests

21 The LORD said to Moses, “Speak to the
priests, the sons of Aaron, and say to
them: ‘A priest must not make himself ceremonially unclean for any of his people who die, 2ex-
cept for a close relative, such as his mother or
father, his son or daughter, his brother, 3or an
unmarried sister who is dependent on him since
she has no husband—for her he may make himself unclean. 4He must not make himself unclean
for people related to him by marriage,[b] and so
defile himself.
5“ ‘Priests must not shave their heads or shave
off the edges of their beards or cut their bodies.
6They must be holy to their God and must not
profane the name of their God. Because they
present the offerings made to the LORD by fire,
the food of their God, they are to be holy.
7“ ‘They must not marry women defiled by
prostitution or divorced from their husbands, because priests are holy to their God. 8Regard them
as holy, because they offer up the food of your
God. Consider them holy, because I the LORD am
holy—I who make you holy.[c]
9“ ‘If a priest’s daughter defiles herself by becoming a prostitute, she disgraces her father; she
must be burned in the fire.
10“ ‘The high priest, the one among his brothers who has had the anointing oil poured on his
head and who has been ordained to wear the
priestly garments, must not let his hair become
unkempt[d] or tear his clothes. 11He must not
enter a place where there is a dead body. He
must not make himself unclean, even for his father or mother, 12nor leave the sanctuary of his
God or desecrate it, because he has been dedicated by the anointing oil of his God. I am the LORD.
13“ ‘The woman he marries must be a virgin.
14He must not marry a widow, a divorced woman, or a woman defiled by prostitution, but only
a virgin from his own people, 15so he will not
defile his offspring among his people. I am the
LORD, who makes him holy.[e]’ ”
16The LORD said to Moses, 17“Say to Aaron:
‘For the generations to come none of your
descendants who has a defect may come near to
offer the food of his God. 18No man who has any
defect may come near: no man who is blind or

[a]26 Or *be my holy ones* [b]4 Or *unclean as a leader among his people* [c]8 Or *who sanctify you*; or *who set you apart as holy*
[d]10 Or *not uncover his head* [e]15 Or *who sanctifies him*; or *who sets him apart as holy*

lame, disfigured or deformed; 19no man with a
crippled foot or hand, 20or who is hunchbacked
or dwarfed, or who has any eye defect, or who
has festering or running sores or damaged testi-
cles. 21No descendant of Aaron the priest who
has any defect is to come near to present the
offerings made to the LORD by fire. He has a defect; he must not come near to offer the food of
his God. 22He may eat the most holy food of his
God, as well as the holy food; 23yet because of his
defect, he must not go near the curtain or approach the altar, and so desecrate my sanctuary.
I am the LORD, who makes them holy.[a]' "
24So Moses told this to Aaron and his sons and
to all the Israelites.

22 The LORD said to Moses, 2"Tell Aaron and
his sons to treat with respect the sacred
offerings the Israelites consecrate to me, so they
will not profane my holy name. I am the LORD.
3"Say to them: 'For the generations to come, if
any of your descendants is ceremonially unclean
and yet comes near the sacred offerings that the
Israelites consecrate to the LORD, that person
must be cut off from my presence. I am the LORD.
4" 'If a descendant of Aaron has an infectious
skin disease[b] or a bodily discharge, he may not
eat the sacred offerings until he is cleansed. He
will also be unclean if he touches something defiled by a corpse or by anyone who has an emission of semen, 5or if he touches any crawling
thing that makes him unclean, or any person who
makes him unclean, whatever the uncleanness
may be. 6The one who touches any such thing
will be unclean till evening. He must not eat any
of the sacred offerings unless he has bathed himself with water. 7When the sun goes down, he
will be clean, and after that he may eat the sacred
offerings, for they are his food. 8He must not eat
anything found dead or torn by wild animals, and
so become unclean through it. I am the LORD.
9" 'The priests are to keep my requirements so
that they do not become guilty and die for treating them with contempt. I am the LORD, who
makes them holy.[c]
10" 'No one outside a priest's family may eat
the sacred offering, nor may the guest of a priest
or his hired worker eat it. 11But if a priest buys a
slave with money, or if a slave is born in his
household, that slave may eat his food. 12If a
priest's daughter marries anyone other than a
priest, she may not eat any of the sacred contributions. 13But if a priest's daughter becomes a widow or is divorced, yet has no children, and she
returns to live in her father's house as in her
youth, she may eat of her father's food. No unauthorized person, however, may eat any of it.
14" 'If anyone eats a sacred offering by mistake,
he must make restitution to the priest for the
offering and add a fifth of the value to it. 15The
priests must not desecrate the sacred offerings
the Israelites present to the LORD 16by allowing
them to eat the sacred offerings and so bring
upon them guilt requiring payment. I am the
LORD, who makes them holy.' "

Unacceptable Sacrifices

17The LORD said to Moses, 18"Speak to Aaron
and his sons and to all the Israelites and say to
them: 'If any of you—either an Israelite or an
alien living in Israel—presents a gift for a burnt
offering to the LORD, either to fulfill a vow or as
a freewill offering, 19you must present a male
without defect from the cattle, sheep or goats in
order that it may be accepted on your behalf.
20Do not bring anything with a defect, because it
will not be accepted on your behalf. 21When anyone brings from the herd or flock a fellowship
offering[d] to the LORD to fulfill a special vow or
as a freewill offering, it must be without defect or
blemish to be acceptable. 22Do not offer to the
LORD the blind, the injured or the maimed, or
anything with warts or festering or running
sores. Do not place any of these on the altar as an
offering made to the LORD by fire. 23You may,
however, present as a freewill offering an ox[e] or
a sheep that is deformed or stunted, but it will
not be accepted in fulfillment of a vow. 24You
must not offer to the LORD an animal whose testi-
cles are bruised, crushed, torn or cut. You must
not do this in your own land, 25and you must not
accept such animals from the hand of a foreigner
and offer them as the food of your God. They will
not be accepted on your behalf, because they are
deformed and have defects.' "
26The LORD said to Moses, 27"When a calf, a
lamb or a goat is born, it is to remain with its
mother for seven days. From the eighth day on,
it will be acceptable as an offering made to the
LORD by fire. 28Do not slaughter a cow or a sheep
and its young on the same day.
29"When you sacrifice a thank offering to the
LORD, sacrifice it in such a way that it will be
accepted on your behalf. 30It must be eaten that
same day; leave none of it till morning. I am the
LORD.
31"Keep my commands and follow them. I am
the LORD. 32Do not profane my holy name. I must
be acknowledged as holy by the Israelites. I am
the LORD, who makes[f] you holy[g] 33and who

a23 Or *who sanctifies them*; or *who sets them apart as holy* b4 Traditionally *leprosy*; the Hebrew word was used for various diseases affecting the skin—not necessarily leprosy. c9 Or *who sanctifies them*; or *who sets them apart as holy*; also in verse 16 d21 Traditionally *peace offering* e23 The Hebrew word can include both male and female. f32 Or *made* g32 Or *who sanctifies you*; or *who sets you apart as holy* brought you out of Egypt to be your God. I am the LORD.”

23

The LORD said to Moses, [2]“Speak to the Israelites and say to them: ‘These are my appointed feasts, the appointed feasts of the LORD, which you are to proclaim as sacred assemblies.

The Sabbath

[3]“ ‘There are six days when you may work, but the seventh day is a Sabbath of rest, a day of sacred assembly. You are not to do any work; wherever you live, it is a Sabbath to the LORD.

The Passover and Unleavened Bread

[4]“ ‘These are the LORD’s appointed feasts, the sacred assemblies you are to proclaim at their appointed times: [5]The LORD’s Passover begins at twilight on the fourteenth day of the first month. [6]On the fifteenth day of that month the LORD’s Feast of Unleavened Bread begins; for seven days you must eat bread made without yeast. [7]On the first day hold a sacred assembly and do no regular work. [8]For seven days present an offering made to the LORD by fire. And on the seventh day hold a sacred assembly and do no regular work.’ ”

Firstfruits

[9]The LORD said to Moses, [10]“Speak to the Israelites and say to them: ‘When you enter the land I am going to give you and you reap its harvest, bring to the priest a sheaf of the first grain you harvest. [11]He is to wave the sheaf before the LORD so it will be accepted on your behalf; the priest is to wave it on the day after the Sabbath. [12]On the day you wave the sheaf, you must sacrifice as a burnt offering to the LORD a lamb a year old without defect, [13]together with its grain offering of two-tenths of an ephah[a] of fine flour mixed with oil—an offering made to the LORD by fire, a pleasing aroma—and its drink offering of a quarter of a hin[b] of wine. [14]You must not eat any bread, or roasted or new grain, until the very day you bring this offering to your God. This is to be a lasting ordinance for the generations to come, wherever you live.

Feast of Weeks

[15]“ ‘From the day after the Sabbath, the day you brought the sheaf of the wave offering, count off seven full weeks. [16]Count off fifty days up to the day after the seventh Sabbath, and then present an offering of new grain to the LORD. [17]From wherever you live, bring two loaves made of two-tenths of an ephah of fine flour, baked with yeast, as a wave offering of firstfruits to the LORD. [18]Present with this bread seven male lambs, each a year old and without defect, one young bull and two rams. They will be a burnt offering to the LORD, together with their grain offerings and drink offerings—an offering made by fire, an aroma pleasing to the LORD. [19]Then sacrifice one male goat for a sin offering and two lambs, each a year old, for a fellowship offering.[c] [20]The priest is to wave the two lambs before the LORD as a wave offering, together with the bread of the firstfruits. They are a sacred offering to the LORD for the priest. [21]On that same day you are to proclaim a sacred assembly and do no regular work. This is to be a lasting ordinance for the generations to come, wherever you live.

[22]“ ‘When you reap the harvest of your land, do not reap to the very edges of your field or gather the gleanings of your harvest. Leave them for the poor and the alien. I am the LORD your God.’ ”

Feast of Trumpets

[23]The LORD said to Moses, [24]“Say to the Israelites: ‘On the first day of the seventh month you are to have a day of rest, a sacred assembly commemorated with trumpet blasts. [25]Do no regular work, but present an offering made to the LORD by fire.’ ”

Day of Atonement

[26]The LORD said to Moses, [27]“The tenth day of this seventh month is the Day of Atonement. Hold a sacred assembly and deny yourselves,[d] and present an offering made to the LORD by fire. [28]Do no work on that day, because it is the Day of Atonement, when atonement is made for you before the LORD your God. [29]Anyone who does not deny himself on that day must be cut off from his people. [30]I will destroy from among his people anyone who does any work on that day. [31]You shall do no work at all. This is to be a lasting ordinance for the generations to come, wherever you live. [32]It is a sabbath of rest for you, and you must deny yourselves. From the evening of the ninth day of the month until the following evening you are to observe your sabbath.”

Feast of Tabernacles

[33]The LORD said to Moses, [34]“Say to the Israelites: ‘On the fifteenth day of the seventh month the LORD’s Feast of Tabernacles begins, and it lasts for seven days. [35]The first day is a sacred assembly; do no regular work. [36]For seven days

[a] *13* That is, probably about 4 quarts (about 4.5 liters); also in verse 17 [b] *13* That is, probably about 1 quart (about 1 liter)
[c] *19* Traditionally *peace offering* [d] *27* Or *and fast*; also in verses 29 and 32

present offerings made to the LORD by fire, and on the eighth day hold a sacred assembly and present an offering made to the LORD by fire. It is the closing assembly; do no regular work.

37(" 'These are the LORD's appointed feasts, which you are to proclaim as sacred assemblies for bringing offerings made to the LORD by fire—the burnt offerings and grain offerings, sacrifices and drink offerings required for each day. 38These offerings are in addition to those for the LORD's Sabbaths and[a] in addition to your gifts and whatever you have vowed and all the freewill offerings you give to the LORD.)

39" 'So beginning with the fifteenth day of the seventh month, after you have gathered the crops of the land, celebrate the festival to the LORD for seven days; the first day is a day of rest, and the eighth day also is a day of rest. 40On the first day you are to take choice fruit from the trees, and palm fronds, leafy branches and poplars, and rejoice before the LORD your God for seven days. 41Celebrate this as a festival to the LORD for seven days each year. This is to be a lasting ordinance for the generations to come; celebrate it in the seventh month. 42Live in booths for seven days: All native-born Israelites are to live in booths 43so your descendants will know that I had the Israelites live in booths when I brought them out of Egypt. I am the LORD your God.' "

44So Moses announced to the Israelites the appointed feasts of the LORD.

Oil and Bread Set Before the LORD

24 The LORD said to Moses, 2"Command the Israelites to bring you clear oil of pressed olives for the light so that the lamps may be kept burning continually. 3Outside the curtain of the Testimony in the Tent of Meeting, Aaron is to tend the lamps before the LORD from evening till morning, continually. This is to be a lasting ordinance for the generations to come. 4The lamps on the pure gold lampstand before the LORD must be tended continually.

5"Take fine flour and bake twelve loaves of bread, using two-tenths of an ephah[b] for each loaf. 6Set them in two rows, six in each row, on the table of pure gold before the LORD. 7Along each row put some pure incense as a memorial portion to represent the bread and to be an offering made to the LORD by fire. 8This bread is to be set out before the LORD regularly, Sabbath after Sabbath, on behalf of the Israelites, as a lasting covenant. 9It belongs to Aaron and his sons, who are to eat it in a holy place, because it is a most holy part of their regular share of the offerings made to the LORD by fire."

A Blasphemer Stoned

10Now the son of an Israelite mother and an Egyptian father went out among the Israelites, and a fight broke out in the camp between him and an Israelite. 11The son of the Israelite woman blasphemed the Name with a curse; so they brought him to Moses. (His mother's name was Shelomith, the daughter of Dibri the Danite.) 12They put him in custody until the will of the LORD should be made clear to them.

13Then the LORD said to Moses: 14"Take the blasphemer outside the camp. All those who heard him are to lay their hands on his head, and the entire assembly is to stone him. 15Say to the Israelites: 'If anyone curses his God, he will be held responsible; 16anyone who blasphemes the name of the LORD must be put to death. The entire assembly must stone him. Whether an alien or native-born, when he blasphemes the Name, he must be put to death.

17" 'If anyone takes the life of a human being, he must be put to death. 18Anyone who takes the life of someone's animal must make restitution—life for life. 19If anyone injures his neighbor, whatever he has done must be done to him: 20fracture for fracture, eye for eye, tooth for tooth. As he has injured the other, so he is to be injured. 21Whoever kills an animal must make restitution, but whoever kills a man must be put to death. 22You are to have the same law for the alien and the native-born. I am the LORD your God.' "

23Then Moses spoke to the Israelites, and they took the blasphemer outside the camp and stoned him. The Israelites did as the LORD commanded Moses.

The Sabbath Year

25 The LORD said to Moses on Mount Sinai, 2"Speak to the Israelites and say to them: 'When you enter the land I am going to give you, the land itself must observe a sabbath to the LORD. 3For six years sow your fields, and for six years prune your vineyards and gather their crops. 4But in the seventh year the land is to have a sabbath of rest, a sabbath to the LORD. Do not sow your fields or prune your vineyards. 5Do not reap what grows of itself or harvest the grapes of your untended vines. The land is to have a year of rest. 6Whatever the land yields during the sabbath year will be food for you—for yourself, your manservant and maidservant, and the hired worker and temporary resident who live among you, 7as well as for your livestock and the wild animals in your land. Whatever the land produces may be eaten.

[a]38 Or *These feasts are in addition to the LORD's Sabbaths, and these offerings are* [b]5 That is, probably about 4 quarts (about 4.5 liters)

The Year of Jubilee

8“ ‘Count off seven sabbaths of years—seven
times seven years—so that the seven sabbaths
of years amount to a period of forty-nine years.
9Then have the trumpet sounded everywhere on
the tenth day of the seventh month; on the Day
of Atonement sound the trumpet throughout
your land. 10Consecrate the fiftieth year and proclaim liberty throughout the land to all its inhabitants. It shall be a jubilee for you; each one of you
is to return to his family property and each to his
own clan. 11The fiftieth year shall be a jubilee for
you; do not sow and do not reap what grows of
itself or harvest the untended vines. 12For it is a
jubilee and is to be holy for you; eat only what is
taken directly from the fields.

13“ ‘In this Year of Jubilee everyone is to return
to his own property.

14“ ‘If you sell land to one of your countrymen
or buy any from him, do not take advantage of
each other. 15You are to buy from your countryman on the basis of the number of years since the
Jubilee. And he is to sell to you on the basis of the
number of years left for harvesting crops. 16When
the years are many, you are to increase the price,
and when the years are few, you are to decrease
the price, because what he is really selling you is
the number of crops. 17Do not take advantage of
each other, but fear your God. I am the LORD your
God.

18“ ‘Follow my decrees and be careful to obey
my laws, and you will live safely in the land.
19Then the land will yield its fruit, and you will
eat your fill and live there in safety. 20You may
ask, “What will we eat in the seventh year if we
do not plant or harvest our crops?” 21I will send
you such a blessing in the sixth year that the land
will yield enough for three years. 22While you
plant during the eighth year, you will eat from
the old crop and will continue to eat from it until
the harvest of the ninth year comes in.

23“ ‘The land must not be sold permanently,
because the land is mine and you are but aliens
and my tenants. 24Throughout the country that
you hold as a possession, you must provide for
the redemption of the land.

25“ ‘If one of your countrymen becomes poor
and sells some of his property, his nearest relative is to come and redeem what his countryman
has sold. 26If, however, a man has no one to
redeem it for him but he himself prospers and
acquires sufficient means to redeem it, 27he is to
determine the value for the years since he sold it
and refund the balance to the man to whom he
sold it; he can then go back to his own property.
28But if he does not acquire the means to repay
him, what he sold will remain in the possession
of the buyer until the Year of Jubilee. It will be
returned in the Jubilee, and he can then go back
to his property.

29“ ‘If a man sells a house in a walled city, he
retains the right of redemption a full year after its
sale. During that time he may redeem it. 30If it is
not redeemed before a full year has passed, the
house in the walled city shall belong permanently
to the buyer and his descendants. It is not to be
returned in the Jubilee. 31But houses in villages
without walls around them are to be considered
as open country. They can be redeemed, and they
are to be returned in the Jubilee.

32“ ‘The Levites always have the right to redeem their houses in the Levitical towns, which
they possess. 33So the property of the Levites is
redeemable—that is, a house sold in any town
they hold—and is to be returned in the Jubilee,
because the houses in the towns of the Levites
are their property among the Israelites. 34But the
pastureland belonging to their towns must not be
sold; it is their permanent possession.

35“ ‘If one of your countrymen becomes poor
and is unable to support himself among you, help
him as you would an alien or a temporary resident, so he can continue to live among you. 36Do
not take interest of any kind[a] from him, but fear
your God, so that your countryman may continue
to live among you. 37You must not lend him money at interest or sell him food at a profit. 38I am
the LORD your God, who brought you out of Egypt
to give you the land of Canaan and to be your
God.

39“ ‘If one of your countrymen becomes poor
among you and sells himself to you, do not make
him work as a slave. 40He is to be treated as a
hired worker or a temporary resident among you;
he is to work for you until the Year of Jubilee.
41Then he and his children are to be released,
and he will go back to his own clan and to the
property of his forefathers. 42Because the Israelites are my servants, whom I brought out of
Egypt, they must not be sold as slaves. 43Do not
rule over them ruthlessly, but fear your God.

44“ ‘Your male and female slaves are to come
from the nations around you; from them you may
buy slaves. 45You may also buy some of the temporary residents living among you and members
of their clans born in your country, and they will
become your property. 46You can will them to
your children as inherited property and can make
them slaves for life, but you must not rule over
your fellow Israelites ruthlessly.

47“ ‘If an alien or a temporary resident among
you becomes rich and one of your countrymen
becomes poor and sells himself to the alien living

[a]*36* Or *take excessive interest*; similarly in verse 37

among you or to a member of the alien’s clan,
48he retains the right of redemption after he has
sold himself. One of his relatives may redeem
him: 49An uncle or a cousin or any blood relative
in his clan may redeem him. Or if he prospers, he
may redeem himself. 50He and his buyer are to
count the time from the year he sold himself up
to the Year of Jubilee. The price for his release is
to be based on the rate paid to a hired man for
that number of years. 51If many years remain, he
must pay for his redemption a larger share of the
price paid for him. 52If only a few years remain
until the Year of Jubilee, he is to compute that
and pay for his redemption accordingly. 53He is to
be treated as a man hired from year to year; you
must see to it that his owner does not rule over
him ruthlessly.
54“ ‘Even if he is not redeemed in any of these
ways, he and his children are to be released in
the Year of Jubilee, 55for the Israelites belong to
me as servants. They are my servants, whom I
brought out of Egypt. I am the LORD your God.

Reward for Obedience

26 “ ‘Do not make idols or set up an image or
a sacred stone for yourselves, and do not
place a carved stone in your land to bow down
before it. I am the LORD your God.
2“ ‘Observe my Sabbaths and have reverence
for my sanctuary. I am the LORD.
3“ ‘If you follow my decrees and are careful to
obey my commands, 4I will send you rain in its
season, and the ground will yield its crops and
the trees of the field their fruit. 5Your threshing
will continue until grape harvest and the grape
harvest will continue until planting, and you will
eat all the food you want and live in safety in your
land.
6“ ‘I will grant peace in the land, and you will
lie down and no one will make you afraid. I will
remove savage beasts from the land, and the
sword will not pass through your country. 7You
will pursue your enemies, and they will fall by
the sword before you. 8Five of you will chase a
hundred, and a hundred of you will chase ten
thousand, and your enemies will fall by the sword
before you.
9“ ‘I will look on you with favor and make you
fruitful and increase your numbers, and I will
keep my covenant with you. 10You will still be
eating last year’s harvest when you will have to
move it out to make room for the new. 11I will
put my dwelling place[a] among you, and I will
not abhor you. 12I will walk among you and be
your God, and you will be my people. 13I am the
LORD your God, who brought you out of Egypt so
that you would no longer be slaves to the Egyptians; I broke the bars of your yoke and enabled
you to walk with heads held high.

Punishment for Disobedience

14“ ‘But if you will not listen to me and carry
out all these commands, 15and if you reject my
decrees and abhor my laws and fail to carry out
all my commands and so violate my covenant,
16then I will do this to you: I will bring upon you
sudden terror, wasting diseases and fever that
will destroy your sight and drain away your life.
You will plant seed in vain, because your enemies
will eat it. 17I will set my face against you so that
you will be defeated by your enemies; those who
hate you will rule over you, and you will flee even
when no one is pursuing you.
18“ ‘If after all this you will not listen to me, I
will punish you for your sins seven times over. 19I
will break down your stubborn pride and make
the sky above you like iron and the ground beneath you like bronze. 20Your strength will be
spent in vain, because your soil will not yield its
crops, nor will the trees of the land yield their
fruit.
21“ ‘If you remain hostile toward me and refuse
to listen to me, I will multiply your afflictions
seven times over, as your sins deserve. 22I will
send wild animals against you, and they will rob
you of your children, destroy your cattle and
make you so few in number that your roads will
be deserted.
23“ ‘If in spite of these things you do not accept
my correction but continue to be hostile toward
me, 24I myself will be hostile toward you and will
afflict you for your sins seven times over. 25And
I will bring the sword upon you to avenge the
breaking of the covenant. When you withdraw
into your cities, I will send a plague among you,
and you will be given into enemy hands. 26When
I cut off your supply of bread, ten women will be
able to bake your bread in one oven, and they
will dole out the bread by weight. You will eat,
but you will not be satisfied.
27“ ‘If in spite of this you still do not listen to
me but continue to be hostile toward me, 28then
in my anger I will be hostile toward you, and I
myself will punish you for your sins seven times
over. 29You will eat the flesh of your sons and the
flesh of your daughters. 30I will destroy your high
places, cut down your incense altars and pile
your dead bodies on the lifeless forms of your
idols, and I will abhor you. 31I will turn your
cities into ruins and lay waste your sanctuaries,
and I will take no delight in the pleasing aroma of
your offerings. 32I will lay waste the land, so that
your enemies who live there will be appalled. 33I
will scatter you among the nations and will draw

a 11 Or *my tabernacle*

out my sword and pursue you. Your land will
be laid waste, and your cities will lie in ruins.
34Then the land will enjoy its sabbath years all
the time that it lies desolate and you are in the
country of your enemies; then the land will rest
and enjoy its sabbaths. 35All the time that it lies
desolate, the land will have the rest it did not
have during the sabbaths you lived in it.

36" 'As for those of you who are left, I will
make their hearts so fearful in the lands of their
enemies that the sound of a windblown leaf will
put them to flight. They will run as though fleeing from the sword, and they will fall, even
though no one is pursuing them. 37They will
stumble over one another as though fleeing from
the sword, even though no one is pursuing them.
So you will not be able to stand before your enemies. 38You will perish among the nations; the
land of your enemies will devour you. 39Those of
you who are left will waste away in the lands of
their enemies because of their sins; also because
of their fathers' sins they will waste away.

40" 'But if they will confess their sins and the
sins of their fathers—their treachery against me
and their hostility toward me, 41which made me
hostile toward them so that I sent them into the
land of their enemies—then when their uncircumcised hearts are humbled and they pay for
their sin, 42I will remember my covenant with
Jacob and my covenant with Isaac and my covenant with Abraham, and I will remember the
land. 43For the land will be deserted by them and
will enjoy its sabbaths while it lies desolate without them. They will pay for their sins because
they rejected my laws and abhorred my decrees.
44Yet in spite of this, when they are in the land
of their enemies, I will not reject them or abhor
them so as to destroy them completely, breaking
my covenant with them. I am the LORD their
God. 45But for their sake I will remember the
covenant with their ancestors whom I brought
out of Egypt in the sight of the nations to be their
God. I am the LORD.' "

46These are the decrees, the laws and the regulations that the LORD established on Mount Sinai between himself and the Israelites through
Moses.

Redeeming What Is the LORD's

27 The LORD said to Moses, 2"Speak to the
Israelites and say to them: 'If anyone
makes a special vow to dedicate persons to the
LORD by giving equivalent values, 3set the value
of a male between the ages of twenty and sixty at
fifty shekels[a] of silver, according to the sanctuary shekel[b]; 4and if it is a female, set her value
at thirty shekels.[c] 5If it is a person between the
ages of five and twenty, set the value of a male at
twenty shekels[d] and of a female at ten shekels.[e] 6If it is a person between one month and
five years, set the value of a male at five shekels[f]
of silver and that of a female at three shekels[g] of
silver. 7If it is a person sixty years old or more, set
the value of a male at fifteen shekels[h] and of a
female at ten shekels. 8If anyone making the vow
is too poor to pay the specified amount, he is to
present the person to the priest, who will set the
value for him according to what the man making
the vow can afford.

9" 'If what he vowed is an animal that is acceptable as an offering to the LORD, such an animal given to the LORD becomes holy. 10He must
not exchange it or substitute a good one for a bad
one, or a bad one for a good one; if he should
substitute one animal for another, both it and the
substitute become holy. 11If what he vowed is a
ceremonially unclean animal—one that is not acceptable as an offering to the LORD—the animal
must be presented to the priest, 12who will judge
its quality as good or bad. Whatever value the
priest then sets, that is what it will be. 13If the
owner wishes to redeem the animal, he must add
a fifth to its value.

14" 'If a man dedicates his house as something
holy to the LORD, the priest will judge its quality
as good or bad. Whatever value the priest then
sets, so it will remain. 15If the man who dedicates
his house redeems it, he must add a fifth to its
value, and the house will again become his.

16" 'If a man dedicates to the LORD part of his
family land, its value is to be set according to the
amount of seed required for it—fifty shekels of
silver to a homer[i] of barley seed. 17If he dedicates his field during the Year of Jubilee, the value that has been set remains. 18But if he dedicates his field after the Jubilee, the priest will
determine the value according to the number of
years that remain until the next Year of Jubilee,
and its set value will be reduced. 19If the man
who dedicates the field wishes to redeem it, he
must add a fifth to its value, and the field will
again become his. 20If, however, he does not redeem the field, or if he has sold it to someone
else, it can never be redeemed. 21When the field
is released in the Jubilee, it will become holy, like
a field devoted to the LORD; it will become the
property of the priests.[j]

22" 'If a man dedicates to the LORD a field he

[a] *3* That is, about 1 1/4 pounds (about 0.6 kilogram); also in verse 16 [b] *3* That is, about 2/5 ounce (about 11.5 grams); also in verse 25 [c] *4* That is, about 12 ounces (about 0.3 kilogram) [d] *5* That is, about 8 ounces (about 0.2 kilogram) [e] *5* That is, about 4 ounces (about 110 grams); also in verse 7 [f] *6* That is, about 2 ounces (about 55 grams) [g] *6* That is, about 1 1/4 ounces (about 35 grams) [h] *7* That is, about 6 ounces (about 170 grams) [i] *16* That is, probably about 6 bushels (about 220 liters) [j] *21* Or *priest*

has bought, which is not part of his family land,
23the priest will determine its value up to the
Year of Jubilee, and the man must pay its value on
that day as something holy to the LORD. 24In the
Year of Jubilee the field will revert to the person
from whom he bought it, the one whose land it
was. 25Every value is to be set according to the
sanctuary shekel, twenty gerahs to the shekel.

26" 'No one, however, may dedicate the firstborn of an animal, since the firstborn already belongs to the LORD; whether an ox[a] or a sheep, it
is the LORD's. 27If it is one of the unclean animals,
he may buy it back at its set value, adding a fifth
of the value to it. If he does not redeem it, it is to
be sold at its set value.

28" 'But nothing that a man owns and devotes[b] to the LORD—whether man or animal or
family land—may be sold or redeemed; everything so devoted is most holy to the LORD.

29" 'No person devoted to destruction[c] may
be ransomed; he must be put to death.

30" 'A tithe of everything from the land,
whether grain from the soil or fruit from the
trees, belongs to the LORD; it is holy to the LORD.
31If a man redeems any of his tithe, he must add
a fifth of the value to it. 32The entire tithe of the
herd and flock—every tenth animal that passes
under the shepherd's rod—will be holy to the
LORD. 33He must not pick out the good from the
bad or make any substitution. If he does make a
substitution, both the animal and its substitute
become holy and cannot be redeemed.' "

34These are the commands the LORD gave Moses on Mount Sinai for the Israelites.

[a]26 The Hebrew word can include both male and female. [b]28 The Hebrew term refers to the irrevocable giving over of things or persons to the LORD. [c]29 The Hebrew term refers to the irrevocable giving over of things or persons to the LORD, often by totally destroying them.

Introduction to NUMBERS

Personal Reading Plan

❒ Numbers 1:1–54	❒ Numbers 11:1–12:16	❒ Numbers 25:1–26:65
❒ Numbers 2:1–3:51	❒ Numbers 13:1–14:45	❒ Numbers 27:1–28:8
❒ Numbers 4:1–49	❒ Numbers 15:1–16:50	❒ Numbers 28:9–29:40
❒ Numbers 5:1–6:27	❒ Numbers 17:1–19:22	❒ Numbers 30:1–31:54
❒ Numbers 7:1–89	❒ Numbers 20:1–21:20	❒ Numbers 32:1–42
❒ Numbers 8:1–9:14	❒ Numbers 21:21–22:41	❒ Numbers 33:1–34:29
❒ Numbers 9:15–10:36	❒ Numbers 23:1–24:25	❒ Numbers 35:1–36:13

Author

Moses is assumed to be the author and editor of most of the first five books of the Old Testament (the Pentateuch).

Date

It is difficult to set a firm date for the writing of the Pentateuch. Conservative estimates place it in either the fifteenth century or thirteenth century B.C., depending on when the Exodus occurred.

Theme

God's faithfulness despite Israel's rebellion, resulting in 40 years of misery and mercy.

Historical Background

The name of this book in the English Bible is derived from the census-taking and the mustering of the Israelite army in preparation for invading the promised land. This is detailed in chapters 1–4 and 26. The title of the book in the Hebrew Bible, meaning "in the desert" or "in the wilderness" is actually much more descriptive. The book of Numbers relates the story of the 40 years during which Israel journeyed from Mount Sinai to the edge of Canaan. This was a time of great turmoil for Israel in which the people expressed not gratitude for deliverance from Egypt, but rebellion against God. Consequently, they lived out their lives in the desert.

Characteristics

Arranged around the Israelites' wilderness wanderings, the book chronicles God's actions in leading his people toward the land of promise. What makes these actions truly remarkable is that they establish God's faithfulness in spite of the people's rebellious nature. The central human figure in all this is Moses. He combines his many talents with a humble spirit to act as intermediary between his God and his people. The book of Numbers provides us with a dramatic portrait of Moses, the Israelites, and God as they struggle to turn the disaster of the wilderness wanderings into success.

Passages for General Group Study

12:1–15	Miriam and Aaron Oppose Moses
13:26–14:10,26–45	Spying on the Promised Land

The Census

1 The LORD spoke to Moses in the Tent of
Meeting in the Desert of Sinai on the first
day of the second month of the second year after
the Israelites came out of Egypt. He said: 2"Take
a census of the whole Israelite community by
their clans and families, listing every man by
name, one by one. 3You and Aaron are to number
by their divisions all the men in Israel twenty
years old or more who are able to serve in the
army. 4One man from each tribe, each the head
of his family, is to help you. 5These are the names
of the men who are to assist you:

from Reuben, Elizur son of Shedeur;
6from Simeon, Shelumiel son of Zurishaddai;
7from Judah, Nahshon son of Amminadab;
8from Issachar, Nethanel son of Zuar;
9from Zebulun, Eliab son of Helon;
10from the sons of Joseph:
from Ephraim, Elishama son of Ammihud;
from Manasseh, Gamaliel son of Pedahzur;
11from Benjamin, Abidan son of Gideoni;
12from Dan, Ahiezer son of Ammishaddai;
13from Asher, Pagiel son of Ocran;
14from Gad, Eliasaph son of Deuel;
15from Naphtali, Ahira son of Enan."

16These were the men appointed from the
community, the leaders of their ancestral tribes.
They were the heads of the clans of Israel.

17Moses and Aaron took these men whose
names had been given, 18and they called the
whole community together on the first day of the
second month. The people indicated their ancestry by their clans and families, and the men twenty years old or more were listed by name, one by
one, 19as the LORD commanded Moses. And so he
counted them in the Desert of Sinai:

20From the descendants of Reuben the firstborn son of Israel:
All the men twenty years old or more who were able to serve in the army were listed by name, one by one, according to the records of their clans and
families. 21The number from the tribe of
Reuben was 46,500.

22From the descendants of Simeon:
All the men twenty years old or more who were able to serve in the army were counted and listed by name, one by one, according to the records of their
clans and families. 23The number from
the tribe of Simeon was 59,300.

24From the descendants of Gad:
All the men twenty years old or more who were able to serve in the army were listed by name, according to the
records of their clans and families. 25The
number from the tribe of Gad was 45,650.

26From the descendants of Judah:
All the men twenty years old or more who were able to serve in the army were listed by name, according to the
records of their clans and families. 27The
number from the tribe of Judah was 74,600.

28From the descendants of Issachar:
All the men twenty years old or more who were able to serve in the army were listed by name, according to the
records of their clans and families. 29The
number from the tribe of Issachar was 54,400.

30From the descendants of Zebulun:
All the men twenty years old or more who were able to serve in the army were listed by name, according to the
records of their clans and families. 31The
number from the tribe of Zebulun was 57,400.

32From the sons of Joseph:
From the descendants of Ephraim:
All the men twenty years old or more who were able to serve in the army were listed by name, according to the
records of their clans and families. 33The
number from the tribe of Ephraim was 40,500.

34From the descendants of Manasseh:
All the men twenty years old or more who were able to serve in the army were listed by name, according to the
records of their clans and families. 35The
number from the tribe of Manasseh was 32,200.

36From the descendants of Benjamin:
All the men twenty years old or more who were able to serve in the army were listed by name, according to the
records of their clans and families. 37The
number from the tribe of Benjamin was 35,400.

38From the descendants of Dan:
All the men twenty years old or more who were able to serve in the army were listed by name, according to the
records of their clans and families. 39The
number from the tribe of Dan was 62,700.

40From the descendants of Asher:

All the men twenty years old or more who were able to serve in the army were listed by name, according to the records of their clans and families. 41The number from the tribe of Asher was 41,500.

42From the descendants of Naphtali:

All the men twenty years old or more who were able to serve in the army were listed by name, according to the records of their clans and families. 43The number from the tribe of Naphtali was 53,400.

44These were the men counted by Moses and Aaron and the twelve leaders of Israel, each one representing his family. 45All the Israelites twenty years old or more who were able to serve in Israel's army were counted according to their families. 46The total number was 603,550.

47The families of the tribe of Levi, however, were not counted along with the others. 48The LORD had said to Moses: 49"You must not count the tribe of Levi or include them in the census of the other Israelites. 50Instead, appoint the Levites to be in charge of the tabernacle of the Testimony—over all its furnishings and everything belonging to it. They are to carry the tabernacle and all its furnishings; they are to take care of it and encamp around it. 51Whenever the tabernacle is to move, the Levites are to take it down, and whenever the tabernacle is to be set up, the Levites shall do it. Anyone else who goes near it shall be put to death. 52The Israelites are to set up their tents by divisions, each man in his own camp under his own standard. 53The Levites, however, are to set up their tents around the tabernacle of the Testimony so that wrath will not fall on the Israelite community. The Levites are to be responsible for the care of the tabernacle of the Testimony."

54The Israelites did all this just as the LORD commanded Moses.

The Arrangement of the Tribal Camps

2 The LORD said to Moses and Aaron: 2"The Israelites are to camp around the Tent of Meeting some distance from it, each man under his standard with the banners of his family."

3On the east, toward the sunrise, the divisions of the camp of Judah are to encamp under their standard. The leader of the people of Judah is Nahshon son of Amminadab. 4His division numbers 74,600.

5The tribe of Issachar will camp next to them. The leader of the people of Issachar is Nethanel son of Zuar. 6His division numbers 54,400.

7The tribe of Zebulun will be next. The leader of the people of Zebulun is Eliab son of Helon. 8His division numbers 57,400.

9All the men assigned to the camp of Judah, according to their divisions, number 186,400. They will set out first.

10On the south will be the divisions of the camp of Reuben under their standard. The leader of the people of Reuben is Elizur son of Shedeur. 11His division numbers 46,500.

12The tribe of Simeon will camp next to them. The leader of the people of Simeon is Shelumiel son of Zurishaddai. 13His division numbers 59,300.

14The tribe of Gad will be next. The leader of the people of Gad is Eliasaph son of Deuel.[a] 15His division numbers 45,650.

16All the men assigned to the camp of Reuben, according to their divisions, number 151,450. They will set out second.

17Then the Tent of Meeting and the camp of the Levites will set out in the middle of the camps. They will set out in the same order as they encamp, each in his own place under his standard.

18On the west will be the divisions of the camp of Ephraim under their standard. The leader of the people of Ephraim is Elishama son of Ammihud. 19His division numbers 40,500.

20The tribe of Manasseh will be next to them. The leader of the people of Manasseh is Gamaliel son of Pedahzur. 21His division numbers 32,200.

22The tribe of Benjamin will be next. The leader of the people of Benjamin is Abidan son of Gideoni. 23His division numbers 35,400.

24All the men assigned to the camp of Ephraim, according to their divisions, number 108,100. They will set out third.

25On the north will be the divisions of the camp of Dan, under their standard. The leader of the people of Dan is Ahiezer son of Ammishaddai. 26His division numbers 62,700.

27The tribe of Asher will camp next to them. The leader of the people of Asher is Pagiel son of Ocran. 28His division numbers 41,500.

[a] *14* Many manuscripts of the Masoretic Text, Samaritan Pentateuch and Vulgate (see also Num. 1:14); most manuscripts of the Masoretic Text *Reuel*

29The tribe of Naphtali will be next. The
leader of the people of Naphtali is Ahira son
of Enan. 30His division numbers 53,400.
31All the men assigned to the camp of
Dan number 157,600. They will set out
last, under their standards.

32These are the Israelites, counted according to their families. All those in the
camps, by their divisions, number 603,550.
33The Levites, however, were not counted
along with the other Israelites, as the LORD
commanded Moses.

34So the Israelites did everything the LORD
commanded Moses; that is the way they encamped under their standards, and that is the
way they set out, each with his clan and family.

The Levites

3 This is the account of the family of Aaron and
Moses at the time the LORD talked with Moses on Mount Sinai.
2The names of the sons of Aaron were Nadab
the firstborn and Abihu, Eleazar and Ithamar.
3Those were the names of Aaron's sons, the
anointed priests, who were ordained to serve as
priests. 4Nadab and Abihu, however, fell dead
before the LORD when they made an offering with
unauthorized fire before him in the Desert of Sinai. They had no sons; so only Eleazar and Ithamar served as priests during the lifetime of their
father Aaron.
5The LORD said to Moses, 6"Bring the tribe of
Levi and present them to Aaron the priest to assist him. 7They are to perform duties for him and
for the whole community at the Tent of Meeting
by doing the work of the tabernacle. 8They are to
take care of all the furnishings of the Tent of
Meeting, fulfilling the obligations of the Israelites
by doing the work of the tabernacle. 9Give the
Levites to Aaron and his sons; they are the Israelites who are to be given wholly to him.[a] 10Ap-
point Aaron and his sons to serve as priests; anyone else who approaches the sanctuary must be
put to death."
11The LORD also said to Moses, 12"I have taken
the Levites from among the Israelites in place of
the first male offspring of every Israelite woman.
The Levites are mine, 13for all the firstborn are
mine. When I struck down all the firstborn in
Egypt, I set apart for myself every firstborn in
Israel, whether man or animal. They are to be
mine. I am the LORD."
14The LORD said to Moses in the Desert of
Sinai, 15"Count the Levites by their families and
clans. Count every male a month old or more."
16So Moses counted them, as he was commanded
by the word of the LORD.
17These were the names of the sons of Levi:
Gershon, Kohath and Merari.
18These were the names of the Gershonite
clans:
Libni and Shimei.
19The Kohathite clans:
Amram, Izhar, Hebron and Uzziel.
20The Merarite clans:
Mahli and Mushi.
These were the Levite clans, according to their
families.

21To Gershon belonged the clans of the Lib-
nites and Shimeites; these were the Gershonite
clans. 22The number of all the males a month old
or more who were counted was 7,500. 23The
Gershonite clans were to camp on the west, behind the tabernacle. 24The leader of the families
of the Gershonites was Eliasaph son of Lael. 25At
the Tent of Meeting the Gershonites were responsible for the care of the tabernacle and tent,
its coverings, the curtain at the entrance to the
Tent of Meeting, 26the curtains of the courtyard,
the curtain at the entrance to the courtyard surrounding the tabernacle and altar, and the
ropes—and everything related to their use.

27To Kohath belonged the clans of the Amramites, Izharites, Hebronites and Uzzielites; these
were the Kohathite clans. 28The number of all
the males a month old or more was 8,600.[b] The
Kohathites were responsible for the care of the
sanctuary. 29The Kohathite clans were to camp
on the south side of the tabernacle. 30The leader
of the families of the Kohathite clans was Elizaphan son of Uzziel. 31They were responsible for
the care of the ark, the table, the lampstand, the
altars, the articles of the sanctuary used in ministering, the curtain, and everything related to
their use. 32The chief leader of the Levites was
Eleazar son of Aaron, the priest. He was appointed over those who were responsible for the care
of the sanctuary.

33To Merari belonged the clans of the Mahlites
and the Mushites; these were the Merarite clans.
34The number of all the males a month old or
more who were counted was 6,200. 35The leader of the families of the Merarite clans was Zuriel
son of Abihail; they were to camp on the north
side of the tabernacle. 36The Merarites were appointed to take care of the frames of the tabernacle, its crossbars, posts, bases, all its equipment,
and everything related to their use, 37as well as

[a] 9 Most manuscripts of the Masoretic Text; some manuscripts of the Masoretic Text, Samaritan Pentateuch and Septuagint (see also Num. 8:16) *to me* [b] 28 Hebrew; some Septuagint manuscripts *8,300*

the posts of the surrounding courtyard with their bases, tent pegs and ropes.

38 Moses and Aaron and his sons were to camp to the east of the tabernacle, toward the sunrise, in front of the Tent of Meeting. They were responsible for the care of the sanctuary on behalf of the Israelites. Anyone else who approached the sanctuary was to be put to death.

39 The total number of Levites counted at the LORD's command by Moses and Aaron according to their clans, including every male a month old or more, was 22,000.

40 The LORD said to Moses, "Count all the firstborn Israelite males who are a month old or more and make a list of their names. 41 Take the Levites for me in place of all the firstborn of the Israelites, and the livestock of the Levites in place of all the firstborn of the livestock of the Israelites. I am the LORD."

42 So Moses counted all the firstborn of the Israelites, as the LORD commanded him. 43 The total number of firstborn males a month old or more, listed by name, was 22,273.

44 The LORD also said to Moses, 45 "Take the Levites in place of all the firstborn of Israel, and the livestock of the Levites in place of their livestock. The Levites are to be mine. I am the LORD. 46 To redeem the 273 firstborn Israelites who exceed the number of the Levites, 47 collect five shekels[a] for each one, according to the sanctuary shekel, which weighs twenty gerahs. 48 Give the money for the redemption of the additional Israelites to Aaron and his sons."

49 So Moses collected the redemption money from those who exceeded the number redeemed by the Levites. 50 From the firstborn of the Israelites he collected silver weighing 1,365 shekels,[b] according to the sanctuary shekel. 51 Moses gave the redemption money to Aaron and his sons, as he was commanded by the word of the LORD.

The Kohathites

4 The LORD said to Moses and Aaron: 2 "Take a census of the Kohathite branch of the Levites by their clans and families. 3 Count all the men from thirty to fifty years of age who come to serve in the work in the Tent of Meeting.

4 "This is the work of the Kohathites in the Tent of Meeting: the care of the most holy things. 5 When the camp is to move, Aaron and his sons are to go in and take down the shielding curtain and cover the ark of the Testimony with it. 6 Then they are to cover this with hides of sea cows,[c] spread a cloth of solid blue over that and put the poles in place.

7 "Over the table of the Presence they are to spread a blue cloth and put on it the plates, dishes and bowls, and the jars for drink offerings; the bread that is continually there is to remain on it. 8 Over these they are to spread a scarlet cloth, cover that with hides of sea cows and put its poles in place.

9 "They are to take a blue cloth and cover the lampstand that is for light, together with its lamps, its wick trimmers and trays, and all its jars for the oil used to supply it. 10 Then they are to wrap it and all its accessories in a covering of hides of sea cows and put it on a carrying frame.

11 "Over the gold altar they are to spread a blue cloth and cover that with hides of sea cows and put its poles in place.

12 "They are to take all the articles used for ministering in the sanctuary, wrap them in a blue cloth, cover that with hides of sea cows and put them on a carrying frame.

13 "They are to remove the ashes from the bronze altar and spread a purple cloth over it. 14 Then they are to place on it all the utensils used for ministering at the altar, including the firepans, meat forks, shovels and sprinkling bowls. Over it they are to spread a covering of hides of sea cows and put its poles in place.

15 "After Aaron and his sons have finished covering the holy furnishings and all the holy articles, and when the camp is ready to move, the Kohathites are to come to do the carrying. But they must not touch the holy things or they will die. The Kohathites are to carry those things that are in the Tent of Meeting.

16 "Eleazar son of Aaron, the priest, is to have charge of the oil for the light, the fragrant incense, the regular grain offering and the anointing oil. He is to be in charge of the entire tabernacle and everything in it, including its holy furnishings and articles."

17 The LORD said to Moses and Aaron, 18 "See that the Kohathite tribal clans are not cut off from the Levites. 19 So that they may live and not die when they come near the most holy things, do this for them: Aaron and his sons are to go into the sanctuary and assign to each man his work and what he is to carry. 20 But the Kohathites must not go in to look at the holy things, even for a moment, or they will die."

The Gershonites

21 The LORD said to Moses, 22 "Take a census also of the Gershonites by their families and clans. 23 Count all the men from thirty to fifty

[a] 47 That is, about 2 ounces (about 55 grams) [b] 50 That is, about 35 pounds (about 15.5 kilograms) [c] 6 That is, dugongs; also in verses 8, 10, 11, 12, 14 and 25

years of age who come to serve in the work at the Tent of Meeting.

24“This is the service of the Gershonite clans as they work and carry burdens: 25They are to carry the curtains of the tabernacle, the Tent of Meeting, its covering and the outer covering of hides of sea cows, the curtains for the entrance to the Tent of Meeting, 26the curtains of the courtyard surrounding the tabernacle and altar, the curtain for the entrance, the ropes and all the equipment used in its service. The Gershonites are to do all that needs to be done with these things. 27All their service, whether carrying or doing other work, is to be done under the direction of Aaron and his sons. You shall assign to them as their responsibility all they are to carry. 28This is the service of the Gershonite clans at the Tent of Meeting. Their duties are to be under the direction of Ithamar son of Aaron, the priest.

The Merarites

29“Count the Merarites by their clans and families. 30Count all the men from thirty to fifty years of age who come to serve in the work at the Tent of Meeting. 31This is their duty as they perform service at the Tent of Meeting: to carry the frames of the tabernacle, its crossbars, posts and bases, 32as well as the posts of the surrounding courtyard with their bases, tent pegs, ropes, all their equipment and everything related to their use. Assign to each man the specific things he is to carry. 33This is the service of the Merarite clans as they work at the Tent of Meeting under the direction of Ithamar son of Aaron, the priest.”

The Numbering of the Levite Clans

34Moses, Aaron and the leaders of the community counted the Kohathites by their clans and families. 35All the men from thirty to fifty years of age who came to serve in the work in the Tent of Meeting, 36counted by clans, were 2,750. 37This was the total of all those in the Kohathite clans who served in the Tent of Meeting. Moses and Aaron counted them according to the LORD’s command through Moses.

38The Gershonites were counted by their clans and families. 39All the men from thirty to fifty years of age who came to serve in the work at the Tent of Meeting, 40counted by their clans and families, were 2,630. 41This was the total of those in the Gershonite clans who served at the Tent of Meeting. Moses and Aaron counted them according to the LORD’s command.

42The Merarites were counted by their clans and families. 43All the men from thirty to fifty years of age who came to serve in the work at the Tent of Meeting, 44counted by their clans, were 3,200. 45This was the total of those in the Merarite clans. Moses and Aaron counted them according to the LORD’s command through Moses.

46So Moses, Aaron and the leaders of Israel counted all the Levites by their clans and families. 47All the men from thirty to fifty years of age who came to do the work of serving and carrying the Tent of Meeting 48numbered 8,580. 49At the LORD’s command through Moses, each was assigned his work and told what to carry.

Thus they were counted, as the LORD commanded Moses.

The Purity of the Camp

5 The LORD said to Moses, 2“Command the Israelites to send away from the camp anyone who has an infectious skin disease[a] or a discharge of any kind, or who is ceremonially unclean because of a dead body. 3Send away male and female alike; send them outside the camp so they will not defile their camp, where I dwell among them.” 4The Israelites did this; they sent them outside the camp. They did just as the LORD had instructed Moses.

Restitution for Wrongs

5The LORD said to Moses, 6“Say to the Israelites: ‘When a man or woman wrongs another in any way[b] and so is unfaithful to the LORD, that person is guilty 7and must confess the sin he has committed. He must make full restitution for his wrong, add one fifth to it and give it all to the person he has wronged. 8But if that person has no close relative to whom restitution can be made for the wrong, the restitution belongs to the LORD and must be given to the priest, along with the ram with which atonement is made for him. 9All the sacred contributions the Israelites bring to a priest will belong to him. 10Each man’s sacred gifts are his own, but what he gives to the priest will belong to the priest.’ ”

The Test for an Unfaithful Wife

11Then the LORD said to Moses, 12“Speak to the Israelites and say to them: ‘If a man’s wife goes astray and is unfaithful to him 13by sleeping with another man, and this is hidden from her husband and her impurity is undetected (since there is no witness against her and she has not been caught in the act), 14and if feelings of jealousy come over her husband and he suspects his wife and she is impure—or if he is jealous and suspects her even though she is not impure—15then he is to take his wife to the priest. He must also take an offering of a tenth of an

a2 Traditionally *leprosy*; the Hebrew word was used for various diseases affecting the skin—not necessarily leprosy. *b6* Or *woman commits any wrong common to mankind* ephah[a] of barley flour on her behalf. He must not pour oil on it or put incense on it, because it is a grain offering for jealousy, a reminder offering to draw attention to guilt.

16" 'The priest shall bring her and have her stand before the LORD. 17Then he shall take some holy water in a clay jar and put some dust from the tabernacle floor into the water. 18After the priest has had the woman stand before the LORD, he shall loosen her hair and place in her hands the reminder offering, the grain offering for jealousy, while he himself holds the bitter water that brings a curse. 19Then the priest shall put the woman under oath and say to her, "If no other man has slept with you and you have not gone astray and become impure while married to your husband, may this bitter water that brings a curse not harm you. 20But if you have gone astray while married to your husband and you have defiled yourself by sleeping with a man other than your husband"— 21here the priest is to put the woman under this curse of the oath—"may the LORD cause your people to curse and denounce you when he causes your thigh to waste away and your abdomen to swell.[b] 22May this water that brings a curse enter your body so that your abdomen swells and your thigh wastes away.[c]"

" 'Then the woman is to say, "Amen. So be it."

23" 'The priest is to write these curses on a scroll and then wash them off into the bitter water. 24He shall have the woman drink the bitter water that brings a curse, and this water will enter her and cause bitter suffering. 25The priest is to take from her hands the grain offering for jealousy, wave it before the LORD and bring it to the altar. 26The priest is then to take a handful of the grain offering as a memorial offering and burn it on the altar; after that, he is to have the woman drink the water. 27If she has defiled herself and been unfaithful to her husband, then when she is made to drink the water that brings a curse, it will go into her and cause bitter suffering; her abdomen will swell and her thigh waste away,[d] and she will become accursed among her people. 28If, however, the woman has not defiled herself and is free from impurity, she will be cleared of guilt and will be able to have children.

29" 'This, then, is the law of jealousy when a woman goes astray and defiles herself while married to her husband, 30or when feelings of jealousy come over a man because he suspects his wife. The priest is to have her stand before the LORD and is to apply this entire law to her. 31The husband will be innocent of any wrongdoing, but the woman will bear the consequences of her sin.' "

The Nazirite

6 The LORD said to Moses, 2"Speak to the Israelites and say to them: 'If a man or woman wants to make a special vow, a vow of separation to the LORD as a Nazirite, 3he must abstain from wine and other fermented drink and must not drink vinegar made from wine or from other fermented drink. He must not drink grape juice or eat grapes or raisins. 4As long as he is a Nazirite, he must not eat anything that comes from the grapevine, not even the seeds or skins.

5" 'During the entire period of his vow of separation no razor may be used on his head. He must be holy until the period of his separation to the LORD is over; he must let the hair of his head grow long. 6Throughout the period of his separation to the LORD he must not go near a dead body. 7Even if his own father or mother or brother or sister dies, he must not make himself ceremonially unclean on account of them, because the symbol of his separation to God is on his head. 8Throughout the period of his separation he is consecrated to the LORD.

9" 'If someone dies suddenly in his presence, thus defiling the hair he has dedicated, he must shave his head on the day of his cleansing—the seventh day. 10Then on the eighth day he must bring two doves or two young pigeons to the priest at the entrance to the Tent of Meeting. 11The priest is to offer one as a sin offering and the other as a burnt offering to make atonement for him because he sinned by being in the presence of the dead body. That same day he is to consecrate his head. 12He must dedicate himself to the LORD for the period of his separation and must bring a year-old male lamb as a guilt offering. The previous days do not count, because he became defiled during his separation.

13" 'Now this is the law for the Nazirite when the period of his separation is over. He is to be brought to the entrance to the Tent of Meeting. 14There he is to present his offerings to the LORD: a year-old male lamb without defect for a burnt offering, a year-old ewe lamb without defect for a sin offering, a ram without defect for a fellowship offering,[e] 15together with their grain offerings and drink offerings, and a basket of bread made without yeast—cakes made of fine flour mixed with oil, and wafers spread with oil.

16" 'The priest is to present them before the LORD and make the sin offering and the burnt offering. 17He is to present the basket of unleavened bread and is to sacrifice the ram as a fellowship offering to the LORD, together with its grain offering and drink offering.

[a] 15 That is, probably about 2 quarts (about 2 liters) [b] 21 Or *causes you to have a miscarrying womb and barrenness*
[c] 22 Or *body and cause you to be barren and have a miscarrying womb* [d] 27 Or *suffering; she will have barrenness and a miscarrying womb* [e] 14 Traditionally *peace offering*; also in verses 17 and 18

18“ ‘Then at the entrance to the Tent of Meeting, the Nazirite must shave off the hair that he dedicated. He is to take the hair and put it in the fire that is under the sacrifice of the fellowship offering.

19“ ‘After the Nazirite has shaved off the hair of his dedication, the priest is to place in his hands a boiled shoulder of the ram, and a cake and a wafer from the basket, both made without yeast. 20The priest shall then wave them before the LORD as a wave offering; they are holy and belong to the priest, together with the breast that was waved and the thigh that was presented. After that, the Nazirite may drink wine.

21“ ‘This is the law of the Nazirite who vows his offering to the LORD in accordance with his separation, in addition to whatever else he can afford. He must fulfill the vow he has made, according to the law of the Nazirite.’ ”

The Priestly Blessing

22The LORD said to Moses, 23“Tell Aaron and his sons, ‘This is how you are to bless the Israelites. Say to them:

24“ ‘ “The LORD bless you
and keep you;
25the LORD make his face shine upon you
and be gracious to you;
26the LORD turn his face toward you
and give you peace.” ’

27“So they will put my name on the Israelites, and I will bless them.”

Offerings at the Dedication of the Tabernacle

7 When Moses finished setting up the tabernacle, he anointed it and consecrated it and all its furnishings. He also anointed and consecrated the altar and all its utensils. 2Then the leaders of Israel, the heads of families who were the tribal leaders in charge of those who were counted, made offerings. 3They brought as their gifts before the LORD six covered carts and twelve oxen—an ox from each leader and a cart from every two. These they presented before the tabernacle.

4The LORD said to Moses, 5“Accept these from them, that they may be used in the work at the Tent of Meeting. Give them to the Levites as each man’s work requires.”

6So Moses took the carts and oxen and gave them to the Levites. 7He gave two carts and four oxen to the Gershonites, as their work required, 8and he gave four carts and eight oxen to the Merarites, as their work required. They were all under the direction of Ithamar son of Aaron, the priest. 9But Moses did not give any to the Kohathites, because they were to carry on their shoulders the holy things, for which they were responsible.

10When the altar was anointed, the leaders brought their offerings for its dedication and presented them before the altar. 11For the LORD had said to Moses, “Each day one leader is to bring his offering for the dedication of the altar.”

12The one who brought his offering on the first day was Nahshon son of Amminadab of the tribe of Judah.

13His offering was one silver plate weighing a hundred and thirty shekels,[a] and one silver sprinkling bowl weighing seventy shekels,[b] both according to the sanctuary shekel, each filled with fine flour mixed with oil as a grain offering; 14one gold dish weighing ten shekels,[c] filled with incense; 15one young bull, one ram and one male lamb a year old, for a burnt offering; 16one male goat for a sin offering; 17and two oxen, five rams, five male goats and five male lambs a year old, to be sacrificed as a fellowship offering.[d] This was the offering of Nahshon son of Amminadab.

18On the second day Nethanel son of Zuar, the leader of Issachar, brought his offering.

19The offering he brought was one silver plate weighing a hundred and thirty shekels, and one silver sprinkling bowl weighing seventy shekels, both according to the sanctuary shekel, each filled with fine flour mixed with oil as a grain offering; 20one gold dish weighing ten shekels, filled with incense; 21one young bull, one ram and one male lamb a year old, for a burnt offering; 22one male goat for a sin offering; 23and two oxen, five rams, five male goats and five male lambs a year old, to be sacrificed as a fellowship offering. This was the offering of Nethanel son of Zuar.

24On the third day, Eliab son of Helon, the leader of the people of Zebulun, brought his offering.

25His offering was one silver plate weighing a hundred and thirty shekels, and one silver sprinkling bowl weighing seventy shekels, both according to the sanctuary shekel, each filled with fine flour mixed with oil as a grain offering; 26one gold dish weighing ten shekels, filled with incense; 27one young bull, one ram and one male lamb a

[a] *13* That is, about 3 1/4 pounds (about 1.5 kilograms); also elsewhere in this chapter [b] *13* That is, about 1 3/4 pounds (about 0.8 kilogram); also elsewhere in this chapter [c] *14* That is, about 4 ounces (about 110 grams); also elsewhere in this chapter
[d] *17* Traditionally *peace offering*; also elsewhere in this chapter

year old, for a burnt offering; 28one male
goat for a sin offering; 29and two oxen, five
rams, five male goats and five male lambs a
year old, to be sacrificed as a fellowship offering. This was the offering of Eliab son of
Helon.

30On the fourth day Elizur son of Shedeur, the
leader of the people of Reuben, brought his offering.

31His offering was one silver plate weighing
a hundred and thirty shekels, and one silver
sprinkling bowl weighing seventy shekels,
both according to the sanctuary shekel,
each filled with fine flour mixed with oil as
a grain offering; 32one gold dish weighing
ten shekels, filled with incense; 33one
young bull, one ram and one male lamb a
year old, for a burnt offering; 34one male
goat for a sin offering; 35and two oxen, five
rams, five male goats and five male lambs a
year old, to be sacrificed as a fellowship offering. This was the offering of Elizur son of
Shedeur.

36On the fifth day Shelumiel son of Zurishaddai,
the leader of the people of Simeon, brought his
offering.

37His offering was one silver plate weighing
a hundred and thirty shekels, and one silver
sprinkling bowl weighing seventy shekels,
both according to the sanctuary shekel,
each filled with fine flour mixed with oil as
a grain offering; 38one gold dish weighing
ten shekels, filled with incense; 39one
young bull, one ram and one male lamb a
year old, for a burnt offering; 40one male
goat for a sin offering; 41and two oxen, five
rams, five male goats and five male lambs a
year old, to be sacrificed as a fellowship offering. This was the offering of Shelumiel
son of Zurishaddai.

42On the sixth day Eliasaph son of Deuel, the
leader of the people of Gad, brought his offering.

43His offering was one silver plate weighing
a hundred and thirty shekels, and one silver
sprinkling bowl weighing seventy shekels,
both according to the sanctuary shekel,
each filled with fine flour mixed with oil as
a grain offering; 44one gold dish weighing
ten shekels, filled with incense; 45one
young bull, one ram and one male lamb a
year old, for a burnt offering; 46one male
goat for a sin offering; 47and two oxen, five
rams, five male goats and five male lambs a
year old, to be sacrificed as a fellowship offering. This was the offering of Eliasaph son
of Deuel.

48On the seventh day Elishama son of Ammihud,
the leader of the people of Ephraim, brought his
offering.

49His offering was one silver plate weighing
a hundred and thirty shekels, and one silver
sprinkling bowl weighing seventy shekels,
both according to the sanctuary shekel,
each filled with fine flour mixed with oil as
a grain offering; 50one gold dish weighing
ten shekels, filled with incense; 51one
young bull, one ram and one male lamb a
year old, for a burnt offering; 52one male
goat for a sin offering; 53and two oxen, five
rams, five male goats and five male lambs a
year old, to be sacrificed as a fellowship offering. This was the offering of Elishama son
of Ammihud.

54On the eighth day Gamaliel son of Pedahzur,
the leader of the people of Manasseh, brought his
offering.

55His offering was one silver plate weighing
a hundred and thirty shekels, and one silver
sprinkling bowl weighing seventy shekels,
both according to the sanctuary shekel,
each filled with fine flour mixed with oil as
a grain offering; 56one gold dish weighing
ten shekels, filled with incense; 57one
young bull, one ram and one male lamb a
year old, for a burnt offering; 58one male
goat for a sin offering; 59and two oxen, five
rams, five male goats and five male lambs a
year old, to be sacrificed as a fellowship offering. This was the offering of Gamaliel son
of Pedahzur.

60On the ninth day Abidan son of Gideoni, the
leader of the people of Benjamin, brought his
offering.

61His offering was one silver plate weighing
a hundred and thirty shekels, and one silver
sprinkling bowl weighing seventy shekels,
both according to the sanctuary shekel,
each filled with fine flour mixed with oil as
a grain offering; 62one gold dish weighing
ten shekels, filled with incense; 63one
young bull, one ram and one male lamb a
year old, for a burnt offering; 64one male
goat for a sin offering; 65and two oxen, five
rams, five male goats and five male lambs a
year old, to be sacrificed as a fellowship offering. This was the offering of Abidan son
of Gideoni.

66On the tenth day Ahiezer son of Ammishaddai,
the leader of the people of Dan, brought his offering.

67His offering was one silver plate weighing
a hundred and thirty shekels, and one silver
sprinkling bowl weighing seventy shekels,
both according to the sanctuary shekel,

each filled with fine flour mixed with oil as
a grain offering; 68one gold dish weighing
ten shekels, filled with incense; 69one
young bull, one ram and one male lamb a
year old, for a burnt offering; 70one male
goat for a sin offering; 71and two oxen, five
rams, five male goats and five male lambs a
year old, to be sacrificed as a fellowship offering. This was the offering of Ahiezer son
of Ammishaddai.

72On the eleventh day Pagiel son of Ocran, the
leader of the people of Asher, brought his offering.

73His offering was one silver plate weighing
a hundred and thirty shekels, and one silver
sprinkling bowl weighing seventy shekels,
both according to the sanctuary shekel,
each filled with fine flour mixed with oil as
a grain offering; 74one gold dish weighing
ten shekels, filled with incense; 75one
young bull, one ram and one male lamb a
year old, for a burnt offering; 76one male
goat for a sin offering; 77and two oxen, five
rams, five male goats and five male lambs a
year old, to be sacrificed as a fellowship offering. This was the offering of Pagiel son of
Ocran.

78On the twelfth day Ahira son of Enan, the leader of the people of Naphtali, brought his offering.

79His offering was one silver plate weighing
a hundred and thirty shekels, and one silver
sprinkling bowl weighing seventy shekels,
both according to the sanctuary shekel,
each filled with fine flour mixed with oil as
a grain offering; 80one gold dish weighing
ten shekels, filled with incense; 81one
young bull, one ram and one male lamb a
year old, for a burnt offering; 82one male
goat for a sin offering; 83and two oxen, five
rams, five male goats and five male lambs a
year old, to be sacrificed as a fellowship offering. This was the offering of Ahira son of
Enan.

84These were the offerings of the Israelite leaders for the dedication of the altar when it was
anointed: twelve silver plates, twelve silver sprinkling bowls and twelve gold dishes. 85Each silver
plate weighed a hundred and thirty shekels, and
each sprinkling bowl seventy shekels. Altogether,
the silver dishes weighed two thousand four hundred shekels,[a] according to the sanctuary shekel. 86The twelve gold dishes filled with incense
weighed ten shekels each, according to the sanctuary shekel. Altogether, the gold dishes weighed
a hundred and twenty shekels.[b] 87The total
number of animals for the burnt offering came to
twelve young bulls, twelve rams and twelve male
lambs a year old, together with their grain offering. Twelve male goats were used for the sin
offering. 88The total number of animals for the
sacrifice of the fellowship offering came to
twenty-four oxen, sixty rams, sixty male goats
and sixty male lambs a year old. These were the
offerings for the dedication of the altar after it
was anointed.

89When Moses entered the Tent of Meeting to
speak with the LORD, he heard the voice speaking
to him from between the two cherubim above
the atonement cover on the ark of the Testimony.
And he spoke with him.

Setting Up the Lamps

8 The LORD said to Moses, 2"Speak to Aaron
and say to him, 'When you set up the seven
lamps, they are to light the area in front of the
lampstand.' "

3Aaron did so; he set up the lamps so that they
faced forward on the lampstand, just as the LORD
commanded Moses. 4This is how the lampstand
was made: It was made of hammered gold—from
its base to its blossoms. The lampstand was made
exactly like the pattern the LORD had shown Moses.

The Setting Apart of the Levites

5The LORD said to Moses: 6"Take the Levites
from among the other Israelites and make them
ceremonially clean. 7To purify them, do this:
Sprinkle the water of cleansing on them; then
have them shave their whole bodies and wash
their clothes, and so purify themselves. 8Have
them take a young bull with its grain offering of
fine flour mixed with oil; then you are to take a
second young bull for a sin offering. 9Bring the
Levites to the front of the Tent of Meeting and
assemble the whole Israelite community. 10You
are to bring the Levites before the LORD, and the
Israelites are to lay their hands on them. 11Aaron
is to present the Levites before the LORD as a
wave offering from the Israelites, so that they
may be ready to do the work of the LORD.

12"After the Levites lay their hands on the
heads of the bulls, use the one for a sin offering
to the LORD and the other for a burnt offering, to
make atonement for the Levites. 13Have the Levites stand in front of Aaron and his sons and
then present them as a wave offering to the LORD.
14In this way you are to set the Levites apart from
the other Israelites, and the Levites will be mine.

15"After you have purified the Levites and presented them as a wave offering, they are to come
to do their work at the Tent of Meeting. 16They

[a]85 That is, about 60 pounds (about 28 kilograms) [b]86 That is, about 3 pounds (about 1.4 kilograms)

are the Israelites who are to be given wholly to
me. I have taken them as my own in place of the
firstborn, the first male offspring from every Israelite woman. 17Every firstborn male in Israel,
whether man or animal, is mine. When I struck
down all the firstborn in Egypt, I set them apart
for myself. 18And I have taken the Levites in
place of all the firstborn sons in Israel. 19Of all the
Israelites, I have given the Levites as gifts to Aaron and his sons to do the work at the Tent of
Meeting on behalf of the Israelites and to make
atonement for them so that no plague will strike
the Israelites when they go near the sanctuary."

20Moses, Aaron and the whole Israelite community did with the Levites just as the LORD commanded Moses. 21The Levites purified themselves and washed their clothes. Then Aaron
presented them as a wave offering before the
LORD and made atonement for them to purify
them. 22After that, the Levites came to do their
work at the Tent of Meeting under the supervision of Aaron and his sons. They did with the
Levites just as the LORD commanded Moses.

23The LORD said to Moses, 24"This applies to
the Levites: Men twenty-five years old or more
shall come to take part in the work at the Tent of
Meeting, 25but at the age of fifty, they must retire
from their regular service and work no longer.
26They may assist their brothers in performing
their duties at the Tent of Meeting, but they
themselves must not do the work. This, then, is
how you are to assign the responsibilities of the
Levites."

The Passover

9 The LORD spoke to Moses in the Desert of
Sinai in the first month of the second year
after they came out of Egypt. He said, 2"Have the
Israelites celebrate the Passover at the appointed
time. 3Celebrate it at the appointed time, at twilight on the fourteenth day of this month, in accordance with all its rules and regulations."

4So Moses told the Israelites to celebrate the
Passover, 5and they did so in the Desert of Sinai
at twilight on the fourteenth day of the first
month. The Israelites did everything just as the
LORD commanded Moses.

6But some of them could not celebrate the
Passover on that day because they were ceremonially unclean on account of a dead body. So
they came to Moses and Aaron that same day
7and said to Moses, "We have become unclean
because of a dead body, but why should we be
kept from presenting the LORD's offering with the
other Israelites at the appointed time?"

8Moses answered them, "Wait until I find out
what the LORD commands concerning you."

9Then the LORD said to Moses, 10"Tell the Israelites: 'When any of you or your descendants are
unclean because of a dead body or are away on a
journey, they may still celebrate the LORD's Passover. 11They are to celebrate it on the fourteenth
day of the second month at twilight. They are to
eat the lamb, together with unleavened bread
and bitter herbs. 12They must not leave any of it
till morning or break any of its bones. When they
celebrate the Passover, they must follow all the
regulations. 13But if a man who is ceremonially
clean and not on a journey fails to celebrate the
Passover, that person must be cut off from his
people because he did not present the LORD's
offering at the appointed time. That man will
bear the consequences of his sin.

14" 'An alien living among you who wants to
celebrate the LORD's Passover must do so in accordance with its rules and regulations. You must
have the same regulations for the alien and the
native-born.' "

The Cloud Above the Tabernacle

15On the day the tabernacle, the Tent of the
Testimony, was set up, the cloud covered it.
From evening till morning the cloud above the
tabernacle looked like fire. 16That is how it continued to be; the cloud covered it, and at night it
looked like fire. 17Whenever the cloud lifted from
above the Tent, the Israelites set out; wherever
the cloud settled, the Israelites encamped. 18At
the LORD's command the Israelites set out, and
at his command they encamped. As long as the
cloud stayed over the tabernacle, they remained
in camp. 19When the cloud remained over the
tabernacle a long time, the Israelites obeyed the
LORD's order and did not set out. 20Sometimes
the cloud was over the tabernacle only a few
days; at the LORD's command they would encamp, and then at his command they would set
out. 21Sometimes the cloud stayed only from evening till morning, and when it lifted in the morning, they set out. Whether by day or by night,
whenever the cloud lifted, they set out. 22Wheth-
er the cloud stayed over the tabernacle for two
days or a month or a year, the Israelites would
remain in camp and not set out; but when it
lifted, they would set out. 23At the LORD's command they encamped, and at the LORD's command they set out. They obeyed the LORD's order, in accordance with his command through
Moses.

The Silver Trumpets

10 The LORD said to Moses: 2"Make two
trumpets of hammered silver, and use
them for calling the community together and for
having the camps set out. 3When both are sounded, the whole community is to assemble before
you at the entrance to the Tent of Meeting. 4If
only one is sounded, the leaders—the heads of

the clans of Israel—are to assemble before you.
5When a trumpet blast is sounded, the tribes
camping on the east are to set out. 6At the sounding of a second blast, the camps on the south are
to set out. The blast will be the signal for setting
out. 7To gather the assembly, blow the trumpets,
but not with the same signal.
8"The sons of Aaron, the priests, are to blow
the trumpets. This is to be a lasting ordinance for
you and the generations to come. 9When you go
into battle in your own land against an enemy
who is oppressing you, sound a blast on the trumpets. Then you will be remembered by the LORD
your God and rescued from your enemies. 10Also
at your times of rejoicing—your appointed feasts
and New Moon festivals—you are to sound the
trumpets over your burnt offerings and fellowship offerings,[a] and they will be a memorial for
you before your God. I am the LORD your God."

The Israelites Leave Sinai

11On the twentieth day of the second month of
the second year, the cloud lifted from above the
tabernacle of the Testimony. 12Then the Israelites set out from the Desert of Sinai and traveled
from place to place until the cloud came to rest
in the Desert of Paran. 13They set out, this first
time, at the LORD's command through Moses.
14The divisions of the camp of Judah went
first, under their standard. Nahshon son of Amminadab was in command. 15Nethanel son of
Zuar was over the division of the tribe of Issachar, 16and Eliab son of Helon was over the division of the tribe of Zebulun. 17Then the tabernacle was taken down, and the Gershonites and
Merarites, who carried it, set out.
18The divisions of the camp of Reuben went
next, under their standard. Elizur son of Shedeur
was in command. 19Shelumiel son of Zurishaddai
was over the division of the tribe of Simeon,
20and Eliasaph son of Deuel was over the division
of the tribe of Gad. 21Then the Kohathites set out,
carrying the holy things. The tabernacle was to
be set up before they arrived.
22The divisions of the camp of Ephraim went
next, under their standard. Elishama son of Ammihud was in command. 23Gamaliel son of Pedahzur was over the division of the tribe of Manasseh, 24and Abidan son of Gideoni was over
the division of the tribe of Benjamin.
25Finally, as the rear guard for all the units, the
divisions of the camp of Dan set out, under their
standard. Ahiezer son of Ammishaddai was in
command. 26Pagiel son of Ocran was over the
division of the tribe of Asher, 27and Ahira son of
Enan was over the division of the tribe of Naphtali. 28This was the order of march for the Israelite
divisions as they set out.
29Now Moses said to Hobab son of Reuel the
Midianite, Moses' father-in-law, "We are setting
out for the place about which the LORD said, 'I
will give it to you.' Come with us and we will
treat you well, for the LORD has promised good
things to Israel."
30He answered, "No, I will not go; I am going
back to my own land and my own people."
31But Moses said, "Please do not leave us. You
know where we should camp in the desert, and
you can be our eyes. 32If you come with us, we
will share with you whatever good things the
LORD gives us."
33So they set out from the mountain of the
LORD and traveled for three days. The ark of the
covenant of the LORD went before them during
those three days to find them a place to rest.
34The cloud of the LORD was over them by day
when they set out from the camp.
35Whenever the ark set out, Moses said,

"Rise up, O LORD!
May your enemies be scattered;
may your foes flee before you."

36Whenever it came to rest, he said,

"Return, O LORD,
to the countless thousands of Israel."

Fire From the LORD

11 Now the people complained about their
hardships in the hearing of the LORD, and
when he heard them his anger was aroused.
Then fire from the LORD burned among them and
consumed some of the outskirts of the camp.
2When the people cried out to Moses, he prayed
to the LORD and the fire died down. 3So that place
was called Taberah,[b] because fire from the LORD
had burned among them.

Quail From the LORD

4The rabble with them began to crave other
food, and again the Israelites started wailing and
said, "If only we had meat to eat! 5We remember
the fish we ate in Egypt at no cost—also the
cucumbers, melons, leeks, onions and garlic.
6But now we have lost our appetite; we never see
anything but this manna!"
7The manna was like coriander seed and
looked like resin. 8The people went around gathering it, and then ground it in a handmill or
crushed it in a mortar. They cooked it in a pot or
made it into cakes. And it tasted like something
made with olive oil. 9When the dew settled on
the camp at night, the manna also came down.

[a] *10* Traditionally *peace offerings* [b] *3* *Taberah* means *burning.*

10Moses heard the people of every family wailing, each at the entrance to his tent. The LORD
became exceedingly angry, and Moses was troubled. 11He asked the LORD, "Why have you
brought this trouble on your servant? What have
I done to displease you that you put the burden
of all these people on me? 12Did I conceive all
these people? Did I give them birth? Why do you
tell me to carry them in my arms, as a nurse
carries an infant, to the land you promised on
oath to their forefathers? 13Where can I get meat
for all these people? They keep wailing to me,
'Give us meat to eat!' 14I cannot carry all these
people by myself; the burden is too heavy for me.
15If this is how you are going to treat me, put me
to death right now—if I have found favor in your
eyes—and do not let me face my own ruin."
16The LORD said to Moses: "Bring me seventy
of Israel's elders who are known to you as leaders
and officials among the people. Have them come
to the Tent of Meeting, that they may stand there
with you. 17I will come down and speak with you
there, and I will take of the Spirit that is on you
and put the Spirit on them. They will help
you carry the burden of the people so that you
will not have to carry it alone.
18"Tell the people: 'Consecrate yourselves in
preparation for tomorrow, when you will eat
meat. The LORD heard you when you wailed, "If
only we had meat to eat! We were better off in
Egypt!" Now the LORD will give you meat, and
you will eat it. 19You will not eat it for just one
day, or two days, or five, ten or twenty days,
20but for a whole month—until it comes out of
your nostrils and you loathe it—because you
have rejected the LORD, who is among you, and
have wailed before him, saying, "Why did we
ever leave Egypt?" ' "
21But Moses said, "Here I am among six hundred thousand men on foot, and you say, 'I will
give them meat to eat for a whole month!'
22Would they have enough if flocks and herds
were slaughtered for them? Would they have
enough if all the fish in the sea were caught for
them?"
23The LORD answered Moses, "Is the LORD's
arm too short? You will now see whether or not
what I say will come true for you."
24So Moses went out and told the people what
the LORD had said. He brought together seventy
of their elders and had them stand around the
Tent. 25Then the LORD came down in the cloud
and spoke with him, and he took of the Spirit that
was on him and put the Spirit on the seventy
elders. When the Spirit rested on them, they
prophesied, but they did not do so again.[a]
26However, two men, whose names were Eldad and Medad, had remained in the camp. They
were listed among the elders, but did not go out
to the Tent. Yet the Spirit also rested on them,
and they prophesied in the camp. 27A young man
ran and told Moses, "Eldad and Medad are prophesying in the camp."
28Joshua son of Nun, who had been Moses'
aide since youth, spoke up and said, "Moses, my
lord, stop them!"
29But Moses replied, "Are you jealous for my
sake? I wish that all the LORD's people were
prophets and that the LORD would put his Spirit
on them!" 30Then Moses and the elders of Israel
returned to the camp.
31Now a wind went out from the LORD and
drove quail in from the sea. It brought them[b]
down all around the camp to about three feet[c]
above the ground, as far as a day's walk in any
direction. 32All that day and night and all the next
day the people went out and gathered quail. No
one gathered less than ten homers.[d] Then they
spread them out all around the camp. 33But while
the meat was still between their teeth and before
it could be consumed, the anger of the LORD
burned against the people, and he struck them
with a severe plague. 34Therefore the place was
named Kibroth Hattaavah,[e] because there they
buried the people who had craved other food.
35From Kibroth Hattaavah the people traveled
to Hazeroth and stayed there.

Miriam and Aaron Oppose Moses

12 Miriam and Aaron began to talk against
Moses because of his Cushite wife, for he
had married a Cushite. 2"Has the LORD spoken
only through Moses?" they asked. "Hasn't he also
spoken through us?" And the LORD heard this.
3(Now Moses was a very humble man, more
humble than anyone else on the face of the
earth.)
4At once the LORD said to Moses, Aaron and
Miriam, "Come out to the Tent of Meeting, all
three of you." So the three of them came out.
5Then the LORD came down in a pillar of cloud;
he stood at the entrance to the Tent and summoned Aaron and Miriam. When both of them
stepped forward, 6he said, "Listen to my words:

"When a prophet of the LORD is among you,
    I reveal myself to him in visions,
    I speak to him in dreams.
7But this is not true of my servant Moses;
    he is faithful in all my house.
8With him I speak face to face,
    clearly and not in riddles;
    he sees the form of the LORD.

[a]25 Or *prophesied and continued to do so* [b]31 Or *They flew* [c]31 Hebrew *two cubits* (about 1 meter) [d]32 That is, probably about 60 bushels (about 2.2 kiloliters) [e]34 *Kibroth Hattaavah* means *graves of craving.*

Why then were you not afraid
to speak against my servant Moses?"

[9]The anger of the LORD burned against them, and he left them.

NUMBERS 12:1–15

1. What person in your family deserves the "Most Humble" award?
2. What person in this group deserves that award? Why?
3. On family issues, are you and your brothers/sisters generally together or divided?
4. If you had been Moses, how would you have felt when you found out your own brother and sister were bad-mouthing you?
5. Do you think God was too hard on Miriam? If you had been in charge, how would you have dealt with her?
6. How do you expect God to punish you when you mess up?
7. What have you learned from this story that you need to put into practice? How can this group help?

[10]When the cloud lifted from above the Tent,
there stood Miriam—leprous,[a] like snow. Aaron turned toward her and saw that she had leprosy; [11]and he said to Moses, "Please, my lord, do
not hold against us the sin we have so foolishly
committed. [12]Do not let her be like a stillborn
infant coming from its mother's womb with its
flesh half eaten away."
[13]So Moses cried out to the LORD, "O God,
please heal her!"
[14]The LORD replied to Moses, "If her father
had spit in her face, would she not have been in
disgrace for seven days? Confine her outside the
camp for seven days; after that she can be
brought back." [15]So Miriam was confined outside
the camp for seven days, and the people did not
move on till she was brought back.
[16]After that, the people left Hazeroth and encamped in the Desert of Paran.

Exploring Canaan

13 The LORD said to Moses, [2]"Send some
men to explore the land of Canaan, which
I am giving to the Israelites. From each ancestral
tribe send one of its leaders."
[3]So at the LORD's command Moses sent them
out from the Desert of Paran. All of them were
leaders of the Israelites. [4]These are their names:

from the tribe of Reuben, Shammua son of Zaccur;
[5]from the tribe of Simeon, Shaphat son of Hori;
[6]from the tribe of Judah, Caleb son of Jephunneh;
[7]from the tribe of Issachar, Igal son of Joseph;
[8]from the tribe of Ephraim, Hoshea son of Nun;
[9]from the tribe of Benjamin, Palti son of Raphu;
[10]from the tribe of Zebulun, Gaddiel son of Sodi;
[11]from the tribe of Manasseh (a tribe of Joseph), Gaddi son of Susi;
[12]from the tribe of Dan, Ammiel son of Gemalli;
[13]from the tribe of Asher, Sethur son of Michael;
[14]from the tribe of Naphtali, Nahbi son of Vophsi;
[15]from the tribe of Gad, Geuel son of Maki.

[16]These are the names of the men Moses sent to

[a]*10* The Hebrew word was used for various diseases affecting the skin—not necessarily leprosy.

12:1 *Miriam and Aaron.* Moses' sister and brother. ***Cushite wife.*** Moses' wife Zipporah may be referred to here; if so, the term "Cushite" is used in contempt of her Midianite ancestry. It is more likely, however, that the reference is to a new wife taken by Moses, perhaps after the death of his first wife. The criticism of the woman was really an excuse to attack Moses' prophetic gift and his special relationship with God.

12:2 *Hasn't he also spoken through us?* Of course he had. Micah 6:4 speaks of Moses, Aaron and Miriam as God's gracious provision for Israel. The prophetic gifting of the 70 elders (11:24–30) seems to have been the immediate provocation for the attack of Miriam and Aaron on their brother.

12:3 Perhaps a later addition to the text, stating the great unfairness of the charges.

12:6–8 The point of the poem is clear: True prophetic vision is from the Lord, but in the case of Moses his position and faithfulness enhance his special relationship with God.

12:10 *leprous.* See NIV text note. Miriam, the principal offender, has become an outcast, as she now suffers from a skin disease that would exclude her from the community of Israel (see 5:1–4).

12:11 *Please, my lord.* Aaron's repentance is touching, both in its intensity and in his concern for his (and Moses') sister.

12:14 *disgrace for seven days.* An act of public rebuke (see Deut. 25:9) demands a period of public shame.

explore the land. (Moses gave Hoshea son of Nun the name Joshua.)

[17]When Moses sent them to explore Canaan, he said, "Go up through the Negev and on into the hill country. [18]See what the land is like and whether the people who live there are strong or weak, few or many. [19]What kind of land do they live in? Is it good or bad? What kind of towns do they live in? Are they unwalled or fortified? [20]How is the soil? Is it fertile or poor? Are there trees on it or not? Do your best to bring back some of the fruit of the land." (It was the season for the first ripe grapes.)

[21]So they went up and explored the land from the Desert of Zin as far as Rehob, toward Lebo[a] Hamath. [22]They went up through the Negev and came to Hebron, where Ahiman, Sheshai and Talmai, the descendants of Anak, lived. (Hebron had been built seven years before Zoan in Egypt.) [23]When they reached the Valley of Eshcol,[b] they cut off a branch bearing a single cluster of grapes. Two of them carried it on a pole between them, along with some pomegranates and figs. [24]That place was called the Valley of Eshcol because of the cluster of grapes the Israelites cut off there. [25]At the end of forty days they returned from exploring the land.

Report on the Exploration

[26]They came back to Moses and Aaron and the whole Israelite community at Kadesh in the Desert of Paran. There they reported to them and to the whole assembly and showed them the fruit of the land. [27]They gave Moses this account: "We went into the land to which you sent us, and it does flow with milk and honey! Here is its fruit. [28]But the people who live there are powerful, and the cities are fortified and very large. We even saw descendants of Anak there. [29]The Amalekites live in the Negev; the Hittites, Jebusites and Amorites live in the hill country; and the Canaanites live near the sea and along the Jordan."

[30]Then Caleb silenced the people before Moses and said, "We should go up and take possession of the land, for we can certainly do it."

[31]But the men who had gone up with him said, "We can't attack those people; they are stronger than we are." [32]And they spread among the Israelites a bad report about the land they had explored. They said, "The land we explored devours those living in it. All the people we saw there are of great size. [33]We saw the Nephilim there (the descendants of Anak come from the Nephilim). We seemed like grasshoppers in our own eyes, and we looked the same to them."

NUMBERS 13:26–14:10,26–45

1. Are you more likely to stop and ask directions if you are lost or drive around until you find your way?
2. Out of your family/friends, who is the greatest optimist? Who is the pessimist?
3. If you had to make a big decision about the future direction of your life, who would you turn to for advice?
4. Why would Israel turn "chicken" when God had already demonstrated he could overcome powerful forces?
5. When you realize you have blown it, what are you likely to do: Cover things up? Patch things up? Blow it off? Simply take the consequences?
6. What "giants" are you facing now: Circumstances? Fears? Decisions? Certain people?
7. What spiritual challenge is God calling you to explore? How can this group help you in prayer?

[a]21 Or *toward the entrance to* [b]23 *Eshcol* means *cluster*; also in verse 24.

13:26–29 ***came back.*** At the people's bidding, the Lord had Moses send a representative from the 12 tribes of Israel to spy out Canaan (Deut. 1:22; Num. 13:1–2). The first part of the spies' "majority report" was truthful, but the goodness of the land was offset in their fearful eyes by the powerful peoples living there. Their words became exaggerations and distortions, to the point of "We seemed like grasshoppers" (v. 33).

13:30 Only Caleb and Joshua gave a report on the promised land prompted by faith.

14:9 ***the LORD is with us.*** There are no walls, fortifications, giants and certainly no gods that can withstand God's people.

14:28 ***I will do to you the very things I heard you say.*** They had said they would rather die in the desert (v. 2) than be led into Canaan to die by the sword. All those 20 years old or more (except Caleb and Joshua) would die in the desert (vv. 29–30). Only their children would survive (v. 31)—the children that the people said God would allow to die in the desert (v. 3).

14:34 The 40 days of the travels of the spies became the numerical pattern for the Israelites' suffering: for 40 years they would recount their misjudgment.

14:40 ***We will go up.*** Now, too late, the people determine to go up to the land they had refused. Such a course of action was doomed to failure. Not only was the Lord not with them; he was against them (v. 41). Their subsequent defeat (v. 45) was another judgment the rebellious people brought down upon their own heads.

The People Rebel

14 That night all the people of the community raised their voices and wept aloud. 2All
the Israelites grumbled against Moses and Aaron,
and the whole assembly said to them, "If only we
had died in Egypt! Or in this desert! 3Why is the
LORD bringing us to this land only to let us fall by
the sword? Our wives and children will be taken
as plunder. Wouldn't it be better for us to go back
to Egypt?" 4And they said to each other, "We
should choose a leader and go back to Egypt."
5Then Moses and Aaron fell facedown in front
of the whole Israelite assembly gathered there.
6Joshua son of Nun and Caleb son of Jephunneh,
who were among those who had explored the
land, tore their clothes 7and said to the entire
Israelite assembly, "The land we passed through
and explored is exceedingly good. 8If the LORD is
pleased with us, he will lead us into that land, a
land flowing with milk and honey, and will give
it to us. 9Only do not rebel against the LORD. And
do not be afraid of the people of the land, because
we will swallow them up. Their protection is
gone, but the LORD is with us. Do not be afraid of
them."
10But the whole assembly talked about stoning
them. Then the glory of the LORD appeared at the
Tent of Meeting to all the Israelites. 11The LORD
said to Moses, "How long will these people treat
me with contempt? How long will they refuse to
believe in me, in spite of all the miraculous signs
I have performed among them? 12I will strike
them down with a plague and destroy them, but
I will make you into a nation greater and stronger
than they."
13Moses said to the LORD, "Then the Egyptians
will hear about it! By your power you brought
these people up from among them. 14And they
will tell the inhabitants of this land about it. They
have already heard that you, O LORD, are with
these people and that you, O LORD, have been
seen face to face, that your cloud stays over them,
and that you go before them in a pillar of cloud by
day and a pillar of fire by night. 15If you put these
people to death all at one time, the nations who
have heard this report about you will say, 16'The
LORD was not able to bring these people into the
land he promised them on oath; so he slaughtered them in the desert.'
17"Now may the Lord's strength be displayed,
just as you have declared: 18'The LORD is slow to
anger, abounding in love and forgiving sin and
rebellion. Yet he does not leave the guilty unpunished; he punishes the children for the sin of the
fathers to the third and fourth generation.' 19In
accordance with your great love, forgive the sin
of these people, just as you have pardoned them
from the time they left Egypt until now."
20The LORD replied, "I have forgiven them, as
you asked. 21Nevertheless, as surely as I live and
as surely as the glory of the LORD fills the whole
earth, 22not one of the men who saw my glory
and the miraculous signs I performed in Egypt
and in the desert but who disobeyed me and tested me ten times— 23not one of them will ever
see the land I promised on oath to their forefathers. No one who has treated me with contempt
will ever see it. 24But because my servant Caleb
has a different spirit and follows me wholeheartedly, I will bring him into the land he went to,
and his descendants will inherit it. 25Since the
Amalekites and Canaanites are living in the valleys, turn back tomorrow and set out toward the
desert along the route to the Red Sea.[a]"
26The LORD said to Moses and Aaron: 27"How
long will this wicked community grumble against
me? I have heard the complaints of these grumbling Israelites. 28So tell them, 'As surely as I live,
declares the LORD, I will do to you the very things
I heard you say: 29In this desert your bodies will
fall—every one of you twenty years old or more
who was counted in the census and who has
grumbled against me. 30Not one of you will enter
the land I swore with uplifted hand to make your
home, except Caleb son of Jephunneh and Joshua
son of Nun. 31As for your children that you said
would be taken as plunder, I will bring them in
to enjoy the land you have rejected. 32But you—
your bodies will fall in this desert. 33Your children will be shepherds here for forty years, suffering for your unfaithfulness, until the last of
your bodies lies in the desert. 34For forty years—
one year for each of the forty days you explored
the land—you will suffer for your sins and know
what it is like to have me against you.' 35I, the
LORD, have spoken, and I will surely do these
things to this whole wicked community, which
has banded together against me. They will meet
their end in this desert; here they will die."
36So the men Moses had sent to explore the
land, who returned and made the whole community grumble against him by spreading a bad report about it— 37these men responsible for
spreading the bad report about the land were
struck down and died of a plague before the
LORD. 38Of the men who went to explore the
land, only Joshua son of Nun and Caleb son of
Jephunneh survived.
39When Moses reported this to all the Israelites, they mourned bitterly. 40Early the next
morning they went up toward the high hill country. "We have sinned," they said. "We will go up
to the place the LORD promised."

a25 Hebrew *Yam Suph*; that is, Sea of Reeds

41But Moses said, "Why are you disobeying the LORD's command? This will not succeed! 42Do not go up, because the LORD is not with you. You will be defeated by your enemies, 43for the Amalekites and Canaanites will face you there. Because you have turned away from the LORD, he will not be with you and you will fall by the sword."

44Nevertheless, in their presumption they went up toward the high hill country, though neither Moses nor the ark of the LORD's covenant moved from the camp. 45Then the Amalekites and Canaanites who lived in that hill country came down and attacked them and beat them down all the way to Hormah.

Supplementary Offerings

15 The LORD said to Moses, 2"Speak to the Israelites and say to them: 'After you enter the land I am giving you as a home 3and you present to the LORD offerings made by fire, from the herd or the flock, as an aroma pleasing to the LORD—whether burnt offerings or sacrifices, for special vows or freewill offerings or festival offerings— 4then the one who brings his offering shall present to the LORD a grain offering of a tenth of an ephah[a] of fine flour mixed with a quarter of a hin[b] of oil. 5With each lamb for the burnt offering or the sacrifice, prepare a quarter of a hin of wine as a drink offering.

6" 'With a ram prepare a grain offering of two-tenths of an ephah[c] of fine flour mixed with a third of a hin[d] of oil, 7and a third of a hin of wine as a drink offering. Offer it as an aroma pleasing to the LORD.

8" 'When you prepare a young bull as a burnt offering or sacrifice, for a special vow or a fellowship offering[e] to the LORD, 9bring with the bull a grain offering of three-tenths of an ephah[f] of fine flour mixed with half a hin[g] of oil. 10Also bring half a hin of wine as a drink offering. It will be an offering made by fire, an aroma pleasing to the LORD. 11Each bull or ram, each lamb or young goat, is to be prepared in this manner. 12Do this for each one, for as many as you prepare.

13" 'Everyone who is native-born must do these things in this way when he brings an offering made by fire as an aroma pleasing to the LORD. 14For the generations to come, whenever an alien or anyone else living among you presents an offering made by fire as an aroma pleasing to the LORD, he must do exactly as you do. 15The community is to have the same rules for you and for the alien living among you; this is a lasting ordinance for the generations to come. You and the alien shall be the same before the LORD: 16The same laws and regulations will apply both to you and to the alien living among you.' "

17The LORD said to Moses, 18"Speak to the Israelites and say to them: 'When you enter the land to which I am taking you 19and you eat the food of the land, present a portion as an offering to the LORD. 20Present a cake from the first of your ground meal and present it as an offering from the threshing floor. 21Throughout the generations to come you are to give this offering to the LORD from the first of your ground meal.

Offerings for Unintentional Sins

22" 'Now if you unintentionally fail to keep any of these commands the LORD gave Moses— 23any of the LORD's commands to you through him, from the day the LORD gave them and continuing through the generations to come— 24and if this is done unintentionally without the community being aware of it, then the whole community is to offer a young bull for a burnt offering as an aroma pleasing to the LORD, along with its prescribed grain offering and drink offering, and a male goat for a sin offering. 25The priest is to make atonement for the whole Israelite community, and they will be forgiven, for it was not intentional and they have brought to the LORD for their wrong an offering made by fire and a sin offering. 26The whole Israelite community and the aliens living among them will be forgiven, because all the people were involved in the unintentional wrong.

27" 'But if just one person sins unintentionally, he must bring a year-old female goat for a sin offering. 28The priest is to make atonement before the LORD for the one who erred by sinning unintentionally, and when atonement has been made for him, he will be forgiven. 29One and the same law applies to everyone who sins unintentionally, whether he is a native-born Israelite or an alien.

30" 'But anyone who sins defiantly, whether native-born or alien, blasphemes the LORD, and that person must be cut off from his people. 31Because he has despised the LORD's word and broken his commands, that person must surely be cut off; his guilt remains on him.' "

The Sabbath-Breaker Put to Death

32While the Israelites were in the desert, a man was found gathering wood on the Sabbath day. 33Those who found him gathering wood brought him to Moses and Aaron and the whole assembly, 34and they kept him in custody, be-

[a]4 That is, probably about 2 quarts (about 2 liters) [b]4 That is, probably about 1 quart (about 1 liter); also in verse 5 [c]6 That is, probably about 4 quarts (about 4.5 liters) [d]6 That is, probably about 1 1/4 quarts (about 1.2 liters); also in verse 7 [e]8 Traditionally *peace offering* [f]9 That is, probably about 6 quarts (about 6.5 liters) [g]9 That is, probably about 2 quarts (about 2 liters); also in verse 10

cause it was not clear what should be done to
him. 35Then the LORD said to Moses, "The man
must die. The whole assembly must stone him
outside the camp." 36So the assembly took him
outside the camp and stoned him to death, as the
LORD commanded Moses.

Tassels on Garments

37The LORD said to Moses, 38"Speak to the Israelites and say to them: 'Throughout the generations to come you are to make tassels on the
corners of your garments, with a blue cord on
each tassel. 39You will have these tassels to look
at and so you will remember all the commands of
the LORD, that you may obey them and not prostitute yourselves by going after the lusts of your
own hearts and eyes. 40Then you will remember
to obey all my commands and will be consecrated
to your God. 41I am the LORD your God, who
brought you out of Egypt to be your God. I am the
LORD your God.' "

Korah, Dathan and Abiram

16 Korah son of Izhar, the son of Kohath, the
son of Levi, and certain Reubenites—
Dathan and Abiram, sons of Eliab, and On son of
Peleth—became insolent[a] 2and rose up against
Moses. With them were 250 Israelite men, well-
known community leaders who had been appointed members of the council. 3They came as a
group to oppose Moses and Aaron and said to
them, "You have gone too far! The whole community is holy, every one of them, and the LORD
is with them. Why then do you set yourselves
above the LORD's assembly?"

4When Moses heard this, he fell facedown.
5Then he said to Korah and all his followers: "In
the morning the LORD will show who belongs to
him and who is holy, and he will have that person come near him. The man he chooses he will
cause to come near him. 6You, Korah, and all
your followers are to do this: Take censers 7and
tomorrow put fire and incense in them before the
LORD. The man the LORD chooses will be the one
who is holy. You Levites have gone too far!"

8Moses also said to Korah, "Now listen, you
Levites! 9Isn't it enough for you that the God of
Israel has separated you from the rest of the Israelite community and brought you near himself to
do the work at the LORD's tabernacle and to stand
before the community and minister to them?
10He has brought you and all your fellow Levites
near himself, but now you are trying to get the
priesthood too. 11It is against the LORD that you
and all your followers have banded together.
Who is Aaron that you should grumble against
him?"

12Then Moses summoned Dathan and Abiram,
the sons of Eliab. But they said, "We will not
come! 13Isn't it enough that you have brought us
up out of a land flowing with milk and honey to
kill us in the desert? And now you also want to
lord it over us? 14Moreover, you haven't brought
us into a land flowing with milk and honey or
given us an inheritance of fields and vineyards.
Will you gouge out the eyes of[b] these men? No,
we will not come!"

15Then Moses became very angry and said to
the LORD, "Do not accept their offering. I have
not taken so much as a donkey from them, nor
have I wronged any of them."

16Moses said to Korah, "You and all your
followers are to appear before the LORD
tomorrow—you and they and Aaron. 17Each man
is to take his censer and put incense in it—250
censers in all—and present it before the LORD.
You and Aaron are to present your censers also."
18So each man took his censer, put fire and incense in it, and stood with Moses and Aaron at
the entrance to the Tent of Meeting. 19When Korah had gathered all his followers in opposition to
them at the entrance to the Tent of Meeting, the
glory of the LORD appeared to the entire assembly. 20The LORD said to Moses and Aaron, 21"Separate yourselves from this assembly so I can put
an end to them at once."

22But Moses and Aaron fell facedown and
cried out, "O God, God of the spirits of all mankind, will you be angry with the entire assembly
when only one man sins?"

23Then the LORD said to Moses, 24"Say to the
assembly, 'Move away from the tents of Korah,
Dathan and Abiram.' "

25Moses got up and went to Dathan and Abiram, and the elders of Israel followed him. 26He
warned the assembly, "Move back from the tents
of these wicked men! Do not touch anything belonging to them, or you will be swept away because of all their sins." 27So they moved away
from the tents of Korah, Dathan and Abiram. Dathan and Abiram had come out and were standing with their wives, children and little ones at
the entrances to their tents.

28Then Moses said, "This is how you will
know that the LORD has sent me to do all these
things and that it was not my idea: 29If these men
die a natural death and experience only what
usually happens to men, then the LORD has not
sent me. 30But if the LORD brings about something totally new, and the earth opens its mouth
and swallows them, with everything that belongs
to them, and they go down alive into the grave,[c]
then you will know that these men have treated
the LORD with contempt."

[a] 1 Or *Peleth—took* ⌞*men*⌟ [b] 14 Or *you make slaves of*; or *you deceive* [c] 30 Hebrew *Sheol*; also in verse 33

31As soon as he finished saying all this, the ground under them split apart 32and the earth opened its mouth and swallowed them, with their households and all Korah's men and all their possessions. 33They went down alive into the grave, with everything they owned; the earth closed over them, and they perished and were gone from the community. 34At their cries, all the Israelites around them fled, shouting, "The earth is going to swallow us too!"

35And fire came out from the LORD and consumed the 250 men who were offering the incense.

36The LORD said to Moses, 37"Tell Eleazar son of Aaron, the priest, to take the censers out of the smoldering remains and scatter the coals some distance away, for the censers are holy— 38the censers of the men who sinned at the cost of their lives. Hammer the censers into sheets to overlay the altar, for they were presented before the LORD and have become holy. Let them be a sign to the Israelites."

39So Eleazar the priest collected the bronze censers brought by those who had been burned up, and he had them hammered out to overlay the altar, 40as the LORD directed him through Moses. This was to remind the Israelites that no one except a descendant of Aaron should come to burn incense before the LORD, or he would become like Korah and his followers.

41The next day the whole Israelite community grumbled against Moses and Aaron. "You have killed the LORD's people," they said.

42But when the assembly gathered in opposition to Moses and Aaron and turned toward the Tent of Meeting, suddenly the cloud covered it and the glory of the LORD appeared. 43Then Moses and Aaron went to the front of the Tent of Meeting, 44and the LORD said to Moses, 45"Get away from this assembly so I can put an end to them at once." And they fell facedown.

46Then Moses said to Aaron, "Take your censer and put incense in it, along with fire from the altar, and hurry to the assembly to make atonement for them. Wrath has come out from the LORD; the plague has started." 47So Aaron did as Moses said, and ran into the midst of the assembly. The plague had already started among the people, but Aaron offered the incense and made atonement for them. 48He stood between the living and the dead, and the plague stopped. 49But 14,700 people died from the plague, in addition to those who had died because of Korah. 50Then Aaron returned to Moses at the entrance to the Tent of Meeting, for the plague had stopped.

The Budding of Aaron's Staff

17 The LORD said to Moses, 2"Speak to the Israelites and get twelve staffs from them, one from the leader of each of their ancestral tribes. Write the name of each man on his staff. 3On the staff of Levi write Aaron's name, for there must be one staff for the head of each ancestral tribe. 4Place them in the Tent of Meeting in front of the Testimony, where I meet with you. 5The staff belonging to the man I choose will sprout, and I will rid myself of this constant grumbling against you by the Israelites."

6So Moses spoke to the Israelites, and their leaders gave him twelve staffs, one for the leader of each of their ancestral tribes, and Aaron's staff was among them. 7Moses placed the staffs before the LORD in the Tent of the Testimony.

8The next day Moses entered the Tent of the Testimony and saw that Aaron's staff, which represented the house of Levi, had not only sprouted but had budded, blossomed and produced almonds. 9Then Moses brought out all the staffs from the LORD's presence to all the Israelites. They looked at them, and each man took his own staff.

10The LORD said to Moses, "Put back Aaron's staff in front of the Testimony, to be kept as a sign to the rebellious. This will put an end to their grumbling against me, so that they will not die." 11Moses did just as the LORD commanded him.

12The Israelites said to Moses, "We will die! We are lost, we are all lost! 13Anyone who even comes near the tabernacle of the LORD will die. Are we all going to die?"

Duties of Priests and Levites

18 The LORD said to Aaron, "You, your sons and your father's family are to bear the responsibility for offenses against the sanctuary, and you and your sons alone are to bear the responsibility for offenses against the priesthood. 2Bring your fellow Levites from your ancestral tribe to join you and assist you when you and your sons minister before the Tent of the Testimony. 3They are to be responsible to you and are to perform all the duties of the Tent, but they must not go near the furnishings of the sanctuary or the altar, or both they and you will die. 4They are to join you and be responsible for the care of the Tent of Meeting—all the work at the Tent—and no one else may come near where you are.

5"You are to be responsible for the care of the sanctuary and the altar, so that wrath will not fall on the Israelites again. 6I myself have selected your fellow Levites from among the Israelites as a gift to you, dedicated to the LORD to do the work at the Tent of Meeting. 7But only you and your sons may serve as priests in connection with everything at the altar and inside the curtain. I am giving you the service of the priesthood as a gift. Anyone else who comes near the sanctuary must be put to death."

Offerings for Priests and Levites

8Then the LORD said to Aaron, "I myself have
put you in charge of the offerings presented to
me; all the holy offerings the Israelites give me I
give to you and your sons as your portion and
regular share. 9You are to have the part of the
most holy offerings that is kept from the fire.
From all the gifts they bring me as most holy
offerings, whether grain or sin or guilt offerings,
that part belongs to you and your sons. 10Eat it as
something most holy; every male shall eat it. You
must regard it as holy.

11"This also is yours: whatever is set aside
from the gifts of all the wave offerings of the
Israelites. I give this to you and your sons and
daughters as your regular share. Everyone in your
household who is ceremonially clean may eat it.

12"I give you all the finest olive oil and all the
finest new wine and grain they give the LORD as
the firstfruits of their harvest. 13All the land's
firstfruits that they bring to the LORD will be
yours. Everyone in your household who is ceremonially clean may eat it.

14"Everything in Israel that is devoted[a] to the
LORD is yours. 15The first offspring of every
womb, both man and animal, that is offered to
the LORD is yours. But you must redeem every
firstborn son and every firstborn male of unclean
animals. 16When they are a month old, you must
redeem them at the redemption price set at five
shekels[b] of silver, according to the sanctuary
shekel, which weighs twenty gerahs.

17"But you must not redeem the firstborn of an
ox, a sheep or a goat; they are holy. Sprinkle their
blood on the altar and burn their fat as an offering
made by fire, an aroma pleasing to the LORD.
18Their meat is to be yours, just as the breast of
the wave offering and the right thigh are yours.
19Whatever is set aside from the holy offerings
the Israelites present to the LORD I give to you
and your sons and daughters as your regular
share. It is an everlasting covenant of salt before
the LORD for both you and your offspring."

20The LORD said to Aaron, "You will have no
inheritance in their land, nor will you have any
share among them; I am your share and your
inheritance among the Israelites.

21"I give to the Levites all the tithes in Israel as
their inheritance in return for the work they do
while serving at the Tent of Meeting. 22From
now on the Israelites must not go near the Tent
of Meeting, or they will bear the consequences of
their sin and will die. 23It is the Levites who are
to do the work at the Tent of Meeting and bear
the responsibility for offenses against it. This is a
lasting ordinance for the generations to come.
They will receive no inheritance among the Israelites. 24Instead, I give to the Levites as their
inheritance the tithes that the Israelites present
as an offering to the LORD. That is why I said
concerning them: 'They will have no inheritance
among the Israelites.'"

25The LORD said to Moses, 26"Speak to the Levites and say to them: 'When you receive from
the Israelites the tithe I give you as your inheritance, you must present a tenth of that tithe as
the LORD's offering. 27Your offering will be reckoned to you as grain from the threshing floor or
juice from the winepress. 28In this way you also
will present an offering to the LORD from all the
tithes you receive from the Israelites. From these
tithes you must give the LORD's portion to Aaron
the priest. 29You must present as the LORD's portion the best and holiest part of everything given
to you.'

30"Say to the Levites: 'When you present the
best part, it will be reckoned to you as the product of the threshing floor or the winepress. 31You
and your households may eat the rest of it anywhere, for it is your wages for your work at the
Tent of Meeting. 32By presenting the best part of
it you will not be guilty in this matter; then you
will not defile the holy offerings of the Israelites,
and you will not die.'"

The Water of Cleansing

19 The LORD said to Moses and Aaron:
2"This is a requirement of the law that
the LORD has commanded: Tell the Israelites to
bring you a red heifer without defect or blemish
and that has never been under a yoke. 3Give it to
Eleazar the priest; it is to be taken outside the
camp and slaughtered in his presence. 4Then Eleazar the priest is to take some of its blood on his
finger and sprinkle it seven times toward the
front of the Tent of Meeting. 5While he watches,
the heifer is to be burned—its hide, flesh, blood
and offal. 6The priest is to take some cedar wood,
hyssop and scarlet wool and throw them onto the
burning heifer. 7After that, the priest must wash
his clothes and bathe himself with water. He may
then come into the camp, but he will be ceremonially unclean till evening. 8The man who
burns it must also wash his clothes and bathe
with water, and he too will be unclean till evening.

9"A man who is clean shall gather up the ashes
of the heifer and put them in a ceremonially
clean place outside the camp. They shall be kept
by the Israelite community for use in the water of
cleansing; it is for purification from sin. 10The
man who gathers up the ashes of the heifer must

a14 The Hebrew term refers to the irrevocable giving over of things or persons to the LORD. b16 That is, about 2 ounces (about 55 grams)

also wash his clothes, and he too will be unclean
till evening. This will be a lasting ordinance both
for the Israelites and for the aliens living among
them.
11“Whoever touches the dead body of anyone
will be unclean for seven days. 12He must purify
himself with the water on the third day and on
the seventh day; then he will be clean. But if he
does not purify himself on the third and seventh
days, he will not be clean. 13Whoever touches
the dead body of anyone and fails to purify himself defiles the LORD's tabernacle. That person
must be cut off from Israel. Because the water of
cleansing has not been sprinkled on him, he is
unclean; his uncleanness remains on him.
14“This is the law that applies when a person
dies in a tent: Anyone who enters the tent and
anyone who is in it will be unclean for seven
days, 15and every open container without a lid
fastened on it will be unclean.
16“Anyone out in the open who touches someone who has been killed with a sword or someone who has died a natural death, or anyone who
touches a human bone or a grave, will be unclean
for seven days.
17“For the unclean person, put some ashes
from the burned purification offering into a jar
and pour fresh water over them. 18Then a man
who is ceremonially clean is to take some hyssop,
dip it in the water and sprinkle the tent and all
the furnishings and the people who were there.
He must also sprinkle anyone who has touched a
human bone or a grave or someone who has been
killed or someone who has died a natural death.
19The man who is clean is to sprinkle the unclean
person on the third and seventh days, and on the
seventh day he is to purify him. The person being
cleansed must wash his clothes and bathe with
water, and that evening he will be clean. 20But if
a person who is unclean does not purify himself,
he must be cut off from the community, because
he has defiled the sanctuary of the LORD. The
water of cleansing has not been sprinkled on
him, and he is unclean. 21This is a lasting ordinance for them.
“The man who sprinkles the water of cleansing must also wash his clothes, and anyone who
touches the water of cleansing will be unclean
till evening. 22Anything that an unclean person
touches becomes unclean, and anyone who
touches it becomes unclean till evening.”

Water From the Rock

20 In the first month the whole Israelite
community arrived at the Desert of Zin,
and they stayed at Kadesh. There Miriam died
and was buried.
2Now there was no water for the community,
and the people gathered in opposition to Moses
and Aaron. 3They quarreled with Moses and said,
“If only we had died when our brothers fell dead
before the LORD! 4Why did you bring the LORD's
community into this desert, that we and our livestock should die here? 5Why did you bring us up
out of Egypt to this terrible place? It has no grain
or figs, grapevines or pomegranates. And there is
no water to drink!”
6Moses and Aaron went from the assembly to
the entrance to the Tent of Meeting and fell facedown, and the glory of the LORD appeared to
them. 7The LORD said to Moses, 8“Take the staff,
and you and your brother Aaron gather the assembly together. Speak to that rock before their
eyes and it will pour out its water. You will bring
water out of the rock for the community so they
and their livestock can drink.”
9So Moses took the staff from the LORD's presence, just as he commanded him. 10He and Aaron
gathered the assembly together in front of the
rock and Moses said to them, “Listen, you rebels,
must we bring you water out of this rock?”
11Then Moses raised his arm and struck the rock
twice with his staff. Water gushed out, and the
community and their livestock drank.
12But the LORD said to Moses and Aaron, “Because you did not trust in me enough to honor
me as holy in the sight of the Israelites, you will
not bring this community into the land I give
them.”
13These were the waters of Meribah,[a] where
the Israelites quarreled with the LORD and where
he showed himself holy among them.

Edom Denies Israel Passage

14Moses sent messengers from Kadesh to the
king of Edom, saying:

“This is what your brother Israel says:
You know about all the hardships that have
come upon us. 15Our forefathers went
down into Egypt, and we lived there many
years. The Egyptians mistreated us and our
fathers, 16but when we cried out to the
LORD, he heard our cry and sent an angel
and brought us out of Egypt.
“Now we are here at Kadesh, a town on
the edge of your territory. 17Please let us
pass through your country. We will not go
through any field or vineyard, or drink water from any well. We will travel along the
king's highway and not turn to the right or
to the left until we have passed through
your territory.”

18But Edom answered:

[a] 13 *Meribah* means *quarreling*.

"You may not pass through here; if you try, we will march out and attack you with the sword."

19The Israelites replied:

"We will go along the main road, and if we or our livestock drink any of your water, we will pay for it. We only want to pass through on foot—nothing else."

20Again they answered:

"You may not pass through."

Then Edom came out against them with a large and powerful army. 21Since Edom refused to let them go through their territory, Israel turned away from them.

The Death of Aaron

22The whole Israelite community set out from Kadesh and came to Mount Hor. 23At Mount Hor, near the border of Edom, the LORD said to Moses and Aaron, 24"Aaron will be gathered to his people. He will not enter the land I give the Israelites, because both of you rebelled against my command at the waters of Meribah. 25Get Aaron and his son Eleazar and take them up Mount Hor. 26Remove Aaron's garments and put them on his son Eleazar, for Aaron will be gathered to his people; he will die there."

27Moses did as the LORD commanded: They went up Mount Hor in the sight of the whole community. 28Moses removed Aaron's garments and put them on his son Eleazar. And Aaron died there on top of the mountain. Then Moses and Eleazar came down from the mountain, 29and when the whole community learned that Aaron had died, the entire house of Israel mourned for him thirty days.

Arad Destroyed

21 When the Canaanite king of Arad, who lived in the Negev, heard that Israel was coming along the road to Atharim, he attacked the Israelites and captured some of them. 2Then Israel made this vow to the LORD: "If you will deliver these people into our hands, we will totally destroy[a] their cities." 3The LORD listened to Israel's plea and gave the Canaanites over to them. They completely destroyed them and their towns; so the place was named Hormah.[b]

The Bronze Snake

4They traveled from Mount Hor along the route to the Red Sea,[c] to go around Edom. But the people grew impatient on the way; 5they spoke against God and against Moses, and said, "Why have you brought us up out of Egypt to die in the desert? There is no bread! There is no water! And we detest this miserable food!"

6Then the LORD sent venomous snakes among them; they bit the people and many Israelites died. 7The people came to Moses and said, "We sinned when we spoke against the LORD and against you. Pray that the LORD will take the snakes away from us." So Moses prayed for the people.

8The LORD said to Moses, "Make a snake and put it up on a pole; anyone who is bitten can look at it and live." 9So Moses made a bronze snake and put it up on a pole. Then when anyone was bitten by a snake and looked at the bronze snake, he lived.

The Journey to Moab

10The Israelites moved on and camped at Oboth. 11Then they set out from Oboth and camped in Iye Abarim, in the desert that faces Moab toward the sunrise. 12From there they moved on and camped in the Zered Valley. 13They set out from there and camped alongside the Arnon, which is in the desert extending into Amorite territory. The Arnon is the border of Moab, between Moab and the Amorites. 14That is why the Book of the Wars of the LORD says:

". . . Waheb in Suphah[d] and the ravines,
the Arnon 15and[e] the slopes of the ravines
that lead to the site of Ar
and lie along the border of Moab."

16From there they continued on to Beer, the well where the LORD said to Moses, "Gather the people together and I will give them water."

17Then Israel sang this song:

"Spring up, O well!
Sing about it,
18about the well that the princes dug,
that the nobles of the people sank—
the nobles with scepters and staffs."

Then they went from the desert to Mattanah, 19from Mattanah to Nahaliel, from Nahaliel to Bamoth, 20and from Bamoth to the valley in Moab where the top of Pisgah overlooks the wasteland.

Defeat of Sihon and Og

21Israel sent messengers to say to Sihon king of the Amorites:

22"Let us pass through your country. We

a2 The Hebrew term refers to the irrevocable giving over of things or persons to the LORD, often by totally destroying them; also in verse 3. b3 *Hormah* means *destruction.* c4 Hebrew *Yam Suph*; that is, Sea of Reeds d14 The meaning of the Hebrew for this phrase is uncertain. e14,15 Or *"I have been given from Suphah and the ravines / of the Arnon* 15*to* will not turn aside into any field or vineyard, or drink water from any well. We will travel along the king's highway until we have passed through your territory."

23But Sihon would not let Israel pass through his territory. He mustered his entire army and marched out into the desert against Israel. When he reached Jahaz, he fought with Israel. 24Israel, however, put him to the sword and took over his land from the Arnon to the Jabbok, but only as far as the Ammonites, because their border was fortified. 25Israel captured all the cities of the Amorites and occupied them, including Heshbon and all its surrounding settlements. 26Heshbon was the city of Sihon king of the Amorites, who had fought against the former king of Moab and had taken from him all his land as far as the Arnon.

27That is why the poets say:

"Come to Heshbon and let it be rebuilt;
 let Sihon's city be restored.
28"Fire went out from Heshbon,
 a blaze from the city of Sihon.
It consumed Ar of Moab,
 the citizens of Arnon's heights.
29Woe to you, O Moab!
 You are destroyed, O people of Chemosh!
He has given up his sons as fugitives
 and his daughters as captives
 to Sihon king of the Amorites.
30"But we have overthrown them;
 Heshbon is destroyed all the way to Dibon.
We have demolished them as far as Nophah,
 which extends to Medeba."

31So Israel settled in the land of the Amorites.

32After Moses had sent spies to Jazer, the Israelites captured its surrounding settlements and drove out the Amorites who were there. 33Then they turned and went up along the road toward Bashan, and Og king of Bashan and his whole army marched out to meet them in battle at Edrei.

34The LORD said to Moses, "Do not be afraid of him, for I have handed him over to you, with his whole army and his land. Do to him what you did to Sihon king of the Amorites, who reigned in Heshbon."

35So they struck him down, together with his sons and his whole army, leaving them no survivors. And they took possession of his land.

Balak Summons Balaam

22 Then the Israelites traveled to the plains of Moab and camped along the Jordan across from Jericho.[a]

2Now Balak son of Zippor saw all that Israel had done to the Amorites, 3and Moab was terrified because there were so many people. Indeed, Moab was filled with dread because of the Israelites.

4The Moabites said to the elders of Midian, "This horde is going to lick up everything around us, as an ox licks up the grass of the field."

So Balak son of Zippor, who was king of Moab at that time, 5sent messengers to summon Balaam son of Beor, who was at Pethor, near the River,[b] in his native land. Balak said:

"A people has come out of Egypt; they cover the face of the land and have settled next to me. 6Now come and put a curse on these people, because they are too powerful for me. Perhaps then I will be able to defeat them and drive them out of the country. For I know that those you bless are blessed, and those you curse are cursed."

7The elders of Moab and Midian left, taking with them the fee for divination. When they came to Balaam, they told him what Balak had said.

8"Spend the night here," Balaam said to them, "and I will bring you back the answer the LORD gives me." So the Moabite princes stayed with him.

9God came to Balaam and asked, "Who are these men with you?"

10Balaam said to God, "Balak son of Zippor, king of Moab, sent me this message: 11'A people that has come out of Egypt covers the face of the land. Now come and put a curse on them for me. Perhaps then I will be able to fight them and drive them away.'"

12But God said to Balaam, "Do not go with them. You must not put a curse on those people, because they are blessed."

13The next morning Balaam got up and said to Balak's princes, "Go back to your own country, for the LORD has refused to let me go with you."

14So the Moabite princes returned to Balak and said, "Balaam refused to come with us."

15Then Balak sent other princes, more numerous and more distinguished than the first. 16They came to Balaam and said:

"This is what Balak son of Zippor says: Do not let anything keep you from coming to me, 17because I will reward you handsomely and do whatever you say. Come and put a curse on these people for me."

[a] *1* Hebrew *Jordan of Jericho*; possibly an ancient name for the Jordan River [b] *5* That is, the Euphrates

18 But Balaam answered them, "Even if Balak
gave me his palace filled with silver and gold, I
could not do anything great or small to go beyond
the command of the LORD my God. 19 Now stay
here tonight as the others did, and I will find out
what else the LORD will tell me."

20 That night God came to Balaam and said,
"Since these men have come to summon you, go
with them, but do only what I tell you."

Balaam's Donkey

21 Balaam got up in the morning, saddled his
donkey and went with the princes of Moab. 22 But
God was very angry when he went, and the angel
of the LORD stood in the road to oppose him.
Balaam was riding on his donkey, and his two
servants were with him. 23 When the donkey saw
the angel of the LORD standing in the road with a
drawn sword in his hand, she turned off the road
into a field. Balaam beat her to get her back on
the road.

24 Then the angel of the LORD stood in a narrow
path between two vineyards, with walls on both
sides. 25 When the donkey saw the angel of the
LORD, she pressed close to the wall, crushing Balaam's foot against it. So he beat her again.

26 Then the angel of the LORD moved on ahead
and stood in a narrow place where there was no
room to turn, either to the right or to the left.
27 When the donkey saw the angel of the LORD,
she lay down under Balaam, and he was angry
and beat her with his staff. 28 Then the LORD
opened the donkey's mouth, and she said to Balaam, "What have I done to you to make you beat
me these three times?"

29 Balaam answered the donkey, "You have
made a fool of me! If I had a sword in my hand,
I would kill you right now."

30 The donkey said to Balaam, "Am I not your
own donkey, which you have always ridden, to
this day? Have I been in the habit of doing this to
you?"

"No," he said.

31 Then the LORD opened Balaam's eyes, and
he saw the angel of the LORD standing in the road
with his sword drawn. So he bowed low and fell
facedown.

32 The angel of the LORD asked him, "Why have
you beaten your donkey these three times? I have
come here to oppose you because your path is a
reckless one before me.[a] 33 The donkey saw me
and turned away from me these three times. If
she had not turned away, I would certainly have
killed you by now, but I would have spared
her."

34 Balaam said to the angel of the LORD, "I have
sinned. I did not realize you were standing in the
road to oppose me. Now if you are displeased, I
will go back."

35 The angel of the LORD said to Balaam, "Go
with the men, but speak only what I tell you." So
Balaam went with the princes of Balak.

36 When Balak heard that Balaam was coming,
he went out to meet him at the Moabite town on
the Arnon border, at the edge of his territory.
37 Balak said to Balaam, "Did I not send you an
urgent summons? Why didn't you come to me?
Am I really not able to reward you?"

38 "Well, I have come to you now," Balaam
replied. "But can I say just anything? I must speak
only what God puts in my mouth."

39 Then Balaam went with Balak to Kiriath Hu-
zoth. 40 Balak sacrificed cattle and sheep, and
gave some to Balaam and the princes who were
with him. 41 The next morning Balak took Balaam
up to Bamoth Baal, and from there he saw part of
the people.

Balaam's First Oracle

23 Balaam said, "Build me seven altars here,
and prepare seven bulls and seven rams
for me." 2 Balak did as Balaam said, and the two
of them offered a bull and a ram on each altar.

3 Then Balaam said to Balak, "Stay here beside
your offering while I go aside. Perhaps the LORD
will come to meet with me. Whatever he reveals
to me I will tell you." Then he went off to a
barren height.

4 God met with him, and Balaam said, "I have
prepared seven altars, and on each altar I have
offered a bull and a ram."

5 The LORD put a message in Balaam's mouth
and said, "Go back to Balak and give him this
message."

6 So he went back to him and found him standing beside his offering, with all the princes of
Moab. 7 Then Balaam uttered his oracle:

"Balak brought me from Aram,
  the king of Moab from the eastern
    mountains.
'Come,' he said, 'curse Jacob for me;
  come, denounce Israel.'
8 How can I curse
  those whom God has not cursed?
How can I denounce
  those whom the LORD has not denounced?
9 From the rocky peaks I see them,
  from the heights I view them.
I see a people who live apart
  and do not consider themselves one of the
    nations.

a 32 The meaning of the Hebrew for this clause is uncertain.

[10]Who can count the dust of Jacob
or number the fourth part of Israel?
Let me die the death of the righteous,
and may my end be like theirs!"

[11]Balak said to Balaam, "What have you done
to me? I brought you to curse my enemies, but
you have done nothing but bless them!"
[12]He answered, "Must I not speak what the
LORD puts in my mouth?"

Balaam's Second Oracle

[13]Then Balak said to him, "Come with me to
another place where you can see them; you will
see only a part but not all of them. And from
there, curse them for me." [14]So he took him to
the field of Zophim on the top of Pisgah, and
there he built seven altars and offered a bull and
a ram on each altar.
[15]Balaam said to Balak, "Stay here beside your
offering while I meet with him over there."
[16]The LORD met with Balaam and put a message in his mouth and said, "Go back to Balak and
give him this message."
[17]So he went to him and found him standing
beside his offering, with the princes of Moab.
Balak asked him, "What did the LORD say?"
[18]Then he uttered his oracle:

"Arise, Balak, and listen;
hear me, son of Zippor.
[19]God is not a man, that he should lie,
nor a son of man, that he should change
his mind.
Does he speak and then not act?
Does he promise and not fulfill?
[20]I have received a command to bless;
he has blessed, and I cannot change it.

[21]"No misfortune is seen in Jacob,
no misery observed in Israel.[a]
The LORD their God is with them;
the shout of the King is among them.
[22]God brought them out of Egypt;
they have the strength of a wild ox.
[23]There is no sorcery against Jacob,
no divination against Israel.
It will now be said of Jacob
and of Israel, 'See what God has done!'
[24]The people rise like a lioness;
they rouse themselves like a lion
that does not rest till he devours his prey
and drinks the blood of his victims."

[25]Then Balak said to Balaam, "Neither curse
them at all nor bless them at all!"
[26]Balaam answered, "Did I not tell you I must
do whatever the LORD says?"

Balaam's Third Oracle

[27]Then Balak said to Balaam, "Come, let me
take you to another place. Perhaps it will please
God to let you curse them for me from there."
[28]And Balak took Balaam to the top of Peor, overlooking the wasteland.
[29]Balaam said, "Build me seven altars here,
and prepare seven bulls and seven rams for me."
[30]Balak did as Balaam had said, and offered a bull
and a ram on each altar.

24 Now when Balaam saw that it pleased the
LORD to bless Israel, he did not resort to
sorcery as at other times, but turned his face toward the desert. [2]When Balaam looked out and
saw Israel encamped tribe by tribe, the Spirit of
God came upon him [3]and he uttered his oracle:

"The oracle of Balaam son of Beor,
the oracle of one whose eye sees clearly,
[4]the oracle of one who hears the words of
God,
who sees a vision from the Almighty,[b]
who falls prostrate, and whose eyes are
opened:

[5]"How beautiful are your tents, O Jacob,
your dwelling places, O Israel!

[6]"Like valleys they spread out,
like gardens beside a river,
like aloes planted by the LORD,
like cedars beside the waters.
[7]Water will flow from their buckets;
their seed will have abundant water.

"Their king will be greater than Agag;
their kingdom will be exalted.

[8]"God brought them out of Egypt;
they have the strength of a wild ox.
They devour hostile nations
and break their bones in pieces;
with their arrows they pierce them.
[9]Like a lion they crouch and lie down,
like a lioness—who dares to rouse them?

"May those who bless you be blessed
and those who curse you be cursed!"

[10]Then Balak's anger burned against Balaam.
He struck his hands together and said to him, "I
summoned you to curse my enemies, but you
have blessed them these three times. [11]Now
leave at once and go home! I said I would reward
you handsomely, but the LORD has kept you from
being rewarded."
[12]Balaam answered Balak, "Did I not tell the
messengers you sent me, [13]'Even if Balak gave
me his palace filled with silver and gold, I could
not do anything of my own accord, good or bad,

[a]21 Or *He has not looked on Jacob's offenses / or on the wrongs found in Israel.* [b]4 Hebrew *Shaddai*; also in verse 16

to go beyond the command of the LORD—and I
must say only what the LORD says'? 14Now I am
going back to my people, but come, let me warn
you of what this people will do to your people in
days to come."

Balaam's Fourth Oracle

15Then he uttered his oracle:

"The oracle of Balaam son of Beor,
the oracle of one whose eye sees clearly,
16the oracle of one who hears the words of God,
who has knowledge from the Most High,
who sees a vision from the Almighty,
who falls prostrate, and whose eyes are opened:
17"I see him, but not now;
I behold him, but not near.
A star will come out of Jacob;
a scepter will rise out of Israel.
He will crush the foreheads of Moab,
the skulls[a] of[b] all the sons of Sheth.[c]
18Edom will be conquered;
Seir, his enemy, will be conquered,
but Israel will grow strong.
19A ruler will come out of Jacob
and destroy the survivors of the city."

Balaam's Final Oracles

20Then Balaam saw Amalek and uttered his
oracle:

"Amalek was first among the nations,
but he will come to ruin at last."

21Then he saw the Kenites and uttered his
oracle:

"Your dwelling place is secure,
your nest is set in a rock;
22yet you Kenites will be destroyed
when Asshur takes you captive."

23Then he uttered his oracle:

"Ah, who can live when God does this?[d]
24 Ships will come from the shores of Kittim;
they will subdue Asshur and Eber,
but they too will come to ruin."

25Then Balaam got up and returned home and
Balak went his own way.

Moab Seduces Israel

25 While Israel was staying in Shittim, the
men began to indulge in sexual immorality with Moabite women, 2who invited them to
the sacrifices to their gods. The people ate and
bowed down before these gods. 3So Israel joined
in worshiping the Baal of Peor. And the LORD's
anger burned against them.
4The LORD said to Moses, "Take all the leaders
of these people, kill them and expose them in
broad daylight before the LORD, so that the
LORD's fierce anger may turn away from Israel."
5So Moses said to Israel's judges, "Each of you
must put to death those of your men who have
joined in worshiping the Baal of Peor."
6Then an Israelite man brought to his family a
Midianite woman right before the eyes of Moses
and the whole assembly of Israel while they were
weeping at the entrance to the Tent of Meeting.
7When Phinehas son of Eleazar, the son of Aaron,
the priest, saw this, he left the assembly, took a
spear in his hand 8and followed the Israelite into
the tent. He drove the spear through both of
them—through the Israelite and into the woman's body. Then the plague against the Israelites
was stopped; 9but those who died in the plague
numbered 24,000.
10The LORD said to Moses, 11"Phinehas son of
Eleazar, the son of Aaron, the priest, has turned
my anger away from the Israelites; for he was as
zealous as I am for my honor among them, so that
in my zeal I did not put an end to them. 12There-
fore tell him I am making my covenant of peace
with him. 13He and his descendants will have a
covenant of a lasting priesthood, because he was
zealous for the honor of his God and made atonement for the Israelites."
14The name of the Israelite who was killed
with the Midianite woman was Zimri son of Salu,
the leader of a Simeonite family. 15And the name
of the Midianite woman who was put to death
was Cozbi daughter of Zur, a tribal chief of a
Midianite family.
16The LORD said to Moses, 17"Treat the Midianites as enemies and kill them, 18because they
treated you as enemies when they deceived you
in the affair of Peor and their sister Cozbi, the
daughter of a Midianite leader, the woman who
was killed when the plague came as a result of
Peor."

The Second Census

26 After the plague the LORD said to Moses
and Eleazar son of Aaron, the priest,
2"Take a census of the whole Israelite community
by families—all those twenty years old or more
who are able to serve in the army of Israel." 3So
on the plains of Moab by the Jordan across from
Jericho,[e] Moses and Eleazar the priest spoke

[a] 17 Samaritan Pentateuch (see also Jer. 48:45); the meaning of the word in the Masoretic Text is uncertain. [b] 17 Or possibly *Moab, / batter* [c] 17 Or *all the noisy boasters* [d] 23 Masoretic Text; with a different word division of the Hebrew *A people will gather from the north.* [e] 3 Hebrew *Jordan of Jericho*; possibly an ancient name for the Jordan River; also in verse 63

with them and said, 4"Take a census of the men twenty years old or more, as the LORD commanded Moses."

These were the Israelites who came out of Egypt:

5The descendants of Reuben, the firstborn son of Israel, were:
through Hanoch, the Hanochite clan;
through Pallu, the Palluite clan;
6through Hezron, the Hezronite clan;
through Carmi, the Carmite clan.
7These were the clans of Reuben; those numbered were 43,730.

8The son of Pallu was Eliab,
9and the sons of Eliab were Nemuel, Dathan and Abiram. The same Dathan and Abiram were the community officials who rebelled against Moses and Aaron and were among Korah's followers when they rebelled against the LORD.
10The earth opened its mouth and swallowed them along with Korah, whose followers died when the fire devoured the 250 men. And they served as a warning sign.
11The line of Korah, however, did not die out.

12The descendants of Simeon by their clans were:
through Nemuel, the Nemuelite clan;
through Jamin, the Jaminite clan;
through Jakin, the Jakinite clan;
13through Zerah, the Zerahite clan;
through Shaul, the Shaulite clan.
14These were the clans of Simeon; there were 22,200 men.

15The descendants of Gad by their clans were:
through Zephon, the Zephonite clan;
through Haggi, the Haggite clan;
through Shuni, the Shunite clan;
16through Ozni, the Oznite clan;
through Eri, the Erite clan;
17through Arodi,[a] the Arodite clan;
through Areli, the Arelite clan.
18These were the clans of Gad; those numbered were 40,500.

19Er and Onan were sons of Judah, but they died in Canaan.
20The descendants of Judah by their clans were:
through Shelah, the Shelanite clan;
through Perez, the Perezite clan;
through Zerah, the Zerahite clan.
21The descendants of Perez were:
through Hezron, the Hezronite clan;
through Hamul, the Hamulite clan.
22These were the clans of Judah; those numbered were 76,500.

23The descendants of Issachar by their clans were:
through Tola, the Tolaite clan;
through Puah, the Puite[b] clan;
24through Jashub, the Jashubite clan;
through Shimron, the Shimronite clan.
25These were the clans of Issachar; those numbered were 64,300.

26The descendants of Zebulun by their clans were:
through Sered, the Seredite clan;
through Elon, the Elonite clan;
through Jahleel, the Jahleelite clan.
27These were the clans of Zebulun; those numbered were 60,500.

28The descendants of Joseph by their clans through Manasseh and Ephraim were:

29The descendants of Manasseh:
through Makir, the Makirite clan (Makir was the father of Gilead);
through Gilead, the Gileadite clan.
30These were the descendants of Gilead:
through Iezer, the Iezerite clan;
through Helek, the Helekite clan;
31through Asriel, the Asrielite clan;
through Shechem, the Shechemite clan;
32through Shemida, the Shemidaite clan;
through Hepher, the Hepherite clan.
33(Zelophehad son of Hepher had no sons; he had only daughters, whose names were Mahlah, Noah, Hoglah, Milcah and Tirzah.)
34These were the clans of Manasseh; those numbered were 52,700.

35These were the descendants of Ephraim by their clans:
through Shuthelah, the Shuthelahite clan;
through Beker, the Bekerite clan;
through Tahan, the Tahanite clan.
36These were the descendants of Shuthelah:
through Eran, the Eranite clan.
37These were the clans of Ephraim; those numbered were 32,500.

These were the descendants of Joseph by their clans.

38The descendants of Benjamin by their clans were:
through Bela, the Belaite clan;
through Ashbel, the Ashbelite clan;
through Ahiram, the Ahiramite clan;
39through Shupham,[c] the Shuphamite clan;
through Hupham, the Huphamite clan.

[a]17 Samaritan Pentateuch and Syriac (see also Gen. 46:16); Masoretic Text *Arod* [b]23 Samaritan Pentateuch, Septuagint, Vulgate and Syriac (see also 1 Chron. 7:1); Masoretic Text *through Puvah, the Punite* [c]39 A few manuscripts of the Masoretic Text, Samaritan Pentateuch, Vulgate and Syriac (see also Septuagint); most manuscripts of the Masoretic Text *Shephupham*

40 The descendants of Bela through Ard and
Naaman were:
through Ard,[a] the Ardite clan;
through Naaman, the Naamite clan.
41 These were the clans of Benjamin; those numbered were 45,600.

42 These were the descendants of Dan by their
clans:
through Shuham, the Shuhamite clan.
These were the clans of Dan: 43 All of them were
Shuhamite clans; and those numbered were
64,400.

44 The descendants of Asher by their clans were:
through Imnah, the Imnite clan;
through Ishvi, the Ishvite clan;
through Beriah, the Beriite clan;
45 and through the descendants of Beriah:
through Heber, the Heberite clan;
through Malkiel, the Malkielite clan.
46 (Asher had a daughter named Serah.)
47 These were the clans of Asher; those numbered
were 53,400.

48 The descendants of Naphtali by their clans
were:
through Jahzeel, the Jahzeelite clan;
through Guni, the Gunite clan;
49 through Jezer, the Jezerite clan;
through Shillem, the Shillemite clan.
50 These were the clans of Naphtali; those numbered were 45,400.

51 The total number of the men of Israel was
601,730.

52 The LORD said to Moses, 53 "The land is to be
allotted to them as an inheritance based on the
number of names. 54 To a larger group give a larger inheritance, and to a smaller group a smaller
one; each is to receive its inheritance according
to the number of those listed. 55 Be sure that the
land is distributed by lot. What each group inherits will be according to the names for its ancestral
tribe. 56 Each inheritance is to be distributed by
lot among the larger and smaller groups."

57 These were the Levites who were counted by
their clans:
through Gershon, the Gershonite clan;
through Kohath, the Kohathite clan;
through Merari, the Merarite clan.
58 These also were Levite clans:
the Libnite clan,
the Hebronite clan,
the Mahlite clan,
the Mushite clan,
the Korahite clan.
(Kohath was the forefather of Amram; 59 the
name of Amram's wife was Jochebed, a
descendant of Levi, who was born to the
Levites[b] in Egypt. To Amram she bore Aaron, Moses and their sister Miriam. 60 Aaron
was the father of Nadab and Abihu, Eleazar
and Ithamar. 61 But Nadab and Abihu died
when they made an offering before the
LORD with unauthorized fire.)

62 All the male Levites a month old or more numbered 23,000. They were not counted along with
the other Israelites because they received no inheritance among them.

63 These are the ones counted by Moses and
Eleazar the priest when they counted the Israelites on the plains of Moab by the Jordan across
from Jericho. 64 Not one of them was among those
counted by Moses and Aaron the priest when
they counted the Israelites in the Desert of Sinai.
65 For the LORD had told those Israelites they
would surely die in the desert, and not one of
them was left except Caleb son of Jephunneh and
Joshua son of Nun.

Zelophehad's Daughters

27 The daughters of Zelophehad son of Hepher, the son of Gilead, the son of Makir,
the son of Manasseh, belonged to the clans of
Manasseh son of Joseph. The names of the daughters were Mahlah, Noah, Hoglah, Milcah and Tirzah. They approached 2 the entrance to the Tent
of Meeting and stood before Moses, Eleazar the
priest, the leaders and the whole assembly, and
said, 3 "Our father died in the desert. He was not
among Korah's followers, who banded together
against the LORD, but he died for his own sin and
left no sons. 4 Why should our father's name disappear from his clan because he had no son? Give
us property among our father's relatives."
5 So Moses brought their case before the LORD
6 and the LORD said to him, 7 "What Zelophehad's
daughters are saying is right. You must certainly
give them property as an inheritance among their
father's relatives and turn their father's inheritance over to them.
8 "Say to the Israelites, 'If a man dies and leaves
no son, turn his inheritance over to his daughter.
9 If he has no daughter, give his inheritance to his
brothers. 10 If he has no brothers, give his inheritance to his father's brothers. 11 If his father had
no brothers, give his inheritance to the nearest
relative in his clan, that he may possess it. This is
to be a legal requirement for the Israelites, as the
LORD commanded Moses.' "

[a] 40 Samaritan Pentateuch and Vulgate (see also Septuagint); Masoretic Text does not have *through Ard*. [b] 59 Or *Jochebed, a daughter of Levi, who was born to Levi*

Joshua to Succeed Moses

12Then the LORD said to Moses, "Go up this mountain in the Abarim range and see the land I have given the Israelites. 13After you have seen it, you too will be gathered to your people, as your brother Aaron was, 14for when the community rebelled at the waters in the Desert of Zin, both of you disobeyed my command to honor me as holy before their eyes." (These were the waters of Meribah Kadesh, in the Desert of Zin.)

15Moses said to the LORD, 16"May the LORD, the God of the spirits of all mankind, appoint a man over this community 17to go out and come in before them, one who will lead them out and bring them in, so the LORD's people will not be like sheep without a shepherd."

18So the LORD said to Moses, "Take Joshua son of Nun, a man in whom is the spirit,[a] and lay your hand on him. 19Have him stand before Eleazar the priest and the entire assembly and commission him in their presence. 20Give him some of your authority so the whole Israelite community will obey him. 21He is to stand before Eleazar the priest, who will obtain decisions for him by inquiring of the Urim before the LORD. At his command he and the entire community of the Israelites will go out, and at his command they will come in."

22Moses did as the LORD commanded him. He took Joshua and had him stand before Eleazar the priest and the whole assembly. 23Then he laid his hands on him and commissioned him, as the LORD instructed through Moses.

Daily Offerings

28 The LORD said to Moses, 2"Give this command to the Israelites and say to them: 'See that you present to me at the appointed time the food for my offerings made by fire, as an aroma pleasing to me.' 3Say to them: 'This is the offering made by fire that you are to present to the LORD: two lambs a year old without defect, as a regular burnt offering each day. 4Prepare one lamb in the morning and the other at twilight, 5together with a grain offering of a tenth of an ephah[b] of fine flour mixed with a quarter of a hin[c] of oil from pressed olives. 6This is the regular burnt offering instituted at Mount Sinai as a pleasing aroma, an offering made to the LORD by fire. 7The accompanying drink offering is to be a quarter of a hin of fermented drink with each lamb. Pour out the drink offering to the LORD at the sanctuary. 8Prepare the second lamb at twilight, along with the same kind of grain offering and drink offering that you prepare in the morning. This is an offering made by fire, an aroma pleasing to the LORD.

Sabbath Offerings

9" 'On the Sabbath day, make an offering of two lambs a year old without defect, together with its drink offering and a grain offering of two-tenths of an ephah[d] of fine flour mixed with oil. 10This is the burnt offering for every Sabbath, in addition to the regular burnt offering and its drink offering.

Monthly Offerings

11" 'On the first of every month, present to the LORD a burnt offering of two young bulls, one ram and seven male lambs a year old, all without defect. 12With each bull there is to be a grain offering of three-tenths of an ephah[e] of fine flour mixed with oil; with the ram, a grain offering of two-tenths of an ephah of fine flour mixed with oil; 13and with each lamb, a grain offering of a tenth of an ephah of fine flour mixed with oil. This is for a burnt offering, a pleasing aroma, an offering made to the LORD by fire. 14With each bull there is to be a drink offering of half a hin[f] of wine; with the ram, a third of a hin[g]; and with each lamb, a quarter of a hin. This is the monthly burnt offering to be made at each new moon during the year. 15Besides the regular burnt offering with its drink offering, one male goat is to be presented to the LORD as a sin offering.

The Passover

16" 'On the fourteenth day of the first month the LORD's Passover is to be held. 17On the fifteenth day of this month there is to be a festival; for seven days eat bread made without yeast. 18On the first day hold a sacred assembly and do no regular work. 19Present to the LORD an offering made by fire, a burnt offering of two young bulls, one ram and seven male lambs a year old, all without defect. 20With each bull prepare a grain offering of three-tenths of an ephah of fine flour mixed with oil; with the ram, two-tenths; 21and with each of the seven lambs, one-tenth. 22Include one male goat as a sin offering to make atonement for you. 23Prepare these in addition to the regular morning burnt offering. 24In this way prepare the food for the offering made by fire every day for seven days as an aroma pleasing to the LORD; it is to be prepared in addition to the regular burnt offering and its drink offering. 25On

[a] *18* Or *Spirit* [b] *5* That is, probably about 2 quarts (about 2 liters); also in verses 13, 21 and 29 [c] *5* That is, probably about 1 quart (about 1 liter); also in verses 7 and 14 [d] *9* That is, probably about 4 quarts (about 4.5 liters); also in verses 12, 20 and 28 [e] *12* That is, probably about 6 quarts (about 6.5 liters); also in verses 20 and 28 [f] *14* That is, probably about 2 quarts (about 2 liters) [g] *14* That is, probably about 1 1/4 quarts (about 1.2 liters)

the seventh day hold a sacred assembly and do no
regular work.

Feast of Weeks

26“ ‘On the day of firstfruits, when you present
to the LORD an offering of new grain during the
Feast of Weeks, hold a sacred assembly and do no
regular work. 27Present a burnt offering of two
young bulls, one ram and seven male lambs a
year old as an aroma pleasing to the LORD. 28With
each bull there is to be a grain offering of three-
tenths of an ephah of fine flour mixed with oil;
with the ram, two-tenths; 29and with each of the
seven lambs, one-tenth. 30Include one male goat
to make atonement for you. 31Prepare these together with their drink offerings, in addition to
the regular burnt offering and its grain offering.
Be sure the animals are without defect.

Feast of Trumpets

29 “ ‘On the first day of the seventh month
hold a sacred assembly and do no regular
work. It is a day for you to sound the trumpets.
2As an aroma pleasing to the LORD, prepare a
burnt offering of one young bull, one ram and
seven male lambs a year old, all without defect.
3With the bull prepare a grain offering of three-
tenths of an ephah[a] of fine flour mixed with oil;
with the ram, two-tenths[b]; 4and with each of
the seven lambs, one-tenth.[c] 5Include one male
goat as a sin offering to make atonement for you.
6These are in addition to the monthly and daily
burnt offerings with their grain offerings and
drink offerings as specified. They are offerings
made to the LORD by fire—a pleasing aroma.

Day of Atonement

7“ ‘On the tenth day of this seventh month
hold a sacred assembly. You must deny yourselves[d] and do no work. 8Present as an aroma
pleasing to the LORD a burnt offering of one
young bull, one ram and seven male lambs a year
old, all without defect. 9With the bull prepare a
grain offering of three-tenths of an ephah of fine
flour mixed with oil; with the ram, two-tenths;
10and with each of the seven lambs, one-tenth.
11Include one male goat as a sin offering, in addition to the sin offering for atonement and the
regular burnt offering with its grain offering, and
their drink offerings.

Feast of Tabernacles

12“ ‘On the fifteenth day of the seventh month,
hold a sacred assembly and do no regular work.
Celebrate a festival to the LORD for seven days.
13Present an offering made by fire as an aroma
pleasing to the LORD, a burnt offering of thirteen
young bulls, two rams and fourteen male lambs a
year old, all without defect. 14With each of the
thirteen bulls prepare a grain offering of three-
tenths of an ephah of fine flour mixed with oil;
with each of the two rams, two-tenths; 15and
with each of the fourteen lambs, one-tenth. 16In-
clude one male goat as a sin offering, in addition
to the regular burnt offering with its grain offering and drink offering.

17“ ‘On the second day prepare twelve young
bulls, two rams and fourteen male lambs a year
old, all without defect. 18With the bulls, rams and
lambs, prepare their grain offerings and drink offerings according to the number specified. 19In-
clude one male goat as a sin offering, in addition
to the regular burnt offering with its grain offering, and their drink offerings.

20“ ‘On the third day prepare eleven bulls, two
rams and fourteen male lambs a year old, all without defect. 21With the bulls, rams and lambs, prepare their grain offerings and drink offerings according to the number specified. 22Include one
male goat as a sin offering, in addition to the
regular burnt offering with its grain offering and
drink offering.

23“ ‘On the fourth day prepare ten bulls, two
rams and fourteen male lambs a year old, all without defect. 24With the bulls, rams and lambs, prepare their grain offerings and drink offerings according to the number specified. 25Include one
male goat as a sin offering, in addition to the
regular burnt offering with its grain offering and
drink offering.

26“ ‘On the fifth day prepare nine bulls, two
rams and fourteen male lambs a year old, all without defect. 27With the bulls, rams and lambs, prepare their grain offerings and drink offerings according to the number specified. 28Include one
male goat as a sin offering, in addition to the
regular burnt offering with its grain offering and
drink offering.

29“ ‘On the sixth day prepare eight bulls, two
rams and fourteen male lambs a year old, all without defect. 30With the bulls, rams and lambs, prepare their grain offerings and drink offerings according to the number specified. 31Include one
male goat as a sin offering, in addition to the
regular burnt offering with its grain offering and
drink offering.

32“ ‘On the seventh day prepare seven bulls,
two rams and fourteen male lambs a year old, all
without defect. 33With the bulls, rams and lambs,
prepare their grain offerings and drink offerings
according to the number specified. 34Include one
male goat as a sin offering, in addition to the

[a] 3 That is, probably about 6 quarts (about 6.5 liters); also in verses 9 and 14
[b] 3 That is, probably about 4 quarts (about 4.5 liters); also in verses 9 and 14
[c] 4 That is, probably about 2 quarts (about 2 liters); also in verses 10 and 15
[d] 7 Or *must fast*

regular burnt offering with its grain offering and drink offering.

35“ ‘On the eighth day hold an assembly and do no regular work. 36Present an offering made by fire as an aroma pleasing to the LORD, a burnt offering of one bull, one ram and seven male lambs a year old, all without defect. 37With the bull, the ram and the lambs, prepare their grain offerings and drink offerings according to the number specified. 38Include one male goat as a sin offering, in addition to the regular burnt offering with its grain offering and drink offering.

39“ ‘In addition to what you vow and your freewill offerings, prepare these for the LORD at your appointed feasts: your burnt offerings, grain offerings, drink offerings and fellowship offerings.[a]’ ”

40Moses told the Israelites all that the LORD commanded him.

Vows

30 Moses said to the heads of the tribes of Israel: “This is what the LORD commands: 2When a man makes a vow to the LORD or takes an oath to obligate himself by a pledge, he must not break his word but must do everything he said.

3“When a young woman still living in her father’s house makes a vow to the LORD or obligates herself by a pledge 4and her father hears about her vow or pledge but says nothing to her, then all her vows and every pledge by which she obligated herself will stand. 5But if her father forbids her when he hears about it, none of her vows or the pledges by which she obligated herself will stand; the LORD will release her because her father has forbidden her.

6“If she marries after she makes a vow or after her lips utter a rash promise by which she obligates herself 7and her husband hears about it but says nothing to her, then her vows or the pledges by which she obligated herself will stand. 8But if her husband forbids her when he hears about it, he nullifies the vow that obligates her or the rash promise by which she obligates herself, and the LORD will release her.

9“Any vow or obligation taken by a widow or divorced woman will be binding on her.

10“If a woman living with her husband makes a vow or obligates herself by a pledge under oath 11and her husband hears about it but says nothing to her and does not forbid her, then all her vows or the pledges by which she obligated herself will stand. 12But if her husband nullifies them when he hears about them, then none of the vows or pledges that came from her lips will stand. Her husband has nullified them, and the LORD will release her. 13Her husband may confirm or nullify any vow she makes or any sworn pledge to deny herself. 14But if her husband says nothing to her about it from day to day, then he confirms all her vows or the pledges binding on her. He confirms them by saying nothing to her when he hears about them. 15If, however, he nullifies them some time after he hears about them, then he is responsible for her guilt.”

16These are the regulations the LORD gave Moses concerning relationships between a man and his wife, and between a father and his young daughter still living in his house.

Vengeance on the Midianites

31 The LORD said to Moses, 2“Take vengeance on the Midianites for the Israelites. After that, you will be gathered to your people.”

3So Moses said to the people, “Arm some of your men to go to war against the Midianites and to carry out the LORD’s vengeance on them. 4Send into battle a thousand men from each of the tribes of Israel.” 5So twelve thousand men armed for battle, a thousand from each tribe, were supplied from the clans of Israel. 6Moses sent them into battle, a thousand from each tribe, along with Phinehas son of Eleazar, the priest, who took with him articles from the sanctuary and the trumpets for signaling.

7They fought against Midian, as the LORD commanded Moses, and killed every man. 8Among their victims were Evi, Rekem, Zur, Hur and Reba—the five kings of Midian. They also killed Balaam son of Beor with the sword. 9The Israelites captured the Midianite women and children and took all the Midianite herds, flocks and goods as plunder. 10They burned all the towns where the Midianites had settled, as well as all their camps. 11They took all the plunder and spoils, including the people and animals, 12and brought the captives, spoils and plunder to Moses and Eleazar the priest and the Israelite assembly at their camp on the plains of Moab, by the Jordan across from Jericho.[b]

13Moses, Eleazar the priest and all the leaders of the community went to meet them outside the camp. 14Moses was angry with the officers of the army—the commanders of thousands and commanders of hundreds—who returned from the battle.

15“Have you allowed all the women to live?” he asked them. 16“They were the ones who followed Balaam’s advice and were the means of turning the Israelites away from the LORD in what happened at Peor, so that a plague struck the LORD’s people. 17Now kill all the boys. And kill every woman who has slept with a man, 18but

[a] 39 Traditionally *peace offerings*

[b] 12 Hebrew *Jordan of Jericho*; possibly an ancient name for the Jordan River

save for yourselves every girl who has never slept
with a man.
19“All of you who have killed anyone or
touched anyone who was killed must stay outside
the camp seven days. On the third and seventh
days you must purify yourselves and your captives. 20Purify every garment as well as everything made of leather, goat hair or wood.”
21Then Eleazar the priest said to the soldiers
who had gone into battle, “This is the requirement of the law that the LORD gave Moses:
22Gold, silver, bronze, iron, tin, lead 23and anything else that can withstand fire must be put
through the fire, and then it will be clean. But it
must also be purified with the water of cleansing.
And whatever cannot withstand fire must be put
through that water. 24On the seventh day wash
your clothes and you will be clean. Then you may
come into the camp.”

Dividing the Spoils

25The LORD said to Moses, 26“You and Eleazar
the priest and the family heads of the community
are to count all the people and animals that were
captured. 27Divide the spoils between the soldiers who took part in the battle and the rest of
the community. 28From the soldiers who fought
in the battle, set apart as tribute for the LORD one
out of every five hundred, whether persons, cattle, donkeys, sheep or goats. 29Take this tribute
from their half share and give it to Eleazar the
priest as the LORD’s part. 30From the Israelites’
half, select one out of every fifty, whether persons, cattle, donkeys, sheep, goats or other animals. Give them to the Levites, who are responsible for the care of the LORD’s tabernacle.” 31So
Moses and Eleazar the priest did as the LORD
commanded Moses.
32The plunder remaining from the spoils that
the soldiers took was 675,000 sheep, 3372,000
cattle, 3461,000 donkeys 35and 32,000 women
who had never slept with a man.
36The half share of those who fought in the
battle was:

337,500 sheep, 37of which the tribute for
the LORD was 675;
3836,000 cattle, of which the tribute for the
LORD was 72;
3930,500 donkeys, of which the tribute for
the LORD was 61;
4016,000 people, of which the tribute for the
LORD was 32.

41Moses gave the tribute to Eleazar the priest
as the LORD’s part, as the LORD commanded Moses.
42The half belonging to the Israelites, which
Moses set apart from that of the fighting men—
43the community’s half—was 337,500 sheep,
4436,000 cattle, 4530,500 donkeys 46and 16,000
people. 47From the Israelites’ half, Moses selected one out of every fifty persons and animals, as
the LORD commanded him, and gave them to the
Levites, who were responsible for the care of the
LORD’s tabernacle.
48Then the officers who were over the units of
the army—the commanders of thousands and
commanders of hundreds—went to Moses 49and
said to him, “Your servants have counted the soldiers under our command, and not one is missing. 50So we have brought as an offering to the
LORD the gold articles each of us acquired—
armlets, bracelets, signet rings, earrings and
necklaces—to make atonement for ourselves before the LORD.”
51Moses and Eleazar the priest accepted from
them the gold—all the crafted articles. 52All the
gold from the commanders of thousands and
commanders of hundreds that Moses and Eleazar
presented as a gift to the LORD weighed 16,750
shekels.[a] 53Each soldier had taken plunder for
himself. 54Moses and Eleazar the priest accepted
the gold from the commanders of thousands and
commanders of hundreds and brought it into the
Tent of Meeting as a memorial for the Israelites
before the LORD.

The Transjordan Tribes

32 The Reubenites and Gadites, who had
very large herds and flocks, saw that the
lands of Jazer and Gilead were suitable for livestock. 2So they came to Moses and Eleazar the
priest and to the leaders of the community, and
said, 3“Ataroth, Dibon, Jazer, Nimrah, Heshbon,
Elealeh, Sebam, Nebo and Beon— 4the land the
LORD subdued before the people of Israel—are
suitable for livestock, and your servants have livestock. 5If we have found favor in your eyes,” they
said, “let this land be given to your servants as
our possession. Do not make us cross the Jordan.”
6Moses said to the Gadites and Reubenites,
“Shall your countrymen go to war while you sit
here? 7Why do you discourage the Israelites from
going over into the land the LORD has given
them? 8This is what your fathers did when I sent
them from Kadesh Barnea to look over the land.
9After they went up to the Valley of Eshcol and
viewed the land, they discouraged the Israelites
from entering the land the LORD had given them.
10The LORD’s anger was aroused that day and he
swore this oath: 11‘Because they have not followed me wholeheartedly, not one of the men
twenty years old or more who came up out of

a52 That is, about 420 pounds (about 190 kilograms)

Egypt will see the land I promised on oath to
Abraham, Isaac and Jacob— 12not one except Caleb son of Jephunneh the Kenizzite and Joshua
son of Nun, for they followed the LORD wholeheartedly.' 13The LORD's anger burned against Israel and he made them wander in the desert forty
years, until the whole generation of those who
had done evil in his sight was gone.

14"And here you are, a brood of sinners, standing in the place of your fathers and making the
LORD even more angry with Israel. 15If you turn
away from following him, he will again leave all
this people in the desert, and you will be the
cause of their destruction."

16Then they came up to him and said, "We
would like to build pens here for our livestock
and cities for our women and children. 17But we
are ready to arm ourselves and go ahead of the
Israelites until we have brought them to their
place. Meanwhile our women and children will
live in fortified cities, for protection from the inhabitants of the land. 18We will not return to our
homes until every Israelite has received his inheritance. 19We will not receive any inheritance
with them on the other side of the Jordan, because our inheritance has come to us on the east
side of the Jordan."

20Then Moses said to them, "If you will do
this—if you will arm yourselves before the LORD
for battle, 21and if all of you will go armed over
the Jordan before the LORD until he has driven his
enemies out before him— 22then when the land
is subdued before the LORD, you may return and
be free from your obligation to the LORD and to
Israel. And this land will be your possession before the LORD.

23"But if you fail to do this, you will be sinning
against the LORD; and you may be sure that your
sin will find you out. 24Build cities for your wom-
en and children, and pens for your flocks, but do
what you have promised."

25The Gadites and Reubenites said to Moses,
"We your servants will do as our lord commands.
26Our children and wives, our flocks and herds
will remain here in the cities of Gilead. 27But
your servants, every man armed for battle, will
cross over to fight before the LORD, just as our
lord says."

28Then Moses gave orders about them to Eleazar the priest and Joshua son of Nun and to the
family heads of the Israelite tribes. 29He said to
them, "If the Gadites and Reubenites, every man
armed for battle, cross over the Jordan with you
before the LORD, then when the land is subdued
before you, give them the land of Gilead as their
possession. 30But if they do not cross over with
you armed, they must accept their possession
with you in Canaan."

31The Gadites and Reubenites answered,
"Your servants will do what the LORD has said.
32We will cross over before the LORD into Canaan
armed, but the property we inherit will be on this
side of the Jordan."

33Then Moses gave to the Gadites, the Reubenites and the half-tribe of Manasseh son of Joseph the kingdom of Sihon king of the Amorites
and the kingdom of Og king of Bashan—the
whole land with its cities and the territory
around them.

34The Gadites built up Dibon, Ataroth, Aroer,
35Atroth Shophan, Jazer, Jogbehah, 36Beth Nimrah and Beth Haran as fortified cities, and built
pens for their flocks. 37And the Reubenites rebuilt Heshbon, Elealeh and Kiriathaim, 38as well
as Nebo and Baal Meon (these names were
changed) and Sibmah. They gave names to the
cities they rebuilt.

39The descendants of Makir son of Manasseh
went to Gilead, captured it and drove out the
Amorites who were there. 40So Moses gave Gilead to the Makirites, the descendants of Manasseh, and they settled there. 41Jair, a descendant
of Manasseh, captured their settlements and
called them Havvoth Jair.[a] 42And Nobah captured Kenath and its surrounding settlements
and called it Nobah after himself.

Stages in Israel's Journey

33 Here are the stages in the journey of the
Israelites when they came out of Egypt by
divisions under the leadership of Moses and Aaron. 2At the LORD's command Moses recorded the
stages in their journey. This is their journey by
stages:

3The Israelites set out from Rameses on
the fifteenth day of the first month, the day
after the Passover. They marched out boldly
in full view of all the Egyptians, 4who were
burying all their firstborn, whom the LORD
had struck down among them; for the LORD
had brought judgment on their gods.

5The Israelites left Rameses and camped
at Succoth.

6They left Succoth and camped at Etham,
on the edge of the desert.

7They left Etham, turned back to Pi Hahiroth, to the east of Baal Zephon, and
camped near Migdol.

8They left Pi Hahiroth[b] and passed
through the sea into the desert, and when
they had traveled for three days in the
Desert of Etham, they camped at Marah.

a41 Or *them the settlements of Jair* b8 Many manuscripts of the Masoretic Text, Samaritan Pentateuch and Vulgate; most manuscripts of the Masoretic Text *left from before Hahiroth*

9They left Marah and went to Elim,
where there were twelve springs and seventy palm trees, and they camped there.
10They left Elim and camped by the Red
Sea.[a]
11They left the Red Sea and camped in
the Desert of Sin.
12They left the Desert of Sin and camped
at Dophkah.
13They left Dophkah and camped at
Alush.
14They left Alush and camped at Rephidim, where there was no water for the people to drink.
15They left Rephidim and camped in the
Desert of Sinai.
16They left the Desert of Sinai and
camped at Kibroth Hattaavah.
17They left Kibroth Hattaavah and
camped at Hazeroth.
18They left Hazeroth and camped at Rithmah.
19They left Rithmah and camped at Rimmon Perez.
20They left Rimmon Perez and camped at
Libnah.
21They left Libnah and camped at Rissah.
22They left Rissah and camped at Kehelathah.
23They left Kehelathah and camped at
Mount Shepher.
24They left Mount Shepher and camped
at Haradah.
25They left Haradah and camped at Makheloth.
26They left Makheloth and camped at Tahath.
27They left Tahath and camped at Terah.
28They left Terah and camped at Mithcah.
29They left Mithcah and camped at Hashmonah.
30They left Hashmonah and camped at
Moseroth.
31They left Moseroth and camped at
Bene Jaakan.
32They left Bene Jaakan and camped at
Hor Haggidgad.
33They left Hor Haggidgad and camped at
Jotbathah.
34They left Jotbathah and camped at
Abronah.
35They left Abronah and camped at Ezion
Geber.
36They left Ezion Geber and camped at
Kadesh, in the Desert of Zin.
37They left Kadesh and camped at Mount
Hor, on the border of Edom. 38At the LORD's
command Aaron the priest went up Mount
Hor, where he died on the first day of the
fifth month of the fortieth year after the Israelites came out of Egypt. 39Aaron was a
hundred and twenty-three years old when
he died on Mount Hor.
40The Canaanite king of Arad, who lived
in the Negev of Canaan, heard that the Israelites were coming.
41They left Mount Hor and camped at
Zalmonah.
42They left Zalmonah and camped at Punon.
43They left Punon and camped at Oboth.
44They left Oboth and camped at Iye Abarim, on the border of Moab.
45They left Iyim[b] and camped at Dibon
Gad.
46They left Dibon Gad and camped at Almon Diblathaim.
47They left Almon Diblathaim and
camped in the mountains of Abarim, near
Nebo.
48They left the mountains of Abarim and
camped on the plains of Moab by the Jordan
across from Jericho.[c] 49There on the plains
of Moab they camped along the Jordan from
Beth Jeshimoth to Abel Shittim.
50On the plains of Moab by the Jordan across
from Jericho the LORD said to Moses, 51"Speak to
the Israelites and say to them: 'When you cross
the Jordan into Canaan, 52drive out all the inhabitants of the land before you. Destroy all their
carved images and their cast idols, and demolish
all their high places. 53Take possession of the
land and settle in it, for I have given you the land
to possess. 54Distribute the land by lot, according
to your clans. To a larger group give a larger inheritance, and to a smaller group a smaller one.
Whatever falls to them by lot will be theirs. Distribute it according to your ancestral tribes.
55" 'But if you do not drive out the inhabitants
of the land, those you allow to remain will become barbs in your eyes and thorns in your sides.
They will give you trouble in the land where you
will live. 56And then I will do to you what I plan
to do to them.' "

Boundaries of Canaan

34 The LORD said to Moses, 2"Command the
Israelites and say to them: 'When you enter Canaan, the land that will be allotted to you
as an inheritance will have these boundaries:

[a]*10* Hebrew *Yam Suph*; that is, Sea of Reeds; also in verse 11
[b]*45* That is, Iye Abarim
[c]*48* Hebrew *Jordan of Jericho*; possibly an ancient name for the Jordan River; also in verse 50

3“ ‘Your southern side will include some of the Desert of Zin along the border of Edom. On the east, your southern boundary will start from the end of the Salt Sea,[a] 4cross south of Scorpion[b] Pass, continue on to Zin and go south of Kadesh Barnea. Then it will go to Hazar Addar and over to Azmon, 5where it will turn, join the Wadi of Egypt and end at the Sea.[c]

6“ ‘Your western boundary will be the coast of the Great Sea. This will be your boundary on the west.

7“ ‘For your northern boundary, run a line from the Great Sea to Mount Hor 8and from Mount Hor to Lebo[d] Hamath. Then the boundary will go to Zedad, 9continue to Ziphron and end at Hazar Enan. This will be your boundary on the north.

10“ ‘For your eastern boundary, run a line from Hazar Enan to Shepham. 11The boundary will go down from Shepham to Riblah on the east side of Ain and continue along the slopes east of the Sea of Kinnereth.[e] 12Then the boundary will go down along the Jordan and end at the Salt Sea.

“ ‘This will be your land, with its boundaries on every side.’ ”

13Moses commanded the Israelites: “Assign this land by lot as an inheritance. The LORD has ordered that it be given to the nine and a half tribes, 14because the families of the tribe of Reuben, the tribe of Gad and the half-tribe of Manasseh have received their inheritance. 15These two and a half tribes have received their inheritance on the east side of the Jordan of Jericho,[f] toward the sunrise.”

16The LORD said to Moses, 17“These are the names of the men who are to assign the land for you as an inheritance: Eleazar the priest and Joshua son of Nun. 18And appoint one leader from each tribe to help assign the land. 19These are their names:

Caleb son of Jephunneh,
from the tribe of Judah;
20Shemuel son of Ammihud,
from the tribe of Simeon;
21Elidad son of Kislon,
from the tribe of Benjamin;
22Bukki son of Jogli,
the leader from the tribe of Dan;
23Hanniel son of Ephod,
the leader from the tribe of Manasseh son of Joseph;
24Kemuel son of Shiphtan,
the leader from the tribe of Ephraim son of Joseph;
25Elizaphan son of Parnach,
the leader from the tribe of Zebulun;
26Paltiel son of Azzan,
the leader from the tribe of Issachar;
27Ahihud son of Shelomi,
the leader from the tribe of Asher;
28Pedahel son of Ammihud,
the leader from the tribe of Naphtali.”

29These are the men the LORD commanded to assign the inheritance to the Israelites in the land of Canaan.

Towns for the Levites

35 On the plains of Moab by the Jordan across from Jericho,[g] the LORD said to Moses, 2“Command the Israelites to give the Levites towns to live in from the inheritance the Israelites will possess. And give them pasturelands around the towns. 3Then they will have towns to live in and pasturelands for their cattle, flocks and all their other livestock.

4“The pasturelands around the towns that you give the Levites will extend out fifteen hundred feet[h] from the town wall. 5Outside the town, measure three thousand feet[i] on the east side, three thousand on the south side, three thousand on the west and three thousand on the north, with the town in the center. They will have this area as pastureland for the towns.

Cities of Refuge

6“Six of the towns you give the Levites will be cities of refuge, to which a person who has killed someone may flee. In addition, give them forty-two other towns. 7In all you must give the Levites forty-eight towns, together with their pasturelands. 8The towns you give the Levites from the land the Israelites possess are to be given in proportion to the inheritance of each tribe: Take many towns from a tribe that has many, but few from one that has few.”

9Then the LORD said to Moses: 10“Speak to the Israelites and say to them: ‘When you cross the Jordan into Canaan, 11select some towns to be your cities of refuge, to which a person who has killed someone accidentally may flee. 12They will be places of refuge from the avenger, so that a person accused of murder may not die before he stands trial before the assembly. 13These six towns you give will be your cities of refuge. 14Give three on this side of the Jordan and three in Canaan as cities of refuge. 15These six towns will be a place of refuge for Israelites, aliens and any other people living among them, so that any-

[a]3 That is, the Dead Sea; also in verse 12 [b]4 Hebrew *Akrabbim* [c]5 That is, the Mediterranean; also in verses 6 and 7
[d]8 Or *to the entrance to* [e]11 That is, Galilee [f]15 *Jordan of Jericho* was possibly an ancient name for the Jordan River.
[g]1 Hebrew *Jordan of Jericho*; possibly an ancient name for the Jordan River [h]4 Hebrew *a thousand cubits* (about 450 meters)
[i]5 Hebrew *two thousand cubits* (about 900 meters)

one who has killed another accidentally can flee
there.
16“ ‘If a man strikes someone with an iron object so that he dies, he is a murderer; the murderer shall be put to death. 17Or if anyone has a
stone in his hand that could kill, and he strikes
someone so that he dies, he is a murderer; the
murderer shall be put to death. 18Or if anyone
has a wooden object in his hand that could kill,
and he hits someone so that he dies, he is a
murderer; the murderer shall be put to death.
19The avenger of blood shall put the murderer to
death; when he meets him, he shall put him to
death. 20If anyone with malice aforethought
shoves another or throws something at him intentionally so that he dies 21or if in hostility he
hits him with his fist so that he dies, that person
shall be put to death; he is a murderer. The
avenger of blood shall put the murderer to death
when he meets him.
22“ ‘But if without hostility someone suddenly
shoves another or throws something at him unintentionally 23or, without seeing him, drops a
stone on him that could kill him, and he dies,
then since he was not his enemy and he did not
intend to harm him, 24the assembly must judge
between him and the avenger of blood according
to these regulations. 25The assembly must protect
the one accused of murder from the avenger of
blood and send him back to the city of refuge to
which he fled. He must stay there until the death
of the high priest, who was anointed with the
holy oil.
26“ ‘But if the accused ever goes outside the
limits of the city of refuge to which he has fled
27and the avenger of blood finds him outside the
city, the avenger of blood may kill the accused
without being guilty of murder. 28The accused
must stay in his city of refuge until the death of
the high priest; only after the death of the high
priest may he return to his own property.
29“ ‘These are to be legal requirements for you
throughout the generations to come, wherever
you live.
30“ ‘Anyone who kills a person is to be put to
death as a murderer only on the testimony of
witnesses. But no one is to be put to death on the
testimony of only one witness.
31“ ‘Do not accept a ransom for the life of a
murderer, who deserves to die. He must surely
be put to death.
32“ ‘Do not accept a ransom for anyone who
has fled to a city of refuge and so allow him to go
back and live on his own land before the death of
the high priest.
33“ ‘Do not pollute the land where you are.
Bloodshed pollutes the land, and atonement cannot be made for the land on which blood has
been shed, except by the blood of the one who
shed it. 34Do not defile the land where you live
and where I dwell, for I, the LORD, dwell among
the Israelites.’ ”

Inheritance of Zelophehad’s Daughters

36 The family heads of the clan of Gilead son
of Makir, the son of Manasseh, who were
from the clans of the descendants of Joseph, came
and spoke before Moses and the leaders, the
heads of the Israelite families. 2They said, “When
the LORD commanded my lord to give the land as
an inheritance to the Israelites by lot, he ordered
you to give the inheritance of our brother Zelophehad to his daughters. 3Now suppose they
marry men from other Israelite tribes; then their
inheritance will be taken from our ancestral inheritance and added to that of the tribe they marry into. And so part of the inheritance allotted to
us will be taken away. 4When the Year of Jubilee
for the Israelites comes, their inheritance will be
added to that of the tribe into which they marry,
and their property will be taken from the tribal
inheritance of our forefathers.”
5Then at the LORD’s command Moses gave this
order to the Israelites: “What the tribe of the
descendants of Joseph is saying is right. 6This
is what the LORD commands for Zelophehad’s
daughters: They may marry anyone they please as
long as they marry within the tribal clan of their
father. 7No inheritance in Israel is to pass from
tribe to tribe, for every Israelite shall keep the
tribal land inherited from his forefathers. 8Every
daughter who inherits land in any Israelite tribe
must marry someone in her father’s tribal clan, so
that every Israelite will possess the inheritance of
his fathers. 9No inheritance may pass from tribe
to tribe, for each Israelite tribe is to keep the land
it inherits.”
10So Zelophehad’s daughters did as the LORD
commanded Moses. 11Zelophehad’s daughters—
Mahlah, Tirzah, Hoglah, Milcah and Noah—
married their cousins on their father’s side.
12They married within the clans of the descendants of Manasseh son of Joseph, and their inheritance remained in their father’s clan and tribe.
13These are the commands and regulations the
LORD gave through Moses to the Israelites on the
plains of Moab by the Jordan across from Jericho.[a]

[a] 13 Hebrew *Jordan of Jericho*; possibly an ancient name for the Jordan River

Introduction to DEUTERONOMY

Personal Reading Plan

- ❒ Deuteronomy 1:1–46
- ❒ Deuteronomy 2:1–3:20
- ❒ Deuteronomy 3:21–4:49
- ❒ Deuteronomy 5:1–6:25
- ❒ Deuteronomy 7:1–9:6
- ❒ Deuteronomy 9:7–10:22
- ❒ Deuteronomy 11:1–12:32
- ❒ Deuteronomy 13:1–14:29
- ❒ Deuteronomy 15:1–17:7
- ❒ Deuteronomy 17:8–19:21
- ❒ Deuteronomy 20:1–22:12
- ❒ Deuteronomy 22:13–23:14
- ❒ Deuteronomy 23:15–25:19
- ❒ Deuteronomy 26:1–27:26
- ❒ Deuteronomy 28:1–68
- ❒ Deuteronomy 29:1–31:13
- ❒ Deuteronomy 31:14–32:52
- ❒ Deuteronomy 33:1–34:12

Author

Moses is assumed to be the author and editor of most of the first five books of the Old Testament (the Pentateuch).

Date

It is difficult to form a firm date for the writing of the Pentateuch. Conservative estimates place it in either the fifteenth or thirteenth century B.C., depending on when the Exodus occurred.

Theme

God's covenant and Moses' personal plea with Israel.

Historical Background

The events of this book take place on the plains of Moab as the Israelites are poised to enter the promised land. Moses oversees the important task of transferring his leadership to Joshua. At this important juncture in Israel's history, Moses gives his final instructions to the people. Moses' speeches in Deuteronomy actually were a renewal of Israel's covenant with the Lord. In a personal way, much like a sermon, Moses emphasized laws that were particularly appropriate and needed at the time. The book of Deuteronomy ends with an account of Moses' death.

Characteristics

Arranged around three sermons given by Moses (1:1–4:43; 4:44–26:19; 29:1–32:47), the book of Deuteronomy introduces the reader to the great theological themes of Judaism. Hence, we read of a God who acts in history for the redemption of his elect; we confront the Israelite concepts of sin, punishment and reward; and we are introduced to the essential creed of Judaism, "Hear, O Israel: The LORD our God, the LORD is one" (6:4). Behind these themes, and binding them together, is the covenant between God and Israel. It is this covenant which provides the driving force of the message of Deuteronomy, leaving no doubt as to the responsibilities, rewards and punishments inherent in the covenant. Deuteronomy's spiritual emphasis and its call to total commitment to the Lord in worship and obedience inspired references to its message throughout the rest of Scripture.

The Command to Leave Horeb

1 These are the words Moses spoke to all Israel
in the desert east of the Jordan—that is, in
the Arabah—opposite Suph, between Paran and
Tophel, Laban, Hazeroth and Dizahab. 2(It takes
eleven days to go from Horeb to Kadesh Barnea
by the Mount Seir road.)
3In the fortieth year, on the first day of the
eleventh month, Moses proclaimed to the Israelites all that the LORD had commanded him concerning them. 4This was after he had defeated
Sihon king of the Amorites, who reigned in Heshbon, and at Edrei had defeated Og king of Bashan,
who reigned in Ashtaroth.
5East of the Jordan in the territory of Moab,
Moses began to expound this law, saying:

6The LORD our God said to us at Horeb, "You
have stayed long enough at this mountain. 7Break
camp and advance into the hill country of the
Amorites; go to all the neighboring peoples in the
Arabah, in the mountains, in the western foothills, in the Negev and along the coast, to the
land of the Canaanites and to Lebanon, as far as
the great river, the Euphrates. 8See, I have given
you this land. Go in and take possession of the
land that the LORD swore he would give to your
fathers—to Abraham, Isaac and Jacob—and to
their descendants after them."

The Appointment of Leaders

9At that time I said to you, "You are too heavy
a burden for me to carry alone. 10The LORD your
God has increased your numbers so that today
you are as many as the stars in the sky. 11May the
LORD, the God of your fathers, increase you a
thousand times and bless you as he has promised!
12But how can I bear your problems and your
burdens and your disputes all by myself?
13Choose some wise, understanding and respected men from each of your tribes, and I will set
them over you."
14You answered me, "What you propose to do
is good."
15So I took the leading men of your tribes, wise
and respected men, and appointed them to have
authority over you—as commanders of thousands, of hundreds, of fifties and of tens and as
tribal officials. 16And I charged your judges at that
time: Hear the disputes between your brothers
and judge fairly, whether the case is between
brother Israelites or between one of them and an
alien. 17Do not show partiality in judging; hear
both small and great alike. Do not be afraid of any
man, for judgment belongs to God. Bring me any
case too hard for you, and I will hear it. 18And at
that time I told you everything you were to do.

Spies Sent Out

19Then, as the LORD our God commanded us,
we set out from Horeb and went toward the hill
country of the Amorites through all that vast and
dreadful desert that you have seen, and so we
reached Kadesh Barnea. 20Then I said to you,
"You have reached the hill country of the Amorites, which the LORD our God is giving us. 21See,
the LORD your God has given you the land. Go up
and take possession of it as the LORD, the God of
your fathers, told you. Do not be afraid; do not be
discouraged."
22Then all of you came to me and said, "Let us
send men ahead to spy out the land for us and
bring back a report about the route we are to take
and the towns we will come to."
23The idea seemed good to me; so I selected
twelve of you, one man from each tribe. 24They
left and went up into the hill country, and came
to the Valley of Eshcol and explored it. 25Taking
with them some of the fruit of the land, they
brought it down to us and reported, "It is a good
land that the LORD our God is giving us."

Rebellion Against the LORD

26But you were unwilling to go up; you rebelled against the command of the LORD your
God. 27You grumbled in your tents and said,
"The LORD hates us; so he brought us out of Egypt
to deliver us into the hands of the Amorites to
destroy us. 28Where can we go? Our brothers
have made us lose heart. They say, 'The people
are stronger and taller than we are; the cities are
large, with walls up to the sky. We even saw the
Anakites there.' "
29Then I said to you, "Do not be terrified; do
not be afraid of them. 30The LORD your God, who
is going before you, will fight for you, as he did
for you in Egypt, before your very eyes, 31and in
the desert. There you saw how the LORD your
God carried you, as a father carries his son, all the
way you went until you reached this place."
32In spite of this, you did not trust in the LORD
your God, 33who went ahead of you on your journey, in fire by night and in a cloud by day, to
search out places for you to camp and to show
you the way you should go.
34When the LORD heard what you said, he was
angry and solemnly swore: 35"Not a man of this
evil generation shall see the good land I swore to
give your forefathers, 36except Caleb son of Jephunneh. He will see it, and I will give him and
his descendants the land he set his feet on, because he followed the LORD wholeheartedly."
37Because of you the LORD became angry with
me also and said, "You shall not enter it, either.
38But your assistant, Joshua son of Nun, will enter it. Encourage him, because he will lead Israel

to inherit it. 39 And the little ones that you said
would be taken captive, your children who do
not yet know good from bad—they will enter the
land. I will give it to them and they will take
possession of it. 40 But as for you, turn around and
set out toward the desert along the route to the
Red Sea.[a]"
41 Then you replied, "We have sinned against
the LORD. We will go up and fight, as the LORD
our God commanded us." So every one of you put
on his weapons, thinking it easy to go up into the
hill country.
42 But the LORD said to me, "Tell them, 'Do not
go up and fight, because I will not be with you.
You will be defeated by your enemies.' "
43 So I told you, but you would not listen. You
rebelled against the LORD's command and in your
arrogance you marched up into the hill country.
44 The Amorites who lived in those hills came out
against you; they chased you like a swarm of bees
and beat you down from Seir all the way to Hormah. 45 You came back and wept before the LORD,
but he paid no attention to your weeping and
turned a deaf ear to you. 46 And so you stayed in
Kadesh many days—all the time you spent there.

Wanderings in the Desert

2 Then we turned back and set out toward the
desert along the route to the Red Sea,[a] as
the LORD had directed me. For a long time we
made our way around the hill country of Seir.
2 Then the LORD said to me, 3 "You have made
your way around this hill country long enough;
now turn north. 4 Give the people these orders:
'You are about to pass through the territory of
your brothers the descendants of Esau, who live
in Seir. They will be afraid of you, but be very
careful. 5 Do not provoke them to war, for I will
not give you any of their land, not even enough
to put your foot on. I have given Esau the hill
country of Seir as his own. 6 You are to pay them
in silver for the food you eat and the water you
drink.' "
7 The LORD your God has blessed you in all the
work of your hands. He has watched over your
journey through this vast desert. These forty
years the LORD your God has been with you, and
you have not lacked anything.
8 So we went on past our brothers the descendants of Esau, who live in Seir. We turned from
the Arabah road, which comes up from Elath and
Ezion Geber, and traveled along the desert road
of Moab.
9 Then the LORD said to me, "Do not harass the
Moabites or provoke them to war, for I will not
give you any part of their land. I have given Ar to
the descendants of Lot as a possession."
10 (The Emites used to live there—a people
strong and numerous, and as tall as the Anakites.
11 Like the Anakites, they too were considered
Rephaites, but the Moabites called them Emites.
12 Horites used to live in Seir, but the descendants
of Esau drove them out. They destroyed the Horites from before them and settled in their place,
just as Israel did in the land the LORD gave them
as their possession.)
13 And the LORD said, "Now get up and cross
the Zered Valley." So we crossed the valley.
14 Thirty-eight years passed from the time we
left Kadesh Barnea until we crossed the Zered
Valley. By then, that entire generation of fighting
men had perished from the camp, as the LORD
had sworn to them. 15 The LORD's hand was
against them until he had completely eliminated
them from the camp.
16 Now when the last of these fighting men
among the people had died, 17 the LORD said to
me, 18 "Today you are to pass by the region of
Moab at Ar. 19 When you come to the Ammonites, do not harass them or provoke them to war,
for I will not give you possession of any land
belonging to the Ammonites. I have given it as a
possession to the descendants of Lot."
20 (That too was considered a land of the Rephaites, who used to live there; but the Ammonites
called them Zamzummites. 21 They were a people
strong and numerous, and as tall as the Anakites.
The LORD destroyed them from before the Ammonites, who drove them out and settled in their
place. 22 The LORD had done the same for the
descendants of Esau, who lived in Seir, when he
destroyed the Horites from before them. They
drove them out and have lived in their place to
this day. 23 And as for the Avvites who lived in
villages as far as Gaza, the Caphtorites coming
out from Caphtor[b] destroyed them and settled
in their place.)

Defeat of Sihon King of Heshbon

24 "Set out now and cross the Arnon Gorge.
See, I have given into your hand Sihon the Amorite, king of Heshbon, and his country. Begin to
take possession of it and engage him in battle.
25 This very day I will begin to put the terror and
fear of you on all the nations under heaven. They
will hear reports of you and will tremble and be
in anguish because of you."
26 From the desert of Kedemoth I sent messengers to Sihon king of Heshbon offering peace and
saying, 27 "Let us pass through your country. We
will stay on the main road; we will not turn aside
to the right or to the left. 28 Sell us food to eat and
water to drink for their price in silver. Only let us
pass through on foot— 29 as the descendants of

[a] *40,1* Hebrew *Yam Suph*; that is, Sea of Reeds [b] *23* That is, Crete

Esau, who live in Seir, and the Moabites, who live in Ar, did for us—until we cross the Jordan into the land the LORD our God is giving us." 30But Sihon king of Heshbon refused to let us pass through. For the LORD your God had made his spirit stubborn and his heart obstinate in order to give him into your hands, as he has now done.

31The LORD said to me, "See, I have begun to deliver Sihon and his country over to you. Now begin to conquer and possess his land."

32When Sihon and all his army came out to meet us in battle at Jahaz, 33the LORD our God delivered him over to us and we struck him down, together with his sons and his whole army. 34At that time we took all his towns and completely destroyed[a] them—men, women and children. We left no survivors. 35But the livestock and the plunder from the towns we had captured we carried off for ourselves. 36From Aroer on the rim of the Arnon Gorge, and from the town in the gorge, even as far as Gilead, not one town was too strong for us. The LORD our God gave us all of them. 37But in accordance with the command of the LORD our God, you did not encroach on any of the land of the Ammonites, neither the land along the course of the Jabbok nor that around the towns in the hills.

Defeat of Og King of Bashan

3 Next we turned and went up along the road toward Bashan, and Og king of Bashan with his whole army marched out to meet us in battle at Edrei. 2The LORD said to me, "Do not be afraid of him, for I have handed him over to you with his whole army and his land. Do to him what you did to Sihon king of the Amorites, who reigned in Heshbon."

3So the LORD our God also gave into our hands Og king of Bashan and all his army. We struck them down, leaving no survivors. 4At that time we took all his cities. There was not one of the sixty cities that we did not take from them—the whole region of Argob, Og's kingdom in Bashan. 5All these cities were fortified with high walls and with gates and bars, and there were also a great many unwalled villages. 6We completely destroyed[a] them, as we had done with Sihon king of Heshbon, destroying[a] every city—men, women and children. 7But all the livestock and the plunder from their cities we carried off for ourselves.

8So at that time we took from these two kings of the Amorites the territory east of the Jordan, from the Arnon Gorge as far as Mount Hermon. 9(Hermon is called Sirion by the Sidonians; the Amorites call it Senir.) 10We took all the towns on the plateau, and all Gilead, and all Bashan as far as Salecah and Edrei, towns of Og's kingdom in Bashan. 11(Only Og king of Bashan was left of the remnant of the Rephaites. His bed[b] was made of iron and was more than thirteen feet long and six feet wide.[c] It is still in Rabbah of the Ammonites.)

Division of the Land

12Of the land that we took over at that time, I gave the Reubenites and the Gadites the territory north of Aroer by the Arnon Gorge, including half the hill country of Gilead, together with its towns. 13The rest of Gilead and also all of Bashan, the kingdom of Og, I gave to the half tribe of Manasseh. (The whole region of Argob in Bashan used to be known as a land of the Rephaites. 14Jair, a descendant of Manasseh, took the whole region of Argob as far as the border of the Geshurites and the Maacathites; it was named after him, so that to this day Bashan is called Havvoth Jair.[d]) 15And I gave Gilead to Makir. 16But to the Reubenites and the Gadites I gave the territory extending from Gilead down to the Arnon Gorge (the middle of the gorge being the border) and out to the Jabbok River, which is the border of the Ammonites. 17Its western border was the Jordan in the Arabah, from Kinnereth to the Sea of the Arabah (the Salt Sea[e]), below the slopes of Pisgah.

18I commanded you at that time: "The LORD your God has given you this land to take possession of it. But all your able-bodied men, armed for battle, must cross over ahead of your brother Israelites. 19However, your wives, your children and your livestock (I know you have much livestock) may stay in the towns I have given you, 20until the LORD gives rest to your brothers as he has to you, and they too have taken over the land that the LORD your God is giving them, across the Jordan. After that, each of you may go back to the possession I have given you."

Moses Forbidden to Cross the Jordan

21At that time I commanded Joshua: "You have seen with your own eyes all that the LORD your God has done to these two kings. The LORD will do the same to all the kingdoms over there where you are going. 22Do not be afraid of them; the LORD your God himself will fight for you."

23At that time I pleaded with the LORD: 24"O Sovereign LORD, you have begun to show to your servant your greatness and your strong hand. For

[a] *34,6* The Hebrew term refers to the irrevocable giving over of things or persons to the LORD, often by totally destroying them.
[b] *11* Or *sarcophagus* [c] *11* Hebrew *nine cubits long and four cubits wide* (about 4 meters long and 1.8 meters wide)
[d] *14* Or *called the settlements of Jair* [e] *17* That is, the Dead Sea

what god is there in heaven or on earth who can
do the deeds and mighty works you do? 25Let
me go over and see the good land beyond the
Jordan—that fine hill country and Lebanon."
26But because of you the LORD was angry with
me and would not listen to me. "That is enough,"
the LORD said. "Do not speak to me anymore
about this matter. 27Go up to the top of Pisgah
and look west and north and south and east. Look
at the land with your own eyes, since you are not
going to cross this Jordan. 28But commission Joshua, and encourage and strengthen him, for he
will lead this people across and will cause them
to inherit the land that you will see." 29So we
stayed in the valley near Beth Peor.

Obedience Commanded

4 Hear now, O Israel, the decrees and laws I
am about to teach you. Follow them so that
you may live and may go in and take possession
of the land that the LORD, the God of your fathers,
is giving you. 2Do not add to what I command
you and do not subtract from it, but keep the
commands of the LORD your God that I give you.
3You saw with your own eyes what the LORD
did at Baal Peor. The LORD your God destroyed
from among you everyone who followed the Baal
of Peor, 4but all of you who held fast to the LORD
your God are still alive today.
5See, I have taught you decrees and laws as the
LORD my God commanded me, so that you may
follow them in the land you are entering to take
possession of it. 6Observe them carefully, for this
will show your wisdom and understanding to the
nations, who will hear about all these decrees
and say, "Surely this great nation is a wise and
understanding people." 7What other nation is so
great as to have their gods near them the way the
LORD our God is near us whenever we pray to
him? 8And what other nation is so great as to
have such righteous decrees and laws as this
body of laws I am setting before you today?
9Only be careful, and watch yourselves closely
so that you do not forget the things your eyes
have seen or let them slip from your heart as long
as you live. Teach them to your children and to
their children after them. 10Remember the day
you stood before the LORD your God at Horeb,
when he said to me, "Assemble the people before
me to hear my words so that they may learn to
revere me as long as they live in the land and may
teach them to their children." 11You came near
and stood at the foot of the mountain while it
blazed with fire to the very heavens, with black
clouds and deep darkness. 12Then the LORD
spoke to you out of the fire. You heard the sound
of words but saw no form; there was only a voice.
13He declared to you his covenant, the Ten Commandments, which he commanded you to follow
and then wrote them on two stone tablets. 14And
the LORD directed me at that time to teach you
the decrees and laws you are to follow in the land
that you are crossing the Jordan to possess.

Idolatry Forbidden

15You saw no form of any kind the day the
LORD spoke to you at Horeb out of the fire. Therefore watch yourselves very carefully, 16so that
you do not become corrupt and make for yourselves an idol, an image of any shape, whether
formed like a man or a woman, 17or like any
animal on earth or any bird that flies in the air,
18or like any creature that moves along the
ground or any fish in the waters below. 19And
when you look up to the sky and see the sun, the
moon and the stars—all the heavenly array—do
not be enticed into bowing down to them and
worshiping things the LORD your God has apportioned to all the nations under heaven. 20But as
for you, the LORD took you and brought you out
of the iron-smelting furnace, out of Egypt, to be
the people of his inheritance, as you now are.
21The LORD was angry with me because of you,
and he solemnly swore that I would not cross the
Jordan and enter the good land the LORD your
God is giving you as your inheritance. 22I will die
in this land; I will not cross the Jordan; but you
are about to cross over and take possession of that
good land. 23Be careful not to forget the covenant
of the LORD your God that he made with you; do
not make for yourselves an idol in the form of
anything the LORD your God has forbidden. 24For
the LORD your God is a consuming fire, a jealous
God.
25After you have had children and grandchildren and have lived in the land a long time—if
you then become corrupt and make any kind of
idol, doing evil in the eyes of the LORD your God
and provoking him to anger, 26I call heaven and
earth as witnesses against you this day that you
will quickly perish from the land that you are
crossing the Jordan to possess. You will not live
there long but will certainly be destroyed. 27The
LORD will scatter you among the peoples, and
only a few of you will survive among the nations
to which the LORD will drive you. 28There you
will worship man-made gods of wood and stone,
which cannot see or hear or eat or smell. 29But if
from there you seek the LORD your God, you will
find him if you look for him with all your heart
and with all your soul. 30When you are in distress
and all these things have happened to you, then
in later days you will return to the LORD your God
and obey him. 31For the LORD your God is a merciful God; he will not abandon or destroy you or
forget the covenant with your forefathers, which
he confirmed to them by oath.

The LORD Is God

32Ask now about the former days, long before
your time, from the day God created man on the
earth; ask from one end of the heavens to the
other. Has anything so great as this ever happened, or has anything like it ever been heard of?
33Has any other people heard the voice of God[a]
speaking out of fire, as you have, and lived? 34Has
any god ever tried to take for himself one nation
out of another nation, by testings, by miraculous
signs and wonders, by war, by a mighty hand and
an outstretched arm, or by great and awesome
deeds, like all the things the LORD your God did
for you in Egypt before your very eyes?
35You were shown these things so that you
might know that the LORD is God; besides him
there is no other. 36From heaven he made you
hear his voice to discipline you. On earth he
showed you his great fire, and you heard his
words from out of the fire. 37Because he loved
your forefathers and chose their descendants after them, he brought you out of Egypt by his
Presence and his great strength, 38to drive out
before you nations greater and stronger than you
and to bring you into their land to give it to you
for your inheritance, as it is today.
39Acknowledge and take to heart this day that
the LORD is God in heaven above and on the
earth below. There is no other. 40Keep his decrees and commands, which I am giving you today, so that it may go well with you and your
children after you and that you may live long in
the land the LORD your God gives you for all time.

Cities of Refuge

41Then Moses set aside three cities east of the
Jordan, 42to which anyone who had killed a person could flee if he had unintentionally killed his
neighbor without malice aforethought. He could
flee into one of these cities and save his life.
43The cities were these: Bezer in the desert plateau, for the Reubenites; Ramoth in Gilead, for
the Gadites; and Golan in Bashan, for the Manassites.

Introduction to the Law

44This is the law Moses set before the Israelites. 45These are the stipulations, decrees and
laws Moses gave them when they came out of
Egypt 46and were in the valley near Beth Peor
east of the Jordan, in the land of Sihon king of the
Amorites, who reigned in Heshbon and was defeated by Moses and the Israelites as they came
out of Egypt. 47They took possession of his land
and the land of Og king of Bashan, the two Amorite kings east of the Jordan. 48This land extended
from Aroer on the rim of the Arnon Gorge to
Mount Siyon[b] (that is, Hermon), 49and included
all the Arabah east of the Jordan, as far as the Sea
of the Arabah,[c] below the slopes of Pisgah.

The Ten Commandments

5 Moses summoned all Israel and said:
Hear, O Israel, the decrees and laws I declare
in your hearing today. Learn them and be sure to
follow them. 2The LORD our God made a covenant with us at Horeb. 3It was not with our
fathers that the LORD made this covenant, but
with us, with all of us who are alive here today.
4The LORD spoke to you face to face out of the fire
on the mountain. 5(At that time I stood between
the LORD and you to declare to you the word of
the LORD, because you were afraid of the fire and
did not go up the mountain.) And he said:

6"I am the LORD your God, who
brought you out of Egypt, out of the
land of slavery.
7"You shall have no other gods before[d] me.
8"You shall not make for yourself an idol in
the form of anything in heaven above
or on the earth beneath or in the waters below. 9You shall not bow down
to them or worship them; for I, the
LORD your God, am a jealous God,
punishing the children for the sin of
the fathers to the third and fourth
generation of those who hate me,
10but showing love to a thousand
⌊generations⌋ of those who love me
and keep my commandments.
11"You shall not misuse the name of the
LORD your God, for the LORD will not
hold anyone guiltless who misuses
his name.
12"Observe the Sabbath day by keeping it
holy, as the LORD your God has commanded you. 13Six days you shall labor and do all your work, 14but the
seventh day is a Sabbath to the LORD
your God. On it you shall not do any
work, neither you, nor your son or
daughter, nor your manservant or
maidservant, nor your ox, your donkey or any of your animals, nor the
alien within your gates, so that your
manservant and maidservant may
rest, as you do. 15Remember that you
were slaves in Egypt and that the
LORD your God brought you out of
there with a mighty hand and an outstretched arm. Therefore the LORD

a33 Or *of a god* b48 Hebrew; Syriac (see also Deut. 3:9) *Sirion* c49 That is, the Dead Sea d7 Or *besides* your God has commanded you to observe the Sabbath day.

16“Honor your father and your mother, as the
LORD your God has commanded you,
so that you may live long and that it
may go well with you in the land the
LORD your God is giving you.
17“You shall not murder.
18“You shall not commit adultery.
19“You shall not steal.
20“You shall not give false testimony against
your neighbor.
21“You shall not covet your neighbor’s wife.
You shall not set your desire on your
neighbor’s house or land, his manservant or maidservant, his ox or donkey, or anything that belongs to your
neighbor.”

22These are the commandments the LORD proclaimed in a loud voice to your whole assembly there on the mountain from out of the fire, the cloud and the deep darkness; and he added nothing more. Then he wrote them on two stone tablets and gave them to me.
23When you heard the voice out of the darkness, while the mountain was ablaze with fire, all the leading men of your tribes and your elders
came to me. 24And you said, “The LORD our God
has shown us his glory and his majesty, and we have heard his voice from the fire. Today we have seen that a man can live even if God speaks
with him. 25But now, why should we die? This
great fire will consume us, and we will die if we hear the voice of the LORD our God any longer.
26For what mortal man has ever heard the voice
of the living God speaking out of fire, as we have,
and survived? 27Go near and listen to all that
the LORD our God says. Then tell us whatever the LORD our God tells you. We will listen and obey.”
28The LORD heard you when you spoke to me
and the LORD said to me, “I have heard what this people said to you. Everything they said was
good. 29Oh, that their hearts would be inclined to
fear me and keep all my commands always, so that it might go well with them and their children forever!
30“Go, tell them to return to their tents. 31But
you stay here with me so that I may give you all the commands, decrees and laws you are to teach them to follow in the land I am giving them to possess.”
32So be careful to do what the LORD your God
has commanded you; do not turn aside to the
right or to the left. 33Walk in all the way that the
LORD your God has commanded you, so that you may live and prosper and prolong your days in the land that you will possess.

Love the LORD Your God

6 These are the commands, decrees and laws the LORD your God directed me to teach you to observe in the land that you are crossing the Jordan to possess, 2so that you, your children and
their children after them may fear the LORD your God as long as you live by keeping all his decrees and commands that I give you, and so that you
may enjoy long life. 3Hear, O Israel, and be care-
ful to obey so that it may go well with you and that you may increase greatly in a land flowing with milk and honey, just as the LORD, the God of your fathers, promised you.
4Hear, O Israel: The LORD our God, the LORD
is one.[a] 5Love the LORD your God with all your
heart and with all your soul and with all your
strength. 6These commandments that I give you
today are to be upon your hearts. 7Impress them
on your children. Talk about them when you sit at home and when you walk along the road,
when you lie down and when you get up. 8Tie
them as symbols on your hands and bind them on
your foreheads. 9Write them on the doorframes of your houses and on your gates.
10When the LORD your God brings you into the
land he swore to your fathers, to Abraham, Isaac and Jacob, to give you—a land with large, flourishing cities you did not build, 11houses filled
with all kinds of good things you did not provide, wells you did not dig, and vineyards and olive groves you did not plant—then when you eat and
are satisfied, 12be careful that you do not forget
the LORD, who brought you out of Egypt, out of the land of slavery.
13Fear the LORD your God, serve him only and
take your oaths in his name. 14Do not follow other gods, the gods of the peoples around you; 15for
the LORD your God, who is among you, is a jealous God and his anger will burn against you, and he will destroy you from the face of the land.
16Do not test the LORD your God as you did at
Massah. 17Be sure to keep the commands of the
LORD your God and the stipulations and decrees
he has given you. 18Do what is right and good in
the LORD’s sight, so that it may go well with you and you may go in and take over the good land that the LORD promised on oath to your forefathers, 19thrusting out all your enemies before
you, as the LORD said.
20In the future, when your son asks you,
“What is the meaning of the stipulations, decrees and laws the LORD our God has commanded
you?” 21tell him: “We were slaves of Pharaoh in
Egypt, but the LORD brought us out of Egypt with

a4 Or *The LORD our God is one LORD*; or *The LORD is our God, the LORD is one*; or *The LORD is our God, the LORD alone*

a mighty hand. 22Before our eyes the LORD sent
miraculous signs and wonders—great and
terrible—upon Egypt and Pharaoh and his whole
household. 23But he brought us out from there to
bring us in and give us the land that he promised
on oath to our forefathers. 24The LORD commanded us to obey all these decrees and to fear the
LORD our God, so that we might always prosper
and be kept alive, as is the case today. 25And if
we are careful to obey all this law before the LORD
our God, as he has commanded us, that will be
our righteousness."

Driving Out the Nations

7 When the LORD your God brings you into the
land you are entering to possess and drives
out before you many nations—the Hittites, Girgashites, Amorites, Canaanites, Perizzites, Hivites and Jebusites, seven nations larger and
stronger than you— 2and when the LORD your
God has delivered them over to you and you have
defeated them, then you must destroy them totally.[a] Make no treaty with them, and show them
no mercy. 3Do not intermarry with them. Do not
give your daughters to their sons or take their
daughters for your sons, 4for they will turn your
sons away from following me to serve other gods,
and the LORD's anger will burn against you and
will quickly destroy you. 5This is what you are to
do to them: Break down their altars, smash their
sacred stones, cut down their Asherah poles[b]
and burn their idols in the fire. 6For you are a
people holy to the LORD your God. The LORD your
God has chosen you out of all the peoples on the
face of the earth to be his people, his treasured
possession.

7The LORD did not set his affection on you and
choose you because you were more numerous
than other peoples, for you were the fewest of all
peoples. 8But it was because the LORD loved you
and kept the oath he swore to your forefathers
that he brought you out with a mighty hand and
redeemed you from the land of slavery, from the
power of Pharaoh king of Egypt. 9Know therefore
that the LORD your God is God; he is the faithful
God, keeping his covenant of love to a thousand
generations of those who love him and keep his
commands. 10But

those who hate him he will repay to their
face by destruction;
he will not be slow to repay to their face
those who hate him.

11Therefore, take care to follow the commands,
decrees and laws I give you today.

12If you pay attention to these laws and are
careful to follow them, then the LORD your God
will keep his covenant of love with you, as he
swore to your forefathers. 13He will love you and
bless you and increase your numbers. He will
bless the fruit of your womb, the crops of your
land—your grain, new wine and oil—the calves
of your herds and the lambs of your flocks in the
land that he swore to your forefathers to give you.
14You will be blessed more than any other people; none of your men or women will be childless, nor any of your livestock without young.
15The LORD will keep you free from every disease. He will not inflict on you the horrible diseases you knew in Egypt, but he will inflict them
on all who hate you. 16You must destroy all the
peoples the LORD your God gives over to you. Do
not look on them with pity and do not serve their
gods, for that will be a snare to you.

17You may say to yourselves, "These nations
are stronger than we are. How can we drive them
out?" 18But do not be afraid of them; remember
well what the LORD your God did to Pharaoh and
to all Egypt. 19You saw with your own eyes the
great trials, the miraculous signs and wonders,
the mighty hand and outstretched arm, with
which the LORD your God brought you out. The
LORD your God will do the same to all the peoples
you now fear. 20Moreover, the LORD your God
will send the hornet among them until even the
survivors who hide from you have perished. 21Do
not be terrified by them, for the LORD your God,
who is among you, is a great and awesome God.
22The LORD your God will drive out those nations
before you, little by little. You will not be allowed
to eliminate them all at once, or the wild animals
will multiply around you. 23But the LORD your
God will deliver them over to you, throwing
them into great confusion until they are destroyed. 24He will give their kings into your hand,
and you will wipe out their names from under
heaven. No one will be able to stand up against
you; you will destroy them. 25The images of their
gods you are to burn in the fire. Do not covet the
silver and gold on them, and do not take it for
yourselves, or you will be ensnared by it, for it is
detestable to the LORD your God. 26Do not bring
a detestable thing into your house or you, like it,
will be set apart for destruction. Utterly abhor
and detest it, for it is set apart for destruction.

Do Not Forget the LORD

8 Be careful to follow every command I am
giving you today, so that you may live and
increase and may enter and possess the land that
the LORD promised on oath to your forefathers.
2Remember how the LORD your God led you all

[a]2 The Hebrew term refers to the irrevocable giving over of things or persons to the LORD, often by totally destroying them; also in verse 26. [b]5 That is, symbols of the goddess Asherah; here and elsewhere in Deuteronomy

the way in the desert these forty years, to humble
you and to test you in order to know what was in
your heart, whether or not you would keep his
commands. 3He humbled you, causing you to
hunger and then feeding you with manna, which
neither you nor your fathers had known, to teach
you that man does not live on bread alone but on
every word that comes from the mouth of the
LORD. 4Your clothes did not wear out and your
feet did not swell during these forty years. 5Know
then in your heart that as a man disciplines his
son, so the LORD your God disciplines you.
6Observe the commands of the LORD your
God, walking in his ways and revering him. 7For
the LORD your God is bringing you into a good
land—a land with streams and pools of water,
with springs flowing in the valleys and hills; 8a
land with wheat and barley, vines and fig trees,
pomegranates, olive oil and honey; 9a land where
bread will not be scarce and you will lack nothing; a land where the rocks are iron and you can
dig copper out of the hills.
10When you have eaten and are satisfied,
praise the LORD your God for the good land he
has given you. 11Be careful that you do not forget
the LORD your God, failing to observe his commands, his laws and his decrees that I am giving
you this day. 12Otherwise, when you eat and are
satisfied, when you build fine houses and settle
down, 13and when your herds and flocks grow
large and your silver and gold increase and all you
have is multiplied, 14then your heart will become
proud and you will forget the LORD your God,
who brought you out of Egypt, out of the land of
slavery. 15He led you through the vast and dreadful desert, that thirsty and waterless land, with its
venomous snakes and scorpions. He brought you
water out of hard rock. 16He gave you manna to
eat in the desert, something your fathers had never known, to humble and to test you so that in
the end it might go well with you. 17You may say
to yourself, "My power and the strength of my
hands have produced this wealth for me." 18But
remember the LORD your God, for it is he who
gives you the ability to produce wealth, and so
confirms his covenant, which he swore to your
forefathers, as it is today.
19If you ever forget the LORD your God and
follow other gods and worship and bow down to
them, I testify against you today that you will
surely be destroyed. 20Like the nations the LORD
destroyed before you, so you will be destroyed for
not obeying the LORD your God.

Not Because of Israel's Righteousness

9 Hear, O Israel. You are now about to cross
the Jordan to go in and dispossess nations
greater and stronger than you, with large cities
that have walls up to the sky. 2The people are
strong and tall—Anakites! You know about them
and have heard it said: "Who can stand up against
the Anakites?" 3But be assured today that the
LORD your God is the one who goes across ahead
of you like a devouring fire. He will destroy them;
he will subdue them before you. And you will
drive them out and annihilate them quickly, as
the LORD has promised you.
4After the LORD your God has driven them out
before you, do not say to yourself, "The LORD has
brought me here to take possession of this land
because of my righteousness." No, it is on account of the wickedness of these nations that the
LORD is going to drive them out before you. 5It is
not because of your righteousness or your integrity that you are going in to take possession of their
land; but on account of the wickedness of these
nations, the LORD your God will drive them out
before you, to accomplish what he swore to your
fathers, to Abraham, Isaac and Jacob. 6Under-
stand, then, that it is not because of your righteousness that the LORD your God is giving you
this good land to possess, for you are a stiff-
necked people.

The Golden Calf

7Remember this and never forget how you
provoked the LORD your God to anger in the
desert. From the day you left Egypt until you arrived here, you have been rebellious against the
LORD. 8At Horeb you aroused the LORD's wrath so
that he was angry enough to destroy you. 9When
I went up on the mountain to receive the tablets
of stone, the tablets of the covenant that the LORD
had made with you, I stayed on the mountain
forty days and forty nights; I ate no bread and
drank no water. 10The LORD gave me two stone
tablets inscribed by the finger of God. On them
were all the commandments the LORD proclaimed to you on the mountain out of the fire, on
the day of the assembly.
11At the end of the forty days and forty nights,
the LORD gave me the two stone tablets, the tablets of the covenant. 12Then the LORD told me,
"Go down from here at once, because your people whom you brought out of Egypt have become
corrupt. They have turned away quickly from
what I commanded them and have made a cast
idol for themselves."
13And the LORD said to me, "I have seen this
people, and they are a stiff-necked people indeed! 14Let me alone, so that I may destroy them
and blot out their name from under heaven. And
I will make you into a nation stronger and more
numerous than they."
15So I turned and went down from the mountain while it was ablaze with fire. And the two

tablets of the covenant were in my hands.[a] 16When I looked, I saw that you had sinned against the LORD your God; you had made for yourselves an idol cast in the shape of a calf. You had turned aside quickly from the way that the LORD had commanded you. 17So I took the two tablets and threw them out of my hands, breaking them to pieces before your eyes.

18Then once again I fell prostrate before the LORD for forty days and forty nights; I ate no bread and drank no water, because of all the sin you had committed, doing what was evil in the LORD's sight and so provoking him to anger. 19I feared the anger and wrath of the LORD, for he was angry enough with you to destroy you. But again the LORD listened to me. 20And the LORD was angry enough with Aaron to destroy him, but at that time I prayed for Aaron too. 21Also I took that sinful thing of yours, the calf you had made, and burned it in the fire. Then I crushed it and ground it to powder as fine as dust and threw the dust into a stream that flowed down the mountain.

22You also made the LORD angry at Taberah, at Massah and at Kibroth Hattaavah.

23And when the LORD sent you out from Kadesh Barnea, he said, "Go up and take possession of the land I have given you." But you rebelled against the command of the LORD your God. You did not trust him or obey him. 24You have been rebellious against the LORD ever since I have known you.

25I lay prostrate before the LORD those forty days and forty nights because the LORD had said he would destroy you. 26I prayed to the LORD and said, "O Sovereign LORD, do not destroy your people, your own inheritance that you redeemed by your great power and brought out of Egypt with a mighty hand. 27Remember your servants Abraham, Isaac and Jacob. Overlook the stubbornness of this people, their wickedness and their sin. 28Otherwise, the country from which you brought us will say, 'Because the LORD was not able to take them into the land he had promised them, and because he hated them, he brought them out to put them to death in the desert.' 29But they are your people, your inheritance that you brought out by your great power and your outstretched arm."

Tablets Like the First Ones

10 At that time the LORD said to me, "Chisel out two stone tablets like the first ones and come up to me on the mountain. Also make a wooden chest.[b] 2I will write on the tablets the words that were on the first tablets, which you broke. Then you are to put them in the chest."

3So I made the ark out of acacia wood and chiseled out two stone tablets like the first ones, and I went up on the mountain with the two tablets in my hands. 4The LORD wrote on these tablets what he had written before, the Ten Commandments he had proclaimed to you on the mountain, out of the fire, on the day of the assembly. And the LORD gave them to me. 5Then I came back down the mountain and put the tablets in the ark I had made, as the LORD commanded me, and they are there now.

6(The Israelites traveled from the wells of the Jaakanites to Moserah. There Aaron died and was buried, and Eleazar his son succeeded him as priest. 7From there they traveled to Gudgodah and on to Jotbathah, a land with streams of water. 8At that time the LORD set apart the tribe of Levi to carry the ark of the covenant of the LORD, to stand before the LORD to minister and to pronounce blessings in his name, as they still do today. 9That is why the Levites have no share or inheritance among their brothers; the LORD is their inheritance, as the LORD your God told them.)

10Now I had stayed on the mountain forty days and nights, as I did the first time, and the LORD listened to me at this time also. It was not his will to destroy you. 11"Go," the LORD said to me, "and lead the people on their way, so that they may enter and possess the land that I swore to their fathers to give them."

Fear the LORD

12And now, O Israel, what does the LORD your God ask of you but to fear the LORD your God, to walk in all his ways, to love him, to serve the LORD your God with all your heart and with all your soul, 13and to observe the LORD's commands and decrees that I am giving you today for your own good?

14To the LORD your God belong the heavens, even the highest heavens, the earth and everything in it. 15Yet the LORD set his affection on your forefathers and loved them, and he chose you, their descendants, above all the nations, as it is today. 16Circumcise your hearts, therefore, and do not be stiff-necked any longer. 17For the LORD your God is God of gods and Lord of lords, the great God, mighty and awesome, who shows no partiality and accepts no bribes. 18He defends the cause of the fatherless and the widow, and loves the alien, giving him food and clothing. 19And you are to love those who are aliens, for you yourselves were aliens in Egypt. 20Fear the LORD your God and serve him. Hold fast to him and take your oaths in his name. 21He is your praise; he is your God, who performed for you

[a] 15 Or *And I had the two tablets of the covenant with me, one in each hand* [b] 1 That is, an ark

those great and awesome wonders you saw with your own eyes. 22Your forefathers who went down into Egypt were seventy in all, and now the LORD your God has made you as numerous as the stars in the sky.

Love and Obey the LORD

11 Love the LORD your God and keep his requirements, his decrees, his laws and his commands always. 2Remember today that your children were not the ones who saw and experienced the discipline of the LORD your God: his majesty, his mighty hand, his outstretched arm; 3the signs he performed and the things he did in the heart of Egypt, both to Pharaoh king of Egypt and to his whole country; 4what he did to the Egyptian army, to its horses and chariots, how he overwhelmed them with the waters of the Red Sea[a] as they were pursuing you, and how the LORD brought lasting ruin on them. 5It was not your children who saw what he did for you in the desert until you arrived at this place, 6and what he did to Dathan and Abiram, sons of Eliab the Reubenite, when the earth opened its mouth right in the middle of all Israel and swallowed them up with their households, their tents and every living thing that belonged to them. 7But it was your own eyes that saw all these great things the LORD has done.

8Observe therefore all the commands I am giving you today, so that you may have the strength to go in and take over the land that you are crossing the Jordan to possess, 9and so that you may live long in the land that the LORD swore to your forefathers to give to them and their descendants, a land flowing with milk and honey. 10The land you are entering to take over is not like the land of Egypt, from which you have come, where you planted your seed and irrigated it by foot as in a vegetable garden. 11But the land you are crossing the Jordan to take possession of is a land of mountains and valleys that drinks rain from heaven. 12It is a land the LORD your God cares for; the eyes of the LORD your God are continually on it from the beginning of the year to its end.

13So if you faithfully obey the commands I am giving you today—to love the LORD your God and to serve him with all your heart and with all your soul— 14then I will send rain on your land in its season, both autumn and spring rains, so that you may gather in your grain, new wine and oil. 15I will provide grass in the fields for your cattle, and you will eat and be satisfied.

16Be careful, or you will be enticed to turn away and worship other gods and bow down to them. 17Then the LORD's anger will burn against you, and he will shut the heavens so that it will not rain and the ground will yield no produce, and you will soon perish from the good land the LORD is giving you. 18Fix these words of mine in your hearts and minds; tie them as symbols on your hands and bind them on your foreheads. 19Teach them to your children, talking about them when you sit at home and when you walk along the road, when you lie down and when you get up. 20Write them on the doorframes of your houses and on your gates, 21so that your days and the days of your children may be many in the land that the LORD swore to give your forefathers, as many as the days that the heavens are above the earth.

22If you carefully observe all these commands I am giving you to follow—to love the LORD your God, to walk in all his ways and to hold fast to him— 23then the LORD will drive out all these nations before you, and you will dispossess nations larger and stronger than you. 24Every place where you set your foot will be yours: Your territory will extend from the desert to Lebanon, and from the Euphrates River to the western sea.[b] 25No man will be able to stand against you. The LORD your God, as he promised you, will put the terror and fear of you on the whole land, wherever you go.

26See, I am setting before you today a blessing and a curse— 27the blessing if you obey the commands of the LORD your God that I am giving you today; 28the curse if you disobey the commands of the LORD your God and turn from the way that I command you today by following other gods, which you have not known. 29When the LORD your God has brought you into the land you are entering to possess, you are to proclaim on Mount Gerizim the blessings, and on Mount Ebal the curses. 30As you know, these mountains are across the Jordan, west of the road,[c] toward the setting sun, near the great trees of Moreh, in the territory of those Canaanites living in the Arabah in the vicinity of Gilgal. 31You are about to cross the Jordan to enter and take possession of the land the LORD your God is giving you. When you have taken it over and are living there, 32be sure that you obey all the decrees and laws I am setting before you today.

The One Place of Worship

12 These are the decrees and laws you must be careful to follow in the land that the LORD, the God of your fathers, has given you to possess—as long as you live in the land. 2Destroy completely all the places on the high mountains and on the hills and under every spreading tree where the nations you are dispossessing worship their gods. 3Break down their altars, smash their

[a]4 Hebrew *Yam Suph*; that is, Sea of Reeds [b]24 That is, the Mediterranean [c]30 Or *Jordan, westward*

sacred stones and burn their Asherah poles in the fire; cut down the idols of their gods and wipe out their names from those places.

4You must not worship the LORD your God in their way. 5But you are to seek the place the LORD your God will choose from among all your tribes to put his Name there for his dwelling. To that place you must go; 6there bring your burnt offerings and sacrifices, your tithes and special gifts, what you have vowed to give and your freewill offerings, and the firstborn of your herds and flocks. 7There, in the presence of the LORD your God, you and your families shall eat and shall rejoice in everything you have put your hand to, because the LORD your God has blessed you.

8You are not to do as we do here today, everyone as he sees fit, 9since you have not yet reached the resting place and the inheritance the LORD your God is giving you. 10But you will cross the Jordan and settle in the land the LORD your God is giving you as an inheritance, and he will give you rest from all your enemies around you so that you will live in safety. 11Then to the place the LORD your God will choose as a dwelling for his Name—there you are to bring everything I command you: your burnt offerings and sacrifices, your tithes and special gifts, and all the choice possessions you have vowed to the LORD. 12And there rejoice before the LORD your God, you, your sons and daughters, your menservants and maidservants, and the Levites from your towns, who have no allotment or inheritance of their own. 13Be careful not to sacrifice your burnt offerings anywhere you please. 14Offer them only at the place the LORD will choose in one of your tribes, and there observe everything I command you.

15Nevertheless, you may slaughter your animals in any of your towns and eat as much of the meat as you want, as if it were gazelle or deer, according to the blessing the LORD your God gives you. Both the ceremonially unclean and the clean may eat it. 16But you must not eat the blood; pour it out on the ground like water. 17You must not eat in your own towns the tithe of your grain and new wine and oil, or the firstborn of your herds and flocks, or whatever you have vowed to give, or your freewill offerings or special gifts. 18Instead, you are to eat them in the presence of the LORD your God at the place the LORD your God will choose—you, your sons and daughters, your menservants and maidservants, and the Levites from your towns—and you are to rejoice before the LORD your God in everything you put your hand to. 19Be careful not to neglect the Levites as long as you live in your land.

20When the LORD your God has enlarged your territory as he promised you, and you crave meat and say, "I would like some meat," then you may eat as much of it as you want. 21If the place where the LORD your God chooses to put his Name is too far away from you, you may slaughter animals from the herds and flocks the LORD has given you, as I have commanded you, and in your own towns you may eat as much of them as you want. 22Eat them as you would gazelle or deer. Both the ceremonially unclean and the clean may eat. 23But be sure you do not eat the blood, because the blood is the life, and you must not eat the life with the meat. 24You must not eat the blood; pour it out on the ground like water. 25Do not eat it, so that it may go well with you and your children after you, because you will be doing what is right in the eyes of the LORD.

26But take your consecrated things and whatever you have vowed to give, and go to the place the LORD will choose. 27Present your burnt offerings on the altar of the LORD your God, both the meat and the blood. The blood of your sacrifices must be poured beside the altar of the LORD your God, but you may eat the meat. 28Be careful to obey all these regulations I am giving you, so that it may always go well with you and your children after you, because you will be doing what is good and right in the eyes of the LORD your God.

29The LORD your God will cut off before you the nations you are about to invade and dispossess. But when you have driven them out and settled in their land, 30and after they have been destroyed before you, be careful not to be ensnared by inquiring about their gods, saying, "How do these nations serve their gods? We will do the same." 31You must not worship the LORD your God in their way, because in worshiping their gods, they do all kinds of detestable things the LORD hates. They even burn their sons and daughters in the fire as sacrifices to their gods.

32See that you do all I command you; do not add to it or take away from it.

Worshiping Other Gods

13 If a prophet, or one who foretells by dreams, appears among you and announces to you a miraculous sign or wonder, 2and if the sign or wonder of which he has spoken takes place, and he says, "Let us follow other gods" (gods you have not known) "and let us worship them," 3you must not listen to the words of that prophet or dreamer. The LORD your God is testing you to find out whether you love him with all your heart and with all your soul. 4It is the LORD your God you must follow, and him you must revere. Keep his commands and obey him; serve him and hold fast to him. 5That prophet or dreamer must be put to death, because he preached rebellion against the LORD your God, who brought you out of Egypt and redeemed you from the land of slavery; he has tried to turn you

from the way the LORD your God commanded you to follow. You must purge the evil from among you.

[6]If your very own brother, or your son or daughter, or the wife you love, or your closest friend secretly entices you, saying, "Let us go and worship other gods" (gods that neither you nor your fathers have known, [7]gods of the peoples around you, whether near or far, from one end of the land to the other), [8]do not yield to him or listen to him. Show him no pity. Do not spare him or shield him. [9]You must certainly put him to death. Your hand must be the first in putting him to death, and then the hands of all the people. [10]Stone him to death, because he tried to turn you away from the LORD your God, who brought you out of Egypt, out of the land of slavery. [11]Then all Israel will hear and be afraid, and no one among you will do such an evil thing again.

[12]If you hear it said about one of the towns the LORD your God is giving you to live in [13]that wicked men have arisen among you and have led the people of their town astray, saying, "Let us go and worship other gods" (gods you have not known), [14]then you must inquire, probe and investigate it thoroughly. And if it is true and it has been proved that this detestable thing has been done among you, [15]you must certainly put to the sword all who live in that town. Destroy it completely,[a] both its people and its livestock. [16]Gather all the plunder of the town into the middle of the public square and completely burn the town and all its plunder as a whole burnt offering to the LORD your God. It is to remain a ruin forever, never to be rebuilt. [17]None of those condemned things[a] shall be found in your hands, so that the LORD will turn from his fierce anger; he will show you mercy, have compassion on you, and increase your numbers, as he promised on oath to your forefathers, [18]because you obey the LORD your God, keeping all his commands that I am giving you today and doing what is right in his eyes.

Clean and Unclean Food

14 You are the children of the LORD your God. Do not cut yourselves or shave the front of your heads for the dead, [2]for you are a people holy to the LORD your God. Out of all the peoples on the face of the earth, the LORD has chosen you to be his treasured possession.

[3]Do not eat any detestable thing. [4]These are the animals you may eat: the ox, the sheep, the goat, [5]the deer, the gazelle, the roe deer, the wild goat, the ibex, the antelope and the mountain sheep.[b] [6]You may eat any animal that has a split hoof divided in two and that chews the cud. [7]However, of those that chew the cud or that have a split hoof completely divided you may not eat the camel, the rabbit or the coney.[c] Although they chew the cud, they do not have a split hoof; they are ceremonially unclean for you. [8]The pig is also unclean; although it has a split hoof, it does not chew the cud. You are not to eat their meat or touch their carcasses.

[9]Of all the creatures living in the water, you may eat any that has fins and scales. [10]But anything that does not have fins and scales you may not eat; for you it is unclean.

[11]You may eat any clean bird. [12]But these you may not eat: the eagle, the vulture, the black vulture, [13]the red kite, the black kite, any kind of falcon, [14]any kind of raven, [15]the horned owl, the screech owl, the gull, any kind of hawk, [16]the little owl, the great owl, the white owl, [17]the desert owl, the osprey, the cormorant, [18]the stork, any kind of heron, the hoopoe and the bat.

[19]All flying insects that swarm are unclean to you; do not eat them. [20]But any winged creature that is clean you may eat.

[21]Do not eat anything you find already dead. You may give it to an alien living in any of your towns, and he may eat it, or you may sell it to a foreigner. But you are a people holy to the LORD your God.

Do not cook a young goat in its mother's milk.

Tithes

[22]Be sure to set aside a tenth of all that your fields produce each year. [23]Eat the tithe of your grain, new wine and oil, and the firstborn of your herds and flocks in the presence of the LORD your God at the place he will choose as a dwelling for his Name, so that you may learn to revere the LORD your God always. [24]But if that place is too distant and you have been blessed by the LORD your God and cannot carry your tithe (because the place where the LORD will choose to put his Name is so far away), [25]then exchange your tithe for silver, and take the silver with you and go to the place the LORD your God will choose. [26]Use the silver to buy whatever you like: cattle, sheep, wine or other fermented drink, or anything you wish. Then you and your household shall eat there in the presence of the LORD your God and rejoice. [27]And do not neglect the Levites living in your towns, for they have no allotment or inheritance of their own.

[28]At the end of every three years, bring all the tithes of that year's produce and store it in your towns, [29]so that the Levites (who have no allotment or inheritance of their own) and the aliens,

[a] *15,17* The Hebrew term refers to the irrevocable giving over of things or persons to the LORD, often by totally destroying them.
[b] *5* The precise identification of some of the birds and animals in this chapter is uncertain.
[c] *7* That is, the hyrax or rock badger

the fatherless and the widows who live in your
towns may come and eat and be satisfied, and so
that the LORD your God may bless you in all the
work of your hands.

The Year for Canceling Debts

15 At the end of every seven years you must
cancel debts. [2]This is how it is to be done:
Every creditor shall cancel the loan he has made
to his fellow Israelite. He shall not require payment from his fellow Israelite or brother, because
the LORD's time for canceling debts has been proclaimed. [3]You may require payment from a foreigner, but you must cancel any debt your brother owes you. [4]However, there should be no poor
among you, for in the land the LORD your God is
giving you to possess as your inheritance, he will
richly bless you, [5]if only you fully obey the LORD
your God and are careful to follow all these commands I am giving you today. [6]For the LORD your
God will bless you as he has promised, and you
will lend to many nations but will borrow from
none. You will rule over many nations but none
will rule over you.
[7]If there is a poor man among your brothers in
any of the towns of the land that the LORD your
God is giving you, do not be hardhearted or tight-
fisted toward your poor brother. [8]Rather be open-
handed and freely lend him whatever he needs.
[9]Be careful not to harbor this wicked thought:
"The seventh year, the year for canceling debts,
is near," so that you do not show ill will toward
your needy brother and give him nothing. He
may then appeal to the LORD against you, and you
will be found guilty of sin. [10]Give generously to
him and do so without a grudging heart; then
because of this the LORD your God will bless you
in all your work and in everything you put your
hand to. [11]There will always be poor people in
the land. Therefore I command you to be open-
handed toward your brothers and toward the
poor and needy in your land.

Freeing Servants

[12]If a fellow Hebrew, a man or a woman, sells
himself to you and serves you six years, in the
seventh year you must let him go free. [13]And
when you release him, do not send him away
empty-handed. [14]Supply him liberally from your
flock, your threshing floor and your winepress.
Give to him as the LORD your God has blessed
you. [15]Remember that you were slaves in Egypt
and the LORD your God redeemed you. That is
why I give you this command today.
[16]But if your servant says to you, "I do not
want to leave you," because he loves you and
your family and is well off with you, [17]then take
an awl and push it through his ear lobe into the
door, and he will become your servant for life. Do
the same for your maidservant.
[18]Do not consider it a hardship to set your
servant free, because his service to you these six
years has been worth twice as much as that of a
hired hand. And the LORD your God will bless
you in everything you do.

The Firstborn Animals

[19]Set apart for the LORD your God every firstborn male of your herds and flocks. Do not put
the firstborn of your oxen to work, and do not
shear the firstborn of your sheep. [20]Each year you
and your family are to eat them in the presence
of the LORD your God at the place he will choose.
[21]If an animal has a defect, is lame or blind, or
has any serious flaw, you must not sacrifice it to
the LORD your God. [22]You are to eat it in your
own towns. Both the ceremonially unclean and
the clean may eat it, as if it were gazelle or deer.
[23]But you must not eat the blood; pour it out on
the ground like water.

Passover

16 Observe the month of Abib and celebrate
the Passover of the LORD your God, because in the month of Abib he brought you out of
Egypt by night. [2]Sacrifice as the Passover to the
LORD your God an animal from your flock or herd
at the place the LORD will choose as a dwelling for
his Name. [3]Do not eat it with bread made with
yeast, but for seven days eat unleavened bread,
the bread of affliction, because you left Egypt in
haste—so that all the days of your life you may
remember the time of your departure from Egypt.
[4]Let no yeast be found in your possession in all
your land for seven days. Do not let any of the
meat you sacrifice on the evening of the first day
remain until morning.
[5]You must not sacrifice the Passover in any
town the LORD your God gives you [6]except in the
place he will choose as a dwelling for his Name.
There you must sacrifice the Passover in the evening, when the sun goes down, on the anniversa-
ry[a] of your departure from Egypt. [7]Roast it and
eat it at the place the LORD your God will choose.
Then in the morning return to your tents. [8]For
six days eat unleavened bread and on the seventh
day hold an assembly to the LORD your God and
do no work.

Feast of Weeks

[9]Count off seven weeks from the time you begin to put the sickle to the standing grain. [10]Then
celebrate the Feast of Weeks to the LORD your
God by giving a freewill offering in proportion to

[a]6 Or *down, at the time of day*

the blessings the LORD your God has given you. [11]And rejoice before the LORD your God at the place he will choose as a dwelling for his Name—you, your sons and daughters, your menservants and maidservants, the Levites in your towns, and the aliens, the fatherless and the widows living among you. [12]Remember that you were slaves in Egypt, and follow carefully these decrees.

Feast of Tabernacles

[13]Celebrate the Feast of Tabernacles for seven days after you have gathered the produce of your threshing floor and your winepress. [14]Be joyful at your Feast—you, your sons and daughters, your menservants and maidservants, and the Levites, the aliens, the fatherless and the widows who live in your towns. [15]For seven days celebrate the Feast to the LORD your God at the place the LORD will choose. For the LORD your God will bless you in all your harvest and in all the work of your hands, and your joy will be complete.

[16]Three times a year all your men must appear before the LORD your God at the place he will choose: at the Feast of Unleavened Bread, the Feast of Weeks and the Feast of Tabernacles. No man should appear before the LORD emptyhanded: [17]Each of you must bring a gift in proportion to the way the LORD your God has blessed you.

Judges

[18]Appoint judges and officials for each of your tribes in every town the LORD your God is giving you, and they shall judge the people fairly. [19]Do not pervert justice or show partiality. Do not accept a bribe, for a bribe blinds the eyes of the wise and twists the words of the righteous. [20]Follow justice and justice alone, so that you may live and possess the land the LORD your God is giving you.

Worshiping Other Gods

[21]Do not set up any wooden Asherah pole[a] beside the altar you build to the LORD your God, [22]and do not erect a sacred stone, for these the LORD your God hates.

17 Do not sacrifice to the LORD your God an ox or a sheep that has any defect or flaw in it, for that would be detestable to him.

[2]If a man or woman living among you in one of the towns the LORD gives you is found doing evil in the eyes of the LORD your God in violation of his covenant, [3]and contrary to my command has worshiped other gods, bowing down to them or to the sun or the moon or the stars of the sky, [4]and this has been brought to your attention, then you must investigate it thoroughly. If it is true and it has been proved that this detestable thing has been done in Israel, [5]take the man or woman who has done this evil deed to your city gate and stone that person to death. [6]On the testimony of two or three witnesses a man shall be put to death, but no one shall be put to death on the testimony of only one witness. [7]The hands of the witnesses must be the first in putting him to death, and then the hands of all the people. You must purge the evil from among you.

Law Courts

[8]If cases come before your courts that are too difficult for you to judge—whether bloodshed, lawsuits or assaults—take them to the place the LORD your God will choose. [9]Go to the priests, who are Levites, and to the judge who is in office at that time. Inquire of them and they will give you the verdict. [10]You must act according to the decisions they give you at the place the LORD will choose. Be careful to do everything they direct you to do. [11]Act according to the law they teach you and the decisions they give you. Do not turn aside from what they tell you, to the right or to the left. [12]The man who shows contempt for the judge or for the priest who stands ministering there to the LORD your God must be put to death. You must purge the evil from Israel. [13]All the people will hear and be afraid, and will not be contemptuous again.

The King

[14]When you enter the land the LORD your God is giving you and have taken possession of it and settled in it, and you say, "Let us set a king over us like all the nations around us," [15]be sure to appoint over you the king the LORD your God chooses. He must be from among your own brothers. Do not place a foreigner over you, one who is not a brother Israelite. [16]The king, moreover, must not acquire great numbers of horses for himself or make the people return to Egypt to get more of them, for the LORD has told you, "You are not to go back that way again." [17]He must not take many wives, or his heart will be led astray. He must not accumulate large amounts of silver and gold.

[18]When he takes the throne of his kingdom, he is to write for himself on a scroll a copy of this law, taken from that of the priests, who are Levites. [19]It is to be with him, and he is to read it all the days of his life so that he may learn to revere the LORD his God and follow carefully all the words of this law and these decrees [20]and not consider himself better than his brothers and turn from the law to the right or to the left. Then

[a]21 Or *Do not plant any tree dedicated to Asherah*

he and his descendants will reign a long time
over his kingdom in Israel.

Offerings for Priests and Levites

18 The priests, who are Levites—indeed the
whole tribe of Levi—are to have no allotment or inheritance with Israel. They shall live
on the offerings made to the LORD by fire, for that
is their inheritance. 2They shall have no inheritance among their brothers; the LORD is their
inheritance, as he promised them.
3This is the share due the priests from the
people who sacrifice a bull or a sheep: the shoulder, the jowls and the inner parts. 4You are to
give them the firstfruits of your grain, new wine
and oil, and the first wool from the shearing of
your sheep, 5for the LORD your God has chosen
them and their descendants out of all your tribes
to stand and minister in the LORD's name always.
6If a Levite moves from one of your towns
anywhere in Israel where he is living, and comes
in all earnestness to the place the LORD will
choose, 7he may minister in the name of the
LORD his God like all his fellow Levites who serve
there in the presence of the LORD. 8He is to share
equally in their benefits, even though he has received money from the sale of family possessions.

Detestable Practices

9When you enter the land the LORD your God
is giving you, do not learn to imitate the detestable ways of the nations there. 10Let no one be
found among you who sacrifices his son or daughter in[a] the fire, who practices divination or sorcery, interprets omens, engages in witchcraft,
11or casts spells, or who is a medium or spiritist
or who consults the dead. 12Anyone who does
these things is detestable to the LORD, and because of these detestable practices the LORD your
God will drive out those nations before you.
13You must be blameless before the LORD your
God.

The Prophet

14The nations you will dispossess listen to
those who practice sorcery or divination. But as
for you, the LORD your God has not permitted you
to do so. 15The LORD your God will raise up for
you a prophet like me from among your own
brothers. You must listen to him. 16For this is
what you asked of the LORD your God at Horeb on
the day of the assembly when you said, "Let us
not hear the voice of the LORD our God nor see
this great fire anymore, or we will die."
17The LORD said to me: "What they say is
good. 18I will raise up for them a prophet like you
from among their brothers; I will put my words in
his mouth, and he will tell them everything I
command him. 19If anyone does not listen to my
words that the prophet speaks in my name, I
myself will call him to account. 20But a prophet
who presumes to speak in my name anything I
have not commanded him to say, or a prophet
who speaks in the name of other gods, must be
put to death."
21You may say to yourselves, "How can we
know when a message has not been spoken by
the LORD?" 22If what a prophet proclaims in the
name of the LORD does not take place or come
true, that is a message the LORD has not spoken.
That prophet has spoken presumptuously. Do not
be afraid of him.

Cities of Refuge

19 When the LORD your God has destroyed
the nations whose land he is giving you,
and when you have driven them out and settled
in their towns and houses, 2then set aside for
yourselves three cities centrally located in the
land the LORD your God is giving you to possess.
3Build roads to them and divide into three parts
the land the LORD your God is giving you as an
inheritance, so that anyone who kills a man may
flee there.
4This is the rule concerning the man who kills
another and flees there to save his life—one who
kills his neighbor unintentionally, without malice
aforethought. 5For instance, a man may go into
the forest with his neighbor to cut wood, and as
he swings his ax to fell a tree, the head may fly
off and hit his neighbor and kill him. That man
may flee to one of these cities and save his life.
6Otherwise, the avenger of blood might pursue
him in a rage, overtake him if the distance is too
great, and kill him even though he is not deserving of death, since he did it to his neighbor without malice aforethought. 7This is why I command
you to set aside for yourselves three cities.
8If the LORD your God enlarges your territory,
as he promised on oath to your forefathers, and
gives you the whole land he promised them, 9be-
cause you carefully follow all these laws I command you today—to love the LORD your God and
to walk always in his ways—then you are to set
aside three more cities. 10Do this so that innocent blood will not be shed in your land, which
the LORD your God is giving you as your inheritance, and so that you will not be guilty of bloodshed.
11But if a man hates his neighbor and lies in
wait for him, assaults and kills him, and then
flees to one of these cities, 12the elders of his
town shall send for him, bring him back from the
city, and hand him over to the avenger of blood

[a]10 Or *who makes his son or daughter pass through*

to die. 13Show him no pity. You must purge from
Israel the guilt of shedding innocent blood, so
that it may go well with you.
14Do not move your neighbor's boundary
stone set up by your predecessors in the inheritance you receive in the land the LORD your God
is giving you to possess.

Witnesses

15One witness is not enough to convict a man
accused of any crime or offense he may have
committed. A matter must be established by the
testimony of two or three witnesses.
16If a malicious witness takes the stand to accuse a man of a crime, 17the two men involved in
the dispute must stand in the presence of the
LORD before the priests and the judges who are in
office at the time. 18The judges must make a thorough investigation, and if the witness proves to
be a liar, giving false testimony against his brother, 19then do to him as he intended to do to his
brother. You must purge the evil from among
you. 20The rest of the people will hear of this and
be afraid, and never again will such an evil thing
be done among you. 21Show no pity: life for life,
eye for eye, tooth for tooth, hand for hand, foot
for foot.

Going to War

20 When you go to war against your enemies
and see horses and chariots and an army
greater than yours, do not be afraid of them, because the LORD your God, who brought you up
out of Egypt, will be with you. 2When you are
about to go into battle, the priest shall come forward and address the army. 3He shall say: "Hear,
O Israel, today you are going into battle against
your enemies. Do not be fainthearted or afraid;
do not be terrified or give way to panic before
them. 4For the LORD your God is the one who
goes with you to fight for you against your enemies to give you victory."
5The officers shall say to the army: "Has anyone built a new house and not dedicated it? Let
him go home, or he may die in battle and someone else may dedicate it. 6Has anyone planted a
vineyard and not begun to enjoy it? Let him go
home, or he may die in battle and someone else
enjoy it. 7Has anyone become pledged to a woman and not married her? Let him go home, or he
may die in battle and someone else marry her."
8Then the officers shall add, "Is any man afraid or
fainthearted? Let him go home so that his brothers will not become disheartened too." 9When
the officers have finished speaking to the army,
they shall appoint commanders over it.
10When you march up to attack a city, make its
people an offer of peace. 11If they accept and
open their gates, all the people in it shall be subject to forced labor and shall work for you. 12If
they refuse to make peace and they engage you in
battle, lay siege to that city. 13When the LORD
your God delivers it into your hand, put to the
sword all the men in it. 14As for the women, the
children, the livestock and everything else in
the city, you may take these as plunder for yourselves. And you may use the plunder the LORD
your God gives you from your enemies. 15This is
how you are to treat all the cities that are at a
distance from you and do not belong to the nations nearby.
16However, in the cities of the nations the
LORD your God is giving you as an inheritance, do
not leave alive anything that breathes. 17Com-
pletely destroy[a] them—the Hittites, Amorites,
Canaanites, Perizzites, Hivites and Jebusites—as
the LORD your God has commanded you. 18Other-
wise, they will teach you to follow all the detestable things they do in worshiping their gods, and
you will sin against the LORD your God.
19When you lay siege to a city for a long time,
fighting against it to capture it, do not destroy its
trees by putting an ax to them, because you can
eat their fruit. Do not cut them down. Are the
trees of the field people, that you should besiege
them?[b] 20However, you may cut down trees
that you know are not fruit trees and use them to
build siege works until the city at war with you
falls.

Atonement for an Unsolved Murder

21 If a man is found slain, lying in a field in
the land the LORD your God is giving you
to possess, and it is not known who killed him,
2your elders and judges shall go out and measure
the distance from the body to the neighboring
towns. 3Then the elders of the town nearest the
body shall take a heifer that has never been
worked and has never worn a yoke 4and lead her
down to a valley that has not been plowed or
planted and where there is a flowing stream.
There in the valley they are to break the heifer's
neck. 5The priests, the sons of Levi, shall step
forward, for the LORD your God has chosen them
to minister and to pronounce blessings in the
name of the LORD and to decide all cases of dispute and assault. 6Then all the elders of the town
nearest the body shall wash their hands over the
heifer whose neck was broken in the valley, 7and
they shall declare: "Our hands did not shed this
blood, nor did our eyes see it done. 8Accept this
atonement for your people Israel, whom you have

[a]17 The Hebrew term refers to the irrevocable giving over of things or persons to the LORD, often by totally destroying them.
[b]19 Or *down to use in the siege, for the fruit trees are for the benefit of man.*

redeemed, O LORD, and do not hold your people
guilty of the blood of an innocent man." And the
bloodshed will be atoned for. 9So you will purge
from yourselves the guilt of shedding innocent
blood, since you have done what is right in the
eyes of the LORD.

Marrying a Captive Woman

10When you go to war against your enemies
and the LORD your God delivers them into your
hands and you take captives, 11if you notice
among the captives a beautiful woman and are
attracted to her, you may take her as your wife.
12Bring her into your home and have her shave
her head, trim her nails 13and put aside the
clothes she was wearing when captured. After
she has lived in your house and mourned her
father and mother for a full month, then you may
go to her and be her husband and she shall be
your wife. 14If you are not pleased with her, let
her go wherever she wishes. You must not sell
her or treat her as a slave, since you have dishonored her.

The Right of the Firstborn

15If a man has two wives, and he loves one but
not the other, and both bear him sons but the
firstborn is the son of the wife he does not love,
16when he wills his property to his sons, he must
not give the rights of the firstborn to the son of
the wife he loves in preference to his actual firstborn, the son of the wife he does not love. 17He
must acknowledge the son of his unloved wife as
the firstborn by giving him a double share of all
he has. That son is the first sign of his father's
strength. The right of the firstborn belongs to
him.

A Rebellious Son

18If a man has a stubborn and rebellious son
who does not obey his father and mother and will
not listen to them when they discipline him,
19his father and mother shall take hold of him
and bring him to the elders at the gate of his
town. 20They shall say to the elders, "This son of
ours is stubborn and rebellious. He will not obey
us. He is a profligate and a drunkard." 21Then all
the men of his town shall stone him to death. You
must purge the evil from among you. All Israel
will hear of it and be afraid.

Various Laws

22If a man guilty of a capital offense is put to
death and his body is hung on a tree, 23you must
not leave his body on the tree overnight. Be sure
to bury him that same day, because anyone who
is hung on a tree is under God's curse. You must
not desecrate the land the LORD your God is giving you as an inheritance.

22 If you see your brother's ox or sheep
straying, do not ignore it but be sure to
take it back to him. 2If the brother does not live
near you or if you do not know who he is, take it
home with you and keep it until he comes looking for it. Then give it back to him. 3Do the same
if you find your brother's donkey or his cloak or
anything he loses. Do not ignore it.

4If you see your brother's donkey or his ox
fallen on the road, do not ignore it. Help him get
it to its feet.

5A woman must not wear men's clothing, nor
a man wear women's clothing, for the LORD your
God detests anyone who does this.

6If you come across a bird's nest beside the
road, either in a tree or on the ground, and the
mother is sitting on the young or on the eggs, do
not take the mother with the young. 7You may
take the young, but be sure to let the mother go,
so that it may go well with you and you may have
a long life.

8When you build a new house, make a parapet
around your roof so that you may not bring the
guilt of bloodshed on your house if someone falls
from the roof.

9Do not plant two kinds of seed in your vineyard; if you do, not only the crops you plant but
also the fruit of the vineyard will be defiled.[a]

10Do not plow with an ox and a donkey yoked
together.

11Do not wear clothes of wool and linen woven together.

12Make tassels on the four corners of the cloak
you wear.

Marriage Violations

13If a man takes a wife and, after lying with
her, dislikes her 14and slanders her and gives her
a bad name, saying, "I married this woman, but
when I approached her, I did not find proof of her
virginity," 15then the girl's father and mother
shall bring proof that she was a virgin to the town
elders at the gate. 16The girl's father will say to
the elders, "I gave my daughter in marriage to
this man, but he dislikes her. 17Now he has slandered her and said, 'I did not find your daughter
to be a virgin.' But here is the proof of my daughter's virginity." Then her parents shall display the
cloth before the elders of the town, 18and the
elders shall take the man and punish him. 19They
shall fine him a hundred shekels of silver[b] and
give them to the girl's father, because this man
has given an Israelite virgin a bad name. She shall
continue to be his wife; he must not divorce her
as long as he lives.

[a] 9 Or *be forfeited to the sanctuary*
[b] 19 That is, about 2 1/2 pounds (about 1 kilogram)

20If, however, the charge is true and no proof of the girl's virginity can be found, 21she shall be brought to the door of her father's house and there the men of her town shall stone her to death. She has done a disgraceful thing in Israel by being promiscuous while still in her father's house. You must purge the evil from among you.

22If a man is found sleeping with another man's wife, both the man who slept with her and the woman must die. You must purge the evil from Israel.

23If a man happens to meet in a town a virgin pledged to be married and he sleeps with her, 24you shall take both of them to the gate of that town and stone them to death—the girl because she was in a town and did not scream for help, and the man because he violated another man's wife. You must purge the evil from among you.

25But if out in the country a man happens to meet a girl pledged to be married and rapes her, only the man who has done this shall die. 26Do nothing to the girl; she has committed no sin deserving death. This case is like that of someone who attacks and murders his neighbor, 27for the man found the girl out in the country, and though the betrothed girl screamed, there was no one to rescue her.

28If a man happens to meet a virgin who is not pledged to be married and rapes her and they are discovered, 29he shall pay the girl's father fifty shekels of silver.[a] He must marry the girl, for he has violated her. He can never divorce her as long as he lives.

30A man is not to marry his father's wife; he must not dishonor his father's bed.

Exclusion From the Assembly

23 No one who has been emasculated by crushing or cutting may enter the assembly of the LORD.

2No one born of a forbidden marriage[b] nor any of his descendants may enter the assembly of the LORD, even down to the tenth generation.

3No Ammonite or Moabite or any of his descendants may enter the assembly of the LORD, even down to the tenth generation. 4For they did not come to meet you with bread and water on your way when you came out of Egypt, and they hired Balaam son of Beor from Pethor in Aram Naharaim[c] to pronounce a curse on you. 5However, the LORD your God would not listen to Balaam but turned the curse into a blessing for you, because the LORD your God loves you. 6Do not seek a treaty of friendship with them as long as you live.

7Do not abhor an Edomite, for he is your brother. Do not abhor an Egyptian, because you lived as an alien in his country. 8The third generation of children born to them may enter the assembly of the LORD.

Uncleanness in the Camp

9When you are encamped against your enemies, keep away from everything impure. 10If one of your men is unclean because of a nocturnal emission, he is to go outside the camp and stay there. 11But as evening approaches he is to wash himself, and at sunset he may return to the camp.

12Designate a place outside the camp where you can go to relieve yourself. 13As part of your equipment have something to dig with, and when you relieve yourself, dig a hole and cover up your excrement. 14For the LORD your God moves about in your camp to protect you and to deliver your enemies to you. Your camp must be holy, so that he will not see among you anything indecent and turn away from you.

Miscellaneous Laws

15If a slave has taken refuge with you, do not hand him over to his master. 16Let him live among you wherever he likes and in whatever town he chooses. Do not oppress him.

17No Israelite man or woman is to become a shrine prostitute. 18You must not bring the earnings of a female prostitute or of a male prostitute[d] into the house of the LORD your God to pay any vow, because the LORD your God detests them both.

19Do not charge your brother interest, whether on money or food or anything else that may earn interest. 20You may charge a foreigner interest, but not a brother Israelite, so that the LORD your God may bless you in everything you put your hand to in the land you are entering to possess.

21If you make a vow to the LORD your God, do not be slow to pay it, for the LORD your God will certainly demand it of you and you will be guilty of sin. 22But if you refrain from making a vow, you will not be guilty. 23Whatever your lips utter you must be sure to do, because you made your vow freely to the LORD your God with your own mouth.

24If you enter your neighbor's vineyard, you may eat all the grapes you want, but do not put any in your basket. 25If you enter your neighbor's grainfield, you may pick kernels with your hands, but you must not put a sickle to his standing grain.

[a] *29* That is, about 1 1/4 pounds (about 0.6 kilogram) [b] *2* Or *one of illegitimate birth* [c] *4* That is, Northwest Mesopotamia
[d] *18* Hebrew *of a dog*

24 If a man marries a woman who becomes displeasing to him because he finds something indecent about her, and he writes her a certificate of divorce, gives it to her and sends her from his house, 2and if after she leaves his house she becomes the wife of another man, 3and her second husband dislikes her and writes her a certificate of divorce, gives it to her and sends her from his house, or if he dies, 4then her first husband, who divorced her, is not allowed to marry her again after she has been defiled. That would be detestable in the eyes of the LORD. Do not bring sin upon the land the LORD your God is giving you as an inheritance.

5If a man has recently married, he must not be sent to war or have any other duty laid on him. For one year he is to be free to stay at home and bring happiness to the wife he has married.

6Do not take a pair of millstones—not even the upper one—as security for a debt, because that would be taking a man's livelihood as security.

7If a man is caught kidnapping one of his brother Israelites and treats him as a slave or sells him, the kidnapper must die. You must purge the evil from among you.

8In cases of leprous[a] diseases be very careful to do exactly as the priests, who are Levites, instruct you. You must follow carefully what I have commanded them. 9Remember what the LORD your God did to Miriam along the way after you came out of Egypt.

10When you make a loan of any kind to your neighbor, do not go into his house to get what he is offering as a pledge. 11Stay outside and let the man to whom you are making the loan bring the pledge out to you. 12If the man is poor, do not go to sleep with his pledge in your possession. 13Return his cloak to him by sunset so that he may sleep in it. Then he will thank you, and it will be regarded as a righteous act in the sight of the LORD your God.

14Do not take advantage of a hired man who is poor and needy, whether he is a brother Israelite or an alien living in one of your towns. 15Pay him his wages each day before sunset, because he is poor and is counting on it. Otherwise he may cry to the LORD against you, and you will be guilty of sin.

16Fathers shall not be put to death for their children, nor children put to death for their fathers; each is to die for his own sin.

17Do not deprive the alien or the fatherless of justice, or take the cloak of the widow as a pledge. 18Remember that you were slaves in Egypt and the LORD your God redeemed you from there. That is why I command you to do this.

19When you are harvesting in your field and you overlook a sheaf, do not go back to get it. Leave it for the alien, the fatherless and the widow, so that the LORD your God may bless you in all the work of your hands. 20When you beat the olives from your trees, do not go over the branches a second time. Leave what remains for the alien, the fatherless and the widow. 21When you harvest the grapes in your vineyard, do not go over the vines again. Leave what remains for the alien, the fatherless and the widow. 22Remember that you were slaves in Egypt. That is why I command you to do this.

25 When men have a dispute, they are to take it to court and the judges will decide the case, acquitting the innocent and condemning the guilty. 2If the guilty man deserves to be beaten, the judge shall make him lie down and have him flogged in his presence with the number of lashes his crime deserves, 3but he must not give him more than forty lashes. If he is flogged more than that, your brother will be degraded in your eyes.

4Do not muzzle an ox while it is treading out the grain.

5If brothers are living together and one of them dies without a son, his widow must not marry outside the family. Her husband's brother shall take her and marry her and fulfill the duty of a brother-in-law to her. 6The first son she bears shall carry on the name of the dead brother so that his name will not be blotted out from Israel.

7However, if a man does not want to marry his brother's wife, she shall go to the elders at the town gate and say, "My husband's brother refuses to carry on his brother's name in Israel. He will not fulfill the duty of a brother-in-law to me." 8Then the elders of his town shall summon him and talk to him. If he persists in saying, "I do not want to marry her," 9his brother's widow shall go up to him in the presence of the elders, take off one of his sandals, spit in his face and say, "This is what is done to the man who will not build up his brother's family line." 10That man's line shall be known in Israel as The Family of the Unsandaled.

11If two men are fighting and the wife of one of them comes to rescue her husband from his assailant, and she reaches out and seizes him by his private parts, 12you shall cut off her hand. Show her no pity.

13Do not have two differing weights in your bag—one heavy, one light. 14Do not have two differing measures in your house—one large, one small. 15You must have accurate and honest weights and measures, so that you may live long

[a]8 The Hebrew word was used for various diseases affecting the skin—not necessarily leprosy.

in the land the LORD your God is giving you. 16For the LORD your God detests anyone who does these things, anyone who deals dishonestly.

17Remember what the Amalekites did to you along the way when you came out of Egypt. 18When you were weary and worn out, they met you on your journey and cut off all who were lagging behind; they had no fear of God. 19When the LORD your God gives you rest from all the enemies around you in the land he is giving you to possess as an inheritance, you shall blot out the memory of Amalek from under heaven. Do not forget!

Firstfruits and Tithes

26 When you have entered the land the LORD your God is giving you as an inheritance and have taken possession of it and settled in it, 2take some of the firstfruits of all that you produce from the soil of the land the LORD your God is giving you and put them in a basket. Then go to the place the LORD your God will choose as a dwelling for his Name 3and say to the priest in office at the time, "I declare today to the LORD your God that I have come to the land the LORD swore to our forefathers to give us." 4The priest shall take the basket from your hands and set it down in front of the altar of the LORD your God. 5Then you shall declare before the LORD your God: "My father was a wandering Aramean, and he went down into Egypt with a few people and lived there and became a great nation, powerful and numerous. 6But the Egyptians mistreated us and made us suffer, putting us to hard labor. 7Then we cried out to the LORD, the God of our fathers, and the LORD heard our voice and saw our misery, toil and oppression. 8So the LORD brought us out of Egypt with a mighty hand and an outstretched arm, with great terror and with miraculous signs and wonders. 9He brought us to this place and gave us this land, a land flowing with milk and honey; 10and now I bring the firstfruits of the soil that you, O LORD, have given me." Place the basket before the LORD your God and bow down before him. 11And you and the Levites and the aliens among you shall rejoice in all the good things the LORD your God has given to you and your household.

12When you have finished setting aside a tenth of all your produce in the third year, the year of the tithe, you shall give it to the Levite, the alien, the fatherless and the widow, so that they may eat in your towns and be satisfied. 13Then say to the LORD your God: "I have removed from my house the sacred portion and have given it to the Levite, the alien, the fatherless and the widow, according to all you commanded. I have not turned aside from your commands nor have I forgotten any of them. 14I have not eaten any of the sacred portion while I was in mourning, nor have I removed any of it while I was unclean, nor have I offered any of it to the dead. I have obeyed the LORD my God; I have done everything you commanded me. 15Look down from heaven, your holy dwelling place, and bless your people Israel and the land you have given us as you promised on oath to our forefathers, a land flowing with milk and honey."

Follow the LORD's Commands

16The LORD your God commands you this day to follow these decrees and laws; carefully observe them with all your heart and with all your soul. 17You have declared this day that the LORD is your God and that you will walk in his ways, that you will keep his decrees, commands and laws, and that you will obey him. 18And the LORD has declared this day that you are his people, his treasured possession as he promised, and that you are to keep all his commands. 19He has declared that he will set you in praise, fame and honor high above all the nations he has made and that you will be a people holy to the LORD your God, as he promised.

The Altar on Mount Ebal

27 Moses and the elders of Israel commanded the people: "Keep all these commands that I give you today. 2When you have crossed the Jordan into the land the LORD your God is giving you, set up some large stones and coat them with plaster. 3Write on them all the words of this law when you have crossed over to enter the land the LORD your God is giving you, a land flowing with milk and honey, just as the LORD, the God of your fathers, promised you. 4And when you have crossed the Jordan, set up these stones on Mount Ebal, as I command you today, and coat them with plaster. 5Build there an altar to the LORD your God, an altar of stones. Do not use any iron tool upon them. 6Build the altar of the LORD your God with fieldstones and offer burnt offerings on it to the LORD your God. 7Sacrifice fellowship offerings[a] there, eating them and rejoicing in the presence of the LORD your God. 8And you shall write very clearly all the words of this law on these stones you have set up."

Curses From Mount Ebal

9Then Moses and the priests, who are Levites, said to all Israel, "Be silent, O Israel, and listen! You have now become the people of the LORD your God. 10Obey the LORD your God and follow his commands and decrees that I give you today."

a7 Traditionally *peace offerings*

11 On the same day Moses commanded the
people:
12 When you have crossed the Jordan, these
tribes shall stand on Mount Gerizim to bless the
people: Simeon, Levi, Judah, Issachar, Joseph and
Benjamin. 13 And these tribes shall stand on
Mount Ebal to pronounce curses: Reuben, Gad,
Asher, Zebulun, Dan and Naphtali.
14 The Levites shall recite to all the people of
Israel in a loud voice:

15 "Cursed is the man who carves an image or casts an idol—a thing detestable to
the LORD, the work of the craftsman's
hands—and sets it up in secret."
Then all the people shall say, "Amen!"
16 "Cursed is the man who dishonors his
father or his mother."
Then all the people shall say, "Amen!"
17 "Cursed is the man who moves his
neighbor's boundary stone."
Then all the people shall say, "Amen!"
18 "Cursed is the man who leads the blind
astray on the road."
Then all the people shall say, "Amen!"
19 "Cursed is the man who withholds justice from the alien, the fatherless or the
widow."
Then all the people shall say, "Amen!"
20 "Cursed is the man who sleeps with
his father's wife, for he dishonors his father's bed."
Then all the people shall say, "Amen!"
21 "Cursed is the man who has sexual relations with any animal."
Then all the people shall say, "Amen!"
22 "Cursed is the man who sleeps with
his sister, the daughter of his father or the
daughter of his mother."
Then all the people shall say, "Amen!"
23 "Cursed is the man who sleeps with
his mother-in-law."
Then all the people shall say, "Amen!"
24 "Cursed is the man who kills his neighbor secretly."
Then all the people shall say, "Amen!"
25 "Cursed is the man who accepts a
bribe to kill an innocent person."
Then all the people shall say, "Amen!"
26 "Cursed is the man who does not uphold the words of this law by carrying them
out."
Then all the people shall say, "Amen!"

Blessings for Obedience

28 If you fully obey the LORD your God and
carefully follow all his commands I give
you today, the LORD your God will set you high
above all the nations on earth. 2 All these blessings will come upon you and accompany you if
you obey the LORD your God:

3 You will be blessed in the city and
blessed in the country.
4 The fruit of your womb will be blessed,
and the crops of your land and the young of
your livestock—the calves of your herds
and the lambs of your flocks.
5 Your basket and your kneading trough
will be blessed.
6 You will be blessed when you come in
and blessed when you go out.

7 The LORD will grant that the enemies who
rise up against you will be defeated before you.
They will come at you from one direction but flee
from you in seven.
8 The LORD will send a blessing on your barns
and on everything you put your hand to. The
LORD your God will bless you in the land he is
giving you.
9 The LORD will establish you as his holy people, as he promised you on oath, if you keep the
commands of the LORD your God and walk in his
ways. 10 Then all the peoples on earth will see
that you are called by the name of the LORD, and
they will fear you. 11 The LORD will grant you
abundant prosperity—in the fruit of your womb,
the young of your livestock and the crops of your
ground—in the land he swore to your forefathers
to give you.
12 The LORD will open the heavens, the storehouse of his bounty, to send rain on your land in
season and to bless all the work of your hands.
You will lend to many nations but will borrow
from none. 13 The LORD will make you the head,
not the tail. If you pay attention to the commands
of the LORD your God that I give you this day and
carefully follow them, you will always be at the
top, never at the bottom. 14 Do not turn aside
from any of the commands I give you today, to
the right or to the left, following other gods and
serving them.

Curses for Disobedience

15 However, if you do not obey the LORD your
God and do not carefully follow all his commands
and decrees I am giving you today, all these
curses will come upon you and overtake you:

16 You will be cursed in the city and
cursed in the country.
17 Your basket and your kneading trough
will be cursed.
18 The fruit of your womb will be cursed,
and the crops of your land, and the calves of
your herds and the lambs of your flocks.
19 You will be cursed when you come in
and cursed when you go out.

20The LORD will send on you curses, confusion and rebuke in everything you put your hand to, until you are destroyed and come to sudden ruin because of the evil you have done in forsaking him.[a] 21The LORD will plague you with diseases until he has destroyed you from the land you are entering to possess. 22The LORD will strike you with wasting disease, with fever and inflammation, with scorching heat and drought, with blight and mildew, which will plague you until you perish. 23The sky over your head will be bronze, the ground beneath you iron. 24The LORD will turn the rain of your country into dust and powder; it will come down from the skies until you are destroyed.

25The LORD will cause you to be defeated before your enemies. You will come at them from one direction but flee from them in seven, and you will become a thing of horror to all the kingdoms on earth. 26Your carcasses will be food for all the birds of the air and the beasts of the earth, and there will be no one to frighten them away. 27The LORD will afflict you with the boils of Egypt and with tumors, festering sores and the itch, from which you cannot be cured. 28The LORD will afflict you with madness, blindness and confusion of mind. 29At midday you will grope about like a blind man in the dark. You will be unsuccessful in everything you do; day after day you will be oppressed and robbed, with no one to rescue you.

30You will be pledged to be married to a woman, but another will take her and ravish her. You will build a house, but you will not live in it. You will plant a vineyard, but you will not even begin to enjoy its fruit. 31Your ox will be slaughtered before your eyes, but you will eat none of it. Your donkey will be forcibly taken from you and will not be returned. Your sheep will be given to your enemies, and no one will rescue them. 32Your sons and daughters will be given to another nation, and you will wear out your eyes watching for them day after day, powerless to lift a hand. 33A people that you do not know will eat what your land and labor produce, and you will have nothing but cruel oppression all your days. 34The sights you see will drive you mad. 35The LORD will afflict your knees and legs with painful boils that cannot be cured, spreading from the soles of your feet to the top of your head.

36The LORD will drive you and the king you set over you to a nation unknown to you or your fathers. There you will worship other gods, gods of wood and stone. 37You will become a thing of horror and an object of scorn and ridicule to all the nations where the LORD will drive you.

38You will sow much seed in the field but you will harvest little, because locusts will devour it. 39You will plant vineyards and cultivate them but you will not drink the wine or gather the grapes, because worms will eat them. 40You will have olive trees throughout your country but you will not use the oil, because the olives will drop off. 41You will have sons and daughters but you will not keep them, because they will go into captivity. 42Swarms of locusts will take over all your trees and the crops of your land.

43The alien who lives among you will rise above you higher and higher, but you will sink lower and lower. 44He will lend to you, but you will not lend to him. He will be the head, but you will be the tail.

45All these curses will come upon you. They will pursue you and overtake you until you are destroyed, because you did not obey the LORD your God and observe the commands and decrees he gave you. 46They will be a sign and a wonder to you and your descendants forever. 47Because you did not serve the LORD your God joyfully and gladly in the time of prosperity, 48therefore in hunger and thirst, in nakedness and dire poverty, you will serve the enemies the LORD sends against you. He will put an iron yoke on your neck until he has destroyed you.

49The LORD will bring a nation against you from far away, from the ends of the earth, like an eagle swooping down, a nation whose language you will not understand, 50a fierce-looking nation without respect for the old or pity for the young. 51They will devour the young of your livestock and the crops of your land until you are destroyed. They will leave you no grain, new wine or oil, nor any calves of your herds or lambs of your flocks until you are ruined. 52They will lay siege to all the cities throughout your land until the high fortified walls in which you trust fall down. They will besiege all the cities throughout the land the LORD your God is giving you.

53Because of the suffering that your enemy will inflict on you during the siege, you will eat the fruit of the womb, the flesh of the sons and daughters the LORD your God has given you. 54Even the most gentle and sensitive man among you will have no compassion on his own brother or the wife he loves or his surviving children, 55and he will not give to one of them any of the flesh of his children that he is eating. It will be all he has left because of the suffering your enemy will inflict on you during the siege of all your cities. 56The most gentle and sensitive woman among you—so sensitive and gentle that she would not venture to touch the ground with the sole of her foot—will begrudge the husband she loves and her own son or daughter 57the after-

[a]20 Hebrew *me*

birth from her womb and the children she bears.
For she intends to eat them secretly during the
siege and in the distress that your enemy will
inflict on you in your cities.
58If you do not carefully follow all the words of
this law, which are written in this book, and do
not revere this glorious and awesome name—the
LORD your God— 59the LORD will send fearful
plagues on you and your descendants, harsh and
prolonged disasters, and severe and lingering illnesses. 60He will bring upon you all the diseases
of Egypt that you dreaded, and they will cling to
you. 61The LORD will also bring on you every kind
of sickness and disaster not recorded in this Book
of the Law, until you are destroyed. 62You who
were as numerous as the stars in the sky will be
left but few in number, because you did not obey
the LORD your God. 63Just as it pleased the LORD
to make you prosper and increase in number, so
it will please him to ruin and destroy you. You
will be uprooted from the land you are entering
to possess.
64Then the LORD will scatter you among all
nations, from one end of the earth to the other.
There you will worship other gods—gods of
wood and stone, which neither you nor your fathers have known. 65Among those nations you
will find no repose, no resting place for the sole
of your foot. There the LORD will give you an
anxious mind, eyes weary with longing, and a
despairing heart. 66You will live in constant suspense, filled with dread both night and day, never sure of your life. 67In the morning you will say,
"If only it were evening!" and in the evening, "If
only it were morning!"—because of the terror
that will fill your hearts and the sights that your
eyes will see. 68The LORD will send you back in
ships to Egypt on a journey I said you should
never make again. There you will offer yourselves
for sale to your enemies as male and female
slaves, but no one will buy you.

Renewal of the Covenant

29 These are the terms of the covenant the
LORD commanded Moses to make with
the Israelites in Moab, in addition to the covenant he had made with them at Horeb.
2Moses summoned all the Israelites and said to
them:
Your eyes have seen all that the LORD did in
Egypt to Pharaoh, to all his officials and to all his
land. 3With your own eyes you saw those great
trials, those miraculous signs and great wonders.
4But to this day the LORD has not given you a
mind that understands or eyes that see or ears
that hear. 5During the forty years that I led you
through the desert, your clothes did not wear
out, nor did the sandals on your feet. 6You ate no
bread and drank no wine or other fermented
drink. I did this so that you might know that I am
the LORD your God.
7When you reached this place, Sihon king of
Heshbon and Og king of Bashan came out to fight
against us, but we defeated them. 8We took their
land and gave it as an inheritance to the Reubenites, the Gadites and the half-tribe of Manasseh.
9Carefully follow the terms of this covenant, so
that you may prosper in everything you do. 10All
of you are standing today in the presence of the
LORD your God—your leaders and chief men,
your elders and officials, and all the other men of
Israel, 11together with your children and your
wives, and the aliens living in your camps who
chop your wood and carry your water. 12You are
standing here in order to enter into a covenant
with the LORD your God, a covenant the LORD is
making with you this day and sealing with an
oath, 13to confirm you this day as his people, that
he may be your God as he promised you and as
he swore to your fathers, Abraham, Isaac and
Jacob. 14I am making this covenant, with its oath,
not only with you 15who are standing here with
us today in the presence of the LORD our God but
also with those who are not here today.
16You yourselves know how we lived in Egypt
and how we passed through the countries on the
way here. 17You saw among them their detestable images and idols of wood and stone, of silver
and gold. 18Make sure there is no man or woman,
clan or tribe among you today whose heart turns
away from the LORD our God to go and worship
the gods of those nations; make sure there is no
root among you that produces such bitter poison.
19When such a person hears the words of this
oath, he invokes a blessing on himself and therefore thinks, "I will be safe, even though I persist
in going my own way." This will bring disaster on
the watered land as well as the dry.[a] 20The LORD
will never be willing to forgive him; his wrath
and zeal will burn against that man. All the
curses written in this book will fall upon him,
and the LORD will blot out his name from under
heaven. 21The LORD will single him out from all
the tribes of Israel for disaster, according to all
the curses of the covenant written in this Book of
the Law.
22Your children who follow you in later generations and foreigners who come from distant
lands will see the calamities that have fallen on
the land and the diseases with which the LORD
has afflicted it. 23The whole land will be a burning waste of salt and sulfur—nothing planted,
nothing sprouting, no vegetation growing on it. It

a 19 Or *way, in order to add drunkenness to thirst."*

will be like the destruction of Sodom and Gomorrah, Admah and Zeboiim, which the LORD overthrew in fierce anger. 24All the nations will ask:
“Why has the LORD done this to this land? Why
this fierce, burning anger?”
25And the answer will be: “It is because this
people abandoned the covenant of the LORD, the
God of their fathers, the covenant he made with
them when he brought them out of Egypt. 26They
went off and worshiped other gods and bowed
down to them, gods they did not know, gods he
had not given them. 27Therefore the LORD’s anger burned against this land, so that he brought
on it all the curses written in this book. 28In
furious anger and in great wrath the LORD uprooted them from their land and thrust them into
another land, as it is now.”
29The secret things belong to the LORD our
God, but the things revealed belong to us and to
our children forever, that we may follow all the
words of this law.

Prosperity After Turning to the LORD

30 When all these blessings and curses I
have set before you come upon you and
you take them to heart wherever the LORD your
God disperses you among the nations, 2and when
you and your children return to the LORD your
God and obey him with all your heart and with all
your soul according to everything I command you
today, 3then the LORD your God will restore your
fortunes[a] and have compassion on you and gather you again from all the nations where he scattered you. 4Even if you have been banished to the
most distant land under the heavens, from there
the LORD your God will gather you and bring you
back. 5He will bring you to the land that belonged
to your fathers, and you will take possession of it.
He will make you more prosperous and numerous than your fathers. 6The LORD your God will
circumcise your hearts and the hearts of your
descendants, so that you may love him with all
your heart and with all your soul, and live. 7The
LORD your God will put all these curses on your
enemies who hate and persecute you. 8You will
again obey the LORD and follow all his commands
I am giving you today. 9Then the LORD your God
will make you most prosperous in all the work of
your hands and in the fruit of your womb, the
young of your livestock and the crops of your
land. The LORD will again delight in you and
make you prosperous, just as he delighted in your
fathers, 10if you obey the LORD your God and
keep his commands and decrees that are written
in this Book of the Law and turn to the LORD your
God with all your heart and with all your soul.

The Offer of Life or Death

11Now what I am commanding you today is
not too difficult for you or beyond your reach. 12It
is not up in heaven, so that you have to ask,
“Who will ascend into heaven to get it and proclaim it to us so we may obey it?” 13Nor is it
beyond the sea, so that you have to ask, “Who
will cross the sea to get it and proclaim it to us so
we may obey it?” 14No, the word is very near
you; it is in your mouth and in your heart so you
may obey it.
15See, I set before you today life and prosperity, death and destruction. 16For I command you
today to love the LORD your God, to walk in his
ways, and to keep his commands, decrees and
laws; then you will live and increase, and the
LORD your God will bless you in the land you are
entering to possess.
17But if your heart turns away and you are not
obedient, and if you are drawn away to bow
down to other gods and worship them, 18I declare to you this day that you will certainly be
destroyed. You will not live long in the land you
are crossing the Jordan to enter and possess.
19This day I call heaven and earth as witnesses
against you that I have set before you life and
death, blessings and curses. Now choose life, so
that you and your children may live 20and that
you may love the LORD your God, listen to his
voice, and hold fast to him. For the LORD is your
life, and he will give you many years in the land
he swore to give to your fathers, Abraham, Isaac
and Jacob.

Joshua to Succeed Moses

31 Then Moses went out and spoke these
words to all Israel: 2“I am now a hundred
and twenty years old and I am no longer able to
lead you. The LORD has said to me, ‘You shall not
cross the Jordan.’ 3The LORD your God himself
will cross over ahead of you. He will destroy
these nations before you, and you will take possession of their land. Joshua also will cross over
ahead of you, as the LORD said. 4And the LORD
will do to them what he did to Sihon and Og, the
kings of the Amorites, whom he destroyed along
with their land. 5The LORD will deliver them to
you, and you must do to them all that I have
commanded you. 6Be strong and courageous. Do
not be afraid or terrified because of them, for the
LORD your God goes with you; he will never leave
you nor forsake you.”
7Then Moses summoned Joshua and said to
him in the presence of all Israel, “Be strong and
courageous, for you must go with this people into
the land that the LORD swore to their forefathers

[a]3 Or *will bring you back from captivity*

to give them, and you must divide it among them
as their inheritance. 8The LORD himself goes before you and will be with you; he will never leave
you nor forsake you. Do not be afraid; do not be
discouraged."

The Reading of the Law

9So Moses wrote down this law and gave it to
the priests, the sons of Levi, who carried the ark
of the covenant of the LORD, and to all the elders
of Israel. 10Then Moses commanded them: "At
the end of every seven years, in the year for canceling debts, during the Feast of Tabernacles,
11when all Israel comes to appear before the
LORD your God at the place he will choose, you
shall read this law before them in their hearing.
12Assemble the people—men, women and children, and the aliens living in your towns—so
they can listen and learn to fear the LORD your
God and follow carefully all the words of this law.
13Their children, who do not know this law, must
hear it and learn to fear the LORD your God as
long as you live in the land you are crossing the
Jordan to possess."

Israel's Rebellion Predicted

14The LORD said to Moses, "Now the day of
your death is near. Call Joshua and present yourselves at the Tent of Meeting, where I will commission him." So Moses and Joshua came and
presented themselves at the Tent of Meeting.
15Then the LORD appeared at the Tent in a
pillar of cloud, and the cloud stood over the entrance to the Tent. 16And the LORD said to Moses:
"You are going to rest with your fathers, and
these people will soon prostitute themselves to
the foreign gods of the land they are entering.
They will forsake me and break the covenant I
made with them. 17On that day I will become
angry with them and forsake them; I will hide my
face from them, and they will be destroyed. Many
disasters and difficulties will come upon them,
and on that day they will ask, 'Have not these
disasters come upon us because our God is not
with us?' 18And I will certainly hide my face on
that day because of all their wickedness in turning to other gods.
19"Now write down for yourselves this song
and teach it to the Israelites and have them sing
it, so that it may be a witness for me against
them. 20When I have brought them into the land
flowing with milk and honey, the land I promised
on oath to their forefathers, and when they eat
their fill and thrive, they will turn to other gods
and worship them, rejecting me and breaking my
covenant. 21And when many disasters and difficulties come upon them, this song will testify
against them, because it will not be forgotten by
their descendants. I know what they are disposed
to do, even before I bring them into the land I
promised them on oath." 22So Moses wrote down
this song that day and taught it to the Israelites.
23The LORD gave this command to Joshua son
of Nun: "Be strong and courageous, for you will
bring the Israelites into the land I promised them
on oath, and I myself will be with you."
24After Moses finished writing in a book the
words of this law from beginning to end, 25he
gave this command to the Levites who carried
the ark of the covenant of the LORD: 26"Take this
Book of the Law and place it beside the ark of the
covenant of the LORD your God. There it will
remain as a witness against you. 27For I know
how rebellious and stiff-necked you are. If you
have been rebellious against the LORD while I am
still alive and with you, how much more will you
rebel after I die! 28Assemble before me all the
elders of your tribes and all your officials, so that
I can speak these words in their hearing and call
heaven and earth to testify against them. 29For I
know that after my death you are sure to become
utterly corrupt and to turn from the way I have
commanded you. In days to come, disaster will
fall upon you because you will do evil in the sight
of the LORD and provoke him to anger by what
your hands have made."

The Song of Moses

30And Moses recited the words of this song
from beginning to end in the hearing of the
whole assembly of Israel:

32 Listen, O heavens, and I will speak;
hear, O earth, the words of my mouth.
2Let my teaching fall like rain
and my words descend like dew,
like showers on new grass,
like abundant rain on tender plants.

3I will proclaim the name of the LORD.
Oh, praise the greatness of our God!
4He is the Rock, his works are perfect,
and all his ways are just.
A faithful God who does no wrong,
upright and just is he.
5They have acted corruptly toward him;
to their shame they are no longer his
children,
but a warped and crooked generation.[a]
6Is this the way you repay the LORD,
O foolish and unwise people?
Is he not your Father, your Creator,[b]
who made you and formed you?
7Remember the days of old;

[a]5 Or *Corrupt are they and not his children, / a generation warped and twisted to their shame* [b]6 Or *Father, who bought you*

consider the generations long past.
Ask your father and he will tell you,
your elders, and they will explain to you.
8 When the Most High gave the nations their inheritance,
when he divided all mankind,
he set up boundaries for the peoples
according to the number of the sons of Israel.[a]
9 For the LORD's portion is his people,
Jacob his allotted inheritance.

10 In a desert land he found him,
in a barren and howling waste.
He shielded him and cared for him;
he guarded him as the apple of his eye,
11 like an eagle that stirs up its nest
and hovers over its young,
that spreads its wings to catch them
and carries them on its pinions.
12 The LORD alone led him;
no foreign god was with him.

13 He made him ride on the heights of the land
and fed him with the fruit of the fields.
He nourished him with honey from the rock,
and with oil from the flinty crag,
14 with curds and milk from herd and flock
and with fattened lambs and goats,
with choice rams of Bashan
and the finest kernels of wheat.
You drank the foaming blood of the grape.

15 Jeshurun[b] grew fat and kicked;
filled with food, he became heavy and sleek.
He abandoned the God who made him
and rejected the Rock his Savior.
16 They made him jealous with their foreign gods
and angered him with their detestable idols.
17 They sacrificed to demons, which are not God—
gods they had not known,
gods that recently appeared,
gods your fathers did not fear.
18 You deserted the Rock, who fathered you;
you forgot the God who gave you birth.

19 The LORD saw this and rejected them
because he was angered by his sons and daughters.
20 "I will hide my face from them," he said,
"and see what their end will be;
for they are a perverse generation,
children who are unfaithful.
21 They made me jealous by what is no god
and angered me with their worthless idols.
I will make them envious by those who are not a people;
I will make them angry by a nation that has no understanding.
22 For a fire has been kindled by my wrath,
one that burns to the realm of death[c] below.
It will devour the earth and its harvests
and set afire the foundations of the mountains.

23 "I will heap calamities upon them
and spend my arrows against them.
24 I will send wasting famine against them,
consuming pestilence and deadly plague;
I will send against them the fangs of wild beasts,
the venom of vipers that glide in the dust.
25 In the street the sword will make them childless;
in their homes terror will reign.
Young men and young women will perish,
infants and gray-haired men.
26 I said I would scatter them
and blot out their memory from mankind,
27 but I dreaded the taunt of the enemy,
lest the adversary misunderstand
and say, 'Our hand has triumphed;
the LORD has not done all this.' "

28 They are a nation without sense,
there is no discernment in them.
29 If only they were wise and would understand this
and discern what their end will be!
30 How could one man chase a thousand,
or two put ten thousand to flight,
unless their Rock had sold them,
unless the LORD had given them up?
31 For their rock is not like our Rock,
as even our enemies concede.
32 Their vine comes from the vine of Sodom
and from the fields of Gomorrah.
Their grapes are filled with poison,
and their clusters with bitterness.
33 Their wine is the venom of serpents,
the deadly poison of cobras.

34 "Have I not kept this in reserve
and sealed it in my vaults?
35 It is mine to avenge; I will repay.
In due time their foot will slip;
their day of disaster is near
and their doom rushes upon them."

36 The LORD will judge his people
and have compassion on his servants

a8 Masoretic Text; Dead Sea Scrolls (see also Septuagint) *sons of God*
b15 *Jeshurun* means *the upright one*, that is, Israel.
c22 Hebrew *to Sheol*

when he sees their strength is gone
and no one is left, slave or free.
37He will say: "Now where are their gods,
the rock they took refuge in,
38the gods who ate the fat of their sacrifices
and drank the wine of their drink
offerings?
Let them rise up to help you!
Let them give you shelter!

39"See now that I myself am He!
There is no god besides me.
I put to death and I bring to life,
I have wounded and I will heal,
and no one can deliver out of my hand.
40I lift my hand to heaven and declare:
As surely as I live forever,
41when I sharpen my flashing sword
and my hand grasps it in judgment,
I will take vengeance on my adversaries
and repay those who hate me.
42I will make my arrows drunk with blood,
while my sword devours flesh:
the blood of the slain and the captives,
the heads of the enemy leaders."

43Rejoice, O nations, with his people,[a,b]
for he will avenge the blood of his
servants;
he will take vengeance on his enemies
and make atonement for his land and
people.

44Moses came with Joshua[c] son of Nun and
spoke all the words of this song in the hearing of
the people. 45When Moses finished reciting all
these words to all Israel, 46he said to them, "Take
to heart all the words I have solemnly declared to
you this day, so that you may command your
children to obey carefully all the words of this
law. 47They are not just idle words for you—they
are your life. By them you will live long in the
land you are crossing the Jordan to possess."

Moses to Die on Mount Nebo

48On that same day the LORD told Moses,
49"Go up into the Abarim Range to Mount Nebo
in Moab, across from Jericho, and view Canaan,
the land I am giving the Israelites as their own
possession. 50There on the mountain that you
have climbed you will die and be gathered to
your people, just as your brother Aaron died on
Mount Hor and was gathered to his people.
51This is because both of you broke faith with me
in the presence of the Israelites at the waters of
Meribah Kadesh in the Desert of Zin and because
you did not uphold my holiness among the Israelites. 52Therefore, you will see the land only from
a distance; you will not enter the land I am giving
to the people of Israel."

Moses Blesses the Tribes

33 This is the blessing that Moses the man of
God pronounced on the Israelites before
his death. 2He said:

"The LORD came from Sinai
and dawned over them from Seir;
he shone forth from Mount Paran.
He came with[d] myriads of holy ones
from the south, from his mountain
slopes.[e]
3Surely it is you who love the people;
all the holy ones are in your hand.
At your feet they all bow down,
and from you receive instruction,
4the law that Moses gave us,
the possession of the assembly of Jacob.
5He was king over Jeshurun[f]
when the leaders of the people assembled,
along with the tribes of Israel.

6"Let Reuben live and not die,
nor[g] his men be few."

7And this he said about Judah:

"Hear, O LORD, the cry of Judah;
bring him to his people.
With his own hands he defends his cause.
Oh, be his help against his foes!"

8About Levi he said:

"Your Thummim and Urim belong
to the man you favored.
You tested him at Massah;
you contended with him at the waters of
Meribah.
9He said of his father and mother,
'I have no regard for them.'
He did not recognize his brothers
or acknowledge his own children,
but he watched over your word
and guarded your covenant.
10He teaches your precepts to Jacob
and your law to Israel.
He offers incense before you
and whole burnt offerings on your altar.
11Bless all his skills, O LORD,
and be pleased with the work of his
hands.
Smite the loins of those who rise up against
him;
strike his foes till they rise no more."

a43 Or *Make his people rejoice, O nations* b43 Masoretic Text; Dead Sea Scrolls (see also Septuagint) *people, / and let all the angels worship him /* c44 Hebrew *Hoshea,* a variant of *Joshua* d2 Or *from* e2 The meaning of the Hebrew for this phrase is uncertain. f5 *Jeshurun* means *the upright one,* that is, Israel; also in verse 26. g6 Or *but let*

12About Benjamin he said:

"Let the beloved of the LORD rest secure in
him,
for he shields him all day long,
and the one the LORD loves rests between
his shoulders."

13About Joseph he said:

"May the LORD bless his land
with the precious dew from heaven above
and with the deep waters that lie below;
14with the best the sun brings forth
and the finest the moon can yield;
15with the choicest gifts of the ancient
mountains
and the fruitfulness of the everlasting hills;
16with the best gifts of the earth and its
fullness
and the favor of him who dwelt in the
burning bush.
Let all these rest on the head of Joseph,
on the brow of the prince among[a] his
brothers.
17In majesty he is like a firstborn bull;
his horns are the horns of a wild ox.
With them he will gore the nations,
even those at the ends of the earth.
Such are the ten thousands of Ephraim;
such are the thousands of Manasseh."

18About Zebulun he said:

"Rejoice, Zebulun, in your going out,
and you, Issachar, in your tents.
19They will summon peoples to the mountain
and there offer sacrifices of righteousness;
they will feast on the abundance of the seas,
on the treasures hidden in the sand."

20About Gad he said:

"Blessed is he who enlarges Gad's domain!
Gad lives there like a lion,
tearing at arm or head.
21He chose the best land for himself;
the leader's portion was kept for him.
When the heads of the people assembled,
he carried out the LORD's righteous will,
and his judgments concerning Israel."

22About Dan he said:

"Dan is a lion's cub,
springing out of Bashan."

23About Naphtali he said:

"Naphtali is abounding with the favor of the
LORD
and is full of his blessing;
he will inherit southward to the lake."

24About Asher he said:

"Most blessed of sons is Asher;
let him be favored by his brothers,
and let him bathe his feet in oil.
25The bolts of your gates will be iron and
bronze,
and your strength will equal your days.

26"There is no one like the God of Jeshurun,
who rides on the heavens to help you
and on the clouds in his majesty.
27The eternal God is your refuge,
and underneath are the everlasting arms.
He will drive out your enemy before you,
saying, 'Destroy him!'
28So Israel will live in safety alone;
Jacob's spring is secure
in a land of grain and new wine,
where the heavens drop dew.
29Blessed are you, O Israel!
Who is like you,
a people saved by the LORD?
He is your shield and helper
and your glorious sword.
Your enemies will cower before you,
and you will trample down their high
places.[b]"

The Death of Moses

34 Then Moses climbed Mount Nebo from
the plains of Moab to the top of Pisgah,
across from Jericho. There the LORD showed him
the whole land—from Gilead to Dan, 2all of
Naphtali, the territory of Ephraim and Manasseh,
all the land of Judah as far as the western sea,[c]
3the Negev and the whole region from the Valley
of Jericho, the City of Palms, as far as Zoar. 4Then
the LORD said to him, "This is the land I promised
on oath to Abraham, Isaac and Jacob when I said,
'I will give it to your descendants.' I have let you
see it with your eyes, but you will not cross over
into it."
5And Moses the servant of the LORD died there
in Moab, as the LORD had said. 6He buried him[d]
in Moab, in the valley opposite Beth Peor, but to
this day no one knows where his grave is. 7Moses
was a hundred and twenty years old when he
died, yet his eyes were not weak nor his strength
gone. 8The Israelites grieved for Moses in the
plains of Moab thirty days, until the time of
weeping and mourning was over.
9Now Joshua son of Nun was filled with the
spirit[e] of wisdom because Moses had laid his

[a] 16 Or *of the one separated from* [b] 29 Or *will tread upon their bodies* [c] 2 That is, the Mediterranean [d] 6 Or *He was buried* [e] 9 Or *Spirit*

hands on him. So the Israelites listened to him
and did what the LORD had commanded Moses.
10 Since then, no prophet has risen in Israel
like Moses, whom the LORD knew face to face,
11 who did all those miraculous signs and wonders
the LORD sent him to do in Egypt—to Pharaoh
and to all his officials and to his whole land.
12 For
no one has ever shown the mighty power or performed the awesome deeds that Moses did in the sight of all Israel.

Introduction to JOSHUA

Personal Reading Plan

- ❒ Joshua 1:1–2:24
- ❒ Joshua 3:1–4:24
- ❒ Joshua 5:1–6:27
- ❒ Joshua 7:1–8:35
- ❒ Joshua 9:1–10:43
- ❒ Joshua 11:1–12:24
- ❒ Joshua 13:1–14:15
- ❒ Joshua 15:1–16:10
- ❒ Joshua 17:1–18:28
- ❒ Joshua 19:1–20:9
- ❒ Joshua 21:1–22:34
- ❒ Joshua 23:1–24:33

Author

The author is not identified. The book is named for its main character, Joshua, successor to Moses.

Date

Suggested dates for Joshua range from c. 1405 to 1250 B.C.

Theme

Obedience brings long-awaited victory in the promised land.

Historical Background

Having led the children of Israel to the entrance of the promised land, Moses is forbidden to guide them in. His servant and aide, Joshua, is chosen by God to take the people in, lead them to victory over their enemies, and divide the land among them. Joshua's training has included accompanying Moses partially up Mount Sinai, being the captain of the army under Moses' direction, and being sent as a spy into Canaan. He was one of only two spies who believed Israel could possess the land by God's enablement. The book of Joshua opens with the Israelites camped on the east side of the Jordan River. Through Joshua, the Lord commands the people to pass through the Jordan on dry ground. After recounting the series of military victories and allotments of land for the 12 tribes, the book concludes with Joshua's charge to the people before his death.

Characteristics

This book has inspired many hymns and spirituals because of the "good news" character of Joshua's successful leadership of Israel and because of God's active involvement in history. We see this most obviously in the "book of war" (chapters 1–11), which chronicles a series of battles, with victory going to the strong and courageous (a theme repeated at least eight times in God's call to Joshua). When the Israelites do what God calls them to do, they defeat the enemy. When they disobey, they are unable to win. The less action-packed "book of distribution" (chapters 12–24) mostly details allocation of the conquered land.

Passage for Topical Group Study

5:13–6:21 WAR The Fall of Jericho

See the Lesson Plans in the front of this Bible.

Passage for General Group Study

3:14–4:24 Crossing the Jordan

The LORD Commands Joshua

1 After the death of Moses the servant of the
LORD, the LORD said to Joshua son of Nun,
Moses' aide: 2“Moses my servant is dead. Now
then, you and all these people, get ready to cross
the Jordan River into the land I am about to give
to them—to the Israelites. 3I will give you every
place where you set your foot, as I promised Moses. 4Your territory will extend from the desert
to Lebanon, and from the great river, the
Euphrates—all the Hittite country—to the Great
Sea[a] on the west. 5No one will be able to stand
up against you all the days of your life. As I was
with Moses, so I will be with you; I will never
leave you nor forsake you.

6“Be strong and courageous, because you will
lead these people to inherit the land I swore to
their forefathers to give them. 7Be strong and
very courageous. Be careful to obey all the law
my servant Moses gave you; do not turn from it
to the right or to the left, that you may be successful wherever you go. 8Do not let this Book of the
Law depart from your mouth; meditate on it day
and night, so that you may be careful to do everything written in it. Then you will be prosperous
and successful. 9Have I not commanded you? Be
strong and courageous. Do not be terrified; do
not be discouraged, for the LORD your God will be
with you wherever you go.”

10So Joshua ordered the officers of the people:
11“Go through the camp and tell the people, ‘Get
your supplies ready. Three days from now you
will cross the Jordan here to go in and take possession of the land the LORD your God is giving
you for your own.’ ”

12But to the Reubenites, the Gadites and the
half-tribe of Manasseh, Joshua said, 13“Remember the command that Moses the servant of the
LORD gave you: ‘The LORD your God is giving you
rest and has granted you this land.’ 14Your wives,
your children and your livestock may stay in the
land that Moses gave you east of the Jordan, but
all your fighting men, fully armed, must cross
over ahead of your brothers. You are to help your
brothers 15until the LORD gives them rest, as he
has done for you, and until they too have taken
possession of the land that the LORD your God is
giving them. After that, you may go back and
occupy your own land, which Moses the servant
of the LORD gave you east of the Jordan toward
the sunrise.”

16Then they answered Joshua, “Whatever you
have commanded us we will do, and wherever
you send us we will go. 17Just as we fully obeyed
Moses, so we will obey you. Only may the LORD
your God be with you as he was with Moses.
18Whoever rebels against your word and does not
obey your words, whatever you may command
them, will be put to death. Only be strong and
courageous!”

Rahab and the Spies

2 Then Joshua son of Nun secretly sent two
spies from Shittim. “Go, look over the land,”
he said, “especially Jericho.” So they went and
entered the house of a prostitute[b] named Rahab
and stayed there.

2The king of Jericho was told, “Look! Some of
the Israelites have come here tonight to spy out
the land.” 3So the king of Jericho sent this message to Rahab: “Bring out the men who came to
you and entered your house, because they have
come to spy out the whole land.”

4But the woman had taken the two men and
hidden them. She said, “Yes, the men came to
me, but I did not know where they had come
from. 5At dusk, when it was time to close the city
gate, the men left. I don't know which way they
went. Go after them quickly. You may catch up
with them.” 6(But she had taken them up to the
roof and hidden them under the stalks of flax she
had laid out on the roof.) 7So the men set out in
pursuit of the spies on the road that leads to the
fords of the Jordan, and as soon as the pursuers
had gone out, the gate was shut.

8Before the spies lay down for the night, she
went up on the roof 9and said to them, “I know
that the LORD has given this land to you and that
a great fear of you has fallen on us, so that all who
live in this country are melting in fear because of
you. 10We have heard how the LORD dried up the
water of the Red Sea[c] for you when you came
out of Egypt, and what you did to Sihon and Og,
the two kings of the Amorites east of the Jordan,
whom you completely destroyed.[d] 11When we
heard of it, our hearts melted and everyone's
courage failed because of you, for the LORD your
God is God in heaven above and on the earth
below. 12Now then, please swear to me by the
LORD that you will show kindness to my family,
because I have shown kindness to you. Give me
a sure sign 13that you will spare the lives of my
father and mother, my brothers and sisters, and
all who belong to them, and that you will save us
from death.”

14“Our lives for your lives!” the men assured
her. “If you don't tell what we are doing, we will
treat you kindly and faithfully when the LORD
gives us the land.”

15So she let them down by a rope through the
window, for the house she lived in was part of
the city wall. 16Now she had said to them, “Go to

[a]4 That is, the Mediterranean [b]1 Or possibly *an innkeeper* [c]10 Hebrew *Yam Suph*; that is, Sea of Reeds
[d]10 The Hebrew term refers to the irrevocable giving over of things or persons to the LORD, often by totally destroying them.

the hills so the pursuers will not find you. Hide
yourselves there three days until they return, and
then go on your way."
17The men said to her, "This oath you made us
swear will not be binding on us 18unless, when
we enter the land, you have tied this scarlet cord
in the window through which you let us down,
and unless you have brought your father and
mother, your brothers and all your family into
your house. 19If anyone goes outside your house
into the street, his blood will be on his own head;
we will not be responsible. As for anyone who is
in the house with you, his blood will be on our
head if a hand is laid on him. 20But if you tell
what we are doing, we will be released from the
oath you made us swear."
21"Agreed," she replied. "Let it be as you say."
So she sent them away and they departed. And
she tied the scarlet cord in the window.
22When they left, they went into the hills and
stayed there three days, until the pursuers had
searched all along the road and returned without
finding them. 23Then the two men started back.
They went down out of the hills, forded the river
and came to Joshua son of Nun and told him
everything that had happened to them. 24They
said to Joshua, "The LORD has surely given the
whole land into our hands; all the people are
melting in fear because of us."

Crossing the Jordan

3 Early in the morning Joshua and all the Israelites set out from Shittim and went to the
Jordan, where they camped before crossing over.
2After three days the officers went throughout
the camp, 3giving orders to the people: "When
you see the ark of the covenant of the LORD your
God, and the priests, who are Levites, carrying it,
you are to move out from your positions and follow it. 4Then you will know which way to go,
since you have never been this way before. But
keep a distance of about a thousand yards[a] between you and the ark; do not go near it."
5Joshua told the people, "Consecrate yourselves, for tomorrow the LORD will do amazing
things among you."
6Joshua said to the priests, "Take up the ark of
the covenant and pass on ahead of the people."
So they took it up and went ahead of them.
7And the LORD said to Joshua, "Today I will
begin to exalt you in the eyes of all Israel, so they
may know that I am with you as I was with Moses. 8Tell the priests who carry the ark of the
covenant: 'When you reach the edge of the Jordan's waters, go and stand in the river.' "
9Joshua said to the Israelites, "Come here and
listen to the words of the LORD your God. 10This
is how you will know that the living God is
among you and that he will certainly drive out
before you the Canaanites, Hittites, Hivites, Perizzites, Girgashites, Amorites and Jebusites.
11See, the ark of the covenant of the Lord of all
the earth will go into the Jordan ahead of you.
12Now then, choose twelve men from the tribes
of Israel, one from each tribe. 13And as soon as
the priests who carry the ark of the LORD—the
Lord of all the earth—set foot in the Jordan, its
waters flowing downstream will be cut off and
stand up in a heap."
14So when the people broke camp to cross the
Jordan, the priests carrying the ark of the covenant went ahead of them. 15Now the Jordan is at
flood stage all during harvest. Yet as soon as the
priests who carried the ark reached the Jordan
and their feet touched the water's edge, 16the
water from upstream stopped flowing. It piled up
in a heap a great distance away, at a town called
Adam in the vicinity of Zarethan, while the water
flowing down to the Sea of the Arabah (the Salt
Sea[b]) was completely cut off. So the people
crossed over opposite Jericho. 17The priests who
carried the ark of the covenant of the LORD stood
firm on dry ground in the middle of the Jordan,
while all Israel passed by until the whole nation
had completed the crossing on dry ground.
4 When the whole nation had finished crossing the Jordan, the LORD said to Joshua,
2"Choose twelve men from among the people,
one from each tribe, 3and tell them to take up
twelve stones from the middle of the Jordan from
right where the priests stood and to carry them
over with you and put them down at the place
where you stay tonight."
4So Joshua called together the twelve men he
had appointed from the Israelites, one from each
tribe, 5and said to them, "Go over before the ark
of the LORD your God into the middle of the Jordan. Each of you is to take up a stone on his
shoulder, according to the number of the tribes of
the Israelites, 6to serve as a sign among you. In
the future, when your children ask you, 'What do
these stones mean?' 7tell them that the flow of
the Jordan was cut off before the ark of the covenant of the LORD. When it crossed the Jordan,
the waters of the Jordan were cut off. These
stones are to be a memorial to the people of Israel
forever."
8So the Israelites did as Joshua commanded
them. They took twelve stones from the middle
of the Jordan, according to the number of the
tribes of the Israelites, as the LORD had told Joshua; and they carried them over with them to their
camp, where they put them down. 9Joshua set up

[a]4 Hebrew *about two thousand cubits* (about 900 meters)
[b]16 That is, the Dead Sea

the twelve stones that had been[a] in the middle
of the Jordan at the spot where the priests who
carried the ark of the covenant had stood. And
they are there to this day.
10 Now the priests who carried the ark remained standing in the middle of the Jordan until
everything the LORD had commanded Joshua was
done by the people, just as Moses had directed
Joshua. The people hurried over, 11 and as soon as
all of them had crossed, the ark of the LORD and
the priests came to the other side while the people watched. 12 The men of Reuben, Gad and the
half-tribe of Manasseh crossed over, armed, in
front of the Israelites, as Moses had directed
them. 13 About forty thousand armed for battle
crossed over before the LORD to the plains of Jericho for war.
14 That day the LORD exalted Joshua in the sight
of all Israel; and they revered him all the days of
his life, just as they had revered Moses.
15 Then the LORD said to Joshua, 16 "Command
the priests carrying the ark of the Testimony to
come up out of the Jordan."
17 So Joshua commanded the priests, "Come
up out of the Jordan."
18 And the priests came up out of the river carrying the ark of the covenant of the LORD. No
sooner had they set their feet on the dry ground
than the waters of the Jordan returned to their
place and ran at flood stage as before.
19 On the tenth day of the first month the people went up from the Jordan and camped at Gilgal
on the eastern border of Jericho. 20 And Joshua set
up at Gilgal the twelve stones they had taken out
of the Jordan. 21 He said to the Israelites, "In the
future when your descendants ask their fathers,
'What do these stones mean?' 22 tell them, 'Israel
crossed the Jordan on dry ground.' 23 For the
LORD your God dried up the Jordan before you
until you had crossed over. The LORD your God
did to the Jordan just what he had done to the
Red Sea[b] when he dried it up before us until we
had crossed over. 24 He did this so that all the
peoples of the earth might know that the hand of
the LORD is powerful and so that you might always fear the LORD your God."

Circumcision at Gilgal

5 Now when all the Amorite kings west of the
Jordan and all the Canaanite kings along the
coast heard how the LORD had dried up the Jordan before the Israelites until we had crossed
over, their hearts melted and they no longer had
the courage to face the Israelites.
2 At that time the LORD said to Joshua, "Make
flint knives and circumcise the Israelites again."
3 So Joshua made flint knives and circumcised the
Israelites at Gibeath Haaraloth.[c]
4 Now this is why he did so: All those who

JOSHUA 3:14–4:24

1. What is the biggest river in your state?
2. What kind of souvenir do you collect to remember special times: T-shirt? Post-cards? Some other kind of keepsake?
3. Which of your parents' childhood memories have you heard over and over?
4. If you were one of the priests in this story, how would you feel about marching into a river?
5. What is something God has done for you that's worth commemorating?
6. What do you do, or what can you do, to "remember" things God has done for you?
7. Close in prayer by having the members of the group complete this sentence: Thank you God for ___________.

[a] 9 Or *Joshua also set up twelve stones* [b] 23 Hebrew *Yam Suph*; that is, Sea of Reeds [c] 3 *Gibeath Haaraloth* means *hill of foreskins.*

Forty years after the Israelites left Egypt, the day to enter the promised land finally came. However, they had to cross the Jordan River—during flood season no less. But God told Joshua, Moses' successor, that a miracle was about to happen.

3:16 *piled up in a heap.* It is possible that God used a physical means (such as a landslide) to dam up the Jordan at the place called Adam, nearly 20 miles upstream. (As recently as 1927 a blockage of water in this area was recorded that lasted over 20 hours.) But even so, the miraculous element is not diminished.

4:9 *Joshua set up the twelve stones.* Each tribe brought a stone for the monument from the riverbed to the new campsite at Gilgal, and Joshua constructed the monument there. An alternative translation suggests Joshua set up a second pile in the middle of the river (see NIV text note).

4:14 *the LORD exalted Joshua in the sight of all Israel.* A prime objective for the divine intervention at the Jordan was to validate the leadership of Joshua. With a miraculous event so much like that of the crossing of the Red Sea, Joshua's position as the Lord's servant would be shown to be comparable to that of Moses.

4:24 *so that all ... might know.* God's revelation of his power to Israel was a public event that all the Canaanites heard about (see 5:1), just as they had heard of the Red Sea crossing. ***fear the LORD.*** Worship and serve him according to his commandments.

came out of Egypt—all the men of military age—
died in the desert on the way after leaving Egypt.
5All the people that came out had been circumcised, but all the people born in the desert during
the journey from Egypt had not. 6The Israelites
had moved about in the desert forty years until all
the men who were of military age when they left
Egypt had died, since they had not obeyed the
LORD. For the LORD had sworn to them that they
would not see the land that he had solemnly
promised their fathers to give us, a land flowing
with milk and honey. 7So he raised up their sons
in their place, and these were the ones Joshua
circumcised. They were still uncircumcised because they had not been circumcised on the way.
8And after the whole nation had been circumcised, they remained where they were in camp
until they were healed.
9Then the LORD said to Joshua, "Today I have
rolled away the reproach of Egypt from you." So
the place has been called Gilgal[a] to this day.
10On the evening of the fourteenth day of the
month, while camped at Gilgal on the plains of
Jericho, the Israelites celebrated the Passover.
11The day after the Passover, that very day, they
ate some of the produce of the land: unleavened
bread and roasted grain. 12The manna stopped
the day after[b] they ate this food from the land;
there was no longer any manna for the Israelites,
but that year they ate of the produce of Canaan.

The Fall of Jericho

13Now when Joshua was near Jericho, he
looked up and saw a man standing in front of him
with a drawn sword in his hand. Joshua went up
to him and asked, "Are you for us or for our
enemies?"
14"Neither," he replied, "but as commander of
the army of the LORD I have now come." Then
Joshua fell facedown to the ground in reverence,
and asked him, "What message does my Lord[c]
have for his servant?"
15The commander of the LORD's army replied,
"Take off your sandals, for the place where you
are standing is holy." And Joshua did so.

6 Now Jericho was tightly shut up because of
the Israelites. No one went out and no one
came in.

> ***JOSHUA 5:13–6:21***
>
> 1. Were you ever in a fight as a kid?
> 2. Growing up, what were you taught about fighting: Turn the other cheek? Stand up for yourself?
> 3. What do you think of violent movies or television shows?
> 4. What do you think now about war and killing?
> 5. If you were a soldier in Joshua's army, how would you feel about your orders?
> 6. This was clearly the Lord's battle. How do you think God feels about war now (see note on 6:17)?
> 7. What battles are you facing today? Pray for one another.

2Then the LORD said to Joshua, "See, I have
delivered Jericho into your hands, along with its
king and its fighting men. 3March around the city
once with all the armed men. Do this for six days.
4Have seven priests carry trumpets of rams'
horns in front of the ark. On the seventh day,
march around the city seven times, with the
priests blowing the trumpets. 5When you hear
them sound a long blast on the trumpets, have all
the people give a loud shout; then the wall of the
city will collapse and the people will go up, every
man straight in."
6So Joshua son of Nun called the priests and
said to them, "Take up the ark of the covenant of

a9 *Gilgal* sounds like the Hebrew for *roll.* b12 Or *the day* c14 Or *lord*

5:13 The Israelites have just crossed the Jordan River and entered the promised land. ***Joshua was near Jericho.*** The leader of God's army went to scout the nearest Canaanite stronghold, but another warrior was already on the scene.

5:14 ***Neither.*** Joshua and Israel must know their place—it is not that God is on their side; rather, they must fight God's battles. ***commander of the army of the LORD.*** God has sent the commander of his heavenly armies to take charge of the battle on earth.

6:4 ***trumpets of rams' horns.*** Instruments not of music but of signaling, in both religious and military contexts (which appear to come together here). The trumpets were to be sounded (v. 8), as on the seventh day, announcing the presence of the Lord. ***ark.*** The ark of the Lord is made the center of focus, highlighting the fact that it was the Lord himself who besieged the city.

6:17 ***devoted.*** See NIV text note. The ban placed all of Jericho's inhabitants under the curse of death and all of the city's treasures that could not be destroyed under consignment to the Lord's house (v. 19). The Lord's triumph over the Canaanites testified to the world that the God of Israel is the one true and living God, whose claim on the world is absolute. The question of the Christian response to war has been greatly debated. Some see the history of the OT as justification for acceptance of at least some warfare. Others see Jesus and the NT as introducing a radically new ethic, based on love (see Matt. 5:38–48).

the LORD and have seven priests carry trumpets in front of it." 7And he ordered the people, "Advance! March around the city, with the armed guard going ahead of the ark of the LORD."

8When Joshua had spoken to the people, the seven priests carrying the seven trumpets before the LORD went forward, blowing their trumpets, and the ark of the LORD's covenant followed them. 9The armed guard marched ahead of the priests who blew the trumpets, and the rear guard followed the ark. All this time the trumpets were sounding. 10But Joshua had commanded the people, "Do not give a war cry, do not raise your voices, do not say a word until the day I tell you to shout. Then shout!" 11So he had the ark of the LORD carried around the city, circling it once. Then the people returned to camp and spent the night there.

12Joshua got up early the next morning and the priests took up the ark of the LORD. 13The seven priests carrying the seven trumpets went forward, marching before the ark of the LORD and blowing the trumpets. The armed men went ahead of them and the rear guard followed the ark of the LORD, while the trumpets kept sounding. 14So on the second day they marched around the city once and returned to the camp. They did this for six days.

15On the seventh day, they got up at daybreak and marched around the city seven times in the same manner, except that on that day they circled the city seven times. 16The seventh time around, when the priests sounded the trumpet blast, Joshua commanded the people, "Shout! For the LORD has given you the city! 17The city and all that is in it are to be devoted[a] to the LORD. Only Rahab the prostitute[b] and all who are with her in her house shall be spared, because she hid the spies we sent. 18But keep away from the devoted things, so that you will not bring about your own destruction by taking any of them. Otherwise you will make the camp of Israel liable to destruction and bring trouble on it. 19All the silver and gold and the articles of bronze and iron are sacred to the LORD and must go into his treasury."

20When the trumpets sounded, the people shouted, and at the sound of the trumpet, when the people gave a loud shout, the wall collapsed; so every man charged straight in, and they took the city. 21They devoted the city to the LORD and destroyed with the sword every living thing in it—men and women, young and old, cattle, sheep and donkeys.

22Joshua said to the two men who had spied out the land, "Go into the prostitute's house and bring her out and all who belong to her, in accordance with your oath to her." 23So the young men who had done the spying went in and brought out Rahab, her father and mother and brothers and all who belonged to her. They brought out her entire family and put them in a place outside the camp of Israel.

24Then they burned the whole city and everything in it, but they put the silver and gold and the articles of bronze and iron into the treasury of the LORD's house. 25But Joshua spared Rahab the prostitute, with her family and all who belonged to her, because she hid the men Joshua had sent as spies to Jericho—and she lives among the Israelites to this day.

26At that time Joshua pronounced this solemn oath: "Cursed before the LORD is the man who undertakes to rebuild this city, Jericho:

"At the cost of his firstborn son
  will he lay its foundations;
at the cost of his youngest
  will he set up its gates."

27So the LORD was with Joshua, and his fame spread throughout the land.

Achan's Sin

7 But the Israelites acted unfaithfully in regard to the devoted things[c]; Achan son of Carmi, the son of Zimri,[d] the son of Zerah, of the tribe of Judah, took some of them. So the LORD's anger burned against Israel.

2Now Joshua sent men from Jericho to Ai, which is near Beth Aven to the east of Bethel, and told them, "Go up and spy out the region." So the men went up and spied out Ai.

3When they returned to Joshua, they said, "Not all the people will have to go up against Ai. Send two or three thousand men to take it and do not weary all the people, for only a few men are there." 4So about three thousand men went up; but they were routed by the men of Ai, 5who killed about thirty-six of them. They chased the Israelites from the city gate as far as the stone quarries[e] and struck them down on the slopes. At this the hearts of the people melted and became like water.

6Then Joshua tore his clothes and fell facedown to the ground before the ark of the LORD, remaining there till evening. The elders of Israel did the same, and sprinkled dust on their heads. 7And Joshua said, "Ah, Sovereign LORD, why did you ever bring this people across the Jordan to deliver us into the hands of the Amorites to destroy us? If only we had been content to stay on

a 17 The Hebrew term refers to the irrevocable giving over of things or persons to the LORD, often by totally destroying them; also in verses 18 and 21. b 17 Or possibly *innkeeper*; also in verses 22 and 25 c 1 The Hebrew term refers to the irrevocable giving over of things or persons to the LORD, often by totally destroying them; also in verses 11, 12, 13 and 15. d 1 See Septuagint and 1 Chron. 2:6; Hebrew *Zabdi*; also in verses 17 and 18. e 5 Or *as far as Shebarim* the other side of the Jordan! 8O Lord, what can I say, now that Israel has been routed by its enemies? 9The Canaanites and the other people of the country will hear about this and they will surround us and wipe out our name from the earth. What then will you do for your own great name?"

10The LORD said to Joshua, "Stand up! What are you doing down on your face? 11Israel has sinned; they have violated my covenant, which I commanded them to keep. They have taken some of the devoted things; they have stolen, they have lied, they have put them with their own possessions. 12That is why the Israelites cannot stand against their enemies; they turn their backs and run because they have been made liable to destruction. I will not be with you anymore unless you destroy whatever among you is devoted to destruction.

13"Go, consecrate the people. Tell them, 'Consecrate yourselves in preparation for tomorrow; for this is what the LORD, the God of Israel, says: That which is devoted is among you, O Israel. You cannot stand against your enemies until you remove it.

14" 'In the morning, present yourselves tribe by tribe. The tribe that the LORD takes shall come forward clan by clan; the clan that the LORD takes shall come forward family by family; and the family that the LORD takes shall come forward man by man. 15He who is caught with the devoted things shall be destroyed by fire, along with all that belongs to him. He has violated the covenant of the LORD and has done a disgraceful thing in Israel!' "

16Early the next morning Joshua had Israel come forward by tribes, and Judah was taken. 17The clans of Judah came forward, and he took the Zerahites. He had the clan of the Zerahites come forward by families, and Zimri was taken. 18Joshua had his family come forward man by man, and Achan son of Carmi, the son of Zimri, the son of Zerah, of the tribe of Judah, was taken.

19Then Joshua said to Achan, "My son, give glory to the LORD,[a] the God of Israel, and give him the praise.[b] Tell me what you have done; do not hide it from me."

20Achan replied, "It is true! I have sinned against the LORD, the God of Israel. This is what I have done: 21When I saw in the plunder a beautiful robe from Babylonia,[c] two hundred shekels[d] of silver and a wedge of gold weighing fifty shekels,[e] I coveted them and took them. They are hidden in the ground inside my tent, with the silver underneath."

22So Joshua sent messengers, and they ran to the tent, and there it was, hidden in his tent, with the silver underneath. 23They took the things from the tent, brought them to Joshua and all the Israelites and spread them out before the LORD.

24Then Joshua, together with all Israel, took Achan son of Zerah, the silver, the robe, the gold wedge, his sons and daughters, his cattle, donkeys and sheep, his tent and all that he had, to the Valley of Achor. 25Joshua said, "Why have you brought this trouble on us? The LORD will bring trouble on you today."

Then all Israel stoned him, and after they had stoned the rest, they burned them. 26Over Achan they heaped up a large pile of rocks, which remains to this day. Then the LORD turned from his fierce anger. Therefore that place has been called the Valley of Achor[f] ever since.

Ai Destroyed

8 Then the LORD said to Joshua, "Do not be afraid; do not be discouraged. Take the whole army with you, and go up and attack Ai. For I have delivered into your hands the king of Ai, his people, his city and his land. 2You shall do to Ai and its king as you did to Jericho and its king, except that you may carry off their plunder and livestock for yourselves. Set an ambush behind the city."

3So Joshua and the whole army moved out to attack Ai. He chose thirty thousand of his best fighting men and sent them out at night 4with these orders: "Listen carefully. You are to set an ambush behind the city. Don't go very far from it. All of you be on the alert. 5I and all those with me will advance on the city, and when the men come out against us, as they did before, we will flee from them. 6They will pursue us until we have lured them away from the city, for they will say, 'They are running away from us as they did before.' So when we flee from them, 7you are to rise up from ambush and take the city. The LORD your God will give it into your hand. 8When you have taken the city, set it on fire. Do what the LORD has commanded. See to it; you have my orders."

9Then Joshua sent them off, and they went to the place of ambush and lay in wait between Bethel and Ai, to the west of Ai—but Joshua spent that night with the people.

10Early the next morning Joshua mustered his men, and he and the leaders of Israel marched before them to Ai. 11The entire force that was with him marched up and approached the city and arrived in front of it. They set up camp north of Ai, with the valley between them and the city. 12Joshua had taken about five thousand men and

[a] 19 A solemn charge to tell the truth [b] 19 Or *and confess to him* [c] 21 Hebrew *Shinar* [d] 21 That is, about 5 pounds (about 2.3 kilograms) [e] 21 That is, about 1 1/4 pounds (about 0.6 kilogram) [f] 26 *Achor* means *trouble.*

set them in ambush between Bethel and Ai, to
the west of the city. 13They had the soldiers take
up their positions—all those in the camp to the
north of the city and the ambush to the west of
it. That night Joshua went into the valley.

14When the king of Ai saw this, he and all the
men of the city hurried out early in the morning
to meet Israel in battle at a certain place overlooking the Arabah. But he did not know that an
ambush had been set against him behind the city.
15Joshua and all Israel let themselves be driven
back before them, and they fled toward the
desert. 16All the men of Ai were called to pursue
them, and they pursued Joshua and were lured
away from the city. 17Not a man remained in Ai
or Bethel who did not go after Israel. They left the
city open and went in pursuit of Israel.

18Then the LORD said to Joshua, "Hold out toward Ai the javelin that is in your hand, for into
your hand I will deliver the city." So Joshua held
out his javelin toward Ai. 19As soon as he did this,
the men in the ambush rose quickly from their
position and rushed forward. They entered the
city and captured it and quickly set it on fire.

20The men of Ai looked back and saw the
smoke of the city rising against the sky, but they
had no chance to escape in any direction, for the
Israelites who had been fleeing toward the desert
had turned back against their pursuers. 21For
when Joshua and all Israel saw that the ambush
had taken the city and that smoke was going up
from the city, they turned around and attacked
the men of Ai. 22The men of the ambush also
came out of the city against them, so that they
were caught in the middle, with Israelites on
both sides. Israel cut them down, leaving them
neither survivors nor fugitives. 23But they took
the king of Ai alive and brought him to Joshua.

24When Israel had finished killing all the men
of Ai in the fields and in the desert where they
had chased them, and when every one of them
had been put to the sword, all the Israelites returned to Ai and killed those who were in it.
25Twelve thousand men and women fell that
day—all the people of Ai. 26For Joshua did not
draw back the hand that held out his javelin until
he had destroyed[a] all who lived in Ai. 27But
Israel did carry off for themselves the livestock
and plunder of this city, as the LORD had instructed Joshua.

28So Joshua burned Ai and made it a permanent heap of ruins, a desolate place to this day.
29He hung the king of Ai on a tree and left him
there until evening. At sunset, Joshua ordered
them to take his body from the tree and throw it
down at the entrance of the city gate. And they
raised a large pile of rocks over it, which remains
to this day.

The Covenant Renewed at Mount Ebal

30Then Joshua built on Mount Ebal an altar to
the LORD, the God of Israel, 31as Moses the servant of the LORD had commanded the Israelites.
He built it according to what is written in the
Book of the Law of Moses—an altar of uncut
stones, on which no iron tool had been used. On
it they offered to the LORD burnt offerings and
sacrificed fellowship offerings.[b] 32There, in the
presence of the Israelites, Joshua copied on
stones the law of Moses, which he had written.
33All Israel, aliens and citizens alike, with their
elders, officials and judges, were standing on
both sides of the ark of the covenant of the LORD,
facing those who carried it—the priests, who
were Levites. Half of the people stood in front
of Mount Gerizim and half of them in front of
Mount Ebal, as Moses the servant of the LORD
had formerly commanded when he gave instructions to bless the people of Israel.

34Afterward, Joshua read all the words of the
law—the blessings and the curses—just as it is
written in the Book of the Law. 35There was not
a word of all that Moses had commanded that
Joshua did not read to the whole assembly of
Israel, including the women and children, and
the aliens who lived among them.

The Gibeonite Deception

9 Now when all the kings west of the Jordan
heard about these things—those in the hill
country, in the western foothills, and along the
entire coast of the Great Sea[c] as far as Lebanon
(the kings of the Hittites, Amorites, Canaanites,
Perizzites, Hivites and Jebusites)— 2they came
together to make war against Joshua and Israel.

3However, when the people of Gibeon heard
what Joshua had done to Jericho and Ai, 4they
resorted to a ruse: They went as a delegation
whose donkeys were loaded[d] with worn-out
sacks and old wineskins, cracked and mended.
5The men put worn and patched sandals on their
feet and wore old clothes. All the bread of their
food supply was dry and moldy. 6Then they went
to Joshua in the camp at Gilgal and said to him
and the men of Israel, "We have come from a
distant country; make a treaty with us."

7The men of Israel said to the Hivites, "But
perhaps you live near us. How then can we make
a treaty with you?"

8"We are your servants," they said to Joshua.

[a] *26* The Hebrew term refers to the irrevocable giving over of things or persons to the LORD, often by totally destroying them.
[b] *31* Traditionally *peace offerings* [c] *1* That is, the Mediterranean [d] *4* Most Hebrew manuscripts; some Hebrew manuscripts, Vulgate and Syriac (see also Septuagint) *They prepared provisions and loaded their donkeys*

But Joshua asked, "Who are you and where do you come from?"

9They answered: "Your servants have come from a very distant country because of the fame of the LORD your God. For we have heard reports of him: all that he did in Egypt, 10and all that he did to the two kings of the Amorites east of the Jordan—Sihon king of Heshbon, and Og king of Bashan, who reigned in Ashtaroth. 11And our elders and all those living in our country said to us, 'Take provisions for your journey; go and meet them and say to them, "We are your servants; make a treaty with us." ' 12This bread of ours was warm when we packed it at home on the day we left to come to you. But now see how dry and moldy it is. 13And these wineskins that we filled were new, but see how cracked they are. And our clothes and sandals are worn out by the very long journey."

14The men of Israel sampled their provisions but did not inquire of the LORD. 15Then Joshua made a treaty of peace with them to let them live, and the leaders of the assembly ratified it by oath.

16Three days after they made the treaty with the Gibeonites, the Israelites heard that they were neighbors, living near them. 17So the Israelites set out and on the third day came to their cities: Gibeon, Kephirah, Beeroth and Kiriath Jearim. 18But the Israelites did not attack them, because the leaders of the assembly had sworn an oath to them by the LORD, the God of Israel.

The whole assembly grumbled against the leaders, 19but all the leaders answered, "We have given them our oath by the LORD, the God of Israel, and we cannot touch them now. 20This is what we will do to them: We will let them live, so that wrath will not fall on us for breaking the oath we swore to them." 21They continued, "Let them live, but let them be woodcutters and water carriers for the entire community." So the leaders' promise to them was kept.

22Then Joshua summoned the Gibeonites and said, "Why did you deceive us by saying, 'We live a long way from you,' while actually you live near us? 23You are now under a curse: You will never cease to serve as woodcutters and water carriers for the house of my God."

24They answered Joshua, "Your servants were clearly told how the LORD your God had commanded his servant Moses to give you the whole land and to wipe out all its inhabitants from before you. So we feared for our lives because of you, and that is why we did this. 25We are now in your hands. Do to us whatever seems good and right to you."

26So Joshua saved them from the Israelites, and they did not kill them. 27That day he made the Gibeonites woodcutters and water carriers for the community and for the altar of the LORD at the place the LORD would choose. And that is what they are to this day.

The Sun Stands Still

10 Now Adoni-Zedek king of Jerusalem heard that Joshua had taken Ai and totally destroyed[a] it, doing to Ai and its king as he had done to Jericho and its king, and that the people of Gibeon had made a treaty of peace with Israel and were living near them. 2He and his people were very much alarmed at this, because Gibeon was an important city, like one of the royal cities; it was larger than Ai, and all its men were good fighters. 3So Adoni-Zedek king of Jerusalem appealed to Hoham king of Hebron, Piram king of Jarmuth, Japhia king of Lachish and Debir king of Eglon. 4"Come up and help me attack Gibeon," he said, "because it has made peace with Joshua and the Israelites."

5Then the five kings of the Amorites—the kings of Jerusalem, Hebron, Jarmuth, Lachish and Eglon—joined forces. They moved up with all their troops and took up positions against Gibeon and attacked it.

6The Gibeonites then sent word to Joshua in the camp at Gilgal: "Do not abandon your servants. Come up to us quickly and save us! Help us, because all the Amorite kings from the hill country have joined forces against us."

7So Joshua marched up from Gilgal with his entire army, including all the best fighting men. 8The LORD said to Joshua, "Do not be afraid of them; I have given them into your hand. Not one of them will be able to withstand you."

9After an all-night march from Gilgal, Joshua took them by surprise. 10The LORD threw them into confusion before Israel, who defeated them in a great victory at Gibeon. Israel pursued them along the road going up to Beth Horon and cut them down all the way to Azekah and Makkedah. 11As they fled before Israel on the road down from Beth Horon to Azekah, the LORD hurled large hailstones down on them from the sky, and more of them died from the hailstones than were killed by the swords of the Israelites.

12On the day the LORD gave the Amorites over to Israel, Joshua said to the LORD in the presence of Israel:

"O sun, stand still over Gibeon,
O moon, over the Valley of Aijalon."

13So the sun stood still,
and the moon stopped,

a 1 The Hebrew term refers to the irrevocable giving over of things or persons to the LORD, often by totally destroying them; also in verses 28, 35, 37, 39 and 40.

till the nation avenged itself on[a] its
enemies,
as it is written in the Book of Jashar.
The sun stopped in the middle of the sky and
delayed going down about a full day. 14 There has
never been a day like it before or since, a day
when the LORD listened to a man. Surely the
LORD was fighting for Israel!
15 Then Joshua returned with all Israel to the
camp at Gilgal.

Five Amorite Kings Killed

16 Now the five kings had fled and hidden in
the cave at Makkedah. 17 When Joshua was told
that the five kings had been found hiding in the
cave at Makkedah, 18 he said, "Roll large rocks up
to the mouth of the cave, and post some men
there to guard it. 19 But don't stop! Pursue your
enemies, attack them from the rear and don't let
them reach their cities, for the LORD your God
has given them into your hand."
20 So Joshua and the Israelites destroyed them
completely—almost to a man—but the few who
were left reached their fortified cities. 21 The
whole army then returned safely to Joshua in the
camp at Makkedah, and no one uttered a word
against the Israelites.
22 Joshua said, "Open the mouth of the cave
and bring those five kings out to me." 23 So they
brought the five kings out of the cave—the kings
of Jerusalem, Hebron, Jarmuth, Lachish and Eglon. 24 When they had brought these kings to
Joshua, he summoned all the men of Israel and
said to the army commanders who had come
with him, "Come here and put your feet on the
necks of these kings." So they came forward and
placed their feet on their necks.
25 Joshua said to them, "Do not be afraid; do
not be discouraged. Be strong and courageous.
This is what the LORD will do to all the enemies
you are going to fight." 26 Then Joshua struck and
killed the kings and hung them on five trees, and
they were left hanging on the trees until evening.
27 At sunset Joshua gave the order and they
took them down from the trees and threw them
into the cave where they had been hiding. At the
mouth of the cave they placed large rocks, which
are there to this day.
28 That day Joshua took Makkedah. He put the
city and its king to the sword and totally destroyed everyone in it. He left no survivors. And
he did to the king of Makkedah as he had done to
the king of Jericho.

Southern Cities Conquered

29 Then Joshua and all Israel with him moved
on from Makkedah to Libnah and attacked it.
30 The LORD also gave that city and its king into
Israel's hand. The city and everyone in it Joshua
put to the sword. He left no survivors there. And
he did to its king as he had done to the king of
Jericho.
31 Then Joshua and all Israel with him moved
on from Libnah to Lachish; he took up positions
against it and attacked it. 32 The LORD handed
Lachish over to Israel, and Joshua took it on the
second day. The city and everyone in it he put
to the sword, just as he had done to Libnah.
33 Meanwhile, Horam king of Gezer had come up
to help Lachish, but Joshua defeated him and his
army—until no survivors were left.
34 Then Joshua and all Israel with him moved
on from Lachish to Eglon; they took up positions
against it and attacked it. 35 They captured it that
same day and put it to the sword and totally destroyed everyone in it, just as they had done to
Lachish.
36 Then Joshua and all Israel with him went up
from Eglon to Hebron and attacked it. 37 They
took the city and put it to the sword, together
with its king, its villages and everyone in it. They
left no survivors. Just as at Eglon, they totally
destroyed it and everyone in it.
38 Then Joshua and all Israel with him turned
around and attacked Debir. 39 They took the city,
its king and its villages, and put them to the
sword. Everyone in it they totally destroyed.
They left no survivors. They did to Debir and its
king as they had done to Libnah and its king and
to Hebron.
40 So Joshua subdued the whole region, including the hill country, the Negev, the western foothills and the mountain slopes, together with all
their kings. He left no survivors. He totally destroyed all who breathed, just as the LORD, the
God of Israel, had commanded. 41 Joshua subdued
them from Kadesh Barnea to Gaza and from the
whole region of Goshen to Gibeon. 42 All these
kings and their lands Joshua conquered in one
campaign, because the LORD, the God of Israel,
fought for Israel.
43 Then Joshua returned with all Israel to the
camp at Gilgal.

Northern Kings Defeated

11 When Jabin king of Hazor heard of this,
he sent word to Jobab king of Madon, to
the kings of Shimron and Acshaph, 2 and to the
northern kings who were in the mountains, in
the Arabah south of Kinnereth, in the western
foothills and in Naphoth Dor[b] on the west; 3 to
the Canaanites in the east and west; to the Amorites, Hittites, Perizzites and Jebusites in the hill

[a] 13 Or *nation triumphed over* [b] 2 Or *in the heights of Dor*

country; and to the Hivites below Hermon in the region of Mizpah. 4They came out with all their troops and a large number of horses and chariots—a huge army, as numerous as the sand on the seashore. 5All these kings joined forces and made camp together at the Waters of Merom, to fight against Israel.

6The LORD said to Joshua, "Do not be afraid of them, because by this time tomorrow I will hand all of them over to Israel, slain. You are to hamstring their horses and burn their chariots."

7So Joshua and his whole army came against them suddenly at the Waters of Merom and attacked them, 8and the LORD gave them into the hand of Israel. They defeated them and pursued them all the way to Greater Sidon, to Misrephoth Maim, and to the Valley of Mizpah on the east, until no survivors were left. 9Joshua did to them as the LORD had directed: He hamstrung their horses and burned their chariots.

10At that time Joshua turned back and captured Hazor and put its king to the sword. (Hazor had been the head of all these kingdoms.) 11Everyone in it they put to the sword. They totally destroyed[a] them, not sparing anything that breathed, and he burned up Hazor itself.

12Joshua took all these royal cities and their kings and put them to the sword. He totally destroyed them, as Moses the servant of the LORD had commanded. 13Yet Israel did not burn any of the cities built on their mounds—except Hazor, which Joshua burned. 14The Israelites carried off for themselves all the plunder and livestock of these cities, but all the people they put to the sword until they completely destroyed them, not sparing anyone that breathed. 15As the LORD commanded his servant Moses, so Moses commanded Joshua, and Joshua did it; he left nothing undone of all that the LORD commanded Moses.

16So Joshua took this entire land: the hill country, all the Negev, the whole region of Goshen, the western foothills, the Arabah and the mountains of Israel with their foothills, 17from Mount Halak, which rises toward Seir, to Baal Gad in the Valley of Lebanon below Mount Hermon. He captured all their kings and struck them down, putting them to death. 18Joshua waged war against all these kings for a long time. 19Except for the Hivites living in Gibeon, not one city made a treaty of peace with the Israelites, who took them all in battle. 20For it was the LORD himself who hardened their hearts to wage war against Israel, so that he might destroy them totally, exterminating them without mercy, as the LORD had commanded Moses.

21At that time Joshua went and destroyed the Anakites from the hill country: from Hebron, Debir and Anab, from all the hill country of Judah, and from all the hill country of Israel. Joshua totally destroyed them and their towns. 22No Anakites were left in Israelite territory; only in Gaza, Gath and Ashdod did any survive. 23So Joshua took the entire land, just as the LORD had directed Moses, and he gave it as an inheritance to Israel according to their tribal divisions.

Then the land had rest from war.

List of Defeated Kings

12 These are the kings of the land whom the Israelites had defeated and whose territory they took over east of the Jordan, from the Arnon Gorge to Mount Hermon, including all the eastern side of the Arabah:

2Sihon king of the Amorites,
who reigned in Heshbon. He ruled from Aroer on the rim of the Arnon Gorge—from the middle of the gorge—to the Jabbok River, which is the border of the Ammonites. This included half of Gilead. 3He also ruled over the eastern Arabah from the Sea of Kinnereth[b] to the Sea of the Arabah (the Salt Sea[c]), to Beth Jeshimoth, and then southward below the slopes of Pisgah.

4And the territory of Og king of Bashan,
one of the last of the Rephaites, who reigned in Ashtaroth and Edrei. 5He ruled over Mount Hermon, Salecah, all of Bashan to the border of the people of Geshur and Maacah, and half of Gilead to the border of Sihon king of Heshbon.

6Moses, the servant of the LORD, and the Israelites conquered them. And Moses the servant of the LORD gave their land to the Reubenites, the Gadites and the half-tribe of Manasseh to be their possession.

7These are the kings of the land that Joshua and the Israelites conquered on the west side of the Jordan, from Baal Gad in the Valley of Lebanon to Mount Halak, which rises toward Seir (their lands Joshua gave as an inheritance to the tribes of Israel according to their tribal divisions— 8the hill country, the western foothills, the Arabah, the mountain slopes, the desert and the Negev—the lands of the Hittites, Amorites, Canaanites, Perizzites, Hivites and Jebusites):

9the king of Jericho	one
the king of Ai (near Bethel)	one
10the king of Jerusalem	one
the king of Hebron	one

a11 The Hebrew term refers to the irrevocable giving over of things or persons to the LORD, often by totally destroying them; also in verses 12, 20 and 21. b3 That is, Galilee c3 That is, the Dead Sea

11the king of Jarmuth one
the king of Lachish one
12the king of Eglon one
the king of Gezer one
13the king of Debir one
the king of Geder one
14the king of Hormah one
the king of Arad one
15the king of Libnah one
the king of Adullam one
16the king of Makkedah one
the king of Bethel one
17the king of Tappuah one
the king of Hepher one
18the king of Aphek one
the king of Lasharon one
19the king of Madon one
the king of Hazor one
20the king of Shimron Meron one
the king of Acshaph one
21the king of Taanach one
the king of Megiddo one
22the king of Kedesh one
the king of Jokneam in Carmel one
23the king of Dor (in Naphoth Dor[a]) one
the king of Goyim in Gilgal one
24the king of Tirzah one
thirty-one kings in all.

Land Still to Be Taken

13 When Joshua was old and well advanced
in years, the LORD said to him, "You are
very old, and there are still very large areas of
land to be taken over.

2"This is the land that remains: all the regions of the Philistines and Geshurites:
3from the Shihor River on the east of Egypt
to the territory of Ekron on the north, all of
it counted as Canaanite (the territory of the
five Philistine rulers in Gaza, Ashdod, Ashkelon, Gath and Ekron—that of the Avvites); 4from the south, all the land of the
Canaanites, from Arah of the Sidonians as
far as Aphek, the region of the Amorites,
5the area of the Gebalites[b]; and all Lebanon to the east, from Baal Gad below Mount
Hermon to Lebo[c] Hamath.

6"As for all the inhabitants of the mountain
regions from Lebanon to Misrephoth Maim, that
is, all the Sidonians, I myself will drive them out
before the Israelites. Be sure to allocate this land
to Israel for an inheritance, as I have instructed
you, 7and divide it as an inheritance among the
nine tribes and half of the tribe of Manasseh."

Division of the Land East of the Jordan

8The other half of Manasseh,[d] the Reubenites
and the Gadites had received the inheritance that
Moses had given them east of the Jordan, as he,
the servant of the LORD, had assigned it to them.

9It extended from Aroer on the rim of the
Arnon Gorge, and from the town in the
middle of the gorge, and included the whole
plateau of Medeba as far as Dibon, 10and all
the towns of Sihon king of the Amorites,
who ruled in Heshbon, out to the border of
the Ammonites. 11It also included Gilead,
the territory of the people of Geshur and
Maacah, all of Mount Hermon and all Bashan as far as Salecah— 12that is, the whole
kingdom of Og in Bashan, who had reigned
in Ashtaroth and Edrei and had survived as
one of the last of the Rephaites. Moses had
defeated them and taken over their land.
13But the Israelites did not drive out the
people of Geshur and Maacah, so they continue to live among the Israelites to this day.

14But to the tribe of Levi he gave no inheritance, since the offerings made by fire to the
LORD, the God of Israel, are their inheritance, as
he promised them.

15This is what Moses had given to the tribe of
Reuben, clan by clan:

16The territory from Aroer on the rim of the
Arnon Gorge, and from the town in the
middle of the gorge, and the whole plateau
past Medeba 17to Heshbon and all its towns
on the plateau, including Dibon, Bamoth
Baal, Beth Baal Meon, 18Jahaz, Kedemoth,
Mephaath, 19Kiriathaim, Sibmah, Zereth
Shahar on the hill in the valley, 20Beth Peor,
the slopes of Pisgah, and Beth Jeshimoth
21—all the towns on the plateau and the
entire realm of Sihon king of the Amorites,
who ruled at Heshbon. Moses had defeated
him and the Midianite chiefs, Evi, Rekem,
Zur, Hur and Reba—princes allied with
Sihon—who lived in that country. 22In addition to those slain in battle, the Israelites
had put to the sword Balaam son of Beor,
who practiced divination. 23The boundary
of the Reubenites was the bank of the Jordan. These towns and their villages were
the inheritance of the Reubenites, clan by
clan.

24This is what Moses had given to the tribe of
Gad, clan by clan:

25The territory of Jazer, all the towns of Gil-

[a]23 Or *in the heights of Dor* [b]5 That is, the area of Byblos [c]5 Or *to the entrance to* [d]8 Hebrew *With it* (that is, with the other half of Manasseh)

ead and half the Ammonite country as far as Aroer, near Rabbah; 26and from Heshbon to Ramath Mizpah and Betonim, and from Mahanaim to the territory of Debir; 27and in the valley, Beth Haram, Beth Nimrah, Succoth and Zaphon with the rest of the realm of Sihon king of Heshbon (the east side of the Jordan, the territory up to the end of the Sea of Kinnereth[a]). 28These towns and their villages were the inheritance of the Gadites, clan by clan.

29This is what Moses had given to the half-tribe of Manasseh, that is, to half the family of the descendants of Manasseh, clan by clan:

30The territory extending from Mahanaim and including all of Bashan, the entire realm of Og king of Bashan—all the settlements of Jair in Bashan, sixty towns, 31half of Gilead, and Ashtaroth and Edrei (the royal cities of Og in Bashan). This was for the descendants of Makir son of Manasseh—for half of the sons of Makir, clan by clan.

32This is the inheritance Moses had given when he was in the plains of Moab across the Jordan east of Jericho. 33But to the tribe of Levi, Moses had given no inheritance; the LORD, the God of Israel, is their inheritance, as he promised them.

Division of the Land West of the Jordan

14 Now these are the areas the Israelites received as an inheritance in the land of Canaan, which Eleazar the priest, Joshua son of Nun and the heads of the tribal clans of Israel allotted to them. 2Their inheritances were assigned by lot to the nine-and-a-half tribes, as the LORD had commanded through Moses. 3Moses had granted the two-and-a-half tribes their inheritance east of the Jordan but had not granted the Levites an inheritance among the rest, 4for the sons of Joseph had become two tribes—Manasseh and Ephraim. The Levites received no share of the land but only towns to live in, with pasturelands for their flocks and herds. 5So the Israelites divided the land, just as the LORD had commanded Moses.

Hebron Given to Caleb

6Now the men of Judah approached Joshua at Gilgal, and Caleb son of Jephunneh the Kenizzite said to him, "You know what the LORD said to Moses the man of God at Kadesh Barnea about you and me. 7I was forty years old when Moses the servant of the LORD sent me from Kadesh Barnea to explore the land. And I brought him back a report according to my convictions, 8but my brothers who went up with me made the hearts of the people melt with fear. I, however, followed the LORD my God wholeheartedly. 9So on that day Moses swore to me, 'The land on which your feet have walked will be your inheritance and that of your children forever, because you have followed the LORD my God wholeheartedly.'[b]

10"Now then, just as the LORD promised, he has kept me alive for forty-five years since the time he said this to Moses, while Israel moved about in the desert. So here I am today, eighty-five years old! 11I am still as strong today as the day Moses sent me out; I'm just as vigorous to go out to battle now as I was then. 12Now give me this hill country that the LORD promised me that day. You yourself heard then that the Anakites were there and their cities were large and fortified, but, the LORD helping me, I will drive them out just as he said."

13Then Joshua blessed Caleb son of Jephunneh and gave him Hebron as his inheritance. 14So Hebron has belonged to Caleb son of Jephunneh the Kenizzite ever since, because he followed the LORD, the God of Israel, wholeheartedly. 15(Hebron used to be called Kiriath Arba after Arba, who was the greatest man among the Anakites.)

Then the land had rest from war.

Allotment for Judah

15 The allotment for the tribe of Judah, clan by clan, extended down to the territory of Edom, to the Desert of Zin in the extreme south.

2Their southern boundary started from the bay at the southern end of the Salt Sea,[c] 3crossed south of Scorpion[d] Pass, continued on to Zin and went over to the south of Kadesh Barnea. Then it ran past Hezron up to Addar and curved around to Karka. 4It then passed along to Azmon and joined the Wadi of Egypt, ending at the sea. This is their[e] southern boundary.

5The eastern boundary is the Salt Sea as far as the mouth of the Jordan.

The northern boundary started from the bay of the sea at the mouth of the Jordan, 6went up to Beth Hoglah and continued north of Beth Arabah to the Stone of Bohan son of Reuben. 7The boundary then went up to Debir from the Valley of Achor and turned north to Gilgal, which faces the Pass of Adummim south of the gorge. It continued along to the waters of En Shemesh and came out at En Rogel. 8Then it ran up the Valley of Ben Hinnom along the southern

[a] *27* That is, Galilee [b] *9* Deut. 1:36 [c] *2* That is, the Dead Sea; also in verse 5 [d] *3* Hebrew *Akrabbim*
[e] *4* Hebrew *your*

slope of the Jebusite city (that is, Jerusalem). From there it climbed to the top of the hill west of the Hinnom Valley at the northern end of the Valley of Rephaim. 9From the hilltop the boundary headed toward the spring of the waters of Nephtoah, came out at the towns of Mount Ephron and went down toward Baalah (that is, Kiriath Jearim). 10Then it curved westward from Baalah to Mount Seir, ran along the northern slope of Mount Jearim (that is, Kesalon), continued down to Beth Shemesh and crossed to Timnah. 11It went to the northern slope of Ekron, turned toward Shikkeron, passed along to Mount Baalah and reached Jabneel. The boundary ended at the sea.

12The western boundary is the coastline of the Great Sea.[a]

These are the boundaries around the people of Judah by their clans.

13In accordance with the LORD's command to him, Joshua gave to Caleb son of Jephunneh a portion in Judah—Kiriath Arba, that is, Hebron. (Arba was the forefather of Anak.) 14From Hebron Caleb drove out the three Anakites—Sheshai, Ahiman and Talmai—descendants of Anak. 15From there he marched against the people living in Debir (formerly called Kiriath Sepher). 16And Caleb said, "I will give my daughter Acsah in marriage to the man who attacks and captures Kiriath Sepher." 17Othniel son of Kenaz, Caleb's brother, took it; so Caleb gave his daughter Acsah to him in marriage.

18One day when she came to Othniel, she urged him[b] to ask her father for a field. When she got off her donkey, Caleb asked her, "What can I do for you?"

19She replied, "Do me a special favor. Since you have given me land in the Negev, give me also springs of water." So Caleb gave her the upper and lower springs.

20This is the inheritance of the tribe of Judah, clan by clan:

21The southernmost towns of the tribe of Judah in the Negev toward the boundary of Edom were:

Kabzeel, Eder, Jagur, 22Kinah, Dimonah, Adadah, 23Kedesh, Hazor, Ithnan, 24Ziph, Telem, Bealoth, 25Hazor Hadattah, Kerioth Hezron (that is, Hazor), 26Amam, Shema, Moladah, 27Hazar Gaddah, Heshmon, Beth Pelet, 28Hazar Shual, Beersheba, Biziothiah, 29Baalah, Iim, Ezem, 30Eltolad, Kesil, Hormah, 31Ziklag, Madmannah, Sansannah, 32Lebaoth, Shilhim, Ain and Rimmon—a total of twenty-nine towns and their villages.

33In the western foothills:

Eshtaol, Zorah, Ashnah, 34Zanoah, En Gannim, Tappuah, Enam, 35Jarmuth, Adullam, Socoh, Azekah, 36Shaaraim, Adithaim and Gederah (or Gederothaim)[c]—fourteen towns and their villages.

37Zenan, Hadashah, Migdal Gad, 38Dilean, Mizpah, Joktheel, 39Lachish, Bozkath, Eglon, 40Cabbon, Lahmas, Kitlish, 41Gederoth, Beth Dagon, Naamah and Makkedah—sixteen towns and their villages.

42Libnah, Ether, Ashan, 43Iphtah, Ashnah, Nezib, 44Keilah, Aczib and Mareshah—nine towns and their villages.

45Ekron, with its surrounding settlements and villages; 46west of Ekron, all that were in the vicinity of Ashdod, together with their villages; 47Ashdod, its surrounding settlements and villages; and Gaza, its settlements and villages, as far as the Wadi of Egypt and the coastline of the Great Sea.

48In the hill country:

Shamir, Jattir, Socoh, 49Dannah, Kiriath Sannah (that is, Debir), 50Anab, Eshtemoh, Anim, 51Goshen, Holon and Giloh—eleven towns and their villages.

52Arab, Dumah, Eshan, 53Janim, Beth Tappuah, Aphekah, 54Humtah, Kiriath Arba (that is, Hebron) and Zior—nine towns and their villages.

55Maon, Carmel, Ziph, Juttah, 56Jezreel, Jokdeam, Zanoah, 57Kain, Gibeah and Timnah—ten towns and their villages.

58Halhul, Beth Zur, Gedor, 59Maarath, Beth Anoth and Eltekon—six towns and their villages.

60Kiriath Baal (that is, Kiriath Jearim) and Rabbah—two towns and their villages.

61In the desert:

Beth Arabah, Middin, Secacah, 62Nibshan, the City of Salt and En Gedi—six towns and their villages.

63Judah could not dislodge the Jebusites, who were living in Jerusalem; to this day the Jebusites live there with the people of Judah.

Allotment for Ephraim and Manasseh

16 The allotment for Joseph began at the Jordan of Jericho,[d] east of the waters of Jericho, and went up from there through the desert into the hill country of

[a] 12 That is, the Mediterranean; also in verse 47
[b] 18 Hebrew and some Septuagint manuscripts; other Septuagint manuscripts (see also note at Judges 1:14) *Othniel, he urged her*
[c] 36 Or *Gederah and Gederothaim*
[d] 1 *Jordan of Jericho* was possibly an ancient name for the Jordan River.

Bethel. 2It went on from Bethel (that is,
Luz),[a] crossed over to the territory of the
Arkites in Ataroth, 3descended westward to
the territory of the Japhletites as far as the
region of Lower Beth Horon and on to Gezer, ending at the sea.
4So Manasseh and Ephraim, the descendants of
Joseph, received their inheritance.

5This was the territory of Ephraim, clan by clan:
The boundary of their inheritance went
from Ataroth Addar in the east to Upper
Beth Horon 6and continued to the sea. From
Micmethath on the north it curved eastward to Taanath Shiloh, passing by it to Janoah on the east. 7Then it went down from
Janoah to Ataroth and Naarah, touched Jericho and came out at the Jordan. 8From Tappuah the border went west to the Kanah
Ravine and ended at the sea. This was the
inheritance of the tribe of the Ephraimites,
clan by clan. 9It also included all the towns
and their villages that were set aside for the
Ephraimites within the inheritance of the
Manassites.
10They did not dislodge the Canaanites living in
Gezer; to this day the Canaanites live among the
people of Ephraim but are required to do forced
labor.

17 This was the allotment for the tribe of
Manasseh as Joseph's firstborn, that is,
for Makir, Manasseh's firstborn. Makir was the
ancestor of the Gileadites, who had received Gilead and Bashan because the Makirites were great
soldiers. 2So this allotment was for the rest of the
people of Manasseh—the clans of Abiezer, Helek, Asriel, Shechem, Hepher and Shemida.
These are the other male descendants of Manasseh son of Joseph by their clans.
3Now Zelophehad son of Hepher, the son of
Gilead, the son of Makir, the son of Manasseh,
had no sons but only daughters, whose names
were Mahlah, Noah, Hoglah, Milcah and Tirzah.
4They went to Eleazar the priest, Joshua son of
Nun, and the leaders and said, "The LORD commanded Moses to give us an inheritance among
our brothers." So Joshua gave them an inheritance along with the brothers of their father, according to the LORD's command. 5Manasseh's
share consisted of ten tracts of land besides Gilead and Bashan east of the Jordan, 6because the
daughters of the tribe of Manasseh received an
inheritance among the sons. The land of Gilead
belonged to the rest of the descendants of Manasseh.
7The territory of Manasseh extended
from Asher to Micmethath east of Shechem.
The boundary ran southward from there to
include the people living at En Tappuah.
8(Manasseh had the land of Tappuah, but
Tappuah itself, on the boundary of Manasseh, belonged to the Ephraimites.) 9Then
the boundary continued south to the Kanah
Ravine. There were towns belonging to
Ephraim lying among the towns of Manasseh, but the boundary of Manasseh was the
northern side of the ravine and ended at the
sea. 10On the south the land belonged to
Ephraim, on the north to Manasseh. The
territory of Manasseh reached the sea and
bordered Asher on the north and Issachar
on the east.
11Within Issachar and Asher, Manasseh
also had Beth Shan, Ibleam and the people
of Dor, Endor, Taanach and Megiddo, together with their surrounding settlements
(the third in the list is Naphoth[b]).
12Yet the Manassites were not able to occupy
these towns, for the Canaanites were determined
to live in that region. 13However, when the Israelites grew stronger, they subjected the Canaanites to forced labor but did not drive them out
completely.
14The people of Joseph said to Joshua, "Why
have you given us only one allotment and one
portion for an inheritance? We are a numerous
people and the LORD has blessed us abundantly."
15"If you are so numerous," Joshua answered,
"and if the hill country of Ephraim is too small for
you, go up into the forest and clear land for yourselves there in the land of the Perizzites and
Rephaites."
16The people of Joseph replied, "The hill country is not enough for us, and all the Canaanites
who live in the plain have iron chariots, both
those in Beth Shan and its settlements and those
in the Valley of Jezreel."
17But Joshua said to the house of Joseph—to
Ephraim and Manasseh—"You are numerous
and very powerful. You will have not only one
allotment 18but the forested hill country as well.
Clear it, and its farthest limits will be yours;
though the Canaanites have iron chariots and
though they are strong, you can drive them out."

Division of the Rest of the Land

18 The whole assembly of the Israelites gathered at Shiloh and set up the Tent of
Meeting there. The country was brought under
their control, 2but there were still seven Israelite
tribes who had not yet received their inheritance.
3So Joshua said to the Israelites: "How long
will you wait before you begin to take possession

[a] 2 Septuagint; Hebrew *Bethel to Luz*
[b] 11 That is, Naphoth Dor

of the land that the LORD, the God of your fathers,
has given you? 4Appoint three men from each
tribe. I will send them out to make a survey of the
land and to write a description of it, according to
the inheritance of each. Then they will return to
me. 5You are to divide the land into seven parts.
Judah is to remain in its territory on the south and
the house of Joseph in its territory on the north.
6After you have written descriptions of the seven
parts of the land, bring them here to me and I
will cast lots for you in the presence of the
LORD our God. 7The Levites, however, do not get
a portion among you, because the priestly service
of the LORD is their inheritance. And Gad, Reuben and the half-tribe of Manasseh have already
received their inheritance on the east side of the
Jordan. Moses the servant of the LORD gave it to
them."

8As the men started on their way to map out
the land, Joshua instructed them, "Go and make
a survey of the land and write a description of it.
Then return to me, and I will cast lots for you
here at Shiloh in the presence of the LORD." 9So
the men left and went through the land. They
wrote its description on a scroll, town by town,
in seven parts, and returned to Joshua in the camp
at Shiloh. 10Joshua then cast lots for them in Shiloh in the presence of the LORD, and there he
distributed the land to the Israelites according to
their tribal divisions.

Allotment for Benjamin

11The lot came up for the tribe of Benjamin, clan
by clan. Their allotted territory lay between the
tribes of Judah and Joseph:

12On the north side their boundary began at the Jordan, passed the northern slope
of Jericho and headed west into the hill
country, coming out at the desert of Beth
Aven. 13From there it crossed to the south
slope of Luz (that is, Bethel) and went down
to Ataroth Addar on the hill south of Lower
Beth Horon.

14From the hill facing Beth Horon on the
south the boundary turned south along the
western side and came out at Kiriath Baal
(that is, Kiriath Jearim), a town of the people of Judah. This was the western side.

15The southern side began at the outskirts of Kiriath Jearim on the west, and the
boundary came out at the spring of the waters of Nephtoah. 16The boundary went
down to the foot of the hill facing the Valley
of Ben Hinnom, north of the Valley of Rephaim. It continued down the Hinnom Valley
along the southern slope of the Jebusite city
and so to En Rogel. 17It then curved north,
went to En Shemesh, continued to Geliloth,
which faces the Pass of Adummim, and ran
down to the Stone of Bohan son of Reuben.
18It continued to the northern slope of Beth
Arabah[a] and on down into the Arabah. 19It
then went to the northern slope of Beth
Hoglah and came out at the northern bay of
the Salt Sea,[b] at the mouth of the Jordan in
the south. This was the southern boundary.

20The Jordan formed the boundary on the
eastern side.

These were the boundaries that marked out the
inheritance of the clans of Benjamin on all sides.

21The tribe of Benjamin, clan by clan, had the
following cities:

Jericho, Beth Hoglah, Emek Keziz, 22Beth
Arabah, Zemaraim, Bethel, 23Avvim, Parah,
Ophrah, 24Kephar Ammoni, Ophni and
Geba—twelve towns and their villages.

25Gibeon, Ramah, Beeroth, 26Mizpah,
Kephirah, Mozah, 27Rekem, Irpeel, Taralah,
28Zelah, Haeleph, the Jebusite city (that is,
Jerusalem), Gibeah and Kiriath—fourteen
towns and their villages.

This was the inheritance of Benjamin for its
clans.

Allotment for Simeon

19 The second lot came out for the tribe of
Simeon, clan by clan. Their inheritance
lay within the territory of Judah. 2It included:

Beersheba (or Sheba),[c] Moladah, 3Ha-
zar Shual, Balah, Ezem, 4Eltolad, Bethul,
Hormah, 5Ziklag, Beth Marcaboth, Hazar
Susah, 6Beth Lebaoth and Sharuhen—
thirteen towns and their villages;

7Ain, Rimmon, Ether and Ashan—four
towns and their villages— 8and all the villages around these towns as far as Baalath
Beer (Ramah in the Negev).

This was the inheritance of the tribe of the Simeonites, clan by clan. 9The inheritance of the Simeonites was taken from the share of Judah, because Judah's portion was more than they
needed. So the Simeonites received their inheritance within the territory of Judah.

Allotment for Zebulun

10The third lot came up for Zebulun, clan by clan:

The boundary of their inheritance went
as far as Sarid. 11Going west it ran to Mara-
lah, touched Dabbesheth, and extended to
the ravine near Jokneam. 12It turned east
from Sarid toward the sunrise to the territory of Kisloth Tabor and went on to Daberath

[a] 18 Septuagint; Hebrew *slope facing the Arabah* [b] 19 That is, the Dead Sea [c] 2 Or *Beersheba, Sheba*; 1 Chron. 4:28 does not have *Sheba*.

and up to Japhia. [13]Then it continued eastward to Gath Hepher and Eth Kazin; it came
out at Rimmon and turned toward Neah.
[14]There the boundary went around on the
north to Hannathon and ended at the Valley
of Iphtah El. [15]Included were Kattath, Nahalal, Shimron, Idalah and Bethlehem. There
were twelve towns and their villages.
[16]These towns and their villages were the inheritance of Zebulun, clan by clan.

Allotment for Issachar

[17]The fourth lot came out for Issachar, clan by
clan. [18]Their territory included:
Jezreel, Kesulloth, Shunem, [19]Haphara-
im, Shion, Anaharath, [20]Rabbith, Kishion,
Ebez, [21]Remeth, En Gannim, En Haddah
and Beth Pazzez. [22]The boundary touched
Tabor, Shahazumah and Beth Shemesh, and
ended at the Jordan. There were sixteen
towns and their villages.
[23]These towns and their villages were the inheritance of the tribe of Issachar, clan by clan.

Allotment for Asher

[24]The fifth lot came out for the tribe of Asher,
clan by clan. [25]Their territory included:
Helkath, Hali, Beten, Acshaph, [26]Allam-
melech, Amad and Mishal. On the west the
boundary touched Carmel and Shihor Lib-
nath. [27]It then turned east toward Beth Dagon, touched Zebulun and the Valley of Iphtah El, and went north to Beth Emek and
Neiel, passing Cabul on the left. [28]It went to
Abdon,[a] Rehob, Hammon and Kanah, as
far as Greater Sidon. [29]The boundary then
turned back toward Ramah and went to the
fortified city of Tyre, turned toward Hosah
and came out at the sea in the region of
Aczib, [30]Ummah, Aphek and Rehob. There
were twenty-two towns and their villages.
[31]These towns and their villages were the inheritance of the tribe of Asher, clan by clan.

Allotment for Naphtali

[32]The sixth lot came out for Naphtali, clan by
clan:
[33]Their boundary went from Heleph and
the large tree in Zaanannim, passing Adami
Nekeb and Jabneel to Lakkum and ending
at the Jordan. [34]The boundary ran west
through Aznoth Tabor and came out at Huk-
kok. It touched Zebulun on the south, Asher
on the west and the Jordan[b] on the east.
[35]The fortified cities were Ziddim, Zer,
Hammath, Rakkath, Kinnereth, [36]Adamah,
Ramah, Hazor, [37]Kedesh, Edrei, En Hazor,
[38]Iron, Migdal El, Horem, Beth Anath and
Beth Shemesh. There were nineteen towns
and their villages.
[39]These towns and their villages were the inheritance of the tribe of Naphtali, clan by clan.

Allotment for Dan

[40]The seventh lot came out for the tribe of Dan,
clan by clan. [41]The territory of their inheritance
included:
Zorah, Eshtaol, Ir Shemesh, [42]Shaalab-
bin, Aijalon, Ithlah, [43]Elon, Timnah, Ekron,
[44]Eltekeh, Gibbethon, Baalath, [45]Jehud,
Bene Berak, Gath Rimmon, [46]Me Jarkon
and Rakkon, with the area facing Joppa.
[47](But the Danites had difficulty taking possession of their territory, so they went up and attacked Leshem, took it, put it to the sword and
occupied it. They settled in Leshem and named it
Dan after their forefather.)
[48]These towns and their villages were the inheritance of the tribe of Dan, clan by clan.

Allotment for Joshua

[49]When they had finished dividing the land
into its allotted portions, the Israelites gave Joshua son of Nun an inheritance among them, [50]as
the LORD had commanded. They gave him the
town he asked for—Timnath Serah[c] in the hill
country of Ephraim. And he built up the town
and settled there.
[51]These are the territories that Eleazar the
priest, Joshua son of Nun and the heads of the
tribal clans of Israel assigned by lot at Shiloh in
the presence of the LORD at the entrance to the
Tent of Meeting. And so they finished dividing
the land.

Cities of Refuge

20 Then the LORD said to Joshua: [2]"Tell the
Israelites to designate the cities of refuge,
as I instructed you through Moses, [3]so that anyone who kills a person accidentally and unintentionally may flee there and find protection from
the avenger of blood.
[4]"When he flees to one of these cities, he is to
stand in the entrance of the city gate and state his
case before the elders of that city. Then they are
to admit him into their city and give him a place
to live with them. [5]If the avenger of blood pursues him, they must not surrender the one accused, because he killed his neighbor unintentionally and without malice aforethought. [6]He is
to stay in that city until he has stood trial before
the assembly and until the death of the high

[a]*28* Some Hebrew manuscripts (see also Joshua 21:30); most Hebrew manuscripts *Ebron* [b]*34* Septuagint; Hebrew *west, and Judah, the Jordan,* [c]*50* Also known as *Timnath Heres* (see Judges 2:9)

priest who is serving at that time. Then he may
go back to his own home in the town from which
he fled."
7So they set apart Kedesh in Galilee in the hill
country of Naphtali, Shechem in the hill country
of Ephraim, and Kiriath Arba (that is, Hebron) in
the hill country of Judah. 8On the east side of the
Jordan of Jericho[a] they designated Bezer in the
desert on the plateau in the tribe of Reuben, Ramoth in Gilead in the tribe of Gad, and Golan in
Bashan in the tribe of Manasseh. 9Any of the
Israelites or any alien living among them who
killed someone accidentally could flee to these
designated cities and not be killed by the avenger
of blood prior to standing trial before the assembly.

Towns for the Levites

21 Now the family heads of the Levites approached Eleazar the priest, Joshua son of
Nun, and the heads of the other tribal families
of Israel 2at Shiloh in Canaan and said to them,
"The LORD commanded through Moses that you
give us towns to live in, with pasturelands for our
livestock." 3So, as the LORD had commanded, the
Israelites gave the Levites the following towns
and pasturelands out of their own inheritance:
4The first lot came out for the Kohathites, clan
by clan. The Levites who were descendants of
Aaron the priest were allotted thirteen towns
from the tribes of Judah, Simeon and Benjamin.
5The rest of Kohath's descendants were allotted
ten towns from the clans of the tribes of Ephraim,
Dan and half of Manasseh.
6The descendants of Gershon were allotted
thirteen towns from the clans of the tribes of
Issachar, Asher, Naphtali and the half-tribe of
Manasseh in Bashan.
7The descendants of Merari, clan by clan, received twelve towns from the tribes of Reuben,
Gad and Zebulun.
8So the Israelites allotted to the Levites these
towns and their pasturelands, as the LORD had
commanded through Moses.
9From the tribes of Judah and Simeon they allotted the following towns by name 10(these towns
were assigned to the descendants of Aaron who
were from the Kohathite clans of the Levites,
because the first lot fell to them):
11They gave them Kiriath Arba (that is,
Hebron), with its surrounding pastureland,
in the hill country of Judah. (Arba was the
forefather of Anak.) 12But the fields and villages around the city they had given to Caleb son of Jephunneh as his possession.
13So to the descendants of Aaron the
priest they gave Hebron (a city of refuge
for one accused of murder), Libnah, 14Jattir,
Eshtemoa, 15Holon, Debir, 16Ain, Juttah and
Beth Shemesh, together with their pasturelands—nine towns from these two
tribes.
17And from the tribe of Benjamin they
gave them Gibeon, Geba, 18Anathoth and
Almon, together with their pasturelands—
four towns.
19All the towns for the priests, the descendants of
Aaron, were thirteen, together with their pasturelands.
20The rest of the Kohathite clans of the Levites
were allotted towns from the tribe of Ephraim:
21In the hill country of Ephraim they
were given Shechem (a city of refuge for
one accused of murder) and Gezer, 22Kibza-
im and Beth Horon, together with their pasturelands—four towns.
23Also from the tribe of Dan they received Eltekeh, Gibbethon, 24Aijalon and
Gath Rimmon, together with their pasturelands—four towns.
25From half the tribe of Manasseh they
received Taanach and Gath Rimmon, together with their pasturelands—two towns.
26All these ten towns and their pasturelands
were given to the rest of the Kohathite clans.
27The Levite clans of the Gershonites were given:
from the half-tribe of Manasseh,
Golan in Bashan (a city of refuge for one
accused of murder) and Be Eshtarah, together with their pasturelands—two towns;
28from the tribe of Issachar,
Kishion, Daberath, 29Jarmuth and En Gannim, together with their pasturelands—
four towns;
30from the tribe of Asher,
Mishal, Abdon, 31Helkath and Rehob, together with their pasturelands—four towns;
32from the tribe of Naphtali,
Kedesh in Galilee (a city of refuge for one
accused of murder), Hammoth Dor and Kar-
tan, together with their pasturelands—
three towns.
33All the towns of the Gershonite clans were thirteen, together with their pasturelands.
34The Merarite clans (the rest of the Levites)
were given:
from the tribe of Zebulun,
Jokneam, Kartah, 35Dimnah and Nahalal,
together with their pasturelands—four
towns;

[a]8 *Jordan of Jericho* was possibly an ancient name for the Jordan River.

36from the tribe of Reuben,
Bezer, Jahaz, 37Kedemoth and Mephaath,
together with their pasturelands—four
towns;
38from the tribe of Gad,
Ramoth in Gilead (a city of refuge for
one accused of murder), Mahanaim, 39Hesh-
bon and Jazer, together with their pasturelands—four towns in all.
40All the towns allotted to the Merarite clans,
who were the rest of the Levites, were twelve.
41The towns of the Levites in the territory held
by the Israelites were forty-eight in all, together
with their pasturelands. 42Each of these towns
had pasturelands surrounding it; this was true for
all these towns.

43So the LORD gave Israel all the land he had
sworn to give their forefathers, and they took
possession of it and settled there. 44The LORD
gave them rest on every side, just as he had
sworn to their forefathers. Not one of their enemies withstood them; the LORD handed all their
enemies over to them. 45Not one of all the LORD's
good promises to the house of Israel failed; every
one was fulfilled.

Eastern Tribes Return Home

22 Then Joshua summoned the Reubenites,
the Gadites and the half-tribe of Manasseh 2and said to them, "You have done all that
Moses the servant of the LORD commanded, and
you have obeyed me in everything I commanded.
3For a long time now—to this very day—you
have not deserted your brothers but have carried
out the mission the LORD your God gave you.
4Now that the LORD your God has given your
brothers rest as he promised, return to your
homes in the land that Moses the servant of the
LORD gave you on the other side of the Jordan.
5But be very careful to keep the commandment
and the law that Moses the servant of the LORD
gave you: to love the LORD your God, to walk in
all his ways, to obey his commands, to hold fast
to him and to serve him with all your heart and
all your soul."
6Then Joshua blessed them and sent them
away, and they went to their homes. 7(To the
half-tribe of Manasseh Moses had given land in
Bashan, and to the other half of the tribe Joshua
gave land on the west side of the Jordan with
their brothers.) When Joshua sent them home,
he blessed them, 8saying, "Return to your homes
with your great wealth—with large herds of livestock, with silver, gold, bronze and iron, and a
great quantity of clothing—and divide with your
brothers the plunder from your enemies."
9So the Reubenites, the Gadites and the half-
tribe of Manasseh left the Israelites at Shiloh in
Canaan to return to Gilead, their own land,
which they had acquired in accordance with the
command of the LORD through Moses.
10When they came to Geliloth near the Jordan
in the land of Canaan, the Reubenites, the Gadites and the half-tribe of Manasseh built an imposing altar there by the Jordan. 11And when the
Israelites heard that they had built the altar on
the border of Canaan at Geliloth near the Jordan
on the Israelite side, 12the whole assembly of Israel gathered at Shiloh to go to war against them.
13So the Israelites sent Phinehas son of Eleazar, the priest, to the land of Gilead—to Reuben,
Gad and the half-tribe of Manasseh. 14With him
they sent ten of the chief men, one for each of the
tribes of Israel, each the head of a family division
among the Israelite clans.
15When they went to Gilead—to Reuben, Gad
and the half-tribe of Manasseh—they said to
them: 16"The whole assembly of the LORD says:
'How could you break faith with the God of Israel
like this? How could you turn away from the
LORD and build yourselves an altar in rebellion
against him now? 17Was not the sin of Peor
enough for us? Up to this very day we have not
cleansed ourselves from that sin, even though a
plague fell on the community of the LORD! 18And
are you now turning away from the LORD?
" 'If you rebel against the LORD today, tomorrow he will be angry with the whole community
of Israel. 19If the land you possess is defiled, come
over to the LORD's land, where the LORD's tabernacle stands, and share the land with us. But do
not rebel against the LORD or against us by building an altar for yourselves, other than the altar
of the LORD our God. 20When Achan son of Zerah acted unfaithfully regarding the devoted
things,[a] did not wrath come upon the whole
community of Israel? He was not the only one
who died for his sin.' "
21Then Reuben, Gad and the half-tribe of Manasseh replied to the heads of the clans of Israel:
22"The Mighty One, God, the LORD! The Mighty
One, God, the LORD! He knows! And let Israel
know! If this has been in rebellion or disobedience to the LORD, do not spare us this day. 23If we
have built our own altar to turn away from the
LORD and to offer burnt offerings and grain offerings, or to sacrifice fellowship offerings[b] on it,
may the LORD himself call us to account.
24"No! We did it for fear that some day your
descendants might say to ours, 'What do you
have to do with the LORD, the God of Israel?
25The LORD has made the Jordan a boundary be-

[a] 20 The Hebrew term refers to the irrevocable giving over of things or persons to the LORD, often by totally destroying them.
[b] 23 Traditionally *peace offerings*; also in verse 27

tween us and you—you Reubenites and Gadites!
You have no share in the LORD.’ So your descendants might cause ours to stop fearing the LORD.
26“That is why we said, ‘Let us get ready and
build an altar—but not for burnt offerings or sacrifices.’ 27On the contrary, it is to be a witness
between us and you and the generations that follow, that we will worship the LORD at his sanctuary with our burnt offerings, sacrifices and fellowship offerings. Then in the future your
descendants will not be able to say to ours, ‘You
have no share in the LORD.’
28“And we said, ‘If they ever say this to us, or
to our descendants, we will answer: Look at the
replica of the LORD’s altar, which our fathers
built, not for burnt offerings and sacrifices, but as
a witness between us and you.’
29“Far be it from us to rebel against the LORD
and turn away from him today by building an
altar for burnt offerings, grain offerings and sacrifices, other than the altar of the LORD our God
that stands before his tabernacle.”
30When Phinehas the priest and the leaders of
the community—the heads of the clans of the
Israelites—heard what Reuben, Gad and Manasseh had to say, they were pleased. 31And Phinehas son of Eleazar, the priest, said to Reuben, Gad
and Manasseh, “Today we know that the LORD is
with us, because you have not acted unfaithfully
toward the LORD in this matter. Now you have
rescued the Israelites from the LORD’s hand.”
32Then Phinehas son of Eleazar, the priest,
and the leaders returned to Canaan from their
meeting with the Reubenites and Gadites in Gilead and reported to the Israelites. 33They were
glad to hear the report and praised God. And they
talked no more about going to war against them
to devastate the country where the Reubenites
and the Gadites lived.
34And the Reubenites and the Gadites gave the
altar this name: A Witness Between Us that the
LORD is God.

Joshua’s Farewell to the Leaders

23 After a long time had passed and the LORD
had given Israel rest from all their enemies around them, Joshua, by then old and well
advanced in years, 2summoned all Israel—their
elders, leaders, judges and officials—and said to
them: “I am old and well advanced in years. 3You
yourselves have seen everything the LORD your
God has done to all these nations for your sake;
it was the LORD your God who fought for you.
4Remember how I have allotted as an inheritance
for your tribes all the land of the nations that
remain—the nations I conquered—between the
Jordan and the Great Sea[a] in the west. 5The
LORD your God himself will drive them out of
your way. He will push them out before you, and
you will take possession of their land, as the LORD
your God promised you.
6“Be very strong; be careful to obey all that is
written in the Book of the Law of Moses, without
turning aside to the right or to the left. 7Do not
associate with these nations that remain among
you; do not invoke the names of their gods or
swear by them. You must not serve them or bow
down to them. 8But you are to hold fast to the
LORD your God, as you have until now.
9“The LORD has driven out before you great
and powerful nations; to this day no one has been
able to withstand you. 10One of you routs a thousand, because the LORD your God fights for you,
just as he promised. 11So be very careful to love
the LORD your God.
12“But if you turn away and ally yourselves
with the survivors of these nations that remain
among you and if you intermarry with them and
associate with them, 13then you may be sure that
the LORD your God will no longer drive out these
nations before you. Instead, they will become
snares and traps for you, whips on your backs and
thorns in your eyes, until you perish from this
good land, which the LORD your God has given
you.
14“Now I am about to go the way of all the
earth. You know with all your heart and soul that
not one of all the good promises the LORD your
God gave you has failed. Every promise has been
fulfilled; not one has failed. 15But just as every
good promise of the LORD your God has come
true, so the LORD will bring on you all the evil he
has threatened, until he has destroyed you from
this good land he has given you. 16If you violate
the covenant of the LORD your God, which he
commanded you, and go and serve other gods
and bow down to them, the LORD’s anger will
burn against you, and you will quickly perish
from the good land he has given you.”

The Covenant Renewed at Shechem

24 Then Joshua assembled all the tribes of
Israel at Shechem. He summoned the elders, leaders, judges and officials of Israel, and
they presented themselves before God.
2Joshua said to all the people, “This is what the
LORD, the God of Israel, says: ‘Long ago your forefathers, including Terah the father of Abraham
and Nahor, lived beyond the River[b] and worshiped other gods. 3But I took your father Abraham from the land beyond the River and led him
throughout Canaan and gave him many descendants. I gave him Isaac, 4and to Isaac I gave Jacob
and Esau. I assigned the hill country of Seir to

[a]4 That is, the Mediterranean [b]2 That is, the Euphrates; also in verses 3, 14 and 15

Esau, but Jacob and his sons went down to Egypt.
5“ ‘Then I sent Moses and Aaron, and I afflicted the Egyptians by what I did there, and I
brought you out. 6When I brought your fathers
out of Egypt, you came to the sea, and the Egyptians pursued them with chariots and horsemen[a] as far as the Red Sea.[b] 7But they cried to
the LORD for help, and he put darkness between
you and the Egyptians; he brought the sea over
them and covered them. You saw with your own
eyes what I did to the Egyptians. Then you lived
in the desert for a long time.
8“ ‘I brought you to the land of the Amorites
who lived east of the Jordan. They fought against
you, but I gave them into your hands. I destroyed
them from before you, and you took possession of
their land. 9When Balak son of Zippor, the king of
Moab, prepared to fight against Israel, he sent for
Balaam son of Beor to put a curse on you. 10But
I would not listen to Balaam, so he blessed you
again and again, and I delivered you out of his
hand.
11“ ‘Then you crossed the Jordan and came to
Jericho. The citizens of Jericho fought against
you, as did also the Amorites, Perizzites, Canaanites, Hittites, Girgashites, Hivites and Jebusites,
but I gave them into your hands. 12I sent the
hornet ahead of you, which drove them out before you—also the two Amorite kings. You did
not do it with your own sword and bow. 13So I
gave you a land on which you did not toil and
cities you did not build; and you live in them and
eat from vineyards and olive groves that you did
not plant.’
14“Now fear the LORD and serve him with all
faithfulness. Throw away the gods your forefathers worshiped beyond the River and in Egypt,
and serve the LORD. 15But if serving the LORD
seems undesirable to you, then choose for yourselves this day whom you will serve, whether the
gods your forefathers served beyond the River, or
the gods of the Amorites, in whose land you are
living. But as for me and my household, we will
serve the LORD.”
16Then the people answered, “Far be it from
us to forsake the LORD to serve other gods! 17It
was the LORD our God himself who brought us
and our fathers up out of Egypt, from that land of
slavery, and performed those great signs before
our eyes. He protected us on our entire journey
and among all the nations through which we
traveled. 18And the LORD drove out before us all
the nations, including the Amorites, who lived in
the land. We too will serve the LORD, because he
is our God.”
19Joshua said to the people, “You are not able
to serve the LORD. He is a holy God; he is a
jealous God. He will not forgive your rebellion
and your sins. 20If you forsake the LORD and serve
foreign gods, he will turn and bring disaster on
you and make an end of you, after he has been
good to you.”
21But the people said to Joshua, “No! We will
serve the LORD.”
22Then Joshua said, “You are witnesses against
yourselves that you have chosen to serve the
LORD.”
“Yes, we are witnesses,” they replied.
23“Now then,” said Joshua, “throw away the
foreign gods that are among you and yield your
hearts to the LORD, the God of Israel.”
24And the people said to Joshua, “We will
serve the LORD our God and obey him.”
25On that day Joshua made a covenant for the
people, and there at Shechem he drew up for
them decrees and laws. 26And Joshua recorded
these things in the Book of the Law of God. Then
he took a large stone and set it up there under the
oak near the holy place of the LORD.
27“See!” he said to all the people. “This stone
will be a witness against us. It has heard all the
words the LORD has said to us. It will be a witness
against you if you are untrue to your God.”

Buried in the Promised Land

28Then Joshua sent the people away, each to
his own inheritance.
29After these things, Joshua son of Nun, the
servant of the LORD, died at the age of a hundred
and ten. 30And they buried him in the land of his
inheritance, at Timnath Serah[c] in the hill country of Ephraim, north of Mount Gaash.
31Israel served the LORD throughout the lifetime of Joshua and of the elders who outlived him
and who had experienced everything the LORD
had done for Israel.
32And Joseph's bones, which the Israelites had
brought up from Egypt, were buried at Shechem
in the tract of land that Jacob bought for a hundred pieces of silver[d] from the sons of Hamor,
the father of Shechem. This became the inheritance of Joseph's descendants.
33And Eleazar son of Aaron died and was buried at Gibeah, which had been allotted to his son
Phinehas in the hill country of Ephraim.

a6 Or *charioteers* b6 Hebrew *Yam Suph*; that is, Sea of Reeds c30 Also known as *Timnath Heres* (see Judges 2:9)
d32 Hebrew *hundred kesitahs*; a kesitah was a unit of money of unknown weight and value.

Introduction to JUDGES

Personal Reading Plan

❐ Judges 1:1–2:5	❐ Judges 7:1–8:35	❐ Judges 15:1–16:31
❐ Judges 2:6–3:31	❐ Judges 9:1–57	❐ Judges 17:1–18:31
❐ Judges 4:1–5:31	❐ Judges 10:1–11:40	❐ Judges 19:1–30
❐ Judges 6:1–40	❐ Judges 12:1–14:20	❐ Judges 20:1–21:25

Author

The author of Judges is not designated in the book. Some view Samuel as the author, but this is uncertain.

Date

The exact date of authorship is unknown, but Judges may have been written during the early period of the reign of David (c. 1000–980 B.C.). The action recorded here spans the period between the conquest and the monarchy of Israel.

Theme

God is merciful and long-suffering despite the sin of his people.

Historical Background

The title of the book describes Israel's leaders from Joshua to the time when Israel had kings. Two to three hundred years lapse between the conquest of Canaan (after Joshua's death) and the rise of Saul (c. 1050 B.C.). During this time Israel was a loose confederation of tribes spread throughout the promised land. This area was heavily influenced by Canaanite culture and religion. Hence, Israel is repeatedly drawn away from worshiping the Lord in their desire to have a king like their neighbors (17:6; 18:1; 19:1; 21:25).

Characteristics

Once in Canaan, all the Israelites needed to do was obey God; instead, they followed the sinful example of the Canaanites. Their disobedience resulted in a cycle observed throughout the book (see 2:11–19): (1) There is apostasy or rebellion by God's people; (2) God raises up foreign oppressors to chasten his people; (3) A cry of distress goes up from the Israelites; (4) God raises up a "deliverer" or "judge" who takes up arms to defend the homeland and rescue the repentant people. The Lord's covenant faithfulness arises out of these repeated cycles. The book of Judges shows that even in dark, chaotic times, God is in control.

Passage for Topical Group Study

14:1–20 DATING—THE WRONG WAY Samson's Marriage

See the Lesson Plans in the front of this Bible.

Passages for General Group Study

7:1–25	Gideon Defeats the Midianites
16:1–22	Samson and Delilah
16:23–31	Samson's Death

Israel Fights the Remaining Canaanites

1 After the death of Joshua, the Israelites asked
the LORD, "Who will be the first to go up and
fight for us against the Canaanites?"
2The LORD answered, "Judah is to go; I have
given the land into their hands."
3Then the men of Judah said to the Simeonites
their brothers, "Come up with us into the territory allotted to us, to fight against the Canaanites.
We in turn will go with you into yours." So the
Simeonites went with them.
4When Judah attacked, the LORD gave the Canaanites and Perizzites into their hands and they
struck down ten thousand men at Bezek. 5It was
there that they found Adoni-Bezek and fought
against him, putting to rout the Canaanites and
Perizzites. 6Adoni-Bezek fled, but they chased
him and caught him, and cut off his thumbs and
big toes.
7Then Adoni-Bezek said, "Seventy kings with
their thumbs and big toes cut off have picked up
scraps under my table. Now God has paid me
back for what I did to them." They brought him
to Jerusalem, and he died there.
8The men of Judah attacked Jerusalem also and
took it. They put the city to the sword and set it
on fire.
9After that, the men of Judah went down to
fight against the Canaanites living in the hill
country, the Negev and the western foothills.
10They advanced against the Canaanites living in
Hebron (formerly called Kiriath Arba) and defeated Sheshai, Ahiman and Talmai.
11From there they advanced against the people
living in Debir (formerly called Kiriath Sepher).
12And Caleb said, "I will give my daughter Acsah
in marriage to the man who attacks and captures
Kiriath Sepher." 13Othniel son of Kenaz, Caleb's
younger brother, took it; so Caleb gave his daughter Acsah to him in marriage.
14One day when she came to Othniel, she
urged him[a] to ask her father for a field. When
she got off her donkey, Caleb asked her, "What
can I do for you?"
15She replied, "Do me a special favor. Since
you have given me land in the Negev, give me
also springs of water." Then Caleb gave her the
upper and lower springs.
16The descendants of Moses' father-in-law,
the Kenite, went up from the City of Palms[b]
with the men of Judah to live among the people of the Desert of Judah in the Negev near
Arad.
17Then the men of Judah went with the Simeonites their brothers and attacked the Canaanites
living in Zephath, and they totally destroyed[c]
the city. Therefore it was called Hormah.[d] 18The
men of Judah also took[e] Gaza, Ashkelon and
Ekron—each city with its territory.
19The LORD was with the men of Judah. They
took possession of the hill country, but they were
unable to drive the people from the plains, because they had iron chariots. 20As Moses had
promised, Hebron was given to Caleb, who drove
from it the three sons of Anak. 21The Benjamites,
however, failed to dislodge the Jebusites, who
were living in Jerusalem; to this day the Jebusites
live there with the Benjamites.
22Now the house of Joseph attacked Bethel,
and the LORD was with them. 23When they sent
men to spy out Bethel (formerly called Luz), 24the
spies saw a man coming out of the city and they
said to him, "Show us how to get into the city
and we will see that you are treated well." 25So
he showed them, and they put the city to the
sword but spared the man and his whole family.
26He then went to the land of the Hittites, where
he built a city and called it Luz, which is its name
to this day.
27But Manasseh did not drive out the people of
Beth Shan or Taanach or Dor or Ibleam or Megiddo and their surrounding settlements, for the Canaanites were determined to live in that land.
28When Israel became strong, they pressed the
Canaanites into forced labor but never drove
them out completely. 29Nor did Ephraim drive
out the Canaanites living in Gezer, but the Canaanites continued to live there among them.
30Neither did Zebulun drive out the Canaanites
living in Kitron or Nahalol, who remained among
them; but they did subject them to forced labor.
31Nor did Asher drive out those living in Acco or
Sidon or Ahlab or Aczib or Helbah or Aphek or
Rehob, 32and because of this the people of Asher
lived among the Canaanite inhabitants of the
land. 33Neither did Naphtali drive out those living in Beth Shemesh or Beth Anath; but the
Naphtalites too lived among the Canaanite inhabitants of the land, and those living in Beth Shemesh and Beth Anath became forced laborers for
them. 34The Amorites confined the Danites to
the hill country, not allowing them to come down
into the plain. 35And the Amorites were determined also to hold out in Mount Heres, Aijalon
and Shaalbim, but when the power of the house
of Joseph increased, they too were pressed into
forced labor. 36The boundary of the Amorites was
from Scorpion[f] Pass to Sela and beyond.

[a] *14* Hebrew; Septuagint and Vulgate *Othniel, he urged her* [b] *16* That is, Jericho [c] *17* The Hebrew term refers to the irrevocable giving over of things or persons to the LORD, often by totally destroying them. [d] *17* *Hormah* means *destruction.*
[e] *18* Hebrew; Septuagint *Judah did not take* [f] *36* Hebrew *Akrabbim*

The Angel of the LORD at Bokim

2 The angel of the LORD went up from Gilgal to
Bokim and said, "I brought you up out of
Egypt and led you into the land that I swore to
give to your forefathers. I said, 'I will never break
my covenant with you, 2and you shall not make
a covenant with the people of this land, but you
shall break down their altars.' Yet you have disobeyed me. Why have you done this? 3Now
therefore I tell you that I will not drive them out
before you; they will be ⌊thorns⌋ in your sides and
their gods will be a snare to you."
4When the angel of the LORD had spoken these
things to all the Israelites, the people wept aloud,
5and they called that place Bokim.[a] There they
offered sacrifices to the LORD.

Disobedience and Defeat

6After Joshua had dismissed the Israelites, they
went to take possession of the land, each to his
own inheritance. 7The people served the LORD
throughout the lifetime of Joshua and of the elders who outlived him and who had seen all the
great things the LORD had done for Israel.
8Joshua son of Nun, the servant of the LORD,
died at the age of a hundred and ten. 9And they
buried him in the land of his inheritance, at Timnath Heres[b] in the hill country of Ephraim,
north of Mount Gaash.
10After that whole generation had been gathered to their fathers, another generation grew up,
who knew neither the LORD nor what he had
done for Israel. 11Then the Israelites did evil in
the eyes of the LORD and served the Baals. 12They
forsook the LORD, the God of their fathers, who
had brought them out of Egypt. They followed
and worshiped various gods of the peoples
around them. They provoked the LORD to anger
13because they forsook him and served Baal and
the Ashtoreths. 14In his anger against Israel the
LORD handed them over to raiders who plundered them. He sold them to their enemies all
around, whom they were no longer able to resist.
15Whenever Israel went out to fight, the hand of
the LORD was against them to defeat them, just as
he had sworn to them. They were in great distress.
16Then the LORD raised up judges,[c] who
saved them out of the hands of these raiders.
17Yet they would not listen to their judges but
prostituted themselves to other gods and worshiped them. Unlike their fathers, they quickly
turned from the way in which their fathers had
walked, the way of obedience to the LORD's commands. 18Whenever the LORD raised up a judge
for them, he was with the judge and saved them
out of the hands of their enemies as long as the
judge lived; for the LORD had compassion on
them as they groaned under those who oppressed
and afflicted them. 19But when the judge died,
the people returned to ways even more corrupt
than those of their fathers, following other gods
and serving and worshiping them. They refused
to give up their evil practices and stubborn ways.
20Therefore the LORD was very angry with Israel and said, "Because this nation has violated the
covenant that I laid down for their forefathers
and has not listened to me, 21I will no longer
drive out before them any of the nations Joshua
left when he died. 22I will use them to test Israel
and see whether they will keep the way of the
LORD and walk in it as their forefathers did."
23The LORD had allowed those nations to remain;
he did not drive them out at once by giving them
into the hands of Joshua.

3 These are the nations the LORD left to test all
those Israelites who had not experienced
any of the wars in Canaan 2(he did this only to
teach warfare to the descendants of the Israelites
who had not had previous battle experience):
3the five rulers of the Philistines, all the Canaanites, the Sidonians, and the Hivites living in the
Lebanon mountains from Mount Baal Hermon to
Lebo[d] Hamath. 4They were left to test the Israelites to see whether they would obey the LORD's
commands, which he had given their forefathers
through Moses.
5The Israelites lived among the Canaanites,
Hittites, Amorites, Perizzites, Hivites and Jebusites. 6They took their daughters in marriage and
gave their own daughters to their sons, and
served their gods.

Othniel

7The Israelites did evil in the eyes of the LORD;
they forgot the LORD their God and served the
Baals and the Asherahs. 8The anger of the LORD
burned against Israel so that he sold them into
the hands of Cushan-Rishathaim king of Aram
Naharaim,[e] to whom the Israelites were subject
for eight years. 9But when they cried out to the
LORD, he raised up for them a deliverer, Othniel
son of Kenaz, Caleb's younger brother, who
saved them. 10The Spirit of the LORD came upon
him, so that he became Israel's judge[f] and went
to war. The LORD gave Cushan-Rishathaim king
of Aram into the hands of Othniel, who overpowered him. 11So the land had peace for forty years,
until Othniel son of Kenaz died.

Ehud

12Once again the Israelites did evil in the eyes

---

a5 *Bokim* means *weepers.* b9 Also known as *Timnath Serah* (see Joshua 19:50 and 24:30) c16 Or *leaders*; similarly in verses 17-19 d3 Or *to the entrance to* e8 That is, Northwest Mesopotamia f10 Or *leader* of the LORD, and because they did this evil the LORD gave Eglon king of Moab power over Israel. [13]Getting the Ammonites and Amalekites to join him, Eglon came and attacked Israel, and they took possession of the City of Palms.[a] [14]The Israelites were subject to Eglon king of Moab for eighteen years.

[15]Again the Israelites cried out to the LORD, and he gave them a deliverer—Ehud, a left-handed man, the son of Gera the Benjamite. The Israelites sent him with tribute to Eglon king of Moab. [16]Now Ehud had made a double-edged sword about a foot and a half[b] long, which he strapped to his right thigh under his clothing. [17]He presented the tribute to Eglon king of Moab, who was a very fat man. [18]After Ehud had presented the tribute, he sent on their way the men who had carried it. [19]At the idols[c] near Gilgal he himself turned back and said, "I have a secret message for you, O king."

The king said, "Quiet!" And all his attendants left him.

[20]Ehud then approached him while he was sitting alone in the upper room of his summer palace[d] and said, "I have a message from God for you." As the king rose from his seat, [21]Ehud reached with his left hand, drew the sword from his right thigh and plunged it into the king's belly. [22]Even the handle sank in after the blade, which came out his back. Ehud did not pull the sword out, and the fat closed in over it. [23]Then Ehud went out to the porch[e]; he shut the doors of the upper room behind him and locked them.

[24]After he had gone, the servants came and found the doors of the upper room locked. They said, "He must be relieving himself in the inner room of the house." [25]They waited to the point of embarrassment, but when he did not open the doors of the room, they took a key and unlocked them. There they saw their lord fallen to the floor, dead.

[26]While they waited, Ehud got away. He passed by the idols and escaped to Seirah. [27]When he arrived there, he blew a trumpet in the hill country of Ephraim, and the Israelites went down with him from the hills, with him leading them.

[28]"Follow me," he ordered, "for the LORD has given Moab, your enemy, into your hands." So they followed him down and, taking possession of the fords of the Jordan that led to Moab, they allowed no one to cross over. [29]At that time they struck down about ten thousand Moabites, all vigorous and strong; not a man escaped. [30]That day Moab was made subject to Israel, and the land had peace for eighty years.

Shamgar

[31]After Ehud came Shamgar son of Anath, who struck down six hundred Philistines with an oxgoad. He too saved Israel.

Deborah

4 After Ehud died, the Israelites once again did evil in the eyes of the LORD. [2]So the LORD sold them into the hands of Jabin, a king of Canaan, who reigned in Hazor. The commander of his army was Sisera, who lived in Harosheth Haggoyim. [3]Because he had nine hundred iron chariots and had cruelly oppressed the Israelites for twenty years, they cried to the LORD for help.

[4]Deborah, a prophetess, the wife of Lappidoth, was leading[f] Israel at that time. [5]She held court under the Palm of Deborah between Ramah and Bethel in the hill country of Ephraim, and the Israelites came to her to have their disputes decided. [6]She sent for Barak son of Abinoam from Kedesh in Naphtali and said to him, "The LORD, the God of Israel, commands you: 'Go, take with you ten thousand men of Naphtali and Zebulun and lead the way to Mount Tabor. [7]I will lure Sisera, the commander of Jabin's army, with his chariots and his troops to the Kishon River and give him into your hands.'"

[8]Barak said to her, "If you go with me, I will go; but if you don't go with me, I won't go."

[9]"Very well," Deborah said, "I will go with you. But because of the way you are going about this,[g] the honor will not be yours, for the LORD will hand Sisera over to a woman." So Deborah went with Barak to Kedesh, [10]where he summoned Zebulun and Naphtali. Ten thousand men followed him, and Deborah also went with him.

[11]Now Heber the Kenite had left the other Kenites, the descendants of Hobab, Moses' brother-in-law,[h] and pitched his tent by the great tree in Zaanannim near Kedesh.

[12]When they told Sisera that Barak son of Abinoam had gone up to Mount Tabor, [13]Sisera gathered together his nine hundred iron chariots and all the men with him, from Harosheth Haggoyim to the Kishon River.

[14]Then Deborah said to Barak, "Go! This is the day the LORD has given Sisera into your hands. Has not the LORD gone ahead of you?" So Barak went down Mount Tabor, followed by ten thousand men. [15]At Barak's advance, the LORD routed Sisera and all his chariots and army by the sword, and Sisera abandoned his chariot and fled on foot.

a13 That is, Jericho b16 Hebrew *a cubit* (about 0.5 meter) c19 Or *the stone quarries*; also in verse 26
d20 The meaning of the Hebrew for this phrase is uncertain. e23 The meaning of the Hebrew for this word is uncertain.
f4 Traditionally *judging* g9 Or *But on the expedition you are undertaking* h11 Or *father-in-law*

16But Barak pursued the chariots and army as far as Harosheth Haggoyim. All the troops of Sisera fell by the sword; not a man was left.

17Sisera, however, fled on foot to the tent of Jael, the wife of Heber the Kenite, because there were friendly relations between Jabin king of Hazor and the clan of Heber the Kenite.

18Jael went out to meet Sisera and said to him, "Come, my lord, come right in. Don't be afraid." So he entered her tent, and she put a covering over him.

19"I'm thirsty," he said. "Please give me some water." She opened a skin of milk, gave him a drink, and covered him up.

20"Stand in the doorway of the tent," he told her. "If someone comes by and asks you, 'Is anyone here?' say 'No.'"

21But Jael, Heber's wife, picked up a tent peg and a hammer and went quietly to him while he lay fast asleep, exhausted. She drove the peg through his temple into the ground, and he died.

22Barak came by in pursuit of Sisera, and Jael went out to meet him. "Come," she said, "I will show you the man you're looking for." So he went in with her, and there lay Sisera with the tent peg through his temple—dead.

23On that day God subdued Jabin, the Canaanite king, before the Israelites. 24And the hand of the Israelites grew stronger and stronger against Jabin, the Canaanite king, until they destroyed him.

The Song of Deborah

5 On that day Deborah and Barak son of Abinoam sang this song:

2"When the princes in Israel take the lead,
when the people willingly offer
themselves—
praise the LORD!

3"Hear this, you kings! Listen, you rulers!
I will sing to[a] the LORD, I will sing;
I will make music to[b] the LORD, the God
of Israel.

4"O LORD, when you went out from Seir,
when you marched from the land of Edom,
the earth shook, the heavens poured,
the clouds poured down water.
5The mountains quaked before the LORD, the
One of Sinai,
before the LORD, the God of Israel.

6"In the days of Shamgar son of Anath,
in the days of Jael, the roads were
abandoned;
travelers took to winding paths.
7Village life[c] in Israel ceased,
ceased until I,[d] Deborah, arose,
arose a mother in Israel.
8When they chose new gods,
war came to the city gates,
and not a shield or spear was seen
among forty thousand in Israel.
9My heart is with Israel's princes,
with the willing volunteers among the
people.
Praise the LORD!

10"You who ride on white donkeys,
sitting on your saddle blankets,
and you who walk along the road,
consider 11the voice of the singers[e] at the
watering places.
They recite the righteous acts of the LORD,
the righteous acts of his warriors[f] in
Israel.

"Then the people of the LORD
went down to the city gates.
12'Wake up, wake up, Deborah!
Wake up, wake up, break out in song!
Arise, O Barak!
Take captive your captives, O son of
Abinoam.'

13"Then the men who were left
came down to the nobles;
the people of the LORD
came to me with the mighty.
14Some came from Ephraim, whose roots were
in Amalek;
Benjamin was with the people who
followed you.
From Makir captains came down,
from Zebulun those who bear a
commander's staff.
15The princes of Issachar were with Deborah;
yes, Issachar was with Barak,
rushing after him into the valley.
In the districts of Reuben
there was much searching of heart.
16Why did you stay among the campfires[g]
to hear the whistling for the flocks?
In the districts of Reuben
there was much searching of heart.
17Gilead stayed beyond the Jordan.
And Dan, why did he linger by the ships?
Asher remained on the coast
and stayed in his coves.
18The people of Zebulun risked their very lives;
so did Naphtali on the heights of the field.

19"Kings came, they fought;
the kings of Canaan fought

a3 Or *of* b3 Or / *with song I will praise* c7 Or *Warriors* d7 Or *you* e11 Or *archers*; the meaning of the Hebrew for this word is uncertain. f11 Or *villagers* g16 Or *saddlebags*

at Taanach by the waters of Megiddo,
but they carried off no silver, no plunder.
20 From the heavens the stars fought,
from their courses they fought against
Sisera.
21 The river Kishon swept them away,
the age-old river, the river Kishon.
March on, my soul; be strong!
22 Then thundered the horses' hoofs—
galloping, galloping go his mighty steeds.
23 'Curse Meroz,' said the angel of the LORD.
'Curse its people bitterly,
because they did not come to help the LORD,
to help the LORD against the mighty.'

24 "Most blessed of women be Jael,
the wife of Heber the Kenite,
most blessed of tent-dwelling women.
25 He asked for water, and she gave him milk;
in a bowl fit for nobles she brought him
curdled milk.
26 Her hand reached for the tent peg,
her right hand for the workman's hammer.
She struck Sisera, she crushed his head,
she shattered and pierced his temple.
27 At her feet he sank,
he fell; there he lay.
At her feet he sank, he fell;
where he sank, there he fell—dead.

28 "Through the window peered Sisera's
mother;
behind the lattice she cried out,
'Why is his chariot so long in coming?
Why is the clatter of his chariots delayed?'
29 The wisest of her ladies answer her;
indeed, she keeps saying to herself,
30 'Are they not finding and dividing the spoils:
a girl or two for each man,
colorful garments as plunder for Sisera,
colorful garments embroidered,
highly embroidered garments for my
neck—
all this as plunder?'

31 "So may all your enemies perish, O LORD!
But may they who love you be like the
sun
when it rises in its strength."

Then the land had peace forty years.

Gideon

6 Again the Israelites did evil in the eyes of the
LORD, and for seven years he gave them into
the hands of the Midianites. 2 Because the power
of Midian was so oppressive, the Israelites prepared shelters for themselves in mountain clefts,
caves and strongholds. 3 Whenever the Israelites
planted their crops, the Midianites, Amalekites
and other eastern peoples invaded the country.
4 They camped on the land and ruined the crops
all the way to Gaza and did not spare a living
thing for Israel, neither sheep nor cattle nor donkeys. 5 They came up with their livestock and
their tents like swarms of locusts. It was impossible to count the men and their camels; they invaded the land to ravage it. 6 Midian so impover-
ished the Israelites that they cried out to the
LORD for help.

7 When the Israelites cried to the LORD because
of Midian, 8 he sent them a prophet, who said,
"This is what the LORD, the God of Israel, says: I
brought you up out of Egypt, out of the land of
slavery. 9 I snatched you from the power of Egypt
and from the hand of all your oppressors. I drove
them from before you and gave you their land. 10 I
said to you, 'I am the LORD your God; do not
worship the gods of the Amorites, in whose land
you live.' But you have not listened to me."

11 The angel of the LORD came and sat down
under the oak in Ophrah that belonged to Joash
the Abiezrite, where his son Gideon was threshing wheat in a winepress to keep it from the
Midianites. 12 When the angel of the LORD appeared to Gideon, he said, "The LORD is with
you, mighty warrior."

13 "But sir," Gideon replied, "if the LORD is
with us, why has all this happened to us? Where
are all his wonders that our fathers told us about
when they said, 'Did not the LORD bring us up
out of Egypt?' But now the LORD has abandoned
us and put us into the hand of Midian."

14 The LORD turned to him and said, "Go in the
strength you have and save Israel out of Midian's
hand. Am I not sending you?"

15 "But Lord,[a]" Gideon asked, "how can I
save Israel? My clan is the weakest in Manasseh,
and I am the least in my family."

16 The LORD answered, "I will be with you, and
you will strike down all the Midianites together."

17 Gideon replied, "If now I have found favor in
your eyes, give me a sign that it is really you
talking to me. 18 Please do not go away until I
come back and bring my offering and set it before
you."

And the LORD said, "I will wait until you return."

19 Gideon went in, prepared a young goat, and
from an ephah[b] of flour he made bread without
yeast. Putting the meat in a basket and its broth
in a pot, he brought them out and offered them
to him under the oak.

20 The angel of God said to him, "Take the
meat and the unleavened bread, place them on

[a] 15 Or *sir* [b] 19 That is, probably about 3/5 bushel (about 22 liters)

this rock, and pour out the broth." And Gideon did so. 21With the tip of the staff that was in his hand, the angel of the LORD touched the meat and the unleavened bread. Fire flared from the rock, consuming the meat and the bread. And the angel of the LORD disappeared. 22When Gideon realized that it was the angel of the LORD, he exclaimed, "Ah, Sovereign LORD! I have seen the angel of the LORD face to face!"

23But the LORD said to him, "Peace! Do not be afraid. You are not going to die."

24So Gideon built an altar to the LORD there and called it The LORD is Peace. To this day it stands in Ophrah of the Abiezrites.

25That same night the LORD said to him, "Take the second bull from your father's herd, the one seven years old.[a] Tear down your father's altar to Baal and cut down the Asherah pole[b] beside it. 26Then build a proper kind of[c] altar to the LORD your God on the top of this height. Using the wood of the Asherah pole that you cut down, offer the second[d] bull as a burnt offering."

27So Gideon took ten of his servants and did as the LORD told him. But because he was afraid of his family and the men of the town, he did it at night rather than in the daytime.

28In the morning when the men of the town got up, there was Baal's altar, demolished, with the Asherah pole beside it cut down and the second bull sacrificed on the newly built altar!

29They asked each other, "Who did this?"

When they carefully investigated, they were told, "Gideon son of Joash did it."

30The men of the town demanded of Joash, "Bring out your son. He must die, because he has broken down Baal's altar and cut down the Asherah pole beside it."

31But Joash replied to the hostile crowd around him, "Are you going to plead Baal's cause? Are you trying to save him? Whoever fights for him shall be put to death by morning! If Baal really is a god, he can defend himself when someone breaks down his altar." 32So that day they called Gideon "Jerub-Baal,[e]" saying, "Let Baal contend with him," because he broke down Baal's altar.

33Now all the Midianites, Amalekites and other eastern peoples joined forces and crossed over the Jordan and camped in the Valley of Jezreel. 34Then the Spirit of the LORD came upon Gideon, and he blew a trumpet, summoning the Abiezrites to follow him. 35He sent messengers throughout Manasseh, calling them to arms, and also into Asher, Zebulun and Naphtali, so that they too went up to meet them.

36Gideon said to God, "If you will save Israel by my hand as you have promised— 37look, I will place a wool fleece on the threshing floor. If there is dew only on the fleece and all the ground is dry, then I will know that you will save Israel by my hand, as you said." 38And that is what happened. Gideon rose early the next day; he squeezed the fleece and wrung out the dew—a bowlful of water.

39Then Gideon said to God, "Do not be angry with me. Let me make just one more request. Allow me one more test with the fleece. This time make the fleece dry and the ground covered with dew." 40That night God did so. Only the fleece was dry; all the ground was covered with dew.

Gideon Defeats the Midianites

7 Early in the morning, Jerub-Baal (that is, Gideon) and all his men camped at the spring of Harod. The camp of Midian was north of them in the valley near the hill of Moreh. 2The LORD said to Gideon, "You have too many men for me to deliver Midian into their hands. In order that Israel may not boast against me that her own strength has saved her, 3announce now to the people, 'Anyone who trembles with fear may turn back and leave Mount Gilead.'" So twenty-two thousand men left, while ten thousand remained.

4But the LORD said to Gideon, "There are still too many men. Take them down to the water, and I will sift them for you there. If I say, 'This one shall go with you,' he shall go; but if I say, 'This one shall not go with you,' he shall not go."

5So Gideon took the men down to the water. There the LORD told him, "Separate those who lap the water with their tongues like a dog from those who kneel down to drink." 6Three hundred men lapped with their hands to their mouths. All the rest got down on their knees to drink.

7The LORD said to Gideon, "With the three hundred men that lapped I will save you and give the Midianites into your hands. Let all the other men go, each to his own place." 8So Gideon sent the rest of the Israelites to their tents but kept the three hundred, who took over the provisions and trumpets of the others.

Now the camp of Midian lay below him in the valley. 9During that night the LORD said to Gideon, "Get up, go down against the camp, because I am going to give it into your hands. 10If you are afraid to attack, go down to the camp with your servant Purah 11and listen to what they are say-

[a]25 Or *Take a full-grown, mature bull from your father's herd* [b]25 That is, a symbol of the goddess Asherah; here and elsewhere in Judges [c]26 Or *build with layers of stone an* [d]26 Or *full-grown*; also in verse 28 [e]32 *Jerub-Baal* means *let Baal contend.*

ing. Afterward, you will be encouraged to attack
the camp." So he and Purah his servant went
down to the outposts of the camp. 12The Midianites, the Amalekites and all the other eastern peoples had settled in the valley, thick as locusts.
Their camels could no more be counted than the
sand on the seashore.

JUDGES 7:1–25

1. What is the biggest "upset victory" you can recall?
2. Do you usually root for the favored team or the underdog?
3. How would you feel if you had been Gideon when God asked him to cut his army down to 300?
4. What was God trying to prove when he asked Gideon to cut down his army?
5. In your school, what is the spiritual battle where you feel the forces of God are outnumbered?
6. In your own life what is a battle you face?
7. How can this group pray for you this week?

13Gideon arrived just as a man was telling a
friend his dream. "I had a dream," he was saying.
"A round loaf of barley bread came tumbling into
the Midianite camp. It struck the tent with such
force that the tent overturned and collapsed."
14His friend responded, "This can be nothing
other than the sword of Gideon son of Joash, the
Israelite. God has given the Midianites and the
whole camp into his hands."
15When Gideon heard the dream and its interpretation, he worshiped God. He returned to the
camp of Israel and called out, "Get up! The LORD
has given the Midianite camp into your hands."
16Dividing the three hundred men into three
companies, he placed trumpets and empty jars in
the hands of all of them, with torches inside.
17"Watch me," he told them. "Follow my lead.
When I get to the edge of the camp, do exactly as
I do. 18When I and all who are with me blow our
trumpets, then from all around the camp blow
yours and shout, 'For the LORD and for Gideon.' "
19Gideon and the hundred men with him
reached the edge of the camp at the beginning of
the middle watch, just after they had changed the
guard. They blew their trumpets and broke the
jars that were in their hands. 20The three companies blew the trumpets and smashed the jars.
Grasping the torches in their left hands and holding in their right hands the trumpets they were to
blow, they shouted, "A sword for the LORD and
for Gideon!" 21While each man held his position
around the camp, all the Midianites ran, crying
out as they fled.
22When the three hundred trumpets sounded,
the LORD caused the men throughout the camp to
turn on each other with their swords. The army
fled to Beth Shittah toward Zererah as far as the
border of Abel Meholah near Tabbath. 23Israel-
ites from Naphtali, Asher and all Manasseh were
called out, and they pursued the Midianites.
24Gideon sent messengers throughout the hill
country of Ephraim, saying, "Come down against
the Midianites and seize the waters of the Jordan
ahead of them as far as Beth Barah."
So all the men of Ephraim were called out and
they took the waters of the Jordan as far as Beth
Barah. 25They also captured two of the Midianite
leaders, Oreb and Zeeb. They killed Oreb at the
rock of Oreb, and Zeeb at the winepress of Zeeb.
They pursued the Midianites and brought the
heads of Oreb and Zeeb to Gideon, who was by
the Jordan.

Zebah and Zalmunna

8 Now the Ephraimites asked Gideon, "Why
have you treated us like this? Why didn't you
call us when you went to fight Midian?" And they
criticized him sharply.

Rather reluctantly, Gideon has accepted God's call to lead Israel against her oppressors—the Midianites.

7:1–8 As supreme commander of Israel, the Lord reduced the army so that Israel would know that the victory was by his power, not theirs. The apostle Paul recognized that God's grace and power are made perfect in human weakness. "For when I am weak, then I am strong" (2 Cor. 12:7–10).

7:3 ***may turn back.*** Those who were afraid to fight the Lord's battle were not to go out with his army so that they would not demoralize the others (Deut. 20:8).

7:6 ***lapped.*** The 300 remained on their feet, prepared for any emergency.

7:8–14 God provided Gideon with encouraging intelligence information for the battle.

7:13–14 Revelations by dreams are frequently mentioned in the OT. This, however, is an unusual instance in which both the dreamer and the interpreter are non-Israelites. ***round loaf of barley.*** Since barley was considered an inferior grain and only half the value of wheat, it is a fitting symbol for Israel, which was inferior in numbers.

7:22–23 ***three hundred trumpets.*** Normally only a comparatively small number of men in an army carried trumpets. ***turn on each other.*** The Midianites believed the enemy had entered their camp. ***were called out.*** Encouraged by the turn of events, many of those who had left now joined the battle.

2But he answered them, "What have I accomplished compared to you? Aren't the gleanings of
Ephraim's grapes better than the full grape harvest of Abiezer? 3God gave Oreb and Zeeb, the
Midianite leaders, into your hands. What was I
able to do compared to you?" At this, their resentment against him subsided.

4Gideon and his three hundred men, exhausted yet keeping up the pursuit, came to the Jordan
and crossed it. 5He said to the men of Succoth,
"Give my troops some bread; they are worn out,
and I am still pursuing Zebah and Zalmunna, the
kings of Midian."

6But the officials of Succoth said, "Do you already have the hands of Zebah and Zalmunna in
your possession? Why should we give bread to
your troops?"

7Then Gideon replied, "Just for that, when the
LORD has given Zebah and Zalmunna into my
hand, I will tear your flesh with desert thorns and
briers."

8From there he went up to Peniel[a] and made
the same request of them, but they answered as
the men of Succoth had. 9So he said to the men
of Peniel, "When I return in triumph, I will tear
down this tower."

10Now Zebah and Zalmunna were in Karkor
with a force of about fifteen thousand men, all
that were left of the armies of the eastern peoples; a hundred and twenty thousand swordsmen
had fallen. 11Gideon went up by the route of the
nomads east of Nobah and Jogbehah and fell upon
the unsuspecting army. 12Zebah and Zalmunna,
the two kings of Midian, fled, but he pursued
them and captured them, routing their entire
army.

13Gideon son of Joash then returned from the
battle by the Pass of Heres. 14He caught a young
man of Succoth and questioned him, and the
young man wrote down for him the names of the
seventy-seven officials of Succoth, the elders of
the town. 15Then Gideon came and said to the
men of Succoth, "Here are Zebah and Zalmunna,
about whom you taunted me by saying, 'Do you
already have the hands of Zebah and Zalmunna in
your possession? Why should we give bread to
your exhausted men?' " 16He took the elders of
the town and taught the men of Succoth a lesson
by punishing them with desert thorns and briers.
17He also pulled down the tower of Peniel and
killed the men of the town.

18Then he asked Zebah and Zalmunna, "What
kind of men did you kill at Tabor?"

"Men like you," they answered, "each one
with the bearing of a prince."

19Gideon replied, "Those were my brothers,
the sons of my own mother. As surely as the
LORD lives, if you had spared their lives, I would
not kill you." 20Turning to Jether, his oldest son,
he said, "Kill them!" But Jether did not draw his
sword, because he was only a boy and was afraid.

21Zebah and Zalmunna said, "Come, do it
yourself. 'As is the man, so is his strength.' " So
Gideon stepped forward and killed them, and
took the ornaments off their camels' necks.

Gideon's Ephod

22The Israelites said to Gideon, "Rule over
us—you, your son and your grandson—because
you have saved us out of the hand of Midian."

23But Gideon told them, "I will not rule over
you, nor will my son rule over you. The LORD will
rule over you." 24And he said, "I do have one
request, that each of you give me an earring from
your share of the plunder." (It was the custom of
the Ishmaelites to wear gold earrings.)

25They answered, "We'll be glad to give
them." So they spread out a garment, and each
man threw a ring from his plunder onto it. 26The
weight of the gold rings he asked for came to
seventeen hundred shekels,[b] not counting the
ornaments, the pendants and the purple garments worn by the kings of Midian or the chains
that were on their camels' necks. 27Gideon made
the gold into an ephod, which he placed in Ophrah, his town. All Israel prostituted themselves
by worshiping it there, and it became a snare to
Gideon and his family.

Gideon's Death

28Thus Midian was subdued before the Israelites and did not raise its head again. During Gideon's lifetime, the land enjoyed peace forty years.

29Jerub-Baal son of Joash went back home to
live. 30He had seventy sons of his own, for he had
many wives. 31His concubine, who lived in Shechem, also bore him a son, whom he named
Abimelech. 32Gideon son of Joash died at a good
old age and was buried in the tomb of his father
Joash in Ophrah of the Abiezrites.

33No sooner had Gideon died than the Israelites again prostituted themselves to the Baals.
They set up Baal-Berith as their god and 34did not
remember the LORD their God, who had rescued
them from the hands of all their enemies on every side. 35They also failed to show kindness to
the family of Jerub-Baal (that is, Gideon) for all
the good things he had done for them.

Abimelech

9 Abimelech son of Jerub-Baal went to his
mother's brothers in Shechem and said to
them and to all his mother's clan, 2"Ask all the
citizens of Shechem, 'Which is better for you: to

[a]8 Hebrew *Penuel,* a variant of *Peniel*; also in verses 9 and 17

[b]26 That is, about 43 pounds (about 19.5 kilograms)

have all seventy of Jerub-Baal's sons rule over
you, or just one man?' Remember, I am your flesh
and blood."
3When the brothers repeated all this to the
citizens of Shechem, they were inclined to follow
Abimelech, for they said, "He is our brother."
4They gave him seventy shekels[a] of silver from
the temple of Baal-Berith, and Abimelech used it
to hire reckless adventurers, who became his followers. 5He went to his father's home in Ophrah
and on one stone murdered his seventy brothers,
the sons of Jerub-Baal. But Jotham, the youngest
son of Jerub-Baal, escaped by hiding. 6Then all
the citizens of Shechem and Beth Millo gathered
beside the great tree at the pillar in Shechem to
crown Abimelech king.
7When Jotham was told about this, he climbed
up on the top of Mount Gerizim and shouted to
them, "Listen to me, citizens of Shechem, so that
God may listen to you. 8One day the trees went
out to anoint a king for themselves. They said to
the olive tree, 'Be our king.'
9"But the olive tree answered, 'Should I give
up my oil, by which both gods and men are honored, to hold sway over the trees?'
10"Next, the trees said to the fig tree, 'Come
and be our king.'
11"But the fig tree replied, 'Should I give up
my fruit, so good and sweet, to hold sway over
the trees?'
12"Then the trees said to the vine, 'Come and
be our king.'
13"But the vine answered, 'Should I give up
my wine, which cheers both gods and men, to
hold sway over the trees?'
14"Finally all the trees said to the thornbush,
'Come and be our king.'
15"The thornbush said to the trees, 'If you
really want to anoint me king over you, come and
take refuge in my shade; but if not, then let fire
come out of the thornbush and consume the cedars of Lebanon!'
16"Now if you have acted honorably and in
good faith when you made Abimelech king, and
if you have been fair to Jerub-Baal and his family,
and if you have treated him as he deserves—
17and to think that my father fought for you,
risked his life to rescue you from the hand of
Midian 18(but today you have revolted against my
father's family, murdered his seventy sons on a
single stone, and made Abimelech, the son of his
slave girl, king over the citizens of Shechem because he is your brother)— 19if then you have
acted honorably and in good faith toward Jerub-
Baal and his family today, may Abimelech be your
joy, and may you be his, too! 20But if you have
not, let fire come out from Abimelech and consume you, citizens of Shechem and Beth Millo,
and let fire come out from you, citizens of Shechem and Beth Millo, and consume Abimelech!"
21Then Jotham fled, escaping to Beer, and he
lived there because he was afraid of his brother
Abimelech.
22After Abimelech had governed Israel three
years, 23God sent an evil spirit between Abimelech and the citizens of Shechem, who acted
treacherously against Abimelech. 24God did this
in order that the crime against Jerub-Baal's seventy sons, the shedding of their blood, might be
avenged on their brother Abimelech and on the
citizens of Shechem, who had helped him murder his brothers. 25In opposition to him these
citizens of Shechem set men on the hilltops to
ambush and rob everyone who passed by, and
this was reported to Abimelech.
26Now Gaal son of Ebed moved with his brothers into Shechem, and its citizens put their confidence in him. 27After they had gone out into the
fields and gathered the grapes and trodden them,
they held a festival in the temple of their god.
While they were eating and drinking, they cursed
Abimelech. 28Then Gaal son of Ebed said, "Who
is Abimelech, and who is Shechem, that we
should be subject to him? Isn't he Jerub-Baal's
son, and isn't Zebul his deputy? Serve the men of
Hamor, Shechem's father! Why should we serve
Abimelech? 29If only this people were under my
command! Then I would get rid of him. I would
say to Abimelech, 'Call out your whole army!'"[b]
30When Zebul the governor of the city heard
what Gaal son of Ebed said, he was very angry.
31Under cover he sent messengers to Abimelech,
saying, "Gaal son of Ebed and his brothers have
come to Shechem and are stirring up the city
against you. 32Now then, during the night you
and your men should come and lie in wait in
the fields. 33In the morning at sunrise, advance
against the city. When Gaal and his men come
out against you, do whatever your hand finds
to do."
34So Abimelech and all his troops set out by
night and took up concealed positions near Shechem in four companies. 35Now Gaal son of Ebed
had gone out and was standing at the entrance to
the city gate just as Abimelech and his soldiers
came out from their hiding place.
36When Gaal saw them, he said to Zebul,
"Look, people are coming down from the tops of
the mountains!"
Zebul replied, "You mistake the shadows of
the mountains for men."
37But Gaal spoke up again: "Look, people are

[a]4 That is, about 1 3/4 pounds (about 0.8 kilogram) [b]29 Septuagint; Hebrew *him." Then he said to Abimelech, "Call out your whole army!"*

coming down from the center of the land, and
a company is coming from the direction of the
soothsayers' tree."

38Then Zebul said to him, "Where is your big
talk now, you who said, 'Who is Abimelech that
we should be subject to him?' Aren't these the
men you ridiculed? Go out and fight them!"

39So Gaal led out[a] the citizens of Shechem
and fought Abimelech. 40Abimelech chased him,
and many fell wounded in the flight—all the way
to the entrance to the gate. 41Abimelech stayed
in Arumah, and Zebul drove Gaal and his brothers out of Shechem.

42The next day the people of Shechem went
out to the fields, and this was reported to Abimelech. 43So he took his men, divided them into
three companies and set an ambush in the fields.
When he saw the people coming out of the city,
he rose to attack them. 44Abimelech and the
companies with him rushed forward to a position
at the entrance to the city gate. Then two companies rushed upon those in the fields and struck
them down. 45All that day Abimelech pressed his
attack against the city until he had captured it
and killed its people. Then he destroyed the city
and scattered salt over it.

46On hearing this, the citizens in the tower of
Shechem went into the stronghold of the temple
of El-Berith. 47When Abimelech heard that they
had assembled there, 48he and all his men went
up Mount Zalmon. He took an ax and cut off
some branches, which he lifted to his shoulders.
He ordered the men with him, "Quick! Do what
you have seen me do!" 49So all the men cut
branches and followed Abimelech. They piled
them against the stronghold and set it on fire over
the people inside. So all the people in the tower
of Shechem, about a thousand men and women,
also died.

50Next Abimelech went to Thebez and besieged it and captured it. 51Inside the city, however, was a strong tower, to which all the men
and women—all the people of the city—fled.
They locked themselves in and climbed up on the
tower roof. 52Abimelech went to the tower and
stormed it. But as he approached the entrance to
the tower to set it on fire, 53a woman dropped
an upper millstone on his head and cracked his
skull.

54Hurriedly he called to his armor-bearer,
"Draw your sword and kill me, so that they can't
say, 'A woman killed him.'" So his servant ran
him through, and he died. 55When the Israelites
saw that Abimelech was dead, they went home.

56Thus God repaid the wickedness that Abimelech had done to his father by murdering his seventy brothers. 57God also made the men of Shechem pay for all their wickedness. The curse of
Jotham son of Jerub-Baal came on them.

Tola

10 After the time of Abimelech a man of Issachar, Tola son of Puah, the son of Dodo,
rose to save Israel. He lived in Shamir, in the hill
country of Ephraim. 2He led[b] Israel twenty-
three years; then he died, and was buried in Shamir.

Jair

3He was followed by Jair of Gilead, who led
Israel twenty-two years. 4He had thirty sons, who
rode thirty donkeys. They controlled thirty towns
in Gilead, which to this day are called Havvoth
Jair.[c] 5When Jair died, he was buried in Kamon.

Jephthah

6Again the Israelites did evil in the eyes of the
LORD. They served the Baals and the Ashtoreths,
and the gods of Aram, the gods of Sidon, the gods
of Moab, the gods of the Ammonites and the gods
of the Philistines. And because the Israelites forsook the LORD and no longer served him, 7he
became angry with them. He sold them into the
hands of the Philistines and the Ammonites,
8who that year shattered and crushed them. For
eighteen years they oppressed all the Israelites on
the east side of the Jordan in Gilead, the land of
the Amorites. 9The Ammonites also crossed the
Jordan to fight against Judah, Benjamin and the
house of Ephraim; and Israel was in great distress. 10Then the Israelites cried out to the LORD,
"We have sinned against you, forsaking our God
and serving the Baals."

11The LORD replied, "When the Egyptians, the
Amorites, the Ammonites, the Philistines, 12the
Sidonians, the Amalekites and the Maonites[d]
oppressed you and you cried to me for help, did
I not save you from their hands? 13But you have
forsaken me and served other gods, so I will no
longer save you. 14Go and cry out to the gods you
have chosen. Let them save you when you are in
trouble!"

15But the Israelites said to the LORD, "We have
sinned. Do with us whatever you think best, but
please rescue us now." 16Then they got rid of the
foreign gods among them and served the LORD.
And he could bear Israel's misery no longer.

17When the Ammonites were called to arms
and camped in Gilead, the Israelites assembled
and camped at Mizpah. 18The leaders of the people of Gilead said to each other, "Whoever will

[a]39 Or *Gaal went out in the sight of* [b]2 Traditionally *judged*; also in verse 3 [c]4 Or *called the settlements of Jair*
[d]12 Hebrew; some Septuagint manuscripts *Midianites*

launch the attack against the Ammonites will be
the head of all those living in Gilead."

11 Jephthah the Gileadite was a mighty warrior. His father was Gilead; his mother
was a prostitute. [2]Gilead's wife also bore him
sons, and when they were grown up, they drove
Jephthah away. "You are not going to get any
inheritance in our family," they said, "because
you are the son of another woman." [3]So Jephthah
fled from his brothers and settled in the land of
Tob, where a group of adventurers gathered
around him and followed him.

[4]Some time later, when the Ammonites made
war on Israel, [5]the elders of Gilead went to get
Jephthah from the land of Tob. [6]"Come," they
said, "be our commander, so we can fight the
Ammonites."

[7]Jephthah said to them, "Didn't you hate me
and drive me from my father's house? Why do
you come to me now, when you're in trouble?"

[8]The elders of Gilead said to him, "Nevertheless, we are turning to you now; come with us to
fight the Ammonites, and you will be our head
over all who live in Gilead."

[9]Jephthah answered, "Suppose you take me
back to fight the Ammonites and the LORD gives
them to me—will I really be your head?"

[10]The elders of Gilead replied, "The LORD is
our witness; we will certainly do as you say."
[11]So Jephthah went with the elders of Gilead, and
the people made him head and commander over
them. And he repeated all his words before the
LORD in Mizpah.

[12]Then Jephthah sent messengers to the Ammonite king with the question: "What do you
have against us that you have attacked our country?"

[13]The king of the Ammonites answered Jephthah's messengers, "When Israel came up out of
Egypt, they took away my land from the Arnon to
the Jabbok, all the way to the Jordan. Now give it
back peaceably."

[14]Jephthah sent back messengers to the Ammonite king, [15]saying:

"This is what Jephthah says: Israel did not
take the land of Moab or the land of the
Ammonites. [16]But when they came up out
of Egypt, Israel went through the desert to
the Red Sea[a] and on to Kadesh. [17]Then
Israel sent messengers to the king of Edom,
saying, 'Give us permission to go through
your country,' but the king of Edom would
not listen. They sent also to the king of
Moab, and he refused. So Israel stayed at
Kadesh.

[18]"Next they traveled through the desert,
skirted the lands of Edom and Moab, passed
along the eastern side of the country of
Moab, and camped on the other side of the
Arnon. They did not enter the territory of
Moab, for the Arnon was its border.

[19]"Then Israel sent messengers to Sihon
king of the Amorites, who ruled in Heshbon, and said to him, 'Let us pass through
your country to our own place.' [20]Sihon,
however, did not trust Israel[b] to pass
through his territory. He mustered all his
men and encamped at Jahaz and fought
with Israel.

[21]"Then the LORD, the God of Israel, gave
Sihon and all his men into Israel's hands,
and they defeated them. Israel took over all
the land of the Amorites who lived in that
country, [22]capturing all of it from the Arnon
to the Jabbok and from the desert to the
Jordan.

[23]"Now since the LORD, the God of Israel, has driven the Amorites out before his
people Israel, what right have you to take it
over? [24]Will you not take what your god
Chemosh gives you? Likewise, whatever
the LORD our God has given us, we will
possess. [25]Are you better than Balak son of
Zippor, king of Moab? Did he ever quarrel
with Israel or fight with them? [26]For three
hundred years Israel occupied Heshbon,
Aroer, the surrounding settlements and all
the towns along the Arnon. Why didn't you
retake them during that time? [27]I have not
wronged you, but you are doing me wrong
by waging war against me. Let the LORD, the
Judge,[c] decide the dispute this day between the Israelites and the Ammonites."

[28]The king of Ammon, however, paid no attention to the message Jephthah sent him.

[29]Then the Spirit of the LORD came upon Jephthah. He crossed Gilead and Manasseh, passed
through Mizpah of Gilead, and from there he advanced against the Ammonites. [30]And Jephthah
made a vow to the LORD: "If you give the Ammonites into my hands, [31]whatever comes out of
the door of my house to meet me when I return
in triumph from the Ammonites will be the
LORD's, and I will sacrifice it as a burnt offering."

[32]Then Jephthah went over to fight the Ammonites, and the LORD gave them into his hands.
[33]He devastated twenty towns from Aroer to the
vicinity of Minnith, as far as Abel Keramim. Thus
Israel subdued Ammon.

[34]When Jephthah returned to his home in Mizpah, who should come out to meet him but his

[a]16 Hebrew *Yam Suph*; that is, Sea of Reeds [b]20 Or *however, would not make an agreement for Israel* [c]27 Or *Ruler*

daughter, dancing to the sound of tambourines!
She was an only child. Except for her he had
neither son nor daughter. 35When he saw her, he
tore his clothes and cried, "Oh! My daughter!
You have made me miserable and wretched, because I have made a vow to the LORD that I cannot break."
36"My father," she replied, "you have given
your word to the LORD. Do to me just as you
promised, now that the LORD has avenged you of
your enemies, the Ammonites. 37But grant me
this one request," she said. "Give me two
months to roam the hills and weep with my
friends, because I will never marry."
38"You may go," he said. And he let her go for
two months. She and the girls went into the hills
and wept because she would never marry. 39Af-
ter the two months, she returned to her father
and he did to her as he had vowed. And she was
a virgin.

From this comes the Israelite custom 40that
each year the young women of Israel go out for
four days to commemorate the daughter of Jephthah the Gileadite.

Jephthah and Ephraim

12 The men of Ephraim called out their
forces, crossed over to Zaphon and said to
Jephthah, "Why did you go to fight the Ammonites without calling us to go with you? We're
going to burn down your house over your head."
2Jephthah answered, "I and my people were
engaged in a great struggle with the Ammonites,
and although I called, you didn't save me out of
their hands. 3When I saw that you wouldn't help,
I took my life in my hands and crossed over to
fight the Ammonites, and the LORD gave me the
victory over them. Now why have you come up
today to fight me?"
4Jephthah then called together the men of Gilead and fought against Ephraim. The Gileadites
struck them down because the Ephraimites had
said, "You Gileadites are renegades from Ephraim and Manasseh." 5The Gileadites captured the
fords of the Jordan leading to Ephraim, and whenever a survivor of Ephraim said, "Let me cross
over," the men of Gilead asked him, "Are you an
Ephraimite?" If he replied, "No," 6they said, "All
right, say 'Shibboleth.'" If he said, "Sibboleth,"
because he could not pronounce the word correctly, they seized him and killed him at the fords
of the Jordan. Forty-two thousand Ephraimites
were killed at that time.
7Jephthah led[a] Israel six years. Then Jephthah the Gileadite died, and was buried in a town
in Gilead.

Ibzan, Elon and Abdon

8After him, Ibzan of Bethlehem led Israel. 9He
had thirty sons and thirty daughters. He gave his
daughters away in marriage to those outside his
clan, and for his sons he brought in thirty young
women as wives from outside his clan. Ibzan led
Israel seven years. 10Then Ibzan died, and was
buried in Bethlehem.
11After him, Elon the Zebulunite led Israel ten
years. 12Then Elon died, and was buried in Aijalon in the land of Zebulun.
13After him, Abdon son of Hillel, from Pirathon, led Israel. 14He had forty sons and thirty
grandsons, who rode on seventy donkeys. He led
Israel eight years. 15Then Abdon son of Hillel
died, and was buried at Pirathon in Ephraim, in
the hill country of the Amalekites.

The Birth of Samson

13 Again the Israelites did evil in the eyes of
the LORD, so the LORD delivered them
into the hands of the Philistines for forty years.
2A certain man of Zorah, named Manoah, from
the clan of the Danites, had a wife who was sterile and remained childless. 3The angel of the
LORD appeared to her and said, "You are sterile
and childless, but you are going to conceive and
have a son. 4Now see to it that you drink no wine
or other fermented drink and that you do not eat
anything unclean, 5because you will conceive
and give birth to a son. No razor may be used on
his head, because the boy is to be a Nazirite, set
apart to God from birth, and he will begin the
deliverance of Israel from the hands of the Philistines."
6Then the woman went to her husband and
told him, "A man of God came to me. He looked
like an angel of God, very awesome. I didn't ask
him where he came from, and he didn't tell me
his name. 7But he said to me, 'You will conceive
and give birth to a son. Now then, drink no wine
or other fermented drink and do not eat anything
unclean, because the boy will be a Nazirite of
God from birth until the day of his death.'"
8Then Manoah prayed to the LORD: "O Lord, I
beg you, let the man of God you sent to us come
again to teach us how to bring up the boy who is
to be born."
9God heard Manoah, and the angel of God
came again to the woman while she was out in
the field; but her husband Manoah was not with
her. 10The woman hurried to tell her husband,
"He's here! The man who appeared to me the
other day!"
11Manoah got up and followed his wife. When

[a] 7 Traditionally *judged*; also in verses 8-14

he came to the man, he said, "Are you the one
who talked to my wife?"
"I am," he said.
12So Manoah asked him, "When your words
are fulfilled, what is to be the rule for the boy's
life and work?"
13The angel of the LORD answered, "Your wife
must do all that I have told her. 14She must not
eat anything that comes from the grapevine, nor
drink any wine or other fermented drink nor eat
anything unclean. She must do everything I have
commanded her."
15Manoah said to the angel of the LORD, "We
would like you to stay until we prepare a young
goat for you."
16The angel of the LORD replied, "Even though
you detain me, I will not eat any of your food. But
if you prepare a burnt offering, offer it to the
LORD." (Manoah did not realize that it was the
angel of the LORD.)
17Then Manoah inquired of the angel of the
LORD, "What is your name, so that we may honor
you when your word comes true?"
18He replied, "Why do you ask my name? It is
beyond understanding.[a]" 19Then Manoah took
a young goat, together with the grain offering,
and sacrificed it on a rock to the LORD. And the
LORD did an amazing thing while Manoah and his
wife watched: 20As the flame blazed up from the
altar toward heaven, the angel of the LORD ascended in the flame. Seeing this, Manoah and his
wife fell with their faces to the ground. 21When
the angel of the LORD did not show himself again
to Manoah and his wife, Manoah realized that it
was the angel of the LORD.
22"We are doomed to die!" he said to his wife.
"We have seen God!"
23But his wife answered, "If the LORD had
meant to kill us, he would not have accepted a
burnt offering and grain offering from our hands,
nor shown us all these things or now told us
this."
24The woman gave birth to a boy and named
him Samson. He grew and the LORD blessed him,
25and the Spirit of the LORD began to stir him
while he was in Mahaneh Dan, between Zorah
and Eshtaol.

Samson's Marriage

14 Samson went down to Timnah and saw
there a young Philistine woman. 2When
he returned, he said to his father and mother, "I
have seen a Philistine woman in Timnah; now
get her for me as my wife."
3His father and mother replied, "Isn't there

JUDGES 14:1–20

1. When it comes to dating, do you prefer playing the field, going steady or just being friends?
2. In choosing a date, what is more important: Body build? Looks? Brains? Personality? Bank account?
3. What do you think about the way Samson's mom and dad tried to get involved in Samson's dating decisions (v. 3)?
4. How do your parents feel about the people you date or run around with?
5. What do you do when you discover that a boyfriend or girlfriend is not what you expected them to be?
6. On a scale of 1 (never) to 10 (all the time), how often do you find yourself getting into friendships or dating relationships that are a mistake?
7. When it comes to guarding yourself against bad choices in dating, what could this group do to help you?

[a]18 Or *is wonderful*

Before Samson was born, the Lord told his parents he would be "set apart" and used by God in delivering Israel from the oppression of their enemies the Philistines.

14:1 *young Philistine woman.* The disappointment of Samson's parents (v. 3) is understandable in light of the prohibition against marriage with the peoples of Canaan (Deut. 7:1–4; see Judg. 3:5–6).

14:2 *get her for me.* As the head of the family, the father exercised authority in all matters, often including the choice of wives for his sons (12:9; Gen. 24:1–4).

14:4 *this was from the LORD.* God uses even the sinful weaknesses of men to accomplish his purposes and bring praise to his name (Gen. 50:20; Acts 2:23).

14:12 *riddle.* The use of riddles at special occasions was popular in the ancient world.

14:16 *don't really love me.* Delilah would later use the same tactics to trick Samson (16:15).

14:18 *my heifer.* Samson's wife (see v. 15). Since heifers were not used for plowing, Samson is accusing them of unfairness.

14:19 *Spirit ... came upon him.* Verse 6 also. The Holy Spirit gave Samson incredible strength. God's purposes for Samson included humbling the Philistines (13:5). ***Ashkelon.*** A principal city of the Philistines.

14:20 *friend.* See 15:2; probably the young man who had attended Samson, in all likelihood one of his 30 companions (v. 11).

an acceptable woman among your relatives or
among all our people? Must you go to the uncircumcised Philistines to get a wife?"
But Samson said to his father, "Get her for me.
She's the right one for me." 4(His parents did not
know that this was from the LORD, who was seeking an occasion to confront the Philistines; for at
that time they were ruling over Israel.) 5Samson
went down to Timnah together with his father
and mother. As they approached the vineyards of
Timnah, suddenly a young lion came roaring toward him. 6The Spirit of the LORD came upon
him in power so that he tore the lion apart with
his bare hands as he might have torn a young
goat. But he told neither his father nor his mother what he had done. 7Then he went down and
talked with the woman, and he liked her.
8Some time later, when he went back to marry
her, he turned aside to look at the lion's carcass.
In it was a swarm of bees and some honey,
9which he scooped out with his hands and ate as
he went along. When he rejoined his parents, he
gave them some, and they too ate it. But he did
not tell them that he had taken the honey from
the lion's carcass.
10Now his father went down to see the woman. And Samson made a feast there, as was customary for bridegrooms. 11When he appeared, he
was given thirty companions.
12"Let me tell you a riddle," Samson said to
them. "If you can give me the answer within the
seven days of the feast, I will give you thirty linen
garments and thirty sets of clothes. 13If you can't
tell me the answer, you must give me thirty linen
garments and thirty sets of clothes."
"Tell us your riddle," they said. "Let's
hear it."
14He replied,

"Out of the eater, something to eat;
out of the strong, something sweet."

For three days they could not give the answer.
15On the fourth[a] day, they said to Samson's
wife, "Coax your husband into explaining the
riddle for us, or we will burn you and your father's household to death. Did you invite us here
to rob us?"
16Then Samson's wife threw herself on him,
sobbing, "You hate me! You don't really love me.
You've given my people a riddle, but you haven't
told me the answer."
"I haven't even explained it to my father or
mother," he replied, "so why should I explain it
to you?" 17She cried the whole seven days of the
feast. So on the seventh day he finally told her,
because she continued to press him. She in turn
explained the riddle to her people.
18Before sunset on the seventh day the men of
the town said to him,

"What is sweeter than honey?
What is stronger than a lion?"

Samson said to them,

"If you had not plowed with my heifer,
you would not have solved my riddle."

19Then the Spirit of the LORD came upon him
in power. He went down to Ashkelon, struck
down thirty of their men, stripped them of their
belongings and gave their clothes to those who
had explained the riddle. Burning with anger, he
went up to his father's house. 20And Samson's
wife was given to the friend who had attended
him at his wedding.

Samson's Vengeance on the Philistines

15 Later on, at the time of wheat harvest,
Samson took a young goat and went to
visit his wife. He said, "I'm going to my wife's
room." But her father would not let him go in.
2"I was so sure you thoroughly hated her," he
said, "that I gave her to your friend. Isn't her
younger sister more attractive? Take her instead."
3Samson said to them, "This time I have a
right to get even with the Philistines; I will really
harm them." 4So he went out and caught three
hundred foxes and tied them tail to tail in pairs.
He then fastened a torch to every pair of tails, 5lit
the torches and let the foxes loose in the standing
grain of the Philistines. He burned up the shocks
and standing grain, together with the vineyards
and olive groves.
6When the Philistines asked, "Who did this?"
they were told, "Samson, the Timnite's son-in-
law, because his wife was given to his friend."
So the Philistines went up and burned her and
her father to death. 7Samson said to them, "Since
you've acted like this, I won't stop until I get my
revenge on you." 8He attacked them viciously
and slaughtered many of them. Then he went
down and stayed in a cave in the rock of Etam.
9The Philistines went up and camped in Judah,
spreading out near Lehi. 10The men of Judah
asked, "Why have you come to fight us?"
"We have come to take Samson prisoner,"
they answered, "to do to him as he did to us."
11Then three thousand men from Judah went
down to the cave in the rock of Etam and said to
Samson, "Don't you realize that the Philistines
are rulers over us? What have you done to us?"
He answered, "I merely did to them what they
did to me."

a 15 Some Septuagint manuscripts and Syriac; Hebrew *seventh*

12They said to him, “We’ve come to tie you up
and hand you over to the Philistines.”
Samson said, “Swear to me that you won’t kill
me yourselves.”
13“Agreed,” they answered. “We will only tie
you up and hand you over to them. We will not
kill you.” So they bound him with two new ropes
and led him up from the rock. 14As he approached Lehi, the Philistines came toward him
shouting. The Spirit of the LORD came upon him
in power. The ropes on his arms became like
charred flax, and the bindings dropped from his
hands. 15Finding a fresh jawbone of a donkey, he
grabbed it and struck down a thousand men.
16Then Samson said,

“With a donkey’s jawbone
  I have made donkeys of them.[a]
With a donkey’s jawbone
  I have killed a thousand men.”

17When he finished speaking, he threw away the
jawbone; and the place was called Ramath
Lehi.[b]
18Because he was very thirsty, he cried out to
the LORD, “You have given your servant this great
victory. Must I now die of thirst and fall into
the hands of the uncircumcised?” 19Then God
opened up the hollow place in Lehi, and water
came out of it. When Samson drank, his strength
returned and he revived. So the spring was called
En Hakkore,[c] and it is still there in Lehi.
20Samson led[d] Israel for twenty years in the
days of the Philistines.

Samson and Delilah

16 One day Samson went to Gaza, where he
saw a prostitute. He went in to spend the
night with her. 2The people of Gaza were told,
“Samson is here!” So they surrounded the place
and lay in wait for him all night at the city gate.
They made no move during the night, saying, “At
dawn we’ll kill him.”
3But Samson lay there only until the middle of
the night. Then he got up and took hold of the
doors of the city gate, together with the two
posts, and tore them loose, bar and all. He lifted
them to his shoulders and carried them to the top
of the hill that faces Hebron.
4Some time later, he fell in love with a woman
in the Valley of Sorek whose name was Delilah.
5The rulers of the Philistines went to her and
said, “See if you can lure him into showing you
the secret of his great strength and how we can
overpower him so we may tie him up and subdue
him. Each one of us will give you eleven hundred
shekels[e] of silver.”
6So Delilah said to Samson, “Tell me the secret
of your great strength and how you can be tied up
and subdued.”

JUDGES 16:1–22

1. When was your hair the shortest? Longest? Craziest?
2. How do you feel when a celebrity you admire does things they shouldn’t?
3. Have you ever told someone a personal secret only to discover they have told others? How did you feel?
4. What caused Samson to go back to Delilah again and again, knowing that she would betray him?
5. What was the worst thing that Samson lost: His hair? His eyes? His honor? His lover? His Lord?
6. What one weakness of yours is in danger of taking away your spiritual strength?
7. Spiritually, what are you struggling to overcome? How can this group pray for you?

[a]*16* Or *made a heap or two*; the Hebrew for *donkey* sounds like the Hebrew for *heap.* [b]*17* *Ramath Lehi* means *jawbone hill.* [c]*19* *En Hakkore* means *caller’s spring.* [d]*20* Traditionally *judged* [e]*5* That is, about 28 pounds (about 13 kilograms)

16:1 ***Gaza.*** An important Philistine seaport. ***prostitute.*** While Samson certainly possessed physical strength, he lacked moral strength, which ultimately led to his ruin.

16:2 ***we’ll kill him.*** Samson’s exploits against the Philistines, Israel’s enemy, had incited the Philistines against him.

16:5 ***Delilah.*** Samson is again attracted to a Philistine woman (see ch. 14). ***subdue him.*** The Philistines were not interested in killing him quickly; they sought revenge by a prolonged period of torture. ***eleven hundred shekels.*** A very large amount of money.

16:19–20 ***his strength left him ... the LORD had left him.*** The source of Samson’s strength was ultimately God himself. Having his hair cut off was a violation of Samson’s Nazirite vows (13:5) and a renunciation of the Lord’s visible presence in his life.

16:20 ***he did not know that the LORD had left him.*** One of the most tragic statements in the Bible. Samson was unaware that he had betrayed his calling. He had permitted a Philistine woman to rob him of the sign of his special consecration to the Lord. God’s champion, by his own volition, lay asleep and helpless in the arms of his lover.

16:21 ***gouged out his eyes.*** Brutal treatment of prisoners of war to humiliate and incapacitate them was common. ***to Gaza.*** In shame and weakness, Samson was made to do the lowly labor of grinding grain in the place where he had displayed great strength (vv. 1–3).

7Samson answered her, "If anyone ties me
with seven fresh thongs[a] that have not been
dried, I'll become as weak as any other man."
8Then the rulers of the Philistines brought her
seven fresh thongs that had not been dried, and
she tied him with them. 9With men hidden in
the room, she called to him, "Samson, the Philistines are upon you!" But he snapped the thongs
as easily as a piece of string snaps when it comes
close to a flame. So the secret of his strength was
not discovered.
10Then Delilah said to Samson, "You have
made a fool of me; you lied to me. Come now, tell
me how you can be tied."
11He said, "If anyone ties me securely with
new ropes that have never been used, I'll become
as weak as any other man."
12So Delilah took new ropes and tied him with
them. Then, with men hidden in the room, she
called to him, "Samson, the Philistines are upon
you!" But he snapped the ropes off his arms as if
they were threads.
13Delilah then said to Samson, "Until now,
you have been making a fool of me and lying to
me. Tell me how you can be tied."

He replied, "If you weave the seven braids of
my head into the fabric ⌞on the loom⌟ and tighten
it with the pin, I'll become as weak as any other
man." So while he was sleeping, Delilah took the
seven braids of his head, wove them into the
fabric 14and[b] tightened it with the pin.

Again she called to him, "Samson, the Philistines are upon you!" He awoke from his sleep and
pulled up the pin and the loom, with the fabric.
15Then she said to him, "How can you say, 'I
love you,' when you won't confide in me? This is
the third time you have made a fool of me and
haven't told me the secret of your great
strength." 16With such nagging she prodded him
day after day until he was tired to death.
17So he told her everything. "No razor has
ever been used on my head," he said, "because I
have been a Nazirite set apart to God since birth.
If my head were shaved, my strength would leave
me, and I would become as weak as any other
man."
18When Delilah saw that he had told her everything, she sent word to the rulers of the Philistines, "Come back once more; he has told me
everything." So the rulers of the Philistines returned with the silver in their hands. 19Having put
him to sleep on her lap, she called a man to
shave off the seven braids of his hair, and so
began to subdue him.[c] And his strength left
him.
20Then she called, "Samson, the Philistines are
upon you!"

JUDGES 16:23–31

1. What is the saddest funeral you have attended?
2. Who is the strongest (physically, intellectually, emotionally or spiritually) person you know?
3. What would you say to a little boy who says, "I want to grow up to be like Samson"?
4. Samson had both strengths and weaknesses. What do you see as your greatest strength? Your greatest weakness?
5. How would you describe Samson's life if you had to write his obituary?
6. What do you want to be said about you in your obituary?
7. Like Samson, if you could pray for just one thing to happen, what would that be? Pray as a group.

[a]7 Or *bowstrings*; also in verses 8 and 9 [b]13,14 Some Septuagint manuscripts; Hebrew *"⌞I can⌟ if you weave the seven braids of my head into the fabric ⌞on the loom⌟." 14So she* [c]19 Hebrew; some Septuagint manuscripts *and he began to weaken*

Samson—the great champion of Israel—had been captured by the Philistines, blinded, shackled and relegated to the menial task of grinding grain (16:21).

16:23 ***Dagon.*** Though the Philistines worshiped many Canaanite gods, their most popular deities appear to have been Dagon and Baal-Zebub. ***Our god has delivered.*** It was common to attribute a victory to the national deities. While the Philistines were celebrating, through Samson the Lord was about to halt their false worship.

16:27 ***on the roof.*** The temple complex probably surrounded an open court and had a flat roof where a large number of people had gathered to get a glimpse of the fallen and humiliated champion.

16:30 ***pushed.*** Samson pushed the wooden pillars from their stone bases. Archaeologists have discovered a Philistine temple with a pair of closely spaced pillar bases. ***killed many more.*** Samson previously had slain well over 1,000 people (see 15:15; see also 14:19; 15:8).

16:31 ***led Israel twenty years.*** Samson typifies the nation of Israel—born by special divine provision, consecrated to the Lord from birth and endowed with unique power among his fellowmen. The likeness is even more remarkable in light of his foolish chasing of foreign women, some of ill repute, until he was cleverly subdued by one of them. In this he exemplified Israel, who during the period of the judges constantly prostituted herself to Canaanite gods to her own destruction.

He awoke from his sleep and thought, "I'll go out as before and shake myself free." But he did not know that the LORD had left him.

21 Then the Philistines seized him, gouged out his eyes and took him down to Gaza. Binding him with bronze shackles, they set him to grinding in the prison. 22 But the hair on his head began to grow again after it had been shaved.

The Death of Samson

23 Now the rulers of the Philistines assembled to offer a great sacrifice to Dagon their god and to celebrate, saying, "Our god has delivered Samson, our enemy, into our hands."

24 When the people saw him, they praised their god, saying,

"Our god has delivered our enemy
    into our hands,
the one who laid waste our land
    and multiplied our slain."

25 While they were in high spirits, they shouted, "Bring out Samson to entertain us." So they called Samson out of the prison, and he performed for them.

When they stood him among the pillars, 26 Samson said to the servant who held his hand, "Put me where I can feel the pillars that support the temple, so that I may lean against them." 27 Now the temple was crowded with men and women; all the rulers of the Philistines were there, and on the roof were about three thousand men and women watching Samson perform. 28 Then Samson prayed to the LORD, "O Sovereign LORD, remember me. O God, please strengthen me just once more, and let me with one blow get revenge on the Philistines for my two eyes." 29 Then Samson reached toward the two central pillars on which the temple stood. Bracing himself against them, his right hand on the one and his left hand on the other, 30 Samson said, "Let me die with the Philistines!" Then he pushed with all his might, and down came the temple on the rulers and all the people in it. Thus he killed many more when he died than while he lived.

31 Then his brothers and his father's whole family went down to get him. They brought him back and buried him between Zorah and Eshtaol in the tomb of Manoah his father. He had led[a] Israel twenty years.

Micah's Idols

17 Now a man named Micah from the hill country of Ephraim 2 said to his mother, "The eleven hundred shekels[b] of silver that were taken from you and about which I heard you utter a curse—I have that silver with me; I took it."

Then his mother said, "The LORD bless you, my son!"

3 When he returned the eleven hundred shekels of silver to his mother, she said, "I solemnly consecrate my silver to the LORD for my son to make a carved image and a cast idol. I will give it back to you."

4 So he returned the silver to his mother, and she took two hundred shekels[c] of silver and gave them to a silversmith, who made them into the image and the idol. And they were put in Micah's house.

5 Now this man Micah had a shrine, and he made an ephod and some idols and installed one of his sons as his priest. 6 In those days Israel had no king; everyone did as he saw fit.

7 A young Levite from Bethlehem in Judah, who had been living within the clan of Judah, 8 left that town in search of some other place to stay. On his way[d] he came to Micah's house in the hill country of Ephraim.

9 Micah asked him, "Where are you from?"

"I'm a Levite from Bethlehem in Judah," he said, "and I'm looking for a place to stay."

10 Then Micah said to him, "Live with me and be my father and priest, and I'll give you ten shekels[e] of silver a year, your clothes and your food." 11 So the Levite agreed to live with him, and the young man was to him like one of his sons. 12 Then Micah installed the Levite, and the young man became his priest and lived in his house. 13 And Micah said, "Now I know that the LORD will be good to me, since this Levite has become my priest."

Danites Settle in Laish

18 In those days Israel had no king. And in those days the tribe of the Danites was seeking a place of their own where they might settle, because they had not yet come into an inheritance among the tribes of Israel. 2 So the Danites sent five warriors from Zorah and Eshtaol to spy out the land and explore it. These men represented all their clans. They told them, "Go, explore the land."

The men entered the hill country of Ephraim and came to the house of Micah, where they spent the night. 3 When they were near Micah's house, they recognized the voice of the young Levite; so they turned in there and asked him, "Who brought you here? What are you doing in this place? Why are you here?"

[a] 31 Traditionally *judged* [b] 2 That is, about 28 pounds (about 13 kilograms) [c] 4 That is, about 5 pounds (about 2.3 kilograms)
[d] 8 Or *To carry on his profession* [e] 10 That is, about 4 ounces (about 110 grams)

4 He told them what Micah had done for him, and said, "He has hired me and I am his priest."

5 Then they said to him, "Please inquire of God to learn whether our journey will be successful."

6 The priest answered them, "Go in peace. Your journey has the LORD's approval."

7 So the five men left and came to Laish, where they saw that the people were living in safety, like the Sidonians, unsuspecting and secure. And since their land lacked nothing, they were prosperous.[a] Also, they lived a long way from the Sidonians and had no relationship with anyone else.[b]

8 When they returned to Zorah and Eshtaol, their brothers asked them, "How did you find things?"

9 They answered, "Come on, let's attack them! We have seen that the land is very good. Aren't you going to do something? Don't hesitate to go there and take it over. 10 When you get there, you will find an unsuspecting people and a spacious land that God has put into your hands, a land that lacks nothing whatever."

11 Then six hundred men from the clan of the Danites, armed for battle, set out from Zorah and Eshtaol. 12 On their way they set up camp near Kiriath Jearim in Judah. This is why the place west of Kiriath Jearim is called Mahaneh Dan[c] to this day. 13 From there they went on to the hill country of Ephraim and came to Micah's house.

14 Then the five men who had spied out the land of Laish said to their brothers, "Do you know that one of these houses has an ephod, other household gods, a carved image and a cast idol? Now you know what to do." 15 So they turned in there and went to the house of the young Levite at Micah's place and greeted him. 16 The six hundred Danites, armed for battle, stood at the entrance to the gate. 17 The five men who had spied out the land went inside and took the carved image, the ephod, the other household gods and the cast idol while the priest and the six hundred armed men stood at the entrance to the gate.

18 When these men went into Micah's house and took the carved image, the ephod, the other household gods and the cast idol, the priest said to them, "What are you doing?"

19 They answered him, "Be quiet! Don't say a word. Come with us, and be our father and priest. Isn't it better that you serve a tribe and clan in Israel as priest rather than just one man's household?" 20 Then the priest was glad. He took the ephod, the other household gods and the carved image and went along with the people. 21 Putting their little children, their livestock and their possessions in front of them, they turned away and left.

22 When they had gone some distance from Micah's house, the men who lived near Micah were called together and overtook the Danites. 23 As they shouted after them, the Danites turned and said to Micah, "What's the matter with you that you called out your men to fight?"

24 He replied, "You took the gods I made, and my priest, and went away. What else do I have? How can you ask, 'What's the matter with you?' "

25 The Danites answered, "Don't argue with us, or some hot-tempered men will attack you, and you and your family will lose your lives." 26 So the Danites went their way, and Micah, seeing that they were too strong for him, turned around and went back home.

27 Then they took what Micah had made, and his priest, and went on to Laish, against a peaceful and unsuspecting people. They attacked them with the sword and burned down their city. 28 There was no one to rescue them because they lived a long way from Sidon and had no relationship with anyone else. The city was in a valley near Beth Rehob.

The Danites rebuilt the city and settled there. 29 They named it Dan after their forefather Dan, who was born to Israel—though the city used to be called Laish. 30 There the Danites set up for themselves the idols, and Jonathan son of Gershom, the son of Moses,[d] and his sons were priests for the tribe of Dan until the time of the captivity of the land. 31 They continued to use the idols Micah had made, all the time the house of God was in Shiloh.

A Levite and His Concubine

19 In those days Israel had no king. Now a Levite who lived in a remote area in the hill country of Ephraim took a concubine from Bethlehem in Judah. 2 But she was unfaithful to him. She left him and went back to her father's house in Bethlehem, Judah. After she had been there four months, 3 her husband went to her to persuade her to return. He had with him his servant and two donkeys. She took him into her father's house, and when her father saw him, he gladly welcomed him. 4 His father-in-law, the girl's father, prevailed upon him to stay; so he remained with him three days, eating and drinking, and sleeping there.

5 On the fourth day they got up early and he prepared to leave, but the girl's father said to his son-in-law, "Refresh yourself with something to

[a] 7 The meaning of the Hebrew for this clause is uncertain. [b] 7 Hebrew; some Septuagint manuscripts *with the Arameans*
[c] 12 *Mahaneh Dan* means *Dan's camp.* [d] 30 An ancient Hebrew scribal tradition, some Septuagint manuscripts and Vulgate; Masoretic Text *Manasseh*

eat; then you can go." 6So the two of them sat
down to eat and drink together. Afterward the
girl's father said, "Please stay tonight and enjoy
yourself." 7And when the man got up to go, his
father-in-law persuaded him, so he stayed there
that night. 8On the morning of the fifth day,
when he rose to go, the girl's father said, "Refresh yourself. Wait till afternoon!" So the two of
them ate together.
9Then when the man, with his concubine and
his servant, got up to leave, his father-in-law, the
girl's father, said, "Now look, it's almost evening.
Spend the night here; the day is nearly over. Stay
and enjoy yourself. Early tomorrow morning you
can get up and be on your way home." 10But,
unwilling to stay another night, the man left and
went toward Jebus (that is, Jerusalem), with his
two saddled donkeys and his concubine.
11When they were near Jebus and the day was
almost gone, the servant said to his master,
"Come, let's stop at this city of the Jebusites and
spend the night."
12His master replied, "No. We won't go into
an alien city, whose people are not Israelites. We
will go on to Gibeah." 13He added, "Come, let's
try to reach Gibeah or Ramah and spend the
night in one of those places." 14So they went on,
and the sun set as they neared Gibeah in Benjamin. 15There they stopped to spend the night.
They went and sat in the city square, but no one
took them into his home for the night.
16That evening an old man from the hill country of Ephraim, who was living in Gibeah (the
men of the place were Benjamites), came in from
his work in the fields. 17When he looked and saw
the traveler in the city square, the old man asked,
"Where are you going? Where did you come
from?"
18He answered, "We are on our way from
Bethlehem in Judah to a remote area in the hill
country of Ephraim where I live. I have been to
Bethlehem in Judah and now I am going to the
house of the LORD. No one has taken me into his
house. 19We have both straw and fodder for our
donkeys and bread and wine for ourselves your
servants—me, your maidservant, and the young
man with us. We don't need anything."
20"You are welcome at my house," the old
man said. "Let me supply whatever you need.
Only don't spend the night in the square." 21So
he took him into his house and fed his donkeys.
After they had washed their feet, they had something to eat and drink.
22While they were enjoying themselves, some
of the wicked men of the city surrounded the
house. Pounding on the door, they shouted to the
old man who owned the house, "Bring out
the man who came to your house so we can have
sex with him."
23The owner of the house went outside and
said to them, "No, my friends, don't be so vile.
Since this man is my guest, don't do this disgraceful thing. 24Look, here is my virgin daughter, and
his concubine. I will bring them out to you now,
and you can use them and do to them whatever
you wish. But to this man, don't do such a disgraceful thing."
25But the men would not listen to him. So the
man took his concubine and sent her outside to
them, and they raped her and abused her
throughout the night, and at dawn they let her
go. 26At daybreak the woman went back to the
house where her master was staying, fell down at
the door and lay there until daylight.
27When her master got up in the morning and
opened the door of the house and stepped out to
continue on his way, there lay his concubine,
fallen in the doorway of the house, with her
hands on the threshold. 28He said to her, "Get
up; let's go." But there was no answer. Then the
man put her on his donkey and set out for home.
29When he reached home, he took a knife and
cut up his concubine, limb by limb, into twelve
parts and sent them into all the areas of Israel.
30Everyone who saw it said, "Such a thing has
never been seen or done, not since the day the
Israelites came up out of Egypt. Think about it!
Consider it! Tell us what to do!"

Israelites Fight the Benjamites

20 Then all the Israelites from Dan to Beersheba and from the land of Gilead came
out as one man and assembled before the LORD
in Mizpah. 2The leaders of all the people of the
tribes of Israel took their places in the assembly
of the people of God, four hundred thousand soldiers armed with swords. 3(The Benjamites heard
that the Israelites had gone up to Mizpah.) Then
the Israelites said, "Tell us how this awful thing
happened."
4So the Levite, the husband of the murdered
woman, said, "I and my concubine came to Gibeah in Benjamin to spend the night. 5During the
night the men of Gibeah came after me and surrounded the house, intending to kill me. They
raped my concubine, and she died. 6I took my
concubine, cut her into pieces and sent one piece
to each region of Israel's inheritance, because
they committed this lewd and disgraceful act in
Israel. 7Now, all you Israelites, speak up and give
your verdict."
8All the people rose as one man, saying, "None
of us will go home. No, not one of us will return
to his house. 9But now this is what we'll do to
Gibeah: We'll go up against it as the lot directs.
10We'll take ten men out of every hundred from
all the tribes of Israel, and a hundred from a thousand, and a thousand from ten thousand, to get

provisions for the army. Then, when the army
arrives at Gibeah[a] in Benjamin, it can give them
what they deserve for all this vileness done in
Israel." 11So all the men of Israel got together and
united as one man against the city.

12The tribes of Israel sent men throughout the
tribe of Benjamin, saying, "What about this awful
crime that was committed among you? 13Now
surrender those wicked men of Gibeah so that
we may put them to death and purge the evil
from Israel."

But the Benjamites would not listen to their
fellow Israelites. 14From their towns they came
together at Gibeah to fight against the Israelites.
15At once the Benjamites mobilized twenty-six
thousand swordsmen from their towns, in addition to seven hundred chosen men from those
living in Gibeah. 16Among all these soldiers there
were seven hundred chosen men who were left-
handed, each of whom could sling a stone at a
hair and not miss.

17Israel, apart from Benjamin, mustered four
hundred thousand swordsmen, all of them fighting men.

18The Israelites went up to Bethel[b] and inquired of God. They said, "Who of us shall go first
to fight against the Benjamites?"

The LORD replied, "Judah shall go first."

19The next morning the Israelites got up and
pitched camp near Gibeah. 20The men of Israel
went out to fight the Benjamites and took up
battle positions against them at Gibeah. 21The
Benjamites came out of Gibeah and cut down
twenty-two thousand Israelites on the battlefield
that day. 22But the men of Israel encouraged one
another and again took up their positions where
they had stationed themselves the first day. 23The
Israelites went up and wept before the LORD until
evening, and they inquired of the LORD. They
said, "Shall we go up again to battle against the
Benjamites, our brothers?"

The LORD answered, "Go up against them."

24Then the Israelites drew near to Benjamin
the second day. 25This time, when the Benjamites came out from Gibeah to oppose them,
they cut down another eighteen thousand Israelites, all of them armed with swords.

26Then the Israelites, all the people, went up
to Bethel, and there they sat weeping before the
LORD. They fasted that day until evening and presented burnt offerings and fellowship offerings[c]
to the LORD. 27And the Israelites inquired of the
LORD. (In those days the ark of the covenant of
God was there, 28with Phinehas son of Eleazar,
the son of Aaron, ministering before it.) They
asked, "Shall we go up again to battle with Benjamin our brother, or not?"

The LORD responded, "Go, for tomorrow I will
give them into your hands."

29Then Israel set an ambush around Gibeah.
30They went up against the Benjamites on the
third day and took up positions against Gibeah as
they had done before. 31The Benjamites came out
to meet them and were drawn away from the
city. They began to inflict casualties on the Israelites as before, so that about thirty men fell in the
open field and on the roads—the one leading to
Bethel and the other to Gibeah.

32While the Benjamites were saying, "We are
defeating them as before," the Israelites were
saying, "Let's retreat and draw them away from
the city to the roads."

33All the men of Israel moved from their places
and took up positions at Baal Tamar, and the Israelite ambush charged out of its place on the
west[d] of Gibeah.[e] 34Then ten thousand of Israel's finest men made a frontal attack on Gibeah.
The fighting was so heavy that the Benjamites did
not realize how near disaster was. 35The LORD
defeated Benjamin before Israel, and on that day
the Israelites struck down 25,100 Benjamites, all
armed with swords. 36Then the Benjamites saw
that they were beaten.

Now the men of Israel had given way before
Benjamin, because they relied on the ambush
they had set near Gibeah. 37The men who had
been in ambush made a sudden dash into Gibeah, spread out and put the whole city to the
sword. 38The men of Israel had arranged with the
ambush that they should send up a great cloud of
smoke from the city, 39and then the men of Israel
would turn in the battle.

The Benjamites had begun to inflict casualties
on the men of Israel (about thirty), and they said,
"We are defeating them as in the first battle."
40But when the column of smoke began to rise
from the city, the Benjamites turned and saw the
smoke of the whole city going up into the sky.
41Then the men of Israel turned on them, and the
men of Benjamin were terrified, because they realized that disaster had come upon them. 42So
they fled before the Israelites in the direction of
the desert, but they could not escape the battle.
And the men of Israel who came out of the towns
cut them down there. 43They surrounded the
Benjamites, chased them and easily[f] overran
them in the vicinity of Gibeah on the east. 44Eigh-
teen thousand Benjamites fell, all of them valiant
fighters. 45As they turned and fled toward the
desert to the rock of Rimmon, the Israelites cut

[a] 10 One Hebrew manuscript; most Hebrew manuscripts *Geba,* a variant of *Gibeah*
[b] 18 Or *to the house of God*; also in verse 26
[c] 26 Traditionally *peace offerings*
[d] 33 Some Septuagint manuscripts and Vulgate; the meaning of the Hebrew for this word is uncertain.
[e] 33 Hebrew *Geba,* a variant of *Gibeah*
[f] 43 The meaning of the Hebrew for this word is uncertain.

down five thousand men along the roads. They
kept pressing after the Benjamites as far as Gidom
and struck down two thousand more.
46On that day twenty-five thousand Benjamite
swordsmen fell, all of them valiant fighters. 47But
six hundred men turned and fled into the desert
to the rock of Rimmon, where they stayed four
months. 48The men of Israel went back to Benjamin and put all the towns to the sword, including
the animals and everything else they found. All
the towns they came across they set on fire.

Wives for the Benjamites

21 The men of Israel had taken an oath at
Mizpah: "Not one of us will give his
daughter in marriage to a Benjamite."
2The people went to Bethel,[a] where they sat
before God until evening, raising their voices and
weeping bitterly. 3"O LORD, the God of Israel,"
they cried, "why has this happened to Israel?
Why should one tribe be missing from Israel today?"
4Early the next day the people built an altar
and presented burnt offerings and fellowship offerings.[b]
5Then the Israelites asked, "Who from all the
tribes of Israel has failed to assemble before the
LORD?" For they had taken a solemn oath that
anyone who failed to assemble before the LORD at
Mizpah should certainly be put to death.
6Now the Israelites grieved for their brothers,
the Benjamites. "Today one tribe is cut off from
Israel," they said. 7"How can we provide wives
for those who are left, since we have taken an
oath by the LORD not to give them any of our
daughters in marriage?" 8Then they asked,
"Which one of the tribes of Israel failed to assemble before the LORD at Mizpah?" They discovered
that no one from Jabesh Gilead had come to the
camp for the assembly. 9For when they counted
the people, they found that none of the people of
Jabesh Gilead were there.
10So the assembly sent twelve thousand fighting men with instructions to go to Jabesh Gilead
and put to the sword those living there, including
the women and children. 11"This is what you are
to do," they said. "Kill every male and every
woman who is not a virgin." 12They found among
the people living in Jabesh Gilead four hundred
young women who had never slept with a man,
and they took them to the camp at Shiloh in
Canaan.
13Then the whole assembly sent an offer of
peace to the Benjamites at the rock of Rimmon.
14So the Benjamites returned at that time and
were given the women of Jabesh Gilead who had
been spared. But there were not enough for all of
them.
15The people grieved for Benjamin, because
the LORD had made a gap in the tribes of Israel.
16And the elders of the assembly said, "With the
women of Benjamin destroyed, how shall we provide wives for the men who are left? 17The Benjamite survivors must have heirs," they said, "so
that a tribe of Israel will not be wiped out. 18We
can't give them our daughters as wives, since we
Israelites have taken this oath: 'Cursed be anyone
who gives a wife to a Benjamite.' 19But look,
there is the annual festival of the LORD in Shiloh,
to the north of Bethel, and east of the road that
goes from Bethel to Shechem, and to the south of
Lebonah."
20So they instructed the Benjamites, saying,
"Go and hide in the vineyards 21and watch.
When the girls of Shiloh come out to join in the
dancing, then rush from the vineyards and each
of you seize a wife from the girls of Shiloh and go
to the land of Benjamin. 22When their fathers or
brothers complain to us, we will say to them, 'Do
us a kindness by helping them, because we did
not get wives for them during the war, and you
are innocent, since you did not give your daughters to them.' "
23So that is what the Benjamites did. While the
girls were dancing, each man caught one and
carried her off to be his wife. Then they returned
to their inheritance and rebuilt the towns and
settled in them.
24At that time the Israelites left that place and
went home to their tribes and clans, each to his
own inheritance.
25In those days Israel had no king; everyone
did as he saw fit.

[a]2 Or *to the house of God* [b]4 Traditionally *peace offerings*

Introduction to
RUTH

Personal Reading Plan

❒ Ruth 1:1–22
❒ Ruth 2:1–23
❒ Ruth 3:1–18
❒ Ruth 4:1–22

Author

The author of Ruth is unknown.

Date

The date of composition is difficult to fix, though it was probably written during the period of the Israelite monarchy (c. 1000–722 B.C.). An early date is likely, as suggested by the fact that the genealogy in 4:17–22 ends with David.

Theme

Divine providence and human loyalty in the life of one family. The legal procedure of kinsman-redeemer also serves to illustrate the larger biblical theme of redemption.

Historical Background

The action of the book of Ruth is set in the tumultuous period of the judges (c. 1100 B.C.). In a time of foreign oppression and spiritual decline, this encouraging story takes place at a temporary time of peace and presents a picture of genuine faith. It may be that the book's original intention was to provide a politically important genealogy for David (4:17–22). The story goes to great lengths to legitimize his Moabite connections. This was important since Moabite women were considered immoral by many in Israel (see Gen. 19:30–38; Num. 25:1–3). Modern readers of Ruth, unfamiliar with the background of the "kinsman-redeemer" motif, will also want to read about the plight of bereft widows and disenfranchised poor people, and how the next of kin was obliged to extend the family name (see Deut. 25:5–10) and redeem their lost property (see Lev. 25:23–28).

Characteristics

This book does not drive home its points, but subtly weaves them into the form of a story. In style, with its condensed action and plot twists, the book of Ruth is like a modern short story. The author has taken the changing fortunes of a single family and created a work of art. The book is interesting for its contrast to the book of Judges. Though set during the time of the judges, the story of Ruth does not present the dramatic acts of God; in fact, God is not often mentioned in the book. Nonetheless, implied throughout is the quiet and tangible presence of God superintending the action of the story.

Above all, this is a book about a loving and righteous woman. The author takes an outsider of questionable background, Ruth, and shows her to be a person about whom God is vitally concerned. Throughout the book, Ruth displays an unconditional loyalty to her desolate mother-in-law, Naomi. In her love, and in Boaz's kindness to these two widows, we see an illustration of God's self-giving love.

Naomi and Ruth

1 In the days when the judges ruled,[a] there
was a famine in the land, and a man from
Bethlehem in Judah, together with his wife and
two sons, went to live for a while in the country
of Moab. 2 The man's name was Elimelech, his
wife's name Naomi, and the names of his two
sons were Mahlon and Kilion. They were Eph-
rathites from Bethlehem, Judah. And they went
to Moab and lived there.
3 Now Elimelech, Naomi's husband, died, and
she was left with her two sons. 4 They married
Moabite women, one named Orpah and the other Ruth. After they had lived there about ten
years, 5 both Mahlon and Kilion also died, and
Naomi was left without her two sons and her
husband.
6 When she heard in Moab that the LORD
had come to the aid of his people by providing
food for them, Naomi and her daughters-in-law
prepared to return home from there. 7 With her
two daughters-in-law she left the place where
she had been living and set out on the road that
would take them back to the land of Judah.
8 Then Naomi said to her two daughters-in-
law, "Go back, each of you, to your mother's
home. May the LORD show kindness to you, as
you have shown to your dead and to me. 9 May
the LORD grant that each of you will find rest in
the home of another husband."
Then she kissed them and they wept aloud
10 and said to her, "We will go back with you to
your people."
11 But Naomi said, "Return home, my daughters. Why would you come with me? Am I going
to have any more sons, who could become your
husbands? 12 Return home, my daughters; I am
too old to have another husband. Even if I
thought there was still hope for me—even if I
had a husband tonight and then gave birth to
sons— 13 would you wait until they grew up?
Would you remain unmarried for them? No, my
daughters. It is more bitter for me than for you,
because the LORD's hand has gone out
against me!"
14 At this they wept again. Then Orpah kissed
her mother-in-law good-by, but Ruth clung to
her.
15 "Look," said Naomi, "your sister-in-law is
going back to her people and her gods. Go back
with her."
16 But Ruth replied, "Don't urge me to leave
you or to turn back from you. Where you go I will
go, and where you stay I will stay. Your people
will be my people and your God my God.
17 Where you die I will die, and there I will be
buried. May the LORD deal with me, be it ever so
severely, if anything but death separates you and
me." 18 When Naomi realized that Ruth was determined to go with her, she stopped urging her.
19 So the two women went on until they came
to Bethlehem. When they arrived in Bethlehem,
the whole town was stirred because of them, and
the women exclaimed, "Can this be Naomi?"
20 "Don't call me Naomi,[b]" she told them.
"Call me Mara,[c] because the Almighty[d] has
made my life very bitter. 21 I went away full, but
the LORD has brought me back empty. Why call
me Naomi? The LORD has afflicted[e] me; the Almighty has brought misfortune upon me."
22 So Naomi returned from Moab accompanied
by Ruth the Moabitess, her daughter-in-law, arriving in Bethlehem as the barley harvest was
beginning.

Ruth Meets Boaz

2 Now Naomi had a relative on her husband's
side, from the clan of Elimelech, a man of
standing, whose name was Boaz.
2 And Ruth the Moabitess said to Naomi, "Let
me go to the fields and pick up the leftover grain
behind anyone in whose eyes I find favor."
Naomi said to her, "Go ahead, my daughter."
3 So she went out and began to glean in the fields
behind the harvesters. As it turned out, she
found herself working in a field belonging to
Boaz, who was from the clan of Elimelech.
4 Just then Boaz arrived from Bethlehem and
greeted the harvesters, "The LORD be with you!"
"The LORD bless you!" they called back.
5 Boaz asked the foreman of his harvesters,
"Whose young woman is that?"
6 The foreman replied, "She is the Moabitess
who came back from Moab with Naomi. 7 She
said, 'Please let me glean and gather among the
sheaves behind the harvesters.' She went into
the field and has worked steadily from morning
till now, except for a short rest in the shelter."
8 So Boaz said to Ruth, "My daughter, listen to
me. Don't go and glean in another field and don't
go away from here. Stay here with my servant
girls. 9 Watch the field where the men are harvesting, and follow along after the girls. I have
told the men not to touch you. And whenever
you are thirsty, go and get a drink from the water
jars the men have filled."
10 At this, she bowed down with her face to the
ground. She exclaimed, "Why have I found such
favor in your eyes that you notice me—a foreigner?"

[a] *1* Traditionally *judged* [b] *20* *Naomi* means *pleasant*; also in verse 21. [c] *20* *Mara* means *bitter.* [d] *20* Hebrew *Shaddai*; also in verse 21 [e] *21* Or *has testified against*

11 Boaz replied, "I've been told all about what you have done for your mother-in-law since the death of your husband—how you left your father and mother and your homeland and came to live with a people you did not know before. 12 May the LORD repay you for what you have done. May you be richly rewarded by the LORD, the God of Israel, under whose wings you have come to take refuge."

13 "May I continue to find favor in your eyes, my lord," she said. "You have given me comfort and have spoken kindly to your servant—though I do not have the standing of one of your servant girls."

14 At mealtime Boaz said to her, "Come over here. Have some bread and dip it in the wine vinegar."

When she sat down with the harvesters, he offered her some roasted grain. She ate all she wanted and had some left over. 15 As she got up to glean, Boaz gave orders to his men, "Even if she gathers among the sheaves, don't embarrass her. 16 Rather, pull out some stalks for her from the bundles and leave them for her to pick up, and don't rebuke her."

17 So Ruth gleaned in the field until evening. Then she threshed the barley she had gathered, and it amounted to about an ephah.[a] 18 She carried it back to town, and her mother-in-law saw how much she had gathered. Ruth also brought out and gave her what she had left over after she had eaten enough.

19 Her mother-in-law asked her, "Where did you glean today? Where did you work? Blessed be the man who took notice of you!"

Then Ruth told her mother-in-law about the one at whose place she had been working. "The name of the man I worked with today is Boaz," she said.

20 "The LORD bless him!" Naomi said to her daughter-in-law. "He has not stopped showing his kindness to the living and the dead." She added, "That man is our close relative; he is one of our kinsman-redeemers."

21 Then Ruth the Moabitess said, "He even said to me, 'Stay with my workers until they finish harvesting all my grain.' "

22 Naomi said to Ruth her daughter-in-law, "It will be good for you, my daughter, to go with his girls, because in someone else's field you might be harmed."

23 So Ruth stayed close to the servant girls of Boaz to glean until the barley and wheat harvests were finished. And she lived with her mother-in-law.

Ruth and Boaz at the Threshing Floor

3 One day Naomi her mother-in-law said to her, "My daughter, should I not try to find a home[b] for you, where you will be well provided for? 2 Is not Boaz, with whose servant girls you have been, a kinsman of ours? Tonight he will be winnowing barley on the threshing floor. 3 Wash and perfume yourself, and put on your best clothes. Then go down to the threshing floor, but don't let him know you are there until he has finished eating and drinking. 4 When he lies down, note the place where he is lying. Then go and uncover his feet and lie down. He will tell you what to do."

5 "I will do whatever you say," Ruth answered. 6 So she went down to the threshing floor and did everything her mother-in-law told her to do.

7 When Boaz had finished eating and drinking and was in good spirits, he went over to lie down at the far end of the grain pile. Ruth approached quietly, uncovered his feet and lay down. 8 In the middle of the night something startled the man, and he turned and discovered a woman lying at his feet.

9 "Who are you?" he asked.

"I am your servant Ruth," she said. "Spread the corner of your garment over me, since you are a kinsman-redeemer."

10 "The LORD bless you, my daughter," he replied. "This kindness is greater than that which you showed earlier: You have not run after the younger men, whether rich or poor. 11 And now, my daughter, don't be afraid. I will do for you all you ask. All my fellow townsmen know that you are a woman of noble character. 12 Although it is true that I am near of kin, there is a kinsman-redeemer nearer than I. 13 Stay here for the night, and in the morning if he wants to redeem, good; let him redeem. But if he is not willing, as surely as the LORD lives I will do it. Lie here until morning."

14 So she lay at his feet until morning, but got up before anyone could be recognized; and he said, "Don't let it be known that a woman came to the threshing floor."

15 He also said, "Bring me the shawl you are wearing and hold it out." When she did so, he poured into it six measures of barley and put it on her. Then he[c] went back to town.

16 When Ruth came to her mother-in-law, Naomi asked, "How did it go, my daughter?"

Then she told her everything Boaz had done for her 17 and added, "He gave me these six measures of barley, saying, 'Don't go back to your mother-in-law empty-handed.' "

18 Then Naomi said, "Wait, my daughter, until

[a] *17* That is, probably about 3/5 bushel (about 22 liters) [b] *1* Hebrew *find rest* (see Ruth 1:9) [c] *15* Most Hebrew manuscripts; many Hebrew manuscripts, Vulgate and Syriac *she*

you find out what happens. For the man will not
rest until the matter is settled today."

Boaz Marries Ruth

4 Meanwhile Boaz went up to the town gate
and sat there. When the kinsman-redeemer
he had mentioned came along, Boaz said, "Come
over here, my friend, and sit down." So he went
over and sat down.
2Boaz took ten of the elders of the town and
said, "Sit here," and they did so. 3Then he said to
the kinsman-redeemer, "Naomi, who has come
back from Moab, is selling the piece of land that
belonged to our brother Elimelech. 4I thought I
should bring the matter to your attention and
suggest that you buy it in the presence of these
seated here and in the presence of the elders of
my people. If you will redeem it, do so. But if
you[a] will not, tell me, so I will know. For no one
has the right to do it except you, and I am next
in line."
"I will redeem it," he said.
5Then Boaz said, "On the day you buy the land
from Naomi and from Ruth the Moabitess, you
acquire[b] the dead man's widow, in order to
maintain the name of the dead with his property."
6At this, the kinsman-redeemer said, "Then I
cannot redeem it because I might endanger my
own estate. You redeem it yourself. I cannot
do it."
7(Now in earlier times in Israel, for the redemption and transfer of property to become final, one party took off his sandal and gave it to
the other. This was the method of legalizing
transactions in Israel.)
8So the kinsman-redeemer said to Boaz, "Buy
it yourself." And he removed his sandal.
9Then Boaz announced to the elders and all
the people, "Today you are witnesses that I have
bought from Naomi all the property of Elimelech,
Kilion and Mahlon. 10I have also acquired Ruth
the Moabitess, Mahlon's widow, as my wife, in
order to maintain the name of the dead with his
property, so that his name will not disappear
from among his family or from the town records.
Today you are witnesses!"
11Then the elders and all those at the gate said,
"We are witnesses. May the LORD make the
woman who is coming into your home like Rachel and Leah, who together built up the house of
Israel. May you have standing in Ephrathah and
be famous in Bethlehem. 12Through the offspring
the LORD gives you by this young woman, may
your family be like that of Perez, whom Tamar
bore to Judah."

The Genealogy of David

13So Boaz took Ruth and she became his wife.
Then he went to her, and the LORD enabled her
to conceive, and she gave birth to a son. 14The
women said to Naomi: "Praise be to the LORD,
who this day has not left you without a kinsman-
redeemer. May he become famous throughout
Israel! 15He will renew your life and sustain you
in your old age. For your daughter-in-law, who
loves you and who is better to you than seven
sons, has given him birth."
16Then Naomi took the child, laid him in her
lap and cared for him. 17The women living there
said, "Naomi has a son." And they named him
Obed. He was the father of Jesse, the father of
David.
18This, then, is the family line of Perez:

Perez was the father of Hezron,
19Hezron the father of Ram,
Ram the father of Amminadab,
20Amminadab the father of Nahshon,
Nahshon the father of Salmon,[c]
21Salmon the father of Boaz,
Boaz the father of Obed,
22Obed the father of Jesse,
and Jesse the father of David.

[a]4 Many Hebrew manuscripts, Septuagint, Vulgate and Syriac; most Hebrew manuscripts *he* [b]5 Hebrew; Vulgate and Syriac *Naomi, you acquire Ruth the Moabitess,* [c]20 A few Hebrew manuscripts, some Septuagint manuscripts and Vulgate (see also verse 21 and Septuagint of 1 Chron. 2:11); most Hebrew manuscripts *Salma*

Introduction to 1 SAMUEL

Personal Reading Plan

❐ 1 Samuel 1:1–2:11	❐ 1 Samuel 12:1–13:15	❐ 1 Samuel 21:1–22:23
❐ 1 Samuel 2:12–3:21	❐ 1 Samuel 13:16–14:52	❐ 1 Samuel 23:1–24:22
❐ 1 Samuel 4:1–5:12	❐ 1 Samuel 15:1–16:23	❐ 1 Samuel 25:1–44
❐ 1 Samuel 6:1–7:17	❐ 1 Samuel 17:1–58	❐ 1 Samuel 26:1–27:12
❐ 1 Samuel 8:1–10:8	❐ 1 Samuel 18:1–19:24	❐ 1 Samuel 28:1–29:11
❐ 1 Samuel 10:9–11:15	❐ 1 Samuel 20:1–42	❐ 1 Samuel 30:1–31:13

Author

The author of 1 Samuel is not known with certainty. Perhaps a compiler drew from materials written by others such as Samuel, Gad and Nathan (see 1 Chron. 29:29) in order to produce the final rendition. Note that 1 and 2 Samuel were originally composed as one unit.

Date

The date of authorship is uncertain, though it is possible that this two-volume book was written around the time of Solomon's death (c. 930 B.C.).

Theme

The king-maker (Samuel) and the first king (Saul).

Historical Background and Characteristics

The first book of Samuel narrates a major transition in the life of Israel—the shift from government under judges to a monarchy. Samuel, the last judge, anoints Saul as Israel's first king (c. 1050 B.C.). He later anoints David as the king who will take Saul's place.

This historical book highlights the lives of three central figures: Samuel, Saul and David. Sad elements abound: Eli's sons rebel; faithless Israel rejects her great King; Saul self-destructs in his vicious pursuit of David, reaching his lowest point when he consults a witch. But bright notes also punctuate this sordid story: Samuel stands firm and godly as the prophet of God who is ever faithful to his Lord; David (with soul mate Jonathan) appears youthful, courageous, popular and abounding in faith in the mighty God of Israel. In the context of almost constant warfare, trust in God is either conspicuously present or conspicuously absent. God is seen as the rejected King, the Revealer of the unknown, the Judge of the rebellious, as well as the Deliverer of his people.

Passages for Topical Group Study

17:20–50	SELF-CONFIDENCE	David and Goliath
18:1–16	FRIENDSHIPS JEALOUSY	Saul's Jealousy of David
20:1–13,18–42	TRUST	David and Jonathan
31:1–13	ASSISTED SUICIDE	Saul Takes His Life

See the Lesson Plans in the front of this Bible.

Passages for General Group Study

3:1–14	The Lord Calls Samuel
8:1–22	Israel Asks for a King
13:1–15	Samuel Rebukes Saul
16:1–13	Samuel Anoints David
24:1–22	David Spares Saul's Life

The Birth of Samuel

1 There was a certain man from Ramathaim, a
Zuphite[a] from the hill country of Ephraim,
whose name was Elkanah son of Jeroham, the son
of Elihu, the son of Tohu, the son of Zuph, an
Ephraimite. 2He had two wives; one was called
Hannah and the other Peninnah. Peninnah had
children, but Hannah had none.
3Year after year this man went up from his
town to worship and sacrifice to the LORD Almighty at Shiloh, where Hophni and Phinehas,
the two sons of Eli, were priests of the LORD.
4Whenever the day came for Elkanah to sacrifice,
he would give portions of the meat to his wife
Peninnah and to all her sons and daughters. 5But
to Hannah he gave a double portion because he
loved her, and the LORD had closed her womb.
6And because the LORD had closed her womb,
her rival kept provoking her in order to irritate
her. 7This went on year after year. Whenever
Hannah went up to the house of the LORD, her
rival provoked her till she wept and would not
eat. 8Elkanah her husband would say to her,
"Hannah, why are you weeping? Why don't you
eat? Why are you downhearted? Don't I mean
more to you than ten sons?"
9Once when they had finished eating and
drinking in Shiloh, Hannah stood up. Now Eli the
priest was sitting on a chair by the doorpost of
the LORD's temple.[b] 10In bitterness of soul Hannah wept much and prayed to the LORD. 11And
she made a vow, saying, "O LORD Almighty, if
you will only look upon your servant's misery and
remember me, and not forget your servant but
give her a son, then I will give him to the LORD
for all the days of his life, and no razor will ever
be used on his head."
12As she kept on praying to the LORD, Eli observed her mouth. 13Hannah was praying in her
heart, and her lips were moving but her voice
was not heard. Eli thought she was drunk 14and
said to her, "How long will you keep on getting
drunk? Get rid of your wine."
15"Not so, my lord," Hannah replied, "I am a
woman who is deeply troubled. I have not been
drinking wine or beer; I was pouring out my soul
to the LORD. 16Do not take your servant for a
wicked woman; I have been praying here out of
my great anguish and grief."
17Eli answered, "Go in peace, and may the
God of Israel grant you what you have asked of
him."
18She said, "May your servant find favor in
your eyes." Then she went her way and ate something, and her face was no longer downcast.
19Early the next morning they arose and worshiped before the LORD and then went back to
their home at Ramah. Elkanah lay with Hannah
his wife, and the LORD remembered her. 20So in
the course of time Hannah conceived and gave
birth to a son. She named him Samuel,[c] saying,
"Because I asked the LORD for him."

Hannah Dedicates Samuel

21When the man Elkanah went up with all his
family to offer the annual sacrifice to the LORD
and to fulfill his vow, 22Hannah did not go. She
said to her husband, "After the boy is weaned, I
will take him and present him before the LORD,
and he will live there always."
23"Do what seems best to you," Elkanah her
husband told her. "Stay here until you have
weaned him; only may the LORD make good his[d]
word." So the woman stayed at home and nursed
her son until she had weaned him.
24After he was weaned, she took the boy with
her, young as he was, along with a three-year-old
bull,[e] an ephah[f] of flour and a skin of wine,
and brought him to the house of the LORD at
Shiloh. 25When they had slaughtered the bull,
they brought the boy to Eli, 26and she said to him,
"As surely as you live, my lord, I am the woman
who stood here beside you praying to the LORD.
27I prayed for this child, and the LORD has granted me what I asked of him. 28So now I give him
to the LORD. For his whole life he will be given
over to the LORD." And he worshiped the LORD
there.

Hannah's Prayer

2 Then Hannah prayed and said:

"My heart rejoices in the LORD;
in the LORD my horn[g] is lifted high.
My mouth boasts over my enemies,
for I delight in your deliverance.

2"There is no one holy[h] like the LORD;
there is no one besides you;
there is no Rock like our God.

3"Do not keep talking so proudly
or let your mouth speak such arrogance,
for the LORD is a God who knows,
and by him deeds are weighed.

4"The bows of the warriors are broken,
but those who stumbled are armed with
strength.

[a] 1 Or *from Ramathaim Zuphim* [b] 9 That is, tabernacle [c] 20 *Samuel* sounds like the Hebrew for *heard of God.*
[d] 23 Masoretic Text; Dead Sea Scrolls, Septuagint and Syriac *your* [e] 24 Dead Sea Scrolls, Septuagint and Syriac; Masoretic Text *with three bulls* [f] 24 That is, probably about 3/5 bushel (about 22 liters) [g] 1 *Horn* here symbolizes strength; also in verse 10.
[h] 2 Or *no Holy One*

5Those who were full hire themselves out for
food,
but those who were hungry hunger no
more.
She who was barren has borne seven
children,
but she who has had many sons pines
away.
6"The LORD brings death and makes alive;
he brings down to the grave[a] and raises
up.
7The LORD sends poverty and wealth;
he humbles and he exalts.
8He raises the poor from the dust
and lifts the needy from the ash heap;
he seats them with princes
and has them inherit a throne of honor.

"For the foundations of the earth are the
LORD's;
upon them he has set the world.
9He will guard the feet of his saints,
but the wicked will be silenced in
darkness.

"It is not by strength that one prevails;
10 those who oppose the LORD will be
shattered.
He will thunder against them from heaven;
the LORD will judge the ends of the earth.

"He will give strength to his king
and exalt the horn of his anointed."

11Then Elkanah went home to Ramah, but the
boy ministered before the LORD under Eli the
priest.

Eli's Wicked Sons

12Eli's sons were wicked men; they had no
regard for the LORD. 13Now it was the practice of
the priests with the people that whenever anyone offered a sacrifice and while the meat was
being boiled, the servant of the priest would
come with a three-pronged fork in his hand. 14He
would plunge it into the pan or kettle or caldron
or pot, and the priest would take for himself
whatever the fork brought up. This is how they
treated all the Israelites who came to Shiloh.
15But even before the fat was burned, the servant
of the priest would come and say to the man who
was sacrificing, "Give the priest some meat to
roast; he won't accept boiled meat from you, but
only raw."
16If the man said to him, "Let the fat be burned
up first, and then take whatever you want," the
servant would then answer, "No, hand it over
now; if you don't, I'll take it by force."
17This sin of the young men was very great in
the LORD's sight, for they[b] were treating the
LORD's offering with contempt.
18But Samuel was ministering before the
LORD—a boy wearing a linen ephod. 19Each year
his mother made him a little robe and took it to
him when she went up with her husband to offer
the annual sacrifice. 20Eli would bless Elkanah
and his wife, saying, "May the LORD give you
children by this woman to take the place of the
one she prayed for and gave to the LORD." Then
they would go home. 21And the LORD was gracious to Hannah; she conceived and gave birth to
three sons and two daughters. Meanwhile, the
boy Samuel grew up in the presence of the LORD.
22Now Eli, who was very old, heard about everything his sons were doing to all Israel and how
they slept with the women who served at the
entrance to the Tent of Meeting. 23So he said to
them, "Why do you do such things? I hear from
all the people about these wicked deeds of yours.
24No, my sons; it is not a good report that I hear
spreading among the LORD's people. 25If a man
sins against another man, God[c] may mediate for
him; but if a man sins against the LORD, who will
intercede for him?" His sons, however, did not
listen to their father's rebuke, for it was the
LORD's will to put them to death.
26And the boy Samuel continued to grow in
stature and in favor with the LORD and with men.

Prophecy Against the House of Eli

27Now a man of God came to Eli and said to
him, "This is what the LORD says: 'Did I not clearly reveal myself to your father's house when they
were in Egypt under Pharaoh? 28I chose your father out of all the tribes of Israel to be my priest,
to go up to my altar, to burn incense, and to wear
an ephod in my presence. I also gave your father's house all the offerings made with fire by
the Israelites. 29Why do you[d] scorn my sacrifice
and offering that I prescribed for my dwelling?
Why do you honor your sons more than me by
fattening yourselves on the choice parts of every
offering made by my people Israel?'
30"Therefore the LORD, the God of Israel, declares: 'I promised that your house and your father's house would minister before me forever.'
But now the LORD declares: 'Far be it from me!
Those who honor me I will honor, but those who
despise me will be disdained. 31The time is coming when I will cut short your strength and the
strength of your father's house, so that there will
not be an old man in your family line 32and
you will see distress in my dwelling. Although
good will be done to Israel, in your family line
there will never be an old man. 33Every one of

[a]6 Hebrew *Sheol* [b]17 Or *men* [c]25 Or *the judges* [d]29 The Hebrew is plural.

you that I do not cut off from my altar will be spared only to blind your eyes with tears and to grieve your heart, and all your descendants will die in the prime of life.

34“ ‘And what happens to your two sons, Hophni and Phinehas, will be a sign to you—they will both die on the same day. 35I will raise up for myself a faithful priest, who will do according to what is in my heart and mind. I will firmly establish his house, and he will minister before my anointed one always. 36Then everyone left in your family line will come and bow down before him for a piece of silver and a crust of bread and plead, “Appoint me to some priestly office so I can have food to eat.” ’ ”

The LORD Calls Samuel

3 The boy Samuel ministered before the LORD under Eli. In those days the word of the LORD was rare; there were not many visions.

2One night Eli, whose eyes were becoming so weak that he could barely see, was lying down in his usual place. 3The lamp of God had not yet gone out, and Samuel was lying down in the temple[a] of the LORD, where the ark of God was. 4Then the LORD called Samuel.

Samuel answered, “Here I am.” 5And he ran to Eli and said, “Here I am; you called me.”

But Eli said, “I did not call; go back and lie down.” So he went and lay down.

6Again the LORD called, “Samuel!” And Samuel got up and went to Eli and said, “Here I am; you called me.”

“My son,” Eli said, “I did not call; go back and lie down.”

7Now Samuel did not yet know the LORD: The word of the LORD had not yet been revealed to him.

8The LORD called Samuel a third time, and Samuel got up and went to Eli and said, “Here I am; you called me.”

Then Eli realized that the LORD was calling the boy. 9So Eli told Samuel, “Go and lie down, and if he calls you, say, ‘Speak, LORD, for your servant is listening.’ ” So Samuel went and lay down in his place.

10The LORD came and stood there, calling as at the other times, “Samuel! Samuel!”

Then Samuel said, “Speak, for your servant is listening.”

11And the LORD said to Samuel: “See, I am about to do something in Israel that will make the ears of everyone who hears of it tingle. 12At that time I will carry out against Eli everything I spoke against his family—from beginning to end. 13For I told him that I would judge his family forever because of the sin he knew about; his sons made themselves contemptible,[b] and he failed to restrain them. 14Therefore, I swore to the house of Eli, ‘The guilt of Eli’s house will never be atoned for by sacrifice or offering.’ ”

1 SAMUEL 3:1–14

1. Who in your family is usually first to answer the phone? Who hogs the phone?
2. Are you a light or heavy sleeper? What does it take to wake you?
3. If you were Samuel, how many times would God have to call to get your attention: Once? Three times? More?
4. How would you feel if the Lord audibly called you by name?
5. Are your prayers more like “Speak Lord, for your servant listens” or “Listen Lord, for your servant speaks”?
6. How are you and God communicating right now?
7. Close in silence. Listen for God’s call.

[a]3 That is, tabernacle [b]13 Masoretic Text; an ancient Hebrew scribal tradition and Septuagint *sons blasphemed God*

As a child, Samuel had been brought by his parents to grow up and serve in the house of the Lord with Eli, the high priest.

3:1 ***boy.*** Samuel is now no longer a little child (see 2:21,26). The Jewish historian Josephus places his age at 12 years; he may have been older. ***the word of the LORD was rare.*** During the entire period of the judges there were few prophets and few revelations in Israel.

3:3 ***The lamp of God had not yet gone out.*** The reference is to the golden lampstand, which stood opposite the table of the bread of the Presence (Ex. 25:31–40) in the Holy Place. For the lamp to be permitted to go out before morning was a violation of regulations in the Law of Moses.

3:5 ***Eli said.*** Eli’s failure to recognize at once that the Lord had called Samuel may be indicative of his own unfamiliarity with the Lord.

3:7 ***did not yet know the LORD.*** In the sense of having a direct experience of him, such as receiving a revelation from God (see the last half of the verse).

3:11–14 The Lord’s first revelation to Samuel repeats the message Eli had already received from the “man of God” (2:27–3:6), thus confirming the fact that the youth had indeed received a revelation from God. The Lord would bring judgment to both Eli and his sons for the young priests’ sinful behavior (see 2:22).

15 Samuel lay down until morning and then
opened the doors of the house of the LORD. He
was afraid to tell Eli the vision, 16 but Eli called
him and said, "Samuel, my son."
Samuel answered, "Here I am."
17 "What was it he said to you?" Eli asked. "Do
not hide it from me. May God deal with you, be
it ever so severely, if you hide from me anything
he told you." 18 So Samuel told him everything,
hiding nothing from him. Then Eli said, "He is
the LORD; let him do what is good in his eyes."
19 The LORD was with Samuel as he grew up,
and he let none of his words fall to the ground.
20 And all Israel from Dan to Beersheba recognized that Samuel was attested as a prophet of
the LORD. 21 The LORD continued to appear at Shiloh, and there he revealed himself to Samuel
through his word.

4 And Samuel's word came to all Israel.

The Philistines Capture the Ark

Now the Israelites went out to fight against the
Philistines. The Israelites camped at Ebenezer,
and the Philistines at Aphek. 2 The Philistines deployed their forces to meet Israel, and as the battle spread, Israel was defeated by the Philistines,
who killed about four thousand of them on the
battlefield. 3 When the soldiers returned to camp,
the elders of Israel asked, "Why did the LORD
bring defeat upon us today before the Philistines?
Let us bring the ark of the LORD's covenant from
Shiloh, so that it[a] may go with us and save us
from the hand of our enemies."
4 So the people sent men to Shiloh, and they
brought back the ark of the covenant of the LORD
Almighty, who is enthroned between the cherubim. And Eli's two sons, Hophni and Phinehas,
were there with the ark of the covenant of God.
5 When the ark of the LORD's covenant came
into the camp, all Israel raised such a great shout
that the ground shook. 6 Hearing the uproar, the
Philistines asked, "What's all this shouting in the
Hebrew camp?"
When they learned that the ark of the LORD
had come into the camp, 7 the Philistines were
afraid. "A god has come into the camp," they
said. "We're in trouble! Nothing like this has
happened before. 8 Woe to us! Who will deliver
us from the hand of these mighty gods? They are
the gods who struck the Egyptians with all kinds
of plagues in the desert. 9 Be strong, Philistines!
Be men, or you will be subject to the Hebrews, as
they have been to you. Be men, and fight!"
10 So the Philistines fought, and the Israelites
were defeated and every man fled to his tent. The
slaughter was very great; Israel lost thirty thousand foot soldiers. 11 The ark of God was captured, and Eli's two sons, Hophni and Phinehas,
died.

Death of Eli

12 That same day a Benjamite ran from the battle line and went to Shiloh, his clothes torn and
dust on his head. 13 When he arrived, there was
Eli sitting on his chair by the side of the road,
watching, because his heart feared for the ark of
God. When the man entered the town and told
what had happened, the whole town sent up a
cry.
14 Eli heard the outcry and asked, "What is the
meaning of this uproar?"
The man hurried over to Eli, 15 who was
ninety-eight years old and whose eyes were set
so that he could not see. 16 He told Eli, "I have
just come from the battle line; I fled from it this
very day."
Eli asked, "What happened, my son?"
17 The man who brought the news replied, "Israel fled before the Philistines, and the army has
suffered heavy losses. Also your two sons, Hophni and Phinehas, are dead, and the ark of God has
been captured."
18 When he mentioned the ark of God, Eli fell
backward off his chair by the side of the gate. His
neck was broken and he died, for he was an old
man and heavy. He had led[b] Israel forty years.
19 His daughter-in-law, the wife of Phinehas,
was pregnant and near the time of delivery.
When she heard the news that the ark of God had
been captured and that her father-in-law and her
husband were dead, she went into labor and gave
birth, but was overcome by her labor pains. 20 As
she was dying, the women attending her said,
"Don't despair; you have given birth to a son."
But she did not respond or pay any attention.
21 She named the boy Ichabod,[c] saying, "The
glory has departed from Israel"—because of the
capture of the ark of God and the deaths of her
father-in-law and her husband. 22 She said, "The
glory has departed from Israel, for the ark of God
has been captured."

The Ark in Ashdod and Ekron

5 After the Philistines had captured the ark of
God, they took it from Ebenezer to Ashdod.
2 Then they carried the ark into Dagon's temple
and set it beside Dagon. 3 When the people of
Ashdod rose early the next day, there was Dagon,
fallen on his face on the ground before the ark of
the LORD! They took Dagon and put him back in
his place. 4 But the following morning when they
rose, there was Dagon, fallen on his face on the
ground before the ark of the LORD! His head and

[a] 3 Or *he* [b] 18 Traditionally *judged* [c] 21 *Ichabod* means *no glory.*

hands had been broken off and were lying on the
threshold; only his body remained. 5That is why
to this day neither the priests of Dagon nor any
others who enter Dagon's temple at Ashdod step
on the threshold.

6The LORD's hand was heavy upon the people
of Ashdod and its vicinity; he brought devastation
upon them and afflicted them with tumors.[a]
7When the men of Ashdod saw what was happening, they said, "The ark of the god of Israel
must not stay here with us, because his hand is
heavy upon us and upon Dagon our god." 8So
they called together all the rulers of the Philistines and asked them, "What shall we do with
the ark of the god of Israel?"

They answered, "Have the ark of the god of
Israel moved to Gath." So they moved the ark of
the God of Israel.

9But after they had moved it, the LORD's hand
was against that city, throwing it into a great
panic. He afflicted the people of the city, both
young and old, with an outbreak of tumors.[b]
10So they sent the ark of God to Ekron.

As the ark of God was entering Ekron, the
people of Ekron cried out, "They have brought
the ark of the god of Israel around to us to kill us
and our people." 11So they called together all the
rulers of the Philistines and said, "Send the ark of
the god of Israel away; let it go back to its own
place, or it[c] will kill us and our people." For
death had filled the city with panic; God's hand
was very heavy upon it. 12Those who did not die
were afflicted with tumors, and the outcry of the
city went up to heaven.

The Ark Returned to Israel

6 When the ark of the LORD had been in Philistine territory seven months, 2the Philistines
called for the priests and the diviners and said,
"What shall we do with the ark of the LORD? Tell
us how we should send it back to its place."

3They answered, "If you return the ark of the
god of Israel, do not send it away empty, but by
all means send a guilt offering to him. Then you
will be healed, and you will know why his hand
has not been lifted from you."

4The Philistines asked, "What guilt offering
should we send to him?"

They replied, "Five gold tumors and five gold
rats, according to the number of the Philistine
rulers, because the same plague has struck both
you and your rulers. 5Make models of the tumors
and of the rats that are destroying the country,
and pay honor to Israel's god. Perhaps he will lift
his hand from you and your gods and your land.
6Why do you harden your hearts as the Egyptians
and Pharaoh did? When he[d] treated them harshly, did they not send the Israelites out so they
could go on their way?

7"Now then, get a new cart ready, with two
cows that have calved and have never been
yoked. Hitch the cows to the cart, but take their
calves away and pen them up. 8Take the ark of
the LORD and put it on the cart, and in a chest
beside it put the gold objects you are sending
back to him as a guilt offering. Send it on its way,
9but keep watching it. If it goes up to its own
territory, toward Beth Shemesh, then the LORD
has brought this great disaster on us. But if it does
not, then we will know that it was not his hand
that struck us and that it happened to us by
chance."

10So they did this. They took two such cows
and hitched them to the cart and penned up their
calves. 11They placed the ark of the LORD on the
cart and along with it the chest containing the
gold rats and the models of the tumors. 12Then
the cows went straight up toward Beth Shemesh,
keeping on the road and lowing all the way; they
did not turn to the right or to the left. The rulers
of the Philistines followed them as far as the border of Beth Shemesh.

13Now the people of Beth Shemesh were harvesting their wheat in the valley, and when they
looked up and saw the ark, they rejoiced at the
sight. 14The cart came to the field of Joshua of
Beth Shemesh, and there it stopped beside a large
rock. The people chopped up the wood of the cart
and sacrificed the cows as a burnt offering to the
LORD. 15The Levites took down the ark of the
LORD, together with the chest containing the gold
objects, and placed them on the large rock. On
that day the people of Beth Shemesh offered
burnt offerings and made sacrifices to the LORD.
16The five rulers of the Philistines saw all this and
then returned that same day to Ekron.

17These are the gold tumors the Philistines
sent as a guilt offering to the LORD—one each for
Ashdod, Gaza, Ashkelon, Gath and Ekron. 18And
the number of the gold rats was according to the
number of Philistine towns belonging to the five
rulers—the fortified towns with their country villages. The large rock, on which[e] they set the ark
of the LORD, is a witness to this day in the field
of Joshua of Beth Shemesh.

19But God struck down some of the men of
Beth Shemesh, putting seventy[f] of them to
death because they had looked into the ark of the
LORD. The people mourned because of the heavy
blow the LORD had dealt them, 20and the men of

[a]6 Hebrew; Septuagint and Vulgate *tumors. And rats appeared in their land, and death and destruction were throughout the city*
[b]9 Or *with tumors in the groin* (see Septuagint)
[c]11 Or *he*
[d]6 That is, God
[e]18 A few Hebrew manuscripts (see also Septuagint); most Hebrew manuscripts *villages as far as Greater Abel, where*
[f]19 A few Hebrew manuscripts; most Hebrew manuscripts and Septuagint *50,070*

Beth Shemesh asked, "Who can stand in the presence of the LORD, this holy God? To whom will the ark go up from here?"

21 Then they sent messengers to the people of Kiriath Jearim, saying, "The Philistines have returned the ark of the LORD. Come down and take it up to your place."

7 1 So the men of Kiriath Jearim came and took up the ark of the LORD. They took it to Abinadab's house on the hill and consecrated Eleazar his son to guard the ark of the LORD.

Samuel Subdues the Philistines at Mizpah

2 It was a long time, twenty years in all, that the ark remained at Kiriath Jearim, and all the people of Israel mourned and sought after the LORD. 3 And Samuel said to the whole house of Israel, "If you are returning to the LORD with all your hearts, then rid yourselves of the foreign gods and the Ashtoreths and commit yourselves to the LORD and serve him only, and he will deliver you out of the hand of the Philistines." 4 So the Israelites put away their Baals and Ashtoreths, and served the LORD only.

5 Then Samuel said, "Assemble all Israel at Mizpah and I will intercede with the LORD for you." 6 When they had assembled at Mizpah, they drew water and poured it out before the LORD. On that day they fasted and there they confessed, "We have sinned against the LORD." And Samuel was leader[a] of Israel at Mizpah.

7 When the Philistines heard that Israel had assembled at Mizpah, the rulers of the Philistines came up to attack them. And when the Israelites heard of it, they were afraid because of the Philistines. 8 They said to Samuel, "Do not stop crying out to the LORD our God for us, that he may rescue us from the hand of the Philistines." 9 Then Samuel took a suckling lamb and offered it up as a whole burnt offering to the LORD. He cried out to the LORD on Israel's behalf, and the LORD answered him.

10 While Samuel was sacrificing the burnt offering, the Philistines drew near to engage Israel in battle. But that day the LORD thundered with loud thunder against the Philistines and threw them into such a panic that they were routed before the Israelites. 11 The men of Israel rushed out of Mizpah and pursued the Philistines, slaughtering them along the way to a point below Beth Car.

12 Then Samuel took a stone and set it up between Mizpah and Shen. He named it Ebenezer,[b] saying, "Thus far has the LORD helped us." 13 So the Philistines were subdued and did not invade Israelite territory again.

Throughout Samuel's lifetime, the hand of the LORD was against the Philistines. 14 The towns from Ekron to Gath that the Philistines had captured from Israel were restored to her, and Israel delivered the neighboring territory from the power of the Philistines. And there was peace between Israel and the Amorites.

15 Samuel continued as judge over Israel all the days of his life. 16 From year to year he went on a circuit from Bethel to Gilgal to Mizpah, judging Israel in all those places. 17 But he always went back to Ramah, where his home was, and there he also judged Israel. And he built an altar there to the LORD.

Israel Asks for a King

8 When Samuel grew old, he appointed his sons as judges for Israel. 2 The name of his firstborn was Joel and the name of his second was Abijah, and they served at Beersheba. 3 But his sons did not walk in his ways. They turned aside after dishonest gain and accepted bribes and perverted justice.

4 So all the elders of Israel gathered together and came to Samuel at Ramah. 5 They said to him, "You are old, and your sons do not walk in your ways; now appoint a king to lead[c] us, such as all the other nations have."

6 But when they said, "Give us a king to lead us," this displeased Samuel; so he prayed to the LORD. 7 And the LORD told him: "Listen to all that the people are saying to you; it is not you they have rejected, but they have rejected me as their king. 8 As they have done from the day I brought them up out of Egypt until this day, forsaking me and serving other gods, so they are doing to you. 9 Now listen to them; but warn them solemnly and let them know what the king who will reign over them will do."

10 Samuel told all the words of the LORD to the people who were asking him for a king. 11 He said, "This is what the king who will reign over you will do: He will take your sons and make them serve with his chariots and horses, and they will run in front of his chariots. 12 Some he will assign to be commanders of thousands and commanders of fifties, and others to plow his ground and reap his harvest, and still others to make weapons of war and equipment for his chariots. 13 He will take your daughters to be perfumers and cooks and bakers. 14 He will take the best of your fields and vineyards and olive groves and give them to his attendants. 15 He will take a tenth of your grain and of your vintage and give it to his officials and attendants. 16 Your menservants and maidservants and the best of your cat-

[a] 6 Traditionally *judge* [b] 12 *Ebenezer* means *stone of help* [c] 5 Traditionally *judge*; also in verses 6 and 20.

tle[a] and donkeys he will take for his own use.
17He will take a tenth of your flocks, and you
yourselves will become his slaves. 18When that
day comes, you will cry out for relief from the
king you have chosen, and the LORD will not answer you in that day."
19But the people refused to listen to Samuel.
"No!" they said. "We want a king over us. 20Then
we will be like all the other nations, with a king
to lead us and to go out before us and fight our
battles."
21When Samuel heard all that the people said,
he repeated it before the LORD. 22The LORD answered, "Listen to them and give them a king."
Then Samuel said to the men of Israel, "Everyone go back to his town."

1 SAMUEL 8:1–22

1. When did your parents let you start choosing your own clothes? Deciding on your own hairstyle?
2. What influences your buying habits the most: Your parents? Friends? TV?
3. If you heard Samuel's warnings about what a king would do, how much do you think your mind would have changed?
4. When have you wanted something "just like" what someone else had? What was it? Did you get it?
5. When you pray and ask God for "things," how do you think God feels about what you ask for?
6. Who or what is "king" in your life right now?
7. Close in prayer together. Pray to desire the things of God (see 1 John 5:14).

Samuel Anoints Saul

9 There was a Benjamite, a man of standing,
whose name was Kish son of Abiel, the son
of Zeror, the son of Becorath, the son of Aphiah
of Benjamin. 2He had a son named Saul, an
impressive young man without equal among
the Israelites—a head taller than any of the
others.
3Now the donkeys belonging to Saul's father
Kish were lost, and Kish said to his son Saul,
"Take one of the servants with you and go and
look for the donkeys." 4So he passed through the
hill country of Ephraim and through the area
around Shalisha, but they did not find them. They
went on into the district of Shaalim, but the donkeys were not there. Then he passed through
the territory of Benjamin, but they did not find
them.
5When they reached the district of Zuph, Saul
said to the servant who was with him, "Come,
let's go back, or my father will stop thinking
about the donkeys and start worrying about us."
6But the servant replied, "Look, in this town
there is a man of God; he is highly respected,
and everything he says comes true. Let's go
there now. Perhaps he will tell us what way to
take."
7Saul said to his servant, "If we go, what can
we give the man? The food in our sacks is gone.
We have no gift to take to the man of God. What
do we have?"
8The servant answered him again. "Look," he
said, "I have a quarter of a shekel[b] of silver. I
will give it to the man of God so that he will tell
us what way to take." 9(Formerly in Israel, if a
man went to inquire of God, he would say,
"Come, let us go to the seer," because the prophet of today used to be called a seer.)
10"Good," Saul said to his servant. "Come,
let's go." So they set out for the town where the
man of God was.
11As they were going up the hill to the town,
they met some girls coming out to draw water,
and they asked them, "Is the seer here?"

[a] 16 Septuagint; Hebrew *young men* [b] 8 That is, about 1/10 ounce (about 3 grams)

For the years since God led the Israelites out of Egypt and into the promised land, Israel had been without a king. Rather, the nation had been led by "judges"—individuals called by God not only to judicial functions, but also to rally the people in times of spiritual and military crises.

8:5 ***appoint a king to lead us.*** The elders cite Samuel's age and the misconduct of his sons as justifications for their request for a king. It soon becomes apparent, however, that the more basic reason for their request was a desire to be like the surrounding nations—to have a human king as a symbol of national power and unity who would lead them in battle and guarantee their security (see v. 20).

8:7 ***it is not you they have rejected, but they have rejected me as their king.*** The sin of Israel in their request for a king (see 10:19; 12:16–19) did not rest in any evil inherent in kingship itself, but rather in the kind of kingship the people envisioned and their reasons for desiring it. In requesting a king "like all the other nations" (v. 20) they broke the covenant, rejecting the Lord, who himself was pledged to be their savior and deliverer, and forgot his constant provision for their protection in the past (10:18; 12:8–11).

8:11 ***what the king who will reign over you will do.*** Using a description of the policies of contemporary Canaanite kings (vv. 11–17), Samuel warns the people of the burdens associated with the type of kingship they long for.

12“He is,” they answered. “He’s ahead of you.
Hurry now; he has just come to our town today,
for the people have a sacrifice at the high place.
13As soon as you enter the town, you will find
him before he goes up to the high place to eat.
The people will not begin eating until he comes,
because he must bless the sacrifice; afterward,
those who are invited will eat. Go up now; you
should find him about this time.”
14They went up to the town, and as they were
entering it, there was Samuel, coming toward
them on his way up to the high place.
15Now the day before Saul came, the LORD had
revealed this to Samuel: 16“About this time tomorrow I will send you a man from the land of
Benjamin. Anoint him leader over my people Israel; he will deliver my people from the hand of
the Philistines. I have looked upon my people, for
their cry has reached me.”
17When Samuel caught sight of Saul, the LORD
said to him, “This is the man I spoke to you
about; he will govern my people.”
18Saul approached Samuel in the gateway and
asked, “Would you please tell me where the
seer’s house is?”
19“I am the seer,” Samuel replied. “Go up
ahead of me to the high place, for today you are
to eat with me, and in the morning I will let you
go and will tell you all that is in your heart. 20As
for the donkeys you lost three days ago, do not
worry about them; they have been found. And to
whom is all the desire of Israel turned, if not to
you and all your father’s family?”
21Saul answered, “But am I not a Benjamite,
from the smallest tribe of Israel, and is not my
clan the least of all the clans of the tribe of Benjamin? Why do you say such a thing to me?”
22Then Samuel brought Saul and his servant
into the hall and seated them at the head of those
who were invited—about thirty in number.
23Samuel said to the cook, “Bring the piece of
meat I gave you, the one I told you to lay aside.”
24So the cook took up the leg with what was
on it and set it in front of Saul. Samuel said,
“Here is what has been kept for you. Eat, because
it was set aside for you for this occasion, from the
time I said, ‘I have invited guests.’” And Saul
dined with Samuel that day.
25After they came down from the high place to
the town, Samuel talked with Saul on the roof of
his house. 26They rose about daybreak and Samuel called to Saul on the roof, “Get ready, and
I will send you on your way.” When Saul got
ready, he and Samuel went outside together.
27As they were going down to the edge of the
town, Samuel said to Saul, “Tell the servant to go
on ahead of us”—and the servant did so—“but
you stay here awhile, so that I may give you a
message from God.”

10 Then Samuel took a flask of oil and
poured it on Saul’s head and kissed him,
saying, “Has not the LORD anointed you leader
over his inheritance?[a] 2When you leave me today, you will meet two men near Rachel’s tomb,
at Zelzah on the border of Benjamin. They will
say to you, ‘The donkeys you set out to look for
have been found. And now your father has
stopped thinking about them and is worried
about you. He is asking, “What shall I do about
my son?”’
3“Then you will go on from there until you
reach the great tree of Tabor. Three men going
up to God at Bethel will meet you there. One will
be carrying three young goats, another three
loaves of bread, and another a skin of wine.
4They will greet you and offer you two loaves of
bread, which you will accept from them.
5“After that you will go to Gibeah of God,
where there is a Philistine outpost. As you approach the town, you will meet a procession of
prophets coming down from the high place with
lyres, tambourines, flutes and harps being played
before them, and they will be prophesying. 6The
Spirit of the LORD will come upon you in power,
and you will prophesy with them; and you will be
changed into a different person. 7Once these
signs are fulfilled, do whatever your hand finds to
do, for God is with you.
8“Go down ahead of me to Gilgal. I will surely
come down to you to sacrifice burnt offerings and
fellowship offerings,[b] but you must wait seven
days until I come to you and tell you what you are
to do.”

Saul Made King

9As Saul turned to leave Samuel, God changed
Saul’s heart, and all these signs were fulfilled that
day. 10When they arrived at Gibeah, a procession
of prophets met him; the Spirit of God came upon
him in power, and he joined in their prophesying. 11When all those who had formerly known
him saw him prophesying with the prophets,
they asked each other, “What is this that has
happened to the son of Kish? Is Saul also among
the prophets?”
12A man who lived there answered, “And who
is their father?” So it became a saying: “Is Saul
also among the prophets?” 13After Saul stopped
prophesying, he went to the high place.

[a] *1* Hebrew; Septuagint and Vulgate *over his people Israel? You will reign over the LORD’s people and save them from the power of their enemies round about. And this will be a sign to you that the LORD has anointed you leader over his inheritance:*
[b] *8* Traditionally *peace offerings*

14Now Saul's uncle asked him and his servant, "Where have you been?"

"Looking for the donkeys," he said. "But when we saw they were not to be found, we went to Samuel."

15Saul's uncle said, "Tell me what Samuel said to you."

16Saul replied, "He assured us that the donkeys had been found." But he did not tell his uncle what Samuel had said about the kingship.

17Samuel summoned the people of Israel to the LORD at Mizpah 18and said to them, "This is what the LORD, the God of Israel, says: 'I brought Israel up out of Egypt, and I delivered you from the power of Egypt and all the kingdoms that oppressed you.' 19But you have now rejected your God, who saves you out of all your calamities and distresses. And you have said, 'No, set a king over us.' So now present yourselves before the LORD by your tribes and clans."

20When Samuel brought all the tribes of Israel near, the tribe of Benjamin was chosen. 21Then he brought forward the tribe of Benjamin, clan by clan, and Matri's clan was chosen. Finally Saul son of Kish was chosen. But when they looked for him, he was not to be found. 22So they inquired further of the LORD, "Has the man come here yet?"

And the LORD said, "Yes, he has hidden himself among the baggage."

23They ran and brought him out, and as he stood among the people he was a head taller than any of the others. 24Samuel said to all the people, "Do you see the man the LORD has chosen? There is no one like him among all the people."

Then the people shouted, "Long live the king!"

25Samuel explained to the people the regulations of the kingship. He wrote them down on a scroll and deposited it before the LORD. Then Samuel dismissed the people, each to his own home.

26Saul also went to his home in Gibeah, accompanied by valiant men whose hearts God had touched. 27But some troublemakers said, "How can this fellow save us?" They despised him and brought him no gifts. But Saul kept silent.

Saul Rescues the City of Jabesh

11 Nahash the Ammonite went up and besieged Jabesh Gilead. And all the men of Jabesh said to him, "Make a treaty with us, and we will be subject to you."

2But Nahash the Ammonite replied, "I will make a treaty with you only on the condition that I gouge out the right eye of every one of you and so bring disgrace on all Israel."

3The elders of Jabesh said to him, "Give us seven days so we can send messengers throughout Israel; if no one comes to rescue us, we will surrender to you."

4When the messengers came to Gibeah of Saul and reported these terms to the people, they all wept aloud. 5Just then Saul was returning from the fields, behind his oxen, and he asked, "What is wrong with the people? Why are they weeping?" Then they repeated to him what the men of Jabesh had said.

6When Saul heard their words, the Spirit of God came upon him in power, and he burned with anger. 7He took a pair of oxen, cut them into pieces, and sent the pieces by messengers throughout Israel, proclaiming, "This is what will be done to the oxen of anyone who does not follow Saul and Samuel." Then the terror of the LORD fell on the people, and they turned out as one man. 8When Saul mustered them at Bezek, the men of Israel numbered three hundred thousand and the men of Judah thirty thousand.

9They told the messengers who had come, "Say to the men of Jabesh Gilead, 'By the time the sun is hot tomorrow, you will be delivered.'" When the messengers went and reported this to the men of Jabesh, they were elated. 10They said to the Ammonites, "Tomorrow we will surrender to you, and you can do to us whatever seems good to you."

11The next day Saul separated his men into three divisions; during the last watch of the night they broke into the camp of the Ammonites and slaughtered them until the heat of the day. Those who survived were scattered, so that no two of them were left together.

Saul Confirmed as King

12The people then said to Samuel, "Who was it that asked, 'Shall Saul reign over us?' Bring these men to us and we will put them to death."

13But Saul said, "No one shall be put to death today, for this day the LORD has rescued Israel."

14Then Samuel said to the people, "Come, let us go to Gilgal and there reaffirm the kingship." 15So all the people went to Gilgal and confirmed Saul as king in the presence of the LORD. There they sacrificed fellowship offerings[a] before the LORD, and Saul and all the Israelites held a great celebration.

Samuel's Farewell Speech

12 Samuel said to all Israel, "I have listened to everything you said to me and have set a king over you. 2Now you have a king as your leader. As for me, I am old and gray, and my sons are here with you. I have been your leader from

a 15 Traditionally *peace offerings*

my youth until this day. [3]Here I stand. Testify against me in the presence of the LORD and his anointed. Whose ox have I taken? Whose donkey have I taken? Whom have I cheated? Whom have I oppressed? From whose hand have I accepted a bribe to make me shut my eyes? If I have done any of these, I will make it right."

[4]"You have not cheated or oppressed us," they replied. "You have not taken anything from anyone's hand."

[5]Samuel said to them, "The LORD is witness against you, and also his anointed is witness this day, that you have not found anything in my hand."

"He is witness," they said.

[6]Then Samuel said to the people, "It is the LORD who appointed Moses and Aaron and brought your forefathers up out of Egypt. [7]Now then, stand here, because I am going to confront you with evidence before the LORD as to all the righteous acts performed by the LORD for you and your fathers.

[8]"After Jacob entered Egypt, they cried to the LORD for help, and the LORD sent Moses and Aaron, who brought your forefathers out of Egypt and settled them in this place.

[9]"But they forgot the LORD their God; so he sold them into the hand of Sisera, the commander of the army of Hazor, and into the hands of the Philistines and the king of Moab, who fought against them. [10]They cried out to the LORD and said, 'We have sinned; we have forsaken the LORD and served the Baals and the Ashtoreths. But now deliver us from the hands of our enemies, and we will serve you.' [11]Then the LORD sent Jerub-Baal,[a] Barak,[b] Jephthah and Samuel,[c] and he delivered you from the hands of your enemies on every side, so that you lived securely.

[12]"But when you saw that Nahash king of the Ammonites was moving against you, you said to me, 'No, we want a king to rule over us'—even though the LORD your God was your king. [13]Now here is the king you have chosen, the one you asked for; see, the LORD has set a king over you. [14]If you fear the LORD and serve and obey him and do not rebel against his commands, and if both you and the king who reigns over you follow the LORD your God—good! [15]But if you do not obey the LORD, and if you rebel against his commands, his hand will be against you, as it was against your fathers.

[16]"Now then, stand still and see this great thing the LORD is about to do before your eyes! [17]Is it not wheat harvest now? I will call upon the LORD to send thunder and rain. And you will realize what an evil thing you did in the eyes of the LORD when you asked for a king."

[18]Then Samuel called upon the LORD, and that same day the LORD sent thunder and rain. So all the people stood in awe of the LORD and of Samuel.

[19]The people all said to Samuel, "Pray to the LORD your God for your servants so that we will not die, for we have added to all our other sins the evil of asking for a king."

[20]"Do not be afraid," Samuel replied. "You have done all this evil; yet do not turn away from the LORD, but serve the LORD with all your heart. [21]Do not turn away after useless idols. They can do you no good, nor can they rescue you, because they are useless. [22]For the sake of his great name the LORD will not reject his people, because the LORD was pleased to make you his own. [23]As for me, far be it from me that I should sin against the LORD by failing to pray for you. And I will teach you the way that is good and right. [24]But be sure to fear the LORD and serve him faithfully with all your heart; consider what great things he has done for you. [25]Yet if you persist in doing evil, both you and your king will be swept away."

Samuel Rebukes Saul

13 Saul was ⌞thirty⌟[d] years old when he became king, and he reigned over Israel ⌞forty-⌟[e] two years.

[2]Saul[f] chose three thousand men from Israel; two thousand were with him at Micmash and in the hill country of Bethel, and a thousand were with Jonathan at Gibeah in Benjamin. The rest of the men he sent back to their homes.

[3]Jonathan attacked the Philistine outpost at Geba, and the Philistines heard about it. Then Saul had the trumpet blown throughout the land and said, "Let the Hebrews hear!" [4]So all Israel heard the news: "Saul has attacked the Philistine outpost, and now Israel has become a stench to the Philistines." And the people were summoned to join Saul at Gilgal.

[5]The Philistines assembled to fight Israel, with three thousand[g] chariots, six thousand charioteers, and soldiers as numerous as the sand on the seashore. They went up and camped at Micmash, east of Beth Aven. [6]When the men of Israel saw that their situation was critical and that their army was hard pressed, they hid in caves and thickets, among the rocks, and in pits and cisterns. [7]Some Hebrews even crossed the Jordan to the land of Gad and Gilead.

Saul remained at Gilgal, and all the troops with

[a] *11* Also called *Gideon* [b] *11* Some Septuagint manuscripts and Syriac; Hebrew *Bedan* [c] *11* Hebrew; some Septuagint manuscripts and Syriac *Samson* [d] *1* A few late manuscripts of the Septuagint; Hebrew does not have *thirty.* [e] *1* See the round number in Acts 13:21; Hebrew does not have *forty-.* [f] *1,2* Or *and when he had reigned over Israel two years,* [2]*he* [g] *5* Some Septuagint manuscripts and Syriac; Hebrew *thirty thousand*

him were quaking with fear. 8He waited seven days, the time set by Samuel; but Samuel did not come to Gilgal, and Saul's men began to scatter. 9So he said, "Bring me the burnt offering and the fellowship offerings.[a]" And Saul offered up the burnt offering. 10Just as he finished making the offering, Samuel arrived, and Saul went out to greet him.

11"What have you done?" asked Samuel.

Saul replied, "When I saw that the men were scattering, and that you did not come at the set time, and that the Philistines were assembling at Micmash, 12I thought, 'Now the Philistines will come down against me at Gilgal, and I have not sought the LORD's favor.' So I felt compelled to offer the burnt offering."

13"You acted foolishly," Samuel said. "You have not kept the command the LORD your God gave you; if you had, he would have established your kingdom over Israel for all time. 14But now your kingdom will not endure; the LORD has sought out a man after his own heart and appointed him leader of his people, because you have not kept the LORD's command."

15Then Samuel left Gilgal[b] and went up to Gibeah in Benjamin, and Saul counted the men who were with him. They numbered about six hundred.

Israel Without Weapons

16Saul and his son Jonathan and the men with them were staying in Gibeah[c] in Benjamin, while the Philistines camped at Micmash. 17Raiding parties went out from the Philistine camp in three detachments. One turned toward Ophrah in the vicinity of Shual, 18another toward Beth Horon, and the third toward the borderland overlooking the Valley of Zeboim facing the desert.

19Not a blacksmith could be found in the whole land of Israel, because the Philistines had said, "Otherwise the Hebrews will make swords or spears!" 20So all Israel went down to the Philistines to have their plowshares, mattocks, axes and sickles[d] sharpened. 21The price was two thirds of a shekel[e] for sharpening plowshares and mattocks, and a third of a shekel[f] for sharpening forks and axes and for repointing goads.

22So on the day of the battle not a soldier with Saul and Jonathan had a sword or spear in his hand; only Saul and his son Jonathan had them.

Jonathan Attacks the Philistines

23Now a detachment of Philistines had gone

1 SAMUEL 13:1–15

1. How many "tardies" have you had this school year? Are you generally late or on time for your scheduled appointments?
2. What's something you hate waiting for: A red light? The bathroom?
3. In decision making, are you more likely to act impulsively and risk making a bad choice, or hold back and miss an opportunity?
4. How do Saul's reasons for deciding to sacrifice (vv. 11–12) sound to you? How do you feel about his punishment (vv. 13–14; see note on v. 14)?
5. When has a hastily made decision cost you dearly?
6. How hard is it for you to admit when you are wrong?
7. How can the group pray for you this week? Close in prayer.

a9 Traditionally *peace offerings* *b15* Hebrew; Septuagint *Gilgal and went his way; the rest of the people went after Saul to meet the army, and they went out of Gilgal* *c16* Two Hebrew manuscripts; most Hebrew manuscripts *Geba,* a variant of *Gibeah* *d20* Septuagint; Hebrew *plowshares* *e21* Hebrew *pim;* that is, about 1/4 ounce (about 8 grams) *f21* That is, about 1/8 ounce (about 4 grams)

Through the prophet Samuel, Saul has just been installed as Israel's first king. After leading the people to victory over the Ammonites, Saul (with the help of his son Jonathan) now faces the Philistines.

13:8 *time set by Samuel.* See 10:8. Saul is fully aware that Samuel's previous instructions had reference to this gathering at Gilgal. ***Saul's men began to scatter.*** The seven-day delay heightened the fear of the Israelite soldiers. The troops were reduced from 3,000 (v. 2) to 600 (v. 15).

13:9 *Saul offered up the burnt offering.* Samuel had promised to make these offerings himself (10:8) before Israel went to battle (see 7:7–9), and he had directed Saul to await his arrival and instructions.

13:13 *You acted foolishly.* The foolish and sinful aspect of Saul's act was that he thought he could strengthen Israel's chances against the Philistines while disregarding the instruction of the Lord's prophet Samuel. ***You have not kept the command the LORD your God gave you.*** Saul was to recognize the word of the prophet Samuel as the word of the Lord (see 3:20; 15:1; Ex. 20:18–19). In disobeying Samuel's instructions, Saul violated a fundamental requirement of his theocratic office. His kingship was not to function independently of the Law and the prophets.

13:14 *your kingdom will not endure.* Saul will not be followed by his sons; there will be no dynasty bearing his name. Saul's position will be given to another. There is a striking parallel in God's word to Eli (2:30).

14 out to the pass at Micmash. [1]One day Jonathan son of Saul said to the young man
bearing his armor, "Come, let's go over to the
Philistine outpost on the other side." But he did
not tell his father.
[2]Saul was staying on the outskirts of Gibeah
under a pomegranate tree in Migron. With him
were about six hundred men, [3]among whom was
Ahijah, who was wearing an ephod. He was a son
of Ichabod's brother Ahitub son of Phinehas, the
son of Eli, the LORD's priest in Shiloh. No one was
aware that Jonathan had left.
[4]On each side of the pass that Jonathan intended to cross to reach the Philistine outpost was a
cliff; one was called Bozez, and the other Seneh.
[5]One cliff stood to the north toward Micmash,
the other to the south toward Geba.
[6]Jonathan said to his young armor-bearer,
"Come, let's go over to the outpost of those uncircumcised fellows. Perhaps the LORD will act in
our behalf. Nothing can hinder the LORD from
saving, whether by many or by few."
[7]"Do all that you have in mind," his armor-
bearer said. "Go ahead; I am with you heart and
soul."
[8]Jonathan said, "Come, then; we will cross
over toward the men and let them see us. [9]If they
say to us, 'Wait there until we come to you,' we
will stay where we are and not go up to them.
[10]But if they say, 'Come up to us,' we will climb
up, because that will be our sign that the LORD
has given them into our hands."
[11]So both of them showed themselves to the
Philistine outpost. "Look!" said the Philistines.
"The Hebrews are crawling out of the holes they
were hiding in." [12]The men of the outpost shouted to Jonathan and his armor-bearer, "Come up
to us and we'll teach you a lesson."
So Jonathan said to his armor-bearer, "Climb
up after me; the LORD has given them into the
hand of Israel."
[13]Jonathan climbed up, using his hands and
feet, with his armor-bearer right behind him.
The Philistines fell before Jonathan, and his
armor-bearer followed and killed behind him.
[14]In that first attack Jonathan and his armor-
bearer killed some twenty men in an area of
about half an acre.[a]

Israel Routs the Philistines

[15]Then panic struck the whole army—those in
the camp and field, and those in the outposts and
raiding parties—and the ground shook. It was a
panic sent by God.[b]
[16]Saul's lookouts at Gibeah in Benjamin saw
the army melting away in all directions. [17]Then
Saul said to the men who were with him, "Muster the forces and see who has left us." When
they did, it was Jonathan and his armor-bearer
who were not there.
[18]Saul said to Ahijah, "Bring the ark of God."
(At that time it was with the Israelites.)[c]
[19]While Saul was talking to the priest, the tumult
in the Philistine camp increased more and more.
So Saul said to the priest, "Withdraw your hand."
[20]Then Saul and all his men assembled and
went to the battle. They found the Philistines in
total confusion, striking each other with their
swords. [21]Those Hebrews who had previously
been with the Philistines and had gone up with
them to their camp went over to the Israelites
who were with Saul and Jonathan. [22]When all the
Israelites who had hidden in the hill country of
Ephraim heard that the Philistines were on the
run, they joined the battle in hot pursuit. [23]So
the LORD rescued Israel that day, and the battle
moved on beyond Beth Aven.

Jonathan Eats Honey

[24]Now the men of Israel were in distress that
day, because Saul had bound the people under an
oath, saying, "Cursed be any man who eats food
before evening comes, before I have avenged myself on my enemies!" So none of the troops tasted
food.
[25]The entire army[d] entered the woods, and
there was honey on the ground. [26]When they
went into the woods, they saw the honey oozing
out, yet no one put his hand to his mouth, because they feared the oath. [27]But Jonathan had
not heard that his father had bound the people
with the oath, so he reached out the end of the
staff that was in his hand and dipped it into the
honeycomb. He raised his hand to his mouth, and
his eyes brightened.[e] [28]Then one of the soldiers
told him, "Your father bound the army under a
strict oath, saying, 'Cursed be any man who eats
food today!' That is why the men are faint."
[29]Jonathan said, "My father has made trouble
for the country. See how my eyes brightened[f]
when I tasted a little of this honey. [30]How much
better it would have been if the men had eaten
today some of the plunder they took from their
enemies. Would not the slaughter of the Philistines have been even greater?"
[31]That day, after the Israelites had struck
down the Philistines from Micmash to Aijalon,
they were exhausted. [32]They pounced on the
plunder and, taking sheep, cattle and calves, they
butchered them on the ground and ate them,

[a] 14 Hebrew *half a yoke*; a "yoke" was the land plowed by a yoke of oxen in one day. [b] 15 Or *a terrible panic* [c] 18 Hebrew; Septuagint *"Bring the ephod." (At that time he wore the ephod before the Israelites.)* [d] 25 Or *Now all the people of the land* [e] 27 Or *his strength was renewed* [f] 29 Or *my strength was renewed*

together with the blood. 33Then someone said
to Saul, "Look, the men are sinning against the
LORD by eating meat that has blood in it."
"You have broken faith," he said. "Roll a large
stone over here at once." 34Then he said, "Go out
among the men and tell them, 'Each of you bring
me your cattle and sheep, and slaughter them
here and eat them. Do not sin against the LORD
by eating meat with blood still in it.'"
So everyone brought his ox that night and
slaughtered it there. 35Then Saul built an altar to
the LORD; it was the first time he had done this.
36Saul said, "Let us go down after the Philistines by night and plunder them till dawn, and let
us not leave one of them alive."
"Do whatever seems best to you," they replied.
But the priest said, "Let us inquire of God
here."
37So Saul asked God, "Shall I go down after
the Philistines? Will you give them into Israel's
hand?" But God did not answer him that day.
38Saul therefore said, "Come here, all you who
are leaders of the army, and let us find out what
sin has been committed today. 39As surely as the
LORD who rescues Israel lives, even if it lies with
my son Jonathan, he must die." But not one of
the men said a word.
40Saul then said to all the Israelites, "You stand
over there; I and Jonathan my son will stand over
here."
"Do what seems best to you," the men replied.
41Then Saul prayed to the LORD, the God of
Israel, "Give me the right answer."[a] And Jonathan and Saul were taken by lot, and the men
were cleared. 42Saul said, "Cast the lot between
me and Jonathan my son." And Jonathan was
taken.
43Then Saul said to Jonathan, "Tell me what
you have done."
So Jonathan told him, "I merely tasted a little
honey with the end of my staff. And now must I
die?"
44Saul said, "May God deal with me, be it ever
so severely, if you do not die, Jonathan."
45But the men said to Saul, "Should Jonathan
die—he who has brought about this great deliverance in Israel? Never! As surely as the LORD
lives, not a hair of his head will fall to the ground,
for he did this today with God's help." So the
men rescued Jonathan, and he was not put to
death.
46Then Saul stopped pursuing the Philistines,
and they withdrew to their own land.
47After Saul had assumed rule over Israel, he
fought against their enemies on every side:
Moab, the Ammonites, Edom, the kings[b] of Zobah, and the Philistines. Wherever he turned, he
inflicted punishment on them.[c] 48He fought val-
iantly and defeated the Amalekites, delivering Israel from the hands of those who had plundered
them.

Saul's Family

49Saul's sons were Jonathan, Ishvi and Malki-
Shua. The name of his older daughter was Merab,
and that of the younger was Michal. 50His wife's
name was Ahinoam daughter of Ahimaaz. The
name of the commander of Saul's army was Abner son of Ner, and Ner was Saul's uncle. 51Saul's
father Kish and Abner's father Ner were sons of
Abiel.
52All the days of Saul there was bitter war with
the Philistines, and whenever Saul saw a mighty
or brave man, he took him into his service.

The LORD Rejects Saul as King

15 Samuel said to Saul, "I am the one the
LORD sent to anoint you king over his people Israel; so listen now to the message from the
LORD. 2This is what the LORD Almighty says: 'I
will punish the Amalekites for what they did to
Israel when they waylaid them as they came up
from Egypt. 3Now go, attack the Amalekites and
totally destroy[d] everything that belongs to them.
Do not spare them; put to death men and wom-
en, children and infants, cattle and sheep, camels
and donkeys.'"
4So Saul summoned the men and mustered
them at Telaim—two hundred thousand foot soldiers and ten thousand men from Judah. 5Saul
went to the city of Amalek and set an ambush in
the ravine. 6Then he said to the Kenites, "Go
away, leave the Amalekites so that I do not destroy you along with them; for you showed kindness to all the Israelites when they came up out
of Egypt." So the Kenites moved away from the
Amalekites.
7Then Saul attacked the Amalekites all the way
from Havilah to Shur, to the east of Egypt. 8He
took Agag king of the Amalekites alive, and all his
people he totally destroyed with the sword. 9But
Saul and the army spared Agag and the best of the
sheep and cattle, the fat calves[e] and lambs—
everything that was good. These they were unwilling to destroy completely, but everything that
was despised and weak they totally destroyed.
10Then the word of the LORD came to Samuel:

[a] 41 Hebrew; Septuagint *"Why have you not answered your servant today? If the fault is in me or my son Jonathan, respond with Urim, but if the men of Israel are at fault, respond with Thummim."* [b] 47 Masoretic Text; Dead Sea Scrolls and Septuagint *king* [c] 47 Hebrew; Septuagint *he was victorious* [d] 3 The Hebrew term refers to the irrevocable giving over of things or persons to the LORD, often by totally destroying them; also in verses 8, 9, 15, 18, 20 and 21. [e] 9 Or *the grown bulls*; the meaning of the Hebrew for this phrase is uncertain.

11 "I am grieved that I have made Saul king, because he has turned away from me and has not
carried out my instructions." Samuel was troubled, and he cried out to the LORD all that night.
12 Early in the morning Samuel got up and
went to meet Saul, but he was told, "Saul has
gone to Carmel. There he has set up a monument
in his own honor and has turned and gone on
down to Gilgal."
13 When Samuel reached him, Saul said, "The
LORD bless you! I have carried out the LORD's
instructions."
14 But Samuel said, "What then is this bleating
of sheep in my ears? What is this lowing of cattle
that I hear?"
15 Saul answered, "The soldiers brought them
from the Amalekites; they spared the best of the
sheep and cattle to sacrifice to the LORD your
God, but we totally destroyed the rest."
16 "Stop!" Samuel said to Saul. "Let me tell you
what the LORD said to me last night."
"Tell me," Saul replied.
17 Samuel said, "Although you were once small
in your own eyes, did you not become the head
of the tribes of Israel? The LORD anointed you
king over Israel.
18 And he sent you on a mission,
saying, 'Go and completely destroy those wicked
people, the Amalekites; make war on them until
you have wiped them out.'
19 Why did you not
obey the LORD? Why did you pounce on the plunder and do evil in the eyes of the LORD?"
20 "But I did obey the LORD," Saul said. "I went
on the mission the LORD assigned me. I completely destroyed the Amalekites and brought back
Agag their king.
21 The soldiers took sheep and
cattle from the plunder, the best of what was
devoted to God, in order to sacrifice them to the
LORD your God at Gilgal."
22 But Samuel replied:

"Does the LORD delight in burnt offerings
and sacrifices
as much as in obeying the voice of the
LORD?
To obey is better than sacrifice,
and to heed is better than the fat of rams.
23 For rebellion is like the sin of divination,
and arrogance like the evil of idolatry.
Because you have rejected the word of the
LORD,
he has rejected you as king."

24 Then Saul said to Samuel, "I have sinned. I
violated the LORD's command and your instructions. I was afraid of the people and so I gave in
to them.
25 Now I beg you, forgive my sin and
come back with me, so that I may worship the
LORD."
26 But Samuel said to him, "I will not go back
with you. You have rejected the word of the
LORD, and the LORD has rejected you as king over
Israel!"
27 As Samuel turned to leave, Saul caught hold
of the hem of his robe, and it tore.
28 Samuel said
to him, "The LORD has torn the kingdom of Israel
from you today and has given it to one of your
neighbors—to one better than you.
29 He who is
the Glory of Israel does not lie or change his
mind; for he is not a man, that he should change
his mind."
30 Saul replied, "I have sinned. But please hon-
or me before the elders of my people and before
Israel; come back with me, so that I may worship
the LORD your God."
31 So Samuel went back with
Saul, and Saul worshiped the LORD.
32 Then Samuel said, "Bring me Agag king of
the Amalekites."
Agag came to him confidently,[a] thinking,
"Surely the bitterness of death is past."
33 But Samuel said,

"As your sword has made women childless,
so will your mother be childless among
women."

And Samuel put Agag to death before the LORD at
Gilgal.
34 Then Samuel left for Ramah, but Saul went
up to his home in Gibeah of Saul.
35 Until the day
Samuel died, he did not go to see Saul again,
though Samuel mourned for him. And the LORD
was grieved that he had made Saul king over
Israel.

Samuel Anoints David

16 The LORD said to Samuel, "How long will
you mourn for Saul, since I have rejected
him as king over Israel? Fill your horn with oil
and be on your way; I am sending you to Jesse of
Bethlehem. I have chosen one of his sons to be
king."
2 But Samuel said, "How can I go? Saul will
hear about it and kill me."
The LORD said, "Take a heifer with you and
say, 'I have come to sacrifice to the LORD.'
3 Invite
Jesse to the sacrifice, and I will show you what to
do. You are to anoint for me the one I indicate."
4 Samuel did what the LORD said. When he arrived at Bethlehem, the elders of the town trembled when they met him. They asked, "Do you
come in peace?"
5 Samuel replied, "Yes, in peace; I have come
to sacrifice to the LORD. Consecrate yourselves
and come to the sacrifice with me." Then he
consecrated Jesse and his sons and invited them
to the sacrifice.

[a] 32 Or *him trembling, yet*

6When they arrived, Samuel saw Eliab and
thought, "Surely the LORD's anointed stands here
before the LORD."
7But the LORD said to Samuel, "Do not consider his appearance or his height, for I have rejected him. The LORD does not look at the things man
looks at. Man looks at the outward appearance,
but the LORD looks at the heart."

1 Samuel 16:1–13

1. Where are you in the birth order of your family: The oldest? Youngest? In the middle? Who gets favored when it comes to chores? Curfews?
2. When the elementary kids picked teams on the playground, how long did it usually take you to get chosen?
3. What do you look for in a date: Looks? Brains? Personality?
4. Who is a person you know who you would nominate to be "King/Queen"? Based on what qualities?
5. Why do you think God skipped over the older brothers and chose David?
6. God looks at the heart (v. 7). On a scale of 1 (weak) to 10 (strong), how's your heart right now?
7. Share a prayer request with the group. Close in prayer.

8Then Jesse called Abinadab and had him pass
in front of Samuel. But Samuel said, "The LORD
has not chosen this one either." 9Jesse then had
Shammah pass by, but Samuel said, "Nor has the
LORD chosen this one." 10Jesse had seven of his
sons pass before Samuel, but Samuel said to him,
"The LORD has not chosen these." 11So he asked
Jesse, "Are these all the sons you have?"

"There is still the youngest," Jesse answered, "but he is tending the sheep."

Samuel said, "Send for him; we will not sit down[a] until he arrives."

12So he sent and had him brought in. He was
ruddy, with a fine appearance and handsome features.

Then the LORD said, "Rise and anoint him; he is the one."

13So Samuel took the horn of oil and anointed
him in the presence of his brothers, and from
that day on the Spirit of the LORD came upon
David in power. Samuel then went to Ramah.

David in Saul's Service

14Now the Spirit of the LORD had departed
from Saul, and an evil[b] spirit from the LORD
tormented him.

15Saul's attendants said to him, "See, an evil
spirit from God is tormenting you. 16Let our lord
command his servants here to search for someone who can play the harp. He will play when the
evil spirit from God comes upon you, and you
will feel better."

17So Saul said to his attendants, "Find someone who plays well and bring him to me."

18One of the servants answered, "I have seen
a son of Jesse of Bethlehem who knows how to
play the harp. He is a brave man and a warrior.
He speaks well and is a fine-looking man. And
the LORD is with him."

19Then Saul sent messengers to Jesse and said,
"Send me your son David, who is with the
sheep." 20So Jesse took a donkey loaded with
bread, a skin of wine and a young goat and sent
them with his son David to Saul.

21David came to Saul and entered his service.
Saul liked him very much, and David became one
of his armor-bearers. 22Then Saul sent word to
Jesse, saying, "Allow David to remain in my service, for I am pleased with him."

[a] *11* Some Septuagint manuscripts; Hebrew *not gather around*

[b] *14* Or *injurious*; also in verses 15, 16 and 23

16:1 God had led the prophet Samuel to anoint Saul as Israel's king. Now God tells Samuel it is time to anoint a new king. ***Bethlehem.*** A town five miles south of Jerusalem. It was later to become renowned as the "town of David" and the birthplace of Christ (Mic. 5:2; Luke 2:4–7).

16:2 ***Saul will hear about it and kill me.*** The road from Ramah, where Samuel was (15:34), to Bethlehem passed through Gibeah of Saul. Saul already knew that the Lord had chosen someone to replace him as king (see 15:28). Samuel fears that jealousy will incite Saul to violence. Later incidents demonstrate that Samuel's fears were well-founded. ***say, 'I have come to sacrifice to the LORD.'*** This response is true but incomplete, and it was intended to deceive Saul.

16:3 ***anoint.*** Signifying separation to God and his equipping for a particular task.

16:7 ***his appearance or his height.*** Samuel is not to focus on these outward features, which had characterized Saul (see 9:2). ***the LORD looks at the heart.*** God is concerned with the inner disposition and character (see 1 Chron. 28:9; Luke 16:15).

16:11 ***he is tending the sheep.*** The Lord's chosen one is a shepherd (Ps. 78:71–72).

16:13 ***in the presence of his brothers.*** The small circle of witnesses to David's anointing assured its confidentiality, but also provided ample testimony for the future that David had been anointed by Samuel and was not merely usurping Saul's office.

23 Whenever the spirit from God came upon Saul, David would take his harp and play. Then relief would come to Saul; he would feel better, and the evil spirit would leave him.

David and Goliath

17 Now the Philistines gathered their forces for war and assembled at Socoh in Judah. They pitched camp at Ephes Dammim, between Socoh and Azekah. 2 Saul and the Israelites assembled and camped in the Valley of Elah and drew up their battle line to meet the Philistines. 3 The Philistines occupied one hill and the Israelites another, with the valley between them.

4 A champion named Goliath, who was from Gath, came out of the Philistine camp. He was over nine feet[a] tall. 5 He had a bronze helmet on his head and wore a coat of scale armor of bronze weighing five thousand shekels[b]; 6 on his legs he wore bronze greaves, and a bronze javelin was slung on his back. 7 His spear shaft was like a weaver's rod, and its iron point weighed six hundred shekels.[c] His shield bearer went ahead of him.

8 Goliath stood and shouted to the ranks of Israel, "Why do you come out and line up for battle? Am I not a Philistine, and are you not the servants of Saul? Choose a man and have him come down to me. 9 If he is able to fight and kill me, we will become your subjects; but if I overcome him and kill him, you will become our subjects and serve us." 10 Then the Philistine said, "This day I defy the ranks of Israel! Give me a man and let us fight each other." 11 On hearing the Philistine's words, Saul and all the Israelites were dismayed and terrified.

12 Now David was the son of an Ephrathite named Jesse, who was from Bethlehem in Judah. Jesse had eight sons, and in Saul's time he was old and well advanced in years. 13 Jesse's three oldest sons had followed Saul to the war: The firstborn was Eliab; the second, Abinadab; and the third, Shammah. 14 David was the youngest. The three oldest followed Saul, 15 but David went back and forth from Saul to tend his father's sheep at Bethlehem.

16 For forty days the Philistine came forward every morning and evening and took his stand.

17 Now Jesse said to his son David, "Take this ephah[d] of roasted grain and these ten loaves of bread for your brothers and hurry to their camp. 18 Take along these ten cheeses to the commander of their unit.[e] See how your brothers are and bring back some assurance[f] from them. 19 They are with Saul and all the men of Israel in the Valley of Elah, fighting against the Philistines."

20 Early in the morning David left the flock with a shepherd, loaded up and set out, as Jesse had directed. He reached the camp as the army was going out to its battle positions, shouting the war cry. 21 Israel and the Philistines were drawing up their lines facing each other. 22 David left his things with the keeper of supplies, ran to the battle lines and greeted his brothers. 23 As he was talking with them, Goliath, the Philistine champion from Gath, stepped out from his lines and shouted his usual defiance, and David heard it. 24 When the Israelites saw the man, they all ran from him in great fear.

25 Now the Israelites had been saying, "Do you see how this man keeps coming out? He comes out to defy Israel. The king will give great wealth to the man who kills him. He will also give him his daughter in marriage and will exempt his father's family from taxes in Israel."

26 David asked the men standing near him, "What will be done for the man who kills this Philistine and removes this disgrace from Israel? Who is this uncircumcised Philistine that he should defy the armies of the living God?"

27 They repeated to him what they had been saying and told him, "This is what will be done for the man who kills him."

28 When Eliab, David's oldest brother, heard him speaking with the men, he burned with anger at him and asked, "Why have you come down here? And with whom did you leave those few sheep in the desert? I know how conceited you are and how wicked your heart is; you came down only to watch the battle."

29 "Now what have I done?" said David. "Can't I even speak?" 30 He then turned away to someone else and brought up the same matter, and the men answered him as before. 31 What David said was overheard and reported to Saul, and Saul sent for him.

32 David said to Saul, "Let no one lose heart on account of this Philistine; your servant will go and fight him."

33 Saul replied, "You are not able to go out against this Philistine and fight him; you are only a boy, and he has been a fighting man from his youth."

34 But David said to Saul, "Your servant has been keeping his father's sheep. When a lion or a bear came and carried off a sheep from the flock, 35 I went after it, struck it and rescued the sheep from its mouth. When it turned on me, I seized it by its hair, struck it and killed it. 36 Your

[a] *4* Hebrew *was six cubits and a span* (about 3 meters) [b] *5* That is, about 125 pounds (about 57 kilograms) [c] *7* That is, about 15 pounds (about 7 kilograms) [d] *17* That is, probably about 3/5 bushel (about 22 liters) [e] *18* Hebrew *thousand*
[f] *18* Or *some token*; or *some pledge of spoils*

servant has killed both the lion and the bear; this
uncircumcised Philistine will be like one of them,
because he has defied the armies of the living
God. 37The LORD who delivered me from the paw
of the lion and the paw of the bear will deliver
me from the hand of this Philistine."
Saul said to David, "Go, and the LORD be with
you."
38Then Saul dressed David in his own tunic.
He put a coat of armor on him and a bronze
helmet on his head. 39David fastened on his
sword over the tunic and tried walking around,
because he was not used to them.

1 SAMUEL 17:20–50

1. When you were a child, who were the bullies in your life?
2. What is the closest you or a team you were on came to being totally outmatched against an opponent?
3. How do you feel when someone casts doubts on your abilities? How do you react when you are told you can't do something?
4. Read aloud verses 26,34–37 and 45–47. What are you able to tell about David's personality?
5. What gives you confidence: Size? Strength? Age? Smarts? Looks? Faith?
6. What "giant" are you now facing? What do you need the most for the fight: Faith in God? Confidence in yourself? Support from others?
7. Name one way you will take a stand for God this week. How can the group support you in prayer?

"I cannot go in these," he said to Saul, "because I am not used to them." So he took them
off. 40Then he took his staff in his hand, chose
five smooth stones from the stream, put them in
the pouch of his shepherd's bag and, with his
sling in his hand, approached the Philistine.
41Meanwhile, the Philistine, with his shield
bearer in front of him, kept coming closer to David. 42He looked David over and saw that he was
only a boy, ruddy and handsome, and he despised
him. 43He said to David, "Am I a dog, that you
come at me with sticks?" And the Philistine
cursed David by his gods. 44"Come here," he
said, "and I'll give your flesh to the birds of the
air and the beasts of the field!"
45David said to the Philistine, "You come
against me with sword and spear and javelin, but
I come against you in the name of the LORD Almighty, the God of the armies of Israel, whom
you have defied. 46This day the LORD will hand
you over to me, and I'll strike you down and cut
off your head. Today I will give the carcasses of
the Philistine army to the birds of the air and the
beasts of the earth, and the whole world will
know that there is a God in Israel. 47All those
gathered here will know that it is not by sword or
spear that the LORD saves; for the battle is the
LORD's, and he will give all of you into our
hands."
48As the Philistine moved closer to attack him,
David ran quickly toward the battle line to meet
him. 49Reaching into his bag and taking out a
stone, he slung it and struck the Philistine on the
forehead. The stone sank into his forehead, and
he fell facedown on the ground.
50So David triumphed over the Philistine
with a sling and a stone; without a sword in his
hand he struck down the Philistine and killed
him.
51David ran and stood over him. He took hold
of the Philistine's sword and drew it from the
scabbard. After he killed him, he cut off his head
with the sword.
When the Philistines saw that their hero was
dead, they turned and ran. 52Then the men of
Israel and Judah surged forward with a shout and

Israel's army had drawn up a battle line with the Philistines. Each day Goliath—the 9-foot Philistine champion—came forward to defy the Israelites and challenge them to send a representative to fight him.

17:24 ***great fear.*** The fear of Saul and the Israelite army betrays a loss of faith in the covenant promises of the Lord (see Ex. 23:22; Deut. 3:22; 20:1–4). Their fear demonstrates that the Israelite search for security in a human king (apart from trust in the Lord) had failed.

17:32–33 ***Let no one lose heart on account of this Philistine.*** David's confidence does not rest in his own power but in the power of the living God (see vv. 37,47), whose honor has been violated by the Philistines. ***You are not able.*** Saul does not take into account God's power.

17:40 ***his staff.*** God's newly appointed shepherd of his people goes to defend the Lord's threatened and frightened flock. ***stones.*** Usually round and smooth and somewhat larger than a baseball. When hurled by a master slinger, they probably traveled at close to 100 miles per hour.

17:45–46 ***in the name of the LORD Almighty.*** David's strength was his reliance on the Lord. ***the whole world will know.*** The victory David anticipates will demonstrate God's power to all the world.

17:47 ***the battle is the LORD's.*** Both armies will be shown the error of placing trust in human devices for personal or national security.

pursued the Philistines to the entrance of Gath[a] and to the gates of Ekron. Their dead were strewn along the Shaaraim road to Gath and Ekron. 53When the Israelites returned from chasing the Philistines, they plundered their camp. 54David took the Philistine's head and brought it to Jerusalem, and he put the Philistine's weapons in his own tent.

55As Saul watched David going out to meet the Philistine, he said to Abner, commander of the army, "Abner, whose son is that young man?"

Abner replied, "As surely as you live, O king, I don't know."

56The king said, "Find out whose son this young man is."

57As soon as David returned from killing the Philistine, Abner took him and brought him before Saul, with David still holding the Philistine's head.

58"Whose son are you, young man?" Saul asked him.

David said, "I am the son of your servant Jesse of Bethlehem."

Saul's Jealousy of David

18 After David had finished talking with Saul, Jonathan became one in spirit with David, and he loved him as himself. 2From that day Saul kept David with him and did not let him return to his father's house. 3And Jonathan made a covenant with David because he loved him as himself. 4Jonathan took off the robe he was wearing and gave it to David, along with his tunic, and even his sword, his bow and his belt.

5Whatever Saul sent him to do, David did it so successfully[b] that Saul gave him a high rank in the army. This pleased all the people, and Saul's officers as well.

6When the men were returning home after David had killed the Philistine, the women came out from all the towns of Israel to meet King Saul with singing and dancing, with joyful songs and with tambourines and lutes. 7As they danced, they sang:

"Saul has slain his thousands,
and David his tens of thousands."

8Saul was very angry; this refrain galled him. "They have credited David with tens of thousands," he thought, "but me with only thousands. What more can he get but the kingdom?" 9And from that time on Saul kept a jealous eye on David.

10The next day an evil[c] spirit from God came forcefully upon Saul. He was prophesying in his house, while David was playing the harp, as he usually did. Saul had a spear in his hand 11and he hurled it, saying to himself, "I'll pin David to the wall." But David eluded him twice.

1 Samuel 18:1–16

1. Who was your best friend in grade school? Did you ever swap or give each other stuff?
2. What qualities do you look for when you choose a friend?
3. What is the status symbol in your school that causes the most jealousy: Clothes? Cars? Popularity?
4. What was it about Jonathan that made him such a good friend to David?
5. How do you react when you are not given the credit you think you deserve?
6. What's your biggest barrier to having closer friendships: Acting like you don't need them? Jealousy? Hiding your feelings?
7. How would you like the group to pray for you this week?

[a] *52* Some Septuagint manuscripts; Hebrew *a valley* [b] *5* Or *wisely* [c] *10* Or *injurious*

Young David has recently experienced two events which would drastically change his life: He was anointed by the prophet Samuel—without King Saul's knowledge—to be Israel's next king; then he courageously defeated Goliath the giant.

18:1 *one in spirit.* One of the greatest examples of friendship in the Bible is that of David and Saul's son Jonathan.

18:3–4 *Jonathan made a covenant.* The initiative to pledge mutual loyalty and friendship comes from Jonathan. With the items Jonathan gave, he ratifies the covenant in an act that symbolizes giving himself to David. His act may even signify his recognition that David was to assume his place as successor to Saul (23:17).

18:7 *David his tens of thousands.* In accord with the usage of parallels in Hebrew poetry, this was the women's way of saying, "Saul and David have slain thousands." It is a measure of Saul's insecurity and jealousy that he read their intentions incorrectly and took offense. His resentment may have been initially triggered by the mention of David's name alongside his own.

18:10 *evil spirit from God.* Evil spirits are subject to God's control and operate only within divinely determined boundaries (compare 2 Sam. 24:1 with 1 Chron. 21:1). ***prophesying.*** The Hebrew for this word is sometimes used to indicate uncontrolled ecstatic behavior and is best understood in that sense here. ***as he usually did.*** See 16:14,23.

12 Saul was afraid of David, because the LORD was with David but had left Saul. 13 So he sent David away from him and gave him command over a thousand men, and David led the troops in their campaigns. 14 In everything he did he had great success,[a] because the LORD was with him. 15 When Saul saw how successful[b] he was, he was afraid of him. 16 But all Israel and Judah loved David, because he led them in their campaigns.

17 Saul said to David, "Here is my older daughter Merab. I will give her to you in marriage; only serve me bravely and fight the battles of the LORD." For Saul said to himself, "I will not raise a hand against him. Let the Philistines do that!"

18 But David said to Saul, "Who am I, and what is my family or my father's clan in Israel, that I should become the king's son-in-law?" 19 So[c] when the time came for Merab, Saul's daughter, to be given to David, she was given in marriage to Adriel of Meholah.

20 Now Saul's daughter Michal was in love with David, and when they told Saul about it, he was pleased. 21 "I will give her to him," he thought, "so that she may be a snare to him and so that the hand of the Philistines may be against him." So Saul said to David, "Now you have a second opportunity to become my son-in-law."

22 Then Saul ordered his attendants: "Speak to David privately and say, 'Look, the king is pleased with you, and his attendants all like you; now become his son-in-law.'"

23 They repeated these words to David. But David said, "Do you think it is a small matter to become the king's son-in-law? I'm only a poor man and little known."

24 When Saul's servants told him what David had said, 25 Saul replied, "Say to David, 'The king wants no other price for the bride than a hundred Philistine foreskins, to take revenge on his enemies.'" Saul's plan was to have David fall by the hands of the Philistines.

26 When the attendants told David these things, he was pleased to become the king's son-in-law. So before the allotted time elapsed, 27 David and his men went out and killed two hundred Philistines. He brought their foreskins and presented the full number to the king so that he might become the king's son-in-law. Then Saul gave him his daughter Michal in marriage.

28 When Saul realized that the LORD was with David and that his daughter Michal loved David, 29 Saul became still more afraid of him, and he remained his enemy the rest of his days.

30 The Philistine commanders continued to go out to battle, and as often as they did, David met with more success[d] than the rest of Saul's officers, and his name became well known.

Saul Tries to Kill David

19 Saul told his son Jonathan and all the attendants to kill David. But Jonathan was very fond of David 2 and warned him, "My father Saul is looking for a chance to kill you. Be on your guard tomorrow morning; go into hiding and stay there. 3 I will go out and stand with my father in the field where you are. I'll speak to him about you and will tell you what I find out."

4 Jonathan spoke well of David to Saul his father and said to him, "Let not the king do wrong to his servant David; he has not wronged you, and what he has done has benefited you greatly. 5 He took his life in his hands when he killed the Philistine. The LORD won a great victory for all Israel, and you saw it and were glad. Why then would you do wrong to an innocent man like David by killing him for no reason?"

6 Saul listened to Jonathan and took this oath: "As surely as the LORD lives, David will not be put to death."

7 So Jonathan called David and told him the whole conversation. He brought him to Saul, and David was with Saul as before.

8 Once more war broke out, and David went out and fought the Philistines. He struck them with such force that they fled before him.

9 But an evil[e] spirit from the LORD came upon Saul as he was sitting in his house with his spear in his hand. While David was playing the harp, 10 Saul tried to pin him to the wall with his spear, but David eluded him as Saul drove the spear into the wall. That night David made good his escape.

11 Saul sent men to David's house to watch it and to kill him in the morning. But Michal, David's wife, warned him, "If you don't run for your life tonight, tomorrow you'll be killed." 12 So Michal let David down through a window, and he fled and escaped. 13 Then Michal took an idol[f] and laid it on the bed, covering it with a garment and putting some goats' hair at the head.

14 When Saul sent the men to capture David, Michal said, "He is ill."

15 Then Saul sent the men back to see David and told them, "Bring him up to me in his bed so that I may kill him." 16 But when the men entered, there was the idol in the bed, and at the head was some goats' hair.

17 Saul said to Michal, "Why did you deceive me like this and send my enemy away so that he escaped?"

Michal told him, "He said to me, 'Let me get away. Why should I kill you?'"

[a] 14 Or *he was very wise* [b] 15 Or *wise* [c] 19 Or *However,* [d] 30 Or *David acted more wisely* [e] 9 Or *injurious*
[f] 13 Hebrew *teraphim*; also in verse 16

18When David had fled and made his escape, he went to Samuel at Ramah and told him all that Saul had done to him. Then he and Samuel went to Naioth and stayed there. 19Word came to Saul: "David is in Naioth at Ramah"; 20so he sent men to capture him. But when they saw a group of prophets prophesying, with Samuel standing there as their leader, the Spirit of God came upon Saul's men and they also prophesied. 21Saul was told about it, and he sent more men, and they prophesied too. Saul sent men a third time, and they also prophesied. 22Finally, he himself left for Ramah and went to the great cistern at Secu. And he asked, "Where are Samuel and David?"

"Over in Naioth at Ramah," they said.

23So Saul went to Naioth at Ramah. But the Spirit of God came even upon him, and he walked along prophesying until he came to Naioth. 24He stripped off his robes and also prophesied in Samuel's presence. He lay that way all that day and night. This is why people say, "Is Saul also among the prophets?"

David and Jonathan

20 Then David fled from Naioth at Ramah and went to Jonathan and asked, "What have I done? What is my crime? How have I wronged your father, that he is trying to take my life?"

2"Never!" Jonathan replied. "You are not going to die! Look, my father doesn't do anything, great or small, without confiding in me. Why would he hide this from me? It's not so!"

3But David took an oath and said, "Your father knows very well that I have found favor in your eyes, and he has said to himself, 'Jonathan must not know this or he will be grieved.' Yet as surely as the LORD lives and as you live, there is only a step between me and death."

4Jonathan said to David, "Whatever you want me to do, I'll do for you."

5So David said, "Look, tomorrow is the New Moon festival, and I am supposed to dine with the king; but let me go and hide in the field until the evening of the day after tomorrow. 6If your father misses me at all, tell him, 'David earnestly asked my permission to hurry to Bethlehem, his hometown, because an annual sacrifice is being made there for his whole clan.' 7If he says, 'Very well,' then your servant is safe. But if he loses his temper, you can be sure that he is determined to harm me. 8As for you, show kindness to your servant, for you have brought him into a covenant with you before the LORD. If I am guilty, then kill me yourself! Why hand me over to your father?"

1 Samuel 20:1–13,18–42

1. What secret ways of communicating have you tried with a friend: Secret handshake? Sign language? Passing notes?
2. Generally speaking, do you think the average guy on the street can be trusted?
3. Do you tend to accept people quickly or wait until they prove themselves?
4. Whom can you trust with anything?
5. If you had to choose between your family or your best friend, whom would you choose?
6. How hard is it for you to trust this group with the heavy stuff in your life? What could help?
7. Close in prayer.

9"Never!" Jonathan said. "If I had the least inkling that my father was determined to harm you, wouldn't I tell you?"

10David asked, "Who will tell me if your father answers you harshly?"

11"Come," Jonathan said, "let's go out into the field." So they went there together.

12Then Jonathan said to David: "By the LORD, the God of Israel, I will surely sound out my fa-

---

20:1 After escaping Saul's attempts to kill him, David goes to his friend Jonathan.

20:8 ***covenant.*** David reminds Jonathan of the covenant they had made earlier (see note on 18:3–4).

20:11 ***let's go out into the field.*** Jonathan takes action to save his friend David. Cain had said the same to Abel, but in order to kill him (Gen. 4:8).

20:30 ***son of a perverse and rebellious woman.*** The Hebrew idiom intends to characterize Jonathan, not his mother.

20:31 ***neither you nor your kingdom will be established.*** Saul is now convinced that David will succeed him if David is not killed, and he is incapable of understanding Jonathan's lack of concern for his own succession to the throne.

20:33 ***hurled his spear.*** As he had done with David (18:11; 19:10). Here is a tragic picture of how pathetic Saul had become.

20:41 ***kissed each other.*** Men in that culture were not hesitant to express love for each other.

20:42 ***between your descendants and my descendants.*** See verses 14–15. Jonathan realizes that the Lord would make David Israel's next king. As it was quite common for the first ruler of a new dynasty to secure his position by murdering all potential claimants to the throne from the preceding dynasty, David and Jonathan mutually agreed that such would not be the case (see 2 Sam. 9:3–7; 21:7).

ther by this time the day after tomorrow! If he is
favorably disposed toward you, will I not send
you word and let you know? 13But if my father is
inclined to harm you, may the LORD deal with
me, be it ever so severely, if I do not let you know
and send you away safely. May the LORD be with
you as he has been with my father. 14But show
me unfailing kindness like that of the LORD as
long as I live, so that I may not be killed, 15and do
not ever cut off your kindness from my family—
not even when the LORD has cut off every one of
David's enemies from the face of the earth."

16So Jonathan made a covenant with the house
of David, saying, "May the LORD call David's enemies to account." 17And Jonathan had David reaffirm his oath out of love for him, because he
loved him as he loved himself.

18Then Jonathan said to David: "Tomorrow is
the New Moon festival. You will be missed, because your seat will be empty. 19The day after
tomorrow, toward evening, go to the place where
you hid when this trouble began, and wait by the
stone Ezel. 20I will shoot three arrows to the side
of it, as though I were shooting at a target. 21Then
I will send a boy and say, 'Go, find the arrows.'
If I say to him, 'Look, the arrows are on this side
of you; bring them here,' then come, because, as
surely as the LORD lives, you are safe; there is no
danger. 22But if I say to the boy, 'Look, the arrows
are beyond you,' then you must go, because the
LORD has sent you away. 23And about the matter
you and I discussed—remember, the LORD is witness between you and me forever."

24So David hid in the field, and when the New
Moon festival came, the king sat down to eat.
25He sat in his customary place by the wall, opposite Jonathan,[a] and Abner sat next to Saul, but
David's place was empty. 26Saul said nothing that
day, for he thought, "Something must have happened to David to make him ceremonially
unclean—surely he is unclean." 27But the next
day, the second day of the month, David's place
was empty again. Then Saul said to his son Jonathan, "Why hasn't the son of Jesse come to the
meal, either yesterday or today?"

28Jonathan answered, "David earnestly asked
me for permission to go to Bethlehem. 29He said,
'Let me go, because our family is observing a
sacrifice in the town and my brother has ordered
me to be there. If I have found favor in your eyes,
let me get away to see my brothers.' That is why
he has not come to the king's table."

30Saul's anger flared up at Jonathan and he said
to him, "You son of a perverse and rebellious
woman! Don't I know that you have sided with
the son of Jesse to your own shame and to the
shame of the mother who bore you? 31As long as
the son of Jesse lives on this earth, neither you
nor your kingdom will be established. Now send
and bring him to me, for he must die!"

32"Why should he be put to death? What has
he done?" Jonathan asked his father. 33But Saul
hurled his spear at him to kill him. Then Jonathan knew that his father intended to kill David.

34Jonathan got up from the table in fierce anger; on that second day of the month he did not
eat, because he was grieved at his father's shameful treatment of David.

35In the morning Jonathan went out to the
field for his meeting with David. He had a small
boy with him, 36and he said to the boy, "Run and
find the arrows I shoot." As the boy ran, he shot
an arrow beyond him. 37When the boy came to
the place where Jonathan's arrow had fallen, Jonathan called out after him, "Isn't the arrow beyond you?" 38Then he shouted, "Hurry! Go
quickly! Don't stop!" The boy picked up the arrow and returned to his master. 39(The boy knew
nothing of all this; only Jonathan and David
knew.) 40Then Jonathan gave his weapons to the
boy and said, "Go, carry them back to town."

41After the boy had gone, David got up from
the south side ⌞of the stone⌟ and bowed down
before Jonathan three times, with his face to the
ground. Then they kissed each other and wept
together—but David wept the most.

42Jonathan said to David, "Go in peace, for we
have sworn friendship with each other in the
name of the LORD, saying, 'The LORD is witness
between you and me, and between your descendants and my descendants forever.'" Then David
left, and Jonathan went back to the town.

David at Nob

21 David went to Nob, to Ahimelech the
priest. Ahimelech trembled when he met
him, and asked, "Why are you alone? Why is no
one with you?"

2David answered Ahimelech the priest, "The
king charged me with a certain matter and said to
me, 'No one is to know anything about your mission and your instructions.' As for my men, I
have told them to meet me at a certain place.
3Now then, what do you have on hand? Give me
five loaves of bread, or whatever you can find."

4But the priest answered David, "I don't have
any ordinary bread on hand; however, there is
some consecrated bread here—provided the
men have kept themselves from women."

5David replied, "Indeed women have been
kept from us, as usual whenever[b] I set out. The
men's things[c] are holy even on missions that
are not holy. How much more so today!" 6So the
priest gave him the consecrated bread, since

[a]25 Septuagint; Hebrew *wall. Jonathan arose*
[b]5 Or *from us in the past few days since*
[c]5 Or *bodies*

there was no bread there except the bread of the
Presence that had been removed from before the
LORD and replaced by hot bread on the day it was
taken away.
[7]Now one of Saul's servants was there that
day, detained before the LORD; he was Doeg the
Edomite, Saul's head shepherd.
[8]David asked Ahimelech, "Don't you have a
spear or a sword here? I haven't brought my
sword or any other weapon, because the king's
business was urgent."
[9]The priest replied, "The sword of Goliath the
Philistine, whom you killed in the Valley of Elah,
is here; it is wrapped in a cloth behind the ephod.
If you want it, take it; there is no sword here but
that one."
David said, "There is none like it; give it
to me."

David at Gath

[10]That day David fled from Saul and went to
Achish king of Gath. [11]But the servants of Achish
said to him, "Isn't this David, the king of the
land? Isn't he the one they sing about in their
dances:

" 'Saul has slain his thousands,
and David his tens of thousands'?"

[12]David took these words to heart and was
very much afraid of Achish king of Gath. [13]So he
pretended to be insane in their presence; and
while he was in their hands he acted like a madman, making marks on the doors of the gate and
letting saliva run down his beard.
[14]Achish said to his servants, "Look at the
man! He is insane! Why bring him to me? [15]Am I
so short of madmen that you have to bring this
fellow here to carry on like this in front of me?
Must this man come into my house?"

David at Adullam and Mizpah

22 David left Gath and escaped to the cave of
Adullam. When his brothers and his father's household heard about it, they went down
to him there. [2]All those who were in distress or
in debt or discontented gathered around him,
and he became their leader. About four hundred
men were with him.
[3]From there David went to Mizpah in Moab
and said to the king of Moab, "Would you let my
father and mother come and stay with you until
I learn what God will do for me?" [4]So he left
them with the king of Moab, and they stayed
with him as long as David was in the stronghold.
[5]But the prophet Gad said to David, "Do not
stay in the stronghold. Go into the land of Judah."
So David left and went to the forest of Hereth.

Saul Kills the Priests of Nob

[6]Now Saul heard that David and his men had
been discovered. And Saul, spear in hand, was
seated under the tamarisk tree on the hill at Gibeah, with all his officials standing around him.
[7]Saul said to them, "Listen, men of Benjamin!
Will the son of Jesse give all of you fields and
vineyards? Will he make all of you commanders
of thousands and commanders of hundreds? [8]Is
that why you have all conspired against me? No
one tells me when my son makes a covenant with
the son of Jesse. None of you is concerned about
me or tells me that my son has incited my servant
to lie in wait for me, as he does today."
[9]But Doeg the Edomite, who was standing
with Saul's officials, said, "I saw the son of Jesse
come to Ahimelech son of Ahitub at Nob.
[10]Ahimelech inquired of the LORD for him; he
also gave him provisions and the sword of Goliath
the Philistine."
[11]Then the king sent for the priest Ahimelech
son of Ahitub and his father's whole family, who
were the priests at Nob, and they all came to the
king. [12]Saul said, "Listen now, son of Ahitub."
"Yes, my lord," he answered.
[13]Saul said to him, "Why have you conspired
against me, you and the son of Jesse, giving him
bread and a sword and inquiring of God for him,
so that he has rebelled against me and lies in wait
for me, as he does today?"
[14]Ahimelech answered the king, "Who of all
your servants is as loyal as David, the king's son-
in-law, captain of your bodyguard and highly respected in your household? [15]Was that day the
first time I inquired of God for him? Of course
not! Let not the king accuse your servant or any
of his father's family, for your servant knows
nothing at all about this whole affair."
[16]But the king said, "You will surely die, Ahimelech, you and your father's whole family."
[17]Then the king ordered the guards at his side:
"Turn and kill the priests of the LORD, because
they too have sided with David. They knew he
was fleeing, yet they did not tell me."
But the king's officials were not willing to raise
a hand to strike the priests of the LORD.
[18]The king then ordered Doeg, "You turn and
strike down the priests." So Doeg the Edomite
turned and struck them down. That day he killed
eighty-five men who wore the linen ephod. [19]He
also put to the sword Nob, the town of the
priests, with its men and women, its children and
infants, and its cattle, donkeys and sheep.
[20]But Abiathar, a son of Ahimelech son of Ahitub, escaped and fled to join David. [21]He told
David that Saul had killed the priests of the LORD.
[22]Then David said to Abiathar: "That day, when
Doeg the Edomite was there, I knew he would be

sure to tell Saul. I am responsible for the death of your father's whole family. [23]Stay with me; don't be afraid; the man who is seeking your life is seeking mine also. You will be safe with me."

David Saves Keilah

23 When David was told, "Look, the Philistines are fighting against Keilah and are looting the threshing floors," [2]he inquired of the LORD, saying, "Shall I go and attack these Philistines?"

The LORD answered him, "Go, attack the Philistines and save Keilah."

[3]But David's men said to him, "Here in Judah we are afraid. How much more, then, if we go to Keilah against the Philistine forces!"

[4]Once again David inquired of the LORD, and the LORD answered him, "Go down to Keilah, for I am going to give the Philistines into your hand." [5]So David and his men went to Keilah, fought the Philistines and carried off their livestock. He inflicted heavy losses on the Philistines and saved the people of Keilah. [6](Now Abiathar son of Ahimelech had brought the ephod down with him when he fled to David at Keilah.)

Saul Pursues David

[7]Saul was told that David had gone to Keilah, and he said, "God has handed him over to me, for David has imprisoned himself by entering a town with gates and bars." [8]And Saul called up all his forces for battle, to go down to Keilah to besiege David and his men.

[9]When David learned that Saul was plotting against him, he said to Abiathar the priest, "Bring the ephod." [10]David said, "O LORD, God of Israel, your servant has heard definitely that Saul plans to come to Keilah and destroy the town on account of me. [11]Will the citizens of Keilah surrender me to him? Will Saul come down, as your servant has heard? O LORD, God of Israel, tell your servant."

And the LORD said, "He will."

[12]Again David asked, "Will the citizens of Keilah surrender me and my men to Saul?"

And the LORD said, "They will."

[13]So David and his men, about six hundred in number, left Keilah and kept moving from place to place. When Saul was told that David had escaped from Keilah, he did not go there.

[14]David stayed in the desert strongholds and in the hills of the Desert of Ziph. Day after day Saul searched for him, but God did not give David into his hands.

[15]While David was at Horesh in the Desert of Ziph, he learned that Saul had come out to take his life. [16]And Saul's son Jonathan went to David at Horesh and helped him find strength in God. [17]"Don't be afraid," he said. "My father Saul will not lay a hand on you. You will be king over Israel, and I will be second to you. Even my father Saul knows this." [18]The two of them made a covenant before the LORD. Then Jonathan went home, but David remained at Horesh.

[19]The Ziphites went up to Saul at Gibeah and said, "Is not David hiding among us in the strongholds at Horesh, on the hill of Hakilah, south of Jeshimon? [20]Now, O king, come down whenever it pleases you to do so, and we will be responsible for handing him over to the king."

[21]Saul replied, "The LORD bless you for your concern for me. [22]Go and make further preparation. Find out where David usually goes and who has seen him there. They tell me he is very crafty. [23]Find out about all the hiding places he uses and come back to me with definite information.[a] Then I will go with you; if he is in the area, I will track him down among all the clans of Judah."

[24]So they set out and went to Ziph ahead of Saul. Now David and his men were in the Desert of Maon, in the Arabah south of Jeshimon. [25]Saul and his men began the search, and when David was told about it, he went down to the rock and stayed in the Desert of Maon. When Saul heard this, he went into the Desert of Maon in pursuit of David.

[26]Saul was going along one side of the mountain, and David and his men were on the other side, hurrying to get away from Saul. As Saul and his forces were closing in on David and his men to capture them, [27]a messenger came to Saul, saying, "Come quickly! The Philistines are raiding the land." [28]Then Saul broke off his pursuit of David and went to meet the Philistines. That is why they call this place Sela Hammahlekoth.[b] [29]And David went up from there and lived in the strongholds of En Gedi.

David Spares Saul's Life

24 After Saul returned from pursuing the Philistines, he was told, "David is in the Desert of En Gedi." [2]So Saul took three thousand chosen men from all Israel and set out to look for David and his men near the Crags of the Wild Goats.

[3]He came to the sheep pens along the way; a cave was there, and Saul went in to relieve himself. David and his men were far back in the cave. [4]The men said, "This is the day the LORD spoke of when he said[c] to you, 'I will give your enemy into your hands for you to deal with as you wish.'" Then David crept up unnoticed and cut off a corner of Saul's robe.

[5]Afterward, David was conscience-stricken for

[a]23 Or *me at Nacon* [b]28 *Sela Hammahlekoth* means *rock of parting.* [c]4 Or *"Today the LORD is saying*

having cut off a corner of his robe. 6He said to his
men, "The LORD forbid that I should do such a
thing to my master, the LORD's anointed, or lift
my hand against him; for he is the anointed of the
LORD." 7With these words David rebuked his
men and did not allow them to attack Saul. And
Saul left the cave and went his way.

1 Samuel 24:1–22

1. When you were growing up, where was the "hide out" in your neighborhood?
2. Do those in authority over you get your respect automatically or do they have to earn it?
3. In this dog-eat-dog real world, is it practical to "turn the other cheek"?
4. If you were David and the man who was out to kill you walked into your cave, what would you do?
5. When seeking justice, is it right to take the law into your own hands?
6. What situation are you in where you have to "stand tall" and not take advantage of your opponent's weakness?
7. What is your biggest struggle in relating to persons in authority? How can the group pray for you?

8Then David went out of the cave and called
out to Saul, "My lord the king!" When Saul
looked behind him, David bowed down and prostrated himself with his face to the ground. 9He
said to Saul, "Why do you listen when men say,
'David is bent on harming you'? 10This day you
have seen with your own eyes how the LORD
delivered you into my hands in the cave. Some
urged me to kill you, but I spared you; I said, 'I
will not lift my hand against my master, because
he is the LORD's anointed.' 11See, my father, look
at this piece of your robe in my hand! I cut off the
corner of your robe but did not kill you. Now
understand and recognize that I am not guilty
of wrongdoing or rebellion. I have not wronged
you, but you are hunting me down to take my
life. 12May the LORD judge between you and me.
And may the LORD avenge the wrongs you have
done to me, but my hand will not touch you. 13As
the old saying goes, 'From evildoers come evil
deeds,' so my hand will not touch you.
14"Against whom has the king of Israel come
out? Whom are you pursuing? A dead dog? A flea?
15May the LORD be our judge and decide between
us. May he consider my cause and uphold it; may
he vindicate me by delivering me from your
hand."
16When David finished saying this, Saul asked,
"Is that your voice, David my son?" And he wept
aloud. 17"You are more righteous than I," he
said. "You have treated me well, but I have treated you badly. 18You have just now told me of the
good you did to me; the LORD delivered me into
your hands, but you did not kill me. 19When a
man finds his enemy, does he let him get away
unharmed? May the LORD reward you well for
the way you treated me today. 20I know that you
will surely be king and that the kingdom of Israel
will be established in your hands. 21Now swear
to me by the LORD that you will not cut off my
descendants or wipe out my name from my father's family."
22So David gave his oath to Saul. Then Saul
returned home, but David and his men went up
to the stronghold.

David, Nabal and Abigail

25 Now Samuel died, and all Israel assembled and mourned for him; and they buried him at his home in Ramah.
Then David moved down into the Desert of
Maon.[a] 2A certain man in Maon, who had prop-

[a] 1 Some Septuagint manuscripts; Hebrew *Paran*

Saul has been pursuing David in an attempt to kill him to keep David (who has been chosen by God) from replacing Saul as Israel's king.

24:4 *This is the day the Lord spoke of when he said.* There is no previous record of the divine revelation alluded to here by David's men. Perhaps this was their own interpretation of the anointing of David to replace Saul (16:13–14) or of assurances given to David that he would survive Saul's vendetta against him and ultimately become king (see 23:17).

24:6 *for he is the anointed of the Lord.* Because Saul's royal office carried divine sanction by virtue of his anointing, David is determined not to seize the kingship from Saul but to leave its disposition to the Lord who gave it (vv. 12,15; 26:10).

24:11 *my father.* Saul was David's father-in-law (18:27).

24:16 *he wept aloud.* Saul experiences temporary remorse (26:21) for his actions against David but quickly reverts to his former determination to kill him (26:2).

24:21 *not cut off my descendants.* See note on 20:42.

24:22 *stronghold.* An inaccessible place. This may have been a specific fortress, but more likely it was a reference to a geographical area in which it was very easy to hide. From previous experience David did not place any confidence in Saul's words of repentance.

erty there at Carmel, was very wealthy. He had a
thousand goats and three thousand sheep, which
he was shearing in Carmel. 3His name was Nabal
and his wife's name was Abigail. She was an intelligent and beautiful woman, but her husband,
a Calebite, was surly and mean in his dealings.
4While David was in the desert, he heard that
Nabal was shearing sheep. 5So he sent ten young
men and said to them, "Go up to Nabal at Carmel
and greet him in my name. 6Say to him: 'Long life
to you! Good health to you and your household!
And good health to all that is yours!
7" 'Now I hear that it is sheep-shearing time.
When your shepherds were with us, we did not
mistreat them, and the whole time they were at
Carmel nothing of theirs was missing. 8Ask your
own servants and they will tell you. Therefore be
favorable toward my young men, since we come
at a festive time. Please give your servants and
your son David whatever you can find for
them.' "
9When David's men arrived, they gave Nabal
this message in David's name. Then they waited.
10Nabal answered David's servants, "Who is
this David? Who is this son of Jesse? Many servants are breaking away from their masters these
days. 11Why should I take my bread and water,
and the meat I have slaughtered for my shearers,
and give it to men coming from who knows
where?"
12David's men turned around and went back.
When they arrived, they reported every word.
13David said to his men, "Put on your swords!"
So they put on their swords, and David put on
his. About four hundred men went up with David, while two hundred stayed with the supplies.
14One of the servants told Nabal's wife Abigail:
"David sent messengers from the desert to give
our master his greetings, but he hurled insults at
them. 15Yet these men were very good to us.
They did not mistreat us, and the whole time we
were out in the fields near them nothing was
missing. 16Night and day they were a wall around
us all the time we were herding our sheep near
them. 17Now think it over and see what you can
do, because disaster is hanging over our master
and his whole household. He is such a wicked
man that no one can talk to him."
18Abigail lost no time. She took two hundred
loaves of bread, two skins of wine, five dressed
sheep, five seahs[a] of roasted grain, a hundred
cakes of raisins and two hundred cakes of pressed
figs, and loaded them on donkeys. 19Then she
told her servants, "Go on ahead; I'll follow you."
But she did not tell her husband Nabal.
20As she came riding her donkey into a mountain ravine, there were David and his men descending toward her, and she met them. 21David
had just said, "It's been useless—all my watching
over this fellow's property in the desert so that
nothing of his was missing. He has paid me back
evil for good. 22May God deal with David,[b] be it
ever so severely, if by morning I leave alive one
male of all who belong to him!"
23When Abigail saw David, she quickly got off
her donkey and bowed down before David with
her face to the ground. 24She fell at his feet and
said: "My lord, let the blame be on me alone.
Please let your servant speak to you; hear what
your servant has to say. 25May my lord pay no
attention to that wicked man Nabal. He is just
like his name—his name is Fool, and folly goes
with him. But as for me, your servant, I did not
see the men my master sent.
26"Now since the LORD has kept you, my master, from bloodshed and from avenging yourself
with your own hands, as surely as the LORD lives
and as you live, may your enemies and all who
intend to harm my master be like Nabal. 27And
let this gift, which your servant has brought to
my master, be given to the men who follow you.
28Please forgive your servant's offense, for the
LORD will certainly make a lasting dynasty for my
master, because he fights the LORD's battles. Let
no wrongdoing be found in you as long as you
live. 29Even though someone is pursuing you to
take your life, the life of my master will be bound
securely in the bundle of the living by the LORD
your God. But the lives of your enemies he will
hurl away as from the pocket of a sling. 30When
the LORD has done for my master every good
thing he promised concerning him and has appointed him leader over Israel, 31my master will
not have on his conscience the staggering burden
of needless bloodshed or of having avenged himself. And when the LORD has brought my master
success, remember your servant."
32David said to Abigail, "Praise be to the LORD,
the God of Israel, who has sent you today to meet
me. 33May you be blessed for your good judgment
and for keeping me from bloodshed this day and
from avenging myself with my own hands. 34Oth-
erwise, as surely as the LORD, the God of Israel,
lives, who has kept me from harming you, if you
had not come quickly to meet me, not one male
belonging to Nabal would have been left alive by
daybreak."
35Then David accepted from her hand what
she had brought him and said, "Go home in
peace. I have heard your words and granted your
request."
36When Abigail went to Nabal, he was in the
house holding a banquet like that of a king. He
was in high spirits and very drunk. So she told

[a] *18* That is, probably about a bushel (about 37 liters) [b] *22* Some Septuagint manuscripts; Hebrew *with David's enemies*

him nothing until daybreak. 37Then in the morning, when Nabal was sober, his wife told him all these things, and his heart failed him and he became like a stone. 38About ten days later, the LORD struck Nabal and he died.

39When David heard that Nabal was dead, he said, "Praise be to the LORD, who has upheld my cause against Nabal for treating me with contempt. He has kept his servant from doing wrong and has brought Nabal's wrongdoing down on his own head."

Then David sent word to Abigail, asking her to become his wife. 40His servants went to Carmel and said to Abigail, "David has sent us to you to take you to become his wife."

41She bowed down with her face to the ground and said, "Here is your maidservant, ready to serve you and wash the feet of my master's servants." 42Abigail quickly got on a donkey and, attended by her five maids, went with David's messengers and became his wife. 43David had also married Ahinoam of Jezreel, and they both were his wives. 44But Saul had given his daughter Michal, David's wife, to Paltiel[a] son of Laish, who was from Gallim.

David Again Spares Saul's Life

26 The Ziphites went to Saul at Gibeah and said, "Is not David hiding on the hill of Hakilah, which faces Jeshimon?"

2So Saul went down to the Desert of Ziph, with his three thousand chosen men of Israel, to search there for David. 3Saul made his camp beside the road on the hill of Hakilah facing Jeshimon, but David stayed in the desert. When he saw that Saul had followed him there, 4he sent out scouts and learned that Saul had definitely arrived.[b]

5Then David set out and went to the place where Saul had camped. He saw where Saul and Abner son of Ner, the commander of the army, had lain down. Saul was lying inside the camp, with the army encamped around him.

6David then asked Ahimelech the Hittite and Abishai son of Zeruiah, Joab's brother, "Who will go down into the camp with me to Saul?"

"I'll go with you," said Abishai.

7So David and Abishai went to the army by night, and there was Saul, lying asleep inside the camp with his spear stuck in the ground near his head. Abner and the soldiers were lying around him.

8Abishai said to David, "Today God has delivered your enemy into your hands. Now let me pin him to the ground with one thrust of my spear; I won't strike him twice."

9But David said to Abishai, "Don't destroy him! Who can lay a hand on the LORD's anointed and be guiltless? 10As surely as the LORD lives," he said, "the LORD himself will strike him; either his time will come and he will die, or he will go into battle and perish. 11But the LORD forbid that I should lay a hand on the LORD's anointed. Now get the spear and water jug that are near his head, and let's go."

12So David took the spear and water jug near Saul's head, and they left. No one saw or knew about it, nor did anyone wake up. They were all sleeping, because the LORD had put them into a deep sleep.

13Then David crossed over to the other side and stood on top of the hill some distance away; there was a wide space between them. 14He called out to the army and to Abner son of Ner, "Aren't you going to answer me, Abner?"

Abner replied, "Who are you who calls to the king?"

15David said, "You're a man, aren't you? And who is like you in Israel? Why didn't you guard your lord the king? Someone came to destroy your lord the king. 16What you have done is not good. As surely as the LORD lives, you and your men deserve to die, because you did not guard your master, the LORD's anointed. Look around you. Where are the king's spear and water jug that were near his head?"

17Saul recognized David's voice and said, "Is that your voice, David my son?"

David replied, "Yes it is, my lord the king." 18And he added, "Why is my lord pursuing his servant? What have I done, and what wrong am I guilty of? 19Now let my lord the king listen to his servant's words. If the LORD has incited you against me, then may he accept an offering. If, however, men have done it, may they be cursed before the LORD! They have now driven me from my share in the LORD's inheritance and have said, 'Go, serve other gods.' 20Now do not let my blood fall to the ground far from the presence of the LORD. The king of Israel has come out to look for a flea—as one hunts a partridge in the mountains."

21Then Saul said, "I have sinned. Come back, David my son. Because you considered my life precious today, I will not try to harm you again. Surely I have acted like a fool and have erred greatly."

22"Here is the king's spear," David answered. "Let one of your young men come over and get it. 23The LORD rewards every man for his righteousness and faithfulness. The LORD delivered you into my hands today, but I would not lay a hand on the LORD's anointed. 24As surely as I valued

[a]44 Hebrew *Palti*, a variant of *Paltiel* [b]4 Or *had come to Nacon*

your life today, so may the LORD value my life and deliver me from all trouble."

25Then Saul said to David, "May you be blessed, my son David; you will do great things and surely triumph."

So David went on his way, and Saul returned home.

David Among the Philistines

27 But David thought to himself, "One of these days I will be destroyed by the hand of Saul. The best thing I can do is to escape to the land of the Philistines. Then Saul will give up searching for me anywhere in Israel, and I will slip out of his hand."

2So David and the six hundred men with him left and went over to Achish son of Maoch king of Gath. 3David and his men settled in Gath with Achish. Each man had his family with him, and David had his two wives: Ahinoam of Jezreel and Abigail of Carmel, the widow of Nabal. 4When Saul was told that David had fled to Gath, he no longer searched for him.

5Then David said to Achish, "If I have found favor in your eyes, let a place be assigned to me in one of the country towns, that I may live there. Why should your servant live in the royal city with you?"

6So on that day Achish gave him Ziklag, and it has belonged to the kings of Judah ever since. 7David lived in Philistine territory a year and four months.

8Now David and his men went up and raided the Geshurites, the Girzites and the Amalekites. (From ancient times these peoples had lived in the land extending to Shur and Egypt.) 9Whenever David attacked an area, he did not leave a man or woman alive, but took sheep and cattle, donkeys and camels, and clothes. Then he returned to Achish.

10When Achish asked, "Where did you go raiding today?" David would say, "Against the Negev of Judah" or "Against the Negev of Jerahmeel" or "Against the Negev of the Kenites." 11He did not leave a man or woman alive to be brought to Gath, for he thought, "They might inform on us and say, 'This is what David did.'" And such was his practice as long as he lived in Philistine territory. 12Achish trusted David and said to himself, "He has become so odious to his people, the Israelites, that he will be my servant forever."

Saul and the Witch of Endor

28 In those days the Philistines gathered their forces to fight against Israel. Achish said to David, "You must understand that you and your men will accompany me in the army."

2David said, "Then you will see for yourself what your servant can do."

Achish replied, "Very well, I will make you my bodyguard for life."

3Now Samuel was dead, and all Israel had mourned for him and buried him in his own town of Ramah. Saul had expelled the mediums and spiritists from the land.

4The Philistines assembled and came and set up camp at Shunem, while Saul gathered all the Israelites and set up camp at Gilboa. 5When Saul saw the Philistine army, he was afraid; terror filled his heart. 6He inquired of the LORD, but the LORD did not answer him by dreams or Urim or prophets. 7Saul then said to his attendants, "Find me a woman who is a medium, so I may go and inquire of her."

"There is one in Endor," they said.

8So Saul disguised himself, putting on other clothes, and at night he and two men went to the woman. "Consult a spirit for me," he said, "and bring up for me the one I name."

9But the woman said to him, "Surely you know what Saul has done. He has cut off the mediums and spiritists from the land. Why have you set a trap for my life to bring about my death?"

10Saul swore to her by the LORD, "As surely as the LORD lives, you will not be punished for this."

11Then the woman asked, "Whom shall I bring up for you?"

"Bring up Samuel," he said.

12When the woman saw Samuel, she cried out at the top of her voice and said to Saul, "Why have you deceived me? You are Saul!"

13The king said to her, "Don't be afraid. What do you see?"

The woman said, "I see a spirit[a] coming up out of the ground."

14"What does he look like?" he asked.

"An old man wearing a robe is coming up," she said.

Then Saul knew it was Samuel, and he bowed down and prostrated himself with his face to the ground.

15Samuel said to Saul, "Why have you disturbed me by bringing me up?"

"I am in great distress," Saul said. "The Philistines are fighting against me, and God has turned away from me. He no longer answers me, either by prophets or by dreams. So I have called on you to tell me what to do."

16Samuel said, "Why do you consult me, now that the LORD has turned away from you and become your enemy? 17The LORD has done what he predicted through me. The LORD has torn the kingdom out of your hands and given it to one of your neighbors—to David. 18Because you did not

[a]13 Or *see spirits*; or *see gods*

obey the LORD or carry out his fierce wrath against the Amalekites, the LORD has done this to you today. [19]The LORD will hand over both Israel and you to the Philistines, and tomorrow you and your sons will be with me. The LORD will also hand over the army of Israel to the Philistines."

[20]Immediately Saul fell full length on the ground, filled with fear because of Samuel's words. His strength was gone, for he had eaten nothing all that day and night.

[21]When the woman came to Saul and saw that he was greatly shaken, she said, "Look, your maidservant has obeyed you. I took my life in my hands and did what you told me to do. [22]Now please listen to your servant and let me give you some food so you may eat and have the strength to go on your way."

[23]He refused and said, "I will not eat."

But his men joined the woman in urging him, and he listened to them. He got up from the ground and sat on the couch.

[24]The woman had a fattened calf at the house, which she butchered at once. She took some flour, kneaded it and baked bread without yeast. [25]Then she set it before Saul and his men, and they ate. That same night they got up and left.

Achish Sends David Back to Ziklag

29 The Philistines gathered all their forces at Aphek, and Israel camped by the spring in Jezreel. [2]As the Philistine rulers marched with their units of hundreds and thousands, David and his men were marching at the rear with Achish. [3]The commanders of the Philistines asked, "What about these Hebrews?"

Achish replied, "Is this not David, who was an officer of Saul king of Israel? He has already been with me for over a year, and from the day he left Saul until now, I have found no fault in him."

[4]But the Philistine commanders were angry with him and said, "Send the man back, that he may return to the place you assigned him. He must not go with us into battle, or he will turn against us during the fighting. How better could he regain his master's favor than by taking the heads of our own men? [5]Isn't this the David they sang about in their dances:

"'Saul has slain his thousands,
and David his tens of thousands'?"

[6]So Achish called David and said to him, "As surely as the LORD lives, you have been reliable, and I would be pleased to have you serve with me in the army. From the day you came to me until now, I have found no fault in you, but the rulers don't approve of you. [7]Turn back and go in peace; do nothing to displease the Philistine rulers."

[8]"But what have I done?" asked David. "What have you found against your servant from the day I came to you until now? Why can't I go and fight against the enemies of my lord the king?"

[9]Achish answered, "I know that you have been as pleasing in my eyes as an angel of God; nevertheless, the Philistine commanders have said, 'He must not go up with us into battle.' [10]Now get up early, along with your master's servants who have come with you, and leave in the morning as soon as it is light."

[11]So David and his men got up early in the morning to go back to the land of the Philistines, and the Philistines went up to Jezreel.

David Destroys the Amalekites

30 David and his men reached Ziklag on the third day. Now the Amalekites had raided the Negev and Ziklag. They had attacked Ziklag and burned it, [2]and had taken captive the women and all who were in it, both young and old. They killed none of them, but carried them off as they went on their way.

[3]When David and his men came to Ziklag, they found it destroyed by fire and their wives and sons and daughters taken captive. [4]So David and his men wept aloud until they had no strength left to weep. [5]David's two wives had been captured—Ahinoam of Jezreel and Abigail, the widow of Nabal of Carmel. [6]David was greatly distressed because the men were talking of stoning him; each one was bitter in spirit because of his sons and daughters. But David found strength in the LORD his God.

[7]Then David said to Abiathar the priest, the son of Ahimelech, "Bring me the ephod." Abiathar brought it to him, [8]and David inquired of the LORD, "Shall I pursue this raiding party? Will I overtake them?"

"Pursue them," he answered. "You will certainly overtake them and succeed in the rescue."

[9]David and the six hundred men with him came to the Besor Ravine, where some stayed behind, [10]for two hundred men were too exhausted to cross the ravine. But David and four hundred men continued the pursuit.

[11]They found an Egyptian in a field and brought him to David. They gave him water to drink and food to eat— [12]part of a cake of pressed figs and two cakes of raisins. He ate and was revived, for he had not eaten any food or drunk any water for three days and three nights.

[13]David asked him, "To whom do you belong, and where do you come from?"

He said, "I am an Egyptian, the slave of an Amalekite. My master abandoned me when I became ill three days ago. [14]We raided the Negev of the Kerethites and the territory belonging to Judah and the Negev of Caleb. And we burned Ziklag."

15David asked him, "Can you lead me down to
this raiding party?"
He answered, "Swear to me before God that
you will not kill me or hand me over to my master, and I will take you down to them."
16He led David down, and there they were,
scattered over the countryside, eating, drinking
and reveling because of the great amount of plunder they had taken from the land of the Philistines and from Judah. 17David fought them from
dusk until the evening of the next day, and none
of them got away, except four hundred young
men who rode off on camels and fled. 18David
recovered everything the Amalekites had taken,
including his two wives. 19Nothing was missing:
young or old, boy or girl, plunder or anything else
they had taken. David brought everything back.
20He took all the flocks and herds, and his men
drove them ahead of the other livestock, saying,
"This is David's plunder."
21Then David came to the two hundred men
who had been too exhausted to follow him and
who were left behind at the Besor Ravine. They
came out to meet David and the people with him.
As David and his men approached, he greeted
them. 22But all the evil men and troublemakers
among David's followers said, "Because they did
not go out with us, we will not share with them
the plunder we recovered. However, each man
may take his wife and children and go."
23David replied, "No, my brothers, you must
not do that with what the LORD has given us. He
has protected us and handed over to us the forces
that came against us. 24Who will listen to what
you say? The share of the man who stayed with
the supplies is to be the same as that of him who
went down to the battle. All will share alike."
25David made this a statute and ordinance for
Israel from that day to this.
26When David arrived in Ziklag, he sent some
of the plunder to the elders of Judah, who were
his friends, saying, "Here is a present for you
from the plunder of the LORD's enemies."
27He sent it to those who were in Bethel, Ramoth Negev and Jattir; 28to those in Aroer, Siph-
moth, Eshtemoa 29and Racal; to those in the
towns of the Jerahmeelites and the Kenites; 30to
those in Hormah, Bor Ashan, Athach 31and Hebron; and to those in all the other places where
David and his men had roamed.

Saul Takes His Life

31 Now the Philistines fought against Israel;
the Israelites fled before them, and many
fell slain on Mount Gilboa. 2The Philistines
pressed hard after Saul and his sons, and they
killed his sons Jonathan, Abinadab and Malki-
Shua. 3The fighting grew fierce around Saul, and
when the archers overtook him, they wounded
him critically.
4Saul said to his armor-bearer, "Draw your
sword and run me through, or these uncircum-

1 SAMUEL 31:1–13

1. What is your first memory about death: A pet or other animal? A friend or relative? A famous person in the news?
2. How old were you then? What do you remember most about this?
3. What would you do if your wounded king and commander in chief told you to "Draw your sword and run me through"? Would you do it?
4. How do you feel about euthanasia and assisted suicide? How do you think God feels?
5. What would you say to someone who was hurting so much that they longed to die?
6. How do you feel talking about death?
7. What can you do to really make your life count? How can your group pray for you in that regard?

King Saul's life had been driven by intense jealousy of David, whom the Lord has chosen as Saul's replacement. In this story, Saul's sad life comes to a sad end.

31:1–2 ***Philistines.*** See 14:52. The Philistines engaged in continual struggle with Israel for permanent control of the promised land in the southern and central regions. ***killed his sons.*** Saul's only surviving son, Ish-Bosheth, was afterward promoted by Abner, the commander of Saul's army (who somehow survived the battle), to succeed his father as king (2 Sam. 2:8–9).

31:4 ***abuse me.*** A practice that was not uncommon; previously the Philistines had mutilated and humiliated Samson after his capture (see Judg. 16:23–25). ***took his own sword and fell on it.*** The culmination of a long process of self-destruction.

31:6 ***all his men.*** Those who had served around him in his administration, except Abner (see note on 31:1–2).

31:9 ***They cut off his head.*** David had done the same to Goliath. ***sent messengers throughout the land.*** Probably bearing Saul's head and armor as proof of their victory.

31:10 ***They put his armor in the temple.*** Symbolic of ascribing the victory to the Philistine gods.

31:12 The men of Jabesh Gilead had not forgotten how Saul had come to their defense (ch. 11). ***burned them.*** Probably to prevent further abuse of the bodies.

cised fellows will come and run me through and
abuse me."
But his armor-bearer was terrified and would
not do it; so Saul took his own sword and fell on
it. [5]When the armor-bearer saw that Saul was
dead, he too fell on his sword and died with him.
[6]So Saul and his three sons and his armor-bearer
and all his men died together that same day.
[7]When the Israelites along the valley and
those across the Jordan saw that the Israelite
army had fled and that Saul and his sons had died,
they abandoned their towns and fled. And the
Philistines came and occupied them.
[8]The next day, when the Philistines came to
strip the dead, they found Saul and his three sons
fallen on Mount Gilboa. [9]They cut off his head
and stripped off his armor, and they sent messengers throughout the land of the Philistines to proclaim the news in the temple of their idols and
among their people. [10]They put his armor in the
temple of the Ashtoreths and fastened his body to
the wall of Beth Shan.
[11]When the people of Jabesh Gilead heard of
what the Philistines had done to Saul, [12]all their
valiant men journeyed through the night to Beth
Shan. They took down the bodies of Saul and his
sons from the wall of Beth Shan and went to
Jabesh, where they burned them. [13]Then they
took their bones and buried them under a tamarisk tree at Jabesh, and they fasted seven days.

Introduction to
2 SAMUEL

Personal Reading Plan

❒ 2 Samuel 1:1–27
❒ 2 Samuel 2:1–3:5
❒ 2 Samuel 3:6–39
❒ 2 Samuel 4:1–5:25
❒ 2 Samuel 6:1–23
❒ 2 Samuel 7:1–8:18
❒ 2 Samuel 9:1–10:19
❒ 2 Samuel 11:1–27
❒ 2 Samuel 12:1–31
❒ 2 Samuel 13:1–39
❒ 2 Samuel 14:1–33
❒ 2 Samuel 15:1–16:14
❒ 2 Samuel 16:15–17:29
❒ 2 Samuel 18:1–19:8a
❒ 2 Samuel 19:8b–20:25
❒ 2 Samuel 21:1–22:51
❒ 2 Samuel 23:1–39
❒ 2 Samuel 24:1–25

Author

The author is not known with certainty. Perhaps a compiler drew from materials written by others such as Samuel, Gad and Nathan (see 1 Chron. 29:29) in order to produce the final rendition. Note that 1 and 2 Samuel were originally composed as one unit.

Date

The date of authorship is uncertain, though it is possible that this two-volume book was written around the time of Solomon's death (c. 930 B.C.).

Theme

The life and times of King David.

Historical Background

David had been on the run from Saul. Now that Saul has died, David is able to take his rightful place on the throne over all of Israel, but only after he emerges triumphant from a political power struggle. Surrounding nations, especially the Philistines, still pose the threat of war; however, Israel is militarily strong under David's victorious reign.

Characteristics

Second Samuel continues the historical narrative of 1 Samuel, where David's youth and troublesome exile were the focus. Now in "volume two" David reigns as Saul's successor and he must heal and unify the war-torn country. Chapters 1–10 narrate the prosperous early reign of David. He is anointed king over Judah and then over all Israel. He also sustains victory after victory on the battlefield. David's adultery with Bathsheba (chapters 11–12), however, marks a turning point in the book. In the chapters which follow, the "sword never departs from David's house" (12:10). Throughout the book, God forms the backdrop as the One who establishes David upon the throne of Israel and gives him victory over his enemies.

Passages for Topical Group Study

11:1–27	LUST / PORNOGRAPHY	David and Bathsheba
12:1–14	ACCOUNTABILITY	Nathan Rebukes David
12:15–25	ABORTION	David Grieves
13:1–22	DATE RAPE	Amnon Rapes Tamar
13:23–39	GRUDGES	Absalom Kills Amnon

See the Lesson Plans in the front of this Bible.

David Hears of Saul's Death

1 After the death of Saul, David returned from
defeating the Amalekites and stayed in Ziklag
two days. 2On the third day a man arrived from
Saul's camp, with his clothes torn and with dust
on his head. When he came to David, he fell to
the ground to pay him honor.
3"Where have you come from?" David asked
him.
He answered, "I have escaped from the Israelite camp."
4"What happened?" David asked. "Tell me."
He said, "The men fled from the battle. Many
of them fell and died. And Saul and his son Jonathan are dead."
5Then David said to the young man who
brought him the report, "How do you know that
Saul and his son Jonathan are dead?"
6"I happened to be on Mount Gilboa," the
young man said, "and there was Saul, leaning on
his spear, with the chariots and riders almost
upon him. 7When he turned around and saw me,
he called out to me, and I said, 'What can I do?'
8"He asked me, 'Who are you?'
" 'An Amalekite,' I answered.
9"Then he said to me, 'Stand over me and kill
me! I am in the throes of death, but I'm still
alive.'
10"So I stood over him and killed him, because
I knew that after he had fallen he could not survive. And I took the crown that was on his head
and the band on his arm and have brought them
here to my lord."
11Then David and all the men with him took
hold of their clothes and tore them. 12They
mourned and wept and fasted till evening for Saul
and his son Jonathan, and for the army of the
LORD and the house of Israel, because they had
fallen by the sword.
13David said to the young man who brought
him the report, "Where are you from?"
"I am the son of an alien, an Amalekite," he
answered.
14David asked him, "Why were you not afraid
to lift your hand to destroy the LORD's anointed?"
15Then David called one of his men and said,
"Go, strike him down!" So he struck him down,
and he died. 16For David had said to him, "Your
blood be on your own head. Your own mouth
testified against you when you said, 'I killed the
LORD's anointed.' "

David's Lament for Saul and Jonathan

17David took up this lament concerning Saul
and his son Jonathan, 18and ordered that the men
of Judah be taught this lament of the bow (it is
written in the Book of Jashar):

19"Your glory, O Israel, lies slain on your heights.
How the mighty have fallen!

20"Tell it not in Gath,
proclaim it not in the streets of Ashkelon,
lest the daughters of the Philistines be glad,
lest the daughters of the uncircumcised rejoice.

21"O mountains of Gilboa,
may you have neither dew nor rain,
nor fields that yield offerings ⌞of grain⌟.
For there the shield of the mighty was defiled,
the shield of Saul—no longer rubbed with oil.
22From the blood of the slain,
from the flesh of the mighty,
the bow of Jonathan did not turn back,
the sword of Saul did not return unsatisfied.

23"Saul and Jonathan—
in life they were loved and gracious,
and in death they were not parted.
They were swifter than eagles,
they were stronger than lions.

24"O daughters of Israel,
weep for Saul,
who clothed you in scarlet and finery,
who adorned your garments with ornaments of gold.

25"How the mighty have fallen in battle!
Jonathan lies slain on your heights.
26I grieve for you, Jonathan my brother;
you were very dear to me.
Your love for me was wonderful,
more wonderful than that of women.

27"How the mighty have fallen!
The weapons of war have perished!"

David Anointed King Over Judah

2 In the course of time, David inquired of the
LORD. "Shall I go up to one of the towns of
Judah?" he asked.
The LORD said, "Go up."
David asked, "Where shall I go?"
"To Hebron," the LORD answered.
2So David went up there with his two wives,
Ahinoam of Jezreel and Abigail, the widow of
Nabal of Carmel. 3David also took the men who
were with him, each with his family, and they
settled in Hebron and its towns. 4Then the men
of Judah came to Hebron and there they anointed
David king over the house of Judah.
When David was told that it was the men of
Jabesh Gilead who had buried Saul, 5he sent messengers to the men of Jabesh Gilead to say to

them, "The LORD bless you for showing this kindness to Saul your master by burying him. 6May
the LORD now show you kindness and faithfulness, and I too will show you the same favor
because you have done this. 7Now then, be
strong and brave, for Saul your master is dead,
and the house of Judah has anointed me king over
them."

War Between the Houses of David and Saul

8Meanwhile, Abner son of Ner, the commander of Saul's army, had taken Ish-Bosheth son of
Saul and brought him over to Mahanaim. 9He
made him king over Gilead, Ashuri[a] and Jezreel,
and also over Ephraim, Benjamin and all Israel.
10Ish-Bosheth son of Saul was forty years old
when he became king over Israel, and he reigned
two years. The house of Judah, however, followed David. 11The length of time David was
king in Hebron over the house of Judah was sev-
en years and six months.
12Abner son of Ner, together with the men of
Ish-Bosheth son of Saul, left Mahanaim and went
to Gibeon. 13Joab son of Zeruiah and David's men
went out and met them at the pool of Gibeon.
One group sat down on one side of the pool and
one group on the other side.
14Then Abner said to Joab, "Let's have some of
the young men get up and fight hand to hand in
front of us."
"All right, let them do it," Joab said.
15So they stood up and were counted off—
twelve men for Benjamin and Ish-Bosheth son of
Saul, and twelve for David. 16Then each man
grabbed his opponent by the head and thrust his
dagger into his opponent's side, and they fell
down together. So that place in Gibeon was
called Helkath Hazzurim.[b]
17The battle that day was very fierce, and Abner and the men of Israel were defeated by David's men.
18The three sons of Zeruiah were there: Joab,
Abishai and Asahel. Now Asahel was as fleet-
footed as a wild gazelle. 19He chased Abner, turning neither to the right nor to the left as he pursued him. 20Abner looked behind him and asked,
"Is that you, Asahel?"
"It is," he answered.
21Then Abner said to him, "Turn aside to the
right or to the left; take on one of the young men
and strip him of his weapons." But Asahel would
not stop chasing him.
22Again Abner warned Asahel, "Stop chasing
me! Why should I strike you down? How could I
look your brother Joab in the face?"
23But Asahel refused to give up the pursuit; so
Abner thrust the butt of his spear into Asahel's
stomach, and the spear came out through his
back. He fell there and died on the spot. And
every man stopped when he came to the place
where Asahel had fallen and died.
24But Joab and Abishai pursued Abner, and as
the sun was setting, they came to the hill of Ammah, near Giah on the way to the wasteland of
Gibeon. 25Then the men of Benjamin rallied behind Abner. They formed themselves into a
group and took their stand on top of a hill.
26Abner called out to Joab, "Must the sword
devour forever? Don't you realize that this will
end in bitterness? How long before you order
your men to stop pursuing their brothers?"
27Joab answered, "As surely as God lives, if
you had not spoken, the men would have continued the pursuit of their brothers until morning.[c]"
28So Joab blew the trumpet, and all the men
came to a halt; they no longer pursued Israel, nor
did they fight anymore.
29All that night Abner and his men marched
through the Arabah. They crossed the Jordan,
continued through the whole Bithron[d] and
came to Mahanaim.
30Then Joab returned from pursuing Abner
and assembled all his men. Besides Asahel,
nineteen of David's men were found missing.
31But David's men had killed three hundred and
sixty Benjamites who were with Abner. 32They
took Asahel and buried him in his father's
tomb at Bethlehem. Then Joab and his men
marched all night and arrived at Hebron by daybreak.

3 The war between the house of Saul and the
house of David lasted a long time. David
grew stronger and stronger, while the house of
Saul grew weaker and weaker.
2Sons were born to David in Hebron:
His firstborn was Amnon the son of
Ahinoam of Jezreel;
3his second, Kileab the son of Abigail the
widow of Nabal of Carmel;
the third, Absalom the son of Maacah
daughter of Talmai king of Geshur;
4the fourth, Adonijah the son of Haggith;
the fifth, Shephatiah the son of Abital;
5and the sixth, Ithream the son of David's
wife Eglah.
These were born to David in Hebron.

a9 Or *Asher* b16 *Helkath Hazzurim* means *field of daggers* or *field of hostilities.* c27 Or *spoken this morning, the men would not have taken up the pursuit of their brothers*; or *spoken, the men would have given up the pursuit of their brothers by morning*
d29 Or *morning*; or *ravine*; the meaning of the Hebrew for this word is uncertain.

Abner Goes Over to David

6During the war between the house of Saul
and the house of David, Abner had been
strengthening his own position in the house of
Saul. 7Now Saul had had a concubine named Rizpah daughter of Aiah. And Ish-Bosheth said to
Abner, "Why did you sleep with my father's concubine?"

8Abner was very angry because of what Ish-
Bosheth said and he answered, "Am I a dog's
head—on Judah's side? This very day I am loyal
to the house of your father Saul and to his family
and friends. I haven't handed you over to David.
Yet now you accuse me of an offense involving
this woman! 9May God deal with Abner, be it
ever so severely, if I do not do for David what the
LORD promised him on oath 10and transfer the
kingdom from the house of Saul and establish
David's throne over Israel and Judah from Dan to
Beersheba." 11Ish-Bosheth did not dare to say
another word to Abner, because he was afraid of
him.

12Then Abner sent messengers on his behalf to
say to David, "Whose land is it? Make an agreement with me, and I will help you bring all Israel
over to you."

13"Good," said David. "I will make an agreement with you. But I demand one thing of you:
Do not come into my presence unless you bring
Michal daughter of Saul when you come to see
me." 14Then David sent messengers to Ish-
Bosheth son of Saul, demanding, "Give me my
wife Michal, whom I betrothed to myself for the
price of a hundred Philistine foreskins."

15So Ish-Bosheth gave orders and had her tak-
en away from her husband Paltiel son of Laish.
16Her husband, however, went with her, weeping behind her all the way to Bahurim. Then
Abner said to him, "Go back home!" So he went
back.

17Abner conferred with the elders of Israel and
said, "For some time you have wanted to make
David your king. 18Now do it! For the LORD promised David, 'By my servant David I will rescue my
people Israel from the hand of the Philistines and
from the hand of all their enemies.' "

19Abner also spoke to the Benjamites in person. Then he went to Hebron to tell David everything that Israel and the whole house of Benjamin wanted to do. 20When Abner, who had
twenty men with him, came to David at Hebron,
David prepared a feast for him and his men.
21Then Abner said to David, "Let me go at once
and assemble all Israel for my lord the king,
so that they may make a compact with you, and
that you may rule over all that your heart desires." So David sent Abner away, and he went in
peace.

Joab Murders Abner

22Just then David's men and Joab returned
from a raid and brought with them a great deal of
plunder. But Abner was no longer with David in
Hebron, because David had sent him away, and
he had gone in peace. 23When Joab and all the
soldiers with him arrived, he was told that Abner
son of Ner had come to the king and that the king
had sent him away and that he had gone in peace.

24So Joab went to the king and said, "What
have you done? Look, Abner came to you. Why
did you let him go? Now he is gone! 25You know
Abner son of Ner; he came to deceive you and
observe your movements and find out everything
you are doing."

26Joab then left David and sent messengers after Abner, and they brought him back from the
well of Sirah. But David did not know it. 27Now
when Abner returned to Hebron, Joab took him
aside into the gateway, as though to speak with
him privately. And there, to avenge the blood of
his brother Asahel, Joab stabbed him in the stomach, and he died.

28Later, when David heard about this, he said,
"I and my kingdom are forever innocent before
the LORD concerning the blood of Abner son of
Ner. 29May his blood fall upon the head of Joab
and upon all his father's house! May Joab's house
never be without someone who has a running
sore or leprosy[a] or who leans on a crutch or
who falls by the sword or who lacks food."

30(Joab and his brother Abishai murdered Abner because he had killed their brother Asahel in
the battle at Gibeon.)

31Then David said to Joab and all the people
with him, "Tear your clothes and put on sackcloth and walk in mourning in front of Abner."
King David himself walked behind the bier.
32They buried Abner in Hebron, and the king
wept aloud at Abner's tomb. All the people wept
also.

33The king sang this lament for Abner:

"Should Abner have died as the lawless die?
34 Your hands were not bound,
your feet were not fettered.
You fell as one falls before wicked men."

And all the people wept over him again.

35Then they all came and urged David to eat
something while it was still day; but David took
an oath, saying, "May God deal with me, be it
ever so severely, if I taste bread or anything else
before the sun sets!"

36All the people took note and were pleased;

[a]29 The Hebrew word was used for various diseases affecting the skin—not necessarily leprosy.

indeed, everything the king did pleased them. 37So on that day all the people and all Israel knew that the king had no part in the murder of Abner son of Ner.

38Then the king said to his men, "Do you not realize that a prince and a great man has fallen in Israel this day? 39And today, though I am the anointed king, I am weak, and these sons of Zeruiah are too strong for me. May the LORD repay the evildoer according to his evil deeds!"

Ish-Bosheth Murdered

4 When Ish-Bosheth son of Saul heard that Abner had died in Hebron, he lost courage, and all Israel became alarmed. 2Now Saul's son had two men who were leaders of raiding bands. One was named Baanah and the other Recab; they were sons of Rimmon the Beerothite from the tribe of Benjamin—Beeroth is considered part of Benjamin, 3because the people of Beeroth fled to Gittaim and have lived there as aliens to this day.

4(Jonathan son of Saul had a son who was lame in both feet. He was five years old when the news about Saul and Jonathan came from Jezreel. His nurse picked him up and fled, but as she hurried to leave, he fell and became crippled. His name was Mephibosheth.)

5Now Recab and Baanah, the sons of Rimmon the Beerothite, set out for the house of Ish-Bosheth, and they arrived there in the heat of the day while he was taking his noonday rest. 6They went into the inner part of the house as if to get some wheat, and they stabbed him in the stomach. Then Recab and his brother Baanah slipped away.

7They had gone into the house while he was lying on the bed in his bedroom. After they stabbed and killed him, they cut off his head. Taking it with them, they traveled all night by way of the Arabah. 8They brought the head of Ish-Bosheth to David at Hebron and said to the king, "Here is the head of Ish-Bosheth son of Saul, your enemy, who tried to take your life. This day the LORD has avenged my lord the king against Saul and his offspring."

9David answered Recab and his brother Baanah, the sons of Rimmon the Beerothite, "As surely as the LORD lives, who has delivered me out of all trouble, 10when a man told me, 'Saul is dead,' and thought he was bringing good news, I seized him and put him to death in Ziklag. That was the reward I gave him for his news! 11How much more—when wicked men have killed an innocent man in his own house and on his own bed—should I not now demand his blood from your hand and rid the earth of you!"

12So David gave an order to his men, and they killed them. They cut off their hands and feet and hung the bodies by the pool in Hebron. But they took the head of Ish-Bosheth and buried it in Abner's tomb at Hebron.

David Becomes King Over Israel

5 All the tribes of Israel came to David at Hebron and said, "We are your own flesh and blood. 2In the past, while Saul was king over us, you were the one who led Israel on their military campaigns. And the LORD said to you, 'You will shepherd my people Israel, and you will become their ruler.' "

3When all the elders of Israel had come to King David at Hebron, the king made a compact with them at Hebron before the LORD, and they anointed David king over Israel.

4David was thirty years old when he became king, and he reigned forty years. 5In Hebron he reigned over Judah seven years and six months, and in Jerusalem he reigned over all Israel and Judah thirty-three years.

David Conquers Jerusalem

6The king and his men marched to Jerusalem to attack the Jebusites, who lived there. The Jebusites said to David, "You will not get in here; even the blind and the lame can ward you off." They thought, "David cannot get in here." 7Nevertheless, David captured the fortress of Zion, the City of David.

8On that day, David said, "Anyone who conquers the Jebusites will have to use the water shaft[a] to reach those 'lame and blind' who are David's enemies.[b]" That is why they say, "The 'blind and lame' will not enter the palace."

9David then took up residence in the fortress and called it the City of David. He built up the area around it, from the supporting terraces[c] inward. 10And he became more and more powerful, because the LORD God Almighty was with him.

11Now Hiram king of Tyre sent messengers to David, along with cedar logs and carpenters and stonemasons, and they built a palace for David. 12And David knew that the LORD had established him as king over Israel and had exalted his kingdom for the sake of his people Israel.

13After he left Hebron, David took more concubines and wives in Jerusalem, and more sons and daughters were born to him. 14These are the names of the children born to him there: Shammua, Shobab, Nathan, Solomon, 15Ibhar, Elishua, Nepheg, Japhia, 16Elishama, Eliada and Eliphelet.

David Defeats the Philistines

17When the Philistines heard that David had

[a]8 Or *use scaling hooks* [b]8 Or *are hated by David* [c]9 Or *the Millo*

been anointed king over Israel, they went up in full force to search for him, but David heard about it and went down to the stronghold. 18 Now the Philistines had come and spread out in the Valley of Rephaim; 19 so David inquired of the LORD, "Shall I go and attack the Philistines? Will you hand them over to me?"

The LORD answered him, "Go, for I will surely hand the Philistines over to you."

20 So David went to Baal Perazim, and there he defeated them. He said, "As waters break out, the LORD has broken out against my enemies before me." So that place was called Baal Perazim.[a] 21 The Philistines abandoned their idols there, and David and his men carried them off.

22 Once more the Philistines came up and spread out in the Valley of Rephaim; 23 so David inquired of the LORD, and he answered, "Do not go straight up, but circle around behind them and attack them in front of the balsam trees. 24 As soon as you hear the sound of marching in the tops of the balsam trees, move quickly, because that will mean the LORD has gone out in front of you to strike the Philistine army." 25 So David did as the LORD commanded him, and he struck down the Philistines all the way from Gibeon[b] to Gezer.

The Ark Brought to Jerusalem

6 David again brought together out of Israel chosen men, thirty thousand in all. 2 He and all his men set out from Baalah of Judah[c] to bring up from there the ark of God, which is called by the Name,[d] the name of the LORD Almighty, who is enthroned between the cherubim that are on the ark. 3 They set the ark of God on a new cart and brought it from the house of Abinadab, which was on the hill. Uzzah and Ahio, sons of Abinadab, were guiding the new cart 4 with the ark of God on it,[e] and Ahio was walking in front of it. 5 David and the whole house of Israel were celebrating with all their might before the LORD, with songs[f] and with harps, lyres, tambourines, sistrums and cymbals.

6 When they came to the threshing floor of Nacon, Uzzah reached out and took hold of the ark of God, because the oxen stumbled. 7 The LORD's anger burned against Uzzah because of his irreverent act; therefore God struck him down and he died there beside the ark of God.

8 Then David was angry because the LORD's wrath had broken out against Uzzah, and to this day that place is called Perez Uzzah.[g]

9 David was afraid of the LORD that day and said, "How can the ark of the LORD ever come to me?" 10 He was not willing to take the ark of the LORD to be with him in the City of David. Instead, he took it aside to the house of Obed-Edom the Gittite. 11 The ark of the LORD remained in the house of Obed-Edom the Gittite for three months, and the LORD blessed him and his entire household.

12 Now King David was told, "The LORD has blessed the household of Obed-Edom and everything he has, because of the ark of God." So David went down and brought up the ark of God from the house of Obed-Edom to the City of David with rejoicing. 13 When those who were carrying the ark of the LORD had taken six steps, he sacrificed a bull and a fattened calf. 14 David, wearing a linen ephod, danced before the LORD with all his might, 15 while he and the entire house of Israel brought up the ark of the LORD with shouts and the sound of trumpets.

16 As the ark of the LORD was entering the City of David, Michal daughter of Saul watched from a window. And when she saw King David leaping and dancing before the LORD, she despised him in her heart.

17 They brought the ark of the LORD and set it in its place inside the tent that David had pitched for it, and David sacrificed burnt offerings and fellowship offerings[h] before the LORD. 18 After he had finished sacrificing the burnt offerings and fellowship offerings, he blessed the people in the name of the LORD Almighty. 19 Then he gave a loaf of bread, a cake of dates and a cake of raisins to each person in the whole crowd of Israelites, both men and women. And all the people went to their homes.

20 When David returned home to bless his household, Michal daughter of Saul came out to meet him and said, "How the king of Israel has distinguished himself today, disrobing in the sight of the slave girls of his servants as any vulgar fellow would!"

21 David said to Michal, "It was before the LORD, who chose me rather than your father or anyone from his house when he appointed me ruler over the LORD's people Israel—I will celebrate before the LORD. 22 I will become even more undignified than this, and I will be humiliated in my own eyes. But by these slave girls you spoke of, I will be held in honor."

23 And Michal daughter of Saul had no children to the day of her death.

[a] 20 *Baal Perazim* means *the lord who breaks out.* [b] 25 Septuagint (see also 1 Chron. 14:16); Hebrew *Geba* [c] 2 That is, Kiriath Jearim; Hebrew *Baale Judah*, a variant of *Baalah of Judah* [d] 2 Hebrew; Septuagint and Vulgate do not have *the Name.* [e] 3,4 Dead Sea Scrolls and some Septuagint manuscripts; Masoretic Text *cart* 4*and they brought it with the ark of God from the house of Abinadab, which was on the hill* [f] 5 See Dead Sea Scrolls, Septuagint and 1 Chronicles 13:8; Masoretic Text *celebrating before the LORD with all kinds of instruments made of pine.* [g] 8 *Perez Uzzah* means *outbreak against Uzzah.* [h] 17 Traditionally *peace offerings*; also in verse 18

God's Promise to David

7 After the king was settled in his palace and the LORD had given him rest from all his enemies around him, 2he said to Nathan the prophet, "Here I am, living in a palace of cedar, while the ark of God remains in a tent."

3Nathan replied to the king, "Whatever you have in mind, go ahead and do it, for the LORD is with you."

4That night the word of the LORD came to Nathan, saying:

5"Go and tell my servant David, 'This is what the LORD says: Are you the one to build me a house to dwell in? 6I have not dwelt in a house from the day I brought the Israelites up out of Egypt to this day. I have been moving from place to place with a tent as my dwelling. 7Wherever I have moved with all the Israelites, did I ever say to any of their rulers whom I commanded to shepherd my people Israel, "Why have you not built me a house of cedar?" '

8"Now then, tell my servant David, 'This is what the LORD Almighty says: I took you from the pasture and from following the flock to be ruler over my people Israel. 9I have been with you wherever you have gone, and I have cut off all your enemies from before you. Now I will make your name great, like the names of the greatest men of the earth. 10And I will provide a place for my people Israel and will plant them so that they can have a home of their own and no longer be disturbed. Wicked people will not oppress them anymore, as they did at the beginning 11and have done ever since the time I appointed leaders[a] over my people Israel. I will also give you rest from all your enemies.

" 'The LORD declares to you that the LORD himself will establish a house for you: 12When your days are over and you rest with your fathers, I will raise up your offspring to succeed you, who will come from your own body, and I will establish his kingdom. 13He is the one who will build a house for my Name, and I will establish the throne of his kingdom forever. 14I will be his father, and he will be my son. When he does wrong, I will punish him with the rod of men, with floggings inflicted by men. 15But my love will never be taken away from him, as I took it away from Saul, whom I removed from before you. 16Your house and your kingdom will endure forever before me[b]; your throne will be established forever.' "

17Nathan reported to David all the words of this entire revelation.

David's Prayer

18Then King David went in and sat before the LORD, and he said:

"Who am I, O Sovereign LORD, and what is my family, that you have brought me this far? 19And as if this were not enough in your sight, O Sovereign LORD, you have also spoken about the future of the house of your servant. Is this your usual way of dealing with man, O Sovereign LORD?

20"What more can David say to you? For you know your servant, O Sovereign LORD. 21For the sake of your word and according to your will, you have done this great thing and made it known to your servant.

22"How great you are, O Sovereign LORD! There is no one like you, and there is no God but you, as we have heard with our own ears. 23And who is like your people Israel—the one nation on earth that God went out to redeem as a people for himself, and to make a name for himself, and to perform great and awesome wonders by driving out nations and their gods from before your people, whom you redeemed from Egypt?[c] 24You have established your people Israel as your very own forever, and you, O LORD, have become their God.

25"And now, LORD God, keep forever the promise you have made concerning your servant and his house. Do as you promised, 26so that your name will be great forever. Then men will say, 'The LORD Almighty is God over Israel!' And the house of your servant David will be established before you.

27"O LORD Almighty, God of Israel, you have revealed this to your servant, saying, 'I will build a house for you.' So your servant has found courage to offer you this prayer. 28O Sovereign LORD, you are God! Your words are trustworthy, and you have promised these good things to your servant. 29Now be pleased to bless the house of your servant, that it may continue forever in your sight; for you, O Sovereign LORD, have spoken, and with your blessing the house of your servant will be blessed forever."

[a]*11* Traditionally *judges* [b]*16* Some Hebrew manuscripts and Septuagint; most Hebrew manuscripts *you* [c]*23* See Septuagint and 1 Chron. 17:21; Hebrew *wonders for your land and before your people, whom you redeemed from Egypt, from the nations and their gods.*

David's Victories

8 In the course of time, David defeated the Philistines and subdued them, and he took Metheg Ammah from the control of the Philistines.

2David also defeated the Moabites. He made them lie down on the ground and measured them off with a length of cord. Every two lengths of them were put to death, and the third length was allowed to live. So the Moabites became subject to David and brought tribute.

3Moreover, David fought Hadadezer son of Rehob, king of Zobah, when he went to restore his control along the Euphrates River. 4David captured a thousand of his chariots, seven thousand charioteers[a] and twenty thousand foot soldiers. He hamstrung all but a hundred of the chariot horses.

5When the Arameans of Damascus came to help Hadadezer king of Zobah, David struck down twenty-two thousand of them. 6He put garrisons in the Aramean kingdom of Damascus, and the Arameans became subject to him and brought tribute. The LORD gave David victory wherever he went.

7David took the gold shields that belonged to the officers of Hadadezer and brought them to Jerusalem. 8From Tebah[b] and Berothai, towns that belonged to Hadadezer, King David took a great quantity of bronze.

9When Tou[c] king of Hamath heard that David had defeated the entire army of Hadadezer, 10he sent his son Joram[d] to King David to greet him and congratulate him on his victory in battle over Hadadezer, who had been at war with Tou. Joram brought with him articles of silver and gold and bronze.

11King David dedicated these articles to the LORD, as he had done with the silver and gold from all the nations he had subdued: 12Edom[e] and Moab, the Ammonites and the Philistines, and Amalek. He also dedicated the plunder taken from Hadadezer son of Rehob, king of Zobah.

13And David became famous after he returned from striking down eighteen thousand Edomites[f] in the Valley of Salt.

14He put garrisons throughout Edom, and all the Edomites became subject to David. The LORD gave David victory wherever he went.

David's Officials

15David reigned over all Israel, doing what was just and right for all his people. 16Joab son of Zeruiah was over the army; Jehoshaphat son of Ahilud was recorder; 17Zadok son of Ahitub and Ahimelech son of Abiathar were priests; Seraiah was secretary; 18Benaiah son of Jehoiada was over the Kerethites and Pelethites; and David's sons were royal advisers.[g]

David and Mephibosheth

9 David asked, "Is there anyone still left of the house of Saul to whom I can show kindness for Jonathan's sake?"

2Now there was a servant of Saul's household named Ziba. They called him to appear before David, and the king said to him, "Are you Ziba?"

"Your servant," he replied.

3The king asked, "Is there no one still left of the house of Saul to whom I can show God's kindness?"

Ziba answered the king, "There is still a son of Jonathan; he is crippled in both feet."

4"Where is he?" the king asked.

Ziba answered, "He is at the house of Makir son of Ammiel in Lo Debar."

5So King David had him brought from Lo Debar, from the house of Makir son of Ammiel.

6When Mephibosheth son of Jonathan, the son of Saul, came to David, he bowed down to pay him honor.

David said, "Mephibosheth!"

"Your servant," he replied.

7"Don't be afraid," David said to him, "for I will surely show you kindness for the sake of your father Jonathan. I will restore to you all the land that belonged to your grandfather Saul, and you will always eat at my table."

8Mephibosheth bowed down and said, "What is your servant, that you should notice a dead dog like me?"

9Then the king summoned Ziba, Saul's servant, and said to him, "I have given your master's grandson everything that belonged to Saul and his family. 10You and your sons and your servants are to farm the land for him and bring in the crops, so that your master's grandson may be provided for. And Mephibosheth, grandson of your master, will always eat at my table." (Now Ziba had fifteen sons and twenty servants.)

11Then Ziba said to the king, "Your servant will do whatever my lord the king commands his servant to do." So Mephibosheth ate at David's[h] table like one of the king's sons.

12Mephibosheth had a young son named Mica, and all the members of Ziba's household were servants of Mephibosheth. 13And Mephibosheth

[a] 4 Septuagint (see also Dead Sea Scrolls and 1 Chron. 18:4); Masoretic Text *captured seventeen hundred of his charioteers*
[b] 8 See some Septuagint manuscripts (see also 1 Chron. 18:8); Hebrew *Betah.*
[c] 9 Hebrew *Toi,* a variant of *Tou;* also in verse 10
[d] 10 A variant of *Hadoram*
[e] 12 Some Hebrew manuscripts, Septuagint and Syriac (see also 1 Chron. 18:11); most Hebrew manuscripts *Aram*
[f] 13 A few Hebrew manuscripts, Septuagint and Syriac (see also 1 Chron. 18:12); most Hebrew manuscripts *Aram* (that is, Arameans)
[g] 18 Or *were priests*
[h] 11 Septuagint; Hebrew *my*

lived in Jerusalem, because he always ate at the
king's table, and he was crippled in both feet.

David Defeats the Ammonites

10 In the course of time, the king of the Ammonites died, and his son Hanun succeeded him as king. [2]David thought, "I will show
kindness to Hanun son of Nahash, just as his
father showed kindness to me." So David sent a
delegation to express his sympathy to Hanun concerning his father.
When David's men came to the land of the
Ammonites, [3]the Ammonite nobles said to Hanun their lord, "Do you think David is honoring
your father by sending men to you to express
sympathy? Hasn't David sent them to you to explore the city and spy it out and overthrow it?"
[4]So Hanun seized David's men, shaved off half of
each man's beard, cut off their garments in the
middle at the buttocks, and sent them away.
[5]When David was told about this, he sent messengers to meet the men, for they were greatly
humiliated. The king said, "Stay at Jericho till
your beards have grown, and then come back."
[6]When the Ammonites realized that they had
become a stench in David's nostrils, they hired
twenty thousand Aramean foot soldiers from
Beth Rehob and Zobah, as well as the king of
Maacah with a thousand men, and also twelve
thousand men from Tob.
[7]On hearing this, David sent Joab out with the
entire army of fighting men. [8]The Ammonites
came out and drew up in battle formation at the
entrance to their city gate, while the Arameans of
Zobah and Rehob and the men of Tob and Maacah were by themselves in the open country.
[9]Joab saw that there were battle lines in front
of him and behind him; so he selected some of
the best troops in Israel and deployed them
against the Arameans. [10]He put the rest of the
men under the command of Abishai his brother
and deployed them against the Ammonites.
[11]Joab said, "If the Arameans are too strong for
me, then you are to come to my rescue; but if the
Ammonites are too strong for you, then I will
come to rescue you. [12]Be strong and let us fight
bravely for our people and the cities of our God.
The LORD will do what is good in his sight."
[13]Then Joab and the troops with him advanced
to fight the Arameans, and they fled before him.
[14]When the Ammonites saw that the Arameans
were fleeing, they fled before Abishai and went
inside the city. So Joab returned from fighting the
Ammonites and came to Jerusalem.
[15]After the Arameans saw that they had been
routed by Israel, they regrouped. [16]Hadadezer
had Arameans brought from beyond the River[a];
they went to Helam, with Shobach the commander of Hadadezer's army leading them.
[17]When David was told of this, he gathered all
Israel, crossed the Jordan and went to Helam.
The Arameans formed their battle lines to meet
David and fought against him. [18]But they fled
before Israel, and David killed seven hundred of
their charioteers and forty thousand of their foot
soldiers.[b] He also struck down Shobach the
commander of their army, and he died there.
[19]When all the kings who were vassals of Hadadezer saw that they had been defeated by Israel,
they made peace with the Israelites and became
subject to them.
So the Arameans were afraid to help the Ammonites anymore.

David and Bathsheba

11 In the spring, at the time when kings go
off to war, David sent Joab out with the
king's men and the whole Israelite army. They
destroyed the Ammonites and besieged Rabbah.
But David remained in Jerusalem.
[2]One evening David got up from his bed and
walked around on the roof of the palace. From
the roof he saw a woman bathing. The woman
was very beautiful, [3]and David sent someone to
find out about her. The man said, "Isn't this Bathsheba, the daughter of Eliam and the wife of Uriah the Hittite?" [4]Then David sent messengers to
get her. She came to him, and he slept with her.
(She had purified herself from her uncleanness.)
Then[c] she went back home. [5]The woman conceived and sent word to David, saying, "I am
pregnant."
[6]So David sent this word to Joab: "Send me
Uriah the Hittite." And Joab sent him to David.
[7]When Uriah came to him, David asked him how
Joab was, how the soldiers were and how the war
was going. [8]Then David said to Uriah, "Go down
to your house and wash your feet." So Uriah left
the palace, and a gift from the king was sent after
him. [9]But Uriah slept at the entrance to the palace with all his master's servants and did not go
down to his house.
[10]When David was told, "Uriah did not go
home," he asked him, "Haven't you just come
from a distance? Why didn't you go home?"
[11]Uriah said to David, "The ark and Israel and
Judah are staying in tents, and my master Joab
and my lord's men are camped in the open fields.
How could I go to my house to eat and drink and
lie with my wife? As surely as you live, I will not
do such a thing!"
[12]Then David said to him, "Stay here one more

[a]*16* That is, the Euphrates [b]*18* Some Septuagint manuscripts (see also 1 Chron. 19:18); Hebrew *horsemen* [c]*4* Or *with her. When she purified herself from her uncleanness,*

day, and tomorrow I will send you back." So Uriah remained in Jerusalem that day and the next.
13At David's invitation, he ate and drank with
him, and David made him drunk. But in the evening Uriah went out to sleep on his mat among
his master's servants; he did not go home.

> ### 2 SAMUEL 11:1–27
>
> 1. Are you more likely to get hooked on chocolate, soaps, video games or the Internet?
> 2. What has the biggest impact on the morals in your school: TV? Church? Magazines? Movies? Parents? Other?
> 3. What has the biggest influence on your morals?
> 4. When did David's thoughts or actions become sin? What is the line between "looking" and "lusting"?
> 5. What have you found helpful in dealing with temptation?
> 6. Where do you need to set some boundaries for what you are going to watch, read and see?
> 7. How can this group help you resist lust/pornography? Pray together.

14In the morning David wrote a letter to Joab
and sent it with Uriah. 15In it he wrote, "Put
Uriah in the front line where the fighting is fierc-
est. Then withdraw from him so he will be struck
down and die."
16So while Joab had the city under siege, he
put Uriah at a place where he knew the strongest
defenders were. 17When the men of the city
came out and fought against Joab, some of the
men in David's army fell; moreover, Uriah the
Hittite died.
18Joab sent David a full account of the battle.
19He instructed the messenger: "When you have
finished giving the king this account of the battle,
20the king's anger may flare up, and he may ask
you, 'Why did you get so close to the city to fight?
Didn't you know they would shoot arrows from
the wall? 21Who killed Abimelech son of Jerub-
Besheth[a]? Didn't a woman throw an upper millstone on him from the wall, so that he died in
Thebez? Why did you get so close to the wall?' If
he asks you this, then say to him, 'Also, your
servant Uriah the Hittite is dead.' "
22The messenger set out, and when he arrived
he told David everything Joab had sent him to
say. 23The messenger said to David, "The men
overpowered us and came out against us in the
open, but we drove them back to the entrance to
the city gate. 24Then the archers shot arrows at
your servants from the wall, and some of the
king's men died. Moreover, your servant Uriah
the Hittite is dead."
25David told the messenger, "Say this to Joab:
'Don't let this upset you; the sword devours one
as well as another. Press the attack against the
city and destroy it.' Say this to encourage Joab."
26When Uriah's wife heard that her husband
was dead, she mourned for him. 27After the time
of mourning was over, David had her brought to
his house, and she became his wife and bore him
a son. But the thing David had done displeased
the LORD.

Nathan Rebukes David

12 The LORD sent Nathan to David. When he
came to him, he said, "There were two
men in a certain town, one rich and the other
poor. 2The rich man had a very large number of
sheep and cattle, 3but the poor man had nothing
except one little ewe lamb he had bought. He
raised it, and it grew up with him and his children. It shared his food, drank from his cup and

[a]21 Also known as *Jerub-Baal* (that is, Gideon)

Everything has been going King David's way. He has acquired the admiration of all Israel, numerous wives and children, great military victories, and God's promise of a perpetual heir on the throne.

11:1–2 ***the time when kings go off to war.*** Directly after the grain harvest in April and May. David relaxed while his comrades fought his battles. ***walked around on the roof.*** The roofs were flat. David probably went there to enjoy the cool evening air.

11:4 ***David sent messengers to get her.*** Through this action David eventually becomes guilty of breaking the sixth, seventh, ninth and tenth commandments (Ex. 20:13–17). ***She came to him, and he slept with her.*** Bathsheba appears to have been an unprotesting partner in this adulterous relationship with David.

11:5 ***I am pregnant.*** Bathsheba leaves the next step up to David. The Law prescribed the death penalty for both of them (Deut. 22:22), as they well knew.

11:6–12 David twice attempts to get Uriah to sleep with Bathsheba so that Uriah will think his wife's baby is his. But Uriah shows far more honor than David (v. 11).

11:15 ***so he will be struck down and die.*** Unsuccessful in making it appear Uriah was the father of Bathsheba's child, David plotted Uriah's death so he could marry Bathsheba himself as soon as possible.

11:27 ***the thing David had done displeased the LORD.*** See note on verse 4.

even slept in his arms. It was like a daughter to him.

4“Now a traveler came to the rich man, but the rich man refrained from taking one of his own sheep or cattle to prepare a meal for the traveler who had come to him. Instead, he took the ewe lamb that belonged to the poor man and prepared it for the one who had come to him.”

2 SAMUEL 12:1–14

1. Have you ever been caught with your hand in the cookie jar? How did you react?
2. What's closest to your standard of justice: Lock 'em up or rehabilitate?
3. What teacher or coach do you admire because they were willing to tell you what you needed to hear even though it hurt?
4. Is it easier for you to see your own faults—or someone else's?
5. Would you confront a friend if you thought they were doing something wrong?
6. If someone sees something wrong in your life, do you want them to talk to you about it or keep it to themselves?
7. How would you feel about making yourself accountable to someone (maybe this group), giving them permission to challenge you when you need it?

5David burned with anger against the man and said to Nathan, “As surely as the LORD lives, the man who did this deserves to die! 6He must pay for that lamb four times over, because he did such a thing and had no pity.”

7Then Nathan said to David, “You are the man! This is what the LORD, the God of Israel, says: ‘I anointed you king over Israel, and I delivered you from the hand of Saul. 8I gave your master's house to you, and your master's wives into your arms. I gave you the house of Israel and Judah. And if all this had been too little, I would have given you even more. 9Why did you despise the word of the LORD by doing what is evil in his eyes? You struck down Uriah the Hittite with the sword and took his wife to be your own. You killed him with the sword of the Ammonites. 10Now, therefore, the sword will never depart from your house, because you despised me and took the wife of Uriah the Hittite to be your own.’

11“This is what the LORD says: ‘Out of your own household I am going to bring calamity upon you. Before your very eyes I will take your wives and give them to one who is close to you, and he will lie with your wives in broad daylight. 12You did it in secret, but I will do this thing in broad daylight before all Israel.’ ”

13Then David said to Nathan, “I have sinned against the LORD.”

Nathan replied, “The LORD has taken away your sin. You are not going to die. 14But because by doing this you have made the enemies of the LORD show utter contempt,[a] the son born to you will die.”

15After Nathan had gone home, the LORD struck the child that Uriah's wife had borne to David, and he became ill. 16David pleaded with God for the child. He fasted and went into his house and spent the nights lying on the ground. 17The elders of his household stood beside him to get him up from the ground, but he refused, and he would not eat any food with them.

18On the seventh day the child died. David's servants were afraid to tell him that the child was dead, for they thought, “While the child was still living, we spoke to David but he would not listen to us. How can we tell him the child is dead? He may do something desperate.”

19David noticed that his servants were whispering among themselves and he realized the child was dead. “Is the child dead?” he asked.

[a]14 Masoretic Text; an ancient Hebrew scribal tradition *this you have shown utter contempt for the LORD*

The previous chapter records David's great sin: his adultery with Bathsheba, his attempts to cover up the fact he got her pregnant—ending with his ordering her husband's murder, and then taking Bathsheba as his wife.

12:1 ***The LORD sent.*** Prophets like Nathan were messengers from the Lord. Here the Great King sends his emissary to rebuke and announce judgment on the king he had enthroned over his people. ***There were two men.*** Nathan begins one of the most striking parables in the Old Testament.

12:5–6 ***burned with anger.*** David didn't see himself in the story, though in his strong reaction he may have been projecting his own repressed guilt. ***deserves to die.*** Without knowing it, David was pronouncing judgment on himself. According to Moses' Law, David did indeed deserve to die. ***four times over.*** In agreement with the requirements of Exodus 22:1.

12:9 ***You killed him.*** David is held responsible for Uriah's death.

12:10–12 These judgments against David were fulfilled when three of his sons came to violent deaths, and when his son Absalom conspired to seize the kingship.

12:13 ***I have sinned against the LORD.*** David recognizes his guilt and confesses his sin in response to Nathan's rebuke. ***The LORD ... away your sin.*** David experienced the joy of knowing his sin was forgiven. ***You are not going to die.*** The Lord, in his grace, released David from the customary death penalty for adultery and murder.

"Yes," they replied, "he is dead."
20Then David got up from the ground. After
he had washed, put on lotions and changed his
clothes, he went into the house of the LORD and
worshiped. Then he went to his own house, and
at his request they served him food, and he ate.

2 SAMUEL 12:15–25

1. What do you do when you're really upset: Do you eat? Not eat? Not sleep?
2. How do the students in your school look upon premarital sex? Abortion?
3. What do the teachers in your school say about birth control? Abortion?
4. If a friend of yours got pregnant and came to you for help, what would you advise?
5. If your friend had already had an abortion, what would you say to this person?
6. How hard is it for you to ask for and accept God's forgiveness?
7. What could you/your church do to help kids in your school who have had an abortion?

21His servants asked him, "Why are you acting
this way? While the child was alive, you fasted
and wept, but now that the child is dead, you get
up and eat!"
22He answered, "While the child was still
alive, I fasted and wept. I thought, 'Who knows?
The LORD may be gracious to me and let the child
live.' 23But now that he is dead, why should I
fast? Can I bring him back again? I will go to him,
but he will not return to me."
24Then David comforted his wife Bathsheba,
and he went to her and lay with her. She gave
birth to a son, and they named him Solomon. The
LORD loved him; 25and because the LORD loved
him, he sent word through Nathan the prophet to
name him Jedidiah.[a]
26Meanwhile Joab fought against Rabbah of
the Ammonites and captured the royal citadel.
27Joab then sent messengers to David, saying, "I
have fought against Rabbah and taken its water
supply. 28Now muster the rest of the troops and
besiege the city and capture it. Otherwise I will
take the city, and it will be named after me."
29So David mustered the entire army and went
to Rabbah, and attacked and captured it. 30He
took the crown from the head of their king[b]—
its weight was a talent[c] of gold, and it was set
with precious stones—and it was placed on David's head. He took a great quantity of plunder
from the city 31and brought out the people who
were there, consigning them to labor with saws
and with iron picks and axes, and he made them
work at brickmaking.[d] He did this to all the
Ammonite towns. Then David and his entire
army returned to Jerusalem.

Amnon and Tamar

13 In the course of time, Amnon son of David fell in love with Tamar, the beautiful
sister of Absalom son of David.
2Amnon became frustrated to the point of illness on account of his sister Tamar, for she was
a virgin, and it seemed impossible for him to do
anything to her.
3Now Amnon had a friend named Jonadab son
of Shimeah, David's brother. Jonadab was a very
shrewd man. 4He asked Amnon, "Why do you,
the king's son, look so haggard morning after
morning? Won't you tell me?"
Amnon said to him, "I'm in love with Tamar,
my brother Absalom's sister."
5"Go to bed and pretend to be ill," Jonadab
said. "When your father comes to see you, say to
him, 'I would like my sister Tamar to come and

[a]25 *Jedidiah* means *loved by the LORD.* [b]30 Or *of Milcom* (that is, Molech) [c]30 That is, about 75 pounds (about 34 kilograms) [d]31 The meaning of the Hebrew for this clause is uncertain.

King David committed adultery with Bathsheba while her husband was off fighting the king's battles. When she became pregnant, David attempted to cover up his sin—even having her husband killed in battle. David married Bathsheba, who bore him a son. God sent Nathan to confront David about his sin and David immediately repented. David would be spared the decreed death penalty for his sins. But Nathan stated, "the son born to you will die" (12:14).

12:18 *the child died.* Nathan pronounced several judgments on David for his sin (see note on 12:10–12). Nathan's final pronouncement was the first to find fulfillment: the child of the adulterous union died. Here the sins of the father were certainly visited on the child (Num. 14:18). Yet the good news is that God clearly forgave David's genuine confession (v. 13; see Ps. 51). And because of Christ, "If we confess our sins, he is faithful and just and will forgive us our sins" (1 John 1:9).

12:20 *he went into the house of the LORD and worshiped.* In this way David clearly demonstrated his humble acceptance of the disciplinary results of his sin.

12:25 *Jedidiah.* The giving of the name (meaning loved by the Lord) suggests that God's special favor rested on him from his birth. The name also contained an echo of David's name, providing assurance to David. Solomon is a form of the word *shalom,* which means peace. God promised his rule would be one of peace (1 Chron. 22:9).

give me something to eat. Let her prepare the
food in my sight so I may watch her and then eat
it from her hand.' "
[6]So Amnon lay down and pretended to be ill.

2 SAMUEL 13:1–22

1. When have you pretended to be sick? Did you get caught?
2. Have you ever been lovesick over someone who didn't like you?
3. What advice would you have given Amnon about Tamar?
4. In your school, what is said about date rape? Have you known of someone who was raped?
5. Could you ever forgive someone who raped your sister?
6. Where do you draw the line for yourself to guard against going too far?
7. How can this group pray for you this week? Close in prayer.

When the king came to see him, Amnon said to
him, "I would like my sister Tamar to come and
make some special bread in my sight, so I may eat
from her hand."
[7]David sent word to Tamar at the palace: "Go
to the house of your brother Amnon and prepare
some food for him." [8]So Tamar went to the house
of her brother Amnon, who was lying down. She
took some dough, kneaded it, made the bread in
his sight and baked it. [9]Then she took the pan
and served him the bread, but he refused to eat.
"Send everyone out of here," Amnon said. So
everyone left him. [10]Then Amnon said to Tamar,
"Bring the food here into my bedroom so I may
eat from your hand." And Tamar took the bread
she had prepared and brought it to her brother
Amnon in his bedroom. [11]But when she took it to
him to eat, he grabbed her and said, "Come to
bed with me, my sister."
[12]"Don't, my brother!" she said to him. "Don't
force me. Such a thing should not be done in
Israel! Don't do this wicked thing. [13]What about
me? Where could I get rid of my disgrace? And
what about you? You would be like one of the
wicked fools in Israel. Please speak to the king;
he will not keep me from being married to you."
[14]But he refused to listen to her, and since he was
stronger than she, he raped her.
[15]Then Amnon hated her with intense hatred.
In fact, he hated her more than he had loved her.
Amnon said to her, "Get up and get out!"
[16]"No!" she said to him. "Sending me away
would be a greater wrong than what you have
already done to me."
But he refused to listen to her. [17]He called his
personal servant and said, "Get this woman out
of here and bolt the door after her." [18]So his
servant put her out and bolted the door after her.
She was wearing a richly ornamented[a] robe, for
this was the kind of garment the virgin daughters
of the king wore. [19]Tamar put ashes on her head
and tore the ornamented[b] robe she was wearing. She put her hand on her head and went
away, weeping aloud as she went.
[20]Her brother Absalom said to her, "Has that
Amnon, your brother, been with you? Be quiet
now, my sister; he is your brother. Don't take
this thing to heart." And Tamar lived in her
brother Absalom's house, a desolate woman.
[21]When King David heard all this, he was furious. [22]Absalom never said a word to Amnon, either good or bad; he hated Amnon because he
had disgraced his sister Tamar.

Absalom Kills Amnon

[23]Two years later, when Absalom's sheep-
shearers were at Baal Hazor near the border of
Ephraim, he invited all the king's sons to come

[a] *18* The meaning of the Hebrew for this phrase is uncertain. [b] *19* The meaning of the Hebrew for this word is uncertain.

As a result of King David's sins, the Lord said through the prophet Nathan that David would reap great calamity from his own household. Now the trouble begins.

13:1 ***Amnon.*** David's oldest son, whose mother was Ahinoam (3:2). ***Tamar.*** David's daughter by Maacah (3:3), who was Absalom's full sister.

13:13 ***what about you?*** Among other things, Tamar points out that Amnon's action would jeopardize his position as crown prince and heir to the throne. ***he will not keep me from being married to you.*** Possibly a futile attempt by Tamar to escape Amnon's immediate designs rather than a serious suggestion, since such a marriage was prohibited in Israel (Lev. 18:9; 20:17).

13:15 ***Amnon hated her.*** The reversal in Amnon's feelings toward Tamar demonstrates that his former "love" (v. 1) was nothing but lust.

13:16 ***Sending me away would be a greater wrong.*** No longer a virgin, she could not be offered to another husband.

13:21 ***he was furious.*** Although David was incensed by Amnon's rape of Tamar, there is no record that he took any punitive action against him. Perhaps the memory of his own sin with Bathsheba adversely affected his handling of the matter. Whatever the reason, David abdicated his responsibility both as king and as father. This disciplinary leniency toward his sons led to the death of Amnon and the revolts of Absalom and Adonijah.

there. [24]Absalom went to the king and said,
"Your servant has had shearers come. Will the
king and his officials please join me?"
[25]"No, my son," the king replied. "All of us
should not go; we would only be a burden to
you." Although Absalom urged him, he still refused to go, but gave him his blessing.

2 Samuel 13:23–39

1. In your school, who is your school's biggest rival in sports? Has this competition ever gotten out of control?
2. How do your family or friends know when you are mad at one of them?
3. What was the result of Absalom's grudge that he carried for two years? Do you think Absalom's actions were right or wrong?
4. How do you feel when you see a wrong go unpunished?
5. In your own life, where do you need to let God do the punishing and get on with your life?
6. In what relationship do you have the biggest problem turning over your anger to God?
7. How would you like the group to remember you in prayer now and this coming week?

[26]Then Absalom said, "If not, please let my
brother Amnon come with us."
The king asked him, "Why should he go with
you?" [27]But Absalom urged him, so he sent with
him Amnon and the rest of the king's sons.
[28]Absalom ordered his men, "Listen! When
Amnon is in high spirits from drinking wine and
I say to you, 'Strike Amnon down,' then kill him.
Don't be afraid. Have not I given you this order?
Be strong and brave." [29]So Absalom's men did to
Amnon what Absalom had ordered. Then all the
king's sons got up, mounted their mules and fled.
[30]While they were on their way, the report
came to David: "Absalom has struck down all the
king's sons; not one of them is left." [31]The king
stood up, tore his clothes and lay down on the
ground; and all his servants stood by with their
clothes torn.
[32]But Jonadab son of Shimeah, David's brother, said, "My lord should not think that they
killed all the princes; only Amnon is dead. This
has been Absalom's expressed intention ever
since the day Amnon raped his sister Tamar.
[33]My lord the king should not be concerned
about the report that all the king's sons are dead.
Only Amnon is dead."
[34]Meanwhile, Absalom had fled.
Now the man standing watch looked up and
saw many people on the road west of him, coming down the side of the hill. The watchman
went and told the king, "I see men in the direction of Horonaim, on the side of the hill."[a]
[35]Jonadab said to the king, "See, the king's
sons are here; it has happened just as your servant said."
[36]As he finished speaking, the king's sons
came in, wailing loudly. The king, too, and all his
servants wept very bitterly.
[37]Absalom fled and went to Talmai son of Ammihud, the king of Geshur. But King David
mourned for his son every day.
[38]After Absalom fled and went to Geshur, he
stayed there three years. [39]And the spirit of the
king[b] longed to go to Absalom, for he was consoled concerning Amnon's death.

Absalom Returns to Jerusalem

14 Joab son of Zeruiah knew that the king's
heart longed for Absalom. [2]So Joab sent
someone to Tekoa and had a wise woman

a34 Septuagint; Hebrew does not have this sentence. *b39* Dead Sea Scrolls and some Septuagint manuscripts; Masoretic Text *But ⌞the spirit of⌟ David the king*

The Lord pronounced that King David would experience tragedy within his family because of his sins of adultery and murder. That prophecy began to be fulfilled when David's oldest son Amnon raped David's daughter Tamar (Amnon's half sister). The king, though furious, did nothing about Amnon's offense. However, David's second oldest son Absalom (Tamar's full brother) hated Amnon for what he did. Without saying a word at the time (13:22), Absalom now takes action after two years.

13:23 ***he invited all the king's sons.*** The time of sheepshearing was a festive occasion (see 1 Sam. 25:4,8).

13:26 ***let my brother Amnon come.*** Upon David's refusal of the invitation, Absalom diplomatically requested that Amnon, the crown prince and oldest son, be his representative. ***Why should he go with you?*** David's question suggests some misgivings because of the strained relationship between the two half brothers (13:22).

13:28 ***kill him.*** Absalom carefully planned for the murder of his half brother in violation of Eastern hospitality. In the wicked acts of Amnon and Absalom, David's sons became guilty of sexual immorality and murder, as their father had before them.

13:37–39 ***Absalom fled and went to ... Geshur.*** To see Talmai, Absalom's grandfather (see 3:3). ***the spirit of the king longed to go to Absalom.*** With Absalom a refugee, David had lost both of his oldest living sons.

brought from there. He said to her, "Pretend you
are in mourning. Dress in mourning clothes, and
don't use any cosmetic lotions. Act like a woman
who has spent many days grieving for the dead.
3Then go to the king and speak these words to
him." And Joab put the words in her mouth.
4When the woman from Tekoa went[a] to the
king, she fell with her face to the ground to pay
him honor, and she said, "Help me, O king!"
5The king asked her, "What is troubling you?"
She said, "I am indeed a widow; my husband
is dead. 6I your servant had two sons. They got
into a fight with each other in the field, and no
one was there to separate them. One struck the
other and killed him. 7Now the whole clan has
risen up against your servant; they say, 'Hand
over the one who struck his brother down, so
that we may put him to death for the life of his
brother whom he killed; then we will get rid of
the heir as well.' They would put out the only
burning coal I have left, leaving my husband neither name nor descendant on the face of the
earth."
8The king said to the woman, "Go home, and
I will issue an order in your behalf."
9But the woman from Tekoa said to him, "My
lord the king, let the blame rest on me and on my
father's family, and let the king and his throne be
without guilt."
10The king replied, "If anyone says anything to
you, bring him to me, and he will not bother you
again."
11She said, "Then let the king invoke the LORD
his God to prevent the avenger of blood from
adding to the destruction, so that my son will not
be destroyed."
"As surely as the LORD lives," he said, "not
one hair of your son's head will fall to the
ground."
12Then the woman said, "Let your servant
speak a word to my lord the king."
"Speak," he replied.
13The woman said, "Why then have you devised a thing like this against the people of God?
When the king says this, does he not convict
himself, for the king has not brought back his
banished son? 14Like water spilled on the ground,
which cannot be recovered, so we must die. But
God does not take away life; instead, he devises
ways so that a banished person may not remain
estranged from him.
15"And now I have come to say this to my lord
the king because the people have made me
afraid. Your servant thought, 'I will speak to the
king; perhaps he will do what his servant asks.
16Perhaps the king will agree to deliver his servant from the hand of the man who is trying to
cut off both me and my son from the inheritance
God gave us.'
17"And now your servant says, 'May the word
of my lord the king bring me rest, for my lord the
king is like an angel of God in discerning good
and evil. May the LORD your God be with you.'"
18Then the king said to the woman, "Do not
keep from me the answer to what I am going to
ask you."
"Let my lord the king speak," the woman said.
19The king asked, "Isn't the hand of Joab with
you in all this?"
The woman answered, "As surely as you live,
my lord the king, no one can turn to the right or
to the left from anything my lord the king says.
Yes, it was your servant Joab who instructed me
to do this and who put all these words into the
mouth of your servant. 20Your servant Joab did
this to change the present situation. My lord has
wisdom like that of an angel of God—he knows
everything that happens in the land."
21The king said to Joab, "Very well, I will do it.
Go, bring back the young man Absalom."
22Joab fell with his face to the ground to pay
him honor, and he blessed the king. Joab said,
"Today your servant knows that he has found
favor in your eyes, my lord the king, because the
king has granted his servant's request."
23Then Joab went to Geshur and brought Absalom back to Jerusalem. 24But the king said, "He
must go to his own house; he must not see my
face." So Absalom went to his own house and did
not see the face of the king.
25In all Israel there was not a man so highly
praised for his handsome appearance as Absalom.
From the top of his head to the sole of his foot
there was no blemish in him. 26Whenever he cut
the hair of his head—he used to cut his hair from
time to time when it became too heavy for him—
he would weigh it, and its weight was two hundred shekels[b] by the royal standard.
27Three sons and a daughter were born to Absalom. The daughter's name was Tamar, and she
became a beautiful woman.
28Absalom lived two years in Jerusalem without seeing the king's face. 29Then Absalom sent
for Joab in order to send him to the king, but Joab
refused to come to him. So he sent a second time,
but he refused to come. 30Then he said to his
servants, "Look, Joab's field is next to mine, and
he has barley there. Go and set it on fire." So
Absalom's servants set the field on fire.
31Then Joab did go to Absalom's house and he
said to him, "Why have your servants set my field
on fire?"

[a]4 Many Hebrew manuscripts, Septuagint, Vulgate and Syriac; most Hebrew manuscripts *spoke*
[b]26 That is, about 5 pounds (about 2.3 kilograms)

32 Absalom said to Joab, "Look, I sent word to
you and said, 'Come here so I can send you to the
king to ask, "Why have I come from Geshur? It
would be better for me if I were still there!" '
Now then, I want to see the king's face, and
if I am guilty of anything, let him put me to
death."
33 So Joab went to the king and told him this.
Then the king summoned Absalom, and he came
in and bowed down with his face to the ground
before the king. And the king kissed Absalom.

Absalom's Conspiracy

15 In the course of time, Absalom provided
himself with a chariot and horses and
with fifty men to run ahead of him. 2 He would
get up early and stand by the side of the road
leading to the city gate. Whenever anyone came
with a complaint to be placed before the king for
a decision, Absalom would call out to him, "What
town are you from?" He would answer, "Your
servant is from one of the tribes of Israel." 3 Then
Absalom would say to him, "Look, your claims
are valid and proper, but there is no representative of the king to hear you." 4 And Absalom
would add, "If only I were appointed judge in the
land! Then everyone who has a complaint or case
could come to me and I would see that he gets
justice."
5 Also, whenever anyone approached him to
bow down before him, Absalom would reach out
his hand, take hold of him and kiss him. 6 Absalom behaved in this way toward all the Israelites
who came to the king asking for justice, and so he
stole the hearts of the men of Israel.
7 At the end of four[a] years, Absalom said to
the king, "Let me go to Hebron and fulfill a vow
I made to the LORD. 8 While your servant was
living at Geshur in Aram, I made this vow: 'If the
LORD takes me back to Jerusalem, I will worship
the LORD in Hebron.[b]' "
9 The king said to him, "Go in peace." So he
went to Hebron.
10 Then Absalom sent secret messengers
throughout the tribes of Israel to say, "As soon as
you hear the sound of the trumpets, then say,
'Absalom is king in Hebron.' " 11 Two hundred
men from Jerusalem had accompanied Absalom.
They had been invited as guests and went quite
innocently, knowing nothing about the matter.
12 While Absalom was offering sacrifices, he also
sent for Ahithophel the Gilonite, David's counsel-
or, to come from Giloh, his hometown. And so
the conspiracy gained strength, and Absalom's
following kept on increasing.

David Flees

13 A messenger came and told David, "The
hearts of the men of Israel are with Absalom."
14 Then David said to all his officials who were
with him in Jerusalem, "Come! We must flee, or
none of us will escape from Absalom. We must
leave immediately, or he will move quickly to
overtake us and bring ruin upon us and put the
city to the sword."
15 The king's officials answered him, "Your servants are ready to do whatever our lord the king
chooses."
16 The king set out, with his entire household
following him; but he left ten concubines to take
care of the palace. 17 So the king set out, with all
the people following him, and they halted at a
place some distance away. 18 All his men marched
past him, along with all the Kerethites and Pelethites; and all the six hundred Gittites who had
accompanied him from Gath marched before the
king.
19 The king said to Ittai the Gittite, "Why
should you come along with us? Go back and stay
with King Absalom. You are a foreigner, an exile
from your homeland. 20 You came only yesterday.
And today shall I make you wander about with
us, when I do not know where I am going? Go
back, and take your countrymen. May kindness
and faithfulness be with you."
21 But Ittai replied to the king, "As surely as the
LORD lives, and as my lord the king lives, wherever my lord the king may be, whether it means
life or death, there will your servant be."
22 David said to Ittai, "Go ahead, march on." So
Ittai the Gittite marched on with all his men and
the families that were with him.
23 The whole countryside wept aloud as all the
people passed by. The king also crossed the Kidron Valley, and all the people moved on toward
the desert.
24 Zadok was there, too, and all the Levites
who were with him were carrying the ark of the
covenant of God. They set down the ark of God,
and Abiathar offered sacrifices[c] until all the people had finished leaving the city.
25 Then the king said to Zadok, "Take the ark
of God back into the city. If I find favor in the
LORD's eyes, he will bring me back and let me see
it and his dwelling place again. 26 But if he says,
'I am not pleased with you,' then I am ready; let
him do to me whatever seems good to him."
27 The king also said to Zadok the priest,
"Aren't you a seer? Go back to the city in peace,
with your son Ahimaaz and Jonathan son of Abiathar. You and Abiathar take your two sons with
you. 28 I will wait at the fords in the desert until

[a] 7 Some Septuagint manuscripts, Syriac and Josephus; Hebrew *forty* [b] 8 Some Septuagint manuscripts; Hebrew does not have *in Hebron.* [c] 24 Or *Abiathar went up*

word comes from you to inform me." 29So Zadok
and Abiathar took the ark of God back to Jerusalem and stayed there.
30But David continued up the Mount of Olives,
weeping as he went; his head was covered and
he was barefoot. All the people with him covered
their heads too and were weeping as they went
up. 31Now David had been told, "Ahithophel is
among the conspirators with Absalom." So David
prayed, "O LORD, turn Ahithophel's counsel into
foolishness."
32When David arrived at the summit, where
people used to worship God, Hushai the Arkite
was there to meet him, his robe torn and dust on
his head. 33David said to him, "If you go with me,
you will be a burden to me. 34But if you return to
the city and say to Absalom, 'I will be your servant, O king; I was your father's servant in the
past, but now I will be your servant,' then you
can help me by frustrating Ahithophel's advice.
35Won't the priests Zadok and Abiathar be there
with you? Tell them anything you hear in the
king's palace. 36Their two sons, Ahimaaz son of
Zadok and Jonathan son of Abiathar, are there
with them. Send them to me with anything you
hear."
37So David's friend Hushai arrived at Jerusalem as Absalom was entering the city.

David and Ziba

16 When David had gone a short distance
beyond the summit, there was Ziba, the
steward of Mephibosheth, waiting to meet him.
He had a string of donkeys saddled and loaded
with two hundred loaves of bread, a hundred
cakes of raisins, a hundred cakes of figs and a skin
of wine.
2The king asked Ziba, "Why have you brought
these?"
Ziba answered, "The donkeys are for the
king's household to ride on, the bread and fruit
are for the men to eat, and the wine is to refresh
those who become exhausted in the desert."
3The king then asked, "Where is your master's
grandson?"
Ziba said to him, "He is staying in Jerusalem,
because he thinks, 'Today the house of Israel will
give me back my grandfather's kingdom.'"
4Then the king said to Ziba, "All that belonged
to Mephibosheth is now yours."
"I humbly bow," Ziba said. "May I find favor in
your eyes, my lord the king."

Shimei Curses David

5As King David approached Bahurim, a man
from the same clan as Saul's family came out from
there. His name was Shimei son of Gera, and he
cursed as he came out. 6He pelted David and all
the king's officials with stones, though all the
troops and the special guard were on David's
right and left. 7As he cursed, Shimei said, "Get
out, get out, you man of blood, you scoundrel!
8The LORD has repaid you for all the blood you
shed in the household of Saul, in whose place you
have reigned. The LORD has handed the kingdom
over to your son Absalom. You have come to ruin
because you are a man of blood!"
9Then Abishai son of Zeruiah said to the king,
"Why should this dead dog curse my lord the
king? Let me go over and cut off his head."
10But the king said, "What do you and I have
in common, you sons of Zeruiah? If he is cursing
because the LORD said to him, 'Curse David,'
who can ask, 'Why do you do this?'"
11David then said to Abishai and all his officials, "My son, who is of my own flesh, is trying
to take my life. How much more, then, this Benjamite! Leave him alone; let him curse, for the
LORD has told him to. 12It may be that the LORD
will see my distress and repay me with good for
the cursing I am receiving today."
13So David and his men continued along the
road while Shimei was going along the hillside
opposite him, cursing as he went and throwing
stones at him and showering him with dirt. 14The
king and all the people with him arrived at their
destination exhausted. And there he refreshed
himself.

The Advice of Hushai and Ahithophel

15Meanwhile, Absalom and all the men of Israel came to Jerusalem, and Ahithophel was with
him. 16Then Hushai the Arkite, David's friend,
went to Absalom and said to him, "Long live the
king! Long live the king!"
17Absalom asked Hushai, "Is this the love you
show your friend? Why didn't you go with your
friend?"
18Hushai said to Absalom, "No, the one chosen by the LORD, by these people, and by all the
men of Israel—his I will be, and I will remain
with him. 19Furthermore, whom should I serve?
Should I not serve the son? Just as I served your
father, so I will serve you."
20Absalom said to Ahithophel, "Give us your
advice. What should we do?"
21Ahithophel answered, "Lie with your father's concubines whom he left to take care of
the palace. Then all Israel will hear that you have
made yourself a stench in your father's nostrils,
and the hands of everyone with you will be
strengthened." 22So they pitched a tent for Absalom on the roof, and he lay with his father's concubines in the sight of all Israel.
23Now in those days the advice Ahithophel
gave was like that of one who inquires of God.
That was how both David and Absalom regarded
all of Ahithophel's advice.

17 Ahithophel said to Absalom, "I would[a]
choose twelve thousand men and set out
tonight in pursuit of David. 2I would[b] attack him
while he is weary and weak. I would[b] strike him
with terror, and then all the people with him will
flee. I would[b] strike down only the king 3and
bring all the people back to you. The death of the
man you seek will mean the return of all; all the
people will be unharmed." 4This plan seemed
good to Absalom and to all the elders of Israel.
5But Absalom said, "Summon also Hushai the
Arkite, so we can hear what he has to say."
6When Hushai came to him, Absalom said,
"Ahithophel has given this advice. Should we do
what he says? If not, give us your opinion."
7Hushai replied to Absalom, "The advice
Ahithophel has given is not good this time. 8You
know your father and his men; they are fighters,
and as fierce as a wild bear robbed of her cubs.
Besides, your father is an experienced fighter; he
will not spend the night with the troops. 9Even
now, he is hidden in a cave or some other place.
If he should attack your troops first,[c] whoever
hears about it will say, 'There has been a slaughter among the troops who follow Absalom.'
10Then even the bravest soldier, whose heart is
like the heart of a lion, will melt with fear, for all
Israel knows that your father is a fighter and that
those with him are brave.
11"So I advise you: Let all Israel, from Dan
to Beersheba—as numerous as the sand on the
seashore—be gathered to you, with you yourself
leading them into battle. 12Then we will attack
him wherever he may be found, and we will fall
on him as dew settles on the ground. Neither he
nor any of his men will be left alive. 13If he withdraws into a city, then all Israel will bring ropes
to that city, and we will drag it down to the valley
until not even a piece of it can be found."
14Absalom and all the men of Israel said, "The
advice of Hushai the Arkite is better than that of
Ahithophel." For the LORD had determined to
frustrate the good advice of Ahithophel in order
to bring disaster on Absalom.
15Hushai told Zadok and Abiathar, the priests,
"Ahithophel has advised Absalom and the elders
of Israel to do such and such, but I have advised
them to do so and so. 16Now send a message
immediately and tell David, 'Do not spend the
night at the fords in the desert; cross over without fail, or the king and all the people with him
will be swallowed up.'"
17Jonathan and Ahimaaz were staying at En
Rogel. A servant girl was to go and inform them,
and they were to go and tell King David, for they
could not risk being seen entering the city. 18But
a young man saw them and told Absalom. So the
two of them left quickly and went to the house of
a man in Bahurim. He had a well in his courtyard,
and they climbed down into it. 19His wife took a
covering and spread it out over the opening of the
well and scattered grain over it. No one knew
anything about it.
20When Absalom's men came to the woman at
the house, they asked, "Where are Ahimaaz and
Jonathan?"
The woman answered them, "They crossed
over the brook."[d] The men searched but found
no one, so they returned to Jerusalem.
21After the men had gone, the two climbed out
of the well and went to inform King David. They
said to him, "Set out and cross the river at once;
Ahithophel has advised such and such against
you." 22So David and all the people with him set
out and crossed the Jordan. By daybreak, no one
was left who had not crossed the Jordan.
23When Ahithophel saw that his advice had
not been followed, he saddled his donkey and set
out for his house in his hometown. He put his
house in order and then hanged himself. So he
died and was buried in his father's tomb.
24David went to Mahanaim, and Absalom
crossed the Jordan with all the men of Israel.
25Absalom had appointed Amasa over the army in
place of Joab. Amasa was the son of a man named
Jether,[e] an Israelite[f] who had married Abigail,[g] the daughter of Nahash and sister of Zeruiah the mother of Joab. 26The Israelites and Absalom camped in the land of Gilead.
27When David came to Mahanaim, Shobi son
of Nahash from Rabbah of the Ammonites, and
Makir son of Ammiel from Lo Debar, and Barzillai
the Gileadite from Rogelim 28brought bedding
and bowls and articles of pottery. They also
brought wheat and barley, flour and roasted
grain, beans and lentils,[h] 29honey and curds,
sheep, and cheese from cows' milk for David and
his people to eat. For they said, "The people have
become hungry and tired and thirsty in the
desert."

Absalom's Death

18 David mustered the men who were with
him and appointed over them commanders of thousands and commanders of hundreds.
2David sent the troops out—a third under the
command of Joab, a third under Joab's brother
Abishai son of Zeruiah, and a third under Ittai the
Gittite. The king told the troops, "I myself will
surely march out with you."

[a]1 Or *Let me* [b]2 Or *will* [c]9 Or *When some of the men fall at the first attack* [d]20 Or *"They passed by the sheep pen toward the water."* [e]25 Hebrew *Ithra,* a variant of *Jether* [f]25 Hebrew and some Septuagint manuscripts; other Septuagint manuscripts (see also 1 Chron. 2:17) *Ishmaelite* or *Jezreelite* [g]25 Hebrew *Abigal,* a variant of *Abigail* [h]28 Most Septuagint manuscripts and Syriac; Hebrew *lentils, and roasted grain*

3But the men said, "You must not go out; if we are forced to flee, they won't care about us. Even if half of us die, they won't care; but you are worth ten thousand of us.[a] It would be better now for you to give us support from the city."

4The king answered, "I will do whatever seems best to you."

So the king stood beside the gate while all the men marched out in units of hundreds and of thousands. 5The king commanded Joab, Abishai and Ittai, "Be gentle with the young man Absalom for my sake." And all the troops heard the king giving orders concerning Absalom to each of the commanders.

6The army marched into the field to fight Israel, and the battle took place in the forest of Ephraim. 7There the army of Israel was defeated by David's men, and the casualties that day were great—twenty thousand men. 8The battle spread out over the whole countryside, and the forest claimed more lives that day than the sword.

9Now Absalom happened to meet David's men. He was riding his mule, and as the mule went under the thick branches of a large oak, Absalom's head got caught in the tree. He was left hanging in midair, while the mule he was riding kept on going.

10When one of the men saw this, he told Joab, "I just saw Absalom hanging in an oak tree."

11Joab said to the man who had told him this, "What! You saw him? Why didn't you strike him to the ground right there? Then I would have had to give you ten shekels[b] of silver and a warrior's belt."

12But the man replied, "Even if a thousand shekels[c] were weighed out into my hands, I would not lift my hand against the king's son. In our hearing the king commanded you and Abishai and Ittai, 'Protect the young man Absalom for my sake.[d]' 13And if I had put my life in jeopardy[e]—and nothing is hidden from the king—you would have kept your distance from me."

14Joab said, "I'm not going to wait like this for you." So he took three javelins in his hand and plunged them into Absalom's heart while Absalom was still alive in the oak tree. 15And ten of Joab's armor-bearers surrounded Absalom, struck him and killed him.

16Then Joab sounded the trumpet, and the troops stopped pursuing Israel, for Joab halted them. 17They took Absalom, threw him into a big pit in the forest and piled up a large heap of rocks over him. Meanwhile, all the Israelites fled to their homes.

18During his lifetime Absalom had taken a pillar and erected it in the King's Valley as a monument to himself, for he thought, "I have no son to carry on the memory of my name." He named the pillar after himself, and it is called Absalom's Monument to this day.

David Mourns

19Now Ahimaaz son of Zadok said, "Let me run and take the news to the king that the LORD has delivered him from the hand of his enemies."

20"You are not the one to take the news today," Joab told him. "You may take the news another time, but you must not do so today, because the king's son is dead."

21Then Joab said to a Cushite, "Go, tell the king what you have seen." The Cushite bowed down before Joab and ran off.

22Ahimaaz son of Zadok again said to Joab, "Come what may, please let me run behind the Cushite."

But Joab replied, "My son, why do you want to go? You don't have any news that will bring you a reward."

23He said, "Come what may, I want to run."

So Joab said, "Run!" Then Ahimaaz ran by way of the plain[f] and outran the Cushite.

24While David was sitting between the inner and outer gates, the watchman went up to the roof of the gateway by the wall. As he looked out, he saw a man running alone. 25The watchman called out to the king and reported it.

The king said, "If he is alone, he must have good news." And the man came closer and closer.

26Then the watchman saw another man running, and he called down to the gatekeeper, "Look, another man running alone!"

The king said, "He must be bringing good news, too."

27The watchman said, "It seems to me that the first one runs like Ahimaaz son of Zadok."

"He's a good man," the king said. "He comes with good news."

28Then Ahimaaz called out to the king, "All is well!" He bowed down before the king with his face to the ground and said, "Praise be to the LORD your God! He has delivered up the men who lifted their hands against my lord the king."

29The king asked, "Is the young man Absalom safe?"

Ahimaaz answered, "I saw great confusion just as Joab was about to send the king's servant and me, your servant, but I don't know what it was."

[a] *3* Two Hebrew manuscripts, some Septuagint manuscripts and Vulgate; most Hebrew manuscripts *care; for now there are ten thousand like us* [b] *11* That is, about 4 ounces (about 115 grams) [c] *12* That is, about 25 pounds (about 11 kilograms) [d] *12* A few Hebrew manuscripts, Septuagint, Vulgate and Syriac; most Hebrew manuscripts may be translated *Absalom, whoever you may be.*
[e] *13* Or *Otherwise, if I had acted treacherously toward him* [f] *23* That is, the plain of the Jordan

30The king said, "Stand aside and wait here." So he stepped aside and stood there.

31Then the Cushite arrived and said, "My lord the king, hear the good news! The LORD has delivered you today from all who rose up against you."

32The king asked the Cushite, "Is the young man Absalom safe?"

The Cushite replied, "May the enemies of my lord the king and all who rise up to harm you be like that young man."

33The king was shaken. He went up to the room over the gateway and wept. As he went, he said: "O my son Absalom! My son, my son Absalom! If only I had died instead of you—O Absalom, my son, my son!"

19 Joab was told, "The king is weeping and mourning for Absalom." 2And for the whole army the victory that day was turned into mourning, because on that day the troops heard it said, "The king is grieving for his son." 3The men stole into the city that day as men steal in who are ashamed when they flee from battle. 4The king covered his face and cried aloud, "O my son Absalom! O Absalom, my son, my son!"

5Then Joab went into the house to the king and said, "Today you have humiliated all your men, who have just saved your life and the lives of your sons and daughters and the lives of your wives and concubines. 6You love those who hate you and hate those who love you. You have made it clear today that the commanders and their men mean nothing to you. I see that you would be pleased if Absalom were alive today and all of us were dead. 7Now go out and encourage your men. I swear by the LORD that if you don't go out, not a man will be left with you by nightfall. This will be worse for you than all the calamities that have come upon you from your youth till now."

8So the king got up and took his seat in the gateway. When the men were told, "The king is sitting in the gateway," they all came before him.

David Returns to Jerusalem

Meanwhile, the Israelites had fled to their homes. 9Throughout the tribes of Israel, the people were all arguing with each other, saying, "The king delivered us from the hand of our enemies; he is the one who rescued us from the hand of the Philistines. But now he has fled the country because of Absalom; 10and Absalom, whom we anointed to rule over us, has died in battle. So why do you say nothing about bringing the king back?"

11King David sent this message to Zadok and Abiathar, the priests: "Ask the elders of Judah, 'Why should you be the last to bring the king back to his palace, since what is being said throughout Israel has reached the king at his quarters? 12You are my brothers, my own flesh and blood. So why should you be the last to bring back the king?' 13And say to Amasa, 'Are you not my own flesh and blood? May God deal with me, be it ever so severely, if from now on you are not the commander of my army in place of Joab.'"

14He won over the hearts of all the men of Judah as though they were one man. They sent word to the king, "Return, you and all your men." 15Then the king returned and went as far as the Jordan.

Now the men of Judah had come to Gilgal to go out and meet the king and bring him across the Jordan. 16Shimei son of Gera, the Benjamite from Bahurim, hurried down with the men of Judah to meet King David. 17With him were a thousand Benjamites, along with Ziba, the steward of Saul's household, and his fifteen sons and twenty servants. They rushed to the Jordan, where the king was. 18They crossed at the ford to take the king's household over and to do whatever he wished.

When Shimei son of Gera crossed the Jordan, he fell prostrate before the king 19and said to him, "May my lord not hold me guilty. Do not remember how your servant did wrong on the day my lord the king left Jerusalem. May the king put it out of his mind. 20For I your servant know that I have sinned, but today I have come here as the first of the whole house of Joseph to come down and meet my lord the king."

21Then Abishai son of Zeruiah said, "Shouldn't Shimei be put to death for this? He cursed the LORD's anointed."

22David replied, "What do you and I have in common, you sons of Zeruiah? This day you have become my adversaries! Should anyone be put to death in Israel today? Do I not know that today I am king over Israel?" 23So the king said to Shimei, "You shall not die." And the king promised him on oath.

24Mephibosheth, Saul's grandson, also went down to meet the king. He had not taken care of his feet or trimmed his mustache or washed his clothes from the day the king left until the day he returned safely. 25When he came from Jerusalem to meet the king, the king asked him, "Why didn't you go with me, Mephibosheth?"

26He said, "My lord the king, since I your servant am lame, I said, 'I will have my donkey saddled and will ride on it, so I can go with the king.' But Ziba my servant betrayed me. 27And he has slandered your servant to my lord the king. My lord the king is like an angel of God; so do whatever pleases you. 28All my grandfather's descendants deserved nothing but death from my lord the king, but you gave your servant a place among those who eat at your table. So what right do I have to make any more appeals to the king?"

29The king said to him, "Why say more? I order you and Ziba to divide the fields."
30Mephibosheth said to the king, "Let him
take everything, now that my lord the king has
arrived home safely."
31Barzillai the Gileadite also came down from
Rogelim to cross the Jordan with the king and to
send him on his way from there. 32Now Barzillai
was a very old man, eighty years of age. He had
provided for the king during his stay in Mahanaim, for he was a very wealthy man. 33The king
said to Barzillai, "Cross over with me and stay
with me in Jerusalem, and I will provide for you."
34But Barzillai answered the king, "How many
more years will I live, that I should go up to
Jerusalem with the king? 35I am now eighty years
old. Can I tell the difference between what is
good and what is not? Can your servant taste
what he eats and drinks? Can I still hear the
voices of men and women singers? Why should
your servant be an added burden to my lord the
king? 36Your servant will cross over the Jordan
with the king for a short distance, but why should
the king reward me in this way? 37Let your servant return, that I may die in my own town near
the tomb of my father and mother. But here is
your servant Kimham. Let him cross over with
my lord the king. Do for him whatever pleases
you."
38The king said, "Kimham shall cross over
with me, and I will do for him whatever pleases
you. And anything you desire from me I will do
for you."
39So all the people crossed the Jordan, and
then the king crossed over. The king kissed Barzillai and gave him his blessing, and Barzillai returned to his home.
40When the king crossed over to Gilgal, Kimham crossed with him. All the troops of Judah
and half the troops of Israel had taken the king
over.
41Soon all the men of Israel were coming to
the king and saying to him, "Why did our brothers, the men of Judah, steal the king away and
bring him and his household across the Jordan,
together with all his men?"
42All the men of Judah answered the men of
Israel, "We did this because the king is closely
related to us. Why are you angry about it? Have
we eaten any of the king's provisions? Have we
taken anything for ourselves?"
43Then the men of Israel answered the men of
Judah, "We have ten shares in the king; and besides, we have a greater claim on David than you
have. So why do you treat us with contempt?
Were we not the first to speak of bringing back
our king?"
But the men of Judah responded even more
harshly than the men of Israel.

Sheba Rebels Against David

20 Now a troublemaker named Sheba son of
Bicri, a Benjamite, happened to be there.
He sounded the trumpet and shouted,

"We have no share in David,
no part in Jesse's son!
Every man to his tent, O Israel!"

2So all the men of Israel deserted David to
follow Sheba son of Bicri. But the men of Judah
stayed by their king all the way from the Jordan
to Jerusalem.
3When David returned to his palace in Jerusalem, he took the ten concubines he had left to
take care of the palace and put them in a house
under guard. He provided for them, but did not
lie with them. They were kept in confinement till
the day of their death, living as widows.
4Then the king said to Amasa, "Summon the
men of Judah to come to me within three days,
and be here yourself." 5But when Amasa went to
summon Judah, he took longer than the time the
king had set for him.
6David said to Abishai, "Now Sheba son of
Bicri will do us more harm than Absalom did.
Take your master's men and pursue him, or he
will find fortified cities and escape from us." 7So
Joab's men and the Kerethites and Pelethites and
all the mighty warriors went out under the command of Abishai. They marched out from Jerusalem to pursue Sheba son of Bicri.
8While they were at the great rock in Gibeon,
Amasa came to meet them. Joab was wearing
his military tunic, and strapped over it at his
waist was a belt with a dagger in its sheath.
As he stepped forward, it dropped out of its
sheath.
9Joab said to Amasa, "How are you, my brother?" Then Joab took Amasa by the beard with his
right hand to kiss him. 10Amasa was not on his
guard against the dagger in Joab's hand, and Joab
plunged it into his belly, and his intestines spilled
out on the ground. Without being stabbed again,
Amasa died. Then Joab and his brother Abishai
pursued Sheba son of Bicri.
11One of Joab's men stood beside Amasa and
said, "Whoever favors Joab, and whoever is for
David, let him follow Joab!" 12Amasa lay wallowing in his blood in the middle of the road, and the
man saw that all the troops came to a halt there.
When he realized that everyone who came up to
Amasa stopped, he dragged him from the road
into a field and threw a garment over him. 13Af-
ter Amasa had been removed from the road, all
the men went on with Joab to pursue Sheba son
of Bicri.
14Sheba passed through all the tribes of Israel

to Abel Beth Maacah[a] and through the entire region of the Berites, who gathered together and followed him. 15All the troops with Joab came and besieged Sheba in Abel Beth Maacah. They built a siege ramp up to the city, and it stood against the outer fortifications. While they were battering the wall to bring it down, 16a wise woman called from the city, "Listen! Listen! Tell Joab to come here so I can speak to him." 17He went toward her, and she asked, "Are you Joab?"

"I am," he answered.

She said, "Listen to what your servant has to say."

"I'm listening," he said.

18She continued, "Long ago they used to say, 'Get your answer at Abel,' and that settled it. 19We are the peaceful and faithful in Israel. You are trying to destroy a city that is a mother in Israel. Why do you want to swallow up the LORD's inheritance?"

20"Far be it from me!" Joab replied, "Far be it from me to swallow up or destroy! 21That is not the case. A man named Sheba son of Bicri, from the hill country of Ephraim, has lifted up his hand against the king, against David. Hand over this one man, and I'll withdraw from the city."

The woman said to Joab, "His head will be thrown to you from the wall."

22Then the woman went to all the people with her wise advice, and they cut off the head of Sheba son of Bicri and threw it to Joab. So he sounded the trumpet, and his men dispersed from the city, each returning to his home. And Joab went back to the king in Jerusalem.

23Joab was over Israel's entire army; Benaiah son of Jehoiada was over the Kerethites and Pelethites; 24Adoniram[b] was in charge of forced labor; Jehoshaphat son of Ahilud was recorder; 25Sheva was secretary; Zadok and Abiathar were priests; 26and Ira the Jairite was David's priest.

The Gibeonites Avenged

21 During the reign of David, there was a famine for three successive years; so David sought the face of the LORD. The LORD said, "It is on account of Saul and his blood-stained house; it is because he put the Gibeonites to death."

2The king summoned the Gibeonites and spoke to them. (Now the Gibeonites were not a part of Israel but were survivors of the Amorites; the Israelites had sworn to ⌊spare⌋ them, but Saul in his zeal for Israel and Judah had tried to annihilate them.) 3David asked the Gibeonites, "What shall I do for you? How shall I make amends so that you will bless the LORD's inheritance?"

4The Gibeonites answered him, "We have no right to demand silver or gold from Saul or his family, nor do we have the right to put anyone in Israel to death."

"What do you want me to do for you?" David asked.

5They answered the king, "As for the man who destroyed us and plotted against us so that we have been decimated and have no place anywhere in Israel, 6let seven of his male descendants be given to us to be killed and exposed before the LORD at Gibeah of Saul—the LORD's chosen one."

So the king said, "I will give them to you."

7The king spared Mephibosheth son of Jonathan, the son of Saul, because of the oath before the LORD between David and Jonathan son of Saul. 8But the king took Armoni and Mephibosheth, the two sons of Aiah's daughter Rizpah, whom she had borne to Saul, together with the five sons of Saul's daughter Merab,[c] whom she had borne to Adriel son of Barzillai the Meholathite. 9He handed them over to the Gibeonites, who killed and exposed them on a hill before the LORD. All seven of them fell together; they were put to death during the first days of the harvest, just as the barley harvest was beginning.

10Rizpah daughter of Aiah took sackcloth and spread it out for herself on a rock. From the beginning of the harvest till the rain poured down from the heavens on the bodies, she did not let the birds of the air touch them by day or the wild animals by night. 11When David was told what Aiah's daughter Rizpah, Saul's concubine, had done, 12he went and took the bones of Saul and his son Jonathan from the citizens of Jabesh Gilead. (They had taken them secretly from the public square at Beth Shan, where the Philistines had hung them after they struck Saul down on Gilboa.) 13David brought the bones of Saul and his son Jonathan from there, and the bones of those who had been killed and exposed were gathered up.

14They buried the bones of Saul and his son Jonathan in the tomb of Saul's father Kish, at Zela in Benjamin, and did everything the king commanded. After that, God answered prayer in behalf of the land.

Wars Against the Philistines

15Once again there was a battle between the Philistines and Israel. David went down with his men to fight against the Philistines, and he be-

[a] 14 Or *Abel, even Beth Maacah*; also in verse 15 [b] 24 Some Septuagint manuscripts (see also 1 Kings 4:6 and 5:14); Hebrew *Adoram* [c] 8 Two Hebrew manuscripts, some Septuagint manuscripts and Syriac (see also 1 Samuel 18:19); most Hebrew and Septuagint manuscripts *Michal*

came exhausted. 16And Ishbi-Benob, one of the
descendants of Rapha, whose bronze spearhead
weighed three hundred shekels[a] and who was
armed with a new ⌊sword⌋, said he would kill
David. 17But Abishai son of Zeruiah came to David's rescue; he struck the Philistine down and
killed him. Then David's men swore to him, saying, "Never again will you go out with us to battle, so that the lamp of Israel will not be extinguished."
18In the course of time, there was another battle with the Philistines, at Gob. At that time Sibbecai the Hushathite killed Saph, one of the
descendants of Rapha.
19In another battle with the Philistines at Gob,
Elhanan son of Jaare-Oregim[b] the Bethlehemite
killed Goliath[c] the Gittite, who had a spear with
a shaft like a weaver's rod.
20In still another battle, which took place at
Gath, there was a huge man with six fingers on
each hand and six toes on each foot—twenty-
four in all. He also was descended from Rapha.
21When he taunted Israel, Jonathan son of Shimeah, David's brother, killed him.
22These four were descendants of Rapha in
Gath, and they fell at the hands of David and his
men.

David's Song of Praise

22 David sang to the LORD the words of this
song when the LORD delivered him from
the hand of all his enemies and from the hand of
Saul. 2He said:

"The LORD is my rock, my fortress and my
deliverer;
3 my God is my rock, in whom I take
refuge,
my shield and the horn[d] of my salvation.
He is my stronghold, my refuge and my
savior—
from violent men you save me.
4I call to the LORD, who is worthy of praise,
and I am saved from my enemies.

5"The waves of death swirled about me;
the torrents of destruction overwhelmed
me.
6The cords of the grave[e] coiled around me;
the snares of death confronted me.
7In my distress I called to the LORD;
I called out to my God.
From his temple he heard my voice;
my cry came to his ears.

8"The earth trembled and quaked,
the foundations of the heavens[f] shook;
they trembled because he was angry.
9Smoke rose from his nostrils;
consuming fire came from his mouth,
burning coals blazed out of it.
10He parted the heavens and came down;
dark clouds were under his feet.
11He mounted the cherubim and flew;
he soared[g] on the wings of the wind.
12He made darkness his canopy around him—
the dark[h] rain clouds of the sky.
13Out of the brightness of his presence
bolts of lightning blazed forth.
14The LORD thundered from heaven;
the voice of the Most High resounded.
15He shot arrows and scattered ⌊the enemies⌋,
bolts of lightning and routed them.
16The valleys of the sea were exposed
and the foundations of the earth laid bare
at the rebuke of the LORD,
at the blast of breath from his nostrils.

17"He reached down from on high and took
hold of me;
he drew me out of deep waters.
18He rescued me from my powerful enemy,
from my foes, who were too strong for
me.
19They confronted me in the day of my
disaster,
but the LORD was my support.
20He brought me out into a spacious place;
he rescued me because he delighted in
me.

21"The LORD has dealt with me according to
my righteousness;
according to the cleanness of my hands he
has rewarded me.
22For I have kept the ways of the LORD;
I have not done evil by turning from my
God.
23All his laws are before me;
I have not turned away from his decrees.
24I have been blameless before him
and have kept myself from sin.
25The LORD has rewarded me according to my
righteousness,
according to my cleanness[i] in his sight.

26"To the faithful you show yourself faithful,
to the blameless you show yourself
blameless,

[a]16 That is, about 7 1/2 pounds (about 3.5 kilograms) [b]19 Or *son of Jair the weaver* [c]19 Hebrew and Septuagint; 1 Chron. 20:5 *son of Jair killed Lahmi the brother of Goliath* [d]3 *Horn* here symbolizes strength. [e]6 Hebrew *Sheol* [f]8 Hebrew; Vulgate and Syriac (see also Psalm 18:7) *mountains* [g]11 Many Hebrew manuscripts (see also Psalm 18:10); most Hebrew manuscripts *appeared* [h]12 Septuagint and Vulgate (see also Psalm 18:11); Hebrew *massed* [i]25 Hebrew; Septuagint and Vulgate (see also Psalm 18:24) *to the cleanness of my hands*

27 to the pure you show yourself pure,
but to the crooked you show yourself shrewd.
28 You save the humble,
but your eyes are on the haughty to bring them low.
29 You are my lamp, O LORD;
the LORD turns my darkness into light.
30 With your help I can advance against a troop[a];
with my God I can scale a wall.

31 "As for God, his way is perfect;
the word of the LORD is flawless.
He is a shield
for all who take refuge in him.
32 For who is God besides the LORD?
And who is the Rock except our God?
33 It is God who arms me with strength[b]
and makes my way perfect.
34 He makes my feet like the feet of a deer;
he enables me to stand on the heights.
35 He trains my hands for battle;
my arms can bend a bow of bronze.
36 You give me your shield of victory;
you stoop down to make me great.
37 You broaden the path beneath me,
so that my ankles do not turn.

38 "I pursued my enemies and crushed them;
I did not turn back till they were destroyed.
39 I crushed them completely, and they could not rise;
they fell beneath my feet.
40 You armed me with strength for battle;
you made my adversaries bow at my feet.
41 You made my enemies turn their backs in flight,
and I destroyed my foes.
42 They cried for help, but there was no one to save them—
to the LORD, but he did not answer.
43 I beat them as fine as the dust of the earth;
I pounded and trampled them like mud in the streets.

44 "You have delivered me from the attacks of my people;
you have preserved me as the head of nations.
People I did not know are subject to me,
45 and foreigners come cringing to me;
as soon as they hear me, they obey me.
46 They all lose heart;
they come trembling[c] from their strongholds.

47 "The LORD lives! Praise be to my Rock!
Exalted be God, the Rock, my Savior!
48 He is the God who avenges me,
who puts the nations under me,
49 who sets me free from my enemies.
You exalted me above my foes;
from violent men you rescued me.
50 Therefore I will praise you, O LORD, among the nations;
I will sing praises to your name.
51 He gives his king great victories;
he shows unfailing kindness to his anointed,
to David and his descendants forever."

The Last Words of David

23 These are the last words of David:

"The oracle of David son of Jesse,
the oracle of the man exalted by the Most High,
the man anointed by the God of Jacob,
Israel's singer of songs[d]:

2 "The Spirit of the LORD spoke through me;
his word was on my tongue.
3 The God of Israel spoke,
the Rock of Israel said to me:
'When one rules over men in righteousness,
when he rules in the fear of God,
4 he is like the light of morning at sunrise
on a cloudless morning,
like the brightness after rain
that brings the grass from the earth.'
5 "Is not my house right with God?
Has he not made with me an everlasting covenant,
arranged and secured in every part?
Will he not bring to fruition my salvation
and grant me my every desire?
6 But evil men are all to be cast aside like thorns,
which are not gathered with the hand.
7 Whoever touches thorns
uses a tool of iron or the shaft of a spear;
they are burned up where they lie."

David's Mighty Men

8 These are the names of David's mighty men:
Josheb-Basshebeth,[e] a Tahkemonite,[f] was
chief of the Three; he raised his spear against

[a]30 Or *can run through a barricade* [b]33 Dead Sea Scrolls, some Septuagint manuscripts, Vulgate and Syriac (see also Psalm 18:32); Masoretic Text *who is my strong refuge* [c]46 Some Septuagint manuscripts and Vulgate (see also Psalm 18:45); Masoretic Text *they arm themselves.* [d]1 Or *Israel's beloved singer* [e]8 Hebrew; some Septuagint manuscripts suggest *Ish-Bosheth,* that is, *Esh-Baal* (see also 1 Chron. 11:11 *Jashobeam*). [f]8 Probably a variant of *Hacmonite* (see 1 Chron. 11:11)

eight hundred men, whom he killed[a] in one
encounter.

9Next to him was Eleazar son of Dodai the
Ahohite. As one of the three mighty men, he was
with David when they taunted the Philistines
gathered ⌞at Pas Dammim⌟[b] for battle. Then the
men of Israel retreated, 10but he stood his ground
and struck down the Philistines till his hand grew
tired and froze to the sword. The LORD brought
about a great victory that day. The troops returned to Eleazar, but only to strip the dead.

11Next to him was Shammah son of Agee the
Hararite. When the Philistines banded together
at a place where there was a field full of lentils,
Israel's troops fled from them. 12But Shammah
took his stand in the middle of the field. He defended it and struck the Philistines down, and
the LORD brought about a great victory.

13During harvest time, three of the thirty chief
men came down to David at the cave of Adullam,
while a band of Philistines was encamped in the
Valley of Rephaim. 14At that time David was in
the stronghold, and the Philistine garrison was at
Bethlehem. 15David longed for water and said,
"Oh, that someone would get me a drink of water
from the well near the gate of Bethlehem!" 16So
the three mighty men broke through the Philistine lines, drew water from the well near the gate
of Bethlehem and carried it back to David. But he
refused to drink it; instead, he poured it out before the LORD. 17"Far be it from me, O LORD, to
do this!" he said. "Is it not the blood of men who
went at the risk of their lives?" And David would
not drink it.

Such were the exploits of the three mighty
men.

18Abishai the brother of Joab son of Zeruiah
was chief of the Three.[c] He raised his spear
against three hundred men, whom he killed, and
so he became as famous as the Three. 19Was he
not held in greater honor than the Three? He
became their commander, even though he was
not included among them.

20Benaiah son of Jehoiada was a valiant fighter
from Kabzeel, who performed great exploits. He
struck down two of Moab's best men. He also
went down into a pit on a snowy day and killed
a lion. 21And he struck down a huge Egyptian.
Although the Egyptian had a spear in his hand,
Benaiah went against him with a club. He
snatched the spear from the Egyptian's hand and
killed him with his own spear. 22Such were the
exploits of Benaiah son of Jehoiada; he too was as
famous as the three mighty men. 23He was held
in greater honor than any of the Thirty, but he
was not included among the Three. And David
put him in charge of his bodyguard.

24Among the Thirty were:
Asahel the brother of Joab,
Elhanan son of Dodo from Bethlehem,
25Shammah the Harodite,
Elika the Harodite,
26Helez the Paltite,
Ira son of Ikkesh from Tekoa,
27Abiezer from Anathoth,
Mebunnai[d] the Hushathite,
28Zalmon the Ahohite,
Maharai the Netophathite,
29Heled[e] son of Baanah the Netophathite,
Ithai son of Ribai from Gibeah in Benjamin,
30Benaiah the Pirathonite,
Hiddai[f] from the ravines of Gaash,
31Abi-Albon the Arbathite,
Azmaveth the Barhumite,
32Eliahba the Shaalbonite,
the sons of Jashen,
Jonathan 33son of[g] Shammah the Hararite,
Ahiam son of Sharar[h] the Hararite,
34Eliphelet son of Ahasbai the Maacathite,
Eliam son of Ahithophel the Gilonite,
35Hezro the Carmelite,
Paarai the Arbite,
36Igal son of Nathan from Zobah,
the son of Hagri,[i]
37Zelek the Ammonite,
Naharai the Beerothite, the armor-bearer
of Joab son of Zeruiah,
38Ira the Ithrite,
Gareb the Ithrite
39and Uriah the Hittite.
There were thirty-seven in all.

David Counts the Fighting Men

24 Again the anger of the LORD burned
against Israel, and he incited David
against them, saying, "Go and take a census of
Israel and Judah."

2So the king said to Joab and the army commanders[j] with him, "Go throughout the tribes
of Israel from Dan to Beersheba and enroll the

[a]8 Some Septuagint manuscripts (see also 1 Chron. 11:11); Hebrew and other Septuagint manuscripts *Three; it was Adino the Eznite who killed eight hundred men* [b]9 See 1 Chron. 11:13; Hebrew *gathered there.* [c]18 Most Hebrew manuscripts (see also 1 Chron. 11:20); two Hebrew manuscripts and Syriac *Thirty* [d]27 Hebrew; some Septuagint manuscripts (see also 1 Chron. 11:29) *Sibbecai* [e]29 Some Hebrew manuscripts and Vulgate (see also 1 Chron. 11:30); most Hebrew manuscripts *Heleb* [f]30 Hebrew; some Septuagint manuscripts (see also 1 Chron. 11:32) *Hurai* [g]33 Some Septuagint manuscripts (see also 1 Chron. 11:34); Hebrew does not have *son of.* [h]33 Hebrew; some Septuagint manuscripts (see also 1 Chron. 11:35) *Sacar* [i]36 Some Septuagint manuscripts (see also 1 Chron. 11:38); Hebrew *Haggadi* [j]2 Septuagint (see also verse 4 and 1 Chron. 21:2); Hebrew *Joab the army commander*

fighting men, so that I may know how many
there are."
3 But Joab replied to the king, "May the LORD
your God multiply the troops a hundred times
over, and may the eyes of my lord the king see it.
But why does my lord the king want to do such
a thing?"
4 The king's word, however, overruled Joab
and the army commanders; so they left the presence of the king to enroll the fighting men of
Israel.
5 After crossing the Jordan, they camped near
Aroer, south of the town in the gorge, and then
went through Gad and on to Jazer. 6 They went to
Gilead and the region of Tahtim Hodshi, and on
to Dan Jaan and around toward Sidon. 7 Then they
went toward the fortress of Tyre and all the
towns of the Hivites and Canaanites. Finally, they
went on to Beersheba in the Negev of Judah.
8 After they had gone through the entire land,
they came back to Jerusalem at the end of nine
months and twenty days.
9 Joab reported the number of the fighting men
to the king: In Israel there were eight hundred
thousand able-bodied men who could handle a
sword, and in Judah five hundred thousand.
10 David was conscience-stricken after he had
counted the fighting men, and he said to the
LORD, "I have sinned greatly in what I have done.
Now, O LORD, I beg you, take away the guilt of
your servant. I have done a very foolish thing."
11 Before David got up the next morning, the
word of the LORD had come to Gad the prophet,
David's seer: 12 "Go and tell David, 'This is what
the LORD says: I am giving you three options.
Choose one of them for me to carry out against
you.' "
13 So Gad went to David and said to him, "Shall
there come upon you three[a] years of famine in
your land? Or three months of fleeing from your
enemies while they pursue you? Or three days of
plague in your land? Now then, think it over and
decide how I should answer the one who
sent me."
14 David said to Gad, "I am in deep distress. Let
us fall into the hands of the LORD, for his mercy
is great; but do not let me fall into the hands of
men."
15 So the LORD sent a plague on Israel from that
morning until the end of the time designated,
and seventy thousand of the people from Dan to
Beersheba died. 16 When the angel stretched out
his hand to destroy Jerusalem, the LORD was
grieved because of the calamity and said to the
angel who was afflicting the people, "Enough!
Withdraw your hand." The angel of the LORD was
then at the threshing floor of Araunah the Jebusite.
17 When David saw the angel who was striking
down the people, he said to the LORD, "I am the
one who has sinned and done wrong. These are
but sheep. What have they done? Let your hand
fall upon me and my family."

David Builds an Altar

18 On that day Gad went to David and said to
him, "Go up and build an altar to the LORD on the
threshing floor of Araunah the Jebusite." 19 So David went up, as the LORD had commanded
through Gad. 20 When Araunah looked and saw
the king and his men coming toward him, he
went out and bowed down before the king with
his face to the ground.
21 Araunah said, "Why has my lord the king
come to his servant?"
"To buy your threshing floor," David answered, "so I can build an altar to the LORD, that
the plague on the people may be stopped."
22 Araunah said to David, "Let my lord the king
take whatever pleases him and offer it up. Here
are oxen for the burnt offering, and here are
threshing sledges and ox yokes for the wood. 23 O
king, Araunah gives all this to the king." Araunah
also said to him, "May the LORD your God accept
you."
24 But the king replied to Araunah, "No, I insist
on paying you for it. I will not sacrifice to the
LORD my God burnt offerings that cost me nothing."
So David bought the threshing floor and the
oxen and paid fifty shekels[b] of silver for them.
25 David built an altar to the LORD there and sacrificed burnt offerings and fellowship offerings.[c]
Then the LORD answered prayer in behalf of the
land, and the plague on Israel was stopped.

[a] *13* Septuagint (see also 1 Chron. 21:12); Hebrew *seven*
[b] *24* That is, about 1 1/4 pounds (about 0.6 kilogram)
[c] *25* Traditionally *peace offerings*

Introduction to
1 KINGS

Personal Reading Plan

- ❐ 1 Kings 1:1–53
- ❐ 1 Kings 2:1–46
- ❐ 1 Kings 3:1–4:19
- ❐ 1 Kings 4:20–5:18
- ❐ 1 Kings 6:1–38
- ❐ 1 Kings 7:1–51
- ❐ 1 Kings 8:1–66
- ❐ 1 Kings 9:1–10:13
- ❐ 1 Kings 10:14–11:25
- ❐ 1 Kings 11:26–12:33
- ❐ 1 Kings 13:1–14:20
- ❐ 1 Kings 14:21–15:32
- ❐ 1 Kings 15:33–16:34
- ❐ 1 Kings 17:1–24
- ❐ 1 Kings 18:1–46
- ❐ 1 Kings 19:1–20:34
- ❐ 1 Kings 20:35–21:29
- ❐ 1 Kings 22:1–53

Author

The author of 1 and 2 Kings is not known, but the three literary sources that are named suggest multiple authors and editors: "the Annals of Solomon" (1 Kings 11:41); "the Annals of the Kings of Israel" (1 Kings 14:19; 2 Kings 15:31); and "the Annals of the Kings of Judah" (1 Kings 14:29; 2 Kings 24:5).

Date

The account of Jehoiachin's release from prison in 2 Kings 25:27–30 means that the final form of Kings was written after 561 B.C. Nonetheless, the source materials could have been written at the time of the events they describe. These events span almost 400 years.

Theme

Israel's golden age—its coronation and corrosion.

Historical Background

Solomon reaps the reward of David's military success. He inherits peace and security and so launches Israel's "Golden Age." Following Solomon's death, the division of the country into the two separate nations of Israel and Judah brings an end to this era of strength. Both nations then enter a period of decline.

Characteristics

The atmosphere in the early chapters of 1 Kings is one of grandeur as Solomon's wealth, wisdom and fame is set forth. But Solomon's end is most pitiful, as he turns to foreign wives and their false gods. Jeroboam follows suit, as do other kings of northern Israel and southern Judah. All told, 19 kings in the North and 20 rulers in the South are alternately profiled in 1 Kings. Tracking the rise and fall of both kingdoms can be confusing, but it helps to remember that none of Israel's kings were faithful to God during this time, while only half of Judah's rulers showed any faithfulness.

Passages for Topical Group Study

3:16–28	DECISIONS	Solomon's Wise Ruling
10:23–11:13	NO COMPROMISE	Solomon's Splendor; Solomon's Wives

See the Lesson Plans in the front of this Bible.

Passages for General Group Study

12:1–24	The Kingdom is Divided
18:16–40	Elijah and the Prophets of Baal

Adonijah Sets Himself Up as King

1 When King David was old and well advanced in years, he could not keep warm even when they put covers over him. 2 So his servants said to him, "Let us look for a young virgin to attend the king and take care of him. She can lie beside him so that our lord the king may keep warm."

3 Then they searched throughout Israel for a beautiful girl and found Abishag, a Shunammite, and brought her to the king. 4 The girl was very beautiful; she took care of the king and waited on him, but the king had no intimate relations with her.

5 Now Adonijah, whose mother was Haggith, put himself forward and said, "I will be king." So he got chariots and horses[a] ready, with fifty men to run ahead of him. 6 (His father had never interfered with him by asking, "Why do you behave as you do?" He was also very handsome and was born next after Absalom.)

7 Adonijah conferred with Joab son of Zeruiah and with Abiathar the priest, and they gave him their support. 8 But Zadok the priest, Benaiah son of Jehoiada, Nathan the prophet, Shimei and Rei[b] and David's special guard did not join Adonijah.

9 Adonijah then sacrificed sheep, cattle and fattened calves at the Stone of Zoheleth near En Rogel. He invited all his brothers, the king's sons, and all the men of Judah who were royal officials, 10 but he did not invite Nathan the prophet or Benaiah or the special guard or his brother Solomon.

11 Then Nathan asked Bathsheba, Solomon's mother, "Have you not heard that Adonijah, the son of Haggith, has become king without our lord David's knowing it? 12 Now then, let me advise you how you can save your own life and the life of your son Solomon. 13 Go in to King David and say to him, 'My lord the king, did you not swear to me your servant: "Surely Solomon your son shall be king after me, and he will sit on my throne"? Why then has Adonijah become king?' 14 While you are still there talking to the king, I will come in and confirm what you have said."

15 So Bathsheba went to see the aged king in his room, where Abishag the Shunammite was attending him. 16 Bathsheba bowed low and knelt before the king.

"What is it you want?" the king asked.

17 She said to him, "My lord, you yourself swore to me your servant by the LORD your God: 'Solomon your son shall be king after me, and he will sit on my throne.' 18 But now Adonijah has become king, and you, my lord the king, do not know about it. 19 He has sacrificed great numbers of cattle, fattened calves, and sheep, and has invited all the king's sons, Abiathar the priest and Joab the commander of the army, but he has not invited Solomon your servant. 20 My lord the king, the eyes of all Israel are on you, to learn from you who will sit on the throne of my lord the king after him. 21 Otherwise, as soon as my lord the king is laid to rest with his fathers, I and my son Solomon will be treated as criminals."

22 While she was still speaking with the king, Nathan the prophet arrived. 23 And they told the king, "Nathan the prophet is here." So he went before the king and bowed with his face to the ground.

24 Nathan said, "Have you, my lord the king, declared that Adonijah shall be king after you, and that he will sit on your throne? 25 Today he has gone down and sacrificed great numbers of cattle, fattened calves, and sheep. He has invited all the king's sons, the commanders of the army and Abiathar the priest. Right now they are eating and drinking with him and saying, 'Long live King Adonijah!' 26 But me your servant, and Zadok the priest, and Benaiah son of Jehoiada, and your servant Solomon he did not invite. 27 Is this something my lord the king has done without letting his servants know who should sit on the throne of my lord the king after him?"

David Makes Solomon King

28 Then King David said, "Call in Bathsheba." So she came into the king's presence and stood before him.

29 The king then took an oath: "As surely as the LORD lives, who has delivered me out of every trouble, 30 I will surely carry out today what I swore to you by the LORD, the God of Israel: Solomon your son shall be king after me, and he will sit on my throne in my place."

31 Then Bathsheba bowed low with her face to the ground and, kneeling before the king, said, "May my lord King David live forever!"

32 King David said, "Call in Zadok the priest, Nathan the prophet and Benaiah son of Jehoiada." When they came before the king, 33 he said to them: "Take your lord's servants with you and set Solomon my son on my own mule and take him down to Gihon. 34 There have Zadok the priest and Nathan the prophet anoint him king over Israel. Blow the trumpet and shout, 'Long live King Solomon!' 35 Then you are to go up with him, and he is to come and sit on my throne and reign in my place. I have appointed him ruler over Israel and Judah."

36 Benaiah son of Jehoiada answered the king,

[a] 5 Or *charioteers* [b] 8 Or *and his friends*

"Amen! May the LORD, the God of my lord the
king, so declare it. 37As the LORD was with my
lord the king, so may he be with Solomon to
make his throne even greater than the throne of
my lord King David!"

38So Zadok the priest, Nathan the prophet, Benaiah son of Jehoiada, the Kerethites and the Pelethites went down and put Solomon on King David's mule and escorted him to Gihon. 39Zadok
the priest took the horn of oil from the sacred
tent and anointed Solomon. Then they sounded
the trumpet and all the people shouted, "Long
live King Solomon!" 40And all the people went up
after him, playing flutes and rejoicing greatly, so
that the ground shook with the sound.

41Adonijah and all the guests who were with
him heard it as they were finishing their feast.
On hearing the sound of the trumpet, Joab asked,
"What's the meaning of all the noise in the city?"

42Even as he was speaking, Jonathan son of
Abiathar the priest arrived. Adonijah said, "Come
in. A worthy man like you must be bringing good
news."

43"Not at all!" Jonathan answered. "Our lord
King David has made Solomon king. 44The king
has sent with him Zadok the priest, Nathan the
prophet, Benaiah son of Jehoiada, the Kerethites
and the Pelethites, and they have put him on the
king's mule, 45and Zadok the priest and Nathan
the prophet have anointed him king at Gihon.
From there they have gone up cheering, and the
city resounds with it. That's the noise you hear.
46Moreover, Solomon has taken his seat on the
royal throne. 47Also, the royal officials have come
to congratulate our lord King David, saying, 'May
your God make Solomon's name more famous
than yours and his throne greater than yours!'
And the king bowed in worship on his bed 48and
said, 'Praise be to the LORD, the God of Israel,
who has allowed my eyes to see a successor on
my throne today.'"

49At this, all Adonijah's guests rose in alarm
and dispersed. 50But Adonijah, in fear of Solomon, went and took hold of the horns of the altar.
51Then Solomon was told, "Adonijah is afraid of
King Solomon and is clinging to the horns of the
altar. He says, 'Let King Solomon swear to me
today that he will not put his servant to death
with the sword.'"

52Solomon replied, "If he shows himself to be
a worthy man, not a hair of his head will fall to
the ground; but if evil is found in him, he will
die." 53Then King Solomon sent men, and they
brought him down from the altar. And Adonijah
came and bowed down to King Solomon, and
Solomon said, "Go to your home."

David's Charge to Solomon

2 When the time drew near for David to die,
he gave a charge to Solomon his son.
2"I am about to go the way of all the earth," he
said. "So be strong, show yourself a man, 3and
observe what the LORD your God requires: Walk
in his ways, and keep his decrees and commands,
his laws and requirements, as written in the Law
of Moses, so that you may prosper in all you do
and wherever you go, 4and that the LORD may
keep his promise to me: 'If your descendants
watch how they live, and if they walk faithfully
before me with all their heart and soul, you will
never fail to have a man on the throne of Israel.'

5"Now you yourself know what Joab son of
Zeruiah did to me—what he did to the two commanders of Israel's armies, Abner son of Ner and
Amasa son of Jether. He killed them, shedding
their blood in peacetime as if in battle, and with
that blood stained the belt around his waist and
the sandals on his feet. 6Deal with him according
to your wisdom, but do not let his gray head go
down to the grave[a] in peace.

7"But show kindness to the sons of Barzillai of
Gilead and let them be among those who eat at
your table. They stood by me when I fled from
your brother Absalom.

8"And remember, you have with you Shimei
son of Gera, the Benjamite from Bahurim, who
called down bitter curses on me the day I went to
Mahanaim. When he came down to meet me at
the Jordan, I swore to him by the LORD: 'I will not
put you to death by the sword.' 9But now, do not
consider him innocent. You are a man of wisdom;
you will know what to do to him. Bring his gray
head down to the grave in blood."

10Then David rested with his fathers and was
buried in the City of David. 11He had reigned
forty years over Israel—seven years in Hebron
and thirty-three in Jerusalem. 12So Solomon sat
on the throne of his father David, and his rule
was firmly established.

Solomon's Throne Established

13Now Adonijah, the son of Haggith, went to
Bathsheba, Solomon's mother. Bathsheba asked
him, "Do you come peacefully?"

He answered, "Yes, peacefully." 14Then he
added, "I have something to say to you."

"You may say it," she replied.

15"As you know," he said, "the kingdom was
mine. All Israel looked to me as their king. But
things changed, and the kingdom has gone to my
brother; for it has come to him from the LORD.
16Now I have one request to make of you. Do not
refuse me."

[a]6 Hebrew *Sheol*; also in verse 9

"You may make it," she said.
17So he continued, "Please ask King Solomon—he will not refuse you—to give me Abishag the Shunammite as my wife."
18"Very well," Bathsheba replied, "I will speak
to the king for you."
19When Bathsheba went to King Solomon to
speak to him for Adonijah, the king stood up to
meet her, bowed down to her and sat down on
his throne. He had a throne brought for the
king's mother, and she sat down at his right
hand.
20"I have one small request to make of you,"
she said. "Do not refuse me."
The king replied, "Make it, my mother; I will
not refuse you."
21So she said, "Let Abishag the Shunammite
be given in marriage to your brother Adonijah."
22King Solomon answered his mother, "Why
do you request Abishag the Shunammite for Adonijah? You might as well request the kingdom for
him—after all, he is my older brother—yes, for
him and for Abiathar the priest and Joab son of
Zeruiah!"
23Then King Solomon swore by the LORD:
"May God deal with me, be it ever so severely, if
Adonijah does not pay with his life for this request! 24And now, as surely as the LORD lives—
he who has established me securely on the
throne of my father David and has founded a
dynasty for me as he promised—Adonijah shall
be put to death today!" 25So King Solomon gave
orders to Benaiah son of Jehoiada, and he struck
down Adonijah and he died.
26To Abiathar the priest the king said, "Go
back to your fields in Anathoth. You deserve to
die, but I will not put you to death now, because
you carried the ark of the Sovereign LORD before
my father David and shared all my father's hardships." 27So Solomon removed Abiathar from the
priesthood of the LORD, fulfilling the word the
LORD had spoken at Shiloh about the house of Eli.
28When the news reached Joab, who had conspired with Adonijah though not with Absalom,
he fled to the tent of the LORD and took hold of
the horns of the altar. 29King Solomon was told
that Joab had fled to the tent of the LORD and was
beside the altar. Then Solomon ordered Benaiah
son of Jehoiada, "Go, strike him down!"
30So Benaiah entered the tent of the LORD and
said to Joab, "The king says, 'Come out!'"
But he answered, "No, I will die here."
Benaiah reported to the king, "This is how
Joab answered me."
31Then the king commanded Benaiah, "Do as
he says. Strike him down and bury him, and so
clear me and my father's house of the guilt of the
innocent blood that Joab shed. 32The LORD will
repay him for the blood he shed, because without
the knowledge of my father David he attacked
two men and killed them with the sword. Both of
them—Abner son of Ner, commander of Israel's
army, and Amasa son of Jether, commander of
Judah's army—were better men and more upright than he. 33May the guilt of their blood rest
on the head of Joab and his descendants forever.
But on David and his descendants, his house and
his throne, may there be the LORD's peace forever."
34So Benaiah son of Jehoiada went up and
struck down Joab and killed him, and he was
buried on his own land[a] in the desert. 35The
king put Benaiah son of Jehoiada over the army in
Joab's position and replaced Abiathar with Zadok
the priest.
36Then the king sent for Shimei and said to
him, "Build yourself a house in Jerusalem and
live there, but do not go anywhere else. 37The
day you leave and cross the Kidron Valley, you
can be sure you will die; your blood will be on
your own head."
38Shimei answered the king, "What you say is
good. Your servant will do as my lord the king has
said." And Shimei stayed in Jerusalem for a long
time.
39But three years later, two of Shimei's slaves
ran off to Achish son of Maacah, king of Gath,
and Shimei was told, "Your slaves are in Gath."
40At this, he saddled his donkey and went to
Achish at Gath in search of his slaves. So Shimei
went away and brought the slaves back from
Gath.
41When Solomon was told that Shimei had
gone from Jerusalem to Gath and had returned,
42the king summoned Shimei and said to him,
"Did I not make you swear by the LORD and warn
you, 'On the day you leave to go anywhere else,
you can be sure you will die'? At that time you
said to me, 'What you say is good. I will obey.'
43Why then did you not keep your oath to the
LORD and obey the command I gave you?"
44The king also said to Shimei, "You know in
your heart all the wrong you did to my father
David. Now the LORD will repay you for your
wrongdoing. 45But King Solomon will be blessed,
and David's throne will remain secure before the
LORD forever."
46Then the king gave the order to Benaiah son
of Jehoiada, and he went out and struck Shimei
down and killed him.
The kingdom was now firmly established in
Solomon's hands.

[a]34 Or *buried in his tomb*

Solomon Asks for Wisdom

3 Solomon made an alliance with Pharaoh king of Egypt and married his daughter. He brought her to the City of David until he finished building his palace and the temple of the LORD, and the wall around Jerusalem. 2The people, however, were still sacrificing at the high places, because a temple had not yet been built for the Name of the LORD. 3Solomon showed his love for the LORD by walking according to the statutes of his father David, except that he offered sacrifices and burned incense on the high places.

4The king went to Gibeon to offer sacrifices, for that was the most important high place, and Solomon offered a thousand burnt offerings on that altar. 5At Gibeon the LORD appeared to Solomon during the night in a dream, and God said, "Ask for whatever you want me to give you."

6Solomon answered, "You have shown great kindness to your servant, my father David, because he was faithful to you and righteous and upright in heart. You have continued this great kindness to him and have given him a son to sit on his throne this very day.

7"Now, O LORD my God, you have made your servant king in place of my father David. But I am only a little child and do not know how to carry out my duties. 8Your servant is here among the people you have chosen, a great people, too numerous to count or number. 9So give your servant a discerning heart to govern your people and to distinguish between right and wrong. For who is able to govern this great people of yours?"

10The Lord was pleased that Solomon had asked for this. 11So God said to him, "Since you have asked for this and not for long life or wealth for yourself, nor have asked for the death of your enemies but for discernment in administering justice, 12I will do what you have asked. I will give you a wise and discerning heart, so that there will never have been anyone like you, nor will there ever be. 13Moreover, I will give you what you have not asked for—both riches and honor—so that in your lifetime you will have no equal among kings. 14And if you walk in my ways and obey my statutes and commands as David your father did, I will give you a long life." 15Then Solomon awoke—and he realized it had been a dream.

He returned to Jerusalem, stood before the ark of the Lord's covenant and sacrificed burnt offerings and fellowship offerings.[a] Then he gave a feast for all his court.

A Wise Ruling

16Now two prostitutes came to the king and stood before him. 17One of them said, "My lord, this woman and I live in the same house. I had a baby while she was there with me. 18The third day after my child was born, this woman also had a baby. We were alone; there was no one in the house but the two of us.

19"During the night this woman's son died because she lay on him. 20So she got up in the middle of the night and took my son from my side while I your servant was asleep. She put him by her breast and put her dead son by my breast. 21The next morning, I got up to nurse my son—and he was dead! But when I looked at him closely in the morning light, I saw that it wasn't the son I had borne."

22The other woman said, "No! The living one is my son; the dead one is yours."

But the first one insisted, "No! The dead one is yours; the living one is mine." And so they argued before the king.

23The king said, "This one says, 'My son is alive and your son is dead,' while that one says, 'No! Your son is dead and mine is alive.' "

24Then the king said, "Bring me a sword." So they brought a sword for the king. 25He then gave an order: "Cut the living child in two and give half to one and half to the other."

26The woman whose son was alive was filled with compassion for her son and said to the king, "Please, my lord, give her the living baby! Don't kill him!"

But the other said, "Neither I nor you shall have him. Cut him in two!"

[a] *15* Traditionally *peace offerings*

Solomon, David's son by Bathsheba, has just succeeded his father as Israel's king (at about 20 years of age). God comes to Solomon in a dream and offers him anything he desires. Solomon responds with an unusual answer—he wants wisdom! The Lord is very pleased and not only grants him his request, but promises him great riches, honor and a long life. Unfortunately, Solomon did not remain obedient to the covenant as his father David had, and he did not live to be much more than 60 years of age (11:6,42).

3:16–28 The wisdom which God had given Solomon is now demonstrated in a typical case. It is wisdom in the practical sense, but is nevertheless attributed to God (v. 28).

3:16 ***two prostitutes.*** It is not known if they were Israelites or Jebusites—possibly the latter. ***came to the king.*** It was possible for Israelites (and others within the realm) to bypass lower judicial officials (Deut. 16:18) and appeal directly to the king (see 2 Kings 8:3; 2 Sam. 15:2).

3:17 ***live in the same house.*** Brothels were common in ancient Near Eastern cities.

3:22 This verse includes, as does the entire story, intimate details of the argument before the king.

3:28 ***they saw that he had wisdom from God.*** This episode strikingly demonstrated that the Lord had answered Solomon's prayer for a discerning heart (vv. 9,12).

27 Then the king gave his ruling: "Give the living baby to the first woman. Do not kill him; she
is his mother."
28 When all Israel heard the verdict the king
had given, they held the king in awe, because
they saw that he had wisdom from God to administer justice.

1 Kings 3:16–28

1. How did your parents settle disputes between you and your brother(s)/sister(s)?
2. Who did you favor in the last presidential election? Are you more likely to vote like your parents or your friends?
3. If God said to you, "Ask for whatever you want me to give you," what would you ask for?
4. How do you feel about the way Solomon handled the case of the two women? Why did his strategy work?
5. How do you go about making decisions: Consult others? Pray? Go with your gut feeling?
6. What has been the toughest decision you've had to make lately? Do you feel now that your decision was wise?
7. What decision are you facing right now that you need the "wisdom of Solomon"? Pray accordingly as a group.

(Study notes on page 330)

Solomon's Officials and Governors

4 So King Solomon ruled over all Israel. 2 And
these were his chief officials:

Azariah son of Zadok—the priest;
3 Elihoreph and Ahijah, sons of Shisha—secretaries;
Jehoshaphat son of Ahilud—recorder;
4 Benaiah son of Jehoiada—commander in chief;
Zadok and Abiathar—priests;
5 Azariah son of Nathan—in charge of the district officers;
Zabud son of Nathan—a priest and personal adviser to the king;
6 Ahishar—in charge of the palace;
Adoniram son of Abda—in charge of forced labor.

7 Solomon also had twelve district governors
over all Israel, who supplied provisions for the
king and the royal household. Each one had to
provide supplies for one month in the year.
8 These are their names:

Ben-Hur—in the hill country of Ephraim;
9 Ben-Deker—in Makaz, Shaalbim, Beth Shemesh and Elon Bethhanan;
10 Ben-Hesed—in Arubboth (Socoh and all the land of Hepher were his);
11 Ben-Abinadab—in Naphoth Dor[a] (he was married to Taphath daughter of Solomon);
12 Baana son of Ahilud—in Taanach and Megiddo, and in all of Beth Shan next to Zarethan below Jezreel, from Beth Shan to Abel Meholah across to Jokmeam;
13 Ben-Geber—in Ramoth Gilead (the settlements of Jair son of Manasseh in Gilead were his, as well as the district of Argob in Bashan and its sixty large walled cities with bronze gate bars);
14 Ahinadab son of Iddo—in Mahanaim;
15 Ahimaaz—in Naphtali (he had married Basemath daughter of Solomon);
16 Baana son of Hushai—in Asher and in Aloth;
17 Jehoshaphat son of Paruah—in Issachar;
18 Shimei son of Ela—in Benjamin;
19 Geber son of Uri—in Gilead (the country of Sihon king of the Amorites and the country of Og king of Bashan). He was the only governor over the district.

Solomon's Daily Provisions

20 The people of Judah and Israel were as numerous as the sand on the seashore; they ate,
they drank and they were happy. 21 And Solomon
ruled over all the kingdoms from the River[b] to
the land of the Philistines, as far as the border of
Egypt. These countries brought tribute and were
Solomon's subjects all his life.
22 Solomon's daily provisions were thirty
cors[c] of fine flour and sixty cors[d] of meal, 23 ten
head of stall-fed cattle, twenty of pasture-fed cattle and a hundred sheep and goats, as well as
deer, gazelles, roebucks and choice fowl. 24 For he
ruled over all the kingdoms west of the River,
from Tiphsah to Gaza, and had peace on all sides.
25 During Solomon's lifetime Judah and Israel,
from Dan to Beersheba, lived in safety, each man
under his own vine and fig tree.

[a] *11* Or *in the heights of Dor* [b] *21* That is, the Euphrates; also in verse 24 [c] *22* That is, probably about 185 bushels (about 6.6 kiloliters) [d] *22* That is, probably about 375 bushels (about 13.2 kiloliters)

26Solomon had four[a] thousand stalls for chariot horses, and twelve thousand horses.[b]

27The district officers, each in his month, supplied provisions for King Solomon and all who came to the king's table. They saw to it that nothing was lacking. 28They also brought to the proper place their quotas of barley and straw for the chariot horses and the other horses.

Solomon's Wisdom

29God gave Solomon wisdom and very great insight, and a breadth of understanding as measureless as the sand on the seashore. 30Solomon's wisdom was greater than the wisdom of all the men of the East, and greater than all the wisdom of Egypt. 31He was wiser than any other man, including Ethan the Ezrahite—wiser than Heman, Calcol and Darda, the sons of Mahol. And his fame spread to all the surrounding nations. 32He spoke three thousand proverbs and his songs numbered a thousand and five. 33He described plant life, from the cedar of Lebanon to the hyssop that grows out of walls. He also taught about animals and birds, reptiles and fish. 34Men of all nations came to listen to Solomon's wisdom, sent by all the kings of the world, who had heard of his wisdom.

Preparations for Building the Temple

5 When Hiram king of Tyre heard that Solomon had been anointed king to succeed his father David, he sent his envoys to Solomon, because he had always been on friendly terms with David. 2Solomon sent back this message to Hiram:

3"You know that because of the wars waged against my father David from all sides, he could not build a temple for the Name of the LORD his God until the LORD put his enemies under his feet. 4But now the LORD my God has given me rest on every side, and there is no adversary or disaster. 5I intend, therefore, to build a temple for the Name of the LORD my God, as the LORD told my father David, when he said, 'Your son whom I will put on the throne in your place will build the temple for my Name.'

6"So give orders that cedars of Lebanon be cut for me. My men will work with yours, and I will pay you for your men whatever wages you set. You know that we have no one so skilled in felling timber as the Sidonians."

7When Hiram heard Solomon's message, he was greatly pleased and said, "Praise be to the LORD today, for he has given David a wise son to rule over this great nation."

8So Hiram sent word to Solomon:

"I have received the message you sent me and will do all you want in providing the cedar and pine logs. 9My men will haul them down from Lebanon to the sea, and I will float them in rafts by sea to the place you specify. There I will separate them and you can take them away. And you are to grant my wish by providing food for my royal household."

10In this way Hiram kept Solomon supplied with all the cedar and pine logs he wanted, 11and Solomon gave Hiram twenty thousand cors[c] of wheat as food for his household, in addition to twenty thousand baths[d,e] of pressed olive oil. Solomon continued to do this for Hiram year after year. 12The LORD gave Solomon wisdom, just as he had promised him. There were peaceful relations between Hiram and Solomon, and the two of them made a treaty.

13King Solomon conscripted laborers from all Israel—thirty thousand men. 14He sent them off to Lebanon in shifts of ten thousand a month, so that they spent one month in Lebanon and two months at home. Adoniram was in charge of the forced labor. 15Solomon had seventy thousand carriers and eighty thousand stonecutters in the hills, 16as well as thirty-three hundred[f] foremen who supervised the project and directed the workmen. 17At the king's command they removed from the quarry large blocks of quality stone to provide a foundation of dressed stone for the temple. 18The craftsmen of Solomon and Hiram and the men of Gebal[g] cut and prepared the timber and stone for the building of the temple.

Solomon Builds the Temple

6 In the four hundred and eightieth[h] year after the Israelites had come out of Egypt, in the fourth year of Solomon's reign over Israel, in the month of Ziv, the second month, he began to build the temple of the LORD.

2The temple that King Solomon built for the LORD was sixty cubits long, twenty wide and thirty high.[i] 3The portico at the front of the main hall of the temple extended the width of the tem-

[a]*26* Some Septuagint manuscripts (see also 2 Chron. 9:25); Hebrew *forty* [b]*26* Or *charioteers* [c]*11* That is, probably about 125,000 bushels (about 4,400 kiloliters) [d]*11* Septuagint (see also 2 Chron. 2:10); Hebrew *twenty cors* [e]*11* That is, about 115,000 gallons (about 440 kiloliters) [f]*16* Hebrew; some Septuagint manuscripts (see also 2 Chron. 2:2, 18) *thirty-six hundred* [g]*18* That is, Byblos [h]*1* Hebrew; Septuagint *four hundred and fortieth* [i]*2* That is, about 90 feet (about 27 meters) long and 30 feet (about 9 meters) wide and 45 feet (about 13.5 meters) high

ple, that is twenty cubits,[a] and projected ten cubits[b] from the front of the temple. 4He made narrow clerestory windows in the temple. 5Against the walls of the main hall and inner sanctuary he built a structure around the building, in which there were side rooms. 6The lowest floor was five cubits[c] wide, the middle floor six cubits[d] and the third floor seven.[e] He made offset ledges around the outside of the temple so that nothing would be inserted into the temple walls.

7In building the temple, only blocks dressed at the quarry were used, and no hammer, chisel or any other iron tool was heard at the temple site while it was being built.

8The entrance to the lowest[f] floor was on the south side of the temple; a stairway led up to the middle level and from there to the third. 9So he built the temple and completed it, roofing it with beams and cedar planks. 10And he built the side rooms all along the temple. The height of each was five cubits, and they were attached to the temple by beams of cedar.

11The word of the LORD came to Solomon: 12"As for this temple you are building, if you follow my decrees, carry out my regulations and keep all my commands and obey them, I will fulfill through you the promise I gave to David your father. 13And I will live among the Israelites and will not abandon my people Israel."

14So Solomon built the temple and completed it. 15He lined its interior walls with cedar boards, paneling them from the floor of the temple to the ceiling, and covered the floor of the temple with planks of pine. 16He partitioned off twenty cubits[a] at the rear of the temple with cedar boards from floor to ceiling to form within the temple an inner sanctuary, the Most Holy Place. 17The main hall in front of this room was forty cubits[g] long. 18The inside of the temple was cedar, carved with gourds and open flowers. Everything was cedar; no stone was to be seen.

19He prepared the inner sanctuary within the temple to set the ark of the covenant of the LORD there. 20The inner sanctuary was twenty cubits long, twenty wide and twenty high.[h] He overlaid the inside with pure gold, and he also overlaid the altar of cedar. 21Solomon covered the inside of the temple with pure gold, and he extended gold chains across the front of the inner sanctuary, which was overlaid with gold. 22So he overlaid the whole interior with gold. He also overlaid with gold the altar that belonged to the inner sanctuary.

23In the inner sanctuary he made a pair of cherubim of olive wood, each ten cubits[b] high. 24One wing of the first cherub was five cubits long, and the other wing five cubits—ten cubits from wing tip to wing tip. 25The second cherub also measured ten cubits, for the two cherubim were identical in size and shape. 26The height of each cherub was ten cubits. 27He placed the cherubim inside the innermost room of the temple, with their wings spread out. The wing of one cherub touched one wall, while the wing of the other touched the other wall, and their wings touched each other in the middle of the room. 28He overlaid the cherubim with gold.

29On the walls all around the temple, in both the inner and outer rooms, he carved cherubim, palm trees and open flowers. 30He also covered the floors of both the inner and outer rooms of the temple with gold.

31For the entrance of the inner sanctuary he made doors of olive wood with five-sided jambs. 32And on the two olive wood doors he carved cherubim, palm trees and open flowers, and overlaid the cherubim and palm trees with beaten gold. 33In the same way he made four-sided jambs of olive wood for the entrance to the main hall. 34He also made two pine doors, each having two leaves that turned in sockets. 35He carved cherubim, palm trees and open flowers on them and overlaid them with gold hammered evenly over the carvings.

36And he built the inner courtyard of three courses of dressed stone and one course of trimmed cedar beams.

37The foundation of the temple of the LORD was laid in the fourth year, in the month of Ziv. 38In the eleventh year in the month of Bul, the eighth month, the temple was finished in all its details according to its specifications. He had spent seven years building it.

Solomon Builds His Palace

7 It took Solomon thirteen years, however, to complete the construction of his palace. 2He built the Palace of the Forest of Lebanon a hundred cubits long, fifty wide and thirty high,[i] with four rows of cedar columns supporting trimmed cedar beams. 3It was roofed with cedar above the beams that rested on the columns—forty-five beams, fifteen to a row. 4Its windows were placed high in sets of three, facing each other. 5All the doorways had rectangular frames; they were in the front part in sets of three, facing each other.[j]

[a] 3,16 That is, about 30 feet (about 9 meters) [b] 3,23 That is, about 15 feet (about 4.5 meters) [c] 6 That is, about 7 1/2 feet (about 2.3 meters); also in verses 10 and 24 [d] 6 That is, about 9 feet (about 2.7 meters) [e] 6 That is, about 10 1/2 feet (about 3.1 meters) [f] 8 Septuagint; Hebrew *middle* [g] 17 That is, about 60 feet (about 18 meters) [h] 20 That is, about 30 feet (about 9 meters) long, wide and high [i] 2 That is, about 150 feet (about 46 meters) long, 75 feet (about 23 meters) wide and 45 feet (about 13.5 meters) high [j] 5 The meaning of the Hebrew for this verse is uncertain.

6 He made a colonnade fifty cubits long and thirty wide.[a] In front of it was a portico, and in front of that were pillars and an overhanging roof. 7 He built the throne hall, the Hall of Justice, where he was to judge, and he covered it with cedar from floor to ceiling.[b] 8 And the palace in which he was to live, set farther back, was similar in design. Solomon also made a palace like this hall for Pharaoh's daughter, whom he had married.

9 All these structures, from the outside to the great courtyard and from foundation to eaves, were made of blocks of high-grade stone cut to size and trimmed with a saw on their inner and outer faces. 10 The foundations were laid with large stones of good quality, some measuring ten cubits[c] and some eight.[d] 11 Above were high-grade stones, cut to size, and cedar beams. 12 The great courtyard was surrounded by a wall of three courses of dressed stone and one course of trimmed cedar beams, as was the inner courtyard of the temple of the LORD with its portico.

The Temple's Furnishings

13 King Solomon sent to Tyre and brought Huram,[e] 14 whose mother was a widow from the tribe of Naphtali and whose father was a man of Tyre and a craftsman in bronze. Huram was highly skilled and experienced in all kinds of bronze work. He came to King Solomon and did all the work assigned to him.

15 He cast two bronze pillars, each eighteen cubits high and twelve cubits around,[f] by line. 16 He also made two capitals of cast bronze to set on the tops of the pillars; each capital was five cubits[g] high. 17 A network of interwoven chains festooned the capitals on top of the pillars, seven for each capital. 18 He made pomegranates in two rows[h] encircling each network to decorate the capitals on top of the pillars.[i] He did the same for each capital. 19 The capitals on top of the pillars in the portico were in the shape of lilies, four cubits[j] high. 20 On the capitals of both pillars, above the bowl-shaped part next to the network, were the two hundred pomegranates in rows all around. 21 He erected the pillars at the portico of the temple. The pillar to the south he named Jakin[k] and the one to the north Boaz.[l] 22 The capitals on top were in the shape of lilies. And so the work on the pillars was completed.

23 He made the Sea of cast metal, circular in shape, measuring ten cubits[c] from rim to rim and five cubits high. It took a line of thirty cubits[m] to measure around it. 24 Below the rim, gourds encircled it—ten to a cubit. The gourds were cast in two rows in one piece with the Sea.

25 The Sea stood on twelve bulls, three facing north, three facing west, three facing south and three facing east. The Sea rested on top of them, and their hindquarters were toward the center. 26 It was a handbreadth[n] in thickness, and its rim was like the rim of a cup, like a lily blossom. It held two thousand baths.[o]

27 He also made ten movable stands of bronze; each was four cubits long, four wide and three high.[p] 28 This is how the stands were made: They had side panels attached to uprights. 29 On the panels between the uprights were lions, bulls and cherubim—and on the uprights as well. Above and below the lions and bulls were wreaths of hammered work. 30 Each stand had four bronze wheels with bronze axles, and each had a basin resting on four supports, cast with wreaths on each side. 31 On the inside of the stand there was an opening that had a circular frame one cubit[q] deep. This opening was round, and with its basework it measured a cubit and a half.[r] Around its opening there was engraving. The panels of the stands were square, not round. 32 The four wheels were under the panels, and the axles of the wheels were attached to the stand. The diameter of each wheel was a cubit and a half. 33 The wheels were made like chariot wheels; the axles, rims, spokes and hubs were all of cast metal.

34 Each stand had four handles, one on each corner, projecting from the stand. 35 At the top of the stand there was a circular band half a cubit[s] deep. The supports and panels were attached to the top of the stand. 36 He engraved cherubim, lions and palm trees on the surfaces of the supports and on the panels, in every available space, with wreaths all around. 37 This is the way he made the ten stands. They were all cast in the same molds and were identical in size and shape.

38 He then made ten bronze basins, each holding forty baths[t] and measuring four cubits

[a] *6* That is, about 75 feet (about 23 meters) long and 45 feet (about 13.5 meters) wide [b] *7* Vulgate and Syriac; Hebrew *floor* [c] *10,23* That is, about 15 feet (about 4.5 meters) [d] *10* That is, about 12 feet (about 3.6 meters) [e] *13* Hebrew *Hiram,* a variant of *Huram;* also in verses 40 and 45 [f] *15* That is, about 27 feet (about 8.1 meters) high and 18 feet (about 5.4 meters) around [g] *16* That is, about 7 1/2 feet (about 2.3 meters); also in verse 23 [h] *18* Two Hebrew manuscripts and Septuagint; most Hebrew manuscripts *made the pillars, and there were two rows* [i] *18* Many Hebrew manuscripts and Syriac; most Hebrew manuscripts *pomegranates* [j] *19* That is, about 6 feet (about 1.8 meters); also in verse 38 [k] *21* *Jakin* probably means *he establishes.* [l] *21* *Boaz* probably means *in him is strength.* [m] *23* That is, about 45 feet (about 13.5 meters) [n] *26* That is, about 3 inches (about 8 centimeters) [o] *26* That is, probably about 11,500 gallons (about 44 kiloliters); the Septuagint does not have this sentence. [p] *27* That is, about 6 feet (about 1.8 meters) long and wide and about 4 1/2 feet (about 1.3 meters) high [q] *31* That is, about 1 1/2 feet (about 0.5 meter) [r] *31* That is, about 2 1/4 feet (about 0.7 meter); also in verse 32 [s] *35* That is, about 3/4 foot (about 0.2 meter) [t] *38* That is, about 230 gallons (about 880 liters)

across, one basin to go on each of the ten stands.
39He placed five of the stands on the south side
of the temple and five on the north. He placed
the Sea on the south side, at the southeast corner
of the temple. 40He also made the basins and
shovels and sprinkling bowls.

So Huram finished all the work he had undertaken for King Solomon in the temple of the LORD:

41the two pillars;
the two bowl-shaped capitals on top of the pillars;
the two sets of network decorating the two bowl-shaped capitals on top of the pillars;
42the four hundred pomegranates for the two sets of network (two rows of pomegranates for each network, decorating the bowl-shaped capitals on top of the pillars);
43the ten stands with their ten basins;
44the Sea and the twelve bulls under it;
45the pots, shovels and sprinkling bowls.

All these objects that Huram made for King
Solomon for the temple of the LORD were of burnished bronze. 46The king had them cast in clay
molds in the plain of the Jordan between Succoth
and Zarethan. 47Solomon left all these things unweighed, because there were so many; the
weight of the bronze was not determined.

48Solomon also made all the furnishings that
were in the LORD's temple:

the golden altar;
the golden table on which was the bread of the Presence;
49the lampstands of pure gold (five on the right and five on the left, in front of the inner sanctuary);
the gold floral work and lamps and tongs;
50the pure gold basins, wick trimmers, sprinkling bowls, dishes and censers;
and the gold sockets for the doors of the innermost room, the Most Holy Place, and also for the doors of the main hall of the temple.

51When all the work King Solomon had done
for the temple of the LORD was finished, he
brought in the things his father David had
dedicated—the silver and gold and the
furnishings—and he placed them in the treasuries of the LORD's temple.

The Ark Brought to the Temple

8 Then King Solomon summoned into his presence at Jerusalem the elders of Israel, all the
heads of the tribes and the chiefs of the Israelite
families, to bring up the ark of the LORD's covenant from Zion, the City of David. 2All the men
of Israel came together to King Solomon at the
time of the festival in the month of Ethanim, the
seventh month.

3When all the elders of Israel had arrived, the
priests took up the ark, 4and they brought up the
ark of the LORD and the Tent of Meeting and all
the sacred furnishings in it. The priests and Levites carried them up, 5and King Solomon and
the entire assembly of Israel that had gathered
about him were before the ark, sacrificing so
many sheep and cattle that they could not be
recorded or counted.

6The priests then brought the ark of the LORD's
covenant to its place in the inner sanctuary of the
temple, the Most Holy Place, and put it beneath
the wings of the cherubim. 7The cherubim
spread their wings over the place of the ark and
overshadowed the ark and its carrying poles.
8These poles were so long that their ends could
be seen from the Holy Place in front of the inner
sanctuary, but not from outside the Holy Place;
and they are still there today. 9There was nothing
in the ark except the two stone tablets that Moses had placed in it at Horeb, where the LORD
made a covenant with the Israelites after they
came out of Egypt.

10When the priests withdrew from the Holy
Place, the cloud filled the temple of the LORD.
11And the priests could not perform their service
because of the cloud, for the glory of the LORD
filled his temple.

12Then Solomon said, "The LORD has said that
he would dwell in a dark cloud; 13I have indeed
built a magnificent temple for you, a place for you
to dwell forever."

14While the whole assembly of Israel was
standing there, the king turned around and
blessed them. 15Then he said:

"Praise be to the LORD, the God of Israel,
who with his own hand has fulfilled what
he promised with his own mouth to my father David. For he said, 16'Since the day I
brought my people Israel out of Egypt, I
have not chosen a city in any tribe of Israel
to have a temple built for my Name to be
there, but I have chosen David to rule my
people Israel.'

17"My father David had it in his heart to
build a temple for the Name of the LORD,
the God of Israel. 18But the LORD said to my
father David, 'Because it was in your heart
to build a temple for my Name, you did well
to have this in your heart. 19Nevertheless,
you are not the one to build the temple,
but your son, who is your own flesh and
blood—he is the one who will build the
temple for my Name.'

20“The LORD has kept the promise he
made: I have succeeded David my father
and now I sit on the throne of Israel, just as
the LORD promised, and I have built the
temple for the Name of the LORD, the God
of Israel. 21I have provided a place there for
the ark, in which is the covenant of the
LORD that he made with our fathers when
he brought them out of Egypt.”

Solomon’s Prayer of Dedication

22Then Solomon stood before the altar of the
LORD in front of the whole assembly of Israel,
spread out his hands toward heaven 23and said:

“O LORD, God of Israel, there is no God
like you in heaven above or on earth
below—you who keep your covenant of
love with your servants who continue
wholeheartedly in your way. 24You have
kept your promise to your servant David my
father; with your mouth you have promised
and with your hand you have fulfilled it—as
it is today.

25“Now LORD, God of Israel, keep for
your servant David my father the promises
you made to him when you said, ‘You shall
never fail to have a man to sit before me on
the throne of Israel, if only your sons are
careful in all they do to walk before me as
you have done.’ 26And now, O God of Israel, let your word that you promised your
servant David my father come true.

27“But will God really dwell on earth?
The heavens, even the highest heaven, cannot contain you. How much less this temple
I have built! 28Yet give attention to your
servant’s prayer and his plea for mercy,
O LORD my God. Hear the cry and the
prayer that your servant is praying in your
presence this day. 29May your eyes be open
toward this temple night and day, this place
of which you said, ‘My Name shall be
there,’ so that you will hear the prayer your
servant prays toward this place. 30Hear the
supplication of your servant and of your
people Israel when they pray toward this
place. Hear from heaven, your dwelling
place, and when you hear, forgive.

31“When a man wrongs his neighbor and
is required to take an oath and he comes
and swears the oath before your altar in this
temple, 32then hear from heaven and act.
Judge between your servants, condemning
the guilty and bringing down on his own
head what he has done. Declare the innocent not guilty, and so establish his innocence.

33“When your people Israel have been
defeated by an enemy because they have
sinned against you, and when they turn
back to you and confess your name, praying
and making supplication to you in this temple, 34then hear from heaven and forgive
the sin of your people Israel and bring them
back to the land you gave to their fathers.

35“When the heavens are shut up and
there is no rain because your people have
sinned against you, and when they pray toward this place and confess your name and
turn from their sin because you have afflicted them, 36then hear from heaven and forgive the sin of your servants, your people
Israel. Teach them the right way to live, and
send rain on the land you gave your people
for an inheritance.

37“When famine or plague comes to the
land, or blight or mildew, locusts or grasshoppers, or when an enemy besieges them
in any of their cities, whatever disaster or
disease may come, 38and when a prayer or
plea is made by any of your people Israel—
each one aware of the afflictions of his own
heart, and spreading out his hands toward
this temple— 39then hear from heaven,
your dwelling place. Forgive and act; deal
with each man according to all he does,
since you know his heart (for you alone
know the hearts of all men), 40so that they
will fear you all the time they live in the
land you gave our fathers.

41“As for the foreigner who does not belong to your people Israel but has come
from a distant land because of your name—
42for men will hear of your great name and
your mighty hand and your outstretched
arm—when he comes and prays toward
this temple, 43then hear from heaven, your
dwelling place, and do whatever the foreigner asks of you, so that all the peoples of
the earth may know your name and fear
you, as do your own people Israel, and may
know that this house I have built bears your
Name.

44“When your people go to war against
their enemies, wherever you send them,
and when they pray to the LORD toward the
city you have chosen and the temple I have
built for your Name, 45then hear from heav-
en their prayer and their plea, and uphold
their cause.

46“When they sin against you—for there
is no one who does not sin—and you become angry with them and give them over
to the enemy, who takes them captive to his
own land, far away or near; 47and if they
have a change of heart in the land where
they are held captive, and repent and plead

with you in the land of their conquerors and
say, 'We have sinned, we have done wrong,
we have acted wickedly'; 48 and if they turn
back to you with all their heart and soul in
the land of their enemies who took them
captive, and pray to you toward the land you
gave their fathers, toward the city you have
chosen and the temple I have built for your
Name; 49 then from heaven, your dwelling
place, hear their prayer and their plea, and
uphold their cause. 50 And forgive your people, who have sinned against you; forgive all
the offenses they have committed against
you, and cause their conquerors to show
them mercy; 51 for they are your people and
your inheritance, whom you brought out of
Egypt, out of that iron-smelting furnace.

52 "May your eyes be open to your servant's plea and to the plea of your people
Israel, and may you listen to them whenever they cry out to you. 53 For you singled
them out from all the nations of the world to
be your own inheritance, just as you declared through your servant Moses when
you, O Sovereign LORD, brought our fathers
out of Egypt."

54 When Solomon had finished all these
prayers and supplications to the LORD, he rose
from before the altar of the LORD, where he had
been kneeling with his hands spread out toward
heaven. 55 He stood and blessed the whole assembly of Israel in a loud voice, saying:

56 "Praise be to the LORD, who has given
rest to his people Israel just as he promised.
Not one word has failed of all the good
promises he gave through his servant Moses. 57 May the LORD our God be with us as
he was with our fathers; may he never leave
us nor forsake us. 58 May he turn our hearts
to him, to walk in all his ways and to keep
the commands, decrees and regulations he
gave our fathers. 59 And may these words of
mine, which I have prayed before the LORD,
be near to the LORD our God day and night,
that he may uphold the cause of his servant
and the cause of his people Israel according
to each day's need, 60 so that all the peoples
of the earth may know that the LORD is God
and that there is no other. 61 But your hearts
must be fully committed to the LORD our
God, to live by his decrees and obey his
commands, as at this time."

The Dedication of the Temple

62 Then the king and all Israel with him offered
sacrifices before the LORD. 63 Solomon offered a
sacrifice of fellowship offerings[a] to the LORD:
twenty-two thousand cattle and a hundred and
twenty thousand sheep and goats. So the king
and all the Israelites dedicated the temple of the
LORD.

64 On that same day the king consecrated the
middle part of the courtyard in front of the temple of the LORD, and there he offered burnt offerings, grain offerings and the fat of the fellowship
offerings, because the bronze altar before the
LORD was too small to hold the burnt offerings,
the grain offerings and the fat of the fellowship
offerings.

65 So Solomon observed the festival at that
time, and all Israel with him—a vast assembly,
people from Lebo[b] Hamath to the Wadi of
Egypt. They celebrated it before the LORD our
God for seven days and seven days more, fourteen days in all. 66 On the following day he sent
the people away. They blessed the king and then
went home, joyful and glad in heart for all the
good things the LORD had done for his servant
David and his people Israel.

The LORD Appears to Solomon

9 When Solomon had finished building the
temple of the LORD and the royal palace, and
had achieved all he had desired to do, 2 the LORD
appeared to him a second time, as he had appeared to him at Gibeon. 3 The LORD said to him:

"I have heard the prayer and plea you
have made before me; I have consecrated
this temple, which you have built, by putting my Name there forever. My eyes and
my heart will always be there.

4 "As for you, if you walk before me in
integrity of heart and uprightness, as David
your father did, and do all I command and
observe my decrees and laws, 5 I will establish your royal throne over Israel forever, as
I promised David your father when I said,
'You shall never fail to have a man on the
throne of Israel.'

6 "But if you[c] or your sons turn away
from me and do not observe the commands
and decrees I have given you[c] and go off to
serve other gods and worship them, 7 then I
will cut off Israel from the land I have given
them and will reject this temple I have consecrated for my Name. Israel will then become a byword and an object of ridicule
among all peoples. 8 And though this temple
is now imposing, all who pass by will be
appalled and will scoff and say, 'Why has
the LORD done such a thing to this land and
to this temple?' 9 People will answer, 'Be-

[a]63 Traditionally *peace offerings*; also in verse 64 [b]65 Or *from the entrance to* [c]6 The Hebrew is plural.

cause they have forsaken the LORD their God, who brought their fathers out of Egypt, and have embraced other gods, worshiping and serving them—that is why the LORD brought all this disaster on them.' "

Solomon's Other Activities

[10]At the end of twenty years, during which Solomon built these two buildings—the temple of the LORD and the royal palace— [11]King Solomon gave twenty towns in Galilee to Hiram king of Tyre, because Hiram had supplied him with all the cedar and pine and gold he wanted. [12]But when Hiram went from Tyre to see the towns that Solomon had given him, he was not pleased with them. [13]"What kind of towns are these you have given me, my brother?" he asked. And he called them the Land of Cabul,[a] a name they have to this day. [14]Now Hiram had sent to the king 120 talents[b] of gold.

[15]Here is the account of the forced labor King Solomon conscripted to build the LORD's temple, his own palace, the supporting terraces,[c] the wall of Jerusalem, and Hazor, Megiddo and Gezer. [16](Pharaoh king of Egypt had attacked and captured Gezer. He had set it on fire. He killed its Canaanite inhabitants and then gave it as a wedding gift to his daughter, Solomon's wife. [17]And Solomon rebuilt Gezer.) He built up Lower Beth Horon, [18]Baalath, and Tadmor[d] in the desert, within his land, [19]as well as all his store cities and the towns for his chariots and for his horses[e]—whatever he desired to build in Jerusalem, in Lebanon and throughout all the territory he ruled.

[20]All the people left from the Amorites, Hittites, Perizzites, Hivites and Jebusites (these peoples were not Israelites), [21]that is, their descendants remaining in the land, whom the Israelites could not exterminate[f]—these Solomon conscripted for his slave labor force, as it is to this day. [22]But Solomon did not make slaves of any of the Israelites; they were his fighting men, his government officials, his officers, his captains, and the commanders of his chariots and charioteers. [23]They were also the chief officials in charge of Solomon's projects—550 officials supervising the men who did the work.

[24]After Pharaoh's daughter had come up from the City of David to the palace Solomon had built for her, he constructed the supporting terraces.

[25]Three times a year Solomon sacrificed burnt offerings and fellowship offerings[g] on the altar he had built for the LORD, burning incense before the LORD along with them, and so fulfilled the temple obligations.

[26]King Solomon also built ships at Ezion Geber, which is near Elath in Edom, on the shore of the Red Sea.[h] [27]And Hiram sent his men—sailors who knew the sea—to serve in the fleet with Solomon's men. [28]They sailed to Ophir and brought back 420 talents[i] of gold, which they delivered to King Solomon.

The Queen of Sheba Visits Solomon

10 When the queen of Sheba heard about the fame of Solomon and his relation to the name of the LORD, she came to test him with hard questions. [2]Arriving at Jerusalem with a very great caravan—with camels carrying spices, large quantities of gold, and precious stones—she came to Solomon and talked with him about all that she had on her mind. [3]Solomon answered all her questions; nothing was too hard for the king to explain to her. [4]When the queen of Sheba saw all the wisdom of Solomon and the palace he had built, [5]the food on his table, the seating of his officials, the attending servants in their robes, his cupbearers, and the burnt offerings he made at[j] the temple of the LORD, she was overwhelmed.

[6]She said to the king, "The report I heard in my own country about your achievements and your wisdom is true. [7]But I did not believe these things until I came and saw with my own eyes. Indeed, not even half was told me; in wisdom and wealth you have far exceeded the report I heard. [8]How happy your men must be! How happy your officials, who continually stand before you and hear your wisdom! [9]Praise be to the LORD your God, who has delighted in you and placed you on the throne of Israel. Because of the LORD's eternal love for Israel, he has made you king, to maintain justice and righteousness."

[10]And she gave the king 120 talents[b] of gold, large quantities of spices, and precious stones. Never again were so many spices brought in as those the queen of Sheba gave to King Solomon.

[11](Hiram's ships brought gold from Ophir; and from there they brought great cargoes of almugwood[k] and precious stones. [12]The king used the almugwood to make supports for the temple of the LORD and for the royal palace, and to make harps and lyres for the musicians. So much almugwood has never been imported or seen since that day.)

[13]King Solomon gave the queen of Sheba all she desired and asked for, besides what he had given her out of his royal bounty. Then she left

[a]13 *Cabul* sounds like the Hebrew for *good-for-nothing.* [b]14,10 That is, about 4 1/2 tons (about 4 metric tons) [c]15 Or *the Millo*; also in verse 24 [d]18 The Hebrew may also be read *Tamar.* [e]19 Or *charioteers* [f]21 The Hebrew term refers to the irrevocable giving over of things or persons to the LORD, often by totally destroying them. [g]25 Traditionally *peace offerings* [h]26 Hebrew *Yam Suph*; that is, Sea of Reeds [i]28 That is, about 16 tons (about 14.5 metric tons) [j]5 Or *the ascent by which he went up to* [k]11 Probably a variant of *algumwood*; also in verse 12

and returned with her retinue to her own country.

Solomon's Splendor

14The weight of the gold that Solomon received yearly was 666 talents,[a] 15not including
the revenues from merchants and traders and
from all the Arabian kings and the governors of
the land.
16King Solomon made two hundred large
shields of hammered gold; six hundred bekas[b]
of gold went into each shield. 17He also made
three hundred small shields of hammered gold,
with three minas[c] of gold in each shield. The
king put them in the Palace of the Forest of Lebanon.
18Then the king made a great throne inlaid
with ivory and overlaid with fine gold. 19The
throne had six steps, and its back had a rounded
top. On both sides of the seat were armrests,
with a lion standing beside each of them.
20Twelve lions stood on the six steps, one at either end of each step. Nothing like it had ever
been made for any other kingdom. 21All King Solomon's goblets were gold, and all the household
articles in the Palace of the Forest of Lebanon
were pure gold. Nothing was made of silver, because silver was considered of little value in Solomon's days. 22The king had a fleet of trading
ships[d] at sea along with the ships of Hiram.
Once every three years it returned, carrying gold,
silver and ivory, and apes and baboons.
23King Solomon was greater in riches and wisdom than all the other kings of the earth. 24The
whole world sought audience with Solomon to
hear the wisdom God had put in his heart. 25Year
after year, everyone who came brought a gift—
articles of silver and gold, robes, weapons and
spices, and horses and mules.
26Solomon accumulated chariots and horses;
he had fourteen hundred chariots and twelve
thousand horses,[e] which he kept in the chariot
cities and also with him in Jerusalem. 27The king
made silver as common in Jerusalem as stones,
and cedar as plentiful as sycamore-fig trees in the
foothills. 28Solomon's horses were imported from
Egypt[f] and from Kue[g]—the royal merchants
purchased them from Kue. 29They imported a
chariot from Egypt for six hundred shekels[h] of
silver, and a horse for a hundred and fifty.[c] They
also exported them to all the kings of the Hittites
and of the Arameans.

1 Kings 10:23–11:13

1. Finish the sentence: "The one with the most toys ______________": (a) wins, (b) sins, (c) is lucky, (d) must be God's favorite.

2. Guys: What would you do if you had 700 wives and 300 concubines?

   Girls: What would you do if you had to share your husband with 699 other women?

3. What was Solomon's biggest problem: His wealth? His women? His will? His worship?

4. Have you ever dated someone with an entirely different religious background? How did that affect your faith?

5. In what area of your life are you most vulnerable to compromise? What have you found helpful in resisting compromise?

6. How would you like the group to pray for you?

[a]*14* That is, about 25 tons (about 23 metric tons) [b]*16* That is, about 7 1/2 pounds (about 3.5 kilograms) [c]*17,29* That is, about 3 3/4 pounds (about 1.7 kilograms) [d]*22* Hebrew *of ships of Tarshish* [e]*26* Or *charioteers* [f]*28* Or possibly *Muzur*, a region in Cilicia; also in verse 29 [g]*28* Probably *Cilicia* [h]*29* That is, about 15 pounds (about 7 kilograms)

10:23 *Solomon was greater in riches and wisdom.* As a gift from God (3:12–13). However, Solomon's accumulation of horses (10:26), large amounts of silver and gold (10:21,27), and many wives (11:3) was in violation of Mosaic law (Deut. 17:16–17).

11:1–2 *loved many foreign women.* Many of Solomon's marriages were no doubt for the purpose of sealing international relationships with various kingdoms, large and small—a common practice in the ancient Near East. But this violated not only Deuteronomy 17:17 with respect to the multiplicity of wives, but also the prohibition against taking wives from the pagan peoples among whom Israel settled (see Deut. 7:1–3; Josh. 23:12–13). As warned, Solomon's heart turned "after their gods."

11:4 *his heart was not fully devoted to the Lord his God.* In sad contradiction to Solomon's own charge to Israel at the dedication of the temple (8:61). The atmosphere of paganism and idolatry introduced into Solomon's court by his foreign wives gradually led Solomon into compromising religious practices.

11:6 *as David his father had done.* Although David committed grievous sins, he was repentant and he was never involved in idolatrous worship.

11:11 *not kept my covenant.* Solomon had broken the most basic demands of the covenant (see Ex. 20:2–5) and thereby severely undermined the entire covenant relationship between God and his people.

Solomon's Wives

11 King Solomon, however, loved many foreign women besides Pharaoh's daughter—Moabites, Ammonites, Edomites, Sidonians and Hittites. 2They were from nations about which the LORD had told the Israelites, "You must not intermarry with them, because they will surely turn your hearts after their gods." Nevertheless, Solomon held fast to them in love. 3He had seven hundred wives of royal birth and three hundred concubines, and his wives led him astray. 4As Solomon grew old, his wives turned his heart after other gods, and his heart was not fully devoted to the LORD his God, as the heart of David his father had been. 5He followed Ashtoreth the goddess of the Sidonians, and Molech[a] the detestable god of the Ammonites. 6So Solomon did evil in the eyes of the LORD; he did not follow the LORD completely, as David his father had done.

7On a hill east of Jerusalem, Solomon built a high place for Chemosh the detestable god of Moab, and for Molech the detestable god of the Ammonites. 8He did the same for all his foreign wives, who burned incense and offered sacrifices to their gods.

9The LORD became angry with Solomon because his heart had turned away from the LORD, the God of Israel, who had appeared to him twice. 10Although he had forbidden Solomon to follow other gods, Solomon did not keep the LORD's command. 11So the LORD said to Solomon, "Since this is your attitude and you have not kept my covenant and my decrees, which I commanded you, I will most certainly tear the kingdom away from you and give it to one of your subordinates. 12Nevertheless, for the sake of David your father, I will not do it during your lifetime. I will tear it out of the hand of your son. 13Yet I will not tear the whole kingdom from him, but will give him one tribe for the sake of David my servant and for the sake of Jerusalem, which I have chosen."

Solomon's Adversaries

14Then the LORD raised up against Solomon an adversary, Hadad the Edomite, from the royal line of Edom. 15Earlier when David was fighting with Edom, Joab the commander of the army, who had gone up to bury the dead, had struck down all the men in Edom. 16Joab and all the Israelites stayed there for six months, until they had destroyed all the men in Edom. 17But Hadad, still only a boy, fled to Egypt with some Edomite officials who had served his father. 18They set out from Midian and went to Paran. Then taking men from Paran with them, they went to Egypt, to Pharaoh king of Egypt, who gave Hadad a house and land and provided him with food.

19Pharaoh was so pleased with Hadad that he gave him a sister of his own wife, Queen Tahpenes, in marriage. 20The sister of Tahpenes bore him a son named Genubath, whom Tahpenes brought up in the royal palace. There Genubath lived with Pharaoh's own children.

21While he was in Egypt, Hadad heard that David rested with his fathers and that Joab the commander of the army was also dead. Then Hadad said to Pharaoh, "Let me go, that I may return to my own country."

22"What have you lacked here that you want to go back to your own country?" Pharaoh asked.

"Nothing," Hadad replied, "but do let me go!"

23And God raised up against Solomon another adversary, Rezon son of Eliada, who had fled from his master, Hadadezer king of Zobah. 24He gathered men around him and became the leader of a band of rebels when David destroyed the forces[b] ⌊of Zobah⌋; the rebels went to Damascus, where they settled and took control. 25Rezon was Israel's adversary as long as Solomon lived, adding to the trouble caused by Hadad. So Rezon ruled in Aram and was hostile toward Israel.

Jeroboam Rebels Against Solomon

26Also, Jeroboam son of Nebat rebelled against the king. He was one of Solomon's officials, an Ephraimite from Zeredah, and his mother was a widow named Zeruah.

27Here is the account of how he rebelled against the king: Solomon had built the supporting terraces[c] and had filled in the gap in the wall of the city of David his father. 28Now Jeroboam was a man of standing, and when Solomon saw how well the young man did his work, he put him in charge of the whole labor force of the house of Joseph.

29About that time Jeroboam was going out of Jerusalem, and Ahijah the prophet of Shiloh met him on the way, wearing a new cloak. The two of them were alone out in the country, 30and Ahijah took hold of the new cloak he was wearing and tore it into twelve pieces. 31Then he said to Jeroboam, "Take ten pieces for yourself, for this is what the LORD, the God of Israel, says: 'See, I am going to tear the kingdom out of Solomon's hand and give you ten tribes. 32But for the sake of my servant David and the city of Jerusalem, which I have chosen out of all the tribes of Israel, he will have one tribe. 33I will do this because they have[d] forsaken me and worshiped Ashtoreth the goddess of the Sidonians, Chemosh the god of

[a] 5 Hebrew *Milcom*; also in verse 33 [b] 24 Hebrew *destroyed them* [c] 27 Or *the Millo* [d] 33 Hebrew; Septuagint, Vulgate and Syriac *because he has*

the Moabites, and Molech the god of the Ammonites, and have not walked in my ways, nor done
what is right in my eyes, nor kept my statutes and
laws as David, Solomon's father, did.
34"'But I will not take the whole kingdom out
of Solomon's hand; I have made him ruler all the
days of his life for the sake of David my servant,
whom I chose and who observed my commands
and statutes. 35I will take the kingdom from his
son's hands and give you ten tribes. 36I will give
one tribe to his son so that David my servant may
always have a lamp before me in Jerusalem, the
city where I chose to put my Name. 37However,
as for you, I will take you, and you will rule over
all that your heart desires; you will be king over
Israel. 38If you do whatever I command you and
walk in my ways and do what is right in my eyes
by keeping my statutes and commands, as David
my servant did, I will be with you. I will build you
a dynasty as enduring as the one I built for David
and will give Israel to you. 39I will humble David's descendants because of this, but not forever.'"
40Solomon tried to kill Jeroboam, but Jeroboam
fled to Egypt, to Shishak the king, and stayed
there until Solomon's death.

Solomon's Death

41As for the other events of Solomon's reign—
all he did and the wisdom he displayed—are they
not written in the book of the annals of Solomon?
42Solomon reigned in Jerusalem over all Israel
forty years. 43Then he rested with his fathers and
was buried in the city of David his father. And
Rehoboam his son succeeded him as king.

Israel Rebels Against Rehoboam

12 Rehoboam went to Shechem, for all the
Israelites had gone there to make him
king. 2When Jeroboam son of Nebat heard this
(he was still in Egypt, where he had fled from
King Solomon), he returned from[a] Egypt. 3So
they sent for Jeroboam, and he and the whole
assembly of Israel went to Rehoboam and said to
him: 4"Your father put a heavy yoke on us, but
now lighten the harsh labor and the heavy yoke
he put on us, and we will serve you."
5Rehoboam answered, "Go away for three
days and then come back to me." So the people
went away.

1 Kings 12:1–24

1. What issue divides the students in your school? Where do you stand on this issue?
2. What was the best or worst advice your best friend ever gave you?
3. Why do you think Rehoboam chose his friends' advice: He didn't trust old people? He gave in to peer pressure? He didn't want to look like a wimp? God made him?
4. If a parent and a friend both give you advice, who will you most likely listen to? Why?
5. Where do you usually go for advice? What do you do if you don't like what you hear?
6. Since giving your life to God, what has changed in the way you see things? In the way you make decisions?
7. Close in prayer.

6Then King Rehoboam consulted the elders
who had served his father Solomon during his
lifetime. "How would you advise me to answer
these people?" he asked.
7They replied, "If today you will be a servant
to these people and serve them and give them a
favorable answer, they will always be your servants."
8But Rehoboam rejected the advice the elders

[a]2 Or *he remained in*

Before Solomon died, God told him that—due to his spiritual disobedience—he would lose most of the kingdom. However, for the sake of his father David, this would happen to his son. A prophet also promised Jeroboam he would later rule the northern tribes. The southern tribe of Judah naturally accepted David and his descendants since they were from that tribe. Now Rehoboam has succeeded his father Solomon as king, and travels to Shechem in hopes of receiving the continued support of the northern tribes.

12:4 ***put a heavy yoke on us.*** Smoldering discontent with Solomon's heavy taxation and conscription of labor and military forces flared up into strong expression.

12:11 ***scorpions.*** Metal-spiked leather lashes. Not only will governmental burdens on the people be increased, but the punishment for not complying with the government's directives will also be intensified.

12:14 ***followed the advice of the young men.*** Rehoboam's answer reflects an oppressive spirit completely contrary to the covenantal character of Israelite kingship (see Deut. 17:14–20).

12:15 ***this turn of events was from the Lord.*** By this statement the writer of Kings does not condone either the foolish act of Rehoboam or the revolutionary spirit of the northern tribes, but he reminds the reader that all these things occurred to bring about the divinely announced punishment on the house of David for Solomon's idolatry and breach of the covenant (11:9–13).

gave him and consulted the young men who had grown up with him and were serving him. 9 He asked them, "What is your advice? How should we answer these people who say to me, 'Lighten the yoke your father put on us'?"

10 The young men who had grown up with him replied, "Tell these people who have said to you, 'Your father put a heavy yoke on us, but make our yoke lighter'—tell them, 'My little finger is thicker than my father's waist. 11 My father laid on you a heavy yoke; I will make it even heavier. My father scourged you with whips; I will scourge you with scorpions.' "

12 Three days later Jeroboam and all the people returned to Rehoboam, as the king had said, "Come back to me in three days." 13 The king answered the people harshly. Rejecting the advice given him by the elders, 14 he followed the advice of the young men and said, "My father made your yoke heavy; I will make it even heavier. My father scourged you with whips; I will scourge you with scorpions." 15 So the king did not listen to the people, for this turn of events was from the LORD, to fulfill the word the LORD had spoken to Jeroboam son of Nebat through Ahijah the Shilonite.

16 When all Israel saw that the king refused to listen to them, they answered the king:

"What share do we have in David,
  what part in Jesse's son?
To your tents, O Israel!
  Look after your own house, O David!"

So the Israelites went home. 17 But as for the Israelites who were living in the towns of Judah, Rehoboam still ruled over them.

18 King Rehoboam sent out Adoniram,[a] who was in charge of forced labor, but all Israel stoned him to death. King Rehoboam, however, managed to get into his chariot and escape to Jerusalem. 19 So Israel has been in rebellion against the house of David to this day.

20 When all the Israelites heard that Jeroboam had returned, they sent and called him to the assembly and made him king over all Israel. Only the tribe of Judah remained loyal to the house of David.

21 When Rehoboam arrived in Jerusalem, he mustered the whole house of Judah and the tribe of Benjamin—a hundred and eighty thousand fighting men—to make war against the house of Israel and to regain the kingdom for Rehoboam son of Solomon.

22 But this word of God came to Shemaiah the man of God: 23 "Say to Rehoboam son of Solomon king of Judah, to the whole house of Judah and Benjamin, and to the rest of the people, 24 'This is what the LORD says: Do not go up to fight against your brothers, the Israelites. Go home, every one of you, for this is my doing.' " So they obeyed the word of the LORD and went home again, as the LORD had ordered.

Golden Calves at Bethel and Dan

25 Then Jeroboam fortified Shechem in the hill country of Ephraim and lived there. From there he went out and built up Peniel.[b]

26 Jeroboam thought to himself, "The kingdom will now likely revert to the house of David. 27 If these people go up to offer sacrifices at the temple of the LORD in Jerusalem, they will again give their allegiance to their lord, Rehoboam king of Judah. They will kill me and return to King Rehoboam."

28 After seeking advice, the king made two golden calves. He said to the people, "It is too much for you to go up to Jerusalem. Here are your gods, O Israel, who brought you up out of Egypt." 29 One he set up in Bethel, and the other in Dan. 30 And this thing became a sin; the people went even as far as Dan to worship the one there.

31 Jeroboam built shrines on high places and appointed priests from all sorts of people, even though they were not Levites. 32 He instituted a festival on the fifteenth day of the eighth month, like the festival held in Judah, and offered sacrifices on the altar. This he did in Bethel, sacrificing to the calves he had made. And at Bethel he also installed priests at the high places he had made. 33 On the fifteenth day of the eighth month, a month of his own choosing, he offered sacrifices on the altar he had built at Bethel. So he instituted the festival for the Israelites and went up to the altar to make offerings.

The Man of God From Judah

13 By the word of the LORD a man of God came from Judah to Bethel, as Jeroboam was standing by the altar to make an offering. 2 He cried out against the altar by the word of the LORD: "O altar, altar! This is what the LORD says: 'A son named Josiah will be born to the house of David. On you he will sacrifice the priests of the high places who now make offerings here, and human bones will be burned on you.' " 3 That same day the man of God gave a sign: "This is the sign the LORD has declared: The altar will be split apart and the ashes on it will be poured out."

4 When King Jeroboam heard what the man of God cried out against the altar at Bethel, he stretched out his hand from the altar and said, "Seize him!" But the hand he stretched out to-

[a] *18* Some Septuagint manuscripts and Syriac (see also 1 Kings 4:6 and 5:14); Hebrew *Adoram*
[b] *25* Hebrew *Penuel,* a variant of *Peniel*

ward the man shriveled up, so that he could not pull it back. 5Also, the altar was split apart and its ashes poured out according to the sign given by the man of God by the word of the LORD.

6Then the king said to the man of God, "Intercede with the LORD your God and pray for me that my hand may be restored." So the man of God interceded with the LORD, and the king's hand was restored and became as it was before.

7The king said to the man of God, "Come home with me and have something to eat, and I will give you a gift."

8But the man of God answered the king, "Even if you were to give me half your possessions, I would not go with you, nor would I eat bread or drink water here. 9For I was commanded by the word of the LORD: 'You must not eat bread or drink water or return by the way you came.'" 10So he took another road and did not return by the way he had come to Bethel.

11Now there was a certain old prophet living in Bethel, whose sons came and told him all that the man of God had done there that day. They also told their father what he had said to the king. 12Their father asked them, "Which way did he go?" And his sons showed him which road the man of God from Judah had taken. 13So he said to his sons, "Saddle the donkey for me." And when they had saddled the donkey for him, he mounted it 14and rode after the man of God. He found him sitting under an oak tree and asked, "Are you the man of God who came from Judah?"

"I am," he replied.

15So the prophet said to him, "Come home with me and eat."

16The man of God said, "I cannot turn back and go with you, nor can I eat bread or drink water with you in this place. 17I have been told by the word of the LORD: 'You must not eat bread or drink water there or return by the way you came.'"

18The old prophet answered, "I too am a prophet, as you are. And an angel said to me by the word of the LORD: 'Bring him back with you to your house so that he may eat bread and drink water.'" (But he was lying to him.) 19So the man of God returned with him and ate and drank in his house.

20While they were sitting at the table, the word of the LORD came to the old prophet who had brought him back. 21He cried out to the man of God who had come from Judah, "This is what the LORD says: 'You have defied the word of the LORD and have not kept the command the LORD your God gave you. 22You came back and ate bread and drank water in the place where he told you not to eat or drink. Therefore your body will not be buried in the tomb of your fathers.'"

23When the man of God had finished eating and drinking, the prophet who had brought him back saddled his donkey for him. 24As he went on his way, a lion met him on the road and killed him, and his body was thrown down on the road, with both the donkey and the lion standing beside it. 25Some people who passed by saw the body thrown down there, with the lion standing beside the body, and they went and reported it in the city where the old prophet lived.

26When the prophet who had brought him back from his journey heard of it, he said, "It is the man of God who defied the word of the LORD. The LORD has given him over to the lion, which has mauled him and killed him, as the word of the LORD had warned him."

27The prophet said to his sons, "Saddle the donkey for me," and they did so. 28Then he went out and found the body thrown down on the road, with the donkey and the lion standing beside it. The lion had neither eaten the body nor mauled the donkey. 29So the prophet picked up the body of the man of God, laid it on the donkey, and brought it back to his own city to mourn for him and bury him. 30Then he laid the body in his own tomb, and they mourned over him and said, "Oh, my brother!"

31After burying him, he said to his sons, "When I die, bury me in the grave where the man of God is buried; lay my bones beside his bones. 32For the message he declared by the word of the LORD against the altar in Bethel and against all the shrines on the high places in the towns of Samaria will certainly come true."

33Even after this, Jeroboam did not change his evil ways, but once more appointed priests for the high places from all sorts of people. Anyone who wanted to become a priest he consecrated for the high places. 34This was the sin of the house of Jeroboam that led to its downfall and to its destruction from the face of the earth.

Ahijah's Prophecy Against Jeroboam

14 At that time Abijah son of Jeroboam became ill, 2and Jeroboam said to his wife, "Go, disguise yourself, so you won't be recognized as the wife of Jeroboam. Then go to Shiloh. Ahijah the prophet is there—the one who told me I would be king over this people. 3Take ten loaves of bread with you, some cakes and a jar of honey, and go to him. He will tell you what will happen to the boy." 4So Jeroboam's wife did what he said and went to Ahijah's house in Shiloh.

Now Ahijah could not see; his sight was gone because of his age. 5But the LORD had told Ahijah, "Jeroboam's wife is coming to ask you about her son, for he is ill, and you are to give her such and such an answer. When she arrives, she will pretend to be someone else."

6So when Ahijah heard the sound of her foot-

steps at the door, he said, "Come in, wife of
Jeroboam. Why this pretense? I have been sent to
you with bad news. 7 Go, tell Jeroboam that this
is what the LORD, the God of Israel, says: 'I raised
you up from among the people and made you a
leader over my people Israel. 8 I tore the kingdom
away from the house of David and gave it to you,
but you have not been like my servant David,
who kept my commands and followed me with all
his heart, doing only what was right in my eyes.
9 You have done more evil than all who lived before you. You have made for yourself other gods,
idols made of metal; you have provoked me to
anger and thrust me behind your back.

10 " 'Because of this, I am going to bring disaster on the house of Jeroboam. I will cut off from
Jeroboam every last male in Israel—slave or free.
I will burn up the house of Jeroboam as one burns
dung, until it is all gone. 11 Dogs will eat those
belonging to Jeroboam who die in the city, and
the birds of the air will feed on those who die in
the country. The LORD has spoken!'

12 "As for you, go back home. When you set
foot in your city, the boy will die. 13 All Israel will
mourn for him and bury him. He is the only one
belonging to Jeroboam who will be buried, because he is the only one in the house of Jeroboam
in whom the LORD, the God of Israel, has found
anything good.

14 "The LORD will raise up for himself a king
over Israel who will cut off the family of Jeroboam. This is the day! What? Yes, even now.[a]
15 And the LORD will strike Israel, so that it will be
like a reed swaying in the water. He will uproot
Israel from this good land that he gave to their
forefathers and scatter them beyond the River,[b]
because they provoked the LORD to anger by making Asherah poles.[c] 16 And he will give Israel up
because of the sins Jeroboam has committed and
has caused Israel to commit."

17 Then Jeroboam's wife got up and left and
went to Tirzah. As soon as she stepped over the
threshold of the house, the boy died. 18 They buried him, and all Israel mourned for him, as the
LORD had said through his servant the prophet
Ahijah.

19 The other events of Jeroboam's reign, his
wars and how he ruled, are written in the book
of the annals of the kings of Israel. 20 He reigned
for twenty-two years and then rested with his
fathers. And Nadab his son succeeded him as
king.

Rehoboam King of Judah

21 Rehoboam son of Solomon was king in Judah. He was forty-one years old when he became
king, and he reigned seventeen years in Jerusalem, the city the LORD had chosen out of all the
tribes of Israel in which to put his Name. His
mother's name was Naamah; she was an Ammonite.

22 Judah did evil in the eyes of the LORD. By the
sins they committed they stirred up his jealous
anger more than their fathers had done. 23 They
also set up for themselves high places, sacred
stones and Asherah poles on every high hill and
under every spreading tree. 24 There were even
male shrine prostitutes in the land; the people
engaged in all the detestable practices of the nations the LORD had driven out before the Israelites.

25 In the fifth year of King Rehoboam, Shishak
king of Egypt attacked Jerusalem. 26 He carried off
the treasures of the temple of the LORD and the
treasures of the royal palace. He took everything,
including all the gold shields Solomon had made.
27 So King Rehoboam made bronze shields to replace them and assigned these to the commanders of the guard on duty at the entrance to the
royal palace. 28 Whenever the king went to the
LORD's temple, the guards bore the shields, and
afterward they returned them to the guardroom.

29 As for the other events of Rehoboam's reign,
and all he did, are they not written in the book of
the annals of the kings of Judah? 30 There was
continual warfare between Rehoboam and Jeroboam. 31 And Rehoboam rested with his fathers
and was buried with them in the City of David.
His mother's name was Naamah; she was an Ammonite. And Abijah[d] his son succeeded him as
king.

Abijah King of Judah

15 In the eighteenth year of the reign of Jeroboam son of Nebat, Abijah[e] became king
of Judah, 2 and he reigned in Jerusalem three
years. His mother's name was Maacah daughter
of Abishalom.[f]

3 He committed all the sins his father had done
before him; his heart was not fully devoted to the
LORD his God, as the heart of David his forefather
had been. 4 Nevertheless, for David's sake the
LORD his God gave him a lamp in Jerusalem by
raising up a son to succeed him and by making
Jerusalem strong. 5 For David had done what was
right in the eyes of the LORD and had not failed to
keep any of the LORD's commands all the days of
his life—except in the case of Uriah the Hittite.

[a] *14* The meaning of the Hebrew for this sentence is uncertain. [b] *15* That is, the Euphrates [c] *15* That is, symbols of the goddess Asherah; here and elsewhere in 1 Kings [d] *31* Some Hebrew manuscripts and Septuagint (see also 2 Chron. 12:16); most Hebrew manuscripts *Abijam* [e] *1* Some Hebrew manuscripts and Septuagint (see also 2 Chron. 12:16); most Hebrew manuscripts *Abijam*; also in verses 7 and 8 [f] *2* A variant of *Absalom*; also in verse 10

6 There was war between Rehoboam[a] and Jeroboam throughout ⌞Abijah's⌟ lifetime. 7 As for the other events of Abijah's reign, and all he did, are they not written in the book of the annals of the kings of Judah? There was war between Abijah and Jeroboam. 8 And Abijah rested with his fathers and was buried in the City of David. And Asa his son succeeded him as king.

Asa King of Judah

9 In the twentieth year of Jeroboam king of Israel, Asa became king of Judah, 10 and he reigned in Jerusalem forty-one years. His grandmother's name was Maacah daughter of Abishalom.

11 Asa did what was right in the eyes of the LORD, as his father David had done. 12 He expelled the male shrine prostitutes from the land and got rid of all the idols his fathers had made. 13 He even deposed his grandmother Maacah from her position as queen mother, because she had made a repulsive Asherah pole. Asa cut the pole down and burned it in the Kidron Valley. 14 Although he did not remove the high places, Asa's heart was fully committed to the LORD all his life. 15 He brought into the temple of the LORD the silver and gold and the articles that he and his father had dedicated.

16 There was war between Asa and Baasha king of Israel throughout their reigns. 17 Baasha king of Israel went up against Judah and fortified Ramah to prevent anyone from leaving or entering the territory of Asa king of Judah.

18 Asa then took all the silver and gold that was left in the treasuries of the LORD's temple and of his own palace. He entrusted it to his officials and sent them to Ben-Hadad son of Tabrimmon, the son of Hezion, the king of Aram, who was ruling in Damascus. 19 "Let there be a treaty between me and you," he said, "as there was between my father and your father. See, I am sending you a gift of silver and gold. Now break your treaty with Baasha king of Israel so he will withdraw from me."

20 Ben-Hadad agreed with King Asa and sent the commanders of his forces against the towns of Israel. He conquered Ijon, Dan, Abel Beth Maacah and all Kinnereth in addition to Naphtali. 21 When Baasha heard this, he stopped building Ramah and withdrew to Tirzah. 22 Then King Asa issued an order to all Judah—no one was exempt—and they carried away from Ramah the stones and timber Baasha had been using there. With them King Asa built up Geba in Benjamin, and also Mizpah.

23 As for all the other events of Asa's reign, all his achievements, all he did and the cities he built, are they not written in the book of the annals of the kings of Judah? In his old age, however, his feet became diseased. 24 Then Asa rested with his fathers and was buried with them in the city of his father David. And Jehoshaphat his son succeeded him as king.

Nadab King of Israel

25 Nadab son of Jeroboam became king of Israel in the second year of Asa king of Judah, and he reigned over Israel two years. 26 He did evil in the eyes of the LORD, walking in the ways of his father and in his sin, which he had caused Israel to commit.

27 Baasha son of Ahijah of the house of Issachar plotted against him, and he struck him down at Gibbethon, a Philistine town, while Nadab and all Israel were besieging it. 28 Baasha killed Nadab in the third year of Asa king of Judah and succeeded him as king.

29 As soon as he began to reign, he killed Jeroboam's whole family. He did not leave Jeroboam anyone that breathed, but destroyed them all, according to the word of the LORD given through his servant Ahijah the Shilonite— 30 because of the sins Jeroboam had committed and had caused Israel to commit, and because he provoked the LORD, the God of Israel, to anger.

31 As for the other events of Nadab's reign, and all he did, are they not written in the book of the annals of the kings of Israel? 32 There was war between Asa and Baasha king of Israel throughout their reigns.

Baasha King of Israel

33 In the third year of Asa king of Judah, Baasha son of Ahijah became king of all Israel in Tirzah, and he reigned twenty-four years. 34 He did evil in the eyes of the LORD, walking in the ways of Jeroboam and in his sin, which he had caused Israel to commit.

16 Then the word of the LORD came to Jehu son of Hanani against Baasha: 2 "I lifted you up from the dust and made you leader of my people Israel, but you walked in the ways of Jeroboam and caused my people Israel to sin and to provoke me to anger by their sins. 3 So I am about to consume Baasha and his house, and I will make your house like that of Jeroboam son of Nebat. 4 Dogs will eat those belonging to Baasha who die in the city, and the birds of the air will feed on those who die in the country."

5 As for the other events of Baasha's reign, what he did and his achievements, are they not written in the book of the annals of the kings of Israel? 6 Baasha rested with his fathers and was buried in Tirzah. And Elah his son succeeded him as king.

[a] 6 Most Hebrew manuscripts; some Hebrew manuscripts and Syriac *Abijam* (that is, Abijah)

[7]Moreover, the word of the LORD came
through the prophet Jehu son of Hanani to Baasha and his house, because of all the evil he had
done in the eyes of the LORD, provoking him to
anger by the things he did, and becoming like the
house of Jeroboam—and also because he destroyed it.

Elah King of Israel

[8]In the twenty-sixth year of Asa king of Judah,
Elah son of Baasha became king of Israel, and he
reigned in Tirzah two years.
[9]Zimri, one of his officials, who had command
of half his chariots, plotted against him. Elah was
in Tirzah at the time, getting drunk in the home
of Arza, the man in charge of the palace at Tirzah.
[10]Zimri came in, struck him down and killed him
in the twenty-seventh year of Asa king of Judah.
Then he succeeded him as king.
[11]As soon as he began to reign and was seated
on the throne, he killed off Baasha's whole family. He did not spare a single male, whether relative or friend. [12]So Zimri destroyed the whole
family of Baasha, in accordance with the word
of the LORD spoken against Baasha through the
prophet Jehu— [13]because of all the sins Baasha
and his son Elah had committed and had caused
Israel to commit, so that they provoked the LORD,
the God of Israel, to anger by their worthless
idols.
[14]As for the other events of Elah's reign, and
all he did, are they not written in the book of the
annals of the kings of Israel?

Zimri King of Israel

[15]In the twenty-seventh year of Asa king of
Judah, Zimri reigned in Tirzah seven days. The
army was encamped near Gibbethon, a Philistine
town. [16]When the Israelites in the camp heard
that Zimri had plotted against the king and murdered him, they proclaimed Omri, the commander of the army, king over Israel that very day
there in the camp. [17]Then Omri and all the Israelites with him withdrew from Gibbethon and
laid siege to Tirzah. [18]When Zimri saw that the
city was taken, he went into the citadel of the
royal palace and set the palace on fire around
him. So he died, [19]because of the sins he had
committed, doing evil in the eyes of the LORD and
walking in the ways of Jeroboam and in the sin he
had committed and had caused Israel to commit.
[20]As for the other events of Zimri's reign, and
the rebellion he carried out, are they not written
in the book of the annals of the kings of Israel?

Omri King of Israel

[21]Then the people of Israel were split into two
factions; half supported Tibni son of Ginath for
king, and the other half supported Omri. [22]But
Omri's followers proved stronger than those of
Tibni son of Ginath. So Tibni died and Omri became king.
[23]In the thirty-first year of Asa king of Judah,
Omri became king of Israel, and he reigned
twelve years, six of them in Tirzah. [24]He bought
the hill of Samaria from Shemer for two talents[a]
of silver and built a city on the hill, calling it
Samaria, after Shemer, the name of the former
owner of the hill.
[25]But Omri did evil in the eyes of the LORD and
sinned more than all those before him. [26]He
walked in all the ways of Jeroboam son of Nebat
and in his sin, which he had caused Israel to
commit, so that they provoked the LORD, the God
of Israel, to anger by their worthless idols.
[27]As for the other events of Omri's reign, what
he did and the things he achieved, are they not
written in the book of the annals of the kings of
Israel? [28]Omri rested with his fathers and was
buried in Samaria. And Ahab his son succeeded
him as king.

Ahab Becomes King of Israel

[29]In the thirty-eighth year of Asa king of Judah, Ahab son of Omri became king of Israel, and
he reigned in Samaria over Israel twenty-two
years. [30]Ahab son of Omri did more evil in the
eyes of the LORD than any of those before him.
[31]He not only considered it trivial to commit the
sins of Jeroboam son of Nebat, but he also married Jezebel daughter of Ethbaal king of the Sidonians, and began to serve Baal and worship him.
[32]He set up an altar for Baal in the temple of Baal
that he built in Samaria. [33]Ahab also made an
Asherah pole and did more to provoke the LORD,
the God of Israel, to anger than did all the kings
of Israel before him.
[34]In Ahab's time, Hiel of Bethel rebuilt Jericho. He laid its foundations at the cost of his
firstborn son Abiram, and he set up its gates at
the cost of his youngest son Segub, in accordance
with the word of the LORD spoken by Joshua son
of Nun.

Elijah Fed by Ravens

17 Now Elijah the Tishbite, from Tishbe[b] in
Gilead, said to Ahab, "As the LORD, the
God of Israel, lives, whom I serve, there will be
neither dew nor rain in the next few years except
at my word."
[2]Then the word of the LORD came to Elijah:
[3]"Leave here, turn eastward and hide in the Kerith Ravine, east of the Jordan. [4]You will drink

[a]24 That is, about 150 pounds (about 70 kilograms) [b]1 Or *Tishbite, of the settlers*

from the brook, and I have ordered the ravens to feed you there."

5So he did what the LORD had told him. He went to the Kerith Ravine, east of the Jordan, and stayed there. 6The ravens brought him bread and meat in the morning and bread and meat in the evening, and he drank from the brook.

The Widow at Zarephath

7Some time later the brook dried up because there had been no rain in the land. 8Then the word of the LORD came to him: 9"Go at once to Zarephath of Sidon and stay there. I have commanded a widow in that place to supply you with food." 10So he went to Zarephath. When he came to the town gate, a widow was there gathering sticks. He called to her and asked, "Would you bring me a little water in a jar so I may have a drink?" 11As she was going to get it, he called, "And bring me, please, a piece of bread."

12"As surely as the LORD your God lives," she replied, "I don't have any bread—only a handful of flour in a jar and a little oil in a jug. I am gathering a few sticks to take home and make a meal for myself and my son, that we may eat it—and die."

13Elijah said to her, "Don't be afraid. Go home and do as you have said. But first make a small cake of bread for me from what you have and bring it to me, and then make something for yourself and your son. 14For this is what the LORD, the God of Israel, says: 'The jar of flour will not be used up and the jug of oil will not run dry until the day the LORD gives rain on the land.' "

15She went away and did as Elijah had told her. So there was food every day for Elijah and for the woman and her family. 16For the jar of flour was not used up and the jug of oil did not run dry, in keeping with the word of the LORD spoken by Elijah.

17Some time later the son of the woman who owned the house became ill. He grew worse and worse, and finally stopped breathing. 18She said to Elijah, "What do you have against me, man of God? Did you come to remind me of my sin and kill my son?"

19"Give me your son," Elijah replied. He took him from her arms, carried him to the upper room where he was staying, and laid him on his bed. 20Then he cried out to the LORD, "O LORD my God, have you brought tragedy also upon this widow I am staying with, by causing her son to die?" 21Then he stretched himself out on the boy three times and cried to the LORD, "O LORD my God, let this boy's life return to him!"

22The LORD heard Elijah's cry, and the boy's life returned to him, and he lived. 23Elijah picked up the child and carried him down from the room into the house. He gave him to his mother and said, "Look, your son is alive!"

24Then the woman said to Elijah, "Now I know that you are a man of God and that the word of the LORD from your mouth is the truth."

Elijah and Obadiah

18 After a long time, in the third year, the word of the LORD came to Elijah: "Go and present yourself to Ahab, and I will send rain on the land." 2So Elijah went to present himself to Ahab.

Now the famine was severe in Samaria, 3and Ahab had summoned Obadiah, who was in charge of his palace. (Obadiah was a devout believer in the LORD. 4While Jezebel was killing off the LORD's prophets, Obadiah had taken a hundred prophets and hidden them in two caves, fifty in each, and had supplied them with food and water.) 5Ahab had said to Obadiah, "Go through the land to all the springs and valleys. Maybe we can find some grass to keep the horses and mules alive so we will not have to kill any of our animals." 6So they divided the land they were to cover, Ahab going in one direction and Obadiah in another.

7As Obadiah was walking along, Elijah met him. Obadiah recognized him, bowed down to the ground, and said, "Is it really you, my lord Elijah?"

8"Yes," he replied. "Go tell your master, 'Elijah is here.' "

9"What have I done wrong," asked Obadiah, "that you are handing your servant over to Ahab to be put to death? 10As surely as the LORD your God lives, there is not a nation or kingdom where my master has not sent someone to look for you. And whenever a nation or kingdom claimed you were not there, he made them swear they could not find you. 11But now you tell me to go to my master and say, 'Elijah is here.' 12I don't know where the Spirit of the LORD may carry you when I leave you. If I go and tell Ahab and he doesn't find you, he will kill me. Yet I your servant have worshiped the LORD since my youth. 13Haven't you heard, my lord, what I did while Jezebel was killing the prophets of the LORD? I hid a hundred of the LORD's prophets in two caves, fifty in each, and supplied them with food and water. 14And now you tell me to go to my master and say, 'Elijah is here.' He will kill me!"

15Elijah said, "As the LORD Almighty lives, whom I serve, I will surely present myself to Ahab today."

Elijah on Mount Carmel

16So Obadiah went to meet Ahab and told him,

and Ahab went to meet Elijah. [17]When he saw Elijah, he said to him, "Is that you, you troubler of Israel?"

[18]"I have not made trouble for Israel," Elijah replied. "But you and your father's family have. You have abandoned the LORD's commands and have followed the Baals. [19]Now summon the people from all over Israel to meet me on Mount Carmel. And bring the four hundred and fifty prophets of Baal and the four hundred prophets of Asherah, who eat at Jezebel's table."

1 Kings 18:16–40

1. Have you ever had an accident involving fire? What happened?
2. If the *New York Times* sent a team to your school to interview the students, what would they report as the "religion" of your school?
3. Who are the "false prophets" that the students listen to? What impact do these people have on their values?
4. How would you have felt if you were there when "the fire of the Lord fell and burned up the sacrifice, the wood, the stones and the soil, and also licked up the water in the trench" (v. 38)?
5. What convinces you that God is more powerful than anything else: Mighty miracles? His Word? Changed lives? Changes in your own life?
6. If you knew you had the support of your group, what cause would you like to take on? What could your whole group take on?
7. How can this group pray for you this week? Close in prayer.

[20]So Ahab sent word throughout all Israel and assembled the prophets on Mount Carmel. [21]Elijah went before the people and said, "How long will you waver between two opinions? If the LORD is God, follow him; but if Baal is God, follow him."

But the people said nothing.

[22]Then Elijah said to them, "I am the only one of the LORD's prophets left, but Baal has four hundred and fifty prophets. [23]Get two bulls for us. Let them choose one for themselves, and let them cut it into pieces and put it on the wood but not set fire to it. I will prepare the other bull and put it on the wood but not set fire to it. [24]Then you call on the name of your god, and I will call on the name of the LORD. The god who answers by fire—he is God."

Then all the people said, "What you say is good."

[25]Elijah said to the prophets of Baal, "Choose one of the bulls and prepare it first, since there are so many of you. Call on the name of your god, but do not light the fire." [26]So they took the bull given them and prepared it.

Then they called on the name of Baal from morning till noon. "O Baal, answer us!" they shouted. But there was no response; no one answered. And they danced around the altar they had made.

[27]At noon Elijah began to taunt them. "Shout louder!" he said. "Surely he is a god! Perhaps he is deep in thought, or busy, or traveling. Maybe he is sleeping and must be awakened." [28]So they shouted louder and slashed themselves with swords and spears, as was their custom, until their blood flowed. [29]Midday passed, and they continued their frantic prophesying until the time for the evening sacrifice. But there was no response, no one answered, no one paid attention.

[30]Then Elijah said to all the people, "Come here to me." They came to him, and he repaired the altar of the LORD, which was in ruins. [31]Elijah took twelve stones, one for each of the tribes descended from Jacob, to whom the word of the LORD had come, saying, "Your name shall be Israel." [32]With the stones he built an altar in the

---

After announcing to wicked King Ahab the beginning of a severe drought, the prophet Elijah left Israel. Now, about three years later, Elijah returns.

18:17–18 ***you troubler of Israel.*** Ahab holds Elijah accountable for the drought. But Elijah counters that the real source of Israel's trouble was Ahab's idolatry.

18:19 ***Jezebel's table.*** The prophets of the false gods Baal and Asherah were provided for by Ahab's wicked wife Jezebel.

18:21 How long will you waver? Elijah placed a clear choice before the people. He drew a sharp contrast between the worship of the Lord and that of Baal, to eliminate the apostate idea that both deities could be worshiped in a mixed way.

18:26–29 ***danced around the altar.*** The ecstatic cultic dance was part of the pagan ritual intended to arouse the deity to perform some desired action. ***until their blood flowed.*** Self-inflicted wounds, as a symbol of self-sacrifice, were strictly forbidden in the Law of Moses (Deut. 14:1). ***frantic prophesying.*** Indicative of ecstatic raving, in which the ritual reached its climax.

18:36 ***prayed.*** Elijah's simple but earnest prayer stands in sharp contrast to the frantic activity of the Baal prophets.

18:40 ***slaughtered there.*** Elijah, acting on the authority of the Lord, who sent him, carried out the sentence pronounced in the Mosaic Law for prophets of pagan gods (see Deut. 17:2–5).

name of the LORD, and he dug a trench around it
large enough to hold two seahs[a] of seed. 33He
arranged the wood, cut the bull into pieces and
laid it on the wood. Then he said to them, "Fill
four large jars with water and pour it on the offering and on the wood."
34"Do it again," he said, and they did it again.
"Do it a third time," he ordered, and they did
it the third time. 35The water ran down around
the altar and even filled the trench.
36At the time of sacrifice, the prophet Elijah
stepped forward and prayed: "O LORD, God of
Abraham, Isaac and Israel, let it be known today
that you are God in Israel and that I am your
servant and have done all these things at your
command. 37Answer me, O LORD, answer me, so
these people will know that you, O LORD, are
God, and that you are turning their hearts back
again."
38Then the fire of the LORD fell and burned up
the sacrifice, the wood, the stones and the soil,
and also licked up the water in the trench.
39When all the people saw this, they fell prostrate and cried, "The LORD—he is God! The
LORD—he is God!"
40Then Elijah commanded them, "Seize the
prophets of Baal. Don't let anyone get away!"
They seized them, and Elijah had them brought
down to the Kishon Valley and slaughtered there.
41And Elijah said to Ahab, "Go, eat and drink,
for there is the sound of a heavy rain." 42So Ahab
went off to eat and drink, but Elijah climbed to
the top of Carmel, bent down to the ground and
put his face between his knees.
43"Go and look toward the sea," he told his
servant. And he went up and looked.
"There is nothing there," he said.
Seven times Elijah said, "Go back."
44The seventh time the servant reported, "A
cloud as small as a man's hand is rising from the
sea."
So Elijah said, "Go and tell Ahab, 'Hitch up
your chariot and go down before the rain stops
you.' "
45Meanwhile, the sky grew black with clouds,
the wind rose, a heavy rain came on and Ahab
rode off to Jezreel. 46The power of the LORD came
upon Elijah and, tucking his cloak into his belt,
he ran ahead of Ahab all the way to Jezreel.

Elijah Flees to Horeb

19 Now Ahab told Jezebel everything Elijah
had done and how he had killed all the
prophets with the sword. 2So Jezebel sent a messenger to Elijah to say, "May the gods deal with
me, be it ever so severely, if by this time tomorrow I do not make your life like that of one of
them."
3Elijah was afraid[b] and ran for his life. When
he came to Beersheba in Judah, he left his servant
there, 4while he himself went a day's journey
into the desert. He came to a broom tree, sat
down under it and prayed that he might die. "I
have had enough, LORD," he said. "Take my life;
I am no better than my ancestors." 5Then he lay
down under the tree and fell asleep.
All at once an angel touched him and said,
"Get up and eat." 6He looked around, and there
by his head was a cake of bread baked over hot
coals, and a jar of water. He ate and drank and
then lay down again.
7The angel of the LORD came back a second
time and touched him and said, "Get up and eat,
for the journey is too much for you." 8So he got
up and ate and drank. Strengthened by that food,
he traveled forty days and forty nights until he
reached Horeb, the mountain of God. 9There he
went into a cave and spent the night.

The LORD Appears to Elijah

And the word of the LORD came to him: "What
are you doing here, Elijah?"
10He replied, "I have been very zealous for the
LORD God Almighty. The Israelites have rejected
your covenant, broken down your altars, and put
your prophets to death with the sword. I am the
only one left, and now they are trying to kill me
too."
11The LORD said, "Go out and stand on the
mountain in the presence of the LORD, for the
LORD is about to pass by."
Then a great and powerful wind tore the
mountains apart and shattered the rocks before
the LORD, but the LORD was not in the wind.
After the wind there was an earthquake, but the
LORD was not in the earthquake. 12After the
earthquake came a fire, but the LORD was not in
the fire. And after the fire came a gentle whisper.
13When Elijah heard it, he pulled his cloak over
his face and went out and stood at the mouth of
the cave.
Then a voice said to him, "What are you doing
here, Elijah?"
14He replied, "I have been very zealous for the
LORD God Almighty. The Israelites have rejected
your covenant, broken down your altars, and put
your prophets to death with the sword. I am the
only one left, and now they are trying to kill me
too."
15The LORD said to him, "Go back the way you
came, and go to the Desert of Damascus. When
you get there, anoint Hazael king over Aram.
16Also, anoint Jehu son of Nimshi king over Isra-

[a] 32 That is, probably about 13 quarts (about 15 liters)
[b] 3 Or *Elijah saw*

el, and anoint Elisha son of Shaphat from Abel Meholah to succeed you as prophet. 17Jehu will put to death any who escape the sword of Hazael, and Elisha will put to death any who escape the sword of Jehu. 18Yet I reserve seven thousand in Israel—all whose knees have not bowed down to Baal and all whose mouths have not kissed him."

The Call of Elisha

19So Elijah went from there and found Elisha son of Shaphat. He was plowing with twelve yoke of oxen, and he himself was driving the twelfth pair. Elijah went up to him and threw his cloak around him. 20Elisha then left his oxen and ran after Elijah. "Let me kiss my father and mother good-by," he said, "and then I will come with you."

"Go back," Elijah replied. "What have I done to you?"

21So Elisha left him and went back. He took his yoke of oxen and slaughtered them. He burned the plowing equipment to cook the meat and gave it to the people, and they ate. Then he set out to follow Elijah and became his attendant.

Ben-Hadad Attacks Samaria

20 Now Ben-Hadad king of Aram mustered his entire army. Accompanied by thirty-two kings with their horses and chariots, he went up and besieged Samaria and attacked it. 2He sent messengers into the city to Ahab king of Israel, saying, "This is what Ben-Hadad says: 3'Your silver and gold are mine, and the best of your wives and children are mine.' "

4The king of Israel answered, "Just as you say, my lord the king. I and all I have are yours."

5The messengers came again and said, "This is what Ben-Hadad says: 'I sent to demand your silver and gold, your wives and your children. 6But about this time tomorrow I am going to send my officials to search your palace and the houses of your officials. They will seize everything you value and carry it away.' "

7The king of Israel summoned all the elders of the land and said to them, "See how this man is looking for trouble! When he sent for my wives and my children, my silver and my gold, I did not refuse him."

8The elders and the people all answered, "Don't listen to him or agree to his demands."

9So he replied to Ben-Hadad's messengers, "Tell my lord the king, 'Your servant will do all you demanded the first time, but this demand I cannot meet.' " They left and took the answer back to Ben-Hadad.

10Then Ben-Hadad sent another message to Ahab: "May the gods deal with me, be it ever so severely, if enough dust remains in Samaria to give each of my men a handful."

11The king of Israel answered, "Tell him: 'One who puts on his armor should not boast like one who takes it off.' "

12Ben-Hadad heard this message while he and the kings were drinking in their tents,[a] and he ordered his men: "Prepare to attack." So they prepared to attack the city.

Ahab Defeats Ben-Hadad

13Meanwhile a prophet came to Ahab king of Israel and announced, "This is what the LORD says: 'Do you see this vast army? I will give it into your hand today, and then you will know that I am the LORD.' "

14"But who will do this?" asked Ahab.

The prophet replied, "This is what the LORD says: 'The young officers of the provincial commanders will do it.' "

"And who will start the battle?" he asked.

The prophet answered, "You will."

15So Ahab summoned the young officers of the provincial commanders, 232 men. Then he assembled the rest of the Israelites, 7,000 in all. 16They set out at noon while Ben-Hadad and the 32 kings allied with him were in their tents getting drunk. 17The young officers of the provincial commanders went out first.

Now Ben-Hadad had dispatched scouts, who reported, "Men are advancing from Samaria."

18He said, "If they have come out for peace, take them alive; if they have come out for war, take them alive."

19The young officers of the provincial commanders marched out of the city with the army behind them 20and each one struck down his opponent. At that, the Arameans fled, with the Israelites in pursuit. But Ben-Hadad king of Aram escaped on horseback with some of his horsemen. 21The king of Israel advanced and overpowered the horses and chariots and inflicted heavy losses on the Arameans.

22Afterward, the prophet came to the king of Israel and said, "Strengthen your position and see what must be done, because next spring the king of Aram will attack you again."

23Meanwhile, the officials of the king of Aram advised him, "Their gods are gods of the hills. That is why they were too strong for us. But if we fight them on the plains, surely we will be stronger than they. 24Do this: Remove all the kings from their commands and replace them with other officers. 25You must also raise an army like the one you lost—horse for horse and chariot for chariot—so we can fight Israel on the plains.

[a] *12* Or *in Succoth*; also in verse 16

Then surely we will be stronger than they." He agreed with them and acted accordingly.

26The next spring Ben-Hadad mustered the Arameans and went up to Aphek to fight against Israel. 27When the Israelites were also mustered and given provisions, they marched out to meet them. The Israelites camped opposite them like two small flocks of goats, while the Arameans covered the countryside.

28The man of God came up and told the king of Israel, "This is what the LORD says: 'Because the Arameans think the LORD is a god of the hills and not a god of the valleys, I will deliver this vast army into your hands, and you will know that I am the LORD.' "

29For seven days they camped opposite each other, and on the seventh day the battle was joined. The Israelites inflicted a hundred thousand casualties on the Aramean foot soldiers in one day. 30The rest of them escaped to the city of Aphek, where the wall collapsed on twenty-seven thousand of them. And Ben-Hadad fled to the city and hid in an inner room.

31His officials said to him, "Look, we have heard that the kings of the house of Israel are merciful. Let us go to the king of Israel with sackcloth around our waists and ropes around our heads. Perhaps he will spare your life."

32Wearing sackcloth around their waists and ropes around their heads, they went to the king of Israel and said, "Your servant Ben-Hadad says: 'Please let me live.' "

The king answered, "Is he still alive? He is my brother."

33The men took this as a good sign and were quick to pick up his word. "Yes, your brother Ben-Hadad!" they said.

"Go and get him," the king said. When Ben-Hadad came out, Ahab had him come up into his chariot.

34"I will return the cities my father took from your father," Ben-Hadad offered. "You may set up your own market areas in Damascus, as my father did in Samaria."

⌊Ahab said,⌋ "On the basis of a treaty I will set you free." So he made a treaty with him, and let him go.

A Prophet Condemns Ahab

35By the word of the LORD one of the sons of the prophets said to his companion, "Strike me with your weapon," but the man refused.

36So the prophet said, "Because you have not obeyed the LORD, as soon as you leave me a lion will kill you." And after the man went away, a lion found him and killed him.

37The prophet found another man and said, "Strike me, please." So the man struck him and wounded him. 38Then the prophet went and stood by the road waiting for the king. He disguised himself with his headband down over his eyes. 39As the king passed by, the prophet called out to him, "Your servant went into the thick of the battle, and someone came to me with a captive and said, 'Guard this man. If he is missing, it will be your life for his life, or you must pay a talent[a] of silver.' 40While your servant was busy here and there, the man disappeared."

"That is your sentence," the king of Israel said. "You have pronounced it yourself."

41Then the prophet quickly removed the headband from his eyes, and the king of Israel recognized him as one of the prophets. 42He said to the king, "This is what the LORD says: 'You have set free a man I had determined should die.[b] Therefore it is your life for his life, your people for his people.' " 43Sullen and angry, the king of Israel went to his palace in Samaria.

Naboth's Vineyard

21 Some time later there was an incident involving a vineyard belonging to Naboth the Jezreelite. The vineyard was in Jezreel, close to the palace of Ahab king of Samaria. 2Ahab said to Naboth, "Let me have your vineyard to use for a vegetable garden, since it is close to my palace. In exchange I will give you a better vineyard or, if you prefer, I will pay you whatever it is worth."

3But Naboth replied, "The LORD forbid that I should give you the inheritance of my fathers."

4So Ahab went home, sullen and angry because Naboth the Jezreelite had said, "I will not give you the inheritance of my fathers." He lay on his bed sulking and refused to eat.

5His wife Jezebel came in and asked him, "Why are you so sullen? Why won't you eat?"

6He answered her, "Because I said to Naboth the Jezreelite, 'Sell me your vineyard; or if you prefer, I will give you another vineyard in its place.' But he said, 'I will not give you my vineyard.' "

7Jezebel his wife said, "Is this how you act as king over Israel? Get up and eat! Cheer up. I'll get you the vineyard of Naboth the Jezreelite."

8So she wrote letters in Ahab's name, placed his seal on them, and sent them to the elders and nobles who lived in Naboth's city with him. 9In those letters she wrote:

> "Proclaim a day of fasting and seat Naboth in a prominent place among the people. 10But seat two scoundrels opposite him and have them testify that he has cursed

[a]39 That is, about 75 pounds (about 34 kilograms) [b]42 The Hebrew term refers to the irrevocable giving over of things or persons to the LORD, often by totally destroying them.

both God and the king. Then take him out and stone him to death."

11So the elders and nobles who lived in Naboth's city did as Jezebel directed in the letters she had written to them. 12They proclaimed a fast and seated Naboth in a prominent place among the people. 13Then two scoundrels came and sat opposite him and brought charges against Naboth before the people, saying, "Naboth has cursed both God and the king." So they took him outside the city and stoned him to death. 14Then they sent word to Jezebel: "Naboth has been stoned and is dead."

15As soon as Jezebel heard that Naboth had been stoned to death, she said to Ahab, "Get up and take possession of the vineyard of Naboth the Jezreelite that he refused to sell you. He is no longer alive, but dead." 16When Ahab heard that Naboth was dead, he got up and went down to take possession of Naboth's vineyard.

17Then the word of the LORD came to Elijah the Tishbite: 18"Go down to meet Ahab king of Israel, who rules in Samaria. He is now in Naboth's vineyard, where he has gone to take possession of it. 19Say to him, 'This is what the LORD says: Have you not murdered a man and seized his property?' Then say to him, 'This is what the LORD says: In the place where dogs licked up Naboth's blood, dogs will lick up your blood—yes, yours!' "

20Ahab said to Elijah, "So you have found me, my enemy!"

"I have found you," he answered, "because you have sold yourself to do evil in the eyes of the LORD. 21'I am going to bring disaster on you. I will consume your descendants and cut off from Ahab every last male in Israel—slave or free. 22I will make your house like that of Jeroboam son of Nebat and that of Baasha son of Ahijah, because you have provoked me to anger and have caused Israel to sin.'

23"And also concerning Jezebel the LORD says: 'Dogs will devour Jezebel by the wall of[a] Jezreel.'

24"Dogs will eat those belonging to Ahab who die in the city, and the birds of the air will feed on those who die in the country."

25(There was never a man like Ahab, who sold himself to do evil in the eyes of the LORD, urged on by Jezebel his wife. 26He behaved in the vilest manner by going after idols, like the Amorites the LORD drove out before Israel.)

27When Ahab heard these words, he tore his clothes, put on sackcloth and fasted. He lay in sackcloth and went around meekly.

28Then the word of the LORD came to Elijah the Tishbite: 29"Have you noticed how Ahab has humbled himself before me? Because he has humbled himself, I will not bring this disaster in his day, but I will bring it on his house in the days of his son."

Micaiah Prophesies Against Ahab

22 For three years there was no war between Aram and Israel. 2But in the third year Jehoshaphat king of Judah went down to see the king of Israel. 3The king of Israel had said to his officials, "Don't you know that Ramoth Gilead belongs to us and yet we are doing nothing to retake it from the king of Aram?"

4So he asked Jehoshaphat, "Will you go with me to fight against Ramoth Gilead?"

Jehoshaphat replied to the king of Israel, "I am as you are, my people as your people, my horses as your horses." 5But Jehoshaphat also said to the king of Israel, "First seek the counsel of the LORD."

6So the king of Israel brought together the prophets—about four hundred men—and asked them, "Shall I go to war against Ramoth Gilead, or shall I refrain?"

"Go," they answered, "for the Lord will give it into the king's hand."

7But Jehoshaphat asked, "Is there not a prophet of the LORD here whom we can inquire of?"

8The king of Israel answered Jehoshaphat, "There is still one man through whom we can inquire of the LORD, but I hate him because he never prophesies anything good about me, but always bad. He is Micaiah son of Imlah."

"The king should not say that," Jehoshaphat replied.

9So the king of Israel called one of his officials and said, "Bring Micaiah son of Imlah at once."

10Dressed in their royal robes, the king of Israel and Jehoshaphat king of Judah were sitting on their thrones at the threshing floor by the entrance of the gate of Samaria, with all the prophets prophesying before them. 11Now Zedekiah son of Kenaanah had made iron horns and he declared, "This is what the LORD says: 'With these you will gore the Arameans until they are destroyed.' "

12All the other prophets were prophesying the same thing. "Attack Ramoth Gilead and be victorious," they said, "for the LORD will give it into the king's hand."

13The messenger who had gone to summon Micaiah said to him, "Look, as one man the other prophets are predicting success for the king. Let your word agree with theirs, and speak favorably."

14But Micaiah said, "As surely as the LORD

a23 Most Hebrew manuscripts; a few Hebrew manuscripts, Vulgate and Syriac (see also 2 Kings 9:26) *the plot of ground at* lives, I can tell him only what the LORD tells me."

15 When he arrived, the king asked him, "Micaiah, shall we go to war against Ramoth Gilead, or shall I refrain?"

"Attack and be victorious," he answered, "for the LORD will give it into the king's hand."

16 The king said to him, "How many times must I make you swear to tell me nothing but the truth in the name of the LORD?"

17 Then Micaiah answered, "I saw all Israel scattered on the hills like sheep without a shepherd, and the LORD said, 'These people have no master. Let each one go home in peace.' "

18 The king of Israel said to Jehoshaphat, "Didn't I tell you that he never prophesies anything good about me, but only bad?"

19 Micaiah continued, "Therefore hear the word of the LORD: I saw the LORD sitting on his throne with all the host of heaven standing around him on his right and on his left. 20 And the LORD said, 'Who will entice Ahab into attacking Ramoth Gilead and going to his death there?'

"One suggested this, and another that. 21 Finally, a spirit came forward, stood before the LORD and said, 'I will entice him.'

22 " 'By what means?' the LORD asked.

" 'I will go out and be a lying spirit in the mouths of all his prophets,' he said.

" 'You will succeed in enticing him,' said the LORD. 'Go and do it.'

23 "So now the LORD has put a lying spirit in the mouths of all these prophets of yours. The LORD has decreed disaster for you."

24 Then Zedekiah son of Kenaanah went up and slapped Micaiah in the face. "Which way did the spirit from[a] the LORD go when he went from me to speak to you?" he asked.

25 Micaiah replied, "You will find out on the day you go to hide in an inner room."

26 The king of Israel then ordered, "Take Micaiah and send him back to Amon the ruler of the city and to Joash the king's son 27 and say, 'This is what the king says: Put this fellow in prison and give him nothing but bread and water until I return safely.' "

28 Micaiah declared, "If you ever return safely, the LORD has not spoken through me." Then he added, "Mark my words, all you people!"

Ahab Killed at Ramoth Gilead

29 So the king of Israel and Jehoshaphat king of Judah went up to Ramoth Gilead. 30 The king of Israel said to Jehoshaphat, "I will enter the battle in disguise, but you wear your royal robes." So the king of Israel disguised himself and went into battle.

31 Now the king of Aram had ordered his thirty-two chariot commanders, "Do not fight with anyone, small or great, except the king of Israel." 32 When the chariot commanders saw Jehoshaphat, they thought, "Surely this is the king of Israel." So they turned to attack him, but when Jehoshaphat cried out, 33 the chariot commanders saw that he was not the king of Israel and stopped pursuing him.

34 But someone drew his bow at random and hit the king of Israel between the sections of his armor. The king told his chariot driver, "Wheel around and get me out of the fighting. I've been wounded." 35 All day long the battle raged, and the king was propped up in his chariot facing the Arameans. The blood from his wound ran onto the floor of the chariot, and that evening he died. 36 As the sun was setting, a cry spread through the army: "Every man to his town; everyone to his land!"

37 So the king died and was brought to Samaria, and they buried him there. 38 They washed the chariot at a pool in Samaria (where the prostitutes bathed),[b] and the dogs licked up his blood, as the word of the LORD had declared.

39 As for the other events of Ahab's reign, including all he did, the palace he built and inlaid with ivory, and the cities he fortified, are they not written in the book of the annals of the kings of Israel? 40 Ahab rested with his fathers. And Ahaziah his son succeeded him as king.

Jehoshaphat King of Judah

41 Jehoshaphat son of Asa became king of Judah in the fourth year of Ahab king of Israel. 42 Jehoshaphat was thirty-five years old when he became king, and he reigned in Jerusalem twenty-five years. His mother's name was Azubah daughter of Shilhi. 43 In everything he walked in the ways of his father Asa and did not stray from them; he did what was right in the eyes of the LORD. The high places, however, were not removed, and the people continued to offer sacrifices and burn incense there. 44 Jehoshaphat was also at peace with the king of Israel.

45 As for the other events of Jehoshaphat's reign, the things he achieved and his military exploits, are they not written in the book of the annals of the kings of Judah? 46 He rid the land of the rest of the male shrine prostitutes who remained there even after the reign of his father Asa. 47 There was then no king in Edom; a deputy ruled.

48 Now Jehoshaphat built a fleet of trading ships[c] to go to Ophir for gold, but they never set sail—they were wrecked at Ezion Geber. 49 At that time Ahaziah son of Ahab said to Jehosha-

a 24 Or *Spirit of*   b 38 Or *Samaria and cleaned the weapons*   c 48 Hebrew *of ships of Tarshish*

phat, "Let my men sail with your men," but Jehoshaphat refused.
[50]Then Jehoshaphat rested with his fathers
and was buried with them in the city of David his
father. And Jehoram his son succeeded him.

Ahaziah King of Israel

[51]Ahaziah son of Ahab became king of Israel in
Samaria in the seventeenth year of Jehoshaphat
king of Judah, and he reigned over Israel two
years. [52]He did evil in the eyes of the LORD, because he walked in the ways of his father and
mother and in the ways of Jeroboam son of Nebat, who caused Israel to sin. [53]He served and
worshiped Baal and provoked the LORD, the God
of Israel, to anger, just as his father had done.

Introduction to
2 KINGS

Personal Reading Plan

❒ 2 Kings 1:1–2:25	❒ 2 Kings 9:14–10:17	❒ 2 Kings 18:1–37
❒ 2 Kings 3:1–27	❒ 2 Kings 10:18–11:21	❒ 2 Kings 19:1–37
❒ 2 Kings 4:1–44	❒ 2 Kings 12:1–13:25	❒ 2 Kings 20:1–21:26
❒ 2 Kings 5:1–6:23	❒ 2 Kings 14:1–15:12	❒ 2 Kings 22:1–23:30
❒ 2 Kings 6:24–8:6	❒ 2 Kings 15:13–16:20	❒ 2 Kings 23:31–24:17
❒ 2 Kings 8:7–9:13	❒ 2 Kings 17:1–41	❒ 2 Kings 24:18–25:30

Author

The author of 1 and 2 Kings is not known, but the three literary sources that are named suggest multiple authors and editors: "the Annals of Solomon" (1 Kings 11:41); "the Annals of the Kings of Israel" (1 Kings 14:19; 2 Kings 15:31); and "the Annals of the Kings of Judah" (1 Kings 14:29; 2 Kings 24:5).

Date

The account of Jehoiachin's release from prison in 2 Kings 25:27–30 means that the final form of Kings was written after 561 B.C. Nonetheless, the source materials could have been written at the time of the events they describe. These events span almost 400 years.

Theme

Israel's and Judah's spiral to destruction.

Historical Background

The divided kingdoms of Israel and Judah continue their political and moral decline. They are oppressed by their enemies, particularly Aram (Syria). Second Kings gives witness to the rise of Assyrian power which crushes Israel's capital, Samaria, in 722 B.C. (2 Kings 17). The Babylonians succeeded the Assyrians as the dominant power in the region. It was at their hands, in 586 B.C., that Judah's capital, Jerusalem, suffered a fate similar to that of Samaria (2 Kings 25).

Characteristics

Second Kings completes the historical narrative begun in 1 Kings. It chronicles the succession of kings in both the northern kingdom of Israel and the southern kingdom of Judah. The verdict upon most of these kings is sadly repetitive: They "did evil in the eyes of the Lord." Elisha succeeds the great prophet, Elijah, and is "doubly blessed" with God's Spirit.

Passage for Topical Group Study

4:1–7	FINANCIAL PROBLEMS	Elisha and the Widow's Oil

See the Lesson Plans in the front of this Bible.

Passages for General Group Study

5:1–16	Naaman Healed of Leprosy
6:8–23	Elisha and the Chariots of Fire

The Lord*'s Judgment on Ahaziah*

1 After Ahab's death, Moab rebelled against Israel. [2]Now Ahaziah had fallen through the lattice of his upper room in Samaria and injured himself. So he sent messengers, saying to them, "Go and consult Baal-Zebub, the god of Ekron, to see if I will recover from this injury."

[3]But the angel of the Lord said to Elijah the Tishbite, "Go up and meet the messengers of the king of Samaria and ask them, 'Is it because there is no God in Israel that you are going off to consult Baal-Zebub, the god of Ekron?' [4]Therefore this is what the Lord says: 'You will not leave the bed you are lying on. You will certainly die!' " So Elijah went.

[5]When the messengers returned to the king, he asked them, "Why have you come back?"

[6]"A man came to meet us," they replied. "And he said to us, 'Go back to the king who sent you and tell him, "This is what the Lord says: Is it because there is no God in Israel that you are sending men to consult Baal-Zebub, the god of Ekron? Therefore you will not leave the bed you are lying on. You will certainly die!" ' "

[7]The king asked them, "What kind of man was it who came to meet you and told you this?"

[8]They replied, "He was a man with a garment of hair and with a leather belt around his waist."

The king said, "That was Elijah the Tishbite."

[9]Then he sent to Elijah a captain with his company of fifty men. The captain went up to Elijah, who was sitting on the top of a hill, and said to him, "Man of God, the king says, 'Come down!' "

[10]Elijah answered the captain, "If I am a man of God, may fire come down from heaven and consume you and your fifty men!" Then fire fell from heaven and consumed the captain and his men.

[11]At this the king sent to Elijah another captain with his fifty men. The captain said to him, "Man of God, this is what the king says, 'Come down at once!' "

[12]"If I am a man of God," Elijah replied, "may fire come down from heaven and consume you and your fifty men!" Then the fire of God fell from heaven and consumed him and his fifty men.

[13]So the king sent a third captain with his fifty men. This third captain went up and fell on his knees before Elijah. "Man of God," he begged, "please have respect for my life and the lives of these fifty men, your servants! [14]See, fire has fallen from heaven and consumed the first two captains and all their men. But now have respect for my life!"

[15]The angel of the Lord said to Elijah, "Go down with him; do not be afraid of him." So Elijah got up and went down with him to the king.

[16]He told the king, "This is what the Lord says: Is it because there is no God in Israel for you to consult that you have sent messengers to consult Baal-Zebub, the god of Ekron? Because you have done this, you will never leave the bed you are lying on. You will certainly die!" [17]So he died, according to the word of the Lord that Elijah had spoken.

Because Ahaziah had no son, Joram[a] succeeded him as king in the second year of Jehoram son of Jehoshaphat king of Judah. [18]As for all the other events of Ahaziah's reign, and what he did, are they not written in the book of the annals of the kings of Israel?

Elijah Taken Up to Heaven

2 When the Lord was about to take Elijah up to heaven in a whirlwind, Elijah and Elisha were on their way from Gilgal. [2]Elijah said to Elisha, "Stay here; the Lord has sent me to Bethel."

But Elisha said, "As surely as the Lord lives and as you live, I will not leave you." So they went down to Bethel.

[3]The company of the prophets at Bethel came out to Elisha and asked, "Do you know that the Lord is going to take your master from you today?"

"Yes, I know," Elisha replied, "but do not speak of it."

[4]Then Elijah said to him, "Stay here, Elisha; the Lord has sent me to Jericho."

And he replied, "As surely as the Lord lives and as you live, I will not leave you." So they went to Jericho.

[5]The company of the prophets at Jericho went up to Elisha and asked him, "Do you know that the Lord is going to take your master from you today?"

"Yes, I know," he replied, "but do not speak of it."

[6]Then Elijah said to him, "Stay here; the Lord has sent me to the Jordan."

And he replied, "As surely as the Lord lives and as you live, I will not leave you." So the two of them walked on.

[7]Fifty men of the company of the prophets went and stood at a distance, facing the place where Elijah and Elisha had stopped at the Jordan. [8]Elijah took his cloak, rolled it up and struck the water with it. The water divided to the right and to the left, and the two of them crossed over on dry ground.

[9]When they had crossed, Elijah said to Elisha,

[a] 17 Hebrew *Jehoram,* a variant of *Joram*

"Tell me, what can I do for you before I am taken
from you?"
"Let me inherit a double portion of your spirit," Elisha replied.
[10]"You have asked a difficult thing," Elijah
said, "yet if you see me when I am taken from
you, it will be yours—otherwise not."
[11]As they were walking along and talking together, suddenly a chariot of fire and horses of
fire appeared and separated the two of them, and
Elijah went up to heaven in a whirlwind. [12]Elisha
saw this and cried out, "My father! My father!
The chariots and horsemen of Israel!" And Elisha
saw him no more. Then he took hold of his own
clothes and tore them apart.
[13]He picked up the cloak that had fallen from
Elijah and went back and stood on the bank of the
Jordan. [14]Then he took the cloak that had fallen
from him and struck the water with it. "Where
now is the LORD, the God of Elijah?" he asked.
When he struck the water, it divided to the right
and to the left, and he crossed over.
[15]The company of the prophets from Jericho,
who were watching, said, "The spirit of Elijah is
resting on Elisha." And they went to meet him
and bowed to the ground before him. [16]"Look,"
they said, "we your servants have fifty able men.
Let them go and look for your master. Perhaps
the Spirit of the LORD has picked him up and set
him down on some mountain or in some valley."
"No," Elisha replied, "do not send them."
[17]But they persisted until he was too ashamed
to refuse. So he said, "Send them." And they sent
fifty men, who searched for three days but did
not find him. [18]When they returned to Elisha,
who was staying in Jericho, he said to them,
"Didn't I tell you not to go?"

Healing of the Water

[19]The men of the city said to Elisha, "Look, our
lord, this town is well situated, as you can see,
but the water is bad and the land is unproductive."
[20]"Bring me a new bowl," he said, "and put
salt in it." So they brought it to him.
[21]Then he went out to the spring and threw
the salt into it, saying, "This is what the LORD
says: 'I have healed this water. Never again will
it cause death or make the land unproductive.' "
[22]And the water has remained wholesome to this
day, according to the word Elisha had spoken.

Elisha Is Jeered

[23]From there Elisha went up to Bethel. As he
was walking along the road, some youths came
out of the town and jeered at him. "Go on up, you
baldhead!" they said. "Go on up, you baldhead!"
[24]He turned around, looked at them and called
down a curse on them in the name of the LORD.
Then two bears came out of the woods and
mauled forty-two of the youths. [25]And he went
on to Mount Carmel and from there returned to
Samaria.

Moab Revolts

3 Joram[a] son of Ahab became king of Israel in
Samaria in the eighteenth year of Jehoshaphat king of Judah, and he reigned twelve years.
[2]He did evil in the eyes of the LORD, but not as
his father and mother had done. He got rid of the
sacred stone of Baal that his father had made.
[3]Nevertheless he clung to the sins of Jeroboam
son of Nebat, which he had caused Israel to commit; he did not turn away from them.
[4]Now Mesha king of Moab raised sheep, and
he had to supply the king of Israel with a hundred
thousand lambs and with the wool of a hundred
thousand rams. [5]But after Ahab died, the king of
Moab rebelled against the king of Israel. [6]So at
that time King Joram set out from Samaria and
mobilized all Israel. [7]He also sent this message to
Jehoshaphat king of Judah: "The king of Moab
has rebelled against me. Will you go with me to
fight against Moab?"
"I will go with you," he replied. "I am as you
are, my people as your people, my horses as your
horses."
[8]"By what route shall we attack?" he asked.
"Through the Desert of Edom," he answered.
[9]So the king of Israel set out with the king of
Judah and the king of Edom. After a roundabout
march of seven days, the army had no more water for themselves or for the animals with them.
[10]"What!" exclaimed the king of Israel. "Has
the LORD called us three kings together only to
hand us over to Moab?"
[11]But Jehoshaphat asked, "Is there no prophet
of the LORD here, that we may inquire of the
LORD through him?"
An officer of the king of Israel answered, "Elisha son of Shaphat is here. He used to pour water
on the hands of Elijah.[b]"
[12]Jehoshaphat said, "The word of the LORD is
with him." So the king of Israel and Jehoshaphat
and the king of Edom went down to him.
[13]Elisha said to the king of Israel, "What do we
have to do with each other? Go to the prophets
of your father and the prophets of your mother."
"No," the king of Israel answered, "because it
was the LORD who called us three kings together
to hand us over to Moab."
[14]Elisha said, "As surely as the LORD Almighty
lives, whom I serve, if I did not have respect
for the presence of Jehoshaphat king of Judah, I

[a] *1* Hebrew *Jehoram,* a variant of *Joram*; also in verse 6
[b] *11* That is, he was Elijah's personal servant.

would not look at you or even notice you. 15But now bring me a harpist."

While the harpist was playing, the hand of the LORD came upon Elisha 16and he said, "This is what the LORD says: Make this valley full of ditches. 17For this is what the LORD says: You will see neither wind nor rain, yet this valley will be filled with water, and you, your cattle and your other animals will drink. 18This is an easy thing in the eyes of the LORD; he will also hand Moab over to you. 19You will overthrow every fortified city and every major town. You will cut down every good tree, stop up all the springs, and ruin every good field with stones."

20The next morning, about the time for offering the sacrifice, there it was—water flowing from the direction of Edom! And the land was filled with water.

21Now all the Moabites had heard that the kings had come to fight against them; so every man, young and old, who could bear arms was called up and stationed on the border. 22When they got up early in the morning, the sun was shining on the water. To the Moabites across the way, the water looked red—like blood. 23"That's blood!" they said. "Those kings must have fought and slaughtered each other. Now to the plunder, Moab!"

24But when the Moabites came to the camp of Israel, the Israelites rose up and fought them until they fled. And the Israelites invaded the land and slaughtered the Moabites. 25They destroyed the towns, and each man threw a stone on every good field until it was covered. They stopped up all the springs and cut down every good tree. Only Kir Hareseth was left with its stones in place, but men armed with slings surrounded it and attacked it as well.

26When the king of Moab saw that the battle had gone against him, he took with him seven hundred swordsmen to break through to the king of Edom, but they failed. 27Then he took his firstborn son, who was to succeed him as king, and offered him as a sacrifice on the city wall. The fury against Israel was great; they withdrew and returned to their own land.

The Widow's Oil

4 The wife of a man from the company of the prophets cried out to Elisha, "Your servant my husband is dead, and you know that he revered the LORD. But now his creditor is coming to take my two boys as his slaves."

2Elisha replied to her, "How can I help you? Tell me, what do you have in your house?"

2 KINGS 4:1–7

1. As a kid did you receive an allowance? How much? How did it compare to what your friends got?
2. When it comes to money are you more of a spender or saver?
3. What's the primary source of your means right now: Job? Parents? None! Other?
4. Is there any connection between how you feel spiritually—rich to poor—and the balance in your bank account?
5. If your faith was a bucket of oil, how would you describe it: Bone dry? Running low? Getting refilled? Full and overflowing?
6. If God could work a miracle in your life right now, what would you want him to do?
7. Share prayer requests and close in prayer.

"Your servant has nothing there at all," she said, "except a little oil."

3Elisha said, "Go around and ask all your neighbors for empty jars. Don't ask for just a few. 4Then go inside and shut the door behind you and your sons. Pour oil into all the jars, and as each is filled, put it to one side."

5She left him and afterward shut the door behind her and her sons. They brought the jars

---

Elisha had recently succeeded Elijah as Israel's leading prophet. Like his predecessor, Elisha performed several miracles like the one in this story.

4:1 ***company of the prophets.*** Devoted religious communities that sprang up in the face of general indifference and apostasy. It seems likely that they were known as prophets because their religious practices (sometimes ecstatic) were called prophesying (1 Sam. 10:5–6,10–11). The relationship of the Lord's great prophets (such as Elisha) to these communities was understandably a close one, the Lord's prophets probably being their spiritual mentors. ***to take my two boys as his slaves.*** Servitude as a means of paying one's debt by labor was permitted in the Law of Moses (Lev. 25:39–41). It appears that this practice was much abused, even though the Law limited the term of such bondage and also required that those so held be treated as hired workers.

4:2–7 What seems like an elaborate method of meeting a financial need required the woman to put her faith into action following the prophet's instructions. She did not hesitate to respond in faith and obedience, and she saw God turn her limited resources into bountiful provisions.

4:4 ***shut the door behind you.*** The impending miracle was not intended to be a public sensation, but to demonstrate privately God's mercy and grace to this widow.

to her and she kept pouring. 6When all the jars
were full, she said to her son, "Bring me another
one."

But he replied, "There is not a jar left." Then
the oil stopped flowing.

7She went and told the man of God, and he
said, "Go, sell the oil and pay your debts. You and
your sons can live on what is left."

The Shunammite's Son Restored to Life

8One day Elisha went to Shunem. And a well-
to-do woman was there, who urged him to stay
for a meal. So whenever he came by, he stopped
there to eat. 9She said to her husband, "I know
that this man who often comes our way is a holy
man of God. 10Let's make a small room on the
roof and put in it a bed and a table, a chair and
a lamp for him. Then he can stay there whenever
he comes to us."

11One day when Elisha came, he went up to
his room and lay down there. 12He said to his
servant Gehazi, "Call the Shunammite." So he
called her, and she stood before him. 13Elisha
said to him, "Tell her, 'You have gone to all this
trouble for us. Now what can be done for you?
Can we speak on your behalf to the king or the
commander of the army?'"

She replied, "I have a home among my own
people."

14"What can be done for her?" Elisha asked.

Gehazi said, "Well, she has no son and her
husband is old."

15Then Elisha said, "Call her." So he called
her, and she stood in the doorway. 16"About this
time next year," Elisha said, "you will hold a son
in your arms."

"No, my lord," she objected. "Don't mislead
your servant, O man of God!"

17But the woman became pregnant, and the
next year about that same time she gave birth to
a son, just as Elisha had told her.

18The child grew, and one day he went out
to his father, who was with the reapers. 19"My
head! My head!" he said to his father.

His father told a servant, "Carry him to his
mother." 20After the servant had lifted him up
and carried him to his mother, the boy sat on her
lap until noon, and then he died. 21She went up
and laid him on the bed of the man of God, then
shut the door and went out.

22She called her husband and said, "Please
send me one of the servants and a donkey so I can
go to the man of God quickly and return."

23"Why go to him today?" he asked. "It's not
the New Moon or the Sabbath."

"It's all right," she said.

24She saddled the donkey and said to her servant, "Lead on; don't slow down for me unless I
tell you." 25So she set out and came to the man
of God at Mount Carmel.

When he saw her in the distance, the man of
God said to his servant Gehazi, "Look! There's
the Shunammite! 26Run to meet her and ask her,
'Are you all right? Is your husband all right? Is
your child all right?'"

"Everything is all right," she said.

27When she reached the man of God at the
mountain, she took hold of his feet. Gehazi came
over to push her away, but the man of God said,
"Leave her alone! She is in bitter distress, but the
LORD has hidden it from me and has not told me
why."

28"Did I ask you for a son, my lord?" she said.
"Didn't I tell you, 'Don't raise my hopes'?"

29Elisha said to Gehazi, "Tuck your cloak into
your belt, take my staff in your hand and run. If
you meet anyone, do not greet him, and if anyone
greets you, do not answer. Lay my staff on the
boy's face."

30But the child's mother said, "As surely as the
LORD lives and as you live, I will not leave you."
So he got up and followed her.

31Gehazi went on ahead and laid the staff on
the boy's face, but there was no sound or response. So Gehazi went back to meet Elisha and
told him, "The boy has not awakened."

32When Elisha reached the house, there was
the boy lying dead on his couch. 33He went in,
shut the door on the two of them and prayed to
the LORD. 34Then he got on the bed and lay upon
the boy, mouth to mouth, eyes to eyes, hands to
hands. As he stretched himself out upon him, the
boy's body grew warm. 35Elisha turned away and
walked back and forth in the room and then got
on the bed and stretched out upon him once
more. The boy sneezed seven times and opened
his eyes.

36Elisha summoned Gehazi and said, "Call the
Shunammite." And he did. When she came, he
said, "Take your son." 37She came in, fell at his
feet and bowed to the ground. Then she took her
son and went out.

Death in the Pot

38Elisha returned to Gilgal and there was a
famine in that region. While the company of the
prophets was meeting with him, he said to his
servant, "Put on the large pot and cook some
stew for these men."

39One of them went out into the fields to gather herbs and found a wild vine. He gathered some
of its gourds and filled the fold of his cloak. When
he returned, he cut them up into the pot of stew,
though no one knew what they were. 40The stew
was poured out for the men, but as they began to
eat it, they cried out, "O man of God, there is
death in the pot!" And they could not eat it.

41 Elisha said, "Get some flour." He put it into
the pot and said, "Serve it to the people to eat."
And there was nothing harmful in the pot.

Feeding of a Hundred

42 A man came from Baal Shalishah, bringing
the man of God twenty loaves of barley bread
baked from the first ripe grain, along with some
heads of new grain. "Give it to the people to eat,"
Elisha said.
43 "How can I set this before a hundred men?"
his servant asked.
But Elisha answered, "Give it to the people to
eat. For this is what the LORD says: 'They will eat
and have some left over.' " 44 Then he set it before
them, and they ate and had some left over, according to the word of the LORD.

Naaman Healed of Leprosy

5 Now Naaman was commander of the army of
the king of Aram. He was a great man in the
sight of his master and highly regarded, because
through him the LORD had given victory to Aram.
He was a valiant soldier, but he had leprosy.[a]
2 Now bands from Aram had gone out and had
taken captive a young girl from Israel, and she
served Naaman's wife. 3 She said to her mistress,
"If only my master would see the prophet who is
in Samaria! He would cure him of his leprosy."
4 Naaman went to his master and told him
what the girl from Israel had said. 5 "By all means,
go," the king of Aram replied. "I will send a letter
to the king of Israel." So Naaman left, taking with
him ten talents[b] of silver, six thousand shekels[c] of gold and ten sets of clothing. 6 The letter
that he took to the king of Israel read: "With this
letter I am sending my servant Naaman to you so
that you may cure him of his leprosy."
7 As soon as the king of Israel read the letter,
he tore his robes and said, "Am I God? Can I kill
and bring back to life? Why does this fellow send
someone to me to be cured of his leprosy? See
how he is trying to pick a quarrel with me!"
8 When Elisha the man of God heard that the
king of Israel had torn his robes, he sent him this
message: "Why have you torn your robes? Have
the man come to me and he will know that there
is a prophet in Israel." 9 So Naaman went with his
horses and chariots and stopped at the door of
Elisha's house. 10 Elisha sent a messenger to say
to him, "Go, wash yourself seven times in the
Jordan, and your flesh will be restored and you
will be cleansed."

2 KINGS 5:1–16

1. What is the sickest you have ever been?
2. Does your family have any "home remedies" to cure the hiccups, a cold or something else?
3. What is the closest you have come to seeing a physical healing?
4. Who is the Elisha in your life, the one who invited you to try God's way?
5. What did it take to convince you, like Naaman, that there is only one God?
6. Is your faith in God stronger today than it was one year ago?
7. Where do you need "healing" in your life? Close by praying together for each other.

11 But Naaman went away angry and said, "I
thought that he would surely come out to me and
stand and call on the name of the LORD his God,
wave his hand over the spot and cure me of my
leprosy. 12 Are not Abana and Pharpar, the rivers
of Damascus, better than any of the waters of
Israel? Couldn't I wash in them and be
cleansed?" So he turned and went off in a rage.

[a] *1* The Hebrew word was used for various diseases affecting the skin—not necessarily leprosy; also in verses 3, 6, 7, 11 and 27.
[b] *5* That is, about 750 pounds (about 340 kilograms) [c] *5* That is, about 150 pounds (about 70 kilograms)

When this story takes place, the people of Aram and Israel were officially at peace, though border skirmishes weren't unusual.

5:2 *a young girl from Israel.* In sharp contrast to the king in Israel (v. 7), this young girl held captive in Aram was very much aware of God's saving presence with his people through his servant Elisha, and she selflessly shared that knowledge with her Aramean captors.

5:6 *so that you may cure him of his leprosy.* The king of Aram assumed that the prophet described by the Israelite slave girl (vv. 2–3) was subject to the authority of the king and that his services could be bought with a large gift. He thought he could buy God's blessings with worldly wealth.

5:10 *wash yourself seven times in the Jordan.* The instruction is designed to demonstrate to Naaman that healing would come by the power of the God of Israel, but only if he obeyed the Lord's prophet. Naaman was to wash in the muddy waters of the Jordan River, demonstrating that there was no natural connection between the washing and the desired healing.

5:11 *wave his hand.* Naaman expected to be healed by the magical technique of the prophet rather than by God's power working in connection with his own obedience.

5:16 *I will not accept a thing.* Elisha did not seek monetary gain for proclaiming the word of the Lord. Naaman was healed solely by divine grace, not by Elisha's power.

13Naaman's servants went to him and said,
"My father, if the prophet had told you to do
some great thing, would you not have done it?
How much more, then, when he tells you, 'Wash
and be cleansed'!" 14So he went down and
dipped himself in the Jordan seven times, as the
man of God had told him, and his flesh was restored and became clean like that of a young boy.
15Then Naaman and all his attendants went
back to the man of God. He stood before him and
said, "Now I know that there is no God in all the
world except in Israel. Please accept now a gift
from your servant."
16The prophet answered, "As surely as the
LORD lives, whom I serve, I will not accept a
thing." And even though Naaman urged him, he
refused.
17"If you will not," said Naaman, "please let
me, your servant, be given as much earth as a
pair of mules can carry, for your servant will never again make burnt offerings and sacrifices to
any other god but the LORD. 18But may the LORD
forgive your servant for this one thing: When my
master enters the temple of Rimmon to bow
down and he is leaning on my arm and I bow
there also—when I bow down in the temple of
Rimmon, may the LORD forgive your servant for
this."
19"Go in peace," Elisha said.
After Naaman had traveled some distance,
20Gehazi, the servant of Elisha the man of God,
said to himself, "My master was too easy on Naaman, this Aramean, by not accepting from him
what he brought. As surely as the LORD lives, I
will run after him and get something from him."
21So Gehazi hurried after Naaman. When Naaman saw him running toward him, he got down
from the chariot to meet him. "Is everything all
right?" he asked.
22"Everything is all right," Gehazi answered.
"My master sent me to say, 'Two young men
from the company of the prophets have just come
to me from the hill country of Ephraim. Please
give them a talent[a] of silver and two sets of
clothing.'"
23"By all means, take two talents," said Naaman. He urged Gehazi to accept them, and then
tied up the two talents of silver in two bags, with
two sets of clothing. He gave them to two of his
servants, and they carried them ahead of Gehazi.
24When Gehazi came to the hill, he took the
things from the servants and put them away in
the house. He sent the men away and they left.
25Then he went in and stood before his master
Elisha.
"Where have you been, Gehazi?" Elisha asked.
"Your servant didn't go anywhere," Gehazi answered.
26But Elisha said to him, "Was not my spirit
with you when the man got down from his chariot to meet you? Is this the time to take money, or
to accept clothes, olive groves, vineyards, flocks,
herds, or menservants and maidservants? 27Naa-
man's leprosy will cling to you and to your
descendants forever." Then Gehazi went from
Elisha's presence and he was leprous, as white as
snow.

An Axhead Floats

6 The company of the prophets said to Elisha,
"Look, the place where we meet with you is
too small for us. 2Let us go to the Jordan, where
each of us can get a pole; and let us build a place
there for us to live."
And he said, "Go."
3Then one of them said, "Won't you please
come with your servants?"
"I will," Elisha replied. 4And he went with
them.
They went to the Jordan and began to cut
down trees. 5As one of them was cutting down a
tree, the iron axhead fell into the water. "Oh, my
lord," he cried out, "it was borrowed!"
6The man of God asked, "Where did it fall?"
When he showed him the place, Elisha cut a stick
and threw it there, and made the iron float. 7"Lift
it out," he said. Then the man reached out his
hand and took it.

Elisha Traps Blinded Arameans

8Now the king of Aram was at war with Israel.
After conferring with his officers, he said, "I will
set up my camp in such and such a place."
9The man of God sent word to the king of
Israel: "Beware of passing that place, because the
Arameans are going down there." 10So the king
of Israel checked on the place indicated by the
man of God. Time and again Elisha warned the
king, so that he was on his guard in such places.
11This enraged the king of Aram. He summoned his officers and demanded of them, "Will
you not tell me which of us is on the side of the
king of Israel?"
12"None of us, my lord the king," said one of
his officers, "but Elisha, the prophet who is in
Israel, tells the king of Israel the very words you
speak in your bedroom."
13"Go, find out where he is," the king ordered,
"so I can send men and capture him." The report
came back: "He is in Dothan." 14Then he sent
horses and chariots and a strong force there.
They went by night and surrounded the city.
15When the servant of the man of God got up

a22 That is, about 75 pounds (about 34 kilograms)

and went out early the next morning, an army with horses and chariots had surrounded the city. "Oh, my lord, what shall we do?" the servant asked.

2 Kings 6:8–23

1. Recall a time when you got really lost. How did you find your way?
2. Which of the five senses would be the worst to lose?
3. How would you feel if your bedroom (see v. 12) or telephone was bugged?
4. If you, like Elisha, had captured the enemy, what would you have done to your prisoners?
5. How much are you aware of the "angels" that surround you, protecting you from the evil one?
6. Elisha's kindness towards the enemy worked (see v. 23). In what relationship do you need to change strategy and apply some kindness?
7. Share something you are thankful for and close in prayer.

16 "Don't be afraid," the prophet answered. "Those who are with us are more than those who are with them."

17 And Elisha prayed, "O LORD, open his eyes so he may see." Then the LORD opened the servant's eyes, and he looked and saw the hills full of horses and chariots of fire all around Elisha.

18 As the enemy came down toward him, Elisha prayed to the LORD, "Strike these people with blindness." So he struck them with blindness, as Elisha had asked.

19 Elisha told them, "This is not the road and this is not the city. Follow me, and I will lead you to the man you are looking for." And he led them to Samaria.

20 After they entered the city, Elisha said, "LORD, open the eyes of these men so they can see." Then the LORD opened their eyes and they looked, and there they were, inside Samaria.

21 When the king of Israel saw them, he asked Elisha, "Shall I kill them, my father? Shall I kill them?"

22 "Do not kill them," he answered. "Would you kill men you have captured with your own sword or bow? Set food and water before them so that they may eat and drink and then go back to their master." 23 So he prepared a great feast for them, and after they had finished eating and drinking, he sent them away, and they returned to their master. So the bands from Aram stopped raiding Israel's territory.

Famine in Besieged Samaria

24 Some time later, Ben-Hadad king of Aram mobilized his entire army and marched up and laid siege to Samaria. 25 There was a great famine in the city; the siege lasted so long that a donkey's head sold for eighty shekels[a] of silver, and a quarter of a cab[b] of seed pods[c] for five shekels.[d]

26 As the king of Israel was passing by on the wall, a woman cried to him, "Help me, my lord the king!"

27 The king replied, "If the LORD does not help you, where can I get help for you? From the threshing floor? From the winepress?" 28 Then he asked her, "What's the matter?"

She answered, "This woman said to me, 'Give up your son so we may eat him today, and tomorrow we'll eat my son.' 29 So we cooked my son and ate him. The next day I said to her, 'Give up

[a]25 That is, about 2 pounds (about 1 kilogram) [b]25 That is, probably about 1/2 pint (about 0.3 liter) [c]25 Or *of dove's dung*
[d]25 That is, about 2 ounces (about 55 grams)

6:9 ***man of God.*** Elisha (see v. 10). ***king of Israel.*** Probably Joram (see 3:1; 9:24).

6:11 ***which of us is on the side ... of Israel?*** Repeated evidence that Israel possessed advance knowledge of Aramean military plans led the king of Aram to suspect that there was a traitor among his top officials.

6:16 ***Those who are with us are more than those who are with them.*** Elisha knew that there was greater strength in the unseen reality of the hosts of heaven than in the visible reality of the Aramean forces (see 2 Chron. 32:7–8; Ps. 34:7; 1 John 4:4).

6:17–18 ***saw the hills full of horses and chariots.*** In response to Elisha's prayer, his servant was able to see the protecting might of the heavenly hosts gathered about them (see Matt. 26:53). ***Strike these people with blindness.*** Elisha had prayed for the servant's eyes to be opened to the unseen reality of the heavenly hosts; now he prays for the eyes of the Aramean soldiers to be closed to earthly reality (see Gen. 19:11).

6:19–20 ***to the man.*** Technically, Elisha's statement was not an untruth, since Elisha accompanied them. God's power working through Elisha turned the intended captors into captives—inside the capital of Israel!

6:22 ***Do not kill them.*** In reality the Aramean soldiers had been taken captive by the power of the Lord, not by military means. God's purpose was to demonstrate to them and their king and to the Israelites and their king that Israel's national security ultimately was grounded in the Lord.

your son so we may eat him,' but she had hidden
him."
30When the king heard the woman's words,
he tore his robes. As he went along the wall, the
people looked, and there, underneath, he had
sackcloth on his body. 31He said, "May God deal
with me, be it ever so severely, if the head of
Elisha son of Shaphat remains on his shoulders
today!"
32Now Elisha was sitting in his house, and the
elders were sitting with him. The king sent a
messenger ahead, but before he arrived, Elisha
said to the elders, "Don't you see how this murderer is sending someone to cut off my head?
Look, when the messenger comes, shut the door
and hold it shut against him. Is not the sound of
his master's footsteps behind him?"
33While he was still talking to them, the messenger came down to him. And ⌞the king⌟ said,
"This disaster is from the LORD. Why should I
wait for the LORD any longer?"

7 Elisha said, "Hear the word of the LORD. This
is what the LORD says: About this time tomorrow, a seah[a] of flour will sell for a shekel[b]
and two seahs[c] of barley for a shekel at the gate
of Samaria."
2The officer on whose arm the king was leaning said to the man of God, "Look, even if the
LORD should open the floodgates of the heavens,
could this happen?"
"You will see it with your own eyes," answered Elisha, "but you will not eat any of it!"

The Siege Lifted

3Now there were four men with leprosy[d] at
the entrance of the city gate. They said to each
other, "Why stay here until we die? 4If we say,
'We'll go into the city'—the famine is there, and
we will die. And if we stay here, we will die. So
let's go over to the camp of the Arameans and
surrender. If they spare us, we live; if they kill us,
then we die."
5At dusk they got up and went to the camp of
the Arameans. When they reached the edge of
the camp, not a man was there, 6for the Lord had
caused the Arameans to hear the sound of chariots and horses and a great army, so that they said
to one another, "Look, the king of Israel has hired
the Hittite and Egyptian kings to attack us!" 7So
they got up and fled in the dusk and abandoned
their tents and their horses and donkeys. They
left the camp as it was and ran for their lives.
8The men who had leprosy reached the edge
of the camp and entered one of the tents. They
ate and drank, and carried away silver, gold and
clothes, and went off and hid them. They returned and entered another tent and took some
things from it and hid them also.
9Then they said to each other, "We're not doing right. This is a day of good news and we are
keeping it to ourselves. If we wait until daylight,
punishment will overtake us. Let's go at once and
report this to the royal palace."
10So they went and called out to the city gatekeepers and told them, "We went into the Aramean camp and not a man was there—not a
sound of anyone—only tethered horses and donkeys, and the tents left just as they were." 11The
gatekeepers shouted the news, and it was reported within the palace.
12The king got up in the night and said to his
officers, "I will tell you what the Arameans have
done to us. They know we are starving; so they
have left the camp to hide in the countryside,
thinking, 'They will surely come out, and then
we will take them alive and get into the city.'"
13One of his officers answered, "Have some
men take five of the horses that are left in the
city. Their plight will be like that of all the Israelites left here—yes, they will only be like all these
Israelites who are doomed. So let us send them to
find out what happened."
14So they selected two chariots with their
horses, and the king sent them after the Aramean
army. He commanded the drivers, "Go and find
out what has happened." 15They followed them
as far as the Jordan, and they found the whole
road strewn with the clothing and equipment the
Arameans had thrown away in their headlong
flight. So the messengers returned and reported
to the king. 16Then the people went out and plundered the camp of the Arameans. So a seah of
flour sold for a shekel, and two seahs of barley
sold for a shekel, as the LORD had said.
17Now the king had put the officer on whose
arm he leaned in charge of the gate, and the
people trampled him in the gateway, and he died,
just as the man of God had foretold when the
king came down to his house. 18It happened as
the man of God had said to the king: "About this
time tomorrow, a seah of flour will sell for a shekel and two seahs of barley for a shekel at the gate
of Samaria."
19The officer had said to the man of God,
"Look, even if the LORD should open the floodgates of the heavens, could this happen?" The
man of God had replied, "You will see it with
your own eyes, but you will not eat any of it!"
20And that is exactly what happened to him, for

[a]1 That is, probably about 7 quarts (about 7.3 liters); also in verses 16 and 18 [b]1 That is, about 2/5 ounce (about 11 grams); also in verses 16 and 18 [c]1 That is, probably about 13 quarts (about 15 liters); also in verses 16 and 18 [d]3 The Hebrew word is used for various diseases affecting the skin—not necessarily leprosy; also in verse 8.

the people trampled him in the gateway, and he died.

The Shunammite's Land Restored

8 Now Elisha had said to the woman whose son he had restored to life, "Go away with your family and stay for a while wherever you can, because the LORD has decreed a famine in the land that will last seven years." 2The woman proceeded to do as the man of God said. She and her family went away and stayed in the land of the Philistines seven years.

3At the end of the seven years she came back from the land of the Philistines and went to the king to beg for her house and land. 4The king was talking to Gehazi, the servant of the man of God, and had said, "Tell me about all the great things Elisha has done." 5Just as Gehazi was telling the king how Elisha had restored the dead to life, the woman whose son Elisha had brought back to life came to beg the king for her house and land.

Gehazi said, "This is the woman, my lord the king, and this is her son whom Elisha restored to life." 6The king asked the woman about it, and she told him.

Then he assigned an official to her case and said to him, "Give back everything that belonged to her, including all the income from her land from the day she left the country until now."

Hazael Murders Ben-Hadad

7Elisha went to Damascus, and Ben-Hadad king of Aram was ill. When the king was told, "The man of God has come all the way up here," 8he said to Hazael, "Take a gift with you and go to meet the man of God. Consult the LORD through him; ask him, 'Will I recover from this illness?' "

9Hazael went to meet Elisha, taking with him as a gift forty camel-loads of all the finest wares of Damascus. He went in and stood before him, and said, "Your son Ben-Hadad king of Aram has sent me to ask, 'Will I recover from this illness?' "

10Elisha answered, "Go and say to him, 'You will certainly recover'; but[a] the LORD has revealed to me that he will in fact die." 11He stared at him with a fixed gaze until Hazael felt ashamed. Then the man of God began to weep.

12"Why is my lord weeping?" asked Hazael.

"Because I know the harm you will do to the Israelites," he answered. "You will set fire to their fortified places, kill their young men with the sword, dash their little children to the ground, and rip open their pregnant women."

13Hazael said, "How could your servant, a mere dog, accomplish such a feat?"

"The LORD has shown me that you will become king of Aram," answered Elisha.

14Then Hazael left Elisha and returned to his master. When Ben-Hadad asked, "What did Elisha say to you?" Hazael replied, "He told me that you would certainly recover." 15But the next day he took a thick cloth, soaked it in water and spread it over the king's face, so that he died. Then Hazael succeeded him as king.

Jehoram King of Judah

16In the fifth year of Joram son of Ahab king of Israel, when Jehoshaphat was king of Judah, Jehoram son of Jehoshaphat began his reign as king of Judah. 17He was thirty-two years old when he became king, and he reigned in Jerusalem eight years. 18He walked in the ways of the kings of Israel, as the house of Ahab had done, for he married a daughter of Ahab. He did evil in the eyes of the LORD. 19Nevertheless, for the sake of his servant David, the LORD was not willing to destroy Judah. He had promised to maintain a lamp for David and his descendants forever.

20In the time of Jehoram, Edom rebelled against Judah and set up its own king. 21So Jehoram[b] went to Zair with all his chariots. The Edomites surrounded him and his chariot commanders, but he rose up and broke through by night; his army, however, fled back home. 22To this day Edom has been in rebellion against Judah. Libnah revolted at the same time.

23As for the other events of Jehoram's reign, and all he did, are they not written in the book of the annals of the kings of Judah? 24Jehoram rested with his fathers and was buried with them in the City of David. And Ahaziah his son succeeded him as king.

Ahaziah King of Judah

25In the twelfth year of Joram son of Ahab king of Israel, Ahaziah son of Jehoram king of Judah began to reign. 26Ahaziah was twenty-two years old when he became king, and he reigned in Jerusalem one year. His mother's name was Athaliah, a granddaughter of Omri king of Israel. 27He walked in the ways of the house of Ahab and did evil in the eyes of the LORD, as the house of Ahab had done, for he was related by marriage to Ahab's family.

28Ahaziah went with Joram son of Ahab to war against Hazael king of Aram at Ramoth Gilead. The Arameans wounded Joram; 29so King Joram returned to Jezreel to recover from the wounds the Arameans had inflicted on him at Ramoth[c] in his battle with Hazael king of Aram.

Then Ahaziah son of Jehoram king of Judah

[a] 10 The Hebrew may also be read *Go and say, 'You will certainly not recover,' for.* [b] 21 Hebrew *Joram,* a variant of *Jehoram;* also in verses 23 and 24 [c] 29 Hebrew *Ramah,* a variant of *Ramoth*

went down to Jezreel to see Joram son of Ahab, because he had been wounded.

Jehu Anointed King of Israel

9 The prophet Elisha summoned a man from the company of the prophets and said to him, "Tuck your cloak into your belt, take this flask of oil with you and go to Ramoth Gilead. 2When you get there, look for Jehu son of Jehoshaphat, the son of Nimshi. Go to him, get him away from his companions and take him into an inner room. 3Then take the flask and pour the oil on his head and declare, 'This is what the LORD says: I anoint you king over Israel.' Then open the door and run; don't delay!"

4So the young man, the prophet, went to Ramoth Gilead. 5When he arrived, he found the army officers sitting together. "I have a message for you, commander," he said.

"For which of us?" asked Jehu.

"For you, commander," he replied.

6Jehu got up and went into the house. Then the prophet poured the oil on Jehu's head and declared, "This is what the LORD, the God of Israel, says: 'I anoint you king over the LORD's people Israel. 7You are to destroy the house of Ahab your master, and I will avenge the blood of my servants the prophets and the blood of all the LORD's servants shed by Jezebel. 8The whole house of Ahab will perish. I will cut off from Ahab every last male in Israel—slave or free. 9I will make the house of Ahab like the house of Jeroboam son of Nebat and like the house of Baasha son of Ahijah. 10As for Jezebel, dogs will devour her on the plot of ground at Jezreel, and no one will bury her.'" Then he opened the door and ran.

11When Jehu went out to his fellow officers, one of them asked him, "Is everything all right? Why did this madman come to you?"

"You know the man and the sort of things he says," Jehu replied.

12"That's not true!" they said. "Tell us."

Jehu said, "Here is what he told me: 'This is what the LORD says: I anoint you king over Israel.'"

13They hurried and took their cloaks and spread them under him on the bare steps. Then they blew the trumpet and shouted, "Jehu is king!"

Jehu Kills Joram and Ahaziah

14So Jehu son of Jehoshaphat, the son of Nimshi, conspired against Joram. (Now Joram and all Israel had been defending Ramoth Gilead against Hazael king of Aram, 15but King Joram[a] had returned to Jezreel to recover from the wounds the Arameans had inflicted on him in the battle with Hazael king of Aram.) Jehu said, "If this is the way you feel, don't let anyone slip out of the city to go and tell the news in Jezreel." 16Then he got into his chariot and rode to Jezreel, because Joram was resting there and Ahaziah king of Judah had gone down to see him.

17When the lookout standing on the tower in Jezreel saw Jehu's troops approaching, he called out, "I see some troops coming."

"Get a horseman," Joram ordered. "Send him to meet them and ask, 'Do you come in peace?'"

18The horseman rode off to meet Jehu and said, "This is what the king says: 'Do you come in peace?'"

"What do you have to do with peace?" Jehu replied. "Fall in behind me."

The lookout reported, "The messenger has reached them, but he isn't coming back."

19So the king sent out a second horseman. When he came to them he said, "This is what the king says: 'Do you come in peace?'"

Jehu replied, "What do you have to do with peace? Fall in behind me."

20The lookout reported, "He has reached them, but he isn't coming back either. The driving is like that of Jehu son of Nimshi—he drives like a madman."

21"Hitch up my chariot," Joram ordered. And when it was hitched up, Joram king of Israel and Ahaziah king of Judah rode out, each in his own chariot, to meet Jehu. They met him at the plot of ground that had belonged to Naboth the Jezreelite. 22When Joram saw Jehu he asked, "Have you come in peace, Jehu?"

"How can there be peace," Jehu replied, "as long as all the idolatry and witchcraft of your mother Jezebel abound?"

23Joram turned about and fled, calling out to Ahaziah, "Treachery, Ahaziah!"

24Then Jehu drew his bow and shot Joram between the shoulders. The arrow pierced his heart and he slumped down in his chariot. 25Jehu said to Bidkar, his chariot officer, "Pick him up and throw him on the field that belonged to Naboth the Jezreelite. Remember how you and I were riding together in chariots behind Ahab his father when the LORD made this prophecy about him: 26'Yesterday I saw the blood of Naboth and the blood of his sons, declares the LORD, and I will surely make you pay for it on this plot of ground, declares the LORD.'[b] Now then, pick him up and throw him on that plot, in accordance with the word of the LORD."

27When Ahaziah king of Judah saw what had happened, he fled up the road to Beth Haggan.[c]

[a] 15 Hebrew *Jehoram,* a variant of *Joram;* also in verses 17 and 21-24 [b] 26 See 1 Kings 21:19. [c] 27 Or *fled by way of the garden house*

Jehu chased him, shouting, "Kill him too!" They
wounded him in his chariot on the way up to Gur
near Ibleam, but he escaped to Megiddo and died
there. 28His servants took him by chariot to Jerusalem and buried him with his fathers in his
tomb in the City of David. 29(In the eleventh year
of Joram son of Ahab, Ahaziah had become king
of Judah.)

Jezebel Killed

30Then Jehu went to Jezreel. When Jezebel
heard about it, she painted her eyes, arranged her
hair and looked out of a window. 31As Jehu entered the gate, she asked, "Have you come in
peace, Zimri, you murderer of your master?"[a]
32He looked up at the window and called out,
"Who is on my side? Who?" Two or three eunuchs looked down at him. 33"Throw her down!"
Jehu said. So they threw her down, and some of
her blood spattered the wall and the horses as
they trampled her underfoot.
34Jehu went in and ate and drank. "Take care
of that cursed woman," he said, "and bury her,
for she was a king's daughter." 35But when they
went out to bury her, they found nothing except
her skull, her feet and her hands. 36They went
back and told Jehu, who said, "This is the word
of the LORD that he spoke through his servant
Elijah the Tishbite: On the plot of ground at Jezreel dogs will devour Jezebel's flesh.[b] 37Jezebel's
body will be like refuse on the ground in the plot
at Jezreel, so that no one will be able to say, 'This
is Jezebel.'"

Ahab's Family Killed

10 Now there were in Samaria seventy sons
of the house of Ahab. So Jehu wrote letters and sent them to Samaria: to the officials of
Jezreel,[c] to the elders and to the guardians of
Ahab's children. He said, 2"As soon as this letter
reaches you, since your master's sons are with
you and you have chariots and horses, a fortified
city and weapons, 3choose the best and most
worthy of your master's sons and set him on his
father's throne. Then fight for your master's
house."
4But they were terrified and said, "If two kings
could not resist him, how can we?"
5So the palace administrator, the city governor, the elders and the guardians sent this message to Jehu: "We are your servants and we will
do anything you say. We will not appoint anyone
as king; you do whatever you think best."
6Then Jehu wrote them a second letter, saying,
"If you are on my side and will obey me, take the
heads of your master's sons and come to me in
Jezreel by this time tomorrow."
Now the royal princes, seventy of them, were
with the leading men of the city, who were rear-
ing them. 7When the letter arrived, these men
took the princes and slaughtered all seventy of
them. They put their heads in baskets and sent
them to Jehu in Jezreel. 8When the messenger
arrived, he told Jehu, "They have brought the
heads of the princes."
Then Jehu ordered, "Put them in two piles at
the entrance of the city gate until morning."
9The next morning Jehu went out. He stood
before all the people and said, "You are innocent.
It was I who conspired against my master and
killed him, but who killed all these? 10Know
then, that not a word the LORD has spoken
against the house of Ahab will fail. The LORD has
done what he promised through his servant Elijah." 11So Jehu killed everyone in Jezreel who
remained of the house of Ahab, as well as all his
chief men, his close friends and his priests, leaving him no survivor.
12Jehu then set out and went toward Samaria.
At Beth Eked of the Shepherds, 13he met some
relatives of Ahaziah king of Judah and asked,
"Who are you?"
They said, "We are relatives of Ahaziah, and
we have come down to greet the families of the
king and of the queen mother."
14"Take them alive!" he ordered. So they took
them alive and slaughtered them by the well of
Beth Eked—forty-two men. He left no survivor.
15After he left there, he came upon Jehonadab
son of Recab, who was on his way to meet him.
Jehu greeted him and said, "Are you in accord
with me, as I am with you?"
"I am," Jehonadab answered.
"If so," said Jehu, "give me your hand." So he
did, and Jehu helped him up into the chariot.
16Jehu said, "Come with me and see my zeal for
the LORD." Then he had him ride along in his
chariot.
17When Jehu came to Samaria, he killed all
who were left there of Ahab's family; he destroyed them, according to the word of the LORD
spoken to Elijah.

Ministers of Baal Killed

18Then Jehu brought all the people together
and said to them, "Ahab served Baal a little; Jehu
will serve him much. 19Now summon all the
prophets of Baal, all his ministers and all his
priests. See that no one is missing, because I am
going to hold a great sacrifice for Baal. Anyone
who fails to come will no longer live." But Jehu

[a] 31 Or *"Did Zimri have peace, who murdered his master?"* [b] 36 See 1 Kings 21:23. [c] 1 Hebrew; some Septuagint manuscripts and Vulgate *of the city*

was acting deceptively in order to destroy the
ministers of Baal.
20 Jehu said, "Call an assembly in honor of
Baal." So they proclaimed it. 21 Then he sent
word throughout Israel, and all the ministers of
Baal came; not one stayed away. They crowded
into the temple of Baal until it was full from one
end to the other. 22 And Jehu said to the keeper of
the wardrobe, "Bring robes for all the ministers
of Baal." So he brought out robes for them.
23 Then Jehu and Jehonadab son of Recab went
into the temple of Baal. Jehu said to the ministers
of Baal, "Look around and see that no servants of
the LORD are here with you—only ministers of
Baal." 24 So they went in to make sacrifices and
burnt offerings. Now Jehu had posted eighty men
outside with this warning: "If one of you lets any
of the men I am placing in your hands escape, it
will be your life for his life."
25 As soon as Jehu had finished making the
burnt offering, he ordered the guards and officers: "Go in and kill them; let no one escape." So
they cut them down with the sword. The guards
and officers threw the bodies out and then entered the inner shrine of the temple of Baal.
26 They brought the sacred stone out of the temple of Baal and burned it. 27 They demolished the
sacred stone of Baal and tore down the temple of
Baal, and people have used it for a latrine to this
day.
28 So Jehu destroyed Baal worship in Israel.
29 However, he did not turn away from the sins of
Jeroboam son of Nebat, which he had caused Israel to commit—the worship of the golden calves
at Bethel and Dan.
30 The LORD said to Jehu, "Because you have
done well in accomplishing what is right in my
eyes and have done to the house of Ahab all I had
in mind to do, your descendants will sit on the
throne of Israel to the fourth generation." 31 Yet
Jehu was not careful to keep the law of the LORD,
the God of Israel, with all his heart. He did not
turn away from the sins of Jeroboam, which he
had caused Israel to commit.
32 In those days the LORD began to reduce the
size of Israel. Hazael overpowered the Israelites
throughout their territory 33 east of the Jordan in
all the land of Gilead (the region of Gad, Reuben
and Manasseh), from Aroer by the Arnon Gorge
through Gilead to Bashan.
34 As for the other events of Jehu's reign, all he
did, and all his achievements, are they not written in the book of the annals of the kings of
Israel?
35 Jehu rested with his fathers and was buried
in Samaria. And Jehoahaz his son succeeded him
as king. 36 The time that Jehu reigned over Israel
in Samaria was twenty-eight years.

Athaliah and Joash

11 When Athaliah the mother of Ahaziah
saw that her son was dead, she proceeded
to destroy the whole royal family. 2 But Jehosheba, the daughter of King Jehoram[a] and sister of
Ahaziah, took Joash son of Ahaziah and stole him
away from among the royal princes, who were
about to be murdered. She put him and his nurse
in a bedroom to hide him from Athaliah; so he
was not killed. 3 He remained hidden with his
nurse at the temple of the LORD for six years
while Athaliah ruled the land.
4 In the seventh year Jehoiada sent for the commanders of units of a hundred, the Carites and
the guards and had them brought to him at the
temple of the LORD. He made a covenant with
them and put them under oath at the temple of
the LORD. Then he showed them the king's son.
5 He commanded them, saying, "This is what you
are to do: You who are in the three companies
that are going on duty on the Sabbath—a third of
you guarding the royal palace, 6 a third at the Sur
Gate, and a third at the gate behind the guard,
who take turns guarding the temple— 7 and you
who are in the other two companies that normally go off Sabbath duty are all to guard the temple
for the king. 8 Station yourselves around the king,
each man with his weapon in his hand. Anyone
who approaches your ranks[b] must be put to
death. Stay close to the king wherever he goes."
9 The commanders of units of a hundred did
just as Jehoiada the priest ordered. Each one took
his men—those who were going on duty on the
Sabbath and those who were going off duty—and
came to Jehoiada the priest. 10 Then he gave the
commanders the spears and shields that had belonged to King David and that were in the temple
of the LORD. 11 The guards, each with his weapon
in his hand, stationed themselves around the
king—near the altar and the temple, from the
south side to the north side of the temple.
12 Jehoiada brought out the king's son and put
the crown on him; he presented him with a copy
of the covenant and proclaimed him king. They
anointed him, and the people clapped their hands
and shouted, "Long live the king!"
13 When Athaliah heard the noise made by the
guards and the people, she went to the people at
the temple of the LORD. 14 She looked and there
was the king, standing by the pillar, as the custom was. The officers and the trumpeters were
beside the king, and all the people of the land
were rejoicing and blowing trumpets. Then Atha-

[a] 2 Hebrew *Joram*, a variant of *Jehoram* [b] 8 Or *approaches the precincts*

liah tore her robes and called out, "Treason! Treason!"

15 Jehoiada the priest ordered the commanders of units of a hundred, who were in charge of the troops: "Bring her out between the ranks[a] and put to the sword anyone who follows her." For the priest had said, "She must not be put to death in the temple of the LORD." 16 So they seized her as she reached the place where the horses enter the palace grounds, and there she was put to death.

17 Jehoiada then made a covenant between the LORD and the king and people that they would be the LORD's people. He also made a covenant between the king and the people. 18 All the people of the land went to the temple of Baal and tore it down. They smashed the altars and idols to pieces and killed Mattan the priest of Baal in front of the altars.

Then Jehoiada the priest posted guards at the temple of the LORD. 19 He took with him the commanders of hundreds, the Carites, the guards and all the people of the land, and together they brought the king down from the temple of the LORD and went into the palace, entering by way of the gate of the guards. The king then took his place on the royal throne, 20 and all the people of the land rejoiced. And the city was quiet, because Athaliah had been slain with the sword at the palace.

21 Joash[b] was seven years old when he began to reign.

Joash Repairs the Temple

12 In the seventh year of Jehu, Joash[c] became king, and he reigned in Jerusalem forty years. His mother's name was Zibiah; she was from Beersheba. 2 Joash did what was right in the eyes of the LORD all the years Jehoiada the priest instructed him. 3 The high places, however, were not removed; the people continued to offer sacrifices and burn incense there.

4 Joash said to the priests, "Collect all the money that is brought as sacred offerings to the temple of the LORD—the money collected in the census, the money received from personal vows and the money brought voluntarily to the temple. 5 Let every priest receive the money from one of the treasurers, and let it be used to repair whatever damage is found in the temple."

6 But by the twenty-third year of King Joash the priests still had not repaired the temple. 7 Therefore King Joash summoned Jehoiada the priest and the other priests and asked them, "Why aren't you repairing the damage done to the temple? Take no more money from your treasurers, but hand it over for repairing the temple." 8 The priests agreed that they would not collect any more money from the people and that they would not repair the temple themselves.

9 Jehoiada the priest took a chest and bored a hole in its lid. He placed it beside the altar, on the right side as one enters the temple of the LORD. The priests who guarded the entrance put into the chest all the money that was brought to the temple of the LORD. 10 Whenever they saw that there was a large amount of money in the chest, the royal secretary and the high priest came, counted the money that had been brought into the temple of the LORD and put it into bags. 11 When the amount had been determined, they gave the money to the men appointed to supervise the work on the temple. With it they paid those who worked on the temple of the LORD—the carpenters and builders, 12 the masons and stonecutters. They purchased timber and dressed stone for the repair of the temple of the LORD, and met all the other expenses of restoring the temple.

13 The money brought into the temple was not spent for making silver basins, wick trimmers, sprinkling bowls, trumpets or any other articles of gold or silver for the temple of the LORD; 14 it was paid to the workmen, who used it to repair the temple. 15 They did not require an accounting from those to whom they gave the money to pay the workers, because they acted with complete honesty. 16 The money from the guilt offerings and sin offerings was not brought into the temple of the LORD; it belonged to the priests.

17 About this time Hazael king of Aram went up and attacked Gath and captured it. Then he turned to attack Jerusalem. 18 But Joash king of Judah took all the sacred objects dedicated by his fathers—Jehoshaphat, Jehoram and Ahaziah, the kings of Judah—and the gifts he himself had dedicated and all the gold found in the treasuries of the temple of the LORD and of the royal palace, and he sent them to Hazael king of Aram, who then withdrew from Jerusalem.

19 As for the other events of the reign of Joash, and all he did, are they not written in the book of the annals of the kings of Judah? 20 His officials conspired against him and assassinated him at Beth Millo, on the road down to Silla. 21 The officials who murdered him were Jozabad son of Shimeath and Jehozabad son of Shomer. He died and was buried with his fathers in the City of David. And Amaziah his son succeeded him as king.

[a] *15* Or *out from the precincts* [b] *21* Hebrew *Jehoash,* a variant of *Joash* [c] *1* Hebrew *Jehoash,* a variant of *Joash*; also in verses 2, 4, 6, 7 and 18

Jehoahaz King of Israel

13 In the twenty-third year of Joash son of Ahaziah king of Judah, Jehoahaz son of Jehu became king of Israel in Samaria, and he reigned seventeen years. 2He did evil in the eyes of the LORD by following the sins of Jeroboam son of Nebat, which he had caused Israel to commit, and he did not turn away from them. 3So the LORD's anger burned against Israel, and for a long time he kept them under the power of Hazael king of Aram and Ben-Hadad his son.

4Then Jehoahaz sought the LORD's favor, and the LORD listened to him, for he saw how severely the king of Aram was oppressing Israel. 5The LORD provided a deliverer for Israel, and they escaped from the power of Aram. So the Israelites lived in their own homes as they had before. 6But they did not turn away from the sins of the house of Jeroboam, which he had caused Israel to commit; they continued in them. Also, the Asherah pole[a] remained standing in Samaria.

7Nothing had been left of the army of Jehoahaz except fifty horsemen, ten chariots and ten thousand foot soldiers, for the king of Aram had destroyed the rest and made them like the dust at threshing time.

8As for the other events of the reign of Jehoahaz, all he did and his achievements, are they not written in the book of the annals of the kings of Israel? 9Jehoahaz rested with his fathers and was buried in Samaria. And Jehoash[b] his son succeeded him as king.

Jehoash King of Israel

10In the thirty-seventh year of Joash king of Judah, Jehoash son of Jehoahaz became king of Israel in Samaria, and he reigned sixteen years. 11He did evil in the eyes of the LORD and did not turn away from any of the sins of Jeroboam son of Nebat, which he had caused Israel to commit; he continued in them.

12As for the other events of the reign of Jehoash, all he did and his achievements, including his war against Amaziah king of Judah, are they not written in the book of the annals of the kings of Israel? 13Jehoash rested with his fathers, and Jeroboam succeeded him on the throne. Jehoash was buried in Samaria with the kings of Israel.

14Now Elisha was suffering from the illness from which he died. Jehoash king of Israel went down to see him and wept over him. "My father! My father!" he cried. "The chariots and horsemen of Israel!"

15Elisha said, "Get a bow and some arrows," and he did so. 16"Take the bow in your hands," he said to the king of Israel. When he had taken it, Elisha put his hands on the king's hands.

17"Open the east window," he said, and he opened it. "Shoot!" Elisha said, and he shot. "The LORD's arrow of victory, the arrow of victory over Aram!" Elisha declared. "You will completely destroy the Arameans at Aphek."

18Then he said, "Take the arrows," and the king took them. Elisha told him, "Strike the ground." He struck it three times and stopped. 19The man of God was angry with him and said, "You should have struck the ground five or six times; then you would have defeated Aram and completely destroyed it. But now you will defeat it only three times."

20Elisha died and was buried.

Now Moabite raiders used to enter the country every spring. 21Once while some Israelites were burying a man, suddenly they saw a band of raiders; so they threw the man's body into Elisha's tomb. When the body touched Elisha's bones, the man came to life and stood up on his feet.

22Hazael king of Aram oppressed Israel throughout the reign of Jehoahaz. 23But the LORD was gracious to them and had compassion and showed concern for them because of his covenant with Abraham, Isaac and Jacob. To this day he has been unwilling to destroy them or banish them from his presence.

24Hazael king of Aram died, and Ben-Hadad his son succeeded him as king. 25Then Jehoash son of Jehoahaz recaptured from Ben-Hadad son of Hazael the towns he had taken in battle from his father Jehoahaz. Three times Jehoash defeated him, and so he recovered the Israelite towns.

Amaziah King of Judah

14 In the second year of Jehoash[c] son of Jehoahaz king of Israel, Amaziah son of Joash king of Judah began to reign. 2He was twenty-five years old when he became king, and he reigned in Jerusalem twenty-nine years. His mother's name was Jehoaddin; she was from Jerusalem. 3He did what was right in the eyes of the LORD, but not as his father David had done. In everything he followed the example of his father Joash. 4The high places, however, were not removed; the people continued to offer sacrifices and burn incense there.

5After the kingdom was firmly in his grasp, he executed the officials who had murdered his father the king. 6Yet he did not put the sons of the assassins to death, in accordance with what is written in the Book of the Law of Moses where the LORD commanded: "Fathers shall not be put to death for their children, nor children put to

a 6 That is, a symbol of the goddess Asherah; here and elsewhere in 2 Kings *b* 9 Hebrew *Joash,* a variant of *Jehoash*; also in verses 12-14 and 25 *c* 1 Hebrew *Joash,* a variant of *Jehoash*; also in verses 13, 23 and 27 death for their fathers; each is to die for his own sins."[a]

7He was the one who defeated ten thousand Edomites in the Valley of Salt and captured Sela in battle, calling it Joktheel, the name it has to this day.

8Then Amaziah sent messengers to Jehoash son of Jehoahaz, the son of Jehu, king of Israel, with the challenge: "Come, meet me face to face."

9But Jehoash king of Israel replied to Amaziah king of Judah: "A thistle in Lebanon sent a message to a cedar in Lebanon, 'Give your daughter to my son in marriage.' Then a wild beast in Lebanon came along and trampled the thistle underfoot. 10You have indeed defeated Edom and now you are arrogant. Glory in your victory, but stay at home! Why ask for trouble and cause your own downfall and that of Judah also?"

11Amaziah, however, would not listen, so Jehoash king of Israel attacked. He and Amaziah king of Judah faced each other at Beth Shemesh in Judah. 12Judah was routed by Israel, and every man fled to his home. 13Jehoash king of Israel captured Amaziah king of Judah, the son of Joash, the son of Ahaziah, at Beth Shemesh. Then Jehoash went to Jerusalem and broke down the wall of Jerusalem from the Ephraim Gate to the Corner Gate—a section about six hundred feet long.[b] 14He took all the gold and silver and all the articles found in the temple of the LORD and in the treasuries of the royal palace. He also took hostages and returned to Samaria.

15As for the other events of the reign of Jehoash, what he did and his achievements, including his war against Amaziah king of Judah, are they not written in the book of the annals of the kings of Israel? 16Jehoash rested with his fathers and was buried in Samaria with the kings of Israel. And Jeroboam his son succeeded him as king.

17Amaziah son of Joash king of Judah lived for fifteen years after the death of Jehoash son of Jehoahaz king of Israel. 18As for the other events of Amaziah's reign, are they not written in the book of the annals of the kings of Judah?

19They conspired against him in Jerusalem, and he fled to Lachish, but they sent men after him to Lachish and killed him there. 20He was brought back by horse and was buried in Jerusalem with his fathers, in the City of David.

21Then all the people of Judah took Azariah,[c] who was sixteen years old, and made him king in place of his father Amaziah. 22He was the one who rebuilt Elath and restored it to Judah after Amaziah rested with his fathers.

Jeroboam II King of Israel

23In the fifteenth year of Amaziah son of Joash king of Judah, Jeroboam son of Jehoash king of Israel became king in Samaria, and he reigned forty-one years. 24He did evil in the eyes of the LORD and did not turn away from any of the sins of Jeroboam son of Nebat, which he had caused Israel to commit. 25He was the one who restored the boundaries of Israel from Lebo[d] Hamath to the Sea of the Arabah,[e] in accordance with the word of the LORD, the God of Israel, spoken through his servant Jonah son of Amittai, the prophet from Gath Hepher.

26The LORD had seen how bitterly everyone in Israel, whether slave or free, was suffering; there was no one to help them. 27And since the LORD had not said he would blot out the name of Israel from under heaven, he saved them by the hand of Jeroboam son of Jehoash.

28As for the other events of Jeroboam's reign, all he did, and his military achievements, including how he recovered for Israel both Damascus and Hamath, which had belonged to Yaudi,[f] are they not written in the book of the annals of the kings of Israel? 29Jeroboam rested with his fathers, the kings of Israel. And Zechariah his son succeeded him as king.

Azariah King of Judah

15 In the twenty-seventh year of Jeroboam king of Israel, Azariah son of Amaziah king of Judah began to reign. 2He was sixteen years old when he became king, and he reigned in Jerusalem fifty-two years. His mother's name was Jecoliah; she was from Jerusalem. 3He did what was right in the eyes of the LORD, just as his father Amaziah had done. 4The high places, however, were not removed; the people continued to offer sacrifices and burn incense there.

5The LORD afflicted the king with leprosy[g] until the day he died, and he lived in a separate house.[h] Jotham the king's son had charge of the palace and governed the people of the land.

6As for the other events of Azariah's reign, and all he did, are they not written in the book of the annals of the kings of Judah? 7Azariah rested with his fathers and was buried near them in the City of David. And Jotham his son succeeded him as king.

Zechariah King of Israel

8In the thirty-eighth year of Azariah king of Judah, Zechariah son of Jeroboam became king of Israel in Samaria, and he reigned six months. 9He did evil in the eyes of the LORD, as his fathers had

[a] 6 Deut. 24:16 [b] 13 Hebrew *four hundred cubits* (about 180 meters) [c] 21 Also called *Uzziah* [d] 25 Or *from the entrance to* [e] 25 That is, the Dead Sea [f] 28 Or *Judah* [g] 5 The Hebrew word was used for various diseases affecting the skin—not necessarily leprosy. [h] 5 Or *in a house where he was relieved of responsibility*

done. He did not turn away from the sins of Jeroboam son of Nebat, which he had caused Israel to
commit.
10 Shallum son of Jabesh conspired against
Zechariah. He attacked him in front of the people,[a] assassinated him and succeeded him as
king. 11 The other events of Zechariah's reign are
written in the book of the annals of the kings of
Israel. 12 So the word of the LORD spoken to Jehu
was fulfilled: "Your descendants will sit on the
throne of Israel to the fourth generation."[b]

Shallum King of Israel

13 Shallum son of Jabesh became king in the
thirty-ninth year of Uzziah king of Judah, and he
reigned in Samaria one month. 14 Then Menahem
son of Gadi went from Tirzah up to Samaria. He
attacked Shallum son of Jabesh in Samaria, assassinated him and succeeded him as king.
15 The other events of Shallum's reign, and the
conspiracy he led, are written in the book of the
annals of the kings of Israel.
16 At that time Menahem, starting out from Tirzah, attacked Tiphsah and everyone in the city
and its vicinity, because they refused to open
their gates. He sacked Tiphsah and ripped open
all the pregnant women.

Menahem King of Israel

17 In the thirty-ninth year of Azariah king of
Judah, Menahem son of Gadi became king of Israel, and he reigned in Samaria ten years. 18 He did
evil in the eyes of the LORD. During his entire
reign he did not turn away from the sins of Jeroboam son of Nebat, which he had caused Israel to
commit.
19 Then Pul[c] king of Assyria invaded the land,
and Menahem gave him a thousand talents[d] of
silver to gain his support and strengthen his own
hold on the kingdom. 20 Menahem exacted this
money from Israel. Every wealthy man had to
contribute fifty shekels[e] of silver to be given to
the king of Assyria. So the king of Assyria withdrew and stayed in the land no longer.
21 As for the other events of Menahem's reign,
and all he did, are they not written in the book of
the annals of the kings of Israel? 22 Menahem rested with his fathers. And Pekahiah his son succeeded him as king.

Pekahiah King of Israel

23 In the fiftieth year of Azariah king of Judah,
Pekahiah son of Menahem became king of Israel
in Samaria, and he reigned two years. 24 Pekahiah
did evil in the eyes of the LORD. He did not turn
away from the sins of Jeroboam son of Nebat,
which he had caused Israel to commit. 25 One of
his chief officers, Pekah son of Remaliah, conspired against him. Taking fifty men of Gilead
with him, he assassinated Pekahiah, along with
Argob and Arieh, in the citadel of the royal palace
at Samaria. So Pekah killed Pekahiah and succeeded him as king.
26 The other events of Pekahiah's reign, and all
he did, are written in the book of the annals of
the kings of Israel.

Pekah King of Israel

27 In the fifty-second year of Azariah king of
Judah, Pekah son of Remaliah became king of
Israel in Samaria, and he reigned twenty years.
28 He did evil in the eyes of the LORD. He did not
turn away from the sins of Jeroboam son of Nebat, which he had caused Israel to commit.
29 In the time of Pekah king of Israel, Tiglath-
Pileser king of Assyria came and took Ijon, Abel
Beth Maacah, Janoah, Kedesh and Hazor. He took
Gilead and Galilee, including all the land of
Naphtali, and deported the people to Assyria.
30 Then Hoshea son of Elah conspired against Pekah son of Remaliah. He attacked and assassinated him, and then succeeded him as king in the
twentieth year of Jotham son of Uzziah.
31 As for the other events of Pekah's reign, and
all he did, are they not written in the book of the
annals of the kings of Israel?

Jotham King of Judah

32 In the second year of Pekah son of Remaliah
king of Israel, Jotham son of Uzziah king of Judah
began to reign. 33 He was twenty-five years old
when he became king, and he reigned in Jerusalem sixteen years. His mother's name was Jeru-
sha daughter of Zadok. 34 He did what was right in
the eyes of the LORD, just as his father Uzziah had
done. 35 The high places, however, were not removed; the people continued to offer sacrifices
and burn incense there. Jotham rebuilt the Upper
Gate of the temple of the LORD.
36 As for the other events of Jotham's reign,
and what he did, are they not written in the book
of the annals of the kings of Judah? 37 (In those
days the LORD began to send Rezin king of Aram
and Pekah son of Remaliah against Judah.) 38 Jotham rested with his fathers and was buried with
them in the City of David, the city of his father.
And Ahaz his son succeeded him as king.

Ahaz King of Judah

16 In the seventeenth year of Pekah son of
Remaliah, Ahaz son of Jotham king of Judah began to reign. 2 Ahaz was twenty years old

[a] *10* Hebrew; some Septuagint manuscripts *in Ibleam* [b] *12* 2 Kings 10:30 [c] *19* Also called *Tiglath-Pileser* [d] *19* That is, about 37 tons (about 34 metric tons) [e] *20* That is, about 1 1/4 pounds (about 0.6 kilogram)

when he became king, and he reigned in Jerusalem sixteen years. Unlike David his father, he did
not do what was right in the eyes of the LORD his
God. 3He walked in the ways of the kings of Israel
and even sacrificed his son in[a] the fire, following the detestable ways of the nations the LORD
had driven out before the Israelites. 4He offered
sacrifices and burned incense at the high places,
on the hilltops and under every spreading tree.
5Then Rezin king of Aram and Pekah son of
Remaliah king of Israel marched up to fight
against Jerusalem and besieged Ahaz, but they
could not overpower him. 6At that time, Rezin
king of Aram recovered Elath for Aram by driving
out the men of Judah. Edomites then moved into
Elath and have lived there to this day.
7Ahaz sent messengers to say to Tiglath-
Pileser king of Assyria, "I am your servant and
vassal. Come up and save me out of the hand of
the king of Aram and of the king of Israel, who
are attacking me." 8And Ahaz took the silver and
gold found in the temple of the LORD and in the
treasuries of the royal palace and sent it as a gift
to the king of Assyria. 9The king of Assyria com-
plied by attacking Damascus and capturing it. He
deported its inhabitants to Kir and put Rezin to
death.
10Then King Ahaz went to Damascus to meet
Tiglath-Pileser king of Assyria. He saw an altar in
Damascus and sent to Uriah the priest a sketch of
the altar, with detailed plans for its construction.
11So Uriah the priest built an altar in accordance
with all the plans that King Ahaz had sent from
Damascus and finished it before King Ahaz returned. 12When the king came back from Damascus and saw the altar, he approached it and presented offerings[b] on it. 13He offered up his
burnt offering and grain offering, poured out his
drink offering, and sprinkled the blood of his fellowship offerings[c] on the altar. 14The bronze
altar that stood before the LORD he brought from
the front of the temple—from between the new
altar and the temple of the LORD—and put it on
the north side of the new altar.
15King Ahaz then gave these orders to Uriah
the priest: "On the large new altar, offer the
morning burnt offering and the evening grain offering, the king's burnt offering and his grain offering, and the burnt offering of all the people of
the land, and their grain offering and their drink
offering. Sprinkle on the altar all the blood of the
burnt offerings and sacrifices. But I will use the
bronze altar for seeking guidance." 16And Uriah
the priest did just as King Ahaz had ordered.
17King Ahaz took away the side panels and
removed the basins from the movable stands. He
removed the Sea from the bronze bulls that supported it and set it on a stone base. 18He took
away the Sabbath canopy[d] that had been built at
the temple and removed the royal entryway outside the temple of the LORD, in deference to the
king of Assyria.
19As for the other events of the reign of Ahaz,
and what he did, are they not written in the book
of the annals of the kings of Judah? 20Ahaz rested
with his fathers and was buried with them in the
City of David. And Hezekiah his son succeeded
him as king.

Hoshea Last King of Israel

17 In the twelfth year of Ahaz king of Judah,
Hoshea son of Elah became king of Israel
in Samaria, and he reigned nine years. 2He did
evil in the eyes of the LORD, but not like the kings
of Israel who preceded him.
3Shalmaneser king of Assyria came up to attack
Hoshea, who had been Shalmaneser's vassal and
had paid him tribute. 4But the king of Assyria
discovered that Hoshea was a traitor, for he had
sent envoys to So[e] king of Egypt, and he no
longer paid tribute to the king of Assyria, as he
had done year by year. Therefore Shalmaneser
seized him and put him in prison. 5The king of
Assyria invaded the entire land, marched against
Samaria and laid siege to it for three years. 6In the
ninth year of Hoshea, the king of Assyria captured Samaria and deported the Israelites to Assyria. He settled them in Halah, in Gozan on the
Habor River and in the towns of the Medes.

Israel Exiled Because of Sin

7All this took place because the Israelites had
sinned against the LORD their God, who had
brought them up out of Egypt from under the
power of Pharaoh king of Egypt. They worshiped
other gods 8and followed the practices of the nations the LORD had driven out before them, as
well as the practices that the kings of Israel had
introduced. 9The Israelites secretly did things
against the LORD their God that were not right.
From watchtower to fortified city they built
themselves high places in all their towns. 10They
set up sacred stones and Asherah poles on every
high hill and under every spreading tree. 11At
every high place they burned incense, as the nations whom the LORD had driven out before them
had done. They did wicked things that provoked
the LORD to anger. 12They worshiped idols,
though the LORD had said, "You shall not do
this."[f] 13The LORD warned Israel and Judah
through all his prophets and seers: "Turn from
your evil ways. Observe my commands and de-

[a]3 Or *even made his son pass through* [b]12 Or *and went up* [c]13 Traditionally *peace offerings* [d]18 Or *the dais of his throne* (see Septuagint) [e]4 Or *to Sais, to the*; *So* is possibly an abbreviation for *Osorkon*. [f]12 Exodus 20:4, 5

crees, in accordance with the entire Law that I
commanded your fathers to obey and that I delivered to you through my servants the prophets."
14But they would not listen and were as stiff-
necked as their fathers, who did not trust in the
LORD their God. 15They rejected his decrees and
the covenant he had made with their fathers and
the warnings he had given them. They followed
worthless idols and themselves became worthless. They imitated the nations around them although the LORD had ordered them, "Do not do
as they do," and they did the things the LORD had
forbidden them to do.
16They forsook all the commands of the LORD
their God and made for themselves two idols cast
in the shape of calves, and an Asherah pole. They
bowed down to all the starry hosts, and they worshiped Baal. 17They sacrificed their sons and
daughters in[a] the fire. They practiced divination
and sorcery and sold themselves to do evil in the
eyes of the LORD, provoking him to anger.
18So the LORD was very angry with Israel and
removed them from his presence. Only the tribe
of Judah was left, 19and even Judah did not keep
the commands of the LORD their God. They followed the practices Israel had introduced.
20Therefore the LORD rejected all the people of
Israel; he afflicted them and gave them into the
hands of plunderers, until he thrust them from
his presence.
21When he tore Israel away from the house of
David, they made Jeroboam son of Nebat their
king. Jeroboam enticed Israel away from following the LORD and caused them to commit a great
sin. 22The Israelites persisted in all the sins of
Jeroboam and did not turn away from them 23un-
til the LORD removed them from his presence,
as he had warned through all his servants the
prophets. So the people of Israel were taken from
their homeland into exile in Assyria, and they are
still there.

Samaria Resettled

24The king of Assyria brought people from Babylon, Cuthah, Avva, Hamath and Sepharvaim and
settled them in the towns of Samaria to replace
the Israelites. They took over Samaria and lived
in its towns. 25When they first lived there, they
did not worship the LORD; so he sent lions among
them and they killed some of the people. 26It was
reported to the king of Assyria: "The people you
deported and resettled in the towns of Samaria do
not know what the god of that country requires.
He has sent lions among them, which are killing
them off, because the people do not know what
he requires."
27Then the king of Assyria gave this order:
"Have one of the priests you took captive from
Samaria go back to live there and teach the people what the god of the land requires." 28So one
of the priests who had been exiled from Samaria
came to live in Bethel and taught them how to
worship the LORD.
29Nevertheless, each national group made its
own gods in the several towns where they settled, and set them up in the shrines the people of
Samaria had made at the high places. 30The men
from Babylon made Succoth Benoth, the men
from Cuthah made Nergal, and the men from
Hamath made Ashima; 31the Avvites made Nib-
haz and Tartak, and the Sepharvites burned their
children in the fire as sacrifices to Adrammelech
and Anammelech, the gods of Sepharvaim.
32They worshiped the LORD, but they also appointed all sorts of their own people to officiate
for them as priests in the shrines at the high
places. 33They worshiped the LORD, but they also
served their own gods in accordance with the
customs of the nations from which they had been
brought.
34To this day they persist in their former practices. They neither worship the LORD nor adhere
to the decrees and ordinances, the laws and commands that the LORD gave the descendants of Jacob, whom he named Israel. 35When the LORD
made a covenant with the Israelites, he commanded them: "Do not worship any other gods or
bow down to them, serve them or sacrifice to
them. 36But the LORD, who brought you up out of
Egypt with mighty power and outstretched arm,
is the one you must worship. To him you shall
bow down and to him offer sacrifices. 37You must
always be careful to keep the decrees and ordinances, the laws and commands he wrote for
you. Do not worship other gods. 38Do not forget
the covenant I have made with you, and do not
worship other gods. 39Rather, worship the LORD
your God; it is he who will deliver you from the
hand of all your enemies."
40They would not listen, however, but persisted in their former practices. 41Even while these
people were worshiping the LORD, they were
serving their idols. To this day their children and
grandchildren continue to do as their fathers did.

Hezekiah King of Judah

18 In the third year of Hoshea son of Elah
king of Israel, Hezekiah son of Ahaz king
of Judah began to reign. 2He was twenty-five
years old when he became king, and he reigned
in Jerusalem twenty-nine years. His mother's
name was Abijah[b] daughter of Zechariah. 3He
did what was right in the eyes of the LORD, just
as his father David had done. 4He removed the

[a] 17 Or *They made their sons and daughters pass through*
[b] 2 Hebrew *Abi,* a variant of *Abijah*

high places, smashed the sacred stones and cut down the Asherah poles. He broke into pieces the bronze snake Moses had made, for up to that time the Israelites had been burning incense to it. (It was called[a] Nehushtan.[b])

5Hezekiah trusted in the LORD, the God of Israel. There was no one like him among all the kings of Judah, either before him or after him. 6He held fast to the LORD and did not cease to follow him; he kept the commands the LORD had given Moses. 7And the LORD was with him; he was successful in whatever he undertook. He rebelled against the king of Assyria and did not serve him. 8From watchtower to fortified city, he defeated the Philistines, as far as Gaza and its territory.

9In King Hezekiah's fourth year, which was the seventh year of Hoshea son of Elah king of Israel, Shalmaneser king of Assyria marched against Samaria and laid siege to it. 10At the end of three years the Assyrians took it. So Samaria was captured in Hezekiah's sixth year, which was the ninth year of Hoshea king of Israel. 11The king of Assyria deported Israel to Assyria and settled them in Halah, in Gozan on the Habor River and in towns of the Medes. 12This happened because they had not obeyed the LORD their God, but had violated his covenant—all that Moses the servant of the LORD commanded. They neither listened to the commands nor carried them out.

13In the fourteenth year of King Hezekiah's reign, Sennacherib king of Assyria attacked all the fortified cities of Judah and captured them. 14So Hezekiah king of Judah sent this message to the king of Assyria at Lachish: "I have done wrong. Withdraw from me, and I will pay whatever you demand of me." The king of Assyria exacted from Hezekiah king of Judah three hundred talents[c] of silver and thirty talents[d] of gold. 15So Hezekiah gave him all the silver that was found in the temple of the LORD and in the treasuries of the royal palace.

16At this time Hezekiah king of Judah stripped off the gold with which he had covered the doors and doorposts of the temple of the LORD, and gave it to the king of Assyria.

Sennacherib Threatens Jerusalem

17The king of Assyria sent his supreme commander, his chief officer and his field commander with a large army, from Lachish to King Hezekiah at Jerusalem. They came up to Jerusalem and stopped at the aqueduct of the Upper Pool, on the road to the Washerman's Field. 18They called for the king; and Eliakim son of Hilkiah the palace administrator, Shebna the secretary, and Joah son of Asaph the recorder went out to them.

19The field commander said to them, "Tell Hezekiah:

" 'This is what the great king, the king of Assyria, says: On what are you basing this confidence of yours? 20You say you have strategy and military strength—but you speak only empty words. On whom are you depending, that you rebel against me? 21Look now, you are depending on Egypt, that splintered reed of a staff, which pierces a man's hand and wounds him if he leans on it! Such is Pharaoh king of Egypt to all who depend on him. 22And if you say to me, "We are depending on the LORD our God"—isn't he the one whose high places and altars Hezekiah removed, saying to Judah and Jerusalem, "You must worship before this altar in Jerusalem"?

23" 'Come now, make a bargain with my master, the king of Assyria: I will give you two thousand horses—if you can put riders on them! 24How can you repulse one officer of the least of my master's officials, even though you are depending on Egypt for chariots and horsemen[e]? 25Furthermore, have I come to attack and destroy this place without word from the LORD? The LORD himself told me to march against this country and destroy it.' "

26Then Eliakim son of Hilkiah, and Shebna and Joah said to the field commander, "Please speak to your servants in Aramaic, since we understand it. Don't speak to us in Hebrew in the hearing of the people on the wall."

27But the commander replied, "Was it only to your master and you that my master sent me to say these things, and not to the men sitting on the wall—who, like you, will have to eat their own filth and drink their own urine?"

28Then the commander stood and called out in Hebrew: "Hear the word of the great king, the king of Assyria! 29This is what the king says: Do not let Hezekiah deceive you. He cannot deliver you from my hand. 30Do not let Hezekiah persuade you to trust in the LORD when he says, 'The LORD will surely deliver us; this city will not be given into the hand of the king of Assyria.'

31"Do not listen to Hezekiah. This is what the king of Assyria says: Make peace with me and come out to me. Then every one of you will eat from his own vine and fig tree and drink water from his own cistern, 32until I come and take you to a land like your own, a land of grain and new wine, a land of bread and vineyards, a land of olive trees and honey. Choose life and not death!

[a]4 Or *He called it* [b]4 *Nehushtan* sounds like the Hebrew for *bronze* and *snake* and *unclean thing.* [c]14 That is, about 11 tons (about 10 metric tons) [d]14 That is, about 1 ton (about 1 metric ton) [e]24 Or *charioteers*

"Do not listen to Hezekiah, for he is misleading you when he says, 'The LORD will deliver us.' 33Has the god of any nation ever delivered his land from the hand of the king of Assyria? 34Where are the gods of Hamath and Arpad? Where are the gods of Sepharvaim, Hena and Ivvah? Have they rescued Samaria from my hand? 35Who of all the gods of these countries has been able to save his land from me? How then can the LORD deliver Jerusalem from my hand?"

36But the people remained silent and said nothing in reply, because the king had commanded, "Do not answer him."

37Then Eliakim son of Hilkiah the palace administrator, Shebna the secretary and Joah son of Asaph the recorder went to Hezekiah, with their clothes torn, and told him what the field commander had said.

Jerusalem's Deliverance Foretold

19 When King Hezekiah heard this, he tore his clothes and put on sackcloth and went into the temple of the LORD. 2He sent Eliakim the palace administrator, Shebna the secretary and the leading priests, all wearing sackcloth, to the prophet Isaiah son of Amoz. 3They told him, "This is what Hezekiah says: This day is a day of distress and rebuke and disgrace, as when children come to the point of birth and there is no strength to deliver them. 4It may be that the LORD your God will hear all the words of the field commander, whom his master, the king of Assyria, has sent to ridicule the living God, and that he will rebuke him for the words the LORD your God has heard. Therefore pray for the remnant that still survives."

5When King Hezekiah's officials came to Isaiah, 6Isaiah said to them, "Tell your master, 'This is what the LORD says: Do not be afraid of what you have heard—those words with which the underlings of the king of Assyria have blasphemed me. 7Listen! I am going to put such a spirit in him that when he hears a certain report, he will return to his own country, and there I will have him cut down with the sword.' "

8When the field commander heard that the king of Assyria had left Lachish, he withdrew and found the king fighting against Libnah.

9Now Sennacherib received a report that Tirhakah, the Cushite[a] king ⌊of Egypt⌋, was marching out to fight against him. So he again sent messengers to Hezekiah with this word: 10"Say to Hezekiah king of Judah: Do not let the god you depend on deceive you when he says, 'Jerusalem will not be handed over to the king of Assyria.' 11Surely you have heard what the kings of Assyria have done to all the countries, destroying them completely. And will you be delivered? 12Did the gods of the nations that were destroyed by my forefathers deliver them: the gods of Gozan, Haran, Rezeph and the people of Eden who were in Tel Assar? 13Where is the king of Hamath, the king of Arpad, the king of the city of Sepharvaim, or of Hena or Ivvah?"

Hezekiah's Prayer

14Hezekiah received the letter from the messengers and read it. Then he went up to the temple of the LORD and spread it out before the LORD. 15And Hezekiah prayed to the LORD: "O LORD, God of Israel, enthroned between the cherubim, you alone are God over all the kingdoms of the earth. You have made heaven and earth. 16Give ear, O LORD, and hear; open your eyes, O LORD, and see; listen to the words Sennacherib has sent to insult the living God.

17"It is true, O LORD, that the Assyrian kings have laid waste these nations and their lands. 18They have thrown their gods into the fire and destroyed them, for they were not gods but only wood and stone, fashioned by men's hands. 19Now, O LORD our God, deliver us from his hand, so that all kingdoms on earth may know that you alone, O LORD, are God."

Isaiah Prophesies Sennacherib's Fall

20Then Isaiah son of Amoz sent a message to Hezekiah: "This is what the LORD, the God of Israel, says: I have heard your prayer concerning Sennacherib king of Assyria. 21This is the word that the LORD has spoken against him:

" 'The Virgin Daughter of Zion
despises you and mocks you.
The Daughter of Jerusalem
tosses her head as you flee.
22Who is it you have insulted and blasphemed?
Against whom have you raised your voice
and lifted your eyes in pride?
Against the Holy One of Israel!
23By your messengers
you have heaped insults on the Lord.
And you have said,
"With my many chariots
I have ascended the heights of the mountains,
the utmost heights of Lebanon.
I have cut down its tallest cedars,
the choicest of its pines.
I have reached its remotest parts,
the finest of its forests.
24I have dug wells in foreign lands
and drunk the water there.

[a]9 That is, from the upper Nile region

With the soles of my feet
I have dried up all the streams of Egypt.”
25“ ‘Have you not heard?
Long ago I ordained it.
In days of old I planned it;
now I have brought it to pass,
that you have turned fortified cities
into piles of stone.
26Their people, drained of power,
are dismayed and put to shame.
They are like plants in the field,
like tender green shoots,
like grass sprouting on the roof,
scorched before it grows up.

27“ ‘But I know where you stay
and when you come and go
and how you rage against me.
28Because you rage against me
and your insolence has reached my ears,
I will put my hook in your nose
and my bit in your mouth,
and I will make you return
by the way you came.’

29“This will be the sign for you, O Hezekiah:

“This year you will eat what grows by itself,
and the second year what springs from
that.
But in the third year sow and reap,
plant vineyards and eat their fruit.
30Once more a remnant of the house of Judah
will take root below and bear fruit above.
31For out of Jerusalem will come a remnant,
and out of Mount Zion a band of survivors.

The zeal of the LORD Almighty will accomplish
this.

32“Therefore this is what the LORD says concerning the king of Assyria:

“He will not enter this city
or shoot an arrow here.
He will not come before it with shield
or build a siege ramp against it.
33By the way that he came he will return;
he will not enter this city,
declares the LORD.
34I will defend this city and save it,
for my sake and for the sake of David my
servant.”

35That night the angel of the LORD went out
and put to death a hundred and eighty-five thousand men in the Assyrian camp. When the people
got up the next morning—there were all the
dead bodies! 36So Sennacherib king of Assyria
broke camp and withdrew. He returned to Nineveh and stayed there.
37One day, while he was worshiping in the
temple of his god Nisroch, his sons Adrammelech
and Sharezer cut him down with the sword, and
they escaped to the land of Ararat. And Esarhaddon his son succeeded him as king.

Hezekiah’s Illness

20 In those days Hezekiah became ill and
was at the point of death. The prophet
Isaiah son of Amoz went to him and said, “This
is what the LORD says: Put your house in order,
because you are going to die; you will not recover.”

2Hezekiah turned his face to the wall and
prayed to the LORD, 3“Remember, O LORD, how
I have walked before you faithfully and with
wholehearted devotion and have done what is
good in your eyes.” And Hezekiah wept bitterly.
4Before Isaiah had left the middle court, the
word of the LORD came to him: 5“Go back and tell
Hezekiah, the leader of my people, ‘This is what
the LORD, the God of your father David, says: I
have heard your prayer and seen your tears; I will
heal you. On the third day from now you will go
up to the temple of the LORD. 6I will add fifteen
years to your life. And I will deliver you and this
city from the hand of the king of Assyria. I will
defend this city for my sake and for the sake of
my servant David.’ ”
7Then Isaiah said, “Prepare a poultice of figs.”
They did so and applied it to the boil, and he
recovered.
8Hezekiah had asked Isaiah, “What will be the
sign that the LORD will heal me and that I will go
up to the temple of the LORD on the third day
from now?”
9Isaiah answered, “This is the LORD’s sign to
you that the LORD will do what he has promised:
Shall the shadow go forward ten steps, or shall it
go back ten steps?”
10“It is a simple matter for the shadow to go
forward ten steps,” said Hezekiah. “Rather, have
it go back ten steps.”
11Then the prophet Isaiah called upon the
LORD, and the LORD made the shadow go back the
ten steps it had gone down on the stairway of
Ahaz.

Envoys From Babylon

12At that time Merodach-Baladan son of Baladan king of Babylon sent Hezekiah letters and a
gift, because he had heard of Hezekiah’s illness.
13Hezekiah received the messengers and showed
them all that was in his storehouses—the silver,
the gold, the spices and the fine oil—his armory
and everything found among his treasures. There
was nothing in his palace or in all his kingdom
that Hezekiah did not show them.
14Then Isaiah the prophet went to King Heze-

kiah and asked, "What did those men say, and where did they come from?"

"From a distant land," Hezekiah replied. "They came from Babylon."

[15]The prophet asked, "What did they see in your palace?"

"They saw everything in my palace," Hezekiah said. "There is nothing among my treasures that I did not show them."

[16]Then Isaiah said to Hezekiah, "Hear the word of the LORD: [17]The time will surely come when everything in your palace, and all that your fathers have stored up until this day, will be carried off to Babylon. Nothing will be left, says the LORD. [18]And some of your descendants, your own flesh and blood, that will be born to you, will be taken away, and they will become eunuchs in the palace of the king of Babylon."

[19]"The word of the LORD you have spoken is good," Hezekiah replied. For he thought, "Will there not be peace and security in my lifetime?"

[20]As for the other events of Hezekiah's reign, all his achievements and how he made the pool and the tunnel by which he brought water into the city, are they not written in the book of the annals of the kings of Judah? [21]Hezekiah rested with his fathers. And Manasseh his son succeeded him as king.

Manasseh King of Judah

21 Manasseh was twelve years old when he became king, and he reigned in Jerusalem fifty-five years. His mother's name was Hephzibah. [2]He did evil in the eyes of the LORD, following the detestable practices of the nations the LORD had driven out before the Israelites. [3]He rebuilt the high places his father Hezekiah had destroyed; he also erected altars to Baal and made an Asherah pole, as Ahab king of Israel had done. He bowed down to all the starry hosts and worshiped them. [4]He built altars in the temple of the LORD, of which the LORD had said, "In Jerusalem I will put my Name." [5]In both courts of the temple of the LORD, he built altars to all the starry hosts. [6]He sacrificed his own son in[a] the fire, practiced sorcery and divination, and consulted mediums and spiritists. He did much evil in the eyes of the LORD, provoking him to anger.

[7]He took the carved Asherah pole he had made and put it in the temple, of which the LORD had said to David and to his son Solomon, "In this temple and in Jerusalem, which I have chosen out of all the tribes of Israel, I will put my Name forever. [8]I will not again make the feet of the Israelites wander from the land I gave their forefathers, if only they will be careful to do everything I commanded them and will keep the whole Law that my servant Moses gave them." [9]But the people did not listen. Manasseh led them astray, so that they did more evil than the nations the LORD had destroyed before the Israelites.

[10]The LORD said through his servants the prophets: [11]"Manasseh king of Judah has committed these detestable sins. He has done more evil than the Amorites who preceded him and has led Judah into sin with his idols. [12]Therefore this is what the LORD, the God of Israel, says: I am going to bring such disaster on Jerusalem and Judah that the ears of everyone who hears of it will tingle. [13]I will stretch out over Jerusalem the measuring line used against Samaria and the plumb line used against the house of Ahab. I will wipe out Jerusalem as one wipes a dish, wiping it and turning it upside down. [14]I will forsake the remnant of my inheritance and hand them over to their enemies. They will be looted and plundered by all their foes, [15]because they have done evil in my eyes and have provoked me to anger from the day their forefathers came out of Egypt until this day."

[16]Moreover, Manasseh also shed so much innocent blood that he filled Jerusalem from end to end—besides the sin that he had caused Judah to commit, so that they did evil in the eyes of the LORD.

[17]As for the other events of Manasseh's reign, and all he did, including the sin he committed, are they not written in the book of the annals of the kings of Judah? [18]Manasseh rested with his fathers and was buried in his palace garden, the garden of Uzza. And Amon his son succeeded him as king.

Amon King of Judah

[19]Amon was twenty-two years old when he became king, and he reigned in Jerusalem two years. His mother's name was Meshullemeth daughter of Haruz; she was from Jotbah. [20]He did evil in the eyes of the LORD, as his father Manasseh had done. [21]He walked in all the ways of his father; he worshiped the idols his father had worshiped, and bowed down to them. [22]He forsook the LORD, the God of his fathers, and did not walk in the way of the LORD.

[23]Amon's officials conspired against him and assassinated the king in his palace. [24]Then the people of the land killed all who had plotted against King Amon, and they made Josiah his son king in his place.

[25]As for the other events of Amon's reign, and what he did, are they not written in the book of the annals of the kings of Judah? [26]He was buried

[a]6 Or *He made his own son pass through*

in his grave in the garden of Uzza. And Josiah his
son succeeded him as king.

The Book of the Law Found

22 Josiah was eight years old when he became king, and he reigned in Jerusalem
thirty-one years. His mother's name was Jedidah
daughter of Adaiah; she was from Bozkath. 2He
did what was right in the eyes of the LORD and
walked in all the ways of his father David, not
turning aside to the right or to the left.
3In the eighteenth year of his reign, King Josiah sent the secretary, Shaphan son of Azaliah, the
son of Meshullam, to the temple of the LORD. He
said: 4"Go up to Hilkiah the high priest and have
him get ready the money that has been brought
into the temple of the LORD, which the doorkeepers have collected from the people. 5Have them
entrust it to the men appointed to supervise the
work on the temple. And have these men pay the
workers who repair the temple of the LORD—
6the carpenters, the builders and the masons.
Also have them purchase timber and dressed
stone to repair the temple. 7But they need not
account for the money entrusted to them, because they are acting faithfully."
8Hilkiah the high priest said to Shaphan the
secretary, "I have found the Book of the Law in
the temple of the LORD." He gave it to Shaphan,
who read it. 9Then Shaphan the secretary went
to the king and reported to him: "Your officials
have paid out the money that was in the temple
of the LORD and have entrusted it to the workers
and supervisors at the temple." 10Then Shaphan
the secretary informed the king, "Hilkiah the
priest has given me a book." And Shaphan read
from it in the presence of the king.
11When the king heard the words of the Book
of the Law, he tore his robes. 12He gave these
orders to Hilkiah the priest, Ahikam son of Shaphan, Acbor son of Micaiah, Shaphan the secretary and Asaiah the king's attendant: 13"Go and
inquire of the LORD for me and for the people and
for all Judah about what is written in this book
that has been found. Great is the LORD's anger
that burns against us because our fathers have
not obeyed the words of this book; they have not
acted in accordance with all that is written there
concerning us."
14Hilkiah the priest, Ahikam, Acbor, Shaphan
and Asaiah went to speak to the prophetess Huldah, who was the wife of Shallum son of Tikvah,
the son of Harhas, keeper of the wardrobe. She
lived in Jerusalem, in the Second District.
15She said to them, "This is what the LORD,
the God of Israel, says: Tell the man who sent you
to me, 16'This is what the LORD says: I am going
to bring disaster on this place and its people,
according to everything written in the book the
king of Judah has read. 17Because they have forsaken me and burned incense to other gods and
provoked me to anger by all the idols their hands
have made,[a] my anger will burn against this
place and will not be quenched.' 18Tell the king
of Judah, who sent you to inquire of the LORD,
'This is what the LORD, the God of Israel, says
concerning the words you heard: 19Because your
heart was responsive and you humbled yourself
before the LORD when you heard what I have
spoken against this place and its people, that they
would become accursed and laid waste, and because you tore your robes and wept in my presence, I have heard you, declares the LORD.
20Therefore I will gather you to your fathers, and
you will be buried in peace. Your eyes will not
see all the disaster I am going to bring on this
place.'"
So they took her answer back to the king.

Josiah Renews the Covenant

23 Then the king called together all the elders of Judah and Jerusalem. 2He went up
to the temple of the LORD with the men of Judah,
the people of Jerusalem, the priests and the
prophets—all the people from the least to the
greatest. He read in their hearing all the words of
the Book of the Covenant, which had been found
in the temple of the LORD. 3The king stood by the
pillar and renewed the covenant in the presence
of the LORD—to follow the LORD and keep his
commands, regulations and decrees with all his
heart and all his soul, thus confirming the words
of the covenant written in this book. Then all the
people pledged themselves to the covenant.
4The king ordered Hilkiah the high priest, the
priests next in rank and the doorkeepers to remove from the temple of the LORD all the articles
made for Baal and Asherah and all the starry
hosts. He burned them outside Jerusalem in the
fields of the Kidron Valley and took the ashes to
Bethel. 5He did away with the pagan priests appointed by the kings of Judah to burn incense on
the high places of the towns of Judah and on
those around Jerusalem—those who burned incense to Baal, to the sun and moon, to the constellations and to all the starry hosts. 6He took the
Asherah pole from the temple of the LORD to the
Kidron Valley outside Jerusalem and burned it
there. He ground it to powder and scattered the
dust over the graves of the common people. 7He
also tore down the quarters of the male shrine
prostitutes, which were in the temple of the
LORD and where women did weaving for Asherah.

[a]17 Or *by everything they have done*

8 Josiah brought all the priests from the towns of Judah and desecrated the high places, from Geba to Beersheba, where the priests had burned incense. He broke down the shrines[a] at the gates—at the entrance to the Gate of Joshua, the city governor, which is on the left of the city gate. 9 Although the priests of the high places did not serve at the altar of the LORD in Jerusalem, they ate unleavened bread with their fellow priests.

10 He desecrated Topheth, which was in the Valley of Ben Hinnom, so no one could use it to sacrifice his son or daughter in[b] the fire to Molech. 11 He removed from the entrance to the temple of the LORD the horses that the kings of Judah had dedicated to the sun. They were in the court near the room of an official named Nathan-Melech. Josiah then burned the chariots dedicated to the sun.

12 He pulled down the altars the kings of Judah had erected on the roof near the upper room of Ahaz, and the altars Manasseh had built in the two courts of the temple of the LORD. He removed them from there, smashed them to pieces and threw the rubble into the Kidron Valley. 13 The king also desecrated the high places that were east of Jerusalem on the south of the Hill of Corruption—the ones Solomon king of Israel had built for Ashtoreth the vile goddess of the Sidonians, for Chemosh the vile god of Moab, and for Molech[c] the detestable god of the people of Ammon. 14 Josiah smashed the sacred stones and cut down the Asherah poles and covered the sites with human bones.

15 Even the altar at Bethel, the high place made by Jeroboam son of Nebat, who had caused Israel to sin—even that altar and high place he demolished. He burned the high place and ground it to powder, and burned the Asherah pole also. 16 Then Josiah looked around, and when he saw the tombs that were there on the hillside, he had the bones removed from them and burned on the altar to defile it, in accordance with the word of the LORD proclaimed by the man of God who foretold these things.

17 The king asked, "What is that tombstone I see?"

The men of the city said, "It marks the tomb of the man of God who came from Judah and pronounced against the altar of Bethel the very things you have done to it."

18 "Leave it alone," he said. "Don't let anyone disturb his bones." So they spared his bones and those of the prophet who had come from Samaria.

19 Just as he had done at Bethel, Josiah removed and defiled all the shrines at the high places that the kings of Israel had built in the towns of Samaria that had provoked the LORD to anger. 20 Josiah slaughtered all the priests of those high places on the altars and burned human bones on them. Then he went back to Jerusalem.

21 The king gave this order to all the people: "Celebrate the Passover to the LORD your God, as it is written in this Book of the Covenant." 22 Not since the days of the judges who led Israel, nor throughout the days of the kings of Israel and the kings of Judah, had any such Passover been observed. 23 But in the eighteenth year of King Josiah, this Passover was celebrated to the LORD in Jerusalem.

24 Furthermore, Josiah got rid of the mediums and spiritists, the household gods, the idols and all the other detestable things seen in Judah and Jerusalem. This he did to fulfill the requirements of the law written in the book that Hilkiah the priest had discovered in the temple of the LORD. 25 Neither before nor after Josiah was there a king like him who turned to the LORD as he did—with all his heart and with all his soul and with all his strength, in accordance with all the Law of Moses.

26 Nevertheless, the LORD did not turn away from the heat of his fierce anger, which burned against Judah because of all that Manasseh had done to provoke him to anger. 27 So the LORD said, "I will remove Judah also from my presence as I removed Israel, and I will reject Jerusalem, the city I chose, and this temple, about which I said, 'There shall my Name be.'[d]"

28 As for the other events of Josiah's reign, and all he did, are they not written in the book of the annals of the kings of Judah?

29 While Josiah was king, Pharaoh Neco king of Egypt went up to the Euphrates River to help the king of Assyria. King Josiah marched out to meet him in battle, but Neco faced him and killed him at Megiddo. 30 Josiah's servants brought his body in a chariot from Megiddo to Jerusalem and buried him in his own tomb. And the people of the land took Jehoahaz son of Josiah and anointed him and made him king in place of his father.

Jehoahaz King of Judah

31 Jehoahaz was twenty-three years old when he became king, and he reigned in Jerusalem three months. His mother's name was Hamutal daughter of Jeremiah; she was from Libnah. 32 He did evil in the eyes of the LORD, just as his fathers had done. 33 Pharaoh Neco put him in chains at Riblah in the land of Hamath[e] so that he might not reign in Jerusalem, and he imposed on Judah

[a] 8 Or *high places* [b] 10 Or *to make his son or daughter pass through* [c] 13 Hebrew *Milcom* [d] 27 1 Kings 8:29
[e] 33 Hebrew; Septuagint (see also 2 Chron. 36:3) *Neco at Riblah in Hamath removed him*

a levy of a hundred talents[a] of silver and a talent[b] of gold. [34]Pharaoh Neco made Eliakim son of Josiah king in place of his father Josiah and changed Eliakim's name to Jehoiakim. But he took Jehoahaz and carried him off to Egypt, and there he died. [35]Jehoiakim paid Pharaoh Neco the silver and gold he demanded. In order to do so, he taxed the land and exacted the silver and gold from the people of the land according to their assessments.

Jehoiakim King of Judah

[36]Jehoiakim was twenty-five years old when he became king, and he reigned in Jerusalem eleven years. His mother's name was Zebidah daughter of Pedaiah; she was from Rumah. [37]And he did evil in the eyes of the LORD, just as his fathers had done.

24 During Jehoiakim's reign, Nebuchadnezzar king of Babylon invaded the land, and Jehoiakim became his vassal for three years. But then he changed his mind and rebelled against Nebuchadnezzar. [2]The LORD sent Babylonian,[c] Aramean, Moabite and Ammonite raiders against him. He sent them to destroy Judah, in accordance with the word of the LORD proclaimed by his servants the prophets. [3]Surely these things happened to Judah according to the LORD's command, in order to remove them from his presence because of the sins of Manasseh and all he had done, [4]including the shedding of innocent blood. For he had filled Jerusalem with innocent blood, and the LORD was not willing to forgive.

[5]As for the other events of Jehoiakim's reign, and all he did, are they not written in the book of the annals of the kings of Judah? [6]Jehoiakim rested with his fathers. And Jehoiachin his son succeeded him as king.

[7]The king of Egypt did not march out from his own country again, because the king of Babylon had taken all his territory, from the Wadi of Egypt to the Euphrates River.

Jehoiachin King of Judah

[8]Jehoiachin was eighteen years old when he became king, and he reigned in Jerusalem three months. His mother's name was Nehushta daughter of Elnathan; she was from Jerusalem. [9]He did evil in the eyes of the LORD, just as his father had done.

[10]At that time the officers of Nebuchadnezzar king of Babylon advanced on Jerusalem and laid siege to it, [11]and Nebuchadnezzar himself came up to the city while his officers were besieging it. [12]Jehoiachin king of Judah, his mother, his attendants, his nobles and his officials all surrendered to him.

In the eighth year of the reign of the king of Babylon, he took Jehoiachin prisoner. [13]As the LORD had declared, Nebuchadnezzar removed all the treasures from the temple of the LORD and from the royal palace, and took away all the gold articles that Solomon king of Israel had made for the temple of the LORD. [14]He carried into exile all Jerusalem: all the officers and fighting men, and all the craftsmen and artisans—a total of ten thousand. Only the poorest people of the land were left.

[15]Nebuchadnezzar took Jehoiachin captive to Babylon. He also took from Jerusalem to Babylon the king's mother, his wives, his officials and the leading men of the land. [16]The king of Babylon also deported to Babylon the entire force of seven thousand fighting men, strong and fit for war, and a thousand craftsmen and artisans. [17]He made Mattaniah, Jehoiachin's uncle, king in his place and changed his name to Zedekiah.

Zedekiah King of Judah

[18]Zedekiah was twenty-one years old when he became king, and he reigned in Jerusalem eleven years. His mother's name was Hamutal daughter of Jeremiah; she was from Libnah. [19]He did evil in the eyes of the LORD, just as Jehoiakim had done. [20]It was because of the LORD's anger that all this happened to Jerusalem and Judah, and in the end he thrust them from his presence.

The Fall of Jerusalem

Now Zedekiah rebelled against the king of Babylon.

25 So in the ninth year of Zedekiah's reign, on the tenth day of the tenth month, Nebuchadnezzar king of Babylon marched against Jerusalem with his whole army. He encamped outside the city and built siege works all around it. [2]The city was kept under siege until the eleventh year of King Zedekiah. [3]By the ninth day of the ⌞fourth⌟[d] month the famine in the city had become so severe that there was no food for the people to eat. [4]Then the city wall was broken through, and the whole army fled at night through the gate between the two walls near the king's garden, though the Babylonians[e] were surrounding the city. They fled toward the Arabah,[f] [5]but the Babylonian[g] army pursued the king and overtook him in the plains of Jericho. All his soldiers were separated from him and scattered, [6]and he was captured. He was taken to the king of Babylon at Riblah, where sentence was

[a] *33* That is, about 3 3/4 tons (about 3.4 metric tons) [b] *33* That is, about 75 pounds (about 34 kilograms) [c] *2* Or *Chaldean* [d] *3* See Jer. 52:6. [e] *4* Or *Chaldeans*; also in verses 13, 25 and 26 [f] *4* Or *the Jordan Valley* [g] *5* Or *Chaldean*; also in verses 10 and 24

pronounced on him. 7They killed the sons of Zedekiah before his eyes. Then they put out his eyes,
bound him with bronze shackles and took him to
Babylon.
8On the seventh day of the fifth month, in the
nineteenth year of Nebuchadnezzar king of Babylon, Nebuzaradan commander of the imperial
guard, an official of the king of Babylon, came to
Jerusalem. 9He set fire to the temple of the LORD,
the royal palace and all the houses of Jerusalem.
Every important building he burned down. 10The
whole Babylonian army, under the commander of
the imperial guard, broke down the walls around
Jerusalem. 11Nebuzaradan the commander of the
guard carried into exile the people who remained
in the city, along with the rest of the populace
and those who had gone over to the king of Babylon. 12But the commander left behind some of
the poorest people of the land to work the vineyards and fields.
13The Babylonians broke up the bronze pillars,
the movable stands and the bronze Sea that were
at the temple of the LORD and they carried the
bronze to Babylon. 14They also took away the
pots, shovels, wick trimmers, dishes and all
the bronze articles used in the temple service.
15The commander of the imperial guard took
away the censers and sprinkling bowls—all that
were made of pure gold or silver.
16The bronze from the two pillars, the Sea and
the movable stands, which Solomon had made for
the temple of the LORD, was more than could be
weighed. 17Each pillar was twenty-seven feet[a]
high. The bronze capital on top of one pillar was
four and a half feet[b] high and was decorated
with a network and pomegranates of bronze all
around. The other pillar, with its network, was
similar.
18The commander of the guard took as prisoners Seraiah the chief priest, Zephaniah the priest
next in rank and the three doorkeepers. 19Of
those still in the city, he took the officer in charge
of the fighting men and five royal advisers. He
also took the secretary who was chief officer in
charge of conscripting the people of the land and
sixty of his men who were found in the city.
20Nebuzaradan the commander took them all and
brought them to the king of Babylon at Riblah.
21There at Riblah, in the land of Hamath, the king
had them executed.
So Judah went into captivity, away from her
land.
22Nebuchadnezzar king of Babylon appointed
Gedaliah son of Ahikam, the son of Shaphan, to
be over the people he had left behind in Judah.
23When all the army officers and their men heard
that the king of Babylon had appointed Gedaliah
as governor, they came to Gedaliah at Mizpah—
Ishmael son of Nethaniah, Johanan son of Kareah, Seraiah son of Tanhumeth the Netophathite,
Jaazaniah the son of the Maacathite, and their
men. 24Gedaliah took an oath to reassure them
and their men. "Do not be afraid of the Babylonian officials," he said. "Settle down in the land
and serve the king of Babylon, and it will go well
with you."
25In the seventh month, however, Ishmael son
of Nethaniah, the son of Elishama, who was of
royal blood, came with ten men and assassinated
Gedaliah and also the men of Judah and the Babylonians who were with him at Mizpah. 26At this,
all the people from the least to the greatest, together with the army officers, fled to Egypt for
fear of the Babylonians.

Jehoiachin Released

27In the thirty-seventh year of the exile of Jehoiachin king of Judah, in the year Evil-
Merodach[c] became king of Babylon, he released
Jehoiachin from prison on the twenty-seventh
day of the twelfth month. 28He spoke kindly to
him and gave him a seat of honor higher than
those of the other kings who were with him in
Babylon. 29So Jehoiachin put aside his prison
clothes and for the rest of his life ate regularly at
the king's table. 30Day by day the king gave Jehoiachin a regular allowance as long as he lived.

[a] *17* Hebrew *eighteen cubits* (about 8.1 meters) [b] *17* Hebrew *three cubits* (about 1.3 meters) [c] *27* Also called *Amel-Marduk*

Introduction to
1 CHRONICLES

Personal Reading Plan

❐ 1 Chronicles 1:1–54	❐ 1 Chronicles 8:1–40	❐ 1 Chronicles 17:1–27
❐ 1 Chronicles 2:1–55	❐ 1 Chronicles 9:1–44	❐ 1 Chronicles 18:1–19:19
❐ 1 Chronicles 3:1–24	❐ 1 Chronicles 10:1–11:9	❐ 1 Chronicles 20:1–22:1
❐ 1 Chronicles 4:1–43	❐ 1 Chronicles 11:10–47	❐ 1 Chronicles 22:2–23:32
❐ 1 Chronicles 5:1–26	❐ 1 Chronicles 12:1–40	❐ 1 Chronicles 24:1–25:31
❐ 1 Chronicles 6:1–30	❐ 1 Chronicles 13:1–14:17	❐ 1 Chronicles 26:1–27:34
❐ 1 Chronicles 6:31–80	❐ 1 Chronicles 15:1–16:6	❐ 1 Chronicles 28:1–21
❐ 1 Chronicles 7:1–40	❐ 1 Chronicles 16:7–43	❐ 1 Chronicles 29:1–30

Author

Jewish tradition suggests Ezra as author. This may well be the case, but there is no firm evidence.

Date

First Chronicles was probably written toward the end of the fifth century B.C. or a little later. The actions narrated in the book are centered primarily in the reign of David (c. 1011–971 B.C.).

Theme

A family record to remind exiled and returning Israelites of God's chosen king and their place in the restored Jerusalem.

Historical Background

The reign of David was the golden age of Jewish history. The country was united and military victories allowed David to enlarge his territory. He introduced new administrative organization which brought stability and prosperity. He brought the ark of the covenant to Jerusalem and restructured the tabernacle worship.

Characteristics

In his recounting of history long past, the author relied on many written sources. About half of his work was taken from Samuel and Kings and the rest he drew from the Pentateuch, Judges, Ruth, Psalms, Isaiah, Jeremiah, Lamentations and Zechariah (though he used different versions of these books than those preserved in the later standardized Hebrew texts). Chapters 1–9 trace Israel's family record back to Adam. God is very much behind the scenes selecting a people for himself. Chapters 10–29 record the history of David's reign from the viewpoint of the chronicler's priestly interests. His concern is not the ups and downs of one man, but the lasting achievements of David—the monarchy and the temple. David is seen as God's chosen king around whom the welfare of the nation revolves. The chronicler omits much of the personal and family detail recorded in 2 Samuel. Instead, he records the nature of David's reorganization of worship in Jerusalem—detailing his appointments of not only priests, but singers, musicians and gatekeepers.

Historical Records From Adam to Abraham

To Noah's Sons

1 Adam, Seth, Enosh, 2 Kenan, Mahalalel, Jared, 3 Enoch, Methuselah, Lamech, Noah.

4 The sons of Noah:[a]
Shem, Ham and Japheth.

The Japhethites

5 The sons[b] of Japheth:
Gomer, Magog, Madai, Javan, Tubal, Meshech and Tiras.
6 The sons of Gomer:
Ashkenaz, Riphath[c] and Togarmah.
7 The sons of Javan:
Elishah, Tarshish, the Kittim and the Rodanim.

The Hamites

8 The sons of Ham:
Cush, Mizraim,[d] Put and Canaan.
9 The sons of Cush:
Seba, Havilah, Sabta, Raamah and Sabteca.
The sons of Raamah:
Sheba and Dedan.
10 Cush was the father[e] of
Nimrod, who grew to be a mighty warrior on earth.
11 Mizraim was the father of
the Ludites, Anamites, Lehabites, Naphtuhites, 12 Pathrusites, Casluhites (from whom the Philistines came) and Caphtorites.
13 Canaan was the father of
Sidon his firstborn,[f] and of the Hittites, 14 Jebusites, Amorites, Girgashites, 15 Hivites, Arkites, Sinites, 16 Arvadites, Zemarites and Hamathites.

The Semites

17 The sons of Shem:
Elam, Asshur, Arphaxad, Lud and Aram.
The sons of Aram[g]:
Uz, Hul, Gether and Meshech.
18 Arphaxad was the father of Shelah,
and Shelah the father of Eber.
19 Two sons were born to Eber:
One was named Peleg,[h] because in his time the earth was divided; his brother was named Joktan.
20 Joktan was the father of
Almodad, Sheleph, Hazarmaveth, Jerah, 21 Hadoram, Uzal, Diklah, 22 Obal,[i] Abimael, Sheba, 23 Ophir, Havilah and Jobab. All these were sons of Joktan.

24 Shem, Arphaxad,[j] Shelah,
25 Eber, Peleg, Reu,
26 Serug, Nahor, Terah
27 and Abram (that is, Abraham).

The Family of Abraham

28 The sons of Abraham:
Isaac and Ishmael.

Descendants of Hagar

29 These were their descendants:
Nebaioth the firstborn of Ishmael, Kedar, Adbeel, Mibsam, 30 Mishma, Dumah, Massa, Hadad, Tema, 31 Jetur, Naphish and Kedemah. These were the sons of Ishmael.

Descendants of Keturah

32 The sons born to Keturah, Abraham's concubine:
Zimran, Jokshan, Medan, Midian, Ishbak and Shuah.
The sons of Jokshan:
Sheba and Dedan.
33 The sons of Midian:
Ephah, Epher, Hanoch, Abida and Eldaah.
All these were descendants of Keturah.

Descendants of Sarah

34 Abraham was the father of Isaac.
The sons of Isaac:
Esau and Israel.

Esau's Sons

35 The sons of Esau:
Eliphaz, Reuel, Jeush, Jalam and Korah.
36 The sons of Eliphaz:
Teman, Omar, Zepho,[k] Gatam and Kenaz;
by Timna: Amalek.[l]
37 The sons of Reuel:
Nahath, Zerah, Shammah and Mizzah.

[a] 4 Septuagint; Hebrew does not have *The sons of Noah:* [b] 5 *Sons* may mean *descendants* or *successors* or *nations*; also in verses 6-10, 17 and 20. [c] 6 Many Hebrew manuscripts and Vulgate (see also Septuagint and Gen. 10:3); most Hebrew manuscripts *Diphath* [d] 8 That is, Egypt; also in verse 11 [e] 10 *Father* may mean *ancestor* or *predecessor* or *founder*; also in verses 11, 13, 18 and 20. [f] 13 Or *of the Sidonians, the foremost* [g] 17 One Hebrew manuscript and some Septuagint manuscripts (see also Gen. 10:23); most Hebrew manuscripts do not have this line. [h] 19 *Peleg* means *division.* [i] 22 Some Hebrew manuscripts and Syriac (see also Gen. 10:28); most Hebrew manuscripts *Ebal* [j] 24 Hebrew; some Septuagint manuscripts *Arphaxad, Cainan* (see also note at Gen. 11:10) [k] 36 Many Hebrew manuscripts, some Septuagint manuscripts and Syriac (see also Gen. 36:11); most Hebrew manuscripts *Zephi* [l] 36 Some Septuagint manuscripts (see also Gen. 36:12); Hebrew *Gatam, Kenaz, Timna and Amalek*

The People of Seir in Edom

38The sons of Seir:
Lotan, Shobal, Zibeon, Anah, Dishon, Ezer and Dishan.
39The sons of Lotan:
Hori and Homam. Timna was Lotan's sister.
40The sons of Shobal:
Alvan,[a] Manahath, Ebal, Shepho and Onam.
The sons of Zibeon:
Aiah and Anah.
41The son of Anah:
Dishon.
The sons of Dishon:
Hemdan,[b] Eshban, Ithran and Keran.
42The sons of Ezer:
Bilhan, Zaavan and Akan.[c]
The sons of Dishan[d]:
Uz and Aran.

The Rulers of Edom

43These were the kings who reigned in Edom before any Israelite king reigned[e]:
Bela son of Beor, whose city was named Dinhabah.
44When Bela died, Jobab son of Zerah from Bozrah succeeded him as king.
45When Jobab died, Husham from the land of the Temanites succeeded him as king.
46When Husham died, Hadad son of Bedad, who defeated Midian in the country of Moab, succeeded him as king. His city was named Avith.
47When Hadad died, Samlah from Masrekah succeeded him as king.
48When Samlah died, Shaul from Rehoboth on the river[f] succeeded him as king.
49When Shaul died, Baal-Hanan son of Acbor succeeded him as king.
50When Baal-Hanan died, Hadad succeeded him as king. His city was named Pau,[g] and his wife's name was Mehetabel daughter of Matred, the daughter of Me-Zahab.
51Hadad also died.

The chiefs of Edom were:
Timna, Alvah, Jetheth,
52Oholibamah, Elah, Pinon,
53Kenaz, Teman, Mibzar,
54Magdiel and Iram. These were the chiefs of Edom.

Israel's Sons

2 These were the sons of Israel:
Reuben, Simeon, Levi, Judah, Issachar, Zebulun,
2Dan, Joseph, Benjamin, Naphtali, Gad and Asher.

Judah

To Hezron's Sons

3The sons of Judah:
Er, Onan and Shelah. These three were born to him by a Canaanite woman, the daughter of Shua. Er, Judah's firstborn, was wicked in the LORD's sight; so the LORD put him to death.
4Tamar, Judah's daughter-in-law, bore him Perez and Zerah. Judah had five sons in all.

5The sons of Perez:
Hezron and Hamul.
6The sons of Zerah:
Zimri, Ethan, Heman, Calcol and Darda[h]—five in all.
7The son of Carmi:
Achar,[i] who brought trouble on Israel by violating the ban on taking devoted things.[j]
8The son of Ethan:
Azariah.
9The sons born to Hezron were:
Jerahmeel, Ram and Caleb.[k]

From Ram Son of Hezron

10Ram was the father of
Amminadab, and Amminadab the father of Nahshon, the leader of the people of Judah.
11Nahshon was the father of Salmon,[l] Salmon the father of Boaz,
12Boaz the father of Obed and Obed the father of Jesse.
13Jesse was the father of
Eliab his firstborn; the second son was Abinadab, the third Shimea,
14the fourth Nethanel, the fifth Raddai,
15the sixth Ozem and the seventh David.
16Their sisters were Zeruiah and Abigail. Zeruiah's three sons were Abishai, Joab and Asahel.
17Abigail was the mother of Amasa, whose father was Jether the Ishmaelite.

[a] 40 Many Hebrew manuscripts and some Septuagint manuscripts (see also Gen. 36:23); most Hebrew manuscripts *Alian*
[b] 41 Many Hebrew manuscripts and some Septuagint manuscripts (see also Gen. 36:26); most Hebrew manuscripts *Hamran*
[c] 42 Many Hebrew and Septuagint manuscripts (see also Gen. 36:27); most Hebrew manuscripts *Zaavan, Jaakan*
[d] 42 Hebrew *Dishon,* a variant of *Dishan*
[e] 43 Or *before an Israelite king reigned over them*
[f] 48 Possibly the Euphrates
[g] 50 Many Hebrew manuscripts, some Septuagint manuscripts, Vulgate and Syriac (see also Gen. 36:39); most Hebrew manuscripts *Pai*
[h] 6 Many Hebrew manuscripts, some Septuagint manuscripts and Syriac (see also 1 Kings 4:31); most Hebrew manuscripts *Dara*
[i] 7 *Achar* means *trouble*; *Achar* is called *Achan* in Joshua.
[j] 7 The Hebrew term refers to the irrevocable giving over of things or persons to the LORD, often by totally destroying them.
[k] 9 Hebrew *Kelubai,* a variant of *Caleb*
[l] 11 Septuagint (see also Ruth 4:21); Hebrew *Salma*

Caleb Son of Hezron

18 Caleb son of Hezron had children by his
wife Azubah (and by Jerioth). These
were her sons: Jesher, Shobab and Ar-
don. 19 When Azubah died, Caleb married Ephrath, who bore him Hur. 20 Hur
was the father of Uri, and Uri the father
of Bezalel.

21 Later, Hezron lay with the daughter of Makir the father of Gilead (he had married
her when he was sixty years old), and
she bore him Segub. 22 Segub was the
father of Jair, who controlled twenty-
three towns in Gilead. 23 (But Geshur
and Aram captured Havvoth Jair,[a] as
well as Kenath with its surrounding
settlements—sixty towns.) All these
were descendants of Makir the father of
Gilead.

24 After Hezron died in Caleb Ephrathah, Abijah the wife of Hezron bore him Ashhur
the father[b] of Tekoa.

Jerahmeel Son of Hezron

25 The sons of Jerahmeel the firstborn of Hezron:
Ram his firstborn, Bunah, Oren, Ozem
and[c] Ahijah. 26 Jerahmeel had another
wife, whose name was Atarah; she was
the mother of Onam.

27 The sons of Ram the firstborn of Jerahmeel:
Maaz, Jamin and Eker.

28 The sons of Onam:
Shammai and Jada.
The sons of Shammai:
Nadab and Abishur.

29 Abishur's wife was named Abihail, who
bore him Ahban and Molid.

30 The sons of Nadab:
Seled and Appaim. Seled died without
children.

31 The son of Appaim:
Ishi, who was the father of Sheshan.
Sheshan was the father of Ahlai.

32 The sons of Jada, Shammai's brother:
Jether and Jonathan. Jether died without
children.

33 The sons of Jonathan:
Peleth and Zaza.
These were the descendants of Jerahmeel.

34 Sheshan had no sons—only daughters.
He had an Egyptian servant named Jarha. 35 Sheshan gave his daughter in marriage to his servant Jarha, and she bore
him Attai.

36 Attai was the father of Nathan,
Nathan the father of Zabad,
37 Zabad the father of Ephlal,
Ephlal the father of Obed,
38 Obed the father of Jehu,
Jehu the father of Azariah,
39 Azariah the father of Helez,
Helez the father of Eleasah,
40 Eleasah the father of Sismai,
Sismai the father of Shallum,
41 Shallum the father of Jekamiah,
and Jekamiah the father of Elishama.

The Clans of Caleb

42 The sons of Caleb the brother of Jerahmeel:
Mesha his firstborn, who was the father
of Ziph, and his son Mareshah,[d] who
was the father of Hebron.

43 The sons of Hebron:
Korah, Tappuah, Rekem and Shema.
44 Shema was the father of Raham, and
Raham the father of Jorkeam. Rekem
was the father of Shammai. 45 The son of
Shammai was Maon, and Maon was the
father of Beth Zur.

46 Caleb's concubine Ephah was the mother
of Haran, Moza and Gazez. Haran was
the father of Gazez.

47 The sons of Jahdai:
Regem, Jotham, Geshan, Pelet, Ephah
and Shaaph.

48 Caleb's concubine Maacah was the mother
of Sheber and Tirhanah. 49 She also gave
birth to Shaaph the father of Madmannah and to Sheva the father of Macbe-
nah and Gibea. Caleb's daughter was
Acsah. 50 These were the descendants of
Caleb.

The sons of Hur the firstborn of Ephrathah:
Shobal the father of Kiriath Jearim, 51 Salma the father of Bethlehem, and Hareph
the father of Beth Gader.

52 The descendants of Shobal the father of
Kiriath Jearim were:
Haroeh, half the Manahathites, 53 and
the clans of Kiriath Jearim: the Ithrites,
Puthites, Shumathites and Mishraites.
From these descended the Zorathites
and Eshtaolites.

54 The descendants of Salma:
Bethlehem, the Netophathites, Atroth
Beth Joab, half the Manahathites, the
Zorites, 55 and the clans of scribes[e] who

[a] 23 Or *captured the settlements of Jair* [b] 24 *Father* may mean *civic leader* or *military leader*; also in verses 42, 45, 49-52 and possibly elsewhere. [c] 25 Or *Oren and Ozem, by* [d] 42 The meaning of the Hebrew for this phrase is uncertain.
[e] 55 Or *of the Sopherites*

lived at Jabez: the Tirathites, Shimeathites and Sucathites. These are the Kenites who came from Hammath, the father of the house of Recab.[a]

The Sons of David

3 These were the sons of David born to him in Hebron:
The firstborn was Amnon the son of Ahinoam of Jezreel;
the second, Daniel the son of Abigail of Carmel;
2 the third, Absalom the son of Maacah daughter of Talmai king of Geshur;
the fourth, Adonijah the son of Haggith;
3 the fifth, Shephatiah the son of Abital;
and the sixth, Ithream, by his wife Eglah.
4 These six were born to David in Hebron, where he reigned seven years and six months.

David reigned in Jerusalem thirty-three years,
5 and these were the children born to him there:
Shammua,[b] Shobab, Nathan and Solomon. These four were by Bathsheba[c]
daughter of Ammiel. 6 There were also
Ibhar, Elishua,[d] Eliphelet, 7 Nogah, Nepheg, Japhia, 8 Elishama, Eliada and
Eliphelet—nine in all. 9 All these were
the sons of David, besides his sons by his concubines. And Tamar was their sister.

The Kings of Judah

10 Solomon's son was Rehoboam,
Abijah his son,
Asa his son,
Jehoshaphat his son,
11 Jehoram[e] his son,
Ahaziah his son,
Joash his son,
12 Amaziah his son,
Azariah his son,
Jotham his son,
13 Ahaz his son,
Hezekiah his son,
Manasseh his son,
14 Amon his son,
Josiah his son.
15 The sons of Josiah:
Johanan the firstborn,
Jehoiakim the second son,
Zedekiah the third,
Shallum the fourth.
16 The successors of Jehoiakim:
Jehoiachin[f] his son,
and Zedekiah.

The Royal Line After the Exile

17 The descendants of Jehoiachin the captive:
Shealtiel his son, 18 Malkiram, Pedaiah, Shenazzar, Jekamiah, Hoshama and Nedabiah.
19 The sons of Pedaiah:
Zerubbabel and Shimei.
The sons of Zerubbabel:
Meshullam and Hananiah.
Shelomith was their sister.
20 There were also five others:
Hashubah, Ohel, Berekiah, Hasadiah and Jushab-Hesed.
21 The descendants of Hananiah:
Pelatiah and Jeshaiah, and the sons of Rephaiah, of Arnan, of Obadiah and of Shecaniah.
22 The descendants of Shecaniah:
Shemaiah and his sons:
Hattush, Igal, Bariah, Neariah and Shaphat—six in all.
23 The sons of Neariah:
Elioenai, Hizkiah and Azrikam—three in all.
24 The sons of Elioenai:
Hodaviah, Eliashib, Pelaiah, Akkub, Johanan, Delaiah and Anani—seven in all.

Other Clans of Judah

4 The descendants of Judah:
Perez, Hezron, Carmi, Hur and Shobal.
2 Reaiah son of Shobal was the father of Jahath, and Jahath the father of Ahumai and Lahad. These were the clans of the Zorathites.
3 These were the sons[g] of Etam:
Jezreel, Ishma and Idbash. Their sister
was named Hazzelelponi. 4 Penuel was
the father of Gedor, and Ezer the father of Hushah.
These were the descendants of Hur, the firstborn of Ephrathah and father[h] of Bethlehem.
5 Ashhur the father of Tekoa had two wives, Helah and Naarah.
6 Naarah bore him Ahuzzam, Hepher, Temeni and Haahashtari. These were the descendants of Naarah.
7 The sons of Helah:
Zereth, Zohar, Ethnan, 8 and Koz, who

[a] 55 Or *father of Beth Recab* [b] 5 Hebrew *Shimea,* a variant of *Shammua* [c] 5 One Hebrew manuscript and Vulgate (see also Septuagint and 2 Samuel 11:3); most Hebrew manuscripts *Bathshua* [d] 6 Two Hebrew manuscripts (see also 2 Samuel 5:15 and 1 Chron. 14:5); most Hebrew manuscripts *Elishama* [e] 11 Hebrew *Joram,* a variant of *Jehoram* [f] 16 Hebrew *Jeconiah,* a variant of *Jehoiachin*; also in verse 17 [g] 3 Some Septuagint manuscripts (see also Vulgate); Hebrew *father* [h] 4 *Father* may mean *civic leader* or *military leader*; also in verses 12, 14, 17, 18 and possibly elsewhere.

was the father of Anub and Hazzobebah
and of the clans of Aharhel son of Harum.

9Jabez was more honorable than his brothers.
His mother had named him Jabez,[a] saying, "I
gave birth to him in pain." 10Jabez cried out to
the God of Israel, "Oh, that you would bless me
and enlarge my territory! Let your hand be with
me, and keep me from harm so that I will be free
from pain." And God granted his request.

11Kelub, Shuhah's brother, was the father of
Mehir, who was the father of Eshton.
12Eshton was the father of Beth Rapha,
Paseah and Tehinnah the father of Ir Nahash.[b] These were the men of Recah.

13The sons of Kenaz:
Othniel and Seraiah.
The sons of Othniel:
Hathath and Meonothai.[c] 14Meonothai
was the father of Ophrah.
Seraiah was the father of Joab,
the father of Ge Harashim.[d] It was
called this because its people were
craftsmen.

15The sons of Caleb son of Jephunneh:
Iru, Elah and Naam.
The son of Elah:
Kenaz.

16The sons of Jehallelel:
Ziph, Ziphah, Tiria and Asarel.

17The sons of Ezrah:
Jether, Mered, Epher and Jalon. One of
Mered's wives gave birth to Miriam,
Shammai and Ishbah the father of Eshtemoa. 18(His Judean wife gave birth to
Jered the father of Gedor, Heber the father of Soco, and Jekuthiel the father of
Zanoah.) These were the children of
Pharaoh's daughter Bithiah, whom Mered had married.

19The sons of Hodiah's wife, the sister of Naham:
the father of Keilah the Garmite, and
Eshtemoa the Maacathite.

20The sons of Shimon:
Amnon, Rinnah, Ben-Hanan and Tilon.
The descendants of Ishi:
Zoheth and Ben-Zoheth.

21The sons of Shelah son of Judah:
Er the father of Lecah, Laadah the father
of Mareshah and the clans of the linen
workers at Beth Ashbea, 22Jokim, the
men of Cozeba, and Joash and Saraph,
who ruled in Moab and Jashubi Lehem.
(These records are from ancient times.)
23They were the potters who lived at
Netaim and Gederah; they stayed there
and worked for the king.

Simeon

24The descendants of Simeon:
Nemuel, Jamin, Jarib, Zerah and Shaul;
25Shallum was Shaul's son, Mibsam his
son and Mishma his son.

26The descendants of Mishma:
Hammuel his son, Zaccur his son and
Shimei his son.

27Shimei had sixteen sons and six daughters,
but his brothers did not have many children; so
their entire clan did not become as numerous as
the people of Judah. 28They lived in Beersheba,
Moladah, Hazar Shual, 29Bilhah, Ezem, Tolad,
30Bethuel, Hormah, Ziklag, 31Beth Marcaboth,
Hazar Susim, Beth Biri and Shaaraim. These were
their towns until the reign of David. 32Their surrounding villages were Etam, Ain, Rimmon, Token and Ashan—five towns— 33and all the villages around these towns as far as Baalath.[e]
These were their settlements. And they kept a
genealogical record.

34Meshobab, Jamlech, Joshah son of Amaziah, 35Joel, Jehu son of Joshibiah, the son of
Seraiah, the son of Asiel, 36also Elioenai,
Jaakobah, Jeshohaiah, Asaiah, Adiel, Jesimiel, Benaiah, 37and Ziza son of Shiphi, the
son of Allon, the son of Jedaiah, the son of
Shimri, the son of Shemaiah.

38The men listed above by name were leaders
of their clans. Their families increased greatly,
39and they went to the outskirts of Gedor to the
east of the valley in search of pasture for their
flocks. 40They found rich, good pasture, and the
land was spacious, peaceful and quiet. Some
Hamites had lived there formerly.

41The men whose names were listed came in
the days of Hezekiah king of Judah. They attacked
the Hamites in their dwellings and also the Meunites who were there and completely destroyed[f] them, as is evident to this day. Then
they settled in their place, because there was
pasture for their flocks. 42And five hundred of
these Simeonites, led by Pelatiah, Neariah, Rephaiah and Uzziel, the sons of Ishi, invaded the
hill country of Seir. 43They killed the remaining
Amalekites who had escaped, and they have lived
there to this day.

[a] 9 *Jabez* sounds like the Hebrew for *pain.* [b] 12 Or *of the city of Nahash* [c] 13 Some Septuagint manuscripts and Vulgate; Hebrew does not have *and Meonothai.* [d] 14 *Ge Harashim* means *valley of craftsmen.* [e] 33 Some Septuagint manuscripts (see also Joshua 19:8); Hebrew *Baal* [f] 41 The Hebrew term refers to the irrevocable giving over of things or persons to the LORD, often by totally destroying them.

Reuben

5 The sons of Reuben the firstborn of Israel (he
was the firstborn, but when he defiled his
father's marriage bed, his rights as firstborn were
given to the sons of Joseph son of Israel; so he
could not be listed in the genealogical record in
accordance with his birthright, [2]and though Judah was the strongest of his brothers and a ruler
came from him, the rights of the firstborn belonged to Joseph)— [3]the sons of Reuben the firstborn of Israel:

Hanoch, Pallu, Hezron and Carmi.

[4]The descendants of Joel:

Shemaiah his son, Gog his son,
Shimei his son, [5]Micah his son,
Reaiah his son, Baal his son,
[6]and Beerah his son, whom Tiglath-
Pileser[a] king of Assyria took into exile.
Beerah was a leader of the Reubenites.

[7]Their relatives by clans, listed according to
their genealogical records:

Jeiel the chief, Zechariah, [8]and Bela son
of Azaz, the son of Shema, the son of
Joel. They settled in the area from Aroer
to Nebo and Baal Meon. [9]To the east
they occupied the land up to the edge of
the desert that extends to the Euphrates
River, because their livestock had increased in Gilead.

[10]During Saul's reign they waged war
against the Hagrites, who were defeated at
their hands; they occupied the dwellings of
the Hagrites throughout the entire region
east of Gilead.

Gad

[11]The Gadites lived next to them in Bashan,
as far as Salecah:

[12]Joel was the chief, Shapham the second,
then Janai and Shaphat, in Bashan.

[13]Their relatives, by families, were:

Michael, Meshullam, Sheba, Jorai, Ja-
can, Zia and Eber—seven in all.

[14]These were the sons of Abihail son of
Huri, the son of Jaroah, the son of Gilead, the son of Michael, the son of Je-
shishai, the son of Jahdo, the son of Buz.

[15]Ahi son of Abdiel, the son of Guni, was
head of their family.

[16]The Gadites lived in Gilead, in Bashan and
its outlying villages, and on all the pasturelands of Sharon as far as they extended.

[17]All these were entered in the genealogical
records during the reigns of Jotham king of Judah
and Jeroboam king of Israel.

[18]The Reubenites, the Gadites and the half-
tribe of Manasseh had 44,760 men ready for military service—able-bodied men who could handle
shield and sword, who could use a bow, and who
were trained for battle. [19]They waged war against
the Hagrites, Jetur, Naphish and Nodab. [20]They
were helped in fighting them, and God handed
the Hagrites and all their allies over to them,
because they cried out to him during the battle.
He answered their prayers, because they trusted
in him. [21]They seized the livestock of the
Hagrites—fifty thousand camels, two hundred fifty thousand sheep and two thousand donkeys.
They also took one hundred thousand people captive, [22]and many others fell slain, because the
battle was God's. And they occupied the land
until the exile.

The Half-Tribe of Manasseh

[23]The people of the half-tribe of Manasseh
were numerous; they settled in the land from
Bashan to Baal Hermon, that is, to Senir (Mount
Hermon).

[24]These were the heads of their families:
Epher, Ishi, Eliel, Azriel, Jeremiah, Hodaviah and
Jahdiel. They were brave warriors, famous men,
and heads of their families. [25]But they were unfaithful to the God of their fathers and prostituted
themselves to the gods of the peoples of the land,
whom God had destroyed before them. [26]So the
God of Israel stirred up the spirit of Pul king of
Assyria (that is, Tiglath-Pileser king of Assyria),
who took the Reubenites, the Gadites and the
half-tribe of Manasseh into exile. He took them
to Halah, Habor, Hara and the river of Gozan,
where they are to this day.

Levi

6 The sons of Levi:

Gershon, Kohath and Merari.

[2]The sons of Kohath:

Amram, Izhar, Hebron and Uzziel.

[3]The children of Amram:

Aaron, Moses and Miriam.

The sons of Aaron:

Nadab, Abihu, Eleazar and Ithamar.
[4]Eleazar was the father of Phinehas,
Phinehas the father of Abishua,
[5]Abishua the father of Bukki,
Bukki the father of Uzzi,
[6]Uzzi the father of Zerahiah,
Zerahiah the father of Meraioth,
[7]Meraioth the father of Amariah,
Amariah the father of Ahitub,
[8]Ahitub the father of Zadok,

[a]6 Hebrew *Tilgath-Pilneser*, a variant of *Tiglath-Pileser*; also in verse 26

Zadok the father of Ahimaaz,
9 Ahimaaz the father of Azariah,
Azariah the father of Johanan,
10 Johanan the father of Azariah (it was he who served as priest in the temple Solomon built in Jerusalem),
11 Azariah the father of Amariah,
Amariah the father of Ahitub,
12 Ahitub the father of Zadok,
Zadok the father of Shallum,
13 Shallum the father of Hilkiah,
Hilkiah the father of Azariah,
14 Azariah the father of Seraiah,
and Seraiah the father of Jehozadak.

15 Jehozadak was deported when the LORD sent Judah and Jerusalem into exile by the hand of Nebuchadnezzar.

16 The sons of Levi:
Gershon,[a] Kohath and Merari.
17 These are the names of the sons of Gershon:
Libni and Shimei.
18 The sons of Kohath:
Amram, Izhar, Hebron and Uzziel.
19 The sons of Merari:
Mahli and Mushi.
These are the clans of the Levites listed according to their fathers:
20 Of Gershon:
Libni his son, Jehath his son,
Zimmah his son, 21 Joah his son,
Iddo his son, Zerah his son
and Jeatherai his son.
22 The descendants of Kohath:
Amminadab his son, Korah his son,
Assir his son, 23 Elkanah his son,
Ebiasaph his son, Assir his son,
24 Tahath his son, Uriel his son,
Uzziah his son and Shaul his son.
25 The descendants of Elkanah:
Amasai, Ahimoth,
26 Elkanah his son,[b] Zophai his son,
Nahath his son, 27 Eliab his son,
Jeroham his son, Elkanah his son
and Samuel his son.[c]
28 The sons of Samuel:
Joel[d] the firstborn
and Abijah the second son.
29 The descendants of Merari:
Mahli, Libni his son,
Shimei his son, Uzzah his son,
30 Shimea his son, Haggiah his son
and Asaiah his son.

The Temple Musicians

31 These are the men David put in charge of the
music in the house of the LORD after the ark came
to rest there. 32 They ministered with music before the tabernacle, the Tent of Meeting, until
Solomon built the temple of the LORD in Jerusalem. They performed their duties according to
the regulations laid down for them.
33 Here are the men who served, together with
their sons:

From the Kohathites:
Heman, the musician,
the son of Joel, the son of Samuel,
34 the son of Elkanah, the son of Jeroham,
the son of Eliel, the son of Toah,
35 the son of Zuph, the son of Elkanah,
the son of Mahath, the son of Amasai,
36 the son of Elkanah, the son of Joel,
the son of Azariah, the son of Zephaniah,
37 the son of Tahath, the son of Assir,
the son of Ebiasaph, the son of Korah,
38 the son of Izhar, the son of Kohath,
the son of Levi, the son of Israel;
39 and Heman's associate Asaph, who served at his right hand:
Asaph son of Berekiah, the son of Shimea,
40 the son of Michael, the son of Baaseiah,[e]
the son of Malkijah, 41 the son of Ethni,
the son of Zerah, the son of Adaiah,
42 the son of Ethan, the son of Zimmah,
the son of Shimei, 43 the son of Jahath,
the son of Gershon, the son of Levi;
44 and from their associates, the Merarites, at his left hand:
Ethan son of Kishi, the son of Abdi,
the son of Malluch, 45 the son of Hashabiah,
the son of Amaziah, the son of Hilkiah,
46 the son of Amzi, the son of Bani,
the son of Shemer, 47 the son of Mahli,
the son of Mushi, the son of Merari,
the son of Levi.

48 Their fellow Levites were assigned to all the
other duties of the tabernacle, the house of God.
49 But Aaron and his descendants were the ones
who presented offerings on the altar of burnt offering and on the altar of incense in connection
with all that was done in the Most Holy Place,
making atonement for Israel, in accordance with

[a] 16 Hebrew *Gershom,* a variant of *Gershon;* also in verses 17, 20, 43, 62 and 71
[b] 26 Some Hebrew manuscripts, Septuagint and Syriac; most Hebrew manuscripts *Ahimoth 26and Elkanah. The sons of Elkanah:*
[c] 27 Some Septuagint manuscripts (see also 1 Samuel 1:19,20 and 1 Chron. 6:33,34); Hebrew does not have *and Samuel his son.*
[d] 28 Some Septuagint manuscripts and Syriac (see also 1 Samuel 8:2 and 1 Chron. 6:33); Hebrew does not have *Joel.*
[e] 40 Most Hebrew manuscripts; some Hebrew manuscripts, one Septuagint manuscript and Syriac *Maaseiah*

all that Moses the servant of God had commanded.
50 These were the descendants of Aaron:
Eleazar his son, Phinehas his son,
Abishua his son, 51 Bukki his son,
Uzzi his son, Zerahiah his son,
52 Meraioth his son, Amariah his son,
Ahitub his son, 53 Zadok his son
and Ahimaaz his son.

54 These were the locations of their settlements
allotted as their territory (they were assigned to
the descendants of Aaron who were from the
Kohathite clan, because the first lot was for
them):
55 They were given Hebron in Judah with
its surrounding pasturelands. 56 But the
fields and villages around the city were giv-
en to Caleb son of Jephunneh.
57 So the descendants of Aaron were giv-
en Hebron (a city of refuge), and Libnah,[a]
Jattir, Eshtemoa, 58 Hilen, Debir, 59 Ashan,
Juttah[b] and Beth Shemesh, together with
their pasturelands. 60 And from the tribe of
Benjamin they were given Gibeon,[c] Geba,
Alemeth and Anathoth, together with their
pasturelands.
These towns, which were distributed
among the Kohathite clans, were thirteen in
all.
61 The rest of Kohath's descendants were allotted ten towns from the clans of half the tribe of
Manasseh.
62 The descendants of Gershon, clan by clan,
were allotted thirteen towns from the tribes of
Issachar, Asher and Naphtali, and from the part
of the tribe of Manasseh that is in Bashan.
63 The descendants of Merari, clan by clan,
were allotted twelve towns from the tribes of
Reuben, Gad and Zebulun.
64 So the Israelites gave the Levites these towns
and their pasturelands. 65 From the tribes of Judah, Simeon and Benjamin they allotted the previously named towns.
66 Some of the Kohathite clans were given as
their territory towns from the tribe of Ephraim.
67 In the hill country of Ephraim they
were given Shechem (a city of refuge), and
Gezer,[d] 68 Jokmeam, Beth Horon, 69 Aijalon
and Gath Rimmon, together with their pasturelands.
70 And from half the tribe of Manasseh
the Israelites gave Aner and Bileam, together with their pasturelands, to the rest of the
Kohathite clans.

71 The Gershonites received the following:
From the clan of the half-tribe of Manasseh
they received Golan in Bashan and also
Ashtaroth, together with their pasturelands;
72 from the tribe of Issachar
they received Kedesh, Daberath, 73 Ramoth and Anem, together with their
pasturelands;
74 from the tribe of Asher
they received Mashal, Abdon, 75 Hukok
and Rehob, together with their pasturelands;
76 and from the tribe of Naphtali
they received Kedesh in Galilee, Hammon and Kiriathaim, together with their
pasturelands.

77 The Merarites (the rest of the Levites) received the following:
From the tribe of Zebulun
they received Jokneam, Kartah,[e] Rim-
mono and Tabor, together with their
pasturelands;
78 from the tribe of Reuben across the Jordan
east of Jericho
they received Bezer in the desert, Jahzah, 79 Kedemoth and Mephaath, together with their pasturelands;
80 and from the tribe of Gad
they received Ramoth in Gilead, Mahanaim, 81 Heshbon and Jazer, together
with their pasturelands.

Issachar

7 The sons of Issachar:
Tola, Puah, Jashub and Shimron—four
in all.
2 The sons of Tola:
Uzzi, Rephaiah, Jeriel, Jahmai, Ibsam
and Samuel—heads of their families.
During the reign of David, the descendants of Tola listed as fighting men in
their genealogy numbered 22,600.
3 The son of Uzzi:
Izrahiah.
The sons of Izrahiah:
Michael, Obadiah, Joel and Isshiah. All
five of them were chiefs. 4 According to
their family genealogy, they had 36,000
men ready for battle, for they had many
wives and children.
5 The relatives who were fighting men belonging to all the clans of Issachar, as
listed in their genealogy, were 87,000
in all.

[a] 57 See Joshua 21:13; Hebrew *given the cities of refuge: Hebron, Libnah.* [b] 59 Syriac (see also Septuagint and Joshua 21:16); Hebrew does not have *Juttah.* [c] 60 See Joshua 21:17; Hebrew does not have *Gibeon.* [d] 67 See Joshua 21:21; Hebrew *given the cities of refuge: Shechem, Gezer.* [e] 77 See Septuagint and Joshua 21:34; Hebrew does not have *Jokneam, Kartah.*

Benjamin

6Three sons of Benjamin:
Bela, Beker and Jediael.
7The sons of Bela:
Ezbon, Uzzi, Uzziel, Jerimoth and Iri, heads of families—five in all. Their genealogical record listed 22,034 fighting men.
8The sons of Beker:
Zemirah, Joash, Eliezer, Elioenai, Omri, Jeremoth, Abijah, Anathoth and Alemeth. All these were the sons of Beker.
9Their genealogical record listed the heads of families and 20,200 fighting men.
10The son of Jediael:
Bilhan.
The sons of Bilhan:
Jeush, Benjamin, Ehud, Kenaanah, Zethan, Tarshish and Ahishahar.
11All these sons of Jediael were heads of families. There were 17,200 fighting men ready to go out to war.
12The Shuppites and Huppites were the descendants of Ir, and the Hushites the descendants of Aher.

Naphtali

13The sons of Naphtali:
Jahziel, Guni, Jezer and Shillem[a]—the descendants of Bilhah.

Manasseh

14The descendants of Manasseh:
Asriel was his descendant through his Aramean concubine. She gave birth to Makir the father of Gilead.
15Makir took a wife from among the Huppites and Shuppites. His sister's name was Maacah.
Another descendant was named Zelophehad, who had only daughters.
16Makir's wife Maacah gave birth to a son and named him Peresh. His brother was named Sheresh, and his sons were Ulam and Rakem.
17The son of Ulam:
Bedan.
These were the sons of Gilead son of Makir, the son of Manasseh.
18His sister Hammoleketh gave birth to Ishhod, Abiezer and Mahlah.
19The sons of Shemida were:
Ahian, Shechem, Likhi and Aniam.

Ephraim

20The descendants of Ephraim:
Shuthelah, Bered his son,
Tahath his son, Eleadah his son,
Tahath his son,
21Zabad his son
and Shuthelah his son.
Ezer and Elead were killed by the native-born men of Gath, when they went down to seize their livestock.
22Their father Ephraim mourned for them many days, and his relatives came to comfort him.
23Then he lay with his wife again, and she became pregnant and gave birth to a son. He named him Beriah,[b] because there had been misfortune in his family.
24His daughter was Sheerah, who built Lower and Upper Beth Horon as well as Uzzen Sheerah.
25Rephah was his son, Resheph his son,[c]
Telah his son, Tahan his son,
26Ladan his son, Ammihud his son,
Elishama his son,
27Nun his son
and Joshua his son.
28Their lands and settlements included Bethel and its surrounding villages, Naaran to the east, Gezer and its villages to the west, and Shechem and its villages all the way to Ayyah and its villages.
29Along the borders of Manasseh were Beth Shan, Taanach, Megiddo and Dor, together with their villages. The descendants of Joseph son of Israel lived in these towns.

Asher

30The sons of Asher:
Imnah, Ishvah, Ishvi and Beriah. Their sister was Serah.
31The sons of Beriah:
Heber and Malkiel, who was the father of Birzaith.
32Heber was the father of Japhlet, Shomer and Hotham and of their sister Shua.
33The sons of Japhlet:
Pasach, Bimhal and Ashvath.
These were Japhlet's sons.
34The sons of Shomer:
Ahi, Rohgah,[d] Hubbah and Aram.
35The sons of his brother Helem:
Zophah, Imna, Shelesh and Amal.
36The sons of Zophah:
Suah, Harnepher, Shual, Beri, Imrah,
37Bezer, Hod, Shamma, Shilshah, Ithran[e] and Beera.
38The sons of Jether:
Jephunneh, Pispah and Ara.
39The sons of Ulla:

a 13 Some Hebrew and Septuagint manuscripts (see also Gen. 46:24 and Num. 26:49); most Hebrew manuscripts *Shallum*
b 23 *Beriah* sounds like the Hebrew for *misfortune.* c 25 Some Septuagint manuscripts; Hebrew does not have *his son.*
d 34 Or *of his brother Shomer: Rohgah* e 37 Possibly a variant of *Jether*

Arah, Hanniel and Rizia.
[40]All these were descendants of Asher—heads of families, choice men, brave warriors and outstanding leaders. The number of men ready for battle, as listed in their genealogy, was 26,000.

The Genealogy of Saul the Benjamite

8 Benjamin was the father of Bela his firstborn,
Ashbel the second son, Aharah the third,
[2]Nohah the fourth and Rapha the fifth.
[3]The sons of Bela were:
Addar, Gera, Abihud,[a] [4]Abishua, Naaman, Ahoah, [5]Gera, Shephuphan and Huram.
[6]These were the descendants of Ehud, who were heads of families of those living in Geba and were deported to Manahath:
[7]Naaman, Ahijah, and Gera, who deported them and who was the father of Uzza and Ahihud.
[8]Sons were born to Shaharaim in Moab after he had divorced his wives Hushim and Baara. [9]By his wife Hodesh he had Jobab, Zibia, Mesha, Malcam, [10]Jeuz, Sakia and Mirmah. These were his sons, heads of families. [11]By Hushim he had Abitub and Elpaal.
[12]The sons of Elpaal:
Eber, Misham, Shemed (who built Ono and Lod with its surrounding villages), [13]and Beriah and Shema, who were heads of families of those living in Aijalon and who drove out the inhabitants of Gath.
[14]Ahio, Shashak, Jeremoth, [15]Zebadiah, Arad, Eder, [16]Michael, Ishpah and Joha were the sons of Beriah.
[17]Zebadiah, Meshullam, Hizki, Heber, [18]Ishmerai, Izliah and Jobab were the sons of Elpaal.
[19]Jakim, Zicri, Zabdi, [20]Elienai, Zillethai, Eliel, [21]Adaiah, Beraiah and Shimrath were the sons of Shimei.
[22]Ishpan, Eber, Eliel, [23]Abdon, Zicri, Hanan, [24]Hananiah, Elam, Anthothijah, [25]Iphdeiah and Penuel were the sons of Shashak.
[26]Shamsherai, Shehariah, Athaliah, [27]Jaareshiah, Elijah and Zicri were the sons of Jeroham.
[28]All these were heads of families, chiefs as listed in their genealogy, and they lived in Jerusalem.
[29]Jeiel[b] the father[c] of Gibeon lived in Gibeon.
His wife's name was Maacah, [30]and his firstborn son was Abdon, followed by Zur, Kish, Baal, Ner,[d] Nadab, [31]Gedor, Ahio, Zeker [32]and Mikloth, who was the father of Shimeah. They too lived near their relatives in Jerusalem.
[33]Ner was the father of Kish, Kish the father of Saul, and Saul the father of Jonathan, Malki-Shua, Abinadab and Esh-Baal.[e]
[34]The son of Jonathan:
Merib-Baal,[f] who was the father of Micah.
[35]The sons of Micah:
Pithon, Melech, Tarea and Ahaz.
[36]Ahaz was the father of Jehoaddah, Jehoaddah was the father of Alemeth, Azmaveth and Zimri, and Zimri was the father of Moza. [37]Moza was the father of Binea; Raphah was his son, Eleasah his son and Azel his son.
[38]Azel had six sons, and these were their names:
Azrikam, Bokeru, Ishmael, Sheariah, Obadiah and Hanan. All these were the sons of Azel.
[39]The sons of his brother Eshek:
Ulam his firstborn, Jeush the second son and Eliphelet the third. [40]The sons of Ulam were brave warriors who could handle the bow. They had many sons and grandsons—150 in all.
All these were the descendants of Benjamin.

9 All Israel was listed in the genealogies recorded in the book of the kings of Israel.

The People in Jerusalem

The people of Judah were taken captive to Babylon because of their unfaithfulness. [2]Now the first to resettle on their own property in their own towns were some Israelites, priests, Levites and temple servants.
[3]Those from Judah, from Benjamin, and from Ephraim and Manasseh who lived in Jerusalem were:
[4]Uthai son of Ammihud, the son of Omri, the son of Imri, the son of Bani, a descendant of Perez son of Judah.
[5]Of the Shilonites:
Asaiah the firstborn and his sons.
[6]Of the Zerahites:
Jeuel.

[a]3 Or *Gera the father of Ehud* [b]29 Some Septuagint manuscripts (see also 1 Chron. 9:35); Hebrew does not have *Jeiel.* [c]29 *Father* may mean *civic leader* or *military leader.* [d]30 Some Septuagint manuscripts (see also 1 Chron. 9:36); Hebrew does not have *Ner.* [e]33 Also known as *Ish-Bosheth* [f]34 Also known as *Mephibosheth*

The people from Judah numbered 690.
7 Of the Benjamites:
Sallu son of Meshullam, the son of Hodaviah, the son of Hassenuah;
8 Ibneiah son of Jeroham; Elah son of
Uzzi, the son of Micri; and Meshullam
son of Shephatiah, the son of Reuel, the
son of Ibnijah.
9 The people from Benjamin, as listed in
their genealogy, numbered 956. All
these men were heads of their families.
10 Of the priests:
Jedaiah; Jehoiarib; Jakin;
11 Azariah son of Hilkiah, the son of Meshullam, the son of Zadok, the son of
Meraioth, the son of Ahitub, the official
in charge of the house of God;
12 Adaiah son of Jeroham, the son of Pashhur, the son of Malkijah; and Maasai son
of Adiel, the son of Jahzerah, the son of
Meshullam, the son of Meshillemith,
the son of Immer.
13 The priests, who were heads of families,
numbered 1,760. They were able men,
responsible for ministering in the house
of God.
14 Of the Levites:
Shemaiah son of Hasshub, the son of Azrikam, the son of Hashabiah, a Merarite;
15 Bakbakkar, Heresh, Galal and Mattaniah son of Mica, the son of Zicri, the son
of Asaph; 16 Obadiah son of Shemaiah,
the son of Galal, the son of Jeduthun;
and Berekiah son of Asa, the son of Elkanah, who lived in the villages of the Netophathites.
17 The gatekeepers:
Shallum, Akkub, Talmon, Ahiman and
their brothers, Shallum their chief 18 being stationed at the King's Gate on the
east, up to the present time. These were
the gatekeepers belonging to the camp
of the Levites. 19 Shallum son of Kore,
the son of Ebiasaph, the son of Korah,
and his fellow gatekeepers from his family (the Korahites) were responsible for
guarding the thresholds of the Tent[a]
just as their fathers had been responsible for guarding the entrance to the
dwelling of the LORD. 20 In earlier times
Phinehas son of Eleazar was in charge of
the gatekeepers, and the LORD was with
him. 21 Zechariah son of Meshelemiah
was the gatekeeper at the entrance to
the Tent of Meeting.

22 Altogether, those chosen to be gatekeepers
at the thresholds numbered 212. They were registered by genealogy in their villages. The gatekeepers had been assigned to their positions of
trust by David and Samuel the seer. 23 They and
their descendants were in charge of guarding the
gates of the house of the LORD—the house called
the Tent. 24 The gatekeepers were on the four
sides: east, west, north and south. 25 Their brothers in their villages had to come from time to
time and share their duties for seven-day periods.
26 But the four principal gatekeepers, who were
Levites, were entrusted with the responsibility
for the rooms and treasuries in the house of God.
27 They would spend the night stationed around
the house of God, because they had to guard it;
and they had charge of the key for opening it each
morning.

28 Some of them were in charge of the articles
used in the temple service; they counted them
when they were brought in and when they were
taken out. 29 Others were assigned to take care of
the furnishings and all the other articles of the
sanctuary, as well as the flour and wine, and the
oil, incense and spices. 30 But some of the priests
took care of mixing the spices. 31 A Levite named
Mattithiah, the firstborn son of Shallum the Korahite, was entrusted with the responsibility for
baking the offering bread. 32 Some of their Kohathite brothers were in charge of preparing for
every Sabbath the bread set out on the table.

33 Those who were musicians, heads of Levite
families, stayed in the rooms of the temple and
were exempt from other duties because they
were responsible for the work day and night.

34 All these were heads of Levite families,
chiefs as listed in their genealogy, and they lived
in Jerusalem.

The Genealogy of Saul

35 Jeiel the father[b] of Gibeon lived in Gibeon.
His wife's name was Maacah, 36 and his
firstborn son was Abdon, followed by
Zur, Kish, Baal, Ner, Nadab, 37 Gedor,
Ahio, Zechariah and Mikloth. 38 Mikloth
was the father of Shimeam. They too
lived near their relatives in Jerusalem.
39 Ner was the father of Kish, Kish the father
of Saul, and Saul the father of Jonathan,
Malki-Shua, Abinadab and Esh-Baal.[c]
40 The son of Jonathan:
Merib-Baal,[d] who was the father of Micah.
41 The sons of Micah:

[a] 19 That is, the temple; also in verses 21 and 23 [b] 35 *Father* may mean *civic leader* or *military leader.* [c] 39 Also known as *Ish-Bosheth* [d] 40 Also known as *Mephibosheth*

Pithon, Melech, Tahrea and Ahaz.[a]
42 Ahaz was the father of Jadah, Jadah[b]
was the father of Alemeth, Azmaveth
and Zimri, and Zimri was the father of
Moza. 43 Moza was the father of Binea;
Rephaiah was his son, Eleasah his son
and Azel his son.
44 Azel had six sons, and these were their
names:
Azrikam, Bokeru, Ishmael, Sheariah,
Obadiah and Hanan. These were the
sons of Azel.

Saul Takes His Life

10 Now the Philistines fought against Israel;
the Israelites fled before them, and many
fell slain on Mount Gilboa. 2 The Philistines
pressed hard after Saul and his sons, and they
killed his sons Jonathan, Abinadab and Malki-
Shua. 3 The fighting grew fierce around Saul, and
when the archers overtook him, they wounded
him.
4 Saul said to his armor-bearer, "Draw your
sword and run me through, or these uncircumcised fellows will come and abuse me."
But his armor-bearer was terrified and would
not do it; so Saul took his own sword and fell on
it. 5 When the armor-bearer saw that Saul was
dead, he too fell on his sword and died. 6 So Saul
and his three sons died, and all his house died
together.
7 When all the Israelites in the valley saw that
the army had fled and that Saul and his sons had
died, they abandoned their towns and fled. And
the Philistines came and occupied them.
8 The next day, when the Philistines came to
strip the dead, they found Saul and his sons fallen
on Mount Gilboa. 9 They stripped him and took
his head and his armor, and sent messengers
throughout the land of the Philistines to proclaim
the news among their idols and their people.
10 They put his armor in the temple of their gods
and hung up his head in the temple of Dagon.
11 When all the inhabitants of Jabesh Gilead
heard of everything the Philistines had done to
Saul, 12 all their valiant men went and took the
bodies of Saul and his sons and brought them to
Jabesh. Then they buried their bones under the
great tree in Jabesh, and they fasted seven days.
13 Saul died because he was unfaithful to the
LORD; he did not keep the word of the LORD and
even consulted a medium for guidance, 14 and did
not inquire of the LORD. So the LORD put him to
death and turned the kingdom over to David son
of Jesse.

David Becomes King Over Israel

11 All Israel came together to David at Hebron and said, "We are your own flesh
and blood. 2 In the past, even while Saul was king,
you were the one who led Israel on their military
campaigns. And the LORD your God said to you,
'You will shepherd my people Israel, and you will
become their ruler.' "
3 When all the elders of Israel had come to King
David at Hebron, he made a compact with them
at Hebron before the LORD, and they anointed
David king over Israel, as the LORD had promised
through Samuel.

David Conquers Jerusalem

4 David and all the Israelites marched to Jerusalem (that is, Jebus). The Jebusites who lived there
5 said to David, "You will not get in here." Nevertheless, David captured the fortress of Zion, the
City of David.
6 David had said, "Whoever leads the attack on
the Jebusites will become commander-in-chief."
Joab son of Zeruiah went up first, and so he received the command.
7 David then took up residence in the fortress,
and so it was called the City of David. 8 He built
up the city around it, from the supporting terraces[c] to the surrounding wall, while Joab restored the rest of the city. 9 And David became
more and more powerful, because the LORD Almighty was with him.

David's Mighty Men

10 These were the chiefs of David's mighty
men—they, together with all Israel, gave his
kingship strong support to extend it over the
whole land, as the LORD had promised— 11 this is
the list of David's mighty men:
Jashobeam,[d] a Hacmonite, was chief of the
officers[e]; he raised his spear against three hundred men, whom he killed in one encounter.
12 Next to him was Eleazar son of Dodai the
Ahohite, one of the three mighty men. 13 He was
with David at Pas Dammim when the Philistines
gathered there for battle. At a place where there
was a field full of barley, the troops fled from the
Philistines. 14 But they took their stand in the
middle of the field. They defended it and struck
the Philistines down, and the LORD brought about
a great victory.
15 Three of the thirty chiefs came down to David to the rock at the cave of Adullam, while a
band of Philistines was encamped in the Valley of
Rephaim. 16 At that time David was in the stronghold, and the Philistine garrison was at Bethle-

[a] 41 Vulgate and Syriac (see also Septuagint and 1 Chron. 8:35); Hebrew does not have *and Ahaz.* [b] 42 Some Hebrew manuscripts and Septuagint (see also 1 Chron. 8:36); most Hebrew manuscripts *Jarah, Jarah* [c] 8 Or *the Millo* [d] 11 Possibly a variant of *Jashob-Baal* [e] 11 Or *Thirty*; some Septuagint manuscripts *Three* (see also 2 Samuel 23:8)

hem. 17David longed for water and said, "Oh,
that someone would get me a drink of water from
the well near the gate of Bethlehem!" 18So the
Three broke through the Philistine lines, drew
water from the well near the gate of Bethlehem
and carried it back to David. But he refused to
drink it; instead, he poured it out before the
LORD. 19"God forbid that I should do this!" he
said. "Should I drink the blood of these men who
went at the risk of their lives?" Because they
risked their lives to bring it back, David would
not drink it.

Such were the exploits of the three mighty
men.

20Abishai the brother of Joab was chief of the
Three. He raised his spear against three hundred
men, whom he killed, and so he became as famous as the Three. 21He was doubly honored
above the Three and became their commander,
even though he was not included among them.

22Benaiah son of Jehoiada was a valiant fighter
from Kabzeel, who performed great exploits. He
struck down two of Moab's best men. He also
went down into a pit on a snowy day and killed
a lion. 23And he struck down an Egyptian who
was seven and a half feet[a] tall. Although the
Egyptian had a spear like a weaver's rod in his
hand, Benaiah went against him with a club. He
snatched the spear from the Egyptian's hand and
killed him with his own spear. 24Such were the
exploits of Benaiah son of Jehoiada; he too was as
famous as the three mighty men. 25He was held
in greater honor than any of the Thirty, but he
was not included among the Three. And David
put him in charge of his bodyguard.

26The mighty men were:
Asahel the brother of Joab,
Elhanan son of Dodo from Bethlehem,
27Shammoth the Harorite,
Helez the Pelonite,
28Ira son of Ikkesh from Tekoa,
Abiezer from Anathoth,
29Sibbecai the Hushathite,
Ilai the Ahohite,
30Maharai the Netophathite,
Heled son of Baanah the Netophathite,
31Ithai son of Ribai from Gibeah in Benjamin,
Benaiah the Pirathonite,
32Hurai from the ravines of Gaash,
Abiel the Arbathite,
33Azmaveth the Baharumite,
Eliahba the Shaalbonite,
34the sons of Hashem the Gizonite,
Jonathan son of Shagee the Hararite,
35Ahiam son of Sacar the Hararite,
Eliphal son of Ur,
36Hepher the Mekerathite,
Ahijah the Pelonite,
37Hezro the Carmelite,
Naarai son of Ezbai,
38Joel the brother of Nathan,
Mibhar son of Hagri,
39Zelek the Ammonite,
Naharai the Berothite, the armor-bearer
of Joab son of Zeruiah,
40Ira the Ithrite,
Gareb the Ithrite,
41Uriah the Hittite,
Zabad son of Ahlai,
42Adina son of Shiza the Reubenite, who
was chief of the Reubenites, and the
thirty with him,
43Hanan son of Maacah,
Joshaphat the Mithnite,
44Uzzia the Ashterathite,
Shama and Jeiel the sons of Hotham the
Aroerite,
45Jediael son of Shimri,
his brother Joha the Tizite,
46Eliel the Mahavite,
Jeribai and Joshaviah the sons of El-
naam,
Ithmah the Moabite,
47Eliel, Obed and Jaasiel the Mezobaite.

Warriors Join David

12 These were the men who came to David
at Ziklag, while he was banished from the
presence of Saul son of Kish (they were among
the warriors who helped him in battle; 2they
were armed with bows and were able to shoot
arrows or to sling stones right-handed or left-
handed; they were kinsmen of Saul from the tribe
of Benjamin):

3Ahiezer their chief and Joash the sons of
Shemaah the Gibeathite; Jeziel and Pelet
the sons of Azmaveth; Beracah, Jehu the
Anathothite, 4and Ishmaiah the Gibeonite,
a mighty man among the Thirty, who was a
leader of the Thirty; Jeremiah, Jahaziel, Johanan, Jozabad the Gederathite, 5Eluzai,
Jerimoth, Bealiah, Shemariah and Shephatiah the Haruphite; 6Elkanah, Isshiah, Azarel,
Joezer and Jashobeam the Korahites; 7and
Joelah and Zebadiah the sons of Jeroham
from Gedor.

8Some Gadites defected to David at his stronghold in the desert. They were brave warriors,
ready for battle and able to handle the shield and
spear. Their faces were the faces of lions, and
they were as swift as gazelles in the mountains.

[a]23 Hebrew *five cubits* (about 2.3 meters)

9 Ezer was the chief,
Obadiah the second in command, Eliab the
third,
10 Mishmannah the fourth, Jeremiah the fifth,
11 Attai the sixth, Eliel the seventh,
12 Johanan the eighth, Elzabad the ninth,
13 Jeremiah the tenth and Macbannai the
eleventh.
14 These Gadites were army commanders; the
least was a match for a hundred, and the greatest
for a thousand. 15 It was they who crossed the
Jordan in the first month when it was overflowing all its banks, and they put to flight everyone
living in the valleys, to the east and to the west.
16 Other Benjamites and some men from Judah
also came to David in his stronghold. 17 David
went out to meet them and said to them, "If you
have come to me in peace, to help me, I am ready
to have you unite with me. But if you have come
to betray me to my enemies when my hands are
free from violence, may the God of our fathers
see it and judge you."
18 Then the Spirit came upon Amasai, chief of
the Thirty, and he said:

"We are yours, O David!
We are with you, O son of Jesse!
Success, success to you,
and success to those who help you,
for your God will help you."

So David received them and made them leaders of his raiding bands.
19 Some of the men of Manasseh defected to
David when he went with the Philistines to fight
against Saul. (He and his men did not help the
Philistines because, after consultation, their rulers sent him away. They said, "It will cost us our
heads if he deserts to his master Saul.") 20 When
David went to Ziklag, these were the men of Manasseh who defected to him: Adnah, Jozabad, Jediael, Michael, Jozabad, Elihu and Zillethai, leaders of units of a thousand in Manasseh. 21 They
helped David against raiding bands, for all of
them were brave warriors, and they were commanders in his army. 22 Day after day men came
to help David, until he had a great army, like the
army of God.[a]

Others Join David at Hebron

23 These are the numbers of the men armed
for battle who came to David at Hebron to turn
Saul's kingdom over to him, as the LORD had said:
24 men of Judah, carrying shield and spear—
6,800 armed for battle;
25 men of Simeon, warriors ready for battle—
7,100;
26 men of Levi—4,600, 27 including Jehoiada,
leader of the family of Aaron, with
3,700 men, 28 and Zadok, a brave young
warrior, with 22 officers from his family;
29 men of Benjamin, Saul's kinsmen—3,000,
most of whom had remained loyal to
Saul's house until then;
30 men of Ephraim, brave warriors, famous in
their own clans—20,800;
31 men of half the tribe of Manasseh, designated by name to come and make David
king—18,000;
32 men of Issachar, who understood the times
and knew what Israel should do—200
chiefs, with all their relatives under
their command;
33 men of Zebulun, experienced soldiers prepared for battle with every type of weapon, to help David with undivided
loyalty—50,000;
34 men of Naphtali—1,000 officers, together
with 37,000 men carrying shields and
spears;
35 men of Dan, ready for battle—28,600;
36 men of Asher, experienced soldiers prepared for battle—40,000;
37 and from east of the Jordan, men of Reuben, Gad and the half-tribe of Manasseh, armed with every type of weapon—
120,000.
38 All these were fighting men who volunteered to serve in the ranks. They came to Hebron fully determined to make David king over all
Israel. All the rest of the Israelites were also of
one mind to make David king. 39 The men spent
three days there with David, eating and drinking,
for their families had supplied provisions for
them. 40 Also, their neighbors from as far away as
Issachar, Zebulun and Naphtali came bringing
food on donkeys, camels, mules and oxen. There
were plentiful supplies of flour, fig cakes, raisin
cakes, wine, oil, cattle and sheep, for there was
joy in Israel.

Bringing Back the Ark

13 David conferred with each of his officers,
the commanders of thousands and commanders of hundreds. 2 He then said to the whole
assembly of Israel, "If it seems good to you and if
it is the will of the LORD our God, let us send
word far and wide to the rest of our brothers
throughout the territories of Israel, and also to
the priests and Levites who are with them in
their towns and pasturelands, to come and join
us. 3 Let us bring the ark of our God back to us,
for we did not inquire of[b] it[c] during the reign of

[a] 22 Or *a great and mighty army* [b] 3 Or *we neglected* [c] 3 Or *him*

Saul." 4The whole assembly agreed to do this, because it seemed right to all the people.

5So David assembled all the Israelites, from the Shihor River in Egypt to Lebo[a] Hamath, to bring the ark of God from Kiriath Jearim. 6David and all the Israelites with him went to Baalah of Judah (Kiriath Jearim) to bring up from there the ark of God the LORD, who is enthroned between the cherubim—the ark that is called by the Name.

7They moved the ark of God from Abinadab's house on a new cart, with Uzzah and Ahio guiding it. 8David and all the Israelites were celebrating with all their might before God, with songs and with harps, lyres, tambourines, cymbals and trumpets.

9When they came to the threshing floor of Kidon, Uzzah reached out his hand to steady the ark, because the oxen stumbled. 10The LORD's anger burned against Uzzah, and he struck him down because he had put his hand on the ark. So he died there before God.

11Then David was angry because the LORD's wrath had broken out against Uzzah, and to this day that place is called Perez Uzzah.[b]

12David was afraid of God that day and asked, "How can I ever bring the ark of God to me?" 13He did not take the ark to be with him in the City of David. Instead, he took it aside to the house of Obed-Edom the Gittite. 14The ark of God remained with the family of Obed-Edom in his house for three months, and the LORD blessed his household and everything he had.

David's House and Family

14 Now Hiram king of Tyre sent messengers to David, along with cedar logs, stonemasons and carpenters to build a palace for him. 2And David knew that the LORD had established him as king over Israel and that his kingdom had been highly exalted for the sake of his people Israel.

3In Jerusalem David took more wives and became the father of more sons and daughters. 4These are the names of the children born to him there: Shammua, Shobab, Nathan, Solomon, 5Ibhar, Elishua, Elpelet, 6Nogah, Nepheg, Japhia, 7Elishama, Beeliada[c] and Eliphelet.

David Defeats the Philistines

8When the Philistines heard that David had been anointed king over all Israel, they went up in full force to search for him, but David heard about it and went out to meet them. 9Now the Philistines had come and raided the Valley of Rephaim; 10so David inquired of God: "Shall I go and attack the Philistines? Will you hand them over to me?"

The LORD answered him, "Go, I will hand them over to you."

11So David and his men went up to Baal Perazim, and there he defeated them. He said, "As waters break out, God has broken out against my enemies by my hand." So that place was called Baal Perazim.[d] 12The Philistines had abandoned their gods there, and David gave orders to burn them in the fire.

13Once more the Philistines raided the valley; 14so David inquired of God again, and God answered him, "Do not go straight up, but circle around them and attack them in front of the balsam trees. 15As soon as you hear the sound of marching in the tops of the balsam trees, move out to battle, because that will mean God has gone out in front of you to strike the Philistine army." 16So David did as God commanded him, and they struck down the Philistine army, all the way from Gibeon to Gezer.

17So David's fame spread throughout every land, and the LORD made all the nations fear him.

The Ark Brought to Jerusalem

15 After David had constructed buildings for himself in the City of David, he prepared a place for the ark of God and pitched a tent for it. 2Then David said, "No one but the Levites may carry the ark of God, because the LORD chose them to carry the ark of the LORD and to minister before him forever."

3David assembled all Israel in Jerusalem to bring up the ark of the LORD to the place he had prepared for it. 4He called together the descendants of Aaron and the Levites:

5From the descendants of Kohath,
  Uriel the leader and 120 relatives;
6from the descendants of Merari,
  Asaiah the leader and 220 relatives;
7from the descendants of Gershon,[e]
  Joel the leader and 130 relatives;
8from the descendants of Elizaphan,
  Shemaiah the leader and 200 relatives;
9from the descendants of Hebron,
  Eliel the leader and 80 relatives;
10from the descendants of Uzziel,
  Amminadab the leader and 112 relatives.

11Then David summoned Zadok and Abiathar the priests, and Uriel, Asaiah, Joel, Shemaiah, Eliel and Amminadab the Levites. 12He said to them, "You are the heads of the Levitical families; you and your fellow Levites are to consecrate yourselves and bring up the ark of the LORD, the

[a] 5 Or *to the entrance to*
[b] 11 *Perez Uzzah* means *outbreak against Uzzah.*
[c] 7 A variant of *Eliada*
[d] 11 *Baal Perazim* means *the lord who breaks out.*
[e] 7 Hebrew *Gershom,* a variant of *Gershon*

God of Israel, to the place I have prepared for it.
13It was because you, the Levites, did not bring it
up the first time that the LORD our God broke out
in anger against us. We did not inquire of him
about how to do it in the prescribed way." 14So
the priests and Levites consecrated themselves in
order to bring up the ark of the LORD, the God of
Israel. 15And the Levites carried the ark of God
with the poles on their shoulders, as Moses had
commanded in accordance with the word of the
LORD.

16David told the leaders of the Levites to appoint their brothers as singers to sing joyful
songs, accompanied by musical instruments:
lyres, harps and cymbals.

17So the Levites appointed Heman son of Joel;
from his brothers, Asaph son of Berekiah; and
from their brothers the Merarites, Ethan son of
Kushaiah; 18and with them their brothers next in
rank: Zechariah,[a] Jaaziel, Shemiramoth, Jehiel,
Unni, Eliab, Benaiah, Maaseiah, Mattithiah,
Eliphelehu, Mikneiah, Obed-Edom and Jeiel,[b]
the gatekeepers.

19The musicians Heman, Asaph and Ethan
were to sound the bronze cymbals; 20Zechariah,
Aziel, Shemiramoth, Jehiel, Unni, Eliab, Maaseiah and Benaiah were to play the lyres according
to *alamoth*,[c] 21and Mattithiah, Eliphelehu, Mikneiah, Obed-Edom, Jeiel and Azaziah were to
play the harps, directing according to *sheminith*.[c] 22Kenaniah the head Levite was in charge
of the singing; that was his responsibility because
he was skillful at it.

23Berekiah and Elkanah were to be doorkeepers for the ark. 24Shebaniah, Joshaphat, Nethanel, Amasai, Zechariah, Benaiah and Eliezer the
priests were to blow trumpets before the ark of
God. Obed-Edom and Jehiah were also to be
doorkeepers for the ark.

25So David and the elders of Israel and the
commanders of units of a thousand went to bring
up the ark of the covenant of the LORD from the
house of Obed-Edom, with rejoicing. 26Because
God had helped the Levites who were carrying
the ark of the covenant of the LORD, seven bulls
and seven rams were sacrificed. 27Now David
was clothed in a robe of fine linen, as were all the
Levites who were carrying the ark, and as were
the singers, and Kenaniah, who was in charge of
the singing of the choirs. David also wore a linen
ephod. 28So all Israel brought up the ark of the
covenant of the LORD with shouts, with the
sounding of rams' horns and trumpets, and of
cymbals, and the playing of lyres and harps.

29As the ark of the covenant of the LORD was
entering the City of David, Michal daughter of
Saul watched from a window. And when she saw
King David dancing and celebrating, she despised
him in her heart.

16 They brought the ark of God and set it
inside the tent that David had pitched for
it, and they presented burnt offerings and fellowship offerings[d] before God. 2After David had finished sacrificing the burnt offerings and fellowship offerings, he blessed the people in the name
of the LORD. 3Then he gave a loaf of bread, a cake
of dates and a cake of raisins to each Israelite man
and woman.

4He appointed some of the Levites to minister
before the ark of the LORD, to make petition, to
give thanks, and to praise the LORD, the God of
Israel: 5Asaph was the chief, Zechariah second,
then Jeiel, Shemiramoth, Jehiel, Mattithiah, Eliab, Benaiah, Obed-Edom and Jeiel. They were to
play the lyres and harps, Asaph was to sound the
cymbals, 6and Benaiah and Jahaziel the priests
were to blow the trumpets regularly before the
ark of the covenant of God.

David's Psalm of Thanks

7That day David first committed to Asaph and
his associates this psalm of thanks to the LORD:

8Give thanks to the LORD, call on his name;
make known among the nations what he
has done.
9Sing to him, sing praise to him;
tell of all his wonderful acts.
10Glory in his holy name;
let the hearts of those who seek the LORD
rejoice.
11Look to the LORD and his strength;
seek his face always.
12Remember the wonders he has done,
his miracles, and the judgments he
pronounced,
13O descendants of Israel his servant,
O sons of Jacob, his chosen ones.
14He is the LORD our God;
his judgments are in all the earth.
15He remembers[e] his covenant forever,
the word he commanded, for a thousand
generations,
16the covenant he made with Abraham,
the oath he swore to Isaac.
17He confirmed it to Jacob as a decree,
to Israel as an everlasting covenant:
18"To you I will give the land of Canaan
as the portion you will inherit."

[a] *18* Three Hebrew manuscripts and most Septuagint manuscripts (see also verse 20 and 1 Chron. 16:5); most Hebrew manuscripts *Zechariah son and* or *Zechariah, Ben and* [b] *18* Hebrew; Septuagint (see also verse 21) *Jeiel and Azaziah* [c] *20,21* Probably a musical term [d] *1* Traditionally *peace offerings*; also in verse 2 [e] *15* Some Septuagint manuscripts (see also Psalm 105:8); Hebrew *Remember*

19When they were but few in number,
few indeed, and strangers in it,
20they[a] wandered from nation to nation,
from one kingdom to another.
21He allowed no man to oppress them;
for their sake he rebuked kings:
22"Do not touch my anointed ones;
do my prophets no harm."

23Sing to the LORD, all the earth;
proclaim his salvation day after day.
24Declare his glory among the nations,
his marvelous deeds among all peoples.
25For great is the LORD and most worthy of
praise;
he is to be feared above all gods.
26For all the gods of the nations are idols,
but the LORD made the heavens.
27Splendor and majesty are before him;
strength and joy in his dwelling place.
28Ascribe to the LORD, O families of nations,
ascribe to the LORD glory and strength,
29 ascribe to the LORD the glory due his
name.
Bring an offering and come before him;
worship the LORD in the splendor of his[b]
holiness.
30Tremble before him, all the earth!
The world is firmly established; it cannot
be moved.
31Let the heavens rejoice, let the earth be glad;
let them say among the nations, "The
LORD reigns!"
32Let the sea resound, and all that is in it;
let the fields be jubilant, and everything in
them!
33Then the trees of the forest will sing,
they will sing for joy before the LORD,
for he comes to judge the earth.

34Give thanks to the LORD, for he is good;
his love endures forever.
35Cry out, "Save us, O God our Savior;
gather us and deliver us from the nations,
that we may give thanks to your holy name,
that we may glory in your praise."
36Praise be to the LORD, the God of Israel,
from everlasting to everlasting.

Then all the people said "Amen" and "Praise the
LORD."

37David left Asaph and his associates before
the ark of the covenant of the LORD to minister
there regularly, according to each day's requirements. 38He also left Obed-Edom and his sixty-
eight associates to minister with them. Obed-
Edom son of Jeduthun, and also Hosah, were
gatekeepers.
39David left Zadok the priest and his fellow
priests before the tabernacle of the LORD at the
high place in Gibeon 40to present burnt offerings
to the LORD on the altar of burnt offering regularly, morning and evening, in accordance with everything written in the Law of the LORD, which
he had given Israel. 41With them were Heman
and Jeduthun and the rest of those chosen and
designated by name to give thanks to the LORD,
"for his love endures forever." 42Heman and Jeduthun were responsible for the sounding of the
trumpets and cymbals and for the playing of the
other instruments for sacred song. The sons of
Jeduthun were stationed at the gate.
43Then all the people left, each for his own
home, and David returned home to bless his family.

God's Promise to David

17 After David was settled in his palace, he
said to Nathan the prophet, "Here I am,
living in a palace of cedar, while the ark of the
covenant of the LORD is under a tent."
2Nathan replied to David, "Whatever you have
in mind, do it, for God is with you."
3That night the word of God came to Nathan,
saying:

4"Go and tell my servant David, 'This is
what the LORD says: You are not the one to
build me a house to dwell in. 5I have not
dwelt in a house from the day I brought
Israel up out of Egypt to this day. I have
moved from one tent site to another, from
one dwelling place to another. 6Wherever
I have moved with all the Israelites, did I
ever say to any of their leaders[c] whom
I commanded to shepherd my people, "Why
have you not built me a house of cedar?" '
7"Now then, tell my servant David, 'This
is what the LORD Almighty says: I took you
from the pasture and from following the
flock, to be ruler over my people Israel. 8I
have been with you wherever you have
gone, and I have cut off all your enemies
from before you. Now I will make your
name like the names of the greatest men of
the earth. 9And I will provide a place for my
people Israel and will plant them so that
they can have a home of their own and no
longer be disturbed. Wicked people will not
oppress them anymore, as they did at the
beginning 10and have done ever since the

a *18-20* One Hebrew manuscript, Septuagint and Vulgate (see also Psalm 105:12); most Hebrew manuscripts *inherit, / 19though you are but few in number, / few indeed, and strangers in it." / 20They* b *29* Or *LORD with the splendor of* c *6* Traditionally *judges;* also in verse 10

time I appointed leaders over my people Israel. I will also subdue all your enemies.
"'I declare to you that the LORD will build
a house for you: 11When your days are over
and you go to be with your fathers, I will
raise up your offspring to succeed you, one
of your own sons, and I will establish his
kingdom. 12He is the one who will build a
house for me, and I will establish his throne
forever. 13I will be his father, and he will be
my son. I will never take my love away from
him, as I took it away from your predecessor. 14I will set him over my house and my
kingdom forever; his throne will be established forever.'"

15Nathan reported to David all the words of
this entire revelation.

David's Prayer

16Then King David went in and sat before the
LORD, and he said:

"Who am I, O LORD God, and what is my
family, that you have brought me this far?
17And as if this were not enough in your
sight, O God, you have spoken about the
future of the house of your servant. You
have looked on me as though I were the
most exalted of men, O LORD God.

18"What more can David say to you for
honoring your servant? For you know your
servant, 19O LORD. For the sake of your servant and according to your will, you have
done this great thing and made known all
these great promises.

20"There is no one like you, O LORD, and
there is no God but you, as we have heard
with our own ears. 21And who is like your
people Israel—the one nation on earth
whose God went out to redeem a people for
himself, and to make a name for yourself,
and to perform great and awesome wonders
by driving out nations from before your people, whom you redeemed from Egypt?
22You made your people Israel your very
own forever, and you, O LORD, have become their God.

23"And now, LORD, let the promise you
have made concerning your servant and his
house be established forever. Do as you
promised, 24so that it will be established
and that your name will be great forever.
Then men will say, 'The LORD Almighty, the
God over Israel, is Israel's God!' And the
house of your servant David will be established before you.

25"You, my God, have revealed to your
servant that you will build a house for him.
So your servant has found courage to pray
to you. 26O LORD, you are God! You have
promised these good things to your servant.
27Now you have been pleased to bless the
house of your servant, that it may continue
forever in your sight; for you, O LORD, have
blessed it, and it will be blessed forever."

David's Victories

18 In the course of time, David defeated the
Philistines and subdued them, and he
took Gath and its surrounding villages from the
control of the Philistines.

2David also defeated the Moabites, and they
became subject to him and brought tribute.

3Moreover, David fought Hadadezer king of
Zobah, as far as Hamath, when he went to establish his control along the Euphrates River. 4David
captured a thousand of his chariots, seven thousand charioteers and twenty thousand foot soldiers. He hamstrung all but a hundred of the
chariot horses.

5When the Arameans of Damascus came to
help Hadadezer king of Zobah, David struck
down twenty-two thousand of them. 6He put garrisons in the Aramean kingdom of Damascus, and
the Arameans became subject to him and brought
tribute. The LORD gave David victory everywhere
he went.

7David took the gold shields carried by the
officers of Hadadezer and brought them to Jerusalem. 8From Tebah[a] and Cun, towns that belonged to Hadadezer, David took a great quantity
of bronze, which Solomon used to make the
bronze Sea, the pillars and various bronze articles.

9When Tou king of Hamath heard that David
had defeated the entire army of Hadadezer king
of Zobah, 10he sent his son Hadoram to King David to greet him and congratulate him on his
victory in battle over Hadadezer, who had been
at war with Tou. Hadoram brought all kinds of
articles of gold and silver and bronze.

11King David dedicated these articles to the
LORD, as he had done with the silver and gold
he had taken from all these nations: Edom and
Moab, the Ammonites and the Philistines, and
Amalek.

12Abishai son of Zeruiah struck down eighteen
thousand Edomites in the Valley of Salt. 13He put
garrisons in Edom, and all the Edomites became
subject to David. The LORD gave David victory
everywhere he went.

David's Officials

14David reigned over all Israel, doing what was

a8 Hebrew *Tibhath,* a variant of *Tebah*

just and right for all his people. 15Joab son of
Zeruiah was over the army; Jehoshaphat son of
Ahilud was recorder; 16Zadok son of Ahitub and
Ahimelech[a] son of Abiathar were priests; Shav-
sha was secretary; 17Benaiah son of Jehoiada was
over the Kerethites and Pelethites; and David's
sons were chief officials at the king's side.

The Battle Against the Ammonites

19 In the course of time, Nahash king of the
Ammonites died, and his son succeeded
him as king. 2David thought, "I will show kindness to Hanun son of Nahash, because his father
showed kindness to me." So David sent a delegation to express his sympathy to Hanun concerning his father.

When David's men came to Hanun in the land
of the Ammonites to express sympathy to him,
3the Ammonite nobles said to Hanun, "Do you
think David is honoring your father by sending
men to you to express sympathy? Haven't his
men come to you to explore and spy out the
country and overthrow it?" 4So Hanun seized David's men, shaved them, cut off their garments in
the middle at the buttocks, and sent them away.
5When someone came and told David about
the men, he sent messengers to meet them, for
they were greatly humiliated. The king said,
"Stay at Jericho till your beards have grown, and
then come back."
6When the Ammonites realized that they had
become a stench in David's nostrils, Hanun and
the Ammonites sent a thousand talents[b] of silver to hire chariots and charioteers from Aram
Naharaim,[c] Aram Maacah and Zobah. 7They
hired thirty-two thousand chariots and charioteers, as well as the king of Maacah with his
troops, who came and camped near Medeba,
while the Ammonites were mustered from their
towns and moved out for battle.
8On hearing this, David sent Joab out with the
entire army of fighting men. 9The Ammonites
came out and drew up in battle formation at the
entrance to their city, while the kings who had
come were by themselves in the open country.
10Joab saw that there were battle lines in front
of him and behind him; so he selected some of
the best troops in Israel and deployed them
against the Arameans. 11He put the rest of the
men under the command of Abishai his brother,
and they were deployed against the Ammonites.
12Joab said, "If the Arameans are too strong for
me, then you are to rescue me; but if the Ammonites are too strong for you, then I will rescue
you. 13Be strong and let us fight bravely for our
people and the cities of our God. The LORD will
do what is good in his sight."
14Then Joab and the troops with him advanced
to fight the Arameans, and they fled before him.
15When the Ammonites saw that the Arameans
were fleeing, they too fled before his brother
Abishai and went inside the city. So Joab went
back to Jerusalem.
16After the Arameans saw that they had been
routed by Israel, they sent messengers and had
Arameans brought from beyond the River,[d] with
Shophach the commander of Hadadezer's army
leading them.
17When David was told of this, he gathered
all Israel and crossed the Jordan; he advanced
against them and formed his battle lines opposite
them. David formed his lines to meet the Arameans in battle, and they fought against him. 18But
they fled before Israel, and David killed seven
thousand of their charioteers and forty thousand
of their foot soldiers. He also killed Shophach the
commander of their army.
19When the vassals of Hadadezer saw that they
had been defeated by Israel, they made peace
with David and became subject to him.

So the Arameans were not willing to help the
Ammonites anymore.

The Capture of Rabbah

20 In the spring, at the time when kings go
off to war, Joab led out the armed forces.
He laid waste the land of the Ammonites and
went to Rabbah and besieged it, but David remained in Jerusalem. Joab attacked Rabbah and
left it in ruins. 2David took the crown from the
head of their king[e]—its weight was found to be
a talent[f] of gold, and it was set with precious
stones—and it was placed on David's head. He
took a great quantity of plunder from the city
3and brought out the people who were there,
consigning them to labor with saws and with iron
picks and axes. David did this to all the Ammonite towns. Then David and his entire army returned to Jerusalem.

War With the Philistines

4In the course of time, war broke out with the
Philistines, at Gezer. At that time Sibbecai the
Hushathite killed Sippai, one of the descendants
of the Rephaites, and the Philistines were subju-
gated.
5In another battle with the Philistines, Elhanan son of Jair killed Lahmi the brother of Goliath
the Gittite, who had a spear with a shaft like a
weaver's rod.

[a] 16 Some Hebrew manuscripts, Vulgate and Syriac (see also 2 Samuel 8:17); most Hebrew manuscripts *Abimelech* [b] 6 That is, about 37 tons (about 34 metric tons) [c] 6 That is, Northwest Mesopotamia [d] 16 That is, the Euphrates [e] 2 Or *of Milcom,* that is, Molech [f] 2 That is, about 75 pounds (about 34 kilograms)

6In still another battle, which took place at
Gath, there was a huge man with six fingers on
each hand and six toes on each foot—twenty-
four in all. He also was descended from Rapha.
7When he taunted Israel, Jonathan son of Shimea, David's brother, killed him.
8These were descendants of Rapha in Gath,
and they fell at the hands of David and his men.

David Numbers the Fighting Men

21 Satan rose up against Israel and incited
David to take a census of Israel. 2So David
said to Joab and the commanders of the troops,
"Go and count the Israelites from Beersheba to
Dan. Then report back to me so that I may know
how many there are."
3But Joab replied, "May the LORD multiply his
troops a hundred times over. My lord the king,
are they not all my lord's subjects? Why does my
lord want to do this? Why should he bring guilt
on Israel?"
4The king's word, however, overruled Joab; so
Joab left and went throughout Israel and then
came back to Jerusalem. 5Joab reported the number of the fighting men to David: In all Israel
there were one million one hundred thousand
men who could handle a sword, including four
hundred and seventy thousand in Judah.
6But Joab did not include Levi and Benjamin in
the numbering, because the king's command was
repulsive to him. 7This command was also evil in
the sight of God; so he punished Israel.
8Then David said to God, "I have sinned greatly by doing this. Now, I beg you, take away the
guilt of your servant. I have done a very foolish
thing."
9The LORD said to Gad, David's seer, 10"Go
and tell David, 'This is what the LORD says: I am
giving you three options. Choose one of them for
me to carry out against you.'"
11So Gad went to David and said to him, "This
is what the LORD says: 'Take your choice: 12three
years of famine, three months of being swept
away[a] before your enemies, with their swords
overtaking you, or three days of the sword of the
LORD—days of plague in the land, with the angel
of the LORD ravaging every part of Israel.' Now
then, decide how I should answer the one who
sent me."
13David said to Gad, "I am in deep distress. Let
me fall into the hands of the LORD, for his mercy
is very great; but do not let me fall into the hands
of men."
14So the LORD sent a plague on Israel, and seventy thousand men of Israel fell dead. 15And God
sent an angel to destroy Jerusalem. But as the
angel was doing so, the LORD saw it and was
grieved because of the calamity and said to the
angel who was destroying the people, "Enough!
Withdraw your hand." The angel of the LORD was
then standing at the threshing floor of Araunah[b]
the Jebusite.
16David looked up and saw the angel of the
LORD standing between heaven and earth, with a
drawn sword in his hand extended over Jerusalem. Then David and the elders, clothed in sackcloth, fell facedown.
17David said to God, "Was it not I who ordered
the fighting men to be counted? I am the one
who has sinned and done wrong. These are but
sheep. What have they done? O LORD my God,
let your hand fall upon me and my family, but do
not let this plague remain on your people."
18Then the angel of the LORD ordered Gad to
tell David to go up and build an altar to the LORD
on the threshing floor of Araunah the Jebusite.
19So David went up in obedience to the word that
Gad had spoken in the name of the LORD.
20While Araunah was threshing wheat, he
turned and saw the angel; his four sons who were
with him hid themselves. 21Then David approached, and when Araunah looked and saw
him, he left the threshing floor and bowed down
before David with his face to the ground.
22David said to him, "Let me have the site of
your threshing floor so I can build an altar to the
LORD, that the plague on the people may be
stopped. Sell it to me at the full price."
23Araunah said to David, "Take it! Let my lord
the king do whatever pleases him. Look, I will
give the oxen for the burnt offerings, the threshing sledges for the wood, and the wheat for the
grain offering. I will give all this."
24But King David replied to Araunah, "No, I
insist on paying the full price. I will not take for
the LORD what is yours, or sacrifice a burnt offering that costs me nothing."
25So David paid Araunah six hundred shek-
els[c] of gold for the site. 26David built an altar to
the LORD there and sacrificed burnt offerings and
fellowship offerings.[d] He called on the LORD,
and the LORD answered him with fire from heav-
en on the altar of burnt offering.
27Then the LORD spoke to the angel, and he
put his sword back into its sheath. 28At that time,
when David saw that the LORD had answered
him on the threshing floor of Araunah the Jebusite, he offered sacrifices there. 29The tabernacle
of the LORD, which Moses had made in the
desert, and the altar of burnt offering were at that
time on the high place at Gibeon. 30But David
could not go before it to inquire of God, because

[a]12 Hebrew; Septuagint and Vulgate (see also 2 Samuel 24:13) *of fleeing* [b]15 Hebrew *Ornan,* a variant of *Araunah;* also in verses 18-28 [c]25 That is, about 15 pounds (about 7 kilograms) [d]26 Traditionally *peace offerings*

he was afraid of the sword of the angel of the
LORD.
22 Then David said, "The house of the LORD
God is to be here, and also the altar of
burnt offering for Israel."

Preparations for the Temple

2So David gave orders to assemble the aliens
living in Israel, and from among them he appointed stonecutters to prepare dressed stone for
building the house of God. 3He provided a large
amount of iron to make nails for the doors of the
gateways and for the fittings, and more bronze
than could be weighed. 4He also provided more
cedar logs than could be counted, for the Sidonians and Tyrians had brought large numbers of
them to David.
5David said, "My son Solomon is young and
inexperienced, and the house to be built for the
LORD should be of great magnificence and fame
and splendor in the sight of all the nations.
Therefore I will make preparations for it." So David made extensive preparations before his
death.
6Then he called for his son Solomon and
charged him to build a house for the LORD, the
God of Israel. 7David said to Solomon: "My son,
I had it in my heart to build a house for the Name
of the LORD my God. 8But this word of the LORD
came to me: 'You have shed much blood and
have fought many wars. You are not to build a
house for my Name, because you have shed
much blood on the earth in my sight. 9But you
will have a son who will be a man of peace and
rest, and I will give him rest from all his enemies
on every side. His name will be Solomon,[a] and
I will grant Israel peace and quiet during his
reign. 10He is the one who will build a house for
my Name. He will be my son, and I will be his
father. And I will establish the throne of his kingdom over Israel forever.'
11"Now, my son, the LORD be with you, and
may you have success and build the house of the
LORD your God, as he said you would. 12May
the LORD give you discretion and understanding
when he puts you in command over Israel, so
that you may keep the law of the LORD your God.
13Then you will have success if you are careful to
observe the decrees and laws that the LORD gave
Moses for Israel. Be strong and courageous. Do
not be afraid or discouraged.
14"I have taken great pains to provide for the
temple of the LORD a hundred thousand talents[b]
of gold, a million talents[c] of silver, quantities of
bronze and iron too great to be weighed, and
wood and stone. And you may add to them. 15You
have many workmen: stonecutters, masons and
carpenters, as well as men skilled in every kind
of work 16in gold and silver, bronze and iron—
craftsmen beyond number. Now begin the work,
and the LORD be with you."
17Then David ordered all the leaders of Israel
to help his son Solomon. 18He said to them, "Is
not the LORD your God with you? And has he not
granted you rest on every side? For he has handed the inhabitants of the land over to me, and the
land is subject to the LORD and to his people.
19Now devote your heart and soul to seeking the
LORD your God. Begin to build the sanctuary of
the LORD God, so that you may bring the ark of
the covenant of the LORD and the sacred articles
belonging to God into the temple that will be
built for the Name of the LORD."

The Levites

23 When David was old and full of years, he
made his son Solomon king over Israel.
2He also gathered together all the leaders of
Israel, as well as the priests and Levites. 3The
Levites thirty years old or more were counted,
and the total number of men was thirty-eight
thousand. 4David said, "Of these, twenty-four
thousand are to supervise the work of the temple
of the LORD and six thousand are to be officials
and judges. 5Four thousand are to be gatekeepers
and four thousand are to praise the LORD with the
musical instruments I have provided for that purpose."
6David divided the Levites into groups corresponding to the sons of Levi: Gershon, Kohath
and Merari.

Gershonites

7Belonging to the Gershonites:
Ladan and Shimei.
8The sons of Ladan:
Jehiel the first, Zetham and Joel—three
in all.
9The sons of Shimei:
Shelomoth, Haziel and Haran—three in
all.
These were the heads of the families of
Ladan.
10And the sons of Shimei:
Jahath, Ziza,[d] Jeush and Beriah.
These were the sons of Shimei—four in
all.
11Jahath was the first and Ziza the second,
but Jeush and Beriah did not have many

[a] 9 *Solomon* sounds like and may be derived from the Hebrew for *peace.*
[b] 14 That is, about 3,750 tons (about 3,450 metric tons)
[c] 14 That is, about 37,500 tons (about 34,500 metric tons)
[d] 10 One Hebrew manuscript, Septuagint and Vulgate (see also verse 11); most Hebrew manuscripts *Zina*

sons; so they were counted as one family
with one assignment.

Kohathites

12The sons of Kohath:
Amram, Izhar, Hebron and Uzziel—four
in all.
13The sons of Amram:
Aaron and Moses.
Aaron was set apart, he and his descendants forever, to consecrate the most
holy things, to offer sacrifices before the
LORD, to minister before him and to pronounce blessings in his name forever.
14The sons of Moses the man of God
were counted as part of the tribe of Levi.
15The sons of Moses:
Gershom and Eliezer.
16The descendants of Gershom:
Shubael was the first.
17The descendants of Eliezer:
Rehabiah was the first.
Eliezer had no other sons, but the sons
of Rehabiah were very numerous.
18The sons of Izhar:
Shelomith was the first.
19The sons of Hebron:
Jeriah the first, Amariah the second, Jahaziel the third and Jekameam the
fourth.
20The sons of Uzziel:
Micah the first and Isshiah the second.

Merarites

21The sons of Merari:
Mahli and Mushi.
The sons of Mahli:
Eleazar and Kish.
22Eleazar died without having sons: he
had only daughters. Their cousins, the
sons of Kish, married them.
23The sons of Mushi:
Mahli, Eder and Jerimoth—three in all.

24These were the descendants of Levi by their
families—the heads of families as they were registered under their names and counted individu-
ally, that is, the workers twenty years old or more
who served in the temple of the LORD. 25For David had said, "Since the LORD, the God of Israel,
has granted rest to his people and has come to
dwell in Jerusalem forever, 26the Levites no longer need to carry the tabernacle or any of the articles used in its service." 27According to the last
instructions of David, the Levites were counted
from those twenty years old or more.

28The duty of the Levites was to help Aaron's
descendants in the service of the temple of the
LORD: to be in charge of the courtyards, the side
rooms, the purification of all sacred things and
the performance of other duties at the house of
God. 29They were in charge of the bread set out
on the table, the flour for the grain offerings, the
unleavened wafers, the baking and the mixing,
and all measurements of quantity and size.
30They were also to stand every morning to thank
and praise the LORD. They were to do the same
in the evening 31and whenever burnt offerings
were presented to the LORD on Sabbaths and at
New Moon festivals and at appointed feasts. They
were to serve before the LORD regularly in the
proper number and in the way prescribed for
them.

32And so the Levites carried out their responsibilities for the Tent of Meeting, for the Holy
Place and, under their brothers the descendants
of Aaron, for the service of the temple of the
LORD.

The Divisions of Priests

24 These were the divisions of the sons of
Aaron:
The sons of Aaron were Nadab, Abihu, Eleazar
and Ithamar. 2But Nadab and Abihu died before
their father did, and they had no sons; so Eleazar
and Ithamar served as the priests. 3With the help
of Zadok a descendant of Eleazar and Ahimelech
a descendant of Ithamar, David separated them
into divisions for their appointed order of ministering. 4A larger number of leaders were found
among Eleazar's descendants than among Ithamar's, and they were divided accordingly: sixteen heads of families from Eleazar's descendants
and eight heads of families from Ithamar's
descendants. 5They divided them impartially by
drawing lots, for there were officials of the sanctuary and officials of God among the descendants
of both Eleazar and Ithamar.

6The scribe Shemaiah son of Nethanel, a Levite, recorded their names in the presence of the
king and of the officials: Zadok the priest, Ahimelech son of Abiathar and the heads of families of
the priests and of the Levites—one family being
taken from Eleazar and then one from Ithamar.

7The first lot fell to Jehoiarib,
the second to Jedaiah,
8the third to Harim,
the fourth to Seorim,
9the fifth to Malkijah,
the sixth to Mijamin,
10the seventh to Hakkoz,
the eighth to Abijah,
11the ninth to Jeshua,
the tenth to Shecaniah,
12the eleventh to Eliashib,
the twelfth to Jakim,
13the thirteenth to Huppah,

the fourteenth to Jeshebeab,
14the fifteenth to Bilgah,
the sixteenth to Immer,
15the seventeenth to Hezir,
the eighteenth to Happizzez,
16the nineteenth to Pethahiah,
the twentieth to Jehezkel,
17the twenty-first to Jakin,
the twenty-second to Gamul,
18the twenty-third to Delaiah
and the twenty-fourth to Maaziah.

19This was their appointed order of ministering when they entered the temple of the LORD, according to the regulations prescribed for them by their forefather Aaron, as the LORD, the God of Israel, had commanded him.

The Rest of the Levites

20As for the rest of the descendants of Levi:
from the sons of Amram: Shubael;
from the sons of Shubael: Jehdeiah.
21As for Rehabiah, from his sons:
Isshiah was the first.
22From the Izharites: Shelomoth;
from the sons of Shelomoth: Jahath.
23The sons of Hebron: Jeriah the first,[a] Amariah the second, Jahaziel the third and Jekameam the fourth.
24The son of Uzziel: Micah;
from the sons of Micah: Shamir.
25The brother of Micah: Isshiah;
from the sons of Isshiah: Zechariah.
26The sons of Merari: Mahli and Mushi.
The son of Jaaziah: Beno.
27The sons of Merari:
from Jaaziah: Beno, Shoham, Zaccur and Ibri.
28From Mahli: Eleazar, who had no sons.
29From Kish: the son of Kish:
Jerahmeel.
30And the sons of Mushi: Mahli, Eder and Jerimoth.

These were the Levites, according to their families.
31They also cast lots, just as their brothers the descendants of Aaron did, in the presence of King David and of Zadok, Ahimelech, and the heads of families of the priests and of the Levites. The families of the oldest brother were treated the same as those of the youngest.

The Singers

25 David, together with the commanders of the army, set apart some of the sons of Asaph, Heman and Jeduthun for the ministry of prophesying, accompanied by harps, lyres and cymbals. Here is the list of the men who performed this service:

2From the sons of Asaph:
Zaccur, Joseph, Nethaniah and Asarelah. The sons of Asaph were under the supervision of Asaph, who prophesied under the king's supervision.
3As for Jeduthun, from his sons:
Gedaliah, Zeri, Jeshaiah, Shimei,[b] Hashabiah and Mattithiah, six in all, under the supervision of their father Jeduthun, who prophesied, using the harp in thanking and praising the LORD.
4As for Heman, from his sons:
Bukkiah, Mattaniah, Uzziel, Shubael and Jerimoth; Hananiah, Hanani, Eliathah, Giddalti and Romamti-Ezer; Joshbekashah, Mallothi, Hothir and Mahazioth.
5All these were sons of Heman the king's seer. They were given him through the promises of God to exalt him.[c] God gave Heman fourteen sons and three daughters.

6All these men were under the supervision of their fathers for the music of the temple of the LORD, with cymbals, lyres and harps, for the ministry at the house of God. Asaph, Jeduthun and Heman were under the supervision of the king.
7Along with their relatives—all of them trained and skilled in music for the LORD—they numbered 288.
8Young and old alike, teacher as well as student, cast lots for their duties.

9The first lot, which was for Asaph, fell to Joseph,
his sons and relatives,[d] 12[e]
the second to Gedaliah,
he and his relatives and sons, 12
10the third to Zaccur,
his sons and relatives, 12
11the fourth to Izri,[f]
his sons and relatives, 12
12the fifth to Nethaniah,
his sons and relatives, 12
13the sixth to Bukkiah,
his sons and relatives, 12
14the seventh to Jesarelah,[g]
his sons and relatives, 12
15the eighth to Jeshaiah,
his sons and relatives, 12
16the ninth to Mattaniah,
his sons and relatives, 12
17the tenth to Shimei,
his sons and relatives, 12

[a]23 Two Hebrew manuscripts and some Septuagint manuscripts (see also 1 Chron. 23:19); most Hebrew manuscripts *The sons of Jeriah:* [b]3 One Hebrew manuscript and some Septuagint manuscripts (see also verse 17); most Hebrew manuscripts do not have *Shimei.* [c]5 Hebrew *exalt the horn* [d]9 See Septuagint; Hebrew does not have *his sons and relatives.* [e]9 See the total in verse 7; Hebrew does not have *twelve.* [f]11 A variant of *Zeri* [g]14 A variant of *Asarelah*

18the eleventh to Azarel,[a]
his sons and relatives, 12
19the twelfth to Hashabiah,
his sons and relatives, 12
20the thirteenth to Shubael,
his sons and relatives, 12
21the fourteenth to Mattithiah,
his sons and relatives, 12
22the fifteenth to Jerimoth,
his sons and relatives, 12
23the sixteenth to Hananiah,
his sons and relatives, 12
24the seventeenth to Joshbekashah,
his sons and relatives, 12
25the eighteenth to Hanani,
his sons and relatives, 12
26the nineteenth to Mallothi,
his sons and relatives, 12
27the twentieth to Eliathah,
his sons and relatives, 12
28the twenty-first to Hothir,
his sons and relatives, 12
29the twenty-second to Giddalti,
his sons and relatives, 12
30the twenty-third to Mahazioth,
his sons and relatives, 12
31the twenty-fourth to Romamti-Ezer,
his sons and relatives, 12

The Gatekeepers

26 The divisions of the gatekeepers:

From the Korahites: Meshelemiah son of Kore, one of the sons of Asaph.
2Meshelemiah had sons:
Zechariah the firstborn,
Jediael the second,
Zebadiah the third,
Jathniel the fourth,
3Elam the fifth,
Jehohanan the sixth
and Eliehoenai the seventh.
4Obed-Edom also had sons:
Shemaiah the firstborn,
Jehozabad the second,
Joah the third,
Sacar the fourth,
Nethanel the fifth,
5Ammiel the sixth,
Issachar the seventh
and Peullethai the eighth.
(For God had blessed Obed-Edom.)

6His son Shemaiah also had sons, who were
leaders in their father's family because
they were very capable men. 7The sons
of Shemaiah: Othni, Rephael, Obed and
Elzabad; his relatives Elihu and Semaki-
ah were also able men. 8All these were
descendants of Obed-Edom; they and
their sons and their relatives were capable men with the strength to do the
work—descendants of Obed-Edom, 62
in all.
9Meshelemiah had sons and relatives, who
were able men—18 in all.

10Hosah the Merarite had sons: Shimri the
first (although he was not the firstborn,
his father had appointed him the first),
11Hilkiah the second, Tabaliah the third
and Zechariah the fourth. The sons and
relatives of Hosah were 13 in all.

12These divisions of the gatekeepers, through
their chief men, had duties for ministering in the
temple of the LORD, just as their relatives had.
13Lots were cast for each gate, according to their
families, young and old alike.
14The lot for the East Gate fell to Shelemiah.[b]
Then lots were cast for his son Zechariah, a wise
counselor, and the lot for the North Gate fell to
him. 15The lot for the South Gate fell to Obed-
Edom, and the lot for the storehouse fell to his
sons. 16The lots for the West Gate and the Shalle-
keth Gate on the upper road fell to Shuppim and
Hosah.

Guard was alongside of guard: 17There were
six Levites a day on the east, four a day on the
north, four a day on the south and two at a time
at the storehouse. 18As for the court to the west,
there were four at the road and two at the court
itself.
19These were the divisions of the gatekeepers
who were descendants of Korah and Merari.

The Treasurers and Other Officials

20Their fellow Levites were[c] in charge of the
treasuries of the house of God and the treasuries
for the dedicated things.
21The descendants of Ladan, who were Gershonites through Ladan and who were heads of
families belonging to Ladan the Gershonite, were
Jehieli, 22the sons of Jehieli, Zetham and his
brother Joel. They were in charge of the treasuries of the temple of the LORD.
23From the Amramites, the Izharites, the Hebronites and the Uzzielites:

24Shubael, a descendant of Gershom son of
Moses, was the officer in charge of the
treasuries. 25His relatives through Eliezer: Rehabiah his son, Jeshaiah his son,
Joram his son, Zicri his son and Shelomith his son. 26Shelomith and his rela-

a18 A variant of *Uzziel* b14 A variant of *Meshelemiah* c20 Septuagint; Hebrew *As for the Levites, Ahijah was*

tives were in charge of all the treasuries
for the things dedicated by King David,
by the heads of families who were the
commanders of thousands and commanders of hundreds, and by the other
army commanders. 27Some of the plunder taken in battle they dedicated for the
repair of the temple of the LORD. 28And
everything dedicated by Samuel the seer
and by Saul son of Kish, Abner son of
Ner and Joab son of Zeruiah, and all the
other dedicated things were in the care
of Shelomith and his relatives.
29From the Izharites: Kenaniah and his sons
were assigned duties away from the
temple, as officials and judges over Israel.
30From the Hebronites: Hashabiah and his
relatives—seventeen hundred able
men—were responsible in Israel west of
the Jordan for all the work of the LORD
and for the king's service. 31As for the
Hebronites, Jeriah was their chief according to the genealogical records of
their families. In the fortieth year of David's reign a search was made in the
records, and capable men among the
Hebronites were found at Jazer in Gilead. 32Jeriah had twenty-seven hundred
relatives, who were able men and heads
of families, and King David put them in
charge of the Reubenites, the Gadites
and the half-tribe of Manasseh for every
matter pertaining to God and for the affairs of the king.

Army Divisions

27 This is the list of the Israelites—heads of
families, commanders of thousands and
commanders of hundreds, and their officers, who
served the king in all that concerned the army
divisions that were on duty month by month
throughout the year. Each division consisted of
24,000 men.

2In charge of the first division, for the first
month, was Jashobeam son of Zabdiel.
There were 24,000 men in his division. 3He
was a descendant of Perez and chief of all
the army officers for the first month.
4In charge of the division for the second month
was Dodai the Ahohite; Mikloth was the
leader of his division. There were 24,000
men in his division.
5The third army commander, for the third
month, was Benaiah son of Jehoiada the
priest. He was chief and there were 24,000
men in his division. 6This was the Benaiah
who was a mighty man among the Thirty
and was over the Thirty. His son Ammiza-
bad was in charge of his division.
7The fourth, for the fourth month, was Asahel
the brother of Joab; his son Zebadiah was his
successor. There were 24,000 men in his
division.
8The fifth, for the fifth month, was the commander Shamhuth the Izrahite. There were
24,000 men in his division.
9The sixth, for the sixth month, was Ira the son
of Ikkesh the Tekoite. There were 24,000
men in his division.
10The seventh, for the seventh month, was Helez
the Pelonite, an Ephraimite. There were
24,000 men in his division.
11The eighth, for the eighth month, was Sibbecai
the Hushathite, a Zerahite. There were
24,000 men in his division.
12The ninth, for the ninth month, was Abiezer
the Anathothite, a Benjamite. There were
24,000 men in his division.
13The tenth, for the tenth month, was Maharai
the Netophathite, a Zerahite. There were
24,000 men in his division.
14The eleventh, for the eleventh month, was Benaiah the Pirathonite, an Ephraimite. There
were 24,000 men in his division.
15The twelfth, for the twelfth month, was Heldai
the Netophathite, from the family of Othniel. There were 24,000 men in his division.

Officers of the Tribes

16The officers over the tribes of Israel:
over the Reubenites: Eliezer son of Zicri;
over the Simeonites: Shephatiah son of Maacah;
17over Levi: Hashabiah son of Kemuel;
over Aaron: Zadok;
18over Judah: Elihu, a brother of David;
over Issachar: Omri son of Michael;
19over Zebulun: Ishmaiah son of Obadiah;
over Naphtali: Jerimoth son of Azriel;
20over the Ephraimites: Hoshea son of Azaziah;
over half the tribe of Manasseh: Joel son of
Pedaiah;
21over the half-tribe of Manasseh in Gilead:
Iddo son of Zechariah;
over Benjamin: Jaasiel son of Abner;
22over Dan: Azarel son of Jeroham.
These were the officers over the tribes of Israel.

23David did not take the number of the men
twenty years old or less, because the LORD had
promised to make Israel as numerous as the stars
in the sky. 24Joab son of Zeruiah began to count

the men but did not finish. Wrath came on Israel
on account of this numbering, and the number
was not entered in the book[a] of the annals of
King David.

The King's Overseers

25Azmaveth son of Adiel was in charge of the
royal storehouses.
Jonathan son of Uzziah was in charge of the
storehouses in the outlying districts, in the
towns, the villages and the watchtowers.
26Ezri son of Kelub was in charge of the field
workers who farmed the land.
27Shimei the Ramathite was in charge of the
vineyards.
Zabdi the Shiphmite was in charge of the produce of the vineyards for the wine vats.
28Baal-Hanan the Gederite was in charge of
the olive and sycamore-fig trees in the western
foothills.
Joash was in charge of the supplies of olive oil.
29Shitrai the Sharonite was in charge of the
herds grazing in Sharon.
Shaphat son of Adlai was in charge of the
herds in the valleys.
30Obil the Ishmaelite was in charge of the
camels.
Jehdeiah the Meronothite was in charge of the
donkeys.
31Jaziz the Hagrite was in charge of the flocks.
All these were the officials in charge of King
David's property.

32Jonathan, David's uncle, was a counselor, a
man of insight and a scribe. Jehiel son of Hacmo-
ni took care of the king's sons.
33Ahithophel was the king's counselor.
Hushai the Arkite was the king's friend.
34Ahithophel was succeeded by Jehoiada son of
Benaiah and by Abiathar.
Joab was the commander of the royal army.

David's Plans for the Temple

28 David summoned all the officials of Israel
to assemble at Jerusalem: the officers over
the tribes, the commanders of the divisions in the
service of the king, the commanders of thousands
and commanders of hundreds, and the officials in
charge of all the property and livestock belonging
to the king and his sons, together with the palace
officials, the mighty men and all the brave warriors.
2King David rose to his feet and said: "Listen
to me, my brothers and my people. I had it in my
heart to build a house as a place of rest for the ark
of the covenant of the LORD, for the footstool of
our God, and I made plans to build it. 3But God
said to me, 'You are not to build a house for my
Name, because you are a warrior and have shed
blood.'
4"Yet the LORD, the God of Israel, chose me
from my whole family to be king over Israel forever. He chose Judah as leader, and from the house
of Judah he chose my family, and from my father's sons he was pleased to make me king over
all Israel. 5Of all my sons—and the LORD has
given me many—he has chosen my son Solomon
to sit on the throne of the kingdom of the LORD
over Israel. 6He said to me: 'Solomon your son is
the one who will build my house and my courts,
for I have chosen him to be my son, and I will be
his father. 7I will establish his kingdom forever if
he is unswerving in carrying out my commands
and laws, as is being done at this time.'
8"So now I charge you in the sight of all Israel
and of the assembly of the LORD, and in the
hearing of our God: Be careful to follow all the
commands of the LORD your God, that you may
possess this good land and pass it on as an
inheritance to your descendants forever.
9"And you, my son Solomon, acknowledge the
God of your father, and serve him with wholehearted devotion and with a willing mind, for the
LORD searches every heart and understands every
motive behind the thoughts. If you seek him, he
will be found by you; but if you forsake him, he
will reject you forever. 10Consider now, for the
LORD has chosen you to build a temple as a sanctuary. Be strong and do the work."
11Then David gave his son Solomon the plans
for the portico of the temple, its buildings, its
storerooms, its upper parts, its inner rooms and
the place of atonement. 12He gave him the plans
of all that the Spirit had put in his mind for the
courts of the temple of the LORD and all the surrounding rooms, for the treasuries of the temple
of God and for the treasuries for the dedicated
things. 13He gave him instructions for the divisions of the priests and Levites, and for all the
work of serving in the temple of the LORD, as well
as for all the articles to be used in its service.
14He designated the weight of gold for all the gold
articles to be used in various kinds of service, and
the weight of silver for all the silver articles to be
used in various kinds of service: 15the weight of
gold for the gold lampstands and their lamps,
with the weight for each lampstand and its
lamps; and the weight of silver for each silver
lampstand and its lamps, according to the use of
each lampstand; 16the weight of gold for each
table for consecrated bread; the weight of silver
for the silver tables; 17the weight of pure gold
for the forks, sprinkling bowls and pitchers; the

[a] *24* Septuagint; Hebrew *number*

weight of gold for each gold dish; the weight of
silver for each silver dish; 18 and the weight of the
refined gold for the altar of incense. He also gave
him the plan for the chariot, that is, the cherubim
of gold that spread their wings and shelter the ark
of the covenant of the LORD.
19 "All this," David said, "I have in writing
from the hand of the LORD upon me, and he gave
me understanding in all the details of the plan."
20 David also said to Solomon his son, "Be
strong and courageous, and do the work. Do not
be afraid or discouraged, for the LORD God, my
God, is with you. He will not fail you or forsake
you until all the work for the service of the temple of the LORD is finished. 21 The divisions of the
priests and Levites are ready for all the work on
the temple of God, and every willing man skilled
in any craft will help you in all the work. The
officials and all the people will obey your every
command."

Gifts for Building the Temple

29 Then King David said to the whole assembly: "My son Solomon, the one whom
God has chosen, is young and inexperienced.
The task is great, because this palatial structure is
not for man but for the LORD God. 2 With all my
resources I have provided for the temple of my
God—gold for the gold work, silver for the silver,
bronze for the bronze, iron for the iron and wood
for the wood, as well as onyx for the settings,
turquoise,[a] stones of various colors, and all
kinds of fine stone and marble—all of these in
large quantities. 3 Besides, in my devotion to the
temple of my God I now give my personal treasures of gold and silver for the temple of my God,
over and above everything I have provided for
this holy temple: 4 three thousand talents[b] of
gold (gold of Ophir) and seven thousand talents[c]
of refined silver, for the overlaying of the walls of
the buildings, 5 for the gold work and the silver
work, and for all the work to be done by the
craftsmen. Now, who is willing to consecrate
himself today to the LORD?"
6 Then the leaders of families, the officers of
the tribes of Israel, the commanders of thousands
and commanders of hundreds, and the officials in
charge of the king's work gave willingly. 7 They
gave toward the work on the temple of God five
thousand talents[d] and ten thousand darics[e] of
gold, ten thousand talents[f] of silver, eighteen
thousand talents[g] of bronze and a hundred thousand talents[h] of iron. 8 Any who had precious
stones gave them to the treasury of the temple of
the LORD in the custody of Jehiel the Gershonite.
9 The people rejoiced at the willing response of
their leaders, for they had given freely and wholeheartedly to the LORD. David the king also rejoiced greatly.

David's Prayer

10 David praised the LORD in the presence of
the whole assembly, saying,

"Praise be to you, O LORD,
  God of our father Israel,
  from everlasting to everlasting.
11 Yours, O LORD, is the greatness and the power
  and the glory and the majesty and the splendor,
  for everything in heaven and earth is yours.
Yours, O LORD, is the kingdom;
  you are exalted as head over all.
12 Wealth and honor come from you;
  you are the ruler of all things.
In your hands are strength and power
  to exalt and give strength to all.
13 Now, our God, we give you thanks,
  and praise your glorious name.

14 "But who am I, and who are my people, that
we should be able to give as generously as this?
Everything comes from you, and we have given
you only what comes from your hand. 15 We are
aliens and strangers in your sight, as were all our
forefathers. Our days on earth are like a shadow,
without hope. 16 O LORD our God, as for all this
abundance that we have provided for building
you a temple for your Holy Name, it comes from
your hand, and all of it belongs to you. 17 I know,
my God, that you test the heart and are pleased
with integrity. All these things have I given willingly and with honest intent. And now I have
seen with joy how willingly your people who are
here have given to you. 18 O LORD, God of our
fathers Abraham, Isaac and Israel, keep this desire in the hearts of your people forever, and keep
their hearts loyal to you. 19 And give my son Solomon the wholehearted devotion to keep your
commands, requirements and decrees and to do
everything to build the palatial structure for
which I have provided."
20 Then David said to the whole assembly,
"Praise the LORD your God." So they all praised
the LORD, the God of their fathers; they bowed
low and fell prostrate before the LORD and the
king.

[a] 2 The meaning of the Hebrew for this word is uncertain. [b] 4 That is, about 110 tons (about 100 metric tons) [c] 4 That is, about 260 tons (about 240 metric tons) [d] 7 That is, about 190 tons (about 170 metric tons) [e] 7 That is, about 185 pounds (about 84 kilograms) [f] 7 That is, about 375 tons (about 345 metric tons) [g] 7 That is, about 675 tons (about 610 metric tons) [h] 7 That is, about 3,750 tons (about 3,450 metric tons)

Solomon Acknowledged as King

21The next day they made sacrifices to the LORD and presented burnt offerings to him: a thousand bulls, a thousand rams and a thousand male lambs, together with their drink offerings, and other sacrifices in abundance for all Israel.
22They ate and drank with great joy in the presence of the LORD that day.

Then they acknowledged Solomon son of David as king a second time, anointing him before the LORD to be ruler and Zadok to be priest. 23So Solomon sat on the throne of the LORD as king in place of his father David. He prospered and all Israel obeyed him. 24All the officers and mighty men, as well as all of King David's sons, pledged their submission to King Solomon.

25The LORD highly exalted Solomon in the sight of all Israel and bestowed on him royal splendor such as no king over Israel ever had before.

The Death of David

26David son of Jesse was king over all Israel.
27He ruled over Israel forty years—seven in Hebron and thirty-three in Jerusalem. 28He died at a good old age, having enjoyed long life, wealth and honor. His son Solomon succeeded him as king.

29As for the events of King David's reign, from beginning to end, they are written in the records of Samuel the seer, the records of Nathan the prophet and the records of Gad the seer, 30together with the details of his reign and power, and the circumstances that surrounded him and Israel and the kingdoms of all the other lands.

Introduction to
2 CHRONICLES

Personal Reading Plan

❐ 2 Chronicles 1:1–3:17
❐ 2 Chronicles 4:1–6:11
❐ 2 Chronicles 6:12–7:10
❐ 2 Chronicles 7:11–9:12
❐ 2 Chronicles 9:13–11:4
❐ 2 Chronicles 11:5–14:1
❐ 2 Chronicles 14:2–16:14
❐ 2 Chronicles 17:1–18:27
❐ 2 Chronicles 18:28–20:30
❐ 2 Chronicles 20:31–22:9
❐ 2 Chronicles 22:10–24:16
❐ 2 Chronicles 24:17–25:28
❐ 2 Chronicles 26:1–28:27
❐ 2 Chronicles 29:1–36
❐ 2 Chronicles 30:1–31:21
❐ 2 Chronicles 32:1–33:25
❐ 2 Chronicles 34:1–33
❐ 2 Chronicles 35:1–36:23

Author

Jewish tradition suggests Ezra as author. This may well be the case, but there is no firm evidence.

Date

Second Chronicles was probably written toward the end of the fifth century B.C. or a little later. The events narrated span 970–538 B.C.

Theme

Kingship and worship in Judah from Solomon to the Exile.

Historical Background

After the glory days of Israel under Solomon, warfare and unrest divide the nation, the people forsake temple worship for idols, and they lose their national identity when Jerusalem is totally destroyed in 586 B.C. Along the way, the southern kingdom of Judah is led into slow decline by evil kings and, alternately, into periods of spiritual reformation and restored national pride by Asa, Jehoshaphat, Uzziah, Hezekiah and Josiah. Judah's slow decline (and the chronicler's account) ends with the Exile, but a "postscript" gives us a brief glimpse of future restoration.

Characteristics

The major interests of 1 Chronicles—the Davidic dynasty and the temple worship—are continued in 2 Chronicles. Compared to the colorful stories in the books of Samuel and Kings, the chronicler has written a blander account. The stains of David's or Solomon's past are not given attention. Instead, the great wealth, worldwide acclaim, political stability, and magnificent temple get full-page treatment (chapters 1–9). Each king is evaluated on the basis of his response to God, especially as to worship of God and obedience to the Law. Those who introduce reforms are given top billing and the nature of their reforms is described in some detail.

Some of the details included in 2 Chronicles that are not mentioned in Samuel and Kings are: (1) God giving the plans for both the tabernacle and temple; (2) the spoils of war being used as building materials for both tabernacle and temple; (3) the people generously contributing for both structures; and (4) the glory cloud appearing at the dedication of both structures.

Solomon Asks for Wisdom

1 Solomon son of David established himself firmly over his kingdom, for the LORD his God was with him and made him exceedingly great.

[2]Then Solomon spoke to all Israel—to the commanders of thousands and commanders of hundreds, to the judges and to all the leaders in Israel, the heads of families— [3]and Solomon and the whole assembly went to the high place at Gibeon, for God's Tent of Meeting was there, which Moses the LORD's servant had made in the desert. [4]Now David had brought up the ark of God from Kiriath Jearim to the place he had prepared for it, because he had pitched a tent for it in Jerusalem. [5]But the bronze altar that Bezalel son of Uri, the son of Hur, had made was in Gibeon in front of the tabernacle of the LORD; so Solomon and the assembly inquired of him there. [6]Solomon went up to the bronze altar before the LORD in the Tent of Meeting and offered a thousand burnt offerings on it.

[7]That night God appeared to Solomon and said to him, "Ask for whatever you want me to give you."

[8]Solomon answered God, "You have shown great kindness to David my father and have made me king in his place. [9]Now, LORD God, let your promise to my father David be confirmed, for you have made me king over a people who are as numerous as the dust of the earth. [10]Give me wisdom and knowledge, that I may lead this people, for who is able to govern this great people of yours?"

[11]God said to Solomon, "Since this is your heart's desire and you have not asked for wealth, riches or honor, nor for the death of your enemies, and since you have not asked for a long life but for wisdom and knowledge to govern my people over whom I have made you king, [12]therefore wisdom and knowledge will be given you. And I will also give you wealth, riches and honor, such as no king who was before you ever had and none after you will have."

[13]Then Solomon went to Jerusalem from the high place at Gibeon, from before the Tent of Meeting. And he reigned over Israel.

[14]Solomon accumulated chariots and horses; he had fourteen hundred chariots and twelve thousand horses,[a] which he kept in the chariot cities and also with him in Jerusalem. [15]The king made silver and gold as common in Jerusalem as stones, and cedar as plentiful as sycamore-fig trees in the foothills. [16]Solomon's horses were imported from Egypt[b] and from Kue[c]—the royal merchants purchased them from Kue. [17]They imported a chariot from Egypt for six hundred shekels[d] of silver, and a horse for a hundred and fifty.[e] They also exported them to all the kings of the Hittites and of the Arameans.

Preparations for Building the Temple

2 Solomon gave orders to build a temple for the Name of the LORD and a royal palace for himself. [2]He conscripted seventy thousand men as carriers and eighty thousand as stonecutters in the hills and thirty-six hundred as foremen over them.

[3]Solomon sent this message to Hiram[f] king of Tyre:

"Send me cedar logs as you did for my father David when you sent him cedar to build a palace to live in. [4]Now I am about to build a temple for the Name of the LORD my God and to dedicate it to him for burning fragrant incense before him, for setting out the consecrated bread regularly, and for making burnt offerings every morning and evening and on Sabbaths and New Moons and at the appointed feasts of the LORD our God. This is a lasting ordinance for Israel.

[5]"The temple I am going to build will be great, because our God is greater than all other gods. [6]But who is able to build a temple for him, since the heavens, even the highest heavens, cannot contain him? Who then am I to build a temple for him, except as a place to burn sacrifices before him?

[7]"Send me, therefore, a man skilled to work in gold and silver, bronze and iron, and in purple, crimson and blue yarn, and experienced in the art of engraving, to work in Judah and Jerusalem with my skilled craftsmen, whom my father David provided.

[8]"Send me also cedar, pine and algum[g] logs from Lebanon, for I know that your men are skilled in cutting timber there. My men will work with yours [9]to provide me with plenty of lumber, because the temple I build must be large and magnificent. [10]I will give your servants, the woodsmen who cut the timber, twenty thousand cors[h] of ground wheat, twenty thousand cors of barley, twenty thousand baths[i] of wine and twenty thousand baths of olive oil."

[11]Hiram king of Tyre replied by letter to Solomon:

[a] *14* Or *charioteers* [b] *16* Or possibly *Muzur,* a region in Cilicia; also in verse 17 [c] *16* Probably Cilicia [d] *17* That is, about 15 pounds (about 7 kilograms) [e] *17* That is, about 3 3/4 pounds (about 1.7 kilograms) [f] *3* Hebrew *Huram,* a variant of *Hiram*; also in verses 11 and 12 [g] *8* Probably a variant of *almug*; possibly juniper [h] *10* That is, probably about 125,000 bushels (about 4,400 kiloliters) [i] *10* That is, probably about 115,000 gallons (about 440 kiloliters)

"Because the LORD loves his people, he has made you their king."

12 And Hiram added:

"Praise be to the LORD, the God of Israel, who made heaven and earth! He has given King David a wise son, endowed with intelligence and discernment, who will build a temple for the LORD and a palace for himself.

13 "I am sending you Huram-Abi, a man of great skill, 14 whose mother was from Dan and whose father was from Tyre. He is trained to work in gold and silver, bronze and iron, stone and wood, and with purple and blue and crimson yarn and fine linen. He is experienced in all kinds of engraving and can execute any design given to him. He will work with your craftsmen and with those of my lord, David your father.

15 "Now let my lord send his servants the wheat and barley and the olive oil and wine he promised, 16 and we will cut all the logs from Lebanon that you need and will float them in rafts by sea down to Joppa. You can then take them up to Jerusalem."

17 Solomon took a census of all the aliens who were in Israel, after the census his father David had taken; and they were found to be 153,600. 18 He assigned 70,000 of them to be carriers and 80,000 to be stonecutters in the hills, with 3,600 foremen over them to keep the people working.

Solomon Builds the Temple

3 Then Solomon began to build the temple of the LORD in Jerusalem on Mount Moriah, where the LORD had appeared to his father David. It was on the threshing floor of Araunah[a] the Jebusite, the place provided by David. 2 He began building on the second day of the second month in the fourth year of his reign.

3 The foundation Solomon laid for building the temple of God was sixty cubits long and twenty cubits wide[b] (using the cubit of the old standard). 4 The portico at the front of the temple was twenty cubits[c] long across the width of the building and twenty cubits[d] high.

He overlaid the inside with pure gold. 5 He paneled the main hall with pine and covered it with fine gold and decorated it with palm tree and chain designs. 6 He adorned the temple with precious stones. And the gold he used was gold of Parvaim. 7 He overlaid the ceiling beams, doorframes, walls and doors of the temple with gold, and he carved cherubim on the walls.

8 He built the Most Holy Place, its length corresponding to the width of the temple—twenty cubits long and twenty cubits wide. He overlaid the inside with six hundred talents[e] of fine gold. 9 The gold nails weighed fifty shekels.[f] He also overlaid the upper parts with gold.

10 In the Most Holy Place he made a pair of sculptured cherubim and overlaid them with gold. 11 The total wingspan of the cherubim was twenty cubits. One wing of the first cherub was five cubits[g] long and touched the temple wall, while its other wing, also five cubits long, touched the wing of the other cherub. 12 Similarly one wing of the second cherub was five cubits long and touched the other temple wall, and its other wing, also five cubits long, touched the wing of the first cherub. 13 The wings of these cherubim extended twenty cubits. They stood on their feet, facing the main hall.[h]

14 He made the curtain of blue, purple and crimson yarn and fine linen, with cherubim worked into it.

15 In the front of the temple he made two pillars, which ⌞together⌟ were thirty-five cubits[i] long, each with a capital on top measuring five cubits. 16 He made interwoven chains[j] and put them on top of the pillars. He also made a hundred pomegranates and attached them to the chains. 17 He erected the pillars in the front of the temple, one to the south and one to the north. The one to the south he named Jakin[k] and the one to the north Boaz.[l]

The Temple's Furnishings

4 He made a bronze altar twenty cubits long, twenty cubits wide and ten cubits high.[m] 2 He made the Sea of cast metal, circular in shape, measuring ten cubits from rim to rim and five cubits[n] high. It took a line of thirty cubits[o] to measure around it. 3 Below the rim, figures of bulls encircled it—ten to a cubit.[p] The bulls were cast in two rows in one piece with the Sea.

4 The Sea stood on twelve bulls, three facing north, three facing west, three facing south and three facing east. The Sea rested on top of them, and their hindquarters were toward the center.

a 1 Hebrew *Ornan,* a variant of *Araunah* b 3 That is, about 90 feet (about 27 meters) long and 30 feet (about 9 meters) wide c 4 That is, about 30 feet (about 9 meters); also in verses 8, 11 and 13 d 4 Some Septuagint and Syriac manuscripts; Hebrew *and a hundred and twenty* e 8 That is, about 23 tons (about 21 metric tons) f 9 That is, about 1 1/4 pounds (about 0.6 kilogram) g 11 That is, about 7 1/2 feet (about 2.3 meters); also in verse 15 h 13 Or *facing inward* i 15 That is, about 52 feet (about 16 meters) j 16 Or possibly *made chains in the inner sanctuary*; the meaning of the Hebrew for this phrase is uncertain. k 17 *Jakin* probably means *he establishes.* l 17 *Boaz* probably means *in him is strength.* m 1 That is, about 30 feet (about 9 meters) long and wide, and about 15 feet (about 4.5 meters) high n 2 That is, about 7 1/2 feet (about 2.3 meters) o 2 That is, about 45 feet (about 13.5 meters) p 3 That is, about 1 1/2 feet (about 0.5 meter)

5It was a handbreadth[a] in thickness, and its rim
was like the rim of a cup, like a lily blossom. It
held three thousand baths.[b]
6He then made ten basins for washing and
placed five on the south side and five on the
north. In them the things to be used for the burnt
offerings were rinsed, but the Sea was to be used
by the priests for washing.
7He made ten gold lampstands according to
the specifications for them and placed them in
the temple, five on the south side and five on the
north.
8He made ten tables and placed them in the
temple, five on the south side and five on the
north. He also made a hundred gold sprinkling
bowls.
9He made the courtyard of the priests, and the
large court and the doors for the court, and overlaid the doors with bronze. 10He placed the Sea
on the south side, at the southeast corner.
11He also made the pots and shovels and sprinkling bowls.
So Huram finished the work he had undertak-
en for King Solomon in the temple of God:

12the two pillars;
the two bowl-shaped capitals on top of the
pillars;
the two sets of network decorating the two
bowl-shaped capitals on top of the pillars;
13the four hundred pomegranates for the two
sets of network (two rows of pomegranates for each network, decorating the
bowl-shaped capitals on top of the pillars);
14the stands with their basins;
15the Sea and the twelve bulls under it;
16the pots, shovels, meat forks and all related
articles.

All the objects that Huram-Abi made for King
Solomon for the temple of the LORD were of polished bronze. 17The king had them cast in clay
molds in the plain of the Jordan between Succoth
and Zarethan.[c] 18All these things that Solomon
made amounted to so much that the weight of
the bronze was not determined.
19Solomon also made all the furnishings that
were in God's temple:

the golden altar;
the tables on which was the bread of the
Presence;
20the lampstands of pure gold with their
lamps, to burn in front of the inner sanctuary as prescribed;
21the gold floral work and lamps and tongs
(they were solid gold);
22the pure gold wick trimmers, sprinkling
bowls, dishes and censers; and the gold
doors of the temple: the inner doors to
the Most Holy Place and the doors of the
main hall.

5 When all the work Solomon had done for the
temple of the LORD was finished, he brought
in the things his father David had dedicated—the
silver and gold and all the furnishings—and he
placed them in the treasuries of God's temple.

The Ark Brought to the Temple

2Then Solomon summoned to Jerusalem the
elders of Israel, all the heads of the tribes and the
chiefs of the Israelite families, to bring up the ark
of the LORD's covenant from Zion, the City of
David. 3And all the men of Israel came together
to the king at the time of the festival in the seventh month.
4When all the elders of Israel had arrived, the
Levites took up the ark, 5and they brought up the
ark and the Tent of Meeting and all the sacred
furnishings in it. The priests, who were Levites,
carried them up; 6and King Solomon and the entire assembly of Israel that had gathered about
him were before the ark, sacrificing so many
sheep and cattle that they could not be recorded
or counted.
7The priests then brought the ark of the
LORD's covenant to its place in the inner sanctuary of the temple, the Most Holy Place, and put it
beneath the wings of the cherubim. 8The cherubim spread their wings over the place of the ark
and covered the ark and its carrying poles.
9These poles were so long that their ends, extending from the ark, could be seen from in front
of the inner sanctuary, but not from outside the
Holy Place; and they are still there today. 10There
was nothing in the ark except the two tablets that
Moses had placed in it at Horeb, where the LORD
made a covenant with the Israelites after they
came out of Egypt.
11The priests then withdrew from the Holy
Place. All the priests who were there had consecrated themselves, regardless of their divisions.
12All the Levites who were musicians—Asaph,
Heman, Jeduthun and their sons and relatives—
stood on the east side of the altar, dressed in fine
linen and playing cymbals, harps and lyres. They
were accompanied by 120 priests sounding trumpets. 13The trumpeters and singers joined in unison, as with one voice, to give praise and thanks
to the LORD. Accompanied by trumpets, cymbals

[a] *5* That is, about 3 inches (about 8 centimeters) [b] *5* That is, about 17,500 gallons (about 66 kiloliters) [c] *17* Hebrew *Zeredatha,* a variant of *Zarethan*

and other instruments, they raised their voices in
praise to the LORD and sang:

"He is good;
his love endures forever."

Then the temple of the LORD was filled with a
cloud, 14and the priests could not perform their
service because of the cloud, for the glory of the
LORD filled the temple of God.

6 Then Solomon said, "The LORD has said that
he would dwell in a dark cloud; 2I have built
a magnificent temple for you, a place for you to
dwell forever."
3While the whole assembly of Israel was standing there, the king turned around and blessed
them. 4Then he said:

"Praise be to the LORD, the God of Israel,
who with his hands has fulfilled what he
promised with his mouth to my father David. For he said, 5'Since the day I brought
my people out of Egypt, I have not chosen a
city in any tribe of Israel to have a temple
built for my Name to be there, nor have I
chosen anyone to be the leader over my
people Israel. 6But now I have chosen Jerusalem for my Name to be there, and I have
chosen David to rule my people Israel.'
7"My father David had it in his heart to
build a temple for the Name of the LORD,
the God of Israel. 8But the LORD said to my
father David, 'Because it was in your heart
to build a temple for my Name, you did well
to have this in your heart. 9Nevertheless,
you are not the one to build the temple,
but your son, who is your own flesh and
blood—he is the one who will build the
temple for my Name.'
10"The LORD has kept the promise he
made. I have succeeded David my father
and now I sit on the throne of Israel, just as
the LORD promised, and I have built the
temple for the Name of the LORD, the God
of Israel. 11There I have placed the ark, in
which is the covenant of the LORD that he
made with the people of Israel."

Solomon's Prayer of Dedication

12Then Solomon stood before the altar of the
LORD in front of the whole assembly of Israel and
spread out his hands. 13Now he had made a
bronze platform, five cubits[a] long, five cubits
wide and three cubits[b] high, and had placed it
in the center of the outer court. He stood on the
platform and then knelt down before the whole
assembly of Israel and spread out his hands toward heaven. 14He said:

"O LORD, God of Israel, there is no God
like you in heaven or on earth—you who
keep your covenant of love with your servants who continue wholeheartedly in your
way. 15You have kept your promise to your
servant David my father; with your mouth
you have promised and with your hand you
have fulfilled it—as it is today.
16"Now LORD, God of Israel, keep for
your servant David my father the promises
you made to him when you said, 'You shall
never fail to have a man to sit before me on
the throne of Israel, if only your sons are
careful in all they do to walk before me according to my law, as you have done.'
17And now, O LORD, God of Israel, let your
word that you promised your servant David
come true.
18"But will God really dwell on earth
with men? The heavens, even the highest
heavens, cannot contain you. How much
less this temple I have built! 19Yet give attention to your servant's prayer and his plea
for mercy, O LORD my God. Hear the cry
and the prayer that your servant is praying
in your presence. 20May your eyes be open
toward this temple day and night, this place
of which you said you would put your Name
there. May you hear the prayer your servant
prays toward this place. 21Hear the supplications of your servant and of your people Israel when they pray toward this place. Hear
from heaven, your dwelling place; and
when you hear, forgive.
22"When a man wrongs his neighbor and
is required to take an oath and he comes
and swears the oath before your altar in this
temple, 23then hear from heaven and act.
Judge between your servants, repaying the
guilty by bringing down on his own head
what he has done. Declare the innocent not
guilty and so establish his innocence.
24"When your people Israel have been
defeated by an enemy because they have
sinned against you and when they turn back
and confess your name, praying and making
supplication before you in this temple,
25then hear from heaven and forgive the sin
of your people Israel and bring them back to
the land you gave to them and their fathers.
26"When the heavens are shut up and
there is no rain because your people have
sinned against you, and when they pray toward this place and confess your name and
turn from their sin because you have afflicted them, 27then hear from heaven and forgive the sin of your servants, your people

[a] *13* That is, about 7 1/2 feet (about 2.3 meters)
[b] *13* That is, about 4 1/2 feet (about 1.3 meters)

Israel. Teach them the right way to live, and
send rain on the land you gave your people
for an inheritance.
28“When famine or plague comes to the
land, or blight or mildew, locusts or grasshoppers, or when enemies besiege them in
any of their cities, whatever disaster or disease may come, 29and when a prayer or plea
is made by any of your people Israel—each
one aware of his afflictions and pains, and
spreading out his hands toward this
temple— 30then hear from heaven, your
dwelling place. Forgive, and deal with each
man according to all he does, since you
know his heart (for you alone know the
hearts of men), 31so that they will fear you
and walk in your ways all the time they live
in the land you gave our fathers.
32“As for the foreigner who does not belong to your people Israel but has come
from a distant land because of your great
name and your mighty hand and your outstretched arm—when he comes and prays
toward this temple, 33then hear from heav-
en, your dwelling place, and do whatever
the foreigner asks of you, so that all the
peoples of the earth may know your name
and fear you, as do your own people Israel,
and may know that this house I have built
bears your Name.
34“When your people go to war against
their enemies, wherever you send them,
and when they pray to you toward this city
you have chosen and the temple I have built
for your Name, 35then hear from heaven
their prayer and their plea, and uphold their
cause.
36“When they sin against you—for there
is no one who does not sin—and you become angry with them and give them over
to the enemy, who takes them captive to a
land far away or near; 37and if they have a
change of heart in the land where they are
held captive, and repent and plead with you
in the land of their captivity and say, ‘We
have sinned, we have done wrong and acted wickedly’; 38and if they turn back to you
with all their heart and soul in the land of
their captivity where they were taken, and
pray toward the land you gave their fathers,
toward the city you have chosen and toward
the temple I have built for your Name;
39then from heaven, your dwelling place,
hear their prayer and their pleas, and uphold their cause. And forgive your people,
who have sinned against you.
40“Now, my God, may your eyes be open
and your ears attentive to the prayers offered in this place.

41“Now arise, O LORD God, and come to
your resting place,
you and the ark of your might.
May your priests, O LORD God, be
clothed with salvation,
may your saints rejoice in your
goodness.
42O LORD God, do not reject your
anointed one.
Remember the great love promised to
David your servant.”

The Dedication of the Temple

7 When Solomon finished praying, fire came
down from heaven and consumed the burnt
offering and the sacrifices, and the glory of the
LORD filled the temple. 2The priests could not
enter the temple of the LORD because the glory of
the LORD filled it. 3When all the Israelites saw the
fire coming down and the glory of the LORD above
the temple, they knelt on the pavement with
their faces to the ground, and they worshiped
and gave thanks to the LORD, saying,

“He is good;
his love endures forever.”

4Then the king and all the people offered sacrifices before the LORD. 5And King Solomon offered
a sacrifice of twenty-two thousand head of cattle
and a hundred and twenty thousand sheep and
goats. So the king and all the people dedicated
the temple of God. 6The priests took their positions, as did the Levites with the LORD’s musical
instruments, which King David had made for
praising the LORD and which were used when he
gave thanks, saying, “His love endures forever.”
Opposite the Levites, the priests blew their trumpets, and all the Israelites were standing.
7Solomon consecrated the middle part of the
courtyard in front of the temple of the LORD, and
there he offered burnt offerings and the fat of the
fellowship offerings,[a] because the bronze altar
he had made could not hold the burnt offerings,
the grain offerings and the fat portions.
8So Solomon observed the festival at that time
for seven days, and all Israel with him—a vast
assembly, people from Lebo[b] Hamath to the
Wadi of Egypt. 9On the eighth day they held an
assembly, for they had celebrated the dedication
of the altar for seven days and the festival for
seven days more. 10On the twenty-third day of
the seventh month he sent the people to their
homes, joyful and glad in heart for the good

[a] 7 Traditionally *peace offerings*   [b] 8 Or *from the entrance to*

things the LORD had done for David and Solomon
and for his people Israel.

The LORD Appears to Solomon

11When Solomon had finished the temple of
the LORD and the royal palace, and had succeeded
in carrying out all he had in mind to do in the
temple of the LORD and in his own palace, 12the
LORD appeared to him at night and said:

"I have heard your prayer and have chosen this place for myself as a temple for
sacrifices.

13"When I shut up the heavens so that
there is no rain, or command locusts to devour the land or send a plague among my
people, 14if my people, who are called by
my name, will humble themselves and pray
and seek my face and turn from their wicked ways, then will I hear from heaven and
will forgive their sin and will heal their
land. 15Now my eyes will be open and my
ears attentive to the prayers offered in this
place. 16I have chosen and consecrated this
temple so that my Name may be there forever. My eyes and my heart will always be
there.

17"As for you, if you walk before me as
David your father did, and do all I command, and observe my decrees and laws, 18I
will establish your royal throne, as I covenanted with David your father when I said,
'You shall never fail to have a man to rule
over Israel.'

19"But if you[a] turn away and forsake the
decrees and commands I have given you[a]
and go off to serve other gods and worship
them, 20then I will uproot Israel from my
land, which I have given them, and will
reject this temple I have consecrated for my
Name. I will make it a byword and an object
of ridicule among all peoples. 21And though
this temple is now so imposing, all who pass
by will be appalled and say, 'Why has the
LORD done such a thing to this land and
to this temple?' 22People will answer, 'Because they have forsaken the LORD, the God
of their fathers, who brought them out of
Egypt, and have embraced other gods, worshiping and serving them—that is why he
brought all this disaster on them.'"

Solomon's Other Activities

8 At the end of twenty years, during which
Solomon built the temple of the LORD and his
own palace, 2Solomon rebuilt the villages that
Hiram[b] had given him, and settled Israelites in
them. 3Solomon then went to Hamath Zobah and
captured it. 4He also built up Tadmor in the
desert and all the store cities he had built in
Hamath. 5He rebuilt Upper Beth Horon and Lower Beth Horon as fortified cities, with walls and
with gates and bars, 6as well as Baalath and all his
store cities, and all the cities for his chariots and
for his horses[c]—whatever he desired to build in
Jerusalem, in Lebanon and throughout all the territory he ruled.

7All the people left from the Hittites, Amorites, Perizzites, Hivites and Jebusites (these peoples were not Israelites), 8that is, their descendants remaining in the land, whom the Israelites
had not destroyed—these Solomon conscripted
for his slave labor force, as it is to this day. 9But
Solomon did not make slaves of the Israelites for
his work; they were his fighting men, commanders of his captains, and commanders of his chariots and charioteers. 10They were also King Solomon's chief officials—two hundred and fifty
officials supervising the men.

11Solomon brought Pharaoh's daughter up
from the City of David to the palace he had built
for her, for he said, "My wife must not live in the
palace of David king of Israel, because the places
the ark of the LORD has entered are holy."

12On the altar of the LORD that he had built in
front of the portico, Solomon sacrificed burnt offerings to the LORD, 13according to the daily requirement for offerings commanded by Moses for
Sabbaths, New Moons and the three annual
feasts—the Feast of Unleavened Bread, the Feast
of Weeks and the Feast of Tabernacles. 14In keeping with the ordinance of his father David, he
appointed the divisions of the priests for their
duties, and the Levites to lead the praise and to
assist the priests according to each day's requirement. He also appointed the gatekeepers by divisions for the various gates, because this was what
David the man of God had ordered. 15They did
not deviate from the king's commands to the
priests or to the Levites in any matter, including
that of the treasuries.

16All Solomon's work was carried out, from
the day the foundation of the temple of the LORD
was laid until its completion. So the temple of the
LORD was finished.

17Then Solomon went to Ezion Geber and
Elath on the coast of Edom. 18And Hiram sent
him ships commanded by his own officers, men
who knew the sea. These, with Solomon's men,
sailed to Ophir and brought back four hundred
and fifty talents[d] of gold, which they delivered
to King Solomon.

[a] *19* The Hebrew is plural. [b] *2* Hebrew *Huram,* a variant of *Hiram*; also in verse 18 [c] *6* Or *charioteers* [d] *18* That is, about 17 tons (about 16 metric tons)

The Queen of Sheba Visits Solomon

9 When the queen of Sheba heard of Solomon's fame, she came to Jerusalem to test him with hard questions. Arriving with a very great caravan—with camels carrying spices, large quantities of gold, and precious stones—she came to Solomon and talked with him about all she had on her mind. 2Solomon answered all her questions; nothing was too hard for him to explain to her. 3When the queen of Sheba saw the wisdom of Solomon, as well as the palace he had built, 4the food on his table, the seating of his officials, the attending servants in their robes, the cupbearers in their robes and the burnt offerings he made at[a] the temple of the LORD, she was overwhelmed.

5She said to the king, "The report I heard in my own country about your achievements and your wisdom is true. 6But I did not believe what they said until I came and saw with my own eyes. Indeed, not even half the greatness of your wisdom was told me; you have far exceeded the report I heard. 7How happy your men must be! How happy your officials, who continually stand before you and hear your wisdom! 8Praise be to the LORD your God, who has delighted in you and placed you on his throne as king to rule for the LORD your God. Because of the love of your God for Israel and his desire to uphold them forever, he has made you king over them, to maintain justice and righteousness."

9Then she gave the king 120 talents[b] of gold, large quantities of spices, and precious stones. There had never been such spices as those the queen of Sheba gave to King Solomon.

10(The men of Hiram and the men of Solomon brought gold from Ophir; they also brought algumwood[c] and precious stones. 11The king used the algumwood to make steps for the temple of the LORD and for the royal palace, and to make harps and lyres for the musicians. Nothing like them had ever been seen in Judah.)

12King Solomon gave the queen of Sheba all she desired and asked for; he gave her more than she had brought to him. Then she left and returned with her retinue to her own country.

Solomon's Splendor

13The weight of the gold that Solomon received yearly was 666 talents,[d] 14not including the revenues brought in by merchants and traders. Also all the kings of Arabia and the governors of the land brought gold and silver to Solomon.

15King Solomon made two hundred large shields of hammered gold; six hundred bekas[e] of hammered gold went into each shield. 16He also made three hundred small shields of hammered gold, with three hundred bekas[f] of gold in each shield. The king put them in the Palace of the Forest of Lebanon.

17Then the king made a great throne inlaid with ivory and overlaid with pure gold. 18The throne had six steps, and a footstool of gold was attached to it. On both sides of the seat were armrests, with a lion standing beside each of them. 19Twelve lions stood on the six steps, one at either end of each step. Nothing like it had ever been made for any other kingdom. 20All King Solomon's goblets were gold, and all the household articles in the Palace of the Forest of Lebanon were pure gold. Nothing was made of silver, because silver was considered of little value in Solomon's day. 21The king had a fleet of trading ships[g] manned by Hiram's[h] men. Once every three years it returned, carrying gold, silver and ivory, and apes and baboons.

22King Solomon was greater in riches and wisdom than all the other kings of the earth. 23All the kings of the earth sought audience with Solomon to hear the wisdom God had put in his heart. 24Year after year, everyone who came brought a gift—articles of silver and gold, and robes, weapons and spices, and horses and mules.

25Solomon had four thousand stalls for horses and chariots, and twelve thousand horses,[i] which he kept in the chariot cities and also with him in Jerusalem. 26He ruled over all the kings from the River[j] to the land of the Philistines, as far as the border of Egypt. 27The king made silver as common in Jerusalem as stones, and cedar as plentiful as sycamore-fig trees in the foothills. 28Solomon's horses were imported from Egypt[k] and from all other countries.

Solomon's Death

29As for the other events of Solomon's reign, from beginning to end, are they not written in the records of Nathan the prophet, in the prophecy of Ahijah the Shilonite and in the visions of Iddo the seer concerning Jeroboam son of Nebat? 30Solomon reigned in Jerusalem over all Israel forty years. 31Then he rested with his fathers and was buried in the city of David his father. And Rehoboam his son succeeded him as king.

Israel Rebels Against Rehoboam

10 Rehoboam went to Shechem, for all the Israelites had gone there to make him

[a] 4 Or *the ascent by which he went up to* [b] 9 That is, about 4 1/2 tons (about 4 metric tons) [c] 10 Probably a variant of *almugwood* [d] 13 That is, about 25 tons (about 23 metric tons) [e] 15 That is, about 7 1/2 pounds (about 3.5 kilograms) [f] 16 That is, about 3 3/4 pounds (about 1.7 kilograms) [g] 21 Hebrew *of ships that could go to Tarshish* [h] 21 Hebrew *Huram,* a variant of *Hiram* [i] 25 Or *charioteers* [j] 26 That is, the Euphrates [k] 28 Or possibly *Muzur,* a region in Cilicia

king. 2When Jeroboam son of Nebat heard this
(he was in Egypt, where he had fled from King
Solomon), he returned from Egypt. 3So they sent
for Jeroboam, and he and all Israel went to Rehoboam and said to him: 4"Your father put a heavy
yoke on us, but now lighten the harsh labor and
the heavy yoke he put on us, and we will serve
you."
5Rehoboam answered, "Come back to me in
three days." So the people went away.
6Then King Rehoboam consulted the elders
who had served his father Solomon during his
lifetime. "How would you advise me to answer
these people?" he asked.
7They replied, "If you will be kind to these
people and please them and give them a favorable
answer, they will always be your servants."
8But Rehoboam rejected the advice the elders
gave him and consulted the young men who had
grown up with him and were serving him. 9He
asked them, "What is your advice? How should
we answer these people who say to me, 'Lighten
the yoke your father put on us'?"
10The young men who had grown up with him
replied, "Tell the people who have said to you,
'Your father put a heavy yoke on us, but make our
yoke lighter'—tell them, 'My little finger is thicker than my father's waist. 11My father laid on you
a heavy yoke; I will make it even heavier. My
father scourged you with whips; I will scourge
you with scorpions.'"
12Three days later Jeroboam and all the people
returned to Rehoboam, as the king had said,
"Come back to me in three days." 13The king
answered them harshly. Rejecting the advice of
the elders, 14he followed the advice of the young
men and said, "My father made your yoke heavy;
I will make it even heavier. My father scourged
you with whips; I will scourge you with scorpions." 15So the king did not listen to the people,
for this turn of events was from God, to fulfill the
word the LORD had spoken to Jeroboam son of
Nebat through Ahijah the Shilonite.
16When all Israel saw that the king refused to
listen to them, they answered the king:

"What share do we have in David,
what part in Jesse's son?
To your tents, O Israel!
Look after your own house, O David!"

So all the Israelites went home. 17But as for the
Israelites who were living in the towns of Judah,
Rehoboam still ruled over them.
18King Rehoboam sent out Adoniram,[a] who
was in charge of forced labor, but the Israelites
stoned him to death. King Rehoboam, however,
managed to get into his chariot and escape to
Jerusalem. 19So Israel has been in rebellion
against the house of David to this day.

11 When Rehoboam arrived in Jerusalem, he
mustered the house of Judah and
Benjamin—a hundred and eighty thousand fighting men—to make war against Israel and to regain the kingdom for Rehoboam.
2But this word of the LORD came to Shemaiah
the man of God: 3"Say to Rehoboam son of Solomon king of Judah and to all the Israelites in
Judah and Benjamin, 4'This is what the LORD
says: Do not go up to fight against your brothers.
Go home, every one of you, for this is my doing.'" So they obeyed the words of the LORD and
turned back from marching against Jeroboam.

Rehoboam Fortifies Judah

5Rehoboam lived in Jerusalem and built up
towns for defense in Judah: 6Bethlehem, Etam,
Tekoa, 7Beth Zur, Soco, Adullam, 8Gath, Mareshah, Ziph, 9Adoraim, Lachish, Azekah, 10Zorah,
Aijalon and Hebron. These were fortified cities in
Judah and Benjamin. 11He strengthened their defenses and put commanders in them, with supplies of food, olive oil and wine. 12He put shields
and spears in all the cities, and made them very
strong. So Judah and Benjamin were his.
13The priests and Levites from all their districts throughout Israel sided with him. 14The
Levites even abandoned their pasturelands and
property, and came to Judah and Jerusalem because Jeroboam and his sons had rejected them as
priests of the LORD. 15And he appointed his own
priests for the high places and for the goat and
calf idols he had made. 16Those from every tribe
of Israel who set their hearts on seeking the
LORD, the God of Israel, followed the Levites to
Jerusalem to offer sacrifices to the LORD, the God
of their fathers. 17They strengthened the kingdom of Judah and supported Rehoboam son of
Solomon three years, walking in the ways of David and Solomon during this time.

Rehoboam's Family

18Rehoboam married Mahalath, who was the
daughter of David's son Jerimoth and of Abihail,
the daughter of Jesse's son Eliab. 19She bore him
sons: Jeush, Shemariah and Zaham. 20Then he
married Maacah daughter of Absalom, who bore
him Abijah, Attai, Ziza and Shelomith. 21Rehobo-
am loved Maacah daughter of Absalom more than
any of his other wives and concubines. In all,
he had eighteen wives and sixty concubines,
twenty-eight sons and sixty daughters.
22Rehoboam appointed Abijah son of Maacah
to be the chief prince among his brothers, in
order to make him king. 23He acted wisely, dis-

[a]*18* Hebrew *Hadoram,* a variant of *Adoniram*

persing some of his sons throughout the districts of Judah and Benjamin, and to all the fortified cities. He gave them abundant provisions and took many wives for them.

Shishak Attacks Jerusalem

12 After Rehoboam's position as king was established and he had become strong, he and all Israel[a] with him abandoned the law of the LORD. 2Because they had been unfaithful to the LORD, Shishak king of Egypt attacked Jerusalem in the fifth year of King Rehoboam. 3With twelve hundred chariots and sixty thousand horsemen and the innumerable troops of Libyans, Sukkites and Cushites[b] that came with him from Egypt, 4he captured the fortified cities of Judah and came as far as Jerusalem.

5Then the prophet Shemaiah came to Rehoboam and to the leaders of Judah who had assembled in Jerusalem for fear of Shishak, and he said to them, "This is what the LORD says, 'You have abandoned me; therefore, I now abandon you to Shishak.' "

6The leaders of Israel and the king humbled themselves and said, "The LORD is just."

7When the LORD saw that they humbled themselves, this word of the LORD came to Shemaiah: "Since they have humbled themselves, I will not destroy them but will soon give them deliverance. My wrath will not be poured out on Jerusalem through Shishak. 8They will, however, become subject to him, so that they may learn the difference between serving me and serving the kings of other lands."

9When Shishak king of Egypt attacked Jerusalem, he carried off the treasures of the temple of the LORD and the treasures of the royal palace. He took everything, including the gold shields Solomon had made. 10So King Rehoboam made bronze shields to replace them and assigned these to the commanders of the guard on duty at the entrance to the royal palace. 11Whenever the king went to the LORD's temple, the guards went with him, bearing the shields, and afterward they returned them to the guardroom.

12Because Rehoboam humbled himself, the LORD's anger turned from him, and he was not totally destroyed. Indeed, there was some good in Judah.

13King Rehoboam established himself firmly in Jerusalem and continued as king. He was forty-one years old when he became king, and he reigned seventeen years in Jerusalem, the city the LORD had chosen out of all the tribes of Israel in which to put his Name. His mother's name was Naamah; she was an Ammonite. 14He did evil because he had not set his heart on seeking the LORD.

15As for the events of Rehoboam's reign, from beginning to end, are they not written in the records of Shemaiah the prophet and of Iddo the seer that deal with genealogies? There was continual warfare between Rehoboam and Jeroboam. 16Rehoboam rested with his fathers and was buried in the City of David. And Abijah his son succeeded him as king.

Abijah King of Judah

13 In the eighteenth year of the reign of Jeroboam, Abijah became king of Judah, 2and he reigned in Jerusalem three years. His mother's name was Maacah,[c] a daughter[d] of Uriel of Gibeah.

There was war between Abijah and Jeroboam. 3Abijah went into battle with a force of four hundred thousand able fighting men, and Jeroboam drew up a battle line against him with eight hundred thousand able troops.

4Abijah stood on Mount Zemaraim, in the hill country of Ephraim, and said, "Jeroboam and all Israel, listen to me! 5Don't you know that the LORD, the God of Israel, has given the kingship of Israel to David and his descendants forever by a covenant of salt? 6Yet Jeroboam son of Nebat, an official of Solomon son of David, rebelled against his master. 7Some worthless scoundrels gathered around him and opposed Rehoboam son of Solomon when he was young and indecisive and not strong enough to resist them.

8"And now you plan to resist the kingdom of the LORD, which is in the hands of David's descendants. You are indeed a vast army and have with you the golden calves that Jeroboam made to be your gods. 9But didn't you drive out the priests of the LORD, the sons of Aaron, and the Levites, and make priests of your own as the peoples of other lands do? Whoever comes to consecrate himself with a young bull and seven rams may become a priest of what are not gods.

10"As for us, the LORD is our God, and we have not forsaken him. The priests who serve the LORD are sons of Aaron, and the Levites assist them. 11Every morning and evening they present burnt offerings and fragrant incense to the LORD. They set out the bread on the ceremonially clean table and light the lamps on the gold lampstand every evening. We are observing the requirements of the LORD our God. But you have forsaken him. 12God is with us; he is our leader. His priests with their trumpets will sound the battle cry against you. Men of Israel, do not fight against

[a] *1* That is, Judah, as frequently in 2 Chronicles [b] *3* That is, people from the upper Nile region [c] *2* Most Septuagint manuscripts and Syriac (see also 2 Chron. 11:20 and 1 Kings 15:2); Hebrew *Micaiah* [d] *2* Or *granddaughter*

the LORD, the God of your fathers, for you will not succeed."

13Now Jeroboam had sent troops around to the rear, so that while he was in front of Judah the ambush was behind them. 14Judah turned and saw that they were being attacked at both front and rear. Then they cried out to the LORD. The priests blew their trumpets 15and the men of Judah raised the battle cry. At the sound of their battle cry, God routed Jeroboam and all Israel before Abijah and Judah. 16The Israelites fled before Judah, and God delivered them into their hands. 17Abijah and his men inflicted heavy losses on them, so that there were five hundred thousand casualties among Israel's able men. 18The men of Israel were subdued on that occasion, and the men of Judah were victorious because they relied on the LORD, the God of their fathers.

19Abijah pursued Jeroboam and took from him the towns of Bethel, Jeshanah and Ephron, with their surrounding villages. 20Jeroboam did not regain power during the time of Abijah. And the LORD struck him down and he died.

21But Abijah grew in strength. He married fourteen wives and had twenty-two sons and sixteen daughters.

22The other events of Abijah's reign, what he did and what he said, are written in the annotations of the prophet Iddo.

14 And Abijah rested with his fathers and was buried in the City of David. Asa his son succeeded him as king, and in his days the country was at peace for ten years.

Asa King of Judah

2Asa did what was good and right in the eyes of the LORD his God. 3He removed the foreign altars and the high places, smashed the sacred stones and cut down the Asherah poles.[a] 4He commanded Judah to seek the LORD, the God of their fathers, and to obey his laws and commands. 5He removed the high places and incense altars in every town in Judah, and the kingdom was at peace under him. 6He built up the fortified cities of Judah, since the land was at peace. No one was at war with him during those years, for the LORD gave him rest.

7"Let us build up these towns," he said to Judah, "and put walls around them, with towers, gates and bars. The land is still ours, because we have sought the LORD our God; we sought him and he has given us rest on every side." So they built and prospered.

8Asa had an army of three hundred thousand men from Judah, equipped with large shields and with spears, and two hundred and eighty thousand from Benjamin, armed with small shields and with bows. All these were brave fighting men.

9Zerah the Cushite marched out against them with a vast army[b] and three hundred chariots, and came as far as Mareshah. 10Asa went out to meet him, and they took up battle positions in the Valley of Zephathah near Mareshah.

11Then Asa called to the LORD his God and said, "LORD, there is no one like you to help the powerless against the mighty. Help us, O LORD our God, for we rely on you, and in your name we have come against this vast army. O LORD, you are our God; do not let man prevail against you."

12The LORD struck down the Cushites before Asa and Judah. The Cushites fled, 13and Asa and his army pursued them as far as Gerar. Such a great number of Cushites fell that they could not recover; they were crushed before the LORD and his forces. The men of Judah carried off a large amount of plunder. 14They destroyed all the villages around Gerar, for the terror of the LORD had fallen upon them. They plundered all these villages, since there was much booty there. 15They also attacked the camps of the herdsmen and carried off droves of sheep and goats and camels. Then they returned to Jerusalem.

Asa's Reform

15 The Spirit of God came upon Azariah son of Oded. 2He went out to meet Asa and said to him, "Listen to me, Asa and all Judah and Benjamin. The LORD is with you when you are with him. If you seek him, he will be found by you, but if you forsake him, he will forsake you. 3For a long time Israel was without the true God, without a priest to teach and without the law. 4But in their distress they turned to the LORD, the God of Israel, and sought him, and he was found by them. 5In those days it was not safe to travel about, for all the inhabitants of the lands were in great turmoil. 6One nation was being crushed by another and one city by another, because God was troubling them with every kind of distress. 7But as for you, be strong and do not give up, for your work will be rewarded."

8When Asa heard these words and the prophecy of Azariah son of[c] Oded the prophet, he took courage. He removed the detestable idols from the whole land of Judah and Benjamin and from the towns he had captured in the hills of Ephraim. He repaired the altar of the LORD that was in front of the portico of the LORD's temple.

[a]3 That is, symbols of the goddess Asherah; here and elsewhere in 2 Chronicles [b]9 Hebrew *with an army of a thousand thousands* or *with an army of thousands upon thousands* [c]8 Vulgate and Syriac (see also Septuagint and verse 1); Hebrew does not have *Azariah son of.*

9 Then he assembled all Judah and Benjamin
and the people from Ephraim, Manasseh and
Simeon who had settled among them, for large
numbers had come over to him from Israel when
they saw that the LORD his God was with him.
10 They assembled at Jerusalem in the third
month of the fifteenth year of Asa's reign. 11 At
that time they sacrificed to the LORD seven hundred head of cattle and seven thousand sheep and
goats from the plunder they had brought back.
12 They entered into a covenant to seek the LORD,
the God of their fathers, with all their heart and
soul. 13 All who would not seek the LORD, the God
of Israel, were to be put to death, whether small
or great, man or woman. 14 They took an oath to
the LORD with loud acclamation, with shouting
and with trumpets and horns. 15 All Judah rejoiced about the oath because they had sworn it
wholeheartedly. They sought God eagerly, and he
was found by them. So the LORD gave them rest
on every side.
16 King Asa also deposed his grandmother Maacah from her position as queen mother, because
she had made a repulsive Asherah pole. Asa cut
the pole down, broke it up and burned it in the
Kidron Valley. 17 Although he did not remove the
high places from Israel, Asa's heart was fully committed ⌞to the LORD⌟ all his life. 18 He brought into
the temple of God the silver and gold and the
articles that he and his father had dedicated.
19 There was no more war until the thirty-fifth
year of Asa's reign.

Asa's Last Years

16 In the thirty-sixth year of Asa's reign Baasha king of Israel went up against Judah
and fortified Ramah to prevent anyone from leaving or entering the territory of Asa king of Judah.
2 Asa then took the silver and gold out of the
treasuries of the LORD's temple and of his own
palace and sent it to Ben-Hadad king of Aram,
who was ruling in Damascus. 3 "Let there be a
treaty between me and you," he said, "as there
was between my father and your father. See, I am
sending you silver and gold. Now break your treaty with Baasha king of Israel so he will withdraw
from me."
4 Ben-Hadad agreed with King Asa and sent the
commanders of his forces against the towns of
Israel. They conquered Ijon, Dan, Abel Maim[a]
and all the store cities of Naphtali. 5 When Baasha
heard this, he stopped building Ramah and abandoned his work. 6 Then King Asa brought all the
men of Judah, and they carried away from Ramah
the stones and timber Baasha had been using.
With them he built up Geba and Mizpah.
7 At that time Hanani the seer came to Asa king
of Judah and said to him: "Because you relied on
the king of Aram and not on the LORD your God,
the army of the king of Aram has escaped from
your hand. 8 Were not the Cushites[b] and Libyans
a mighty army with great numbers of chariots
and horsemen[c]? Yet when you relied on the
LORD, he delivered them into your hand. 9 For the
eyes of the LORD range throughout the earth to
strengthen those whose hearts are fully committed to him. You have done a foolish thing, and
from now on you will be at war."
10 Asa was angry with the seer because of this;
he was so enraged that he put him in prison. At
the same time Asa brutally oppressed some of the
people.
11 The events of Asa's reign, from beginning to
end, are written in the book of the kings of Judah
and Israel. 12 In the thirty-ninth year of his reign
Asa was afflicted with a disease in his feet.
Though his disease was severe, even in his illness
he did not seek help from the LORD, but only
from the physicians. 13 Then in the forty-first year
of his reign Asa died and rested with his fathers.
14 They buried him in the tomb that he had cut
out for himself in the City of David. They laid him
on a bier covered with spices and various blended perfumes, and they made a huge fire in his
honor.

Jehoshaphat King of Judah

17 Jehoshaphat his son succeeded him as
king and strengthened himself against Israel. 2 He stationed troops in all the fortified cities
of Judah and put garrisons in Judah and in the
towns of Ephraim that his father Asa had captured.
3 The LORD was with Jehoshaphat because in
his early years he walked in the ways his father
David had followed. He did not consult the Baals
4 but sought the God of his father and followed his
commands rather than the practices of Israel.
5 The LORD established the kingdom under his
control; and all Judah brought gifts to Jehoshaphat, so that he had great wealth and honor. 6 His
heart was devoted to the ways of the LORD; furthermore, he removed the high places and the
Asherah poles from Judah.
7 In the third year of his reign he sent his officials Ben-Hail, Obadiah, Zechariah, Nethanel and
Micaiah to teach in the towns of Judah. 8 With
them were certain Levites—Shemaiah, Nethaniah, Zebadiah, Asahel, Shemiramoth, Jehonathan,
Adonijah, Tobijah and Tob-Adonijah—and the
priests Elishama and Jehoram. 9 They taught
throughout Judah, taking with them the Book of

[a] 4 Also known as *Abel Beth Maacah* [b] 8 That is, people from the upper Nile region [c] 8 Or *charioteers*

the Law of the LORD; they went around to all the towns of Judah and taught the people.

10The fear of the LORD fell on all the kingdoms of the lands surrounding Judah, so that they did not make war with Jehoshaphat. 11Some Philistines brought Jehoshaphat gifts and silver as tribute, and the Arabs brought him flocks: seven thousand seven hundred rams and seven thousand seven hundred goats.

12Jehoshaphat became more and more powerful; he built forts and store cities in Judah 13and had large supplies in the towns of Judah. He also kept experienced fighting men in Jerusalem. 14Their enrollment by families was as follows:

From Judah, commanders of units of 1,000:
Adnah the commander, with 300,000 fighting men;
15next, Jehohanan the commander, with 280,000;
16next, Amasiah son of Zicri, who volunteered himself for the service of the LORD, with 200,000.
17From Benjamin:
Eliada, a valiant soldier, with 200,000 men armed with bows and shields;
18next, Jehozabad, with 180,000 men armed for battle.

19These were the men who served the king, besides those he stationed in the fortified cities throughout Judah.

Micaiah Prophesies Against Ahab

18 Now Jehoshaphat had great wealth and honor, and he allied himself with Ahab by marriage. 2Some years later he went down to visit Ahab in Samaria. Ahab slaughtered many sheep and cattle for him and the people with him and urged him to attack Ramoth Gilead. 3Ahab king of Israel asked Jehoshaphat king of Judah, "Will you go with me against Ramoth Gilead?"

Jehoshaphat replied, "I am as you are, and my people as your people; we will join you in the war." 4But Jehoshaphat also said to the king of Israel, "First seek the counsel of the LORD."

5So the king of Israel brought together the prophets—four hundred men—and asked them, "Shall we go to war against Ramoth Gilead, or shall I refrain?"

"Go," they answered, "for God will give it into the king's hand."

6But Jehoshaphat asked, "Is there not a prophet of the LORD here whom we can inquire of?"

7The king of Israel answered Jehoshaphat, "There is still one man through whom we can inquire of the LORD, but I hate him because he never prophesies anything good about me, but always bad. He is Micaiah son of Imlah."

"The king should not say that," Jehoshaphat replied.

8So the king of Israel called one of his officials and said, "Bring Micaiah son of Imlah at once."

9Dressed in their royal robes, the king of Israel and Jehoshaphat king of Judah were sitting on their thrones at the threshing floor by the entrance to the gate of Samaria, with all the prophets prophesying before them. 10Now Zedekiah son of Kenaanah had made iron horns, and he declared, "This is what the LORD says: 'With these you will gore the Arameans until they are destroyed.'"

11All the other prophets were prophesying the same thing. "Attack Ramoth Gilead and be victorious," they said, "for the LORD will give it into the king's hand."

12The messenger who had gone to summon Micaiah said to him, "Look, as one man the other prophets are predicting success for the king. Let your word agree with theirs, and speak favorably."

13But Micaiah said, "As surely as the LORD lives, I can tell him only what my God says."

14When he arrived, the king asked him, "Micaiah, shall we go to war against Ramoth Gilead, or shall I refrain?"

"Attack and be victorious," he answered, "for they will be given into your hand."

15The king said to him, "How many times must I make you swear to tell me nothing but the truth in the name of the LORD?"

16Then Micaiah answered, "I saw all Israel scattered on the hills like sheep without a shepherd, and the LORD said, 'These people have no master. Let each one go home in peace.'"

17The king of Israel said to Jehoshaphat, "Didn't I tell you that he never prophesies anything good about me, but only bad?"

18Micaiah continued, "Therefore hear the word of the LORD: I saw the LORD sitting on his throne with all the host of heaven standing on his right and on his left. 19And the LORD said, 'Who will entice Ahab king of Israel into attacking Ramoth Gilead and going to his death there?'

"One suggested this, and another that. 20Finally, a spirit came forward, stood before the LORD and said, 'I will entice him.'

" 'By what means?' the LORD asked.

21" 'I will go and be a lying spirit in the mouths of all his prophets,' he said.

" 'You will succeed in enticing him,' said the LORD. 'Go and do it.'

22"So now the LORD has put a lying spirit in the mouths of these prophets of yours. The LORD has decreed disaster for you."

23Then Zedekiah son of Kenaanah went up and slapped Micaiah in the face. "Which way did

the spirit from[a] the LORD go when he went from
me to speak to you?" he asked.
[24]Micaiah replied, "You will find out on the
day you go to hide in an inner room."
[25]The king of Israel then ordered, "Take Micaiah and send him back to Amon the ruler of the
city and to Joash the king's son, [26]and say, 'This
is what the king says: Put this fellow in prison
and give him nothing but bread and water until
I return safely.'"
[27]Micaiah declared, "If you ever return safely,
the LORD has not spoken through me." Then he
added, "Mark my words, all you people!"

Ahab Killed at Ramoth Gilead

[28]So the king of Israel and Jehoshaphat king of
Judah went up to Ramoth Gilead. [29]The king of
Israel said to Jehoshaphat, "I will enter the battle
in disguise, but you wear your royal robes." So
the king of Israel disguised himself and went into
battle.
[30]Now the king of Aram had ordered his chariot commanders, "Do not fight with anyone, small
or great, except the king of Israel." [31]When the
chariot commanders saw Jehoshaphat, they
thought, "This is the king of Israel." So they
turned to attack him, but Jehoshaphat cried out,
and the LORD helped him. God drew them away
from him, [32]for when the chariot commanders
saw that he was not the king of Israel, they
stopped pursuing him.
[33]But someone drew his bow at random and
hit the king of Israel between the sections of his
armor. The king told the chariot driver, "Wheel
around and get me out of the fighting. I've been
wounded." [34]All day long the battle raged, and
the king of Israel propped himself up in his chariot facing the Arameans until evening. Then at
sunset he died.

19 When Jehoshaphat king of Judah returned
safely to his palace in Jerusalem, [2]Jehu
the seer, the son of Hanani, went out to meet him
and said to the king, "Should you help the wicked
and love[b] those who hate the LORD? Because of
this, the wrath of the LORD is upon you. [3]There
is, however, some good in you, for you have rid
the land of the Asherah poles and have set your
heart on seeking God."

Jehoshaphat Appoints Judges

[4]Jehoshaphat lived in Jerusalem, and he went
out again among the people from Beersheba to
the hill country of Ephraim and turned them back
to the LORD, the God of their fathers. [5]He appointed judges in the land, in each of the fortified
cities of Judah. [6]He told them, "Consider carefully what you do, because you are not judging for
man but for the LORD, who is with you whenever
you give a verdict. [7]Now let the fear of the LORD
be upon you. Judge carefully, for with the LORD
our God there is no injustice or partiality or brib-
ery."
[8]In Jerusalem also, Jehoshaphat appointed
some of the Levites, priests and heads of Israelite
families to administer the law of the LORD and to
settle disputes. And they lived in Jerusalem. [9]He
gave them these orders: "You must serve faithfully and wholeheartedly in the fear of the LORD.
[10]In every case that comes before you from your
fellow countrymen who live in the cities—
whether bloodshed or other concerns of the law,
commands, decrees or ordinances—you are to
warn them not to sin against the LORD; otherwise
his wrath will come on you and your brothers. Do
this, and you will not sin.
[11]"Amariah the chief priest will be over you in
any matter concerning the LORD, and Zebadiah
son of Ishmael, the leader of the tribe of Judah,
will be over you in any matter concerning the
king, and the Levites will serve as officials before
you. Act with courage, and may the LORD be with
those who do well."

Jehoshaphat Defeats Moab and Ammon

20 After this, the Moabites and Ammonites
with some of the Meunites[c] came to
make war on Jehoshaphat.
[2]Some men came and told Jehoshaphat, "A
vast army is coming against you from Edom,[d]
from the other side of the Sea.[e] It is already in
Hazazon Tamar" (that is, En Gedi). [3]Alarmed,
Jehoshaphat resolved to inquire of the LORD, and
he proclaimed a fast for all Judah. [4]The people of
Judah came together to seek help from the LORD;
indeed, they came from every town in Judah to
seek him.
[5]Then Jehoshaphat stood up in the assembly of
Judah and Jerusalem at the temple of the LORD in
the front of the new courtyard [6]and said:

"O LORD, God of our fathers, are you not
the God who is in heaven? You rule over all
the kingdoms of the nations. Power and
might are in your hand, and no one can
withstand you. [7]O our God, did you not
drive out the inhabitants of this land before
your people Israel and give it forever to the
descendants of Abraham your friend? [8]They
have lived in it and have built in it a sanctuary for your Name, saying, [9]'If calamity
comes upon us, whether the sword of judgment, or plague or famine, we will stand in
your presence before this temple that bears

[a]23 Or *Spirit of* [b]2 Or *and make alliances with* [c]1 Some Septuagint manuscripts; Hebrew *Ammonites* [d]2 One Hebrew manuscript; most Hebrew manuscripts, Septuagint and Vulgate *Aram* [e]2 That is, the Dead Sea

your Name and will cry out to you in our distress, and you will hear us and save us.'

10"But now here are men from Ammon, Moab and Mount Seir, whose territory you would not allow Israel to invade when they came from Egypt; so they turned away from them and did not destroy them. 11See how they are repaying us by coming to drive us out of the possession you gave us as an inheritance. 12O our God, will you not judge them? For we have no power to face this vast army that is attacking us. We do not know what to do, but our eyes are upon you."

13All the men of Judah, with their wives and children and little ones, stood there before the LORD.

14Then the Spirit of the LORD came upon Jahaziel son of Zechariah, the son of Benaiah, the son of Jeiel, the son of Mattaniah, a Levite and descendant of Asaph, as he stood in the assembly.

15He said: "Listen, King Jehoshaphat and all who live in Judah and Jerusalem! This is what the LORD says to you: 'Do not be afraid or discouraged because of this vast army. For the battle is not yours, but God's. 16Tomorrow march down against them. They will be climbing up by the Pass of Ziz, and you will find them at the end of the gorge in the Desert of Jeruel. 17You will not have to fight this battle. Take up your positions; stand firm and see the deliverance the LORD will give you, O Judah and Jerusalem. Do not be afraid; do not be discouraged. Go out to face them tomorrow, and the LORD will be with you.' "

18Jehoshaphat bowed with his face to the ground, and all the people of Judah and Jerusalem fell down in worship before the LORD. 19Then some Levites from the Kohathites and Korahites stood up and praised the LORD, the God of Israel, with very loud voice.

20Early in the morning they left for the Desert of Tekoa. As they set out, Jehoshaphat stood and said, "Listen to me, Judah and people of Jerusalem! Have faith in the LORD your God and you will be upheld; have faith in his prophets and you will be successful." 21After consulting the people, Jehoshaphat appointed men to sing to the LORD and to praise him for the splendor of his[a] holiness as they went out at the head of the army, saying:

"Give thanks to the LORD,
for his love endures forever."

22As they began to sing and praise, the LORD set ambushes against the men of Ammon and Moab and Mount Seir who were invading Judah, and they were defeated. 23The men of Ammon and Moab rose up against the men from Mount Seir to destroy and annihilate them. After they finished slaughtering the men from Seir, they helped to destroy one another.

24When the men of Judah came to the place that overlooks the desert and looked toward the vast army, they saw only dead bodies lying on the ground; no one had escaped. 25So Jehoshaphat and his men went to carry off their plunder, and they found among them a great amount of equipment and clothing[b] and also articles of value—more than they could take away. There was so much plunder that it took three days to collect it. 26On the fourth day they assembled in the Valley of Beracah, where they praised the LORD. This is why it is called the Valley of Beracah[c] to this day.

27Then, led by Jehoshaphat, all the men of Judah and Jerusalem returned joyfully to Jerusalem, for the LORD had given them cause to rejoice over their enemies. 28They entered Jerusalem and went to the temple of the LORD with harps and lutes and trumpets.

29The fear of God came upon all the kingdoms of the countries when they heard how the LORD had fought against the enemies of Israel. 30And the kingdom of Jehoshaphat was at peace, for his God had given him rest on every side.

The End of Jehoshaphat's Reign

31So Jehoshaphat reigned over Judah. He was thirty-five years old when he became king of Judah, and he reigned in Jerusalem twenty-five years. His mother's name was Azubah daughter of Shilhi. 32He walked in the ways of his father Asa and did not stray from them; he did what was right in the eyes of the LORD. 33The high places, however, were not removed, and the people still had not set their hearts on the God of their fathers.

34The other events of Jehoshaphat's reign, from beginning to end, are written in the annals of Jehu son of Hanani, which are recorded in the book of the kings of Israel.

35Later, Jehoshaphat king of Judah made an alliance with Ahaziah king of Israel, who was guilty of wickedness. 36He agreed with him to construct a fleet of trading ships.[d] After these were built at Ezion Geber, 37Eliezer son of Dodavahu of Mareshah prophesied against Jehoshaphat, saying, "Because you have made an alliance with Ahaziah, the LORD will destroy what you have made." The ships were wrecked and were not able to set sail to trade.[e]

[a]21 Or *him with the splendor of* [b]25 Some Hebrew manuscripts and Vulgate; most Hebrew manuscripts *corpses* [c]26 *Beracah* means *praise.* [d]36 Hebrew *of ships that could go to Tarshish* [e]37 Hebrew *sail for Tarshish*

21 Then Jehoshaphat rested with his fathers and was buried with them in the City of David. And Jehoram his son succeeded him as king. [2]Jehoram's brothers, the sons of Jehoshaphat, were Azariah, Jehiel, Zechariah, Azariahu, Michael and Shephatiah. All these were sons of Jehoshaphat king of Israel.[a] [3]Their father had given them many gifts of silver and gold and articles of value, as well as fortified cities in Judah, but he had given the kingdom to Jehoram because he was his firstborn son.

Jehoram King of Judah

[4]When Jehoram established himself firmly over his father's kingdom, he put all his brothers to the sword along with some of the princes of Israel. [5]Jehoram was thirty-two years old when he became king, and he reigned in Jerusalem eight years. [6]He walked in the ways of the kings of Israel, as the house of Ahab had done, for he married a daughter of Ahab. He did evil in the eyes of the LORD. [7]Nevertheless, because of the covenant the LORD had made with David, the LORD was not willing to destroy the house of David. He had promised to maintain a lamp for him and his descendants forever.

[8]In the time of Jehoram, Edom rebelled against Judah and set up its own king. [9]So Jehoram went there with his officers and all his chariots. The Edomites surrounded him and his chariot commanders, but he rose up and broke through by night. [10]To this day Edom has been in rebellion against Judah.

Libnah revolted at the same time, because Jehoram had forsaken the LORD, the God of his fathers. [11]He had also built high places on the hills of Judah and had caused the people of Jerusalem to prostitute themselves and had led Judah astray.

[12]Jehoram received a letter from Elijah the prophet, which said:

"This is what the LORD, the God of your father David, says: 'You have not walked in the ways of your father Jehoshaphat or of Asa king of Judah. [13]But you have walked in the ways of the kings of Israel, and you have led Judah and the people of Jerusalem to prostitute themselves, just as the house of Ahab did. You have also murdered your own brothers, members of your father's house, men who were better than you. [14]So now the LORD is about to strike your people, your sons, your wives and everything that is yours, with a heavy blow. [15]You yourself will be very ill with a lingering disease of the bowels, until the disease causes your bowels to come out.' "

[16]The LORD aroused against Jehoram the hostility of the Philistines and of the Arabs who lived near the Cushites. [17]They attacked Judah, invaded it and carried off all the goods found in the king's palace, together with his sons and wives. Not a son was left to him except Ahaziah,[b] the youngest.

[18]After all this, the LORD afflicted Jehoram with an incurable disease of the bowels. [19]In the course of time, at the end of the second year, his bowels came out because of the disease, and he died in great pain. His people made no fire in his honor, as they had for his fathers.

[20]Jehoram was thirty-two years old when he became king, and he reigned in Jerusalem eight years. He passed away, to no one's regret, and was buried in the City of David, but not in the tombs of the kings.

Ahaziah King of Judah

22 The people of Jerusalem made Ahaziah, Jehoram's youngest son, king in his place, since the raiders, who came with the Arabs into the camp, had killed all the older sons. So Ahaziah son of Jehoram king of Judah began to reign. [2]Ahaziah was twenty-two[c] years old when he became king, and he reigned in Jerusalem one year. His mother's name was Athaliah, a granddaughter of Omri.

[3]He too walked in the ways of the house of Ahab, for his mother encouraged him in doing wrong. [4]He did evil in the eyes of the LORD, as the house of Ahab had done, for after his father's death they became his advisers, to his undoing. [5]He also followed their counsel when he went with Joram[d] son of Ahab king of Israel to war against Hazael king of Aram at Ramoth Gilead. The Arameans wounded Joram; [6]so he returned to Jezreel to recover from the wounds they had inflicted on him at Ramoth[e] in his battle with Hazael king of Aram.

Then Ahaziah[f] son of Jehoram king of Judah went down to Jezreel to see Joram son of Ahab because he had been wounded.

[7]Through Ahaziah's visit to Joram, God brought about Ahaziah's downfall. When Ahaziah arrived, he went out with Joram to meet Jehu son of Nimshi, whom the LORD had anointed to destroy the house of Ahab. [8]While Jehu was executing judgment on the house of Ahab, he found the princes of Judah and the sons of Ahaziah's

a2 That is, Judah, as frequently in 2 Chronicles b17 Hebrew *Jehoahaz,* a variant of *Ahaziah* c2 Some Septuagint manuscripts and Syriac (see also 2 Kings 8:26); Hebrew *forty-two* d5 Hebrew *Jehoram,* a variant of *Joram;* also in verses 6 and 7 e6 Hebrew *Ramah,* a variant of *Ramoth* f6 Some Hebrew manuscripts, Septuagint, Vulgate and Syriac (see also 2 Kings 8:29); most Hebrew manuscripts *Azariah*

relatives, who had been attending Ahaziah, and
he killed them. 9He then went in search of Ahaziah, and his men captured him while he was hiding in Samaria. He was brought to Jehu and put
to death. They buried him, for they said, "He was
a son of Jehoshaphat, who sought the LORD with
all his heart." So there was no one in the house
of Ahaziah powerful enough to retain the kingdom.

Athaliah and Joash

10When Athaliah the mother of Ahaziah saw
that her son was dead, she proceeded to destroy
the whole royal family of the house of Judah.
11But Jehosheba,[a] the daughter of King Jehoram, took Joash son of Ahaziah and stole him
away from among the royal princes who were
about to be murdered and put him and his nurse
in a bedroom. Because Jehosheba,[a] the daughter
of King Jehoram and wife of the priest Jehoiada,
was Ahaziah's sister, she hid the child from Athaliah so she could not kill him. 12He remained
hidden with them at the temple of God for six
years while Athaliah ruled the land.

23 In the seventh year Jehoiada showed his
strength. He made a covenant with the
commanders of units of a hundred: Azariah son of
Jeroham, Ishmael son of Jehohanan, Azariah son
of Obed, Maaseiah son of Adaiah, and Elishaphat
son of Zicri. 2They went throughout Judah and
gathered the Levites and the heads of Israelite
families from all the towns. When they came to
Jerusalem, 3the whole assembly made a covenant
with the king at the temple of God.

Jehoiada said to them, "The king's son shall
reign, as the LORD promised concerning the
descendants of David. 4Now this is what you are
to do: A third of you priests and Levites who are
going on duty on the Sabbath are to keep watch
at the doors, 5a third of you at the royal palace
and a third at the Foundation Gate, and all the
other men are to be in the courtyards of the temple of the LORD. 6No one is to enter the temple of
the LORD except the priests and Levites on duty;
they may enter because they are consecrated, but
all the other men are to guard what the LORD has
assigned to them.[b] 7The Levites are to station
themselves around the king, each man with his
weapons in his hand. Anyone who enters the
temple must be put to death. Stay close to the
king wherever he goes."

8The Levites and all the men of Judah did just
as Jehoiada the priest ordered. Each one took his
men—those who were going on duty on the Sabbath and those who were going off duty—for Jehoiada the priest had not released any of the divisions. 9Then he gave the commanders of units of
a hundred the spears and the large and small
shields that had belonged to King David and that
were in the temple of God. 10He stationed all the
men, each with his weapon in his hand, around
the king—near the altar and the temple, from the
south side to the north side of the temple.

11Jehoiada and his sons brought out the king's
son and put the crown on him; they presented
him with a copy of the covenant and proclaimed
him king. They anointed him and shouted, "Long
live the king!"

12When Athaliah heard the noise of the people
running and cheering the king, she went to them
at the temple of the LORD. 13She looked, and
there was the king, standing by his pillar at the
entrance. The officers and the trumpeters were
beside the king, and all the people of the land
were rejoicing and blowing trumpets, and singers
with musical instruments were leading the
praises. Then Athaliah tore her robes and shouted, "Treason! Treason!"

14Jehoiada the priest sent out the commanders
of units of a hundred, who were in charge of the
troops, and said to them: "Bring her out between
the ranks[c] and put to the sword anyone who
follows her." For the priest had said, "Do not put
her to death at the temple of the LORD." 15So they
seized her as she reached the entrance of the
Horse Gate on the palace grounds, and there they
put her to death.

16Jehoiada then made a covenant that he and
the people and the king[d] would be the LORD's
people. 17All the people went to the temple of
Baal and tore it down. They smashed the altars
and idols and killed Mattan the priest of Baal in
front of the altars.

18Then Jehoiada placed the oversight of the
temple of the LORD in the hands of the priests,
who were Levites, to whom David had made assignments in the temple, to present the burnt
offerings of the LORD as written in the Law of
Moses, with rejoicing and singing, as David had
ordered. 19He also stationed doorkeepers at the
gates of the LORD's temple so that no one who
was in any way unclean might enter.

20He took with him the commanders of hundreds, the nobles, the rulers of the people and all
the people of the land and brought the king down
from the temple of the LORD. They went into the
palace through the Upper Gate and seated the
king on the royal throne, 21and all the people of
the land rejoiced. And the city was quiet, because
Athaliah had been slain with the sword.

[a] 11 Hebrew *Jehoshabeath,* a variant of *Jehosheba* [b] 6 Or *to observe the LORD's command* ⌞*not to enter*⌟ [c] 14 Or *out from the precincts* [d] 16 Or *covenant between* ⌞*the LORD*⌟ *and the people and the king that they* (see 2 Kings 11:17)

Joash Repairs the Temple

24 Joash was seven years old when he became king, and he reigned in Jerusalem forty years. His mother's name was Zibiah; she was from Beersheba. [2]Joash did what was right in the eyes of the LORD all the years of Jehoiada the priest. [3]Jehoiada chose two wives for him, and he had sons and daughters.

[4]Some time later Joash decided to restore the temple of the LORD. [5]He called together the priests and Levites and said to them, "Go to the towns of Judah and collect the money due annually from all Israel, to repair the temple of your God. Do it now." But the Levites did not act at once.

[6]Therefore the king summoned Jehoiada the chief priest and said to him, "Why haven't you required the Levites to bring in from Judah and Jerusalem the tax imposed by Moses the servant of the LORD and by the assembly of Israel for the Tent of the Testimony?"

[7]Now the sons of that wicked woman Athaliah had broken into the temple of God and had used even its sacred objects for the Baals.

[8]At the king's command, a chest was made and placed outside, at the gate of the temple of the LORD. [9]A proclamation was then issued in Judah and Jerusalem that they should bring to the LORD the tax that Moses the servant of God had required of Israel in the desert. [10]All the officials and all the people brought their contributions gladly, dropping them into the chest until it was full. [11]Whenever the chest was brought in by the Levites to the king's officials and they saw that there was a large amount of money, the royal secretary and the officer of the chief priest would come and empty the chest and carry it back to its place. They did this regularly and collected a great amount of money. [12]The king and Jehoiada gave it to the men who carried out the work required for the temple of the LORD. They hired masons and carpenters to restore the LORD's temple, and also workers in iron and bronze to repair the temple.

[13]The men in charge of the work were diligent, and the repairs progressed under them. They rebuilt the temple of God according to its original design and reinforced it. [14]When they had finished, they brought the rest of the money to the king and Jehoiada, and with it were made articles for the LORD's temple: articles for the service and for the burnt offerings, and also dishes and other objects of gold and silver. As long as Jehoiada lived, burnt offerings were presented continually in the temple of the LORD.

[15]Now Jehoiada was old and full of years, and he died at the age of a hundred and thirty. [16]He was buried with the kings in the City of David, because of the good he had done in Israel for God and his temple.

The Wickedness of Joash

[17]After the death of Jehoiada, the officials of Judah came and paid homage to the king, and he listened to them. [18]They abandoned the temple of the LORD, the God of their fathers, and worshiped Asherah poles and idols. Because of their guilt, God's anger came upon Judah and Jerusalem. [19]Although the LORD sent prophets to the people to bring them back to him, and though they testified against them, they would not listen.

[20]Then the Spirit of God came upon Zechariah son of Jehoiada the priest. He stood before the people and said, "This is what God says: 'Why do you disobey the LORD's commands? You will not prosper. Because you have forsaken the LORD, he has forsaken you.' "

[21]But they plotted against him, and by order of the king they stoned him to death in the courtyard of the LORD's temple. [22]King Joash did not remember the kindness Zechariah's father Jehoiada had shown him but killed his son, who said as he lay dying, "May the LORD see this and call you to account."

[23]At the turn of the year,[a] the army of Aram marched against Joash; it invaded Judah and Jerusalem and killed all the leaders of the people. They sent all the plunder to their king in Damascus. [24]Although the Aramean army had come with only a few men, the LORD delivered into their hands a much larger army. Because Judah had forsaken the LORD, the God of their fathers, judgment was executed on Joash. [25]When the Arameans withdrew, they left Joash severely wounded. His officials conspired against him for murdering the son of Jehoiada the priest, and they killed him in his bed. So he died and was buried in the City of David, but not in the tombs of the kings.

[26]Those who conspired against him were Zabad,[b] son of Shimeath an Ammonite woman, and Jehozabad, son of Shimrith[c] a Moabite woman. [27]The account of his sons, the many prophecies about him, and the record of the restoration of the temple of God are written in the annotations on the book of the kings. And Amaziah his son succeeded him as king.

Amaziah King of Judah

25 Amaziah was twenty-five years old when he became king, and he reigned in Jerusalem twenty-nine years. His mother's name was

[a]23 Probably in the spring [b]26 A variant of *Jozabad* [c]26 A variant of *Shomer*

Jehoaddin[a]; she was from Jerusalem. 2He did what was right in the eyes of the LORD, but not wholeheartedly. 3After the kingdom was firmly in his control, he executed the officials who had murdered his father the king. 4Yet he did not put their sons to death, but acted in accordance with what is written in the Law, in the Book of Moses, where the LORD commanded: "Fathers shall not be put to death for their children, nor children put to death for their fathers; each is to die for his own sins."[b]

5Amaziah called the people of Judah together and assigned them according to their families to commanders of thousands and commanders of hundreds for all Judah and Benjamin. He then mustered those twenty years old or more and found that there were three hundred thousand men ready for military service, able to handle the spear and shield. 6He also hired a hundred thousand fighting men from Israel for a hundred talents[c] of silver.

7But a man of God came to him and said, "O king, these troops from Israel must not march with you, for the LORD is not with Israel—not with any of the people of Ephraim. 8Even if you go and fight courageously in battle, God will overthrow you before the enemy, for God has the power to help or to overthrow."

9Amaziah asked the man of God, "But what about the hundred talents I paid for these Israelite troops?"

The man of God replied, "The LORD can give you much more than that."

10So Amaziah dismissed the troops who had come to him from Ephraim and sent them home. They were furious with Judah and left for home in a great rage.

11Amaziah then marshaled his strength and led his army to the Valley of Salt, where he killed ten thousand men of Seir. 12The army of Judah also captured ten thousand men alive, took them to the top of a cliff and threw them down so that all were dashed to pieces.

13Meanwhile the troops that Amaziah had sent back and had not allowed to take part in the war raided Judean towns from Samaria to Beth Horon. They killed three thousand people and carried off great quantities of plunder.

14When Amaziah returned from slaughtering the Edomites, he brought back the gods of the people of Seir. He set them up as his own gods, bowed down to them and burned sacrifices to them. 15The anger of the LORD burned against Amaziah, and he sent a prophet to him, who said, "Why do you consult this people's gods, which could not save their own people from your hand?"

16While he was still speaking, the king said to him, "Have we appointed you an adviser to the king? Stop! Why be struck down?"

So the prophet stopped but said, "I know that God has determined to destroy you, because you have done this and have not listened to my counsel."

17After Amaziah king of Judah consulted his advisers, he sent this challenge to Jehoash[d] son of Jehoahaz, the son of Jehu, king of Israel: "Come, meet me face to face."

18But Jehoash king of Israel replied to Amaziah king of Judah: "A thistle in Lebanon sent a message to a cedar in Lebanon, 'Give your daughter to my son in marriage.' Then a wild beast in Lebanon came along and trampled the thistle underfoot. 19You say to yourself that you have defeated Edom, and now you are arrogant and proud. But stay at home! Why ask for trouble and cause your own downfall and that of Judah also?"

20Amaziah, however, would not listen, for God so worked that he might hand them over to ⌞Jehoash⌟, because they sought the gods of Edom. 21So Jehoash king of Israel attacked. He and Amaziah king of Judah faced each other at Beth Shemesh in Judah. 22Judah was routed by Israel, and every man fled to his home. 23Jehoash king of Israel captured Amaziah king of Judah, the son of Joash, the son of Ahaziah,[e] at Beth Shemesh. Then Jehoash brought him to Jerusalem and broke down the wall of Jerusalem from the Ephraim Gate to the Corner Gate—a section about six hundred feet[f] long. 24He took all the gold and silver and all the articles found in the temple of God that had been in the care of Obed-Edom, together with the palace treasures and the hostages, and returned to Samaria.

25Amaziah son of Joash king of Judah lived for fifteen years after the death of Jehoash son of Jehoahaz king of Israel. 26As for the other events of Amaziah's reign, from beginning to end, are they not written in the book of the kings of Judah and Israel? 27From the time that Amaziah turned away from following the LORD, they conspired against him in Jerusalem and he fled to Lachish, but they sent men after him to Lachish and killed him there. 28He was brought back by horse and was buried with his fathers in the City of Judah.

Uzziah King of Judah

26 Then all the people of Judah took Uzziah,[g] who was sixteen years old, and made him king in place of his father Amaziah.

[a] *1* Hebrew *Jehoaddan,* a variant of *Jehoaddin* [b] *4* Deut. 24:16 [c] *6* That is, about 3 3/4 tons (about 3.4 metric tons); also in verse 9 [d] *17* Hebrew *Joash,* a variant of *Jehoash*; also in verses 18, 21, 23 and 25 [e] *23* Hebrew *Jehoahaz,* a variant of *Ahaziah* [f] *23* Hebrew *four hundred cubits* (about 180 meters) [g] *1* Also called *Azariah*

2He was the one who rebuilt Elath and restored
it to Judah after Amaziah rested with his fathers.
3Uzziah was sixteen years old when he became king, and he reigned in Jerusalem fifty-two
years. His mother's name was Jecoliah; she was
from Jerusalem. 4He did what was right in the
eyes of the LORD, just as his father Amaziah had
done. 5He sought God during the days of Zechariah, who instructed him in the fear[a] of God. As
long as he sought the LORD, God gave him success.

6He went to war against the Philistines and
broke down the walls of Gath, Jabneh and Ashdod. He then rebuilt towns near Ashdod and elsewhere among the Philistines. 7God helped him
against the Philistines and against the Arabs who
lived in Gur Baal and against the Meunites. 8The
Ammonites brought tribute to Uzziah, and his
fame spread as far as the border of Egypt, because
he had become very powerful.

9Uzziah built towers in Jerusalem at the Corner Gate, at the Valley Gate and at the angle of
the wall, and he fortified them. 10He also built
towers in the desert and dug many cisterns, because he had much livestock in the foothills and
in the plain. He had people working his fields and
vineyards in the hills and in the fertile lands, for
he loved the soil.

11Uzziah had a well-trained army, ready to go
out by divisions according to their numbers as
mustered by Jeiel the secretary and Maaseiah the
officer under the direction of Hananiah, one of
the royal officials. 12The total number of family
leaders over the fighting men was 2,600. 13Un-
der their command was an army of 307,500 men
trained for war, a powerful force to support the
king against his enemies. 14Uzziah provided
shields, spears, helmets, coats of armor, bows
and slingstones for the entire army. 15In Jerusalem he made machines designed by skillful men
for use on the towers and on the corner defenses
to shoot arrows and hurl large stones. His fame
spread far and wide, for he was greatly helped
until he became powerful.

16But after Uzziah became powerful, his pride
led to his downfall. He was unfaithful to the LORD
his God, and entered the temple of the LORD to
burn incense on the altar of incense. 17Azariah
the priest with eighty other courageous priests of
the LORD followed him in. 18They confronted him
and said, "It is not right for you, Uzziah, to burn
incense to the LORD. That is for the priests, the
descendants of Aaron, who have been consecrated to burn incense. Leave the sanctuary, for you
have been unfaithful; and you will not be honored by the LORD God."

19Uzziah, who had a censer in his hand ready
to burn incense, became angry. While he was
raging at the priests in their presence before the
incense altar in the LORD's temple, leprosy[b]
broke out on his forehead. 20When Azariah the
chief priest and all the other priests looked at
him, they saw that he had leprosy on his forehead, so they hurried him out. Indeed, he himself
was eager to leave, because the LORD had afflicted him.

21King Uzziah had leprosy until the day he
died. He lived in a separate house[c]—leprous,
and excluded from the temple of the LORD. Jotham his son had charge of the palace and governed the people of the land.

22The other events of Uzziah's reign, from beginning to end, are recorded by the prophet Isaiah son of Amoz. 23Uzziah rested with his fathers
and was buried near them in a field for burial that
belonged to the kings, for people said, "He had
leprosy." And Jotham his son succeeded him as
king.

Jotham King of Judah

27 Jotham was twenty-five years old when
he became king, and he reigned in Jerusalem sixteen years. His mother's name was Jeru-
sha daughter of Zadok. 2He did what was right in
the eyes of the LORD, just as his father Uzziah had
done, but unlike him he did not enter the temple
of the LORD. The people, however, continued
their corrupt practices. 3Jotham rebuilt the Upper
Gate of the temple of the LORD and did extensive
work on the wall at the hill of Ophel. 4He built
towns in the Judean hills and forts and towers in
the wooded areas.

5Jotham made war on the king of the Ammonites and conquered them. That year the Ammonites paid him a hundred talents[d] of silver, ten
thousand cors[e] of wheat and ten thousand cors
of barley. The Ammonites brought him the same
amount also in the second and third years.

6Jotham grew powerful because he walked
steadfastly before the LORD his God.

7The other events in Jotham's reign, including
all his wars and the other things he did, are written in the book of the kings of Israel and Judah.
8He was twenty-five years old when he became
king, and he reigned in Jerusalem sixteen years.
9Jotham rested with his fathers and was buried in
the City of David. And Ahaz his son succeeded
him as king.

[a]5 Many Hebrew manuscripts, Septuagint and Syriac; other Hebrew manuscripts *vision*
[b]19 The Hebrew word was used for various diseases affecting the skin—not necessarily leprosy; also in verses 20, 21 and 23.
[c]21 Or *in a house where he was relieved of responsibilities*
[d]5 That is, about 3 3/4 tons (about 3.4 metric tons)
[e]5 That is, probably about 62,000 bushels (about 2,200 kiloliters)

Ahaz King of Judah

28 Ahaz was twenty years old when he became king, and he reigned in Jerusalem
sixteen years. Unlike David his father, he did not
do what was right in the eyes of the LORD. 2He
walked in the ways of the kings of Israel and also
made cast idols for worshiping the Baals. 3He
burned sacrifices in the Valley of Ben Hinnom
and sacrificed his sons in the fire, following the
detestable ways of the nations the LORD had driv-
en out before the Israelites. 4He offered sacrifices
and burned incense at the high places, on the
hilltops and under every spreading tree.
5Therefore the LORD his God handed him over
to the king of Aram. The Arameans defeated him
and took many of his people as prisoners and
brought them to Damascus.
He was also given into the hands of the king of
Israel, who inflicted heavy casualties on him. 6In
one day Pekah son of Remaliah killed a hundred
and twenty thousand soldiers in Judah—because
Judah had forsaken the LORD, the God of their
fathers. 7Zicri, an Ephraimite warrior, killed Maaseiah the king's son, Azrikam the officer in
charge of the palace, and Elkanah, second to the
king. 8The Israelites took captive from their kinsmen two hundred thousand wives, sons and
daughters. They also took a great deal of plunder,
which they carried back to Samaria.
9But a prophet of the LORD named Oded was
there, and he went out to meet the army when it
returned to Samaria. He said to them, "Because
the LORD, the God of your fathers, was angry with
Judah, he gave them into your hand. But you
have slaughtered them in a rage that reaches to
heaven. 10And now you intend to make the men
and women of Judah and Jerusalem your slaves.
But aren't you also guilty of sins against the LORD
your God? 11Now listen to me! Send back your
fellow countrymen you have taken as prisoners,
for the LORD's fierce anger rests on you."
12Then some of the leaders in Ephraim—
Azariah son of Jehohanan, Berekiah son of Meshillemoth, Jehizkiah son of Shallum, and Amasa
son of Hadlai—confronted those who were arriving from the war. 13"You must not bring those
prisoners here," they said, "or we will be guilty
before the LORD. Do you intend to add to our sin
and guilt? For our guilt is already great, and his
fierce anger rests on Israel."
14So the soldiers gave up the prisoners and
plunder in the presence of the officials and all the
assembly. 15The men designated by name took
the prisoners, and from the plunder they clothed
all who were naked. They provided them with
clothes and sandals, food and drink, and healing
balm. All those who were weak they put on donkeys. So they took them back to their fellow
countrymen at Jericho, the City of Palms, and
returned to Samaria.
16At that time King Ahaz sent to the king[a] of
Assyria for help. 17The Edomites had again come
and attacked Judah and carried away prisoners,
18while the Philistines had raided towns in the
foothills and in the Negev of Judah. They captured and occupied Beth Shemesh, Aijalon and
Gederoth, as well as Soco, Timnah and Gimzo,
with their surrounding villages. 19The LORD had
humbled Judah because of Ahaz king of Israel,[b]
for he had promoted wickedness in Judah and
had been most unfaithful to the LORD. 20Tiglath-
Pileser[c] king of Assyria came to him, but he
gave him trouble instead of help. 21Ahaz took
some of the things from the temple of the LORD
and from the royal palace and from the princes
and presented them to the king of Assyria, but
that did not help him.
22In his time of trouble King Ahaz became
even more unfaithful to the LORD. 23He offered
sacrifices to the gods of Damascus, who had defeated him; for he thought, "Since the gods of the
kings of Aram have helped them, I will sacrifice
to them so they will help me." But they were his
downfall and the downfall of all Israel.
24Ahaz gathered together the furnishings from
the temple of God and took them away.[d] He
shut the doors of the LORD's temple and set up
altars at every street corner in Jerusalem. 25In
every town in Judah he built high places to burn
sacrifices to other gods and provoked the LORD,
the God of his fathers, to anger.
26The other events of his reign and all his
ways, from beginning to end, are written in the
book of the kings of Judah and Israel. 27Ahaz
rested with his fathers and was buried in the city
of Jerusalem, but he was not placed in the tombs
of the kings of Israel. And Hezekiah his son succeeded him as king.

Hezekiah Purifies the Temple

29 Hezekiah was twenty-five years old when
he became king, and he reigned in Jerusalem twenty-nine years. His mother's name was
Abijah daughter of Zechariah. 2He did what was
right in the eyes of the LORD, just as his father
David had done.
3In the first month of the first year of his reign,
he opened the doors of the temple of the LORD
and repaired them. 4He brought in the priests
and the Levites, assembled them in the square on
the east side 5and said: "Listen to me, Levites!
Consecrate yourselves now and consecrate the

a *16* One Hebrew manuscript, Septuagint and Vulgate (see also 2 Kings 16:7); most Hebrew manuscripts *kings* b *19* That is, Judah, as frequently in 2 Chronicles c *20* Hebrew *Tilgath-Pilneser,* a variant of *Tiglath-Pileser* d *24* Or *and cut them up*

temple of the LORD, the God of your fathers. Remove all defilement from the sanctuary. 6Our fathers were unfaithful; they did evil in the eyes of
the LORD our God and forsook him. They turned
their faces away from the LORD's dwelling place
and turned their backs on him. 7They also shut
the doors of the portico and put out the lamps.
They did not burn incense or present any burnt
offerings at the sanctuary to the God of Israel.
8Therefore, the anger of the LORD has fallen on
Judah and Jerusalem; he has made them an object
of dread and horror and scorn, as you can see
with your own eyes. 9This is why our fathers
have fallen by the sword and why our sons and
daughters and our wives are in captivity. 10Now
I intend to make a covenant with the LORD, the
God of Israel, so that his fierce anger will turn
away from us. 11My sons, do not be negligent
now, for the LORD has chosen you to stand before
him and serve him, to minister before him and to
burn incense."

12Then these Levites set to work:

from the Kohathites,
 Mahath son of Amasai and Joel son of Azariah;
from the Merarites,
 Kish son of Abdi and Azariah son of Jehallelel;
from the Gershonites,
 Joah son of Zimmah and Eden son of Joah;
13from the descendants of Elizaphan,
 Shimri and Jeiel;
from the descendants of Asaph,
 Zechariah and Mattaniah;
14from the descendants of Heman,
 Jehiel and Shimei;
from the descendants of Jeduthun,
 Shemaiah and Uzziel.

15When they had assembled their brothers and
consecrated themselves, they went in to purify
the temple of the LORD, as the king had ordered,
following the word of the LORD. 16The priests
went into the sanctuary of the LORD to purify it.
They brought out to the courtyard of the LORD's
temple everything unclean that they found in the
temple of the LORD. The Levites took it and carried it out to the Kidron Valley. 17They began the
consecration on the first day of the first month,
and by the eighth day of the month they reached
the portico of the LORD. For eight more days they
consecrated the temple of the LORD itself, finishing on the sixteenth day of the first month.

18Then they went in to King Hezekiah and
reported: "We have purified the entire temple of
the LORD, the altar of burnt offering with all its
utensils, and the table for setting out the consecrated bread, with all its articles. 19We have prepared and consecrated all the articles that King
Ahaz removed in his unfaithfulness while he was
king. They are now in front of the LORD's altar."

20Early the next morning King Hezekiah gathered the city officials together and went up to the
temple of the LORD. 21They brought seven bulls,
seven rams, seven male lambs and seven male
goats as a sin offering for the kingdom, for the
sanctuary and for Judah. The king commanded
the priests, the descendants of Aaron, to offer
these on the altar of the LORD. 22So they slaughtered the bulls, and the priests took the blood and
sprinkled it on the altar; next they slaughtered
the rams and sprinkled their blood on the altar;
then they slaughtered the lambs and sprinkled
their blood on the altar. 23The goats for the sin
offering were brought before the king and the
assembly, and they laid their hands on them.
24The priests then slaughtered the goats and presented their blood on the altar for a sin offering
to atone for all Israel, because the king had ordered the burnt offering and the sin offering for
all Israel.

25He stationed the Levites in the temple of the
LORD with cymbals, harps and lyres in the way
prescribed by David and Gad the king's seer and
Nathan the prophet; this was commanded by the
LORD through his prophets. 26So the Levites stood
ready with David's instruments, and the priests
with their trumpets.

27Hezekiah gave the order to sacrifice the
burnt offering on the altar. As the offering began,
singing to the LORD began also, accompanied by
trumpets and the instruments of David king of
Israel. 28The whole assembly bowed in worship,
while the singers sang and the trumpeters
played. All this continued until the sacrifice of
the burnt offering was completed.

29When the offerings were finished, the king
and everyone present with him knelt down and
worshiped. 30King Hezekiah and his officials ordered the Levites to praise the LORD with the
words of David and of Asaph the seer. So they
sang praises with gladness and bowed their heads
and worshiped.

31Then Hezekiah said, "You have now dedicated yourselves to the LORD. Come and bring sacrifices and thank offerings to the temple of the
LORD." So the assembly brought sacrifices and
thank offerings, and all whose hearts were willing brought burnt offerings.

32The number of burnt offerings the assembly
brought was seventy bulls, a hundred rams and
two hundred male lambs—all of them for burnt
offerings to the LORD. 33The animals consecrated
as sacrifices amounted to six hundred bulls and
three thousand sheep and goats. 34The priests,
however, were too few to skin all the burnt offerings; so their kinsmen the Levites helped them
until the task was finished and until other priests

had been consecrated, for the Levites had been more conscientious in consecrating themselves than the priests had been. 35There were burnt offerings in abundance, together with the fat of the fellowship offerings[a] and the drink offerings that accompanied the burnt offerings.

So the service of the temple of the LORD was reestablished. 36Hezekiah and all the people rejoiced at what God had brought about for his people, because it was done so quickly.

Hezekiah Celebrates the Passover

30 Hezekiah sent word to all Israel and Judah and also wrote letters to Ephraim and Manasseh, inviting them to come to the temple of the LORD in Jerusalem and celebrate the Passover to the LORD, the God of Israel. 2The king and his officials and the whole assembly in Jerusalem decided to celebrate the Passover in the second month. 3They had not been able to celebrate it at the regular time because not enough priests had consecrated themselves and the people had not assembled in Jerusalem. 4The plan seemed right both to the king and to the whole assembly. 5They decided to send a proclamation throughout Israel, from Beersheba to Dan, calling the people to come to Jerusalem and celebrate the Passover to the LORD, the God of Israel. It had not been celebrated in large numbers according to what was written.

6At the king's command, couriers went throughout Israel and Judah with letters from the king and from his officials, which read:

> "People of Israel, return to the LORD, the God of Abraham, Isaac and Israel, that he may return to you who are left, who have escaped from the hand of the kings of Assyria. 7Do not be like your fathers and brothers, who were unfaithful to the LORD, the God of their fathers, so that he made them an object of horror, as you see. 8Do not be stiff-necked, as your fathers were; submit to the LORD. Come to the sanctuary, which he has consecrated forever. Serve the LORD your God, so that his fierce anger will turn away from you. 9If you return to the LORD, then your brothers and your children will be shown compassion by their captors and will come back to this land, for the LORD your God is gracious and compassionate. He will not turn his face from you if you return to him."

10The couriers went from town to town in Ephraim and Manasseh, as far as Zebulun, but the people scorned and ridiculed them. 11Nevertheless, some men of Asher, Manasseh and Zebulun humbled themselves and went to Jerusalem. 12Also in Judah the hand of God was on the people to give them unity of mind to carry out what the king and his officials had ordered, following the word of the LORD.

13A very large crowd of people assembled in Jerusalem to celebrate the Feast of Unleavened Bread in the second month. 14They removed the altars in Jerusalem and cleared away the incense altars and threw them into the Kidron Valley.

15They slaughtered the Passover lamb on the fourteenth day of the second month. The priests and the Levites were ashamed and consecrated themselves and brought burnt offerings to the temple of the LORD. 16Then they took up their regular positions as prescribed in the Law of Moses the man of God. The priests sprinkled the blood handed to them by the Levites. 17Since many in the crowd had not consecrated themselves, the Levites had to kill the Passover lambs for all those who were not ceremonially clean and could not consecrate ⌊their lambs⌋ to the LORD. 18Although most of the many people who came from Ephraim, Manasseh, Issachar and Zebulun had not purified themselves, yet they ate the Passover, contrary to what was written. But Hezekiah prayed for them, saying, "May the LORD, who is good, pardon everyone 19who sets his heart on seeking God—the LORD, the God of his fathers—even if he is not clean according to the rules of the sanctuary." 20And the LORD heard Hezekiah and healed the people.

21The Israelites who were present in Jerusalem celebrated the Feast of Unleavened Bread for seven days with great rejoicing, while the Levites and priests sang to the LORD every day, accompanied by the LORD's instruments of praise.[b]

22Hezekiah spoke encouragingly to all the Levites, who showed good understanding of the service of the LORD. For the seven days they ate their assigned portion and offered fellowship offerings[a] and praised the LORD, the God of their fathers.

23The whole assembly then agreed to celebrate the festival seven more days; so for another seven days they celebrated joyfully. 24Hezekiah king of Judah provided a thousand bulls and seven thousand sheep and goats for the assembly, and the officials provided them with a thousand bulls and ten thousand sheep and goats. A great number of priests consecrated themselves. 25The entire assembly of Judah rejoiced, along with the priests and Levites and all who had assembled from Israel, including the aliens who had come from Israel and those who lived in Judah. 26There

[a] 35,22 Traditionally *peace offerings* [b] 21 Or *priests praised the LORD every day with resounding instruments belonging to the LORD*

was great joy in Jerusalem, for since the days of
Solomon son of David king of Israel there had
been nothing like this in Jerusalem. 27The priests
and the Levites stood to bless the people, and
God heard them, for their prayer reached heav-
en, his holy dwelling place.

31 When all this had ended, the Israelites
who were there went out to the towns of
Judah, smashed the sacred stones and cut down
the Asherah poles. They destroyed the high
places and the altars throughout Judah and Benjamin and in Ephraim and Manasseh. After they
had destroyed all of them, the Israelites returned
to their own towns and to their own property.

Contributions for Worship

2Hezekiah assigned the priests and Levites to
divisions—each of them according to their duties
as priests or Levites—to offer burnt offerings and
fellowship offerings,[a] to minister, to give thanks
and to sing praises at the gates of the LORD's
dwelling. 3The king contributed from his own
possessions for the morning and evening burnt
offerings and for the burnt offerings on the Sabbaths, New Moons and appointed feasts as written in the Law of the LORD. 4He ordered the
people living in Jerusalem to give the portion due
the priests and Levites so they could devote
themselves to the Law of the LORD. 5As soon as
the order went out, the Israelites generously gave
the firstfruits of their grain, new wine, oil and
honey and all that the fields produced. They
brought a great amount, a tithe of everything.
6The men of Israel and Judah who lived in the
towns of Judah also brought a tithe of their herds
and flocks and a tithe of the holy things dedicated
to the LORD their God, and they piled them in
heaps. 7They began doing this in the third month
and finished in the seventh month. 8When Hezekiah and his officials came and saw the heaps,
they praised the LORD and blessed his people Israel.
9Hezekiah asked the priests and Levites about
the heaps; 10and Azariah the chief priest, from
the family of Zadok, answered, "Since the people
began to bring their contributions to the temple
of the LORD, we have had enough to eat and
plenty to spare, because the LORD has blessed his
people, and this great amount is left over."
11Hezekiah gave orders to prepare storerooms
in the temple of the LORD, and this was done.
12Then they faithfully brought in the contributions, tithes and dedicated gifts. Conaniah, a Levite, was in charge of these things, and his brother Shimei was next in rank. 13Jehiel, Azaziah,
Nahath, Asahel, Jerimoth, Jozabad, Eliel, Ismaki-
ah, Mahath and Benaiah were supervisors under
Conaniah and Shimei his brother, by appointment of King Hezekiah and Azariah the official in
charge of the temple of God.
14Kore son of Imnah the Levite, keeper of the
East Gate, was in charge of the freewill offerings
given to God, distributing the contributions made
to the LORD and also the consecrated gifts.
15Eden, Miniamin, Jeshua, Shemaiah, Amariah
and Shecaniah assisted him faithfully in the
towns of the priests, distributing to their fellow
priests according to their divisions, old and young
alike.
16In addition, they distributed to the males
three years old or more whose names were in the
genealogical records—all who would enter the
temple of the LORD to perform the daily duties of
their various tasks, according to their responsibilities and their divisions. 17And they distributed
to the priests enrolled by their families in the
genealogical records and likewise to the Levites
twenty years old or more, according to their responsibilities and their divisions. 18They included all the little ones, the wives, and the sons and
daughters of the whole community listed in these
genealogical records. For they were faithful in
consecrating themselves.
19As for the priests, the descendants of Aaron,
who lived on the farm lands around their towns
or in any other towns, men were designated by
name to distribute portions to every male among
them and to all who were recorded in the genealogies of the Levites.
20This is what Hezekiah did throughout Judah,
doing what was good and right and faithful before
the LORD his God. 21In everything that he undertook in the service of God's temple and in obedience to the law and the commands, he sought his
God and worked wholeheartedly. And so he prospered.

Sennacherib Threatens Jerusalem

32 After all that Hezekiah had so faithfully
done, Sennacherib king of Assyria came
and invaded Judah. He laid siege to the fortified
cities, thinking to conquer them for himself.
2When Hezekiah saw that Sennacherib had come
and that he intended to make war on Jerusalem,
3he consulted with his officials and military staff
about blocking off the water from the springs outside the city, and they helped him. 4A large force
of men assembled, and they blocked all the
springs and the stream that flowed through the
land. "Why should the kings[b] of Assyria come
and find plenty of water?" they said. 5Then he
worked hard repairing all the broken sections of
the wall and building towers on it. He built another wall outside that one and reinforced the

[a]2 Traditionally *peace offerings* [b]4 Hebrew; Septuagint and Syriac *king*

supporting terraces[a] of the City of David. He
also made large numbers of weapons and shields.
6He appointed military officers over the people
and assembled them before him in the square at
the city gate and encouraged them with these
words: 7"Be strong and courageous. Do not be
afraid or discouraged because of the king of Assyria and the vast army with him, for there is a
greater power with us than with him. 8With him
is only the arm of flesh, but with us is the LORD
our God to help us and to fight our battles." And
the people gained confidence from what Hezekiah the king of Judah said.
9Later, when Sennacherib king of Assyria and
all his forces were laying siege to Lachish, he sent
his officers to Jerusalem with this message for
Hezekiah king of Judah and for all the people of
Judah who were there:

10"This is what Sennacherib king of Assyria says: On what are you basing your confidence, that you remain in Jerusalem under
siege? 11When Hezekiah says, 'The LORD
our God will save us from the hand of the
king of Assyria,' he is misleading you, to let
you die of hunger and thirst. 12Did not Hezekiah himself remove this god's high places
and altars, saying to Judah and Jerusalem,
'You must worship before one altar and
burn sacrifices on it'?
13"Do you not know what I and my fathers have done to all the peoples of the
other lands? Were the gods of those nations
ever able to deliver their land from my
hand? 14Who of all the gods of these nations
that my fathers destroyed has been able to
save his people from me? How then can
your god deliver you from my hand? 15Now
do not let Hezekiah deceive you and mislead you like this. Do not believe him, for
no god of any nation or kingdom has been
able to deliver his people from my hand or
the hand of my fathers. How much less will
your god deliver you from my hand!"

16Sennacherib's officers spoke further against
the LORD God and against his servant Hezekiah.
17The king also wrote letters insulting the LORD,
the God of Israel, and saying this against him:
"Just as the gods of the peoples of the other lands
did not rescue their people from my hand, so the
god of Hezekiah will not rescue his people from
my hand." 18Then they called out in Hebrew to
the people of Jerusalem who were on the wall, to
terrify them and make them afraid in order
to capture the city. 19They spoke about the God
of Jerusalem as they did about the gods of the
other peoples of the world—the work of men's
hands.
20King Hezekiah and the prophet Isaiah son of
Amoz cried out in prayer to heaven about this.
21And the LORD sent an angel, who annihilated
all the fighting men and the leaders and officers
in the camp of the Assyrian king. So he withdrew
to his own land in disgrace. And when he went
into the temple of his god, some of his sons cut
him down with the sword.
22So the LORD saved Hezekiah and the people
of Jerusalem from the hand of Sennacherib king
of Assyria and from the hand of all others. He
took care of them[b] on every side. 23Many
brought offerings to Jerusalem for the LORD and
valuable gifts for Hezekiah king of Judah. From
then on he was highly regarded by all the nations.

Hezekiah's Pride, Success and Death

24In those days Hezekiah became ill and was at
the point of death. He prayed to the LORD, who
answered him and gave him a miraculous sign.
25But Hezekiah's heart was proud and he did not
respond to the kindness shown him; therefore
the LORD's wrath was on him and on Judah and
Jerusalem. 26Then Hezekiah repented of the
pride of his heart, as did the people of Jerusalem;
therefore the LORD's wrath did not come upon
them during the days of Hezekiah.
27Hezekiah had very great riches and honor,
and he made treasuries for his silver and gold and
for his precious stones, spices, shields and all
kinds of valuables. 28He also made buildings to
store the harvest of grain, new wine and oil; and
he made stalls for various kinds of cattle, and
pens for the flocks. 29He built villages and acquired great numbers of flocks and herds, for God
had given him very great riches.
30It was Hezekiah who blocked the upper out-
let of the Gihon spring and channeled the water
down to the west side of the City of David. He
succeeded in everything he undertook. 31But
when envoys were sent by the rulers of Babylon
to ask him about the miraculous sign that had
occurred in the land, God left him to test him and
to know everything that was in his heart.
32The other events of Hezekiah's reign and his
acts of devotion are written in the vision of the
prophet Isaiah son of Amoz in the book of the
kings of Judah and Israel. 33Hezekiah rested with
his fathers and was buried on the hill where the
tombs of David's descendants are. All Judah and
the people of Jerusalem honored him when he
died. And Manasseh his son succeeded him as
king.

[a]*5* Or *the Millo* [b]*22* Hebrew; Septuagint and Vulgate *He gave them rest*

Manasseh King of Judah

33 Manasseh was twelve years old when he became king, and he reigned in Jerusalem fifty-five years. 2He did evil in the eyes of the LORD, following the detestable practices of the nations the LORD had driven out before the Israelites. 3He rebuilt the high places his father Hezekiah had demolished; he also erected altars to the Baals and made Asherah poles. He bowed down to all the starry hosts and worshiped them. 4He built altars in the temple of the LORD, of which the LORD had said, "My Name will remain in Jerusalem forever." 5In both courts of the temple of the LORD, he built altars to all the starry hosts. 6He sacrificed his sons in[a] the fire in the Valley of Ben Hinnom, practiced sorcery, divination and witchcraft, and consulted mediums and spiritists. He did much evil in the eyes of the LORD, provoking him to anger.

7He took the carved image he had made and put it in God's temple, of which God had said to David and to his son Solomon, "In this temple and in Jerusalem, which I have chosen out of all the tribes of Israel, I will put my Name forever. 8I will not again make the feet of the Israelites leave the land I assigned to your forefathers, if only they will be careful to do everything I commanded them concerning all the laws, decrees and ordinances given through Moses." 9But Manasseh led Judah and the people of Jerusalem astray, so that they did more evil than the nations the LORD had destroyed before the Israelites.

10The LORD spoke to Manasseh and his people, but they paid no attention. 11So the LORD brought against them the army commanders of the king of Assyria, who took Manasseh prisoner, put a hook in his nose, bound him with bronze shackles and took him to Babylon. 12In his distress he sought the favor of the LORD his God and humbled himself greatly before the God of his fathers. 13And when he prayed to him, the LORD was moved by his entreaty and listened to his plea; so he brought him back to Jerusalem and to his kingdom. Then Manasseh knew that the LORD is God.

14Afterward he rebuilt the outer wall of the City of David, west of the Gihon spring in the valley, as far as the entrance of the Fish Gate and encircling the hill of Ophel; he also made it much higher. He stationed military commanders in all the fortified cities in Judah.

15He got rid of the foreign gods and removed the image from the temple of the LORD, as well as all the altars he had built on the temple hill and in Jerusalem; and he threw them out of the city. 16Then he restored the altar of the LORD and sacrificed fellowship offerings[b] and thank offerings on it, and told Judah to serve the LORD, the God of Israel. 17The people, however, continued to sacrifice at the high places, but only to the LORD their God.

18The other events of Manasseh's reign, including his prayer to his God and the words the seers spoke to him in the name of the LORD, the God of Israel, are written in the annals of the kings of Israel.[c] 19His prayer and how God was moved by his entreaty, as well as all his sins and unfaithfulness, and the sites where he built high places and set up Asherah poles and idols before he humbled himself—all are written in the records of the seers.[d] 20Manasseh rested with his fathers and was buried in his palace. And Amon his son succeeded him as king.

Amon King of Judah

21Amon was twenty-two years old when he became king, and he reigned in Jerusalem two years. 22He did evil in the eyes of the LORD, as his father Manasseh had done. Amon worshiped and offered sacrifices to all the idols Manasseh had made. 23But unlike his father Manasseh, he did not humble himself before the LORD; Amon increased his guilt.

24Amon's officials conspired against him and assassinated him in his palace. 25Then the people of the land killed all who had plotted against King Amon, and they made Josiah his son king in his place.

Josiah's Reforms

34 Josiah was eight years old when he became king, and he reigned in Jerusalem thirty-one years. 2He did what was right in the eyes of the LORD and walked in the ways of his father David, not turning aside to the right or to the left.

3In the eighth year of his reign, while he was still young, he began to seek the God of his father David. In his twelfth year he began to purge Judah and Jerusalem of high places, Asherah poles, carved idols and cast images. 4Under his direction the altars of the Baals were torn down; he cut to pieces the incense altars that were above them, and smashed the Asherah poles, the idols and the images. These he broke to pieces and scattered over the graves of those who had sacrificed to them. 5He burned the bones of the priests on their altars, and so he purged Judah and Jerusalem. 6In the towns of Manasseh, Ephraim and Simeon, as far as Naphtali, and in the ruins around them, 7he tore down the altars and the Asherah poles and crushed the idols to

[a] 6 Or *He made his sons pass through* [b] 16 Traditionally *peace offerings* [c] 18 That is, Judah, as frequently in 2 Chronicles
[d] 19 One Hebrew manuscript and Septuagint; most Hebrew manuscripts *of Hozai*

powder and cut to pieces all the incense altars
throughout Israel. Then he went back to Jerusalem.
8 In the eighteenth year of Josiah's reign, to
purify the land and the temple, he sent Shaphan
son of Azaliah and Maaseiah the ruler of the city,
with Joah son of Joahaz, the recorder, to repair
the temple of the LORD his God.
9 They went to Hilkiah the high priest and gave
him the money that had been brought into the
temple of God, which the Levites who were the
doorkeepers had collected from the people of Manasseh, Ephraim and the entire remnant of Israel
and from all the people of Judah and Benjamin
and the inhabitants of Jerusalem. 10 Then they entrusted it to the men appointed to supervise the
work on the LORD's temple. These men paid the
workers who repaired and restored the temple.
11 They also gave money to the carpenters and
builders to purchase dressed stone, and timber
for joists and beams for the buildings that the
kings of Judah had allowed to fall into ruin.
12 The men did the work faithfully. Over them
to direct them were Jahath and Obadiah, Levites
descended from Merari, and Zechariah and Meshullam, descended from Kohath. The Levites—
all who were skilled in playing musical
instruments— 13 had charge of the laborers and
supervised all the workers from job to job. Some
of the Levites were secretaries, scribes and doorkeepers.

The Book of the Law Found

14 While they were bringing out the money
that had been taken into the temple of the LORD,
Hilkiah the priest found the Book of the Law of
the LORD that had been given through Moses.
15 Hilkiah said to Shaphan the secretary, "I have
found the Book of the Law in the temple of the
LORD." He gave it to Shaphan.
16 Then Shaphan took the book to the king and
reported to him: "Your officials are doing everything that has been committed to them. 17 They
have paid out the money that was in the temple
of the LORD and have entrusted it to the supervisors and workers." 18 Then Shaphan the secretary
informed the king, "Hilkiah the priest has given
me a book." And Shaphan read from it in the
presence of the king.
19 When the king heard the words of the Law,
he tore his robes. 20 He gave these orders to Hilkiah, Ahikam son of Shaphan, Abdon son of Micah,[a] Shaphan the secretary and Asaiah the
king's attendant: 21 "Go and inquire of the LORD
for me and for the remnant in Israel and Judah
about what is written in this book that has been
found. Great is the LORD's anger that is poured
out on us because our fathers have not kept the
word of the LORD; they have not acted in accordance with all that is written in this book."
22 Hilkiah and those the king had sent with
him[b] went to speak to the prophetess Huldah,
who was the wife of Shallum son of Tokhath,[c]
the son of Hasrah,[d] keeper of the wardrobe. She
lived in Jerusalem, in the Second District.
23 She said to them, "This is what the LORD,
the God of Israel, says: Tell the man who sent you
to me, 24 'This is what the LORD says: I am going
to bring disaster on this place and its people—all
the curses written in the book that has been read
in the presence of the king of Judah. 25 Because
they have forsaken me and burned incense to
other gods and provoked me to anger by all that
their hands have made,[e] my anger will be
poured out on this place and will not be
quenched.' 26 Tell the king of Judah, who sent you
to inquire of the LORD, 'This is what the LORD,
the God of Israel, says concerning the words you
heard: 27 Because your heart was responsive and
you humbled yourself before God when you
heard what he spoke against this place and its
people, and because you humbled yourself before
me and tore your robes and wept in my presence,
I have heard you, declares the LORD. 28 Now I will
gather you to your fathers, and you will be buried
in peace. Your eyes will not see all the disaster I
am going to bring on this place and on those who
live here.'"
So they took her answer back to the king.
29 Then the king called together all the elders
of Judah and Jerusalem. 30 He went up to the temple of the LORD with the men of Judah, the people
of Jerusalem, the priests and the Levites—all the
people from the least to the greatest. He read in
their hearing all the words of the Book of the
Covenant, which had been found in the temple
of the LORD. 31 The king stood by his pillar and
renewed the covenant in the presence of the
LORD—to follow the LORD and keep his commands, regulations and decrees with all his heart
and all his soul, and to obey the words of the
covenant written in this book.
32 Then he had everyone in Jerusalem and Benjamin pledge themselves to it; the people of Jerusalem did this in accordance with the covenant of
God, the God of their fathers.
33 Josiah removed all the detestable idols from
all the territory belonging to the Israelites, and he

[a] 20 Also called *Acbor son of Micaiah* [b] 22 One Hebrew manuscript, Vulgate and Syriac; most Hebrew manuscripts do not have *had sent with him.* [c] 22 Also called *Tikvah* [d] 22 Also called *Harhas* [e] 25 Or *by everything they have done*

had all who were present in Israel serve the LORD their God. As long as he lived, they did not fail to follow the LORD, the God of their fathers.

Josiah Celebrates the Passover

35 Josiah celebrated the Passover to the LORD in Jerusalem, and the Passover lamb was slaughtered on the fourteenth day of the first month. 2He appointed the priests to their duties and encouraged them in the service of the LORD's temple. 3He said to the Levites, who instructed all Israel and who had been consecrated to the LORD: "Put the sacred ark in the temple that Solomon son of David king of Israel built. It is not to be carried about on your shoulders. Now serve the LORD your God and his people Israel. 4Prepare yourselves by families in your divisions, according to the directions written by David king of Israel and by his son Solomon.

5"Stand in the holy place with a group of Levites for each subdivision of the families of your fellow countrymen, the lay people. 6Slaughter the Passover lambs, consecrate yourselves and prepare ⌊the lambs⌋ for your fellow countrymen, doing what the LORD commanded through Moses."

7Josiah provided for all the lay people who were there a total of thirty thousand sheep and goats for the Passover offerings, and also three thousand cattle—all from the king's own possessions.

8His officials also contributed voluntarily to the people and the priests and Levites. Hilkiah, Zechariah and Jehiel, the administrators of God's temple, gave the priests twenty-six hundred Passover offerings and three hundred cattle. 9Also Conaniah along with Shemaiah and Nethanel, his brothers, and Hashabiah, Jeiel and Jozabad, the leaders of the Levites, provided five thousand Passover offerings and five hundred head of cattle for the Levites.

10The service was arranged and the priests stood in their places with the Levites in their divisions as the king had ordered. 11The Passover lambs were slaughtered, and the priests sprinkled the blood handed to them, while the Levites skinned the animals. 12They set aside the burnt offerings to give them to the subdivisions of the families of the people to offer to the LORD, as is written in the Book of Moses. They did the same with the cattle. 13They roasted the Passover animals over the fire as prescribed, and boiled the holy offerings in pots, caldrons and pans and served them quickly to all the people. 14After this, they made preparations for themselves and for the priests, because the priests, the descendants of Aaron, were sacrificing the burnt offerings and the fat portions until nightfall. So the Levites made preparations for themselves and for the Aaronic priests.

15The musicians, the descendants of Asaph, were in the places prescribed by David, Asaph, Heman and Jeduthun the king's seer. The gatekeepers at each gate did not need to leave their posts, because their fellow Levites made the preparations for them.

16So at that time the entire service of the LORD was carried out for the celebration of the Passover and the offering of burnt offerings on the altar of the LORD, as King Josiah had ordered. 17The Israelites who were present celebrated the Passover at that time and observed the Feast of Unleavened Bread for seven days. 18The Passover had not been observed like this in Israel since the days of the prophet Samuel; and none of the kings of Israel had ever celebrated such a Passover as did Josiah, with the priests, the Levites and all Judah and Israel who were there with the people of Jerusalem. 19This Passover was celebrated in the eighteenth year of Josiah's reign.

The Death of Josiah

20After all this, when Josiah had set the temple in order, Neco king of Egypt went up to fight at Carchemish on the Euphrates, and Josiah marched out to meet him in battle. 21But Neco sent messengers to him, saying, "What quarrel is there between you and me, O king of Judah? It is not you I am attacking at this time, but the house with which I am at war. God has told me to hurry; so stop opposing God, who is with me, or he will destroy you."

22Josiah, however, would not turn away from him, but disguised himself to engage him in battle. He would not listen to what Neco had said at God's command but went to fight him on the plain of Megiddo.

23Archers shot King Josiah, and he told his officers, "Take me away; I am badly wounded." 24So they took him out of his chariot, put him in the other chariot he had and brought him to Jerusalem, where he died. He was buried in the tombs of his fathers, and all Judah and Jerusalem mourned for him.

25Jeremiah composed laments for Josiah, and to this day all the men and women singers commemorate Josiah in the laments. These became a tradition in Israel and are written in the Laments.

26The other events of Josiah's reign and his acts of devotion, according to what is written in the Law of the LORD— 27all the events, from beginning to end, are written in the book of the kings of Israel and Judah.

36 1And the people of the land took Jehoahaz son of Josiah and made him king in Jerusalem in place of his father.

Jehoahaz King of Judah

2Jehoahaz[a] was twenty-three years old when
he became king, and he reigned in Jerusalem
three months. 3The king of Egypt dethroned him
in Jerusalem and imposed on Judah a levy of a
hundred talents[b] of silver and a talent[c] of gold.
4The king of Egypt made Eliakim, a brother of
Jehoahaz, king over Judah and Jerusalem and
changed Eliakim's name to Jehoiakim. But Neco
took Eliakim's brother Jehoahaz and carried him
off to Egypt.

Jehoiakim King of Judah

5Jehoiakim was twenty-five years old when he
became king, and he reigned in Jerusalem eleven
years. He did evil in the eyes of the LORD his God.
6Nebuchadnezzar king of Babylon attacked him
and bound him with bronze shackles to take him
to Babylon. 7Nebuchadnezzar also took to Babylon articles from the temple of the LORD and put
them in his temple[d] there.

8The other events of Jehoiakim's reign, the
detestable things he did and all that was found
against him, are written in the book of the kings
of Israel and Judah. And Jehoiachin his son succeeded him as king.

Jehoiachin King of Judah

9Jehoiachin was eighteen[e] years old when he
became king, and he reigned in Jerusalem three
months and ten days. He did evil in the eyes of
the LORD. 10In the spring, King Nebuchadnezzar
sent for him and brought him to Babylon, together with articles of value from the temple of the
LORD, and he made Jehoiachin's uncle,[f] Zedekiah, king over Judah and Jerusalem.

Zedekiah King of Judah

11Zedekiah was twenty-one years old when he
became king, and he reigned in Jerusalem eleven
years. 12He did evil in the eyes of the LORD his
God and did not humble himself before Jeremiah
the prophet, who spoke the word of the LORD.
13He also rebelled against King Nebuchadnezzar,
who had made him take an oath in God's name.
He became stiff-necked and hardened his heart
and would not turn to the LORD, the God of Israel. 14Furthermore, all the leaders of the priests
and the people became more and more unfaithful, following all the detestable practices of the
nations and defiling the temple of the LORD,
which he had consecrated in Jerusalem.

The Fall of Jerusalem

15The LORD, the God of their fathers, sent
word to them through his messengers again and
again, because he had pity on his people and on
his dwelling place. 16But they mocked God's messengers, despised his words and scoffed at his
prophets until the wrath of the LORD was aroused
against his people and there was no remedy.
17He brought up against them the king of the
Babylonians,[g] who killed their young men with
the sword in the sanctuary, and spared neither
young man nor young woman, old man or aged.
God handed all of them over to Nebuchadnezzar.
18He carried to Babylon all the articles from the
temple of God, both large and small, and the treasures of the LORD's temple and the treasures of
the king and his officials. 19They set fire to God's
temple and broke down the wall of Jerusalem;
they burned all the palaces and destroyed everything of value there.

20He carried into exile to Babylon the remnant, who escaped from the sword, and they became servants to him and his sons until the kingdom of Persia came to power. 21The land enjoyed
its sabbath rests; all the time of its desolation it
rested, until the seventy years were completed in
fulfillment of the word of the LORD spoken by
Jeremiah.

22In the first year of Cyrus king of Persia, in
order to fulfill the word of the LORD spoken by
Jeremiah, the LORD moved the heart of Cyrus
king of Persia to make a proclamation throughout
his realm and to put it in writing:

23"This is what Cyrus king of Persia says:

> " 'The LORD, the God of heaven, has giv-
> en me all the kingdoms of the earth and he
> has appointed me to build a temple for him
> at Jerusalem in Judah. Anyone of his people
> among you—may the LORD his God be with
> him, and let him go up.' "

a2 Hebrew *Joahaz,* a variant of *Jehoahaz*; also in verse 4 *b3* That is, about 3 3/4 tons (about 3.4 metric tons) *c3* That is, about 75 pounds (about 34 kilograms) *d7* Or *palace* *e9* One Hebrew manuscript, some Septuagint manuscripts and Syriac (see also 2 Kings 24:8); most Hebrew manuscripts *eight* *f10* Hebrew *brother,* that is, relative (see 2 Kings 24:17) *g17* Or *Chaldeans*

Introduction to EZRA

Personal Reading Plan

❐ Ezra 1:1–11	❐ Ezra 5:1–17	❐ Ezra 8:1–36
❐ Ezra 2:1–70	❐ Ezra 6:1–22	❐ Ezra 9:1–15
❐ Ezra 3:1–4:24	❐ Ezra 7:1–28	❐ Ezra 10:1–44

Author

The book is named for the principal character, Ezra, but it does not state its author. Whoever it was may have also helped to compile the book of Nehemiah and perhaps 1 and 2 Chronicles, as these books share many common characteristics:

1. A fondness for lists, for the descriptions of religious festivals and for the phrases "heads of families" and "the house of God."
2. The prominence of Levites and temple personnel.
3. The almost exclusive use of the Hebrew words for "singer," "gatekeeper" and "temple servants."

Date

With an unstated author, precise dating is difficult to determine. The events narrated cover the years c. 538–458 B.C.

Theme

Beginning again, by building the second temple.

Historical Background

Originally this work was one book along with Nehemiah. In the Latin Bible, Ezra and Nehemiah are entitled 1 and 2 Esdras. This book chronicles the restoration of Israel after 70 years of captivity in Babylon. This is accomplished through the help of three Persian kings (Cyrus, Darius and Artaxerxes I). Cyrus was an enlightened king who reversed the oppressive policies of his Assyrian and Babylonian predecessors and encouraged the return of the exiles and the rebirth of their religion. The traditional view is that Ezra arrived in Jerusalem in the seventh year of the reign of Artaxerxes I (458 B.C.) and Nehemiah in the twentieth year of the reign (445 B.C.).

Characteristics

This book weaves together various lists, the first-person and third-person memoirs of Ezra and official documents. These include: (1) the decree of Cyrus (1:2–4); (2) the accusation against the Jews (4:11–16); (3) the response of Artaxerxes (4:17–22); (4) the letter of Tattenai to Darius (5:7–17); (5) a memo (6:2b–5); (6) Darius' reply to Tattenai (6:6–12); and (7) a letter from Artaxerxes I to Ezra (7:12–26). God is shown using Persian kings and Jewish leaders both to bless and to discipline his people. Ezra is often seen as the "father of Judaism" because he promotes a way of life renewed by and centered on unswerving allegiance to the Torah. Ezra's policies saved Judaism from oblivion in this crucial period of transition.

Cyrus Helps the Exiles to Return

1 In the first year of Cyrus king of Persia, in
order to fulfill the word of the LORD spoken
by Jeremiah, the LORD moved the heart of Cyrus
king of Persia to make a proclamation throughout
his realm and to put it in writing:
[2]"This is what Cyrus king of Persia says:
"'The LORD, the God of heaven, has giv-
en me all the kingdoms of the earth and he
has appointed me to build a temple for him
at Jerusalem in Judah. [3]Anyone of his people among you—may his God be with him,
and let him go up to Jerusalem in Judah and
build the temple of the LORD, the God of
Israel, the God who is in Jerusalem. [4]And
the people of any place where survivors
may now be living are to provide him with
silver and gold, with goods and livestock,
and with freewill offerings for the temple of
God in Jerusalem.'"
[5]Then the family heads of Judah and Benjamin,
and the priests and Levites—everyone whose
heart God had moved—prepared to go up and
build the house of the LORD in Jerusalem. [6]All
their neighbors assisted them with articles of silver and gold, with goods and livestock, and with
valuable gifts, in addition to all the freewill offerings. [7]Moreover, King Cyrus brought out the articles belonging to the temple of the LORD, which
Nebuchadnezzar had carried away from Jerusalem and had placed in the temple of his god.[a]
[8]Cyrus king of Persia had them brought by Mithredath the treasurer, who counted them out to
Sheshbazzar the prince of Judah.
[9]This was the inventory:

gold dishes	30
silver dishes	1,000
silver pans[b]	29
[10]gold bowls	30
matching silver bowls	410
other articles	1,000

[11]In all, there were 5,400 articles of gold and
of silver. Sheshbazzar brought all these along
when the exiles came up from Babylon to Jerusalem.

The List of the Exiles Who Returned

2 Now these are the people of the province
who came up from the captivity of the exiles,
whom Nebuchadnezzar king of Babylon had tak-
en captive to Babylon (they returned to Jerusalem
and Judah, each to his own town, [2]in company
with Zerubbabel, Jeshua, Nehemiah, Seraiah, Re-
elaiah, Mordecai, Bilshan, Mispar, Bigvai, Rehum
and Baanah):

The list of the men of the people of Israel:

[3]the descendants of Parosh	2,172
[4]of Shephatiah	372
[5]of Arah	775
[6]of Pahath-Moab (through the line of Jeshua and Joab)	2,812
[7]of Elam	1,254
[8]of Zattu	945
[9]of Zaccai	760
[10]of Bani	642
[11]of Bebai	623
[12]of Azgad	1,222
[13]of Adonikam	666
[14]of Bigvai	2,056
[15]of Adin	454
[16]of Ater (through Hezekiah)	98
[17]of Bezai	323
[18]of Jorah	112
[19]of Hashum	223
[20]of Gibbar	95
[21]the men of Bethlehem	123
[22]of Netophah	56
[23]of Anathoth	128
[24]of Azmaveth	42
[25]of Kiriath Jearim,[c] Kephirah and Beeroth	743
[26]of Ramah and Geba	621
[27]of Micmash	122
[28]of Bethel and Ai	223
[29]of Nebo	52
[30]of Magbish	156
[31]of the other Elam	1,254
[32]of Harim	320
[33]of Lod, Hadid and Ono	725
[34]of Jericho	345
[35]of Senaah	3,630

[36]The priests:

the descendants of Jedaiah (through the family of Jeshua)	973
[37]of Immer	1,052
[38]of Pashhur	1,247
[39]of Harim	1,017

[40]The Levites:

the descendants of Jeshua and Kadmiel (through the line of Hodaviah)	74

[41]The singers:

the descendants of Asaph	128

[42]The gatekeepers of the temple:

the descendants of

[a]7 Or *gods* [b]9 The meaning of the Hebrew for this word is uncertain. [c]25 See Septuagint (see also Neh. 7:29); Hebrew *Kiriath Arim.*

Shallum, Ater, Talmon,
Akkub, Hatita and Shobai 139

43The temple servants:

the descendants of
Ziha, Hasupha, Tabbaoth,
44Keros, Siaha, Padon,
45Lebanah, Hagabah, Akkub,
46Hagab, Shalmai, Hanan,
47Giddel, Gahar, Reaiah,
48Rezin, Nekoda, Gazzam,
49Uzza, Paseah, Besai,
50Asnah, Meunim, Nephussim,
51Bakbuk, Hakupha, Harhur,
52Bazluth, Mehida, Harsha,
53Barkos, Sisera, Temah,
54Neziah and Hatipha

55The descendants of the servants of Solomon:

the descendants of
Sotai, Hassophereth, Peruda,
56Jaala, Darkon, Giddel,
57Shephatiah, Hattil,
Pokereth-Hazzebaim and Ami

58The temple servants and the
descendants of the servants of
Solomon 392

59The following came up from the towns of Tel Melah, Tel Harsha, Kerub, Addon and Immer, but they could not show that their families were descended from Israel:

60The descendants of
Delaiah, Tobiah and Nekoda 652

61And from among the priests:

The descendants of
Hobaiah, Hakkoz and Barzillai (a man who had married a daughter of Barzillai the Gileadite and was called by that name).

62These searched for their family records, but they could not find them and so were excluded from the priesthood as unclean. 63The governor ordered them not to eat any of the most sacred food until there was a priest ministering with the Urim and Thummim.

64The whole company numbered 42,360, 65besides their 7,337 menservants and maidservants; and they also had 200 men and women singers. 66They had 736 horses, 245 mules, 67435 camels and 6,720 donkeys.

68When they arrived at the house of the LORD in Jerusalem, some of the heads of the families gave freewill offerings toward the rebuilding of the house of God on its site. 69According to their ability they gave to the treasury for this work 61,000 drachmas[a] of gold, 5,000 minas[b] of silver and 100 priestly garments.

70The priests, the Levites, the singers, the gatekeepers and the temple servants settled in their own towns, along with some of the other people, and the rest of the Israelites settled in their towns.

Rebuilding the Altar

3 When the seventh month came and the Israelites had settled in their towns, the people
assembled as one man in Jerusalem. 2Then Jeshua son of Jozadak and his fellow priests and Zerubbabel son of Shealtiel and his associates began
to build the altar of the God of Israel to sacrifice
burnt offerings on it, in accordance with what is
written in the Law of Moses the man of God.
3Despite their fear of the peoples around them,
they built the altar on its foundation and sacrificed burnt offerings on it to the LORD, both the
morning and evening sacrifices. 4Then in accordance with what is written, they celebrated the
Feast of Tabernacles with the required number of
burnt offerings prescribed for each day. 5After
that, they presented the regular burnt offerings,
the New Moon sacrifices and the sacrifices for all
the appointed sacred feasts of the LORD, as well as
those brought as freewill offerings to the LORD.
6On the first day of the seventh month they began to offer burnt offerings to the LORD, though
the foundation of the LORD's temple had not yet
been laid.

Rebuilding the Temple

7Then they gave money to the masons and
carpenters, and gave food and drink and oil to the
people of Sidon and Tyre, so that they would
bring cedar logs by sea from Lebanon to Joppa, as
authorized by Cyrus king of Persia.
8In the second month of the second year after
their arrival at the house of God in Jerusalem,
Zerubbabel son of Shealtiel, Jeshua son of Jozadak
and the rest of their brothers (the priests and the
Levites and all who had returned from the captivity to Jerusalem) began the work, appointing Levites twenty years of age and older to supervise
the building of the house of the LORD. 9Jeshua
and his sons and brothers and Kadmiel and his
sons (descendants of Hodaviah[c]) and the sons
of Henadad and their sons and brothers—all

[a]69 That is, about 1,100 pounds (about 500 kilograms) [b]69 That is, about 3 tons (about 2.9 metric tons) [c]9 Hebrew *Yehudah,* probably a variant of *Hodaviah*

Levites—joined together in supervising those
working on the house of God.
10When the builders laid the foundation of the
temple of the LORD, the priests in their vestments
and with trumpets, and the Levites (the sons of
Asaph) with cymbals, took their places to praise
the LORD, as prescribed by David king of Israel.
11With praise and thanksgiving they sang to the
LORD:

"He is good;
his love to Israel endures forever."

And all the people gave a great shout of praise to
the LORD, because the foundation of the house of
the LORD was laid. 12But many of the older priests
and Levites and family heads, who had seen the
former temple, wept aloud when they saw the
foundation of this temple being laid, while many
others shouted for joy. 13No one could distinguish the sound of the shouts of joy from the
sound of weeping, because the people made so
much noise. And the sound was heard far away.

Opposition to the Rebuilding

4 When the enemies of Judah and Benjamin
heard that the exiles were building a temple
for the LORD, the God of Israel, 2they came to
Zerubbabel and to the heads of the families and
said, "Let us help you build because, like you, we
seek your God and have been sacrificing to him
since the time of Esarhaddon king of Assyria,
who brought us here."
3But Zerubbabel, Jeshua and the rest of the
heads of the families of Israel answered, "You
have no part with us in building a temple to our
God. We alone will build it for the LORD, the God
of Israel, as King Cyrus, the king of Persia, commanded us."
4Then the peoples around them set out to discourage the people of Judah and make them
afraid to go on building.[a] 5They hired counselors to work against them and frustrate their plans
during the entire reign of Cyrus king of Persia
and down to the reign of Darius king of Persia.

Later Opposition Under Xerxes and Artaxerxes

6At the beginning of the reign of Xerxes,[b]
they lodged an accusation against the people of
Judah and Jerusalem.
7And in the days of Artaxerxes king of Persia,
Bishlam, Mithredath, Tabeel and the rest of his
associates wrote a letter to Artaxerxes. The letter
was written in Aramaic script and in the Aramaic
language.[c,d]

8Rehum the commanding officer and Shimshai
the secretary wrote a letter against Jerusalem to
Artaxerxes the king as follows:

9Rehum the commanding officer and Shimshai the secretary, together with the rest of
their associates—the judges and officials
over the men from Tripolis, Persia,[e] Erech
and Babylon, the Elamites of Susa, 10and the
other people whom the great and honorable
Ashurbanipal[f] deported and settled in the
city of Samaria and elsewhere in Trans-
Euphrates.

11(This is a copy of the letter they sent him.)

To King Artaxerxes,
From your servants, the men of Trans-
Euphrates:

12The king should know that the Jews
who came up to us from you have gone to
Jerusalem and are rebuilding that rebellious
and wicked city. They are restoring the
walls and repairing the foundations.
13Furthermore, the king should know
that if this city is built and its walls are
restored, no more taxes, tribute or duty will
be paid, and the royal revenues will suffer.
14Now since we are under obligation to the
palace and it is not proper for us to see the
king dishonored, we are sending this message to inform the king, 15so that a search
may be made in the archives of your predecessors. In these records you will find that
this city is a rebellious city, troublesome to
kings and provinces, a place of rebellion
from ancient times. That is why this city
was destroyed. 16We inform the king that if
this city is built and its walls are restored,
you will be left with nothing in Trans-
Euphrates.

17The king sent this reply:

To Rehum the commanding officer, Shimshai the secretary and the rest of their associates living in Samaria and elsewhere in
Trans-Euphrates:

Greetings.

18The letter you sent us has been read
and translated in my presence. 19I issued an
order and a search was made, and it was
found that this city has a long history of
revolt against kings and has been a place of
rebellion and sedition. 20Jerusalem has had

[a]4 Or *and troubled them as they built* [b]6 Hebrew *Ahasuerus,* a variant of Xerxes' Persian name [c]7 Or *written in Aramaic and translated* [d]7 The text of Ezra 4:8—6:18 is in Aramaic. [e]9 Or *officials, magistrates and governors over the men from* [f]10 Aramaic *Osnappar,* a variant of *Ashurbanipal*

powerful kings ruling over the whole of Trans-Euphrates, and taxes, tribute and duty were paid to them. 21Now issue an order to these men to stop work, so that this city will not be rebuilt until I so order. 22Be careful not to neglect this matter. Why let this threat grow, to the detriment of the royal interests?

23As soon as the copy of the letter of King Artaxerxes was read to Rehum and Shimshai the secretary and their associates, they went immediately to the Jews in Jerusalem and compelled them by force to stop.

24Thus the work on the house of God in Jerusalem came to a standstill until the second year of the reign of Darius king of Persia.

Tattenai's Letter to Darius

5 Now Haggai the prophet and Zechariah the prophet, a descendant of Iddo, prophesied to the Jews in Judah and Jerusalem in the name of the God of Israel, who was over them. 2Then Zerubbabel son of Shealtiel and Jeshua son of Jozadak set to work to rebuild the house of God in Jerusalem. And the prophets of God were with them, helping them.

3At that time Tattenai, governor of Trans-Euphrates, and Shethar-Bozenai and their associates went to them and asked, "Who authorized you to rebuild this temple and restore this structure?" 4They also asked, "What are the names of the men constructing this building?"[a] 5But the eye of their God was watching over the elders of the Jews, and they were not stopped until a report could go to Darius and his written reply be received.

6This is a copy of the letter that Tattenai, governor of Trans-Euphrates, and Shethar-Bozenai and their associates, the officials of Trans-Euphrates, sent to King Darius. 7The report they sent him read as follows:

To King Darius:

Cordial greetings.

8The king should know that we went to the district of Judah, to the temple of the great God. The people are building it with large stones and placing the timbers in the walls. The work is being carried on with diligence and is making rapid progress under their direction.

9We questioned the elders and asked them, "Who authorized you to rebuild this temple and restore this structure?" 10We also asked them their names, so that we could write down the names of their leaders for your information.

11This is the answer they gave us:

"We are the servants of the God of heaven and earth, and we are rebuilding the temple that was built many years ago, one that a great king of Israel built and finished. 12But because our fathers angered the God of heaven, he handed them over to Nebuchadnezzar the Chaldean, king of Babylon, who destroyed this temple and deported the people to Babylon.

13"However, in the first year of Cyrus king of Babylon, King Cyrus issued a decree to rebuild this house of God. 14He even removed from the temple[b] of Babylon the gold and silver articles of the house of God, which Nebuchadnezzar had taken from the temple in Jerusalem and brought to the temple[b] in Babylon.

"Then King Cyrus gave them to a man named Sheshbazzar, whom he had appointed governor, 15and he told him, 'Take these articles and go and deposit them in the temple in Jerusalem. And rebuild the house of God on its site.' 16So this Sheshbazzar came and laid the foundations of the house of God in Jerusalem. From that day to the present it has been under construction but is not yet finished."

17Now if it pleases the king, let a search be made in the royal archives of Babylon to see if King Cyrus did in fact issue a decree to rebuild this house of God in Jerusalem. Then let the king send us his decision in this matter.

The Decree of Darius

6 King Darius then issued an order, and they searched in the archives stored in the treasury at Babylon. 2A scroll was found in the citadel of Ecbatana in the province of Media, and this was written on it:

Memorandum:

3In the first year of King Cyrus, the king issued a decree concerning the temple of God in Jerusalem:

Let the temple be rebuilt as a place to present sacrifices, and let its foundations be laid. It is to be ninety feet[c] high and ninety feet wide, 4with three courses of large stones and one of timbers. The costs are to

[a] 4 See Septuagint; Aramaic *4We told them the names of the men constructing this building.* [b] 14 Or *palace* [c] 3 Aramaic *sixty cubits* (about 27 meters)

be paid by the royal treasury. [5]Also, the gold
and silver articles of the house of God,
which Nebuchadnezzar took from the temple in Jerusalem and brought to Babylon,
are to be returned to their places in the
temple in Jerusalem; they are to be deposited in the house of God.

[6]Now then, Tattenai, governor of Trans-
Euphrates, and Shethar-Bozenai and you,
their fellow officials of that province, stay
away from there. [7]Do not interfere with the
work on this temple of God. Let the governor of the Jews and the Jewish elders rebuild this house of God on its site.

[8]Moreover, I hereby decree what you are
to do for these elders of the Jews in the
construction of this house of God:

The expenses of these men are to be fully
paid out of the royal treasury, from the revenues of Trans-Euphrates, so that the work
will not stop. [9]Whatever is needed—young
bulls, rams, male lambs for burnt offerings
to the God of heaven, and wheat, salt, wine
and oil, as requested by the priests in
Jerusalem—must be given them daily without fail, [10]so that they may offer sacrifices
pleasing to the God of heaven and pray for
the well-being of the king and his sons.

[11]Furthermore, I decree that if anyone
changes this edict, a beam is to be pulled
from his house and he is to be lifted up and
impaled on it. And for this crime his house
is to be made a pile of rubble. [12]May God,
who has caused his Name to dwell there,
overthrow any king or people who lifts a
hand to change this decree or to destroy this
temple in Jerusalem.

I Darius have decreed it. Let it be carried
out with diligence.

Completion and Dedication of the Temple

[13]Then, because of the decree King Darius had
sent, Tattenai, governor of Trans-Euphrates, and
Shethar-Bozenai and their associates carried it
out with diligence. [14]So the elders of the Jews
continued to build and prosper under the preaching of Haggai the prophet and Zechariah, a
descendant of Iddo. They finished building the
temple according to the command of the God of
Israel and the decrees of Cyrus, Darius and Artaxerxes, kings of Persia. [15]The temple was completed on the third day of the month Adar, in the
sixth year of the reign of King Darius.

[16]Then the people of Israel—the priests, the
Levites and the rest of the exiles—celebrated the
dedication of the house of God with joy. [17]For the
dedication of this house of God they offered a
hundred bulls, two hundred rams, four hundred
male lambs and, as a sin offering for all Israel,
twelve male goats, one for each of the tribes of
Israel. [18]And they installed the priests in their
divisions and the Levites in their groups for the
service of God at Jerusalem, according to what is
written in the Book of Moses.

The Passover

[19]On the fourteenth day of the first month, the
exiles celebrated the Passover. [20]The priests and
Levites had purified themselves and were all ceremonially clean. The Levites slaughtered the
Passover lamb for all the exiles, for their brothers
the priests and for themselves. [21]So the Israelites
who had returned from the exile ate it, together
with all who had separated themselves from the
unclean practices of their Gentile neighbors in
order to seek the LORD, the God of Israel. [22]For
seven days they celebrated with joy the Feast of
Unleavened Bread, because the LORD had filled
them with joy by changing the attitude of the
king of Assyria, so that he assisted them in the
work on the house of God, the God of Israel.

Ezra Comes to Jerusalem

7 After these things, during the reign of Artaxerxes king of Persia, Ezra son of Seraiah, the
son of Azariah, the son of Hilkiah, [2]the son of
Shallum, the son of Zadok, the son of Ahitub,
[3]the son of Amariah, the son of Azariah, the son
of Meraioth, [4]the son of Zerahiah, the son of
Uzzi, the son of Bukki, [5]the son of Abishua, the
son of Phinehas, the son of Eleazar, the son of
Aaron the chief priest— [6]this Ezra came up from
Babylon. He was a teacher well versed in the Law
of Moses, which the LORD, the God of Israel, had
given. The king had granted him everything he
asked, for the hand of the LORD his God was on
him. [7]Some of the Israelites, including priests,
Levites, singers, gatekeepers and temple servants, also came up to Jerusalem in the seventh
year of King Artaxerxes.

[8]Ezra arrived in Jerusalem in the fifth month of
the seventh year of the king. [9]He had begun his
journey from Babylon on the first day of the first
month, and he arrived in Jerusalem on the first
day of the fifth month, for the gracious hand of
his God was on him. [10]For Ezra had devoted himself to the study and observance of the Law of the
LORD, and to teaching its decrees and laws in
Israel.

King Artaxerxes' Letter to Ezra

[11]This is a copy of the letter King Artaxerxes
had given to Ezra the priest and teacher, a man
learned in matters concerning the commands and
decrees of the LORD for Israel:

[12a]Artaxerxes, king of kings,

To Ezra the priest, a teacher of the Law of
the God of heaven:

Greetings.

[13]Now I decree that any of the Israelites
in my kingdom, including priests and Levites, who wish to go to Jerusalem with you,
may go. [14]You are sent by the king and his
seven advisers to inquire about Judah and
Jerusalem with regard to the Law of your
God, which is in your hand. [15]Moreover,
you are to take with you the silver and gold
that the king and his advisers have freely
given to the God of Israel, whose dwelling is
in Jerusalem, [16]together with all the silver
and gold you may obtain from the province
of Babylon, as well as the freewill offerings
of the people and priests for the temple of
their God in Jerusalem. [17]With this money
be sure to buy bulls, rams and male lambs,
together with their grain offerings and drink
offerings, and sacrifice them on the altar of
the temple of your God in Jerusalem.
[18]You and your brother Jews may then do
whatever seems best with the rest of the
silver and gold, in accordance with the will
of your God. [19]Deliver to the God of Jerusalem all the articles entrusted to you for worship in the temple of your God. [20]And anything else needed for the temple of your
God that you may have occasion to supply,
you may provide from the royal treasury.
[21]Now I, King Artaxerxes, order all the
treasurers of Trans-Euphrates to provide
with diligence whatever Ezra the priest, a
teacher of the Law of the God of heaven,
may ask of you— [22]up to a hundred talents[b] of silver, a hundred cors[c] of wheat,
a hundred baths[d] of wine, a hundred
baths[d] of olive oil, and salt without limit.
[23]Whatever the God of heaven has prescribed, let it be done with diligence for the
temple of the God of heaven. Why should
there be wrath against the realm of the king
and of his sons? [24]You are also to know that
you have no authority to impose taxes, tribute or duty on any of the priests, Levites,
singers, gatekeepers, temple servants or
other workers at this house of God.
[25]And you, Ezra, in accordance with the
wisdom of your God, which you possess,
appoint magistrates and judges to administer justice to all the people of Trans-
Euphrates—all who know the laws of your
God. And you are to teach any who do not
know them. [26]Whoever does not obey the
law of your God and the law of the king
must surely be punished by death, banishment, confiscation of property, or imprisonment.

[27]Praise be to the LORD, the God of our fathers,
who has put it into the king's heart to bring hon-
or to the house of the LORD in Jerusalem in this
way [28]and who has extended his good favor to
me before the king and his advisers and all the
king's powerful officials. Because the hand of the
LORD my God was on me, I took courage and
gathered leading men from Israel to go up
with me.

List of the Family Heads Returning With Ezra

8 These are the family heads and those registered with them who came up with me from
Babylon during the reign of King Artaxerxes:

[2]of the descendants of Phinehas, Gershom;
of the descendants of Ithamar, Daniel;
of the descendants of David, Hattush [3]of
the descendants of Shecaniah;

of the descendants of Parosh, Zechariah,
and with him were registered 150 men;
[4]of the descendants of Pahath-Moab, Eliehoenai son of Zerahiah, and with him 200
men;
[5]of the descendants of Zattu,[e] Shecaniah
son of Jahaziel, and with him 300 men;
[6]of the descendants of Adin, Ebed son of
Jonathan, and with him 50 men;
[7]of the descendants of Elam, Jeshaiah son of
Athaliah, and with him 70 men;
[8]of the descendants of Shephatiah, Zebadiah
son of Michael, and with him 80 men;
[9]of the descendants of Joab, Obadiah son of
Jehiel, and with him 218 men;
[10]of the descendants of Bani,[f] Shelomith
son of Josiphiah, and with him 160
men;
[11]of the descendants of Bebai, Zechariah son
of Bebai, and with him 28 men;
[12]of the descendants of Azgad, Johanan son
of Hakkatan, and with him 110 men;
[13]of the descendants of Adonikam, the last
ones, whose names were Eliphelet, Jeuel and Shemaiah, and with them 60
men;

[a] *12* The text of Ezra 7:12-26 is in Aramaic. [b] *22* That is, about 3 3/4 tons (about 3.4 metric tons) [c] *22* That is, probably about 600 bushels (about 22 kiloliters) [d] *22* That is, probably about 600 gallons (about 2.2 kiloliters) [e] *5* Some Septuagint manuscripts (also 1 Esdras 8:32); Hebrew does not have *Zattu.* [f] *10* Some Septuagint manuscripts (also 1 Esdras 8:36); Hebrew does not have *Bani.*

14of the descendants of Bigvai, Uthai and Zaccur, and with them 70 men.

The Return to Jerusalem

15I assembled them at the canal that flows toward Ahava, and we camped there three days.
When I checked among the people and the
priests, I found no Levites there. 16So I summoned Eliezer, Ariel, Shemaiah, Elnathan, Jarib,
Elnathan, Nathan, Zechariah and Meshullam,
who were leaders, and Joiarib and Elnathan, who
were men of learning, 17and I sent them to Iddo,
the leader in Casiphia. I told them what to say to
Iddo and his kinsmen, the temple servants in
Casiphia, so that they might bring attendants to
us for the house of our God. 18Because the gracious hand of our God was on us, they brought us
Sherebiah, a capable man, from the descendants
of Mahli son of Levi, the son of Israel, and Sherebiah's sons and brothers, 18 men; 19and Hashabiah, together with Jeshaiah from the descendants
of Merari, and his brothers and nephews, 20
men. 20They also brought 220 of the temple
servants—a body that David and the officials had
established to assist the Levites. All were registered by name.

21There, by the Ahava Canal, I proclaimed a
fast, so that we might humble ourselves before
our God and ask him for a safe journey for us and
our children, with all our possessions. 22I was
ashamed to ask the king for soldiers and horsemen to protect us from enemies on the road,
because we had told the king, "The gracious
hand of our God is on everyone who looks to
him, but his great anger is against all who forsake
him." 23So we fasted and petitioned our God
about this, and he answered our prayer.

24Then I set apart twelve of the leading priests,
together with Sherebiah, Hashabiah and ten of
their brothers, 25and I weighed out to them the
offering of silver and gold and the articles that
the king, his advisers, his officials and all Israel
present there had donated for the house of our
God. 26I weighed out to them 650 talents[a] of
silver, silver articles weighing 100 talents,[b] 100
talents[b] of gold, 2720 bowls of gold valued at
1,000 darics,[c] and two fine articles of polished
bronze, as precious as gold.

28I said to them, "You as well as these articles
are consecrated to the LORD. The silver and gold
are a freewill offering to the LORD, the God of
your fathers. 29Guard them carefully until you
weigh them out in the chambers of the house of
the LORD in Jerusalem before the leading priests
and the Levites and the family heads of Israel."
30Then the priests and Levites received the silver
and gold and sacred articles that had been
weighed out to be taken to the house of our God
in Jerusalem.

31On the twelfth day of the first month we set
out from the Ahava Canal to go to Jerusalem. The
hand of our God was on us, and he protected us
from enemies and bandits along the way. 32So we
arrived in Jerusalem, where we rested three days.

33On the fourth day, in the house of our God,
we weighed out the silver and gold and the sacred articles into the hands of Meremoth son of
Uriah, the priest. Eleazar son of Phinehas was
with him, and so were the Levites Jozabad son of
Jeshua and Noadiah son of Binnui. 34Everything
was accounted for by number and weight, and
the entire weight was recorded at that time.

35Then the exiles who had returned from captivity sacrificed burnt offerings to the God of Israel: twelve bulls for all Israel, ninety-six rams,
seventy-seven male lambs and, as a sin offering,
twelve male goats. All this was a burnt offering to
the LORD. 36They also delivered the king's orders
to the royal satraps and to the governors of Trans-
Euphrates, who then gave assistance to the people and to the house of God.

Ezra's Prayer About Intermarriage

9 After these things had been done, the leaders came to me and said, "The people of
Israel, including the priests and the Levites, have
not kept themselves separate from the neighboring peoples with their detestable practices, like
those of the Canaanites, Hittites, Perizzites, Jebusites, Ammonites, Moabites, Egyptians and Amorites. 2They have taken some of their daughters
as wives for themselves and their sons, and have
mingled the holy race with the peoples around
them. And the leaders and officials have led the
way in this unfaithfulness."

3When I heard this, I tore my tunic and cloak,
pulled hair from my head and beard and sat down
appalled. 4Then everyone who trembled at the
words of the God of Israel gathered around me
because of this unfaithfulness of the exiles. And
I sat there appalled until the evening sacrifice.

5Then, at the evening sacrifice, I rose from my
self-abasement, with my tunic and cloak torn,
and fell on my knees with my hands spread out to
the LORD my God 6and prayed:

"O my God, I am too ashamed and disgraced to lift up my face to you, my God,
because our sins are higher than our heads
and our guilt has reached to the heavens.
7From the days of our forefathers until now,
our guilt has been great. Because of our
sins, we and our kings and our priests have

[a]*26* That is, about 25 tons (about 22 metric tons) [b]*26* That is, about 3 3/4 tons (about 3.4 metric tons) [c]*27* That is, about 19 pounds (about 8.5 kilograms)

been subjected to the sword and captivity,
to pillage and humiliation at the hand of
foreign kings, as it is today.
8“But now, for a brief moment, the LORD
our God has been gracious in leaving us a
remnant and giving us a firm place in his
sanctuary, and so our God gives light to our
eyes and a little relief in our bondage.
9Though we are slaves, our God has not
deserted us in our bondage. He has shown
us kindness in the sight of the kings of Persia: He has granted us new life to rebuild
the house of our God and repair its ruins,
and he has given us a wall of protection in
Judah and Jerusalem.
10“But now, O our God, what can we say
after this? For we have disregarded the commands 11you gave through your servants the
prophets when you said: ‘The land you are
entering to possess is a land polluted by the
corruption of its peoples. By their detestable
practices they have filled it with their impurity from one end to the other. 12Therefore,
do not give your daughters in marriage to
their sons or take their daughters for your
sons. Do not seek a treaty of friendship with
them at any time, that you may be strong
and eat the good things of the land and
leave it to your children as an everlasting
inheritance.’
13“What has happened to us is a result of
our evil deeds and our great guilt, and yet,
our God, you have punished us less than
our sins have deserved and have given us a
remnant like this. 14Shall we again break
your commands and intermarry with the
peoples who commit such detestable practices? Would you not be angry enough with
us to destroy us, leaving us no remnant or
survivor? 15O LORD, God of Israel, you are
righteous! We are left this day as a remnant.
Here we are before you in our guilt, though
because of it not one of us can stand in your
presence.”

The People’s Confession of Sin

10 While Ezra was praying and confessing,
weeping and throwing himself down
before the house of God, a large crowd of
Israelites—men, women and children—
gathered around him. They too wept bitterly.
2Then Shecaniah son of Jehiel, one of the descendants of Elam, said to Ezra, “We have been unfaithful to our God by marrying foreign women
from the peoples around us. But in spite of this,
there is still hope for Israel. 3Now let us make a
covenant before our God to send away all these
women and their children, in accordance with
the counsel of my lord and of those who fear the
commands of our God. Let it be done according
to the Law. 4Rise up; this matter is in your hands.
We will support you, so take courage and do it.”
5So Ezra rose up and put the leading priests
and Levites and all Israel under oath to do what
had been suggested. And they took the oath.
6Then Ezra withdrew from before the house of
God and went to the room of Jehohanan son of
Eliashib. While he was there, he ate no food and
drank no water, because he continued to mourn
over the unfaithfulness of the exiles.
7A proclamation was then issued throughout
Judah and Jerusalem for all the exiles to assemble
in Jerusalem. 8Anyone who failed to appear within three days would forfeit all his property, in
accordance with the decision of the officials and
elders, and would himself be expelled from the
assembly of the exiles.
9Within the three days, all the men of Judah
and Benjamin had gathered in Jerusalem. And on
the twentieth day of the ninth month, all the
people were sitting in the square before the
house of God, greatly distressed by the occasion
and because of the rain. 10Then Ezra the priest
stood up and said to them, “You have been unfaithful; you have married foreign women, adding
to Israel’s guilt. 11Now make confession to the
LORD, the God of your fathers, and do his will.
Separate yourselves from the peoples around you
and from your foreign wives.”
12The whole assembly responded with a loud
voice: “You are right! We must do as you say.
13But there are many people here and it is the
rainy season; so we cannot stand outside. Besides, this matter cannot be taken care of in a day
or two, because we have sinned greatly in this
thing. 14Let our officials act for the whole assembly. Then let everyone in our towns who has
married a foreign woman come at a set time,
along with the elders and judges of each town,
until the fierce anger of our God in this matter is
turned away from us.” 15Only Jonathan son of
Asahel and Jahzeiah son of Tikvah, supported by
Meshullam and Shabbethai the Levite, opposed
this.
16So the exiles did as was proposed. Ezra the
priest selected men who were family heads, one
from each family division, and all of them designated by name. On the first day of the tenth
month they sat down to investigate the cases,
17and by the first day of the first month they
finished dealing with all the men who had married foreign women.

Those Guilty of Intermarriage

18Among the descendants of the priests, the
following had married foreign women:

From the descendants of Jeshua son of Joza-

dak, and his brothers: Maaseiah, Eliezer,
Jarib and Gedaliah. 19(They all gave their
hands in pledge to put away their wives,
and for their guilt they each presented a
ram from the flock as a guilt offering.)

20From the descendants of Immer:
Hanani and Zebadiah.

21From the descendants of Harim:
Maaseiah, Elijah, Shemaiah, Jehiel and Uzziah.

22From the descendants of Pashhur:
Elioenai, Maaseiah, Ishmael, Nethanel, Jozabad and Elasah.

23Among the Levites:

Jozabad, Shimei, Kelaiah (that is, Kelita), Pethahiah, Judah and Eliezer.

24From the singers:
Eliashib.

From the gatekeepers:
Shallum, Telem and Uri.

25And among the other Israelites:

From the descendants of Parosh:
Ramiah, Izziah, Malkijah, Mijamin, Eleazar, Malkijah and Benaiah.

26From the descendants of Elam:
Mattaniah, Zechariah, Jehiel, Abdi, Jeremoth and Elijah.

27From the descendants of Zattu:
Elioenai, Eliashib, Mattaniah, Jeremoth, Zabad and Aziza.

28From the descendants of Bebai:
Jehohanan, Hananiah, Zabbai and Athlai.

29From the descendants of Bani:
Meshullam, Malluch, Adaiah, Jashub, Sheal and Jeremoth.

30From the descendants of Pahath-Moab:
Adna, Kelal, Benaiah, Maaseiah, Mattaniah, Bezalel, Binnui and Manasseh.

31From the descendants of Harim:
Eliezer, Ishijah, Malkijah, Shemaiah,
Shimeon, 32Benjamin, Malluch and
Shemariah.

33From the descendants of Hashum:
Mattenai, Mattattah, Zabad, Eliphelet, Jeremai, Manasseh and Shimei.

34From the descendants of Bani:
Maadai, Amram, Uel, 35Benaiah, Bede-
iah, Keluhi, 36Vaniah, Meremoth, Eliashib, 37Mattaniah, Mattenai and Jaasu.

38From the descendants of Binnui:[a]
Shimei, 39Shelemiah, Nathan, Adaiah,
40Macnadebai, Shashai, Sharai, 41Aza-
rel, Shelemiah, Shemariah, 42Shallum,
Amariah and Joseph.

43From the descendants of Nebo:
Jeiel, Mattithiah, Zabad, Zebina, Jaddai, Joel and Benaiah.

44All these had married foreign women, and some of them had children by these wives.[b]

[a]*37,38* See Septuagint (also 1 Esdras 9:34); Hebrew *Jaasu 38and Bani and Binnui,* [b]*44* Or *and they sent them away with their children*

Introduction to
NEHEMIAH

Personal Reading Plan

❐ Nehemiah 1:1–2:20
❐ Nehemiah 3:1–32
❐ Nehemiah 4:1–23
❐ Nehemiah 5:1–6:14
❐ Nehemiah 6:15–7:73a
❐ Nehemiah 7:73b–8:18
❐ Nehemiah 9:1–37
❐ Nehemiah 9:38–10:39
❐ Nehemiah 11:1–36
❐ Nehemiah 12:1–26
❐ Nehemiah 12:27–47
❐ Nehemiah 13:1–31

Author

The book is named for the principal character, Nehemiah, but it does not state its author. Whoever it was may have also helped to compile the book of Ezra and perhaps 1 and 2 Chronicles, as these books share many common characteristics:

1. A fondness for lists, for the descriptions of religious festivals and for the phrases “heads of families” and “the house of God.”

2. The prominence of Levites and temple personnel.

3. The almost exclusive use of the Hebrew words for “singer,” “gatekeeper” and “temple servants.”

Date

With an unstated author, precise dating is difficult to determine. The events narrated cover the years c. 445–432 B.C.

Theme

Restoration of the second temple and revival of the people, providing a legacy of God-given leadership principles.

Historical Background

Originally this work was one book along with Ezra. In the Latin Bible, Ezra and Nehemiah are entitled 1 and 2 Esdras. This book complements Ezra in reporting the restoration of Israel after 70 years of captivity in Babylon. Nehemiah’s distress over the broken-down walls of Jerusalem (1:3) is probably caused by the episode in Ezra 4:7–23. Ezra’s return had revived spiritual and nationalistic fervor in God’s people so that they worked to rebuild the walls of Jerusalem (chapters 8–9). But the completion of that task apparently fell to governor Nehemiah, a man dedicated to God.

Characteristics

This book weaves together various lists with first-person and third-person memoirs of Nehemiah, who is the lead actor in this drama. Some of the most moving prayers outside the Psalms are found here (1:5–11; 9:5b–37). With plot twists akin to a modern short story, Nehemiah describes the rebuilding of the Jerusalem walls. The physical condition of the walls (chapters 1–7) parallels the spiritual condition of the people. As the walls are restored, the people are rehabilitated (chapters 8–13).

Nehemiah's Prayer

1 The words of Nehemiah son of Hacaliah:
In the month of Kislev in the twentieth year,
while I was in the citadel of Susa, [2]Hanani, one
of my brothers, came from Judah with some other
men, and I questioned them about the Jewish
remnant that survived the exile, and also about
Jerusalem.
[3]They said to me, "Those who survived the
exile and are back in the province are in great
trouble and disgrace. The wall of Jerusalem is
broken down, and its gates have been burned
with fire."
[4]When I heard these things, I sat down and
wept. For some days I mourned and fasted and
prayed before the God of heaven. [5]Then I said:

"O LORD, God of heaven, the great and
awesome God, who keeps his covenant of
love with those who love him and obey his
commands, [6]let your ear be attentive and
your eyes open to hear the prayer your servant is praying before you day and night for
your servants, the people of Israel. I confess
the sins we Israelites, including myself and
my father's house, have committed against
you. [7]We have acted very wickedly toward
you. We have not obeyed the commands,
decrees and laws you gave your servant Moses.
[8]"Remember the instruction you gave
your servant Moses, saying, 'If you are unfaithful, I will scatter you among the nations, [9]but if you return to me and obey my
commands, then even if your exiled people
are at the farthest horizon, I will gather
them from there and bring them to the
place I have chosen as a dwelling for my
Name.'
[10]"They are your servants and your people, whom you redeemed by your great
strength and your mighty hand. [11]O Lord,
let your ear be attentive to the prayer of this
your servant and to the prayer of your servants who delight in revering your name.
Give your servant success today by granting
him favor in the presence of this man."

I was cupbearer to the king.

Artaxerxes Sends Nehemiah to Jerusalem

2 In the month of Nisan in the twentieth year
of King Artaxerxes, when wine was brought
for him, I took the wine and gave it to the king.
I had not been sad in his presence before; [2]so the
king asked me, "Why does your face look so sad
when you are not ill? This can be nothing but
sadness of heart."
I was very much afraid, [3]but I said to the king,
"May the king live forever! Why should my face
not look sad when the city where my fathers are
buried lies in ruins, and its gates have been destroyed by fire?"
[4]The king said to me, "What is it you want?"
Then I prayed to the God of heaven, [5]and I
answered the king, "If it pleases the king and if
your servant has found favor in his sight, let him
send me to the city in Judah where my fathers are
buried so that I can rebuild it."
[6]Then the king, with the queen sitting beside
him, asked me, "How long will your journey take,
and when will you get back?" It pleased the king
to send me; so I set a time.
[7]I also said to him, "If it pleases the king, may
I have letters to the governors of Trans-
Euphrates, so that they will provide me safe-
conduct until I arrive in Judah? [8]And may I have
a letter to Asaph, keeper of the king's forest, so
he will give me timber to make beams for the
gates of the citadel by the temple and for the city
wall and for the residence I will occupy?" And
because the gracious hand of my God was upon
me, the king granted my requests. [9]So I went to
the governors of Trans-Euphrates and gave them
the king's letters. The king had also sent army
officers and cavalry with me.
[10]When Sanballat the Horonite and Tobiah the
Ammonite official heard about this, they were
very much disturbed that someone had come to
promote the welfare of the Israelites.

Nehemiah Inspects Jerusalem's Walls

[11]I went to Jerusalem, and after staying there
three days [12]I set out during the night with a few
men. I had not told anyone what my God had put
in my heart to do for Jerusalem. There were no
mounts with me except the one I was riding on.
[13]By night I went out through the Valley Gate
toward the Jackal[a] Well and the Dung Gate, examining the walls of Jerusalem, which had been
broken down, and its gates, which had been destroyed by fire. [14]Then I moved on toward the
Fountain Gate and the King's Pool, but there was
not enough room for my mount to get through;
[15]so I went up the valley by night, examining
the wall. Finally, I turned back and reentered
through the Valley Gate. [16]The officials did not
know where I had gone or what I was doing,
because as yet I had said nothing to the Jews or
the priests or nobles or officials or any others
who would be doing the work.
[17]Then I said to them, "You see the trouble we
are in: Jerusalem lies in ruins, and its gates have

[a]13 Or *Serpent* or *Fig*

been burned with fire. Come, let us rebuild the
wall of Jerusalem, and we will no longer be in
disgrace." 18 I also told them about the gracious
hand of my God upon me and what the king had
said to me.

They replied, "Let us start rebuilding." So they
began this good work.

19 But when Sanballat the Horonite, Tobiah the
Ammonite official and Geshem the Arab heard
about it, they mocked and ridiculed us. "What is
this you are doing?" they asked. "Are you rebelling against the king?"

20 I answered them by saying, "The God of
heaven will give us success. We his servants will
start rebuilding, but as for you, you have no share
in Jerusalem or any claim or historic right to it."

Builders of the Wall

3 Eliashib the high priest and his fellow priests
went to work and rebuilt the Sheep Gate.
They dedicated it and set its doors in place, building as far as the Tower of the Hundred, which
they dedicated, and as far as the Tower of Hananel. 2 The men of Jericho built the adjoining section, and Zaccur son of Imri built next to them.

3 The Fish Gate was rebuilt by the sons of Has-
senaah. They laid its beams and put its doors and
bolts and bars in place. 4 Meremoth son of Uriah,
the son of Hakkoz, repaired the next section.
Next to him Meshullam son of Berekiah, the son
of Meshezabel, made repairs, and next to him
Zadok son of Baana also made repairs. 5 The next
section was repaired by the men of Tekoa, but
their nobles would not put their shoulders to the
work under their supervisors.[a]

6 The Jeshanah[b] Gate was repaired by Joiada
son of Paseah and Meshullam son of Besodeiah.
They laid its beams and put its doors and bolts
and bars in place. 7 Next to them, repairs were
made by men from Gibeon and Mizpah—
Melatiah of Gibeon and Jadon of Meronoth—
places under the authority of the governor of
Trans-Euphrates. 8 Uzziel son of Harhaiah, one of
the goldsmiths, repaired the next section; and
Hananiah, one of the perfume-makers, made repairs next to that. They restored[c] Jerusalem as
far as the Broad Wall. 9 Rephaiah son of Hur, ruler
of a half-district of Jerusalem, repaired the next
section. 10 Adjoining this, Jedaiah son of Haru-
maph made repairs opposite his house, and Hattush son of Hashabneiah made repairs next to
him. 11 Malkijah son of Harim and Hasshub son of
Pahath-Moab repaired another section and the
Tower of the Ovens. 12 Shallum son of Hallohesh,
ruler of a half-district of Jerusalem, repaired the
next section with the help of his daughters.

13 The Valley Gate was repaired by Hanun and
the residents of Zanoah. They rebuilt it and put
its doors and bolts and bars in place. They also
repaired five hundred yards[d] of the wall as far as
the Dung Gate.

14 The Dung Gate was repaired by Malkijah son
of Recab, ruler of the district of Beth Hakkerem.
He rebuilt it and put its doors and bolts and bars
in place.

15 The Fountain Gate was repaired by Shallun
son of Col-Hozeh, ruler of the district of Mizpah.
He rebuilt it, roofing it over and putting its doors
and bolts and bars in place. He also repaired the
wall of the Pool of Siloam,[e] by the King's Garden, as far as the steps going down from the City
of David. 16 Beyond him, Nehemiah son of Azbuk,
ruler of a half-district of Beth Zur, made repairs
up to a point opposite the tombs[f] of David, as
far as the artificial pool and the House of the
Heroes.

17 Next to him, the repairs were made by the
Levites under Rehum son of Bani. Beside him,
Hashabiah, ruler of half the district of Keilah, carried out repairs for his district. 18 Next to him, the
repairs were made by their countrymen under
Binnui[g] son of Henadad, ruler of the other half-
district of Keilah. 19 Next to him, Ezer son of Jeshua, ruler of Mizpah, repaired another section,
from a point facing the ascent to the armory as far
as the angle. 20 Next to him, Baruch son of Zabbai
zealously repaired another section, from the angle to the entrance of the house of Eliashib the
high priest. 21 Next to him, Meremoth son of Uriah, the son of Hakkoz, repaired another section,
from the entrance of Eliashib's house to the end
of it.

22 The repairs next to him were made by the
priests from the surrounding region. 23 Beyond
them, Benjamin and Hasshub made repairs in
front of their house; and next to them, Azariah
son of Maaseiah, the son of Ananiah, made repairs beside his house. 24 Next to him, Binnui son
of Henadad repaired another section, from Azariah's house to the angle and the corner, 25 and
Palal son of Uzai worked opposite the angle and
the tower projecting from the upper palace near
the court of the guard. Next to him, Pedaiah son
of Parosh 26 and the temple servants living on the
hill of Ophel made repairs up to a point opposite
the Water Gate toward the east and the projecting tower. 27 Next to them, the men of Tekoa

[a] 5 Or *their Lord* or *the governor* [b] 6 Or *Old* [c] 8 Or *They left out part of* [d] 13 Hebrew *a thousand cubits* (about 450 meters) [e] 15 Hebrew *Shelah,* a variant of *Shiloah,* that is, Siloam [f] 16 Hebrew; Septuagint, some Vulgate manuscripts and Syriac *tomb* [g] 18 Two Hebrew manuscripts and Syriac (see also Septuagint and verse 24); most Hebrew manuscripts *Bavvai*

repaired another section, from the great projecting tower to the wall of Ophel.

28 Above the Horse Gate, the priests made repairs, each in front of his own house. 29 Next to them, Zadok son of Immer made repairs opposite his house. Next to him, Shemaiah son of Shecaniah, the guard at the East Gate, made repairs. 30 Next to him, Hananiah son of Shelemiah, and Hanun, the sixth son of Zalaph, repaired another section. Next to them, Meshullam son of Berekiah made repairs opposite his living quarters. 31 Next to him, Malkijah, one of the goldsmiths, made repairs as far as the house of the temple servants and the merchants, opposite the Inspection Gate, and as far as the room above the corner; 32 and between the room above the corner and the Sheep Gate the goldsmiths and merchants made repairs.

Opposition to the Rebuilding

4 When Sanballat heard that we were rebuilding the wall, he became angry and was greatly incensed. He ridiculed the Jews, 2 and in the presence of his associates and the army of Samaria, he said, "What are those feeble Jews doing? Will they restore their wall? Will they offer sacrifices? Will they finish in a day? Can they bring the stones back to life from those heaps of rubble—burned as they are?"

3 Tobiah the Ammonite, who was at his side, said, "What they are building—if even a fox climbed up on it, he would break down their wall of stones!"

4 Hear us, O our God, for we are despised. Turn their insults back on their own heads. Give them over as plunder in a land of captivity. 5 Do not cover up their guilt or blot out their sins from your sight, for they have thrown insults in the face of[a] the builders.

6 So we rebuilt the wall till all of it reached half its height, for the people worked with all their heart.

7 But when Sanballat, Tobiah, the Arabs, the Ammonites and the men of Ashdod heard that the repairs to Jerusalem's walls had gone ahead and that the gaps were being closed, they were very angry. 8 They all plotted together to come and fight against Jerusalem and stir up trouble against it. 9 But we prayed to our God and posted a guard day and night to meet this threat.

10 Meanwhile, the people in Judah said, "The strength of the laborers is giving out, and there is so much rubble that we cannot rebuild the wall."

11 Also our enemies said, "Before they know it or see us, we will be right there among them and will kill them and put an end to the work."

12 Then the Jews who lived near them came and told us ten times over, "Wherever you turn, they will attack us."

13 Therefore I stationed some of the people behind the lowest points of the wall at the exposed places, posting them by families, with their swords, spears and bows. 14 After I looked things over, I stood up and said to the nobles, the officials and the rest of the people, "Don't be afraid of them. Remember the Lord, who is great and awesome, and fight for your brothers, your sons and your daughters, your wives and your homes."

15 When our enemies heard that we were aware of their plot and that God had frustrated it, we all returned to the wall, each to his own work.

16 From that day on, half of my men did the work, while the other half were equipped with spears, shields, bows and armor. The officers posted themselves behind all the people of Judah 17 who were building the wall. Those who carried materials did their work with one hand and held a weapon in the other, 18 and each of the builders wore his sword at his side as he worked. But the man who sounded the trumpet stayed with me.

19 Then I said to the nobles, the officials and the rest of the people, "The work is extensive and spread out, and we are widely separated from each other along the wall. 20 Wherever you hear the sound of the trumpet, join us there. Our God will fight for us!"

21 So we continued the work with half the men holding spears, from the first light of dawn till the stars came out. 22 At that time I also said to the people, "Have every man and his helper stay inside Jerusalem at night, so they can serve us as guards by night and workmen by day." 23 Neither I nor my brothers nor my men nor the guards with me took off our clothes; each had his weapon, even when he went for water.[b]

Nehemiah Helps the Poor

5 Now the men and their wives raised a great outcry against their Jewish brothers. 2 Some were saying, "We and our sons and daughters are numerous; in order for us to eat and stay alive, we must get grain."

3 Others were saying, "We are mortgaging our fields, our vineyards and our homes to get grain during the famine."

4 Still others were saying, "We have had to borrow money to pay the king's tax on our fields and vineyards. 5 Although we are of the same flesh and blood as our countrymen and though our sons are as good as theirs, yet we have to subject

[a] 5 Or *have provoked you to anger before*
[b] 23 The meaning of the Hebrew for this clause is uncertain.

our sons and daughters to slavery. Some of our
daughters have already been enslaved, but we are
powerless, because our fields and our vineyards
belong to others."
6 When I heard their outcry and these charges,
I was very angry. 7 I pondered them in my mind
and then accused the nobles and officials. I told
them, "You are exacting usury from your own
countrymen!" So I called together a large meeting
to deal with them 8 and said: "As far as possible,
we have bought back our Jewish brothers who
were sold to the Gentiles. Now you are selling
your brothers, only for them to be sold back to
us!" They kept quiet, because they could find
nothing to say.
9 So I continued, "What you are doing is not
right. Shouldn't you walk in the fear of our God
to avoid the reproach of our Gentile enemies? 10 I
and my brothers and my men are also lending the
people money and grain. But let the exacting of
usury stop! 11 Give back to them immediately
their fields, vineyards, olive groves and houses,
and also the usury you are charging them—the
hundredth part of the money, grain, new wine
and oil."
12 "We will give it back," they said. "And we
will not demand anything more from them. We
will do as you say."
Then I summoned the priests and made the
nobles and officials take an oath to do what they
had promised. 13 I also shook out the folds of my
robe and said, "In this way may God shake out of
his house and possessions every man who does
not keep this promise. So may such a man be
shaken out and emptied!"
At this the whole assembly said, "Amen," and
praised the LORD. And the people did as they had
promised.
14 Moreover, from the twentieth year of King
Artaxerxes, when I was appointed to be their
governor in the land of Judah, until his thirty-
second year—twelve years—neither I nor my
brothers ate the food allotted to the governor.
15 But the earlier governors—those preceding
me—placed a heavy burden on the people and
took forty shekels[a] of silver from them in addition to food and wine. Their assistants also lorded
it over the people. But out of reverence for God
I did not act like that. 16 Instead, I devoted myself
to the work on this wall. All my men were assembled there for the work; we[b] did not acquire any
land.
17 Furthermore, a hundred and fifty Jews and
officials ate at my table, as well as those who
came to us from the surrounding nations. 18 Each
day one ox, six choice sheep and some poultry
were prepared for me, and every ten days an
abundant supply of wine of all kinds. In spite of
all this, I never demanded the food allotted to the
governor, because the demands were heavy on
these people.
19 Remember me with favor, O my God, for all
I have done for these people.

Further Opposition to the Rebuilding

6 When word came to Sanballat, Tobiah, Geshem the Arab and the rest of our enemies
that I had rebuilt the wall and not a gap was left
in it—though up to that time I had not set the
doors in the gates— 2 Sanballat and Geshem sent
me this message: "Come, let us meet together in
one of the villages[c] on the plain of Ono."
But they were scheming to harm me; 3 so I sent
messengers to them with this reply: "I am carrying on a great project and cannot go down. Why
should the work stop while I leave it and go down
to you?" 4 Four times they sent me the same message, and each time I gave them the same answer.
5 Then, the fifth time, Sanballat sent his aide to
me with the same message, and in his hand was
an unsealed letter 6 in which was written:

> "It is reported among the nations—and
> Geshem[d] says it is true—that you and the
> Jews are plotting to revolt, and therefore
> you are building the wall. Moreover, ac-
> cording to these reports you are about to
> become their king 7 and have even appoint-
> ed prophets to make this proclamation
> about you in Jerusalem: 'There is a king in
> Judah!' Now this report will get back to the
> king; so come, let us confer together."

8 I sent him this reply: "Nothing like what you
are saying is happening; you are just making it up
out of your head."
9 They were all trying to frighten us, thinking,
"Their hands will get too weak for the work, and
it will not be completed."
⌞But I prayed,⌟ "Now strengthen my hands."
10 One day I went to the house of Shemaiah
son of Delaiah, the son of Mehetabel, who was
shut in at his home. He said, "Let us meet in the
house of God, inside the temple, and let us close
the temple doors, because men are coming to kill
you—by night they are coming to kill you."
11 But I said, "Should a man like me run away?
Or should one like me go into the temple to save
his life? I will not go!" 12 I realized that God had
not sent him, but that he had prophesied against
me because Tobiah and Sanballat had hired him.
13 He had been hired to intimidate me so that I

[a] *15* That is, about 1 pound (about 0.5 kilogram) [b] *16* Most Hebrew manuscripts; some Hebrew manuscripts, Septuagint, Vulgate and Syriac *I* [c] *2* Or *in Kephirim* [d] *6* Hebrew *Gashmu,* a variant of *Geshem*

would commit a sin by doing this, and then they
would give me a bad name to discredit me.

14 Remember Tobiah and Sanballat, O my God,
because of what they have done; remember also
the prophetess Noadiah and the rest of the prophets who have been trying to intimidate me.

The Completion of the Wall

15 So the wall was completed on the twenty-
fifth of Elul, in fifty-two days. 16 When all our
enemies heard about this, all the surrounding nations were afraid and lost their self-confidence,
because they realized that this work had been
done with the help of our God.

17 Also, in those days the nobles of Judah were
sending many letters to Tobiah, and replies from
Tobiah kept coming to them. 18 For many in Judah
were under oath to him, since he was son-in-law
to Shecaniah son of Arah, and his son Jehohanan
had married the daughter of Meshullam son of
Berekiah. 19 Moreover, they kept reporting to me
his good deeds and then telling him what I said.
And Tobiah sent letters to intimidate me.

7 After the wall had been rebuilt and I had set
the doors in place, the gatekeepers and the
singers and the Levites were appointed. 2 I put in
charge of Jerusalem my brother Hanani, along
with[a] Hananiah the commander of the citadel,
because he was a man of integrity and feared God
more than most men do. 3 I said to them, "The
gates of Jerusalem are not to be opened until the
sun is hot. While the gatekeepers are still on
duty, have them shut the doors and bar them.
Also appoint residents of Jerusalem as guards,
some at their posts and some near their own
houses."

The List of the Exiles Who Returned

4 Now the city was large and spacious, but
there were few people in it, and the houses had
not yet been rebuilt. 5 So my God put it into my
heart to assemble the nobles, the officials and the
common people for registration by families. I
found the genealogical record of those who had
been the first to return. This is what I found
written there:

6 These are the people of the province
who came up from the captivity of the exiles whom Nebuchadnezzar king of Babylon
had taken captive (they returned to Jerusalem and Judah, each to his own town, 7 in
company with Zerubbabel, Jeshua, Nehemiah, Azariah, Raamiah, Nahamani, Mordecai, Bilshan, Mispereth, Bigvai, Nehum and
Baanah):

The list of the men of Israel:

8 the descendants of Parosh 2,172
9 of Shephatiah 372
10 of Arah 652
11 of Pahath-Moab (through the line of Jeshua and Joab) 2,818
12 of Elam 1,254
13 of Zattu 845
14 of Zaccai 760
15 of Binnui 648
16 of Bebai 628
17 of Azgad 2,322
18 of Adonikam 667
19 of Bigvai 2,067
20 of Adin 655
21 of Ater (through Hezekiah) 98
22 of Hashum 328
23 of Bezai 324
24 of Hariph 112
25 of Gibeon 95

26 the men of Bethlehem and Netophah 188
27 of Anathoth 128
28 of Beth Azmaveth 42
29 of Kiriath Jearim, Kephirah and Beeroth 743
30 of Ramah and Geba 621
31 of Micmash 122
32 of Bethel and Ai 123
33 of the other Nebo 52
34 of the other Elam 1,254
35 of Harim 320
36 of Jericho 345
37 of Lod, Hadid and Ono 721
38 of Senaah 3,930

39 The priests:

the descendants of Jedaiah (through the family of Jeshua) 973
40 of Immer 1,052
41 of Pashhur 1,247
42 of Harim 1,017

43 The Levites:

the descendants of Jeshua (through Kadmiel through the line of Hodaviah) 74

44 The singers:

the descendants of Asaph 148

45 The gatekeepers:

the descendants of Shallum, Ater, Talmon, Akkub, Hatita and Shobai 138

[a] 2 Or *Hanani, that is,*

46 The temple servants:

the descendants of
Ziha, Hasupha, Tabbaoth,
47 Keros, Sia, Padon,
48 Lebana, Hagaba, Shalmai,
49 Hanan, Giddel, Gahar,
50 Reaiah, Rezin, Nekoda,
51 Gazzam, Uzza, Paseah,
52 Besai, Meunim, Nephussim,
53 Bakbuk, Hakupha, Harhur,
54 Bazluth, Mehida, Harsha,
55 Barkos, Sisera, Temah,
56 Neziah and Hatipha

57 The descendants of the servants of Solomon:

the descendants of
Sotai, Sophereth, Perida,
58 Jaala, Darkon, Giddel,
59 Shephatiah, Hattil,
Pokereth-Hazzebaim and Amon

60 The temple servants and the descendants of the servants of Solomon 392

61 The following came up from the towns
of Tel Melah, Tel Harsha, Kerub, Addon and
Immer, but they could not show that their
families were descended from Israel:

62 the descendants of
Delaiah, Tobiah and Nekoda 642

63 And from among the priests:

the descendants of
Hobaiah, Hakkoz and Barzillai (a man who had married a daughter of Barzillai the Gileadite and was called by that name).

64 These searched for their family
records, but they could not find them and so
were excluded from the priesthood as unclean. 65 The governor, therefore, ordered
them not to eat any of the most sacred food
until there should be a priest ministering
with the Urim and Thummim.

66 The whole company numbered
42,360, 67 besides their 7,337 menservants
and maidservants; and they also had 245
men and women singers. 68 There were 736
horses, 245 mules,[a] 69 435 camels and
6,720 donkeys.

70 Some of the heads of the families contributed to the work. The governor gave to
the treasury 1,000 drachmas[b] of gold, 50
bowls and 530 garments for priests. 71 Some
of the heads of the families gave to the treasury for the work 20,000 drachmas[c] of
gold and 2,200 minas[d] of silver. 72 The total given by the rest of the people was
20,000 drachmas of gold, 2,000 minas[e] of
silver and 67 garments for priests.

73 The priests, the Levites, the gatekeepers, the singers and the temple servants,
along with certain of the people and the rest
of the Israelites, settled in their own towns.

Ezra Reads the Law

8 When the seventh month came and the Israelites had settled in their towns, 1 all the people assembled as one man in the square before the Water Gate. They told Ezra the scribe to
bring out the Book of the Law of Moses, which
the LORD had commanded for Israel.
2 So on the first day of the seventh month Ezra
the priest brought the Law before the assembly,
which was made up of men and women and all
who were able to understand. 3 He read it aloud
from daybreak till noon as he faced the square
before the Water Gate in the presence of the
men, women and others who could understand.
And all the people listened attentively to the
Book of the Law.
4 Ezra the scribe stood on a high wooden platform built for the occasion. Beside him on his
right stood Mattithiah, Shema, Anaiah, Uriah,
Hilkiah and Maaseiah; and on his left were Pedaiah, Mishael, Malkijah, Hashum, Hashbaddanah,
Zechariah and Meshullam.
5 Ezra opened the book. All the people could
see him because he was standing above them;
and as he opened it, the people all stood up. 6 Ezra
praised the LORD, the great God; and all the people lifted their hands and responded, "Amen!
Amen!" Then they bowed down and worshiped
the LORD with their faces to the ground.
7 The Levites—Jeshua, Bani, Sherebiah, Jamin,
Akkub, Shabbethai, Hodiah, Maaseiah, Kelita,
Azariah, Jozabad, Hanan and Pelaiah—instructed
the people in the Law while the people were
standing there. 8 They read from the Book of the
Law of God, making it clear[f] and giving the
meaning so that the people could understand
what was being read.
9 Then Nehemiah the governor, Ezra the priest
and scribe, and the Levites who were instructing
the people said to them all, "This day is sacred to
the LORD your God. Do not mourn or weep." For
all the people had been weeping as they listened
to the words of the Law.

[a] *68* Some Hebrew manuscripts (see also Ezra 2:66); most Hebrew manuscripts do not have this verse. [b] *70* That is, about 19 pounds (about 8.5 kilograms) [c] *71* That is, about 375 pounds (about 170 kilograms); also in verse 72 [d] *71* That is, about 1 1/3 tons (about 1.2 metric tons) [e] *72* That is, about 1 1/4 tons (about 1.1 metric tons) [f] *8* Or *God, translating it*

10Nehemiah said, "Go and enjoy choice food
and sweet drinks, and send some to those who
have nothing prepared. This day is sacred to our
Lord. Do not grieve, for the joy of the LORD is
your strength."
11The Levites calmed all the people, saying,
"Be still, for this is a sacred day. Do not grieve."
12Then all the people went away to eat and
drink, to send portions of food and to celebrate
with great joy, because they now understood the
words that had been made known to them.
13On the second day of the month, the heads
of all the families, along with the priests and the
Levites, gathered around Ezra the scribe to give
attention to the words of the Law. 14They found
written in the Law, which the LORD had commanded through Moses, that the Israelites were
to live in booths during the feast of the seventh
month 15and that they should proclaim this word
and spread it throughout their towns and in Jerusalem: "Go out into the hill country and bring
back branches from olive and wild olive trees,
and from myrtles, palms and shade trees, to make
booths"—as it is written.[a]
16So the people went out and brought back
branches and built themselves booths on their
own roofs, in their courtyards, in the courts of
the house of God and in the square by the Water
Gate and the one by the Gate of Ephraim. 17The
whole company that had returned from exile
built booths and lived in them. From the days of
Joshua son of Nun until that day, the Israelites
had not celebrated it like this. And their joy was
very great.
18Day after day, from the first day to the last,
Ezra read from the Book of the Law of God. They
celebrated the feast for seven days, and on the
eighth day, in accordance with the regulation,
there was an assembly.

The Israelites Confess Their Sins

9 On the twenty-fourth day of the same
month, the Israelites gathered together, fasting and wearing sackcloth and having dust on
their heads. 2Those of Israelite descent had separated themselves from all foreigners. They stood
in their places and confessed their sins and the
wickedness of their fathers. 3They stood where
they were and read from the Book of the Law of
the LORD their God for a quarter of the day, and
spent another quarter in confession and in worshiping the LORD their God. 4Standing on the
stairs were the Levites—Jeshua, Bani, Kadmiel,
Shebaniah, Bunni, Sherebiah, Bani and Kenani—
who called with loud voices to the LORD their
God. 5And the Levites—Jeshua, Kadmiel, Bani,
Hashabneiah, Sherebiah, Hodiah, Shebaniah and
Pethahiah—said: "Stand up and praise the LORD
your God, who is from everlasting to everlasting.[b]"

"Blessed be your glorious name, and may
it be exalted above all blessing and praise.
6You alone are the LORD. You made the
heavens, even the highest heavens, and all
their starry host, the earth and all that is on
it, the seas and all that is in them. You give
life to everything, and the multitudes of
heaven worship you.
7"You are the LORD God, who chose
Abram and brought him out of Ur of the
Chaldeans and named him Abraham. 8You
found his heart faithful to you, and you
made a covenant with him to give to his
descendants the land of the Canaanites, Hittites, Amorites, Perizzites, Jebusites and
Girgashites. You have kept your promise because you are righteous.
9"You saw the suffering of our forefathers
in Egypt; you heard their cry at the Red
Sea.[c] 10You sent miraculous signs and
wonders against Pharaoh, against all his officials and all the people of his land, for you
knew how arrogantly the Egyptians treated
them. You made a name for yourself, which
remains to this day. 11You divided the sea
before them, so that they passed through it
on dry ground, but you hurled their pursuers into the depths, like a stone into mighty
waters. 12By day you led them with a pillar
of cloud, and by night with a pillar of fire to
give them light on the way they were to
take.
13"You came down on Mount Sinai; you
spoke to them from heaven. You gave them
regulations and laws that are just and right,
and decrees and commands that are good.
14You made known to them your holy Sabbath and gave them commands, decrees and
laws through your servant Moses. 15In their
hunger you gave them bread from heaven
and in their thirst you brought them water
from the rock; you told them to go in and
take possession of the land you had sworn
with uplifted hand to give them.
16"But they, our forefathers, became arrogant and stiff-necked, and did not obey
your commands. 17They refused to listen
and failed to remember the miracles you
performed among them. They became stiff-
necked and in their rebellion appointed a
leader in order to return to their slavery.
But you are a forgiving God, gracious and
compassionate, slow to anger and abound-

[a] *15* See Lev. 23:37-40. [b] *5* Or *God for ever and ever* [c] *9* Hebrew *Yam Suph*; that is, Sea of Reeds

ing in love. Therefore you did not desert them, [18]even when they cast for themselves an image of a calf and said, 'This is your god, who brought you up out of Egypt,' or when they committed awful blasphemies.

[19]"Because of your great compassion you did not abandon them in the desert. By day the pillar of cloud did not cease to guide them on their path, nor the pillar of fire by night to shine on the way they were to take. [20]You gave your good Spirit to instruct them. You did not withhold your manna from their mouths, and you gave them water for their thirst. [21]For forty years you sustained them in the desert; they lacked nothing, their clothes did not wear out nor did their feet become swollen.

[22]"You gave them kingdoms and nations, allotting to them even the remotest frontiers. They took over the country of Sihon[a] king of Heshbon and the country of Og king of Bashan. [23]You made their sons as numerous as the stars in the sky, and you brought them into the land that you told their fathers to enter and possess. [24]Their sons went in and took possession of the land. You subdued before them the Canaanites, who lived in the land; you handed the Canaanites over to them, along with their kings and the peoples of the land, to deal with them as they pleased. [25]They captured fortified cities and fertile land; they took possession of houses filled with all kinds of good things, wells already dug, vineyards, olive groves and fruit trees in abundance. They ate to the full and were well-nourished; they reveled in your great goodness.

[26]"But they were disobedient and rebelled against you; they put your law behind their backs. They killed your prophets, who had admonished them in order to turn them back to you; they committed awful blasphemies. [27]So you handed them over to their enemies, who oppressed them. But when they were oppressed they cried out to you. From heaven you heard them, and in your great compassion you gave them deliverers, who rescued them from the hand of their enemies.

[28]"But as soon as they were at rest, they again did what was evil in your sight. Then you abandoned them to the hand of their enemies so that they ruled over them. And when they cried out to you again, you heard from heaven, and in your compassion you delivered them time after time.

[29]"You warned them to return to your law, but they became arrogant and disobeyed your commands. They sinned against your ordinances, by which a man will live if he obeys them. Stubbornly they turned their backs on you, became stiff-necked and refused to listen. [30]For many years you were patient with them. By your Spirit you admonished them through your prophets. Yet they paid no attention, so you handed them over to the neighboring peoples. [31]But in your great mercy you did not put an end to them or abandon them, for you are a gracious and merciful God.

[32]"Now therefore, O our God, the great, mighty and awesome God, who keeps his covenant of love, do not let all this hardship seem trifling in your eyes—the hardship that has come upon us, upon our kings and leaders, upon our priests and prophets, upon our fathers and all your people, from the days of the kings of Assyria until today. [33]In all that has happened to us, you have been just; you have acted faithfully, while we did wrong. [34]Our kings, our leaders, our priests and our fathers did not follow your law; they did not pay attention to your commands or the warnings you gave them. [35]Even while they were in their kingdom, enjoying your great goodness to them in the spacious and fertile land you gave them, they did not serve you or turn from their evil ways.

[36]"But see, we are slaves today, slaves in the land you gave our forefathers so they could eat its fruit and the other good things it produces. [37]Because of our sins, its abundant harvest goes to the kings you have placed over us. They rule over our bodies and our cattle as they please. We are in great distress.

The Agreement of the People

[38]"In view of all this, we are making a binding agreement, putting it in writing, and our leaders, our Levites and our priests are affixing their seals to it."

10 Those who sealed it were:

Nehemiah the governor, the son of Hacaliah.

Zedekiah, [2]Seraiah, Azariah, Jeremiah,
[3]Pashhur, Amariah, Malkijah,
[4]Hattush, Shebaniah, Malluch,
[5]Harim, Meremoth, Obadiah,
[6]Daniel, Ginnethon, Baruch,

[a]22 One Hebrew manuscript and Septuagint; most Hebrew manuscripts *Sihon, that is, the country of the*

7Meshullam, Abijah, Mijamin,
8Maaziah, Bilgai and Shemaiah.
These were the priests.

9The Levites:

Jeshua son of Azaniah, Binnui of the sons of
Henadad, Kadmiel,
10and their associates: Shebaniah,
Hodiah, Kelita, Pelaiah, Hanan,
11Mica, Rehob, Hashabiah,
12Zaccur, Sherebiah, Shebaniah,
13Hodiah, Bani and Beninu.

14The leaders of the people:

Parosh, Pahath-Moab, Elam, Zattu, Bani,
15Bunni, Azgad, Bebai,
16Adonijah, Bigvai, Adin,
17Ater, Hezekiah, Azzur,
18Hodiah, Hashum, Bezai,
19Hariph, Anathoth, Nebai,
20Magpiash, Meshullam, Hezir,
21Meshezabel, Zadok, Jaddua,
22Pelatiah, Hanan, Anaiah,
23Hoshea, Hananiah, Hasshub,
24Hallohesh, Pilha, Shobek,
25Rehum, Hashabnah, Maaseiah,
26Ahiah, Hanan, Anan,
27Malluch, Harim and Baanah.

28"The rest of the people—priests, Levites, gatekeepers, singers, temple servants
and all who separated themselves from the
neighboring peoples for the sake of the Law
of God, together with their wives and all
their sons and daughters who are able to
understand— 29all these now join their
brothers the nobles, and bind themselves
with a curse and an oath to follow the Law
of God given through Moses the servant of
God and to obey carefully all the commands,
regulations and decrees of the LORD our
Lord.

30"We promise not to give our daughters
in marriage to the peoples around us or take
their daughters for our sons.

31"When the neighboring peoples bring
merchandise or grain to sell on the Sabbath,
we will not buy from them on the Sabbath
or on any holy day. Every seventh year we
will forgo working the land and will cancel
all debts.

32"We assume the responsibility for carrying out the commands to give a third of a
shekel[a] each year for the service of the
house of our God: 33for the bread set out on
the table; for the regular grain offerings and
burnt offerings; for the offerings on the Sabbaths, New Moon festivals and appointed
feasts; for the holy offerings; for sin offerings to make atonement for Israel; and for
all the duties of the house of our God.

34"We—the priests, the Levites and the
people—have cast lots to determine when
each of our families is to bring to the house
of our God at set times each year a contribution of wood to burn on the altar of the
LORD our God, as it is written in the Law.

35"We also assume responsibility for
bringing to the house of the LORD each year
the firstfruits of our crops and of every fruit
tree.

36"As it is also written in the Law, we
will bring the firstborn of our sons and of
our cattle, of our herds and of our flocks to
the house of our God, to the priests ministering there.

37"Moreover, we will bring to the storerooms of the house of our God, to the
priests, the first of our ground meal, of our
⌞grain⌟ offerings, of the fruit of all our trees
and of our new wine and oil. And we will
bring a tithe of our crops to the Levites, for
it is the Levites who collect the tithes in all
the towns where we work. 38A priest descended from Aaron is to accompany the
Levites when they receive the tithes, and
the Levites are to bring a tenth of the tithes
up to the house of our God, to the storerooms of the treasury. 39The people of Israel, including the Levites, are to bring their
contributions of grain, new wine and oil to
the storerooms where the articles for the
sanctuary are kept and where the ministering priests, the gatekeepers and the singers
stay.

"We will not neglect the house of our
God."

The New Residents of Jerusalem

11 Now the leaders of the people settled in
Jerusalem, and the rest of the people cast
lots to bring one out of every ten to live in Jerusalem, the holy city, while the remaining nine were
to stay in their own towns. 2The people commended all the men who volunteered to live in
Jerusalem.

3These are the provincial leaders who settled
in Jerusalem (now some Israelites, priests, Levites, temple servants and descendants of Solomon's servants lived in the towns of Judah, each
on his own property in the various towns, 4while
other people from both Judah and Benjamin lived
in Jerusalem):

a32 That is, about 1/8 ounce (about 4 grams)

From the descendants of Judah:

Athaiah son of Uzziah, the son of Zechariah,
the son of Amariah, the son of Shephatiah,
the son of Mahalalel, a descendant of Perez;
5and Maaseiah son of Baruch, the son of
Col-Hozeh, the son of Hazaiah, the son of
Adaiah, the son of Joiarib, the son of Zechariah, a descendant of Shelah. 6The descendants of Perez who lived in Jerusalem totaled 468 able men.

7From the descendants of Benjamin:

Sallu son of Meshullam, the son of Joed, the
son of Pedaiah, the son of Kolaiah, the son
of Maaseiah, the son of Ithiel, the son of
Jeshaiah, 8and his followers, Gabbai and
Sallai—928 men. 9Joel son of Zicri was
their chief officer, and Judah son of Hassenuah was over the Second District of the
city.

10From the priests:

Jedaiah; the son of Joiarib; Jakin; 11Seraiah
son of Hilkiah, the son of Meshullam, the
son of Zadok, the son of Meraioth, the son
of Ahitub, supervisor in the house of God,
12and their associates, who carried on work
for the temple—822 men; Adaiah son of
Jeroham, the son of Pelaliah, the son of
Amzi, the son of Zechariah, the son of Pashhur, the son of Malkijah, 13and his associates, who were heads of families—242
men; Amashsai son of Azarel, the son of
Ahzai, the son of Meshillemoth, the son of
Immer, 14and his[a] associates, who were
able men—128. Their chief officer was
Zabdiel son of Haggedolim.

15From the Levites:

Shemaiah son of Hasshub, the son of Azrikam, the son of Hashabiah, the son of Bunni; 16Shabbethai and Jozabad, two of the
heads of the Levites, who had charge of the
outside work of the house of God; 17Matta-
niah son of Mica, the son of Zabdi, the son
of Asaph, the director who led in thanksgiving and prayer; Bakbukiah, second among
his associates; and Abda son of Shammua,
the son of Galal, the son of Jeduthun. 18The
Levites in the holy city totaled 284.

19The gatekeepers:

Akkub, Talmon and their associates, who
kept watch at the gates—172 men.

20The rest of the Israelites, with the priests
and Levites, were in all the towns of Judah, each
on his ancestral property.

21The temple servants lived on the hill of
Ophel, and Ziha and Gishpa were in charge of
them.

22The chief officer of the Levites in Jerusalem
was Uzzi son of Bani, the son of Hashabiah, the
son of Mattaniah, the son of Mica. Uzzi was one
of Asaph's descendants, who were the singers
responsible for the service of the house of God.
23The singers were under the king's orders,
which regulated their daily activity.

24Pethahiah son of Meshezabel, one of the
descendants of Zerah son of Judah, was the king's
agent in all affairs relating to the people.

25As for the villages with their fields, some of
the people of Judah lived in Kiriath Arba and its
surrounding settlements, in Dibon and its settlements, in Jekabzeel and its villages, 26in Jeshua,
in Moladah, in Beth Pelet, 27in Hazar Shual, in
Beersheba and its settlements, 28in Ziklag, in Me-
conah and its settlements, 29in En Rimmon, in
Zorah, in Jarmuth, 30Zanoah, Adullam and their
villages, in Lachish and its fields, and in Azekah
and its settlements. So they were living all the
way from Beersheba to the Valley of Hinnom.

31The descendants of the Benjamites from
Geba lived in Micmash, Aija, Bethel and its settlements, 32in Anathoth, Nob and Ananiah, 33in Hazor, Ramah and Gittaim, 34in Hadid, Zeboim and
Neballat, 35in Lod and Ono, and in the Valley of
the Craftsmen.

36Some of the divisions of the Levites of Judah
settled in Benjamin.

Priests and Levites

12 These were the priests and Levites who
returned with Zerubbabel son of Shealtiel
and with Jeshua:

Seraiah, Jeremiah, Ezra,
2Amariah, Malluch, Hattush,
3Shecaniah, Rehum, Meremoth,
4Iddo, Ginnethon,[b] Abijah,
5Mijamin,[c] Moadiah, Bilgah,
6Shemaiah, Joiarib, Jedaiah,
7Sallu, Amok, Hilkiah and Jedaiah.

These were the leaders of the priests and their
associates in the days of Jeshua.

8The Levites were Jeshua, Binnui, Kadmiel,
Sherebiah, Judah, and also Mattaniah, who, together with his associates, was in charge of the
songs of thanksgiving. 9Bakbukiah and Unni,
their associates, stood opposite them in the services.

10Jeshua was the father of Joiakim, Joiakim the
father of Eliashib, Eliashib the father of Joiada,

[a] 14 Most Septuagint manuscripts; Hebrew *their* [b] 4 Many Hebrew manuscripts and Vulgate (see also Neh. 12:16); most Hebrew manuscripts *Ginnethoi* [c] 5 A variant of *Miniamin*

11Joiada the father of Jonathan, and Jonathan the
father of Jaddua.
12In the days of Joiakim, these were the heads
of the priestly families:

of Seraiah's family, Meraiah;
of Jeremiah's, Hananiah;
13of Ezra's, Meshullam;
of Amariah's, Jehohanan;
14of Malluch's, Jonathan;
of Shecaniah's,[a] Joseph;
15of Harim's, Adna;
of Meremoth's,[b] Helkai;
16of Iddo's, Zechariah;
of Ginnethon's, Meshullam;
17of Abijah's, Zicri;
of Miniamin's and of Moadiah's, Piltai;
18of Bilgah's, Shammua;
of Shemaiah's, Jehonathan;
19of Joiarib's, Mattenai;
of Jedaiah's, Uzzi;
20of Sallu's, Kallai;
of Amok's, Eber;
21of Hilkiah's, Hashabiah;
of Jedaiah's, Nethanel.

22The family heads of the Levites in the days of
Eliashib, Joiada, Johanan and Jaddua, as well as
those of the priests, were recorded in the reign of
Darius the Persian. 23The family heads among the
descendants of Levi up to the time of Johanan son
of Eliashib were recorded in the book of the annals. 24And the leaders of the Levites were Hashabiah, Sherebiah, Jeshua son of Kadmiel, and
their associates, who stood opposite them to give
praise and thanksgiving, one section responding
to the other, as prescribed by David the man of
God.
25Mattaniah, Bakbukiah, Obadiah, Meshullam,
Talmon and Akkub were gatekeepers who guarded the storerooms at the gates. 26They served in
the days of Joiakim son of Jeshua, the son of Jozadak, and in the days of Nehemiah the governor
and of Ezra the priest and scribe.

Dedication of the Wall of Jerusalem

27At the dedication of the wall of Jerusalem,
the Levites were sought out from where they
lived and were brought to Jerusalem to celebrate
joyfully the dedication with songs of thanksgiving
and with the music of cymbals, harps and lyres.
28The singers also were brought together from
the region around Jerusalem—from the villages
of the Netophathites, 29from Beth Gilgal, and
from the area of Geba and Azmaveth, for the
singers had built villages for themselves around
Jerusalem. 30When the priests and Levites had
purified themselves ceremonially, they purified
the people, the gates and the wall.
31I had the leaders of Judah go up on top[c] of
the wall. I also assigned two large choirs to give
thanks. One was to proceed on top[d] of the wall
to the right, toward the Dung Gate. 32Hoshaiah
and half the leaders of Judah followed them,
33along with Azariah, Ezra, Meshullam, 34Judah,
Benjamin, Shemaiah, Jeremiah, 35as well as some
priests with trumpets, and also Zechariah son of
Jonathan, the son of Shemaiah, the son of Mattaniah, the son of Micaiah, the son of Zaccur, the
son of Asaph, 36and his associates—Shemaiah,
Azarel, Milalai, Gilalai, Maai, Nethanel, Judah
and Hanani—with musical instruments ⌞pre-
scribed by⌟ David the man of God. Ezra the scribe
led the procession. 37At the Fountain Gate they
continued directly up the steps of the City of
David on the ascent to the wall and passed above
the house of David to the Water Gate on the
east.
38The second choir proceeded in the opposite
direction. I followed them on top[e] of the wall,
together with half the people—past the Tower of
the Ovens to the Broad Wall, 39over the Gate of
Ephraim, the Jeshanah[f] Gate, the Fish Gate, the
Tower of Hananel and the Tower of the Hundred,
as far as the Sheep Gate. At the Gate of the Guard
they stopped.
40The two choirs that gave thanks then took
their places in the house of God; so did I, together with half the officials, 41as well as the
priests—Eliakim, Maaseiah, Miniamin, Micaiah,
Elioenai, Zechariah and Hananiah with their
trumpets— 42and also Maaseiah, Shemaiah, Eleazar, Uzzi, Jehohanan, Malkijah, Elam and Ezer.
The choirs sang under the direction of Jezrahiah.
43And on that day they offered great sacrifices,
rejoicing because God had given them great joy.
The women and children also rejoiced. The
sound of rejoicing in Jerusalem could be heard far
away.
44At that time men were appointed to be in
charge of the storerooms for the contributions,
firstfruits and tithes. From the fields around the
towns they were to bring into the storerooms the
portions required by the Law for the priests and
the Levites, for Judah was pleased with the ministering priests and Levites. 45They performed the
service of their God and the service of purification, as did also the singers and gatekeepers, according to the commands of David and his son
Solomon. 46For long ago, in the days of David and

[a] *14* Very many Hebrew manuscripts, some Septuagint manuscripts and Syriac (see also Neh. 12:3); most Hebrew manuscripts *Shebaniah's* [b] *15* Some Septuagint manuscripts (see also Neh. 12:3); Hebrew *Meraioth's* [c] *31* Or *go alongside* [d] *31* Or *proceed alongside* [e] *38* Or *them alongside* [f] *39* Or *Old*

Asaph, there had been directors for the singers
and for the songs of praise and thanksgiving to
God. 47So in the days of Zerubbabel and of Nehemiah, all Israel contributed the daily portions for
the singers and gatekeepers. They also set aside
the portion for the other Levites, and the Levites
set aside the portion for the descendants of
Aaron.

Nehemiah's Final Reforms

13 On that day the Book of Moses was read
aloud in the hearing of the people and
there it was found written that no Ammonite or
Moabite should ever be admitted into the assembly of God, 2because they had not met the Israelites with food and water but had hired Balaam to
call a curse down on them. (Our God, however,
turned the curse into a blessing.) 3When the people heard this law, they excluded from Israel all
who were of foreign descent.

4Before this, Eliashib the priest had been put
in charge of the storerooms of the house of our
God. He was closely associated with Tobiah, 5and
he had provided him with a large room formerly
used to store the grain offerings and incense and
temple articles, and also the tithes of grain, new
wine and oil prescribed for the Levites, singers
and gatekeepers, as well as the contributions for
the priests.

6But while all this was going on, I was not in
Jerusalem, for in the thirty-second year of Artaxerxes king of Babylon I had returned to the king.
Some time later I asked his permission 7and came
back to Jerusalem. Here I learned about the evil
thing Eliashib had done in providing Tobiah a
room in the courts of the house of God. 8I was
greatly displeased and threw all Tobiah's household goods out of the room. 9I gave orders to
purify the rooms, and then I put back into them
the equipment of the house of God, with the
grain offerings and the incense.

10I also learned that the portions assigned to
the Levites had not been given to them, and that
all the Levites and singers responsible for the
service had gone back to their own fields. 11So I
rebuked the officials and asked them, "Why is the
house of God neglected?" Then I called them together and stationed them at their posts.

12All Judah brought the tithes of grain, new
wine and oil into the storerooms. 13I put Shelemiah the priest, Zadok the scribe, and a Levite
named Pedaiah in charge of the storerooms and
made Hanan son of Zaccur, the son of Mattaniah,
their assistant, because these men were considered trustworthy. They were made responsible
for distributing the supplies to their brothers.

14Remember me for this, O my God, and do
not blot out what I have so faithfully done for the
house of my God and its services.

15In those days I saw men in Judah treading
winepresses on the Sabbath and bringing in grain
and loading it on donkeys, together with wine,
grapes, figs and all other kinds of loads. And they
were bringing all this into Jerusalem on the Sabbath. Therefore I warned them against selling
food on that day. 16Men from Tyre who lived in
Jerusalem were bringing in fish and all kinds of
merchandise and selling them in Jerusalem on
the Sabbath to the people of Judah. 17I rebuked
the nobles of Judah and said to them, "What is
this wicked thing you are doing—desecrating the
Sabbath day? 18Didn't your forefathers do the
same things, so that our God brought all this calamity upon us and upon this city? Now you are
stirring up more wrath against Israel by desecrating the Sabbath."

19When evening shadows fell on the gates of
Jerusalem before the Sabbath, I ordered the doors
to be shut and not opened until the Sabbath was
over. I stationed some of my own men at the
gates so that no load could be brought in on the
Sabbath day. 20Once or twice the merchants and
sellers of all kinds of goods spent the night outside Jerusalem. 21But I warned them and said,
"Why do you spend the night by the wall? If you
do this again, I will lay hands on you." From that
time on they no longer came on the Sabbath.
22Then I commanded the Levites to purify themselves and go and guard the gates in order to keep
the Sabbath day holy.

Remember me for this also, O my God, and
show mercy to me according to your great love.

23Moreover, in those days I saw men of Judah
who had married women from Ashdod, Ammon
and Moab. 24Half of their children spoke the language of Ashdod or the language of one of the
other peoples, and did not know how to speak
the language of Judah. 25I rebuked them and
called curses down on them. I beat some of the
men and pulled out their hair. I made them take
an oath in God's name and said: "You are not to
give your daughters in marriage to their sons, nor
are you to take their daughters in marriage for
your sons or for yourselves. 26Was it not because
of marriages like these that Solomon king of Israel
sinned? Among the many nations there was no
king like him. He was loved by his God, and God
made him king over all Israel, but even he was
led into sin by foreign women. 27Must we hear
now that you too are doing all this terrible wickedness and are being unfaithful to our God by
marrying foreign women?"

28One of the sons of Joiada son of Eliashib the high priest was son-in-law to Sanballat the Horonite. And I drove him away from me.

29Remember them, O my God, because they defiled the priestly office and the covenant of the priesthood and of the Levites.

30So I purified the priests and the Levites of everything foreign, and assigned them duties, each to his own task. 31I also made provision for contributions of wood at designated times, and for the firstfruits.

Remember me with favor, O my God.

Introduction to
ESTHER

Personal Reading Plan

- ❐ Esther 1:1–22
- ❐ Esther 2:1–23
- ❐ Esther 3:1–4:17
- ❐ Esther 5:1–6:14
- ❐ Esther 7:1–8:17
- ❐ Esther 9:1–10:3

Author

The author is unknown, but was most likely a Jewish nationalist who was a resident of a Persian city. Some suggest that Mordecai is the author.

Date

The writing of Esther was no earlier than the reign of Xerxes (c. 486–465 B.C.), and probably no later than 331 B.C., when the Persian Empire fell to Greece.

Theme

The providence of God in the free decisions of people, especially in delivering the Jews under Xerxes; also a profile in human courage.

Historical Background

More than a generation had passed since Cyrus defeated the Babylonians and allowed the Jews to return to Israel. Still, many Jews remained spread throughout the known world, making their home among their captors. The book of Esther features some of these expatriates. It is noteworthy that Artaxerxes, the son of Xerxes, was king during Nehemiah's time. He may have been influenced by Queen Esther in his handling of the Jews (see Neh. 2:6).

Characteristics

The book of Esther recounts how the Feast of Purim came to be celebrated—a feast still observed today by Jews in memory of the Lord's sovereign, providential care of his people. The story revolves around 10 banquets (1:3–4; 1:5–8; 1:9; 2:18; 3:15; 5:1–8; 7:1–10; 8:17; 9:17; 9:18–32). The banquets culminate in the double celebration of the Feast of Purim. Interestingly, the book of Esther does not directly name God. This conspicuous lack of any reference to God focuses attention on what he is doing constantly, behind the scenes, to effect deliverance for the Jews. Esther is a literary masterpiece which reads like a modern suspense novel, complete with plot twists, coincidence, irony, intrigue, revenge and plenty of feasting.

Passage for Topical Group Study

2:1–18	POPULARITY APPEARANCE	Esther Chosen Queen

See the Lesson Plans in the front of this Bible.

Queen Vashti Deposed

1 This is what happened during the time of
Xerxes,[a] the Xerxes who ruled over 127
provinces stretching from India to Cush[b]: 2At
that time King Xerxes reigned from his royal
throne in the citadel of Susa, 3and in the third
year of his reign he gave a banquet for all his
nobles and officials. The military leaders of Persia
and Media, the princes, and the nobles of the
provinces were present.
4For a full 180 days he displayed the vast
wealth of his kingdom and the splendor and glory
of his majesty. 5When these days were over, the
king gave a banquet, lasting seven days, in the
enclosed garden of the king's palace, for all
the people from the least to the greatest, who
were in the citadel of Susa. 6The garden had
hangings of white and blue linen, fastened with
cords of white linen and purple material to silver
rings on marble pillars. There were couches of
gold and silver on a mosaic pavement of porphy-
ry, marble, mother-of-pearl and other costly
stones. 7Wine was served in goblets of gold, each
one different from the other, and the royal wine
was abundant, in keeping with the king's liberality. 8By the king's command each guest was allowed to drink in his own way, for the king instructed all the wine stewards to serve each man
what he wished.
9Queen Vashti also gave a banquet for the
women in the royal palace of King Xerxes.
10On the seventh day, when King Xerxes was
in high spirits from wine, he commanded the
seven eunuchs who served him—Mehuman, Biz-
tha, Harbona, Bigtha, Abagtha, Zethar and
Carcas— 11to bring before him Queen Vashti,
wearing her royal crown, in order to display her
beauty to the people and nobles, for she was lovely to look at. 12But when the attendants delivered
the king's command, Queen Vashti refused to
come. Then the king became furious and burned
with anger.
13Since it was customary for the king to consult experts in matters of law and justice, he
spoke with the wise men who understood the
times 14and were closest to the king—Carshena,
Shethar, Admatha, Tarshish, Meres, Marsena and
Memucan, the seven nobles of Persia and Media
who had special access to the king and were
highest in the kingdom.
15"According to law, what must be done to
Queen Vashti?" he asked. "She has not obeyed
the command of King Xerxes that the eunuchs
have taken to her."
16Then Memucan replied in the presence of
the king and the nobles, "Queen Vashti has done
wrong, not only against the king but also against
all the nobles and the peoples of all the provinces
of King Xerxes. 17For the queen's conduct will
become known to all the women, and so they will
despise their husbands and say, 'King Xerxes
commanded Queen Vashti to be brought before
him, but she would not come.' 18This very day
the Persian and Median women of the nobility
who have heard about the queen's conduct will
respond to all the king's nobles in the same way.
There will be no end of disrespect and discord.
19"Therefore, if it pleases the king, let him
issue a royal decree and let it be written in the
laws of Persia and Media, which cannot be repealed, that Vashti is never again to enter the
presence of King Xerxes. Also let the king give
her royal position to someone else who is better
than she. 20Then when the king's edict is proclaimed throughout all his vast realm, all the
women will respect their husbands, from the
least to the greatest."
21The king and his nobles were pleased with
this advice, so the king did as Memucan proposed. 22He sent dispatches to all parts of the
kingdom, to each province in its own script and
to each people in its own language, proclaiming
in each people's tongue that every man should be
ruler over his own household.

Esther Made Queen

2 Later when the anger of King Xerxes had
subsided, he remembered Vashti and what
she had done and what he had decreed about
her. 2Then the king's personal attendants proposed, "Let a search be made for beautiful young
virgins for the king. 3Let the king appoint commissioners in every province of his realm to bring
all these beautiful girls into the harem at the citadel of Susa. Let them be placed under the care of
Hegai, the king's eunuch, who is in charge of the
women; and let beauty treatments be given to
them. 4Then let the girl who pleases the king be
queen instead of Vashti." This advice appealed to
the king, and he followed it.
5Now there was in the citadel of Susa a Jew of
the tribe of Benjamin, named Mordecai son of
Jair, the son of Shimei, the son of Kish, 6who had
been carried into exile from Jerusalem by Nebuchadnezzar king of Babylon, among those taken
captive with Jehoiachin[c] king of Judah. 7Morde-
cai had a cousin named Hadassah, whom he had
brought up because she had neither father nor
mother. This girl, who was also known as Esther,
was lovely in form and features, and Mordecai
had taken her as his own daughter when her
father and mother died.

[a] 1 Hebrew *Ahasuerus,* a variant of Xerxes' Persian name; here and throughout Esther [b] 1 That is, the upper Nile region
[c] 6 Hebrew *Jeconiah,* a variant of *Jehoiachin*

8When the king's order and edict had been proclaimed, many girls were brought to the citadel of Susa and put under the care of Hegai. Esther also was taken to the king's palace and entrusted to Hegai, who had charge of the harem.

Esther 2:1–18

1. What do you think of beauty contests: Are they great? Harmless? Insulting? Stupid?
2. How many times a day do you look in the mirror? What are you looking for?
3. In your school, who is the popular crowd? To hang out with this crowd, what do you have to do? Wear? Say?
4. Besides being "lovely in form and features," what else did Esther have going for her?
5. What makes a person beautiful to God? How is this different from the world's standard (see 1 Samuel 16:7)?
6. In your relationship with God right now, how do you feel: Chosen? Rejected? Pleasing?
7. What beautiful inner qualities do you see in the people in your group? Have one person at a time listen while others affirm that person.

9The girl pleased him and won his favor. Immediately he provided her with her beauty treatments and special food. He assigned to her seven maids selected from the king's palace and moved her and her maids into the best place in the harem.

10Esther had not revealed her nationality and family background, because Mordecai had forbidden her to do so. 11Every day he walked back and forth near the courtyard of the harem to find out how Esther was and what was happening to her.

12Before a girl's turn came to go in to King Xerxes, she had to complete twelve months of beauty treatments prescribed for the women, six months with oil of myrrh and six with perfumes and cosmetics. 13And this is how she would go to the king: Anything she wanted was given her to take with her from the harem to the king's palace. 14In the evening she would go there and in the morning return to another part of the harem to the care of Shaashgaz, the king's eunuch who was in charge of the concubines. She would not return to the king unless he was pleased with her and summoned her by name.

15When the turn came for Esther (the girl Mordecai had adopted, the daughter of his uncle Abihail) to go to the king, she asked for nothing other than what Hegai, the king's eunuch who was in charge of the harem, suggested. And Esther won the favor of everyone who saw her. 16She was taken to King Xerxes in the royal residence in the tenth month, the month of Tebeth, in the seventh year of his reign.

17Now the king was attracted to Esther more than to any of the other women, and she won his favor and approval more than any of the other virgins. So he set a royal crown on her head and made her queen instead of Vashti. 18And the king gave a great banquet, Esther's banquet, for all his nobles and officials. He proclaimed a holiday throughout the provinces and distributed gifts with royal liberality.

Mordecai Uncovers a Conspiracy

19When the virgins were assembled a second time, Mordecai was sitting at the king's gate. 20But Esther had kept secret her family background and nationality just as Mordecai had told her to do, for she continued to follow Mordecai's instructions as she had done when he was bringing her up.

21During the time Mordecai was sitting at the

This story takes place in Susa, one of the capital cities of the Persian Empire. King Xerxes has deposed Queen Vashti for refusing a request he had made of her (see 1:10–12). Introduced in this chapter are Mordecai and Esther—Jews whose ancestors had been taken into exile from Israel years before.

2:2 ***Let a search be made for beautiful young virgins for the king.*** To add to his harem and to provide candidates for a new queen (see 1:19; v. 4).

2:7 ***Hadassah.*** Esther's Hebrew name. Many Jewish exiles had two names (Dan. 1:7). In concealing her nationality and family background (v. 10), Esther would have kept her Hebrew name secret. The author used her Persian name because that was how she would have been known, even among the Jews.

2:8 ***Esther also was taken.*** Neither she nor Mordecai, her cousin and adopted father (see v. 15), would have had any choice in the matter.

2:10 ***Mordecai had forbidden her.*** Mordecai insisted that Esther conceal her Jewish identity because he was aware that her background could put her at a disadvantage, likely even in danger, due to potential anti-Jewish attitudes (clearly demonstrated later in the book).

2:14 ***to another part of the harem.*** To the chambers of the concubines.

2:17 Esther's tenure as queen continued at least through the events of the book.

king's gate, Bigthana[a] and Teresh, two of the king's officers who guarded the doorway, became angry and conspired to assassinate King Xerxes. 22But Mordecai found out about the plot and told Queen Esther, who in turn reported it to the king, giving credit to Mordecai. 23And when the report was investigated and found to be true, the two officials were hanged on a gallows.[b] All this was recorded in the book of the annals in the presence of the king.

Haman's Plot to Destroy the Jews

3 After these events, King Xerxes honored Haman son of Hammedatha, the Agagite, elevating him and giving him a seat of honor higher than that of all the other nobles. 2All the royal officials at the king's gate knelt down and paid honor to Haman, for the king had commanded this concerning him. But Mordecai would not kneel down or pay him honor.

3Then the royal officials at the king's gate asked Mordecai, "Why do you disobey the king's command?" 4Day after day they spoke to him but he refused to comply. Therefore they told Haman about it to see whether Mordecai's behavior would be tolerated, for he had told them he was a Jew.

5When Haman saw that Mordecai would not kneel down or pay him honor, he was enraged. 6Yet having learned who Mordecai's people were, he scorned the idea of killing only Mordecai. Instead Haman looked for a way to destroy all Mordecai's people, the Jews, throughout the whole kingdom of Xerxes.

7In the twelfth year of King Xerxes, in the first month, the month of Nisan, they cast the *pur* (that is, the lot) in the presence of Haman to select a day and month. And the lot fell on[c] the twelfth month, the month of Adar.

8Then Haman said to King Xerxes, "There is a certain people dispersed and scattered among the peoples in all the provinces of your kingdom whose customs are different from those of all other people and who do not obey the king's laws; it is not in the king's best interest to tolerate them. 9If it pleases the king, let a decree be issued to destroy them, and I will put ten thousand talents[d] of silver into the royal treasury for the men who carry out this business."

10So the king took his signet ring from his finger and gave it to Haman son of Hammedatha, the Agagite, the enemy of the Jews. 11"Keep the money," the king said to Haman, "and do with the people as you please."

12Then on the thirteenth day of the first month the royal secretaries were summoned. They wrote out in the script of each province and in the language of each people all Haman's orders to the king's satraps, the governors of the various provinces and the nobles of the various peoples. These were written in the name of King Xerxes himself and sealed with his own ring. 13Dispatches were sent by couriers to all the king's provinces with the order to destroy, kill and annihilate all the Jews—young and old, women and little children—on a single day, the thirteenth day of the twelfth month, the month of Adar, and to plunder their goods. 14A copy of the text of the edict was to be issued as law in every province and made known to the people of every nationality so they would be ready for that day.

15Spurred on by the king's command, the couriers went out, and the edict was issued in the citadel of Susa. The king and Haman sat down to drink, but the city of Susa was bewildered.

Mordecai Persuades Esther to Help

4 When Mordecai learned of all that had been done, he tore his clothes, put on sackcloth and ashes, and went out into the city, wailing loudly and bitterly. 2But he went only as far as the king's gate, because no one clothed in sackcloth was allowed to enter it. 3In every province to which the edict and order of the king came, there was great mourning among the Jews, with fasting, weeping and wailing. Many lay in sackcloth and ashes.

4When Esther's maids and eunuchs came and told her about Mordecai, she was in great distress. She sent clothes for him to put on instead of his sackcloth, but he would not accept them. 5Then Esther summoned Hathach, one of the king's eunuchs assigned to attend her, and ordered him to find out what was troubling Mordecai and why.

6So Hathach went out to Mordecai in the open square of the city in front of the king's gate. 7Mordecai told him everything that had happened to him, including the exact amount of money Haman had promised to pay into the royal treasury for the destruction of the Jews. 8He also gave him a copy of the text of the edict for their annihilation, which had been published in Susa, to show to Esther and explain it to her, and he told him to urge her to go into the king's presence to beg for mercy and plead with him for her people.

9Hathach went back and reported to Esther what Mordecai had said. 10Then she instructed him to say to Mordecai, 11"All the king's officials and the people of the royal provinces know that

[a] 21 Hebrew *Bigthan,* a variant of *Bigthana* [b] 23 Or *were hung* (or *impaled*) *on poles*; similarly elsewhere in Esther
[c] 7 Septuagint; Hebrew does not have *And the lot fell on.* [d] 9 That is, about 375 tons (about 345 metric tons)

for any man or woman who approaches the king in the inner court without being summoned the king has but one law: that he be put to death. The only exception to this is for the king to extend the gold scepter to him and spare his life. But thirty days have passed since I was called to go to the king."

12When Esther's words were reported to Mordecai, 13he sent back this answer: "Do not think that because you are in the king's house you alone of all the Jews will escape. 14For if you remain silent at this time, relief and deliverance for the Jews will arise from another place, but you and your father's family will perish. And who knows but that you have come to royal position for such a time as this?"

15Then Esther sent this reply to Mordecai: 16"Go, gather together all the Jews who are in Susa, and fast for me. Do not eat or drink for three days, night or day. I and my maids will fast as you do. When this is done, I will go to the king, even though it is against the law. And if I perish, I perish."

17So Mordecai went away and carried out all of Esther's instructions.

Esther's Request to the King

5 On the third day Esther put on her royal robes and stood in the inner court of the palace, in front of the king's hall. The king was sitting on his royal throne in the hall, facing the entrance. 2When he saw Queen Esther standing in the court, he was pleased with her and held out to her the gold scepter that was in his hand. So Esther approached and touched the tip of the scepter.

3Then the king asked, "What is it, Queen Esther? What is your request? Even up to half the kingdom, it will be given you."

4"If it pleases the king," replied Esther, "let the king, together with Haman, come today to a banquet I have prepared for him."

5"Bring Haman at once," the king said, "so that we may do what Esther asks."

So the king and Haman went to the banquet Esther had prepared. 6As they were drinking wine, the king again asked Esther, "Now what is your petition? It will be given you. And what is your request? Even up to half the kingdom, it will be granted."

7Esther replied, "My petition and my request is this: 8If the king regards me with favor and if it pleases the king to grant my petition and fulfill my request, let the king and Haman come tomorrow to the banquet I will prepare for them. Then I will answer the king's question."

Haman's Rage Against Mordecai

9Haman went out that day happy and in high spirits. But when he saw Mordecai at the king's gate and observed that he neither rose nor showed fear in his presence, he was filled with rage against Mordecai. 10Nevertheless, Haman restrained himself and went home.

Calling together his friends and Zeresh, his wife, 11Haman boasted to them about his vast wealth, his many sons, and all the ways the king had honored him and how he had elevated him above the other nobles and officials. 12"And that's not all," Haman added. "I'm the only person Queen Esther invited to accompany the king to the banquet she gave. And she has invited me along with the king tomorrow. 13But all this gives me no satisfaction as long as I see that Jew Mordecai sitting at the king's gate."

14His wife Zeresh and all his friends said to him, "Have a gallows built, seventy-five feet[a] high, and ask the king in the morning to have Mordecai hanged on it. Then go with the king to the dinner and be happy." This suggestion delighted Haman, and he had the gallows built.

Mordecai Honored

6 That night the king could not sleep; so he ordered the book of the chronicles, the record of his reign, to be brought in and read to him. 2It was found recorded there that Mordecai had exposed Bigthana and Teresh, two of the king's officers who guarded the doorway, who had conspired to assassinate King Xerxes.

3"What honor and recognition has Mordecai received for this?" the king asked.

"Nothing has been done for him," his attendants answered.

4The king said, "Who is in the court?" Now Haman had just entered the outer court of the palace to speak to the king about hanging Mordecai on the gallows he had erected for him.

5His attendants answered, "Haman is standing in the court."

"Bring him in," the king ordered.

6When Haman entered, the king asked him, "What should be done for the man the king delights to honor?"

Now Haman thought to himself, "Who is there that the king would rather honor than me?" 7So he answered the king, "For the man the king delights to honor, 8have them bring a royal robe the king has worn and a horse the king has ridden, one with a royal crest placed on its head. 9Then let the robe and horse be entrusted to one of the king's most noble princes. Let them robe the man the king delights to honor, and lead him

a 14 Hebrew *fifty cubits* (about 23 meters)

on the horse through the city streets, proclaiming
before him, 'This is what is done for the man the
king delights to honor!' "
10"Go at once," the king commanded Haman.
"Get the robe and the horse and do just as you
have suggested for Mordecai the Jew, who sits at
the king's gate. Do not neglect anything you have
recommended."
11So Haman got the robe and the horse. He
robed Mordecai, and led him on horseback
through the city streets, proclaiming before him,
"This is what is done for the man the king delights to honor!"
12Afterward Mordecai returned to the king's
gate. But Haman rushed home, with his head
covered in grief, 13and told Zeresh his wife and
all his friends everything that had happened to
him.
His advisers and his wife Zeresh said to him,
"Since Mordecai, before whom your downfall has
started, is of Jewish origin, you cannot stand
against him—you will surely come to ruin!"
14While they were still talking with him, the
king's eunuchs arrived and hurried Haman away
to the banquet Esther had prepared.

Haman Hanged

7 So the king and Haman went to dine with
Queen Esther, 2and as they were drinking
wine on that second day, the king again asked,
"Queen Esther, what is your petition? It will be
given you. What is your request? Even up to half
the kingdom, it will be granted."
3Then Queen Esther answered, "If I have
found favor with you, O king, and if it pleases
your majesty, grant me my life—this is my petition. And spare my people—this is my request.
4For I and my people have been sold for destruction and slaughter and annihilation. If we had
merely been sold as male and female slaves, I
would have kept quiet, because no such distress
would justify disturbing the king.[a]"
5King Xerxes asked Queen Esther, "Who is
he? Where is the man who has dared to do such
a thing?"
6Esther said, "The adversary and enemy is this
vile Haman."
Then Haman was terrified before the king and
queen. 7The king got up in a rage, left his wine
and went out into the palace garden. But Haman,
realizing that the king had already decided his
fate, stayed behind to beg Queen Esther for his
life.
8Just as the king returned from the palace garden to the banquet hall, Haman was falling on the
couch where Esther was reclining.
The king exclaimed, "Will he even molest the
queen while she is with me in the house?"
As soon as the word left the king's mouth, they
covered Haman's face. 9Then Harbona, one of
the eunuchs attending the king, said, "A gallows
seventy-five feet[b] high stands by Haman's
house. He had it made for Mordecai, who spoke
up to help the king."
The king said, "Hang him on it!" 10So they
hanged Haman on the gallows he had prepared
for Mordecai. Then the king's fury subsided.

The King's Edict in Behalf of the Jews

8 That same day King Xerxes gave Queen Esther the estate of Haman, the enemy of the
Jews. And Mordecai came into the presence of
the king, for Esther had told how he was related
to her. 2The king took off his signet ring, which
he had reclaimed from Haman, and presented it
to Mordecai. And Esther appointed him over Haman's estate.
3Esther again pleaded with the king, falling at
his feet and weeping. She begged him to put an
end to the evil plan of Haman the Agagite, which
he had devised against the Jews. 4Then the king
extended the gold scepter to Esther and she arose
and stood before him.
5"If it pleases the king," she said, "and if he
regards me with favor and thinks it the right
thing to do, and if he is pleased with me, let an
order be written overruling the dispatches that
Haman son of Hammedatha, the Agagite, devised
and wrote to destroy the Jews in all the king's
provinces. 6For how can I bear to see disaster fall
on my people? How can I bear to see the destruction of my family?"
7King Xerxes replied to Queen Esther and to
Mordecai the Jew, "Because Haman attacked the
Jews, I have given his estate to Esther, and they
have hanged him on the gallows. 8Now write
another decree in the king's name in behalf of
the Jews as seems best to you, and seal it with the
king's signet ring—for no document written in
the king's name and sealed with his ring can be
revoked."
9At once the royal secretaries were
summoned—on the twenty-third day of the third
month, the month of Sivan. They wrote out all
Mordecai's orders to the Jews, and to the satraps,
governors and nobles of the 127 provinces
stretching from India to Cush.[c] These orders
were written in the script of each province and
the language of each people and also to the Jews
in their own script and language. 10Mordecai
wrote in the name of King Xerxes, sealed the
dispatches with the king's signet ring, and sent

[a]4 Or *quiet, but the compensation our adversary offers cannot be compared with the loss the king would suffer* [b]9 Hebrew *fifty cubits* (about 23 meters) [c]9 That is, the upper Nile region

them by mounted couriers, who rode fast horses especially bred for the king.

11The king's edict granted the Jews in every city the right to assemble and protect themselves; to destroy, kill and annihilate any armed force of any nationality or province that might attack them and their women and children; and to plunder the property of their enemies. 12The day appointed for the Jews to do this in all the provinces of King Xerxes was the thirteenth day of the twelfth month, the month of Adar. 13A copy of the text of the edict was to be issued as law in every province and made known to the people of every nationality so that the Jews would be ready on that day to avenge themselves on their enemies.

14The couriers, riding the royal horses, raced out, spurred on by the king's command. And the edict was also issued in the citadel of Susa.

15Mordecai left the king's presence wearing royal garments of blue and white, a large crown of gold and a purple robe of fine linen. And the city of Susa held a joyous celebration. 16For the Jews it was a time of happiness and joy, gladness and honor. 17In every province and in every city, wherever the edict of the king went, there was joy and gladness among the Jews, with feasting and celebrating. And many people of other nationalities became Jews because fear of the Jews had seized them.

Triumph of the Jews

9 On the thirteenth day of the twelfth month, the month of Adar, the edict commanded by the king was to be carried out. On this day the enemies of the Jews had hoped to overpower them, but now the tables were turned and the Jews got the upper hand over those who hated them. 2The Jews assembled in their cities in all the provinces of King Xerxes to attack those seeking their destruction. No one could stand against them, because the people of all the other nationalities were afraid of them. 3And all the nobles of the provinces, the satraps, the governors and the king's administrators helped the Jews, because fear of Mordecai had seized them. 4Mordecai was prominent in the palace; his reputation spread throughout the provinces, and he became more and more powerful.

5The Jews struck down all their enemies with the sword, killing and destroying them, and they did what they pleased to those who hated them. 6In the citadel of Susa, the Jews killed and destroyed five hundred men. 7They also killed Parshandatha, Dalphon, Aspatha, 8Poratha, Adalia, Aridatha, 9Parmashta, Arisai, Aridai and Vaizatha, 10the ten sons of Haman son of Hammedatha, the enemy of the Jews. But they did not lay their hands on the plunder.

11The number of those slain in the citadel of Susa was reported to the king that same day. 12The king said to Queen Esther, "The Jews have killed and destroyed five hundred men and the ten sons of Haman in the citadel of Susa. What have they done in the rest of the king's provinces? Now what is your petition? It will be given you. What is your request? It will also be granted."

13"If it pleases the king," Esther answered, "give the Jews in Susa permission to carry out this day's edict tomorrow also, and let Haman's ten sons be hanged on gallows."

14So the king commanded that this be done. An edict was issued in Susa, and they hanged the ten sons of Haman. 15The Jews in Susa came together on the fourteenth day of the month of Adar, and they put to death in Susa three hundred men, but they did not lay their hands on the plunder.

16Meanwhile, the remainder of the Jews who were in the king's provinces also assembled to protect themselves and get relief from their enemies. They killed seventy-five thousand of them but did not lay their hands on the plunder. 17This happened on the thirteenth day of the month of Adar, and on the fourteenth they rested and made it a day of feasting and joy.

Purim Celebrated

18The Jews in Susa, however, had assembled on the thirteenth and fourteenth, and then on the fifteenth they rested and made it a day of feasting and joy.

19That is why rural Jews—those living in villages—observe the fourteenth of the month of Adar as a day of joy and feasting, a day for giving presents to each other.

20Mordecai recorded these events, and he sent letters to all the Jews throughout the provinces of King Xerxes, near and far, 21to have them celebrate annually the fourteenth and fifteenth days of the month of Adar 22as the time when the Jews got relief from their enemies, and as the month when their sorrow was turned into joy and their mourning into a day of celebration. He wrote them to observe the days as days of feasting and joy and giving presents of food to one another and gifts to the poor.

23So the Jews agreed to continue the celebration they had begun, doing what Mordecai had written to them. 24For Haman son of Hammedatha, the Agagite, the enemy of all the Jews, had plotted against the Jews to destroy them and had cast the *pur* (that is, the lot) for their ruin and destruction. 25But when the plot came to the

king's attention,[a] he issued written orders that
the evil scheme Haman had devised against the
Jews should come back onto his own head, and
that he and his sons should be hanged on the
gallows. 26(Therefore these days were called Purim, from the word *pur*.) Because of everything
written in this letter and because of what they
had seen and what had happened to them, 27the
Jews took it upon themselves to establish the custom that they and their descendants and all who
join them should without fail observe these two
days every year, in the way prescribed and at the
time appointed. 28These days should be remembered and observed in every generation by every
family, and in every province and in every city.
And these days of Purim should never cease to be
celebrated by the Jews, nor should the memory of
them die out among their descendants.
29So Queen Esther, daughter of Abihail, along
with Mordecai the Jew, wrote with full authority
to confirm this second letter concerning Purim.
30And Mordecai sent letters to all the Jews in the
127 provinces of the kingdom of Xerxes—words
of goodwill and assurance— 31to establish these
days of Purim at their designated times, as Mordecai the Jew and Queen Esther had decreed for
them, and as they had established for themselves
and their descendants in regard to their times of
fasting and lamentation. 32Esther's decree confirmed these regulations about Purim, and it was
written down in the records.

The Greatness of Mordecai

10 King Xerxes imposed tribute throughout
the empire, to its distant shores. 2And all
his acts of power and might, together with a full
account of the greatness of Mordecai to which
the king had raised him, are they not written in
the book of the annals of the kings of Media and
Persia? 3Mordecai the Jew was second in rank to
King Xerxes, preeminent among the Jews, and
held in high esteem by his many fellow Jews,
because he worked for the good of his people and
spoke up for the welfare of all the Jews.

[a]25 Or *when Esther came before the king*

Introduction to JOB

Personal Reading Plan

❒ Job 1:1–2:13	❒ Job 18:1–19:29	❒ Job 32:1–33:33
❒ Job 3:1–5:27	❒ Job 20:1–21:34	❒ Job 34:1–37
❒ Job 6:1–7:21	❒ Job 22:1–30	❒ Job 35:1–37:24
❒ Job 8:1–22	❒ Job 23:1–25:6	❒ Job 38:1–41
❒ Job 9:1–11:20	❒ Job 26:1–28:28	❒ Job 39:1–30
❒ Job 12:1–14:22	❒ Job 29:1–30:31	❒ Job 40:1–41:34
❒ Job 15:1–17:16	❒ Job 31:1–40	❒ Job 42:1–17

Author

The writer is not Job himself, but an Israelite who is otherwise unknown.

Date

The events described may have taken place in the patriarchal age, but the book was probably not written in its present form until much later, possibly 600–400 B.C.

Theme

The justice of God in the light of human suffering.

Historical Background

Since there is little significant detail given, the precise situation cannot be established with certainty.

Characteristics

The opening verses set the stage for this well-crafted drama. Job is a wealthy, leading citizen, reputed to be very wise. When he loses herds, house and family and is struck down with a painful illness, we see an example in one life of the forms of suffering which afflict so many in our world. As a clue to Job's apparent alienation from God, the reader is shown that Satan, as accuser, is actively driving a wedge between God and his beloved. If Job proves to be righteous only because "it pays," then Satan wins his bet with God. Job's friends do not have the benefit of this insight, but their theology (and Job's) is quite biblical:

1. God is almighty.
2. God is just.
3. No human is entirely innocent in God's eyes.

Therefore, say his friends, Job's suffering must be retribution for some sin—a logical answer, but not at all consoling to Job in his despair. Finally, all are silenced, as God breaks in, but he gives no "solution" except to point to his greatness, glory and power. For the most profound insight, we turn to the Cross where God takes on himself human suffering and thus defeats it forever—a solution only hinted at in the book of Job.

Passage for Topical Group Study

1:6–22 TRAGEDY and DISASTER Job's First Test

See the Lesson Plans in the front of this Bible.

Prologue

1 In the land of Uz there lived a man whose
name was Job. This man was blameless and
upright; he feared God and shunned evil. 2He had
seven sons and three daughters, 3and he owned
seven thousand sheep, three thousand camels,
five hundred yoke of oxen and five hundred donkeys, and had a large number of servants. He
was the greatest man among all the people of the
East.
4His sons used to take turns holding feasts in
their homes, and they would invite their three
sisters to eat and drink with them. 5When a period of feasting had run its course, Job would send
and have them purified. Early in the morning he
would sacrifice a burnt offering for each of them,
thinking, "Perhaps my children have sinned and
cursed God in their hearts." This was Job's regular custom.

Job's First Test

6One day the angels[a] came to present themselves before the LORD, and Satan[b] also came
with them. 7The LORD said to Satan, "Where
have you come from?"
Satan answered the LORD, "From roaming
through the earth and going back and forth in it."
8Then the LORD said to Satan, "Have you considered my servant Job? There is no one on earth
like him; he is blameless and upright, a man who
fears God and shuns evil."
9"Does Job fear God for nothing?" Satan replied. 10"Have you not put a hedge around him
and his household and everything he has? You
have blessed the work of his hands, so that his
flocks and herds are spread throughout the land.
11But stretch out your hand and strike everything he has, and he will surely curse you to your
face."
12The LORD said to Satan, "Very well, then,
everything he has is in your hands, but on the
man himself do not lay a finger."
Then Satan went out from the presence of the
LORD.
13One day when Job's sons and daughters
were feasting and drinking wine at the oldest
brother's house, 14a messenger came to Job and
said, "The oxen were plowing and the donkeys
were grazing nearby, 15and the Sabeans attacked
and carried them off. They put the servants to the
sword, and I am the only one who has escaped to
tell you!"
16While he was still speaking, another messenger came and said, "The fire of God fell from the
sky and burned up the sheep and the servants,
and I am the only one who has escaped to tell
you!"

JOB 1:6–22

1. What is the worst thing that has happened to someone you know?
2. What funeral was the hardest for you to attend?
3. If you suddenly lost all your money, possessions and family, what would be your first response: Anger at God? Anger at Satan? Loss of faith? Peaceful acceptance?
4. What's the worst personal tragedy you've experienced?
5. How did your tragedy affect your belief in a loving God?
6. If your friend was going through "grief and loss," what would you share from your own experience?
7. Right now, what trial or test would you like this group to remember in prayer?

[a]6 Hebrew *the sons of God* [b]6 *Satan* means *accuser.*

Though the book of Job was written much later, Job himself probably lived during the time of the patriarchs of the book of Genesis. Job 1:1 refers to him as a "blameless and upright" man.

1:6 ***angels came to present themselves.*** They came as members of the heavenly council who stand in the presence of God. ***Satan.*** Literally "the accuser."

1:8–9 ***Have you considered my servant Job?*** The Lord, not Satan, initiates the dialogue that leads to the testing of Job. He holds up Job as one against whom "the accuser" can lodge no accusation. ***Does Job fear God for nothing?*** "The accuser" boldly accuses the man God commends: He says Job's righteousness, in which God delights, is self-serving—the heart of Satan's attack on God and his faithful servant in the book of Job. ***hedge.*** This symbolizes protection (see Isa. 5:5; contrast Job 3:23).

1:12 Satan, the accuser, is given power to afflict (v. 12a) but is kept on a leash (v. 12b). In all his evil among men (vv. 15,17) or in nature (vv. 16,19), Satan is mighty but still under God's power (compare 1 Chron. 21:1 with 2 Sam. 24:1).

1:20–21 ***At this, Job got up.*** He is silent until his children are killed. ***tore his robe and shaved his head.*** In mourning. ***The LORD gave and the LORD has taken away.*** Job's faith leads him to see the sovereign God's hand at work, and that gives him comfort even in the face of calamity.

17While he was still speaking, another messenger came and said, "The Chaldeans formed three raiding parties and swept down on your camels and carried them off. They put the servants to the sword, and I am the only one who has escaped to tell you!"

18While he was still speaking, yet another messenger came and said, "Your sons and daughters were feasting and drinking wine at the oldest brother's house, 19when suddenly a mighty wind swept in from the desert and struck the four corners of the house. It collapsed on them and they are dead, and I am the only one who has escaped to tell you!"

20At this, Job got up and tore his robe and shaved his head. Then he fell to the ground in worship 21and said:

"Naked I came from my mother's womb,
and naked I will depart.[a]
The LORD gave and the LORD has taken away;
may the name of the LORD be praised."

22In all this, Job did not sin by charging God with wrongdoing.

Job's Second Test

2 On another day the angels[b] came to present themselves before the LORD, and Satan also came with them to present himself before him. 2And the LORD said to Satan, "Where have you come from?"

Satan answered the LORD, "From roaming through the earth and going back and forth in it."

3Then the LORD said to Satan, "Have you considered my servant Job? There is no one on earth like him; he is blameless and upright, a man who fears God and shuns evil. And he still maintains his integrity, though you incited me against him to ruin him without any reason."

4"Skin for skin!" Satan replied. "A man will give all he has for his own life. 5But stretch out your hand and strike his flesh and bones, and he will surely curse you to your face."

6The LORD said to Satan, "Very well, then, he is in your hands; but you must spare his life."

7So Satan went out from the presence of the LORD and afflicted Job with painful sores from the soles of his feet to the top of his head. 8Then Job took a piece of broken pottery and scraped himself with it as he sat among the ashes.

9His wife said to him, "Are you still holding on to your integrity? Curse God and die!"

10He replied, "You are talking like a foolish[c] woman. Shall we accept good from God, and not trouble?"

In all this, Job did not sin in what he said.

Job's Three Friends

11When Job's three friends, Eliphaz the Temanite, Bildad the Shuhite and Zophar the Naamathite, heard about all the troubles that had come upon him, they set out from their homes and met together by agreement to go and sympathize with him and comfort him. 12When they saw him from a distance, they could hardly recognize him; they began to weep aloud, and they tore their robes and sprinkled dust on their heads. 13Then they sat on the ground with him for seven days and seven nights. No one said a word to him, because they saw how great his suffering was.

Job Speaks

3 After this, Job opened his mouth and cursed the day of his birth. 2He said:

3"May the day of my birth perish,
and the night it was said, 'A boy is born!'
4That day—may it turn to darkness;
may God above not care about it;
may no light shine upon it.
5May darkness and deep shadow[d] claim it once more;
may a cloud settle over it;
may blackness overwhelm its light.
6That night—may thick darkness seize it;
may it not be included among the days of the year
nor be entered in any of the months.
7May that night be barren;
may no shout of joy be heard in it.
8May those who curse days[e] curse that day,
those who are ready to rouse Leviathan.
9May its morning stars become dark;
may it wait for daylight in vain
and not see the first rays of dawn,
10for it did not shut the doors of the womb on me
to hide trouble from my eyes.

11"Why did I not perish at birth,
and die as I came from the womb?
12Why were there knees to receive me
and breasts that I might be nursed?
13For now I would be lying down in peace;
I would be asleep and at rest
14with kings and counselors of the earth,
who built for themselves places now lying in ruins,
15with rulers who had gold,
who filled their houses with silver.
16Or why was I not hidden in the ground like a stillborn child,

[a]21 Or *will return there* [b]1 Hebrew *the sons of God* [c]10 The Hebrew word rendered *foolish* denotes moral deficiency.
[d]5 Or *and the shadow of death* [e]8 Or *the sea*

like an infant who never saw the light of day?
17 There the wicked cease from turmoil,
and there the weary are at rest.
18 Captives also enjoy their ease;
they no longer hear the slave driver's shout.
19 The small and the great are there,
and the slave is freed from his master.

20 "Why is light given to those in misery,
and life to the bitter of soul,
21 to those who long for death that does not come,
who search for it more than for hidden treasure,
22 who are filled with gladness
and rejoice when they reach the grave?
23 Why is life given to a man
whose way is hidden,
whom God has hedged in?
24 For sighing comes to me instead of food;
my groans pour out like water.
25 What I feared has come upon me;
what I dreaded has happened to me.
26 I have no peace, no quietness;
I have no rest, but only turmoil."

Eliphaz

4 Then Eliphaz the Temanite replied:

2 "If someone ventures a word with you, will you be impatient?
But who can keep from speaking?
3 Think how you have instructed many,
how you have strengthened feeble hands.
4 Your words have supported those who stumbled;
you have strengthened faltering knees.
5 But now trouble comes to you, and you are discouraged;
it strikes you, and you are dismayed.
6 Should not your piety be your confidence
and your blameless ways your hope?

7 "Consider now: Who, being innocent, has ever perished?
Where were the upright ever destroyed?
8 As I have observed, those who plow evil
and those who sow trouble reap it.
9 At the breath of God they are destroyed;
at the blast of his anger they perish.
10 The lions may roar and growl,
yet the teeth of the great lions are broken.
11 The lion perishes for lack of prey,
and the cubs of the lioness are scattered.

12 "A word was secretly brought to me,
my ears caught a whisper of it.
13 Amid disquieting dreams in the night,
when deep sleep falls on men,
14 fear and trembling seized me
and made all my bones shake.
15 A spirit glided past my face,
and the hair on my body stood on end.
16 It stopped,
but I could not tell what it was.
A form stood before my eyes,
and I heard a hushed voice:
17 'Can a mortal be more righteous than God?
Can a man be more pure than his Maker?
18 If God places no trust in his servants,
if he charges his angels with error,
19 how much more those who live in houses of clay,
whose foundations are in the dust,
who are crushed more readily than a moth!
20 Between dawn and dusk they are broken to pieces;
unnoticed, they perish forever.
21 Are not the cords of their tent pulled up,
so that they die without wisdom?'[a]

5 "Call if you will, but who will answer you?
To which of the holy ones will you turn?
2 Resentment kills a fool,
and envy slays the simple.
3 I myself have seen a fool taking root,
but suddenly his house was cursed.
4 His children are far from safety,
crushed in court without a defender.
5 The hungry consume his harvest,
taking it even from among thorns,
and the thirsty pant after his wealth.
6 For hardship does not spring from the soil,
nor does trouble sprout from the ground.
7 Yet man is born to trouble
as surely as sparks fly upward.

8 "But if it were I, I would appeal to God;
I would lay my cause before him.
9 He performs wonders that cannot be fathomed,
miracles that cannot be counted.
10 He bestows rain on the earth;
he sends water upon the countryside.
11 The lowly he sets on high,
and those who mourn are lifted to safety.
12 He thwarts the plans of the crafty,
so that their hands achieve no success.
13 He catches the wise in their craftiness,
and the schemes of the wily are swept away.
14 Darkness comes upon them in the daytime;
at noon they grope as in the night.

a21 Some interpreters end the quotation after verse 17.

15He saves the needy from the sword in their
mouth;
he saves them from the clutches of the
powerful.
16So the poor have hope,
and injustice shuts its mouth.

17"Blessed is the man whom God corrects;
so do not despise the discipline of the
Almighty.[a]
18For he wounds, but he also binds up;
he injures, but his hands also heal.
19From six calamities he will rescue you;
in seven no harm will befall you.
20In famine he will ransom you from death,
and in battle from the stroke of the sword.
21You will be protected from the lash of the
tongue,
and need not fear when destruction
comes.
22You will laugh at destruction and famine,
and need not fear the beasts of the earth.
23For you will have a covenant with the stones
of the field,
and the wild animals will be at peace with
you.
24You will know that your tent is secure;
you will take stock of your property and
find nothing missing.
25You will know that your children will be
many,
and your descendants like the grass of the
earth.
26You will come to the grave in full vigor,
like sheaves gathered in season.

27"We have examined this, and it is true.
So hear it and apply it to yourself."

Job

6 Then Job replied:

2"If only my anguish could be weighed
and all my misery be placed on the scales!
3It would surely outweigh the sand of the
seas—
no wonder my words have been
impetuous.
4The arrows of the Almighty are in me,
my spirit drinks in their poison;
God's terrors are marshaled against me.
5Does a wild donkey bray when it has grass,
or an ox bellow when it has fodder?
6Is tasteless food eaten without salt,
or is there flavor in the white of an egg[b]?
7I refuse to touch it;
such food makes me ill.

8"Oh, that I might have my request,
that God would grant what I hope for,
9that God would be willing to crush me,
to let loose his hand and cut me off!
10Then I would still have this consolation—
my joy in unrelenting pain—
that I had not denied the words of the
Holy One.

11"What strength do I have, that I should still
hope?
What prospects, that I should be patient?
12Do I have the strength of stone?
Is my flesh bronze?
13Do I have any power to help myself,
now that success has been driven from
me?

14"A despairing man should have the devotion
of his friends,
even though he forsakes the fear of the
Almighty.
15But my brothers are as undependable as
intermittent streams,
as the streams that overflow
16when darkened by thawing ice
and swollen with melting snow,
17but that cease to flow in the dry season,
and in the heat vanish from their
channels.
18Caravans turn aside from their routes;
they go up into the wasteland and perish.
19The caravans of Tema look for water,
the traveling merchants of Sheba look in
hope.
20They are distressed, because they had been
confident;
they arrive there, only to be disappointed.
21Now you too have proved to be of no help;
you see something dreadful and are afraid.
22Have I ever said, 'Give something on my
behalf,
pay a ransom for me from your wealth,
23deliver me from the hand of the enemy,
ransom me from the clutches of the
ruthless'?

24"Teach me, and I will be quiet;
show me where I have been wrong.
25How painful are honest words!
But what do your arguments prove?
26Do you mean to correct what I say,
and treat the words of a despairing man as
wind?
27You would even cast lots for the fatherless
and barter away your friend.

28"But now be so kind as to look at me.
Would I lie to your face?

[a]*17* Hebrew *Shaddai*; here and throughout Job [b]*6* The meaning of the Hebrew for this phrase is uncertain.

29Relent, do not be unjust;
reconsider, for my integrity is at stake.[a]
30Is there any wickedness on my lips?
Can my mouth not discern malice?

7 "Does not man have hard service on earth?
Are not his days like those of a hired man?
2Like a slave longing for the evening shadows,
or a hired man waiting eagerly for his wages,
3so I have been allotted months of futility,
and nights of misery have been assigned to me.
4When I lie down I think, 'How long before I get up?'
The night drags on, and I toss till dawn.
5My body is clothed with worms and scabs,
my skin is broken and festering.

6"My days are swifter than a weaver's shuttle,
and they come to an end without hope.
7Remember, O God, that my life is but a breath;
my eyes will never see happiness again.
8The eye that now sees me will see me no longer;
you will look for me, but I will be no more.
9As a cloud vanishes and is gone,
so he who goes down to the grave[b] does not return.
10He will never come to his house again;
his place will know him no more.

11"Therefore I will not keep silent;
I will speak out in the anguish of my spirit,
I will complain in the bitterness of my soul.
12Am I the sea, or the monster of the deep,
that you put me under guard?
13When I think my bed will comfort me
and my couch will ease my complaint,
14even then you frighten me with dreams
and terrify me with visions,
15so that I prefer strangling and death,
rather than this body of mine.
16I despise my life; I would not live forever.
Let me alone; my days have no meaning.

17"What is man that you make so much of him,
that you give him so much attention,
18that you examine him every morning
and test him every moment?
19Will you never look away from me,
or let me alone even for an instant?
20If I have sinned, what have I done to you,
O watcher of men?
Why have you made me your target?
Have I become a burden to you?[c]
21Why do you not pardon my offenses
and forgive my sins?
For I will soon lie down in the dust;
you will search for me, but I will be no more."

Bildad

8 Then Bildad the Shuhite replied:

2"How long will you say such things?
Your words are a blustering wind.
3Does God pervert justice?
Does the Almighty pervert what is right?
4When your children sinned against him,
he gave them over to the penalty of their sin.
5But if you will look to God
and plead with the Almighty,
6if you are pure and upright,
even now he will rouse himself on your behalf
and restore you to your rightful place.
7Your beginnings will seem humble,
so prosperous will your future be.

8"Ask the former generations
and find out what their fathers learned,
9for we were born only yesterday and know nothing,
and our days on earth are but a shadow.
10Will they not instruct you and tell you?
Will they not bring forth words from their understanding?
11Can papyrus grow tall where there is no marsh?
Can reeds thrive without water?
12While still growing and uncut,
they wither more quickly than grass.
13Such is the destiny of all who forget God;
so perishes the hope of the godless.
14What he trusts in is fragile[d];
what he relies on is a spider's web.
15He leans on his web, but it gives way;
he clings to it, but it does not hold.
16He is like a well-watered plant in the sunshine,
spreading its shoots over the garden;
17it entwines its roots around a pile of rocks
and looks for a place among the stones.
18But when it is torn from its spot,

a29 Or *my righteousness still stands* b9 Hebrew *Sheol* c20 A few manuscripts of the Masoretic Text, an ancient Hebrew scribal tradition and Septuagint; most manuscripts of the Masoretic Text *I have become a burden to myself.* d14 The meaning of the Hebrew for this word is uncertain.

that place disowns it and says, 'I never
saw you.'
19Surely its life withers away,
and[a] from the soil other plants grow.

20"Surely God does not reject a blameless man
or strengthen the hands of evildoers.
21He will yet fill your mouth with laughter
and your lips with shouts of joy.
22Your enemies will be clothed in shame,
and the tents of the wicked will be no
more."

Job

9 Then Job replied:

2"Indeed, I know that this is true.
But how can a mortal be righteous before
God?
3Though one wished to dispute with him,
he could not answer him one time out of a
thousand.
4His wisdom is profound, his power is vast.
Who has resisted him and come out
unscathed?
5He moves mountains without their knowing
it
and overturns them in his anger.
6He shakes the earth from its place
and makes its pillars tremble.
7He speaks to the sun and it does not shine;
he seals off the light of the stars.
8He alone stretches out the heavens
and treads on the waves of the sea.
9He is the Maker of the Bear and Orion,
the Pleiades and the constellations of the
south.
10He performs wonders that cannot be
fathomed,
miracles that cannot be counted.
11When he passes me, I cannot see him;
when he goes by, I cannot perceive him.
12If he snatches away, who can stop him?
Who can say to him, 'What are you
doing?'
13God does not restrain his anger;
even the cohorts of Rahab cowered at his
feet.

14"How then can I dispute with him?
How can I find words to argue with him?
15Though I were innocent, I could not answer
him;
I could only plead with my Judge for
mercy.
16Even if I summoned him and he responded,
I do not believe he would give me a
hearing.
17He would crush me with a storm
and multiply my wounds for no reason.
18He would not let me regain my breath
but would overwhelm me with misery.
19If it is a matter of strength, he is mighty!
And if it is a matter of justice, who will
summon him[b]?
20Even if I were innocent, my mouth would
condemn me;
if I were blameless, it would pronounce
me guilty.

21"Although I am blameless,
I have no concern for myself;
I despise my own life.
22It is all the same; that is why I say,
'He destroys both the blameless and the
wicked.'
23When a scourge brings sudden death,
he mocks the despair of the innocent.
24When a land falls into the hands of the
wicked,
he blindfolds its judges.
If it is not he, then who is it?

25"My days are swifter than a runner;
they fly away without a glimpse of joy.
26They skim past like boats of papyrus,
like eagles swooping down on their prey.
27If I say, 'I will forget my complaint,
I will change my expression, and smile,'
28I still dread all my sufferings,
for I know you will not hold me innocent.
29Since I am already found guilty,
why should I struggle in vain?
30Even if I washed myself with soap[c]
and my hands with washing soda,
31you would plunge me into a slime pit
so that even my clothes would detest me.

32"He is not a man like me that I might
answer him,
that we might confront each other in
court.
33If only there were someone to arbitrate
between us,
to lay his hand upon us both,
34someone to remove God's rod from me,
so that his terror would frighten me no
more.
35Then I would speak up without fear of him,
but as it now stands with me, I cannot.

10 "I loathe my very life;
therefore I will give free rein to my
complaint
and speak out in the bitterness of my soul.
2I will say to God: Do not condemn me,

a19 Or *Surely all the joy it has / is that* b19 See Septuagint; Hebrew *me.* c30 Or *snow*

but tell me what charges you have against
me.
3Does it please you to oppress me,
to spurn the work of your hands,
while you smile on the schemes of the
wicked?
4Do you have eyes of flesh?
Do you see as a mortal sees?
5Are your days like those of a mortal
or your years like those of a man,
6that you must search out my faults
and probe after my sin—
7though you know that I am not guilty
and that no one can rescue me from your
hand?

8"Your hands shaped me and made me.
Will you now turn and destroy me?
9Remember that you molded me like clay.
Will you now turn me to dust again?
10Did you not pour me out like milk
and curdle me like cheese,
11clothe me with skin and flesh
and knit me together with bones and
sinews?
12You gave me life and showed me kindness,
and in your providence watched over my
spirit.

13"But this is what you concealed in your
heart,
and I know that this was in your mind:
14If I sinned, you would be watching me
and would not let my offense go
unpunished.
15If I am guilty—woe to me!
Even if I am innocent, I cannot lift my
head,
for I am full of shame
and drowned in[a] my affliction.
16If I hold my head high, you stalk me like a
lion
and again display your awesome power
against me.
17You bring new witnesses against me
and increase your anger toward me;
your forces come against me wave upon
wave.

18"Why then did you bring me out of the
womb?
I wish I had died before any eye saw me.
19If only I had never come into being,
or had been carried straight from the
womb to the grave!
20Are not my few days almost over?
Turn away from me so I can have a
moment's joy
21before I go to the place of no return,
to the land of gloom and deep shadow,[b]
22to the land of deepest night,
of deep shadow and disorder,
where even the light is like darkness."

Zophar

11 Then Zophar the Naamathite replied:

2"Are all these words to go unanswered?
Is this talker to be vindicated?
3Will your idle talk reduce men to silence?
Will no one rebuke you when you mock?
4You say to God, 'My beliefs are flawless
and I am pure in your sight.'
5Oh, how I wish that God would speak,
that he would open his lips against you
6and disclose to you the secrets of wisdom,
for true wisdom has two sides.
Know this: God has even forgotten some
of your sin.

7"Can you fathom the mysteries of God?
Can you probe the limits of the Almighty?
8They are higher than the heavens—what can
you do?
They are deeper than the depths of the
grave[c]—what can you know?
9Their measure is longer than the earth
and wider than the sea.

10"If he comes along and confines you in
prison
and convenes a court, who can oppose
him?
11Surely he recognizes deceitful men;
and when he sees evil, does he not take
note?
12But a witless man can no more become wise
than a wild donkey's colt can be born a
man.[d]

13"Yet if you devote your heart to him
and stretch out your hands to him,
14if you put away the sin that is in your hand
and allow no evil to dwell in your tent,
15then you will lift up your face without
shame;
you will stand firm and without fear.
16You will surely forget your trouble,
recalling it only as waters gone by.
17Life will be brighter than noonday,
and darkness will become like morning.
18You will be secure, because there is hope;
you will look about you and take your rest
in safety.
19You will lie down, with no one to make you
afraid,

[a]*15* Or *and aware of* [b]*21* Or *and the shadow of death*; also in verse 22 [c]*8* Hebrew *than Sheol* [d]*12* Or *wild donkey can be born tame*

and many will court your favor.
20But the eyes of the wicked will fail,
and escape will elude them;
their hope will become a dying gasp."

Job

12 Then Job replied:
2"Doubtless you are the people,
and wisdom will die with you!
3But I have a mind as well as you;
I am not inferior to you.
Who does not know all these things?

4"I have become a laughingstock to my friends,
though I called upon God and he answered—
a mere laughingstock, though righteous and blameless!
5Men at ease have contempt for misfortune
as the fate of those whose feet are slipping.
6The tents of marauders are undisturbed,
and those who provoke God are secure—
those who carry their god in their hands.[a]

7"But ask the animals, and they will teach you,
or the birds of the air, and they will tell you;
8or speak to the earth, and it will teach you,
or let the fish of the sea inform you.
9Which of all these does not know
that the hand of the LORD has done this?
10In his hand is the life of every creature
and the breath of all mankind.
11Does not the ear test words
as the tongue tastes food?
12Is not wisdom found among the aged?
Does not long life bring understanding?

13"To God belong wisdom and power;
counsel and understanding are his.
14What he tears down cannot be rebuilt;
the man he imprisons cannot be released.
15If he holds back the waters, there is drought;
if he lets them loose, they devastate the land.
16To him belong strength and victory;
both deceived and deceiver are his.
17He leads counselors away stripped
and makes fools of judges.
18He takes off the shackles put on by kings
and ties a loincloth[b] around their waist.
19He leads priests away stripped
and overthrows men long established.
20He silences the lips of trusted advisers
and takes away the discernment of elders.
21He pours contempt on nobles
and disarms the mighty.
22He reveals the deep things of darkness
and brings deep shadows into the light.
23He makes nations great, and destroys them;
he enlarges nations, and disperses them.
24He deprives the leaders of the earth of their reason;
he sends them wandering through a trackless waste.
25They grope in darkness with no light;
he makes them stagger like drunkards.

13 "My eyes have seen all this,
my ears have heard and understood it.
2What you know, I also know;
I am not inferior to you.
3But I desire to speak to the Almighty
and to argue my case with God.
4You, however, smear me with lies;
you are worthless physicians, all of you!
5If only you would be altogether silent!
For you, that would be wisdom.
6Hear now my argument;
listen to the plea of my lips.
7Will you speak wickedly on God's behalf?
Will you speak deceitfully for him?
8Will you show him partiality?
Will you argue the case for God?
9Would it turn out well if he examined you?
Could you deceive him as you might deceive men?
10He would surely rebuke you
if you secretly showed partiality.
11Would not his splendor terrify you?
Would not the dread of him fall on you?
12Your maxims are proverbs of ashes;
your defenses are defenses of clay.

13"Keep silent and let me speak;
then let come to me what may.
14Why do I put myself in jeopardy
and take my life in my hands?
15Though he slay me, yet will I hope in him;
I will surely[c] defend my ways to his face.
16Indeed, this will turn out for my deliverance,
for no godless man would dare come before him!
17Listen carefully to my words;
let your ears take in what I say.
18Now that I have prepared my case,
I know I will be vindicated.
19Can anyone bring charges against me?
If so, I will be silent and die.

20"Only grant me these two things, O God,

a6 Or *secure / in what God's hand brings them have no hope — / yet I will*
b18 Or *shackles of kings / and ties a belt*
c15 Or *He will surely slay me; I*

and then I will not hide from you:
21Withdraw your hand far from me,
and stop frightening me with your terrors.
22Then summon me and I will answer,
or let me speak, and you reply.
23How many wrongs and sins have I
committed?
Show me my offense and my sin.
24Why do you hide your face
and consider me your enemy?
25Will you torment a windblown leaf?
Will you chase after dry chaff?
26For you write down bitter things against me
and make me inherit the sins of my youth.
27You fasten my feet in shackles;
you keep close watch on all my paths
by putting marks on the soles of my feet.

28"So man wastes away like something rotten,
like a garment eaten by moths.

14 "Man born of woman
is of few days and full of trouble.
2He springs up like a flower and withers
away;
like a fleeting shadow, he does not
endure.
3Do you fix your eye on such a one?
Will you bring him[a] before you for
judgment?
4Who can bring what is pure from the
impure?
No one!
5Man's days are determined;
you have decreed the number of his
months
and have set limits he cannot exceed.
6So look away from him and let him alone,
till he has put in his time like a hired
man.

7"At least there is hope for a tree:
If it is cut down, it will sprout again,
and its new shoots will not fail.
8Its roots may grow old in the ground
and its stump die in the soil,
9yet at the scent of water it will bud
and put forth shoots like a plant.
10But man dies and is laid low;
he breathes his last and is no more.
11As water disappears from the sea
or a riverbed becomes parched and dry,
12so man lies down and does not rise;
till the heavens are no more, men will not
awake
or be roused from their sleep.

13"If only you would hide me in the grave[b]
and conceal me till your anger has passed!
If only you would set me a time
and then remember me!
14If a man dies, will he live again?
All the days of my hard service
I will wait for my renewal[c] to come.
15You will call and I will answer you;
you will long for the creature your hands
have made.
16Surely then you will count my steps
but not keep track of my sin.
17My offenses will be sealed up in a bag;
you will cover over my sin.

18"But as a mountain erodes and crumbles
and as a rock is moved from its place,
19as water wears away stones
and torrents wash away the soil,
so you destroy man's hope.
20You overpower him once for all, and he is
gone;
you change his countenance and send him
away.
21If his sons are honored, he does not know it;
if they are brought low, he does not see it.
22He feels but the pain of his own body
and mourns only for himself."

Eliphaz

15 Then Eliphaz the Temanite replied:

2"Would a wise man answer with empty
notions
or fill his belly with the hot east wind?
3Would he argue with useless words,
with speeches that have no value?
4But you even undermine piety
and hinder devotion to God.
5Your sin prompts your mouth;
you adopt the tongue of the crafty.
6Your own mouth condemns you, not mine;
your own lips testify against you.

7"Are you the first man ever born?
Were you brought forth before the hills?
8Do you listen in on God's council?
Do you limit wisdom to yourself?
9What do you know that we do not know?
What insights do you have that we do not
have?
10The gray-haired and the aged are on our
side,
men even older than your father.
11Are God's consolations not enough for you,
words spoken gently to you?
12Why has your heart carried you away,
and why do your eyes flash,
13so that you vent your rage against God

[a]3 Septuagint, Vulgate and Syriac; Hebrew *me* [b]13 Hebrew *Sheol* [c]14 Or *release*

and pour out such words from your
mouth?

14"What is man, that he could be pure,
or one born of woman, that he could be
righteous?
15If God places no trust in his holy ones,
if even the heavens are not pure in his
eyes,
16how much less man, who is vile and corrupt,
who drinks up evil like water!

17"Listen to me and I will explain to you;
let me tell you what I have seen,
18what wise men have declared,
hiding nothing received from their fathers
19(to whom alone the land was given
when no alien passed among them):
20All his days the wicked man suffers torment,
the ruthless through all the years stored
up for him.
21Terrifying sounds fill his ears;
when all seems well, marauders attack
him.
22He despairs of escaping the darkness;
he is marked for the sword.
23He wanders about—food for vultures[a];
he knows the day of darkness is at hand.
24Distress and anguish fill him with terror;
they overwhelm him, like a king poised to
attack,
25because he shakes his fist at God
and vaunts himself against the Almighty,
26defiantly charging against him
with a thick, strong shield.

27"Though his face is covered with fat
and his waist bulges with flesh,
28he will inhabit ruined towns
and houses where no one lives,
houses crumbling to rubble.
29He will no longer be rich and his wealth will
not endure,
nor will his possessions spread over the
land.
30He will not escape the darkness;
a flame will wither his shoots,
and the breath of God's mouth will carry
him away.
31Let him not deceive himself by trusting what
is worthless,
for he will get nothing in return.
32Before his time he will be paid in full,
and his branches will not flourish.
33He will be like a vine stripped of its unripe
grapes,
like an olive tree shedding its blossoms.
34For the company of the godless will be
barren,
and fire will consume the tents of those
who love bribes.
35They conceive trouble and give birth to evil;
their womb fashions deceit."

Job

16

Then Job replied:

2"I have heard many things like these;
miserable comforters are you all!
3Will your long-winded speeches never end?
What ails you that you keep on arguing?
4I also could speak like you,
if you were in my place;
I could make fine speeches against you
and shake my head at you.
5But my mouth would encourage you;
comfort from my lips would bring you
relief.

6"Yet if I speak, my pain is not relieved;
and if I refrain, it does not go away.
7Surely, O God, you have worn me out;
you have devastated my entire household.
8You have bound me—and it has become a
witness;
my gauntness rises up and testifies against
me.
9God assails me and tears me in his anger
and gnashes his teeth at me;
my opponent fastens on me his piercing
eyes.
10Men open their mouths to jeer at me;
they strike my cheek in scorn
and unite together against me.
11God has turned me over to evil men
and thrown me into the clutches of the
wicked.
12All was well with me, but he shattered me;
he seized me by the neck and crushed me.
He has made me his target;
13 his archers surround me.
Without pity, he pierces my kidneys
and spills my gall on the ground.
14Again and again he bursts upon me;
he rushes at me like a warrior.

15"I have sewed sackcloth over my skin
and buried my brow in the dust.
16My face is red with weeping,
deep shadows ring my eyes;
17yet my hands have been free of violence
and my prayer is pure.

18"O earth, do not cover my blood;
may my cry never be laid to rest!

[a]23 Or *about, looking for food*

19 Even now my witness is in heaven;
my advocate is on high.
20 My intercessor is my friend[a]
as my eyes pour out tears to God;
21 on behalf of a man he pleads with God
as a man pleads for his friend.

22 "Only a few years will pass
before I go on the journey of no return.

17 1 My spirit is broken,
my days are cut short,
the grave awaits me.
2 Surely mockers surround me;
my eyes must dwell on their hostility.

3 "Give me, O God, the pledge you demand.
Who else will put up security for me?
4 You have closed their minds to
understanding;
therefore you will not let them triumph.
5 If a man denounces his friends for reward,
the eyes of his children will fail.

6 "God has made me a byword to everyone,
a man in whose face people spit.
7 My eyes have grown dim with grief;
my whole frame is but a shadow.
8 Upright men are appalled at this;
the innocent are aroused against the
ungodly.
9 Nevertheless, the righteous will hold to their
ways,
and those with clean hands will grow
stronger.

10 "But come on, all of you, try again!
I will not find a wise man among you.
11 My days have passed, my plans are shattered,
and so are the desires of my heart.
12 These men turn night into day;
in the face of darkness they say, 'Light is
near.'
13 If the only home I hope for is the grave,[b]
if I spread out my bed in darkness,
14 if I say to corruption, 'You are my father,'
and to the worm, 'My mother' or 'My
sister,'
15 where then is my hope?
Who can see any hope for me?
16 Will it go down to the gates of death[b]?
Will we descend together into the dust?"

Bildad

18 Then Bildad the Shuhite replied:

2 "When will you end these speeches?
Be sensible, and then we can talk.
3 Why are we regarded as cattle
and considered stupid in your sight?
4 You who tear yourself to pieces in your
anger,
is the earth to be abandoned for your
sake?
Or must the rocks be moved from their
place?

5 "The lamp of the wicked is snuffed out;
the flame of his fire stops burning.
6 The light in his tent becomes dark;
the lamp beside him goes out.
7 The vigor of his step is weakened;
his own schemes throw him down.
8 His feet thrust him into a net
and he wanders into its mesh.
9 A trap seizes him by the heel;
a snare holds him fast.
10 A noose is hidden for him on the ground;
a trap lies in his path.
11 Terrors startle him on every side
and dog his every step.
12 Calamity is hungry for him;
disaster is ready for him when he falls.
13 It eats away parts of his skin;
death's firstborn devours his limbs.
14 He is torn from the security of his tent
and marched off to the king of terrors.
15 Fire resides[c] in his tent;
burning sulfur is scattered over his
dwelling.
16 His roots dry up below
and his branches wither above.
17 The memory of him perishes from the earth;
he has no name in the land.
18 He is driven from light into darkness
and is banished from the world.
19 He has no offspring or descendants among
his people,
no survivor where once he lived.
20 Men of the west are appalled at his fate;
men of the east are seized with horror.
21 Surely such is the dwelling of an evil man;
such is the place of one who knows not
God."

Job

19 Then Job replied:

2 "How long will you torment me
and crush me with words?
3 Ten times now you have reproached me;
shamelessly you attack me.
4 If it is true that I have gone astray,
my error remains my concern alone.
5 If indeed you would exalt yourselves above
me
and use my humiliation against me,

a20 Or *My friends treat me with scorn* b13,16 Hebrew *Sheol* c15 Or *Nothing he had remains*

6 then know that God has wronged me
and drawn his net around me.

7 "Though I cry, 'I've been wronged!' I get no response;
though I call for help, there is no justice.
8 He has blocked my way so I cannot pass;
he has shrouded my paths in darkness.
9 He has stripped me of my honor
and removed the crown from my head.
10 He tears me down on every side till I am gone;
he uproots my hope like a tree.
11 His anger burns against me;
he counts me among his enemies.
12 His troops advance in force;
they build a siege ramp against me
and encamp around my tent.

13 "He has alienated my brothers from me;
my acquaintances are completely estranged from me.
14 My kinsmen have gone away;
my friends have forgotten me.
15 My guests and my maidservants count me a stranger;
they look upon me as an alien.
16 I summon my servant, but he does not answer,
though I beg him with my own mouth.
17 My breath is offensive to my wife;
I am loathsome to my own brothers.
18 Even the little boys scorn me;
when I appear, they ridicule me.
19 All my intimate friends detest me;
those I love have turned against me.
20 I am nothing but skin and bones;
I have escaped with only the skin of my teeth.[a]

21 "Have pity on me, my friends, have pity,
for the hand of God has struck me.
22 Why do you pursue me as God does?
Will you never get enough of my flesh?

23 "Oh, that my words were recorded,
that they were written on a scroll,
24 that they were inscribed with an iron tool on[b] lead,
or engraved in rock forever!
25 I know that my Redeemer[c] lives,
and that in the end he will stand upon the earth.[d]
26 And after my skin has been destroyed,
yet[e] in[f] my flesh I will see God;
27 I myself will see him
with my own eyes—I, and not another.
How my heart yearns within me!

28 "If you say, 'How we will hound him,
since the root of the trouble lies in him,[g]'
29 you should fear the sword yourselves;
for wrath will bring punishment by the sword,
and then you will know that there is judgment.[h]"

Zophar

20 Then Zophar the Naamathite replied:

2 "My troubled thoughts prompt me to answer
because I am greatly disturbed.
3 I hear a rebuke that dishonors me,
and my understanding inspires me to reply.

4 "Surely you know how it has been from of old,
ever since man[i] was placed on the earth,
5 that the mirth of the wicked is brief,
the joy of the godless lasts but a moment.
6 Though his pride reaches to the heavens
and his head touches the clouds,
7 he will perish forever, like his own dung;
those who have seen him will say, 'Where is he?'
8 Like a dream he flies away, no more to be found,
banished like a vision of the night.
9 The eye that saw him will not see him again;
his place will look on him no more.
10 His children must make amends to the poor;
his own hands must give back his wealth.
11 The youthful vigor that fills his bones
will lie with him in the dust.

12 "Though evil is sweet in his mouth
and he hides it under his tongue,
13 though he cannot bear to let it go
and keeps it in his mouth,
14 yet his food will turn sour in his stomach;
it will become the venom of serpents within him.
15 He will spit out the riches he swallowed;
God will make his stomach vomit them up.
16 He will suck the poison of serpents;
the fangs of an adder will kill him.
17 He will not enjoy the streams,
the rivers flowing with honey and cream.
18 What he toiled for he must give back uneaten;

[a] 20 Or *only my gums* [b] 24 Or *and* [c] 25 Or *defender* [d] 25 Or *upon my grave* [e] 26 Or *And after I awake, / though this ⌊body⌋ has been destroyed, / then* [f] 26 Or */ apart from* [g] 28 Many Hebrew manuscripts, Septuagint and Vulgate; most Hebrew manuscripts *me* [h] 29 Or */ that you may come to know the Almighty* [i] 4 Or *Adam*

he will not enjoy the profit from his
trading.
19 For he has oppressed the poor and left them
destitute;
he has seized houses he did not build.

20 "Surely he will have no respite from his
craving;
he cannot save himself by his treasure.
21 Nothing is left for him to devour;
his prosperity will not endure.
22 In the midst of his plenty, distress will
overtake him;
the full force of misery will come upon
him.
23 When he has filled his belly,
God will vent his burning anger against
him
and rain down his blows upon him.
24 Though he flees from an iron weapon,
a bronze-tipped arrow pierces him.
25 He pulls it out of his back,
the gleaming point out of his liver.
Terrors will come over him;
26 total darkness lies in wait for his treasures.
A fire unfanned will consume him
and devour what is left in his tent.
27 The heavens will expose his guilt;
the earth will rise up against him.
28 A flood will carry off his house,
rushing waters[a] on the day of God's
wrath.
29 Such is the fate God allots the wicked,
the heritage appointed for them by God."

Job

21 Then Job replied:

2 "Listen carefully to my words;
let this be the consolation you give me.
3 Bear with me while I speak,
and after I have spoken, mock on.

4 "Is my complaint directed to man?
Why should I not be impatient?
5 Look at me and be astonished;
clap your hand over your mouth.
6 When I think about this, I am terrified;
trembling seizes my body.
7 Why do the wicked live on,
growing old and increasing in power?
8 They see their children established around
them,
their offspring before their eyes.
9 Their homes are safe and free from fear;
the rod of God is not upon them.
10 Their bulls never fail to breed;
their cows calve and do not miscarry.
11 They send forth their children as a flock;
their little ones dance about.
12 They sing to the music of tambourine and
harp;
they make merry to the sound of the flute.
13 They spend their years in prosperity
and go down to the grave[b] in peace.[c]
14 Yet they say to God, 'Leave us alone!
We have no desire to know your ways.
15 Who is the Almighty, that we should serve
him?
What would we gain by praying to him?'
16 But their prosperity is not in their own
hands,
so I stand aloof from the counsel of the
wicked.

17 "Yet how often is the lamp of the wicked
snuffed out?
How often does calamity come upon them,
the fate God allots in his anger?
18 How often are they like straw before the
wind,
like chaff swept away by a gale?
19 ⌊It is said,⌋ 'God stores up a man's
punishment for his sons.'
Let him repay the man himself, so that he
will know it!
20 Let his own eyes see his destruction;
let him drink of the wrath of the
Almighty.[d]
21 For what does he care about the family he
leaves behind
when his allotted months come to an end?

22 "Can anyone teach knowledge to God,
since he judges even the highest?
23 One man dies in full vigor,
completely secure and at ease,
24 his body[e] well nourished,
his bones rich with marrow.
25 Another man dies in bitterness of soul,
never having enjoyed anything good.
26 Side by side they lie in the dust,
and worms cover them both.

27 "I know full well what you are thinking,
the schemes by which you would wrong
me.
28 You say, 'Where now is the great man's
house,
the tents where wicked men lived?'
29 Have you never questioned those who travel?
Have you paid no regard to their
accounts—

[a] *28* Or *The possessions in his house will be carried off, / washed away* [b] *13* Hebrew *Sheol* [c] *13* Or *in an instant*
[d] *17-20* Verses 17 and 18 may be taken as exclamations and 19 and 20 as declarations. [e] *24* The meaning of the Hebrew for this word is uncertain.

30 that the evil man is spared from the day of calamity,
that he is delivered from[a] the day of wrath?
31 Who denounces his conduct to his face?
Who repays him for what he has done?
32 He is carried to the grave,
and watch is kept over his tomb.
33 The soil in the valley is sweet to him;
all men follow after him,
and a countless throng goes[b] before him.

34 "So how can you console me with your nonsense?
Nothing is left of your answers but falsehood!"

Eliphaz

22 Then Eliphaz the Temanite replied:
2 "Can a man be of benefit to God?
Can even a wise man benefit him?
3 What pleasure would it give the Almighty if you were righteous?
What would he gain if your ways were blameless?

4 "Is it for your piety that he rebukes you
and brings charges against you?
5 Is not your wickedness great?
Are not your sins endless?
6 You demanded security from your brothers for no reason;
you stripped men of their clothing, leaving them naked.
7 You gave no water to the weary
and you withheld food from the hungry,
8 though you were a powerful man, owning land—
an honored man, living on it.
9 And you sent widows away empty-handed
and broke the strength of the fatherless.
10 That is why snares are all around you,
why sudden peril terrifies you,
11 why it is so dark you cannot see,
and why a flood of water covers you.

12 "Is not God in the heights of heaven?
And see how lofty are the highest stars!
13 Yet you say, 'What does God know?
Does he judge through such darkness?
14 Thick clouds veil him, so he does not see us
as he goes about in the vaulted heavens.'
15 Will you keep to the old path
that evil men have trod?
16 They were carried off before their time,
their foundations washed away by a flood.
17 They said to God, 'Leave us alone!
What can the Almighty do to us?'
18 Yet it was he who filled their houses with good things,
so I stand aloof from the counsel of the wicked.

19 "The righteous see their ruin and rejoice;
the innocent mock them, saying,
20 'Surely our foes are destroyed,
and fire devours their wealth.'

21 "Submit to God and be at peace with him;
in this way prosperity will come to you.
22 Accept instruction from his mouth
and lay up his words in your heart.
23 If you return to the Almighty, you will be restored:
If you remove wickedness far from your tent
24 and assign your nuggets to the dust,
your gold of Ophir to the rocks in the ravines,
25 then the Almighty will be your gold,
the choicest silver for you.
26 Surely then you will find delight in the Almighty
and will lift up your face to God.
27 You will pray to him, and he will hear you,
and you will fulfill your vows.
28 What you decide on will be done,
and light will shine on your ways.
29 When men are brought low and you say, 'Lift them up!'
then he will save the downcast.
30 He will deliver even one who is not innocent,
who will be delivered through the cleanness of your hands."

Job

23 Then Job replied:
2 "Even today my complaint is bitter;
his hand[c] is heavy in spite of[d] my groaning.
3 If only I knew where to find him;
if only I could go to his dwelling!
4 I would state my case before him
and fill my mouth with arguments.
5 I would find out what he would answer me,
and consider what he would say.
6 Would he oppose me with great power?
No, he would not press charges against me.
7 There an upright man could present his case before him,

[a] 30 Or *man is reserved for the day of calamity, / that he is brought forth to* [b] 33 Or / *as a countless throng went*
[c] 2 Septuagint and Syriac; Hebrew / *the hand on me* [d] 2 Or *heavy on me in*

and I would be delivered forever from my
judge.
8 "But if I go to the east, he is not there;
if I go to the west, I do not find him.
9 When he is at work in the north, I do not
see him;
when he turns to the south, I catch no
glimpse of him.
10 But he knows the way that I take;
when he has tested me, I will come forth
as gold.
11 My feet have closely followed his steps;
I have kept to his way without turning
aside.
12 I have not departed from the commands of
his lips;
I have treasured the words of his mouth
more than my daily bread.

13 "But he stands alone, and who can oppose
him?
He does whatever he pleases.
14 He carries out his decree against me,
and many such plans he still has in store.
15 That is why I am terrified before him;
when I think of all this, I fear him.
16 God has made my heart faint;
the Almighty has terrified me.
17 Yet I am not silenced by the darkness,
by the thick darkness that covers my face.

24 "Why does the Almighty not set times
for judgment?
Why must those who know him look in
vain for such days?
2 Men move boundary stones;
they pasture flocks they have stolen.
3 They drive away the orphan's donkey
and take the widow's ox in pledge.
4 They thrust the needy from the path
and force all the poor of the land into
hiding.
5 Like wild donkeys in the desert,
the poor go about their labor of foraging
food;
the wasteland provides food for their
children.
6 They gather fodder in the fields
and glean in the vineyards of the wicked.
7 Lacking clothes, they spend the night naked;
they have nothing to cover themselves in
the cold.
8 They are drenched by mountain rains
and hug the rocks for lack of shelter.
9 The fatherless child is snatched from the
breast;
the infant of the poor is seized for a debt.
10 Lacking clothes, they go about naked;
they carry the sheaves, but still go hungry.
11 They crush olives among the terraces[a];
they tread the winepresses, yet suffer
thirst.
12 The groans of the dying rise from the city,
and the souls of the wounded cry out for
help.
But God charges no one with wrongdoing.

13 "There are those who rebel against the light,
who do not know its ways
or stay in its paths.
14 When daylight is gone, the murderer rises up
and kills the poor and needy;
in the night he steals forth like a thief.
15 The eye of the adulterer watches for dusk;
he thinks, 'No eye will see me,'
and he keeps his face concealed.
16 In the dark, men break into houses,
but by day they shut themselves in;
they want nothing to do with the light.
17 For all of them, deep darkness is their
morning[b];
they make friends with the terrors of
darkness.[c]

18 "Yet they are foam on the surface of the
water;
their portion of the land is cursed,
so that no one goes to the vineyards.
19 As heat and drought snatch away the melted
snow,
so the grave[d] snatches away those who
have sinned.
20 The womb forgets them,
the worm feasts on them;
evil men are no longer remembered
but are broken like a tree.
21 They prey on the barren and childless
woman,
and to the widow show no kindness.
22 But God drags away the mighty by his
power;
though they become established, they have
no assurance of life.
23 He may let them rest in a feeling of security,
but his eyes are on their ways.
24 For a little while they are exalted, and then
they are gone;
they are brought low and gathered up like
all others;
they are cut off like heads of grain.

25 "If this is not so, who can prove me false
and reduce my words to nothing?"

[a] 11 Or *olives between the millstones*; the meaning of the Hebrew for this word is uncertain. [b] 17 Or *them, their morning is like the shadow of death* [c] 17 Or *of the shadow of death* [d] 19 Hebrew *Sheol*

Bildad

25 Then Bildad the Shuhite replied:

2"Dominion and awe belong to God;
he establishes order in the heights of heaven.
3Can his forces be numbered?
Upon whom does his light not rise?
4How then can a man be righteous before God?
How can one born of woman be pure?
5If even the moon is not bright
and the stars are not pure in his eyes,
6how much less man, who is but a maggot—
a son of man, who is only a worm!"

Job

26 Then Job replied:

2"How you have helped the powerless!
How you have saved the arm that is feeble!
3What advice you have offered to one without wisdom!
And what great insight you have displayed!
4Who has helped you utter these words?
And whose spirit spoke from your mouth?

5"The dead are in deep anguish,
those beneath the waters and all that live in them.
6Death[a] is naked before God;
Destruction[b] lies uncovered.
7He spreads out the northern ⌞skies⌟ over empty space;
he suspends the earth over nothing.
8He wraps up the waters in his clouds,
yet the clouds do not burst under their weight.
9He covers the face of the full moon,
spreading his clouds over it.
10He marks out the horizon on the face of the waters
for a boundary between light and darkness.
11The pillars of the heavens quake,
aghast at his rebuke.
12By his power he churned up the sea;
by his wisdom he cut Rahab to pieces.
13By his breath the skies became fair;
his hand pierced the gliding serpent.
14And these are but the outer fringe of his works;
how faint the whisper we hear of him!
Who then can understand the thunder of his power?"

27 And Job continued his discourse:

2"As surely as God lives, who has denied me justice,
the Almighty, who has made me taste bitterness of soul,
3as long as I have life within me,
the breath of God in my nostrils,
4my lips will not speak wickedness,
and my tongue will utter no deceit.
5I will never admit you are in the right;
till I die, I will not deny my integrity.
6I will maintain my righteousness and never let go of it;
my conscience will not reproach me as long as I live.

7"May my enemies be like the wicked,
my adversaries like the unjust!
8For what hope has the godless when he is cut off,
when God takes away his life?
9Does God listen to his cry
when distress comes upon him?
10Will he find delight in the Almighty?
Will he call upon God at all times?

11"I will teach you about the power of God;
the ways of the Almighty I will not conceal.
12You have all seen this yourselves.
Why then this meaningless talk?

13"Here is the fate God allots to the wicked,
the heritage a ruthless man receives from the Almighty:
14However many his children, their fate is the sword;
his offspring will never have enough to eat.
15The plague will bury those who survive him,
and their widows will not weep for them.
16Though he heaps up silver like dust
and clothes like piles of clay,
17what he lays up the righteous will wear,
and the innocent will divide his silver.
18The house he builds is like a moth's cocoon,
like a hut made by a watchman.
19He lies down wealthy, but will do so no more;
when he opens his eyes, all is gone.
20Terrors overtake him like a flood;
a tempest snatches him away in the night.
21The east wind carries him off, and he is gone;
it sweeps him out of his place.
22It hurls itself against him without mercy
as he flees headlong from its power.

[a]6 Hebrew *Sheol* [b]6 Hebrew *Abaddon*

23It claps its hands in derision
and hisses him out of his place.

28 "There is a mine for silver
and a place where gold is refined.
2Iron is taken from the earth,
and copper is smelted from ore.
3Man puts an end to the darkness;
he searches the farthest recesses
for ore in the blackest darkness.
4Far from where people dwell he cuts a shaft,
in places forgotten by the foot of man;
far from men he dangles and sways.
5The earth, from which food comes,
is transformed below as by fire;
6sapphires[a] come from its rocks,
and its dust contains nuggets of gold.
7No bird of prey knows that hidden path,
no falcon's eye has seen it.
8Proud beasts do not set foot on it,
and no lion prowls there.
9Man's hand assaults the flinty rock
and lays bare the roots of the mountains.
10He tunnels through the rock;
his eyes see all its treasures.
11He searches[b] the sources of the rivers
and brings hidden things to light.

12"But where can wisdom be found?
Where does understanding dwell?
13Man does not comprehend its worth;
it cannot be found in the land of the living.
14The deep says, 'It is not in me';
the sea says, 'It is not with me.'
15It cannot be bought with the finest gold,
nor can its price be weighed in silver.
16It cannot be bought with the gold of Ophir,
with precious onyx or sapphires.
17Neither gold nor crystal can compare with it,
nor can it be had for jewels of gold.
18Coral and jasper are not worthy of mention;
the price of wisdom is beyond rubies.
19The topaz of Cush cannot compare with it;
it cannot be bought with pure gold.

20"Where then does wisdom come from?
Where does understanding dwell?
21It is hidden from the eyes of every living thing,
concealed even from the birds of the air.
22Destruction[c] and Death say,
'Only a rumor of it has reached our ears.'
23God understands the way to it
and he alone knows where it dwells,
24for he views the ends of the earth
and sees everything under the heavens.
25When he established the force of the wind
and measured out the waters,
26when he made a decree for the rain
and a path for the thunderstorm,
27then he looked at wisdom and appraised it;
he confirmed it and tested it.
28And he said to man,
'The fear of the Lord—that is wisdom,
and to shun evil is understanding.'"

29 Job continued his discourse:

2"How I long for the months gone by,
for the days when God watched over me,
3when his lamp shone upon my head
and by his light I walked through darkness!
4Oh, for the days when I was in my prime,
when God's intimate friendship blessed my house,
5when the Almighty was still with me
and my children were around me,
6when my path was drenched with cream
and the rock poured out for me streams of olive oil.

7"When I went to the gate of the city
and took my seat in the public square,
8the young men saw me and stepped aside
and the old men rose to their feet;
9the chief men refrained from speaking
and covered their mouths with their hands;
10the voices of the nobles were hushed,
and their tongues stuck to the roof of their mouths.
11Whoever heard me spoke well of me,
and those who saw me commended me,
12because I rescued the poor who cried for help,
and the fatherless who had none to assist him.
13The man who was dying blessed me;
I made the widow's heart sing.
14I put on righteousness as my clothing;
justice was my robe and my turban.
15I was eyes to the blind
and feet to the lame.
16I was a father to the needy;
I took up the case of the stranger.
17I broke the fangs of the wicked
and snatched the victims from their teeth.

18"I thought, 'I will die in my own house,
my days as numerous as the grains of sand.
19My roots will reach to the water,
and the dew will lie all night on my branches.

[a]6 Or *lapis lazuli*; also in verse 16 [b]11 Septuagint, Aquila and Vulgate; Hebrew *He dams up* [c]22 Hebrew *Abaddon*

20My glory will remain fresh in me,
the bow ever new in my hand.'

21"Men listened to me expectantly,
waiting in silence for my counsel.
22After I had spoken, they spoke no more;
my words fell gently on their ears.
23They waited for me as for showers
and drank in my words as the spring rain.
24When I smiled at them, they scarcely
believed it;
the light of my face was precious to
them.[a]
25I chose the way for them and sat as their
chief;
I dwelt as a king among his troops;
I was like one who comforts mourners.

30 "But now they mock me,
men younger than I,
whose fathers I would have disdained
to put with my sheep dogs.
2Of what use was the strength of their hands
to me,
since their vigor had gone from them?
3Haggard from want and hunger,
they roamed[b] the parched land
in desolate wastelands at night.
4In the brush they gathered salt herbs,
and their food[c] was the root of the
broom tree.
5They were banished from their fellow men,
shouted at as if they were thieves.
6They were forced to live in the dry stream
beds,
among the rocks and in holes in the
ground.
7They brayed among the bushes
and huddled in the undergrowth.
8A base and nameless brood,
they were driven out of the land.

9"And now their sons mock me in song;
I have become a byword among them.
10They detest me and keep their distance;
they do not hesitate to spit in my face.
11Now that God has unstrung my bow and
afflicted me,
they throw off restraint in my presence.
12On my right the tribe[d] attacks;
they lay snares for my feet,
they build their siege ramps against me.
13They break up my road;
they succeed in destroying me—
without anyone's helping them.[e]
14They advance as through a gaping breach;
amid the ruins they come rolling in.
15Terrors overwhelm me;
my dignity is driven away as by the wind,
my safety vanishes like a cloud.

16"And now my life ebbs away;
days of suffering grip me.
17Night pierces my bones;
my gnawing pains never rest.
18In his great power ⌞God⌟ becomes like
clothing to me[f];
he binds me like the neck of my garment.
19He throws me into the mud,
and I am reduced to dust and ashes.

20"I cry out to you, O God, but you do not
answer;
I stand up, but you merely look at me.
21You turn on me ruthlessly;
with the might of your hand you attack
me.
22You snatch me up and drive me before the
wind;
you toss me about in the storm.
23I know you will bring me down to death,
to the place appointed for all the living.

24"Surely no one lays a hand on a broken man
when he cries for help in his distress.
25Have I not wept for those in trouble?
Has not my soul grieved for the poor?
26Yet when I hoped for good, evil came;
when I looked for light, then came
darkness.
27The churning inside me never stops;
days of suffering confront me.
28I go about blackened, but not by the sun;
I stand up in the assembly and cry for
help.
29I have become a brother of jackals,
a companion of owls.
30My skin grows black and peels;
my body burns with fever.
31My harp is tuned to mourning,
and my flute to the sound of wailing.

31 "I made a covenant with my eyes
not to look lustfully at a girl.
2For what is man's lot from God above,
his heritage from the Almighty on high?
3Is it not ruin for the wicked,
disaster for those who do wrong?
4Does he not see my ways
and count my every step?

5"If I have walked in falsehood
or my foot has hurried after deceit—
6let God weigh me in honest scales
and he will know that I am blameless—

[a]24 The meaning of the Hebrew for this clause is uncertain. [b]3 Or *gnawed* [c]4 Or *fuel* [d]12 The meaning of the Hebrew for this word is uncertain. [e]13 Or *me. / 'No one can help him,' ⌞they say⌟.* [f]18 Hebrew; Septuagint ⌞*God*⌟ *grasps my clothing*

7if my steps have turned from the path,
if my heart has been led by my eyes,
or if my hands have been defiled,
8then may others eat what I have sown,
and may my crops be uprooted.

9"If my heart has been enticed by a woman,
or if I have lurked at my neighbor's door,
10then may my wife grind another man's grain,
and may other men sleep with her.
11For that would have been shameful,
a sin to be judged.
12It is a fire that burns to Destruction[a];
it would have uprooted my harvest.

13"If I have denied justice to my menservants
and maidservants
when they had a grievance against me,
14what will I do when God confronts me?
What will I answer when called to
account?
15Did not he who made me in the womb make
them?
Did not the same one form us both within
our mothers?

16"If I have denied the desires of the poor
or let the eyes of the widow grow weary,
17if I have kept my bread to myself,
not sharing it with the fatherless—
18but from my youth I reared him as would a
father,
and from my birth I guided the widow—
19if I have seen anyone perishing for lack of
clothing,
or a needy man without a garment,
20and his heart did not bless me
for warming him with the fleece from my
sheep,
21if I have raised my hand against the
fatherless,
knowing that I had influence in court,
22then let my arm fall from the shoulder,
let it be broken off at the joint.
23For I dreaded destruction from God,
and for fear of his splendor I could not do
such things.

24"If I have put my trust in gold
or said to pure gold, 'You are my security,'
25if I have rejoiced over my great wealth,
the fortune my hands had gained,
26if I have regarded the sun in its radiance
or the moon moving in splendor,
27so that my heart was secretly enticed
and my hand offered them a kiss of
homage,
28then these also would be sins to be judged,
for I would have been unfaithful to God on
high.

29"If I have rejoiced at my enemy's misfortune
or gloated over the trouble that came to
him—
30I have not allowed my mouth to sin
by invoking a curse against his life—
31if the men of my household have never said,
'Who has not had his fill of Job's meat?'—
32but no stranger had to spend the night in the
street,
for my door was always open to the
traveler—
33if I have concealed my sin as men do,[b]
by hiding my guilt in my heart
34because I so feared the crowd
and so dreaded the contempt of the clans
that I kept silent and would not go outside

35("Oh, that I had someone to hear me!
I sign now my defense—let the Almighty
answer me;
let my accuser put his indictment in
writing.
36Surely I would wear it on my shoulder,
I would put it on like a crown.
37I would give him an account of my every
step;
like a prince I would approach him.)—

38"if my land cries out against me
and all its furrows are wet with tears,
39if I have devoured its yield without payment
or broken the spirit of its tenants,
40then let briers come up instead of wheat
and weeds instead of barley."

The words of Job are ended.

Elihu

32 So these three men stopped answering
Job, because he was righteous in his own
eyes. 2But Elihu son of Barakel the Buzite, of the
family of Ram, became very angry with Job for
justifying himself rather than God. 3He was also
angry with the three friends, because they had
found no way to refute Job, and yet had condemned him.[c] 4Now Elihu had waited before
speaking to Job because they were older than he.
5But when he saw that the three men had nothing more to say, his anger was aroused.
6So Elihu son of Barakel the Buzite said:

"I am young in years,
and you are old;
that is why I was fearful,
not daring to tell you what I know.
7I thought, 'Age should speak;

a12 Hebrew *Abaddon* b33 Or *as Adam did* c3 Masoretic Text; an ancient Hebrew scribal tradition *Job, and so had condemned God*

advanced years should teach wisdom.'
8 But it is the spirit[a] in a man,
the breath of the Almighty, that gives him understanding.
9 It is not only the old[b] who are wise,
not only the aged who understand what is right.

10 "Therefore I say: Listen to me;
I too will tell you what I know.
11 I waited while you spoke,
I listened to your reasoning;
while you were searching for words,
12 I gave you my full attention.
But not one of you has proved Job wrong;
none of you has answered his arguments.
13 Do not say, 'We have found wisdom;
let God refute him, not man.'
14 But Job has not marshaled his words against me,
and I will not answer him with your arguments.

15 "They are dismayed and have no more to say;
words have failed them.
16 Must I wait, now that they are silent,
now that they stand there with no reply?
17 I too will have my say;
I too will tell what I know.
18 For I am full of words,
and the spirit within me compels me;
19 inside I am like bottled-up wine,
like new wineskins ready to burst.
20 I must speak and find relief;
I must open my lips and reply.
21 I will show partiality to no one,
nor will I flatter any man;
22 for if I were skilled in flattery,
my Maker would soon take me away.

33 "But now, Job, listen to my words;
pay attention to everything I say.
2 I am about to open my mouth;
my words are on the tip of my tongue.
3 My words come from an upright heart;
my lips sincerely speak what I know.
4 The Spirit of God has made me;
the breath of the Almighty gives me life.
5 Answer me then, if you can;
prepare yourself and confront me.
6 I am just like you before God;
I too have been taken from clay.
7 No fear of me should alarm you,
nor should my hand be heavy upon you.

8 "But you have said in my hearing—
I heard the very words—
9 'I am pure and without sin;
I am clean and free from guilt.
10 Yet God has found fault with me;
he considers me his enemy.
11 He fastens my feet in shackles;
he keeps close watch on all my paths.'

12 "But I tell you, in this you are not right,
for God is greater than man.
13 Why do you complain to him
that he answers none of man's words[c]?
14 For God does speak—now one way, now another—
though man may not perceive it.
15 In a dream, in a vision of the night,
when deep sleep falls on men
as they slumber in their beds,
16 he may speak in their ears
and terrify them with warnings,
17 to turn man from wrongdoing
and keep him from pride,
18 to preserve his soul from the pit,[d]
his life from perishing by the sword.[e]
19 Or a man may be chastened on a bed of pain
with constant distress in his bones,
20 so that his very being finds food repulsive
and his soul loathes the choicest meal.
21 His flesh wastes away to nothing,
and his bones, once hidden, now stick out.
22 His soul draws near to the pit,[f]
and his life to the messengers of death.[g]
23 "Yet if there is an angel on his side
as a mediator, one out of a thousand,
to tell a man what is right for him,
24 to be gracious to him and say,
'Spare him from going down to the pit[h];
I have found a ransom for him'—
25 then his flesh is renewed like a child's;
it is restored as in the days of his youth.
26 He prays to God and finds favor with him,
he sees God's face and shouts for joy;
he is restored by God to his righteous state.
27 Then he comes to men and says,
'I sinned, and perverted what was right,
but I did not get what I deserved.
28 He redeemed my soul from going down to the pit,[i]
and I will live to enjoy the light.'

29 "God does all these things to a man—
twice, even three times—
30 to turn back his soul from the pit,[j]
that the light of life may shine on him.

[a] 8 Or *Spirit*; also in verse 18 [b] 9 Or *many*; or *great* [c] 13 Or *that he does not answer for any of his actions*
[d] 18 Or *preserve him from the grave* [e] 18 Or *from crossing the River* [f] 22 Or *He draws near to the grave* [g] 22 Or *to the dead* [h] 24 Or *grave* [i] 28 Or *redeemed me from going down to the grave* [j] 30 Or *turn him back from the grave*

31 "Pay attention, Job, and listen to me;
be silent, and I will speak.
32 If you have anything to say, answer me;
speak up, for I want you to be cleared.
33 But if not, then listen to me;
be silent, and I will teach you wisdom."

34

Then Elihu said:

2 "Hear my words, you wise men;
listen to me, you men of learning.
3 For the ear tests words
as the tongue tastes food.
4 Let us discern for ourselves what is right;
let us learn together what is good.

5 "Job says, 'I am innocent,
but God denies me justice.
6 Although I am right,
I am considered a liar;
although I am guiltless,
his arrow inflicts an incurable wound.'
7 What man is like Job,
who drinks scorn like water?
8 He keeps company with evildoers;
he associates with wicked men.
9 For he says, 'It profits a man nothing
when he tries to please God.'

10 "So listen to me, you men of understanding.
Far be it from God to do evil,
from the Almighty to do wrong.
11 He repays a man for what he has done;
he brings upon him what his conduct
deserves.
12 It is unthinkable that God would do wrong,
that the Almighty would pervert justice.
13 Who appointed him over the earth?
Who put him in charge of the whole
world?
14 If it were his intention
and he withdrew his spirit[a] and breath,
15 all mankind would perish together
and man would return to the dust.

16 "If you have understanding, hear this;
listen to what I say.
17 Can he who hates justice govern?
Will you condemn the just and mighty
One?
18 Is he not the One who says to kings, 'You
are worthless,'
and to nobles, 'You are wicked,'
19 who shows no partiality to princes
and does not favor the rich over the poor,
for they are all the work of his hands?
20 They die in an instant, in the middle of the
night;
the people are shaken and they pass away;
the mighty are removed without human
hand.

21 "His eyes are on the ways of men;
he sees their every step.
22 There is no dark place, no deep shadow,
where evildoers can hide.
23 God has no need to examine men further,
that they should come before him for
judgment.
24 Without inquiry he shatters the mighty
and sets up others in their place.
25 Because he takes note of their deeds,
he overthrows them in the night and they
are crushed.
26 He punishes them for their wickedness
where everyone can see them,
27 because they turned from following him
and had no regard for any of his ways.
28 They caused the cry of the poor to come
before him,
so that he heard the cry of the needy.
29 But if he remains silent, who can condemn
him?
If he hides his face, who can see him?
Yet he is over man and nation alike,
30 to keep a godless man from ruling,
from laying snares for the people.

31 "Suppose a man says to God,
'I am guilty but will offend no more.
32 Teach me what I cannot see;
if I have done wrong, I will not do so
again.'
33 Should God then reward you on your terms,
when you refuse to repent?
You must decide, not I;
so tell me what you know.

34 "Men of understanding declare,
wise men who hear me say to me,
35 'Job speaks without knowledge;
his words lack insight.'
36 Oh, that Job might be tested to the utmost
for answering like a wicked man!
37 To his sin he adds rebellion;
scornfully he claps his hands among us
and multiplies his words against God."

35

Then Elihu said:

2 "Do you think this is just?
You say, 'I will be cleared by God.[b]'
3 Yet you ask him, 'What profit is it to me,[c]
and what do I gain by not sinning?'

4 "I would like to reply to you
and to your friends with you.

[a] 14 Or *Spirit* [b] 2 Or *My righteousness is more than God's* [c] 3 Or *you*

5Look up at the heavens and see;
gaze at the clouds so high above you.
6If you sin, how does that affect him?
If your sins are many, what does that do to him?
7If you are righteous, what do you give to him,
or what does he receive from your hand?
8Your wickedness affects only a man like yourself,
and your righteousness only the sons of men.

9"Men cry out under a load of oppression;
they plead for relief from the arm of the powerful.
10But no one says, 'Where is God my Maker,
who gives songs in the night,
11who teaches more to us than to[a] the beasts of the earth
and makes us wiser than[b] the birds of the air?'
12He does not answer when men cry out
because of the arrogance of the wicked.
13Indeed, God does not listen to their empty plea;
the Almighty pays no attention to it.
14How much less, then, will he listen
when you say that you do not see him,
that your case is before him
and you must wait for him,
15and further, that his anger never punishes
and he does not take the least notice of wickedness.[c]
16So Job opens his mouth with empty talk;
without knowledge he multiplies words."

36

Elihu continued:

2"Bear with me a little longer and I will show you
that there is more to be said in God's behalf.
3I get my knowledge from afar;
I will ascribe justice to my Maker.
4Be assured that my words are not false;
one perfect in knowledge is with you.

5"God is mighty, but does not despise men;
he is mighty, and firm in his purpose.
6He does not keep the wicked alive
but gives the afflicted their rights.
7He does not take his eyes off the righteous;
he enthrones them with kings
and exalts them forever.
8But if men are bound in chains,
held fast by cords of affliction,
9he tells them what they have done—
that they have sinned arrogantly.
10He makes them listen to correction
and commands them to repent of their evil.
11If they obey and serve him,
they will spend the rest of their days in prosperity
and their years in contentment.
12But if they do not listen,
they will perish by the sword[d]
and die without knowledge.

13"The godless in heart harbor resentment;
even when he fetters them, they do not cry for help.
14They die in their youth,
among male prostitutes of the shrines.
15But those who suffer he delivers in their suffering;
he speaks to them in their affliction.

16"He is wooing you from the jaws of distress
to a spacious place free from restriction,
to the comfort of your table laden with choice food.
17But now you are laden with the judgment due the wicked;
judgment and justice have taken hold of you.
18Be careful that no one entices you by riches;
do not let a large bribe turn you aside.
19Would your wealth
or even all your mighty efforts
sustain you so you would not be in distress?
20Do not long for the night,
to drag people away from their homes.[e]
21Beware of turning to evil,
which you seem to prefer to affliction.

22"God is exalted in his power.
Who is a teacher like him?
23Who has prescribed his ways for him,
or said to him, 'You have done wrong'?
24Remember to extol his work,
which men have praised in song.
25All mankind has seen it;
men gaze on it from afar.
26How great is God—beyond our understanding!
The number of his years is past finding out.

27"He draws up the drops of water,
which distill as rain to the streams[f];

a11 Or *teaches us by* b11 Or *us wise by* c15 Symmachus, Theodotion and Vulgate; the meaning of the Hebrew for this word is uncertain. d12 Or *will cross the River* e20 The meaning of the Hebrew for verses 18-20 is uncertain. f27 Or *distill from the mist as rain*

28the clouds pour down their moisture
and abundant showers fall on mankind.
29Who can understand how he spreads out the clouds,
how he thunders from his pavilion?
30See how he scatters his lightning about him,
bathing the depths of the sea.
31This is the way he governs[a] the nations
and provides food in abundance.
32He fills his hands with lightning
and commands it to strike its mark.
33His thunder announces the coming storm;
even the cattle make known its approach.[b]

37 "At this my heart pounds
and leaps from its place.
2Listen! Listen to the roar of his voice,
to the rumbling that comes from his mouth.
3He unleashes his lightning beneath the whole heaven
and sends it to the ends of the earth.
4After that comes the sound of his roar;
he thunders with his majestic voice.
When his voice resounds,
he holds nothing back.
5God's voice thunders in marvelous ways;
he does great things beyond our understanding.
6He says to the snow, 'Fall on the earth,'
and to the rain shower, 'Be a mighty downpour.'
7So that all men he has made may know his work,
he stops every man from his labor.[c]
8The animals take cover;
they remain in their dens.
9The tempest comes out from its chamber,
the cold from the driving winds.
10The breath of God produces ice,
and the broad waters become frozen.
11He loads the clouds with moisture;
he scatters his lightning through them.
12At his direction they swirl around
over the face of the whole earth
to do whatever he commands them.
13He brings the clouds to punish men,
or to water his earth[d] and show his love.
14"Listen to this, Job;
stop and consider God's wonders.
15Do you know how God controls the clouds
and makes his lightning flash?
16Do you know how the clouds hang poised,
those wonders of him who is perfect in knowledge?
17You who swelter in your clothes
when the land lies hushed under the south wind,
18can you join him in spreading out the skies,
hard as a mirror of cast bronze?
19"Tell us what we should say to him;
we cannot draw up our case because of our darkness.
20Should he be told that I want to speak?
Would any man ask to be swallowed up?
21Now no one can look at the sun,
bright as it is in the skies
after the wind has swept them clean.
22Out of the north he comes in golden splendor;
God comes in awesome majesty.
23The Almighty is beyond our reach and exalted in power;
in his justice and great righteousness, he does not oppress.
24Therefore, men revere him,
for does he not have regard for all the wise in heart?[e]"

The LORD Speaks

38 Then the LORD answered Job out of the storm. He said:
2"Who is this that darkens my counsel
with words without knowledge?
3Brace yourself like a man;
I will question you,
and you shall answer me.
4"Where were you when I laid the earth's foundation?
Tell me, if you understand.
5Who marked off its dimensions? Surely you know!
Who stretched a measuring line across it?
6On what were its footings set,
or who laid its cornerstone—
7while the morning stars sang together
and all the angels[f] shouted for joy?
8"Who shut up the sea behind doors
when it burst forth from the womb,
9when I made the clouds its garment
and wrapped it in thick darkness,
10when I fixed limits for it
and set its doors and bars in place,
11when I said, 'This far you may come and no farther;
here is where your proud waves halt'?

[a]31 Or *nourishes* [b]33 Or *announces his coming— / the One zealous against evil* [c]7 Or / *he fills all men with fear by his power* [d]13 Or *to favor them* [e]24 Or *for he does not have regard for any who think they are wise.* [f]7 Hebrew *the sons of God*

12"Have you ever given orders to the morning,
or shown the dawn its place,
13that it might take the earth by the edges
and shake the wicked out of it?
14The earth takes shape like clay under a seal;
its features stand out like those of a
garment.
15The wicked are denied their light,
and their upraised arm is broken.

16"Have you journeyed to the springs of the
sea
or walked in the recesses of the deep?
17Have the gates of death been shown to you?
Have you seen the gates of the shadow of
death[a]?
18Have you comprehended the vast expanses of
the earth?
Tell me, if you know all this.

19"What is the way to the abode of light?
And where does darkness reside?
20Can you take them to their places?
Do you know the paths to their dwellings?
21Surely you know, for you were already born!
You have lived so many years!

22"Have you entered the storehouses of the
snow
or seen the storehouses of the hail,
23which I reserve for times of trouble,
for days of war and battle?
24What is the way to the place where the
lightning is dispersed,
or the place where the east winds are
scattered over the earth?
25Who cuts a channel for the torrents of rain,
and a path for the thunderstorm,
26to water a land where no man lives,
a desert with no one in it,
27to satisfy a desolate wasteland
and make it sprout with grass?
28Does the rain have a father?
Who fathers the drops of dew?
29From whose womb comes the ice?
Who gives birth to the frost from the
heavens
30when the waters become hard as stone,
when the surface of the deep is frozen?

31"Can you bind the beautiful[b] Pleiades?
Can you loose the cords of Orion?
32Can you bring forth the constellations in
their seasons[c]
or lead out the Bear[d] with its cubs?
33Do you know the laws of the heavens?
Can you set up ⌞God's[e]⌟ dominion over
the earth?

34"Can you raise your voice to the clouds
and cover yourself with a flood of water?
35Do you send the lightning bolts on their
way?
Do they report to you, 'Here we are'?
36Who endowed the heart[f] with wisdom
or gave understanding to the mind[f]?
37Who has the wisdom to count the clouds?
Who can tip over the water jars of the
heavens
38when the dust becomes hard
and the clods of earth stick together?

39"Do you hunt the prey for the lioness
and satisfy the hunger of the lions
40when they crouch in their dens
or lie in wait in a thicket?
41Who provides food for the raven
when its young cry out to God
and wander about for lack of food?

39

"Do you know when the mountain
goats give birth?
Do you watch when the doe bears her
fawn?
2Do you count the months till they bear?
Do you know the time they give birth?
3They crouch down and bring forth their
young;
their labor pains are ended.
4Their young thrive and grow strong in the
wilds;
they leave and do not return.

5"Who let the wild donkey go free?
Who untied his ropes?
6I gave him the wasteland as his home,
the salt flats as his habitat.
7He laughs at the commotion in the town;
he does not hear a driver's shout.
8He ranges the hills for his pasture
and searches for any green thing.

9"Will the wild ox consent to serve you?
Will he stay by your manger at night?
10Can you hold him to the furrow with a
harness?
Will he till the valleys behind you?
11Will you rely on him for his great strength?
Will you leave your heavy work to him?
12Can you trust him to bring in your grain
and gather it to your threshing floor?

13"The wings of the ostrich flap joyfully,
but they cannot compare with the pinions
and feathers of the stork.
14She lays her eggs on the ground

[a] 17 Or *gates of deep shadows* [b] 31 Or *the twinkling*; or *the chains of the* [c] 32 Or *the morning star in its season*
[d] 32 Or *out Leo* [e] 33 Or *his*; or *their* [f] 36 The meaning of the Hebrew for this word is uncertain.

and lets them warm in the sand,
15unmindful that a foot may crush them,
that some wild animal may trample them.
16She treats her young harshly, as if they were not hers;
she cares not that her labor was in vain,
17for God did not endow her with wisdom
or give her a share of good sense.
18Yet when she spreads her feathers to run,
she laughs at horse and rider.

19"Do you give the horse his strength
or clothe his neck with a flowing mane?
20Do you make him leap like a locust,
striking terror with his proud snorting?
21He paws fiercely, rejoicing in his strength,
and charges into the fray.
22He laughs at fear, afraid of nothing;
he does not shy away from the sword.
23The quiver rattles against his side,
along with the flashing spear and lance.
24In frenzied excitement he eats up the ground;
he cannot stand still when the trumpet sounds.
25At the blast of the trumpet he snorts, 'Aha!'
He catches the scent of battle from afar,
the shout of commanders and the battle cry.

26"Does the hawk take flight by your wisdom
and spread his wings toward the south?
27Does the eagle soar at your command
and build his nest on high?
28He dwells on a cliff and stays there at night;
a rocky crag is his stronghold.
29From there he seeks out his food;
his eyes detect it from afar.
30His young ones feast on blood,
and where the slain are, there is he."

40 The LORD said to Job:

2"Will the one who contends with the Almighty correct him?
Let him who accuses God answer him!"

3Then Job answered the LORD:

4"I am unworthy—how can I reply to you?
I put my hand over my mouth.
5I spoke once, but I have no answer—
twice, but I will say no more."

6Then the LORD spoke to Job out of the storm:

7"Brace yourself like a man;
I will question you,
and you shall answer me.

8"Would you discredit my justice?
Would you condemn me to justify yourself?
9Do you have an arm like God's,
and can your voice thunder like his?
10Then adorn yourself with glory and splendor,
and clothe yourself in honor and majesty.
11Unleash the fury of your wrath,
look at every proud man and bring him low,
12look at every proud man and humble him,
crush the wicked where they stand.
13Bury them all in the dust together;
shroud their faces in the grave.
14Then I myself will admit to you
that your own right hand can save you.

15"Look at the behemoth,[a]
which I made along with you
and which feeds on grass like an ox.
16What strength he has in his loins,
what power in the muscles of his belly!
17His tail[b] sways like a cedar;
the sinews of his thighs are close-knit.
18His bones are tubes of bronze,
his limbs like rods of iron.
19He ranks first among the works of God,
yet his Maker can approach him with his sword.
20The hills bring him their produce,
and all the wild animals play nearby.
21Under the lotus plants he lies,
hidden among the reeds in the marsh.
22The lotuses conceal him in their shadow;
the poplars by the stream surround him.
23When the river rages, he is not alarmed;
he is secure, though the Jordan should surge against his mouth.
24Can anyone capture him by the eyes,[c]
or trap him and pierce his nose?

41 "Can you pull in the leviathan[d] with a fishhook
or tie down his tongue with a rope?
2Can you put a cord through his nose
or pierce his jaw with a hook?
3Will he keep begging you for mercy?
Will he speak to you with gentle words?
4Will he make an agreement with you
for you to take him as your slave for life?
5Can you make a pet of him like a bird
or put him on a leash for your girls?

[a]15 Possibly the hippopotamus or the elephant [b]17 Possibly trunk [c]24 Or *by a water hole* [d]1 Possibly the crocodile

[6]Will traders barter for him?
Will they divide him up among the merchants?
[7]Can you fill his hide with harpoons
or his head with fishing spears?
[8]If you lay a hand on him,
you will remember the struggle and never do it again!
[9]Any hope of subduing him is false;
the mere sight of him is overpowering.
[10]No one is fierce enough to rouse him.
Who then is able to stand against me?
[11]Who has a claim against me that I must pay?
Everything under heaven belongs to me.

[12]"I will not fail to speak of his limbs,
his strength and his graceful form.
[13]Who can strip off his outer coat?
Who would approach him with a bridle?
[14]Who dares open the doors of his mouth,
ringed about with his fearsome teeth?
[15]His back has[a] rows of shields
tightly sealed together;
[16]each is so close to the next
that no air can pass between.
[17]They are joined fast to one another;
they cling together and cannot be parted.
[18]His snorting throws out flashes of light;
his eyes are like the rays of dawn.
[19]Firebrands stream from his mouth;
sparks of fire shoot out.
[20]Smoke pours from his nostrils
as from a boiling pot over a fire of reeds.
[21]His breath sets coals ablaze,
and flames dart from his mouth.
[22]Strength resides in his neck;
dismay goes before him.
[23]The folds of his flesh are tightly joined;
they are firm and immovable.
[24]His chest is hard as rock,
hard as a lower millstone.
[25]When he rises up, the mighty are terrified;
they retreat before his thrashing.
[26]The sword that reaches him has no effect,
nor does the spear or the dart or the javelin.
[27]Iron he treats like straw
and bronze like rotten wood.
[28]Arrows do not make him flee;
slingstones are like chaff to him.
[29]A club seems to him but a piece of straw;
he laughs at the rattling of the lance.
[30]His undersides are jagged potsherds,
leaving a trail in the mud like a threshing sledge.
[31]He makes the depths churn like a boiling caldron
and stirs up the sea like a pot of ointment.
[32]Behind him he leaves a glistening wake;
one would think the deep had white hair.
[33]Nothing on earth is his equal—
a creature without fear.
[34]He looks down on all that are haughty;
he is king over all that are proud."

Job

42 Then Job replied to the LORD:

[2]"I know that you can do all things;
no plan of yours can be thwarted.
[3]⌊You asked,⌋ 'Who is this that obscures my counsel without knowledge?'
Surely I spoke of things I did not understand,
things too wonderful for me to know.

[4]⌊"You said,⌋ 'Listen now, and I will speak;
I will question you,
and you shall answer me.'
[5]My ears had heard of you
but now my eyes have seen you.
[6]Therefore I despise myself
and repent in dust and ashes."

Epilogue

[7]After the LORD had said these things to Job,
he said to Eliphaz the Temanite, "I am angry with
you and your two friends, because you have not
spoken of me what is right, as my servant Job has.
[8]So now take seven bulls and seven rams and go
to my servant Job and sacrifice a burnt offering
for yourselves. My servant Job will pray for you,
and I will accept his prayer and not deal with you
according to your folly. You have not spoken of
me what is right, as my servant Job has." [9]So
Eliphaz the Temanite, Bildad the Shuhite and Zophar the Naamathite did what the LORD told
them; and the LORD accepted Job's prayer.

[10]After Job had prayed for his friends, the LORD
made him prosperous again and gave him twice
as much as he had before. [11]All his brothers and
sisters and everyone who had known him before
came and ate with him in his house. They comforted and consoled him over all the trouble the
LORD had brought upon him, and each one gave
him a piece of silver[b] and a gold ring.

[12]The LORD blessed the latter part of Job's life
more than the first. He had fourteen thousand

[a] 15 Or *His pride is his* [b] 11 Hebrew *him a kesitah*; a kesitah was a unit of money of unknown weight and value.

sheep, six thousand camels, a thousand yoke of
oxen and a thousand donkeys. 13And he also
had seven sons and three daughters. 14The first
daughter he named Jemimah, the second Keziah
and the third Keren-Happuch. 15Nowhere in all
the land were there found women as beautiful as
Job's daughters, and their father granted them
an inheritance along with their brothers.
16After this, Job lived a hundred and forty
years; he saw his children and their children to
the fourth generation. 17And so he died, old and
full of years.

Introduction to
PSALMS

Personal Reading Plan

- ❒ Psalms 1–7
- ❒ Psalms 8–14
- ❒ Psalms 15–18
- ❒ Psalms 19–23
- ❒ Psalms 24–29
- ❒ Psalms 30–33
- ❒ Psalms 34–36
- ❒ Psalms 37–39
- ❒ Psalms 40–44
- ❒ Psalms 45–49
- ❒ Psalms 50–54
- ❒ Psalms 55–60
- ❒ Psalms 61–66
- ❒ Psalms 67–69
- ❒ Psalms 70–72
- ❒ Psalms 73–77
- ❒ Psalms 78–79
- ❒ Psalms 80–83
- ❒ Psalms 84–88
- ❒ Psalms 89–90
- ❒ Psalms 91–95
- ❒ Psalms 96–100
- ❒ Psalms 101–103
- ❒ Psalms 104–105
- ❒ Psalms 106–107
- ❒ Psalms 108–112
- ❒ Psalms 113–118
- ❒ Psalm 119:1–88
- ❒ Psalm 119:89–176
- ❒ Psalms 120–129
- ❒ Psalms 130–137
- ❒ Psalms 138–144
- ❒ Psalms 145–150

Author

King David (e.g. Ps. 3), King Solomon (Pss. 72; 127), the sons of Korah (Pss. 42–49; 84–85; 87–88), Asaph (Pss. 50; 73–83), Heman (Ps. 88), Ethan (Ps. 89), and Moses (Ps. 90) all have psalms attributed to them. Many psalms are anonymous.

Date

Although composed over centuries (c. 1400–400 B.C.), the Psalms may well have been collected and arranged in their present form as the "hymn book" of Israel sometime in the fourth or third century B.C.

Theme

The range of human response to God and his world.

Historical Background

The book of Psalms is a collection of various smaller groupings of psalms that were used in Israel's worship over the centuries. Some psalms were associated with certain feasts (Ps. 130, Yom Kippur; Ps. 135, Passover), others with the Sabbath (Pss. 92–100), and others for confession (Pss. 32; 51) or praise (Pss. 111–118; 146–150).

Characteristics

The moods of the various psalms embrace the whole range of human experience from exuberant praise (Ps. 145) to despair (Ps. 42); from intense anger (Ps. 137) and doubt about God's care (Ps. 73); to hope for a future based precisely upon God's care (Ps. 23). They can help us express emotions that otherwise we might not have words for, or feel right about. The Psalms catch the reality of our up-and-down relationship with God, but they also move us steadily along the path of knowing God.

Passages for Topical Group Study

23:1–6	DEATH and DYING	"The Lord is my shepherd"
46:1–11	WAR	"God is our refuge and strength"
139:1–24	ABORTION	"You knit me together in my mother's womb"

See the Lesson Plans in the front of this Bible.

BOOK I
Psalms 1–41

Psalm 1

1 Blessed is the man
who does not walk in the counsel of the wicked
or stand in the way of sinners
or sit in the seat of mockers.
2 But his delight is in the law of the LORD,
and on his law he meditates day and night.
3 He is like a tree planted by streams of water,
which yields its fruit in season
and whose leaf does not wither.
Whatever he does prospers.

4 Not so the wicked!
They are like chaff
that the wind blows away.
5 Therefore the wicked will not stand in the judgment,
nor sinners in the assembly of the righteous.

6 For the LORD watches over the way of the righteous,
but the way of the wicked will perish.

Psalm 2

1 Why do the nations conspire[a]
and the peoples plot in vain?
2 The kings of the earth take their stand
and the rulers gather together
against the LORD
and against his Anointed One.[b]
3 "Let us break their chains," they say,
"and throw off their fetters."

4 The One enthroned in heaven laughs;
the Lord scoffs at them.
5 Then he rebukes them in his anger
and terrifies them in his wrath, saying,
6 "I have installed my King[c]
on Zion, my holy hill."

7 I will proclaim the decree of the LORD:

He said to me, "You are my Son[d];
today I have become your Father.[e]
8 Ask of me,
and I will make the nations your inheritance,
the ends of the earth your possession.
9 You will rule them with an iron scepter[f];
you will dash them to pieces like pottery."
10 Therefore, you kings, be wise;
be warned, you rulers of the earth.
11 Serve the LORD with fear
and rejoice with trembling.
12 Kiss the Son, lest he be angry
and you be destroyed in your way,
for his wrath can flare up in a moment.
Blessed are all who take refuge in him.

Psalm 3

A psalm of David. When he fled from his son Absalom.

1 O LORD, how many are my foes!
How many rise up against me!
2 Many are saying of me,
"God will not deliver him." *Selah*[g]

3 But you are a shield around me, O LORD;
you bestow glory on me and lift[h] up my head.
4 To the LORD I cry aloud,
and he answers me from his holy hill. *Selah*

5 I lie down and sleep;
I wake again, because the LORD sustains me.
6 I will not fear the tens of thousands
drawn up against me on every side.

7 Arise, O LORD!
Deliver me, O my God!
Strike all my enemies on the jaw;
break the teeth of the wicked.

8 From the LORD comes deliverance.
May your blessing be on your people. *Selah*

Psalm 4

For the director of music. With stringed instruments. A psalm of David.

1 Answer me when I call to you,
O my righteous God.
Give me relief from my distress;
be merciful to me and hear my prayer.

2 How long, O men, will you turn my glory into shame[i]?
How long will you love delusions and seek false gods[j]? *Selah*
3 Know that the LORD has set apart the godly for himself;
the LORD will hear when I call to him.

a 1 Hebrew; Septuagint *rage* b 2 Or *anointed one* c 6 Or *king* d 7 Or *son*; also in verse 12 e 7 Or *have begotten you* f 9 Or *will break them with a rod of iron* g 2 A word of uncertain meaning, occurring frequently in the Psalms; possibly a musical term h 3 Or *LORD, / my Glorious One, who lifts* i 2 Or *you dishonor my Glorious One* j 2 Or *seek lies*

4In your anger do not sin;
when you are on your beds,
search your hearts and be silent. *Selah*
5Offer right sacrifices
and trust in the LORD.

6Many are asking, "Who can show us any good?"
Let the light of your face shine upon us, O LORD.
7You have filled my heart with greater joy
than when their grain and new wine abound.
8I will lie down and sleep in peace,
for you alone, O LORD,
make me dwell in safety.

Psalm 5

For the director of music. For flutes. A psalm of David.

1Give ear to my words, O LORD,
consider my sighing.
2Listen to my cry for help,
my King and my God,
for to you I pray.
3In the morning, O LORD, you hear my voice;
in the morning I lay my requests before you
and wait in expectation.

4You are not a God who takes pleasure in evil;
with you the wicked cannot dwell.
5The arrogant cannot stand in your presence;
you hate all who do wrong.
6You destroy those who tell lies;
bloodthirsty and deceitful men
the LORD abhors.

7But I, by your great mercy,
will come into your house;
in reverence will I bow down
toward your holy temple.
8Lead me, O LORD, in your righteousness
because of my enemies—
make straight your way before me.

9Not a word from their mouth can be trusted;
their heart is filled with destruction.
Their throat is an open grave;
with their tongue they speak deceit.
10Declare them guilty, O God!
Let their intrigues be their downfall.
Banish them for their many sins,
for they have rebelled against you.

11But let all who take refuge in you be glad;
let them ever sing for joy.
Spread your protection over them,
that those who love your name may rejoice in you.
12For surely, O LORD, you bless the righteous;
you surround them with your favor as with a shield.

Psalm 6

For the director of music. With stringed instruments. According to *sheminith.*[a] A psalm of David.

1O LORD, do not rebuke me in your anger
or discipline me in your wrath.
2Be merciful to me, LORD, for I am faint;
O LORD, heal me, for my bones are in agony.
3My soul is in anguish.
How long, O LORD, how long?

4Turn, O LORD, and deliver me;
save me because of your unfailing love.
5No one remembers you when he is dead.
Who praises you from the grave[b]?

6I am worn out from groaning;
all night long I flood my bed with weeping
and drench my couch with tears.
7My eyes grow weak with sorrow;
they fail because of all my foes.

8Away from me, all you who do evil,
for the LORD has heard my weeping.
9The LORD has heard my cry for mercy;
the LORD accepts my prayer.
10All my enemies will be ashamed and dismayed;
they will turn back in sudden disgrace.

Psalm 7

A *shiggaion*[c] of David, which he sang to the LORD concerning Cush, a Benjamite.

1O LORD my God, I take refuge in you;
save and deliver me from all who pursue me,
2or they will tear me like a lion
and rip me to pieces with no one to rescue me.

3O LORD my God, if I have done this
and there is guilt on my hands—
4if I have done evil to him who is at peace with me
or without cause have robbed my foe—
5then let my enemy pursue and overtake me;
let him trample my life to the ground
and make me sleep in the dust. *Selah*

[a]Title: Probably a musical term [b]5 Hebrew *Sheol* [c]Title: Probably a literary or musical term

6Arise, O LORD, in your anger;
rise up against the rage of my enemies.
Awake, my God; decree justice.
7Let the assembled peoples gather around you.
Rule over them from on high;
8 let the LORD judge the peoples.
Judge me, O LORD, according to my righteousness,
according to my integrity, O Most High.
9O righteous God,
who searches minds and hearts,
bring to an end the violence of the wicked
and make the righteous secure.

10My shield[a] is God Most High,
who saves the upright in heart.
11God is a righteous judge,
a God who expresses his wrath every day.
12If he does not relent,
he[b] will sharpen his sword;
he will bend and string his bow.
13He has prepared his deadly weapons;
he makes ready his flaming arrows.

14He who is pregnant with evil
and conceives trouble gives birth to disillusionment.
15He who digs a hole and scoops it out
falls into the pit he has made.
16The trouble he causes recoils on himself;
his violence comes down on his own head.

17I will give thanks to the LORD because of his righteousness
and will sing praise to the name of the LORD Most High.

Psalm 8

For the director of music. According to *gittith*.[c] A psalm of David.

1O LORD, our Lord,
how majestic is your name in all the earth!

You have set your glory
above the heavens.
2From the lips of children and infants
you have ordained praise[d]
because of your enemies,
to silence the foe and the avenger.

3When I consider your heavens,
the work of your fingers,
the moon and the stars,
which you have set in place,
4what is man that you are mindful of him,
the son of man that you care for him?
5You made him a little lower than the heavenly beings[e]
and crowned him with glory and honor.

6You made him ruler over the works of your hands;
you put everything under his feet:
7all flocks and herds,
and the beasts of the field,
8the birds of the air,
and the fish of the sea,
all that swim the paths of the seas.

9O LORD, our Lord,
how majestic is your name in all the earth!

Psalm 9[f]

For the director of music. To ⌊the tune of⌋ "The Death of the Son." A psalm of David.

1I will praise you, O LORD, with all my heart;
I will tell of all your wonders.
2I will be glad and rejoice in you;
I will sing praise to your name, O Most High.

3My enemies turn back;
they stumble and perish before you.
4For you have upheld my right and my cause;
you have sat on your throne, judging righteously.
5You have rebuked the nations and destroyed the wicked;
you have blotted out their name for ever and ever.
6Endless ruin has overtaken the enemy,
you have uprooted their cities;
even the memory of them has perished.

7The LORD reigns forever;
he has established his throne for judgment.
8He will judge the world in righteousness;
he will govern the peoples with justice.
9The LORD is a refuge for the oppressed,
a stronghold in times of trouble.
10Those who know your name will trust in you,
for you, LORD, have never forsaken those who seek you.

11Sing praises to the LORD, enthroned in Zion;
proclaim among the nations what he has done.
12For he who avenges blood remembers;
he does not ignore the cry of the afflicted.

a10 Or *sovereign* b12 Or *If a man does not repent, / God* cTitle: Probably a musical term d2 Or *strength*
e5 Or *than God* fPsalms 9 and 10 may have been originally a single acrostic poem, the stanzas of which begin with the successive letters of the Hebrew alphabet. In the Septuagint they constitute one psalm.

13O LORD, see how my enemies persecute me!
Have mercy and lift me up from the gates of death,
14that I may declare your praises
in the gates of the Daughter of Zion
and there rejoice in your salvation.
15The nations have fallen into the pit they have dug;
their feet are caught in the net they have hidden.
16The LORD is known by his justice;
the wicked are ensnared by the work of their hands. *Higgaion.*[a] *Selah*
17The wicked return to the grave,[b]
all the nations that forget God.
18But the needy will not always be forgotten,
nor the hope of the afflicted ever perish.

19Arise, O LORD, let not man triumph;
let the nations be judged in your presence.
20Strike them with terror, O LORD;
let the nations know they are but men. *Selah*

Psalm 10[c]

1Why, O LORD, do you stand far off?
Why do you hide yourself in times of trouble?
2In his arrogance the wicked man hunts down the weak,
who are caught in the schemes he devises.
3He boasts of the cravings of his heart;
he blesses the greedy and reviles the LORD.
4In his pride the wicked does not seek him;
in all his thoughts there is no room for God.
5His ways are always prosperous;
he is haughty and your laws are far from him;
he sneers at all his enemies.
6He says to himself, "Nothing will shake me;
I'll always be happy and never have trouble."
7His mouth is full of curses and lies and threats;
trouble and evil are under his tongue.
8He lies in wait near the villages;
from ambush he murders the innocent,
watching in secret for his victims.
9He lies in wait like a lion in cover;
he lies in wait to catch the helpless;
he catches the helpless and drags them off in his net.
10His victims are crushed, they collapse;
they fall under his strength.
11He says to himself, "God has forgotten;
he covers his face and never sees."

12Arise, LORD! Lift up your hand, O God.
Do not forget the helpless.
13Why does the wicked man revile God?
Why does he say to himself,
"He won't call me to account"?
14But you, O God, do see trouble and grief;
you consider it to take it in hand.
The victim commits himself to you;
you are the helper of the fatherless.
15Break the arm of the wicked and evil man;
call him to account for his wickedness
that would not be found out.
16The LORD is King for ever and ever;
the nations will perish from his land.
17You hear, O LORD, the desire of the afflicted;
you encourage them, and you listen to their cry,
18defending the fatherless and the oppressed,
in order that man, who is of the earth,
may terrify no more.

Psalm 11

For the director of music. Of David.

1In the LORD I take refuge.
How then can you say to me:
"Flee like a bird to your mountain.
2For look, the wicked bend their bows;
they set their arrows against the strings
to shoot from the shadows
at the upright in heart.
3When the foundations are being destroyed,
what can the righteous do[d]?"

4The LORD is in his holy temple;
the LORD is on his heavenly throne.
He observes the sons of men;
his eyes examine them.
5The LORD examines the righteous,
but the wicked[e] and those who love violence
his soul hates.
6On the wicked he will rain
fiery coals and burning sulfur;
a scorching wind will be their lot.
7For the LORD is righteous,
he loves justice;
upright men will see his face.

[a]16 Or *Meditation*; possibly a musical notation [b]17 Hebrew *Sheol* [c]Psalms 9 and 10 may have been originally a single acrostic poem, the stanzas of which begin with the successive letters of the Hebrew alphabet. In the Septuagint they constitute one psalm. [d]3 Or *what is the Righteous One doing* [e]5 Or *The LORD, the Righteous One, examines the wicked, /*

Psalm 12

For the director of music. According to *sheminith.*[a] A psalm of David.

1Help, LORD, for the godly are no more;
the faithful have vanished from among men.
2Everyone lies to his neighbor;
their flattering lips speak with deception.

3May the LORD cut off all flattering lips
and every boastful tongue
4that says, "We will triumph with our tongues;
we own our lips[b]—who is our master?"

5"Because of the oppression of the weak
and the groaning of the needy,
I will now arise," says the LORD.
"I will protect them from those who malign them."
6And the words of the LORD are flawless,
like silver refined in a furnace of clay,
purified seven times.

7O LORD, you will keep us safe
and protect us from such people forever.
8The wicked freely strut about
when what is vile is honored among men.

Psalm 13

For the director of music. A psalm of David.

1How long, O LORD? Will you forget me forever?
How long will you hide your face from me?
2How long must I wrestle with my thoughts
and every day have sorrow in my heart?
How long will my enemy triumph over me?

3Look on me and answer, O LORD my God.
Give light to my eyes, or I will sleep in death;
4my enemy will say, "I have overcome him,"
and my foes will rejoice when I fall.

5But I trust in your unfailing love;
my heart rejoices in your salvation.
6I will sing to the LORD,
for he has been good to me.

Psalm 14

For the director of music. Of David.

1The fool[c] says in his heart,
"There is no God."
They are corrupt, their deeds are vile;
there is no one who does good.

2The LORD looks down from heaven
on the sons of men
to see if there are any who understand,
any who seek God.
3All have turned aside,
they have together become corrupt;
there is no one who does good,
not even one.

4Will evildoers never learn—
those who devour my people as men eat bread
and who do not call on the LORD?
5There they are, overwhelmed with dread,
for God is present in the company of the righteous.
6You evildoers frustrate the plans of the poor,
but the LORD is their refuge.

7Oh, that salvation for Israel would come out of Zion!
When the LORD restores the fortunes of his people,
let Jacob rejoice and Israel be glad!

Psalm 15

A psalm of David.

1LORD, who may dwell in your sanctuary?
Who may live on your holy hill?

2He whose walk is blameless
and who does what is righteous,
who speaks the truth from his heart
3 and has no slander on his tongue,
who does his neighbor no wrong
and casts no slur on his fellowman,
4who despises a vile man
but honors those who fear the LORD,
who keeps his oath
even when it hurts,
5who lends his money without usury
and does not accept a bribe against the innocent.

He who does these things
will never be shaken.

[a]Title: Probably a musical term [b]4 Or / *our lips are our plowshares* [c]1 The Hebrew words rendered *fool* in Psalms denote one who is morally deficient.

Psalm 16

A *miktam*[a] of David.

1Keep me safe, O God,
for in you I take refuge.

2I said to the LORD, "You are my Lord;
apart from you I have no good thing."
3As for the saints who are in the land,
they are the glorious ones in whom is all my delight.[b]
4The sorrows of those will increase
who run after other gods.
I will not pour out their libations of blood
or take up their names on my lips.

5LORD, you have assigned me my portion and my cup;
you have made my lot secure.
6The boundary lines have fallen for me in pleasant places;
surely I have a delightful inheritance.

7I will praise the LORD, who counsels me;
even at night my heart instructs me.
8I have set the LORD always before me.
Because he is at my right hand,
I will not be shaken.

9Therefore my heart is glad and my tongue rejoices;
my body also will rest secure,
10because you will not abandon me to the grave,[c]
nor will you let your Holy One[d] see decay.
11You have made[e] known to me the path of life;
you will fill me with joy in your presence,
with eternal pleasures at your right hand.

Psalm 17

A prayer of David.

1Hear, O LORD, my righteous plea;
listen to my cry.
Give ear to my prayer—
it does not rise from deceitful lips.
2May my vindication come from you;
may your eyes see what is right.

3Though you probe my heart and examine me at night,
though you test me, you will find nothing;
I have resolved that my mouth will not sin.
4As for the deeds of men—
by the word of your lips
I have kept myself
from the ways of the violent.
5My steps have held to your paths;
my feet have not slipped.

6I call on you, O God, for you will answer me;
give ear to me and hear my prayer.
7Show the wonder of your great love,
you who save by your right hand
those who take refuge in you from their foes.
8Keep me as the apple of your eye;
hide me in the shadow of your wings
9from the wicked who assail me,
from my mortal enemies who surround me.

10They close up their callous hearts,
and their mouths speak with arrogance.
11They have tracked me down, they now surround me,
with eyes alert, to throw me to the ground.
12They are like a lion hungry for prey,
like a great lion crouching in cover.

13Rise up, O LORD, confront them, bring them down;
rescue me from the wicked by your sword.
14O LORD, by your hand save me from such men,
from men of this world whose reward is in this life.
You still the hunger of those you cherish;
their sons have plenty,
and they store up wealth for their children.
15And I—in righteousness I will see your face;
when I awake, I will be satisfied with seeing your likeness.

Psalm 18

For the director of music. Of David the servant of the LORD. He sang to the LORD the words of this song when the LORD delivered him from the hand of all his enemies and from the hand of Saul. He said:

1I love you, O LORD, my strength.

2The LORD is my rock, my fortress and my deliverer;
my God is my rock, in whom I take refuge.

[a]Title: Probably a literary or musical term [b]3 Or *As for the pagan priests who are in the land / and the nobles in whom all delight, I said:* [c]10 Hebrew *Sheol* [d]10 Or *your faithful one* [e]11 Or *You will make*

He is my shield and the horn[a] of my
salvation, my stronghold.
3I call to the LORD, who is worthy of praise,
and I am saved from my enemies.

4The cords of death entangled me;
the torrents of destruction overwhelmed
me.
5The cords of the grave[b] coiled around me;
the snares of death confronted me.
6In my distress I called to the LORD;
I cried to my God for help.
From his temple he heard my voice;
my cry came before him, into his ears.

7The earth trembled and quaked,
and the foundations of the mountains
shook;
they trembled because he was angry.
8Smoke rose from his nostrils;
consuming fire came from his mouth,
burning coals blazed out of it.
9He parted the heavens and came down;
dark clouds were under his feet.
10He mounted the cherubim and flew;
he soared on the wings of the wind.
11He made darkness his covering, his canopy
around him—
the dark rain clouds of the sky.
12Out of the brightness of his presence clouds
advanced,
with hailstones and bolts of lightning.
13The LORD thundered from heaven;
the voice of the Most High resounded.[c]
14He shot his arrows and scattered ⌞the
enemies⌟,
great bolts of lightning and routed them.
15The valleys of the sea were exposed
and the foundations of the earth laid bare
at your rebuke, O LORD,
at the blast of breath from your nostrils.

16He reached down from on high and took
hold of me;
he drew me out of deep waters.
17He rescued me from my powerful enemy,
from my foes, who were too strong for
me.
18They confronted me in the day of my
disaster,
but the LORD was my support.
19He brought me out into a spacious place;
he rescued me because he delighted in
me.
20The LORD has dealt with me according to my
righteousness;
according to the cleanness of my hands he
has rewarded me.
21For I have kept the ways of the LORD;
I have not done evil by turning from my
God.
22All his laws are before me;
I have not turned away from his decrees.
23I have been blameless before him
and have kept myself from sin.
24The LORD has rewarded me according to my
righteousness,
according to the cleanness of my hands in
his sight.

25To the faithful you show yourself faithful,
to the blameless you show yourself
blameless,
26to the pure you show yourself pure,
but to the crooked you show yourself
shrewd.
27You save the humble
but bring low those whose eyes are
haughty.
28You, O LORD, keep my lamp burning;
my God turns my darkness into light.
29With your help I can advance against a
troop[d];
with my God I can scale a wall.

30As for God, his way is perfect;
the word of the LORD is flawless.
He is a shield
for all who take refuge in him.
31For who is God besides the LORD?
And who is the Rock except our God?
32It is God who arms me with strength
and makes my way perfect.
33He makes my feet like the feet of a deer;
he enables me to stand on the heights.
34He trains my hands for battle;
my arms can bend a bow of bronze.
35You give me your shield of victory,
and your right hand sustains me;
you stoop down to make me great.
36You broaden the path beneath me,
so that my ankles do not turn.

37I pursued my enemies and overtook them;
I did not turn back till they were
destroyed.
38I crushed them so that they could not rise;
they fell beneath my feet.
39You armed me with strength for battle;
you made my adversaries bow at my feet.
40You made my enemies turn their backs in
flight,
and I destroyed my foes.

[a]2 *Horn* here symbolizes strength. [b]5 Hebrew *Sheol* [c]13 Some Hebrew manuscripts and Septuagint (see also 2 Samuel 22:14); most Hebrew manuscripts *resounded, / amid hailstones and bolts of lightning* [d]29 Or *can run through a barricade*

41They cried for help, but there was no one to save them—
to the LORD, but he did not answer.
42I beat them as fine as dust borne on the wind;
I poured them out like mud in the streets.

43You have delivered me from the attacks of the people;
you have made me the head of nations;
people I did not know are subject to me.
44As soon as they hear me, they obey me;
foreigners cringe before me.
45They all lose heart;
they come trembling from their strongholds.

46The LORD lives! Praise be to my Rock!
Exalted be God my Savior!
47He is the God who avenges me,
who subdues nations under me,
48 who saves me from my enemies.
You exalted me above my foes;
from violent men you rescued me.
49Therefore I will praise you among the nations, O LORD;
I will sing praises to your name.
50He gives his king great victories;
he shows unfailing kindness to his anointed,
to David and his descendants forever.

Psalm 19

For the director of music. A psalm of David.

1The heavens declare the glory of God;
the skies proclaim the work of his hands.
2Day after day they pour forth speech;
night after night they display knowledge.
3There is no speech or language
where their voice is not heard.[a]
4Their voice[b] goes out into all the earth,
their words to the ends of the world.

In the heavens he has pitched a tent for the sun,
5 which is like a bridegroom coming forth from his pavilion,
like a champion rejoicing to run his course.
6It rises at one end of the heavens
and makes its circuit to the other;
nothing is hidden from its heat.

7The law of the LORD is perfect,
reviving the soul.
The statutes of the LORD are trustworthy,
making wise the simple.
8The precepts of the LORD are right,
giving joy to the heart.
The commands of the LORD are radiant,
giving light to the eyes.
9The fear of the LORD is pure,
enduring forever.
The ordinances of the LORD are sure
and altogether righteous.
10They are more precious than gold,
than much pure gold;
they are sweeter than honey,
than honey from the comb.
11By them is your servant warned;
in keeping them there is great reward.

12Who can discern his errors?
Forgive my hidden faults.
13Keep your servant also from willful sins;
may they not rule over me.
Then will I be blameless,
innocent of great transgression.

14May the words of my mouth and the meditation of my heart
be pleasing in your sight,
O LORD, my Rock and my Redeemer.

Psalm 20

For the director of music. A psalm of David.

1May the LORD answer you when you are in distress;
may the name of the God of Jacob protect you.
2May he send you help from the sanctuary
and grant you support from Zion.
3May he remember all your sacrifices
and accept your burnt offerings. *Selah*
4May he give you the desire of your heart
and make all your plans succeed.
5We will shout for joy when you are victorious
and will lift up our banners in the name of our God.

May the LORD grant all your requests.

6Now I know that the LORD saves his anointed;
he answers him from his holy heaven
with the saving power of his right hand.
7Some trust in chariots and some in horses,
but we trust in the name of the LORD our God.
8They are brought to their knees and fall,
but we rise up and stand firm.

[a] 3 Or *They have no speech, there are no words; / no sound is heard from them* [b] 4 Septuagint, Jerome and Syriac; Hebrew *line*

9 O LORD, save the king!
Answer[a] us when we call!

Psalm 21

For the director of music. A psalm of David.

1 O LORD, the king rejoices in your strength.
How great is his joy in the victories you give!
2 You have granted him the desire of his heart
and have not withheld the request of his lips. *Selah*
3 You welcomed him with rich blessings
and placed a crown of pure gold on his head.
4 He asked you for life, and you gave it to him—
length of days, for ever and ever.
5 Through the victories you gave, his glory is great;
you have bestowed on him splendor and majesty.
6 Surely you have granted him eternal blessings
and made him glad with the joy of your presence.
7 For the king trusts in the LORD;
through the unfailing love of the Most High
he will not be shaken.
8 Your hand will lay hold on all your enemies;
your right hand will seize your foes.
9 At the time of your appearing
you will make them like a fiery furnace.
In his wrath the LORD will swallow them up,
and his fire will consume them.
10 You will destroy their descendants from the earth,
their posterity from mankind.
11 Though they plot evil against you
and devise wicked schemes, they cannot succeed;
12 for you will make them turn their backs
when you aim at them with drawn bow.
13 Be exalted, O LORD, in your strength;
we will sing and praise your might.

Psalm 22

For the director of music. To ⌊the tune of⌋ "The Doe of the Morning." A psalm of David.

1 My God, my God, why have you forsaken me?
Why are you so far from saving me,
so far from the words of my groaning?
2 O my God, I cry out by day, but you do not answer,
by night, and am not silent.
3 Yet you are enthroned as the Holy One;
you are the praise of Israel.[b]
4 In you our fathers put their trust;
they trusted and you delivered them.
5 They cried to you and were saved;
in you they trusted and were not disappointed.

6 But I am a worm and not a man,
scorned by men and despised by the people.
7 All who see me mock me;
they hurl insults, shaking their heads:
8 "He trusts in the LORD;
let the LORD rescue him.
Let him deliver him,
since he delights in him."

9 Yet you brought me out of the womb;
you made me trust in you
even at my mother's breast.
10 From birth I was cast upon you;
from my mother's womb you have been my God.
11 Do not be far from me,
for trouble is near
and there is no one to help.

12 Many bulls surround me;
strong bulls of Bashan encircle me.
13 Roaring lions tearing their prey
open their mouths wide against me.
14 I am poured out like water,
and all my bones are out of joint.
My heart has turned to wax;
it has melted away within me.
15 My strength is dried up like a potsherd,
and my tongue sticks to the roof of my mouth;
you lay me[c] in the dust of death.
16 Dogs have surrounded me;
a band of evil men has encircled me,
they have pierced[d] my hands and my feet.
17 I can count all my bones;
people stare and gloat over me.
18 They divide my garments among them
and cast lots for my clothing.

19 But you, O LORD, be not far off;
O my Strength, come quickly to help me.
20 Deliver my life from the sword,
my precious life from the power of the dogs.
21 Rescue me from the mouth of the lions;

[a] 9 Or *save! / O King, answer* [b] 3 Or *Yet you are holy, / enthroned on the praises of Israel* [c] 15 Or */ I am laid*
[d] 16 Some Hebrew manuscripts, Septuagint and Syriac; most Hebrew manuscripts */ like the lion,*

save[a] me from the horns of the wild
oxen.
22 I will declare your name to my brothers;
in the congregation I will praise you.
23 You who fear the LORD, praise him!
All you descendants of Jacob, honor him!
Revere him, all you descendants of Israel!
24 For he has not despised or disdained
the suffering of the afflicted one;
he has not hidden his face from him
but has listened to his cry for help.
25 From you comes the theme of my praise in
the great assembly;
before those who fear you[b] will I fulfill
my vows.
26 The poor will eat and be satisfied;
they who seek the LORD will praise him—
may your hearts live forever!
27 All the ends of the earth
will remember and turn to the LORD,
and all the families of the nations
will bow down before him,
28 for dominion belongs to the LORD
and he rules over the nations.
29 All the rich of the earth will feast and
worship;
all who go down to the dust will kneel
before him—
those who cannot keep themselves alive.
30 Posterity will serve him;
future generations will be told about the
Lord.
31 They will proclaim his righteousness
to a people yet unborn—
for he has done it.

Psalm 23

A psalm of David.

1 The LORD is my shepherd, I shall not be in
want.
2 He makes me lie down in green pastures,
he leads me beside quiet waters,
3 he restores my soul.
He guides me in paths of righteousness
for his name's sake.
4 Even though I walk

PSALM 23:1–6

1. What is the closest you have come to living on a farm and looking after animals?
2. Where do you like to go for some peace and quiet?
3. What do you believe happens to someone when they die?
4. What is the closest you have come to "the valley of the shadow of death"?
5. On a scale of 1 (no fear) to 10 (very afraid), how do you feel about dying?
6. If you were to die tonight would you have the same confidence as the psalmist, David, that you "will dwell in the house of the Lord forever"? Why or why not?
7. Which benefit of having the Lord as your shepherd do you need the most right now: Peace? Guidance? Protection? Comfort?
8. How can your group pray for you?

through the valley of the shadow of
death,[c]
I will fear no evil,
for you are with me;
your rod and your staff,
they comfort me.
5 You prepare a table before me
in the presence of my enemies.

[a] 21 Or / *you have heard* [b] 25 Hebrew *him* [c] 4 Or *through the darkest valley*

Perhaps the most beloved passage in all the Bible, this psalm is a profession of joyful trust in the Lord. David (the shepherd turned king) acknowledges that the Lord is his Shepherd-King. For the Lord as the shepherd of Israel, see Psalm 100:3 and Ezekiel 34:11–16. For Jesus as the shepherd of his people, see John 10:14–15.

23:1 ***not be in want.*** On the contrary, David will enjoy "goodness" all his life (v. 6).

23:2 ***lie down.*** The shepherd brings contented and secure rest (see Ezek. 34:14–15). ***green pastures.*** A symbol for all that makes life flourish (see John 10:9). ***leads me.*** Like a shepherd (see Isa. 40:11). ***quiet waters.*** Waters that provide refreshment and well-being (see Isa. 49:10).

23:4 ***through the valley of the shadow of death.*** In summer, efficient shepherds lead their sheep into the high country. Though this is the time of greatest danger—from floods, rock slides, poisonous snakes and predators—it is also the time of greatest intimacy between sheep and shepherd. ***rod.*** Instrument of authority (as in Ps. 2:9); used also by shepherds for counting, guiding, rescuing, and protecting sheep from predators. ***staff.*** Instrument of support used by shepherds to guide and "comfort" sheep.

23:5 ***prepare a table.*** Though surrounded by enemies, David could feast in security. ***anoint my head with oil.*** Customary treatment of an honored guest at a banquet (see Luke 7:46). ***cup.*** Of the Lord's banquet.

You anoint my head with oil;
my cup overflows.
6 Surely goodness and love will follow me
all the days of my life,
and I will dwell in the house of the LORD
forever.

Psalm 24

Of David. A psalm.

1 The earth is the LORD's, and everything in it,
the world, and all who live in it;
2 for he founded it upon the seas
and established it upon the waters.

3 Who may ascend the hill of the LORD?
Who may stand in his holy place?
4 He who has clean hands and a pure heart,
who does not lift up his soul to an idol
or swear by what is false.[a]
5 He will receive blessing from the LORD
and vindication from God his Savior.
6 Such is the generation of those who seek him,
who seek your face, O God of Jacob.[b] *Selah*

7 Lift up your heads, O you gates;
be lifted up, you ancient doors,
that the King of glory may come in.
8 Who is this King of glory?
The LORD strong and mighty,
the LORD mighty in battle.
9 Lift up your heads, O you gates;
lift them up, you ancient doors,
that the King of glory may come in.
10 Who is he, this King of glory?
The LORD Almighty—
he is the King of glory. *Selah*

Psalm 25[c]

Of David.

1 To you, O LORD, I lift up my soul;
2 in you I trust, O my God.
Do not let me be put to shame,
nor let my enemies triumph over me.
3 No one whose hope is in you
will ever be put to shame,
but they will be put to shame
who are treacherous without excuse.

4 Show me your ways, O LORD,
teach me your paths;
5 guide me in your truth and teach me,
for you are God my Savior,
and my hope is in you all day long.
6 Remember, O LORD, your great mercy and love,
for they are from of old.
7 Remember not the sins of my youth
and my rebellious ways;
according to your love remember me,
for you are good, O LORD.

8 Good and upright is the LORD;
therefore he instructs sinners in his ways.
9 He guides the humble in what is right
and teaches them his way.
10 All the ways of the LORD are loving and faithful
for those who keep the demands of his covenant.
11 For the sake of your name, O LORD,
forgive my iniquity, though it is great.
12 Who, then, is the man that fears the LORD?
He will instruct him in the way chosen for him.
13 He will spend his days in prosperity,
and his descendants will inherit the land.
14 The LORD confides in those who fear him;
he makes his covenant known to them.
15 My eyes are ever on the LORD,
for only he will release my feet from the snare.

16 Turn to me and be gracious to me,
for I am lonely and afflicted.
17 The troubles of my heart have multiplied;
free me from my anguish.
18 Look upon my affliction and my distress
and take away all my sins.
19 See how my enemies have increased
and how fiercely they hate me!
20 Guard my life and rescue me;
let me not be put to shame,
for I take refuge in you.
21 May integrity and uprightness protect me,
because my hope is in you.

22 Redeem Israel, O God,
from all their troubles!

Psalm 26

Of David.

1 Vindicate me, O LORD,
for I have led a blameless life;
I have trusted in the LORD
without wavering.
2 Test me, O LORD, and try me,
examine my heart and my mind;
3 for your love is ever before me,

[a] 4 Or *swear falsely* [b] 6 Two Hebrew manuscripts and Syriac (see also Septuagint); most Hebrew manuscripts *face, Jacob*
[c] This psalm is an acrostic poem, the verses of which begin with the successive letters of the Hebrew alphabet.

and I walk continually in your truth.
4I do not sit with deceitful men,
nor do I consort with hypocrites;
5I abhor the assembly of evildoers
and refuse to sit with the wicked.
6I wash my hands in innocence,
and go about your altar, O LORD,
7proclaiming aloud your praise
and telling of all your wonderful deeds.
8I love the house where you live, O LORD,
the place where your glory dwells.

9Do not take away my soul along with sinners,
my life with bloodthirsty men,
10in whose hands are wicked schemes,
whose right hands are full of bribes.
11But I lead a blameless life;
redeem me and be merciful to me.

12My feet stand on level ground;
in the great assembly I will praise the LORD.

Psalm 27

Of David.

1The LORD is my light and my salvation—
whom shall I fear?
The LORD is the stronghold of my life—
of whom shall I be afraid?
2When evil men advance against me
to devour my flesh,[a]
when my enemies and my foes attack me,
they will stumble and fall.
3Though an army besiege me,
my heart will not fear;
though war break out against me,
even then will I be confident.

4One thing I ask of the LORD,
this is what I seek:
that I may dwell in the house of the LORD
all the days of my life,
to gaze upon the beauty of the LORD
and to seek him in his temple.
5For in the day of trouble
he will keep me safe in his dwelling;
he will hide me in the shelter of his tabernacle
and set me high upon a rock.
6Then my head will be exalted
above the enemies who surround me;
at his tabernacle will I sacrifice with shouts of joy;
I will sing and make music to the LORD.

7Hear my voice when I call, O LORD;
be merciful to me and answer me.
8My heart says of you, "Seek his[b] face!"
Your face, LORD, I will seek.
9Do not hide your face from me,
do not turn your servant away in anger;
you have been my helper.
Do not reject me or forsake me,
O God my Savior.
10Though my father and mother forsake me,
the LORD will receive me.
11Teach me your way, O LORD;
lead me in a straight path
because of my oppressors.
12Do not turn me over to the desire of my foes,
for false witnesses rise up against me,
breathing out violence.

13I am still confident of this:
I will see the goodness of the LORD
in the land of the living.
14Wait for the LORD;
be strong and take heart
and wait for the LORD.

Psalm 28

Of David.

1To you I call, O LORD my Rock;
do not turn a deaf ear to me.
For if you remain silent,
I will be like those who have gone down to the pit.
2Hear my cry for mercy
as I call to you for help,
as I lift up my hands
toward your Most Holy Place.

3Do not drag me away with the wicked,
with those who do evil,
who speak cordially with their neighbors
but harbor malice in their hearts.
4Repay them for their deeds
and for their evil work;
repay them for what their hands have done
and bring back upon them what they deserve.
5Since they show no regard for the works of the LORD
and what his hands have done,
he will tear them down
and never build them up again.

6Praise be to the LORD,
for he has heard my cry for mercy.
7The LORD is my strength and my shield;
my heart trusts in him, and I am helped.

[a] 2 Or *to slander me* [b] 8 Or *To you, O my heart, he has said, "Seek my*

My heart leaps for joy
and I will give thanks to him in song.

8The LORD is the strength of his people,
a fortress of salvation for his anointed one.
9Save your people and bless your inheritance;
be their shepherd and carry them forever.

Psalm 29

A psalm of David.

1Ascribe to the LORD, O mighty ones,
ascribe to the LORD glory and strength.
2Ascribe to the LORD the glory due his name;
worship the LORD in the splendor of his[a] holiness.

3The voice of the LORD is over the waters;
the God of glory thunders,
the LORD thunders over the mighty waters.
4The voice of the LORD is powerful;
the voice of the LORD is majestic.
5The voice of the LORD breaks the cedars;
the LORD breaks in pieces the cedars of Lebanon.
6He makes Lebanon skip like a calf,
Sirion[b] like a young wild ox.
7The voice of the LORD strikes
with flashes of lightning.
8The voice of the LORD shakes the desert;
the LORD shakes the Desert of Kadesh.
9The voice of the LORD twists the oaks[c]
and strips the forests bare.
And in his temple all cry, "Glory!"

10The LORD sits[d] enthroned over the flood;
the LORD is enthroned as King forever.
11The LORD gives strength to his people;
the LORD blesses his people with peace.

Psalm 30

A psalm. A song. For the dedication of the temple.[e] Of David.

1I will exalt you, O LORD,
for you lifted me out of the depths
and did not let my enemies gloat over me.
2O LORD my God, I called to you for help
and you healed me.
3O LORD, you brought me up from the grave[f];
you spared me from going down into the pit.

4Sing to the LORD, you saints of his;
praise his holy name.
5For his anger lasts only a moment,
but his favor lasts a lifetime;
weeping may remain for a night,
but rejoicing comes in the morning.

6When I felt secure, I said,
"I will never be shaken."
7O LORD, when you favored me,
you made my mountain[g] stand firm;
but when you hid your face,
I was dismayed.

8To you, O LORD, I called;
to the Lord I cried for mercy:
9"What gain is there in my destruction,[h]
in my going down into the pit?
Will the dust praise you?
Will it proclaim your faithfulness?
10Hear, O LORD, and be merciful to me;
O LORD, be my help."

11You turned my wailing into dancing;
you removed my sackcloth and clothed me with joy,
12that my heart may sing to you and not be silent.
O LORD my God, I will give you thanks forever.

Psalm 31

For the director of music. A psalm of David.

1In you, O LORD, I have taken refuge;
let me never be put to shame;
deliver me in your righteousness.
2Turn your ear to me,
come quickly to my rescue;
be my rock of refuge,
a strong fortress to save me.
3Since you are my rock and my fortress,
for the sake of your name lead and guide me.
4Free me from the trap that is set for me,
for you are my refuge.
5Into your hands I commit my spirit;
redeem me, O LORD, the God of truth.

6I hate those who cling to worthless idols;
I trust in the LORD.
7I will be glad and rejoice in your love,
for you saw my affliction
and knew the anguish of my soul.
8You have not handed me over to the enemy
but have set my feet in a spacious place.

9Be merciful to me, O LORD, for I am in distress;
my eyes grow weak with sorrow,
my soul and my body with grief.

a2 Or *LORD with the splendor of* b6 That is, Mount Hermon c9 Or *LORD makes the deer give birth* d10 Or sat
eTitle: Or *palace* f3 Hebrew *Sheol* g7 Or *hill country* h9 Or *there if I am silenced*

10My life is consumed by anguish
and my years by groaning;
my strength fails because of my affliction,[a]
and my bones grow weak.
11Because of all my enemies,
I am the utter contempt of my neighbors;
I am a dread to my friends—
those who see me on the street flee from me.
12I am forgotten by them as though I were dead;
I have become like broken pottery.
13For I hear the slander of many;
there is terror on every side;
they conspire against me
and plot to take my life.

14But I trust in you, O LORD;
I say, "You are my God."
15My times are in your hands;
deliver me from my enemies
and from those who pursue me.
16Let your face shine on your servant;
save me in your unfailing love.
17Let me not be put to shame, O LORD,
for I have cried out to you;
but let the wicked be put to shame
and lie silent in the grave.[b]
18Let their lying lips be silenced,
for with pride and contempt
they speak arrogantly against the righteous.

19How great is your goodness,
which you have stored up for those who fear you,
which you bestow in the sight of men
on those who take refuge in you.
20In the shelter of your presence you hide them
from the intrigues of men;
in your dwelling you keep them safe
from accusing tongues.

21Praise be to the LORD,
for he showed his wonderful love to me
when I was in a besieged city.
22In my alarm I said,
"I am cut off from your sight!"
Yet you heard my cry for mercy
when I called to you for help.

23Love the LORD, all his saints!
The LORD preserves the faithful,
but the proud he pays back in full.
24Be strong and take heart,
all you who hope in the LORD.

Psalm 32

Of David. A *maskil.*[c]

1Blessed is he
whose transgressions are forgiven,
whose sins are covered.
2Blessed is the man
whose sin the LORD does not count against him
and in whose spirit is no deceit.

3When I kept silent,
my bones wasted away
through my groaning all day long.
4For day and night
your hand was heavy upon me;
my strength was sapped
as in the heat of summer. *Selah*
5Then I acknowledged my sin to you
and did not cover up my iniquity.
I said, "I will confess
my transgressions to the LORD"—
and you forgave
the guilt of my sin. *Selah*

6Therefore let everyone who is godly pray to you
while you may be found;
surely when the mighty waters rise,
they will not reach him.
7You are my hiding place;
you will protect me from trouble
and surround me with songs of deliverance. *Selah*

8I will instruct you and teach you in the way you should go;
I will counsel you and watch over you.
9Do not be like the horse or the mule,
which have no understanding
but must be controlled by bit and bridle
or they will not come to you.
10Many are the woes of the wicked,
but the LORD's unfailing love
surrounds the man who trusts in him.

11Rejoice in the LORD and be glad, you righteous;
sing, all you who are upright in heart!

Psalm 33

1Sing joyfully to the LORD, you righteous;
it is fitting for the upright to praise him.
2Praise the LORD with the harp;
make music to him on the ten-stringed lyre.
3Sing to him a new song;
play skillfully, and shout for joy.

[a] 10 Or *guilt*   [b] 17 Hebrew *Sheol*   [c] Title: Probably a literary or musical term

4For the word of the LORD is right and true;
he is faithful in all he does.
5The LORD loves righteousness and justice;
the earth is full of his unfailing love.

6By the word of the LORD were the heavens made,
their starry host by the breath of his mouth.
7He gathers the waters of the sea into jars[a];
he puts the deep into storehouses.
8Let all the earth fear the LORD;
let all the people of the world revere him.
9For he spoke, and it came to be;
he commanded, and it stood firm.
10The LORD foils the plans of the nations;
he thwarts the purposes of the peoples.
11But the plans of the LORD stand firm forever,
the purposes of his heart through all generations.

12Blessed is the nation whose God is the LORD,
the people he chose for his inheritance.
13From heaven the LORD looks down
and sees all mankind;
14from his dwelling place he watches
all who live on earth—
15he who forms the hearts of all,
who considers everything they do.
16No king is saved by the size of his army;
no warrior escapes by his great strength.
17A horse is a vain hope for deliverance;
despite all its great strength it cannot save.
18But the eyes of the LORD are on those who fear him,
on those whose hope is in his unfailing love,
19to deliver them from death
and keep them alive in famine.

20We wait in hope for the LORD;
he is our help and our shield.
21In him our hearts rejoice,
for we trust in his holy name.
22May your unfailing love rest upon us,
O LORD,
even as we put our hope in you.

Psalm 34[b]

Of David. When he pretended to be insane before Abimelech, who drove him away, and he left.

1I will extol the LORD at all times;
his praise will always be on my lips.
2My soul will boast in the LORD;
let the afflicted hear and rejoice.
3Glorify the LORD with me;
let us exalt his name together.

4I sought the LORD, and he answered me;
he delivered me from all my fears.
5Those who look to him are radiant;
their faces are never covered with shame.
6This poor man called, and the LORD heard him;
he saved him out of all his troubles.
7The angel of the LORD encamps around those who fear him,
and he delivers them.

8Taste and see that the LORD is good;
blessed is the man who takes refuge in him.
9Fear the LORD, you his saints,
for those who fear him lack nothing.
10The lions may grow weak and hungry,
but those who seek the LORD lack no good thing.

11Come, my children, listen to me;
I will teach you the fear of the LORD.
12Whoever of you loves life
and desires to see many good days,
13keep your tongue from evil
and your lips from speaking lies.
14Turn from evil and do good;
seek peace and pursue it.

15The eyes of the LORD are on the righteous
and his ears are attentive to their cry;
16the face of the LORD is against those who do evil,
to cut off the memory of them from the earth.

17The righteous cry out, and the LORD hears them;
he delivers them from all their troubles.
18The LORD is close to the brokenhearted
and saves those who are crushed in spirit.

19A righteous man may have many troubles,
but the LORD delivers him from them all;
20he protects all his bones,
not one of them will be broken.

21Evil will slay the wicked;
the foes of the righteous will be condemned.
22The LORD redeems his servants;
no one will be condemned who takes refuge in him.

[a] 7 Or *sea as into a heap* [b] This psalm is an acrostic poem, the verses of which begin with the successive letters of the Hebrew alphabet.

Psalm 35

Of David.

1Contend, O LORD, with those who contend
with me;
fight against those who fight against me.
2Take up shield and buckler;
arise and come to my aid.
3Brandish spear and javelin[a]
against those who pursue me.
Say to my soul,
"I am your salvation."

4May those who seek my life
be disgraced and put to shame;
may those who plot my ruin
be turned back in dismay.
5May they be like chaff before the wind,
with the angel of the LORD driving them
away;
6may their path be dark and slippery,
with the angel of the LORD pursuing them.
7Since they hid their net for me without cause
and without cause dug a pit for me,
8may ruin overtake them by surprise—
may the net they hid entangle them,
may they fall into the pit, to their ruin.
9Then my soul will rejoice in the LORD
and delight in his salvation.
10My whole being will exclaim,
"Who is like you, O LORD?
You rescue the poor from those too strong for
them,
the poor and needy from those who rob
them."

11Ruthless witnesses come forward;
they question me on things I know
nothing about.
12They repay me evil for good
and leave my soul forlorn.
13Yet when they were ill, I put on sackcloth
and humbled myself with fasting.
When my prayers returned to me
unanswered,
14 I went about mourning
as though for my friend or brother.
I bowed my head in grief
as though weeping for my mother.
15But when I stumbled, they gathered in glee;
attackers gathered against me when I was
unaware.
They slandered me without ceasing.
16Like the ungodly they maliciously mocked[b];
they gnashed their teeth at me.
17O Lord, how long will you look on?
Rescue my life from their ravages,
my precious life from these lions.
18I will give you thanks in the great assembly;
among throngs of people I will praise you.

19Let not those gloat over me
who are my enemies without cause;
let not those who hate me without reason
maliciously wink the eye.
20They do not speak peaceably,
but devise false accusations
against those who live quietly in the land.
21They gape at me and say, "Aha! Aha!
With our own eyes we have seen it."

22O LORD, you have seen this; be not silent.
Do not be far from me, O Lord.
23Awake, and rise to my defense!
Contend for me, my God and Lord.
24Vindicate me in your righteousness, O LORD
my God;
do not let them gloat over me.
25Do not let them think, "Aha, just what we
wanted!"
or say, "We have swallowed him up."

26May all who gloat over my distress
be put to shame and confusion;
may all who exalt themselves over me
be clothed with shame and disgrace.
27May those who delight in my vindication
shout for joy and gladness;
may they always say, "The LORD be exalted,
who delights in the well-being of his
servant."
28My tongue will speak of your righteousness
and of your praises all day long.

Psalm 36

For the director of music. Of David the servant
of the LORD.

1An oracle is within my heart
concerning the sinfulness of the wicked:[c]
There is no fear of God
before his eyes.
2For in his own eyes he flatters himself
too much to detect or hate his sin.
3The words of his mouth are wicked and
deceitful;
he has ceased to be wise and to do good.
4Even on his bed he plots evil;
he commits himself to a sinful course
and does not reject what is wrong.
5Your love, O LORD, reaches to the heavens,
your faithfulness to the skies.

a3 Or *and block the way* b16 Septuagint; Hebrew may mean *ungodly circle of mockers.* c1 Or *heart: / Sin proceeds from the wicked.*

6Your righteousness is like the mighty
mountains,
your justice like the great deep.
O LORD, you preserve both man and beast.
7 How priceless is your unfailing love!
Both high and low among men
find[a] refuge in the shadow of your wings.
8They feast on the abundance of your house;
you give them drink from your river of
delights.
9For with you is the fountain of life;
in your light we see light.

10Continue your love to those who know you,
your righteousness to the upright in heart.
11May the foot of the proud not come against
me,
nor the hand of the wicked drive me
away.
12See how the evildoers lie fallen—
thrown down, not able to rise!

Psalm 37[b]

Of David.

1Do not fret because of evil men
or be envious of those who do wrong;
2for like the grass they will soon wither,
like green plants they will soon die away.

3Trust in the LORD and do good;
dwell in the land and enjoy safe pasture.
4Delight yourself in the LORD
and he will give you the desires of your
heart.

5Commit your way to the LORD;
trust in him and he will do this:
6He will make your righteousness shine like
the dawn,
the justice of your cause like the noonday
sun.

7Be still before the LORD and wait patiently for
him;
do not fret when men succeed in their
ways,
when they carry out their wicked
schemes.

8Refrain from anger and turn from wrath;
do not fret—it leads only to evil.
9For evil men will be cut off,
but those who hope in the LORD will
inherit the land.

10A little while, and the wicked will be no
more;
though you look for them, they will not be
found.
11But the meek will inherit the land
and enjoy great peace.

12The wicked plot against the righteous
and gnash their teeth at them;
13but the Lord laughs at the wicked,
for he knows their day is coming.

14The wicked draw the sword
and bend the bow
to bring down the poor and needy,
to slay those whose ways are upright.
15But their swords will pierce their own hearts,
and their bows will be broken.

16Better the little that the righteous have
than the wealth of many wicked;
17for the power of the wicked will be broken,
but the LORD upholds the righteous.

18The days of the blameless are known to the
LORD,
and their inheritance will endure forever.
19In times of disaster they will not wither;
in days of famine they will enjoy plenty.

20But the wicked will perish:
The LORD's enemies will be like the
beauty of the fields,
they will vanish—vanish like smoke.

21The wicked borrow and do not repay,
but the righteous give generously;
22those the LORD blesses will inherit the land,
but those he curses will be cut off.

23If the LORD delights in a man's way,
he makes his steps firm;
24though he stumble, he will not fall,
for the LORD upholds him with his hand.

25I was young and now I am old,
yet I have never seen the righteous
forsaken
or their children begging bread.
26They are always generous and lend freely;
their children will be blessed.

27Turn from evil and do good;
then you will dwell in the land forever.
28For the LORD loves the just
and will not forsake his faithful ones.

They will be protected forever,
but the offspring of the wicked will be cut
off;
29the righteous will inherit the land
and dwell in it forever.

[a]7 Or *love, O God! / Men find*; or *love! / Both heavenly beings and men / find*

[b]This psalm is an acrostic poem, the stanzas of which begin with the successive letters of the Hebrew alphabet.

30The mouth of the righteous man utters wisdom,
and his tongue speaks what is just.
31The law of his God is in his heart;
his feet do not slip.

32The wicked lie in wait for the righteous,
seeking their very lives;
33but the LORD will not leave them in their power
or let them be condemned when brought to trial.

34Wait for the LORD
and keep his way.
He will exalt you to inherit the land;
when the wicked are cut off, you will see it.

35I have seen a wicked and ruthless man
flourishing like a green tree in its native soil,
36but he soon passed away and was no more;
though I looked for him, he could not be found.

37Consider the blameless, observe the upright;
there is a future[a] for the man of peace.
38But all sinners will be destroyed;
the future[b] of the wicked will be cut off.

39The salvation of the righteous comes from the LORD;
he is their stronghold in time of trouble.
40The LORD helps them and delivers them;
he delivers them from the wicked and saves them,
because they take refuge in him.

Psalm 38

A psalm of David. A petition.

1O LORD, do not rebuke me in your anger
or discipline me in your wrath.
2For your arrows have pierced me,
and your hand has come down upon me.
3Because of your wrath there is no health in my body;
my bones have no soundness because of my sin.
4My guilt has overwhelmed me
like a burden too heavy to bear.

5My wounds fester and are loathsome
because of my sinful folly.
6I am bowed down and brought very low;
all day long I go about mourning.
7My back is filled with searing pain;
there is no health in my body.
8I am feeble and utterly crushed;
I groan in anguish of heart.

9All my longings lie open before you, O Lord;
my sighing is not hidden from you.
10My heart pounds, my strength fails me;
even the light has gone from my eyes.
11My friends and companions avoid me
because of my wounds;
my neighbors stay far away.
12Those who seek my life set their traps,
those who would harm me talk of my ruin;
all day long they plot deception.

13I am like a deaf man, who cannot hear,
like a mute, who cannot open his mouth;
14I have become like a man who does not hear,
whose mouth can offer no reply.
15I wait for you, O LORD;
you will answer, O Lord my God.
16For I said, "Do not let them gloat
or exalt themselves over me when my foot slips."

17For I am about to fall,
and my pain is ever with me.
18I confess my iniquity;
I am troubled by my sin.
19Many are those who are my vigorous enemies;
those who hate me without reason are numerous.
20Those who repay my good with evil
slander me when I pursue what is good.

21O LORD, do not forsake me;
be not far from me, O my God.
22Come quickly to help me,
O Lord my Savior.

Psalm 39

For the director of music. For Jeduthun. A psalm of David.

1I said, "I will watch my ways
and keep my tongue from sin;
I will put a muzzle on my mouth
as long as the wicked are in my presence."
2But when I was silent and still,
not even saying anything good,
my anguish increased.
3My heart grew hot within me,
and as I meditated, the fire burned;
then I spoke with my tongue:

4"Show me, O LORD, my life's end
and the number of my days;

[a]37 Or *there will be posterity* [b]38 Or *posterity*

let me know how fleeting is my life.
5You have made my days a mere handbreadth;
the span of my years is as nothing before you.
Each man's life is but a breath. *Selah*
6Man is a mere phantom as he goes to and fro:
He bustles about, but only in vain;
he heaps up wealth, not knowing who will get it.

7"But now, Lord, what do I look for?
My hope is in you.
8Save me from all my transgressions;
do not make me the scorn of fools.
9I was silent; I would not open my mouth,
for you are the one who has done this.
10Remove your scourge from me;
I am overcome by the blow of your hand.
11You rebuke and discipline men for their sin;
you consume their wealth like a moth—
each man is but a breath. *Selah*

12"Hear my prayer, O LORD,
listen to my cry for help;
be not deaf to my weeping.
For I dwell with you as an alien,
a stranger, as all my fathers were.
13Look away from me, that I may rejoice again
before I depart and am no more."

Psalm 40

For the director of music. Of David. A psalm.

1I waited patiently for the LORD;
he turned to me and heard my cry.
2He lifted me out of the slimy pit,
out of the mud and mire;
he set my feet on a rock
and gave me a firm place to stand.
3He put a new song in my mouth,
a hymn of praise to our God.
Many will see and fear
and put their trust in the LORD.

4Blessed is the man
who makes the LORD his trust,
who does not look to the proud,
to those who turn aside to false gods.[a]
5Many, O LORD my God,
are the wonders you have done.
The things you planned for us
no one can recount to you;
were I to speak and tell of them,
they would be too many to declare.

6Sacrifice and offering you did not desire,
but my ears you have pierced[b,c];
burnt offerings and sin offerings
you did not require.
7Then I said, "Here I am, I have come—
it is written about me in the scroll.[d]
8I desire to do your will, O my God;
your law is within my heart."

9I proclaim righteousness in the great assembly;
I do not seal my lips,
as you know, O LORD.
10I do not hide your righteousness in my heart;
I speak of your faithfulness and salvation.
I do not conceal your love and your truth
from the great assembly.

11Do not withhold your mercy from me, O LORD;
may your love and your truth always protect me.
12For troubles without number surround me;
my sins have overtaken me, and I cannot see.
They are more than the hairs of my head,
and my heart fails within me.

13Be pleased, O LORD, to save me;
O LORD, come quickly to help me.
14May all who seek to take my life
be put to shame and confusion;
may all who desire my ruin
be turned back in disgrace.
15May those who say to me, "Aha! Aha!"
be appalled at their own shame.
16But may all who seek you
rejoice and be glad in you;
may those who love your salvation always say,
"The LORD be exalted!"
17Yet I am poor and needy;
may the Lord think of me.
You are my help and my deliverer;
O my God, do not delay.

Psalm 41

For the director of music. A psalm of David.

1Blessed is he who has regard for the weak;
the LORD delivers him in times of trouble.
2The LORD will protect him and preserve his life;
he will bless him in the land
and not surrender him to the desire of his foes.

a4 Or *to falsehood* b6 Hebrew; Septuagint *but a body you have prepared for me* (see also Symmachus and Theodotion)
c6 Or *opened* d7 Or *come / with the scroll written for me*

3The LORD will sustain him on his sickbed
and restore him from his bed of illness.

4I said, "O LORD, have mercy on me;
heal me, for I have sinned against you."
5My enemies say of me in malice,
"When will he die and his name perish?"
6Whenever one comes to see me,
he speaks falsely, while his heart gathers slander;
then he goes out and spreads it abroad.

7All my enemies whisper together against me;
they imagine the worst for me, saying,
8"A vile disease has beset him;
he will never get up from the place where he lies."
9Even my close friend, whom I trusted,
he who shared my bread,
has lifted up his heel against me.

10But you, O LORD, have mercy on me;
raise me up, that I may repay them.
11I know that you are pleased with me,
for my enemy does not triumph over me.
12In my integrity you uphold me
and set me in your presence forever.

13Praise be to the LORD, the God of Israel,
from everlasting to everlasting.
Amen and Amen.

BOOK II

Psalms 42–72

Psalm 42[a]

For the director of music. A *maskil*[b] of the Sons of Korah.

1As the deer pants for streams of water,
so my soul pants for you, O God.
2My soul thirsts for God, for the living God.
When can I go and meet with God?
3My tears have been my food
day and night,
while men say to me all day long,
"Where is your God?"
4These things I remember
as I pour out my soul:
how I used to go with the multitude,
leading the procession to the house of God,
with shouts of joy and thanksgiving
among the festive throng.

5Why are you downcast, O my soul?
Why so disturbed within me?
Put your hope in God,
for I will yet praise him,
my Savior and 6my God.

My[c] soul is downcast within me;
therefore I will remember you
from the land of the Jordan,
the heights of Hermon—from Mount Mizar.
7Deep calls to deep
in the roar of your waterfalls;
all your waves and breakers
have swept over me.

8By day the LORD directs his love,
at night his song is with me—
a prayer to the God of my life.

9I say to God my Rock,
"Why have you forgotten me?
Why must I go about mourning,
oppressed by the enemy?"
10My bones suffer mortal agony
as my foes taunt me,
saying to me all day long,
"Where is your God?"

11Why are you downcast, O my soul?
Why so disturbed within me?
Put your hope in God,
for I will yet praise him,
my Savior and my God.

Psalm 43[a]

1Vindicate me, O God,
and plead my cause against an ungodly nation;
rescue me from deceitful and wicked men.
2You are God my stronghold.
Why have you rejected me?
Why must I go about mourning,
oppressed by the enemy?
3Send forth your light and your truth,
let them guide me;
let them bring me to your holy mountain,
to the place where you dwell.
4Then will I go to the altar of God,
to God, my joy and my delight.
I will praise you with the harp,
O God, my God.

5Why are you downcast, O my soul?
Why so disturbed within me?
Put your hope in God,
for I will yet praise him,
my Savior and my God.

[a]In many Hebrew manuscripts Psalms 42 and 43 constitute one psalm. [b]Title: Probably a literary or musical term [c]5,6 A few Hebrew manuscripts, Septuagint and Syriac; most Hebrew manuscripts *praise him for his saving help. / 6O my God, my*

Psalm 44

For the director of music. Of the Sons of Korah. A *maskil.*[a]

1We have heard with our ears, O God;
our fathers have told us
what you did in their days,
in days long ago.
2With your hand you drove out the nations
and planted our fathers;
you crushed the peoples
and made our fathers flourish.
3It was not by their sword that they won the land,
nor did their arm bring them victory;
it was your right hand, your arm,
and the light of your face, for you loved them.

4You are my King and my God,
who decrees[b] victories for Jacob.
5Through you we push back our enemies;
through your name we trample our foes.
6I do not trust in my bow,
my sword does not bring me victory;
7but you give us victory over our enemies,
you put our adversaries to shame.
8In God we make our boast all day long,
and we will praise your name forever.
Selah

9But now you have rejected and humbled us;
you no longer go out with our armies.
10You made us retreat before the enemy,
and our adversaries have plundered us.
11You gave us up to be devoured like sheep
and have scattered us among the nations.
12You sold your people for a pittance,
gaining nothing from their sale.

13You have made us a reproach to our neighbors,
the scorn and derision of those around us.
14You have made us a byword among the nations;
the peoples shake their heads at us.
15My disgrace is before me all day long,
and my face is covered with shame
16at the taunts of those who reproach and revile me,
because of the enemy, who is bent on revenge.

17All this happened to us,
though we had not forgotten you
or been false to your covenant.
18Our hearts had not turned back;
our feet had not strayed from your path.
19But you crushed us and made us a haunt for jackals
and covered us over with deep darkness.

20If we had forgotten the name of our God
or spread out our hands to a foreign god,
21would not God have discovered it,
since he knows the secrets of the heart?
22Yet for your sake we face death all day long;
we are considered as sheep to be slaughtered.

23Awake, O Lord! Why do you sleep?
Rouse yourself! Do not reject us forever.
24Why do you hide your face
and forget our misery and oppression?

25We are brought down to the dust;
our bodies cling to the ground.
26Rise up and help us;
redeem us because of your unfailing love.

Psalm 45

For the director of music. To ⌞the tune of⌟ "Lilies." Of the Sons of Korah. A *maskil.*[a] A wedding song.

1My heart is stirred by a noble theme
as I recite my verses for the king;
my tongue is the pen of a skillful writer.

2You are the most excellent of men
and your lips have been anointed with grace,
since God has blessed you forever.
3Gird your sword upon your side, O mighty one;
clothe yourself with splendor and majesty.
4In your majesty ride forth victoriously
in behalf of truth, humility and righteousness;
let your right hand display awesome deeds.
5Let your sharp arrows pierce the hearts of the king's enemies;
let the nations fall beneath your feet.
6Your throne, O God, will last for ever and ever;
a scepter of justice will be the scepter of your kingdom.
7You love righteousness and hate wickedness;
therefore God, your God, has set you above your companions
by anointing you with the oil of joy.
8All your robes are fragrant with myrrh and aloes and cassia;
from palaces adorned with ivory
the music of the strings makes you glad.

[a]Title: Probably a literary or musical term [b]4 Septuagint, Aquila and Syriac; Hebrew *King, O God; / command*

9Daughters of kings are among your honored
women;
at your right hand is the royal bride in
gold of Ophir.

10Listen, O daughter, consider and give ear:
Forget your people and your father's
house.
11The king is enthralled by your beauty;
honor him, for he is your lord.
12The Daughter of Tyre will come with a
gift,[a]
men of wealth will seek your favor.

13All glorious is the princess within ⌞her
chamber⌟;
her gown is interwoven with gold.
14In embroidered garments she is led to the
king;
her virgin companions follow her
and are brought to you.
15They are led in with joy and gladness;
they enter the palace of the king.

16Your sons will take the place of your fathers;
you will make them princes throughout
the land.
17I will perpetuate your memory through all
generations;
therefore the nations will praise you for
ever and ever.

Psalm 46

For the director of music. Of the Sons of Korah.
According to *alamoth.*[b] A song.

1God is our refuge and strength,
an ever-present help in trouble.
2Therefore we will not fear, though the earth
give way
and the mountains fall into the heart of
the sea,
3though its waters roar and foam
and the mountains quake with their
surging. *Selah*

4There is a river whose streams make glad the
city of God,
the holy place where the Most High
dwells.
5God is within her, she will not fall;
God will help her at break of day.
6Nations are in uproar, kingdoms fall;
he lifts his voice, the earth melts.

7The LORD Almighty is with us;
the God of Jacob is our fortress. *Selah*

8Come and see the works of the LORD,

PSALM 46:1–11

1. Who is the "tower of strength" in your family?
2. What is the worst disaster you've ever been in: Earthquake? Tornado? Hurricane? Flood? Your room?
3. If you were called to battle, what friend would you want on your side?
4. What's harder for you: To be still or to know (believe in) God?
5. Name some conflicts/wars happening in the world today. How is God involved?
6. If God is in control (see vv. 8–10), why does he let wars and other tragedies occur?
7. What storm or battle are you facing? What is the answer in this psalm for that situation?
8. Practice being still. Close in silence before God for five minutes.

[a] *12* Or *A Tyrian robe is among the gifts*
[b] Title: Probably a musical term

Psalm 46 is a celebration of the security of Jerusalem as the city of God (and the inspiration of Martin Luther's great hymn, "A Mighty Fortress Is Our God").

46:1–3 A triumphant confession of fearless trust in God. The described upheaval is probably imagery for great threats to Israel's existence, especially from her enemies (see vv. 6,8–10).

46:5 ***at break of day.*** When attacks against cities were likely to be launched. God's help comes when we most need it.

46:8–10 A declaration of the blessed effects of God's triumph over the nations.

46:8 ***Come and see.*** An invitation to see God's victories in the world. ***desolations he has brought.*** Evil and injustice are conquered by God's judgment.

46:9 Fighting and killing will come to an end when God exerts his power. There will be no more attacks against his city. This verse probably also speaks of universal peace. For the Messiah's universal victory see Isaiah 9:2–7.

46:10 God's voice breaks through, as he addresses the nations (see v. 6). ***I will be exalted among the nations.*** God's mighty acts in behalf of his people will bring him universal recognition, a major theme in the Psalms and elsewhere in the Old Testament. This has proven to be supremely true of God's climactic saving act through Jesus Christ—to be brought to complete fruition at his return.

the desolations he has brought on the
earth.
9He makes wars cease to the ends of the
earth;
he breaks the bow and shatters the spear,
he burns the shields[a] with fire.
10"Be still, and know that I am God;
I will be exalted among the nations,
I will be exalted in the earth."
11The LORD Almighty is with us;
the God of Jacob is our fortress. *Selah*

Psalm 47

For the director of music. Of the Sons of Korah.
A psalm.

1Clap your hands, all you nations;
shout to God with cries of joy.
2How awesome is the LORD Most High,
the great King over all the earth!
3He subdued nations under us,
peoples under our feet.
4He chose our inheritance for us,
the pride of Jacob, whom he loved. *Selah*

5God has ascended amid shouts of joy,
the LORD amid the sounding of trumpets.
6Sing praises to God, sing praises;
sing praises to our King, sing praises.

7For God is the King of all the earth;
sing to him a psalm[b] of praise.
8God reigns over the nations;
God is seated on his holy throne.
9The nobles of the nations assemble
as the people of the God of Abraham,
for the kings[c] of the earth belong to God;
he is greatly exalted.

Psalm 48

A song. A psalm of the Sons of Korah.

1Great is the LORD, and most worthy of praise,
in the city of our God, his holy mountain.
2It is beautiful in its loftiness,
the joy of the whole earth.
Like the utmost heights of Zaphon[d] is
Mount Zion,
the[e] city of the Great King.
3God is in her citadels;
he has shown himself to be her fortress.

4When the kings joined forces,
when they advanced together,
5they saw ⌞her⌟ and were astounded;
they fled in terror.
6Trembling seized them there,
pain like that of a woman in labor.
7You destroyed them like ships of Tarshish
shattered by an east wind.

8As we have heard,
so have we seen
in the city of the LORD Almighty,
in the city of our God:
God makes her secure forever. *Selah*

9Within your temple, O God,
we meditate on your unfailing love.
10Like your name, O God,
your praise reaches to the ends of the
earth;
your right hand is filled with
righteousness.
11Mount Zion rejoices,
the villages of Judah are glad
because of your judgments.

12Walk about Zion, go around her,
count her towers,
13consider well her ramparts,
view her citadels,
that you may tell of them to the next
generation.
14For this God is our God for ever and ever;
he will be our guide even to the end.

Psalm 49

For the director of music. Of the Sons of Korah.
A psalm.

1Hear this, all you peoples;
listen, all who live in this world,
2both low and high,
rich and poor alike:
3My mouth will speak words of wisdom;
the utterance from my heart will give
understanding.
4I will turn my ear to a proverb;
with the harp I will expound my riddle:

5Why should I fear when evil days come,
when wicked deceivers surround me—
6those who trust in their wealth
and boast of their great riches?
7No man can redeem the life of another
or give to God a ransom for him—
8the ransom for a life is costly,
no payment is ever enough—
9that he should live on forever
and not see decay.
10For all can see that wise men die;
the foolish and the senseless alike perish

[a]9 Or *chariots* [b]7 Or *a maskil* (probably a literary or musical term) [c]9 Or *shields* [d]2 *Zaphon* can refer to a sacred mountain or the direction north. [e]2 Or *earth, / Mount Zion, on the northern side / of the*

and leave their wealth to others.
11Their tombs will remain their houses[a]
forever,
their dwellings for endless generations,
though they had[b] named lands after
themselves.

12But man, despite his riches, does not endure;
he is[c] like the beasts that perish.

13This is the fate of those who trust in
themselves,
and of their followers, who approve their
sayings. *Selah*
14Like sheep they are destined for the grave,[d]
and death will feed on them.
The upright will rule over them in the
morning;
their forms will decay in the grave,[d]
far from their princely mansions.
15But God will redeem my life[e] from the
grave;
he will surely take me to himself. *Selah*

16Do not be overawed when a man grows rich,
when the splendor of his house increases;
17for he will take nothing with him when he
dies,
his splendor will not descend with him.
18Though while he lived he counted himself
blessed—
and men praise you when you prosper—
19he will join the generation of his fathers,
who will never see the light ⌊of life⌋.

20A man who has riches without understanding
is like the beasts that perish.

Psalm 50

A psalm of Asaph.

1The Mighty One, God, the LORD,
speaks and summons the earth
from the rising of the sun to the place
where it sets.
2From Zion, perfect in beauty,
God shines forth.
3Our God comes and will not be silent;
a fire devours before him,
and around him a tempest rages.
4He summons the heavens above,
and the earth, that he may judge his
people:
5"Gather to me my consecrated ones,
who made a covenant with me by
sacrifice."
6And the heavens proclaim his righteousness,
for God himself is judge. *Selah*

7"Hear, O my people, and I will speak,
O Israel, and I will testify against you:
I am God, your God.
8I do not rebuke you for your sacrifices
or your burnt offerings, which are ever
before me.
9I have no need of a bull from your stall
or of goats from your pens,
10for every animal of the forest is mine,
and the cattle on a thousand hills.
11I know every bird in the mountains,
and the creatures of the field are mine.
12If I were hungry I would not tell you,
for the world is mine, and all that is in it.
13Do I eat the flesh of bulls
or drink the blood of goats?
14Sacrifice thank offerings to God,
fulfill your vows to the Most High,
15and call upon me in the day of trouble;
I will deliver you, and you will honor me."

16But to the wicked, God says:

"What right have you to recite my laws
or take my covenant on your lips?
17You hate my instruction
and cast my words behind you.
18When you see a thief, you join with him;
you throw in your lot with adulterers.
19You use your mouth for evil
and harness your tongue to deceit.
20You speak continually against your brother
and slander your own mother's son.
21These things you have done and I kept silent;
you thought I was altogether[f] like you.
But I will rebuke you
and accuse you to your face.

22"Consider this, you who forget God,
or I will tear you to pieces, with none to
rescue:
23He who sacrifices thank offerings honors me,
and he prepares the way
so that I may show him[g] the salvation of
God."

Psalm 51

For the director of music. A psalm of David.
When the prophet Nathan came to him after
David had committed adultery with Bathsheba.

1Have mercy on me, O God,
according to your unfailing love;
according to your great compassion

[a] *11* Septuagint and Syriac; Hebrew *In their thoughts their houses will remain* [b] *11* Or / *for they have* [c] *12* Hebrew; Septuagint and Syriac read verse 12 the same as verse 20. [d] *14* Hebrew *Sheol*; also in verse 15 [e] *15* Or *soul* [f] *21* Or *thought the 'I AM' was* [g] *23* Or *and to him who considers his way / I will show*

blot out my transgressions.
2Wash away all my iniquity
and cleanse me from my sin.

3For I know my transgressions,
and my sin is always before me.
4Against you, you only, have I sinned
and done what is evil in your sight,
so that you are proved right when you speak
and justified when you judge.
5Surely I was sinful at birth,
sinful from the time my mother conceived me.
6Surely you desire truth in the inner parts[a];
you teach[b] me wisdom in the inmost place.

7Cleanse me with hyssop, and I will be clean;
wash me, and I will be whiter than snow.
8Let me hear joy and gladness;
let the bones you have crushed rejoice.
9Hide your face from my sins
and blot out all my iniquity.

10Create in me a pure heart, O God,
and renew a steadfast spirit within me.
11Do not cast me from your presence
or take your Holy Spirit from me.
12Restore to me the joy of your salvation
and grant me a willing spirit, to sustain me.

13Then I will teach transgressors your ways,
and sinners will turn back to you.
14Save me from bloodguilt, O God,
the God who saves me,
and my tongue will sing of your righteousness.
15O Lord, open my lips,
and my mouth will declare your praise.
16You do not delight in sacrifice, or I would bring it;
you do not take pleasure in burnt offerings.
17The sacrifices of God are[c] a broken spirit;
a broken and contrite heart,
O God, you will not despise.

18In your good pleasure make Zion prosper;
build up the walls of Jerusalem.
19Then there will be righteous sacrifices,
whole burnt offerings to delight you;
then bulls will be offered on your altar.

Psalm 52

For the director of music. A *maskil*[d] of David. When Doeg the Edomite had gone to Saul and told him: "David has gone to the house of Ahimelech."

1Why do you boast of evil, you mighty man?
Why do you boast all day long,
you who are a disgrace in the eyes of God?
2Your tongue plots destruction;
it is like a sharpened razor,
you who practice deceit.
3You love evil rather than good,
falsehood rather than speaking the truth.
Selah
4You love every harmful word,
O you deceitful tongue!

5Surely God will bring you down to everlasting ruin:
He will snatch you up and tear you from your tent;
he will uproot you from the land of the living. *Selah*
6The righteous will see and fear;
they will laugh at him, saying,
7"Here now is the man
who did not make God his stronghold
but trusted in his great wealth
and grew strong by destroying others!"

8But I am like an olive tree
flourishing in the house of God;
I trust in God's unfailing love
for ever and ever.
9I will praise you forever for what you have done;
in your name I will hope, for your name is good.
I will praise you in the presence of your saints.

Psalm 53

For the director of music. According to *mahalath*.[e] A *maskil*[d] of David.

1The fool says in his heart,
"There is no God."
They are corrupt, and their ways are vile;
there is no one who does good.

2God looks down from heaven
on the sons of men
to see if there are any who understand,
any who seek God.
3Everyone has turned away,

[a]6 The meaning of the Hebrew for this phrase is uncertain. [b]6 Or *you desired . . . ; / you taught* [c]17 Or *My sacrifice, O God, is* [d]Title: Probably a literary or musical term [e]Title: Probably a musical term

they have together become corrupt;
there is no one who does good,
not even one.

4Will the evildoers never learn—
those who devour my people as men eat bread
and who do not call on God?
5There they were, overwhelmed with dread,
where there was nothing to dread.
God scattered the bones of those who attacked you;
you put them to shame, for God despised them.

6Oh, that salvation for Israel would come out of Zion!
When God restores the fortunes of his people,
let Jacob rejoice and Israel be glad!

Psalm 54

For the director of music. With stringed instruments. A *maskil*[a] of David. When the Ziphites had gone to Saul and said, "Is not David hiding among us?"

1Save me, O God, by your name;
vindicate me by your might.
2Hear my prayer, O God;
listen to the words of my mouth.

3Strangers are attacking me;
ruthless men seek my life—
men without regard for God. *Selah*
4Surely God is my help;
the Lord is the one who sustains me.

5Let evil recoil on those who slander me;
in your faithfulness destroy them.

6I will sacrifice a freewill offering to you;
I will praise your name, O LORD,
for it is good.
7For he has delivered me from all my troubles,
and my eyes have looked in triumph on my foes.

Psalm 55

For the director of music. With stringed instruments. A *maskil*[a] of David.

1Listen to my prayer, O God,
do not ignore my plea;
2 hear me and answer me.
My thoughts trouble me and I am distraught
3 at the voice of the enemy,
at the stares of the wicked;
for they bring down suffering upon me
and revile me in their anger.

4My heart is in anguish within me;
the terrors of death assail me.
5Fear and trembling have beset me;
horror has overwhelmed me.
6I said, "Oh, that I had the wings of a dove!
I would fly away and be at rest—
7I would flee far away
and stay in the desert; *Selah*
8I would hurry to my place of shelter,
far from the tempest and storm."

9Confuse the wicked, O Lord, confound their speech,
for I see violence and strife in the city.
10Day and night they prowl about on its walls;
malice and abuse are within it.
11Destructive forces are at work in the city;
threats and lies never leave its streets.

12If an enemy were insulting me,
I could endure it;
if a foe were raising himself against me,
I could hide from him.
13But it is you, a man like myself,
my companion, my close friend,
14with whom I once enjoyed sweet fellowship
as we walked with the throng at the house of God.

15Let death take my enemies by surprise;
let them go down alive to the grave,[b]
for evil finds lodging among them.

16But I call to God,
and the LORD saves me.
17Evening, morning and noon
I cry out in distress,
and he hears my voice.
18He ransoms me unharmed
from the battle waged against me,
even though many oppose me.
19God, who is enthroned forever,
will hear them and afflict them— *Selah*
men who never change their ways
and have no fear of God.

20My companion attacks his friends;
he violates his covenant.
21His speech is smooth as butter,
yet war is in his heart;
his words are more soothing than oil,
yet they are drawn swords.

[a] Title: Probably a literary or musical term [b] 15 Hebrew *Sheol*

22 Cast your cares on the LORD
and he will sustain you;
he will never let the righteous fall.
23 But you, O God, will bring down the wicked
into the pit of corruption;
bloodthirsty and deceitful men
will not live out half their days.

But as for me, I trust in you.

Psalm 56

For the director of music. To ⌊the tune of⌋ "A Dove on Distant Oaks." Of David. A *miktam.*[a] When the Philistines had seized him in Gath.

1 Be merciful to me, O God, for men hotly
pursue me;
all day long they press their attack.
2 My slanderers pursue me all day long;
many are attacking me in their pride.

3 When I am afraid,
I will trust in you.
4 In God, whose word I praise,
in God I trust; I will not be afraid.
What can mortal man do to me?

5 All day long they twist my words;
they are always plotting to harm me.
6 They conspire, they lurk,
they watch my steps,
eager to take my life.

7 On no account let them escape;
in your anger, O God, bring down the
nations.
8 Record my lament;
list my tears on your scroll[b]—
are they not in your record?

9 Then my enemies will turn back
when I call for help.
By this I will know that God is for me.
10 In God, whose word I praise,
in the LORD, whose word I praise—
11 in God I trust; I will not be afraid.
What can man do to me?

12 I am under vows to you, O God;
I will present my thank offerings to
you.
13 For you have delivered me[c] from death
and my feet from stumbling,
that I may walk before God
in the light of life.[d]

Psalm 57

For the director of music. ⌊To the tune of⌋ "Do Not Destroy." Of David. A *miktam.*[a] When he had fled from Saul into the cave.

1 Have mercy on me, O God, have mercy on
me,
for in you my soul takes refuge.
I will take refuge in the shadow of your
wings
until the disaster has passed.

2 I cry out to God Most High,
to God, who fulfills ⌊his purpose⌋ for me.
3 He sends from heaven and saves me,
rebuking those who hotly pursue
me; *Selah*
God sends his love and his faithfulness.

4 I am in the midst of lions;
I lie among ravenous beasts—
men whose teeth are spears and arrows,
whose tongues are sharp swords.

5 Be exalted, O God, above the heavens;
let your glory be over all the earth.

6 They spread a net for my feet—
I was bowed down in distress.
They dug a pit in my path—
but they have fallen into it themselves.
Selah

7 My heart is steadfast, O God,
my heart is steadfast;
I will sing and make music.
8 Awake, my soul!
Awake, harp and lyre!
I will awaken the dawn.

9 I will praise you, O Lord, among the nations;
I will sing of you among the peoples.
10 For great is your love, reaching to the
heavens;
your faithfulness reaches to the skies.

11 Be exalted, O God, above the heavens;
let your glory be over all the earth.

Psalm 58

For the director of music. ⌊To the tune of⌋ "Do Not Destroy." Of David. A *miktam.*[a]

1 Do you rulers indeed speak justly?
Do you judge uprightly among men?
2 No, in your heart you devise injustice,
and your hands mete out violence on the
earth.

[a] Title: Probably a literary or musical term [b] 8 Or / *put my tears in your wineskin* [c] 13 Or *my soul* [d] 13 Or *the land of the living*

3Even from birth the wicked go astray;
from the womb they are wayward and speak lies.
4Their venom is like the venom of a snake,
like that of a cobra that has stopped its ears,
5that will not heed the tune of the charmer,
however skillful the enchanter may be.

6Break the teeth in their mouths, O God;
tear out, O LORD, the fangs of the lions!
7Let them vanish like water that flows away;
when they draw the bow, let their arrows be blunted.
8Like a slug melting away as it moves along,
like a stillborn child, may they not see the sun.

9Before your pots can feel ⌞the heat of⌟ the thorns—
whether they be green or dry—the wicked will be swept away.[a]
10The righteous will be glad when they are avenged,
when they bathe their feet in the blood of the wicked.
11Then men will say,
"Surely the righteous still are rewarded;
surely there is a God who judges the earth."

Psalm 59

For the director of music. ⌞To the tune of⌟ "Do Not Destroy." Of David. A *miktam.*[b] When Saul had sent men to watch David's house in order to kill him.

1Deliver me from my enemies, O God;
protect me from those who rise up against me.
2Deliver me from evildoers
and save me from bloodthirsty men.

3See how they lie in wait for me!
Fierce men conspire against me
for no offense or sin of mine, O LORD.
4I have done no wrong, yet they are ready to attack me.
Arise to help me; look on my plight!
5O LORD God Almighty, the God of Israel,
rouse yourself to punish all the nations;
show no mercy to wicked traitors. *Selah*

6They return at evening,
snarling like dogs,
and prowl about the city.
7See what they spew from their mouths—
they spew out swords from their lips,
and they say, "Who can hear us?"
8But you, O LORD, laugh at them;
you scoff at all those nations.

9O my Strength, I watch for you;
you, O God, are my fortress, 10my loving God.

God will go before me
and will let me gloat over those who slander me.
11But do not kill them, O Lord our shield,[c]
or my people will forget.
In your might make them wander about,
and bring them down.
12For the sins of their mouths,
for the words of their lips,
let them be caught in their pride.
For the curses and lies they utter,
13 consume them in wrath,
consume them till they are no more.
Then it will be known to the ends of the earth
that God rules over Jacob. *Selah*

14They return at evening,
snarling like dogs,
and prowl about the city.
15They wander about for food
and howl if not satisfied.
16But I will sing of your strength,
in the morning I will sing of your love;
for you are my fortress,
my refuge in times of trouble.

17O my Strength, I sing praise to you;
you, O God, are my fortress, my loving God.

Psalm 60

For the director of music. To ⌞the tune of⌟ "The Lily of the Covenant." A *miktam*[b] of David. For teaching. When he fought Aram Naharaim[d] and Aram Zobah,[e] and when Joab returned and struck down twelve thousand Edomites in the Valley of Salt.

1You have rejected us, O God, and burst forth upon us;
you have been angry—now restore us!
2You have shaken the land and torn it open;
mend its fractures, for it is quaking.
3You have shown your people desperate times;
you have given us wine that makes us stagger.

[a]9 The meaning of the Hebrew for this verse is uncertain. [b]Title: Probably a literary or musical term [c]11 Or *sovereign*
[d]Title: That is, Arameans of Northwest Mesopotamia [e]Title: That is, Arameans of central Syria

4But for those who fear you, you have raised a banner
to be unfurled against the bow. *Selah*

5Save us and help us with your right hand,
that those you love may be delivered.
6God has spoken from his sanctuary:
"In triumph I will parcel out Shechem
and measure off the Valley of Succoth.
7Gilead is mine, and Manasseh is mine;
Ephraim is my helmet,
Judah my scepter.
8Moab is my washbasin,
upon Edom I toss my sandal;
over Philistia I shout in triumph."

9Who will bring me to the fortified city?
Who will lead me to Edom?
10Is it not you, O God, you who have rejected us
and no longer go out with our armies?
11Give us aid against the enemy,
for the help of man is worthless.
12With God we will gain the victory,
and he will trample down our enemies.

Psalm 61

For the director of music. With stringed instruments. Of David.

1Hear my cry, O God;
listen to my prayer.

2From the ends of the earth I call to you,
I call as my heart grows faint;
lead me to the rock that is higher than I.
3For you have been my refuge,
a strong tower against the foe.

4I long to dwell in your tent forever
and take refuge in the shelter of your wings. *Selah*
5For you have heard my vows, O God;
you have given me the heritage of those who fear your name.

6Increase the days of the king's life,
his years for many generations.
7May he be enthroned in God's presence forever;
appoint your love and faithfulness to protect him.

8Then will I ever sing praise to your name
and fulfill my vows day after day.

Psalm 62

For the director of music. For Jeduthun. A psalm of David.

1My soul finds rest in God alone;
my salvation comes from him.
2He alone is my rock and my salvation;
he is my fortress, I will never be shaken.

3How long will you assault a man?
Would all of you throw him down—
this leaning wall, this tottering fence?
4They fully intend to topple him
from his lofty place;
they take delight in lies.
With their mouths they bless,
but in their hearts they curse. *Selah*

5Find rest, O my soul, in God alone;
my hope comes from him.
6He alone is my rock and my salvation;
he is my fortress, I will not be shaken.
7My salvation and my honor depend on God[a];
he is my mighty rock, my refuge.
8Trust in him at all times, O people;
pour out your hearts to him,
for God is our refuge. *Selah*

9Lowborn men are but a breath,
the highborn are but a lie;
if weighed on a balance, they are nothing;
together they are only a breath.
10Do not trust in extortion
or take pride in stolen goods;
though your riches increase,
do not set your heart on them.

11One thing God has spoken,
two things have I heard:
that you, O God, are strong,
12 and that you, O Lord, are loving.
Surely you will reward each person
according to what he has done.

Psalm 63

A psalm of David. When he was in the Desert of Judah.

1O God, you are my God,
earnestly I seek you;
my soul thirsts for you,
my body longs for you,
in a dry and weary land
where there is no water.

2I have seen you in the sanctuary
and beheld your power and your glory.

[a]7 Or / *God Most High is my salvation and my honor*

3Because your love is better than life,
my lips will glorify you.
4I will praise you as long as I live,
and in your name I will lift up my hands.
5My soul will be satisfied as with the richest of foods;
with singing lips my mouth will praise you.

6On my bed I remember you;
I think of you through the watches of the night.
7Because you are my help,
I sing in the shadow of your wings.
8My soul clings to you;
your right hand upholds me.

9They who seek my life will be destroyed;
they will go down to the depths of the earth.
10They will be given over to the sword
and become food for jackals.

11But the king will rejoice in God;
all who swear by God's name will praise him,
while the mouths of liars will be silenced.

Psalm 64

For the director of music. A psalm of David.

1Hear me, O God, as I voice my complaint;
protect my life from the threat of the enemy.
2Hide me from the conspiracy of the wicked,
from that noisy crowd of evildoers.

3They sharpen their tongues like swords
and aim their words like deadly arrows.
4They shoot from ambush at the innocent man;
they shoot at him suddenly, without fear.

5They encourage each other in evil plans,
they talk about hiding their snares;
they say, "Who will see them[a]?"
6They plot injustice and say,
"We have devised a perfect plan!"
Surely the mind and heart of man are cunning.

7But God will shoot them with arrows;
suddenly they will be struck down.
8He will turn their own tongues against them
and bring them to ruin;
all who see them will shake their heads in scorn.
9All mankind will fear;
they will proclaim the works of God
and ponder what he has done.
10Let the righteous rejoice in the LORD
and take refuge in him;
let all the upright in heart praise him!

Psalm 65

For the director of music. A psalm of David. A song.

1Praise awaits[b] you, O God, in Zion;
to you our vows will be fulfilled.
2O you who hear prayer,
to you all men will come.
3When we were overwhelmed by sins,
you forgave[c] our transgressions.
4Blessed are those you choose
and bring near to live in your courts!
We are filled with the good things of your house,
of your holy temple.

5You answer us with awesome deeds of righteousness,
O God our Savior,
the hope of all the ends of the earth
and of the farthest seas,
6who formed the mountains by your power,
having armed yourself with strength,
7who stilled the roaring of the seas,
the roaring of their waves,
and the turmoil of the nations.
8Those living far away fear your wonders;
where morning dawns and evening fades
you call forth songs of joy.

9You care for the land and water it;
you enrich it abundantly.
The streams of God are filled with water
to provide the people with grain,
for so you have ordained it.[d]
10You drench its furrows
and level its ridges;
you soften it with showers
and bless its crops.
11You crown the year with your bounty,
and your carts overflow with abundance.
12The grasslands of the desert overflow;
the hills are clothed with gladness.
13The meadows are covered with flocks
and the valleys are mantled with grain;
they shout for joy and sing.

[a]5 Or *us* [b]1 Or *befits*; the meaning of the Hebrew for this word is uncertain. [c]3 Or *made atonement for* [d]9 Or *for that is how you prepare the land*

Psalm 66

For the director of music. A song. A psalm.

1Shout with joy to God, all the earth!
2 Sing the glory of his name;
make his praise glorious!
3Say to God, "How awesome are your deeds!
So great is your power
that your enemies cringe before you.
4All the earth bows down to you;
they sing praise to you,
they sing praise to your name." *Selah*

5Come and see what God has done,
how awesome his works in man's behalf!
6He turned the sea into dry land,
they passed through the waters on foot—
come, let us rejoice in him.
7He rules forever by his power,
his eyes watch the nations—
let not the rebellious rise up against him. *Selah*

8Praise our God, O peoples,
let the sound of his praise be heard;
9he has preserved our lives
and kept our feet from slipping.
10For you, O God, tested us;
you refined us like silver.
11You brought us into prison
and laid burdens on our backs.
12You let men ride over our heads;
we went through fire and water,
but you brought us to a place of abundance.

13I will come to your temple with burnt offerings
and fulfill my vows to you—
14vows my lips promised and my mouth spoke
when I was in trouble.
15I will sacrifice fat animals to you
and an offering of rams;
I will offer bulls and goats. *Selah*

16Come and listen, all you who fear God;
let me tell you what he has done for me.
17I cried out to him with my mouth;
his praise was on my tongue.
18If I had cherished sin in my heart,
the Lord would not have listened;
19but God has surely listened
and heard my voice in prayer.
20Praise be to God,
who has not rejected my prayer
or withheld his love from me!

Psalm 67

For the director of music. With stringed instruments. A psalm. A song.

1May God be gracious to us and bless us
and make his face shine upon us, *Selah*
2that your ways may be known on earth,
your salvation among all nations.

3May the peoples praise you, O God;
may all the peoples praise you.
4May the nations be glad and sing for joy,
for you rule the peoples justly
and guide the nations of the earth. *Selah*
5May the peoples praise you, O God;
may all the peoples praise you.

6Then the land will yield its harvest,
and God, our God, will bless us.
7God will bless us,
and all the ends of the earth will fear him.

Psalm 68

For the director of music. Of David. A psalm. A song.

1May God arise, may his enemies be scattered;
may his foes flee before him.
2As smoke is blown away by the wind,
may you blow them away;
as wax melts before the fire,
may the wicked perish before God.
3But may the righteous be glad
and rejoice before God;
may they be happy and joyful.

4Sing to God, sing praise to his name,
extol him who rides on the clouds[a]—
his name is the LORD—
and rejoice before him.
5A father to the fatherless, a defender of widows,
is God in his holy dwelling.
6God sets the lonely in families,[b]
he leads forth the prisoners with singing;
but the rebellious live in a sun-scorched land.

7When you went out before your people, O God,
when you marched through the wasteland, *Selah*

8the earth shook,
the heavens poured down rain,
before God, the One of Sinai,
before God, the God of Israel.
9You gave abundant showers, O God;

[a]4 Or / *prepare the way for him who rides through the deserts*
[b]6 Or *the desolate in a homeland*

you refreshed your weary inheritance.
10Your people settled in it,
and from your bounty, O God, you provided for the poor.

11The Lord announced the word,
and great was the company of those who proclaimed it:
12"Kings and armies flee in haste;
in the camps men divide the plunder.
13Even while you sleep among the campfires,[a]
the wings of ⌞my⌟ dove are sheathed with silver,
its feathers with shining gold."
14When the Almighty[b] scattered the kings in the land,
it was like snow fallen on Zalmon.

15The mountains of Bashan are majestic mountains;
rugged are the mountains of Bashan.
16Why gaze in envy, O rugged mountains,
at the mountain where God chooses to reign,
where the LORD himself will dwell forever?
17The chariots of God are tens of thousands
and thousands of thousands;
the Lord ⌞has come⌟ from Sinai into his sanctuary.
18When you ascended on high,
you led captives in your train;
you received gifts from men,
even from[c] the rebellious—
that you,[d] O LORD God, might dwell there.

19Praise be to the Lord, to God our Savior,
who daily bears our burdens. *Selah*
20Our God is a God who saves;
from the Sovereign LORD comes escape from death.

21Surely God will crush the heads of his enemies,
the hairy crowns of those who go on in their sins.
22The Lord says, "I will bring them from Bashan;
I will bring them from the depths of the sea,
23that you may plunge your feet in the blood of your foes,
while the tongues of your dogs have their share."

24Your procession has come into view, O God,
the procession of my God and King into the sanctuary.
25In front are the singers, after them the musicians;
with them are the maidens playing tambourines.
26Praise God in the great congregation;
praise the LORD in the assembly of Israel.
27There is the little tribe of Benjamin, leading them,
there the great throng of Judah's princes,
and there the princes of Zebulun and of Naphtali.

28Summon your power, O God[e];
show us your strength, O God, as you have done before.
29Because of your temple at Jerusalem
kings will bring you gifts.
30Rebuke the beast among the reeds,
the herd of bulls among the calves of the nations.
Humbled, may it bring bars of silver.
Scatter the nations who delight in war.
31Envoys will come from Egypt;
Cush[f] will submit herself to God.

32Sing to God, O kingdoms of the earth,
sing praise to the Lord, *Selah*
33to him who rides the ancient skies above,
who thunders with mighty voice.
34Proclaim the power of God,
whose majesty is over Israel,
whose power is in the skies.
35You are awesome, O God, in your sanctuary;
the God of Israel gives power and strength to his people.

Praise be to God!

Psalm 69

For the director of music. To ⌞the tune of⌟ "Lilies." Of David.

1Save me, O God,
for the waters have come up to my neck.
2I sink in the miry depths,
where there is no foothold.
I have come into the deep waters;
the floods engulf me.
3I am worn out calling for help;
my throat is parched.
My eyes fail,
looking for my God.
4Those who hate me without reason
outnumber the hairs of my head;

[a]13 Or *saddlebags* [b]14 Hebrew *Shaddai* [c]18 Or *gifts for men, / even* [d]18 Or *they* [e]28 Many Hebrew manuscripts, Septuagint and Syriac; most Hebrew manuscripts *Your God has summoned power for you* [f]31 That is, the upper Nile region

many are my enemies without cause,
those who seek to destroy me.
I am forced to restore
what I did not steal.

5 You know my folly, O God;
my guilt is not hidden from you.

6 May those who hope in you
not be disgraced because of me,
O Lord, the LORD Almighty;
may those who seek you
not be put to shame because of me,
O God of Israel.
7 For I endure scorn for your sake,
and shame covers my face.
8 I am a stranger to my brothers,
an alien to my own mother's sons;
9 for zeal for your house consumes me,
and the insults of those who insult you fall on me.
10 When I weep and fast,
I must endure scorn;
11 when I put on sackcloth,
people make sport of me.
12 Those who sit at the gate mock me,
and I am the song of the drunkards.

13 But I pray to you, O LORD,
in the time of your favor;
in your great love, O God,
answer me with your sure salvation.
14 Rescue me from the mire,
do not let me sink;
deliver me from those who hate me,
from the deep waters.
15 Do not let the floodwaters engulf me
or the depths swallow me up
or the pit close its mouth over me.
16 Answer me, O LORD, out of the goodness of your love;
in your great mercy turn to me.
17 Do not hide your face from your servant;
answer me quickly, for I am in trouble.
18 Come near and rescue me;
redeem me because of my foes.
19 You know how I am scorned, disgraced and shamed;
all my enemies are before you.
20 Scorn has broken my heart
and has left me helpless;
I looked for sympathy, but there was none,
for comforters, but I found none.
21 They put gall in my food
and gave me vinegar for my thirst.
22 May the table set before them become a snare;
may it become retribution and[a] a trap.
23 May their eyes be darkened so they cannot see,
and their backs be bent forever.
24 Pour out your wrath on them;
let your fierce anger overtake them.
25 May their place be deserted;
let there be no one to dwell in their tents.
26 For they persecute those you wound
and talk about the pain of those you hurt.
27 Charge them with crime upon crime;
do not let them share in your salvation.
28 May they be blotted out of the book of life
and not be listed with the righteous.

29 I am in pain and distress;
may your salvation, O God, protect me.

30 I will praise God's name in song
and glorify him with thanksgiving.
31 This will please the LORD more than an ox,
more than a bull with its horns and hoofs.
32 The poor will see and be glad—
you who seek God, may your hearts live!
33 The LORD hears the needy
and does not despise his captive people.

34 Let heaven and earth praise him,
the seas and all that move in them,
35 for God will save Zion
and rebuild the cities of Judah.
Then people will settle there and possess it;
36 the children of his servants will inherit it,
and those who love his name will dwell there.

Psalm 70

For the director of music. Of David. A petition.

1 Hasten, O God, to save me;
O LORD, come quickly to help me.
2 May those who seek my life
be put to shame and confusion;
may all who desire my ruin
be turned back in disgrace.
3 May those who say to me, "Aha! Aha!"
turn back because of their shame.
4 But may all who seek you
rejoice and be glad in you;
may those who love your salvation always say,
"Let God be exalted!"
5 Yet I am poor and needy;
come quickly to me, O God.
You are my help and my deliverer;
O LORD, do not delay.

[a] 22 Or *snare / and their fellowship become*

Psalm 71

1In you, O LORD, I have taken refuge;
let me never be put to shame.
2Rescue me and deliver me in your righteousness;
turn your ear to me and save me.
3Be my rock of refuge,
to which I can always go;
give the command to save me,
for you are my rock and my fortress.
4Deliver me, O my God, from the hand of the wicked,
from the grasp of evil and cruel men.

5For you have been my hope, O Sovereign LORD,
my confidence since my youth.
6From birth I have relied on you;
you brought me forth from my mother's womb.
I will ever praise you.
7I have become like a portent to many,
but you are my strong refuge.
8My mouth is filled with your praise,
declaring your splendor all day long.

9Do not cast me away when I am old;
do not forsake me when my strength is gone.
10For my enemies speak against me;
those who wait to kill me conspire together.
11They say, "God has forsaken him;
pursue him and seize him,
for no one will rescue him."
12Be not far from me, O God;
come quickly, O my God, to help me.
13May my accusers perish in shame;
may those who want to harm me
be covered with scorn and disgrace.

14But as for me, I will always have hope;
I will praise you more and more.
15My mouth will tell of your righteousness,
of your salvation all day long,
though I know not its measure.
16I will come and proclaim your mighty acts,
O Sovereign LORD;
I will proclaim your righteousness, yours alone.
17Since my youth, O God, you have taught me,
and to this day I declare your marvelous deeds.
18Even when I am old and gray,
do not forsake me, O God,
till I declare your power to the next generation,
your might to all who are to come.

19Your righteousness reaches to the skies, O God,
you who have done great things.
Who, O God, is like you?
20Though you have made me see troubles, many and bitter,
you will restore my life again;
from the depths of the earth
you will again bring me up.
21You will increase my honor
and comfort me once again.

22I will praise you with the harp
for your faithfulness, O my God;
I will sing praise to you with the lyre,
O Holy One of Israel.
23My lips will shout for joy
when I sing praise to you—
I, whom you have redeemed.
24My tongue will tell of your righteous acts
all day long,
for those who wanted to harm me
have been put to shame and confusion.

Psalm 72

Of Solomon.

1Endow the king with your justice, O God,
the royal son with your righteousness.
2He will[a] judge your people in righteousness,
your afflicted ones with justice.
3The mountains will bring prosperity to the people,
the hills the fruit of righteousness.
4He will defend the afflicted among the people
and save the children of the needy;
he will crush the oppressor.

5He will endure[b] as long as the sun,
as long as the moon, through all generations.
6He will be like rain falling on a mown field,
like showers watering the earth.
7In his days the righteous will flourish;
prosperity will abound till the moon is no more.

8He will rule from sea to sea
and from the River[c] to the ends of the earth.[d]
9The desert tribes will bow before him
and his enemies will lick the dust.
10The kings of Tarshish and of distant shores

a2 Or *May he*; similarly in verses 3-11 and 17 b5 Septuagint; Hebrew *You will be feared* c8 That is, the Euphrates
d8 Or *the end of the land*

will bring tribute to him;
the kings of Sheba and Seba
will present him gifts.
11 All kings will bow down to him
and all nations will serve him.

12 For he will deliver the needy who cry out,
the afflicted who have no one to help.
13 He will take pity on the weak and the needy
and save the needy from death.
14 He will rescue them from oppression and violence,
for precious is their blood in his sight.

15 Long may he live!
May gold from Sheba be given him.
May people ever pray for him
and bless him all day long.
16 Let grain abound throughout the land;
on the tops of the hills may it sway.
Let its fruit flourish like Lebanon;
let it thrive like the grass of the field.
17 May his name endure forever;
may it continue as long as the sun.

All nations will be blessed through him,
and they will call him blessed.

18 Praise be to the LORD God, the God of Israel,
who alone does marvelous deeds.
19 Praise be to his glorious name forever;
may the whole earth be filled with his glory.
Amen and Amen.

20 This concludes the prayers of David son of Jesse.

BOOK III

Psalms 73–89

Psalm 73

A psalm of Asaph.

1 Surely God is good to Israel,
to those who are pure in heart.

2 But as for me, my feet had almost slipped;
I had nearly lost my foothold.
3 For I envied the arrogant
when I saw the prosperity of the wicked.

4 They have no struggles;
their bodies are healthy and strong.[a]
5 They are free from the burdens common to man;
they are not plagued by human ills.
6 Therefore pride is their necklace;
they clothe themselves with violence.
7 From their callous hearts comes iniquity[b];
the evil conceits of their minds know no limits.
8 They scoff, and speak with malice;
in their arrogance they threaten oppression.
9 Their mouths lay claim to heaven,
and their tongues take possession of the earth.
10 Therefore their people turn to them
and drink up waters in abundance.[c]
11 They say, "How can God know?
Does the Most High have knowledge?"
12 This is what the wicked are like—
always carefree, they increase in wealth.

13 Surely in vain have I kept my heart pure;
in vain have I washed my hands in innocence.
14 All day long I have been plagued;
I have been punished every morning.

15 If I had said, "I will speak thus,"
I would have betrayed your children.
16 When I tried to understand all this,
it was oppressive to me
17 till I entered the sanctuary of God;
then I understood their final destiny.

18 Surely you place them on slippery ground;
you cast them down to ruin.
19 How suddenly are they destroyed,
completely swept away by terrors!
20 As a dream when one awakes,
so when you arise, O Lord,
you will despise them as fantasies.

21 When my heart was grieved
and my spirit embittered,
22 I was senseless and ignorant;
I was a brute beast before you.

23 Yet I am always with you;
you hold me by my right hand.
24 You guide me with your counsel,
and afterward you will take me into glory.
25 Whom have I in heaven but you?
And earth has nothing I desire besides you.
26 My flesh and my heart may fail,
but God is the strength of my heart
and my portion forever.

27 Those who are far from you will perish;
you destroy all who are unfaithful to you.
28 But as for me, it is good to be near God.

[a] 4 With a different word division of the Hebrew; Masoretic Text *struggles at their death; / their bodies are healthy* [b] 7 Syriac (see also Septuagint); Hebrew *Their eyes bulge with fat* [c] 10 The meaning of the Hebrew for this verse is uncertain.

I have made the Sovereign LORD my
refuge;
I will tell of all your deeds.

Psalm 74

A *maskil*[a] of Asaph.

1Why have you rejected us forever, O God?
Why does your anger smolder against the
sheep of your pasture?
2Remember the people you purchased of old,
the tribe of your inheritance, whom you
redeemed—
Mount Zion, where you dwelt.
3Turn your steps toward these everlasting
ruins,
all this destruction the enemy has brought
on the sanctuary.
4Your foes roared in the place where you met
with us;
they set up their standards as signs.
5They behaved like men wielding axes
to cut through a thicket of trees.
6They smashed all the carved paneling
with their axes and hatchets.
7They burned your sanctuary to the ground;
they defiled the dwelling place of your
Name.
8They said in their hearts, "We will crush
them completely!"
They burned every place where God was
worshiped in the land.
9We are given no miraculous signs;
no prophets are left,
and none of us knows how long this will
be.
10How long will the enemy mock you, O God?
Will the foe revile your name forever?
11Why do you hold back your hand, your right
hand?
Take it from the folds of your garment and
destroy them!
12But you, O God, are my king from of old;
you bring salvation upon the earth.
13It was you who split open the sea by your
power;
you broke the heads of the monster in the
waters.
14It was you who crushed the heads of
Leviathan
and gave him as food to the creatures of
the desert.
15It was you who opened up springs and
streams;
you dried up the ever flowing rivers.
16The day is yours, and yours also the night;
you established the sun and moon.
17It was you who set all the boundaries of the
earth;
you made both summer and winter.
18Remember how the enemy has mocked you,
O LORD,
how foolish people have reviled your
name.
19Do not hand over the life of your dove to
wild beasts;
do not forget the lives of your afflicted
people forever.
20Have regard for your covenant,
because haunts of violence fill the dark
places of the land.
21Do not let the oppressed retreat in disgrace;
may the poor and needy praise your name.
22Rise up, O God, and defend your cause;
remember how fools mock you all day
long.
23Do not ignore the clamor of your adversaries,
the uproar of your enemies, which rises
continually.

Psalm 75

For the director of music. ⌞To the tune of⌟ "Do Not Destroy." A psalm of Asaph. A song.

1We give thanks to you, O God,
we give thanks, for your Name is near;
men tell of your wonderful deeds.
2You say, "I choose the appointed time;
it is I who judge uprightly.
3When the earth and all its people quake,
it is I who hold its pillars firm. *Selah*
4To the arrogant I say, 'Boast no more,'
and to the wicked, 'Do not lift up your
horns.
5Do not lift your horns against heaven;
do not speak with outstretched neck.' "
6No one from the east or the west
or from the desert can exalt a man.
7But it is God who judges:
He brings one down, he exalts another.
8In the hand of the LORD is a cup
full of foaming wine mixed with spices;
he pours it out, and all the wicked of the
earth
drink it down to its very dregs.
9As for me, I will declare this forever;
I will sing praise to the God of Jacob.
10I will cut off the horns of all the wicked,

[a]Title: Probably a literary or musical term

but the horns of the righteous will be
lifted up.

Psalm 76

For the director of music. With stringed instruments. A psalm of Asaph. A song.

1In Judah God is known;
his name is great in Israel.
2His tent is in Salem,
his dwelling place in Zion.
3There he broke the flashing arrows,
the shields and the swords, the weapons
of war. *Selah*

4You are resplendent with light,
more majestic than mountains rich with
game.
5Valiant men lie plundered,
they sleep their last sleep;
not one of the warriors
can lift his hands.
6At your rebuke, O God of Jacob,
both horse and chariot lie still.
7You alone are to be feared.
Who can stand before you when you are
angry?
8From heaven you pronounced judgment,
and the land feared and was quiet—
9when you, O God, rose up to judge,
to save all the afflicted of the land. *Selah*
10Surely your wrath against men brings you
praise,
and the survivors of your wrath are
restrained.[a]
11Make vows to the LORD your God and fulfill
them;
let all the neighboring lands
bring gifts to the One to be feared.
12He breaks the spirit of rulers;
he is feared by the kings of the earth.

Psalm 77

For the director of music. For Jeduthun. Of Asaph. A psalm.

1I cried out to God for help;
I cried out to God to hear me.
2When I was in distress, I sought the Lord;
at night I stretched out untiring hands
and my soul refused to be comforted.

3I remembered you, O God, and I groaned;
I mused, and my spirit grew faint. *Selah*
4You kept my eyes from closing;
I was too troubled to speak.
5I thought about the former days,
the years of long ago;
6I remembered my songs in the night.
My heart mused and my spirit inquired:

7"Will the Lord reject forever?
Will he never show his favor again?
8Has his unfailing love vanished forever?
Has his promise failed for all time?
9Has God forgotten to be merciful?
Has he in anger withheld his
compassion?" *Selah*

10Then I thought, "To this I will appeal:
the years of the right hand of the Most
High."
11I will remember the deeds of the LORD;
yes, I will remember your miracles of long
ago.
12I will meditate on all your works
and consider all your mighty deeds.

13Your ways, O God, are holy.
What god is so great as our God?
14You are the God who performs miracles;
you display your power among the
peoples.
15With your mighty arm you redeemed your
people,
the descendants of Jacob and Joseph. *Selah*

16The waters saw you, O God,
the waters saw you and writhed;
the very depths were convulsed.
17The clouds poured down water,
the skies resounded with thunder;
your arrows flashed back and forth.
18Your thunder was heard in the whirlwind,
your lightning lit up the world;
the earth trembled and quaked.
19Your path led through the sea,
your way through the mighty waters,
though your footprints were not seen.

20You led your people like a flock
by the hand of Moses and Aaron.

Psalm 78

A *maskil*[b] of Asaph.

1O my people, hear my teaching;
listen to the words of my mouth.
2I will open my mouth in parables,
I will utter hidden things, things from of
old—
3what we have heard and known,
what our fathers have told us.

[a] 10 Or *Surely the wrath of men brings you praise, / and with the remainder of wrath you arm yourself* [b] Title: Probably a literary or musical term

4We will not hide them from their children;
we will tell the next generation
the praiseworthy deeds of the LORD,
his power, and the wonders he has done.
5He decreed statutes for Jacob
and established the law in Israel,
which he commanded our forefathers
to teach their children,
6so the next generation would know them,
even the children yet to be born,
and they in turn would tell their children.
7Then they would put their trust in God
and would not forget his deeds
but would keep his commands.
8They would not be like their forefathers—
a stubborn and rebellious generation,
whose hearts were not loyal to God,
whose spirits were not faithful to him.

9The men of Ephraim, though armed with bows,
turned back on the day of battle;
10they did not keep God's covenant
and refused to live by his law.
11They forgot what he had done,
the wonders he had shown them.
12He did miracles in the sight of their fathers
in the land of Egypt, in the region of Zoan.
13He divided the sea and led them through;
he made the water stand firm like a wall.
14He guided them with the cloud by day
and with light from the fire all night.
15He split the rocks in the desert
and gave them water as abundant as the seas;
16he brought streams out of a rocky crag
and made water flow down like rivers.
17But they continued to sin against him,
rebelling in the desert against the Most High.
18They willfully put God to the test
by demanding the food they craved.
19They spoke against God, saying,
"Can God spread a table in the desert?
20When he struck the rock, water gushed out,
and streams flowed abundantly.
But can he also give us food?
Can he supply meat for his people?"
21When the LORD heard them, he was very angry;
his fire broke out against Jacob,
and his wrath rose against Israel,
22for they did not believe in God
or trust in his deliverance.
23Yet he gave a command to the skies above
and opened the doors of the heavens;
24he rained down manna for the people to eat,
he gave them the grain of heaven.
25Men ate the bread of angels;
he sent them all the food they could eat.
26He let loose the east wind from the heavens
and led forth the south wind by his power.
27He rained meat down on them like dust,
flying birds like sand on the seashore.
28He made them come down inside their camp,
all around their tents.
29They ate till they had more than enough,
for he had given them what they craved.
30But before they turned from the food they craved,
even while it was still in their mouths,
31God's anger rose against them;
he put to death the sturdiest among them,
cutting down the young men of Israel.

32In spite of all this, they kept on sinning;
in spite of his wonders, they did not believe.
33So he ended their days in futility
and their years in terror.
34Whenever God slew them, they would seek him;
they eagerly turned to him again.
35They remembered that God was their Rock,
that God Most High was their Redeemer.
36But then they would flatter him with their mouths,
lying to him with their tongues;
37their hearts were not loyal to him,
they were not faithful to his covenant.
38Yet he was merciful;
he forgave their iniquities
and did not destroy them.
Time after time he restrained his anger
and did not stir up his full wrath.
39He remembered that they were but flesh,
a passing breeze that does not return.

40How often they rebelled against him in the desert
and grieved him in the wasteland!
41Again and again they put God to the test;
they vexed the Holy One of Israel.
42They did not remember his power—
the day he redeemed them from the oppressor,
43the day he displayed his miraculous signs in Egypt,
his wonders in the region of Zoan.
44He turned their rivers to blood;
they could not drink from their streams.
45He sent swarms of flies that devoured them,
and frogs that devastated them.
46He gave their crops to the grasshopper,
their produce to the locust.
47He destroyed their vines with hail
and their sycamore-figs with sleet.
48He gave over their cattle to the hail,

their livestock to bolts of lightning.
49He unleashed against them his hot anger,
his wrath, indignation and hostility—
a band of destroying angels.
50He prepared a path for his anger;
he did not spare them from death
but gave them over to the plague.
51He struck down all the firstborn of Egypt,
the firstfruits of manhood in the tents of
Ham.
52But he brought his people out like a flock;
he led them like sheep through the desert.
53He guided them safely, so they were
unafraid;
but the sea engulfed their enemies.
54Thus he brought them to the border of his
holy land,
to the hill country his right hand had
taken.
55He drove out nations before them
and allotted their lands to them as an
inheritance;
he settled the tribes of Israel in their
homes.

56But they put God to the test
and rebelled against the Most High;
they did not keep his statutes.
57Like their fathers they were disloyal and
faithless,
as unreliable as a faulty bow.
58They angered him with their high places;
they aroused his jealousy with their idols.
59When God heard them, he was very angry;
he rejected Israel completely.
60He abandoned the tabernacle of Shiloh,
the tent he had set up among men.
61He sent ⌊the ark of⌋ his might into captivity,
his splendor into the hands of the enemy.
62He gave his people over to the sword;
he was very angry with his inheritance.
63Fire consumed their young men,
and their maidens had no wedding songs;
64their priests were put to the sword,
and their widows could not weep.

65Then the Lord awoke as from sleep,
as a man wakes from the stupor of wine.
66He beat back his enemies;
he put them to everlasting shame.
67Then he rejected the tents of Joseph,
he did not choose the tribe of Ephraim;
68but he chose the tribe of Judah,
Mount Zion, which he loved.
69He built his sanctuary like the heights,
like the earth that he established forever.
70He chose David his servant
and took him from the sheep pens;
71from tending the sheep he brought him
to be the shepherd of his people Jacob,
of Israel his inheritance.
72And David shepherded them with integrity of
heart;
with skillful hands he led them.

Psalm 79

A psalm of Asaph.

1O God, the nations have invaded your
inheritance;
they have defiled your holy temple,
they have reduced Jerusalem to rubble.
2They have given the dead bodies of your
servants
as food to the birds of the air,
the flesh of your saints to the beasts of the
earth.
3They have poured out blood like water
all around Jerusalem,
and there is no one to bury the dead.
4We are objects of reproach to our neighbors,
of scorn and derision to those around us.

5How long, O LORD? Will you be angry
forever?
How long will your jealousy burn like fire?
6Pour out your wrath on the nations
that do not acknowledge you,
on the kingdoms
that do not call on your name;
7for they have devoured Jacob
and destroyed his homeland.
8Do not hold against us the sins of the fathers;
may your mercy come quickly to meet us,
for we are in desperate need.
9Help us, O God our Savior,
for the glory of your name;
deliver us and forgive our sins
for your name's sake.
10Why should the nations say,
"Where is their God?"
Before our eyes, make known among the
nations
that you avenge the outpoured blood of
your servants.
11May the groans of the prisoners come before
you;
by the strength of your arm
preserve those condemned to die.
12Pay back into the laps of our neighbors seven
times
the reproach they have hurled at you,
O Lord.
13Then we your people, the sheep of your
pasture,
will praise you forever;

from generation to generation
we will recount your praise.

Psalm 80

For the director of music. To ⌊the tune of⌋ "The Lilies of the Covenant." Of Asaph. A psalm.

1Hear us, O Shepherd of Israel,
you who lead Joseph like a flock;
you who sit enthroned between the cherubim, shine forth
2 before Ephraim, Benjamin and Manasseh.
Awaken your might;
come and save us.

3Restore us, O God;
make your face shine upon us,
that we may be saved.

4O LORD God Almighty,
how long will your anger smolder
against the prayers of your people?
5You have fed them with the bread of tears;
you have made them drink tears by the bowlful.
6You have made us a source of contention to our neighbors,
and our enemies mock us.

7Restore us, O God Almighty;
make your face shine upon us,
that we may be saved.

8You brought a vine out of Egypt;
you drove out the nations and planted it.
9You cleared the ground for it,
and it took root and filled the land.
10The mountains were covered with its shade,
the mighty cedars with its branches.
11It sent out its boughs to the Sea,[a]
its shoots as far as the River.[b]

12Why have you broken down its walls
so that all who pass by pick its grapes?
13Boars from the forest ravage it
and the creatures of the field feed on it.
14Return to us, O God Almighty!
Look down from heaven and see!
Watch over this vine,
15 the root your right hand has planted,
the son[c] you have raised up for yourself.

16Your vine is cut down, it is burned with fire;
at your rebuke your people perish.
17Let your hand rest on the man at your right hand,
the son of man you have raised up for yourself.
18Then we will not turn away from you;
revive us, and we will call on your name.

19Restore us, O LORD God Almighty;
make your face shine upon us,
that we may be saved.

Psalm 81

For the director of music. According to *gittith*.[d] Of Asaph.

1Sing for joy to God our strength;
shout aloud to the God of Jacob!
2Begin the music, strike the tambourine,
play the melodious harp and lyre.

3Sound the ram's horn at the New Moon,
and when the moon is full, on the day of our Feast;
4this is a decree for Israel,
an ordinance of the God of Jacob.
5He established it as a statute for Joseph
when he went out against Egypt,
where we heard a language we did not understand.[e]

6He says, "I removed the burden from their shoulders;
their hands were set free from the basket.
7In your distress you called and I rescued you,
I answered you out of a thundercloud;
I tested you at the waters of Meribah.
Selah

8"Hear, O my people, and I will warn you—
if you would but listen to me, O Israel!
9You shall have no foreign god among you;
you shall not bow down to an alien god.
10I am the LORD your God,
who brought you up out of Egypt.
Open wide your mouth and I will fill it.

11"But my people would not listen to me;
Israel would not submit to me.
12So I gave them over to their stubborn hearts
to follow their own devices.

13"If my people would but listen to me,
if Israel would follow my ways,
14how quickly would I subdue their enemies
and turn my hand against their foes!
15Those who hate the LORD would cringe before him,
and their punishment would last forever.
16But you would be fed with the finest of wheat;
with honey from the rock I would satisfy you."

[a] *11* Probably the Mediterranean [b] *11* That is, the Euphrates [c] *15* Or *branch* [d] Title: Probably a musical term
[e] *5* Or */ and we heard a voice we had not known*

Psalm 82

A psalm of Asaph.

1God presides in the great assembly;
he gives judgment among the "gods":
2"How long will you[a] defend the unjust
and show partiality to the wicked? *Selah*
3Defend the cause of the weak and fatherless;
maintain the rights of the poor and oppressed.
4Rescue the weak and needy;
deliver them from the hand of the wicked.

5"They know nothing, they understand nothing.
They walk about in darkness;
all the foundations of the earth are shaken.

6"I said, 'You are "gods";
you are all sons of the Most High.'
7But you will die like mere men;
you will fall like every other ruler."

8Rise up, O God, judge the earth,
for all the nations are your inheritance.

Psalm 83

A song. A psalm of Asaph.

1O God, do not keep silent;
be not quiet, O God, be not still.
2See how your enemies are astir,
how your foes rear their heads.
3With cunning they conspire against your people;
they plot against those you cherish.
4"Come," they say, "let us destroy them as a nation,
that the name of Israel be remembered no more."

5With one mind they plot together;
they form an alliance against you—
6the tents of Edom and the Ishmaelites,
of Moab and the Hagrites,
7Gebal,[b] Ammon and Amalek,
Philistia, with the people of Tyre.
8Even Assyria has joined them
to lend strength to the descendants of Lot. *Selah*

9Do to them as you did to Midian,
as you did to Sisera and Jabin at the river Kishon,
10who perished at Endor
and became like refuse on the ground.
11Make their nobles like Oreb and Zeeb,
all their princes like Zebah and Zalmunna,
12who said, "Let us take possession
of the pasturelands of God."

13Make them like tumbleweed, O my God,
like chaff before the wind.
14As fire consumes the forest
or a flame sets the mountains ablaze,
15so pursue them with your tempest
and terrify them with your storm.
16Cover their faces with shame
so that men will seek your name, O LORD.

17May they ever be ashamed and dismayed;
may they perish in disgrace.
18Let them know that you, whose name is the LORD—
that you alone are the Most High over all the earth.

Psalm 84

For the director of music. According to *gittith*.[c] Of the Sons of Korah. A psalm.

1How lovely is your dwelling place,
O LORD Almighty!
2My soul yearns, even faints,
for the courts of the LORD;
my heart and my flesh cry out
for the living God.

3Even the sparrow has found a home,
and the swallow a nest for herself,
where she may have her young—
a place near your altar,
O LORD Almighty, my King and my God.
4Blessed are those who dwell in your house;
they are ever praising you. *Selah*

5Blessed are those whose strength is in you,
who have set their hearts on pilgrimage.
6As they pass through the Valley of Baca,
they make it a place of springs;
the autumn rains also cover it with pools.[d]
7They go from strength to strength,
till each appears before God in Zion.

8Hear my prayer, O LORD God Almighty;
listen to me, O God of Jacob. *Selah*
9Look upon our shield,[e] O God;
look with favor on your anointed one.

10Better is one day in your courts
than a thousand elsewhere;
I would rather be a doorkeeper in the house of my God
than dwell in the tents of the wicked.
11For the LORD God is a sun and shield;
the LORD bestows favor and honor;

[a]2 The Hebrew is plural. [b]7 That is, Byblos [c]Title: Probably a musical term [d]6 Or *blessings* [e]9 Or *sovereign*

no good thing does he withhold
from those whose walk is blameless.

12 O LORD Almighty,
blessed is the man who trusts in you.

Psalm 85

For the director of music. Of the Sons of Korah. A psalm.

1 You showed favor to your land, O LORD;
you restored the fortunes of Jacob.
2 You forgave the iniquity of your people
and covered all their sins. *Selah*
3 You set aside all your wrath
and turned from your fierce anger.

4 Restore us again, O God our Savior,
and put away your displeasure toward us.
5 Will you be angry with us forever?
Will you prolong your anger through all generations?
6 Will you not revive us again,
that your people may rejoice in you?
7 Show us your unfailing love, O LORD,
and grant us your salvation.

8 I will listen to what God the LORD will say;
he promises peace to his people, his saints—
but let them not return to folly.
9 Surely his salvation is near those who fear him,
that his glory may dwell in our land.
10 Love and faithfulness meet together;
righteousness and peace kiss each other.
11 Faithfulness springs forth from the earth,
and righteousness looks down from heaven.
12 The LORD will indeed give what is good,
and our land will yield its harvest.
13 Righteousness goes before him
and prepares the way for his steps.

Psalm 86

A prayer of David.

1 Hear, O LORD, and answer me,
for I am poor and needy.
2 Guard my life, for I am devoted to you.
You are my God; save your servant
who trusts in you.
3 Have mercy on me, O Lord,
for I call to you all day long.
4 Bring joy to your servant,
for to you, O Lord,
I lift up my soul.
5 You are forgiving and good, O Lord,
abounding in love to all who call to you.
6 Hear my prayer, O LORD;
listen to my cry for mercy.
7 In the day of my trouble I will call to you,
for you will answer me.
8 Among the gods there is none like you, O Lord;
no deeds can compare with yours.
9 All the nations you have made
will come and worship before you, O Lord;
they will bring glory to your name.
10 For you are great and do marvelous deeds;
you alone are God.
11 Teach me your way, O LORD,
and I will walk in your truth;
give me an undivided heart,
that I may fear your name.
12 I will praise you, O Lord my God, with all my heart;
I will glorify your name forever.
13 For great is your love toward me;
you have delivered me from the depths of the grave.[a]
14 The arrogant are attacking me, O God;
a band of ruthless men seeks my life—
men without regard for you.
15 But you, O Lord, are a compassionate and gracious God,
slow to anger, abounding in love and faithfulness.
16 Turn to me and have mercy on me;
grant your strength to your servant
and save the son of your maidservant.[b]
17 Give me a sign of your goodness,
that my enemies may see it and be put to shame,
for you, O LORD, have helped me and comforted me.

Psalm 87

Of the Sons of Korah. A psalm. A song.

1 He has set his foundation on the holy mountain;
2 the LORD loves the gates of Zion
more than all the dwellings of Jacob.
3 Glorious things are said of you,
O city of God: *Selah*
4 "I will record Rahab[c] and Babylon
among those who acknowledge me—
Philistia too, and Tyre, along with Cush[d]—

a13 Hebrew *Sheol* b16 Or *save your faithful son* c4 A poetic name for Egypt d4 That is, the upper Nile region

and will say, 'This[a] one was born in
Zion.'"
5Indeed, of Zion it will be said,
"This one and that one were born in her,
and the Most High himself will establish
her."
6The LORD will write in the register of the
peoples:
"This one was born in Zion." *Selah*
7As they make music they will sing,
"All my fountains are in you."

Psalm 88

A song. A psalm of the Sons of Korah. For the director of music. According to *mahalath leannoth.*[b] A *maskil*[c] of Heman the Ezrahite.

1O LORD, the God who saves me,
day and night I cry out before you.
2May my prayer come before you;
turn your ear to my cry.
3For my soul is full of trouble
and my life draws near the grave.[d]
4I am counted among those who go down to
the pit;
I am like a man without strength.
5I am set apart with the dead,
like the slain who lie in the grave,
whom you remember no more,
who are cut off from your care.
6You have put me in the lowest pit,
in the darkest depths.
7Your wrath lies heavily upon me;
you have overwhelmed me with all your
waves. *Selah*
8You have taken from me my closest friends
and have made me repulsive to them.
I am confined and cannot escape;
9 my eyes are dim with grief.
I call to you, O LORD, every day;
I spread out my hands to you.
10Do you show your wonders to the dead?
Do those who are dead rise up and praise
you? *Selah*
11Is your love declared in the grave,
your faithfulness in Destruction[e]?
12Are your wonders known in the place of
darkness,
or your righteous deeds in the land of
oblivion?
13But I cry to you for help, O LORD;
in the morning my prayer comes before
you.
14Why, O LORD, do you reject me
and hide your face from me?
15From my youth I have been afflicted and
close to death;
I have suffered your terrors and am in
despair.
16Your wrath has swept over me;
your terrors have destroyed me.
17All day long they surround me like a flood;
they have completely engulfed me.
18You have taken my companions and loved
ones from me;
the darkness is my closest friend.

Psalm 89

A *maskil*[c] of Ethan the Ezrahite.

1I will sing of the LORD's great love forever;
with my mouth I will make your
faithfulness known through all
generations.
2I will declare that your love stands firm
forever,
that you established your faithfulness in
heaven itself.
3You said, "I have made a covenant with my
chosen one,
I have sworn to David my servant,
4'I will establish your line forever
and make your throne firm through all
generations.'" *Selah*
5The heavens praise your wonders, O LORD,
your faithfulness too, in the assembly of
the holy ones.
6For who in the skies above can compare with
the LORD?
Who is like the LORD among the heavenly
beings?
7In the council of the holy ones God is greatly
feared;
he is more awesome than all who
surround him.
8O LORD God Almighty, who is like you?
You are mighty, O LORD, and your
faithfulness surrounds you.
9You rule over the surging sea;
when its waves mount up, you still them.
10You crushed Rahab like one of the slain;
with your strong arm you scattered your
enemies.

[a]4 Or *"O Rahab and Babylon, / Philistia, Tyre and Cush, / I will record concerning those who acknowledge me: / 'This* [b]Title: Possibly a tune, "The Suffering of Affliction" [c]Title: Probably a literary or musical term [d]3 Hebrew *Sheol* [e]11 Hebrew *Abaddon*

11The heavens are yours, and yours also the
earth;
you founded the world and all that is in it.
12You created the north and the south;
Tabor and Hermon sing for joy at your
name.
13Your arm is endued with power;
your hand is strong, your right hand
exalted.

14Righteousness and justice are the foundation
of your throne;
love and faithfulness go before you.
15Blessed are those who have learned to
acclaim you,
who walk in the light of your presence,
O LORD.
16They rejoice in your name all day long;
they exult in your righteousness.
17For you are their glory and strength,
and by your favor you exalt our horn.[a]
18Indeed, our shield[b] belongs to the LORD,
our king to the Holy One of Israel.

19Once you spoke in a vision,
to your faithful people you said:
"I have bestowed strength on a warrior;
I have exalted a young man from among
the people.
20I have found David my servant;
with my sacred oil I have anointed him.
21My hand will sustain him;
surely my arm will strengthen him.
22No enemy will subject him to tribute;
no wicked man will oppress him.
23I will crush his foes before him
and strike down his adversaries.
24My faithful love will be with him,
and through my name his horn[c] will be
exalted.
25I will set his hand over the sea,
his right hand over the rivers.
26He will call out to me, 'You are my Father,
my God, the Rock my Savior.'
27I will also appoint him my firstborn,
the most exalted of the kings of the earth.
28I will maintain my love to him forever,
and my covenant with him will never fail.
29I will establish his line forever,
his throne as long as the heavens endure.

30"If his sons forsake my law
and do not follow my statutes,
31if they violate my decrees
and fail to keep my commands,
32I will punish their sin with the rod,
their iniquity with flogging;
33but I will not take my love from him,
nor will I ever betray my faithfulness.
34I will not violate my covenant
or alter what my lips have uttered.
35Once for all, I have sworn by my holiness—
and I will not lie to David—
36that his line will continue forever
and his throne endure before me like the
sun;
37it will be established forever like the moon,
the faithful witness in the sky." *Selah*

38But you have rejected, you have spurned,
you have been very angry with your
anointed one.
39You have renounced the covenant with your
servant
and have defiled his crown in the dust.
40You have broken through all his walls
and reduced his strongholds to ruins.
41All who pass by have plundered him;
he has become the scorn of his neighbors.
42You have exalted the right hand of his foes;
you have made all his enemies rejoice.
43You have turned back the edge of his sword
and have not supported him in battle.
44You have put an end to his splendor
and cast his throne to the ground.
45You have cut short the days of his youth;
you have covered him with a mantle of
shame. *Selah*

46How long, O LORD? Will you hide yourself
forever?
How long will your wrath burn like fire?
47Remember how fleeting is my life.
For what futility you have created all
men!
48What man can live and not see death,
or save himself from the power of the
grave[d]? *Selah*
49O Lord, where is your former great love,
which in your faithfulness you swore to
David?
50Remember, Lord, how your servant has[e]
been mocked,
how I bear in my heart the taunts of all
the nations,
51the taunts with which your enemies have
mocked, O LORD,
with which they have mocked every step
of your anointed one.

52Praise be to the LORD forever!
Amen and Amen.

[a]17 *Horn* here symbolizes strong one. [b]18 Or *sovereign* [c]24 *Horn* here symbolizes strength. [d]48 Hebrew *Sheol*
[e]50 Or *your servants have*

BOOK IV

Psalms 90–106

Psalm 90

A prayer of Moses the man of God.

1 Lord, you have been our dwelling place
throughout all generations.
2 Before the mountains were born
or you brought forth the earth and the world,
from everlasting to everlasting you are God.

3 You turn men back to dust,
saying, "Return to dust, O sons of men."
4 For a thousand years in your sight
are like a day that has just gone by,
or like a watch in the night.
5 You sweep men away in the sleep of death;
they are like the new grass of the morning—
6 though in the morning it springs up new,
by evening it is dry and withered.

7 We are consumed by your anger
and terrified by your indignation.
8 You have set our iniquities before you,
our secret sins in the light of your presence.
9 All our days pass away under your wrath;
we finish our years with a moan.
10 The length of our days is seventy years—
or eighty, if we have the strength;
yet their span[a] is but trouble and sorrow,
for they quickly pass, and we fly away.

11 Who knows the power of your anger?
For your wrath is as great as the fear that is due you.
12 Teach us to number our days aright,
that we may gain a heart of wisdom.

13 Relent, O LORD! How long will it be?
Have compassion on your servants.
14 Satisfy us in the morning with your unfailing love,
that we may sing for joy and be glad all our days.
15 Make us glad for as many days as you have afflicted us,
for as many years as we have seen trouble.
16 May your deeds be shown to your servants,
your splendor to their children.
17 May the favor[b] of the Lord our God rest upon us;
establish the work of our hands for us—
yes, establish the work of our hands.

Psalm 91

1 He who dwells in the shelter of the Most High
will rest in the shadow of the Almighty.[c]
2 I will say[d] of the LORD, "He is my refuge and my fortress,
my God, in whom I trust."

3 Surely he will save you from the fowler's snare
and from the deadly pestilence.
4 He will cover you with his feathers,
and under his wings you will find refuge;
his faithfulness will be your shield and rampart.
5 You will not fear the terror of night,
nor the arrow that flies by day,
6 nor the pestilence that stalks in the darkness,
nor the plague that destroys at midday.
7 A thousand may fall at your side,
ten thousand at your right hand,
but it will not come near you.
8 You will only observe with your eyes
and see the punishment of the wicked.

9 If you make the Most High your dwelling—
even the LORD, who is my refuge—
10 then no harm will befall you,
no disaster will come near your tent.
11 For he will command his angels concerning you
to guard you in all your ways;
12 they will lift you up in their hands,
so that you will not strike your foot against a stone.
13 You will tread upon the lion and the cobra;
you will trample the great lion and the serpent.

14 "Because he loves me," says the LORD, "I will rescue him;
I will protect him, for he acknowledges my name.
15 He will call upon me, and I will answer him;
I will be with him in trouble,
I will deliver him and honor him.
16 With long life will I satisfy him
and show him my salvation."

[a] 10 Or *yet the best of them* [b] 17 Or *beauty* [c] 1 Hebrew *Shaddai* [d] 2 Or *He says*

Psalm 92

A psalm. A song. For the Sabbath day.

1It is good to praise the LORD
and make music to your name, O Most High,
2to proclaim your love in the morning
and your faithfulness at night,
3to the music of the ten-stringed lyre
and the melody of the harp.

4For you make me glad by your deeds, O LORD;
I sing for joy at the works of your hands.
5How great are your works, O LORD,
how profound your thoughts!
6The senseless man does not know,
fools do not understand,
7that though the wicked spring up like grass
and all evildoers flourish,
they will be forever destroyed.

8But you, O LORD, are exalted forever.

9For surely your enemies, O LORD,
surely your enemies will perish;
all evildoers will be scattered.
10You have exalted my horn[a] like that of a wild ox;
fine oils have been poured upon me.
11My eyes have seen the defeat of my adversaries;
my ears have heard the rout of my wicked foes.

12The righteous will flourish like a palm tree,
they will grow like a cedar of Lebanon;
13planted in the house of the LORD,
they will flourish in the courts of our God.
14They will still bear fruit in old age,
they will stay fresh and green,
15proclaiming, "The LORD is upright;
he is my Rock, and there is no wickedness in him."

Psalm 93

1The LORD reigns, he is robed in majesty;
the LORD is robed in majesty
and is armed with strength.
The world is firmly established;
it cannot be moved.
2Your throne was established long ago;
you are from all eternity.

3The seas have lifted up, O LORD,
the seas have lifted up their voice;
the seas have lifted up their pounding waves.
4Mightier than the thunder of the great waters,
mightier than the breakers of the sea—
the LORD on high is mighty.

5Your statutes stand firm;
holiness adorns your house
for endless days, O LORD.

Psalm 94

1O LORD, the God who avenges,
O God who avenges, shine forth.
2Rise up, O Judge of the earth;
pay back to the proud what they deserve.
3How long will the wicked, O LORD,
how long will the wicked be jubilant?

4They pour out arrogant words;
all the evildoers are full of boasting.
5They crush your people, O LORD;
they oppress your inheritance.
6They slay the widow and the alien;
they murder the fatherless.
7They say, "The LORD does not see;
the God of Jacob pays no heed."

8Take heed, you senseless ones among the people;
you fools, when will you become wise?
9Does he who implanted the ear not hear?
Does he who formed the eye not see?
10Does he who disciplines nations not punish?
Does he who teaches man lack knowledge?
11The LORD knows the thoughts of man;
he knows that they are futile.

12Blessed is the man you discipline, O LORD,
the man you teach from your law;
13you grant him relief from days of trouble,
till a pit is dug for the wicked.
14For the LORD will not reject his people;
he will never forsake his inheritance.
15Judgment will again be founded on righteousness,
and all the upright in heart will follow it.

16Who will rise up for me against the wicked?
Who will take a stand for me against evildoers?
17Unless the LORD had given me help,
I would soon have dwelt in the silence of death.
18When I said, "My foot is slipping,"
your love, O LORD, supported me.
19When anxiety was great within me,
your consolation brought joy to my soul.
20Can a corrupt throne be allied with you—

[a] 10 *Horn* here symbolizes strength.

one that brings on misery by its decrees?
21They band together against the righteous
and condemn the innocent to death.
22But the LORD has become my fortress,
and my God the rock in whom I take refuge.
23He will repay them for their sins
and destroy them for their wickedness;
the LORD our God will destroy them.

Psalm 95

1Come, let us sing for joy to the LORD;
let us shout aloud to the Rock of our salvation.
2Let us come before him with thanksgiving
and extol him with music and song.

3For the LORD is the great God,
the great King above all gods.
4In his hand are the depths of the earth,
and the mountain peaks belong to him.
5The sea is his, for he made it,
and his hands formed the dry land.

6Come, let us bow down in worship,
let us kneel before the LORD our Maker;
7for he is our God
and we are the people of his pasture,
the flock under his care.

Today, if you hear his voice,
8 do not harden your hearts as you did at Meribah,[a]
as you did that day at Massah[b] in the desert,
9where your fathers tested and tried me,
though they had seen what I did.
10For forty years I was angry with that generation;
I said, "They are a people whose hearts go astray,
and they have not known my ways."
11So I declared on oath in my anger,
"They shall never enter my rest."

Psalm 96

1Sing to the LORD a new song;
sing to the LORD, all the earth.
2Sing to the LORD, praise his name;
proclaim his salvation day after day.
3Declare his glory among the nations,
his marvelous deeds among all peoples.

4For great is the LORD and most worthy of praise;
he is to be feared above all gods.
5For all the gods of the nations are idols,
but the LORD made the heavens.
6Splendor and majesty are before him;
strength and glory are in his sanctuary.

7Ascribe to the LORD, O families of nations,
ascribe to the LORD glory and strength.
8Ascribe to the LORD the glory due his name;
bring an offering and come into his courts.
9Worship the LORD in the splendor of his[c] holiness;
tremble before him, all the earth.

10Say among the nations, "The LORD reigns."
The world is firmly established, it cannot be moved;
he will judge the peoples with equity.
11Let the heavens rejoice, let the earth be glad;
let the sea resound, and all that is in it;
12 let the fields be jubilant, and everything in them.
Then all the trees of the forest will sing for joy;
13 they will sing before the LORD, for he comes,
he comes to judge the earth.
He will judge the world in righteousness
and the peoples in his truth.

Psalm 97

1The LORD reigns, let the earth be glad;
let the distant shores rejoice.

2Clouds and thick darkness surround him;
righteousness and justice are the foundation of his throne.
3Fire goes before him
and consumes his foes on every side.
4His lightning lights up the world;
the earth sees and trembles.
5The mountains melt like wax before the LORD,
before the Lord of all the earth.
6The heavens proclaim his righteousness,
and all the peoples see his glory.

7All who worship images are put to shame,
those who boast in idols—
worship him, all you gods!

8Zion hears and rejoices
and the villages of Judah are glad
because of your judgments, O LORD.
9For you, O LORD, are the Most High over all the earth;
you are exalted far above all gods.

10Let those who love the LORD hate evil,
for he guards the lives of his faithful ones
and delivers them from the hand of the wicked.

[a]8 *Meribah* means *quarreling.* [b]8 *Massah* means *testing.* [c]9 Or *LORD with the splendor of*

11Light is shed upon the righteous
and joy on the upright in heart.
12Rejoice in the LORD, you who are righteous,
and praise his holy name.

Psalm 98

A psalm.

1Sing to the LORD a new song,
for he has done marvelous things;
his right hand and his holy arm
have worked salvation for him.
2The LORD has made his salvation known
and revealed his righteousness to the nations.
3He has remembered his love
and his faithfulness to the house of Israel;
all the ends of the earth have seen
the salvation of our God.

4Shout for joy to the LORD, all the earth,
burst into jubilant song with music;
5make music to the LORD with the harp,
with the harp and the sound of singing,
6with trumpets and the blast of the ram's horn—
shout for joy before the LORD, the King.

7Let the sea resound, and everything in it,
the world, and all who live in it.
8Let the rivers clap their hands,
let the mountains sing together for joy;
9let them sing before the LORD,
for he comes to judge the earth.
He will judge the world in righteousness
and the peoples with equity.

Psalm 99

1The LORD reigns,
let the nations tremble;
he sits enthroned between the cherubim,
let the earth shake.
2Great is the LORD in Zion;
he is exalted over all the nations.
3Let them praise your great and awesome name—
he is holy.

4The King is mighty, he loves justice—
you have established equity;
in Jacob you have done
what is just and right.
5Exalt the LORD our God
and worship at his footstool;
he is holy.

6Moses and Aaron were among his priests,
Samuel was among those who called on his name;
they called on the LORD
and he answered them.
7He spoke to them from the pillar of cloud;
they kept his statutes and the decrees he gave them.

8O LORD our God,
you answered them;
you were to Israel[a] a forgiving God,
though you punished their misdeeds.[b]
9Exalt the LORD our God
and worship at his holy mountain,
for the LORD our God is holy.

Psalm 100

A psalm. For giving thanks.

1Shout for joy to the LORD, all the earth.
2 Worship the LORD with gladness;
come before him with joyful songs.
3Know that the LORD is God.
It is he who made us, and we are his[c];
we are his people, the sheep of his pasture.

4Enter his gates with thanksgiving
and his courts with praise;
give thanks to him and praise his name.
5For the LORD is good and his love endures forever;
his faithfulness continues through all generations.

Psalm 101

Of David. A psalm.

1I will sing of your love and justice;
to you, O LORD, I will sing praise.
2I will be careful to lead a blameless life—
when will you come to me?

I will walk in my house
with blameless heart.
3I will set before my eyes
no vile thing.

The deeds of faithless men I hate;
they will not cling to me.
4Men of perverse heart shall be far from me;
I will have nothing to do with evil.
5Whoever slanders his neighbor in secret,
him will I put to silence;
whoever has haughty eyes and a proud heart,
him will I not endure.
6My eyes will be on the faithful in the land,

[a]8 Hebrew *them* [b]8 Or */ an avenger of the wrongs done to them* [c]3 Or *and not we ourselves*

that they may dwell with me;
he whose walk is blameless
will minister to me.

7No one who practices deceit
will dwell in my house;
no one who speaks falsely
will stand in my presence.

8Every morning I will put to silence
all the wicked in the land;
I will cut off every evildoer
from the city of the LORD.

Psalm 102

A prayer of an afflicted man. When he is faint and pours out his lament before the LORD.

1Hear my prayer, O LORD;
let my cry for help come to you.
2Do not hide your face from me
when I am in distress.
Turn your ear to me;
when I call, answer me quickly.

3For my days vanish like smoke;
my bones burn like glowing embers.
4My heart is blighted and withered like grass;
I forget to eat my food.
5Because of my loud groaning
I am reduced to skin and bones.
6I am like a desert owl,
like an owl among the ruins.
7I lie awake; I have become
like a bird alone on a roof.
8All day long my enemies taunt me;
those who rail against me use my name as a curse.
9For I eat ashes as my food
and mingle my drink with tears
10because of your great wrath,
for you have taken me up and thrown me aside.
11My days are like the evening shadow;
I wither away like grass.

12But you, O LORD, sit enthroned forever;
your renown endures through all generations.
13You will arise and have compassion on Zion,
for it is time to show favor to her;
the appointed time has come.
14For her stones are dear to your servants;
her very dust moves them to pity.
15The nations will fear the name of the LORD,
all the kings of the earth will revere your glory.
16For the LORD will rebuild Zion
and appear in his glory.
17He will respond to the prayer of the destitute;
he will not despise their plea.

18Let this be written for a future generation,
that a people not yet created may praise the LORD:
19"The LORD looked down from his sanctuary on high,
from heaven he viewed the earth,
20to hear the groans of the prisoners
and release those condemned to death."
21So the name of the LORD will be declared in Zion
and his praise in Jerusalem
22when the peoples and the kingdoms
assemble to worship the LORD.

23In the course of my life[a] he broke my strength;
he cut short my days.
24So I said:
"Do not take me away, O my God, in the midst of my days;
your years go on through all generations.
25In the beginning you laid the foundations of the earth,
and the heavens are the work of your hands.
26They will perish, but you remain;
they will all wear out like a garment.
Like clothing you will change them
and they will be discarded.
27But you remain the same,
and your years will never end.
28The children of your servants will live in your presence;
their descendants will be established before you."

Psalm 103

Of David.

1Praise the LORD, O my soul;
all my inmost being, praise his holy name.
2Praise the LORD, O my soul,
and forget not all his benefits—
3who forgives all your sins
and heals all your diseases,
4who redeems your life from the pit
and crowns you with love and compassion,
5who satisfies your desires with good things
so that your youth is renewed like the eagle's.

6The LORD works righteousness
and justice for all the oppressed.

[a]23 Or *By his power*

7He made known his ways to Moses,
his deeds to the people of Israel:
8The LORD is compassionate and gracious,
slow to anger, abounding in love.
9He will not always accuse,
nor will he harbor his anger forever;
10he does not treat us as our sins deserve
or repay us according to our iniquities.
11For as high as the heavens are above the earth,
so great is his love for those who fear him;
12as far as the east is from the west,
so far has he removed our transgressions from us.
13As a father has compassion on his children,
so the LORD has compassion on those who fear him;
14for he knows how we are formed,
he remembers that we are dust.
15As for man, his days are like grass,
he flourishes like a flower of the field;
16the wind blows over it and it is gone,
and its place remembers it no more.
17But from everlasting to everlasting
the LORD's love is with those who fear him,
and his righteousness with their children's children—
18with those who keep his covenant
and remember to obey his precepts.
19The LORD has established his throne in heaven,
and his kingdom rules over all.
20Praise the LORD, you his angels,
you mighty ones who do his bidding,
who obey his word.
21Praise the LORD, all his heavenly hosts,
you his servants who do his will.
22Praise the LORD, all his works
everywhere in his dominion.

Praise the LORD, O my soul.

Psalm 104

1Praise the LORD, O my soul.

O LORD my God, you are very great;
you are clothed with splendor and majesty.
2He wraps himself in light as with a garment;
he stretches out the heavens like a tent
3 and lays the beams of his upper chambers on their waters.
He makes the clouds his chariot
and rides on the wings of the wind.
4He makes winds his messengers,[a]
flames of fire his servants.
5He set the earth on its foundations;
it can never be moved.
6You covered it with the deep as with a garment;
the waters stood above the mountains.
7But at your rebuke the waters fled,
at the sound of your thunder they took to flight;
8they flowed over the mountains,
they went down into the valleys,
to the place you assigned for them.
9You set a boundary they cannot cross;
never again will they cover the earth.

10He makes springs pour water into the ravines;
it flows between the mountains.
11They give water to all the beasts of the field;
the wild donkeys quench their thirst.
12The birds of the air nest by the waters;
they sing among the branches.
13He waters the mountains from his upper chambers;
the earth is satisfied by the fruit of his work.
14He makes grass grow for the cattle,
and plants for man to cultivate—
bringing forth food from the earth:
15wine that gladdens the heart of man,
oil to make his face shine,
and bread that sustains his heart.
16The trees of the LORD are well watered,
the cedars of Lebanon that he planted.
17There the birds make their nests;
the stork has its home in the pine trees.
18The high mountains belong to the wild goats;
the crags are a refuge for the coneys.[b]

19The moon marks off the seasons,
and the sun knows when to go down.
20You bring darkness, it becomes night,
and all the beasts of the forest prowl.
21The lions roar for their prey
and seek their food from God.
22The sun rises, and they steal away;
they return and lie down in their dens.
23Then man goes out to his work,
to his labor until evening.

24How many are your works, O LORD!
In wisdom you made them all;
the earth is full of your creatures.
25There is the sea, vast and spacious,
teeming with creatures beyond number—
living things both large and small.
26There the ships go to and fro,
and the leviathan, which you formed to frolic there.

a4 Or *angels* b18 That is, the hyrax or rock badger

27These all look to you
to give them their food at the proper time.
28When you give it to them,
they gather it up;
when you open your hand,
they are satisfied with good things.
29When you hide your face,
they are terrified;
when you take away their breath,
they die and return to the dust.
30When you send your Spirit,
they are created,
and you renew the face of the earth.

31May the glory of the LORD endure forever;
may the LORD rejoice in his works—
32he who looks at the earth, and it trembles,
who touches the mountains, and they smoke.
33I will sing to the LORD all my life;
I will sing praise to my God as long as I live.
34May my meditation be pleasing to him,
as I rejoice in the LORD.
35But may sinners vanish from the earth
and the wicked be no more.

Praise the LORD, O my soul.
Praise the LORD.[a]

Psalm 105

1Give thanks to the LORD, call on his name;
make known among the nations what he has done.
2Sing to him, sing praise to him;
tell of all his wonderful acts.
3Glory in his holy name;
let the hearts of those who seek the LORD rejoice.
4Look to the LORD and his strength;
seek his face always.

5Remember the wonders he has done,
his miracles, and the judgments he pronounced,
6O descendants of Abraham his servant,
O sons of Jacob, his chosen ones.
7He is the LORD our God;
his judgments are in all the earth.

8He remembers his covenant forever,
the word he commanded, for a thousand generations,
9the covenant he made with Abraham,
the oath he swore to Isaac.
10He confirmed it to Jacob as a decree,
to Israel as an everlasting covenant:
11"To you I will give the land of Canaan
as the portion you will inherit."

12When they were but few in number,
few indeed, and strangers in it,
13they wandered from nation to nation,
from one kingdom to another.
14He allowed no one to oppress them;
for their sake he rebuked kings:
15"Do not touch my anointed ones;
do my prophets no harm."

16He called down famine on the land
and destroyed all their supplies of food;
17and he sent a man before them—
Joseph, sold as a slave.
18They bruised his feet with shackles,
his neck was put in irons,
19till what he foretold came to pass,
till the word of the LORD proved him true.
20The king sent and released him,
the ruler of peoples set him free.
21He made him master of his household,
ruler over all he possessed,
22to instruct his princes as he pleased
and teach his elders wisdom.

23Then Israel entered Egypt;
Jacob lived as an alien in the land of Ham.
24The LORD made his people very fruitful;
he made them too numerous for their foes,
25whose hearts he turned to hate his people,
to conspire against his servants.
26He sent Moses his servant,
and Aaron, whom he had chosen.
27They performed his miraculous signs among them,
his wonders in the land of Ham.
28He sent darkness and made the land dark—
for had they not rebelled against his words?
29He turned their waters into blood,
causing their fish to die.
30Their land teemed with frogs,
which went up into the bedrooms of their rulers.
31He spoke, and there came swarms of flies,
and gnats throughout their country.
32He turned their rain into hail,
with lightning throughout their land;
33he struck down their vines and fig trees
and shattered the trees of their country.
34He spoke, and the locusts came,
grasshoppers without number;
35they ate up every green thing in their land,
ate up the produce of their soil.

[a]*35* Hebrew *Hallelu Yah*; in the Septuagint this line stands at the beginning of Psalm 105.

36Then he struck down all the firstborn in their land,
the firstfruits of all their manhood.
37He brought out Israel, laden with silver and gold,
and from among their tribes no one faltered.
38Egypt was glad when they left,
because dread of Israel had fallen on them.
39He spread out a cloud as a covering,
and a fire to give light at night.
40They asked, and he brought them quail
and satisfied them with the bread of heaven.
41He opened the rock, and water gushed out;
like a river it flowed in the desert.

42For he remembered his holy promise
given to his servant Abraham.
43He brought out his people with rejoicing,
his chosen ones with shouts of joy;
44he gave them the lands of the nations,
and they fell heir to what others had toiled for—
45that they might keep his precepts
and observe his laws.

Praise the LORD.[a]

Psalm 106

1Praise the LORD.[b]

Give thanks to the LORD, for he is good;
his love endures forever.
2Who can proclaim the mighty acts of the LORD
or fully declare his praise?
3Blessed are they who maintain justice,
who constantly do what is right.
4Remember me, O LORD, when you show favor to your people,
come to my aid when you save them,
5that I may enjoy the prosperity of your chosen ones,
that I may share in the joy of your nation
and join your inheritance in giving praise.

6We have sinned, even as our fathers did;
we have done wrong and acted wickedly.
7When our fathers were in Egypt,
they gave no thought to your miracles;
they did not remember your many kindnesses,
and they rebelled by the sea, the Red Sea.[c]
8Yet he saved them for his name's sake,
to make his mighty power known.
9He rebuked the Red Sea, and it dried up;
he led them through the depths as through a desert.
10He saved them from the hand of the foe;
from the hand of the enemy he redeemed them.
11The waters covered their adversaries;
not one of them survived.
12Then they believed his promises
and sang his praise.

13But they soon forgot what he had done
and did not wait for his counsel.
14In the desert they gave in to their craving;
in the wasteland they put God to the test.
15So he gave them what they asked for,
but sent a wasting disease upon them.

16In the camp they grew envious of Moses
and of Aaron, who was consecrated to the LORD.
17The earth opened up and swallowed Dathan;
it buried the company of Abiram.
18Fire blazed among their followers;
a flame consumed the wicked.

19At Horeb they made a calf
and worshiped an idol cast from metal.
20They exchanged their Glory
for an image of a bull, which eats grass.
21They forgot the God who saved them,
who had done great things in Egypt,
22miracles in the land of Ham
and awesome deeds by the Red Sea.
23So he said he would destroy them—
had not Moses, his chosen one,
stood in the breach before him
to keep his wrath from destroying them.

24Then they despised the pleasant land;
they did not believe his promise.
25They grumbled in their tents
and did not obey the LORD.
26So he swore to them with uplifted hand
that he would make them fall in the desert,
27make their descendants fall among the nations
and scatter them throughout the lands.

28They yoked themselves to the Baal of Peor
and ate sacrifices offered to lifeless gods;
29they provoked the LORD to anger by their wicked deeds,
and a plague broke out among them.
30But Phinehas stood up and intervened,
and the plague was checked.
31This was credited to him as righteousness
for endless generations to come.

[a] *45* Hebrew *Hallelu Yah* [b] *1* Hebrew *Hallelu Yah*; also in verse 48 [c] *7* Hebrew *Yam Suph*; that is, Sea of Reeds; also in verses 9 and 22

32By the waters of Meribah they angered the
LORD,
and trouble came to Moses because of
them;
33for they rebelled against the Spirit of God,
and rash words came from Moses' lips.[a]

34They did not destroy the peoples
as the LORD had commanded them,
35but they mingled with the nations
and adopted their customs.
36They worshiped their idols,
which became a snare to them.
37They sacrificed their sons
and their daughters to demons.
38They shed innocent blood,
the blood of their sons and daughters,
whom they sacrificed to the idols of Canaan,
and the land was desecrated by their
blood.
39They defiled themselves by what they did;
by their deeds they prostituted themselves.

40Therefore the LORD was angry with his
people
and abhorred his inheritance.
41He handed them over to the nations,
and their foes ruled over them.
42Their enemies oppressed them
and subjected them to their power.
43Many times he delivered them,
but they were bent on rebellion
and they wasted away in their sin.

44But he took note of their distress
when he heard their cry;
45for their sake he remembered his covenant
and out of his great love he relented.
46He caused them to be pitied
by all who held them captive.

47Save us, O LORD our God,
and gather us from the nations,
that we may give thanks to your holy name
and glory in your praise.

48Praise be to the LORD, the God of Israel,
from everlasting to everlasting.
Let all the people say, "Amen!"

Praise the LORD.

BOOK V

Psalms 107–150

Psalm 107

1Give thanks to the LORD, for he is good;
his love endures forever.
2Let the redeemed of the LORD say this—
those he redeemed from the hand of the
foe,
3those he gathered from the lands,
from east and west, from north and
south.[b]

4Some wandered in desert wastelands,
finding no way to a city where they could
settle.
5They were hungry and thirsty,
and their lives ebbed away.
6Then they cried out to the LORD in their
trouble,
and he delivered them from their distress.
7He led them by a straight way
to a city where they could settle.
8Let them give thanks to the LORD for his
unfailing love
and his wonderful deeds for men,
9for he satisfies the thirsty
and fills the hungry with good things.

10Some sat in darkness and the deepest gloom,
prisoners suffering in iron chains,
11for they had rebelled against the words of
God
and despised the counsel of the Most
High.
12So he subjected them to bitter labor;
they stumbled, and there was no one to
help.
13Then they cried to the LORD in their trouble,
and he saved them from their distress.
14He brought them out of darkness and the
deepest gloom
and broke away their chains.
15Let them give thanks to the LORD for his
unfailing love
and his wonderful deeds for men,
16for he breaks down gates of bronze
and cuts through bars of iron.

17Some became fools through their rebellious
ways
and suffered affliction because of their
iniquities.
18They loathed all food
and drew near the gates of death.
19Then they cried to the LORD in their trouble,
and he saved them from their distress.
20He sent forth his word and healed them;
he rescued them from the grave.
21Let them give thanks to the LORD for his
unfailing love
and his wonderful deeds for men.
22Let them sacrifice thank offerings
and tell of his works with songs of joy.

23Others went out on the sea in ships;

[a] 33 Or *against his spirit, / and rash words came from his lips*
[b] 3 Hebrew *north and the sea*

they were merchants on the mighty
waters.
24They saw the works of the LORD,
his wonderful deeds in the deep.
25For he spoke and stirred up a tempest
that lifted high the waves.
26They mounted up to the heavens and went
down to the depths;
in their peril their courage melted away.
27They reeled and staggered like drunken men;
they were at their wits' end.
28Then they cried out to the LORD in their
trouble,
and he brought them out of their distress.
29He stilled the storm to a whisper;
the waves of the sea were hushed.
30They were glad when it grew calm,
and he guided them to their desired
haven.
31Let them give thanks to the LORD for his
unfailing love
and his wonderful deeds for men.
32Let them exalt him in the assembly of the
people
and praise him in the council of the
elders.

33He turned rivers into a desert,
flowing springs into thirsty ground,
34and fruitful land into a salt waste,
because of the wickedness of those who
lived there.
35He turned the desert into pools of water
and the parched ground into flowing
springs;
36there he brought the hungry to live,
and they founded a city where they could
settle.
37They sowed fields and planted vineyards
that yielded a fruitful harvest;
38he blessed them, and their numbers greatly
increased,
and he did not let their herds diminish.

39Then their numbers decreased, and they
were humbled
by oppression, calamity and sorrow;
40he who pours contempt on nobles
made them wander in a trackless waste.
41But he lifted the needy out of their affliction
and increased their families like flocks.
42The upright see and rejoice,
but all the wicked shut their mouths.

43Whoever is wise, let him heed these things
and consider the great love of the LORD.

Psalm 108

A song. A psalm of David.

1My heart is steadfast, O God;
I will sing and make music with all my
soul.
2Awake, harp and lyre!
I will awaken the dawn.
3I will praise you, O LORD, among the nations;
I will sing of you among the peoples.
4For great is your love, higher than the
heavens;
your faithfulness reaches to the skies.
5Be exalted, O God, above the heavens,
and let your glory be over all the earth.

6Save us and help us with your right hand,
that those you love may be delivered.
7God has spoken from his sanctuary:
"In triumph I will parcel out Shechem
and measure off the Valley of Succoth.
8Gilead is mine, Manasseh is mine;
Ephraim is my helmet,
Judah my scepter.
9Moab is my washbasin,
upon Edom I toss my sandal;
over Philistia I shout in triumph."

10Who will bring me to the fortified city?
Who will lead me to Edom?
11Is it not you, O God, you who have rejected
us
and no longer go out with our armies?
12Give us aid against the enemy,
for the help of man is worthless.
13With God we will gain the victory,
and he will trample down our enemies.

Psalm 109

For the director of music. Of David. A psalm.

1O God, whom I praise,
do not remain silent,
2for wicked and deceitful men
have opened their mouths against me;
they have spoken against me with lying
tongues.
3With words of hatred they surround me;
they attack me without cause.
4In return for my friendship they accuse me,
but I am a man of prayer.
5They repay me evil for good,
and hatred for my friendship.

6Appoint[a] an evil man[b] to oppose him;
let an accuser[c] stand at his right hand.
7When he is tried, let him be found guilty,

[a]6 Or ⌊They say:⌋ "Appoint (with quotation marks at the end of verse 19) [b]6 Or *the Evil One* [c]6 Or *let Satan*

and may his prayers condemn him.
8May his days be few;
may another take his place of leadership.
9May his children be fatherless
and his wife a widow.
10May his children be wandering beggars;
may they be driven[a] from their ruined homes.
11May a creditor seize all he has;
may strangers plunder the fruits of his labor.
12May no one extend kindness to him
or take pity on his fatherless children.
13May his descendants be cut off,
their names blotted out from the next generation.
14May the iniquity of his fathers be remembered before the LORD;
may the sin of his mother never be blotted out.
15May their sins always remain before the LORD,
that he may cut off the memory of them from the earth.

16For he never thought of doing a kindness,
but hounded to death the poor
and the needy and the brokenhearted.
17He loved to pronounce a curse—
may it[b] come on him;
he found no pleasure in blessing—
may it be[c] far from him.
18He wore cursing as his garment;
it entered into his body like water,
into his bones like oil.
19May it be like a cloak wrapped about him,
like a belt tied forever around him.
20May this be the LORD's payment to my accusers,
to those who speak evil of me.

21But you, O Sovereign LORD,
deal well with me for your name's sake;
out of the goodness of your love, deliver me.
22For I am poor and needy,
and my heart is wounded within me.
23I fade away like an evening shadow;
I am shaken off like a locust.
24My knees give way from fasting;
my body is thin and gaunt.
25I am an object of scorn to my accusers;
when they see me, they shake their heads.

26Help me, O LORD my God;
save me in accordance with your love.
27Let them know that it is your hand,
that you, O LORD, have done it.
28They may curse, but you will bless;
when they attack they will be put to shame,
but your servant will rejoice.
29My accusers will be clothed with disgrace
and wrapped in shame as in a cloak.

30With my mouth I will greatly extol the LORD;
in the great throng I will praise him.
31For he stands at the right hand of the needy one,
to save his life from those who condemn him.

Psalm 110

Of David. A psalm.

1The LORD says to my Lord:
"Sit at my right hand
until I make your enemies
a footstool for your feet."

2The LORD will extend your mighty scepter from Zion;
you will rule in the midst of your enemies.
3Your troops will be willing
on your day of battle.
Arrayed in holy majesty,
from the womb of the dawn
you will receive the dew of your youth.[d]

4The LORD has sworn
and will not change his mind:
"You are a priest forever,
in the order of Melchizedek."
5The Lord is at your right hand;
he will crush kings on the day of his wrath.
6He will judge the nations, heaping up the dead
and crushing the rulers of the whole earth.
7He will drink from a brook beside the way[e];
therefore he will lift up his head.

Psalm 111[f]

1Praise the LORD.[g]

I will extol the LORD with all my heart
in the council of the upright and in the assembly.

2Great are the works of the LORD;
they are pondered by all who delight in them.
3Glorious and majestic are his deeds,

[a]10 Septuagint; Hebrew *sought* [b]17 Or *curse, / and it has* [c]17 Or *blessing, / and it is* [d]3 Or */ your young men will come to you like the dew* [e]7 Or */ The One who grants succession will set him in authority* [f]This psalm is an acrostic poem, the lines of which begin with the successive letters of the Hebrew alphabet. [g]1 Hebrew *Hallelu Yah*

and his righteousness endures forever.
4He has caused his wonders to be
remembered;
the LORD is gracious and compassionate.
5He provides food for those who fear him;
he remembers his covenant forever.
6He has shown his people the power of his
works,
giving them the lands of other nations.
7The works of his hands are faithful and just;
all his precepts are trustworthy.
8They are steadfast for ever and ever,
done in faithfulness and uprightness.
9He provided redemption for his people;
he ordained his covenant forever—
holy and awesome is his name.

10The fear of the LORD is the beginning of
wisdom;
all who follow his precepts have good
understanding.
To him belongs eternal praise.

Psalm 112[a]

1Praise the LORD.[b]

Blessed is the man who fears the LORD,
who finds great delight in his commands.

2His children will be mighty in the land;
the generation of the upright will be
blessed.
3Wealth and riches are in his house,
and his righteousness endures forever.
4Even in darkness light dawns for the upright,
for the gracious and compassionate and
righteous man.[c]
5Good will come to him who is generous and
lends freely,
who conducts his affairs with justice.
6Surely he will never be shaken;
a righteous man will be remembered
forever.
7He will have no fear of bad news;
his heart is steadfast, trusting in the LORD.
8His heart is secure, he will have no fear;
in the end he will look in triumph on his
foes.
9He has scattered abroad his gifts to the poor,
his righteousness endures forever;
his horn[d] will be lifted high in honor.

10The wicked man will see and be vexed,
he will gnash his teeth and waste away;
the longings of the wicked will come to
nothing.

Psalm 113

1Praise the LORD.[e]

Praise, O servants of the LORD,
praise the name of the LORD.
2Let the name of the LORD be praised,
both now and forevermore.
3From the rising of the sun to the place where
it sets,
the name of the LORD is to be praised.

4The LORD is exalted over all the nations,
his glory above the heavens.
5Who is like the LORD our God,
the One who sits enthroned on high,
6who stoops down to look
on the heavens and the earth?

7He raises the poor from the dust
and lifts the needy from the ash heap;
8he seats them with princes,
with the princes of their people.
9He settles the barren woman in her home
as a happy mother of children.

Praise the LORD.

Psalm 114

1When Israel came out of Egypt,
the house of Jacob from a people of foreign
tongue,
2Judah became God's sanctuary,
Israel his dominion.

3The sea looked and fled,
the Jordan turned back;
4the mountains skipped like rams,
the hills like lambs.

5Why was it, O sea, that you fled,
O Jordan, that you turned back,
6you mountains, that you skipped like rams,
you hills, like lambs?

7Tremble, O earth, at the presence of the
Lord,
at the presence of the God of Jacob,
8who turned the rock into a pool,
the hard rock into springs of water.

Psalm 115

1Not to us, O LORD, not to us
but to your name be the glory,
because of your love and faithfulness.

2Why do the nations say,
"Where is their God?"
3Our God is in heaven;

[a] This psalm is an acrostic poem, the lines of which begin with the successive letters of the Hebrew alphabet. [b] *1* Hebrew *Hallelu Yah* [c] *4* Or */ for ⌊the LORD⌋ is gracious and compassionate and righteous* [d] *9* *Horn* here symbolizes dignity. [e] *1* Hebrew *Hallelu Yah*; also in verse 9

he does whatever pleases him.
4But their idols are silver and gold,
made by the hands of men.
5They have mouths, but cannot speak,
eyes, but they cannot see;
6they have ears, but cannot hear,
noses, but they cannot smell;
7they have hands, but cannot feel,
feet, but they cannot walk;
nor can they utter a sound with their
throats.
8Those who make them will be like them,
and so will all who trust in them.

9O house of Israel, trust in the LORD—
he is their help and shield.
10O house of Aaron, trust in the LORD—
he is their help and shield.
11You who fear him, trust in the LORD—
he is their help and shield.

12The LORD remembers us and will bless us:
He will bless the house of Israel,
he will bless the house of Aaron,
13he will bless those who fear the LORD—
small and great alike.

14May the LORD make you increase,
both you and your children.
15May you be blessed by the LORD,
the Maker of heaven and earth.

16The highest heavens belong to the LORD,
but the earth he has given to man.
17It is not the dead who praise the LORD,
those who go down to silence;
18it is we who extol the LORD,
both now and forevermore.

Praise the LORD.[a]

Psalm 116

1I love the LORD, for he heard my voice;
he heard my cry for mercy.
2Because he turned his ear to me,
I will call on him as long as I live.
3The cords of death entangled me,
the anguish of the grave[b] came upon me;
I was overcome by trouble and sorrow.
4Then I called on the name of the LORD:
"O LORD, save me!"
5The LORD is gracious and righteous;
our God is full of compassion.
6The LORD protects the simplehearted;
when I was in great need, he saved me.
7Be at rest once more, O my soul,
for the LORD has been good to you.
8For you, O LORD, have delivered my soul
from death,
my eyes from tears,
my feet from stumbling,
9that I may walk before the LORD
in the land of the living.
10I believed; therefore[c] I said,
"I am greatly afflicted."
11And in my dismay I said,
"All men are liars."

12How can I repay the LORD
for all his goodness to me?
13I will lift up the cup of salvation
and call on the name of the LORD.
14I will fulfill my vows to the LORD
in the presence of all his people.
15Precious in the sight of the LORD
is the death of his saints.
16O LORD, truly I am your servant;
I am your servant, the son of your
maidservant[d];
you have freed me from my chains.

17I will sacrifice a thank offering to you
and call on the name of the LORD.
18I will fulfill my vows to the LORD
in the presence of all his people,
19in the courts of the house of the LORD—
in your midst, O Jerusalem.

Praise the LORD.[a]

Psalm 117

1Praise the LORD, all you nations;
extol him, all you peoples.
2For great is his love toward us,
and the faithfulness of the LORD endures
forever.
Praise the LORD.[a]

Psalm 118

1Give thanks to the LORD, for he is good;
his love endures forever.

2Let Israel say:
"His love endures forever."
3Let the house of Aaron say:
"His love endures forever."
4Let those who fear the LORD say:
"His love endures forever."

5In my anguish I cried to the LORD,
and he answered by setting me free.
6The LORD is with me; I will not be afraid.
What can man do to me?

[a] 18,19,2 Hebrew *Hallelu Yah* [b] 3 Hebrew *Sheol* [c] 10 Or *believed even when* [d] 16 Or *servant, your faithful son*

7The LORD is with me; he is my helper.
I will look in triumph on my enemies.

8It is better to take refuge in the LORD
than to trust in man.
9It is better to take refuge in the LORD
than to trust in princes.

10All the nations surrounded me,
but in the name of the LORD I cut them off.
11They surrounded me on every side,
but in the name of the LORD I cut them off.
12They swarmed around me like bees,
but they died out as quickly as burning thorns;
in the name of the LORD I cut them off.

13I was pushed back and about to fall,
but the LORD helped me.
14The LORD is my strength and my song;
he has become my salvation.

15Shouts of joy and victory
resound in the tents of the righteous:
"The LORD's right hand has done mighty things!
16 The LORD's right hand is lifted high;
the LORD's right hand has done mighty things!"

17I will not die but live,
and will proclaim what the LORD has done.
18The LORD has chastened me severely,
but he has not given me over to death.

19Open for me the gates of righteousness;
I will enter and give thanks to the LORD.
20This is the gate of the LORD
through which the righteous may enter.
21I will give you thanks, for you answered me;
you have become my salvation.

22The stone the builders rejected
has become the capstone;
23the LORD has done this,
and it is marvelous in our eyes.
24This is the day the LORD has made;
let us rejoice and be glad in it.

25O LORD, save us;
O LORD, grant us success.
26Blessed is he who comes in the name of the LORD.
From the house of the LORD we bless you.[a]
27The LORD is God,
and he has made his light shine upon us.
With boughs in hand, join in the festal procession
up[b] to the horns of the altar.

28You are my God, and I will give you thanks;
you are my God, and I will exalt you.

29Give thanks to the LORD, for he is good;
his love endures forever.

Psalm 119[c]

א Aleph

1Blessed are they whose ways are blameless,
who walk according to the law of the LORD.
2Blessed are they who keep his statutes
and seek him with all their heart.
3They do nothing wrong;
they walk in his ways.
4You have laid down precepts
that are to be fully obeyed.
5Oh, that my ways were steadfast
in obeying your decrees!
6Then I would not be put to shame
when I consider all your commands.
7I will praise you with an upright heart
as I learn your righteous laws.
8I will obey your decrees;
do not utterly forsake me.

ב Beth

9How can a young man keep his way pure?
By living according to your word.
10I seek you with all my heart;
do not let me stray from your commands.
11I have hidden your word in my heart
that I might not sin against you.
12Praise be to you, O LORD;
teach me your decrees.
13With my lips I recount
all the laws that come from your mouth.
14I rejoice in following your statutes
as one rejoices in great riches.
15I meditate on your precepts
and consider your ways.
16I delight in your decrees;
I will not neglect your word.

ג Gimel

17Do good to your servant, and I will live;
I will obey your word.
18Open my eyes that I may see
wonderful things in your law.
19I am a stranger on earth;
do not hide your commands from me.
20My soul is consumed with longing

[a]26 The Hebrew is plural. [b]27 Or *Bind the festal sacrifice with ropes / and take it* [c]This psalm is an acrostic poem; the verses of each stanza begin with the same letter of the Hebrew alphabet.

for your laws at all times.
21 You rebuke the arrogant, who are cursed
and who stray from your commands.
22 Remove from me scorn and contempt,
for I keep your statutes.
23 Though rulers sit together and slander me,
your servant will meditate on your
decrees.
24 Your statutes are my delight;
they are my counselors.

ד Daleth

25 I am laid low in the dust;
preserve my life according to your word.
26 I recounted my ways and you answered me;
teach me your decrees.
27 Let me understand the teaching of your
precepts;
then I will meditate on your wonders.
28 My soul is weary with sorrow;
strengthen me according to your word.
29 Keep me from deceitful ways;
be gracious to me through your law.
30 I have chosen the way of truth;
I have set my heart on your laws.
31 I hold fast to your statutes, O LORD;
do not let me be put to shame.
32 I run in the path of your commands,
for you have set my heart free.

ה He

33 Teach me, O LORD, to follow your decrees;
then I will keep them to the end.
34 Give me understanding, and I will keep your
law
and obey it with all my heart.
35 Direct me in the path of your commands,
for there I find delight.
36 Turn my heart toward your statutes
and not toward selfish gain.
37 Turn my eyes away from worthless things;
preserve my life according to your word.[a]
38 Fulfill your promise to your servant,
so that you may be feared.
39 Take away the disgrace I dread,
for your laws are good.
40 How I long for your precepts!
Preserve my life in your righteousness.

ו Waw

41 May your unfailing love come to me,
O LORD,
your salvation according to your promise;
42 then I will answer the one who taunts me,
for I trust in your word.
43 Do not snatch the word of truth from my
mouth,
for I have put my hope in your laws.
44 I will always obey your law,
for ever and ever.
45 I will walk about in freedom,
for I have sought out your precepts.
46 I will speak of your statutes before kings
and will not be put to shame,
47 for I delight in your commands
because I love them.
48 I lift up my hands to[b] your commands,
which I love,
and I meditate on your decrees.

ז Zayin

49 Remember your word to your servant,
for you have given me hope.
50 My comfort in my suffering is this:
Your promise preserves my life.
51 The arrogant mock me without restraint,
but I do not turn from your law.
52 I remember your ancient laws, O LORD,
and I find comfort in them.
53 Indignation grips me because of the wicked,
who have forsaken your law.
54 Your decrees are the theme of my song
wherever I lodge.
55 In the night I remember your name, O LORD,
and I will keep your law.
56 This has been my practice:
I obey your precepts.

ח Heth

57 You are my portion, O LORD;
I have promised to obey your words.
58 I have sought your face with all my heart;
be gracious to me according to your
promise.
59 I have considered my ways
and have turned my steps to your statutes.
60 I will hasten and not delay
to obey your commands.
61 Though the wicked bind me with ropes,
I will not forget your law.
62 At midnight I rise to give you thanks
for your righteous laws.
63 I am a friend to all who fear you,
to all who follow your precepts.
64 The earth is filled with your love, O LORD;
teach me your decrees.

ט Teth

65 Do good to your servant
according to your word, O LORD.
66 Teach me knowledge and good judgment,

[a] 37 Two manuscripts of the Masoretic Text and Dead Sea Scrolls; most manuscripts of the Masoretic Text *life in your way*
[b] 48 Or *for*

for I believe in your commands.
67Before I was afflicted I went astray,
but now I obey your word.
68You are good, and what you do is good;
teach me your decrees.
69Though the arrogant have smeared me with lies,
I keep your precepts with all my heart.
70Their hearts are callous and unfeeling,
but I delight in your law.
71It was good for me to be afflicted
so that I might learn your decrees.
72The law from your mouth is more precious to me
than thousands of pieces of silver and gold.

י Yodh

73Your hands made me and formed me;
give me understanding to learn your commands.
74May those who fear you rejoice when they see me,
for I have put my hope in your word.
75I know, O LORD, that your laws are righteous,
and in faithfulness you have afflicted me.
76May your unfailing love be my comfort,
according to your promise to your servant.
77Let your compassion come to me that I may live,
for your law is my delight.
78May the arrogant be put to shame for wronging me without cause;
but I will meditate on your precepts.
79May those who fear you turn to me,
those who understand your statutes.
80May my heart be blameless toward your decrees,
that I may not be put to shame.

כ Kaph

81My soul faints with longing for your salvation,
but I have put my hope in your word.
82My eyes fail, looking for your promise;
I say, "When will you comfort me?"
83Though I am like a wineskin in the smoke,
I do not forget your decrees.
84How long must your servant wait?
When will you punish my persecutors?
85The arrogant dig pitfalls for me,
contrary to your law.
86All your commands are trustworthy;
help me, for men persecute me without cause.
87They almost wiped me from the earth,
but I have not forsaken your precepts.
88Preserve my life according to your love,
and I will obey the statutes of your mouth.

ל Lamedh

89Your word, O LORD, is eternal;
it stands firm in the heavens.
90Your faithfulness continues through all generations;
you established the earth, and it endures.
91Your laws endure to this day,
for all things serve you.
92If your law had not been my delight,
I would have perished in my affliction.
93I will never forget your precepts,
for by them you have preserved my life.
94Save me, for I am yours;
I have sought out your precepts.
95The wicked are waiting to destroy me,
but I will ponder your statutes.
96To all perfection I see a limit;
but your commands are boundless.

מ Mem

97Oh, how I love your law!
I meditate on it all day long.
98Your commands make me wiser than my enemies,
for they are ever with me.
99I have more insight than all my teachers,
for I meditate on your statutes.
100I have more understanding than the elders,
for I obey your precepts.
101I have kept my feet from every evil path
so that I might obey your word.
102I have not departed from your laws,
for you yourself have taught me.
103How sweet are your words to my taste,
sweeter than honey to my mouth!
104I gain understanding from your precepts;
therefore I hate every wrong path.

נ Nun

105Your word is a lamp to my feet
and a light for my path.
106I have taken an oath and confirmed it,
that I will follow your righteous laws.
107I have suffered much;
preserve my life, O LORD, according to your word.
108Accept, O LORD, the willing praise of my mouth,
and teach me your laws.
109Though I constantly take my life in my hands,
I will not forget your law.
110The wicked have set a snare for me,
but I have not strayed from your precepts.
111Your statutes are my heritage forever;
they are the joy of my heart.
112My heart is set on keeping your decrees
to the very end.

ס Samekh

113 I hate double-minded men,
but I love your law.
114 You are my refuge and my shield;
I have put my hope in your word.
115 Away from me, you evildoers,
that I may keep the commands of my God!
116 Sustain me according to your promise, and I will live;
do not let my hopes be dashed.
117 Uphold me, and I will be delivered;
I will always have regard for your decrees.
118 You reject all who stray from your decrees,
for their deceitfulness is in vain.
119 All the wicked of the earth you discard like dross;
therefore I love your statutes.
120 My flesh trembles in fear of you;
I stand in awe of your laws.

ע Ayin

121 I have done what is righteous and just;
do not leave me to my oppressors.
122 Ensure your servant's well-being;
let not the arrogant oppress me.
123 My eyes fail, looking for your salvation,
looking for your righteous promise.
124 Deal with your servant according to your love
and teach me your decrees.
125 I am your servant; give me discernment
that I may understand your statutes.
126 It is time for you to act, O LORD;
your law is being broken.
127 Because I love your commands
more than gold, more than pure gold,
128 and because I consider all your precepts right,
I hate every wrong path.

פ Pe

129 Your statutes are wonderful;
therefore I obey them.
130 The unfolding of your words gives light;
it gives understanding to the simple.
131 I open my mouth and pant,
longing for your commands.
132 Turn to me and have mercy on me,
as you always do to those who love your name.
133 Direct my footsteps according to your word;
let no sin rule over me.
134 Redeem me from the oppression of men,
that I may obey your precepts.
135 Make your face shine upon your servant
and teach me your decrees.
136 Streams of tears flow from my eyes,
for your law is not obeyed.

צ Tsadhe

137 Righteous are you, O LORD,
and your laws are right.
138 The statutes you have laid down are righteous;
they are fully trustworthy.
139 My zeal wears me out,
for my enemies ignore your words.
140 Your promises have been thoroughly tested,
and your servant loves them.
141 Though I am lowly and despised,
I do not forget your precepts.
142 Your righteousness is everlasting
and your law is true.
143 Trouble and distress have come upon me,
but your commands are my delight.
144 Your statutes are forever right;
give me understanding that I may live.

ק Qoph

145 I call with all my heart; answer me, O LORD,
and I will obey your decrees.
146 I call out to you; save me
and I will keep your statutes.
147 I rise before dawn and cry for help;
I have put my hope in your word.
148 My eyes stay open through the watches of the night,
that I may meditate on your promises.
149 Hear my voice in accordance with your love;
preserve my life, O LORD, according to your laws.
150 Those who devise wicked schemes are near,
but they are far from your law.
151 Yet you are near, O LORD,
and all your commands are true.
152 Long ago I learned from your statutes
that you established them to last forever.

ר Resh

153 Look upon my suffering and deliver me,
for I have not forgotten your law.
154 Defend my cause and redeem me;
preserve my life according to your promise.
155 Salvation is far from the wicked,
for they do not seek out your decrees.
156 Your compassion is great, O LORD;
preserve my life according to your laws.
157 Many are the foes who persecute me,
but I have not turned from your statutes.
158 I look on the faithless with loathing,
for they do not obey your word.
159 See how I love your precepts;
preserve my life, O LORD, according to your love.
160 All your words are true;
all your righteous laws are eternal.

ש Sin and Shin

161Rulers persecute me without cause,
but my heart trembles at your word.
162I rejoice in your promise
like one who finds great spoil.
163I hate and abhor falsehood
but I love your law.
164Seven times a day I praise you
for your righteous laws.
165Great peace have they who love your law,
and nothing can make them stumble.
166I wait for your salvation, O LORD,
and I follow your commands.
167I obey your statutes,
for I love them greatly.
168I obey your precepts and your statutes,
for all my ways are known to you.

ת Taw

169May my cry come before you, O LORD;
give me understanding according to your word.
170May my supplication come before you;
deliver me according to your promise.
171May my lips overflow with praise,
for you teach me your decrees.
172May my tongue sing of your word,
for all your commands are righteous.
173May your hand be ready to help me,
for I have chosen your precepts.
174I long for your salvation, O LORD,
and your law is my delight.
175Let me live that I may praise you,
and may your laws sustain me.
176I have strayed like a lost sheep.
Seek your servant,
for I have not forgotten your commands.

Psalm 120

A song of ascents.

1I call on the LORD in my distress,
and he answers me.
2Save me, O LORD, from lying lips
and from deceitful tongues.

3What will he do to you,
and what more besides, O deceitful tongue?
4He will punish you with a warrior's sharp arrows,
with burning coals of the broom tree.

5Woe to me that I dwell in Meshech,
that I live among the tents of Kedar!
6Too long have I lived
among those who hate peace.
7I am a man of peace;
but when I speak, they are for war.

Psalm 121

A song of ascents.

1I lift up my eyes to the hills—
where does my help come from?
2My help comes from the LORD,
the Maker of heaven and earth.

3He will not let your foot slip—
he who watches over you will not slumber;
4indeed, he who watches over Israel
will neither slumber nor sleep.

5The LORD watches over you—
the LORD is your shade at your right hand;
6the sun will not harm you by day,
nor the moon by night.

7The LORD will keep you from all harm—
he will watch over your life;
8the LORD will watch over your coming and going
both now and forevermore.

Psalm 122

A song of ascents. Of David.

1I rejoiced with those who said to me,
"Let us go to the house of the LORD."
2Our feet are standing
in your gates, O Jerusalem.

3Jerusalem is built like a city
that is closely compacted together.
4That is where the tribes go up,
the tribes of the LORD,
to praise the name of the LORD
according to the statute given to Israel.
5There the thrones for judgment stand,
the thrones of the house of David.

6Pray for the peace of Jerusalem:
"May those who love you be secure.
7May there be peace within your walls
and security within your citadels."
8For the sake of my brothers and friends,
I will say, "Peace be within you."
9For the sake of the house of the LORD our God,
I will seek your prosperity.

Psalm 123

A song of ascents.

[1]I lift up my eyes to you,
to you whose throne is in heaven.
[2]As the eyes of slaves look to the hand of their master,
as the eyes of a maid look to the hand of her mistress,
so our eyes look to the LORD our God,
till he shows us his mercy.

[3]Have mercy on us, O LORD, have mercy on us,
for we have endured much contempt.
[4]We have endured much ridicule from the proud,
much contempt from the arrogant.

Psalm 124

A song of ascents. Of David.

[1]If the LORD had not been on our side—
let Israel say—
[2]if the LORD had not been on our side
when men attacked us,
[3]when their anger flared against us,
they would have swallowed us alive;
[4]the flood would have engulfed us,
the torrent would have swept over us,
[5]the raging waters
would have swept us away.

[6]Praise be to the LORD,
who has not let us be torn by their teeth.
[7]We have escaped like a bird
out of the fowler's snare;
the snare has been broken,
and we have escaped.
[8]Our help is in the name of the LORD,
the Maker of heaven and earth.

Psalm 125

A song of ascents.

[1]Those who trust in the LORD are like Mount Zion,
which cannot be shaken but endures forever.
[2]As the mountains surround Jerusalem,
so the LORD surrounds his people
both now and forevermore.

[3]The scepter of the wicked will not remain
over the land allotted to the righteous,
for then the righteous might use
their hands to do evil.
[4]Do good, O LORD, to those who are good,
to those who are upright in heart.
[5]But those who turn to crooked ways
the LORD will banish with the evildoers.

Peace be upon Israel.

Psalm 126

A song of ascents.

[1]When the LORD brought back the captives to[a] Zion,
we were like men who dreamed.[b]
[2]Our mouths were filled with laughter,
our tongues with songs of joy.
Then it was said among the nations,
"The LORD has done great things for them."
[3]The LORD has done great things for us,
and we are filled with joy.

[4]Restore our fortunes,[c] O LORD,
like streams in the Negev.
[5]Those who sow in tears
will reap with songs of joy.
[6]He who goes out weeping,
carrying seed to sow,
will return with songs of joy,
carrying sheaves with him.

Psalm 127

A song of ascents. Of Solomon.

[1]Unless the LORD builds the house,
its builders labor in vain.
Unless the LORD watches over the city,
the watchmen stand guard in vain.
[2]In vain you rise early
and stay up late,
toiling for food to eat—
for he grants sleep to[d] those he loves.

[3]Sons are a heritage from the LORD,
children a reward from him.
[4]Like arrows in the hands of a warrior
are sons born in one's youth.
[5]Blessed is the man
whose quiver is full of them.
They will not be put to shame
when they contend with their enemies in the gate.

[a] 1 Or *LORD restored the fortunes of* [b] 1 Or *men restored to health* [c] 4 Or *Bring back our captives* [d] 2 Or *eat— / for while they sleep he provides for*

Psalm 128

A song of ascents.

1Blessed are all who fear the LORD,
who walk in his ways.
2You will eat the fruit of your labor;
blessings and prosperity will be yours.
3Your wife will be like a fruitful vine
within your house;
your sons will be like olive shoots
around your table.
4Thus is the man blessed
who fears the LORD.

5May the LORD bless you from Zion
all the days of your life;
may you see the prosperity of Jerusalem,
6 and may you live to see your children's
children.

Peace be upon Israel.

Psalm 129

A song of ascents.

1They have greatly oppressed me from my
youth—
let Israel say—
2they have greatly oppressed me from my
youth,
but they have not gained the victory over
me.
3Plowmen have plowed my back
and made their furrows long.
4But the LORD is righteous;
he has cut me free from the cords of the
wicked.

5May all who hate Zion
be turned back in shame.
6May they be like grass on the roof,
which withers before it can grow;
7with it the reaper cannot fill his hands,
nor the one who gathers fill his arms.
8May those who pass by not say,
"The blessing of the LORD be upon you;
we bless you in the name of the LORD."

Psalm 130

A song of ascents.

1Out of the depths I cry to you, O LORD;
2 O Lord, hear my voice.
Let your ears be attentive
to my cry for mercy.

3If you, O LORD, kept a record of sins,
O Lord, who could stand?
4But with you there is forgiveness;
therefore you are feared.

5I wait for the LORD, my soul waits,
and in his word I put my hope.
6My soul waits for the Lord
more than watchmen wait for the
morning,
more than watchmen wait for the
morning.

7O Israel, put your hope in the LORD,
for with the LORD is unfailing love
and with him is full redemption.
8He himself will redeem Israel
from all their sins.

Psalm 131

A song of ascents. Of David.

1My heart is not proud, O LORD,
my eyes are not haughty;
I do not concern myself with great matters
or things too wonderful for me.
2But I have stilled and quieted my soul;
like a weaned child with its mother,
like a weaned child is my soul within me.

3O Israel, put your hope in the LORD
both now and forevermore.

Psalm 132

A song of ascents.

1O LORD, remember David
and all the hardships he endured.

2He swore an oath to the LORD
and made a vow to the Mighty One of
Jacob:
3"I will not enter my house
or go to my bed—
4I will allow no sleep to my eyes,
no slumber to my eyelids,
5till I find a place for the LORD,
a dwelling for the Mighty One of Jacob."

6We heard it in Ephrathah,
we came upon it in the fields of Jaar[a]:[b]
7"Let us go to his dwelling place;
let us worship at his footstool—
8arise, O LORD, and come to your resting
place,
you and the ark of your might.
9May your priests be clothed with
righteousness;
may your saints sing for joy."

[a]6 That is, Kiriath Jearim [b]6 Or *heard of it in Ephrathah, / we found it in the fields of Jaar.* (And no quotes around verses 7-9)

10For the sake of David your servant,
do not reject your anointed one.

11The LORD swore an oath to David,
a sure oath that he will not revoke:
"One of your own descendants
I will place on your throne—
12if your sons keep my covenant
and the statutes I teach them,
then their sons will sit
on your throne for ever and ever."

13For the LORD has chosen Zion,
he has desired it for his dwelling:
14"This is my resting place for ever and ever;
here I will sit enthroned, for I have
desired it—
15I will bless her with abundant provisions;
her poor will I satisfy with food.
16I will clothe her priests with salvation,
and her saints will ever sing for joy.

17"Here I will make a horn[a] grow for David
and set up a lamp for my anointed one.
18I will clothe his enemies with shame,
but the crown on his head will be
resplendent."

Psalm 133

A song of ascents. Of David.

1How good and pleasant it is
when brothers live together in unity!
2It is like precious oil poured on the head,
running down on the beard,
running down on Aaron's beard,
down upon the collar of his robes.
3It is as if the dew of Hermon
were falling on Mount Zion.
For there the LORD bestows his blessing,
even life forevermore.

Psalm 134

A song of ascents.

1Praise the LORD, all you servants of the LORD
who minister by night in the house of the
LORD.
2Lift up your hands in the sanctuary
and praise the LORD.

3May the LORD, the Maker of heaven and
earth,
bless you from Zion.

Psalm 135

1Praise the LORD.[b]

Praise the name of the LORD;
praise him, you servants of the LORD,
2you who minister in the house of the LORD,
in the courts of the house of our God.

3Praise the LORD, for the LORD is good;
sing praise to his name, for that is
pleasant.
4For the LORD has chosen Jacob to be his
own,
Israel to be his treasured possession.

5I know that the LORD is great,
that our Lord is greater than all gods.
6The LORD does whatever pleases him,
in the heavens and on the earth,
in the seas and all their depths.
7He makes clouds rise from the ends of the
earth;
he sends lightning with the rain
and brings out the wind from his
storehouses.

8He struck down the firstborn of Egypt,
the firstborn of men and animals.
9He sent his signs and wonders into your
midst, O Egypt,
against Pharaoh and all his servants.
10He struck down many nations
and killed mighty kings—
11Sihon king of the Amorites,
Og king of Bashan
and all the kings of Canaan—
12and he gave their land as an inheritance,
an inheritance to his people Israel.

13Your name, O LORD, endures forever,
your renown, O LORD, through all
generations.
14For the LORD will vindicate his people
and have compassion on his servants.

15The idols of the nations are silver and gold,
made by the hands of men.
16They have mouths, but cannot speak,
eyes, but they cannot see;
17they have ears, but cannot hear,
nor is there breath in their mouths.
18Those who make them will be like them,
and so will all who trust in them.

19O house of Israel, praise the LORD;
O house of Aaron, praise the LORD;
20O house of Levi, praise the LORD;
you who fear him, praise the LORD.

[a] 17 *Horn* here symbolizes strong one, that is, king.

[b] 1 Hebrew *Hallelu Yah*; also in verses 3 and 21

21Praise be to the LORD from Zion,
to him who dwells in Jerusalem.

Praise the LORD.

Psalm 136

1Give thanks to the LORD, for he is good.
His love endures forever.
2Give thanks to the God of gods.
His love endures forever.
3Give thanks to the Lord of lords:
His love endures forever.

4to him who alone does great wonders,
His love endures forever.
5who by his understanding made the heavens,
His love endures forever.
6who spread out the earth upon the waters,
His love endures forever.
7who made the great lights—
His love endures forever.
8the sun to govern the day,
His love endures forever.
9the moon and stars to govern the night;
His love endures forever.

10to him who struck down the firstborn of Egypt
His love endures forever.
11and brought Israel out from among them
His love endures forever.
12with a mighty hand and outstretched arm;
His love endures forever.

13to him who divided the Red Sea[a] asunder
His love endures forever.
14and brought Israel through the midst of it,
His love endures forever.
15but swept Pharaoh and his army into the Red Sea;
His love endures forever.

16to him who led his people through the desert,
His love endures forever.
17who struck down great kings,
His love endures forever.
18and killed mighty kings—
His love endures forever.
19Sihon king of the Amorites
His love endures forever.
20and Og king of Bashan—
His love endures forever.
21and gave their land as an inheritance,
His love endures forever.
22an inheritance to his servant Israel;
His love endures forever.

23to the One who remembered us in our low estate
His love endures forever.
24and freed us from our enemies,
His love endures forever.
25and who gives food to every creature.
His love endures forever.

26Give thanks to the God of heaven.
His love endures forever.

Psalm 137

1By the rivers of Babylon we sat and wept
when we remembered Zion.
2There on the poplars
we hung our harps,
3for there our captors asked us for songs,
our tormentors demanded songs of joy;
they said, "Sing us one of the songs of Zion!"

4How can we sing the songs of the LORD
while in a foreign land?
5If I forget you, O Jerusalem,
may my right hand forget ⌞its skill⌟.
6May my tongue cling to the roof of my mouth
if I do not remember you,
if I do not consider Jerusalem
my highest joy.

7Remember, O LORD, what the Edomites did
on the day Jerusalem fell.
"Tear it down," they cried,
"tear it down to its foundations!"
8O Daughter of Babylon, doomed to destruction,
happy is he who repays you
for what you have done to us—
9he who seizes your infants
and dashes them against the rocks.

Psalm 138

Of David.

1I will praise you, O LORD, with all my heart;
before the "gods" I will sing your praise.
2I will bow down toward your holy temple
and will praise your name
for your love and your faithfulness,
for you have exalted above all things
your name and your word.
3When I called, you answered me;
you made me bold and stouthearted.

4May all the kings of the earth praise you,
O LORD,

[a] 13 Hebrew *Yam Suph*; that is, Sea of Reeds; also in verse 15

when they hear the words of your mouth.
5 May they sing of the ways of the LORD,
for the glory of the LORD is great.

6 Though the LORD is on high, he looks upon
the lowly,
but the proud he knows from afar.
7 Though I walk in the midst of trouble,
you preserve my life;
you stretch out your hand against the anger
of my foes,
with your right hand you save me.
8 The LORD will fulfill ⌊his purpose⌋ for me;
your love, O LORD, endures forever—
do not abandon the works of your hands.

Psalm 139

For the director of music. Of David. A psalm.

1 O LORD, you have searched me
and you know me.
2 You know when I sit and when I rise;
you perceive my thoughts from afar.
3 You discern my going out and my lying
down;
you are familiar with all my ways.
4 Before a word is on my tongue
you know it completely, O LORD.

5 You hem me in—behind and before;
you have laid your hand upon me.
6 Such knowledge is too wonderful for me,
too lofty for me to attain.

7 Where can I go from your Spirit?
Where can I flee from your presence?
8 If I go up to the heavens, you are there;
if I make my bed in the depths,[a] you are
there.
9 If I rise on the wings of the dawn,
if I settle on the far side of the sea,
10 even there your hand will guide me,
your right hand will hold me fast.

11 If I say, "Surely the darkness will hide me
and the light become night around me,"
12 even the darkness will not be dark to you;
the night will shine like the day,
for darkness is as light to you.

13 For you created my inmost being;

PSALM 139:1–24

1. As a child, were you afraid of the dark? Did you sleep with a night light?
2. Who knows you so well that they know what you are going to say before you even say it?
3. Without naming names, do you know of someone who has had an abortion?
4. How do you feel about abortion?
5. How does this psalm make you feel about yourself and your value to God?
6. How does it make you feel to know you can't go anywhere that God isn't (see vv. 7–8)?
7. How can "knowing God is there" and that he loves you (see Rom. 8:38–39) be an encouragement when you've done something that makes you feel apart from God?
8. Close in prayer by praying together verses 23 and 24 of this psalm.

you knit me together in my mother's
womb.
14 I praise you because I am fearfully and
wonderfully made;
your works are wonderful,
I know that full well.
15 My frame was not hidden from you

[a] 8 Hebrew *Sheol*

Psalm 139 is a prayer of David for God to examine his heart and see its true devotion.

139:1–6 God, you know me perfectly, far beyond my knowledge of myself: my every action (v. 2a) and undertaking (v. 3a), the manner in which I pursue them (v. 3b), my thoughts before they are fully crystallized (v. 2b), and my words before they are uttered (v. 4). When David says, "You hem me in" (v. 5), he wasn't feeling oppressed or lacking in freedom. Rather, he was grateful that wherever he turned he found God.

139:7–12 There is no hiding from you. David did not actually want to flee from God's presence, but was asking rhetorical questions (v. 7) to make the point that God is omnipresent—he can be found everywhere. Just as the whole creation offers no hiding place (vv. 8–9), neither does even the darkness (vv. 11–12).

139:13–16 You yourself put me together in the womb and ordained the span of my life before I was born. Poetic language is used to convey that God is involved in every detail of our lives, including our beginning and end. These verses give assurance that God is personally concerned for every human being—even before birth.

139:19–22 My zeal for you sets me against all your adversaries. David reflects jealous impatience with God's patience toward the wicked, but leaves judgment to God.

139:23–24 Examine me, see the integrity of my devotion and keep me true. It is no light matter to be examined by God.

when I was made in the secret place.
When I was woven together in the depths of the earth,
16 your eyes saw my unformed body.
All the days ordained for me
were written in your book
before one of them came to be.

17 How precious to[a] me are your thoughts, O God!
How vast is the sum of them!
18 Were I to count them,
they would outnumber the grains of sand.
When I awake,
I am still with you.

19 If only you would slay the wicked, O God!
Away from me, you bloodthirsty men!
20 They speak of you with evil intent;
your adversaries misuse your name.
21 Do I not hate those who hate you, O LORD,
and abhor those who rise up against you?
22 I have nothing but hatred for them;
I count them my enemies.

23 Search me, O God, and know my heart;
test me and know my anxious thoughts.
24 See if there is any offensive way in me,
and lead me in the way everlasting.

Psalm 140

For the director of music. A psalm of David.

1 Rescue me, O LORD, from evil men;
protect me from men of violence,
2 who devise evil plans in their hearts
and stir up war every day.
3 They make their tongues as sharp as a serpent's;
the poison of vipers is on their lips. *Selah*

4 Keep me, O LORD, from the hands of the wicked;
protect me from men of violence
who plan to trip my feet.
5 Proud men have hidden a snare for me;
they have spread out the cords of their net
and have set traps for me along my path. *Selah*

6 O LORD, I say to you, "You are my God."
Hear, O LORD, my cry for mercy.
7 O Sovereign LORD, my strong deliverer,
who shields my head in the day of battle—
8 do not grant the wicked their desires, O LORD;
do not let their plans succeed,
or they will become proud. *Selah*

9 Let the heads of those who surround me
be covered with the trouble their lips have caused.
10 Let burning coals fall upon them;
may they be thrown into the fire,
into miry pits, never to rise.
11 Let slanderers not be established in the land;
may disaster hunt down men of violence.

12 I know that the LORD secures justice for the poor
and upholds the cause of the needy.
13 Surely the righteous will praise your name
and the upright will live before you.

Psalm 141

A psalm of David.

1 O LORD, I call to you; come quickly to me.
Hear my voice when I call to you.
2 May my prayer be set before you like incense;
may the lifting up of my hands be like the evening sacrifice.

3 Set a guard over my mouth, O LORD;
keep watch over the door of my lips.
4 Let not my heart be drawn to what is evil,
to take part in wicked deeds
with men who are evildoers;
let me not eat of their delicacies.

5 Let a righteous man[b] strike me—it is a kindness;
let him rebuke me—it is oil on my head.
My head will not refuse it.

Yet my prayer is ever against the deeds of evildoers;
6 their rulers will be thrown down from the cliffs,
and the wicked will learn that my words were well spoken.
7 ⌞They will say,⌟ "As one plows and breaks up the earth,
so our bones have been scattered at the mouth of the grave.[c]"

8 But my eyes are fixed on you, O Sovereign LORD;
in you I take refuge—do not give me over to death.
9 Keep me from the snares they have laid for me,
from the traps set by evildoers.
10 Let the wicked fall into their own nets,
while I pass by in safety.

[a] 17 Or *concerning* [b] 5 Or *Let the Righteous One* [c] 7 Hebrew *Sheol*

Psalm 142

A *maskil*[a] of David. When he was in the cave. A prayer.

1 I cry aloud to the LORD;
I lift up my voice to the LORD for mercy.
2 I pour out my complaint before him;
before him I tell my trouble.

3 When my spirit grows faint within me,
it is you who know my way.
In the path where I walk
men have hidden a snare for me.
4 Look to my right and see;
no one is concerned for me.
I have no refuge;
no one cares for my life.

5 I cry to you, O LORD;
I say, "You are my refuge,
my portion in the land of the living."
6 Listen to my cry,
for I am in desperate need;
rescue me from those who pursue me,
for they are too strong for me.
7 Set me free from my prison,
that I may praise your name.

Then the righteous will gather about me
because of your goodness to me.

Psalm 143

A psalm of David.

1 O LORD, hear my prayer,
listen to my cry for mercy;
in your faithfulness and righteousness
come to my relief.
2 Do not bring your servant into judgment,
for no one living is righteous before you.

3 The enemy pursues me,
he crushes me to the ground;
he makes me dwell in darkness
like those long dead.
4 So my spirit grows faint within me;
my heart within me is dismayed.
5 I remember the days of long ago;
I meditate on all your works
and consider what your hands have done.
6 I spread out my hands to you;
my soul thirsts for you like a parched land.
Selah

7 Answer me quickly, O LORD;
my spirit fails.
Do not hide your face from me
or I will be like those who go down to the pit.
8 Let the morning bring me word of your unfailing love,
for I have put my trust in you.
Show me the way I should go,
for to you I lift up my soul.
9 Rescue me from my enemies, O LORD,
for I hide myself in you.
10 Teach me to do your will,
for you are my God;
may your good Spirit
lead me on level ground.

11 For your name's sake, O LORD, preserve my life;
in your righteousness, bring me out of trouble.
12 In your unfailing love, silence my enemies;
destroy all my foes,
for I am your servant.

Psalm 144

Of David.

1 Praise be to the LORD my Rock,
who trains my hands for war,
my fingers for battle.
2 He is my loving God and my fortress,
my stronghold and my deliverer,
my shield, in whom I take refuge,
who subdues peoples[b] under me.

3 O LORD, what is man that you care for him,
the son of man that you think of him?
4 Man is like a breath;
his days are like a fleeting shadow.

5 Part your heavens, O LORD, and come down;
touch the mountains, so that they smoke.
6 Send forth lightning and scatter ⌊the enemies⌋;
shoot your arrows and rout them.
7 Reach down your hand from on high;
deliver me and rescue me
from the mighty waters,
from the hands of foreigners
8 whose mouths are full of lies,
whose right hands are deceitful.

9 I will sing a new song to you, O God;
on the ten-stringed lyre I will make music to you,
10 to the One who gives victory to kings,
who delivers his servant David from the deadly sword.

11 Deliver me and rescue me

[a] Title: Probably a literary or musical term [b] 2 Many manuscripts of the Masoretic Text, Dead Sea Scrolls, Aquila, Jerome and Syriac; most manuscripts of the Masoretic Text *subdues my people*

from the hands of foreigners
whose mouths are full of lies,
whose right hands are deceitful.

12 Then our sons in their youth
will be like well-nurtured plants,
and our daughters will be like pillars
carved to adorn a palace.
13 Our barns will be filled
with every kind of provision.
Our sheep will increase by thousands,
by tens of thousands in our fields;
14 our oxen will draw heavy loads.[a]
There will be no breaching of walls,
no going into captivity,
no cry of distress in our streets.
15 Blessed are the people of whom this is true;
blessed are the people whose God is the
LORD.

Psalm 145[b]

A psalm of praise. Of David.

1 I will exalt you, my God the King;
I will praise your name for ever and ever.
2 Every day I will praise you
and extol your name for ever and ever.

3 Great is the LORD and most worthy of praise;
his greatness no one can fathom.
4 One generation will commend your works to
another;
they will tell of your mighty acts.
5 They will speak of the glorious splendor of
your majesty,
and I will meditate on your wonderful
works.[c]
6 They will tell of the power of your awesome
works,
and I will proclaim your great deeds.
7 They will celebrate your abundant goodness
and joyfully sing of your righteousness.

8 The LORD is gracious and compassionate,
slow to anger and rich in love.
9 The LORD is good to all;
he has compassion on all he has made.
10 All you have made will praise you, O LORD;
your saints will extol you.
11 They will tell of the glory of your kingdom
and speak of your might,
12 so that all men may know of your mighty
acts
and the glorious splendor of your kingdom.
13 Your kingdom is an everlasting kingdom,
and your dominion endures through all
generations.

The LORD is faithful to all his promises
and loving toward all he has made.[d]
14 The LORD upholds all those who fall
and lifts up all who are bowed down.
15 The eyes of all look to you,
and you give them their food at the proper
time.
16 You open your hand
and satisfy the desires of every living
thing.

17 The LORD is righteous in all his ways
and loving toward all he has made.
18 The LORD is near to all who call on him,
to all who call on him in truth.
19 He fulfills the desires of those who fear him;
he hears their cry and saves them.
20 The LORD watches over all who love him,
but all the wicked he will destroy.

21 My mouth will speak in praise of the LORD.
Let every creature praise his holy name
for ever and ever.

Psalm 146

1 Praise the LORD.[e]

Praise the LORD, O my soul.
2 I will praise the LORD all my life;
I will sing praise to my God as long as I
live.

3 Do not put your trust in princes,
in mortal men, who cannot save.
4 When their spirit departs, they return to the
ground;
on that very day their plans come to
nothing.

5 Blessed is he whose help is the God of Jacob,
whose hope is in the LORD his God,
6 the Maker of heaven and earth,
the sea, and everything in them—
the LORD, who remains faithful forever.
7 He upholds the cause of the oppressed
and gives food to the hungry.
The LORD sets prisoners free,
8 the LORD gives sight to the blind,
the LORD lifts up those who are bowed
down,
the LORD loves the righteous.
9 The LORD watches over the alien

[a] 14 Or *our chieftains will be firmly established* [b] This psalm is an acrostic poem, the verses of which (including verse 13b) begin with the successive letters of the Hebrew alphabet. [c] 5 Dead Sea Scrolls and Syriac (see also Septuagint); Masoretic Text *On the glorious splendor of your majesty / and on your wonderful works I will meditate* [d] 13 One manuscript of the Masoretic Text, Dead Sea Scrolls and Syriac (see also Septuagint); most manuscripts of the Masoretic Text do not have the last two lines of verse 13. [e] 1 Hebrew *Hallelu Yah*; also in verse 10

and sustains the fatherless and the widow,
but he frustrates the ways of the wicked.

10 The LORD reigns forever,
your God, O Zion, for all generations.

Praise the LORD.

Psalm 147

1 Praise the LORD.[a]

How good it is to sing praises to our God,
how pleasant and fitting to praise him!

2 The LORD builds up Jerusalem;
he gathers the exiles of Israel.
3 He heals the brokenhearted
and binds up their wounds.

4 He determines the number of the stars
and calls them each by name.
5 Great is our Lord and mighty in power;
his understanding has no limit.
6 The LORD sustains the humble
but casts the wicked to the ground.

7 Sing to the LORD with thanksgiving;
make music to our God on the harp.
8 He covers the sky with clouds;
he supplies the earth with rain
and makes grass grow on the hills.
9 He provides food for the cattle
and for the young ravens when they call.

10 His pleasure is not in the strength of the
horse,
nor his delight in the legs of a man;
11 the LORD delights in those who fear him,
who put their hope in his unfailing love.

12 Extol the LORD, O Jerusalem;
praise your God, O Zion,
13 for he strengthens the bars of your gates
and blesses your people within you.
14 He grants peace to your borders
and satisfies you with the finest of wheat.

15 He sends his command to the earth;
his word runs swiftly.
16 He spreads the snow like wool
and scatters the frost like ashes.
17 He hurls down his hail like pebbles.
Who can withstand his icy blast?
18 He sends his word and melts them;
he stirs up his breezes, and the waters
flow.

19 He has revealed his word to Jacob,
his laws and decrees to Israel.
20 He has done this for no other nation;
they do not know his laws.

Praise the LORD.

Psalm 148

1 Praise the LORD.[b]

Praise the LORD from the heavens,
praise him in the heights above.
2 Praise him, all his angels,
praise him, all his heavenly hosts.
3 Praise him, sun and moon,
praise him, all you shining stars.
4 Praise him, you highest heavens
and you waters above the skies.
5 Let them praise the name of the LORD,
for he commanded and they were created.
6 He set them in place for ever and ever;
he gave a decree that will never pass
away.

7 Praise the LORD from the earth,
you great sea creatures and all ocean
depths,
8 lightning and hail, snow and clouds,
stormy winds that do his bidding,
9 you mountains and all hills,
fruit trees and all cedars,
10 wild animals and all cattle,
small creatures and flying birds,
11 kings of the earth and all nations,
you princes and all rulers on earth,
12 young men and maidens,
old men and children.

13 Let them praise the name of the LORD,
for his name alone is exalted;
his splendor is above the earth and the
heavens.
14 He has raised up for his people a horn,[c]
the praise of all his saints,
of Israel, the people close to his heart.

Praise the LORD.

Psalm 149

1 Praise the LORD.[d]

Sing to the LORD a new song,
his praise in the assembly of the saints.

2 Let Israel rejoice in their Maker;
let the people of Zion be glad in their
King.
3 Let them praise his name with dancing

a 1 Hebrew *Hallelu Yah*; also in verse 20 b 1 Hebrew *Hallelu Yah*; also in verse 14 c 14 *Horn* here symbolizes strong one, that is, king. d 1 Hebrew *Hallelu Yah*; also in verse 9

and make music to him with tambourine
and harp.
4For the LORD takes delight in his people;
he crowns the humble with salvation.
5Let the saints rejoice in this honor
and sing for joy on their beds.

6May the praise of God be in their mouths
and a double-edged sword in their hands,
7to inflict vengeance on the nations
and punishment on the peoples,
8to bind their kings with fetters,
their nobles with shackles of iron,
9to carry out the sentence written against
them.
This is the glory of all his saints.

Praise the LORD.

Psalm 150

1Praise the LORD.[a]

Praise God in his sanctuary;
praise him in his mighty heavens.
2Praise him for his acts of power;
praise him for his surpassing greatness.
3Praise him with the sounding of the trumpet,
praise him with the harp and lyre,
4praise him with tambourine and dancing,
praise him with the strings and flute,
5praise him with the clash of cymbals,
praise him with resounding cymbals.

6Let everything that has breath praise the
LORD.

Praise the LORD.

a 1 Hebrew *Hallelu Yah*; also in verse 6

Introduction to PROVERBS

Personal Reading Plan

- ❒ Proverbs 1:1–2:22
- ❒ Proverbs 3:1–4:27
- ❒ Proverbs 5:1–6:35
- ❒ Proverbs 7:1–8:36
- ❒ Proverbs 9:1–10:32
- ❒ Proverbs 11:1–12:28
- ❒ Proverbs 13:1–14:35
- ❒ Proverbs 15:1–16:33
- ❒ Proverbs 17:1–18:24
- ❒ Proverbs 19:1–20:30
- ❒ Proverbs 21:1–22:29
- ❒ Proverbs 23:1–24:29
- ❒ Proverbs 25:1–26:28
- ❒ Proverbs 27:1–28:28
- ❒ Proverbs 29:1–31:31

Author

Proverbs has multiple authors and compilers who are named in the section subtitles. Solomon (1:1–22:16; 25:1–29:27) is the most prominent of these, and the introduction to the entire work (1:1–7) is attributed to him. The group of authors entitled "the wise" (22:17–24:34) may have been royal scribes. The sayings of Agur (ch. 30) and Lemuel (ch. 31) conclude the book.

Date

Solomon reigned in Israel c. 970–930 B.C. During that time he wrote thousands of proverbs and songs (1 Kings 4:32). The final compilation of this work occurred after Hezekiah's time (25:1), more than 200 years later, and very possibly as late as 500 B.C.

Theme

To impart moral wisdom and uncommon sense for right living.

Historical Background

Following Solomon's ascension to the throne of Israel, the Lord appeared to him in a dream and offered him the desire of his heart (1 Kings 3:1–28; 4:29–34)—wisdom. The book of Proverbs collects this God-given wisdom in poetic figures of speech, along with the trusted sayings of wise men, accumulated over 200-plus years. Given the international nature of Solomon's court and Israel's mixing with its neighbors, it is not surprising that many parallels to the Proverbs have been found in extra-biblical texts.

Characteristics

Following the book of Psalms, which focuses on our devotional life, we find the book of Proverbs which focuses on our practical life. The English word "proverb" means a brief saying in place of many words. The Hebrew word for proverb, however, has a much broader meaning including longer sentences and discourses. The book of Proverbs is a part of the Wisdom Literature of the Hebrews. Drawn from the everyday life of common people, these proverbs are couched in figurative, poetic speech laced with analogies and similes. Therefore, Proverbs leave a visual as well as verbal impact upon the reader.

As the introduction states, Proverbs was written to give "knowledge and discretion to the young" (1:4). The repeated references to "my son" (1:8,10; 2:1; 3:1; 4:1; 5:1) focus on guiding the young to make righteous and moral choices. Because these proverbs were written particularly for instruction, they are frequently given in the form of a command.

Prologue: Purpose and Theme

1 The proverbs of Solomon son of David, king of Israel:

2for attaining wisdom and discipline;
for understanding words of insight;
3for acquiring a disciplined and prudent life,
doing what is right and just and fair;
4for giving prudence to the simple,
knowledge and discretion to the young—
5let the wise listen and add to their learning,
and let the discerning get guidance—
6for understanding proverbs and parables,
the sayings and riddles of the wise.

7The fear of the LORD is the beginning of knowledge,
but fools[a] despise wisdom and discipline.

Exhortations to Embrace Wisdom

Warning Against Enticement

8Listen, my son, to your father's instruction
and do not forsake your mother's teaching.
9They will be a garland to grace your head
and a chain to adorn your neck.

10My son, if sinners entice you,
do not give in to them.
11If they say, "Come along with us;
let's lie in wait for someone's blood,
let's waylay some harmless soul;
12let's swallow them alive, like the grave,[b]
and whole, like those who go down to the pit;
13we will get all sorts of valuable things
and fill our houses with plunder;
14throw in your lot with us,
and we will share a common purse"—
15my son, do not go along with them,
do not set foot on their paths;
16for their feet rush into sin,
they are swift to shed blood.
17How useless to spread a net
in full view of all the birds!
18These men lie in wait for their own blood;
they waylay only themselves!
19Such is the end of all who go after ill-gotten gain;
it takes away the lives of those who get it.

Warning Against Rejecting Wisdom

20Wisdom calls aloud in the street,
she raises her voice in the public squares;
21at the head of the noisy streets[c] she cries out,
in the gateways of the city she makes her speech:

22"How long will you simple ones[d] love your simple ways?
How long will mockers delight in mockery
and fools hate knowledge?
23If you had responded to my rebuke,
I would have poured out my heart to you
and made my thoughts known to you.
24But since you rejected me when I called
and no one gave heed when I stretched out my hand,
25since you ignored all my advice
and would not accept my rebuke,
26I in turn will laugh at your disaster;
I will mock when calamity overtakes you—
27when calamity overtakes you like a storm,
when disaster sweeps over you like a whirlwind,
when distress and trouble overwhelm you.

28"Then they will call to me but I will not answer;
they will look for me but will not find me.
29Since they hated knowledge
and did not choose to fear the LORD,
30since they would not accept my advice
and spurned my rebuke,
31they will eat the fruit of their ways
and be filled with the fruit of their schemes.
32For the waywardness of the simple will kill them,
and the complacency of fools will destroy them;
33but whoever listens to me will live in safety
and be at ease, without fear of harm."

Moral Benefits of Wisdom

2 My son, if you accept my words
and store up my commands within you,
2turning your ear to wisdom
and applying your heart to understanding,
3and if you call out for insight
and cry aloud for understanding,
4and if you look for it as for silver
and search for it as for hidden treasure,
5then you will understand the fear of the LORD
and find the knowledge of God.
6For the LORD gives wisdom,
and from his mouth come knowledge and understanding.
7He holds victory in store for the upright,

[a]7 The Hebrew words rendered *fool* in Proverbs, and often elsewhere in the Old Testament, denote one who is morally deficient.
[b]12 Hebrew *Sheol*
[c]21 Hebrew; Septuagint / *on the tops of the walls*
[d]22 The Hebrew word rendered *simple* in Proverbs generally denotes one without moral direction and inclined to evil.

he is a shield to those whose walk is
blameless,
8for he guards the course of the just
and protects the way of his faithful ones.

9Then you will understand what is right and
just
and fair—every good path.
10For wisdom will enter your heart,
and knowledge will be pleasant to your
soul.
11Discretion will protect you,
and understanding will guard you.

12Wisdom will save you from the ways of
wicked men,
from men whose words are perverse,
13who leave the straight paths
to walk in dark ways,
14who delight in doing wrong
and rejoice in the perverseness of evil,
15whose paths are crooked
and who are devious in their ways.

16It will save you also from the adulteress,
from the wayward wife with her seductive
words,
17who has left the partner of her youth
and ignored the covenant she made before
God.[a]
18For her house leads down to death
and her paths to the spirits of the dead.
19None who go to her return
or attain the paths of life.

20Thus you will walk in the ways of good men
and keep to the paths of the righteous.
21For the upright will live in the land,
and the blameless will remain in it;
22but the wicked will be cut off from the land,
and the unfaithful will be torn from it.

Further Benefits of Wisdom

3 My son, do not forget my teaching,
but keep my commands in your heart,
2for they will prolong your life many years
and bring you prosperity.

3Let love and faithfulness never leave you;
bind them around your neck,
write them on the tablet of your heart.
4Then you will win favor and a good name
in the sight of God and man.

5Trust in the LORD with all your heart
and lean not on your own understanding;
6in all your ways acknowledge him,
and he will make your paths straight.[b]

7Do not be wise in your own eyes;
fear the LORD and shun evil.
8This will bring health to your body
and nourishment to your bones.

9Honor the LORD with your wealth,
with the firstfruits of all your crops;
10then your barns will be filled to overflowing,
and your vats will brim over with new
wine.

11My son, do not despise the LORD's discipline
and do not resent his rebuke,
12because the LORD disciplines those he loves,
as a father[c] the son he delights in.

13Blessed is the man who finds wisdom,
the man who gains understanding,
14for she is more profitable than silver
and yields better returns than gold.
15She is more precious than rubies;
nothing you desire can compare with her.
16Long life is in her right hand;
in her left hand are riches and honor.
17Her ways are pleasant ways,
and all her paths are peace.
18She is a tree of life to those who embrace
her;
those who lay hold of her will be blessed.

19By wisdom the LORD laid the earth's
foundations,
by understanding he set the heavens in
place;
20by his knowledge the deeps were divided,
and the clouds let drop the dew.

21My son, preserve sound judgment and
discernment,
do not let them out of your sight;
22they will be life for you,
an ornament to grace your neck.
23Then you will go on your way in safety,
and your foot will not stumble;
24when you lie down, you will not be afraid;
when you lie down, your sleep will be
sweet.
25Have no fear of sudden disaster
or of the ruin that overtakes the wicked,
26for the LORD will be your confidence
and will keep your foot from being snared.

27Do not withhold good from those who
deserve it,
when it is in your power to act.
28Do not say to your neighbor,
"Come back later; I'll give it tomorrow"—
when you now have it with you.

29Do not plot harm against your neighbor,
who lives trustfully near you.

a17 Or *covenant of her God*   b6 Or *will direct your paths*   c12 Hebrew; Septuagint / *and he punishes*

30 Do not accuse a man for no reason—
when he has done you no harm.
31 Do not envy a violent man
or choose any of his ways,
32 for the LORD detests a perverse man
but takes the upright into his confidence.
33 The LORD's curse is on the house of the wicked,
but he blesses the home of the righteous.
34 He mocks proud mockers
but gives grace to the humble.
35 The wise inherit honor,
but fools he holds up to shame.

Wisdom Is Supreme

4 Listen, my sons, to a father's instruction;
pay attention and gain understanding.
2 I give you sound learning,
so do not forsake my teaching.
3 When I was a boy in my father's house,
still tender, and an only child of my mother,
4 he taught me and said,
"Lay hold of my words with all your heart;
keep my commands and you will live.
5 Get wisdom, get understanding;
do not forget my words or swerve from them.
6 Do not forsake wisdom, and she will protect you;
love her, and she will watch over you.
7 Wisdom is supreme; therefore get wisdom.
Though it cost all you have,[a] get understanding.
8 Esteem her, and she will exalt you;
embrace her, and she will honor you.
9 She will set a garland of grace on your head
and present you with a crown of splendor."
10 Listen, my son, accept what I say,
and the years of your life will be many.
11 I guide you in the way of wisdom
and lead you along straight paths.
12 When you walk, your steps will not be hampered;
when you run, you will not stumble.
13 Hold on to instruction, do not let it go;
guard it well, for it is your life.
14 Do not set foot on the path of the wicked
or walk in the way of evil men.
15 Avoid it, do not travel on it;
turn from it and go on your way.
16 For they cannot sleep till they do evil;
they are robbed of slumber till they make someone fall.
17 They eat the bread of wickedness
and drink the wine of violence.
18 The path of the righteous is like the first gleam of dawn,
shining ever brighter till the full light of day.
19 But the way of the wicked is like deep darkness;
they do not know what makes them stumble.
20 My son, pay attention to what I say;
listen closely to my words.
21 Do not let them out of your sight,
keep them within your heart;
22 for they are life to those who find them
and health to a man's whole body.
23 Above all else, guard your heart,
for it is the wellspring of life.
24 Put away perversity from your mouth;
keep corrupt talk far from your lips.
25 Let your eyes look straight ahead,
fix your gaze directly before you.
26 Make level[b] paths for your feet
and take only ways that are firm.
27 Do not swerve to the right or the left;
keep your foot from evil.

Warning Against Adultery

5 My son, pay attention to my wisdom,
listen well to my words of insight,
2 that you may maintain discretion
and your lips may preserve knowledge.
3 For the lips of an adulteress drip honey,
and her speech is smoother than oil;
4 but in the end she is bitter as gall,
sharp as a double-edged sword.
5 Her feet go down to death;
her steps lead straight to the grave.[c]
6 She gives no thought to the way of life;
her paths are crooked, but she knows it not.
7 Now then, my sons, listen to me;
do not turn aside from what I say.
8 Keep to a path far from her,
do not go near the door of her house,
9 lest you give your best strength to others
and your years to one who is cruel,
10 lest strangers feast on your wealth
and your toil enrich another man's house.
11 At the end of your life you will groan,
when your flesh and body are spent.
12 You will say, "How I hated discipline!
How my heart spurned correction!
13 I would not obey my teachers
or listen to my instructors.

[a] 7 Or *Whatever else you get* [b] 26 Or *Consider the* [c] 5 Hebrew *Sheol*

14I have come to the brink of utter ruin
in the midst of the whole assembly."

15Drink water from your own cistern,
running water from your own well.
16Should your springs overflow in the streets,
your streams of water in the public
squares?
17Let them be yours alone,
never to be shared with strangers.
18May your fountain be blessed,
and may you rejoice in the wife of your
youth.
19A loving doe, a graceful deer—
may her breasts satisfy you always,
may you ever be captivated by her love.
20Why be captivated, my son, by an adulteress?
Why embrace the bosom of another man's
wife?

21For a man's ways are in full view of the
LORD,
and he examines all his paths.
22The evil deeds of a wicked man ensnare him;
the cords of his sin hold him fast.
23He will die for lack of discipline,
led astray by his own great folly.

Warnings Against Folly

6 My son, if you have put up security for
your neighbor,
if you have struck hands in pledge for
another,
2if you have been trapped by what you said,
ensnared by the words of your mouth,
3then do this, my son, to free yourself,
since you have fallen into your neighbor's
hands:
Go and humble yourself;
press your plea with your neighbor!
4Allow no sleep to your eyes,
no slumber to your eyelids.
5Free yourself, like a gazelle from the hand of
the hunter,
like a bird from the snare of the fowler.

6Go to the ant, you sluggard;
consider its ways and be wise!
7It has no commander,
no overseer or ruler,
8yet it stores its provisions in summer
and gathers its food at harvest.

9How long will you lie there, you sluggard?
When will you get up from your sleep?
10A little sleep, a little slumber,
a little folding of the hands to rest—
11and poverty will come on you like a bandit
and scarcity like an armed man.[a]

12A scoundrel and villain,
who goes about with a corrupt mouth,
13 who winks with his eye,
signals with his feet
and motions with his fingers,
14 who plots evil with deceit in his heart—
he always stirs up dissension.
15Therefore disaster will overtake him in an
instant;
he will suddenly be destroyed—without
remedy.

16There are six things the LORD hates,
seven that are detestable to him:
17 haughty eyes,
a lying tongue,
hands that shed innocent blood,
18 a heart that devises wicked schemes,
feet that are quick to rush into evil,
19 a false witness who pours out lies
and a man who stirs up dissension
among brothers.

Warning Against Adultery

20My son, keep your father's commands
and do not forsake your mother's teaching.
21Bind them upon your heart forever;
fasten them around your neck.
22When you walk, they will guide you;
when you sleep, they will watch over you;
when you awake, they will speak to you.
23For these commands are a lamp,
this teaching is a light,
and the corrections of discipline
are the way to life,
24keeping you from the immoral woman,
from the smooth tongue of the wayward
wife.
25Do not lust in your heart after her beauty
or let her captivate you with her eyes,
26for the prostitute reduces you to a loaf of
bread,
and the adulteress preys upon your very
life.
27Can a man scoop fire into his lap
without his clothes being burned?
28Can a man walk on hot coals
without his feet being scorched?
29So is he who sleeps with another man's wife;
no one who touches her will go
unpunished.

30Men do not despise a thief if he steals
to satisfy his hunger when he is starving.
31Yet if he is caught, he must pay sevenfold,
though it costs him all the wealth of his
house.

[a] 11 Or *like a vagrant / and scarcity like a beggar*

32But a man who commits adultery lacks judgment;
whoever does so destroys himself.
33Blows and disgrace are his lot,
and his shame will never be wiped away;
34for jealousy arouses a husband's fury,
and he will show no mercy when he takes revenge.
35He will not accept any compensation;
he will refuse the bribe, however great it is.

Warning Against the Adulteress

7 My son, keep my words
and store up my commands within you.
2Keep my commands and you will live;
guard my teachings as the apple of your eye.
3Bind them on your fingers;
write them on the tablet of your heart.
4Say to wisdom, "You are my sister,"
and call understanding your kinsman;
5they will keep you from the adulteress,
from the wayward wife with her seductive words.

6At the window of my house
I looked out through the lattice.
7I saw among the simple,
I noticed among the young men,
a youth who lacked judgment.
8He was going down the street near her corner,
walking along in the direction of her house
9at twilight, as the day was fading,
as the dark of night set in.

10Then out came a woman to meet him,
dressed like a prostitute and with crafty intent.
11(She is loud and defiant,
her feet never stay at home;
12now in the street, now in the squares,
at every corner she lurks.)
13She took hold of him and kissed him
and with a brazen face she said:

14"I have fellowship offerings[a] at home;
today I fulfilled my vows.
15So I came out to meet you;
I looked for you and have found you!
16I have covered my bed
with colored linens from Egypt.
17I have perfumed my bed
with myrrh, aloes and cinnamon.
18Come, let's drink deep of love till morning;
let's enjoy ourselves with love!
19My husband is not at home;
he has gone on a long journey.
20He took his purse filled with money
and will not be home till full moon."

21With persuasive words she led him astray;
she seduced him with her smooth talk.
22All at once he followed her
like an ox going to the slaughter,
like a deer[b] stepping into a noose[c]
23 till an arrow pierces his liver,
like a bird darting into a snare,
little knowing it will cost him his life.

24Now then, my sons, listen to me;
pay attention to what I say.
25Do not let your heart turn to her ways
or stray into her paths.
26Many are the victims she has brought down;
her slain are a mighty throng.
27Her house is a highway to the grave,[d]
leading down to the chambers of death.

Wisdom's Call

8 Does not wisdom call out?
Does not understanding raise her voice?
2On the heights along the way,
where the paths meet, she takes her stand;
3beside the gates leading into the city,
at the entrances, she cries aloud:
4"To you, O men, I call out;
I raise my voice to all mankind.
5You who are simple, gain prudence;
you who are foolish, gain understanding.
6Listen, for I have worthy things to say;
I open my lips to speak what is right.
7My mouth speaks what is true,
for my lips detest wickedness.
8All the words of my mouth are just;
none of them is crooked or perverse.
9To the discerning all of them are right;
they are faultless to those who have knowledge.
10Choose my instruction instead of silver,
knowledge rather than choice gold,
11for wisdom is more precious than rubies,
and nothing you desire can compare with her.

12"I, wisdom, dwell together with prudence;
I possess knowledge and discretion.
13To fear the LORD is to hate evil;
I hate pride and arrogance,
evil behavior and perverse speech.
14Counsel and sound judgment are mine;

a 14 Traditionally *peace offerings* b 22 Syriac (see also Septuagint); Hebrew *fool* c 22 The meaning of the Hebrew for this line is uncertain. d 27 Hebrew *Sheol*

I have understanding and power.
[15]By me kings reign
and rulers make laws that are just;
[16]by me princes govern,
and all nobles who rule on earth.[a]
[17]I love those who love me,
and those who seek me find me.
[18]With me are riches and honor,
enduring wealth and prosperity.
[19]My fruit is better than fine gold;
what I yield surpasses choice silver.
[20]I walk in the way of righteousness,
along the paths of justice,
[21]bestowing wealth on those who love me
and making their treasuries full.

[22]"The LORD brought me forth as the first of his works,[b,c]
before his deeds of old;
[23]I was appointed[d] from eternity,
from the beginning, before the world began.
[24]When there were no oceans, I was given birth,
when there were no springs abounding with water;
[25]before the mountains were settled in place,
before the hills, I was given birth,
[26]before he made the earth or its fields
or any of the dust of the world.
[27]I was there when he set the heavens in place,
when he marked out the horizon on the face of the deep,
[28]when he established the clouds above
and fixed securely the fountains of the deep,
[29]when he gave the sea its boundary
so the waters would not overstep his command,
and when he marked out the foundations of the earth.
[30] Then I was the craftsman at his side.
I was filled with delight day after day,
rejoicing always in his presence,
[31]rejoicing in his whole world
and delighting in mankind.

[32]"Now then, my sons, listen to me;
blessed are those who keep my ways.
[33]Listen to my instruction and be wise;
do not ignore it.
[34]Blessed is the man who listens to me,
watching daily at my doors,
waiting at my doorway.
[35]For whoever finds me finds life
and receives favor from the LORD.
[36]But whoever fails to find me harms himself;
all who hate me love death."

Invitations of Wisdom and of Folly

9 Wisdom has built her house;
she has hewn out its seven pillars.
[2]She has prepared her meat and mixed her wine;
she has also set her table.
[3]She has sent out her maids, and she calls
from the highest point of the city.
[4]"Let all who are simple come in here!"
she says to those who lack judgment.
[5]"Come, eat my food
and drink the wine I have mixed.
[6]Leave your simple ways and you will live;
walk in the way of understanding.

[7]"Whoever corrects a mocker invites insult;
whoever rebukes a wicked man incurs abuse.
[8]Do not rebuke a mocker or he will hate you;
rebuke a wise man and he will love you.
[9]Instruct a wise man and he will be wiser still;
teach a righteous man and he will add to his learning.

[10]"The fear of the LORD is the beginning of wisdom,
and knowledge of the Holy One is understanding.
[11]For through me your days will be many,
and years will be added to your life.
[12]If you are wise, your wisdom will reward you;
if you are a mocker, you alone will suffer."

[13]The woman Folly is loud;
she is undisciplined and without knowledge.
[14]She sits at the door of her house,
on a seat at the highest point of the city,
[15]calling out to those who pass by,
who go straight on their way.
[16]"Let all who are simple come in here!"
she says to those who lack judgment.
[17]"Stolen water is sweet;
food eaten in secret is delicious!"
[18]But little do they know that the dead are there,
that her guests are in the depths of the grave.[e]

[a]*16* Many Hebrew manuscripts and Septuagint; most Hebrew manuscripts *and nobles—all righteous rulers* [b]*22* Or *way*; or *dominion* [c]*22* Or *The LORD possessed me at the beginning of his work*; or *The LORD brought me forth at the beginning of his work* [d]*23* Or *fashioned* [e]*18* Hebrew *Sheol*

Proverbs of Solomon

10 The proverbs of Solomon:

A wise son brings joy to his father,
but a foolish son grief to his mother.

2 Ill-gotten treasures are of no value,
but righteousness delivers from death.

3 The LORD does not let the righteous go
hungry
but he thwarts the craving of the wicked.

4 Lazy hands make a man poor,
but diligent hands bring wealth.

5 He who gathers crops in summer is a wise
son,
but he who sleeps during harvest is a
disgraceful son.

6 Blessings crown the head of the righteous,
but violence overwhelms the mouth of the
wicked.[a]

7 The memory of the righteous will be a
blessing,
but the name of the wicked will rot.

8 The wise in heart accept commands,
but a chattering fool comes to ruin.

9 The man of integrity walks securely,
but he who takes crooked paths will be
found out.

10 He who winks maliciously causes grief,
and a chattering fool comes to ruin.

11 The mouth of the righteous is a fountain of
life,
but violence overwhelms the mouth of the
wicked.

12 Hatred stirs up dissension,
but love covers over all wrongs.

13 Wisdom is found on the lips of the
discerning,
but a rod is for the back of him who lacks
judgment.

14 Wise men store up knowledge,
but the mouth of a fool invites ruin.

15 The wealth of the rich is their fortified city,
but poverty is the ruin of the poor.

16 The wages of the righteous bring them life,
but the income of the wicked brings them
punishment.

17 He who heeds discipline shows the way to
life,
but whoever ignores correction leads
others astray.

18 He who conceals his hatred has lying lips,
and whoever spreads slander is a fool.

19 When words are many, sin is not absent,
but he who holds his tongue is wise.

20 The tongue of the righteous is choice silver,
but the heart of the wicked is of little
value.

21 The lips of the righteous nourish many,
but fools die for lack of judgment.

22 The blessing of the LORD brings wealth,
and he adds no trouble to it.

23 A fool finds pleasure in evil conduct,
but a man of understanding delights in
wisdom.

24 What the wicked dreads will overtake him;
what the righteous desire will be granted.

25 When the storm has swept by, the wicked
are gone,
but the righteous stand firm forever.

26 As vinegar to the teeth and smoke to the
eyes,
so is a sluggard to those who send him.

27 The fear of the LORD adds length to life,
but the years of the wicked are cut short.

28 The prospect of the righteous is joy,
but the hopes of the wicked come to
nothing.

29 The way of the LORD is a refuge for the
righteous,
but it is the ruin of those who do evil.

30 The righteous will never be uprooted,
but the wicked will not remain in the
land.

31 The mouth of the righteous brings forth
wisdom,
but a perverse tongue will be cut out.

32 The lips of the righteous know what is
fitting,
but the mouth of the wicked only what is
perverse.

11 The LORD abhors dishonest scales,
but accurate weights are his delight.

2 When pride comes, then comes disgrace,
but with humility comes wisdom.

3 The integrity of the upright guides them,

[a] 6 Or *but the mouth of the wicked conceals violence*; also in verse 11

but the unfaithful are destroyed by their
duplicity.

4 Wealth is worthless in the day of wrath,
but righteousness delivers from death.

5 The righteousness of the blameless makes a
straight way for them,
but the wicked are brought down by their
own wickedness.

6 The righteousness of the upright delivers
them,
but the unfaithful are trapped by evil
desires.

7 When a wicked man dies, his hope perishes;
all he expected from his power comes to
nothing.

8 The righteous man is rescued from trouble,
and it comes on the wicked instead.

9 With his mouth the godless destroys his
neighbor,
but through knowledge the righteous
escape.

10 When the righteous prosper, the city rejoices;
when the wicked perish, there are shouts
of joy.

11 Through the blessing of the upright a city is
exalted,
but by the mouth of the wicked it is
destroyed.

12 A man who lacks judgment derides his
neighbor,
but a man of understanding holds his
tongue.

13 A gossip betrays a confidence,
but a trustworthy man keeps a secret.

14 For lack of guidance a nation falls,
but many advisers make victory sure.

15 He who puts up security for another will
surely suffer,
but whoever refuses to strike hands in
pledge is safe.

16 A kindhearted woman gains respect,
but ruthless men gain only wealth.

17 A kind man benefits himself,
but a cruel man brings trouble on himself.

18 The wicked man earns deceptive wages,
but he who sows righteousness reaps a
sure reward.

19 The truly righteous man attains life,
but he who pursues evil goes to his death.

20 The LORD detests men of perverse heart
but he delights in those whose ways are
blameless.

21 Be sure of this: The wicked will not go
unpunished,
but those who are righteous will go free.

22 Like a gold ring in a pig's snout
is a beautiful woman who shows no
discretion.

23 The desire of the righteous ends only in
good,
but the hope of the wicked only in wrath.

24 One man gives freely, yet gains even more;
another withholds unduly, but comes to
poverty.

25 A generous man will prosper;
he who refreshes others will himself be
refreshed.

26 People curse the man who hoards grain,
but blessing crowns him who is willing to
sell.

27 He who seeks good finds goodwill,
but evil comes to him who searches for it.

28 Whoever trusts in his riches will fall,
but the righteous will thrive like a green
leaf.

29 He who brings trouble on his family will
inherit only wind,
and the fool will be servant to the wise.

30 The fruit of the righteous is a tree of life,
and he who wins souls is wise.

31 If the righteous receive their due on earth,
how much more the ungodly and the
sinner!

12 Whoever loves discipline loves
knowledge,
but he who hates correction is stupid.

2 A good man obtains favor from the LORD,
but the LORD condemns a crafty man.

3 A man cannot be established through
wickedness,
but the righteous cannot be uprooted.

4 A wife of noble character is her husband's
crown,
but a disgraceful wife is like decay in his
bones.

5 The plans of the righteous are just,
but the advice of the wicked is deceitful.

6 The words of the wicked lie in wait for
blood,

but the speech of the upright rescues
them.

7Wicked men are overthrown and are no
more,
but the house of the righteous stands firm.

8A man is praised according to his wisdom,
but men with warped minds are despised.

9Better to be a nobody and yet have a servant
than pretend to be somebody and have no
food.

10A righteous man cares for the needs of his
animal,
but the kindest acts of the wicked are
cruel.

11He who works his land will have abundant
food,
but he who chases fantasies lacks
judgment.

12The wicked desire the plunder of evil men,
but the root of the righteous flourishes.

13An evil man is trapped by his sinful talk,
but a righteous man escapes trouble.

14From the fruit of his lips a man is filled with
good things
as surely as the work of his hands rewards
him.

15The way of a fool seems right to him,
but a wise man listens to advice.

16A fool shows his annoyance at once,
but a prudent man overlooks an insult.

17A truthful witness gives honest testimony,
but a false witness tells lies.

18Reckless words pierce like a sword,
but the tongue of the wise brings healing.

19Truthful lips endure forever,
but a lying tongue lasts only a moment.

20There is deceit in the hearts of those who
plot evil,
but joy for those who promote peace.

21No harm befalls the righteous,
but the wicked have their fill of trouble.

22The LORD detests lying lips,
but he delights in men who are truthful.

23A prudent man keeps his knowledge to
himself,
but the heart of fools blurts out folly.

24Diligent hands will rule,
but laziness ends in slave labor.

25An anxious heart weighs a man down,
but a kind word cheers him up.

26A righteous man is cautious in friendship,[a]
but the way of the wicked leads them
astray.

27The lazy man does not roast[b] his game,
but the diligent man prizes his
possessions.

28In the way of righteousness there is life;
along that path is immortality.

13 A wise son heeds his father's
instruction,
but a mocker does not listen to rebuke.

2From the fruit of his lips a man enjoys good
things,
but the unfaithful have a craving for
violence.

3He who guards his lips guards his life,
but he who speaks rashly will come to
ruin.

4The sluggard craves and gets nothing,
but the desires of the diligent are fully
satisfied.

5The righteous hate what is false,
but the wicked bring shame and disgrace.

6Righteousness guards the man of integrity,
but wickedness overthrows the sinner.

7One man pretends to be rich, yet has
nothing;
another pretends to be poor, yet has great
wealth.

8A man's riches may ransom his life,
but a poor man hears no threat.

9The light of the righteous shines brightly,
but the lamp of the wicked is snuffed out.

10Pride only breeds quarrels,
but wisdom is found in those who take
advice.

11Dishonest money dwindles away,
but he who gathers money little by little
makes it grow.

12Hope deferred makes the heart sick,
but a longing fulfilled is a tree of life.

13He who scorns instruction will pay for it,
but he who respects a command is
rewarded.

14The teaching of the wise is a fountain of life,
turning a man from the snares of death.

[a]*26* Or *man is a guide to his neighbor* [b]*27* The meaning of the Hebrew for this word is uncertain.

15Good understanding wins favor,
but the way of the unfaithful is hard.[a]

16Every prudent man acts out of knowledge,
but a fool exposes his folly.

17A wicked messenger falls into trouble,
but a trustworthy envoy brings healing.

18He who ignores discipline comes to poverty
and shame,
but whoever heeds correction is honored.

19A longing fulfilled is sweet to the soul,
but fools detest turning from evil.

20He who walks with the wise grows wise,
but a companion of fools suffers harm.

21Misfortune pursues the sinner,
but prosperity is the reward of the
righteous.

22A good man leaves an inheritance for his
children's children,
but a sinner's wealth is stored up for the
righteous.

23A poor man's field may produce abundant
food,
but injustice sweeps it away.

24He who spares the rod hates his son,
but he who loves him is careful to
discipline him.

25The righteous eat to their hearts' content,
but the stomach of the wicked goes
hungry.

14 The wise woman builds her house,
but with her own hands the foolish one
tears hers down.

2He whose walk is upright fears the LORD,
but he whose ways are devious despises
him.

3A fool's talk brings a rod to his back,
but the lips of the wise protect them.

4Where there are no oxen, the manger is
empty,
but from the strength of an ox comes an
abundant harvest.

5A truthful witness does not deceive,
but a false witness pours out lies.

6The mocker seeks wisdom and finds none,
but knowledge comes easily to the
discerning.

7Stay away from a foolish man,
for you will not find knowledge on his
lips.

8The wisdom of the prudent is to give thought
to their ways,
but the folly of fools is deception.

9Fools mock at making amends for sin,
but goodwill is found among the upright.

10Each heart knows its own bitterness,
and no one else can share its joy.

11The house of the wicked will be destroyed,
but the tent of the upright will flourish.

12There is a way that seems right to a man,
but in the end it leads to death.

13Even in laughter the heart may ache,
and joy may end in grief.

14The faithless will be fully repaid for their
ways,
and the good man rewarded for his.

15A simple man believes anything,
but a prudent man gives thought to his
steps.

16A wise man fears the LORD and shuns evil,
but a fool is hotheaded and reckless.

17A quick-tempered man does foolish things,
and a crafty man is hated.

18The simple inherit folly,
but the prudent are crowned with
knowledge.

19Evil men will bow down in the presence of
the good,
and the wicked at the gates of the
righteous.

20The poor are shunned even by their
neighbors,
but the rich have many friends.

21He who despises his neighbor sins,
but blessed is he who is kind to the
needy.

22Do not those who plot evil go astray?
But those who plan what is good find[b]
love and faithfulness.

23All hard work brings a profit,
but mere talk leads only to poverty.

24The wealth of the wise is their crown,
but the folly of fools yields folly.

25A truthful witness saves lives,
but a false witness is deceitful.

[a] *15* Or *unfaithful does not endure* [b] *22* Or *show*

26 He who fears the LORD has a secure fortress,
and for his children it will be a refuge.

27 The fear of the LORD is a fountain of life,
turning a man from the snares of death.

28 A large population is a king's glory,
but without subjects a prince is ruined.

29 A patient man has great understanding,
but a quick-tempered man displays folly.

30 A heart at peace gives life to the body,
but envy rots the bones.

31 He who oppresses the poor shows contempt for their Maker,
but whoever is kind to the needy honors God.

32 When calamity comes, the wicked are brought down,
but even in death the righteous have a refuge.

33 Wisdom reposes in the heart of the discerning
and even among fools she lets herself be known.[a]

34 Righteousness exalts a nation,
but sin is a disgrace to any people.

35 A king delights in a wise servant,
but a shameful servant incurs his wrath.

15 A gentle answer turns away wrath,
but a harsh word stirs up anger.

2 The tongue of the wise commends knowledge,
but the mouth of the fool gushes folly.

3 The eyes of the LORD are everywhere,
keeping watch on the wicked and the good.

4 The tongue that brings healing is a tree of life,
but a deceitful tongue crushes the spirit.

5 A fool spurns his father's discipline,
but whoever heeds correction shows prudence.

6 The house of the righteous contains great treasure,
but the income of the wicked brings them trouble.

7 The lips of the wise spread knowledge;
not so the hearts of fools.

8 The LORD detests the sacrifice of the wicked,
but the prayer of the upright pleases him.

9 The LORD detests the way of the wicked
but he loves those who pursue righteousness.

10 Stern discipline awaits him who leaves the path;
he who hates correction will die.

11 Death and Destruction[b] lie open before the LORD—
how much more the hearts of men!

12 A mocker resents correction;
he will not consult the wise.

13 A happy heart makes the face cheerful,
but heartache crushes the spirit.

14 The discerning heart seeks knowledge,
but the mouth of a fool feeds on folly.

15 All the days of the oppressed are wretched,
but the cheerful heart has a continual feast.

16 Better a little with the fear of the LORD
than great wealth with turmoil.

17 Better a meal of vegetables where there is love
than a fattened calf with hatred.

18 A hot-tempered man stirs up dissension,
but a patient man calms a quarrel.

19 The way of the sluggard is blocked with thorns,
but the path of the upright is a highway.

20 A wise son brings joy to his father,
but a foolish man despises his mother.

21 Folly delights a man who lacks judgment,
but a man of understanding keeps a straight course.

22 Plans fail for lack of counsel,
but with many advisers they succeed.

23 A man finds joy in giving an apt reply—
and how good is a timely word!

24 The path of life leads upward for the wise
to keep him from going down to the grave.[c]

25 The LORD tears down the proud man's house
but he keeps the widow's boundaries intact.

26 The LORD detests the thoughts of the wicked,
but those of the pure are pleasing to him.

27 A greedy man brings trouble to his family,
but he who hates bribes will live.

[a] 33 Hebrew; Septuagint and Syriac / *but in the heart of fools she is not known*
[b] 11 Hebrew *Sheol and Abaddon*
[c] 24 Hebrew *Sheol*

28The heart of the righteous weighs its
answers,
but the mouth of the wicked gushes evil.

29The LORD is far from the wicked
but he hears the prayer of the righteous.

30A cheerful look brings joy to the heart,
and good news gives health to the bones.

31He who listens to a life-giving rebuke
will be at home among the wise.

32He who ignores discipline despises himself,
but whoever heeds correction gains
understanding.

33The fear of the LORD teaches a man
wisdom,[a]
and humility comes before honor.

16 To man belong the plans of the heart,
but from the LORD comes the reply of
the tongue.

2All a man's ways seem innocent to him,
but motives are weighed by the LORD.

3Commit to the LORD whatever you do,
and your plans will succeed.

4The LORD works out everything for his own
ends—
even the wicked for a day of disaster.

5The LORD detests all the proud of heart.
Be sure of this: They will not go
unpunished.

6Through love and faithfulness sin is atoned
for;
through the fear of the LORD a man avoids
evil.

7When a man's ways are pleasing to the LORD,
he makes even his enemies live at peace
with him.

8Better a little with righteousness
than much gain with injustice.

9In his heart a man plans his course,
but the LORD determines his steps.

10The lips of a king speak as an oracle,
and his mouth should not betray justice.

11Honest scales and balances are from the
LORD;
all the weights in the bag are of his
making.

12Kings detest wrongdoing,
for a throne is established through
righteousness.

13Kings take pleasure in honest lips;
they value a man who speaks the truth.

14A king's wrath is a messenger of death,
but a wise man will appease it.

15When a king's face brightens, it means life;
his favor is like a rain cloud in spring.

16How much better to get wisdom than gold,
to choose understanding rather than silver!

17The highway of the upright avoids evil;
he who guards his way guards his life.

18Pride goes before destruction,
a haughty spirit before a fall.

19Better to be lowly in spirit and among the
oppressed
than to share plunder with the proud.

20Whoever gives heed to instruction prospers,
and blessed is he who trusts in the LORD.

21The wise in heart are called discerning,
and pleasant words promote instruction.[b]

22Understanding is a fountain of life to those
who have it,
but folly brings punishment to fools.

23A wise man's heart guides his mouth,
and his lips promote instruction.[c]

24Pleasant words are a honeycomb,
sweet to the soul and healing to the
bones.

25There is a way that seems right to a man,
but in the end it leads to death.

26The laborer's appetite works for him;
his hunger drives him on.

27A scoundrel plots evil,
and his speech is like a scorching fire.

28A perverse man stirs up dissension,
and a gossip separates close friends.

29A violent man entices his neighbor
and leads him down a path that is not
good.

30He who winks with his eye is plotting
perversity;
he who purses his lips is bent on evil.

31Gray hair is a crown of splendor;
it is attained by a righteous life.

32Better a patient man than a warrior,
a man who controls his temper than one
who takes a city.

[a]33 Or *Wisdom teaches the fear of the LORD* [b]21 Or *words make a man persuasive* [c]23 Or *mouth / and makes his lips persuasive*

[33]The lot is cast into the lap,
but its every decision is from the LORD.

17 Better a dry crust with peace and quiet
than a house full of feasting,[a] with strife.

[2]A wise servant will rule over a disgraceful son,
and will share the inheritance as one of the brothers.

[3]The crucible for silver and the furnace for gold,
but the LORD tests the heart.

[4]A wicked man listens to evil lips;
a liar pays attention to a malicious tongue.

[5]He who mocks the poor shows contempt for their Maker;
whoever gloats over disaster will not go unpunished.

[6]Children's children are a crown to the aged,
and parents are the pride of their children.

[7]Arrogant[b] lips are unsuited to a fool—
how much worse lying lips to a ruler!

[8]A bribe is a charm to the one who gives it;
wherever he turns, he succeeds.

[9]He who covers over an offense promotes love,
but whoever repeats the matter separates close friends.

[10]A rebuke impresses a man of discernment
more than a hundred lashes a fool.

[11]An evil man is bent only on rebellion;
a merciless official will be sent against him.

[12]Better to meet a bear robbed of her cubs
than a fool in his folly.

[13]If a man pays back evil for good,
evil will never leave his house.

[14]Starting a quarrel is like breaching a dam;
so drop the matter before a dispute breaks out.

[15]Acquitting the guilty and condemning the innocent—
the LORD detests them both.

[16]Of what use is money in the hand of a fool,
since he has no desire to get wisdom?

[17]A friend loves at all times,
and a brother is born for adversity.

[18]A man lacking in judgment strikes hands in pledge
and puts up security for his neighbor.

[19]He who loves a quarrel loves sin;
he who builds a high gate invites destruction.

[20]A man of perverse heart does not prosper;
he whose tongue is deceitful falls into trouble.

[21]To have a fool for a son brings grief;
there is no joy for the father of a fool.

[22]A cheerful heart is good medicine,
but a crushed spirit dries up the bones.

[23]A wicked man accepts a bribe in secret
to pervert the course of justice.

[24]A discerning man keeps wisdom in view,
but a fool's eyes wander to the ends of the earth.

[25]A foolish son brings grief to his father
and bitterness to the one who bore him.

[26]It is not good to punish an innocent man,
or to flog officials for their integrity.

[27]A man of knowledge uses words with restraint,
and a man of understanding is even-tempered.

[28]Even a fool is thought wise if he keeps silent,
and discerning if he holds his tongue.

18 An unfriendly man pursues selfish ends;
he defies all sound judgment.

[2]A fool finds no pleasure in understanding
but delights in airing his own opinions.

[3]When wickedness comes, so does contempt,
and with shame comes disgrace.

[4]The words of a man's mouth are deep waters,
but the fountain of wisdom is a bubbling brook.

[5]It is not good to be partial to the wicked
or to deprive the innocent of justice.

[6]A fool's lips bring him strife,
and his mouth invites a beating.

[7]A fool's mouth is his undoing,
and his lips are a snare to his soul.

[8]The words of a gossip are like choice morsels;
they go down to a man's inmost parts.

[a]*1* Hebrew *sacrifices* [b]*7* Or *Eloquent*

9One who is slack in his work
is brother to one who destroys.

10The name of the LORD is a strong tower;
the righteous run to it and are safe.

11The wealth of the rich is their fortified city;
they imagine it an unscalable wall.

12Before his downfall a man's heart is proud,
but humility comes before honor.

13He who answers before listening—
that is his folly and his shame.

14A man's spirit sustains him in sickness,
but a crushed spirit who can bear?

15The heart of the discerning acquires
knowledge;
the ears of the wise seek it out.

16A gift opens the way for the giver
and ushers him into the presence of the
great.

17The first to present his case seems right,
till another comes forward and questions
him.

18Casting the lot settles disputes
and keeps strong opponents apart.

19An offended brother is more unyielding than
a fortified city,
and disputes are like the barred gates of a
citadel.

20From the fruit of his mouth a man's stomach
is filled;
with the harvest from his lips he is
satisfied.

21The tongue has the power of life and death,
and those who love it will eat its fruit.

22He who finds a wife finds what is good
and receives favor from the LORD.

23A poor man pleads for mercy,
but a rich man answers harshly.

24A man of many companions may come to
ruin,
but there is a friend who sticks closer than
a brother.

19 Better a poor man whose walk is
blameless
than a fool whose lips are perverse.

2It is not good to have zeal without
knowledge,
nor to be hasty and miss the way.

3A man's own folly ruins his life,
yet his heart rages against the LORD.

4Wealth brings many friends,
but a poor man's friend deserts him.

5A false witness will not go unpunished,
and he who pours out lies will not go free.

6Many curry favor with a ruler,
and everyone is the friend of a man who
gives gifts.

7A poor man is shunned by all his relatives—
how much more do his friends avoid him!
Though he pursues them with pleading,
they are nowhere to be found.[a]

8He who gets wisdom loves his own soul;
he who cherishes understanding prospers.

9A false witness will not go unpunished,
and he who pours out lies will perish.

10It is not fitting for a fool to live in luxury—
how much worse for a slave to rule over
princes!

11A man's wisdom gives him patience;
it is to his glory to overlook an offense.

12A king's rage is like the roar of a lion,
but his favor is like dew on the grass.

13A foolish son is his father's ruin,
and a quarrelsome wife is like a constant
dripping.

14Houses and wealth are inherited from
parents,
but a prudent wife is from the LORD.

15Laziness brings on deep sleep,
and the shiftless man goes hungry.

16He who obeys instructions guards his life,
but he who is contemptuous of his ways
will die.

17He who is kind to the poor lends to the
LORD,
and he will reward him for what he has
done.

18Discipline your son, for in that there is hope;
do not be a willing party to his death.

19A hot-tempered man must pay the penalty;
if you rescue him, you will have to do it
again.

20Listen to advice and accept instruction,
and in the end you will be wise.

21Many are the plans in a man's heart,
but it is the LORD's purpose that prevails.

[a]7 The meaning of the Hebrew for this sentence is uncertain.

22What a man desires is unfailing love[a];
better to be poor than a liar.

23The fear of the LORD leads to life:
Then one rests content, untouched by trouble.

24The sluggard buries his hand in the dish;
he will not even bring it back to his mouth!

25Flog a mocker, and the simple will learn prudence;
rebuke a discerning man, and he will gain knowledge.

26He who robs his father and drives out his mother
is a son who brings shame and disgrace.

27Stop listening to instruction, my son,
and you will stray from the words of knowledge.

28A corrupt witness mocks at justice,
and the mouth of the wicked gulps down evil.

29Penalties are prepared for mockers,
and beatings for the backs of fools.

20 Wine is a mocker and beer a brawler;
whoever is led astray by them is not wise.

2A king's wrath is like the roar of a lion;
he who angers him forfeits his life.

3It is to a man's honor to avoid strife,
but every fool is quick to quarrel.

4A sluggard does not plow in season;
so at harvest time he looks but finds nothing.

5The purposes of a man's heart are deep waters,
but a man of understanding draws them out.

6Many a man claims to have unfailing love,
but a faithful man who can find?

7The righteous man leads a blameless life;
blessed are his children after him.

8When a king sits on his throne to judge,
he winnows out all evil with his eyes.

9Who can say, "I have kept my heart pure;
I am clean and without sin"?

10Differing weights and differing measures—
the LORD detests them both.

11Even a child is known by his actions,
by whether his conduct is pure and right.

12Ears that hear and eyes that see—
the LORD has made them both.

13Do not love sleep or you will grow poor;
stay awake and you will have food to spare.

14"It's no good, it's no good!" says the buyer;
then off he goes and boasts about his purchase.

15Gold there is, and rubies in abundance,
but lips that speak knowledge are a rare jewel.

16Take the garment of one who puts up security for a stranger;
hold it in pledge if he does it for a wayward woman.

17Food gained by fraud tastes sweet to a man,
but he ends up with a mouth full of gravel.

18Make plans by seeking advice;
if you wage war, obtain guidance.

19A gossip betrays a confidence;
so avoid a man who talks too much.

20If a man curses his father or mother,
his lamp will be snuffed out in pitch darkness.

21An inheritance quickly gained at the beginning
will not be blessed at the end.

22Do not say, "I'll pay you back for this wrong!"
Wait for the LORD, and he will deliver you.

23The LORD detests differing weights,
and dishonest scales do not please him.

24A man's steps are directed by the LORD.
How then can anyone understand his own way?

25It is a trap for a man to dedicate something rashly
and only later to consider his vows.

26A wise king winnows out the wicked;
he drives the threshing wheel over them.

27The lamp of the LORD searches the spirit of a man[b];
it searches out his inmost being.

28Love and faithfulness keep a king safe;
through love his throne is made secure.

[a]22 Or *A man's greed is his shame* [b]27 Or *The spirit of man is the LORD's lamp*

29The glory of young men is their strength,
gray hair the splendor of the old.

30Blows and wounds cleanse away evil,
and beatings purge the inmost being.

21 The king's heart is in the hand of the LORD;
he directs it like a watercourse wherever he pleases.

2All a man's ways seem right to him,
but the LORD weighs the heart.

3To do what is right and just
is more acceptable to the LORD than sacrifice.

4Haughty eyes and a proud heart,
the lamp of the wicked, are sin!

5The plans of the diligent lead to profit
as surely as haste leads to poverty.

6A fortune made by a lying tongue
is a fleeting vapor and a deadly snare.[a]

7The violence of the wicked will drag them away,
for they refuse to do what is right.

8The way of the guilty is devious,
but the conduct of the innocent is upright.

9Better to live on a corner of the roof
than share a house with a quarrelsome wife.

10The wicked man craves evil;
his neighbor gets no mercy from him.

11When a mocker is punished, the simple gain wisdom;
when a wise man is instructed, he gets knowledge.

12The Righteous One[b] takes note of the house of the wicked
and brings the wicked to ruin.

13If a man shuts his ears to the cry of the poor,
he too will cry out and not be answered.

14A gift given in secret soothes anger,
and a bribe concealed in the cloak pacifies great wrath.

15When justice is done, it brings joy to the righteous
but terror to evildoers.

16A man who strays from the path of understanding
comes to rest in the company of the dead.

17He who loves pleasure will become poor;
whoever loves wine and oil will never be rich.

18The wicked become a ransom for the righteous,
and the unfaithful for the upright.

19Better to live in a desert
than with a quarrelsome and ill-tempered wife.

20In the house of the wise are stores of choice food and oil,
but a foolish man devours all he has.

21He who pursues righteousness and love
finds life, prosperity[c] and honor.

22A wise man attacks the city of the mighty
and pulls down the stronghold in which they trust.

23He who guards his mouth and his tongue
keeps himself from calamity.

24The proud and arrogant man—"Mocker" is his name;
he behaves with overweening pride.

25The sluggard's craving will be the death of him,
because his hands refuse to work.

26All day long he craves for more,
but the righteous give without sparing.

27The sacrifice of the wicked is detestable—
how much more so when brought with evil intent!

28A false witness will perish,
and whoever listens to him will be destroyed forever.[d]

29A wicked man puts up a bold front,
but an upright man gives thought to his ways.

30There is no wisdom, no insight, no plan
that can succeed against the LORD.

31The horse is made ready for the day of battle,
but victory rests with the LORD.

22 A good name is more desirable than great riches;
to be esteemed is better than silver or gold.

2Rich and poor have this in common:
The LORD is the Maker of them all.

3A prudent man sees danger and takes refuge,
but the simple keep going and suffer for it.

[a]6 Some Hebrew manuscripts, Septuagint and Vulgate; most Hebrew manuscripts *vapor for those who seek death* [b]12 Or *The righteous man* [c]21 Or *righteousness* [d]28 Or / *but the words of an obedient man will live on*

4Humility and the fear of the LORD
bring wealth and honor and life.

5In the paths of the wicked lie thorns and snares,
but he who guards his soul stays far from them.

6Train[a] a child in the way he should go,
and when he is old he will not turn from it.

7The rich rule over the poor,
and the borrower is servant to the lender.

8He who sows wickedness reaps trouble,
and the rod of his fury will be destroyed.

9A generous man will himself be blessed,
for he shares his food with the poor.

10Drive out the mocker, and out goes strife;
quarrels and insults are ended.

11He who loves a pure heart and whose speech is gracious
will have the king for his friend.

12The eyes of the LORD keep watch over knowledge,
but he frustrates the words of the unfaithful.

13The sluggard says, "There is a lion outside!"
or, "I will be murdered in the streets!"

14The mouth of an adulteress is a deep pit;
he who is under the LORD's wrath will fall into it.

15Folly is bound up in the heart of a child,
but the rod of discipline will drive it far from him.

16He who oppresses the poor to increase his wealth
and he who gives gifts to the rich—both come to poverty.

Sayings of the Wise

17Pay attention and listen to the sayings of the wise;
apply your heart to what I teach,
18for it is pleasing when you keep them in your heart
and have all of them ready on your lips.
19So that your trust may be in the LORD,
I teach you today, even you.
20Have I not written thirty[b] sayings for you,
sayings of counsel and knowledge,
21teaching you true and reliable words,
so that you can give sound answers
to him who sent you?

22Do not exploit the poor because they are poor
and do not crush the needy in court,
23for the LORD will take up their case
and will plunder those who plunder them.
24Do not make friends with a hot-tempered man,
do not associate with one easily angered,
25or you may learn his ways
and get yourself ensnared.

26Do not be a man who strikes hands in pledge
or puts up security for debts;
27if you lack the means to pay,
your very bed will be snatched from under you.

28Do not move an ancient boundary stone
set up by your forefathers.

29Do you see a man skilled in his work?
He will serve before kings;
he will not serve before obscure men.

23 When you sit to dine with a ruler,
note well what[c] is before you,
2and put a knife to your throat
if you are given to gluttony.
3Do not crave his delicacies,
for that food is deceptive.

4Do not wear yourself out to get rich;
have the wisdom to show restraint.
5Cast but a glance at riches, and they are gone,
for they will surely sprout wings
and fly off to the sky like an eagle.

6Do not eat the food of a stingy man,
do not crave his delicacies;
7for he is the kind of man
who is always thinking about the cost.[d]
"Eat and drink," he says to you,
but his heart is not with you.
8You will vomit up the little you have eaten
and will have wasted your compliments.

9Do not speak to a fool,
for he will scorn the wisdom of your words.

10Do not move an ancient boundary stone
or encroach on the fields of the fatherless,
11for their Defender is strong;
he will take up their case against you.

12Apply your heart to instruction
and your ears to words of knowledge.

[a] 6 Or *Start* [b] 20 Or *not formerly written*; or *not written excellent* [c] 1 Or *who* [d] 7 Or *for as he thinks within himself, / so he is*; or *for as he puts on a feast, / so he is*

13Do not withhold discipline from a child;
if you punish him with the rod, he will not die.
14Punish him with the rod
and save his soul from death.[a]

15My son, if your heart is wise,
then my heart will be glad;
16my inmost being will rejoice
when your lips speak what is right.

17Do not let your heart envy sinners,
but always be zealous for the fear of the LORD.
18There is surely a future hope for you,
and your hope will not be cut off.

19Listen, my son, and be wise,
and keep your heart on the right path.
20Do not join those who drink too much wine
or gorge themselves on meat,
21for drunkards and gluttons become poor,
and drowsiness clothes them in rags.

22Listen to your father, who gave you life,
and do not despise your mother when she is old.
23Buy the truth and do not sell it;
get wisdom, discipline and understanding.
24The father of a righteous man has great joy;
he who has a wise son delights in him.
25May your father and mother be glad;
may she who gave you birth rejoice!

26My son, give me your heart
and let your eyes keep to my ways,
27for a prostitute is a deep pit
and a wayward wife is a narrow well.
28Like a bandit she lies in wait,
and multiplies the unfaithful among men.

29Who has woe? Who has sorrow?
Who has strife? Who has complaints?
Who has needless bruises? Who has bloodshot eyes?
30Those who linger over wine,
who go to sample bowls of mixed wine.
31Do not gaze at wine when it is red,
when it sparkles in the cup,
when it goes down smoothly!
32In the end it bites like a snake
and poisons like a viper.
33Your eyes will see strange sights
and your mind imagine confusing things.
34You will be like one sleeping on the high seas,
lying on top of the rigging.
35"They hit me," you will say, "but I'm not hurt!
They beat me, but I don't feel it!
When will I wake up
so I can find another drink?"

24 Do not envy wicked men,
do not desire their company;
2for their hearts plot violence,
and their lips talk about making trouble.

3By wisdom a house is built,
and through understanding it is established;
4through knowledge its rooms are filled
with rare and beautiful treasures.
5A wise man has great power,
and a man of knowledge increases strength;
6for waging war you need guidance,
and for victory many advisers.

7Wisdom is too high for a fool;
in the assembly at the gate he has nothing to say.

8He who plots evil
will be known as a schemer.
9The schemes of folly are sin,
and men detest a mocker.

10If you falter in times of trouble,
how small is your strength!

11Rescue those being led away to death;
hold back those staggering toward slaughter.
12If you say, "But we knew nothing about this,"
does not he who weighs the heart perceive it?
Does not he who guards your life know it?
Will he not repay each person according to what he has done?

13Eat honey, my son, for it is good;
honey from the comb is sweet to your taste.
14Know also that wisdom is sweet to your soul;
if you find it, there is a future hope for you,
and your hope will not be cut off.

15Do not lie in wait like an outlaw against a righteous man's house,
do not raid his dwelling place;
16for though a righteous man falls seven times,
he rises again,
but the wicked are brought down by calamity.

17Do not gloat when your enemy falls;
when he stumbles, do not let your heart rejoice,

a14 Hebrew *Sheol*

18or the LORD will see and disapprove
and turn his wrath away from him.

19Do not fret because of evil men
or be envious of the wicked,
20for the evil man has no future hope,
and the lamp of the wicked will be snuffed out.

21Fear the LORD and the king, my son,
and do not join with the rebellious,
22for those two will send sudden destruction upon them,
and who knows what calamities they can bring?

Further Sayings of the Wise

23These also are sayings of the wise:

To show partiality in judging is not good:
24Whoever says to the guilty, "You are innocent"—
peoples will curse him and nations denounce him.
25But it will go well with those who convict the guilty,
and rich blessing will come upon them.

26An honest answer
is like a kiss on the lips.

27Finish your outdoor work
and get your fields ready;
after that, build your house.

28Do not testify against your neighbor without cause,
or use your lips to deceive.
29Do not say, "I'll do to him as he has done to me;
I'll pay that man back for what he did."

30I went past the field of the sluggard,
past the vineyard of the man who lacks judgment;
31thorns had come up everywhere,
the ground was covered with weeds,
and the stone wall was in ruins.
32I applied my heart to what I observed
and learned a lesson from what I saw:
33A little sleep, a little slumber,
a little folding of the hands to rest—
34and poverty will come on you like a bandit
and scarcity like an armed man.[a]

More Proverbs of Solomon

25 These are more proverbs of Solomon, copied by the men of Hezekiah king of Judah:

2It is the glory of God to conceal a matter;
to search out a matter is the glory of kings.

3As the heavens are high and the earth is deep,
so the hearts of kings are unsearchable.

4Remove the dross from the silver,
and out comes material for[b] the silversmith;
5remove the wicked from the king's presence,
and his throne will be established through righteousness.

6Do not exalt yourself in the king's presence,
and do not claim a place among great men;
7it is better for him to say to you, "Come up here,"
than for him to humiliate you before a nobleman.

What you have seen with your eyes
8 do not bring[c] hastily to court,
for what will you do in the end
if your neighbor puts you to shame?

9If you argue your case with a neighbor,
do not betray another man's confidence,
10or he who hears it may shame you
and you will never lose your bad reputation.

11A word aptly spoken
is like apples of gold in settings of silver.
12Like an earring of gold or an ornament of fine gold
is a wise man's rebuke to a listening ear.

13Like the coolness of snow at harvest time
is a trustworthy messenger to those who send him;
he refreshes the spirit of his masters.

14Like clouds and wind without rain
is a man who boasts of gifts he does not give.

15Through patience a ruler can be persuaded,
and a gentle tongue can break a bone.

16If you find honey, eat just enough—
too much of it, and you will vomit.
17Seldom set foot in your neighbor's house—
too much of you, and he will hate you.

18Like a club or a sword or a sharp arrow
is the man who gives false testimony against his neighbor.

19Like a bad tooth or a lame foot

[a]34 Or *like a vagrant / and scarcity like a beggar* [b]4 Or *comes a vessel from* [c]7,8 Or *nobleman / on whom you had set your eyes. / 8Do not go*

is reliance on the unfaithful in times of
trouble.

20Like one who takes away a garment on a
cold day,
or like vinegar poured on soda,
is one who sings songs to a heavy heart.

21If your enemy is hungry, give him food to
eat;
if he is thirsty, give him water to drink.

22In doing this, you will heap burning coals on
his head,
and the LORD will reward you.

23As a north wind brings rain,
so a sly tongue brings angry looks.

24Better to live on a corner of the roof
than share a house with a quarrelsome
wife.

25Like cold water to a weary soul
is good news from a distant land.

26Like a muddied spring or a polluted well
is a righteous man who gives way to the
wicked.

27It is not good to eat too much honey,
nor is it honorable to seek one's own
honor.

28Like a city whose walls are broken down
is a man who lacks self-control.

26 Like snow in summer or rain in
harvest,
honor is not fitting for a fool.

2Like a fluttering sparrow or a darting
swallow,
an undeserved curse does not come to
rest.

3A whip for the horse, a halter for the
donkey,
and a rod for the backs of fools!

4Do not answer a fool according to his folly,
or you will be like him yourself.

5Answer a fool according to his folly,
or he will be wise in his own eyes.

6Like cutting off one's feet or drinking
violence
is the sending of a message by the hand of
a fool.

7Like a lame man's legs that hang limp
is a proverb in the mouth of a fool.

8Like tying a stone in a sling
is the giving of honor to a fool.

9Like a thornbush in a drunkard's hand
is a proverb in the mouth of a fool.

10Like an archer who wounds at random
is he who hires a fool or any passer-by.

11As a dog returns to its vomit,
so a fool repeats his folly.

12Do you see a man wise in his own eyes?
There is more hope for a fool than for
him.

13The sluggard says, "There is a lion in the
road,
a fierce lion roaming the streets!"

14As a door turns on its hinges,
so a sluggard turns on his bed.

15The sluggard buries his hand in the dish;
he is too lazy to bring it back to his
mouth.

16The sluggard is wiser in his own eyes
than seven men who answer discreetly.

17Like one who seizes a dog by the ears
is a passer-by who meddles in a quarrel
not his own.

18Like a madman shooting
firebrands or deadly arrows
19is a man who deceives his neighbor
and says, "I was only joking!"

20Without wood a fire goes out;
without gossip a quarrel dies down.

21As charcoal to embers and as wood to fire,
so is a quarrelsome man for kindling strife.

22The words of a gossip are like choice
morsels;
they go down to a man's inmost parts.

23Like a coating of glaze[a] over earthenware
are fervent lips with an evil heart.

24A malicious man disguises himself with his
lips,
but in his heart he harbors deceit.

25Though his speech is charming, do not
believe him,
for seven abominations fill his heart.

26His malice may be concealed by deception,
but his wickedness will be exposed in the
assembly.

27If a man digs a pit, he will fall into it;
if a man rolls a stone, it will roll back on
him.

28A lying tongue hates those it hurts,
and a flattering mouth works ruin.

a23 With a different word division of the Hebrew; Masoretic Text *of silver dross*

27 Do not boast about tomorrow,
for you do not know what a day may
bring forth.

2Let another praise you, and not your own
mouth;
someone else, and not your own lips.

3Stone is heavy and sand a burden,
but provocation by a fool is heavier than
both.

4Anger is cruel and fury overwhelming,
but who can stand before jealousy?

5Better is open rebuke
than hidden love.

6Wounds from a friend can be trusted,
but an enemy multiplies kisses.

7He who is full loathes honey,
but to the hungry even what is bitter
tastes sweet.

8Like a bird that strays from its nest
is a man who strays from his home.

9Perfume and incense bring joy to the heart,
and the pleasantness of one's friend
springs from his earnest counsel.

10Do not forsake your friend and the friend of
your father,
and do not go to your brother's house
when disaster strikes you—
better a neighbor nearby than a brother far
away.

11Be wise, my son, and bring joy to my heart;
then I can answer anyone who treats me
with contempt.

12The prudent see danger and take refuge,
but the simple keep going and suffer for it.

13Take the garment of one who puts up
security for a stranger;
hold it in pledge if he does it for a
wayward woman.

14If a man loudly blesses his neighbor early in
the morning,
it will be taken as a curse.

15A quarrelsome wife is like
a constant dripping on a rainy day;
16restraining her is like restraining the wind
or grasping oil with the hand.

17As iron sharpens iron,
so one man sharpens another.

18He who tends a fig tree will eat its fruit,
and he who looks after his master will be
honored.

19As water reflects a face,
so a man's heart reflects the man.

20Death and Destruction[a] are never satisfied,
and neither are the eyes of man.

21The crucible for silver and the furnace for
gold,
but man is tested by the praise he
receives.

22Though you grind a fool in a mortar,
grinding him like grain with a pestle,
you will not remove his folly from him.

23Be sure you know the condition of your
flocks,
give careful attention to your herds;
24for riches do not endure forever,
and a crown is not secure for all
generations.
25When the hay is removed and new growth
appears
and the grass from the hills is gathered in,
26the lambs will provide you with clothing,
and the goats with the price of a field.
27You will have plenty of goats' milk
to feed you and your family
and to nourish your servant girls.

28 The wicked man flees though no one
pursues,
but the righteous are as bold as a lion.

2When a country is rebellious, it has many
rulers,
but a man of understanding and
knowledge maintains order.

3A ruler[b] who oppresses the poor
is like a driving rain that leaves no crops.

4Those who forsake the law praise the
wicked,
but those who keep the law resist them.

5Evil men do not understand justice,
but those who seek the LORD understand
it fully.

6Better a poor man whose walk is blameless
than a rich man whose ways are perverse.

7He who keeps the law is a discerning son,
but a companion of gluttons disgraces his
father.

8He who increases his wealth by exorbitant
interest

a20 Hebrew *Sheol and Abaddon* b3 Or *A poor man*

amasses it for another, who will be kind to
the poor.

9If anyone turns a deaf ear to the law,
even his prayers are detestable.

10He who leads the upright along an evil path
will fall into his own trap,
but the blameless will receive a good
inheritance.

11A rich man may be wise in his own eyes,
but a poor man who has discernment sees
through him.

12When the righteous triumph, there is great
elation;
but when the wicked rise to power, men
go into hiding.

13He who conceals his sins does not prosper,
but whoever confesses and renounces
them finds mercy.

14Blessed is the man who always fears the
LORD,
but he who hardens his heart falls into
trouble.

15Like a roaring lion or a charging bear
is a wicked man ruling over a helpless
people.

16A tyrannical ruler lacks judgment,
but he who hates ill-gotten gain will enjoy
a long life.

17A man tormented by the guilt of murder
will be a fugitive till death;
let no one support him.

18He whose walk is blameless is kept safe,
but he whose ways are perverse will
suddenly fall.

19He who works his land will have abundant
food,
but the one who chases fantasies will have
his fill of poverty.

20A faithful man will be richly blessed,
but one eager to get rich will not go
unpunished.

21To show partiality is not good—
yet a man will do wrong for a piece of
bread.

22A stingy man is eager to get rich
and is unaware that poverty awaits him.

23He who rebukes a man will in the end gain
more favor
than he who has a flattering tongue.

24He who robs his father or mother
and says, "It's not wrong"—
he is partner to him who destroys.

25A greedy man stirs up dissension,
but he who trusts in the LORD will
prosper.

26He who trusts in himself is a fool,
but he who walks in wisdom is kept safe.

27He who gives to the poor will lack nothing,
but he who closes his eyes to them
receives many curses.

28When the wicked rise to power, people go
into hiding;
but when the wicked perish, the righteous
thrive.

29 A man who remains stiff-necked after
many rebukes
will suddenly be destroyed—without
remedy.

2When the righteous thrive, the people
rejoice;
when the wicked rule, the people groan.

3A man who loves wisdom brings joy to his
father,
but a companion of prostitutes squanders
his wealth.

4By justice a king gives a country stability,
but one who is greedy for bribes tears it
down.

5Whoever flatters his neighbor
is spreading a net for his feet.

6An evil man is snared by his own sin,
but a righteous one can sing and be glad.

7The righteous care about justice for the poor,
but the wicked have no such concern.

8Mockers stir up a city,
but wise men turn away anger.

9If a wise man goes to court with a fool,
the fool rages and scoffs, and there is no
peace.

10Bloodthirsty men hate a man of integrity
and seek to kill the upright.

11A fool gives full vent to his anger,
but a wise man keeps himself under
control.

12If a ruler listens to lies,
all his officials become wicked.

13The poor man and the oppressor have this in
common:
The LORD gives sight to the eyes of both.

14 If a king judges the poor with fairness,
his throne will always be secure.

15 The rod of correction imparts wisdom,
but a child left to himself disgraces his mother.

16 When the wicked thrive, so does sin,
but the righteous will see their downfall.

17 Discipline your son, and he will give you peace;
he will bring delight to your soul.

18 Where there is no revelation, the people cast off restraint;
but blessed is he who keeps the law.

19 A servant cannot be corrected by mere words;
though he understands, he will not respond.

20 Do you see a man who speaks in haste?
There is more hope for a fool than for him.

21 If a man pampers his servant from youth,
he will bring grief[a] in the end.

22 An angry man stirs up dissension,
and a hot-tempered one commits many sins.

23 A man's pride brings him low,
but a man of lowly spirit gains honor.

24 The accomplice of a thief is his own enemy;
he is put under oath and dare not testify.

25 Fear of man will prove to be a snare,
but whoever trusts in the LORD is kept safe.

26 Many seek an audience with a ruler,
but it is from the LORD that man gets justice.

27 The righteous detest the dishonest;
the wicked detest the upright.

Sayings of Agur

30 The sayings of Agur son of Jakeh—an oracle[b]:

This man declared to Ithiel,
to Ithiel and to Ucal:[c]

2 "I am the most ignorant of men;
I do not have a man's understanding.
3 I have not learned wisdom,
nor have I knowledge of the Holy One.
4 Who has gone up to heaven and come down?
Who has gathered up the wind in the hollow of his hands?
Who has wrapped up the waters in his cloak?
Who has established all the ends of the earth?
What is his name, and the name of his son?
Tell me if you know!

5 "Every word of God is flawless;
he is a shield to those who take refuge in him.
6 Do not add to his words,
or he will rebuke you and prove you a liar.

7 "Two things I ask of you, O LORD;
do not refuse me before I die:
8 Keep falsehood and lies far from me;
give me neither poverty nor riches,
but give me only my daily bread.
9 Otherwise, I may have too much and disown you
and say, 'Who is the LORD?'
Or I may become poor and steal,
and so dishonor the name of my God.

10 "Do not slander a servant to his master,
or he will curse you, and you will pay for it.

11 "There are those who curse their fathers
and do not bless their mothers;
12 those who are pure in their own eyes
and yet are not cleansed of their filth;
13 those whose eyes are ever so haughty,
whose glances are so disdainful;
14 those whose teeth are swords
and whose jaws are set with knives
to devour the poor from the earth,
the needy from among mankind.

15 "The leech has two daughters.
'Give! Give!' they cry.

"There are three things that are never satisfied,
four that never say, 'Enough!':
16 the grave,[d] the barren womb,
land, which is never satisfied with water,
and fire, which never says, 'Enough!'

17 "The eye that mocks a father,
that scorns obedience to a mother,
will be pecked out by the ravens of the valley,
will be eaten by the vultures.

18 "There are three things that are too amazing for me,
four that I do not understand:
19 the way of an eagle in the sky,

[a] 21 The meaning of the Hebrew for this word is uncertain. [b] 1 Or *Jakeh of Massa* [c] 1 Masoretic Text; with a different word division of the Hebrew *declared, "I am weary, O God; / I am weary, O God, and faint.* [d] 16 Hebrew *Sheol*

the way of a snake on a rock,
the way of a ship on the high seas,
and the way of a man with a maiden.
20"This is the way of an adulteress:
She eats and wipes her mouth
and says, 'I've done nothing wrong.'

21"Under three things the earth trembles,
under four it cannot bear up:
22a servant who becomes king,
a fool who is full of food,
23an unloved woman who is married,
and a maidservant who displaces her mistress.

24"Four things on earth are small,
yet they are extremely wise:
25Ants are creatures of little strength,
yet they store up their food in the summer;
26coneys[a] are creatures of little power,
yet they make their home in the crags;
27locusts have no king,
yet they advance together in ranks;
28a lizard can be caught with the hand,
yet it is found in kings' palaces.

29"There are three things that are stately in their stride,
four that move with stately bearing:
30a lion, mighty among beasts,
who retreats before nothing;
31a strutting rooster, a he-goat,
and a king with his army around him.[b]

32"If you have played the fool and exalted yourself,
or if you have planned evil,
clap your hand over your mouth!
33For as churning the milk produces butter,
and as twisting the nose produces blood,
so stirring up anger produces strife."

Sayings of King Lemuel

31 The sayings of King Lemuel—an oracle[c] his mother taught him:

2"O my son, O son of my womb,
O son of my vows,[d]
3do not spend your strength on women,
your vigor on those who ruin kings.

4"It is not for kings, O Lemuel—
not for kings to drink wine,
not for rulers to crave beer,
5lest they drink and forget what the law decrees,
and deprive all the oppressed of their rights.
6Give beer to those who are perishing,
wine to those who are in anguish;
7let them drink and forget their poverty
and remember their misery no more.

8"Speak up for those who cannot speak for themselves,
for the rights of all who are destitute.
9Speak up and judge fairly;
defend the rights of the poor and needy."

Epilogue: The Wife of Noble Character

10[e]A wife of noble character who can find?
She is worth far more than rubies.
11Her husband has full confidence in her
and lacks nothing of value.
12She brings him good, not harm,
all the days of her life.
13She selects wool and flax
and works with eager hands.
14She is like the merchant ships,
bringing her food from afar.
15She gets up while it is still dark;
she provides food for her family
and portions for her servant girls.
16She considers a field and buys it;
out of her earnings she plants a vineyard.
17She sets about her work vigorously;
her arms are strong for her tasks.
18She sees that her trading is profitable,
and her lamp does not go out at night.
19In her hand she holds the distaff
and grasps the spindle with her fingers.
20She opens her arms to the poor
and extends her hands to the needy.
21When it snows, she has no fear for her household;
for all of them are clothed in scarlet.
22She makes coverings for her bed;
she is clothed in fine linen and purple.
23Her husband is respected at the city gate,
where he takes his seat among the elders of the land.
24She makes linen garments and sells them,
and supplies the merchants with sashes.
25She is clothed with strength and dignity;
she can laugh at the days to come.
26She speaks with wisdom,
and faithful instruction is on her tongue.
27She watches over the affairs of her household
and does not eat the bread of idleness.

[a] *26* That is, the hyrax or rock badger [b] *31* Or *king secure against revolt* [c] *1* Or *of Lemuel king of Massa, which* [d] *2* Or */ the answer to my prayers* [e] *10* Verses 10-31 are an acrostic, each verse beginning with a successive letter of the Hebrew alphabet.

28Her children arise and call her blessed;
her husband also, and he praises her:
29"Many women do noble things,
but you surpass them all."
30Charm is deceptive, and beauty is fleeting;
but a woman who fears the LORD is to be praised.
31Give her the reward she has earned,
and let her works bring her praise at the city gate.

Introduction to
ECCLESIASTES

Personal Reading Plan

- ❒ Ecclesiastes 1:1–2:16
- ❒ Ecclesiastes 2:17–4:12
- ❒ Ecclesiastes 4:13–6:12
- ❒ Ecclesiastes 7:1–8:17
- ❒ Ecclesiastes 9:1–10:20
- ❒ Ecclesiastes 11:1–12:14

Author

The writing of Ecclesiastes is traditionally attributed to Solomon (see 1:1,12), though no writer is named in the book. However, Ecclesiastes may have been the product of a writer from a later period who felt that his teaching was akin to the great wisdom which Solomon possessed.

Date

The book may perhaps be dated after the return from exile, in the fifth century B.C. If Solomon is the author, the book would date from c. 950 B.C.

Theme

Life not focused on God is purposeless and meaningless. Without him, nothing can satisfy (2:25). With him, all of life is to be enjoyed to the full (2:26; 11:8).

Historical Background

With so little information available about the author or date, it is difficult to place Ecclesiastes into a historical context. One possibility is that it was produced by a wisdom movement in Judaism that was responsible for collecting stories and sayings.

Characteristics

This book has always raised questions concerning its appropriateness in the Old Testament canon (the authoritative list of books accepted as Holy Scripture). Its apparent pessimism and questioning of beliefs that are central to Judaism and Christianity has led many to reject or ignore it. Others have tried to explain it as what Solomon would have said on an "off" day, or suggest that it clearly demonstrates the futility of the agnostic and therefore acts as a warning against such a position. It may be, however, that the work is a foil against which we discern our tendency to overestimate or overspiritualize our relationship with God. The book is unsparingly forthright in recording the author's desperate search for meaning. While he might be accused of overstating his case, hints of his true piety are evident (see 7:29), and the conclusion challenges the reader to obey God (12:13–14).

Near the end of the book, young people are specifically addressed (11:7–12:8). Youth are challenged to "let your heart give you joy in the days of your youth" (11:9). The author exhorts to "remember your Creator in the days of your youth" (12:1)—because without focusing on God, "Everything is meaningless" (12:8).

Everything Is Meaningless

1 The words of the Teacher,[a] son of David, king in Jerusalem:

2"Meaningless! Meaningless!"
says the Teacher.
"Utterly meaningless!
Everything is meaningless."

3What does man gain from all his labor
at which he toils under the sun?
4Generations come and generations go,
but the earth remains forever.
5The sun rises and the sun sets,
and hurries back to where it rises.
6The wind blows to the south
and turns to the north;
round and round it goes,
ever returning on its course.
7All streams flow into the sea,
yet the sea is never full.
To the place the streams come from,
there they return again.
8All things are wearisome,
more than one can say.
The eye never has enough of seeing,
nor the ear its fill of hearing.
9What has been will be again,
what has been done will be done again;
there is nothing new under the sun.
10Is there anything of which one can say,
"Look! This is something new"?
It was here already, long ago;
it was here before our time.
11There is no remembrance of men of old,
and even those who are yet to come
will not be remembered
by those who follow.

Wisdom Is Meaningless

12I, the Teacher, was king over Israel in Jerusalem. 13I devoted myself to study and to explore by
wisdom all that is done under heaven. What a
heavy burden God has laid on men! 14I have seen
all the things that are done under the sun; all of
them are meaningless, a chasing after the wind.

15What is twisted cannot be straightened;
what is lacking cannot be counted.

16I thought to myself, "Look, I have grown and
increased in wisdom more than anyone who has
ruled over Jerusalem before me; I have experienced much of wisdom and knowledge." 17Then
I applied myself to the understanding of wisdom,
and also of madness and folly, but I learned that
this, too, is a chasing after the wind.

18For with much wisdom comes much sorrow;
the more knowledge, the more grief.

Pleasures Are Meaningless

2 I thought in my heart, "Come now, I will test
you with pleasure to find out what is good."
But that also proved to be meaningless. 2"Laughter," I said, "is foolish. And what does pleasure
accomplish?" 3I tried cheering myself with wine,
and embracing folly—my mind still guiding me
with wisdom. I wanted to see what was worthwhile for men to do under heaven during the few
days of their lives.

4I undertook great projects: I built houses for
myself and planted vineyards. 5I made gardens
and parks and planted all kinds of fruit trees in
them. 6I made reservoirs to water groves of flourishing trees. 7I bought male and female slaves
and had other slaves who were born in my house.
I also owned more herds and flocks than anyone
in Jerusalem before me. 8I amassed silver and
gold for myself, and the treasure of kings and
provinces. I acquired men and women singers,
and a harem[b] as well—the delights of the heart
of man. 9I became greater by far than anyone
in Jerusalem before me. In all this my wisdom
stayed with me.

10I denied myself nothing my eyes desired;
I refused my heart no pleasure.
My heart took delight in all my work,
and this was the reward for all my labor.
11Yet when I surveyed all that my hands had done
and what I had toiled to achieve,
everything was meaningless, a chasing after the wind;
nothing was gained under the sun.

Wisdom and Folly Are Meaningless

12Then I turned my thoughts to consider wisdom,
and also madness and folly.
What more can the king's successor do
than what has already been done?
13I saw that wisdom is better than folly,
just as light is better than darkness.
14The wise man has eyes in his head,
while the fool walks in the darkness;
but I came to realize
that the same fate overtakes them both.

15Then I thought in my heart,

"The fate of the fool will overtake me also.
What then do I gain by being wise?"
I said in my heart,
"This too is meaningless."

[a] *1* Or *leader of the assembly*; also in verses 2 and 12 [b] *8* The meaning of the Hebrew for this phrase is uncertain.

16 For the wise man, like the fool, will not be
long remembered;
in days to come both will be forgotten.
Like the fool, the wise man too must die!

Toil Is Meaningless

17 So I hated life, because the work that is done
under the sun was grievous to me. All of it is
meaningless, a chasing after the wind. 18 I hated
all the things I had toiled for under the sun, because I must leave them to the one who comes
after me. 19 And who knows whether he will be a
wise man or a fool? Yet he will have control over
all the work into which I have poured my effort
and skill under the sun. This too is meaningless.
20 So my heart began to despair over all my toilsome labor under the sun. 21 For a man may do
his work with wisdom, knowledge and skill, and
then he must leave all he owns to someone who
has not worked for it. This too is meaningless and
a great misfortune. 22 What does a man get for all
the toil and anxious striving with which he labors
under the sun? 23 All his days his work is pain and
grief; even at night his mind does not rest. This
too is meaningless.

24 A man can do nothing better than to eat and
drink and find satisfaction in his work. This too,
I see, is from the hand of God, 25 for without him,
who can eat or find enjoyment? 26 To the man
who pleases him, God gives wisdom, knowledge
and happiness, but to the sinner he gives the task
of gathering and storing up wealth to hand it over
to the one who pleases God. This too is meaningless, a chasing after the wind.

A Time for Everything

3 There is a time for everything,
and a season for every activity under
heaven:

2 a time to be born and a time to die,
a time to plant and a time to uproot,
3 a time to kill and a time to heal,
a time to tear down and a time to build,
4 a time to weep and a time to laugh,
a time to mourn and a time to dance,
5 a time to scatter stones and a time to
gather them,
a time to embrace and a time to refrain,
6 a time to search and a time to give up,
a time to keep and a time to throw away,
7 a time to tear and a time to mend,
a time to be silent and a time to speak,
8 a time to love and a time to hate,
a time for war and a time for peace.

9 What does the worker gain from his toil? 10 I
have seen the burden God has laid on men. 11 He
has made everything beautiful in its time. He has
also set eternity in the hearts of men; yet they
cannot fathom what God has done from beginning to end. 12 I know that there is nothing better
for men than to be happy and do good while they
live. 13 That everyone may eat and drink, and find
satisfaction in all his toil—this is the gift of God.
14 I know that everything God does will endure
forever; nothing can be added to it and nothing
taken from it. God does it so that men will revere
him.

15 Whatever is has already been,
and what will be has been before;
and God will call the past to account.[a]

16 And I saw something else under the sun:

In the place of judgment—wickedness was
there,
in the place of justice—wickedness was
there.

17 I thought in my heart,

"God will bring to judgment
both the righteous and the wicked,
for there will be a time for every activity,
a time for every deed."

18 I also thought, "As for men, God tests them
so that they may see that they are like the animals. 19 Man's fate is like that of the animals; the
same fate awaits them both: As one dies, so dies
the other. All have the same breath[b]; man has
no advantage over the animal. Everything is
meaningless. 20 All go to the same place; all come
from dust, and to dust all return. 21 Who knows if
the spirit of man rises upward and if the spirit of
the animal[c] goes down into the earth?"

22 So I saw that there is nothing better for a
man than to enjoy his work, because that is his
lot. For who can bring him to see what will happen after him?

Oppression, Toil, Friendlessness

4 Again I looked and saw all the oppression
that was taking place under the sun:

I saw the tears of the oppressed—
and they have no comforter;
power was on the side of their oppressors—
and they have no comforter.
2 And I declared that the dead,
who had already died,
are happier than the living,
who are still alive.
3 But better than both
is he who has not yet been,

[a] *15* Or *God calls back the past* [b] *19* Or *spirit* [c] *21* Or *Who knows the spirit of man, which rises upward, or the spirit of the animal, which*

who has not seen the evil
that is done under the sun.

4And I saw that all labor and all achievement spring from man's envy of his neighbor. This too is meaningless, a chasing after the wind.

5The fool folds his hands
and ruins himself.
6Better one handful with tranquillity
than two handfuls with toil
and chasing after the wind.

7Again I saw something meaningless under the sun:

8There was a man all alone;
he had neither son nor brother.
There was no end to his toil,
yet his eyes were not content with his wealth.
"For whom am I toiling," he asked,
"and why am I depriving myself of enjoyment?"
This too is meaningless—
a miserable business!

9Two are better than one,
because they have a good return for their work:
10If one falls down,
his friend can help him up.
But pity the man who falls
and has no one to help him up!
11Also, if two lie down together, they will keep warm.
But how can one keep warm alone?
12Though one may be overpowered,
two can defend themselves.
A cord of three strands is not quickly broken.

Advancement Is Meaningless

13Better a poor but wise youth than an old but foolish king who no longer knows how to take warning. 14The youth may have come from prison to the kingship, or he may have been born in poverty within his kingdom. 15I saw that all who lived and walked under the sun followed the youth, the king's successor. 16There was no end to all the people who were before them. But those who came later were not pleased with the successor. This too is meaningless, a chasing after the wind.

Stand in Awe of God

5 Guard your steps when you go to the house of God. Go near to listen rather than to offer the sacrifice of fools, who do not know that they do wrong.

2Do not be quick with your mouth,
do not be hasty in your heart
to utter anything before God.
God is in heaven
and you are on earth,
so let your words be few.
3As a dream comes when there are many cares,
so the speech of a fool when there are many words.

4When you make a vow to God, do not delay
in fulfilling it. He has no pleasure in fools; fulfill
your vow. 5It is better not to vow than to make
a vow and not fulfill it. 6Do not let your mouth
lead you into sin. And do not protest to the ⌊temple⌋ messenger, "My vow was a mistake." Why should God be angry at what you say and destroy the work of your hands? 7Much dreaming and
many words are meaningless. Therefore stand in awe of God.

Riches Are Meaningless

8If you see the poor oppressed in a district, and justice and rights denied, do not be surprised at such things; for one official is eyed by a higher one, and over them both are others higher still.
9The increase from the land is taken by all; the king himself profits from the fields.

10Whoever loves money never has money enough;
whoever loves wealth is never satisfied with his income.
This too is meaningless.

11As goods increase,
so do those who consume them.
And what benefit are they to the owner
except to feast his eyes on them?

12The sleep of a laborer is sweet,
whether he eats little or much,
but the abundance of a rich man
permits him no sleep.

13I have seen a grievous evil under the sun:

wealth hoarded to the harm of its owner,
14 or wealth lost through some misfortune,
so that when he has a son
there is nothing left for him.
15Naked a man comes from his mother's womb,
and as he comes, so he departs.
He takes nothing from his labor
that he can carry in his hand.

16This too is a grievous evil:

As a man comes, so he departs,
and what does he gain,
since he toils for the wind?
17All his days he eats in darkness,
with great frustration, affliction and anger.

18 Then I realized that it is good and proper for
a man to eat and drink, and to find satisfaction in
his toilsome labor under the sun during the few
days of life God has given him—for this is his lot.
19 Moreover, when God gives any man wealth
and possessions, and enables him to enjoy them,
to accept his lot and be happy in his work—this
is a gift of God. 20 He seldom reflects on the days
of his life, because God keeps him occupied with
gladness of heart.

6 I have seen another evil under the sun, and
it weighs heavily on men: 2 God gives a man
wealth, possessions and honor, so that he lacks
nothing his heart desires, but God does not enable him to enjoy them, and a stranger enjoys
them instead. This is meaningless, a grievous
evil.

3 A man may have a hundred children and live
many years; yet no matter how long he lives, if he
cannot enjoy his prosperity and does not receive
proper burial, I say that a stillborn child is better
off than he. 4 It comes without meaning, it departs in darkness, and in darkness its name is
shrouded. 5 Though it never saw the sun or knew
anything, it has more rest than does that man—
6 even if he lives a thousand years twice over but
fails to enjoy his prosperity. Do not all go to the
same place?

7 All man's efforts are for his mouth,
yet his appetite is never satisfied.
8 What advantage has a wise man
over a fool?
What does a poor man gain
by knowing how to conduct himself before
others?
9 Better what the eye sees
than the roving of the appetite.
This too is meaningless,
a chasing after the wind.

10 Whatever exists has already been named,
and what man is has been known;
no man can contend
with one who is stronger than he.
11 The more the words,
the less the meaning,
and how does that profit anyone?

12 For who knows what is good for a man in
life, during the few and meaningless days he
passes through like a shadow? Who can tell him
what will happen under the sun after he is gone?

Wisdom

7 A good name is better than fine perfume,
and the day of death better than the day of
birth.
2 It is better to go to a house of mourning
than to go to a house of feasting,
for death is the destiny of every man;
the living should take this to heart.
3 Sorrow is better than laughter,
because a sad face is good for the heart.
4 The heart of the wise is in the house of
mourning,
but the heart of fools is in the house of
pleasure.
5 It is better to heed a wise man's rebuke
than to listen to the song of fools.
6 Like the crackling of thorns under the pot,
so is the laughter of fools.
This too is meaningless.

7 Extortion turns a wise man into a fool,
and a bribe corrupts the heart.

8 The end of a matter is better than its
beginning,
and patience is better than pride.
9 Do not be quickly provoked in your spirit,
for anger resides in the lap of fools.

10 Do not say, "Why were the old days better
than these?"
For it is not wise to ask such questions.

11 Wisdom, like an inheritance, is a good thing
and benefits those who see the sun.
12 Wisdom is a shelter
as money is a shelter,
but the advantage of knowledge is this:
that wisdom preserves the life of its
possessor.

13 Consider what God has done:

Who can straighten
what he has made crooked?
14 When times are good, be happy;
but when times are bad, consider:
God has made the one
as well as the other.
Therefore, a man cannot discover
anything about his future.

15 In this meaningless life of mine I have seen
both of these:

a righteous man perishing in his
righteousness,
and a wicked man living long in his
wickedness.
16 Do not be overrighteous,
neither be overwise—
why destroy yourself?
17 Do not be overwicked,
and do not be a fool—
why die before your time?
18 It is good to grasp the one
and not let go of the other.

The man who fears God will avoid all
⌞extremes⌟.[a]
19Wisdom makes one wise man more powerful
than ten rulers in a city.
20There is not a righteous man on earth
who does what is right and never sins.
21Do not pay attention to every word people
say,
or you may hear your servant cursing
you—
22for you know in your heart
that many times you yourself have cursed
others.

23All this I tested by wisdom and I said,

"I am determined to be wise"—
but this was beyond me.
24Whatever wisdom may be,
it is far off and most profound—
who can discover it?
25So I turned my mind to understand,
to investigate and to search out wisdom
and the scheme of things
and to understand the stupidity of
wickedness
and the madness of folly.
26I find more bitter than death
the woman who is a snare,
whose heart is a trap
and whose hands are chains.
The man who pleases God will escape her,
but the sinner she will ensnare.

27"Look," says the Teacher,[b] "this is what I
have discovered:

"Adding one thing to another to discover the
scheme of things—
28 while I was still searching
but not finding—
I found one ⌞upright⌟ man among a thousand,
but not one ⌞upright⌟ woman among them
all.
29This only have I found:
God made mankind upright,
but men have gone in search of many
schemes."

8 Who is like the wise man?
Who knows the explanation of things?
Wisdom brightens a man's face
and changes its hard appearance.

Obey the King

2Obey the king's command, I say, because you
took an oath before God. 3Do not be in a hurry to
leave the king's presence. Do not stand up for a
bad cause, for he will do whatever he pleases.
4Since a king's word is supreme, who can say to
him, "What are you doing?"

5Whoever obeys his command will come to no
harm,
and the wise heart will know the proper
time and procedure.
6For there is a proper time and procedure for
every matter,
though a man's misery weighs heavily
upon him.
7Since no man knows the future,
who can tell him what is to come?
8No man has power over the wind to contain
it[c];
so no one has power over the day of his
death.
As no one is discharged in time of war,
so wickedness will not release those who
practice it.

9All this I saw, as I applied my mind to everything done under the sun. There is a time when
a man lords it over others to his own[d] hurt.
10Then too, I saw the wicked buried—those who
used to come and go from the holy place and
receive praise[e] in the city where they did this.
This too is meaningless.

11When the sentence for a crime is not quickly
carried out, the hearts of the people are filled
with schemes to do wrong. 12Although a wicked
man commits a hundred crimes and still lives a
long time, I know that it will go better with God-
fearing men, who are reverent before God. 13Yet
because the wicked do not fear God, it will not go
well with them, and their days will not lengthen
like a shadow.

14There is something else meaningless that occurs on earth: righteous men who get what the
wicked deserve, and wicked men who get what
the righteous deserve. This too, I say, is meaningless. 15So I commend the enjoyment of life, because nothing is better for a man under the sun
than to eat and drink and be glad. Then joy will
accompany him in his work all the days of the life
God has given him under the sun.

16When I applied my mind to know wisdom
and to observe man's labor on earth—his eyes
not seeing sleep day or night— 17then I saw all
that God has done. No one can comprehend what
goes on under the sun. Despite all his efforts to
search it out, man cannot discover its meaning.
Even if a wise man claims he knows, he cannot
really comprehend it.

a *18* Or *will follow them both* b *27* Or *leader of the assembly* c *8* Or *over his spirit to retain it* d *9* Or *to their*
e *10* Some Hebrew manuscripts and Septuagint (Aquila); most Hebrew manuscripts *and are forgotten*

A Common Destiny for All

9 So I reflected on all this and concluded that
the righteous and the wise and what they do
are in God's hands, but no man knows whether
love or hate awaits him. 2All share a common
destiny—the righteous and the wicked, the good
and the bad,[a] the clean and the unclean, those
who offer sacrifices and those who do not.

As it is with the good man,
so with the sinner;
as it is with those who take oaths,
so with those who are afraid to take them.

3This is the evil in everything that happens
under the sun: The same destiny overtakes all.
The hearts of men, moreover, are full of evil and
there is madness in their hearts while they live,
and afterward they join the dead. 4Anyone who is
among the living has hope[b]—even a live dog is
better off than a dead lion!

5For the living know that they will die,
but the dead know nothing;
they have no further reward,
and even the memory of them is forgotten.
6Their love, their hate
and their jealousy have long since
vanished;
never again will they have a part
in anything that happens under the sun.

7Go, eat your food with gladness, and drink
your wine with a joyful heart, for it is now that
God favors what you do. 8Always be clothed in
white, and always anoint your head with oil. 9En-
joy life with your wife, whom you love, all the
days of this meaningless life that God has given
you under the sun—all your meaningless days.
For this is your lot in life and in your toilsome
labor under the sun. 10Whatever your hand finds
to do, do it with all your might, for in the grave,[c]
where you are going, there is neither working
nor planning nor knowledge nor wisdom.

11I have seen something else under the sun:

The race is not to the swift
or the battle to the strong,
nor does food come to the wise
or wealth to the brilliant
or favor to the learned;
but time and chance happen to them all.

12Moreover, no man knows when his hour
will come:

As fish are caught in a cruel net,
or birds are taken in a snare,
so men are trapped by evil times
that fall unexpectedly upon them.

Wisdom Better Than Folly

13I also saw under the sun this example of
wisdom that greatly impressed me: 14There was
once a small city with only a few people in it. And
a powerful king came against it, surrounded it
and built huge siegeworks against it. 15Now there
lived in that city a man poor but wise, and he
saved the city by his wisdom. But nobody remembered that poor man. 16So I said, "Wisdom is
better than strength." But the poor man's wisdom is despised, and his words are no longer
heeded.

17The quiet words of the wise are more to be
heeded
than the shouts of a ruler of fools.
18Wisdom is better than weapons of war,
but one sinner destroys much good.

10 As dead flies give perfume a bad smell,
so a little folly outweighs wisdom and
honor.
2The heart of the wise inclines to the right,
but the heart of the fool to the left.
3Even as he walks along the road,
the fool lacks sense
and shows everyone how stupid he is.
4If a ruler's anger rises against you,
do not leave your post;
calmness can lay great errors to rest.

5There is an evil I have seen under the sun,
the sort of error that arises from a ruler:
6Fools are put in many high positions,
while the rich occupy the low ones.
7I have seen slaves on horseback,
while princes go on foot like slaves.

8Whoever digs a pit may fall into it;
whoever breaks through a wall may be
bitten by a snake.
9Whoever quarries stones may be injured by
them;
whoever splits logs may be endangered by
them.

10If the ax is dull
and its edge unsharpened,
more strength is needed
but skill will bring success.

11If a snake bites before it is charmed,
there is no profit for the charmer.

12Words from a wise man's mouth are
gracious,
but a fool is consumed by his own lips.

[a]2 Septuagint (Aquila), Vulgate and Syriac; Hebrew does not have *and the bad.* [b]4 Or *What then is to be chosen? With all who live, there is hope* [c]10 Hebrew *Sheol*

13 At the beginning his words are folly;
at the end they are wicked madness—
14 and the fool multiplies words.

No one knows what is coming—
who can tell him what will happen after him?
15 A fool's work wearies him;
he does not know the way to town.

16 Woe to you, O land whose king was a servant[a]
and whose princes feast in the morning.
17 Blessed are you, O land whose king is of noble birth
and whose princes eat at a proper time—
for strength and not for drunkenness.

18 If a man is lazy, the rafters sag;
if his hands are idle, the house leaks.

19 A feast is made for laughter,
and wine makes life merry,
but money is the answer for everything.

20 Do not revile the king even in your thoughts,
or curse the rich in your bedroom,
because a bird of the air may carry your words,
and a bird on the wing may report what you say.

Bread Upon the Waters

11 Cast your bread upon the waters,
for after many days you will find it again.
2 Give portions to seven, yes to eight,
for you do not know what disaster may come upon the land.

3 If clouds are full of water,
they pour rain upon the earth.
Whether a tree falls to the south or to the north,
in the place where it falls, there will it lie.
4 Whoever watches the wind will not plant;
whoever looks at the clouds will not reap.

5 As you do not know the path of the wind,
or how the body is formed[b] in a mother's womb,
so you cannot understand the work of God,
the Maker of all things.

6 Sow your seed in the morning,
and at evening let not your hands be idle,
for you do not know which will succeed,
whether this or that,
or whether both will do equally well.

Remember Your Creator While Young

7 Light is sweet,
and it pleases the eyes to see the sun.
8 However many years a man may live,
let him enjoy them all.
But let him remember the days of darkness,
for they will be many.
Everything to come is meaningless.

9 Be happy, young man, while you are young,
and let your heart give you joy in the days of your youth.
Follow the ways of your heart
and whatever your eyes see,
but know that for all these things
God will bring you to judgment.
10 So then, banish anxiety from your heart
and cast off the troubles of your body,
for youth and vigor are meaningless.

12 Remember your Creator
in the days of your youth,
before the days of trouble come
and the years approach when you will say,
"I find no pleasure in them"—
2 before the sun and the light
and the moon and the stars grow dark,
and the clouds return after the rain;
3 when the keepers of the house tremble,
and the strong men stoop,
when the grinders cease because they are few,
and those looking through the windows grow dim;
4 when the doors to the street are closed
and the sound of grinding fades;
when men rise up at the sound of birds,
but all their songs grow faint;
5 when men are afraid of heights
and of dangers in the streets;
when the almond tree blossoms
and the grasshopper drags himself along
and desire no longer is stirred.
Then man goes to his eternal home
and mourners go about the streets.

6 Remember him—before the silver cord is severed,
or the golden bowl is broken;
before the pitcher is shattered at the spring,
or the wheel broken at the well,
7 and the dust returns to the ground it came from,
and the spirit returns to God who gave it.

8 "Meaningless! Meaningless!" says the Teacher.[c]
"Everything is meaningless!"

[a] 16 Or *king is a child* also in verses 9 and 10
[b] 5 Or *know how life* (or *the spirit*) */ enters the body being formed*
[c] 8 Or *the leader of the assembly*;

The Conclusion of the Matter

[9]Not only was the Teacher wise, but also he
imparted knowledge to the people. He pondered
and searched out and set in order many proverbs.
[10]The Teacher searched to find just the right
words, and what he wrote was upright and true.

[11]The words of the wise are like goads, their
collected sayings like firmly embedded nails—
given by one Shepherd. [12]Be warned, my son, of
anything in addition to them.

Of making many books there is no end, and
much study wearies the body.

[13]Now all has been heard;
here is the conclusion of the matter:
Fear God and keep his commandments,
for this is the whole ⌞duty⌟ of man.
[14]For God will bring every deed into
judgment,
including every hidden thing,
whether it is good or evil.

Introduction to
SONG OF SONGS

Personal Reading Plan

- ❐ Song of Songs 1:1–2:13
- ❐ Song of Songs 2:14–3:11
- ❐ Song of Songs 4:1–16
- ❐ Song of Songs 5:1–16
- ❐ Song of Songs 6:1–7:9a
- ❐ Song of Songs 7:9b–8:14

Author

Traditionally, King Solomon is thought to be the author of this book. However, its title, "Solomon's Song of Songs" (1:1), can mean a song *by, for* or *about* Solomon. For this and other reasons, the identity of the author remains an open question.

Date

Song of Songs was perhaps written during Solomon's reign, c. 970–930 B.C., but the presence of non-Hebrew words or expressions suggests a later date for the final editing.

Theme

A celebration of love between a man and woman which is akin to God's love for his people.

Historical Background

Solomon's dynasty, his unsurpassed wisdom and wealth, and his many wives and concubines are thought-provoking contrasts to the simple rustic purity of the Song of Songs.

Characteristics

Interpretations of this "best of all songs" vary widely. Some view it literally, as a human love poem about King Solomon and his bride. Others see a third character in a triangle of relationships: a shepherd figure who is the true lover and who wins the Shulammite girl's hand over against the advances of Solomon. Some understand the book to be an anthology of unrelated love poems, with no overall story to tell. Many interpret this lovers' song as an allegory, depicting either God's love for Israel or Christ's love for his bride, the church. Still others think that the song makes no such connection to God's love, but that it is only natural that the wonders of human love inspire thoughts of its divine source. Readers are sometimes surprised to find an explicit love song in the Bible, hence the many attempts to spiritualize away its occasionally erotic lyrics, though the sensual expressions of the poem easily get lost or confused in the translation. Another problem in understanding the Song of Songs has to do with the frequent change of voice and scene. The captions in the text are designed to help follow the lovers' dialogue.

Passage for Topical Group Study

1:1–2:7 SEXUALITY Lyrics of Love From Solomon

See the Lesson Plans in the front of this Bible.

1 Solomon's Song of Songs.

Beloved[a]

2Let him kiss me with the kisses of his
mouth—
for your love is more delightful than
wine.
3Pleasing is the fragrance of your perfumes;
your name is like perfume poured out.
No wonder the maidens love you!
4Take me away with you—let us hurry!
Let the king bring me into his chambers.

> ### SONG OF SONGS 1:1–2:7
>
> 1. Girls: What celebrity fits your idea of a "Prince Charming"?
>
>   Guys: What celebrity fits your idea of a "Dream Girl"?
> 2. How did your parents handle the subject of sex with you?
> 3. When did you start being interested in the opposite sex?
> 4. What do you think of this couple's exchange of compliments?
> 5. Why do you think God included a book about romance and sex in the Bible?
> 6. What do you think the beloved meant when she said, "Do not arouse or awaken love until it so desires" (see note on 2:7)?
> 7. How can the group pray for you as you consider your own romantic desires?

Friends

We rejoice and delight in you[b];
we will praise your love more than wine.

Beloved

How right they are to adore you!

5Dark am I, yet lovely,
O daughters of Jerusalem,
dark like the tents of Kedar,
like the tent curtains of Solomon.[c]
6Do not stare at me because I am dark,
because I am darkened by the sun.
My mother's sons were angry with me
and made me take care of the vineyards;
my own vineyard I have neglected.
7Tell me, you whom I love, where you graze
your flock
and where you rest your sheep at midday.
Why should I be like a veiled woman
beside the flocks of your friends?

Friends

8If you do not know, most beautiful of
women,
follow the tracks of the sheep
and graze your young goats
by the tents of the shepherds.

Lover

9I liken you, my darling, to a mare
harnessed to one of the chariots of
Pharaoh.
10Your cheeks are beautiful with earrings,
your neck with strings of jewels.
11We will make you earrings of gold,
studded with silver.

Beloved

12While the king was at his table,
my perfume spread its fragrance.
13My lover is to me a sachet of myrrh
resting between my breasts.

[a]Primarily on the basis of the gender of the Hebrew pronouns used, male and female speakers are indicated in the margins by the captions *Lover* and *Beloved* respectively. The words of others are marked *Friends*. In some instances the divisions and their captions are debatable. [b]4 The Hebrew is masculine singular. [c]5 Or *Salma*

Many have wondered why a poem about romance and sexual intimacy is found in the Bible. Some suggest it be taken symbolically, as an illustration of God's love. While there is value in that approach, Song of Songs (which means the greatest of songs) is a beautiful picture of romantic love, and its sensual words celebrate sexuality as a gift from God. There are three voices in the poem: (1) the Lover—probably King Solomon, who wrote 1,005 songs (1 Kings 4:32); (2) the Beloved—the king's young bride; (3) the Friends—observers of the romance (who were probably the maidens of v. 3 and the daughters of Jerusalem in v. 5).

1:6 ***dark.*** Not considered desirable. More privileged girls didn't have to work outside in the sun, in the fields or vineyards. ***my own vineyard.*** Her body (see 8:12; 2:15). Vineyard is an apt metaphor since it yields wine, and the excitements of love are compared with those produced by wine (see v. 2; 4:10). The beloved is also compared to a garden, yielding precious fruits for her lover.

1:9 A flattering comparison: the beloved's beauty attracts attention the way a mare would among the Egyptian chariot stallions.

2:4 ***his banner.*** The king's love is displayed for all to see, like a large military banner.

2:7 A recurring refrain, always spoken by the beloved in a context of physical intimacy with her lover. ***until it so desires.*** Out of the beloved's experience of love comes wise admonition that sexual intimacy can't be forced. Love and lust are not the same.

14My lover is to me a cluster of henna
blossoms
from the vineyards of En Gedi.

Lover

15How beautiful you are, my darling!
Oh, how beautiful!
Your eyes are doves.

Beloved

16How handsome you are, my lover!
Oh, how charming!
And our bed is verdant.

Lover

17The beams of our house are cedars;
our rafters are firs.

Beloved[a]

2 I am a rose[b] of Sharon,
a lily of the valleys.

Lover

2Like a lily among thorns
is my darling among the maidens.

Beloved

3Like an apple tree among the trees of the
forest
is my lover among the young men.
I delight to sit in his shade,
and his fruit is sweet to my taste.
4He has taken me to the banquet hall,
and his banner over me is love.
5Strengthen me with raisins,
refresh me with apples,
for I am faint with love.
6His left arm is under my head,
and his right arm embraces me.
7Daughters of Jerusalem, I charge you
by the gazelles and by the does of the
field:
Do not arouse or awaken love
until it so desires.
8Listen! My lover!
Look! Here he comes,
leaping across the mountains,
bounding over the hills.
9My lover is like a gazelle or a young stag.
Look! There he stands behind our wall,
gazing through the windows,
peering through the lattice.
10My lover spoke and said to me,
"Arise, my darling,
my beautiful one, and come with me.
11See! The winter is past;
the rains are over and gone.
12Flowers appear on the earth;
the season of singing has come,
the cooing of doves
is heard in our land.
13The fig tree forms its early fruit;
the blossoming vines spread their
fragrance.
Arise, come, my darling;
my beautiful one, come with me."

Lover

14My dove in the clefts of the rock,
in the hiding places on the mountainside,
show me your face,
let me hear your voice;
for your voice is sweet,
and your face is lovely.
15Catch for us the foxes,
the little foxes
that ruin the vineyards,
our vineyards that are in bloom.

Beloved

16My lover is mine and I am his;
he browses among the lilies.
17Until the day breaks
and the shadows flee,
turn, my lover,
and be like a gazelle
or like a young stag
on the rugged hills.[c]

3 All night long on my bed
I looked for the one my heart loves;
I looked for him but did not find him.
2I will get up now and go about the city,
through its streets and squares;
I will search for the one my heart loves.
So I looked for him but did not find him.
3The watchmen found me
as they made their rounds in the city.
"Have you seen the one my heart loves?"
4Scarcely had I passed them
when I found the one my heart loves.
I held him and would not let him go
till I had brought him to my mother's
house,
to the room of the one who conceived me.
5Daughters of Jerusalem, I charge you
by the gazelles and by the does of the
field:
Do not arouse or awaken love
until it so desires.
6Who is this coming up from the desert
like a column of smoke,
perfumed with myrrh and incense

a *1* Or *Lover* b *1* Possibly a member of the crocus family c *17* Or *the hills of Bether*

made from all the spices of the merchant?
7Look! It is Solomon's carriage,
escorted by sixty warriors,
the noblest of Israel,
8all of them wearing the sword,
all experienced in battle,
each with his sword at his side,
prepared for the terrors of the night.
9King Solomon made for himself the carriage;
he made it of wood from Lebanon.
10Its posts he made of silver,
its base of gold.
Its seat was upholstered with purple,
its interior lovingly inlaid
by[a] the daughters of Jerusalem.
11Come out, you daughters of Zion,
and look at King Solomon wearing the crown,
the crown with which his mother crowned him
on the day of his wedding,
the day his heart rejoiced.

Lover

4 How beautiful you are, my darling!
Oh, how beautiful!
Your eyes behind your veil are doves.
Your hair is like a flock of goats
descending from Mount Gilead.
2Your teeth are like a flock of sheep just shorn,
coming up from the washing.
Each has its twin;
not one of them is alone.
3Your lips are like a scarlet ribbon;
your mouth is lovely.
Your temples behind your veil
are like the halves of a pomegranate.
4Your neck is like the tower of David,
built with elegance[b];
on it hang a thousand shields,
all of them shields of warriors.
5Your two breasts are like two fawns,
like twin fawns of a gazelle
that browse among the lilies.
6Until the day breaks
and the shadows flee,
I will go to the mountain of myrrh
and to the hill of incense.
7All beautiful you are, my darling;
there is no flaw in you.

8Come with me from Lebanon, my bride,
come with me from Lebanon.
Descend from the crest of Amana,
from the top of Senir, the summit of Hermon,
from the lions' dens
and the mountain haunts of the leopards.
9You have stolen my heart, my sister, my bride;
you have stolen my heart
with one glance of your eyes,
with one jewel of your necklace.
10How delightful is your love, my sister, my bride!
How much more pleasing is your love than wine,
and the fragrance of your perfume than any spice!
11Your lips drop sweetness as the honeycomb, my bride;
milk and honey are under your tongue.
The fragrance of your garments is like that of Lebanon.
12You are a garden locked up, my sister, my bride;
you are a spring enclosed, a sealed fountain.
13Your plants are an orchard of pomegranates
with choice fruits,
with henna and nard,
14 nard and saffron,
calamus and cinnamon,
with every kind of incense tree,
with myrrh and aloes
and all the finest spices.
15You are[c] a garden fountain,
a well of flowing water
streaming down from Lebanon.

Beloved

16Awake, north wind,
and come, south wind!
Blow on my garden,
that its fragrance may spread abroad.
Let my lover come into his garden
and taste its choice fruits.

Lover

5 I have come into my garden, my sister, my bride;
I have gathered my myrrh with my spice.
I have eaten my honeycomb and my honey;
I have drunk my wine and my milk.

Friends

Eat, O friends, and drink;
drink your fill, O lovers.

Beloved

2I slept but my heart was awake.
Listen! My lover is knocking:

[a] 10 Or *its inlaid interior a gift of love / from* (spoken by the *Beloved*)
[b] 4 The meaning of the Hebrew for this word is uncertain.
[c] 15 Or *I am*

"Open to me, my sister, my darling,
my dove, my flawless one.
My head is drenched with dew,
my hair with the dampness of the night."
3 I have taken off my robe—
must I put it on again?
I have washed my feet—
must I soil them again?
4 My lover thrust his hand through the
latch-opening;
my heart began to pound for him.
5 I arose to open for my lover,
and my hands dripped with myrrh,
my fingers with flowing myrrh,
on the handles of the lock.
6 I opened for my lover,
but my lover had left; he was gone.
My heart sank at his departure.[a]
I looked for him but did not find him.
I called him but he did not answer.
7 The watchmen found me
as they made their rounds in the city.
They beat me, they bruised me;
they took away my cloak,
those watchmen of the walls!
8 O daughters of Jerusalem, I charge you—
if you find my lover,
what will you tell him?
Tell him I am faint with love.

Friends

9 How is your beloved better than others,
most beautiful of women?
How is your beloved better than others,
that you charge us so?

Beloved

10 My lover is radiant and ruddy,
outstanding among ten thousand.
11 His head is purest gold;
his hair is wavy
and black as a raven.
12 His eyes are like doves
by the water streams,
washed in milk,
mounted like jewels.
13 His cheeks are like beds of spice
yielding perfume.
His lips are like lilies
dripping with myrrh.
14 His arms are rods of gold
set with chrysolite.
His body is like polished ivory
decorated with sapphires.[b]
15 His legs are pillars of marble
set on bases of pure gold.
His appearance is like Lebanon,
choice as its cedars.
16 His mouth is sweetness itself;
he is altogether lovely.
This is my lover, this my friend,
O daughters of Jerusalem.

Friends

6 Where has your lover gone,
most beautiful of women?
Which way did your lover turn,
that we may look for him with you?

Beloved

2 My lover has gone down to his garden,
to the beds of spices,
to browse in the gardens
and to gather lilies.
3 I am my lover's and my lover is mine;
he browses among the lilies.

Lover

4 You are beautiful, my darling, as Tirzah,
lovely as Jerusalem,
majestic as troops with banners.
5 Turn your eyes from me;
they overwhelm me.
Your hair is like a flock of goats
descending from Gilead.
6 Your teeth are like a flock of sheep
coming up from the washing.
Each has its twin,
not one of them is alone.
7 Your temples behind your veil
are like the halves of a pomegranate.
8 Sixty queens there may be,
and eighty concubines,
and virgins beyond number;
9 but my dove, my perfect one, is unique,
the only daughter of her mother,
the favorite of the one who bore her.
The maidens saw her and called her blessed;
the queens and concubines praised her.

Friends

10 Who is this that appears like the dawn,
fair as the moon, bright as the sun,
majestic as the stars in procession?

Lover

11 I went down to the grove of nut trees
to look at the new growth in the valley,
to see if the vines had budded
or the pomegranates were in bloom.
12 Before I realized it,

[a] 6 Or *heart had gone out to him when he spoke* [b] 14 Or *lapis lazuli*

my desire set me among the royal chariots
of my people.[a]

Friends

13Come back, come back, O Shulammite;
come back, come back, that we may gaze
on you!

Lover

Why would you gaze on the Shulammite
as on the dance of Mahanaim?

7 How beautiful your sandaled feet,
O prince's daughter!
Your graceful legs are like jewels,
the work of a craftsman's hands.
2Your navel is a rounded goblet
that never lacks blended wine.
Your waist is a mound of wheat
encircled by lilies.
3Your breasts are like two fawns,
twins of a gazelle.
4Your neck is like an ivory tower.
Your eyes are the pools of Heshbon
by the gate of Bath Rabbim.
Your nose is like the tower of Lebanon
looking toward Damascus.
5Your head crowns you like Mount Carmel.
Your hair is like royal tapestry;
the king is held captive by its tresses.
6How beautiful you are and how pleasing,
O love, with your delights!
7Your stature is like that of the palm,
and your breasts like clusters of fruit.
8I said, "I will climb the palm tree;
I will take hold of its fruit."
May your breasts be like the clusters of the
vine,
the fragrance of your breath like apples,
9and your mouth like the best wine.

Beloved

May the wine go straight to my lover,
flowing gently over lips and teeth.[b]
10I belong to my lover,
and his desire is for me.
11Come, my lover, let us go to the countryside,
let us spend the night in the villages.[c]
12Let us go early to the vineyards
to see if the vines have budded,
if their blossoms have opened,
and if the pomegranates are in bloom—
there I will give you my love.
13The mandrakes send out their fragrance,
and at our door is every delicacy,
both new and old,
that I have stored up for you, my lover.

8 If only you were to me like a brother,
who was nursed at my mother's breasts!
Then, if I found you outside,
I would kiss you,
and no one would despise me.
2I would lead you
and bring you to my mother's house—
she who has taught me.
I would give you spiced wine to drink,
the nectar of my pomegranates.
3His left arm is under my head
and his right arm embraces me.
4Daughters of Jerusalem, I charge you:
Do not arouse or awaken love
until it so desires.

Friends

5Who is this coming up from the desert
leaning on her lover?

Beloved

Under the apple tree I roused you;
there your mother conceived you,
there she who was in labor gave you birth.
6Place me like a seal over your heart,
like a seal on your arm;
for love is as strong as death,
its jealousy[d] unyielding as the grave.[e]
It burns like blazing fire,
like a mighty flame.[f]
7Many waters cannot quench love;
rivers cannot wash it away.
If one were to give
all the wealth of his house for love,
it[g] would be utterly scorned.

Friends

8We have a young sister,
and her breasts are not yet grown.
What shall we do for our sister
for the day she is spoken for?
9If she is a wall,
we will build towers of silver on her.
If she is a door,
we will enclose her with panels of cedar.

Beloved

10I am a wall,
and my breasts are like towers.
Thus I have become in his eyes

[a]12 Or *among the chariots of Amminadab*; or *among the chariots of the people of the prince* [b]9 Septuagint, Aquila, Vulgate and Syriac; Hebrew *lips of sleepers* [c]11 Or *henna bushes* [d]6 Or *ardor* [e]6 Hebrew *Sheol* [f]6 Or / *like the very flame of the LORD* [g]7 Or *he*

like one bringing contentment.
11 Solomon had a vineyard in Baal Hamon;
he let out his vineyard to tenants.
Each was to bring for its fruit
a thousand shekels[a] of silver.
12 But my own vineyard is mine to give;
the thousand shekels are for you,
O Solomon,
and two hundred[b] are for those who tend
its fruit.

Lover

13 You who dwell in the gardens
with friends in attendance,
let me hear your voice!

Beloved

14 Come away, my lover,
and be like a gazelle
or like a young stag
on the spice-laden mountains.

[a] *11* That is, about 25 pounds (about 11.5 kilograms); also in verse 12
[b] *12* That is, about 5 pounds (about 2.3 kilograms)

Introduction to
ISAIAH

Personal Reading Plan

❒ Isaiah 1:1–2:22
❒ Isaiah 3:1–5:30
❒ Isaiah 6:1–8:22
❒ Isaiah 9:1–10:34
❒ Isaiah 11:1–14:23
❒ Isaiah 14:24–18:7
❒ Isaiah 19:1–22:25
❒ Isaiah 23:1–25:12
❒ Isaiah 26:1–28:29
❒ Isaiah 29:1–30:33
❒ Isaiah 31:1–34:17
❒ Isaiah 35:1–37:38
❒ Isaiah 38:1–40:31
❒ Isaiah 41:1–42:25
❒ Isaiah 43:1–44:23
❒ Isaiah 44:24–47:15
❒ Isaiah 48:1–49:26
❒ Isaiah 50:1–52:12
❒ Isaiah 52:13–55:13
❒ Isaiah 56:1–58:14
❒ Isaiah 59:1–60:22
❒ Isaiah 61:1–63:6
❒ Isaiah 63:7–65:16
❒ Isaiah 65:17–66:24

Author

In the opening verse of the book, the author is declared to be Isaiah son of Amoz (see also 2:1; 13:1). Chapters 1–39 ("The Book of Judgment") reflect for the most part the kingdom of Isaiah's day, but chapters 40–66 ("The Book of Comfort") envision the return from exile (536 B.C.) and the coming kingdom of God. Some believe that these visionary chapters may have been written later by others following in Isaiah's steps.

Date

Isaiah ministered in Judah c. 740–681 B.C.

Theme

The sovereign Lord, judging and redeeming the whole earth.

Historical Background

Assyria, the invincible superpower of the day, was threatening Jerusalem with conquest (2 Kings 15–20; 2 Chron. 26–32). Isaiah saw in this the culmination of God's judgment against the widespread apostasy of Judah under King Ahaz. He predicted the fall of Jerusalem (which happened in 586 B.C.). The only hope for escape, Isaiah declared, was God's intervention, not political alliances, material wealth, or religious pretense. Chapters 40–66 focus on events 150–200 years after Isaiah's day, foretelling God's deliverance of his people from their Babylonian captors (in 538 B.C.) and prefiguring the greater deliverance from sin through Christ.

Characteristics

As a prophet, poet and politician, Isaiah was a giant in his day, respected in royal circles despite his unpopular message. Known for his beautiful images and profound insights into the nature of God (whom Isaiah calls "The Holy One of Israel"), the prophet Isaiah is quoted in the New Testament more than all other prophets combined. Isaiah's use of fire as a symbol of punishment (1:31), his references to the "holy mountain" of Jerusalem (2:2–4), and his mention of the highway to Jerusalem (11:16) are images that recur throughout the book.

1 The vision concerning Judah and Jerusalem
that Isaiah son of Amoz saw during the
reigns of Uzziah, Jotham, Ahaz and Hezekiah,
kings of Judah.

A Rebellious Nation

2 Hear, O heavens! Listen, O earth!
For the LORD has spoken:
"I reared children and brought them up,
but they have rebelled against me.
3 The ox knows his master,
the donkey his owner's manger,
but Israel does not know,
my people do not understand."

4 Ah, sinful nation,
a people loaded with guilt,
a brood of evildoers,
children given to corruption!
They have forsaken the LORD;
they have spurned the Holy One of Israel
and turned their backs on him.
5 Why should you be beaten anymore?
Why do you persist in rebellion?
Your whole head is injured,
your whole heart afflicted.
6 From the sole of your foot to the top of your
head
there is no soundness—
only wounds and welts
and open sores,
not cleansed or bandaged
or soothed with oil.

7 Your country is desolate,
your cities burned with fire;
your fields are being stripped by foreigners
right before you,
laid waste as when overthrown by
strangers.
8 The Daughter of Zion is left
like a shelter in a vineyard,
like a hut in a field of melons,
like a city under siege.
9 Unless the LORD Almighty
had left us some survivors,
we would have become like Sodom,
we would have been like Gomorrah.

10 Hear the word of the LORD,
you rulers of Sodom;
listen to the law of our God,
you people of Gomorrah!
11 "The multitude of your sacrifices—
what are they to me?" says the LORD.
"I have more than enough of burnt offerings,
of rams and the fat of fattened animals;
I have no pleasure
in the blood of bulls and lambs and goats.
12 When you come to appear before me,
who has asked this of you,
this trampling of my courts?
13 Stop bringing meaningless offerings!
Your incense is detestable to me.
New Moons, Sabbaths and convocations—
I cannot bear your evil assemblies.
14 Your New Moon festivals and your appointed
feasts
my soul hates.
They have become a burden to me;
I am weary of bearing them.
15 When you spread out your hands in prayer,
I will hide my eyes from you;
even if you offer many prayers,
I will not listen.
Your hands are full of blood;
16 wash and make yourselves clean.
Take your evil deeds
out of my sight!
Stop doing wrong,
17 learn to do right!
Seek justice,
encourage the oppressed.[a]
Defend the cause of the fatherless,
plead the case of the widow.

18 "Come now, let us reason together,"
says the LORD.
"Though your sins are like scarlet,
they shall be as white as snow;
though they are red as crimson,
they shall be like wool.
19 If you are willing and obedient,
you will eat the best from the land;
20 but if you resist and rebel,
you will be devoured by the sword."
For the mouth of the LORD
has spoken.

21 See how the faithful city
has become a harlot!
She once was full of justice;
righteousness used to dwell in her—
but now murderers!
22 Your silver has become dross,
your choice wine is diluted with water.
23 Your rulers are rebels,
companions of thieves;
they all love bribes
and chase after gifts.
They do not defend the cause of the
fatherless;
the widow's case does not come before
them.
24 Therefore the Lord, the LORD Almighty,
the Mighty One of Israel, declares:

[a] *17* Or / *rebuke the oppressor*

"Ah, I will get relief from my foes
and avenge myself on my enemies.
25 I will turn my hand against you;
I will thoroughly purge away your dross
and remove all your impurities.
26 I will restore your judges as in days of old,
your counselors as at the beginning.
Afterward you will be called
the City of Righteousness,
the Faithful City."

27 Zion will be redeemed with justice,
her penitent ones with righteousness.
28 But rebels and sinners will both be broken,
and those who forsake the LORD will perish.

29 "You will be ashamed because of the sacred oaks
in which you have delighted;
you will be disgraced because of the gardens
that you have chosen.
30 You will be like an oak with fading leaves,
like a garden without water.
31 The mighty man will become tinder
and his work a spark;
both will burn together,
with no one to quench the fire."

The Mountain of the LORD

2 This is what Isaiah son of Amoz saw concerning Judah and Jerusalem:

2 In the last days

the mountain of the LORD's temple will be established
as chief among the mountains;
it will be raised above the hills,
and all nations will stream to it.

3 Many peoples will come and say,

"Come, let us go up to the mountain of the LORD,
to the house of the God of Jacob.
He will teach us his ways,
so that we may walk in his paths."
The law will go out from Zion,
the word of the LORD from Jerusalem.
4 He will judge between the nations
and will settle disputes for many peoples.
They will beat their swords into plowshares
and their spears into pruning hooks.
Nation will not take up sword against nation,
nor will they train for war anymore.
5 Come, O house of Jacob,
let us walk in the light of the LORD.

The Day of the LORD

6 You have abandoned your people,
the house of Jacob.
They are full of superstitions from the East;
they practice divination like the Philistines
and clasp hands with pagans.
7 Their land is full of silver and gold;
there is no end to their treasures.
Their land is full of horses;
there is no end to their chariots.
8 Their land is full of idols;
they bow down to the work of their hands,
to what their fingers have made.
9 So man will be brought low
and mankind humbled—
do not forgive them.[a]

10 Go into the rocks,
hide in the ground
from dread of the LORD
and the splendor of his majesty!
11 The eyes of the arrogant man will be humbled
and the pride of men brought low;
the LORD alone will be exalted in that day.

12 The LORD Almighty has a day in store
for all the proud and lofty,
for all that is exalted
(and they will be humbled),
13 for all the cedars of Lebanon, tall and lofty,
and all the oaks of Bashan,
14 for all the towering mountains
and all the high hills,
15 for every lofty tower
and every fortified wall,
16 for every trading ship[b]
and every stately vessel.
17 The arrogance of man will be brought low
and the pride of men humbled;
the LORD alone will be exalted in that day,
18 and the idols will totally disappear.

19 Men will flee to caves in the rocks
and to holes in the ground
from dread of the LORD
and the splendor of his majesty,
when he rises to shake the earth.
20 In that day men will throw away
to the rodents and bats
their idols of silver and idols of gold,
which they made to worship.
21 They will flee to caverns in the rocks
and to the overhanging crags
from dread of the LORD
and the splendor of his majesty,
when he rises to shake the earth.

a9 Or *not raise them up* b16 Hebrew *every ship of Tarshish*

22 Stop trusting in man,
who has but a breath in his nostrils.
Of what account is he?

Judgment on Jerusalem and Judah

3 See now, the Lord,
the LORD Almighty,
is about to take from Jerusalem and Judah
both supply and support:
all supplies of food and all supplies of water,
2 the hero and warrior,
the judge and prophet,
the soothsayer and elder,
3 the captain of fifty and man of rank,
the counselor, skilled craftsman and clever enchanter.

4 I will make boys their officials;
mere children will govern them.
5 People will oppress each other—
man against man, neighbor against neighbor.
The young will rise up against the old,
the base against the honorable.

6 A man will seize one of his brothers
at his father's home, and say,
"You have a cloak, you be our leader;
take charge of this heap of ruins!"
7 But in that day he will cry out,
"I have no remedy.
I have no food or clothing in my house;
do not make me the leader of the people."

8 Jerusalem staggers,
Judah is falling;
their words and deeds are against the LORD,
defying his glorious presence.
9 The look on their faces testifies against them;
they parade their sin like Sodom;
they do not hide it.
Woe to them!
They have brought disaster upon themselves.

10 Tell the righteous it will be well with them,
for they will enjoy the fruit of their deeds.
11 Woe to the wicked! Disaster is upon them!
They will be paid back for what their hands have done.

12 Youths oppress my people,
women rule over them.
O my people, your guides lead you astray;
they turn you from the path.

13 The LORD takes his place in court;
he rises to judge the people.
14 The LORD enters into judgment
against the elders and leaders of his people:
"It is you who have ruined my vineyard;
the plunder from the poor is in your houses.
15 What do you mean by crushing my people
and grinding the faces of the poor?"
declares the Lord,
the LORD Almighty.

16 The LORD says,
"The women of Zion are haughty,
walking along with outstretched necks,
flirting with their eyes,
tripping along with mincing steps,
with ornaments jingling on their ankles.
17 Therefore the Lord will bring sores on the heads of the women of Zion;
the LORD will make their scalps bald."

18 In that day the Lord will snatch away their
finery: the bangles and headbands and crescent
necklaces, 19 the earrings and bracelets and veils,
20 the headdresses and ankle chains and sashes,
the perfume bottles and charms, 21 the signet
rings and nose rings, 22 the fine robes and the
capes and cloaks, the purses 23 and mirrors, and
the linen garments and tiaras and shawls.

24 Instead of fragrance there will be a stench;
instead of a sash, a rope;
instead of well-dressed hair, baldness;
instead of fine clothing, sackcloth;
instead of beauty, branding.
25 Your men will fall by the sword,
your warriors in battle.
26 The gates of Zion will lament and mourn;
destitute, she will sit on the ground.

4 In that day seven women
will take hold of one man
and say, "We will eat our own food
and provide our own clothes;
only let us be called by your name.
Take away our disgrace!"

The Branch of the LORD

2 In that day the Branch of the LORD will be
beautiful and glorious, and the fruit of the land
will be the pride and glory of the survivors in
Israel. 3 Those who are left in Zion, who remain
in Jerusalem, will be called holy, all who are recorded among the living in Jerusalem. 4 The Lord
will wash away the filth of the women of Zion; he
will cleanse the bloodstains from Jerusalem by a
spirit[a] of judgment and a spirit[a] of fire. 5 Then
the LORD will create over all of Mount Zion and
over those who assemble there a cloud of smoke
by day and a glow of flaming fire by night; over all
the glory will be a canopy. 6 It will be a shelter

[a] 4 Or *the Spirit*

and shade from the heat of the day, and a refuge and hiding place from the storm and rain.

The Song of the Vineyard

5 I will sing for the one I love
a song about his vineyard:
My loved one had a vineyard
on a fertile hillside.
2He dug it up and cleared it of stones
and planted it with the choicest vines.
He built a watchtower in it
and cut out a winepress as well.
Then he looked for a crop of good grapes,
but it yielded only bad fruit.

3"Now you dwellers in Jerusalem and men of Judah,
judge between me and my vineyard.
4What more could have been done for my vineyard
than I have done for it?
When I looked for good grapes,
why did it yield only bad?
5Now I will tell you
what I am going to do to my vineyard:
I will take away its hedge,
and it will be destroyed;
I will break down its wall,
and it will be trampled.
6I will make it a wasteland,
neither pruned nor cultivated,
and briers and thorns will grow there.
I will command the clouds
not to rain on it."
7The vineyard of the LORD Almighty
is the house of Israel,
and the men of Judah
are the garden of his delight.
And he looked for justice, but saw bloodshed;
for righteousness, but heard cries of distress.

Woes and Judgments

8Woe to you who add house to house
and join field to field
till no space is left
and you live alone in the land.

9The LORD Almighty has declared in my hearing:

"Surely the great houses will become desolate,
the fine mansions left without occupants.
10A ten-acre[a] vineyard will produce only a bath[b] of wine,
a homer[c] of seed only an ephah[d] of grain."

11Woe to those who rise early in the morning
to run after their drinks,
who stay up late at night
till they are inflamed with wine.
12They have harps and lyres at their banquets,
tambourines and flutes and wine,
but they have no regard for the deeds of the LORD,
no respect for the work of his hands.
13Therefore my people will go into exile
for lack of understanding;
their men of rank will die of hunger
and their masses will be parched with thirst.
14Therefore the grave[e] enlarges its appetite
and opens its mouth without limit;
into it will descend their nobles and masses
with all their brawlers and revelers.
15So man will be brought low
and mankind humbled,
the eyes of the arrogant humbled.
16But the LORD Almighty will be exalted by his justice,
and the holy God will show himself holy
by his righteousness.
17Then sheep will graze as in their own pasture;
lambs will feed[f] among the ruins of the rich.
18Woe to those who draw sin along with cords of deceit,
and wickedness as with cart ropes,
19to those who say, "Let God hurry,
let him hasten his work
so we may see it.
Let it approach,
let the plan of the Holy One of Israel come,
so we may know it."

20Woe to those who call evil good
and good evil,
who put darkness for light
and light for darkness,
who put bitter for sweet
and sweet for bitter.

21Woe to those who are wise in their own eyes
and clever in their own sight.

22Woe to those who are heroes at drinking wine
and champions at mixing drinks,
23who acquit the guilty for a bribe,

[a]10 Hebrew *ten-yoke,* that is, the land plowed by 10 yoke of oxen in one day [b]10 That is, probably about 6 gallons (about 22 liters) [c]10 That is, probably about 6 bushels (about 220 liters) [d]10 That is, probably about 3/5 bushel (about 22 liters) [e]14 Hebrew *Sheol* [f]17 Septuagint; Hebrew / *strangers will eat*

but deny justice to the innocent.
24 Therefore, as tongues of fire lick up straw
and as dry grass sinks down in the flames,
so their roots will decay
and their flowers blow away like dust;
for they have rejected the law of the LORD Almighty
and spurned the word of the Holy One of Israel.
25 Therefore the LORD's anger burns against his people;
his hand is raised and he strikes them down.
The mountains shake,
and the dead bodies are like refuse in the streets.

Yet for all this, his anger is not turned away,
his hand is still upraised.

26 He lifts up a banner for the distant nations,
he whistles for those at the ends of the earth.
Here they come,
swiftly and speedily!
27 Not one of them grows tired or stumbles,
not one slumbers or sleeps;
not a belt is loosened at the waist,
not a sandal thong is broken.
28 Their arrows are sharp,
all their bows are strung;
their horses' hoofs seem like flint,
their chariot wheels like a whirlwind.
29 Their roar is like that of the lion,
they roar like young lions;
they growl as they seize their prey
and carry it off with no one to rescue.
30 In that day they will roar over it
like the roaring of the sea.
And if one looks at the land,
he will see darkness and distress;
even the light will be darkened by the clouds.

Isaiah's Commission

6 In the year that King Uzziah died, I saw the
Lord seated on a throne, high and exalted,
and the train of his robe filled the temple. 2 Above
him were seraphs, each with six wings: With two
wings they covered their faces, with two they
covered their feet, and with two they were flying.
3 And they were calling to one another:

"Holy, holy, holy is the LORD Almighty;
the whole earth is full of his glory."

4 At the sound of their voices the doorposts and
thresholds shook and the temple was filled with
smoke.
5 "Woe to me!" I cried. "I am ruined! For I am
a man of unclean lips, and I live among a people
of unclean lips, and my eyes have seen the King,
the LORD Almighty."
6 Then one of the seraphs flew to me with a
live coal in his hand, which he had taken with
tongs from the altar. 7 With it he touched my
mouth and said, "See, this has touched your lips;
your guilt is taken away and your sin atoned for."
8 Then I heard the voice of the Lord saying,
"Whom shall I send? And who will go for us?"
And I said, "Here am I. Send me!"
9 He said, "Go and tell this people:

" 'Be ever hearing, but never understanding;
be ever seeing, but never perceiving.'
10 Make the heart of this people calloused;
make their ears dull
and close their eyes.[a]
Otherwise they might see with their eyes,
hear with their ears,
understand with their hearts,
and turn and be healed."

11 Then I said, "For how long, O Lord?"
And he answered:

"Until the cities lie ruined
and without inhabitant,
until the houses are left deserted
and the fields ruined and ravaged,
12 until the LORD has sent everyone far away
and the land is utterly forsaken.
13 And though a tenth remains in the land,
it will again be laid waste.
But as the terebinth and oak
leave stumps when they are cut down,
so the holy seed will be the stump in the land."

The Sign of Immanuel

7 When Ahaz son of Jotham, the son of Uzziah,
was king of Judah, King Rezin of Aram and
Pekah son of Remaliah king of Israel marched up
to fight against Jerusalem, but they could not
overpower it.
2 Now the house of David was told, "Aram has
allied itself with[b] Ephraim"; so the hearts of
Ahaz and his people were shaken, as the trees of
the forest are shaken by the wind.
3 Then the LORD said to Isaiah, "Go out, you
and your son Shear-Jashub,[c] to meet Ahaz at the
end of the aqueduct of the Upper Pool, on the
road to the Washerman's Field. 4 Say to him, 'Be
careful, keep calm and don't be afraid. Do not

[a] 9,10 Hebrew; Septuagint *'You will be ever hearing, but never understanding; / you will be ever seeing, but never perceiving.' / 10 This people's heart has become calloused; / they hardly hear with their ears, / and they have closed their eyes* [b] 2 Or *has set up camp in* [c] 3 *Shear-Jashub* means *a remnant will return.*

lose heart because of these two smoldering stubs
of firewood—because of the fierce anger of Rezin
and Aram and of the son of Remaliah. 5Aram,
Ephraim and Remaliah's son have plotted your
ruin, saying, 6"Let us invade Judah; let us tear it
apart and divide it among ourselves, and make
the son of Tabeel king over it." 7Yet this is what
the Sovereign LORD says:

" 'It will not take place,
 it will not happen,
8for the head of Aram is Damascus,
 and the head of Damascus is only Rezin.
Within sixty-five years
 Ephraim will be too shattered to be a
 people.
9The head of Ephraim is Samaria,
 and the head of Samaria is only Remaliah's
 son.
If you do not stand firm in your faith,
 you will not stand at all.' "

10Again the LORD spoke to Ahaz, 11"Ask the
LORD your God for a sign, whether in the deepest
depths or in the highest heights."
12But Ahaz said, "I will not ask; I will not put
the LORD to the test."
13Then Isaiah said, "Hear now, you house of
David! Is it not enough to try the patience of
men? Will you try the patience of my God also?
14Therefore the Lord himself will give you[a] a
sign: The virgin will be with child and will give
birth to a son, and[b] will call him Immanuel.[c]
15He will eat curds and honey when he knows
enough to reject the wrong and choose the right.
16But before the boy knows enough to reject the
wrong and choose the right, the land of the two
kings you dread will be laid waste. 17The LORD
will bring on you and on your people and on the
house of your father a time unlike any since
Ephraim broke away from Judah—he will bring
the king of Assyria."
18In that day the LORD will whistle for flies
from the distant streams of Egypt and for bees
from the land of Assyria. 19They will all come and
settle in the steep ravines and in the crevices in
the rocks, on all the thornbushes and at all the
water holes. 20In that day the Lord will use a
razor hired from beyond the River[d]—the king of
Assyria—to shave your head and the hair of your
legs, and to take off your beards also. 21In that
day, a man will keep alive a young cow and two
goats. 22And because of the abundance of the
milk they give, he will have curds to eat. All who
remain in the land will eat curds and honey. 23In
that day, in every place where there were a thousand vines worth a thousand silver shekels,[e]
there will be only briers and thorns. 24Men will
go there with bow and arrow, for the land will be
covered with briers and thorns. 25As for all the
hills once cultivated by the hoe, you will no longer go there for fear of the briers and thorns; they
will become places where cattle are turned loose
and where sheep run.

Assyria, the LORD's Instrument

8 The LORD said to me, "Take a large scroll and
write on it with an ordinary pen: Maher-
Shalal-Hash-Baz.[f] 2And I will call in Uriah the
priest and Zechariah son of Jeberekiah as reliable
witnesses for me."
3Then I went to the prophetess, and she conceived and gave birth to a son. And the LORD said
to me, "Name him Maher-Shalal-Hash-Baz. 4Be-
fore the boy knows how to say 'My father' or 'My
mother,' the wealth of Damascus and the plunder
of Samaria will be carried off by the king of Assyria."
5The LORD spoke to me again:

6"Because this people has rejected
 the gently flowing waters of Shiloah
and rejoices over Rezin
 and the son of Remaliah,
7therefore the Lord is about to bring against
 them
 the mighty floodwaters of the River[d]—
 the king of Assyria with all his pomp.
It will overflow all its channels,
 run over all its banks
8and sweep on into Judah, swirling over it,
 passing through it and reaching up to the
 neck.
Its outspread wings will cover the breadth of
 your land,
 O Immanuel[c]!"

9Raise the war cry,[g] you nations, and be
 shattered!
 Listen, all you distant lands.
Prepare for battle, and be shattered!
 Prepare for battle, and be shattered!
10Devise your strategy, but it will be thwarted;
 propose your plan, but it will not stand,
for God is with us.[h]

Fear God

11The LORD spoke to me with his strong hand
upon me, warning me not to follow the way of
this people. He said:

12"Do not call conspiracy

[a] 14 The Hebrew is plural. [b] 14 Masoretic Text; Dead Sea Scrolls *and he* or *and they* [c] 14,8 *Immanuel* means *God with us.*
[d] 20,7 That is, the Euphrates [e] 23 That is, about 25 pounds (about 11.5 kilograms) [f] 1 *Maher-Shalal-Hash-Baz* means *quick to the plunder, swift to the spoil*; also in verse 3. [g] 9 Or *Do your worst* [h] 10 Hebrew *Immanuel*

everything that these people call
conspiracy[a];
do not fear what they fear,
and do not dread it.
13The LORD Almighty is the one you are to
regard as holy,
he is the one you are to fear,
he is the one you are to dread,
14and he will be a sanctuary;
but for both houses of Israel he will be
a stone that causes men to stumble
and a rock that makes them fall.
And for the people of Jerusalem he will be
a trap and a snare.
15Many of them will stumble;
they will fall and be broken,
they will be snared and captured."

16Bind up the testimony
and seal up the law among my disciples.
17I will wait for the LORD,
who is hiding his face from the house of
Jacob.
I will put my trust in him.

18Here am I, and the children the LORD has
given me. We are signs and symbols in Israel
from the LORD Almighty, who dwells on Mount
Zion.
19When men tell you to consult mediums and
spiritists, who whisper and mutter, should not a
people inquire of their God? Why consult the
dead on behalf of the living? 20To the law and to
the testimony! If they do not speak according to
this word, they have no light of dawn. 21Dis-
tressed and hungry, they will roam through the
land; when they are famished, they will become
enraged and, looking upward, will curse their
king and their God. 22Then they will look toward
the earth and see only distress and darkness and
fearful gloom, and they will be thrust into utter
darkness.

To Us a Child Is Born

9 Nevertheless, there will be no more gloom
for those who were in distress. In the past he
humbled the land of Zebulun and the land of
Naphtali, but in the future he will honor Galilee
of the Gentiles, by the way of the sea, along the
Jordan—

2The people walking in darkness
have seen a great light;
on those living in the land of the shadow of
death[b]
a light has dawned.
3You have enlarged the nation
and increased their joy;
they rejoice before you
as people rejoice at the harvest,
as men rejoice
when dividing the plunder.
4For as in the day of Midian's defeat,
you have shattered
the yoke that burdens them,
the bar across their shoulders,
the rod of their oppressor.
5Every warrior's boot used in battle
and every garment rolled in blood
will be destined for burning,
will be fuel for the fire.
6For to us a child is born,
to us a son is given,
and the government will be on his
shoulders.
And he will be called
Wonderful Counselor,[c] Mighty God,
Everlasting Father, Prince of Peace.
7Of the increase of his government and peace
there will be no end.
He will reign on David's throne
and over his kingdom,
establishing and upholding it
with justice and righteousness
from that time on and forever.
The zeal of the LORD Almighty
will accomplish this.

The LORD's Anger Against Israel

8The Lord has sent a message against Jacob;
it will fall on Israel.
9All the people will know it—
Ephraim and the inhabitants of Samaria—
who say with pride
and arrogance of heart,
10"The bricks have fallen down,
but we will rebuild with dressed stone;
the fig trees have been felled,
but we will replace them with cedars."
11But the LORD has strengthened Rezin's foes
against them
and has spurred their enemies on.
12Arameans from the east and Philistines from
the west
have devoured Israel with open mouth.

Yet for all this, his anger is not turned away,
his hand is still upraised.

13But the people have not returned to him who
struck them,
nor have they sought the LORD Almighty.
14So the LORD will cut off from Israel both
head and tail,
both palm branch and reed in a single day;

[a] 12 Or *Do not call for a treaty / every time these people call for a treaty* [b] 2 Or *land of darkness* [c] 6 Or *Wonderful, Counselor*

15the elders and prominent men are the head,
the prophets who teach lies are the tail.
16Those who guide this people mislead them,
and those who are guided are led astray.
17Therefore the Lord will take no pleasure in the young men,
nor will he pity the fatherless and widows,
for everyone is ungodly and wicked,
every mouth speaks vileness.

Yet for all this, his anger is not turned away,
his hand is still upraised.

18Surely wickedness burns like a fire;
it consumes briers and thorns,
it sets the forest thickets ablaze,
so that it rolls upward in a column of smoke.
19By the wrath of the LORD Almighty
the land will be scorched
and the people will be fuel for the fire;
no one will spare his brother.
20On the right they will devour,
but still be hungry;
on the left they will eat,
but not be satisfied.
Each will feed on the flesh of his own offspring[a]:
21 Manasseh will feed on Ephraim, and Ephraim on Manasseh;
together they will turn against Judah.

Yet for all this, his anger is not turned away,
his hand is still upraised.

10 Woe to those who make unjust laws,
to those who issue oppressive decrees,
2to deprive the poor of their rights
and withhold justice from the oppressed of my people,
making widows their prey
and robbing the fatherless.
3What will you do on the day of reckoning,
when disaster comes from afar?
To whom will you run for help?
Where will you leave your riches?
4Nothing will remain but to cringe among the captives
or fall among the slain.

Yet for all this, his anger is not turned away,
his hand is still upraised.

God's Judgment on Assyria

5"Woe to the Assyrian, the rod of my anger,
in whose hand is the club of my wrath!
6I send him against a godless nation,
I dispatch him against a people who anger me,
to seize loot and snatch plunder,
and to trample them down like mud in the streets.
7But this is not what he intends,
this is not what he has in mind;
his purpose is to destroy,
to put an end to many nations.
8'Are not my commanders all kings?' he says.
9 'Has not Calno fared like Carchemish?
Is not Hamath like Arpad,
and Samaria like Damascus?
10As my hand seized the kingdoms of the idols,
kingdoms whose images excelled those of Jerusalem and Samaria—
11shall I not deal with Jerusalem and her images
as I dealt with Samaria and her idols?'"

12When the Lord has finished all his work
against Mount Zion and Jerusalem, he will say, "I
will punish the king of Assyria for the willful
pride of his heart and the haughty look in his
eyes. 13For he says:

"'By the strength of my hand I have done this,
and by my wisdom, because I have understanding.
I removed the boundaries of nations,
I plundered their treasures;
like a mighty one I subdued[b] their kings.
14As one reaches into a nest,
so my hand reached for the wealth of the nations;
as men gather abandoned eggs,
so I gathered all the countries;
not one flapped a wing,
or opened its mouth to chirp.'"

15Does the ax raise itself above him who swings it,
or the saw boast against him who uses it?
As if a rod were to wield him who lifts it up,
or a club brandish him who is not wood!
16Therefore, the Lord, the LORD Almighty,
will send a wasting disease upon his sturdy warriors;
under his pomp a fire will be kindled
like a blazing flame.
17The Light of Israel will become a fire,
their Holy One a flame;
in a single day it will burn and consume
his thorns and his briers.
18The splendor of his forests and fertile fields
it will completely destroy,
as when a sick man wastes away.

a20 Or *arm* b13 Or / *I subdued the mighty,*

19 And the remaining trees of his forests will be so few
that a child could write them down.

The Remnant of Israel

20 In that day the remnant of Israel,
the survivors of the house of Jacob,
will no longer rely on him
who struck them down
but will truly rely on the LORD,
the Holy One of Israel.
21 A remnant will return,[a] a remnant of Jacob
will return to the Mighty God.
22 Though your people, O Israel, be like the sand by the sea,
only a remnant will return.
Destruction has been decreed,
overwhelming and righteous.
23 The Lord, the LORD Almighty, will carry out
the destruction decreed upon the whole land.

24 Therefore, this is what the Lord, the LORD Almighty, says:

"O my people who live in Zion,
do not be afraid of the Assyrians,
who beat you with a rod
and lift up a club against you, as Egypt did.
25 Very soon my anger against you will end
and my wrath will be directed to their destruction."
26 The LORD Almighty will lash them with a whip,
as when he struck down Midian at the rock of Oreb;
and he will raise his staff over the waters,
as he did in Egypt.
27 In that day their burden will be lifted from your shoulders,
their yoke from your neck;
the yoke will be broken
because you have grown so fat.[b]

28 They enter Aiath;
they pass through Migron;
they store supplies at Micmash.
29 They go over the pass, and say,
"We will camp overnight at Geba."
Ramah trembles;
Gibeah of Saul flees.
30 Cry out, O Daughter of Gallim!
Listen, O Laishah!
Poor Anathoth!
31 Madmenah is in flight;
the people of Gebim take cover.
32 This day they will halt at Nob;
they will shake their fist
at the mount of the Daughter of Zion,
at the hill of Jerusalem.

33 See, the Lord, the LORD Almighty,
will lop off the boughs with great power.
The lofty trees will be felled,
the tall ones will be brought low.
34 He will cut down the forest thickets with an ax;
Lebanon will fall before the Mighty One.

The Branch From Jesse

11 A shoot will come up from the stump of Jesse;
from his roots a Branch will bear fruit.
2 The Spirit of the LORD will rest on him—
the Spirit of wisdom and of understanding,
the Spirit of counsel and of power,
the Spirit of knowledge and of the fear of the LORD—
3 and he will delight in the fear of the LORD.

He will not judge by what he sees with his eyes,
or decide by what he hears with his ears;
4 but with righteousness he will judge the needy,
with justice he will give decisions for the poor of the earth.
He will strike the earth with the rod of his mouth;
with the breath of his lips he will slay the wicked.
5 Righteousness will be his belt
and faithfulness the sash around his waist.

6 The wolf will live with the lamb,
the leopard will lie down with the goat,
the calf and the lion and the yearling[c] together;
and a little child will lead them.
7 The cow will feed with the bear,
their young will lie down together,
and the lion will eat straw like the ox.
8 The infant will play near the hole of the cobra,
and the young child put his hand into the viper's nest.
9 They will neither harm nor destroy
on all my holy mountain,
for the earth will be full of the knowledge of the LORD
as the waters cover the sea.

10 In that day the Root of Jesse will stand as a
banner for the peoples; the nations will rally to
him, and his place of rest will be glorious. 11 In

[a] 21 Hebrew *shear-jashub*; also in verse 22 [b] 27 Hebrew; Septuagint *broken / from your shoulders* [c] 6 Hebrew; Septuagint *lion will feed*

that day the Lord will reach out his hand a second time to reclaim the remnant that is left of his people from Assyria, from Lower Egypt, from Upper Egypt,[a] from Cush,[b] from Elam, from Babylonia,[c] from Hamath and from the islands of the sea.

12He will raise a banner for the nations
and gather the exiles of Israel;
he will assemble the scattered people of Judah
from the four quarters of the earth.
13Ephraim's jealousy will vanish,
and Judah's enemies[d] will be cut off;
Ephraim will not be jealous of Judah,
nor Judah hostile toward Ephraim.
14They will swoop down on the slopes of Philistia to the west;
together they will plunder the people to the east.
They will lay hands on Edom and Moab,
and the Ammonites will be subject to them.
15The LORD will dry up
the gulf of the Egyptian sea;
with a scorching wind he will sweep his hand
over the Euphrates River.[e]
He will break it up into seven streams
so that men can cross over in sandals.
16There will be a highway for the remnant of his people
that is left from Assyria,
as there was for Israel
when they came up from Egypt.

Songs of Praise

12 In that day you will say:

"I will praise you, O LORD.
Although you were angry with me,
your anger has turned away
and you have comforted me.
2Surely God is my salvation;
I will trust and not be afraid.
The LORD, the LORD, is my strength and my song;
he has become my salvation."
3With joy you will draw water
from the wells of salvation.

4In that day you will say:

"Give thanks to the LORD, call on his name;
make known among the nations what he has done,
and proclaim that his name is exalted.
5Sing to the LORD, for he has done glorious things;
let this be known to all the world.
6Shout aloud and sing for joy, people of Zion,
for great is the Holy One of Israel among you."

A Prophecy Against Babylon

13 An oracle concerning Babylon that Isaiah son of Amoz saw:

2Raise a banner on a bare hilltop,
shout to them;
beckon to them
to enter the gates of the nobles.
3I have commanded my holy ones;
I have summoned my warriors to carry out my wrath—
those who rejoice in my triumph.
4Listen, a noise on the mountains,
like that of a great multitude!
Listen, an uproar among the kingdoms,
like nations massing together!
The LORD Almighty is mustering
an army for war.
5They come from faraway lands,
from the ends of the heavens—
the LORD and the weapons of his wrath—
to destroy the whole country.

6Wail, for the day of the LORD is near;
it will come like destruction from the Almighty.[f]
7Because of this, all hands will go limp,
every man's heart will melt.
8Terror will seize them,
pain and anguish will grip them;
they will writhe like a woman in labor.
They will look aghast at each other,
their faces aflame.

9See, the day of the LORD is coming
—a cruel day, with wrath and fierce anger—
to make the land desolate
and destroy the sinners within it.
10The stars of heaven and their constellations
will not show their light.
The rising sun will be darkened
and the moon will not give its light.
11I will punish the world for its evil,
the wicked for their sins.
I will put an end to the arrogance of the haughty
and will humble the pride of the ruthless.
12I will make man scarcer than pure gold,
more rare than the gold of Ophir.

a11 Hebrew *from Pathros* b11 That is, the upper Nile region c11 Hebrew *Shinar* d13 Or *hostility* e15 Hebrew *the River* f6 Hebrew *Shaddai*

13Therefore I will make the heavens tremble;
and the earth will shake from its place
at the wrath of the LORD Almighty,
in the day of his burning anger.
14Like a hunted gazelle,
like sheep without a shepherd,
each will return to his own people,
each will flee to his native land.
15Whoever is captured will be thrust through;
all who are caught will fall by the sword.
16Their infants will be dashed to pieces before their eyes;
their houses will be looted and their wives ravished.

17See, I will stir up against them the Medes,
who do not care for silver
and have no delight in gold.
18Their bows will strike down the young men;
they will have no mercy on infants
nor will they look with compassion on children.
19Babylon, the jewel of kingdoms,
the glory of the Babylonians'[a] pride,
will be overthrown by God
like Sodom and Gomorrah.
20She will never be inhabited
or lived in through all generations;
no Arab will pitch his tent there,
no shepherd will rest his flocks there.
21But desert creatures will lie there,
jackals will fill her houses;
there the owls will dwell,
and there the wild goats will leap about.
22Hyenas will howl in her strongholds,
jackals in her luxurious palaces.
Her time is at hand,
and her days will not be prolonged.

14 The LORD will have compassion on Jacob;
once again he will choose Israel
and will settle them in their own land.
Aliens will join them
and unite with the house of Jacob.
2Nations will take them
and bring them to their own place.
And the house of Israel will possess the nations
as menservants and maidservants in the LORD's land.
They will make captives of their captors
and rule over their oppressors.

3On the day the LORD gives you relief from
suffering and turmoil and cruel bondage, 4you
will take up this taunt against the king of Babylon:

How the oppressor has come to an end!
How his fury[b] has ended!
5The LORD has broken the rod of the wicked,
the scepter of the rulers,
6which in anger struck down peoples
with unceasing blows,
and in fury subdued nations
with relentless aggression.
7All the lands are at rest and at peace;
they break into singing.
8Even the pine trees and the cedars of Lebanon
exult over you and say,
"Now that you have been laid low,
no woodsman comes to cut us down."
9The grave[c] below is all astir
to meet you at your coming;
it rouses the spirits of the departed to greet you—
all those who were leaders in the world;
it makes them rise from their thrones—
all those who were kings over the nations.
10They will all respond,
they will say to you,
"You also have become weak, as we are;
you have become like us."
11All your pomp has been brought down to the grave,
along with the noise of your harps;
maggots are spread out beneath you
and worms cover you.

12How you have fallen from heaven,
O morning star, son of the dawn!
You have been cast down to the earth,
you who once laid low the nations!
13You said in your heart,
"I will ascend to heaven;
I will raise my throne
above the stars of God;
I will sit enthroned on the mount of assembly,
on the utmost heights of the sacred mountain.[d]
14I will ascend above the tops of the clouds;
I will make myself like the Most High."
15But you are brought down to the grave,
to the depths of the pit.

16Those who see you stare at you,
they ponder your fate:
"Is this the man who shook the earth
and made kingdoms tremble,
17the man who made the world a desert,

[a] 19 Or *Chaldeans'* [b] 4 Dead Sea Scrolls, Septuagint and Syriac; the meaning of the word in the Masoretic Text is uncertain. [c] 9 Hebrew *Sheol*; also in verses 11 and 15 [d] 13 Or *the north*; Hebrew *Zaphon*

who overthrew its cities
and would not let his captives go home?"
18All the kings of the nations lie in state,
each in his own tomb.
19But you are cast out of your tomb
like a rejected branch;
you are covered with the slain,
with those pierced by the sword,
those who descend to the stones of the pit.
Like a corpse trampled underfoot,
20 you will not join them in burial,
for you have destroyed your land
and killed your people.

The offspring of the wicked
will never be mentioned again.
21Prepare a place to slaughter his sons
for the sins of their forefathers;
they are not to rise to inherit the land
and cover the earth with their cities.
22"I will rise up against them,"
declares the LORD Almighty.
"I will cut off from Babylon her name and survivors,
her offspring and descendants,"
declares the LORD.
23"I will turn her into a place for owls
and into swampland;
I will sweep her with the broom of destruction,"
declares the LORD Almighty.

A Prophecy Against Assyria

24The LORD Almighty has sworn,
"Surely, as I have planned, so it will be,
and as I have purposed, so it will stand.
25I will crush the Assyrian in my land;
on my mountains I will trample him down.
His yoke will be taken from my people,
and his burden removed from their shoulders."

26This is the plan determined for the whole world;
this is the hand stretched out over all nations.
27For the LORD Almighty has purposed, and who can thwart him?
His hand is stretched out, and who can turn it back?

A Prophecy Against the Philistines

28This oracle came in the year King Ahaz died:

29Do not rejoice, all you Philistines,
that the rod that struck you is broken;
from the root of that snake will spring up a viper,
its fruit will be a darting, venomous serpent.
30The poorest of the poor will find pasture,
and the needy will lie down in safety.
But your root I will destroy by famine;
it will slay your survivors.

31Wail, O gate! Howl, O city!
Melt away, all you Philistines!
A cloud of smoke comes from the north,
and there is not a straggler in its ranks.
32What answer shall be given
to the envoys of that nation?
"The LORD has established Zion,
and in her his afflicted people will find refuge."

A Prophecy Against Moab

15 An oracle concerning Moab:

Ar in Moab is ruined,
destroyed in a night!
Kir in Moab is ruined,
destroyed in a night!
2Dibon goes up to its temple,
to its high places to weep;
Moab wails over Nebo and Medeba.
Every head is shaved
and every beard cut off.
3In the streets they wear sackcloth;
on the roofs and in the public squares
they all wail,
prostrate with weeping.
4Heshbon and Elealeh cry out,
their voices are heard all the way to Jahaz.
Therefore the armed men of Moab cry out,
and their hearts are faint.

5My heart cries out over Moab;
her fugitives flee as far as Zoar,
as far as Eglath Shelishiyah.
They go up the way to Luhith,
weeping as they go;
on the road to Horonaim
they lament their destruction.
6The waters of Nimrim are dried up
and the grass is withered;
the vegetation is gone
and nothing green is left.
7So the wealth they have acquired and stored up
they carry away over the Ravine of the Poplars.
8Their outcry echoes along the border of Moab;
their wailing reaches as far as Eglaim,
their lamentation as far as Beer Elim.

9Dimon's[a] waters are full of blood,
but I will bring still more upon
Dimon[a]—
a lion upon the fugitives of Moab
and upon those who remain in the land.

16 Send lambs as tribute
to the ruler of the land,
from Sela, across the desert,
to the mount of the Daughter of Zion.
2Like fluttering birds
pushed from the nest,
so are the women of Moab
at the fords of the Arnon.

3"Give us counsel,
render a decision.
Make your shadow like night—
at high noon.
Hide the fugitives,
do not betray the refugees.
4Let the Moabite fugitives stay with you;
be their shelter from the destroyer."

The oppressor will come to an end,
and destruction will cease;
the aggressor will vanish from the land.
5In love a throne will be established;
in faithfulness a man will sit on it—
one from the house[b] of David—
one who in judging seeks justice
and speeds the cause of righteousness.

6We have heard of Moab's pride—
her overweening pride and conceit,
her pride and her insolence—
but her boasts are empty.
7Therefore the Moabites wail,
they wail together for Moab.
Lament and grieve
for the men[c] of Kir Hareseth.
8The fields of Heshbon wither,
the vines of Sibmah also.
The rulers of the nations
have trampled down the choicest vines,
which once reached Jazer
and spread toward the desert.
Their shoots spread out
and went as far as the sea.
9So I weep, as Jazer weeps,
for the vines of Sibmah.
O Heshbon, O Elealeh,
I drench you with tears!
The shouts of joy over your ripened fruit
and over your harvests have been stilled.
10Joy and gladness are taken away from the
orchards;
no one sings or shouts in the vineyards;
no one treads out wine at the presses,
for I have put an end to the shouting.
11My heart laments for Moab like a harp,
my inmost being for Kir Hareseth.
12When Moab appears at her high place,
she only wears herself out;
when she goes to her shrine to pray,
it is to no avail.

13This is the word the LORD has already spo
ken concerning Moab. 14But now the LORD says
"Within three years, as a servant bound by con
tract would count them, Moab's splendor and al
her many people will be despised, and her survi
vors will be very few and feeble."

An Oracle Against Damascus

17 An oracle concerning Damascus:

"See, Damascus will no longer be a city
but will become a heap of ruins.
2The cities of Aroer will be deserted
and left to flocks, which will lie down,
with no one to make them afraid.
3The fortified city will disappear from Ephraim,
and royal power from Damascus;
the remnant of Aram will be
like the glory of the Israelites,"
declares the LORD Almighty.

4"In that day the glory of Jacob will fade;
the fat of his body will waste away.
5It will be as when a reaper gathers the
standing grain
and harvests the grain with his arm—
as when a man gleans heads of grain
in the Valley of Rephaim.
6Yet some gleanings will remain,
as when an olive tree is beaten,
leaving two or three olives on the topmost
branches,
four or five on the fruitful boughs,"
declares the LORD,
the God of Israel.

7In that day men will look to their Maker
and turn their eyes to the Holy One of
Israel.
8They will not look to the altars,
the work of their hands,
and they will have no regard for the Asherah
poles[d]
and the incense altars their fingers have
made.

9In that day their strong cities, which they left
because of the Israelites, will be like places aban-

[a]9 Masoretic Text; Dead Sea Scrolls, some Septuagint manuscripts and Vulgate *Dibon* [b]5 Hebrew *tent* [c]7 Or "*raisin cakes*," a wordplay [d]8 That is, symbols of the goddess Asherah

doned to thickets and undergrowth. And all will be desolation.

[10]You have forgotten God your Savior;
you have not remembered the Rock, your fortress.
Therefore, though you set out the finest plants
and plant imported vines,
[11]though on the day you set them out, you make them grow,
and on the morning when you plant them, you bring them to bud,
yet the harvest will be as nothing
in the day of disease and incurable pain.
[12]Oh, the raging of many nations—
they rage like the raging sea!
Oh, the uproar of the peoples—
they roar like the roaring of great waters!
[13]Although the peoples roar like the roar of surging waters,
when he rebukes them they flee far away,
driven before the wind like chaff on the hills,
like tumbleweed before a gale.
[14]In the evening, sudden terror!
Before the morning, they are gone!
This is the portion of those who loot us,
the lot of those who plunder us.

A Prophecy Against Cush

18 Woe to the land of whirring wings[a]
along the rivers of Cush,[b]
[2]which sends envoys by sea
in papyrus boats over the water.

Go, swift messengers,
to a people tall and smooth-skinned,
to a people feared far and wide,
an aggressive nation of strange speech,
whose land is divided by rivers.

[3]All you people of the world,
you who live on the earth,
when a banner is raised on the mountains,
you will see it,
and when a trumpet sounds,
you will hear it.
[4]This is what the LORD says to me:
"I will remain quiet and will look on from my dwelling place,
like shimmering heat in the sunshine,
like a cloud of dew in the heat of harvest."
[5]For, before the harvest, when the blossom is gone
and the flower becomes a ripening grape,
he will cut off the shoots with pruning knives,
and cut down and take away the spreading branches.
[6]They will all be left to the mountain birds of prey
and to the wild animals;
the birds will feed on them all summer,
the wild animals all winter.

[7]At that time gifts will be brought to the LORD Almighty

from a people tall and smooth-skinned,
from a people feared far and wide,
an aggressive nation of strange speech,
whose land is divided by rivers—

the gifts will be brought to Mount Zion, the place of the Name of the LORD Almighty.

A Prophecy About Egypt

19 An oracle concerning Egypt:

See, the LORD rides on a swift cloud
and is coming to Egypt.
The idols of Egypt tremble before him,
and the hearts of the Egyptians melt within them.

[2]"I will stir up Egyptian against Egyptian—
brother will fight against brother,
neighbor against neighbor,
city against city,
kingdom against kingdom.
[3]The Egyptians will lose heart,
and I will bring their plans to nothing;
they will consult the idols and the spirits of the dead,
the mediums and the spiritists.
[4]I will hand the Egyptians over
to the power of a cruel master,
and a fierce king will rule over them,"
declares the Lord, the LORD Almighty.

[5]The waters of the river will dry up,
and the riverbed will be parched and dry.
[6]The canals will stink;
the streams of Egypt will dwindle and dry up.
The reeds and rushes will wither,
[7] also the plants along the Nile,
at the mouth of the river.
Every sown field along the Nile
will become parched, will blow away and be no more.
[8]The fishermen will groan and lament,
all who cast hooks into the Nile;
those who throw nets on the water
will pine away.

[a]1 Or *of locusts* [b]1 That is, the upper Nile region

9Those who work with combed flax will despair,
the weavers of fine linen will lose hope.
10The workers in cloth will be dejected,
and all the wage earners will be sick at heart.

11The officials of Zoan are nothing but fools;
the wise counselors of Pharaoh give senseless advice.
How can you say to Pharaoh,
"I am one of the wise men,
a disciple of the ancient kings"?

12Where are your wise men now?
Let them show you and make known
what the LORD Almighty
has planned against Egypt.
13The officials of Zoan have become fools,
the leaders of Memphis[a] are deceived;
the cornerstones of her peoples
have led Egypt astray.
14The LORD has poured into them
a spirit of dizziness;
they make Egypt stagger in all that she does,
as a drunkard staggers around in his vomit.
15There is nothing Egypt can do—
head or tail, palm branch or reed.

16In that day the Egyptians will be like women.
They will shudder with fear at the uplifted hand
that the LORD Almighty raises against them.
17And the land of Judah will bring terror to the
Egyptians; everyone to whom Judah is mentioned
will be terrified, because of what the LORD Almighty is planning against them.
18In that day five cities in Egypt will speak the
language of Canaan and swear allegiance to the
LORD Almighty. One of them will be called the
City of Destruction.[b]
19In that day there will be an altar to the LORD
in the heart of Egypt, and a monument to the
LORD at its border. 20It will be a sign and witness
to the LORD Almighty in the land of Egypt. When
they cry out to the LORD because of their oppressors, he will send them a savior and defender,
and he will rescue them. 21So the LORD will make
himself known to the Egyptians, and in that day
they will acknowledge the LORD. They will worship with sacrifices and grain offerings; they will
make vows to the LORD and keep them. 22The
LORD will strike Egypt with a plague; he will
strike them and heal them. They will turn to the
LORD, and he will respond to their pleas and heal
them.
23In that day there will be a highway from
Egypt to Assyria. The Assyrians will go to Egypt
and the Egyptians to Assyria. The Egyptians and
Assyrians will worship together. 24In that day Israel will be the third, along with Egypt and Assyria, a blessing on the earth. 25The LORD Almighty
will bless them, saying, "Blessed be Egypt my
people, Assyria my handiwork, and Israel my inheritance."

A Prophecy Against Egypt and Cush

20 In the year that the supreme commander,
sent by Sargon king of Assyria, came to
Ashdod and attacked and captured it— 2at that
time the LORD spoke through Isaiah son of Amoz.
He said to him, "Take off the sackcloth from your
body and the sandals from your feet." And he did
so, going around stripped and barefoot.
3Then the LORD said, "Just as my servant Isaiah has gone stripped and barefoot for three
years, as a sign and portent against Egypt and
Cush,[c] 4so the king of Assyria will lead away
stripped and barefoot the Egyptian captives and
Cushite exiles, young and old, with buttocks
bared—to Egypt's shame. 5Those who trusted in
Cush and boasted in Egypt will be afraid and put
to shame. 6In that day the people who live on this
coast will say, 'See what has happened to those
we relied on, those we fled to for help and deliverance from the king of Assyria! How then can
we escape?' "

A Prophecy Against Babylon

21 An oracle concerning the Desert by the Sea:

Like whirlwinds sweeping through the southland,
an invader comes from the desert,
from a land of terror.
2A dire vision has been shown to me:
The traitor betrays, the looter takes loot.
Elam, attack! Media, lay siege!
I will bring to an end all the groaning she caused.
3At this my body is racked with pain,
pangs seize me, like those of a woman in labor;
I am staggered by what I hear,
I am bewildered by what I see.
4My heart falters,
fear makes me tremble;
the twilight I longed for
has become a horror to me.

5They set the tables,
they spread the rugs,
they eat, they drink!

[a] 13 Hebrew *Noph* [b] 18 Most manuscripts of the Masoretic Text; some manuscripts of the Masoretic Text, Dead Sea Scrolls and Vulgate *City of the Sun* (that is, Heliopolis) [c] 3 That is, the upper Nile region; also in verse 5

Get up, you officers,
oil the shields!

6This is what the Lord says to me:

"Go, post a lookout
and have him report what he sees.
7When he sees chariots
with teams of horses,
riders on donkeys
or riders on camels,
let him be alert,
fully alert."

8And the lookout[a] shouted,

"Day after day, my lord, I stand on the watchtower;
every night I stay at my post.
9Look, here comes a man in a chariot
with a team of horses.
And he gives back the answer:
'Babylon has fallen, has fallen!
All the images of its gods
lie shattered on the ground!' "

10O my people, crushed on the threshing floor,
I tell you what I have heard
from the LORD Almighty,
from the God of Israel.

A Prophecy Against Edom

11An oracle concerning Dumah[b]:

Someone calls to me from Seir,
"Watchman, what is left of the night?
Watchman, what is left of the night?"
12The watchman replies,
"Morning is coming, but also the night.
If you would ask, then ask;
and come back yet again."

A Prophecy Against Arabia

13An oracle concerning Arabia:

You caravans of Dedanites,
who camp in the thickets of Arabia,
14 bring water for the thirsty;
you who live in Tema,
bring food for the fugitives.
15They flee from the sword,
from the drawn sword,
from the bent bow
and from the heat of battle.

16This is what the Lord says to me: "Within
one year, as a servant bound by contract would
count it, all the pomp of Kedar will come to an
end. 17The survivors of the bowmen, the warriors of Kedar, will be few." The LORD, the God
of Israel, has spoken.

A Prophecy About Jerusalem

22 An oracle concerning the Valley of Vision:

What troubles you now,
that you have all gone up on the roofs,
2O town full of commotion,
O city of tumult and revelry?
Your slain were not killed by the sword,
nor did they die in battle.
3All your leaders have fled together;
they have been captured without using the bow.
All you who were caught were taken prisoner together,
having fled while the enemy was still far away.
4Therefore I said, "Turn away from me;
let me weep bitterly.
Do not try to console me
over the destruction of my people."

5The Lord, the LORD Almighty, has a day
of tumult and trampling and terror
in the Valley of Vision,
a day of battering down walls
and of crying out to the mountains.
6Elam takes up the quiver,
with her charioteers and horses;
Kir uncovers the shield.
7Your choicest valleys are full of chariots,
and horsemen are posted at the city gates;
8 the defenses of Judah are stripped away.

And you looked in that day
to the weapons in the Palace of the Forest;
9you saw that the City of David
had many breaches in its defenses;
you stored up water
in the Lower Pool.
10You counted the buildings in Jerusalem
and tore down houses to strengthen the wall.
11You built a reservoir between the two walls
for the water of the Old Pool,
but you did not look to the One who made it,
or have regard for the One who planned it long ago.

12The Lord, the LORD Almighty,
called you on that day
to weep and to wail,
to tear out your hair and put on sackcloth.
13But see, there is joy and revelry,
slaughtering of cattle and killing of sheep,
eating of meat and drinking of wine!

[a]8 Dead Sea Scrolls and Syriac; Masoretic Text *A lion* [b]11 *Dumah* means *silence* or *stillness*, a wordplay on *Edom*.

"Let us eat and drink," you say,
"for tomorrow we die!"

14 The LORD Almighty has revealed this in my
hearing: "Till your dying day this sin will not be
atoned for," says the Lord, the LORD Almighty.

15 This is what the Lord, the LORD Almighty,
says:

"Go, say to this steward,
to Shebna, who is in charge of the palace:
16 What are you doing here and who gave you
permission
to cut out a grave for yourself here,
hewing your grave on the height
and chiseling your resting place in the
rock?

17 "Beware, the LORD is about to take firm hold
of you
and hurl you away, O you mighty man.
18 He will roll you up tightly like a ball
and throw you into a large country.
There you will die
and there your splendid chariots will
remain—
you disgrace to your master's house!
19 I will depose you from your office,
and you will be ousted from your position.

20 "In that day I will summon my servant, Eliakim son of Hilkiah. 21 I will clothe him with your
robe and fasten your sash around him and hand
your authority over to him. He will be a father to
those who live in Jerusalem and to the house of
Judah. 22 I will place on his shoulder the key to
the house of David; what he opens no one can
shut, and what he shuts no one can open. 23 I will
drive him like a peg into a firm place; he will be
a seat[a] of honor for the house of his father. 24 All
the glory of his family will hang on him: its offspring and offshoots—all its lesser vessels, from
the bowls to all the jars.

25 "In that day," declares the LORD Almighty,
"the peg driven into the firm place will give way;
it will be sheared off and will fall, and the load
hanging on it will be cut down." The LORD has
spoken.

A Prophecy About Tyre

23 An oracle concerning Tyre:

Wail, O ships of Tarshish!
For Tyre is destroyed
and left without house or harbor.
From the land of Cyprus[b]
word has come to them.

2 Be silent, you people of the island
and you merchants of Sidon,
whom the seafarers have enriched.
3 On the great waters
came the grain of the Shihor;
the harvest of the Nile[c] was the revenue of
Tyre,
and she became the marketplace of the
nations.

4 Be ashamed, O Sidon, and you, O fortress of
the sea,
for the sea has spoken:
"I have neither been in labor nor given birth;
I have neither reared sons nor brought up
daughters."
5 When word comes to Egypt,
they will be in anguish at the report from
Tyre.

6 Cross over to Tarshish;
wail, you people of the island.
7 Is this your city of revelry,
the old, old city,
whose feet have taken her
to settle in far-off lands?
8 Who planned this against Tyre,
the bestower of crowns,
whose merchants are princes,
whose traders are renowned in the earth?
9 The LORD Almighty planned it,
to bring low the pride of all glory
and to humble all who are renowned on
the earth.

10 Till[d] your land as along the Nile,
O Daughter of Tarshish,
for you no longer have a harbor.
11 The LORD has stretched out his hand over
the sea
and made its kingdoms tremble.
He has given an order concerning
Phoenicia[e]
that her fortresses be destroyed.
12 He said, "No more of your reveling,
O Virgin Daughter of Sidon, now crushed!

"Up, cross over to Cyprus[b];
even there you will find no rest."
13 Look at the land of the Babylonians,[f]
this people that is now of no account!
The Assyrians have made it
a place for desert creatures;
they raised up their siege towers,

[a] 23 Or *throne* [b] 1,12 Hebrew *Kittim* [c] 2,3 Masoretic Text; one Dead Sea Scroll *Sidon, / who cross over the sea; / your envoys* 3*are on the great waters. / The grain of the Shihor, / the harvest of the Nile,* [d] 10 Dead Sea Scrolls and some Septuagint manuscripts; Masoretic Text *Go through* [e] 11 Hebrew *Canaan* [f] 13 Or *Chaldeans*

they stripped its fortresses bare
and turned it into a ruin.

14Wail, you ships of Tarshish;
your fortress is destroyed!

15At that time Tyre will be forgotten for seventy years, the span of a king's life. But at the end of these seventy years, it will happen to Tyre as in the song of the prostitute:

16"Take up a harp, walk through the city,
O prostitute forgotten;
play the harp well, sing many a song,
so that you will be remembered."

17At the end of seventy years, the LORD will deal with Tyre. She will return to her hire as a prostitute and will ply her trade with all the kingdoms on the face of the earth. 18Yet her profit and her earnings will be set apart for the LORD; they will not be stored up or hoarded. Her profits will go to those who live before the LORD, for abundant food and fine clothes.

The LORD's Devastation of the Earth

24 See, the LORD is going to lay waste the earth
and devastate it;
he will ruin its face
and scatter its inhabitants—
2it will be the same
for priest as for people,
for master as for servant,
for mistress as for maid,
for seller as for buyer,
for borrower as for lender,
for debtor as for creditor.
3The earth will be completely laid waste
and totally plundered.
The LORD has spoken this word.

4The earth dries up and withers,
the world languishes and withers,
the exalted of the earth languish.
5The earth is defiled by its people;
they have disobeyed the laws,
violated the statutes
and broken the everlasting covenant.
6Therefore a curse consumes the earth;
its people must bear their guilt.
Therefore earth's inhabitants are burned up,
and very few are left.
7The new wine dries up and the vine withers;
all the merrymakers groan.
8The gaiety of the tambourines is stilled,
the noise of the revelers has stopped,
the joyful harp is silent.
9No longer do they drink wine with a song;
the beer is bitter to its drinkers.
10The ruined city lies desolate;
the entrance to every house is barred.
11In the streets they cry out for wine;
all joy turns to gloom,
all gaiety is banished from the earth.
12The city is left in ruins,
its gate is battered to pieces.
13So will it be on the earth
and among the nations,
as when an olive tree is beaten,
or as when gleanings are left after the grape harvest.

14They raise their voices, they shout for joy;
from the west they acclaim the LORD's majesty.
15Therefore in the east give glory to the LORD;
exalt the name of the LORD, the God of Israel,
in the islands of the sea.
16From the ends of the earth we hear singing:
"Glory to the Righteous One."

But I said, "I waste away, I waste away!
Woe to me!
The treacherous betray!
With treachery the treacherous betray!"
17Terror and pit and snare await you,
O people of the earth.
18Whoever flees at the sound of terror
will fall into a pit;
whoever climbs out of the pit
will be caught in a snare.

The floodgates of the heavens are opened,
the foundations of the earth shake.
19The earth is broken up,
the earth is split asunder,
the earth is thoroughly shaken.
20The earth reels like a drunkard,
it sways like a hut in the wind;
so heavy upon it is the guilt of its rebellion
that it falls—never to rise again.

21In that day the LORD will punish
the powers in the heavens above
and the kings on the earth below.
22They will be herded together
like prisoners bound in a dungeon;
they will be shut up in prison
and be punished[a] after many days.
23The moon will be abashed, the sun ashamed;
for the LORD Almighty will reign
on Mount Zion and in Jerusalem,
and before its elders, gloriously.

a *22* Or *released*

Praise to the LORD

25 O LORD, you are my God;
I will exalt you and praise your name,
for in perfect faithfulness
you have done marvelous things,
things planned long ago.
2 You have made the city a heap of rubble,
the fortified town a ruin,
the foreigners' stronghold a city no more;
it will never be rebuilt.
3 Therefore strong peoples will honor you;
cities of ruthless nations will revere you.
4 You have been a refuge for the poor,
a refuge for the needy in his distress,
a shelter from the storm
and a shade from the heat.
For the breath of the ruthless
is like a storm driving against a wall
5 and like the heat of the desert.
You silence the uproar of foreigners;
as heat is reduced by the shadow of a cloud,
so the song of the ruthless is stilled.

6 On this mountain the LORD Almighty will prepare
a feast of rich food for all peoples,
a banquet of aged wine—
the best of meats and the finest of wines.
7 On this mountain he will destroy
the shroud that enfolds all peoples,
the sheet that covers all nations;
8 he will swallow up death forever.
The Sovereign LORD will wipe away the tears
from all faces;
he will remove the disgrace of his people
from all the earth.
The LORD has spoken.

9 In that day they will say,

"Surely this is our God;
we trusted in him, and he saved us.
This is the LORD, we trusted in him;
let us rejoice and be glad in his salvation."

10 The hand of the LORD will rest on this mountain;
but Moab will be trampled under him
as straw is trampled down in the manure.
11 They will spread out their hands in it,
as a swimmer spreads out his hands to swim.
God will bring down their pride
despite the cleverness[a] of their hands.
12 He will bring down your high fortified walls
and lay them low;
he will bring them down to the ground,
to the very dust.

A Song of Praise

26 In that day this song will be sung in the land of Judah:

We have a strong city;
God makes salvation
its walls and ramparts.
2 Open the gates
that the righteous nation may enter,
the nation that keeps faith.
3 You will keep in perfect peace
him whose mind is steadfast,
because he trusts in you.
4 Trust in the LORD forever,
for the LORD, the LORD, is the Rock eternal.
5 He humbles those who dwell on high,
he lays the lofty city low;
he levels it to the ground
and casts it down to the dust.
6 Feet trample it down—
the feet of the oppressed,
the footsteps of the poor.
7 The path of the righteous is level;
O upright One, you make the way of the righteous smooth.
8 Yes, LORD, walking in the way of your laws,[b]
we wait for you;
your name and renown
are the desire of our hearts.
9 My soul yearns for you in the night;
in the morning my spirit longs for you.
When your judgments come upon the earth,
the people of the world learn righteousness.
10 Though grace is shown to the wicked,
they do not learn righteousness;
even in a land of uprightness they go on doing evil
and regard not the majesty of the LORD.
11 O LORD, your hand is lifted high,
but they do not see it.
Let them see your zeal for your people and be put to shame;
let the fire reserved for your enemies consume them.
12 LORD, you establish peace for us;
all that we have accomplished you have done for us.
13 O LORD, our God, other lords besides you have ruled over us,
but your name alone do we honor.

[a] 11 The meaning of the Hebrew for this word is uncertain.
[b] 8 Or *judgments*

14They are now dead, they live no more;
those departed spirits do not rise.
You punished them and brought them to ruin;
you wiped out all memory of them.
15You have enlarged the nation, O LORD;
you have enlarged the nation.
You have gained glory for yourself;
you have extended all the borders of the land.

16LORD, they came to you in their distress;
when you disciplined them,
they could barely whisper a prayer.[a]
17As a woman with child and about to give birth
writhes and cries out in her pain,
so were we in your presence, O LORD.
18We were with child, we writhed in pain,
but we gave birth to wind.
We have not brought salvation to the earth;
we have not given birth to people of the world.

19But your dead will live;
their bodies will rise.
You who dwell in the dust,
wake up and shout for joy.
Your dew is like the dew of the morning;
the earth will give birth to her dead.

20Go, my people, enter your rooms
and shut the doors behind you;
hide yourselves for a little while
until his wrath has passed by.
21See, the LORD is coming out of his dwelling
to punish the people of the earth for their sins.
The earth will disclose the blood shed upon her;
she will conceal her slain no longer.

Deliverance of Israel

27 In that day,
the LORD will punish with his sword,
his fierce, great and powerful sword,
Leviathan the gliding serpent,
Leviathan the coiling serpent;
he will slay the monster of the sea.

2In that day—

"Sing about a fruitful vineyard:
3 I, the LORD, watch over it;
I water it continually.
I guard it day and night
so that no one may harm it.
4 I am not angry.
If only there were briers and thorns confronting me!
I would march against them in battle;
I would set them all on fire.
5Or else let them come to me for refuge;
let them make peace with me,
yes, let them make peace with me."

6In days to come Jacob will take root,
Israel will bud and blossom
and fill all the world with fruit.

7Has ⌞the LORD⌟ struck her
as he struck down those who struck her?
Has she been killed
as those were killed who killed her?
8By warfare[b] and exile you contend with her—
with his fierce blast he drives her out,
as on a day the east wind blows.
9By this, then, will Jacob's guilt be atoned for,
and this will be the full fruitage of the removal of his sin:
When he makes all the altar stones
to be like chalk stones crushed to pieces,
no Asherah poles[c] or incense altars
will be left standing.
10The fortified city stands desolate,
an abandoned settlement, forsaken like the desert;
there the calves graze,
there they lie down;
they strip its branches bare.
11When its twigs are dry, they are broken off
and women come and make fires with them.
For this is a people without understanding;
so their Maker has no compassion on them,
and their Creator shows them no favor.

12In that day the LORD will thresh from the
flowing Euphrates[d] to the Wadi of Egypt, and
you, O Israelites, will be gathered up one by one.
13And in that day a great trumpet will sound.
Those who were perishing in Assyria and those
who were exiled in Egypt will come and worship
the LORD on the holy mountain in Jerusalem.

Woe to Ephraim

28 Woe to that wreath, the pride of Ephraim's drunkards,
to the fading flower, his glorious beauty,
set on the head of a fertile valley—
to that city, the pride of those laid low by wine!
2See, the Lord has one who is powerful and strong.

[a] 16 The meaning of the Hebrew for this clause is uncertain. [b] 8 See Septuagint; the meaning of the Hebrew for this word is uncertain. [c] 9 That is, symbols of the goddess Asherah [d] 12 Hebrew *River*

Like a hailstorm and a destructive wind,
like a driving rain and a flooding downpour,
he will throw it forcefully to the ground.
3That wreath, the pride of Ephraim's drunkards,
will be trampled underfoot.
4That fading flower, his glorious beauty,
set on the head of a fertile valley,
will be like a fig ripe before harvest—
as soon as someone sees it and takes it in his hand,
he swallows it.
5In that day the LORD Almighty
will be a glorious crown,
a beautiful wreath
for the remnant of his people.
6He will be a spirit of justice
to him who sits in judgment,
a source of strength
to those who turn back the battle at the gate.

7And these also stagger from wine
and reel from beer:
Priests and prophets stagger from beer
and are befuddled with wine;
they reel from beer,
they stagger when seeing visions,
they stumble when rendering decisions.
8All the tables are covered with vomit
and there is not a spot without filth.

9"Who is it he is trying to teach?
To whom is he explaining his message?
To children weaned from their milk,
to those just taken from the breast?
10For it is:
Do and do, do and do,
rule on rule, rule on rule[a];
a little here, a little there."
11Very well then, with foreign lips and strange tongues
God will speak to this people,
12to whom he said,
"This is the resting place, let the weary rest";
and, "This is the place of repose"—
but they would not listen.
13So then, the word of the LORD to them will become:
Do and do, do and do,
rule on rule, rule on rule;
a little here, a little there—
so that they will go and fall backward,
be injured and snared and captured.

14Therefore hear the word of the LORD, you scoffers
who rule this people in Jerusalem.
15You boast, "We have entered into a covenant with death,
with the grave[b] we have made an agreement.
When an overwhelming scourge sweeps by,
it cannot touch us,
for we have made a lie our refuge
and falsehood[c] our hiding place."

16So this is what the Sovereign LORD says:
"See, I lay a stone in Zion,
a tested stone,
a precious cornerstone for a sure foundation;
the one who trusts will never be dismayed.
17I will make justice the measuring line
and righteousness the plumb line;
hail will sweep away your refuge, the lie,
and water will overflow your hiding place.
18Your covenant with death will be annulled;
your agreement with the grave will not stand.
When the overwhelming scourge sweeps by,
you will be beaten down by it.
19As often as it comes it will carry you away;
morning after morning, by day and by night,
it will sweep through."

The understanding of this message
will bring sheer terror.
20The bed is too short to stretch out on,
the blanket too narrow to wrap around you.
21The LORD will rise up as he did at Mount Perazim,
he will rouse himself as in the Valley of Gibeon—
to do his work, his strange work,
and perform his task, his alien task.
22Now stop your mocking,
or your chains will become heavier;
the Lord, the LORD Almighty, has told me
of the destruction decreed against the whole land.

23Listen and hear my voice;
pay attention and hear what I say.
24When a farmer plows for planting, does he plow continually?
Does he keep on breaking up and harrowing the soil?
25When he has leveled the surface,

[a] *10* Hebrew */ sav lasav sav lasav / kav lakav kav lakav* (possibly meaningless sounds; perhaps a mimicking of the prophet's words); also in verse 13
[b] *15* Hebrew *Sheol*; also in verse 18
[c] *15* Or *false gods*

does he not sow caraway and scatter
cummin?
Does he not plant wheat in its place,[a]
barley in its plot,[a]
and spelt in its field?
26His God instructs him
and teaches him the right way.

27Caraway is not threshed with a sledge,
nor is a cartwheel rolled over cummin;
caraway is beaten out with a rod,
and cummin with a stick.
28Grain must be ground to make bread;
so one does not go on threshing it forever.
Though he drives the wheels of his threshing
cart over it,
his horses do not grind it.
29All this also comes from the LORD Almighty,
wonderful in counsel and magnificent in
wisdom.

Woe to David's City

29 Woe to you, Ariel, Ariel,
the city where David settled!
Add year to year
and let your cycle of festivals go on.
2Yet I will besiege Ariel;
she will mourn and lament,
she will be to me like an altar hearth.[b]
3I will encamp against you all around;
I will encircle you with towers
and set up my siege works against you.
4Brought low, you will speak from the ground;
your speech will mumble out of the dust.
Your voice will come ghostlike from the
earth;
out of the dust your speech will whisper.
5But your many enemies will become like fine
dust,
the ruthless hordes like blown chaff.
Suddenly, in an instant,
6 the LORD Almighty will come
with thunder and earthquake and great noise,
with windstorm and tempest and flames of
a devouring fire.
7Then the hordes of all the nations that fight
against Ariel,
that attack her and her fortress and
besiege her,
will be as it is with a dream,
with a vision in the night—
8as when a hungry man dreams that he is
eating,
but he awakens, and his hunger remains;
as when a thirsty man dreams that he is
drinking,
but he awakens faint, with his thirst
unquenched.
So will it be with the hordes of all the
nations
that fight against Mount Zion.

9Be stunned and amazed,
blind yourselves and be sightless;
be drunk, but not from wine,
stagger, but not from beer.
10The LORD has brought over you a deep sleep:
He has sealed your eyes (the prophets);
he has covered your heads (the seers).

11For you this whole vision is nothing but
words sealed in a scroll. And if you give the scroll
to someone who can read, and say to him, "Read
this, please," he will answer, "I can't; it is
sealed." 12Or if you give the scroll to someone
who cannot read, and say, "Read this, please," he
will answer, "I don't know how to read."

13The Lord says:
"These people come near to me with their
mouth
and honor me with their lips,
but their hearts are far from me.
Their worship of me
is made up only of rules taught by men.[c]
14Therefore once more I will astound these
people
with wonder upon wonder;
the wisdom of the wise will perish,
the intelligence of the intelligent will
vanish."
15Woe to those who go to great depths
to hide their plans from the LORD,
who do their work in darkness and think,
"Who sees us? Who will know?"
16You turn things upside down,
as if the potter were thought to be like the
clay!
Shall what is formed say to him who formed
it,
"He did not make me"?
Can the pot say of the potter,
"He knows nothing"?

17In a very short time, will not Lebanon be
turned into a fertile field
and the fertile field seem like a forest?
18In that day the deaf will hear the words of
the scroll,
and out of gloom and darkness
the eyes of the blind will see.
19Once more the humble will rejoice in the
LORD;

[a]25 The meaning of the Hebrew for this word is uncertain. [b]2 The Hebrew for *altar hearth* sounds like the Hebrew for *Ariel.*
[c]13 Hebrew; Septuagint *They worship me in vain; / their teachings are but rules taught by men*

the needy will rejoice in the Holy One of Israel.
20The ruthless will vanish,
the mockers will disappear,
and all who have an eye for evil will be cut down—
21those who with a word make a man out to be guilty,
who ensnare the defender in court
and with false testimony deprive the innocent of justice.

22Therefore this is what the LORD, who redeemed Abraham, says to the house of Jacob:

"No longer will Jacob be ashamed;
no longer will their faces grow pale.
23When they see among them their children,
the work of my hands,
they will keep my name holy;
they will acknowledge the holiness of the Holy One of Jacob,
and will stand in awe of the God of Israel.
24Those who are wayward in spirit will gain understanding;
those who complain will accept instruction."

Woe to the Obstinate Nation

30 "Woe to the obstinate children,"
declares the LORD,
"to those who carry out plans that are not mine,
forming an alliance, but not by my Spirit,
heaping sin upon sin;
2who go down to Egypt
without consulting me;
who look for help to Pharaoh's protection,
to Egypt's shade for refuge.
3But Pharaoh's protection will be to your shame,
Egypt's shade will bring you disgrace.
4Though they have officials in Zoan
and their envoys have arrived in Hanes,
5everyone will be put to shame
because of a people useless to them,
who bring neither help nor advantage,
but only shame and disgrace."

6An oracle concerning the animals of the
Negev:

Through a land of hardship and distress,
of lions and lionesses,
of adders and darting snakes,
the envoys carry their riches on donkeys' backs,
their treasures on the humps of camels,
to that unprofitable nation,
7 to Egypt, whose help is utterly useless.
Therefore I call her
Rahab the Do-Nothing.

8Go now, write it on a tablet for them,
inscribe it on a scroll,
that for the days to come
it may be an everlasting witness.
9These are rebellious people, deceitful children,
children unwilling to listen to the LORD's instruction.
10They say to the seers,
"See no more visions!"
and to the prophets,
"Give us no more visions of what is right!
Tell us pleasant things,
prophesy illusions.
11Leave this way,
get off this path,
and stop confronting us
with the Holy One of Israel!"

12Therefore, this is what the Holy One of Israel says:

"Because you have rejected this message,
relied on oppression
and depended on deceit,
13this sin will become for you
like a high wall, cracked and bulging,
that collapses suddenly, in an instant.
14It will break in pieces like pottery,
shattered so mercilessly
that among its pieces not a fragment will be found
for taking coals from a hearth
or scooping water out of a cistern."

15This is what the Sovereign LORD, the Holy
One of Israel, says:

"In repentance and rest is your salvation,
in quietness and trust is your strength,
but you would have none of it.
16You said, 'No, we will flee on horses.'
Therefore you will flee!
You said, 'We will ride off on swift horses.'
Therefore your pursuers will be swift!
17A thousand will flee
at the threat of one;
at the threat of five
you will all flee away,
till you are left
like a flagstaff on a mountaintop,
like a banner on a hill."

18Yet the LORD longs to be gracious to you;
he rises to show you compassion.
For the LORD is a God of justice.
Blessed are all who wait for him!

19O people of Zion, who live in Jerusalem, you

will weep no more. How gracious he will be
when you cry for help! As soon as he hears, he
will answer you. 20Although the Lord gives you
the bread of adversity and the water of affliction,
your teachers will be hidden no more; with your
own eyes you will see them. 21Whether you turn
to the right or to the left, your ears will hear a
voice behind you, saying, "This is the way; walk
in it." 22Then you will defile your idols overlaid
with silver and your images covered with gold;
you will throw them away like a menstrual cloth
and say to them, "Away with you!"

23He will also send you rain for the seed you
sow in the ground, and the food that comes from
the land will be rich and plentiful. In that day
your cattle will graze in broad meadows. 24The
oxen and donkeys that work the soil will eat fodder and mash, spread out with fork and shovel.
25In the day of great slaughter, when the towers
fall, streams of water will flow on every high
mountain and every lofty hill. 26The moon will
shine like the sun, and the sunlight will be seven
times brighter, like the light of seven full days,
when the LORD binds up the bruises of his people
and heals the wounds he inflicted.

27See, the Name of the LORD comes from afar,
with burning anger and dense clouds of smoke;
his lips are full of wrath,
and his tongue is a consuming fire.
28His breath is like a rushing torrent,
rising up to the neck.
He shakes the nations in the sieve of destruction;
he places in the jaws of the peoples
a bit that leads them astray.
29And you will sing
as on the night you celebrate a holy festival;
your hearts will rejoice
as when people go up with flutes
to the mountain of the LORD,
to the Rock of Israel.
30The LORD will cause men to hear his majestic voice
and will make them see his arm coming down
with raging anger and consuming fire,
with cloudburst, thunderstorm and hail.
31The voice of the LORD will shatter Assyria;
with his scepter he will strike them down.
32Every stroke the LORD lays on them
with his punishing rod
will be to the music of tambourines and harps,
as he fights them in battle with the blows of his arm.
33Topheth has long been prepared;
it has been made ready for the king.
Its fire pit has been made deep and wide,
with an abundance of fire and wood;
the breath of the LORD,
like a stream of burning sulfur,
sets it ablaze.

Woe to Those Who Rely on Egypt

31 Woe to those who go down to Egypt for help,
who rely on horses,
who trust in the multitude of their chariots
and in the great strength of their horsemen,
but do not look to the Holy One of Israel,
or seek help from the LORD.
2Yet he too is wise and can bring disaster;
he does not take back his words.
He will rise up against the house of the wicked,
against those who help evildoers.
3But the Egyptians are men and not God;
their horses are flesh and not spirit.
When the LORD stretches out his hand,
he who helps will stumble,
he who is helped will fall;
both will perish together.

4This is what the LORD says to me:
"As a lion growls,
a great lion over his prey—
and though a whole band of shepherds
is called together against him,
he is not frightened by their shouts
or disturbed by their clamor—
so the LORD Almighty will come down
to do battle on Mount Zion and on its heights.
5Like birds hovering overhead,
the LORD Almighty will shield Jerusalem;
he will shield it and deliver it,
he will 'pass over' it and will rescue it."

6Return to him you have so greatly revolted
against, O Israelites. 7For in that day every one of
you will reject the idols of silver and gold your
sinful hands have made.

8"Assyria will fall by a sword that is not of man;
a sword, not of mortals, will devour them.
They will flee before the sword
and their young men will be put to forced labor.
9Their stronghold will fall because of terror;
at sight of the battle standard their commanders will panic,"
declares the LORD,
whose fire is in Zion,
whose furnace is in Jerusalem.

The Kingdom of Righteousness

32 See, a king will reign in righteousness
and rulers will rule with justice.
2Each man will be like a shelter from the wind
and a refuge from the storm,
like streams of water in the desert
and the shadow of a great rock in a thirsty land.

3Then the eyes of those who see will no longer be closed,
and the ears of those who hear will listen.
4The mind of the rash will know and understand,
and the stammering tongue will be fluent and clear.
5No longer will the fool be called noble
nor the scoundrel be highly respected.
6For the fool speaks folly,
his mind is busy with evil:
He practices ungodliness
and spreads error concerning the LORD;
the hungry he leaves empty
and from the thirsty he withholds water.
7The scoundrel's methods are wicked,
he makes up evil schemes
to destroy the poor with lies,
even when the plea of the needy is just.
8But the noble man makes noble plans,
and by noble deeds he stands.

The Women of Jerusalem

9You women who are so complacent,
rise up and listen to me;
you daughters who feel secure,
hear what I have to say!
10In little more than a year
you who feel secure will tremble;
the grape harvest will fail,
and the harvest of fruit will not come.
11Tremble, you complacent women;
shudder, you daughters who feel secure!
Strip off your clothes,
put sackcloth around your waists.
12Beat your breasts for the pleasant fields,
for the fruitful vines
13and for the land of my people,
a land overgrown with thorns and briers—
yes, mourn for all houses of merriment
and for this city of revelry.
14The fortress will be abandoned,
the noisy city deserted;
citadel and watchtower will become a wasteland forever,
the delight of donkeys, a pasture for flocks,
15till the Spirit is poured upon us from on high,
and the desert becomes a fertile field,
and the fertile field seems like a forest.
16Justice will dwell in the desert
and righteousness live in the fertile field.
17The fruit of righteousness will be peace;
the effect of righteousness will be
quietness and confidence forever.
18My people will live in peaceful dwelling places,
in secure homes,
in undisturbed places of rest.
19Though hail flattens the forest
and the city is leveled completely,
20how blessed you will be,
sowing your seed by every stream,
and letting your cattle and donkeys range free.

Distress and Help

33 Woe to you, O destroyer,
you who have not been destroyed!
Woe to you, O traitor,
you who have not been betrayed!
When you stop destroying,
you will be destroyed;
when you stop betraying,
you will be betrayed.

2O LORD, be gracious to us;
we long for you.
Be our strength every morning,
our salvation in time of distress.
3At the thunder of your voice, the peoples flee;
when you rise up, the nations scatter.
4Your plunder, O nations, is harvested as by young locusts;
like a swarm of locusts men pounce on it.

5The LORD is exalted, for he dwells on high;
he will fill Zion with justice and righteousness.
6He will be the sure foundation for your times,
a rich store of salvation and wisdom and knowledge;
the fear of the LORD is the key to this treasure.[a]

7Look, their brave men cry aloud in the streets;
the envoys of peace weep bitterly.
8The highways are deserted,
no travelers are on the roads.
The treaty is broken,
its witnesses[b] are despised,

[a]6 Or *is a treasure from him* [b]8 Dead Sea Scrolls; Masoretic Text / *the cities*

no one is respected.
9The land mourns[a] and wastes away,
Lebanon is ashamed and withers;
Sharon is like the Arabah,
and Bashan and Carmel drop their leaves.
10"Now will I arise," says the LORD.
"Now will I be exalted;
now will I be lifted up.
11You conceive chaff,
you give birth to straw;
your breath is a fire that consumes you.
12The peoples will be burned as if to lime;
like cut thornbushes they will be set
ablaze."

13You who are far away, hear what I have
done;
you who are near, acknowledge my power!
14The sinners in Zion are terrified;
trembling grips the godless:
"Who of us can dwell with the consuming
fire?
Who of us can dwell with everlasting
burning?"
15He who walks righteously
and speaks what is right,
who rejects gain from extortion
and keeps his hand from accepting bribes,
who stops his ears against plots of murder
and shuts his eyes against contemplating
evil—
16this is the man who will dwell on the
heights,
whose refuge will be the mountain
fortress.
His bread will be supplied,
and water will not fail him.

17Your eyes will see the king in his beauty
and view a land that stretches afar.
18In your thoughts you will ponder the former
terror:
"Where is that chief officer?
Where is the one who took the revenue?
Where is the officer in charge of the
towers?"
19You will see those arrogant people no more,
those people of an obscure speech,
with their strange, incomprehensible
tongue.

20Look upon Zion, the city of our festivals;
your eyes will see Jerusalem,
a peaceful abode, a tent that will not be
moved;
its stakes will never be pulled up,
nor any of its ropes broken.
21There the LORD will be our Mighty One.
It will be like a place of broad rivers and
streams.
No galley with oars will ride them,
no mighty ship will sail them.
22For the LORD is our judge,
the LORD is our lawgiver,
the LORD is our king;
it is he who will save us.

23Your rigging hangs loose:
The mast is not held secure,
the sail is not spread.
Then an abundance of spoils will be divided
and even the lame will carry off plunder.
24No one living in Zion will say, "I am ill";
and the sins of those who dwell there will
be forgiven.

Judgment Against the Nations

34 Come near, you nations, and listen;
pay attention, you peoples!
Let the earth hear, and all that is in it,
the world, and all that comes out of it!
2The LORD is angry with all nations;
his wrath is upon all their armies.
He will totally destroy[b] them,
he will give them over to slaughter.
3Their slain will be thrown out,
their dead bodies will send up a stench;
the mountains will be soaked with their
blood.
4All the stars of the heavens will be dissolved
and the sky rolled up like a scroll;
all the starry host will fall
like withered leaves from the vine,
like shriveled figs from the fig tree.

5My sword has drunk its fill in the heavens;
see, it descends in judgment on Edom,
the people I have totally destroyed.
6The sword of the LORD is bathed in blood,
it is covered with fat—
the blood of lambs and goats,
fat from the kidneys of rams.
For the LORD has a sacrifice in Bozrah
and a great slaughter in Edom.
7And the wild oxen will fall with them,
the bull calves and the great bulls.
Their land will be drenched with blood,
and the dust will be soaked with fat.

8For the LORD has a day of vengeance,
a year of retribution, to uphold Zion's
cause.
9Edom's streams will be turned into pitch,
her dust into burning sulfur;
her land will become blazing pitch!

[a] 9 Or *dries up* [b] 2 The Hebrew term refers to the irrevocable giving over of things or persons to the LORD, often by totally destroying them; also in verse 5.

10 It will not be quenched night and day;
its smoke will rise forever.
From generation to generation it will lie
desolate;
no one will ever pass through it again.
11 The desert owl[a] and screech owl[a] will
possess it;
the great owl[a] and the raven will nest
there.
God will stretch out over Edom
the measuring line of chaos
and the plumb line of desolation.
12 Her nobles will have nothing there to be
called a kingdom,
all her princes will vanish away.
13 Thorns will overrun her citadels,
nettles and brambles her strongholds.
She will become a haunt for jackals,
a home for owls.
14 Desert creatures will meet with hyenas,
and wild goats will bleat to each other;
there the night creatures will also repose
and find for themselves places of rest.
15 The owl will nest there and lay eggs,
she will hatch them, and care for her
young under the shadow of her
wings;
there also the falcons will gather,
each with its mate.

16 Look in the scroll of the LORD and read:

None of these will be missing,
not one will lack her mate.
For it is his mouth that has given the order,
and his Spirit will gather them together.
17 He allots their portions;
his hand distributes them by measure.
They will possess it forever
and dwell there from generation to
generation.

Joy of the Redeemed

35 The desert and the parched land will be
glad;
the wilderness will rejoice and blossom.
Like the crocus, 2 it will burst into bloom;
it will rejoice greatly and shout for joy.
The glory of Lebanon will be given to it,
the splendor of Carmel and Sharon;
they will see the glory of the LORD,
the splendor of our God.

3 Strengthen the feeble hands,
steady the knees that give way;
4 say to those with fearful hearts,
"Be strong, do not fear;
your God will come,
he will come with vengeance;
with divine retribution
he will come to save you."

5 Then will the eyes of the blind be opened
and the ears of the deaf unstopped.
6 Then will the lame leap like a deer,
and the mute tongue shout for joy.
Water will gush forth in the wilderness
and streams in the desert.
7 The burning sand will become a pool,
the thirsty ground bubbling springs.
In the haunts where jackals once lay,
grass and reeds and papyrus will grow.

8 And a highway will be there;
it will be called the Way of Holiness.
The unclean will not journey on it;
it will be for those who walk in that Way;
wicked fools will not go about on it.[b]
9 No lion will be there,
nor will any ferocious beast get up on it;
they will not be found there.
But only the redeemed will walk there,
10 and the ransomed of the LORD will return.
They will enter Zion with singing;
everlasting joy will crown their heads.
Gladness and joy will overtake them,
and sorrow and sighing will flee away.

Sennacherib Threatens Jerusalem

36 In the fourteenth year of King Hezekiah's
reign, Sennacherib king of Assyria attacked all the fortified cities of Judah and captured them. 2 Then the king of Assyria sent his
field commander with a large army from Lachish
to King Hezekiah at Jerusalem. When the commander stopped at the aqueduct of the Upper
Pool, on the road to the Washerman's Field, 3 Eliakim son of Hilkiah the palace administrator,
Shebna the secretary, and Joah son of Asaph the
recorder went out to him.
4 The field commander said to them, "Tell Hezekiah,

" 'This is what the great king, the king of
Assyria, says: On what are you basing this
confidence of yours? 5 You say you have
strategy and military strength—but you
speak only empty words. On whom are you
depending, that you rebel against me?
6 Look now, you are depending on Egypt,
that splintered reed of a staff, which pierces
a man's hand and wounds him if he leans
on it! Such is Pharaoh king of Egypt to all
who depend on him. 7 And if you say to
me, "We are depending on the LORD our

[a] *11* The precise identification of these birds is uncertain.
[b] *8* Or / *the simple will not stray from it*

God"—isn't he the one whose high places
and altars Hezekiah removed, saying to Judah and Jerusalem, "You must worship before this altar"?
8" 'Come now, make a bargain with my
master, the king of Assyria: I will give you
two thousand horses—if you can put riders
on them! 9How then can you repulse one
officer of the least of my master's officials,
even though you are depending on Egypt for
chariots and horsemen? 10Furthermore,
have I come to attack and destroy this land
without the LORD? The LORD himself told
me to march against this country and destroy it.' "

11Then Eliakim, Shebna and Joah said to the
field commander, "Please speak to your servants
in Aramaic, since we understand it. Don't speak
to us in Hebrew in the hearing of the people on
the wall."
12But the commander replied, "Was it only to
your master and you that my master sent me to
say these things, and not to the men sitting on
the wall—who, like you, will have to eat their
own filth and drink their own urine?"
13Then the commander stood and called out in
Hebrew, "Hear the words of the great king, the
king of Assyria! 14This is what the king says: Do
not let Hezekiah deceive you. He cannot deliver
you! 15Do not let Hezekiah persuade you to trust
in the LORD when he says, 'The LORD will surely
deliver us; this city will not be given into the
hand of the king of Assyria.'
16"Do not listen to Hezekiah. This is what the
king of Assyria says: Make peace with me and
come out to me. Then every one of you will eat
from his own vine and fig tree and drink water
from his own cistern, 17until I come and take you
to a land like your own—a land of grain and new
wine, a land of bread and vineyards.
18"Do not let Hezekiah mislead you when he
says, 'The LORD will deliver us.' Has the god of
any nation ever delivered his land from the hand
of the king of Assyria? 19Where are the gods of
Hamath and Arpad? Where are the gods of Sepharvaim? Have they rescued Samaria from my
hand? 20Who of all the gods of these countries
has been able to save his land from me? How
then can the LORD deliver Jerusalem from my
hand?"
21But the people remained silent and said
nothing in reply, because the king had commanded, "Do not answer him."
22Then Eliakim son of Hilkiah the palace administrator, Shebna the secretary, and Joah son of
Asaph the recorder went to Hezekiah, with their
clothes torn, and told him what the field commander had said.

Jerusalem's Deliverance Foretold

37 When King Hezekiah heard this, he tore
his clothes and put on sackcloth and went
into the temple of the LORD. 2He sent Eliakim the
palace administrator, Shebna the secretary, and
the leading priests, all wearing sackcloth, to the
prophet Isaiah son of Amoz. 3They told him,
"This is what Hezekiah says: This day is a day of
distress and rebuke and disgrace, as when children come to the point of birth and there is no
strength to deliver them. 4It may be that the
LORD your God will hear the words of the field
commander, whom his master, the king of Assyria, has sent to ridicule the living God, and that he
will rebuke him for the words the LORD your God
has heard. Therefore pray for the remnant that
still survives."
5When King Hezekiah's officials came to Isaiah, 6Isaiah said to them, "Tell your master, 'This
is what the LORD says: Do not be afraid of what
you have heard—those words with which the
underlings of the king of Assyria have blasphemed me. 7Listen! I am going to put a spirit in
him so that when he hears a certain report, he
will return to his own country, and there I will
have him cut down with the sword.' "
8When the field commander heard that the
king of Assyria had left Lachish, he withdrew and
found the king fighting against Libnah.
9Now Sennacherib received a report that Tirhakah, the Cushite[a] king ⌞of Egypt⌟, was marching out to fight against him. When he heard it, he
sent messengers to Hezekiah with this word:
10"Say to Hezekiah king of Judah: Do not let the
god you depend on deceive you when he says,
'Jerusalem will not be handed over to the king of
Assyria.' 11Surely you have heard what the kings
of Assyria have done to all the countries, destroying them completely. And will you be delivered?
12Did the gods of the nations that were destroyed
by my forefathers deliver them—the gods of Gozan, Haran, Rezeph and the people of Eden who
were in Tel Assar? 13Where is the king of Hamath, the king of Arpad, the king of the city of
Sepharvaim, or of Hena or Ivvah?"

Hezekiah's Prayer

14Hezekiah received the letter from the messengers and read it. Then he went up to the temple of the LORD and spread it out before the LORD.
15And Hezekiah prayed to the LORD: 16"O LORD
Almighty, God of Israel, enthroned between the
cherubim, you alone are God over all the kingdoms of the earth. You have made heaven and

[a] 9 That is, from the upper Nile region

earth. 17 Give ear, O LORD, and hear; open your
eyes, O LORD, and see; listen to all the words
Sennacherib has sent to insult the living God.
18 "It is true, O LORD, that the Assyrian kings
have laid waste all these peoples and their lands.
19 They have thrown their gods into the fire and
destroyed them, for they were not gods but only
wood and stone, fashioned by human hands.
20 Now, O LORD our God, deliver us from his
hand, so that all kingdoms on earth may know
that you alone, O LORD, are God.[a]"

Sennacherib's Fall

21 Then Isaiah son of Amoz sent a message to
Hezekiah: "This is what the LORD, the God of
Israel, says: Because you have prayed to me concerning Sennacherib king of Assyria, 22 this is the
word the LORD has spoken against him:

"The Virgin Daughter of Zion
despises and mocks you.
The Daughter of Jerusalem
tosses her head as you flee.
23 Who is it you have insulted and blasphemed?
Against whom have you raised your voice
and lifted your eyes in pride?
Against the Holy One of Israel!
24 By your messengers
you have heaped insults on the Lord.
And you have said,
'With my many chariots
I have ascended the heights of the mountains,
the utmost heights of Lebanon.
I have cut down its tallest cedars,
the choicest of its pines.
I have reached its remotest heights,
the finest of its forests.
25 I have dug wells in foreign lands[b]
and drunk the water there.
With the soles of my feet
I have dried up all the streams of Egypt.'
26 "Have you not heard?
Long ago I ordained it.
In days of old I planned it;
now I have brought it to pass,
that you have turned fortified cities
into piles of stone.
27 Their people, drained of power,
are dismayed and put to shame.
They are like plants in the field,
like tender green shoots,
like grass sprouting on the roof,
scorched[c] before it grows up.
28 "But I know where you stay
and when you come and go
and how you rage against me.
29 Because you rage against me
and because your insolence has reached my ears,
I will put my hook in your nose
and my bit in your mouth,
and I will make you return
by the way you came.

30 "This will be the sign for you, O Hezekiah:

"This year you will eat what grows by itself,
and the second year what springs from that.
But in the third year sow and reap,
plant vineyards and eat their fruit.
31 Once more a remnant of the house of Judah
will take root below and bear fruit above.
32 For out of Jerusalem will come a remnant,
and out of Mount Zion a band of survivors.
The zeal of the LORD Almighty
will accomplish this.

33 "Therefore this is what the LORD says concerning the king of Assyria:

"He will not enter this city
or shoot an arrow here.
He will not come before it with shield
or build a siege ramp against it.
34 By the way that he came he will return;
he will not enter this city,"
declares the LORD.
35 "I will defend this city and save it,
for my sake and for the sake of David my servant!"

36 Then the angel of the LORD went out and put
to death a hundred and eighty-five thousand men
in the Assyrian camp. When the people got up
the next morning—there were all the dead bodies! 37 So Sennacherib king of Assyria broke camp
and withdrew. He returned to Nineveh and
stayed there.
38 One day, while he was worshiping in the
temple of his god Nisroch, his sons Adrammelech
and Sharezer cut him down with the sword, and
they escaped to the land of Ararat. And Esarhaddon his son succeeded him as king.

Hezekiah's Illness

38 In those days Hezekiah became ill and
was at the point of death. The prophet
Isaiah son of Amoz went to him and said, "This
is what the LORD says: Put your house in order,
because you are going to die; you will not recover."

a 20 Dead Sea Scrolls (see also 2 Kings 19:19); Masoretic Text *alone are the LORD* b 25 Dead Sea Scrolls (see also 2 Kings 19:24); Masoretic Text does not have *in foreign lands.* c 27 Some manuscripts of the Masoretic Text, Dead Sea Scrolls and some Septuagint manuscripts (see also 2 Kings 19:26); most manuscripts of the Masoretic Text *roof / and terraced fields*

2Hezekiah turned his face to the wall and
prayed to the LORD, 3"Remember, O LORD, how
I have walked before you faithfully and with
wholehearted devotion and have done what is
good in your eyes." And Hezekiah wept bitterly.
4Then the word of the LORD came to Isaiah:
5"Go and tell Hezekiah, 'This is what the LORD,
the God of your father David, says: I have heard
your prayer and seen your tears; I will add fifteen
years to your life. 6And I will deliver you and this
city from the hand of the king of Assyria. I will
defend this city.

7" 'This is the LORD's sign to you that the LORD
will do what he has promised: 8I will make the
shadow cast by the sun go back the ten steps it
has gone down on the stairway of Ahaz.' " So the
sunlight went back the ten steps it had gone
down.

9A writing of Hezekiah king of Judah after his illness and recovery:

10I said, "In the prime of my life
must I go through the gates of death[a]
and be robbed of the rest of my years?"
11I said, "I will not again see the LORD,
the LORD, in the land of the living;
no longer will I look on mankind,
or be with those who now dwell in this world.[b]
12Like a shepherd's tent my house
has been pulled down and taken from me.
Like a weaver I have rolled up my life,
and he has cut me off from the loom;
day and night you made an end of me.
13I waited patiently till dawn,
but like a lion he broke all my bones;
day and night you made an end of me.
14I cried like a swift or thrush,
I moaned like a mourning dove.
My eyes grew weak as I looked to the heavens.
I am troubled; O Lord, come to my aid!"

15But what can I say?
He has spoken to me, and he himself has done this.
I will walk humbly all my years
because of this anguish of my soul.
16Lord, by such things men live;
and my spirit finds life in them too.
You restored me to health
and let me live.
17Surely it was for my benefit
that I suffered such anguish.
In your love you kept me
from the pit of destruction;
you have put all my sins
behind your back.
18For the grave[a] cannot praise you,
death cannot sing your praise;
those who go down to the pit
cannot hope for your faithfulness.
19The living, the living—they praise you,
as I am doing today;
fathers tell their children
about your faithfulness.

20The LORD will save me,
and we will sing with stringed instruments
all the days of our lives
in the temple of the LORD.

21Isaiah had said, "Prepare a poultice of figs
and apply it to the boil, and he will recover."
22Hezekiah had asked, "What will be the sign
that I will go up to the temple of the LORD?"

Envoys From Babylon

39 At that time Merodach-Baladan son of
Baladan king of Babylon sent Hezekiah
letters and a gift, because he had heard of his
illness and recovery. 2Hezekiah received the envoys gladly and showed them what was in his
storehouses—the silver, the gold, the spices, the
fine oil, his entire armory and everything found
among his treasures. There was nothing in his
palace or in all his kingdom that Hezekiah did not
show them.

3Then Isaiah the prophet went to King Hezekiah and asked, "What did those men say, and
where did they come from?"

"From a distant land," Hezekiah replied. "They came to me from Babylon."

4The prophet asked, "What did they see in
your palace?"

"They saw everything in my palace," Hezekiah said. "There is nothing among my treasures that I did not show them."

5Then Isaiah said to Hezekiah, "Hear the word
of the LORD Almighty: 6The time will surely come
when everything in your palace, and all that your
fathers have stored up until this day, will be carried off to Babylon. Nothing will be left, says the
LORD. 7And some of your descendants, your own
flesh and blood who will be born to you, will be
taken away, and they will become eunuchs in the
palace of the king of Babylon."

8"The word of the LORD you have spoken is
good," Hezekiah replied. For he thought, "There
will be peace and security in my lifetime."

Comfort for God's People

40 Comfort, comfort my people,
says your God.
2Speak tenderly to Jerusalem,

[a] *10,18* Hebrew *Sheol* [b] *11* A few Hebrew manuscripts; most Hebrew manuscripts *in the place of cessation*

and proclaim to her
that her hard service has been completed,
that her sin has been paid for,
that she has received from the LORD's hand
double for all her sins.

3A voice of one calling:
"In the desert prepare
the way for the LORD[a];
make straight in the wilderness
a highway for our God.[b]
4Every valley shall be raised up,
every mountain and hill made low;
the rough ground shall become level,
the rugged places a plain.
5And the glory of the LORD will be revealed,
and all mankind together will see it.
For the mouth of the LORD
has spoken."

6A voice says, "Cry out."
And I said, "What shall I cry?"

"All men are like grass,
and all their glory is like the flowers of the field.
7The grass withers and the flowers fall,
because the breath of the LORD blows on them.
Surely the people are grass.
8The grass withers and the flowers fall,
but the word of our God stands forever."

9You who bring good tidings to Zion,
go up on a high mountain.
You who bring good tidings to Jerusalem,[c]
lift up your voice with a shout,
lift it up, do not be afraid;
say to the towns of Judah,
"Here is your God!"
10See, the Sovereign LORD comes with power,
and his arm rules for him.
See, his reward is with him,
and his recompense accompanies him.
11He tends his flock like a shepherd:
He gathers the lambs in his arms
and carries them close to his heart;
he gently leads those that have young.

12Who has measured the waters in the hollow of his hand,
or with the breadth of his hand marked off the heavens?
Who has held the dust of the earth in a basket,
or weighed the mountains on the scales
and the hills in a balance?
13Who has understood the mind[d] of the LORD,
or instructed him as his counselor?
14Whom did the LORD consult to enlighten him,
and who taught him the right way?
Who was it that taught him knowledge
or showed him the path of understanding?

15Surely the nations are like a drop in a bucket;
they are regarded as dust on the scales;
he weighs the islands as though they were fine dust.
16Lebanon is not sufficient for altar fires,
nor its animals enough for burnt offerings.
17Before him all the nations are as nothing;
they are regarded by him as worthless
and less than nothing.

18To whom, then, will you compare God?
What image will you compare him to?
19As for an idol, a craftsman casts it,
and a goldsmith overlays it with gold
and fashions silver chains for it.
20A man too poor to present such an offering
selects wood that will not rot.
He looks for a skilled craftsman
to set up an idol that will not topple.

21Do you not know?
Have you not heard?
Has it not been told you from the beginning?
Have you not understood since the earth was founded?
22He sits enthroned above the circle of the earth,
and its people are like grasshoppers.
He stretches out the heavens like a canopy,
and spreads them out like a tent to live in.
23He brings princes to naught
and reduces the rulers of this world to nothing.
24No sooner are they planted,
no sooner are they sown,
no sooner do they take root in the ground,
than he blows on them and they wither,
and a whirlwind sweeps them away like chaff.

25"To whom will you compare me?
Or who is my equal?" says the Holy One.
26Lift your eyes and look to the heavens:
Who created all these?
He who brings out the starry host one by one,
and calls them each by name.

a3 Or *A voice of one calling in the desert: / "Prepare the way for the LORD* b3 Hebrew; Septuagint *make straight the paths of our God* c9 Or *O Zion, bringer of good tidings, / go up on a high mountain. / O Jerusalem, bringer of good tidings*
d13 Or *Spirit*; or *spirit*

Because of his great power and mighty
strength,
not one of them is missing.
27Why do you say, O Jacob,
and complain, O Israel,
"My way is hidden from the LORD;
my cause is disregarded by my God"?
28Do you not know?
Have you not heard?
The LORD is the everlasting God,
the Creator of the ends of the earth.
He will not grow tired or weary,
and his understanding no one can fathom.
29He gives strength to the weary
and increases the power of the weak.
30Even youths grow tired and weary,
and young men stumble and fall;
31but those who hope in the LORD
will renew their strength.
They will soar on wings like eagles;
they will run and not grow weary,
they will walk and not be faint.

The Helper of Israel

41 "Be silent before me, you islands!
Let the nations renew their strength!
Let them come forward and speak;
let us meet together at the place of
judgment.

2"Who has stirred up one from the east,
calling him in righteousness to his
service[a]?
He hands nations over to him
and subdues kings before him.
He turns them to dust with his sword,
to windblown chaff with his bow.
3He pursues them and moves on unscathed,
by a path his feet have not traveled before.
4Who has done this and carried it through,
calling forth the generations from the
beginning?
I, the LORD—with the first of them
and with the last—I am he."

5The islands have seen it and fear;
the ends of the earth tremble.
They approach and come forward;
6 each helps the other
and says to his brother, "Be strong!"
7The craftsman encourages the goldsmith,
and he who smooths with the hammer
spurs on him who strikes the anvil.
He says of the welding, "It is good."
He nails down the idol so it will not
topple.

8"But you, O Israel, my servant,
Jacob, whom I have chosen,
you descendants of Abraham my friend,
9I took you from the ends of the earth,
from its farthest corners I called you.
I said, 'You are my servant';
I have chosen you and have not rejected
you.
10So do not fear, for I am with you;
do not be dismayed, for I am your God.
I will strengthen you and help you;
I will uphold you with my righteous right
hand.

11"All who rage against you
will surely be ashamed and disgraced;
those who oppose you
will be as nothing and perish.
12Though you search for your enemies,
you will not find them.
Those who wage war against you
will be as nothing at all.
13For I am the LORD, your God,
who takes hold of your right hand
and says to you, Do not fear;
I will help you.
14Do not be afraid, O worm Jacob,
O little Israel,
for I myself will help you," declares the
LORD,
your Redeemer, the Holy One of Israel.
15"See, I will make you into a threshing sledge,
new and sharp, with many teeth.
You will thresh the mountains and crush
them,
and reduce the hills to chaff.
16You will winnow them, the wind will pick
them up,
and a gale will blow them away.
But you will rejoice in the LORD
and glory in the Holy One of Israel.

17"The poor and needy search for water,
but there is none;
their tongues are parched with thirst.
But I the LORD will answer them;
I, the God of Israel, will not forsake them.
18I will make rivers flow on barren heights,
and springs within the valleys.
I will turn the desert into pools of water,
and the parched ground into springs.
19I will put in the desert
the cedar and the acacia, the myrtle and
the olive.
I will set pines in the wasteland,
the fir and the cypress together,
20so that people may see and know,
may consider and understand,

[a]2 Or / *whom victory meets at every step*

that the hand of the LORD has done this,
that the Holy One of Israel has created it.

21 "Present your case," says the LORD.
"Set forth your arguments," says Jacob's King.
22 "Bring in ⌞ your idols⌟ to tell us
what is going to happen.
Tell us what the former things were,
so that we may consider them
and know their final outcome.
Or declare to us the things to come,
23 tell us what the future holds,
so we may know that you are gods.
Do something, whether good or bad,
so that we will be dismayed and filled with fear.
24 But you are less than nothing
and your works are utterly worthless;
he who chooses you is detestable.

25 "I have stirred up one from the north, and he comes—
one from the rising sun who calls on my name.
He treads on rulers as if they were mortar,
as if he were a potter treading the clay.
26 Who told of this from the beginning, so we could know,
or beforehand, so we could say, 'He was right'?
No one told of this,
no one foretold it,
no one heard any words from you.
27 I was the first to tell Zion, 'Look, here they are!'
I gave to Jerusalem a messenger of good tidings.
28 I look but there is no one—
no one among them to give counsel,
no one to give answer when I ask them.
29 See, they are all false!
Their deeds amount to nothing;
their images are but wind and confusion.

The Servant of the LORD

42 "Here is my servant, whom I uphold,
my chosen one in whom I delight;
I will put my Spirit on him
and he will bring justice to the nations.
2 He will not shout or cry out,
or raise his voice in the streets.
3 A bruised reed he will not break,
and a smoldering wick he will not snuff out.
In faithfulness he will bring forth justice;
4 he will not falter or be discouraged
till he establishes justice on earth.
In his law the islands will put their hope."

5 This is what God the LORD says—
he who created the heavens and stretched them out,
who spread out the earth and all that comes out of it,
who gives breath to its people,
and life to those who walk on it:
6 "I, the LORD, have called you in righteousness;
I will take hold of your hand.
I will keep you and will make you
to be a covenant for the people
and a light for the Gentiles,
7 to open eyes that are blind,
to free captives from prison
and to release from the dungeon those who sit in darkness.

8 "I am the LORD; that is my name!
I will not give my glory to another
or my praise to idols.
9 See, the former things have taken place,
and new things I declare;
before they spring into being
I announce them to you."

Song of Praise to the LORD

10 Sing to the LORD a new song,
his praise from the ends of the earth,
you who go down to the sea, and all that is in it,
you islands, and all who live in them.
11 Let the desert and its towns raise their voices;
let the settlements where Kedar lives rejoice.
Let the people of Sela sing for joy;
let them shout from the mountaintops.
12 Let them give glory to the LORD
and proclaim his praise in the islands.
13 The LORD will march out like a mighty man,
like a warrior he will stir up his zeal;
with a shout he will raise the battle cry
and will triumph over his enemies.

14 "For a long time I have kept silent,
I have been quiet and held myself back.
But now, like a woman in childbirth,
I cry out, I gasp and pant.
15 I will lay waste the mountains and hills
and dry up all their vegetation;
I will turn rivers into islands
and dry up the pools.
16 I will lead the blind by ways they have not known,
along unfamiliar paths I will guide them;
I will turn the darkness into light before them
and make the rough places smooth.
These are the things I will do;

I will not forsake them.
17But those who trust in idols,
who say to images, 'You are our gods,'
will be turned back in utter shame.

Israel Blind and Deaf

18"Hear, you deaf;
look, you blind, and see!
19Who is blind but my servant,
and deaf like the messenger I send?
Who is blind like the one committed to me,
blind like the servant of the LORD?
20You have seen many things, but have paid no attention;
your ears are open, but you hear nothing."
21It pleased the LORD
for the sake of his righteousness
to make his law great and glorious.
22But this is a people plundered and looted,
all of them trapped in pits
or hidden away in prisons.
They have become plunder,
with no one to rescue them;
they have been made loot,
with no one to say, "Send them back."

23Which of you will listen to this
or pay close attention in time to come?
24Who handed Jacob over to become loot,
and Israel to the plunderers?
Was it not the LORD,
against whom we have sinned?
For they would not follow his ways;
they did not obey his law.
25So he poured out on them his burning anger,
the violence of war.
It enveloped them in flames, yet they did not understand;
it consumed them, but they did not take it to heart.

Israel's Only Savior

43 But now, this is what the LORD says—
he who created you, O Jacob,
he who formed you, O Israel:
"Fear not, for I have redeemed you;
I have summoned you by name; you are mine.
2When you pass through the waters,
I will be with you;
and when you pass through the rivers,
they will not sweep over you.
When you walk through the fire,
you will not be burned;
the flames will not set you ablaze.
3For I am the LORD, your God,
the Holy One of Israel, your Savior;
I give Egypt for your ransom,
Cush[a] and Seba in your stead.
4Since you are precious and honored in my sight,
and because I love you,
I will give men in exchange for you,
and people in exchange for your life.
5Do not be afraid, for I am with you;
I will bring your children from the east
and gather you from the west.
6I will say to the north, 'Give them up!'
and to the south, 'Do not hold them back.'
Bring my sons from afar
and my daughters from the ends of the earth—
7everyone who is called by my name,
whom I created for my glory,
whom I formed and made."

8Lead out those who have eyes but are blind,
who have ears but are deaf.
9All the nations gather together
and the peoples assemble.
Which of them foretold this
and proclaimed to us the former things?
Let them bring in their witnesses to prove they were right,
so that others may hear and say, "It is true."
10"You are my witnesses," declares the LORD,
"and my servant whom I have chosen,
so that you may know and believe me
and understand that I am he.
Before me no god was formed,
nor will there be one after me.
11I, even I, am the LORD,
and apart from me there is no savior.
12I have revealed and saved and proclaimed—
I, and not some foreign god among you.
You are my witnesses," declares the LORD,
"that I am God.
13 Yes, and from ancient days I am he.
No one can deliver out of my hand.
When I act, who can reverse it?"

God's Mercy and Israel's Unfaithfulness

14This is what the LORD says—
your Redeemer, the Holy One of Israel:
"For your sake I will send to Babylon
and bring down as fugitives all the Babylonians,[b]
in the ships in which they took pride.
15I am the LORD, your Holy One,
Israel's Creator, your King."

16This is what the LORD says—
he who made a way through the sea,
a path through the mighty waters,

[a]3 That is, the upper Nile region [b]14 Or *Chaldeans*

17who drew out the chariots and horses,
the army and reinforcements together,
and they lay there, never to rise again,
extinguished, snuffed out like a wick:
18"Forget the former things;
do not dwell on the past.
19See, I am doing a new thing!
Now it springs up; do you not perceive it?
I am making a way in the desert
and streams in the wasteland.
20The wild animals honor me,
the jackals and the owls,
because I provide water in the desert
and streams in the wasteland,
to give drink to my people, my chosen,
21 the people I formed for myself
that they may proclaim my praise.

22"Yet you have not called upon me, O Jacob,
you have not wearied yourselves for me,
O Israel.
23You have not brought me sheep for burnt
offerings,
nor honored me with your sacrifices.
I have not burdened you with grain offerings
nor wearied you with demands for
incense.
24You have not bought any fragrant calamus for
me,
or lavished on me the fat of your
sacrifices.
But you have burdened me with your sins
and wearied me with your offenses.

25"I, even I, am he who blots out
your transgressions, for my own sake,
and remembers your sins no more.
26Review the past for me,
let us argue the matter together;
state the case for your innocence.
27Your first father sinned;
your spokesmen rebelled against me.
28So I will disgrace the dignitaries of your
temple,
and I will consign Jacob to destruction[a]
and Israel to scorn.

Israel the Chosen

44 "But now listen, O Jacob, my servant,
Israel, whom I have chosen.
2This is what the LORD says—
he who made you, who formed you in the
womb,
and who will help you:
Do not be afraid, O Jacob, my servant,
Jeshurun, whom I have chosen.
3For I will pour water on the thirsty land,
and streams on the dry ground;
I will pour out my Spirit on your offspring,
and my blessing on your descendants.
4They will spring up like grass in a meadow,
like poplar trees by flowing streams.
5One will say, 'I belong to the LORD';
another will call himself by the name of
Jacob;
still another will write on his hand, 'The
LORD'S,'
and will take the name Israel.

The LORD, Not Idols

6"This is what the LORD says—
Israel's King and Redeemer, the LORD
Almighty:
I am the first and I am the last;
apart from me there is no God.
7Who then is like me? Let him proclaim it.
Let him declare and lay out before me
what has happened since I established my
ancient people,
and what is yet to come—
yes, let him foretell what will come.
8Do not tremble, do not be afraid.
Did I not proclaim this and foretell it long
ago?
You are my witnesses. Is there any God
besides me?
No, there is no other Rock; I know not
one."

9All who make idols are nothing,
and the things they treasure are worthless.
Those who would speak up for them are
blind;
they are ignorant, to their own shame.
10Who shapes a god and casts an idol,
which can profit him nothing?
11He and his kind will be put to shame;
craftsmen are nothing but men.
Let them all come together and take their
stand;
they will be brought down to terror and
infamy.

12The blacksmith takes a tool
and works with it in the coals;
he shapes an idol with hammers,
he forges it with the might of his arm.
He gets hungry and loses his strength;
he drinks no water and grows faint.
13The carpenter measures with a line
and makes an outline with a marker;
he roughs it out with chisels
and marks it with compasses.
He shapes it in the form of man,
of man in all his glory,
that it may dwell in a shrine.

[a]28 The Hebrew term refers to the irrevocable giving over of things or persons to the LORD, often by totally destroying them.

14He cut down cedars,
or perhaps took a cypress or oak.
He let it grow among the trees of the forest,
or planted a pine, and the rain made it grow.
15It is man's fuel for burning;
some of it he takes and warms himself,
he kindles a fire and bakes bread.
But he also fashions a god and worships it;
he makes an idol and bows down to it.
16Half of the wood he burns in the fire;
over it he prepares his meal,
he roasts his meat and eats his fill.
He also warms himself and says,
"Ah! I am warm; I see the fire."
17From the rest he makes a god, his idol;
he bows down to it and worships.
He prays to it and says,
"Save me; you are my god."
18They know nothing, they understand nothing;
their eyes are plastered over so they cannot see,
and their minds closed so they cannot understand.
19No one stops to think,
no one has the knowledge or understanding to say,
"Half of it I used for fuel;
I even baked bread over its coals,
I roasted meat and I ate.
Shall I make a detestable thing from what is left?
Shall I bow down to a block of wood?"
20He feeds on ashes, a deluded heart misleads him;
he cannot save himself, or say,
"Is not this thing in my right hand a lie?"

21"Remember these things, O Jacob,
for you are my servant, O Israel.
I have made you, you are my servant;
O Israel, I will not forget you.
22I have swept away your offenses like a cloud,
your sins like the morning mist.
Return to me,
for I have redeemed you."

23Sing for joy, O heavens, for the LORD has done this;
shout aloud, O earth beneath.
Burst into song, you mountains,
you forests and all your trees,
for the LORD has redeemed Jacob,
he displays his glory in Israel.

Jerusalem to Be Inhabited

24"This is what the LORD says—
your Redeemer, who formed you in the womb:

I am the LORD,
who has made all things,
who alone stretched out the heavens,
who spread out the earth by myself,

25who foils the signs of false prophets
and makes fools of diviners,
who overthrows the learning of the wise
and turns it into nonsense,
26who carries out the words of his servants
and fulfills the predictions of his messengers,

who says of Jerusalem, 'It shall be inhabited,'
of the towns of Judah, 'They shall be built,'
and of their ruins, 'I will restore them,'
27who says to the watery deep, 'Be dry,
and I will dry up your streams,'
28who says of Cyrus, 'He is my shepherd
and will accomplish all that I please;
he will say of Jerusalem, "Let it be rebuilt,"
and of the temple, "Let its foundations be laid." '

45 "This is what the LORD says to his anointed,
to Cyrus, whose right hand I take hold of
to subdue nations before him
and to strip kings of their armor,
to open doors before him
so that gates will not be shut:
2I will go before you
and will level the mountains[a];
I will break down gates of bronze
and cut through bars of iron.
3I will give you the treasures of darkness,
riches stored in secret places,
so that you may know that I am the LORD,
the God of Israel, who summons you by name.
4For the sake of Jacob my servant,
of Israel my chosen,
I summon you by name
and bestow on you a title of honor,
though you do not acknowledge me.
5I am the LORD, and there is no other;
apart from me there is no God.
I will strengthen you,
though you have not acknowledged me,
6so that from the rising of the sun
to the place of its setting
men may know there is none besides me.
I am the LORD, and there is no other.

[a]2 Dead Sea Scrolls and Septuagint; the meaning of the word in the Masoretic Text is uncertain.

7I form the light and create darkness,
I bring prosperity and create disaster;
I, the LORD, do all these things.

8"You heavens above, rain down
righteousness;
let the clouds shower it down.
Let the earth open wide,
let salvation spring up,
let righteousness grow with it;
I, the LORD, have created it.

9"Woe to him who quarrels with his Maker,
to him who is but a potsherd among the
potsherds on the ground.
Does the clay say to the potter,
'What are you making?'
Does your work say,
'He has no hands'?
10Woe to him who says to his father,
'What have you begotten?'
or to his mother,
'What have you brought to birth?'

11"This is what the LORD says—
the Holy One of Israel, and its Maker:
Concerning things to come,
do you question me about my children,
or give me orders about the work of my
hands?
12It is I who made the earth
and created mankind upon it.
My own hands stretched out the heavens;
I marshaled their starry hosts.
13I will raise up Cyrus[a] in my righteousness:
I will make all his ways straight.
He will rebuild my city
and set my exiles free,
but not for a price or reward,
says the LORD Almighty."

14This is what the LORD says:

"The products of Egypt and the merchandise
of Cush,[b]
and those tall Sabeans—
they will come over to you
and will be yours;
they will trudge behind you,
coming over to you in chains.
They will bow down before you
and plead with you, saying,
'Surely God is with you, and there is no
other;
there is no other god.'"

15Truly you are a God who hides himself,
O God and Savior of Israel.
16All the makers of idols will be put to shame
and disgraced;
they will go off into disgrace together.
17But Israel will be saved by the LORD
with an everlasting salvation;
you will never be put to shame or disgraced,
to ages everlasting.

18For this is what the LORD says—
he who created the heavens,
he is God;
he who fashioned and made the earth,
he founded it;
he did not create it to be empty,
but formed it to be inhabited—
he says:
"I am the LORD,
and there is no other.
19I have not spoken in secret,
from somewhere in a land of darkness;
I have not said to Jacob's descendants,
'Seek me in vain.'
I, the LORD, speak the truth;
I declare what is right.

20"Gather together and come;
assemble, you fugitives from the nations.
Ignorant are those who carry about idols of
wood,
who pray to gods that cannot save.
21Declare what is to be, present it—
let them take counsel together.
Who foretold this long ago,
who declared it from the distant past?
Was it not I, the LORD?
And there is no God apart from me,
a righteous God and a Savior;
there is none but me.

22"Turn to me and be saved,
all you ends of the earth;
for I am God, and there is no other.
23By myself I have sworn,
my mouth has uttered in all integrity
a word that will not be revoked:
Before me every knee will bow;
by me every tongue will swear.
24They will say of me, 'In the LORD alone
are righteousness and strength.'"
All who have raged against him
will come to him and be put to shame.
25But in the LORD all the descendants of Israel
will be found righteous and will exult.

Gods of Babylon

46 Bel bows down, Nebo stoops low;
their idols are borne by beasts of
burden.[c]
The images that are carried about are
burdensome,

[a] 13 Hebrew *him* [b] 14 That is, the upper Nile region [c] 1 Or *are but beasts and cattle*

a burden for the weary.
2They stoop and bow down together;
unable to rescue the burden,
they themselves go off into captivity.

3"Listen to me, O house of Jacob,
all you who remain of the house of Israel,
you whom I have upheld since you were conceived,
and have carried since your birth.
4Even to your old age and gray hairs
I am he, I am he who will sustain you.
I have made you and I will carry you;
I will sustain you and I will rescue you.

5"To whom will you compare me or count me equal?
To whom will you liken me that we may be compared?
6Some pour out gold from their bags
and weigh out silver on the scales;
they hire a goldsmith to make it into a god,
and they bow down and worship it.
7They lift it to their shoulders and carry it;
they set it up in its place, and there it stands.
From that spot it cannot move.
Though one cries out to it, it does not answer;
it cannot save him from his troubles.

8"Remember this, fix it in mind,
take it to heart, you rebels.
9Remember the former things, those of long ago;
I am God, and there is no other;
I am God, and there is none like me.
10I make known the end from the beginning,
from ancient times, what is still to come.
I say: My purpose will stand,
and I will do all that I please.
11From the east I summon a bird of prey;
from a far-off land, a man to fulfill my purpose.
What I have said, that will I bring about;
what I have planned, that will I do.
12Listen to me, you stubborn-hearted,
you who are far from righteousness.
13I am bringing my righteousness near,
it is not far away;
and my salvation will not be delayed.
I will grant salvation to Zion,
my splendor to Israel.

The Fall of Babylon

47 "Go down, sit in the dust,
Virgin Daughter of Babylon;
sit on the ground without a throne,
Daughter of the Babylonians.[a]
No more will you be called
tender or delicate.
2Take millstones and grind flour;
take off your veil.
Lift up your skirts, bare your legs,
and wade through the streams.
3Your nakedness will be exposed
and your shame uncovered.
I will take vengeance;
I will spare no one."

4Our Redeemer—the LORD Almighty is his name—
is the Holy One of Israel.

5"Sit in silence, go into darkness,
Daughter of the Babylonians;
no more will you be called
queen of kingdoms.
6I was angry with my people
and desecrated my inheritance;
I gave them into your hand,
and you showed them no mercy.
Even on the aged
you laid a very heavy yoke.
7You said, 'I will continue forever—
the eternal queen!'
But you did not consider these things
or reflect on what might happen.

8"Now then, listen, you wanton creature,
lounging in your security
and saying to yourself,
'I am, and there is none besides me.
I will never be a widow
or suffer the loss of children.'
9Both of these will overtake you
in a moment, on a single day:
loss of children and widowhood.
They will come upon you in full measure,
in spite of your many sorceries
and all your potent spells.
10You have trusted in your wickedness
and have said, 'No one sees me.'
Your wisdom and knowledge mislead you
when you say to yourself,
'I am, and there is none besides me.'
11Disaster will come upon you,
and you will not know how to conjure it away.
A calamity will fall upon you
that you cannot ward off with a ransom;
a catastrophe you cannot foresee
will suddenly come upon you.

12"Keep on, then, with your magic spells
and with your many sorceries,

[a] 1 Or *Chaldeans*; also in verse 5

which you have labored at since
childhood.
Perhaps you will succeed,
perhaps you will cause terror.
13 All the counsel you have received has only
worn you out!
Let your astrologers come forward,
those stargazers who make predictions month
by month,
let them save you from what is coming
upon you.
14 Surely they are like stubble;
the fire will burn them up.
They cannot even save themselves
from the power of the flame.
Here are no coals to warm anyone;
here is no fire to sit by.
15 That is all they can do for you—
these you have labored with
and trafficked with since childhood.
Each of them goes on in his error;
there is not one that can save you.

Stubborn Israel

48 "Listen to this, O house of Jacob,
you who are called by the name of
Israel
and come from the line of Judah,
you who take oaths in the name of the LORD
and invoke the God of Israel—
but not in truth or righteousness—
2 you who call yourselves citizens of the holy
city
and rely on the God of Israel—
the LORD Almighty is his name:
3 I foretold the former things long ago,
my mouth announced them and I made
them known;
then suddenly I acted, and they came to
pass.
4 For I knew how stubborn you were;
the sinews of your neck were iron,
your forehead was bronze.
5 Therefore I told you these things long ago;
before they happened I announced them
to you
so that you could not say,
'My idols did them;
my wooden image and metal god ordained
them.'
6 You have heard these things; look at them
all.
Will you not admit them?
"From now on I will tell you of new things,
of hidden things unknown to you.
7 They are created now, and not long ago;
you have not heard of them before today.
So you cannot say,
'Yes, I knew of them.'
8 You have neither heard nor understood;
from of old your ear has not been open.
Well do I know how treacherous you are;
you were called a rebel from birth.
9 For my own name's sake I delay my wrath;
for the sake of my praise I hold it back
from you,
so as not to cut you off.
10 See, I have refined you, though not as silver;
I have tested you in the furnace of
affliction.
11 For my own sake, for my own sake, I do this.
How can I let myself be defamed?
I will not yield my glory to another.

Israel Freed

12 "Listen to me, O Jacob,
Israel, whom I have called:
I am he;
I am the first and I am the last.
13 My own hand laid the foundations of the
earth,
and my right hand spread out the heavens;
when I summon them,
they all stand up together.
14 "Come together, all of you, and listen:
Which of ⌞the idols⌟ has foretold these
things?
The LORD's chosen ally
will carry out his purpose against Babylon;
his arm will be against the Babylonians.[a]
15 I, even I, have spoken;
yes, I have called him.
I will bring him,
and he will succeed in his mission.
16 "Come near me and listen to this:
"From the first announcement I have not
spoken in secret;
at the time it happens, I am there."
And now the Sovereign LORD has sent me,
with his Spirit.
17 This is what the LORD says—
your Redeemer, the Holy One of Israel:
"I am the LORD your God,
who teaches you what is best for you,
who directs you in the way you should go.
18 If only you had paid attention to my
commands,
your peace would have been like a river,
your righteousness like the waves of the
sea.

a 14 Or *Chaldeans*; also in verse 20

19Your descendants would have been like the
sand,
your children like its numberless grains;
their name would never be cut off
nor destroyed from before me."

20Leave Babylon,
flee from the Babylonians!
Announce this with shouts of joy
and proclaim it.
Send it out to the ends of the earth;
say, "The LORD has redeemed his servant
Jacob."
21They did not thirst when he led them
through the deserts;
he made water flow for them from the
rock;
he split the rock
and water gushed out.

22"There is no peace," says the LORD, "for the
wicked."

The Servant of the LORD

49 Listen to me, you islands;
hear this, you distant nations:
Before I was born the LORD called me;
from my birth he has made mention of my
name.
2He made my mouth like a sharpened sword,
in the shadow of his hand he hid me;
he made me into a polished arrow
and concealed me in his quiver.
3He said to me, "You are my servant,
Israel, in whom I will display my
splendor."
4But I said, "I have labored to no purpose;
I have spent my strength in vain and for
nothing.
Yet what is due me is in the LORD's hand,
and my reward is with my God."

5And now the LORD says—
he who formed me in the womb to be his
servant
to bring Jacob back to him
and gather Israel to himself,
for I am honored in the eyes of the LORD
and my God has been my strength—
6he says:
"It is too small a thing for you to be my
servant
to restore the tribes of Jacob
and bring back those of Israel I have kept.
I will also make you a light for the Gentiles,
that you may bring my salvation to the
ends of the earth."

7This is what the LORD says—
the Redeemer and Holy One of Israel—
to him who was despised and abhorred by
the nation,
to the servant of rulers:
"Kings will see you and rise up,
princes will see and bow down,
because of the LORD, who is faithful,
the Holy One of Israel, who has chosen
you."

Restoration of Israel

8This is what the LORD says:

"In the time of my favor I will answer you,
and in the day of salvation I will help you;
I will keep you and will make you
to be a covenant for the people,
to restore the land
and to reassign its desolate inheritances,
9to say to the captives, 'Come out,'
and to those in darkness, 'Be free!'

"They will feed beside the roads
and find pasture on every barren hill.
10They will neither hunger nor thirst,
nor will the desert heat or the sun beat
upon them.
He who has compassion on them will guide
them
and lead them beside springs of water.
11I will turn all my mountains into roads,
and my highways will be raised up.
12See, they will come from afar—
some from the north, some from the west,
some from the region of Aswan.[a]"

13Shout for joy, O heavens;
rejoice, O earth;
burst into song, O mountains!
For the LORD comforts his people
and will have compassion on his afflicted
ones.

14But Zion said, "The LORD has forsaken me,
the Lord has forgotten me."

15"Can a mother forget the baby at her breast
and have no compassion on the child she
has borne?
Though she may forget,
I will not forget you!
16See, I have engraved you on the palms of my
hands;
your walls are ever before me.
17Your sons hasten back,

a12 Dead Sea Scrolls; Masoretic Text *Sinim*

and those who laid you waste depart from
you.
18Lift up your eyes and look around;
all your sons gather and come to you.
As surely as I live," declares the LORD,
"you will wear them all as ornaments;
you will put them on, like a bride.

19"Though you were ruined and made desolate
and your land laid waste,
now you will be too small for your people,
and those who devoured you will be far
away.
20The children born during your bereavement
will yet say in your hearing,
'This place is too small for us;
give us more space to live in.'
21Then you will say in your heart,
'Who bore me these?
I was bereaved and barren;
I was exiled and rejected.
Who brought these up?
I was left all alone,
but these—where have they come from?'"

22This is what the Sovereign LORD says:

"See, I will beckon to the Gentiles,
I will lift up my banner to the peoples;
they will bring your sons in their arms
and carry your daughters on their
shoulders.
23Kings will be your foster fathers,
and their queens your nursing mothers.
They will bow down before you with their
faces to the ground;
they will lick the dust at your feet.
Then you will know that I am the LORD;
those who hope in me will not be
disappointed."

24Can plunder be taken from warriors,
or captives rescued from the fierce[a]?
25But this is what the LORD says:

"Yes, captives will be taken from warriors,
and plunder retrieved from the fierce;
I will contend with those who contend with
you,
and your children I will save.
26I will make your oppressors eat their own
flesh;
they will be drunk on their own blood, as
with wine.
Then all mankind will know
that I, the LORD, am your Savior,
your Redeemer, the Mighty One of Jacob."

Israel's Sin and the Servant's Obedience

50 This is what the LORD says:

"Where is your mother's certificate of
divorce
with which I sent her away?
Or to which of my creditors
did I sell you?
Because of your sins you were sold;
because of your transgressions your
mother was sent away.
2When I came, why was there no one?
When I called, why was there no one to
answer?
Was my arm too short to ransom you?
Do I lack the strength to rescue you?
By a mere rebuke I dry up the sea,
I turn rivers into a desert;
their fish rot for lack of water
and die of thirst.
3I clothe the sky with darkness
and make sackcloth its covering."

4The Sovereign LORD has given me an
instructed tongue,
to know the word that sustains the weary.
He wakens me morning by morning,
wakens my ear to listen like one being
taught.
5The Sovereign LORD has opened my ears,
and I have not been rebellious;
I have not drawn back.
6I offered my back to those who beat me,
my cheeks to those who pulled out my
beard;
I did not hide my face
from mocking and spitting.
7Because the Sovereign LORD helps me,
I will not be disgraced.
Therefore have I set my face like flint,
and I know I will not be put to shame.
8He who vindicates me is near.
Who then will bring charges against me?
Let us face each other!
Who is my accuser?
Let him confront me!
9It is the Sovereign LORD who helps me.
Who is he that will condemn me?
They will all wear out like a garment;
the moths will eat them up.

10Who among you fears the LORD
and obeys the word of his servant?
Let him who walks in the dark,
who has no light,
trust in the name of the LORD
and rely on his God.

[a]24 Dead Sea Scrolls, Vulgate and Syriac (see also Septuagint and verse 25); Masoretic Text *righteous*

11But now, all you who light fires
and provide yourselves with flaming
torches,
go, walk in the light of your fires
and of the torches you have set ablaze.
This is what you shall receive from my hand:
You will lie down in torment.

Everlasting Salvation for Zion

51 "Listen to me, you who pursue
righteousness
and who seek the LORD:
Look to the rock from which you were cut
and to the quarry from which you were
hewn;
2look to Abraham, your father,
and to Sarah, who gave you birth.
When I called him he was but one,
and I blessed him and made him many.
3The LORD will surely comfort Zion
and will look with compassion on all her
ruins;
he will make her deserts like Eden,
her wastelands like the garden of the
LORD.
Joy and gladness will be found in her,
thanksgiving and the sound of singing.

4"Listen to me, my people;
hear me, my nation:
The law will go out from me;
my justice will become a light to the
nations.
5My righteousness draws near speedily,
my salvation is on the way,
and my arm will bring justice to the
nations.
The islands will look to me
and wait in hope for my arm.
6Lift up your eyes to the heavens,
look at the earth beneath;
the heavens will vanish like smoke,
the earth will wear out like a garment
and its inhabitants die like flies.
But my salvation will last forever,
my righteousness will never fail.

7"Hear me, you who know what is right,
you people who have my law in your
hearts:
Do not fear the reproach of men
or be terrified by their insults.
8For the moth will eat them up like a
garment;
the worm will devour them like wool.
But my righteousness will last forever,
my salvation through all generations."

9Awake, awake! Clothe yourself with strength,
O arm of the LORD;
awake, as in days gone by,
as in generations of old.
Was it not you who cut Rahab to pieces,
who pierced that monster through?
10Was it not you who dried up the sea,
the waters of the great deep,
who made a road in the depths of the sea
so that the redeemed might cross over?
11The ransomed of the LORD will return.
They will enter Zion with singing;
everlasting joy will crown their heads.
Gladness and joy will overtake them,
and sorrow and sighing will flee away.

12"I, even I, am he who comforts you.
Who are you that you fear mortal men,
the sons of men, who are but grass,
13that you forget the LORD your Maker,
who stretched out the heavens
and laid the foundations of the earth,
that you live in constant terror every day
because of the wrath of the oppressor,
who is bent on destruction?
For where is the wrath of the oppressor?
14 The cowering prisoners will soon be set
free;
they will not die in their dungeon,
nor will they lack bread.
15For I am the LORD your God,
who churns up the sea so that its waves
roar—
the LORD Almighty is his name.
16I have put my words in your mouth
and covered you with the shadow of my
hand—
I who set the heavens in place,
who laid the foundations of the earth,
and who say to Zion, 'You are my
people.'"

The Cup of the LORD's Wrath

17Awake, awake!
Rise up, O Jerusalem,
you who have drunk from the hand of the
LORD
the cup of his wrath,
you who have drained to its dregs
the goblet that makes men stagger.
18Of all the sons she bore
there was none to guide her;
of all the sons she reared
there was none to take her by the hand.
19These double calamities have come upon
you—
who can comfort you?—
ruin and destruction, famine and sword—

who can[a] console you?
20Your sons have fainted;
they lie at the head of every street,
like antelope caught in a net.
They are filled with the wrath of the LORD
and the rebuke of your God.

21Therefore hear this, you afflicted one,
made drunk, but not with wine.
22This is what your Sovereign LORD says,
your God, who defends his people:
"See, I have taken out of your hand
the cup that made you stagger;
from that cup, the goblet of my wrath,
you will never drink again.
23I will put it into the hands of your
tormentors,
who said to you,
'Fall prostrate that we may walk over you.'
And you made your back like the ground,
like a street to be walked over."

52 Awake, awake, O Zion,
clothe yourself with strength.
Put on your garments of splendor,
O Jerusalem, the holy city.
The uncircumcised and defiled
will not enter you again.
2Shake off your dust;
rise up, sit enthroned, O Jerusalem.
Free yourself from the chains on your neck,
O captive Daughter of Zion.

3For this is what the LORD says:

"You were sold for nothing,
and without money you will be
redeemed."

4For this is what the Sovereign LORD says:

"At first my people went down to Egypt to
live;
lately, Assyria has oppressed them.

5"And now what do I have here?" declares the LORD.

"For my people have been taken away for
nothing,
and those who rule them mock,[b]"
declares the LORD.
"And all day long
my name is constantly blasphemed.
6Therefore my people will know my name;
therefore in that day they will know
that it is I who foretold it.
Yes, it is I."

7How beautiful on the mountains
are the feet of those who bring good news,
who proclaim peace,
who bring good tidings,
who proclaim salvation,
who say to Zion,
"Your God reigns!"
8Listen! Your watchmen lift up their voices;
together they shout for joy.
When the LORD returns to Zion,
they will see it with their own eyes.
9Burst into songs of joy together,
you ruins of Jerusalem,
for the LORD has comforted his people,
he has redeemed Jerusalem.
10The LORD will lay bare his holy arm
in the sight of all the nations,
and all the ends of the earth will see
the salvation of our God.

11Depart, depart, go out from there!
Touch no unclean thing!
Come out from it and be pure,
you who carry the vessels of the LORD.
12But you will not leave in haste
or go in flight;
for the LORD will go before you,
the God of Israel will be your rear guard.

The Suffering and Glory of the Servant

13See, my servant will act wisely[c];
he will be raised and lifted up and highly
exalted.
14Just as there were many who were appalled
at him[d]—
his appearance was so disfigured beyond
that of any man
and his form marred beyond human
likeness—
15so will he sprinkle many nations,[e]
and kings will shut their mouths because
of him.
For what they were not told, they will see,
and what they have not heard, they will
understand.

53 Who has believed our message
and to whom has the arm of the LORD
been revealed?
2He grew up before him like a tender shoot,
and like a root out of dry ground.
He had no beauty or majesty to attract us to
him,
nothing in his appearance that we should
desire him.
3He was despised and rejected by men,
a man of sorrows, and familiar with
suffering.

[a]19 Dead Sea Scrolls, Septuagint, Vulgate and Syriac; Masoretic Text / *how can I wail* [b]5 Dead Sea Scrolls and Vulgate; Masoretic Text [c]13 Or *will prosper* [d]14 Hebrew *you* [e]15 Hebrew; Septuagint *so will many nations marvel at him*

Like one from whom men hide their faces
he was despised, and we esteemed him
not.

4 Surely he took up our infirmities
and carried our sorrows,
yet we considered him stricken by God,
smitten by him, and afflicted.
5 But he was pierced for our transgressions,
he was crushed for our iniquities;
the punishment that brought us peace was
upon him,
and by his wounds we are healed.
6 We all, like sheep, have gone astray,
each of us has turned to his own way;
and the LORD has laid on him
the iniquity of us all.

7 He was oppressed and afflicted,
yet he did not open his mouth;
he was led like a lamb to the slaughter,
and as a sheep before her shearers is
silent,
so he did not open his mouth.
8 By oppression[a] and judgment he was taken
away.
And who can speak of his descendants?
For he was cut off from the land of the
living;
for the transgression of my people he was
stricken.[b]
9 He was assigned a grave with the wicked,
and with the rich in his death,
though he had done no violence,
nor was any deceit in his mouth.

10 Yet it was the LORD's will to crush him and
cause him to suffer,
and though the LORD makes[c] his life a
guilt offering,
he will see his offspring and prolong his
days,
and the will of the LORD will prosper in
his hand.
11 After the suffering of his soul,
he will see the light ⌞of life⌟[d] and be
satisfied[e];
by his knowledge[f] my righteous servant will
justify many,
and he will bear their iniquities.
12 Therefore I will give him a portion among
the great,[g]
and he will divide the spoils with the
strong,[h]
because he poured out his life unto death,
and was numbered with the transgressors.
For he bore the sin of many,
and made intercession for the
transgressors.

The Future Glory of Zion

54 "Sing, O barren woman,
you who never bore a child;
burst into song, shout for joy,
you who were never in labor;
because more are the children of the desolate
woman
than of her who has a husband,"
says the LORD.
2 "Enlarge the place of your tent,
stretch your tent curtains wide,
do not hold back;
lengthen your cords,
strengthen your stakes.
3 For you will spread out to the right and to
the left;
your descendants will dispossess nations
and settle in their desolate cities.

4 "Do not be afraid; you will not suffer shame.
Do not fear disgrace; you will not be
humiliated.
You will forget the shame of your youth
and remember no more the reproach of
your widowhood.
5 For your Maker is your husband—
the LORD Almighty is his name—
the Holy One of Israel is your Redeemer;
he is called the God of all the earth.
6 The LORD will call you back
as if you were a wife deserted and
distressed in spirit—
a wife who married young,
only to be rejected," says your God.
7 "For a brief moment I abandoned you,
but with deep compassion I will bring you
back.
8 In a surge of anger
I hid my face from you for a moment,
but with everlasting kindness
I will have compassion on you,"
says the LORD your Redeemer.
9 "To me this is like the days of Noah,
when I swore that the waters of Noah
would never again cover the earth.
So now I have sworn not to be angry with
you,
never to rebuke you again.
10 Though the mountains be shaken
and the hills be removed,

[a] 8 Or *From arrest* [b] 8 Or *away. / Yet who of his generation considered / that he was cut off from the land of the living / for the transgression of my people, / to whom the blow was due?* [c] 10 Hebrew *though you make* [d] 11 Dead Sea Scrolls (see also Septuagint); Masoretic Text does not have *the light ⌞of life⌟* [e] 11 Or (with Masoretic Text) *11He will see the result of the suffering of his soul / and be satisfied* [f] 11 Or *by knowledge of him* [g] 12 Or *many* [h] 12 Or *numerous*

yet my unfailing love for you will not be
shaken
nor my covenant of peace be removed,"
says the LORD, who has compassion on
you.

11"O afflicted city, lashed by storms and not
comforted,
I will build you with stones of turquoise,[a]
your foundations with sapphires.[b]
12I will make your battlements of rubies,
your gates of sparkling jewels,
and all your walls of precious stones.
13All your sons will be taught by the LORD,
and great will be your children's peace.
14In righteousness you will be established:
Tyranny will be far from you;
you will have nothing to fear.
Terror will be far removed;
it will not come near you.
15If anyone does attack you, it will not be my
doing;
whoever attacks you will surrender to you.

16"See, it is I who created the blacksmith
who fans the coals into flame
and forges a weapon fit for its work.
And it is I who have created the destroyer to
work havoc;
17 no weapon forged against you will prevail,
and you will refute every tongue that
accuses you.
This is the heritage of the servants of the
LORD,
and this is their vindication from me,"
declares the LORD.

Invitation to the Thirsty

55 "Come, all you who are thirsty,
come to the waters;
and you who have no money,
come, buy and eat!
Come, buy wine and milk
without money and without cost.
2Why spend money on what is not bread,
and your labor on what does not satisfy?
Listen, listen to me, and eat what is good,
and your soul will delight in the richest of
fare.
3Give ear and come to me;
hear me, that your soul may live.
I will make an everlasting covenant with you,
my faithful love promised to David.
4See, I have made him a witness to the
peoples,
a leader and commander of the peoples.
5Surely you will summon nations you know
not,
and nations that do not know you will
hasten to you,
because of the LORD your God,
the Holy One of Israel,
for he has endowed you with splendor."

6Seek the LORD while he may be found;
call on him while he is near.
7Let the wicked forsake his way
and the evil man his thoughts.
Let him turn to the LORD, and he will have
mercy on him,
and to our God, for he will freely pardon.

8"For my thoughts are not your thoughts,
neither are your ways my ways,"
declares the LORD.
9"As the heavens are higher than the earth,
so are my ways higher than your ways
and my thoughts than your thoughts.
10As the rain and the snow
come down from heaven,
and do not return to it
without watering the earth
and making it bud and flourish,
so that it yields seed for the sower and
bread for the eater,
11so is my word that goes out from my mouth:
It will not return to me empty,
but will accomplish what I desire
and achieve the purpose for which I sent
it.
12You will go out in joy
and be led forth in peace;
the mountains and hills
will burst into song before you,
and all the trees of the field
will clap their hands.
13Instead of the thornbush will grow the pine
tree,
and instead of briers the myrtle will grow.
This will be for the LORD's renown,
for an everlasting sign,
which will not be destroyed."

Salvation for Others

56 This is what the LORD says:

"Maintain justice
and do what is right,
for my salvation is close at hand
and my righteousness will soon be
revealed.
2Blessed is the man who does this,
the man who holds it fast,
who keeps the Sabbath without desecrating
it,
and keeps his hand from doing any evil."

[a] 11 The meaning of the Hebrew for this word is uncertain. [b] 11 Or *lapis lazuli*

3Let no foreigner who has bound himself to
the LORD say,
"The LORD will surely exclude me from his
people."
And let not any eunuch complain,
"I am only a dry tree."

4For this is what the LORD says:

"To the eunuchs who keep my Sabbaths,
who choose what pleases me
and hold fast to my covenant—
5to them I will give within my temple and its
walls
a memorial and a name
better than sons and daughters;
I will give them an everlasting name
that will not be cut off.
6And foreigners who bind themselves to the
LORD
to serve him,
to love the name of the LORD,
and to worship him,
all who keep the Sabbath without desecrating
it
and who hold fast to my covenant—
7these I will bring to my holy mountain
and give them joy in my house of prayer.
Their burnt offerings and sacrifices
will be accepted on my altar;
for my house will be called
a house of prayer for all nations."
8The Sovereign LORD declares—
he who gathers the exiles of Israel:
"I will gather still others to them
besides those already gathered."

God's Accusation Against the Wicked

9Come, all you beasts of the field,
come and devour, all you beasts of the
forest!
10Israel's watchmen are blind,
they all lack knowledge;
they are all mute dogs,
they cannot bark;
they lie around and dream,
they love to sleep.
11They are dogs with mighty appetites;
they never have enough.
They are shepherds who lack understanding;
they all turn to their own way,
each seeks his own gain.
12"Come," each one cries, "let me get wine!
Let us drink our fill of beer!
And tomorrow will be like today,
or even far better."

57 The righteous perish,
and no one ponders it in his heart;
devout men are taken away,
and no one understands
that the righteous are taken away
to be spared from evil.
2Those who walk uprightly
enter into peace;
they find rest as they lie in death.

3"But you—come here, you sons of a
sorceress,
you offspring of adulterers and prostitutes!
4Whom are you mocking?
At whom do you sneer
and stick out your tongue?
Are you not a brood of rebels,
the offspring of liars?
5You burn with lust among the oaks
and under every spreading tree;
you sacrifice your children in the ravines
and under the overhanging crags.
6⌞The idols⌟ among the smooth stones of the
ravines are your portion;
they, they are your lot.
Yes, to them you have poured out drink
offerings
and offered grain offerings.
In the light of these things, should I
relent?
7You have made your bed on a high and lofty
hill;
there you went up to offer your sacrifices.
8Behind your doors and your doorposts
you have put your pagan symbols.
Forsaking me, you uncovered your bed,
you climbed into it and opened it wide;
you made a pact with those whose beds you
love,
and you looked on their nakedness.
9You went to Molech[a] with olive oil
and increased your perfumes.
You sent your ambassadors[b] far away;
you descended to the grave[c] itself!
10You were wearied by all your ways,
but you would not say, 'It is hopeless.'
You found renewal of your strength,
and so you did not faint.

11"Whom have you so dreaded and feared
that you have been false to me,
and have neither remembered me
nor pondered this in your hearts?
Is it not because I have long been silent
that you do not fear me?
12I will expose your righteousness and your
works,
and they will not benefit you.

[a]9 Or *to the king* [b]9 Or *idols* [c]9 Hebrew *Sheol*

13When you cry out for help,
let your collection ⌊of idols⌋ save you!
The wind will carry all of them off,
a mere breath will blow them away.
But the man who makes me his refuge
will inherit the land
and possess my holy mountain."

Comfort for the Contrite

14And it will be said:

"Build up, build up, prepare the road!
Remove the obstacles out of the way of my people."
15For this is what the high and lofty One says—
he who lives forever, whose name is holy:
"I live in a high and holy place,
but also with him who is contrite and lowly in spirit,
to revive the spirit of the lowly
and to revive the heart of the contrite.
16I will not accuse forever,
nor will I always be angry,
for then the spirit of man would grow faint before me—
the breath of man that I have created.
17I was enraged by his sinful greed;
I punished him, and hid my face in anger,
yet he kept on in his willful ways.
18I have seen his ways, but I will heal him;
I will guide him and restore comfort to him,
19 creating praise on the lips of the mourners in Israel.
Peace, peace, to those far and near,"
says the LORD. "And I will heal them."
20But the wicked are like the tossing sea,
which cannot rest,
whose waves cast up mire and mud.
21"There is no peace," says my God, "for the wicked."

True Fasting

58 "Shout it aloud, do not hold back.
Raise your voice like a trumpet.
Declare to my people their rebellion
and to the house of Jacob their sins.
2For day after day they seek me out;
they seem eager to know my ways,
as if they were a nation that does what is right
and has not forsaken the commands of its God.
They ask me for just decisions
and seem eager for God to come near them.
3'Why have we fasted,' they say,
'and you have not seen it?
Why have we humbled ourselves,
and you have not noticed?'

"Yet on the day of your fasting, you do as you please
and exploit all your workers.
4Your fasting ends in quarreling and strife,
and in striking each other with wicked fists.
You cannot fast as you do today
and expect your voice to be heard on high.
5Is this the kind of fast I have chosen,
only a day for a man to humble himself?
Is it only for bowing one's head like a reed
and for lying on sackcloth and ashes?
Is that what you call a fast,
a day acceptable to the LORD?

6"Is not this the kind of fasting I have chosen:
to loose the chains of injustice
and untie the cords of the yoke,
to set the oppressed free
and break every yoke?
7Is it not to share your food with the hungry
and to provide the poor wanderer with shelter—
when you see the naked, to clothe him,
and not to turn away from your own flesh and blood?
8Then your light will break forth like the dawn,
and your healing will quickly appear;
then your righteousness[a] will go before you,
and the glory of the LORD will be your rear guard.
9Then you will call, and the LORD will answer;
you will cry for help, and he will say: Here am I.

"If you do away with the yoke of oppression,
with the pointing finger and malicious talk,
10and if you spend yourselves in behalf of the hungry
and satisfy the needs of the oppressed,
then your light will rise in the darkness,
and your night will become like the noonday.
11The LORD will guide you always;
he will satisfy your needs in a sun-scorched land
and will strengthen your frame.
You will be like a well-watered garden,
like a spring whose waters never fail.
12Your people will rebuild the ancient ruins

[a]8 *Or your righteous One*

and will raise up the age-old foundations;
you will be called Repairer of Broken Walls,
Restorer of Streets with Dwellings.

13"If you keep your feet from breaking the Sabbath
and from doing as you please on my holy day,
if you call the Sabbath a delight
and the LORD's holy day honorable,
and if you honor it by not going your own way
and not doing as you please or speaking idle words,
14then you will find your joy in the LORD,
and I will cause you to ride on the heights of the land
and to feast on the inheritance of your father Jacob."
The mouth of the LORD has spoken.

Sin, Confession and Redemption

59 Surely the arm of the LORD is not too short to save,
nor his ear too dull to hear.
2But your iniquities have separated
you from your God;
your sins have hidden his face from you,
so that he will not hear.
3For your hands are stained with blood,
your fingers with guilt.
Your lips have spoken lies,
and your tongue mutters wicked things.
4No one calls for justice;
no one pleads his case with integrity.
They rely on empty arguments and speak lies;
they conceive trouble and give birth to evil.
5They hatch the eggs of vipers
and spin a spider's web.
Whoever eats their eggs will die,
and when one is broken, an adder is hatched.
6Their cobwebs are useless for clothing;
they cannot cover themselves with what they make.
Their deeds are evil deeds,
and acts of violence are in their hands.
7Their feet rush into sin;
they are swift to shed innocent blood.
Their thoughts are evil thoughts;
ruin and destruction mark their ways.
8The way of peace they do not know;
there is no justice in their paths.
They have turned them into crooked roads;
no one who walks in them will know peace.

9So justice is far from us,
and righteousness does not reach us.
We look for light, but all is darkness;
for brightness, but we walk in deep shadows.
10Like the blind we grope along the wall,
feeling our way like men without eyes.
At midday we stumble as if it were twilight;
among the strong, we are like the dead.
11We all growl like bears;
we moan mournfully like doves.
We look for justice, but find none;
for deliverance, but it is far away.

12For our offenses are many in your sight,
and our sins testify against us.
Our offenses are ever with us,
and we acknowledge our iniquities:
13rebellion and treachery against the LORD,
turning our backs on our God,
fomenting oppression and revolt,
uttering lies our hearts have conceived.
14So justice is driven back,
and righteousness stands at a distance;
truth has stumbled in the streets,
honesty cannot enter.
15Truth is nowhere to be found,
and whoever shuns evil becomes a prey.

The LORD looked and was displeased
that there was no justice.
16He saw that there was no one,
he was appalled that there was no one to intervene;
so his own arm worked salvation for him,
and his own righteousness sustained him.
17He put on righteousness as his breastplate,
and the helmet of salvation on his head;
he put on the garments of vengeance
and wrapped himself in zeal as in a cloak.
18According to what they have done,
so will he repay
wrath to his enemies
and retribution to his foes;
he will repay the islands their due.
19From the west, men will fear the name of the LORD,
and from the rising of the sun, they will revere his glory.
For he will come like a pent-up flood
that the breath of the LORD drives along.[a]

20"The Redeemer will come to Zion,
to those in Jacob who repent of their sins,"
declares the LORD.

[a] 19 Or *When the enemy comes in like a flood, / the Spirit of the LORD will put him to flight*

21"As for me, this is my covenant with them," says the LORD. "My Spirit, who is on you, and my words that I have put in your mouth will not depart from your mouth, or from the mouths of your children, or from the mouths of their descendants from this time on and forever," says the LORD.

The Glory of Zion

60 "Arise, shine, for your light has come,
and the glory of the LORD rises upon you.
2See, darkness covers the earth
and thick darkness is over the peoples,
but the LORD rises upon you
and his glory appears over you.
3Nations will come to your light,
and kings to the brightness of your dawn.

4"Lift up your eyes and look about you:
All assemble and come to you;
your sons come from afar,
and your daughters are carried on the arm.
5Then you will look and be radiant,
your heart will throb and swell with joy;
the wealth on the seas will be brought to you,
to you the riches of the nations will come.
6Herds of camels will cover your land,
young camels of Midian and Ephah.
And all from Sheba will come,
bearing gold and incense
and proclaiming the praise of the LORD.
7All Kedar's flocks will be gathered to you,
the rams of Nebaioth will serve you;
they will be accepted as offerings on my altar,
and I will adorn my glorious temple.

8"Who are these that fly along like clouds,
like doves to their nests?
9Surely the islands look to me;
in the lead are the ships of Tarshish,[a]
bringing your sons from afar,
with their silver and gold,
to the honor of the LORD your God,
the Holy One of Israel,
for he has endowed you with splendor.

10"Foreigners will rebuild your walls,
and their kings will serve you.
Though in anger I struck you,
in favor I will show you compassion.
11Your gates will always stand open,
they will never be shut, day or night,
so that men may bring you the wealth of the nations—
their kings led in triumphal procession.
12For the nation or kingdom that will not serve you will perish;
it will be utterly ruined.

13"The glory of Lebanon will come to you,
the pine, the fir and the cypress together,
to adorn the place of my sanctuary;
and I will glorify the place of my feet.
14The sons of your oppressors will come bowing before you;
all who despise you will bow down at your feet
and will call you the City of the LORD,
Zion of the Holy One of Israel.

15"Although you have been forsaken and hated,
with no one traveling through,
I will make you the everlasting pride
and the joy of all generations.
16You will drink the milk of nations
and be nursed at royal breasts.
Then you will know that I, the LORD, am your Savior,
your Redeemer, the Mighty One of Jacob.
17Instead of bronze I will bring you gold,
and silver in place of iron.
Instead of wood I will bring you bronze,
and iron in place of stones.
I will make peace your governor
and righteousness your ruler.
18No longer will violence be heard in your land,
nor ruin or destruction within your borders,
but you will call your walls Salvation
and your gates Praise.
19The sun will no more be your light by day,
nor will the brightness of the moon shine on you,
for the LORD will be your everlasting light,
and your God will be your glory.
20Your sun will never set again,
and your moon will wane no more;
the LORD will be your everlasting light,
and your days of sorrow will end.
21Then will all your people be righteous
and they will possess the land forever.
They are the shoot I have planted,
the work of my hands,
for the display of my splendor.
22The least of you will become a thousand,
the smallest a mighty nation.
I am the LORD;
in its time I will do this swiftly."

The Year of the LORD's Favor

61 The Spirit of the Sovereign LORD is on me,

[a] 9 Or *the trading ships*

because the LORD has anointed me
to preach good news to the poor.
He has sent me to bind up the brokenhearted,
to proclaim freedom for the captives
and release from darkness for the prisoners,[a]
2 to proclaim the year of the LORD's favor
and the day of vengeance of our God,
to comfort all who mourn,
3 and provide for those who grieve in Zion—
to bestow on them a crown of beauty
instead of ashes,
the oil of gladness
instead of mourning,
and a garment of praise
instead of a spirit of despair.
They will be called oaks of righteousness,
a planting of the LORD
for the display of his splendor.

4 They will rebuild the ancient ruins
and restore the places long devastated;
they will renew the ruined cities
that have been devastated for generations.
5 Aliens will shepherd your flocks;
foreigners will work your fields and vineyards.
6 And you will be called priests of the LORD,
you will be named ministers of our God.
You will feed on the wealth of nations,
and in their riches you will boast.

7 Instead of their shame
my people will receive a double portion,
and instead of disgrace
they will rejoice in their inheritance;
and so they will inherit a double portion in their land,
and everlasting joy will be theirs.

8 "For I, the LORD, love justice;
I hate robbery and iniquity.
In my faithfulness I will reward them
and make an everlasting covenant with them.
9 Their descendants will be known among the nations
and their offspring among the peoples.
All who see them will acknowledge
that they are a people the LORD has blessed."

10 I delight greatly in the LORD;
my soul rejoices in my God.
For he has clothed me with garments of salvation
and arrayed me in a robe of righteousness,
as a bridegroom adorns his head like a priest,
and as a bride adorns herself with her jewels.
11 For as the soil makes the sprout come up
and a garden causes seeds to grow,
so the Sovereign LORD will make righteousness and praise
spring up before all nations.

Zion's New Name

62 For Zion's sake I will not keep silent,
for Jerusalem's sake I will not remain quiet,
till her righteousness shines out like the dawn,
her salvation like a blazing torch.
2 The nations will see your righteousness,
and all kings your glory;
you will be called by a new name
that the mouth of the LORD will bestow.
3 You will be a crown of splendor in the LORD's hand,
a royal diadem in the hand of your God.
4 No longer will they call you Deserted,
or name your land Desolate.
But you will be called Hephzibah,[b]
and your land Beulah[c];
for the LORD will take delight in you,
and your land will be married.
5 As a young man marries a maiden,
so will your sons[d] marry you;
as a bridegroom rejoices over his bride,
so will your God rejoice over you.

6 I have posted watchmen on your walls,
O Jerusalem;
they will never be silent day or night.
You who call on the LORD,
give yourselves no rest,
7 and give him no rest till he establishes Jerusalem
and makes her the praise of the earth.

8 The LORD has sworn by his right hand
and by his mighty arm:
"Never again will I give your grain
as food for your enemies,
and never again will foreigners drink the new wine
for which you have toiled;
9 but those who harvest it will eat it
and praise the LORD,
and those who gather the grapes will drink it
in the courts of my sanctuary."

10 Pass through, pass through the gates!
Prepare the way for the people.
Build up, build up the highway!

[a] *1* Hebrew; Septuagint *the blind* [b] *4* *Hephzibah* means *my delight is in her.* [c] *4* *Beulah* means *married.* [d] *5* Or *Builder*

Remove the stones.
Raise a banner for the nations.

11The LORD has made proclamation
to the ends of the earth:
"Say to the Daughter of Zion,
'See, your Savior comes!
See, his reward is with him,
and his recompense accompanies him.'"
12They will be called the Holy People,
the Redeemed of the LORD;
and you will be called Sought After,
the City No Longer Deserted.

God's Day of Vengeance and Redemption

63 Who is this coming from Edom,
from Bozrah, with his garments stained crimson?
Who is this, robed in splendor,
striding forward in the greatness of his strength?

"It is I, speaking in righteousness,
mighty to save."

2Why are your garments red,
like those of one treading the winepress?

3"I have trodden the winepress alone;
from the nations no one was with me.
I trampled them in my anger
and trod them down in my wrath;
their blood spattered my garments,
and I stained all my clothing.
4For the day of vengeance was in my heart,
and the year of my redemption has come.
5I looked, but there was no one to help,
I was appalled that no one gave support;
so my own arm worked salvation for me,
and my own wrath sustained me.
6I trampled the nations in my anger;
in my wrath I made them drunk
and poured their blood on the ground."

Praise and Prayer

7I will tell of the kindnesses of the LORD,
the deeds for which he is to be praised,
according to all the LORD has done for us—
yes, the many good things he has done
for the house of Israel,
according to his compassion and many kindnesses.
8He said, "Surely they are my people,
sons who will not be false to me";
and so he became their Savior.
9In all their distress he too was distressed,
and the angel of his presence saved them.
In his love and mercy he redeemed them;
he lifted them up and carried them
all the days of old.
10Yet they rebelled
and grieved his Holy Spirit.
So he turned and became their enemy
and he himself fought against them.

11Then his people recalled[a] the days of old,
the days of Moses and his people—
where is he who brought them through the sea,
with the shepherd of his flock?
Where is he who set
his Holy Spirit among them,
12who sent his glorious arm of power
to be at Moses' right hand,
who divided the waters before them,
to gain for himself everlasting renown,
13who led them through the depths?
Like a horse in open country,
they did not stumble;
14like cattle that go down to the plain,
they were given rest by the Spirit of the LORD.
This is how you guided your people
to make for yourself a glorious name.

15Look down from heaven and see
from your lofty throne, holy and glorious.
Where are your zeal and your might?
Your tenderness and compassion are withheld from us.
16But you are our Father,
though Abraham does not know us
or Israel acknowledge us;
you, O LORD, are our Father,
our Redeemer from of old is your name.
17Why, O LORD, do you make us wander from your ways
and harden our hearts so we do not revere you?
Return for the sake of your servants,
the tribes that are your inheritance.
18For a little while your people possessed your holy place,
but now our enemies have trampled down your sanctuary.
19We are yours from of old;
but you have not ruled over them,
they have not been called by your name.[b]

64 Oh, that you would rend the heavens
and come down,
that the mountains would tremble before you!
2As when fire sets twigs ablaze
and causes water to boil,

[a] 11 Or *But may he recall* [b] 19 Or *We are like those you have never ruled, / like those never called by your name*

come down to make your name known to
your enemies
and cause the nations to quake before you!
3For when you did awesome things that we
did not expect,
you came down, and the mountains
trembled before you.
4Since ancient times no one has heard,
no ear has perceived,
no eye has seen any God besides you,
who acts on behalf of those who wait for
him.
5You come to the help of those who gladly do
right,
who remember your ways.
But when we continued to sin against them,
you were angry.
How then can we be saved?
6All of us have become like one who is
unclean,
and all our righteous acts are like filthy
rags;
we all shrivel up like a leaf,
and like the wind our sins sweep us away.
7No one calls on your name
or strives to lay hold of you;
for you have hidden your face from us
and made us waste away because of our
sins.
8Yet, O LORD, you are our Father.
We are the clay, you are the potter;
we are all the work of your hand.
9Do not be angry beyond measure, O LORD;
do not remember our sins forever.
Oh, look upon us, we pray,
for we are all your people.
10Your sacred cities have become a desert;
even Zion is a desert, Jerusalem a
desolation.
11Our holy and glorious temple, where our
fathers praised you,
has been burned with fire,
and all that we treasured lies in ruins.
12After all this, O LORD, will you hold yourself
back?
Will you keep silent and punish us beyond
measure?

Judgment and Salvation

65 "I revealed myself to those who did not
ask for me;
I was found by those who did not seek
me.
To a nation that did not call on my name,
I said, 'Here am I, here am I.'
2All day long I have held out my hands
to an obstinate people,
who walk in ways not good,
pursuing their own imaginations—
3a people who continually provoke me
to my very face,
offering sacrifices in gardens
and burning incense on altars of brick;
4who sit among the graves
and spend their nights keeping secret vigil;
who eat the flesh of pigs,
and whose pots hold broth of unclean
meat;
5who say, 'Keep away; don't come near me,
for I am too sacred for you!'
Such people are smoke in my nostrils,
a fire that keeps burning all day.

6"See, it stands written before me:
I will not keep silent but will pay back in
full;
I will pay it back into their laps—
7both your sins and the sins of your fathers,"
says the LORD.
"Because they burned sacrifices on the
mountains
and defied me on the hills,
I will measure into their laps
the full payment for their former deeds."

8This is what the LORD says:

"As when juice is still found in a cluster of
grapes
and men say, 'Don't destroy it,
there is yet some good in it,'
so will I do in behalf of my servants;
I will not destroy them all.
9I will bring forth descendants from Jacob,
and from Judah those who will possess my
mountains;
my chosen people will inherit them,
and there will my servants live.
10Sharon will become a pasture for flocks,
and the Valley of Achor a resting place for
herds,
for my people who seek me.
11"But as for you who forsake the LORD
and forget my holy mountain,
who spread a table for Fortune
and fill bowls of mixed wine for Destiny,
12I will destine you for the sword,
and you will all bend down for the
slaughter;
for I called but you did not answer,
I spoke but you did not listen.
You did evil in my sight
and chose what displeases me."

13Therefore this is what the Sovereign LORD
says:

"My servants will eat,
but you will go hungry;

my servants will drink,
but you will go thirsty;
my servants will rejoice,
but you will be put to shame.
14My servants will sing
out of the joy of their hearts,
but you will cry out
from anguish of heart
and wail in brokenness of spirit.
15You will leave your name
to my chosen ones as a curse;
the Sovereign LORD will put you to death,
but to his servants he will give another name.
16Whoever invokes a blessing in the land
will do so by the God of truth;
he who takes an oath in the land
will swear by the God of truth.
For the past troubles will be forgotten
and hidden from my eyes.

New Heavens and a New Earth

17"Behold, I will create
new heavens and a new earth.
The former things will not be remembered,
nor will they come to mind.
18But be glad and rejoice forever
in what I will create,
for I will create Jerusalem to be a delight
and its people a joy.
19I will rejoice over Jerusalem
and take delight in my people;
the sound of weeping and of crying
will be heard in it no more.
20"Never again will there be in it
an infant who lives but a few days,
or an old man who does not live out his years;
he who dies at a hundred
will be thought a mere youth;
he who fails to reach[a] a hundred
will be considered accursed.
21They will build houses and dwell in them;
they will plant vineyards and eat their fruit.
22No longer will they build houses and others live in them,
or plant and others eat.
For as the days of a tree,
so will be the days of my people;
my chosen ones will long enjoy
the works of their hands.
23They will not toil in vain
or bear children doomed to misfortune;
for they will be a people blessed by the LORD,
they and their descendants with them.
24Before they call I will answer;
while they are still speaking I will hear.
25The wolf and the lamb will feed together,
and the lion will eat straw like the ox,
but dust will be the serpent's food.
They will neither harm nor destroy
on all my holy mountain,"
says the LORD.

Judgment and Hope

66 This is what the LORD says:
"Heaven is my throne,
and the earth is my footstool.
Where is the house you will build for me?
Where will my resting place be?
2Has not my hand made all these things,
and so they came into being?"
declares the LORD.

"This is the one I esteem:
he who is humble and contrite in spirit,
and trembles at my word.
3But whoever sacrifices a bull
is like one who kills a man,
and whoever offers a lamb,
like one who breaks a dog's neck;
whoever makes a grain offering
is like one who presents pig's blood,
and whoever burns memorial incense,
like one who worships an idol.
They have chosen their own ways,
and their souls delight in their abominations;
4so I also will choose harsh treatment for them
and will bring upon them what they dread.
For when I called, no one answered,
when I spoke, no one listened.
They did evil in my sight
and chose what displeases me."
5Hear the word of the LORD,
you who tremble at his word:
"Your brothers who hate you,
and exclude you because of my name,
have said,
'Let the LORD be glorified,
that we may see your joy!'
Yet they will be put to shame.
6Hear that uproar from the city,
hear that noise from the temple!
It is the sound of the LORD
repaying his enemies all they deserve.
7"Before she goes into labor,

[a]20 Or *the sinner who reaches*

she gives birth;
before the pains come upon her,
she delivers a son.
8Who has ever heard of such a thing?
Who has ever seen such things?
Can a country be born in a day
or a nation be brought forth in a moment?
Yet no sooner is Zion in labor
than she gives birth to her children.
9Do I bring to the moment of birth
and not give delivery?" says the LORD.
"Do I close up the womb
when I bring to delivery?" says your God.
10"Rejoice with Jerusalem and be glad for her,
all you who love her;
rejoice greatly with her,
all you who mourn over her.
11For you will nurse and be satisfied
at her comforting breasts;
you will drink deeply
and delight in her overflowing
abundance."

12For this is what the LORD says:

"I will extend peace to her like a river,
and the wealth of nations like a flooding
stream;
you will nurse and be carried on her arm
and dandled on her knees.
13As a mother comforts her child,
so will I comfort you;
and you will be comforted over
Jerusalem."

14When you see this, your heart will rejoice
and you will flourish like grass;
the hand of the LORD will be made known to
his servants,
but his fury will be shown to his foes.
15See, the LORD is coming with fire,
and his chariots are like a whirlwind;
he will bring down his anger with fury,
and his rebuke with flames of fire.
16For with fire and with his sword
the LORD will execute judgment upon all
men,
and many will be those slain by the LORD.

17"Those who consecrate and purify themselves to go into the gardens, following the one in
the midst of[a] those who eat the flesh of pigs and
rats and other abominable things—they will
meet their end together," declares the LORD.
18"And I, because of their actions and their
imaginations, am about to come[b] and gather all
nations and tongues, and they will come and see
my glory.
19"I will set a sign among them, and I will send
some of those who survive to the nations—to
Tarshish, to the Libyans[c] and Lydians (famous
as archers), to Tubal and Greece, and to the distant islands that have not heard of my fame or
seen my glory. They will proclaim my glory
among the nations. 20And they will bring all your
brothers, from all the nations, to my holy mountain in Jerusalem as an offering to the LORD—on
horses, in chariots and wagons, and on mules and
camels," says the LORD. "They will bring them, as
the Israelites bring their grain offerings, to the
temple of the LORD in ceremonially clean vessels.
21And I will select some of them also to be priests
and Levites," says the LORD.
22"As the new heavens and the new earth that
I make will endure before me," declares the
LORD, "so will your name and descendants endure. 23From one New Moon to another and from
one Sabbath to another, all mankind will come
and bow down before me," says the LORD.
24"And they will go out and look upon the dead
bodies of those who rebelled against me; their
worm will not die, nor will their fire be
quenched, and they will be loathsome to all mankind."

a17 Or *gardens behind one of your temples, and* b18 The meaning of the Hebrew for this clause is uncertain. c19 Some Septuagint manuscripts *Put* (Libyans); Hebrew *Pul*

Introduction to
JEREMIAH

Personal Reading Plan

❒ Jeremiah 1:1–3:5	❒ Jeremiah 21:1–23:8	❒ Jeremiah 38:1–40:6
❒ Jeremiah 3:6–4:31	❒ Jeremiah 23:9–25:14	❒ Jeremiah 40:7–43:13
❒ Jeremiah 5:1–6:30	❒ Jeremiah 25:15–26:24	❒ Jeremiah 44:1–46:28
❒ Jeremiah 7:1–9:26	❒ Jeremiah 27:1–29:32	❒ Jeremiah 47:1–48:47
❒ Jeremiah 10:1–12:17	❒ Jeremiah 30:1–31:40	❒ Jeremiah 49:1–39
❒ Jeremiah 13:1–15:21	❒ Jeremiah 32:1–33:26	❒ Jeremiah 50:1–46
❒ Jeremiah 16:1–17:27	❒ Jeremiah 34:1–35:19	❒ Jeremiah 51:1–64
❒ Jeremiah 18:1–20:18	❒ Jeremiah 36:1–37:21	❒ Jeremiah 52:1–34

Author

These are the words of Jeremiah, who was both a prophet and a priest. They were written down by his secretary Baruch (36:4–32) who may have been the one to put the book in its final form.

Date

Events recorded here span the years 626–585 B.C. The book was compiled sometime later. Jeremiah's ministry was immediately preceded by that of Zephaniah. Habakkuk, Obadiah and Ezekiel were possibly contemporaries of Jeremiah.

Theme

God is just and must punish sin. But God in his grace promises Israel restoration and covenant renewal.

Historical Background

The prophet Jeremiah ministered in the context of three major kings. Under King Josiah (640–609 B.C.), Jeremiah was free to preach and join in Josiah's reform movement. Under King Jehoiakim (609–598 B.C.), Jeremiah fell out of royal favor and experienced frequent imprisonments. Under King Zedekiah (597–586 B.C.), Jeremiah was treated more kindly but still had to fear for his life. The judgment that Jeremiah announced was brought about by King Nebuchadnezzar of Babylon. He besieged Jerusalem three times, culminating in the sacking of Jerusalem in 586 B.C. and a full-scale exile of Jews to Babylon. Jewish tradition asserts that while Jeremiah was living in exile in Egypt he was put to death by being stoned (see Heb. 11:37).

Characteristics

The book is constructed thematically, not chronologically. In it Jeremiah speaks his mind—a most disturbed and distressed mind. He complains to God about the job allotted to him more than any other prophet. Jeremiah denounces Judah's kings for their folly and weakness and the people for going their own way. Equally a part of his message, however, is a God of love who is determined to mold a people worthy of his name, and who compelled Jeremiah to announce that the divine wrath had 70 years as its bounds. After that—forgiveness and cleansing would come—bringing a new day in which all expectations would be fulfilled in a manner transcending all God's mercies of old.

1 The words of Jeremiah son of Hilkiah, one of
the priests at Anathoth in the territory of
Benjamin. 2The word of the LORD came to him in
the thirteenth year of the reign of Josiah son of
Amon king of Judah, 3and through the reign of
Jehoiakim son of Josiah king of Judah, down to
the fifth month of the eleventh year of Zedekiah
son of Josiah king of Judah, when the people of
Jerusalem went into exile.

The Call of Jeremiah

4The word of the LORD came to me, saying,

5"Before I formed you in the womb I knew[a]
you,
before you were born I set you apart;
I appointed you as a prophet to the
nations."

6"Ah, Sovereign LORD," I said, "I do not know
how to speak; I am only a child."
7But the LORD said to me, "Do not say, 'I am
only a child.' You must go to everyone I send you
to and say whatever I command you. 8Do not be
afraid of them, for I am with you and will rescue
you," declares the LORD.
9Then the LORD reached out his hand and
touched my mouth and said to me, "Now, I have
put my words in your mouth. 10See, today I appoint you over nations and kingdoms to uproot
and tear down, to destroy and overthrow, to
build and to plant."
11The word of the LORD came to me: "What do
you see, Jeremiah?"

"I see the branch of an almond tree," I replied.
12The LORD said to me, "You have seen correctly, for I am watching[b] to see that my word
is fulfilled."
13The word of the LORD came to me again:
"What do you see?"

"I see a boiling pot, tilting away from the north," I answered.
14The LORD said to me, "From the north disas-
ter will be poured out on all who live in the land.
15I am about to summon all the peoples of the
northern kingdoms," declares the LORD.

"Their kings will come and set up their
thrones
in the entrance of the gates of Jerusalem;
they will come against all her surrounding
walls
and against all the towns of Judah.
16I will pronounce my judgments on my people
because of their wickedness in forsaking
me,
in burning incense to other gods
and in worshiping what their hands have
made.

17"Get yourself ready! Stand up and say to
them whatever I command you. Do not be terrified by them, or I will terrify you before them.
18Today I have made you a fortified city, an iron
pillar and a bronze wall to stand against the
whole land—against the kings of Judah, its officials, its priests and the people of the land.
19They will fight against you but will not overcome you, for I am with you and will rescue you,"
declares the LORD.

Israel Forsakes God

2 The word of the LORD came to me: 2"Go and
proclaim in the hearing of Jerusalem:

"'I remember the devotion of your youth,
how as a bride you loved me
and followed me through the desert,
through a land not sown.
3Israel was holy to the LORD,
the firstfruits of his harvest;
all who devoured her were held guilty,
and disaster overtook them,'"
declares the LORD.

4Hear the word of the LORD, O house of
Jacob,
all you clans of the house of Israel.

5This is what the LORD says:

"What fault did your fathers find in me,
that they strayed so far from me?
They followed worthless idols
and became worthless themselves.
6They did not ask, 'Where is the LORD,
who brought us up out of Egypt
and led us through the barren wilderness,
through a land of deserts and rifts,
a land of drought and darkness,[c]
a land where no one travels and no one
lives?'
7I brought you into a fertile land
to eat its fruit and rich produce.
But you came and defiled my land
and made my inheritance detestable.
8The priests did not ask,
'Where is the LORD?'
Those who deal with the law did not know
me;
the leaders rebelled against me.
The prophets prophesied by Baal,
following worthless idols.

9"Therefore I bring charges against you
again,"
declares the LORD.

[a]5 Or *chose* [b]12 The Hebrew for *watching* sounds like the Hebrew for *almond tree.* [c]6 Or *and the shadow of death*

"And I will bring charges against your
children's children.
10Cross over to the coasts of Kittim[a] and look,
send to Kedar[b] and observe closely;
see if there has ever been anything like this:
11Has a nation ever changed its gods?
(Yet they are not gods at all.)
But my people have exchanged their[c] Glory
for worthless idols.
12Be appalled at this, O heavens,
and shudder with great horror,"
declares the LORD.
13"My people have committed two sins:
They have forsaken me,
the spring of living water,
and have dug their own cisterns,
broken cisterns that cannot hold water.
14Is Israel a servant, a slave by birth?
Why then has he become plunder?
15Lions have roared;
they have growled at him.
They have laid waste his land;
his towns are burned and deserted.
16Also, the men of Memphis[d] and Tahpanhes
have shaved the crown of your head.[e]
17Have you not brought this on yourselves
by forsaking the LORD your God
when he led you in the way?
18Now why go to Egypt
to drink water from the Shihor[f]?
And why go to Assyria
to drink water from the River[g]?
19Your wickedness will punish you;
your backsliding will rebuke you.
Consider then and realize
how evil and bitter it is for you
when you forsake the LORD your God
and have no awe of me,"
declares the Lord,
the LORD Almighty.

20"Long ago you broke off your yoke
and tore off your bonds;
you said, 'I will not serve you!'
Indeed, on every high hill
and under every spreading tree
you lay down as a prostitute.
21I had planted you like a choice vine
of sound and reliable stock.
How then did you turn against me
into a corrupt, wild vine?
22Although you wash yourself with soda
and use an abundance of soap,
the stain of your guilt is still before me,"
declares the Sovereign LORD.
23"How can you say, 'I am not defiled;
I have not run after the Baals'?
See how you behaved in the valley;
consider what you have done.
You are a swift she-camel
running here and there,
24a wild donkey accustomed to the desert,
sniffing the wind in her craving—
in her heat who can restrain her?
Any males that pursue her need not tire
themselves;
at mating time they will find her.
25Do not run until your feet are bare
and your throat is dry.
But you said, 'It's no use!
I love foreign gods,
and I must go after them.'

26"As a thief is disgraced when he is caught,
so the house of Israel is disgraced—
they, their kings and their officials,
their priests and their prophets.
27They say to wood, 'You are my father,'
and to stone, 'You gave me birth.'
They have turned their backs to me
and not their faces;
yet when they are in trouble, they say,
'Come and save us!'
28Where then are the gods you made for
yourselves?
Let them come if they can save you
when you are in trouble!
For you have as many gods
as you have towns, O Judah.

29"Why do you bring charges against me?
You have all rebelled against me,"
declares the LORD.
30"In vain I punished your people;
they did not respond to correction.
Your sword has devoured your prophets
like a ravening lion.

31"You of this generation, consider the word of
the LORD:

"Have I been a desert to Israel
or a land of great darkness?
Why do my people say, 'We are free to roam;
we will come to you no more'?
32Does a maiden forget her jewelry,
a bride her wedding ornaments?
Yet my people have forgotten me,
days without number.
33How skilled you are at pursuing love!
Even the worst of women can learn from
your ways.
34On your clothes men find

a10 That is, Cyprus and western coastlands b10 The home of Bedouin tribes in the Syro-Arabian desert c11 Masoretic Text; an ancient Hebrew scribal tradition *my* d16 Hebrew *Noph* e16 Or *have cracked your skull* f18 That is, a branch of the Nile g18 That is, the Euphrates

INTERACTIVE EXERCISES

8 CATEGORIES OF ACTIVITIES FOR KICKING-OFF YOUR MEETING:

- **AWARENESS** "Who am I?"
- **RELATIONSHIPS** "How do I relate to others?"
- **CHOICES** "How do I decide what's right?"
- **STRESS** "How do I deal with the pressure?"
- **ISSUES** "How do I respond to hot topics?"
- **CRISES** "How can I get through tough times?"
- **BELIEFS** "What is Christianity all about?"
- **DISCIPLESHIP** "How do I live out my faith?"

4 BASIC GROUP STRUCTURES FOR MORE EFFECTIVE ACTIVITIES:

- **TWOSOMES**
- **FOURSOMES**
- **CIRCLE OF EIGHT**
- **WAGON WHEEL**

TABLE OF CONTENTS

BIBLICAL INVENTORIES

CASE STUDIES

SCRIPTURE REFLECTIONS

AFFIRMATION EXERCISES

EVALUATION

I Am Somebody Who …

Rotate around the group, one person reading the first item, the next person reading the second item, etc. Before answering, let everyone in the group try to GUESS what the answer would be: "Yes" ... "No" ... or "Maybe." After everyone has guessed, explain the answer. Anyone who guessed right gets 10 points. When every item on the list has been read, the person with the most points WINS.

I AM SOMEBODY WHO ...

	YES	NO	MAYBE
blushes at a compliment	❑	❑	❑
sings in the shower	❑	❑	❑
will tell someone their fly is open	❑	❑	❑
slurps my soup	❑	❑	❑
loves crossword puzzles	❑	❑	❑
hates flying	❑	❑	❑
watches soap operas.	❑	❑	❑
is afraid of the dark	❑	❑	❑
sleeps until the last second	❑	❑	❑
has traveled overseas	❑	❑	❑
reads the sports page	❑	❑	❑
saves for a rainy day	❑	❑	❑
sleeps with a teddy bear	❑	❑	❑
tells a friend they have bad breath	❑	❑	❑
likes to play practical jokes	❑	❑	❑
eats dessert first	❑	❑	❑
often watches cartoons	❑	❑	❑
loves liver	❑	❑	❑
can touch my tongue to my nose	❑	❑	❑
sleeps on a water bed	❑	❑	❑
has had their tonsils out.	❑	❑	❑
enjoys classical music	❑	❑	❑
is an only child	❑	❑	❑
likes to dress up	❑	❑	❑
plays chess regularly	❑	❑	❑
frequently stays up all night	❑	❑	❑
moved recently	❑	❑	❑
plays the guitar	❑	❑	❑
does a lot of rollerblading	❑	❑	❑

BACK TO BACK

Pair off and sit back to back. Let one person guess out loud what their partner would do in each situation: "yes" ... "no" ... or "maybe." Give yourself 10 points for every correct guess. Then reverse roles and let your partner guess about you in these situations. Total your scores to find the winner.

MY PARTNER IS SOMEONE WHO WOULD:	YES	NO	MAYBE
1. Yell at a referee?	❑	❑	❑
2. Go to the restroom if the movie got scary?	❑	❑	❑
3. Spend most of their money on video games?	❑	❑	❑
4. Cut school to do something fun?	❑	❑	❑
5. Buy the latest fashions?	❑	❑	❑
6. Rather participate in a sport than watch one?	❑	❑	❑
7. Choose vanilla ice cream over jamoca almond fudge?	❑	❑	❑
8. Rather ride a motorcycle than a horse?	❑	❑	❑
9. Choose ESPN over MTV?	❑	❑	❑
10. Prefer to own a Jeep more than a Mercedes Benz?	❑	❑	❑

MY TEMPERAMENT

Get together in groups of 2 to 4 and explain how you see yourself in the eight categories below. In each category, circle which statement is closest to the way you think or act. Go down the list one item at a time letting everyone share their response for each category.

ON SHOWING MY FEELINGS:
Big boys/girls don't cry. ________________ I love you, man!

ON INTENSITY:
Chill out. ________________ Just do it.

ON BEING GENTLE AND KIND:
Nice guys finish last. ________________ You say "Jump"; I say "How high?"

ON SPIRITUAL DESIRE:
Don't go overboard. ________________ Full speed ahead.

ON CARING FOR OTHER PEOPLE:
Not my problem. ________________ He ain't heavy; he's my brother.

ON BEING OPEN AND HONEST:
Mind your own business. ________________ Lay it on the line.

ON HANDLING CONFLICT:
Peace at any price. ________________ I don't get mad; I get even.

KWIZ

Form groups of 4 to 8 people. Everyone in the group chooses one of the categories. One person at a time will read aloud the questions in their category—pausing to let others guess before revealing the answer. For each correct answer, the guesser receives the dollar amount for that question. After everyone is finished, add up your winnings and see who has the most money.

SPORTING EVENTS

FOR $1—I would prefer:
- ❑ to watch a sports event
- ❑ to play a sport

FOR $2—At a live sporting event, I am more likely to:
- ❑ yell at the ref ❑ do the wave
- ❑ paint my face and act crazy

FOR $3—My favorite ballpark food is:
- ❑ hot dogs ❑ nachos
- ❑ peanuts ❑ pretzels

FOR $4—One sport I would never try is:
- ❑ bungee jumping ❑ ski jumping
- ❑ motorcross racing ❑ sky surfing
- ❑ scuba diving ❑ snowboarding

OUTDOORS

FOR $1—I would rather go to the:
- ❑ mountains ❑ beach

FOR $2—I would rather stay in a:
- ❑ tent ❑ motor home
- ❑ cabin ❑ hotel

FOR $3—When I go camping I prefer to:
- ❑ go hiking ❑ go swimming
- ❑ take photographs ❑ do nothing

FOR $4—My favorite camping food is:
- ❑ hot chocolate
- ❑ trail mix
- ❑ hot dogs cooked over a campfire
- ❑ roasted marshmallows
- ❑ hot, spicy chili

DRIVING

FOR $1—I could best be described as:
- ❑ Cautious Casey ❑ Racey Randy

FOR $2—I am probably more likely to:
- ❑ speed
- ❑ roll through a stop sign
- ❑ zoom through a yellow light

FOR $3—I got my last speeding ticket:
- ❑ within the last month
- ❑ within the last six months
- ❑ over a year ago
- ❑ never

FOR $4—My pet peeve when driving is:
- ❑ people who don't use a turn signal
- ❑ rush hour traffic
- ❑ speeders in residential neighborhoods
- ❑ slow traffic in the left lane
- ❑ Sunday drivers

PETS

FOR $1—In my opinion, the cutest animal is:
- ❑ a puppy ❑ a kitten

FOR $2—If I could choose a dog, I'd select:
- ❑ a frisky, little dog
- ❑ a big, playful dog
- ❑ a lovable, lazy dog

FOR $3—What bugs me most about having a pet is:
- ❑ cleaning up the mess
- ❑ when they are noisy
- ❑ finding hair or feathers everywhere
- ❑ when they scratch things

FOR $4—My favorite unusual type of pet is:
- ❑ a snake ❑ a parrot
- ❑ a pot-bellied pig ❑ a gerbil
- ❑ a lizard ❑ a monkey

HABITS

FOR $1—I am more likely to squeeze the toothpaste:
- ❑ in the middle
- ❑ from the end

FOR $2—If I am lost, I will probably
- ❑ stop and ask directions
- ❑ check the map
- ❑ find the way by driving around

FOR $3—I read the newspaper starting with the:
- ❑ front page
- ❑ funnies
- ❑ entertainment
- ❑ sports

FOR $4—When I undress at night, I put my clothes:
- ❑ on a hanger in the closet
- ❑ folded neatly over a chair
- ❑ into a hamper or clothes basket
- ❑ on the floor

SHOWS

FOR $1—I am more likely to:
- ❑ go see a first-run movie
- ❑ rent a video at home

FOR $2—On TV, my first choice is:
- ❑ news
- ❑ sports
- ❑ sitcoms

FOR $3—If a show gets scary, I will usually:
- ❑ go to the restroom
- ❑ close my eyes
- ❑ clutch a friend
- ❑ love it

FOR $4—In movies, I prefer:
- ❑ comedies
- ❑ serious drama
- ❑ action films
- ❑ Disney animations

FOOD

FOR $1—I prefer to eat at a:
- ❑ fast-food restaurant
- ❑ fancy restaurant

FOR $2—On the menu, I look for something:
- ❑ familiar
- ❑ different
- ❑ way-out

FOR $3—When eating chicken, my preference is a:
- ❑ drumstick
- ❑ breast
- ❑ wing
- ❑ gizzard

FOR $4—I draw the line when it come to eating:
- ❑ frog legs
- ❑ sushi
- ❑ Rocky Mountain oysters

CLOTHES

FOR $1—I'm more likely to shop at:
- ❑ Walmart
- ❑ Neiman Marcus

FOR $2—I feel more comfortable wearing:
- ❑ formal clothes
- ❑ sport clothes
- ❑ casual clothes
- ❑ grubbies

FOR $3—In buying clothes, I look first for:
- ❑ fashion/style
- ❑ name brand
- ❑ price
- ❑ quality

FOR $4—In buying clothes, I usually:
- ❑ shop all day for a bargain
- ❑ choose one store but try on everything
- ❑ buy the first thing I try on
- ❑ buy without trying it on

How Was Your Day?

What was your day like today? In groups of 4 to 8, use one of the characters below to help you describe your day to the group. Feel free to elaborate.

GREEK TRAGEDY
It was classic, not a dry eye in the house.

SOAP OPERA
I didn't think these things could happen, until it happened to me.

EPISODE OF THREE STOOGES
I was Larry, trapped between Curley and Moe.

ACTION ADVENTURE
When I rode onto the scene, everybody noticed.

LATE NIGHT NEWS
It might as well have been broadcast over the airwaves.

BIBLE EPIC
Cecil B. DeMille couldn't have done it any better.

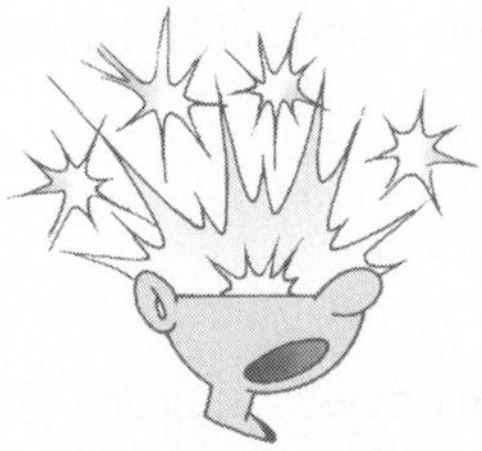

FIREWORKS DISPLAY
It was spectacular.

BORING LECTURE
The biggest challenge of the day was staying awake.

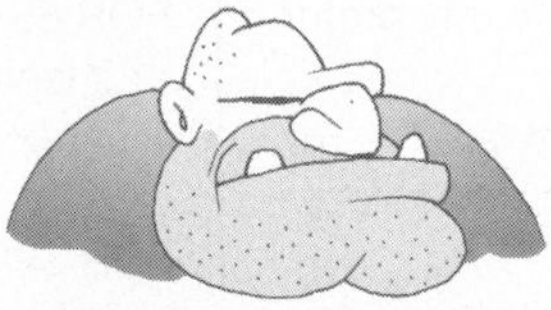

PROFESSIONAL WRESTLING MATCH
I feel as if Hulk Hogan's been coming after me.

SCOUTING REPORT

Get together with 2 or 3 people from your group and work together on the scouting report below. Taking one category at a time, check your one or two best points. See if the others agree with you ... and let them add one more that you did not mention. Then do the next person's list. Do this for all three categories.

MENTAL	EMOTIONAL	SPIRITUAL
___intelligence	___warmth	___compassion
___creativity	___sensitivity	___joyfulness
___good judgment	___consistency	___serenity
___self-confidence	___enthusiasm	___dedication
___common sense	___patience	___gentleness
___determination	___self-control	___generosity
___sense of humor	___cheerfulness	___humility
___perception	___dependability	___discipline
___comprehension	___balance	___faith
___good memory	___peacefulness	___courage

LIFESTYLE CHECKUP

How healthy is your lifestyle? Taking one line at a time, mark an ***"X"*** where you would rate yourself for each of the areas. Share the results of your checkup with your group.

DIET / NUTRITION
health food ____ junk food

EXERCISE / PHYSICAL ACTIVITY
marathon runner ____ couch potato

SLEEPING HABITS
"Good morning, Lord!" ____ "O Lord, it's morning!"

TOBACCO
Mr. Clean ____ Joe Camel

STRESS / HYPERACTIVITY
Garfield ____ Tazmanian Devil

MENTAL ALERTNESS
Road Runner ____ Wile E. Coyote

OVERALL FITNESS / VITALITY
Energizer Bunny ____ dead battery

THE GRAND TOTAL

Fill each box with the correct number and then total your score. When everyone is finished, go around the group and explain how you got your total. You can also determine who has the highest and lowest totals.

☐	x	☐	=	☐
Number of hours you sleep		Number of push-ups you can do		
☐	–	☐	=	☐
Number of times sent to principal's office		Number of speeding tickets you've received		
☐	÷	☐	=	☐
Number of hours spent watching TV daily		Number of books you read this year for fun		
☐	+	☐	=	☐
Number of states you have lived in		Number of brothers and sisters you have (including stepbrothers and stepsisters)		

☐

GRAND TOTAL

My Daily Routine

Everybody gets 24 hours a day. It's how you use those hours that counts. Get together with 1 to 3 people and finish the sentences below. Take turns explaining to each other your daily routine. In a usual day ..."

1. I get up around ...
2. It takes me about _______ minutes to dress and get ready.
3. For breakfast I usually have ...
4. I leave for school around ...
5. The way I usually get to school is by ...
6. For lunch, I usually have ...
7. After school, I usually ...
8. If I have some free time before supper, I usually ...
9. It usually takes me about _______ hour(s) to do my homework.
10. If I have a test the next day, I usually start studying around ...
11. If I don't have any homework, I usually ...
12. In a typical day, I watch about _______ hour(s) of TV.
13. In a typical day, I spend about _______ minutes on the phone.
14. In a typical day, I check my look in the mirror ______ times.
15. I usually go to bed around ...
16. It takes me about ______ minutes to fall asleep.

You Are What You Eat

Get together in groups of 8, sitting in the shape of the Wagonwheel above—four people back to back in the center and four people across from them on the outside of the circle. Everyone shares with the person across from them the answer to the first three questions about your eating habits. After two minutes, the four people on the outside move left (clockwise) to form new pairs. Now everyone answers the next three questions. Shift again to answer questions 7 to 9, and again to answer 10 to 12. Keep it moving—spending only about two minutes with each partner.

1. My favorite food is ...
2. My favorite place to eat out is ...
3. My favorite dessert is ...
4. I draw the line when it comes to eating ...
5. If I could visit another part of the world to taste their food, I would go to ...
6. My idea of a midnight snack is ...
7. On a first date, I would probably eat at ...
8. If this was a really special occasion, I might take this person to ...
9. My favorite meal of the year with my family is ...
10. If I could order something "way out" at a restaurant, I might order ...
11. The most bizarre thing I ever ate was ...
12. The food that best describes my personality in the morning is ...

My Coat of Arms

Get together with one other person and share about your family strengths, using the Coat of Arms below (Part 1). Explain how you would fill in the Coat of Arms with five things about your parents and yourself. Then use the half-finished sentences that follow (Part 2) to comment on what your partner said.

Part 1:

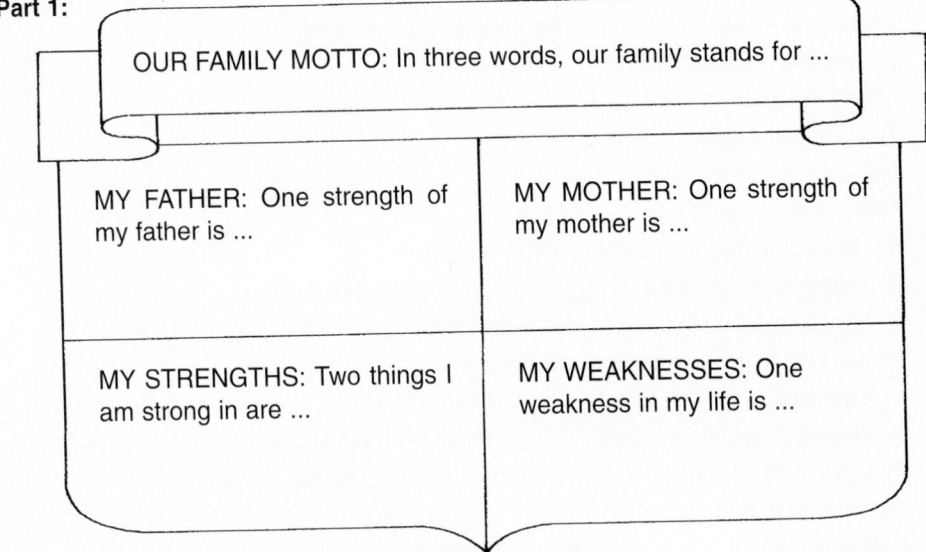

OUR FAMILY MOTTO: In three words, our family stands for ...

MY FATHER: One strength of my father is ...	MY MOTHER: One strength of my mother is ...
MY STRENGTHS: Two things I am strong in are ...	MY WEAKNESSES: One weakness in my life is ...

Part 2: FEEDBACK FROM YOUR PARTNER:

1. I really like what you said about ...
2. If I could add one more strength that I have seen in you, it would be ...

Four Facts / One Lie

Here's a chance to share some significant facts about yourself and have fun doing it. In groups of 4 to 8, ask one person to finish the five sentences below—making one of the five a lie. (Try to keep a straight face.) Then, let the others in the group try to guess which fact is a lie. When everyone has guessed, ask the person to explain which fact was the lie ... and what would be an honest answer. Continue around the group until everyone has had a chance to share.

1. At age 7, my favorite TV show was ...
2. At age 9, my hero was ...
3. At age 10, I wanted to be a ...
4. At age 12, my favorite music was ...
5. Right now, my favorite pastime is ...

FAMILY EXPECTATIONS

Our family background is an important factor determining who we are. Take turns answering the following questions about your family and share them in groups of 2 to 4.

I FEEL LIKE MY PARENTS LOOK UPON ME AS ...

- ❑ a troublesome kid
- ❑ a helpless baby
- ❑ a scapegoat
- ❑ glue
- ❑ a security blanket
- ❑ a capable adult
- ❑ their pride and joy
- ❑ a liability
- ❑ a disappointment
- ❑ invisible
- ❑ a wonderful person
- ❑ good stock
- ❑ a continuation of themselves
- ❑ the family name

I FEEL LIKE MY PARENTS EXPECT ME TO BE ...

- ❑ the next president
- ❑ a doctor
- ❑ an incredible success
- ❑ a minister
- ❑ completely obedient
- ❑ just like them
- ❑ the next Albert Einstein
- ❑ perfect
- ❑ a golden boy/girl
- ❑ a great athlete
- ❑ independent
- ❑ self-sufficient
- ❑ a compensation for their failures
- ❑ whatever makes me happy

TAKE YOUR CHOICE

Get together with 1 to 3 people and do this quiz together. Take one question at a time, letting the others try to guess your answer before you share.

IN MY FREE TIME, I WOULD RATHER:
a. read
b. watch TV
c. listen to music

AT NIGHT, I PUT MY CLOTHES:
a. on the floor
b. on a hanger
c. folded over a chair

WHEN I RELAX, I LIKE TO:
a. be alone
b. be in a crowd
c. be with friends

FOR AN AWARD, I WOULD RATHER GET:
a. a Nobel prize
b. an Oscar
c. an Olympic gold medal

IN BUYING CLOTHES, I LOOK FOR:
a. cost
b. fashion / style
c. quality

WHEN EATING CHICKEN, I PREFER:
a. white meat
b. dark meat
c. the gizzard

FOR WHEELS, I PREFER:
a. a sports car
b. a truck
c. anything that runs

FOR A VACATION, I WOULD CHOOSE:
a. a Caribbean cruise
b. going to Europe
c. going to Disney World

FOR A MOVIE, I WOULD CHOOSE:
a. comedy
b. drama
c. action adventure

I WOULD LIKE TO MARRY SOMEONE:
a. rich
b. attractive
c. with a good personality

Mr. / Miss America Contest

Get together with 1 to 3 people from your group and discuss the exercise below. Taking one category at a time, put an **"X"** somewhere in between the two extremes to indicate how you see yourself. For instance, on ATHLETICISM you might put the **"X"** in the middle because you are in between the two extremes.

ATHLETICISM
Most Valuable Player ______________________________ Bench Warmer

MANNERS
Mr. / Miss Manners ______________________________ Rude Dude

FITNESS
Mr. / Miss Universe ______________________________ Couch Potato

SENSITIVITY
I'm listening ______________________________ I can't hear you

FASHION
All dressed up ______________________________ Grubbies

NEATNESS
Mr. / Miss Clean ______________________________ Mr. / Miss Messy

SEX APPEAL
Homecoming king / queen ______________________________ Home alone on Friday night

911 Phone Numbers

Get together with one other person and work on this exercise together. Read the five situations below and think of the telephone number or the person you would call for each situation.

CRISIS SITUATION:	PERSON / PHONE NUMBER TO CALL:
1. You just received a break-up letter. You need someone to talk to.	______________
2. You are at a crossroads in your life. You need some good counsel.	______________
3. You had a big fight with your parents. You need to talk to someone who understands.	______________
4. You just found out you have a serious disease. You need someone to pray for you.	______________
5. Someone you thought was your friend has been spreading rumors about you. You need advice about what to do.	______________

My Favorite Things

Pair off with one other person (preferably someone that you do NOT know very well) and work together on this exercise. Read over the list below and choose the top five things you like to do. Then, compare your list with your partner's list.

MY TOP FIVE

_____ Playing sports
_____ Watching TV
_____ Hiking / biking
_____ Listening to music
_____ Shopping
_____ Talking on the phone
_____ Working out
_____ Spending time alone
_____ Spending time with friends
_____ Playing on my computer
_____ Reading
_____ Working on my car / bike
_____ Going to the beach / mountains
_____ Going to the movies
_____ Going to parties
_____ Working on my hobby
_____ Playing a musical instrument
_____ Playing with my pet
_____ Going on vacation
_____ Going to sporting events

Medical History

Have everyone in your group stay together for this ice-breaker. Here are some "highly scientific," but not so rare "diseases." As someone reads the descriptions one at a time, raise your hand if that's part of *your* "medical history"!

INTERNET-ITIS—staring at a monitor for hours while typing messages to people you've never met.

MONOTONE-EOSIS—a sure sign of this disease is when people move away from you like you have the plague when you sing "The Star Spangled Banner."

CHOCO-HOLISM—snarling when people suggest you share your "chocolate decadence" dessert.

MALL-ITIS—a strong compulsion to spend many hours (and many dollars!) at the mall.

ESPN DEFICIENCY SYNDROME—going into convulsions when you haven't heard the sports scores in too long a time.

HAVEIGOTAGREATPERSONFORYOU-APHOBIA—fear of friends who are anxious to set you up with a member of the opposite sex.

CHANNELSURF-EOSIS—cramps in your index finger from having to push the remote control buttons so much—often makes you bed or couch-ridden.

INVOLUNTARY LEADFOOT REFLEX—a physiological phenomenon that results in "keeping the pedal to the metal" while driving.

WHATAGREATKID-APHOBIA—fear of the motives of parents when they compliment you.

Wallet Scavenger Hunt

Get together with 1 to 3 people and work on this exercise together. If you have a wallet or purse, use the first set of questions below. If you do not have your wallet or purse with you, use the second set of questions below.

This is run like a scavenger hunt. You get two minutes in silence to go through your possessions or think about your answers. Then, you break the silence and "show and tell" what you have found. For instance, "the thing I have had for the LONGEST TIME is ... this picture of me when I was a baby." Now, take two minutes in silence to find the items on this scavenger hunt.

WALLET OR PURSE LIST OF ITEMS (finish each sentence):

1. The thing I have had for the LONGEST TIME is ...
2. The thing that has SENTIMENTAL VALUE is ...
3. The thing that reminds me of a FUN TIME is ...
4. The most REVEALING thing about me is ...

IF YOU DON'T HAVE YOUR WALLET OR PURSE (finish each sentence):

1. The most EXPENSIVE thing I am wearing is ...
2. The CHEAPEST thing I am wearing is ...
3. The one thing that I CARRY with me all the time is ...
4. The thing I wear that has SENTIMENTAL VALUE is ...

A Bunch of Bests

Get together in groups of about 4. Think of the "bests" in your life using the following suggestions. Choose two or three items from the list below to talk about the highlights from your past.

1. The best friend I ever had was ...
2. The best teacher I ever had was ...
3. The best concert I ever went to was ...
4. The best game I ever went to was ...
5. The best babysitter I ever had was ...
6. The best class in school I ever had was ...
7. The best pet I ever had was ...
8. The best birthday I ever had was ...
9. The best vacation I ever had was ...
10. The best book I ever read or movie I ever saw was ...

Places in My Life

On the map below, place the corresponding letter to indicate these five significant places in your journey. Gather in groups of 2 to 4. Then go around and have everyone explain their selections.

B = Where I was born

C = Where I spent most of my childhood

V = My favorite vacation

H = Where I would like to go on my honeymoon

G = Where God became real to me—more than just a name

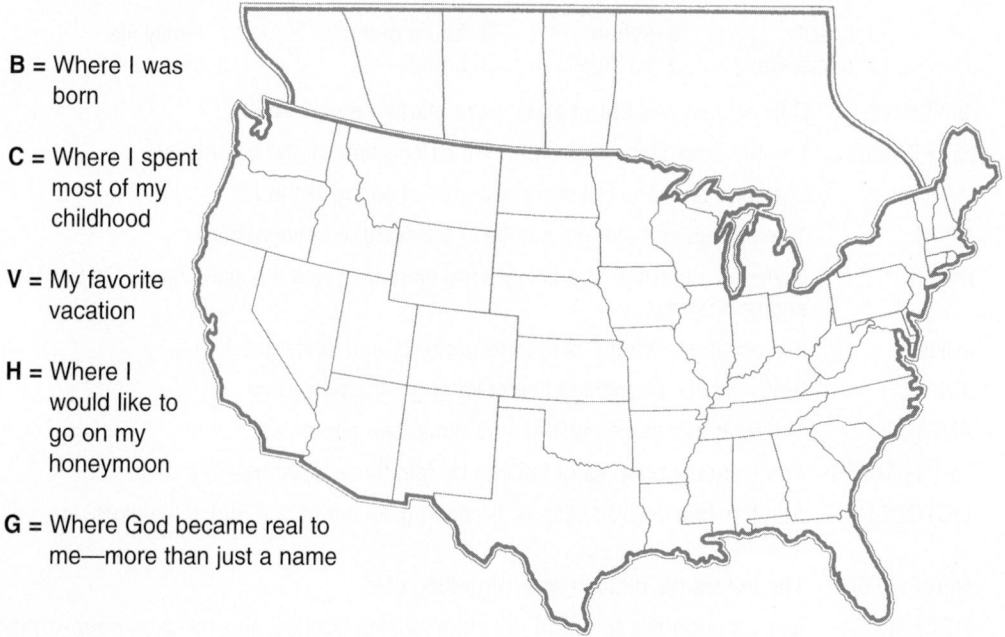

The Dating Game

Get together with one other person and interview each other for a feature story about your attitudes about dating for People. The interview questions to ask are below.

1. What is your "nickname"? What do your friends call you?
2. When you were 7 years old, who was your hero?
3. Who was your first "true love"? The little boy or girl next door?
4. What TV show or movie did you like because it showed a dating relationship that you admired?
5. What TV show or movie did you not like because it showed dating relationships that were not attractive to you?
6. When it comes to dating, what do you look for in a date?
7. When it comes to going with someone, what do you look for in that person?
8. When it comes to marriage, what would you look for in a mate?

How's the Weather?

Consider all the different areas of your life. Choose two or three areas and assign a month of the year to each area. Get together in groups of 2 to 4 and share what season it is in these areas of your life. Feel free to explain why you chose what you did.

❑ health	❑ school	❑ future outlook	❑ family life
❑ social life	❑ spiritual	❑ emotional	❑ friendships

JANUARY: Cold and snowy, but at least we're starting a new year.

FEBRUARY: The bleakest time of the year; I'm getting tired of the color gray.

MARCH: Cold and blustery, but there is a sniff of spring in the air.

APRIL: Tumultuous and stormy, but life is breaking out everywhere.

MAY: Spring has sprung! The flowers are blooming, and the skies are full of sunlight and cool breezes.

JUNE: It's pleasantly warm, things are growing, and life is good.

JULY: Boy, it's hot—everything is smoldering and oppressive.

AUGUST: The heat has settled in; we sure could use some rain.

SEPTEMBER: The first cool breezes of fall can be felt; there is change in the air.

OCTOBER: Autumn has arrived; life is beginning to hibernate, but the colors are still beautiful.

NOVEMBER: The leaves have fallen and it's getting cold.

DECEMBER: Even though it's cold and desolate-looking outside, the holidays keep things festive.

Comfort Zones

There are people in the world who go for all the gusto they can. Others simply try to keep their waters as calm as possible. Where are you on the risk scale? Taking one line at a time, place an "**X**" on the following lines and share your responses with each other.

go skysurfing ______________________________ go bowling

spend my inheritance ______________________________ put the money in the bank

take a lap around the track with an Indy driver ______________________________ sit in the stands

lead a group ______________________________ go with the crowd

study hard for a test ______________________________ wing it

say what I think ______________________________ keep my opinions to myself

explore the city ______________________________ stay close to home

watch a suspense thriller ______________________________ watch a Disney animation

God has full control of my future. ______________________________ I'm scared to death to think of my future.

FRIENDSHIP SURVEY

Get into groups of 2 to 4 and discuss your preferences in choosing friends. On the first category—PERSONALITY—put an ***"X"*** on the line somewhere in between the two extremes and explain why. Then, let your partners explain where they marked themselves and why. Then, move to the next category, etc. ... through the list.

PERSONALITY
similar to mine ______________________________ different from mine

COMMUNICATION
motormouth ______________________________ quiet as a mouse

TEMPERAMENT
laid-back ______________________________ intense

COMPATIBILITY
like doing the same things ______________ not afraid to disagree and go their own way

LOYALTY
go along with me through thick and thin ______________ challenge me when I need it

SELF-ESTEEM
put themselves down all the time ______________ brag about themselves all the time

RELATIONSHIP TO THEIR FAMILY
speak highly of their parents ______________ always complaining about their parents

MORAL STANDARDS
wild and free ______________________________ stick to the rules

RELATIONSHIP TO A CHURCH
couldn't care less ______________________________ very committed

ATTITUDE ABOUT LIFE
optimistic ______________________________ pessimistic

CHOOSING FRIENDS

Get together with 1 to 3 people from your group and look over the list of qualities that you look for in a friend. See if you can agree on the top five.

___ right clothes
___ nice smile
___ honesty
___ generosity
___ spiritual depth
___ shares personally
___ good looks
___ solid family
___ plenty of money
___ plenty of time for me
___ cool car or truck
___ same music taste
___ good personality
___ big house
___ great sense of humor
___ popularity
___ laid-back
___ loyalty
___ common interests
___ straight morals
___ athletic interest
___ similar background
___ academic interest
___ fun to be with

My Risk Quotient

Gather with 1 to 3 people from your group and discuss your "risk quotient." The test below is a fun way to figure out how much of a risk-taker you really are. First, complete the questionnaire. Then figure out your score.

1. In playing Monopoly, I usually:
   a. play it safe / stash my cash
   b. stay cool and hold back a little
   c. go for broke—gambling everything

2. With my parents, I usually:
   a. do exactly as I'm asked
   b. test my boundaries a little
   c. do my own thing despite the cost

3. On a menu, I usually pick:
   a. something familiar that I know I like
   b. something that's a little different
   c. something way out that I've never tried

4. At a party, I usually:
   a. stick with my friends
   b. mingle with some strangers
   c. see how many new people I can meet

5. In starting a relationship, I usually:
   a. let the other person do the talking
   b. meet the other person halfway
   c. take the initiative

6. I would prefer my life to have:
   a. no risks and lots of safety
   b. some risks and some safety
   c. lots of risks and little safety

Scoring: Give yourself 1 point for every "a," 2 points for every "b," and 3 points for every "c." Then circle the total on the line below to get your risk quotient.

PLAY IT SAFE — **TAKE A CHANCE**

6 7 8 9 10 11 12 13 14 15 16 17

A Slice of Life

Get together in groups of 2 to 4. As you think about all the different things you do in your life, do you consider your time well managed? How much of your time is spent in activities like:

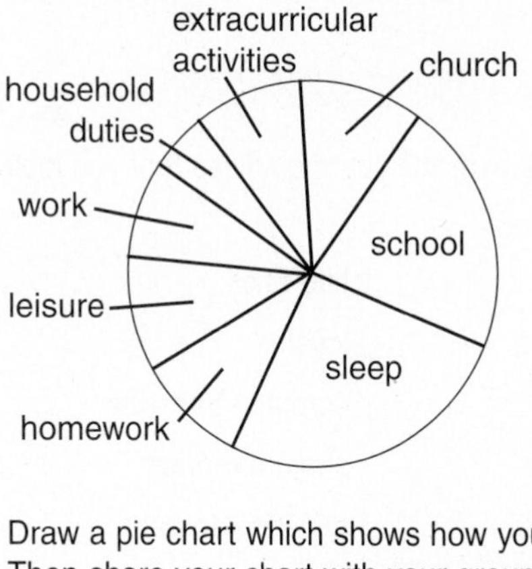

school
sleep
leisure
church
work
household duties
homework
extracurricular activities
etc.

Draw a pie chart which shows how your time is spent right now. Then share your chart with your group.

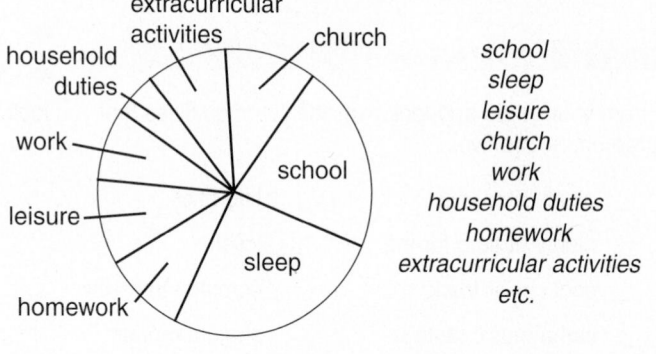

WOW, SO-SO, OR HO-HUM

If you had to rank each activity WOW ... SO-SO ... or HO-HUM, how would you do it? Get together with 1 to 3 other people and go over the list together.

		WOW	SO-SO	HO-HUM
1.	Spending a day with the president of the United States	___	___	___
2.	Having a date with the best-looking person in school	___	___	___
3.	Having $1,000 to spend on clothes	___	___	___
4.	Having a computer do all my homework	___	___	___
5.	Owning the latest hot car	___	___	___
6.	Having a continual supply of junk food at my disposal	___	___	___
7.	Getting the lead in a movie	___	___	___
8.	Making the Olympic team	___	___	___
9.	Being the lead singer in a rock group	___	___	___
10.	Getting two seats on the 50-yard line at the Super Bowl	___	___	___

DOWN MEMORY LANE

Have groups of 8 get in the shape of the Wagonwheel above—four people back to back in the center and four people across from them on the outside of the circle. The four who are on the inside finish statement #1, and the four who are on the outside finish statement #2. Then the four on the outside move left (clockwise) to form new pairs. Those on the inside answer #3, and those on the outside answer #4. Then shift again ... and keep rotating until you've completed all the statements. Each time you rotate, the inside person goes first, answering the odd-numbered statements; then the outside partner answers the even-numbered statements. Keep it moving—spending less than one minute on each rotation. Here's your chance to take a walk down memory lane—to your elementary school years.

I REMEMBER ...

1. My favorite subject in grade school:
2. The person I went to when I got hurt:
3. My first pet:
4. The chore I hated to do:
5. My first big trip or vacation:
6. My favorite room in the house:
7. The adult who took time to play with me:
8. The fun thing we often did as a family:
9. My favorite thing to do on a summer day:
10. The person who helped me with homework:
11. The first thing I can remember wanting to be when I grew up:
12. My favorite thing to eat:
13. My favorite uncle or aunt:
14. The first person of the opposite sex I thought was cute:
15. The best Christmas present I received:
16. The friend who got in trouble with me:

My Childhood Supper Table

Get together with 1 to 3 people and share some things in your life at age 7. Focus on your supper table—the place where you ate your nightly meal. Let your partner interview you like a talk show host—*This Is Your Life.* Switch roles until everyone has been interviewed.

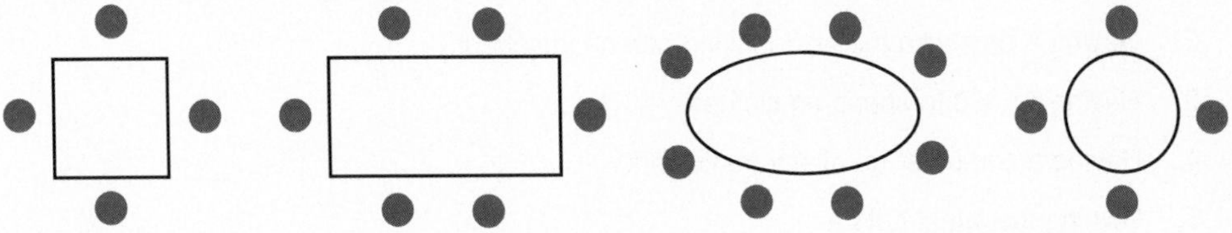

1. When you were 7 years old, where were you living?
2. What was the shape of the table where you ate your evening meal? Round? Square? Rectangle?
3. How often did you eat together as a family? All of the time? Most of the time? About half of the time? Seldom? Almost never?
4. Where did you sit? Who else was at the table and where did they sit?
5. Who did most of the talking? About what usually?
6. How would you describe the typical atmosphere at the table? Relaxed? Tense? Quiet? Exciting? Crazy? Rushed? Dull? Peaceful?
7. Did anyone say the "blessing"? If so, who?
8. Who reached out to you and always included you in the conversation?
9. What is your favorite or best memory of your childhood supper table?

Fun Money

Imagine that a rich aunt or uncle just gave you $5000. Decide how much you would spend in each of the following categories. Get together in groups of up to 8 and compare your results. To make it more fun, see if the others can guess which category you spent the most in before you share your answers.

______ clothes

______ sports equipment

______ gas

______ going out with friends

______ dates

______ savings

______ concert tickets

______ my hobby

______ video games

______ my family

______ sporting events tickets

______ music

______ skiing

______ church

Things That Drive You Crazy

Here's a list of things that drive a lot of people crazy. Do they drive you crazy, too? Take turns reading the different lines (person #1 reads line 1, person #2, line 2, and so on). Let others guess your answer before sharing your response.

	YES	NO	SOMETIMES
people who constantly channel-surf	❑	❑	❑
an annoying song that gets stuck in your head	❑	❑	❑
dripping faucet	❑	❑	❑
someone talking during a movie	❑	❑	❑
losing one sock	❑	❑	❑
not enough toilet paper	❑	❑	❑
someone who is always late	❑	❑	❑
someone who sings in the car	❑	❑	❑
boring teacher	❑	❑	❑
a motormouth	❑	❑	❑
preempting of a television program	❑	❑	❑
an itch you can't reach	❑	❑	❑
screeching chalk on a chalkboard	❑	❑	❑
a pen that won't work	❑	❑	❑
people who smack their gum	❑	❑	❑
people who crack their knuckles	❑	❑	❑
backseat drivers	❑	❑	❑
people who chew with their mouths open	❑	❑	❑
someone leaving the toilet seat up	❑	❑	❑

Assessing the Future

Get together with 1 or 2 others and take turns interviewing each other about the future.

1. Which phrase would best describe your philosophy about facing the future?
   - ❑ "I don't want to grow up!"
   - ❑ "Back to the Future!"
   - ❑ "You can't go home again."
   - ❑ "One day at a time, Sweet Jesus."
   - ❑ "Climb Every Mountain" (from The Sound of Music)
   - ❑ "He who isn't busy being born is busy dying."
   - ❑ "The future belongs to those who plan for it."
   - ❑ "I don't know what the future holds, but I know who holds the future."
   - ❑ "Every day in every way, things are getting better."
   - ❑ "The future's so bright, I've got to wear shades!"

2. What would you like to be doing when you're 40 years old?

3. What is one thing you expect to have in the future which you do not have now?

MY PEOPLE TREE

Get together in groups of about 8. In this drawing, which child do you identify with—or which one portrays you right now? Share with your group which child you would choose, and why. You can also use this as an affirmation exercise, by assigning each person in your group to a child in the picture.

Some of My Feelings

Get together with 1 to 3 people in your group and explain how you would finish each of the half-finished sentences below. Do one sentence at a time.

1. For me, school is going ...
2. If I am bored at a party, I will usually ...
3. At halftime in a basketball game when my team is way behind, I would probably ...
4. My outlook on life right now is ...
5. When I get frustrated at home, I usually ...
6. When I see a handsome guy/beautiful girl, I usually say ...
7. The best thing happening in my life right now is ...
8. My biggest concern or worry right now is ...

Headache Survey

In groups of about 4, work on the headache survey below. For each headache, decide together whether the situation is a 1-aspirin, 2-aspirin or a 3-aspirin headache.

	1 aspirin	2 aspirin	3 aspirin
not having enough money	❑	❑	❑
curfew / rules at home	❑	❑	❑
braces	❑	❑	❑
Sunday school / religion class	❑	❑	❑
girls / guys	❑	❑	❑
losing my driver's license	❑	❑	❑
getting into college	❑	❑	❑
arguing with my parents	❑	❑	❑
sitting alone in school cafeteria	❑	❑	❑
people I don't get along with at school	❑	❑	❑
death of a friend	❑	❑	❑
worrying about my parents getting divorced	❑	❑	❑
grades	❑	❑	❑
getting a job	❑	❑	❑
getting up in the morning	❑	❑	❑
violence at school	❑	❑	❑

LAY IT ON THE LINE

Get together with 1 to 3 people and explain where you stand on these issues. For instance, on FEMINISM you might put yourself in the middle, because you are equal distance between the two positions on feminism. Go through the categories one at a time by placing an ***"X"*** on the lines, with each person sharing their answer.

ON FEMINISM
A woman's place is in the home. ______________________ A woman's place is in the House of Representatives!

ON LAW AND ORDER
Lock the "losers" up. ______________________ Educate and rehabilitate them.

ON DRUGS
Just say no. ______________________ Make them legal.

ON ABORTION
People should have a choice. ______________________ Fetuses have rights too.

ON CONDOMS
Kids have got to learn to protect themselves. ______________ They encourage promiscuity.

ON PORNOGRAPHY
It's a first amendment freedom. ____________ We can't let such "freedom" destroy society.

ON SMOKING
It's my right. ______________________ Your right to smoke stops at my nose.

OUR UN-CALLING

Get together in groups of about 8 and have fun discussing your future. To recognize your calling in life, perhaps it might help to eliminate some lines of work you would *not* like to do. Look over the list below and choose the three WORST options for a future career.

- ❑ crowd control officer at a rock concert
- ❑ organizer of paperwork for Congress
- ❑ day care center director
- ❑ researcher studying the spawning habits of Alaskan salmon
- ❑ toy assembly person for a local toy store over the holidays
- ❑ middle / high school principal
- ❑ nurse's aide at a home for retired Sumo wrestlers
- ❑ referee at a mud wrestling match
- ❑ official physician for the National Association of Hypochondriacs
- ❑ chief animal control officer at a reptile zoo
- ❑ pump operator for portable toilet company
- ❑ other:______________________________

Ups and Downs

Our lives have their good times and their bad times. In groups of about 4, help the others get to know you better by charting your life. From your birth to the present, draw a graph line showing the ups and downs—the high points and low points—in your life. Feel free to explain some of these ups and downs to your group.

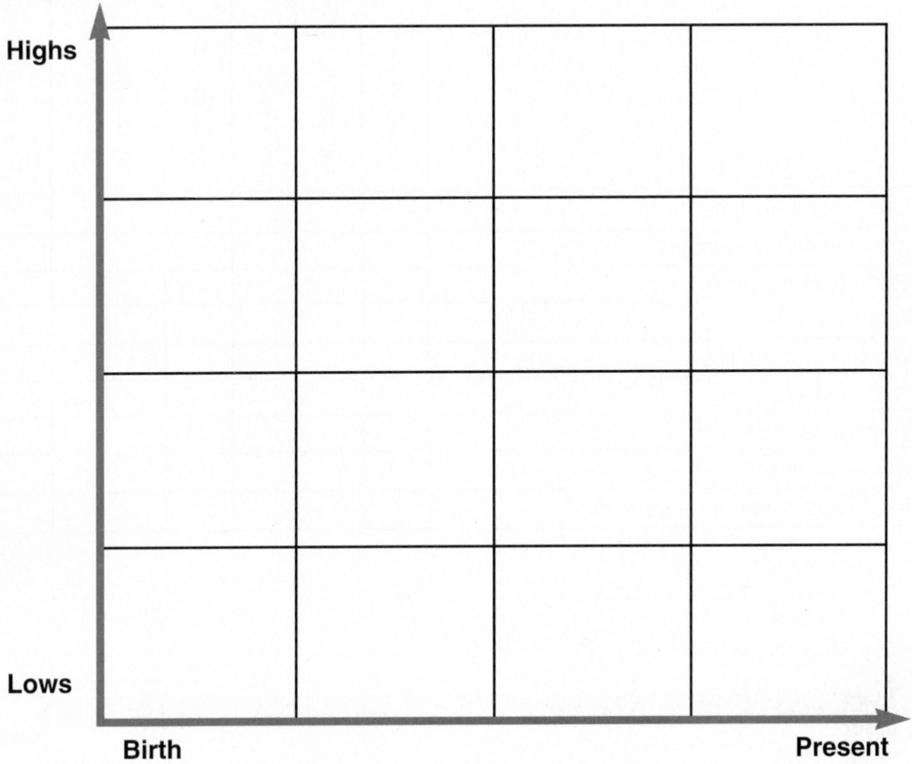

Robinson Crusoe

Imagine that you are going to be Robinson Crusoe for a year and live on a deserted tropical island. Get together in groups of up to 8 and discuss the question below.

Besides adequate food and clothing, you can choose three of the following items to take with you. Which will you choose?

- ❑ lots of novels
- ❑ a CD player and lots of CDs
- ❑ a Jeep Grand Cherokee
- ❑ a solar-powered curling iron
- ❑ exercise equipment
- ❑ a cellular phone
- ❑ a rifle
- ❑ a bed
- ❑ a Bible
- ❑ a surfboard
- ❑ a battery-powered TV / satellite dish
- ❑ a pet
- ❑ a first-aid kit
- ❑ a deck of cards

Who Influences You?

Get together with 1 to 3 people and discuss who influences you most in making decisions in your life. In each category, check one or two columns—either parents, brother / sister, friends, teachers, church / youth group or TV / movies / music. Take one category at a time

WHO INFLUENCES ...	my parents	my brother / sister	my friends	my teachers	my church/ youth group	TV / movies / music
How I spend my time						
How I spend my money						
What I feed my mind						
What I wear						
Where I draw the line						
What I believe						
What I want out of life						
How I see myself						
How I handle fear, failure and guilt						

The Life Raft

Get together in groups of up to 8 and work together on the exercise below. Here are the instructions. There is a group of 12 people stranded on a deserted island. A raft is available, but it can only accommodate 8. Four people will have to stay. Your group has been asked to choose the 8 who get the life raft. Read over the list below, and decide who you will choose.

___ Pop musician on drugs (sleeps around)
___ *Playboy* centerfold model (divorced twice)
___ Medical doctor, Protestant (performs abortions)
___ Environmental engineer (single mother)
___ Police officer, Irish Catholic (father of six)
___ All-Pro football player (helps inner city kids)
___ Millionaire (generous giver in your church)
___ Scientist (Black man, specializing in AIDS research)
___ Teacher (Native American, working on a reservation)
___ Communist student (devoted to revolution in South America)
___ Black Muslim (outspoken against "white imperialism")
___ Roman Catholic priest (started home for unwed mothers)

PRECIOUS TIME

God has given us a precious gift: the time to live. Maybe that's why now is called "the present." Answer the following questions about precious time and share your answers in your group of 4.

MY IDEA OF A GREAT TIME IS:

- ❑ going to a party
- ❑ going to a cool concert
- ❑ hanging out at the mall
- ❑ watching a good movie / TV show
- ❑ watching an exciting sports event
- ❑ fishing or hiking
- ❑ going out on a date
- ❑ playing my favorite sport
- ❑ eating my favorite food
- ❑ playing video / computer games
- ❑ curling up with a good book

THESE THINGS MAKE A BAD DAY FOR ME:

- ❑ crummy weather
- ❑ Mondays
- ❑ bad hair
- ❑ being broke
- ❑ getting a bad grade
- ❑ when my team loses
- ❑ boring classes or work
- ❑ hassles with parents
- ❑ conflict with a friend
- ❑ dating problems

IF I KNEW I HAD THREE MONTHS TO LIVE, I WOULD:

- ❑ do exactly what I'm doing now
- ❑ party, party, party
- ❑ see the world
- ❑ spend all my money
- ❑ give everything away
- ❑ be very angry
- ❑ love everyone more
- ❑ climb Mt. Everest
- ❑ spend more time with friends
- ❑ spend more time with family
- ❑ do all I can for God

original cartoon by Robert Shull

DREAM CAREER

What would you do if you could choose any career? Look at the list below and choose two: (1) your first choice and (2) your last choice. Feel free to choose a career that is not listed. Get in groups of up to 8, and let other group members take turns guessing what you have selected.

POLICE OFFICER:
A brave upholder of the law in an exciting fight against criminals.

ACTOR / ACTRESS:
A glamorous movie star who gets big money to appear on the silver screen.

HIGH-POWERED ATTORNEY:
An eloquent, intelligent spokesperson of the law who defends the innocent in the courtroom.

POLITICIAN:
A high-profile public servant who can whip out a clever deal or an inspiring speech at the drop of a hat.

FASHION MODEL:
A jet-setting career for those with charm and an alluring smile.

TEACHER:
The educator who inspires students to expand their horizons and appreciate the world.

BANKER:
The respected lender who can help someone fulfill their greatest dreams.

MISSIONARY:
The bold preacher who is willing to go around the world to share the Gospel.

PSYCHOLOGIST:
The trusted counselor who helps people come to peace with themselves.

ASTRONAUT:
A daring outer space pilot and extraterrestrial scientist.

MINISTER:
A beloved servant who takes care of a congregation's spiritual needs.

RACE CAR DRIVER:
A courageous competitor who tears around the track at 200 mph.

VETERINARIAN:
The beloved animal doctor everyone trusts with their pets and livestock.

NOVELIST:
The fiction writer who can produce best-sellers that everyone talks about.

SOCIAL WORKER:
The steward of government resources who strives to help the unfortunate get back on their feet.

DOCTOR:
The family physician who is a trusted healer, devoted listener and close friend.

JET PILOT:
Streaking across the sky in a screaming jet, ready to defend the nation.

COMPUTER JOCKEY:
The computer whiz who boldly writes software programs that no one has written before.

Money and Success

The apostle Paul said that "the love of money is a root of all kinds of evil" (1 Tim. 6:10). There is no doubt that money can play a powerful role in our life. The same is true for success. Get in groups of 4 and share your answers to the three questions below.

Your group can learn a lot about each other by discussing your answers to these questions about money and success.

MY ATTITUDE ABOUT MONEY IS:

- ❑ It should be saved.
- ❑ Spend, spend, spend!
- ❑ It's something I need more of.
- ❑ It's a necessary evil.
- ❑ It's a source of arguments.
- ❑ It's a source of fun.
- ❑ It's a resource for freedom.

MY FEELINGS ABOUT "GETTING AHEAD" ARE:

- ❑ Look out for #1.
- ❑ What else is there in life?
- ❑ It's a high priority.
- ❑ Keep a balanced life instead.
- ❑ Don't neglect your family.
- ❑ It's not worth it.

MY IDEA OF A SUCCESSFUL PERSON IS:

- ❑ Mother Teresa
- ❑ Martin Luther King, Jr.
- ❑ Bill Gates
- ❑ Billy Graham
- ❑ The president
- ❑ Michael Jordan
- ❑ Amy Grant
- ❑ other:_______________

original cartoon by Robert Shull

Problem Survey

Get together with one other person and discuss how you would rank the problems young people face today—from 1 (greatest) to 15 (least). Put your ranking in the left column and your partner's ranking in the right column. If you would like, share with your partner the greatest problem *you* face, so he or she can pray for you.

YOUR RANKING		YOUR PARTNER'S
____	Conflict with teachers at school	____
____	Gangs and violence	____
____	Parents splitting up	____
____	Use of alcohol / drugs	____
____	Feelings of loneliness and need for friendship	____
____	TV programs and movies that promote lousy morals	____
____	Family problems	____
____	Uncertain future and goals	____
____	Cliques in school	____
____	Teen pregnancy and the threat of sexual diseases like AIDS	____
____	Not knowing how to handle anger	____
____	Peer pressure	____
____	Disillusionment with or apathy toward church / faith	____
____	Grades in school	____
____	Abusive relationships	____

Sharing Dreams

Here's your chance to dream about your future. Get together in groups of 4 and interview each other on your future plans. Below is a list of interview questions. Each person in the group can choose one or two questions from the list below to ask the person being interviewed.

1. What would you like to be doing five years from now?
2. Where would you like to be living in five years?
3. In 10 years, how much money would you like to be making?
4. What is it going to take for you to get to where you want to be in 10 years?
5. What values would you look for in the person you will marry?
6. What kind of spiritual commitment would you want the person you marry to have?
7. How many children would you like to have? Boys or girls?
8. When are you going to allow your children to start dating?
9. Are you going to send your children to a private school or a public school?
10. Are you going to be more or less strict with your kids than your parents have been with you?
11. Will it be easier to get along with your parent(s) when you have a family of your own?

Stress Test

This is one test where everyone would like to have a low score! Circle the events you have experienced within the past year. Total your score. If it's more than 150 points, you're probably living under a lot of stress. Get together in groups of about 4 to share your scores and compare the types of stress you're each under.

EVENT	STRESS POINTS
Death of parent	100
Death of family member	75
Death of friend	65
Divorce of parents	60
Breakup with girl/boyfriend	55
Major personal injury or illness	53
Failed a class	50
Got in trouble at school	45
Lost your driver's license	40
Moved to a new community	37
Failed a big test	35
Conflict with parents	33
Changed schools	30
Got in a fight with a friend	27
Health or financial problem in family	23
Forgot to do your homework	20
Had a "bad hair day"	10
Found a zit on your nose	5
Your Total	________

Warm Memories

Get together in groups of up to 4. Each of you answer the first question. Then, go around again on question #2, etc. through the four questions.

1. Where were you living between the ages of 7 and 12, and what was your favorite thing to do on a warm summer day?

2. What is the worst storm you can remember? Where was your favorite place to hide during bad storms?

3. What was the center of warmth in your life when you were a child? (It could be a place in the house, a time of year, a person, etc.)

4. When did God become a "warm" person to you, and how did that happen?

Old-Fashioned Auction

Get together in groups of 8 or more. Just like an old-fashioned farm auction, conduct an auction in your group—starting each item at $50. Everybody starts out with $1,000. SELECT AN AUCTIONEER—This person can also get in on the bidding. Remember, start the bidding on each item at $50. Then, write the winning bid in the left column and the winner's name in the right column. Remember, you only have $1,000 to spend for the whole game. AUCTIONEER: Start off by asking: "Who will give me $50 for two Super Bowl tickets on the 50-yard line?" ... and keep going until you have a winner. Have fun!

WINNING BID		WINNER'S NAME
$______	Two Super Bowl tickets on the 50-yard line	____________
$______	All-expense-paid vacation for four to Disney World	____________
$______	Big screen TV with surround sound	____________
$______	Date with your favorite celebrity.	____________
$______	Freedom from household chores for one year	____________
$______	Complete new wardrobe of latest fashions.	____________
$______	Assurance of a college degree	____________
$______	Backstage passes with your favorite band	____________
$______	Season pass to ski resort of my choice	____________
$______	A role in a major motion picture	____________
$______	Six months of no hassles with your parents	____________
$______	A brand new, shiny red Corvette	____________
$______	Five-minute shopping spree in a music / electronics store	____________
$______	One year off to do anything you want	____________

WILD PREDICTIONS

Get in groups of 8 or more. Try to match the people in your group to the crazy forecasts below. (Don't take it too seriously; it's meant to be fun!) Read out loud the first item and ask everyone to call out the name of the person who is most likely to accomplish this feat. Then, read the next item and ask everyone to make a new prediction, etc.

THE PERSON IN OUR GROUP MOST LIKELY TO ...

rollerblade across the country

become most famous pet psychologist in Beverly Hills

win the *MAD Magazine* award for worst jokes

become the first woman to win the Indianapolis 500

appear on the cover of *Muscle & Fitness Magazine*

replace Regis Philbin on the *Regis and Kathie Lee Show*

replace Vanna White on *Wheel of Fortune*

win the tattoo contest at the Harley-Davidson National Convention

win the Iditarod dogsled race in Alaska

become a stuntperson for Mountain Dew commercials

make a fortune on portable toilet rentals

become the salesperson of the year for athletic shoes

write a best-selling novel based on their love life

set a world record for marathon dancing

get listed in the *Guinness Book of World Records* for the messiest car

become a millionaire by age 30

CHRISTIAN BASICS

How do you view the Christian faith? Get in groups of about 4 people. Answer these questions—one topic at a time. Feel free to discuss your answers with your group. You may check more than one answer on each question.

This ice-breaker is intended to let people talk freely about their feelings on these religious subjects without worrying about "right or wrong" answers.

I SEE PRAYER AS:

- ❑ wishful thinking
- ❑ a psychological exercise
- ❑ a direct line to God
- ❑ powerful
- ❑ magic
- ❑ a daily practice
- ❑ a life saver
- ❑ positive thinking
- ❑ the key to my sanity

I THINK OF JESUS AS:

- ❑ a great guy
- ❑ a courageous rabbi
- ❑ a wise teacher
- ❑ one of many teachers
- ❑ a miracle worker
- ❑ a great example
- ❑ a Jewish rebel
- ❑ confused
- ❑ my Savior
- ❑ my best friend

I VIEW THE CHURCH AS:

- ❑ scary
- ❑ too traditional
- ❑ boring
- ❑ hard to relate to
- ❑ friendly
- ❑ uplifting
- ❑ fun
- ❑ always asking for money
- ❑ a safe place
- ❑ confusing because of the different denominations

I SEE THE BIBLE AS:

- ❑ hard to understand
- ❑ old-fashioned
- ❑ inspiring
- ❑ full of promises
- ❑ hard to apply
- ❑ the secret to life
- ❑ full of violence
- ❑ having too many pages
- ❑ too far removed from our culture

I VIEW CHRISTIANS AS:

- ❑ the salt of the earth
- ❑ hypocrites
- ❑ fanatics
- ❑ too conservative
- ❑ just like everyone else
- ❑ world changers
- ❑ God's people
- ❑ more loving
- ❑ goody-two-shoes

WHEN I THINK ABOUT THE CROSS I FEEL:

- ❑ squeamish
- ❑ relieved
- ❑ skeptical
- ❑ unsure
- ❑ angry
- ❑ grateful
- ❑ inspired
- ❑ humbled
- ❑ hopeful
- ❑ nothing

My Last Will and Testament

Get together with 1 to 3 people from your group and discuss the funeral arrangements below, choosing from the multiple-choice options. Let your partners interview you.

HOW WOULD YOU CHOOSE TO DIE?
- ❑ prolong life as long as possible with support systems
- ❑ die naturally in a hospital, with pain relievers if needed
- ❑ die at home without medical care, but with family

WHAT FUNERAL WOULD YOU CHOOSE?
- ❑ big funeral with lots of flowers
- ❑ small funeral, money to charity
- ❑ no funeral, just family at grave

WHAT WOULD YOU WANT ON YOUR TOMBSTONE?
- ❑ the words from my favorite song
- ❑ something about my life
- ❑ just my date of birth and death

HOW WOULD YOU LIKE TO BE REMEMBERED?
- ❑ someone who cared for people
- ❑ someone who loved God
- ❑ someone who lived life to the fullest

HOW WOULD YOU WANT YOUR BODY TREATED?
- ❑ cremated
- ❑ given to science / organ donation
- ❑ buried intact

IF YOU HAD ANY MONEY, WHERE WOULD YOU LIKE IT TO GO?
- ❑ to my family
- ❑ to a charity
- ❑ to a memorial in my honor

Parent Problems

Gather in groups of about 4. Have each person answer the first question. Then go around on the second question and the third question.

1. What was the funniest thing you ever did that got you in trouble with your parents?

2. What important thing have you learned in conflicts with your parents?
   - ❑ Always apologize (even if you're right!).
   - ❑ It's best to talk it out.
   - ❑ Even parents can be wrong sometimes.
   - ❑ What your parents don't know won't hurt them (or you either!).
   - ❑ Listening to each other clears up many conflicts.
   - ❑ It's better to face a conflict and get it over with than to try to hide or ignore it.
   - ❑ other:______________________________

3. In your normal style of handling conflict, which are you more like?
   - ❑ an ostrich—I hide my head in the sand until it goes away.
   - ❑ a cat—I timidly slip away, then scratch up the couch when no one's looking.
   - ❑ a hawk—I fly above it all and pick my targets.
   - ❑ a fox—I use my brains to win.
   - ❑ a dolphin—I can fight if necessary, but would rather swim away.
   - ❑ other:______________________________

Brain Food

Congratulations! You have won a gift certificate for a free class at a local junior college. You get to take any course they offer! Form groups of 4 to 8 people. Have someone read out loud the first course description and then ask those who would be interested in that class to raise their hands. Take turns reading the courses down through the list. When you're done, have everyone choose their FIRST and LAST choices for a course.

ARCHAEOLOGY 714: "Bones Down Under: The study of aboriginal fossils in Australia." Professor: C. Dundee. Prerequisite: Archaeology 602, "Providing Data for Your Professor's Latest Book." Shovels provided.

BIRD-WATCHING 101: "Birds Are Our Friends." In this introductory course you will learn what a bird looks like, how many wings it has, and how to identify a feather. BYOB (Bring your own binoculars). Prerequisite: none. Tests: none. Term papers: none. Professor: none.

POLITICAL SCIENCE 403: "The Management of a Bureaucracy." An introduction to bureaucratic language, form making and standing in line. Special segments will include "How to get a driver's license" and "You can't fight city hall until you can find a parking place." Professor: Ann R. Kay. Prerequisite: Surviving enrollment or equivalent.

CALCULUS 555: "The Mathematics of Chaos." This class meets in several different locations at several different times and is taught by several different professors. Prerequisites: Literature 101, Ceramics and Physical Education.

CREATIVE WRITING 201: "The Limerick." There once was a student in school/Who thought he was totally cool/Then he took this class/And he did not pass/Now everyone thinks he's a fool. Professor: Dr. Seuss. Prerequisite: Creative Writing 121, "The Food Label."

SOCIOLOGY 313: "TV Viewing in America." A fascinating sociological study of television viewing at its finest. Special sections will focus on becoming an expert couch potato, snacking and viewing habits, and channel surfing. The art of reciting lines from classic reruns will also be addressed. Professor: Mr. Potato Head. Prerequisite: Sociology 213: "Relating to Your Nintendo."

RADIO, TELEVISION AND FILM 202: "Movie Snacks." This class is a serious investigation of popcorn, goo-goo clusters, Whoppers and Good'n Fruity in the 20th century American film experience. Professor: Dr. Hitchcock. Prerequisite: Radio, Television and Film 132, "Finding a Seat at the Theatre."

CAR REPAIR 401: "Automotive Electronics." This course is for serious students only. The first part of the semester will be devoted to setting the buttons on your car radio. The second part of the course will focus on how to use intermittent wipers. Professor: Tim "The Tool Man" Taylor. Prerequisite: Home Repair 401, "Setting the Clock on Your VCR" or equivalent.

Hallowed Inhibitions

Pair off with someone else and take turns sharing your answer to each question below. Try to guess your partner's answer before they tell you what it is. For every right guess, give yourself 10 points.

"I AM SOMEONE WHO WOULD ..."

	YES	NO	MAYBE
pig out on chocolate	❑	❑	❑
go to the 10-item express lane with 14 items	❑	❑	❑
come home *after* curfew	❑	❑	❑
blush at the mention of sex	❑	❑	❑
cry at the movies	❑	❑	❑
lie about my age	❑	❑	❑
forge my parent's signature	❑	❑	❑
t.p. a friend's house	❑	❑	❑
try skydiving	❑	❑	❑
go to a ballet / opera	❑	❑	❑
forget my gym clothes ... on purpose	❑	❑	❑
go on a blind date	❑	❑	❑
sneak into a movie or concert without paying	❑	❑	❑
belch in public	❑	❑	❑

The Old Neighborhood

Get together with 1 to 3 people and share about your "old neighborhood." If you have moved a lot, talk about the neighborhood where you spent the most time, or the one which was your favorite. On the other hand, you may still be living in your "old neighborhood." Take turns sharing with your group where your "old neighborhood" is located, and your responses to the following.

1. My "old neighborhood" was more like:
   - ❑ Sesame Street—urban and multicultural
   - ❑ Family Matters—distinctively ethnic
   - ❑ Home Improvement—suburban housing with a common cultural background
   - ❑ Dr. Quinn, Medicine Woman—spread out but close-knit

2. Share your responses to as many of the following questions as you have time for:
   - ❑ Where did the kids gather in your neighborhood?
   - ❑ What were your favorite things to do together?
   - ❑ What were the special places—the best places to climb trees, skateboard or rollerblade, hide from adults, etc.?
   - ❑ Where were the "danger spots"—the yards with mean dogs, the "grumpy old Mr. Wilson" who didn't like kids, the "haunted" houses or boarded-up buildings?
   - ❑ Who was the Dennis the Menace who always got into trouble or got you into trouble?
   - ❑ Who was the "Steve Erkel"—the kid who really stood out from the rest of the crowd?

Like Music to My Ears

Have everyone in your group stay together for this ice-breaker. In each of the following pairs, which sound is more likely to be "music to your ears"? For each pair, circle one of the choices. Then have one person read the first pair. Everyone who circled "the crackling of a campfire" gets up and moves to the left side of the room. All of those who circled "the sounds of city traffic at night" move to the right side of the room. Have fun going down the list this way.

the crackling of a campfire	the sounds of city traffic at night
the cry of "play ball!"	waves crashing against the shore
the clatter of a roller coaster	the beat coming through the stereo
the ring of the telephone	the ring of a cash register
the gurgling of a mountain stream	the buzz of a crowd just before a concert
the purr of a kitten	the hum of a well-tuned engine
the school lunch bell	the school dismissal bell

Competition vs. Cooperation

Are you more likely to compete or cooperate in each of the situations below? Gather in groups of about 4 and take turns going first as you go down this list:

	COMPETE	COOPERATE
playing a game of pick-up ball with friends	❑	❑
playing on a school sports team	❑	❑
working with a group at school on a project	❑	❑
playing a board game	❑	❑
taking the lead with a group of friends	❑	❑
discussing an issue in class	❑	❑
driving the family car	❑	❑
using the telephone	❑	❑
making a decision as a family	❑	❑

Emotional Dashboard

How are you feeling today? Check your gauges on your emotional dashboard. Use the drawing below to mark where you are emotionally. How high are your stress, frustration and friendship levels? Is your love tank full or empty? How many miles per hour is your enthusiasm running? What gear is your optimism transmission in?

Fill in the gauges and take turns sharing in groups of about 4 how you are feeling.

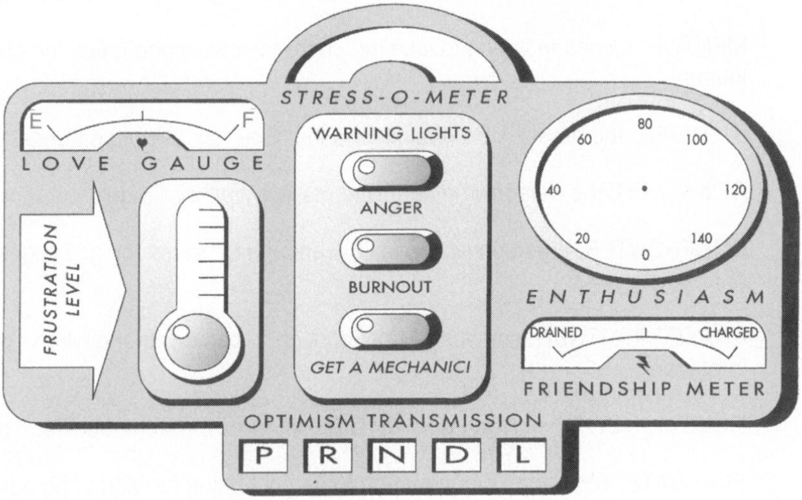

Final Jeopardy

Form groups of 4 to 8 people. Imagine you've entered the final round of *Jeopardy!* with $4,000. Your opponents have $4,500 and $5,000. How much of your $4,000 would you risk if the final category would be each of the following? Write down an amount on the first line and then take turns sharing your answers with your group. Repeat this procedure down the list of categories.

______________ understanding the opposite sex

______________ current rock groups

______________ auto mechanics

______________ spelling

______________ names in the Old Testament

______________ current movies

______________ famous football players

______________ world geography

POWER PEOPLE

Some people in your life have a powerful effect on you. Different kinds of "power people" are listed below. Fill in the names of at least three of the "power people" in your life. Then get together in groups of about 4 and share your answers with each other.

__________ LISTENER: the person who will always hear what I have to say without trying to change me

__________ ENCOURAGER: someone who helps me look on the bright side of things

__________ MENTOR: someone willing to take me under their wing and guide me on my life's journey

__________ INSPIRER: the person who reminds me that God has everything under control

__________ CONSOLER: the person who can calm me down when life gets out of control

__________ CONFRONTER: a person who loves me enough to tell me things I might not want to hear

__________ PRAYER PARTNER: someone I trust enough to come with me when I go to God in prayer

__________ ROLE MODEL: the person I want to be like in my actions, character and reputation

__________ PLAYMATE: someone I can count on to do something fun and bring out the child in me

__________ DREAMER: that special person who will listen to and appreciate my dreams

I DREAM OF GENIE

If you could have three wishes, which three would you choose from the list below? Get together with 1 to 3 people and share your choices with the group.

❑ WIN THE LOTTERY: never have to work
❑ ROMANCE: an active and exciting love life
❑ SECURE AND REWARDING JOB: lifetime guarantee with benefits
❑ PERFECT BODY: appearance that stands out in a crowd
❑ STRESS-FREE LIFE: no pain, no struggle, no tension
❑ POPULARITY: everybody knocking at my door to spend time with me
❑ CLOSE FAMILY: no hassles, lots of love and support
❑ GOOD HEALTH: long life, full of vigor and vitality
❑ ONE DEEP, ABIDING FRIENDSHIP: someone who will always be there
❑ SUCCESS: fame and recognition in your chosen field
❑ STRONG, SPIRITUAL FAITH: a deep, satisfying relationship with God

LIFE SIGNS

Get together in groups of about 4 and spend some time thinking about your lives in terms of traffic signs. Have each person share their response to the first question. Then go around on the second question and the third question.

1. If you were to select a traffic sign to tell how you've been seeking to live your life, what sign would it be?
   - ❑ "Merge"—because I've been trying to get along with everyone
   - ❑ "Slow"—because I've been seeking to slow down and experience more of life
   - ❑ "Keep Right"—because I'm trying to keep my life on the right track
   - ❑ "One Way"—because I'm seeking to be more decisive in my life
   - ❑ "Yield"—because I'm seeking to yield my life to God
   - ❑ "Children Playing"—because I'm trying to let out the "little kid" in me
   - ❑ "Under Construction"—because I'm changing so much

2. What sign are you displaying in your relationship with others?
   - ❑ "No Trespassing!"—because I keep people at a distance
   - ❑ "Help Wanted"—because I'm reaching out for support
   - ❑ "One Way"—because I'm not always tolerant of differences
   - ❑ "Open 24 Hours"—because I'm always available to others
   - ❑ "Keep Right"—because I encourage others to do what is right
   - ❑ "No Vacancy"—because there's no room in my life for anyone else right now

3. If God were to give you a "traffic ticket" right now for how you are living your life, what would it be for?
   - ❑ "Speeding"—not slowing down enough to really live
   - ❑ "Failing to Yield"—trying to do things my own way
   - ❑ "Blocking Traffic"—I feel I've gotten in the way of others who are doing more.
   - ❑ "Illegal U-Turn"—I have been trying to live in the past.
   - ❑ "Driving the Wrong Way on a One-Way Street"—I need to turn my life around.

My Roles

Get together in groups of about 4. From the list below, check the different roles you fill in your life. After sharing your answers with the group, take turns answering the questions below.

I AM A / AN …

❏ Brother	❏ Writer	❏ Skier
❏ Sister	❏ Boyfriend	❏ Actor / Actress
❏ Student	❏ Girlfriend	❏ Rollerblader
❏ Friend	❏ Babysitter	❏ Pet owner
❏ Employee	❏ Youth group member	❏ Club member
❏ Singer	❏ Volunteer	❏ Hobbyist
❏ Athlete	❏ Automobile operator	❏ Health nut
❏ Sports fan	❏ Musician	❏ Computer whiz

Which of these is the most fun?

… the most challenging? … the most rewarding? … the most frustrating?

Music in My Life

Get together with 1 to 3 people. Put an ***"X"*** on the first line below—somewhere between the two extremes—to indicate how you are feeling right now. Share your answers with each other, and then repeat this process down the list. If you feel comfortable, briefly explain why you put the ***"X"*** where you did.

1. In my emotional life, I'm feeling like ...
   "Blues in the Night" ________________________ "Celebrate!"

2. In my family life, I'm feeling like ...
   "Love Stinks" ________________________ "The Sound of Music"

3. In my attitude toward school or work, I'm feeling like ...
   "Take This Job and Shove It" ________________________ "Be True to Your School"

4. In my spiritual life, I'm feeling like ...
   "Sounds of Silence" ________________________ "Hallelujah Chorus"

5. In my close relationships, I'm feeling like ...
   "Love Is a Battlefield" ________________________ "I'll Be There for You" (Theme from *Friends*)

6. As I look toward the future, I'm feeling like ...
   "Help!" ________________________ "The Future's So Bright I Gotta Wear Shades"

PREFERENCES

Divide into groups of up to 4 people each. Go down this exercise, one line at a time. Share your preferences with each other by choosing one of the two options on each line. For more fun, let your group guess your answer first.

I PREFER:

spending the day inside . . . . spending the day outside
one-topping pizza . . . . pizza with the works
a home-cooked meal . . . . eating out
playing sports . . . . watching sports
skiing in the mountains . . . . sunning by the sea
going to the movies . . . . renting a video
lots of friends . . . . one close friend

I WOULD CHOOSE:

traveling by plane . . . . traveling by car
a leisurely life . . . . daily challenges
sitting on the bench on a winning team . . . . playing every game on a losing team
a stand-up roller coaster . . . . the carousel
a challenging job with no security . . . . a boring job with lots of security
living in the city . . . . living in the country

LIVING UNDER THE INFLUENCE

Form groups of up to 4. Before sharing your answers, silently read over the list and check on the left side the three most important things in your life right now. Then jot down on the right side one of three codes to indicate how much influence your relationship with Jesus has on these three areas of your life.

D = My relationship with Jesus DIRECTLY influences this.
I = My relationship with Jesus INDIRECTLY influences this.
N = My relationship with Jesus has NOTHING to do with this.

CHOICES (check three): **INFLUENCE**

______ Being accepted by my peers / friends . . . . _______
______ Getting along at home . . . . _______
______ Feeling good about myself . . . . _______
______ Dating . . . . _______
______ Going to heaven . . . . _______
______ Getting good grades . . . . _______
______ Knowing what is right . . . . _______
______ Having a job / car . . . . _______
______ Knowing who I am and what I want to do in life . . . . _______

What Are Your Values?

How do your values affect the decisions you make? Get together with 1 to 3 people and share your answers with each other—going through the questions one at a time.

1. When it comes to making a tough decision, I generally:
   - ❑ struggle for days
   - ❑ wait to see what someone else will do
   - ❑ never ask for advice
   - ❑ take myself on a long walk
   - ❑ make a snap decision
   - ❑ ask for advice
   - ❑ hope it will go away

2. The hardest decisions for me are usually when (rank top three):
   - ___ money is involved
   - ___ my reputation is on the line
   - ___ my moral values are involved
   - ___ friendship is involved
   - ___ my popularity is at stake

3. The biggest fear I have to deal with in standing up for what I believe is:
   - ❑ being laughed at
   - ❑ getting someone else in trouble
   - ❑ losing my friends
   - ❑ standing alone
   - ❑ being wrong
   - ❑ other:____________________

4. In my home, my parents have stressed that morality is:
   - ❑ a very individual thing
   - ❑ the mark of a gentleman / lady
   - ❑ dependent upon the circumstances
   - ❑ a matter of black and white
   - ❑ a byproduct of Christianity
   - ❑ other:____________________

There are many tough situations in life that call for decisions. You may take one of a variety of actions or do nothing. What would you do in each situation below?

1. You don't agree with the behavior of a friend. What do you do?
   - ❑ ignore it
   - ❑ stop running around with him/her
   - ❑ confront him/her about it
   - ❑ talk to someone else about it

2. You are the friend of someone who has been deliberately omitted from a party. What do you do?
   - ❑ ignore the offense and go
   - ❑ refuse to go
   - ❑ call and ask why

3. Your friends are going to a beer party and you're invited. What do you do?
   - ❑ tell them I don't drink
   - ❑ go along but don't drink
   - ❑ tell their parents
   - ❑ make some excuse
   - ❑ join the party

4. Your best friend never studies. It's exam time and he wants to cheat off your paper. He'll flunk if you don't let him. What do you do?
   - ❑ let him copy
   - ❑ quietly explain my feelings about cheating
   - ❑ refuse him but offer to help him study for the next exam
   - ❑ tell the teacher
   - ❑ cover my paper

How's Your Love Life?

The best-known passage in the Bible about love is 1 Corinthians 13—the "love chapter." The personal inventory below is taken from this passage. Get into groups of about 4. Turn to 1 Corinthians 13:4–7 (p. 1066) and have someone read the verses out loud. Then, let one person read the first phrase. Go around the group and have everyone pick a number between 1 (failure) and 10 (success). Have someone else read the next phrase, etc. through the inventory.

Love is patient: I don't take out my frustrations on those I love. I am calm under pressure and careful with my tongue.

1 2 3 4 5 6 7 8 9 10

Love is kind: I go out of my way to say nice words and do thoughtful things for others.

1 2 3 4 5 6 7 8 9 10

Love does not envy: I am not envious of others' gifts and abilities or of what they have. Neither am I jealous with my time toward those who need me.

1 2 3 4 5 6 7 8 9 10

Love does not boast: I don't consider my role any more important than those I love—or talk like "I know better."

1 2 3 4 5 6 7 8 9 10

Love is not proud: I don't think of myself as better than those I love; or better at sports, music, academics, etc.

1 2 3 4 5 6 7 8 9 10

Love is not rude: I don't make cutting or crude remarks when I don't get my way—or become silent and withdrawn.

1 2 3 4 5 6 7 8 9 10

Love is not self-seeking: I don't put myself first. I try to give those I love spiritual and emotional support.

1 2 3 4 5 6 7 8 9 10

Love is not easily angered: I don't let little things bother me, especially with those I love. I have a muffler on my mouth.

1 2 3 4 5 6 7 8 9 10

Love keeps no record of wrongs: I don't keep score of the number of times those I love have said something or done something that upset me, and I don't bring it up when we have conflict.

1 2 3 4 5 6 7 8 9 10

Love does not delight in evil: There is a difference between acceptance and approval. I accept those I love, but I do not have to approve of everything they do.

1 2 3 4 5 6 7 8 9 10

Love rejoices with the truth: With a compassionate spirit, I will say what needs to be said to someone, even if it might be difficult. I seek the truth in my own life and encourage others to do the same.

1 2 3 4 5 6 7 8 9 10

Love always protects: I am always there for those I love—even when they upset me—seeking to comfort and care as Christ would.

1 2 3 4 5 6 7 8 9 10

Love always trusts: I believe in those I love and I believe in God. And I am willing to let God do the shaping and molding.

1 2 3 4 5 6 7 8 9 10

Love always hopes: I am good at expecting the best and thinking the best about those I love. I always give those I love the benefit of the doubt.

1 2 3 4 5 6 7 8 9 10

Love always perseveres: I am committed to those I love and I am prepared to see that commitment through to the end.

1 2 3 4 5 6 7 8 9 10

The Armor of God

Scripture doesn't promise Christians an easy life. In Ephesians 6, the apostle Paul calls the Christian life a struggle and compares the spiritual equipment of a Christian to a Roman soldier fully dressed for battle.

Get into groups of about 4 to take the personal inventory below. Turn to Ephesians 6:10–18 (pp. 1106–1107) and have someone read the Scripture out loud. Then, let one person read the first piece of equipment and its application. Go around the group and have everyone give a number from 1 (very low) to 10 (very high), and explain why you gave yourself this number. Have someone else read the next piece of equipment and application, etc. until you've completed the inventory.

Belt of truth: I am prepared to stake my life on the fact that Jesus Christ is the Son of God. I have thought through what I believe, and I am willing to take a stand.

1 2 3 4 5 6 7 8 9 10

Breastplate of righteousness: I am prepared to put my life where my mouth is—in clean and right living—with genuine integrity—as Christ did. I am serious about being God's man or God's woman.

1 2 3 4 5 6 7 8 9 10

Feet fitted with the readiness that comes from the gospel of peace: I am willing to publicly affirm my faith in Christ—at school, work or wherever. I find it easy to talk about my personal faith.

1 2 3 4 5 6 7 8 9 10

Shield of faith: I am prepared to step out with Christ—to risk my life, my fortune and my future for him whatever the cost or consequences. And through faith, I am taking a stand against the "evil one."

1 2 3 4 5 6 7 8 9 10

Helmet of salvation: I know that I am part of the family of God because of Jesus Christ. I have a strong inner peace because I am at peace with God.

1 2 3 4 5 6 7 8 9 10

Sword of the Spirit, which is the word of God: I actively seek to know more about God and his will for my life through an ongoing study of his guidebook, the Bible. I discipline myself to reflect on it daily.

1 2 3 4 5 6 7 8 9 10

Prayer: I set aside time regularly to talk with God and to let him speak to me. I consciously try to submit every decision in my life to God.

1 2 3 4 5 6 7 8 9 10

A High Standard

In writing to the early Christians in Rome, the apostle Paul gave them a big challenge—to stand tall for Christ. Gather in groups of about 4 to take the personal inventory below. Turn to Romans 12:9–21 (pp. 1045–1046) and have someone read the Scripture out loud. Then, let one person read the phrase and the paraphrase. Go around the group and have everyone give a number from 1 (very low) to 10 (very high) to indicate how they measure themselves in that area. Have someone else read the next phrase, etc. until you've completed the inventory.

Love must be sincere: I am able to really give myself to others; not in some phony way, but with real meaning.

1 2 3 4 5 6 7 8 9 10

Hate what is evil; cling to what is good: I am learning to stand up for my convictions; to say no to something I know is wrong and yes to God.

1 2 3 4 5 6 7 8 9 10

Be devoted to one another in brotherly love: I am learning how to reach out and hug my Christian brothers and sisters warmly—in the right way—and for purely spiritual reasons.

1 2 3 4 5 6 7 8 9 10

Keep your spiritual fervor, serving the Lord: I am eager and enthusiastic to do anything I can for Christ because my heart is full of gratitude for what he has done for me.

1 2 3 4 5 6 7 8 9 10

Be joyful in hope: I am experiencing a new freedom that overflows in praise because I know God is in control.

1 2 3 4 5 6 7 8 9 10

Patient in affliction: Problems don't always get me down. I can take the heat. Under pressure I can stay cool.

1 2 3 4 5 6 7 8 9 10

Faithful in prayer: I have learned to turn over every need to Christ and to share every decision I have to make with him. I have learned to "wait on God" and let him work things out.

1 2 3 4 5 6 7 8 9 10

Share with God's people who are in need. Practice hospitality: I have learned that my possessions, my time, my whole being belongs to God—to be shared with those in need.

1 2 3 4 5 6 7 8 9 10

Bless those who persecute you: I have learned to respond with kindness to those who put me down—and to pray on their behalf. I am no longer defensive about my life.

1 2 3 4 5 6 7 8 9 10

Rejoice with those who rejoice; mourn with those who mourn: I celebrate life when others are rejoicing, and grieve openly when others are hurting. I am not afraid to show my feelings.

1 2 3 4 5 6 7 8 9 10

A Case Study on Violence

Get together in groups of about 4 and discuss the following case study. Start out by having one person read the case study out loud; then discuss each question as a group.

CASE STUDY:
Jake is 15 and an only child. He spends a lot of time at the video arcade playing the martial arts combat and shoot'em up games with friends. His dad has been long gone since the divorce several years ago; and his mom is gone a lot with her career. Although a bright student, Jake is bored with school and is not really sure he wants to grow up and be "successful" like his parents. Jake begins to hang out late at night with some guys from school, as they cruise around town looking for excitement. They begin doing a little shoplifting, vandalism, graffiti, and sneaking into the porno flicks downtown. Pretty soon that becomes boring too. One night they see a girl from school who hangs with the "in" crowd walking to her car in a secluded lot. One of the guys says, "Hey, let's have some fun with the babe." They start by playing keep-away with her purse until the young woman starts fighting back. A couple of the guys begin to retaliate, mocking her attempts to defend herself. Before it's over some of the guys are taking turns beating and raping her. Jake watches, trying to be cool while inside he knows this is wrong; but fear of rejection, ridicule and physical harm keep him silent. These guys are not just poor, underprivileged kids who grew up in violent and abusive neighborhoods; some are above average students and enjoy the "good" life.

DISCUSSION QUESTIONS:

1. Why did Jake get involved with this group of guys?
   - ❑ He was into shoplifting.
   - ❑ He was bored.
   - ❑ He wanted to feel accepted.
   - ❑ He wanted to belong to a tough gang and hurt someone.
   - ❑ other:____

2. What or who is to blame for Jake's involvement in the group and the things the guys did? Explain.
   - ❑ Jake
   - ❑ Jake's youth group
   - ❑ Jake's parents
   - ❑ the guys in the group
   - ❑ other:____

3. What effect do you think that the video games and other forms of entertainment had on Jake's actions and attitudes? Explain.
   - ❑ little effect
   - ❑ some effect
   - ❑ big effect

4. If you were a part of the jury who tried these guys for what they did to the girl, what do you think should happen to them, especially Jake?

A Case Study on Depression and Suicide

Get together in groups of about 4 and discuss the following case study. Start out by having one person read the case study out loud; then discuss each question as a group.

CASE STUDY:

Bill was the president of the sophomore class, captain of the junior varsity football team and an honor student. Bill was the most popular kid in his class, but one night he put the barrel of a shotgun in his mouth and pulled the trigger. Looking back, his friends say they might have been able to do something if they had known what to look for. He was the youngest in a family of very gifted and successful children. And the family had high expectations for him—which he said he could not live up to.

His older sister was killed the year before in an automobile accident. His friends thought it was just the grieving process when he spoke about "going to see his sister soon." And his favorite comment when he was disappointed or frustrated in a dating relationship was, "I'm going to kill myself."

DISCUSSION QUESTIONS:

1. If you had been a close friend of Bill's and you heard him speaking this way, what would you do?
   - ❏ probably ignore it
   - ❏ assume he was only joking
   - ❏ ask him what he was really saying
   - ❏ tell a counselor about it
   - ❏ see to it that he gets help at the risk of offending him

2. If you thought Bill should get help but feared you were going to "break his confidence," what would you do?
   - ❏ tell someone without telling Bill
   - ❏ tell Bill first that I was going to tell someone
   - ❏ get Bill together with his parents and tell them
   - ❏ I don't know what I would do.

3. If Bill was in your youth group, what would you do?
   - ❏ open up about the situation to the whole group
   - ❏ tell the youth leader
   - ❏ tell Bill first that I was going to tell the youth leader
   - ❏ just be a friend to Bill
   - ❏ I don't know.

A Case Study on Sex

Get together in groups of about 4 girls or 4 guys. The first case study is for the girls, and the second one is for the guys. Start out by having one person read the case study out loud; then discuss each question in your group of 4.

CASE STUDY #1: FOR GIRLS

Mary wasn't a Christian in junior high when she got involved with guys. She had a rich fantasy life and enjoyed visualizing herself in sexual experiences with guys. She was quiet at school, but fun to be with, and made it easy or challenging for guys to touch her. She could play hard to get, or give guys the come on, depending on her mood and desires. She knew how to dress to attract their attention, yet still be accepted by the girls. She had lost count of the guys she had made it with, and had no intention of giving any of that up.

When she gave her life to Christ, she figured that it was the attitude about Christ, not all the do's and don'ts, that was important, that "love" was the most important principle, and that she could witness in the back seat of a car as easily as anywhere else.

But to her surprise she found all of that changing. It was not an instant miracle, but it was totally the process of God working on her and in her mind and heart. Changes began to take place from the inside out. One action, one attitude, one thought at a time ... over many months.

CASE STUDY #2: FOR GUYS

In Sam's life, lust was not always a problem. It took hold a little at a time. When he was 7, he had his first encounter with sex. Out of curiosity he and a young girl touched and explored each other. Lusts were aroused in him at that early age.

Sam began to think about this experience. He focused his mind on these thoughts and desires. The more he thought about the opposite sex, the stronger his feelings became. In junior high he began looking at "girlie" magazines. He read pornographic stories about sexual conquests. As the thoughts and actions ran unchecked, lustful habit patterns began to form in his life. Sexual fantasy and pornography became a way of life and he couldn't seem to help himself. These reinforced the lustful pattern of thinking. When he saw cute girls, he visualized them like the girls in the magazine. He began to focus on parts of their bodies instead of seeing them as whole people. As time went on, the bondage became stronger. He talked about girls differently, and kept looking forward to when he himself would be the conqueror.

Sam could never get moral victory over lust until he understood why he was lusting. His youth director at church helped him understand that he did not lust primarily for the sexual pleasure it brought him, but because he was getting temporary acceptance and satisfaction from these thoughts and habits.

DISCUSSION QUESTIONS:

1. How do you feel about Mary or Sam?
2. If you were Mary or Sam's friend, how would you treat them?
3. How do you think Mary and Sam should deal with the feelings of failure and guilt for the stuff they have done?
4. What could you share from your own experience that might help Mary or Sam?
5. Do these case studies lead you to some questions or concerns? Is there someone you could share them with?

Thanks Bunches!

Giving thanks is a great thing to do, even if there's no turkey in front of us. This exercise provides an opportunity for you to say "thank you" to God. Get together in groups of 8 or more. Looking at the list below, choose those things you are thankful for and share your answers with the group.

I AM THANKFUL FOR MY ...

family	neighborhood	sense of purpose
church	home	calling
school	nationality	mind
heritage	pets	emotions
faith	accomplishments	education
spiritual gifts	creativity	job
friends	health	reputation
talents	appearance	car
hobby	character	memories
wisdom	courage	future

Next choose a Bible verse from the list below. Then go around the circle and have everyone read the verse they selected.

Give thanks to the Lord, call on his name; make known among the nations what he has done. Give thanks to the Lord, for he is good; his love endures forever.
1 Chronicles 16:8,34

I will give thanks to the Lord because of his righteousness and will sing praise to the name of the Lord Most High. *Psalm 7:17*

I will praise you, O Lord, with all my heart; I will tell of all your wonders. I will be glad and rejoice in you; I will sing praise to your name, O Most High.
Psalm 9:1–2

Enter his gates with thanksgiving and his courts with praise; give thanks to him and praise his name. *Psalm 100:4*

Let them give thanks to the Lord for his unfailing love and his wonderful deeds for men. Let them sacrifice thank offerings and tell of his works with songs of joy.
Psalm 107:21–22

Do not be anxious about anything, but in everything, by prayer and petition, with thanksgiving, present your requests to God. *Philippians 4:6*

After everyone has shared what they are thankful for and a Bible verse, close with a prayer of thanksgiving.

Pick a Promise

Gather in groups of 8 or more. Take your pick of the Scripture promises listed below. Tell the group why you chose the one you did.

You can also personalize the promise. After you have chosen a verse, restate it in first-person language. For example, if you personalized the first verse listed below, it would sound like this: "Therefore, if I am in Christ, I am a new creation; the old has gone, the new has come!"

Therefore, if anyone is in Christ, he is a new creation; the old has gone, the new has come!
2 Corinthians 5:17

... being confident of this, that he who began a good work in you will carry it on to completion until the day of Christ Jesus. *Philippians 1:6*

"Call to me and I will answer you and tell you great and unsearchable things you do not know."
Jeremiah 33:3

And God is able to make all grace abound to you, so that in all things at all times, having all that you need, you will abound in every good work.
2 Corinthians 9:8

I can do everything through him who gives me strength. *Philippians 4:13*

And we know that in all things God works for the good of those who love him, who have been called according to his purpose. *Romans 8:28*

"Ask and it will be given to you; seek and you will find; knock and the door will be opened to you. For everyone who asks receives; he who seek finds; and to him who knocks, the door will be opened." *Matthew 7:7–8*

No temptation has seized you except what is common to man. And God is faithful; he will not let you be tempted beyond what you can bear. But when you are tempted, he will also provide a way out so that you can stand up under it.
1 Corinthians 10:13

"Here I am! I stand at the door and knock. If anyone hears my voice and opens the door, I will come in and eat with him, and he with me." *Revelation 3:20*

"Peace I leave with you; my peace I give you. I do not give to you as the world gives. Do not let your hearts be troubled and do not be afraid." *John 14:27*

Trust in the Lord with all your heart and lean not on your own understanding; in all your ways acknowledge him, and he will make your paths straight. *Proverbs 3:5–6*

The Lord will keep you from all harm—he will watch over your life; the Lord will watch over your coming and going both now and forevermore. *Psalm 121:7–8*

You and Me, Partner

Get in groups of 8 or more. Think of the people in your group as you read over the list of activities below. If you had to choose someone from your group to be your partner, who would you choose to do these activities with? Jot down each person's name beside the activity you have chosen for them. You can use each person's name only once and you have to use everyone's name once (therefore, you won't be writing a name in every blank). Then, let one person listen to what the others chose for them. Move to the next person, etc. around your group.

WHO WOULD YOU CHOOSE FOR THE FOLLOWING?

_______________ENDURANCE DANCE CONTEST partner

_______________BOBSLED RACE partner for the Olympics

_______________MONDAY NIGHT FOOTBALL ANNOUNCER teammate

_______________TRAPEZE ACT partner

_______________MY UNDERSTUDY for my debut in a Broadway musical

_______________TAG-TEAM partner for a professional wrestling match

_______________BEST MAN or MAID OF HONOR at my wedding

_______________SECRET UNDERCOVER AGENT copartner

_______________BODYGUARD for me when I strike it rich

_______________MOUNTAIN CLIMBING partner in climbing Mt. Everest

_______________ASTRONAUT to fly the space shuttle while I walk in space

_______________SAND CASTLE TOURNAMENT building partner

_______________PIT CREW foreman for entry in Indianapolis 500

_______________AUTHOR of a book about my love life

_______________SURGEON to operate on me for a life-threatening cancer

_______________TWO-ON-TWO BEACH VOLLEYBALL teammate

_______________NEW BUSINESS START-UP partner

_______________HEAVY-DUTY PRAYER partner

VALUED VALUES

Get together in groups of 8 or more. Below is a list of qualities based on positive values. Think about the members of your group and jot down their names next to the value that describes them best. You can use each person's name only once and you have to use everyone's name once (therefore, you won't be writing a name in every blank). Ask one person to listen while the others explain which value they selected for that individual. Then go to the next person and do the same until everyone is affirmed.

_______________PURE IN HEART: Your life is marked with integrity before God and other people.

_______________PEACEMAKER: You have a gift from God to help people overcome their differences.

_______________TRANSPARENT: You can be yourself without any pretenses and let the light of Christ shine through you.

_______________FAITHFUL: You are faithful to uphold God's morality even under pressure.

_______________MERCIFUL / COMPASSIONATE: You have the ability to feel what others feel—to be happy or to hurt with them.

_______________MEEK / GENTLE: You can be outwardly tender because you are inwardly strong.

_______________SPIRITUALLY HUNGRY: I admire the longing in your heart for a growing, genuine relationship with God.

_______________ALWAYS LOVING: You have a Christlike capacity to love others unconditionally—no matter what.

_______________COMMUNITY BUILDER: God uses you as a bond to bring people together in unity.

_______________HUMBLE: I admire the quiet way you demonstrate what humility is all about.

_______________GENEROUS: You give freely, not for attention or praise—but for the simple joy of giving.

_______________CONTENTED: You know your worth is based on who you are rather than on what you have.

_______________JOYFUL: Regardless of the circumstances, you have a smile on your face and a positive outlook about life.

_______________PATIENT: You never seem to be in a hurry or to get irritated by others.

BROADWAY JOBS

Get together in groups of 8 or more. Imagine for a moment that your group has been chosen to produce a Broadway show, and you had to choose people from your group for all of the jobs for this production. Have someone read out loud the job description for the first job below—PRODUCER. Then, let everyone in your group call out the name of the person in your group who would best fit this job. (You don't have to agree.) Then read the job description for the next job and let everyone nominate another person. Repeat this process through the list.

PRODUCER: Typical Hollywood business tycoon; extravagant, big-spender, big-production magnate.

DIRECTOR: Creative, imaginative brains who coordinates the production and draws the best out of others.

HEROINE: Beautiful, captivating, everybody's heart throb; defenseless when men are around, but nobody's fool.

HERO: Tough, macho, champion of the underdog, knight in shining armor, defender of truth.

COMEDIAN: Childlike, happy-go-lucky, outrageously funny, keeps everyone laughing.

CHARACTER PERSON: Rugged individualist, outrageously different, colorful, adds spice to any surrounding.

FALL GUY: Easy-going, nonchalant character who wins the hearts of everyone by being the "foil" of the heavy characters.

TECHNICAL DIRECTOR: The genius for "sound and lights"; creates the perfect atmosphere.

COMPOSER OF LYRICS: Communicates in music what everybody understands; heavy into feelings, moods, outbursts of energy.

PUBLICITY AGENT: Advertising and public relations expert; knows all the angles, good at one-liners, a flair for "hot" news.

VILLAIN: The "bad guy" who really is the heavy for the plot, forces others to think, challenges traditional values; out to destroy anything artificial or hypocritical.

AUTHOR: Shy, aloof; very much in touch with feelings, sensitive to people, puts into words what others only feel.

STAGEHAND: Supportive, behind-the-scenes person who makes things run smoothly; patient and tolerant.

THANK YOU

Gather together in groups of 8 or more. Below is a list of animals. Read over the list and pick one that best describes how you feel about this group. Take turns sharing your answers as a way of saying "thank you" to the group.

WILD EAGLE: You have helped me discover my spiritual wings and helped me soar like an eagle—spiritually.

HAPPY HIPPOPOTAMUS: You have helped me surface and bask in the warm sunshine of God's love.

LANKY LEOPARD: You have helped me look closely at myself and see some spots, and you still accept me the way I am.

SAFARI ELEPHANT: You have helped me get started on the exciting adventure of the Christian life.

COLORFUL PEACOCK: You have helped me see the new person that Christ has made me—something beautiful and special.

PLAYFUL PORPOISE: You have helped me laugh at some of my problems and realize that I am not alone.

OSTRICH IN LOVE: You have helped me get my head out of the sand, enjoy life and have fun.

TOWERING GIRAFFE: You have helped me hold my head up and feel confident about my faith.

ROARING LION: You have helped me stand up for what I believe and speak out for my faith.

DANCING BEAR: You have helped me celebrate life and show my friends that the Christian life can be fun.

ALL-WEATHER DUCK: You have helped me appreciate the storms that I am going through—and to sing in the rain.

Thank You!

You Remind Me of Jesus

Get together in groups of 8 or more. Every Christian reflects the character of Jesus in some way. As your group has gotten to know each other, you can begin to see how each person demonstrates Christ in their very own personality. Go around the circle and have each person listen while others take turns telling that person what they notice in him or her that reminds them of Jesus. You may also want to tell them why you selected what you did.

YOU REMIND ME OF:

JESUS THE HEALER: You seem to be able to touch someone's life with your compassion and help make them whole.

JESUS THE SERVANT: There's nothing that you wouldn't do for someone.

JESUS THE PREACHER: You share your faith in a way that challenges and inspires people.

JESUS THE LEADER: As Jesus had a plan for the disciples, you are able to lead others in a way that honors God.

JESUS THE REBEL: By doing the unexpected, you remind me of Jesus' way of revealing God in unique, surprising ways.

JESUS THE RECONCILER: Like Jesus, you have the ability to be a peacemaker between others.

JESUS THE TEACHER: You have a gift for bringing light and understanding to God's Word.

JESUS THE CRITIC: You have the courage to say what needs to be said, even if it isn't always popular.

JESUS THE SACRIFICE: Like Jesus, you seem to be willing to sacrifice anything to glorify God.

MY GROUP IS ...

Get together in groups of 8 or more. How would you describe your group? Choose one of the images below which best describes your group, then share why you chose the one you did.

AN ORCHARD. Because of this group, I feel like a strong, healthy apple tree that's growing and producing fruit.

A BIRD'S NEST. I know how a baby bird feels, because being a part of this group makes me feel cared for and protected.

A TEEPEE. We couldn't stand tall and provide warmth and shelter if we didn't lean on each other.

A THINK TANK. This group must be full of geniuses! We seem to be able to understand every issue and creatively work out every problem.

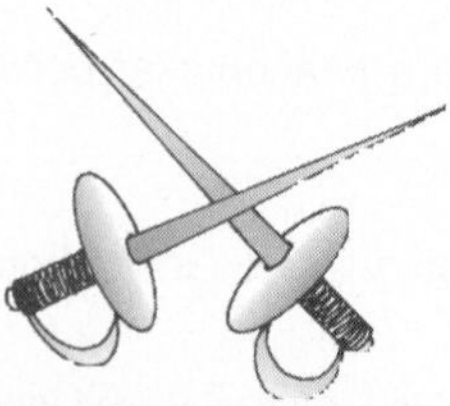

THE MUSKETEERS. It's "All for one and one for all" with this group. I always feel like I belong and I'm part of a great team.

THE BRADY BUNCH. I feel like I'm part of one big happy family. We're not perfect, but we're committed to each other.

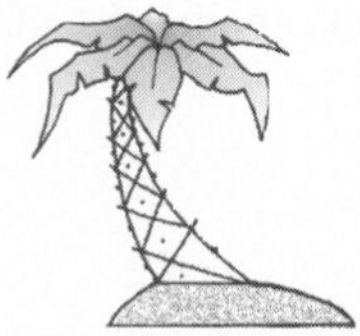

AN OASIS. While the rest of the world can be like a harsh desert, this group is a refreshing stop on the journey of life.

A LITTER OF PUPPIES. You are fun, friendly and enthusiastic. I feel full of energy every time we are together.

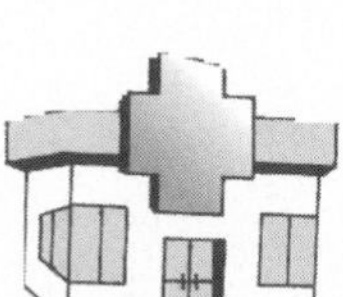

AN E.R. UNIT. This group is like a hospital. I came in hurting and now I feel so much better—thanks to a bunch of great friends.

Automotive Affirmation

Get together in groups of 8 or more. Use this list of automotive items to affirm the contribution of each person in your group. Have someone read out loud the first item—BATTERY. Then, let everyone in the group call out the name of the person in your group who best fits this description. (You don't all have to agree.) Then read the next item, etc., down through the list.

BATTERY: A dependable "die-hard"—provides the "juice" for everything to happen.

SPARK PLUG: Gets things started. Makes sure there is "fire," even on cold mornings.

OIL: "The razor's edge" to protect against engine wear-out, provide longer mileage, and reduce friction for fast-moving parts.

SHOCK ABSORBER: Cushions heavy bumps. Makes for an easy, comfortable ride.

RADIO: The "music machine," making the trip fun and enjoyable. Adds a little "rock 'n' roll" for a good time.

MUFFLER: Reduces the engine's roar to a cat's "purr," even at high speeds over rough terrain.

CUP HOLDER: The servant, always meeting a need.

SUB WOOFER: The strong voice in the crowd. When they talk, people listen.

TRANSMISSION: Converts the energy into motion, enables the engine to slip from one speed to another without stripping the gears.

SEAT BELT / AIR BAG: Restrains or protects others when there is a possibility of them getting hurt.

GASOLINE: Liquid fuel that is consumed, giving away its own life for the energy to keep things moving.

WINDSHIELD: Keeps the vision clear, protects from debris and flying objects.

ANIMAL AFFIRMATION

Get together in groups of 8 or more. Which animal in the list below reminds you of each member's personality? Have one person listen while others share which animal reminds them of that person. Go around the group until everyone has been affirmed.

PLAYFUL PORPOISE: intelligent, lively, the life of the party

CUDDLY TEDDY BEAR: lovable, warm, brings out the "heart" in all of us

PUPPY DOG: fun-loving, irresistible, disarming, childlike

MOTHER HEN: caring, sensitive, always on the lookout for the well-being of others

WILD EAGLE: untamed, noble, independent, cherishes freedom and the wide-open spaces

FAITHFUL SHEEP DOG: loyal, dependable, devoted, always there when you need someone

HUNGRY CHEETAH: unassuming, sleek, on the prowl—usually gets their prey

WISE OLD OWL: quiet and thoughtful, with the appearance of being in deep contemplation

GRACEFUL SWAN: majestic, smooth-sailing, unruffled—always in command of the situation

PEACEFUL DOVE: calm, behind-the-scenes peacemaker in the midst of storms

COLORFUL PEACOCK: fun, outrageous, flashy

TIRELESS TURTLE: slow and steady, persistent plodder—but willing to stick their neck out at times

HONEY BEE: energetic, tireless worker

INNOCENT LAMB: with a gentle, peaceful spirit

This Little Light of Yours

Get together in groups of 8 or more. What kind of light best describes each of the members of your group? Focus on one group member at a time and share what light you would choose for him or her.

FLASHLIGHT: You showed insight that brought light into an area that has been dark for me.

SUNLIGHT: You bring warmth and life to others.

WARNING LIGHT: You gave some needed cautions, without which I or the group may have gotten into trouble.

CANDLELIGHT: You help provide a relaxed, gentle mood.

LIGHTHOUSE BEAM: You showed us the way when we got "lost in the fog."

NEON LIGHT: You bring color and personality to the group.

PORCH LIGHT: You were the light that said, "You are welcome here!"

NIGHT-LIGHT: You made some scary things seem less scary.

FIREPLACE LIGHT: You bring people together around your warmth and crackling flames.

MOONLIGHT: You reflect well the light of the Son.

The Giving Game

Get together in groups of about 4. This game is a beautiful way to express your love and appreciation for one another. Follow the three steps below.

1. Ask everyone to sit in silence and ask themselves this question, "If I could give something of myself to each person in this group ... that expresses my feelings right now for them, what would I want to give each person that they could keep for the rest of their lives?" (This is for keeps.)

2. Still in silence, take out your purse or wallet ... or things in your pockets ... and try to find symbols or tokens of the real thing you would like to give this person. For instance:

   - ❑ picture of my family—to remember the times we have shared together
   - ❑ a ticket stub to a concert—to remember the music that we enjoy in Christ
   - ❑ a Band-Aid—for the "little hurts" that come along in life

   Remember, you need ONE gift (a different gift) for each person—a token or symbol of the real gift.

3. Ask one person to listen while the others go around and explain their gift and hand it to this person. The person who receives the gift is to say "Thanks." Nothing more.

Repeat this procedure until everyone in your group has been given their gifts. In the giving and receiving of gifts, you are able to say two things: (1) What I have appreciated most about you, and (2) What I want you to keep as a token of our friendship—for the rest of your life.

GROUP EVALUATION

Get together in groups of 8 or more. Sometimes a group needs to stop and give themselves a checkup. Go down this list one question at a time, and let everyone share their response.

Mark each question by circling a number:

1 = never
2 = rarely
3 = sometimes
4 = most of the time
5 = always

After everyone has answered the questions, the group could have an open discussion about their opinions of the group. Keep in mind that no group is perfect and every group needs time to grow and mature.

GENERALLY SPEAKING, I FEEL LIKE THIS GROUP:

understands what I am trying to say	1	2	3	4	5
encourages my comments and opinions	1	2	3	4	5
accepts me for who I am	1	2	3	4	5
feels free to let me know when I'm bugging them	1	2	3	4	5
helps me understand God better	1	2	3	4	5
includes me in what's going on	1	2	3	4	5
can tell when something is bothering me	1	2	3	4	5
gives me support	1	2	3	4	5
encourages me to grow in my Christian faith	1	2	3	4	5
succeeds with problem solving	1	2	3	4	5
is fulfilling its total potential	1	2	3	4	5

the lifeblood of the innocent poor,
though you did not catch them breaking in.
Yet in spite of all this
35 you say, 'I am innocent;
he is not angry with me.'
But I will pass judgment on you
because you say, 'I have not sinned.'
36 Why do you go about so much,
changing your ways?
You will be disappointed by Egypt
as you were by Assyria.
37 You will also leave that place
with your hands on your head,
for the LORD has rejected those you trust;
you will not be helped by them.

3 "If a man divorces his wife
and she leaves him and marries another man,
should he return to her again?
Would not the land be completely defiled?
But you have lived as a prostitute with many lovers—
would you now return to me?"
declares the LORD.
2 "Look up to the barren heights and see.
Is there any place where you have not been ravished?
By the roadside you sat waiting for lovers,
sat like a nomad[a] in the desert.
You have defiled the land
with your prostitution and wickedness.
3 Therefore the showers have been withheld,
and no spring rains have fallen.
Yet you have the brazen look of a prostitute;
you refuse to blush with shame.
4 Have you not just called to me:
'My Father, my friend from my youth,
5 will you always be angry?
Will your wrath continue forever?'
This is how you talk,
but you do all the evil you can."

Unfaithful Israel

6 During the reign of King Josiah, the LORD said
to me, "Have you seen what faithless Israel has
done? She has gone up on every high hill and
under every spreading tree and has committed
adultery there. 7 I thought that after she had done
all this she would return to me but she did not,
and her unfaithful sister Judah saw it. 8 I gave
faithless Israel her certificate of divorce and sent
her away because of all her adulteries. Yet I saw
that her unfaithful sister Judah had no fear; she
also went out and committed adultery. 9 Because
Israel's immorality mattered so little to her, she
defiled the land and committed adultery with
stone and wood. 10 In spite of all this, her unfaithful
sister Judah did not return to me with all her
heart, but only in pretense," declares the LORD.
11 The LORD said to me, "Faithless Israel is
more righteous than unfaithful Judah. 12 Go, proclaim
this message toward the north:

" 'Return, faithless Israel,' declares the LORD,
'I will frown on you no longer,
for I am merciful,' declares the LORD,
'I will not be angry forever.
13 Only acknowledge your guilt—
you have rebelled against the LORD your God,
you have scattered your favors to foreign gods
under every spreading tree,
and have not obeyed me,' "
declares the LORD.

14 "Return, faithless people," declares the
LORD, "for I am your husband. I will choose
you—one from a town and two from a clan—and
bring you to Zion. 15 Then I will give you shepherds
after my own heart, who will lead you with
knowledge and understanding. 16 In those days,
when your numbers have increased greatly in the
land," declares the LORD, "men will no longer
say, 'The ark of the covenant of the LORD.' It will
never enter their minds or be remembered; it
will not be missed, nor will another one be made.
17 At that time they will call Jerusalem The
Throne of the LORD, and all nations will gather in
Jerusalem to honor the name of the LORD. No
longer will they follow the stubbornness of their
evil hearts. 18 In those days the house of Judah
will join the house of Israel, and together they
will come from a northern land to the land I gave
your forefathers as an inheritance.
19 "I myself said,

" 'How gladly would I treat you like sons
and give you a desirable land,
the most beautiful inheritance of any nation.'
I thought you would call me 'Father'
and not turn away from following me.
20 But like a woman unfaithful to her husband,
so you have been unfaithful to me,
O house of Israel,"
declares the LORD.

21 A cry is heard on the barren heights,
the weeping and pleading of the people of Israel,
because they have perverted their ways
and have forgotten the LORD their God.

[a] 2 Or *an Arab*

22"Return, faithless people;
I will cure you of backsliding."

"Yes, we will come to you,
for you are the LORD our God.
23Surely the ⌊idolatrous⌋ commotion on the hills
and mountains is a deception;
surely in the LORD our God
is the salvation of Israel.
24From our youth shameful gods have consumed
the fruits of our fathers' labor—
their flocks and herds,
their sons and daughters.
25Let us lie down in our shame,
and let our disgrace cover us.
We have sinned against the LORD our God,
both we and our fathers;
from our youth till this day
we have not obeyed the LORD our God."

4 "If you will return, O Israel,
return to me,"
declares the LORD.
"If you put your detestable idols out of my sight
and no longer go astray,
2and if in a truthful, just and righteous way
you swear, 'As surely as the LORD lives,'
then the nations will be blessed by him
and in him they will glory."

3This is what the LORD says to the men of
Judah and to Jerusalem:

"Break up your unplowed ground
and do not sow among thorns.
4Circumcise yourselves to the LORD,
circumcise your hearts,
you men of Judah and people of Jerusalem,
or my wrath will break out and burn like fire
because of the evil you have done—
burn with no one to quench it.

Disaster From the North

5"Announce in Judah and proclaim in Jerusalem and say:
'Sound the trumpet throughout the land!'
Cry aloud and say:
'Gather together!
Let us flee to the fortified cities!'
6Raise the signal to go to Zion!
Flee for safety without delay!
For I am bringing disaster from the north,
even terrible destruction."

7A lion has come out of his lair;
a destroyer of nations has set out.
He has left his place
to lay waste your land.
Your towns will lie in ruins
without inhabitant.
8So put on sackcloth,
lament and wail,
for the fierce anger of the LORD
has not turned away from us.

9"In that day," declares the LORD,
"the king and the officials will lose heart,
the priests will be horrified,
and the prophets will be appalled."

10Then I said, "Ah, Sovereign LORD, how completely you have deceived this people and Jerusalem by saying, 'You will have peace,' when the
sword is at our throats."
11At that time this people and Jerusalem will
be told, "A scorching wind from the barren
heights in the desert blows toward my people,
but not to winnow or cleanse; 12a wind too strong
for that comes from me.[a] Now I pronounce my
judgments against them."

13Look! He advances like the clouds,
his chariots come like a whirlwind,
his horses are swifter than eagles.
Woe to us! We are ruined!
14O Jerusalem, wash the evil from your heart
and be saved.
How long will you harbor wicked thoughts?
15A voice is announcing from Dan,
proclaiming disaster from the hills of Ephraim.
16"Tell this to the nations,
proclaim it to Jerusalem:
'A besieging army is coming from a distant land,
raising a war cry against the cities of Judah.
17They surround her like men guarding a field,
because she has rebelled against me,' "
declares the LORD.
18"Your own conduct and actions
have brought this upon you.
This is your punishment.
How bitter it is!
How it pierces to the heart!"

19Oh, my anguish, my anguish!
I writhe in pain.
Oh, the agony of my heart!
My heart pounds within me,
I cannot keep silent.
For I have heard the sound of the trumpet;
I have heard the battle cry.
20Disaster follows disaster;

[a]12 Or *comes at my command*

the whole land lies in ruins.
In an instant my tents are destroyed,
my shelter in a moment.
21 How long must I see the battle standard
and hear the sound of the trumpet?

22 "My people are fools;
they do not know me.
They are senseless children;
they have no understanding.
They are skilled in doing evil;
they know not how to do good."

23 I looked at the earth,
and it was formless and empty;
and at the heavens,
and their light was gone.
24 I looked at the mountains,
and they were quaking;
all the hills were swaying.
25 I looked, and there were no people;
every bird in the sky had flown away.
26 I looked, and the fruitful land was a desert;
all its towns lay in ruins
before the LORD, before his fierce anger.

27 This is what the LORD says:

"The whole land will be ruined,
though I will not destroy it completely.
28 Therefore the earth will mourn
and the heavens above grow dark,
because I have spoken and will not relent,
I have decided and will not turn back."

29 At the sound of horsemen and archers
every town takes to flight.
Some go into the thickets;
some climb up among the rocks.
All the towns are deserted;
no one lives in them.

30 What are you doing, O devastated one?
Why dress yourself in scarlet
and put on jewels of gold?
Why shade your eyes with paint?
You adorn yourself in vain.
Your lovers despise you;
they seek your life.

31 I hear a cry as of a woman in labor,
a groan as of one bearing her first child—
the cry of the Daughter of Zion gasping for breath,
stretching out her hands and saying,
"Alas! I am fainting;
my life is given over to murderers."

Not One Is Upright

5 "Go up and down the streets of Jerusalem,
look around and consider,
search through her squares.
If you can find but one person
who deals honestly and seeks the truth,
I will forgive this city.
2 Although they say, 'As surely as the LORD lives,'
still they are swearing falsely."
3 O LORD, do not your eyes look for truth?
You struck them, but they felt no pain;
you crushed them, but they refused correction.
They made their faces harder than stone
and refused to repent.
4 I thought, "These are only the poor;
they are foolish,
for they do not know the way of the LORD,
the requirements of their God.
5 So I will go to the leaders
and speak to them;
surely they know the way of the LORD,
the requirements of their God."
But with one accord they too had broken off the yoke
and torn off the bonds.
6 Therefore a lion from the forest will attack them,
a wolf from the desert will ravage them,
a leopard will lie in wait near their towns
to tear to pieces any who venture out,
for their rebellion is great
and their backslidings many.

7 "Why should I forgive you?
Your children have forsaken me
and sworn by gods that are not gods.
I supplied all their needs,
yet they committed adultery
and thronged to the houses of prostitutes.
8 They are well-fed, lusty stallions,
each neighing for another man's wife.
9 Should I not punish them for this?"
declares the LORD.
"Should I not avenge myself
on such a nation as this?

10 "Go through her vineyards and ravage them,
but do not destroy them completely.
Strip off her branches,
for these people do not belong to the LORD.
11 The house of Israel and the house of Judah
have been utterly unfaithful to me,"
declares the LORD.

12 They have lied about the LORD;
they said, "He will do nothing!
No harm will come to us;
we will never see sword or famine.
13 The prophets are but wind
and the word is not in them;
so let what they say be done to them."

14Therefore this is what the LORD God Almighty says:

"Because the people have spoken these
words,
I will make my words in your mouth a fire
and these people the wood it consumes.
15O house of Israel," declares the LORD,
"I am bringing a distant nation against
you—
an ancient and enduring nation,
a people whose language you do not know,
whose speech you do not understand.
16Their quivers are like an open grave;
all of them are mighty warriors.
17They will devour your harvests and food,
devour your sons and daughters;
they will devour your flocks and herds,
devour your vines and fig trees.
With the sword they will destroy
the fortified cities in which you trust.

18"Yet even in those days," declares the LORD,
"I will not destroy you completely. 19And when
the people ask, 'Why has the LORD our God done
all this to us?' you will tell them, 'As you have
forsaken me and served foreign gods in your own
land, so now you will serve foreigners in a land
not your own.'

20"Announce this to the house of Jacob
and proclaim it in Judah:
21Hear this, you foolish and senseless people,
who have eyes but do not see,
who have ears but do not hear:
22Should you not fear me?" declares the LORD.
"Should you not tremble in my presence?
I made the sand a boundary for the sea,
an everlasting barrier it cannot cross.
The waves may roll, but they cannot prevail;
they may roar, but they cannot cross it.
23But these people have stubborn and
rebellious hearts;
they have turned aside and gone away.
24They do not say to themselves,
'Let us fear the LORD our God,
who gives autumn and spring rains in season,
who assures us of the regular weeks of
harvest.'
25Your wrongdoings have kept these away;
your sins have deprived you of good.

26"Among my people are wicked men
who lie in wait like men who snare birds
and like those who set traps to catch men.
27Like cages full of birds,
their houses are full of deceit;
they have become rich and powerful
28 and have grown fat and sleek.
Their evil deeds have no limit;
they do not plead the case of the fatherless
to win it,
they do not defend the rights of the poor.
29Should I not punish them for this?"
declares the LORD.
"Should I not avenge myself
on such a nation as this?

30"A horrible and shocking thing
has happened in the land:
31The prophets prophesy lies,
the priests rule by their own authority,
and my people love it this way.
But what will you do in the end?

Jerusalem Under Siege

6 "Flee for safety, people of Benjamin!
Flee from Jerusalem!
Sound the trumpet in Tekoa!
Raise the signal over Beth Hakkerem!
For disaster looms out of the north,
even terrible destruction.
2I will destroy the Daughter of Zion,
so beautiful and delicate.
3Shepherds with their flocks will come against
her;
they will pitch their tents around her,
each tending his own portion."

4"Prepare for battle against her!
Arise, let us attack at noon!
But, alas, the daylight is fading,
and the shadows of evening grow long.
5So arise, let us attack at night
and destroy her fortresses!"

6This is what the LORD Almighty says:

"Cut down the trees
and build siege ramps against Jerusalem.
This city must be punished;
it is filled with oppression.
7As a well pours out its water,
so she pours out her wickedness.
Violence and destruction resound in her;
her sickness and wounds are ever before
me.
8Take warning, O Jerusalem,
or I will turn away from you
and make your land desolate
so no one can live in it."

9This is what the LORD Almighty says:

"Let them glean the remnant of Israel
as thoroughly as a vine;
pass your hand over the branches again,
like one gathering grapes."

10To whom can I speak and give warning?
Who will listen to me?

Their ears are closed[a]
so they cannot hear.
The word of the LORD is offensive to them;
they find no pleasure in it.
11But I am full of the wrath of the LORD,
and I cannot hold it in.

"Pour it out on the children in the street
and on the young men gathered together;
both husband and wife will be caught in it,
and the old, those weighed down with years.
12Their houses will be turned over to others,
together with their fields and their wives,
when I stretch out my hand
against those who live in the land,"
declares the LORD.

13"From the least to the greatest,
all are greedy for gain;
prophets and priests alike,
all practice deceit.
14They dress the wound of my people
as though it were not serious.
'Peace, peace,' they say,
when there is no peace.
15Are they ashamed of their loathsome conduct?
No, they have no shame at all;
they do not even know how to blush.
So they will fall among the fallen;
they will be brought down when I punish them,"
says the LORD.

16This is what the LORD says:

"Stand at the crossroads and look;
ask for the ancient paths,
ask where the good way is, and walk in it,
and you will find rest for your souls.
But you said, 'We will not walk in it.'
17I appointed watchmen over you and said,
'Listen to the sound of the trumpet!'
But you said, 'We will not listen.'
18Therefore hear, O nations;
observe, O witnesses,
what will happen to them.
19Hear, O earth:
I am bringing disaster on this people,
the fruit of their schemes,
because they have not listened to my words
and have rejected my law.
20What do I care about incense from Sheba
or sweet calamus from a distant land?
Your burnt offerings are not acceptable;
your sacrifices do not please me."

21Therefore this is what the LORD says:

"I will put obstacles before this people.
Fathers and sons alike will stumble over them;
neighbors and friends will perish."

22This is what the LORD says:

"Look, an army is coming
from the land of the north;
a great nation is being stirred up
from the ends of the earth.
23They are armed with bow and spear;
they are cruel and show no mercy.
They sound like the roaring sea
as they ride on their horses;
they come like men in battle formation
to attack you, O Daughter of Zion."

24We have heard reports about them,
and our hands hang limp.
Anguish has gripped us,
pain like that of a woman in labor.
25Do not go out to the fields
or walk on the roads,
for the enemy has a sword,
and there is terror on every side.
26O my people, put on sackcloth
and roll in ashes;
mourn with bitter wailing
as for an only son,
for suddenly the destroyer
will come upon us.

27"I have made you a tester of metals
and my people the ore,
that you may observe
and test their ways.
28They are all hardened rebels,
going about to slander.
They are bronze and iron;
they all act corruptly.
29The bellows blow fiercely
to burn away the lead with fire,
but the refining goes on in vain;
the wicked are not purged out.
30They are called rejected silver,
because the LORD has rejected them."

False Religion Worthless

7 This is the word that came to Jeremiah from
the LORD: 2"Stand at the gate of the LORD's
house and there proclaim this message:
"'Hear the word of the LORD, all you people of
Judah who come through these gates to worship
the LORD. 3This is what the LORD Almighty, the
God of Israel, says: Reform your ways and your
actions, and I will let you live in this place. 4Do
not trust in deceptive words and say, "This is the
temple of the LORD, the temple of the LORD, the

[a]10 Hebrew *uncircumcised*

temple of the LORD!" 5If you really change your
ways and your actions and deal with each other
justly, 6if you do not oppress the alien, the fatherless or the widow and do not shed innocent blood
in this place, and if you do not follow other gods
to your own harm, 7then I will let you live in this
place, in the land I gave your forefathers for ever
and ever. 8But look, you are trusting in deceptive
words that are worthless.

9" 'Will you steal and murder, commit adultery
and perjury,[a] burn incense to Baal and follow
other gods you have not known, 10and then come
and stand before me in this house, which bears
my Name, and say, "We are safe"—safe to do all
these detestable things? 11Has this house, which
bears my Name, become a den of robbers to you?
But I have been watching! declares the LORD.

12" 'Go now to the place in Shiloh where I first
made a dwelling for my Name, and see what I did
to it because of the wickedness of my people
Israel. 13While you were doing all these things,
declares the LORD, I spoke to you again and again,
but you did not listen; I called you, but you did
not answer. 14Therefore, what I did to Shiloh I
will now do to the house that bears my Name,
the temple you trust in, the place I gave to you
and your fathers. 15I will thrust you from my presence, just as I did all your brothers, the people of
Ephraim.'

16"So do not pray for this people nor offer any
plea or petition for them; do not plead with me,
for I will not listen to you. 17Do you not see what
they are doing in the towns of Judah and in the
streets of Jerusalem? 18The children gather wood,
the fathers light the fire, and the women knead
the dough and make cakes of bread for the Queen
of Heaven. They pour out drink offerings to other
gods to provoke me to anger. 19But am I the one
they are provoking? declares the LORD. Are they
not rather harming themselves, to their own
shame?

20" 'Therefore this is what the Sovereign LORD
says: My anger and my wrath will be poured out
on this place, on man and beast, on the trees of
the field and on the fruit of the ground, and it will
burn and not be quenched.

21" 'This is what the LORD Almighty, the God
of Israel, says: Go ahead, add your burnt offerings
to your other sacrifices and eat the meat yourselves! 22For when I brought your forefathers out
of Egypt and spoke to them, I did not just give
them commands about burnt offerings and sacrifices, 23but I gave them this command: Obey me,
and I will be your God and you will be my people.
Walk in all the ways I command you, that it may
go well with you. 24But they did not listen or pay
attention; instead, they followed the stubborn in-
clinations of their evil hearts. They went backward and not forward. 25From the time your forefathers left Egypt until now, day after day, again
and again I sent you my servants the prophets.
26But they did not listen to me or pay attention.
They were stiff-necked and did more evil than
their forefathers.'

27"When you tell them all this, they will not
listen to you; when you call to them, they will not
answer. 28Therefore say to them, 'This is the nation that has not obeyed the LORD its God or
responded to correction. Truth has perished; it
has vanished from their lips. 29Cut off your hair
and throw it away; take up a lament on the barren heights, for the LORD has rejected and abandoned this generation that is under his wrath.

The Valley of Slaughter

30" 'The people of Judah have done evil in my
eyes, declares the LORD. They have set up their
detestable idols in the house that bears my Name
and have defiled it. 31They have built the high
places of Topheth in the Valley of Ben Hinnom
to burn their sons and daughters in the fire—
something I did not command, nor did it enter
my mind. 32So beware, the days are coming, declares the LORD, when people will no longer call
it Topheth or the Valley of Ben Hinnom, but the
Valley of Slaughter, for they will bury the dead in
Topheth until there is no more room. 33Then the
carcasses of this people will become food for the
birds of the air and the beasts of the earth, and
there will be no one to frighten them away. 34I
will bring an end to the sounds of joy and gladness and to the voices of bride and bridegroom in
the towns of Judah and the streets of Jerusalem,
for the land will become desolate.

8 " 'At that time, declares the LORD, the bones
of the kings and officials of Judah, the bones
of the priests and prophets, and the bones of the
people of Jerusalem will be removed from their
graves. 2They will be exposed to the sun and the
moon and all the stars of the heavens, which they
have loved and served and which they have followed and consulted and worshiped. They will
not be gathered up or buried, but will be like
refuse lying on the ground. 3Wherever I banish
them, all the survivors of this evil nation will
prefer death to life, declares the LORD Almighty.'

Sin and Punishment

4"Say to them, 'This is what the LORD says:

" 'When men fall down, do they not get up?
When a man turns away, does he not
return?
5Why then have these people turned away?

[a] 9 Or *and swear by false gods*

Why does Jerusalem always turn away?
They cling to deceit;
they refuse to return.
6 I have listened attentively,
but they do not say what is right.
No one repents of his wickedness,
saying, "What have I done?"
Each pursues his own course
like a horse charging into battle.
7 Even the stork in the sky
knows her appointed seasons,
and the dove, the swift and the thrush
observe the time of their migration.
But my people do not know
the requirements of the LORD.

8 " 'How can you say, "We are wise,
for we have the law of the LORD,"
when actually the lying pen of the scribes
has handled it falsely?
9 The wise will be put to shame;
they will be dismayed and trapped.
Since they have rejected the word of the LORD,
what kind of wisdom do they have?
10 Therefore I will give their wives to other men
and their fields to new owners.
From the least to the greatest,
all are greedy for gain;
prophets and priests alike,
all practice deceit.
11 They dress the wound of my people
as though it were not serious.
"Peace, peace," they say,
when there is no peace.
12 Are they ashamed of their loathsome conduct?
No, they have no shame at all;
they do not even know how to blush.
So they will fall among the fallen;
they will be brought down when they are punished,
says the LORD.

13 " 'I will take away their harvest,
declares the LORD.
There will be no grapes on the vine.
There will be no figs on the tree,
and their leaves will wither.
What I have given them
will be taken from them.[a]' "

14 "Why are we sitting here?
Gather together!
Let us flee to the fortified cities
and perish there!
For the LORD our God has doomed us to perish
and given us poisoned water to drink,
because we have sinned against him.
15 We hoped for peace
but no good has come,
for a time of healing
but there was only terror.
16 The snorting of the enemy's horses
is heard from Dan;
at the neighing of their stallions
the whole land trembles.
They have come to devour
the land and everything in it,
the city and all who live there."

17 "See, I will send venomous snakes among you,
vipers that cannot be charmed,
and they will bite you,"
declares the LORD.

18 O my Comforter[b] in sorrow,
my heart is faint within me.
19 Listen to the cry of my people
from a land far away:
"Is the LORD not in Zion?
Is her King no longer there?"

"Why have they provoked me to anger with their images,
with their worthless foreign idols?"

20 "The harvest is past,
the summer has ended,
and we are not saved."

21 Since my people are crushed, I am crushed;
I mourn, and horror grips me.
22 Is there no balm in Gilead?
Is there no physician there?
Why then is there no healing
for the wound of my people?

9 1 Oh, that my head were a spring of water
and my eyes a fountain of tears!
I would weep day and night
for the slain of my people.
2 Oh, that I had in the desert
a lodging place for travelers,
so that I might leave my people
and go away from them;
for they are all adulterers,
a crowd of unfaithful people.

3 "They make ready their tongue
like a bow, to shoot lies;
it is not by truth
that they triumph[c] in the land.
They go from one sin to another;

[a] 13 The meaning of the Hebrew for this sentence is uncertain.
[b] 18 The meaning of the Hebrew for this word is uncertain.
[c] 3 Or *lies; / they are not valiant for truth*

they do not acknowledge me,"
declares the LORD.
4"Beware of your friends;
do not trust your brothers.
For every brother is a deceiver,[a]
and every friend a slanderer.
5Friend deceives friend,
and no one speaks the truth.
They have taught their tongues to lie;
they weary themselves with sinning.
6You[b] live in the midst of deception;
in their deceit they refuse to acknowledge me,"
declares the LORD.

7Therefore this is what the LORD Almighty says:

"See, I will refine and test them,
for what else can I do
because of the sin of my people?
8Their tongue is a deadly arrow;
it speaks with deceit.
With his mouth each speaks cordially to his neighbor,
but in his heart he sets a trap for him.
9Should I not punish them for this?"
declares the LORD.
"Should I not avenge myself
on such a nation as this?"

10I will weep and wail for the mountains
and take up a lament concerning the desert pastures.
They are desolate and untraveled,
and the lowing of cattle is not heard.
The birds of the air have fled
and the animals are gone.
11"I will make Jerusalem a heap of ruins,
a haunt of jackals;
and I will lay waste the towns of Judah
so no one can live there."

12What man is wise enough to understand
this? Who has been instructed by the LORD and
can explain it? Why has the land been ruined and
laid waste like a desert that no one can cross?
13The LORD said, "It is because they have forsaken my law, which I set before them; they have
not obeyed me or followed my law. 14Instead,
they have followed the stubbornness of their
hearts; they have followed the Baals, as their fathers taught them." 15Therefore, this is what the
LORD Almighty, the God of Israel, says: "See, I
will make this people eat bitter food and drink
poisoned water. 16I will scatter them among nations that neither they nor their fathers have
known, and I will pursue them with the sword
until I have destroyed them."

17This is what the LORD Almighty says:

"Consider now! Call for the wailing women to come;
send for the most skillful of them.
18Let them come quickly
and wail over us
till our eyes overflow with tears
and water streams from our eyelids.
19The sound of wailing is heard from Zion:
'How ruined we are!
How great is our shame!
We must leave our land
because our houses are in ruins.'"
20Now, O women, hear the word of the LORD;
open your ears to the words of his mouth.
Teach your daughters how to wail;
teach one another a lament.
21Death has climbed in through our windows
and has entered our fortresses;
it has cut off the children from the streets
and the young men from the public squares.

22Say, "This is what the LORD declares:

" 'The dead bodies of men will lie
like refuse on the open field,
like cut grain behind the reaper,
with no one to gather them.' "

23This is what the LORD says:

"Let not the wise man boast of his wisdom
or the strong man boast of his strength
or the rich man boast of his riches,
24but let him who boasts boast about this:
that he understands and knows me,
that I am the LORD, who exercises kindness,
justice and righteousness on earth,
for in these I delight,"
declares the LORD.

25"The days are coming," declares the LORD,
"when I will punish all who are circumcised only
in the flesh— 26Egypt, Judah, Edom, Ammon,
Moab and all who live in the desert in distant
places.[c] For all these nations are really uncircumcised, and even the whole house of Israel is
uncircumcised in heart."

God and Idols

10 Hear what the LORD says to you, O house
of Israel. 2This is what the LORD says:

"Do not learn the ways of the nations
or be terrified by signs in the sky,

[a]4 Or *a deceiving Jacob* [b]6 That is, Jeremiah (the Hebrew is singular) [c]26 Or *desert and who clip the hair by their foreheads*

though the nations are terrified by them.
3For the customs of the peoples are worthless;
they cut a tree out of the forest,
and a craftsman shapes it with his chisel.
4They adorn it with silver and gold;
they fasten it with hammer and nails
so it will not totter.
5Like a scarecrow in a melon patch,
their idols cannot speak;
they must be carried
because they cannot walk.
Do not fear them;
they can do no harm
nor can they do any good."

6No one is like you, O LORD;
you are great,
and your name is mighty in power.
7Who should not revere you,
O King of the nations?
This is your due.
Among all the wise men of the nations
and in all their kingdoms,
there is no one like you.
8They are all senseless and foolish;
they are taught by worthless wooden idols.
9Hammered silver is brought from Tarshish
and gold from Uphaz.
What the craftsman and goldsmith have made
is then dressed in blue and purple—
all made by skilled workers.
10But the LORD is the true God;
he is the living God, the eternal King.
When he is angry, the earth trembles;
the nations cannot endure his wrath.

11"Tell them this: 'These gods, who did not make the heavens and the earth, will perish from the earth and from under the heavens.' "[a]

12But God made the earth by his power;
he founded the world by his wisdom
and stretched out the heavens by his understanding.
13When he thunders, the waters in the heavens roar;
he makes clouds rise from the ends of the earth.
He sends lightning with the rain
and brings out the wind from his storehouses.

14Everyone is senseless and without knowledge;
every goldsmith is shamed by his idols.
His images are a fraud;
they have no breath in them.
15They are worthless, the objects of mockery;
when their judgment comes, they will perish.
16He who is the Portion of Jacob is not like these,
for he is the Maker of all things,
including Israel, the tribe of his inheritance—
the LORD Almighty is his name.

Coming Destruction

17Gather up your belongings to leave the land,
you who live under siege.
18For this is what the LORD says:
"At this time I will hurl out
those who live in this land;
I will bring distress on them
so that they may be captured."

19Woe to me because of my injury!
My wound is incurable!
Yet I said to myself,
"This is my sickness, and I must endure it."
20My tent is destroyed;
all its ropes are snapped.
My sons are gone from me and are no more;
no one is left now to pitch my tent
or to set up my shelter.
21The shepherds are senseless
and do not inquire of the LORD;
so they do not prosper
and all their flock is scattered.
22Listen! The report is coming—
a great commotion from the land of the north!
It will make the towns of Judah desolate,
a haunt of jackals.

Jeremiah's Prayer

23I know, O LORD, that a man's life is not his own;
it is not for man to direct his steps.
24Correct me, LORD, but only with justice—
not in your anger,
lest you reduce me to nothing.
25Pour out your wrath on the nations
that do not acknowledge you,
on the peoples who do not call on your name.
For they have devoured Jacob;
they have devoured him completely
and destroyed his homeland.

The Covenant Is Broken

11 This is the word that came to Jeremiah
from the LORD: 2"Listen to the terms of
this covenant and tell them to the people of Judah

a11 The text of this verse is in Aramaic.

and to those who live in Jerusalem. 3Tell them
that this is what the LORD, the God of Israel, says:
'Cursed is the man who does not obey the terms
of this covenant— 4the terms I commanded your
forefathers when I brought them out of Egypt, out
of the iron-smelting furnace.' I said, 'Obey me
and do everything I command you, and you will
be my people, and I will be your God. 5Then I
will fulfill the oath I swore to your forefathers, to
give them a land flowing with milk and honey'—
the land you possess today."

I answered, "Amen, LORD."

6The LORD said to me, "Proclaim all these
words in the towns of Judah and in the streets of
Jerusalem: 'Listen to the terms of this covenant
and follow them. 7From the time I brought your
forefathers up from Egypt until today, I warned
them again and again, saying, "Obey me." 8But
they did not listen or pay attention; instead, they
followed the stubbornness of their evil hearts. So
I brought on them all the curses of the covenant
I had commanded them to follow but that they
did not keep.' "

9Then the LORD said to me, "There is a conspiracy among the people of Judah and those who
live in Jerusalem. 10They have returned to the
sins of their forefathers, who refused to listen
to my words. They have followed other gods to
serve them. Both the house of Israel and the
house of Judah have broken the covenant I made
with their forefathers. 11Therefore this is what
the LORD says: 'I will bring on them a disaster
they cannot escape. Although they cry out to me,
I will not listen to them. 12The towns of Judah
and the people of Jerusalem will go and cry out to
the gods to whom they burn incense, but they
will not help them at all when disaster strikes.
13You have as many gods as you have towns, O
Judah; and the altars you have set up to burn
incense to that shameful god Baal are as many as
the streets of Jerusalem.'

14"Do not pray for this people nor offer any
plea or petition for them, because I will not listen
when they call to me in the time of their distress.

15"What is my beloved doing in my temple
as she works out her evil schemes with
many?
Can consecrated meat avert ⌊your
punishment⌋?
When you engage in your wickedness,
then you rejoice.[a] "

16The LORD called you a thriving olive tree
with fruit beautiful in form.
But with the roar of a mighty storm
he will set it on fire,
and its branches will be broken.

17The LORD Almighty, who planted you, has decreed disaster for you, because the house of Israel
and the house of Judah have done evil and provoked me to anger by burning incense to Baal.

Plot Against Jeremiah

18Because the LORD revealed their plot to me,
I knew it, for at that time he showed me what
they were doing. 19I had been like a gentle lamb
led to the slaughter; I did not realize that they
had plotted against me, saying,

"Let us destroy the tree and its fruit;
let us cut him off from the land of the
living,
that his name be remembered no more."
20But, O LORD Almighty, you who judge
righteously
and test the heart and mind,
let me see your vengeance upon them,
for to you I have committed my cause.

21"Therefore this is what the LORD says about
the men of Anathoth who are seeking your life
and saying, 'Do not prophesy in the name of the
LORD or you will die by our hands'— 22therefore
this is what the LORD Almighty says: 'I will punish them. Their young men will die by the sword,
their sons and daughters by famine. 23Not even a
remnant will be left to them, because I will bring
disaster on the men of Anathoth in the year of
their punishment.' "

Jeremiah's Complaint

12 You are always righteous, O LORD,
when I bring a case before you.
Yet I would speak with you about your
justice:
Why does the way of the wicked prosper?
Why do all the faithless live at ease?
2You have planted them, and they have taken
root;
they grow and bear fruit.
You are always on their lips
but far from their hearts.
3Yet you know me, O LORD;
you see me and test my thoughts about
you.
Drag them off like sheep to be butchered!
Set them apart for the day of slaughter!
4How long will the land lie parched[b]
and the grass in every field be withered?
Because those who live in it are wicked,
the animals and birds have perished.
Moreover, the people are saying,
"He will not see what happens to us."

[a] 15 Or *Could consecrated meat avert your punishment? / Then you would rejoice* [b] 4 Or *land mourn*

God's Answer

5 "If you have raced with men on foot
and they have worn you out,
how can you compete with horses?
If you stumble in safe country,[a]
how will you manage in the thickets by[b]
the Jordan?
6 Your brothers, your own family—
even they have betrayed you;
they have raised a loud cry against you.
Do not trust them,
though they speak well of you.

7 "I will forsake my house,
abandon my inheritance;
I will give the one I love
into the hands of her enemies.
8 My inheritance has become to me
like a lion in the forest.
She roars at me;
therefore I hate her.
9 Has not my inheritance become to me
like a speckled bird of prey
that other birds of prey surround and
attack?
Go and gather all the wild beasts;
bring them to devour.
10 Many shepherds will ruin my vineyard
and trample down my field;
they will turn my pleasant field
into a desolate wasteland.
11 It will be made a wasteland,
parched and desolate before me;
the whole land will be laid waste
because there is no one who cares.
12 Over all the barren heights in the desert
destroyers will swarm,
for the sword of the LORD will devour
from one end of the land to the other;
no one will be safe.
13 They will sow wheat but reap thorns;
they will wear themselves out but gain
nothing.
So bear the shame of your harvest
because of the LORD's fierce anger."

14 This is what the LORD says: "As for all my
wicked neighbors who seize the inheritance I
gave my people Israel, I will uproot them from
their lands and I will uproot the house of Judah
from among them. 15 But after I uproot them, I
will again have compassion and will bring each of
them back to his own inheritance and his own
country. 16 And if they learn well the ways of my
people and swear by my name, saying, 'As surely
as the LORD lives'—even as they once taught my
people to swear by Baal—then they will be established among my people. 17 But if any nation does
not listen, I will completely uproot and destroy
it," declares the LORD.

A Linen Belt

13 This is what the LORD said to me: "Go and buy a linen belt and put it around your waist, but do not let it touch water." 2 So I bought
a belt, as the LORD directed, and put it around my
waist.

3 Then the word of the LORD came to me a
second time: 4 "Take the belt you bought and are
wearing around your waist, and go now to Perath[c] and hide it there in a crevice in the rocks."
5 So I went and hid it at Perath, as the LORD
told me.

6 Many days later the LORD said to me, "Go
now to Perath and get the belt I told you to hide
there." 7 So I went to Perath and dug up the belt
and took it from the place where I had hidden it,
but now it was ruined and completely useless.

8 Then the word of the LORD came to me:
9 "This is what the LORD says: 'In the same way I
will ruin the pride of Judah and the great pride of
Jerusalem. 10 These wicked people, who refuse to
listen to my words, who follow the stubbornness
of their hearts and go after other gods to serve
and worship them, will be like this belt—
completely useless! 11 For as a belt is bound
around a man's waist, so I bound the whole
house of Israel and the whole house of Judah to
me,' declares the LORD, 'to be my people for my
renown and praise and honor. But they have not
listened.'

Wineskins

12 "Say to them: 'This is what the LORD, the
God of Israel, says: Every wineskin should be
filled with wine.' And if they say to you, 'Don't
we know that every wineskin should be filled
with wine?' 13 then tell them, 'This is what the
LORD says: I am going to fill with drunkenness all
who live in this land, including the kings who sit
on David's throne, the priests, the prophets and
all those living in Jerusalem. 14 I will smash them
one against the other, fathers and sons alike, declares the LORD. I will allow no pity or mercy or
compassion to keep me from destroying them.'"

Threat of Captivity

15 Hear and pay attention,
do not be arrogant,
for the LORD has spoken.
16 Give glory to the LORD your God
before he brings the darkness,
before your feet stumble
on the darkening hills.

[a] 5 Or *If you put your trust in a land of safety* [b] 5 Or *the flooding of* [c] 4 Or possibly *the Euphrates*; also in verses 5-7

You hope for light,
but he will turn it to thick darkness
and change it to deep gloom.
17 But if you do not listen,
I will weep in secret
because of your pride;
my eyes will weep bitterly,
overflowing with tears,
because the LORD's flock will be taken captive.

18 Say to the king and to the queen mother,
"Come down from your thrones,
for your glorious crowns
will fall from your heads."
19 The cities in the Negev will be shut up,
and there will be no one to open them.
All Judah will be carried into exile,
carried completely away.

20 Lift up your eyes and see
those who are coming from the north.
Where is the flock that was entrusted to you,
the sheep of which you boasted?
21 What will you say when ⌞the LORD⌟ sets over you
those you cultivated as your special allies?
Will not pain grip you
like that of a woman in labor?
22 And if you ask yourself,
"Why has this happened to me?"—
it is because of your many sins
that your skirts have been torn off
and your body mistreated.
23 Can the Ethiopian[a] change his skin
or the leopard its spots?
Neither can you do good
who are accustomed to doing evil.
24 "I will scatter you like chaff
driven by the desert wind.
25 This is your lot,
the portion I have decreed for you,"
declares the LORD,
"because you have forgotten me
and trusted in false gods.
26 I will pull up your skirts over your face
that your shame may be seen—
27 your adulteries and lustful neighings,
your shameless prostitution!
I have seen your detestable acts
on the hills and in the fields.
Woe to you, O Jerusalem!
How long will you be unclean?"

Drought, Famine, Sword

14 This is the word of the LORD to Jeremiah concerning the drought:

2 "Judah mourns,
her cities languish;
they wail for the land,
and a cry goes up from Jerusalem.
3 The nobles send their servants for water;
they go to the cisterns
but find no water.
They return with their jars unfilled;
dismayed and despairing,
they cover their heads.
4 The ground is cracked
because there is no rain in the land;
the farmers are dismayed
and cover their heads.
5 Even the doe in the field
deserts her newborn fawn
because there is no grass.
6 Wild donkeys stand on the barren heights
and pant like jackals;
their eyesight fails
for lack of pasture."

7 Although our sins testify against us,
O LORD, do something for the sake of your name.
For our backsliding is great;
we have sinned against you.
8 O Hope of Israel,
its Savior in times of distress,
why are you like a stranger in the land,
like a traveler who stays only a night?
9 Why are you like a man taken by surprise,
like a warrior powerless to save?
You are among us, O LORD,
and we bear your name;
do not forsake us!

10 This is what the LORD says about this people:

"They greatly love to wander;
they do not restrain their feet.
So the LORD does not accept them;
he will now remember their wickedness
and punish them for their sins."

11 Then the LORD said to me, "Do not pray for
the well-being of this people. 12 Although they
fast, I will not listen to their cry; though they
offer burnt offerings and grain offerings, I will not
accept them. Instead, I will destroy them with
the sword, famine and plague."
13 But I said, "Ah, Sovereign LORD, the prophets keep telling them, 'You will not see the sword
or suffer famine. Indeed, I will give you lasting
peace in this place.' "
14 Then the LORD said to me, "The prophets are
prophesying lies in my name. I have not sent
them or appointed them or spoken to them. They
are prophesying to you false visions, divinations,

[a] 23 Hebrew *Cushite* (probably a person from the upper Nile region)

idolatries[a] and the delusions of their own
minds. 15Therefore, this is what the LORD says
about the prophets who are prophesying in my
name: I did not send them, yet they are saying,
'No sword or famine will touch this land.' Those
same prophets will perish by sword and famine.
16And the people they are prophesying to will be
thrown out into the streets of Jerusalem because
of the famine and sword. There will be no one
to bury them or their wives, their sons or their
daughters. I will pour out on them the calamity
they deserve.

17"Speak this word to them:

"'Let my eyes overflow with tears
night and day without ceasing;
for my virgin daughter—my people—
has suffered a grievous wound,
a crushing blow.
18If I go into the country,
I see those slain by the sword;
if I go into the city,
I see the ravages of famine.
Both prophet and priest
have gone to a land they know not.'"
19Have you rejected Judah completely?
Do you despise Zion?
Why have you afflicted us
so that we cannot be healed?
We hoped for peace
but no good has come,
for a time of healing
but there is only terror.
20O LORD, we acknowledge our wickedness
and the guilt of our fathers;
we have indeed sinned against you.
21For the sake of your name do not despise us;
do not dishonor your glorious throne.
Remember your covenant with us
and do not break it.
22Do any of the worthless idols of the nations
bring rain?
Do the skies themselves send down
showers?
No, it is you, O LORD our God.
Therefore our hope is in you,
for you are the one who does all this.

15 Then the LORD said to me: "Even if Moses
and Samuel were to stand before me, my
heart would not go out to this people. Send them
away from my presence! Let them go! 2And if
they ask you, 'Where shall we go?' tell them,
'This is what the LORD says:

"'Those destined for death, to death;
those for the sword, to the sword;
those for starvation, to starvation;
those for captivity, to captivity.'

3"I will send four kinds of destroyers against
them," declares the LORD, "the sword to kill and
the dogs to drag away and the birds of the air and
the beasts of the earth to devour and destroy. 4I
will make them abhorrent to all the kingdoms of
the earth because of what Manasseh son of Hezekiah king of Judah did in Jerusalem.

5"Who will have pity on you, O Jerusalem?
Who will mourn for you?
Who will stop to ask how you are?
6You have rejected me," declares the LORD.
"You keep on backsliding.
So I will lay hands on you and destroy you;
I can no longer show compassion.
7I will winnow them with a winnowing fork
at the city gates of the land.
I will bring bereavement and destruction on
my people,
for they have not changed their ways.
8I will make their widows more numerous
than the sand of the sea.
At midday I will bring a destroyer
against the mothers of their young men;
suddenly I will bring down on them
anguish and terror.
9The mother of seven will grow faint
and breathe her last.
Her sun will set while it is still day;
she will be disgraced and humiliated.
I will put the survivors to the sword
before their enemies,"
declares the LORD.

10Alas, my mother, that you gave me birth,
a man with whom the whole land strives
and contends!
I have neither lent nor borrowed,
yet everyone curses me.

11The LORD said,

"Surely I will deliver you for a good purpose;
surely I will make your enemies plead
with you
in times of disaster and times of distress.
12"Can a man break iron—
iron from the north—or bronze?
13Your wealth and your treasures
I will give as plunder, without charge,
because of all your sins
throughout your country.
14I will enslave you to your enemies
in[b] a land you do not know,

[a] 14 Or *visions, worthless divinations*   [b] 14 Some Hebrew manuscripts, Septuagint and Syriac (see also Jer. 17:4); most Hebrew manuscripts *I will cause your enemies to bring you / into*

for my anger will kindle a fire
that will burn against you."

15You understand, O LORD;
remember me and care for me.
Avenge me on my persecutors.
You are long-suffering—do not take me
away;
think of how I suffer reproach for your
sake.
16When your words came, I ate them;
they were my joy and my heart's delight,
for I bear your name,
O LORD God Almighty.
17I never sat in the company of revelers,
never made merry with them;
I sat alone because your hand was on me
and you had filled me with indignation.
18Why is my pain unending
and my wound grievous and incurable?
Will you be to me like a deceptive brook,
like a spring that fails?

19Therefore this is what the LORD says:

"If you repent, I will restore you
that you may serve me;
if you utter worthy, not worthless, words,
you will be my spokesman.
Let this people turn to you,
but you must not turn to them.
20I will make you a wall to this people,
a fortified wall of bronze;
they will fight against you
but will not overcome you,
for I am with you
to rescue and save you,"
declares the LORD.
21"I will save you from the hands of the
wicked
and redeem you from the grasp of the
cruel."

Day of Disaster

16 Then the word of the LORD came to me:
2"You must not marry and have sons or
daughters in this place." 3For this is what the
LORD says about the sons and daughters born in
this land and about the women who are their
mothers and the men who are their fathers:
4"They will die of deadly diseases. They will not
be mourned or buried but will be like refuse lying
on the ground. They will perish by sword and
famine, and their dead bodies will become food
for the birds of the air and the beasts of the
earth."
5For this is what the LORD says: "Do not enter
a house where there is a funeral meal; do not go
to mourn or show sympathy, because I have withdrawn my blessing, my love and my pity from this
people," declares the LORD. 6"Both high and low
will die in this land. They will not be buried or
mourned, and no one will cut himself or shave
his head for them. 7No one will offer food to
comfort those who mourn for the dead—not
even for a father or a mother—nor will anyone
give them a drink to console them.
8"And do not enter a house where there is
feasting and sit down to eat and drink. 9For this
is what the LORD Almighty, the God of Israel,
says: Before your eyes and in your days I will
bring an end to the sounds of joy and gladness
and to the voices of bride and bridegroom in this
place.
10"When you tell these people all this and they
ask you, 'Why has the LORD decreed such a great
disaster against us? What wrong have we done?
What sin have we committed against the LORD
our God?' 11then say to them, 'It is because your
fathers forsook me,' declares the LORD, 'and followed other gods and served and worshiped
them. They forsook me and did not keep my law.
12But you have behaved more wickedly than your
fathers. See how each of you is following the
stubbornness of his evil heart instead of obeying
me. 13So I will throw you out of this land into a
land neither you nor your fathers have known,
and there you will serve other gods day and
night, for I will show you no favor.'
14"However, the days are coming," declares
the LORD, "when men will no longer say, 'As
surely as the LORD lives, who brought the Israelites up out of Egypt,' 15but they will say, 'As
surely as the LORD lives, who brought the Israelites up out of the land of the north and out of all
the countries where he had banished them.' For
I will restore them to the land I gave their forefathers.
16"But now I will send for many fishermen,"
declares the LORD, "and they will catch them.
After that I will send for many hunters, and they
will hunt them down on every mountain and hill
and from the crevices of the rocks. 17My eyes are
on all their ways; they are not hidden from me,
nor is their sin concealed from my eyes. 18I will
repay them double for their wickedness and their
sin, because they have defiled my land with the
lifeless forms of their vile images and have filled
my inheritance with their detestable idols."

19O LORD, my strength and my fortress,
my refuge in time of distress,
to you the nations will come
from the ends of the earth and say,
"Our fathers possessed nothing but false
gods,
worthless idols that did them no good.
20Do men make their own gods?
Yes, but they are not gods!"

21"Therefore I will teach them—
this time I will teach them
my power and might.
Then they will know
that my name is the LORD.

17 "Judah's sin is engraved with an iron tool,
inscribed with a flint point,
on the tablets of their hearts
and on the horns of their altars.
2Even their children remember
their altars and Asherah poles[a]
beside the spreading trees
and on the high hills.
3My mountain in the land
and your[b] wealth and all your treasures
I will give away as plunder,
together with your high places,
because of sin throughout your country.
4Through your own fault you will lose
the inheritance I gave you.
I will enslave you to your enemies
in a land you do not know,
for you have kindled my anger,
and it will burn forever."

5This is what the LORD says:

"Cursed is the one who trusts in man,
who depends on flesh for his strength
and whose heart turns away from the LORD.
6He will be like a bush in the wastelands;
he will not see prosperity when it comes.
He will dwell in the parched places of the desert,
in a salt land where no one lives.

7"But blessed is the man who trusts in the LORD,
whose confidence is in him.
8He will be like a tree planted by the water
that sends out its roots by the stream.
It does not fear when heat comes;
its leaves are always green.
It has no worries in a year of drought
and never fails to bear fruit."

9The heart is deceitful above all things
and beyond cure.
Who can understand it?

10"I the LORD search the heart
and examine the mind,
to reward a man according to his conduct,
according to what his deeds deserve."
11Like a partridge that hatches eggs it did not lay
is the man who gains riches by unjust means.
When his life is half gone, they will desert him,
and in the end he will prove to be a fool.

12A glorious throne, exalted from the beginning,
is the place of our sanctuary.
13O LORD, the hope of Israel,
all who forsake you will be put to shame.
Those who turn away from you will be written in the dust
because they have forsaken the LORD,
the spring of living water.

14Heal me, O LORD, and I will be healed;
save me and I will be saved,
for you are the one I praise.
15They keep saying to me,
"Where is the word of the LORD?
Let it now be fulfilled!"
16I have not run away from being your shepherd;
you know I have not desired the day of despair.
What passes my lips is open before you.
17Do not be a terror to me;
you are my refuge in the day of disaster.
18Let my persecutors be put to shame,
but keep me from shame;
let them be terrified,
but keep me from terror.
Bring on them the day of disaster;
destroy them with double destruction.

Keeping the Sabbath Holy

19This is what the LORD said to me: "Go and
stand at the gate of the people, through which
the kings of Judah go in and out; stand also at all
the other gates of Jerusalem. 20Say to them, 'Hear
the word of the LORD, O kings of Judah and all
people of Judah and everyone living in Jerusalem
who come through these gates. 21This is what the
LORD says: Be careful not to carry a load on the
Sabbath day or bring it through the gates of Jerusalem.
22Do not bring a load out of your houses or
do any work on the Sabbath, but keep the Sabbath
day holy, as I commanded your forefathers.
23Yet they did not listen or pay attention; they
were stiff-necked and would not listen or respond
to discipline. 24But if you are careful to
obey me, declares the LORD, and bring no load
through the gates of this city on the Sabbath, but
keep the Sabbath day holy by not doing any work
on it, 25then kings who sit on David's throne will
come through the gates of this city with their
officials. They and their officials will come riding

[a]2 That is, symbols of the goddess Asherah
[b]2,3 Or *hills* / 3*and the mountains of the land. / Your*

in chariots and on horses, accompanied by the
men of Judah and those living in Jerusalem, and
this city will be inhabited forever. 26People will
come from the towns of Judah and the villages
around Jerusalem, from the territory of Benjamin
and the western foothills, from the hill country
and the Negev, bringing burnt offerings and sacrifices, grain offerings, incense and thank offerings
to the house of the LORD. 27But if you do not obey
me to keep the Sabbath day holy by not carrying
any load as you come through the gates of Jerusalem on the Sabbath day, then I will kindle an
unquenchable fire in the gates of Jerusalem that
will consume her fortresses.' "

At the Potter's House

18 This is the word that came to Jeremiah
from the LORD: 2"Go down to the potter's
house, and there I will give you my message." 3So
I went down to the potter's house, and I saw him
working at the wheel. 4But the pot he was shaping from the clay was marred in his hands; so the
potter formed it into another pot, shaping it as
seemed best to him.

5Then the word of the LORD came to me: 6"O
house of Israel, can I not do with you as this
potter does?" declares the LORD. "Like clay in the
hand of the potter, so are you in my hand, O
house of Israel. 7If at any time I announce that a
nation or kingdom is to be uprooted, torn down
and destroyed, 8and if that nation I warned repents of its evil, then I will relent and not inflict
on it the disaster I had planned. 9And if at another time I announce that a nation or kingdom is to
be built up and planted, 10and if it does evil in my
sight and does not obey me, then I will reconsider the good I had intended to do for it.

11"Now therefore say to the people of Judah
and those living in Jerusalem, 'This is what the
LORD says: Look! I am preparing a disaster for you
and devising a plan against you. So turn from
your evil ways, each one of you, and reform your
ways and your actions.' 12But they will reply, 'It's
no use. We will continue with our own plans;
each of us will follow the stubbornness of his evil
heart.' "

13Therefore this is what the LORD says:

"Inquire among the nations:
  Who has ever heard anything like this?
A most horrible thing has been done
  by Virgin Israel.
14Does the snow of Lebanon
  ever vanish from its rocky slopes?
Do its cool waters from distant sources
  ever cease to flow?[a]
15Yet my people have forgotten me;
  they burn incense to worthless idols,
which made them stumble in their ways
  and in the ancient paths.
They made them walk in bypaths
  and on roads not built up.
16Their land will be laid waste,
  an object of lasting scorn;
all who pass by will be appalled
  and will shake their heads.
17Like a wind from the east,
  I will scatter them before their enemies;
I will show them my back and not my face
  in the day of their disaster."

18They said, "Come, let's make plans against
Jeremiah; for the teaching of the law by the priest
will not be lost, nor will counsel from the wise,
nor the word from the prophets. So come, let's
attack him with our tongues and pay no attention
to anything he says."

19Listen to me, O LORD;
  hear what my accusers are saying!
20Should good be repaid with evil?
  Yet they have dug a pit for me.
Remember that I stood before you
  and spoke in their behalf
  to turn your wrath away from them.
21So give their children over to famine;
  hand them over to the power of the
    sword.
Let their wives be made childless and
    widows;
  let their men be put to death,
  their young men slain by the sword in
    battle.
22Let a cry be heard from their houses
  when you suddenly bring invaders against
    them,
for they have dug a pit to capture me
  and have hidden snares for my feet.
23But you know, O LORD,
  all their plots to kill me.
Do not forgive their crimes
  or blot out their sins from your sight.
Let them be overthrown before you;
  deal with them in the time of your anger.

19 This is what the LORD says: "Go and buy
a clay jar from a potter. Take along some
of the elders of the people and of the priests 2and
go out to the Valley of Ben Hinnom, near the
entrance of the Potsherd Gate. There proclaim
the words I tell you, 3and say, 'Hear the word of
the LORD, O kings of Judah and people of Jerusalem. This is what the LORD Almighty, the God of
Israel, says: Listen! I am going to bring a disaster
on this place that will make the ears of everyone

[a] 14 The meaning of the Hebrew for this sentence is uncertain.

who hears of it tingle. 4For they have forsaken me
and made this a place of foreign gods; they have
burned sacrifices in it to gods that neither they
nor their fathers nor the kings of Judah ever
knew, and they have filled this place with the
blood of the innocent. 5They have built the high
places of Baal to burn their sons in the fire as
offerings to Baal—something I did not command
or mention, nor did it enter my mind. 6So beware, the days are coming, declares the LORD,
when people will no longer call this place Topheth or the Valley of Ben Hinnom, but the Valley of Slaughter.

7" 'In this place I will ruin[a] the plans of Judah
and Jerusalem. I will make them fall by the sword
before their enemies, at the hands of those who
seek their lives, and I will give their carcasses as
food to the birds of the air and the beasts of the
earth. 8I will devastate this city and make it an
object of scorn; all who pass by will be appalled
and will scoff because of all its wounds. 9I will
make them eat the flesh of their sons and daughters, and they will eat one another's flesh during
the stress of the siege imposed on them by the
enemies who seek their lives.'

10"Then break the jar while those who go with
you are watching, 11and say to them, 'This is
what the LORD Almighty says: I will smash this
nation and this city just as this potter's jar is
smashed and cannot be repaired. They will bury
the dead in Topheth until there is no more room.
12This is what I will do to this place and to those
who live here, declares the LORD. I will make this
city like Topheth. 13The houses in Jerusalem and
those of the kings of Judah will be defiled like
this place, Topheth—all the houses where they
burned incense on the roofs to all the starry hosts
and poured out drink offerings to other gods.' "

14Jeremiah then returned from Topheth,
where the LORD had sent him to prophesy, and
stood in the court of the LORD's temple and said
to all the people, 15"This is what the LORD Almighty, the God of Israel, says: 'Listen! I am going to bring on this city and the villages around
it every disaster I pronounced against them, because they were stiff-necked and would not listen
to my words.' "

Jeremiah and Pashhur

20 When the priest Pashhur son of Immer,
the chief officer in the temple of the
LORD, heard Jeremiah prophesying these things,
2he had Jeremiah the prophet beaten and put in
the stocks at the Upper Gate of Benjamin at the
LORD's temple. 3The next day, when Pashhur released him from the stocks, Jeremiah said to him,
"The LORD's name for you is not Pashhur, but
Magor-Missabib.[b] 4For this is what the LORD
says: 'I will make you a terror to yourself and to
all your friends; with your own eyes you will see
them fall by the sword of their enemies. I will
hand all Judah over to the king of Babylon, who
will carry them away to Babylon or put them to
the sword. 5I will hand over to their enemies all
the wealth of this city—all its products, all its
valuables and all the treasures of the kings of
Judah. They will take it away as plunder and carry
it off to Babylon. 6And you, Pashhur, and all who
live in your house will go into exile to Babylon.
There you will die and be buried, you and all your
friends to whom you have prophesied lies.' "

Jeremiah's Complaint

7O LORD, you deceived[c] me, and I was
deceived[c];
you overpowered me and prevailed.
I am ridiculed all day long;
everyone mocks me.
8Whenever I speak, I cry out
proclaiming violence and destruction.
So the word of the LORD has brought me
insult and reproach all day long.
9But if I say, "I will not mention him
or speak any more in his name,"
his word is in my heart like a fire,
a fire shut up in my bones.
I am weary of holding it in;
indeed, I cannot.
10I hear many whispering,
"Terror on every side!
Report him! Let's report him!"
All my friends
are waiting for me to slip, saying,
"Perhaps he will be deceived;
then we will prevail over him
and take our revenge on him."

11But the LORD is with me like a mighty
warrior;
so my persecutors will stumble and not
prevail.
They will fail and be thoroughly disgraced;
their dishonor will never be forgotten.
12O LORD Almighty, you who examine the
righteous
and probe the heart and mind,
let me see your vengeance upon them,
for to you I have committed my cause.
13Sing to the LORD!
Give praise to the LORD!
He rescues the life of the needy
from the hands of the wicked.

[a] *7* The Hebrew for *ruin* sounds like the Hebrew for *jar* (see verses 1 and 10).
[b] *3* *Magor-Missabib* means *terror on every side.*
[c] *7* Or *persuaded*

14Cursed be the day I was born!
May the day my mother bore me not be blessed!
15Cursed be the man who brought my father the news,
who made him very glad, saying,
"A child is born to you—a son!"
16May that man be like the towns
the LORD overthrew without pity.
May he hear wailing in the morning,
a battle cry at noon.
17For he did not kill me in the womb,
with my mother as my grave,
her womb enlarged forever.
18Why did I ever come out of the womb
to see trouble and sorrow
and to end my days in shame?

God Rejects Zedekiah's Request

21 The word came to Jeremiah from the LORD when King Zedekiah sent to him Pashhur son of Malkijah and the priest Zephaniah son of Maaseiah. They said: 2"Inquire now of the LORD for us because Nebuchadnezzar[a] king of Babylon is attacking us. Perhaps the LORD will perform wonders for us as in times past so that he will withdraw from us."

3But Jeremiah answered them, "Tell Zedekiah, 4'This is what the LORD, the God of Israel, says: I am about to turn against you the weapons of war that are in your hands, which you are using to fight the king of Babylon and the Babylonians[b] who are outside the wall besieging you. And I will gather them inside this city. 5I myself will fight against you with an outstretched hand and a mighty arm in anger and fury and great wrath. 6I will strike down those who live in this city—both men and animals—and they will die of a terrible plague. 7After that, declares the LORD, I will hand over Zedekiah king of Judah, his officials and the people in this city who survive the plague, sword and famine, to Nebuchadnezzar king of Babylon and to their enemies who seek their lives. He will put them to the sword; he will show them no mercy or pity or compassion.'

8"Furthermore, tell the people, 'This is what the LORD says: See, I am setting before you the way of life and the way of death. 9Whoever stays in this city will die by the sword, famine or plague. But whoever goes out and surrenders to the Babylonians who are besieging you will live; he will escape with his life. 10I have determined to do this city harm and not good, declares the LORD. It will be given into the hands of the king of Babylon, and he will destroy it with fire.'

11"Moreover, say to the royal house of Judah, 'Hear the word of the LORD; 12O house of David, this is what the LORD says:

" 'Administer justice every morning;
rescue from the hand of his oppressor
the one who has been robbed,
or my wrath will break out and burn like fire
because of the evil you have done—
burn with no one to quench it.
13I am against you, ⌞Jerusalem,⌟
you who live above this valley
on the rocky plateau,
declares the LORD—
you who say, "Who can come against us?
Who can enter our refuge?"
14I will punish you as your deeds deserve,
declares the LORD.
I will kindle a fire in your forests
that will consume everything around you.' "

Judgment Against Evil Kings

22 This is what the LORD says: "Go down to the palace of the king of Judah and proclaim this message there: 2'Hear the word of the LORD, O king of Judah, you who sit on David's throne—you, your officials and your people who come through these gates. 3This is what the LORD says: Do what is just and right. Rescue from the hand of his oppressor the one who has been robbed. Do no wrong or violence to the alien, the fatherless or the widow, and do not shed innocent blood in this place. 4For if you are careful to carry out these commands, then kings who sit on David's throne will come through the gates of this palace, riding in chariots and on horses, accompanied by their officials and their people. 5But if you do not obey these commands, declares the LORD, I swear by myself that this palace will become a ruin.' "

6For this is what the LORD says about the palace of the king of Judah:

"Though you are like Gilead to me,
like the summit of Lebanon,
I will surely make you like a desert,
like towns not inhabited.
7I will send destroyers against you,
each man with his weapons,
and they will cut up your fine cedar beams
and throw them into the fire.

8"People from many nations will pass by this city and will ask one another, 'Why has the LORD done such a thing to this great city?' 9And the answer will be: 'Because they have forsaken the

[a]2 Hebrew *Nebuchadrezzar,* of which *Nebuchadnezzar* is a variant; here and often in Jeremiah and Ezekiel [b]4 Or *Chaldeans*; also in verse 9

covenant of the LORD their God and have worshiped and served other gods.' "

10Do not weep for the dead ⌊king⌋ or mourn
his loss;
rather, weep bitterly for him who is
exiled,
because he will never return
nor see his native land again.

11For this is what the LORD says about Shallum[a]
son of Josiah, who succeeded his father as king of
Judah but has gone from this place: "He will never return. 12He will die in the place where they
have led him captive; he will not see this land
again."

13"Woe to him who builds his palace by
unrighteousness,
his upper rooms by injustice,
making his countrymen work for nothing,
not paying them for their labor.
14He says, 'I will build myself a great palace
with spacious upper rooms.'
So he makes large windows in it,
panels it with cedar
and decorates it in red.

15"Does it make you a king
to have more and more cedar?
Did not your father have food and drink?
He did what was right and just,
so all went well with him.
16He defended the cause of the poor and
needy,
and so all went well.
Is that not what it means to know me?"
declares the LORD.
17"But your eyes and your heart
are set only on dishonest gain,
on shedding innocent blood
and on oppression and extortion."

18Therefore this is what the LORD says about Jehoiakim son of Josiah king of Judah:

"They will not mourn for him:
'Alas, my brother! Alas, my sister!'
They will not mourn for him:
'Alas, my master! Alas, his splendor!'
19He will have the burial of a donkey—
dragged away and thrown
outside the gates of Jerusalem."

20"Go up to Lebanon and cry out,
let your voice be heard in Bashan,
cry out from Abarim,
for all your allies are crushed.
21I warned you when you felt secure,
but you said, 'I will not listen!'
This has been your way from your youth;
you have not obeyed me.
22The wind will drive all your shepherds away,
and your allies will go into exile.
Then you will be ashamed and disgraced
because of all your wickedness.
23You who live in 'Lebanon,[b]'
who are nestled in cedar buildings,
how you will groan when pangs come upon
you,
pain like that of a woman in labor!

24"As surely as I live," declares the LORD,
"even if you, Jehoiachin[c] son of Jehoiakim king
of Judah, were a signet ring on my right hand, I
would still pull you off. 25I will hand you over to
those who seek your life, those you fear—to Nebuchadnezzar king of Babylon and to the Babylonians.[d] 26I will hurl you and the mother who gave
you birth into another country, where neither of
you was born, and there you both will die. 27You
will never come back to the land you long to
return to."

28Is this man Jehoiachin a despised, broken
pot,
an object no one wants?
Why will he and his children be hurled out,
cast into a land they do not know?
29O land, land, land,
hear the word of the LORD!
30This is what the LORD says:
"Record this man as if childless,
a man who will not prosper in his lifetime,
for none of his offspring will prosper,
none will sit on the throne of David
or rule anymore in Judah."

The Righteous Branch

23 "Woe to the shepherds who are destroying and scattering the sheep of my pasture!" declares the LORD. 2Therefore this is what
the LORD, the God of Israel, says to the shepherds
who tend my people: "Because you have scattered my flock and driven them away and have
not bestowed care on them, I will bestow punishment on you for the evil you have done," declares
the LORD. 3"I myself will gather the remnant of
my flock out of all the countries where I have
driven them and will bring them back to their
pasture, where they will be fruitful and increase
in number. 4I will place shepherds over them
who will tend them, and they will no longer be
afraid or terrified, nor will any be missing," declares the LORD.

5"The days are coming," declares the LORD,

[a] *11* Also called *Jehoahaz* also in verse 28 [b] *23* That is, the palace in Jerusalem (see 1 Kings 7:2) [c] *24* Hebrew *Coniah,* a variant of *Jehoiachin;* [d] *25* Or *Chaldeans*

"when I will raise up to David[a] a
righteous Branch,
a King who will reign wisely
and do what is just and right in the land.
6In his days Judah will be saved
and Israel will live in safety.
This is the name by which he will be called:
The LORD Our Righteousness.

7"So then, the days are coming," declares the
LORD, "when people will no longer say, 'As surely
as the LORD lives, who brought the Israelites up
out of Egypt,' 8but they will say, 'As surely as the
LORD lives, who brought the descendants of Israel
up out of the land of the north and out of all the
countries where he had banished them.' Then
they will live in their own land."

Lying Prophets

9Concerning the prophets:
My heart is broken within me;
all my bones tremble.
I am like a drunken man,
like a man overcome by wine,
because of the LORD
and his holy words.
10The land is full of adulterers;
because of the curse[b] the land lies
parched[c]
and the pastures in the desert are
withered.
The ⌞prophets⌟ follow an evil course
and use their power unjustly.
11"Both prophet and priest are godless;
even in my temple I find their
wickedness,"
declares the LORD.
12"Therefore their path will become slippery;
they will be banished to darkness
and there they will fall.
I will bring disaster on them
in the year they are punished,"
declares the LORD.
13"Among the prophets of Samaria
I saw this repulsive thing:
They prophesied by Baal
and led my people Israel astray.
14And among the prophets of Jerusalem
I have seen something horrible:
They commit adultery and live a lie.
They strengthen the hands of evildoers,
so that no one turns from his wickedness.
They are all like Sodom to me;
the people of Jerusalem are like
Gomorrah."

15Therefore, this is what the LORD Almighty
says concerning the prophets:

"I will make them eat bitter food
and drink poisoned water,
because from the prophets of Jerusalem
ungodliness has spread throughout the
land."

16This is what the LORD Almighty says:
"Do not listen to what the prophets are
prophesying to you;
they fill you with false hopes.
They speak visions from their own minds,
not from the mouth of the LORD.
17They keep saying to those who despise me,
'The LORD says: You will have peace.'
And to all who follow the stubbornness of
their hearts
they say, 'No harm will come to you.'
18But which of them has stood in the council
of the LORD
to see or to hear his word?
Who has listened and heard his word?
19See, the storm of the LORD
will burst out in wrath,
a whirlwind swirling down
on the heads of the wicked.
20The anger of the LORD will not turn back
until he fully accomplishes
the purposes of his heart.
In days to come
you will understand it clearly.
21I did not send these prophets,
yet they have run with their message;
I did not speak to them,
yet they have prophesied.
22But if they had stood in my council,
they would have proclaimed my words to
my people
and would have turned them from their evil
ways
and from their evil deeds.

23"Am I only a God nearby,"
declares the LORD,
"and not a God far away?
24Can anyone hide in secret places
so that I cannot see him?"
declares the LORD.
"Do not I fill heaven and earth?"
declares the LORD.

25"I have heard what the prophets say who
prophesy lies in my name. They say, 'I had a
dream! I had a dream!' 26How long will this continue in the hearts of these lying prophets, who
prophesy the delusions of their own minds?

[a] 5 Or *up from David's line* [b] 10 Or *because of these things* [c] 10 Or *land mourns*

27 They think the dreams they tell one another
will make my people forget my name, just as their
fathers forgot my name through Baal worship.
28 Let the prophet who has a dream tell his
dream, but let the one who has my word speak it
faithfully. For what has straw to do with grain?"
declares the LORD. 29 "Is not my word like fire,"
declares the LORD, "and like a hammer that
breaks a rock in pieces?
30 "Therefore," declares the LORD, "I am
against the prophets who steal from one another
words supposedly from me. 31 Yes," declares the
LORD, "I am against the prophets who wag their
own tongues and yet declare, 'The LORD declares.' 32 Indeed, I am against those who prophesy false dreams," declares the LORD. "They tell
them and lead my people astray with their reckless lies, yet I did not send or appoint them. They
do not benefit these people in the least," declares
the LORD.

False Oracles and False Prophets

33 "When these people, or a prophet or a
priest, ask you, 'What is the oracle[a] of the
LORD?' say to them, 'What oracle?[b] I will forsake
you, declares the LORD.' 34 If a prophet or a priest
or anyone else claims, 'This is the oracle of the
LORD,' I will punish that man and his household.
35 This is what each of you keeps on saying to his
friend or relative: 'What is the LORD's answer?' or
'What has the LORD spoken?' 36 But you must not
mention 'the oracle of the LORD' again, because
every man's own word becomes his oracle and so
you distort the words of the living God, the LORD
Almighty, our God. 37 This is what you keep saying to a prophet: 'What is the LORD's answer to
you?' or 'What has the LORD spoken?' 38 Although
you claim, 'This is the oracle of the LORD,' this is
what the LORD says: You used the words, 'This is
the oracle of the LORD,' even though I told you
that you must not claim, 'This is the oracle of the
LORD.' 39 Therefore, I will surely forget you and
cast you out of my presence along with the city I
gave to you and your fathers. 40 I will bring upon
you everlasting disgrace—everlasting shame that
will not be forgotten."

Two Baskets of Figs

24 After Jehoiachin[c] son of Jehoiakim king
of Judah and the officials, the craftsmen
and the artisans of Judah were carried into exile
from Jerusalem to Babylon by Nebuchadnezzar
king of Babylon, the LORD showed me two baskets of figs placed in front of the temple of the
LORD. 2 One basket had very good figs, like those
that ripen early; the other basket had very poor
figs, so bad they could not be eaten.
3 Then the LORD asked me, "What do you see,
Jeremiah?"
"Figs," I answered. "The good ones are very
good, but the poor ones are so bad they cannot be
eaten."
4 Then the word of the LORD came to me:
5 "This is what the LORD, the God of Israel, says:
'Like these good figs, I regard as good the exiles
from Judah, whom I sent away from this place
to the land of the Babylonians.[d] 6 My eyes will
watch over them for their good, and I will bring
them back to this land. I will build them up and
not tear them down; I will plant them and not
uproot them. 7 I will give them a heart to know
me, that I am the LORD. They will be my people,
and I will be their God, for they will return to me
with all their heart.
8 " 'But like the poor figs, which are so bad they
cannot be eaten,' says the LORD, 'so will I deal
with Zedekiah king of Judah, his officials and the
survivors from Jerusalem, whether they remain
in this land or live in Egypt. 9 I will make them
abhorrent and an offense to all the kingdoms of
the earth, a reproach and a byword, an object of
ridicule and cursing, wherever I banish them. 10 I
will send the sword, famine and plague against
them until they are destroyed from the land I
gave to them and their fathers.' "

Seventy Years of Captivity

25 The word came to Jeremiah concerning
all the people of Judah in the fourth year
of Jehoiakim son of Josiah king of Judah, which
was the first year of Nebuchadnezzar king of Babylon. 2 So Jeremiah the prophet said to all the
people of Judah and to all those living in Jerusalem: 3 For twenty-three years—from the thirteenth year of Josiah son of Amon king of Judah
until this very day—the word of the LORD has
come to me and I have spoken to you again and
again, but you have not listened.
4 And though the LORD has sent all his servants
the prophets to you again and again, you have not
listened or paid any attention. 5 They said, "Turn
now, each of you, from your evil ways and your
evil practices, and you can stay in the land the
LORD gave to you and your fathers for ever and
ever. 6 Do not follow other gods to serve and worship them; do not provoke me to anger with what
your hands have made. Then I will not harm
you."
7 "But you did not listen to me," declares the
LORD, "and you have provoked me with what

[a] *33* Or *burden* (see Septuagint and Vulgate) [b] *33* Hebrew; Septuagint and Vulgate *'You are the burden.* (The Hebrew for *oracle* and *burden* is the same.) [c] *1* Hebrew *Jeconiah,* a variant of *Jehoiachin* [d] *5* Or *Chaldeans*

your hands have made, and you have brought
harm to yourselves."
8Therefore the LORD Almighty says this: "Because you have not listened to my words, 9I will
summon all the peoples of the north and my servant Nebuchadnezzar king of Babylon," declares
the LORD, "and I will bring them against this land
and its inhabitants and against all the surrounding nations. I will completely destroy[a] them and
make them an object of horror and scorn, and an
everlasting ruin. 10I will banish from them the
sounds of joy and gladness, the voices of bride
and bridegroom, the sound of millstones and the
light of the lamp. 11This whole country will become a desolate wasteland, and these nations will
serve the king of Babylon seventy years.
12"But when the seventy years are fulfilled, I
will punish the king of Babylon and his nation,
the land of the Babylonians,[b] for their guilt,"
declares the LORD, "and will make it desolate
forever. 13I will bring upon that land all the
things I have spoken against it, all that are written in this book and prophesied by Jeremiah
against all the nations. 14They themselves will be
enslaved by many nations and great kings; I will
repay them according to their deeds and the
work of their hands."

The Cup of God's Wrath

15This is what the LORD, the God of Israel, said
to me: "Take from my hand this cup filled with
the wine of my wrath and make all the nations to
whom I send you drink it. 16When they drink
it, they will stagger and go mad because of the
sword I will send among them."
17So I took the cup from the LORD's hand and
made all the nations to whom he sent me drink
it: 18Jerusalem and the towns of Judah, its kings
and officials, to make them a ruin and an object
of horror and scorn and cursing, as they are today; 19Pharaoh king of Egypt, his attendants, his
officials and all his people, 20and all the foreign
people there; all the kings of Uz; all the kings of
the Philistines (those of Ashkelon, Gaza, Ekron,
and the people left at Ashdod); 21Edom, Moab
and Ammon; 22all the kings of Tyre and Sidon;
the kings of the coastlands across the sea; 23De-
dan, Tema, Buz and all who are in distant
places[c]; 24all the kings of Arabia and all the
kings of the foreign people who live in the desert;
25all the kings of Zimri, Elam and Media; 26and all
the kings of the north, near and far, one after the
other—all the kingdoms on the face of the earth.
And after all of them, the king of Sheshach[d] will
drink it too.

27"Then tell them, 'This is what the LORD Almighty, the God of Israel, says: Drink, get drunk
and vomit, and fall to rise no more because of the
sword I will send among you.' 28But if they refuse
to take the cup from your hand and drink, tell
them, 'This is what the LORD Almighty says: You
must drink it! 29See, I am beginning to bring disaster on the city that bears my Name, and will
you indeed go unpunished? You will not go unpunished, for I am calling down a sword upon
all who live on the earth, declares the LORD Almighty.'
30"Now prophesy all these words against them
and say to them:

" 'The LORD will roar from on high;
he will thunder from his holy dwelling
and roar mightily against his land.
He will shout like those who tread the
grapes,
shout against all who live on the earth.
31The tumult will resound to the ends of the
earth,
for the LORD will bring charges against the
nations;
he will bring judgment on all mankind
and put the wicked to the sword,' "
declares the LORD.

32This is what the LORD Almighty says:

"Look! Disaster is spreading
from nation to nation;
a mighty storm is rising
from the ends of the earth."

33At that time those slain by the LORD will be
everywhere—from one end of the earth to the
other. They will not be mourned or gathered up
or buried, but will be like refuse lying on the
ground.

34Weep and wail, you shepherds;
roll in the dust, you leaders of the flock.
For your time to be slaughtered has come;
you will fall and be shattered like fine
pottery.
35The shepherds will have nowhere to flee,
the leaders of the flock no place to escape.
36Hear the cry of the shepherds,
the wailing of the leaders of the flock,
for the LORD is destroying their pasture.
37The peaceful meadows will be laid waste
because of the fierce anger of the LORD.
38Like a lion he will leave his lair,
and their land will become desolate
because of the sword[e] of the oppressor
and because of the LORD's fierce anger.

[a] 9 The Hebrew term refers to the irrevocable giving over of things or persons to the LORD, often by totally destroying them.
[b] 12 Or *Chaldeans* [c] 23 Or *who clip the hair by their foreheads* [d] 26 *Sheshach* is a cryptogram for Babylon. [e] 38 Some Hebrew manuscripts and Septuagint (see also Jer. 46:16 and 50:16); most Hebrew manuscripts *anger*

Jeremiah Threatened With Death

26 Early in the reign of Jehoiakim son of Josiah king of Judah, this word came from the
LORD: 2"This is what the LORD says: Stand in the
courtyard of the LORD's house and speak to all
the people of the towns of Judah who come to
worship in the house of the LORD. Tell them everything I command you; do not omit a word.
3Perhaps they will listen and each will turn from
his evil way. Then I will relent and not bring on
them the disaster I was planning because of the
evil they have done. 4Say to them, 'This is what
the LORD says: If you do not listen to me and
follow my law, which I have set before you, 5and
if you do not listen to the words of my servants
the prophets, whom I have sent to you again and
again (though you have not listened), 6then I will
make this house like Shiloh and this city an object of cursing among all the nations of the
earth.' "
7The priests, the prophets and all the people
heard Jeremiah speak these words in the house of
the LORD. 8But as soon as Jeremiah finished telling all the people everything the LORD had commanded him to say, the priests, the prophets and
all the people seized him and said, "You must
die! 9Why do you prophesy in the LORD's name
that this house will be like Shiloh and this city
will be desolate and deserted?" And all the people crowded around Jeremiah in the house of the
LORD.
10When the officials of Judah heard about
these things, they went up from the royal palace
to the house of the LORD and took their places
at the entrance of the New Gate of the LORD's
house. 11Then the priests and the prophets said
to the officials and all the people, "This man
should be sentenced to death because he has
prophesied against this city. You have heard it
with your own ears!"
12Then Jeremiah said to all the officials and
all the people: "The LORD sent me to prophesy
against this house and this city all the things you
have heard. 13Now reform your ways and your
actions and obey the LORD your God. Then the
LORD will relent and not bring the disaster he has
pronounced against you. 14As for me, I am in
your hands; do with me whatever you think is
good and right. 15Be assured, however, that if you
put me to death, you will bring the guilt of innocent blood on yourselves and on this city and on
those who live in it, for in truth the LORD has sent
me to you to speak all these words in your hearing."
16Then the officials and all the people said to
the priests and the prophets, "This man should
not be sentenced to death! He has spoken to us
in the name of the LORD our God."
17Some of the elders of the land stepped forward and said to the entire assembly of people,
18"Micah of Moresheth prophesied in the days of
Hezekiah king of Judah. He told all the people of
Judah, 'This is what the LORD Almighty says:

" 'Zion will be plowed like a field,
Jerusalem will become a heap of rubble,
the temple hill a mound overgrown with
thickets.'[a]

19"Did Hezekiah king of Judah or anyone else in
Judah put him to death? Did not Hezekiah fear
the LORD and seek his favor? And did not the
LORD relent, so that he did not bring the disaster
he pronounced against them? We are about to
bring a terrible disaster on ourselves!"
20(Now Uriah son of Shemaiah from Kiriath
Jearim was another man who prophesied in the
name of the LORD; he prophesied the same things
against this city and this land as Jeremiah did.
21When King Jehoiakim and all his officers and
officials heard his words, the king sought to put
him to death. But Uriah heard of it and fled in
fear to Egypt. 22King Jehoiakim, however, sent
Elnathan son of Acbor to Egypt, along with some
other men. 23They brought Uriah out of Egypt
and took him to King Jehoiakim, who had him
struck down with a sword and his body thrown
into the burial place of the common people.)
24Furthermore, Ahikam son of Shaphan supported Jeremiah, and so he was not handed over
to the people to be put to death.

Judah to Serve Nebuchadnezzar

27 Early in the reign of Zedekiah[b] son of
Josiah king of Judah, this word came to
Jeremiah from the LORD: 2This is what the LORD
said to me: "Make a yoke out of straps and crossbars and put it on your neck. 3Then send word to
the kings of Edom, Moab, Ammon, Tyre and Sidon through the envoys who have come to Jerusalem to Zedekiah king of Judah. 4Give them a
message for their masters and say, 'This is what
the LORD Almighty, the God of Israel, says: "Tell
this to your masters: 5With my great power and
outstretched arm I made the earth and its people
and the animals that are on it, and I give it to
anyone I please. 6Now I will hand all your countries over to my servant Nebuchadnezzar king of
Babylon; I will make even the wild animals subject to him. 7All nations will serve him and his
son and his grandson until the time for his land
comes; then many nations and great kings will
subjugate him.

[a] *18* Micah 3:12 [b] *1* A few Hebrew manuscripts and Syriac (see also Jer. 27:3, 12 and 28:1); most Hebrew manuscripts *Jehoiakim*
(Most Septuagint manuscripts do not have this verse.)

8“ ‘ “If, however, any nation or kingdom will
not serve Nebuchadnezzar king of Babylon or
bow its neck under his yoke, I will punish that
nation with the sword, famine and plague, declares the LORD, until I destroy it by his hand. 9So
do not listen to your prophets, your diviners,
your interpreters of dreams, your mediums or
your sorcerers who tell you, ‘You will not serve
the king of Babylon.’ 10They prophesy lies to you
that will only serve to remove you far from your
lands; I will banish you and you will perish. 11But
if any nation will bow its neck under the yoke of
the king of Babylon and serve him, I will let that
nation remain in its own land to till it and to live
there, declares the LORD.” ’ ”

12I gave the same message to Zedekiah king of
Judah. I said, “Bow your neck under the yoke of
the king of Babylon; serve him and his people,
and you will live. 13Why will you and your people
die by the sword, famine and plague with which
the LORD has threatened any nation that will not
serve the king of Babylon? 14Do not listen to the
words of the prophets who say to you, ‘You will
not serve the king of Babylon,’ for they are prophesying lies to you. 15‘I have not sent them,’ declares the LORD. ‘They are prophesying lies in my
name. Therefore, I will banish you and you will
perish, both you and the prophets who prophesy
to you.’ ”

16Then I said to the priests and all these people, “This is what the LORD says: Do not listen to
the prophets who say, ‘Very soon now the articles from the LORD’s house will be brought back
from Babylon.’ They are prophesying lies to you.
17Do not listen to them. Serve the king of Babylon, and you will live. Why should this city become a ruin? 18If they are prophets and have the
word of the LORD, let them plead with the LORD
Almighty that the furnishings remaining in the
house of the LORD and in the palace of the king
of Judah and in Jerusalem not be taken to Babylon. 19For this is what the LORD Almighty says
about the pillars, the Sea, the movable stands and
the other furnishings that are left in this city,
20which Nebuchadnezzar king of Babylon did not
take away when he carried Jehoiachin[a] son of
Jehoiakim king of Judah into exile from Jerusalem
to Babylon, along with all the nobles of Judah and
Jerusalem— 21yes, this is what the LORD Almighty, the God of Israel, says about the things
that are left in the house of the LORD and in the
palace of the king of Judah and in Jerusalem:
22‘They will be taken to Babylon and there they
will remain until the day I come for them,’ declares the LORD. ‘Then I will bring them back and
restore them to this place.’ ”

The False Prophet Hananiah

28 In the fifth month of that same year, the
fourth year, early in the reign of Zedekiah
king of Judah, the prophet Hananiah son of Azzur, who was from Gibeon, said to me in the
house of the LORD in the presence of the priests
and all the people: 2“This is what the LORD Almighty, the God of Israel, says: ‘I will break the
yoke of the king of Babylon. 3Within two years I
will bring back to this place all the articles of the
LORD’s house that Nebuchadnezzar king of Babylon removed from here and took to Babylon. 4I
will also bring back to this place Jehoiachin[a] son
of Jehoiakim king of Judah and all the other exiles
from Judah who went to Babylon,’ declares the
LORD, ‘for I will break the yoke of the king of
Babylon.’ ”

5Then the prophet Jeremiah replied to the
prophet Hananiah before the priests and all the
people who were standing in the house of the
LORD. 6He said, “Amen! May the LORD do so!
May the LORD fulfill the words you have prophesied by bringing the articles of the LORD’s house
and all the exiles back to this place from Babylon.
7Nevertheless, listen to what I have to say in your
hearing and in the hearing of all the people:
8From early times the prophets who preceded
you and me have prophesied war, disaster and
plague against many countries and great kingdoms. 9But the prophet who prophesies peace
will be recognized as one truly sent by the LORD
only if his prediction comes true.”

10Then the prophet Hananiah took the yoke off
the neck of the prophet Jeremiah and broke it,
11and he said before all the people, “This is what
the LORD says: ‘In the same way will I break the
yoke of Nebuchadnezzar king of Babylon off the
neck of all the nations within two years.’ ” At
this, the prophet Jeremiah went on his way.

12Shortly after the prophet Hananiah had broken the yoke off the neck of the prophet Jeremiah, the word of the LORD came to Jeremiah:
13“Go and tell Hananiah, ‘This is what the LORD
says: You have broken a wooden yoke, but in its
place you will get a yoke of iron. 14This is what
the LORD Almighty, the God of Israel, says: I will
put an iron yoke on the necks of all these nations
to make them serve Nebuchadnezzar king of Babylon, and they will serve him. I will even give
him control over the wild animals.’ ”

15Then the prophet Jeremiah said to Hananiah
the prophet, “Listen, Hananiah! The LORD has
not sent you, yet you have persuaded this nation
to trust in lies. 16Therefore, this is what the LORD
says: ‘I am about to remove you from the face of
the earth. This very year you are going to die,

[a]20,4 Hebrew *Jeconiah,* a variant of *Jehoiachin*

because you have preached rebellion against the
LORD.'"
17In the seventh month of that same year,
Hananiah the prophet died.

A Letter to the Exiles

29 This is the text of the letter that the
prophet Jeremiah sent from Jerusalem to
the surviving elders among the exiles and to the
priests, the prophets and all the other people
Nebuchadnezzar had carried into exile from Jerusalem to Babylon. 2(This was after King Jehoiachin[a] and the queen mother, the court officials
and the leaders of Judah and Jerusalem, the
craftsmen and the artisans had gone into exile
from Jerusalem.) 3He entrusted the letter to Elasah son of Shaphan and to Gemariah son of Hilkiah, whom Zedekiah king of Judah sent to King
Nebuchadnezzar in Babylon. It said:

4This is what the LORD Almighty, the
God of Israel, says to all those I carried into
exile from Jerusalem to Babylon: 5"Build
houses and settle down; plant gardens and
eat what they produce. 6Marry and have
sons and daughters; find wives for your sons
and give your daughters in marriage, so that
they too may have sons and daughters. Increase in number there; do not decrease.
7Also, seek the peace and prosperity of the
city to which I have carried you into exile.
Pray to the LORD for it, because if it prospers, you too will prosper." 8Yes, this is
what the LORD Almighty, the God of Israel,
says: "Do not let the prophets and diviners
among you deceive you. Do not listen to the
dreams you encourage them to have. 9They
are prophesying lies to you in my name. I
have not sent them," declares the LORD.

10This is what the LORD says: "When seventy years are completed for Babylon, I will
come to you and fulfill my gracious promise
to bring you back to this place. 11For I know
the plans I have for you," declares the LORD,
"plans to prosper you and not to harm you,
plans to give you hope and a future. 12Then
you will call upon me and come and pray to
me, and I will listen to you. 13You will seek
me and find me when you seek me with all
your heart. 14I will be found by you," declares the LORD, "and will bring you back
from captivity.[b] I will gather you from all
the nations and places where I have banished you," declares the LORD, "and will
bring you back to the place from which I
carried you into exile."

15You may say, "The LORD has raised up
prophets for us in Babylon," 16but this is
what the LORD says about the king who sits
on David's throne and all the people who
remain in this city, your countrymen who
did not go with you into exile— 17yes, this
is what the LORD Almighty says: "I will send
the sword, famine and plague against them
and I will make them like poor figs that are
so bad they cannot be eaten. 18I will pursue
them with the sword, famine and plague
and will make them abhorrent to all the
kingdoms of the earth and an object of cursing and horror, of scorn and reproach,
among all the nations where I drive them.
19For they have not listened to my words,"
declares the LORD, "words that I sent to
them again and again by my servants the
prophets. And you exiles have not listened
either," declares the LORD.

20Therefore, hear the word of the LORD,
all you exiles whom I have sent away from
Jerusalem to Babylon. 21This is what the
LORD Almighty, the God of Israel, says about
Ahab son of Kolaiah and Zedekiah son of
Maaseiah, who are prophesying lies to you
in my name: "I will hand them over to Nebuchadnezzar king of Babylon, and he will
put them to death before your very eyes.
22Because of them, all the exiles from Judah
who are in Babylon will use this curse: 'The
LORD treat you like Zedekiah and Ahab,
whom the king of Babylon burned in the
fire.' 23For they have done outrageous
things in Israel; they have committed adultery with their neighbors' wives and in my
name have spoken lies, which I did not tell
them to do. I know it and am a witness to
it," declares the LORD.

Message to Shemaiah

24Tell Shemaiah the Nehelamite, 25"This is
what the LORD Almighty, the God of Israel, says:
You sent letters in your own name to all the people in Jerusalem, to Zephaniah son of Maaseiah
the priest, and to all the other priests. You said to
Zephaniah, 26'The LORD has appointed you priest
in place of Jehoiada to be in charge of the house
of the LORD; you should put any madman who
acts like a prophet into the stocks and neck-irons.
27So why have you not reprimanded Jeremiah
from Anathoth, who poses as a prophet among
you? 28He has sent this message to us in Babylon:
It will be a long time. Therefore build houses and
settle down; plant gardens and eat what they produce.'"

29Zephaniah the priest, however, read the letter to Jeremiah the prophet. 30Then the word of

[a]2 Hebrew *Jeconiah,* a variant of *Jehoiachin* [b]14 Or *will restore your fortunes*

the LORD came to Jeremiah: 31“Send this message
to all the exiles: ‘This is what the LORD says about
Shemaiah the Nehelamite: Because Shemaiah has
prophesied to you, even though I did not send
him, and has led you to believe a lie, 32this is
what the LORD says: I will surely punish Shemaiah the Nehelamite and his descendants. He will
have no one left among this people, nor will he
see the good things I will do for my people, declares the LORD, because he has preached rebellion against me.’ ”

Restoration of Israel

30 This is the word that came to Jeremiah
from the LORD: 2“This is what the LORD,
the God of Israel, says: ‘Write in a book all the
words I have spoken to you. 3The days are coming,’ declares the LORD, ‘when I will bring my
people Israel and Judah back from captivity[a] and
restore them to the land I gave their forefathers
to possess,’ says the LORD.”

4These are the words the LORD spoke concerning Israel and Judah: 5“This is what the LORD
says:

“ ‘Cries of fear are heard—
terror, not peace.
6Ask and see:
Can a man bear children?
Then why do I see every strong man
with his hands on his stomach like a
woman in labor,
every face turned deathly pale?
7How awful that day will be!
None will be like it.
It will be a time of trouble for Jacob,
but he will be saved out of it.

8“ ‘In that day,’ declares the LORD Almighty,
‘I will break the yoke off their necks
and will tear off their bonds;
no longer will foreigners enslave them.
9Instead, they will serve the LORD their God
and David their king,
whom I will raise up for them.

10“ ‘So do not fear, O Jacob my servant;
do not be dismayed, O Israel,’
declares the LORD.
‘I will surely save you out of a distant place,
your descendants from the land of their
exile.
Jacob will again have peace and security,
and no one will make him afraid.
11I am with you and will save you,’
declares the LORD.
‘Though I completely destroy all the nations
among which I scatter you,
I will not completely destroy you.
I will discipline you but only with justice;
I will not let you go entirely unpunished.’

12“This is what the LORD says:

“ ‘Your wound is incurable,
your injury beyond healing.
13There is no one to plead your cause,
no remedy for your sore,
no healing for you.
14All your allies have forgotten you;
they care nothing for you.
I have struck you as an enemy would
and punished you as would the cruel,
because your guilt is so great
and your sins so many.
15Why do you cry out over your wound,
your pain that has no cure?
Because of your great guilt and many sins
I have done these things to you.

16“ ‘But all who devour you will be devoured;
all your enemies will go into exile.
Those who plunder you will be plundered;
all who make spoil of you I will despoil.
17But I will restore you to health
and heal your wounds,’
declares the LORD,
‘because you are called an outcast,
Zion for whom no one cares.’

18“This is what the LORD says:

“ ‘I will restore the fortunes of Jacob’s tents
and have compassion on his dwellings;
the city will be rebuilt on her ruins,
and the palace will stand in its proper
place.
19From them will come songs of thanksgiving
and the sound of rejoicing.
I will add to their numbers,
and they will not be decreased;
I will bring them honor,
and they will not be disdained.
20Their children will be as in days of old,
and their community will be established
before me;
I will punish all who oppress them.
21Their leader will be one of their own;
their ruler will arise from among them.
I will bring him near and he will come close
to me,
for who is he who will devote himself
to be close to me?’
declares the LORD.
22“ ‘So you will be my people,
and I will be your God.’ ”
23See, the storm of the LORD

a3 Or *will restore the fortunes of my people Israel and Judah*

will burst out in wrath,
a driving wind swirling down
on the heads of the wicked.
24The fierce anger of the LORD will not turn back
until he fully accomplishes
the purposes of his heart.
In days to come
you will understand this.

31 "At that time," declares the LORD, "I will be the God of all the clans of Israel, and they will be my people."
2This is what the LORD says:

"The people who survive the sword
will find favor in the desert;
I will come to give rest to Israel."

3The LORD appeared to us in the past,[a] saying:

"I have loved you with an everlasting love;
I have drawn you with loving-kindness.
4I will build you up again
and you will be rebuilt, O Virgin Israel.
Again you will take up your tambourines
and go out to dance with the joyful.
5Again you will plant vineyards
on the hills of Samaria;
the farmers will plant them
and enjoy their fruit.
6There will be a day when watchmen cry out
on the hills of Ephraim,
'Come, let us go up to Zion,
to the LORD our God.'"

7This is what the LORD says:

"Sing with joy for Jacob;
shout for the foremost of the nations.
Make your praises heard, and say,
'O LORD, save your people,
the remnant of Israel.'
8See, I will bring them from the land of the north
and gather them from the ends of the earth.
Among them will be the blind and the lame,
expectant mothers and women in labor;
a great throng will return.
9They will come with weeping;
they will pray as I bring them back.
I will lead them beside streams of water
on a level path where they will not stumble,
because I am Israel's father,
and Ephraim is my firstborn son.
10"Hear the word of the LORD, O nations;
proclaim it in distant coastlands:
'He who scattered Israel will gather them
and will watch over his flock like a shepherd.'
11For the LORD will ransom Jacob
and redeem them from the hand of those stronger than they.
12They will come and shout for joy on the heights of Zion;
they will rejoice in the bounty of the LORD—
the grain, the new wine and the oil,
the young of the flocks and herds.
They will be like a well-watered garden,
and they will sorrow no more.
13Then maidens will dance and be glad,
young men and old as well.
I will turn their mourning into gladness;
I will give them comfort and joy instead of sorrow.
14I will satisfy the priests with abundance,
and my people will be filled with my bounty,"
declares the LORD.

15This is what the LORD says:

"A voice is heard in Ramah,
mourning and great weeping,
Rachel weeping for her children
and refusing to be comforted,
because her children are no more."

16This is what the LORD says:

"Restrain your voice from weeping
and your eyes from tears,
for your work will be rewarded,"
declares the LORD.
"They will return from the land of the enemy.
17So there is hope for your future,"
declares the LORD.
"Your children will return to their own land.

18"I have surely heard Ephraim's moaning:
'You disciplined me like an unruly calf,
and I have been disciplined.
Restore me, and I will return,
because you are the LORD my God.
19After I strayed,
I repented;
after I came to understand,
I beat my breast.
I was ashamed and humiliated
because I bore the disgrace of my youth.'
20Is not Ephraim my dear son,
the child in whom I delight?

a3 Or *LORD has appeared to us from afar*

Though I often speak against him,
I still remember him.
Therefore my heart yearns for him;
I have great compassion for him,"
declares the LORD.
21"Set up road signs;
put up guideposts.
Take note of the highway,
the road that you take.
Return, O Virgin Israel,
return to your towns.
22How long will you wander,
O unfaithful daughter?
The LORD will create a new thing on earth—
a woman will surround[a] a man."

23This is what the LORD Almighty, the God of
Israel, says: "When I bring them back from captivity,[b] the people in the land of Judah and in
its towns will once again use these words: 'The
LORD bless you, O righteous dwelling, O sacred
mountain.' 24People will live together in Judah
and all its towns—farmers and those who move
about with their flocks. 25I will refresh the weary
and satisfy the faint."

26At this I awoke and looked around. My sleep
had been pleasant to me.

27"The days are coming," declares the LORD,
"when I will plant the house of Israel and the
house of Judah with the offspring of men and of
animals. 28Just as I watched over them to uproot
and tear down, and to overthrow, destroy and
bring disaster, so I will watch over them to build
and to plant," declares the LORD. 29"In those days
people will no longer say,

'The fathers have eaten sour grapes,
and the children's teeth are set on edge.'

30Instead, everyone will die for his own sin; whoever eats sour grapes—his own teeth will be set
on edge.

31"The time is coming," declares the LORD,
"when I will make a new covenant
with the house of Israel
and with the house of Judah.
32It will not be like the covenant
I made with their forefathers
when I took them by the hand
to lead them out of Egypt,
because they broke my covenant,
though I was a husband to[c] them,[d]"
declares the LORD.
33"This is the covenant I will make with the
house of Israel
after that time," declares the LORD.
"I will put my law in their minds
and write it on their hearts.
I will be their God,
and they will be my people.
34No longer will a man teach his neighbor,
or a man his brother, saying, 'Know the
LORD,'
because they will all know me,
from the least of them to the greatest,"
declares the LORD.
"For I will forgive their wickedness
and will remember their sins no more."

35This is what the LORD says,

he who appoints the sun
to shine by day,
who decrees the moon and stars
to shine by night,
who stirs up the sea
so that its waves roar—
the LORD Almighty is his name:
36"Only if these decrees vanish from my sight,"
declares the LORD,
"will the descendants of Israel ever cease
to be a nation before me."

37This is what the LORD says:

"Only if the heavens above can be measured
and the foundations of the earth below be
searched out
will I reject all the descendants of Israel
because of all they have done,"
declares the LORD.

38"The days are coming," declares the LORD,
"when this city will be rebuilt for me from the
Tower of Hananel to the Corner Gate. 39The measuring line will stretch from there straight to the
hill of Gareb and then turn to Goah. 40The whole
valley where dead bodies and ashes are thrown,
and all the terraces out to the Kidron Valley on
the east as far as the corner of the Horse Gate,
will be holy to the LORD. The city will never again
be uprooted or demolished."

Jeremiah Buys a Field

32 This is the word that came to Jeremiah
from the LORD in the tenth year of Zedekiah king of Judah, which was the eighteenth year
of Nebuchadnezzar. 2The army of the king of Babylon was then besieging Jerusalem, and Jeremiah
the prophet was confined in the courtyard of the
guard in the royal palace of Judah.

3Now Zedekiah king of Judah had imprisoned
him there, saying, "Why do you prophesy as you
do? You say, 'This is what the LORD says: I am
about to hand this city over to the king of Babylon, and he will capture it. 4Zedekiah king of

[a]22 Or *will go about ⌞seeking⌟*; or *will protect* [b]23 Or *I restore their fortunes* [c]32 Hebrew; Septuagint and Syriac / *and I turned away from* [d]32 Or *was their master*

Judah will not escape out of the hands of the
Babylonians[a] but will certainly be handed over
to the king of Babylon, and will speak with him
face to face and see him with his own eyes. 5He
will take Zedekiah to Babylon, where he will remain until I deal with him, declares the LORD. If
you fight against the Babylonians, you will not
succeed.' "

6Jeremiah said, "The word of the LORD came to
me: 7Hanamel son of Shallum your uncle is going
to come to you and say, 'Buy my field at Anathoth, because as nearest relative it is your right
and duty to buy it.'

8"Then, just as the LORD had said, my cousin
Hanamel came to me in the courtyard of the
guard and said, 'Buy my field at Anathoth in the
territory of Benjamin. Since it is your right to
redeem it and possess it, buy it for yourself.'

"I knew that this was the word of the LORD;
9so I bought the field at Anathoth from my cousin
Hanamel and weighed out for him seventeen
shekels[b] of silver. 10I signed and sealed the
deed, had it witnessed, and weighed out the silver on the scales. 11I took the deed of purchase—
the sealed copy containing the terms and conditions, as well as the unsealed copy— 12and I gave
this deed to Baruch son of Neriah, the son of
Mahseiah, in the presence of my cousin Hanamel
and of the witnesses who had signed the deed
and of all the Jews sitting in the courtyard of the
guard.

13"In their presence I gave Baruch these instructions: 14'This is what the LORD Almighty,
the God of Israel, says: Take these documents,
both the sealed and unsealed copies of the deed
of purchase, and put them in a clay jar so they
will last a long time. 15For this is what the LORD
Almighty, the God of Israel, says: Houses, fields
and vineyards will again be bought in this land.'

16"After I had given the deed of purchase to
Baruch son of Neriah, I prayed to the LORD:

17"Ah, Sovereign LORD, you have made the
heavens and the earth by your great power
and outstretched arm. Nothing is too hard
for you. 18You show love to thousands but
bring the punishment for the fathers' sins
into the laps of their children after them.
O great and powerful God, whose name is
the LORD Almighty, 19great are your purposes and mighty are your deeds. Your eyes
are open to all the ways of men; you reward
everyone according to his conduct and as
his deeds deserve. 20You performed miraculous signs and wonders in Egypt and have
continued them to this day, both in Israel
and among all mankind, and have gained
the renown that is still yours. 21You brought
your people Israel out of Egypt with signs
and wonders, by a mighty hand and an outstretched arm and with great terror. 22You
gave them this land you had sworn to give
their forefathers, a land flowing with milk
and honey. 23They came in and took possession of it, but they did not obey you or follow your law; they did not do what you
commanded them to do. So you brought all
this disaster upon them.

24"See how the siege ramps are built up
to take the city. Because of the sword, famine and plague, the city will be handed over
to the Babylonians who are attacking it.
What you said has happened, as you now
see. 25And though the city will be handed
over to the Babylonians, you, O Sovereign
LORD, say to me, 'Buy the field with silver
and have the transaction witnessed.' "

26Then the word of the LORD came to Jeremiah: 27"I am the LORD, the God of all mankind. Is
anything too hard for me? 28Therefore, this is
what the LORD says: I am about to hand this city
over to the Babylonians and to Nebuchadnezzar
king of Babylon, who will capture it. 29The Babylonians who are attacking this city will come in
and set it on fire; they will burn it down, along
with the houses where the people provoked me
to anger by burning incense on the roofs to Baal
and by pouring out drink offerings to other gods.

30"The people of Israel and Judah have done
nothing but evil in my sight from their youth;
indeed, the people of Israel have done nothing
but provoke me with what their hands have
made, declares the LORD. 31From the day it was
built until now, this city has so aroused my anger
and wrath that I must remove it from my sight.
32The people of Israel and Judah have provoked
me by all the evil they have done—they, their
kings and officials, their priests and prophets, the
men of Judah and the people of Jerusalem. 33They
turned their backs to me and not their faces;
though I taught them again and again, they would
not listen or respond to discipline. 34They set up
their abominable idols in the house that bears my
Name and defiled it. 35They built high places for
Baal in the Valley of Ben Hinnom to sacrifice
their sons and daughters[c] to Molech, though I
never commanded, nor did it enter my mind, that
they should do such a detestable thing and so
make Judah sin.

36"You are saying about this city, 'By the
sword, famine and plague it will be handed over
to the king of Babylon'; but this is what the LORD,
the God of Israel, says: 37I will surely gather them

a4 Or *Chaldeans*; also in verses 5, 24, 25, 28, 29 and 43
b9 That is, about 7 ounces (about 200 grams)
c35 Or *to make their sons and daughters pass through ⌊the fire⌋*

from all the lands where I banish them in my
furious anger and great wrath; I will bring them
back to this place and let them live in safety.
38They will be my people, and I will be their God.
39I will give them singleness of heart and action,
so that they will always fear me for their own
good and the good of their children after them.
40I will make an everlasting covenant with them:
I will never stop doing good to them, and I will
inspire them to fear me, so that they will never
turn away from me. 41I will rejoice in doing them
good and will assuredly plant them in this land
with all my heart and soul.

42"This is what the LORD says: As I have
brought all this great calamity on this people, so
I will give them all the prosperity I have promised
them. 43Once more fields will be bought in this
land of which you say, 'It is a desolate waste,
without men or animals, for it has been handed
over to the Babylonians.' 44Fields will be bought
for silver, and deeds will be signed, sealed and
witnessed in the territory of Benjamin, in the
villages around Jerusalem, in the towns of Judah
and in the towns of the hill country, of the western foothills and of the Negev, because I will
restore their fortunes,[a] declares the LORD."

Promise of Restoration

33 While Jeremiah was still confined in the
courtyard of the guard, the word of the
LORD came to him a second time: 2"This is what
the LORD says, he who made the earth, the LORD
who formed it and established it—the LORD is his
name: 3'Call to me and I will answer you and tell
you great and unsearchable things you do not
know.' 4For this is what the LORD, the God of
Israel, says about the houses in this city and the
royal palaces of Judah that have been torn down
to be used against the siege ramps and the sword
5in the fight with the Babylonians[b]: 'They will
be filled with the dead bodies of the men I will
slay in my anger and wrath. I will hide my face
from this city because of all its wickedness.

6" 'Nevertheless, I will bring health and healing to it; I will heal my people and will let them
enjoy abundant peace and security. 7I will bring
Judah and Israel back from captivity[c] and will
rebuild them as they were before. 8I will cleanse
them from all the sin they have committed
against me and will forgive all their sins of rebellion against me. 9Then this city will bring me
renown, joy, praise and honor before all nations
on earth that hear of all the good things I do for
it; and they will be in awe and will tremble at the
abundant prosperity and peace I provide for it.'

10"This is what the LORD says: 'You say about
this place, "It is a desolate waste, without men
or animals." Yet in the towns of Judah and the
streets of Jerusalem that are deserted, inhabited
by neither men nor animals, there will be heard
once more 11the sounds of joy and gladness, the
voices of bride and bridegroom, and the voices of
those who bring thank offerings to the house of
the LORD, saying,

"Give thanks to the LORD Almighty,
for the LORD is good;
his love endures forever."

For I will restore the fortunes of the land as they
were before,' says the LORD.

12"This is what the LORD Almighty says: 'In
this place, desolate and without men or animals—in all its towns there will again be pastures for shepherds to rest their flocks. 13In the
towns of the hill country, of the western foothills
and of the Negev, in the territory of Benjamin, in
the villages around Jerusalem and in the towns of
Judah, flocks will again pass under the hand of
the one who counts them,' says the LORD.

14" 'The days are coming,' declares the LORD,
'when I will fulfill the gracious promise I made to
the house of Israel and to the house of Judah.

15" 'In those days and at that time
I will make a righteous Branch sprout from
David's line;
he will do what is just and right in the
land.
16In those days Judah will be saved
and Jerusalem will live in safety.
This is the name by which it[d] will be
called:
The LORD Our Righteousness.'

17For this is what the LORD says: 'David will never fail to have a man to sit on the throne of the
house of Israel, 18nor will the priests, who are
Levites, ever fail to have a man to stand before
me continually to offer burnt offerings, to burn
grain offerings and to present sacrifices.' "

19The word of the LORD came to Jeremiah:
20"This is what the LORD says: 'If you can break
my covenant with the day and my covenant with
the night, so that day and night no longer come
at their appointed time, 21then my covenant with
David my servant—and my covenant with the
Levites who are priests ministering before me—
can be broken and David will no longer have a
descendant to reign on his throne. 22I will make
the descendants of David my servant and the Levites who minister before me as countless as the
stars of the sky and as measureless as the sand on
the seashore.' "

[a]44 Or *will bring them back from captivity* [b]5 Or *Chaldeans* [c]7 Or *will restore the fortunes of Judah and Israel*
[d]16 Or *he*

23The word of the LORD came to Jeremiah:
24"Have you not noticed that these people are
saying, 'The LORD has rejected the two kingdoms[a] he chose'? So they despise my people
and no longer regard them as a nation. 25This is
what the LORD says: 'If I have not established my
covenant with day and night and the fixed laws of
heaven and earth, 26then I will reject the descendants of Jacob and David my servant and will not
choose one of his sons to rule over the descendants of Abraham, Isaac and Jacob. For I will restore their fortunes[b] and have compassion on
them.' "

Warning to Zedekiah

34 While Nebuchadnezzar king of Babylon
and all his army and all the kingdoms and
peoples in the empire he ruled were fighting
against Jerusalem and all its surrounding towns,
this word came to Jeremiah from the LORD:
2"This is what the LORD, the God of Israel, says:
Go to Zedekiah king of Judah and tell him, 'This
is what the LORD says: I am about to hand this
city over to the king of Babylon, and he will burn
it down. 3You will not escape from his grasp but
will surely be captured and handed over to him.
You will see the king of Babylon with your own
eyes, and he will speak with you face to face. And
you will go to Babylon.
4" 'Yet hear the promise of the LORD,
O Zedekiah king of Judah. This is what the LORD
says concerning you: You will not die by the
sword; 5you will die peacefully. As people made
a funeral fire in honor of your fathers, the former
kings who preceded you, so they will make a fire
in your honor and lament, "Alas, O master!" I
myself make this promise, declares the LORD.' "
6Then Jeremiah the prophet told all this to
Zedekiah king of Judah, in Jerusalem, 7while the
army of the king of Babylon was fighting against
Jerusalem and the other cities of Judah that were
still holding out—Lachish and Azekah. These
were the only fortified cities left in Judah.

Freedom for Slaves

8The word came to Jeremiah from the LORD
after King Zedekiah had made a covenant with all
the people in Jerusalem to proclaim freedom for
the slaves. 9Everyone was to free his Hebrew
slaves, both male and female; no one was to hold
a fellow Jew in bondage. 10So all the officials and
people who entered into this covenant agreed
that they would free their male and female slaves
and no longer hold them in bondage. They
agreed, and set them free. 11But afterward they
changed their minds and took back the slaves
they had freed and enslaved them again.
12Then the word of the LORD came to Jeremiah: 13"This is what the LORD, the God of Israel,
says: I made a covenant with your forefathers
when I brought them out of Egypt, out of the land
of slavery. I said, 14'Every seventh year each of
you must free any fellow Hebrew who has sold
himself to you. After he has served you six years,
you must let him go free.'[c] Your fathers, however, did not listen to me or pay attention to me.
15Recently you repented and did what is right in
my sight: Each of you proclaimed freedom to his
countrymen. You even made a covenant before
me in the house that bears my Name. 16But now
you have turned around and profaned my name;
each of you has taken back the male and female
slaves you had set free to go where they wished.
You have forced them to become your slaves
again.
17"Therefore, this is what the LORD says: You
have not obeyed me; you have not proclaimed
freedom for your fellow countrymen. So I now
proclaim 'freedom' for you, declares the LORD—
'freedom' to fall by the sword, plague and famine.
I will make you abhorrent to all the kingdoms of
the earth. 18The men who have violated my covenant and have not fulfilled the terms of the covenant they made before me, I will treat like the
calf they cut in two and then walked between its
pieces. 19The leaders of Judah and Jerusalem, the
court officials, the priests and all the people of the
land who walked between the pieces of the calf,
20I will hand over to their enemies who seek
their lives. Their dead bodies will become food
for the birds of the air and the beasts of the earth.
21"I will hand Zedekiah king of Judah and his
officials over to their enemies who seek their
lives, to the army of the king of Babylon, which
has withdrawn from you. 22I am going to give the
order, declares the LORD, and I will bring them
back to this city. They will fight against it, take it
and burn it down. And I will lay waste the towns
of Judah so no one can live there."

The Recabites

35 This is the word that came to Jeremiah
from the LORD during the reign of Jehoiakim son of Josiah king of Judah: 2"Go to the Rec-
abite family and invite them to come to one of the
side rooms of the house of the LORD and give
them wine to drink."
3So I went to get Jaazaniah son of Jeremiah,
the son of Habazziniah, and his brothers and all
his sons—the whole family of the Recabites. 4I
brought them into the house of the LORD, into
the room of the sons of Hanan son of Igdaliah the
man of God. It was next to the room of the officials, which was over that of Maaseiah son of

[a]24 Or *families* [b]26 Or *will bring them back from captivity* [c]14 Deut. 15:12

Shallum the doorkeeper. 5 Then I set bowls full of
wine and some cups before the men of the Recab-
ite family and said to them, "Drink some wine."
6 But they replied, "We do not drink wine, because our forefather Jonadab son of Recab gave us
this command: 'Neither you nor your descendants must ever drink wine. 7 Also you must never build houses, sow seed or plant vineyards; you
must never have any of these things, but must
always live in tents. Then you will live a long
time in the land where you are nomads.' 8 We
have obeyed everything our forefather Jonadab
son of Recab commanded us. Neither we nor our
wives nor our sons and daughters have ever
drunk wine 9 or built houses to live in or had
vineyards, fields or crops. 10 We have lived in
tents and have fully obeyed everything our forefather Jonadab commanded us. 11 But when Nebuchadnezzar king of Babylon invaded this land, we
said, 'Come, we must go to Jerusalem to escape
the Babylonian[a] and Aramean armies.' So we
have remained in Jerusalem."
12 Then the word of the LORD came to Jeremiah, saying: 13 "This is what the LORD Almighty,
the God of Israel, says: Go and tell the men of
Judah and the people of Jerusalem, 'Will you not
learn a lesson and obey my words?' declares the
LORD. 14 'Jonadab son of Recab ordered his sons
not to drink wine and this command has been
kept. To this day they do not drink wine, because
they obey their forefather's command. But I have
spoken to you again and again, yet you have not
obeyed me. 15 Again and again I sent all my servants the prophets to you. They said, "Each of
you must turn from your wicked ways and reform
your actions; do not follow other gods to serve
them. Then you will live in the land I have given
to you and your fathers." But you have not paid
attention or listened to me. 16 The descendants of
Jonadab son of Recab have carried out the command their forefather gave them, but these people have not obeyed me.'
17 "Therefore, this is what the LORD God Almighty, the God of Israel, says: 'Listen! I am going to bring on Judah and on everyone living in
Jerusalem every disaster I pronounced against
them. I spoke to them, but they did not listen; I
called to them, but they did not answer.' "
18 Then Jeremiah said to the family of the Recabites, "This is what the LORD Almighty, the God
of Israel, says: 'You have obeyed the command of
your forefather Jonadab and have followed all his
instructions and have done everything he ordered.' 19 Therefore, this is what the LORD Almighty, the God of Israel, says: 'Jonadab son of
Recab will never fail to have a man to
serve me.' "

Jehoiakim Burns Jeremiah's Scroll

36 In the fourth year of Jehoiakim son of Josiah king of Judah, this word came to Jeremiah from the LORD: 2 "Take a scroll and write on
it all the words I have spoken to you concerning
Israel, Judah and all the other nations from the
time I began speaking to you in the reign of Josiah
till now. 3 Perhaps when the people of Judah hear
about every disaster I plan to inflict on them,
each of them will turn from his wicked way; then
I will forgive their wickedness and their sin."
4 So Jeremiah called Baruch son of Neriah, and
while Jeremiah dictated all the words the LORD
had spoken to him, Baruch wrote them on the
scroll. 5 Then Jeremiah told Baruch, "I am restrict-
ed; I cannot go to the LORD's temple. 6 So you go
to the house of the LORD on a day of fasting and
read to the people from the scroll the words of
the LORD that you wrote as I dictated. Read them
to all the people of Judah who come in from their
towns. 7 Perhaps they will bring their petition before the LORD, and each will turn from his wicked
ways, for the anger and wrath pronounced
against this people by the LORD are great."
8 Baruch son of Neriah did everything Jeremiah
the prophet told him to do; at the LORD's temple
he read the words of the LORD from the scroll. 9 In
the ninth month of the fifth year of Jehoiakim son
of Josiah king of Judah, a time of fasting before
the LORD was proclaimed for all the people in
Jerusalem and those who had come from the
towns of Judah. 10 From the room of Gemariah
son of Shaphan the secretary, which was in the
upper courtyard at the entrance of the New Gate
of the temple, Baruch read to all the people at the
LORD's temple the words of Jeremiah from the
scroll.
11 When Micaiah son of Gemariah, the son of
Shaphan, heard all the words of the LORD from
the scroll, 12 he went down to the secretary's
room in the royal palace, where all the officials
were sitting: Elishama the secretary, Delaiah son
of Shemaiah, Elnathan son of Acbor, Gemariah
son of Shaphan, Zedekiah son of Hananiah, and
all the other officials. 13 After Micaiah told them
everything he had heard Baruch read to the people from the scroll, 14 all the officials sent Jehudi
son of Nethaniah, the son of Shelemiah, the son
of Cushi, to say to Baruch, "Bring the scroll from
which you have read to the people and come." So
Baruch son of Neriah went to them with the
scroll in his hand. 15 They said to him, "Sit down,
please, and read it to us."
So Baruch read it to them. 16 When they heard
all these words, they looked at each other in fear
and said to Baruch, "We must report all these

[a] 11 Or *Chaldean*

words to the king." 17Then they asked Baruch, "Tell us, how did you come to write all this? Did Jeremiah dictate it?"

18"Yes," Baruch replied, "he dictated all these words to me, and I wrote them in ink on the scroll."

19Then the officials said to Baruch, "You and Jeremiah, go and hide. Don't let anyone know where you are."

20After they put the scroll in the room of Elishama the secretary, they went to the king in the courtyard and reported everything to him. 21The king sent Jehudi to get the scroll, and Jehudi brought it from the room of Elishama the secretary and read it to the king and all the officials standing beside him. 22It was the ninth month and the king was sitting in the winter apartment, with a fire burning in the firepot in front of him. 23Whenever Jehudi had read three or four columns of the scroll, the king cut them off with a scribe's knife and threw them into the firepot, until the entire scroll was burned in the fire. 24The king and all his attendants who heard all these words showed no fear, nor did they tear their clothes. 25Even though Elnathan, Delaiah and Gemariah urged the king not to burn the scroll, he would not listen to them. 26Instead, the king commanded Jerahmeel, a son of the king, Seraiah son of Azriel and Shelemiah son of Abdeel to arrest Baruch the scribe and Jeremiah the prophet. But the LORD had hidden them.

27After the king burned the scroll containing the words that Baruch had written at Jeremiah's dictation, the word of the LORD came to Jeremiah: 28"Take another scroll and write on it all the words that were on the first scroll, which Jehoiakim king of Judah burned up. 29Also tell Jehoiakim king of Judah, 'This is what the LORD says: You burned that scroll and said, "Why did you write on it that the king of Babylon would certainly come and destroy this land and cut off both men and animals from it?" 30Therefore, this is what the LORD says about Jehoiakim king of Judah: He will have no one to sit on the throne of David; his body will be thrown out and exposed to the heat by day and the frost by night. 31I will punish him and his children and his attendants for their wickedness; I will bring on them and those living in Jerusalem and the people of Judah every disaster I pronounced against them, because they have not listened.' "

32So Jeremiah took another scroll and gave it to the scribe Baruch son of Neriah, and as Jeremiah dictated, Baruch wrote on it all the words of the scroll that Jehoiakim king of Judah had burned in the fire. And many similar words were added to them.

Jeremiah in Prison

37 Zedekiah son of Josiah was made king of Judah by Nebuchadnezzar king of Babylon; he reigned in place of Jehoiachin[a] son of Jehoiakim. 2Neither he nor his attendants nor the people of the land paid any attention to the words the LORD had spoken through Jeremiah the prophet.

3King Zedekiah, however, sent Jehucal son of Shelemiah with the priest Zephaniah son of Maaseiah to Jeremiah the prophet with this message: "Please pray to the LORD our God for us."

4Now Jeremiah was free to come and go among the people, for he had not yet been put in prison. 5Pharaoh's army had marched out of Egypt, and when the Babylonians[b] who were besieging Jerusalem heard the report about them, they withdrew from Jerusalem.

6Then the word of the LORD came to Jeremiah the prophet: 7"This is what the LORD, the God of Israel, says: Tell the king of Judah, who sent you to inquire of me, 'Pharaoh's army, which has marched out to support you, will go back to its own land, to Egypt. 8Then the Babylonians will return and attack this city; they will capture it and burn it down.'

9"This is what the LORD says: Do not deceive yourselves, thinking, 'The Babylonians will surely leave us.' They will not! 10Even if you were to defeat the entire Babylonian[c] army that is attacking you and only wounded men were left in their tents, they would come out and burn this city down."

11After the Babylonian army had withdrawn from Jerusalem because of Pharaoh's army, 12Jeremiah started to leave the city to go to the territory of Benjamin to get his share of the property among the people there. 13But when he reached the Benjamin Gate, the captain of the guard, whose name was Irijah son of Shelemiah, the son of Hananiah, arrested him and said, "You are deserting to the Babylonians!"

14"That's not true!" Jeremiah said. "I am not deserting to the Babylonians." But Irijah would not listen to him; instead, he arrested Jeremiah and brought him to the officials. 15They were angry with Jeremiah and had him beaten and imprisoned in the house of Jonathan the secretary, which they had made into a prison.

16Jeremiah was put into a vaulted cell in a dungeon, where he remained a long time. 17Then King Zedekiah sent for him and had him

[a] *1* Hebrew *Coniah,* a variant of *Jehoiachin* [b] *5* Or *Chaldeans*; also in verses 8, 9, 13 and 14 [c] *10* Or *Chaldean*; also in verse 11

brought to the palace, where he asked him privately, "Is there any word from the LORD?"

"Yes," Jeremiah replied, "you will be handed over to the king of Babylon."

18Then Jeremiah said to King Zedekiah, "What crime have I committed against you or your officials or this people, that you have put me in prison? 19Where are your prophets who prophesied to you, 'The king of Babylon will not attack you or this land'? 20But now, my lord the king, please listen. Let me bring my petition before you: Do not send me back to the house of Jonathan the secretary, or I will die there."

21King Zedekiah then gave orders for Jeremiah to be placed in the courtyard of the guard and given bread from the street of the bakers each day until all the bread in the city was gone. So Jeremiah remained in the courtyard of the guard.

Jeremiah Thrown Into a Cistern

38 Shephatiah son of Mattan, Gedaliah son of Pashhur, Jehucal[a] son of Shelemiah, and Pashhur son of Malkijah heard what Jeremiah was telling all the people when he said, 2"This is what the LORD says: 'Whoever stays in this city will die by the sword, famine or plague, but whoever goes over to the Babylonians[b] will live. He will escape with his life; he will live.' 3And this is what the LORD says: 'This city will certainly be handed over to the army of the king of Babylon, who will capture it.'"

4Then the officials said to the king, "This man should be put to death. He is discouraging the soldiers who are left in this city, as well as all the people, by the things he is saying to them. This man is not seeking the good of these people but their ruin."

5"He is in your hands," King Zedekiah answered. "The king can do nothing to oppose you."

6So they took Jeremiah and put him into the cistern of Malkijah, the king's son, which was in the courtyard of the guard. They lowered Jeremiah by ropes into the cistern; it had no water in it, only mud, and Jeremiah sank down into the mud.

7But Ebed-Melech, a Cushite,[c] an official[d] in the royal palace, heard that they had put Jeremiah into the cistern. While the king was sitting in the Benjamin Gate, 8Ebed-Melech went out of the palace and said to him, 9"My lord the king, these men have acted wickedly in all they have done to Jeremiah the prophet. They have thrown him into a cistern, where he will starve to death when there is no longer any bread in the city."

10Then the king commanded Ebed-Melech the Cushite, "Take thirty men from here with you and lift Jeremiah the prophet out of the cistern before he dies."

11So Ebed-Melech took the men with him and went to a room under the treasury in the palace. He took some old rags and worn-out clothes from there and let them down with ropes to Jeremiah in the cistern. 12Ebed-Melech the Cushite said to Jeremiah, "Put these old rags and worn-out clothes under your arms to pad the ropes." Jeremiah did so, 13and they pulled him up with the ropes and lifted him out of the cistern. And Jeremiah remained in the courtyard of the guard.

Zedekiah Questions Jeremiah Again

14Then King Zedekiah sent for Jeremiah the prophet and had him brought to the third entrance to the temple of the LORD. "I am going to ask you something," the king said to Jeremiah. "Do not hide anything from me."

15Jeremiah said to Zedekiah, "If I give you an answer, will you not kill me? Even if I did give you counsel, you would not listen to me."

16But King Zedekiah swore this oath secretly to Jeremiah: "As surely as the LORD lives, who has given us breath, I will neither kill you nor hand you over to those who are seeking your life."

17Then Jeremiah said to Zedekiah, "This is what the LORD God Almighty, the God of Israel, says: 'If you surrender to the officers of the king of Babylon, your life will be spared and this city will not be burned down; you and your family will live. 18But if you will not surrender to the officers of the king of Babylon, this city will be handed over to the Babylonians and they will burn it down; you yourself will not escape from their hands.'"

19King Zedekiah said to Jeremiah, "I am afraid of the Jews who have gone over to the Babylonians, for the Babylonians may hand me over to them and they will mistreat me."

20"They will not hand you over," Jeremiah replied. "Obey the LORD by doing what I tell you. Then it will go well with you, and your life will be spared. 21But if you refuse to surrender, this is what the LORD has revealed to me: 22All the women left in the palace of the king of Judah will be brought out to the officials of the king of Babylon. Those women will say to you:

"'They misled you and overcame you—
  those trusted friends of yours.
Your feet are sunk in the mud;
  your friends have deserted you.'

23"All your wives and children will be brought out to the Babylonians. You yourself will not es-

[a] *1* Hebrew *Jucal*, a variant of *Jehucal* [b] *2* Or *Chaldeans*; also in verses 18, 19 and 23 [c] *7* Probably from the upper Nile region [d] *7* Or *a eunuch*

cape from their hands but will be captured by the king of Babylon; and this city will[a] be burned down."

[24]Then Zedekiah said to Jeremiah, "Do not let anyone know about this conversation, or you may die. [25]If the officials hear that I talked with you, and they come to you and say, 'Tell us what you said to the king and what the king said to you; do not hide it from us or we will kill you,' [26]then tell them, 'I was pleading with the king not to send me back to Jonathan's house to die there.'"

[27]All the officials did come to Jeremiah and question him, and he told them everything the king had ordered him to say. So they said no more to him, for no one had heard his conversation with the king.

[28]And Jeremiah remained in the courtyard of the guard until the day Jerusalem was captured.

The Fall of Jerusalem

39 This is how Jerusalem was taken: [1]In the ninth year of Zedekiah king of Judah, in the tenth month, Nebuchadnezzar king of Babylon marched against Jerusalem with his whole army and laid siege to it. [2]And on the ninth day of the fourth month of Zedekiah's eleventh year, the city wall was broken through. [3]Then all the officials of the king of Babylon came and took seats in the Middle Gate: Nergal-Sharezer of Samgar, Nebo-Sarsekim[b] a chief officer, Nergal-Sharezer a high official and all the other officials of the king of Babylon. [4]When Zedekiah king of Judah and all the soldiers saw them, they fled; they left the city at night by way of the king's garden, through the gate between the two walls, and headed toward the Arabah.[c]

[5]But the Babylonian[d] army pursued them and overtook Zedekiah in the plains of Jericho. They captured him and took him to Nebuchadnezzar king of Babylon at Riblah in the land of Hamath, where he pronounced sentence on him. [6]There at Riblah the king of Babylon slaughtered the sons of Zedekiah before his eyes and also killed all the nobles of Judah. [7]Then he put out Zedekiah's eyes and bound him with bronze shackles to take him to Babylon.

[8]The Babylonians[e] set fire to the royal palace and the houses of the people and broke down the walls of Jerusalem. [9]Nebuzaradan commander of the imperial guard carried into exile to Babylon the people who remained in the city, along with those who had gone over to him, and the rest of the people. [10]But Nebuzaradan the commander of the guard left behind in the land of Judah some of the poor people, who owned nothing; and at that time he gave them vineyards and fields.

[11]Now Nebuchadnezzar king of Babylon had given these orders about Jeremiah through Nebuzaradan commander of the imperial guard: [12]"Take him and look after him; don't harm him but do for him whatever he asks." [13]So Nebuzaradan the commander of the guard, Nebushazban a chief officer, Nergal-Sharezer a high official and all the other officers of the king of Babylon [14]sent and had Jeremiah taken out of the courtyard of the guard. They turned him over to Gedaliah son of Ahikam, the son of Shaphan, to take him back to his home. So he remained among his own people.

[15]While Jeremiah had been confined in the courtyard of the guard, the word of the LORD came to him: [16]"Go and tell Ebed-Melech the Cushite, 'This is what the LORD Almighty, the God of Israel, says: I am about to fulfill my words against this city through disaster, not prosperity. At that time they will be fulfilled before your eyes. [17]But I will rescue you on that day, declares the LORD; you will not be handed over to those you fear. [18]I will save you; you will not fall by the sword but will escape with your life, because you trust in me, declares the LORD.'"

Jeremiah Freed

40 The word came to Jeremiah from the LORD after Nebuzaradan commander of the imperial guard had released him at Ramah. He had found Jeremiah bound in chains among all the captives from Jerusalem and Judah who were being carried into exile to Babylon. [2]When the commander of the guard found Jeremiah, he said to him, "The LORD your God decreed this disaster for this place. [3]And now the LORD has brought it about; he has done just as he said he would. All this happened because you people sinned against the LORD and did not obey him. [4]But today I am freeing you from the chains on your wrists. Come with me to Babylon, if you like, and I will look after you; but if you do not want to, then don't come. Look, the whole country lies before you; go wherever you please." [5]However, before Jeremiah turned to go,[f] Nebuzaradan added, "Go back to Gedaliah son of Ahikam, the son of Shaphan, whom the king of Babylon has appointed over the towns of Judah, and live with him among the people, or go anywhere else you please."

Then the commander gave him provisions and a present and let him go. [6]So Jeremiah went to Gedaliah son of Ahikam at Mizpah and stayed with him among the people who were left behind in the land.

[a]23 Or *and you will cause this city to* [b]3 Or *Nergal-Sharezer, Samgar-Nebo, Sarsekim* [c]4 Or *the Jordan Valley* [d]5 Or *Chaldean* [e]8 Or *Chaldeans* [f]5 Or *Jeremiah answered*

Gedaliah Assassinated

7When all the army officers and their men who were still in the open country heard that the king of Babylon had appointed Gedaliah son of Ahikam as governor over the land and had put him in charge of the men, women and children who were the poorest in the land and who had not been carried into exile to Babylon, 8they came to Gedaliah at Mizpah—Ishmael son of Nethaniah, Johanan and Jonathan the sons of Kareah, Seraiah son of Tanhumeth, the sons of Ephai the Netophathite, and Jaazaniah[a] the son of the Maacathite, and their men. 9Gedaliah son of Ahikam, the son of Shaphan, took an oath to reassure them and their men. "Do not be afraid to serve the Babylonians,[b]" he said. "Settle down in the land and serve the king of Babylon, and it will go well with you. 10I myself will stay at Mizpah to represent you before the Babylonians who come to us, but you are to harvest the wine, summer fruit and oil, and put them in your storage jars, and live in the towns you have taken over."

11When all the Jews in Moab, Ammon, Edom and all the other countries heard that the king of Babylon had left a remnant in Judah and had appointed Gedaliah son of Ahikam, the son of Shaphan, as governor over them, 12they all came back to the land of Judah, to Gedaliah at Mizpah, from all the countries where they had been scattered. And they harvested an abundance of wine and summer fruit.

13Johanan son of Kareah and all the army officers still in the open country came to Gedaliah at Mizpah 14and said to him, "Don't you know that Baalis king of the Ammonites has sent Ishmael son of Nethaniah to take your life?" But Gedaliah son of Ahikam did not believe them.

15Then Johanan son of Kareah said privately to Gedaliah in Mizpah, "Let me go and kill Ishmael son of Nethaniah, and no one will know it. Why should he take your life and cause all the Jews who are gathered around you to be scattered and the remnant of Judah to perish?"

16But Gedaliah son of Ahikam said to Johanan son of Kareah, "Don't do such a thing! What you are saying about Ishmael is not true."

41 In the seventh month Ishmael son of Nethaniah, the son of Elishama, who was of royal blood and had been one of the king's officers, came with ten men to Gedaliah son of Ahikam at Mizpah. While they were eating together there, 2Ishmael son of Nethaniah and the ten men who were with him got up and struck down Gedaliah son of Ahikam, the son of Shaphan, with the sword, killing the one whom the king of Babylon had appointed as governor over the land. 3Ishmael also killed all the Jews who were with Gedaliah at Mizpah, as well as the Babylonian[c] soldiers who were there.

4The day after Gedaliah's assassination, before anyone knew about it, 5eighty men who had shaved off their beards, torn their clothes and cut themselves came from Shechem, Shiloh and Samaria, bringing grain offerings and incense with them to the house of the LORD. 6Ishmael son of Nethaniah went out from Mizpah to meet them, weeping as he went. When he met them, he said, "Come to Gedaliah son of Ahikam." 7When they went into the city, Ishmael son of Nethaniah and the men who were with him slaughtered them and threw them into a cistern. 8But ten of them said to Ishmael, "Don't kill us! We have wheat and barley, oil and honey, hidden in a field." So he let them alone and did not kill them with the others. 9Now the cistern where he threw all the bodies of the men he had killed along with Gedaliah was the one King Asa had made as part of his defense against Baasha king of Israel. Ishmael son of Nethaniah filled it with the dead.

10Ishmael made captives of all the rest of the people who were in Mizpah—the king's daughters along with all the others who were left there, over whom Nebuzaradan commander of the imperial guard had appointed Gedaliah son of Ahikam. Ishmael son of Nethaniah took them captive and set out to cross over to the Ammonites.

11When Johanan son of Kareah and all the army officers who were with him heard about all the crimes Ishmael son of Nethaniah had committed, 12they took all their men and went to fight Ishmael son of Nethaniah. They caught up with him near the great pool in Gibeon. 13When all the people Ishmael had with him saw Johanan son of Kareah and the army officers who were with him, they were glad. 14All the people Ishmael had taken captive at Mizpah turned and went over to Johanan son of Kareah. 15But Ishmael son of Nethaniah and eight of his men escaped from Johanan and fled to the Ammonites.

Flight to Egypt

16Then Johanan son of Kareah and all the army officers who were with him led away all the survivors from Mizpah whom he had recovered from Ishmael son of Nethaniah after he had assassinated Gedaliah son of Ahikam: the soldiers, women, children and court officials he had brought from Gibeon. 17And they went on, stopping at Geruth Kimham near Bethlehem on their way to Egypt 18to escape the Babylonians.[d] They were afraid of them because Ishmael son of Nethaniah had killed Gedaliah son of Ahikam, whom the king of

[a] 8 Hebrew *Jezaniah,* a variant of *Jaazaniah* [b] 9 Or *Chaldeans*; also in verse 10 [c] 3 Or *Chaldean* [d] 18 Or *Chaldeans*

Babylon had appointed as governor over the land.
42 Then all the army officers, including Johanan son of Kareah and Jezaniah[a] son of
Hoshaiah, and all the people from the least to the
greatest approached 2Jeremiah the prophet and
said to him, "Please hear our petition and pray to
the LORD your God for this entire remnant. For as
you now see, though we were once many, now
only a few are left. 3Pray that the LORD your God
will tell us where we should go and what we
should do."
4"I have heard you," replied Jeremiah the
prophet. "I will certainly pray to the LORD your
God as you have requested; I will tell you everything the LORD says and will keep nothing back
from you."
5Then they said to Jeremiah, "May the LORD
be a true and faithful witness against us if we do
not act in accordance with everything the LORD
your God sends you to tell us. 6Whether it is
favorable or unfavorable, we will obey the LORD
our God, to whom we are sending you, so that it
will go well with us, for we will obey the LORD
our God."
7Ten days later the word of the LORD came to
Jeremiah. 8So he called together Johanan son of
Kareah and all the army officers who were with
him and all the people from the least to the greatest. 9He said to them, "This is what the LORD, the
God of Israel, to whom you sent me to present
your petition, says: 10'If you stay in this land, I
will build you up and not tear you down; I will
plant you and not uproot you, for I am grieved
over the disaster I have inflicted on you. 11Do not
be afraid of the king of Babylon, whom you now
fear. Do not be afraid of him, declares the LORD,
for I am with you and will save you and deliver
you from his hands. 12I will show you compassion
so that he will have compassion on you and restore you to your land.'
13"However, if you say, 'We will not stay in
this land,' and so disobey the LORD your God,
14and if you say, 'No, we will go and live in Egypt,
where we will not see war or hear the trumpet or
be hungry for bread,' 15then hear the word of the
LORD, O remnant of Judah. This is what the LORD
Almighty, the God of Israel, says: 'If you are determined to go to Egypt and you do go to settle
there, 16then the sword you fear will overtake
you there, and the famine you dread will follow
you into Egypt, and there you will die. 17Indeed,
all who are determined to go to Egypt to settle
there will die by the sword, famine and plague;
not one of them will survive or escape the disaster I will bring on them.' 18This is what the LORD
Almighty, the God of Israel, says: 'As my anger
and wrath have been poured out on those who
lived in Jerusalem, so will my wrath be poured
out on you when you go to Egypt. You will be an
object of cursing and horror, of condemnation
and reproach; you will never see this place
again.'
19"O remnant of Judah, the LORD has told you,
'Do not go to Egypt.' Be sure of this: I warn you
today 20that you made a fatal mistake[b] when you
sent me to the LORD your God and said, 'Pray to
the LORD our God for us; tell us everything he
says and we will do it.' 21I have told you today,
but you still have not obeyed the LORD your God
in all he sent me to tell you. 22So now, be sure
of this: You will die by the sword, famine and
plague in the place where you want to go to settle."
43 When Jeremiah finished telling the people all the words of the LORD their God—
everything the LORD had sent him to tell them—
2Azariah son of Hoshaiah and Johanan son of Kareah and all the arrogant men said to Jeremiah,
"You are lying! The LORD our God has not sent
you to say, 'You must not go to Egypt to settle
there.' 3But Baruch son of Neriah is inciting you
against us to hand us over to the Babylonians,[c]
so they may kill us or carry us into exile to Babylon."
4So Johanan son of Kareah and all the army
officers and all the people disobeyed the LORD's
command to stay in the land of Judah. 5Instead,
Johanan son of Kareah and all the army officers
led away all the remnant of Judah who had come
back to live in the land of Judah from all the
nations where they had been scattered. 6They
also led away all the men, women and children
and the king's daughters whom Nebuzaradan
commander of the imperial guard had left with
Gedaliah son of Ahikam, the son of Shaphan, and
Jeremiah the prophet and Baruch son of Neriah.
7So they entered Egypt in disobedience to the
LORD and went as far as Tahpanhes.
8In Tahpanhes the word of the LORD came to
Jeremiah: 9"While the Jews are watching, take
some large stones with you and bury them in clay
in the brick pavement at the entrance to Pharaoh's palace in Tahpanhes. 10Then say to them,
'This is what the LORD Almighty, the God of Israel, says: I will send for my servant Nebuchadnezzar king of Babylon, and I will set his throne over
these stones I have buried here; he will spread
his royal canopy above them. 11He will come and
attack Egypt, bringing death to those destined for
death, captivity to those destined for captivity,
and the sword to those destined for the sword.
12He[d] will set fire to the temples of the gods of
Egypt; he will burn their temples and take their
gods captive. As a shepherd wraps his garment

[a] *1* Hebrew; Septuagint (see also 43:2) *Azariah* [b] *20* Or *you erred in your hearts* [c] *3* Or *Chaldeans* [d] *12* Or *I*

around him, so will he wrap Egypt around himself and depart from there unscathed. 13There in the temple of the sun[a] in Egypt he will demolish the sacred pillars and will burn down the temples of the gods of Egypt.' "

Disaster Because of Idolatry

44 This word came to Jeremiah concerning all the Jews living in Lower Egypt—in Migdol, Tahpanhes and Memphis[b]—and in Upper Egypt[c]: 2"This is what the LORD Almighty, the God of Israel, says: You saw the great disaster I brought on Jerusalem and on all the towns of Judah. Today they lie deserted and in ruins 3because of the evil they have done. They provoked me to anger by burning incense and by worshiping other gods that neither they nor you nor your fathers ever knew. 4Again and again I sent my servants the prophets, who said, 'Do not do this detestable thing that I hate!' 5But they did not listen or pay attention; they did not turn from their wickedness or stop burning incense to other gods. 6Therefore, my fierce anger was poured out; it raged against the towns of Judah and the streets of Jerusalem and made them the desolate ruins they are today.

7"Now this is what the LORD God Almighty, the God of Israel, says: Why bring such great disaster on yourselves by cutting off from Judah the men and women, the children and infants, and so leave yourselves without a remnant? 8Why provoke me to anger with what your hands have made, burning incense to other gods in Egypt, where you have come to live? You will destroy yourselves and make yourselves an object of cursing and reproach among all the nations on earth. 9Have you forgotten the wickedness committed by your fathers and by the kings and queens of Judah and the wickedness committed by you and your wives in the land of Judah and the streets of Jerusalem? 10To this day they have not humbled themselves or shown reverence, nor have they followed my law and the decrees I set before you and your fathers.

11"Therefore, this is what the LORD Almighty, the God of Israel, says: I am determined to bring disaster on you and to destroy all Judah. 12I will take away the remnant of Judah who were determined to go to Egypt to settle there. They will all perish in Egypt; they will fall by the sword or die from famine. From the least to the greatest, they will die by sword or famine. They will become an object of cursing and horror, of condemnation and reproach. 13I will punish those who live in Egypt with the sword, famine and plague, as I punished Jerusalem. 14None of the remnant of Judah who have gone to live in Egypt will escape or survive to return to the land of Judah, to which they long to return and live; none will return except a few fugitives."

15Then all the men who knew that their wives were burning incense to other gods, along with all the women who were present—a large assembly—and all the people living in Lower and Upper Egypt,[d] said to Jeremiah, 16"We will not listen to the message you have spoken to us in the name of the LORD! 17We will certainly do everything we said we would: We will burn incense to the Queen of Heaven and will pour out drink offerings to her just as we and our fathers, our kings and our officials did in the towns of Judah and in the streets of Jerusalem. At that time we had plenty of food and were well off and suffered no harm. 18But ever since we stopped burning incense to the Queen of Heaven and pouring out drink offerings to her, we have had nothing and have been perishing by sword and famine."

19The women added, "When we burned incense to the Queen of Heaven and poured out drink offerings to her, did not our husbands know that we were making cakes like her image and pouring out drink offerings to her?"

20Then Jeremiah said to all the people, both men and women, who were answering him, 21"Did not the LORD remember and think about the incense burned in the towns of Judah and the streets of Jerusalem by you and your fathers, your kings and your officials and the people of the land? 22When the LORD could no longer endure your wicked actions and the detestable things you did, your land became an object of cursing and a desolate waste without inhabitants, as it is today. 23Because you have burned incense and have sinned against the LORD and have not obeyed him or followed his law or his decrees or his stipulations, this disaster has come upon you, as you now see."

24Then Jeremiah said to all the people, including the women, "Hear the word of the LORD, all you people of Judah in Egypt. 25This is what the LORD Almighty, the God of Israel, says: You and your wives have shown by your actions what you promised when you said, 'We will certainly carry out the vows we made to burn incense and pour out drink offerings to the Queen of Heaven.'

"Go ahead then, do what you promised! Keep your vows! 26But hear the word of the LORD, all Jews living in Egypt: 'I swear by my great name,' says the LORD, 'that no one from Judah living anywhere in Egypt will ever again invoke my name or swear, "As surely as the Sovereign LORD lives." 27For I am watching over them for harm, not for good; the Jews in Egypt will perish by sword and famine until they are all destroyed.

[a] 13 Or *in Heliopolis* [b] 1 Hebrew *Noph* [c] 1 Hebrew *in Pathros* [d] 15 Hebrew *in Egypt and Pathros*

28Those who escape the sword and return to the
land of Judah from Egypt will be very few. Then
the whole remnant of Judah who came to live in
Egypt will know whose word will stand—mine
or theirs.
29"'This will be the sign to you that I will
punish you in this place,' declares the LORD, 'so
that you will know that my threats of harm
against you will surely stand.' 30This is what the
LORD says: 'I am going to hand Pharaoh Hophra
king of Egypt over to his enemies who seek his
life, just as I handed Zedekiah king of Judah over
to Nebuchadnezzar king of Babylon, the enemy
who was seeking his life.'"

A Message to Baruch

45 This is what Jeremiah the prophet told
Baruch son of Neriah in the fourth year of
Jehoiakim son of Josiah king of Judah, after Baruch had written on a scroll the words Jeremiah
was then dictating: 2"This is what the LORD, the
God of Israel, says to you, Baruch: 3You said,
'Woe to me! The LORD has added sorrow to my
pain; I am worn out with groaning and find no
rest.'"
4⌊The LORD said,⌋ "Say this to him: 'This is
what the LORD says: I will overthrow what I have
built and uproot what I have planted, throughout
the land. 5Should you then seek great things for
yourself? Seek them not. For I will bring disaster
on all people, declares the LORD, but wherever
you go I will let you escape with your life.'"

A Message About Egypt

46 This is the word of the LORD that came to
Jeremiah the prophet concerning the nations:

2Concerning Egypt:

This is the message against the army of Pharaoh Neco king of Egypt, which was defeated at
Carchemish on the Euphrates River by Nebuchadnezzar king of Babylon in the fourth year of
Jehoiakim son of Josiah king of Judah:

3"Prepare your shields, both large and small,
and march out for battle!
4Harness the horses,
mount the steeds!
Take your positions
with helmets on!
Polish your spears,
put on your armor!
5What do I see?
They are terrified,
they are retreating,
their warriors are defeated.
They flee in haste
without looking back,
and there is terror on every side,"
declares the LORD.
6"The swift cannot flee
nor the strong escape.
In the north by the River Euphrates
they stumble and fall.

7"Who is this that rises like the Nile,
like rivers of surging waters?
8Egypt rises like the Nile,
like rivers of surging waters.
She says, 'I will rise and cover the earth;
I will destroy cities and their people.'
9Charge, O horses!
Drive furiously, O charioteers!
March on, O warriors—
men of Cush[a] and Put who carry shields,
men of Lydia who draw the bow.
10But that day belongs to the Lord, the LORD
Almighty—
a day of vengeance, for vengeance on his
foes.
The sword will devour till it is satisfied,
till it has quenched its thirst with blood.
For the Lord, the LORD Almighty, will offer
sacrifice
in the land of the north by the River
Euphrates.

11"Go up to Gilead and get balm,
O Virgin Daughter of Egypt.
But you multiply remedies in vain;
there is no healing for you.
12The nations will hear of your shame;
your cries will fill the earth.
One warrior will stumble over another;
both will fall down together."

13This is the message the LORD spoke to Jeremiah the prophet about the coming of Nebuchadnezzar king of Babylon to attack Egypt:

14"Announce this in Egypt, and proclaim it in
Migdol;
proclaim it also in Memphis[b] and
Tahpanhes:
'Take your positions and get ready,
for the sword devours those around you.'
15Why will your warriors be laid low?
They cannot stand, for the LORD will push
them down.
16They will stumble repeatedly;
they will fall over each other.
They will say, 'Get up, let us go back
to our own people and our native lands,
away from the sword of the oppressor.'
17There they will exclaim,

[a] 9 That is, the upper Nile region [b] 14 Hebrew *Noph*; also in verse 19

'Pharaoh king of Egypt is only a loud
noise;
he has missed his opportunity.'
18"As surely as I live," declares the King,
whose name is the LORD Almighty,
"one will come who is like Tabor among the
mountains,
like Carmel by the sea.
19Pack your belongings for exile,
you who live in Egypt,
for Memphis will be laid waste
and lie in ruins without inhabitant.

20"Egypt is a beautiful heifer,
but a gadfly is coming
against her from the north.
21The mercenaries in her ranks
are like fattened calves.
They too will turn and flee together,
they will not stand their ground,
for the day of disaster is coming upon them,
the time for them to be punished.
22Egypt will hiss like a fleeing serpent
as the enemy advances in force;
they will come against her with axes,
like men who cut down trees.
23They will chop down her forest,"
declares the LORD,
"dense though it be.
They are more numerous than locusts,
they cannot be counted.
24The Daughter of Egypt will be put to shame,
handed over to the people of the north."

25The LORD Almighty, the God of Israel, says:
"I am about to bring punishment on Amon god of
Thebes,[a] on Pharaoh, on Egypt and her gods
and her kings, and on those who rely on Pharaoh.
26I will hand them over to those who seek their
lives, to Nebuchadnezzar king of Babylon and his
officers. Later, however, Egypt will be inhabited
as in times past," declares the LORD.

27"Do not fear, O Jacob my servant;
do not be dismayed, O Israel.
I will surely save you out of a distant place,
your descendants from the land of their
exile.
Jacob will again have peace and security,
and no one will make him afraid.
28Do not fear, O Jacob my servant,
for I am with you," declares the LORD.
"Though I completely destroy all the nations
among which I scatter you,
I will not completely destroy you.
I will discipline you but only with justice;
I will not let you go entirely unpunished."

A Message About the Philistines

47 This is the word of the LORD that came to
Jeremiah the prophet concerning the Philistines before Pharaoh attacked Gaza:

2This is what the LORD says:

"See how the waters are rising in the north;
they will become an overflowing torrent.
They will overflow the land and everything
in it,
the towns and those who live in them.
The people will cry out;
all who dwell in the land will wail
3at the sound of the hoofs of galloping steeds,
at the noise of enemy chariots
and the rumble of their wheels.
Fathers will not turn to help their children;
their hands will hang limp.
4For the day has come
to destroy all the Philistines
and to cut off all survivors
who could help Tyre and Sidon.
The LORD is about to destroy the Philistines,
the remnant from the coasts of Caphtor.[b]
5Gaza will shave her head in mourning;
Ashkelon will be silenced.
O remnant on the plain,
how long will you cut yourselves?
6" 'Ah, sword of the LORD,' ⌞you cry,⌟
'how long till you rest?
Return to your scabbard;
cease and be still.'
7But how can it rest
when the LORD has commanded it,
when he has ordered it
to attack Ashkelon and the coast?"

A Message About Moab

48 Concerning Moab:

This is what the LORD Almighty, the God of
Israel, says:

"Woe to Nebo, for it will be ruined.
Kiriathaim will be disgraced and captured;
the stronghold[c] will be disgraced and
shattered.
2Moab will be praised no more;
in Heshbon[d] men will plot her downfall:
'Come, let us put an end to that nation.'
You too, O Madmen,[e] will be silenced;
the sword will pursue you.
3Listen to the cries from Horonaim,
cries of great havoc and destruction.
4Moab will be broken;
her little ones will cry out.[f]

[a] 25 Hebrew *No* [b] 4 That is, Crete [c] 1 Or / *Misgab* [d] 2 The Hebrew for *Heshbon* sounds like the Hebrew for *plot*.
[e] 2 The name of the Moabite town Madmen sounds like the Hebrew for *be silenced*. [f] 4 Hebrew; Septuagint / *proclaim it to Zoar*

5 They go up the way to Luhith,
weeping bitterly as they go;
on the road down to Horonaim
anguished cries over the destruction are heard.
6 Flee! Run for your lives;
become like a bush[a] in the desert.
7 Since you trust in your deeds and riches,
you too will be taken captive,
and Chemosh will go into exile,
together with his priests and officials.
8 The destroyer will come against every town,
and not a town will escape.
The valley will be ruined
and the plateau destroyed,
because the LORD has spoken.
9 Put salt on Moab,
for she will be laid waste[b];
her towns will become desolate,
with no one to live in them.

10 "A curse on him who is lax in doing the LORD's work!
A curse on him who keeps his sword from bloodshed!

11 "Moab has been at rest from youth,
like wine left on its dregs,
not poured from one jar to another—
she has not gone into exile.
So she tastes as she did,
and her aroma is unchanged.
12 But days are coming,"
declares the LORD,
"when I will send men who pour from jars,
and they will pour her out;
they will empty her jars
and smash her jugs.
13 Then Moab will be ashamed of Chemosh,
as the house of Israel was ashamed
when they trusted in Bethel.

14 "How can you say, 'We are warriors,
men valiant in battle'?
15 Moab will be destroyed and her towns invaded;
her finest young men will go down in the slaughter,"
declares the King, whose name is the LORD Almighty.
16 "The fall of Moab is at hand;
her calamity will come quickly.
17 Mourn for her, all who live around her,
all who know her fame;
say, 'How broken is the mighty scepter,
how broken the glorious staff!'

18 "Come down from your glory
and sit on the parched ground,
O inhabitants of the Daughter of Dibon,
for he who destroys Moab
will come up against you
and ruin your fortified cities.
19 Stand by the road and watch,
you who live in Aroer.
Ask the man fleeing and the woman escaping,
ask them, 'What has happened?'
20 Moab is disgraced, for she is shattered.
Wail and cry out!
Announce by the Arnon
that Moab is destroyed.
21 Judgment has come to the plateau—
to Holon, Jahzah and Mephaath,
22 to Dibon, Nebo and Beth Diblathaim,
23 to Kiriathaim, Beth Gamul and Beth Meon,
24 to Kerioth and Bozrah—
to all the towns of Moab, far and near.
25 Moab's horn[c] is cut off;
her arm is broken,"
declares the LORD.

26 "Make her drunk,
for she has defied the LORD.
Let Moab wallow in her vomit;
let her be an object of ridicule.
27 Was not Israel the object of your ridicule?
Was she caught among thieves,
that you shake your head in scorn
whenever you speak of her?
28 Abandon your towns and dwell among the rocks,
you who live in Moab.
Be like a dove that makes its nest
at the mouth of a cave.

29 "We have heard of Moab's pride—
her overweening pride and conceit,
her pride and arrogance
and the haughtiness of her heart.
30 I know her insolence but it is futile,"
declares the LORD,
"and her boasts accomplish nothing.
31 Therefore I wail over Moab,
for all Moab I cry out,
I moan for the men of Kir Hareseth.
32 I weep for you, as Jazer weeps,
O vines of Sibmah.
Your branches spread as far as the sea;
they reached as far as the sea of Jazer.
The destroyer has fallen
on your ripened fruit and grapes.
33 Joy and gladness are gone
from the orchards and fields of Moab.
I have stopped the flow of wine from the presses;
no one treads them with shouts of joy.

[a] 6 Or *like Aroer* [b] 9 Or *Give wings to Moab, / for she will fly away* [c] 25 *Horn* here symbolizes strength.

Although there are shouts,
they are not shouts of joy.
34"The sound of their cry rises
from Heshbon to Elealeh and Jahaz,
from Zoar as far as Horonaim and Eglath
Shelishiyah,
for even the waters of Nimrim are dried
up.
35In Moab I will put an end
to those who make offerings on the high
places
and burn incense to their gods,"
declares the LORD.
36"So my heart laments for Moab like a flute;
it laments like a flute for the men of Kir
Hareseth.
The wealth they acquired is gone.
37Every head is shaved
and every beard cut off;
every hand is slashed
and every waist is covered with sackcloth.
38On all the roofs in Moab
and in the public squares
there is nothing but mourning,
for I have broken Moab
like a jar that no one wants,"
declares the LORD.
39"How shattered she is! How they wail!
How Moab turns her back in shame!
Moab has become an object of ridicule,
an object of horror to all those around
her."

40This is what the LORD says:

"Look! An eagle is swooping down,
spreading its wings over Moab.
41Kerioth[a] will be captured
and the strongholds taken.
In that day the hearts of Moab's warriors
will be like the heart of a woman in labor.
42Moab will be destroyed as a nation
because she defied the LORD.
43Terror and pit and snare await you,
O people of Moab,"
declares the LORD.
44"Whoever flees from the terror
will fall into a pit,
whoever climbs out of the pit
will be caught in a snare;
for I will bring upon Moab
the year of her punishment,"
declares the LORD.

45"In the shadow of Heshbon
the fugitives stand helpless,
for a fire has gone out from Heshbon,
a blaze from the midst of Sihon;
it burns the foreheads of Moab,
the skulls of the noisy boasters.
46Woe to you, O Moab!
The people of Chemosh are destroyed;
your sons are taken into exile
and your daughters into captivity.
47"Yet I will restore the fortunes of Moab
in days to come,"
declares the LORD.

Here ends the judgment on Moab.

A Message About Ammon

49 Concerning the Ammonites:

This is what the LORD says:

"Has Israel no sons?
Has she no heirs?
Why then has Molech[b] taken possession of
Gad?
Why do his people live in its towns?
2But the days are coming,"
declares the LORD,
"when I will sound the battle cry
against Rabbah of the Ammonites;
it will become a mound of ruins,
and its surrounding villages will be set on fire.
Then Israel will drive out
those who drove her out,"
says the LORD.
3"Wail, O Heshbon, for Ai is destroyed!
Cry out, O inhabitants of Rabbah!
Put on sackcloth and mourn;
rush here and there inside the walls,
for Molech will go into exile,
together with his priests and officials.
4Why do you boast of your valleys,
boast of your valleys so fruitful?
O unfaithful daughter,
you trust in your riches and say,
'Who will attack me?'
5I will bring terror on you
from all those around you,"
declares the Lord,
the LORD Almighty.
"Every one of you will be driven away,
and no one will gather the fugitives.

6"Yet afterward, I will restore the fortunes of
the Ammonites,"
declares the LORD.

A Message About Edom

7Concerning Edom:

This is what the LORD Almighty says:

"Is there no longer wisdom in Teman?

[a]41 Or *The cities* [b]1 Or *their king*; Hebrew *malcam*; also in verse 3

Has counsel perished from the prudent?
Has their wisdom decayed?
8Turn and flee, hide in deep caves,
you who live in Dedan,
for I will bring disaster on Esau
at the time I punish him.
9If grape pickers came to you,
would they not leave a few grapes?
If thieves came during the night,
would they not steal only as much as they wanted?
10But I will strip Esau bare;
I will uncover his hiding places,
so that he cannot conceal himself.
His children, relatives and neighbors will perish,
and he will be no more.
11Leave your orphans; I will protect their lives.
Your widows too can trust in me."

12This is what the LORD says: "If those who do
not deserve to drink the cup must drink it, why
should you go unpunished? You will not go unpunished, but must drink it. 13I swear by myself,"
declares the LORD, "that Bozrah will become a
ruin and an object of horror, of reproach and of
cursing; and all its towns will be in ruins forever."

14I have heard a message from the LORD:
An envoy was sent to the nations to say,
"Assemble yourselves to attack it!
Rise up for battle!"

15"Now I will make you small among the nations,
despised among men.
16The terror you inspire
and the pride of your heart have deceived you,
you who live in the clefts of the rocks,
who occupy the heights of the hill.
Though you build your nest as high as the eagle's,
from there I will bring you down,"
declares the LORD.
17"Edom will become an object of horror;
all who pass by will be appalled and will scoff
because of all its wounds.
18As Sodom and Gomorrah were overthrown,
along with their neighboring towns,"
says the LORD,
"so no one will live there;
no man will dwell in it.

19"Like a lion coming up from Jordan's thickets
to a rich pastureland,
I will chase Edom from its land in an instant.
Who is the chosen one I will appoint for this?
Who is like me and who can challenge me?
And what shepherd can stand against me?"
20Therefore, hear what the LORD has planned against Edom,
what he has purposed against those who live in Teman:
The young of the flock will be dragged away;
he will completely destroy their pasture because of them.
21At the sound of their fall the earth will tremble;
their cry will resound to the Red Sea.[a]
22Look! An eagle will soar and swoop down,
spreading its wings over Bozrah.
In that day the hearts of Edom's warriors
will be like the heart of a woman in labor.

A Message About Damascus

23Concerning Damascus:

"Hamath and Arpad are dismayed,
for they have heard bad news.
They are disheartened,
troubled like[b] the restless sea.
24Damascus has become feeble,
she has turned to flee
and panic has gripped her;
anguish and pain have seized her,
pain like that of a woman in labor.
25Why has the city of renown not been abandoned,
the town in which I delight?
26Surely, her young men will fall in the streets;
all her soldiers will be silenced in that day,"
declares the LORD Almighty.
27"I will set fire to the walls of Damascus;
it will consume the fortresses of Ben-Hadad."

A Message About Kedar and Hazor

28Concerning Kedar and the kingdoms of Hazor, which Nebuchadnezzar king of Babylon attacked:

This is what the LORD says:

"Arise, and attack Kedar
and destroy the people of the East.
29Their tents and their flocks will be taken;
their shelters will be carried off
with all their goods and camels.
Men will shout to them,
'Terror on every side!'

30"Flee quickly away!

[a]21 Hebrew *Yam Suph*; that is, Sea of Reeds [b]23 Hebrew *on* or *by*

Stay in deep caves, you who live in
Hazor,"
declares the LORD.
"Nebuchadnezzar king of Babylon has plotted
against you;
he has devised a plan against you.
31 "Arise and attack a nation at ease,
which lives in confidence,"
declares the LORD,
"a nation that has neither gates nor bars;
its people live alone.
32 Their camels will become plunder,
and their large herds will be booty.
I will scatter to the winds those who are in
distant places[a]
and will bring disaster on them from every
side,"
declares the LORD.
33 "Hazor will become a haunt of jackals,
a desolate place forever.
No one will live there;
no man will dwell in it."

A Message About Elam

34 This is the word of the LORD that came to
Jeremiah the prophet concerning Elam, early in
the reign of Zedekiah king of Judah:

35 This is what the LORD Almighty says:

"See, I will break the bow of Elam,
the mainstay of their might.
36 I will bring against Elam the four winds
from the four quarters of the heavens;
I will scatter them to the four winds,
and there will not be a nation
where Elam's exiles do not go.
37 I will shatter Elam before their foes,
before those who seek their lives;
I will bring disaster upon them,
even my fierce anger,"
declares the LORD.
"I will pursue them with the sword
until I have made an end of them.
38 I will set my throne in Elam
and destroy her king and officials,"
declares the LORD.

39 "Yet I will restore the fortunes of Elam
in days to come,"
declares the LORD.

A Message About Babylon

50 This is the word the LORD spoke through
Jeremiah the prophet concerning Babylon
and the land of the Babylonians[b]:

2 "Announce and proclaim among the nations,
lift up a banner and proclaim it;
keep nothing back, but say,
'Babylon will be captured;
Bel will be put to shame,
Marduk filled with terror.
Her images will be put to shame
and her idols filled with terror.'
3 A nation from the north will attack her
and lay waste her land.
No one will live in it;
both men and animals will flee away.

4 "In those days, at that time,"
declares the LORD,
"the people of Israel and the people of Judah
together
will go in tears to seek the LORD their
God.
5 They will ask the way to Zion
and turn their faces toward it.
They will come and bind themselves to the
LORD
in an everlasting covenant
that will not be forgotten.

6 "My people have been lost sheep;
their shepherds have led them astray
and caused them to roam on the
mountains.
They wandered over mountain and hill
and forgot their own resting place.
7 Whoever found them devoured them;
their enemies said, 'We are not guilty,
for they sinned against the LORD, their true
pasture,
the LORD, the hope of their fathers.'

8 "Flee out of Babylon;
leave the land of the Babylonians,
and be like the goats that lead the flock.
9 For I will stir up and bring against Babylon
an alliance of great nations from the land
of the north.
They will take up their positions against her,
and from the north she will be captured.
Their arrows will be like skilled warriors
who do not return empty-handed.
10 So Babylonia[c] will be plundered;
all who plunder her will have their fill,"
declares the LORD.

11 "Because you rejoice and are glad,
you who pillage my inheritance,
because you frolic like a heifer threshing
grain
and neigh like stallions,
12 your mother will be greatly ashamed;
she who gave you birth will be disgraced.
She will be the least of the nations—

[a] 32 Or *who clip the hair by their foreheads* [b] 1 Or *Chaldeans*; also in verses 8, 25, 35 and 45 [c] 10 Or *Chaldea*

a wilderness, a dry land, a desert.
13 Because of the LORD's anger she will not be inhabited
but will be completely desolate.
All who pass Babylon will be horrified and scoff
because of all her wounds.

14 "Take up your positions around Babylon,
all you who draw the bow.
Shoot at her! Spare no arrows,
for she has sinned against the LORD.
15 Shout against her on every side!
She surrenders, her towers fall,
her walls are torn down.
Since this is the vengeance of the LORD,
take vengeance on her;
do to her as she has done to others.
16 Cut off from Babylon the sower,
and the reaper with his sickle at harvest.
Because of the sword of the oppressor
let everyone return to his own people,
let everyone flee to his own land.

17 "Israel is a scattered flock
that lions have chased away.
The first to devour him
was the king of Assyria;
the last to crush his bones
was Nebuchadnezzar king of Babylon."

18 Therefore this is what the LORD Almighty, the God of Israel, says:

"I will punish the king of Babylon and his land
as I punished the king of Assyria.
19 But I will bring Israel back to his own pasture
and he will graze on Carmel and Bashan;
his appetite will be satisfied
on the hills of Ephraim and Gilead.
20 In those days, at that time,"
declares the LORD,
"search will be made for Israel's guilt,
but there will be none,
and for the sins of Judah,
but none will be found,
for I will forgive the remnant I spare.

21 "Attack the land of Merathaim
and those who live in Pekod.
Pursue, kill and completely destroy[a] them,"
declares the LORD.

"Do everything I have commanded you.
22 The noise of battle is in the land,
the noise of great destruction!
23 How broken and shattered
is the hammer of the whole earth!
How desolate is Babylon
among the nations!
24 I set a trap for you, O Babylon,
and you were caught before you knew it;
you were found and captured
because you opposed the LORD.
25 The LORD has opened his arsenal
and brought out the weapons of his wrath,
for the Sovereign LORD Almighty has work to do
in the land of the Babylonians.
26 Come against her from afar.
Break open her granaries;
pile her up like heaps of grain.
Completely destroy her
and leave her no remnant.
27 Kill all her young bulls;
let them go down to the slaughter!
Woe to them! For their day has come,
the time for them to be punished.
28 Listen to the fugitives and refugees from Babylon
declaring in Zion
how the LORD our God has taken vengeance,
vengeance for his temple.

29 "Summon archers against Babylon,
all those who draw the bow.
Encamp all around her;
let no one escape.
Repay her for her deeds;
do to her as she has done.
For she has defied the LORD,
the Holy One of Israel.
30 Therefore, her young men will fall in the streets;
all her soldiers will be silenced in that day,"
declares the LORD.

31 "See, I am against you, O arrogant one,"
declares the Lord, the LORD Almighty,
"for your day has come,
the time for you to be punished.
32 The arrogant one will stumble and fall
and no one will help her up;
I will kindle a fire in her towns
that will consume all who are around her."

33 This is what the LORD Almighty says:

"The people of Israel are oppressed,
and the people of Judah as well.
All their captors hold them fast,
refusing to let them go.
34 Yet their Redeemer is strong;
the LORD Almighty is his name.
He will vigorously defend their cause

[a] 21 The Hebrew term refers to the irrevocable giving over of things or persons to the LORD, often by totally destroying them; also in verse 26.

so that he may bring rest to their land,
but unrest to those who live in Babylon.

35 "A sword against the Babylonians!"
declares the LORD—
"against those who live in Babylon
and against her officials and wise men!
36 A sword against her false prophets!
They will become fools.
A sword against her warriors!
They will be filled with terror.
37 A sword against her horses and chariots
and all the foreigners in her ranks!
They will become women.
A sword against her treasures!
They will be plundered.
38 A drought on[a] her waters!
They will dry up.
For it is a land of idols,
idols that will go mad with terror.

39 "So desert creatures and hyenas will live there,
and there the owl will dwell.
It will never again be inhabited
or lived in from generation to generation.
40 As God overthrew Sodom and Gomorrah
along with their neighboring towns,"
declares the LORD,
"so no one will live there;
no man will dwell in it.

41 "Look! An army is coming from the north;
a great nation and many kings
are being stirred up from the ends of the earth.
42 They are armed with bows and spears;
they are cruel and without mercy.
They sound like the roaring sea
as they ride on their horses;
they come like men in battle formation
to attack you, O Daughter of Babylon.
43 The king of Babylon has heard reports about them,
and his hands hang limp.
Anguish has gripped him,
pain like that of a woman in labor.
44 Like a lion coming up from Jordan's thickets
to a rich pastureland,
I will chase Babylon from its land in an instant.
Who is the chosen one I will appoint for this?
Who is like me and who can challenge me?
And what shepherd can stand against me?"
45 Therefore, hear what the LORD has planned against Babylon,
what he has purposed against the land of the Babylonians:
The young of the flock will be dragged away;
he will completely destroy their pasture because of them.
46 At the sound of Babylon's capture the earth will tremble;
its cry will resound among the nations.

51 This is what the LORD says:

"See, I will stir up the spirit of a destroyer
against Babylon and the people of Leb Kamai.[b]
2 I will send foreigners to Babylon
to winnow her and to devastate her land;
they will oppose her on every side
in the day of her disaster.
3 Let not the archer string his bow,
nor let him put on his armor.
Do not spare her young men;
completely destroy[c] her army.
4 They will fall down slain in Babylon,[d]
fatally wounded in her streets.
5 For Israel and Judah have not been forsaken
by their God, the LORD Almighty,
though their land[e] is full of guilt
before the Holy One of Israel.

6 "Flee from Babylon!
Run for your lives!
Do not be destroyed because of her sins.
It is time for the LORD's vengeance;
he will pay her what she deserves.
7 Babylon was a gold cup in the LORD's hand;
she made the whole earth drunk.
The nations drank her wine;
therefore they have now gone mad.
8 Babylon will suddenly fall and be broken.
Wail over her!
Get balm for her pain;
perhaps she can be healed.

9 " 'We would have healed Babylon,
but she cannot be healed;
let us leave her and each go to his own land,
for her judgment reaches to the skies,
it rises as high as the clouds.'
10 " 'The LORD has vindicated us;
come, let us tell in Zion
what the LORD our God has done.'

11 "Sharpen the arrows,
take up the shields!

[a] 38 Or *A sword against* [b] 1 *Leb Kamai* is a cryptogram for Chaldea, that is, Babylonia. [c] 3 The Hebrew term refers to the irrevocable giving over of things or persons to the LORD, often by totally destroying them. [d] 4 Or *Chaldea* [e] 5 Or */ and the land ⌞of the Babylonians⌟*

The LORD has stirred up the kings of the Medes,
because his purpose is to destroy Babylon.
The LORD will take vengeance,
vengeance for his temple.
12 Lift up a banner against the walls of Babylon!
Reinforce the guard,
station the watchmen,
prepare an ambush!
The LORD will carry out his purpose,
his decree against the people of Babylon.
13 You who live by many waters
and are rich in treasures,
your end has come,
the time for you to be cut off.
14 The LORD Almighty has sworn by himself:
I will surely fill you with men, as with a swarm of locusts,
and they will shout in triumph over you.

15 "He made the earth by his power;
he founded the world by his wisdom
and stretched out the heavens by his understanding.
16 When he thunders, the waters in the heavens roar;
he makes clouds rise from the ends of the earth.
He sends lightning with the rain
and brings out the wind from his storehouses.

17 "Every man is senseless and without knowledge;
every goldsmith is shamed by his idols.
His images are a fraud;
they have no breath in them.
18 They are worthless, the objects of mockery;
when their judgment comes, they will perish.
19 He who is the Portion of Jacob is not like these,
for he is the Maker of all things,
including the tribe of his inheritance—
the LORD Almighty is his name.

20 "You are my war club,
my weapon for battle—
with you I shatter nations,
with you I destroy kingdoms,
21 with you I shatter horse and rider,
with you I shatter chariot and driver,
22 with you I shatter man and woman,
with you I shatter old man and youth,
with you I shatter young man and maiden,
23 with you I shatter shepherd and flock,
with you I shatter farmer and oxen,
with you I shatter governors and officials.

24 "Before your eyes I will repay Babylon and all who live in Babylonia[a] for all the wrong they have done in Zion," declares the LORD.

25 "I am against you, O destroying mountain,
you who destroy the whole earth,"
declares the LORD.
"I will stretch out my hand against you,
roll you off the cliffs,
and make you a burned-out mountain.
26 No rock will be taken from you for a cornerstone,
nor any stone for a foundation,
for you will be desolate forever,"
declares the LORD.

27 "Lift up a banner in the land!
Blow the trumpet among the nations!
Prepare the nations for battle against her;
summon against her these kingdoms:
Ararat, Minni and Ashkenaz.
Appoint a commander against her;
send up horses like a swarm of locusts.
28 Prepare the nations for battle against her—
the kings of the Medes,
their governors and all their officials,
and all the countries they rule.
29 The land trembles and writhes,
for the LORD's purposes against Babylon stand—
to lay waste the land of Babylon
so that no one will live there.
30 Babylon's warriors have stopped fighting;
they remain in their strongholds.
Their strength is exhausted;
they have become like women.
Her dwellings are set on fire;
the bars of her gates are broken.
31 One courier follows another
and messenger follows messenger
to announce to the king of Babylon
that his entire city is captured,
32 the river crossings seized,
the marshes set on fire,
and the soldiers terrified."

33 This is what the LORD Almighty, the God of Israel, says:

"The Daughter of Babylon is like a threshing floor
at the time it is trampled;
the time to harvest her will soon come."

34 "Nebuchadnezzar king of Babylon has devoured us,
he has thrown us into confusion,
he has made us an empty jar.
Like a serpent he has swallowed us

[a] *24* Or *Chaldea*; also in verse 35

and filled his stomach with our delicacies,
and then has spewed us out.
35May the violence done to our flesh[a] be
upon Babylon,"
say the inhabitants of Zion.
"May our blood be on those who live in
Babylonia,"
says Jerusalem.

36Therefore, this is what the LORD says:

"See, I will defend your cause
and avenge you;
I will dry up her sea
and make her springs dry.
37Babylon will be a heap of ruins,
a haunt of jackals,
an object of horror and scorn,
a place where no one lives.
38Her people all roar like young lions,
they growl like lion cubs.
39But while they are aroused,
I will set out a feast for them
and make them drunk,
so that they shout with laughter—
then sleep forever and not awake,"
declares the LORD.
40"I will bring them down
like lambs to the slaughter,
like rams and goats.

41"How Sheshach[b] will be captured,
the boast of the whole earth seized!
What a horror Babylon will be
among the nations!
42The sea will rise over Babylon;
its roaring waves will cover her.
43Her towns will be desolate,
a dry and desert land,
a land where no one lives,
through which no man travels.
44I will punish Bel in Babylon
and make him spew out what he has
swallowed.
The nations will no longer stream to him.
And the wall of Babylon will fall.

45"Come out of her, my people!
Run for your lives!
Run from the fierce anger of the LORD.
46Do not lose heart or be afraid
when rumors are heard in the land;
one rumor comes this year, another the next,
rumors of violence in the land
and of ruler against ruler.
47For the time will surely come
when I will punish the idols of Babylon;
her whole land will be disgraced
and her slain will all lie fallen within her.
48Then heaven and earth and all that is in
them
will shout for joy over Babylon,
for out of the north
destroyers will attack her,"
declares the LORD.

49"Babylon must fall because of Israel's slain,
just as the slain in all the earth
have fallen because of Babylon.
50You who have escaped the sword,
leave and do not linger!
Remember the LORD in a distant land,
and think on Jerusalem."

51"We are disgraced,
for we have been insulted
and shame covers our faces,
because foreigners have entered
the holy places of the LORD's house."

52"But days are coming," declares the LORD,
"when I will punish her idols,
and throughout her land
the wounded will groan.
53Even if Babylon reaches the sky
and fortifies her lofty stronghold,
I will send destroyers against her,"
declares the LORD.

54"The sound of a cry comes from Babylon,
the sound of great destruction
from the land of the Babylonians.[c]
55The LORD will destroy Babylon;
he will silence her noisy din.
Waves ⌊of enemies⌋ will rage like great
waters;
the roar of their voices will resound.
56A destroyer will come against Babylon;
her warriors will be captured,
and their bows will be broken.
For the LORD is a God of retribution;
he will repay in full.
57I will make her officials and wise men drunk,
her governors, officers and warriors as
well;
they will sleep forever and not awake,"
declares the King, whose name is the
LORD Almighty.

58This is what the LORD Almighty says:

"Babylon's thick wall will be leveled
and her high gates set on fire;
the peoples exhaust themselves for nothing,
the nations' labor is only fuel for the
flames."

59This is the message Jeremiah gave to the staff
officer Seraiah son of Neriah, the son of Mahse-

[a]35 Or *done to us and to our children* [b]41 *Sheshach* is a cryptogram for Babylon. [c]54 Or *Chaldeans*

iah, when he went to Babylon with Zedekiah king of Judah in the fourth year of his reign. 60Jeremiah had written on a scroll about all the disasters that would come upon Babylon—all that had been recorded concerning Babylon. 61He said to Seraiah, "When you get to Babylon, see that you read all these words aloud. 62Then say, 'O LORD, you have said you will destroy this place, so that neither man nor animal will live in it; it will be desolate forever.' 63When you finish reading this scroll, tie a stone to it and throw it into the Euphrates. 64Then say, 'So will Babylon sink to rise no more because of the disaster I will bring upon her. And her people will fall.' "

The words of Jeremiah end here.

The Fall of Jerusalem

52 Zedekiah was twenty-one years old when he became king, and he reigned in Jerusalem eleven years. His mother's name was Hamutal daughter of Jeremiah; she was from Libnah. 2He did evil in the eyes of the LORD, just as Jehoiakim had done. 3It was because of the LORD's anger that all this happened to Jerusalem and Judah, and in the end he thrust them from his presence.

Now Zedekiah rebelled against the king of Babylon.

4So in the ninth year of Zedekiah's reign, on the tenth day of the tenth month, Nebuchadnezzar king of Babylon marched against Jerusalem with his whole army. They camped outside the city and built siege works all around it. 5The city was kept under siege until the eleventh year of King Zedekiah.

6By the ninth day of the fourth month the famine in the city had become so severe that there was no food for the people to eat. 7Then the city wall was broken through, and the whole army fled. They left the city at night through the gate between the two walls near the king's garden, though the Babylonians[a] were surrounding the city. They fled toward the Arabah,[b] 8but the Babylonian[c] army pursued King Zedekiah and overtook him in the plains of Jericho. All his soldiers were separated from him and scattered, 9and he was captured.

He was taken to the king of Babylon at Riblah in the land of Hamath, where he pronounced sentence on him. 10There at Riblah the king of Babylon slaughtered the sons of Zedekiah before his eyes; he also killed all the officials of Judah. 11Then he put out Zedekiah's eyes, bound him with bronze shackles and took him to Babylon, where he put him in prison till the day of his death.

12On the tenth day of the fifth month, in the nineteenth year of Nebuchadnezzar king of Babylon, Nebuzaradan commander of the imperial guard, who served the king of Babylon, came to Jerusalem. 13He set fire to the temple of the LORD, the royal palace and all the houses of Jerusalem. Every important building he burned down. 14The whole Babylonian army under the commander of the imperial guard broke down all the walls around Jerusalem. 15Nebuzaradan the commander of the guard carried into exile some of the poorest people and those who remained in the city, along with the rest of the craftsmen[d] and those who had gone over to the king of Babylon. 16But Nebuzaradan left behind the rest of the poorest people of the land to work the vineyards and fields.

17The Babylonians broke up the bronze pillars, the movable stands and the bronze Sea that were at the temple of the LORD and they carried all the bronze to Babylon. 18They also took away the pots, shovels, wick trimmers, sprinkling bowls, dishes and all the bronze articles used in the temple service. 19The commander of the imperial guard took away the basins, censers, sprinkling bowls, pots, lampstands, dishes and bowls used for drink offerings—all that were made of pure gold or silver.

20The bronze from the two pillars, the Sea and the twelve bronze bulls under it, and the movable stands, which King Solomon had made for the temple of the LORD, was more than could be weighed. 21Each of the pillars was eighteen cubits high and twelve cubits in circumference[e]; each was four fingers thick, and hollow. 22The bronze capital on top of the one pillar was five cubits[f] high and was decorated with a network and pomegranates of bronze all around. The other pillar, with its pomegranates, was similar. 23There were ninety-six pomegranates on the sides; the total number of pomegranates above the surrounding network was a hundred.

24The commander of the guard took as prisoners Seraiah the chief priest, Zephaniah the priest next in rank and the three doorkeepers. 25Of those still in the city, he took the officer in charge of the fighting men, and seven royal advisers. He also took the secretary who was chief officer in charge of conscripting the people of the land and sixty of his men who were found in the city. 26Nebuzaradan the commander took them all and brought them to the king of Babylon at

[a] 7 Or *Chaldeans*; also in verse 17 [b] 7 Or *the Jordan Valley* [c] 8 Or *Chaldean*; also in verse 14 [d] 15 Or *populace* [e] 21 That is, about 27 feet (about 8.1 meters) high and 18 feet (about 5.4 meters) in circumference [f] 22 That is, about 7 1/2 feet (about 2.3 meters)

Riblah. 27There at Riblah, in the land of Hamath,
the king had them executed.

So Judah went into captivity, away from her
land. 28This is the number of the people Nebuchadnezzar carried into exile:

in the seventh year, 3,023 Jews;
29in Nebuchadnezzar's eighteenth year,
832 people from Jerusalem;
30in his twenty-third year,
745 Jews taken into exile by Nebuzaradan the commander of the imperial guard.

There were 4,600 people in all.

Jehoiachin Released

31In the thirty-seventh year of the exile of Jehoiachin king of Judah, in the year Evil-
Merodach[a] became king of Babylon, he released
Jehoiachin king of Judah and freed him from prison on the twenty-fifth day of the twelfth month.
32He spoke kindly to him and gave him a seat of
honor higher than those of the other kings who
were with him in Babylon. 33So Jehoiachin put
aside his prison clothes and for the rest of his life
ate regularly at the king's table. 34Day by day the
king of Babylon gave Jehoiachin a regular allowance as long as he lived, till the day of his death.

a31 Also called *Amel-Marduk*

Introduction to LAMENTATIONS

Personal Reading Plan

- ❒ Lamentations 1:1–22
- ❒ Lamentations 2:1–22
- ❒ Lamentations 3:1–33
- ❒ Lamentations 3:34–66
- ❒ Lamentations 4:1–22
- ❒ Lamentations 5:1–22

Author

Early Jewish and Christian tradition ascribes this anonymous book to Jeremiah. Although likely, the evidence for this view is not certain. It is clear, however, that the author was an eyewitness to the fall of Jerusalem and Judah's forced exile to Babylon.

Date

Lamentations was probably written between 586 B.C. (the fall of Jerusalem) and 516 B.C. (the dedication of the rebuilt temple).

Theme

Grief over Judah's fall and Jerusalem's destruction.

Historical Background

Jerusalem laid under siege by Babylon for 18 months. Outside the city, the Babylonians captured and killed many of the people of Judah. While inside the city, disease and famine claimed many more. Reflecting on these stark days, and then the fall of Jerusalem, Lamentations depicts the incredible grief and loss accompanying the invasion and destruction of Jerusalem—including the temple—and the exile of Judah's residents.

Characteristics

Lamentations is a good example of ancient Near Eastern "dirge" poetry which was read aloud at funerals. It is used by Jews wailing at the Western Wall, even to this day. The author of this book crafted his theological lessons and channeled his emotions to fit his lament into an "acrostic" poem. (An acrostic poem is one in which the verses each begin with the successive 22 letters of the Hebrew alphabet.) An interesting thematic parallel to Lamentations is the book of Job (see the introduction page for Job). Job grieves over the calamity which has struck him on a personal level, while the author of Lamentations pours out his grief over the destruction of the city of Jerusalem. Whereas Job has done nothing to deserve his disaster and thus wonders how God can be just, the poet of Lamentations readily confesses that Judah is guilty and that God is just. Lamentations provides a sad "post-mortem" on the prophetic warnings that Judah had repeatedly (and fatally) ignored. Though appalled at the severity of the national destruction, the poet still trusts God. Having confessed the people's sin, the poet desperately hopes that the God who brings grief will also renew mercy (see 3:21–33; 5:21–22). Because of its profound reflection on the problem of suffering (which finds no easy answers, but is content to trust God's mercy), Lamentations, like Job, has inspired Christian devotion and hymn-writing.

1 [a] How deserted lies the city,
once so full of people!
How like a widow is she,
who once was great among the nations!
She who was queen among the provinces
has now become a slave.

2 Bitterly she weeps at night,
tears are upon her cheeks.
Among all her lovers
there is none to comfort her.
All her friends have betrayed her;
they have become her enemies.

3 After affliction and harsh labor,
Judah has gone into exile.
She dwells among the nations;
she finds no resting place.
All who pursue her have overtaken her
in the midst of her distress.

4 The roads to Zion mourn,
for no one comes to her appointed feasts.
All her gateways are desolate,
her priests groan,
her maidens grieve,
and she is in bitter anguish.

5 Her foes have become her masters;
her enemies are at ease.
The LORD has brought her grief
because of her many sins.
Her children have gone into exile,
captive before the foe.

6 All the splendor has departed
from the Daughter of Zion.
Her princes are like deer
that find no pasture;
in weakness they have fled
before the pursuer.

7 In the days of her affliction and wandering
Jerusalem remembers all the treasures
that were hers in days of old.
When her people fell into enemy hands,
there was no one to help her.
Her enemies looked at her
and laughed at her destruction.

8 Jerusalem has sinned greatly
and so has become unclean.
All who honored her despise her,
for they have seen her nakedness;
she herself groans
and turns away.

9 Her filthiness clung to her skirts;
she did not consider her future.
Her fall was astounding;
there was none to comfort her.
"Look, O LORD, on my affliction,
for the enemy has triumphed."

10 The enemy laid hands
on all her treasures;
she saw pagan nations
enter her sanctuary—
those you had forbidden
to enter your assembly.

11 All her people groan
as they search for bread;
they barter their treasures for food
to keep themselves alive.
"Look, O LORD, and consider,
for I am despised."

12 "Is it nothing to you, all you who pass by?
Look around and see.
Is any suffering like my suffering
that was inflicted on me,
that the LORD brought on me
in the day of his fierce anger?

13 "From on high he sent fire,
sent it down into my bones.
He spread a net for my feet
and turned me back.
He made me desolate,
faint all the day long.

14 "My sins have been bound into a yoke[b];
by his hands they were woven together.
They have come upon my neck
and the Lord has sapped my strength.
He has handed me over
to those I cannot withstand.

15 "The Lord has rejected
all the warriors in my midst;
he has summoned an army against me
to[c] crush my young men.
In his winepress the Lord has trampled
the Virgin Daughter of Judah.

16 "This is why I weep
and my eyes overflow with tears.
No one is near to comfort me,
no one to restore my spirit.
My children are destitute
because the enemy has prevailed."

17 Zion stretches out her hands,
but there is no one to comfort her.
The LORD has decreed for Jacob
that his neighbors become his foes;
Jerusalem has become
an unclean thing among them.

18 "The LORD is righteous,

[a] This chapter is an acrostic poem, the verses of which begin with the successive letters of the Hebrew alphabet. [b] *14* Most Hebrew manuscripts; Septuagint *He kept watch over my sins* [c] *15* Or *has set a time for me / when he will*

yet I rebelled against his command.
Listen, all you peoples;
look upon my suffering.
My young men and maidens
have gone into exile.

19 "I called to my allies
but they betrayed me.
My priests and my elders
perished in the city
while they searched for food
to keep themselves alive.

20 "See, O LORD, how distressed I am!
I am in torment within,
and in my heart I am disturbed,
for I have been most rebellious.
Outside, the sword bereaves;
inside, there is only death.

21 "People have heard my groaning,
but there is no one to comfort me.
All my enemies have heard of my distress;
they rejoice at what you have done.
May you bring the day you have announced
so they may become like me.

22 "Let all their wickedness come before you;
deal with them
as you have dealt with me
because of all my sins.
My groans are many
and my heart is faint."

2 [a] How the Lord has covered the Daughter of Zion
with the cloud of his anger[b]!
He has hurled down the splendor of Israel
from heaven to earth;
he has not remembered his footstool
in the day of his anger.

2 Without pity the Lord has swallowed up
all the dwellings of Jacob;
in his wrath he has torn down
the strongholds of the Daughter of Judah.
He has brought her kingdom and its princes
down to the ground in dishonor.

3 In fierce anger he has cut off
every horn[c] of Israel.
He has withdrawn his right hand
at the approach of the enemy.
He has burned in Jacob like a flaming fire
that consumes everything around it.

4 Like an enemy he has strung his bow;
his right hand is ready.
Like a foe he has slain
all who were pleasing to the eye;
he has poured out his wrath like fire
on the tent of the Daughter of Zion.

5 The Lord is like an enemy;
he has swallowed up Israel.
He has swallowed up all her palaces
and destroyed her strongholds.
He has multiplied mourning and lamentation
for the Daughter of Judah.

6 He has laid waste his dwelling like a garden;
he has destroyed his place of meeting.
The LORD has made Zion forget
her appointed feasts and her Sabbaths;
in his fierce anger he has spurned
both king and priest.

7 The Lord has rejected his altar
and abandoned his sanctuary.
He has handed over to the enemy
the walls of her palaces;
they have raised a shout in the house of the LORD
as on the day of an appointed feast.

8 The LORD determined to tear down
the wall around the Daughter of Zion.
He stretched out a measuring line
and did not withhold his hand from destroying.
He made ramparts and walls lament;
together they wasted away.

9 Her gates have sunk into the ground;
their bars he has broken and destroyed.
Her king and her princes are exiled among the nations,
the law is no more,
and her prophets no longer find
visions from the LORD.

10 The elders of the Daughter of Zion
sit on the ground in silence;
they have sprinkled dust on their heads
and put on sackcloth.
The young women of Jerusalem
have bowed their heads to the ground.

11 My eyes fail from weeping,
I am in torment within,
my heart is poured out on the ground
because my people are destroyed,
because children and infants faint
in the streets of the city.

12 They say to their mothers,
"Where is bread and wine?"
as they faint like wounded men

[a] This chapter is an acrostic poem, the verses of which begin with the successive letters of the Hebrew alphabet. [b] 1 Or *How the Lord in his anger / has treated the Daughter of Zion with contempt* [c] 3 Or */ all the strength*; or *every king*; *horn* here symbolizes strength.

in the streets of the city,
as their lives ebb away
in their mothers' arms.

13What can I say for you?
With what can I compare you,
O Daughter of Jerusalem?
To what can I liken you,
that I may comfort you,
O Virgin Daughter of Zion?
Your wound is as deep as the sea.
Who can heal you?

14The visions of your prophets
were false and worthless;
they did not expose your sin
to ward off your captivity.
The oracles they gave you
were false and misleading.

15All who pass your way
clap their hands at you;
they scoff and shake their heads
at the Daughter of Jerusalem:
"Is this the city that was called
the perfection of beauty,
the joy of the whole earth?"

16All your enemies open their mouths
wide against you;
they scoff and gnash their teeth
and say, "We have swallowed her up.
This is the day we have waited for;
we have lived to see it."

17The LORD has done what he planned;
he has fulfilled his word,
which he decreed long ago.
He has overthrown you without pity,
he has let the enemy gloat over you,
he has exalted the horn[a] of your foes.

18The hearts of the people
cry out to the Lord.
O wall of the Daughter of Zion,
let your tears flow like a river
day and night;
give yourself no relief,
your eyes no rest.

19Arise, cry out in the night,
as the watches of the night begin;
pour out your heart like water
in the presence of the Lord.
Lift up your hands to him
for the lives of your children,
who faint from hunger
at the head of every street.

20"Look, O LORD, and consider:
Whom have you ever treated like this?
Should women eat their offspring,
the children they have cared for?
Should priest and prophet be killed
in the sanctuary of the Lord?

21"Young and old lie together
in the dust of the streets;
my young men and maidens
have fallen by the sword.
You have slain them in the day of your
anger;
you have slaughtered them without pity.

22"As you summon to a feast day,
so you summoned against me terrors on
every side.
In the day of the LORD's anger
no one escaped or survived;
those I cared for and reared,
my enemy has destroyed."

3[b] I am the man who has seen affliction
by the rod of his wrath.
2He has driven me away and made me walk
in darkness rather than light;
3indeed, he has turned his hand against me
again and again, all day long.

4He has made my skin and my flesh grow old
and has broken my bones.
5He has besieged me and surrounded me
with bitterness and hardship.
6He has made me dwell in darkness
like those long dead.

7He has walled me in so I cannot escape;
he has weighed me down with chains.
8Even when I call out or cry for help,
he shuts out my prayer.
9He has barred my way with blocks of stone;
he has made my paths crooked.

10Like a bear lying in wait,
like a lion in hiding,
11he dragged me from the path and mangled
me
and left me without help.
12He drew his bow
and made me the target for his arrows.

13He pierced my heart
with arrows from his quiver.
14I became the laughingstock of all my people;
they mock me in song all day long.
15He has filled me with bitter herbs
and sated me with gall.

16He has broken my teeth with gravel;
he has trampled me in the dust.

[a] *17 Horn* here symbolizes strength. [b] This chapter is an acrostic poem; the verses of each stanza begin with the successive letters of the Hebrew alphabet, and the verses within each stanza begin with the same letter.

17I have been deprived of peace;
I have forgotten what prosperity is.
18So I say, "My splendor is gone
and all that I had hoped from the LORD."

19I remember my affliction and my wandering,
the bitterness and the gall.
20I well remember them,
and my soul is downcast within me.
21Yet this I call to mind
and therefore I have hope:

22Because of the LORD's great love we are not consumed,
for his compassions never fail.
23They are new every morning;
great is your faithfulness.
24I say to myself, "The LORD is my portion;
therefore I will wait for him."

25The LORD is good to those whose hope is in him,
to the one who seeks him;
26it is good to wait quietly
for the salvation of the LORD.
27It is good for a man to bear the yoke
while he is young.

28Let him sit alone in silence,
for the LORD has laid it on him.
29Let him bury his face in the dust—
there may yet be hope.
30Let him offer his cheek to one who would strike him,
and let him be filled with disgrace.

31For men are not cast off
by the Lord forever.
32Though he brings grief, he will show compassion,
so great is his unfailing love.
33For he does not willingly bring affliction
or grief to the children of men.

34To crush underfoot
all prisoners in the land,
35to deny a man his rights
before the Most High,
36to deprive a man of justice—
would not the Lord see such things?

37Who can speak and have it happen
if the Lord has not decreed it?
38Is it not from the mouth of the Most High
that both calamities and good things come?
39Why should any living man complain
when punished for his sins?

40Let us examine our ways and test them,
and let us return to the LORD.
41Let us lift up our hearts and our hands
to God in heaven, and say:
42"We have sinned and rebelled
and you have not forgiven.

43"You have covered yourself with anger and pursued us;
you have slain without pity.
44You have covered yourself with a cloud
so that no prayer can get through.
45You have made us scum and refuse
among the nations.

46"All our enemies have opened their mouths
wide against us.
47We have suffered terror and pitfalls,
ruin and destruction."
48Streams of tears flow from my eyes
because my people are destroyed.

49My eyes will flow unceasingly,
without relief,
50until the LORD looks down
from heaven and sees.
51What I see brings grief to my soul
because of all the women of my city.

52Those who were my enemies without cause
hunted me like a bird.
53They tried to end my life in a pit
and threw stones at me;
54the waters closed over my head,
and I thought I was about to be cut off.

55I called on your name, O LORD,
from the depths of the pit.
56You heard my plea: "Do not close your ears
to my cry for relief."
57You came near when I called you,
and you said, "Do not fear."

58O Lord, you took up my case;
you redeemed my life.
59You have seen, O LORD, the wrong done to me.
Uphold my cause!
60You have seen the depth of their vengeance,
all their plots against me.

61O LORD, you have heard their insults,
all their plots against me—
62what my enemies whisper and mutter
against me all day long.
63Look at them! Sitting or standing,
they mock me in their songs.

64Pay them back what they deserve, O LORD,
for what their hands have done.
65Put a veil over their hearts,
and may your curse be on them!
66Pursue them in anger and destroy them
from under the heavens of the LORD.

4 [a] How the gold has lost its luster,
the fine gold become dull!
The sacred gems are scattered
at the head of every street.

2 How the precious sons of Zion,
once worth their weight in gold,
are now considered as pots of clay,
the work of a potter's hands!

3 Even jackals offer their breasts
to nurse their young,
but my people have become heartless
like ostriches in the desert.

4 Because of thirst the infant's tongue
sticks to the roof of its mouth;
the children beg for bread,
but no one gives it to them.

5 Those who once ate delicacies
are destitute in the streets.
Those nurtured in purple
now lie on ash heaps.

6 The punishment of my people
is greater than that of Sodom,
which was overthrown in a moment
without a hand turned to help her.

7 Their princes were brighter than snow
and whiter than milk,
their bodies more ruddy than rubies,
their appearance like sapphires.[b]

8 But now they are blacker than soot;
they are not recognized in the streets.
Their skin has shriveled on their bones;
it has become as dry as a stick.

9 Those killed by the sword are better off
than those who die of famine;
racked with hunger, they waste away
for lack of food from the field.

10 With their own hands compassionate women
have cooked their own children,
who became their food
when my people were destroyed.

11 The LORD has given full vent to his wrath;
he has poured out his fierce anger.
He kindled a fire in Zion
that consumed her foundations.

12 The kings of the earth did not believe,
nor did any of the world's people,
that enemies and foes could enter
the gates of Jerusalem.

13 But it happened because of the sins of her
prophets
and the iniquities of her priests,
who shed within her
the blood of the righteous.

14 Now they grope through the streets
like men who are blind.
They are so defiled with blood
that no one dares to touch their garments.

15 "Go away! You are unclean!" men cry to
them.
"Away! Away! Don't touch us!"
When they flee and wander about,
people among the nations say,
"They can stay here no longer."

16 The LORD himself has scattered them;
he no longer watches over them.
The priests are shown no honor,
the elders no favor.

17 Moreover, our eyes failed,
looking in vain for help;
from our towers we watched
for a nation that could not save us.

18 Men stalked us at every step,
so we could not walk in our streets.
Our end was near, our days were numbered,
for our end had come.

19 Our pursuers were swifter
than eagles in the sky;
they chased us over the mountains
and lay in wait for us in the desert.

20 The LORD's anointed, our very life breath,
was caught in their traps.
We thought that under his shadow
we would live among the nations.

21 Rejoice and be glad, O Daughter of Edom,
you who live in the land of Uz.
But to you also the cup will be passed;
you will be drunk and stripped naked.

22 O Daughter of Zion, your punishment will
end;
he will not prolong your exile.
But, O Daughter of Edom, he will punish
your sin
and expose your wickedness.

5 Remember, O LORD, what has happened
to us;
look, and see our disgrace.
2 Our inheritance has been turned over to
aliens,
our homes to foreigners.
3 We have become orphans and fatherless,
our mothers like widows.

[a] This chapter is an acrostic poem, the verses of which begin with the successive letters of the Hebrew alphabet. [b] 7 Or *lapis lazuli*

4We must buy the water we drink;
our wood can be had only at a price.
5Those who pursue us are at our heels;
we are weary and find no rest.
6We submitted to Egypt and Assyria
to get enough bread.
7Our fathers sinned and are no more,
and we bear their punishment.
8Slaves rule over us,
and there is none to free us from their hands.
9We get our bread at the risk of our lives
because of the sword in the desert.
10Our skin is hot as an oven,
feverish from hunger.
11Women have been ravished in Zion,
and virgins in the towns of Judah.
12Princes have been hung up by their hands;
elders are shown no respect.
13Young men toil at the millstones;
boys stagger under loads of wood.
14The elders are gone from the city gate;
the young men have stopped their music.
15Joy is gone from our hearts;
our dancing has turned to mourning.
16The crown has fallen from our head.
Woe to us, for we have sinned!
17Because of this our hearts are faint,
because of these things our eyes grow dim
18for Mount Zion, which lies desolate,
with jackals prowling over it.

19You, O LORD, reign forever;
your throne endures from generation to generation.
20Why do you always forget us?
Why do you forsake us so long?
21Restore us to yourself, O LORD, that we may return;
renew our days as of old
22unless you have utterly rejected us
and are angry with us beyond measure.

Introduction to
EZEKIEL

Personal Reading Plan

❐ Ezekiel 1:1–3:15	❐ Ezekiel 19:1–20:49	❐ Ezekiel 34:1–35:15
❐ Ezekiel 3:16–5:17	❐ Ezekiel 21:1–22:31	❐ Ezekiel 36:1–37:14
❐ Ezekiel 6:1–8:18	❐ Ezekiel 23:1–49	❐ Ezekiel 37:15–39:29
❐ Ezekiel 9:1–11:25	❐ Ezekiel 24:1–25:17	❐ Ezekiel 40:1–47
❐ Ezekiel 12:1–13:23	❐ Ezekiel 26:1–27:36	❐ Ezekiel 40:48–42:20
❐ Ezekiel 14:1–15:8	❐ Ezekiel 28:1–29:21	❐ Ezekiel 43:1–44:31
❐ Ezekiel 16:1–63	❐ Ezekiel 30:1–31:18	❐ Ezekiel 45:1–46:24
❐ Ezekiel 17:1–18:32	❐ Ezekiel 32:1–33:33	❐ Ezekiel 47:1–48:35

Author

The writer is Ezekiel, a Jewish priest and prophet, exiled in Babylon. He was a man of broad knowledge, not only of his own traditions but also of international affairs and history.

Date

Ezekiel's prophecies can be dated with precision, more than any other prophet. His first dates from 593 B.C., seven years before the fall of Jerusalem; his last from 571 B.C. The book of Ezekiel contains more dates than any other Old Testament prophetic book. In addition, archaeologists (from Babylonian records) and astronomists (from accurate dating of eclipses referred to in ancient archives), provide precise modern calendar equivalents.

Theme

God acts in the events of human history so that everyone may come to know him and find new life in him.

Historical Background

Like his contemporary Jeremiah, Ezekiel prophesied in politically volatile times. After Israel was destroyed by the Assyrians in 722 B.C., only the southern kingdom of Judah was left. Assyria lost its domination in 612 B.C. and was replaced as a world power by Babylon. Judah was a subservient state of Babylon, but rebelled, hoping for Egypt's support. Egypt proved unreliable and Judah was subdued by King Nebuchadnezzar of Babylon in 605 and again in 598–597 B.C. He took thousands of Jews captive each time. Among those in the second wave of exiles was Ezekiel.

Characteristics

Ezekiel is a book of heavenly visions, poems, parables and dramatically acted-out prophetic symbolism. However, to get the people's attention, God uses more than Ezekiel's vivid images and symbolic actions. He allows the people to suffer. But Ezekiel's message of imminent doom turns to ultimate hope in the end. There is symmetry in the book with, (1) the vision of the desecrated temple balanced by that of the restored temple, (2) the message of God's anger balanced by the truth of God's mercy, and (3) the appointment of Ezekiel as a watchman of judgment balanced by his role as a watchman of consolation. In writing to the Jews in exile, Ezekiel communicated that the God of Israel was God even in idolatrous Babylon. Ezekiel both warned the people that their own idolatry would be judged, and offered them the encouragement that the Lord would return them to their homeland.

The Living Creatures and the Glory of the LORD

1 In the[a] thirtieth year, in the fourth month on the fifth day, while I was among the exiles by the Kebar River, the heavens were opened and I saw visions of God.

2On the fifth of the month—it was the fifth year of the exile of King Jehoiachin— 3the word of the LORD came to Ezekiel the priest, the son of Buzi,[b] by the Kebar River in the land of the Babylonians.[c] There the hand of the LORD was upon him.

4I looked, and I saw a windstorm coming out of the north—an immense cloud with flashing lightning and surrounded by brilliant light. The center of the fire looked like glowing metal, 5and in the fire was what looked like four living creatures. In appearance their form was that of a man, 6but each of them had four faces and four wings. 7Their legs were straight; their feet were like those of a calf and gleamed like burnished bronze. 8Under their wings on their four sides they had the hands of a man. All four of them had faces and wings, 9and their wings touched one another. Each one went straight ahead; they did not turn as they moved.

10Their faces looked like this: Each of the four had the face of a man, and on the right side each had the face of a lion, and on the left the face of an ox; each also had the face of an eagle. 11Such were their faces. Their wings were spread out upward; each had two wings, one touching the wing of another creature on either side, and two wings covering its body. 12Each one went straight ahead. Wherever the spirit would go, they would go, without turning as they went. 13The appearance of the living creatures was like burning coals of fire or like torches. Fire moved back and forth among the creatures; it was bright, and lightning flashed out of it. 14The creatures sped back and forth like flashes of lightning.

15As I looked at the living creatures, I saw a wheel on the ground beside each creature with its four faces. 16This was the appearance and structure of the wheels: They sparkled like chrysolite, and all four looked alike. Each appeared to be made like a wheel intersecting a wheel. 17As they moved, they would go in any one of the four directions the creatures faced; the wheels did not turn about[d] as the creatures went. 18Their rims were high and awesome, and all four rims were full of eyes all around.

19When the living creatures moved, the wheels beside them moved; and when the living creatures rose from the ground, the wheels also rose. 20Wherever the spirit would go, they would go, and the wheels would rise along with them, because the spirit of the living creatures was in the wheels. 21When the creatures moved, they also moved; when the creatures stood still, they also stood still; and when the creatures rose from the ground, the wheels rose along with them, because the spirit of the living creatures was in the wheels.

22Spread out above the heads of the living creatures was what looked like an expanse, sparkling like ice, and awesome. 23Under the expanse their wings were stretched out one toward the other, and each had two wings covering its body. 24When the creatures moved, I heard the sound of their wings, like the roar of rushing waters, like the voice of the Almighty,[e] like the tumult of an army. When they stood still, they lowered their wings.

25Then there came a voice from above the expanse over their heads as they stood with lowered wings. 26Above the expanse over their heads was what looked like a throne of sapphire,[f] and high above on the throne was a figure like that of a man. 27I saw that from what appeared to be his waist up he looked like glowing metal, as if full of fire, and that from there down he looked like fire; and brilliant light surrounded him. 28Like the appearance of a rainbow in the clouds on a rainy day, so was the radiance around him.

This was the appearance of the likeness of the glory of the LORD. When I saw it, I fell facedown, and I heard the voice of one speaking.

Ezekiel's Call

2 He said to me, "Son of man, stand up on your feet and I will speak to you." 2As he spoke, the Spirit came into me and raised me to my feet, and I heard him speaking to me.

3He said: "Son of man, I am sending you to the Israelites, to a rebellious nation that has rebelled against me; they and their fathers have been in revolt against me to this very day. 4The people to whom I am sending you are obstinate and stubborn. Say to them, 'This is what the Sovereign LORD says.' 5And whether they listen or fail to listen—for they are a rebellious house—they will know that a prophet has been among them. 6And you, son of man, do not be afraid of them or their words. Do not be afraid, though briers and thorns are all around you and you live among scorpions. Do not be afraid of what they say or terrified by them, though they are a rebellious house. 7You must speak my words to them, whether they listen or fail to listen, for they are rebellious. 8But you, son of man, listen to what

a1 Or ⌊my⌋ b3 Or *Ezekiel son of Buzi the priest* c3 Or *Chaldeans* d17 Or *aside* e24 Hebrew *Shaddai*
f26 Or *lapis lazuli*

I say to you. Do not rebel like that rebellious
house; open your mouth and eat what I give
you."
[9]Then I looked, and I saw a hand stretched out
to me. In it was a scroll, [10]which he unrolled
before me. On both sides of it were written
words of lament and mourning and woe.

3 And he said to me, "Son of man, eat what is
before you, eat this scroll; then go and speak
to the house of Israel." [2]So I opened my mouth,
and he gave me the scroll to eat.
[3]Then he said to me, "Son of man, eat this
scroll I am giving you and fill your stomach with
it." So I ate it, and it tasted as sweet as honey in
my mouth.
[4]He then said to me: "Son of man, go now to
the house of Israel and speak my words to them.
[5]You are not being sent to a people of obscure
speech and difficult language, but to the house of
Israel— [6]not to many peoples of obscure speech
and difficult language, whose words you cannot
understand. Surely if I had sent you to them, they
would have listened to you. [7]But the house of
Israel is not willing to listen to you because they
are not willing to listen to me, for the whole
house of Israel is hardened and obstinate. [8]But I
will make you as unyielding and hardened as they
are. [9]I will make your forehead like the hardest
stone, harder than flint. Do not be afraid of them
or terrified by them, though they are a rebellious
house."
[10]And he said to me, "Son of man, listen carefully and take to heart all the words I speak to
you. [11]Go now to your countrymen in exile and
speak to them. Say to them, 'This is what the
Sovereign LORD says,' whether they listen or fail
to listen."
[12]Then the Spirit lifted me up, and I heard
behind me a loud rumbling sound—May the glory of the LORD be praised in his dwelling place!—
[13]the sound of the wings of the living creatures
brushing against each other and the sound of the
wheels beside them, a loud rumbling sound.
[14]The Spirit then lifted me up and took me away,
and I went in bitterness and in the anger of my
spirit, with the strong hand of the LORD upon me.
[15]I came to the exiles who lived at Tel Abib near
the Kebar River. And there, where they were
living, I sat among them for seven days—
overwhelmed.

Warning to Israel

[16]At the end of seven days the word of the
LORD came to me: [17]"Son of man, I have made
you a watchman for the house of Israel; so hear
the word I speak and give them warning from
me. [18]When I say to a wicked man, 'You will
surely die,' and you do not warn him or speak out
to dissuade him from his evil ways in order to
save his life, that wicked man will die for[a] his
sin, and I will hold you accountable for his blood.
[19]But if you do warn the wicked man and he does
not turn from his wickedness or from his evil
ways, he will die for his sin; but you will have
saved yourself.
[20]"Again, when a righteous man turns from
his righteousness and does evil, and I put a stumbling block before him, he will die. Since you did
not warn him, he will die for his sin. The righteous things he did will not be remembered, and
I will hold you accountable for his blood. [21]But if
you do warn the righteous man not to sin and he
does not sin, he will surely live because he took
warning, and you will have saved yourself."
[22]The hand of the LORD was upon me there,
and he said to me, "Get up and go out to the
plain, and there I will speak to you." [23]So I got up
and went out to the plain. And the glory of the
LORD was standing there, like the glory I had seen
by the Kebar River, and I fell facedown.
[24]Then the Spirit came into me and raised me
to my feet. He spoke to me and said: "Go, shut
yourself inside your house. [25]And you, son of
man, they will tie with ropes; you will be bound
so that you cannot go out among the people. [26]I
will make your tongue stick to the roof of your
mouth so that you will be silent and unable to
rebuke them, though they are a rebellious house.
[27]But when I speak to you, I will open your
mouth and you shall say to them, 'This is what
the Sovereign LORD says.' Whoever will listen let
him listen, and whoever will refuse let him refuse; for they are a rebellious house.

Siege of Jerusalem Symbolized

4 "Now, son of man, take a clay tablet, put it
in front of you and draw the city of Jerusalem
on it. [2]Then lay siege to it: Erect siege works
against it, build a ramp up to it, set up camps
against it and put battering rams around it. [3]Then
take an iron pan, place it as an iron wall between
you and the city and turn your face toward it. It
will be under siege, and you shall besiege it. This
will be a sign to the house of Israel.
[4]"Then lie on your left side and put the sin of
the house of Israel upon yourself.[b] You are to
bear their sin for the number of days you lie on
your side. [5]I have assigned you the same number
of days as the years of their sin. So for 390 days
you will bear the sin of the house of Israel.
[6]"After you have finished this, lie down again,
this time on your right side, and bear the sin of
the house of Judah. I have assigned you 40 days,
a day for each year. [7]Turn your face toward the

[a] *18* Or *in*; also in verses 19 and 20 [b] *4* Or *your side*

siege of Jerusalem and with bared arm prophesy
against her. 8I will tie you up with ropes so that
you cannot turn from one side to the other until
you have finished the days of your siege.
9"Take wheat and barley, beans and lentils,
millet and spelt; put them in a storage jar and use
them to make bread for yourself. You are to eat
it during the 390 days you lie on your side.
10Weigh out twenty shekels[a] of food to eat each
day and eat it at set times. 11Also measure out a
sixth of a hin[b] of water and drink it at set times.
12Eat the food as you would a barley cake; bake it
in the sight of the people, using human excrement for fuel." 13The LORD said, "In this way the
people of Israel will eat defiled food among the
nations where I will drive them."
14Then I said, "Not so, Sovereign LORD! I have
never defiled myself. From my youth until now I
have never eaten anything found dead or torn by
wild animals. No unclean meat has ever entered
my mouth."
15"Very well," he said, "I will let you bake
your bread over cow manure instead of human
excrement."
16He then said to me: "Son of man, I will cut
off the supply of food in Jerusalem. The people
will eat rationed food in anxiety and drink rationed water in despair, 17for food and water will
be scarce. They will be appalled at the sight of
each other and will waste away because of[c]
their sin.

5 "Now, son of man, take a sharp sword and
use it as a barber's razor to shave your head
and your beard. Then take a set of scales and
divide up the hair. 2When the days of your siege
come to an end, burn a third of the hair with fire
inside the city. Take a third and strike it with the
sword all around the city. And scatter a third to
the wind. For I will pursue them with drawn
sword. 3But take a few strands of hair and tuck
them away in the folds of your garment. 4Again,
take a few of these and throw them into the fire
and burn them up. A fire will spread from there
to the whole house of Israel.
5"This is what the Sovereign LORD says: This is
Jerusalem, which I have set in the center of the
nations, with countries all around her. 6Yet in
her wickedness she has rebelled against my laws
and decrees more than the nations and countries
around her. She has rejected my laws and has not
followed my decrees.
7"Therefore this is what the Sovereign LORD
says: You have been more unruly than the nations around you and have not followed my decrees or kept my laws. You have not even[d] conformed to the standards of the nations around
you.
8"Therefore this is what the Sovereign LORD
says: I myself am against you, Jerusalem, and I
will inflict punishment on you in the sight of the
nations. 9Because of all your detestable idols, I
will do to you what I have never done before and
will never do again. 10Therefore in your midst
fathers will eat their children, and children will
eat their fathers. I will inflict punishment on you
and will scatter all your survivors to the winds.
11Therefore as surely as I live, declares the Sovereign LORD, because you have defiled my sanctuary with all your vile images and detestable practices, I myself will withdraw my favor; I will not
look on you with pity or spare you. 12A third of
your people will die of the plague or perish by
famine inside you; a third will fall by the sword
outside your walls; and a third I will scatter to the
winds and pursue with drawn sword.
13"Then my anger will cease and my wrath
against them will subside, and I will be avenged.
And when I have spent my wrath upon them,
they will know that I the LORD have spoken in my
zeal.
14"I will make you a ruin and a reproach
among the nations around you, in the sight of
all who pass by. 15You will be a reproach and a
taunt, a warning and an object of horror to the
nations around you when I inflict punishment on
you in anger and in wrath and with stinging rebuke. I the LORD have spoken. 16When I shoot at
you with my deadly and destructive arrows of
famine, I will shoot to destroy you. I will bring
more and more famine upon you and cut off your
supply of food. 17I will send famine and wild
beasts against you, and they will leave you childless. Plague and bloodshed will sweep through
you, and I will bring the sword against you. I the
LORD have spoken."

A Prophecy Against the Mountains of Israel

6 The word of the LORD came to me: 2"Son
of man, set your face against the mountains
of Israel; prophesy against them 3and say:
'O mountains of Israel, hear the word of the Sovereign LORD. This is what the Sovereign LORD
says to the mountains and hills, to the ravines
and valleys: I am about to bring a sword against
you, and I will destroy your high places. 4Your
altars will be demolished and your incense altars
will be smashed; and I will slay your people in
front of your idols. 5I will lay the dead bodies of
the Israelites in front of their idols, and I will
scatter your bones around your altars. 6Wherever
you live, the towns will be laid waste and the

[a] 10 That is, about 8 ounces (about 0.2 kilogram) [b] 11 That is, about 2/3 quart (about 0.6 liter) [c] 17 Or *away in*
[d] 7 Most Hebrew manuscripts; some Hebrew manuscripts and Syriac *You have*

high places demolished, so that your altars will be
laid waste and devastated, your idols smashed
and ruined, your incense altars broken down,
and what you have made wiped out. 7Your people will fall slain among you, and you will know
that I am the LORD.
8" 'But I will spare some, for some of you will
escape the sword when you are scattered among
the lands and nations. 9Then in the nations
where they have been carried captive, those who
escape will remember me—how I have been
grieved by their adulterous hearts, which have
turned away from me, and by their eyes, which
have lusted after their idols. They will loathe
themselves for the evil they have done and for all
their detestable practices. 10And they will know
that I am the LORD; I did not threaten in vain to
bring this calamity on them.
11" 'This is what the Sovereign LORD says:
Strike your hands together and stamp your feet
and cry out "Alas!" because of all the wicked and
detestable practices of the house of Israel, for
they will fall by the sword, famine and plague.
12He that is far away will die of the plague, and
he that is near will fall by the sword, and he that
survives and is spared will die of famine. So will
I spend my wrath upon them. 13And they will
know that I am the LORD, when their people lie
slain among their idols around their altars, on
every high hill and on all the mountaintops, under every spreading tree and every leafy oak—
places where they offered fragrant incense to all
their idols. 14And I will stretch out my hand
against them and make the land a desolate waste
from the desert to Diblah[a]—wherever they live.
Then they will know that I am the LORD.' "

The End Has Come

7 The word of the LORD came to me: 2"Son of
man, this is what the Sovereign LORD says to
the land of Israel: The end! The end has come
upon the four corners of the land. 3The end is
now upon you and I will unleash my anger
against you. I will judge you according to your
conduct and repay you for all your detestable
practices. 4I will not look on you with pity or
spare you; I will surely repay you for your conduct and the detestable practices among you.
Then you will know that I am the LORD.
5"This is what the Sovereign LORD says: Disaster! An unheard-of[b] disaster is coming. 6The
end has come! The end has come! It has roused
itself against you. It has come! 7Doom has come
upon you—you who dwell in the land. The time
has come, the day is near; there is panic, not joy,
upon the mountains. 8I am about to pour out my
wrath on you and spend my anger against you; I
will judge you according to your conduct and repay you for all your detestable practices. 9I will
not look on you with pity or spare you; I will
repay you in accordance with your conduct and
the detestable practices among you. Then you
will know that it is I the LORD who strikes the
blow.
10"The day is here! It has come! Doom has
burst forth, the rod has budded, arrogance has
blossomed! 11Violence has grown into[c] a rod to
punish wickedness; none of the people will be
left, none of that crowd—no wealth, nothing of
value. 12The time has come, the day has arrived.
Let not the buyer rejoice nor the seller grieve, for
wrath is upon the whole crowd. 13The seller will
not recover the land he has sold as long as both
of them live, for the vision concerning the whole
crowd will not be reversed. Because of their sins,
not one of them will preserve his life. 14Though
they blow the trumpet and get everything ready,
no one will go into battle, for my wrath is upon
the whole crowd.
15"Outside is the sword, inside are plague and
famine; those in the country will die by the
sword, and those in the city will be devoured by
famine and plague. 16All who survive and escape
will be in the mountains, moaning like doves of
the valleys, each because of his sins. 17Every
hand will go limp, and every knee will become as
weak as water. 18They will put on sackcloth and
be clothed with terror. Their faces will be covered with shame and their heads will be shaved.
19They will throw their silver into the streets,
and their gold will be an unclean thing. Their
silver and gold will not be able to save them in
the day of the LORD's wrath. They will not satisfy
their hunger or fill their stomachs with it, for it
has made them stumble into sin. 20They were
proud of their beautiful jewelry and used it to
make their detestable idols and vile images.
Therefore I will turn these into an unclean thing
for them. 21I will hand it all over as plunder to
foreigners and as loot to the wicked of the earth,
and they will defile it. 22I will turn my face away
from them, and they will desecrate my treasured
place; robbers will enter it and desecrate it.
23"Prepare chains, because the land is full of
bloodshed and the city is full of violence. 24I will
bring the most wicked of the nations to take possession of their houses; I will put an end to the
pride of the mighty, and their sanctuaries will be
desecrated. 25When terror comes, they will seek
peace, but there will be none. 26Calamity upon
calamity will come, and rumor upon rumor. They
will try to get a vision from the prophet; the

[a] *14* Most Hebrew manuscripts; a few Hebrew manuscripts *Riblah* [b] *5* Most Hebrew manuscripts; some Hebrew manuscripts and Syriac *Disaster after* [c] *11* Or *The violent one has become*

teaching of the law by the priest will be lost, as will the counsel of the elders. 27The king will mourn, the prince will be clothed with despair, and the hands of the people of the land will tremble. I will deal with them according to their conduct, and by their own standards I will judge them. Then they will know that I am the LORD."

Idolatry in the Temple

8 In the sixth year, in the sixth month on the fifth day, while I was sitting in my house and the elders of Judah were sitting before me, the hand of the Sovereign LORD came upon me there. 2I looked, and I saw a figure like that of a man.[a] From what appeared to be his waist down he was like fire, and from there up his appearance was as bright as glowing metal. 3He stretched out what looked like a hand and took me by the hair of my head. The Spirit lifted me up between earth and heaven and in visions of God he took me to Jerusalem, to the entrance to the north gate of the inner court, where the idol that provokes to jealousy stood. 4And there before me was the glory of the God of Israel, as in the vision I had seen in the plain.

5Then he said to me, "Son of man, look toward the north." So I looked, and in the entrance north of the gate of the altar I saw this idol of jealousy.

6And he said to me, "Son of man, do you see what they are doing—the utterly detestable things the house of Israel is doing here, things that will drive me far from my sanctuary? But you will see things that are even more detestable."

7Then he brought me to the entrance to the court. I looked, and I saw a hole in the wall. 8He said to me, "Son of man, now dig into the wall." So I dug into the wall and saw a doorway there.

9And he said to me, "Go in and see the wicked and detestable things they are doing here." 10So I went in and looked, and I saw portrayed all over the walls all kinds of crawling things and detestable animals and all the idols of the house of Israel. 11In front of them stood seventy elders of the house of Israel, and Jaazaniah son of Shaphan was standing among them. Each had a censer in his hand, and a fragrant cloud of incense was rising.

12He said to me, "Son of man, have you seen what the elders of the house of Israel are doing in the darkness, each at the shrine of his own idol? They say, 'The LORD does not see us; the LORD has forsaken the land.'" 13Again, he said, "You will see them doing things that are even more detestable."

14Then he brought me to the entrance to the north gate of the house of the LORD, and I saw women sitting there, mourning for Tammuz. 15He said to me, "Do you see this, son of man? You will see things that are even more detestable than this."

16He then brought me into the inner court of the house of the LORD, and there at the entrance to the temple, between the portico and the altar, were about twenty-five men. With their backs toward the temple of the LORD and their faces toward the east, they were bowing down to the sun in the east.

17He said to me, "Have you seen this, son of man? Is it a trivial matter for the house of Judah to do the detestable things they are doing here? Must they also fill the land with violence and continually provoke me to anger? Look at them putting the branch to their nose! 18Therefore I will deal with them in anger; I will not look on them with pity or spare them. Although they shout in my ears, I will not listen to them."

Idolaters Killed

9 Then I heard him call out in a loud voice, "Bring the guards of the city here, each with a weapon in his hand." 2And I saw six men coming from the direction of the upper gate, which faces north, each with a deadly weapon in his hand. With them was a man clothed in linen who had a writing kit at his side. They came in and stood beside the bronze altar.

3Now the glory of the God of Israel went up from above the cherubim, where it had been, and moved to the threshold of the temple. Then the LORD called to the man clothed in linen who had the writing kit at his side 4and said to him, "Go throughout the city of Jerusalem and put a mark on the foreheads of those who grieve and lament over all the detestable things that are done in it."

5As I listened, he said to the others, "Follow him through the city and kill, without showing pity or compassion. 6Slaughter old men, young men and maidens, women and children, but do not touch anyone who has the mark. Begin at my sanctuary." So they began with the elders who were in front of the temple.

7Then he said to them, "Defile the temple and fill the courts with the slain. Go!" So they went out and began killing throughout the city. 8While they were killing and I was left alone, I fell facedown, crying out, "Ah, Sovereign LORD! Are you going to destroy the entire remnant of Israel in this outpouring of your wrath on Jerusalem?"

9He answered me, "The sin of the house of Israel and Judah is exceedingly great; the land is full of bloodshed and the city is full of injustice. They say, 'The LORD has forsaken the land; the LORD does not see.' 10So I will not look on them

a2 Or *saw a fiery figure*

with pity or spare them, but I will bring down on their own heads what they have done."

11Then the man in linen with the writing kit at his side brought back word, saying, "I have done as you commanded."

The Glory Departs From the Temple

10 I looked, and I saw the likeness of a throne of sapphire[a] above the expanse that was over the heads of the cherubim. 2The LORD said to the man clothed in linen, "Go in among the wheels beneath the cherubim. Fill your hands with burning coals from among the cherubim and scatter them over the city." And as I watched, he went in.

3Now the cherubim were standing on the south side of the temple when the man went in, and a cloud filled the inner court. 4Then the glory of the LORD rose from above the cherubim and moved to the threshold of the temple. The cloud filled the temple, and the court was full of the radiance of the glory of the LORD. 5The sound of the wings of the cherubim could be heard as far away as the outer court, like the voice of God Almighty[b] when he speaks.

6When the LORD commanded the man in linen, "Take fire from among the wheels, from among the cherubim," the man went in and stood beside a wheel. 7Then one of the cherubim reached out his hand to the fire that was among them. He took up some of it and put it into the hands of the man in linen, who took it and went out. 8(Under the wings of the cherubim could be seen what looked like the hands of a man.)

9I looked, and I saw beside the cherubim four wheels, one beside each of the cherubim; the wheels sparkled like chrysolite. 10As for their appearance, the four of them looked alike; each was like a wheel intersecting a wheel. 11As they moved, they would go in any one of the four directions the cherubim faced; the wheels did not turn about[c] as the cherubim went. The cherubim went in whatever direction the head faced, without turning as they went. 12Their entire bodies, including their backs, their hands and their wings, were completely full of eyes, as were their four wheels. 13I heard the wheels being called "the whirling wheels." 14Each of the cherubim had four faces: One face was that of a cherub, the second the face of a man, the third the face of a lion, and the fourth the face of an eagle.

15Then the cherubim rose upward. These were the living creatures I had seen by the Kebar River. 16When the cherubim moved, the wheels beside them moved; and when the cherubim spread their wings to rise from the ground, the wheels did not leave their side. 17When the cherubim stood still, they also stood still; and when the cherubim rose, they rose with them, because the spirit of the living creatures was in them.

18Then the glory of the LORD departed from over the threshold of the temple and stopped above the cherubim. 19While I watched, the cherubim spread their wings and rose from the ground, and as they went, the wheels went with them. They stopped at the entrance to the east gate of the LORD's house, and the glory of the God of Israel was above them.

20These were the living creatures I had seen beneath the God of Israel by the Kebar River, and I realized that they were cherubim. 21Each had four faces and four wings, and under their wings was what looked like the hands of a man. 22Their faces had the same appearance as those I had seen by the Kebar River. Each one went straight ahead.

Judgment on Israel's Leaders

11 Then the Spirit lifted me up and brought me to the gate of the house of the LORD that faces east. There at the entrance to the gate were twenty-five men, and I saw among them Jaazaniah son of Azzur and Pelatiah son of Benaiah, leaders of the people. 2The LORD said to me, "Son of man, these are the men who are plotting evil and giving wicked advice in this city. 3They say, 'Will it not soon be time to build houses?[d] This city is a cooking pot, and we are the meat.' 4Therefore prophesy against them; prophesy, son of man."

5Then the Spirit of the LORD came upon me, and he told me to say: "This is what the LORD says: That is what you are saying, O house of Israel, but I know what is going through your mind. 6You have killed many people in this city and filled its streets with the dead.

7"Therefore this is what the Sovereign LORD says: The bodies you have thrown there are the meat and this city is the pot, but I will drive you out of it. 8You fear the sword, and the sword is what I will bring against you, declares the Sovereign LORD. 9I will drive you out of the city and hand you over to foreigners and inflict punishment on you. 10You will fall by the sword, and I will execute judgment on you at the borders of Israel. Then you will know that I am the LORD. 11This city will not be a pot for you, nor will you be the meat in it; I will execute judgment on you at the borders of Israel. 12And you will know that I am the LORD, for you have not followed my decrees or kept my laws but have conformed to the standards of the nations around you."

13Now as I was prophesying, Pelatiah son of Benaiah died. Then I fell facedown and cried out

[a] *1* Or *lapis lazuli* [b] *5* Hebrew *El-Shaddai* [c] *11* Or *aside* [d] *3* Or *This is not the time to build houses.*

in a loud voice, "Ah, Sovereign LORD! Will you
completely destroy the remnant of Israel?"
14The word of the LORD came to me: 15"Son of
man, your brothers—your brothers who are your
blood relatives[a] and the whole house of Israel—
are those of whom the people of Jerusalem have
said, 'They are[b] far away from the LORD; this
land was given to us as our possession.'

Promised Return of Israel

16"Therefore say: 'This is what the Sovereign
LORD says: Although I sent them far away among
the nations and scattered them among the countries, yet for a little while I have been a sanctuary
for them in the countries where they have gone.'
17"Therefore say: 'This is what the Sovereign
LORD says: I will gather you from the nations and
bring you back from the countries where you
have been scattered, and I will give you back the
land of Israel again.'
18"They will return to it and remove all its vile
images and detestable idols. 19I will give them an
undivided heart and put a new spirit in them; I
will remove from them their heart of stone and
give them a heart of flesh. 20Then they will follow
my decrees and be careful to keep my laws. They
will be my people, and I will be their God. 21But
as for those whose hearts are devoted to their vile
images and detestable idols, I will bring down on
their own heads what they have done, declares
the Sovereign LORD."
22Then the cherubim, with the wheels beside
them, spread their wings, and the glory of the
God of Israel was above them. 23The glory of the
LORD went up from within the city and stopped
above the mountain east of it. 24The Spirit lifted
me up and brought me to the exiles in Babylonia[c] in the vision given by the Spirit of God.
Then the vision I had seen went up from me,
25and I told the exiles everything the LORD had
shown me.

The Exile Symbolized

12 The word of the LORD came to me: 2"Son
of man, you are living among a rebellious
people. They have eyes to see but do not see and
ears to hear but do not hear, for they are a rebellious people.
3"Therefore, son of man, pack your belongings
for exile and in the daytime, as they watch, set
out and go from where you are to another place.
Perhaps they will understand, though they are
a rebellious house. 4During the daytime, while
they watch, bring out your belongings packed for
exile. Then in the evening, while they are watching, go out like those who go into exile. 5While
they watch, dig through the wall and take your
belongings out through it. 6Put them on your
shoulder as they are watching and carry them out
at dusk. Cover your face so that you cannot see
the land, for I have made you a sign to the house
of Israel."
7So I did as I was commanded. During the day
I brought out my things packed for exile. Then
in the evening I dug through the wall with my
hands. I took my belongings out at dusk, carrying
them on my shoulders while they watched.
8In the morning the word of the LORD came to
me: 9"Son of man, did not that rebellious house
of Israel ask you, 'What are you doing?'
10"Say to them, 'This is what the Sovereign
LORD says: This oracle concerns the prince in
Jerusalem and the whole house of Israel who are
there.' 11Say to them, 'I am a sign to you.'
"As I have done, so it will be done to them.
They will go into exile as captives.
12"The prince among them will put his things
on his shoulder at dusk and leave, and a hole will
be dug in the wall for him to go through. He will
cover his face so that he cannot see the land. 13I
will spread my net for him, and he will be caught
in my snare; I will bring him to Babylonia, the
land of the Chaldeans, but he will not see it, and
there he will die. 14I will scatter to the winds all
those around him—his staff and all his troops—
and I will pursue them with drawn sword.
15"They will know that I am the LORD, when
I disperse them among the nations and scatter
them through the countries. 16But I will spare a
few of them from the sword, famine and plague,
so that in the nations where they go they may
acknowledge all their detestable practices. Then
they will know that I am the LORD."
17The word of the LORD came to me: 18"Son of
man, tremble as you eat your food, and shudder
in fear as you drink your water. 19Say to the people of the land: 'This is what the Sovereign LORD
says about those living in Jerusalem and in the
land of Israel: They will eat their food in anxiety
and drink their water in despair, for their land
will be stripped of everything in it because of the
violence of all who live there. 20The inhabited
towns will be laid waste and the land will be
desolate. Then you will know that I am the
LORD.'"
21The word of the LORD came to me: 22"Son of
man, what is this proverb you have in the land of
Israel: 'The days go by and every vision comes to
nothing'? 23Say to them, 'This is what the Sovereign LORD says: I am going to put an end to this
proverb, and they will no longer quote it in Israel.' Say to them, 'The days are near when every

[a] 15 Or *are in exile with you* (see Septuagint and Syriac)
[b] 15 Or *those to whom the people of Jerusalem have said, 'Stay*
[c] 24 Or *Chaldea*

vision will be fulfilled. [24]For there will be no
more false visions or flattering divinations among
the people of Israel. [25]But I the LORD will speak
what I will, and it shall be fulfilled without delay.
For in your days, you rebellious house, I will fulfill whatever I say, declares the Sovereign
LORD.' "

[26]The word of the LORD came to me: [27]"Son of
man, the house of Israel is saying, 'The vision he
sees is for many years from now, and he prophesies about the distant future.'

[28]"Therefore say to them, 'This is what the
Sovereign LORD says: None of my words will be
delayed any longer; whatever I say will be fulfilled, declares the Sovereign LORD.' "

False Prophets Condemned

13 The word of the LORD came to me: [2]"Son
of man, prophesy against the prophets of
Israel who are now prophesying. Say to those
who prophesy out of their own imagination:
'Hear the word of the LORD! [3]This is what the
Sovereign LORD says: Woe to the foolish[a] prophets who follow their own spirit and have seen
nothing! [4]Your prophets, O Israel, are like jackals
among ruins. [5]You have not gone up to the
breaks in the wall to repair it for the house of
Israel so that it will stand firm in the battle on the
day of the LORD. [6]Their visions are false and their
divinations a lie. They say, "The LORD declares,"
when the LORD has not sent them; yet they expect their words to be fulfilled. [7]Have you not
seen false visions and uttered lying divinations
when you say, "The LORD declares," though I
have not spoken?

[8]" 'Therefore this is what the Sovereign LORD
says: Because of your false words and lying visions, I am against you, declares the Sovereign
LORD. [9]My hand will be against the prophets who
see false visions and utter lying divinations. They
will not belong to the council of my people or be
listed in the records of the house of Israel, nor
will they enter the land of Israel. Then you will
know that I am the Sovereign LORD.

[10]" 'Because they lead my people astray, saying, "Peace," when there is no peace, and because, when a flimsy wall is built, they cover it
with whitewash, [11]therefore tell those who cover
it with whitewash that it is going to fall. Rain will
come in torrents, and I will send hailstones hur-
tling down, and violent winds will burst forth.
[12]When the wall collapses, will people not ask
you, "Where is the whitewash you covered it
with?"

[13]" 'Therefore this is what the Sovereign LORD
says: In my wrath I will unleash a violent wind,
and in my anger hailstones and torrents of rain
will fall with destructive fury. [14]I will tear down
the wall you have covered with whitewash and
will level it to the ground so that its foundation
will be laid bare. When it[b] falls, you will be
destroyed in it; and you will know that I am the
LORD. [15]So I will spend my wrath against the wall
and against those who covered it with whitewash. I will say to you, "The wall is gone and so
are those who whitewashed it, [16]those prophets
of Israel who prophesied to Jerusalem and saw
visions of peace for her when there was no peace,
declares the Sovereign LORD." '

[17]"Now, son of man, set your face against the
daughters of your people who prophesy out of
their own imagination. Prophesy against them
[18]and say, 'This is what the Sovereign LORD says:
Woe to the women who sew magic charms on all
their wrists and make veils of various lengths for
their heads in order to ensnare people. Will you
ensnare the lives of my people but preserve your
own? [19]You have profaned me among my people
for a few handfuls of barley and scraps of bread.
By lying to my people, who listen to lies, you
have killed those who should not have died and
have spared those who should not live.

[20]" 'Therefore this is what the Sovereign LORD
says: I am against your magic charms with which
you ensnare people like birds and I will tear them
from your arms; I will set free the people that you
ensnare like birds. [21]I will tear off your veils and
save my people from your hands, and they will no
longer fall prey to your power. Then you will
know that I am the LORD. [22]Because you disheartened the righteous with your lies, when I had
brought them no grief, and because you encouraged the wicked not to turn from their evil ways
and so save their lives, [23]therefore you will no
longer see false visions or practice divination. I
will save my people from your hands. And then
you will know that I am the LORD.' "

Idolaters Condemned

14 Some of the elders of Israel came to me
and sat down in front of me. [2]Then the
word of the LORD came to me: [3]"Son of man,
these men have set up idols in their hearts and
put wicked stumbling blocks before their faces.
Should I let them inquire of me at all? [4]Therefore
speak to them and tell them, 'This is what the
Sovereign LORD says: When any Israelite sets up
idols in his heart and puts a wicked stumbling
block before his face and then goes to a prophet,
I the LORD will answer him myself in keeping
with his great idolatry. [5]I will do this to recapture
the hearts of the people of Israel, who have all
deserted me for their idols.'

[6]"Therefore say to the house of Israel, 'This is

[a]3 Or *wicked* [b]14 Or *the city*

what the Sovereign LORD says: Repent! Turn from
your idols and renounce all your detestable practices!
7“‘When any Israelite or any alien living in
Israel separates himself from me and sets up idols
in his heart and puts a wicked stumbling block
before his face and then goes to a prophet to
inquire of me, I the LORD will answer him myself.
8I will set my face against that man and make him
an example and a byword. I will cut him off from
my people. Then you will know that I am the
LORD.
9“‘And if the prophet is enticed to utter a
prophecy, I the LORD have enticed that prophet,
and I will stretch out my hand against him and
destroy him from among my people Israel. 10They
will bear their guilt—the prophet will be as
guilty as the one who consults him. 11Then the
people of Israel will no longer stray from me, nor
will they defile themselves anymore with all their
sins. They will be my people, and I will be their
God, declares the Sovereign LORD.’”

Judgment Inescapable

12The word of the LORD came to me: 13“Son of
man, if a country sins against me by being unfaithful and I stretch out my hand against it to cut
off its food supply and send famine upon it and
kill its men and their animals, 14even if these
three men—Noah, Daniel[a] and Job—were in it,
they could save only themselves by their righteousness, declares the Sovereign LORD.
15“Or if I send wild beasts through that country and they leave it childless and it becomes
desolate so that no one can pass through it because of the beasts, 16as surely as I live, declares
the Sovereign LORD, even if these three men
were in it, they could not save their own sons or
daughters. They alone would be saved, but the
land would be desolate.
17“Or if I bring a sword against that country
and say, ‘Let the sword pass throughout the
land,’ and I kill its men and their animals, 18as
surely as I live, declares the Sovereign LORD,
even if these three men were in it, they could not
save their own sons or daughters. They alone
would be saved.
19“Or if I send a plague into that land and pour
out my wrath upon it through bloodshed, killing
its men and their animals, 20as surely as I live,
declares the Sovereign LORD, even if Noah, Daniel and Job were in it, they could save neither son
nor daughter. They would save only themselves
by their righteousness.
21“For this is what the Sovereign LORD says:
How much worse will it be when I send against
Jerusalem my four dreadful judgments—sword
and famine and wild beasts and plague—to kill
its men and their animals! 22Yet there will be
some survivors—sons and daughters who will be
brought out of it. They will come to you, and
when you see their conduct and their actions,
you will be consoled regarding the disaster I have
brought upon Jerusalem—every disaster I have
brought upon it. 23You will be consoled when
you see their conduct and their actions, for you
will know that I have done nothing in it without
cause, declares the Sovereign LORD.”

Jerusalem, A Useless Vine

15 The word of the LORD came to me: 2“Son
of man, how is the wood of a vine better
than that of a branch on any of the trees in the
forest? 3Is wood ever taken from it to make anything useful? Do they make pegs from it to hang
things on? 4And after it is thrown on the fire as
fuel and the fire burns both ends and chars the
middle, is it then useful for anything? 5If it was
not useful for anything when it was whole, how
much less can it be made into something useful
when the fire has burned it and it is charred?
6“Therefore this is what the Sovereign LORD
says: As I have given the wood of the vine among
the trees of the forest as fuel for the fire, so will
I treat the people living in Jerusalem. 7I will set
my face against them. Although they have come
out of the fire, the fire will yet consume them.
And when I set my face against them, you will
know that I am the LORD. 8I will make the land
desolate because they have been unfaithful, declares the Sovereign LORD.”

An Allegory of Unfaithful Jerusalem

16 The word of the LORD came to me: 2“Son
of man, confront Jerusalem with her detestable practices 3and say, ‘This is what the Sovereign LORD says to Jerusalem: Your ancestry and
birth were in the land of the Canaanites; your
father was an Amorite and your mother a Hittite.
4On the day you were born your cord was not
cut, nor were you washed with water to make
you clean, nor were you rubbed with salt or
wrapped in cloths. 5No one looked on you with
pity or had compassion enough to do any of these
things for you. Rather, you were thrown out into
the open field, for on the day you were born you
were despised.
6“‘Then I passed by and saw you kicking about
in your blood, and as you lay there in your blood
I said to you, “Live!”[b] 7I made you grow like a
plant of the field. You grew up and developed and

[a] 14 Or *Daniel*; the Hebrew spelling may suggest a person other than the prophet Daniel; also in verse 20. [b] 6 A few Hebrew manuscripts, Septuagint and Syriac; most Hebrew manuscripts *“Live!” And as you lay there in your blood I said to you, “Live!”*

became the most beautiful of jewels.[a] Your breasts were formed and your hair grew, you who were naked and bare.

8"'Later I passed by, and when I looked at you and saw that you were old enough for love, I spread the corner of my garment over you and covered your nakedness. I gave you my solemn oath and entered into a covenant with you, declares the Sovereign LORD, and you became mine.

9"'I bathed[b] you with water and washed the blood from you and put ointments on you. 10I clothed you with an embroidered dress and put leather sandals on you. I dressed you in fine linen and covered you with costly garments. 11I adorned you with jewelry: I put bracelets on your arms and a necklace around your neck, 12and I put a ring on your nose, earrings on your ears and a beautiful crown on your head. 13So you were adorned with gold and silver; your clothes were of fine linen and costly fabric and embroidered cloth. Your food was fine flour, honey and olive oil. You became very beautiful and rose to be a queen. 14And your fame spread among the nations on account of your beauty, because the splendor I had given you made your beauty perfect, declares the Sovereign LORD.

15"'But you trusted in your beauty and used your fame to become a prostitute. You lavished your favors on anyone who passed by and your beauty became his.[c] 16You took some of your garments to make gaudy high places, where you carried on your prostitution. Such things should not happen, nor should they ever occur. 17You also took the fine jewelry I gave you, the jewelry made of my gold and silver, and you made for yourself male idols and engaged in prostitution with them. 18And you took your embroidered clothes to put on them, and you offered my oil and incense before them. 19Also the food I provided for you—the fine flour, olive oil and honey I gave you to eat—you offered as fragrant incense before them. That is what happened, declares the Sovereign LORD.

20"'And you took your sons and daughters whom you bore to me and sacrificed them as food to the idols. Was your prostitution not enough? 21You slaughtered my children and sacrificed them[d] to the idols. 22In all your detestable practices and your prostitution you did not remember the days of your youth, when you were naked and bare, kicking about in your blood.

23"'Woe! Woe to you, declares the Sovereign LORD. In addition to all your other wickedness, 24you built a mound for yourself and made a lofty shrine in every public square. 25At the head of every street you built your lofty shrines and degraded your beauty, offering your body with increasing promiscuity to anyone who passed by. 26You engaged in prostitution with the Egyptians, your lustful neighbors, and provoked me to anger with your increasing promiscuity. 27So I stretched out my hand against you and reduced your territory; I gave you over to the greed of your enemies, the daughters of the Philistines, who were shocked by your lewd conduct. 28You engaged in prostitution with the Assyrians too, because you were insatiable; and even after that, you still were not satisfied. 29Then you increased your promiscuity to include Babylonia,[e] a land of merchants, but even with this you were not satisfied.

30"'How weak-willed you are, declares the Sovereign LORD, when you do all these things, acting like a brazen prostitute! 31When you built your mounds at the head of every street and made your lofty shrines in every public square, you were unlike a prostitute, because you scorned payment.

32"'You adulterous wife! You prefer strangers to your own husband! 33Every prostitute receives a fee, but you give gifts to all your lovers, bribing them to come to you from everywhere for your illicit favors. 34So in your prostitution you are the opposite of others; no one runs after you for your favors. You are the very opposite, for you give payment and none is given to you.

35"'Therefore, you prostitute, hear the word of the LORD! 36This is what the Sovereign LORD says: Because you poured out your wealth[f] and exposed your nakedness in your promiscuity with your lovers, and because of all your detestable idols, and because you gave them your children's blood, 37therefore I am going to gather all your lovers, with whom you found pleasure, those you loved as well as those you hated. I will gather them against you from all around and will strip you in front of them, and they will see all your nakedness. 38I will sentence you to the punishment of women who commit adultery and who shed blood; I will bring upon you the blood vengeance of my wrath and jealous anger. 39Then I will hand you over to your lovers, and they will tear down your mounds and destroy your lofty shrines. They will strip you of your clothes and take your fine jewelry and leave you naked and bare. 40They will bring a mob against you, who will stone you and hack you to pieces with their swords. 41They will burn down your houses and inflict punishment on you in the sight of many women. I will put a stop to your prostitution, and

[a] 7 Or *became mature* [b] 9 Or *I had bathed* [c] 15 Most Hebrew manuscripts; one Hebrew manuscript (see some Septuagint manuscripts) *by. Such a thing should not happen* [d] 21 Or *and made them pass through* ⌊*the fire*⌋ [e] 29 Or *Chaldea* [f] 36 Or *lust*

you will no longer pay your lovers. 42Then my wrath against you will subside and my jealous anger will turn away from you; I will be calm and no longer angry.

43" 'Because you did not remember the days of your youth but enraged me with all these things, I will surely bring down on your head what you have done, declares the Sovereign LORD. Did you not add lewdness to all your other detestable practices?

44" 'Everyone who quotes proverbs will quote this proverb about you: "Like mother, like daughter." 45You are a true daughter of your mother, who despised her husband and her children; and you are a true sister of your sisters, who despised their husbands and their children. Your mother was a Hittite and your father an Amorite. 46Your older sister was Samaria, who lived to the north of you with her daughters; and your younger sister, who lived to the south of you with her daughters, was Sodom. 47You not only walked in their ways and copied their detestable practices, but in all your ways you soon became more depraved than they. 48As surely as I live, declares the Sovereign LORD, your sister Sodom and her daughters never did what you and your daughters have done.

49" 'Now this was the sin of your sister Sodom: She and her daughters were arrogant, overfed and unconcerned; they did not help the poor and needy. 50They were haughty and did detestable things before me. Therefore I did away with them as you have seen. 51Samaria did not commit half the sins you did. You have done more detestable things than they, and have made your sisters seem righteous by all these things you have done. 52Bear your disgrace, for you have furnished some justification for your sisters. Because your sins were more vile than theirs, they appear more righteous than you. So then, be ashamed and bear your disgrace, for you have made your sisters appear righteous.

53" 'However, I will restore the fortunes of Sodom and her daughters and of Samaria and her daughters, and your fortunes along with them, 54so that you may bear your disgrace and be ashamed of all you have done in giving them comfort. 55And your sisters, Sodom with her daughters and Samaria with her daughters, will return to what they were before; and you and your daughters will return to what you were before. 56You would not even mention your sister Sodom in the day of your pride, 57before your wickedness was uncovered. Even so, you are now scorned by the daughters of Edom[a] and all her neighbors and the daughters of the Philistines—all those around you who despise you. 58You will bear the consequences of your lewdness and your detestable practices, declares the LORD.

59" 'This is what the Sovereign LORD says: I will deal with you as you deserve, because you have despised my oath by breaking the covenant. 60Yet I will remember the covenant I made with you in the days of your youth, and I will establish an everlasting covenant with you. 61Then you will remember your ways and be ashamed when you receive your sisters, both those who are older than you and those who are younger. I will give them to you as daughters, but not on the basis of my covenant with you. 62So I will establish my covenant with you, and you will know that I am the LORD. 63Then, when I make atonement for you for all you have done, you will remember and be ashamed and never again open your mouth because of your humiliation, declares the Sovereign LORD.' "

Two Eagles and a Vine

17 The word of the LORD came to me: 2"Son of man, set forth an allegory and tell the house of Israel a parable. 3Say to them, 'This is what the Sovereign LORD says: A great eagle with powerful wings, long feathers and full plumage of varied colors came to Lebanon. Taking hold of the top of a cedar, 4he broke off its topmost shoot and carried it away to a land of merchants, where he planted it in a city of traders.

5" 'He took some of the seed of your land and put it in fertile soil. He planted it like a willow by abundant water, 6and it sprouted and became a low, spreading vine. Its branches turned toward him, but its roots remained under it. So it became a vine and produced branches and put out leafy boughs.

7" 'But there was another great eagle with powerful wings and full plumage. The vine now sent out its roots toward him from the plot where it was planted and stretched out its branches to him for water. 8It had been planted in good soil by abundant water so that it would produce branches, bear fruit and become a splendid vine.'

9"Say to them, 'This is what the Sovereign LORD says: Will it thrive? Will it not be uprooted and stripped of its fruit so that it withers? All its new growth will wither. It will not take a strong arm or many people to pull it up by the roots. 10Even if it is transplanted, will it thrive? Will it not wither completely when the east wind strikes it—wither away in the plot where it grew?' "

11Then the word of the LORD came to me: 12"Say to this rebellious house, 'Do you not know what these things mean?' Say to them: 'The king of Babylon went to Jerusalem and carried off her

[a]57 Many Hebrew manuscripts and Syriac; most Hebrew manuscripts, Septuagint and Vulgate *Aram*

king and her nobles, bringing them back with
him to Babylon. 13Then he took a member of the
royal family and made a treaty with him, putting
him under oath. He also carried away the leading
men of the land, 14so that the kingdom would be
brought low, unable to rise again, surviving only
by keeping his treaty. 15But the king rebelled
against him by sending his envoys to Egypt to get
horses and a large army. Will he succeed? Will he
who does such things escape? Will he break the
treaty and yet escape?

16" 'As surely as I live, declares the Sovereign
LORD, he shall die in Babylon, in the land of the
king who put him on the throne, whose oath he
despised and whose treaty he broke. 17Pharaoh
with his mighty army and great horde will be of
no help to him in war, when ramps are built and
siege works erected to destroy many lives. 18He
despised the oath by breaking the covenant. Because he had given his hand in pledge and yet did
all these things, he shall not escape.

19" 'Therefore this is what the Sovereign LORD
says: As surely as I live, I will bring down on his
head my oath that he despised and my covenant
that he broke. 20I will spread my net for him, and
he will be caught in my snare. I will bring him to
Babylon and execute judgment upon him there
because he was unfaithful to me. 21All his fleeing
troops will fall by the sword, and the survivors
will be scattered to the winds. Then you will
know that I the LORD have spoken.

22" 'This is what the Sovereign LORD says: I
myself will take a shoot from the very top of a
cedar and plant it; I will break off a tender sprig
from its topmost shoots and plant it on a high and
lofty mountain. 23On the mountain heights of Israel I will plant it; it will produce branches and
bear fruit and become a splendid cedar. Birds of
every kind will nest in it; they will find shelter in
the shade of its branches. 24All the trees of the
field will know that I the LORD bring down the
tall tree and make the low tree grow tall. I dry up
the green tree and make the dry tree flourish.

" 'I the LORD have spoken, and I will do it.' "

The Soul Who Sins Will Die

18 The word of the LORD came to me:
2"What do you people mean by quoting
this proverb about the land of Israel:

" 'The fathers eat sour grapes,
and the children's teeth are set on edge'?

3"As surely as I live, declares the Sovereign
LORD, you will no longer quote this proverb in
Israel. 4For every living soul belongs to me, the
father as well as the son—both alike belong to
me. The soul who sins is the one who will die.

5"Suppose there is a righteous man
who does what is just and right.
6He does not eat at the mountain shrines
or look to the idols of the house of Israel.
He does not defile his neighbor's wife
or lie with a woman during her period.
7He does not oppress anyone,
but returns what he took in pledge for a loan.
He does not commit robbery
but gives his food to the hungry
and provides clothing for the naked.
8He does not lend at usury
or take excessive interest.[a]
He withholds his hand from doing wrong
and judges fairly between man and man.
9He follows my decrees
and faithfully keeps my laws.
That man is righteous;
he will surely live,
declares the Sovereign LORD.

10"Suppose he has a violent son, who sheds
blood or does any of these other things[b]
11(though the father has done none of them):

"He eats at the mountain shrines.
He defiles his neighbor's wife.
12He oppresses the poor and needy.
He commits robbery.
He does not return what he took in pledge.
He looks to the idols.
He does detestable things.
13He lends at usury and takes excessive interest.

Will such a man live? He will not! Because he has
done all these detestable things, he will surely be
put to death and his blood will be on his own
head.

14"But suppose this son has a son who sees all
the sins his father commits, and though he sees
them, he does not do such things:

15"He does not eat at the mountain shrines
or look to the idols of the house of Israel.
He does not defile his neighbor's wife.
16He does not oppress anyone
or require a pledge for a loan.
He does not commit robbery
but gives his food to the hungry
and provides clothing for the naked.
17He withholds his hand from sin[c]

[a]8 Or *take interest*; similarly in verses 13 and 17 [b]10 Or *things to a brother* [c]17 Septuagint (see also verse 8); Hebrew *from the poor*

and takes no usury or excessive interest.
He keeps my laws and follows my decrees.
He will not die for his father's sin; he will surely
live. 18But his father will die for his own sin,
because he practiced extortion, robbed his brother and did what was wrong among his people.
19"Yet you ask, 'Why does the son not share
the guilt of his father?' Since the son has done
what is just and right and has been careful to
keep all my decrees, he will surely live. 20The
soul who sins is the one who will die. The son
will not share the guilt of the father, nor will the
father share the guilt of the son. The righteousness of the righteous man will be credited to him,
and the wickedness of the wicked will be charged
against him.
21"But if a wicked man turns away from all the
sins he has committed and keeps all my decrees
and does what is just and right, he will surely
live; he will not die. 22None of the offenses he
has committed will be remembered against him.
Because of the righteous things he has done, he
will live. 23Do I take any pleasure in the death of
the wicked? declares the Sovereign LORD. Rather,
am I not pleased when they turn from their ways
and live?
24"But if a righteous man turns from his righteousness and commits sin and does the same
detestable things the wicked man does, will he
live? None of the righteous things he has done
will be remembered. Because of the unfaithfulness he is guilty of and because of the sins he has
committed, he will die.
25"Yet you say, 'The way of the Lord is not
just.' Hear, O house of Israel: Is my way unjust?
Is it not your ways that are unjust? 26If a righteous man turns from his righteousness and commits sin, he will die for it; because of the sin he
has committed he will die. 27But if a wicked man
turns away from the wickedness he has committed and does what is just and right, he will save
his life. 28Because he considers all the offenses he
has committed and turns away from them, he
will surely live; he will not die. 29Yet the house
of Israel says, 'The way of the Lord is not just.'
Are my ways unjust, O house of Israel? Is it not
your ways that are unjust?
30"Therefore, O house of Israel, I will judge
you, each one according to his ways, declares the
Sovereign LORD. Repent! Turn away from all your
offenses; then sin will not be your downfall. 31Rid
yourselves of all the offenses you have committed, and get a new heart and a new spirit. Why
will you die, O house of Israel? 32For I take no
pleasure in the death of anyone, declares the Sovereign LORD. Repent and live!

A Lament for Israel's Princes

19 "Take up a lament concerning the princes
of Israel 2and say:

"'What a lioness was your mother
among the lions!
She lay down among the young lions
and reared her cubs.
3She brought up one of her cubs,
and he became a strong lion.
He learned to tear the prey
and he devoured men.
4The nations heard about him,
and he was trapped in their pit.
They led him with hooks
to the land of Egypt.
5"'When she saw her hope unfulfilled,
her expectation gone,
she took another of her cubs
and made him a strong lion.
6He prowled among the lions,
for he was now a strong lion.
He learned to tear the prey
and he devoured men.
7He broke down[a] their strongholds
and devastated their towns.
The land and all who were in it
were terrified by his roaring.
8Then the nations came against him,
those from regions round about.
They spread their net for him,
and he was trapped in their pit.
9With hooks they pulled him into a cage
and brought him to the king of Babylon.
They put him in prison,
so his roar was heard no longer
on the mountains of Israel.

10"'Your mother was like a vine in your
vineyard[b]
planted by the water;
it was fruitful and full of branches
because of abundant water.
11Its branches were strong,
fit for a ruler's scepter.
It towered high
above the thick foliage,
conspicuous for its height
and for its many branches.
12But it was uprooted in fury
and thrown to the ground.
The east wind made it shrivel,
it was stripped of its fruit;
its strong branches withered
and fire consumed them.
13Now it is planted in the desert,
in a dry and thirsty land.

[a]7 Targum (see Septuagint); Hebrew *He knew*
[b]10 Two Hebrew manuscripts; most Hebrew manuscripts *your blood*

14 Fire spread from one of its main[a] branches
and consumed its fruit.
No strong branch is left on it
fit for a ruler's scepter.'
This is a lament and is to be used as a lament."

Rebellious Israel

20 In the seventh year, in the fifth month on
the tenth day, some of the elders of Israel
came to inquire of the LORD, and they sat down
in front of me.
2 Then the word of the LORD came to me:
3 "Son of man, speak to the elders of Israel and say
to them, 'This is what the Sovereign LORD says:
Have you come to inquire of me? As surely as I
live, I will not let you inquire of me, declares the
Sovereign LORD.'
4 "Will you judge them? Will you judge them,
son of man? Then confront them with the detestable practices of their fathers 5 and say to them:
'This is what the Sovereign LORD says: On the day
I chose Israel, I swore with uplifted hand to the
descendants of the house of Jacob and revealed
myself to them in Egypt. With uplifted hand I said
to them, "I am the LORD your God." 6 On that day
I swore to them that I would bring them out of
Egypt into a land I had searched out for them, a
land flowing with milk and honey, the most beautiful of all lands. 7 And I said to them, "Each of
you, get rid of the vile images you have set your
eyes on, and do not defile yourselves with the
idols of Egypt. I am the LORD your God."
8 " 'But they rebelled against me and would not
listen to me; they did not get rid of the vile images they had set their eyes on, nor did they
forsake the idols of Egypt. So I said I would pour
out my wrath on them and spend my anger
against them in Egypt. 9 But for the sake of my
name I did what would keep it from being profaned in the eyes of the nations they lived among
and in whose sight I had revealed myself to the
Israelites by bringing them out of Egypt. 10 Therefore I led them out of Egypt and brought them
into the desert. 11 I gave them my decrees and
made known to them my laws, for the man who
obeys them will live by them. 12 Also I gave them
my Sabbaths as a sign between us, so they would
know that I the LORD made them holy.
13 " 'Yet the people of Israel rebelled against me
in the desert. They did not follow my decrees but
rejected my laws—although the man who obeys
them will live by them—and they utterly desecrated my Sabbaths. So I said I would pour out my
wrath on them and destroy them in the desert.
14 But for the sake of my name I did what would
keep it from being profaned in the eyes of the
nations in whose sight I had brought them out.
15 Also with uplifted hand I swore to them in the
desert that I would not bring them into the land
I had given them—a land flowing with milk and
honey, most beautiful of all lands— 16 because
they rejected my laws and did not follow my decrees and desecrated my Sabbaths. For their
hearts were devoted to their idols. 17 Yet I looked
on them with pity and did not destroy them or
put an end to them in the desert. 18 I said to their
children in the desert, "Do not follow the statutes
of your fathers or keep their laws or defile yourselves with their idols. 19 I am the LORD your God;
follow my decrees and be careful to keep my
laws. 20 Keep my Sabbaths holy, that they may be
a sign between us. Then you will know that I am
the LORD your God."
21 " 'But the children rebelled against me: They
did not follow my decrees, they were not careful
to keep my laws—although the man who obeys
them will live by them—and they desecrated my
Sabbaths. So I said I would pour out my wrath on
them and spend my anger against them in the
desert. 22 But I withheld my hand, and for the
sake of my name I did what would keep it from
being profaned in the eyes of the nations in
whose sight I had brought them out. 23 Also with
uplifted hand I swore to them in the desert that
I would disperse them among the nations and
scatter them through the countries, 24 because
they had not obeyed my laws but had rejected my
decrees and desecrated my Sabbaths, and their
eyes ⌞lusted⌟ after their fathers' idols. 25 I also
gave them over to statutes that were not good
and laws they could not live by; 26 I let them become defiled through their gifts—the sacrifice of
every firstborn[b]—that I might fill them with
horror so they would know that I am the LORD.'
27 "Therefore, son of man, speak to the people
of Israel and say to them, 'This is what the Sovereign LORD says: In this also your fathers blasphemed me by forsaking me: 28 When I brought
them into the land I had sworn to give them and
they saw any high hill or any leafy tree, there
they offered their sacrifices, made offerings that
provoked me to anger, presented their fragrant
incense and poured out their drink offerings.
29 Then I said to them: What is this high place you
go to?'" (It is called Bamah[c] to this day.)

Judgment and Restoration

30 "Therefore say to the house of Israel: 'This is
what the Sovereign LORD says: Will you defile
yourselves the way your fathers did and lust after
their vile images? 31 When you offer your gifts—
the sacrifice of your sons in[d] the fire—you con-

[a] 14 Or *from under its* [b] 26 Or *—making every firstborn pass through ⌞the fire⌟* [c] 29 *Bamah* means *high place.*
[d] 31 Or *—making your sons pass through*

tinue to defile yourselves with all your idols to
this day. Am I to let you inquire of me, O house
of Israel? As surely as I live, declares the Sovereign LORD, I will not let you inquire of me.
32“ ‘You say, “We want to be like the nations,
like the peoples of the world, who serve wood
and stone.” But what you have in mind will never
happen. 33As surely as I live, declares the Sovereign LORD, I will rule over you with a mighty
hand and an outstretched arm and with outpoured wrath. 34I will bring you from the nations
and gather you from the countries where you
have been scattered—with a mighty hand and an
outstretched arm and with outpoured wrath. 35I
will bring you into the desert of the nations and
there, face to face, I will execute judgment upon
you. 36As I judged your fathers in the desert of
the land of Egypt, so I will judge you, declares the
Sovereign LORD. 37I will take note of you as you
pass under my rod, and I will bring you into the
bond of the covenant. 38I will purge you of those
who revolt and rebel against me. Although I will
bring them out of the land where they are living,
yet they will not enter the land of Israel. Then
you will know that I am the LORD.
39“ ‘As for you, O house of Israel, this is what
the Sovereign LORD says: Go and serve your idols,
every one of you! But afterward you will surely
listen to me and no longer profane my holy name
with your gifts and idols. 40For on my holy mountain, the high mountain of Israel, declares the
Sovereign LORD, there in the land the entire
house of Israel will serve me, and there I will
accept them. There I will require your offerings
and your choice gifts,[a] along with all your holy
sacrifices. 41I will accept you as fragrant incense
when I bring you out from the nations and gather
you from the countries where you have been
scattered, and I will show myself holy among you
in the sight of the nations. 42Then you will know
that I am the LORD, when I bring you into the
land of Israel, the land I had sworn with uplifted
hand to give to your fathers. 43There you will
remember your conduct and all the actions by
which you have defiled yourselves, and you will
loathe yourselves for all the evil you have done.
44You will know that I am the LORD, when I deal
with you for my name's sake and not according
to your evil ways and your corrupt practices,
O house of Israel, declares the Sovereign LORD.’ ”

Prophecy Against the South

45The word of the LORD came to me: 46“Son
of man, set your face toward the south; preach
against the south and prophesy against the forest
of the southland. 47Say to the southern forest:
‘Hear the word of the LORD. This is what the
Sovereign LORD says: I am about to set fire to you,
and it will consume all your trees, both green and
dry. The blazing flame will not be quenched, and
every face from south to north will be scorched
by it. 48Everyone will see that I the LORD have
kindled it; it will not be quenched.’ ”
49Then I said, “Ah, Sovereign LORD! They are
saying of me, ‘Isn't he just telling parables?’ ”

Babylon, God's Sword of Judgment

21 The word of the LORD came to me: 2“Son
of man, set your face against Jerusalem
and preach against the sanctuary. Prophesy
against the land of Israel 3and say to her: ‘This is
what the LORD says: I am against you. I will draw
my sword from its scabbard and cut off from you
both the righteous and the wicked. 4Because I am
going to cut off the righteous and the wicked, my
sword will be unsheathed against everyone from
south to north. 5Then all people will know that I
the LORD have drawn my sword from its scabbard; it will not return again.’
6“Therefore groan, son of man! Groan before
them with broken heart and bitter grief. 7And
when they ask you, ‘Why are you groaning?’ you
shall say, ‘Because of the news that is coming.
Every heart will melt and every hand go limp;
every spirit will become faint and every knee become as weak as water.’ It is coming! It will surely take place, declares the Sovereign LORD.”
8The word of the LORD came to me: 9“Son of
man, prophesy and say, ‘This is what the Lord
says:

“ ‘A sword, a sword,
  sharpened and polished—
10sharpened for the slaughter,
  polished to flash like lightning!

“ ‘Shall we rejoice in the scepter of my son ⌞Judah⌟? The sword despises every such stick.

11“ ‘The sword is appointed to be polished,
  to be grasped with the hand;
it is sharpened and polished,
  made ready for the hand of the slayer.
12Cry out and wail, son of man,
  for it is against my people;
  it is against all the princes of Israel.
They are thrown to the sword
  along with my people.
Therefore beat your breast.

13“ ‘Testing will surely come. And what if the
scepter ⌞of Judah⌟, which the sword despises,
does not continue? declares the Sovereign LORD.’

14“So then, son of man, prophesy
  and strike your hands together.

[a]40 Or *and the gifts of your firstfruits*

Let the sword strike twice,
even three times.
It is a sword for slaughter—
a sword for great slaughter,
closing in on them from every side.
15So that hearts may melt
and the fallen be many,
I have stationed the sword for slaughter[a]
at all their gates.
Oh! It is made to flash like lightning,
it is grasped for slaughter.
16O sword, slash to the right,
then to the left,
wherever your blade is turned.
17I too will strike my hands together,
and my wrath will subside.
I the LORD have spoken."

18The word of the LORD came to me: 19"Son of
man, mark out two roads for the sword of the
king of Babylon to take, both starting from the
same country. Make a signpost where the road
branches off to the city. 20Mark out one road for
the sword to come against Rabbah of the Ammonites and another against Judah and fortified Jerusalem. 21For the king of Babylon will stop at the
fork in the road, at the junction of the two roads,
to seek an omen: He will cast lots with arrows, he
will consult his idols, he will examine the liver.
22Into his right hand will come the lot for Jerusalem, where he is to set up battering rams, to give
the command to slaughter, to sound the battle
cry, to set battering rams against the gates, to
build a ramp and to erect siege works. 23It will
seem like a false omen to those who have sworn
allegiance to him, but he will remind them of
their guilt and take them captive.

24"Therefore this is what the Sovereign LORD
says: 'Because you people have brought to mind
your guilt by your open rebellion, revealing your
sins in all that you do—because you have done
this, you will be taken captive.

25" 'O profane and wicked prince of Israel,
whose day has come, whose time of punishment
has reached its climax, 26this is what the Sovereign LORD says: Take off the turban, remove the
crown. It will not be as it was: The lowly will be
exalted and the exalted will be brought low. 27A
ruin! A ruin! I will make it a ruin! It will not be
restored until he comes to whom it rightfully belongs; to him I will give it.'

28"And you, son of man, prophesy and say,
'This is what the Sovereign LORD says about the
Ammonites and their insults:

" 'A sword, a sword,
drawn for the slaughter,
polished to consume
and to flash like lightning!
29Despite false visions concerning you
and lying divinations about you,
it will be laid on the necks
of the wicked who are to be slain,
whose day has come,
whose time of punishment has reached its
climax.
30Return the sword to its scabbard.
In the place where you were created,
in the land of your ancestry,
I will judge you.
31I will pour out my wrath upon you
and breathe out my fiery anger against
you;
I will hand you over to brutal men,
men skilled in destruction.
32You will be fuel for the fire,
your blood will be shed in your land,
you will be remembered no more;
for I the LORD have spoken.' "

Jerusalem's Sins

22 The word of the LORD came to me: 2"Son
of man, will you judge her? Will you judge
this city of bloodshed? Then confront her with all
her detestable practices 3and say: 'This is what
the Sovereign LORD says: O city that brings on
herself doom by shedding blood in her midst and
defiles herself by making idols, 4you have become
guilty because of the blood you have shed and
have become defiled by the idols you have made.
You have brought your days to a close, and the
end of your years has come. Therefore I will
make you an object of scorn to the nations and a
laughingstock to all the countries. 5Those who
are near and those who are far away will mock
you, O infamous city, full of turmoil.

6" 'See how each of the princes of Israel who
are in you uses his power to shed blood. 7In you
they have treated father and mother with contempt; in you they have oppressed the alien and
mistreated the fatherless and the widow. 8You
have despised my holy things and desecrated my
Sabbaths. 9In you are slanderous men bent on
shedding blood; in you are those who eat at the
mountain shrines and commit lewd acts. 10In you
are those who dishonor their fathers' bed; in you
are those who violate women during their period, when they are ceremonially unclean. 11In you
one man commits a detestable offense with his
neighbor's wife, another shamefully defiles his
daughter-in-law, and another violates his sister,
his own father's daughter. 12In you men accept
bribes to shed blood; you take usury and excessive interest[b] and make unjust gain from your

[a] *15* Septuagint; the meaning of the Hebrew for this word is uncertain.
[b] *12* Or *usury and interest*

neighbors by extortion. And you have forgotten
me, declares the Sovereign LORD.
13"'I will surely strike my hands together at
the unjust gain you have made and at the blood
you have shed in your midst. 14Will your courage
endure or your hands be strong in the day I deal
with you? I the LORD have spoken, and I will do
it. 15I will disperse you among the nations and
scatter you through the countries; and I will put
an end to your uncleanness. 16When you have
been defiled[a] in the eyes of the nations, you will
know that I am the LORD.'"
17Then the word of the LORD came to me:
18"Son of man, the house of Israel has become
dross to me; all of them are the copper, tin, iron
and lead left inside a furnace. They are but the
dross of silver. 19Therefore this is what the Sovereign LORD says: 'Because you have all become
dross, I will gather you into Jerusalem. 20As men
gather silver, copper, iron, lead and tin into a
furnace to melt it with a fiery blast, so will I
gather you in my anger and my wrath and put you
inside the city and melt you. 21I will gather you
and I will blow on you with my fiery wrath, and
you will be melted inside her. 22As silver is melted in a furnace, so you will be melted inside her,
and you will know that I the LORD have poured
out my wrath upon you.'"
23Again the word of the LORD came to me:
24"Son of man, say to the land, 'You are a land
that has had no rain or showers[b] in the day of
wrath.' 25There is a conspiracy of her princes[c]
within her like a roaring lion tearing its prey;
they devour people, take treasures and precious
things and make many widows within her. 26Her
priests do violence to my law and profane my
holy things; they do not distinguish between the
holy and the common; they teach that there is no
difference between the unclean and the clean;
and they shut their eyes to the keeping of my
Sabbaths, so that I am profaned among them.
27Her officials within her are like wolves tearing
their prey; they shed blood and kill people to
make unjust gain. 28Her prophets whitewash
these deeds for them by false visions and lying
divinations. They say, 'This is what the Sovereign
LORD says'—when the LORD has not spoken.
29The people of the land practice extortion and
commit robbery; they oppress the poor and
needy and mistreat the alien, denying them justice.
30"I looked for a man among them who would
build up the wall and stand before me in the gap
on behalf of the land so I would not have to
destroy it, but I found none. 31So I will pour out
my wrath on them and consume them with my
fiery anger, bringing down on their own heads all
they have done, declares the Sovereign LORD."

Two Adulterous Sisters

23 The word of the LORD came to me: 2"Son
of man, there were two women, daughters of the same mother. 3They became prostitutes in Egypt, engaging in prostitution from their
youth. In that land their breasts were fondled and
their virgin bosoms caressed. 4The older was
named Oholah, and her sister was Oholibah.
They were mine and gave birth to sons and
daughters. Oholah is Samaria, and Oholibah is
Jerusalem.
5"Oholah engaged in prostitution while she
was still mine; and she lusted after her lovers, the
Assyrians—warriors 6clothed in blue, governors
and commanders, all of them handsome young
men, and mounted horsemen. 7She gave herself
as a prostitute to all the elite of the Assyrians and
defiled herself with all the idols of everyone she
lusted after. 8She did not give up the prostitution
she began in Egypt, when during her youth men
slept with her, caressed her virgin bosom and
poured out their lust upon her.
9"Therefore I handed her over to her lovers,
the Assyrians, for whom she lusted. 10They
stripped her naked, took away her sons and
daughters and killed her with the sword. She became a byword among women, and punishment
was inflicted on her.
11"Her sister Oholibah saw this, yet in her lust
and prostitution she was more depraved than her
sister. 12She too lusted after the Assyrians—
governors and commanders, warriors in full
dress, mounted horsemen, all handsome young
men. 13I saw that she too defiled herself; both of
them went the same way.
14"But she carried her prostitution still further. She saw men portrayed on a wall, figures
of Chaldeans[d] portrayed in red, 15with belts
around their waists and flowing turbans on their
heads; all of them looked like Babylonian chariot
officers, natives of Chaldea.[e] 16As soon as she
saw them, she lusted after them and sent messengers to them in Chaldea. 17Then the Babylonians
came to her, to the bed of love, and in their lust
they defiled her. After she had been defiled by
them, she turned away from them in disgust.
18When she carried on her prostitution openly
and exposed her nakedness, I turned away from
her in disgust, just as I had turned away from her
sister. 19Yet she became more and more promiscuous as she recalled the days of her youth, when
she was a prostitute in Egypt. 20There she lusted
after her lovers, whose genitals were like those

[a] 16 Or *When I have allotted you your inheritance* [b] 24 Septuagint; Hebrew *has not been cleansed or rained on*
[c] 25 Septuagint; Hebrew *prophets* [d] 14 Or *Babylonians* [e] 15 Or *Babylonia*; also in verse 16

of donkeys and whose emission was like that of
horses. 21So you longed for the lewdness of your
youth, when in Egypt your bosom was caressed
and your young breasts fondled.[a]
22"Therefore, Oholibah, this is what the Sovereign LORD says: I will stir up your lovers against
you, those you turned away from in disgust, and
I will bring them against you from every side—
23the Babylonians and all the Chaldeans, the men
of Pekod and Shoa and Koa, and all the Assyrians
with them, handsome young men, all of them
governors and commanders, chariot officers and
men of high rank, all mounted on horses. 24They
will come against you with weapons,[b] chariots
and wagons and with a throng of people; they
will take up positions against you on every side
with large and small shields and with helmets. I
will turn you over to them for punishment, and
they will punish you according to their standards.
25I will direct my jealous anger against you, and
they will deal with you in fury. They will cut off
your noses and your ears, and those of you who
are left will fall by the sword. They will take away
your sons and daughters, and those of you who
are left will be consumed by fire. 26They will also
strip you of your clothes and take your fine jewelry. 27So I will put a stop to the lewdness and
prostitution you began in Egypt. You will not look
on these things with longing or remember Egypt
anymore.
28"For this is what the Sovereign LORD says: I
am about to hand you over to those you hate, to
those you turned away from in disgust. 29They
will deal with you in hatred and take away everything you have worked for. They will leave you
naked and bare, and the shame of your prostitution will be exposed. Your lewdness and promiscuity 30have brought this upon you, because you
lusted after the nations and defiled yourself with
their idols. 31You have gone the way of your sister; so I will put her cup into your hand.
32"This is what the Sovereign LORD says:

"You will drink your sister's cup,
a cup large and deep;
it will bring scorn and derision,
for it holds so much.
33You will be filled with drunkenness and
sorrow,
the cup of ruin and desolation,
the cup of your sister Samaria.
34You will drink it and drain it dry;
you will dash it to pieces
and tear your breasts.

I have spoken, declares the Sovereign LORD.

35"Therefore this is what the Sovereign LORD
says: Since you have forgotten me and thrust me
behind your back, you must bear the consequences of your lewdness and prostitution."
36The LORD said to me: "Son of man, will you
judge Oholah and Oholibah? Then confront them
with their detestable practices, 37for they have
committed adultery and blood is on their hands.
They committed adultery with their idols; they
even sacrificed their children, whom they bore to
me,[c] as food for them. 38They have also done
this to me: At that same time they defiled my
sanctuary and desecrated my Sabbaths. 39On the
very day they sacrificed their children to their
idols, they entered my sanctuary and desecrated
it. That is what they did in my house.
40"They even sent messengers for men who
came from far away, and when they arrived you
bathed yourself for them, painted your eyes and
put on your jewelry. 41You sat on an elegant
couch, with a table spread before it on which you
had placed the incense and oil that belonged
to me.
42"The noise of a carefree crowd was around
her; Sabeans[d] were brought from the desert
along with men from the rabble, and they put
bracelets on the arms of the woman and her sister and beautiful crowns on their heads. 43Then
I said about the one worn out by adultery, 'Now
let them use her as a prostitute, for that is all she
is.' 44And they slept with her. As men sleep with
a prostitute, so they slept with those lewd wom-
en, Oholah and Oholibah. 45But righteous men
will sentence them to the punishment of women
who commit adultery and shed blood, because
they are adulterous and blood is on their hands.
46"This is what the Sovereign LORD says: Bring
a mob against them and give them over to terror
and plunder. 47The mob will stone them and cut
them down with their swords; they will kill their
sons and daughters and burn down their houses.
48"So I will put an end to lewdness in the land,
that all women may take warning and not imitate
you. 49You will suffer the penalty for your lewdness and bear the consequences of your sins of
idolatry. Then you will know that I am the Sovereign LORD."

The Cooking Pot

24 In the ninth year, in the tenth month on
the tenth day, the word of the LORD came
to me: 2"Son of man, record this date, this very
date, because the king of Babylon has laid siege
to Jerusalem this very day. 3Tell this rebellious
house a parable and say to them: 'This is what the
Sovereign LORD says:

" 'Put on the cooking pot; put it on

[a] *21* Syriac (see also verse 3); Hebrew *caressed because of your young breasts* [b] *24* The meaning of the Hebrew for this word is uncertain. [c] *37* Or *even made the children they bore to me pass through ⌊the fire⌋* [d] *42* Or *drunkards*

and pour water into it.
4Put into it the pieces of meat,
all the choice pieces—the leg and the
shoulder.
Fill it with the best of these bones;
5 take the pick of the flock.
Pile wood beneath it for the bones;
bring it to a boil
and cook the bones in it.

6" 'For this is what the Sovereign LORD says:

" 'Woe to the city of bloodshed,
to the pot now encrusted,
whose deposit will not go away!
Empty it piece by piece
without casting lots for them.

7" 'For the blood she shed is in her midst:
She poured it on the bare rock;
she did not pour it on the ground,
where the dust would cover it.
8To stir up wrath and take revenge
I put her blood on the bare rock,
so that it would not be covered.

9" 'Therefore this is what the Sovereign LORD
says:

" 'Woe to the city of bloodshed!
I, too, will pile the wood high.
10So heap on the wood
and kindle the fire.
Cook the meat well,
mixing in the spices;
and let the bones be charred.
11Then set the empty pot on the coals
till it becomes hot and its copper glows
so its impurities may be melted
and its deposit burned away.
12It has frustrated all efforts;
its heavy deposit has not been removed,
not even by fire.

13" 'Now your impurity is lewdness. Because
I tried to cleanse you but you would not be
cleansed from your impurity, you will not be
clean again until my wrath against you has subsided.

14" 'I the LORD have spoken. The time has
come for me to act. I will not hold back; I will not
have pity, nor will I relent. You will be judged
according to your conduct and your actions, declares the Sovereign LORD.' "

Ezekiel's Wife Dies

15The word of the LORD came to me: 16"Son of
man, with one blow I am about to take away from
you the delight of your eyes. Yet do not lament or
weep or shed any tears. 17Groan quietly; do not
mourn for the dead. Keep your turban fastened
and your sandals on your feet; do not cover the
lower part of your face or eat the customary food
⌞of mourners⌟."

18So I spoke to the people in the morning, and
in the evening my wife died. The next morning
I did as I had been commanded.

19Then the people asked me, "Won't you tell
us what these things have to do with us?"

20So I said to them, "The word of the LORD
came to me: 21Say to the house of Israel, 'This is
what the Sovereign LORD says: I am about to desecrate my sanctuary—the stronghold in which
you take pride, the delight of your eyes, the object of your affection. The sons and daughters you
left behind will fall by the sword. 22And you will
do as I have done. You will not cover the lower
part of your face or eat the customary food ⌞of
mourners⌟. 23You will keep your turbans on your
heads and your sandals on your feet. You will not
mourn or weep but will waste away because of[a]
your sins and groan among yourselves. 24Ezekiel
will be a sign to you; you will do just as he has
done. When this happens, you will know that I
am the Sovereign LORD.'

25"And you, son of man, on the day I take away
their stronghold, their joy and glory, the delight
of their eyes, their heart's desire, and their sons
and daughters as well— 26on that day a fugitive
will come to tell you the news. 27At that time
your mouth will be opened; you will speak with
him and will no longer be silent. So you will be
a sign to them, and they will know that I am the
LORD."

A Prophecy Against Ammon

25 The word of the LORD came to me: 2"Son
of man, set your face against the Ammonites and prophesy against them. 3Say to them,
'Hear the word of the Sovereign LORD. This is
what the Sovereign LORD says: Because you said
"Aha!" over my sanctuary when it was desecrated and over the land of Israel when it was laid
waste and over the people of Judah when they
went into exile, 4therefore I am going to give you
to the people of the East as a possession. They
will set up their camps and pitch their tents
among you; they will eat your fruit and drink
your milk. 5I will turn Rabbah into a pasture for
camels and Ammon into a resting place for sheep.
Then you will know that I am the LORD. 6For this
is what the Sovereign LORD says: Because you
have clapped your hands and stamped your feet,
rejoicing with all the malice of your heart against
the land of Israel, 7therefore I will stretch out my
hand against you and give you as plunder to the

[a] 23 Or *away in*

nations. I will cut you off from the nations and
exterminate you from the countries. I will destroy you, and you will know that I am the
LORD.’”

A Prophecy Against Moab

8“This is what the Sovereign LORD says: ‘Because Moab and Seir said, “Look, the house of
Judah has become like all the other nations,”
9therefore I will expose the flank of Moab, beginning at its frontier towns—Beth Jeshimoth, Baal
Meon and Kiriathaim—the glory of that land. 10I
will give Moab along with the Ammonites to the
people of the East as a possession, so that the
Ammonites will not be remembered among
the nations; 11and I will inflict punishment on
Moab. Then they will know that I am the LORD.’”

A Prophecy Against Edom

12“This is what the Sovereign LORD says: ‘Because Edom took revenge on the house of Judah
and became very guilty by doing so, 13therefore
this is what the Sovereign LORD says: I will
stretch out my hand against Edom and kill its
men and their animals. I will lay it waste, and
from Teman to Dedan they will fall by the sword.
14I will take vengeance on Edom by the hand of
my people Israel, and they will deal with Edom in
accordance with my anger and my wrath; they
will know my vengeance, declares the Sovereign
LORD.’”

A Prophecy Against Philistia

15“This is what the Sovereign LORD says: ‘Because the Philistines acted in vengeance and took
revenge with malice in their hearts, and with
ancient hostility sought to destroy Judah, 16there-
fore this is what the Sovereign LORD says: I am
about to stretch out my hand against the Philistines, and I will cut off the Kerethites and destroy
those remaining along the coast. 17I will carry out
great vengeance on them and punish them in my
wrath. Then they will know that I am the LORD,
when I take vengeance on them.’”

A Prophecy Against Tyre

26 In the eleventh year, on the first day of
the month, the word of the LORD came to
me: 2“Son of man, because Tyre has said of Jerusalem, ‘Aha! The gate to the nations is broken,
and its doors have swung open to me; now that
she lies in ruins I will prosper,’ 3therefore this is
what the Sovereign LORD says: I am against you,
O Tyre, and I will bring many nations against
you, like the sea casting up its waves. 4They will
destroy the walls of Tyre and pull down her towers; I will scrape away her rubble and make her
a bare rock. 5Out in the sea she will become a
place to spread fishnets, for I have spoken, declares the Sovereign LORD. She will become plunder for the nations, 6and her settlements on the
mainland will be ravaged by the sword. Then
they will know that I am the LORD.

7“For this is what the Sovereign LORD says:
From the north I am going to bring against Tyre
Nebuchadnezzar[a] king of Babylon, king of
kings, with horses and chariots, with horsemen
and a great army. 8He will ravage your settlements on the mainland with the sword; he will
set up siege works against you, build a ramp up
to your walls and raise his shields against you.
9He will direct the blows of his battering rams
against your walls and demolish your towers with
his weapons. 10His horses will be so many that
they will cover you with dust. Your walls will
tremble at the noise of the war horses, wagons
and chariots when he enters your gates as men
enter a city whose walls have been broken
through. 11The hoofs of his horses will trample all
your streets; he will kill your people with the
sword, and your strong pillars will fall to the
ground. 12They will plunder your wealth and loot
your merchandise; they will break down your
walls and demolish your fine houses and throw
your stones, timber and rubble into the sea. 13I
will put an end to your noisy songs, and the music of your harps will be heard no more. 14I will
make you a bare rock, and you will become a
place to spread fishnets. You will never be rebuilt, for I the LORD have spoken, declares the
Sovereign LORD.

15“This is what the Sovereign LORD says to
Tyre: Will not the coastlands tremble at the
sound of your fall, when the wounded groan and
the slaughter takes place in you? 16Then all the
princes of the coast will step down from their
thrones and lay aside their robes and take off
their embroidered garments. Clothed with terror, they will sit on the ground, trembling every
moment, appalled at you. 17Then they will take
up a lament concerning you and say to you:

“‘How you are destroyed, O city of renown,
    peopled by men of the sea!
You were a power on the seas,
    you and your citizens;
you put your terror
    on all who lived there.
18Now the coastlands tremble
    on the day of your fall;
the islands in the sea
    are terrified at your collapse.’

19“This is what the Sovereign LORD says:
When I make you a desolate city, like cities no

[a]7 Hebrew *Nebuchadrezzar,* of which *Nebuchadnezzar* is a variant; here and often in Ezekiel and Jeremiah

longer inhabited, and when I bring the ocean
depths over you and its vast waters cover you,
20then I will bring you down with those who go
down to the pit, to the people of long ago. I will
make you dwell in the earth below, as in ancient
ruins, with those who go down to the pit, and
you will not return or take your place[a] in the
land of the living. 21I will bring you to a horrible
end and you will be no more. You will be sought,
but you will never again be found, declares the
Sovereign LORD."

A Lament for Tyre

27 The word of the LORD came to me: 2"Son
of man, take up a lament concerning
Tyre. 3Say to Tyre, situated at the gateway to the
sea, merchant of peoples on many coasts, 'This is
what the Sovereign LORD says:

" 'You say, O Tyre,
"I am perfect in beauty."
4Your domain was on the high seas;
your builders brought your beauty to perfection.
5They made all your timbers
of pine trees from Senir[b];
they took a cedar from Lebanon
to make a mast for you.
6Of oaks from Bashan
they made your oars;
of cypress wood[c] from the coasts of Cyprus[d]
they made your deck, inlaid with ivory.
7Fine embroidered linen from Egypt was your sail
and served as your banner;
your awnings were of blue and purple
from the coasts of Elishah.
8Men of Sidon and Arvad were your oarsmen;
your skilled men, O Tyre, were aboard as your seamen.
9Veteran craftsmen of Gebal[e] were on board
as shipwrights to caulk your seams.
All the ships of the sea and their sailors
came alongside to trade for your wares.

10" 'Men of Persia, Lydia and Put
served as soldiers in your army.
They hung their shields and helmets on your walls,
bringing you splendor.
11Men of Arvad and Helech
manned your walls on every side;
men of Gammad
were in your towers.
They hung their shields around your walls;
they brought your beauty to perfection.

12" 'Tarshish did business with you because of
your great wealth of goods; they exchanged silver, iron, tin and lead for your merchandise.
13" 'Greece, Tubal and Meshech traded with
you; they exchanged slaves and articles of bronze
for your wares.
14" 'Men of Beth Togarmah exchanged work
horses, war horses and mules for your merchandise.
15" 'The men of Rhodes[f] traded with you, and
many coastlands were your customers; they paid
you with ivory tusks and ebony.
16" 'Aram[g] did business with you because of
your many products; they exchanged turquoise,
purple fabric, embroidered work, fine linen, coral
and rubies for your merchandise.
17" 'Judah and Israel traded with you; they exchanged wheat from Minnith and confections,[h]
honey, oil and balm for your wares.
18" 'Damascus, because of your many products
and great wealth of goods, did business with you
in wine from Helbon and wool from Zahar.
19" 'Danites and Greeks from Uzal bought your
merchandise; they exchanged wrought iron, cassia and calamus for your wares.
20" 'Dedan traded in saddle blankets with you.
21" 'Arabia and all the princes of Kedar were
your customers; they did business with you in
lambs, rams and goats.
22" 'The merchants of Sheba and Raamah traded with you; for your merchandise they exchanged the finest of all kinds of spices and precious stones, and gold.
23" 'Haran, Canneh and Eden and merchants
of Sheba, Asshur and Kilmad traded with you.
24In your marketplace they traded with you beautiful garments, blue fabric, embroidered work
and multicolored rugs with cords twisted and
tightly knotted.

25" 'The ships of Tarshish serve
as carriers for your wares.
You are filled with heavy cargo
in the heart of the sea.
26Your oarsmen take you
out to the high seas.
But the east wind will break you to pieces
in the heart of the sea.
27Your wealth, merchandise and wares,
your mariners, seamen and shipwrights,
your merchants and all your soldiers,
and everyone else on board
will sink into the heart of the sea

a20 Septuagint; Hebrew *return, and I will give glory* b5 That is, Hermon c6 Targum; the Masoretic Text has a different division of the consonants. d6 Hebrew *Kittim* e9 That is, Byblos f15 Septuagint; Hebrew *Dedan* g16 Most Hebrew manuscripts; some Hebrew manuscripts and Syriac *Edom* h17 The meaning of the Hebrew for this word is uncertain.

on the day of your shipwreck.
28 The shorelands will quake
when your seamen cry out.
29 All who handle the oars
will abandon their ships;
the mariners and all the seamen
will stand on the shore.
30 They will raise their voice
and cry bitterly over you;
they will sprinkle dust on their heads
and roll in ashes.
31 They will shave their heads because of you
and will put on sackcloth.
They will weep over you with anguish of soul
and with bitter mourning.
32 As they wail and mourn over you,
they will take up a lament concerning you:
"Who was ever silenced like Tyre,
surrounded by the sea?"
33 When your merchandise went out on the seas,
you satisfied many nations;
with your great wealth and your wares
you enriched the kings of the earth.
34 Now you are shattered by the sea
in the depths of the waters;
your wares and all your company
have gone down with you.
35 All who live in the coastlands
are appalled at you;
their kings shudder with horror
and their faces are distorted with fear.
36 The merchants among the nations hiss at you;
you have come to a horrible end
and will be no more.' "

A Prophecy Against the King of Tyre

28 The word of the LORD came to me: 2 "Son of man, say to the ruler of Tyre, 'This is what the Sovereign LORD says:

" 'In the pride of your heart
you say, "I am a god;
I sit on the throne of a god
in the heart of the seas."
But you are a man and not a god,
though you think you are as wise as a god.
3 Are you wiser than Daniel[a]?
Is no secret hidden from you?
4 By your wisdom and understanding
you have gained wealth for yourself
and amassed gold and silver
in your treasuries.
5 By your great skill in trading
you have increased your wealth,
and because of your wealth
your heart has grown proud.

6 " 'Therefore this is what the Sovereign LORD says:

" 'Because you think you are wise,
as wise as a god,
7 I am going to bring foreigners against you,
the most ruthless of nations;
they will draw their swords against your beauty and wisdom
and pierce your shining splendor.
8 They will bring you down to the pit,
and you will die a violent death
in the heart of the seas.
9 Will you then say, "I am a god,"
in the presence of those who kill you?
You will be but a man, not a god,
in the hands of those who slay you.
10 You will die the death of the uncircumcised
at the hands of foreigners.

I have spoken, declares the Sovereign LORD.' "

11 The word of the LORD came to me: 12 "Son of man, take up a lament concerning the king of Tyre and say to him: 'This is what the Sovereign LORD says:

" 'You were the model of perfection,
full of wisdom and perfect in beauty.
13 You were in Eden,
the garden of God;
every precious stone adorned you:
ruby, topaz and emerald,
chrysolite, onyx and jasper,
sapphire,[b] turquoise and beryl.[c]
Your settings and mountings[d] were made of gold;
on the day you were created they were prepared.
14 You were anointed as a guardian cherub,
for so I ordained you.
You were on the holy mount of God;
you walked among the fiery stones.
15 You were blameless in your ways
from the day you were created
till wickedness was found in you.
16 Through your widespread trade
you were filled with violence,
and you sinned.
So I drove you in disgrace from the mount of God,
and I expelled you, O guardian cherub,
from among the fiery stones.
17 Your heart became proud
on account of your beauty,
and you corrupted your wisdom

[a] 3 Or *Danel*; the Hebrew spelling may suggest a person other than the prophet Daniel. [b] 13 Or *lapis lazuli* [c] 13 The precise identification of some of these precious stones is uncertain. [d] 13 The meaning of the Hebrew for this phrase is uncertain.

because of your splendor.
So I threw you to the earth;
I made a spectacle of you before kings.
18By your many sins and dishonest trade
you have desecrated your sanctuaries.
So I made a fire come out from you,
and it consumed you,
and I reduced you to ashes on the ground
in the sight of all who were watching.
19All the nations who knew you
are appalled at you;
you have come to a horrible end
and will be no more.' "

A Prophecy Against Sidon

20The word of the LORD came to me: 21"Son
of man, set your face against Sidon; prophesy
against her 22and say: 'This is what the Sovereign
LORD says:

" 'I am against you, O Sidon,
and I will gain glory within you.
They will know that I am the LORD,
when I inflict punishment on her
and show myself holy within her.
23I will send a plague upon her
and make blood flow in her streets.
The slain will fall within her,
with the sword against her on every side.
Then they will know that I am the LORD.

24" 'No longer will the people of Israel have
malicious neighbors who are painful briers and
sharp thorns. Then they will know that I am the
Sovereign LORD.
25" 'This is what the Sovereign LORD says:
When I gather the people of Israel from the nations where they have been scattered, I will show
myself holy among them in the sight of the nations. Then they will live in their own land,
which I gave to my servant Jacob. 26They will live
there in safety and will build houses and plant
vineyards; they will live in safety when I inflict
punishment on all their neighbors who maligned
them. Then they will know that I am the LORD
their God.' "

A Prophecy Against Egypt

29 In the tenth year, in the tenth month on
the twelfth day, the word of the LORD
came to me: 2"Son of man, set your face against
Pharaoh king of Egypt and prophesy against him
and against all Egypt. 3Speak to him and say: 'This
is what the Sovereign LORD says:

" 'I am against you, Pharaoh king of Egypt,
you great monster lying among your
streams.
You say, "The Nile is mine;
I made it for myself."
4But I will put hooks in your jaws
and make the fish of your streams stick to
your scales.
I will pull you out from among your streams,
with all the fish sticking to your scales.
5I will leave you in the desert,
you and all the fish of your streams.
You will fall on the open field
and not be gathered or picked up.
I will give you as food
to the beasts of the earth and the birds of
the air.

6Then all who live in Egypt will know that I am
the LORD.
" 'You have been a staff of reed for the house
of Israel. 7When they grasped you with their
hands, you splintered and you tore open their
shoulders; when they leaned on you, you broke
and their backs were wrenched.[a]
8" 'Therefore this is what the Sovereign LORD
says: I will bring a sword against you and kill your
men and their animals. 9Egypt will become a desolate wasteland. Then they will know that I am
the LORD.
" 'Because you said, "The Nile is mine; I made
it," 10therefore I am against you and against your
streams, and I will make the land of Egypt a ruin
and a desolate waste from Migdol to Aswan, as far
as the border of Cush.[b] 11No foot of man or
animal will pass through it; no one will live there
for forty years. 12I will make the land of Egypt
desolate among devastated lands, and her cities
will lie desolate forty years among ruined cities.
And I will disperse the Egyptians among the nations and scatter them through the countries.
13" 'Yet this is what the Sovereign LORD says:
At the end of forty years I will gather the Egyptians from the nations where they were scattered. 14I will bring them back from captivity and
return them to Upper Egypt,[c] the land of their
ancestry. There they will be a lowly kingdom. 15It
will be the lowliest of kingdoms and will never
again exalt itself above the other nations. I will
make it so weak that it will never again rule over
the nations. 16Egypt will no longer be a source of
confidence for the people of Israel but will be a
reminder of their sin in turning to her for help.
Then they will know that I am the Sovereign
LORD.' "

17In the twenty-seventh year, in the first
month on the first day, the word of the LORD
came to me: 18"Son of man, Nebuchadnezzar
king of Babylon drove his army in a hard cam-

[a] 7 Syriac (see also Septuagint and Vulgate); Hebrew *and you caused their backs to stand* [b] 10 That is, the upper Nile region
[c] 14 Hebrew *to Pathros*

paign against Tyre; every head was rubbed bare and every shoulder made raw. Yet he and his army got no reward from the campaign he led against Tyre. 19Therefore this is what the Sovereign LORD says: I am going to give Egypt to Nebuchadnezzar king of Babylon, and he will carry off its wealth. He will loot and plunder the land as pay for his army. 20I have given him Egypt as a reward for his efforts because he and his army did it for me, declares the Sovereign LORD.

21"On that day I will make a horn[a] grow for the house of Israel, and I will open your mouth among them. Then they will know that I am the LORD."

A Lament for Egypt

30 The word of the LORD came to me: 2"Son of man, prophesy and say: 'This is what the Sovereign LORD says:

"'Wail and say,
"Alas for that day!"
3For the day is near,
the day of the LORD is near—
a day of clouds,
a time of doom for the nations.
4A sword will come against Egypt,
and anguish will come upon Cush.[b]
When the slain fall in Egypt,
her wealth will be carried away
and her foundations torn down.

5Cush and Put, Lydia and all Arabia, Libya[c] and the people of the covenant land will fall by the sword along with Egypt.

6"'This is what the LORD says:

"'The allies of Egypt will fall
and her proud strength will fail.
From Migdol to Aswan
they will fall by the sword within her,
declares the Sovereign LORD.
7"'They will be desolate
among desolate lands,
and their cities will lie
among ruined cities.
8Then they will know that I am the LORD,
when I set fire to Egypt
and all her helpers are crushed.

9"'On that day messengers will go out from me in ships to frighten Cush out of her complacency. Anguish will take hold of them on the day of Egypt's doom, for it is sure to come.

10"'This is what the Sovereign LORD says:

"'I will put an end to the hordes of Egypt
by the hand of Nebuchadnezzar king of Babylon.
11He and his army—the most ruthless of nations—
will be brought in to destroy the land.
They will draw their swords against Egypt
and fill the land with the slain.
12I will dry up the streams of the Nile
and sell the land to evil men;
by the hand of foreigners
I will lay waste the land and everything in it.

I the LORD have spoken.

13"'This is what the Sovereign LORD says:

"'I will destroy the idols
and put an end to the images in Memphis.[d]
No longer will there be a prince in Egypt,
and I will spread fear throughout the land.
14I will lay waste Upper Egypt,[e]
set fire to Zoan
and inflict punishment on Thebes.[f]
15I will pour out my wrath on Pelusium,[g]
the stronghold of Egypt,
and cut off the hordes of Thebes.
16I will set fire to Egypt;
Pelusium will writhe in agony.
Thebes will be taken by storm;
Memphis will be in constant distress.
17The young men of Heliopolis[h] and Bubastis[i]
will fall by the sword,
and the cities themselves will go into captivity.
18Dark will be the day at Tahpanhes
when I break the yoke of Egypt;
there her proud strength will come to an end.
She will be covered with clouds,
and her villages will go into captivity.
19So I will inflict punishment on Egypt,
and they will know that I am the LORD.'"

20In the eleventh year, in the first month on the seventh day, the word of the LORD came to me: 21"Son of man, I have broken the arm of Pharaoh king of Egypt. It has not been bound up for healing or put in a splint so as to become strong enough to hold a sword. 22Therefore this is what the Sovereign LORD says: I am against Pharaoh king of Egypt. I will break both his arms, the good arm as well as the broken one, and make the sword fall from his hand. 23I will disperse the Egyptians among the nations and scat-

[a]21 *Horn* here symbolizes strength. [b]4 That is, the upper Nile region; also in verses 5 and 9 [c]5 Hebrew *Cub*
[d]13 Hebrew *Noph*; also in verse 16 [e]14 Hebrew *waste Pathros* [f]14 Hebrew *No*; also in verses 15 and 16
[g]15 Hebrew *Sin*; also in verse 16 [h]17 Hebrew *Awen* (or *On*) [i]17 Hebrew *Pi Beseth*

ter them through the countries. 24 I will strength-
en the arms of the king of Babylon and put my
sword in his hand, but I will break the arms of
Pharaoh, and he will groan before him like a mor-
tally wounded man. 25 I will strengthen the arms
of the king of Babylon, but the arms of Pharaoh
will fall limp. Then they will know that I am the
LORD, when I put my sword into the hand of the
king of Babylon and he brandishes it against
Egypt. 26 I will disperse the Egyptians among the
nations and scatter them through the countries.
Then they will know that I am the LORD."

A Cedar in Lebanon

31 In the eleventh year, in the third month
on the first day, the word of the LORD
came to me: 2 "Son of man, say to Pharaoh king of
Egypt and to his hordes:

" 'Who can be compared with you in
    majesty?
3 Consider Assyria, once a cedar in Lebanon,
  with beautiful branches overshadowing the
    forest;
it towered on high,
  its top above the thick foliage.
4 The waters nourished it,
  deep springs made it grow tall;
their streams flowed
  all around its base
and sent their channels
  to all the trees of the field.
5 So it towered higher
  than all the trees of the field;
its boughs increased
  and its branches grew long,
  spreading because of abundant waters.
6 All the birds of the air
  nested in its boughs,
all the beasts of the field
  gave birth under its branches;
all the great nations
  lived in its shade.
7 It was majestic in beauty,
  with its spreading boughs,
for its roots went down
  to abundant waters.
8 The cedars in the garden of God
  could not rival it,
nor could the pine trees
  equal its boughs,
nor could the plane trees
  compare with its branches—
no tree in the garden of God
  could match its beauty.
9 I made it beautiful
  with abundant branches,
the envy of all the trees of Eden
  in the garden of God.

10 " 'Therefore this is what the Sovereign LORD
says: Because it towered on high, lifting its top
above the thick foliage, and because it was proud
of its height, 11 I handed it over to the ruler of the
nations, for him to deal with according to its
wickedness. I cast it aside, 12 and the most ruthless of foreign nations cut it down and left it. Its
boughs fell on the mountains and in all the valleys; its branches lay broken in all the ravines of
the land. All the nations of the earth came out
from under its shade and left it. 13 All the birds of
the air settled on the fallen tree, and all the beasts
of the field were among its branches. 14 Therefore
no other trees by the waters are ever to tower
proudly on high, lifting their tops above the thick
foliage. No other trees so well-watered are ever
to reach such a height; they are all destined for
death, for the earth below, among mortal men,
with those who go down to the pit.

15 " 'This is what the Sovereign LORD says: On
the day it was brought down to the grave[a] I
covered the deep springs with mourning for it; I
held back its streams, and its abundant waters
were restrained. Because of it I clothed Lebanon
with gloom, and all the trees of the field withered
away. 16 I made the nations tremble at the sound
of its fall when I brought it down to the grave
with those who go down to the pit. Then all the
trees of Eden, the choicest and best of Lebanon,
all the trees that were well-watered, were consoled in the earth below. 17 Those who lived in its
shade, its allies among the nations, had also gone
down to the grave with it, joining those killed by
the sword.

18 " 'Which of the trees of Eden can be compared with you in splendor and majesty? Yet you,
too, will be brought down with the trees of Eden
to the earth below; you will lie among the uncircumcised, with those killed by the sword.

" 'This is Pharaoh and all his hordes, declares
the Sovereign LORD.' "

A Lament for Pharaoh

32 In the twelfth year, in the twelfth month
on the first day, the word of the LORD
came to me: 2 "Son of man, take up a lament
concerning Pharaoh king of Egypt and say to him:

" 'You are like a lion among the nations;
  you are like a monster in the seas
thrashing about in your streams,
  churning the water with your feet
  and muddying the streams.

3 " 'This is what the Sovereign LORD says:

a 15 Hebrew *Sheol*; also in verses 16 and 17

" 'With a great throng of people
I will cast my net over you,
and they will haul you up in my net.
4I will throw you on the land
and hurl you on the open field.
I will let all the birds of the air settle on you
and all the beasts of the earth gorge
themselves on you.
5I will spread your flesh on the mountains
and fill the valleys with your remains.
6I will drench the land with your flowing
blood
all the way to the mountains,
and the ravines will be filled with your
flesh.
7When I snuff you out, I will cover the
heavens
and darken their stars;
I will cover the sun with a cloud,
and the moon will not give its light.
8All the shining lights in the heavens
I will darken over you;
I will bring darkness over your land,
declares the Sovereign LORD.
9I will trouble the hearts of many peoples
when I bring about your destruction
among the nations,
among[a] lands you have not known.
10I will cause many peoples to be appalled at
you,
and their kings will shudder with horror
because of you
when I brandish my sword before them.
On the day of your downfall
each of them will tremble
every moment for his life.

11" 'For this is what the Sovereign LORD says:
" 'The sword of the king of Babylon
will come against you.
12I will cause your hordes to fall
by the swords of mighty men—
the most ruthless of all nations.
They will shatter the pride of Egypt,
and all her hordes will be overthrown.
13I will destroy all her cattle
from beside abundant waters
no longer to be stirred by the foot of man
or muddied by the hoofs of cattle.
14Then I will let her waters settle
and make her streams flow like oil,
declares the Sovereign LORD.
15When I make Egypt desolate
and strip the land of everything in it,
when I strike down all who live there,
then they will know that I am the LORD.'

16"This is the lament they will chant for her.
The daughters of the nations will chant it; for
Egypt and all her hordes they will chant it, de-
clares the Sovereign LORD."

17In the twelfth year, on the fifteenth day of
the month, the word of the LORD came to me:
18"Son of man, wail for the hordes of Egypt and
consign to the earth below both her and the
daughters of mighty nations, with those who go
down to the pit. 19Say to them, 'Are you more
favored than others? Go down and be laid among
the uncircumcised.' 20They will fall among those
killed by the sword. The sword is drawn; let her
be dragged off with all her hordes. 21From within
the grave[b] the mighty leaders will say of Egypt
and her allies, 'They have come down and they
lie with the uncircumcised, with those killed by
the sword.'

22"Assyria is there with her whole army; she is
surrounded by the graves of all her slain, all who
have fallen by the sword. 23Their graves are in
the depths of the pit and her army lies around her
grave. All who had spread terror in the land of
the living are slain, fallen by the sword.

24"Elam is there, with all her hordes around
her grave. All of them are slain, fallen by the
sword. All who had spread terror in the land of
the living went down uncircumcised to the earth
below. They bear their shame with those who go
down to the pit. 25A bed is made for her among
the slain, with all her hordes around her grave.
All of them are uncircumcised, killed by the
sword. Because their terror had spread in the
land of the living, they bear their shame with
those who go down to the pit; they are laid
among the slain.

26"Meshech and Tubal are there, with all their
hordes around their graves. All of them are uncircumcised, killed by the sword because they
spread their terror in the land of the living. 27Do
they not lie with the other uncircumcised warriors who have fallen, who went down to the
grave with their weapons of war, whose swords
were placed under their heads? The punishment
for their sins rested on their bones, though the
terror of these warriors had stalked through the
land of the living.

28"You too, O Pharaoh, will be broken and
will lie among the uncircumcised, with those
killed by the sword.

29"Edom is there, her kings and all her
princes; despite their power, they are laid with
those killed by the sword. They lie with the uncircumcised, with those who go down to the pit.

30"All the princes of the north and all the Sidonians are there; they went down with the slain in

[a]9 Hebrew; Septuagint *bring you into captivity among the nations, / to* [b]21 Hebrew *Sheol*; also in verse 27

disgrace despite the terror caused by their power.
They lie uncircumcised with those killed by the
sword and bear their shame with those who go
down to the pit.
31“Pharaoh—he and all his army—will see
them and he will be consoled for all his hordes
that were killed by the sword, declares the Sovereign LORD. 32Although I had him spread terror in
the land of the living, Pharaoh and all his hordes
will be laid among the uncircumcised, with those
killed by the sword, declares the Sovereign
LORD.”

Ezekiel a Watchman

33 The word of the LORD came to me: 2“Son
of man, speak to your countrymen and
say to them: ‘When I bring the sword against a
land, and the people of the land choose one of
their men and make him their watchman, 3and
he sees the sword coming against the land and
blows the trumpet to warn the people, 4then if
anyone hears the trumpet but does not take
warning and the sword comes and takes his life,
his blood will be on his own head. 5Since he
heard the sound of the trumpet but did not take
warning, his blood will be on his own head. If he
had taken warning, he would have saved himself.
6But if the watchman sees the sword coming and
does not blow the trumpet to warn the people
and the sword comes and takes the life of one of
them, that man will be taken away because of his
sin, but I will hold the watchman accountable for
his blood.’
7“Son of man, I have made you a watchman for
the house of Israel; so hear the word I speak and
give them warning from me. 8When I say to the
wicked, ‘O wicked man, you will surely die,’ and
you do not speak out to dissuade him from his
ways, that wicked man will die for[a] his sin, and
I will hold you accountable for his blood. 9But if
you do warn the wicked man to turn from his
ways and he does not do so, he will die for his
sin, but you will have saved yourself.
10“Son of man, say to the house of Israel, ‘This
is what you are saying: “Our offenses and sins
weigh us down, and we are wasting away because of[b] them. How then can we live?” ’ 11Say
to them, ‘As surely as I live, declares the Sovereign LORD, I take no pleasure in the death of the
wicked, but rather that they turn from their ways
and live. Turn! Turn from your evil ways! Why
will you die, O house of Israel?’
12“Therefore, son of man, say to your countrymen, ‘The righteousness of the righteous man
will not save him when he disobeys, and the
wickedness of the wicked man will not cause him
to fall when he turns from it. The righteous man,
if he sins, will not be allowed to live because of
his former righteousness.’ 13If I tell the righteous
man that he will surely live, but then he trusts in
his righteousness and does evil, none of the righteous things he has done will be remembered; he
will die for the evil he has done. 14And if I say to
the wicked man, ‘You will surely die,’ but he
then turns away from his sin and does what is
just and right— 15if he gives back what he took
in pledge for a loan, returns what he has stolen,
follows the decrees that give life, and does no
evil, he will surely live; he will not die. 16None of
the sins he has committed will be remembered
against him. He has done what is just and right;
he will surely live.
17“Yet your countrymen say, ‘The way of the
Lord is not just.’ But it is their way that is not
just. 18If a righteous man turns from his righteousness and does evil, he will die for it. 19And
if a wicked man turns away from his wickedness
and does what is just and right, he will live by
doing so. 20Yet, O house of Israel, you say, ‘The
way of the Lord is not just.’ But I will judge each
of you according to his own ways.”

Jerusalem’s Fall Explained

21In the twelfth year of our exile, in the tenth
month on the fifth day, a man who had escaped
from Jerusalem came to me and said, “The city
has fallen!” 22Now the evening before the man
arrived, the hand of the LORD was upon me, and
he opened my mouth before the man came to me
in the morning. So my mouth was opened and I
was no longer silent.
23Then the word of the LORD came to me:
24“Son of man, the people living in those ruins in
the land of Israel are saying, ‘Abraham was only
one man, yet he possessed the land. But we are
many; surely the land has been given to us as our
possession.’ 25Therefore say to them, ‘This is
what the Sovereign LORD says: Since you eat meat
with the blood still in it and look to your idols and
shed blood, should you then possess the land?
26You rely on your sword, you do detestable
things, and each of you defiles his neighbor’s
wife. Should you then possess the land?’
27“Say this to them: ‘This is what the Sovereign LORD says: As surely as I live, those who are
left in the ruins will fall by the sword, those out
in the country I will give to the wild animals to
be devoured, and those in strongholds and caves
will die of a plague. 28I will make the land a
desolate waste, and her proud strength will come
to an end, and the mountains of Israel will become desolate so that no one will cross them.
29Then they will know that I am the LORD, when

[a] 8 Or *in*; also in verse 9 [b] 10 Or *away in*

I have made the land a desolate waste because of all the detestable things they have done.’

30“As for you, son of man, your countrymen are talking together about you by the walls and at the doors of the houses, saying to each other, ‘Come and hear the message that has come from the LORD.’ 31My people come to you, as they usually do, and sit before you to listen to your words, but they do not put them into practice. With their mouths they express devotion, but their hearts are greedy for unjust gain. 32Indeed, to them you are nothing more than one who sings love songs with a beautiful voice and plays an instrument well, for they hear your words but do not put them into practice.

33“When all this comes true—and it surely will—then they will know that a prophet has been among them.”

Shepherds and Sheep

34 The word of the LORD came to me: 2“Son of man, prophesy against the shepherds of Israel; prophesy and say to them: ‘This is what the Sovereign LORD says: Woe to the shepherds of Israel who only take care of themselves! Should not shepherds take care of the flock? 3You eat the curds, clothe yourselves with the wool and slaughter the choice animals, but you do not take care of the flock. 4You have not strengthened the weak or healed the sick or bound up the injured. You have not brought back the strays or searched for the lost. You have ruled them harshly and brutally. 5So they were scattered because there was no shepherd, and when they were scattered they became food for all the wild animals. 6My sheep wandered over all the mountains and on every high hill. They were scattered over the whole earth, and no one searched or looked for them.

7“ ‘Therefore, you shepherds, hear the word of the LORD: 8As surely as I live, declares the Sovereign LORD, because my flock lacks a shepherd and so has been plundered and has become food for all the wild animals, and because my shepherds did not search for my flock but cared for themselves rather than for my flock, 9therefore, O shepherds, hear the word of the LORD: 10This is what the Sovereign LORD says: I am against the shepherds and will hold them accountable for my flock. I will remove them from tending the flock so that the shepherds can no longer feed themselves. I will rescue my flock from their mouths, and it will no longer be food for them.

11“ ‘For this is what the Sovereign LORD says: I myself will search for my sheep and look after them. 12As a shepherd looks after his scattered flock when he is with them, so will I look after my sheep. I will rescue them from all the places where they were scattered on a day of clouds and darkness. 13I will bring them out from the nations and gather them from the countries, and I will bring them into their own land. I will pasture them on the mountains of Israel, in the ravines and in all the settlements in the land. 14I will tend them in a good pasture, and the mountain heights of Israel will be their grazing land. There they will lie down in good grazing land, and there they will feed in a rich pasture on the mountains of Israel. 15I myself will tend my sheep and have them lie down, declares the Sovereign LORD. 16I will search for the lost and bring back the strays. I will bind up the injured and strengthen the weak, but the sleek and the strong I will destroy. I will shepherd the flock with justice.

17“ ‘As for you, my flock, this is what the Sovereign LORD says: I will judge between one sheep and another, and between rams and goats. 18Is it not enough for you to feed on the good pasture? Must you also trample the rest of your pasture with your feet? Is it not enough for you to drink clear water? Must you also muddy the rest with your feet? 19Must my flock feed on what you have trampled and drink what you have muddied with your feet?

20“ ‘Therefore this is what the Sovereign LORD says to them: See, I myself will judge between the fat sheep and the lean sheep. 21Because you shove with flank and shoulder, butting all the weak sheep with your horns until you have driven them away, 22I will save my flock, and they will no longer be plundered. I will judge between one sheep and another. 23I will place over them one shepherd, my servant David, and he will tend them; he will tend them and be their shepherd. 24I the LORD will be their God, and my servant David will be prince among them. I the LORD have spoken.

25“ ‘I will make a covenant of peace with them and rid the land of wild beasts so that they may live in the desert and sleep in the forests in safety. 26I will bless them and the places surrounding my hill.[a] I will send down showers in season; there will be showers of blessing. 27The trees of the field will yield their fruit and the ground will yield its crops; the people will be secure in their land. They will know that I am the LORD, when I break the bars of their yoke and rescue them from the hands of those who enslaved them. 28They will no longer be plundered by the nations, nor will wild animals devour them. They will live in safety, and no one will make them afraid. 29I will provide for them a land renowned for its crops, and they will no longer be victims of famine in the land or bear the scorn of the na-

[a]26 Or *I will make them and the places surrounding my hill a blessing*

tions. 30Then they will know that I, the LORD
their God, am with them and that they, the house
of Israel, are my people, declares the Sovereign
LORD. 31You my sheep, the sheep of my pasture,
are people, and I am your God, declares the Sovereign LORD.' "

A Prophecy Against Edom

35 The word of the LORD came to me: 2"Son
of man, set your face against Mount Seir;
prophesy against it 3and say: 'This is what the
Sovereign LORD says: I am against you, Mount
Seir, and I will stretch out my hand against you
and make you a desolate waste. 4I will turn your
towns into ruins and you will be desolate. Then
you will know that I am the LORD.

5" 'Because you harbored an ancient hostility
and delivered the Israelites over to the sword at
the time of their calamity, the time their punishment reached its climax, 6therefore as surely as I
live, declares the Sovereign LORD, I will give you
over to bloodshed and it will pursue you. Since
you did not hate bloodshed, bloodshed will pursue you. 7I will make Mount Seir a desolate waste
and cut off from it all who come and go. 8I will fill
your mountains with the slain; those killed by the
sword will fall on your hills and in your valleys
and in all your ravines. 9I will make you desolate
forever; your towns will not be inhabited. Then
you will know that I am the LORD.

10" 'Because you have said, "These two nations
and countries will be ours and we will take possession of them," even though I the LORD was
there, 11therefore as surely as I live, declares the
Sovereign LORD, I will treat you in accordance
with the anger and jealousy you showed in your
hatred of them and I will make myself known
among them when I judge you. 12Then you will
know that I the LORD have heard all the contemptible things you have said against the mountains of Israel. You said, "They have been laid
waste and have been given over to us to devour."
13You boasted against me and spoke against me
without restraint, and I heard it. 14This is what
the Sovereign LORD says: While the whole earth
rejoices, I will make you desolate. 15Because you
rejoiced when the inheritance of the house of
Israel became desolate, that is how I will treat
you. You will be desolate, O Mount Seir, you and
all of Edom. Then they will know that I am the
LORD.' "

A Prophecy to the Mountains of Israel

36 "Son of man, prophesy to the mountains
of Israel and say, 'O mountains of Israel,
hear the word of the LORD. 2This is what the
Sovereign LORD says: The enemy said of you,
"Aha! The ancient heights have become our possession." ' 3Therefore prophesy and say, 'This is
what the Sovereign LORD says: Because they ravaged and hounded you from every side so that
you became the possession of the rest of the nations and the object of people's malicious talk and
slander, 4therefore, O mountains of Israel, hear
the word of the Sovereign LORD: This is what the
Sovereign LORD says to the mountains and hills,
to the ravines and valleys, to the desolate ruins
and the deserted towns that have been plundered
and ridiculed by the rest of the nations around
you— 5this is what the Sovereign LORD says: In
my burning zeal I have spoken against the rest of
the nations, and against all Edom, for with glee
and with malice in their hearts they made my
land their own possession so that they might
plunder its pastureland.' 6Therefore prophesy
concerning the land of Israel and say to the
mountains and hills, to the ravines and valleys:
'This is what the Sovereign LORD says: I speak in
my jealous wrath because you have suffered the
scorn of the nations. 7Therefore this is what the
Sovereign LORD says: I swear with uplifted hand
that the nations around you will also suffer scorn.

8" 'But you, O mountains of Israel, will produce branches and fruit for my people Israel, for
they will soon come home. 9I am concerned for
you and will look on you with favor; you will be
plowed and sown, 10and I will multiply the number of people upon you, even the whole house of
Israel. The towns will be inhabited and the ruins
rebuilt. 11I will increase the number of men and
animals upon you, and they will be fruitful and
become numerous. I will settle people on you as
in the past and will make you prosper more than
before. Then you will know that I am the LORD.
12I will cause people, my people Israel, to walk
upon you. They will possess you, and you will be
their inheritance; you will never again deprive
them of their children.

13" 'This is what the Sovereign LORD says: Because people say to you, "You devour men and
deprive your nation of its children," 14therefore
you will no longer devour men or make your
nation childless, declares the Sovereign LORD.
15No longer will I make you hear the taunts of the
nations, and no longer will you suffer the scorn of
the peoples or cause your nation to fall, declares
the Sovereign LORD.' "

16Again the word of the LORD came to me:
17"Son of man, when the people of Israel were
living in their own land, they defiled it by their
conduct and their actions. Their conduct was like
a woman's monthly uncleanness in my sight.
18So I poured out my wrath on them because they
had shed blood in the land and because they had
defiled it with their idols. 19I dispersed them
among the nations, and they were scattered
through the countries; I judged them according to
their conduct and their actions. 20And wherever

they went among the nations they profaned my
holy name, for it was said of them, 'These are the
LORD's people, and yet they had to leave his
land.' [21]I had concern for my holy name, which
the house of Israel profaned among the nations
where they had gone.
[22]"Therefore say to the house of Israel, 'This is
what the Sovereign LORD says: It is not for your
sake, O house of Israel, that I am going to do
these things, but for the sake of my holy name,
which you have profaned among the nations
where you have gone. [23]I will show the holiness
of my great name, which has been profaned
among the nations, the name you have profaned
among them. Then the nations will know that I
am the LORD, declares the Sovereign LORD, when
I show myself holy through you before their eyes.
[24]" 'For I will take you out of the nations; I will
gather you from all the countries and bring you
back into your own land. [25]I will sprinkle clean
water on you, and you will be clean; I will cleanse
you from all your impurities and from all your
idols. [26]I will give you a new heart and put a new
spirit in you; I will remove from you your heart of
stone and give you a heart of flesh. [27]And I will
put my Spirit in you and move you to follow my
decrees and be careful to keep my laws. [28]You
will live in the land I gave your forefathers; you
will be my people, and I will be your God. [29]I will
save you from all your uncleanness. I will call for
the grain and make it plentiful and will not bring
famine upon you. [30]I will increase the fruit of the
trees and the crops of the field, so that you will
no longer suffer disgrace among the nations because of famine. [31]Then you will remember your
evil ways and wicked deeds, and you will loathe
yourselves for your sins and detestable practices.
[32]I want you to know that I am not doing this
for your sake, declares the Sovereign LORD. Be
ashamed and disgraced for your conduct,
O house of Israel!
[33]" 'This is what the Sovereign LORD says: On
the day I cleanse you from all your sins, I will
resettle your towns, and the ruins will be rebuilt.
[34]The desolate land will be cultivated instead of
lying desolate in the sight of all who pass through
it. [35]They will say, "This land that was laid waste
has become like the garden of Eden; the cities
that were lying in ruins, desolate and destroyed,
are now fortified and inhabited." [36]Then the nations around you that remain will know that I the
LORD have rebuilt what was destroyed and have
replanted what was desolate. I the LORD have
spoken, and I will do it.'
[37]"This is what the Sovereign LORD says: Once
again I will yield to the plea of the house of Israel
and do this for them: I will make their people as
numerous as sheep, [38]as numerous as the flocks
for offerings at Jerusalem during her appointed
feasts. So will the ruined cities be filled with
flocks of people. Then they will know that I am
the LORD."

The Valley of Dry Bones

37 The hand of the LORD was upon me, and
he brought me out by the Spirit of the
LORD and set me in the middle of a valley; it was
full of bones. [2]He led me back and forth among
them, and I saw a great many bones on the floor
of the valley, bones that were very dry. [3]He asked
me, "Son of man, can these bones live?"
I said, "O Sovereign LORD, you alone know."
[4]Then he said to me, "Prophesy to these bones
and say to them, 'Dry bones, hear the word of the
LORD! [5]This is what the Sovereign LORD says to
these bones: I will make breath[a] enter you, and
you will come to life. [6]I will attach tendons to you
and make flesh come upon you and cover you
with skin; I will put breath in you, and you will
come to life. Then you will know that I am the
LORD.' "
[7]So I prophesied as I was commanded. And as
I was prophesying, there was a noise, a rattling
sound, and the bones came together, bone to
bone. [8]I looked, and tendons and flesh appeared
on them and skin covered them, but there was no
breath in them.
[9]Then he said to me, "Prophesy to the breath;
prophesy, son of man, and say to it, 'This is what
the Sovereign LORD says: Come from the four
winds, O breath, and breathe into these slain,
that they may live.' " [10]So I prophesied as he commanded me, and breath entered them; they came
to life and stood up on their feet—a vast army.
[11]Then he said to me: "Son of man, these
bones are the whole house of Israel. They say,
'Our bones are dried up and our hope is gone; we
are cut off.' [12]Therefore prophesy and say to
them: 'This is what the Sovereign LORD says:
O my people, I am going to open your graves and
bring you up from them; I will bring you back to
the land of Israel. [13]Then you, my people, will
know that I am the LORD, when I open your
graves and bring you up from them. [14]I will put
my Spirit in you and you will live, and I will settle
you in your own land. Then you will know that I
the LORD have spoken, and I have done it, declares the LORD.' "

One Nation Under One King

[15]The word of the LORD came to me: [16]"Son of
man, take a stick of wood and write on it, 'Belonging to Judah and the Israelites associated
with him.' Then take another stick of wood, and

[a]5 The Hebrew for this word can also mean *wind* or *spirit* (see verses 6-14).

write on it, 'Ephraim's stick, belonging to Joseph
and all the house of Israel associated with him.'
17Join them together into one stick so that they
will become one in your hand.
18"When your countrymen ask you, 'Won't
you tell us what you mean by this?' 19say to them,
'This is what the Sovereign LORD says: I am going
to take the stick of Joseph—which is in Ephraim's hand—and of the Israelite tribes associated
with him, and join it to Judah's stick, making
them a single stick of wood, and they will become one in my hand.' 20Hold before their eyes
the sticks you have written on 21and say to them,
'This is what the Sovereign LORD says: I will take
the Israelites out of the nations where they have
gone. I will gather them from all around and
bring them back into their own land. 22I will
make them one nation in the land, on the mountains of Israel. There will be one king over all of
them and they will never again be two nations or
be divided into two kingdoms. 23They will no
longer defile themselves with their idols and vile
images or with any of their offenses, for I will
save them from all their sinful backsliding,[a] and
I will cleanse them. They will be my people, and
I will be their God.
24" 'My servant David will be king over them,
and they will all have one shepherd. They will
follow my laws and be careful to keep my decrees. 25They will live in the land I gave to my
servant Jacob, the land where your fathers lived.
They and their children and their children's children will live there forever, and David my servant will be their prince forever. 26I will make a
covenant of peace with them; it will be an everlasting covenant. I will establish them and increase their numbers, and I will put my sanctuary
among them forever. 27My dwelling place will be
with them; I will be their God, and they will be
my people. 28Then the nations will know that I
the LORD make Israel holy, when my sanctuary is
among them forever.' "

A Prophecy Against Gog

38 The word of the LORD came to me: 2"Son
of man, set your face against Gog, of the
land of Magog, the chief prince of[b] Meshech
and Tubal; prophesy against him 3and say: 'This
is what the Sovereign LORD says: I am against
you, O Gog, chief prince of[c] Meshech and Tubal. 4I will turn you around, put hooks in your
jaws and bring you out with your whole army—
your horses, your horsemen fully armed, and a
great horde with large and small shields, all of
them brandishing their swords. 5Persia, Cush[d]
and Put will be with them, all with shields and
helmets, 6also Gomer with all its troops, and Beth
Togarmah from the far north with all its troops—
the many nations with you.
7" 'Get ready; be prepared, you and all the
hordes gathered about you, and take command
of them. 8After many days you will be called to
arms. In future years you will invade a land that
has recovered from war, whose people were
gathered from many nations to the mountains of
Israel, which had long been desolate. They had
been brought out from the nations, and now all of
them live in safety. 9You and all your troops and
the many nations with you will go up, advancing
like a storm; you will be like a cloud covering the
land.
10" 'This is what the Sovereign LORD says: On
that day thoughts will come into your mind and
you will devise an evil scheme. 11You will say, "I
will invade a land of unwalled villages; I will attack a peaceful and unsuspecting people—all of
them living without walls and without gates and
bars. 12I will plunder and loot and turn my hand
against the resettled ruins and the people gathered from the nations, rich in livestock and
goods, living at the center of the land." 13Sheba
and Dedan and the merchants of Tarshish and all
her villages[e] will say to you, "Have you come to
plunder? Have you gathered your hordes to loot,
to carry off silver and gold, to take away livestock
and goods and to seize much plunder?" '
14"Therefore, son of man, prophesy and say to
Gog: 'This is what the Sovereign LORD says: In
that day, when my people Israel are living in
safety, will you not take notice of it? 15You will
come from your place in the far north, you and
many nations with you, all of them riding on
horses, a great horde, a mighty army. 16You will
advance against my people Israel like a cloud that
covers the land. In days to come, O Gog, I will
bring you against my land, so that the nations
may know me when I show myself holy through
you before their eyes.
17" 'This is what the Sovereign LORD says: Are
you not the one I spoke of in former days by my
servants the prophets of Israel? At that time they
prophesied for years that I would bring you
against them. 18This is what will happen in that
day: When Gog attacks the land of Israel, my hot
anger will be aroused, declares the Sovereign
LORD. 19In my zeal and fiery wrath I declare that
at that time there shall be a great earthquake in
the land of Israel. 20The fish of the sea, the birds
of the air, the beasts of the field, every creature
that moves along the ground, and all the people
on the face of the earth will tremble at my presence. The mountains will be overturned, the

[a] 23 Many Hebrew manuscripts (see also Septuagint); most Hebrew manuscripts *all their dwelling places where they sinned*
[b] 2 Or *the prince of Rosh,* [c] 3 Or *Gog, prince of Rosh,* [d] 5 That is, the upper Nile region [e] 13 Or *her strong lions*

cliffs will crumble and every wall will fall to the
ground. 21 I will summon a sword against Gog on
all my mountains, declares the Sovereign LORD.
Every man's sword will be against his brother. 22 I
will execute judgment upon him with plague and
bloodshed; I will pour down torrents of rain, hailstones and burning sulfur on him and on his
troops and on the many nations with him. 23 And
so I will show my greatness and my holiness, and
I will make myself known in the sight of many
nations. Then they will know that I am the LORD.'

39 "Son of man, prophesy against Gog and
say: 'This is what the Sovereign LORD
says: I am against you, O Gog, chief prince of[a]
Meshech and Tubal. 2 I will turn you around and
drag you along. I will bring you from the far north
and send you against the mountains of Israel.
3 Then I will strike your bow from your left hand
and make your arrows drop from your right hand.
4 On the mountains of Israel you will fall, you and
all your troops and the nations with you. I will
give you as food to all kinds of carrion birds and
to the wild animals. 5 You will fall in the open
field, for I have spoken, declares the Sovereign
LORD. 6 I will send fire on Magog and on those
who live in safety in the coastlands, and they will
know that I am the LORD.

7 " 'I will make known my holy name among
my people Israel. I will no longer let my holy
name be profaned, and the nations will know
that I the LORD am the Holy One in Israel. 8 It is
coming! It will surely take place, declares the
Sovereign LORD. This is the day I have spoken of.

9 " 'Then those who live in the towns of Israel
will go out and use the weapons for fuel and burn
them up—the small and large shields, the bows
and arrows, the war clubs and spears. For seven
years they will use them for fuel. 10 They will not
need to gather wood from the fields or cut it from
the forests, because they will use the weapons for
fuel. And they will plunder those who plundered
them and loot those who looted them, declares
the Sovereign LORD.

11 " 'On that day I will give Gog a burial place
in Israel, in the valley of those who travel east
toward[b] the Sea.[c] It will block the way of travelers, because Gog and all his hordes will be buried there. So it will be called the Valley of Hamon
Gog.[d]

12 " 'For seven months the house of Israel will
be burying them in order to cleanse the land.
13 All the people of the land will bury them, and
the day I am glorified will be a memorable day for
them, declares the Sovereign LORD.

14 " 'Men will be regularly employed to cleanse
the land. Some will go throughout the land and,
in addition to them, others will bury those that
remain on the ground. At the end of the seven
months they will begin their search. 15 As they go
through the land and one of them sees a human
bone, he will set up a marker beside it until the
gravediggers have buried it in the Valley of Hamon Gog. 16 (Also a town called Hamonah[e] will
be there.) And so they will cleanse the land.'

17 "Son of man, this is what the Sovereign
LORD says: Call out to every kind of bird and all
the wild animals: 'Assemble and come together
from all around to the sacrifice I am preparing for
you, the great sacrifice on the mountains of Israel. There you will eat flesh and drink blood.
18 You will eat the flesh of mighty men and drink
the blood of the princes of the earth as if they
were rams and lambs, goats and bulls—all of
them fattened animals from Bashan. 19 At the sacrifice I am preparing for you, you will eat fat till
you are glutted and drink blood till you are drunk.
20 At my table you will eat your fill of horses and
riders, mighty men and soldiers of every kind,'
declares the Sovereign LORD.

21 "I will display my glory among the nations,
and all the nations will see the punishment I
inflict and the hand I lay upon them. 22 From that
day forward the house of Israel will know that I
am the LORD their God. 23 And the nations will
know that the people of Israel went into exile for
their sin, because they were unfaithful to me. So
I hid my face from them and handed them over
to their enemies, and they all fell by the sword.
24 I dealt with them according to their uncleanness and their offenses, and I hid my face from
them.

25 "Therefore this is what the Sovereign LORD
says: I will now bring Jacob back from captivity[f]
and will have compassion on all the people of
Israel, and I will be zealous for my holy name.
26 They will forget their shame and all the unfaithfulness they showed toward me when they lived
in safety in their land with no one to make them
afraid. 27 When I have brought them back from
the nations and have gathered them from the
countries of their enemies, I will show myself
holy through them in the sight of many nations.
28 Then they will know that I am the LORD their
God, for though I sent them into exile among the
nations, I will gather them to their own land, not
leaving any behind. 29 I will no longer hide my
face from them, for I will pour out my Spirit on
the house of Israel, declares the Sovereign LORD."

The New Temple Area

40 In the twenty-fifth year of our exile, at
the beginning of the year, on the tenth of

[a] *1* Or *Gog, prince of Rosh,* [b] *11* Or *of* [c] *11* That is, the Dead Sea [d] *11* *Hamon Gog* means *hordes of Gog.*
[e] *16* *Hamonah* means *horde.* [f] *25* Or *now restore the fortunes of Jacob*

the month, in the fourteenth year after the fall of
the city—on that very day the hand of the LORD
was upon me and he took me there. 2 In visions
of God he took me to the land of Israel and set me
on a very high mountain, on whose south side
were some buildings that looked like a city. 3 He
took me there, and I saw a man whose appearance was like bronze; he was standing in the
gateway with a linen cord and a measuring rod in
his hand. 4 The man said to me, "Son of man, look
with your eyes and hear with your ears and pay
attention to everything I am going to show you,
for that is why you have been brought here. Tell
the house of Israel everything you see."

The East Gate to the Outer Court

5 I saw a wall completely surrounding the temple area. The length of the measuring rod in the
man's hand was six long cubits, each of which
was a cubit[a] and a handbreadth.[b] He measured
the wall; it was one measuring rod thick and one
rod high.
6 Then he went to the gate facing east. He
climbed its steps and measured the threshold of
the gate; it was one rod deep.[c] 7 The alcoves for
the guards were one rod long and one rod wide,
and the projecting walls between the alcoves
were five cubits thick. And the threshold of the
gate next to the portico facing the temple was
one rod deep.
8 Then he measured the portico of the gateway;
9 it[d] was eight cubits deep and its jambs were
two cubits thick. The portico of the gateway faced
the temple.
10 Inside the east gate were three alcoves on
each side; the three had the same measurements,
and the faces of the projecting walls on each side
had the same measurements. 11 Then he measured the width of the entrance to the gateway;
it was ten cubits and its length was thirteen cubits. 12 In front of each alcove was a wall one cubit
high, and the alcoves were six cubits square.
13 Then he measured the gateway from the top of
the rear wall of one alcove to the top of the opposite one; the distance was twenty-five cubits from
one parapet opening to the opposite one. 14 He
measured along the faces of the projecting walls
all around the inside of the gateway—sixty cubits. The measurement was up to the portico[e]
facing the courtyard.[f] 15 The distance from the
entrance of the gateway to the far end of its portico was fifty cubits. 16 The alcoves and the projecting walls inside the gateway were surmounted by
narrow parapet openings all around, as was the
portico; the openings all around faced inward.
The faces of the projecting walls were decorated
with palm trees.

The Outer Court

17 Then he brought me into the outer court.
There I saw some rooms and a pavement that had
been constructed all around the court; there
were thirty rooms along the pavement. 18 It abut-
ted the sides of the gateways and was as wide as
they were long; this was the lower pavement.
19 Then he measured the distance from the inside
of the lower gateway to the outside of the inner
court; it was a hundred cubits on the east side as
well as on the north.

The North Gate

20 Then he measured the length and width of
the gate facing north, leading into the outer
court. 21 Its alcoves—three on each side—its projecting walls and its portico had the same measurements as those of the first gateway. It was
fifty cubits long and twenty-five cubits wide. 22 Its
openings, its portico and its palm tree decora-
tions had the same measurements as those of the
gate facing east. Seven steps led up to it, with its
portico opposite them. 23 There was a gate to the
inner court facing the north gate, just as there
was on the east. He measured from one gate to
the opposite one; it was a hundred cubits.

The South Gate

24 Then he led me to the south side and I saw
a gate facing south. He measured its jambs and its
portico, and they had the same measurements as
the others. 25 The gateway and its portico had
narrow openings all around, like the openings of
the others. It was fifty cubits long and twenty-five
cubits wide. 26 Seven steps led up to it, with its
portico opposite them; it had palm tree decora-
tions on the faces of the projecting walls on each
side. 27 The inner court also had a gate facing
south, and he measured from this gate to the
outer gate on the south side; it was a hundred
cubits.

Gates to the Inner Court

28 Then he brought me into the inner court
through the south gate, and he measured the
south gate; it had the same measurements as the
others. 29 Its alcoves, its projecting walls and its
portico had the same measurements as the others. The gateway and its portico had openings all
around. It was fifty cubits long and twenty-five
cubits wide. 30 (The porticoes of the gateways
around the inner court were twenty-five cubits

[a] 5 The common cubit was about 1 1/2 feet (about 0.5 meter). [b] 5 That is, about 3 inches (about 8 centimeters)
[c] 6 Septuagint; Hebrew *deep, the first threshold, one rod deep* [d] 8,9 Many Hebrew manuscripts, Septuagint, Vulgate and Syriac; most Hebrew manuscripts *gateway facing the temple; it was one rod deep.* [9] *Then he measured the portico of the gateway; it*
[e] 14 Septuagint; Hebrew *projecting wall* [f] 14 The meaning of the Hebrew for this verse is uncertain.

wide and five cubits deep.) 31Its portico faced the outer court; palm trees decorated its jambs, and eight steps led up to it.

32Then he brought me to the inner court on the east side, and he measured the gateway; it had the same measurements as the others. 33Its alcoves, its projecting walls and its portico had the same measurements as the others. The gateway and its portico had openings all around. It was fifty cubits long and twenty-five cubits wide. 34Its portico faced the outer court; palm trees decorated the jambs on either side, and eight steps led up to it.

35Then he brought me to the north gate and measured it. It had the same measurements as the others, 36as did its alcoves, its projecting walls and its portico, and it had openings all around. It was fifty cubits long and twenty-five cubits wide. 37Its portico[a] faced the outer court; palm trees decorated the jambs on either side, and eight steps led up to it.

The Rooms for Preparing Sacrifices

38A room with a doorway was by the portico in each of the inner gateways, where the burnt offerings were washed. 39In the portico of the gateway were two tables on each side, on which the burnt offerings, sin offerings and guilt offerings were slaughtered. 40By the outside wall of the portico of the gateway, near the steps at the entrance to the north gateway were two tables, and on the other side of the steps were two tables. 41So there were four tables on one side of the gateway and four on the other—eight tables in all—on which the sacrifices were slaughtered. 42There were also four tables of dressed stone for the burnt offerings, each a cubit and a half long, a cubit and a half wide and a cubit high. On them were placed the utensils for slaughtering the burnt offerings and the other sacrifices. 43And double-pronged hooks, each a handbreadth long, were attached to the wall all around. The tables were for the flesh of the offerings.

Rooms for the Priests

44Outside the inner gate, within the inner court, were two rooms, one[b] at the side of the north gate and facing south, and another at the side of the south[c] gate and facing north. 45He said to me, "The room facing south is for the priests who have charge of the temple, 46and the room facing north is for the priests who have charge of the altar. These are the sons of Zadok, who are the only Levites who may draw near to the LORD to minister before him."

47Then he measured the court: It was square—a hundred cubits long and a hundred cubits wide. And the altar was in front of the temple.

The Temple

48He brought me to the portico of the temple and measured the jambs of the portico; they were five cubits wide on either side. The width of the entrance was fourteen cubits and its projecting walls were[d] three cubits wide on either side. 49The portico was twenty cubits wide, and twelve[e] cubits from front to back. It was reached by a flight of stairs,[f] and there were pillars on each side of the jambs.

41 Then the man brought me to the outer sanctuary and measured the jambs; the width of the jambs was six cubits[g] on each side.[h] 2The entrance was ten cubits wide, and the projecting walls on each side of it were five cubits wide. He also measured the outer sanctuary; it was forty cubits long and twenty cubits wide.

3Then he went into the inner sanctuary and measured the jambs of the entrance; each was two cubits wide. The entrance was six cubits wide, and the projecting walls on each side of it were seven cubits wide. 4And he measured the length of the inner sanctuary; it was twenty cubits, and its width was twenty cubits across the end of the outer sanctuary. He said to me, "This is the Most Holy Place."

5Then he measured the wall of the temple; it was six cubits thick, and each side room around the temple was four cubits wide. 6The side rooms were on three levels, one above another, thirty on each level. There were ledges all around the wall of the temple to serve as supports for the side rooms, so that the supports were not inserted into the wall of the temple. 7The side rooms all around the temple were wider at each successive level. The structure surrounding the temple was built in ascending stages, so that the rooms widened as one went upward. A stairway went up from the lowest floor to the top floor through the middle floor.

8I saw that the temple had a raised base all around it, forming the foundation of the side rooms. It was the length of the rod, six long cubits. 9The outer wall of the side rooms was five cubits thick. The open area between the side rooms of the temple 10and the ⌊priests'⌋ rooms was twenty cubits wide all around the temple. 11There were entrances to the side rooms from the open area, one on the north and another on

[a] 37 Septuagint (see also verses 31 and 34); Hebrew *jambs* [b] 44 Septuagint; Hebrew *were rooms for singers, which were* [c] 44 Septuagint; Hebrew *east* [d] 48 Septuagint; Hebrew *entrance was* [e] 49 Septuagint; Hebrew *eleven* [f] 49 Hebrew; Septuagint *Ten steps led up to it* [g] 1 The common cubit was about 1 1/2 feet (about 0.5 meter). [h] 1 One Hebrew manuscript and Septuagint; most Hebrew manuscripts *side, the width of the tent*

the south; and the base adjoining the open area
was five cubits wide all around.
12The building facing the temple courtyard on
the west side was seventy cubits wide. The wall
of the building was five cubits thick all around,
and its length was ninety cubits.
13Then he measured the temple; it was a hundred cubits long, and the temple courtyard and
the building with its walls were also a hundred
cubits long. 14The width of the temple courtyard
on the east, including the front of the temple,
was a hundred cubits.
15Then he measured the length of the building
facing the courtyard at the rear of the temple,
including its galleries on each side; it was a hundred cubits.
The outer sanctuary, the inner sanctuary and
the portico facing the court, 16as well as the
thresholds and the narrow windows and galleries
around the three of them—everything beyond
and including the threshold was covered with
wood. The floor, the wall up to the windows, and
the windows were covered. 17In the space above
the outside of the entrance to the inner sanctuary
and on the walls at regular intervals all around
the inner and outer sanctuary 18were carved
cherubim and palm trees. Palm trees alternated
with cherubim. Each cherub had two faces: 19the
face of a man toward the palm tree on one side
and the face of a lion toward the palm tree on the
other. They were carved all around the whole
temple. 20From the floor to the area above the
entrance, cherubim and palm trees were carved
on the wall of the outer sanctuary.
21The outer sanctuary had a rectangular doorframe, and the one at the front of the Most Holy
Place was similar. 22There was a wooden altar
three cubits high and two cubits square[a]; its
corners, its base[b] and its sides were of wood.
The man said to me, "This is the table that is
before the LORD." 23Both the outer sanctuary and
the Most Holy Place had double doors. 24Each
door had two leaves—two hinged leaves for each
door. 25And on the doors of the outer sanctuary
were carved cherubim and palm trees like those
carved on the walls, and there was a wooden
overhang on the front of the portico. 26On the
sidewalls of the portico were narrow windows
with palm trees carved on each side. The side
rooms of the temple also had overhangs.

Rooms for the Priests

42 Then the man led me northward into the
outer court and brought me to the rooms
opposite the temple courtyard and opposite the
outer wall on the north side. 2The building
whose door faced north was a hundred cubits[c]
long and fifty cubits wide. 3Both in the section
twenty cubits from the inner court and in the
section opposite the pavement of the outer court,
gallery faced gallery at the three levels. 4In front
of the rooms was an inner passageway ten cubits
wide and a hundred cubits[d] long. Their doors
were on the north. 5Now the upper rooms were
narrower, for the galleries took more space from
them than from the rooms on the lower and middle floors of the building. 6The rooms on the third
floor had no pillars, as the courts had; so they
were smaller in floor space than those on the
lower and middle floors. 7There was an outer
wall parallel to the rooms and the outer court; it
extended in front of the rooms for fifty cubits.
8While the row of rooms on the side next to the
outer court was fifty cubits long, the row on the
side nearest the sanctuary was a hundred cubits
long. 9The lower rooms had an entrance on the
east side as one enters them from the outer court.
10On the south side[e] along the length of the
wall of the outer court, adjoining the temple
courtyard and opposite the outer wall, were
rooms 11with a passageway in front of them.
These were like the rooms on the north; they had
the same length and width, with similar exits and
dimensions. Similar to the doorways on the north
12were the doorways of the rooms on the south.
There was a doorway at the beginning of the
passageway that was parallel to the corresponding wall extending eastward, by which one enters the rooms.
13Then he said to me, "The north and south
rooms facing the temple courtyard are the
priests' rooms, where the priests who approach
the LORD will eat the most holy offerings.
There they will put the most holy offerings—the
grain offerings, the sin offerings and the guilt
offerings—for the place is holy. 14Once the
priests enter the holy precincts, they are not to go
into the outer court until they leave behind the
garments in which they minister, for these are
holy. They are to put on other clothes before they
go near the places that are for the people."
15When he had finished measuring what was
inside the temple area, he led me out by the east
gate and measured the area all around: 16He measured the east side with the measuring rod; it was
five hundred cubits.[f] 17He measured the north
side; it was five hundred cubits[g] by the measuring rod. 18He measured the south side; it was five
hundred cubits by the measuring rod. 19Then he
turned to the west side and measured; it was five

a22 Septuagint; Hebrew *long* b22 Septuagint; Hebrew *length* c2 The common cubit was about 1 1/2 feet (about 0.5 meter).
d4 Septuagint and Syriac; Hebrew *and one cubit* e10 Septuagint; Hebrew *Eastward* f16 See Septuagint of verse 17; Hebrew
rods; also in verses 18 and 19. g17 Septuagint; Hebrew *rods*

hundred cubits by the measuring rod. [20]So he measured the area on all four sides. It had a wall around it, five hundred cubits long and five hundred cubits wide, to separate the holy from the common.

The Glory Returns to the Temple

43 Then the man brought me to the gate facing east, [2]and I saw the glory of the God of Israel coming from the east. His voice was like the roar of rushing waters, and the land was radiant with his glory. [3]The vision I saw was like the vision I had seen when he[a] came to destroy the city and like the visions I had seen by the Kebar River, and I fell facedown. [4]The glory of the LORD entered the temple through the gate facing east. [5]Then the Spirit lifted me up and brought me into the inner court, and the glory of the LORD filled the temple.

[6]While the man was standing beside me, I heard someone speaking to me from inside the temple. [7]He said: "Son of man, this is the place of my throne and the place for the soles of my feet. This is where I will live among the Israelites forever. The house of Israel will never again defile my holy name—neither they nor their kings—by their prostitution[b] and the lifeless idols[c] of their kings at their high places. [8]When they placed their threshold next to my threshold and their doorposts beside my doorposts, with only a wall between me and them, they defiled my holy name by their detestable practices. So I destroyed them in my anger. [9]Now let them put away from me their prostitution and the lifeless idols of their kings, and I will live among them forever.

[10]"Son of man, describe the temple to the people of Israel, that they may be ashamed of their sins. Let them consider the plan, [11]and if they are ashamed of all they have done, make known to them the design of the temple—its arrangement, its exits and entrances—its whole design and all its regulations[d] and laws. Write these down before them so that they may be faithful to its design and follow all its regulations.

[12]"This is the law of the temple: All the surrounding area on top of the mountain will be most holy. Such is the law of the temple.

The Altar

[13]"These are the measurements of the altar in long cubits, that cubit being a cubit[e] and a handbreadth[f]: Its gutter is a cubit deep and a cubit wide, with a rim of one span[g] around the edge. And this is the height of the altar: [14]From the gutter on the ground up to the lower ledge it is two cubits high and a cubit wide, and from the smaller ledge up to the larger ledge it is four cubits high and a cubit wide. [15]The altar hearth is four cubits high, and four horns project upward from the hearth. [16]The altar hearth is square, twelve cubits long and twelve cubits wide. [17]The upper ledge also is square, fourteen cubits long and fourteen cubits wide, with a rim of half a cubit and a gutter of a cubit all around. The steps of the altar face east."

[18]Then he said to me, "Son of man, this is what the Sovereign LORD says: These will be the regulations for sacrificing burnt offerings and sprinkling blood upon the altar when it is built: [19]You are to give a young bull as a sin offering to the priests, who are Levites, of the family of Zadok, who come near to minister before me, declares the Sovereign LORD. [20]You are to take some of its blood and put it on the four horns of the altar and on the four corners of the upper ledge and all around the rim, and so purify the altar and make atonement for it. [21]You are to take the bull for the sin offering and burn it in the designated part of the temple area outside the sanctuary.

[22]"On the second day you are to offer a male goat without defect for a sin offering, and the altar is to be purified as it was purified with the bull. [23]When you have finished purifying it, you are to offer a young bull and a ram from the flock, both without defect. [24]You are to offer them before the LORD, and the priests are to sprinkle salt on them and sacrifice them as a burnt offering to the LORD.

[25]"For seven days you are to provide a male goat daily for a sin offering; you are also to provide a young bull and a ram from the flock, both without defect. [26]For seven days they are to make atonement for the altar and cleanse it; thus they will dedicate it. [27]At the end of these days, from the eighth day on, the priests are to present your burnt offerings and fellowship offerings[h] on the altar. Then I will accept you, declares the Sovereign LORD."

The Prince, the Levites, the Priests

44 Then the man brought me back to the outer gate of the sanctuary, the one facing east, and it was shut. [2]The LORD said to me, "This gate is to remain shut. It must not be opened; no one may enter through it. It is to remain shut because the LORD, the God of Israel, has entered through it. [3]The prince himself is the only one who may sit inside the gateway to eat in the

[a]3 Some Hebrew manuscripts and Vulgate; most Hebrew manuscripts *I* [b]7 Or *their spiritual adultery*; also in verse 9 [c]7 Or *the corpses*; also in verse 9 [d]11 Some Hebrew manuscripts and Septuagint; most Hebrew manuscripts *regulations and its whole design* [e]13 The common cubit was about 1 1/2 feet (about 0.5 meter). [f]13 That is, about 3 inches (about 8 centimeters) [g]13 That is, about 9 inches (about 22 centimeters) [h]27 Traditionally *peace offerings*

presence of the LORD. He is to enter by way of the portico of the gateway and go out the same way."

4Then the man brought me by way of the north gate to the front of the temple. I looked and saw the glory of the LORD filling the temple of the LORD, and I fell facedown.

5The LORD said to me, "Son of man, look carefully, listen closely and give attention to everything I tell you concerning all the regulations regarding the temple of the LORD. Give attention to the entrance of the temple and all the exits of the sanctuary. 6Say to the rebellious house of Israel, 'This is what the Sovereign LORD says: Enough of your detestable practices, O house of Israel! 7In addition to all your other detestable practices, you brought foreigners uncircumcised in heart and flesh into my sanctuary, desecrating my temple while you offered me food, fat and blood, and you broke my covenant. 8Instead of carrying out your duty in regard to my holy things, you put others in charge of my sanctuary. 9This is what the Sovereign LORD says: No foreigner uncircumcised in heart and flesh is to enter my sanctuary, not even the foreigners who live among the Israelites.

10" 'The Levites who went far from me when Israel went astray and who wandered from me after their idols must bear the consequences of their sin. 11They may serve in my sanctuary, having charge of the gates of the temple and serving in it; they may slaughter the burnt offerings and sacrifices for the people and stand before the people and serve them. 12But because they served them in the presence of their idols and made the house of Israel fall into sin, therefore I have sworn with uplifted hand that they must bear the consequences of their sin, declares the Sovereign LORD. 13They are not to come near to serve me as priests or come near any of my holy things or my most holy offerings; they must bear the shame of their detestable practices. 14Yet I will put them in charge of the duties of the temple and all the work that is to be done in it.

15" 'But the priests, who are Levites and descendants of Zadok and who faithfully carried out the duties of my sanctuary when the Israelites went astray from me, are to come near to minister before me; they are to stand before me to offer sacrifices of fat and blood, declares the Sovereign LORD. 16They alone are to enter my sanctuary; they alone are to come near my table to minister before me and perform my service.

17" 'When they enter the gates of the inner court, they are to wear linen clothes; they must not wear any woolen garment while ministering at the gates of the inner court or inside the temple. 18They are to wear linen turbans on their heads and linen undergarments around their waists. They must not wear anything that makes them perspire. 19When they go out into the outer court where the people are, they are to take off the clothes they have been ministering in and are to leave them in the sacred rooms, and put on other clothes, so that they do not consecrate the people by means of their garments.

20" 'They must not shave their heads or let their hair grow long, but they are to keep the hair of their heads trimmed. 21No priest is to drink wine when he enters the inner court. 22They must not marry widows or divorced women; they may marry only virgins of Israelite descent or widows of priests. 23They are to teach my people the difference between the holy and the common and show them how to distinguish between the unclean and the clean.

24" 'In any dispute, the priests are to serve as judges and decide it according to my ordinances. They are to keep my laws and my decrees for all my appointed feasts, and they are to keep my Sabbaths holy.

25" 'A priest must not defile himself by going near a dead person; however, if the dead person was his father or mother, son or daughter, brother or unmarried sister, then he may defile himself. 26After he is cleansed, he must wait seven days. 27On the day he goes into the inner court of the sanctuary to minister in the sanctuary, he is to offer a sin offering for himself, declares the Sovereign LORD.

28" 'I am to be the only inheritance the priests have. You are to give them no possession in Israel; I will be their possession. 29They will eat the grain offerings, the sin offerings and the guilt offerings; and everything in Israel devoted[a] to the LORD will belong to them. 30The best of all the firstfruits and of all your special gifts will belong to the priests. You are to give them the first portion of your ground meal so that a blessing may rest on your household. 31The priests must not eat anything, bird or animal, found dead or torn by wild animals.

Division of the Land

45 " 'When you allot the land as an inheritance, you are to present to the LORD a portion of the land as a sacred district, 25,000 cubits long and 20,000[b] cubits wide; the entire area will be holy. 2Of this, a section 500 cubits square is to be for the sanctuary, with 50 cubits around it for open land. 3In the sacred district, measure off a section 25,000 cubits[c] long and 10,000 cubits[d] wide. In it will be the sanctuary,

[a]29 The Hebrew term refers to the irrevocable giving over of things or persons to the LORD. [b]1 Septuagint (see also verses 3 and 5 and 48:9); Hebrew *10,000* [c]3 That is, about 7 miles (about 12 kilometers) [d]3 That is, about 3 miles (about 5 kilometers)

the Most Holy Place. 4It will be the sacred portion of the land for the priests, who minister in the sanctuary and who draw near to minister before the LORD. It will be a place for their houses as well as a holy place for the sanctuary. 5An area 25,000 cubits long and 10,000 cubits wide will belong to the Levites, who serve in the temple, as their possession for towns to live in.[a]

6" 'You are to give the city as its property an area 5,000 cubits wide and 25,000 cubits long, adjoining the sacred portion; it will belong to the whole house of Israel.

7" 'The prince will have the land bordering each side of the area formed by the sacred district and the property of the city. It will extend westward from the west side and eastward from the east side, running lengthwise from the western to the eastern border parallel to one of the tribal portions. 8This land will be his possession in Israel. And my princes will no longer oppress my people but will allow the house of Israel to possess the land according to their tribes.

9" 'This is what the Sovereign LORD says: You have gone far enough, O princes of Israel! Give up your violence and oppression and do what is just and right. Stop dispossessing my people, declares the Sovereign LORD. 10You are to use accurate scales, an accurate ephah[b] and an accurate bath.[c] 11The ephah and the bath are to be the same size, the bath containing a tenth of a homer[d] and the ephah a tenth of a homer; the homer is to be the standard measure for both. 12The shekel[e] is to consist of twenty gerahs. Twenty shekels plus twenty-five shekels plus fifteen shekels equal one mina.[f]

Offerings and Holy Days

13" 'This is the special gift you are to offer: a sixth of an ephah from each homer of wheat and a sixth of an ephah from each homer of barley. 14The prescribed portion of oil, measured by the bath, is a tenth of a bath from each cor (which consists of ten baths or one homer, for ten baths are equivalent to a homer). 15Also one sheep is to be taken from every flock of two hundred from the well-watered pastures of Israel. These will be used for the grain offerings, burnt offerings and fellowship offerings[g] to make atonement for the people, declares the Sovereign LORD. 16All the people of the land will participate in this special gift for the use of the prince in Israel. 17It will be the duty of the prince to provide the burnt offerings, grain offerings and drink offerings at the festivals, the New Moons and the Sabbaths—at all the appointed feasts of the house of Israel. He will provide the sin offerings, grain offerings, burnt offerings and fellowship offerings to make atonement for the house of Israel.

18" 'This is what the Sovereign LORD says: In the first month on the first day you are to take a young bull without defect and purify the sanctuary. 19The priest is to take some of the blood of the sin offering and put it on the doorposts of the temple, on the four corners of the upper ledge of the altar and on the gateposts of the inner court. 20You are to do the same on the seventh day of the month for anyone who sins unintentionally or through ignorance; so you are to make atonement for the temple.

21" 'In the first month on the fourteenth day you are to observe the Passover, a feast lasting seven days, during which you shall eat bread made without yeast. 22On that day the prince is to provide a bull as a sin offering for himself and for all the people of the land. 23Every day during the seven days of the Feast he is to provide seven bulls and seven rams without defect as a burnt offering to the LORD, and a male goat for a sin offering. 24He is to provide as a grain offering an ephah for each bull and an ephah for each ram, along with a hin[h] of oil for each ephah.

25" 'During the seven days of the Feast, which begins in the seventh month on the fifteenth day, he is to make the same provision for sin offerings, burnt offerings, grain offerings and oil.

46 " 'This is what the Sovereign LORD says: The gate of the inner court facing east is to be shut on the six working days, but on the Sabbath day and on the day of the New Moon it is to be opened. 2The prince is to enter from the outside through the portico of the gateway and stand by the gatepost. The priests are to sacrifice his burnt offering and his fellowship offerings.[i] He is to worship at the threshold of the gateway and then go out, but the gate will not be shut until evening. 3On the Sabbaths and New Moons the people of the land are to worship in the presence of the LORD at the entrance to that gateway. 4The burnt offering the prince brings to the LORD on the Sabbath day is to be six male lambs and a ram, all without defect. 5The grain offering given with the ram is to be an ephah,[j] and the grain offering with the lambs is to be as much as he pleases, along with a hin[h] of oil for each ephah. 6On the day of the New Moon he is to offer a young bull, six lambs and a ram, all without defect. 7He is to provide as a grain offering one ephah with the bull, one ephah with the ram,

[a]5 Septuagint; Hebrew *temple; they will have as their possession 20 rooms* [b]10 An ephah was a dry measure. [c]10 A bath was a liquid measure. [d]11 A homer was a dry measure. [e]12 A shekel weighed about 2/5 ounce (about 11.5 grams). [f]12 That is, 60 shekels; the common mina was 50 shekels. [g]15 Traditionally *peace offerings*; also in verse 17 [h]24,5 That is, probably about 4 quarts (about 4 liters) [i]2 Traditionally *peace offerings*; also in verse 12 [j]5 That is, probably about 3/5 bushel (about 22 liters)

and with the lambs as much as he wants to give, along with a hin of oil with each ephah. [8]When the prince enters, he is to go in through the portico of the gateway, and he is to come out the same way.

[9]" 'When the people of the land come before the LORD at the appointed feasts, whoever enters by the north gate to worship is to go out the south gate; and whoever enters by the south gate is to go out the north gate. No one is to return through the gate by which he entered, but each is to go out the opposite gate. [10]The prince is to be among them, going in when they go in and going out when they go out.

[11]" 'At the festivals and the appointed feasts, the grain offering is to be an ephah with a bull, an ephah with a ram, and with the lambs as much as one pleases, along with a hin of oil for each ephah. [12]When the prince provides a freewill offering to the LORD—whether a burnt offering or fellowship offerings—the gate facing east is to be opened for him. He shall offer his burnt offering or his fellowship offerings as he does on the Sabbath day. Then he shall go out, and after he has gone out, the gate will be shut.

[13]" 'Every day you are to provide a year-old lamb without defect for a burnt offering to the LORD; morning by morning you shall provide it. [14]You are also to provide with it morning by morning a grain offering, consisting of a sixth of an ephah with a third of a hin of oil to moisten the flour. The presenting of this grain offering to the LORD is a lasting ordinance. [15]So the lamb and the grain offering and the oil shall be provided morning by morning for a regular burnt offering.

[16]" 'This is what the Sovereign LORD says: If the prince makes a gift from his inheritance to one of his sons, it will also belong to his descendants; it is to be their property by inheritance. [17]If, however, he makes a gift from his inheritance to one of his servants, the servant may keep it until the year of freedom; then it will revert to the prince. His inheritance belongs to his sons only; it is theirs. [18]The prince must not take any of the inheritance of the people, driving them off their property. He is to give his sons their inheritance out of his own property, so that none of my people will be separated from his property.' "

[19]Then the man brought me through the entrance at the side of the gate to the sacred rooms facing north, which belonged to the priests, and showed me a place at the western end. [20]He said to me, "This is the place where the priests will cook the guilt offering and the sin offering and bake the grain offering, to avoid bringing them into the outer court and consecrating the people."

[21]He then brought me to the outer court and led me around to its four corners, and I saw in each corner another court. [22]In the four corners of the outer court were enclosed[a] courts, forty cubits long and thirty cubits wide; each of the courts in the four corners was the same size. [23]Around the inside of each of the four courts was a ledge of stone, with places for fire built all around under the ledge. [24]He said to me, "These are the kitchens where those who minister at the temple will cook the sacrifices of the people."

The River From the Temple

47 The man brought me back to the entrance of the temple, and I saw water coming out from under the threshold of the temple toward the east (for the temple faced east). The water was coming down from under the south side of the temple, south of the altar. [2]He then brought me out through the north gate and led me around the outside to the outer gate facing east, and the water was flowing from the south side.

[3]As the man went eastward with a measuring line in his hand, he measured off a thousand cubits[b] and then led me through water that was ankle-deep. [4]He measured off another thousand cubits and led me through water that was knee-deep. He measured off another thousand and led me through water that was up to the waist. [5]He measured off another thousand, but now it was a river that I could not cross, because the water had risen and was deep enough to swim in—a river that no one could cross. [6]He asked me, "Son of man, do you see this?"

Then he led me back to the bank of the river. [7]When I arrived there, I saw a great number of trees on each side of the river. [8]He said to me, "This water flows toward the eastern region and goes down into the Arabah,[c] where it enters the Sea.[d] When it empties into the Sea,[d] the water there becomes fresh. [9]Swarms of living creatures will live wherever the river flows. There will be large numbers of fish, because this water flows there and makes the salt water fresh; so where the river flows everything will live. [10]Fishermen will stand along the shore; from En Gedi to En Eglaim there will be places for spreading nets. The fish will be of many kinds—like the fish of the Great Sea.[e] [11]But the swamps and marshes will not become fresh; they will be left for salt. [12]Fruit trees of all kinds will grow on both banks of the river. Their leaves will not wither, nor will their fruit fail. Every month they will bear, be-

a22 The meaning of the Hebrew for this word is uncertain. *b3* That is, about 1,500 feet (about 450 meters) *c8* Or *the Jordan Valley* *d8* That is, the Dead Sea *e10* That is, the Mediterranean; also in verses 15, 19 and 20

cause the water from the sanctuary flows to
them. Their fruit will serve for food and their
leaves for healing."

The Boundaries of the Land

13This is what the Sovereign LORD says:
"These are the boundaries by which you are to
divide the land for an inheritance among the
twelve tribes of Israel, with two portions for Joseph. 14You are to divide it equally among them.
Because I swore with uplifted hand to give it to
your forefathers, this land will become your inheritance.

15"This is to be the boundary of the land:

"On the north side it will run from the Great
Sea by the Hethlon road past Lebo[a] Hamath to Zedad, 16Berothah[b] and Sibraim
(which lies on the border between Damascus and Hamath), as far as Hazer Hatticon,
which is on the border of Hauran. 17The
boundary will extend from the sea to Hazar
Enan,[c] along the northern border of Damascus, with the border of Hamath to the
north. This will be the north boundary.
18"On the east side the boundary will run between Hauran and Damascus, along the Jordan between Gilead and the land of Israel, to
the eastern sea and as far as Tamar.[d] This
will be the east boundary.
19"On the south side it will run from Tamar as far
as the waters of Meribah Kadesh, then along
the Wadi ⌞of Egypt⌟ to the Great Sea. This
will be the south boundary.
20"On the west side, the Great Sea will be the
boundary to a point opposite Lebo[e] Hamath. This will be the west boundary.

21"You are to distribute this land among yourselves according to the tribes of Israel. 22You are
to allot it as an inheritance for yourselves and for
the aliens who have settled among you and who
have children. You are to consider them as
native-born Israelites; along with you they are to
be allotted an inheritance among the tribes of
Israel. 23In whatever tribe the alien settles, there
you are to give him his inheritance," declares the
Sovereign LORD.

The Division of the Land

48 "These are the tribes, listed by name: At
the northern frontier, Dan will have one
portion; it will follow the Hethlon road to Lebo[f]
Hamath; Hazar Enan and the northern border of
Damascus next to Hamath will be part of its border from the east side to the west side.
2"Asher will have one portion; it will border
the territory of Dan from east to west.
3"Naphtali will have one portion; it will border
the territory of Asher from east to west.
4"Manasseh will have one portion; it will border the territory of Naphtali from east to west.
5"Ephraim will have one portion; it will border
the territory of Manasseh from east to west.
6"Reuben will have one portion; it will border
the territory of Ephraim from east to west.
7"Judah will have one portion; it will border
the territory of Reuben from east to west.
8"Bordering the territory of Judah from east to
west will be the portion you are to present as a
special gift. It will be 25,000 cubits[g] wide, and
its length from east to west will equal one of the
tribal portions; the sanctuary will be in the center
of it.
9"The special portion you are to offer to the
LORD will be 25,000 cubits long and 10,000 cubits[h] wide. 10This will be the sacred portion for
the priests. It will be 25,000 cubits long on the
north side, 10,000 cubits wide on the west side,
10,000 cubits wide on the east side and 25,000
cubits long on the south side. In the center of it
will be the sanctuary of the LORD. 11This will be
for the consecrated priests, the Zadokites, who
were faithful in serving me and did not go astray
as the Levites did when the Israelites went
astray. 12It will be a special gift to them from the
sacred portion of the land, a most holy portion,
bordering the territory of the Levites.
13"Alongside the territory of the priests,
the Levites will have an allotment 25,000 cubits
long and 10,000 cubits wide. Its total length
will be 25,000 cubits and its width 10,000
cubits. 14They must not sell or exchange any of
it. This is the best of the land and must not
pass into other hands, because it is holy to the
LORD.
15"The remaining area, 5,000 cubits wide and
25,000 cubits long, will be for the common use
of the city, for houses and for pastureland. The
city will be in the center of it 16and will have
these measurements: the north side 4,500 cubits, the south side 4,500 cubits, the east side
4,500 cubits, and the west side 4,500 cubits.
17The pastureland for the city will be 250 cubits
on the north, 250 cubits on the south, 250
cubits on the east, and 250 cubits on the west.
18What remains of the area, bordering on the
sacred portion and running the length of it, will

[a] 15 Or *past the entrance to* [b] 15,16 See Septuagint and Ezekiel 48:1; Hebrew *road to go into Zedad, 16Hamath, Berothah*
[c] 17 Hebrew *Enon*, a variant of *Enan* [d] 18 Septuagint and Syriac; Hebrew *Israel. You will measure to the eastern sea*
[e] 20 Or *opposite the entrance to* [f] 1 Or *to the entrance to* [g] 8 That is, about 7 miles (about 12 kilometers) [h] 9 That is,
about 3 miles (about 5 kilometers)

be 10,000 cubits on the east side and 10,000
cubits on the west side. Its produce will supply
food for the workers of the city. 19The workers
from the city who farm it will come from all the
tribes of Israel. 20The entire portion will be a
square, 25,000 cubits on each side. As a special
gift you will set aside the sacred portion, along
with the property of the city.

21"What remains on both sides of the area
formed by the sacred portion and the city property will belong to the prince. It will extend eastward from the 25,000 cubits of the sacred portion to the eastern border, and westward from
the 25,000 cubits to the western border. Both
these areas running the length of the tribal
portions will belong to the prince, and the
sacred portion with the temple sanctuary will be
in the center of them. 22So the property of the
Levites and the property of the city will lie in
the center of the area that belongs to the prince.
The area belonging to the prince will lie between the border of Judah and the border of
Benjamin.

23"As for the rest of the tribes: Benjamin will
have one portion; it will extend from the east
side to the west side.

24"Simeon will have one portion; it will border
the territory of Benjamin from east to west.

25"Issachar will have one portion; it will border the territory of Simeon from east to west.

26"Zebulun will have one portion; it will border the territory of Issachar from east to west.

27"Gad will have one portion; it will border
the territory of Zebulun from east to west.

28"The southern boundary of Gad will run
south from Tamar to the waters of Meribah Kadesh, then along the Wadi ⌞of Egypt⌟ to the Great
Sea.[a]

29"This is the land you are to allot as an inheritance to the tribes of Israel, and these will be
their portions," declares the Sovereign LORD.

The Gates of the City

30"These will be the exits of the city: Beginning on the north side, which is 4,500 cubits
long, 31the gates of the city will be named after
the tribes of Israel. The three gates on the north
side will be the gate of Reuben, the gate of Judah
and the gate of Levi.

32"On the east side, which is 4,500 cubits
long, will be three gates: the gate of Joseph, the
gate of Benjamin and the gate of Dan.

33"On the south side, which measures 4,500
cubits, will be three gates: the gate of Simeon,
the gate of Issachar and the gate of Zebulun.

34"On the west side, which is 4,500 cubits
long, will be three gates: the gate of Gad, the gate
of Asher and the gate of Naphtali.

35"The distance all around will be 18,000 cubits.

"And the name of the city from that time on
will be:

THE LORD IS THERE."

[a]*28* That is, the Mediterranean

Introduction to
DANIEL

Personal Reading Plan

- ❐ Daniel 1:1–2:49
- ❐ Daniel 3:1–4:37
- ❐ Daniel 5:1–6:28
- ❐ Daniel 7:1–8:27
- ❐ Daniel 9:1–11:1
- ❐ Daniel 11:2–12:13

Author

Daniel (whose name means "God is my judge") was an exiled Israelite statesman in the dominating empires of his time.

Date

The date for the writing of this book has been vigorously debated. Scholars who regard the book as genuine predictive prophecy date it c. 530 B.C., near the end of Daniel's life. The events depicted in the life of Daniel and his friends (chapters 1–6) are set in the time of the Babylonian captivity (605–538 B.C.) and the onset of the Persian Empire. The visions (chapters 7–12) look ahead to succeeding history, at least to 160 B.C., and perhaps to events still in the future even today.

Theme

God is sovereign over the kingdoms of men (2:21; 5:21).

Historical Background

In 605 B.C. Nebuchadnezzar took Daniel and other captives to Babylon. Daniel rose quickly to prominence under Nebuchadnezzar. After the king's death, Daniel seems to have fallen from favor only to regain it by interpreting the handwriting on the wall at Belshazzar's feast (5:13–29). With the capture of Babylon by Darius, Daniel maintained his official position, serving under both Darius and Cyrus, the king of Persia.

Characteristics

Daniel is written in the context of the Exile. It calls for a commitment to God's Law amongst the people of God who are suffering persecution (even unto death). Daniel beckons them to awaken and prepare for the unexpected intervention of God into world affairs. Jesus refers to Daniel in his teachings (Matt. 24:15) and quotes from 9:27; 11:31 and 12:11. The book of Revelation draws heavily from Daniel's apocalyptic imagery (in chapters 7–12).

Passages for Topical Group Study

1:1–21	DRUGS / ALCOHOL	Daniel's Training in Babylon
3:1–12,19–27	FAITH	The Image of Gold and the Fiery Furnace

See the Lesson Plans in the front of this Bible.

Passage for General Group Study

6:1–24	Daniel in the Den of Lions

Daniel's Training in Babylon

1 In the third year of the reign of Jehoiakim
king of Judah, Nebuchadnezzar king of Babylon came to Jerusalem and besieged it. 2And the
Lord delivered Jehoiakim king of Judah into his
hand, along with some of the articles from the
temple of God. These he carried off to the temple
of his god in Babylonia[a] and put in the treasure
house of his god.

DANIEL 1:1–21

1. What is your favorite food? Your favorite drink?
2. Could you "survive" on a diet of vegetables and water?
3. Do you know someone who started out "testing" drugs and alcohol and now has a problem?
4. How would your classmates view someone who wouldn't drink, like Daniel?
5. In your own life, where do you draw the line on alcohol use?
6. Our bodies are God's temple (1 Cor. 6:19). What area do you need to work on: Eating habits? Sleeping habits? Exercise habits? Use of alcohol, drugs or tobacco?
7. How can this group help you live a healthier lifestyle? Pray together.

3Then the king ordered Ashpenaz, chief of his
court officials, to bring in some of the Israelites
from the royal family and the nobility— 4young
men without any physical defect, handsome,
showing aptitude for every kind of learning, well
informed, quick to understand, and qualified to
serve in the king's palace. He was to teach them
the language and literature of the Babylonians.[b]
5The king assigned them a daily amount of food
and wine from the king's table. They were to be
trained for three years, and after that they were
to enter the king's service.

6Among these were some from Judah: Daniel,
Hananiah, Mishael and Azariah. 7The chief offi-
cial gave them new names: to Daniel, the name
Belteshazzar; to Hananiah, Shadrach; to Mishael,
Meshach; and to Azariah, Abednego.

8But Daniel resolved not to defile himself with
the royal food and wine, and he asked the chief
official for permission not to defile himself this
way. 9Now God had caused the official to show
favor and sympathy to Daniel, 10but the official
told Daniel, "I am afraid of my lord the king, who
has assigned your[c] food and drink. Why should
he see you looking worse than the other young
men your age? The king would then have my
head because of you."

11Daniel then said to the guard whom the
chief official had appointed over Daniel, Hananiah, Mishael and Azariah, 12"Please test your servants for ten days: Give us nothing but vegetables
to eat and water to drink. 13Then compare our
appearance with that of the young men who eat
the royal food, and treat your servants in accordance with what you see." 14So he agreed to this
and tested them for ten days.

15At the end of the ten days they looked
healthier and better nourished than any of the
young men who ate the royal food. 16So the guard
took away their choice food and the wine they
were to drink and gave them vegetables instead.

17To these four young men God gave knowledge and understanding of all kinds of literature
and learning. And Daniel could understand visions and dreams of all kinds.

18At the end of the time set by the king to
bring them in, the chief official presented them
to Nebuchadnezzar. 19The king talked with
them, and he found none equal to Daniel, Hananiah, Mishael and Azariah; so they entered the

[a] 2 Hebrew *Shinar* [b] 4 Or *Chaldeans* [c] 10 The Hebrew for *your* and *you* in this verse is plural.

1:1–2 Rather than betraying Judah, God was keeping his promise: his covenant with his people promised blessing for obeying him and punishment if they didn't (Deut. 28:45–52). God made certain the nation survived the exile and learned from it.

1:6–7 The four Hebrew exiles were given new names honoring the false gods of Babylon. These young teenagers were probably hostages, and protesting may have meant death both for them and their families back home in Judah.

1:8 ***royal food and wine.*** Israelites considered food from Nebuchadnezzar's table to be contaminated because the first portion of it was offered to idols, which prohibited faithful Jews from eating it (Ex. 34:15). Likewise a portion of the wine was poured out on a pagan altar. Ceremonially unclean animals were used and were neither slaughtered nor prepared according to the regulations of the Law of Moses. ***he asked the chief official for permission not to defile himself.*** Daniel demonstrated the courage of his convictions.

1:12 ***test your servants.*** Daniel used good judgment by offering an alternative instead of rebelling. ***ten.*** Often had the symbolic significance of completeness.

1:17 With God's help, Daniel and his friends mastered the Babylonian literature on astrology and divination by dreams. But in the crucial tests of interpretation and prediction (see 2:3–11; 4:7), all the pagan literature proved worthless. Only by God's special revelation (2:17–28) was Daniel able to interpret correctly.

king's service. 20In every matter of wisdom and
understanding about which the king questioned
them, he found them ten times better than all the
magicians and enchanters in his whole kingdom.
21And Daniel remained there until the first
year of King Cyrus.

Nebuchadnezzar's Dream

2 In the second year of his reign, Nebuchadnezzar had dreams; his mind was troubled
and he could not sleep. 2So the king summoned
the magicians, enchanters, sorcerers and astrologers[a] to tell him what he had dreamed. When
they came in and stood before the king, 3he said
to them, "I have had a dream that troubles me
and I want to know what it means.[b]"
4Then the astrologers answered the king in
Aramaic,[c] "O king, live forever! Tell your servants the dream, and we will interpret it."
5The king replied to the astrologers, "This is
what I have firmly decided: If you do not tell me
what my dream was and interpret it, I will have
you cut into pieces and your houses turned into
piles of rubble. 6But if you tell me the dream and
explain it, you will receive from me gifts and
rewards and great honor. So tell me the dream
and interpret it for me."
7Once more they replied, "Let the king tell his
servants the dream, and we will interpret it."
8Then the king answered, "I am certain that
you are trying to gain time, because you realize
that this is what I have firmly decided: 9If you do
not tell me the dream, there is just one penalty
for you. You have conspired to tell me misleading
and wicked things, hoping the situation will
change. So then, tell me the dream, and I will
know that you can interpret it for me."
10The astrologers answered the king, "There is
not a man on earth who can do what the king
asks! No king, however great and mighty, has
ever asked such a thing of any magician or enchanter or astrologer. 11What the king asks is too
difficult. No one can reveal it to the king except
the gods, and they do not live among men."
12This made the king so angry and furious that
he ordered the execution of all the wise men of
Babylon. 13So the decree was issued to put the
wise men to death, and men were sent to look for
Daniel and his friends to put them to death.
14When Arioch, the commander of the king's
guard, had gone out to put to death the wise men
of Babylon, Daniel spoke to him with wisdom and
tact. 15He asked the king's officer, "Why did the
king issue such a harsh decree?" Arioch then explained the matter to Daniel. 16At this, Daniel
went in to the king and asked for time, so that he
might interpret the dream for him.
17Then Daniel returned to his house and explained the matter to his friends Hananiah, Mishael and Azariah. 18He urged them to plead for
mercy from the God of heaven concerning this
mystery, so that he and his friends might not be
executed with the rest of the wise men of Babylon. 19During the night the mystery was revealed to Daniel in a vision. Then Daniel praised
the God of heaven 20and said:

"Praise be to the name of God for ever and
ever;
wisdom and power are his.
21He changes times and seasons;
he sets up kings and deposes them.
He gives wisdom to the wise
and knowledge to the discerning.
22He reveals deep and hidden things;
he knows what lies in darkness,
and light dwells with him.
23I thank and praise you, O God of my fathers:
You have given me wisdom and power,
you have made known to me what we asked
of you,
you have made known to us the dream of
the king."

Daniel Interprets the Dream

24Then Daniel went to Arioch, whom the king
had appointed to execute the wise men of Babylon, and said to him, "Do not execute the wise
men of Babylon. Take me to the king, and I will
interpret his dream for him."
25Arioch took Daniel to the king at once and
said, "I have found a man among the exiles from
Judah who can tell the king what his dream
means."
26The king asked Daniel (also called Belteshazzar), "Are you able to tell me what I saw in my
dream and interpret it?"
27Daniel replied, "No wise man, enchanter,
magician or diviner can explain to the king the
mystery he has asked about, 28but there is a God
in heaven who reveals mysteries. He has shown
King Nebuchadnezzar what will happen in days
to come. Your dream and the visions that passed
through your mind as you lay on your bed are
these:
29"As you were lying there, O king, your mind
turned to things to come, and the revealer of
mysteries showed you what is going to happen.
30As for me, this mystery has been revealed to
me, not because I have greater wisdom than other living men, but so that you, O king, may know
the interpretation and that you may understand
what went through your mind.
31"You looked, O king, and there before you

[a]2 Or *Chaldeans*; also in verses 4, 5 and 10 [b]3 Or *was* [c]4 The text from here through chapter 7 is in Aramaic.

stood a large statue—an enormous, dazzling statue, awesome in appearance. [32]The head of the statue was made of pure gold, its chest and arms of silver, its belly and thighs of bronze, [33]its legs of iron, its feet partly of iron and partly of baked clay. [34]While you were watching, a rock was cut out, but not by human hands. It struck the statue on its feet of iron and clay and smashed them. [35]Then the iron, the clay, the bronze, the silver and the gold were broken to pieces at the same time and became like chaff on a threshing floor in the summer. The wind swept them away without leaving a trace. But the rock that struck the statue became a huge mountain and filled the whole earth.

[36]"This was the dream, and now we will interpret it to the king. [37]You, O king, are the king of kings. The God of heaven has given you dominion and power and might and glory; [38]in your hands he has placed mankind and the beasts of the field and the birds of the air. Wherever they live, he has made you ruler over them all. You are that head of gold.

[39]"After you, another kingdom will rise, inferior to yours. Next, a third kingdom, one of bronze, will rule over the whole earth. [40]Finally, there will be a fourth kingdom, strong as iron—for iron breaks and smashes everything—and as iron breaks things to pieces, so it will crush and break all the others. [41]Just as you saw that the feet and toes were partly of baked clay and partly of iron, so this will be a divided kingdom; yet it will have some of the strength of iron in it, even as you saw iron mixed with clay. [42]As the toes were partly iron and partly clay, so this kingdom will be partly strong and partly brittle. [43]And just as you saw the iron mixed with baked clay, so the people will be a mixture and will not remain united, any more than iron mixes with clay.

[44]"In the time of those kings, the God of heaven will set up a kingdom that will never be destroyed, nor will it be left to another people. It will crush all those kingdoms and bring them to an end, but it will itself endure forever. [45]This is the meaning of the vision of the rock cut out of a mountain, but not by human hands—a rock that broke the iron, the bronze, the clay, the silver and the gold to pieces.

"The great God has shown the king what will take place in the future. The dream is true and the interpretation is trustworthy."

[46]Then King Nebuchadnezzar fell prostrate before Daniel and paid him honor and ordered that an offering and incense be presented to him. [47]The king said to Daniel, "Surely your God is the God of gods and the Lord of kings and a revealer of mysteries, for you were able to reveal this mystery."

[48]Then the king placed Daniel in a high position and lavished many gifts on him. He made him ruler over the entire province of Babylon and placed him in charge of all its wise men. [49]Moreover, at Daniel's request the king appointed Shadrach, Meshach and Abednego administrators over the province of Babylon, while Daniel himself remained at the royal court.

The Image of Gold and the Fiery Furnace

3 King Nebuchadnezzar made an image of gold, ninety feet high and nine feet[a] wide, and set it up on the plain of Dura in the province of Babylon. [2]He then summoned the satraps, prefects, governors, advisers, treasurers, judges, magistrates and all the other provincial officials to come to the dedication of the image he had set up. [3]So the satraps, prefects, governors, advisers, treasurers, judges, magistrates and all the other provincial officials assembled for the dedication of the image that King Nebuchadnezzar had set up, and they stood before it.

[4]Then the herald loudly proclaimed, "This is what you are commanded to do, O peoples, nations and men of every language: [5]As soon as you hear the sound of the horn, flute, zither, lyre, harp, pipes and all kinds of music, you must fall down and worship the image of gold that King Nebuchadnezzar has set up. [6]Whoever does not fall down and worship will immediately be thrown into a blazing furnace."

[7]Therefore, as soon as they heard the sound of the horn, flute, zither, lyre, harp and all kinds of music, all the peoples, nations and men of every language fell down and worshiped the image of gold that King Nebuchadnezzar had set up.

[8]At this time some astrologers[b] came forward and denounced the Jews. [9]They said to King Nebuchadnezzar, "O king, live forever! [10]You have issued a decree, O king, that everyone who hears the sound of the horn, flute, zither, lyre, harp, pipes and all kinds of music must fall down and worship the image of gold, [11]and that whoever does not fall down and worship will be thrown into a blazing furnace. [12]But there are some Jews whom you have set over the affairs of the province of Babylon—Shadrach, Meshach and Abednego—who pay no attention to you, O king. They neither serve your gods nor worship the image of gold you have set up."

[13]Furious with rage, Nebuchadnezzar summoned Shadrach, Meshach and Abednego. So these men were brought before the king, [14]and Nebuchadnezzar said to them, "Is it true, Sha-

[a] 1 Aramaic *sixty cubits high and six cubits wide* (about 27 meters high and 2.7 meters wide) [b] 8 Or *Chaldeans*

drach, Meshach and Abednego, that you do not serve my gods or worship the image of gold I have set up? 15 Now when you hear the sound of the horn, flute, zither, lyre, harp, pipes and all kinds of music, if you are ready to fall down and worship the image I made, very good. But if you do not worship it, you will be thrown immediately into a blazing furnace. Then what god will be able to rescue you from my hand?"

16 Shadrach, Meshach and Abednego replied to the king, "O Nebuchadnezzar, we do not need to defend ourselves before you in this matter. 17 If we are thrown into the blazing furnace, the God we serve is able to save us from it, and he will rescue us from your hand, O king. 18 But even if he does not, we want you to know, O king, that we will not serve your gods or worship the image of gold you have set up."

19 Then Nebuchadnezzar was furious with Shadrach, Meshach and Abednego, and his attitude toward them changed. He ordered the furnace heated seven times hotter than usual 20 and commanded some of the strongest soldiers in his army to tie up Shadrach, Meshach and Abednego and throw them into the blazing furnace. 21 So these men, wearing their robes, trousers, turbans and other clothes, were bound and thrown into the blazing furnace. 22 The king's command was so urgent and the furnace so hot that the flames of the fire killed the soldiers who took up Shadrach, Meshach and Abednego, 23 and these three men, firmly tied, fell into the blazing furnace.

24 Then King Nebuchadnezzar leaped to his feet in amazement and asked his advisers, "Weren't there three men that we tied up and threw into the fire?"

They replied, "Certainly, O king."

25 He said, "Look! I see four men walking around in the fire, unbound and unharmed, and the fourth looks like a son of the gods."

26 Nebuchadnezzar then approached the opening of the blazing furnace and shouted, "Shadrach, Meshach and Abednego, servants of the Most High God, come out! Come here!"

So Shadrach, Meshach and Abednego came out of the fire, 27 and the satraps, prefects, governors and royal advisers crowded around them. They saw that the fire had not harmed their bodies, nor was a hair of their heads singed; their robes were not scorched, and there was no smell of fire on them.

DANIEL 3:1–12,19–27

1. When you were a kid, who was your hero? What was it about this person that made them your hero?
2. What idols do you face in your school? How are people treated at your school who do not "bow down" to them?
3. What do you admire most about the young Hebrews: Their witness for the Lord? Their faith in God for a miracle? Their trust in God no matter what?
4. What is one "non-negotiable" in your life—something you will not do or say?
5. In many countries, Christians are persecuted. How would your faith stand up if you had to die for it?
6. Where are you being pressured right now to compromise your convictions?
7. Encourage one another. Pray for strong faith in the face of trials.

28 Then Nebuchadnezzar said, "Praise be to the God of Shadrach, Meshach and Abednego, who has sent his angel and rescued his servants! They trusted in him and defied the king's command and were willing to give up their lives rather than serve or worship any god except their own God. 29 Therefore I decree that the people of any nation or language who say anything against the God of

---

3:1–3 ***image of gold.*** Large statues of this kind were not made of solid gold but were plated with gold. ***ninety feet high.*** Including the lofty pedestal on which it no doubt stood. The seven classifications of government officials were to pledge full allegiance to the newly established empire as they stood before the image. The image probably represented the god Nabu, whose name formed the first element in Nebuchadnezzar's name.

3:12 ***They neither serve your gods nor worship the image.*** The three young Jews (see 1:3–7,18–19) obeyed the word of God (Ex. 20:3–5) above the word of the king. Shadrach, Meshach and Abednego had faith in God's ability to rescue them from the fire, though their faith wasn't contingent on that deliverance. Either way, they would remain faithful (vv. 16–18).

3:19 The temperature of the furnace was controlled by the number of bellows forcing air into the fire chamber. Therefore sevenfold intensification was achieved by seven bellows pumping at the same time. But the expression "seven times hotter than usual" may have been figurative for "as hot as possible" (seven signifies completeness).

3:25 ***son of the gods.*** Though some believe the fourth man in the furnace was the preincarnate Son of God, Nebuchadnezzar was speaking as a pagan polytheist and was content to conceive of the fourth figure as a lesser heavenly being (v. 28) sent by the all-powerful God of the Israelites.

Shadrach, Meshach and Abednego be cut into pieces and their houses be turned into piles of rubble, for no other god can save in this way."

30 Then the king promoted Shadrach, Meshach and Abednego in the province of Babylon.

Nebuchadnezzar's Dream of a Tree

4 King Nebuchadnezzar,

To the peoples, nations and men of every language, who live in all the world:

May you prosper greatly!

2 It is my pleasure to tell you about the miraculous signs and wonders that the Most High God has performed for me.

3 How great are his signs,
  how mighty his wonders!
His kingdom is an eternal kingdom;
  his dominion endures from
    generation to generation.

4 I, Nebuchadnezzar, was at home in my palace, contented and prosperous. 5 I had a dream that made me afraid. As I was lying in my bed, the images and visions that passed through my mind terrified me. 6 So I commanded that all the wise men of Babylon be brought before me to interpret the dream for me. 7 When the magicians, enchanters, astrologers[a] and diviners came, I told them the dream, but they could not interpret it for me. 8 Finally, Daniel came into my presence and I told him the dream. (He is called Belteshazzar, after the name of my god, and the spirit of the holy gods is in him.)

9 I said, "Belteshazzar, chief of the magicians, I know that the spirit of the holy gods is in you, and no mystery is too difficult for you. Here is my dream; interpret it for me. 10 These are the visions I saw while lying in my bed: I looked, and there before me stood a tree in the middle of the land. Its height was enormous. 11 The tree grew large and strong and its top touched the sky; it was visible to the ends of the earth. 12 Its leaves were beautiful, its fruit abundant, and on it was food for all. Under it the beasts of the field found shelter, and the birds of the air lived in its branches; from it every creature was fed.

13 "In the visions I saw while lying in my bed, I looked, and there before me was a messenger,[b] a holy one, coming down from heaven. 14 He called in a loud voice: 'Cut down the tree and trim off its branches; strip off its leaves and scatter its fruit. Let the animals flee from under it and the birds from its branches. 15 But let the stump and its roots, bound with iron and bronze, remain in the ground, in the grass of the field.

" 'Let him be drenched with the dew of heaven, and let him live with the animals among the plants of the earth. 16 Let his mind be changed from that of a man and let him be given the mind of an animal, till seven times[c] pass by for him.

17 " 'The decision is announced by messengers, the holy ones declare the verdict, so that the living may know that the Most High is sovereign over the kingdoms of men and gives them to anyone he wishes and sets over them the lowliest of men.'

18 "This is the dream that I, King Nebuchadnezzar, had. Now, Belteshazzar, tell me what it means, for none of the wise men in my kingdom can interpret it for me. But you can, because the spirit of the holy gods is in you."

Daniel Interprets the Dream

19 Then Daniel (also called Belteshazzar) was greatly perplexed for a time, and his thoughts terrified him. So the king said, "Belteshazzar, do not let the dream or its meaning alarm you."

Belteshazzar answered, "My lord, if only the dream applied to your enemies and its meaning to your adversaries! 20 The tree you saw, which grew large and strong, with its top touching the sky, visible to the whole earth, 21 with beautiful leaves and abundant fruit, providing food for all, giving shelter to the beasts of the field, and having nesting places in its branches for the birds of the air— 22 you, O king, are that tree! You have become great and strong; your greatness has grown until it reaches the sky, and your dominion extends to distant parts of the earth.

23 "You, O king, saw a messenger, a holy one, coming down from heaven and saying, 'Cut down the tree and destroy it, but leave the stump, bound with iron and bronze, in the grass of the field, while its roots remain in the ground. Let him be drenched with the dew of heaven; let him live like the wild animals, until seven times pass by for him.'

24 "This is the interpretation, O king, and this is the decree the Most High has issued against my lord the king: 25 You will be driven away from people and will live with the

[a] 7 Or *Chaldeans* [b] 13 Or *watchman*; also in verses 17 and 23 [c] 16 Or *years*; also in verses 23, 25 and 32

wild animals; you will eat grass like cattle and be drenched with the dew of heaven. Seven times will pass by for you until you acknowledge that the Most High is sovereign over the kingdoms of men and gives them to anyone he wishes. 26The command to leave the stump of the tree with its roots means that your kingdom will be restored to you when you acknowledge that Heaven rules. 27Therefore, O king, be pleased to accept my advice: Renounce your sins by doing what is right, and your wickedness by being kind to the oppressed. It may be that then your prosperity will continue."

The Dream Is Fulfilled

28All this happened to King Nebuchadnezzar. 29Twelve months later, as the king was walking on the roof of the royal palace of Babylon, 30he said, "Is not this the great Babylon I have built as the royal residence, by my mighty power and for the glory of my majesty?"

31The words were still on his lips when a voice came from heaven, "This is what is decreed for you, King Nebuchadnezzar: Your royal authority has been taken from you. 32You will be driven away from people and will live with the wild animals; you will eat grass like cattle. Seven times will pass by for you until you acknowledge that the Most High is sovereign over the kingdoms of men and gives them to anyone he wishes."

33Immediately what had been said about Nebuchadnezzar was fulfilled. He was driven away from people and ate grass like cattle. His body was drenched with the dew of heaven until his hair grew like the feathers of an eagle and his nails like the claws of a bird.

34At the end of that time, I, Nebuchadnezzar, raised my eyes toward heaven, and my sanity was restored. Then I praised the Most High; I honored and glorified him who lives forever.

His dominion is an eternal dominion;
  his kingdom endures from generation to
    generation.
35All the peoples of the earth
  are regarded as nothing.
He does as he pleases
  with the powers of heaven
  and the peoples of the earth.
No one can hold back his hand
  or say to him: "What have you done?"

36At the same time that my sanity was restored, my honor and splendor were returned to me for the glory of my kingdom. My advisers and nobles sought me out, and I was restored to my throne and became even greater than before. 37Now I, Nebuchadnezzar, praise and exalt and glorify the King of heaven, because everything he does is right and all his ways are just. And those who walk in pride he is able to humble.

The Writing on the Wall

5 King Belshazzar gave a great banquet for a thousand of his nobles and drank wine with them. 2While Belshazzar was drinking his wine, he gave orders to bring in the gold and silver goblets that Nebuchadnezzar his father[a] had taken from the temple in Jerusalem, so that the king and his nobles, his wives and his concubines might drink from them. 3So they brought in the gold goblets that had been taken from the temple of God in Jerusalem, and the king and his nobles, his wives and his concubines drank from them. 4As they drank the wine, they praised the gods of gold and silver, of bronze, iron, wood and stone.

5Suddenly the fingers of a human hand appeared and wrote on the plaster of the wall, near the lampstand in the royal palace. The king watched the hand as it wrote. 6His face turned pale and he was so frightened that his knees knocked together and his legs gave way.

7The king called out for the enchanters, astrologers[b] and diviners to be brought and said to these wise men of Babylon, "Whoever reads this writing and tells me what it means will be clothed in purple and have a gold chain placed around his neck, and he will be made the third highest ruler in the kingdom."

8Then all the king's wise men came in, but they could not read the writing or tell the king what it meant. 9So King Belshazzar became even more terrified and his face grew more pale. His nobles were baffled.

10The queen,[c] hearing the voices of the king and his nobles, came into the banquet hall. "O king, live forever!" she said. "Don't be alarmed! Don't look so pale! 11There is a man in your kingdom who has the spirit of the holy gods in him. In the time of your father he was found to have insight and intelligence and wisdom like that of the gods. King Nebuchadnezzar your father—your father the king, I say—appointed him chief of the magicians, enchanters, astrologers and diviners. 12This man Daniel, whom the king called Belteshazzar, was found to have a keen mind and knowledge and understanding, and also the ability to interpret dreams, explain

a2 Or *ancestor*; or *predecessor*; also in verses 11, 13 and 18 b7 Or *Chaldeans*; also in verse 11 c10 Or *queen mother*

riddles and solve difficult problems. Call for Daniel, and he will tell you what the writing means."
13So Daniel was brought before the king, and
the king said to him, "Are you Daniel, one of the
exiles my father the king brought from Judah? 14I
have heard that the spirit of the gods is in you
and that you have insight, intelligence and outstanding wisdom. 15The wise men and enchanters were brought before me to read this writing
and tell me what it means, but they could not
explain it. 16Now I have heard that you are able
to give interpretations and to solve difficult problems. If you can read this writing and tell me
what it means, you will be clothed in purple and
have a gold chain placed around your neck, and
you will be made the third highest ruler in the
kingdom."
17Then Daniel answered the king, "You may
keep your gifts for yourself and give your rewards
to someone else. Nevertheless, I will read the
writing for the king and tell him what it means.
18"O king, the Most High God gave your father Nebuchadnezzar sovereignty and greatness
and glory and splendor. 19Because of the high
position he gave him, all the peoples and nations
and men of every language dreaded and feared
him. Those the king wanted to put to death, he
put to death; those he wanted to spare, he
spared; those he wanted to promote, he promoted; and those he wanted to humble, he humbled.
20But when his heart became arrogant and hardened with pride, he was deposed from his royal
throne and stripped of his glory. 21He was driven
away from people and given the mind of an animal; he lived with the wild donkeys and ate grass
like cattle; and his body was drenched with the
dew of heaven, until he acknowledged that the
Most High God is sovereign over the kingdoms of
men and sets over them anyone he wishes.
22"But you his son,[a] O Belshazzar, have not
humbled yourself, though you knew all this. 23In-
stead, you have set yourself up against the Lord
of heaven. You had the goblets from his temple
brought to you, and you and your nobles, your
wives and your concubines drank wine from
them. You praised the gods of silver and gold, of
bronze, iron, wood and stone, which cannot see
or hear or understand. But you did not honor the
God who holds in his hand your life and all your
ways. 24Therefore he sent the hand that wrote
the inscription.
25"This is the inscription that was written:

MENE, MENE, TEKEL, PARSIN[b]

26"This is what these words mean:

Mene[c]: God has numbered the days
of your reign and brought it to an
end.
27*Tekel*[d]: You have been weighed on
the scales and found wanting.
28*Peres*[e]: Your kingdom is divided and
given to the Medes and Per-
sians."

29Then at Belshazzar's command, Daniel was
clothed in purple, a gold chain was placed around
his neck, and he was proclaimed the third highest ruler in the kingdom.
30That very night Belshazzar, king of the Babylonians,[f] was slain, 31and Darius the Mede
took over the kingdom, at the age of sixty-two.

Daniel in the Den of Lions

6 It pleased Darius to appoint 120 satraps to
rule throughout the kingdom, 2with three
administrators over them, one of whom was Daniel. The satraps were made accountable to them
so that the king might not suffer loss. 3Now Daniel so distinguished himself among the administrators and the satraps by his exceptional qualities that the king planned to set him over the
whole kingdom. 4At this, the administrators and
the satraps tried to find grounds for charges
against Daniel in his conduct of government affairs, but they were unable to do so. They could
find no corruption in him, because he was trustworthy and neither corrupt nor negligent. 5Final-
ly these men said, "We will never find any basis
for charges against this man Daniel unless it has
something to do with the law of his God."
6So the administrators and the satraps went as
a group to the king and said: "O King Darius, live
forever! 7The royal administrators, prefects, satraps, advisers and governors have all agreed that
the king should issue an edict and enforce the
decree that anyone who prays to any god or man
during the next thirty days, except to you,
O king, shall be thrown into the lions' den.
8Now, O king, issue the decree and put it in writing so that it cannot be altered—in accordance
with the laws of the Medes and Persians, which
cannot be repealed." 9So King Darius put the decree in writing.
10Now when Daniel learned that the decree
had been published, he went home to his upstairs room where the windows opened toward
Jerusalem. Three times a day he got down on his
knees and prayed, giving thanks to his God, just
as he had done before. 11Then these men went as
a group and found Daniel praying and asking God
for help. 12So they went to the king and spoke to

[a]22 Or *descendant*; or *successor* [b]25 Aramaic *UPARSIN* (that is, *AND PARSIN*) [c]26 *Mene* can mean *numbered* or *mina* (a unit of money). [d]27 *Tekel* can mean *weighed* or *shekel*. [e]28 *Peres* (the singular of *Parsin*) can mean *divided* or *Persia* or *a half mina* or *a half shekel*. [f]30 Or *Chaldeans*

him about his royal decree: "Did you not publish
a decree that during the next thirty days anyone
who prays to any god or man except to you,
O king, would be thrown into the lions' den?"

DANIEL 6:1–24

1. When you were a kid, who tucked you in at night and said prayers with you?
2. When do you pray: Before a test? Before meals? At bedtime? Other?
3. If you were Daniel, would you have continued to pray in public following the king's decree?
4. What saved Daniel: His faith? His innocence? His prayers? The king's prayers? God's faithfulness? Lazy lions?
5. How often do you pray? What do you most often pray for?
6. If you were on trial for being a Christian, what verdict would the evidence require?
7. Like Daniel (vv. 10–11), pray, thanking God and asking for his help.

The king answered, "The decree stands—in
accordance with the laws of the Medes and Persians, which cannot be repealed."
13Then they said to the king, "Daniel, who is
one of the exiles from Judah, pays no attention to
you, O king, or to the decree you put in writing.
He still prays three times a day." 14When the
king heard this, he was greatly distressed; he was
determined to rescue Daniel and made every effort until sundown to save him.
15Then the men went as a group to the king
and said to him, "Remember, O king, that according to the law of the Medes and Persians
no decree or edict that the king issues can be
changed."
16So the king gave the order, and they brought
Daniel and threw him into the lions' den. The
king said to Daniel, "May your God, whom you
serve continually, rescue you!"
17A stone was brought and placed over the
mouth of the den, and the king sealed it with his
own signet ring and with the rings of his nobles,
so that Daniel's situation might not be changed.
18Then the king returned to his palace and spent
the night without eating and without any entertainment being brought to him. And he could not
sleep.
19At the first light of dawn, the king got up and
hurried to the lions' den. 20When he came near
the den, he called to Daniel in an anguished
voice, "Daniel, servant of the living God, has
your God, whom you serve continually, been able
to rescue you from the lions?"
21Daniel answered, "O king, live forever!
22My God sent his angel, and he shut the mouths
of the lions. They have not hurt me, because I
was found innocent in his sight. Nor have I ever
done any wrong before you, O king."
23The king was overjoyed and gave orders to
lift Daniel out of the den. And when Daniel was
lifted from the den, no wound was found on him,
because he had trusted in his God.
24At the king's command, the men who had
falsely accused Daniel were brought in and
thrown into the lions' den, along with their
wives and children. And before they reached the
floor of the den, the lions overpowered them and
crushed all their bones.
25Then King Darius wrote to all the peoples,
nations and men of every language throughout
the land:

"May you prosper greatly!

26"I issue a decree that in every part of
my kingdom people must fear and reverence the God of Daniel.

"For he is the living God
and he endures forever;
his kingdom will not be destroyed,

Daniel, the exiled Israelite, has faithfully served the kings of Babylon. Now, after the Babylonians were conquered by the Medes and Persians, Daniel continues to be a faithful servant.

6:1 ***Darius.*** According to 5:31, "Darius the Mede took over the kingdom." This may have been a local name for King Cyrus, ruler of the Medo-Persian empire that conquered Babylon (see NIV text note on 6:28). Or perhaps Darius was another name for Gubaru, the governor Cyrus put in charge of the newly conquered Babylonian territories.

6:7 The conspirators lied in stating that "all" the royal administrators supported the proposed decree, since they knew that Daniel (totally unaware of the proposal) was the foremost of the three administrators.

6:8 From the Medo-Persian perspective, it was impossible for the law to contradict itself. Overturning a bad decree went beyond just personal embarrassment, because the reigning king *was* the law.

6:10 ***toward Jerusalem.*** Though not required by Scripture, it seems to have been customary for exiled Jews to express their spiritual devotion by praying toward Jerusalem. ***Three times a day.*** See Psalm 55:17.

6:23–24 ***he ... trusted in his God.*** That the lions were ravenously hungry was no obstacle to God's rewarding Daniel's faith by saving his life. ***along with their wives and children.*** In accordance with Persian custom.

his dominion will never end.
27He rescues and he saves;
he performs signs and wonders
in the heavens and on the earth.
He has rescued Daniel
from the power of the lions."

28So Daniel prospered during the reign of Darius and the reign of Cyrus[a] the Persian.

Daniel's Dream of Four Beasts

7 In the first year of Belshazzar king of Babylon, Daniel had a dream, and visions passed through his mind as he was lying on his bed. He wrote down the substance of his dream.

2Daniel said: "In my vision at night I looked, and there before me were the four winds of heaven churning up the great sea. 3Four great beasts, each different from the others, came up out of the sea.

4"The first was like a lion, and it had the wings of an eagle. I watched until its wings were torn off and it was lifted from the ground so that it stood on two feet like a man, and the heart of a man was given to it.

5"And there before me was a second beast, which looked like a bear. It was raised up on one of its sides, and it had three ribs in its mouth between its teeth. It was told, 'Get up and eat your fill of flesh!'

6"After that, I looked, and there before me was another beast, one that looked like a leopard. And on its back it had four wings like those of a bird. This beast had four heads, and it was given authority to rule.

7"After that, in my vision at night I looked, and there before me was a fourth beast—terrifying and frightening and very powerful. It had large iron teeth; it crushed and devoured its victims and trampled underfoot whatever was left. It was different from all the former beasts, and it had ten horns.

8"While I was thinking about the horns, there before me was another horn, a little one, which came up among them; and three of the first horns were uprooted before it. This horn had eyes like the eyes of a man and a mouth that spoke boastfully.

9"As I looked,

"thrones were set in place,
and the Ancient of Days took his seat.
His clothing was as white as snow;
the hair of his head was white like wool.
His throne was flaming with fire,
and its wheels were all ablaze.
10A river of fire was flowing,
coming out from before him.
Thousands upon thousands attended him;
ten thousand times ten thousand stood
before him.
The court was seated,
and the books were opened.

11"Then I continued to watch because of the boastful words the horn was speaking. I kept looking until the beast was slain and its body destroyed and thrown into the blazing fire. 12(The other beasts had been stripped of their authority, but were allowed to live for a period of time.)

13"In my vision at night I looked, and there before me was one like a son of man, coming with the clouds of heaven. He approached the Ancient of Days and was led into his presence. 14He was given authority, glory and sovereign power; all peoples, nations and men of every language worshiped him. His dominion is an everlasting dominion that will not pass away, and his kingdom is one that will never be destroyed.

The Interpretation of the Dream

15"I, Daniel, was troubled in spirit, and the visions that passed through my mind disturbed me. 16I approached one of those standing there and asked him the true meaning of all this.

"So he told me and gave me the interpretation of these things: 17'The four great beasts are four kingdoms that will rise from the earth. 18But the saints of the Most High will receive the kingdom and will possess it forever—yes, for ever and ever.'

19"Then I wanted to know the true meaning of the fourth beast, which was different from all the others and most terrifying, with its iron teeth and bronze claws—the beast that crushed and devoured its victims and trampled underfoot whatever was left. 20I also wanted to know about the ten horns on its head and about the other horn that came up, before which three of them fell—the horn that looked more imposing than the others and that had eyes and a mouth that spoke boastfully. 21As I watched, this horn was waging war against the saints and defeating them, 22until the Ancient of Days came and pronounced judgment in favor of the saints of the Most High, and the time came when they possessed the kingdom.

23"He gave me this explanation: 'The fourth beast is a fourth kingdom that will appear on earth. It will be different from all the other kingdoms and will devour the whole earth, trampling it down and crushing it. 24The ten horns are ten kings who will come from this kingdom. After them another king will arise, different from the

[a]28 Or *Darius, that is, the reign of Cyrus*

earlier ones; he will subdue three kings. 25He
will speak against the Most High and oppress his
saints and try to change the set times and the
laws. The saints will be handed over to him for a
time, times and half a time.[a]
26" 'But the court will sit, and his power will
be taken away and completely destroyed forever.
27Then the sovereignty, power and greatness of
the kingdoms under the whole heaven will be
handed over to the saints, the people of the Most
High. His kingdom will be an everlasting kingdom, and all rulers will worship and obey
him.'
28"This is the end of the matter. I, Daniel, was
deeply troubled by my thoughts, and my face
turned pale, but I kept the matter to myself."

Daniel's Vision of a Ram and a Goat

8 In the third year of King Belshazzar's reign,
I, Daniel, had a vision, after the one that had
already appeared to me. 2In my vision I saw myself in the citadel of Susa in the province of Elam;
in the vision I was beside the Ulai Canal. 3I
looked up, and there before me was a ram with
two horns, standing beside the canal, and the
horns were long. One of the horns was longer
than the other but grew up later. 4I watched the
ram as he charged toward the west and the north
and the south. No animal could stand against
him, and none could rescue from his power. He
did as he pleased and became great.
5As I was thinking about this, suddenly a goat
with a prominent horn between his eyes came
from the west, crossing the whole earth without
touching the ground. 6He came toward the two-
horned ram I had seen standing beside the canal
and charged at him in great rage. 7I saw him
attack the ram furiously, striking the ram and
shattering his two horns. The ram was powerless
to stand against him; the goat knocked him to the
ground and trampled on him, and none could
rescue the ram from his power. 8The goat became very great, but at the height of his power
his large horn was broken off, and in its place
four prominent horns grew up toward the four
winds of heaven.
9Out of one of them came another horn, which
started small but grew in power to the south and
to the east and toward the Beautiful Land. 10It
grew until it reached the host of the heavens, and
it threw some of the starry host down to the earth
and trampled on them. 11It set itself up to be as
great as the Prince of the host; it took away the
daily sacrifice from him, and the place of his sanctuary was brought low. 12Because of rebellion,
the host ⌞of the saints⌟[b] and the daily sacrifice
were given over to it. It prospered in everything
it did, and truth was thrown to the ground.
13Then I heard a holy one speaking, and another holy one said to him, "How long will it take for
the vision to be fulfilled—the vision concerning
the daily sacrifice, the rebellion that causes desolation, and the surrender of the sanctuary and of
the host that will be trampled underfoot?"
14He said to me, "It will take 2,300 evenings
and mornings; then the sanctuary will be recon-
secrated."

The Interpretation of the Vision

15While I, Daniel, was watching the vision and
trying to understand it, there before me stood
one who looked like a man. 16And I heard a
man's voice from the Ulai calling, "Gabriel, tell
this man the meaning of the vision."
17As he came near the place where I was
standing, I was terrified and fell prostrate. "Son
of man," he said to me, "understand that the
vision concerns the time of the end."
18While he was speaking to me, I was in a
deep sleep, with my face to the ground. Then he
touched me and raised me to my feet.
19He said: "I am going to tell you what will
happen later in the time of wrath, because the
vision concerns the appointed time of the end.[c]
20The two-horned ram that you saw represents
the kings of Media and Persia. 21The shaggy goat
is the king of Greece, and the large horn between
his eyes is the first king. 22The four horns that
replaced the one that was broken off represent
four kingdoms that will emerge from his nation
but will not have the same power.
23"In the latter part of their reign, when rebels
have become completely wicked, a stern-faced
king, a master of intrigue, will arise. 24He will
become very strong, but not by his own power.
He will cause astounding devastation and will
succeed in whatever he does. He will destroy the
mighty men and the holy people. 25He will cause
deceit to prosper, and he will consider himself
superior. When they feel secure, he will destroy
many and take his stand against the Prince of
princes. Yet he will be destroyed, but not by human power.
26"The vision of the evenings and mornings
that has been given you is true, but seal up the
vision, for it concerns the distant future."
27I, Daniel, was exhausted and lay ill for several days. Then I got up and went about the king's
business. I was appalled by the vision; it was
beyond understanding.

[a]25 Or *for a year, two years and half a year appointed time*
[b]12 Or *rebellion, the armies*
[c]19 Or *because the end will be at the*

Daniel's Prayer

9 In the first year of Darius son of Xerxes[a] (a
Mede by descent), who was made ruler over
the Babylonian[b] kingdom— 2in the first year of
his reign, I, Daniel, understood from the Scriptures, according to the word of the LORD given to
Jeremiah the prophet, that the desolation of Jerusalem would last seventy years. 3So I turned to
the Lord God and pleaded with him in prayer and
petition, in fasting, and in sackcloth and ashes.
4I prayed to the LORD my God and confessed:

"O Lord, the great and awesome God,
who keeps his covenant of love with all who
love him and obey his commands, 5we have
sinned and done wrong. We have been
wicked and have rebelled; we have turned
away from your commands and laws. 6We
have not listened to your servants the
prophets, who spoke in your name to our
kings, our princes and our fathers, and to all
the people of the land.

7"Lord, you are righteous, but this day
we are covered with shame—the men of
Judah and people of Jerusalem and all Israel,
both near and far, in all the countries where
you have scattered us because of our unfaithfulness to you. 8O LORD, we and our
kings, our princes and our fathers are covered with shame because we have sinned
against you. 9The Lord our God is merciful
and forgiving, even though we have rebelled against him; 10we have not obeyed
the LORD our God or kept the laws he gave
us through his servants the prophets. 11All
Israel has transgressed your law and turned
away, refusing to obey you.

"Therefore the curses and sworn judgments written in the Law of Moses, the servant of God, have been poured out on us,
because we have sinned against you. 12You
have fulfilled the words spoken against us
and against our rulers by bringing upon us
great disaster. Under the whole heaven
nothing has ever been done like what has
been done to Jerusalem. 13Just as it is written in the Law of Moses, all this disaster has
come upon us, yet we have not sought the
favor of the LORD our God by turning from
our sins and giving attention to your truth.
14The LORD did not hesitate to bring the
disaster upon us, for the LORD our God is
righteous in everything he does; yet we
have not obeyed him.

15"Now, O Lord our God, who brought
your people out of Egypt with a mighty hand
and who made for yourself a name that endures to this day, we have sinned, we have
done wrong. 16O Lord, in keeping with all
your righteous acts, turn away your anger
and your wrath from Jerusalem, your city,
your holy hill. Our sins and the iniquities of
our fathers have made Jerusalem and your
people an object of scorn to all those
around us.

17"Now, our God, hear the prayers and
petitions of your servant. For your sake,
O Lord, look with favor on your desolate
sanctuary. 18Give ear, O God, and hear;
open your eyes and see the desolation of the
city that bears your Name. We do not make
requests of you because we are righteous,
but because of your great mercy. 19O Lord,
listen! O Lord, forgive! O Lord, hear and
act! For your sake, O my God, do not delay,
because your city and your people bear your
Name."

The Seventy "Sevens"

20While I was speaking and praying, confessing my sin and the sin of my people Israel and
making my request to the LORD my God for his
holy hill— 21while I was still in prayer, Gabriel,
the man I had seen in the earlier vision, came to
me in swift flight about the time of the evening
sacrifice. 22He instructed me and said to me,
"Daniel, I have now come to give you insight and
understanding. 23As soon as you began to pray,
an answer was given, which I have come to tell
you, for you are highly esteemed. Therefore, consider the message and understand the vision:

24"Seventy 'sevens'[c] are decreed for your
people and your holy city to finish[d] transgression, to put an end to sin, to atone for wickedness, to bring in everlasting righteousness, to seal
up vision and prophecy and to anoint the most
holy.[e]

25"Know and understand this: From the issu-
ing of the decree[f] to restore and rebuild Jerusalem until the Anointed One,[g] the ruler, comes,
there will be seven 'sevens,' and sixty-two 'sevens.' It will be rebuilt with streets and a trench,
but in times of trouble. 26After the sixty-two 'sevens,' the Anointed One will be cut off and will
have nothing.[h] The people of the ruler who will
come will destroy the city and the sanctuary. The
end will come like a flood: War will continue
until the end, and desolations have been decreed.
27He will confirm a covenant with many for one
'seven.'[i] In the middle of the 'seven'[i] he will

[a] 1 Hebrew *Ahasuerus* [b] 1 Or *Chaldean* [c] 24 Or *'weeks'*; also in verses 25 and 26 [d] 24 Or *restrain* [e] 24 Or *Most Holy Place*; or *most holy One* [f] 25 Or *word* [g] 25 Or *an anointed one*; also in verse 26 [h] 26 Or *off and will have no one*; or *off, but not for himself* [i] 27 Or *'week'*

put an end to sacrifice and offering. And on a wing ⌞of the temple⌟ he will set up an abomination that causes desolation, until the end that is decreed is poured out on him.[a]"[b]

Daniel's Vision of a Man

10 In the third year of Cyrus king of Persia, a revelation was given to Daniel (who was called Belteshazzar). Its message was true and it concerned a great war.[c] The understanding of the message came to him in a vision.

[2]At that time I, Daniel, mourned for three weeks. [3]I ate no choice food; no meat or wine touched my lips; and I used no lotions at all until the three weeks were over.

[4]On the twenty-fourth day of the first month, as I was standing on the bank of the great river, the Tigris, [5]I looked up and there before me was a man dressed in linen, with a belt of the finest gold around his waist. [6]His body was like chrysolite, his face like lightning, his eyes like flaming torches, his arms and legs like the gleam of burnished bronze, and his voice like the sound of a multitude.

[7]I, Daniel, was the only one who saw the vision; the men with me did not see it, but such terror overwhelmed them that they fled and hid themselves. [8]So I was left alone, gazing at this great vision; I had no strength left, my face turned deathly pale and I was helpless. [9]Then I heard him speaking, and as I listened to him, I fell into a deep sleep, my face to the ground.

[10]A hand touched me and set me trembling on my hands and knees. [11]He said, "Daniel, you who are highly esteemed, consider carefully the words I am about to speak to you, and stand up, for I have now been sent to you." And when he said this to me, I stood up trembling.

[12]Then he continued, "Do not be afraid, Daniel. Since the first day that you set your mind to gain understanding and to humble yourself before your God, your words were heard, and I have come in response to them. [13]But the prince of the Persian kingdom resisted me twenty-one days. Then Michael, one of the chief princes, came to help me, because I was detained there with the king of Persia. [14]Now I have come to explain to you what will happen to your people in the future, for the vision concerns a time yet to come."

[15]While he was saying this to me, I bowed with my face toward the ground and was speechless. [16]Then one who looked like a man[d] touched my lips, and I opened my mouth and began to speak. I said to the one standing before me, "I am overcome with anguish because of the vision, my lord, and I am helpless. [17]How can I, your servant, talk with you, my lord? My strength is gone and I can hardly breathe."

[18]Again the one who looked like a man touched me and gave me strength. [19]"Do not be afraid, O man highly esteemed," he said. "Peace! Be strong now; be strong."

When he spoke to me, I was strengthened and said, "Speak, my lord, since you have given me strength."

[20]So he said, "Do you know why I have come to you? Soon I will return to fight against the prince of Persia, and when I go, the prince of Greece will come; [21]but first I will tell you what is written in the Book of Truth. (No one supports me against them except Michael, your prince.

11 [1]And in the first year of Darius the Mede, I took my stand to support and protect him.)

The Kings of the South and the North

[2]"Now then, I tell you the truth: Three more kings will appear in Persia, and then a fourth, who will be far richer than all the others. When he has gained power by his wealth, he will stir up everyone against the kingdom of Greece. [3]Then a mighty king will appear, who will rule with great power and do as he pleases. [4]After he has appeared, his empire will be broken up and parceled out toward the four winds of heaven. It will not go to his descendants, nor will it have the power he exercised, because his empire will be uprooted and given to others.

[5]"The king of the South will become strong, but one of his commanders will become even stronger than he and will rule his own kingdom with great power. [6]After some years, they will become allies. The daughter of the king of the South will go to the king of the North to make an alliance, but she will not retain her power, and he and his power[e] will not last. In those days she will be handed over, together with her royal escort and her father[f] and the one who supported her.

[7]"One from her family line will arise to take her place. He will attack the forces of the king of the North and enter his fortress; he will fight against them and be victorious. [8]He will also seize their gods, their metal images and their valuable articles of silver and gold and carry them off to Egypt. For some years he will leave the king of the North alone. [9]Then the king of the North will invade the realm of the king of the South but will retreat to his own country. [10]His sons will

[a]27 Or *it* [b]27 Or *And one who causes desolation will come upon the pinnacle of the abominable ⌞temple⌟, until the end that is decreed is poured out on the desolated ⌞city⌟* [c]1 Or *true and burdensome* [d]16 Most manuscripts of the Masoretic Text; one manuscript of the Masoretic Text, Dead Sea Scrolls and Septuagint *Then something that looked like a man's hand* [e]6 Or *offspring* [f]6 Or *child* (see Vulgate and Syriac)

prepare for war and assemble a great army, which will sweep on like an irresistible flood and carry the battle as far as his fortress.

11“Then the king of the South will march out in a rage and fight against the king of the North, who will raise a large army, but it will be defeated. 12When the army is carried off, the king of the South will be filled with pride and will slaughter many thousands, yet he will not remain triumphant. 13For the king of the North will muster another army, larger than the first; and after several years, he will advance with a huge army fully equipped.

14“In those times many will rise against the king of the South. The violent men among your own people will rebel in fulfillment of the vision, but without success. 15Then the king of the North will come and build up siege ramps and will capture a fortified city. The forces of the South will be powerless to resist; even their best troops will not have the strength to stand. 16The invader will do as he pleases; no one will be able to stand against him. He will establish himself in the Beautiful Land and will have the power to destroy it. 17He will determine to come with the might of his entire kingdom and will make an alliance with the king of the South. And he will give him a daughter in marriage in order to overthrow the kingdom, but his plans[a] will not succeed or help him. 18Then he will turn his attention to the coastlands and will take many of them, but a commander will put an end to his insolence and will turn his insolence back upon him. 19After this, he will turn back toward the fortresses of his own country but will stumble and fall, to be seen no more.

20“His successor will send out a tax collector to maintain the royal splendor. In a few years, however, he will be destroyed, yet not in anger or in battle.

21“He will be succeeded by a contemptible person who has not been given the honor of royalty. He will invade the kingdom when its people feel secure, and he will seize it through intrigue. 22Then an overwhelming army will be swept away before him; both it and a prince of the covenant will be destroyed. 23After coming to an agreement with him, he will act deceitfully, and with only a few people he will rise to power. 24When the richest provinces feel secure, he will invade them and will achieve what neither his fathers nor his forefathers did. He will distribute plunder, loot and wealth among his followers. He will plot the overthrow of fortresses—but only for a time.

25“With a large army he will stir up his strength and courage against the king of the South. The king of the South will wage war with a large and very powerful army, but he will not be able to stand because of the plots devised against him. 26Those who eat from the king's provisions will try to destroy him; his army will be swept away, and many will fall in battle. 27The two kings, with their hearts bent on evil, will sit at the same table and lie to each other, but to no avail, because an end will still come at the appointed time. 28The king of the North will return to his own country with great wealth, but his heart will be set against the holy covenant. He will take action against it and then return to his own country.

29“At the appointed time he will invade the South again, but this time the outcome will be different from what it was before. 30Ships of the western coastlands[b] will oppose him, and he will lose heart. Then he will turn back and vent his fury against the holy covenant. He will return and show favor to those who forsake the holy covenant.

31“His armed forces will rise up to desecrate the temple fortress and will abolish the daily sacrifice. Then they will set up the abomination that causes desolation. 32With flattery he will corrupt those who have violated the covenant, but the people who know their God will firmly resist him.

33“Those who are wise will instruct many, though for a time they will fall by the sword or be burned or captured or plundered. 34When they fall, they will receive a little help, and many who are not sincere will join them. 35Some of the wise will stumble, so that they may be refined, purified and made spotless until the time of the end, for it will still come at the appointed time.

The King Who Exalts Himself

36“The king will do as he pleases. He will exalt and magnify himself above every god and will say unheard-of things against the God of gods. He will be successful until the time of wrath is completed, for what has been determined must take place. 37He will show no regard for the gods of his fathers or for the one desired by women, nor will he regard any god, but will exalt himself above them all. 38Instead of them, he will honor a god of fortresses; a god unknown to his fathers he will honor with gold and silver, with precious stones and costly gifts. 39He will attack the mightiest fortresses with the help of a foreign god and will greatly honor those who acknowledge him. He will make them rulers over many people and will distribute the land at a price.[c]

40“At the time of the end the king of the South will engage him in battle, and the king of the

[a] *17* Or *but she* [b] *30* Hebrew *of Kittim* [c] *39* Or *land for a reward*

North will storm out against him with chariots
and cavalry and a great fleet of ships. He will
invade many countries and sweep through them
like a flood. 41He will also invade the Beautiful
Land. Many countries will fall, but Edom, Moab
and the leaders of Ammon will be delivered from
his hand. 42He will extend his power over many
countries; Egypt will not escape. 43He will gain
control of the treasures of gold and silver and all
the riches of Egypt, with the Libyans and Nubians
in submission. 44But reports from the east and
the north will alarm him, and he will set out in
a great rage to destroy and annihilate many. 45He
will pitch his royal tents between the seas at[a]
the beautiful holy mountain. Yet he will come to
his end, and no one will help him.

The End Times

12 "At that time Michael, the great prince
who protects your people, will arise.
There will be a time of distress such as has not
happened from the beginning of nations until
then. But at that time your people—everyone
whose name is found written in the book—will
be delivered. 2Multitudes who sleep in the dust
of the earth will awake: some to everlasting life,
others to shame and everlasting contempt.
3Those who are wise[b] will shine like the brightness of the heavens, and those who lead many to
righteousness, like the stars for ever and ever.
4But you, Daniel, close up and seal the words of
the scroll until the time of the end. Many will go
here and there to increase knowledge."

5Then I, Daniel, looked, and there before me
stood two others, one on this bank of the river
and one on the opposite bank. 6One of them said
to the man clothed in linen, who was above the
waters of the river, "How long will it be before
these astonishing things are fulfilled?"

7The man clothed in linen, who was above the
waters of the river, lifted his right hand and his
left hand toward heaven, and I heard him swear
by him who lives forever, saying, "It will be for a
time, times and half a time.[c] When the power of
the holy people has been finally broken, all these
things will be completed."

8I heard, but I did not understand. So I asked,
"My lord, what will the outcome of all this be?"

9He replied, "Go your way, Daniel, because
the words are closed up and sealed until the time
of the end. 10Many will be purified, made spotless and refined, but the wicked will continue to
be wicked. None of the wicked will understand,
but those who are wise will understand.

11"From the time that the daily sacrifice is
abolished and the abomination that causes desolation is set up, there will be 1,290 days.
12Blessed is the one who waits for and reaches
the end of the 1,335 days.

13"As for you, go your way till the end. You
will rest, and then at the end of the days you will
rise to receive your allotted inheritance."

a45 Or *the sea and* b3 Or *who impart wisdom* c7 Or *a year, two years and half a year*

Introduction to
HOSEA

Personal Reading Plan

- ❒ Hosea 1:1–2:23
- ❒ Hosea 3:1–5:15
- ❒ Hosea 6:1–8:14
- ❒ Hosea 9:1–10:15
- ❒ Hosea 11:1–12:14
- ❒ Hosea 13:1–14:9

Author

The author is identified as Hosea, son of Beeri—a prophet to the northern kingdom (Israel). He was the only one of the writing prophets to come from Israel, and his prophecy is mainly directed to that kingdom.

Date

Hosea's prophetic career spanned four decades, from the prosperous latter years of Jeroboam II (793–753 B.C.), to the 720s shortly before the fall of Samaria and the exile of Israel.

Theme

God's undying love for his people.

Historical Background

The dominant faith of Israel during Hosea's time was not Mosaic Judaism but a mixture of the worship of the one true God and the local polytheistic Baal religions. Israel was prosperous and complacent under Jeroboam II, but after his death, and a succession of six kings in 30 years, life became increasingly insecure and the nation's resources weakened. Israel stubbornly sought help from other nations instead of from the Lord.

Characteristics

Hosea's language relies heavily upon the covenant stipulations of blessings and curses (see Lev. 26; Deut. 28–32). While reciting the case against Israel and the consequential curses she will face, Hosea interjects God's promise ultimately to restore her to the land and to himself in covenant faithfulness. The beginning of the book (chapters 1–3) tells the story of Hosea's intriguing family situation, which demonstrates his message from God to Israel. First, Hosea obeys the Lord's command to marry an adulterous woman, Gomer. They have three children—each given a name symbolic of Hosea's message. Then, even though Hosea and Gomer are separated by her unfaithfulness, the Lord says to Hosea, "Go, show your love to your wife again" (3:1). This unusual story raises questions. Is the story allegorical or is it meant to be taken literally? The precise nature of Gomer's relationship to Hosea cannot be established with certainty. God's purpose in this "enacted" prophecy is clear, however. Bound to the Lord by covenant, Israel still "prostitutes" herself and bears "children of harlotry." In word and deed, the book of Hosea communicates that despite Israel's faithlessness, God remains faithful and longs to take them back, as Hosea takes back Gomer. This return is described with imagery recalling the exodus from Egypt and settlement in Canaan (see 1:11; 3:5; 14:4–7).

1 The word of the LORD that came to Hosea
son of Beeri during the reigns of Uzziah, Jotham, Ahaz and Hezekiah, kings of Judah, and
during the reign of Jeroboam son of Jehoash[a]
king of Israel:

Hosea's Wife and Children

2When the LORD began to speak through Hosea, the LORD said to him, "Go, take to yourself
an adulterous wife and children of unfaithfulness,
because the land is guilty of the vilest adultery in
departing from the LORD." 3So he married Gomer
daughter of Diblaim, and she conceived and bore
him a son.

4Then the LORD said to Hosea, "Call him Jezreel, because I will soon punish the house of Jehu
for the massacre at Jezreel, and I will put an end
to the kingdom of Israel. 5In that day I will break
Israel's bow in the Valley of Jezreel."

6Gomer conceived again and gave birth to a
daughter. Then the LORD said to Hosea, "Call her
Lo-Ruhamah,[b] for I will no longer show love to
the house of Israel, that I should at all forgive
them. 7Yet I will show love to the house of Judah;
and I will save them—not by bow, sword or battle, or by horses and horsemen, but by the LORD
their God."

8After she had weaned Lo-Ruhamah, Gomer
had another son. 9Then the LORD said, "Call him
Lo-Ammi,[c] for you are not my people, and I am
not your God.

10"Yet the Israelites will be like the sand on
the seashore, which cannot be measured or
counted. In the place where it was said to them,
'You are not my people,' they will be called 'sons
of the living God.' 11The people of Judah and the
people of Israel will be reunited, and they will
appoint one leader and will come up out of the
land, for great will be the day of Jezreel.

2 "Say of your brothers, 'My people,' and of
your sisters, 'My loved one.'

Israel Punished and Restored

2"Rebuke your mother, rebuke her,
for she is not my wife,
and I am not her husband.
Let her remove the adulterous look from her
face
and the unfaithfulness from between her
breasts.
3Otherwise I will strip her naked
and make her as bare as on the day she
was born;
I will make her like a desert,
turn her into a parched land,
and slay her with thirst.
4I will not show my love to her children,
because they are the children of adultery.
5Their mother has been unfaithful
and has conceived them in disgrace.
She said, 'I will go after my lovers,
who give me my food and my water,
my wool and my linen, my oil and my
drink.'
6Therefore I will block her path with
thornbushes;
I will wall her in so that she cannot find
her way.
7She will chase after her lovers but not catch
them;
she will look for them but not find them.
Then she will say,
'I will go back to my husband as at first,
for then I was better off than now.'
8She has not acknowledged that I was the one
who gave her the grain, the new wine and
oil,
who lavished on her the silver and gold—
which they used for Baal.

9"Therefore I will take away my grain when it
ripens,
and my new wine when it is ready.
I will take back my wool and my linen,
intended to cover her nakedness.
10So now I will expose her lewdness
before the eyes of her lovers;
no one will take her out of my hands.
11I will stop all her celebrations:
her yearly festivals, her New Moons,
her Sabbath days—all her appointed feasts.
12I will ruin her vines and her fig trees,
which she said were her pay from her
lovers;
I will make them a thicket,
and wild animals will devour them.
13I will punish her for the days
she burned incense to the Baals;
she decked herself with rings and jewelry,
and went after her lovers,
but me she forgot,"
declares the LORD.

14"Therefore I am now going to allure her;
I will lead her into the desert
and speak tenderly to her.
15There I will give her back her vineyards,
and will make the Valley of Achor[d] a
door of hope.
There she will sing[e] as in the days of her
youth,

[a] *1* Hebrew *Joash,* a variant of *Jehoash* [b] *6* *Lo-Ruhamah* means *not loved.* [c] *9* *Lo-Ammi* means *not my people.*
[d] *15* *Achor* means *trouble.* [e] *15* Or *respond*

as in the day she came up out of Egypt.
16"In that day," declares the LORD,
"you will call me 'my husband';
you will no longer call me 'my master.[a]'
17I will remove the names of the Baals from
her lips;
no longer will their names be invoked.
18In that day I will make a covenant for them
with the beasts of the field and the birds
of the air
and the creatures that move along the
ground.
Bow and sword and battle
I will abolish from the land,
so that all may lie down in safety.
19I will betroth you to me forever;
I will betroth you in[b] righteousness and
justice,
in[c] love and compassion.
20I will betroth you in faithfulness,
and you will acknowledge the LORD.

21"In that day I will respond,"
declares the LORD—
"I will respond to the skies,
and they will respond to the earth;
22and the earth will respond to the grain,
the new wine and oil,
and they will respond to Jezreel.[d]
23I will plant her for myself in the land;
I will show my love to the one I called
'Not my loved one.[e]'
I will say to those called 'Not my people,[f]'
'You are my people';
and they will say, 'You are my God.'"

Hosea's Reconciliation With His Wife

3 The LORD said to me, "Go, show your love to
your wife again, though she is loved by another and is an adulteress. Love her as the LORD
loves the Israelites, though they turn to other
gods and love the sacred raisin cakes."
2So I bought her for fifteen shekels[g] of silver
and about a homer and a lethek[h] of barley.
3Then I told her, "You are to live with[i] me
many days; you must not be a prostitute or be
intimate with any man, and I will live with[i]
you."
4For the Israelites will live many days without
king or prince, without sacrifice or sacred stones,
without ephod or idol. 5Afterward the Israelites
will return and seek the LORD their God and David their king. They will come trembling to the
LORD and to his blessings in the last days.

The Charge Against Israel

4 Hear the word of the LORD, you Israelites,
because the LORD has a charge to bring
against you who live in the land:
"There is no faithfulness, no love,
no acknowledgment of God in the land.
2There is only cursing,[j] lying and murder,
stealing and adultery;
they break all bounds,
and bloodshed follows bloodshed.
3Because of this the land mourns,[k]
and all who live in it waste away;
the beasts of the field and the birds of the air
and the fish of the sea are dying.

4"But let no man bring a charge,
let no man accuse another,
for your people are like those
who bring charges against a priest.
5You stumble day and night,
and the prophets stumble with you.
So I will destroy your mother—
6 my people are destroyed from lack of
knowledge.

"Because you have rejected knowledge,
I also reject you as my priests;
because you have ignored the law of your
God,
I also will ignore your children.
7The more the priests increased,
the more they sinned against me;
they exchanged[l] their[m] Glory for
something disgraceful.
8They feed on the sins of my people
and relish their wickedness.
9And it will be: Like people, like priests.
I will punish both of them for their ways
and repay them for their deeds.

10"They will eat but not have enough;
they will engage in prostitution but not
increase,
because they have deserted the LORD
to give themselves 11to prostitution,
to old wine and new,
which take away the understanding 12of
my people.
They consult a wooden idol
and are answered by a stick of wood.
A spirit of prostitution leads them astray;
they are unfaithful to their God.
13They sacrifice on the mountaintops
and burn offerings on the hills,
under oak, poplar and terebinth,
where the shade is pleasant.

a16 Hebrew *baal* b19 Or *with*; also in verse 20 c19 Or *with* d22 *Jezreel* means *God plants.* e23 Hebrew *Lo-Ruhamah* f23 Hebrew *Lo-Ammi* g2 That is, about 6 ounces (about 170 grams) h2 That is, probably about 10 bushels (about 330 liters) i3 Or *wait for* j2 That is, to pronounce a curse upon k3 Or *dries up* l7 Syriac and an ancient Hebrew scribal tradition; Masoretic Text *I will exchange* m7 Masoretic Text; an ancient Hebrew scribal tradition *my*

Therefore your daughters turn to prostitution
and your daughters-in-law to adultery.
14"I will not punish your daughters
when they turn to prostitution,
nor your daughters-in-law
when they commit adultery,
because the men themselves consort with harlots
and sacrifice with shrine prostitutes—
a people without understanding will come to ruin!

15"Though you commit adultery, O Israel,
let not Judah become guilty.

"Do not go to Gilgal;
do not go up to Beth Aven.[a]
And do not swear, 'As surely as the LORD lives!'
16The Israelites are stubborn,
like a stubborn heifer.
How then can the LORD pasture them
like lambs in a meadow?
17Ephraim is joined to idols;
leave him alone!
18Even when their drinks are gone,
they continue their prostitution;
their rulers dearly love shameful ways.
19A whirlwind will sweep them away,
and their sacrifices will bring them shame.

Judgment Against Israel

5 "Hear this, you priests!
Pay attention, you Israelites!
Listen, O royal house!
This judgment is against you:
You have been a snare at Mizpah,
a net spread out on Tabor.
2The rebels are deep in slaughter.
I will discipline all of them.
3I know all about Ephraim;
Israel is not hidden from me.
Ephraim, you have now turned to prostitution;
Israel is corrupt.

4"Their deeds do not permit them
to return to their God.
A spirit of prostitution is in their heart;
they do not acknowledge the LORD.
5Israel's arrogance testifies against them;
the Israelites, even Ephraim, stumble in their sin;
Judah also stumbles with them.
6When they go with their flocks and herds
to seek the LORD,
they will not find him;
he has withdrawn himself from them.
7They are unfaithful to the LORD;
they give birth to illegitimate children.
Now their New Moon festivals
will devour them and their fields.

8"Sound the trumpet in Gibeah,
the horn in Ramah.
Raise the battle cry in Beth Aven[a];
lead on, O Benjamin.
9Ephraim will be laid waste
on the day of reckoning.
Among the tribes of Israel
I proclaim what is certain.
10Judah's leaders are like those
who move boundary stones.
I will pour out my wrath on them
like a flood of water.
11Ephraim is oppressed,
trampled in judgment,
intent on pursuing idols.[b]
12I am like a moth to Ephraim,
like rot to the people of Judah.

13"When Ephraim saw his sickness,
and Judah his sores,
then Ephraim turned to Assyria,
and sent to the great king for help.
But he is not able to cure you,
not able to heal your sores.
14For I will be like a lion to Ephraim,
like a great lion to Judah.
I will tear them to pieces and go away;
I will carry them off, with no one to rescue them.
15Then I will go back to my place
until they admit their guilt.
And they will seek my face;
in their misery they will earnestly seek me."

Israel Unrepentant

6 "Come, let us return to the LORD.
He has torn us to pieces
but he will heal us;
he has injured us
but he will bind up our wounds.
2After two days he will revive us;
on the third day he will restore us,
that we may live in his presence.
3Let us acknowledge the LORD;
let us press on to acknowledge him.
As surely as the sun rises,
he will appear;
he will come to us like the winter rains,
like the spring rains that water the earth."

4"What can I do with you, Ephraim?

[a] 15,8 *Beth Aven* means *house of wickedness* (a name for Bethel, which means *house of God*). [b] 11 The meaning of the Hebrew for this word is uncertain.

What can I do with you, Judah?
Your love is like the morning mist,
like the early dew that disappears.
5 Therefore I cut you in pieces with my prophets,
I killed you with the words of my mouth;
my judgments flashed like lightning upon you.
6 For I desire mercy, not sacrifice,
and acknowledgment of God rather than burnt offerings.
7 Like Adam,[a] they have broken the covenant—
they were unfaithful to me there.
8 Gilead is a city of wicked men,
stained with footprints of blood.
9 As marauders lie in ambush for a man,
so do bands of priests;
they murder on the road to Shechem,
committing shameful crimes.
10 I have seen a horrible thing
in the house of Israel.
There Ephraim is given to prostitution
and Israel is defiled.

11 "Also for you, Judah,
a harvest is appointed.

"Whenever I would restore the fortunes of my people,
7 1 whenever I would heal Israel,
the sins of Ephraim are exposed
and the crimes of Samaria revealed.
They practice deceit,
thieves break into houses,
bandits rob in the streets;
2 but they do not realize
that I remember all their evil deeds.
Their sins engulf them;
they are always before me.

3 "They delight the king with their wickedness,
the princes with their lies.
4 They are all adulterers,
burning like an oven
whose fire the baker need not stir
from the kneading of the dough till it rises.
5 On the day of the festival of our king
the princes become inflamed with wine,
and he joins hands with the mockers.
6 Their hearts are like an oven;
they approach him with intrigue.
Their passion smolders all night;
in the morning it blazes like a flaming fire.
7 All of them are hot as an oven;
they devour their rulers.
All their kings fall,
and none of them calls on me.

8 "Ephraim mixes with the nations;
Ephraim is a flat cake not turned over.
9 Foreigners sap his strength,
but he does not realize it.
His hair is sprinkled with gray,
but he does not notice.
10 Israel's arrogance testifies against him,
but despite all this
he does not return to the LORD his God
or search for him.

11 "Ephraim is like a dove,
easily deceived and senseless—
now calling to Egypt,
now turning to Assyria.
12 When they go, I will throw my net over them;
I will pull them down like birds of the air.
When I hear them flocking together,
I will catch them.
13 Woe to them,
because they have strayed from me!
Destruction to them,
because they have rebelled against me!
I long to redeem them
but they speak lies against me.
14 They do not cry out to me from their hearts
but wail upon their beds.
They gather together[b] for grain and new wine
but turn away from me.
15 I trained them and strengthened them,
but they plot evil against me.
16 They do not turn to the Most High;
they are like a faulty bow.
Their leaders will fall by the sword
because of their insolent words.
For this they will be ridiculed
in the land of Egypt.

Israel to Reap the Whirlwind

8 "Put the trumpet to your lips!
An eagle is over the house of the LORD
because the people have broken my covenant
and rebelled against my law.
2 Israel cries out to me,
'O our God, we acknowledge you!'
3 But Israel has rejected what is good;
an enemy will pursue him.
4 They set up kings without my consent;
they choose princes without my approval.
With their silver and gold
they make idols for themselves
to their own destruction.
5 Throw out your calf-idol, O Samaria!

[a] 7 Or *As at Adam*; or *Like men* [b] 14 Most Hebrew manuscripts; some Hebrew manuscripts and Septuagint *They slash themselves*

My anger burns against them.
How long will they be incapable of purity?
6 They are from Israel!
This calf—a craftsman has made it;
it is not God.
It will be broken in pieces,
that calf of Samaria.

7 "They sow the wind
and reap the whirlwind.
The stalk has no head;
it will produce no flour.
Were it to yield grain,
foreigners would swallow it up.
8 Israel is swallowed up;
now she is among the nations
like a worthless thing.
9 For they have gone up to Assyria
like a wild donkey wandering alone.
Ephraim has sold herself to lovers.
10 Although they have sold themselves among
the nations,
I will now gather them together.
They will begin to waste away
under the oppression of the mighty king.

11 "Though Ephraim built many altars for sin
offerings,
these have become altars for sinning.
12 I wrote for them the many things of my law,
but they regarded them as something
alien.
13 They offer sacrifices given to me
and they eat the meat,
but the LORD is not pleased with them.
Now he will remember their wickedness
and punish their sins:
They will return to Egypt.
14 Israel has forgotten his Maker
and built palaces;
Judah has fortified many towns.
But I will send fire upon their cities
that will consume their fortresses."

Punishment for Israel

9 Do not rejoice, O Israel;
do not be jubilant like the other nations.
For you have been unfaithful to your God;
you love the wages of a prostitute
at every threshing floor.
2 Threshing floors and winepresses will not
feed the people;
the new wine will fail them.
3 They will not remain in the LORD's land;
Ephraim will return to Egypt
and eat unclean[a] food in Assyria.
4 They will not pour out wine offerings to the
LORD,
nor will their sacrifices please him.
Such sacrifices will be to them like the bread
of mourners;
all who eat them will be unclean.
This food will be for themselves;
it will not come into the temple of the
LORD.

5 What will you do on the day of your
appointed feasts,
on the festival days of the LORD?
6 Even if they escape from destruction,
Egypt will gather them,
and Memphis will bury them.
Their treasures of silver will be taken over by
briers,
and thorns will overrun their tents.
7 The days of punishment are coming,
the days of reckoning are at hand.
Let Israel know this.
Because your sins are so many
and your hostility so great,
the prophet is considered a fool,
the inspired man a maniac.
8 The prophet, along with my God,
is the watchman over Ephraim,[b]
yet snares await him on all his paths,
and hostility in the house of his God.
9 They have sunk deep into corruption,
as in the days of Gibeah.
God will remember their wickedness
and punish them for their sins.

10 "When I found Israel,
it was like finding grapes in the desert;
when I saw your fathers,
it was like seeing the early fruit on the fig
tree.
But when they came to Baal Peor,
they consecrated themselves to that
shameful idol
and became as vile as the thing they
loved.
11 Ephraim's glory will fly away like a bird—
no birth, no pregnancy, no conception.
12 Even if they rear children,
I will bereave them of every one.
Woe to them
when I turn away from them!
13 I have seen Ephraim, like Tyre,
planted in a pleasant place.
But Ephraim will bring out
their children to the slayer."

14 Give them, O LORD—
what will you give them?
Give them wombs that miscarry
and breasts that are dry.

[a] 3 That is, ceremonially unclean [b] 8 Or *The prophet is the watchman over Ephraim, / the people of my God*

15“Because of all their wickedness in Gilgal,
I hated them there.
Because of their sinful deeds,
I will drive them out of my house.
I will no longer love them;
all their leaders are rebellious.
16Ephraim is blighted,
their root is withered,
they yield no fruit.
Even if they bear children,
I will slay their cherished offspring.”

17My God will reject them
because they have not obeyed him;
they will be wanderers among the nations.

10 Israel was a spreading vine;
he brought forth fruit for himself.
As his fruit increased,
he built more altars;
as his land prospered,
he adorned his sacred stones.
2Their heart is deceitful,
and now they must bear their guilt.
The LORD will demolish their altars
and destroy their sacred stones.

3Then they will say, “We have no king
because we did not revere the LORD.
But even if we had a king,
what could he do for us?”
4They make many promises,
take false oaths
and make agreements;
therefore lawsuits spring up
like poisonous weeds in a plowed field.
5The people who live in Samaria fear
for the calf-idol of Beth Aven.[a]
Its people will mourn over it,
and so will its idolatrous priests,
those who had rejoiced over its splendor,
because it is taken from them into exile.
6It will be carried to Assyria
as tribute for the great king.
Ephraim will be disgraced;
Israel will be ashamed of its wooden
idols.[b]
7Samaria and its king will float away
like a twig on the surface of the waters.
8The high places of wickedness[c] will be
destroyed—
it is the sin of Israel.
Thorns and thistles will grow up
and cover their altars.
Then they will say to the mountains, “Cover
us!”
and to the hills, “Fall on us!”

9“Since the days of Gibeah, you have sinned,
O Israel,
and there you have remained.[d]
Did not war overtake
the evildoers in Gibeah?
10When I please, I will punish them;
nations will be gathered against them
to put them in bonds for their double sin.
11Ephraim is a trained heifer
that loves to thresh;
so I will put a yoke
on her fair neck.
I will drive Ephraim,
Judah must plow,
and Jacob must break up the ground.
12Sow for yourselves righteousness,
reap the fruit of unfailing love,
and break up your unplowed ground;
for it is time to seek the LORD,
until he comes
and showers righteousness on you.
13But you have planted wickedness,
you have reaped evil,
you have eaten the fruit of deception.
Because you have depended on your own
strength
and on your many warriors,
14the roar of battle will rise against your
people,
so that all your fortresses will be
devastated—
as Shalman devastated Beth Arbel on the day
of battle,
when mothers were dashed to the ground
with their children.
15Thus will it happen to you, O Bethel,
because your wickedness is great.
When that day dawns,
the king of Israel will be completely
destroyed.

God's Love for Israel

11 “When Israel was a child, I loved him,
and out of Egypt I called my son.
2But the more I[e] called Israel,
the further they went from me.[f]
They sacrificed to the Baals
and they burned incense to images.
3It was I who taught Ephraim to walk,
taking them by the arms;
but they did not realize
it was I who healed them.
4I led them with cords of human kindness,
with ties of love;

[a]5 *Beth Aven* means *house of wickedness* (a name for Bethel, which means *house of God*). [b]6 Or *its counsel* [c]8 Hebrew *aven,* a reference to Beth Aven (a derogatory name for Bethel) [d]9 Or *there a stand was taken* [e]2 Some Septuagint manuscripts; Hebrew *they* [f]2 Septuagint; Hebrew *them*

I lifted the yoke from their neck
and bent down to feed them.

5 "Will they not return to Egypt
and will not Assyria rule over them
because they refuse to repent?
6 Swords will flash in their cities,
will destroy the bars of their gates
and put an end to their plans.
7 My people are determined to turn from me.
Even if they call to the Most High,
he will by no means exalt them.

8 "How can I give you up, Ephraim?
How can I hand you over, Israel?
How can I treat you like Admah?
How can I make you like Zeboiim?
My heart is changed within me;
all my compassion is aroused.
9 I will not carry out my fierce anger,
nor will I turn and devastate Ephraim.
For I am God, and not man—
the Holy One among you.
I will not come in wrath.[a]
10 They will follow the LORD;
he will roar like a lion.
When he roars,
his children will come trembling from the west.
11 They will come trembling
like birds from Egypt,
like doves from Assyria.
I will settle them in their homes,"
declares the LORD.

Israel's Sin

12 Ephraim has surrounded me with lies,
the house of Israel with deceit.
And Judah is unruly against God,
even against the faithful Holy One.

12 1 Ephraim feeds on the wind;
he pursues the east wind all day
and multiplies lies and violence.
He makes a treaty with Assyria
and sends olive oil to Egypt.
2 The LORD has a charge to bring against Judah;
he will punish Jacob[b] according to his ways
and repay him according to his deeds.
3 In the womb he grasped his brother's heel;
as a man he struggled with God.
4 He struggled with the angel and overcame him;
he wept and begged for his favor.
He found him at Bethel
and talked with him there—
5 the LORD God Almighty,
the LORD is his name of renown!
6 But you must return to your God;
maintain love and justice,
and wait for your God always.

7 The merchant uses dishonest scales;
he loves to defraud.
8 Ephraim boasts,
"I am very rich; I have become wealthy.
With all my wealth they will not find in me
any iniquity or sin."

9 "I am the LORD your God,
⌞who brought you⌟ out of[c] Egypt;
I will make you live in tents again,
as in the days of your appointed feasts.
10 I spoke to the prophets,
gave them many visions
and told parables through them."

11 Is Gilead wicked?
Its people are worthless!
Do they sacrifice bulls in Gilgal?
Their altars will be like piles of stones
on a plowed field.
12 Jacob fled to the country of Aram[d];
Israel served to get a wife,
and to pay for her he tended sheep.
13 The LORD used a prophet to bring Israel up from Egypt,
by a prophet he cared for him.
14 But Ephraim has bitterly provoked him to anger;
his Lord will leave upon him the guilt of his bloodshed
and will repay him for his contempt.

The LORD's Anger Against Israel

13 When Ephraim spoke, men trembled;
he was exalted in Israel.
But he became guilty of Baal worship and died.
2 Now they sin more and more;
they make idols for themselves from their silver,
cleverly fashioned images,
all of them the work of craftsmen.
It is said of these people,
"They offer human sacrifice
and kiss[e] the calf-idols."
3 Therefore they will be like the morning mist,
like the early dew that disappears,
like chaff swirling from a threshing floor,
like smoke escaping through a window.

4 "But I am the LORD your God,
⌞who brought you⌟ out of[c] Egypt.

a 9 Or *come against any city* b 2 *Jacob* means *he grasps the heel* (figuratively, *he deceives*). c 9,4 Or *God / ever since you were in* d 12 That is, Northwest Mesopotamia e 2 Or *"Men who sacrifice / kiss*

You shall acknowledge no God but me,
no Savior except me.
5 I cared for you in the desert,
in the land of burning heat.
6 When I fed them, they were satisfied;
when they were satisfied, they became proud;
then they forgot me.
7 So I will come upon them like a lion,
like a leopard I will lurk by the path.
8 Like a bear robbed of her cubs,
I will attack them and rip them open.
Like a lion I will devour them;
a wild animal will tear them apart.

9 "You are destroyed, O Israel,
because you are against me, against your helper.
10 Where is your king, that he may save you?
Where are your rulers in all your towns,
of whom you said,
'Give me a king and princes'?
11 So in my anger I gave you a king,
and in my wrath I took him away.
12 The guilt of Ephraim is stored up,
his sins are kept on record.
13 Pains as of a woman in childbirth come to him,
but he is a child without wisdom;
when the time arrives,
he does not come to the opening of the womb.
14 "I will ransom them from the power of the grave[a];
I will redeem them from death.
Where, O death, are your plagues?
Where, O grave,[a] is your destruction?

"I will have no compassion,
15 even though he thrives among his brothers.
An east wind from the LORD will come,
blowing in from the desert;
his spring will fail
and his well dry up.
His storehouse will be plundered
of all its treasures.
16 The people of Samaria must bear their guilt,
because they have rebelled against their God.
They will fall by the sword;
their little ones will be dashed to the ground,
their pregnant women ripped open."

Repentance to Bring Blessing

14 Return, O Israel, to the LORD your God.
Your sins have been your downfall!
2 Take words with you
and return to the LORD.
Say to him:
"Forgive all our sins
and receive us graciously,
that we may offer the fruit of our lips.[b]
3 Assyria cannot save us;
we will not mount war-horses.
We will never again say 'Our gods'
to what our own hands have made,
for in you the fatherless find compassion."

4 "I will heal their waywardness
and love them freely,
for my anger has turned away from them.
5 I will be like the dew to Israel;
he will blossom like a lily.
Like a cedar of Lebanon
he will send down his roots;
6 his young shoots will grow.
His splendor will be like an olive tree,
his fragrance like a cedar of Lebanon.
7 Men will dwell again in his shade.
He will flourish like the grain.
He will blossom like a vine,
and his fame will be like the wine from Lebanon.
8 O Ephraim, what more have I[c] to do with idols?
I will answer him and care for him.
I am like a green pine tree;
your fruitfulness comes from me."

9 Who is wise? He will realize these things.
Who is discerning? He will understand them.
The ways of the LORD are right;
the righteous walk in them,
but the rebellious stumble in them.

a 14 Hebrew *Sheol* b 2 Or *offer our lips as sacrifices of bulls* c 8 Or *What more has Ephraim*

Introduction to

JOEL

Personal Reading Plan

- ❐ Joel 1:1–20
- ❐ Joel 2:1–17
- ❐ Joel 2:18–32
- ❐ Joel 3:1–21

Author

The author is identified as the prophet Joel, son of Pethuel (1:1). While there are 12 other Old Testament characters with this name, none of them can be identified with this prophet.

Date

The date is uncertain. Joel could have been written as early as the ninth and as late as the fourth century B.C. Since Joel uses quotes or paraphrases from several other prophets and does not refer to either the Babylonian or Assyrian Empire, a later date seems probable—sometime during the Persian period (539–331 B.C.).

Theme

A plague of locusts is a sign of the coming Day of the Lord.

Historical Background

The occasion for Joel's prophetic ministry was a plague of locusts which was consuming Judah. The fact that no historical record of such a plague has endured does not mean this event was simply an allegorical device of the writer. Rather, this underscores the truth that even the worst natural or national disasters fade from memory when attention is turned to something that endures forever—an eternal God and his future kingdom (see 2:28–3:21).

Characteristics

The literary genius of Joel shines through in the book's structure, which flows smoothly from start to finish. Each section relates to what precedes it and what follows it. Hence, it helps to read the whole book in one sitting before studying its parts. The focus of the book is twofold: (1) The ever-present, practical problem of what to do about the locust plague (1:1–2:27); and (2) The future Day of the Lord, of which the current plague is a sign (2:28–3:21). In combining the two—event plus interpretation—Joel is performing the classic function of an Old Testament prophet, that of conveying God's revelation. Likewise, the borrowing of phrases from other prophets to speak a "new word" from the Lord in a new setting shows that Joel was probably an educated person, and had heard, if not read, the prophecies of Micah, Jeremiah and Isaiah. In 2:28–3:21, Joel expands the apocalyptic dimensions of these prophets. In Acts 2, the apostle Peter expounds the meaning of Joel's prophecy. Specifically, Joel's prediction about the outpouring of the Holy Spirit was fulfilled on the Day of Pentecost.

1

The word of the LORD that came to Joel son of Pethuel.

An Invasion of Locusts

2 Hear this, you elders;
listen, all who live in the land.
Has anything like this ever happened in your days
or in the days of your forefathers?
3 Tell it to your children,
and let your children tell it to their children,
and their children to the next generation.
4 What the locust swarm has left
the great locusts have eaten;
what the great locusts have left
the young locusts have eaten;
what the young locusts have left
other locusts[a] have eaten.

5 Wake up, you drunkards, and weep!
Wail, all you drinkers of wine;
wail because of the new wine,
for it has been snatched from your lips.
6 A nation has invaded my land,
powerful and without number;
it has the teeth of a lion,
the fangs of a lioness.
7 It has laid waste my vines
and ruined my fig trees.
It has stripped off their bark
and thrown it away,
leaving their branches white.

8 Mourn like a virgin[b] in sackcloth
grieving for the husband[c] of her youth.
9 Grain offerings and drink offerings
are cut off from the house of the LORD.
The priests are in mourning,
those who minister before the LORD.
10 The fields are ruined,
the ground is dried up[d];
the grain is destroyed,
the new wine is dried up,
the oil fails.
11 Despair, you farmers,
wail, you vine growers;
grieve for the wheat and the barley,
because the harvest of the field is destroyed.
12 The vine is dried up
and the fig tree is withered;
the pomegranate, the palm and the apple tree—
all the trees of the field—are dried up.
Surely the joy of mankind
is withered away.

A Call to Repentance

13 Put on sackcloth, O priests, and mourn;
wail, you who minister before the altar.
Come, spend the night in sackcloth,
you who minister before my God;
for the grain offerings and drink offerings
are withheld from the house of your God.
14 Declare a holy fast;
call a sacred assembly.
Summon the elders
and all who live in the land
to the house of the LORD your God,
and cry out to the LORD.

15 Alas for that day!
For the day of the LORD is near;
it will come like destruction from the Almighty.[e]

16 Has not the food been cut off
before our very eyes—
joy and gladness
from the house of our God?
17 The seeds are shriveled
beneath the clods.[f]
The storehouses are in ruins,
the granaries have been broken down,
for the grain has dried up.
18 How the cattle moan!
The herds mill about
because they have no pasture;
even the flocks of sheep are suffering.

19 To you, O LORD, I call,
for fire has devoured the open pastures
and flames have burned up all the trees of the field.
20 Even the wild animals pant for you;
the streams of water have dried up
and fire has devoured the open pastures.

An Army of Locusts

2

Blow the trumpet in Zion;
sound the alarm on my holy hill.
Let all who live in the land tremble,
for the day of the LORD is coming.
It is close at hand—
2 a day of darkness and gloom,
a day of clouds and blackness.
Like dawn spreading across the mountains
a large and mighty army comes,
such as never was of old
nor ever will be in ages to come.

3 Before them fire devours,
behind them a flame blazes.
Before them the land is like the garden of Eden,

[a] 4 The precise meaning of the four Hebrew words used here for locusts is uncertain. [b] 8 Or *young woman* [c] 8 Or *betrothed*
[d] 10 Or *ground mourns* [e] 15 Hebrew *Shaddai* [f] 17 The meaning of the Hebrew for this word is uncertain.

behind them, a desert waste—
nothing escapes them.
4They have the appearance of horses;
they gallop along like cavalry.
5With a noise like that of chariots
they leap over the mountaintops,
like a crackling fire consuming stubble,
like a mighty army drawn up for battle.

6At the sight of them, nations are in anguish;
every face turns pale.
7They charge like warriors;
they scale walls like soldiers.
They all march in line,
not swerving from their course.
8They do not jostle each other;
each marches straight ahead.
They plunge through defenses
without breaking ranks.
9They rush upon the city;
they run along the wall.
They climb into the houses;
like thieves they enter through the windows.

10Before them the earth shakes,
the sky trembles,
the sun and moon are darkened,
and the stars no longer shine.
11The LORD thunders
at the head of his army;
his forces are beyond number,
and mighty are those who obey his command.
The day of the LORD is great;
it is dreadful.
Who can endure it?

Rend Your Heart

12"Even now," declares the LORD,
"return to me with all your heart,
with fasting and weeping and mourning."

13Rend your heart
and not your garments.
Return to the LORD your God,
for he is gracious and compassionate,
slow to anger and abounding in love,
and he relents from sending calamity.
14Who knows? He may turn and have pity
and leave behind a blessing—
grain offerings and drink offerings
for the LORD your God.

15Blow the trumpet in Zion,
declare a holy fast,
call a sacred assembly.
16Gather the people,
consecrate the assembly;
bring together the elders,
gather the children,
those nursing at the breast.
Let the bridegroom leave his room
and the bride her chamber.
17Let the priests, who minister before the LORD,
weep between the temple porch and the altar.
Let them say, "Spare your people, O LORD.
Do not make your inheritance an object of scorn,
a byword among the nations.
Why should they say among the peoples,
'Where is their God?' "

The LORD's Answer

18Then the LORD will be jealous for his land
and take pity on his people.

19The LORD will reply[a] to them:

"I am sending you grain, new wine and oil,
enough to satisfy you fully;
never again will I make you
an object of scorn to the nations.

20"I will drive the northern army far from you,
pushing it into a parched and barren land,
with its front columns going into the eastern sea[b]
and those in the rear into the western sea.[c]
And its stench will go up;
its smell will rise."

Surely he has done great things.[d]
21 Be not afraid, O land;
be glad and rejoice.
Surely the LORD has done great things.
22 Be not afraid, O wild animals,
for the open pastures are becoming green.
The trees are bearing their fruit;
the fig tree and the vine yield their riches.
23Be glad, O people of Zion,
rejoice in the LORD your God,
for he has given you
the autumn rains in righteousness.[e]
He sends you abundant showers,
both autumn and spring rains, as before.
24The threshing floors will be filled with grain;
the vats will overflow with new wine and oil.

25"I will repay you for the years the locusts have eaten—
the great locust and the young locust,

[a]18,19 Or *LORD was jealous . . . / and took pity . . . / 19The LORD replied* [b]20 That is, the Dead Sea [c]20 That is, the Mediterranean [d]20 Or *rise. / Surely it has done great things."* [e]23 Or */ the teacher for righteousness:*

the other locusts and the locust swarm[a]—
my great army that I sent among you.
26You will have plenty to eat, until you are full,
and you will praise the name of the LORD your God,
who has worked wonders for you;
never again will my people be shamed.
27Then you will know that I am in Israel,
that I am the LORD your God,
and that there is no other;
never again will my people be shamed.

The Day of the LORD

28"And afterward,
I will pour out my Spirit on all people.
Your sons and daughters will prophesy,
your old men will dream dreams,
your young men will see visions.
29Even on my servants, both men and women,
I will pour out my Spirit in those days.
30I will show wonders in the heavens
and on the earth,
blood and fire and billows of smoke.
31The sun will be turned to darkness
and the moon to blood
before the coming of the great and dreadful day of the LORD.
32And everyone who calls
on the name of the LORD will be saved;
for on Mount Zion and in Jerusalem
there will be deliverance,
as the LORD has said,
among the survivors
whom the LORD calls.

The Nations Judged

3 "In those days and at that time,
when I restore the fortunes of Judah and Jerusalem,
2I will gather all nations
and bring them down to the Valley of Jehoshaphat.[b]
There I will enter into judgment against them
concerning my inheritance, my people Israel,
for they scattered my people among the nations
and divided up my land.
3They cast lots for my people
and traded boys for prostitutes;
they sold girls for wine
that they might drink.

4"Now what have you against me, O Tyre and
Sidon and all you regions of Philistia? Are you
repaying me for something I have done? If you
are paying me back, I will swiftly and speedily
return on your own heads what you have done.
5For you took my silver and my gold and carried
off my finest treasures to your temples. 6You sold
the people of Judah and Jerusalem to the Greeks,
that you might send them far from their homeland.
7"See, I am going to rouse them out of the
places to which you sold them, and I will return
on your own heads what you have done. 8I will
sell your sons and daughters to the people of Judah, and they will sell them to the Sabeans, a
nation far away." The LORD has spoken.

9Proclaim this among the nations:
Prepare for war!
Rouse the warriors!
Let all the fighting men draw near and attack.
10Beat your plowshares into swords
and your pruning hooks into spears.
Let the weakling say,
"I am strong!"
11Come quickly, all you nations from every side,
and assemble there.

Bring down your warriors, O LORD!

12"Let the nations be roused;
let them advance into the Valley of Jehoshaphat,
for there I will sit
to judge all the nations on every side.
13Swing the sickle,
for the harvest is ripe.
Come, trample the grapes,
for the winepress is full
and the vats overflow—
so great is their wickedness!"

14Multitudes, multitudes
in the valley of decision!
For the day of the LORD is near
in the valley of decision.
15The sun and moon will be darkened,
and the stars no longer shine.
16The LORD will roar from Zion
and thunder from Jerusalem;
the earth and the sky will tremble.
But the LORD will be a refuge for his people,
a stronghold for the people of Israel.

Blessings for God's People

17"Then you will know that I, the LORD your God,

[a] *25* The precise meaning of the four Hebrew words used here for locusts is uncertain.
[b] *2* *Jehoshaphat* means *the LORD judges*; also in verse 12.

dwell in Zion, my holy hill.
Jerusalem will be holy;
never again will foreigners invade her.

18 "In that day the mountains will drip new wine,
and the hills will flow with milk;
all the ravines of Judah will run with water.
A fountain will flow out of the LORD's house
and will water the valley of acacias.[a]

19 But Egypt will be desolate,
Edom a desert waste,
because of violence done to the people of Judah,
in whose land they shed innocent blood.
20 Judah will be inhabited forever
and Jerusalem through all generations.
21 Their bloodguilt, which I have not pardoned,
I will pardon."

The LORD dwells in Zion!

[a] 18 Or *Valley of Shittim*

Introduction to
AMOS

Personal Reading Plan

- ❒ Amos 1:1–2:5
- ❒ Amos 2:6–3:15
- ❒ Amos 4:1–5:17
- ❒ Amos 5:18–6:14
- ❒ Amos 7:1–8:14
- ❒ Amos 9:1–15

Author

Amos, who came from the small town of Tekoa (six miles south of Bethlehem and 11 miles from Jerusalem), was a citizen of the southern state of Judah, but ministered in the northern state of Israel, alongside the prophet Hosea. Amos was a shepherd (1:1) and fruit farmer (7:14), not a professional prophet. However, his skill with words and the strikingly broad range of his general knowledge of history and the world indicate that he was not just an ignorant peasant.

Date

Amos ministered during the reigns of Uzziah, king of Judah (783–742 B.C.), and Jeroboam II, king of Israel (786–746 B.C.), possibly c. 760–750 B.C.

Theme

God's judgment on injustice.

Historical Background

By 800 B.C. both the northern kingdom (Israel) and the southern kingdom (Judah) had reached new political and military heights. Peace reigned and business was booming. Even religion was on the rise. However, the exterior calm belied Israel's inner disease. Idolatry, extravagant indulgence and a corrupt judicial system ran beneath the surface. In this context, Amos calls for social justice as the foundation for true piety (5:24).

Characteristics

Whereas his contemporary, Hosea, focuses on the love of God and spiritual adultery, Amos focuses on the righteousness of God and social injustice. He often makes his points by use of a simple rhetorical question (e.g., 5:25). Amos speaks as a simple Judean farmer burdened for the materialistic nation of Israel. His prayer averts the total destruction of Israel (7:1–6), and yet his message was most unpopular. However, social acceptance didn't matter to one whose job was not on the line (7:12–15). In Amos, God roars like a lion (1:2) and brings hope only at the end (9:11–15). The book of Amos is constantly shadowed by clouds of judgment as the Lord reacts to the cruel social events in the land. Amos passionately declares both God's concern for the poor and his wrath on those who would exploit them. His message is an uncomfortable one in any age as he challenges us to examine ourselves and our society and to confront injustice wherever we find it.

1 The words of Amos, one of the shepherds of Tekoa—what he saw concerning Israel two years before the earthquake, when Uzziah was king of Judah and Jeroboam son of Jehoash[a] was king of Israel.

2He said:

"The LORD roars from Zion
and thunders from Jerusalem;
the pastures of the shepherds dry up,[b]
and the top of Carmel withers."

Judgment on Israel's Neighbors

3This is what the LORD says:

"For three sins of Damascus,
even for four, I will not turn back ⌞my wrath⌟.
Because she threshed Gilead
with sledges having iron teeth,
4I will send fire upon the house of Hazael
that will consume the fortresses of Ben-Hadad.
5I will break down the gate of Damascus;
I will destroy the king who is in[c] the Valley of Aven[d]
and the one who holds the scepter in Beth Eden.
The people of Aram will go into exile to Kir,"
says the LORD.

6This is what the LORD says:

"For three sins of Gaza,
even for four, I will not turn back ⌞my wrath⌟.
Because she took captive whole communities
and sold them to Edom,
7I will send fire upon the walls of Gaza
that will consume her fortresses.
8I will destroy the king[e] of Ashdod
and the one who holds the scepter in Ashkelon.
I will turn my hand against Ekron,
till the last of the Philistines is dead,"
says the Sovereign LORD.

9This is what the LORD says:

"For three sins of Tyre,
even for four, I will not turn back ⌞my wrath⌟.
Because she sold whole communities of captives to Edom,
disregarding a treaty of brotherhood,
10I will send fire upon the walls of Tyre
that will consume her fortresses."

11This is what the LORD says:

"For three sins of Edom,
even for four, I will not turn back ⌞my wrath⌟.
Because he pursued his brother with a sword,
stifling all compassion,[f]
because his anger raged continually
and his fury flamed unchecked,
12I will send fire upon Teman
that will consume the fortresses of Bozrah."

13This is what the LORD says:

"For three sins of Ammon,
even for four, I will not turn back ⌞my wrath⌟.
Because he ripped open the pregnant women of Gilead
in order to extend his borders,
14I will set fire to the walls of Rabbah
that will consume her fortresses
amid war cries on the day of battle,
amid violent winds on a stormy day.
15Her king[g] will go into exile,
he and his officials together,"
says the LORD.

2 This is what the LORD says:

"For three sins of Moab,
even for four, I will not turn back ⌞my wrath⌟.
Because he burned, as if to lime,
the bones of Edom's king,
2I will send fire upon Moab
that will consume the fortresses of Kerioth.[h]
Moab will go down in great tumult
amid war cries and the blast of the trumpet.
3I will destroy her ruler
and kill all her officials with him,"
says the LORD.

4This is what the LORD says:

"For three sins of Judah,
even for four, I will not turn back ⌞my wrath⌟.
Because they have rejected the law of the LORD
and have not kept his decrees,
because they have been led astray by false gods,[i]
the gods[j] their ancestors followed,

[a] 1 Hebrew *Joash,* a variant of *Jehoash* [b] 2 Or *shepherds mourn* [c] 5 Or *the inhabitants of* [d] 5 Aven means *wickedness.* [e] 8 Or *inhabitants* [f] 11 Or *sword / and destroyed his allies* [g] 15 Or / *Molech*; Hebrew *malcam* [h] 2 Or *of her cities* [i] 4 Or *by lies* [j] 4 Or *lies*

5I will send fire upon Judah
that will consume the fortresses of
Jerusalem."

Judgment on Israel

6This is what the LORD says:

"For three sins of Israel,
even for four, I will not turn back ⌞my
wrath⌟.
They sell the righteous for silver,
and the needy for a pair of sandals.
7They trample on the heads of the poor
as upon the dust of the ground
and deny justice to the oppressed.
Father and son use the same girl
and so profane my holy name.
8They lie down beside every altar
on garments taken in pledge.
In the house of their god
they drink wine taken as fines.

9"I destroyed the Amorite before them,
though he was tall as the cedars
and strong as the oaks.
I destroyed his fruit above
and his roots below.

10"I brought you up out of Egypt,
and I led you forty years in the desert
to give you the land of the Amorites.
11I also raised up prophets from among your
sons
and Nazirites from among your young
men.
Is this not true, people of Israel?"
declares the LORD.
12"But you made the Nazirites drink wine
and commanded the prophets not to
prophesy.

13"Now then, I will crush you
as a cart crushes when loaded with grain.
14The swift will not escape,
the strong will not muster their strength,
and the warrior will not save his life.
15The archer will not stand his ground,
the fleet-footed soldier will not get away,
and the horseman will not save his life.
16Even the bravest warriors
will flee naked on that day,"
declares the LORD.

Witnesses Summoned Against Israel

3 Hear this word the LORD has spoken against you, O people of Israel—against the whole family I brought up out of Egypt:

2"You only have I chosen
of all the families of the earth;
therefore I will punish you
for all your sins."

3Do two walk together
unless they have agreed to do so?
4Does a lion roar in the thicket
when he has no prey?
Does he growl in his den
when he has caught nothing?
5Does a bird fall into a trap on the ground
where no snare has been set?
Does a trap spring up from the earth
when there is nothing to catch?
6When a trumpet sounds in a city,
do not the people tremble?
When disaster comes to a city,
has not the LORD caused it?

7Surely the Sovereign LORD does nothing
without revealing his plan
to his servants the prophets.

8The lion has roared—
who will not fear?
The Sovereign LORD has spoken—
who can but prophesy?

9Proclaim to the fortresses of Ashdod
and to the fortresses of Egypt:
"Assemble yourselves on the mountains of
Samaria;
see the great unrest within her
and the oppression among her people."
10"They do not know how to do right,"
declares the LORD,
"who hoard plunder and loot in their
fortresses."

11Therefore this is what the Sovereign LORD
says:

"An enemy will overrun the land;
he will pull down your strongholds
and plunder your fortresses."

12This is what the LORD says:

"As a shepherd saves from the lion's mouth
only two leg bones or a piece of an ear,
so will the Israelites be saved,
those who sit in Samaria
on the edge of their beds
and in Damascus on their couches.[a]"

13"Hear this and testify against the house of
Jacob," declares the Lord, the LORD God Almighty.

14"On the day I punish Israel for her sins,
I will destroy the altars of Bethel;

[a] 12 The meaning of the Hebrew for this line is uncertain.

the horns of the altar will be cut off
and fall to the ground.
15I will tear down the winter house
along with the summer house;
the houses adorned with ivory will be destroyed
and the mansions will be demolished,"
declares the LORD.

Israel Has Not Returned to God

4 Hear this word, you cows of Bashan on Mount Samaria,
you women who oppress the poor and crush the needy
and say to your husbands, "Bring us some drinks!"
2The Sovereign LORD has sworn by his holiness:
"The time will surely come
when you will be taken away with hooks,
the last of you with fishhooks.
3You will each go straight out
through breaks in the wall,
and you will be cast out toward Harmon,[a]"
declares the LORD.
4"Go to Bethel and sin;
go to Gilgal and sin yet more.
Bring your sacrifices every morning,
your tithes every three years.[b]
5Burn leavened bread as a thank offering
and brag about your freewill offerings—
boast about them, you Israelites,
for this is what you love to do,"
declares the Sovereign LORD.
6"I gave you empty stomachs[c] in every city
and lack of bread in every town,
yet you have not returned to me,"
declares the LORD.
7"I also withheld rain from you
when the harvest was still three months away.
I sent rain on one town,
but withheld it from another.
One field had rain;
another had none and dried up.
8People staggered from town to town for water
but did not get enough to drink,
yet you have not returned to me,"
declares the LORD.
9"Many times I struck your gardens and vineyards,
I struck them with blight and mildew.
Locusts devoured your fig and olive trees,
yet you have not returned to me,"
declares the LORD.
10"I sent plagues among you
as I did to Egypt.
I killed your young men with the sword,
along with your captured horses.
I filled your nostrils with the stench of your camps,
yet you have not returned to me,"
declares the LORD.
11"I overthrew some of you
as I[d] overthrew Sodom and Gomorrah.
You were like a burning stick snatched from the fire,
yet you have not returned to me,"
declares the LORD.
12"Therefore this is what I will do to you, Israel,
and because I will do this to you,
prepare to meet your God, O Israel."
13He who forms the mountains,
creates the wind,
and reveals his thoughts to man,
he who turns dawn to darkness,
and treads the high places of the earth—
the LORD God Almighty is his name.

A Lament and Call to Repentance

5 Hear this word, O house of Israel, this lament I take up concerning you:
2"Fallen is Virgin Israel,
never to rise again,
deserted in her own land,
with no one to lift her up."
3This is what the Sovereign LORD says:
"The city that marches out a thousand strong for Israel
will have only a hundred left;
the town that marches out a hundred strong
will have only ten left."
4This is what the LORD says to the house of Israel:
"Seek me and live;
5 do not seek Bethel,
do not go to Gilgal,
do not journey to Beersheba.
For Gilgal will surely go into exile,
and Bethel will be reduced to nothing.[e]"
6Seek the LORD and live,

[a]3 Masoretic Text; with a different word division of the Hebrew (see Septuagint) *out, O mountain of oppression* [b]4 Or *tithes on the third day* [c]6 Hebrew *you cleanness of teeth* [d]11 Hebrew *God* [e]5 Or *grief*; or *wickedness*; Hebrew *aven*, a reference to Beth Aven (a derogatory name for Bethel)

or he will sweep through the house of
Joseph like a fire;
it will devour,
and Bethel will have no one to quench it.

7 You who turn justice into bitterness
and cast righteousness to the ground
8 (he who made the Pleiades and Orion,
who turns blackness into dawn
and darkens day into night,
who calls for the waters of the sea
and pours them out over the face of the
land—
the LORD is his name—
9 he flashes destruction on the stronghold
and brings the fortified city to ruin),
10 you hate the one who reproves in court
and despise him who tells the truth.

11 You trample on the poor
and force him to give you grain.
Therefore, though you have built stone
mansions,
you will not live in them;
though you have planted lush vineyards,
you will not drink their wine.
12 For I know how many are your offenses
and how great your sins.
You oppress the righteous and take bribes
and you deprive the poor of justice in the
courts.
13 Therefore the prudent man keeps quiet in
such times,
for the times are evil.

14 Seek good, not evil,
that you may live.
Then the LORD God Almighty will be with
you,
just as you say he is.
15 Hate evil, love good;
maintain justice in the courts.
Perhaps the LORD God Almighty will have
mercy
on the remnant of Joseph.

16 Therefore this is what the Lord, the LORD
God Almighty, says:

"There will be wailing in all the streets
and cries of anguish in every public
square.
The farmers will be summoned to weep
and the mourners to wail.
17 There will be wailing in all the vineyards,
for I will pass through your midst,"
says the LORD.

The Day of the LORD

18 Woe to you who long
for the day of the LORD!
Why do you long for the day of the LORD?
That day will be darkness, not light.
19 It will be as though a man fled from a lion
only to meet a bear,
as though he entered his house
and rested his hand on the wall
only to have a snake bite him.
20 Will not the day of the LORD be darkness, not
light—
pitch-dark, without a ray of brightness?

21 "I hate, I despise your religious feasts;
I cannot stand your assemblies.
22 Even though you bring me burnt offerings
and grain offerings,
I will not accept them.
Though you bring choice fellowship
offerings,[a]
I will have no regard for them.
23 Away with the noise of your songs!
I will not listen to the music of your
harps.
24 But let justice roll on like a river,
righteousness like a never-failing stream!

25 "Did you bring me sacrifices and offerings
forty years in the desert, O house of
Israel?
26 You have lifted up the shrine of your king,
the pedestal of your idols,
the star of your god[b]—
which you made for yourselves.
27 Therefore I will send you into exile beyond
Damascus,"
says the LORD, whose name is God
Almighty.

Woe to the Complacent

6 Woe to you who are complacent in Zion,
and to you who feel secure on Mount
Samaria,
you notable men of the foremost nation,
to whom the people of Israel come!
2 Go to Calneh and look at it;
go from there to great Hamath,
and then go down to Gath in Philistia.
Are they better off than your two kingdoms?
Is their land larger than yours?
3 You put off the evil day
and bring near a reign of terror.
4 You lie on beds inlaid with ivory
and lounge on your couches.
You dine on choice lambs
and fattened calves.

[a]22 Traditionally *peace offerings* [b]26 Or *lifted up Sakkuth your king / and Kaiwan your idols, / your star-gods*; Septuagint *lifted up the shrine of Molech / and the star of your god Rephan, / their idols*

5You strum away on your harps like David
and improvise on musical instruments.
6You drink wine by the bowlful
and use the finest lotions,
but you do not grieve over the ruin of
Joseph.
7Therefore you will be among the first to go
into exile;
your feasting and lounging will end.

The LORD Abhors the Pride of Israel

8The Sovereign LORD has sworn by himself—
the LORD God Almighty declares:

"I abhor the pride of Jacob
and detest his fortresses;
I will deliver up the city
and everything in it."

9If ten men are left in one house, they too will
die. 10And if a relative who is to burn the bodies
comes to carry them out of the house and asks
anyone still hiding there, "Is anyone with you?"
and he says, "No," then he will say, "Hush! We
must not mention the name of the LORD."

11For the LORD has given the command,
and he will smash the great house into
pieces
and the small house into bits.
12Do horses run on the rocky crags?
Does one plow there with oxen?
But you have turned justice into poison
and the fruit of righteousness into
bitterness—
13you who rejoice in the conquest of Lo
Debar[a]
and say, "Did we not take Karnaim[b] by
our own strength?"

14For the LORD God Almighty declares,
"I will stir up a nation against you,
O house of Israel,
that will oppress you all the way
from Lebo[c] Hamath to the valley of the
Arabah."

Locusts, Fire and a Plumb Line

7 This is what the Sovereign LORD showed me:
He was preparing swarms of locusts after the
king's share had been harvested and just as the
second crop was coming up. 2When they had
stripped the land clean, I cried out, "Sovereign
LORD, forgive! How can Jacob survive? He is so
small!"
3So the LORD relented.
"This will not happen," the LORD said.
4This is what the Sovereign LORD showed me:
The Sovereign LORD was calling for judgment by
fire; it dried up the great deep and devoured the
land. 5Then I cried out, "Sovereign LORD, I beg
you, stop! How can Jacob survive? He is so
small!"
6So the LORD relented.
"This will not happen either," the Sovereign
LORD said.

7This is what he showed me: The Lord was
standing by a wall that had been built true to
plumb, with a plumb line in his hand. 8And the
LORD asked me, "What do you see, Amos?"
"A plumb line," I replied.
Then the Lord said, "Look, I am setting a
plumb line among my people Israel; I will spare
them no longer.

9"The high places of Isaac will be destroyed
and the sanctuaries of Israel will be
ruined;
with my sword I will rise against the
house of Jeroboam."

Amos and Amaziah

10Then Amaziah the priest of Bethel sent a
message to Jeroboam king of Israel: "Amos is raising a conspiracy against you in the very heart of
Israel. The land cannot bear all his words. 11For
this is what Amos is saying:

" 'Jeroboam will die by the sword,
and Israel will surely go into exile,
away from their native land.' "

12Then Amaziah said to Amos, "Get out, you
seer! Go back to the land of Judah. Earn your
bread there and do your prophesying there.
13Don't prophesy anymore at Bethel, because
this is the king's sanctuary and the temple of the
kingdom."
14Amos answered Amaziah, "I was neither a
prophet nor a prophet's son, but I was a shepherd, and I also took care of sycamore-fig trees.
15But the LORD took me from tending the flock
and said to me, 'Go, prophesy to my people Israel.' 16Now then, hear the word of the LORD. You
say,

" 'Do not prophesy against Israel,
and stop preaching against the house of
Isaac.'

17"Therefore this is what the LORD says:

" 'Your wife will become a prostitute in the
city,
and your sons and daughters will fall by
the sword.
Your land will be measured and divided up,

[a] 13 *Lo Debar* means *nothing.* [b] 13 *Karnaim* means *horns*; *horn* here symbolizes strength. [c] 14 Or *from the entrance to*

and you yourself will die in a pagan[a]
country.
And Israel will certainly go into exile,
away from their native land.' "

A Basket of Ripe Fruit

8 This is what the Sovereign LORD showed me:
a basket of ripe fruit. 2 "What do you see,
Amos?" he asked.
"A basket of ripe fruit," I answered.
Then the LORD said to me, "The time is ripe
for my people Israel; I will spare them no longer.
3 "In that day," declares the Sovereign LORD,
"the songs in the temple will turn to wailing.[b]
Many, many bodies—flung everywhere! Silence!"

4 Hear this, you who trample the needy
and do away with the poor of the land,

5 saying,

"When will the New Moon be over
that we may sell grain,
and the Sabbath be ended
that we may market wheat?"—
skimping the measure,
boosting the price
and cheating with dishonest scales,
6 buying the poor with silver
and the needy for a pair of sandals,
selling even the sweepings with the
wheat.

7 The LORD has sworn by the Pride of Jacob: "I
will never forget anything they have done.

8 "Will not the land tremble for this,
and all who live in it mourn?
The whole land will rise like the Nile;
it will be stirred up and then sink
like the river of Egypt.

9 "In that day," declares the Sovereign LORD,

"I will make the sun go down at noon
and darken the earth in broad daylight.
10 I will turn your religious feasts into mourning
and all your singing into weeping.
I will make all of you wear sackcloth
and shave your heads.
I will make that time like mourning for an
only son
and the end of it like a bitter day.

11 "The days are coming," declares the
Sovereign LORD,
"when I will send a famine through the
land—
not a famine of food or a thirst for water,
but a famine of hearing the words of the
LORD.
12 Men will stagger from sea to sea
and wander from north to east,
searching for the word of the LORD,
but they will not find it.

13 "In that day

"the lovely young women and strong young
men
will faint because of thirst.
14 They who swear by the shame[c] of Samaria,
or say, 'As surely as your god lives,
O Dan,'
or, 'As surely as the god[d] of Beersheba
lives'—
they will fall,
never to rise again."

Israel to Be Destroyed

9 I saw the Lord standing by the altar, and he
said:

"Strike the tops of the pillars
so that the thresholds shake.
Bring them down on the heads of all the
people;
those who are left I will kill with the
sword.
Not one will get away,
none will escape.
2 Though they dig down to the depths of the
grave,[e]
from there my hand will take them.
Though they climb up to the heavens,
from there I will bring them down.
3 Though they hide themselves on the top of
Carmel,
there I will hunt them down and seize
them.
Though they hide from me at the bottom of
the sea,
there I will command the serpent to bite
them.
4 Though they are driven into exile by their
enemies,
there I will command the sword to slay
them.
I will fix my eyes upon them
for evil and not for good."

5 The Lord, the LORD Almighty,
he who touches the earth and it melts,
and all who live in it mourn—
the whole land rises like the Nile,
then sinks like the river of Egypt—

[a] 17 Hebrew *an unclean* [b] 3 Or *"the temple singers will wail* [c] 14 Or *by Ashima*; or *by the idol* [d] 14 Or *power*
[e] 2 Hebrew *to Sheol*

6he who builds his lofty palace[a] in the heavens
and sets its foundation[b] on the earth,
who calls for the waters of the sea
and pours them out over the face of the land—
the LORD is his name.

7"Are not you Israelites
the same to me as the Cushites[c]?"
declares the LORD.
"Did I not bring Israel up from Egypt,
the Philistines from Caphtor[d]
and the Arameans from Kir?

8"Surely the eyes of the Sovereign LORD
are on the sinful kingdom.
I will destroy it
from the face of the earth—
yet I will not totally destroy
the house of Jacob,"
declares the LORD.
9"For I will give the command,
and I will shake the house of Israel
among all the nations
as grain is shaken in a sieve,
and not a pebble will reach the ground.
10All the sinners among my people
will die by the sword,
all those who say,
'Disaster will not overtake or meet us.'

Israel's Restoration

11"In that day I will restore
David's fallen tent.
I will repair its broken places,
restore its ruins,
and build it as it used to be,
12so that they may possess the remnant of Edom
and all the nations that bear my name,[e]"
declares the LORD, who will do these things.

13"The days are coming," declares the LORD,
"when the reaper will be overtaken by the plowman
and the planter by the one treading grapes.
New wine will drip from the mountains
and flow from all the hills.
14I will bring back my exiled[f] people Israel;
they will rebuild the ruined cities and live in them.
They will plant vineyards and drink their wine;
they will make gardens and eat their fruit.
15I will plant Israel in their own land,
never again to be uprooted
from the land I have given them,"
says the LORD your God.

[a] 6 The meaning of the Hebrew for this phrase is uncertain. [b] 6 The meaning of the Hebrew for this word is uncertain.
[c] 7 That is, people from the upper Nile region [d] 7 That is, Crete [e] 12 Hebrew; Septuagint *so that the remnant of men / and all the nations that bear my name may seek* ⌊*the Lord*⌋ [f] 14 Or *will restore the fortunes of my*

Introduction to
OBADIAH

Personal Reading Plan

❒ Obadiah 1–21

Author

This short book is referred to as the "vision of Obadiah" (v. 1). This prophet's name means "the servant of the LORD." While there are 11 other Old Testament characters with this name, none of them can be identified with this prophet.

Date

The date of composition is uncertain, depending upon which of two events in Israel's history correlates with verses 11–14: (1) The Philistine invasion of Jerusalem during the reign of Jehoram (853–841 B.C.; see 2 Chron. 21:8–20), in which case, Obadiah would be a ninth-century contemporary of Elisha; or, (2) The Babylonian campaign against Jerusalem (605–585 B.C.), in which case Obadiah would be a sixth-century contemporary of Jeremiah. The latter seems more likely.

Theme

God's judgment of proud Edom and the restoration of Israel.

Historical Background

The Edomites apparently took advantage of the fall of Jerusalem to Babylon in 586 B.C. They plundered the land and pillaged the homes of survivors. Obadiah speaks God's judgment on Edom for the way they took advantage of "brother Jacob" in his moment of weakness. The term "Edom" is used in the Old Testament for the name of Esau (the brother of Jacob) and for the race made up of his descendants. The area this tribe occupied was originally the land of Seir. It was a rugged, mountainous region that extended from the Dead Sea south to the Gulf of Aqabah. The hatred and hostility between Edom and Israel was long-standing. The history of the blood feud between the two peoples can be traced by a study of the relevant Old Testament passages (see Gen. 27:41–45; 32:1–21; 33; Num. 20:14–21; Deut. 2:1–6; 2 Sam. 8:13–14; 2 Kings 8:20–22; Ezek. 35). Edom was known for sitting smugly in her fortified cities atop rocky clefts, and Obadiah prophesies against her for relying on this for her sense of security. In the fifth century the Edomites were driven out of their own land by the Nabateans. After this, many Edomites moved into southern Palestine.

Characteristics

Obadiah is the shortest book in all of the Old Testament. While other prophets often announced oracles directed at other nations (along with their words for Israel), nearly the whole book of Obadiah consists of the words of a Jewish prophet to another country. In this respect Obadiah is like Nahum, who preached against Nineveh. With respect to language, Obadiah is like Jeremiah (compare vv. 1–9 with Jer. 49:7–22), which suggests interdependence or mutual reliance on an unknown third source. The language of this book is characterized by vivid and striking metaphors (see vv. 4,5,16,18).

[1]The vision of Obadiah.

This is what the Sovereign LORD says about Edom—

We have heard a message from the LORD:
An envoy was sent to the nations to say,
"Rise, and let us go against her for battle"—
[2]"See, I will make you small among the nations;
you will be utterly despised.
[3]The pride of your heart has deceived you,
you who live in the clefts of the rocks[a]
and make your home on the heights,
you who say to yourself,
'Who can bring me down to the ground?'
[4]Though you soar like the eagle
and make your nest among the stars,
from there I will bring you down,"
declares the LORD.
[5]"If thieves came to you,
if robbers in the night—
Oh, what a disaster awaits you—
would they not steal only as much as they wanted?
If grape pickers came to you,
would they not leave a few grapes?
[6]But how Esau will be ransacked,
his hidden treasures pillaged!
[7]All your allies will force you to the border;
your friends will deceive and overpower you;
those who eat your bread will set a trap for you,[b]
but you will not detect it.
[8]"In that day," declares the LORD,
"will I not destroy the wise men of Edom,
men of understanding in the mountains of Esau?
[9]Your warriors, O Teman, will be terrified,
and everyone in Esau's mountains
will be cut down in the slaughter.
[10]Because of the violence against your brother Jacob,
you will be covered with shame;
you will be destroyed forever.
[11]On the day you stood aloof
while strangers carried off his wealth
and foreigners entered his gates
and cast lots for Jerusalem,
you were like one of them.
[12]You should not look down on your brother
in the day of his misfortune,
nor rejoice over the people of Judah
in the day of their destruction,
nor boast so much
in the day of their trouble.
[13]You should not march through the gates of my people
in the day of their disaster,
nor look down on them in their calamity
in the day of their disaster,
nor seize their wealth
in the day of their disaster.
[14]You should not wait at the crossroads
to cut down their fugitives,
nor hand over their survivors
in the day of their trouble.

[15]"The day of the LORD is near
for all nations.
As you have done, it will be done to you;
your deeds will return upon your own head.
[16]Just as you drank on my holy hill,
so all the nations will drink continually;
they will drink and drink
and be as if they had never been.
[17]But on Mount Zion will be deliverance;
it will be holy,
and the house of Jacob
will possess its inheritance.
[18]The house of Jacob will be a fire
and the house of Joseph a flame;
the house of Esau will be stubble,
and they will set it on fire and consume it.
There will be no survivors
from the house of Esau."
The LORD has spoken.
[19]People from the Negev will occupy
the mountains of Esau,
and people from the foothills will possess
the land of the Philistines.
They will occupy the fields of Ephraim and Samaria,
and Benjamin will possess Gilead.
[20]This company of Israelite exiles who are in Canaan
will possess ⌞the land⌟ as far as Zarephath;
the exiles from Jerusalem who are in Sepharad
will possess the towns of the Negev.
[21]Deliverers will go up on[c] Mount Zion
to govern the mountains of Esau.
And the kingdom will be the LORD's.

[a]3 Or *of Sela* [b]7 The meaning of the Hebrew for this clause is uncertain. [c]21 Or *from*

Introduction to
JONAH

Personal Reading Plan

- ❐ Jonah 1:1–17
- ❐ Jonah 2:1–10
- ❐ Jonah 3:1–10
- ❐ Jonah 4:1–11

Author

The story of this book was originally told by the prophet Jonah, though others may have written it down. The author is not identified in the text.

Date

The book was written sometime after Jonah's ministry c. 800–770 B.C., before Nineveh's destruction (612 B.C.) and Samaria's fall (722–721 B.C.).

Theme

God's love for the Gentiles, even Nineveh.

Historical Background

Israel had just restored her northern borders under King Jeroboam II (793–753 B.C.), as Jonah had prophesied (2 Kings 14:25). At this time, Israel was politically secure, spiritually smug and morally corrupt. Nineveh, the city to which Jonah was sent by God, was the capital of Assyria. Assyria was a ruthless empire which threatened tiny Israel, and eventually conquered it in 722 B.C. Nineveh was 500 miles east of Joppa, but Jonah boarded a ship heading 2,000 miles west, revealing how far and fast Jonah wanted to get away from a people he despised. Israelites had many reasons to hate the proud Ninevites, as Nahum points out in a prophecy dedicated exclusively to the Ninevites (see the Introduction to Nahum). Nineveh's repentance and revival under Jonah was short-lived. The second time around for proud, cruel Nineveh resulted in her fall in 612 B.C. She was never heard from again.

Characteristics

Unlike most other Old Testament prophetic books, Jonah gives an account of a single incident in the life of the prophet. The story is briefly told in some 40 verses. His prayer consumes the remaining eight verses. Some regard this book as an imaginative tale, akin to a modern "fish story." Others view Jonah as an allegory or parable, teaching God's universal love. However, the Jews accepted this book as reflecting the experience of the actual prophet Jonah. And Jesus' reference to Jonah (Matt. 12:38–41) substantiates that the book recounts actual events. Jonah's missionary message finds later parallels in the message of Peter (see Acts 10:1–11:18) and Paul (see Rom. 9–11). The theological emphasis in Jonah (on God's universal love, sovereignty and redemption) are equally applicable today.

Passages for General Group Study

1:1–17	Jonah Flees From the Lord
2:1–3:10	Jonah Goes From the Fish to Nineveh
4:1–11	Jonah's Anger at God's Compassion

Jonah Flees From the LORD

1 The word of the LORD came to Jonah son of
Amittai: 2"Go to the great city of Nineveh
and preach against it, because its wickedness has
come up before me."
3But Jonah ran away from the LORD and headed for Tarshish. He went down to Joppa, where
he found a ship bound for that port. After paying
the fare, he went aboard and sailed for Tarshish
to flee from the LORD.

> ### *JONAH 1:1–17*
>
> 1. If you could take a cruise anywhere in the world, where would you go?
> 2. Did you ever try to run away from home? How far did you get?
> 3. In your school, who is the crowd that you would just as soon not have anything to do with?
> 4. What is the most wicked city you have heard about today?
> 5. If God told you to go to this "wicked" city and tell them about Christ, what would you do?
> 6. What is something you think God may be asking of you? How are you going to respond?
> 7. How can this group pray for and help you do what God wants you to do?

4Then the LORD sent a great wind on the sea,
and such a violent storm arose that the ship
threatened to break up. 5All the sailors were
afraid and each cried out to his own god. And
they threw the cargo into the sea to lighten the
ship.
But Jonah had gone below deck, where he lay
down and fell into a deep sleep. 6The captain
went to him and said, "How can you sleep? Get
up and call on your god! Maybe he will take notice of us, and we will not perish."
7Then the sailors said to each other, "Come,
let us cast lots to find out who is responsible for
this calamity." They cast lots and the lot fell on
Jonah.
8So they asked him, "Tell us, who is responsible for making all this trouble for us? What do you
do? Where do you come from? What is your
country? From what people are you?"
9He answered, "I am a Hebrew and I worship
the LORD, the God of heaven, who made the sea
and the land."
10This terrified them and they asked, "What
have you done?" (They knew he was running
away from the LORD, because he had already told
them so.)
11The sea was getting rougher and rougher. So
they asked him, "What should we do to you to
make the sea calm down for us?"
12"Pick me up and throw me into the sea," he
replied, "and it will become calm. I know that it
is my fault that this great storm has come upon
you."
13Instead, the men did their best to row back
to land. But they could not, for the sea grew even
wilder than before. 14Then they cried to the
LORD, "O LORD, please do not let us die for taking
this man's life. Do not hold us accountable for
killing an innocent man, for you, O LORD, have
done as you pleased." 15Then they took Jonah
and threw him overboard, and the raging sea
grew calm. 16At this the men greatly feared the
LORD, and they offered a sacrifice to the LORD and
made vows to him.
17But the LORD provided a great fish to swallow Jonah, and Jonah was inside the fish three
days and three nights.

Jonah's Prayer

2 From inside the fish Jonah prayed to the
LORD his God. 2He said:

1:1–2 *The word of the LORD came.* A common phrase used to indicate the divine source of a prophet's revelation. ***great city of Nineveh.*** The capital of Assyria, the ruthless empire which threatened (and eventually conquered) tiny Israel. Nineveh was over 500 miles from Gath Hepher, Jonah's hometown. ***its wickedness.*** See Nahum 1:11; 2:12–13; 3:1,4,16,19.

1:3 *ran away from the LORD.* The reason is found in 4:2: Jonah did not want to be part of God's gracious compassion toward Nineveh. ***Tarshish.*** Perhaps the city of Tartessus in southwest Spain. By heading in the opposite direction from Nineveh, to what seemed like the end of the world, Jonah intended to escape his divinely appointed task.

1:7 *let us cast lots.* The casting of lots was a custom widely practiced in the ancient Near East. Sticks or marked pebbles were probably drawn from a receptacle. ***lot fell on Jonah.*** By the lot of judgment the Lord exposed the guilty one (see Josh. 7:14–26).

1:17 *a great fish.* The Hebrew here and the Greek of Matthew 12:40 are both general terms for a large fish, not necessarily a whale. ***three days and three nights.*** The phrase used here may, as in the New Testament, refer to a period of time including one full day and parts of two others. The New Testament clearly uses Jonah's experience as a foreshadowing of the burial and resurrection of Jesus, who was entombed for "three days and three nights" (Matt. 12:40; also see Matt. 16:4).

"In my distress I called to the LORD,
and he answered me.
From the depths of the grave[a] I called for help,
and you listened to my cry.
3You hurled me into the deep,
into the very heart of the seas,
and the currents swirled about me;
all your waves and breakers
swept over me.

JONAH 2:1–3:10

1. What is the biggest fish you have ever caught?
2. What was your favorite hiding place as a child?
3. When it comes to listening to God, where would you rank yourself on a scale from 1 (I can't hear you) to 10 (I'm all ears)?
4. What do you think about how the king of Nineveh responded to Jonah's message?
5. What would it take for this to happen in your town?
6. When did God give you a second chance?
7. Where do you need the prayer support of the group this week?

4I said, 'I have been banished
from your sight;
yet I will look again
toward your holy temple.'
5The engulfing waters threatened me,[b]
the deep surrounded me;
seaweed was wrapped around my head.
6To the roots of the mountains I sank down;
the earth beneath barred me in forever.
But you brought my life up from the pit,
O LORD my God.

7"When my life was ebbing away,
I remembered you, LORD,
and my prayer rose to you,
to your holy temple.

8"Those who cling to worthless idols
forfeit the grace that could be theirs.
9But I, with a song of thanksgiving,
will sacrifice to you.
What I have vowed I will make good.
Salvation comes from the LORD."

10And the LORD commanded the fish, and it
vomited Jonah onto dry land.

Jonah Goes to Nineveh

3 Then the word of the LORD came to Jonah
a second time: 2"Go to the great city of
Nineveh and proclaim to it the message I give
you."
3Jonah obeyed the word of the LORD and went
to Nineveh. Now Nineveh was a very important
city—a visit required three days. 4On the first
day, Jonah started into the city. He proclaimed:
"Forty more days and Nineveh will be overturned." 5The Ninevites believed God. They declared a fast, and all of them, from the greatest to
the least, put on sackcloth.
6When the news reached the king of Nineveh,
he rose from his throne, took off his royal robes,
covered himself with sackcloth and sat down in
the dust. 7Then he issued a proclamation in Nineveh:

"By the decree of the king and his nobles:

Do not let any man or beast, herd or
flock, taste anything; do not let them eat or
drink. 8But let man and beast be covered
with sackcloth. Let everyone call urgently
on God. Let them give up their evil ways

[a]2 Hebrew *Sheol* [b]5 Or *waters were at my throat*

2:2–9 A psalm of thanksgiving for deliverance from death in the sea. Jonah recalls his prayer for help as he was sinking into the depths. His gratitude is heightened by his knowledge that he deserved death but that God had shown him extraordinary mercy.

2:9 ***Salvation comes from the LORD.*** The climax of Jonah's thanksgiving prayer. This statement is also central to the book, as salvation comes from the Lord, not from belonging to a particular ethnic group or nationality.

3:2 ***proclaim to it the message I give you.*** A prophet was the bearer of a message from God, not primarily a foreteller of coming events.

3:3 ***Jonah obeyed.*** Reluctantly, still wanting the Ninevites to be destroyed (4:1–5).

3:5 ***believed God.*** This may mean that the Ninevites genuinely turned to the Lord (see Matt. 12:41). At the least they took the prophet's warning seriously and acted accordingly.

3:5–6 ***fast ... sackcloth ... dust.*** Customary signs of humbling oneself in repentance.

3:7–8 Inclusion of the domestic animals was unusual and expressed the urgency with which the Ninevites sought mercy.

3:10 God often responds in mercy to man's repentance by canceling threatened punishment. The Ninevites eventually returned to their wickedness, and the city was destroyed in 612 B.C.—about 150 years after Jonah's ministry.

and their violence. 9Who knows? God may yet relent and with compassion turn from his fierce anger so that we will not perish."

10When God saw what they did and how they turned from their evil ways, he had compassion and did not bring upon them the destruction he had threatened.

Jonah's Anger at the LORD's Compassion

4 But Jonah was greatly displeased and became angry. 2He prayed to the LORD, "O LORD, is this not what I said when I was still at home? That is why I was so quick to flee to Tarshish. I knew that you are a gracious and compassionate God, slow to anger and abounding in love, a God who relents from sending calamity. 3Now, O LORD, take away my life, for it is better for me to die than to live."

4But the LORD replied, "Have you any right to be angry?"

5Jonah went out and sat down at a place east of the city. There he made himself a shelter, sat in its shade and waited to see what would happen to the city. 6Then the LORD God provided a vine and made it grow up over Jonah to give shade for his head to ease his discomfort, and Jonah was very happy about the vine. 7But at dawn the next day God provided a worm, which chewed the vine so that it withered. 8When the sun rose, God provided a scorching east wind, and the sun blazed on Jonah's head so that he grew faint. He wanted to die, and said, "It would be better for me to die than to live."

9But God said to Jonah, "Do you have a right to be angry about the vine?"

"I do," he said. "I am angry enough to die."

10But the LORD said, "You have been concerned about this vine, though you did not tend it or make it grow. It sprang up overnight and died overnight. 11But Nineveh has more than a hundred and twenty thousand people who cannot tell their right hand from their left, and many cattle as well. Should I not be concerned about that great city?"

JONAH 4:1–11

1. When it's real hot out, where do you go and what do you do to cool down?
2. Who is your biggest rival in school sports?
3. Would you be happy if God started to do a great work among the players on that team?
4. When it comes to getting angry, how long is your fuse?
5. What do you think happened to Jonah after this story was over?
6. When have you, like Jonah, been angry at God? Over what? How should you deal with anger (see Eph. 4:26)?
7. Jesus taught, "Love your enemies" (Matt. 5:44). How can this group help you in this?

4:1 ***angry.*** Jonah was angry that God would have compassion on an enemy of Israel. He wanted God's goodness to be shown only to Israelites, not to Gentiles. In contrast to God, who was "slow to anger" (v. 2), Jonah became angry quickly (v. 9 also).

4:3 ***take away my life.*** See 1 Kings 19:4. To Jonah, God's mercy to the Ninevites meant an end to Israel's favored nation standing with him. Jonah shortly before had rejoiced in his deliverance from death, but now that Nineveh lives, he prefers to die.

4:5–6 ***waited to see.*** Jonah still hoped that Nineveh would be destroyed. ***vine.*** Likely a castor oil plant, a shrub growing over 12 feet high with large, shady leaves.

4:10 ***sprang up overnight and died overnight.*** Indicative of fleeting value, as opposed to the value of people, including those of Nineveh.

4:11 ***cannot tell their right hand from their left.*** Like small children, the Ninevites needed God's fatherly compassion. ***many cattle as well.*** God's concern extended even to domestic animals. ***Should I not be concerned ... ?*** The commission God gave Jonah displayed his mercy and compassion to the Ninevites, and his last word emphatically proclaimed that concern for every creature, both man and animal. Jonah and his countrymen traditionally rejoiced in God's special mercies to Israel but wished only his wrath on their enemies. God here rebukes such hardness and proclaims his own generous benevolence.

Introduction to MICAH

Personal Reading Plan

- ❒ Micah 1:1–16
- ❒ Micah 2:1–13
- ❒ Micah 3:1–4:5
- ❒ Micah 4:6–5:15
- ❒ Micah 6:1–16
- ❒ Micah 7:1–20

Author

The author is identified as Micah, a contemporary of Isaiah and Hosea, who was probably from Moresheth Gath (1:14).

Date

These prophecies were given during the reigns of Jotham, Ahaz and Hezekiah (1:1)—kings of Judah who reigned c. 750–686 B.C. Since Micah predicted the fall of Israel's capital, Samaria (1:6–7), which occurred in c. 722 B.C., these prophecies would date from before then.

Theme

A just and merciful God delivers his people from darkness. The lives of God's covenant people should reflect God's standards.

Historical Background

It is helpful to understand the life and times during which Micah prophesied (1:1; see 2 Kings 15:32–20:21). During this dark time when the sins of the nothern kingdom of Israel were being punished by Assyrian invaders, Micah could see that these same activities (idolatry, Baal worship, child sacrifice, sorcery) were creeping south to Judah and Jerusalem. As in the northern kingdom, this led to an increasing gap between the rich and the poor. The poor were oppressed with no recourse to the courts, because of corrupt judges, so Micah champions their cause. Religious life flourished but had little depth or reality. Micah draws a sharp contrast between this "pop religion" and true faith, which involves justice, mercy and walking with God (6:8).

Characteristics

Against this background, judgment is inevitable, says Micah. He stresses that God hates idolatry, injustice, rebellion and empty ritualism. However, judgment will be followed by restoration, which will prepare the way for a new future. Micah emphasizes God's undeserved grace and unstoppable initiative. He had a big view of history, taking in several thousand years at a glance. One moment he is talking about the promised Messiah; in the next fragment of verses he may focus on the imminent invasion of Assyria. Reading these short speeches with their rapid shifts of focus can be confusing. Furthermore, the book of Micah shifts voices frequently—from God to Micah to the rebellious people and back again. Micah and Isaiah have similar literary styles. Both prophets use very descriptive language and many figures of speech. Micah also has a passion for punning, as in 1:10–15 (see NIV text footnotes).

1 The word of the LORD that came to Micah of Moresheth during the reigns of Jotham, Ahaz and Hezekiah, kings of Judah—the vision he saw concerning Samaria and Jerusalem.

2Hear, O peoples, all of you,
listen, O earth and all who are in it,
that the Sovereign LORD may witness against you,
the Lord from his holy temple.

Judgment Against Samaria and Jerusalem

3Look! The LORD is coming from his dwelling place;
he comes down and treads the high places of the earth.
4The mountains melt beneath him
and the valleys split apart,
like wax before the fire,
like water rushing down a slope.
5All this is because of Jacob's transgression,
because of the sins of the house of Israel.
What is Jacob's transgression?
Is it not Samaria?
What is Judah's high place?
Is it not Jerusalem?

6"Therefore I will make Samaria a heap of rubble,
a place for planting vineyards.
I will pour her stones into the valley
and lay bare her foundations.
7All her idols will be broken to pieces;
all her temple gifts will be burned with fire;
I will destroy all her images.
Since she gathered her gifts from the wages of prostitutes,
as the wages of prostitutes they will again be used."

Weeping and Mourning

8Because of this I will weep and wail;
I will go about barefoot and naked.
I will howl like a jackal
and moan like an owl.
9For her wound is incurable;
it has come to Judah.
It[a] has reached the very gate of my people,
even to Jerusalem itself.
10Tell it not in Gath[b];
weep not at all.[c]
In Beth Ophrah[d]
roll in the dust.
11Pass on in nakedness and shame,
you who live in Shaphir.[e]
Those who live in Zaanan[f]
will not come out.
Beth Ezel is in mourning;
its protection is taken from you.
12Those who live in Maroth[g] writhe in pain,
waiting for relief,
because disaster has come from the LORD,
even to the gate of Jerusalem.
13You who live in Lachish,[h]
harness the team to the chariot.
You were the beginning of sin
to the Daughter of Zion,
for the transgressions of Israel
were found in you.
14Therefore you will give parting gifts
to Moresheth Gath.
The town of Aczib[i] will prove deceptive
to the kings of Israel.
15I will bring a conqueror against you
who live in Mareshah.[j]
He who is the glory of Israel
will come to Adullam.
16Shave your heads in mourning
for the children in whom you delight;
make yourselves as bald as the vulture,
for they will go from you into exile.

Man's Plans and God's

2 Woe to those who plan iniquity,
to those who plot evil on their beds!
At morning's light they carry it out
because it is in their power to do it.
2They covet fields and seize them,
and houses, and take them.
They defraud a man of his home,
a fellowman of his inheritance.
3Therefore, the LORD says:
"I am planning disaster against this people,
from which you cannot save yourselves.
You will no longer walk proudly,
for it will be a time of calamity.
4In that day men will ridicule you;
they will taunt you with this mournful song:
'We are utterly ruined;
my people's possession is divided up.
He takes it from me!
He assigns our fields to traitors.'"
5Therefore you will have no one in the assembly of the LORD
to divide the land by lot.

[a]9 Or *He* [b]10 *Gath* sounds like the Hebrew for *tell.* [c]10 Hebrew; Septuagint may suggest *not in Acco.* The Hebrew for *in Acco* sounds like the Hebrew for *weep.* [d]10 *Beth Ophrah* means *house of dust.* [e]11 *Shaphir* means *pleasant.* [f]11 *Zaanan* sounds like the Hebrew for *come out.* [g]12 *Maroth* sounds like the Hebrew for *bitter.* [h]13 *Lachish* sounds like the Hebrew for *team.* [i]14 *Aczib* means *deception.* [j]15 *Mareshah* sounds like the Hebrew for *conqueror.*

False Prophets

6"Do not prophesy," their prophets say.
"Do not prophesy about these things;
disgrace will not overtake us."
7Should it be said, O house of Jacob:
"Is the Spirit of the LORD angry?
Does he do such things?"

"Do not my words do good
to him whose ways are upright?
8Lately my people have risen up
like an enemy.
You strip off the rich robe
from those who pass by without a care,
like men returning from battle.
9You drive the women of my people
from their pleasant homes.
You take away my blessing
from their children forever.
10Get up, go away!
For this is not your resting place,
because it is defiled,
it is ruined, beyond all remedy.
11If a liar and deceiver comes and says,
'I will prophesy for you plenty of wine and beer,'
he would be just the prophet for this people!

Deliverance Promised

12"I will surely gather all of you, O Jacob;
I will surely bring together the remnant of Israel.
I will bring them together like sheep in a pen,
like a flock in its pasture;
the place will throng with people.
13One who breaks open the way will go up before them;
they will break through the gate and go out.
Their king will pass through before them,
the LORD at their head."

Leaders and Prophets Rebuked

3 Then I said,

"Listen, you leaders of Jacob,
you rulers of the house of Israel.
Should you not know justice,
2 you who hate good and love evil;
who tear the skin from my people
and the flesh from their bones;
3who eat my people's flesh,
strip off their skin
and break their bones in pieces;
who chop them up like meat for the pan,
like flesh for the pot?"

4Then they will cry out to the LORD,
but he will not answer them.
At that time he will hide his face from them
because of the evil they have done.

5This is what the LORD says:

"As for the prophets
who lead my people astray,
if one feeds them,
they proclaim 'peace';
if he does not,
they prepare to wage war against him.
6Therefore night will come over you, without visions,
and darkness, without divination.
The sun will set for the prophets,
and the day will go dark for them.
7The seers will be ashamed
and the diviners disgraced.
They will all cover their faces
because there is no answer from God."

8But as for me, I am filled with power,
with the Spirit of the LORD,
and with justice and might,
to declare to Jacob his transgression,
to Israel his sin.
9Hear this, you leaders of the house of Jacob,
you rulers of the house of Israel,
who despise justice
and distort all that is right;
10who build Zion with bloodshed,
and Jerusalem with wickedness.
11Her leaders judge for a bribe,
her priests teach for a price,
and her prophets tell fortunes for money.
Yet they lean upon the LORD and say,
"Is not the LORD among us?
No disaster will come upon us."
12Therefore because of you,
Zion will be plowed like a field,
Jerusalem will become a heap of rubble,
the temple hill a mound overgrown with thickets.

The Mountain of the LORD

4 In the last days

the mountain of the LORD's temple will be established
as chief among the mountains;
it will be raised above the hills,
and peoples will stream to it.

2Many nations will come and say,

"Come, let us go up to the mountain of the LORD,
to the house of the God of Jacob.
He will teach us his ways,

so that we may walk in his paths."
The law will go out from Zion,
the word of the LORD from Jerusalem.
3 He will judge between many peoples
and will settle disputes for strong nations
far and wide.
They will beat their swords into plowshares
and their spears into pruning hooks.
Nation will not take up sword against nation,
nor will they train for war anymore.
4 Every man will sit under his own vine
and under his own fig tree,
and no one will make them afraid,
for the LORD Almighty has spoken.
5 All the nations may walk
in the name of their gods;
we will walk in the name of the LORD
our God for ever and ever.

The LORD's Plan

6 "In that day," declares the LORD,

"I will gather the lame;
I will assemble the exiles
and those I have brought to grief.
7 I will make the lame a remnant,
those driven away a strong nation.
The LORD will rule over them in Mount Zion
from that day and forever.
8 As for you, O watchtower of the flock,
O stronghold[a] of the Daughter of Zion,
the former dominion will be restored to you;
kingship will come to the Daughter of
Jerusalem."

9 Why do you now cry aloud—
have you no king?
Has your counselor perished,
that pain seizes you like that of a woman
in labor?
10 Writhe in agony, O Daughter of Zion,
like a woman in labor,
for now you must leave the city
to camp in the open field.
You will go to Babylon;
there you will be rescued.
There the LORD will redeem you
out of the hand of your enemies.

11 But now many nations
are gathered against you.
They say, "Let her be defiled,
let our eyes gloat over Zion!"
12 But they do not know
the thoughts of the LORD;
they do not understand his plan,
he who gathers them like sheaves to the
threshing floor.
13 "Rise and thresh, O Daughter of Zion,
for I will give you horns of iron;
I will give you hoofs of bronze
and you will break to pieces many
nations."
You will devote their ill-gotten gains to the
LORD,
their wealth to the Lord of all the earth.

A Promised Ruler From Bethlehem

5 Marshal your troops, O city of troops,[b]
for a siege is laid against us.
They will strike Israel's ruler
on the cheek with a rod.

2 "But you, Bethlehem Ephrathah,
though you are small among the clans[c] of
Judah,
out of you will come for me
one who will be ruler over Israel,
whose origins[d] are from of old,
from ancient times.[e]"

3 Therefore Israel will be abandoned
until the time when she who is in labor
gives birth
and the rest of his brothers return
to join the Israelites.

4 He will stand and shepherd his flock
in the strength of the LORD,
in the majesty of the name of the LORD his
God.
And they will live securely, for then his
greatness
will reach to the ends of the earth.
5 And he will be their peace.

Deliverance and Destruction

When the Assyrian invades our land
and marches through our fortresses,
we will raise against him seven shepherds,
even eight leaders of men.
6 They will rule[f] the land of Assyria with the
sword,
the land of Nimrod with drawn sword.[g]
He will deliver us from the Assyrian
when he invades our land
and marches into our borders.

7 The remnant of Jacob will be
in the midst of many peoples
like dew from the LORD,
like showers on the grass,
which do not wait for man
or linger for mankind.
8 The remnant of Jacob will be among the
nations,

[a] 8 Or *hill* [b] 1 Or *Strengthen your walls, O walled city* [c] 2 Or *rulers* [d] 2 Hebrew *goings out* [e] 2 Or *from days of eternity* [f] 6 Or *crush* [g] 6 Or *Nimrod in its gates*

in the midst of many peoples,
like a lion among the beasts of the forest,
like a young lion among flocks of sheep,
which mauls and mangles as it goes,
and no one can rescue.
9Your hand will be lifted up in triumph over
your enemies,
and all your foes will be destroyed.

10"In that day," declares the LORD,

"I will destroy your horses from among you
and demolish your chariots.
11I will destroy the cities of your land
and tear down all your strongholds.
12I will destroy your witchcraft
and you will no longer cast spells.
13I will destroy your carved images
and your sacred stones from among you;
you will no longer bow down
to the work of your hands.
14I will uproot from among you your Asherah
poles[a]
and demolish your cities.
15I will take vengeance in anger and wrath
upon the nations that have not obeyed
me."

The LORD's Case Against Israel

6 Listen to what the LORD says:

"Stand up, plead your case before the
mountains;
let the hills hear what you have to say.
2Hear, O mountains, the LORD's accusation;
listen, you everlasting foundations of the
earth.
For the LORD has a case against his people;
he is lodging a charge against Israel.

3"My people, what have I done to you?
How have I burdened you? Answer me.
4I brought you up out of Egypt
and redeemed you from the land of
slavery.
I sent Moses to lead you,
also Aaron and Miriam.
5My people, remember
what Balak king of Moab counseled
and what Balaam son of Beor answered.
Remember ⌊your journey⌋ from Shittim to
Gilgal,
that you may know the righteous acts of
the LORD."

6With what shall I come before the LORD
and bow down before the exalted God?
Shall I come before him with burnt offerings,
with calves a year old?
7Will the LORD be pleased with thousands of
rams,
with ten thousand rivers of oil?
Shall I offer my firstborn for my
transgression,
the fruit of my body for the sin of my
soul?
8He has showed you, O man, what is good.
And what does the LORD require of you?
To act justly and to love mercy
and to walk humbly with your God.

Israel's Guilt and Punishment

9Listen! The LORD is calling to the city—
and to fear your name is wisdom—
"Heed the rod and the One who appointed
it.[b]
10Am I still to forget, O wicked house,
your ill-gotten treasures
and the short ephah,[c] which is accursed?
11Shall I acquit a man with dishonest scales,
with a bag of false weights?
12Her rich men are violent;
her people are liars
and their tongues speak deceitfully.
13Therefore, I have begun to destroy you,
to ruin you because of your sins.
14You will eat but not be satisfied;
your stomach will still be empty.[d]
You will store up but save nothing,
because what you save I will give to the
sword.
15You will plant but not harvest;
you will press olives but not use the oil on
yourselves,
you will crush grapes but not drink the
wine.
16You have observed the statutes of Omri
and all the practices of Ahab's house,
and you have followed their traditions.
Therefore I will give you over to ruin
and your people to derision;
you will bear the scorn of the nations.[e]"

Israel's Misery

7 What misery is mine!
I am like one who gathers summer fruit
at the gleaning of the vineyard;
there is no cluster of grapes to eat,
none of the early figs that I crave.
2The godly have been swept from the land;
not one upright man remains.
All men lie in wait to shed blood;
each hunts his brother with a net.
3Both hands are skilled in doing evil;

a14 That is, symbols of the goddess Asherah b9 The meaning of the Hebrew for this line is uncertain. c10 An ephah was a dry measure. d14 The meaning of the Hebrew for this word is uncertain. e16 Septuagint; Hebrew *scorn due my people*

the ruler demands gifts,
the judge accepts bribes,
the powerful dictate what they desire—
they all conspire together.
4The best of them is like a brier,
the most upright worse than a thorn hedge.
The day of your watchmen has come,
the day God visits you.
Now is the time of their confusion.
5Do not trust a neighbor;
put no confidence in a friend.
Even with her who lies in your embrace
be careful of your words.
6For a son dishonors his father,
a daughter rises up against her mother,
a daughter-in-law against her mother-in-law—
a man's enemies are the members of his own household.

7But as for me, I watch in hope for the LORD,
I wait for God my Savior;
my God will hear me.

Israel Will Rise

8Do not gloat over me, my enemy!
Though I have fallen, I will rise.
Though I sit in darkness,
the LORD will be my light.
9Because I have sinned against him,
I will bear the LORD's wrath,
until he pleads my case
and establishes my right.
He will bring me out into the light;
I will see his righteousness.
10Then my enemy will see it
and will be covered with shame,
she who said to me,
"Where is the LORD your God?"
My eyes will see her downfall;
even now she will be trampled underfoot
like mire in the streets.

11The day for building your walls will come,
the day for extending your boundaries.
12In that day people will come to you
from Assyria and the cities of Egypt,
even from Egypt to the Euphrates
and from sea to sea
and from mountain to mountain.
13The earth will become desolate because of its inhabitants,
as the result of their deeds.

Prayer and Praise

14Shepherd your people with your staff,
the flock of your inheritance,
which lives by itself in a forest,
in fertile pasturelands.[a]
Let them feed in Bashan and Gilead
as in days long ago.

15"As in the days when you came out of Egypt,
I will show them my wonders."

16Nations will see and be ashamed,
deprived of all their power.
They will lay their hands on their mouths
and their ears will become deaf.
17They will lick dust like a snake,
like creatures that crawl on the ground.
They will come trembling out of their dens;
they will turn in fear to the LORD our God
and will be afraid of you.
18Who is a God like you,
who pardons sin and forgives the transgression
of the remnant of his inheritance?
You do not stay angry forever
but delight to show mercy.
19You will again have compassion on us;
you will tread our sins underfoot
and hurl all our iniquities into the depths of the sea.
20You will be true to Jacob,
and show mercy to Abraham,
as you pledged on oath to our fathers
in days long ago.

a 14 Or *in the middle of Carmel*

Introduction to
NAHUM

Personal Reading Plan

❒ Nahum 1:1–15
❒ Nahum 2:1–13
❒ Nahum 3:1–19

Author

Nahum, "the Elkoshite," who was probably from Judah. Nahum means "comfort" and is related to the name Nehemiah, meaning "The LORD comforts."

Date

Nahum's oracle is dated between the overthrow of Thebes (in 663 B.C.; see 3:8–10) and the fall of Nineveh (in 612 B.C.). It is perhaps near the end of this period since he represents the fall of Nineveh as imminent (2:1; 3:14,19). This would place Nahum during the reign of Josiah and make him a contemporary of Zephaniah and a young Jeremiah.

Theme

The Lord's judgment of Nineveh.

Historical Background

The northern kingdom of Israel had fallen at the hands of the Assyrians c. 722 B.C. The Assyrians were brutally cruel, their kings often being pictured as gloating over the gruesome punishments inflicted on conquered peoples. No wonder the fear and dread of Assyria fell on all her neighbors! About 700 B.C., the Assyrian king Sennacherib made Nineveh, which was the greatest city of its day, the capital of the empire. Jonah had announced Nineveh's doom, but the people repented and were given a "stay of execution" (see the Introduction to Jonah). However, they quickly returned to their evil ways.

Poetic justice and Nineveh's destruction is the focus of Nahum's prophecy. Within a few years, Nahum's prophecies came true. Proud Nineveh fell so hard that it never rose again. Its site was obliterated; it was only rediscovered some 2,500 years later!

Characteristics

Like Obadiah, but unlike the other minor prophets, Nahum does not address his homeland at all, but a foreign city—Nineveh. Still, the book was intended for Jewish readers. While the style of Nahum is that of traditional judgment oracles, the language is poetic, with many metaphors and similes, as well as other vivid images. Each of the three chapters in Nahum is a complete unit in itself. Chapter 1 is in the form of a poem in which Nahum declares the judgment that is to come. Chapter 2 describes the siege and subsequent sack of Nineveh. In chapter 3, Nineveh is described and compared to Thebes. Thebes, the capital of Upper Egypt, was a city like Nineveh that was strong and proud and yet its destruction had come. Thus Nahum shows that the God of Israel is, in fact, the God who controls the fate of all the nations. Nahum's purpose is to lift up the great God of Israel, and thus bring comfort to his people. This book is a powerful indictment of a nation that seeks glory by aggression and oppression. The God of Israel hates violence and pride and "will not leave the guilty unpunished" (1:3).

1 An oracle concerning Nineveh. The book of the vision of Nahum the Elkoshite.

The LORD's Anger Against Nineveh

2The LORD is a jealous and avenging God;
the LORD takes vengeance and is filled with wrath.
The LORD takes vengeance on his foes
and maintains his wrath against his enemies.
3The LORD is slow to anger and great in power;
the LORD will not leave the guilty unpunished.
His way is in the whirlwind and the storm,
and clouds are the dust of his feet.
4He rebukes the sea and dries it up;
he makes all the rivers run dry.
Bashan and Carmel wither
and the blossoms of Lebanon fade.
5The mountains quake before him
and the hills melt away.
The earth trembles at his presence,
the world and all who live in it.
6Who can withstand his indignation?
Who can endure his fierce anger?
His wrath is poured out like fire;
the rocks are shattered before him.
7The LORD is good,
a refuge in times of trouble.
He cares for those who trust in him,
8 but with an overwhelming flood
he will make an end of ⌊Nineveh⌋;
he will pursue his foes into darkness.

9Whatever they plot against the LORD
he[a] will bring to an end;
trouble will not come a second time.
10They will be entangled among thorns
and drunk from their wine;
they will be consumed like dry stubble.[b]
11From you, ⌊O Nineveh,⌋ has one come forth
who plots evil against the LORD
and counsels wickedness.

12This is what the LORD says:

"Although they have allies and are numerous,
they will be cut off and pass away.
Although I have afflicted you, ⌊O Judah,⌋
I will afflict you no more.
13Now I will break their yoke from your neck
and tear your shackles away."

14The LORD has given a command concerning you, ⌊Nineveh⌋:
"You will have no descendants to bear your name.
I will destroy the carved images and cast idols
that are in the temple of your gods.
I will prepare your grave,
for you are vile."

15Look, there on the mountains,
the feet of one who brings good news,
who proclaims peace!
Celebrate your festivals, O Judah,
and fulfill your vows.
No more will the wicked invade you;
they will be completely destroyed.

Nineveh to Fall

2 An attacker advances against you, ⌊Nineveh⌋.
Guard the fortress,
watch the road,
brace yourselves,
marshal all your strength!

2The LORD will restore the splendor of Jacob
like the splendor of Israel,
though destroyers have laid them waste
and have ruined their vines.

3The shields of his soldiers are red;
the warriors are clad in scarlet.
The metal on the chariots flashes
on the day they are made ready;
the spears of pine are brandished.[c]
4The chariots storm through the streets,
rushing back and forth through the squares.
They look like flaming torches;
they dart about like lightning.
5He summons his picked troops,
yet they stumble on their way.
They dash to the city wall;
the protective shield is put in place.
6The river gates are thrown open
and the palace collapses.
7It is decreed[d] that ⌊the city⌋
be exiled and carried away.
Its slave girls moan like doves
and beat upon their breasts.
8Nineveh is like a pool,
and its water is draining away.
"Stop! Stop!" they cry,
but no one turns back.
9Plunder the silver!
Plunder the gold!
The supply is endless,
the wealth from all its treasures!

[a] 9 Or *What do you foes plot against the LORD? / He*
[b] 10 The meaning of the Hebrew for this verse is uncertain.
[c] 3 Hebrew; Septuagint and Syriac / *the horsemen rush to and fro*
[d] 7 The meaning of the Hebrew for this word is uncertain.

10 She is pillaged, plundered, stripped!
Hearts melt, knees give way,
bodies tremble, every face grows pale.

11 Where now is the lions' den,
the place where they fed their young,
where the lion and lioness went,
and the cubs, with nothing to fear?
12 The lion killed enough for his cubs
and strangled the prey for his mate,
filling his lairs with the kill
and his dens with the prey.

13 "I am against you,"
declares the LORD Almighty.
"I will burn up your chariots in smoke,
and the sword will devour your young lions.
I will leave you no prey on the earth.
The voices of your messengers
will no longer be heard."

Woe to Nineveh

3 Woe to the city of blood,
full of lies,
full of plunder,
never without victims!
2 The crack of whips,
the clatter of wheels,
galloping horses
and jolting chariots!
3 Charging cavalry,
flashing swords
and glittering spears!
Many casualties,
piles of dead,
bodies without number,
people stumbling over the corpses—
4 all because of the wanton lust of a harlot,
alluring, the mistress of sorceries,
who enslaved nations by her prostitution
and peoples by her witchcraft.

5 "I am against you," declares the LORD Almighty.
"I will lift your skirts over your face.
I will show the nations your nakedness
and the kingdoms your shame.
6 I will pelt you with filth,
I will treat you with contempt
and make you a spectacle.
7 All who see you will flee from you and say,
'Nineveh is in ruins—who will mourn for her?'
Where can I find anyone to comfort you?"

8 Are you better than Thebes,[a]
situated on the Nile,
with water around her?
The river was her defense,
the waters her wall.
9 Cush[b] and Egypt were her boundless strength;
Put and Libya were among her allies.
10 Yet she was taken captive
and went into exile.
Her infants were dashed to pieces
at the head of every street.
Lots were cast for her nobles,
and all her great men were put in chains.
11 You too will become drunk;
you will go into hiding
and seek refuge from the enemy.
12 All your fortresses are like fig trees
with their first ripe fruit;
when they are shaken,
the figs fall into the mouth of the eater.
13 Look at your troops—
they are all women!
The gates of your land
are wide open to your enemies;
fire has consumed their bars.

14 Draw water for the siege,
strengthen your defenses!
Work the clay,
tread the mortar,
repair the brickwork!
15 There the fire will devour you;
the sword will cut you down
and, like grasshoppers, consume you.
Multiply like grasshoppers,
multiply like locusts!
16 You have increased the number of your merchants
till they are more than the stars of the sky,
but like locusts they strip the land
and then fly away.
17 Your guards are like locusts,
your officials like swarms of locusts
that settle in the walls on a cold day—
but when the sun appears they fly away,
and no one knows where.
18 O king of Assyria, your shepherds[c] slumber;
your nobles lie down to rest.
Your people are scattered on the mountains
with no one to gather them.
19 Nothing can heal your wound;
your injury is fatal.
Everyone who hears the news about you
claps his hands at your fall,
for who has not felt
your endless cruelty?

[a] 8 Hebrew *No Amon* [b] 9 That is, the upper Nile region [c] 18 Or *rulers*

Introduction to
HABAKKUK

Personal Reading Plan

- ❐ Habakkuk 1:1–11
- ❐ Habakkuk 1:12–2:1
- ❐ Habakkuk 2:2–20
- ❐ Habakkuk 3:1–19

Author

The book was written by the prophet Habakkuk, a contemporary of Jeremiah. He was a man of deep faith rooted in the religious traditions of Israel.

Date

Habakkuk was written in the latter part of the seventh century B.C., probably c. 610–605 B.C. Habakkuk, like Jeremiah, probably lived to see the beginning of the fulfillment of his prophecy when Jerusalem was attacked by the Babylonians in 597 B.C.

Theme

Faith triumphs over doubt. Habakkuk wrestles with a problem that faces every age: Why does God seem inactive in the face of evil and injustice?

Historical Background

The northern kingdom (Israel) had fallen to Assyria c. 722 B.C. and now the rising Chaldean Empire (i.e., the second Babylonian Empire) was on the horizon. In Habakkuk's day, the rulers of the southern kingdom (Judah) were known to "do evil in the eyes of the Lord" (see 2 Kings 23:31–24:7). As an agent of judgment in God's hand, the Chaldeans invaded Judah in 605 B.C. The king of Babylon, Nebuchadnezzar, made the Judean king, Jehoiakim, his vassal or puppet ruler. Chapters one and two of Habakkuk are historically rooted in the events preceding and following the 605 B.C. invasion under Nebuchadnezzar's leadership. While 3:1 contains Habakkuk's name, it is less certain as to whether this chapter should be dated at the time of the invasion, or later in the prophet's life.

Characteristics

Habakkuk is unusual in that it contains no prophecy directed to Israel. Instead, it is a dialogue between the prophet and God. The book shares some of the structural and thematic traits of the psalms of lament (e.g. Pss. 13; 44; 74; 80). Complaint and petition are followed by the divine perspective on the problem. Like the psalmist, Habakkuk uses stark poetic images to color and convey his message. Like the psalmist, and unlike all other prophets (who mostly speak on God's behalf to the people), Habakkuk speaks for himself and on behalf of his people directly and only to God. Like Job he receives no answer except that God is God. God is holy, does care and will act as he sees fit, but only in his time.

Habakkuk 2:4—"The righteous will live by [his] faith"—is quoted by several New Testament authors who use it in speaking of faith (see Rom. 1:17; Gal. 3:11; Heb. 10:38). The book of Habakkuk was popular during the time between the Old and New Testaments. A complete commentary on its first two chapters has been found among the Dead Sea Scrolls.

1

The oracle that Habakkuk the prophet received.

Habakkuk's Complaint

2How long, O LORD, must I call for help,
but you do not listen?
Or cry out to you, "Violence!"
but you do not save?
3Why do you make me look at injustice?
Why do you tolerate wrong?
Destruction and violence are before me;
there is strife, and conflict abounds.
4Therefore the law is paralyzed,
and justice never prevails.
The wicked hem in the righteous,
so that justice is perverted.

The LORD's Answer

5"Look at the nations and watch—
and be utterly amazed.
For I am going to do something in your days
that you would not believe,
even if you were told.
6I am raising up the Babylonians,[a]
that ruthless and impetuous people,
who sweep across the whole earth
to seize dwelling places not their own.
7They are a feared and dreaded people;
they are a law to themselves
and promote their own honor.
8Their horses are swifter than leopards,
fiercer than wolves at dusk.
Their cavalry gallops headlong;
their horsemen come from afar.
They fly like a vulture swooping to devour;
9 they all come bent on violence.
Their hordes[b] advance like a desert wind
and gather prisoners like sand.
10They deride kings
and scoff at rulers.
They laugh at all fortified cities;
they build earthen ramps and capture
them.
11Then they sweep past like the wind and go
on—
guilty men, whose own strength is their
god."

Habakkuk's Second Complaint

12O LORD, are you not from everlasting?
My God, my Holy One, we will not die.
O LORD, you have appointed them to execute
judgment;
O Rock, you have ordained them to
punish.
13Your eyes are too pure to look on evil;
you cannot tolerate wrong.
Why then do you tolerate the treacherous?
Why are you silent while the wicked
swallow up those more righteous than
themselves?
14You have made men like fish in the sea,
like sea creatures that have no ruler.
15The wicked foe pulls all of them up with
hooks,
he catches them in his net,
he gathers them up in his dragnet;
and so he rejoices and is glad.
16Therefore he sacrifices to his net
and burns incense to his dragnet,
for by his net he lives in luxury
and enjoys the choicest food.
17Is he to keep on emptying his net,
destroying nations without mercy?

2

I will stand at my watch
and station myself on the ramparts;
I will look to see what he will say to me,
and what answer I am to give to this
complaint.[c]

The LORD's Answer

2Then the LORD replied:

"Write down the revelation
and make it plain on tablets
so that a herald[d] may run with it.
3For the revelation awaits an appointed time;
it speaks of the end
and will not prove false.
Though it linger, wait for it;
it[e] will certainly come and will not delay.

4"See, he is puffed up;
his desires are not upright—
but the righteous will live by his faith[f]—
5indeed, wine betrays him;
he is arrogant and never at rest.
Because he is as greedy as the grave[g]
and like death is never satisfied,
he gathers to himself all the nations
and takes captive all the peoples.

6"Will not all of them taunt him with ridicule
and scorn, saying,

" 'Woe to him who piles up stolen goods
and makes himself wealthy by extortion!
How long must this go on?'
7Will not your debtors[h] suddenly arise?
Will they not wake up and make you
tremble?

a6 Or *Chaldeans* b9 The meaning of the Hebrew for this word is uncertain. c1 Or *and what to answer when I am rebuked*
d2 Or *so that whoever reads it* e3 Or *Though he linger, wait for him; / he* f4 Or *faithfulness* g5 Hebrew *Sheol*
h7 Or *creditors*

Then you will become their victim.
8Because you have plundered many nations,
the peoples who are left will plunder you.
For you have shed man's blood;
you have destroyed lands and cities and everyone in them.

9"Woe to him who builds his realm by unjust gain
to set his nest on high,
to escape the clutches of ruin!
10You have plotted the ruin of many peoples,
shaming your own house and forfeiting your life.
11The stones of the wall will cry out,
and the beams of the woodwork will echo it.

12"Woe to him who builds a city with bloodshed
and establishes a town by crime!
13Has not the LORD Almighty determined
that the people's labor is only fuel for the fire,
that the nations exhaust themselves for nothing?
14For the earth will be filled with the knowledge of the glory of the LORD,
as the waters cover the sea.

15"Woe to him who gives drink to his neighbors,
pouring it from the wineskin till they are drunk,
so that he can gaze on their naked bodies.
16You will be filled with shame instead of glory.
Now it is your turn! Drink and be exposed[a]!
The cup from the LORD's right hand is coming around to you,
and disgrace will cover your glory.
17The violence you have done to Lebanon will overwhelm you,
and your destruction of animals will terrify you.
For you have shed man's blood;
you have destroyed lands and cities and everyone in them.

18"Of what value is an idol, since a man has carved it?
Or an image that teaches lies?
For he who makes it trusts in his own creation;
he makes idols that cannot speak.
19Woe to him who says to wood, 'Come to life!'
Or to lifeless stone, 'Wake up!'
Can it give guidance?
It is covered with gold and silver;
there is no breath in it.
20But the LORD is in his holy temple;
let all the earth be silent before him."

Habakkuk's Prayer

3 A prayer of Habakkuk the prophet. On *shigionoth*.[b]

2LORD, I have heard of your fame;
I stand in awe of your deeds, O LORD.
Renew them in our day,
in our time make them known;
in wrath remember mercy.

3God came from Teman,
the Holy One from Mount Paran. *Selah*[c]
His glory covered the heavens
and his praise filled the earth.
4His splendor was like the sunrise;
rays flashed from his hand,
where his power was hidden.
5Plague went before him;
pestilence followed his steps.
6He stood, and shook the earth;
he looked, and made the nations tremble.
The ancient mountains crumbled
and the age-old hills collapsed.
His ways are eternal.
7I saw the tents of Cushan in distress,
the dwellings of Midian in anguish.

8Were you angry with the rivers, O LORD?
Was your wrath against the streams?
Did you rage against the sea
when you rode with your horses
and your victorious chariots?
9You uncovered your bow,
you called for many arrows. *Selah*
You split the earth with rivers;
10 the mountains saw you and writhed.
Torrents of water swept by;
the deep roared
and lifted its waves on high.
11Sun and moon stood still in the heavens
at the glint of your flying arrows,
at the lightning of your flashing spear.
12In wrath you strode through the earth
and in anger you threshed the nations.
13You came out to deliver your people,
to save your anointed one.
You crushed the leader of the land of wickedness,
you stripped him from head to foot. *Selah*

[a] *16* Masoretic Text; Dead Sea Scrolls, Aquila, Vulgate and Syriac (see also Septuagint) *and stagger* [b] *1* Probably a literary or musical term [c] *3* A word of uncertain meaning; possibly a musical term; also in verses 9 and 13

14With his own spear you pierced his head
when his warriors stormed out to scatter
us,
gloating as though about to devour
the wretched who were in hiding.
15You trampled the sea with your horses,
churning the great waters.

16I heard and my heart pounded,
my lips quivered at the sound;
decay crept into my bones,
and my legs trembled.
Yet I will wait patiently for the day of
calamity
to come on the nation invading us.
17Though the fig tree does not bud
and there are no grapes on the vines,
though the olive crop fails
and the fields produce no food,
though there are no sheep in the pen
and no cattle in the stalls,
18yet I will rejoice in the LORD,
I will be joyful in God my Savior.

19The Sovereign LORD is my strength;
he makes my feet like the feet of a deer,
he enables me to go on the heights.

For the director of music. On my stringed
instruments.

Introduction to ZEPHANIAH

Personal Reading Plan

❒ Zephaniah 1:1–2:3
❒ Zephaniah 2:4–15
❒ Zephaniah 3:1–20

Author

Zephaniah was an aristocrat, a great-great grandson of Hezekiah, the king of Judah from 715 to 686 B.C. (see 1:1).

Date

Zephaniah prophesied during the reign of Josiah (640–609 B.C.). His preaching as recorded here may have contributed to Josiah's reforms, which took place in 621 B.C. This makes Zephaniah an older contemporary and kindred spirit of Jeremiah.

Theme

The coming Day of the Lord.

Historical Background

Zephaniah's twofold message—"gloom and doom" for Judah and its neighbors (1:1–3:8), then the Lord's purging and purifying of a faithful remnant (3:9–20)—is best appreciated within the context of what necessitated this spiritual housecleaning. The historical situation which he addressed is the same pervasive decadence that triggered King Josiah's reform movement (see 2 Chron. 34–35). Josiah was spurred on by the evils of King Manasseh and King Amon, by the rediscovery of Moses' Law, by hearing Jeremiah's early preaching, and quite possibly by Zephaniah's preaching as well. Thus it was that Josiah removed the pagan centers of idol worship. The immediate occasion for Zephaniah's prophecy may have been a century-long invasion of Canaan by the Scythians (a fierce nomadic people). Fulfillment of Zephaniah's prophecy (destruction of Judah) came at the hands of King Nebuchadnezzar of Babylon. He defeated the Assyrians in 612 B.C., thus establishing Babylonian supremacy in the Near East.

Characteristics

Zephaniah consists of several brief oracles or utterances, many heavy with gloom. The prophet foresaw a worldwide catastrophe, but he also saw beyond it. In the prophetic tradition, Zephaniah delivers his message with lament, exhortation and hope. Zephaniah presents a beautiful picture of a God who delights in his people (3:14–20). The prophecies of Zephaniah against the nations are listed below:

Judah:	1:4–2:3
Philistia:	2:4–7
Ammon:	2:8–11
Moab:	2:8–11
Cush:	2:12
Assyria:	2:13–15

1 The word of the LORD that came to Zephaniah son of Cushi, the son of Gedaliah, the son
of Amariah, the son of Hezekiah, during the reign
of Josiah son of Amon king of Judah:

Warning of Coming Destruction

2"I will sweep away everything
from the face of the earth,"
declares the LORD.
3"I will sweep away both men and animals;
I will sweep away the birds of the air
and the fish of the sea.
The wicked will have only heaps of rubble[a]
when I cut off man from the face of the earth,"
declares the LORD.

Against Judah

4"I will stretch out my hand against Judah
and against all who live in Jerusalem.
I will cut off from this place every remnant of Baal,
the names of the pagan and the idolatrous priests—
5those who bow down on the roofs
to worship the starry host,
those who bow down and swear by the LORD
and who also swear by Molech,[b]
6those who turn back from following the LORD
and neither seek the LORD nor inquire of him.
7Be silent before the Sovereign LORD,
for the day of the LORD is near.
The LORD has prepared a sacrifice;
he has consecrated those he has invited.
8On the day of the LORD's sacrifice
I will punish the princes
and the king's sons
and all those clad
in foreign clothes.
9On that day I will punish
all who avoid stepping on the threshold,[c]
who fill the temple of their gods
with violence and deceit.

10"On that day," declares the LORD,
"a cry will go up from the Fish Gate,
wailing from the New Quarter,
and a loud crash from the hills.
11Wail, you who live in the market district[d];
all your merchants will be wiped out,
all who trade with[e] silver will be ruined.
12At that time I will search Jerusalem with lamps
and punish those who are complacent,
who are like wine left on its dregs,
who think, 'The LORD will do nothing,
either good or bad.'
13Their wealth will be plundered,
their houses demolished.
They will build houses
but not live in them;
they will plant vineyards
but not drink the wine.

The Great Day of the LORD

14"The great day of the LORD is near—
near and coming quickly.
Listen! The cry on the day of the LORD will be bitter,
the shouting of the warrior there.
15That day will be a day of wrath,
a day of distress and anguish,
a day of trouble and ruin,
a day of darkness and gloom,
a day of clouds and blackness,
16a day of trumpet and battle cry
against the fortified cities
and against the corner towers.
17I will bring distress on the people
and they will walk like blind men,
because they have sinned against the LORD.
Their blood will be poured out like dust
and their entrails like filth.
18Neither their silver nor their gold
will be able to save them
on the day of the LORD's wrath.
In the fire of his jealousy
the whole world will be consumed,
for he will make a sudden end
of all who live in the earth."

2 Gather together, gather together,
O shameful nation,
2before the appointed time arrives
and that day sweeps on like chaff,
before the fierce anger of the LORD comes upon you,
before the day of the LORD's wrath comes upon you.
3Seek the LORD, all you humble of the land,
you who do what he commands.
Seek righteousness, seek humility;
perhaps you will be sheltered
on the day of the LORD's anger.

Against Philistia

4Gaza will be abandoned
and Ashkelon left in ruins.
At midday Ashdod will be emptied
and Ekron uprooted.
5Woe to you who live by the sea,
O Kerethite people;

[a] 3 The meaning of the Hebrew for this line is uncertain. [b] 5 Hebrew *Malcam,* that is, Milcom [c] 9 See 1 Samuel 5:5.
[d] 11 Or *the Mortar* [e] 11 Or *in*

the word of the LORD is against you,
O Canaan, land of the Philistines.

"I will destroy you,
and none will be left."

6The land by the sea, where the Kerethites[a] dwell,
will be a place for shepherds and sheep pens.
7It will belong to the remnant of the house of Judah;
there they will find pasture.
In the evening they will lie down
in the houses of Ashkelon.
The LORD their God will care for them;
he will restore their fortunes.[b]

Against Moab and Ammon

8"I have heard the insults of Moab
and the taunts of the Ammonites,
who insulted my people
and made threats against their land.
9Therefore, as surely as I live,"
declares the LORD Almighty, the God of Israel,
"surely Moab will become like Sodom,
the Ammonites like Gomorrah—
a place of weeds and salt pits,
a wasteland forever.
The remnant of my people will plunder them;
the survivors of my nation will inherit their land."

10This is what they will get in return for their pride,
for insulting and mocking the people of the LORD Almighty.
11The LORD will be awesome to them
when he destroys all the gods of the land.
The nations on every shore will worship him,
every one in its own land.

Against Cush

12"You too, O Cushites,[c]
will be slain by my sword."

Against Assyria

13He will stretch out his hand against the north
and destroy Assyria,
leaving Nineveh utterly desolate
and dry as the desert.
14Flocks and herds will lie down there,
creatures of every kind.
The desert owl and the screech owl
will roost on her columns.
Their calls will echo through the windows,
rubble will be in the doorways,
the beams of cedar will be exposed.
15This is the carefree city
that lived in safety.
She said to herself,
"I am, and there is none besides me."
What a ruin she has become,
a lair for wild beasts!
All who pass by her scoff
and shake their fists.

The Future of Jerusalem

3 Woe to the city of oppressors,
rebellious and defiled!
2She obeys no one,
she accepts no correction.
She does not trust in the LORD,
she does not draw near to her God.
3Her officials are roaring lions,
her rulers are evening wolves,
who leave nothing for the morning.
4Her prophets are arrogant;
they are treacherous men.
Her priests profane the sanctuary
and do violence to the law.
5The LORD within her is righteous;
he does no wrong.
Morning by morning he dispenses his justice,
and every new day he does not fail,
yet the unrighteous know no shame.

6"I have cut off nations;
their strongholds are demolished.
I have left their streets deserted,
with no one passing through.
Their cities are destroyed;
no one will be left—no one at all.
7I said to the city,
'Surely you will fear me
and accept correction!'
Then her dwelling would not be cut off,
nor all my punishments come upon her.
But they were still eager
to act corruptly in all they did.
8Therefore wait for me," declares the LORD,
"for the day I will stand up to testify.[d]
I have decided to assemble the nations,
to gather the kingdoms
and to pour out my wrath on them—
all my fierce anger.
The whole world will be consumed
by the fire of my jealous anger.

9"Then will I purify the lips of the peoples,
that all of them may call on the name of the LORD

[a] 6 The meaning of the Hebrew for this word is uncertain. [b] 7 Or *will bring back their captives* [c] 12 That is, people from the upper Nile region [d] 8 Septuagint and Syriac; Hebrew *will rise up to plunder*

and serve him shoulder to shoulder.
10 From beyond the rivers of Cush[a]
my worshipers, my scattered people,
will bring me offerings.
11 On that day you will not be put to shame
for all the wrongs you have done to me,
because I will remove from this city
those who rejoice in their pride.
Never again will you be haughty
on my holy hill.
12 But I will leave within you
the meek and humble,
who trust in the name of the LORD.
13 The remnant of Israel will do no wrong;
they will speak no lies,
nor will deceit be found in their mouths.
They will eat and lie down
and no one will make them afraid."

14 Sing, O Daughter of Zion;
shout aloud, O Israel!
Be glad and rejoice with all your heart,
O Daughter of Jerusalem!
15 The LORD has taken away your punishment,
he has turned back your enemy.
The LORD, the King of Israel, is with you;
never again will you fear any harm.
16 On that day they will say to Jerusalem,
"Do not fear, O Zion;
do not let your hands hang limp.
17 The LORD your God is with you,
he is mighty to save.
He will take great delight in you,
he will quiet you with his love,
he will rejoice over you with singing."

18 "The sorrows for the appointed feasts
I will remove from you;
they are a burden and a reproach to
you.[b]
19 At that time I will deal
with all who oppressed you;
I will rescue the lame
and gather those who have been scattered.
I will give them praise and honor
in every land where they were put to
shame.
20 At that time I will gather you;
at that time I will bring you home.
I will give you honor and praise
among all the peoples of the earth
when I restore your fortunes[c]
before your very eyes,"
says the LORD.

a 10 That is, the upper Nile region b 18 Or *"I will gather you who mourn for the appointed feasts; / your reproach is a burden to you* c 20 Or *I bring back your captives*

Introduction to
HAGGAI

Personal Reading Plan

❒ Haggai 1:1–15
❒ Haggai 2:1–23

Author

The author is not identifed, though the book tells of Haggai's ministry and records his oracles. Haggai means "festal," which may suggest that the prophet was born during one of the three Jewish feasts (Unleavened Bread, Pentecost or Weeks and Tabernacles; see Deut. 16:16).

Date

Haggai is quite specific as to the year, month and day of his messages: August 29 (1:1); September 15 (1:15); October 17 (2:1); December 18 (2:10 and 2:20), 520 B.C.

Theme

Rebuilding for results—the blessing is in the doing.

Historical Background

This book is set in the context of the return of the Jews from the Babylonian exile and the subsequent rebuilding of Jerusalem and the temple (see the Introductions to Ezra and Nehemiah). It was through the ministry of Haggai (along with Zechariah) that the rebuilding of the temple began (see Ezra 5:1–2). The problem with getting the building started, it seems, was not just with the neighboring Samaritans who opposed the rebuilding projects (fearing that this would lead to a renewed and politically powerful Jewish state). The real problem had to do with the lethargy of the people. Haggai's aim was to get the people moving on the project. The temple was completed and dedicated four years later in 516 B.C. No other prophet had results as direct, immediate and identifiable as Haggai!

Characteristics

There is only one book in the Old Testament that is shorter than Haggai (Obadiah). Yet in just 38 verses Haggai is able to show the differing consequences of disobedience vs. obedience, as well as point to the coming of the Messiah. Haggai was an older contemporary of Zechariah. Both dealt with the same themes, although in quite different ways (see the Introduction to Zechariah). Haggai was a practical doer, while Zechariah was an apocalyptic visionary. Haggai did not mince words but went right to the point, while Zechariah mixed metaphors in a memorable way. Haggai exhorted the people to get to work on the project at hand (the rebuilding of the temple), while Zechariah encouraged them to put their hope in what lay ahead for them in the distant future (which also served to motivate the people to rebuild the temple, though in a different way). The book records not only his oracles, but also his ministry and the response of the people to it, while in Zechariah the emphasis is on his prophecies (with no indication of response).

Several times Haggai seems to echo other Scriptures (compare 1:6 with Deut. 28:38–39 and 2:17 with Deut. 28:22). The use of "Be strong" three times in 2:4 corresponds with the encouragement given in Joshua 1:6–7,9,18.

A Call to Build the House of the LORD

1 In the second year of King Darius, on the
first day of the sixth month, the word of the
LORD came through the prophet Haggai to Zerubbabel son of Shealtiel, governor of Judah, and to
Joshua[a] son of Jehozadak, the high priest:
2 This is what the LORD Almighty says: "These
people say, 'The time has not yet come for the
LORD's house to be built.' "
3 Then the word of the LORD came through the
prophet Haggai: 4 "Is it a time for you yourselves
to be living in your paneled houses, while this
house remains a ruin?"
5 Now this is what the LORD Almighty says:
"Give careful thought to your ways. 6 You have
planted much, but have harvested little. You eat,
but never have enough. You drink, but never
have your fill. You put on clothes, but are not
warm. You earn wages, only to put them in a
purse with holes in it."
7 This is what the LORD Almighty says: "Give
careful thought to your ways. 8 Go up into the
mountains and bring down timber and build the
house, so that I may take pleasure in it and be
honored," says the LORD. 9 "You expected much,
but see, it turned out to be little. What you
brought home, I blew away. Why?" declares the
LORD Almighty. "Because of my house, which remains a ruin, while each of you is busy with his
own house. 10 Therefore, because of you the heavens have withheld their dew and the earth its
crops. 11 I called for a drought on the fields and
the mountains, on the grain, the new wine, the
oil and whatever the ground produces, on men
and cattle, and on the labor of your hands."

12 Then Zerubbabel son of Shealtiel, Joshua son
of Jehozadak, the high priest, and the whole remnant of the people obeyed the voice of the LORD
their God and the message of the prophet Haggai,
because the LORD their God had sent him. And
the people feared the LORD.
13 Then Haggai, the LORD's messenger, gave
this message of the LORD to the people: "I am
with you," declares the LORD. 14 So the LORD
stirred up the spirit of Zerubbabel son of Shealtiel, governor of Judah, and the spirit of Joshua son
of Jehozadak, the high priest, and the spirit of the
whole remnant of the people. They came and began to work on the house of the LORD Almighty,
their God, 15 on the twenty-fourth day of the
sixth month in the second year of King Darius.

The Promised Glory of the New House

2 On the twenty-first day of the seventh
month, the word of the LORD came through
the prophet Haggai: 2 "Speak to Zerubbabel son of
Shealtiel, governor of Judah, to Joshua son of Jehozadak, the high priest, and to the remnant of
the people. Ask them, 3 'Who of you is left who
saw this house in its former glory? How does it
look to you now? Does it not seem to you like
nothing? 4 But now be strong, O Zerubbabel,' declares the LORD. 'Be strong, O Joshua son of Jehozadak, the high priest. Be strong, all you people of the land,' declares the LORD, 'and work.
For I am with you,' declares the LORD Almighty.
5 'This is what I covenanted with you when you
came out of Egypt. And my Spirit remains among
you. Do not fear.'
6 "This is what the LORD Almighty says: 'In a
little while I will once more shake the heavens
and the earth, the sea and the dry land. 7 I will
shake all nations, and the desired of all nations
will come, and I will fill this house with glory,'
says the LORD Almighty. 8 'The silver is mine and
the gold is mine,' declares the LORD Almighty.
9 'The glory of this present house will be greater
than the glory of the former house,' says the LORD
Almighty. 'And in this place I will grant peace,'
declares the LORD Almighty."

Blessings for a Defiled People

10 On the twenty-fourth day of the ninth
month, in the second year of Darius, the word of
the LORD came to the prophet Haggai: 11 "This is
what the LORD Almighty says: 'Ask the priests
what the law says: 12 If a person carries consecrated meat in the fold of his garment, and that fold
touches some bread or stew, some wine, oil or
other food, does it become consecrated?' "
The priests answered, "No."
13 Then Haggai said, "If a person defiled by
contact with a dead body touches one of these
things, does it become defiled?"
"Yes," the priests replied, "it becomes defiled."
14 Then Haggai said, " 'So it is with this people
and this nation in my sight,' declares the LORD.
'Whatever they do and whatever they offer there
is defiled.
15 " 'Now give careful thought to this from this
day on[b]—consider how things were before one
stone was laid on another in the LORD's temple.
16 When anyone came to a heap of twenty measures, there were only ten. When anyone went to
a wine vat to draw fifty measures, there were
only twenty. 17 I struck all the work of your hands
with blight, mildew and hail, yet you did not turn
to me,' declares the LORD. 18 'From this day on,
from this twenty-fourth day of the ninth month,

[a] 1 A variant of *Jeshua*; here and elsewhere in Haggai
[b] 15 Or *to the days past*

give careful thought to the day when the foundation of the LORD's temple was laid. Give careful thought: 19Is there yet any seed left in the
barn? Until now, the vine and the fig tree, the
pomegranate and the olive tree have not borne
fruit.

"'From this day on I will bless you.'"

Zerubbabel the LORD's Signet Ring

20The word of the LORD came to Haggai a second time on the twenty-fourth day of the month:
21"Tell Zerubbabel governor of Judah that I will
shake the heavens and the earth. 22I will over-
turn royal thrones and shatter the power of the
foreign kingdoms. I will overthrow chariots and
their drivers; horses and their riders will fall,
each by the sword of his brother.

23"'On that day,' declares the LORD Almighty,
'I will take you, my servant Zerubbabel son of
Shealtiel,' declares the LORD, 'and I will make
you like my signet ring, for I have chosen you,'
declares the LORD Almighty."

Introduction to
ZECHARIAH

Personal Reading Plan

- ❐ Zechariah 1:1–2:13
- ❐ Zechariah 3:1–5:11
- ❐ Zechariah 6:1–7:14
- ❐ Zechariah 8:1–9:17
- ❐ Zechariah 10:1–11:17
- ❐ Zechariah 12:1–13:6
- ❐ Zechariah 13:7–14:21

Author

The writer is Zechariah, the prophet and priest who was born in exile and returned from Babylon to Judah in 538 B.C. (1:1; see Ezra 5:1; 6:14).

Date

Zechariah is specific as to the year, month and day of the messages recorded in chapters 1–8. They span the years from 520 to 518 B.C. The date of his final prophecy (chapters 9–14) is uncertain, though it was probably not given until some 40 years later (e.g., after 480 B.C.).

Theme

Rebuilding the temple and the nation of Judah; the Lord's return.

Historical Background

This book is set in the context of the return of the Jews from the Babylonian exile and the subsequent rebuilding of Jerusalem and the temple (see the Introductions to Ezra and Nehemiah). It was through the ministry of Zechariah (along with Haggai) that the rebuilding of the temple began (see Ezra 5:1–2). The temple was completed and dedicated four years later in 516 B.C.

Characteristics

Zechariah was a younger contemporary of Haggai, with a ministry extending well beyond Haggai's, possibly into the reign of Artaxerxes I (465–424 B.C.). Both prophets dealt with the same theme (rebuilding the temple) but in contrasting ways (see the Introduction to Haggai). Zechariah was an apocalyptic visionary, while Haggai was a practical doer. The Book of Zechariah poses a study in contrast between Part I (chapters 1–8) and Part II (chapters 9–14), written some 40 years later. In Part I, Zechariah conveys that when the people of his day see how things ultimately result in their deliverance and God's greater glory, they will be encouraged to take up the temple-rebuilding project. In Part II, he proclaims that rebuilding the temple will point them to the future transformation of God's people into a holy nation. The visions of Zechariah are listed below:

The Horseman Among the Myrtle Trees - 1:7–11
The Four Horns and the Four Craftsmen - 1:18–21
The Man With a Measuring Line - 2:1–13
Clean Garments for the High Priest - 3:1–10
The Gold Lampstand and the Two Olive Trees - 4:1–14
The Flying Scroll - 5:1–4
The Woman in a Basket - 5:5–11
The Four Chariots and the Mountains of Bronze - 6:1–8

A Call to Return to the LORD

1 In the eighth month of the second year of
Darius, the word of the LORD came to the
prophet Zechariah son of Berekiah, the son of
Iddo:
2“The LORD was very angry with your forefathers. 3Therefore tell the people: This is what the
LORD Almighty says: ‘Return to me,’ declares the
LORD Almighty, ‘and I will return to you,’ says
the LORD Almighty. 4Do not be like your forefathers, to whom the earlier prophets proclaimed:
This is what the LORD Almighty says: ‘Turn from
your evil ways and your evil practices.’ But they
would not listen or pay attention to me, declares
the LORD. 5Where are your forefathers now? And
the prophets, do they live forever? 6But did not
my words and my decrees, which I commanded
my servants the prophets, overtake your forefathers?
“Then they repented and said, ‘The LORD Almighty has done to us what our ways and practices deserve, just as he determined to do.’ ”

The Man Among the Myrtle Trees

7On the twenty-fourth day of the eleventh
month, the month of Shebat, in the second year
of Darius, the word of the LORD came to the
prophet Zechariah son of Berekiah, the son of
Iddo.
8During the night I had a vision—and there
before me was a man riding a red horse! He was
standing among the myrtle trees in a ravine. Behind him were red, brown and white horses.
9I asked, “What are these, my lord?”
The angel who was talking with me answered,
“I will show you what they are.”
10Then the man standing among the myrtle
trees explained, “They are the ones the LORD has
sent to go throughout the earth.”
11And they reported to the angel of the LORD,
who was standing among the myrtle trees, “We
have gone throughout the earth and found the
whole world at rest and in peace.”
12Then the angel of the LORD said, “LORD Almighty, how long will you withhold mercy from
Jerusalem and from the towns of Judah, which
you have been angry with these seventy years?”
13So the LORD spoke kind and comforting words
to the angel who talked with me.
14Then the angel who was speaking to me
said, “Proclaim this word: This is what the LORD
Almighty says: ‘I am very jealous for Jerusalem
and Zion, 15but I am very angry with the nations
that feel secure. I was only a little angry, but they
added to the calamity.’
16“Therefore, this is what the LORD says: ‘I will
return to Jerusalem with mercy, and there my
house will be rebuilt. And the measuring line will
be stretched out over Jerusalem,’ declares the
LORD Almighty.
17“Proclaim further: This is what the LORD Almighty says: ‘My towns will again overflow with
prosperity, and the LORD will again comfort Zion
and choose Jerusalem.’ ”

Four Horns and Four Craftsmen

18Then I looked up—and there before me
were four horns! 19I asked the angel who was
speaking to me, “What are these?”
He answered me, “These are the horns that
scattered Judah, Israel and Jerusalem.”
20Then the LORD showed me four craftsmen.
21I asked, “What are these coming to do?”
He answered, “These are the horns that scattered Judah so that no one could raise his head,
but the craftsmen have come to terrify them and
throw down these horns of the nations who lifted
up their horns against the land of Judah to scatter
its people.”

A Man With a Measuring Line

2 Then I looked up—and there before me was
a man with a measuring line in his hand! 2I
asked, “Where are you going?”
He answered me, “To measure Jerusalem, to
find out how wide and how long it is.”
3Then the angel who was speaking to me left,
and another angel came to meet him 4and said to
him: “Run, tell that young man, ‘Jerusalem will
be a city without walls because of the great number of men and livestock in it. 5And I myself will
be a wall of fire around it,’ declares the LORD,
‘and I will be its glory within.’
6“Come! Come! Flee from the land of the
north,” declares the LORD, “for I have scattered
you to the four winds of heaven,” declares the
LORD.
7“Come, O Zion! Escape, you who live in the
Daughter of Babylon!” 8For this is what the LORD
Almighty says: “After he has honored me and has
sent me against the nations that have plundered
you—for whoever touches you touches the apple
of his eye— 9I will surely raise my hand against
them so that their slaves will plunder them.[a]
Then you will know that the LORD Almighty has
sent me.
10“Shout and be glad, O Daughter of Zion. For
I am coming, and I will live among you,” declares
the LORD. 11“Many nations will be joined with
the LORD in that day and will become my people.
I will live among you and you will know that the
LORD Almighty has sent me to you. 12The LORD
will inherit Judah as his portion in the holy land

[a] 8,9 Or *says after . . . eye:* 9“*I . . . plunder them.*”

and will again choose Jerusalem. 13 Be still before
the LORD, all mankind, because he has roused
himself from his holy dwelling."

Clean Garments for the High Priest

3 Then he showed me Joshua[a] the high priest
standing before the angel of the LORD, and
Satan[b] standing at his right side to accuse him.
2 The LORD said to Satan, "The LORD rebuke you,
Satan! The LORD, who has chosen Jerusalem, rebuke you! Is not this man a burning stick
snatched from the fire?"
3 Now Joshua was dressed in filthy clothes as
he stood before the angel. 4 The angel said to
those who were standing before him, "Take off
his filthy clothes."
Then he said to Joshua, "See, I have taken
away your sin, and I will put rich garments on
you."
5 Then I said, "Put a clean turban on his head."
So they put a clean turban on his head and
clothed him, while the angel of the LORD
stood by.
6 The angel of the LORD gave this charge to
Joshua: 7 "This is what the LORD Almighty says: 'If
you will walk in my ways and keep my requirements, then you will govern my house and have
charge of my courts, and I will give you a place
among these standing here.
8 " 'Listen, O high priest Joshua and your associates seated before you, who are men symbolic
of things to come: I am going to bring my servant,
the Branch. 9 See, the stone I have set in front
of Joshua! There are seven eyes[c] on that one
stone, and I will engrave an inscription on it,'
says the LORD Almighty, 'and I will remove the
sin of this land in a single day.
10 " 'In that day each of you will invite his
neighbor to sit under his vine and fig tree,' declares the LORD Almighty."

The Gold Lampstand and the Two Olive Trees

4 Then the angel who talked with me returned
and wakened me, as a man is wakened from
his sleep. 2 He asked me, "What do you see?"
I answered, "I see a solid gold lampstand with
a bowl at the top and seven lights on it, with
seven channels to the lights. 3 Also there are two
olive trees by it, one on the right of the bowl and
the other on its left."
4 I asked the angel who talked with me, "What
are these, my lord?"
5 He answered, "Do you not know what these
are?"
"No, my lord," I replied.
6 So he said to me, "This is the word of the
LORD to Zerubbabel: 'Not by might nor by power,
but by my Spirit,' says the LORD Almighty.
7 "What[d] are you, O mighty mountain? Before Zerubbabel you will become level ground.
Then he will bring out the capstone to shouts of
'God bless it! God bless it!' "
8 Then the word of the LORD came to me:
9 "The hands of Zerubbabel have laid the foundation of this temple; his hands will also complete
it. Then you will know that the LORD Almighty
has sent me to you.
10 "Who despises the day of small things? Men
will rejoice when they see the plumb line in the
hand of Zerubbabel.
"(These seven are the eyes of the LORD, which
range throughout the earth.)"
11 Then I asked the angel, "What are these two
olive trees on the right and the left of the lampstand?"
12 Again I asked him, "What are these two olive branches beside the two gold pipes that pour
out golden oil?"
13 He replied, "Do you not know what these
are?"
"No, my lord," I said.
14 So he said, "These are the two who are
anointed to[e] serve the Lord of all the earth."

The Flying Scroll

5 I looked again—and there before me was a
flying scroll!
2 He asked me, "What do you see?"
I answered, "I see a flying scroll, thirty feet
long and fifteen feet wide.[f]"
3 And he said to me, "This is the curse that is
going out over the whole land; for according to
what it says on one side, every thief will be banished, and according to what it says on the other,
everyone who swears falsely will be banished.
4 The LORD Almighty declares, 'I will send it out,
and it will enter the house of the thief and the
house of him who swears falsely by my name. It
will remain in his house and destroy it, both its
timbers and its stones.' "

The Woman in a Basket

5 Then the angel who was speaking to me came
forward and said to me, "Look up and see what
this is that is appearing."
6 I asked, "What is it?"
He replied, "It is a measuring basket.[g]" And
he added, "This is the iniquity[h] of the people
throughout the land."

a 1 A variant of *Jeshua*; here and elsewhere in Zechariah b 1 *Satan* means *accuser.* c 9 Or *facets* d 7 Or *Who*
e 14 Or *two who bring oil and* f 2 Hebrew *twenty cubits long and ten cubits wide* (about 9 meters long and 4.5 meters wide)
g 6 Hebrew *an ephah*; also in verses 7-11 h 6 Or *appearance*

[7]Then the cover of lead was raised, and there in the basket sat a woman! [8]He said, "This is wickedness," and he pushed her back into the basket and pushed the lead cover down over its mouth.

[9]Then I looked up—and there before me were two women, with the wind in their wings! They had wings like those of a stork, and they lifted up the basket between heaven and earth.

[10]"Where are they taking the basket?" I asked the angel who was speaking to me.

[11]He replied, "To the country of Babylonia[a] to build a house for it. When it is ready, the basket will be set there in its place."

Four Chariots

6 I looked up again—and there before me were four chariots coming out from between two mountains—mountains of bronze! [2]The first chariot had red horses, the second black, [3]the third white, and the fourth dappled—all of them powerful. [4]I asked the angel who was speaking to me, "What are these, my lord?"

[5]The angel answered me, "These are the four spirits[b] of heaven, going out from standing in the presence of the Lord of the whole world. [6]The one with the black horses is going toward the north country, the one with the white horses toward the west,[c] and the one with the dappled horses toward the south."

[7]When the powerful horses went out, they were straining to go throughout the earth. And he said, "Go throughout the earth!" So they went throughout the earth.

[8]Then he called to me, "Look, those going toward the north country have given my Spirit[d] rest in the land of the north."

A Crown for Joshua

[9]The word of the LORD came to me: [10]"Take ⌊silver and gold⌋ from the exiles Heldai, Tobijah and Jedaiah, who have arrived from Babylon. Go the same day to the house of Josiah son of Zephaniah. [11]Take the silver and gold and make a crown, and set it on the head of the high priest, Joshua son of Jehozadak. [12]Tell him this is what the LORD Almighty says: 'Here is the man whose name is the Branch, and he will branch out from his place and build the temple of the LORD. [13]It is he who will build the temple of the LORD, and he will be clothed with majesty and will sit and rule on his throne. And he will be a priest on his throne. And there will be harmony between the two.' [14]The crown will be given to Heldai,[e] Tobijah, Jedaiah and Hen[f] son of Zephaniah as a memorial in the temple of the LORD. [15]Those who are far away will come and help to build the temple of the LORD, and you will know that the LORD Almighty has sent me to you. This will happen if you diligently obey the LORD your God."

Justice and Mercy, Not Fasting

7 In the fourth year of King Darius, the word of the LORD came to Zechariah on the fourth day of the ninth month, the month of Kislev. [2]The people of Bethel had sent Sharezer and Regem-Melech, together with their men, to entreat the LORD [3]by asking the priests of the house of the LORD Almighty and the prophets, "Should I mourn and fast in the fifth month, as I have done for so many years?"

[4]Then the word of the LORD Almighty came to me: [5]"Ask all the people of the land and the priests, 'When you fasted and mourned in the fifth and seventh months for the past seventy years, was it really for me that you fasted? [6]And when you were eating and drinking, were you not just feasting for yourselves? [7]Are these not the words the LORD proclaimed through the earlier prophets when Jerusalem and its surrounding towns were at rest and prosperous, and the Negev and the western foothills were settled?' "

[8]And the word of the LORD came again to Zechariah: [9]"This is what the LORD Almighty says: 'Administer true justice; show mercy and compassion to one another. [10]Do not oppress the widow or the fatherless, the alien or the poor. In your hearts do not think evil of each other.'

[11]"But they refused to pay attention; stubbornly they turned their backs and stopped up their ears. [12]They made their hearts as hard as flint and would not listen to the law or to the words that the LORD Almighty had sent by his Spirit through the earlier prophets. So the LORD Almighty was very angry.

[13]" 'When I called, they did not listen; so when they called, I would not listen,' says the LORD Almighty. [14]'I scattered them with a whirlwind among all the nations, where they were strangers. The land was left so desolate behind them that no one could come or go. This is how they made the pleasant land desolate.' "

The LORD Promises to Bless Jerusalem

8 Again the word of the LORD Almighty came to me. [2]This is what the LORD Almighty says: "I am very jealous for Zion; I am burning with jealousy for her."

[3]This is what the LORD says: "I will return to Zion and dwell in Jerusalem. Then Jerusalem will be called the City of Truth, and the mountain of

[a] 11 Hebrew *Shinar* [b] 5 Or *winds* [c] 6 Or *horses after them* [d] 8 Or *spirit* [e] 14 Syriac; Hebrew *Helem*
[f] 14 Or *and the gracious one, the*

the LORD Almighty will be called the Holy Mountain."
4This is what the LORD Almighty says: "Once
again men and women of ripe old age will sit in
the streets of Jerusalem, each with cane in hand
because of his age. 5The city streets will be filled
with boys and girls playing there."
6This is what the LORD Almighty says: "It may
seem marvelous to the remnant of this people at
that time, but will it seem marvelous to me?"
declares the LORD Almighty.
7This is what the LORD Almighty says: "I will
save my people from the countries of the east and
the west. 8I will bring them back to live in Jerusalem; they will be my people, and I will be faithful
and righteous to them as their God."
9This is what the LORD Almighty says: "You
who now hear these words spoken by the prophets who were there when the foundation was laid
for the house of the LORD Almighty, let your
hands be strong so that the temple may be built.
10Before that time there were no wages for man
or beast. No one could go about his business safely because of his enemy, for I had turned every
man against his neighbor. 11But now I will not
deal with the remnant of this people as I did in
the past," declares the LORD Almighty.
12"The seed will grow well, the vine will yield
its fruit, the ground will produce its crops, and
the heavens will drop their dew. I will give all
these things as an inheritance to the remnant of
this people. 13As you have been an object of cursing among the nations, O Judah and Israel, so
will I save you, and you will be a blessing. Do not
be afraid, but let your hands be strong."
14This is what the LORD Almighty says: "Just as
I had determined to bring disaster upon you and
showed no pity when your fathers angered me,"
says the LORD Almighty, 15"so now I have determined to do good again to Jerusalem and Judah.
Do not be afraid. 16These are the things you are
to do: Speak the truth to each other, and render
true and sound judgment in your courts; 17do not
plot evil against your neighbor, and do not love to
swear falsely. I hate all this," declares the LORD.
18Again the word of the LORD Almighty came
to me. 19This is what the LORD Almighty says:
"The fasts of the fourth, fifth, seventh and tenth
months will become joyful and glad occasions
and happy festivals for Judah. Therefore love
truth and peace."
20This is what the LORD Almighty says: "Many
peoples and the inhabitants of many cities will
yet come, 21and the inhabitants of one city will go
to another and say, 'Let us go at once to entreat
the LORD and seek the LORD Almighty. I myself
am going.' 22And many peoples and powerful nations will come to Jerusalem to seek the LORD
Almighty and to entreat him."
23This is what the LORD Almighty says: "In
those days ten men from all languages and nations will take firm hold of one Jew by the hem
of his robe and say, 'Let us go with you, because
we have heard that God is with you.'"

Judgment on Israel's Enemies

An Oracle

9 The word of the LORD is against the land
of Hadrach
and will rest upon Damascus—
for the eyes of men and all the tribes of
Israel
are on the LORD—[a]
2and upon Hamath too, which borders on it,
and upon Tyre and Sidon, though they are
very skillful.
3Tyre has built herself a stronghold;
she has heaped up silver like dust,
and gold like the dirt of the streets.
4But the Lord will take away her possessions
and destroy her power on the sea,
and she will be consumed by fire.
5Ashkelon will see it and fear;
Gaza will writhe in agony,
and Ekron too, for her hope will wither.
Gaza will lose her king
and Ashkelon will be deserted.
6Foreigners will occupy Ashdod,
and I will cut off the pride of the
Philistines.
7I will take the blood from their mouths,
the forbidden food from between their
teeth.
Those who are left will belong to our God
and become leaders in Judah,
and Ekron will be like the Jebusites.
8But I will defend my house
against marauding forces.
Never again will an oppressor overrun my
people,
for now I am keeping watch.

The Coming of Zion's King

9Rejoice greatly, O Daughter of Zion!
Shout, Daughter of Jerusalem!
See, your king[b] comes to you,
righteous and having salvation,
gentle and riding on a donkey,
on a colt, the foal of a donkey.
10I will take away the chariots from Ephraim
and the war-horses from Jerusalem,
and the battle bow will be broken.
He will proclaim peace to the nations.

[a] 1 Or *Damascus. / For the eye of the LORD is on all mankind, / as well as on the tribes of Israel,* [b] 9 Or *King*

His rule will extend from sea to sea
and from the River[a] to the ends of the earth.[b]
11 As for you, because of the blood of my covenant with you,
I will free your prisoners from the waterless pit.
12 Return to your fortress, O prisoners of hope;
even now I announce that I will restore twice as much to you.
13 I will bend Judah as I bend my bow
and fill it with Ephraim.
I will rouse your sons, O Zion,
against your sons, O Greece,
and make you like a warrior's sword.

The LORD Will Appear

14 Then the LORD will appear over them;
his arrow will flash like lightning.
The Sovereign LORD will sound the trumpet;
he will march in the storms of the south,
15 and the LORD Almighty will shield them.
They will destroy
and overcome with slingstones.
They will drink and roar as with wine;
they will be full like a bowl
used for sprinkling[c] the corners of the altar.
16 The LORD their God will save them on that day
as the flock of his people.
They will sparkle in his land
like jewels in a crown.
17 How attractive and beautiful they will be!
Grain will make the young men thrive,
and new wine the young women.

The LORD Will Care for Judah

10 Ask the LORD for rain in the springtime;
it is the LORD who makes the storm clouds.
He gives showers of rain to men,
and plants of the field to everyone.
2 The idols speak deceit,
diviners see visions that lie;
they tell dreams that are false,
they give comfort in vain.
Therefore the people wander like sheep
oppressed for lack of a shepherd.

3 "My anger burns against the shepherds,
and I will punish the leaders;
for the LORD Almighty will care
for his flock, the house of Judah,
and make them like a proud horse in battle.
4 From Judah will come the cornerstone,
from him the tent peg,
from him the battle bow,
from him every ruler.
5 Together they[d] will be like mighty men
trampling the muddy streets in battle.
Because the LORD is with them,
they will fight and overthrow the horsemen.

6 "I will strengthen the house of Judah
and save the house of Joseph.
I will restore them
because I have compassion on them.
They will be as though
I had not rejected them,
for I am the LORD their God
and I will answer them.
7 The Ephraimites will become like mighty men,
and their hearts will be glad as with wine.
Their children will see it and be joyful;
their hearts will rejoice in the LORD.
8 I will signal for them
and gather them in.
Surely I will redeem them;
they will be as numerous as before.
9 Though I scatter them among the peoples,
yet in distant lands they will remember me.
They and their children will survive,
and they will return.
10 I will bring them back from Egypt
and gather them from Assyria.
I will bring them to Gilead and Lebanon,
and there will not be room enough for them.
11 They will pass through the sea of trouble;
the surging sea will be subdued
and all the depths of the Nile will dry up.
Assyria's pride will be brought down
and Egypt's scepter will pass away.
12 I will strengthen them in the LORD
and in his name they will walk,"
declares the LORD.

11 Open your doors, O Lebanon,
so that fire may devour your cedars!
2 Wail, O pine tree, for the cedar has fallen;
the stately trees are ruined!
Wail, oaks of Bashan;
the dense forest has been cut down!
3 Listen to the wail of the shepherds;
their rich pastures are destroyed!
Listen to the roar of the lions;
the lush thicket of the Jordan is ruined!

[a] 10 That is, the Euphrates [b] 10 Or *the end of the land* [c] 15 Or *bowl, / like* [d] 4,5 Or *ruler, all of them together. / 5They*

Two Shepherds

4This is what the LORD my God says: "Pasture
the flock marked for slaughter. 5Their buyers
slaughter them and go unpunished. Those who
sell them say, 'Praise the LORD, I am rich!' Their
own shepherds do not spare them. 6For I will no
longer have pity on the people of the land," declares the LORD. "I will hand everyone over to his
neighbor and his king. They will oppress the
land, and I will not rescue them from their
hands."

7So I pastured the flock marked for slaughter,
particularly the oppressed of the flock. Then I
took two staffs and called one Favor and the other
Union, and I pastured the flock. 8In one month I
got rid of the three shepherds.

The flock detested me, and I grew weary of
them 9and said, "I will not be your shepherd. Let
the dying die, and the perishing perish. Let those
who are left eat one another's flesh."

10Then I took my staff called Favor and broke
it, revoking the covenant I had made with all the
nations. 11It was revoked on that day, and so the
afflicted of the flock who were watching me
knew it was the word of the LORD.

12I told them, "If you think it best, give me my
pay; but if not, keep it." So they paid me thirty
pieces of silver.

13And the LORD said to me, "Throw it to the
potter"—the handsome price at which they
priced me! So I took the thirty pieces of silver and
threw them into the house of the LORD to the
potter.

14Then I broke my second staff called Union,
breaking the brotherhood between Judah and Israel.

15Then the LORD said to me, "Take again the
equipment of a foolish shepherd. 16For I am going
to raise up a shepherd over the land who will not
care for the lost, or seek the young, or heal the
injured, or feed the healthy, but will eat the meat
of the choice sheep, tearing off their hoofs.

17"Woe to the worthless shepherd,
who deserts the flock!
May the sword strike his arm and his right
eye!
May his arm be completely withered,
his right eye totally blinded!"

Jerusalem's Enemies to Be Destroyed

An Oracle

12 This is the word of the LORD concerning
Israel. The LORD, who stretches out the
heavens, who lays the foundation of the earth,
and who forms the spirit of man within him,
declares: 2"I am going to make Jerusalem a cup
that sends all the surrounding peoples reeling.
Judah will be besieged as well as Jerusalem. 3On
that day, when all the nations of the earth are
gathered against her, I will make Jerusalem an
immovable rock for all the nations. All who try to
move it will injure themselves. 4On that day I
will strike every horse with panic and its rider
with madness," declares the LORD. "I will keep a
watchful eye over the house of Judah, but I will
blind all the horses of the nations. 5Then the
leaders of Judah will say in their hearts, 'The
people of Jerusalem are strong, because the LORD
Almighty is their God.'

6"On that day I will make the leaders of Judah
like a firepot in a woodpile, like a flaming torch
among sheaves. They will consume right and left
all the surrounding peoples, but Jerusalem will
remain intact in her place.

7"The LORD will save the dwellings of Judah
first, so that the honor of the house of David and
of Jerusalem's inhabitants may not be greater
than that of Judah. 8On that day the LORD will
shield those who live in Jerusalem, so that the
feeblest among them will be like David, and the
house of David will be like God, like the Angel of
the LORD going before them. 9On that day I will
set out to destroy all the nations that attack Jerusalem.

Mourning for the One They Pierced

10"And I will pour out on the house of David
and the inhabitants of Jerusalem a spirit[a] of
grace and supplication. They will look on[b] me,
the one they have pierced, and they will mourn
for him as one mourns for an only child, and
grieve bitterly for him as one grieves for a firstborn son. 11On that day the weeping in Jerusalem
will be great, like the weeping of Hadad Rimmon
in the plain of Megiddo. 12The land will mourn,
each clan by itself, with their wives by themselves: the clan of the house of David and their
wives, the clan of the house of Nathan and their
wives, 13the clan of the house of Levi and
their wives, the clan of Shimei and their wives,
14and all the rest of the clans and their wives.

Cleansing From Sin

13 "On that day a fountain will be opened to
the house of David and the inhabitants of
Jerusalem, to cleanse them from sin and impurity.

2"On that day, I will banish the names of the
idols from the land, and they will be remembered
no more," declares the LORD Almighty. "I will
remove both the prophets and the spirit of impurity from the land. 3And if anyone still prophe-

[a]10 Or *the Spirit* [b]10 Or *to*

sies, his father and mother, to whom he was
born, will say to him, 'You must die, because you
have told lies in the LORD's name.' When he
prophesies, his own parents will stab him.
4 "On that day every prophet will be ashamed
of his prophetic vision. He will not put on a
prophet's garment of hair in order to deceive.
5 He will say, 'I am not a prophet. I am a farmer;
the land has been my livelihood since my
youth.[a]' 6 If someone asks him, 'What are these
wounds on your body[b]?' he will answer, 'The
wounds I was given at the house of my friends.'

The Shepherd Struck, the Sheep Scattered

7 "Awake, O sword, against my shepherd,
against the man who is close to me!"
declares the LORD Almighty.
"Strike the shepherd,
and the sheep will be scattered,
and I will turn my hand against the little
ones.
8 In the whole land," declares the LORD,
"two-thirds will be struck down and
perish;
yet one-third will be left in it.
9 This third I will bring into the fire;
I will refine them like silver
and test them like gold.
They will call on my name
and I will answer them;
I will say, 'They are my people,'
and they will say, 'The LORD is our God.'"

The LORD Comes and Reigns

14 A day of the LORD is coming when your
plunder will be divided among you.
2 I will gather all the nations to Jerusalem to
fight against it; the city will be captured, the
houses ransacked, and the women raped. Half of
the city will go into exile, but the rest of the
people will not be taken from the city.
3 Then the LORD will go out and fight against
those nations, as he fights in the day of battle.
4 On that day his feet will stand on the Mount of
Olives, east of Jerusalem, and the Mount of Olives will be split in two from east to west, forming a great valley, with half of the mountain moving north and half moving south. 5 You will flee by
my mountain valley, for it will extend to Azel.
You will flee as you fled from the earthquake[c] in
the days of Uzziah king of Judah. Then the LORD
my God will come, and all the holy ones with
him.
6 On that day there will be no light, no cold or
frost. 7 It will be a unique day, without daytime or
nighttime—a day known to the LORD. When evening comes, there will be light.
8 On that day living water will flow out from
Jerusalem, half to the eastern sea[d] and half to
the western sea,[e] in summer and in winter.
9 The LORD will be king over the whole earth.
On that day there will be one LORD, and his name
the only name.
10 The whole land, from Geba to Rimmon,
south of Jerusalem, will become like the Arabah.
But Jerusalem will be raised up and remain in its
place, from the Benjamin Gate to the site of the
First Gate, to the Corner Gate, and from the Tower of Hananel to the royal winepresses. 11 It will
be inhabited; never again will it be destroyed.
Jerusalem will be secure.
12 This is the plague with which the LORD will
strike all the nations that fought against Jerusalem: Their flesh will rot while they are still standing on their feet, their eyes will rot in their sockets, and their tongues will rot in their mouths.
13 On that day men will be stricken by the LORD
with great panic. Each man will seize the hand of
another, and they will attack each other. 14 Judah
too will fight at Jerusalem. The wealth of all the
surrounding nations will be collected—great
quantities of gold and silver and clothing. 15 A
similar plague will strike the horses and mules,
the camels and donkeys, and all the animals in
those camps.
16 Then the survivors from all the nations that
have attacked Jerusalem will go up year after year
to worship the King, the LORD Almighty, and to
celebrate the Feast of Tabernacles. 17 If any of the
peoples of the earth do not go up to Jerusalem to
worship the King, the LORD Almighty, they will
have no rain. 18 If the Egyptian people do not go
up and take part, they will have no rain. The
LORD[f] will bring on them the plague he inflicts
on the nations that do not go up to celebrate the
Feast of Tabernacles. 19 This will be the punishment of Egypt and the punishment of all the nations that do not go up to celebrate the Feast of
Tabernacles.
20 On that day HOLY TO THE LORD will be inscribed on the bells of the horses, and the cooking pots in the LORD's house will be like the sacred bowls in front of the altar. 21 Every pot in
Jerusalem and Judah will be holy to the LORD
Almighty, and all who come to sacrifice will take
some of the pots and cook in them. And on that
day there will no longer be a Canaanite[g] in the
house of the LORD Almighty.

[a] 5 Or *farmer; a man sold me in my youth* [b] 6 Or *wounds between your hands* [c] 5 Or *5My mountain valley will be blocked and will extend to Azel. It will be blocked as it was blocked because of the earthquake* [d] 8 That is, the Dead Sea [e] 8 That is, the Mediterranean [f] 18 Or *part, then the LORD* [g] 21 Or *merchant*

Introduction to
MALACHI

Personal Reading Plan

- ❐ Malachi 1:1–14
- ❐ Malachi 2:1–16
- ❐ Malachi 2:17–3:18
- ❐ Malachi 4:1–6

Author

This book is ascribed to Malachi, a contemporary of Ezra and Nehemiah. Since the word "Malachi" means "my messenger," some think that this is a title rather than the name of a person. The Greek translation of the Old Testament (the Septuagint) renders "Malachi" in 1:1 as "my messenger." However, the evidence is not conclusive, and there may well have been a specific prophet by this name.

Date

The sins denounced by Nehemiah (see Neh. 13:6–31) correspond closely to the denunciation of Malachi (see 1:6–14; 2:14–16; 3:8–11). Hence, a date may be inferred anytime after Nehemiah returned to Jerusalem the second time, that is, some time later than 433 B.C.

Theme

Repentance and information as prescription to cure the spirit of skepticism and indifference.

Historical Background

In the face of stern opposition, the exiles finished the temple in 516 B.C. under the leadership of Zerubbabel and the prophecy of Haggai. The community was strengthened through the restoration of temple worship by Ezra in 458 B.C. In 445 B.C., Nehemiah returned to Jerusalem, rebuilt the walls, and brought many religious reforms.

Twelve years later, Nehemiah returned to serve the Persian king. With success behind them, the people lapsed into religious indifference. Malachi addresses the sins of a people "just going through the motions" of their faith, doubting the love and justice of God. Malachi was most likely the last prophet until the time of Christ, some 400 years later.

Characteristics

Malachi uses a question-answer form of dialogue to develop his themes. Seven questions or complaints raised by the people are recorded. However, the book is dominated by God's voice, the voice of an effective father (1:6) having to dish out "tough love" to his children. Malachi is written in forceful, lofty prose. He uses repetition (the name "LORD Almighty" occurs 20 times) and vivid images to help the people he is addressing (and his readers) to sense the attitudes of God. When he judges, God will be "like a refiner's fire or a launderer's soap" (3:2), but for the righteous "the sun of righteousness will rise with healing in its wings. And you will go out and leap like calves released from the stall" (4:2).

1 An oracle: The word of the LORD to Israel
through Malachi.[a]

Jacob Loved, Esau Hated

2“I have loved you,” says the LORD.
“But you ask, ‘How have you loved us?’
“Was not Esau Jacob’s brother?” the LORD
says. “Yet I have loved Jacob, 3but Esau I have
hated, and I have turned his mountains into a
wasteland and left his inheritance to the desert
jackals.”
4Edom may say, “Though we have been
crushed, we will rebuild the ruins.”
But this is what the LORD Almighty says: “They
may build, but I will demolish. They will be
called the Wicked Land, a people always under
the wrath of the LORD. 5You will see it with your
own eyes and say, ‘Great is the LORD—even beyond the borders of Israel!’

Blemished Sacrifices

6“A son honors his father, and a servant his
master. If I am a father, where is the honor due
me? If I am a master, where is the respect due
me?” says the LORD Almighty. “It is you,
O priests, who show contempt for my name.
“But you ask, ‘How have we shown contempt
for your name?’
7“You place defiled food on my altar.
“But you ask, ‘How have we defiled you?’
“By saying that the LORD’s table is contemptible. 8When you bring blind animals for sacrifice,
is that not wrong? When you sacrifice crippled or
diseased animals, is that not wrong? Try offering
them to your governor! Would he be pleased with
you? Would he accept you?” says the LORD Almighty.
9“Now implore God to be gracious to us. With
such offerings from your hands, will he accept
you?”—says the LORD Almighty.
10“Oh, that one of you would shut the temple
doors, so that you would not light useless fires on
my altar! I am not pleased with you,” says the
LORD Almighty, “and I will accept no offering
from your hands. 11My name will be great among
the nations, from the rising to the setting of the
sun. In every place incense and pure offerings
will be brought to my name, because my name
will be great among the nations,” says the LORD
Almighty.
12“But you profane it by saying of the Lord’s
table, ‘It is defiled,’ and of its food, ‘It is contemptible.’ 13And you say, ‘What a burden!’ and
you sniff at it contemptuously,” says the LORD
Almighty.
“When you bring injured, crippled or diseased
animals and offer them as sacrifices, should I accept them from your hands?” says the LORD.
14“Cursed is the cheat who has an acceptable
male in his flock and vows to give it, but then
sacrifices a blemished animal to the Lord. For I
am a great king,” says the LORD Almighty, “and
my name is to be feared among the nations.

Admonition for the Priests

2 “And now this admonition is for you,
O priests. 2If you do not listen, and if you do
not set your heart to honor my name,” says the
LORD Almighty, “I will send a curse upon you,
and I will curse your blessings. Yes, I have already cursed them, because you have not set your
heart to honor me.
3“Because of you I will rebuke[b] your descendants[c]; I will spread on your faces the offal from
your festival sacrifices, and you will be carried off
with it. 4And you will know that I have sent you
this admonition so that my covenant with Levi
may continue,” says the LORD Almighty. 5“My
covenant was with him, a covenant of life and
peace, and I gave them to him; this called for
reverence and he revered me and stood in awe of
my name. 6True instruction was in his mouth and
nothing false was found on his lips. He walked
with me in peace and uprightness, and turned
many from sin.
7“For the lips of a priest ought to preserve
knowledge, and from his mouth men should seek
instruction—because he is the messenger of the
LORD Almighty. 8But you have turned from the
way and by your teaching have caused many to
stumble; you have violated the covenant with
Levi,” says the LORD Almighty. 9“So I have caused
you to be despised and humiliated before all the
people, because you have not followed my ways
but have shown partiality in matters of the law.”

Judah Unfaithful

10Have we not all one Father[d]? Did not one
God create us? Why do we profane the covenant
of our fathers by breaking faith with one another?
11Judah has broken faith. A detestable thing
has been committed in Israel and in Jerusalem:
Judah has desecrated the sanctuary the LORD
loves, by marrying the daughter of a foreign god.
12As for the man who does this, whoever he may
be, may the LORD cut him off from the tents of
Jacob[e]—even though he brings offerings to the
LORD Almighty.
13Another thing you do: You flood the LORD’s
altar with tears. You weep and wail because he
no longer pays attention to your offerings or accepts them with pleasure from your hands. 14You

[a] 1 *Malachi* means *my messenger.* [b] 3 Or *cut off* (see Septuagint) [c] 3 Or *will blight your grain* [d] 10 Or *father*
[e] 12 Or *12May the LORD cut off from the tents of Jacob anyone who gives testimony in behalf of the man who does this*

ask, "Why?" It is because the LORD is acting as
the witness between you and the wife of your
youth, because you have broken faith with her,
though she is your partner, the wife of your marriage covenant.
15Has not ⌞the LORD⌟ made them one? In flesh
and spirit they are his. And why one? Because he
was seeking godly offspring.[a] So guard yourself
in your spirit, and do not break faith with the
wife of your youth.
16"I hate divorce," says the LORD God of Israel,
"and I hate a man's covering himself[b] with violence as well as with his garment," says the LORD
Almighty.
So guard yourself in your spirit, and do not
break faith.

The Day of Judgment

17You have wearied the LORD with your
words.
"How have we wearied him?" you ask.
By saying, "All who do evil are good in the
eyes of the LORD, and he is pleased with them" or
"Where is the God of justice?"

3 "See, I will send my messenger, who will
prepare the way before me. Then suddenly
the Lord you are seeking will come to his temple;
the messenger of the covenant, whom you desire, will come," says the LORD Almighty.
2But who can endure the day of his coming?
Who can stand when he appears? For he will be
like a refiner's fire or a launderer's soap. 3He will
sit as a refiner and purifier of silver; he will purify
the Levites and refine them like gold and silver.
Then the LORD will have men who will bring
offerings in righteousness, 4and the offerings of
Judah and Jerusalem will be acceptable to the
LORD, as in days gone by, as in former years.
5"So I will come near to you for judgment. I
will be quick to testify against sorcerers, adulterers and perjurers, against those who defraud laborers of their wages, who oppress the widows
and the fatherless, and deprive aliens of justice,
but do not fear me," says the LORD Almighty.

Robbing God

6"I the LORD do not change. So you,
O descendants of Jacob, are not destroyed. 7Ever
since the time of your forefathers you have
turned away from my decrees and have not kept
them. Return to me, and I will return to you,"
says the LORD Almighty.
"But you ask, 'How are we to return?'
8"Will a man rob God? Yet you rob me.
"But you ask, 'How do we rob you?'
"In tithes and offerings. 9You are under a
curse—the whole nation of you—because you
are robbing me. 10Bring the whole tithe into the
storehouse, that there may be food in my house.
Test me in this," says the LORD Almighty, "and
see if I will not throw open the floodgates of
heaven and pour out so much blessing that you
will not have room enough for it. 11I will prevent
pests from devouring your crops, and the vines in
your fields will not cast their fruit," says the LORD
Almighty. 12"Then all the nations will call you
blessed, for yours will be a delightful land," says
the LORD Almighty.
13"You have said harsh things against me,"
says the LORD.
"Yet you ask, 'What have we said against you?'
14"You have said, 'It is futile to serve God.
What did we gain by carrying out his requirements and going about like mourners before the
LORD Almighty? 15But now we call the arrogant
blessed. Certainly the evildoers prosper, and
even those who challenge God escape.'"
16Then those who feared the LORD talked with
each other, and the LORD listened and heard. A
scroll of remembrance was written in his presence concerning those who feared the LORD and
honored his name.
17"They will be mine," says the LORD Almighty, "in the day when I make up my treasured
possession.[c] I will spare them, just as in compassion a man spares his son who serves him.
18And you will again see the distinction between
the righteous and the wicked, between those
who serve God and those who do not.

The Day of the LORD

4 "Surely the day is coming; it will burn like a
furnace. All the arrogant and every evildoer
will be stubble, and that day that is coming will
set them on fire," says the LORD Almighty. "Not
a root or a branch will be left to them. 2But for
you who revere my name, the sun of righteousness will rise with healing in its wings. And you
will go out and leap like calves released from the
stall. 3Then you will trample down the wicked;
they will be ashes under the soles of your feet on
the day when I do these things," says the LORD
Almighty.
4"Remember the law of my servant Moses, the
decrees and laws I gave him at Horeb for all Israel.
5"See, I will send you the prophet Elijah before
that great and dreadful day of the LORD comes.
6He will turn the hearts of the fathers to their
children, and the hearts of the children to their
fathers; or else I will come and strike the land
with a curse."

[a] *15* Or *15But the one ⌞who is our father⌟ did not do this, not as long as life remained in him. And what was he seeking? An offspring from God* [b] *16* Or *his wife* [c] *17* Or *Almighty, "my treasured possession, in the day when I act*

THE NEW TESTAMENT

Introduction to MATTHEW

Personal Reading Plan

❒ Matthew 1:1–2:23
❒ Matthew 3:1–4:25
❒ Matthew 5:1–48
❒ Matthew 6:1–34
❒ Matthew 7:1–8:17
❒ Matthew 8:18–9:26
❒ Matthew 9:27–10:42
❒ Matthew 11:1–12:21
❒ Matthew 12:22–13:23
❒ Matthew 13:24–58
❒ Matthew 14:1–36
❒ Matthew 15:1–16:12
❒ Matthew 16:13–17:27
❒ Matthew 18:1–19:15
❒ Matthew 19:16–20:34
❒ Matthew 21:1–46
❒ Matthew 22:1–46
❒ Matthew 23:1–39
❒ Matthew 24:1–51
❒ Matthew 25:1–46
❒ Matthew 26:1–46
❒ Matthew 26:47–27:26
❒ Matthew 27:27–66
❒ Matthew 28:1–20

Author

Nowhere is the author named within the first Gospel. There is however, a long tradition that has assigned it to Matthew. Little is known about Matthew except that he was a tax gatherer. As such he would have been bitterly hated by the general populace in Israel—with good reason. For one thing, tax collectors worked for Rome, the oppressor, and therefore were seen as traitors to Israel. For another, tax collectors made their living—and many were quite wealthy—by charging above and beyond what Rome required (only the tax collector knew what was owed). Matthew the tax collector stands in contrast to the poor and middle-class fishermen who composed the main body of the disciples.

Date

When Matthew was written is uncertain, but probably between A.D. 50–70.

Theme

Jesus, the long-promised Messiah and authoritative teacher.

The Synoptic Gospels

The word "synoptic" means, literally, "able to be seen together." It refers to the first three Gospels—Matthew, Mark and Luke—which cover the same events in Jesus' life, often in the same way. A parallel reading of the first three Gospels makes it clear that there is some sort of literary connection between them. The nature of this connection is not absolutely certain, but generally it is assumed that Mark was the first Gospel, that Matthew and Luke had Mark's text before them when they wrote, and that they included some of Mark's material in their own compositions. One reason scholars conclude this is that of the 105 sections of Mark, all but four occur in Matthew or Luke. In fact, Matthew uses 93 of these 105 sections (nearly 90%), including not just the general story but in 51% of the cases Mark's very words. However, Matthew and Luke also share some 200 verses not found in Mark, most of which consist of the teachings of Jesus. This material may have come from an early (but now lost) collection of Jesus' teaching.

In whatever order they were written, it is clear that when the Gospel writers put together their accounts, they did so with a definite purpose in mind. Each selected some stories and left out others to produce an account of Jesus' life that would answer the questions and concerns of his particular audience. Mark probably wrote for Christians in Rome who were suffering under Nero's persecution, and so he told about Jesus who was the suffering Servant. Luke wrote about the Son of Man who came to seek and to save the needy, the lost, the outcasts. Matthew wrote to a Jewish audience and told the story of King Jesus, the Son of David, who came as the long-promised Messiah to claim his throne.

Characteristics

Matthew is the most Jewish of all the Gospels. It was written by a Jew to other Jews to convince them that Jesus was, indeed, the Messiah foretold by OT Scripture. Thus, the author cites numerous OT prophecies which were fulfilled by Jesus. He uses the phrase, "All this took place to fulfill what the Lord had said through the prophets" some 16 times.

The Jewishness of the Gospel is also seen in the fact that Matthew mentions Jewish customs without explanation (e.g., "phylacteries" in 23:5), that he has a very high view of the Law (5:17–20), and that even when recording Jesus' public rebukes, he shows more respect for the teachers of the Law and the Pharisees than any other Gospel writer (23:2).

Yet one of the most interesting features of Matthew is that, although he is so Jewish in his concerns, in his book we discover the universal nature of the Gospel—that it is for all the peoples of the world. This emphasis emerges right at the beginning when the Gentile magi bring gifts to the baby Jesus, and it runs through to the end when Jesus sends his followers out to "make disciples of all nations."

Other features of Matthew include his interests in the church (this is the only Gospel to use the word "church") and his concern about the end times—the second coming of Jesus, the end of the world, and the final judgment (his is the fullest account).

Structure

Matthew is the most orderly in structure of the four Gospel accounts. After an introductory section, the material is organized into five blocks of narrative alternated with five blocks of discourse or teaching. We can see that this is not an accidental arrangement, because Matthew ends each teaching section with a similar statement (compare 7:28; 11:1; 13:53; 19:1 and 26:1).

Passages for Topical Group Study

1:18–25	DIVORCE	An Angel Appears to Joseph
3:1–17	GOD THE FATHER	The Baptism of Jesus
5:1–12	DEVOTIONAL LIFE	The Beatitudes
5:27–30	LUST / PORNOGRAPHY	Adultery and Lust
5:38–48	CAPITAL PUNISHMENT GETTING HURT	Love for Enemies
6:5–18	PRAYER	Prayer and Fasting
6:25–34	THE FUTURE KNOWING GOD'S WILL	Do Not Worry
7:24–29	WEATHERING LIFE'S STORMS	The Wise and Foolish Builders
13:1–23	SETTING PRIORITIES	The Parable of the Sower
14:22–33	FEARS AND HANG-UPS	Jesus Walks on Water
16:13–28	JESUS CHRIST	Christ Must Die
18:21–35	FORGIVENESS	The Parable of the Unmerciful Servant
19:1–12	DIVORCE	Jesus Teaches About Divorce
20:1–16	WORKING ATTITUDES	The Parable of the Workers in the Vineyard
20:20–28	PARENTAL EXPECTATIONS	A Mother's Request
25:1–13	THE SECOND COMING	The Parable of the Ten Virgins
25:14–30	ABILITIES THE FUTURE	The Parable of the Talents
25:31–46	COMPASSION	The Sheep and the Goats
26:47–56	GETTING HURT	Jesus Is Arrested
27:26–31	ABUSE	The Soldiers Mock Jesus
28:1–20	RESURRECTION	Jesus' Resurrection and Great Commission

See the Lesson Plans in the front of this Bible.

The Genealogy of Jesus

1 A record of the genealogy of Jesus Christ the son of David, the son of Abraham:

[2]Abraham was the father of Isaac,
Isaac the father of Jacob,
Jacob the father of Judah and his brothers,
[3]Judah the father of Perez and Zerah, whose mother was Tamar,
Perez the father of Hezron,
Hezron the father of Ram,
[4]Ram the father of Amminadab,
Amminadab the father of Nahshon,
Nahshon the father of Salmon,
[5]Salmon the father of Boaz, whose mother was Rahab,
Boaz the father of Obed, whose mother was Ruth,
Obed the father of Jesse,
[6]and Jesse the father of King David.

David was the father of Solomon, whose mother had been Uriah's wife,
[7]Solomon the father of Rehoboam,
Rehoboam the father of Abijah,
Abijah the father of Asa,
[8]Asa the father of Jehoshaphat,
Jehoshaphat the father of Jehoram,
Jehoram the father of Uzziah,
[9]Uzziah the father of Jotham,
Jotham the father of Ahaz,
Ahaz the father of Hezekiah,
[10]Hezekiah the father of Manasseh,
Manasseh the father of Amon,
Amon the father of Josiah,
[11]and Josiah the father of Jeconiah[a] and his brothers at the time of the exile to Babylon.

[12]After the exile to Babylon:
Jeconiah was the father of Shealtiel,
Shealtiel the father of Zerubbabel,
[13]Zerubbabel the father of Abiud,
Abiud the father of Eliakim,
Eliakim the father of Azor,
[14]Azor the father of Zadok,
Zadok the father of Akim,
Akim the father of Eliud,
[15]Eliud the father of Eleazar,
Eleazar the father of Matthan,
Matthan the father of Jacob,
[16]and Jacob the father of Joseph, the husband of Mary, of whom was born Jesus, who is called Christ.

[17]Thus there were fourteen generations in all from Abraham to David, fourteen from David to the exile to Babylon, and fourteen from the exile to the Christ.[b]

The Birth of Jesus Christ

[18]This is how the birth of Jesus Christ came
about: His mother Mary was pledged to be married to Joseph, but before they came together,
she was found to be with child through the Holy
Spirit. [19]Because Joseph her husband was a righteous man and did not want to expose her to
public disgrace, he had in mind to divorce her
quietly.
[20]But after he had considered this, an angel of
the Lord appeared to him in a dream and said,
"Joseph son of David, do not be afraid to take
Mary home as your wife, because what is conceived in her is from the Holy Spirit. [21]She will
give birth to a son, and you are to give him the
name Jesus,[c] because he will save his people
from their sins."
[22]All this took place to fulfill what the Lord had
said through the prophet: [23]"The virgin will be
with child and will give birth to a son, and they

MATTHEW 1:18–25

1. Do you know how your parents picked your name? What does your name mean?
2. What age do you think is a good age to get married? How long should you be engaged before getting married?
3. How has someone you know been affected by divorce?
4. Joseph "had in mind to divorce" Mary (v. 19). Under what circumstances would you consider divorce?
5. What do you think "the angel of the Lord" would say to someone today who is considering divorce?
6. When did Jesus really become your "Immanuel"—God with you? How are you experiencing Jesus "with you" in your life now?
7. How can this group help you in prayer this week?

(Study notes on page 852)

[a] *11* That is, Jehoiachin; also in verse 12 [b] *17* Or *Messiah*. "The Christ" (Greek) and "the Messiah" (Hebrew) both mean "the Anointed One." [c] *21* *Jesus* is the Greek form of *Joshua*, which means *the LORD saves*.

will call him Immanuel"[a]—which means, "God with us."

24 When Joseph woke up, he did what the angel of the Lord had commanded him and took Mary home as his wife. 25 But he had no union with her until she gave birth to a son. And he gave him the name Jesus.

The Visit of the Magi

2 After Jesus was born in Bethlehem in Judea, during the time of King Herod, Magi[b] from the east came to Jerusalem 2 and asked, "Where is the one who has been born king of the Jews? We saw his star in the east[c] and have come to worship him."

3 When King Herod heard this he was disturbed, and all Jerusalem with him. 4 When he had called together all the people's chief priests and teachers of the law, he asked them where the Christ[d] was to be born. 5 "In Bethlehem in Judea," they replied, "for this is what the prophet has written:

6 " 'But you, Bethlehem, in the land of Judah,
are by no means least among the rulers of Judah;
for out of you will come a ruler
who will be the shepherd of my people Israel.'[e]"

7 Then Herod called the Magi secretly and found out from them the exact time the star had appeared. 8 He sent them to Bethlehem and said, "Go and make a careful search for the child. As soon as you find him, report to me, so that I too may go and worship him."

9 After they had heard the king, they went on their way, and the star they had seen in the east[f] went ahead of them until it stopped over the place where the child was. 10 When they saw the star, they were overjoyed. 11 On coming to the house, they saw the child with his mother Mary, and they bowed down and worshiped him. Then they opened their treasures and presented him with gifts of gold and of incense and of myrrh. 12 And having been warned in a dream not to go back to Herod, they returned to their country by another route.

The Escape to Egypt

13 When they had gone, an angel of the Lord appeared to Joseph in a dream. "Get up," he said, "take the child and his mother and escape to Egypt. Stay there until I tell you, for Herod is going to search for the child to kill him."

14 So he got up, took the child and his mother during the night and left for Egypt, 15 where he stayed until the death of Herod. And so was fulfilled what the Lord had said through the prophet: "Out of Egypt I called my son."[g]

16 When Herod realized that he had been outwitted by the Magi, he was furious, and he gave orders to kill all the boys in Bethlehem and its vicinity who were two years old and under, in accordance with the time he had learned from the Magi. 17 Then what was said through the prophet Jeremiah was fulfilled:

18 "A voice is heard in Ramah,
weeping and great mourning,
Rachel weeping for her children
and refusing to be comforted,
because they are no more."[h]

The Return to Nazareth

19 After Herod died, an angel of the Lord appeared in a dream to Joseph in Egypt 20 and said, "Get up, take the child and his mother and go to the land of Israel, for those who were trying to take the child's life are dead."

21 So he got up, took the child and his mother and went to the land of Israel. 22 But when he heard that Archelaus was reigning in Judea in place of his father Herod, he was afraid to go there. Having been warned in a dream, he withdrew to the district of Galilee, 23 and he went and lived in a town called Nazareth. So was fulfilled what was said through the prophets: "He will be called a Nazarene."

[a] *23* Isaiah 7:14 [b] *1* Traditionally *Wise Men* [c] *2* Or *star when it rose* [d] *4* Or *Messiah* [e] *6* Micah 5:2
[f] *9* Or *seen when it rose* [g] *15* Hosea 11:1 [h] *18* Jer. 31:15

1:18 ***pledged to be married.*** A first-century Jewish marriage had three parts to it: the engagement (which often took place when the couple were children and which was usually arranged by a marriage broker); the betrothal (a one-year period in which the couple were considered virtually "married," though they did not have sexual relations); and the marriage. Mary and Joseph were at the second stage in their relationship. ***she was found to be with child.*** The Law's penalty for sleeping with a woman betrothed to another was death by stoning for both parties (Deut. 22:23–24). ***the Holy Spirit.*** Both Matthew and Luke make it quite clear that the agent in Jesus' birth was the Holy Spirit (see Luke 1:35).

1:19 ***her husband.*** Although the marriage had not yet taken place, a betrothed couple were considered to be husband and wife. ***divorce.*** During betrothal, a divorce was required should either party wish to break off the relationship. ***quietly.*** Joseph would sign the necessary papers, but not have Mary judged publicly.

1:20–21 ***dream.*** Matthew records four other times when dreams were crucial during the birth and childhood of Jesus (2:12–13,19, 22). ***take Mary home as your wife.*** Joseph needed to marry Mary for Jesus to become his legal son and share Joseph's lineage back to David (1:6,16). ***Jesus.*** See NIV text note. ***he will save his people from their sins.*** Jesus did not come as a warrior-messiah who would engage in battle against the oppressors of Israel; he would bring liberation from a far deeper problem, namely sin.

John the Baptist Prepares the Way

3 In those days John the Baptist came, preaching in the Desert of Judea 2and saying, "Repent, for the kingdom of heaven is near." 3This is he who was spoken of through the prophet Isaiah:

"A voice of one calling in the desert,
'Prepare the way for the Lord,
make straight paths for him.' "[a]

4John's clothes were made of camel's hair, and he had a leather belt around his waist. His food was locusts and wild honey. 5People went out to him from Jerusalem and all Judea and the whole region of the Jordan. 6Confessing their sins, they were baptized by him in the Jordan River.

7But when he saw many of the Pharisees and Sadducees coming to where he was baptizing, he said to them: "You brood of vipers! Who warned you to flee from the coming wrath? 8Produce fruit in keeping with repentance. 9And do not think you can say to yourselves, 'We have Abraham as our father.' I tell you that out of these stones God can raise up children for Abraham. 10The ax is already at the root of the trees, and every tree that does not produce good fruit will be cut down and thrown into the fire.

11"I baptize you with[b] water for repentance. But after me will come one who is more powerful than I, whose sandals I am not fit to carry. He will baptize you with the Holy Spirit and with fire. 12His winnowing fork is in his hand, and he will clear his threshing floor, gathering his wheat into the barn and burning up the chaff with unquenchable fire."

The Baptism of Jesus

13Then Jesus came from Galilee to the Jordan to be baptized by John. 14But John tried to deter him, saying, "I need to be baptized by you, and do you come to me?"

15Jesus replied, "Let it be so now; it is proper for us to do this to fulfill all righteousness." Then John consented.

16As soon as Jesus was baptized, he went up out of the water. At that moment heaven was opened, and he saw the Spirit of God descending like a dove and lighting on him. 17And a voice from heaven said, "This is my Son, whom I love; with him I am well pleased."

Matthew 3:1–17

1. Who is the craziest looking man of God you have ever met? Who is the wildest preacher you have heard?
2. What do the students in your school mean when they say the word "God"?
3. Who would you like to hear say, "With you I am well pleased"?
4. Who was the John the Baptist in your life—the person who introduced you to God in a personal way?
5. When you were a child, what was your view of God? How would you describe God now?
6. How would you describe your relationship with your heavenly Father right now?
7. Share something you are thankful to God for and close in prayer.

The Temptation of Jesus

4 Then Jesus was led by the Spirit into the desert to be tempted by the devil. 2After fasting forty days and forty nights, he was hungry. 3The tempter came to him and said, "If you are the Son of God, tell these stones to become bread."

[a] 3 Isaiah 40:3 [b] 11 Or *in*

3:1–12 John the Baptist was an extremely popular figure whose influence spread from Alexandria in Egypt to Asia Minor. All four Gospels stress the importance of his work as the herald of the Messiah.

3:13 ***Then Jesus came.*** Immediately after the ringing witness of John to the one who is coming (3:11–12), Jesus appeared. He is the one to whom John had been pointing.

3:15 It was necessary for Jesus to be baptized and so identify with the sin of the people to bring about salvation ("fulfill all righteousness")—though he himself was without sin (1 Peter 2:22). All of God's righteous requirements for the Messiah were fully met in Jesus. Jesus' baptism launched the beginning of his public ministry, as well as serving as an example to his followers.

3:16–17 All three persons of the Trinity are present at the baptism of Jesus: God the Father whose voice is heard; God the Holy Spirit who descends on Jesus; and God the Son who is affirmed as such by the voice.

3:16 ***like a dove.*** Matthew uses a dove as a symbol of the coming of the Holy Spirit. This is the promised anointing of the Messiah with the Holy Spirit (Isa. 11:2).

3:17 ***voice from heaven.*** These words are an unqualified affirmation of Jesus as he is about to start his ministry. The words of the voice combine Psalm 2:7 and Isaiah 42:1. ***my Son.*** This is a royal title used in the OT to describe Israel's kings who were to exercise God-like rule over the people. ***I am well pleased.*** This phrase is associated with the Servant who suffers while carrying out God's will in the service of Israel (Isa. 42:1). In Jesus, the two OT figures of God's Servant and God's Son are combined.

4 Jesus answered, "It is written: 'Man does not live on bread alone, but on every word that comes from the mouth of God.'[a]"

5 Then the devil took him to the holy city and had him stand on the highest point of the temple. 6 "If you are the Son of God," he said, "throw yourself down. For it is written:

" 'He will command his angels concerning
you,
and they will lift you up in their hands,
so that you will not strike your foot against a
stone.'[b]"

7 Jesus answered him, "It is also written: 'Do not put the Lord your God to the test.'[c]"

8 Again, the devil took him to a very high mountain and showed him all the kingdoms of the world and their splendor. 9 "All this I will give you," he said, "if you will bow down and worship me."

10 Jesus said to him, "Away from me, Satan! For it is written: 'Worship the Lord your God, and serve him only.'[d]"

11 Then the devil left him, and angels came and attended him.

Jesus Begins to Preach

12 When Jesus heard that John had been put in prison, he returned to Galilee. 13 Leaving Nazareth, he went and lived in Capernaum, which was by the lake in the area of Zebulun and Naphtali— 14 to fulfill what was said through the prophet Isaiah:

15 "Land of Zebulun and land of Naphtali,
the way to the sea, along the Jordan,
Galilee of the Gentiles—
16 the people living in darkness
have seen a great light;
on those living in the land of the shadow of
death
a light has dawned."[e]

17 From that time on Jesus began to preach, "Repent, for the kingdom of heaven is near."

The Calling of the First Disciples

18 As Jesus was walking beside the Sea of Galilee, he saw two brothers, Simon called Peter and his brother Andrew. They were casting a net into the lake, for they were fishermen. 19 "Come, follow me," Jesus said, "and I will make you fishers of men." 20 At once they left their nets and followed him.

21 Going on from there, he saw two other brothers, James son of Zebedee and his brother John. They were in a boat with their father Zebedee, preparing their nets. Jesus called them, 22 and immediately they left the boat and their father and followed him.

Jesus Heals the Sick

23 Jesus went throughout Galilee, teaching in their synagogues, preaching the good news of the kingdom, and healing every disease and sickness among the people. 24 News about him spread all over Syria, and people brought to him all who were ill with various diseases, those suffering severe pain, the demon-possessed, those having seizures, and the paralyzed, and he healed them. 25 Large crowds from Galilee, the Decapolis,[f] Jerusalem, Judea and the region across the Jordan followed him.

The Beatitudes

5 Now when he saw the crowds, he went up on a mountainside and sat down. His disciples came to him, 2 and he began to teach them, saying:

MATTHEW 5:1–12

1. Did you eat breakfast this morning? Can you remember what you had? Is breakfast the *most* important meal?
2. What teacher, coach or other person taught you the most about attitude and character?
3. Are you more likely to devote time and energy to your physical fitness or your spiritual fitness?
4. When are you the most receptive to hearing and understanding God's Word: During personal devotions? At church? In group Bible study?
5. On a scale of 1 (not at all) to 10 (totally), how much do you hunger and thirst for righteousness?
6. If God gave you an attitude adjustment, of the eight Beatitudes which "attitude" would need to be worked on the most?
7. What's one thing you could do this coming week to help you live the Beatitudes?
8. How can the group remember you in prayer this week?

(Study notes on page 855)

[a] 4 Deut. 8:3 [b] 6 Psalm 91:11,12 [c] 7 Deut. 6:16 [d] 10 Deut. 6:13 [e] 16 Isaiah 9:1,2 [f] 25 That is, the Ten Cities

3"Blessed are the poor in spirit,
for theirs is the kingdom of heaven.
4Blessed are those who mourn,
for they will be comforted.
5Blessed are the meek,
for they will inherit the earth.
6Blessed are those who hunger and thirst for
righteousness,
for they will be filled.
7Blessed are the merciful,
for they will be shown mercy.
8Blessed are the pure in heart,
for they will see God.
9Blessed are the peacemakers,
for they will be called sons of God.
10Blessed are those who are persecuted
because of righteousness,
for theirs is the kingdom of heaven.

11"Blessed are you when people insult you,
persecute you and falsely say all kinds of evil
against you because of me. 12Rejoice and be glad,
because great is your reward in heaven, for in the
same way they persecuted the prophets who
were before you.

Salt and Light

13"You are the salt of the earth. But if the salt
loses its saltiness, how can it be made salty again?
It is no longer good for anything, except to be
thrown out and trampled by men.
14"You are the light of the world. A city on a
hill cannot be hidden. 15Neither do people light
a lamp and put it under a bowl. Instead they put
it on its stand, and it gives light to everyone in
the house. 16In the same way, let your light shine
before men, that they may see your good deeds
and praise your Father in heaven.

The Fulfillment of the Law

17"Do not think that I have come to abolish
the Law or the Prophets; I have not come to
abolish them but to fulfill them. 18I tell you the
truth, until heaven and earth disappear, not the
smallest letter, not the least stroke of a pen, will
by any means disappear from the Law until everything is accomplished. 19Anyone who breaks one
of the least of these commandments and teaches
others to do the same will be called least in the
kingdom of heaven, but whoever practices and
teaches these commands will be called great in
the kingdom of heaven. 20For I tell you that unless your righteousness surpasses that of the
Pharisees and the teachers of the law, you will
certainly not enter the kingdom of heaven.

Murder

21"You have heard that it was said to the people long ago, 'Do not murder,[a] and anyone who
murders will be subject to judgment.' 22But I tell
you that anyone who is angry with his brother[b]
will be subject to judgment. Again, anyone who
says to his brother, 'Raca,[c]' is answerable to the
Sanhedrin. But anyone who says, 'You fool!' will
be in danger of the fire of hell.
23"Therefore, if you are offering your gift at the
altar and there remember that your brother has
something against you, 24leave your gift there in
front of the altar. First go and be reconciled to
your brother; then come and offer your gift.
25"Settle matters quickly with your adversary
who is taking you to court. Do it while you are
still with him on the way, or he may hand you
over to the judge, and the judge may hand you
over to the officer, and you may be thrown into
prison. 26I tell you the truth, you will not get out
until you have paid the last penny.[d]

Adultery

27"You have heard that it was said, 'Do not
commit adultery.'[e] 28But I tell you that anyone
who looks at a woman lustfully has already committed adultery with her in his heart. 29If your
right eye causes you to sin, gouge it out and
throw it away. It is better for you to lose one part
of your body than for your whole body to be
thrown into hell. 30And if your right hand causes
you to sin, cut it off and throw it away. It is better
for you to lose one part of your body than for your
whole body to go into hell.

[a]21 Exodus 20:13 [b]22 Some manuscripts *brother without cause* [c]22 An Aramaic term of contempt [d]26 Greek *kodrantes* [e]27 Exodus 20:14

The Sermon on the Mount is the first (and longest) of five major teaching sections in Matthew. It is not merely a collection of general ethical principles; it is a focused reflection on what is involved in living in obedience to God.

5:3 *Blessed are.* The Greek word *makarios* refers to those who are to be congratulated or who are fortunate or well-off. It does not mean they are happy or prospering. Instead, whether or not they know or feel it, they are fortunate because their condition reflects that they are in a right relationship to God. ***theirs is the kingdom of heaven.*** God's kingdom, conceived of as a state of peace, fullness, justice and abundance (Isa. 42; 49; 51; 65:17–25) is promised to anyone recognizing his or her need for God. The Beatitudes assert that in Jesus this deliverance has come for all types of people who acknowledge their need and dependence upon God. Such is Jesus' message to any group who would assume that only certified members of that particular religious, racial or ethnic group are heirs to God's kingdom.

5:6 *hunger and thirst for righteousness.* People in Christ's kingdom are marked by a deep-seated, intense need and longing for knowing and living in God's way (see Ps. 42:1–2; Isa. 55:1–2; Matt. 6:33).

5:9 *peacemakers.* Peacemaking is neither a matter of minimizing conflict nor of using force to suppress hostilities. True peacemaking involves seeking heart-to-heart reconciliation between people.

Divorce

31“It has been said, ‘Anyone who divorces his
wife must give her a certificate of divorce.’[a]

> ### *Matthew 5:27–30*
>
> 1. Who told you about the “birds and the bees”? Was the situation awkward? Boring? Interesting? Funny?
> 2. When it comes to “entertainment” where do you draw the line: PG? R-rated? “Adult”?
> 3. Where do you think Jesus would draw the line?
> 4. Jesus used the Word of God to resist temptation (Matt. 4:1–11). What Scripture have you found helpful in cleaning up your thought life?
> 5. In dating, what is a rule you have set for yourself sexually?
> 6. How do you feel about verses 29–30? What point do you think Jesus was trying to make (see note on 5:29–30)?
> 7. What is one thing you would like this group to hold you accountable to in the next week?

32But I tell you that anyone who divorces his
wife, except for marital unfaithfulness, causes
her to become an adulteress, and anyone who
marries the divorced woman commits adultery.

Oaths

33“Again, you have heard that it was said to
the people long ago, ‘Do not break your oath, but
keep the oaths you have made to the Lord.’ 34But
I tell you, Do not swear at all: either by heaven,
for it is God’s throne; 35or by the earth, for it is
his footstool; or by Jerusalem, for it is the city of
the Great King. 36And do not swear by your head,
for you cannot make even one hair white or
black. 37Simply let your ‘Yes’ be ‘Yes,’ and your
‘No,’ ‘No’; anything beyond this comes from the
evil one.

An Eye for an Eye

38“You have heard that it was said, ‘Eye for
eye, and tooth for tooth.’[b] 39But I tell you, Do
not resist an evil person. If someone strikes you
on the right cheek, turn to him the other also.
40And if someone wants to sue you and take your
tunic, let him have your cloak as well. 41If someone forces you to go one mile, go with him two
miles. 42Give to the one who asks you, and do not
turn away from the one who wants to borrow
from you.

Love for Enemies

43“You have heard that it was said, ‘Love your
neighbor[c] and hate your enemy.’ 44But I tell
you: Love your enemies[d] and pray for those who
persecute you, 45that you may be sons of your

[a]31 Deut. 24:1 [b]38 Exodus 21:24; Lev. 24:20; Deut. 19:21 [c]43 Lev. 19:18 [d]44 Some late manuscripts *enemies, bless those who curse you, do good to those who hate you*

Having shown the depth of meaning behind the Law’s prohibition against murder in 5:21–26 (the sixth commandment), Jesus now does the same with the seventh commandment (Ex. 20:14).

5:27–28 ***Do not commit adultery.*** While adultery is defined as having sexual relationships with another person’s spouse, the OT Law also prohibited fornication, incest, bestiality, homosexuality and rape. The prohibition against adultery in the Ten Commandments sums up the various prohibitions against illegitimate sexual acts. ***lustfully.*** Just as anger is at the root of murder (5:21–22), so lust is at the root of adultery. “Jesus’ intention is to prohibit not a natural sexual attraction, but the deliberate harboring of desire for an illicit relationship” (France). ***a woman.*** Probably a married woman is intended, since this is how the Greek word is generally used.

5:29–30 In these statements Jesus is, of course, using exaggeration, deliberately overstating or dramatizing in order to make a point. However, in the early part of the third century, Origen, a prominent theologian, took this literally and emasculated himself. Such actions were prohibited by the Council of Nicea in 325 A.D. The Council understood that Jesus was speaking figuratively to accent his point that radical action must be taken to root out sin in our lives. He commands us to make a conscious, vigilant choice to turn away from sin and those things that draw us toward sin in order to pursue God’s kingdom.

5:38–39 ***“eye for eye.”*** The so-called law of retaliation’s point was usually not to require “eye for eye, and tooth for tooth” but to limit punishment to the extent of the crime. The scribes had transformed this law that set limits on judicial actions into an individual right to carry out revenge in one’s private affairs. ***Do not resist an evil person.*** Jesus dismisses this misinterpretation of the scribes and calls instead for an attitude of non-retaliation.

5:40 The root idea here is not so much the avoidance of litigation as it is the encouragement to act with a generous, loving attitude toward all people.

5:44 ***Love your enemies.*** Jesus expands Leviticus 19:18 to include all people in the call to love others. By this statement, he makes it clear that there is no one who stands outside the circle of love. He, in essence, redefines the whole concept of who one’s neighbor is (see Luke 10:25–37).

5:48 ***be perfect.*** The Greek word used for “perfect” is *teleios,* which means “having attained the end or purpose.” In the creation account God stated: “Let us make man in our image, in our likeness ...” (Gen. 1:26). Thus, men and women are “perfect” when they live out God’s way of love and so demonstrate that they are made in his image. This commandment to be perfect defines the goal toward which God’s children strive. It is not a goal they can ever reach (only God is and can be “perfect”); it is, however, a pattern that becomes the basis of how they seek to live.

Father in heaven. He causes his sun to rise on the
evil and the good, and sends rain on the righteous and the unrighteous. 46If you love those
who love you, what reward will you get? Are not

Matthew 5:38–48

1. What causes you to reach the boiling point: A slow driver in the fast lane? "Technical problems" during your favorite TV show?
2. Who is the peacemaker in your family?
3. When there's a confrontation, are you more like "peace at any price" or "let's have it out now"?
4. In what situation do you find it most difficult to "turn the other cheek"?
5. How do you think Jesus feels about capital punishment?
6. How would you rate your week with a number between 1 (terrible) and 10 (great)?
7. Since turning over your life to God, what effect has this had on your temper and ability to forgive others that hurt you?
8. How can the group pray for you today and in the coming week?

(Study notes on page 856)

even the tax collectors doing that? 47And if you
greet only your brothers, what are you doing
more than others? Do not even pagans do that?
48Be perfect, therefore, as your heavenly Father
is perfect.

Giving to the Needy

6 "Be careful not to do your 'acts of righteousness' before men, to be seen by them. If you
do, you will have no reward from your Father in
heaven.

2"So when you give to the needy, do not announce it with trumpets, as the hypocrites do in
the synagogues and on the streets, to be honored
by men. I tell you the truth, they have received
their reward in full. 3But when you give to the
needy, do not let your left hand know what your
right hand is doing, 4so that your giving may be
in secret. Then your Father, who sees what is
done in secret, will reward you.

Prayer

5"And when you pray, do not be like the hypocrites, for they love to pray standing in the synagogues and on the street corners to be seen by
men. I tell you the truth, they have received their

Matthew 6:5–18

1. When you were a child, who tucked you in and said prayers with you? What's something you prayed for?
2. Who do you admire as a person of prayer?
3. When do you pray: Before meals? In a crisis? Daily in devotions? Before a test?
4. What is something that you pray for on a regular basis?
5. In the Lord's Prayer (vv. 9–13), what seems most important to you?
6. What is the purpose of fasting? What situations have you faced that might be helped by fasting?
7. If you took a full day for prayer and fasting, where would you go and how would you use the time?
8. If you went right now, what would be your most urgent prayer request? How can this group agree with you in prayer?

6:6 ***go into your room, close the door.*** Jesus' point is not to do away with public prayer (which he practiced himself), but to stress that prayer is to be rooted in a desire to commune with God, not in a desire to make a public display. Corporate, public prayer (as shown throughout Jewish and Christian history) is perfectly legitimate when approached with this attitude.

6:8 ***knows ... before you ask.*** This is not meant to indicate that prayer is unimportant, but rather to stress the intimate concern and awareness God has for his people. Prayer serves to nurture the relationship between ourselves and God as it allows us to glimpse God's heart and mind.

6:9–15 The so-called Lord's Prayer consists of three petitions that relate to God and his kingdom and three requests that deal with the everyday needs of life as disciples pursue the kingdom. The prayer suggests the kinds of things that ought to occupy the content of the prayers of God's people.

6:16–18 ***fast.*** Jews fasted on the Day of Atonement as well as at other times (see Deut. 9:9; 1 Sam. 31:13; Ps. 35:13). The issue is not whether disciples should fast, the question is how one goes about fasting. Since the purpose of fasting is to focus one's attention and energy on God, Jesus teaches that his disciples should not fast in a way so as to draw attention to themselves. ***put oil on your head and wash your face.*** Jews put ashes on their heads when fasting. Putting oil on the head and washing the face were reserved for joyous occasions.

reward in full. [6]But when you pray, go into your
room, close the door and pray to your Father,
who is unseen. Then your Father, who sees what
is done in secret, will reward you. [7]And when
you pray, do not keep on babbling like pagans, for
they think they will be heard because of their
many words. [8]Do not be like them, for your Father knows what you need before you ask him.
[9]"This, then, is how you should pray:

" 'Our Father in heaven,
hallowed be your name,
[10]your kingdom come,
your will be done
on earth as it is in heaven.
[11]Give us today our daily bread.
[12]Forgive us our debts,
as we also have forgiven our debtors.
[13]And lead us not into temptation,
but deliver us from the evil one.[a] '

[14]For if you forgive men when they sin against
you, your heavenly Father will also forgive you.
[15]But if you do not forgive men their sins, your
Father will not forgive your sins.

Fasting

[16]"When you fast, do not look somber as the
hypocrites do, for they disfigure their faces to
show men they are fasting. I tell you the truth,
they have received their reward in full. [17]But
when you fast, put oil on your head and wash
your face, [18]so that it will not be obvious to men
that you are fasting, but only to your Father, who
is unseen; and your Father, who sees what is
done in secret, will reward you.

Treasures in Heaven

[19]"Do not store up for yourselves treasures on
earth, where moth and rust destroy, and where
thieves break in and steal. [20]But store up for yourselves treasures in heaven, where moth and rust
do not destroy, and where thieves do not break in
and steal. [21]For where your treasure is, there
your heart will be also.
[22]"The eye is the lamp of the body. If your eyes
are good, your whole body will be full of light.
[23]But if your eyes are bad, your whole body will
be full of darkness. If then the light within you is
darkness, how great is that darkness!
[24]"No one can serve two masters. Either he
will hate the one and love the other, or he will be
devoted to the one and despise the other. You
cannot serve both God and Money.

Do Not Worry

[25]"Therefore I tell you, do not worry about
your life, what you will eat or drink; or about
your body, what you will wear. Is not life more

MATTHEW 6:25–34

1. How long does it take you to get ready in the morning?
2. If someone had judged you by the clothes in your closet, what would they say?
3. Do you tend to plan ahead or take one day at a time?
4. Who is the worrier in your family? Who is cool and collected even in the hardest of times?
5. If your doctor told you that you had to reduce the stress in your life, what would have to change?
6. How can seeking "first his Kingdom" (v. 33) help you know God's will for your life?
7. What is the biggest worry you have about your future? About the coming week?
8. How can this group pray for you regarding these worries?

[a]13 Or *from evil*; some late manuscripts *one, / for yours is the kingdom and the power and the glory forever. Amen.*

By way of illustrating the fact that God takes care of those who follow him, Jesus notes that birds depend upon God for their food, and flowers depend on him for their beautiful adornment. His point is that God's children, who are more valuable than the birds and the flowers, can therefore depend upon God to show the same care for them that he gives to birds and plants. To worry is to show a lack of dependence on God.

6:25 ***do not worry.*** Worry or anxiety is a state of mind. Having chosen God's way, the disciple must not be overly concerned about the demands and pressures that occupy those committed to the other way (materialism).

6:28–29 ***lilies.*** Here represents flowers generally. ***Solomon.*** Solomon, as the third king of Israel, was noted for his fabulous wealth (1 Kings 10:14–29). The folly of being anxious about clothes is revealed in that even the simplest flower is adorned more delicately and attractively than the richest man or woman.

6:31 ***so do not worry.*** What is commended here is not idleness but faith. As verse 33 indicates, the disciples of Jesus are to be busy, but their activity is centered around pursuing God's agenda; they are not to be centered around simply meeting their own needs. They are to be confident that God will meet their needs.

6:34 ***tomorrow.*** Worry generally has to do with the future, about what lies ahead. The disciple is to live one day at a time, and not in dread of what might happen in the future.

important than food, and the body more important than clothes? 26Look at the birds of the air; they do not sow or reap or store away in barns, and yet your heavenly Father feeds them. Are you not much more valuable than they? 27Who of you by worrying can add a single hour to his life[a]?

28"And why do you worry about clothes? See how the lilies of the field grow. They do not labor or spin. 29Yet I tell you that not even Solomon in all his splendor was dressed like one of these. 30If that is how God clothes the grass of the field, which is here today and tomorrow is thrown into the fire, will he not much more clothe you, O you of little faith? 31So do not worry, saying, 'What shall we eat?' or 'What shall we drink?' or 'What shall we wear?' 32For the pagans run after all these things, and your heavenly Father knows that you need them. 33But seek first his kingdom and his righteousness, and all these things will be given to you as well. 34Therefore do not worry about tomorrow, for tomorrow will worry about itself. Each day has enough trouble of its own.

Judging Others

7 "Do not judge, or you too will be judged. 2For in the same way you judge others, you will be judged, and with the measure you use, it will be measured to you.

3"Why do you look at the speck of sawdust in your brother's eye and pay no attention to the plank in your own eye? 4How can you say to your brother, 'Let me take the speck out of your eye,' when all the time there is a plank in your own eye? 5You hypocrite, first take the plank out of your own eye, and then you will see clearly to remove the speck from your brother's eye.

6"Do not give dogs what is sacred; do not throw your pearls to pigs. If you do, they may trample them under their feet, and then turn and tear you to pieces.

Ask, Seek, Knock

7"Ask and it will be given to you; seek and you will find; knock and the door will be opened to you. 8For everyone who asks receives; he who seeks finds; and to him who knocks, the door will be opened.

9"Which of you, if his son asks for bread, will give him a stone? 10Or if he asks for a fish, will give him a snake? 11If you, then, though you are evil, know how to give good gifts to your children, how much more will your Father in heaven give good gifts to those who ask him! 12So in everything, do to others what you would have them do to you, for this sums up the Law and the Prophets.

The Narrow and Wide Gates

13"Enter through the narrow gate. For wide is the gate and broad is the road that leads to destruction, and many enter through it. 14But small is the gate and narrow the road that leads to life, and only a few find it.

A Tree and Its Fruit

15"Watch out for false prophets. They come to you in sheep's clothing, but inwardly they are ferocious wolves. 16By their fruit you will recognize them. Do people pick grapes from thornbushes, or figs from thistles? 17Likewise every good tree bears good fruit, but a bad tree bears bad fruit. 18A good tree cannot bear bad fruit, and a bad tree cannot bear good fruit. 19Every tree that does not bear good fruit is cut down and thrown into the fire. 20Thus, by their fruit you will recognize them.

21"Not everyone who says to me, 'Lord, Lord,' will enter the kingdom of heaven, but only he who does the will of my Father who is in heaven. 22Many will say to me on that day, 'Lord, Lord, did we not prophesy in your name, and in your name drive out demons and perform many miracles?' 23Then I will tell them plainly, 'I never knew you. Away from me, you evildoers!'

The Wise and Foolish Builders

24"Therefore everyone who hears these words of mine and puts them into practice is like a wise man who built his house on the rock. 25The rain came down, the streams rose, and the winds

[a]27 Or *single cubit to his height*

Jesus' Sermon on the Mount, which began in Matthew 5, ends with this parable (vv. 24–27) which dramatically highlights the choice which Jesus confronts his listeners. One must decide either to put Jesus' teaching into practice or face the destruction that is the end result of any other choice. He is the one and only way, truth and life (John 14:6). The two houses in this parable may look alike, but only the one built on a solid foundation (obedience to God) will stand when the storm of God's ultimate accounting comes.

7:24 ***Therefore.*** The parable concludes the argument just presented. Choices about what path to travel (7:13–14), who to listen to (7:15–20), and how to live (7:21–23) all boil down to the ultimate choice of whether or not we will build our lives upon the foundation of Jesus and his teachings.

7:24–27 ***rock / sand.*** Building on sand is easier; and if there is no settling of the land, nor any pressure of wind or water, the house will stand just fine. Palestine was dry most of the year. But in the autumn, rains came and flash floods swept down the ravines. What looks like a fine place to build a house in the dry season may become a raging torrent during flood season. ***rain / streams / winds.*** The storm (repeated exactly) represents both future judgment and the hardships of this life that fall upon believers and nonbelievers alike.

7:28–29 The crowds, present at the beginning of the Sermon, are again brought into the picture. Their amazed reaction stresses the radically new message Jesus brought.

blew and beat against that house; yet it did not
fall, because it had its foundation on the rock.
26But everyone who hears these words of mine
and does not put them into practice is like a foolish man who built his house on sand. 27The rain
came down, the streams rose, and the winds
blew and beat against that house, and it fell with
a great crash."

28When Jesus had finished saying these things,
the crowds were amazed at his teaching, 29be-
cause he taught as one who had authority, and
not as their teachers of the law.

MATTHEW 7:24–29

1. Who is "Mr. Goodwrench" in your family?
2. What is the first thing you ever built? Did it last?
3. Who is the "rock" in your life? What is it about this person that makes them so stable?
4. In this passage, what is Jesus promising to people willing to live by his words?
5. What's the immediate forecast for the "weather" in your life: Sunny? Overcast? Chance for showers?
6. In your spiritual life right now are you standing firm or sinking?
7. How can the group pray for you right now and in the days ahead?

(Study notes on page 859)

The Man With Leprosy

8 When he came down from the mountainside, large crowds followed him. 2A man
with leprosy[a] came and knelt before him and
said, "Lord, if you are willing, you can make me
clean."

3Jesus reached out his hand and touched the
man. "I am willing," he said. "Be clean!" Immediately he was cured[b] of his leprosy. 4Then Jesus
said to him, "See that you don't tell anyone. But
go, show yourself to the priest and offer the gift
Moses commanded, as a testimony to them."

The Faith of the Centurion

5When Jesus had entered Capernaum, a centurion came to him, asking for help. 6"Lord," he
said, "my servant lies at home paralyzed and in
terrible suffering."

7Jesus said to him, "I will go and heal him."
8The centurion replied, "Lord, I do not deserve to have you come under my roof. But just
say the word, and my servant will be healed. 9For
I myself am a man under authority, with soldiers
under me. I tell this one, 'Go,' and he goes; and
that one, 'Come,' and he comes. I say to my servant, 'Do this,' and he does it."

10When Jesus heard this, he was astonished
and said to those following him, "I tell you the
truth, I have not found anyone in Israel with such
great faith. 11I say to you that many will come
from the east and the west, and will take their
places at the feast with Abraham, Isaac and Jacob
in the kingdom of heaven. 12But the subjects of
the kingdom will be thrown outside, into the
darkness, where there will be weeping and
gnashing of teeth."

13Then Jesus said to the centurion, "Go! It will
be done just as you believed it would." And his
servant was healed at that very hour.

Jesus Heals Many

14When Jesus came into Peter's house, he saw
Peter's mother-in-law lying in bed with a fever.
15He touched her hand and the fever left her, and
she got up and began to wait on him.

16When evening came, many who were
demon-possessed were brought to him, and he
drove out the spirits with a word and healed all
the sick. 17This was to fulfill what was spoken
through the prophet Isaiah:

> "He took up our infirmities
> and carried our diseases."[c]

The Cost of Following Jesus

18When Jesus saw the crowd around him, he
gave orders to cross to the other side of the lake.
19Then a teacher of the law came to him and said,
"Teacher, I will follow you wherever you go."

20Jesus replied, "Foxes have holes and birds of
the air have nests, but the Son of Man has no
place to lay his head."

21Another disciple said to him, "Lord, first let
me go and bury my father."

22But Jesus told him, "Follow me, and let the
dead bury their own dead."

Jesus Calms the Storm

23Then he got into the boat and his disciples
followed him. 24Without warning, a furious
storm came up on the lake, so that the waves
swept over the boat. But Jesus was sleeping.

[a]2 The Greek word was used for various diseases affecting the skin—not necessarily leprosy. [b]3 Greek *made clean*
[c]17 Isaiah 53:4

25The disciples went and woke him, saying,
"Lord, save us! We're going to drown!"
26He replied, "You of little faith, why are you
so afraid?" Then he got up and rebuked the
winds and the waves, and it was completely
calm.
27The men were amazed and asked, "What
kind of man is this? Even the winds and the
waves obey him!"

The Healing of Two Demon-possessed Men

28When he arrived at the other side in the
region of the Gadarenes,[a] two demon-possessed
men coming from the tombs met him. They were
so violent that no one could pass that way.
29"What do you want with us, Son of God?" they
shouted. "Have you come here to torture us before the appointed time?"
30Some distance from them a large herd of pigs
was feeding. 31The demons begged Jesus, "If you
drive us out, send us into the herd of pigs."
32He said to them, "Go!" So they came out and
went into the pigs, and the whole herd rushed
down the steep bank into the lake and died in the
water. 33Those tending the pigs ran off, went into
the town and reported all this, including what
had happened to the demon-possessed men.
34Then the whole town went out to meet Jesus.
And when they saw him, they pleaded with him
to leave their region.

Jesus Heals a Paralytic

9 Jesus stepped into a boat, crossed over and
came to his own town. 2Some men brought
to him a paralytic, lying on a mat. When Jesus
saw their faith, he said to the paralytic, "Take
heart, son; your sins are forgiven."
3At this, some of the teachers of the law said
to themselves, "This fellow is blaspheming!"
4Knowing their thoughts, Jesus said, "Why do
you entertain evil thoughts in your hearts?
5Which is easier: to say, 'Your sins are forgiven,'
or to say, 'Get up and walk'? 6But so that you may
know that the Son of Man has authority on earth
to forgive sins. . . ." Then he said to the paralytic,
"Get up, take your mat and go home." 7And the
man got up and went home. 8When the crowd
saw this, they were filled with awe; and they
praised God, who had given such authority to
men.

The Calling of Matthew

9As Jesus went on from there, he saw a man
named Matthew sitting at the tax collector's
booth. "Follow me," he told him, and Matthew
got up and followed him.
10While Jesus was having dinner at Matthew's
house, many tax collectors and "sinners" came
and ate with him and his disciples. 11When the
Pharisees saw this, they asked his disciples,
"Why does your teacher eat with tax collectors
and 'sinners'?"
12On hearing this, Jesus said, "It is not the
healthy who need a doctor, but the sick. 13But go
and learn what this means: 'I desire mercy, not
sacrifice.'[b] For I have not come to call the righteous, but sinners."

Jesus Questioned About Fasting

14Then John's disciples came and asked him,
"How is it that we and the Pharisees fast, but
your disciples do not fast?"
15Jesus answered, "How can the guests of the
bridegroom mourn while he is with them? The
time will come when the bridegroom will be taken from them; then they will fast.
16"No one sews a patch of unshrunk cloth on
an old garment, for the patch will pull away from
the garment, making the tear worse. 17Neither
do men pour new wine into old wineskins. If
they do, the skins will burst, the wine will run
out and the wineskins will be ruined. No, they
pour new wine into new wineskins, and both are
preserved."

A Dead Girl and a Sick Woman

18While he was saying this, a ruler came and
knelt before him and said, "My daughter has just
died. But come and put your hand on her, and
she will live." 19Jesus got up and went with him,
and so did his disciples.
20Just then a woman who had been subject to
bleeding for twelve years came up behind him
and touched the edge of his cloak. 21She said
to herself, "If I only touch his cloak, I will be
healed."
22Jesus turned and saw her. "Take heart,
daughter," he said, "your faith has healed you."
And the woman was healed from that moment.
23When Jesus entered the ruler's house and
saw the flute players and the noisy crowd, 24he
said, "Go away. The girl is not dead but asleep."
But they laughed at him. 25After the crowd had
been put outside, he went in and took the girl by
the hand, and she got up. 26News of this spread
through all that region.

Jesus Heals the Blind and Mute

27As Jesus went on from there, two blind men
followed him, calling out, "Have mercy on us,
Son of David!"
28When he had gone indoors, the blind men
came to him, and he asked them, "Do you believe
that I am able to do this?"

[a] *28* Some manuscripts *Gergesenes*; others *Gerasenes*
[b] *13* Hosea 6:6

"Yes, Lord," they replied.

29Then he touched their eyes and said, "According to your faith will it be done to you"; 30and their sight was restored. Jesus warned them sternly, "See that no one knows about this." 31But they went out and spread the news about him all over that region.

32While they were going out, a man who was demon-possessed and could not talk was brought to Jesus. 33And when the demon was driven out, the man who had been mute spoke. The crowd was amazed and said, "Nothing like this has ever been seen in Israel."

34But the Pharisees said, "It is by the prince of demons that he drives out demons."

The Workers Are Few

35Jesus went through all the towns and villages, teaching in their synagogues, preaching the good news of the kingdom and healing every disease and sickness. 36When he saw the crowds, he had compassion on them, because they were harassed and helpless, like sheep without a shepherd. 37Then he said to his disciples, "The harvest is plentiful but the workers are few. 38Ask the Lord of the harvest, therefore, to send out workers into his harvest field."

Jesus Sends Out the Twelve

10 He called his twelve disciples to him and gave them authority to drive out evil[a] spirits and to heal every disease and sickness.

2These are the names of the twelve apostles: first, Simon (who is called Peter) and his brother Andrew; James son of Zebedee, and his brother John; 3Philip and Bartholomew; Thomas and Matthew the tax collector; James son of Alphaeus, and Thaddaeus; 4Simon the Zealot and Judas Iscariot, who betrayed him.

5These twelve Jesus sent out with the following instructions: "Do not go among the Gentiles or enter any town of the Samaritans. 6Go rather to the lost sheep of Israel. 7As you go, preach this message: 'The kingdom of heaven is near.' 8Heal the sick, raise the dead, cleanse those who have leprosy,[b] drive out demons. Freely you have received, freely give. 9Do not take along any gold or silver or copper in your belts; 10take no bag for the journey, or extra tunic, or sandals or a staff; for the worker is worth his keep.

11"Whatever town or village you enter, search for some worthy person there and stay at his house until you leave. 12As you enter the home, give it your greeting. 13If the home is deserving, let your peace rest on it; if it is not, let your peace return to you. 14If anyone will not welcome you or listen to your words, shake the dust off your feet when you leave that home or town. 15I tell you the truth, it will be more bearable for Sodom and Gomorrah on the day of judgment than for that town. 16I am sending you out like sheep among wolves. Therefore be as shrewd as snakes and as innocent as doves.

17"Be on your guard against men; they will hand you over to the local councils and flog you in their synagogues. 18On my account you will be brought before governors and kings as witnesses to them and to the Gentiles. 19But when they arrest you, do not worry about what to say or how to say it. At that time you will be given what to say, 20for it will not be you speaking, but the Spirit of your Father speaking through you.

21"Brother will betray brother to death, and a father his child; children will rebel against their parents and have them put to death. 22All men will hate you because of me, but he who stands firm to the end will be saved. 23When you are persecuted in one place, flee to another. I tell you the truth, you will not finish going through the cities of Israel before the Son of Man comes.

24"A student is not above his teacher, nor a servant above his master. 25It is enough for the student to be like his teacher, and the servant like his master. If the head of the house has been called Beelzebub,[c] how much more the members of his household!

26"So do not be afraid of them. There is nothing concealed that will not be disclosed, or hidden that will not be made known. 27What I tell you in the dark, speak in the daylight; what is whispered in your ear, proclaim from the roofs. 28Do not be afraid of those who kill the body but cannot kill the soul. Rather, be afraid of the One who can destroy both soul and body in hell. 29Are not two sparrows sold for a penny[d]? Yet not one of them will fall to the ground apart from the will of your Father. 30And even the very hairs of your head are all numbered. 31So don't be afraid; you are worth more than many sparrows.

32"Whoever acknowledges me before men, I will also acknowledge him before my Father in heaven. 33But whoever disowns me before men, I will disown him before my Father in heaven.

34"Do not suppose that I have come to bring peace to the earth. I did not come to bring peace, but a sword. 35For I have come to turn

" 'a man against his father,
a daughter against her mother,
a daughter-in-law against her
mother-in-law—
36 a man's enemies will be the members of
his own household.'[e]

[a]1 Greek *unclean* [b]8 The Greek word was used for various diseases affecting the skin—not necessarily leprosy. [c]25 Greek *Beezeboul* or *Beelzeboul* [d]29 Greek *an assarion* [e]36 Micah 7:6

37“Anyone who loves his father or mother
more than me is not worthy of me; anyone who
loves his son or daughter more than me is not
worthy of me; 38and anyone who does not take
his cross and follow me is not worthy of me.
39Whoever finds his life will lose it, and whoever
loses his life for my sake will find it.
40“He who receives you receives me, and he
who receives me receives the one who sent me.
41Anyone who receives a prophet because he is a
prophet will receive a prophet’s reward, and anyone who receives a righteous man because he is
a righteous man will receive a righteous man’s
reward. 42And if anyone gives even a cup of cold
water to one of these little ones because he is my
disciple, I tell you the truth, he will certainly not
lose his reward.”

Jesus and John the Baptist

11 After Jesus had finished instructing his
twelve disciples, he went on from there
to teach and preach in the towns of Galilee.[a]
2When John heard in prison what Christ was
doing, he sent his disciples 3to ask him, “Are you
the one who was to come, or should we expect
someone else?”
4Jesus replied, “Go back and report to John
what you hear and see: 5The blind receive sight,
the lame walk, those who have leprosy[b] are
cured, the deaf hear, the dead are raised, and the
good news is preached to the poor. 6Blessed is
the man who does not fall away on account
of me.”
7As John’s disciples were leaving, Jesus began
to speak to the crowd about John: “What did you
go out into the desert to see? A reed swayed by
the wind? 8If not, what did you go out to see? A
man dressed in fine clothes? No, those who wear
fine clothes are in kings’ palaces. 9Then what did
you go out to see? A prophet? Yes, I tell you, and
more than a prophet. 10This is the one about
whom it is written:

“ ‘I will send my messenger ahead of you,
who will prepare your way before you.’[c]

11I tell you the truth: Among those born of wom-
en there has not risen anyone greater than John
the Baptist; yet he who is least in the kingdom of
heaven is greater than he. 12From the days of
John the Baptist until now, the kingdom of heav-
en has been forcefully advancing, and forceful
men lay hold of it. 13For all the Prophets and the
Law prophesied until John. 14And if you are willing to accept it, he is the Elijah who was to come.
15He who has ears, let him hear.
16“To what can I compare this generation?
They are like children sitting in the marketplaces
and calling out to others:

17“ ‘We played the flute for you,
and you did not dance;
we sang a dirge,
and you did not mourn.’

18For John came neither eating nor drinking, and
they say, ‘He has a demon.’ 19The Son of Man
came eating and drinking, and they say, ‘Here is
a glutton and a drunkard, a friend of tax collectors
and “sinners.” ’ But wisdom is proved right by
her actions.”

Woe on Unrepentant Cities

20Then Jesus began to denounce the cities in
which most of his miracles had been performed,
because they did not repent. 21“Woe to you, Korazin! Woe to you, Bethsaida! If the miracles that
were performed in you had been performed in
Tyre and Sidon, they would have repented long
ago in sackcloth and ashes. 22But I tell you, it will
be more bearable for Tyre and Sidon on the day
of judgment than for you. 23And you, Capernaum, will you be lifted up to the skies? No, you
will go down to the depths.[d] If the miracles that
were performed in you had been performed in
Sodom, it would have remained to this day. 24But
I tell you that it will be more bearable for Sodom
on the day of judgment than for you.”

Rest for the Weary

25At that time Jesus said, “I praise you, Father,
Lord of heaven and earth, because you have hidden these things from the wise and learned, and
revealed them to little children. 26Yes, Father, for
this was your good pleasure.
27“All things have been committed to me by
my Father. No one knows the Son except the
Father, and no one knows the Father except the
Son and those to whom the Son chooses to reveal
him.
28“Come to me, all you who are weary and
burdened, and I will give you rest. 29Take my
yoke upon you and learn from me, for I am gentle
and humble in heart, and you will find rest for
your souls. 30For my yoke is easy and my burden
is light.”

Lord of the Sabbath

12 At that time Jesus went through the
grainfields on the Sabbath. His disciples
were hungry and began to pick some heads of
grain and eat them. 2When the Pharisees saw
this, they said to him, “Look! Your disciples are
doing what is unlawful on the Sabbath.”

a1 Greek *in their towns* b5 The Greek word was used for various diseases affecting the skin—not necessarily leprosy.
c10 Mal. 3:1 d23 Greek *Hades*

3He answered, "Haven't you read what David
did when he and his companions were hungry?
4He entered the house of God, and he and his
companions ate the consecrated bread—which
was not lawful for them to do, but only for the
priests. 5Or haven't you read in the Law that on
the Sabbath the priests in the temple desecrate
the day and yet are innocent? 6I tell you that
one[a] greater than the temple is here. 7If you had
known what these words mean, 'I desire mercy,
not sacrifice,'[b] you would not have condemned
the innocent. 8For the Son of Man is Lord of the
Sabbath."

9Going on from that place, he went into their
synagogue, 10and a man with a shriveled hand
was there. Looking for a reason to accuse Jesus,
they asked him, "Is it lawful to heal on the Sabbath?"

11He said to them, "If any of you has a sheep
and it falls into a pit on the Sabbath, will you not
take hold of it and lift it out? 12How much more
valuable is a man than a sheep! Therefore it is
lawful to do good on the Sabbath."

13Then he said to the man, "Stretch out your
hand." So he stretched it out and it was completely restored, just as sound as the other. 14But
the Pharisees went out and plotted how they
might kill Jesus.

God's Chosen Servant

15Aware of this, Jesus withdrew from that
place. Many followed him, and he healed all their
sick, 16warning them not to tell who he was.
17This was to fulfill what was spoken through the
prophet Isaiah:

18"Here is my servant whom I have chosen,
the one I love, in whom I delight;
I will put my Spirit on him,
and he will proclaim justice to the nations.
19He will not quarrel or cry out;
no one will hear his voice in the streets.
20A bruised reed he will not break,
and a smoldering wick he will not snuff
out,
till he leads justice to victory.
21 In his name the nations will put their
hope."[c]

Jesus and Beelzebub

22Then they brought him a demon-possessed
man who was blind and mute, and Jesus healed
him, so that he could both talk and see. 23All the
people were astonished and said, "Could this be
the Son of David?"

24But when the Pharisees heard this, they
said, "It is only by Beelzebub,[d] the prince of
demons, that this fellow drives out demons."

25Jesus knew their thoughts and said to them,
"Every kingdom divided against itself will be ruined, and every city or household divided against
itself will not stand. 26If Satan drives out Satan,
he is divided against himself. How then can his
kingdom stand? 27And if I drive out demons by
Beelzebub, by whom do your people drive them
out? So then, they will be your judges. 28But if I
drive out demons by the Spirit of God, then the
kingdom of God has come upon you.

29"Or again, how can anyone enter a strong
man's house and carry off his possessions unless
he first ties up the strong man? Then he can rob
his house.

30"He who is not with me is against me, and
he who does not gather with me scatters. 31And
so I tell you, every sin and blasphemy will be
forgiven men, but the blasphemy against the Spirit will not be forgiven. 32Anyone who speaks a
word against the Son of Man will be forgiven, but
anyone who speaks against the Holy Spirit will
not be forgiven, either in this age or in the age to
come.

33"Make a tree good and its fruit will be good,
or make a tree bad and its fruit will be bad, for a
tree is recognized by its fruit. 34You brood of
vipers, how can you who are evil say anything
good? For out of the overflow of the heart the
mouth speaks. 35The good man brings good
things out of the good stored up in him, and the
evil man brings evil things out of the evil stored
up in him. 36But I tell you that men will have to
give account on the day of judgment for every
careless word they have spoken. 37For by your
words you will be acquitted, and by your words
you will be condemned."

The Sign of Jonah

38Then some of the Pharisees and teachers of
the law said to him, "Teacher, we want to see a
miraculous sign from you."

39He answered, "A wicked and adulterous
generation asks for a miraculous sign! But none
will be given it except the sign of the prophet
Jonah. 40For as Jonah was three days and three
nights in the belly of a huge fish, so the Son of
Man will be three days and three nights in the
heart of the earth. 41The men of Nineveh will
stand up at the judgment with this generation
and condemn it; for they repented at the preaching of Jonah, and now one[e] greater than Jonah
is here. 42The Queen of the South will rise at the
judgment with this generation and condemn it;
for she came from the ends of the earth to listen

[a] *6* Or *something*; also in verses 41 and 42 [b] *7* Hosea 6:6 [c] *21* Isaiah 42:1-4 [d] *24* Greek *Beezeboul* or *Beelzeboul*; also in verse 27 [e] *41* Or *something*; also in verse 42

to Solomon's wisdom, and now one greater than
Solomon is here.
43"When an evil[a] spirit comes out of a man,
it goes through arid places seeking rest and does
not find it. 44Then it says, 'I will return to the
house I left.' When it arrives, it finds the house
unoccupied, swept clean and put in order.
45Then it goes and takes with it seven other spirits more wicked than itself, and they go in and
live there. And the final condition of that man is
worse than the first. That is how it will be with
this wicked generation."

Jesus' Mother and Brothers

46While Jesus was still talking to the crowd,
his mother and brothers stood outside, wanting
to speak to him. 47Someone told him, "Your
mother and brothers are standing outside, wanting to speak to you."[b]
48He replied to him, "Who is my mother, and
who are my brothers?" 49Pointing to his disciples, he said, "Here are my mother and my brothers. 50For whoever does the will of my Father in
heaven is my brother and sister and mother."

The Parable of the Sower

13 That same day Jesus went out of the
house and sat by the lake. 2Such large
crowds gathered around him that he got into a
boat and sat in it, while all the people stood on
the shore. 3Then he told them many things in
parables, saying: "A farmer went out to sow his
seed. 4As he was scattering the seed, some fell
along the path, and the birds came and ate it up.
5Some fell on rocky places, where it did not have
much soil. It sprang up quickly, because the soil
was shallow. 6But when the sun came up, the
plants were scorched, and they withered because
they had no root. 7Other seed fell among thorns,
which grew up and choked the plants. 8Still other
seed fell on good soil, where it produced a crop—
a hundred, sixty or thirty times what was sown.
9He who has ears, let him hear."
10The disciples came to him and asked, "Why
do you speak to the people in parables?"
11He replied, "The knowledge of the secrets of
the kingdom of heaven has been given to you, but
not to them. 12Whoever has will be given more,
and he will have an abundance. Whoever does
not have, even what he has will be taken from
him. 13This is why I speak to them in parables:

"Though seeing, they do not see;
though hearing, they do not hear or
understand.

14In them is fulfilled the prophecy of Isaiah:

" 'You will be ever hearing but never
understanding;
you will be ever seeing but never
perceiving.
15For this people's heart has become calloused;
they hardly hear with their ears,

? MATTHEW 13:1–23

1. Who is the "green thumb" in your family? How are you at making things grow?
2. How do you spend most of your spare time?
3. Who first planted the "seed" of the Gospel in your life? What happened to this seed?
4. Which of the four soils best describes the condition of your heart right now?
5. How often do you make hearing and acting on God's word a priority in your life?
6. What do you need to do to develop strong spiritual roots?
7. What "thorn of worry" is trying to choke your faith? How can this group pray for you about it?

[a]43 Greek *unclean* [b]47 Some manuscripts do not have verse 47.

13:3 *sow his seed.* Farmers would throw seed into the soil by a broadcast method. The indiscriminate sowing of this particular farmer was one of the strange twists that would have captured the hearers' attention.

13:4–8 *path.* Between plots of land the soil was so packed down that seed could not penetrate the soil and germinate. The birds came along and ate up this seed which just sat on the surface. ***rocky places.*** Some of the soil covered a limestone base a few inches beneath the surface. Here seeds would germinate but not have the root system to last. ***thorns.*** As the seed grew here, so would the weeds. Although it lived, such seed would not bear fruit. ***good soil.*** Some seed fell where it was intended and yielded a spectacular crop (10 times what was sown was considered a very good harvest).

13:13–15 These are statements of fact, not pronouncements of judgment. The people's spiritual insensitivity is not caused by Jesus, but it is the reality he must confront when he tries to teach.

13:18–23 Jesus explains the parable pointing to his message of the kingdom. Some are so hardened the seed of the word never even penetrates. Some like what Jesus can give them, but their level of commitment is not deep and they fall away at the hint of trouble or persecution. Others allow the wrong concerns (specifically worries and wealth) to squeeze out their interest in Jesus and his way, preventing them from being fruitful. At last, hearing and understanding come together and bring forth a good crop.

and they have closed their eyes.
Otherwise they might see with their eyes,
hear with their ears,
understand with their hearts
and turn, and I would heal them.'[a]

16 But blessed are your eyes because they see, and
your ears because they hear. 17 For I tell you the
truth, many prophets and righteous men longed
to see what you see but did not see it, and to hear
what you hear but did not hear it.
18 "Listen then to what the parable of the sower means: 19 When anyone hears the message
about the kingdom and does not understand it,
the evil one comes and snatches away what was
sown in his heart. This is the seed sown along the
path. 20 The one who received the seed that fell
on rocky places is the man who hears the word
and at once receives it with joy. 21 But since he
has no root, he lasts only a short time. When
trouble or persecution comes because of the
word, he quickly falls away. 22 The one who received the seed that fell among the thorns is the
man who hears the word, but the worries of this
life and the deceitfulness of wealth choke it, making it unfruitful. 23 But the one who received the
seed that fell on good soil is the man who hears
the word and understands it. He produces a crop,
yielding a hundred, sixty or thirty times what was
sown."

The Parable of the Weeds

24 Jesus told them another parable: "The kingdom of heaven is like a man who sowed good
seed in his field. 25 But while everyone was sleeping, his enemy came and sowed weeds among
the wheat, and went away. 26 When the wheat
sprouted and formed heads, then the weeds also
appeared.
27 "The owner's servants came to him and said,
'Sir, didn't you sow good seed in your field?
Where then did the weeds come from?'
28 " 'An enemy did this,' he replied.
"The servants asked him, 'Do you want us to
go and pull them up?'
29 " 'No,' he answered, 'because while you are
pulling the weeds, you may root up the wheat
with them. 30 Let both grow together until the
harvest. At that time I will tell the harvesters:
First collect the weeds and tie them in bundles to
be burned; then gather the wheat and bring it
into my barn.' "

The Parables of the Mustard Seed and the Yeast

31 He told them another parable: "The kingdom of heaven is like a mustard seed, which a
man took and planted in his field. 32 Though it is
the smallest of all your seeds, yet when it grows,
it is the largest of garden plants and becomes a
tree, so that the birds of the air come and perch
in its branches."
33 He told them still another parable: "The
kingdom of heaven is like yeast that a woman
took and mixed into a large amount[b] of flour
until it worked all through the dough."
34 Jesus spoke all these things to the crowd in
parables; he did not say anything to them without
using a parable. 35 So was fulfilled what was spoken through the prophet:

"I will open my mouth in parables,
I will utter things hidden since the
creation of the world."[c]

The Parable of the Weeds Explained

36 Then he left the crowd and went into the
house. His disciples came to him and said, "Explain to us the parable of the weeds in the field."
37 He answered, "The one who sowed the good
seed is the Son of Man. 38 The field is the world,
and the good seed stands for the sons of the kingdom. The weeds are the sons of the evil one,
39 and the enemy who sows them is the devil. The
harvest is the end of the age, and the harvesters
are angels.
40 "As the weeds are pulled up and burned in
the fire, so it will be at the end of the age. 41 The
Son of Man will send out his angels, and they will
weed out of his kingdom everything that causes
sin and all who do evil. 42 They will throw them
into the fiery furnace, where there will be weeping and gnashing of teeth. 43 Then the righteous
will shine like the sun in the kingdom of their
Father. He who has ears, let him hear.

The Parables of the Hidden Treasure and the Pearl

44 "The kingdom of heaven is like treasure hidden in a field. When a man found it, he hid it
again, and then in his joy went and sold all he had
and bought that field.
45 "Again, the kingdom of heaven is like a merchant looking for fine pearls. 46 When he found
one of great value, he went away and sold everything he had and bought it.

The Parable of the Net

47 "Once again, the kingdom of heaven is like
a net that was let down into the lake and caught
all kinds of fish. 48 When it was full, the fishermen
pulled it up on the shore. Then they sat down and
collected the good fish in baskets, but threw the
bad away. 49 This is how it will be at the end of

[a] *15* Isaiah 6:9,10 [b] *33* Greek *three satas* (probably about 1/2 bushel or 22 liters) [c] *35* Psalm 78:2

the age. The angels will come and separate the wicked from the righteous 50and throw them into the fiery furnace, where there will be weeping and gnashing of teeth.

51"Have you understood all these things?" Jesus asked.

"Yes," they replied.

52He said to them, "Therefore every teacher of the law who has been instructed about the kingdom of heaven is like the owner of a house who brings out of his storeroom new treasures as well as old."

A Prophet Without Honor

53When Jesus had finished these parables, he moved on from there. 54Coming to his hometown, he began teaching the people in their synagogue, and they were amazed. "Where did this man get this wisdom and these miraculous powers?" they asked. 55"Isn't this the carpenter's son? Isn't his mother's name Mary, and aren't his brothers James, Joseph, Simon and Judas? 56Aren't all his sisters with us? Where then did this man get all these things?" 57And they took offense at him.

But Jesus said to them, "Only in his hometown and in his own house is a prophet without honor."

58And he did not do many miracles there because of their lack of faith.

John the Baptist Beheaded

14 At that time Herod the tetrarch heard the reports about Jesus, 2and he said to his attendants, "This is John the Baptist; he has risen from the dead! That is why miraculous powers are at work in him."

3Now Herod had arrested John and bound him and put him in prison because of Herodias, his brother Philip's wife, 4for John had been saying to him: "It is not lawful for you to have her." 5Herod wanted to kill John, but he was afraid of the people, because they considered him a prophet.

6On Herod's birthday the daughter of Herodias danced for them and pleased Herod so much 7that he promised with an oath to give her whatever she asked. 8Prompted by her mother, she said, "Give me here on a platter the head of John the Baptist." 9The king was distressed, but because of his oaths and his dinner guests, he ordered that her request be granted 10and had John beheaded in the prison. 11His head was brought in on a platter and given to the girl, who carried it to her mother. 12John's disciples came and took his body and buried it. Then they went and told Jesus.

Jesus Feeds the Five Thousand

13When Jesus heard what had happened, he withdrew by boat privately to a solitary place. Hearing of this, the crowds followed him on foot from the towns. 14When Jesus landed and saw a large crowd, he had compassion on them and healed their sick.

15As evening approached, the disciples came to him and said, "This is a remote place, and it's already getting late. Send the crowds away, so they can go to the villages and buy themselves some food."

16Jesus replied, "They do not need to go away. You give them something to eat."

17"We have here only five loaves of bread and two fish," they answered.

18"Bring them here to me," he said. 19And he directed the people to sit down on the grass. Taking the five loaves and the two fish and looking up to heaven, he gave thanks and broke the loaves. Then he gave them to the disciples, and the disciples gave them to the people. 20They all ate and were satisfied, and the disciples picked up twelve basketfuls of broken pieces that were left over. 21The number of those who ate was about five thousand men, besides women and children.

Jesus Walks on the Water

22Immediately Jesus made the disciples get

14:25 ***the fourth watch.*** This was the way Roman soldiers marked time. The fourth watch ran from 3:00 to 6:00 a.m. Assuming the disciples set out to sea in the late afternoon, they probably had been struggling at the oars for several hours. ***walking on the lake.*** While it has already been established that Jesus is Lord over the wind and the water (Mark 4:39,41), this is another new action that was well beyond the expectation of the disciples. As miraculous as Jesus walking on water was, his extending this ability to Peter is even more amazing.

14:26 ***a ghost.*** The sea, especially at night, was thought to be a dwelling place for demons. The disciples watched in horror as this figure approached.

14:28 ***if it's you.*** "If" should be understood as "since." Because Peter is sure it is Jesus on the water, he asks permission to join him. He realizes he can only do so on the basis of Jesus' word and authority. Peter's action demonstrates what faith is all about: It is acting with confidence in Jesus even when circumstances seem impossible.

14:30–31 At first it appears Peter was successful in this incredible act. However, the frightening uncertainty of the situation coupled with the power of the wind and waves beating against him led him to doubt Jesus' word; thus, he faltered. ***Lord, save me!*** Peter's cry sums up the cry of all those who find themselves in desperate situations. His hope is solely in Jesus to rescue him from the danger of the sea. ***You of little faith.*** The problem Peter faced was not the circumstances, but inadequate trust in Jesus despite the circumstances.

into the boat and go on ahead of him to the other side, while he dismissed the crowd. 23After he had dismissed them, he went up on a mountainside by himself to pray. When evening came, he was there alone, 24but the boat was already a considerable distance[a] from land, buffeted by the waves because the wind was against it.

25During the fourth watch of the night Jesus went out to them, walking on the lake. 26When the disciples saw him walking on the lake, they were terrified. "It's a ghost," they said, and cried out in fear.

27But Jesus immediately said to them: "Take courage! It is I. Don't be afraid."

28"Lord, if it's you," Peter replied, "tell me to come to you on the water."

29"Come," he said.

Then Peter got down out of the boat, walked on the water and came toward Jesus. 30But when he saw the wind, he was afraid and, beginning to sink, cried out, "Lord, save me!"

31Immediately Jesus reached out his hand and caught him. "You of little faith," he said, "why did you doubt?"

32And when they climbed into the boat, the wind died down. 33Then those who were in the boat worshiped him, saying, "Truly you are the Son of God."

MATTHEW 14:22–33

1. What is something you are afraid of?
2. What is the most daring thing you have ever done?
3. What concerns you most about the future?
4. What made Peter sink: Wind and waves? Waterlogged sandals? Lost confidence? Fear? Lack of faith?
5. What are you facing in your life that you need Jesus to say, "Don't be afraid"?
6. Spiritually, where is God leading you to "step out of the boat and walk on the water"?
7. How can your group help you and support you in prayer as you "step out"?

(Study notes on page 867)

34When they had crossed over, they landed at Gennesaret. 35And when the men of that place recognized Jesus, they sent word to all the surrounding country. People brought all their sick to him 36and begged him to let the sick just touch the edge of his cloak, and all who touched him were healed.

Clean and Unclean

15 Then some Pharisees and teachers of the law came to Jesus from Jerusalem and asked, 2"Why do your disciples break the tradition of the elders? They don't wash their hands before they eat!"

3Jesus replied, "And why do you break the command of God for the sake of your tradition? 4For God said, 'Honor your father and mother'[b] and 'Anyone who curses his father or mother must be put to death.'[c] 5But you say that if a man says to his father or mother, 'Whatever help you might otherwise have received from me is a gift devoted to God,' 6he is not to 'honor his father[d]' with it. Thus you nullify the word of God for the sake of your tradition. 7You hypocrites! Isaiah was right when he prophesied about you:

8" 'These people honor me with their lips,
but their hearts are far from me.
9They worship me in vain;
their teachings are but rules taught by men.'[e]"

10Jesus called the crowd to him and said, "Listen and understand. 11What goes into a man's mouth does not make him 'unclean,' but what comes out of his mouth, that is what makes him 'unclean.' "

12Then the disciples came to him and asked, "Do you know that the Pharisees were offended when they heard this?"

13He replied, "Every plant that my heavenly Father has not planted will be pulled up by the roots. 14Leave them; they are blind guides.[f] If a blind man leads a blind man, both will fall into a pit."

15Peter said, "Explain the parable to us."

16"Are you still so dull?" Jesus asked them. 17"Don't you see that whatever enters the mouth goes into the stomach and then out of the body? 18But the things that come out of the mouth come from the heart, and these make a man 'unclean.' 19For out of the heart come evil thoughts, murder, adultery, sexual immorality, theft, false testimony, slander. 20These are what make a man 'unclean'; but eating with unwashed hands does not make him 'unclean.' "

[a]24 Greek *many stadia* [b]4 Exodus 20:12; Deut. 5:16 [c]4 Exodus 21:17; Lev. 20:9 [d]6 Some manuscripts *father or his mother* [e]9 Isaiah 29:13 [f]14 Some manuscripts *guides of the blind*

The Faith of the Canaanite Woman

21 Leaving that place, Jesus withdrew to the
region of Tyre and Sidon. 22 A Canaanite woman
from that vicinity came to him, crying out, "Lord,
Son of David, have mercy on me! My daughter is
suffering terribly from demon-possession."
23 Jesus did not answer a word. So his disciples
came to him and urged him, "Send her away, for
she keeps crying out after us."
24 He answered, "I was sent only to the lost
sheep of Israel."
25 The woman came and knelt before him.
"Lord, help me!" she said.
26 He replied, "It is not right to take the children's bread and toss it to their dogs."
27 "Yes, Lord," she said, "but even the dogs
eat the crumbs that fall from their masters'
table."
28 Then Jesus answered, "Woman, you have
great faith! Your request is granted." And her
daughter was healed from that very hour.

Jesus Feeds the Four Thousand

29 Jesus left there and went along the Sea of
Galilee. Then he went up on a mountainside and
sat down. 30 Great crowds came to him, bringing
the lame, the blind, the crippled, the mute and
many others, and laid them at his feet; and he
healed them. 31 The people were amazed when
they saw the mute speaking, the crippled made
well, the lame walking and the blind seeing. And
they praised the God of Israel.
32 Jesus called his disciples to him and said, "I
have compassion for these people; they have already been with me three days and have nothing
to eat. I do not want to send them away hungry,
or they may collapse on the way."
33 His disciples answered, "Where could we
get enough bread in this remote place to feed
such a crowd?"
34 "How many loaves do you have?" Jesus
asked.
"Seven," they replied, "and a few small
fish."
35 He told the crowd to sit down on the ground.
36 Then he took the seven loaves and the fish, and
when he had given thanks, he broke them and
gave them to the disciples, and they in turn to the
people. 37 They all ate and were satisfied. Afterward the disciples picked up seven basketfuls of
broken pieces that were left over. 38 The number
of those who ate was four thousand, besides
women and children. 39 After Jesus had sent the
crowd away, he got into the boat and went to the
vicinity of Magadan.

The Demand for a Sign

16 The Pharisees and Sadducees came to
Jesus and tested him by asking him to
show them a sign from heaven.
2 He replied,[a] "When evening comes, you
say, 'It will be fair weather, for the sky is red,'
3 and in the morning, 'Today it will be stormy, for
the sky is red and overcast.' You know how to
interpret the appearance of the sky, but you cannot interpret the signs of the times. 4 A wicked
and adulterous generation looks for a miraculous
sign, but none will be given it except the sign of
Jonah." Jesus then left them and went away.

The Yeast of the Pharisees and Sadducees

5 When they went across the lake, the disciples
forgot to take bread. 6 "Be careful," Jesus said to
them. "Be on your guard against the yeast of the
Pharisees and Sadducees."
7 They discussed this among themselves and
said, "It is because we didn't bring any bread."
8 Aware of their discussion, Jesus asked, "You
of little faith, why are you talking among yourselves about having no bread? 9 Do you still not
understand? Don't you remember the five loaves
for the five thousand, and how many basketfuls
you gathered? 10 Or the seven loaves for the four
thousand, and how many basketfuls you gathered? 11 How is it you don't understand that I was
not talking to you about bread? But be on your
guard against the yeast of the Pharisees and Sadducees." 12 Then they understood that he was not
telling them to guard against the yeast used in
bread, but against the teaching of the Pharisees
and Sadducees.

Peter's Confession of Christ

13 When Jesus came to the region of Caesarea
Philippi, he asked his disciples, "Who do people
say the Son of Man is?"
14 They replied, "Some say John the Baptist;
others say Elijah; and still others, Jeremiah or one
of the prophets."
15 "But what about you?" he asked. "Who do
you say I am?"
16 Simon Peter answered, "You are the
Christ,[b] the Son of the living God."
17 Jesus replied, "Blessed are you, Simon son of
Jonah, for this was not revealed to you by man,
but by my Father in heaven. 18 And I tell you that
you are Peter,[c] and on this rock I will build my
church, and the gates of Hades[d] will not overcome it.[e] 19 I will give you the keys of the kingdom of heaven; whatever you bind on earth will
be[f] bound in heaven, and whatever you loose
on earth will be[f] loosed in heaven." 20 Then he

a2 Some early manuscripts do not have the rest of verse 2 and all of verse 3. b16 Or *Messiah*; also in verse 20 c18 *Peter* means *rock*. d18 Or *hell* e18 Or *not prove stronger than it* f19 Or *have been*

warned his disciples not to tell anyone that he
was the Christ.

Jesus Predicts His Death

21 From that time on Jesus began to explain to
his disciples that he must go to Jerusalem and
suffer many things at the hands of the elders,
chief priests and teachers of the law, and that he
must be killed and on the third day be raised to
life.

MATTHEW 16:13–28

1. What's your favorite TV game show or question-and-answer game?
2. If your best friends were asked what one word best describes you, what would they say?
3. If you asked the average person in your school, "Who is Jesus?" what would they say?
4. Who do you say Jesus is?
5. Who does Jesus himself "say" that he is (see v. 20)?
6. When you hear Jesus' words, "Deny yourself, take up your cross and follow me," what runs through your mind?
7. Quite frankly, what's it going to take to help you get serious about your faith? Pray together.

22 Peter took him aside and began to rebuke
him. "Never, Lord!" he said. "This shall never
happen to you!"
23 Jesus turned and said to Peter, "Get behind
me, Satan! You are a stumbling block to me; you
do not have in mind the things of God, but the
things of men."
24 Then Jesus said to his disciples, "If anyone
would come after me, he must deny himself and
take up his cross and follow me. 25 For whoever
wants to save his life[a] will lose it, but whoever
loses his life for me will find it. 26 What good will
it be for a man if he gains the whole world, yet
forfeits his soul? Or what can a man give in
exchange for his soul? 27 For the Son of Man is going to come in his Father's glory with his angels,
and then he will reward each person according
to what he has done. 28 I tell you the truth,
some who are standing here will not taste death
before they see the Son of Man coming in his
kingdom."

The Transfiguration

17 After six days Jesus took with him Peter,
James and John the brother of James, and
led them up a high mountain by themselves.
2 There he was transfigured before them. His
face shone like the sun, and his clothes became
as white as the light. 3 Just then there appeared
before them Moses and Elijah, talking with
Jesus.
4 Peter said to Jesus, "Lord, it is good for us
to be here. If you wish, I will put up three
shelters—one for you, one for Moses and one for
Elijah."
5 While he was still speaking, a bright cloud
enveloped them, and a voice from the cloud said,
"This is my Son, whom I love; with him I am well
pleased. Listen to him!"
6 When the disciples heard this, they fell facedown to the ground, terrified. 7 But Jesus came
and touched them. "Get up," he said. "Don't be
afraid." 8 When they looked up, they saw no one
except Jesus.
9 As they were coming down the mountain,
Jesus instructed them, "Don't tell anyone what
you have seen, until the Son of Man has been
raised from the dead."
10 The disciples asked him, "Why then do the

a25 The Greek word means either *life* or *soul*; also in verse 26.

16:13 *Son of Man.* This was the title Jesus most often used for himself. Though Daniel 7:13–14 used it as a description of the ruler God had appointed to receive all "authority, glory and sovereign power," it was not a common title for the Messiah at the time.

16:14–16 As opposed to the popular belief that just prior to the coming of the Messiah God would raise up Israel's famous prophets to prepare the way, Peter correctly identifies Jesus not as the forerunner but as the Christ (Greek for "Messiah") himself.

16:18–19 Peter (a nickname meaning "rock"), by way of his confession, becomes the foundation upon which the new people of God will be built. ***bind / loose.*** Not authority to determine, but to announce, guilt or innocence (see 18:18; Acts 5:9).

16:21–28 Jesus' teaching about his suffering, death and resurrection is the reversal of the popular conception of the Messiah as a military hero who would lead a literal army against the Romans. It is through his death that the disciples will discover both what kind of Messiah he actually is and the pattern of discipleship they are to pursue.

16:23 Get behind me, Satan! By urging Jesus to back away from his teaching about suffering, Peter, like Satan, is tempting Jesus with the promise that he can have the whole world without pain (4:8–10).

16:28 Jesus announces that a momentous event demonstrating that God's kingdom has indeed come will soon take place. Six days later (17:1) the Transfiguration occurs.

teachers of the law say that Elijah must come first?"

[11]Jesus replied, "To be sure, Elijah comes and will restore all things. [12]But I tell you, Elijah has already come, and they did not recognize him, but have done to him everything they wished. In the same way the Son of Man is going to suffer at their hands." [13]Then the disciples understood that he was talking to them about John the Baptist.

The Healing of a Boy With a Demon

[14]When they came to the crowd, a man approached Jesus and knelt before him. [15]"Lord, have mercy on my son," he said. "He has seizures and is suffering greatly. He often falls into the fire or into the water. [16]I brought him to your disciples, but they could not heal him."

[17]"O unbelieving and perverse generation," Jesus replied, "how long shall I stay with you? How long shall I put up with you? Bring the boy here to me." [18]Jesus rebuked the demon, and it came out of the boy, and he was healed from that moment.

[19]Then the disciples came to Jesus in private and asked, "Why couldn't we drive it out?"

[20]He replied, "Because you have so little faith. I tell you the truth, if you have faith as small as a mustard seed, you can say to this mountain, 'Move from here to there' and it will move. Nothing will be impossible for you.[a]"

[22]When they came together in Galilee, he said to them, "The Son of Man is going to be betrayed into the hands of men. [23]They will kill him, and on the third day he will be raised to life." And the disciples were filled with grief.

The Temple Tax

[24]After Jesus and his disciples arrived in Capernaum, the collectors of the two-drachma tax came to Peter and asked, "Doesn't your teacher pay the temple tax[b]?"

[25]"Yes, he does," he replied.

When Peter came into the house, Jesus was the first to speak. "What do you think, Simon?" he asked. "From whom do the kings of the earth collect duty and taxes—from their own sons or from others?"

[26]"From others," Peter answered.

"Then the sons are exempt," Jesus said to him. [27]"But so that we may not offend them, go to the lake and throw out your line. Take the first fish you catch; open its mouth and you will find a four-drachma coin. Take it and give it to them for my tax and yours."

The Greatest in the Kingdom of Heaven

18 At that time the disciples came to Jesus and asked, "Who is the greatest in the kingdom of heaven?"

[2]He called a little child and had him stand among them. [3]And he said: "I tell you the truth, unless you change and become like little children, you will never enter the kingdom of heaven. [4]Therefore, whoever humbles himself like this child is the greatest in the kingdom of heaven.

[5]"And whoever welcomes a little child like this in my name welcomes me. [6]But if anyone causes one of these little ones who believe in me to sin, it would be better for him to have a large millstone hung around his neck and to be drowned in the depths of the sea.

[7]"Woe to the world because of the things that cause people to sin! Such things must come, but woe to the man through whom they come! [8]If your hand or your foot causes you to sin, cut it off and throw it away. It is better for you to enter life maimed or crippled than to have two hands or two feet and be thrown into eternal fire. [9]And if your eye causes you to sin, gouge it out and throw it away. It is better for you to enter life with one eye than to have two eyes and be thrown into the fire of hell.

The Parable of the Lost Sheep

[10]"See that you do not look down on one of these little ones. For I tell you that their angels in heaven always see the face of my Father in heaven.[c]

[12]"What do you think? If a man owns a hundred sheep, and one of them wanders away, will he not leave the ninety-nine on the hills and go to look for the one that wandered off? [13]And if he finds it, I tell you the truth, he is happier about that one sheep than about the ninety-nine that did not wander off. [14]In the same way your Father in heaven is not willing that any of these little ones should be lost.

A Brother Who Sins Against You

[15]"If your brother sins against you,[d] go and show him his fault, just between the two of you. If he listens to you, you have won your brother over. [16]But if he will not listen, take one or two others along, so that 'every matter may be established by the testimony of two or three witnesses.'[e] [17]If he refuses to listen to them, tell it to the church; and if he refuses to listen even to the church, treat him as you would a pagan or a tax collector.

[a] *20* Some manuscripts *you.* *21But this kind does not go out except by prayer and fasting.*
[b] *24* Greek *the two drachmas*
[c] *10* Some manuscripts *heaven.* *11The Son of Man came to save what was lost.*
[d] *15* Some manuscripts do not have *against you.*
[e] *16* Deut. 19:15

18“I tell you the truth, whatever you bind on
earth will be[a] bound in heaven, and whatever
you loose on earth will be[a] loosed in heaven.
19“Again, I tell you that if two of you on earth
agree about anything you ask for, it will be done
for you by my Father in heaven. 20For where two
or three come together in my name, there am I
with them.”

The Parable of the Unmerciful Servant

21Then Peter came to Jesus and asked, “Lord,
how many times shall I forgive my brother when
he sins against me? Up to seven times?”
22Jesus answered, “I tell you, not seven times,
but seventy-seven times.[b]
23“Therefore, the kingdom of heaven is like a
king who wanted to settle accounts with his servants. 24As he began the settlement, a man who
owed him ten thousand talents[c] was brought to
him. 25Since he was not able to pay, the master
ordered that he and his wife and his children and
all that he had be sold to repay the debt.
26“The servant fell on his knees before him.
‘Be patient with me,’ he begged, ‘and I will pay
back everything.’ 27The servant’s master took
pity on him, canceled the debt and let him go.
28“But when that servant went out, he found
one of his fellow servants who owed him a hundred denarii.[d] He grabbed him and began to
choke him. ‘Pay back what you owe me!’ he demanded.
29“His fellow servant fell to his knees and
begged him, ‘Be patient with me, and I will pay
you back.’
30“But he refused. Instead, he went off and
had the man thrown into prison until he could
pay the debt. 31When the other servants saw
what had happened, they were greatly distressed
and went and told their master everything that
had happened.
32“Then the master called the servant in. ‘You
wicked servant,’ he said, ‘I canceled all that debt
of yours because you begged me to. 33Shouldn’t
you have had mercy on your fellow servant just as
I had on you?’ 34In anger his master turned him
over to the jailers to be tortured, until he should
pay back all he owed.
35“This is how my heavenly Father will treat
each of you unless you forgive your brother from
your heart.”

MATTHEW 18:21–35

1. To whom do you have to say, “I’m sorry” the most: Parents? Siblings? Teachers? Friends?
2. Are you quick or slow to forgive? When you forgive, do you also forget?
3. Are you more like the master who forgave (v. 27) or the servant who wouldn’t forgive (v. 30)?
4. What does Jesus have to say about forgiveness (see vv. 21–22 and Matt. 6: 14–15)?
5. When it comes to forgiveness, who is the hardest person in your family for you to forgive?
6. Is there someone you need to forgive? What’s keeping you from forgiving them?
7. Pray, thanking God for his forgiveness and for a forgiving spirit towards others.

Divorce

19 When Jesus had finished saying these
things, he left Galilee and went into the
region of Judea to the other side of the Jordan.
2Large crowds followed him, and he healed them
there.
3Some Pharisees came to him to test him.

[a] *18* Or *have been* [b] *22* Or *seventy times seven* [c] *24* That is, millions of dollars [d] *28* That is, a few dollars

---

18:21–22 *seven times.* The rabbis taught that a person ought to be forgiven for a particular offense up to three times. Peter was willing to double the traditional amount plus add one more time for good measure! ***seventy-seven times.*** This could also be understood as seventy times seven. Either way, by taking what Peter thought was a generous offer and multiplying it, Jesus explodes any notion of a limit to forgiveness.

18:23–24 *settle accounts*. Kings would entrust the daily affairs of their kingdom to the management of servants (who were responsible for pursuing the king’s best interest). It was time for an audit. ***ten thousand talents.*** An impossibly high amount, as if a person today was found to be millions (or even billions) of dollars in debt.

18:26–28 I will pay back everything. While it may reflect his sincere desire to save himself and his family, this was an impossible promise. Verse 27 reflects the heart not only of the king, but of God (see Rom. 6:23). ***a hundred denarii.*** Since a denarii was a day’s wage for a laborer, this is a reasonably large amount—though nothing in comparison to the first servant’s debt.

18:33–35 Shouldn’t you have had mercy ... just as I had on you? This is the point of the parable. As recipients of mercy from God, Christ’s disciples are obligated to forgive others continually. In verse 35, the parable is applied to the listeners: As in Matthew 6:14–15, God’s forgiveness of us is to shape the way we forgive others. If it does not, we remain under judgment.

They asked, “Is it lawful for a man to divorce his wife for any and every reason?”

4“Haven't you read,” he replied, “that at the beginning the Creator ‘made them male and female,’[a] 5and said, ‘For this reason a man will leave his father and mother and be united to his wife, and the two will become one flesh’[b]? 6So they are no longer two, but one. Therefore what God has joined together, let man not separate.”

7“Why then,” they asked, “did Moses command that a man give his wife a certificate of divorce and send her away?”

8Jesus replied, “Moses permitted you to divorce your wives because your hearts were hard. But it was not this way from the beginning. 9I tell you that anyone who divorces his wife, except for marital unfaithfulness, and marries another woman commits adultery.”

10The disciples said to him, “If this is the situation between a husband and wife, it is better not to marry.”

11Jesus replied, “Not everyone can accept this word, but only those to whom it has been given. 12For some are eunuchs because they were born that way; others were made that way by men; and others have renounced marriage[c] because of the kingdom of heaven. The one who can accept this should accept it.”

MATTHEW 19:1–12

1. When have you really missed someone? Why were you separated?
2. What married couple do you admire and respect? What qualities in that couple would you like to have in your own marriage some day?
3. How has your life been affected by divorce?
4. What do you think is the main cause of divorce?
5. What do you think Jesus would say is necessary for a couple to have a fulfilling, solid marriage?
6. If your friend was caught in the middle of a divorce of their parents, what advice would you give this person?
7. What can you do now to prepare yourself for a lifelong marriage commitment?
8. How can this group pray for you this week?

The Little Children and Jesus

13Then little children were brought to Jesus for him to place his hands on them and pray for them. But the disciples rebuked those who brought them.

14Jesus said, “Let the little children come to me, and do not hinder them, for the kingdom of heaven belongs to such as these.” 15When he had placed his hands on them, he went on from there.

The Rich Young Man

16Now a man came up to Jesus and asked, “Teacher, what good thing must I do to get eternal life?”

17“Why do you ask me about what is good?” Jesus replied. “There is only One who is good. If you want to enter life, obey the commandments.”

18“Which ones?” the man inquired.

Jesus replied, “ ‘Do not murder, do not commit adultery, do not steal, do not give false testimony, 19honor your father and mother,’[d] and ‘love your neighbor as yourself.’[e]”

[a] *4* Gen. 1:27 [b] *5* Gen. 2:24 [c] *12* Or *have made themselves eunuchs* [d] *19* Exodus 20:12-16; Deut. 5:16-20
[e] *19* Lev. 19:18

19:3 ***test him.*** Since the issue of Herod's divorce and remarriage led to John the Baptist's death (see 14:1–12), it is not by chance that the Pharisees question Jesus about divorce. If he responded affirmatively to this question, it would set him in opposition to John whom the crowds held in high esteem. If he answered negatively, it would set him on a collision course with Herod. Either way, the Pharisees were sure that by posing this question to Jesus they could discredit him.

19:4–6 Rather than being drawn into the argument on the Pharisees' terms, Jesus attacks the way they had twisted Deuteronomy 24:1–4 to justify a casual attitude toward divorce. Jesus quotes from Genesis 1 and 2 to make his point that the original intention of God was that marriage be a permanent union whereby through mutual love a man and a woman grow to experience physical and emotional unity.

19:9 By this teaching, Jesus stresses the importance of faithful relationships to men who viewed relationships in general (and marriage in specific) as a matter of personal convenience.

19:10 The disciples' shocked reaction reveals that Jesus' forbidding of divorce and remarriage went far beyond what rabbis typically taught. Rather than embrace the truth that God's desire for people was faithful, loving, sacrificial relationships with one another, they assumed the only way Jesus' command could be obeyed was if people never married at all.

20“All these I have kept,” the young man said.
“What do I still lack?”
21Jesus answered, “If you want to be perfect,
go, sell your possessions and give to the poor, and
you will have treasure in heaven. Then come,
follow me.”
22When the young man heard this, he went
away sad, because he had great wealth.
23Then Jesus said to his disciples, “I tell you
the truth, it is hard for a rich man to enter the
kingdom of heaven. 24Again I tell you, it is easier
for a camel to go through the eye of a needle than
for a rich man to enter the kingdom of God.”
25When the disciples heard this, they were
greatly astonished and asked, “Who then can be
saved?”
26Jesus looked at them and said, “With man
this is impossible, but with God all things are
possible.”
27Peter answered him, “We have left everything to follow you! What then will there be
for us?”
28Jesus said to them, “I tell you the truth, at
the renewal of all things, when the Son of Man
sits on his glorious throne, you who have followed me will also sit on twelve thrones, judging
the twelve tribes of Israel. 29And everyone who
has left houses or brothers or sisters or father or
mother[a] or children or fields for my sake will
receive a hundred times as much and will inherit
eternal life. 30But many who are first will be last,
and many who are last will be first.

The Parable of the Workers in the Vineyard

20 “For the kingdom of heaven is like a landowner who went out early in the morning
to hire men to work in his vineyard. 2He agreed
to pay them a denarius for the day and sent them
into his vineyard.
3“About the third hour he went out and saw
others standing in the marketplace doing nothing. 4He told them, ‘You also go and work in my
vineyard, and I will pay you whatever is right.’
5So they went.
“He went out again about the sixth hour and
the ninth hour and did the same thing. 6About
the eleventh hour he went out and found still
others standing around. He asked them, ‘Why
have you been standing here all day long doing
nothing?’

MATTHEW 20:1–16

1. When you were a child, what chores were you expected to do? Were you paid?
2. Among your friends, who is likely to end up starting their own business?
3. If you have kids, are you going to give them money or make them work for it?
4. If you were hired in this story at 5 p.m., how would you have felt at pay time (vv. 8–9)? If you were hired at 6 a.m., how would you have felt (vv. 10–12)?
5. In choosing a job, do you look first for pay or personal satisfaction?
6. Do you need an “attitude adjustment” towards work?
7. Read Colossians 3:23 and close in prayer.

7“‘Because no one has hired us,’ they answered.
“He said to them, ‘You also go and work in my
vineyard.’
8“When evening came, the owner of the vineyard said to his foreman, ‘Call the workers and
pay them their wages, beginning with the last
ones hired and going on to the first.’
9“The workers who were hired about the eleventh hour came and each received a denarius.
10So when those came who were hired first, they
expected to receive more. But each one of them

[a]*29* Some manuscripts *mother or wife*

20:1–2 Landowners had full-time servants who took care of the daily needs of the estate, but at certain times (such as planting, pruning or harvest) they would hire day laborers to help with work that the regular servants could not do on their own. At these times, men would gather in the village and hope that they might be hired. ***agreed to pay them.*** The implication is that this was a negotiated agreement. ***a denarius.*** The usual wage for a day's work.

20:3–6 ***third hour.*** 9 a.m. ***sixth hour ... ninth hour.*** Noon and 3 p.m. ***eleventh hour.*** This is 5 p.m. The listeners would have been surprised that the landowner was still hiring people this late in the day.

20:9–12 Probably those hired last agreed to the same arrangement with the landowner as those hired at the third hour—to be paid "whatever is right" (v. 4). As they receive a denarius for an hour's work, they would have been joyfully surprised. Quite naturally, the spirits of the others in line would suddenly rise as they would assume their wages would be based on the same generosity. Instead, as the foreman continues to pay each one a denarius, the earlier workers grow angry at the master. What at first seemed like a just and fair wage to which they could agree (v. 2) now appeared to them unjust and insulting. These grumblers likely represent the Jewish religious leaders who resented Jesus' acceptance of the poor and outcast. The parable stresses that a person's status in the kingdom is a matter of God's grace and not a reward for merit or the longevity of one's work for God.

also received a denarius. 11When they received
it, they began to grumble against the landowner.
12'These men who were hired last worked only
one hour,' they said, 'and you have made them
equal to us who have borne the burden of the
work and the heat of the day.'
13"But he answered one of them, 'Friend, I am
not being unfair to you. Didn't you agree to work
for a denarius? 14Take your pay and go. I want to
give the man who was hired last the same as I
gave you. 15Don't I have the right to do what I
want with my own money? Or are you envious
because I am generous?'
16"So the last will be first, and the first will be
last."

Jesus Again Predicts His Death

17Now as Jesus was going up to Jerusalem, he
took the twelve disciples aside and said to them,
18"We are going up to Jerusalem, and the Son of
Man will be betrayed to the chief priests and the
teachers of the law. They will condemn him to
death 19and will turn him over to the Gentiles to
be mocked and flogged and crucified. On the
third day he will be raised to life!"

A Mother's Request

20Then the mother of Zebedee's sons came to
Jesus with her sons and, kneeling down, asked a
favor of him.
21"What is it you want?" he asked.
She said, "Grant that one of these two sons of
mine may sit at your right and the other at your
left in your kingdom."
22"You don't know what you are asking," Jesus
said to them. "Can you drink the cup I am going
to drink?"
"We can," they answered.
23Jesus said to them, "You will indeed drink
from my cup, but to sit at my right or left is not
for me to grant. These places belong to those for
whom they have been prepared by my Father."
24When the ten heard about this, they were
indignant with the two brothers. 25Jesus called
them together and said, "You know that the rulers of the Gentiles lord it over them, and their
high officials exercise authority over them. 26Not
so with you. Instead, whoever wants to become
great among you must be your servant, 27and
whoever wants to be first must be your slave—
28just as the Son of Man did not come to be
served, but to serve, and to give his life as a
ransom for many."

> ***MATTHEW 20:20–28***
>
> 1. Do your parents ever embarrass you? How?
> 2. What do your parents want you to be "when you grow up"?
> 3. How would you describe your parents' expectations of you: Too high? Too low? Just right?
> 4. If you were one of the brothers in this story, how would you have felt about your mother's request?
> 5. On a scale of 0 (I'm not) to 10 (totally), how well are you living up to your parents' expectations?
> 6. Since becoming a Christian, what expectation do you have of yourself? How well are you meeting this?
> 7. In what way does God want you to be more of a servant? How can your group pray for you?

Two Blind Men Receive Sight

29As Jesus and his disciples were leaving Jericho, a large crowd followed him. 30Two blind
men were sitting by the roadside, and when they
heard that Jesus was going by, they shouted,
"Lord, Son of David, have mercy on us!"
31The crowd rebuked them and told them to

20:20 ***Zebedee's sons.*** James and John, two of Jesus' disciples (see Matt. 4:21–22). Mark has James and John asking the question (Mark 10:35–37). But this isn't contradictory; the brothers and their mother joined in making the request.

20:21 ***right ... left.*** In accordance with the general assumption about the Messiah, the disciples expect that Jesus will come into a position of authority as the new king of Israel and that those who sit on his right and his left will be his chief lieutenants.

20:22–23 ***drink the cup I am going to drink.*** To share Jesus' fate of suffering. ***We can.*** Despite their bold assertion, they do not grasp what he means by this question. They probably assumed he was referring simply to being willing to share in his future which they imagine would be one of power and prestige. Jesus warns them they will share in his experience, but he will not promise them any special status.

20:24 ***they were indignant.*** As self-serving as the request of James and John and their mother had been, the response of the other disciples was not much better. They shared the hope of reigning with Jesus on earth.

20:26–28 Just as he, the Messiah, came to serve, so too must his disciples. Rather than become masters (and exercise authority) they are to become servants (and meet the needs of others). ***ransom.*** A word used most often for the price paid to redeem a slave. ***for many.*** Christ "gave himself as a ransom for all" (1 Tim. 2:6), but only the "many" receive his offer of salvation.

be quiet, but they shouted all the louder, "Lord,
Son of David, have mercy on us!"
32Jesus stopped and called them. "What do you
want me to do for you?" he asked.
33"Lord," they answered, "we want our
sight."
34Jesus had compassion on them and touched
their eyes. Immediately they received their sight
and followed him.

The Triumphal Entry

21 As they approached Jerusalem and came
to Bethphage on the Mount of Olives,
Jesus sent two disciples, 2saying to them, "Go to
the village ahead of you, and at once you will find
a donkey tied there, with her colt by her. Untie
them and bring them to me. 3If anyone says anything to you, tell him that the Lord needs them,
and he will send them right away."
4This took place to fulfill what was spoken
through the prophet:

5"Say to the Daughter of Zion,
'See, your king comes to you,
gentle and riding on a donkey,
on a colt, the foal of a donkey.' "[a]

6The disciples went and did as Jesus had instructed them. 7They brought the donkey and the
colt, placed their cloaks on them, and Jesus sat on
them. 8A very large crowd spread their cloaks on
the road, while others cut branches from the
trees and spread them on the road. 9The crowds
that went ahead of him and those that followed
shouted,

"Hosanna[b] to the Son of David!"

"Blessed is he who comes in the name of the
Lord!"[c]

"Hosanna[b] in the highest!"

10When Jesus entered Jerusalem, the whole
city was stirred and asked, "Who is this?"
11The crowds answered, "This is Jesus, the
prophet from Nazareth in Galilee."

Jesus at the Temple

12Jesus entered the temple area and drove out
all who were buying and selling there. He overturned the tables of the money changers and the
benches of those selling doves. 13"It is written,"
he said to them, " 'My house will be called a
house of prayer,'[d] but you are making it a 'den
of robbers.'[e] "
14The blind and the lame came to him at the
temple, and he healed them. 15But when the
chief priests and the teachers of the law saw the
wonderful things he did and the children shouting in the temple area, "Hosanna to the Son of
David," they were indignant.
16"Do you hear what these children are saying?" they asked him.
"Yes," replied Jesus, "have you never read,

" 'From the lips of children and infants
you have ordained praise'[f]?"

17And he left them and went out of the city to
Bethany, where he spent the night.

The Fig Tree Withers

18Early in the morning, as he was on his way
back to the city, he was hungry. 19Seeing a fig
tree by the road, he went up to it but found
nothing on it except leaves. Then he said to it,
"May you never bear fruit again!" Immediately
the tree withered.
20When the disciples saw this, they were
amazed. "How did the fig tree wither so quickly?" they asked.
21Jesus replied, "I tell you the truth, if you
have faith and do not doubt, not only can you do
what was done to the fig tree, but also you can
say to this mountain, 'Go, throw yourself into the
sea,' and it will be done. 22If you believe, you will
receive whatever you ask for in prayer."

The Authority of Jesus Questioned

23Jesus entered the temple courts, and, while
he was teaching, the chief priests and the elders
of the people came to him. "By what authority
are you doing these things?" they asked. "And
who gave you this authority?"
24Jesus replied, "I will also ask you one question. If you answer me, I will tell you by what
authority I am doing these things. 25John's
baptism—where did it come from? Was it from
heaven, or from men?"
They discussed it among themselves and said,
"If we say, 'From heaven,' he will ask, 'Then why
didn't you believe him?' 26But if we say, 'From
men'—we are afraid of the people, for they all
hold that John was a prophet."
27So they answered Jesus, "We don't know."
Then he said, "Neither will I tell you by what
authority I am doing these things.

The Parable of the Two Sons

28"What do you think? There was a man who
had two sons. He went to the first and said, 'Son,
go and work today in the vineyard.'
29" 'I will not,' he answered, but later he
changed his mind and went.

[a] 5 Zech. 9:9 [b] 9 A Hebrew expression meaning "Save!" which became an exclamation of praise; also in verse 15
[c] 9 Psalm 118:26 [d] 13 Isaiah 56:7 [e] 13 Jer. 7:11 [f] 16 Psalm 8:2

30“Then the father went to the other son and
said the same thing. He answered, ‘I will, sir,’ but
he did not go.
31“Which of the two did what his father
wanted?”
“The first,” they answered.
Jesus said to them, “I tell you the truth, the tax
collectors and the prostitutes are entering the
kingdom of God ahead of you. 32For John came to
you to show you the way of righteousness, and
you did not believe him, but the tax collectors
and the prostitutes did. And even after you saw
this, you did not repent and believe him.

The Parable of the Tenants

33“Listen to another parable: There was a landowner who planted a vineyard. He put a wall
around it, dug a winepress in it and built a watchtower. Then he rented the vineyard to some
farmers and went away on a journey. 34When the
harvest time approached, he sent his servants to
the tenants to collect his fruit.
35“The tenants seized his servants; they beat
one, killed another, and stoned a third. 36Then he
sent other servants to them, more than the first
time, and the tenants treated them the same way.
37Last of all, he sent his son to them. ‘They will
respect my son,’ he said.
38“But when the tenants saw the son, they
said to each other, ‘This is the heir. Come, let’s
kill him and take his inheritance.’ 39So they took
him and threw him out of the vineyard and killed
him.
40“Therefore, when the owner of the vineyard
comes, what will he do to those tenants?”
41“He will bring those wretches to a wretched
end,” they replied, “and he will rent the vineyard
to other tenants, who will give him his share of
the crop at harvest time.”
42Jesus said to them, “Have you never read in
the Scriptures:

“ ‘The stone the builders rejected
has become the capstone[a];
the Lord has done this,
and it is marvelous in our eyes’[b]?

43“Therefore I tell you that the kingdom of
God will be taken away from you and given to a
people who will produce its fruit. 44He who falls
on this stone will be broken to pieces, but he on
whom it falls will be crushed.”[c]
45When the chief priests and the Pharisees
heard Jesus’ parables, they knew he was talking
about them. 46They looked for a way to arrest
him, but they were afraid of the crowd because
the people held that he was a prophet.

The Parable of the Wedding Banquet

22 Jesus spoke to them again in parables,
saying: 2“The kingdom of heaven is like a
king who prepared a wedding banquet for his
son. 3He sent his servants to those who had been
invited to the banquet to tell them to come, but
they refused to come.
4“Then he sent some more servants and said,
‘Tell those who have been invited that I have
prepared my dinner: My oxen and fattened cattle
have been butchered, and everything is ready.
Come to the wedding banquet.’
5“But they paid no attention and went off—
one to his field, another to his business. 6The rest
seized his servants, mistreated them and killed
them. 7The king was enraged. He sent his army
and destroyed those murderers and burned their
city.
8“Then he said to his servants, ‘The wedding
banquet is ready, but those I invited did not deserve to come. 9Go to the street corners and invite to the banquet anyone you find.’ 10So the
servants went out into the streets and gathered
all the people they could find, both good and bad,
and the wedding hall was filled with guests.
11“But when the king came in to see the
guests, he noticed a man there who was not
wearing wedding clothes. 12‘Friend,’ he asked,
‘how did you get in here without wedding
clothes?’ The man was speechless.
13“Then the king told the attendants, ‘Tie him
hand and foot, and throw him outside, into the
darkness, where there will be weeping and
gnashing of teeth.’
14“For many are invited, but few are chosen.”

Paying Taxes to Caesar

15Then the Pharisees went out and laid plans
to trap him in his words. 16They sent their disciples to him along with the Herodians. “Teacher,”
they said, “we know you are a man of integrity
and that you teach the way of God in accordance
with the truth. You aren’t swayed by men, because you pay no attention to who they are.
17Tell us then, what is your opinion? Is it right to
pay taxes to Caesar or not?”
18But Jesus, knowing their evil intent, said,
“You hypocrites, why are you trying to trap me?
19Show me the coin used for paying the tax.”
They brought him a denarius, 20and he asked
them, “Whose portrait is this? And whose inscription?”
21“Caesar’s,” they replied.
Then he said to them, “Give to Caesar what is
Caesar’s, and to God what is God’s.”

[a] 42 Or *cornerstone* [b] 42 Psalm 118:22,23 [c] 44 Some manuscripts do not have verse 44.

22 When they heard this, they were amazed. So they left him and went away.

Marriage at the Resurrection

23 That same day the Sadducees, who say there is no resurrection, came to him with a question. 24 "Teacher," they said, "Moses told us that if a man dies without having children, his brother must marry the widow and have children for him. 25 Now there were seven brothers among us. The first one married and died, and since he had no children, he left his wife to his brother. 26 The same thing happened to the second and third brother, right on down to the seventh. 27 Finally, the woman died. 28 Now then, at the resurrection, whose wife will she be of the seven, since all of them were married to her?"

29 Jesus replied, "You are in error because you do not know the Scriptures or the power of God. 30 At the resurrection people will neither marry nor be given in marriage; they will be like the angels in heaven. 31 But about the resurrection of the dead—have you not read what God said to you, 32 'I am the God of Abraham, the God of Isaac, and the God of Jacob'[a]? He is not the God of the dead but of the living."

33 When the crowds heard this, they were astonished at his teaching.

The Greatest Commandment

34 Hearing that Jesus had silenced the Sadducees, the Pharisees got together. 35 One of them, an expert in the law, tested him with this question: 36 "Teacher, which is the greatest commandment in the Law?"

37 Jesus replied: " 'Love the Lord your God with all your heart and with all your soul and with all your mind.'[b] 38 This is the first and greatest commandment. 39 And the second is like it: 'Love your neighbor as yourself.'[c] 40 All the Law and the Prophets hang on these two commandments."

Whose Son Is the Christ?

41 While the Pharisees were gathered together, Jesus asked them, 42 "What do you think about the Christ[d]? Whose son is he?"

"The son of David," they replied.

43 He said to them, "How is it then that David, speaking by the Spirit, calls him 'Lord'? For he says,

44 " 'The Lord said to my Lord:
"Sit at my right hand
until I put your enemies
under your feet." '[e]

45 If then David calls him 'Lord,' how can he be his son?" 46 No one could say a word in reply, and from that day on no one dared to ask him any more questions.

Seven Woes

23 Then Jesus said to the crowds and to his disciples: 2 "The teachers of the law and the Pharisees sit in Moses' seat. 3 So you must obey them and do everything they tell you. But do not do what they do, for they do not practice what they preach. 4 They tie up heavy loads and put them on men's shoulders, but they themselves are not willing to lift a finger to move them.

5 "Everything they do is done for men to see: They make their phylacteries[f] wide and the tassels on their garments long; 6 they love the place of honor at banquets and the most important seats in the synagogues; 7 they love to be greeted in the marketplaces and to have men call them 'Rabbi.'

8 "But you are not to be called 'Rabbi,' for you have only one Master and you are all brothers. 9 And do not call anyone on earth 'father,' for you have one Father, and he is in heaven. 10 Nor are you to be called 'teacher,' for you have one Teacher, the Christ.[d] 11 The greatest among you will be your servant. 12 For whoever exalts himself will be humbled, and whoever humbles himself will be exalted.

13 "Woe to you, teachers of the law and Pharisees, you hypocrites! You shut the kingdom of heaven in men's faces. You yourselves do not enter, nor will you let those enter who are trying to.[g]

15 "Woe to you, teachers of the law and Pharisees, you hypocrites! You travel over land and sea to win a single convert, and when he becomes one, you make him twice as much a son of hell as you are.

16 "Woe to you, blind guides! You say, 'If anyone swears by the temple, it means nothing; but if anyone swears by the gold of the temple, he is bound by his oath.' 17 You blind fools! Which is greater: the gold, or the temple that makes the gold sacred? 18 You also say, 'If anyone swears by the altar, it means nothing; but if anyone swears by the gift on it, he is bound by his oath.' 19 You blind men! Which is greater: the gift, or the altar that makes the gift sacred? 20 Therefore, he who swears by the altar swears by it and by everything

[a] 32 Exodus 3:6 [b] 37 Deut. 6:5 [c] 39 Lev. 19:18 [d] 42,10 Or *Messiah* [e] 44 Psalm 110:1 [f] 5 That is, boxes containing Scripture verses, worn on forehead and arm [g] 13 Some manuscripts *to.* 14 *Woe to you, teachers of the law and Pharisees, you hypocrites! You devour widows' houses and for a show make lengthy prayers. Therefore you will be punished more severely.*

on it. 21And he who swears by the temple swears
by it and by the one who dwells in it. 22And he
who swears by heaven swears by God's throne
and by the one who sits on it.
23"Woe to you, teachers of the law and Pharisees, you hypocrites! You give a tenth of your
spices—mint, dill and cummin. But you have neglected the more important matters of the law—
justice, mercy and faithfulness. You should have
practiced the latter, without neglecting the former. 24You blind guides! You strain out a gnat but
swallow a camel.
25"Woe to you, teachers of the law and Pharisees, you hypocrites! You clean the outside of the
cup and dish, but inside they are full of greed and
self-indulgence. 26Blind Pharisee! First clean the
inside of the cup and dish, and then the outside
also will be clean.
27"Woe to you, teachers of the law and Pharisees, you hypocrites! You are like whitewashed
tombs, which look beautiful on the outside but
on the inside are full of dead men's bones and
everything unclean. 28In the same way, on the
outside you appear to people as righteous but on
the inside you are full of hypocrisy and wickedness.
29"Woe to you, teachers of the law and Pharisees, you hypocrites! You build tombs for the
prophets and decorate the graves of the righteous. 30And you say, 'If we had lived in the days
of our forefathers, we would not have taken part
with them in shedding the blood of the prophets.' 31So you testify against yourselves that you
are the descendants of those who murdered the
prophets. 32Fill up, then, the measure of the sin
of your forefathers!
33"You snakes! You brood of vipers! How will
you escape being condemned to hell? 34Therefore
I am sending you prophets and wise men and
teachers. Some of them you will kill and crucify;
others you will flog in your synagogues and pursue from town to town. 35And so upon you will
come all the righteous blood that has been shed
on earth, from the blood of righteous Abel to the
blood of Zechariah son of Berekiah, whom you
murdered between the temple and the altar. 36I
tell you the truth, all this will come upon this
generation.
37"O Jerusalem, Jerusalem, you who kill the
prophets and stone those sent to you, how often
I have longed to gather your children together, as
a hen gathers her chicks under her wings, but
you were not willing. 38Look, your house is left to
you desolate. 39For I tell you, you will not see me
again until you say, 'Blessed is he who comes in
the name of the Lord.'[a]"

Signs of the End of the Age

24 Jesus left the temple and was walking
away when his disciples came up to him
to call his attention to its buildings. 2"Do you see
all these things?" he asked. "I tell you the truth,
not one stone here will be left on another; every
one will be thrown down."
3As Jesus was sitting on the Mount of Olives,
the disciples came to him privately. "Tell us,"
they said, "when will this happen, and what will
be the sign of your coming and of the end of the
age?"
4Jesus answered: "Watch out that no one deceives you. 5For many will come in my name,
claiming, 'I am the Christ,[b]' and will deceive
many. 6You will hear of wars and rumors of wars,
but see to it that you are not alarmed. Such things
must happen, but the end is still to come. 7Na-
tion will rise against nation, and kingdom against
kingdom. There will be famines and earthquakes
in various places. 8All these are the beginning of
birth pains.
9"Then you will be handed over to be persecuted and put to death, and you will be hated by
all nations because of me. 10At that time many
will turn away from the faith and will betray and
hate each other, 11and many false prophets will
appear and deceive many people. 12Because of
the increase of wickedness, the love of most will
grow cold, 13but he who stands firm to the end
will be saved. 14And this gospel of the kingdom
will be preached in the whole world as a testimony to all nations, and then the end will come.
15"So when you see standing in the holy place
'the abomination that causes desolation,'[c] spoken of through the prophet Daniel—let the reader understand— 16then let those who are in Judea flee to the mountains. 17Let no one on the
roof of his house go down to take anything out of
the house. 18Let no one in the field go back to get
his cloak. 19How dreadful it will be in those days
for pregnant women and nursing mothers! 20Pray
that your flight will not take place in winter or on
the Sabbath. 21For then there will be great distress, unequaled from the beginning of the world
until now—and never to be equaled again. 22If
those days had not been cut short, no one would
survive, but for the sake of the elect those days
will be shortened. 23At that time if anyone says to
you, 'Look, here is the Christ!' or, 'There he is!'
do not believe it. 24For false Christs and false
prophets will appear and perform great signs and
miracles to deceive even the elect—if that were
possible. 25See, I have told you ahead of time.
26"So if anyone tells you, 'There he is, out in
the desert,' do not go out; or, 'Here he is, in the

[a] *39* Psalm 118:26 [b] *5* Or *Messiah*; also in verse 23 [c] *15* Daniel 9:27; 11:31; 12:11

inner rooms,' do not believe it. 27For as lightning
that comes from the east is visible even in the
west, so will be the coming of the Son of Man.
28Wherever there is a carcass, there the vultures
will gather.
29"Immediately after the distress of those days

"'the sun will be darkened,
and the moon will not give its light;
the stars will fall from the sky,
and the heavenly bodies will be shaken.'[a]

30"At that time the sign of the Son of Man will
appear in the sky, and all the nations of the earth
will mourn. They will see the Son of Man coming
on the clouds of the sky, with power and great
glory. 31And he will send his angels with a loud
trumpet call, and they will gather his elect from
the four winds, from one end of the heavens to
the other.
32"Now learn this lesson from the fig tree: As
soon as its twigs get tender and its leaves come
out, you know that summer is near. 33Even so,
when you see all these things, you know that it[b]
is near, right at the door. 34I tell you the truth,
this generation[c] will certainly not pass away until all these things have happened. 35Heaven and
earth will pass away, but my words will never
pass away.

The Day and Hour Unknown

36"No one knows about that day or hour, not
even the angels in heaven, nor the Son,[d] but
only the Father. 37As it was in the days of Noah,
so it will be at the coming of the Son of Man.
38For in the days before the flood, people were
eating and drinking, marrying and giving in marriage, up to the day Noah entered the ark; 39and
they knew nothing about what would happen until the flood came and took them all away. That is
how it will be at the coming of the Son of Man.
40Two men will be in the field; one will be taken
and the other left. 41Two women will be grinding
with a hand mill; one will be taken and the other
left.
42"Therefore keep watch, because you do not
know on what day your Lord will come. 43But
understand this: If the owner of the house had
known at what time of night the thief was coming, he would have kept watch and would not
have let his house be broken into. 44So you also
must be ready, because the Son of Man will come
at an hour when you do not expect him.
45"Who then is the faithful and wise servant,
whom the master has put in charge of the servants in his household to give them their food at
the proper time? 46It will be good for that servant
whose master finds him doing so when he returns. 47I tell you the truth, he will put him in
charge of all his possessions. 48But suppose that
servant is wicked and says to himself, 'My master
is staying away a long time,' 49and he then begins
to beat his fellow servants and to eat and drink
with drunkards. 50The master of that servant will
come on a day when he does not expect him and
at an hour he is not aware of. 51He will cut him
to pieces and assign him a place with the hypocrites, where there will be weeping and gnashing
of teeth.

The Parable of the Ten Virgins

25 "At that time the kingdom of heaven will
be like ten virgins who took their lamps
and went out to meet the bridegroom. 2Five of
them were foolish and five were wise. 3The foolish ones took their lamps but did not take any oil
with them. 4The wise, however, took oil in jars
along with their lamps. 5The bridegroom was a
long time in coming, and they all became drowsy
and fell asleep.
6"At midnight the cry rang out: 'Here's the
bridegroom! Come out to meet him!'
7"Then all the virgins woke up and trimmed
their lamps. 8The foolish ones said to the wise,
'Give us some of your oil; our lamps are going
out.'
9"'No,' they replied, 'there may not be enough
for both us and you. Instead, go to those who sell
oil and buy some for yourselves.'
10"But while they were on their way to buy
the oil, the bridegroom arrived. The virgins who

[a]*29* Isaiah 13:10; 34:4 [b]*33* Or *he* [c]*34* Or *race* [d]*36* Some manuscripts do not have *nor the Son.*

25:1 ***ten virgins.*** Probably bridesmaids, who were responsible for preparing the bride to meet the bridegroom. ***lamps.*** Weddings typically occurred at night (though the exact time was kept a secret), so lamps would illuminate the bridal procession and add to the celebrative nature of the event. Lamps were likely torches made of rags wrapped around the end of a pole and soaked in oil. Such torches would burn for about 15 minutes before needing to be dipped in oil again. ***meet the bridegroom.*** Weddings usually took place in the house of the groom or his parents. Before the ceremony the groom would go to the bride's home and lead her, along with the villagers, in a procession to the wedding.

25:9 The wise women's refusal to share was not selfish, but simply prudent. They carried only enough for themselves. To share meant everyone would not have sufficient fuel. Likewise, each person needs his or her own relationship with the Lord; such a relationship cannot be obtained by simply being around people who know Christ.

25:10 ***the door was shut.*** The parable moves from a typical wedding to the messianic banquet, as latecomers would not be excluded from a regular wedding party. Emphasizing the urgency of one's response to the Lord, there is a limited time when the "day of salvation" is extended to people.

25:13 A steady theme in the NT teachings about Christ's return. "Watching" is not simply being awake at the time Christ returns, nor is it speculation about the time of his return. It is preparation in the present.

were ready went in with him to the wedding
banquet. And the door was shut.
11 "Later the others also came. 'Sir! Sir!' they
said. 'Open the door for us!'
12 "But he replied, 'I tell you the truth, I don't
know you.'
13 "Therefore keep watch, because you do not
know the day or the hour.

Matthew 25:1–13

1. Are you usually early, late or right on time? What about for this meeting?
2. What happened the last time your electricity went off? How prepared were you?
3. What would you call the refusal of the five girls in this parable to share their oil: Wise? Selfish? Fair? Unfair?
4. Have you tried to live off the "oil" of someone else's faith? If so, whose: Your parents'? Your church's? Your friends'? This group's?
5. How do you feel about Jesus' point that the door to the kingdom gets closed for some (vv. 10–12)?
6. If you knew Jesus will return next week, how would you live your life differently?
7. As you consider Christ's return, how can your group pray for you and hold you accountable?

(Study notes on page 880)

The Parable of the Talents

14 "Again, it will be like a man going on a journey, who called his servants and entrusted his
property to them. 15 To one he gave five talents[a]
of money, to another two talents, and to another
one talent, each according to his ability. Then he
went on his journey. 16 The man who had received the five talents went at once and put his
money to work and gained five more. 17 So also,
the one with the two talents gained two more.
18 But the man who had received the one talent
went off, dug a hole in the ground and hid his
master's money.
19 "After a long time the master of those servants returned and settled accounts with them.
20 The man who had received the five talents
brought the other five. 'Master,' he said, 'you
entrusted me with five talents. See, I have gained
five more.'

Matthew 25:14–30

1. If this group put on a talent show what would you do?
2. What's your best subject or something others say you are good at?
3. Do you have plans to further develop a particular talent for use in the future? What is it? How?
4. Why was the master so hard on the servant with one talent? Does God have the right to your talents?
5. What would you like to be doing five years from now? What are you doing today to get you there?
6. If "the Master" returned today, what would he say about how you've used the talents he gave you?
7. How can this group use its talents together in serving God? Close in prayer.

[a] *15* A talent was worth more than a thousand dollars.

25:14 ***Again.*** Like the preceding parable, the parable of the talents deals with the Lord's return on the Day of Judgment.

25:15 ***talents.*** A talent was originally a unit of weight, but was also used as the name for the highest unit of coinage. The present-day use of "talent" as an ability comes from this parable. ***each according to his ability.*** The master took into account the level of responsibility he felt each one could handle.

25:16–18 Investing money always carries with it the risk that it might be lost. ***dug a hole.*** In the absence of safe deposit boxes, this was not an uncommon occurrence as a way of protecting money from being stolen, but obviously with no investment potential!

25:24–27 ***I was afraid.*** The servant implies that his lack of investment gain is really the fault of the master: He expects too much; he is too frightening. ***You wicked, lazy servant.*** It was not out of justified fear of the master that the servant acted as he did; it was because he didn't have the master's interests at heart. If the servant was so certain of the master's ruthless character, he would have been sure to do something so that he wouldn't have to face the master with nothing to show for himself.

25:28–30 Judgment is pronounced upon the faithless servant, as the capital he had been given is transferred to the faithful servant. We are warned to apply ourselves to the task of serving Jesus. God expects those to whom he has entrusted various gifts to use them faithfully for his purposes.

21“His master replied, ‘Well done, good and
faithful servant! You have been faithful with a
few things; I will put you in charge of many
things. Come and share your master’s happiness!’
22“The man with the two talents also came.
‘Master,’ he said, ‘you entrusted me with two
talents; see, I have gained two more.’
23“His master replied, ‘Well done, good and
faithful servant! You have been faithful with a
few things; I will put you in charge of many
things. Come and share your master’s happiness!’
24“Then the man who had received the one
talent came. ‘Master,’ he said, ‘I knew that you
are a hard man, harvesting where you have not
sown and gathering where you have not scattered seed. 25So I was afraid and went out and hid
your talent in the ground. See, here is what belongs to you.’
26“His master replied, ‘You wicked, lazy servant! So you knew that I harvest where I have not
sown and gather where I have not scattered
seed? 27Well then, you should have put my money on deposit with the bankers, so that when I
returned I would have received it back with interest.
28“ ‘Take the talent from him and give it to the
one who has the ten talents. 29For everyone who
has will be given more, and he will have an abundance. Whoever does not have, even what he has
will be taken from him. 30And throw that worthless servant outside, into the darkness, where
there will be weeping and gnashing of teeth.’

The Sheep and the Goats

31“When the Son of Man comes in his glory,
and all the angels with him, he will sit on his
throne in heavenly glory. 32All the nations will be
gathered before him, and he will separate the
people one from another as a shepherd separates
the sheep from the goats. 33He will put the sheep
on his right and the goats on his left.
34“Then the King will say to those on his right,
‘Come, you who are blessed by my Father; take
your inheritance, the kingdom prepared for you
since the creation of the world. 35For I was hungry and you gave me something to eat, I was
thirsty and you gave me something to drink, I
was a stranger and you invited me in, 36I needed
clothes and you clothed me, I was sick and you
looked after me, I was in prison and you came to
visit me.’
37“Then the righteous will answer him, ‘Lord,
when did we see you hungry and feed you, or
thirsty and give you something to drink? 38When
did we see you a stranger and invite you in, or
needing clothes and clothe you? 39When did we
see you sick or in prison and go to visit you?’

MATTHEW 25:31–46

1. When you were a child, what little prize did you receive that you are still keeping because it meant something?
2. What person has always been there for you when you were hurting or in need?
3. Who would you nominate for “person of the year” in your school or community for being there for hurting people?
4. How would you feel if you were placed in the group of sheep? How would you feel if you were placed in the group of goats?
5. Who do you have the most compassion for? People who are: Homeless? Sick or disabled? Starving? Elderly? Lonely? Prisoners? Refugees?
6. When was the last time you did something for someone hungry, alone, poor, sick or imprisoned?
7. What is something this group can do to help someone in need? Close in prayer.

This passage concludes Matthew’s discourse (24:1–25:46) about the signs of the end of the age, the return of Christ, and the Day of Judgment. This final section is not actually a parable but a description of the scene of final judgment.

25:32 ***All the nations.*** All people will be at this judgment. ***separates the sheep from the goats.*** These animals grazed together during the day, but at night were separated because the goats needed to be in shelters to be protected from the elements.

25:35–40 Why these people are “blessed” (v. 34) is revealed. Throughout their lives they fed the hungry, gave drink to the thirsty, welcomed the stranger, clothed the naked, cared for the sick and visited the prisoners (as opposed to the cursed whose lifestyle reflected unconcern for the needs of others). It is not that they have earned God’s blessing by this lifestyle, but that this lifestyle reflects that they are in a right relationship with God. We are saved by grace not works, but God intends we do good works (Eph. 2:8–10).

25:37–40 ***When did we see you ... ?*** The righteous didn’t act this way because they had some insight regarding the spirit of Christ in the poor. They simply acted with compassion towards those in need. ***these brothers of mine.*** While it is uncertain whether this reflects Christ’s solidarity with all the poor or only those who bear his name, such a debate is like the lawyer questioning just who was really his neighbor (Luke 10:29–37). The point is that the righteous are those who have a heart of compassion for all in need.

40“The King will reply, ‘I tell you the truth,
whatever you did for one of the least of these
brothers of mine, you did for me.’
41“Then he will say to those on his left, ‘Depart from me, you who are cursed, into the eternal fire prepared for the devil and his angels.
42For I was hungry and you gave me nothing to
eat, I was thirsty and you gave me nothing to
drink, 43I was a stranger and you did not invite
me in, I needed clothes and you did not clothe
me, I was sick and in prison and you did not look
after me.’
44“They also will answer, ‘Lord, when did we
see you hungry or thirsty or a stranger or needing
clothes or sick or in prison, and did not help
you?’
45“He will reply, ‘I tell you the truth, whatever
you did not do for one of the least of these, you
did not do for me.’
46“Then they will go away to eternal punishment, but the righteous to eternal life.”

The Plot Against Jesus

26 When Jesus had finished saying all these
things, he said to his disciples, 2“As you
know, the Passover is two days away—and the
Son of Man will be handed over to be crucified.”
3Then the chief priests and the elders of the
people assembled in the palace of the high priest,
whose name was Caiaphas, 4and they plotted to
arrest Jesus in some sly way and kill him. 5“But
not during the Feast,” they said, “or there may be
a riot among the people.”

Jesus Anointed at Bethany

6While Jesus was in Bethany in the home of a
man known as Simon the Leper, 7a woman came
to him with an alabaster jar of very expensive
perfume, which she poured on his head as he
was reclining at the table.
8When the disciples saw this, they were indignant. “Why this waste?” they asked. 9“This perfume could have been sold at a high price and the
money given to the poor.”
10Aware of this, Jesus said to them, “Why are
you bothering this woman? She has done a beautiful thing to me. 11The poor you will always have
with you, but you will not always have me.
12When she poured this perfume on my body,
she did it to prepare me for burial. 13I tell you the
truth, wherever this gospel is preached throughout the world, what she has done will also be
told, in memory of her.”

Judas Agrees to Betray Jesus

14Then one of the Twelve—the one called Judas Iscariot—went to the chief priests 15and
asked, “What are you willing to give me if I hand
him over to you?” So they counted out for him
thirty silver coins. 16From then on Judas watched
for an opportunity to hand him over.

The Lord’s Supper

17On the first day of the Feast of Unleavened
Bread, the disciples came to Jesus and asked,
“Where do you want us to make preparations for
you to eat the Passover?”
18He replied, “Go into the city to a certain man
and tell him, ‘The Teacher says: My appointed
time is near. I am going to celebrate the Passover
with my disciples at your house.’ ” 19So the disciples did as Jesus had directed them and prepared
the Passover.
20When evening came, Jesus was reclining at
the table with the Twelve. 21And while they
were eating, he said, “I tell you the truth, one of
you will betray me.”
22They were very sad and began to say to him
one after the other, “Surely not I, Lord?”
23Jesus replied, “The one who has dipped his
hand into the bowl with me will betray me.
24The Son of Man will go just as it is written
about him. But woe to that man who betrays the
Son of Man! It would be better for him if he had
not been born.”
25Then Judas, the one who would betray him,
said, “Surely not I, Rabbi?”
Jesus answered, “Yes, it is you.”[a]
26While they were eating, Jesus took bread,
gave thanks and broke it, and gave it to his disciples, saying, “Take and eat; this is my body.”
27Then he took the cup, gave thanks and offered it to them, saying, “Drink from it, all of you.
28This is my blood of the[b] covenant, which is
poured out for many for the forgiveness of sins.
29I tell you, I will not drink of this fruit of the vine
from now on until that day when I drink it anew
with you in my Father’s kingdom.”
30When they had sung a hymn, they went out
to the Mount of Olives.

Jesus Predicts Peter’s Denial

31Then Jesus told them, “This very night you
will all fall away on account of me, for it is written:

“ ‘I will strike the shepherd,
and the sheep of the flock will be
scattered.’[c]

32But after I have risen, I will go ahead of you into
Galilee.”
33Peter replied, “Even if all fall away on account of you, I never will.”
34“I tell you the truth,” Jesus answered, “this

[a] 25 Or *“You yourself have said it”* [b] 28 Some manuscripts *the new* [c] 31 Zech. 13:7

very night, before the rooster crows, you will
disown me three times."
35 But Peter declared, "Even if I have to die
with you, I will never disown you." And all the
other disciples said the same.

Gethsemane

36 Then Jesus went with his disciples to a place
called Gethsemane, and he said to them, "Sit
here while I go over there and pray." 37 He took
Peter and the two sons of Zebedee along with
him, and he began to be sorrowful and troubled.
38 Then he said to them, "My soul is overwhelmed with sorrow to the point of death. Stay
here and keep watch with me."
39 Going a little farther, he fell with his face to
the ground and prayed, "My Father, if it is possible, may this cup be taken from me. Yet not as I
will, but as you will."
40 Then he returned to his disciples and found
them sleeping. "Could you men not keep watch
with me for one hour?" he asked Peter. 41 "Watch
and pray so that you will not fall into temptation.
The spirit is willing, but the body is weak."
42 He went away a second time and prayed,
"My Father, if it is not possible for this cup to be
taken away unless I drink it, may your will be
done."
43 When he came back, he again found them
sleeping, because their eyes were heavy. 44 So he
left them and went away once more and prayed
the third time, saying the same thing.
45 Then he returned to the disciples and said to
them, "Are you still sleeping and resting? Look,
the hour is near, and the Son of Man is betrayed
into the hands of sinners. 46 Rise, let us go! Here
comes my betrayer!"

Jesus Arrested

47 While he was still speaking, Judas, one of the
Twelve, arrived. With him was a large crowd
armed with swords and clubs, sent from the chief
priests and the elders of the people. 48 Now the
betrayer had arranged a signal with them: "The
one I kiss is the man; arrest him." 49 Going at
once to Jesus, Judas said, "Greetings, Rabbi!" and
kissed him.
50 Jesus replied, "Friend, do what you came
for."[a]
Then the men stepped forward, seized Jesus
and arrested him. 51 With that, one of Jesus' companions reached for his sword, drew it out and
struck the servant of the high priest, cutting off
his ear.
52 "Put your sword back in its place," Jesus said
to him, "for all who draw the sword will die by

MATTHEW 26:47–56

1. What is the closest you have come to getting arrested?
2. When it comes to relationships, are you more likely to get close quickly or take a long time?
3. On a scale of 1 (low) to 10 (high), how would you rate the following: Your level of loyalty to your friends? Your friends' loyalty to you? Your loyalty to Jesus?
4. How do you think Jesus felt when he saw Judas and an armed mob coming toward him? How would you have reacted?
5. How do you deal with a broken relationship: Have it out? Clam up? Write a letter?
6. In this story Jesus was left by his friends. In what ways do you deny him? What's one way you can stand by Jesus this week?
7. What would you like the group to pray with you about?

[a] 50 Or *"Friend, why have you come?"*

26:47–50 ***While he was still speaking.*** See verses 45–46. ***Rabbi.*** This title was a form of respect. By sharing the same bowl (v. 23—to eat together was a sign of friendship), by his greeting and by his kiss Judas had all the external signs of a warm relationship with Jesus even as he betrayed him. ***arrested him.*** No charge is given.

26:51 ***one of Jesus' companions.*** According to John's Gospel (John 18:10), this was Peter. ***cutting off his ear.*** This is not an indication of Peter's swordsmanship, but of his clumsiness since he undoubtedly was aiming at the man's head! Jesus immediately healed the man (Luke 22:51), which likely diffused the explosiveness of the situation.

26:52–53 ***all who draw the sword will die by the sword.*** Jesus' kingdom will not come about by the use of force. Individuals as well as kingdoms that rely on violence for their existence will one day be destroyed by violence. Jesus will inaugurate God's kingdom by absorbing violence. ***twelve legions of angels.*** A Roman legion had 6,000 soldiers. If force was to be used to establish God's kingdom, Jesus could call on 12 legions of mighty angels rather than relying on the dubious talents of 12 untrained men!

26:54–56 ***the Scriptures be fulfilled.*** In light of verse 56, probably Zechariah 13:7: "Strike the shepherd, and the sheep will be scattered" (see also Ps. 41:9). ***all the disciples deserted him and fled.*** During Jesus' time of prayer in Gethsemane his disciples kept falling asleep (vv. 40–45). Now they abandon him completely.

the sword. 53Do you think I cannot call on my
Father, and he will at once put at my disposal
more than twelve legions of angels? 54But how
then would the Scriptures be fulfilled that say it
must happen in this way?"
55At that time Jesus said to the crowd, "Am I
leading a rebellion, that you have come out with
swords and clubs to capture me? Every day I sat
in the temple courts teaching, and you did not
arrest me. 56But this has all taken place that the
writings of the prophets might be fulfilled." Then
all the disciples deserted him and fled.

Before the Sanhedrin

57Those who had arrested Jesus took him to
Caiaphas, the high priest, where the teachers of
the law and the elders had assembled. 58But Peter followed him at a distance, right up to the
courtyard of the high priest. He entered and sat
down with the guards to see the outcome.
59The chief priests and the whole Sanhedrin
were looking for false evidence against Jesus so
that they could put him to death. 60But they did
not find any, though many false witnesses came
forward.
Finally two came forward 61and declared,
"This fellow said, 'I am able to destroy the temple
of God and rebuild it in three days.'"
62Then the high priest stood up and said to
Jesus, "Are you not going to answer? What is this
testimony that these men are bringing against
you?" 63But Jesus remained silent.
The high priest said to him, "I charge you under oath by the living God: Tell us if you are the
Christ,[a] the Son of God."
64"Yes, it is as you say," Jesus replied. "But I
say to all of you: In the future you will see the Son
of Man sitting at the right hand of the Mighty
One and coming on the clouds of heaven."
65Then the high priest tore his clothes and
said, "He has spoken blasphemy! Why do we
need any more witnesses? Look, now you have
heard the blasphemy. 66What do you think?"
"He is worthy of death," they answered.
67Then they spit in his face and struck him
with their fists. Others slapped him 68and said,
"Prophesy to us, Christ. Who hit you?"

Peter Disowns Jesus

69Now Peter was sitting out in the courtyard,
and a servant girl came to him. "You also were
with Jesus of Galilee," she said.
70But he denied it before them all. "I don't
know what you're talking about," he said.
71Then he went out to the gateway, where
another girl saw him and said to the people there,
"This fellow was with Jesus of Nazareth."
72He denied it again, with an oath: "I don't
know the man!"
73After a little while, those standing there
went up to Peter and said, "Surely you are one of
them, for your accent gives you away."
74Then he began to call down curses on himself and he swore to them, "I don't know the
man!"
Immediately a rooster crowed. 75Then Peter
remembered the word Jesus had spoken: "Before
the rooster crows, you will disown me three
times." And he went outside and wept bitterly.

Judas Hangs Himself

27 Early in the morning, all the chief priests
and the elders of the people came to the
decision to put Jesus to death. 2They bound him,
led him away and handed him over to Pilate, the
governor.
3When Judas, who had betrayed him, saw that
Jesus was condemned, he was seized with remorse and returned the thirty silver coins to the
chief priests and the elders. 4"I have sinned," he
said, "for I have betrayed innocent blood."
"What is that to us?" they replied. "That's
your responsibility."
5So Judas threw the money into the temple
and left. Then he went away and hanged himself.
6The chief priests picked up the coins and
said, "It is against the law to put this into the
treasury, since it is blood money." 7So they decided to use the money to buy the potter's field
as a burial place for foreigners. 8That is why it has
been called the Field of Blood to this day. 9Then
what was spoken by Jeremiah the prophet was
fulfilled: "They took the thirty silver coins, the
price set on him by the people of Israel, 10and
they used them to buy the potter's field, as the
Lord commanded me."[b]

Jesus Before Pilate

11Meanwhile Jesus stood before the governor,
and the governor asked him, "Are you the king of
the Jews?"
"Yes, it is as you say," Jesus replied.
12When he was accused by the chief priests
and the elders, he gave no answer. 13Then Pilate
asked him, "Don't you hear the testimony they
are bringing against you?" 14But Jesus made no
reply, not even to a single charge—to the great
amazement of the governor.
15Now it was the governor's custom at the
Feast to release a prisoner chosen by the crowd.
16At that time they had a notorious prisoner,
called Barabbas. 17So when the crowd had gathered, Pilate asked them, "Which one do you want
me to release to you: Barabbas, or Jesus who is

[a]63 Or *Messiah*; also in verse 68 [b]10 See Zech. 11:12,13; Jer. 19:1-13; 32:6-9.

called Christ?" 18For he knew it was out of envy
that they had handed Jesus over to him.
19While Pilate was sitting on the judge's seat,
his wife sent him this message: "Don't have anything to do with that innocent man, for I have
suffered a great deal today in a dream because of
him."
20But the chief priests and the elders persuaded the crowd to ask for Barabbas and to have
Jesus executed.
21"Which of the two do you want me to release to you?" asked the governor.
"Barabbas," they answered.
22"What shall I do, then, with Jesus who is
called Christ?" Pilate asked.
They all answered, "Crucify him!"
23"Why? What crime has he committed?"
asked Pilate.
But they shouted all the louder, "Crucify him!"
24When Pilate saw that he was getting nowhere, but that instead an uproar was starting,
he took water and washed his hands in front of
the crowd. "I am innocent of this man's blood,"
he said. "It is your responsibility!"
25All the people answered, "Let his blood be
on us and on our children!"
26Then he released Barabbas to them. But he
had Jesus flogged, and handed him over to be
crucified.

The Soldiers Mock Jesus

27Then the governor's soldiers took Jesus into
the Praetorium and gathered the whole company
of soldiers around him. 28They stripped him and
put a scarlet robe on him, 29and then twisted
together a crown of thorns and set it on his head.
They put a staff in his right hand and knelt in
front of him and mocked him. "Hail, king of the
Jews!" they said. 30They spit on him, and took
the staff and struck him on the head again and
again. 31After they had mocked him, they took off
the robe and put his own clothes on him. Then
they led him away to crucify him.

The Crucifixion

32As they were going out, they met a man from
Cyrene, named Simon, and they forced him to
carry the cross. 33They came to a place called
Golgotha (which means The Place of the Skull).
34There they offered Jesus wine to drink, mixed
with gall; but after tasting it, he refused to drink
it. 35When they had crucified him, they divided
up his clothes by casting lots.[a] 36And sitting
down, they kept watch over him there. 37Above
his head they placed the written charge against
him: THIS IS JESUS, THE KING OF THE JEWS. 38Two

MATTHEW 27:26–31

1. Growing up, who were the "bullies" in your life? How did they pick on you? Did you stand up for yourself or someone else who was being bullied?
2. What's the closest you've come to being in a fist-fight? What started it?
3. When have you taken the punishment for someone else? Why did you?
4. How would you counsel a friend who had been abused?
5. How do your sufferings compare to what Jesus went through? How does it make you feel that he suffered for you?
6. Despite the abuse, Jesus forgave (see Luke 23:34). Where do you need to extend forgiveness to someone who's hurt you?
7. How can this group help you in prayer this week?

a35 A few late manuscripts *lots that the word spoken by the prophet might be fulfilled: "They divided my garments among themselves and cast lots for my clothing"* (Psalm 22:18)

27:26 ***Barabbas.*** The Roman governor of Israel typically released a prisoner of the people's choice at the Passover feast. Though Pilate wanted to release Jesus, he finally consented to the crowd's frenzied request to release the notorious murderer Barabbas. ***flogged.*** This was a terrible punishment. Soldiers would lash a naked and bound prisoner with a leather whip into which pieces of bone and lead had been woven. The flesh would be cut to shreds. In itself, this punishment sometimes led to death due to shock and loss of blood.

27:27–31 ***Praetorium.*** The Roman governor's residence in Jerusalem. Here the Roman soldiers mock Jesus, as the Sanhedrin (the Jewish high court) had done before them (see 26:67). The Sanhedrin mocked the idea that he was the Messiah, the soldiers mock the idea that he is king. This whole scene is full of the humiliation of God's Messiah being ridiculed and abused by the oppressors of God's people. ***scarlet robe.*** A Roman soldier's outer cloak, whose color was symbolic of royalty. ***crown of thorns.*** Made from one of Palestine's many prickly plants. ***staff.*** A mock scepter. The robe, crown and scepter were all traditional signs of a king. ***Hail, king of the Jews!*** A taunting salutation corresponding to "Hail, Caesar!" ***spit on him.*** A mockery of the kiss of homage given a king in the Near East. ***Then they led him away to crucify him.*** Crucifixion was the most feared of all punishments in the first-century world. It was cruel in the extreme and totally degrading.

robbers were crucified with him, one on his right
and one on his left. [39]Those who passed by
hurled insults at him, shaking their heads [40]and
saying, "You who are going to destroy the temple
and build it in three days, save yourself! Come
down from the cross, if you are the Son of God!"
[41]In the same way the chief priests, the teachers of the law and the elders mocked him. [42]"He
saved others," they said, "but he can't save himself! He's the King of Israel! Let him come down
now from the cross, and we will believe in him.
[43]He trusts in God. Let God rescue him now if he
wants him, for he said, 'I am the Son of God.'"
[44]In the same way the robbers who were crucified with him also heaped insults on him.

The Death of Jesus

[45]From the sixth hour until the ninth hour
darkness came over all the land. [46]About the
ninth hour Jesus cried out in a loud voice, *"Eloi,
Eloi,*[a] *lama sabachthani?"*—which means, "My
God, my God, why have you forsaken me?"[b]
[47]When some of those standing there heard
this, they said, "He's calling Elijah."
[48]Immediately one of them ran and got a
sponge. He filled it with wine vinegar, put it on
a stick, and offered it to Jesus to drink. [49]The rest
said, "Now leave him alone. Let's see if Elijah
comes to save him."
[50]And when Jesus had cried out again in a loud
voice, he gave up his spirit.
[51]At that moment the curtain of the temple
was torn in two from top to bottom. The earth
shook and the rocks split. [52]The tombs broke
open and the bodies of many holy people who
had died were raised to life. [53]They came out
of the tombs, and after Jesus' resurrection they
went into the holy city and appeared to many
people.
[54]When the centurion and those with him
who were guarding Jesus saw the earthquake and
all that had happened, they were terrified, and
exclaimed, "Surely he was the Son[c] of God!"
[55]Many women were there, watching from a
distance. They had followed Jesus from Galilee to
care for his needs. [56]Among them were Mary
Magdalene, Mary the mother of James and Joses,
and the mother of Zebedee's sons.

The Burial of Jesus

[57]As evening approached, there came a rich
man from Arimathea, named Joseph, who had
himself become a disciple of Jesus. [58]Going to
Pilate, he asked for Jesus' body, and Pilate ordered that it be given to him. [59]Joseph took the
body, wrapped it in a clean linen cloth, [60]and
placed it in his own new tomb that he had cut out
of the rock. He rolled a big stone in front of the
entrance to the tomb and went away. [61]Mary
Magdalene and the other Mary were sitting there
opposite the tomb.

The Guard at the Tomb

[62]The next day, the one after Preparation Day,
the chief priests and the Pharisees went to Pilate.
[63]"Sir," they said, "we remember that while he
was still alive that deceiver said, 'After three days
I will rise again.' [64]So give the order for the tomb
to be made secure until the third day. Otherwise,
his disciples may come and steal the body and tell
the people that he has been raised from the dead.
This last deception will be worse than the first."
[65]"Take a guard," Pilate answered. "Go, make
the tomb as secure as you know how." [66]So they
went and made the tomb secure by putting a seal
on the stone and posting the guard.

The Resurrection

28 After the Sabbath, at dawn on the first
day of the week, Mary Magdalene and the
other Mary went to look at the tomb.
[2]There was a violent earthquake, for an angel
of the Lord came down from heaven and, going to
the tomb, rolled back the stone and sat on it. [3]His
appearance was like lightning, and his clothes
were white as snow. [4]The guards were so afraid
of him that they shook and became like dead
men.
[5]The angel said to the women, "Do not be
afraid, for I know that you are looking for Jesus,

[a]*46* Some manuscripts *Eli, Eli* [b]*46* Psalm 22:1 [c]*54* Or *a son*

28:1–2 *at dawn on the first day of the week.* This scene takes place early on Sunday morning. ***angel of the Lord ... rolled back the stone.*** A tomb like this was cut out of the side of a hill. A large, disc-shaped stone was set in a groove so that it could be fairly easily rolled down to the opening to close it off. Once in place it would have been very difficult for people to push it back up the incline. The stone was rolled away not so that the resurrected Jesus could leave the tomb, but so that his disciples could see that it was empty (v. 6).

28:11–15 *His disciples came during the night and stole him away while we were asleep.* This attempt at "damage control" was weak. The reason the guards were posted was to keep the disciples from stealing the body and concoct a story about resurrection. For a band of frightened men to be able to elude a sleeping Roman guard (Roman guards falling asleep on duty was an offense meriting execution), roll the tombstone uphill without waking anyone, and steal away with the body, stretched the limits of believability.

28:18–20 This passage is known as the Great Commission. All authority in heaven and earth now belongs to Jesus, he sends his disciples to spread his message everywhere with the promise that he himself is with them to the end of time. ***go and make disciples.*** Literally, "as you are going, make disciples." As the apostles go about their business, they are to be teaching people about Jesus and his kingdom. ***with you.*** Matthew ends with the comforting words of him who came to earth to be "God with us" (1:23).

who was crucified. 6He is not here; he has risen, just as he said. Come and see the place where he lay. 7Then go quickly and tell his disciples: 'He has risen from the dead and is going ahead of you into Galilee. There you will see him.' Now I have told you."

MATTHEW 28:1–20

1. What time do you usually get up in the morning? When would you like to get up?
2. As a child, what was your first experience with death? How did you feel?
3. In your school, what do most of the students say about the resurrection of Jesus from the dead?
4. Should the disciples have been surprised that Jesus said (v. 7) he would see them in Galilee (see Matt. 26:32)?
5. When did the fact of the Resurrection start having meaning to you?
6. What difference does the resurrection of Jesus, and your own resurrection one day, make in the way you live your life today?
7. Where do you need to experience Christ "with you" (v. 20) this week? Pray together.

(Study notes on page 887)

8So the women hurried away from the tomb, afraid yet filled with joy, and ran to tell his disciples. 9Suddenly Jesus met them. "Greetings," he said. They came to him, clasped his feet and worshiped him. 10Then Jesus said to them, "Do not be afraid. Go and tell my brothers to go to Galilee; there they will see me."

The Guards' Report

11While the women were on their way, some of the guards went into the city and reported to the chief priests everything that had happened. 12When the chief priests had met with the elders and devised a plan, they gave the soldiers a large sum of money, 13telling them, "You are to say, 'His disciples came during the night and stole him away while we were asleep.' 14If this report gets to the governor, we will satisfy him and keep you out of trouble." 15So the soldiers took the money and did as they were instructed. And this story has been widely circulated among the Jews to this very day.

The Great Commission

16Then the eleven disciples went to Galilee, to the mountain where Jesus had told them to go. 17When they saw him, they worshiped him; but some doubted. 18Then Jesus came to them and said, "All authority in heaven and on earth has been given to me. 19Therefore go and make disciples of all nations, baptizing them in[a] the name of the Father and of the Son and of the Holy Spirit, 20and teaching them to obey everything I have commanded you. And surely I am with you always, to the very end of the age."

[a] *19* Or *into*; see Acts 8:16; 19:5; Romans 6:3; 1 Cor. 1:13; 10:2 and Gal. 3:27.

Introduction to MARK

Personal Reading Plan

- ❒ Mark 1:1–45
- ❒ Mark 2:1–3:6
- ❒ Mark 3:7–35
- ❒ Mark 4:1–20
- ❒ Mark 4:21–41
- ❒ Mark 5:1–20
- ❒ Mark 5:21–43
- ❒ Mark 6:1–29
- ❒ Mark 6:30–56
- ❒ Mark 7:1–37
- ❒ Mark 8:1–26
- ❒ Mark 8:27–9:1
- ❒ Mark 9:2–32
- ❒ Mark 9:33–10:12
- ❒ Mark 10:13–31
- ❒ Mark 10:32–52
- ❒ Mark 11:1–25
- ❒ Mark 11:27–12:12
- ❒ Mark 12:13–44
- ❒ Mark 13:1–37
- ❒ Mark 14:1–31
- ❒ Mark 14:32–72
- ❒ Mark 15:1–41
- ❒ Mark 15:42–16:20

Author

From the Bible, we discover that Mark's full name is John Mark, that his mother's name was Mary, and that their home was used as a meeting place by the disciples. Peter went there directly after his miraculous release from prison (Acts 12:1–17). Consequently, as a young man, Mark was immersed in the life of the newly forming church.

In particular, Mark was close to Peter. Peter referred to him as "my son Mark" (1 Peter 5:13). Many hold that Mark was Peter's secretary and that his Gospel reflects Peter's view of the events. Writing in A.D. 140, Bishop Papias says: "Mark, having become the interpreter of Peter, wrote down accurately all that he remembered of the things said and done by our Lord, but not, however, in order."

Mark was also connected closely with Paul. Along with his cousin Barnabas, Mark accompanied the great apostle on the first missionary journey. Mark, for an unknown reason, left the party at Perga when they turned inland to Asia. Because of this, Paul refused to allow Mark to go on the second missionary journey, so Barnabas went with Mark to Cyprus while Paul teamed up with Silas. For years Mark dropped out of sight. Tradition says he founded the church at Alexandria, Egypt. Eventually, Paul and Mark were reconciled, so much so that Mark became Paul's companion during his imprisonment in a Roman jail.

Date

Mark was written somewhere between A.D. 50–70; probably in the mid-60s.

Theme

Jesus the Messiah, the Son of God.

Historical Background

The 10 years between A.D. 60 and A.D. 70 when Mark wrote his Gospel were not good ones for the Christians living in Rome. For a long time they had hardly been noticed—they were just another exotic religious sect. But then Nero burned down Rome in A.D. 64 and had to find someone to blame. The Christians were nominated, and an era of persecution began. Nero threw them to the animals in the coliseum and burned them as human torches at his garden parties. It is into this atmosphere of persecution, to these Christians who were dying for Jesus' name, that Mark directed his Gospel.

This was the first written account of Jesus' life. Thus it was, according to William Barclay, "the most important book in the world." Mark's collection of previously only word-of-mouth stories was widely circulated and was used by Matthew and Luke when they wrote their Gospels. In fact, all but 24 verses of Mark's Gospel are found in their accounts.

Characteristics

In the shortest of the Gospels, Mark races breathlessly through Jesus' life by connecting together a series of little stories. Yet, despite the way Mark hurries through the material, his account is the richest and most vivid in eyewitness detail. For example, when speaking of Jesus blessing the children, Mark alone tells us that Jesus first took them in his arms (Mark 10:13–16).

In Mark's Gospel there is a very careful and deliberate ordering of the stories. The result is a skillfully crafted outline. In fact, he has told the story of Jesus in a highly skilled and remarkably sophisticated way. This cannot have been easy given the material he had to use. Mark could not sit down and start from scratch to tell Jesus' story. Rather, he had to use the stories everyone knew in the way they knew them. He could not alter them. He was merely the chronicler of the tradition, not the creator of it. The church would not have used his work if it contained questionable tales or if he had mistold stories. No, Mark's creativity under the guidance of the Holy Spirit came at the level of choosing which stories to set next to each other. As you read through the Gospel, be alert to the significance of the sequence of stories as they unfold.

Mark does not put his stories in chronological order as we might expect, given the way history is written today (though overall there is a rough chronology to the story). Instead, he groups his stories thematically. Mark uses several themes, simultaneously. For one thing, it is clear that he has structured his story *geographically.* Jesus' ministry begins to the north in Galilee and then he moves down to Jerusalem, where he is finally killed. Mark also structures the story in terms of *Jesus' unfolding ministry:* preparation, proclamation and completion. There is also an unfolding vision of *who Jesus is.* In broad terms, the first half of the book focuses on the discovery of Jesus as the Messiah, and the second half on the discovery of Jesus as the Son of God. In terms of the *disciples' growing awareness,* they move from experiencing Jesus as an exceptional rabbi, to seeing him as a man of power, and then as the healer of hardened hearts. After Caesarea Philippi and their realization that he is the Messiah, they next know him as a teacher. In Jerusalem during the final week of his life, they come to realize that he is the Son of God.

Passages for Topical Group Study

1:29–39	DEVOTIONAL LIFE	Jesus Heals and Prays
2:1–12	FRIENDS	Jesus Heals a Paralytic
3:20–35	FAMILY INTERFERENCE	Jesus Faces Criticism
4:35–41	WORRY AND ANXIETY	Jesus Calms the Storm
6:14–29	MEDIA / ENTERTAINMENT MUSIC, MOVIES, ETC.	John the Baptist Beheaded
6:30–44	TIME / LEISURE	Jesus Feeds the Five Thousand
10:17–31	POSSESSIONS	The Rich Young Man
10:35–45	SUCCESS / AMBITION COMPETITION	The Request of James and John
11:12–19	ANGER	Jesus Clears the Temple
12:13–17	RELATING TO AUTHORITY	Paying Taxes to Caesar
12:41–44	GIVING	The Widow's Offering
14:32–42	LONELINESS KNOWING GOD'S WILL	Jesus in Gethsemane

See the Lesson Plans in the front of this Bible.

Passages for General Group Study

2:23–3:6	Lord of the Sabbath
5:24–34	Jesus Heals a Bleeding Woman
9:2–13	The Transfiguration
9:14–29	The Healing of a Boy With an Evil Spirit
15:1–15	Jesus Before Pilate

John the Baptist Prepares the Way

1 The beginning of the gospel about Jesus
Christ, the Son of God.[a]

2It is written in Isaiah the prophet:

"I will send my messenger ahead of you,
who will prepare your way"[b]—
3"a voice of one calling in the desert,
'Prepare the way for the Lord,
make straight paths for him.'"[c]

4And so John came, baptizing in the desert region
and preaching a baptism of repentance for the
forgiveness of sins. 5The whole Judean countryside and all the people of Jerusalem went out to
him. Confessing their sins, they were baptized by
him in the Jordan River. 6John wore clothing
made of camel's hair, with a leather belt around
his waist, and he ate locusts and wild honey.
7And this was his message: "After me will come
one more powerful than I, the thongs of whose
sandals I am not worthy to stoop down and untie.
8I baptize you with[d] water, but he will baptize
you with the Holy Spirit."

The Baptism and Temptation of Jesus

9At that time Jesus came from Nazareth in Galilee and was baptized by John in the Jordan. 10As
Jesus was coming up out of the water, he saw
heaven being torn open and the Spirit descending on him like a dove. 11And a voice came from
heaven: "You are my Son, whom I love; with you
I am well pleased."
12At once the Spirit sent him out into the
desert, 13and he was in the desert forty days,
being tempted by Satan. He was with the wild
animals, and angels attended him.

The Calling of the First Disciples

14After John was put in prison, Jesus went into
Galilee, proclaiming the good news of God.
15"The time has come," he said. "The kingdom of
God is near. Repent and believe the good news!"
16As Jesus walked beside the Sea of Galilee, he
saw Simon and his brother Andrew casting a net
into the lake, for they were fishermen. 17"Come,
follow me," Jesus said, "and I will make you fishers of men." 18At once they left their nets and
followed him.
19When he had gone a little farther, he saw
James son of Zebedee and his brother John in a
boat, preparing their nets. 20Without delay he
called them, and they left their father Zebedee in
the boat with the hired men and followed him.

Jesus Drives Out an Evil Spirit

21They went to Capernaum, and when the
Sabbath came, Jesus went into the synagogue and
began to teach. 22The people were amazed at his
teaching, because he taught them as one who had
authority, not as the teachers of the law. 23Just
then a man in their synagogue who was possessed by an evil[e] spirit cried out, 24"What do
you want with us, Jesus of Nazareth? Have you
come to destroy us? I know who you are—the
Holy One of God!"
25"Be quiet!" said Jesus sternly. "Come out of
him!" 26The evil spirit shook the man violently
and came out of him with a shriek.
27The people were all so amazed that they
asked each other, "What is this? A new
teaching—and with authority! He even gives orders to evil spirits and they obey him." 28News
about him spread quickly over the whole region
of Galilee.

Jesus Heals Many

29As soon as they left the synagogue, they
went with James and John to the home of Simon
and Andrew. 30Simon's mother-in-law was in
bed with a fever, and they told Jesus about her.
31So he went to her, took her hand and helped
her up. The fever left her and she began to wait
on them.
32That evening after sunset the people brought
to Jesus all the sick and demon-possessed. 33The
whole town gathered at the door, 34and Jesus
healed many who had various diseases. He also

[a] *1* Some manuscripts do not have *the Son of God.* [b] *2* Mal. 3:1 [c] *3* Isaiah 40:3 [d] *8* Or *in* [e] *23* Greek *unclean*; also in verses 26 and 27

1:29 *home of Simon and Andrew.* After Jesus' baptism and temptation, he immediately launched into his public ministry. Jesus appears to use the home of Simon Peter and his brother Andrew, two of the first disciples, as his base of operations during his ministry in Galilee.

1:31–34 *fever left her.* This was a real, immediate cure. She suffered none of the weakness that normally follows when a fever breaks. ***after sunset the people brought.*** Since both carrying things and healing were forbidden on the Sabbath, they came only after the sun set, signaling the end of the Sabbath. ***would not let the demons speak because they knew who he was.*** Before Jesus could allow himself to be identified, he had to make sure that people knew what kind of Messiah he was. Rather than the warring, nationalistic Messiah the Jews expected, he had come instead to serve, suffer, and ultimately, to die.

1:35 *early in the morning.* Though Jesus had gone through an incredibly demanding day, the next morning finds him praying very early. In the midst of great success, Jesus is quick to acknowledge his dependence on God as the source of his power.

1:36–38 In contrast to Jesus, who sought the Father's will, Peter was simply following the will of the people. It seemed natural to him to remain where Jesus was so appreciated. ***so I can preach there also.*** Refusing to be sidetracked by popular demand, Jesus is determined to carry on his central mission—proclaiming the kingdom of God.

drove out many demons, but he would not let the demons speak because they knew who he was.

Jesus Prays in a Solitary Place

35 Very early in the morning, while it was still dark, Jesus got up, left the house and went off to a solitary place, where he prayed. 36 Simon and his companions went to look for him, 37 and when they found him, they exclaimed: "Everyone is looking for you!"

38 Jesus replied, "Let us go somewhere else—to the nearby villages—so I can preach there also. That is why I have come." 39 So he traveled throughout Galilee, preaching in their synagogues and driving out demons.

MARK 1:29–39

1. Are you a morning person or an evening person?
2. Where do you go when you want to be alone?
3. How often do you spend time alone with God?
4. What do you think Jesus prayed for during his quiet time (v. 35)?
5. What is the greatest obstacle in your devotional life—finding time or having the desire?
6. What goal will you set this week for your quiet time?
7. How can this group help you reach your goal? Pray together.

(Study notes on page 891)

A Man With Leprosy

40 A man with leprosy[a] came to him and begged him on his knees, "If you are willing, you can make me clean."

41 Filled with compassion, Jesus reached out his hand and touched the man. "I am willing," he said. "Be clean!" 42 Immediately the leprosy left him and he was cured.

43 Jesus sent him away at once with a strong warning: 44 "See that you don't tell this to anyone. But go, show yourself to the priest and offer the sacrifices that Moses commanded for your cleansing, as a testimony to them." 45 Instead he went out and began to talk freely, spreading the news. As a result, Jesus could no longer enter a town openly but stayed outside in lonely places. Yet the people still came to him from everywhere.

Jesus Heals a Paralytic

2 A few days later, when Jesus again entered Capernaum, the people heard that he had come home. 2 So many gathered that there was no room left, not even outside the door, and he preached the word to them. 3 Some men came, bringing to him a paralytic, carried by four of them. 4 Since they could not get him to Jesus because of the crowd, they made an opening in the roof above Jesus and, after digging through it, lowered the mat the paralyzed man was lying on. 5 When Jesus saw their faith, he said to the paralytic, "Son, your sins are forgiven."

6 Now some teachers of the law were sitting there, thinking to themselves, 7 "Why does this fellow talk like that? He's blaspheming! Who can forgive sins but God alone?"

8 Immediately Jesus knew in his spirit that this was what they were thinking in their hearts, and he said to them, "Why are you thinking these things? 9 Which is easier: to say to the paralytic, 'Your sins are forgiven,' or to say, 'Get up, take your mat and walk'? 10 But that you may know that the Son of Man has authority on earth to forgive sins. . . ." He said to the paralytic, 11 "I tell

[a] *40* The Greek word was used for various diseases affecting the skin—not necessarily leprosy.

2:1–2 ***come home.*** Capernaum served as Jesus' base for his travels in Galilee. Quite possibly this story took place in Peter and Andrew's house (see 1:21,29). ***So many gathered.*** On Jesus' previous visit to Capernaum (1:21–34) he healed many people. There was great interest when he returned, and the small house quickly filled.

2:3–4 ***Some men.*** Apparently the paralytic had not been healed on Jesus' previous visit. His friends do not want to let this new opportunity pass. ***carried by four of them.*** They probably each took hold of one corner of the paralyzed man's mat. ***an opening in the roof.*** The roof of a typical Palestinian house was flat (it was often used for sleeping) and was reached by an outside ladder or stairway. It was constructed of earth and brushwood that was packed between wooden beams. This type of roof was easily opened up (and could be easily repaired).

2:5 ***your sins are forgiven.*** Jesus first met the man's deepest need: forgiveness. This was not what the crowd expected Jesus to say. They anticipated that he would say, "You are healed." Jesus says this so as to declare to the religious leaders who he is.

2:9 ***Which is easier ... ?*** There is no way to verify if sins have been forgiven, but it is obvious if a lame man walks or not. ***But that you may know.*** If Jesus is able to heal the paralytic the teachers of the Law would have to admit that he had, indeed, forgiven the man's sins since their own theology linked forgiveness and healing. ***to forgive sins.*** The essence of Jesus' ministry.

you, get up, take your mat and go home." 12He
got up, took his mat and walked out in full view
of them all. This amazed everyone and they
praised God, saying, "We have never seen anything like this!"

MARK 2:1–12

1. When was the last time you had to go to the emergency room? Who took you?
2. What four phone numbers do you use most often? Who would you call in a crisis at 3 a.m.?
3. Do you have a friend with a disability? How do you help this person?
4. Why did Jesus forgive the man before healing him?
5. Who were the friends in your life that cared enough to bring you to Jesus?
6. If you could invite one person to join your group, someone who really needs Christ, who would you like to invite? What is keeping you from doing this?
7. Where are you hurting? How can this group help you? Pray for one another.

(Study notes on page 892)

The Calling of Levi

13Once again Jesus went out beside the lake. A
large crowd came to him, and he began to teach
them. 14As he walked along, he saw Levi son of
Alphaeus sitting at the tax collector's booth. "Follow me," Jesus told him, and Levi got up and
followed him.
15While Jesus was having dinner at Levi's
house, many tax collectors and "sinners" were
eating with him and his disciples, for there were
many who followed him. 16When the teachers of
the law who were Pharisees saw him eating with
the "sinners" and tax collectors, they asked his
disciples: "Why does he eat with tax collectors
and 'sinners'?"
17On hearing this, Jesus said to them, "It is not
the healthy who need a doctor, but the sick. I
have not come to call the righteous, but sinners."

Jesus Questioned About Fasting

18Now John's disciples and the Pharisees were
fasting. Some people came and asked Jesus,
"How is it that John's disciples and the disciples
of the Pharisees are fasting, but yours are not?"
19Jesus answered, "How can the guests of the
bridegroom fast while he is with them? They cannot, so long as they have him with them. 20But
the time will come when the bridegroom will be
taken from them, and on that day they will fast.
21"No one sews a patch of unshrunk cloth on
an old garment. If he does, the new piece will
pull away from the old, making the tear worse.
22And no one pours new wine into old wineskins. If he does, the wine will burst the skins,
and both the wine and the wineskins will be
ruined. No, he pours new wine into new wineskins."

Lord of the Sabbath

23One Sabbath Jesus was going through the
grainfields, and as his disciples walked along,
they began to pick some heads of grain. 24The
Pharisees said to him, "Look, why are they doing
what is unlawful on the Sabbath?"

MARK 2:23–3:6

1. When you were a kid, what were you not allowed to do on Sunday because it was the "Sabbath"?
2. In your school, what "rule" do you rebel against?
3. Which of your parents' rules have you broken most often?
4. How do you feel about the Pharisees in these stories?
5. Who do you admire because they know what they believe and are willing to stand by their convictions?
6. What can this group do to help ensure your church is a place more concerned with people's needs than rules and regulations?
7. How can the group help you in prayer this week?

(Study notes on page 894)

25He answered, "Have you never read what
David did when he and his companions were
hungry and in need? 26In the days of Abiathar the
high priest, he entered the house of God and ate
the consecrated bread, which is lawful only for
priests to eat. And he also gave some to his companions."

27Then he said to them, "The Sabbath was
made for man, not man for the Sabbath. 28So the
Son of Man is Lord even of the Sabbath."

3 Another time he went into the synagogue,
and a man with a shriveled hand was there.
2Some of them were looking for a reason to accuse Jesus, so they watched him closely to see if
he would heal him on the Sabbath. 3Jesus said to
the man with the shriveled hand, "Stand up in
front of everyone."

4Then Jesus asked them, "Which is lawful on
the Sabbath: to do good or to do evil, to save life
or to kill?" But they remained silent.

5He looked around at them in anger and, deeply distressed at their stubborn hearts, said to the
man, "Stretch out your hand." He stretched it
out, and his hand was completely restored. 6Then
the Pharisees went out and began to plot with the
Herodians how they might kill Jesus.

Crowds Follow Jesus

7Jesus withdrew with his disciples to the lake,
and a large crowd from Galilee followed. 8When
they heard all he was doing, many people came
to him from Judea, Jerusalem, Idumea, and the regions across the Jordan and around Tyre and Sidon. 9Because of the crowd he told his disciples
to have a small boat ready for him, to keep the
people from crowding him. 10For he had healed
many, so that those with diseases were pushing
forward to touch him. 11Whenever the evil[a]
spirits saw him, they fell down before him and
cried out, "You are the Son of God." 12But he
gave them strict orders not to tell who he was.

The Appointing of the Twelve Apostles

13Jesus went up on a mountainside and called
to him those he wanted, and they came to him.
14He appointed twelve—designating them
apostles[b]—that they might be with him and
that he might send them out to preach 15and to
have authority to drive out demons. 16These are
the twelve he appointed: Simon (to whom he
gave the name Peter); 17James son of Zebedee
and his brother John (to them he gave the name
Boanerges, which means Sons of Thunder); 18An-
drew, Philip, Bartholomew, Matthew, Thomas,
James son of Alphaeus, Thaddaeus, Simon the
Zealot 19and Judas Iscariot, who betrayed him.

Jesus and Beelzebub

20Then Jesus entered a house, and again a
crowd gathered, so that he and his disciples were
not even able to eat. 21When his family heard
about this, they went to take charge of him, for
they said, "He is out of his mind."

22And the teachers of the law who came down
from Jerusalem said, "He is possessed by Beelzebub[c]! By the prince of demons he is driving out
demons."

23So Jesus called them and spoke to them in
parables: "How can Satan drive out Satan? 24If a
kingdom is divided against itself, that kingdom
cannot stand. 25If a house is divided against itself,
that house cannot stand. 26And if Satan opposes
himself and is divided, he cannot stand; his end
has come. 27In fact, no one can enter a strong
man's house and carry off his possessions unless

[a] *11* Greek *unclean*; also in verse 30 [b] *14* Some manuscripts do not have *designating them apostles.* [c] *22* Greek *Beezeboul* or *Beelzeboul*

2:23 *pick some heads of grain.* It was permissible for hungry travellers to pluck and eat grain from a field (Deut. 23:25). The issue is not stealing. What the Pharisees objected to was the "work" (harvesting) this involved, according to Jewish tradition.

2:26–27 *ate the consecrated bread.* David did what was forbidden (1 Sam. 21:1–6; Lev. 24:9), providing a precedent that human need can supercede law. So many Sabbath laws had evolved that the Sabbath had become a burden, not a blessing.

3:2 *if he would heal him on the Sabbath.* An indication the Pharisees accepted Jesus' power to heal. The issue is whether Jesus would do so on the Sabbath in defiance of the oral tradition, which allowed healing only if there was danger to life. Jesus could have waited a day to heal this paralysis.

3:4–5 *to do good or to do evil, to save life or to kill?* Jesus' question is ironic: whereas he was wanting to preserve life by healing, the Pharisees were plotting to kill him (v. 6). ***anger / deeply distressed.*** Jesus felt strongly about the injustice of a system that sacrificed the genuine needs of people for the traditions of men, all in the name of piety.

3:6 *Herodians.* A political group made up of influential Jewish sympathizers of King Herod. They were normally despised by the Pharisees, who considered them traitors (for working with Rome) and irreligious (unclean as a result of their association with Gentiles). However, the Pharisees had no power to kill Jesus. Only the civil authority can do this, and hence the collaboration.

3:20–21 For the first time in Mark, Jesus' family is heard from, though in a surprising role. They think Jesus is out of his mind (literally, "beside himself"), and likely wanted to get him away from his busy schedule.

3:22–30 Sandwiched into the story of his family is this account of how the teachers of the Law explain Jesus' power. ***Beelzebub.*** The prince of demons, or Satan. The teachers of the Law cannot deny his healing and exorcism, and since they know they are God's representatives (and Jesus is not one of them), the only other source of such power is Satan.

3:23–27 Jesus points out the flaw in their argument: the power of Satan cannot be used to undo the power of Satan. He has used his power to bind Satan ("the strong man"), as demonstrated by the fact that he is undoing Satan's works every time he heals or casts out a demon.

3:29 *blasphemes against the Holy Spirit.* Jesus identifies the "unpardonable sin" in verse 30: attributing to Satan the miracles Jesus did in the power of the Holy Spirit. Anxiety about whether one has committed "an eternal sin" is the very demonstration that such a person is still open to the convicting work of the Spirit.

3:34–35 Jesus gives a new definition of family. Kinship is not a matter of heredity, it is a matter of doing God's will (which his natural family is not doing by trying to stop his ministry). Membership in God's spiritual family outweighs that of our human family.

he first ties up the strong man. Then he can rob his house. 28I tell you the truth, all the sins and blasphemies of men will be forgiven them. 29But whoever blasphemes against the Holy Spirit will never be forgiven; he is guilty of an eternal sin."

30He said this because they were saying, "He has an evil spirit."

Jesus' Mother and Brothers

31Then Jesus' mother and brothers arrived. Standing outside, they sent someone in to call him. 32A crowd was sitting around him, and they told him, "Your mother and brothers are outside looking for you."

33"Who are my mother and my brothers?" he asked.

34Then he looked at those seated in a circle around him and said, "Here are my mother and my brothers! 35Whoever does God's will is my brother and sister and mother."

Mark 3:20–35

1. When did you start deciding for yourself on the clothes you would wear? On your hairstyle?
2. What's something you've done that made your family or friends wonder if you were crazy?
3. Right now, how are you feeling about your family? How are they feeling about you?
4. Why do you think Jesus' family thought he was "out of his mind" (v. 21)?
5. On what issue do you most often disagree with your parents? How do you resolve your differences?
6. Where are you in your relationship with the family of God?
7. Close by praying for your families.

(Study notes on page 894)

The Parable of the Sower

4 Again Jesus began to teach by the lake. The crowd that gathered around him was so large that he got into a boat and sat in it out on the lake, while all the people were along the shore at the water's edge. 2He taught them many things by parables, and in his teaching said: 3"Listen! A farmer went out to sow his seed. 4As he was scattering the seed, some fell along the path, and the birds came and ate it up. 5Some fell on rocky places, where it did not have much soil. It sprang up quickly, because the soil was shallow. 6But when the sun came up, the plants were scorched, and they withered because they had no root. 7Other seed fell among thorns, which grew up and choked the plants, so that they did not bear grain. 8Still other seed fell on good soil. It came up, grew and produced a crop, multiplying thirty, sixty, or even a hundred times."

9Then Jesus said, "He who has ears to hear, let him hear."

10When he was alone, the Twelve and the others around him asked him about the parables. 11He told them, "The secret of the kingdom of God has been given to you. But to those on the outside everything is said in parables 12so that,

"'they may be ever seeing but never perceiving,
and ever hearing but never understanding;
otherwise they might turn and be forgiven!'[a]"

13Then Jesus said to them, "Don't you understand this parable? How then will you understand any parable? 14The farmer sows the word. 15Some people are like seed along the path, where the word is sown. As soon as they hear it, Satan comes and takes away the word that was sown in them. 16Others, like seed sown on rocky places, hear the word and at once receive it with joy. 17But since they have no root, they last only a short time. When trouble or persecution comes because of the word, they quickly fall away. 18Still others, like seed sown among thorns, hear the word; 19but the worries of this life, the deceitfulness of wealth and the desires for other things come in and choke the word, making it unfruitful. 20Others, like seed sown on good soil, hear the word, accept it, and produce a crop—thirty, sixty or even a hundred times what was sown."

A Lamp on a Stand

21He said to them, "Do you bring in a lamp to put it under a bowl or a bed? Instead, don't you put it on its stand? 22For whatever is hidden is meant to be disclosed, and whatever is concealed is meant to be brought out into the open. 23If anyone has ears to hear, let him hear."

24"Consider carefully what you hear," he con-

[a] 12 Isaiah 6:9,10

tinued. "With the measure you use, it will be measured to you—and even more. [25]Whoever has will be given more; whoever does not have, even what he has will be taken from him."

The Parable of the Growing Seed

[26]He also said, "This is what the kingdom of God is like. A man scatters seed on the ground. [27]Night and day, whether he sleeps or gets up, the seed sprouts and grows, though he does not know how. [28]All by itself the soil produces grain—first the stalk, then the head, then the full kernel in the head. [29]As soon as the grain is ripe, he puts the sickle to it, because the harvest has come."

The Parable of the Mustard Seed

[30]Again he said, "What shall we say the kingdom of God is like, or what parable shall we use to describe it? [31]It is like a mustard seed, which is the smallest seed you plant in the ground. [32]Yet when planted, it grows and becomes the largest of all garden plants, with such big branches that the birds of the air can perch in its shade."

[33]With many similar parables Jesus spoke the word to them, as much as they could understand. [34]He did not say anything to them without using a parable. But when he was alone with his own disciples, he explained everything.

Jesus Calms the Storm

[35]That day when evening came, he said to his disciples, "Let us go over to the other side." [36]Leaving the crowd behind, they took him along, just as he was, in the boat. There were also other boats with him. [37]A furious squall came up, and the waves broke over the boat, so that it was nearly swamped. [38]Jesus was in the stern, sleeping on a cushion. The disciples woke him and said to him, "Teacher, don't you care if we drown?"

[39]He got up, rebuked the wind and said to the waves, "Quiet! Be still!" Then the wind died down and it was completely calm.

[40]He said to his disciples, "Why are you so afraid? Do you still have no faith?"

[41]They were terrified and asked each other, "Who is this? Even the wind and the waves obey him!"

MARK 4:35–41

1. When you were little, what did you do when there was a big storm?
2. What's the worst storm you've been in?
3. On a scale from 1 (high stress) to 10 (low stress), what is the stress level in your life at the moment?
4. How do you feel about Jesus knowing that "even the wind and the waves obey him" (v. 41)?
5. What brings on most of the storms in your life: Pressures at school? Family problems? Hassles with relationships?
6. What worry do you have that you need Jesus to calm?
7. What have you found helpful when you are anxious? Pray for one another.

The Healing of a Demon-possessed Man

5 They went across the lake to the region of the Gerasenes.[a] [2]When Jesus got out of the boat, a man with an evil[b] spirit came from the tombs to meet him. [3]This man lived in the tombs, and no one could bind him any more, not even with a chain. [4]For he had often been chained hand and foot, but he tore the chains apart and broke the irons on his feet. No one was strong enough to subdue him. [5]Night and day among the

[a] *1* Some manuscripts *Gadarenes*; other manuscripts *Gergesenes*

[b] *2* Greek *unclean*; also in verses 8 and 13

4:37 ***A furious squall.*** The Sea of Galilee was a deep, freshwater lake, 13 miles long and eight miles wide. Fierce winds blew into this bowl-shaped sea, creating savage and unpredictable storms.

4:38 ***sleeping.*** In the OT sleeping peacefully is a sign of trust in the power of God (Ps. 4:8). The fact that Jesus was asleep during a storm is also a sign of his exhaustion from a day of teaching. ***Teacher.*** Up to this point, the disciples understood Jesus to be a rabbi. ***don't you care if we drown?*** They wake Jesus up so he can help them bail out the boat since it was about to be swamped and sink. As their later response indicates (v. 41), they had no expectation he would have any power over the storm.

4:39 Instead of bailing, Jesus commands the wind and the waves to be still and so they are. He has power over the very elements—in the same way that God does (Ps. 65:7; 106:9). ***Be still!*** This is literally, "Be muzzled!" as if the storm were some wild beast needing to be subdued.

4:41 ***terrified.*** Some of the disciples were fishermen who knew how serious their peril was in the face of the storm, so fear for their lives was understandable. But now terror replaces their fear. This is what is felt in the presence of an unknown force or power. It is the response a vision of a demon, angel, ghost or some other strange, supernatural experience would inspire. Once Jesus displays his power, the disciples' fear of the storm turns into fear of Jesus. ***Who is this?*** This is the key question in Mark's Gospel.

tombs and in the hills he would cry out and cut
himself with stones.
6When he saw Jesus from a distance, he ran
and fell on his knees in front of him. 7He shouted
at the top of his voice, "What do you want with
me, Jesus, Son of the Most High God? Swear to
God that you won't torture me!" 8For Jesus had
said to him, "Come out of this man, you evil
spirit!"
9Then Jesus asked him, "What is your name?"
"My name is Legion," he replied, "for we are
many." 10And he begged Jesus again and again
not to send them out of the area.
11A large herd of pigs was feeding on the nearby hillside. 12The demons begged Jesus, "Send us
among the pigs; allow us to go into them." 13He
gave them permission, and the evil spirits came
out and went into the pigs. The herd, about two
thousand in number, rushed down the steep
bank into the lake and were drowned.
14Those tending the pigs ran off and reported
this in the town and countryside, and the people
went out to see what had happened. 15When
they came to Jesus, they saw the man who had
been possessed by the legion of demons, sitting
there, dressed and in his right mind; and they
were afraid. 16Those who had seen it told the
people what had happened to the demon-
possessed man—and told about the pigs as well.
17Then the people began to plead with Jesus to
leave their region.
18As Jesus was getting into the boat, the man
who had been demon-possessed begged to go
with him. 19Jesus did not let him, but said, "Go
home to your family and tell them how much the
Lord has done for you, and how he has had mercy
on you." 20So the man went away and began to
tell in the Decapolis[a] how much Jesus had done
for him. And all the people were amazed.

A Dead Girl and a Sick Woman

21When Jesus had again crossed over by boat
to the other side of the lake, a large crowd gathered around him while he was by the lake.
22Then one of the synagogue rulers, named Jairus, came there. Seeing Jesus, he fell at his feet
23and pleaded earnestly with him, "My little
daughter is dying. Please come and put your
hands on her so that she will be healed and live."
24So Jesus went with him.
A large crowd followed and pressed around
him. 25And a woman was there who had been
subject to bleeding for twelve years. 26She had
suffered a great deal under the care of many doctors and had spent all she had, yet instead of
getting better she grew worse. 27When she heard
about Jesus, she came up behind him in the
crowd and touched his cloak, 28because she
thought, "If I just touch his clothes, I will be
healed." 29Immediately her bleeding stopped and

MARK 5:24–34

1. Whose voice or touch can you recognize in an instant—even in a crowded room?
2. How do you feel about a trip to the doctor's office? Would you rather suffer with pain than go see a doctor?
3. What's the closest you've come to having a chronic health problem that just wouldn't go away?
4. Why was it important to Jesus in verse 31 to know "Who touched me?"
5. Does God still heal? Do you know someone whom God miraculously healed?
6. Where in your life do you need to reach out in faith and touch Jesus?
7. How can this group help you in prayer this week?

[a]20 That is, the Ten Cities

This story is actually sandwiched between the opening and conclusion of the story of Jairus' daughter. The two stories are to be understood in relation to each other. Both deal with females who were second class citizens in the first-century culture; both were religiously unclean (one from bleeding and the other from dying); and both were healed by faith through Jesus' touch.

5:25 *subject to bleeding.* This woman was probably hemorrhaging from the womb. In addition to the obvious physical weakness such a chronic problem would produce, this particular problem rendered her ritually impure (Lev. 15:25–33). As a result, she was not allowed to take part in temple worship, was unable to have sexual relations with her husband, and was not supposed to be in a crowd where others might brush up against her and also become "unclean."

5:28 *just touch his clothes.* The power of a person was thought to be transferred to his or her clothing. Perhaps out of fear of rejection because she was unclean, the woman did not even dare approach Jesus openly. She simply wanted to touch his cloak without drawing any attention to herself.

5:32–34 Jesus insists that the person who touched him reveal herself. Her healing will not be complete without this, since her illness had not only physical but social consequences. Jesus makes it publicly known that she has been healed so that she can once again have a normal relational life. ***Daughter.*** She is indeed a child of God, loved and not under his judgment.

she felt in her body that she was freed from her
suffering.
30At once Jesus realized that power had gone
out from him. He turned around in the crowd and
asked, "Who touched my clothes?"
31"You see the people crowding against you,"
his disciples answered, "and yet you can ask,
'Who touched me?' "
32But Jesus kept looking around to see who
had done it. 33Then the woman, knowing what
had happened to her, came and fell at his feet
and, trembling with fear, told him the whole
truth. 34He said to her, "Daughter, your faith has
healed you. Go in peace and be freed from your
suffering."
35While Jesus was still speaking, some men
came from the house of Jairus, the synagogue
ruler. "Your daughter is dead," they said. "Why
bother the teacher any more?"
36Ignoring what they said, Jesus told the synagogue ruler, "Don't be afraid; just believe."
37He did not let anyone follow him except Peter, James and John the brother of James. 38When
they came to the home of the synagogue ruler,
Jesus saw a commotion, with people crying and
wailing loudly. 39He went in and said to them,
"Why all this commotion and wailing? The child
is not dead but asleep." 40But they laughed at
him.
After he put them all out, he took the child's
father and mother and the disciples who were
with him, and went in where the child was. 41He
took her by the hand and said to her, *"Talitha
koum!"* (which means, "Little girl, I say to you,
get up!"). 42Immediately the girl stood up and
walked around (she was twelve years old). At this
they were completely astonished. 43He gave
strict orders not to let anyone know about this,
and told them to give her something to eat.

A Prophet Without Honor

6 Jesus left there and went to his hometown,
accompanied by his disciples. 2When the
Sabbath came, he began to teach in the synagogue, and many who heard him were amazed.
"Where did this man get these things?" they
asked. "What's this wisdom that has been given
him, that he even does miracles! 3Isn't this the
carpenter? Isn't this Mary's son and the brother
of James, Joseph,[a] Judas and Simon? Aren't his
sisters here with us?" And they took offense at
him.
4Jesus said to them, "Only in his hometown,
among his relatives and in his own house is a
prophet without honor." 5He could not do any
miracles there, except lay his hands on a few sick
people and heal them. 6And he was amazed at
their lack of faith.

Jesus Sends Out the Twelve

Then Jesus went around teaching from village
to village. 7Calling the Twelve to him, he sent
them out two by two and gave them authority
over evil[b] spirits.
8These were his instructions: "Take nothing
for the journey except a staff—no bread, no bag,
no money in your belts. 9Wear sandals but not an
extra tunic. 10Whenever you enter a house, stay
there until you leave that town. 11And if any
place will not welcome you or listen to you,
shake the dust off your feet when you leave, as a
testimony against them."
12They went out and preached that people
should repent. 13They drove out many demons
and anointed many sick people with oil and
healed them.

John the Baptist Beheaded

14King Herod heard about this, for Jesus' name
had become well known. Some were saying,[c]
"John the Baptist has been raised from the dead,
and that is why miraculous powers are at work in
him."
15Others said, "He is Elijah."
And still others claimed, "He is a prophet, like
one of the prophets of long ago."
16But when Herod heard this, he said, "John,
the man I beheaded, has been raised from the
dead!"
17For Herod himself had given orders to have
John arrested, and he had him bound and put
in prison. He did this because of Herodias, his
brother Philip's wife, whom he had married.
18For John had been saying to Herod, "It is not
lawful for you to have your brother's wife." 19So
Herodias nursed a grudge against John and wanted to kill him. But she was not able to, 20because
Herod feared John and protected him, knowing
him to be a righteous and holy man. When Herod
heard John, he was greatly puzzled[d]; yet he
liked to listen to him.
21Finally the opportune time came. On his
birthday Herod gave a banquet for his high officials and military commanders and the leading
men of Galilee. 22When the daughter of Herodias
came in and danced, she pleased Herod and his
dinner guests.
The king said to the girl, "Ask me for anything
you want, and I'll give it to you." 23And he promised her with an oath, "Whatever you ask I will
give you, up to half my kingdom."

[a]3 Greek *Joses*, a variant of *Joseph* [b]7 Greek *unclean* [c]14 Some early manuscripts *He was saying* [d]20 Some early manuscripts *he did many things*

24 She went out and said to her mother, "What
shall I ask for?"
"The head of John the Baptist," she answered.
25 At once the girl hurried in to the king with
the request: "I want you to give me right now the
head of John the Baptist on a platter."

MARK 6:14–29

1. What is the goriest movie you've seen lately? If you gave a movie rating to this story in the Bible, what would it be?
2. What's your favorite musician or group? What kind of influence does their music have on you?
3. Who is *the* John the Baptist at your school—someone not afraid to speak out on issues that are morally wrong?
4. Of the people involved in the death of John the Baptist, who do you hold most responsible?
5. How much influence did Herod's environment (a *wild* party) have on his judgment (see note on 6:22)? How are you influenced by your surroundings?
6. Specifically, where do you draw the line when it comes to movies, music, etc. with sexual and/or violent content?
7. How can the group support you in prayer as you strive to avoid impure words and images?

26 The king was greatly distressed, but because
of his oaths and his dinner guests, he did not
want to refuse her. 27 So he immediately sent an
executioner with orders to bring John's head.
The man went, beheaded John in the prison,
28 and brought back his head on a platter. He presented it to the girl, and she gave it to her mother. 29 On hearing of this, John's disciples came
and took his body and laid it in a tomb.

Jesus Feeds the Five Thousand

30 The apostles gathered around Jesus and reported to him all they had done and taught.
31 Then, because so many people were coming
and going that they did not even have a chance to
eat, he said to them, "Come with me by yourselves to a quiet place and get some rest."
32 So they went away by themselves in a boat
to a solitary place. 33 But many who saw them leaving recognized them and ran on foot from all the
towns and got there ahead of them. 34 When Jesus
landed and saw a large crowd, he had compassion
on them, because they were like sheep without
a shepherd. So he began teaching them many
things.
35 By this time it was late in the day, so his
disciples came to him. "This is a remote place,"
they said, "and it's already very late. 36 Send the
people away so they can go to the surrounding
countryside and villages and buy themselves
something to eat."
37 But he answered, "You give them something
to eat."
They said to him, "That would take eight
months of a man's wages[a]! Are we to go and
spend that much on bread and give it to them to
eat?"
38 "How many loaves do you have?" he asked.
"Go and see."
When they found out, they said, "Five—and
two fish."
39 Then Jesus directed them to have all the people sit down in groups on the green grass. 40 So
they sat down in groups of hundreds and fifties.
41 Taking the five loaves and the two fish and
looking up to heaven, he gave thanks and broke
the loaves. Then he gave them to his disciples to
set before the people. He also divided the two

[a] *37* Greek *take two hundred denarii*

In this parenthetical flashback, Mark describes how John the Baptist died at the hands of Herod. This is the only story in Mark in which Jesus is not the central figure. In this passage the relative powerlessness of Herod (who in reality held all the political power) is contrasted to the great power of Jesus (who had no official status). Two kings and kingdoms are contrasted.

6:14–16 The issue once again is: Who is Jesus? Three answers are proposed. He is John the Baptist come back from the dead (the answer Herod opts for in his guilt); he is Elijah (the assumed forerunner of the Messiah—Mal. 4:5); or he is a new prophet.

6:18 *It is not lawful.* According to Leviticus 18:16 and 20:21, it was not lawful for a man to marry his brother's wife while that brother was still alive, as Herod had done.

6:22 *daughter of Herodias.* Herodias' teenage daughter from her first marriage. According to the historian Josephus, her name was Salome. For a princess to dance publicly before an audience of drunken men was considered shameful. Her dance was undoubtedly highly sensual. ***Ask me for anything you want.*** Through Salome, Herodias succeeds in manipulating Herod by exploiting his lust, drunkenness and tendency to show off. This is the opportunity she has been waiting for (see vv. 19–20).

6:25 *the head of John the Baptist on a platter.* This was a gruesome act: serving John's head on a platter as if it were just another course in the banquet.

fish among them all. 42They all ate and were satisfied, 43and the disciples picked up twelve basketfuls of broken pieces of bread and fish. 44The
number of the men who had eaten was five thousand.

> **?** ***Mark 6:30–44***
>
> 1. What do you like to do to unwind after a busy day?
> 2. What grade would you give to how you manage your time? How could you improve?
> 3. If you could add one hour to your day, what would you use it for?
> 4. The disciples thought they were getting a break (v. 31), but they ended up serving. What does this passage say to you about the use of your free time?
> 5. How much time did you spend with God this week? Where will you schedule time for God this coming week?
> 6. If this group pooled its time and resources, what special project could be accomplished?
> 7. Close by spending time in prayer.

Jesus Walks on the Water

45Immediately Jesus made his disciples get
into the boat and go on ahead of him to Bethsaida, while he dismissed the crowd. 46After leaving
them, he went up on a mountainside to pray.
47When evening came, the boat was in the
middle of the lake, and he was alone on land.
48He saw the disciples straining at the oars, because the wind was against them. About the
fourth watch of the night he went out to them,
walking on the lake. He was about to pass by
them, 49but when they saw him walking on the
lake, they thought he was a ghost. They cried out,
50because they all saw him and were terrified.
Immediately he spoke to them and said, "Take
courage! It is I. Don't be afraid." 51Then he
climbed into the boat with them, and the wind
died down. They were completely amazed, 52for
they had not understood about the loaves; their
hearts were hardened.
53When they had crossed over, they landed at
Gennesaret and anchored there. 54As soon as
they got out of the boat, people recognized Jesus.
55They ran throughout that whole region and carried the sick on mats to wherever they heard he
was. 56And wherever he went—into villages,
towns or countryside—they placed the sick in
the marketplaces. They begged him to let them
touch even the edge of his cloak, and all who
touched him were healed.

Clean and Unclean

7 The Pharisees and some of the teachers of
the law who had come from Jerusalem gathered around Jesus and 2saw some of his disciples
eating food with hands that were "unclean," that
is, unwashed. 3(The Pharisees and all the Jews do
not eat unless they give their hands a ceremonial
washing, holding to the tradition of the elders.
4When they come from the marketplace they do
not eat unless they wash. And they observe many
other traditions, such as the washing of cups,
pitchers and kettles.[a])
5So the Pharisees and teachers of the law
asked Jesus, "Why don't your disciples live according to the tradition of the elders instead of
eating their food with 'unclean' hands?"
6He replied, "Isaiah was right when he prophesied about you hypocrites; as it is written:

" 'These people honor me with their lips,
but their hearts are far from me.
7They worship me in vain;

[a]4 Some early manuscripts *pitchers, kettles and dining couches*

6:30–31 ***apostles.*** An apostle is "one who is sent"; the Twelve have just completed the missionary work Jesus sent them to do (6:7). ***get some rest.*** It is Jesus who insists on rest, even though the opportunity for ministry is great (see also 1:35).

6:33 ***ran on foot.*** The distances wouldn't have been great (the Sea of Galilee was only eight miles at its widest), and perhaps a strong headwind slowed the boat.

6:35–37 The disciples recognize they have a problem on their hands. How are they going to feed the enormous crowd that has gathered? ***Send the people away.*** Not expecting a miracle, this is the disciples' solution. ***You give them something to eat.*** Jesus has quite a different solution in mind. ***eight months of a man's wages.*** See NIV text note. The usual daily wage was one denarius, meaning about 200 denarii would be earned in eight months.

6:42–43 ***satisfied.*** The five loaves and two fish fed everyone not meagerly, but abundantly. Unfortunately, some have tried to explain away this miracle—for instance, by suggesting Jesus and the disciples shared their food and the crowd followed their example. ***twelve basketfuls of broken pieces of bread and fish.*** Jews considered bread a gift from God, and it was required that the scraps of a meal be collected. Each disciple returned with his basket full.

6:44 ***men.*** Literally, "males." When all the women and children are taken into account, this was a huge crowd—far beyond 5,000.

their teachings are but rules taught by
men.'[a]
8You have let go of the commands of God and are
holding on to the traditions of men."
9And he said to them: "You have a fine way of
setting aside the commands of God in order to
observe[b] your own traditions! 10For Moses said,
'Honor your father and your mother,'[c] and,
'Anyone who curses his father or mother must be
put to death.'[d] 11But you say that if a man says
to his father or mother: 'Whatever help you
might otherwise have received from me is Cor-
ban' (that is, a gift devoted to God), 12then you no
longer let him do anything for his father or mother. 13Thus you nullify the word of God by your
tradition that you have handed down. And you do
many things like that."
14Again Jesus called the crowd to him and said,
"Listen to me, everyone, and understand this.
15Nothing outside a man can make him 'unclean'
by going into him. Rather, it is what comes out of
a man that makes him 'unclean.'[e]"
17After he had left the crowd and entered the
house, his disciples asked him about this parable.
18"Are you so dull?" he asked. "Don't you see
that nothing that enters a man from the outside
can make him 'unclean'? 19For it doesn't go into
his heart but into his stomach, and then out of his
body." (In saying this, Jesus declared all foods
"clean.")
20He went on: "What comes out of a man is
what makes him 'unclean.' 21For from within,
out of men's hearts, come evil thoughts, sexual
immorality, theft, murder, adultery, 22greed, malice, deceit, lewdness, envy, slander, arrogance
and folly. 23All these evils come from inside and
make a man 'unclean.'"

The Faith of a Syrophoenician Woman

24Jesus left that place and went to the vicinity
of Tyre.[f] He entered a house and did not want
anyone to know it; yet he could not keep his
presence secret. 25In fact, as soon as she heard
about him, a woman whose little daughter was
possessed by an evil[g] spirit came and fell at his
feet. 26The woman was a Greek, born in Syrian
Phoenicia. She begged Jesus to drive the demon
out of her daughter.
27"First let the children eat all they want," he
told her, "for it is not right to take the children's
bread and toss it to their dogs."
28"Yes, Lord," she replied, "but even the dogs
under the table eat the children's crumbs."
29Then he told her, "For such a reply, you may
go; the demon has left your daughter."
30She went home and found her child lying on
the bed, and the demon gone.

The Healing of a Deaf and Mute Man

31Then Jesus left the vicinity of Tyre and went
through Sidon, down to the Sea of Galilee and
into the region of the Decapolis.[h] 32There some
people brought to him a man who was deaf and
could hardly talk, and they begged him to place
his hand on the man.
33After he took him aside, away from the
crowd, Jesus put his fingers into the man's
ears. Then he spit and touched the man's tongue.
34He looked up to heaven and with a deep sigh
said to him, *"Ephphatha!"* (which means,
"Be opened!"). 35At this, the man's ears were
opened, his tongue was loosened and he began to
speak plainly.
36Jesus commanded them not to tell anyone.
But the more he did so, the more they kept talking about it. 37People were overwhelmed with
amazement. "He has done everything well," they
said. "He even makes the deaf hear and the mute
speak."

Jesus Feeds the Four Thousand

8 During those days another large crowd gathered. Since they had nothing to eat, Jesus
called his disciples to him and said, 2"I have compassion for these people; they have already been
with me three days and have nothing to eat. 3If I
send them home hungry, they will collapse on
the way, because some of them have come a long
distance."
4His disciples answered, "But where in this
remote place can anyone get enough bread to
feed them?"
5"How many loaves do you have?" Jesus asked.
"Seven," they replied.
6He told the crowd to sit down on the ground.
When he had taken the seven loaves and given
thanks, he broke them and gave them to his disciples to set before the people, and they did so.
7They had a few small fish as well; he gave thanks
for them also and told the disciples to distribute
them. 8The people ate and were satisfied. Afterward the disciples picked up seven basketfuls of
broken pieces that were left over. 9About four
thousand men were present. And having sent
them away, 10he got into the boat with his disciples and went to the region of Dalmanutha.
11The Pharisees came and began to question
Jesus. To test him, they asked him for a sign from
heaven. 12He sighed deeply and said, "Why does
this generation ask for a miraculous sign? I tell

[a] *6,7* Isaiah 29:13 [b] *9* Some manuscripts *set up* [c] *10* Exodus 20:12; Deut. 5:16 [d] *10* Exodus 21:17; Lev. 20:9
[e] *15* Some early manuscripts *'unclean.' 16If anyone has ears to hear, let him hear.* [f] *24* Many early manuscripts *Tyre and Sidon*
[g] *25* Greek *unclean* [h] *31* That is, the Ten Cities

you the truth, no sign will be given to it." [13]Then he left them, got back into the boat and crossed to the other side.

The Yeast of the Pharisees and Herod

[14]The disciples had forgotten to bring bread, except for one loaf they had with them in the boat. [15]"Be careful," Jesus warned them. "Watch out for the yeast of the Pharisees and that of Herod."

[16]They discussed this with one another and said, "It is because we have no bread."

[17]Aware of their discussion, Jesus asked them: "Why are you talking about having no bread? Do you still not see or understand? Are your hearts hardened? [18]Do you have eyes but fail to see, and ears but fail to hear? And don't you remember? [19]When I broke the five loaves for the five thousand, how many basketfuls of pieces did you pick up?"

"Twelve," they replied.

[20]"And when I broke the seven loaves for the four thousand, how many basketfuls of pieces did you pick up?"

They answered, "Seven."

[21]He said to them, "Do you still not understand?"

The Healing of a Blind Man at Bethsaida

[22]They came to Bethsaida, and some people brought a blind man and begged Jesus to touch him. [23]He took the blind man by the hand and led him outside the village. When he had spit on the man's eyes and put his hands on him, Jesus asked, "Do you see anything?"

[24]He looked up and said, "I see people; they look like trees walking around."

[25]Once more Jesus put his hands on the man's eyes. Then his eyes were opened, his sight was restored, and he saw everything clearly. [26]Jesus sent him home, saying, "Don't go into the village.[a]"

Peter's Confession of Christ

[27]Jesus and his disciples went on to the villages around Caesarea Philippi. On the way he asked them, "Who do people say I am?"

[28]They replied, "Some say John the Baptist; others say Elijah; and still others, one of the prophets."

[29]"But what about you?" he asked. "Who do you say I am?"

Peter answered, "You are the Christ.[b]"

[30]Jesus warned them not to tell anyone about him.

Jesus Predicts His Death

[31]He then began to teach them that the Son of Man must suffer many things and be rejected by the elders, chief priests and teachers of the law, and that he must be killed and after three days rise again. [32]He spoke plainly about this, and Peter took him aside and began to rebuke him.

[33]But when Jesus turned and looked at his disciples, he rebuked Peter. "Get behind me, Satan!" he said. "You do not have in mind the things of God, but the things of men."

[34]Then he called the crowd to him along with his disciples and said: "If anyone would come after me, he must deny himself and take up his cross and follow me. [35]For whoever wants to save his life[c] will lose it, but whoever loses his life for me and for the gospel will save it. [36]What good is it for a man to gain the whole world, yet forfeit his soul? [37]Or what can a man give in exchange for his soul? [38]If anyone is ashamed of me and my words in this adulterous and sinful generation, the Son of Man will be ashamed of him when he comes in his Father's glory with the holy angels."

9 And he said to them, "I tell you the truth, some who are standing here will not taste death before they see the kingdom of God come with power."

The Transfiguration

[2]After six days Jesus took Peter, James and John with him and led them up a high mountain, where they were all alone. There he was transfigured before them. [3]His clothes became dazzling white, whiter than anyone in the world could bleach them. [4]And there appeared before them Elijah and Moses, who were talking with Jesus.

[5]Peter said to Jesus, "Rabbi, it is good for us to be here. Let us put up three shelters—one for you, one for Moses and one for Elijah." [6](He did not know what to say, they were so frightened.)

[7]Then a cloud appeared and enveloped them, and a voice came from the cloud: "This is my Son, whom I love. Listen to him!"

[8]Suddenly, when they looked around, they no longer saw anyone with them except Jesus.

[9]As they were coming down the mountain, Jesus gave them orders not to tell anyone what they had seen until the Son of Man had risen from the dead. [10]They kept the matter to themselves, discussing what "rising from the dead" meant.

[11]And they asked him, "Why do the teachers of the law say that Elijah must come first?"

[12]Jesus replied, "To be sure, Elijah does come first, and restores all things. Why then is it writ-

[a]26 Some manuscripts *Don't go and tell anyone in the village* [b]29 Or *Messiah.* "The Christ" (Greek) and "the Messiah" (Hebrew) both mean "the Anointed One." [c]35 The Greek word means either *life* or *soul*; also in verse 36.

ten that the Son of Man must suffer much and be
rejected? 13But I tell you, Elijah has come, and
they have done to him everything they wished,
just as it is written about him."

MARK 9:2–13

1. What's the highest place you've ever climbed?
2. Where is a place you have felt especially close to God?
3. If you could choose three friends to go with you on a spiritual retreat, who would you choose? Where would you go?
4. The disciples were told (v. 7), "This is my Son, whom I love. Listen to him!" What is the most effective way for you to listen to God?
5. Who has had the biggest spiritual influence in your life? How?
6. When did Jesus appear to you in a special way? How was his glory revealed to you?
7. How would you describe your relationship with God right now: In the valley? On the mountaintop? Climbing? On the rocks? How can the group pray for you?

The Healing of a Boy With an Evil Spirit

14When they came to the other disciples, they
saw a large crowd around them and the teachers
of the law arguing with them. 15As soon as all the
people saw Jesus, they were overwhelmed with
wonder and ran to greet him.

16"What are you arguing with them about?" he
asked.

17A man in the crowd answered, "Teacher, I
brought you my son, who is possessed by a spirit
that has robbed him of speech. 18Whenever it
seizes him, it throws him to the ground. He
foams at the mouth, gnashes his teeth and becomes rigid. I asked your disciples to drive out
the spirit, but they could not."

19"O unbelieving generation," Jesus replied,
"how long shall I stay with you? How long shall
I put up with you? Bring the boy to me."

20So they brought him. When the spirit saw
Jesus, it immediately threw the boy into a convulsion. He fell to the ground and rolled around,
foaming at the mouth.

21Jesus asked the boy's father, "How long has
he been like this?"

"From childhood," he answered. 22"It has often thrown him into fire or water to kill him.
But if you can do anything, take pity on us and
help us."

23" 'If you can'?" said Jesus. "Everything is possible for him who believes."

24Immediately the boy's father exclaimed, "I
do believe; help me overcome my unbelief!"

25When Jesus saw that a crowd was running to
the scene, he rebuked the evil[a] spirit. "You deaf

[a]25 Greek *unclean*

9:2–3 ***transfigured.*** Meaning "to change one's form." ***dazzling white.*** Brilliant, radiant light is often associated with appearances of God in the OT (Dan. 7:9). The disciples witness Jesus as he is changed into a form just like God.

9:4–5 ***Elijah and Moses.*** These two significant OT figures endorse Jesus and testify to his greatness. ***shelters.*** Peter may have had in mind the huts put up at the Festival of Tabernacles, or the tent of meeting where God met with Moses. At any rate, he seemed eager to find fulfillment of the promised glory then, foregoing the sufferings that Jesus had pronounced necessary.

9:9–10 What must have seemed clear on the mountain became confusing as the disciples walk down. Jesus again mentions his impending death, which seems totally out of context with what they have just experienced. They wonder if there is another meaning to the notion of "rising from the dead." ***not to tell.*** The meaning of this event cannot be understood until Jesus dies and rises again. Then it will be clear what kind of Messiah he is and what it means to be the Son of God.

9:11–13 Elijah was taken to heaven by God (2 Kings 2:9–12). The Jews believed God would send Elijah back before the Messiah appeared (Mal. 4:5). ***Elijah has come.*** In the Transfiguration Elijah does come. However, Elijah has come in a second sense. John the Baptist played the role of Elijah by being the forerunner of the Messiah. ***they have done.*** Elijah and John suffered rejection, and it is no surprise that the Messiah will also.

9:14 Jesus and Peter, James and John descend from the "high" of the Transfiguration (9:2–13) to the valley, where the religious leaders are arguing with the other disciples about their failure to cast out a demon. They go from the experience of God's power and presence to the experience of Satan's power and presence.

9:23 ***'If you can'?*** By this phrase, the man had indicated he was not sure if Jesus can perform such a miracle (after all, his disciples have failed). By highlighting his doubts Jesus pinpoints the real issue: the question is not whether Jesus has the ability to heal (which has been amply demonstrated); the issue is the man's ability to believe.

9:24 ***I do believe; help me overcome my unbelief!*** The problem here is one of *doubt* (being in two minds about an issue) rather than *disbelief* (certainty that something is not true). The father did not disbelieve. After all, he had brought his son to Jesus to be healed (v. 17). His faith has been shaken, however, by the failure of the disciples to heal his son (v. 18) so that now, even though he desperately wants his child to be free of this demon, he wonders if it is possible (v. 22). Belief and unbelief are often mixed, since faith is never perfect.

9:29 ***This kind.*** Suggests that there are different kinds of demons. ***prayer.*** The disciples have been given the authority to cast out demons (6:7) and have, in fact, done so (6:13). However, as this incident makes clear, this power was not their own. It required continuing dependence upon God.

and mute spirit," he said, "I command you, come
out of him and never enter him again."
26The spirit shrieked, convulsed him violently
and came out. The boy looked so much like a
corpse that many said, "He's dead." 27But Jesus
took him by the hand and lifted him to his feet,
and he stood up.
28After Jesus had gone indoors, his disciples
asked him privately, "Why couldn't we drive it
out?"
29He replied, "This kind can come out only by
prayer.[a]"

MARK 9:14–29

1. What was something you did as a child that drove your parents crazy?
2. What's the closest you've come to having a family member who suffered from a disability?
3. This story begins with an argument. What issues, particularly about faith, do you debate the most with others?
4. When have you felt like the father in the story one moment, saying, "I do believe," and the next, "Help me overcome my unbelief" (v. 24)?
5. What kind of doubts hit you the hardest: Faith issues? Self-image issues? Future concerns?
6. What would help silence the doubts you feel: Admitting them? Praying more? Experiencing a miracle? Asking others to pray for you?
7. Take turns sharing what you need Jesus to remove from your life, and pray for one another.

(Study notes on page 903)

30They left that place and passed through Galilee. Jesus did not want anyone to know where
they were, 31because he was teaching his disciples. He said to them, "The Son of Man is going
to be betrayed into the hands of men. They will
kill him, and after three days he will rise." 32But
they did not understand what he meant and were
afraid to ask him about it.

Who Is the Greatest?

33They came to Capernaum. When he was in
the house, he asked them, "What were you arguing about on the road?" 34But they kept quiet
because on the way they had argued about who
was the greatest.
35Sitting down, Jesus called the Twelve and
said, "If anyone wants to be first, he must be the
very last, and the servant of all."
36He took a little child and had him stand
among them. Taking him in his arms, he said to
them, 37"Whoever welcomes one of these little
children in my name welcomes me; and whoever
welcomes me does not welcome me but the one
who sent me."

Whoever Is Not Against Us Is for Us

38"Teacher," said John, "we saw a man driving
out demons in your name and we told him to
stop, because he was not one of us."
39"Do not stop him," Jesus said. "No one who
does a miracle in my name can in the next moment say anything bad about me, 40for whoever
is not against us is for us. 41I tell you the truth,
anyone who gives you a cup of water in my name
because you belong to Christ will certainly not
lose his reward.

Causing to Sin

42"And if anyone causes one of these little
ones who believe in me to sin, it would be better
for him to be thrown into the sea with a large
millstone tied around his neck. 43If your hand
causes you to sin, cut it off. It is better for you to
enter life maimed than with two hands to go into
hell, where the fire never goes out.[b] 45And if
your foot causes you to sin, cut it off. It is better
for you to enter life crippled than to have two feet
and be thrown into hell.[c] 47And if your eye
causes you to sin, pluck it out. It is better for you
to enter the kingdom of God with one eye than to
have two eyes and be thrown into hell, 48where

" 'their worm does not die,
and the fire is not quenched.'[d]

49Everyone will be salted with fire.
50"Salt is good, but if it loses its saltiness, how
can you make it salty again? Have salt in yourselves, and be at peace with each other."

Divorce

10 Jesus then left that place and went into
the region of Judea and across the Jordan.
Again crowds of people came to him, and as was
his custom, he taught them.

[a]29 Some manuscripts *prayer and fasting* [b]43 Some manuscripts *out, 44where / " 'their worm does not die, / and the fire is not quenched.'* [c]45 Some manuscripts *hell, 46where / " 'their worm does not die, / and the fire is not quenched.'* [d]48 Isaiah 66:24

2Some Pharisees came and tested him by asking, "Is it lawful for a man to divorce his wife?"
3"What did Moses command you?" he replied.
4They said, "Moses permitted a man to write
a certificate of divorce and send her away."
5"It was because your hearts were hard that
Moses wrote you this law," Jesus replied. 6"But
at the beginning of creation God 'made them
male and female.'[a] 7'For this reason a man will
leave his father and mother and be united to his
wife,[b] 8and the two will become one flesh.'[c]
So they are no longer two, but one. 9Therefore
what God has joined together, let man not separate."
10When they were in the house again, the disciples asked Jesus about this. 11He answered,
"Anyone who divorces his wife and marries another woman commits adultery against her.
12And if she divorces her husband and marries
another man, she commits adultery."

The Little Children and Jesus

13People were bringing little children to Jesus
to have him touch them, but the disciples rebuked them. 14When Jesus saw this, he was indignant. He said to them, "Let the little children
come to me, and do not hinder them, for the
kingdom of God belongs to such as these. 15I tell
you the truth, anyone who will not receive the
kingdom of God like a little child will never enter
it." 16And he took the children in his arms, put
his hands on them and blessed them.

The Rich Young Man

17As Jesus started on his way, a man ran up
to him and fell on his knees before him. "Good
teacher," he asked, "what must I do to inherit
eternal life?"
18"Why do you call me good?" Jesus answered.
"No one is good—except God alone. 19You know
the commandments: 'Do not murder, do not
commit adultery, do not steal, do not give false
testimony, do not defraud, honor your father and
mother.'[d]"
20"Teacher," he declared, "all these I have
kept since I was a boy."
21Jesus looked at him and loved him. "One
thing you lack," he said. "Go, sell everything you
have and give to the poor, and you will have
treasure in heaven. Then come, follow me."
22At this the man's face fell. He went away
sad, because he had great wealth.

> **MARK 10:17–31**
>
> 1. When it comes to lining up for food, a ride or an event, are you usually first, last or in the middle?
> 2. What is the most valuable thing you own?
> 3. If God asked you to give up all your possessions and be a missionary to Africa, what would you say?
> 4. Why is it so hard (v. 23) for a rich man to enter the kingdom of heaven?
> 5. If Jesus was a student in your school, what would be his style of clothes? What would he do with his spending money?
> 6. If Jesus looked at you like he did the rich man and said, "One thing you lack" (v. 21), what would be that one thing?
> 7. Name one thing you can let go of this week. Pray together.

23Jesus looked around and said to his disciples,
"How hard it is for the rich to enter the kingdom
of God!"
24The disciples were amazed at his words. But
Jesus said again, "Children, how hard it is[e] to
enter the kingdom of God! 25It is easier for a

[a] 6 Gen. 1:27 [b] 7 Some early manuscripts do not have *and be united to his wife.* [c] 8 Gen. 2:24 [d] 19 Exodus 20:12-16; Deut. 5:16-20 [e] 24 Some manuscripts *is for those who trust in riches*

10:17 *a man.* Matthew describes him as young (Matt. 19:20); Luke calls him a ruler (Luke 18:18). ***what must I do ... ?*** His emphasis on earning righteousness is in sharp contrast to Jesus' teaching about receiving it as a gift by faith (10:15).

10:18 In the OT only God is called "good." Jesus was not denying his own goodness, but does the man really grasp what is implied in this title he so easily gives him?

10:21–22 *loved him.* Mark notes Jesus' affection for this sincere young man. ***Go, sell everything.*** By telling him to sell all his goods, it became evident to the young man that his faith was in his possessions, not Jesus. He could remove this obstacle by following Jesus. Christ's command to him was not necessarily intended for all Christians. ***He went away sad.*** The young man's tragic decision demonstrated more love for his wealth than for eternal life.

10:24–25 *amazed.* The disciples are astonished because traditional Jewish wisdom saw wealth as a sign of God's favor (Ps. 128:1–2). ***camel / eye of a needle.*** A humorous illustration of impossibility. The camel was the largest animal in Palestine, and certainly couldn't get through the smallest opening known to most people.

10:27 This is Jesus' point. It is, indeed, impossible for us to make our own way into the kingdom. It is God who grants this gift.

10:30 Discipleship is a mixture of promise and persecution, blessing and suffering.

camel to go through the eye of a needle than for
a rich man to enter the kingdom of God."
26The disciples were even more amazed, and
said to each other, "Who then can be saved?"
27Jesus looked at them and said, "With man
this is impossible, but not with God; all things are
possible with God."
28Peter said to him, "We have left everything
to follow you!"
29"I tell you the truth," Jesus replied, "no one
who has left home or brothers or sisters or mother or father or children or fields for me and the
gospel 30will fail to receive a hundred times as
much in this present age (homes, brothers, sisters, mothers, children and fields—and with
them, persecutions) and in the age to come, eternal life. 31But many who are first will be last, and
the last first."

Jesus Again Predicts His Death

32They were on their way up to Jerusalem,
with Jesus leading the way, and the disciples
were astonished, while those who followed were
afraid. Again he took the Twelve aside and told
them what was going to happen to him. 33"We
are going up to Jerusalem," he said, "and the Son
of Man will be betrayed to the chief priests and
teachers of the law. They will condemn him to
death and will hand him over to the Gentiles,
34who will mock him and spit on him, flog him
and kill him. Three days later he will rise."

The Request of James and John

35Then James and John, the sons of Zebedee,
came to him. "Teacher," they said, "we want you
to do for us whatever we ask."
36"What do you want me to do for you?" he
asked.
37They replied, "Let one of us sit at your right
and the other at your left in your glory."
38"You don't know what you are asking," Jesus
said. "Can you drink the cup I drink or be baptized with the baptism I am baptized with?"
39"We can," they answered.
Jesus said to them, "You will drink the cup I
drink and be baptized with the baptism I am baptized with, 40but to sit at my right or left is not for
me to grant. These places belong to those for
whom they have been prepared."
41When the ten heard about this, they became
indignant with James and John. 42Jesus called

> ### *MARK 10:35–45*
>
> 1. Who is the most competitive person in your family? Do you see competitiveness as a positive or negative quality?
> 2. Who do you know that is a "great" person? What is it that makes them great?
> 3. What would you need to accomplish in your life to consider yourself a success?
> 4. How is Christ's teaching about how to be great (v. 43) different from what others teach?
> 5. Who do you compare yourself against to see if you measure up?
> 6. What could you do this week in your living quarters that would live out your commitment to Christ to be a servant to others?
> 7. Pray about how this group can serve the church.

them together and said, "You know that those
who are regarded as rulers of the Gentiles lord it
over them, and their high officials exercise authority over them. 43Not so with you. Instead,
whoever wants to become great among you must
be your servant, 44and whoever wants to be first
must be slave of all. 45For even the Son of Man
did not come to be served, but to serve, and to
give his life as a ransom for many."

Blind Bartimaeus Receives His Sight

46Then they came to Jericho. As Jesus and his
disciples, together with a large crowd, were leav-

10:35–37 ***James and John.*** Along with Peter, these two brothers were closest to Jesus. Perhaps it is because of this they presume to make such a request. As assumed about the Messiah in those days, they expect that Jesus will come into a position of authority as the new king of Israel. Those who sit on his right and his left will be his chief lieutenants.

10:38–40 Both the cup and the baptism refer to Jesus' upcoming suffering and death. James' and John's leadership will not be expressed through positions of authority, but through suffering and death. ***We can.*** James and John answer too readily Jesus' question as to whether they can share his cup and baptism, thinking perhaps that it is referring to being in fellowship with him.

10:41 ***they became indignant.*** The other disciples get angry. James and John want to have positions ahead of them!

10:42–45 In the same way that Jesus came to serve, so too must his disciples. They are not to seek power and authority over others, but rather they are to serve them.

10:43 Jesus overturns the world's values. ***servant.*** This Greek word (*diakonos,* from which the English word "deacon" is derived) became the most common description of church leaders in the early church.

10:45 In this key verse in Mark's Gospel, Jesus reveals why he must suffer and die: It is to redeem "the many" (in contrast to the one life offered for our "ransom").

ing the city, a blind man, Bartimaeus (that is, the
Son of Timaeus), was sitting by the roadside begging. 47When he heard that it was Jesus of Nazareth, he began to shout, "Jesus, Son of David,
have mercy on me!"
48Many rebuked him and told him to be quiet,
but he shouted all the more, "Son of David, have
mercy on me!"
49Jesus stopped and said, "Call him."
So they called to the blind man, "Cheer up! On
your feet! He's calling you." 50Throwing his cloak
aside, he jumped to his feet and came to Jesus.
51"What do you want me to do for you?" Jesus
asked him.
The blind man said, "Rabbi, I want to see."
52"Go," said Jesus, "your faith has healed
you." Immediately he received his sight and followed Jesus along the road.

The Triumphal Entry

11 As they approached Jerusalem and came
to Bethphage and Bethany at the Mount
of Olives, Jesus sent two of his disciples, 2saying
to them, "Go to the village ahead of you, and just
as you enter it, you will find a colt tied there,
which no one has ever ridden. Untie it and bring
it here. 3If anyone asks you, 'Why are you doing
this?' tell him, 'The Lord needs it and will send
it back here shortly.' "
4They went and found a colt outside in the
street, tied at a doorway. As they untied it, 5some
people standing there asked, "What are you doing, untying that colt?" 6They answered as Jesus
had told them to, and the people let them go.
7When they brought the colt to Jesus and threw
their cloaks over it, he sat on it. 8Many people
spread their cloaks on the road, while others
spread branches they had cut in the fields.
9Those who went ahead and those who followed
shouted,

"Hosanna![a]"

"Blessed is he who comes in the name of the
Lord!"[b]

10"Blessed is the coming kingdom of our father
David!"

"Hosanna in the highest!"

11Jesus entered Jerusalem and went to the
temple. He looked around at everything, but
since it was already late, he went out to Bethany
with the Twelve.

Jesus Clears the Temple

12The next day as they were leaving Bethany,
Jesus was hungry. 13Seeing in the distance a fig
tree in leaf, he went to find out if it had any fruit.
When he reached it, he found nothing but leaves,

Mark 11:12–19

1. What does it take to get you to clean your room?
2. When you see something wrong, are you more likely to act without thinking or think without acting?
3. What's something that makes you mad because it's clearly wrong?
4. In what way had the temple area been made into "a den of robbers" (v. 17)?
5. If Jesus came to your community, what would he clear out first: Your school? Your church? Your house?
6. Where do you need to take a righteous stand? How can you go about this?
7. What's keeping you from taking this stand? How can this group support you? Close in prayer.

[a]9 A Hebrew expression meaning "Save!" which became an exclamation of praise; also in verse 10 [b]9 Psalm 118:25,26

11:13 *fig tree.* On the Mount of Olives, fig trees are in leaf by early April, but they would not have ripe fruit until June, long after Passover. By sandwiching the cleansing of the temple between the two parts of the story of the cursing of the fig tree (vv. 12–14 and vv. 20–25), Mark emphasizes the judgment that both stories illustrate.

11:15–19 Jesus' first act following his triumphal entry into Jerusalem is to go to the temple and (by his actions) call to account the religious leadership of Israel. It is significant that he challenges these leaders in the temple, the very center of their power.

11:15 *buying and selling.* Temple worship centered on animal sacrifice. Merchants working for the high priests' family were profiteering on the religious obligations of the people. ***money changers.*** At Passover, each Jew was required to pay a temple tax of one-half shekel (nearly two days' wages). No other currency was acceptable. Those who changed the various coins into shekels charged exorbitant amounts for this simple act—up to half a day's wage. ***those selling doves.*** A dove was the sacrifice offered by the poorest of people; yet they had to pay the temple vendors some 20 times what a dove cost elsewhere.

11:17 *a house of prayer for all nations.* The outermost area of the temple where these activities were taking place was called the Court of the Gentiles. It was intended to be a place where pious Gentiles could pray. Instead it had been turned into a raucous bazaar where prayer was impossible. ***a den of robbers.*** Both because they took advantage of the people financially and robbed the temple of its sanctity.

because it was not the season for figs. 14Then he
said to the tree, "May no one ever eat fruit from
you again." And his disciples heard him say it.
15On reaching Jerusalem, Jesus entered the
temple area and began driving out those who
were buying and selling there. He overturned the
tables of the money changers and the benches of
those selling doves, 16and would not allow anyone to carry merchandise through the temple
courts. 17And as he taught them, he said, "Is it
not written:

" 'My house will be called
a house of prayer for all nations'[a]?

But you have made it 'a den of robbers.'[b]"
18The chief priests and the teachers of the law
heard this and began looking for a way to kill
him, for they feared him, because the whole
crowd was amazed at his teaching.
19When evening came, they[c] went out of the
city.

The Withered Fig Tree

20In the morning, as they went along, they saw
the fig tree withered from the roots. 21Peter remembered and said to Jesus, "Rabbi, look! The fig
tree you cursed has withered!"
22"Have[d] faith in God," Jesus answered. 23"I
tell you the truth, if anyone says to this mountain,
'Go, throw yourself into the sea,' and does not
doubt in his heart but believes that what he says
will happen, it will be done for him. 24Therefore
I tell you, whatever you ask for in prayer, believe
that you have received it, and it will be yours.
25And when you stand praying, if you hold anything against anyone, forgive him, so that your
Father in heaven may forgive you your sins.[e]"

The Authority of Jesus Questioned

27They arrived again in Jerusalem, and while
Jesus was walking in the temple courts, the chief
priests, the teachers of the law and the elders
came to him. 28"By what authority are you doing
these things?" they asked. "And who gave you
authority to do this?"
29Jesus replied, "I will ask you one question.
Answer me, and I will tell you by what authority
I am doing these things. 30John's baptism—was
it from heaven, or from men? Tell me!"
31They discussed it among themselves and
said, "If we say, 'From heaven,' he will ask,
'Then why didn't you believe him?' 32But if we
say, 'From men' . . . ." (They feared the people,
for everyone held that John really was a prophet.)
33So they answered Jesus, "We don't know."
Jesus said, "Neither will I tell you by what
authority I am doing these things."

The Parable of the Tenants

12 He then began to speak to them in parables: "A man planted a vineyard. He put
a wall around it, dug a pit for the winepress and
built a watchtower. Then he rented the vineyard
to some farmers and went away on a journey. 2At
harvest time he sent a servant to the tenants to
collect from them some of the fruit of the vineyard. 3But they seized him, beat him and sent
him away empty-handed. 4Then he sent another
servant to them; they struck this man on the head
and treated him shamefully. 5He sent still another, and that one they killed. He sent many others;
some of them they beat, others they killed.
6"He had one left to send, a son, whom he
loved. He sent him last of all, saying, 'They will
respect my son.'
7"But the tenants said to one another, 'This is
the heir. Come, let's kill him, and the inheritance
will be ours.' 8So they took him and killed him,
and threw him out of the vineyard.
9"What then will the owner of the vineyard
do? He will come and kill those tenants and give
the vineyard to others. 10Haven't you read this
scripture:

" 'The stone the builders rejected
has become the capstone[f];
11the Lord has done this,
and it is marvelous in our eyes'[g]?"

12Then they looked for a way to arrest him
because they knew he had spoken the parable
against them. But they were afraid of the crowd;
so they left him and went away.

Paying Taxes to Caesar

13Later they sent some of the Pharisees and
Herodians to Jesus to catch him in his words.
14They came to him and said, "Teacher, we know
you are a man of integrity. You aren't swayed by
men, because you pay no attention to who they
are; but you teach the way of God in accordance
with the truth. Is it right to pay taxes to Caesar or
not? 15Should we pay or shouldn't we?"
But Jesus knew their hypocrisy. "Why are you
trying to trap me?" he asked. "Bring me a denarius and let me look at it." 16They brought the coin,
and he asked them, "Whose portrait is this? And
whose inscription?"
"Caesar's," they replied.

[a] 17 Isaiah 56:7 [b] 17 Jer. 7:11 [c] 19 Some early manuscripts *he* [d] 22 Some early manuscripts *If you have*
[e] 25 Some manuscripts *sins.* *26But if you do not forgive, neither will your Father who is in heaven forgive your sins.*
[f] 10 Or *cornerstone* [g] 11 Psalm 118:22,23

17 Then Jesus said to them, "Give to Caesar
what is Caesar's and to God what is God's."
And they were amazed at him.

MARK 12:13–17

1. Whose picture appears on a five dollar bill? Ten? Twenty? Fifty? Hundred?
2. Who has the record for speeding tickets in your group?
3. On a scale of 1 (totally obedient) to 10 (totally rebellious), how would you rate your attitude toward authority?
4. What did Jesus mean when he said, "Give to Caesar what is Caesar's and to God what is God's" (v. 17)?
5. How do you feel about submitting to authority figures when you don't agree with them?
6. If taxes are what you give the government, what do you need to give to God? Are you doing this?
7. Honor your leaders by praying for them.

Marriage at the Resurrection

18 Then the Sadducees, who say there is no
resurrection, came to him with a question.
19 "Teacher," they said, "Moses wrote for us that
if a man's brother dies and leaves a wife but no
children, the man must marry the widow and
have children for his brother. 20 Now there were
seven brothers. The first one married and died
without leaving any children. 21 The second one
married the widow, but he also died, leaving no
child. It was the same with the third. 22 In fact,
none of the seven left any children. Last of all, the
woman died too. 23 At the resurrection[a] whose
wife will she be, since the seven were married to
her?"

24 Jesus replied, "Are you not in error because
you do not know the Scriptures or the power of
God? 25 When the dead rise, they will neither
marry nor be given in marriage; they will be like
the angels in heaven. 26 Now about the dead
rising—have you not read in the book of Moses,
in the account of the bush, how God said to him,
'I am the God of Abraham, the God of Isaac, and
the God of Jacob'[b]? 27 He is not the God of the
dead, but of the living. You are badly mistaken!"

The Greatest Commandment

28 One of the teachers of the law came and
heard them debating. Noticing that Jesus had giv-
en them a good answer, he asked him, "Of all the
commandments, which is the most important?"
29 "The most important one," answered Jesus,
"is this: 'Hear, O Israel, the Lord our God, the
Lord is one.[c] 30 Love the Lord your God with all
your heart and with all your soul and with all
your mind and with all your strength.'[d] 31 The
second is this: 'Love your neighbor as yourself.'[e]
There is no commandment greater than these."
32 "Well said, teacher," the man replied. "You
are right in saying that God is one and there is no
other but him. 33 To love him with all your heart,
with all your understanding and with all your
strength, and to love your neighbor as yourself is
more important than all burnt offerings and sacrifices."
34 When Jesus saw that he had answered wisely, he said to him, "You are not far from the
kingdom of God." And from then on no one
dared ask him any more questions.

Whose Son Is the Christ?

35 While Jesus was teaching in the temple
courts, he asked, "How is it that the teachers of
the law say that the Christ[f] is the son of David?
36 David himself, speaking by the Holy Spirit, declared:

a23 Some manuscripts *resurrection, when men rise from the dead,* b26 Exodus 3:6 c29 Or *the Lord our God is one Lord* d30 Deut. 6:4,5 e31 Lev. 19:18 f35 Or *Messiah*

12:13 *Pharisees and Herodians*. See note on Mark 3:6 for information about this unusual alliance that was formed out of hostility toward Jesus.

12:14 *you are a man of integrity.* By these and other flattering words they hope to catch Jesus off guard. ***taxes to Caesar.*** A poll tax had to be paid to the Romans each year by all adult Jews. This tax was deeply resented. At least one anti-tax rebellion had already been crushed. Many Jews felt that since God was the only rightful ruler of Israel, paying taxes would acknowledge the legitimacy of Caesar's rule.

12:15 *Should we pay or shouldn't we?* If Jesus answered their explosive question by saying the Jews should *not* pay taxes to Caesar, he could be arrested. If he said they *should* pay, he could lose his popular support. ***hypocrisy.*** Jesus knew they were not sincere. This is the essence of hypocrisy: saying one thing while believing another. ***Bring me a denarius.*** Stricter Jews would not even handle these coins. By asking for a coin, Jesus shows that he didn't carry it. A denarius was a coin (worth about 25 cents) bearing the image of Tiberius Caesar and a description of him as "Son of the Divine Augustine"—a man touched by divinity. The denarius was the only coin that could be used to pay the poll tax.

12:17 Jesus' answer is profound. He grants the legitimacy of governments to collect taxes, but at the same time limits the power of governments. One's final loyalty must be to God and not to the state (Acts 5:29).

“ ‘The Lord said to my Lord:
“Sit at my right hand
until I put your enemies
under your feet.” ’[a]
37David himself calls him ‘Lord.’ How then can
he be his son?”
The large crowd listened to him with delight.
38As he taught, Jesus said, “Watch out for the
teachers of the law. They like to walk around
in flowing robes and be greeted in the marketplaces, 39and have the most important seats in
the synagogues and the places of honor at banquets. 40They devour widows’ houses and for a
show make lengthy prayers. Such men will be
punished most severely.”

The Widow’s Offering

41Jesus sat down opposite the place where the
offerings were put and watched the crowd putting their money into the temple treasury. Many
rich people threw in large amounts. 42But a poor
widow came and put in two very small copper
coins,[b] worth only a fraction of a penny.[c]
43Calling his disciples to him, Jesus said, “I tell
you the truth, this poor widow has put more into
the treasury than all the others. 44They all gave
out of their wealth; but she, out of her poverty,
put in everything—all she had to live on.”

Signs of the End of the Age

13 As he was leaving the temple, one of his
disciples said to him, “Look, Teacher!
What massive stones! What magnificent buildings!”
2“Do you see all these great buildings?” replied Jesus. “Not one stone here will be left on
another; every one will be thrown down.”
3As Jesus was sitting on the Mount of Olives
opposite the temple, Peter, James, John and Andrew asked him privately, 4“Tell us, when will
these things happen? And what will be the sign
that they are all about to be fulfilled?”
5Jesus said to them: “Watch out that no one
deceives you. 6Many will come in my name,
claiming, ‘I am he,’ and will deceive many.
7When you hear of wars and rumors of wars, do
not be alarmed. Such things must happen, but
the end is still to come. 8Nation will rise against
nation, and kingdom against kingdom. There will

> ### *Mark 12:41–44*
>
> 1. What was your first job? How much did you make?
> 2. In your wallet or purse, what is your most priceless possession? What makes it so special?
> 3. Who taught you a lot about handling money? About giving?
> 4. What did Jesus mean that this poor widow had given more than all the others (v. 43)?
> 5. In your opinion, why do most people give money to churches? Why do you give? What do you give besides money?
> 6. If you really get serious about God, what will have to change in the way you spend your money?
> 7. How can this group help you in prayer this week?

be earthquakes in various places, and famines.
These are the beginning of birth pains.
9“You must be on your guard. You will be
handed over to the local councils and flogged in
the synagogues. On account of me you will stand
before governors and kings as witnesses to them.
10And the gospel must first be preached to all
nations. 11Whenever you are arrested and
brought to trial, do not worry beforehand about
what to say. Just say whatever is given you at the

[a]36 Psalm 110:1 [b]42 Greek *two lepta* [c]42 Greek *kodrantes*

12:41–44 Mark has just finished recording a series of sharp disputes between Jesus and various religious leaders. Jesus warned his listeners not to be like the teachers of the Law who long for honor and status, while they oppressively “devour widow’s houses” (12:38–40). Now, amidst the rich giving large offerings (probably with the motive of attracting attention to themselves), Jesus affirms the sacrificial giving of one poor widow.

12:41 ***temple treasury.*** This was located in the Court of Women, which was the first of the inner courts of the temple. Both Jewish women and men were allowed in this court, but women were not allowed to go any farther into the temple buildings. It held 13 trumpet-shaped receptacles used to collect donations for the temple.

12:42–43 ***very small copper coins.*** The smallest coins in circulation then, worth 1/400 shekel, or about 1/8 of a cent. ***I tell you the truth.*** Jesus often used this solemn affirmation to add emphasis to his statements (3:28; 10:15).

12:44 Although the poor widow’s offering was quite meager, it was “all she had to live on.” She is a great example of the apostle Paul’s words about giving in 2 Corinthians 8:12: “For if the willingness is there, the gift is acceptable according to what one has, not according to what he does not have.” Regardless of how much we have to give, what matters is the motive of willingness. The value of every gift is relative, and the essence of true giving is sacrifice.

time, for it is not you speaking, but the Holy
Spirit.
12“Brother will betray brother to death, and a
father his child. Children will rebel against their
parents and have them put to death. 13All men
will hate you because of me, but he who stands
firm to the end will be saved.
14“When you see ‘the abomination that causes
desolation’[a] standing where it[b] does not
belong—let the reader understand—then let
those who are in Judea flee to the mountains.
15Let no one on the roof of his house go down or
enter the house to take anything out. 16Let no
one in the field go back to get his cloak. 17How
dreadful it will be in those days for pregnant
women and nursing mothers! 18Pray that this will
not take place in winter, 19because those will be
days of distress unequaled from the beginning,
when God created the world, until now—and
never to be equaled again. 20If the Lord had not
cut short those days, no one would survive. But
for the sake of the elect, whom he has chosen, he
has shortened them. 21At that time if anyone says
to you, ‘Look, here is the Christ[c]!’ or, ‘Look,
there he is!’ do not believe it. 22For false Christs
and false prophets will appear and perform signs
and miracles to deceive the elect—if that were
possible. 23So be on your guard; I have told you
everything ahead of time.
24“But in those days, following that distress,

“ ‘the sun will be darkened,
and the moon will not give its light;
25the stars will fall from the sky,
and the heavenly bodies will be shaken.’[d]

26“At that time men will see the Son of Man
coming in clouds with great power and glory.
27And he will send his angels and gather his elect
from the four winds, from the ends of the earth
to the ends of the heavens.
28“Now learn this lesson from the fig tree: As
soon as its twigs get tender and its leaves come
out, you know that summer is near. 29Even so,
when you see these things happening, you know
that it is near, right at the door. 30I tell you the
truth, this generation[e] will certainly not pass
away until all these things have happened.
31Heaven and earth will pass away, but my words
will never pass away.

The Day and Hour Unknown

32“No one knows about that day or hour, not
even the angels in heaven, nor the Son, but only
the Father. 33Be on guard! Be alert[f]! You do not
know when that time will come. 34It’s like a man
going away: He leaves his house and puts his
servants in charge, each with his assigned task,
and tells the one at the door to keep watch.
35“Therefore keep watch because you do not
know when the owner of the house will come
back—whether in the evening, or at midnight,
or when the rooster crows, or at dawn. 36If he
comes suddenly, do not let him find you sleeping.
37What I say to you, I say to everyone: ‘Watch!’ ”

Jesus Anointed at Bethany

14 Now the Passover and the Feast of Unleavened Bread were only two days away,
and the chief priests and the teachers of the law
were looking for some sly way to arrest Jesus and
kill him. 2“But not during the Feast,” they said,
“or the people may riot.”
3While he was in Bethany, reclining at the
table in the home of a man known as Simon the
Leper, a woman came with an alabaster jar of
very expensive perfume, made of pure nard. She
broke the jar and poured the perfume on his
head.
4Some of those present were saying indignant-
ly to one another, “Why this waste of perfume?
5It could have been sold for more than a year’s
wages[g] and the money given to the poor.” And
they rebuked her harshly.
6“Leave her alone,” said Jesus. “Why are you
bothering her? She has done a beautiful thing to
me. 7The poor you will always have with you,
and you can help them any time you want. But
you will not always have me. 8She did what she
could. She poured perfume on my body beforehand to prepare for my burial. 9I tell you the
truth, wherever the gospel is preached throughout the world, what she has done will also be
told, in memory of her.”
10Then Judas Iscariot, one of the Twelve, went
to the chief priests to betray Jesus to them.
11They were delighted to hear this and promised
to give him money. So he watched for an opportunity to hand him over.

The Lord’s Supper

12On the first day of the Feast of Unleavened
Bread, when it was customary to sacrifice the
Passover lamb, Jesus’ disciples asked him,
“Where do you want us to go and make prepara-
tions for you to eat the Passover?”
13So he sent two of his disciples, telling them,
“Go into the city, and a man carrying a jar of
water will meet you. Follow him. 14Say to the
owner of the house he enters, ‘The Teacher asks:
Where is my guest room, where I may eat the
Passover with my disciples?’ 15He will show you

[a] 14 Daniel 9:27; 11:31; 12:11 [b] 14 Or *he*; also in verse 29 [c] 21 Or *Messiah* [d] 25 Isaiah 13:10; 34:4 [e] 30 Or *race*
[f] 33 Some manuscripts *alert and pray* [g] 5 Greek *than three hundred denarii*

a large upper room, furnished and ready. Make
preparations for us there."
16 The disciples left, went into the city and
found things just as Jesus had told them. So they
prepared the Passover.
17 When evening came, Jesus arrived with the
Twelve. 18 While they were reclining at the table
eating, he said, "I tell you the truth, one of you
will betray me—one who is eating with me."
19 They were saddened, and one by one they
said to him, "Surely not I?"
20 "It is one of the Twelve," he replied, "one
who dips bread into the bowl with me. 21 The Son
of Man will go just as it is written about him. But
woe to that man who betrays the Son of Man! It
would be better for him if he had not been born."
22 While they were eating, Jesus took bread,
gave thanks and broke it, and gave it to his disciples, saying, "Take it; this is my body."
23 Then he took the cup, gave thanks and offered it to them, and they all drank from it.
24 "This is my blood of the[a] covenant, which
is poured out for many," he said to them. 25 "I tell
you the truth, I will not drink again of the fruit of
the vine until that day when I drink it anew in
the kingdom of God."
26 When they had sung a hymn, they went out
to the Mount of Olives.

Jesus Predicts Peter's Denial

27 "You will all fall away," Jesus told them, "for
it is written:

" 'I will strike the shepherd,
and the sheep will be scattered.'[b]

28 But after I have risen, I will go ahead of you into
Galilee."
29 Peter declared, "Even if all fall away, I will
not."
30 "I tell you the truth," Jesus answered,
"today—yes, tonight—before the rooster crows
twice[c] you yourself will disown me three
times."
31 But Peter insisted emphatically, "Even if I
have to die with you, I will never disown you."
And all the others said the same.

Gethsemane

32 They went to a place called Gethsemane,
and Jesus said to his disciples, "Sit here while I
pray." 33 He took Peter, James and John along
with him, and he began to be deeply distressed
and troubled. 34 "My soul is overwhelmed with
sorrow to the point of death," he said to them.
"Stay here and keep watch."
35 Going a little farther, he fell to the ground
and prayed that if possible the hour might pass

MARK 14:32–42

1. When have you fallen asleep at an embarrassing moment: In church? In class? On a date?
2. Where do you go when you're facing a big decision? Do you prefer to be alone at these times or with friends?
3. What is the closest you have come to going through a time of loneliness and anxiety like Jesus did in this story?
4. Jesus told Peter, "Watch and pray" because "the Spirit is willing, but the body is weak" (v. 38). How do these words apply to you?
5. What have you found helpful in determining the will of God in your life?
6. Where in your life right now do you need to submit to God and do his will not yours?
7. How can this group support you in prayer this week?

[a] 24 Some manuscripts *the new* [b] 27 Zech. 13:7 [c] 30 Some early manuscripts do not have *twice.*

Two themes dominate this scene which follows immediately after the Last Supper and just before Jesus' arrest: Jesus' continued obedience to God (despite his dread of what was coming) and the disciples' continued failure to grasp what lay ahead for him.

14:32–33 ***Gethsemane.*** A garden or orchard just outside Jerusalem. ***Peter, James and John.*** Jesus' closest disciples. ***deeply distressed.*** Literally, Jesus is filled with "shuddering awe"—as the full impact of submitting to God's will hits him.

14:34 ***keep watch.*** Though it was late, this was an invitation for the disciples to join Jesus in preparation for the severe trial that was soon to come. While it expresses his desire for human companionship in his time of crisis, it also points out that these men need to prepare themselves as well (v. 38).

14:36 ***Abba.*** This is how a child would address his father: "Daddy." It was not a title that was used in prayer at that time. ***this cup.*** By this image, Jesus acknowledges that his impending death is not simply a human tragedy, but an act of divine judgment. It is this aspect of what he faces that so frightens him. He must drink the cup of God's wrath against sin. ***Yet not what I will, but what you will.*** This is the classic expression of Jesus' submission to God. His personal desire was to avoid the cross, his deeper commitment was to do the Father's will even though it included the cross.

14:38 ***spirit / body.*** When the human spirit is under God's control, it strives against the weakness of the body, or "flesh."

from him. 36“*Abba*,[a] Father,” he said, “everything is possible for you. Take this cup from me.
Yet not what I will, but what you will.”
37Then he returned to his disciples and found
them sleeping. “Simon,” he said to Peter, “are
you asleep? Could you not keep watch for one
hour? 38Watch and pray so that you will not fall
into temptation. The spirit is willing, but the
body is weak.”
39Once more he went away and prayed the
same thing. 40When he came back, he again
found them sleeping, because their eyes were
heavy. They did not know what to say to him.
41Returning the third time, he said to them,
“Are you still sleeping and resting? Enough! The
hour has come. Look, the Son of Man is betrayed
into the hands of sinners. 42Rise! Let us go! Here
comes my betrayer!”

Jesus Arrested

43Just as he was speaking, Judas, one of the
Twelve, appeared. With him was a crowd armed
with swords and clubs, sent from the chief
priests, the teachers of the law, and the elders.
44Now the betrayer had arranged a signal with
them: “The one I kiss is the man; arrest him and
lead him away under guard.” 45Going at once to
Jesus, Judas said, “Rabbi!” and kissed him. 46The
men seized Jesus and arrested him. 47Then one
of those standing near drew his sword and struck
the servant of the high priest, cutting off his ear.
48“Am I leading a rebellion,” said Jesus, “that
you have come out with swords and clubs to capture me? 49Every day I was with you, teaching in
the temple courts, and you did not arrest me. But
the Scriptures must be fulfilled.” 50Then everyone deserted him and fled.
51A young man, wearing nothing but a linen
garment, was following Jesus. When they seized
him, 52he fled naked, leaving his garment behind.

Before the Sanhedrin

53They took Jesus to the high priest, and all the
chief priests, elders and teachers of the law came
together. 54Peter followed him at a distance, right
into the courtyard of the high priest. There he sat
with the guards and warmed himself at the fire.
55The chief priests and the whole Sanhedrin
were looking for evidence against Jesus so that
they could put him to death, but they did not find
any. 56Many testified falsely against him, but
their statements did not agree.
57Then some stood up and gave this false testimony against him: 58“We heard him say, ‘I will
destroy this man-made temple and in three days
will build another, not made by man.’ ” 59Yet
even then their testimony did not agree.
60Then the high priest stood up before them
and asked Jesus, “Are you not going to answer?
What is this testimony that these men are bringing against you?” 61But Jesus remained silent and
gave no answer.
Again the high priest asked him, “Are you the
Christ,[b] the Son of the Blessed One?”
62“I am,” said Jesus. “And you will see the Son
of Man sitting at the right hand of the Mighty
One and coming on the clouds of heaven.”
63The high priest tore his clothes. “Why do we
need any more witnesses?” he asked. 64“You
have heard the blasphemy. What do you think?”
They all condemned him as worthy of death.
65Then some began to spit at him; they blindfolded him, struck him with their fists, and said,
“Prophesy!” And the guards took him and beat
him.

Peter Disowns Jesus

66While Peter was below in the courtyard, one
of the servant girls of the high priest came by.
67When she saw Peter warming himself, she
looked closely at him.
“You also were with that Nazarene, Jesus,”
she said.
68But he denied it. “I don’t know or understand what you’re talking about,” he said, and
went out into the entryway.[c]
69When the servant girl saw him there, she
said again to those standing around, “This fellow
is one of them.” 70Again he denied it.
After a little while, those standing near said to
Peter, “Surely you are one of them, for you are a
Galilean.”
71He began to call down curses on himself, and
he swore to them, “I don’t know this man you’re
talking about.”
72Immediately the rooster crowed the second
time.[d] Then Peter remembered the word Jesus
had spoken to him: “Before the rooster crows
twice[e] you will disown me three times.” And he
broke down and wept.

Jesus Before Pilate

15 Very early in the morning, the chief
priests, with the elders, the teachers of
the law and the whole Sanhedrin, reached a decision. They bound Jesus, led him away and handed him over to Pilate.
2“Are you the king of the Jews?” asked Pilate.
“Yes, it is as you say,” Jesus replied.
3The chief priests accused him of many things.

a*36* Aramaic for *Father* b*61* Or *Messiah* c*68* Some early manuscripts *entryway and the rooster crowed* d*72* Some early manuscripts do not have *the second time.* e*72* Some early manuscripts do not have *twice.*

4So again Pilate asked him, "Aren't you going to
answer? See how many things they are accusing
you of."
5But Jesus still made no reply, and Pilate was
amazed.
6Now it was the custom at the Feast to release
a prisoner whom the people requested. 7A man
called Barabbas was in prison with the insurrec-
tionists who had committed murder in the upris-
ing. 8The crowd came up and asked Pilate to do
for them what he usually did.
9"Do you want me to release to you the king of
the Jews?" asked Pilate, 10knowing it was out of
envy that the chief priests had handed Jesus over
to him. 11But the chief priests stirred up the
crowd to have Pilate release Barabbas instead.
12"What shall I do, then, with the one you call
the king of the Jews?" Pilate asked them.
13"Crucify him!" they shouted.
14"Why? What crime has he committed?"
asked Pilate.
But they shouted all the louder, "Crucify him!"
15Wanting to satisfy the crowd, Pilate released
Barabbas to them. He had Jesus flogged, and
handed him over to be crucified.

MARK 15:1–15

1. If you could choose, what role would you like to take in a high profile court case (judge, jury, expert witness, prosecutor, etc.)?
2. When someone accuses you of something you didn't do, how do you react?
3. What do you remember about the events leading up to Christ's trial before Pilate?
4. Why do you think Jesus didn't answer the charges against him (v. 5)?
5. How does the story of Barabbas illustrate what Christ did for you?
6. Have you come to the point in your life where you've asked Jesus to forgive your sins, realizing he died for you?
7. Close with a time of silent prayer—thank Christ for his sacrifice, confess your need for forgiveness and commit or recommit your life to him.

The Soldiers Mock Jesus

16The soldiers led Jesus away into the palace
(that is, the Praetorium) and called together the
whole company of soldiers. 17They put a purple
robe on him, then twisted together a crown of
thorns and set it on him. 18And they began to call
out to him, "Hail, king of the Jews!" 19Again and
again they struck him on the head with a staff and
spit on him. Falling on their knees, they paid
homage to him. 20And when they had mocked
him, they took off the purple robe and put his
own clothes on him. Then they led him out to
crucify him.

The Crucifixion

21A certain man from Cyrene, Simon, the father of Alexander and Rufus, was passing by on
his way in from the country, and they forced him
to carry the cross. 22They brought Jesus to the
place called Golgotha (which means The Place of
the Skull). 23Then they offered him wine mixed
with myrrh, but he did not take it. 24And they
crucified him. Dividing up his clothes, they cast
lots to see what each would get.
25It was the third hour when they crucified
him. 26The written notice of the charge against
him read: THE KING OF THE JEWS. 27They crucified
two robbers with him, one on his right and one
on his left.[a] 29Those who passed by hurled insults at him, shaking their heads and saying, "So!
You who are going to destroy the temple and

[a] 27 Some manuscripts *left,* 28*and the scripture was fulfilled which says, "He was counted with the lawless ones"* (Isaiah 53:12)

The night before this, Jesus was arrested and brought before the Sanhedrin, the Jewish high court consisting of 71 religious leaders. He was found guilty of blasphemy—a crime deserving of death. The Sanhedrin's power was limited by Roman rule. So now they bring Jesus to Pilate, the Roman governor of the area, requesting his execution.

15:2 ***king of the Jews.*** This is how the Sanhedrin translated the Jewish title "Messiah" so that Pilate would understand it. Put this way, it made Jesus seem guilty of treason (he would appear to be disputing the kingship of Caesar). ***Yes, it is as you say.*** As he accepts the title "the Christ, the Son of the Blessed One" from the Jewish high priest (14:61–62), he also accepts the title "king of the Jews" from the Roman procurator. In both cases, his questioners misunderstood the nature of the title they attribute to Jesus. In both cases, this misunderstanding led to Jesus' condemnation.

15:6–8 ***Barabbas.*** A genuine resistance leader, guilty of murder. The crowd may have gathered to request amnesty for him, as it was Pilate's custom to free a prisoner of the people's choosing at Passover. Pilate tried to manipulate the situation so the people would choose for him to release Jesus.

15:15 ***released Barabbas.*** The death of Jesus (who is innocent) in the place of Barabbas (who is guilty) is a visual statement of substitutionary atonement. ***flogged.*** Soldiers would lash a naked and bound prisoner with a leather thong into which pieces of bone and lead had been woven. ***crucified.*** Crucifixion was the most feared punishment in the first-century world. It was cruel in the extreme and totally degrading.

build it in three days, 30come down from the
cross and save yourself!"
31In the same way the chief priests and the
teachers of the law mocked him among themselves. "He saved others," they said, "but he
can't save himself! 32Let this Christ,[a] this King
of Israel, come down now from the cross, that we
may see and believe." Those crucified with him
also heaped insults on him.

The Death of Jesus

33At the sixth hour darkness came over the
whole land until the ninth hour. 34And at the
ninth hour Jesus cried out in a loud voice, *"Eloi,
Eloi, lama sabachthani?"*—which means, "My
God, my God, why have you forsaken me?"[b]
35When some of those standing near heard
this, they said, "Listen, he's calling Elijah."
36One man ran, filled a sponge with wine vinegar, put it on a stick, and offered it to Jesus to
drink. "Now leave him alone. Let's see if Elijah
comes to take him down," he said.
37With a loud cry, Jesus breathed his last.
38The curtain of the temple was torn in two
from top to bottom. 39And when the centurion,
who stood there in front of Jesus, heard his cry
and[c] saw how he died, he said, "Surely this man
was the Son[d] of God!"
40Some women were watching from a distance. Among them were Mary Magdalene, Mary
the mother of James the younger and of Joses,
and Salome. 41In Galilee these women had followed him and cared for his needs. Many other
women who had come up with him to Jerusalem
were also there.

The Burial of Jesus

42It was Preparation Day (that is, the day before the Sabbath). So as evening approached,
43Joseph of Arimathea, a prominent member of
the Council, who was himself waiting for the
kingdom of God, went boldly to Pilate and asked
for Jesus' body. 44Pilate was surprised to hear that
he was already dead. Summoning the centurion,
he asked him if Jesus had already died. 45When
he learned from the centurion that it was so, he
gave the body to Joseph. 46So Joseph bought some
linen cloth, took down the body, wrapped it in
the linen, and placed it in a tomb cut out of rock.
Then he rolled a stone against the entrance of the
tomb. 47Mary Magdalene and Mary the mother of
Joses saw where he was laid.

The Resurrection

16 When the Sabbath was over, Mary Magdalene, Mary the mother of James, and
Salome bought spices so that they might go to
anoint Jesus' body. 2Very early on the first day of
the week, just after sunrise, they were on their
way to the tomb 3and they asked each other,
"Who will roll the stone away from the entrance
of the tomb?"
4But when they looked up, they saw that the
stone, which was very large, had been rolled
away. 5As they entered the tomb, they saw a
young man dressed in a white robe sitting on the
right side, and they were alarmed.
6"Don't be alarmed," he said. "You are looking
for Jesus the Nazarene, who was crucified. He
has risen! He is not here. See the place where
they laid him. 7But go, tell his disciples and Peter,
'He is going ahead of you into Galilee. There you
will see him, just as he told you.'"
8Trembling and bewildered, the women went
out and fled from the tomb. They said nothing to
anyone, because they were afraid.

[The earliest manuscripts and some other
ancient witnesses do not have Mark 16:9–20.]

9When Jesus rose early on the first day of the
week, he appeared first to Mary Magdalene, out
of whom he had driven seven demons. 10She
went and told those who had been with him and
who were mourning and weeping. 11When they
heard that Jesus was alive and that she had seen
him, they did not believe it.
12Afterward Jesus appeared in a different form
to two of them while they were walking in the
country. 13These returned and reported it to the
rest; but they did not believe them either.
14Later Jesus appeared to the Eleven as they
were eating; he rebuked them for their lack of
faith and their stubborn refusal to believe those
who had seen him after he had risen.
15He said to them, "Go into all the world and
preach the good news to all creation. 16Whoever
believes and is baptized will be saved, but whoever does not believe will be condemned. 17And
these signs will accompany those who believe: In
my name they will drive out demons; they will
speak in new tongues; 18they will pick up snakes
with their hands; and when they drink deadly
poison, it will not hurt them at all; they will place
their hands on sick people, and they will get
well."
19After the Lord Jesus had spoken to them, he
was taken up into heaven and he sat at the right
hand of God. 20Then the disciples went out and
preached everywhere, and the Lord worked with
them and confirmed his word by the signs that
accompanied it.

[a]32 Or *Messiah* [b]34 Psalm 22:1 [c]39 Some manuscripts do not have *heard his cry and* [d]39 Or *a son*

Introduction to
LUKE

Personal Reading Plan

❒ Luke 1:1–38	❒ Luke 8:1–39	❒ Luke 16:1–17:19
❒ Luke 1:39–80	❒ Luke 8:40–9:36	❒ Luke 17:20–18:43
❒ Luke 2:1–52	❒ Luke 9:37–10:24	❒ Luke 19:1–48
❒ Luke 3:1–4:13	❒ Luke 10:25–11:28	❒ Luke 20:1–47
❒ Luke 4:14–5:16	❒ Luke 11:29–12:21	❒ Luke 21:1–38
❒ Luke 5:17–6:11	❒ Luke 12:22–59	❒ Luke 22:1–53
❒ Luke 6:12–7:10	❒ Luke 13:1–14:14	❒ Luke 22:54–23:56
❒ Luke 7:11–50	❒ Luke 14:15–15:32	❒ Luke 24:1–53

Author

Although no author is named in the third Gospel, there is a tradition dating from the second century that Luke was the writer. There is good reason to accept Luke as author simply because he was *not* an apostle, nor was he particularly famous in the first-century church. In fact, he was a Gentile—the only non-Jewish author in the New Testament. Therefore, it is highly unlikely that anyone would have attached his name to this Gospel had he not actually written it.

Internal evidence supports the testimony of tradition. For one thing, it is clear that the same man wrote both the third Gospel and the Book of Acts. Both books are dedicated to Theophilus. The books are similar in style, language and interests. The author of Acts begins by saying, "In my former book," which is surely the Gospel of Luke. Since Acts was traditionally associated with Luke, the evidence that both books came from the same pen strengthens the tradition that Luke wrote the Gospel bearing his name.

It is also interesting to note that the author of the third Gospel uses the language we would expect from a doctor (Luke was a physician). He describes illnesses with more precision than is found in Matthew and Mark (4:38; 5:12). He also omits the comment in Mark 5:26 that the woman who was subject to bleeding "had suffered a great deal under the care of many doctors and had spent all she had, yet instead of getting better she grew worse."

Little is known about Luke from the New Testament except that he was a doctor beloved by Paul (Col. 4:14) and that he was a coworker with Paul (2 Tim. 4:11; Philem. 24). However, in the book of Acts, Luke describes experiences he shared while traveling with Paul, though even here it is Paul, not Luke, who is front and center. One early non-canonical document (writings not included in Holy Scripture), the *Prologue to Luke,* states that Luke was a physician, that he was unmarried and childless, and that he died at the age of 84. Beyond this, we know Luke only through his two eloquent documents published in the New Testament.

Date

There is no strong evidence as to when Luke's Gospel was written. Many scholars date it between A.D. 75 and 85, although this is by no means conclusive. In fact, since Acts ends with Paul awaiting trial in Rome (probably before A.D. 67), if Luke wrote his Gospel before he wrote Acts, then a date in the early A.D. 60s is likely.

The place of writing was most likely Rome, though Achaia, Ephesus and Caesarea are also possibilities. The place to which it was sent depends on where Theophilus lived. By its details about Palestine, the Gospel seems to be written for readers who were unfamiliar with that land. The Christians in Antioch, Achaia and Ephesus are possible recipients of this Gospel.

Theme

Jesus is the Savior of the whole world.

Historical Background

Luke was a Gentile who wrote the story of Jesus for other Gentiles. This fact about the third Gospel gives it its distinctive flavor. The Gentile character of the manuscript begins in the preface, in which Luke dedicates the book to Theophilus, probably a high-ranking Roman government official (the title "most excellent" was normally reserved for such officials). Theophilus was a common name among both Greeks and Jews in New Testament times. It means "friend of God." There have been many theories concerning the identity of Theophilus. We do know that he was an acquaintance of Luke who had been instructed in the Christian way (1:4). He possibly helped Luke with getting his writings copied and distributed.

Luke then dates the conception and birth of John the Baptist and Jesus with reference to the Roman rulers governing at the time (1:5; 2:1–2). Throughout the book, Luke makes a habit of translating Hebrew words into their Greek equivalents so that his Gentile readers will understand. For example, Luke never refers to Jesus as "Rabbi," the Hebrew title for a teacher, but always by the Greek equivalent, "Master." Luke identifies the place where Jesus was crucified not as *Golgotha,* its Hebrew name, but as *Kranion,* the Greek equivalent for "the place of the skull."

The Gentile character of the third Gospel is also seen in its identification of Jesus' lineage. Luke traces him back to Adam, the founder of the human race, and not, as Matthew does, back to Abraham, the founder of the Jewish race. Also, in contrast to Matthew, Luke seldom quotes the Old Testament or demonstrates how Jesus fulfills Old Testament prophecy. This is a Gentile book about the Jewish Messiah who died for the whole world.

Luke writes very carefully. As he indicates in the prologue, his aim is to produce "an orderly account" (1:3), which is exactly what he does. This book gives evidence of his meticulous research. For example, he dates the beginning of John the Baptist's ministry by reference to six historical facts (3:1–2). Another example of Luke's care as a historian is his practice of stating the exact titles of various Roman officials, even though these were notoriously difficult to get straight.

Characteristics

Luke's account of the life of Jesus is a unique document. For one thing, it is the longest book in the New Testament. Therefore, it contains more information about Jesus than any other book in the Bible. For another thing, Luke's Gospel is extraordinarily joyful. It begins and ends with rejoicing (1:46–47 and 24:52–53), and in the account itself, Luke uses the words "joy" (6:23), "laugh" (6:21), and "celebrate" (15:23,32). Luke is also the only writer to record the four great canticles of joy and worship: *Magnificat* (1:46–55), *Benedictus* (1:68–79), *Gloria in Exclesis* (2:14), and *Nunc Dimittis* (2:29–32).

Christ Came for All

Why is Luke so filled with joy? He is overwhelmed with the thought that Jesus is the Savior of the whole world. He is astonished that Jesus came to seek and to save not just his kinsfolk, the Jews, but all people regardless of race, age or culture.

Jesus came, for example, for the Gentiles. This is clear in Luke's Gospel. In Luke, we hear Simeon prophesy that Jesus will be "a light for revelation to the Gentiles" (2:32). We hear Jesus praise the widow at Zarephath and Naaman the Syrian, two Gentiles whose stories are told in the Old Testament (4:25–27), and we hear Jesus single out the faith of a Roman centurion as an example of how people should respond to him (7:9).

Jesus came even for the hated Samaritans. As we see in the parable of the Good Samaritan (10:25–37), he places them on a par with the Jews in regard to God's kingdom. Luke has a lot to say about social outcasts in general. Women, children, and the poor—often treated badly by first-century society—are treated with special compassion by Luke. It is not accidental that Luke alone recounts the birth narratives from *Mary's* point of view. Luke mentions 13 women not named in other Gospel accounts. His special concern for children is clearly seen in his careful record of Jesus' childhood; Luke is the only Gospel writer to record this information. As for the poor, Luke makes it clear that Jesus came to minister to them (4:18; 7:22). Luke also takes great pains to warn about the danger of riches (6:24; 12:13–34; 16:1–31; 21:1–4). From Luke's perspective, then, it does not matter who you are—you are welcome in God's kingdom. How well this is expressed in the beloved parable of the Prodigal Son (15:11–32), which occurs only in Luke's Gospel. In Jesus' own words: "People will come from east and west and north and south, and will take their places at the feast in the kingdom of God" (13:29).

In addition to Luke's universality (Christ has come for all people) and his fascination with people (especially the outcasts), several other themes distinguish Luke. For example, Luke records more of Jesus' teaching about prayer than is found anywhere else in the Bible. He records nine of Jesus' own prayers. Luke also has more to say than the other Gospels about the Holy Spirit (4:1,14; 10:21; 24:49). He will pick up and expand on this emphasis of the Holy Spirit's active ministry in the companion volume to the third Gospel, the book of Acts.

Style

For all the author's care and meticulous nature, Luke's Gospel is no dry, academic document. It sparkles with life and vitality. Luke's portraits of people are particularly vivid and compassionate. People like Zacchaeus and Cleopas, Mary and Martha, Elizabeth and Mary the mother of Jesus all spring to life through his talented pen. Luke's Gospel tells a rare and unforgettable story.

Passages for Topical Group Study

1:26–38	TEEN PREGNANCY	The Birth of Jesus Foretold
2:1–20	ANGELS	The Birth of Jesus
2:41–52	INDEPENDENCE	The Boy Jesus at the Temple
4:1–13	SATAN/OCCULT TEMPTATION	The Temptation of Jesus
4:14–30	REJECTION	Jesus Rejected at Nazareth
5:1–11	GOD'S CALL	The Calling of the First Disciples
7:36–50	GUILT	Jesus Anointed by a Sinful Woman
8:26–39	ADDICTION	The Healing of a Demon-possessed Man
10:25–37	GANGS / VIOLENCE	The Parable of the Good Samaritan
10:38–42	PERSONALITY PRIORITIES	At the Home of Martha and Mary
12:13–21	MONEY FUTURE PLANS	The Parable of the Rich Fool
12:22–34	POSSESSIONS	Where's Your Treasure?
14:25–35	SETTING PRIORITIES	The Cost of Being a Disciple
15:11–32	FAMILY CONFLICTS GOD'S LOVE	The Parable of the Lost (Prodigal) Son
16:19–31	HEAVEN AND HELL	The Rich Man and Lazarus
18:9–14	SELF-IMAGE PRAYER	The Parable of the Pharisee and Tax Collector
19:1–10	UNIQUENESS	Zacchaeus the Tax Collector
22:54–62	FAILURE BLOWING IT	Peter Disowns Jesus
23:26–49	GOD'S FORGIVENESS	Jesus' Crucifixion and Death
24:13–35	SHATTERED DREAMS DEPRESSION	On the Road to Emmaus

See the Lesson Plans in the front of this Bible.

Passages for General Group Study

14:15–24	The Parable of the Great Banquet
17:11–19	Ten Healed of Leprosy
19:28–44	The Triumphal Entry
22:7–23	The Last Supper

Introduction

1 Many have undertaken to draw up an account of the things that have been fulfilled[a] among us, [2]just as they were handed down to us by those who from the first were eyewitnesses and servants of the word. [3]Therefore, since I myself have carefully investigated everything from the beginning, it seemed good also to me to write an orderly account for you, most excellent Theophilus, [4]so that you may know the certainty of the things you have been taught.

The Birth of John the Baptist Foretold

[5]In the time of Herod king of Judea there was a priest named Zechariah, who belonged to the priestly division of Abijah; his wife Elizabeth was also a descendant of Aaron. [6]Both of them were upright in the sight of God, observing all the Lord's commandments and regulations blamelessly. [7]But they had no children, because Elizabeth was barren; and they were both well along in years.

[8]Once when Zechariah's division was on duty and he was serving as priest before God, [9]he was chosen by lot, according to the custom of the priesthood, to go into the temple of the Lord and burn incense. [10]And when the time for the burning of incense came, all the assembled worshipers were praying outside.

[11]Then an angel of the Lord appeared to him, standing at the right side of the altar of incense. [12]When Zechariah saw him, he was startled and was gripped with fear. [13]But the angel said to him: "Do not be afraid, Zechariah; your prayer has been heard. Your wife Elizabeth will bear you a son, and you are to give him the name John. [14]He will be a joy and delight to you, and many will rejoice because of his birth, [15]for he will be great in the sight of the Lord. He is never to take wine or other fermented drink, and he will be filled with the Holy Spirit even from birth.[b] [16]Many of the people of Israel will he bring back to the Lord their God. [17]And he will go on before the Lord, in the spirit and power of Elijah, to turn the hearts of the fathers to their children and the disobedient to the wisdom of the righteous—to make ready a people prepared for the Lord."

[18]Zechariah asked the angel, "How can I be sure of this? I am an old man and my wife is well along in years."

[19]The angel answered, "I am Gabriel. I stand in the presence of God, and I have been sent to speak to you and to tell you this good news. [20]And now you will be silent and not able to speak until the day this happens, because you did not believe my words, which will come true at their proper time."

[21]Meanwhile, the people were waiting for Zechariah and wondering why he stayed so long in the temple. [22]When he came out, he could not speak to them. They realized he had seen a vision in the temple, for he kept making signs to them but remained unable to speak.

[23]When his time of service was completed, he returned home. [24]After this his wife Elizabeth became pregnant and for five months remained in seclusion. [25]"The Lord has done this for me," she said. "In these days he has shown his favor and taken away my disgrace among the people."

The Birth of Jesus Foretold

[26]In the sixth month, God sent the angel Gabriel to Nazareth, a town in Galilee, [27]to a virgin pledged to be married to a man named Joseph, a descendant of David. The virgin's name was Mary. [28]The angel went to her and said, "Greetings, you who are highly favored! The Lord is with you."

[29]Mary was greatly troubled at his words and wondered what kind of greeting this might be. [30]But the angel said to her, "Do not be afraid, Mary, you have found favor with God. [31]You will be with child and give birth to a son, and you are to give him the name Jesus. [32]He will be great and will be called the Son of the Most High. The Lord God will give him the throne of his father David, [33]and he will reign over the house of Jacob forever; his kingdom will never end."

[a] *1* Or *been surely believed* [b] *15* Or *from his mother's womb*

1:26–27 *sixth month.* The sixth month of Elizabeth's pregnancy. Elizabeth, Mary's relative (v. 36), was the mother of John the Baptist. ***pledged to be married.*** Betrothal, usually lasting for about a year, could occur as young as the age of 12. This was a far more binding arrangement than engagements today. Though sexual relations were not permitted, the relationship could be broken only by divorce. ***descendant of David.*** Both Joseph and Mary were descendants of David. The Messiah was to come through the line of David (2 Sam. 7:16).

1:34 *How will this be ... ?* While this question parallels that of Zechariah when he was informed by the angel that his wife Elizabeth would have a child (1:18), it differs in that Mary is not registering doubt as much as wonder.

1:35 *The Holy Spirit will come upon you.* The virgin birth of Jesus traces its roots to the prophecy of the child spoken of in Isaiah 7:14: "The Lord himself will give you a sign: The virgin will be with child and will give birth to a son, and will call him Immanuel." ***the holy one to be born will be called the Son of God.*** While the sonship of verse 32 indicated Jesus' title and role, this reference to Sonship indicates his nature and being as God incarnate.

1:37–38 *For nothing is impossible with God.* The ultimate ground for Mary's faith rests on this fact. ***I am the Lord's servant.*** The rejection, embarrassment and fear that Mary would face as a result of this pregnancy is accepted with this confession of her complete submission to God.

34“How will this be,” Mary asked the angel,
“since I am a virgin?”
35The angel answered, “The Holy Spirit will
come upon you, and the power of the Most High
will overshadow you. So the holy one to be born
will be called[a] the Son of God. 36Even Elizabeth
your relative is going to have a child in her old
age, and she who was said to be barren is in her
sixth month. 37For nothing is impossible with
God.”
38“I am the Lord’s servant,” Mary answered.
“May it be to me as you have said.” Then the
angel left her.

LUKE 1:26–38

1. What have your parents told you about the events surrounding your birth?
2. If an angel told you that you were going to be a parent in nine months, how would you feel?
3. How do people treat unwed teen mothers at your school? Your church? Your community?
4. Mary was young, unmarried and pregnant. What’s one way you or this group could help someone in Mary’s shoes?
5. What is your attitude towards teenagers getting married early?
6. In what area of your life do you need to believe that “nothing is impossible with God” (v. 37)?
7. How can this group help you in prayer this week?

(Study notes on page 919)

Mary Visits Elizabeth

39At that time Mary got ready and hurried to a
town in the hill country of Judea, 40where she
entered Zechariah’s home and greeted Elizabeth.
41When Elizabeth heard Mary’s greeting, the
baby leaped in her womb, and Elizabeth was
filled with the Holy Spirit. 42In a loud voice she
exclaimed: “Blessed are you among women, and
blessed is the child you will bear! 43But why am
I so favored, that the mother of my Lord should
come to me? 44As soon as the sound of your
greeting reached my ears, the baby in my womb
leaped for joy. 45Blessed is she who has believed
that what the Lord has said to her will be accomplished!”

Mary’s Song

46And Mary said:

“My soul glorifies the Lord
47 and my spirit rejoices in God my Savior,
48for he has been mindful
of the humble state of his servant.
From now on all generations will call me
blessed,
49 for the Mighty One has done great things
for me—
holy is his name.
50His mercy extends to those who fear him,
from generation to generation.
51He has performed mighty deeds with his
arm;
he has scattered those who are proud in
their inmost thoughts.
52He has brought down rulers from their
thrones
but has lifted up the humble.
53He has filled the hungry with good things
but has sent the rich away empty.
54He has helped his servant Israel,
remembering to be merciful
55to Abraham and his descendants forever,
even as he said to our fathers.”

56Mary stayed with Elizabeth for about three
months and then returned home.

The Birth of John the Baptist

57When it was time for Elizabeth to have her
baby, she gave birth to a son. 58Her neighbors
and relatives heard that the Lord had shown her
great mercy, and they shared her joy.
59On the eighth day they came to circumcise
the child, and they were going to name him after
his father Zechariah, 60but his mother spoke up
and said, “No! He is to be called John.”
61They said to her, “There is no one among
your relatives who has that name.”
62Then they made signs to his father, to find
out what he would like to name the child. 63He
asked for a writing tablet, and to everyone’s astonishment he wrote, “His name is John.” 64Immediately his mouth was opened and his tongue
was loosed, and he began to speak, praising God.
65The neighbors were all filled with awe, and
throughout the hill country of Judea people were
talking about all these things. 66Everyone who
heard this wondered about it, asking, “What then
is this child going to be?” For the Lord’s hand was
with him.

[a]35 Or *So the child to be born will be called holy,*

Zechariah's Song

67 His father Zechariah was filled with the Holy Spirit and prophesied:

68 "Praise be to the Lord, the God of Israel,
because he has come and has redeemed
his people.
69 He has raised up a horn[a] of salvation for us
in the house of his servant David
70 (as he said through his holy prophets of long
ago),
71 salvation from our enemies
and from the hand of all who hate us—
72 to show mercy to our fathers
and to remember his holy covenant,
73 the oath he swore to our father Abraham:
74 to rescue us from the hand of our enemies,
and to enable us to serve him without fear
75 in holiness and righteousness before him
all our days.

76 And you, my child, will be called a prophet
of the Most High;
for you will go on before the Lord to
prepare the way for him,
77 to give his people the knowledge of salvation
through the forgiveness of their sins,
78 because of the tender mercy of our God,
by which the rising sun will come to us
from heaven
79 to shine on those living in darkness
and in the shadow of death,
to guide our feet into the path of peace."

80 And the child grew and became strong in spirit; and he lived in the desert until he appeared publicly to Israel.

The Birth of Jesus

2 In those days Caesar Augustus issued a decree that a census should be taken of the
entire Roman world. 2 (This was the first census
that took place while Quirinius was governor of
Syria.) 3 And everyone went to his own town to
register.
4 So Joseph also went up from the town of Nazareth in Galilee to Judea, to Bethlehem the town of David, because he belonged to the house and
line of David. 5 He went there to register with

> ### *LUKE 2:1–20*
>
> 1. What's your favorite thing about Christmas?
> 2. When you were a child, what part did you play in the Christmas pageant?
> 3. Suppose your group acted out the Christmas story. Who would you choose to play Joseph? Mary? The innkeeper? The shepherds? The angels?
> 4. What is the closest you've come to experiencing the presence of angels watching over you?
> 5. How would you feel if an angel suddenly appeared to you with a message about God's plan for your life?
> 6. Who was the "angel" that first told you about Jesus? What effect has this good news had on you?
> 7. What would you like the group to pray with you about?

Mary, who was pledged to be married to him and
was expecting a child. 6 While they were there,
the time came for the baby to be born, 7 and she
gave birth to her firstborn, a son. She wrapped him in cloths and placed him in a manger, because there was no room for them in the inn.

The Shepherds and the Angels

8 And there were shepherds living out in the fields nearby, keeping watch over their flocks at

[a] 69 *Horn* here symbolizes strength.

2:1–6 *census.* The Roman Empire ordered people in the various Roman provinces to report every 14 years for a census for tax purposes. Evidently both Joseph and Mary had to make the three- or four-day journey from Nazareth to Bethlehem, the town of their ancestral origin. God used this decree to fulfill the prophecy of Micah 5:2 that the Messiah would be born in Bethlehem.

2:7 *manger.* This was a feeding trough for animals, and is the only indicator that Jesus was born in a stable. A tradition dating back to the second century maintains this was in a cave, perhaps used as a stable.

2:8 *shepherds.* The great announcement of Christ's birth was made to these economically, socially and religiously "low-class" people—not to kings, priests or the wealthy.

2:9 *angel of the Lord.* Popular thought often pictures angels as chubby, cute, naked children, but the Bible represents them as supernatural creatures of enormous power and majesty which cause people to be "terrified." In Scripture, angels serve as God's agents of instruction, judgment and deliverance.

2:10 The angel has not come to frighten them, but to announce God's good news to them. ***all the people.*** The Messiah has come not just for the Jews but for all people. ***Savior ... Christ the Lord.*** The angel gives a full-orbed description of the roles which this child will play.

2:13–14 A great company of angels sings of how Jesus' birth will bring honor to God and peace (personal and relational harmony) to people whom he has called.

night. 9An angel of the Lord appeared to them, and the glory of the Lord shone around them, and they were terrified. 10But the angel said to them, "Do not be afraid. I bring you good news of great joy that will be for all the people. 11Today in the town of David a Savior has been born to you; he is Christ[a] the Lord. 12This will be a sign to you: You will find a baby wrapped in cloths and lying in a manger."

13Suddenly a great company of the heavenly host appeared with the angel, praising God and saying,

14"Glory to God in the highest,
 and on earth peace to men on whom his
  favor rests."

15When the angels had left them and gone into heaven, the shepherds said to one another, "Let's go to Bethlehem and see this thing that has happened, which the Lord has told us about."

16So they hurried off and found Mary and Joseph, and the baby, who was lying in the manger. 17When they had seen him, they spread the word concerning what had been told them about this child, 18and all who heard it were amazed at what the shepherds said to them. 19But Mary treasured up all these things and pondered them in her heart. 20The shepherds returned, glorifying and praising God for all the things they had heard and seen, which were just as they had been told.

Jesus Presented in the Temple

21On the eighth day, when it was time to circumcise him, he was named Jesus, the name the angel had given him before he had been conceived.

22When the time of their purification according to the Law of Moses had been completed, Joseph and Mary took him to Jerusalem to present him to the Lord 23(as it is written in the Law of the Lord, "Every firstborn male is to be consecrated to the Lord"[b]), 24and to offer a sacrifice in keeping with what is said in the Law of the Lord: "a pair of doves or two young pigeons."[c]

25Now there was a man in Jerusalem called Simeon, who was righteous and devout. He was waiting for the consolation of Israel, and the Holy Spirit was upon him. 26It had been revealed to him by the Holy Spirit that he would not die before he had seen the Lord's Christ. 27Moved by the Spirit, he went into the temple courts. When the parents brought in the child Jesus to do for him what the custom of the Law required, 28Simeon took him in his arms and praised God, saying:

29"Sovereign Lord, as you have promised,
 you now dismiss[d] your servant in peace.
30For my eyes have seen your salvation,
31 which you have prepared in the sight of
  all people,
32a light for revelation to the Gentiles
 and for glory to your people Israel."

33The child's father and mother marveled at what was said about him. 34Then Simeon blessed them and said to Mary, his mother: "This child is destined to cause the falling and rising of many in Israel, and to be a sign that will be spoken against, 35so that the thoughts of many hearts will be revealed. And a sword will pierce your own soul too."

36There was also a prophetess, Anna, the daughter of Phanuel, of the tribe of Asher. She was very old; she had lived with her husband seven years after her marriage, 37and then was a widow until she was eighty-four.[e] She never left the temple but worshiped night and day, fasting and praying. 38Coming up to them at that very moment, she gave thanks to God and spoke about the child to all who were looking forward to the redemption of Jerusalem.

39When Joseph and Mary had done everything required by the Law of the Lord, they returned to Galilee to their own town of Nazareth. 40And the child grew and became strong; he was filled with wisdom, and the grace of God was upon him.

The Boy Jesus at the Temple

41Every year his parents went to Jerusalem for the Feast of the Passover. 42When he was twelve years old, they went up to the Feast, according to the custom. 43After the Feast was over, while his parents were returning home, the boy Jesus stayed behind in Jerusalem, but they were unaware of it. 44Thinking he was in their company, they traveled on for a day. Then they began looking for him among their relatives and friends. 45When they did not find him, they went back to Jerusalem to look for him. 46After three days they found him in the temple courts, sitting among the teachers, listening to them and asking them questions. 47Everyone who heard him was amazed at his understanding and his answers. 48When his parents saw him, they were astonished. His mother said to him, "Son, why have you treated us like this? Your father and I have been anxiously searching for you."

49"Why were you searching for me?" he asked. "Didn't you know I had to be in my Fa-

[a]*11* Or *Messiah.* "The Christ" (Greek) and "the Messiah" (Hebrew) both mean "the Anointed One"; also in verse 26.
[b]*23* Exodus 13:2,12 [c]*24* Lev. 12:8 [d]*29* Or *promised, / now dismiss* [e]*37* Or *widow for eighty-four years*

ther's house?" 50But they did not understand what he was saying to them.

51Then he went down to Nazareth with them and was obedient to them. But his mother treasured all these things in her heart. 52And Jesus grew in wisdom and stature, and in favor with God and men.

LUKE 2:41–52

1. Describe a time when you got lost, ran away or were separated from your parents.
2. When did you "graduate" to the adult table at big family dinners?
3. If you were to give your parents a grade on turning over responsibility for your life to you, what grade would you give them?
4. If you have kids, what are you going to do differently in raising them?
5. At what point did you feel grown-up—that you weren't a kid anymore?
6. Jesus grew "in favor with God" (v. 52). What can you do to grow in your relationship with God?
7. How can the group pray for you regarding your relationship with your parents? Your heavenly Father?

John the Baptist Prepares the Way

3 In the fifteenth year of the reign of Tiberius Caesar—when Pontius Pilate was governor of Judea, Herod tetrarch of Galilee, his brother Philip tetrarch of Iturea and Traconitis, and Lysanias tetrarch of Abilene— 2during the high priesthood of Annas and Caiaphas, the word of God came to John son of Zechariah in the desert. 3He went into all the country around the Jordan, preaching a baptism of repentance for the forgiveness of sins. 4As is written in the book of the words of Isaiah the prophet:

"A voice of one calling in the desert,
'Prepare the way for the Lord,
make straight paths for him.
5Every valley shall be filled in,
every mountain and hill made low.
The crooked roads shall become straight,
the rough ways smooth.
6And all mankind will see God's salvation.' "[a]

7John said to the crowds coming out to be baptized by him, "You brood of vipers! Who warned you to flee from the coming wrath? 8Produce fruit in keeping with repentance. And do not begin to say to yourselves, 'We have Abraham as our father.' For I tell you that out of these stones God can raise up children for Abraham. 9The ax is already at the root of the trees, and every tree that does not produce good fruit will be cut down and thrown into the fire."

10"What should we do then?" the crowd asked.

11John answered, "The man with two tunics should share with him who has none, and the one who has food should do the same."

12Tax collectors also came to be baptized. "Teacher," they asked, "what should we do?"

13"Don't collect any more than you are required to," he told them.

14Then some soldiers asked him, "And what should we do?"

He replied, "Don't extort money and don't accuse people falsely—be content with your pay."

15The people were waiting expectantly and were all wondering in their hearts if John might possibly be the Christ.[b] 16John answered them all, "I baptize you with[c] water. But one more powerful than I will come, the thongs of whose sandals I am not worthy to untie. He will baptize you with the Holy Spirit and with fire. 17His winnowing fork is in his hand to clear his threshing

[a] 6 Isaiah 40:3-5 [b] 15 Or *Messiah* [c] 16 Or *in*

2:41–42 While adult males were supposed to go to Jerusalem three times a year for the feasts of Passover, Pentecost and Tabernacles, in practice most only attended the annual Passover celebration. ***twelve years old.*** At age 13, a Jewish boy was expected to take his place in the religious community of Israel. Age 12 would be a time of preparation for assuming the responsibilities of adulthood. It is unclear if this was Jesus' first visit to the temple.

2:43–46 Jewish pilgrims from outside Jerusalem traveled to and from the feast in large caravans. Typically, the women and children would be up front while the men and older boys traveled along behind. It would have been easy during the day for Mary and Joseph to each assume that Jesus was with the other parent or with friends. ***After three days.*** One day traveling away from Jerusalem, a second day coming back and a third day searching for him.

2:48–49 ***astonished.*** Mary's response is not amazement at Jesus' insight, but a motherly one of frustration and concern because of the worry his absence had caused. ***in my Father's house.*** Mary referred to Joseph as "your father." Jesus' answer shows his growing realization of his true Father and of his identity as the Son of God. Though this may have been a gentle rebuke, Jesus was also obedient to his earthly parents (v. 51).

2:52 ***Jesus grew in wisdom.*** Though Jesus was God, he evidently did not have all knowledge and wisdom from birth. He apparently matured like any other boy.

floor and to gather the wheat into his barn, but
he will burn up the chaff with unquenchable
fire." 18And with many other words John exhorted the people and preached the good news to
them.
19But when John rebuked Herod the tetrarch
because of Herodias, his brother's wife, and all
the other evil things he had done, 20Herod added
this to them all: He locked John up in prison.

The Baptism and Genealogy of Jesus

21When all the people were being baptized,
Jesus was baptized too. And as he was praying,
heaven was opened 22and the Holy Spirit descended on him in bodily form like a dove. And
a voice came from heaven: "You are my Son,
whom I love; with you I am well pleased."
23Now Jesus himself was about thirty years old
when he began his ministry. He was the son, so
it was thought, of Joseph,

the son of Heli, 24the son of Matthat,
the son of Levi, the son of Melki,
the son of Jannai, the son of Joseph,
25the son of Mattathias, the son of Amos,
the son of Nahum, the son of Esli,
the son of Naggai, 26the son of Maath,
the son of Mattathias, the son of Semein,
the son of Josech, the son of Joda,
27the son of Joanan, the son of Rhesa,
the son of Zerubbabel, the son of Shealtiel,
the son of Neri, 28the son of Melki,
the son of Addi, the son of Cosam,
the son of Elmadam, the son of Er,
29the son of Joshua, the son of Eliezer,
the son of Jorim, the son of Matthat,
the son of Levi, 30the son of Simeon,
the son of Judah, the son of Joseph,
the son of Jonam, the son of Eliakim,
31the son of Melea, the son of Menna,
the son of Mattatha, the son of Nathan,
the son of David, 32the son of Jesse,
the son of Obed, the son of Boaz,
the son of Salmon,[a] the son of Nahshon,
33the son of Amminadab, the son of Ram,[b]
the son of Hezron, the son of Perez,
the son of Judah, 34the son of Jacob,
the son of Isaac, the son of Abraham,
the son of Terah, the son of Nahor,
35the son of Serug, the son of Reu,
the son of Peleg, the son of Eber,
the son of Shelah, 36the son of Cainan,
the son of Arphaxad, the son of Shem,
the son of Noah, the son of Lamech,
37the son of Methuselah, the son of Enoch,
the son of Jared, the son of Mahalalel,
the son of Kenan, 38the son of Enosh,
the son of Seth, the son of Adam,
the son of God.

The Temptation of Jesus

4 Jesus, full of the Holy Spirit, returned from
the Jordan and was led by the Spirit in the
desert, 2where for forty days he was tempted by
the devil. He ate nothing during those days, and
at the end of them he was hungry.
3The devil said to him, "If you are the Son of
God, tell this stone to become bread."
4Jesus answered, "It is written: 'Man does not
live on bread alone.'[c]"
5The devil led him up to a high place and
showed him in an instant all the kingdoms of the
world. 6And he said to him, "I will give you all
their authority and splendor, for it has been given
to me, and I can give it to anyone I want to. 7So
if you worship me, it will all be yours."
8Jesus answered, "It is written: 'Worship the
Lord your God and serve him only.'[d]"
9The devil led him to Jerusalem and had him
stand on the highest point of the temple. "If you
are the Son of God," he said, "throw yourself
down from here. 10For it is written:

" 'He will command his angels concerning
you
to guard you carefully;
11they will lift you up in their hands,
so that you will not strike your foot against
a stone.'[e]"

[a] 32 Some early manuscripts *Sala* [b] 33 Some manuscripts *Amminadab, the son of Admin, the son of Arni*; other manuscripts vary widely. [c] 4 Deut. 8:3 [d] 8 Deut. 6:13 [e] 11 Psalm 91:11,12

4:1–2 ***led by the Spirit.*** Jesus' temptation was not a result of being apart from the Spirit, but an integral part of the Spirit's preparing him for his mission. ***devil.*** From Genesis 3 on, Scripture represents the devil, or Satan, as a created being who is set in firm opposition to the purposes and people of God.

4:3–4 ***If you are the Son of God.*** "If" should be understood in the sense of "since." Rather than casting doubt on Jesus' deity, Satan is tempting him to use for his own ends his supernatural powers as God's Son. In each instance, Jesus counteracts the temptation with Scripture (see NIV notes).

4:5–8 The second temptation has to do with gaining the kingdoms of the world without the sufferings of the cross. ***given to me.*** Though Satan has power in the world, it is *untrue* that his authority is absolute. Jesus' response shows that, while authority over the nations *was* Jesus' God-given destiny, his allegiance to God precluded bowing to Satan as an easy shortcut.

4:9–12 Finally, Satan tempts Jesus to test God's faithfulness as well as to dramatically draw public attention to himself and his rightful claim as Messiah. This time Satan quotes Scripture also, though he misuses it in order to suggest Jesus do something reckless to prove God's faithfulness. Jesus again asserts his complete trust in his Father, whose word does not need to be tested in foolish ways to find out if it is true.

4:13 Satan's testing of Jesus continued (see Mark 8:33), climaxing at Gethsemane.

12Jesus answered, "It says: 'Do not put the
Lord your God to the test.'[a]"
13When the devil had finished all this tempting, he left him until an opportune time.

LUKE 4:1–13

1. What is the longest you have gone without food?
2. What things go on at your school or in your community that lead you to believe Satan is real?
3. On a scale of 1 (low) to 10 (high), how's your resistance to temptation right now?
4. How did Jesus resist the devil? What have you found helpful in resisting temptation?
5. If Satan wanted to trip you up, where would he likely attack?
6. How tough is it for you to discuss your temptations? How comfortable do you feel sharing like this with the group?
7. Pray for one another regarding the different temptations each person faces.

(Study notes on page 924)

Jesus Rejected at Nazareth

14Jesus returned to Galilee in the power of the
Spirit, and news about him spread through the
whole countryside. 15He taught in their synagogues, and everyone praised him.
16He went to Nazareth, where he had been
brought up, and on the Sabbath day he went into
the synagogue, as was his custom. And he stood
up to read. 17The scroll of the prophet Isaiah was
handed to him. Unrolling it, he found the place
where it is written:

18"The Spirit of the Lord is on me,
because he has anointed me
to preach good news to the poor.
He has sent me to proclaim freedom for the prisoners
and recovery of sight for the blind,
to release the oppressed,
19 to proclaim the year of the Lord's favor."[b]

20Then he rolled up the scroll, gave it back to
the attendant and sat down. The eyes of everyone
in the synagogue were fastened on him, 21and he

LUKE 4:14–30

1. What town did you grow up in? What did you like best/least about your hometown?
2. When was the first time you received a break-up letter? Who comforted you?
3. If you were to go back to the school you previously attended and announced that you were going to be a preacher, what would be said?
4. Jesus said, "no prophet is accepted in his hometown" (v. 24). Why did people in Nazareth reject Jesus?
5. What number between 1 (all spoke well of him) and 10 (throw him from the cliff) best describes your relationships lately?
6. When was the last time you felt rejected? How do you deal with feelings of rejection?
7. What have you found helpful when you feel rejected? Close by praying together.

[a] *12* Deut. 6:16 [b] *19* Isaiah 61:1,2

4:16 ***Nazareth.*** Although Jesus was born in Bethlehem, he was brought up in Nazareth (in the province of Galilee). ***synagogue.*** The focal point of weekly worship and teaching.

4:17–21 The context of this passage that Jesus read from Isaiah was the news that God was going to deliver the Jews from their captivity in Babylon. ***Today this Scripture is fulfilled.*** Isaiah's language regarding restored sight and release from slavery was figurative. Jesus' healings and exorcisms (which had made him so popular) were literal pointers to the truth that the new era of God's deliverance had begun.

4:22 ***All spoke well of him.*** The Greek word which is translated in the positive sense in this verse can also be translated "to speak against." The violent response later in this story (v. 28) shows that the final reaction toward Jesus was decidedly negative. ***Joseph's son.*** This may be a slur, alluding to rumors of Jesus' illegitimacy.

4:25–30 While neither Elijah or Elisha were rejected by their own people, their ministry extended to others outside Israel as well. These stories illustrate that God has never limited his grace only to Israel. Jesus' strong words, which implied that Gentiles were more worthy of God's grace than the people from his hometown, provoked such a strong response that a mob tried to kill him. ***walked right through the crowd.*** Though how Jesus did so is unclear, this illustrates the proper fulfillment of Psalm 91:11–12, which Satan had twisted in his temptation of Jesus (see note on Luke 4:9–12).

began by saying to them, "Today this scripture is fulfilled in your hearing."

22 All spoke well of him and were amazed at the gracious words that came from his lips. "Isn't this Joseph's son?" they asked.

23 Jesus said to them, "Surely you will quote this proverb to me: 'Physician, heal yourself! Do here in your hometown what we have heard that you did in Capernaum.' "

24 "I tell you the truth," he continued, "no prophet is accepted in his hometown. 25 I assure you that there were many widows in Israel in Elijah's time, when the sky was shut for three and a half years and there was a severe famine throughout the land. 26 Yet Elijah was not sent to any of them, but to a widow in Zarephath in the region of Sidon. 27 And there were many in Israel with leprosy[a] in the time of Elisha the prophet, yet not one of them was cleansed—only Naaman the Syrian."

28 All the people in the synagogue were furious when they heard this. 29 They got up, drove him out of the town, and took him to the brow of the hill on which the town was built, in order to throw him down the cliff. 30 But he walked right through the crowd and went on his way.

Jesus Drives Out an Evil Spirit

31 Then he went down to Capernaum, a town in Galilee, and on the Sabbath began to teach the people. 32 They were amazed at his teaching, because his message had authority.

33 In the synagogue there was a man possessed by a demon, an evil[b] spirit. He cried out at the top of his voice, 34 "Ha! What do you want with us, Jesus of Nazareth? Have you come to destroy us? I know who you are—the Holy One of God!"

35 "Be quiet!" Jesus said sternly. "Come out of him!" Then the demon threw the man down before them all and came out without injuring him.

36 All the people were amazed and said to each other, "What is this teaching? With authority and power he gives orders to evil spirits and they come out!" 37 And the news about him spread throughout the surrounding area.

Jesus Heals Many

38 Jesus left the synagogue and went to the home of Simon. Now Simon's mother-in-law was suffering from a high fever, and they asked Jesus to help her. 39 So he bent over her and rebuked the fever, and it left her. She got up at once and began to wait on them.

40 When the sun was setting, the people brought to Jesus all who had various kinds of sickness, and laying his hands on each one, he healed them. 41 Moreover, demons came out of many people, shouting, "You are the Son of God!" But he rebuked them and would not allow them to speak, because they knew he was the Christ.[c]

42 At daybreak Jesus went out to a solitary place. The people were looking for him and when they came to where he was, they tried to keep him from leaving them. 43 But he said, "I must preach the good news of the kingdom of God to the other towns also, because that is why I was sent." 44 And he kept on preaching in the synagogues of Judea.[d]

The Calling of the First Disciples

5 One day as Jesus was standing by the Lake of Gennesaret,[e] with the people crowding around him and listening to the word of God, 2 he saw at the water's edge two boats, left there by the fishermen, who were washing their nets. 3 He got into one of the boats, the one belonging to Simon, and asked him to put out a little from shore. Then he sat down and taught the people from the boat.

4 When he had finished speaking, he said to Simon, "Put out into deep water, and let down[f] the nets for a catch."

5 Simon answered, "Master, we've worked hard all night and haven't caught anything. But because you say so, I will let down the nets."

6 When they had done so, they caught such a

[a] *27* The Greek word was used for various diseases affecting the skin—not necessarily leprosy. [b] *33* Greek *unclean*; also in verse 36 [c] *41* Or *Messiah* [d] *44* Or *the land of the Jews*; some manuscripts *Galilee* [e] *1* That is, Sea of Galilee [f] *4* The Greek verb is plural.

5:1–3 ***Lake of Gennesaret.*** Another name for the Sea of Galilee. ***washing their nets.*** In the morning fishermen would clean and repair the nets which they dragged along behind the boats while fishing throughout the night. ***from the boat.*** Simon Peter's boat served as an ideal speaking platform; Jesus could be set apart from the crowd but still heard and seen.

5:4–7 Jesus' command seemed absolutely foolish since mid-morning was not the time fish would be feeding. These tired men who have worked unsuccessfully all night wonder why in the world they should listen to a religious teacher when it comes to their fishing business! Simon protests, but out of respect for Jesus he consents. In contrast to Simon's doubt, Luke underscores the magnitude of the catch. It was so large that it tore the nets and threatened to sink Simon's boat as well as that of his partners!

5:8 ***Go away from me, Lord.*** The closer people get to God, the more they feel their sinfulness and unworthiness.

5:10–11 ***will catch men.*** The climax of the story is on the significance of the miraculous catch of fish as an illustration of the widespread success that would accompany Jesus' and the apostles' mission of preaching the kingdom of God. ***left everything and followed him.*** A loyalty to Jesus which takes precedence over anything else in life is Luke's way of describing what it means to be a Christian. This was not the first time these men were with Jesus (see John 1:40–42), their loose association now becomes a close fellowship.

large number of fish that their nets began to
break. 7 So they signaled their partners in the other boat to come and help them, and they came
and filled both boats so full that they began to
sink.
8 When Simon Peter saw this, he fell at Jesus'
knees and said, "Go away from me, Lord; I am a
sinful man!" 9 For he and all his companions were
astonished at the catch of fish they had taken,
10 and so were James and John, the sons of Zebedee, Simon's partners.
Then Jesus said to Simon, "Don't be afraid;
from now on you will catch men." 11 So they
pulled their boats up on shore, left everything
and followed him.

LUKE 5:1–11

1. Where is the best fishing spot in your area? What is the biggest fish you've ever caught?
2. What are you "fishing" for now: A job? A car? Good grades? A scholarship? A date?
3. What would you like to be doing five years from now?
4. Consider verse 8. What caused Peter's response? When have you had a similar experience?
5. When is the first time you remember feeling the call of God on your life?
6. Peter, James and John "left everything and followed him" (v. 11). Where is Jesus asking you to follow him? What must you give up to follow him?
7. What would be the greatest thing you would like to do with your life? What is keeping you from doing it? Pray together.

(Study notes on page 926)

The Man With Leprosy

12 While Jesus was in one of the towns, a man
came along who was covered with leprosy.[a]
When he saw Jesus, he fell with his face to the
ground and begged him, "Lord, if you are willing,
you can make me clean."
13 Jesus reached out his hand and touched the
man. "I am willing," he said. "Be clean!" And
immediately the leprosy left him.
14 Then Jesus ordered him, "Don't tell anyone,
but go, show yourself to the priest and offer the
sacrifices that Moses commanded for your cleansing, as a testimony to them."
15 Yet the news about him spread all the more,
so that crowds of people came to hear him and to
be healed of their sicknesses. 16 But Jesus often
withdrew to lonely places and prayed.

Jesus Heals a Paralytic

17 One day as he was teaching, Pharisees and
teachers of the law, who had come from every
village of Galilee and from Judea and Jerusalem,
were sitting there. And the power of the Lord
was present for him to heal the sick. 18 Some men
came carrying a paralytic on a mat and tried to
take him into the house to lay him before Jesus.
19 When they could not find a way to do this because of the crowd, they went up on the roof and
lowered him on his mat through the tiles into the
middle of the crowd, right in front of Jesus.
20 When Jesus saw their faith, he said, "Friend,
your sins are forgiven."
21 The Pharisees and the teachers of the law
began thinking to themselves, "Who is this fellow who speaks blasphemy? Who can forgive sins
but God alone?"
22 Jesus knew what they were thinking and
asked, "Why are you thinking these things in
your hearts? 23 Which is easier: to say, 'Your sins
are forgiven,' or to say, 'Get up and walk'? 24 But
that you may know that the Son of Man has authority on earth to forgive sins . . . ." He said to
the paralyzed man, "I tell you, get up, take your
mat and go home." 25 Immediately he stood up in
front of them, took what he had been lying on
and went home praising God. 26 Everyone was
amazed and gave praise to God. They were filled
with awe and said, "We have seen remarkable
things today."

The Calling of Levi

27 After this, Jesus went out and saw a tax collector by the name of Levi sitting at his tax booth.
"Follow me," Jesus said to him, 28 and Levi got
up, left everything and followed him.
29 Then Levi held a great banquet for Jesus at
his house, and a large crowd of tax collectors and
others were eating with them. 30 But the Pharisees and the teachers of the law who belonged to
their sect complained to his disciples, "Why do
you eat and drink with tax collectors and 'sinners'?"
31 Jesus answered them, "It is not the healthy
who need a doctor, but the sick. 32 I have not
come to call the righteous, but sinners to repentance."

[a] *12* The Greek word was used for various diseases affecting the skin—not necessarily leprosy.

Jesus Questioned About Fasting

33They said to him, "John's disciples often fast
and pray, and so do the disciples of the Pharisees,
but yours go on eating and drinking."
34Jesus answered, "Can you make the guests of
the bridegroom fast while he is with them? 35But
the time will come when the bridegroom will be
taken from them; in those days they will fast."
36He told them this parable: "No one tears a
patch from a new garment and sews it on an old
one. If he does, he will have torn the new garment, and the patch from the new will not match
the old. 37And no one pours new wine into old
wineskins. If he does, the new wine will burst
the skins, the wine will run out and the wineskins will be ruined. 38No, new wine must be
poured into new wineskins. 39And no one after
drinking old wine wants the new, for he says,
'The old is better.'"

Lord of the Sabbath

6 One Sabbath Jesus was going through the
grainfields, and his disciples began to pick
some heads of grain, rub them in their hands and
eat the kernels. 2Some of the Pharisees asked,
"Why are you doing what is unlawful on the Sabbath?"
3Jesus answered them, "Have you never read
what David did when he and his companions
were hungry? 4He entered the house of God, and
taking the consecrated bread, he ate what is lawful only for priests to eat. And he also gave some
to his companions." 5Then Jesus said to them,
"The Son of Man is Lord of the Sabbath."
6On another Sabbath he went into the synagogue and was teaching, and a man was there
whose right hand was shriveled. 7The Pharisees
and the teachers of the law were looking for a
reason to accuse Jesus, so they watched him
closely to see if he would heal on the Sabbath.
8But Jesus knew what they were thinking and
said to the man with the shriveled hand, "Get up
and stand in front of everyone." So he got up and
stood there.
9Then Jesus said to them, "I ask you, which is
lawful on the Sabbath: to do good or to do evil, to
save life or to destroy it?"
10He looked around at them all, and then said
to the man, "Stretch out your hand." He did so,
and his hand was completely restored. 11But they
were furious and began to discuss with one another what they might do to Jesus.

The Twelve Apostles

12One of those days Jesus went out to a mountainside to pray, and spent the night praying to
God. 13When morning came, he called his disciples to him and chose twelve of them, whom
he also designated apostles: 14Simon (whom he
named Peter), his brother Andrew, James, John,
Philip, Bartholomew, 15Matthew, Thomas, James
son of Alphaeus, Simon who was called the Zealot, 16Judas son of James, and Judas Iscariot, who
became a traitor.

Blessings and Woes

17He went down with them and stood on a
level place. A large crowd of his disciples was
there and a great number of people from all over
Judea, from Jerusalem, and from the coast of Tyre
and Sidon, 18who had come to hear him and to be
healed of their diseases. Those troubled by evil[a]
spirits were cured, 19and the people all tried to
touch him, because power was coming from him
and healing them all.
20Looking at his disciples, he said:

"Blessed are you who are poor,
for yours is the kingdom of God.
21Blessed are you who hunger now,
for you will be satisfied.
Blessed are you who weep now,
for you will laugh.
22Blessed are you when men hate you,
when they exclude you and insult you
and reject your name as evil,
because of the Son of Man.

23"Rejoice in that day and leap for joy, because
great is your reward in heaven. For that is how
their fathers treated the prophets.

24"But woe to you who are rich,
for you have already received your
comfort.
25Woe to you who are well fed now,
for you will go hungry.
Woe to you who laugh now,
for you will mourn and weep.
26Woe to you when all men speak well of you,
for that is how their fathers treated the
false prophets.

Love for Enemies

27"But I tell you who hear me: Love your enemies, do good to those who hate you, 28bless
those who curse you, pray for those who mistreat
you. 29If someone strikes you on one cheek, turn
to him the other also. If someone takes your
cloak, do not stop him from taking your tunic.
30Give to everyone who asks you, and if anyone
takes what belongs to you, do not demand it
back. 31Do to others as you would have them do
to you.

[a] *18* Greek *unclean*

32“If you love those who love you, what credit
is that to you? Even ‘sinners’ love those who love
them. 33And if you do good to those who are good
to you, what credit is that to you? Even ‘sinners’
do that. 34And if you lend to those from whom
you expect repayment, what credit is that to you?
Even ‘sinners’ lend to ‘sinners,’ expecting to be
repaid in full. 35But love your enemies, do good
to them, and lend to them without expecting to
get anything back. Then your reward will be
great, and you will be sons of the Most High,
because he is kind to the ungrateful and wicked.
36Be merciful, just as your Father is merciful.

Judging Others

37“Do not judge, and you will not be judged.
Do not condemn, and you will not be condemned. Forgive, and you will be forgiven.
38Give, and it will be given to you. A good measure, pressed down, shaken together and running
over, will be poured into your lap. For with the
measure you use, it will be measured to you.”
39He also told them this parable: “Can a blind
man lead a blind man? Will they not both fall into
a pit? 40A student is not above his teacher, but
everyone who is fully trained will be like his
teacher.
41“Why do you look at the speck of sawdust in
your brother’s eye and pay no attention to the
plank in your own eye? 42How can you say to
your brother, ‘Brother, let me take the speck out
of your eye,’ when you yourself fail to see the
plank in your own eye? You hypocrite, first take
the plank out of your eye, and then you will see
clearly to remove the speck from your brother’s
eye.

A Tree and Its Fruit

43“No good tree bears bad fruit, nor does a bad
tree bear good fruit. 44Each tree is recognized by
its own fruit. People do not pick figs from thornbushes, or grapes from briers. 45The good man
brings good things out of the good stored up in
his heart, and the evil man brings evil things out
of the evil stored up in his heart. For out of the
overflow of his heart his mouth speaks.

The Wise and Foolish Builders

46“Why do you call me, ‘Lord, Lord,’ and do
not do what I say? 47I will show you what he is
like who comes to me and hears my words and
puts them into practice. 48He is like a man building a house, who dug down deep and laid the
foundation on rock. When a flood came, the torrent struck that house but could not shake it,
because it was well built. 49But the one who
hears my words and does not put them into practice is like a man who built a house on the ground
without a foundation. The moment the torrent
struck that house, it collapsed and its destruction
was complete.”

The Faith of the Centurion

7 When Jesus had finished saying all this in the
hearing of the people, he entered Capernaum. 2There a centurion’s servant, whom his master valued highly, was sick and about to die. 3The
centurion heard of Jesus and sent some elders of
the Jews to him, asking him to come and heal his
servant. 4When they came to Jesus, they pleaded
earnestly with him, “This man deserves to have
you do this, 5because he loves our nation and has
built our synagogue.” 6So Jesus went with them.
He was not far from the house when the centurion sent friends to say to him: “Lord, don’t
trouble yourself, for I do not deserve to have you
come under my roof. 7That is why I did not even
consider myself worthy to come to you. But say
the word, and my servant will be healed. 8For I
myself am a man under authority, with soldiers
under me. I tell this one, ‘Go,’ and he goes; and
that one, ‘Come,’ and he comes. I say to my servant, ‘Do this,’ and he does it.”
9When Jesus heard this, he was amazed at
him, and turning to the crowd following him, he
said, “I tell you, I have not found such great faith
even in Israel.” 10Then the men who had been
sent returned to the house and found the servant
well.

Jesus Raises a Widow’s Son

11Soon afterward, Jesus went to a town called
Nain, and his disciples and a large crowd went
along with him. 12As he approached the town
gate, a dead person was being carried out—the
only son of his mother, and she was a widow.
And a large crowd from the town was with her.
13When the Lord saw her, his heart went out to
her and he said, “Don’t cry.”
14Then he went up and touched the coffin, and
those carrying it stood still. He said, “Young man,
I say to you, get up!” 15The dead man sat up and
began to talk, and Jesus gave him back to his
mother.
16They were all filled with awe and praised
God. “A great prophet has appeared among us,”
they said. “God has come to help his people.”
17This news about Jesus spread throughout Judea[a] and the surrounding country.

Jesus and John the Baptist

18John’s disciples told him about all these
things. Calling two of them, 19he sent them to

a17 Or *the land of the Jews*

the Lord to ask, "Are you the one who was to
come, or should we expect someone else?"
20When the men came to Jesus, they said,
"John the Baptist sent us to you to ask, 'Are you
the one who was to come, or should we expect
someone else?'"
21At that very time Jesus cured many who had
diseases, sicknesses and evil spirits, and gave
sight to many who were blind. 22So he replied to
the messengers, "Go back and report to John
what you have seen and heard: The blind receive
sight, the lame walk, those who have leprosy[a]
are cured, the deaf hear, the dead are raised, and
the good news is preached to the poor. 23Blessed
is the man who does not fall away on account
of me."
24After John's messengers left, Jesus began to
speak to the crowd about John: "What did you go
out into the desert to see? A reed swayed by the
wind? 25If not, what did you go out to see? A man
dressed in fine clothes? No, those who wear expensive clothes and indulge in luxury are in palaces. 26But what did you go out to see? A prophet? Yes, I tell you, and more than a prophet.
27This is the one about whom it is written:

> " 'I will send my messenger ahead of you,
> who will prepare your way before you.'[b]

28I tell you, among those born of women there is
no one greater than John; yet the one who is least
in the kingdom of God is greater than he."
29(All the people, even the tax collectors,
when they heard Jesus' words, acknowledged
that God's way was right, because they had been
baptized by John. 30But the Pharisees and experts
in the law rejected God's purpose for themselves,
because they had not been baptized by John.)
31"To what, then, can I compare the people of
this generation? What are they like? 32They are
like children sitting in the marketplace and calling out to each other:

> " 'We played the flute for you,
> and you did not dance;
> we sang a dirge,
> and you did not cry.'

33For John the Baptist came neither eating bread
nor drinking wine, and you say, 'He has a demon.' 34The Son of Man came eating and drinking, and you say, 'Here is a glutton and a drunkard, a friend of tax collectors and "sinners." '
35But wisdom is proved right by all her children."

Jesus Anointed by a Sinful Woman

36Now one of the Pharisees invited Jesus to
have dinner with him, so he went to the Phari-

LUKE 7:36–50

1. Who do you know that you can recognize by the smell of their perfume or cologne?
2. What's something you are "guilty" of: Speeding? Breaking curfew? Borrowing clothes without asking? Other?
3. On a scale of 1 (Simon the Pharisee) to 10 (the woman), how hard is it for you to show your love for Jesus?
4. Why did the woman pour perfume on Jesus' feet, wipe his feet with her hair and kiss his feet?
5. When have you felt guilty and broken like this woman did?
6. When did you come to the place in your life that you experienced forgiveness and release from guilt over sin?
7. Close in silent prayer. Ask God for forgiveness and allow Jesus to wash away your guilt.

[a]*22* The Greek word was used for various diseases affecting the skin—not necessarily leprosy. [b]*27* Mal. 3:1

7:36 *one of the Pharisees.* These strict Jews considered themselves guardians of the Law and subsequent tradition. Why Simon (v. 40) invited Jesus is unclear. His lack of providing common courtesies to his guest—water for his feet, the kiss of peace, and oil on his head (vv. 44–46)—indicates his opinion of Jesus probably was not especially high. He may have even been trying to trap Jesus.

7:37–38 *a woman who had lived a sinful life.* Almost certainly a prostitute. Surely not an invited guest, she evidently had heard Jesus speak and was determined to lead a new life. People ate by reclining on couches with their feet extended away from the table, so she could anoint Jesus' feet without disturbing his eating. The woman's tears show her repentance. For a woman to loose her hair in public was scandalous; using it to dry her tears from Jesus' feet marked her great love and humility.

7:39–47 Simon, seeing only that Jesus violated religious and social codes by allowing such a woman to touch him like this, saw nothing of her repentance or gratitude. Through a brief parable and interpretation, Jesus disarms Simon's silent criticism and highlights his mission of saving those, like this woman, who recognize their sin.

7:47 *for she loved much.* Jesus is not saying the woman is forgiven because she has shown such extravagant love, but that her love expresses the reality of the forgiveness she has received. Jesus states clearly in verse 50 that she was saved by faith.

see's house and reclined at the table. 37When a woman who had lived a sinful life in that town learned that Jesus was eating at the Pharisee's house, she brought an alabaster jar of perfume, 38and as she stood behind him at his feet weeping, she began to wet his feet with her tears. Then she wiped them with her hair, kissed them and poured perfume on them.

39When the Pharisee who had invited him saw this, he said to himself, "If this man were a prophet, he would know who is touching him and what kind of woman she is—that she is a sinner."

40Jesus answered him, "Simon, I have something to tell you."

"Tell me, teacher," he said.

41"Two men owed money to a certain moneylender. One owed him five hundred denarii,[a] and the other fifty. 42Neither of them had the money to pay him back, so he canceled the debts of both. Now which of them will love him more?"

43Simon replied, "I suppose the one who had the bigger debt canceled."

"You have judged correctly," Jesus said.

44Then he turned toward the woman and said to Simon, "Do you see this woman? I came into your house. You did not give me any water for my feet, but she wet my feet with her tears and wiped them with her hair. 45You did not give me a kiss, but this woman, from the time I entered, has not stopped kissing my feet. 46You did not put oil on my head, but she has poured perfume on my feet. 47Therefore, I tell you, her many sins have been forgiven—for she loved much. But he who has been forgiven little loves little."

48Then Jesus said to her, "Your sins are forgiven."

49The other guests began to say among themselves, "Who is this who even forgives sins?"

50Jesus said to the woman, "Your faith has saved you; go in peace."

The Parable of the Sower

8 After this, Jesus traveled about from one town and village to another, proclaiming the good news of the kingdom of God. The Twelve were with him, 2and also some women who had been cured of evil spirits and diseases: Mary (called Magdalene) from whom seven demons had come out; 3Joanna the wife of Cuza, the manager of Herod's household; Susanna; and many others. These women were helping to support them out of their own means.

4While a large crowd was gathering and people were coming to Jesus from town after town, he told this parable: 5"A farmer went out to sow his seed. As he was scattering the seed, some fell along the path; it was trampled on, and the birds of the air ate it up. 6Some fell on rock, and when it came up, the plants withered because they had no moisture. 7Other seed fell among thorns, which grew up with it and choked the plants. 8Still other seed fell on good soil. It came up and yielded a crop, a hundred times more than was sown."

When he said this, he called out, "He who has ears to hear, let him hear."

9His disciples asked him what this parable meant. 10He said, "The knowledge of the secrets of the kingdom of God has been given to you, but to others I speak in parables, so that,

"'though seeing, they may not see;
though hearing, they may not understand.'[b]

11"This is the meaning of the parable: The seed is the word of God. 12Those along the path are the ones who hear, and then the devil comes and takes away the word from their hearts, so that they may not believe and be saved. 13Those on the rock are the ones who receive the word with joy when they hear it, but they have no root. They believe for a while, but in the time of testing they fall away. 14The seed that fell among thorns stands for those who hear, but as they go on their way they are choked by life's worries, riches and pleasures, and they do not mature. 15But the seed on good soil stands for those with a noble and good heart, who hear the word, retain it, and by persevering produce a crop.

A Lamp on a Stand

16"No one lights a lamp and hides it in a jar or puts it under a bed. Instead, he puts it on a stand, so that those who come in can see the light. 17For there is nothing hidden that will not be disclosed, and nothing concealed that will not be known or brought out into the open. 18Therefore consider carefully how you listen. Whoever has will be given more; whoever does not have, even what he thinks he has will be taken from him."

Jesus' Mother and Brothers

19Now Jesus' mother and brothers came to see him, but they were not able to get near him because of the crowd. 20Someone told him, "Your mother and brothers are standing outside, wanting to see you."

21He replied, "My mother and brothers are those who hear God's word and put it into practice."

[a] *41* A denarius was a coin worth about a day's wages. [b] *10* Isaiah 6:9

Jesus Calms the Storm

22One day Jesus said to his disciples, "Let's go
over to the other side of the lake." So they got
into a boat and set out. 23As they sailed, he fell
asleep. A squall came down on the lake, so that
the boat was being swamped, and they were in
great danger.
24The disciples went and woke him, saying,
"Master, Master, we're going to drown!"
He got up and rebuked the wind and the raging waters; the storm subsided, and all was calm.
25"Where is your faith?" he asked his disciples.
In fear and amazement they asked one another, "Who is this? He commands even the winds
and the water, and they obey him."

The Healing of a Demon-possessed Man

26They sailed to the region of the Gerasenes,[a]
which is across the lake from Galilee. 27When
Jesus stepped ashore, he was met by a demon-
possessed man from the town. For a long time
this man had not worn clothes or lived in a
house, but had lived in the tombs. 28When he
saw Jesus, he cried out and fell at his feet, shouting at the top of his voice, "What do you want
with me, Jesus, Son of the Most High God? I beg
you, don't torture me!" 29For Jesus had commanded the evil[b] spirit to come out of the man.
Many times it had seized him, and though he was
chained hand and foot and kept under guard, he
had broken his chains and had been driven by
the demon into solitary places.
30Jesus asked him, "What is your name?"
"Legion," he replied, because many demons
had gone into him. 31And they begged him repeatedly not to order them to go into the Abyss.
32A large herd of pigs was feeding there on the
hillside. The demons begged Jesus to let them go
into them, and he gave them permission. 33When
the demons came out of the man, they went into
the pigs, and the herd rushed down the steep
bank into the lake and was drowned.
34When those tending the pigs saw what had
happened, they ran off and reported this in the
town and countryside, 35and the people went out
to see what had happened. When they came to
Jesus, they found the man from whom the demons had gone out, sitting at Jesus' feet, dressed
and in his right mind; and they were afraid.
36Those who had seen it told the people how the
demon-possessed man had been cured. 37Then
all the people of the region of the Gerasenes
asked Jesus to leave them, because they were
overcome with fear. So he got into the boat and
left.
38The man from whom the demons had gone

Luke 8:26–39

1. What is the scariest place or situation you've ever been in?
2. Are you more likely to get hooked on TV, computer games, cigarettes, candy/pop, coffee or the Internet?
3. In your school, what is the most common addiction?
4. How would you compare the behavior of the demon-possessed man in the story to that of those addicted in your school?
5. Where do you find yourself "in chains" right now: In a relationship? To a habit or addiction? To a stagnant spiritual life?
6. What can this group do to help you: Leave you alone? Hold you accountable? Pray for you?
7. What is one thing "God has done for you" (v. 39)? Who can you share that with this week? Close in prayer.

[a]26 Some manuscripts *Gadarenes*; other manuscripts *Gergesenes*; also in verse 37 [b]29 Greek *unclean*

8:27 *tombs.* Ragged limestone cliffs with their caves and depressions provided natural tombs. The man's nakedness and residence shows the severity of his possession.

8:30–31 *Legion.* The name for a company of Roman soldiers consisting of 6,000 men. The man was occupied by a huge number of demons. When Jesus asked the man his name, the demons spoke, showing they were in control. ***they begged him repeatedly.*** The demons cower in fear before the One they recognize as their Judge.

8:32–37 *pigs.* This must have been an area where Gentiles lived, since Jews considered pigs unclean and were forbidden to eat them (Lev. 11:7–8). This was probably a herd made up of pigs owned by various people in town. ***rushed down the steep bank.*** This scene betrays the evil, death-dealing purpose of the demons in their effect upon creation as opposed to the life-giving effect of Jesus to those who come to him. ***they were afraid.*** It might be expected that the townspeople would rejoice that this man who had terrorized them (v. 29) was healed. But instead they are fearful of Jesus who has the power to overcome the demons and destroy their town herd, even to the extent of asking him to leave.

8:39 *tell.* Jesus had been commanding those he healed *not* to tell others about him. The difference here is that Gentiles, who did not have messianic expectations, would be more able to hear the man's witness for what it was and not read it through a grid of preconceived ideas that would distort the nature of Jesus' mission.

out begged to go with him, but Jesus sent him
away, saying, 39“Return home and tell how much
God has done for you.” So the man went away
and told all over town how much Jesus had done
for him.

A Dead Girl and a Sick Woman

40Now when Jesus returned, a crowd welcomed him, for they were all expecting him.
41Then a man named Jairus, a ruler of the synagogue, came and fell at Jesus’ feet, pleading with
him to come to his house 42because his only
daughter, a girl of about twelve, was dying.

As Jesus was on his way, the crowds almost
crushed him. 43And a woman was there who had
been subject to bleeding for twelve years,[a] but
no one could heal her. 44She came up behind him
and touched the edge of his cloak, and immediately her bleeding stopped.

45“Who touched me?” Jesus asked.

When they all denied it, Peter said, “Master,
the people are crowding and pressing against
you.”

46But Jesus said, “Someone touched me; I
know that power has gone out from me.”

47Then the woman, seeing that she could not
go unnoticed, came trembling and fell at his feet.
In the presence of all the people, she told why
she had touched him and how she had been instantly healed. 48Then he said to her, “Daughter,
your faith has healed you. Go in peace.”

49While Jesus was still speaking, someone
came from the house of Jairus, the synagogue
ruler. “Your daughter is dead,” he said. “Don’t
bother the teacher any more.”

50Hearing this, Jesus said to Jairus, “Don’t be
afraid; just believe, and she will be healed.”

51When he arrived at the house of Jairus, he
did not let anyone go in with him except Peter,
John and James, and the child’s father and mother. 52Meanwhile, all the people were wailing and
mourning for her. “Stop wailing,” Jesus said.
“She is not dead but asleep.”

53They laughed at him, knowing that she was
dead. 54But he took her by the hand and said,
“My child, get up!” 55Her spirit returned, and at
once she stood up. Then Jesus told them to give
her something to eat. 56Her parents were astonished, but he ordered them not to tell anyone
what had happened.

Jesus Sends Out the Twelve

9 When Jesus had called the Twelve together,
he gave them power and authority to drive
out all demons and to cure diseases, 2and he sent
them out to preach the kingdom of God and to
heal the sick. 3He told them: “Take nothing for
the journey—no staff, no bag, no bread, no money, no extra tunic. 4Whatever house you enter,
stay there until you leave that town. 5If people do
not welcome you, shake the dust off your feet
when you leave their town, as a testimony
against them.” 6So they set out and went from
village to village, preaching the gospel and healing people everywhere.

7Now Herod the tetrarch heard about all that
was going on. And he was perplexed, because
some were saying that John had been raised from
the dead, 8others that Elijah had appeared, and
still others that one of the prophets of long ago
had come back to life. 9But Herod said, “I beheaded John. Who, then, is this I hear such things
about?” And he tried to see him.

Jesus Feeds the Five Thousand

10When the apostles returned, they reported
to Jesus what they had done. Then he took them
with him and they withdrew by themselves to a
town called Bethsaida, 11but the crowds learned
about it and followed him. He welcomed them
and spoke to them about the kingdom of God,
and healed those who needed healing.

12Late in the afternoon the Twelve came to
him and said, “Send the crowd away so they can
go to the surrounding villages and countryside
and find food and lodging, because we are in a
remote place here.”

13He replied, “You give them something to
eat.”

They answered, “We have only five loaves of
bread and two fish—unless we go and buy food
for all this crowd.” 14(About five thousand men
were there.)

But he said to his disciples, “Have them sit
down in groups of about fifty each.” 15The disciples did so, and everybody sat down. 16Taking the
five loaves and the two fish and looking up to
heaven, he gave thanks and broke them. Then he
gave them to the disciples to set before the people. 17They all ate and were satisfied, and the
disciples picked up twelve basketfuls of broken
pieces that were left over.

Peter’s Confession of Christ

18Once when Jesus was praying in private and
his disciples were with him, he asked them,
“Who do the crowds say I am?”

19They replied, “Some say John the Baptist;
others say Elijah; and still others, that one of the
prophets of long ago has come back to life.”

20“But what about you?” he asked. “Who do
you say I am?”

Peter answered, “The Christ[b] of God.”

21Jesus strictly warned them not to tell this to

[a] *43* Many manuscripts *years, and she had spent all she had on doctors* [b] *20* Or *Messiah*

anyone. 22And he said, "The Son of Man must suffer many things and be rejected by the elders, chief priests and teachers of the law, and he must be killed and on the third day be raised to life."

23Then he said to them all: "If anyone would come after me, he must deny himself and take up his cross daily and follow me. 24For whoever wants to save his life will lose it, but whoever loses his life for me will save it. 25What good is it for a man to gain the whole world, and yet lose or forfeit his very self? 26If anyone is ashamed of me and my words, the Son of Man will be ashamed of him when he comes in his glory and in the glory of the Father and of the holy angels. 27I tell you the truth, some who are standing here will not taste death before they see the kingdom of God."

The Transfiguration

28About eight days after Jesus said this, he took Peter, John and James with him and went up onto a mountain to pray. 29As he was praying, the appearance of his face changed, and his clothes became as bright as a flash of lightning. 30Two men, Moses and Elijah, 31appeared in glorious splendor, talking with Jesus. They spoke about his departure, which he was about to bring to fulfillment at Jerusalem. 32Peter and his companions were very sleepy, but when they became fully awake, they saw his glory and the two men standing with him. 33As the men were leaving Jesus, Peter said to him, "Master, it is good for us to be here. Let us put up three shelters—one for you, one for Moses and one for Elijah." (He did not know what he was saying.)

34While he was speaking, a cloud appeared and enveloped them, and they were afraid as they entered the cloud. 35A voice came from the cloud, saying, "This is my Son, whom I have chosen; listen to him." 36When the voice had spoken, they found that Jesus was alone. The disciples kept this to themselves, and told no one at that time what they had seen.

The Healing of a Boy With an Evil Spirit

37The next day, when they came down from the mountain, a large crowd met him. 38A man in the crowd called out, "Teacher, I beg you to look at my son, for he is my only child. 39A spirit seizes him and he suddenly screams; it throws him into convulsions so that he foams at the mouth. It scarcely ever leaves him and is destroying him. 40I begged your disciples to drive it out, but they could not."

41"O unbelieving and perverse generation," Jesus replied, "how long shall I stay with you and put up with you? Bring your son here."

42Even while the boy was coming, the demon threw him to the ground in a convulsion. But Jesus rebuked the evil[a] spirit, healed the boy and gave him back to his father. 43And they were all amazed at the greatness of God.

While everyone was marveling at all that Jesus did, he said to his disciples, 44"Listen carefully to what I am about to tell you: The Son of Man is going to be betrayed into the hands of men." 45But they did not understand what this meant. It was hidden from them, so that they did not grasp it, and they were afraid to ask him about it.

Who Will Be the Greatest?

46An argument started among the disciples as to which of them would be the greatest. 47Jesus, knowing their thoughts, took a little child and had him stand beside him. 48Then he said to them, "Whoever welcomes this little child in my name welcomes me; and whoever welcomes me welcomes the one who sent me. For he who is least among you all—he is the greatest."

49"Master," said John, "we saw a man driving out demons in your name and we tried to stop him, because he is not one of us."

50"Do not stop him," Jesus said, "for whoever is not against you is for you."

Samaritan Opposition

51As the time approached for him to be taken up to heaven, Jesus resolutely set out for Jerusalem. 52And he sent messengers on ahead, who went into a Samaritan village to get things ready for him; 53but the people there did not welcome him, because he was heading for Jerusalem. 54When the disciples James and John saw this, they asked, "Lord, do you want us to call fire down from heaven to destroy them[b]?" 55But Jesus turned and rebuked them, 56and[c] they went to another village.

The Cost of Following Jesus

57As they were walking along the road, a man said to him, "I will follow you wherever you go."

58Jesus replied, "Foxes have holes and birds of the air have nests, but the Son of Man has no place to lay his head."

59He said to another man, "Follow me."

But the man replied, "Lord, first let me go and bury my father."

60Jesus said to him, "Let the dead bury their own dead, but you go and proclaim the kingdom of God."

61Still another said, "I will follow you, Lord;

[a]42 Greek *unclean* [b]54 Some manuscripts *them, even as Elijah did* [c]55,56 Some manuscripts *them. And he said, "You do not know what kind of spirit you are of, for the Son of Man did not come to destroy men's lives, but to save them." 56And*

but first let me go back and say good-by to my
family."
62Jesus replied, "No one who puts his hand to
the plow and looks back is fit for service in the
kingdom of God."

Jesus Sends Out the Seventy-two

10 After this the Lord appointed seventy-
two[a] others and sent them two by two
ahead of him to every town and place where he
was about to go. 2He told them, "The harvest is
plentiful, but the workers are few. Ask the Lord
of the harvest, therefore, to send out workers
into his harvest field. 3Go! I am sending you out
like lambs among wolves. 4Do not take a purse or
bag or sandals; and do not greet anyone on the
road.
5"When you enter a house, first say, 'Peace to
this house.' 6If a man of peace is there, your
peace will rest on him; if not, it will return to
you. 7Stay in that house, eating and drinking
whatever they give you, for the worker deserves
his wages. Do not move around from house to
house.
8"When you enter a town and are welcomed,
eat what is set before you. 9Heal the sick who are
there and tell them, 'The kingdom of God is near
you.' 10But when you enter a town and are not
welcomed, go into its streets and say, 11'Even the
dust of your town that sticks to our feet we wipe
off against you. Yet be sure of this: The kingdom of God is near.' 12I tell you, it will be more
bearable on that day for Sodom than for that
town.
13"Woe to you, Korazin! Woe to you, Bethsaida! For if the miracles that were performed in you
had been performed in Tyre and Sidon, they
would have repented long ago, sitting in sackcloth and ashes. 14But it will be more bearable for
Tyre and Sidon at the judgment than for you.
15And you, Capernaum, will you be lifted up to
the skies? No, you will go down to the depths.[b]
16"He who listens to you listens to me; he who
rejects you rejects me; but he who rejects me
rejects him who sent me."
17The seventy-two returned with joy and said,
"Lord, even the demons submit to us in your
name."
18He replied, "I saw Satan fall like lightning
from heaven. 19I have given you authority to
trample on snakes and scorpions and to overcome all the power of the enemy; nothing will
harm you. 20However, do not rejoice that the
spirits submit to you, but rejoice that your names
are written in heaven."
21At that time Jesus, full of joy through the
Holy Spirit, said, "I praise you, Father, Lord of
heaven and earth, because you have hidden these
things from the wise and learned, and revealed
them to little children. Yes, Father, for this was
your good pleasure.
22"All things have been committed to me by
my Father. No one knows who the Son is except
the Father, and no one knows who the Father
is except the Son and those to whom the Son
chooses to reveal him."
23Then he turned to his disciples and said
privately, "Blessed are the eyes that see what
you see. 24For I tell you that many prophets and
kings wanted to see what you see but did not
see it, and to hear what you hear but did not
hear it."

The Parable of the Good Samaritan

25On one occasion an expert in the law stood
up to test Jesus. "Teacher," he asked, "what must
I do to inherit eternal life?"
26"What is written in the Law?" he replied.
"How do you read it?"
27He answered: "'Love the Lord your God
with all your heart and with all your soul and
with all your strength and with all your mind'[c];
and, 'Love your neighbor as yourself.'[d]"
28"You have answered correctly," Jesus replied. "Do this and you will live."
29But he wanted to justify himself, so he asked
Jesus, "And who is my neighbor?"
30In reply Jesus said: "A man was going down
from Jerusalem to Jericho, when he fell into the

[a] 1 Some manuscripts *seventy*; also in verse 17 [b] 15 Greek *Hades* [c] 27 Deut. 6:5 [d] 27 Lev. 19:18

10:25–29 *expert in the law.* This scholar who was well versed in Scripture asks a common question to test this young, uncertified teacher. When the lawyer senses that *he* is being tested rather than Jesus, he tries to regain the initiative by asking the follow-up question, "And who is my neighbor?"

10:30–32 *Jerusalem to Jericho.* The road was notoriously dangerous, running through rocky, desert terrain, which provided places for thieves to mug defenseless travelers. ***priest.*** He may have been concerned that the beaten man was dead; a priest would not want to defile himself by touching a dead man (or a Gentile for that matter). ***Levite.*** These were men assigned to aid the priests in various temple duties. Regulations for Levites weren't quite as stringent as for priests, and it appears he may have stopped and looked at the wounded man. Since he could not identify the man as a neighbor (a Jew) he, too, decided not to get involved.

10:33–35 *Samaritan.* Priests and Levites had distinguished places in Jewish society; Samaritans were despised as spiritual and ethnic half-breeds. This "good Samaritan" was moved by compassion. Whereas the thieves beat, robbed and left the man, the Samaritan bound up his wounds, brought him to safety and promised to return.

10:36–37 *Which ... was a neighbor ... ?* Jesus rephrases the lawyer's question (v. 29). Instead of playing the game of defining who is (and isn't) your neighbor, the true question is, "Am I being a neighbor to the people the Lord places in my path?"

hands of robbers. They stripped him of his
clothes, beat him and went away, leaving him
half dead. 31A priest happened to be going down
the same road, and when he saw the man, he
passed by on the other side. 32So too, a Levite,
when he came to the place and saw him, passed
by on the other side. 33But a Samaritan, as he
traveled, came where the man was; and when he
saw him, he took pity on him. 34He went to him
and bandaged his wounds, pouring on oil and
wine. Then he put the man on his own donkey,
took him to an inn and took care of him. 35The
next day he took out two silver coins[a] and gave
them to the innkeeper. 'Look after him,' he said,
'and when I return, I will reimburse you for any
extra expense you may have.'
36"Which of these three do you think was a
neighbor to the man who fell into the hands of
robbers?"
37The expert in the law replied, "The one who
had mercy on him."
Jesus told him, "Go and do likewise."

At the Home of Martha and Mary

38As Jesus and his disciples were on their way,
he came to a village where a woman named Martha opened her home to him. 39She had a sister
called Mary, who sat at the Lord's feet listening
to what he said. 40But Martha was distracted by

Luke 10:25–37

1. What street or area do you try to avoid after dark because it's a scary place?
2. Have you ever helped a stranger or been helped by a stranger? What happened?
3. How much of a problem are gangs or violence where you live?
4. What's the closest you've come to being beaten or robbed?
5. How would you answer the question the "expert in the law" asked in verse 25?
6. What can you, this group and your church do about gangs and violence in your school or community?
7. Who is someone you can show mercy to this week? Pray for one another.

(Study notes on page 935)

Luke 10:38–42

1. In your family, who does most of the preparation when company comes? What do you do?
2. From the way the two sisters in this passage acted, which one are you more like, laid-back Mary or task-oriented Martha?
3. Of these two sisters, which would you like to have as a friend? An employer? *Guys:* As a date? As a wife? *Girls:* As a roommate?
4. If you could change something about your personality, what would it be?
5. In verse 42 Jesus says, "only one thing is needed." What is that thing?
6. If Jesus dropped in on you, what might he point out that distracts you from more important things in life?
7. Jesus said Martha was "worried and upset about many things" (v. 41). What are you worried or upset about? Close by praying together about those things.

[a]35 Greek *two denarii*

10:38 ***village.*** Bethany, just on the outskirts of Jerusalem, was the home of Martha and Mary and their brother Lazarus (whom Jesus raised from the dead). ***Martha opened her home to him.*** Jesus had a close relationship with this family and frequently enjoyed their hospitality.

10:39 ***Mary, who sat at the Lord's feet.*** While Martha is occupied with providing hospitality for Jesus and his disciples, Mary sits and listens to all he has to say. This was decidedly nontraditional for a woman to do when custom demanded she be busy serving the men. Her position at Jesus' feet is typical of a student eager to learn.

10:40 ***all the preparations.*** For the Jews, hospitality was an important duty for which no effort was spared. To provide for an honored teacher like Jesus and his followers would require a great deal of work. ***Tell her to help me!*** Probably after having asked Mary several times in subtle (or obvious!) ways to help her, Martha finally appeals to Jesus to tell Mary to help her as she ought to. The implication in her question is that it should be obvious to Jesus that the responsibility of being hospitable to him was more important than listening to him!

10:41–42 ***Martha, Martha.*** Jesus' affection and concern for Martha are felt in this repetition of her name. ***only one thing is needed.*** Listening and responding to the word of the kingdom is the single most critical thing in all of life. Mary had "chosen what is better" rather than to be distracted with the less important expectations of hospitality.

all the preparations that had to be made. She
came to him and asked, "Lord, don't you care
that my sister has left me to do the work by
myself? Tell her to help me!"
41"Martha, Martha," the Lord answered, "you
are worried and upset about many things, 42but
only one thing is needed.[a] Mary has chosen
what is better, and it will not be taken away from
her."

Jesus' Teaching on Prayer

11 One day Jesus was praying in a certain
place. When he finished, one of his disciples said to him, "Lord, teach us to pray, just as
John taught his disciples."
2He said to them, "When you pray, say:

"'Father,[b]
hallowed be your name,
your kingdom come.[c]
3Give us each day our daily bread.
4Forgive us our sins,
for we also forgive everyone who sins
against us.[d]
And lead us not into temptation.[e]'"

5Then he said to them, "Suppose one of you
has a friend, and he goes to him at midnight and
says, 'Friend, lend me three loaves of bread, 6be-
cause a friend of mine on a journey has come to
me, and I have nothing to set before him.'
7"Then the one inside answers, 'Don't bother
me. The door is already locked, and my children
are with me in bed. I can't get up and give you
anything.' 8I tell you, though he will not get up
and give him the bread because he is his friend,
yet because of the man's boldness[f] he will get
up and give him as much as he needs.
9"So I say to you: Ask and it will be given to
you; seek and you will find; knock and the door
will be opened to you. 10For everyone who asks
receives; he who seeks finds; and to him who
knocks, the door will be opened.
11"Which of you fathers, if your son asks for[g]
a fish, will give him a snake instead? 12Or if he
asks for an egg, will give him a scorpion? 13If you
then, though you are evil, know how to give good
gifts to your children, how much more will your
Father in heaven give the Holy Spirit to those
who ask him!"

Jesus and Beelzebub

14Jesus was driving out a demon that was
mute. When the demon left, the man who had
been mute spoke, and the crowd was amazed.
15But some of them said, "By Beelzebub,[h] the
prince of demons, he is driving out demons."
16Others tested him by asking for a sign from
heaven.
17Jesus knew their thoughts and said to them:
"Any kingdom divided against itself will be ruined, and a house divided against itself will fall.
18If Satan is divided against himself, how can his
kingdom stand? I say this because you claim that
I drive out demons by Beelzebub. 19Now if I drive
out demons by Beelzebub, by whom do your followers drive them out? So then, they will be your
judges. 20But if I drive out demons by the finger
of God, then the kingdom of God has come to
you.
21"When a strong man, fully armed, guards his
own house, his possessions are safe. 22But when
someone stronger attacks and overpowers him,
he takes away the armor in which the man trusted and divides up the spoils.
23"He who is not with me is against me, and
he who does not gather with me, scatters.
24"When an evil[i] spirit comes out of a man,
it goes through arid places seeking rest and does
not find it. Then it says, 'I will return to the
house I left.' 25When it arrives, it finds the house
swept clean and put in order. 26Then it goes and
takes seven other spirits more wicked than itself,
and they go in and live there. And the final condition of that man is worse than the first."
27As Jesus was saying these things, a woman
in the crowd called out, "Blessed is the mother
who gave you birth and nursed you."
28He replied, "Blessed rather are those who
hear the word of God and obey it."

The Sign of Jonah

29As the crowds increased, Jesus said, "This is
a wicked generation. It asks for a miraculous sign,
but none will be given it except the sign of Jonah.
30For as Jonah was a sign to the Ninevites, so also
will the Son of Man be to this generation. 31The
Queen of the South will rise at the judgment with
the men of this generation and condemn them;
for she came from the ends of the earth to listen
to Solomon's wisdom, and now one[j] greater
than Solomon is here. 32The men of Nineveh will
stand up at the judgment with this generation
and condemn it; for they repented at the preaching of Jonah, and now one greater than Jonah is
here.

[a]42 Some manuscripts *but few things are needed—or only one* [b]2 Some manuscripts *Our Father in heaven* [c]2 Some manuscripts *come. May your will be done on earth as it is in heaven.* [d]4 Greek *everyone who is indebted to us* [e]4 Some manuscripts *temptation but deliver us from the evil one* [f]8 Or *persistence* [g]11 Some manuscripts *for bread, will give him a stone; or if he asks for* [h]15 Greek *Beezeboul* or *Beelzeboul*; also in verses 18 and 19 [i]24 Greek *unclean* [j]31 Or *something*; also in verse 32

The Lamp of the Body

33“No one lights a lamp and puts it in a place where it will be hidden, or under a bowl. Instead he puts it on its stand, so that those who come in may see the light. 34Your eye is the lamp of your body. When your eyes are good, your whole body also is full of light. But when they are bad, your body also is full of darkness. 35See to it, then, that the light within you is not darkness. 36Therefore, if your whole body is full of light, and no part of it dark, it will be completely lighted, as when the light of a lamp shines on you.”

Six Woes

37When Jesus had finished speaking, a Pharisee invited him to eat with him; so he went in and reclined at the table. 38But the Pharisee, noticing that Jesus did not first wash before the meal, was surprised.

39Then the Lord said to him, “Now then, you Pharisees clean the outside of the cup and dish, but inside you are full of greed and wickedness. 40You foolish people! Did not the one who made the outside make the inside also? 41But give what is inside ⌞the dish⌟[a] to the poor, and everything will be clean for you.

42“Woe to you Pharisees, because you give God a tenth of your mint, rue and all other kinds of garden herbs, but you neglect justice and the love of God. You should have practiced the latter without leaving the former undone.

43“Woe to you Pharisees, because you love the most important seats in the synagogues and greetings in the marketplaces.

44“Woe to you, because you are like unmarked graves, which men walk over without knowing it.”

45One of the experts in the law answered him, “Teacher, when you say these things, you insult us also.”

46Jesus replied, “And you experts in the law, woe to you, because you load people down with burdens they can hardly carry, and you yourselves will not lift one finger to help them.

47“Woe to you, because you build tombs for the prophets, and it was your forefathers who killed them. 48So you testify that you approve of what your forefathers did; they killed the prophets, and you build their tombs. 49Because of this, God in his wisdom said, ‘I will send them prophets and apostles, some of whom they will kill and others they will persecute.’ 50Therefore this generation will be held responsible for the blood of all the prophets that has been shed since the beginning of the world, 51from the blood of Abel to the blood of Zechariah, who was killed between the altar and the sanctuary. Yes, I tell you, this generation will be held responsible for it all.

52“Woe to you experts in the law, because you have taken away the key to knowledge. You yourselves have not entered, and you have hindered those who were entering.”

53When Jesus left there, the Pharisees and the teachers of the law began to oppose him fiercely and to besiege him with questions, 54waiting to catch him in something he might say.

Warnings and Encouragements

12 Meanwhile, when a crowd of many thousands had gathered, so that they were trampling on one another, Jesus began to speak first to his disciples, saying: “Be on your guard against the yeast of the Pharisees, which is hypocrisy. 2There is nothing concealed that will not be disclosed, or hidden that will not be made known. 3What you have said in the dark will be heard in the daylight, and what you have whispered in the ear in the inner rooms will be proclaimed from the roofs.

4“I tell you, my friends, do not be afraid of those who kill the body and after that can do no more. 5But I will show you whom you should fear: Fear him who, after the killing of the body, has power to throw you into hell. Yes, I tell you, fear him. 6Are not five sparrows sold for two pennies[b]? Yet not one of them is forgotten by God. 7Indeed, the very hairs of your head are all numbered. Don’t be afraid; you are worth more than many sparrows.

8“I tell you, whoever acknowledges me before men, the Son of Man will also acknowledge him before the angels of God. 9But he who disowns me before men will be disowned before the angels of God. 10And everyone who speaks a word against the Son of Man will be forgiven, but anyone who blasphemes against the Holy Spirit will not be forgiven.

11“When you are brought before synagogues, rulers and authorities, do not worry about how you will defend yourselves or what you will say, 12for the Holy Spirit will teach you at that time what you should say.”

The Parable of the Rich Fool

13Someone in the crowd said to him, “Teacher, tell my brother to divide the inheritance with me.”

14Jesus replied, “Man, who appointed me a judge or an arbiter between you?” 15Then he said to them, “Watch out! Be on your guard against all kinds of greed; a man’s life does not consist in the abundance of his possessions.”

16And he told them this parable: “The ground

[a] 41 Or *what you have*   [b] 6 Greek *two assaria*

of a certain rich man produced a good crop. 17He
thought to himself, 'What shall I do? I have no
place to store my crops.'
18"Then he said, 'This is what I'll do. I will
tear down my barns and build bigger ones, and
there I will store all my grain and my goods.
19And I'll say to myself, "You have plenty of good
things laid up for many years. Take life easy; eat,
drink and be merry." '
20"But God said to him, 'You fool! This very
night your life will be demanded from you. Then
who will get what you have prepared for yourself?'
21"This is how it will be with anyone who
stores up things for himself but is not rich toward
God."

LUKE 12:13–21

1. If you could have fame, fortune or good looks, which would you choose?
2. How important is it to have money at your school?
3. What would you like to be doing 10 years from now? Where would you like to be living?
4. What was Jesus warning us against when he said, "Watch out!" in verse 15?
5. "Take life easy; eat, drink and be merry" (v. 19). What is your attitude towards this philosophy? The attitude of those in your school?
6. In your plans for the future, on a scale of 1 (irrelevant) to 10 (essential), how important is making a lot of money?
7. How can you be "rich toward God" (v. 21)? Share prayer requests and pray together.

Do Not Worry

22Then Jesus said to his disciples: "Therefore I
tell you, do not worry about your life, what you
will eat; or about your body, what you will wear.
23Life is more than food, and the body more than
clothes. 24Consider the ravens: They do not sow
or reap, they have no storeroom or barn; yet God
feeds them. And how much more valuable you
are than birds! 25Who of you by worrying can add
a single hour to his life[a]? 26Since you cannot do
this very little thing, why do you worry about the
rest?
27"Consider how the lilies grow. They do not
labor or spin. Yet I tell you, not even Solomon in
all his splendor was dressed like one of these. 28If
that is how God clothes the grass of the field,
which is here today, and tomorrow is thrown
into the fire, how much more will he clothe you,
O you of little faith! 29And do not set your heart
on what you will eat or drink; do not worry about
it. 30For the pagan world runs after all such

a25 Or *single cubit to his height*

12:13–15 ***Teacher.*** Literally, "Rabbi." As men schooled in the Law, rabbis were often asked to settle legal disputes. ***greed.*** Jesus pinpoints the real motivating factor behind this appeal for justice, then uses a parable as an illustration. ***life.*** Then, as now, a person's happiness and well-being was often thought to be determined by what they owned. Jesus flatly rejects this as a standard for measuring the worth of one's life.

12:19 ***eat, drink and be merry.*** Failing to see his bumper crop as a gift from God to be shared with others, he sees it as his own possession to be used as he pleases.

12:20 The ultimate reality of God's judgment shows that making a priority of seeking wealth for one's own pleasure is meaningless. ***fool!*** A strong word. In the Bible, a fool is someone who lives without regard to God. ***who will get what you have prepared for yourself?*** At death, one's possessions are of no use to them. Also, the rich man may have alienated himself from family and friends, with no one close to him to whom he can pass on an inheritance.

12:21 ***This is how it will be.*** Jesus applies the parable to his listeners. Those who are preoccupied with hoarding material provisions for themselves forfeit life with God and often alienate themselves from others. ***rich toward God.*** Verse 33 reveals that a key element of being rich toward God is making a priority of giving generously to those in need. Disciples can freely give to others because they recognize that God is the provider of all they have and need.

Jesus tells his disciples they must not worry about material goods like food and clothing. Those who worry about such things betray that their priorities are centered on the concerns of this world rather than on God's kingdom.

12:22 ***do not worry.*** Worry is rooted in the fear that I must take care of myself rather than trust God to do so. This prohibition does not mean that disciples need not do anything to feed and clothe themselves: What is commended is faith, not idleness.

12:28 ***you of little faith.*** Faith is reliance on the love, care and power of God. Faith is the opposite of anxiety.

12:31 ***these things will be given to you.*** While the believer may suffer as pointed out in 2 Corinthians 11:27, the promise is that if the disciples concentrate on doing the will of God, then their basic needs will be met by God. They need not grab physical comfort for themselves.

12:33 In light of the inexhaustible resources available to Christ's disciples from God's generosity, they are to give freely to those in need. ***moth.*** Although expensive clothing was a favorite form of wealth, it had the unfortunate drawback of being especially susceptible to insignificant creatures like moths. The treasure of heaven is unassailable (see 1 Peter 1:4).

12:34 A person's heart loyalty is shown by the type of treasure one accumulates. The treasure of one who seeks God's kingdom is found in the hands of the poor to whom he or she has generously given (v. 33).

things, and your Father knows that you need
them. 31But seek his kingdom, and these things
will be given to you as well.
32"Do not be afraid, little flock, for your Father
has been pleased to give you the kingdom. 33Sell
your possessions and give to the poor. Provide
purses for yourselves that will not wear out, a
treasure in heaven that will not be exhausted,
where no thief comes near and no moth destroys.
34For where your treasure is, there your heart
will be also.

LUKE 12:22–34

1. What is the most valuable thing you have in your possession right now?
2. What types of treasure did you collect as a kid? What do you collect now?
3. If a fire started in your home, what three items would you grab first?
4. If you could only keep one thing in your wallet or purse right now, what would you keep?
5. If someone from a Third World country visited your room, what would they think of your values?
6. If you had to adjust your values to be more "kingdom" than physical, what would you have to change?
7. In the last few months, how have you helped others less fortunate than yourself (see v. 33)?
8. How can this group pray for you this week?

(Study notes on page 939)

Watchfulness

35"Be dressed ready for service and keep your
lamps burning, 36like men waiting for their master to return from a wedding banquet, so that
when he comes and knocks they can immediately
open the door for him. 37It will be good for those
servants whose master finds them watching
when he comes. I tell you the truth, he will dress
himself to serve, will have them recline at the
table and will come and wait on them. 38It will be
good for those servants whose master finds them
ready, even if he comes in the second or third
watch of the night. 39But understand this: If the
owner of the house had known at what hour the
thief was coming, he would not have let his
house be broken into. 40You also must be ready,
because the Son of Man will come at an hour
when you do not expect him."
41Peter asked, "Lord, are you telling this parable to us, or to everyone?"
42The Lord answered, "Who then is the faithful and wise manager, whom the master puts in
charge of his servants to give them their food
allowance at the proper time? 43It will be good for
that servant whom the master finds doing so
when he returns. 44I tell you the truth, he will
put him in charge of all his possessions. 45But
suppose the servant says to himself, 'My master
is taking a long time in coming,' and he then
begins to beat the menservants and maidservants
and to eat and drink and get drunk. 46The master
of that servant will come on a day when he does
not expect him and at an hour he is not aware of.
He will cut him to pieces and assign him a place
with the unbelievers.
47"That servant who knows his master's will
and does not get ready or does not do what his
master wants will be beaten with many blows.
48But the one who does not know and does
things deserving punishment will be beaten with
few blows. From everyone who has been given
much, much will be demanded; and from the one
who has been entrusted with much, much more
will be asked.

Not Peace but Division

49"I have come to bring fire on the earth, and
how I wish it were already kindled! 50But I have
a baptism to undergo, and how distressed I am
until it is completed! 51Do you think I came to
bring peace on earth? No, I tell you, but division.
52From now on there will be five in one family
divided against each other, three against two and
two against three. 53They will be divided, father
against son and son against father, mother against
daughter and daughter against mother, mother-
in-law against daughter-in-law and daughter-in-
law against mother-in-law."

Interpreting the Times

54He said to the crowd: "When you see a cloud
rising in the west, immediately you say, 'It's going to rain,' and it does. 55And when the south
wind blows, you say, 'It's going to be hot,' and it
is. 56Hypocrites! You know how to interpret the
appearance of the earth and the sky. How is it
that you don't know how to interpret this present
time?
57"Why don't you judge for yourselves what is
right? 58As you are going with your adversary to

the magistrate, try hard to be reconciled to him on the way, or he may drag you off to the judge, and the judge turn you over to the officer, and the officer throw you into prison. 59I tell you, you will not get out until you have paid the last penny.[a]"

Repent or Perish

13 Now there were some present at that time who told Jesus about the Galileans whose blood Pilate had mixed with their sacrifices. 2Jesus answered, "Do you think that these Galileans were worse sinners than all the other Galileans because they suffered this way? 3I tell you, no! But unless you repent, you too will all perish. 4Or those eighteen who died when the tower in Siloam fell on them—do you think they were more guilty than all the others living in Jerusalem? 5I tell you, no! But unless you repent, you too will all perish."

6Then he told this parable: "A man had a fig tree, planted in his vineyard, and he went to look for fruit on it, but did not find any. 7So he said to the man who took care of the vineyard, 'For three years now I've been coming to look for fruit on this fig tree and haven't found any. Cut it down! Why should it use up the soil?'

8" 'Sir,' the man replied, 'leave it alone for one more year, and I'll dig around it and fertilize it. 9If it bears fruit next year, fine! If not, then cut it down.' "

A Crippled Woman Healed on the Sabbath

10On a Sabbath Jesus was teaching in one of the synagogues, 11and a woman was there who had been crippled by a spirit for eighteen years. She was bent over and could not straighten up at all. 12When Jesus saw her, he called her forward and said to her, "Woman, you are set free from your infirmity." 13Then he put his hands on her, and immediately she straightened up and praised God.

14Indignant because Jesus had healed on the Sabbath, the synagogue ruler said to the people, "There are six days for work. So come and be healed on those days, not on the Sabbath."

15The Lord answered him, "You hypocrites! Doesn't each of you on the Sabbath untie his ox or donkey from the stall and lead it out to give it water? 16Then should not this woman, a daughter of Abraham, whom Satan has kept bound for eighteen long years, be set free on the Sabbath day from what bound her?"

17When he said this, all his opponents were humiliated, but the people were delighted with all the wonderful things he was doing.

The Parables of the Mustard Seed and the Yeast

18Then Jesus asked, "What is the kingdom of God like? What shall I compare it to? 19It is like a mustard seed, which a man took and planted in his garden. It grew and became a tree, and the birds of the air perched in its branches."

20Again he asked, "What shall I compare the kingdom of God to? 21It is like yeast that a woman took and mixed into a large amount[b] of flour until it worked all through the dough."

The Narrow Door

22Then Jesus went through the towns and villages, teaching as he made his way to Jerusalem. 23Someone asked him, "Lord, are only a few people going to be saved?"

He said to them, 24"Make every effort to enter through the narrow door, because many, I tell you, will try to enter and will not be able to. 25Once the owner of the house gets up and closes the door, you will stand outside knocking and pleading, 'Sir, open the door for us.'

"But he will answer, 'I don't know you or where you come from.'

26"Then you will say, 'We ate and drank with you, and you taught in our streets.'

27"But he will reply, 'I don't know you or where you come from. Away from me, all you evildoers!'

28"There will be weeping there, and gnashing of teeth, when you see Abraham, Isaac and Jacob and all the prophets in the kingdom of God, but you yourselves thrown out. 29People will come from east and west and north and south, and will take their places at the feast in the kingdom of God. 30Indeed there are those who are last who will be first, and first who will be last."

Jesus' Sorrow for Jerusalem

31At that time some Pharisees came to Jesus and said to him, "Leave this place and go somewhere else. Herod wants to kill you."

32He replied, "Go tell that fox, 'I will drive out demons and heal people today and tomorrow, and on the third day I will reach my goal.' 33In any case, I must keep going today and tomorrow and the next day—for surely no prophet can die outside Jerusalem!

34"O Jerusalem, Jerusalem, you who kill the prophets and stone those sent to you, how often I have longed to gather your children together, as a hen gathers her chicks under her wings, but you were not willing! 35Look, your house is left to you desolate. I tell you, you will not see me again

[a]59 Greek *lepton* [b]21 Greek *three satas* (probably about 1/2 bushel or 22 liters)

until you say, 'Blessed is he who comes in the name of the Lord.'[a]"

Jesus at a Pharisee's House

14 One Sabbath, when Jesus went to eat in
the house of a prominent Pharisee, he
was being carefully watched. 2There in front of
him was a man suffering from dropsy. 3Jesus
asked the Pharisees and experts in the law, "Is it
lawful to heal on the Sabbath or not?" 4But they
remained silent. So taking hold of the man, he
healed him and sent him away.

5Then he asked them, "If one of you has a
son[b] or an ox that falls into a well on the Sabbath day, will you not immediately pull him out?"
6And they had nothing to say.

7When he noticed how the guests picked the
places of honor at the table, he told them this
parable: 8"When someone invites you to a wedding feast, do not take the place of honor, for a
person more distinguished than you may have
been invited. 9If so, the host who invited both of
you will come and say to you, 'Give this man your
seat.' Then, humiliated, you will have to take the
least important place. 10But when you are invited, take the lowest place, so that when your host
comes, he will say to you, 'Friend, move up to a
better place.' Then you will be honored in the
presence of all your fellow guests. 11For everyone
who exalts himself will be humbled, and he who
humbles himself will be exalted."

12Then Jesus said to his host, "When you give
a luncheon or dinner, do not invite your friends,
your brothers or relatives, or your rich neighbors;
if you do, they may invite you back and so you
will be repaid. 13But when you give a banquet,
invite the poor, the crippled, the lame, the blind,
14and you will be blessed. Although they cannot
repay you, you will be repaid at the resurrection
of the righteous."

The Parable of the Great Banquet

15When one of those at the table with him
heard this, he said to Jesus, "Blessed is the man
who will eat at the feast in the kingdom of God."

16Jesus replied: "A certain man was preparing
a great banquet and invited many guests. 17At the
time of the banquet he sent his servant to tell
those who had been invited, 'Come, for everything is now ready.'

18"But they all alike began to make excuses.
The first said, 'I have just bought a field, and I
must go and see it. Please excuse me.'

19"Another said, 'I have just bought five yoke
of oxen, and I'm on my way to try them out.
Please excuse me.'

20"Still another said, 'I just got married, so I
can't come.'

LUKE 14:15–24

1. What's the most important event you've been invited to?
2. What upcoming party or event have you been invited to? Have you responded to the invitation? How?
3. What's your favorite excuse to get out of going somewhere you don't want to go?
4. In your school, who is more open to Christ—students who grew up with a religious background or those with no religious background?
5. How would you describe your appetite right now for the things of God—from "Really hungry" to "No appetite"?
6. God sent Jesus to invite you to the Great Banquet. How are you going to respond to his invitation?
7. Who would you like to invite to God's banquet? Close by praying for these people.

[a]35 Psalm 118:26 [b]5 Some manuscripts *donkey*

14:15–16 *feast in the kingdom.* The great future messianic banquet. It was typically assumed that this banquet was reserved for righteous Jews only. Jesus' reply used the man's statement to teach a parable about who would and wouldn't enter the kingdom.

14:17 *sent his servant to tell those who had been invited.* In well-to-do circles, invitations to a formal dinner were issued well in advance, but the specific time to arrive was communicated on the day of the event when everything was ready.

14:18–20 *excuses.* These people had accepted the invitation earlier. Now that the feast is actually prepared, however, they offer excuses why they cannot come. ***field.*** Then, as now, a person would not buy property first and look at it later! ***oxen.*** Just as no one today would buy a used car without a test drive, so then a man would not buy a team of oxen unless he had already tried them out. ***married.*** Marriage plans were made far in advance: the man certainly would have known of his marriage plans when he accepted the original invitation to the banquet. All of the "reasons" given were flimsy; in fact, they reflect a social snub.

14:21–24 The kinds of people mentioned in the list in verse 21 were social outcasts and considered spiritually impure. The kingdom of God is precisely for these types of people. Verse 23 likely points to the coming addition of Gentiles in the kingdom as well. Jesus was warning the self-righteous Jews that their refusal to come to the banquet would result in their rejection and the inclusion of those they least expected.

21 “The servant came back and reported this to
his master. Then the owner of the house became
angry and ordered his servant, ‘Go out quickly
into the streets and alleys of the town and bring
in the poor, the crippled, the blind and the lame.’
22 “ ‘Sir,’ the servant said, ‘what you ordered
has been done, but there is still room.’
23 “Then the master told his servant, ‘Go out to
the roads and country lanes and make them come
in, so that my house will be full. 24 I tell you, not
one of those men who were invited will get a
taste of my banquet.’ ”

The Cost of Being a Disciple

25 Large crowds were traveling with Jesus, and
turning to them he said: 26 “If anyone comes to
me and does not hate his father and mother, his
wife and children, his brothers and sisters—yes,
even his own life—he cannot be my disciple.
27 And anyone who does not carry his cross and
follow me cannot be my disciple.
28 “Suppose one of you wants to build a tower.
Will he not first sit down and estimate the cost to
see if he has enough money to complete it? 29 For
if he lays the foundation and is not able to finish
it, everyone who sees it will ridicule him, 30 saying, ‘This fellow began to build and was not able
to finish.’
31 “Or suppose a king is about to go to war
against another king. Will he not first sit down
and consider whether he is able with ten thousand men to oppose the one coming against him
with twenty thousand? 32 If he is not able, he will
send a delegation while the other is still a long
way off and will ask for terms of peace. 33 In the
same way, any of you who does not give up everything he has cannot be my disciple.
34 “Salt is good, but if it loses its saltiness, how
can it be made salty again? 35 It is fit neither for
the soil nor for the manure pile; it is thrown out.
“He who has ears to hear, let him hear.”

The Parable of the Lost Sheep

15 Now the tax collectors and “sinners”
were all gathering around to hear him.
2 But the Pharisees and the teachers of the law
muttered, “This man welcomes sinners and eats
with them.”
3 Then Jesus told them this parable: 4 “Suppose
one of you has a hundred sheep and loses one of
them. Does he not leave the ninety-nine in the
open country and go after the lost sheep until he
finds it? 5 And when he finds it, he joyfully puts it
on his shoulders 6 and goes home. Then he calls
his friends and neighbors together and says, ‘Rejoice with me; I have found my lost sheep.’ 7 I tell

? *LUKE 14:25–35*

1. In a “high-stakes” game, are you more likely to play it safe or gamble everything on the next play?
2. When was the last time you went to buy something and found you didn’t have enough money? How did you feel?
3. What are your top three priorities in life right now: School? Work? Family? Church? Dating? Bible study? Other?
4. Why would Jesus tell us to hate our own families (see note on v. 26)?
5. Do you tend to give Jesus pieces of yourself (certain moments, some lifestyle choices, etc.) or give him your whole self? Which is better? Why?
6. When did you first realize that following Jesus was costly? What price have you had to pay, perhaps with friends or family?
7. On a scale of 1 to 10, how heavy has your “cross” been this past week—1 (“I can barely lift it”) to 10 (“Jesus is carrying it for me”)?
8. How can this group pray for you and help you to “carry your cross”?

14:26 In contrast to the expectant, exuberant nature of the crowds, Jesus introduces a solemn challenge. While the invitation to the kingdom is extended to all, only those who make Jesus their primary loyalty will participate in it. One’s loyalty to Jesus and the kingdom must take precedence over *all* other commitments, including those that people normally take for granted as primary responsibilities. ***hate.*** Jesus often used dramatic, overstated examples to arrest people’s attention and make his point (see Matt. 5:29–30). His use of the word “hate” here is a way of saying that one’s love and loyalty to Jesus must exceed what one naturally has toward one’s family. This idea is stated more positively in Matthew 10:37–38.

14:27 carry his cross. Discipleship’s total commitment is emphasized even more by this idea. ***cross.*** This symbolized the grisly method of Roman execution. While it had a very literal application for some disciples, it is meant as a metaphor emphasizing the need for all of Jesus’ disciples to put to death their own desires and interests for the sake of loyalty to Jesus. This statement echoes the one in Luke 9:23, where Luke inserts the word “daily,” indicating that following Jesus is a day-by-day decision in light of the new pressures and conflicts one continually faces.

14:28–33 Jesus uses three parables to communicate the need for serious consideration of what it means to be his disciple.

14:34 ***Salt is good.*** Good salt was used to preserve and flavor food and, at least in some instances, even as a fertilizer.

you that in the same way there will be more rejoicing in heaven over one sinner who repents than over ninety-nine righteous persons who do not need to repent.

The Parable of the Lost Coin

8"Or suppose a woman has ten silver coins[a] and loses one. Does she not light a lamp, sweep the house and search carefully until she finds it? 9And when she finds it, she calls her friends and neighbors together and says, 'Rejoice with me; I have found my lost coin.' 10In the same way, I tell you, there is rejoicing in the presence of the angels of God over one sinner who repents."

The Parable of the Lost Son

11Jesus continued: "There was a man who had two sons. 12The younger one said to his father, 'Father, give me my share of the estate.' So he divided his property between them.

13"Not long after that, the younger son got together all he had, set off for a distant country and there squandered his wealth in wild living. 14After he had spent everything, there was a severe famine in that whole country, and he began to be in need. 15So he went and hired himself out to a citizen of that country, who sent him to his fields to feed pigs. 16He longed to fill his stomach with the pods that the pigs were eating, but no one gave him anything.

17"When he came to his senses, he said, 'How many of my father's hired men have food to spare, and here I am starving to death! 18I will set out and go back to my father and say to him: Father, I have sinned against heaven and against you. 19I am no longer worthy to be called your son; make me like one of your hired men.' 20So he got up and went to his father.

"But while he was still a long way off, his father saw him and was filled with compassion for him; he ran to his son, threw his arms around him and kissed him.

21"The son said to him, 'Father, I have sinned against heaven and against you. I am no longer worthy to be called your son.[b]'

22"But the father said to his servants, 'Quick! Bring the best robe and put it on him. Put a ring on his finger and sandals on his feet. 23Bring the fattened calf and kill it. Let's have a feast and celebrate. 24For this son of mine was dead and is alive again; he was lost and is found.' So they began to celebrate.

LUKE 15:11–32

1. Where are you in the birth order of your family: Oldest? Youngest? In the middle?
2. When was the first time you thought about leaving home? Did you do it?
3. What would you have done if you had been the father in the Bible story—when the youngest son asked for his inheritance?
4. If you had been the father and had a pretty good idea where the younger son had gone, would you have gone after him?
5. What is the closest you have come to going through a wild period like the young son in this story? What caused you to turn around?
6. On a scale from 1 (not so good) to 10 (great), how is your relationship right now with your parents?
7. If you could compare your spiritual journey to this story, where are you right now: Just leaving home? In a far country? On your way back home? Close in prayer together.

25"Meanwhile, the older son was in the field. When he came near the house, he heard music and dancing. 26So he called one of the servants and asked him what was going on. 27'Your broth-

[a]8 Greek *ten drachmas,* each worth about a day's wages

[b]21 Some early manuscripts *son. Make me like one of your hired men.*

15:11–13 ***give me my share of the estate.*** While a father might divide his property before he died, this son's request would be considered unbelievably callous. The listeners also would have been surprised the father agreed to the request. ***got together all he had.*** The son sold off his share of the estate so he could have cold, hard cash to do with what he wanted (leaving nothing to come back to)! ***wild living.*** Including squandering his money on prostitutes according to verse 30, though perhaps the older brother's bitterness led him to exaggerate.

15:15 ***feed pigs.*** Disgusting work for Jews, who considered pigs ceremonially unclean.

15:20–24 ***his father saw him.*** Implying that the father had been waiting and hoping to one day see his son return. ***I have sinned ... I am no longer worthy to be called your son.*** Although the son may have thought he could earn his way back into some relationship with his father in order to alleviate his own misery, at this point he reflects a true sense of repentance. ***dead and is alive.*** A wonderful picture both of the younger son's return and of salvation through Christ.

15:25–32 The focus of the parable shifts to the older son, who was furious at the treatment his brother received. The father's forgiving love represents God's mercy, while the older brother's resentment is like the attitude of the Pharisees who opposed Jesus. ***I've been slaving for you.*** This son viewed things in terms of a master-slave relationship (like the Pharisees viewed religion), without enjoying the relationship with his father that was available to him.

er has come,' he replied, 'and your father has
killed the fattened calf because he has him back
safe and sound.'
28"The older brother became angry and refused to go in. So his father went out and pleaded
with him. 29But he answered his father, 'Look!
All these years I've been slaving for you and never disobeyed your orders. Yet you never gave me
even a young goat so I could celebrate with my
friends. 30But when this son of yours who has
squandered your property with prostitutes comes
home, you kill the fattened calf for him!'
31" 'My son,' the father said, 'you are always
with me, and everything I have is yours. 32But we
had to celebrate and be glad, because this brother
of yours was dead and is alive again; he was lost
and is found.' "

The Parable of the Shrewd Manager

16 Jesus told his disciples: "There was a rich
man whose manager was accused of wasting his possessions. 2So he called him in and
asked him, 'What is this I hear about you? Give
an account of your management, because you
cannot be manager any longer.'
3"The manager said to himself, 'What shall I
do now? My master is taking away my job. I'm
not strong enough to dig, and I'm ashamed to
beg— 4I know what I'll do so that, when I lose
my job here, people will welcome me into their
houses.'
5"So he called in each one of his master's debtors. He asked the first, 'How much do you owe
my master?'
6" 'Eight hundred gallons[a] of olive oil,' he replied.
"The manager told him, 'Take your bill, sit
down quickly, and make it four hundred.'
7"Then he asked the second, 'And how much
do you owe?'
" 'A thousand bushels[b] of wheat,' he replied.
"He told him, 'Take your bill and make it eight
hundred.'
8"The master commended the dishonest manager because he had acted shrewdly. For the people of this world are more shrewd in dealing with
their own kind than are the people of the light. 9I
tell you, use worldly wealth to gain friends for
yourselves, so that when it is gone, you will be
welcomed into eternal dwellings.
10"Whoever can be trusted with very little can
also be trusted with much, and whoever is dishonest with very little will also be dishonest with
much. 11So if you have not been trustworthy in
handling worldly wealth, who will trust you with
true riches? 12And if you have not been trustworthy with someone else's property, who will give
you property of your own?
13"No servant can serve two masters. Either
he will hate the one and love the other, or he will
be devoted to the one and despise the other. You
cannot serve both God and Money."
14The Pharisees, who loved money, heard all
this and were sneering at Jesus. 15He said to
them, "You are the ones who justify yourselves in
the eyes of men, but God knows your hearts.
What is highly valued among men is detestable in
God's sight.

Additional Teachings

16"The Law and the Prophets were proclaimed
until John. Since that time, the good news of the
kingdom of God is being preached, and everyone
is forcing his way into it. 17It is easier for heaven
and earth to disappear than for the least stroke of
a pen to drop out of the Law.
18"Anyone who divorces his wife and marries
another woman commits adultery, and the man
who marries a divorced woman commits adultery.

The Rich Man and Lazarus

19"There was a rich man who was dressed in
purple and fine linen and lived in luxury every
day. 20At his gate was laid a beggar named Lazarus, covered with sores 21and longing to eat what
fell from the rich man's table. Even the dogs
came and licked his sores.

[a]6 Greek *one hundred batous* (probably about 3 kiloliters) [b]7 Greek *one hundred korous* (probably about 35 kiloliters)

16:19–20 ***a rich man.*** Sometimes called Dives, from the Latin for "rich man." ***purple and fine linen.*** Only the wealthy could afford such garments. ***Lazarus.*** His name means "He whom God helps." This is not the same Lazarus whom Jesus raised from the dead. If Jesus is telling a parable, it is the only time he gave a name to one of its characters. Lazarus was diseased and apparently crippled in that he needed to be brought to the gate of the rich man's house to beg.

16:22–24 After death, the fortune of the two men is dramatically reversed. ***Abraham's side.*** Abraham was the father of the Jews. To be at his side referred to the place where the righteous dead went to await future vindication. ***hell.*** Literally "Hades." This referred to where the wicked went after dying to await final judgment. The rich man's torment is evidence that punishment begins in Hades. ***send Lazarus to ... cool my tongue.*** In his lifetime the rich man never spared a thought for Lazarus, and now, even in Hades, he thinks of Lazarus as there to meet his wants.

16:27–31 ***I have five brothers.*** He shows concern for someone else for the first time. In light of his fate, he urges Abraham to send Lazarus to warn his brothers who are following in his path. Abraham's response is that the witness of the Scripture read weekly in the synagogues is sufficient to show his brothers how they ought to live to please God. ***someone from the dead.*** Perhaps an allusion to Lazarus, but surely to Jesus' own resurrection. No miracle will penetrate the heart of a person closed to God and his word.

22"The time came when the beggar died and
the angels carried him to Abraham's side. The
rich man also died and was buried. 23In hell,[a]
where he was in torment, he looked up and saw
Abraham far away, with Lazarus by his side. 24So
he called to him, 'Father Abraham, have pity on
me and send Lazarus to dip the tip of his finger
in water and cool my tongue, because I am in
agony in this fire.'
25"But Abraham replied, 'Son, remember that
in your lifetime you received your good things,
while Lazarus received bad things, but now he is
comforted here and you are in agony. 26And besides all this, between us and you a great chasm
has been fixed, so that those who want to go from
here to you cannot, nor can anyone cross over
from there to us.'
27"He answered, 'Then I beg you, father, send
Lazarus to my father's house, 28for I have five
brothers. Let him warn them, so that they will
not also come to this place of torment.'
29"Abraham replied, 'They have Moses and
the Prophets; let them listen to them.'

LUKE 16:19–31

1. What did you believe about heaven when you were a child?
2. What is your idea of heaven right now?
3. What do the students in your school think about life after death?
4. When did the belief in heaven and life after death take on a personal meaning in your life?
5. If a friend asked you how you could be sure of a life after death, what would you say?
6. On a scale from 1 (none) to 10 (a whole lot), how much does your belief that there is life after death affect the way you live your life right now?
7. How do you feel about discussing life and death issues with your friends outside of church?
8. In the end, the rich man cared about others (v. 28). Who needs your concern and prayers right now? Pray together.

(Study notes on page 945)

30" 'No, father Abraham,' he said, 'but if someone from the dead goes to them, they will repent.'
31"He said to him, 'If they do not listen to
Moses and the Prophets, they will not be convinced even if someone rises from the dead.' "

Sin, Faith, Duty

17 Jesus said to his disciples: "Things that
cause people to sin are bound to come,
but woe to that person through whom they come.
2It would be better for him to be thrown into the
sea with a millstone tied around his neck than for
him to cause one of these little ones to sin. 3So
watch yourselves.
"If your brother sins, rebuke him, and if he
repents, forgive him. 4If he sins against you seven
times in a day, and seven times comes back to
you and says, 'I repent,' forgive him."
5The apostles said to the Lord, "Increase our
faith!"
6He replied, "If you have faith as small as a
mustard seed, you can say to this mulberry tree,
'Be uprooted and planted in the sea,' and it will
obey you.
7"Suppose one of you had a servant plowing or
looking after the sheep. Would he say to the servant when he comes in from the field, 'Come
along now and sit down to eat'? 8Would he not
rather say, 'Prepare my supper, get yourself ready
and wait on me while I eat and drink; after that
you may eat and drink'? 9Would he thank the
servant because he did what he was told to do?
10So you also, when you have done everything
you were told to do, should say, 'We are unworthy servants; we have only done our duty.' "

Ten Healed of Leprosy

11Now on his way to Jerusalem, Jesus traveled
along the border between Samaria and Galilee.
12As he was going into a village, ten men who
had leprosy[b] met him. They stood at a distance
13and called out in a loud voice, "Jesus, Master,
have pity on us!"
14When he saw them, he said, "Go, show
yourselves to the priests." And as they went, they
were cleansed.
15One of them, when he saw he was healed,
came back, praising God in a loud voice. 16He
threw himself at Jesus' feet and thanked him—
and he was a Samaritan.
17Jesus asked, "Were not all ten cleansed?
Where are the other nine? 18Was no one found to
return and give praise to God except this foreigner?" 19Then he said to him, "Rise and go; your
faith has made you well."

[a] *23* Greek *Hades* [b] *12* The Greek word was used for various diseases affecting the skin—not necessarily leprosy.

LUKE 17:11–19

1. When it comes to writing thank-you notes, how do you do: Always write? Sometimes? Never?
2. Who do you know that is grateful to God for everything?
3. Who are the "lepers" in your school—the people everybody avoids?
4. What would you say if you were asked to help clean restrooms for an AIDS hospice?
5. When it comes to showing gratitude to God, are you more like the one who returned or the nine who didn't?
6. Who is one person you need to thank this week for something they did for you?
7. What do you need to thank God for today? Close with prayers of thanksgiving.

The Coming of the Kingdom of God

20 Once, having been asked by the Pharisees when the kingdom of God would come, Jesus replied, "The kingdom of God does not come with your careful observation, 21 nor will people say, 'Here it is,' or 'There it is,' because the kingdom of God is within[a] you."

22 Then he said to his disciples, "The time is coming when you will long to see one of the days of the Son of Man, but you will not see it. 23 Men will tell you, 'There he is!' or 'Here he is!' Do not go running off after them. 24 For the Son of Man in his day[b] will be like the lightning, which flashes and lights up the sky from one end to the other. 25 But first he must suffer many things and be rejected by this generation.

26 "Just as it was in the days of Noah, so also will it be in the days of the Son of Man. 27 People were eating, drinking, marrying and being given in marriage up to the day Noah entered the ark. Then the flood came and destroyed them all.

28 "It was the same in the days of Lot. People were eating and drinking, buying and selling, planting and building. 29 But the day Lot left Sodom, fire and sulfur rained down from heaven and destroyed them all.

30 "It will be just like this on the day the Son of Man is revealed. 31 On that day no one who is on the roof of his house, with his goods inside, should go down to get them. Likewise, no one in the field should go back for anything. 32 Remember Lot's wife! 33 Whoever tries to keep his life will lose it, and whoever loses his life will preserve it. 34 I tell you, on that night two people will be in one bed; one will be taken and the other left. 35 Two women will be grinding grain together; one will be taken and the other left.[c]"

37 "Where, Lord?" they asked.

He replied, "Where there is a dead body, there the vultures will gather."

The Parable of the Persistent Widow

18 Then Jesus told his disciples a parable to show them that they should always pray and not give up. 2 He said: "In a certain town there was a judge who neither feared God nor cared about men. 3 And there was a widow in that town who kept coming to him with the plea, 'Grant me justice against my adversary.'

4 "For some time he refused. But finally he said to himself, 'Even though I don't fear God or care about men, 5 yet because this widow keeps bothering me, I will see that she gets justice, so that she won't eventually wear me out with her coming!'"

6 And the Lord said, "Listen to what the unjust judge says. 7 And will not God bring about justice for his chosen ones, who cry out to him day and night? Will he keep putting them off? 8 I tell you, he will see that they get justice, and quickly.

[a] *21* Or *among* [b] *24* Some manuscripts do not have *in his day.* [c] *35* Some manuscripts *left.* 36 *Two men will be in the field; one will be taken and the other left.*

17:11–12 between Samaria and Galilee. The Samaritans and Jews lived in a hostile co-existence with one another. Samaritans were despised as ethnic and religious half-breeds who had blended the worship of God with pagan practices. This term was used as an insult to describe a Jew who did not pay strict enough attention to religious tradition. ***leprosy.*** Although this term was used to cover a wide range of skin diseases, no diagnosis was dreaded more than leprosy since it brought not only a slow death and physical disfigurement but also social banishment. ***stood at a distance.*** Lepers were strictly forbidden to approach uninfected people (Lev. 13:45–46).

17:14 In response to their cry, Jesus sends them away to the priests. The Law of Moses required people with skin diseases feared to be leprosy to be examined by a priest who would determine if the infection was clearing up or progressing (Lev. 14:1–7). For Jesus to send them to the priest implied that healing would occur, which is exactly what happened.

17:16–19 *Samaritan.* Presumably the other nine were Jews. Jews didn't usually associate with Samaritans (John 4:9), but leprosy destroyed some social barriers while causing others. Only this man caught the significance of his healing and returned to glorify God because of it. ***your faith has made you well.*** This can also be translated "your faith has saved you." The interest of the other nine was only in the miracle, not the One who performed it. While they received physical healing, this man received salvation as well.

However, when the Son of Man comes, will he find faith on the earth?"

The Parable of the Pharisee and the Tax Collector

9To some who were confident of their own righteousness and looked down on everybody else, Jesus told this parable: 10"Two men went up to the temple to pray, one a Pharisee and the other a tax collector. 11The Pharisee stood up and prayed about[a] himself: 'God, I thank you that I am not like other men—robbers, evildoers, adulterers—or even like this tax collector. 12I fast twice a week and give a tenth of all I get.'

LUKE 18:9–14

1. When it comes to praying out loud, in front of people, how comfortable are you?
2. In your school, what's the "in" crowd? What's the group you *don't* want to be identified with? What "crowd" are you a part of?
3. Are you more likely to build yourself up or tear yourself down?
4. Why did the tax collector in this story go home "justified before God" (v. 14) rather than the Pharisee?
5. Who do you look to as a model for the way to pray? Why?
6. On a scale of 1 (I'm no good) to 10 (I'm special), how do you see yourself? How do you feel God sees you?
7. How do you feel about opening up like this? Close with a time of silent prayer.

13"But the tax collector stood at a distance. He would not even look up to heaven, but beat his breast and said, 'God, have mercy on me, a sinner.'

14"I tell you that this man, rather than the other, went home justified before God. For everyone who exalts himself will be humbled, and he who humbles himself will be exalted."

The Little Children and Jesus

15People were also bringing babies to Jesus to have him touch them. When the disciples saw this, they rebuked them. 16But Jesus called the children to him and said, "Let the little children come to me, and do not hinder them, for the kingdom of God belongs to such as these. 17I tell you the truth, anyone who will not receive the kingdom of God like a little child will never enter it."

The Rich Ruler

18A certain ruler asked him, "Good teacher, what must I do to inherit eternal life?"

19"Why do you call me good?" Jesus answered. "No one is good—except God alone. 20You know the commandments: 'Do not commit adultery, do not murder, do not steal, do not give false testimony, honor your father and mother.'[b]"

21"All these I have kept since I was a boy," he said.

22When Jesus heard this, he said to him, "You still lack one thing. Sell everything you have and give to the poor, and you will have treasure in heaven. Then come, follow me."

23When he heard this, he became very sad, because he was a man of great wealth. 24Jesus looked at him and said, "How hard it is for the rich to enter the kingdom of God! 25Indeed, it is easier for a camel to go through the eye of a needle than for a rich man to enter the kingdom of God."

26Those who heard this asked, "Who then can be saved?"

27Jesus replied, "What is impossible with men is possible with God."

[a] *11* Or *to* [b] *20* Exodus 20:12-16; Deut. 5:16-20

18:10 ***to pray.*** Twice daily, the priests at the temple offered a sacrifice for the sins of the people. At these services, people gathered to pray. Worshipers could also go to the temple for private prayer at any time. ***Pharisee.*** A member of a small, powerful sect whose prime concern was keeping the Law. While modern readers assume the Pharisees are the "bad guys," the original audience of this parable respected them as devout, godly men. ***tax collector.*** Jesus' listeners would have considered a tax collector as vile as a robber or murderer. They were thought to be traitors, because they collaborated with the Roman power in order to gain wealth (usually dishonestly).

18:11 ***God, I thank you.*** To us it is unimaginable that such a prayer might be said in public. Yet it would not be unusual for a religious leader of the time to do so—perhaps as a way to instruct "sinners" in the crowd.

18:13 ***stood at a distance.*** The tax collector stands apart from the crowd, because he is too ashamed to join them. ***have mercy on me, a sinner.*** Rather than appealing to his good works, the tax collector realizes his only hope is in God's mercy.

18:14 ***this man ... went home justified.*** The listeners would have been surprised. How could the Pharisee, the model of righteousness, not be right before God, whereas the hated tax collector is forgiven? The twist in the parable is that righteousness is a matter of humble recognition of sin and dependence on God's grace, rather than a matter of impressing God with one's performance.

28Peter said to him, "We have left all we had
to follow you!"
29"I tell you the truth," Jesus said to them, "no
one who has left home or wife or brothers or
parents or children for the sake of the kingdom of
God 30will fail to receive many times as much in
this age and, in the age to come, eternal life."

Jesus Again Predicts His Death

31Jesus took the Twelve aside and told them,
"We are going up to Jerusalem, and everything
that is written by the prophets about the Son of
Man will be fulfilled. 32He will be handed over to
the Gentiles. They will mock him, insult him,
spit on him, flog him and kill him. 33On the third
day he will rise again."
34The disciples did not understand any of this.
Its meaning was hidden from them, and they did
not know what he was talking about.

A Blind Beggar Receives His Sight

35As Jesus approached Jericho, a blind man
was sitting by the roadside begging. 36When he
heard the crowd going by, he asked what was
happening. 37They told him, "Jesus of Nazareth is
passing by."
38He called out, "Jesus, Son of David, have
mercy on me!"
39Those who led the way rebuked him and
told him to be quiet, but he shouted all the more,
"Son of David, have mercy on me!"
40Jesus stopped and ordered the man to be
brought to him. When he came near, Jesus asked
him, 41"What do you want me to do for you?"
"Lord, I want to see," he replied.
42Jesus said to him, "Receive your sight; your
faith has healed you." 43Immediately he received
his sight and followed Jesus, praising God. When
all the people saw it, they also praised God.

Zacchaeus the Tax Collector

19 Jesus entered Jericho and was passing
through. 2A man was there by the name
of Zacchaeus; he was a chief tax collector and was
wealthy. 3He wanted to see who Jesus was, but
being a short man he could not, because of the
crowd. 4So he ran ahead and climbed a sycamore-
fig tree to see him, since Jesus was coming that
way.
5When Jesus reached the spot, he looked up
and said to him, "Zacchaeus, come down immediately. I must stay at your house today." 6So he
came down at once and welcomed him gladly.
7All the people saw this and began to mutter,
"He has gone to be the guest of a 'sinner.'"
8But Zacchaeus stood up and said to the Lord,
"Look, Lord! Here and now I give half of my
possessions to the poor, and if I have cheated
anybody out of anything, I will pay back four
times the amount."
9Jesus said to him, "Today salvation has come
to this house, because this man, too, is a son of

LUKE 19:1–10

1. What would you consider the ideal height for you?
2. What is the closest encounter you've had with a celebrity? Did this experience change you?
3. Where did Jesus first find you: Up a tree? Out on a limb?
4. In verse 9 Jesus says, "Today salvation has come to this house." How did "salvation" come to Zacchaeus?
5. What is something about you that makes you unique?
6. Zacchaeus realized that he needed to make restitution for cheating people. What wrongs do you need to make right?
7. Close by going around the group having one person at a time sit in silence while others share something that is special or unique about this person.

19:2 ***tax collector.*** These Jews were despised by their countrymen for selling out to the Roman oppressors and cheating their own people in the process. As a chief tax collector, Zacchaeus was probably in charge of a group of tax collectors in a district. ***wealthy.*** Since only the tax collectors knew the rate required by Rome, they could inflate the rate and keep the difference.

19:3–4 ***climbed a sycamore-fig tree.*** This 30- to 40-foot high tree with its short trunk and spreading branches would be easy to climb. Zacchaeus' interest in Jesus, perhaps aroused by reports that this great teacher actually would associate and befriend people like himself, was such that he acted in a most undignified manner!

19:7–8 ***the guest of a "sinner."*** Jesus invited himself to Zacchaeus' house, shocking everyone! Jesus' interest in Zacchaeus prompted a response that exemplified the marks of true discipleship. ***Lord.*** Zacchaeus recognized the need for absolute commitment to Jesus. As a sign of the reality of his repentance and faith, he immediately forsakes money as his main priority, giving half his wealth to the poor and making fourfold restitution to those he had defrauded.

19:9–10 ***son of Abraham.*** Zacchaeus was a true Jew—one who walks in faith like Abraham. Salvation had come to this man whom other Jews considered beyond the reach of God's mercy. ***Son of Man.*** A messianic title Jesus liked to use for himself. ***to seek and to save what was lost.*** This summarizes Jesus' purpose: to bring salvation.

Abraham. 10For the Son of Man came to seek and to save what was lost."

The Parable of the Ten Minas

11While they were listening to this, he went on to tell them a parable, because he was near Jerusalem and the people thought that the kingdom of God was going to appear at once. 12He said: "A man of noble birth went to a distant country to have himself appointed king and then to return. 13So he called ten of his servants and gave them ten minas.[a] 'Put this money to work,' he said, 'until I come back.'

14"But his subjects hated him and sent a delegation after him to say, 'We don't want this man to be our king.'

15"He was made king, however, and returned home. Then he sent for the servants to whom he had given the money, in order to find out what they had gained with it.

16"The first one came and said, 'Sir, your mina has earned ten more.'

17" 'Well done, my good servant!' his master replied. 'Because you have been trustworthy in a very small matter, take charge of ten cities.'

18"The second came and said, 'Sir, your mina has earned five more.'

19"His master answered, 'You take charge of five cities.'

20"Then another servant came and said, 'Sir, here is your mina; I have kept it laid away in a piece of cloth. 21I was afraid of you, because you are a hard man. You take out what you did not put in and reap what you did not sow.'

22"His master replied, 'I will judge you by your own words, you wicked servant! You knew, did you, that I am a hard man, taking out what I did not put in, and reaping what I did not sow? 23Why then didn't you put my money on deposit, so that when I came back, I could have collected it with interest?'

24"Then he said to those standing by, 'Take his mina away from him and give it to the one who has ten minas.'

25" 'Sir,' they said, 'he already has ten!'

26"He replied, 'I tell you that to everyone who has, more will be given, but as for the one who has nothing, even what he has will be taken away. 27But those enemies of mine who did not want me to be king over them—bring them here and kill them in front of me.' "

The Triumphal Entry

28After Jesus had said this, he went on ahead, going up to Jerusalem. 29As he approached Bethphage and Bethany at the hill called the Mount of Olives, he sent two of his disciples, saying to them, 30"Go to the village ahead of you, and as you enter it, you will find a colt tied there, which no one has ever ridden. Untie it and bring it here. 31If anyone asks you, 'Why are you untying it?' tell him, 'The Lord needs it.' "

LUKE 19:28–44

1. When was the last time you really expressed excitement: At a sporting event? A concert? Other?
2. Have you ever been in a parade? What was it like? What's the last parade you saw?
3. Who in this group would you nominate as the grand master of a parade? Why?
4. What kind of reception would Jesus get if he rode into your town?
5. What caused Jesus to weep over Jerusalem (v. 41)?
6. How did Jesus enter your life?
7. How can the group help you in prayer this week?

[a] *13* A mina was about three months' wages.

19:28–30 With Passover just a few days away, Jerusalem would have been filled with travelers. Jesus makes an entrance into the "Holy City" on the first day of this, the last week of his life. ***a colt.*** According to Zechariah 9:9, the Messiah would come riding on a donkey's colt. However, he will not come as a warrior-king (as the people expected) riding a war horse. The donkey's colt symbolizes Jesus' gentleness.

19:35–40 ***spread their cloaks.*** This was a gesture of respect given to kings. The loud shouts of joy were typical of pilgrims on their way to Jerusalem for a feast. However, the real King is, indeed, arriving in the Holy City. ***Blessed is the king.*** In its original setting (Ps. 118:26), this was the acclamation of the people to their king as he came to worship at the temple. Later, the rabbis understood it as a messianic psalm, referring to the One like King David who would usher in the final redemption of Israel. The clear messianic overtones of the disciples' shouts prompt some of the Pharisees to tell Jesus to silence them. In contrast to his previous desire that his identity be kept secret, Jesus asserts that the time has come when it is entirely appropriate he be honored and praised as the King.

19:41–44 Before Jesus enters Jerusalem, he pauses to look out over the city and weep in anticipation of the judgment to come (fulfilled in A.D. 70 when the Romans destroyed Jerusalem). ***the time of God's coming to you.*** In Jesus the Messiah, God came to the Jews; but rather than accept him, his people rejected him.

32Those who were sent ahead went and found
it just as he had told them. 33As they were untying the colt, its owners asked them, "Why are
you untying the colt?"
34They replied, "The Lord needs it."
35They brought it to Jesus, threw their cloaks
on the colt and put Jesus on it. 36As he went
along, people spread their cloaks on the road.
37When he came near the place where the
road goes down the Mount of Olives, the whole
crowd of disciples began joyfully to praise God in
loud voices for all the miracles they had seen:

38"Blessed is the king who comes in the name
of the Lord!"[a]

"Peace in heaven and glory in the highest!"

39Some of the Pharisees in the crowd said to
Jesus, "Teacher, rebuke your disciples!"
40"I tell you," he replied, "if they keep quiet,
the stones will cry out."
41As he approached Jerusalem and saw the
city, he wept over it 42and said, "If you, even you,
had only known on this day what would bring
you peace—but now it is hidden from your eyes.
43The days will come upon you when your enemies will build an embankment against you and
encircle you and hem you in on every side.
44They will dash you to the ground, you and the
children within your walls. They will not leave
one stone on another, because you did not recognize the time of God's coming to you."

Jesus at the Temple

45Then he entered the temple area and began
driving out those who were selling. 46"It is written," he said to them, " 'My house will be a house
of prayer'[b]; but you have made it 'a den of robbers.'[c]"
47Every day he was teaching at the temple. But
the chief priests, the teachers of the law and the
leaders among the people were trying to kill him.
48Yet they could not find any way to do it, because all the people hung on his words.

The Authority of Jesus Questioned

20 One day as he was teaching the people in
the temple courts and preaching the gospel, the chief priests and the teachers of the law,
together with the elders, came up to him. 2"Tell
us by what authority you are doing these things,"
they said. "Who gave you this authority?"
3He replied, "I will also ask you a question.
Tell me, 4John's baptism—was it from heaven, or
from men?"
5They discussed it among themselves and said,
"If we say, 'From heaven,' he will ask, 'Why
didn't you believe him?' 6But if we say, 'From
men,' all the people will stone us, because they
are persuaded that John was a prophet."
7So they answered, "We don't know where it
was from."
8Jesus said, "Neither will I tell you by what
authority I am doing these things."

The Parable of the Tenants

9He went on to tell the people this parable: "A
man planted a vineyard, rented it to some farmers and went away for a long time. 10At harvest
time he sent a servant to the tenants so they
would give him some of the fruit of the vineyard.
But the tenants beat him and sent him away
empty-handed. 11He sent another servant, but
that one also they beat and treated shamefully
and sent away empty-handed. 12He sent still a
third, and they wounded him and threw him out.
13"Then the owner of the vineyard said, 'What
shall I do? I will send my son, whom I love; perhaps they will respect him.'
14"But when the tenants saw him, they talked
the matter over. 'This is the heir,' they said.
'Let's kill him, and the inheritance will be ours.'
15So they threw him out of the vineyard and
killed him.
"What then will the owner of the vineyard do
to them? 16He will come and kill those tenants
and give the vineyard to others."
When the people heard this, they said, "May
this never be!"
17Jesus looked directly at them and asked,
"Then what is the meaning of that which is written:

" 'The stone the builders rejected
has become the capstone[d]'[e]?

18Everyone who falls on that stone will be broken
to pieces, but he on whom it falls will be
crushed."
19The teachers of the law and the chief priests
looked for a way to arrest him immediately, because they knew he had spoken this parable
against them. But they were afraid of the people.

Paying Taxes to Caesar

20Keeping a close watch on him, they sent
spies, who pretended to be honest. They hoped
to catch Jesus in something he said so that they
might hand him over to the power and authority
of the governor. 21So the spies questioned him:
"Teacher, we know that you speak and teach
what is right, and that you do not show partiality
but teach the way of God in accordance with the
truth. 22Is it right for us to pay taxes to Caesar or
not?"

[a]38 Psalm 118:26 [b]46 Isaiah 56:7 [c]46 Jer. 7:11 [d]17 Or *cornerstone* [e]17 Psalm 118:22

23He saw through their duplicity and said to
them, 24"Show me a denarius. Whose portrait
and inscription are on it?"
25"Caesar's," they replied.
He said to them, "Then give to Caesar what is
Caesar's, and to God what is God's."
26They were unable to trap him in what he
had said there in public. And astonished by his
answer, they became silent.

The Resurrection and Marriage

27Some of the Sadducees, who say there is no
resurrection, came to Jesus with a question.
28"Teacher," they said, "Moses wrote for us that
if a man's brother dies and leaves a wife but no
children, the man must marry the widow and
have children for his brother. 29Now there were
seven brothers. The first one married a woman
and died childless. 30The second 31and then the
third married her, and in the same way the seven
died, leaving no children. 32Finally, the woman
died too. 33Now then, at the resurrection whose
wife will she be, since the seven were married to
her?"
34Jesus replied, "The people of this age marry
and are given in marriage. 35But those who are
considered worthy of taking part in that age and
in the resurrection from the dead will neither
marry nor be given in marriage, 36and they can
no longer die; for they are like the angels. They
are God's children, since they are children of the
resurrection. 37But in the account of the bush,
even Moses showed that the dead rise, for he
calls the Lord 'the God of Abraham, and the God
of Isaac, and the God of Jacob.'[a] 38He is not the
God of the dead, but of the living, for to him all
are alive."
39Some of the teachers of the law responded,
"Well said, teacher!" 40And no one dared to ask
him any more questions.

Whose Son Is the Christ?

41Then Jesus said to them, "How is it that they
say the Christ[b] is the Son of David? 42David
himself declares in the Book of Psalms:

" 'The Lord said to my Lord:
"Sit at my right hand
43until I make your enemies
a footstool for your feet." '[c]

44David calls him 'Lord.' How then can he be his
son?"
45While all the people were listening, Jesus
said to his disciples, 46"Beware of the teachers
of the law. They like to walk around in flowing
robes and love to be greeted in the marketplaces
and have the most important seats in the synagogues and the places of honor at banquets.
47They devour widows' houses and for a show
make lengthy prayers. Such men will be punished most severely."

The Widow's Offering

21 As he looked up, Jesus saw the rich putting their gifts into the temple treasury.
2He also saw a poor widow put in two very small
copper coins.[d] 3"I tell you the truth," he said,
"this poor widow has put in more than all the
others. 4All these people gave their gifts out of
their wealth; but she out of her poverty put in all
she had to live on."

Signs of the End of the Age

5Some of his disciples were remarking about
how the temple was adorned with beautiful
stones and with gifts dedicated to God. But Jesus
said, 6"As for what you see here, the time will
come when not one stone will be left on another;
every one of them will be thrown down."
7"Teacher," they asked, "when will these
things happen? And what will be the sign that
they are about to take place?"
8He replied: "Watch out that you are not deceived. For many will come in my name, claiming, 'I am he,' and, 'The time is near.' Do not
follow them. 9When you hear of wars and revolu-
tions, do not be frightened. These things must
happen first, but the end will not come right
away."
10Then he said to them: "Nation will rise
against nation, and kingdom against kingdom.
11There will be great earthquakes, famines and
pestilences in various places, and fearful events
and great signs from heaven.
12"But before all this, they will lay hands on
you and persecute you. They will deliver you to
synagogues and prisons, and you will be brought
before kings and governors, and all on account of
my name. 13This will result in your being witnesses to them. 14But make up your mind not to
worry beforehand how you will defend yourselves. 15For I will give you words and wisdom that none of your adversaries will be able to
resist or contradict. 16You will be betrayed even by
parents, brothers, relatives and friends, and they
will put some of you to death. 17All men will hate
you because of me. 18But not a hair of your head
will perish. 19By standing firm you will gain
life.
20"When you see Jerusalem being surrounded
by armies, you will know that its desolation is
near. 21Then let those who are in Judea flee to

[a] 37 Exodus 3:6 [b] 41 Or *Messiah* [c] 43 Psalm 110:1 [d] 2 Greek *two lepta*

the mountains, let those in the city get out, and
let those in the country not enter the city. 22For
this is the time of punishment in fulfillment of all
that has been written. 23How dreadful it will be
in those days for pregnant women and nursing
mothers! There will be great distress in the land
and wrath against this people. 24They will fall by
the sword and will be taken as prisoners to all the
nations. Jerusalem will be trampled on by the
Gentiles until the times of the Gentiles are fulfilled.

25"There will be signs in the sun, moon and
stars. On the earth, nations will be in anguish
and perplexity at the roaring and tossing of the
sea. 26Men will faint from terror, apprehensive of
what is coming on the world, for the heavenly
bodies will be shaken. 27At that time they will
see the Son of Man coming in a cloud with power
and great glory. 28When these things begin to
take place, stand up and lift up your heads, because your redemption is drawing near."

29He told them this parable: "Look at the fig
tree and all the trees. 30When they sprout leaves,
you can see for yourselves and know that summer is near. 31Even so, when you see these
things happening, you know that the kingdom of
God is near.

32"I tell you the truth, this generation[a] will
certainly not pass away until all these things have
happened. 33Heaven and earth will pass away,
but my words will never pass away.

34"Be careful, or your hearts will be weighed
down with dissipation, drunkenness and the anxieties of life, and that day will close on you unexpectedly like a trap. 35For it will come upon all
those who live on the face of the whole earth.
36Be always on the watch, and pray that you may
be able to escape all that is about to happen, and
that you may be able to stand before the Son of
Man."

37Each day Jesus was teaching at the temple,
and each evening he went out to spend the night
on the hill called the Mount of Olives, 38and all
the people came early in the morning to hear him
at the temple.

[a]32 *Or race*

Judas Agrees to Betray Jesus

22 Now the Feast of Unleavened Bread,
called the Passover, was approaching,
2and the chief priests and the teachers of the law
were looking for some way to get rid of Jesus, for
they were afraid of the people. 3Then Satan entered Judas, called Iscariot, one of the Twelve.
4And Judas went to the chief priests and the officers of the temple guard and discussed with them
how he might betray Jesus. 5They were delighted
and agreed to give him money. 6He consented,
and watched for an opportunity to hand Jesus
over to them when no crowd was present.

The Last Supper

7Then came the day of Unleavened Bread on
which the Passover lamb had to be sacrificed.
8Jesus sent Peter and John, saying, "Go and make
preparations for us to eat the Passover."

9"Where do you want us to prepare for it?"
they asked.

10He replied, "As you enter the city, a man
carrying a jar of water will meet you. Follow him
to the house that he enters, 11and say to the
owner of the house, 'The Teacher asks: Where is
the guest room, where I may eat the Passover
with my disciples?' 12He will show you a large
upper room, all furnished. Make preparations
there."

13They left and found things just as Jesus had
told them. So they prepared the Passover.

14When the hour came, Jesus and his apostles
reclined at the table. 15And he said to them, "I
have eagerly desired to eat this Passover with you
before I suffer. 16For I tell you, I will not eat it
again until it finds fulfillment in the kingdom of
God."

17After taking the cup, he gave thanks and
said, "Take this and divide it among you. 18For I
tell you I will not drink again of the fruit of the
vine until the kingdom of God comes."

19And he took bread, gave thanks and broke it,
and gave it to them, saying, "This is my body
given for you; do this in remembrance of me."
20In the same way, after the supper he took

22:7–13 Jesus had probably made these arrangements ahead of time. ***a man carrying a jar of water.*** Such a person would have been easy to spot since it was highly unusual for a man to carry a jar. Women carried jars, men carried wineskins.

22:15 ***Passover.*** The Passover had a twofold significance. It looked back upon Israel's deliverance from Egypt (Ex. 12)—when the Lord brought death to the Egyptians but "passed over" the Israelites, who marked their houses with the blood of a sacrificial lamb. Secondly, the Passover looked forward to the final redemption that would be ushered in by the Messiah. Jesus is about to fulfill the Passover by being slain as the perfect "Passover lamb" (1 Cor. 5:7). No longer is the OT Passover the supreme act of God's deliverance of his people: From now on this supreme act is the death and resurrection of Jesus.

22:16–18 ***until it finds fulfillment.*** At the final consummation of God's kingdom, when Jesus will renew fellowship with all those who have remembered the Lord's Supper through the ages (see 1 Cor. 11:26).

22:19–20 ***bread.*** Representing Jesus' body, given for us. ***cup.*** Signifying Christ's blood, which represents his life poured out as an atonement for sin. ***covenant.*** A treaty between two parties, often sealed by an animal sacrifice. It refers to the arrangement God made with Israel that was dependent on Israel's obedience. Now a new covenant is established which is dependent on Jesus' obedience and sacrificial death.

the cup, saying, "This cup is the new covenant in my blood, which is poured out for you. 21 But the hand of him who is going to betray me is with mine on the table. 22 The Son of Man will go as it has been decreed, but woe to that man who betrays him." 23 They began to question among themselves which of them it might be who would do this.

Luke 22:7–23

1. What special meals does your family celebrate together: Thanksgiving? Sunday dinner? Birthday suppers?
2. Where do you generally sit for a big meal? Who prepares it? Who serves? Who cleans up? What do you do?
3. How often do you celebrate Communion? What do you do in preparing to receive it?
4. Jesus really wanted to eat this Passover with his disciples (v. 15). How much of what Jesus said and did during this meal did the disciples understand?
5. When did the taking of Communion take on personal meaning to you?
6. If your group has a "last supper" at the end of the year, where would you like it to be? What would you like to do to remember your time together?
7. Share prayer requests. As you pray, remember to thank Christ for giving his life for you.

(Study notes on page 953)

24 Also a dispute arose among them as to which of them was considered to be greatest. 25 Jesus said to them, "The kings of the Gentiles lord it over them; and those who exercise authority over them call themselves Benefactors. 26 But you are not to be like that. Instead, the greatest among you should be like the youngest, and the one who rules like the one who serves. 27 For who is greater, the one who is at the table or the one who serves? Is it not the one who is at the table? But I am among you as one who serves. 28 You are those who have stood by me in my trials. 29 And I confer on you a kingdom, just as my Father conferred one on me, 30 so that you may eat and drink at my table in my kingdom and sit on thrones, judging the twelve tribes of Israel.

31 "Simon, Simon, Satan has asked to sift you[a] as wheat. 32 But I have prayed for you, Simon, that your faith may not fail. And when you have turned back, strengthen your brothers."

33 But he replied, "Lord, I am ready to go with you to prison and to death."

34 Jesus answered, "I tell you, Peter, before the rooster crows today, you will deny three times that you know me."

35 Then Jesus asked them, "When I sent you without purse, bag or sandals, did you lack anything?"

"Nothing," they answered.

36 He said to them, "But now if you have a purse, take it, and also a bag; and if you don't have a sword, sell your cloak and buy one. 37 It is written: 'And he was numbered with the transgressors'[b]; and I tell you that this must be fulfilled in me. Yes, what is written about me is reaching its fulfillment."

38 The disciples said, "See, Lord, here are two swords."

"That is enough," he replied.

Jesus Prays on the Mount of Olives

39 Jesus went out as usual to the Mount of Olives, and his disciples followed him. 40 On reaching the place, he said to them, "Pray that you will not fall into temptation." 41 He withdrew about a stone's throw beyond them, knelt down and prayed, 42 "Father, if you are willing, take this cup from me; yet not my will, but yours be done." 43 An angel from heaven appeared to him and strengthened him. 44 And being in anguish, he prayed more earnestly, and his sweat was like drops of blood falling to the ground.[c]

45 When he rose from prayer and went back to the disciples, he found them asleep, exhausted from sorrow. 46 "Why are you sleeping?" he asked them. "Get up and pray so that you will not fall into temptation."

Jesus Arrested

47 While he was still speaking a crowd came up, and the man who was called Judas, one of the Twelve, was leading them. He approached Jesus to kiss him, 48 but Jesus asked him, "Judas, are you betraying the Son of Man with a kiss?"

49 When Jesus' followers saw what was going to happen, they said, "Lord, should we strike with our swords?" 50 And one of them struck the servant of the high priest, cutting off his right ear. 51 But Jesus answered, "No more of this!" And he touched the man's ear and healed him.

52 Then Jesus said to the chief priests, the offi-

[a] *31* The Greek is plural. [b] *37* Isaiah 53:12 [c] *44* Some early manuscripts do not have verses 43 and 44.

cers of the temple guard, and the elders, who had
come for him, "Am I leading a rebellion, that you
have come with swords and clubs? 53Every day I
was with you in the temple courts, and you did
not lay a hand on me. But this is your hour—
when darkness reigns."

Peter Disowns Jesus

54Then seizing him, they led him away and
took him into the house of the high priest. Peter
followed at a distance. 55But when they had kindled a fire in the middle of the courtyard and had
sat down together, Peter sat down with them.
56A servant girl saw him seated there in the fire-
light. She looked closely at him and said, "This
man was with him."

LUKE 22:54–62

1. Who is someone you admire because they "came back" after a defeat, injury or other setback?
2. How do you usually react to failure: Kick yourself for days? Pray about it? Talk to someone about it? Admit it and move on?
3. When, like Peter, was the last time you really blew it?
4. Peter had just told Jesus he would follow him to death (v. 33). What caused Peter's turnabout?
5. In what ways do you stand up for or deny Christ at your school?
6. What have you found helpful when you feel you have blown it?
7. How can the group help you in prayer this week?

57But he denied it. "Woman, I don't know
him," he said.
58A little later someone else saw him and said,
"You also are one of them."
"Man, I am not!" Peter replied.
59About an hour later another asserted, "Certainly this fellow was with him, for he is a Galilean."
60Peter replied, "Man, I don't know what
you're talking about!" Just as he was speaking,
the rooster crowed. 61The Lord turned and
looked straight at Peter. Then Peter remembered
the word the Lord had spoken to him: "Before
the rooster crows today, you will disown me
three times." 62And he went outside and wept
bitterly.

The Guards Mock Jesus

63The men who were guarding Jesus began
mocking and beating him. 64They blindfolded
him and demanded, "Prophesy! Who hit you?"
65And they said many other insulting things to
him.

Jesus Before Pilate and Herod

66At daybreak the council of the elders of the
people, both the chief priests and teachers of the
law, met together, and Jesus was led before them.
67"If you are the Christ,[a]" they said, "tell us."
Jesus answered, "If I tell you, you will not believe me, 68and if I asked you, you would not
answer. 69But from now on, the Son of Man will
be seated at the right hand of the mighty God."
70They all asked, "Are you then the Son of
God?"
He replied, "You are right in saying I am."
71Then they said, "Why do we need any more
testimony? We have heard it from his own lips."
23 Then the whole assembly rose and led
him off to Pilate. 2And they began to accuse him, saying, "We have found this man sub-
verting our nation. He opposes payment of taxes
to Caesar and claims to be Christ,[b] a king."
3So Pilate asked Jesus, "Are you the king of the
Jews?"

[a] 67 Or *Messiah* [b] 2 Or *Messiah*; also in verses 35 and 39

22:54 *the high priest.* The recognized spiritual head of Israel. Caiaphas was the high priest before whom Jesus came (Matt. 26:57). ***Peter followed at a distance.*** Peter secretly but bravely followed Jesus right to the courtyard of the high priest's house.

22:57 *denied it.* This can mean to refuse to recognize someone or to abandon solidarity with them. Both senses reflect what is going on here, as three times Peter resorts to an outright lie. Later on, this term is used to describe an apostate (2 Tim. 2:12).

22:59–60 *he is a Galilean.* Here in Jerusalem, Peter's accent gave him away as, like Jesus, a Galilean (Matt. 26:73). ***the rooster crowed.*** Roosters in Palestine might crow anytime between midnight until 3 a.m. (which was the reason soldiers called that particular watch "cock-crow").

22:61 *The Lord ... looked straight at Peter.* The other Gospels make it clear that Jesus was interrogated throughout the night by the high priest and at least some members of the Sanhedrin (Matt. 26:57). It may be at this point that Jesus was being transferred from the high priest's house to the meeting place of the full Sanhedrin for his early morning trial, and as Jesus passed through the courtyard he caught Peter's eye.

22:62 *wept.* Peter suddenly realizes what he has done. Despite his vigorous assertion that he would not deny Jesus (v. 33), this is what he had done three times before rather unintimidating people. The look of Jesus and the crowing rooster reveals to him his sin, and he weeps tears of repentance.

"Yes, it is as you say," Jesus replied.
[4]Then Pilate announced to the chief priests
and the crowd, "I find no basis for a charge
against this man."
[5]But they insisted, "He stirs up the people all
over Judea[a] by his teaching. He started in Galilee and has come all the way here."
[6]On hearing this, Pilate asked if the man was
a Galilean. [7]When he learned that Jesus was under Herod's jurisdiction, he sent him to Herod,
who was also in Jerusalem at that time.
[8]When Herod saw Jesus, he was greatly
pleased, because for a long time he had been
wanting to see him. From what he had heard
about him, he hoped to see him perform some
miracle. [9]He plied him with many questions, but
Jesus gave him no answer. [10]The chief priests and
the teachers of the law were standing there, ve-
hemently accusing him. [11]Then Herod and his
soldiers ridiculed and mocked him. Dressing him
in an elegant robe, they sent him back to Pilate.
[12]That day Herod and Pilate became friends—
before this they had been enemies.
[13]Pilate called together the chief priests, the
rulers and the people, [14]and said to them, "You
brought me this man as one who was inciting the
people to rebellion. I have examined him in your
presence and have found no basis for your
charges against him. [15]Neither has Herod, for he
sent him back to us; as you can see, he has done
nothing to deserve death. [16]Therefore, I will punish him and then release him.[b]"
[18]With one voice they cried out, "Away with
this man! Release Barabbas to us!" [19](Barabbas
had been thrown into prison for an insurrection
in the city, and for murder.)
[20]Wanting to release Jesus, Pilate appealed to
them again. [21]But they kept shouting, "Crucify
him! Crucify him!"
[22]For the third time he spoke to them: "Why?
What crime has this man committed? I have
found in him no grounds for the death penalty.
Therefore I will have him punished and then release him."
[23]But with loud shouts they insistently demanded that he be crucified, and their shouts
prevailed. [24]So Pilate decided to grant their demand. [25]He released the man who had been
thrown into prison for insurrection and murder,
the one they asked for, and surrendered Jesus to
their will.

The Crucifixion

[26]As they led him away, they seized Simon
from Cyrene, who was on his way in from the
country, and put the cross on him and made him
carry it behind Jesus. [27]A large number of people
followed him, including women who mourned
and wailed for him. [28]Jesus turned and said to

LUKE 23:26–49

1. Whose death has affected you most?
2. When have you been punished for something you didn't do? How did it feel? Have you ever taken someone else's punishment? Why?
3. Do you know someone who wears or carries a cross? What does this symbol mean to them? What does it mean to you?
4. When Jesus said, "Father, forgive them" (v. 34), who was he asking God to forgive?
5. When did the death of Christ on the cross take on personal meaning to you?
6. What difference has Christ's death and God's forgiveness made in the way you live your life?
7. If you were about to die, how confident would you be that you would be with Jesus in paradise? Why? Close in prayer.

[a]*5* Or *over the land of the Jews* [b]*16* Some manuscripts *him." 17Now he was obliged to release one man to them at the Feast.*

23:26–31 On the way to being crucified, Jesus calls out a warning to the crowd. The real tragedy is not so much what is happening to him, but what will happen to the city and its people when God judges them—in A.D. 70 when Jerusalem was destroyed.

23:33 ***crucified.*** Josephus, the Jewish historian, called crucifixion "the most wretched of all ways of dying." The victim was first stripped. Then his hands were tied or nailed to the cross beam which was lifted to the upright stake already in place. Typically it took several hours before death occurred by asphyxiation, loss of blood and shock.

23:34 ***Father, forgive them.*** Since Jesus died because of the sins of the world, in a sense everyone is responsible. Jesus desired forgiveness for all people, not just for those responsible for his crucifixion.

23:40–43 As always, Jesus reaches out to one who repents. ***paradise.*** The place of bliss after death.

23:44–45 ***darkness came over the whole land.*** This was some sort of supernatural event, showing that the forces of evil were at the height of their power (Luke 22:53). ***curtain of the temple.*** Since it stood as a symbol of the barrier between people and God, its tearing was another supernatural sign of the significance of Jesus' death: It opened the way for all to have immediate and direct access to God (Heb. 10:19–22).

23:46 ***a loud voice.*** Generally, the victim of crucifixion is exhausted and unconscious at the point of death. Jesus voluntarily gives up his life into God's care (see John 10:18).

them, “Daughters of Jerusalem, do not weep for
me; weep for yourselves and for your children.
29For the time will come when you will say,
‘Blessed are the barren women, the wombs that
never bore and the breasts that never nursed!’
30Then

“ ‘they will say to the mountains, “Fall on
us!”
and to the hills, “Cover us!” ’[a]

31For if men do these things when the tree is
green, what will happen when it is dry?”
32Two other men, both criminals, were also
led out with him to be executed. 33When they
came to the place called the Skull, there they
crucified him, along with the criminals—one on
his right, the other on his left. 34Jesus said, “Father, forgive them, for they do not know what
they are doing.”[b] And they divided up his
clothes by casting lots.
35The people stood watching, and the rulers
even sneered at him. They said, “He saved others; let him save himself if he is the Christ of
God, the Chosen One.”
36The soldiers also came up and mocked him.
They offered him wine vinegar 37and said, “If you
are the king of the Jews, save yourself.”
38There was a written notice above him,
which read: THIS IS THE KING OF THE JEWS.
39One of the criminals who hung there hurled
insults at him: “Aren’t you the Christ? Save yourself and us!”
40But the other criminal rebuked him. “Don’t
you fear God,” he said, “since you are under the
same sentence? 41We are punished justly, for we
are getting what our deeds deserve. But this man
has done nothing wrong.”
42Then he said, “Jesus, remember me when
you come into your kingdom.[c]”
43Jesus answered him, “I tell you the truth,
today you will be with me in paradise.”

Jesus’ Death

44It was now about the sixth hour, and darkness came over the whole land until the ninth
hour, 45for the sun stopped shining. And the curtain of the temple was torn in two. 46Jesus called
out with a loud voice, “Father, into your hands I
commit my spirit.” When he had said this, he
breathed his last.
47The centurion, seeing what had happened,
praised God and said, “Surely this was a righteous man.” 48When all the people who had gathered to witness this sight saw what took place,
they beat their breasts and went away. 49But all
those who knew him, including the women who
had followed him from Galilee, stood at a distance, watching these things.

Jesus’ Burial

50Now there was a man named Joseph, a member of the Council, a good and upright man,
51who had not consented to their decision and
action. He came from the Judean town of Arimathea and he was waiting for the kingdom of God.
52Going to Pilate, he asked for Jesus’ body.
53Then he took it down, wrapped it in linen cloth
and placed it in a tomb cut in the rock, one in
which no one had yet been laid. 54It was Preparation Day, and the Sabbath was about to begin.
55The women who had come with Jesus from
Galilee followed Joseph and saw the tomb and
how his body was laid in it. 56Then they went
home and prepared spices and perfumes. But
they rested on the Sabbath in obedience to the
commandment.

The Resurrection

24 On the first day of the week, very early in
the morning, the women took the spices
they had prepared and went to the tomb. 2They
found the stone rolled away from the tomb, 3but
when they entered, they did not find the body
of the Lord Jesus. 4While they were wondering
about this, suddenly two men in clothes that
gleamed like lightning stood beside them. 5In
their fright the women bowed down with their
faces to the ground, but the men said to them,
“Why do you look for the living among the dead?
6He is not here; he has risen! Remember how he
told you, while he was still with you in Galilee:
7‘The Son of Man must be delivered into the
hands of sinful men, be crucified and on the third
day be raised again.’ ” 8Then they remembered
his words.
9When they came back from the tomb, they
told all these things to the Eleven and to all the
others. 10It was Mary Magdalene, Joanna, Mary
the mother of James, and the others with them
who told this to the apostles. 11But they did not
believe the women, because their words seemed
to them like nonsense. 12Peter, however, got up
and ran to the tomb. Bending over, he saw the
strips of linen lying by themselves, and he went
away, wondering to himself what had happened.

On the Road to Emmaus

13Now that same day two of them were going
to a village called Emmaus, about seven miles[d]
from Jerusalem. 14They were talking with each
other about everything that had happened. 15As
they talked and discussed these things with each

[a] 30 Hosea 10:8 [b] 34 Some early manuscripts do not have this sentence. [c] 42 Some manuscripts *come with your kingly power*
[d] 13 Greek *sixty stadia* (about 11 kilometers)

other, Jesus himself came up and walked along
with them; 16but they were kept from recognizing him.
17He asked them, "What are you discussing
together as you walk along?"
They stood still, their faces downcast. 18One of
them, named Cleopas, asked him, "Are you only
a visitor to Jerusalem and do not know the things
that have happened there in these days?"
19"What things?" he asked.
"About Jesus of Nazareth," they replied. "He
was a prophet, powerful in word and deed before
God and all the people. 20The chief priests and
our rulers handed him over to be sentenced to
death, and they crucified him; 21but we had
hoped that he was the one who was going to
redeem Israel. And what is more, it is the third
day since all this took place. 22In addition, some
of our women amazed us. They went to the tomb
early this morning 23but didn't find his body.
They came and told us that they had seen a vision
of angels, who said he was alive. 24Then some of
our companions went to the tomb and found it
just as the women had said, but him they did not
see."
25He said to them, "How foolish you are, and
how slow of heart to believe all that the prophets
have spoken! 26Did not the Christ[a] have to suffer these things and then enter his glory?" 27And
beginning with Moses and all the Prophets, he
explained to them what was said in all the Scriptures concerning himself.
28As they approached the village to which they
were going, Jesus acted as if he were going farther. 29But they urged him strongly, "Stay with
us, for it is nearly evening; the day is almost
over." So he went in to stay with them.
30When he was at the table with them, he took
bread, gave thanks, broke it and began to give it
to them. 31Then their eyes were opened and they
recognized him, and he disappeared from their
sight. 32They asked each other, "Were not our
hearts burning within us while he talked with us
on the road and opened the Scriptures to us?"
33They got up and returned at once to Jerusalem. There they found the Eleven and those with
them, assembled together 34and saying, "It is
true! The Lord has risen and has appeared to
Simon." 35Then the two told what had happened
on the way, and how Jesus was recognized by
them when he broke the bread.

LUKE 24:13–35

1. When you're really down, do you want to be alone or with others? Where do you go to "get away from it all"?
2. What event lately has really gotten you down?
3. When you're down, who knows how to raise your spirits and help you put the pieces back together?
4. When has Jesus come along and walked with you? How were you feeling? How long did it take for you to recognize him?
5. What's the closest you've come to "throwing in the towel" spiritually? What restored your faith and hope?
6. How would you describe your walk with Christ right now?
7. How are you doing—really? How can this group encourage you? Close in prayer.

Jesus Appears to the Disciples

36While they were still talking about this, Jesus
himself stood among them and said to them,
"Peace be with you."
37They were startled and frightened, thinking
they saw a ghost. 38He said to them, "Why are
you troubled, and why do doubts rise in your

[a] 26 Or *Messiah*; also in verse 46

24:13–16 ***two of them.*** Not two of the remaining 11 apostles, but two followers of Jesus who probably lived near Jerusalem and were returning home after Passover. As Jesus came up to them, they were prevented (by God) from recognizing him.

24:18–24 Cleopas speaks of the confusion that filled the minds of all Jesus' followers. How could Jesus, who was shown by miracle after miracle to be a powerful man undoubtedly anointed by God, have met with such a meaningless death? If he was not the Messiah, who was he? If he could not redeem Israel (free them from the Romans, that is), who could? As with Peter, the reality of the empty tomb did not in itself produce faith in these disciples. In fact, after three days, they had lost hope for any miraculous intervention from God.

24:25–27 Jesus rebukes them for their lack of understanding about the OT prophecies regarding the Messiah, and explains how these Scriptures foretold all that had taken place. ***the Christ have to suffer.*** The Messiah's glory was a common expectation of the Jews, but his suffering was not.

24:30–35 ***their eyes were opened.*** Not only to recognize Jesus, but also to understand his words and the Scriptures. ***Jesus was recognized by them when he broke the bread.*** This may be intended as an encouragement to Luke's readers who never saw Jesus during his ministry: While they did not have the opportunity to physically see Jesus, they can "see" him through Scripture and sharing in the Lord's Supper.

minds? 39 Look at my hands and my feet. It is I
myself! Touch me and see; a ghost does not have
flesh and bones, as you see I have."
40 When he had said this, he showed them his
hands and feet. 41 And while they still did not
believe it because of joy and amazement, he
asked them, "Do you have anything here to eat?"
42 They gave him a piece of broiled fish, 43 and he
took it and ate it in their presence.
44 He said to them, "This is what I told you
while I was still with you: Everything must be
fulfilled that is written about me in the Law of
Moses, the Prophets and the Psalms."
45 Then he opened their minds so they could
understand the Scriptures. 46 He told them, "This
is what is written: The Christ will suffer and rise
from the dead on the third day, 47 and repentance
and forgiveness of sins will be preached in his
name to all nations, beginning at Jerusalem.
48 You are witnesses of these things. 49 I am going
to send you what my Father has promised; but
stay in the city until you have been clothed with
power from on high."

The Ascension

50 When he had led them out to the vicinity of
Bethany, he lifted up his hands and blessed them.
51 While he was blessing them, he left them and
was taken up into heaven. 52 Then they worshiped him and returned to Jerusalem with great
joy. 53 And they stayed continually at the temple,
praising God.

Introduction to JOHN

Personal Reading Plan

❐ John 1:1–34	❐ John 8:12–59	❐ John 15:1–16:4
❐ John 1:35–2:25	❐ John 9:1–41	❐ John 16:5–33
❐ John 3:1–36	❐ John 10:1–42	❐ John 17:1–26
❐ John 4:1–42	❐ John 11:1–44	❐ John 18:1–27
❐ John 4:43–5:47	❐ John 11:45–12:19	❐ John 18:28–19:16a
❐ John 6:1–59	❐ John 12:20–50	❐ John 19:16b–42
❐ John 6:60–7:24	❐ John 13:1–38	❐ John 20:1–31
❐ John 7:25–8:11	❐ John 14:1–31	❐ John 21:1–25

Author

The writer of the fourth Gospel does not name himself in the text. Like the other three Gospels, the fourth Gospel is anonymous. The inscription "The Gospel According to John" or "According to John" (as found in some ancient manuscripts) was added to the text by early Christians.

Yet in a curious way the fourth Gospel is less anonymous than the other three because the writer identifies himself in the final chapter by way of a title. He calls himself "the disciple whom Jesus loved" (21:20–24; see also 13:23–25; 19:26–27; 20:2–8; 21:7). Who then is this mysterious disciple who wanted to be known only in terms of his relationship to Jesus?

He must have been one of the 12 original disciples because he was present at the Last Supper (13:23–25; 21:20). In fact, the beloved disciple was "reclining next to" Jesus (13:23). This gives us a valuable clue as to his identity: He was probably one of the three (occasionally four) disciples who were closest to Jesus—Peter, James, John and sometimes Andrew. We know that the person reclining next to Jesus was not Peter, because Peter asked this disciple a question (13:24). The person was probably not Andrew, since Andrew is explicitly named several times in the text (1:40,44; 6:8; 12:22); it would be strange to name a disciple in some places and to list him anonymously in others as "the disciple whom Jesus loved." Most of the other disciples are also named in this Gospel. Some have suggested Lazarus as author of the fourth Gospel because in 11:5 Jesus is said to have loved him, but Lazarus is named in chapters 11–12. Of all the possible candidates, only the sons of Zebedee (James and John) are not named in the fourth Gospel. The beloved disciple could not have been James, since he died at the hands of Herod Agrippa I (Acts 12:2) early in the development of the church, and the fourth Gospel is written years after his death. Therefore, the most likely candidate is his brother, John. Indeed, early church tradition is unanimous that John the apostle, the son of Zebedee, wrote the fourth Gospel. For example, toward the end of the second century Irenaeus wrote: "Afterwards, John, the disciple of the Lord, who also had leaned upon His breast, did himself publish a Gospel during his residence at Ephesus in Asia."

Date

Most scholars agree that John was the last of the four Gospels to be written. It was probably composed in A.D. 80 or 90, though estimates range from the A.D. 50s to 90s.

Theme

Jesus is the giver of life.

Purpose

Why did John write as he did about Jesus? What was his purpose in gathering together this account? Two of his own statements provide the answer to this question. First, John asserts in his first epistle: "This we proclaim concerning the Word of life. The life appeared; we have seen it and testify to it. ... We proclaim to you what we have seen and heard, so that you also may have fellowship with us" (1 John 1:1–3). Second, John states at the end of his Gospel: "These are written that you may believe that Jesus is the Christ, the Son of God, and that by believing you may have life in his name" (John 20:31). John's Gospel, therefore, like the other three Gospels, is a witness document. He tells us Jesus' story so that we will understand who Jesus is, put our faith in him as the unique Son of God, and so experience life in Christ and fellowship with other believers.

Historical Background

What, then, do we know about John the apostle? First, we know that he and his brother James, along with Peter and his brother Andrew, were the first four disciples called by Jesus (Mark 1:16–20). Furthermore, James and John seem inseparable. On only one occasion is John recorded as acting alone (Luke 9:49–50). Together the two brothers want to call down fire on a village (Luke 9:54). Together they earn the title from Jesus of "Sons of Thunder" (Mark 3:17). The two of them request to be seated on Jesus' right and left in the coming kingdom (Mark 10:35–37). They are both with Jesus on the Mount of Transfiguration (Mark 9:2), in Gethsemane (Mark 14:33), and when Jairus' daughter is raised from the dead (Mark 5:37). John is right at the heart of Jesus' life and ministry. He of all the disciples is qualified to give the world a glimpse of Jesus' deepest thoughts and profound concerns.

Characteristics

For those familiar with the Synoptic Gospels (Matthew, Mark, Luke), what strikes one so forcibly about John's Gospel is how *different* it is. Despite their different emphases, the synoptics tell the same story (probably because Matthew and Luke both build upon Mark's account). They are telling one part of Jesus' story. John, however, tells another part of that story. This is not to say that John's account contradicts the synoptics. Rather, John makes explicit what Matthew, Mark and Luke only hint at. He leaves out a lot of material covered in the synoptics, but he adds information about aspects of Jesus' ministry not discussed elsewhere. And he records for us not just Jesus' short, meaningful statements, so prominent in the synoptics, but also his longer discourses.

The Omissions

In John's Gospel, we find no information about Jesus' birth; his baptism is only alluded to; and his temptation is not even mentioned. In the fourth Gospel, Jesus casts out no demons, cures no lepers, almost never speaks in parables, and does not emphasize the idea of the kingdom of God. John does not mention the institution of the Lord's Supper or Jesus' agony in the Garden of Gethsemane.

The Conclusion

Instead, in John's Gospel we are told about portions of Jesus' ministry not discussed in the synoptics. We hear about Jesus' ministry before John the Baptist's imprisonment. We hear of Jesus' visits to Jerusalem before his final visit when he was crucified. Perhaps most importantly, in the fourth Gospel we are given details of Jesus' ministry in Judea (the Synoptic Gospels focus on his Galilean ministry). John's Gospel is particularly rich when it comes to the teachings of Jesus. Here we find his long discourses on great themes such as light, love, life, truth and abiding. Here in the great *I Am* sections we listen to Jesus reveal who he is.

John also records for us some of the most beloved stories about Jesus. Only in the fourth Gospel can we read about the wedding feast at Cana of Galilee (2:1–11), the night visit of Nicodemus (3:1–15), the conversation with the woman at the well (4:1–42), the raising of Lazarus from the dead (11:1–44), and the washing of the disciples' feet (13:1–17). In John's Gospel, we find the bulk of our Lord's teaching about the Holy Spirit, and here the "I" in the Sermon on the Mount in Matthew 5 ("You have heard that it was said ... but I tell you ..."–Matt. 5:21ff) becomes the majestic "I am" who is God's own Son.

Style

John writes in very simple Greek. He does not use a wide range of vocabulary. He often repeats words and phrases. Yet the end is a compelling document whose very simplicity makes it impressive.

The fourth Gospel was written by a man with an adequate but not extensive education in Greek. In fact, some scholars suggest that this Greek sounds acquired, not native. Furthermore, the writing has a strong Jewish flavoring. This is exactly what one would expect of John, the son of Zebedee—a Jew who had lived for a long time in Galilee, an area whose population included more Gentiles than Jews.

Structure

It is not clear how John's Gospel ought to be subdivided. It is an incredibly rich, complex and fluid piece of writing in which various themes operate at different levels.

Still, most scholars agree that John's Gospel begins with a distinct prologue (1:1–18) and then divides into two major parts. The first part of the Gospel concentrates on Jesus' *public ministry.* It is organized around his miracles, "signs" that reveal who he really is. This part covers most of the three years of Jesus' ministry.

In the second part, the focus shifts from the crowds to the disciples and Jesus' *private ministry* among them. The theme in this section is the *glory* that is revealed in Jesus' crucifixion and resurrection. The time period of this part is short: from the Thursday night of the Last Supper through Jesus' postresurrection appearances.

Additional themes run through the book. For example, the material is grouped around the major Jewish feasts. Also, the idea of the passion of Jesus is present throughout.

John recounted events from specially selected days in Jesus' life. These events present a Savior who knows "where I came from and where I am going" (8:14). Jesus' repeated references to the One "who sent me" emphasize he is truly God's Son.

John describes Jesus as the "Word" (1:1–14), the sum of all that God wanted to say to us. God communicated in the only way we could truly understand: by becoming one of us.

Passages for Topical Group Study

2:1–11	PARENTAL DEMANDS	Jesus Changes Water to Wine
3:1–21	ETERNAL LIFE	Jesus Teaches Nicodemus
4:1–26	REACHING OUT	Jesus Talks With a Samaritan Woman
5:1–15	PHYSICAL FITNESS	The Healing at the Pool
8:1–11	PEER PRESSURE MORAL FAILURE	The Woman Caught in Adultery
8:12–20	GOD THE FATHER	The Validity of Jesus' Testimony
9:1–15,24–34	CHRONIC ILLNESS / DISABILITY	Jesus Heals a Man Born Blind
11:17–44	DEATH AND DYING	Jesus Raises Lazarus From the Dead
13:1–17	LOVE A SERVANT'S HEART	Jesus Washes His Disciples' Feet
14:15–27	THE HOLY SPIRIT	Jesus Promises the Holy Spirit
20:1–18	GRIEF AND LOSS	Jesus Appears to Mary Magdalene
20:24–31	DOUBTS	Jesus Appears to Thomas

See the Lesson Plans in the front of this Bible.

Passage for General Group Study

21:1–14 Jesus and the Miraculous Catch of Fish

The Word Became Flesh

1 In the beginning was the Word, and the
Word was with God, and the Word was God.
2He was with God in the beginning.
3Through him all things were made; without
him nothing was made that has been made. 4In
him was life, and that life was the light of men.
5The light shines in the darkness, but the darkness has not understood[a] it.
6There came a man who was sent from God;
his name was John. 7He came as a witness to
testify concerning that light, so that through him
all men might believe. 8He himself was not the
light; he came only as a witness to the light. 9The
true light that gives light to every man was coming into the world.[b]
10He was in the world, and though the world
was made through him, the world did not recognize him. 11He came to that which was his own,
but his own did not receive him. 12Yet to all who
received him, to those who believed in his name,
he gave the right to become children of God—
13children born not of natural descent,[c] nor of
human decision or a husband's will, but born of
God.
14The Word became flesh and made his dwelling among us. We have seen his glory, the glory
of the One and Only,[d] who came from the Father, full of grace and truth.
15John testifies concerning him. He cries out,
saying, "This was he of whom I said, 'He who
comes after me has surpassed me because he was
before me.' " 16From the fullness of his grace we
have all received one blessing after another.
17For the law was given through Moses; grace
and truth came through Jesus Christ. 18No one
has ever seen God, but God the One and
Only,[d,e] who is at the Father's side, has made
him known.

John the Baptist Denies Being the Christ

19Now this was John's testimony when the
Jews of Jerusalem sent priests and Levites to ask
him who he was. 20He did not fail to confess, but
confessed freely, "I am not the Christ.[f]"
21They asked him, "Then who are you? Are
you Elijah?"
He said, "I am not."
"Are you the Prophet?"
He answered, "No."
22Finally they said, "Who are you? Give us an
answer to take back to those who sent us. What
do you say about yourself?"
23John replied in the words of Isaiah the
prophet, "I am the voice of one calling in the
desert, 'Make straight the way for the Lord.' "[g]
24Now some Pharisees who had been sent
25questioned him, "Why then do you baptize if
you are not the Christ, nor Elijah, nor the
Prophet?"
26"I baptize with[h] water," John replied, "but
among you stands one you do not know. 27He is
the one who comes after me, the thongs of whose
sandals I am not worthy to untie."
28This all happened at Bethany on the other
side of the Jordan, where John was baptizing.

Jesus the Lamb of God

29The next day John saw Jesus coming toward
him and said, "Look, the Lamb of God, who takes
away the sin of the world! 30This is the one I
meant when I said, 'A man who comes after me
has surpassed me because he was before me.' 31I
myself did not know him, but the reason I came
baptizing with water was that he might be revealed to Israel."
32Then John gave this testimony: "I saw the
Spirit come down from heaven as a dove and
remain on him. 33I would not have known him,
except that the one who sent me to baptize with
water told me, 'The man on whom you see the
Spirit come down and remain is he who will baptize with the Holy Spirit.' 34I have seen and I
testify that this is the Son of God."

Jesus' First Disciples

35The next day John was there again with two
of his disciples. 36When he saw Jesus passing by,
he said, "Look, the Lamb of God!"
37When the two disciples heard him say this,
they followed Jesus. 38Turning around, Jesus saw
them following and asked, "What do you want?"
They said, "Rabbi" (which means Teacher),
"where are you staying?"
39"Come," he replied, "and you will see."
So they went and saw where he was staying,
and spent that day with him. It was about the
tenth hour.
40Andrew, Simon Peter's brother, was one of
the two who heard what John had said and who
had followed Jesus. 41The first thing Andrew did
was to find his brother Simon and tell him, "We
have found the Messiah" (that is, the Christ).
42And he brought him to Jesus.
Jesus looked at him and said, "You are Simon
son of John. You will be called Cephas" (which,
when translated, is Peter[i]).

[a]5 Or *darkness, and the darkness has not overcome* [b]9 Or *This was the true light that gives light to every man who comes into the world* [c]13 Greek *of bloods* [d]14,18 Or *the Only Begotten* [e]18 Some manuscripts *but the only* (or *only begotten*) *Son* [f]20 Or *Messiah.* "The Christ" (Greek) and "the Messiah" (Hebrew) both mean "the Anointed One"; also in verse 25. [g]23 Isaiah 40:3 [h]26 Or *in;* also in verses 31 and 33 [i]42 Both *Cephas* (Aramaic) and *Peter* (Greek) mean *rock.*

Jesus Calls Philip and Nathanael

43 The next day Jesus decided to leave for Galilee. Finding Philip, he said to him, "Follow me."
44 Philip, like Andrew and Peter, was from the
town of Bethsaida. 45 Philip found Nathanael and
told him, "We have found the one Moses wrote
about in the Law, and about whom the prophets
also wrote—Jesus of Nazareth, the son of Joseph."
46 "Nazareth! Can anything good come from
there?" Nathanael asked.
"Come and see," said Philip.
47 When Jesus saw Nathanael approaching, he
said of him, "Here is a true Israelite, in whom
there is nothing false."
48 "How do you know me?" Nathanael asked.
Jesus answered, "I saw you while you were
still under the fig tree before Philip called you."
49 Then Nathanael declared, "Rabbi, you are
the Son of God; you are the King of Israel."
50 Jesus said, "You believe[a] because I told you
I saw you under the fig tree. You shall see greater
things than that." 51 He then added, "I tell you[b]
the truth, you[b] shall see heaven open, and the
angels of God ascending and descending on the
Son of Man."

Jesus Changes Water to Wine

2 On the third day a wedding took place at
Cana in Galilee. Jesus' mother was there,
2 and Jesus and his disciples had also been invited
to the wedding. 3 When the wine was gone, Jesus'
mother said to him, "They have no more wine."
4 "Dear woman, why do you involve me?"
Jesus replied. "My time has not yet come."
5 His mother said to the servants, "Do whatever he tells you."
6 Nearby stood six stone water jars, the kind
used by the Jews for ceremonial washing, each
holding from twenty to thirty gallons.[c]
7 Jesus said to the servants, "Fill the jars with
water"; so they filled them to the brim.
8 Then he told them, "Now draw some out and
take it to the master of the banquet."
They did so, 9 and the master of the banquet
tasted the water that had been turned into wine.
He did not realize where it had come from,
though the servants who had drawn the water
knew. Then he called the bridegroom aside 10 and
said, "Everyone brings out the choice wine first
and then the cheaper wine after the guests have
had too much to drink; but you have saved the
best till now."
11 This, the first of his miraculous signs, Jesus
performed at Cana in Galilee. He thus revealed
his glory, and his disciples put their faith in him.

JOHN 2:1–11

1. When was the last time one of your parents embarrassed you?
2. Have you ever been at a wedding where things didn't go right? What happened?
3. How often do your parents pressure you to do something you don't want to do? How does this make you feel?
4. This was "the first of his miraculous signs" (v. 11). Why did Mary bring this problem to Jesus? How did Jesus feel about this?
5. What do your parents ask you to do that irritates you the most? How do you deal with differences with your parents? How should you?
6. What is the "wine" level (zest for living) in your life at the moment: Full? Half-full? Empty?
7. What is draining you? How can the group pray for you?

[a] 50 Or *Do you believe . . . ?* [b] 51 The Greek is plural. [c] 6 Greek *two to three metretes* (probably about 75 to 115 liters)

2:1–3 ***wedding.*** Jewish weddings were important social events, a time when all the relatives and townspeople would gather to celebrate, often for up to a week! ***They have no more wine.*** This was a very humiliating social situation. It would reflect badly on the host as someone too miserly to provide adequate refreshments for the guests. Why Jesus' mother approached Jesus with this concern is unknown, since Jesus had not previously done anything to make her expect he could solve the problem. It implies her awareness of his role as the Messiah, and perhaps is an encouragement on her part to start acting the part!

2:4–5 ***Dear woman.*** Not harsh, but unusual for a son to say. ***why do you involve me?*** Since the time for his role as Messiah is at hand, Jesus makes it clear that no other loyalties and relationships will be allowed to dominate that agenda. ***Do whatever he tells you.*** Again, the reason for Mary's confidence in pressing on with this concern is unknown. The phrase does serve to show that the initiative is left with Jesus.

2:6–8 ***twenty to thirty gallons.*** The drinking of wine did not have the associations with alcohol abuse as it does so often today. Jesus' provision of such an ample amount of wine puts him in the place of a host, generously providing for his guests.

2:11 This incident is the first of seven "signs" in John's Gospel. These miracles are meant to demonstrate the glory of God in Jesus. This was the disciples' first glimpse of the light of God's glory in Jesus, and led them to "put their faith in him."

Jesus Clears the Temple

12After this he went down to Capernaum with
his mother and brothers and his disciples. There
they stayed for a few days.
13When it was almost time for the Jewish Passover, Jesus went up to Jerusalem. 14In the temple
courts he found men selling cattle, sheep and
doves, and others sitting at tables exchanging
money. 15So he made a whip out of cords, and
drove all from the temple area, both sheep and
cattle; he scattered the coins of the money changers and overturned their tables. 16To those who
sold doves he said, "Get these out of here! How
dare you turn my Father's house into a market!"
17His disciples remembered that it is written:
"Zeal for your house will consume me."[a]
18Then the Jews demanded of him, "What miraculous sign can you show us to prove your authority to do all this?"
19Jesus answered them, "Destroy this temple,
and I will raise it again in three days."
20The Jews replied, "It has taken forty-six
years to build this temple, and you are going to
raise it in three days?" 21But the temple he had
spoken of was his body. 22After he was raised
from the dead, his disciples recalled what he had
said. Then they believed the Scripture and the
words that Jesus had spoken.
23Now while he was in Jerusalem at the Passover Feast, many people saw the miraculous signs
he was doing and believed in his name.[b] 24But
Jesus would not entrust himself to them, for he
knew all men. 25He did not need man's testimony about man, for he knew what was in a man.

Jesus Teaches Nicodemus

3 Now there was a man of the Pharisees
named Nicodemus, a member of the Jewish
ruling council. 2He came to Jesus at night and
said, "Rabbi, we know you are a teacher who has
come from God. For no one could perform the
miraculous signs you are doing if God were not
with him."
3In reply Jesus declared, "I tell you the truth,
no one can see the kingdom of God unless he is
born again.[c]"
4"How can a man be born when he is old?"
Nicodemus asked. "Surely he cannot enter a second time into his mother's womb to be born!"
5Jesus answered, "I tell you the truth, no one
can enter the kingdom of God unless he is born
of water and the Spirit. 6Flesh gives birth to flesh,
but the Spirit[d] gives birth to spirit. 7You should
not be surprised at my saying, 'You[e] must be
born again.' 8The wind blows wherever it
pleases. You hear its sound, but you cannot tell
where it comes from or where it is going. So it is
with everyone born of the Spirit."

JOHN 3:1–21

1. What is the favorite story your parents tell about the day you were born?
2. When did you find out the real truth about where babies come from? What did you think before this?
3. When did you come to the place in your life that Jesus became more than a stain glass window to you?
4. If your friend asked you to explain what it means to be "born of the Spirit," what would you say?
5. Where are you right now in your spiritual development: New born baby? Terrible two? Toddler? Adolescent? Don't know?
6. What is the next step for you in your spiritual developement?
7. How can the group pray for you this week?

[a] *17* Psalm 69:9 [b] *23* Or *and believed in him* [c] *3* Or *born from above*; also in verse 7 [d] *6* Or *but spirit*
[e] *7* The Greek is plural.

3:1–2 ***Nicodemus.*** A member of the Pharisees and the Sanhedrin, the distinguished Jewish ruling council. ***at night.*** These groups were opposed to Jesus, so Nicodemus likely didn't want to be seen with Jesus in public.

3:3–7 Jesus moves the conversation to essential issues. ***born again.*** This phrase can be translated "born again" (highlighting the major reorientation to life which results from trusting Jesus) or "born from above" (highlighting the fact that spiritual life is a gift from God). As a Pharisee, Nicodemus would believe righteousness was a matter of strictly keeping the Law. By speaking of the need for a new birth, Jesus asserts that his approach to God is all wrong. ***You must be born again.*** "You" is plural, indicating everyone "must" (with no exceptions) turn to Jesus.

3:15 ***eternal life.*** The first use of a phrase found over and over in John's Gospel. Its meaning is not simply tied up with the quantity of time one exists, but much more with the quality of fullness, goodness and perfection of life with God.

3:16–21 These verses sum up the motive, means and result of the Gospel. The Jews spoke of God loving Israel, but they never referred to his relationship with the world as one of love. Because of God's love, he *gave* his Son, in the birth and crucifixion of Jesus.

3:19–20 Just as verses 16–18 sum up the good news of the Gospel, so these verses sum up the human situation which makes the Gospel so necessary. The problem is not a lack of understanding of the light, but a decided preference for the darkness.

9"How can this be?" Nicodemus asked.

10"You are Israel's teacher," said Jesus, "and do you not understand these things? 11I tell you the truth, we speak of what we know, and we testify to what we have seen, but still you people do not accept our testimony. 12I have spoken to you of earthly things and you do not believe; how then will you believe if I speak of heavenly things? 13No one has ever gone into heaven except the one who came from heaven—the Son of Man.[a] 14Just as Moses lifted up the snake in the desert, so the Son of Man must be lifted up, 15that everyone who believes in him may have eternal life.[b]

16"For God so loved the world that he gave his one and only Son,[c] that whoever believes in him shall not perish but have eternal life. 17For God did not send his Son into the world to condemn the world, but to save the world through him. 18Whoever believes in him is not condemned, but whoever does not believe stands condemned already because he has not believed in the name of God's one and only Son.[d] 19This is the verdict: Light has come into the world, but men loved darkness instead of light because their deeds were evil. 20Everyone who does evil hates the light, and will not come into the light for fear that his deeds will be exposed. 21But whoever lives by the truth comes into the light, so that it may be seen plainly that what he has done has been done through God."[e]

John the Baptist's Testimony About Jesus

22After this, Jesus and his disciples went out into the Judean countryside, where he spent some time with them, and baptized. 23Now John also was baptizing at Aenon near Salim, because there was plenty of water, and people were constantly coming to be baptized. 24(This was before John was put in prison.) 25An argument developed between some of John's disciples and a certain Jew[f] over the matter of ceremonial washing. 26They came to John and said to him, "Rabbi, that man who was with you on the other side of the Jordan—the one you testified about—well, he is baptizing, and everyone is going to him."

27To this John replied, "A man can receive only what is given him from heaven. 28You yourselves can testify that I said, 'I am not the Christ[g] but am sent ahead of him.' 29The bride belongs to the bridegroom. The friend who attends the bridegroom waits and listens for him, and is full of joy when he hears the bridegroom's voice. That joy is mine, and it is now complete. 30He must become greater; I must become less.

31"The one who comes from above is above all; the one who is from the earth belongs to the earth, and speaks as one from the earth. The one who comes from heaven is above all. 32He testifies to what he has seen and heard, but no one accepts his testimony. 33The man who has accepted it has certified that God is truthful. 34For the one whom God has sent speaks the words of God, for God[h] gives the Spirit without limit. 35The Father loves the Son and has placed everything in his hands. 36Whoever believes in the Son has eternal life, but whoever rejects the Son will not see life, for God's wrath remains on him."[i]

Jesus Talks With a Samaritan Woman

4 The Pharisees heard that Jesus was gaining and baptizing more disciples than John, 2although in fact it was not Jesus who baptized, but his disciples. 3When the Lord learned of this, he left Judea and went back once more to Galilee.

4Now he had to go through Samaria. 5So he came to a town in Samaria called Sychar, near the plot of ground Jacob had given to his son Joseph. 6Jacob's well was there, and Jesus, tired as he was from the journey, sat down by the well. It was about the sixth hour.

7When a Samaritan woman came to draw water, Jesus said to her, "Will you give me a drink?" 8(His disciples had gone into the town to buy food.)

9The Samaritan woman said to him, "You are a Jew and I am a Samaritan woman. How can you ask me for a drink?" (For Jews do not associate with Samaritans.[j])

10Jesus answered her, "If you knew the gift of God and who it is that asks you for a drink, you would have asked him and he would have given you living water."

11"Sir," the woman said, "you have nothing to draw with and the well is deep. Where can you get this living water? 12Are you greater than our father Jacob, who gave us the well and drank from it himself, as did also his sons and his flocks and herds?"

13Jesus answered, "Everyone who drinks this water will be thirsty again, 14but whoever drinks the water I give him will never thirst. Indeed, the water I give him will become in him a spring of water welling up to eternal life."

15The woman said to him, "Sir, give me this water so that I won't get thirsty and have to keep coming here to draw water."

16He told her, "Go, call your husband and come back."

17"I have no husband," she replied.

a13 Some manuscripts *Man, who is in heaven* b15 Or *believes may have eternal life in him* c16 Or *his only begotten Son* d18 Or *God's only begotten Son* e21 Some interpreters end the quotation after verse 15. f25 Some manuscripts *and certain Jews* g28 Or *Messiah* h34 Greek *he* i36 Some interpreters end the quotation after verse 30. j9 Or *do not use dishes Samaritans have used*

Jesus said to her, "You are right when you say
you have no husband. 18The fact is, you have had
five husbands, and the man you now have is not
your husband. What you have just said is quite
true."

JOHN 4:1–26

1. When you're really thirsty, what quenches your thirst the best?
2. Where is the "watering hole" in your town, the place where *all* the kids gather on Friday night?
3. At your school or in your town, what group is not socially acceptable to associate with? What is your relationship with those people?
4. What kind of water is Jesus talking about in verse 14? What has been your experience with this water?
5. On a scale of 1 (I'm very shy) to 10 (life of the party), how are you at reaching out to others?
6. What could this group do to reach out to the kids hanging out at the "watering hole"?
7. Who is God challenging you to go beyond your comfort zone and reach out to? Pray as a group about that and for those people.

19"Sir," the woman said, "I can see that you
are a prophet. 20Our fathers worshiped on this
mountain, but you Jews claim that the place
where we must worship is in Jerusalem."
21Jesus declared, "Believe me, woman, a time
is coming when you will worship the Father neither on this mountain nor in Jerusalem. 22You
Samaritans worship what you do not know; we
worship what we do know, for salvation is from
the Jews. 23Yet a time is coming and has now
come when the true worshipers will worship the
Father in spirit and truth, for they are the kind of
worshipers the Father seeks. 24God is spirit, and
his worshipers must worship in spirit and in
truth."
25The woman said, "I know that Messiah"
(called Christ) "is coming. When he comes, he
will explain everything to us."
26Then Jesus declared, "I who speak to you
am he."

The Disciples Rejoin Jesus

27Just then his disciples returned and were
surprised to find him talking with a woman. But
no one asked, "What do you want?" or "Why are
you talking with her?"
28Then, leaving her water jar, the woman
went back to the town and said to the people,
29"Come, see a man who told me everything I
ever did. Could this be the Christ[a]?" 30They
came out of the town and made their way toward
him.
31Meanwhile his disciples urged him, "Rabbi,
eat something."
32But he said to them, "I have food to eat that
you know nothing about."
33Then his disciples said to each other, "Could
someone have brought him food?"
34"My food," said Jesus, "is to do the will of
him who sent me and to finish his work. 35Do
you not say, 'Four months more and then the
harvest'? I tell you, open your eyes and look at
the fields! They are ripe for harvest. 36Even now
the reaper draws his wages, even now he harvests the crop for eternal life, so that the sower
and the reaper may be glad together. 37Thus the
saying 'One sows and another reaps' is true. 38I
sent you to reap what you have not worked for.
Others have done the hard work, and you have
reaped the benefits of their labor."

[a]29 Or *Messiah*

4:4 ***he had to go.*** Probably prompted by the suspicion his popularity aroused. ***Samaria.*** A territory sandwiched between the Jewish provinces of Judea and Galilee. Samaritans were a mixed race of Jews and Gentiles. In Jesus' day, strict Jews (who considered Samaritans religious half-breeds), would avoid Samaria entirely by crossing the Jordan River and traveling on its east side.

4:7 This woman represents all that was despised: a woman in a culture that regarded women as second-class; a Samaritan; and, because of her marital track record (v. 18), immoral in the eyes of the Law.

4:19–24 ***mountain.*** This issue was a source of great hostility between Jews and Samaritans. Both claiming OT support for their views, Jewish zealots had destroyed the Samaritan temple on Mt. Gerizim, and Samaritans had retaliated by desecrating the Jerusalem temple. Her statement may be an attempt to test what this "prophet" has to say. ***salvation is from the Jews.*** Because the Messiah would be a Jew. ***true worshipers.*** The barrier between Jewish and Samaritan religion is dismissed. Their concern about location indicates both have missed the point. ***in spirit and truth.*** God's people are to worship God in accordance with how he has revealed himself. The point is not where one worships, but whom.

4:25–26 ***Messiah ... will explain everything.*** Her final attempt to avoid the issue. ***I ... am he.*** Since the Samaritans' concept of the Messiah was less politically charged than the Jews', Jesus laid claim to the title here.

Many Samaritans Believe

[39]Many of the Samaritans from that town believed in him because of the woman's testimony,
"He told me everything I ever did." [40]So when
the Samaritans came to him, they urged him to
stay with them, and he stayed two days. [41]And
because of his words many more became believers.
[42]They said to the woman, "We no longer believe just because of what you said; now we have
heard for ourselves, and we know that this man
really is the Savior of the world."

Jesus Heals the Official's Son

[43]After the two days he left for Galilee. [44](Now
Jesus himself had pointed out that a prophet has
no honor in his own country.) [45]When he arrived
in Galilee, the Galileans welcomed him. They
had seen all that he had done in Jerusalem at the
Passover Feast, for they also had been there.
[46]Once more he visited Cana in Galilee, where
he had turned the water into wine. And there
was a certain royal official whose son lay sick at
Capernaum. [47]When this man heard that Jesus
had arrived in Galilee from Judea, he went to him
and begged him to come and heal his son, who
was close to death.
[48]"Unless you people see miraculous signs and
wonders," Jesus told him, "you will never believe."
[49]The royal official said, "Sir, come down before my child dies."
[50]Jesus replied, "You may go. Your son will
live."
The man took Jesus at his word and departed.
[51]While he was still on the way, his servants met
him with the news that his boy was living.
[52]When he inquired as to the time when his son
got better, they said to him, "The fever left him
yesterday at the seventh hour."
[53]Then the father realized that this was the
exact time at which Jesus had said to him, "Your
son will live." So he and all his household believed.
[54]This was the second miraculous sign that
Jesus performed, having come from Judea to Galilee.

The Healing at the Pool

5 Some time later, Jesus went up to Jerusalem
for a feast of the Jews. [2]Now there is in Jerusalem near the Sheep Gate a pool, which in Aramaic is called Bethesda[a] and which is surrounded by five covered colonnades. [3]Here a great
number of disabled people used to lie—the blind,
the lame, the paralyzed.[b] [5]One who was there

JOHN 5:1–15

1. When you are sick, what do you do to get better?
2. How important is it to you to stay physically fit? What are you doing to keep in shape?
3. What connection is there between your physical and spiritual health?
4. Why did Jesus ask the man if he wanted to get well (see note on 5:5–6)?
5. In what area of your life do you need the most healing: Physical? Emotional? Relational? Spiritual?
6. What is the closest Jesus has come to saying to you, "Get up! Pick up your mat and walk"?
7. How can the group pray for you this week?

[a]2 Some manuscripts *Bethzatha*; other manuscripts *Bethsaida* [b]3 Some less important manuscripts *paralyzed—and they waited for the moving of the waters. [4]From time to time an angel of the Lord would come down and stir up the waters. The first one into the pool after each such disturbance would be cured of whatever disease he had.*

5:3–4 See NIV text note. Verse 4, not found in the best manuscripts of John's Gospel, was likely added by a later copyist as an explanation for why a great number of disabled people waited by the pool.

5:5–6 ***invalid.*** Although John doesn't specify his problem, we assume it was a form of paralysis. ***Do you want to get well?*** An odd but important question. Beggars who were cured could lose their profitable income. This man hadn't asked Jesus to cure him. Maybe he simply lost the will to be cured.

5:7 ***I have no one to help me into the pool when the water is stirred.*** The pool's reputation for bringing healing to the first person to get in when its waters were stirred (v. 4 in NIV text note) explains the man's statement. The man had no prior expectation of Jesus as a healer. He was hopeful only that Jesus might assist him in getting into the water at the next available moment.

5:8–10 Normally Jesus healed in response to faith, but he wasn't limited by someone's lack of faith. Such is the case here with the invalid, who didn't even know who Jesus was (v. 13). ***the law forbids you to carry your mat.*** The rabbis' interpretations rather than the Law of Moses itself forbid carrying any kind of load on the Sabbath.

5:14 ***Stop sinning or something worse may happen.*** Jesus did not accept the common idea that such infirmities as this man had suffered were always the result of personal sin (9:1–3), but his warning does accent that to turn from God is to inherit an eternal fate worse than his illness had been.

had been an invalid for thirty-eight years. 6When
Jesus saw him lying there and learned that he had
been in this condition for a long time, he asked
him, “Do you want to get well?”
7“Sir,” the invalid replied, “I have no one to
help me into the pool when the water is stirred.
While I am trying to get in, someone else goes
down ahead of me.”
8Then Jesus said to him, “Get up! Pick up your
mat and walk.” 9At once the man was cured; he
picked up his mat and walked.
The day on which this took place was a Sabbath, 10and so the Jews said to the man who had
been healed, “It is the Sabbath; the law forbids
you to carry your mat.”
11But he replied, “The man who made me well
said to me, ‘Pick up your mat and walk.’ ”
12So they asked him, “Who is this fellow who
told you to pick it up and walk?”
13The man who was healed had no idea who it
was, for Jesus had slipped away into the crowd
that was there.
14Later Jesus found him at the temple and said
to him, “See, you are well again. Stop sinning or
something worse may happen to you.” 15The
man went away and told the Jews that it was
Jesus who had made him well.

Life Through the Son

16So, because Jesus was doing these things on
the Sabbath, the Jews persecuted him. 17Jesus
said to them, “My Father is always at his work to
this very day, and I, too, am working.” 18For this
reason the Jews tried all the harder to kill him;
not only was he breaking the Sabbath, but he was
even calling God his own Father, making himself
equal with God.
19Jesus gave them this answer: “I tell you the
truth, the Son can do nothing by himself; he can
do only what he sees his Father doing, because
whatever the Father does the Son also does. 20For
the Father loves the Son and shows him all he
does. Yes, to your amazement he will show him
even greater things than these. 21For just as the
Father raises the dead and gives them life, even
so the Son gives life to whom he is pleased to give
it. 22Moreover, the Father judges no one, but has
entrusted all judgment to the Son, 23that all may
honor the Son just as they honor the Father. He
who does not honor the Son does not honor the
Father, who sent him.
24“I tell you the truth, whoever hears my word
and believes him who sent me has eternal life
and will not be condemned; he has crossed over
from death to life. 25I tell you the truth, a time is
coming and has now come when the dead will
hear the voice of the Son of God and those who
hear will live. 26For as the Father has life in himself, so he has granted the Son to have life in
himself. 27And he has given him authority to
judge because he is the Son of Man.
28“Do not be amazed at this, for a time is coming when all who are in their graves will hear his
voice 29and come out—those who have done
good will rise to live, and those who have done
evil will rise to be condemned. 30By myself I can
do nothing; I judge only as I hear, and my judgment is just, for I seek not to please myself but
him who sent me.

Testimonies About Jesus

31“If I testify about myself, my testimony is not
valid. 32There is another who testifies in my favor, and I know that his testimony about me is
valid.
33“You have sent to John and he has testified
to the truth. 34Not that I accept human testimony; but I mention it that you may be saved.
35John was a lamp that burned and gave light,
and you chose for a time to enjoy his light.
36“I have testimony weightier than that of
John. For the very work that the Father has given
me to finish, and which I am doing, testifies that
the Father has sent me. 37And the Father who
sent me has himself testified concerning me. You
have never heard his voice nor seen his form,
38nor does his word dwell in you, for you do not
believe the one he sent. 39You diligently study[a]
the Scriptures because you think that by them
you possess eternal life. These are the Scriptures
that testify about me, 40yet you refuse to come to
me to have life.
41“I do not accept praise from men, 42but
I know you. I know that you do not have the
love of God in your hearts. 43I have come in my
Father’s name, and you do not accept me; but
if someone else comes in his own name, you
will accept him. 44How can you believe if you accept praise from one another, yet make no effort
to obtain the praise that comes from the only
God[b]?
45“But do not think I will accuse you before
the Father. Your accuser is Moses, on whom your
hopes are set. 46If you believed Moses, you would
believe me, for he wrote about me. 47But since
you do not believe what he wrote, how are you
going to believe what I say?”

Jesus Feeds the Five Thousand

6 Some time after this, Jesus crossed to the far
shore of the Sea of Galilee (that is, the Sea of
Tiberias), 2and a great crowd of people followed
him because they saw the miraculous signs he
had performed on the sick. 3Then Jesus went up

[a]39 Or *Study diligently* (the imperative) [b]44 Some early manuscripts *the Only One*

on a mountainside and sat down with his disciples. 4The Jewish Passover Feast was near.
5When Jesus looked up and saw a great crowd
coming toward him, he said to Philip, "Where
shall we buy bread for these people to eat?" 6He
asked this only to test him, for he already had in
mind what he was going to do.
7Philip answered him, "Eight months'
wages[a] would not buy enough bread for each
one to have a bite!"
8Another of his disciples, Andrew, Simon Peter's brother, spoke up, 9"Here is a boy with five
small barley loaves and two small fish, but how
far will they go among so many?"
10Jesus said, "Have the people sit down."
There was plenty of grass in that place, and the
men sat down, about five thousand of them.
11Jesus then took the loaves, gave thanks, and
distributed to those who were seated as much as
they wanted. He did the same with the fish.
12When they had all had enough to eat, he said
to his disciples, "Gather the pieces that are left
over. Let nothing be wasted." 13So they gathered
them and filled twelve baskets with the pieces of
the five barley loaves left over by those who had
eaten.
14After the people saw the miraculous sign
that Jesus did, they began to say, "Surely this is
the Prophet who is to come into the world."
15Jesus, knowing that they intended to come and
make him king by force, withdrew again to a
mountain by himself.

Jesus Walks on the Water

16When evening came, his disciples went
down to the lake, 17where they got into a boat
and set off across the lake for Capernaum. By
now it was dark, and Jesus had not yet joined
them. 18A strong wind was blowing and the waters grew rough. 19When they had rowed three
or three and a half miles,[b] they saw Jesus approaching the boat, walking on the water; and
they were terrified. 20But he said to them, "It is
I; don't be afraid." 21Then they were willing to
take him into the boat, and immediately the boat
reached the shore where they were heading.
22The next day the crowd that had stayed on
the opposite shore of the lake realized that only
one boat had been there, and that Jesus had not
entered it with his disciples, but that they had
gone away alone. 23Then some boats from Tiberias landed near the place where the people had
eaten the bread after the Lord had given thanks.
24Once the crowd realized that neither Jesus nor
his disciples were there, they got into the boats
and went to Capernaum in search of Jesus.

Jesus the Bread of Life

25When they found him on the other side of
the lake, they asked him, "Rabbi, when did you
get here?"
26Jesus answered, "I tell you the truth, you are
looking for me, not because you saw miraculous
signs but because you ate the loaves and had your
fill. 27Do not work for food that spoils, but for
food that endures to eternal life, which the Son of
Man will give you. On him God the Father has
placed his seal of approval."
28Then they asked him, "What must we do to
do the works God requires?"
29Jesus answered, "The work of God is this: to
believe in the one he has sent."
30So they asked him, "What miraculous sign
then will you give that we may see it and believe
you? What will you do? 31Our forefathers ate the
manna in the desert; as it is written: 'He gave
them bread from heaven to eat.'[c]"
32Jesus said to them, "I tell you the truth, it is
not Moses who has given you the bread from
heaven, but it is my Father who gives you the
true bread from heaven. 33For the bread of God
is he who comes down from heaven and gives life
to the world."
34"Sir," they said, "from now on give us this
bread."
35Then Jesus declared, "I am the bread of life.
He who comes to me will never go hungry, and
he who believes in me will never be thirsty.
36But as I told you, you have seen me and still you
do not believe. 37All that the Father gives me will
come to me, and whoever comes to me I will
never drive away. 38For I have come down from
heaven not to do my will but to do the will of him
who sent me. 39And this is the will of him who
sent me, that I shall lose none of all that he has
given me, but raise them up at the last day. 40For
my Father's will is that everyone who looks to the
Son and believes in him shall have eternal life,
and I will raise him up at the last day."
41At this the Jews began to grumble about him
because he said, "I am the bread that came down
from heaven." 42They said, "Is this not Jesus,
the son of Joseph, whose father and mother we
know? How can he now say, 'I came down from
heaven'?"
43"Stop grumbling among yourselves," Jesus
answered. 44"No one can come to me unless the
Father who sent me draws him, and I will raise
him up at the last day. 45It is written in the
Prophets: 'They will all be taught by God.'[d] Everyone who listens to the Father and learns from
him comes to me. 46No one has seen the Father
except the one who is from God; only he has

[a]7 Greek *two hundred denarii* [b]19 Greek *rowed twenty-five or thirty stadia* (about 5 or 6 kilometers) [c]31 Exodus 16:4; Neh. 9:15; Psalm 78:24,25 [d]45 Isaiah 54:13

seen the Father. 47 I tell you the truth, he who
believes has everlasting life. 48 I am the bread of
life. 49 Your forefathers ate the manna in the
desert, yet they died. 50 But here is the bread that
comes down from heaven, which a man may eat
and not die. 51 I am the living bread that came
down from heaven. If anyone eats of this bread,
he will live forever. This bread is my flesh, which
I will give for the life of the world."

52 Then the Jews began to argue sharply among
themselves, "How can this man give us his flesh
to eat?"

53 Jesus said to them, "I tell you the truth, unless you eat the flesh of the Son of Man and drink
his blood, you have no life in you. 54 Whoever
eats my flesh and drinks my blood has eternal
life, and I will raise him up at the last day. 55 For
my flesh is real food and my blood is real drink.
56 Whoever eats my flesh and drinks my blood
remains in me, and I in him. 57 Just as the living
Father sent me and I live because of the Father,
so the one who feeds on me will live because of
me. 58 This is the bread that came down from
heaven. Your forefathers ate manna and died, but
he who feeds on this bread will live forever."
59 He said this while teaching in the synagogue in
Capernaum.

Many Disciples Desert Jesus

60 On hearing it, many of his disciples said,
"This is a hard teaching. Who can accept it?"

61 Aware that his disciples were grumbling
about this, Jesus said to them, "Does this offend
you? 62 What if you see the Son of Man ascend to
where he was before! 63 The Spirit gives life; the
flesh counts for nothing. The words I have spoken to you are spirit[a] and they are life. 64 Yet
there are some of you who do not believe." For
Jesus had known from the beginning which of
them did not believe and who would betray him.
65 He went on to say, "This is why I told you that
no one can come to me unless the Father has
enabled him."

66 From this time many of his disciples turned
back and no longer followed him.

67 "You do not want to leave too, do you?"
Jesus asked the Twelve.

68 Simon Peter answered him, "Lord, to whom
shall we go? You have the words of eternal life.
69 We believe and know that you are the Holy
One of God."

70 Then Jesus replied, "Have I not chosen you,
the Twelve? Yet one of you is a devil!" 71 (He
meant Judas, the son of Simon Iscariot, who,
though one of the Twelve, was later to betray
him.)

Jesus Goes to the Feast of Tabernacles

7 After this, Jesus went around in Galilee, pur-
posely staying away from Judea because the
Jews there were waiting to take his life. 2 But
when the Jewish Feast of Tabernacles was near,
3 Jesus' brothers said to him, "You ought to leave
here and go to Judea, so that your disciples may
see the miracles you do. 4 No one who wants to
become a public figure acts in secret. Since you
are doing these things, show yourself to the
world." 5 For even his own brothers did not believe in him.

6 Therefore Jesus told them, "The right time for
me has not yet come; for you any time is right.
7 The world cannot hate you, but it hates me because I testify that what it does is evil. 8 You go to
the Feast. I am not yet[b] going up to this Feast,
because for me the right time has not yet come."
9 Having said this, he stayed in Galilee.

10 However, after his brothers had left for the
Feast, he went also, not publicly, but in secret.
11 Now at the Feast the Jews were watching for
him and asking, "Where is that man?"

12 Among the crowds there was widespread
whispering about him. Some said, "He is a good
man."

Others replied, "No, he deceives the people."
13 But no one would say anything publicly about
him for fear of the Jews.

Jesus Teaches at the Feast

14 Not until halfway through the Feast did Jesus
go up to the temple courts and begin to teach.
15 The Jews were amazed and asked, "How did
this man get such learning without having studied?"

16 Jesus answered, "My teaching is not my
own. It comes from him who sent me. 17 If anyone chooses to do God's will, he will find out
whether my teaching comes from God or whether I speak on my own. 18 He who speaks on his
own does so to gain honor for himself, but he
who works for the honor of the one who sent him
is a man of truth; there is nothing false about
him. 19 Has not Moses given you the law? Yet not
one of you keeps the law. Why are you trying to
kill me?"

20 "You are demon-possessed," the crowd answered. "Who is trying to kill you?"

21 Jesus said to them, "I did one miracle, and
you are all astonished. 22 Yet, because Moses gave
you circumcision (though actually it did not come
from Moses, but from the patriarchs), you circumcise a child on the Sabbath. 23 Now if a child
can be circumcised on the Sabbath so that the
law of Moses may not be broken, why are you

[a] 63 Or *Spirit* [b] 8 Some early manuscripts do not have *yet.*

angry with me for healing the whole man on the
Sabbath? 24Stop judging by mere appearances,
and make a right judgment."

Is Jesus the Christ?

25At that point some of the people of Jerusalem
began to ask, "Isn't this the man they are trying
to kill? 26Here he is, speaking publicly, and they
are not saying a word to him. Have the authorities really concluded that he is the Christ[a]?
27But we know where this man is from; when the
Christ comes, no one will know where he is
from."

28Then Jesus, still teaching in the temple
courts, cried out, "Yes, you know me, and you
know where I am from. I am not here on my
own, but he who sent me is true. You do not
know him, 29but I know him because I am from
him and he sent me."

30At this they tried to seize him, but no one
laid a hand on him, because his time had not yet
come. 31Still, many in the crowd put their faith in
him. They said, "When the Christ comes, will he
do more miraculous signs than this man?"

32The Pharisees heard the crowd whispering
such things about him. Then the chief priests and
the Pharisees sent temple guards to arrest him.

33Jesus said, "I am with you for only a short
time, and then I go to the one who sent me.
34You will look for me, but you will not find me;
and where I am, you cannot come."

35The Jews said to one another, "Where does
this man intend to go that we cannot find him?
Will he go where our people live scattered among
the Greeks, and teach the Greeks? 36What did he
mean when he said, 'You will look for me, but
you will not find me,' and 'Where I am, you cannot come'?"

37On the last and greatest day of the Feast,
Jesus stood and said in a loud voice, "If anyone is
thirsty, let him come to me and drink. 38Whoever
believes in me, as[b] the Scripture has said,
streams of living water will flow from within
him." 39By this he meant the Spirit, whom those
who believed in him were later to receive. Up to
that time the Spirit had not been given, since
Jesus had not yet been glorified.

40On hearing his words, some of the people
said, "Surely this man is the Prophet."

41Others said, "He is the Christ."

Still others asked, "How can the Christ come
from Galilee? 42Does not the Scripture say that
the Christ will come from David's family[c] and
from Bethlehem, the town where David lived?"
43Thus the people were divided because of Jesus.
44Some wanted to seize him, but no one laid a
hand on him.

Unbelief of the Jewish Leaders

45Finally the temple guards went back to the
chief priests and Pharisees, who asked them,
"Why didn't you bring him in?"

46"No one ever spoke the way this man does,"
the guards declared.

47"You mean he has deceived you also?" the
Pharisees retorted. 48"Has any of the rulers or of
the Pharisees believed in him? 49No! But this
mob that knows nothing of the law—there is a
curse on them."

50Nicodemus, who had gone to Jesus earlier
and who was one of their own number, asked,
51"Does our law condemn anyone without first
hearing him to find out what he is doing?"

52They replied, "Are you from Galilee, too?
Look into it, and you will find that a prophet[d]
does not come out of Galilee."

[The earliest manuscripts and many other ancient witnesses do not have John 7:53–8:11.]

53Then each went to his own home.

8 But Jesus went to the Mount of Olives. 2At
dawn he appeared again in the temple
courts, where all the people gathered around
him, and he sat down to teach them. 3The teach-

[a]26 Or *Messiah*; also in verses 27, 31, 41 and 42
[b]37,38 Or / *If anyone is thirsty, let him come to me. / And let him drink,* [38]*who believes in me. / As*
[c]42 Greek *seed*
[d]52 Two early manuscripts *the Prophet*

This story, undoubtedly reliable as an actual event, may not have been an original part of this Gospel since in early Greek manuscripts it is found in different locations in John and even in other Gospels.

8:3 ***teachers of the law.*** Ordained teachers who served as representatives of Moses to the people in interpreting his Law. They were taught as rabbis and acted as lawyers in legal cases. ***a woman caught in adultery.*** Since adultery cannot be committed alone, one wonders why only the woman was brought. By rights, both parties could be put to death. Verse 6 reveals that the whole situation (including her partner's escape) had been staged to trap Jesus, with the woman as the expendable object in the plot.

8:6 ***using this question as a trap.*** If Jesus allowed stoning he would be in violation of Roman law, which forbid the Jews from carrying out capital punishment. If he tried to release her, he could be faulted for ignoring the Law of Moses. ***write on the ground.*** One can only speculate what Jesus wrote.

8:7 Jesus forces the initiative back on the accusers. By mentioning a stone, he could not be charged with failing to uphold the Law. But the requirement ("without sin") for throwing it kept anyone from stoning her.

8:11 ***neither do I condemn you.*** The woman came face to face with condemnation and death, but was given pardon by the one to whom all judgment has been given. ***leave your life of sin.*** The woman's sin was not condoned. Change is the evidence of God's grace at work in a person's life.

ers of the law and the Pharisees brought in a
woman caught in adultery. They made her stand
before the group 4and said to Jesus, "Teacher,
this woman was caught in the act of adultery. 5In
the Law Moses commanded us to stone such
women. Now what do you say?" 6They were using this question as a trap, in order to have a basis
for accusing him.

> ### *JOHN 8:1–11*
>
> 1. Who influences you the most on the clothes you wear? Your music? Your values?
> 2. To be a part of the "in" crowd at your school, what are you expected to do? Who do you admire for resisting the crowd?
> 3. How do you treat someone who's been caught doing something wrong? How would you want to be treated?
> 4. How does the way Jesus treats this woman help you face your sins?
> 5. When it comes to going against the crowd, who are the hardest people for you to stand up against?
> 6. How should you help a friend who has "blown it" (see also Gal. 6:1)?
> 7. How do you need to stand up for what is right? How can the group pray for you?
>
> (Study notes on page 972)

But Jesus bent down and started to write on
the ground with his finger. 7When they kept on
questioning him, he straightened up and said to
them, "If any one of you is without sin, let him
be the first to throw a stone at her." 8Again he
stooped down and wrote on the ground.
9At this, those who heard began to go away
one at a time, the older ones first, until only Jesus
was left, with the woman still standing there.
10Jesus straightened up and asked her, "Woman,
where are they? Has no one condemned you?"
11"No one, sir," she said.
"Then neither do I condemn you," Jesus declared. "Go now and leave your life of sin."

The Validity of Jesus' Testimony

12When Jesus spoke again to the people, he
said, "I am the light of the world. Whoever follows me will never walk in darkness, but will
have the light of life."

> ### *JOHN 8:12–20*
>
> 1. Who would you say is "the light of your life"?
> 2. When have you witnessed an accident or crime? Were you called to testify as a witness?
> 3. What do you have in common with your dad? What's something important he taught you?
> 4. What do most of the students in your school believe about God?
> 5. If Jesus is the light of the world (v. 12), what is the darkness?
> 6. What does verse 12 mean to you?
> 7. What's something you will do this week to get closer to God?
> 8. How can the group help you in prayer this week?

8:12 ***the light.*** Jesus is light and "God is light" (1 John 1:5). As Christians reflect the light that comes from Jesus and the Father, they too are "the light of the world" (Matt. 5:14; Phil. 2:15). ***darkness.*** The darkness of this world and that of Satan.

8:14 Jesus responds to the Pharisees, and states that he *is* qualified to bear testimony, whereas they are not. Jesus knows both where he came from and where he is going, whereas they know neither.

8:16–18 Jesus makes a second point to the Pharisees and explains that his testimony is not unsupported. The Father is with him, and so he and the Father are the two witnesses required by the Law (Deut. 17:6).

8:16 ***the Father, who sent me.*** Jesus was always thinking of his mission and the work the Father sent him to do. John often mentions this and how Jesus depended on the Father (4:34; 5:30; 8:26; 9:4; 10:37–38; 12:49–50; 14:31; 15:10; 17:4).

8:19 ***If you knew me, you would know my Father also.*** John writes that the Word (Jesus) was with God and was God (1:1). Jesus stresses that the Father is known through the Son and that to know one is to know the other. Since a person's response to Jesus demonstrates his or her true spiritual condition, this is one way that Jesus does, in a real sense, bring judgment (v. 15).

8:20 ***his time.*** Several other times in the Gospel of John (7:6,8,30) Jesus is pictured moving toward the destiny for which he had come: the time of his sacrificial death on the cross (12:23,27; 13:1; 16:32; 17:1).

13The Pharisees challenged him, "Here you
are, appearing as your own witness; your testimony is not valid."
14Jesus answered, "Even if I testify on my own
behalf, my testimony is valid, for I know where I
came from and where I am going. But you have
no idea where I come from or where I am going.
15You judge by human standards; I pass judgment
on no one. 16But if I do judge, my decisions are
right, because I am not alone. I stand with the
Father, who sent me. 17In your own Law it is
written that the testimony of two men is valid. 18I
am one who testifies for myself; my other witness
is the Father, who sent me."
19Then they asked him, "Where is your father?"
"You do not know me or my Father," Jesus
replied. "If you knew me, you would know my
Father also." 20He spoke these words while
teaching in the temple area near the place where
the offerings were put. Yet no one seized him,
because his time had not yet come.
21Once more Jesus said to them, "I am going
away, and you will look for me, and you will die
in your sin. Where I go, you cannot come."
22This made the Jews ask, "Will he kill himself? Is that why he says, 'Where I go, you cannot
come'?"
23But he continued, "You are from below; I am
from above. You are of this world; I am not of this
world. 24I told you that you would die in your
sins; if you do not believe that I am ⌞the one I
claim to be⌟,[a] you will indeed die in your sins."
25"Who are you?" they asked.
"Just what I have been claiming all along,"
Jesus replied. 26"I have much to say in judgment
of you. But he who sent me is reliable, and what
I have heard from him I tell the world."
27They did not understand that he was telling
them about his Father. 28So Jesus said, "When
you have lifted up the Son of Man, then you will
know that I am ⌞the one I claim to be⌟ and that I
do nothing on my own but speak just what the
Father has taught me. 29The one who sent me is
with me; he has not left me alone, for I always do
what pleases him." 30Even as he spoke, many put
their faith in him.

The Children of Abraham

31To the Jews who had believed him, Jesus
said, "If you hold to my teaching, you are really
my disciples. 32Then you will know the truth,
and the truth will set you free."
33They answered him, "We are Abraham's
descendants[b] and have never been slaves of anyone. How can you say that we shall be set free?"
34Jesus replied, "I tell you the truth, everyone
who sins is a slave to sin. 35Now a slave has no
permanent place in the family, but a son belongs
to it forever. 36So if the Son sets you free, you will
be free indeed. 37I know you are Abraham's
descendants. Yet you are ready to kill me, because you have no room for my word. 38I am
telling you what I have seen in the Father's presence, and you do what you have heard from your
father.[c]"
39"Abraham is our father," they answered.
"If you were Abraham's children," said Jesus,
"then you would[d] do the things Abraham did.
40As it is, you are determined to kill me, a man
who has told you the truth that I heard from God.
Abraham did not do such things. 41You are doing
the things your own father does."
"We are not illegitimate children," they protested. "The only Father we have is God himself."

The Children of the Devil

42Jesus said to them, "If God were your Father,
you would love me, for I came from God and now
am here. I have not come on my own; but he sent
me. 43Why is my language not clear to you? Because you are unable to hear what I say. 44You
belong to your father, the devil, and you want to
carry out your father's desire. He was a murderer
from the beginning, not holding to the truth, for
there is no truth in him. When he lies, he speaks
his native language, for he is a liar and the father
of lies. 45Yet because I tell the truth, you do not
believe me! 46Can any of you prove me guilty of
sin? If I am telling the truth, why don't you believe me? 47He who belongs to God hears what
God says. The reason you do not hear is that you
do not belong to God."

The Claims of Jesus About Himself

48The Jews answered him, "Aren't we right
in saying that you are a Samaritan and demon-
possessed?"
49"I am not possessed by a demon," said Jesus,
"but I honor my Father and you dishonor me. 50I
am not seeking glory for myself; but there is one
who seeks it, and he is the judge. 51I tell you the
truth, if anyone keeps my word, he will never see
death."
52At this the Jews exclaimed, "Now we know
that you are demon-possessed! Abraham died
and so did the prophets, yet you say that if anyone keeps your word, he will never taste death.
53Are you greater than our father Abraham? He
died, and so did the prophets. Who do you think
you are?"
54Jesus replied, "If I glorify myself, my glory
means nothing. My Father, whom you claim as

[a] *24* Or *I am he*; also in verse 28 [b] *33* Greek *seed*; also in verse 37 [c] *38* Or *presence. Therefore do what you have heard from the Father.* [d] *39* Some early manuscripts *"If you are Abraham's children," said Jesus, "then*

your God, is the one who glorifies me. [55]Though you do not know him, I know him. If I said I did not, I would be a liar like you, but I do know him and keep his word. [56]Your father Abraham rejoiced at the thought of seeing my day; he saw it and was glad."

[57]"You are not yet fifty years old," the Jews said to him, "and you have seen Abraham!"

[58]"I tell you the truth," Jesus answered, "before Abraham was born, I am!" [59]At this, they picked up stones to stone him, but Jesus hid himself, slipping away from the temple grounds.

Jesus Heals a Man Born Blind

9 As he went along, he saw a man blind from birth. [2]His disciples asked him, "Rabbi, who sinned, this man or his parents, that he was born blind?"

[3]"Neither this man nor his parents sinned," said Jesus, "but this happened so that the work of God might be displayed in his life. [4]As long as it is day, we must do the work of him who sent me. Night is coming, when no one can work. [5]While I am in the world, I am the light of the world."

[6]Having said this, he spit on the ground, made some mud with the saliva, and put it on the man's eyes. [7]"Go," he told him, "wash in the Pool of Siloam" (this word means Sent). So the man went and washed, and came home seeing.

[8]His neighbors and those who had formerly seen him begging asked, "Isn't this the same man who used to sit and beg?" [9]Some claimed that he was.

Others said, "No, he only looks like him."

But he himself insisted, "I am the man."

[10]"How then were your eyes opened?" they demanded.

[11]He replied, "The man they call Jesus made some mud and put it on my eyes. He told me to go to Siloam and wash. So I went and washed, and then I could see."

[12]"Where is this man?" they asked him.

"I don't know," he said.

The Pharisees Investigate the Healing

[13]They brought to the Pharisees the man who had been blind. [14]Now the day on which Jesus had made the mud and opened the man's eyes was a Sabbath. [15]Therefore the Pharisees also asked him how he had received his sight. "He put mud on my eyes," the man replied, "and I washed, and now I see."

John 9:1–15,24–34

1. What is the longest scar you have on your body? How did you get it?
2. Who do you know who has a chronic illness or disability?
3. What's a "disability" you have that causes you problems?
4. How can a weakness in your life turn into an opportunity for God to show his power?
5. In verse 5, Jesus says, "I am the light of the world." How does this story illustrate this?
6. How would you measure your spiritual vision right now: 20-20? Nearsighted? Farsighted? A few blind spots? Legally blind?
7. Share prayer requests and close by praying for one another.

[16]Some of the Pharisees said, "This man is not from God, for he does not keep the Sabbath."

But others asked, "How can a sinner do such miraculous signs?" So they were divided.

[17]Finally they turned again to the blind man, "What have you to say about him? It was your eyes he opened."

The man replied, "He is a prophet."

[18]The Jews still did not believe that he had been blind and had received his sight until they

---

9:2–3 ***who sinned ... ?*** Despite the book of Job, the rabbis taught that a person's misfortune was the result of his or her direct sin or a punishment inherited for the sins of one's parents. Some taught that such handicaps were a punishment for the sin that the child (or its soul) had committed before birth. ***Neither this man nor his parents sinned.*** Jesus clearly denied these beliefs. He is not pronouncing the family as sinless, but is dismissing the disciples' interest in the *cause* of the man's blindness so that he can focus their attention onto its *purpose.*

9:5–8 ***I am the light of the world.*** See 8:12. This story of healing will enact the meaning of that claim. ***spit on the ground, made some mud.*** Likely to provoke a controversy with the Pharisees, who would see this healing on the Sabbath (v. 16) as a violation of their traditions prohibiting "working" on the Sabbath for three reasons: healing a person when the situation was not life-threatening; making mud; and applying ointment to the eye. ***begging.*** At this time a person who was blind or crippled had little choice other than to be a beggar.

9:25 ***One thing I do know.*** The formerly blind man refuses to give in to the prejudice of the Pharisees, but insists their formulations just do not account for his experience.

9:34 ***You were steeped in sin at birth.*** The Pharisees still see the man in the same way Jesus' disciples did in verse 2. However, if his blindness was a result of his being "steeped in sin," how do they account for the fact that he now is able to see?! ***threw him out.*** Probably excommunicating him from Judaism (see v. 22).

sent for the man’s parents. 19“Is this your son?”
they asked. “Is this the one you say was born
blind? How is it that now he can see?”
20“We know he is our son,” the parents answered, “and we know he was born blind. 21But
how he can see now, or who opened his eyes, we
don’t know. Ask him. He is of age; he will speak
for himself.” 22His parents said this because they
were afraid of the Jews, for already the Jews had
decided that anyone who acknowledged that
Jesus was the Christ[a] would be put out of the
synagogue. 23That was why his parents said, “He
is of age; ask him.”
24A second time they summoned the man who
had been blind. “Give glory to God,[b]” they said.
“We know this man is a sinner.”
25He replied, “Whether he is a sinner or not,
I don’t know. One thing I do know. I was blind
but now I see!”
26Then they asked him, “What did he do to
you? How did he open your eyes?”
27He answered, “I have told you already and
you did not listen. Why do you want to hear it
again? Do you want to become his disciples,
too?”
28Then they hurled insults at him and said,
“You are this fellow’s disciple! We are disciples of
Moses! 29We know that God spoke to Moses, but
as for this fellow, we don’t even know where he
comes from.”
30The man answered, “Now that is remarkable! You don’t know where he comes from,
yet he opened my eyes. 31We know that God
does not listen to sinners. He listens to the godly man who does his will. 32Nobody has ever
heard of opening the eyes of a man born blind.
33If this man were not from God, he could do
nothing.”
34To this they replied, “You were steeped in
sin at birth; how dare you lecture us!” And they
threw him out.

Spiritual Blindness

35Jesus heard that they had thrown him out,
and when he found him, he said, “Do you believe
in the Son of Man?”
36“Who is he, sir?” the man asked. “Tell me so
that I may believe in him.”
37Jesus said, “You have now seen him; in fact,
he is the one speaking with you.”
38Then the man said, “Lord, I believe,” and he
worshiped him.
39Jesus said, “For judgment I have come into
this world, so that the blind will see and those
who see will become blind.”
40Some Pharisees who were with him heard
him say this and asked, “What? Are we blind
too?”
41Jesus said, “If you were blind, you would not
be guilty of sin; but now that you claim you can
see, your guilt remains.

The Shepherd and His Flock

10 “I tell you the truth, the man who does
not enter the sheep pen by the gate, but
climbs in by some other way, is a thief and a
robber. 2The man who enters by the gate is the
shepherd of his sheep. 3The watchman opens the
gate for him, and the sheep listen to his voice. He
calls his own sheep by name and leads them out.
4When he has brought out all his own, he goes on
ahead of them, and his sheep follow him because
they know his voice. 5But they will never follow a stranger; in fact, they will run away from
him because they do not recognize a stranger’s
voice.” 6Jesus used this figure of speech, but they
did not understand what he was telling them.
7Therefore Jesus said again, “I tell you the
truth, I am the gate for the sheep. 8All who ever
came before me were thieves and robbers, but
the sheep did not listen to them. 9I am the gate;
whoever enters through me will be saved.[c] He
will come in and go out, and find pasture. 10The
thief comes only to steal and kill and destroy; I
have come that they may have life, and have it to
the full.
11“I am the good shepherd. The good shepherd lays down his life for the sheep. 12The hired
hand is not the shepherd who owns the sheep. So
when he sees the wolf coming, he abandons the
sheep and runs away. Then the wolf attacks the
flock and scatters it. 13The man runs away because he is a hired hand and cares nothing for the
sheep.
14“I am the good shepherd; I know my sheep
and my sheep know me— 15just as the Father
knows me and I know the Father—and I lay
down my life for the sheep. 16I have other sheep
that are not of this sheep pen. I must bring them
also. They too will listen to my voice, and there
shall be one flock and one shepherd. 17The reason my Father loves me is that I lay down my
life—only to take it up again. 18No one takes it
from me, but I lay it down of my own accord. I
have authority to lay it down and authority to
take it up again. This command I received from
my Father.”
19At these words the Jews were again divided.
20Many of them said, “He is demon-possessed
and raving mad. Why listen to him?”
21But others said, “These are not the sayings of
a man possessed by a demon. Can a demon open
the eyes of the blind?”

[a]22 Or *Messiah* [b]24 A solemn charge to tell the truth (see Joshua 7:19) [c]9 Or *kept safe*

The Unbelief of the Jews

22 Then came the Feast of Dedication[a] at Jerusalem. It was winter, 23 and Jesus was in the temple area walking in Solomon's Colonnade. 24 The Jews gathered around him, saying, "How long will you keep us in suspense? If you are the Christ,[b] tell us plainly."

25 Jesus answered, "I did tell you, but you do not believe. The miracles I do in my Father's name speak for me, 26 but you do not believe because you are not my sheep. 27 My sheep listen to my voice; I know them, and they follow me. 28 I give them eternal life, and they shall never perish; no one can snatch them out of my hand. 29 My Father, who has given them to me, is greater than all[c]; no one can snatch them out of my Father's hand. 30 I and the Father are one."

31 Again the Jews picked up stones to stone him, 32 but Jesus said to them, "I have shown you many great miracles from the Father. For which of these do you stone me?"

33 "We are not stoning you for any of these," replied the Jews, "but for blasphemy, because you, a mere man, claim to be God."

34 Jesus answered them, "Is it not written in your Law, 'I have said you are gods'[d]? 35 If he called them 'gods,' to whom the word of God came—and the Scripture cannot be broken—36 what about the one whom the Father set apart as his very own and sent into the world? Why then do you accuse me of blasphemy because I said, 'I am God's Son'? 37 Do not believe me unless I do what my Father does. 38 But if I do it, even though you do not believe me, believe the miracles, that you may know and understand that the Father is in me, and I in the Father." 39 Again they tried to seize him, but he escaped their grasp.

40 Then Jesus went back across the Jordan to the place where John had been baptizing in the early days. Here he stayed 41 and many people came to him. They said, "Though John never performed a miraculous sign, all that John said about this man was true." 42 And in that place many believed in Jesus.

The Death of Lazarus

11 Now a man named Lazarus was sick. He was from Bethany, the village of Mary and her sister Martha. 2 This Mary, whose brother Lazarus now lay sick, was the same one who poured perfume on the Lord and wiped his feet with her hair. 3 So the sisters sent word to Jesus, "Lord, the one you love is sick."

4 When he heard this, Jesus said, "This sickness will not end in death. No, it is for God's glory so that God's Son may be glorified through it." 5 Jesus loved Martha and her sister and Lazarus. 6 Yet when he heard that Lazarus was sick, he stayed where he was two more days.

7 Then he said to his disciples, "Let us go back to Judea."

8 "But Rabbi," they said, "a short while ago the Jews tried to stone you, and yet you are going back there?"

9 Jesus answered, "Are there not twelve hours of daylight? A man who walks by day will not stumble, for he sees by this world's light. 10 It is when he walks by night that he stumbles, for he has no light."

11 After he had said this, he went on to tell them, "Our friend Lazarus has fallen asleep; but I am going there to wake him up."

12 His disciples replied, "Lord, if he sleeps, he will get better." 13 Jesus had been speaking of his death, but his disciples thought he meant natural sleep.

14 So then he told them plainly, "Lazarus is dead, 15 and for your sake I am glad I was not there, so that you may believe. But let us go to him."

16 Then Thomas (called Didymus) said to the rest of the disciples, "Let us also go, that we may die with him."

Jesus Comforts the Sisters

17 On his arrival, Jesus found that Lazarus had already been in the tomb for four days. 18 Bethany was less than two miles[e] from Jerusalem, 19 and many Jews had come to Martha and Mary to comfort them in the loss of their brother. 20 When Martha heard that Jesus was coming, she went out to meet him, but Mary stayed at home.

21 "Lord," Martha said to Jesus, "if you had been here, my brother would not have died. 22 But I know that even now God will give you whatever you ask."

23 Jesus said to her, "Your brother will rise again."

24 Martha answered, "I know he will rise again in the resurrection at the last day."

25 Jesus said to her, "I am the resurrection and the life. He who believes in me will live, even though he dies; 26 and whoever lives and believes in me will never die. Do you believe this?"

27 "Yes, Lord," she told him, "I believe that you are the Christ,[b] the Son of God, who was to come into the world."

28 And after she had said this, she went back and called her sister Mary aside. "The Teacher is

[a] 22 That is, Hanukkah [b] 24,27 Or *Messiah* [c] 29 Many early manuscripts *What my Father has given me is greater than all*
[d] 34 Psalm 82:6 [e] 18 Greek *fifteen stadia* (about 3 kilometers)

here," she said, "and is asking for you." 29When
Mary heard this, she got up quickly and went to
him. 30Now Jesus had not yet entered the village,
but was still at the place where Martha had met
him. 31When the Jews who had been with Mary
in the house, comforting her, noticed how quickly she got up and went out, they followed her,
supposing she was going to the tomb to mourn
there.

John 11:17–44

1. What was the last funeral you attended? What was it like?
2. How do your friends who don't believe in Christ and the resurrection react when someone they know dies?
3. Who's the closest person to you who has died or is dying?
4. How could you use this story (especially verse 25) to help someone who is facing death?
5. When did you come to a personal belief in the resurrection from the dead of all who have put their faith in Christ?
6. What have you found helpful when tragedy strikes and your friends are really hurting?
7. Close in prayer. Lift up and comfort those who are hurting.

32When Mary reached the place where Jesus
was and saw him, she fell at his feet and said,
"Lord, if you had been here, my brother would
not have died."
33When Jesus saw her weeping, and the Jews
who had come along with her also weeping, he
was deeply moved in spirit and troubled.
34"Where have you laid him?" he asked.
"Come and see, Lord," they replied.
35Jesus wept.
36Then the Jews said, "See how he loved
him!"
37But some of them said, "Could not he who
opened the eyes of the blind man have kept this
man from dying?"

Jesus Raises Lazarus From the Dead

38Jesus, once more deeply moved, came to the
tomb. It was a cave with a stone laid across the
entrance. 39"Take away the stone," he said.
"But, Lord," said Martha, the sister of the dead
man, "by this time there is a bad odor, for he has
been there four days."
40Then Jesus said, "Did I not tell you that
if you believed, you would see the glory of
God?"
41So they took away the stone. Then Jesus
looked up and said, "Father, I thank you that you
have heard me. 42I knew that you always hear
me, but I said this for the benefit of the people
standing here, that they may believe that you
sent me."
43When he had said this, Jesus called in a loud
voice, "Lazarus, come out!" 44The dead man
came out, his hands and feet wrapped with strips
of linen, and a cloth around his face.
Jesus said to them, "Take off the grave clothes
and let him go."

The Plot to Kill Jesus

45Therefore many of the Jews who had come
to visit Mary, and had seen what Jesus did, put
their faith in him. 46But some of them went to
the Pharisees and told them what Jesus had done.
47Then the chief priests and the Pharisees called
a meeting of the Sanhedrin.
"What are we accomplishing?" they asked.
"Here is this man performing many miraculous
signs. 48If we let him go on like this, everyone
will believe in him, and then the Romans will

Jesus has received a message from Martha and Mary that their brother was sick (v. 1). Though he dearly loved this family, he did not go immediately upon receiving the message, which the disciples assumed was because the Jewish religious leaders back in Judea had tried to kill him (vv. 5–8). But the real reason was that Jesus' agenda was set neither by himself nor by the desires of those he loves, but by the Father. Along this line, Jesus knew he would be "glorified" (v. 4) both through raising Lazarus from the dead (v. 40) and because this would help set in motion events leading to the cross (vv. 46–53).

11:17 ***four days.*** By the time Jesus reaches Bethany, Lazarus is well and truly dead, so that the body has begun to decompose in the hot middle-eastern climate (see v. 39).

11:25 ***I am the resurrection and the life.*** This claim would jar anyone at a funeral! Jesus focuses Martha's attention, not on the general resurrection (v. 24), but on him as the source of that resurrection. ***will live, even though he dies.*** This is spiritual life that will not end at physical death. Jesus asserts his power over death. Lazarus' resurrection will dramatically validate his claim.

11:33–35 ***her weeping.*** This word indicates "wailing"—a loud expression of grief. ***Jesus wept.*** This word connotes a quiet form of weeping. Being "deeply moved in spirit," Jesus' weeping reflects God's sorrow over the reality of death as it affects his people.

11:44 ***strips of linen.*** Burial customs included wrapping the body with cloth (John 19:40). ***grave clothes.*** In contrast, Jesus' grave clothes were left behind in the tomb (John 20:6–7). Lazarus' coming to life only robbed death for a time: Jesus' resurrection spells the ultimate defeat of death's power.

come and take away both our place[a] and our
nation."
[49]Then one of them, named Caiaphas, who
was high priest that year, spoke up, "You know
nothing at all! [50]You do not realize that it is better
for you that one man die for the people than that
the whole nation perish."
[51]He did not say this on his own, but as high
priest that year he prophesied that Jesus would
die for the Jewish nation, [52]and not only for that
nation but also for the scattered children of God,
to bring them together and make them one. [53]So
from that day on they plotted to take his life.
[54]Therefore Jesus no longer moved about publicly among the Jews. Instead he withdrew to a
region near the desert, to a village called Ephraim, where he stayed with his disciples.
[55]When it was almost time for the Jewish Passover, many went up from the country to Jerusalem for their ceremonial cleansing before the
Passover. [56]They kept looking for Jesus, and as
they stood in the temple area they asked one
another, "What do you think? Isn't he coming to
the Feast at all?" [57]But the chief priests and Pharisees had given orders that if anyone found out
where Jesus was, he should report it so that they
might arrest him.

Jesus Anointed at Bethany

12 Six days before the Passover, Jesus arrived at Bethany, where Lazarus lived,
whom Jesus had raised from the dead. [2]Here a
dinner was given in Jesus' honor. Martha served,
while Lazarus was among those reclining at the
table with him. [3]Then Mary took about a pint[b]
of pure nard, an expensive perfume; she poured
it on Jesus' feet and wiped his feet with her hair.
And the house was filled with the fragrance of
the perfume.
[4]But one of his disciples, Judas Iscariot, who
was later to betray him, objected, [5]"Why wasn't
this perfume sold and the money given to the
poor? It was worth a year's wages.[c]" [6]He did
not say this because he cared about the poor but
because he was a thief; as keeper of the money
bag, he used to help himself to what was put
into it.
[7]"Leave her alone," Jesus replied. "⌞It was in-
tended⌟ that she should save this perfume for the
day of my burial. [8]You will always have the poor
among you, but you will not always have me."
[9]Meanwhile a large crowd of Jews found out
that Jesus was there and came, not only because
of him but also to see Lazarus, whom he had
raised from the dead. [10]So the chief priests made
plans to kill Lazarus as well, [11]for on account of
him many of the Jews were going over to Jesus
and putting their faith in him.

The Triumphal Entry

[12]The next day the great crowd that had come
for the Feast heard that Jesus was on his way to
Jerusalem. [13]They took palm branches and went
out to meet him, shouting,

"Hosanna![d]"

"Blessed is he who comes in the name of the
Lord!"[e]

"Blessed is the King of Israel!"

[14]Jesus found a young donkey and sat upon it, as
it is written,

[15]"Do not be afraid, O Daughter of Zion;
see, your king is coming,
seated on a donkey's colt."[f]

[16]At first his disciples did not understand all
this. Only after Jesus was glorified did they realize that these things had been written about him
and that they had done these things to him.
[17]Now the crowd that was with him when he
called Lazarus from the tomb and raised him from
the dead continued to spread the word. [18]Many
people, because they had heard that he had given
this miraculous sign, went out to meet him. [19]So
the Pharisees said to one another, "See, this is
getting us nowhere. Look how the whole world
has gone after him!"

Jesus Predicts His Death

[20]Now there were some Greeks among those
who went up to worship at the Feast. [21]They
came to Philip, who was from Bethsaida in Galilee, with a request. "Sir," they said, "we would
like to see Jesus." [22]Philip went to tell Andrew;
Andrew and Philip in turn told Jesus.
[23]Jesus replied, "The hour has come for the
Son of Man to be glorified. [24]I tell you the truth,
unless a kernel of wheat falls to the ground and
dies, it remains only a single seed. But if it dies,
it produces many seeds. [25]The man who loves his
life will lose it, while the man who hates his life
in this world will keep it for eternal life. [26]Who-
ever serves me must follow me; and where I am,
my servant also will be. My Father will honor the
one who serves me.
[27]"Now my heart is troubled, and what shall I
say? 'Father, save me from this hour'? No, it was
for this very reason I came to this hour. [28]Father,
glorify your name!"
Then a voice came from heaven, "I have glorified it, and will glorify it again." [29]The crowd that

a48 Or *temple* b3 Greek *a litra* (probably about 0.5 liter) c5 Greek *three hundred denarii* d13 A Hebrew expression meaning "Save!" which became an exclamation of praise e13 Psalm 118:25, 26 f15 Zech. 9:9

was there and heard it said it had thundered;
others said an angel had spoken to him.
30Jesus said, "This voice was for your benefit,
not mine. 31Now is the time for judgment on this
world; now the prince of this world will be driv-
en out. 32But I, when I am lifted up from the
earth, will draw all men to myself." 33He said this
to show the kind of death he was going to die.
34The crowd spoke up, "We have heard from
the Law that the Christ[a] will remain forever, so
how can you say, 'The Son of Man must be lifted
up'? Who is this 'Son of Man'?"
35Then Jesus told them, "You are going to have
the light just a little while longer. Walk while you
have the light, before darkness overtakes you.
The man who walks in the dark does not know
where he is going. 36Put your trust in the light
while you have it, so that you may become sons
of light." When he had finished speaking, Jesus
left and hid himself from them.

The Jews Continue in Their Unbelief

37Even after Jesus had done all these miraculous signs in their presence, they still would not
believe in him. 38This was to fulfill the word of
Isaiah the prophet:

"Lord, who has believed our message
and to whom has the arm of the Lord
been revealed?"[b]

39For this reason they could not believe, because, as Isaiah says elsewhere:

40"He has blinded their eyes
and deadened their hearts,
so they can neither see with their eyes,
nor understand with their hearts,
nor turn—and I would heal them."[c]

41Isaiah said this because he saw Jesus' glory and
spoke about him.
42Yet at the same time many even among the
leaders believed in him. But because of the Pharisees they would not confess their faith for fear
they would be put out of the synagogue; 43for
they loved praise from men more than praise
from God.
44Then Jesus cried out, "When a man believes
in me, he does not believe in me only, but in the
one who sent me. 45When he looks at me, he
sees the one who sent me. 46I have come into the
world as a light, so that no one who believes in
me should stay in darkness.
47"As for the person who hears my words but
does not keep them, I do not judge him. For I
did not come to judge the world, but to save it.
48There is a judge for the one who rejects me and
does not accept my words; that very word which
I spoke will condemn him at the last day. 49For I
did not speak of my own accord, but the Father
who sent me commanded me what to say and
how to say it. 50I know that his command leads to
eternal life. So whatever I say is just what the
Father has told me to say."

Jesus Washes His Disciples' Feet

13 It was just before the Passover Feast.
Jesus knew that the time had come for
him to leave this world and go to the Father.
Having loved his own who were in the world, he
now showed them the full extent of his love.[d]
2The evening meal was being served, and the
devil had already prompted Judas Iscariot, son of
Simon, to betray Jesus. 3Jesus knew that the Father had put all things under his power, and that
he had come from God and was returning to God;
4so he got up from the meal, took off his outer
clothing, and wrapped a towel around his waist.
5After that, he poured water into a basin and
began to wash his disciples' feet, drying them
with the towel that was wrapped around him.

JOHN 13:1–17

1. Who cleans the toilet where you live? When it comes to housework, what's the *last* job you would do?
2. Who do you know whom you would nominate for the "Mother Teresa Award" for loving, tireless service?
3. What service has someone done for you that demonstrated their love? What's something you have done?
4. Why did Jesus wash the disciples' feet? What does he mean by "wash one another's feet" (v. 14)?
5. How would you compare your view of a leader to the model of leadership that Christ demonstrated in this passage?
6. On a scale of 1 (I don't do windows!) to 10 (How may I help you?), rank yourself on having a servant's heart.
7. Who is someone you will show God's love to this week through service? How? Pray together.

(Study notes on page 981)

[a]34 Or *Messiah* [b]38 Isaiah 53:1 [c]40 Isaiah 6:10 [d]1 Or *he loved them to the last*

6He came to Simon Peter, who said to him,
"Lord, are you going to wash my feet?"
7Jesus replied, "You do not realize now what I
am doing, but later you will understand."
8"No," said Peter, "you shall never wash my
feet."
Jesus answered, "Unless I wash you, you have
no part with me."
9"Then, Lord," Simon Peter replied, "not just
my feet but my hands and my head as well!"
10Jesus answered, "A person who has had a
bath needs only to wash his feet; his whole body
is clean. And you are clean, though not every one
of you." 11For he knew who was going to betray
him, and that was why he said not every one was
clean.
12When he had finished washing their feet, he
put on his clothes and returned to his place. "Do
you understand what I have done for you?" he
asked them. 13"You call me 'Teacher' and 'Lord,'
and rightly so, for that is what I am. 14Now that
I, your Lord and Teacher, have washed your feet,
you also should wash one another's feet. 15I have
set you an example that you should do as I have
done for you. 16I tell you the truth, no servant is
greater than his master, nor is a messenger greater than the one who sent him. 17Now that you
know these things, you will be blessed if you do
them.

Jesus Predicts His Betrayal

18"I am not referring to all of you; I know those
I have chosen. But this is to fulfill the scripture:
'He who shares my bread has lifted up his heel
against me.'[a]
19"I am telling you now before it happens, so
that when it does happen you will believe that I
am He. 20I tell you the truth, whoever accepts
anyone I send accepts me; and whoever accepts
me accepts the one who sent me."
21After he had said this, Jesus was troubled in
spirit and testified, "I tell you the truth, one of
you is going to betray me."
22His disciples stared at one another, at a loss
to know which of them he meant. 23One of them,
the disciple whom Jesus loved, was reclining
next to him. 24Simon Peter motioned to this disciple and said, "Ask him which one he means."
25Leaning back against Jesus, he asked him,
"Lord, who is it?"
26Jesus answered, "It is the one to whom I will
give this piece of bread when I have dipped it in
the dish." Then, dipping the piece of bread, he
gave it to Judas Iscariot, son of Simon. 27As soon
as Judas took the bread, Satan entered into him.
"What you are about to do, do quickly," Jesus
told him, 28but no one at the meal understood
why Jesus said this to him. 29Since Judas had
charge of the money, some thought Jesus was
telling him to buy what was needed for the Feast,
or to give something to the poor. 30As soon as
Judas had taken the bread, he went out. And it
was night.

Jesus Predicts Peter's Denial

31When he was gone, Jesus said, "Now is the
Son of Man glorified and God is glorified in him.
32If God is glorified in him,[b] God will glorify the
Son in himself, and will glorify him at once.
33"My children, I will be with you only a little
longer. You will look for me, and just as I told the
Jews, so I tell you now: Where I am going, you
cannot come.
34"A new command I give you: Love one another. As I have loved you, so you must love one
another. 35By this all men will know that you are
my disciples, if you love one another."
36Simon Peter asked him, "Lord, where are
you going?"
Jesus replied, "Where I am going, you cannot
follow now, but you will follow later."
37Peter asked, "Lord, why can't I follow you
now? I will lay down my life for you."
38Then Jesus answered, "Will you really lay
down your life for me? I tell you the truth, before
the rooster crows, you will disown me three
times!

[a] *18* Psalm 41:9 [b] *32* Many early manuscripts do not have *If God is glorified in him.*

13:1 *knew.* Three times in this story John emphasizes the fact that Jesus knew his end was approaching (also vv. 3 and 11). It was in full awareness of his identity and mission that he washed the disciples' feet. His serving would culminate on the cross.

13:4–8 Normally before a meal was served, people's dusty, sandaled feet were washed by the lowest-ranking servant of the household. There was no servant in this instance, and no one else volunteered. Peter, recognizing the impropriety of a master washing the feet of his servant, protests.

13:8–10 *Unless I wash you.* Although it could not be fully understood at the time, the image of being "cleansed" by Jesus became a common picture of what it meant to be forgiven of sin. ***only to wash his feet.*** Jesus uses the picture of a person who, after washing completely, travels somewhere. Upon arrival, only his feet need be washed. ***though not every one of you.*** Jesus was preparing them for his startling announcement in verse 21 that one of them would betray him.

13:12–15 Jesus provides an immediate interpretation of his action. The disciples are to emulate his act of service for one another without regard to titles or status. Though some Christians feel Jesus was instituting an ongoing footwashing ordinance, most see his action as an example.

13:17 *blessed.* "Happy" would be a better choice here. The word carries the sense of emotional joy that the word "happy" conveys. This mutual servanthood of the disciples, precisely because it is concerned with the well-being of others, is what will produce happiness in their community.

Jesus Comforts His Disciples

14 "Do not let your hearts be troubled. Trust in God[a]; trust also in me. [2]In my Father's house are many rooms; if it were not so, I would have told you. I am going there to prepare a place for you. [3]And if I go and prepare a place for you, I will come back and take you to be with me that you also may be where I am. [4]You know the way to the place where I am going."

Jesus the Way to the Father

[5]Thomas said to him, "Lord, we don't know where you are going, so how can we know the way?"

[6]Jesus answered, "I am the way and the truth and the life. No one comes to the Father except through me. [7]If you really knew me, you would know[b] my Father as well. From now on, you do know him and have seen him."

[8]Philip said, "Lord, show us the Father and that will be enough for us."

[9]Jesus answered: "Don't you know me, Philip, even after I have been among you such a long time? Anyone who has seen me has seen the Father. How can you say, 'Show us the Father'? [10]Don't you believe that I am in the Father, and that the Father is in me? The words I say to you are not just my own. Rather, it is the Father, living in me, who is doing his work. [11]Believe me when I say that I am in the Father and the Father is in me; or at least believe on the evidence of the miracles themselves. [12]I tell you the truth, anyone who has faith in me will do what I have been doing. He will do even greater things than these, because I am going to the Father. [13]And I will do whatever you ask in my name, so that the Son may bring glory to the Father. [14]You may ask me for anything in my name, and I will do it.

Jesus Promises the Holy Spirit

[15]"If you love me, you will obey what I command. [16]And I will ask the Father, and he will give you another Counselor to be with you forever— [17]the Spirit of truth. The world cannot accept him, because it neither sees him nor knows him. But you know him, for he lives with you and will be[c] in you. [18]I will not leave you as orphans; I will come to you. [19]Before long, the world will not see me anymore, but you will see me. Because I live, you also will live. [20]On that day you will realize that I am in my Father, and you are in me, and I am in you. [21]Whoever has my commands and obeys them, he is the one

JOHN 14:15–27

1. If you had to go away for a long time, what would you leave your best friend to remember you by?
2. Who would you go to for counsel if you were facing a critical decision that would affect the rest of your life?
3. If you were in charge of a spiritual "boot camp" for the students in your school, what would you drill into these students to help them in the battles they will have to face?
4. What do you learn about the Holy Spirit in verses 16–17 and 25–27?
5. When have you (or someone you know) stood up for the truth (v. 17) even though it was the unpopular thing to do?
6. In your life, what is the difference between how Jesus gives peace (v. 27) and how the world does?
7. On a scale from 1 (smooth sailing) to 10 (furious storm), what is your peace quotient? Where do you need Jesus' peace?
8. How can this group pray for you?

[a] *1* Or *You trust in God and is* [b] *7* Some early manuscripts *If you really have known me, you will know* [c] *17* Some early manuscripts

14:16 *another Counselor.* The Greek term *paraclete* is a rich term for which there is no sufficient English translation. Attempts such as "Counselor" or "Helper" or "Comforter" fail because they emphasize only one of many aspects of the term. "... the Paraclete is a *witness* in defense of Jesus and a *spokesman* for him in the context of his trial ... (he) is a *counselor* of the disciples for he takes Jesus' place among them; (he) is a *teacher* and guide of the disciples and thus their *helper*" (Brown).

14:17 *the Spirit of truth.* As Jesus is the truth (John 14:6), so the one he sends brings truth to the disciples. See also John 16:13.

14:21 *obeys ... loves.* Love for Christ and obeying his commands cannot be separated.

14:26 *will teach you / remind you.* These parallel verbs are two ways of saying the same thing. The purpose of the teaching of the Spirit is not to impart new information, but to remind believers of the truth Jesus taught and helped them apply it to ever-changing situations. This has been illustrated several times in the Gospel of John already (2:22; 7:39; 13:7). Just as Jesus spoke only the words of the Father (v. 24), so the Spirit will speak only the words of Jesus.

14:27 *Peace.* In Ezekiel 37:26 God calls the covenant that he will establish with his people a "covenant of peace." Jesus is instituting this covenant here. His peace involves an invigorating, life-giving fullness, security and purpose that nothing in the world can give.

who loves me. He who loves me will be loved by
my Father, and I too will love him and show
myself to him."
[22]Then Judas (not Judas Iscariot) said, "But,
Lord, why do you intend to show yourself to us
and not to the world?"
[23]Jesus replied, "If anyone loves me, he will
obey my teaching. My Father will love him, and
we will come to him and make our home with
him. [24]He who does not love me will not obey my
teaching. These words you hear are not my own;
they belong to the Father who sent me.
[25]"All this I have spoken while still with you.
[26]But the Counselor, the Holy Spirit, whom the
Father will send in my name, will teach you all
things and will remind you of everything I have
said to you. [27]Peace I leave with you; my peace I
give you. I do not give to you as the world gives.
Do not let your hearts be troubled and do not be
afraid.
[28]"You heard me say, 'I am going away and I
am coming back to you.' If you loved me, you
would be glad that I am going to the Father, for
the Father is greater than I. [29]I have told you now
before it happens, so that when it does happen
you will believe. [30]I will not speak with you
much longer, for the prince of this world is coming. He has no hold on me, [31]but the world must
learn that I love the Father and that I do exactly
what my Father has commanded me.
"Come now; let us leave.

The Vine and the Branches

15 "I am the true vine, and my Father is the
gardener. [2]He cuts off every branch in me
that bears no fruit, while every branch that does
bear fruit he prunes[a] so that it will be even
more fruitful. [3]You are already clean because of
the word I have spoken to you. [4]Remain in me,
and I will remain in you. No branch can bear fruit
by itself; it must remain in the vine. Neither can
you bear fruit unless you remain in me.
[5]"I am the vine; you are the branches. If a man
remains in me and I in him, he will bear much
fruit; apart from me you can do nothing. [6]If anyone does not remain in me, he is like a branch
that is thrown away and withers; such branches
are picked up, thrown into the fire and burned.
[7]If you remain in me and my words remain in
you, ask whatever you wish, and it will be given
you. [8]This is to my Father's glory, that you bear
much fruit, showing yourselves to be my disciples.
[9]"As the Father has loved me, so have I loved
you. Now remain in my love. [10]If you obey my
commands, you will remain in my love, just as I
have obeyed my Father's commands and remain
in his love. [11]I have told you this so that my joy
may be in you and that your joy may be complete.
[12]My command is this: Love each other as I have
loved you. [13]Greater love has no one than this,
that he lay down his life for his friends. [14]You are
my friends if you do what I command. [15]I no
longer call you servants, because a servant does
not know his master's business. Instead, I have
called you friends, for everything that I learned
from my Father I have made known to you. [16]You
did not choose me, but I chose you and appointed
you to go and bear fruit—fruit that will last.
Then the Father will give you whatever you ask
in my name. [17]This is my command: Love each
other.

The World Hates the Disciples

[18]"If the world hates you, keep in mind that it
hated me first. [19]If you belonged to the world, it
would love you as its own. As it is, you do not
belong to the world, but I have chosen you out of
the world. That is why the world hates you. [20]Re-
member the words I spoke to you: 'No servant is
greater than his master.'[b] If they persecuted me,
they will persecute you also. If they obeyed my
teaching, they will obey yours also. [21]They will
treat you this way because of my name, for they
do not know the One who sent me. [22]If I had not
come and spoken to them, they would not be
guilty of sin. Now, however, they have no excuse
for their sin. [23]He who hates me hates my Father
as well. [24]If I had not done among them what no
one else did, they would not be guilty of sin. But
now they have seen these miracles, and yet they
have hated both me and my Father. [25]But this is
to fulfill what is written in their Law: 'They hated
me without reason.'[c]
[26]"When the Counselor comes, whom I will
send to you from the Father, the Spirit of truth
who goes out from the Father, he will testify
about me. [27]And you also must testify, for you
have been with me from the beginning.

16 "All this I have told you so that you will
not go astray. [2]They will put you out of
the synagogue; in fact, a time is coming when
anyone who kills you will think he is offering a
service to God. [3]They will do such things because
they have not known the Father or me. [4]I have
told you this, so that when the time comes you
will remember that I warned you. I did not tell
you this at first because I was with you.

The Work of the Holy Spirit

[5]"Now I am going to him who sent me, yet
none of you asks me, 'Where are you going?'
[6]Because I have said these things, you are filled
with grief. [7]But I tell you the truth: It is for your

[a]2 The Greek for *prunes* also means *cleans*. [b]20 John 13:16 [c]25 Psalms 35:19; 69:4

good that I am going away. Unless I go away, the
Counselor will not come to you; but if I go, I will
send him to you. 8When he comes, he will convict the world of guilt[a] in regard to sin and righteousness and judgment: 9in regard to sin, because men do not believe in me; 10in regard to
righteousness, because I am going to the Father,
where you can see me no longer; 11and in regard
to judgment, because the prince of this world
now stands condemned.
12"I have much more to say to you, more than
you can now bear. 13But when he, the Spirit of
truth, comes, he will guide you into all truth. He
will not speak on his own; he will speak only
what he hears, and he will tell you what is yet to
come. 14He will bring glory to me by taking from
what is mine and making it known to you. 15All
that belongs to the Father is mine. That is why I
said the Spirit will take from what is mine and
make it known to you.
16"In a little while you will see me no more,
and then after a little while you will see me."

The Disciples' Grief Will Turn to Joy

17Some of his disciples said to one another,
"What does he mean by saying, 'In a little while
you will see me no more, and then after a little
while you will see me,' and 'Because I am going
to the Father'?" 18They kept asking, "What does
he mean by 'a little while'? We don't understand
what he is saying."
19Jesus saw that they wanted to ask him about
this, so he said to them, "Are you asking one
another what I meant when I said, 'In a little
while you will see me no more, and then after
a little while you will see me'? 20I tell you the
truth, you will weep and mourn while the world
rejoices. You will grieve, but your grief will turn
to joy. 21A woman giving birth to a child has pain
because her time has come; but when her baby is
born she forgets the anguish because of her joy
that a child is born into the world. 22So with you:
Now is your time of grief, but I will see you again
and you will rejoice, and no one will take away
your joy. 23In that day you will no longer ask me
anything. I tell you the truth, my Father will give
you whatever you ask in my name. 24Until now
you have not asked for anything in my name. Ask
and you will receive, and your joy will be complete.
25"Though I have been speaking figuratively, a
time is coming when I will no longer use this
kind of language but will tell you plainly about my
Father. 26In that day you will ask in my name. I
am not saying that I will ask the Father on your
behalf. 27No, the Father himself loves you because you have loved me and have believed that
I came from God. 28I came from the Father and
entered the world; now I am leaving the world
and going back to the Father."
29Then Jesus' disciples said, "Now you are
speaking clearly and without figures of speech.
30Now we can see that you know all things and
that you do not even need to have anyone ask you
questions. This makes us believe that you came
from God."
31"You believe at last!"[b] Jesus answered.
32"But a time is coming, and has come, when you
will be scattered, each to his own home. You will
leave me all alone. Yet I am not alone, for my
Father is with me.
33"I have told you these things, so that in me
you may have peace. In this world you will have
trouble. But take heart! I have overcome the
world."

Jesus Prays for Himself

17 After Jesus said this, he looked toward
heaven and prayed:
"Father, the time has come. Glorify your
Son, that your Son may glorify you. 2For you
granted him authority over all people that
he might give eternal life to all those you
have given him. 3Now this is eternal life:
that they may know you, the only true God,
and Jesus Christ, whom you have sent. 4I
have brought you glory on earth by completing the work you gave me to do. 5And now,
Father, glorify me in your presence with the
glory I had with you before the world began.

Jesus Prays for His Disciples

6"I have revealed you[c] to those whom
you gave me out of the world. They were
yours; you gave them to me and they have
obeyed your word. 7Now they know that
everything you have given me comes from
you. 8For I gave them the words you gave
me and they accepted them. They knew
with certainty that I came from you, and
they believed that you sent me. 9I pray for
them. I am not praying for the world, but for
those you have given me, for they are yours.
10All I have is yours, and all you have is
mine. And glory has come to me through
them. 11I will remain in the world no longer, but they are still in the world, and I am
coming to you. Holy Father, protect them by
the power of your name—the name you
gave me—so that they may be one as we
are one. 12While I was with them, I protected them and kept them safe by that name

[a] 8 Or *will expose the guilt of the world*   [b] 31 Or *"Do you now believe?"*   [c] 6 Greek *your name*; also in verse 26

you gave me. None has been lost except the
one doomed to destruction so that Scripture
would be fulfilled.
13“I am coming to you now, but I say
these things while I am still in the world, so
that they may have the full measure of my
joy within them. 14I have given them your
word and the world has hated them, for
they are not of the world any more than I
am of the world. 15My prayer is not that you
take them out of the world but that you
protect them from the evil one. 16They are
not of the world, even as I am not of it.
17Sanctify[a] them by the truth; your word is
truth. 18As you sent me into the world, I
have sent them into the world. 19For them
I sanctify myself, that they too may be truly
sanctified.

Jesus Prays for All Believers

20“My prayer is not for them alone. I pray
also for those who will believe in me
through their message, 21that all of them
may be one, Father, just as you are in me
and I am in you. May they also be in us so
that the world may believe that you have
sent me. 22I have given them the glory that
you gave me, that they may be one as we
are one: 23I in them and you in me. May
they be brought to complete unity to let the
world know that you sent me and have
loved them even as you have loved me.
24“Father, I want those you have given
me to be with me where I am, and to see
my glory, the glory you have given me because you loved me before the creation of
the world.
25“Righteous Father, though the world
does not know you, I know you, and they
know that you have sent me. 26I have made
you known to them, and will continue to
make you known in order that the love you
have for me may be in them and that I myself may be in them.”

Jesus Arrested

18 When he had finished praying, Jesus left
with his disciples and crossed the Kidron
Valley. On the other side there was an olive
grove, and he and his disciples went into it.
2Now Judas, who betrayed him, knew the
place, because Jesus had often met there with his
disciples. 3So Judas came to the grove, guiding a
detachment of soldiers and some officials from
the chief priests and Pharisees. They were carrying torches, lanterns and weapons.
4Jesus, knowing all that was going to happen
to him, went out and asked them, “Who is it you
want?”
5“Jesus of Nazareth,” they replied.
“I am he,” Jesus said. (And Judas the traitor
was standing there with them.) 6When Jesus
said, “I am he,” they drew back and fell to the
ground.
7Again he asked them, “Who is it you want?”
And they said, “Jesus of Nazareth.”
8“I told you that I am he,” Jesus answered. “If
you are looking for me, then let these men go.”
9This happened so that the words he had spoken
would be fulfilled: “I have not lost one of those
you gave me.”[b]
10Then Simon Peter, who had a sword, drew it
and struck the high priest’s servant, cutting off
his right ear. (The servant’s name was Malchus.)
11Jesus commanded Peter, “Put your sword
away! Shall I not drink the cup the Father has
given me?”

Jesus Taken to Annas

12Then the detachment of soldiers with its
commander and the Jewish officials arrested
Jesus. They bound him 13and brought him first to
Annas, who was the father-in-law of Caiaphas,
the high priest that year. 14Caiaphas was the one
who had advised the Jews that it would be good
if one man died for the people.

Peter’s First Denial

15Simon Peter and another disciple were following Jesus. Because this disciple was known to
the high priest, he went with Jesus into the high
priest’s courtyard, 16but Peter had to wait outside
at the door. The other disciple, who was known
to the high priest, came back, spoke to the girl on
duty there and brought Peter in.
17“You are not one of his disciples, are you?”
the girl at the door asked Peter.
He replied, “I am not.”
18It was cold, and the servants and officials
stood around a fire they had made to keep warm.
Peter also was standing with them, warming himself.

The High Priest Questions Jesus

19Meanwhile, the high priest questioned Jesus
about his disciples and his teaching.
20“I have spoken openly to the world,” Jesus
replied. “I always taught in synagogues or at the
temple, where all the Jews come together. I said
nothing in secret. 21Why question me? Ask those
who heard me. Surely they know what I said.”
22When Jesus said this, one of the officials
nearby struck him in the face. “Is this the way
you answer the high priest?” he demanded.

[a] *17* Greek *hagiazo (set apart for sacred use* or *make holy)*; also in verse 19 [b] *9* John 6:39

23“If I said something wrong,” Jesus replied, “testify as to what is wrong. But if I spoke the truth, why did you strike me?” 24Then Annas sent him, still bound, to Caiaphas the high priest.[a]

Peter’s Second and Third Denials

25As Simon Peter stood warming himself, he was asked, “You are not one of his disciples, are you?”

He denied it, saying, “I am not.”

26One of the high priest’s servants, a relative of the man whose ear Peter had cut off, challenged him, “Didn’t I see you with him in the olive grove?” 27Again Peter denied it, and at that moment a rooster began to crow.

Jesus Before Pilate

28Then the Jews led Jesus from Caiaphas to the palace of the Roman governor. By now it was early morning, and to avoid ceremonial uncleanness the Jews did not enter the palace; they wanted to be able to eat the Passover. 29So Pilate came out to them and asked, “What charges are you bringing against this man?”

30“If he were not a criminal,” they replied, “we would not have handed him over to you.”

31Pilate said, “Take him yourselves and judge him by your own law.”

“But we have no right to execute anyone,” the Jews objected. 32This happened so that the words Jesus had spoken indicating the kind of death he was going to die would be fulfilled.

33Pilate then went back inside the palace, summoned Jesus and asked him, “Are you the king of the Jews?”

34“Is that your own idea,” Jesus asked, “or did others talk to you about me?”

35“Am I a Jew?” Pilate replied. “It was your people and your chief priests who handed you over to me. What is it you have done?”

36Jesus said, “My kingdom is not of this world. If it were, my servants would fight to prevent my arrest by the Jews. But now my kingdom is from another place.”

37“You are a king, then!” said Pilate.

Jesus answered, “You are right in saying I am a king. In fact, for this reason I was born, and for this I came into the world, to testify to the truth. Everyone on the side of truth listens to me.”

38“What is truth?” Pilate asked. With this he went out again to the Jews and said, “I find no basis for a charge against him. 39But it is your custom for me to release to you one prisoner at the time of the Passover. Do you want me to release ‘the king of the Jews’?”

40They shouted back, “No, not him! Give us Barabbas!” Now Barabbas had taken part in a rebellion.

Jesus Sentenced to Be Crucified

19 Then Pilate took Jesus and had him flogged. 2The soldiers twisted together a crown of thorns and put it on his head. They clothed him in a purple robe 3and went up to him again and again, saying, “Hail, king of the Jews!” And they struck him in the face.

4Once more Pilate came out and said to the Jews, “Look, I am bringing him out to you to let you know that I find no basis for a charge against him.” 5When Jesus came out wearing the crown of thorns and the purple robe, Pilate said to them, “Here is the man!”

6As soon as the chief priests and their officials saw him, they shouted, “Crucify! Crucify!”

But Pilate answered, “You take him and crucify him. As for me, I find no basis for a charge against him.”

7The Jews insisted, “We have a law, and according to that law he must die, because he claimed to be the Son of God.”

8When Pilate heard this, he was even more afraid, 9and he went back inside the palace. “Where do you come from?” he asked Jesus, but Jesus gave him no answer. 10“Do you refuse to speak to me?” Pilate said. “Don’t you realize I have power either to free you or to crucify you?”

11Jesus answered, “You would have no power over me if it were not given to you from above. Therefore the one who handed me over to you is guilty of a greater sin.”

12From then on, Pilate tried to set Jesus free, but the Jews kept shouting, “If you let this man go, you are no friend of Caesar. Anyone who claims to be a king opposes Caesar.”

13When Pilate heard this, he brought Jesus out and sat down on the judge’s seat at a place known as the Stone Pavement (which in Aramaic is Gabbatha). 14It was the day of Preparation of Passover Week, about the sixth hour.

“Here is your king,” Pilate said to the Jews.

15But they shouted, “Take him away! Take him away! Crucify him!”

“Shall I crucify your king?” Pilate asked.

“We have no king but Caesar,” the chief priests answered.

16Finally Pilate handed him over to them to be crucified.

The Crucifixion

So the soldiers took charge of Jesus. 17Carrying his own cross, he went out to the place of the Skull (which in Aramaic is called Golgotha). 18Here they crucified him, and with him two

[a]24 Or *(Now Annas had sent him, still bound, to Caiaphas the high priest.)*

others—one on each side and Jesus in the middle.

[19]Pilate had a notice prepared and fastened to the cross. It read: JESUS OF NAZARETH, THE KING OF THE JEWS. [20]Many of the Jews read this sign, for the place where Jesus was crucified was near the city, and the sign was written in Aramaic, Latin and Greek. [21]The chief priests of the Jews protested to Pilate, "Do not write 'The King of the Jews,' but that this man claimed to be king of the Jews."

[22]Pilate answered, "What I have written, I have written."

[23]When the soldiers crucified Jesus, they took his clothes, dividing them into four shares, one for each of them, with the undergarment remaining. This garment was seamless, woven in one piece from top to bottom.

[24]"Let's not tear it," they said to one another. "Let's decide by lot who will get it."

This happened that the scripture might be fulfilled which said,

"They divided my garments among them
and cast lots for my clothing."[a]

So this is what the soldiers did.

[25]Near the cross of Jesus stood his mother, his mother's sister, Mary the wife of Clopas, and Mary Magdalene. [26]When Jesus saw his mother there, and the disciple whom he loved standing nearby, he said to his mother, "Dear woman, here is your son," [27]and to the disciple, "Here is your mother." From that time on, this disciple took her into his home.

The Death of Jesus

[28]Later, knowing that all was now completed, and so that the Scripture would be fulfilled, Jesus said, "I am thirsty." [29]A jar of wine vinegar was there, so they soaked a sponge in it, put the sponge on a stalk of the hyssop plant, and lifted it to Jesus' lips. [30]When he had received the drink, Jesus said, "It is finished." With that, he bowed his head and gave up his spirit.

[31]Now it was the day of Preparation, and the next day was to be a special Sabbath. Because the Jews did not want the bodies left on the crosses during the Sabbath, they asked Pilate to have the legs broken and the bodies taken down. [32]The soldiers therefore came and broke the legs of the first man who had been crucified with Jesus, and then those of the other. [33]But when they came to Jesus and found that he was already dead, they did not break his legs. [34]Instead, one of the soldiers pierced Jesus' side with a spear, bringing a sudden flow of blood and water. [35]The man who saw it has given testimony, and his testimony is true. He knows that he tells the truth, and he testifies so that you also may believe. [36]These things happened so that the scripture would be fulfilled: "Not one of his bones will be broken,"[b] [37]and, as another scripture says, "They will look on the one they have pierced."[c]

The Burial of Jesus

[38]Later, Joseph of Arimathea asked Pilate for the body of Jesus. Now Joseph was a disciple of Jesus, but secretly because he feared the Jews. With Pilate's permission, he came and took the body away. [39]He was accompanied by Nicodemus, the man who earlier had visited Jesus at night. Nicodemus brought a mixture of myrrh and aloes, about seventy-five pounds.[d] [40]Taking Jesus' body, the two of them wrapped it, with the spices, in strips of linen. This was in accordance with Jewish burial customs. [41]At the place where Jesus was crucified, there was a garden, and in the garden a new tomb, in which no one had ever been laid. [42]Because it was the Jewish day of Preparation and since the tomb was nearby, they laid Jesus there.

The Empty Tomb

20 Early on the first day of the week, while it was still dark, Mary Magdalene went to the tomb and saw that the stone had been removed from the entrance. [2]So she came running to Simon Peter and the other disciple, the one Jesus loved, and said, "They have taken the Lord out of the tomb, and we don't know where they have put him!"

[3]So Peter and the other disciple started for the tomb. [4]Both were running, but the other disciple outran Peter and reached the tomb first. [5]He bent over and looked in at the strips of linen lying there but did not go in. [6]Then Simon Peter, who was behind him, arrived and went into the tomb. He saw the strips of linen lying there, [7]as well as the burial cloth that had been around Jesus' head. The cloth was folded up by itself, separate from the linen. [8]Finally the other disciple, who had reached the tomb first, also went inside. He saw and believed. [9](They still did not understand from Scripture that Jesus had to rise from the dead.)

Jesus Appears to Mary Magdalene

[10]Then the disciples went back to their homes, [11]but Mary stood outside the tomb crying. As she wept, she bent over to look into the tomb [12]and saw two angels in white, seated where Jesus'

[a]24 Psalm 22:18 [b]36 Exodus 12:46; Num. 9:12; Psalm 34:20 [c]37 Zech. 12:10 [d]39 Greek *a hundred litrai* (about 34 kilograms)

body had been, one at the head and the other at
the foot.
13They asked her, "Woman, why are you crying?"

> ### *JOHN 20:1–18*
>
> 1. When was the last time you visited a cemetery? Why?
> 2. Growing up, what was your favorite thing about Easter? What do you like the most about Easter now?
> 3. When was the last time you had a really good cry? What were you upset about?
> 4. What is the first recorded thing Jesus did after he had risen (v. 15)? What does that tell you about him?
> 5. In what way has your faith been shaken or strengthened in times of tragedy?
> 6. In times of grief, what has helped turn your sorrow into joy: Talking to someone? Time alone? Prayer?
> 7. Has your life lately been more like the darkness of Good Friday or the joy of Easter? How can this group pray for you?

"They have taken my Lord away," she said,
"and I don't know where they have put him."
14At this, she turned around and saw Jesus standing there, but she did not realize that it was
Jesus.
15"Woman," he said, "why are you crying?
Who is it you are looking for?"
Thinking he was the gardener, she said, "Sir,
if you have carried him away, tell me where you
have put him, and I will get him."
16Jesus said to her, "Mary."
She turned toward him and cried out in Aramaic, "Rabboni!" (which means Teacher).
17Jesus said, "Do not hold on to me, for I have
not yet returned to the Father. Go instead to my
brothers and tell them, 'I am returning to my
Father and your Father, to my God and your
God.' "
18Mary Magdalene went to the disciples with
the news: "I have seen the Lord!" And she told
them that he had said these things to her.

Jesus Appears to His Disciples

19On the evening of that first day of the week,
when the disciples were together, with the doors
locked for fear of the Jews, Jesus came and stood
among them and said, "Peace be with you!" 20Af-
ter he said this, he showed them his hands and
side. The disciples were overjoyed when they
saw the Lord.
21Again Jesus said, "Peace be with you! As the
Father has sent me, I am sending you." 22And
with that he breathed on them and said, "Receive
the Holy Spirit. 23If you forgive anyone his sins,
they are forgiven; if you do not forgive them, they
are not forgiven."

Jesus Appears to Thomas

24Now Thomas (called Didymus), one of the
Twelve, was not with the disciples when Jesus
came. 25So the other disciples told him, "We
have seen the Lord!"
But he said to them, "Unless I see the nail
marks in his hands and put my finger where the
nails were, and put my hand into his side, I will
not believe it."
26A week later his disciples were in the house
again, and Thomas was with them. Though the
doors were locked, Jesus came and stood among
them and said, "Peace be with you!" 27Then he
said to Thomas, "Put your finger here; see my
hands. Reach out your hand and put it into my
side. Stop doubting and believe."
28Thomas said to him, "My Lord and my God!"
29Then Jesus told him, "Because you have
seen me, you have believed; blessed are those
who have not seen and yet have believed."
30Jesus did many other miraculous signs in the

20:1–2 ***first day of the week.*** Sunday. ***Magdalene.*** From the village of Magdala in Galilee. Though the other Gospels record that a few women went to the tomb, John's focus is only on Mary Magdalene. She was one of several women who traveled with Jesus and the disciples, and at some point had seven demons cast out of her (Luke 8:2). ***the one Jesus loved.*** John. ***have put him.*** Mary had no concept of a resurrection.

20:11 ***crying.*** Meaning "wailing." Given the anguish of watching Jesus on the cross, and the shock of not finding the body in the tomb, Mary's grief and confusion is understandable. Maybe Jesus appeared first to her because she needed him most.

20:14–16 ***she did not realize that it was Jesus.*** Whether she was blinded by her intense grief or if there was some type of transformation in Jesus' appearance that caused Mary's lack of recognition is not known. ***Mary.*** Jesus had said that the Good Shepherd "calls his own sheep by name" and that they "will listen to my voice" (John 10:3,16). When Jesus speaks Mary's name, she immediately recognizes who it is that speaks to her, thus proving her discipleship.

20:17 ***Do not hold on to me.*** After Mary embraced Jesus, expressing the joy and relief of seeing him, he told her she need not cling to him because she would have the chance to see him again. He may also be reminding her that she will "hold on" to him in a far more personal way when he returns to the Father and comes to her in the person of the Holy Spirit (John 16:5–7).

presence of his disciples, which are not recorded
in this book. [31]But these are written that you
may[a] believe that Jesus is the Christ, the Son of
God, and that by believing you may have life in
his name.

JOHN 20:24–31

1. Who is the biggest practical joker you know?
2. Are you more likely to believe what you are told or have to see to believe?
3. When did you come to the place you believed Jesus rose from the dead? Why?
4. How does Jesus deal with Thomas' doubt (v. 27)?
5. How do you answer the skeptic in your school who says the resurrection of Jesus is a myth?
6. What doubts or questions about God are you struggling with right now? What have you found helpful in dealing with doubts?
7. In what area of your life would you like to hear Jesus say, "Peace be with you" (v. 26)? Pray for one another accordingly.

Jesus and the Miraculous Catch of Fish

21 Afterward Jesus appeared again to his disciples, by the Sea of Tiberias.[b] It happened this way: [2]Simon Peter, Thomas (called
Didymus), Nathanael from Cana in Galilee, the
sons of Zebedee, and two other disciples were
together. [3]"I'm going out to fish," Simon Peter
told them, and they said, "We'll go with you." So
they went out and got into the boat, but that
night they caught nothing.
[4]Early in the morning, Jesus stood on the
shore, but the disciples did not realize that it was
Jesus.
[5]He called out to them, "Friends, haven't you
any fish?"
"No," they answered.
[6]He said, "Throw your net on the right side of
the boat and you will find some." When they did,
they were unable to haul the net in because of
the large number of fish.

JOHN 21:1–14

1. What has been your best or worst fishing, camping or hiking experience?
2. What do you like to get away and do?
3. When have you felt really blessed, like your "nets were overflowing"?
4. Why did Peter jump into the lake (v. 7)?
5. What is the closest you have come to giving up your faith? What brought you back?
6. On a scale from 1 (low) to 10 (high), what is the excitement level in your spiritual life right now?
7. How can the group help you in prayer this week?

(Study notes on page 990)

[7]Then the disciple whom Jesus loved said to
Peter, "It is the Lord!" As soon as Simon Peter
heard him say, "It is the Lord," he wrapped his
outer garment around him (for he had taken it
off) and jumped into the water. [8]The other disciples followed in the boat, towing the net full of
fish, for they were not far from shore, about a

[a] *31* Some manuscripts *may continue to*   [b] *1* That is, Sea of Galilee

---

20:24 ***Thomas.*** The Hebrew name from which we get "Thomas" and the Greek name *Didymus* both mean "twin." Although he has become famous for his doubt, he had previously demonstrated that he was a man of faith and loyalty (John 11:16). ***was not with the disciples when Jesus came.*** For some unidentified reason, Thomas was not present Easter evening when the risen Jesus appeared to his disciples (vv. 19–23).

20:25 ***Unless I see ... and put ... I will not believe it.*** This is as extreme as skepticism can get! Luke 24:37–43 shows that the other disciples had also been filled with doubt and skepticism.

20:26–29 ***the doors were locked.*** Probably still "for fear of the Jews," as in verse 19. ***My Lord and my God!*** In this confession of faith, Thomas clearly affirms the divine nature of Jesus. ***blessed are those who have not seen and yet have believed.*** While Thomas would not believe without seeing, Jesus affirms those who believe even though they have not physically seen the resurrected Lord. John's readers (including us!) are not deprived because of never having seen Jesus. Indeed, he will be with future believers through the Spirit (John 14:15–20) just as he was with the apostles.

20:30–31 These words speak of the selection with which the author chose his material (see John 21:25 also), and the evangelistic purpose for which John wrote—that we might *believe* (have faith), and that through that faith we might have *life* in Jesus' name (all that he is and stands for).

hundred yards.[a] 9When they landed, they saw a
fire of burning coals there with fish on it, and
some bread.
10Jesus said to them, "Bring some of the fish
you have just caught."
11Simon Peter climbed aboard and dragged the
net ashore. It was full of large fish, 153, but even
with so many the net was not torn. 12Jesus said
to them, "Come and have breakfast." None of the
disciples dared ask him, "Who are you?" They
knew it was the Lord. 13Jesus came, took the
bread and gave it to them, and did the same with
the fish. 14This was now the third time Jesus
appeared to his disciples after he was raised from
the dead.

Jesus Reinstates Peter

15When they had finished eating, Jesus said to
Simon Peter, "Simon son of John, do you truly
love me more than these?"
"Yes, Lord," he said, "you know that I love
you."
Jesus said, "Feed my lambs."
16Again Jesus said, "Simon son of John, do you
truly love me?"
He answered, "Yes, Lord, you know that I love
you."
Jesus said, "Take care of my sheep."
17The third time he said to him, "Simon son of
John, do you love me?"
Peter was hurt because Jesus asked him the
third time, "Do you love me?" He said, "Lord,
you know all things; you know that I love you."
Jesus said, "Feed my sheep. 18I tell you the
truth, when you were younger you dressed yourself and went where you wanted; but when you
are old you will stretch out your hands, and
someone else will dress you and lead you where
you do not want to go." 19Jesus said this to indicate the kind of death by which Peter would glorify God. Then he said to him, "Follow me!"
20Peter turned and saw that the disciple whom
Jesus loved was following them. (This was the
one who had leaned back against Jesus at the
supper and had said, "Lord, who is going to betray you?") 21When Peter saw him, he asked,
"Lord, what about him?"
22Jesus answered, "If I want him to remain
alive until I return, what is that to you? You must
follow me." 23Because of this, the rumor spread
among the brothers that this disciple would not
die. But Jesus did not say that he would not die;
he only said, "If I want him to remain alive until
I return, what is that to you?"
24This is the disciple who testifies to these
things and who wrote them down. We know that
his testimony is true.
25Jesus did many other things as well. If every
one of them were written down, I suppose that
even the whole world would not have room for
the books that would be written.

[a]8 Greek *about two hundred cubits* (about 90 meters)

21:1 ***Afterward.*** Literally, this is "after these things." We do not know how long after the resurrection this incident took place, but the disciples have had time to journey from Jerusalem to Galilee. ***Sea of Tiberias.*** Another name for the Sea of Galilee.

21:3 ***I'm going out to fish.*** Peter, along with his brother Andrew and James and John (the "sons of Zebedee" in v. 2), were fishermen when Jesus called them (Mark 1:16–20). It is not surprising that they decide to go fishing as they wait for the Lord in Galilee as instructed (Mark 14:28; 16:7). But this also has a symbolic significance. In calling them, Jesus promised to make them "fishers of men" (Mark 1:17). So far this promise has not been fulfilled, just as they would fish all that night and catch nothing. But then Jesus comes and tells them how to fish (v. 6), and they become successful. This is a vivid prediction of the empowerment coming to the disciples.

21:4–7 ***did not realize that it was Jesus.*** Whether they failed to recognize him because it was still somewhat dark or if there was some type of transformation in Jesus' appearance that caused them to be unable to immediately identify him is not told, but verse 12 indicates that the latter is likely. This miraculous catch of fish is very similar to the one recorded at the beginning of Jesus' ministry in Luke 5:1–11. The repetition of such a miracle would underscore their success as fishers of men, and would have special meaning to Peter whose denial of Christ must have plagued him with doubts about his ability to be an apostle.

Introduction to ACTS

Personal Reading Plan

❐ Acts 1:1–26	❐ Acts 9:32–10:23a	❐ Acts 19:1–41
❐ Acts 2:1–47	❐ Acts 10:23b–11:18	❐ Acts 20:1–38
❐ Acts 3:1–4:22	❐ Acts 11:19–12:25	❐ Acts 21:1–36
❐ Acts 4:23–5:16	❐ Acts 13:1–52	❐ Acts 21:37–23:11
❐ Acts 5:17–6:15	❐ Acts 14:1–15:21	❐ Acts 23:12–24:27
❐ Acts 7:1–8:1a	❐ Acts 15:22–16:15	❐ Acts 25:1–26:32
❐ Acts 8:1b–40	❐ Acts 16:16–17:15	❐ Acts 27:1–44
❐ Acts 9:1–31	❐ Acts 17:16–18:28	❐ Acts 28:1–31

Author

Although Luke is nowhere named within Acts as author, there is a strong and ancient tradition that he did, indeed, write this book as a companion piece to the third Gospel. Little is known of Luke. He is mentioned only three times in the New Testament (Col. 4:14; Philem. 24; 2 Tim. 4:11). From these references, it can be deduced that Luke was a physician, a valued companion of Paul and a Gentile.

Luke's medical background is demonstrated by his use of medical terms, especially in his Gospel. For example, in recounting the story of the camel and the needle's eye (Luke 18:25), Luke alone uses the word *belone,* which is the technical word for a surgeon's needle, whereas Matthew and Mark use the Greek word *raphis,* which is the ordinary word for a tailor's or a household needle.

Luke's role as Paul's traveling companion is evident in the book of Acts. In the four so-called *we* sections, the author suddenly switches from saying "They did this" to "We did that" (Acts 16:10–17; 20:5–21:18; 27:1–28:16). At these points in Paul's journeys, Luke joined him as a colleague in ministry.

We learn that Luke was a Gentile from the list of greetings with which Paul concludes Colossians. First, Paul records the greetings sent by "the only Jews among my fellow workers" (Col. 4:10–11). Then in verse 12, he begins a second set of greetings presumably from the Gentiles in the party. Luke's name is included in this latter list.

Date

The final events recorded here took place in early A.D. 60, so Acts must have been compiled after that time.

Theme

The spread of the Gospel to all the known world (1:8).

Historical Background

Why did Luke write the book of Acts? One reason must have been his desire to commend Christianity to the Gentile world in general and to the Roman government in particular. Certainly there was much about Christianity that would have appealed to Gentiles. For one thing, Jesus came for all people and not just for his Jewish kinfolk. So one finds in Acts the same universality present in Luke's Gospel. The Good News about Jesus is not just for Jews but for all people. Not surprisingly, therefore, we find in Acts not only Jews turning to Jesus (3,000 on the Day of Pentecost, see Acts 2:41) but also Gentiles. We see Peter (the apostle to the Jews) welcoming Cornelius, the Roman centurion, into the church. We see Philip preaching to the Samaritans and Jewish believers and evangelizing Gentiles in Antioch. In particular, we find Paul called by Christ to be the apostle to the Gentiles, setting up churches across the Roman Empire. Finally in Acts 15, there is formal affirmation that Gentiles are accepted in the church of Jesus Christ on equal terms with Jews (they do not first have to become Jewish converts). Acts is an eloquent testimony to the universal appeal of Jesus.

Luke's response to the Roman government is fascinating. He seemed to go out of his way to show that Christians were loyal citizens and not lawbreakers and criminals (18:14–16; 19:37; 23:29; 25:25). He also took pains to point out that Roman officials had always treated Christians fairly and courteously (13:12; 18:12–17; 19:31). This was important to state lest Christianity be perceived as a political movement and therefore a threat to the Roman Empire. His writing did, after all, talk about the kingdom and about Jesus as Lord (the imperial title).

However, commending Christianity to Gentiles was probably not Luke's central aim. His main purpose is implicit in 1:8, "But you will receive power when the Holy Spirit comes on you; and you will be my witnesses in Jerusalem, and in all Judea and Samaria, and to the ends of the earth." Luke's aim was to show how, in 30 short years, Christianity had spread from Jerusalem to Rome.

Characteristics

The book of Acts is the bridge between the Gospel and the Epistles. It is no accident that modern Bibles are arranged with the life of Jesus on one side of Acts and the correspondence of the apostles on the other. This is because, on the one hand, Acts completes the story of Jesus. It shows how his life, death and resurrection brought a whole new community into existence: the church. On the other hand, Acts sets the stage for the correspondence to this church; the letters make up the rest of the New Testament. At many points it would be difficult to get the full sense of what the Epistles are saying without the data found in Acts.

Luke tells the story of the development of the church, not by strictly chronicling every event that occurred as the church spread from Jerusalem to Rome—the sheer volume of the data prevented this—but rather by opening a series of windows that allows us to glimpse important (and representative) developments in its growth.

1. Key Figure—The Holy Spirit

One thing that characterizes the entire story is the work of the Holy Spirit. There is little question in Luke's mind how the church spread: The Holy Spirit did it. So we see the church come into being as a result of the baptism of the Holy Spirit (2:38–41). First as only a handful of disciples, it turned suddenly into a full-fledged movement. We then see the Holy Spirit gently but directly guide the early church (13:2 and 16:7). In fact, the presence of the Holy Spirit signals that a church is authentic and not false (19:1–6). Some have suggested that this book ought to have been labeled "The Acts of the Holy Spirit" and not "The Acts of the Apostles"!

2. Leading Roles—Peter and Paul

The title "The Acts of the Apostles" is inaccurate for yet another reason. The whole apostolic band is not really in view here. The book of Acts is the story of only two apostles—Peter and Paul. Peter's story is told first. In the initial 12 chapters, he is the central figure. But in chapter 13, the spotlight shifts to Paul, and he holds center stage until Acts concludes.

The stories of these two men are not dissimilar. In fact, there are a surprising number of common elements. Both heal cripples (3:1–10; 14:8–12); both have the experience of seeing cures brought about in unusual ways (5:15–16; 19:11–12); both bring people back to life (9:36–42; 20:9–12); both meet a sorcerer (8:9–25; 13:6–12); and both are released from prison as the result of a miracle (12:7; 16:26–28).

The reason for this focus on Peter and on Paul is not hard to guess. They were the key leaders of the two main elements of the early church: Peter was the chief apostle to the Jews, while Paul was the chief apostle to the Gentiles. So in hearing their stories, we hear the story of the unfolding of the whole church.

3. Key Sources

Where did Luke get his information about the growth of the church? The source of the second half of the book (chapters 13–28) is clear. Luke got this information directly from his friend and companion Paul. We know Luke was actually with Paul during some of this period (the *we* sections), and he may well have kept a journal. We can also guess that during the long days of travel, and during Paul's confinement in prison, the great apostle probably recounted his many adventures to Luke. But what about the first 12 chapters that center around Peter? Here is where Luke's skill as a historian is especially evident. Luke tells us in his prologue to the third Gospel that he "carefully investigated everything from the beginning" (Luke 1:3). How? Probably by talking to many individuals he may have met through Paul. For example, Luke knew Mark. Both men were with Paul when he wrote Colossians (Col. 4:10,14). From Mark he would have received valuable information about the growth of the church in Jerusalem and about Peter's role in this. (Many feel Mark's Gospel reflects Peter's perspective.) And certainly Luke would have listened to the stories about Peter that were repeated in the churches he visited. Finally, he may well have had access to the official records (written and oral) of the key churches mentioned in the first 12 chapters—the church at Jerusalem (from Mark and others); the church at Caesarea (Philip and his daughters entertained Luke and Paul according to Acts 21:8–9, and Philip was associated with Stephen and the events of Acts 6:1–8:3); and the church at Antioch (many feel Luke's home was Antioch).

4. Keen Historian

Luke's accuracy as a historian was called into question by certain scholars until the archaeological research of Sir William Ramsay demonstrated Luke's exact and detailed knowledge of the political and social conditions of the times. For example, although a number of different titles were given to Roman officials, Luke always seems to have gotten it right. When Paul was in Cyprus (Acts 13:4–7), Luke tells us a proconsul was in charge, although this was only briefly the case. At Malta (Acts 28:1,7), the ruler is correctly called the "chief man" or "chief official." At Ephesus (Acts 19:35), Luke identifies the official who quieted the crowd as the "city clerk." In Thessalonica (Acts 17:6), he identifies the leaders as "city officials," even though this was an unusual office with no parallel elsewhere in the Roman Empire and only recently verified by inscriptions. Luke had the mind of a researcher: He was careful and paid attention to details. Thus, when reading his story of the early church, we have confidence that what Luke tells us is just what happened.

Passages for Topical Group Study

1:12–26	SUICIDE	Matthias Chosen to Replace Judas
2:1–24,36–41	THE HOLY SPIRIT	The Holy Spirit Comes at Pentecost
2:42–47	THE CHURCH	The Fellowship of Believers
3:1–16	SHARING YOUR FAITH	Peter Heals the Crippled Beggar
5:1–11	HONESTY / INTEGRITY	Ananias and Sapphira
6:1–7	SPIRITUAL GIFTS	The Choosing of the Seven
8:26–40	THE BIBLE	Philip and the Ethiopian
9:1–19	CONVERSION	Saul's Conversion
9:20–31	ACCEPTANCE	Saul in Damascus and Jerusalem
10:1–23	CLIQUES	Peter's Vision
	RACISM	
13:1–12	CULTS	Paul Confronts a Sorcerer
15:36–41	LOSING FRIENDS	Disagreement Between Paul and Barnabas
16:22–40	CONTENTMENT	Paul and Silas in Prison
19:23–41	CHOOSING A CAREER	The Riot in Ephesus

See the Lesson Plans in the front of this Bible.

Passages for General Group Study

1:1–11	Jesus Taken Up Into Heaven
12:1–19	Peter's Miraculous Escape From Prison
16:6–10	Paul's Vision of the Man of Macedonia

Jesus Taken Up Into Heaven

1 In my former book, Theophilus, I wrote
about all that Jesus began to do and to teach
2until the day he was taken up to heaven, after
giving instructions through the Holy Spirit to the
apostles he had chosen. 3After his suffering, he
showed himself to these men and gave many con-
vincing proofs that he was alive. He appeared to
them over a period of forty days and spoke about
the kingdom of God. 4On one occasion, while he
was eating with them, he gave them this command: "Do not leave Jerusalem, but wait for the
gift my Father promised, which you have heard
me speak about. 5For John baptized with[a] water, but in a few days you will be baptized with
the Holy Spirit."
6So when they met together, they asked him,
"Lord, are you at this time going to restore the
kingdom to Israel?"
7He said to them: "It is not for you to know the
times or dates the Father has set by his own authority. 8But you will receive power when the
Holy Spirit comes on you; and you will be my
witnesses in Jerusalem, and in all Judea and Samaria, and to the ends of the earth."
9After he said this, he was taken up before
their very eyes, and a cloud hid him from their
sight.
10They were looking intently up into the sky as
he was going, when suddenly two men dressed
in white stood beside them. 11"Men of Galilee,"
they said, "why do you stand here looking into
the sky? This same Jesus, who has been taken
from you into heaven, will come back in the same
way you have seen him go into heaven."

Matthias Chosen to Replace Judas

12Then they returned to Jerusalem from the
hill called the Mount of Olives, a Sabbath day's
walk[b] from the city. 13When they arrived, they
went upstairs to the room where they were staying. Those present were Peter, John, James and
Andrew; Philip and Thomas, Bartholomew and
Matthew; James son of Alphaeus and Simon the
Zealot, and Judas son of James. 14They all joined
together constantly in prayer, along with the
women and Mary the mother of Jesus, and with
his brothers.

Acts 1:1–11

1. What day of the year can you hardly wait for? Why?
2. What long-awaited prize was worth the wait (concert tickets, driver's license, etc.)?
3. How much did the disciples understand about Jesus and his mission at this point in Christ's life?
4. In verse 8 Jesus says, "You will be my witnesses." Where do you feel called to be Christ's witness?
5. What holds you back from spreading the word about Jesus: Lack of knowledge? Lack of concern? Lack of courage?
6. How has your spiritual life been lately: In the pits? On a high?
7. How can this group help you in prayer this week?

15In those days Peter stood up among the believers[c] (a group numbering about a hundred
and twenty) 16and said, "Brothers, the Scripture
had to be fulfilled which the Holy Spirit spoke
long ago through the mouth of David concerning
Judas, who served as guide for those who arrested Jesus— 17he was one of our number and
shared in this ministry."
18(With the reward he got for his wickedness,
Judas bought a field; there he fell headlong, his
body burst open and all his intestines spilled out.

[a]5 Or *in* [b]12 That is, about 3/4 mile (about 1,100 meters) [c]15 Greek *brothers*

1:1 ***my former book.*** The Gospel of Luke. ***Theophilus.*** Both the Gospel of Luke and the book of Acts were addressed to this man, who may have been responsible to see they were copied and distributed. ***all that Jesus began to do and to teach.*** This is a clue to how to view Acts: It is the *continuing* story of the work of Jesus through his Spirit in the life of his body, the church.

1:4–6 ***the gift my Father promised.*** The Holy Spirit (Luke 11:13). ***in a few days.*** This baptism with the Holy Spirit would come 10 days later on the day of Pentecost (2:1–4). ***restore the kingdom to Israel?*** As typical Jews, the disciples expected the Messiah to deliver the people from Roman oppression and set up an earthly kingdom.

1:8 This verse embraces the twin themes of the whole book. Jesus' mission, rather than ending with his ascension, is continued through the work of his Spirit empowering the disciples to bear witness to him. The result of this empowering will be the spread of the Gospel throughout the world—from the heart of Israel (Jerusalem) to the immediate vicinity (Judea) to the despised Samaritans in the adjacent province, to the outermost reaches of the earth.

1:10–11 The ascension is interpreted to the disciples by two angels. They point out that Jesus will indeed return as he taught; therefore, in the meantime, they are not to stand around and wait for him, but to get on with their mission. ***in the same way.*** In clouds and "great glory" (Luke 21:27) and with the same resurrection body.

[19]Everyone in Jerusalem heard about this, so they
called that field in their language Akeldama, that
is, Field of Blood.)
[20]"For," said Peter, "it is written in the book
of Psalms,

"'May his place be deserted;
let there be no one to dwell in it,'[a]

and,

"'May another take his place of
leadership.'[b]

[21]Therefore it is necessary to choose one of the
men who have been with us the whole time the
Lord Jesus went in and out among us, [22]begin-
ning from John's baptism to the time when Jesus
was taken up from us. For one of these must
become a witness with us of his resurrection."
[23]So they proposed two men: Joseph called
Barsabbas (also known as Justus) and Matthias.
[24]Then they prayed, "Lord, you know everyone's
heart. Show us which of these two you have chosen [25]to take over this apostolic ministry, which
Judas left to go where he belongs." [26]Then they
cast lots, and the lot fell to Matthias; so he was
added to the eleven apostles.

Acts 1:12–26

1. If you could add one person to this group right now—who would you invite?
2. If you could choose one place to go with your close friends and deal with some important things in your life, where would you go?
3. How has the tragedy of someone's suicide affected your life?
4. Why did Judas commit suicide?
5. If a friend of yours threatened to commit suicide, what would you do?
6. What have you found helpful when you get really down?
7. What struggles do you (or someone close to you) have that this group can pray for?

The Holy Spirit Comes at Pentecost

2 When the day of Pentecost came, they were
all together in one place. [2]Suddenly a sound
like the blowing of a violent wind came from
heaven and filled the whole house where they
were sitting. [3]They saw what seemed to be
tongues of fire that separated and came to rest on
each of them. [4]All of them were filled with the
Holy Spirit and began to speak in other tongues[c]
as the Spirit enabled them.
[5]Now there were staying in Jerusalem God-
fearing Jews from every nation under heaven.
[6]When they heard this sound, a crowd came together in bewilderment, because each one heard
them speaking in his own language. [7]Utterly
amazed, they asked: "Are not all these men who
are speaking Galileans? [8]Then how is it that each
of us hears them in his own native language?
[9]Parthians, Medes and Elamites; residents of
Mesopotamia, Judea and Cappadocia, Pontus and
Asia, [10]Phrygia and Pamphylia, Egypt and the
parts of Libya near Cyrene; visitors from Rome
[11](both Jews and converts to Judaism); Cretans
and Arabs—we hear them declaring the wonders
of God in our own tongues!" [12]Amazed and perplexed, they asked one another, "What does this
mean?"
[13]Some, however, made fun of them and said,
"They have had too much wine.[d]"

Peter Addresses the Crowd

[14]Then Peter stood up with the Eleven, raised
his voice and addressed the crowd: "Fellow Jews
and all of you who live in Jerusalem, let me ex-

[a]20 Psalm 69:25 [b]20 Psalm 109:8 [c]4 Or *languages*; also in verse 11 [d]13 Or *sweet wine*

1:13 *Judas son of James.* This was not Judas Iscariot. Elsewhere this disciple was called Thaddaeus (Matt. 10:3; Mark 3:18).

1:16–17 *the Scripture had to be fulfilled.* Peter was referring to Psalm 69:25 and Psalm 109:8, quoted in verse 20. After his resurrection, Jesus showed the apostles how the OT pointed to him (Luke 24:27,45). He may have included these psalms in his illumination, and the apostles likely studied the OT to understand more about him. ***one of our number and shared in this ministry.*** The fact that Judas was a disciple and close friend of Jesus, and his identifying Jesus with a kiss, made Judas' betrayal even more despicable (Matt. 26:47–50).

1:18 *reward.* The chief priests gave Judas 30 silver coins (about four months' wages) for betraying Jesus (Matt. 26:14–16). ***body burst open.*** According to Matthew 27:5, Judas hanged himself. There are three possibilities for putting together both accounts: (1) After hanging himself, the rope broke allowing his body to crash to the ground; (2) Some time after hanging himself, the body fell because of decay or someone cutting it down, and in its decomposing condition it burst open; (3) The word "hanged" in Matthew 27:5 actually means "impaled," and the graphic results are told here.

1:26 *cast lots.* By using sticks or stones, they left the choice to God. The practice was common in the OT, but this is the last instance of casting lots in the Bible. The Lord communicated more directly to his people after the coming of the Spirit (ch. 2).

plain this to you; listen carefully to what I say.
15 These men are not drunk, as you suppose. It's
only nine in the morning! 16 No, this is what was
spoken by the prophet Joel:

17 " 'In the last days, God says,
I will pour out my Spirit on all people.
Your sons and daughters will prophesy,
your young men will see visions,
your old men will dream dreams.
18 Even on my servants, both men and women,
I will pour out my Spirit in those days,
and they will prophesy.
19 I will show wonders in the heaven above
and signs on the earth below,
blood and fire and billows of smoke.
20 The sun will be turned to darkness
and the moon to blood
before the coming of the great and
glorious day of the Lord.
21 And everyone who calls
on the name of the Lord will be saved.'[a]

22 "Men of Israel, listen to this: Jesus of Nazareth was a man accredited by God to you by miracles, wonders and signs, which God did among
you through him, as you yourselves know. 23 This
man was handed over to you by God's set purpose and foreknowledge; and you, with the help
of wicked men,[b] put him to death by nailing
him to the cross. 24 But God raised him from the
dead, freeing him from the agony of death, because it was impossible for death to keep its hold
on him. 25 David said about him:

" 'I saw the Lord always before me.
Because he is at my right hand,
I will not be shaken.
26 Therefore my heart is glad and my tongue
rejoices;
my body also will live in hope,
27 because you will not abandon me to the
grave,
nor will you let your Holy One see decay.
28 You have made known to me the paths of
life;
you will fill me with joy in your
presence.'[c]

29 "Brothers, I can tell you confidently that the
patriarch David died and was buried, and his
tomb is here to this day. 30 But he was a prophet
and knew that God had promised him on oath
that he would place one of his descendants on
his throne. 31 Seeing what was ahead, he spoke
of the resurrection of the Christ,[d] that he was
not abandoned to the grave, nor did his body see
decay. 32 God has raised this Jesus to life, and we
are all witnesses of the fact. 33 Exalted to the right
hand of God, he has received from the Father the

Acts 2:1–24,36–41

1. What are you usually doing at 9 a.m. on a Sunday? A weekday? A Saturday?
2. What do the images of wind and fire (vv. 2–3) suggest to you?
3. When are you most aware of the Holy Spirit?
4. Why did God "pour out" his Spirit (see vv. 17–21)?
5. How would you describe your experience with the Holy Spirit right now: On fire? Up in the air? Gone with the wind?
6. Where in your life do you need the power of the Holy Spirit?
7. Through the Spirit, 3,000 people joined the disciples. Who can you invite to join this group? Close by praying together.

[a] *21* Joel 2:28-32 [b] *23* Or *of those not having the law* (that is, Gentiles) [c] *28* Psalm 16:8-11 [d] *31* Or *Messiah.* "The Christ" (Greek) and "the Messiah" (Hebrew) both mean "the Anointed One"; also in verse 36.

2:1 ***Pentecost.*** A feast, a kind of Thanksgiving Day for gathered crops, held 50 days after Passover. ***they.*** Probably all the believers (1:15), not just the apostles.

2:2–4 The Greek word for "wind" and "spirit" is the same, hence the symbolism of the Spirit coming like a great wind. Fire is often associated with divine appearances (Ex. 3:2) as well as judgment and cleansing (see Luke 3:16–17). What "seemed to be tongues of fire" was a fitting description of the empowerment of the disciples to speak God's message with authority and effect.

2:6 ***speaking in his own language.*** Thousands of Jews from all over the Roman Empire would attend Pentecost. People heard the believers speaking in the different languages represented. This phenomenon served as a sign to the crowds of a supernatural event pointing to Jesus.

2:36–37 Peter reaches the dramatic conclusion to his message to the crowd. In light of how Jesus' death, resurrection, ascension and pouring out the Holy Spirit fulfilled the Scriptural witness concerning the Messiah, it is obvious that Jesus *is* the Lord (v. 34) and Messiah (v. 31). ***cut to the heart.*** The horror of the situation sinks in: the long-awaited Messiah was put to death by the very people he was expected to save. The people ask how to escape God's judgment.

2:38 This verse is a classic summary of the response required to become a Christian and the promises associated with that response. ***be baptized ... for the forgiveness of your sins.*** Not that baptism brings forgiveness. Baptism was the outward sign of the inward change of heart and mind showing the desire to be cleansed from sin.

promised Holy Spirit and has poured out what
you now see and hear. 34For David did not ascend
to heaven, and yet he said,

" 'The Lord said to my Lord:
"Sit at my right hand
35until I make your enemies
a footstool for your feet." '[a]

Acts 2:42–47

1. What is the best group you ever belonged to? What made it so special?
2. What is your favorite thing about your church?
3. How is your church, and this group, similar to the fellowship here? How is it different?
4. Why did this group meet every day (v. 46)? How would you feel about going to church daily?
5. On a scale from 1 to 10, how would you compare the closeness in your group to the group of Christians in this passage?
6. If you could change one thing in the group you are in right now, what would you change?
7. Close in prayer by joining hands and asking God to help your church and this group grow as a caring community.

36"Therefore let all Israel be assured of this:
God has made this Jesus, whom you crucified,
both Lord and Christ."
37When the people heard this, they were cut
to the heart and said to Peter and the other apostles, "Brothers, what shall we do?"
38Peter replied, "Repent and be baptized, every one of you, in the name of Jesus Christ for the
forgiveness of your sins. And you will receive the
gift of the Holy Spirit. 39The promise is for you
and your children and for all who are far off—for
all whom the Lord our God will call."
40With many other words he warned them;
and he pleaded with them, "Save yourselves from
this corrupt generation." 41Those who accepted
his message were baptized, and about three thousand were added to their number that day.

The Fellowship of the Believers

42They devoted themselves to the apostles'
teaching and to the fellowship, to the breaking of
bread and to prayer. 43Everyone was filled with
awe, and many wonders and miraculous signs
were done by the apostles. 44All the believers
were together and had everything in common.
45Selling their possessions and goods, they gave
to anyone as he had need. 46Every day they continued to meet together in the temple courts.
They broke bread in their homes and ate together
with glad and sincere hearts, 47praising God and
enjoying the favor of all the people. And the Lord
added to their number daily those who were being saved.

Peter Heals the Crippled Beggar

3 One day Peter and John were going up to the
temple at the time of prayer—at three in the
afternoon. 2Now a man crippled from birth was
being carried to the temple gate called Beautiful,
where he was put every day to beg from those
going into the temple courts. 3When he saw Peter and John about to enter, he asked them for
money. 4Peter looked straight at him, as did John.
Then Peter said, "Look at us!" 5So the man gave
them his attention, expecting to get something
from them.
6Then Peter said, "Silver or gold I do not have,
but what I have I give you. In the name of Jesus
Christ of Nazareth, walk." 7Taking him by the
right hand, he helped him up, and instantly the
man's feet and ankles became strong. 8He

[a]35 Psalm 110:1

2:42 *They.* The fellowship of believers, which had numbered about 120 (Acts 1:15), and as a result of the outpouring of the Holy Spirit on the day of Pentecost had just grown by about 3,000 (v. 41). ***devoted.*** These new converts were not casual about their faith, but saw it as a priority. ***apostles' teaching.*** The foundation of the church's life was the instruction (including primarily what Jesus himself taught) given by the apostles as the representatives of Jesus. ***fellowship.*** The worshiping community of believers. ***the breaking of bread.*** Though used of an ordinary meal in verse 46, the Lord's Supper is referred to here. ***prayer.*** Literally, "the prayers." This may refer to set times and forms of prayer as was the practice of the Jews. The importance of both personal and corporate prayer is emphasized in Acts.

2:43 *wonders / miraculous signs.* Both words clearly indicate that the miracles performed by the apostles (and by Jesus—see Acts 2:22) were not ends in themselves, but pointers to the nature of Jesus' identity, power and mission.

2:44–45 This does not mean they all lived together in a communal setting, but stresses their unity and their commitment to each other's welfare. Generous, voluntary sharing and caring for one another is presented as a natural outworking of having received the grace of God (see also Luke 12:33).

2:46–47 The daily life of the believers is described. Since they were all Jews, it was natural for them to continue meeting in the temple as a place of worship. They joyously fellowshipped together in their homes also.

jumped to his feet and began to walk. Then he
went with them into the temple courts, walking
and jumping, and praising God. 9 When all the
people saw him walking and praising God, 10 they
recognized him as the same man who used to sit
begging at the temple gate called Beautiful, and
they were filled with wonder and amazement at
what had happened to him.

> ### ACTS 3:1–16
>
> 1. What do you do when a beggar asks you for money?
> 2. How would you answer if someone asked you, "Why is your life different?" or "Why do you go to church and stuff?"
> 3. In your school, who do you admire for the way they share their faith?
> 4. Like Peter (v. 6), what do you have that you could share or give to someone in the name of Christ?
> 5. What have you found helpful in sharing your faith?
> 6. Are you more excited about Christ today than you were at this time last year?
> 7. Who is someone "spiritually crippled" that you need to share the love of Christ with? Pray for that person.

Peter Speaks to the Onlookers

11 While the beggar held on to Peter and John,
all the people were astonished and came running
to them in the place called Solomon's Colonnade.
12 When Peter saw this, he said to them: "Men of
Israel, why does this surprise you? Why do you
stare at us as if by our own power or godliness we
had made this man walk? 13 The God of Abraham,
Isaac and Jacob, the God of our fathers, has glorified his servant Jesus. You handed him over to
be killed, and you disowned him before Pilate,
though he had decided to let him go. 14 You disowned the Holy and Righteous One and asked
that a murderer be released to you. 15 You killed
the author of life, but God raised him from the
dead. We are witnesses of this. 16 By faith in the
name of Jesus, this man whom you see and know
was made strong. It is Jesus' name and the faith
that comes through him that has given this complete healing to him, as you can all see.

17 "Now, brothers, I know that you acted in
ignorance, as did your leaders. 18 But this is how
God fulfilled what he had foretold through all the
prophets, saying that his Christ[a] would suffer.
19 Repent, then, and turn to God, so that your sins
may be wiped out, that times of refreshing may
come from the Lord, 20 and that he may send the
Christ, who has been appointed for you—even
Jesus. 21 He must remain in heaven until the time
comes for God to restore everything, as he promised long ago through his holy prophets. 22 For
Moses said, 'The Lord your God will raise up for
you a prophet like me from among your own
people; you must listen to everything he tells
you. 23 Anyone who does not listen to him will be
completely cut off from among his people.'[b]

24 "Indeed, all the prophets from Samuel on, as
many as have spoken, have foretold these days.
25 And you are heirs of the prophets and of the
covenant God made with your fathers. He said
to Abraham, 'Through your offspring all peoples
on earth will be blessed.'[c] 26 When God raised
up his servant, he sent him first to you to bless
you by turning each of you from your wicked
ways."

Peter and John Before the Sanhedrin

4 The priests and the captain of the temple
guard and the Sadducees came up to Peter
and John while they were speaking to the people.

[a] 18 Or *Messiah*; also in verse 20 [b] 23 Deut. 18:15,18,19 [c] 25 Gen. 22:18; 26:4

3:1–2 ***three in the afternoon.*** One of Judaism's stated times of prayer. ***put every day to beg.*** Beggars would gather about the temple in hopes of receiving alms since charity was a major part of Jewish piety.

3:4–5 ***Look at us!*** The man probably simply called out for alms without paying attention to whom he was talking. In contrast, Peter and John break through his impersonal routine by insisting that he pay attention to them. Thus the man's expectations for a generous gift must have been raised.

3:6–10 ***In the name of Jesus.*** By the authority of and presence of Jesus who so often healed the sick, this man is healed. ***walking and jumping, and praising God.*** The former cripple makes no attempt to hide his excitement! The celebration of the man draws a crowd that wonders how it could be that he is suddenly healed.

3:11–12 The miracle provides Peter another opportunity to proclaim Jesus to an interested audience. ***Why do you stare at us ... ?*** As at Pentecost (Acts 2:15), Peter is eager to direct attention away from the immediate phenomenon to the significance behind what has happened. Thus, he backs away from the miracle at hand to focus on Jesus.

3:14–15 Through two stark contrasts, Peter hammers home the enormity of the crime in which the Jewish people at large, in complicity with their leaders, have participated. They rejected the "Holy and Righteous One" (the Messiah) in favor of a murderer, and killed the "author of life" whom God determined to raise from death to life.

2They were greatly disturbed because the apostles were teaching the people and proclaiming in
Jesus the resurrection of the dead. 3They seized
Peter and John, and because it was evening, they
put them in jail until the next day. 4But many
who heard the message believed, and the number of men grew to about five thousand.
5The next day the rulers, elders and teachers
of the law met in Jerusalem. 6Annas the high
priest was there, and so were Caiaphas, John,
Alexander and the other men of the high priest's
family. 7They had Peter and John brought before
them and began to question them: "By what power or what name did you do this?"
8Then Peter, filled with the Holy Spirit, said to
them: "Rulers and elders of the people! 9If we are
being called to account today for an act of kindness shown to a cripple and are asked how he
was healed, 10then know this, you and all the
people of Israel: It is by the name of Jesus Christ
of Nazareth, whom you crucified but whom God
raised from the dead, that this man stands before
you healed. 11He is

" 'the stone you builders rejected,
which has become the capstone.'[a][b]

12Salvation is found in no one else, for there is no
other name under heaven given to men by which
we must be saved."
13When they saw the courage of Peter and
John and realized that they were unschooled, ordinary men, they were astonished and they took
note that these men had been with Jesus. 14But
since they could see the man who had been
healed standing there with them, there was nothing they could say. 15So they ordered them to
withdraw from the Sanhedrin and then conferred
together. 16"What are we going to do with these
men?" they asked. "Everybody living in Jerusalem knows they have done an outstanding miracle, and we cannot deny it. 17But to stop this
thing from spreading any further among the people, we must warn these men to speak no longer
to anyone in this name."
18Then they called them in again and commanded them not to speak or teach at all in the
name of Jesus. 19But Peter and John replied,
"Judge for yourselves whether it is right in God's
sight to obey you rather than God. 20For we cannot help speaking about what we have seen and
heard."
21After further threats they let them go. They
could not decide how to punish them, because all
the people were praising God for what had happened. 22For the man who was miraculously
healed was over forty years old.

The Believers' Prayer

23On their release, Peter and John went back
to their own people and reported all that the
chief priests and elders had said to them. 24When
they heard this, they raised their voices together
in prayer to God. "Sovereign Lord," they said,
"you made the heaven and the earth and the sea,
and everything in them. 25You spoke by the Holy
Spirit through the mouth of your servant, our
father David:

" 'Why do the nations rage
and the peoples plot in vain?
26The kings of the earth take their stand
and the rulers gather together
against the Lord
and against his Anointed One.'[c][d]

27Indeed Herod and Pontius Pilate met together
with the Gentiles and the people[e] of Israel in
this city to conspire against your holy servant
Jesus, whom you anointed. 28They did what your
power and will had decided beforehand should
happen. 29Now, Lord, consider their threats and
enable your servants to speak your word with
great boldness. 30Stretch out your hand to heal
and perform miraculous signs and wonders
through the name of your holy servant Jesus."
31After they prayed, the place where they
were meeting was shaken. And they were all
filled with the Holy Spirit and spoke the word of
God boldly.

The Believers Share Their Possessions

32All the believers were one in heart and
mind. No one claimed that any of his possessions
was his own, but they shared everything they
had. 33With great power the apostles continued
to testify to the resurrection of the Lord Jesus,
and much grace was upon them all. 34There were
no needy persons among them. For from time
to time those who owned lands or houses sold
them, brought the money from the sales 35and
put it at the apostles' feet, and it was distributed
to anyone as he had need.
36Joseph, a Levite from Cyprus, whom the
apostles called Barnabas (which means Son of
Encouragement), 37sold a field he owned and
brought the money and put it at the apostles'
feet.

Ananias and Sapphira

5 Now a man named Ananias, together with
his wife Sapphira, also sold a piece of property. 2With his wife's full knowledge he kept back
part of the money for himself, but brought the
rest and put it at the apostles' feet.

[a] *11* Or *cornerstone* [b] *11* Psalm 118:22 [c] *26* That is, Christ or Messiah [d] *26* Psalm 2:1,2 [e] *27* The Greek is plural.

3Then Peter said, "Ananias, how is it that Satan has so filled your heart that you have lied to the Holy Spirit and have kept for yourself some of the money you received for the land? 4Didn't it belong to you before it was sold? And after it was sold, wasn't the money at your disposal? What made you think of doing such a thing? You have not lied to men but to God."

5When Ananias heard this, he fell down and died. And great fear seized all who heard what had happened. 6Then the young men came forward, wrapped up his body, and carried him out and buried him.

7About three hours later his wife came in, not knowing what had happened. 8Peter asked her, "Tell me, is this the price you and Ananias got for the land?"

"Yes," she said, "that is the price."

9Peter said to her, "How could you agree to test the Spirit of the Lord? Look! The feet of the men who buried your husband are at the door, and they will carry you out also."

10At that moment she fell down at his feet and died. Then the young men came in and, finding her dead, carried her out and buried her beside her husband. 11Great fear seized the whole church and all who heard about these events.

? *Acts 5:1–11*

1. When have you gotten caught with your "hand in the cookie jar"?
2. Describe a time when you told the truth even though it wasn't easy.
3. How do you feel about the severity of punishment in this story?
4. What were Ananias and Sapphira guilty of?
5. In your life, where are you most tempted to be dishonest or lack integrity in some way?
6. On a scale from 1 (totally honest) to 10 (tell lies on a regular basis), how would you rate your honesty quotient right now?
7. How can this group help you walk in integrity? Pray for one another.

The Apostles Heal Many

12The apostles performed many miraculous signs and wonders among the people. And all the believers used to meet together in Solomon's Colonnade. 13No one else dared join them, even though they were highly regarded by the people. 14Nevertheless, more and more men and women believed in the Lord and were added to their number. 15As a result, people brought the sick into the streets and laid them on beds and mats so that at least Peter's shadow might fall on some of them as he passed by. 16Crowds gathered also from the towns around Jerusalem, bringing their sick and those tormented by evil[a] spirits, and all of them were healed.

The Apostles Persecuted

17Then the high priest and all his associates, who were members of the party of the Sadducees, were filled with jealousy. 18They arrested the apostles and put them in the public jail. 19But during the night an angel of the Lord opened the doors of the jail and brought them out. 20"Go, stand in the temple courts," he said, "and tell the people the full message of this new life."

21At daybreak they entered the temple courts, as they had been told, and began to teach the people.

When the high priest and his associates arrived, they called together the Sanhedrin—the full assembly of the elders of Israel—and sent to the jail for the apostles. 22But on arriving at the jail, the officers did not find them there. So they went back and reported, 23"We found the jail securely locked, with the guards standing at the

a16 Greek *unclean*

5:1–4 Following the example of Barnabas and others (4:34–37), Ananias and Sapphira sold some land. They then gave *part* of the proceeds to the apostles while claiming they had given it all. Peter's rebuke (v. 4) makes it plain that their sin was not in keeping back some of the money (which they had every right to do if they chose), but in lying about the fact. This lie showed that, rather than desiring to help the needy like Barnabas and the others, the couple gave what they did to "buy" their way to an elevated status in the community.

5:4 ***What made you think.*** Literally, "to lay to heart." This was not an impulsive act, but the result of careful deliberation prompted and encouraged by Satan (v. 3). ***You have not lied to men but to God.*** Peter's statement is not to minimize the fact that they *did* lie to people, but to highlight the fact that this lie was primarily an affront to God. Their lie showed that they failed to take the Holy Spirit's presence with the community seriously; and their action threatened the trust and integrity that formed the basis of the fellowship among the believers.

5:5–10 Either from heart failure at the surprise exposure of their sin, or from a direct act of God, both Ananias and Sapphira died when their act was revealed. ***test the Spirit of the Lord.*** Their act betrayed their disbelief that the Holy Spirit really knew all that happened. It was crucial at the outset of the church to eliminate any doubt that God could be deceived or even tolerate deceit.

5:11 The result of this incident was that the entire community recognized the seriousness of the presence of God in their midst.

doors; but when we opened them, we found no
one inside." 24On hearing this report, the captain
of the temple guard and the chief priests were
puzzled, wondering what would come of this.
25Then someone came and said, "Look! The
men you put in jail are standing in the temple
courts teaching the people." 26At that, the captain went with his officers and brought the apostles. They did not use force, because they feared
that the people would stone them.
27Having brought the apostles, they made
them appear before the Sanhedrin to be questioned by the high priest. 28"We gave you strict
orders not to teach in this name," he said. "Yet
you have filled Jerusalem with your teaching and
are determined to make us guilty of this man's
blood."
29Peter and the other apostles replied: "We
must obey God rather than men! 30The God of
our fathers raised Jesus from the dead—whom
you had killed by hanging him on a tree. 31God
exalted him to his own right hand as Prince and
Savior that he might give repentance and forgiveness of sins to Israel. 32We are witnesses of these
things, and so is the Holy Spirit, whom God has
given to those who obey him."
33When they heard this, they were furious and
wanted to put them to death. 34But a Pharisee
named Gamaliel, a teacher of the law, who was
honored by all the people, stood up in the Sanhedrin and ordered that the men be put outside for
a little while. 35Then he addressed them: "Men
of Israel, consider carefully what you intend to
do to these men. 36Some time ago Theudas appeared, claiming to be somebody, and about four
hundred men rallied to him. He was killed, all his
followers were dispersed, and it all came to nothing. 37After him, Judas the Galilean appeared in
the days of the census and led a band of people in
revolt. He too was killed, and all his followers
were scattered. 38Therefore, in the present case
I advise you: Leave these men alone! Let them
go! For if their purpose or activity is of human
origin, it will fail. 39But if it is from God, you will
not be able to stop these men; you will only find
yourselves fighting against God."
40His speech persuaded them. They called the
apostles in and had them flogged. Then they ordered them not to speak in the name of Jesus, and
let them go.
41The apostles left the Sanhedrin, rejoicing because they had been counted worthy of suffering
disgrace for the Name. 42Day after day, in the
temple courts and from house to house, they never stopped teaching and proclaiming the good
news that Jesus is the Christ.[a]

The Choosing of the Seven

6 In those days when the number of disciples
was increasing, the Grecian Jews among

Acts 6:1–7

1. If you worked in a restaurant, what job would you like to have?
2. If you had to describe this group in terms of bones, who would be the backbone? Wishbone? Funny bone? Ham bone?
3. How can you tell if someone is "full of the Spirit and wisdom" (v. 3)?
4. What are some spiritual gifts (see 1 Cor. 12:8–10)? What gift do you have?
5. If your youth group were to go on a mission trip to build a church, who would you assign to be the foreman? Carpenter? Landscaper? Decorator? Chauffeur?
6. Let others in the group share what special gift they see that God has given you.
7. What's one way you can use your spiritual gifts this week? Close in prayer.

a*42* Or *Messiah*

6:1 Growing numbers led to this problem centered around questions of fairness in the distribution of food to the poor widows in the church. ***Grecian Jews.*** Jews with a Greek or Hellenistic cultural background who came from outside Palestine and for whom Aramaic and Hebrew were relatively unknown languages. ***Hebraic Jews.*** Jews native to Palestine who spoke Aramaic (and probably Hebrew) and maintained Jewish customs and culture. Since all the apostles were Hebraic Jews, they may have been more aware of the needs of that segment.

6:2 ***the Twelve.*** The apostles at this time were still responsible for the church's spiritual ministry (prayer and the ministry of the word) and physical ministry (caring for the needy). ***wait on tables.*** While many groups use this passage as the basis for the office of deacon, there is no title given to the seven men chosen. However, the Greek verb "to serve" is the root word from which the English word "deacon" comes.

6:3 ***choose seven men.*** The church at large selected them (v. 5), and the apostles commissioned them (v. 6). ***full of the Spirit.*** Indicating an ongoing lifestyle that reflects the presence of Christ. ***and wisdom.*** Proven insight into difficult situations.

6:5–6 The names of the men chosen indicate all seven were Greek-speaking. The complaints came from their ranks, so this would ensure that their concerns were fairly represented. ***laid their hands on them.*** Signifying that the Seven would now be the representatives of the Twelve in the matter over which they were given responsibility.

them complained against the Hebraic Jews because their widows were being overlooked in the daily distribution of food. 2So the Twelve gathered all the disciples together and said, "It would not be right for us to neglect the ministry of the word of God in order to wait on tables. 3Brothers, choose seven men from among you who are known to be full of the Spirit and wisdom. We will turn this responsibility over to them 4and will give our attention to prayer and the ministry of the word."

5This proposal pleased the whole group. They chose Stephen, a man full of faith and of the Holy Spirit; also Philip, Procorus, Nicanor, Timon, Parmenas, and Nicolas from Antioch, a convert to Judaism. 6They presented these men to the apostles, who prayed and laid their hands on them.

7So the word of God spread. The number of disciples in Jerusalem increased rapidly, and a large number of priests became obedient to the faith.

Stephen Seized

8Now Stephen, a man full of God's grace and power, did great wonders and miraculous signs among the people. 9Opposition arose, however, from members of the Synagogue of the Freedmen (as it was called)—Jews of Cyrene and Alexandria as well as the provinces of Cilicia and Asia. These men began to argue with Stephen, 10but they could not stand up against his wisdom or the Spirit by whom he spoke.

11Then they secretly persuaded some men to say, "We have heard Stephen speak words of blasphemy against Moses and against God."

12So they stirred up the people and the elders and the teachers of the law. They seized Stephen and brought him before the Sanhedrin. 13They produced false witnesses, who testified, "This fellow never stops speaking against this holy place and against the law. 14For we have heard him say that this Jesus of Nazareth will destroy this place and change the customs Moses handed down to us."

15All who were sitting in the Sanhedrin looked intently at Stephen, and they saw that his face was like the face of an angel.

Stephen's Speech to the Sanhedrin

7 Then the high priest asked him, "Are these charges true?"

2To this he replied: "Brothers and fathers, listen to me! The God of glory appeared to our father Abraham while he was still in Mesopotamia, before he lived in Haran. 3'Leave your country and your people,' God said, 'and go to the land I will show you.'[a]

4"So he left the land of the Chaldeans and settled in Haran. After the death of his father, God sent him to this land where you are now living. 5He gave him no inheritance here, not even a foot of ground. But God promised him that he and his descendants after him would possess the land, even though at that time Abraham had no child. 6God spoke to him in this way: 'Your descendants will be strangers in a country not their own, and they will be enslaved and mistreated four hundred years. 7But I will punish the nation they serve as slaves,' God said, 'and afterward they will come out of that country and worship me in this place.'[b] 8Then he gave Abraham the covenant of circumcision. And Abraham became the father of Isaac and circumcised him eight days after his birth. Later Isaac became the father of Jacob, and Jacob became the father of the twelve patriarchs.

9"Because the patriarchs were jealous of Joseph, they sold him as a slave into Egypt. But God was with him 10and rescued him from all his troubles. He gave Joseph wisdom and enabled him to gain the goodwill of Pharaoh king of Egypt; so he made him ruler over Egypt and all his palace.

11"Then a famine struck all Egypt and Canaan, bringing great suffering, and our fathers could not find food. 12When Jacob heard that there was grain in Egypt, he sent our fathers on their first visit. 13On their second visit, Joseph told his brothers who he was, and Pharaoh learned about Joseph's family. 14After this, Joseph sent for his father Jacob and his whole family, seventy-five in all. 15Then Jacob went down to Egypt, where he and our fathers died. 16Their bodies were brought back to Shechem and placed in the tomb that Abraham had bought from the sons of Hamor at Shechem for a certain sum of money.

17"As the time drew near for God to fulfill his promise to Abraham, the number of our people in Egypt greatly increased. 18Then another king, who knew nothing about Joseph, became ruler of Egypt. 19He dealt treacherously with our people and oppressed our forefathers by forcing them to throw out their newborn babies so that they would die.

20"At that time Moses was born, and he was no ordinary child.[c] For three months he was cared for in his father's house. 21When he was placed outside, Pharaoh's daughter took him and brought him up as her own son. 22Moses was

[a] 3 Gen. 12:1 [b] 7 Gen. 15:13,14 [c] 20 Or *was fair in the sight of God*

educated in all the wisdom of the Egyptians and
was powerful in speech and action.
23"When Moses was forty years old, he decided to visit his fellow Israelites. 24He saw one of
them being mistreated by an Egyptian, so he
went to his defense and avenged him by killing
the Egyptian. 25Moses thought that his own people would realize that God was using him to rescue them, but they did not. 26The next day Moses
came upon two Israelites who were fighting. He
tried to reconcile them by saying, 'Men, you are
brothers; why do you want to hurt each other?'
27"But the man who was mistreating the other
pushed Moses aside and said, 'Who made you
ruler and judge over us? 28Do you want to kill me
as you killed the Egyptian yesterday?'[a] 29When
Moses heard this, he fled to Midian, where he
settled as a foreigner and had two sons.
30"After forty years had passed, an angel appeared to Moses in the flames of a burning bush
in the desert near Mount Sinai. 31When he saw
this, he was amazed at the sight. As he went over
to look more closely, he heard the Lord's voice:
32'I am the God of your fathers, the God of Abraham, Isaac and Jacob.'[b] Moses trembled with
fear and did not dare to look.
33"Then the Lord said to him, 'Take off your
sandals; the place where you are standing is holy
ground. 34I have indeed seen the oppression of
my people in Egypt. I have heard their groaning
and have come down to set them free. Now
come, I will send you back to Egypt.'[c]
35"This is the same Moses whom they had
rejected with the words, 'Who made you ruler
and judge?' He was sent to be their ruler and
deliverer by God himself, through the angel who
appeared to him in the bush. 36He led them out
of Egypt and did wonders and miraculous signs in
Egypt, at the Red Sea[d] and for forty years in the
desert.
37"This is that Moses who told the Israelites,
'God will send you a prophet like me from your
own people.'[e] 38He was in the assembly in the
desert, with the angel who spoke to him on
Mount Sinai, and with our fathers; and he received living words to pass on to us.
39"But our fathers refused to obey him. Instead, they rejected him and in their hearts
turned back to Egypt. 40They told Aaron, 'Make
us gods who will go before us. As for this fellow
Moses who led us out of Egypt—we don't know
what has happened to him!'[f] 41That was the
time they made an idol in the form of a calf. They
brought sacrifices to it and held a celebration in
honor of what their hands had made. 42But God
turned away and gave them over to the worship
of the heavenly bodies. This agrees with what is
written in the book of the prophets:

"'Did you bring me sacrifices and offerings
forty years in the desert, O house of
Israel?
43You have lifted up the shrine of Molech
and the star of your god Rephan,
the idols you made to worship.
Therefore I will send you into exile'[g]
beyond Babylon.

44"Our forefathers had the tabernacle of the
Testimony with them in the desert. It had been
made as God directed Moses, according to the
pattern he had seen. 45Having received the tabernacle, our fathers under Joshua brought it with
them when they took the land from the nations
God drove out before them. It remained in the
land until the time of David, 46who enjoyed
God's favor and asked that he might provide a
dwelling place for the God of Jacob.[h] 47But it
was Solomon who built the house for him.
48"However, the Most High does not live in
houses made by men. As the prophet says:

49"'Heaven is my throne,
and the earth is my footstool.
What kind of house will you build for me?
says the Lord.
Or where will my resting place be?
50Has not my hand made all these things?'[i]

51"You stiff-necked people, with uncircumcised hearts and ears! You are just like your fathers: You always resist the Holy Spirit! 52Was
there ever a prophet your fathers did not persecute? They even killed those who predicted the
coming of the Righteous One. And now you have
betrayed and murdered him— 53you who have
received the law that was put into effect through
angels but have not obeyed it."

The Stoning of Stephen

54When they heard this, they were furious and
gnashed their teeth at him. 55But Stephen, full of
the Holy Spirit, looked up to heaven and saw the
glory of God, and Jesus standing at the right hand
of God. 56"Look," he said, "I see heaven open
and the Son of Man standing at the right hand of
God."
57At this they covered their ears and, yelling at
the top of their voices, they all rushed at him,
58dragged him out of the city and began to stone
him. Meanwhile, the witnesses laid their clothes
at the feet of a young man named Saul.
59While they were stoning him, Stephen
prayed, "Lord Jesus, receive my spirit." 60Then

[a] 28 Exodus 2:14 [b] 32 Exodus 3:6 [c] 34 Exodus 3:5,7,8,10 [d] 36 That is, Sea of Reeds [e] 37 Deut. 18:15
[f] 40 Exodus 32:1 [g] 43 Amos 5:25-27 [h] 46 Some early manuscripts *the house of Jacob* [i] 50 Isaiah 66:1,2

he fell on his knees and cried out, "Lord, do not
hold this sin against them." When he had said
this, he fell asleep.

8 And Saul was there, giving approval to his
death.

The Church Persecuted and Scattered

On that day a great persecution broke out
against the church at Jerusalem, and all except
the apostles were scattered throughout Judea
and Samaria. 2Godly men buried Stephen and
mourned deeply for him. 3But Saul began to destroy the church. Going from house to house, he
dragged off men and women and put them in
prison.

Philip in Samaria

4Those who had been scattered preached the
word wherever they went. 5Philip went down to
a city in Samaria and proclaimed the Christ[a]
there. 6When the crowds heard Philip and saw
the miraculous signs he did, they all paid close
attention to what he said. 7With shrieks, evil[b]
spirits came out of many, and many paralytics and
cripples were healed. 8So there was great joy in
that city.

Simon the Sorcerer

9Now for some time a man named Simon had
practiced sorcery in the city and amazed all the
people of Samaria. He boasted that he was someone great, 10and all the people, both high and
low, gave him their attention and exclaimed,
"This man is the divine power known as the
Great Power." 11They followed him because he
had amazed them for a long time with his magic.
12But when they believed Philip as he preached
the good news of the kingdom of God and the
name of Jesus Christ, they were baptized, both
men and women. 13Simon himself believed and
was baptized. And he followed Philip everywhere, astonished by the great signs and miracles
he saw.

14When the apostles in Jerusalem heard that
Samaria had accepted the word of God, they sent
Peter and John to them. 15When they arrived,
they prayed for them that they might receive the
Holy Spirit, 16because the Holy Spirit had not yet
come upon any of them; they had simply been
baptized into[c] the name of the Lord Jesus.
17Then Peter and John placed their hands on
them, and they received the Holy Spirit.

18When Simon saw that the Spirit was given at
the laying on of the apostles' hands, he offered
them money 19and said, "Give me also this ability
so that everyone on whom I lay my hands may
receive the Holy Spirit."

20Peter answered: "May your money perish
with you, because you thought you could buy the
gift of God with money! 21You have no part or
share in this ministry, because your heart is not
right before God. 22Repent of this wickedness
and pray to the Lord. Perhaps he will forgive you
for having such a thought in your heart. 23For I
see that you are full of bitterness and captive to
sin."

24Then Simon answered, "Pray to the Lord for
me so that nothing you have said may happen
to me."

25When they had testified and proclaimed the
word of the Lord, Peter and John returned to
Jerusalem, preaching the gospel in many Samaritan villages.

Philip and the Ethiopian

26Now an angel of the Lord said to Philip, "Go
south to the road—the desert road—that goes
down from Jerusalem to Gaza." 27So he started
out, and on his way he met an Ethiopian[d] eunuch, an important official in charge of all the
treasury of Candace, queen of the Ethiopians.
This man had gone to Jerusalem to worship,
28and on his way home was sitting in his chariot
reading the book of Isaiah the prophet. 29The
Spirit told Philip, "Go to that chariot and stay
near it."

30Then Philip ran up to the chariot and heard
the man reading Isaiah the prophet. "Do you understand what you are reading?" Philip asked.

31"How can I," he said, "unless someone explains it to me?" So he invited Philip to come up
and sit with him.

32The eunuch was reading this passage of
Scripture:

"He was led like a sheep to the slaughter,
  and as a lamb before the shearer is silent,
  so he did not open his mouth.
33In his humiliation he was deprived of justice.
  Who can speak of his descendants?
  For his life was taken from the earth."[e]

34The eunuch asked Philip, "Tell me, please,
who is the prophet talking about, himself or
someone else?" 35Then Philip began with that
very passage of Scripture and told him the good
news about Jesus.

36As they traveled along the road, they came to
some water and the eunuch said, "Look, here is
water. Why shouldn't I be baptized?"[f] 38And he
gave orders to stop the chariot. Then both Philip

[a] 5 Or *Messiah* [b] 7 Greek *unclean* [c] 16 Or *in* [d] 27 That is, from the upper Nile region [e] 33 Isaiah 53:7,8
[f] 36 Some late manuscripts *baptized?" 37Philip said, "If you believe with all your heart, you may." The eunuch answered, "I believe that Jesus Christ is the Son of God."*

and the eunuch went down into the water and
Philip baptized him. 39When they came up out of
the water, the Spirit of the Lord suddenly took
Philip away, and the eunuch did not see him
again, but went on his way rejoicing. 40Philip,
however, appeared at Azotus and traveled about,
preaching the gospel in all the towns until he
reached Caesarea.

Saul's Conversion

9 Meanwhile, Saul was still breathing out murderous threats against the Lord's disciples.
He went to the high priest 2and asked him for
letters to the synagogues in Damascus, so that if
he found any there who belonged to the Way,
whether men or women, he might take them as
prisoners to Jerusalem. 3As he neared Damascus
on his journey, suddenly a light from heaven
flashed around him. 4He fell to the ground and
heard a voice say to him, "Saul, Saul, why do you
persecute me?"
5"Who are you, Lord?" Saul asked.
"I am Jesus, whom you are persecuting," he
replied. 6"Now get up and go into the city, and
you will be told what you must do."
7The men traveling with Saul stood there
speechless; they heard the sound but did not see
anyone. 8Saul got up from the ground, but when
he opened his eyes he could see nothing. So they
led him by the hand into Damascus. 9For three
days he was blind, and did not eat or drink anything.

ACTS 8:26–40

1. When did you get your first Bible? Who gave it to you?
2. What is your favorite Bible story or verse?
3. How much time do you spend reading the Bible?
4. Who, like Philip, helped you understand the Bible? What was the most important thing that person taught you?
5. How do you go about studying the Bible for yourself?
6. What goal would you like to set for yourself for Bible reading that you would allow this group to hold you accountable to?
7. How would you describe the road you are traveling on right now: Rough? Smooth? Lonely? Pray for one another.

ACTS 9:1–19

1. When did you "convert" to the hairstyle you now have?
2. How did the Lord first get your attention? How did you respond?
3. Who has been your spiritual mentor in your life—the person who has helped you grow in the faith?
4. How would you compare your experience with Christ to Paul's experience: Similar? Less emotional? Different—but just as real?
5. If Paul came to your school and shared about his conversion experience, how would his story be received?
6. If you had to explain how you met Jesus to one of your friends, what would you say?
7. Since committing your life to Christ, what has been the biggest change? Close in prayer.

(Study notes on page 1006)

8:26 ***Philip.*** One of the Seven chosen to oversee the ministry of distributing aid to the needy in the Jerusalem church (6:5). Now he has become an evangelist, spreading the good news about Jesus (v. 35).

8:27 ***eunuch.*** Eunuchs like this Ethiopian were commonly employed as royal officials. Due to his castration he would not be allowed to participate fully in the temple worship (Deut. 23:1), yet this Gentile was obviously attracted to Judaism. ***Candace.*** A title for the Ethiopian queens.

8:32–35 The eunuch was reading from Isaiah 53:7–8, a key OT passage about the Servant of the Lord. Philip used this as a starting place to explain the Gospel. He undoubtedly referred to other passages about the Servant in Isaiah which point out the Servant's suffering for the sake of others. All of this would have been related to Jesus' ministry, death and resurrection.

8:36–38 ***Why shouldn't I ... ?*** The strict Jew would offer at least one reason why he was ineligible to be considered part of God's people: he was a eunuch. However, he was able to become a full member of Christ's church. This fulfills the prophecy of Isaiah 56:3–7 which anticipates a time when foreigners and eunuchs would be welcomed into God's household. ***Philip baptized him.*** In Acts baptism is associated with acceptance of God's word, belief and repentance.

8:39 ***Spirit of the Lord suddenly took Philip away.*** Whether this was a miraculous act of God or another way of describing a command of the Spirit (v. 29) is uncertain.

10 In Damascus there was a disciple named Ananias. The Lord called to him in a vision, "Ananias!"
"Yes, Lord," he answered.
11 The Lord told him, "Go to the house of Judas
on Straight Street and ask for a man from Tarsus
named Saul, for he is praying. 12 In a vision he has
seen a man named Ananias come and place his
hands on him to restore his sight."
13 "Lord," Ananias answered, "I have heard
many reports about this man and all the harm he
has done to your saints in Jerusalem. 14 And he
has come here with authority from the chief
priests to arrest all who call on your name."
15 But the Lord said to Ananias, "Go! This man
is my chosen instrument to carry my name before
the Gentiles and their kings and before the people of Israel. 16 I will show him how much he
must suffer for my name."
17 Then Ananias went to the house and entered it. Placing his hands on Saul, he said,
"Brother Saul, the Lord—Jesus, who appeared to
you on the road as you were coming here—has
sent me so that you may see again and be filled
with the Holy Spirit." 18 Immediately, something
like scales fell from Saul's eyes, and he could see
again. He got up and was baptized, 19 and after
taking some food, he regained his strength.

Saul in Damascus and Jerusalem

Saul spent several days with the disciples in
Damascus. 20 At once he began to preach in the
synagogues that Jesus is the Son of God. 21 All
those who heard him were astonished and asked,
"Isn't he the man who raised havoc in Jerusalem
among those who call on this name? And hasn't
he come here to take them as prisoners to the
chief priests?" 22 Yet Saul grew more and more
powerful and baffled the Jews living in Damascus
by proving that Jesus is the Christ.[a]
23 After many days had gone by, the Jews conspired to kill him, 24 but Saul learned of their plan.
Day and night they kept close watch on the city
gates in order to kill him. 25 But his followers
took him by night and lowered him in a basket
through an opening in the wall.
26 When he came to Jerusalem, he tried to join
the disciples, but they were all afraid of him, not
believing that he really was a disciple. 27 But Barnabas took him and brought him to the apostles.
He told them how Saul on his journey had seen
the Lord and that the Lord had spoken to him,
and how in Damascus he had preached fearlessly
in the name of Jesus. 28 So Saul stayed with them
and moved about freely in Jerusalem, speaking
boldly in the name of the Lord. 29 He talked and
debated with the Grecian Jews, but they tried to
kill him. 30 When the brothers learned of this,

Acts 9:20–31

1. What clubs, teams, groups or organizations are you a member of?
2. If the meanest person at your school accepted Christ, how would you do at accepting this person?
3. Where do you feel the most accepted? The least?
4. What did Paul do to show he was a Christian? How was he accepted?
5. Who has been a Barnabas to you—encouraging or helping you feel accepted?
6. What do you do to show others you're a Christian? How has this affected how you are accepted by others?
7. Who is someone you could be a Barnabas to this week? Pray for one another.

(Study notes on page 1007)

[a]22 Or *Messiah*

9:1 ***Saul.*** First seen at Stephen's stoning (7:58). Saul (later known as the apostle Paul) trained under the famous rabbi Gamaliel and had great zeal for the Jewish Law (22:3). ***breathing out murderous threats.*** Reflecting the depth of Saul's hatred of Christians. He viewed them as a heretical sect and believed they were determined to undermine the Law of Moses and worship at the temple. Though inflicting the death penalty would have been prohibited by Roman law, he and the Sanhedrin (led by the high priest), did so (22:4; 26:10).

9:2 ***letters.*** The Sanhedrin asked the elders of the synagogue in Damascus (about 150 miles from Jerusalem) to cooperate with Saul, helping him arrest Christians who had fled from Jerusalem. ***the Way.*** Christianity.

9:4–6 ***why do you persecute me?*** Saul's opposition to the church was really directed against its Head. Saul is faced with the fact that he is not honoring God by his activities, but is resisting the One glorified by God. ***I am Jesus.*** Not just a vision, the risen Christ actually appeared to Saul, becoming the basis for him to be an apostle (1 Cor. 9:1).

9:9 This profound experience shattered Saul's previous convictions. Humbled and blinded, he fasted as he awaited what Jesus would do with him next.

9:10–17 The vision Ananias received was the same as the one Saul had of his arrival. Ananias is shocked by Jesus' command to go to the dreaded persecutor. The Lord overruled Ananias with a final command to "Go!" and a description of what Saul's mission would be. ***Brother Saul.*** Without further question, Ananias affirms Saul as part of God's family through the grace of Jesus.

they took him down to Caesarea and sent him off
to Tarsus.
31 Then the church throughout Judea, Galilee
and Samaria enjoyed a time of peace. It was
strengthened; and encouraged by the Holy Spirit,
it grew in numbers, living in the fear of the Lord.

Aeneas and Dorcas

32 As Peter traveled about the country, he went
to visit the saints in Lydda. 33 There he found a
man named Aeneas, a paralytic who had been
bedridden for eight years. 34 "Aeneas," Peter said
to him, "Jesus Christ heals you. Get up and take
care of your mat." Immediately Aeneas got up.
35 All those who lived in Lydda and Sharon saw
him and turned to the Lord.
36 In Joppa there was a disciple named Tabitha
(which, when translated, is Dorcas[a]), who was
always doing good and helping the poor. 37 About
that time she became sick and died, and her body
was washed and placed in an upstairs room.
38 Lydda was near Joppa; so when the disciples
heard that Peter was in Lydda, they sent two men
to him and urged him, "Please come at once!"
39 Peter went with them, and when he arrived
he was taken upstairs to the room. All the widows stood around him, crying and showing him
the robes and other clothing that Dorcas had
made while she was still with them.
40 Peter sent them all out of the room; then he
got down on his knees and prayed. Turning toward the dead woman, he said, "Tabitha, get
up." She opened her eyes, and seeing Peter she
sat up. 41 He took her by the hand and helped her
to her feet. Then he called the believers and the
widows and presented her to them alive. 42 This
became known all over Joppa, and many people
believed in the Lord. 43 Peter stayed in Joppa for
some time with a tanner named Simon.

Cornelius Calls for Peter

10 At Caesarea there was a man named Cornelius, a centurion in what was known as
the Italian Regiment. 2 He and all his family were
devout and God-fearing; he gave generously to
those in need and prayed to God regularly. 3 One
day at about three in the afternoon he had a vision. He distinctly saw an angel of God, who
came to him and said, "Cornelius!"
4 Cornelius stared at him in fear. "What is it,
Lord?" he asked.
The angel answered, "Your prayers and gifts to
the poor have come up as a memorial offering
before God. 5 Now send men to Joppa to bring
back a man named Simon who is called Peter.
6 He is staying with Simon the tanner, whose
house is by the sea."
7 When the angel who spoke to him had gone,
Cornelius called two of his servants and a devout
soldier who was one of his attendants. 8 He told
them everything that had happened and sent
them to Joppa.

Peter's Vision

9 About noon the following day as they were on
their journey and approaching the city, Peter
went up on the roof to pray. 10 He became hungry
and wanted something to eat, and while the meal
was being prepared, he fell into a trance. 11 He
saw heaven opened and something like a large
sheet being let down to earth by its four corners.
12 It contained all kinds of four-footed animals, as
well as reptiles of the earth and birds of the air.
13 Then a voice told him, "Get up, Peter. Kill and
eat."
14 "Surely not, Lord!" Peter replied. "I have
never eaten anything impure or unclean."
15 The voice spoke to him a second time, "Do
not call anything impure that God has made
clean."
16 This happened three times, and immediately
the sheet was taken back to heaven.
17 While Peter was wondering about the meaning of the vision, the men sent by Cornelius
found out where Simon's house was and stopped
at the gate. 18 They called out, asking if Simon
who was known as Peter was staying there.
19 While Peter was still thinking about the vi-

[a]36 Both *Tabitha* (Aramaic) and *Dorcas* (Greek) mean *gazelle*.

Saul, a zealous Pharisee, had been a vehement opponent of Christianity. But while on his way to Damascus to arrest believers, he had a life-changing encounter with the risen Jesus (vv. 3–5). As a result he not only became a Christian himself, but eventually the renowned apostle Paul.

9:20–21 *preach in the synagogues.* That Saul, as a representative from the Sanhedrin (Jewish religious high court), would be invited to speak in the synagogues is not surprising. What was unexpected was his message! The shocked reaction of the Jews in Damascus is understandable given their previous understanding of why Saul came to the city (vv. 1–2).

9:23 *conspired to kill him.* Perhaps under accusations that his teaching was causing an uproar in the Jewish community, the leaders of the synagogue were able to draw upon the help of the local governor in a plot to capture Saul (2 Cor. 11:32–33).

9:26 *the disciples.* This refers to the believers in general. Having been the victim of Saul's violent persecution earlier, the church in Jerusalem was naturally hesitant to believe he had so radically changed.

9:27–28 *Barnabas.* A nickname, meaning "Son of Encouragement," given this good-hearted man (Acts 4:36). How he knew the reality of Saul's story is not explained, but Barnabas clearly risked alienating himself from the church by siding with this former persecutor. Because of Barnabas' endorsement, Saul was accepted in the church.

sion, the Spirit said to him, "Simon, three[a] men
are looking for you. 20 So get up and go down-
stairs. Do not hesitate to go with them, for I have
sent them."

> ### ACTS 10:1–23
>
> 1. Which of these foods would you refuse to eat: Snails? Raw oysters? Pickled pigs' feet? Rocky Mountain oysters?
> 2. If Jesus was a student at your school, what crowd would he eat lunch with?
> 3. If you were put in charge of peacemaking at your school, what would you do? Who would you recruit for your team?
> 4. If a person of another color came to your church, how would this person be accepted? How about in your group?
> 5. In choosing friends, what is the most important thing?
> 6. How can this group reach out beyond cliques and race to include others?
> 7. If God gave you a vision about your attitude toward other people, what would he tell you? Respond to that message in prayer.

21 Peter went down and said to the men, "I'm
the one you're looking for. Why have you come?"
22 The men replied, "We have come from Cornelius the centurion. He is a righteous and God-
fearing man, who is respected by all the Jewish
people. A holy angel told him to have you come
to his house so that he could hear what you have
to say." 23 Then Peter invited the men into the
house to be his guests.

Peter at Cornelius' House

The next day Peter started out with them, and
some of the brothers from Joppa went along.
24 The following day he arrived in Caesarea. Cornelius was expecting them and had called together his relatives and close friends. 25 As Peter entered the house, Cornelius met him and fell at his
feet in reverence. 26 But Peter made him get up.
"Stand up," he said, "I am only a man myself."
27 Talking with him, Peter went inside and
found a large gathering of people. 28 He said to
them: "You are well aware that it is against our
law for a Jew to associate with a Gentile or visit
him. But God has shown me that I should not call
any man impure or unclean. 29 So when I was
sent for, I came without raising any objection.
May I ask why you sent for me?"
30 Cornelius answered: "Four days ago I was in
my house praying at this hour, at three in the
afternoon. Suddenly a man in shining clothes
stood before me 31 and said, 'Cornelius, God has
heard your prayer and remembered your gifts to
the poor. 32 Send to Joppa for Simon who is called
Peter. He is a guest in the home of Simon the
tanner, who lives by the sea.' 33 So I sent for you
immediately, and it was good of you to come.
Now we are all here in the presence of God to
listen to everything the Lord has commanded you
to tell us."
34 Then Peter began to speak: "I now realize
how true it is that God does not show favoritism
35 but accepts men from every nation who fear
him and do what is right. 36 You know the message God sent to the people of Israel, telling the
good news of peace through Jesus Christ, who
is Lord of all. 37 You know what has happened
throughout Judea, beginning in Galilee after the
baptism that John preached— 38 how God anointed Jesus of Nazareth with the Holy Spirit and
power, and how he went around doing good and

[a] 19 One early manuscript *two*; other manuscripts do not have the number.

10:1–2 ***centurion.*** A Roman military officer. ***God-fearing.*** Though Cornelius and his family had not converted to Judaism, they believed in the one true God and respected Jewish moral and ethical teachings.

10:9–12 The scene shifts to Joppa, about 30 miles south of Caesarea, where now it is Peter who is preparing for his daily time of prayer. ***on the roof.*** Roofs were flat and often used as places for people to relax. ***trance.*** God put Peter in a special state of mind where he could readily communicate with him through a vision of a large sheet full of animals. It contained both acceptable animals and those that the Law of Moses forbade the Jews from eating (Lev. 11).

10:15 ***God has made clean.*** In Mark 7:18–19 Jesus laid the groundwork for the pronouncement that food simply was not a spiritual issue. Dietary laws had their place earlier in Jewish history as a means of separating them from their ungodly neighbors, and as an object lesson about holiness. God's ultimate concern is genuine, inward holiness that has nothing to do with external matters such as food and circumcision.

10:17–21 Peter soon would come to see that if God can pronounce foods that were formerly unclean to now be acceptable, he can do the same thing with people. Just as the vision ends, the men sent by Cornelius arrive and inquire about Peter. At the same time, God's Spirit tells him to go with them. Peter would have to be expectant that something especially important was about to occur. Indeed, the centuries-long barrier between Jews and Gentiles is about to be broken as Cornelius and his relatives and close friends would soon be the first Gentiles to become Christians (vv. 44–48).

healing all who were under the power of the
devil, because God was with him.
39“We are witnesses of everything he did in
the country of the Jews and in Jerusalem. They
killed him by hanging him on a tree, 40but God
raised him from the dead on the third day and
caused him to be seen. 41He was not seen by all
the people, but by witnesses whom God had already chosen—by us who ate and drank with
him after he rose from the dead. 42He commanded us to preach to the people and to testify that
he is the one whom God appointed as judge of
the living and the dead. 43All the prophets testify
about him that everyone who believes in him
receives forgiveness of sins through his name.”
44While Peter was still speaking these words,
the Holy Spirit came on all who heard the message. 45The circumcised believers who had come
with Peter were astonished that the gift of the
Holy Spirit had been poured out even on the
Gentiles. 46For they heard them speaking in
tongues[a] and praising God.
Then Peter said, 47“Can anyone keep these
people from being baptized with water? They
have received the Holy Spirit just as we have.”
48So he ordered that they be baptized in the
name of Jesus Christ. Then they asked Peter to
stay with them for a few days.

Peter Explains His Actions

11 The apostles and the brothers throughout
Judea heard that the Gentiles also had received the word of God. 2So when Peter went up
to Jerusalem, the circumcised believers criticized
him 3and said, “You went into the house of uncircumcised men and ate with them.”
4Peter began and explained everything to
them precisely as it had happened: 5“I was in the
city of Joppa praying, and in a trance I saw a
vision. I saw something like a large sheet being
let down from heaven by its four corners, and it
came down to where I was. 6I looked into it and
saw four-footed animals of the earth, wild beasts,
reptiles, and birds of the air. 7Then I heard a
voice telling me, ‘Get up, Peter. Kill and eat.’
8“I replied, ‘Surely not, Lord! Nothing impure
or unclean has ever entered my mouth.’
9“The voice spoke from heaven a second time,
‘Do not call anything impure that God has made
clean.’ 10This happened three times, and then it
was all pulled up to heaven again.
11“Right then three men who had been sent to
me from Caesarea stopped at the house where I
was staying. 12The Spirit told me to have no hesitation about going with them. These six brothers
also went with me, and we entered the man’s
house. 13He told us how he had seen an angel
appear in his house and say, ‘Send to Joppa for
Simon who is called Peter. 14He will bring you a
message through which you and all your household will be saved.’
15“As I began to speak, the Holy Spirit came on
them as he had come on us at the beginning.
16Then I remembered what the Lord had said:
‘John baptized with[b] water, but you will be baptized with the Holy Spirit.’ 17So if God gave them
the same gift as he gave us, who believed in the
Lord Jesus Christ, who was I to think that I could
oppose God?”
18When they heard this, they had no further
objections and praised God, saying, “So then,
God has granted even the Gentiles repentance
unto life.”

The Church in Antioch

19Now those who had been scattered by the
persecution in connection with Stephen traveled
as far as Phoenicia, Cyprus and Antioch, telling
the message only to Jews. 20Some of them, however, men from Cyprus and Cyrene, went to Antioch and began to speak to Greeks also, telling
them the good news about the Lord Jesus. 21The
Lord’s hand was with them, and a great number
of people believed and turned to the Lord.
22News of this reached the ears of the church
at Jerusalem, and they sent Barnabas to Antioch.
23When he arrived and saw the evidence of the
grace of God, he was glad and encouraged them
all to remain true to the Lord with all their
hearts. 24He was a good man, full of the Holy
Spirit and faith, and a great number of people
were brought to the Lord.
25Then Barnabas went to Tarsus to look for
Saul, 26and when he found him, he brought him
to Antioch. So for a whole year Barnabas and Saul
met with the church and taught great numbers of
people. The disciples were called Christians first
at Antioch.
27During this time some prophets came down
from Jerusalem to Antioch. 28One of them,
named Agabus, stood up and through the Spirit
predicted that a severe famine would spread over
the entire Roman world. (This happened during
the reign of Claudius.) 29The disciples, each according to his ability, decided to provide help for
the brothers living in Judea. 30This they did,
sending their gift to the elders by Barnabas and
Saul.

Peter’s Miraculous Escape From Prison

12 It was about this time that King Herod
arrested some who belonged to the
church, intending to persecute them. 2He had
James, the brother of John, put to death with the

[a]46 Or *other languages* [b]16 Or *in*

sword. 3When he saw that this pleased the Jews, he proceeded to seize Peter also. This happened during the Feast of Unleavened Bread. 4After arresting him, he put him in prison, handing him over to be guarded by four squads of four soldiers each. Herod intended to bring him out for public trial after the Passover.

5So Peter was kept in prison, but the church was earnestly praying to God for him.

6The night before Herod was to bring him to trial, Peter was sleeping between two soldiers, bound with two chains, and sentries stood guard at the entrance. 7Suddenly an angel of the Lord appeared and a light shone in the cell. He struck Peter on the side and woke him up. "Quick, get up!" he said, and the chains fell off Peter's wrists.

8Then the angel said to him, "Put on your clothes and sandals." And Peter did so. "Wrap your cloak around you and follow me," the angel told him. 9Peter followed him out of the prison, but he had no idea that what the angel was doing was really happening; he thought he was seeing a vision. 10They passed the first and second guards and came to the iron gate leading to the city. It opened for them by itself, and they went through it. When they had walked the length of one street, suddenly the angel left him.

11Then Peter came to himself and said, "Now I know without a doubt that the Lord sent his angel and rescued me from Herod's clutches and from everything the Jewish people were anticipating."

12When this had dawned on him, he went to the house of Mary the mother of John, also called Mark, where many people had gathered and were praying. 13Peter knocked at the outer entrance, and a servant girl named Rhoda came to answer the door. 14When she recognized Peter's voice, she was so overjoyed she ran back without opening it and exclaimed, "Peter is at the door!"

15"You're out of your mind," they told her. When she kept insisting that it was so, they said, "It must be his angel."

16But Peter kept on knocking, and when they opened the door and saw him, they were astonished. 17Peter motioned with his hand for them to be quiet and described how the Lord had brought him out of prison. "Tell James and the brothers about this," he said, and then he left for another place.

18In the morning, there was no small commotion among the soldiers as to what had become of Peter. 19After Herod had a thorough search made for him and did not find him, he cross-examined the guards and ordered that they be executed.

Acts 12:1–19

1. What's your closest encounter with the police or other law enforcement authority?
2. If your group had to hide from the authorities because of their faith, where would you hide?
3. If one person in this group was put to death and another was thrown in jail, what would that persecution do to your group?
4. The church was praying for Peter (vv. 5,12). Why didn't they believe Peter was at the door?
5. When was a time you felt "imprisoned"? How did God deliver you?
6. If you were arrested by a repressive government for being a Christian, what evidence would there be that you are "guilty"? That you are "innocent"?
7. How can the group help you in prayer this week?

Herod's Death

Then Herod went from Judea to Caesarea and stayed there a while. 20He had been quarreling with the people of Tyre and Sidon; they now joined together and sought an audience with

---

12:1 ***Herod.*** Herod Agrippa I, the Roman representative king—the grandson of Herod the Great, who ruled when Jesus was born, and the nephew of Herod Antipas, who beheaded John the Baptist and questioned Jesus before his death. To further cultivate his popularity with the Jews, he resumed the persecution of the church which had ceased upon Saul's conversion (Acts 9:31).

12:2–4 After receiving support for executing the apostle James, Herod arrested Peter as well. While awaiting trial after Passover, Peter was constantly guarded by four soldiers. Such intense security measures may have been implemented precisely to prevent any "unexplainable" release such as happened when the Jewish religious leaders had imprisoned him earlier (Acts 5:19).

12:7–10 ***a light shone.*** The description of the light, a common symbol of divine glory, underscores that this was a miraculous intervention of God. In a trance-like state, Peter was led by the angel past the guards and through the main door of the prison.

12:12–16 Luke humorously recounts how Peter was left standing at the door while the disciples refused to believe that he could possibly be there! They were astonished, even though they had been "earnestly praying to God for him" (v. 5). ***It must be his angel.*** It was believed that each person had a guardian angel who watched over that individual. Assuming that Peter was killed, the only solution the disciples could come up with was that Peter's angel had taken on Peter's form. ***James.*** Jesus' brother (Mark 6:3), now a leader in the church.

him. Having secured the support of Blastus, a
trusted personal servant of the king, they asked
for peace, because they depended on the king's
country for their food supply.
21On the appointed day Herod, wearing his
royal robes, sat on his throne and delivered a
public address to the people. 22They shouted,
"This is the voice of a god, not of a man." 23Im-
mediately, because Herod did not give praise to
God, an angel of the Lord struck him down, and
he was eaten by worms and died.
24But the word of God continued to increase
and spread.
25When Barnabas and Saul had finished their
mission, they returned from[a] Jerusalem, taking
with them John, also called Mark.

Barnabas and Saul Sent Off

13 In the church at Antioch there were
prophets and teachers: Barnabas, Simeon
called Niger, Lucius of Cyrene, Manaen (who had
been brought up with Herod the tetrarch) and
Saul. 2While they were worshiping the Lord and
fasting, the Holy Spirit said, "Set apart for me
Barnabas and Saul for the work to which I have
called them." 3So after they had fasted and
prayed, they placed their hands on them and sent
them off.

On Cyprus

4The two of them, sent on their way by the
Holy Spirit, went down to Seleucia and sailed
from there to Cyprus. 5When they arrived at Sala-
mis, they proclaimed the word of God in the Jewish synagogues. John was with them as their
helper.
6They traveled through the whole island until
they came to Paphos. There they met a Jewish
sorcerer and false prophet named Bar-Jesus,
7who was an attendant of the proconsul, Sergius
Paulus. The proconsul, an intelligent man, sent
for Barnabas and Saul because he wanted to hear
the word of God. 8But Elymas the sorcerer (for
that is what his name means) opposed them and
tried to turn the proconsul from the faith. 9Then
Saul, who was also called Paul, filled with the
Holy Spirit, looked straight at Elymas and said,
10"You are a child of the devil and an enemy of
everything that is right! You are full of all kinds of
deceit and trickery. Will you never stop pervert-
ing the right ways of the Lord? 11Now the hand
of the Lord is against you. You are going to be
blind, and for a time you will be unable to see the
light of the sun."
Immediately mist and darkness came over
him, and he groped about, seeking someone to
lead him by the hand. 12When the proconsul saw

Acts 13:1–12

1. What was the strangest belief you had when you were a kid?
2. Who are the "false prophets" in your culture who are trying to turn people "from the faith" (v. 8)?
3. What kind of cults or strange beliefs are students at your school involved with?
4. What test do you use to distinguish true teaching from false?
5. What do you do when approached by someone from a cult? How does this compare to how Paul confronted Elymas (vv. 9–10)?
6. How would you describe your spiritual eyesight right now: Blind? 20-20? A few blind spots?
7. Close in prayer. Pray for those you know who have been led astray.

[a] 25 Some manuscripts *to*

13:1–3 *Antioch.* The capital of the Roman province of Syria. The first mostly Gentile church was established here (11:19–26). In the context of prayer and worship, the Spirit calls, and commissions, Saul (Paul) and Barnabas to undertake their first mission.

13:4–5 *Cyprus.* This island in the northeastern Mediterranean was Barnabas' home (Acts 4:36). ***synagogues.*** Throughout most of Paul's travels he made it a point to begin his ministry by preaching in the synagogues in the hope that his Jewish listeners would believe in Jesus as the Messiah.

13:6–8 *Paphos.* The Roman seat of power on Cyprus. ***a Jewish sorcerer.*** The practice of magic was forbidden to Jews. However, outside of Palestine some Jewish religious practices tended to reflect much of the surrounding culture. ***proconsul.*** Provinces like Cyprus that did not require troops to maintain order were administered by the Roman Senate through proconsuls. ***Elymas.*** This name, meaning "sorcerer," "magician," or "wise man," was likely self-assigned.

13:9–10 *Saul.* His Hebrew name. ***Paul.*** His Roman name—which is used exclusively for the "apostle to the Gentiles" from this point. ***child of the devil.*** Though Elymas was also called Bar-Jesus (meaning "son of a savior"), Paul does not hesitate to declare that his opposition to the Gospel means he reflects the characteristics of Satan.

13:11–12 *You are going to be blind.* This was a temporary blindness ("for a time"), meant as a warning for Elymas to repent. Whether or not it had the desired effect is not mentioned. But in combination with Paul's message, it was a miraculous sign that led Sergius Paulus to believe in Christ.

what had happened, he believed, for he was
amazed at the teaching about the Lord.

In Pisidian Antioch

13From Paphos, Paul and his companions
sailed to Perga in Pamphylia, where John left
them to return to Jerusalem. 14From Perga they
went on to Pisidian Antioch. On the Sabbath they
entered the synagogue and sat down. 15After the
reading from the Law and the Prophets, the synagogue rulers sent word to them, saying, "Brothers, if you have a message of encouragement for
the people, please speak."

16Standing up, Paul motioned with his hand
and said: "Men of Israel and you Gentiles who
worship God, listen to me! 17The God of the people of Israel chose our fathers; he made the people prosper during their stay in Egypt, with
mighty power he led them out of that country,
18he endured their conduct[a] for about forty
years in the desert, 19he overthrew seven nations
in Canaan and gave their land to his people as
their inheritance. 20All this took about 450 years.

"After this, God gave them judges until the
time of Samuel the prophet. 21Then the people
asked for a king, and he gave them Saul son of
Kish, of the tribe of Benjamin, who ruled forty
years. 22After removing Saul, he made David
their king. He testified concerning him: 'I have
found David son of Jesse a man after my own
heart; he will do everything I want him to do.'

23"From this man's descendants God has
brought to Israel the Savior Jesus, as he promised.
24Before the coming of Jesus, John preached repentance and baptism to all the people of Israel.
25As John was completing his work, he said:
'Who do you think I am? I am not that one. No,
but he is coming after me, whose sandals I am
not worthy to untie.'

26"Brothers, children of Abraham, and you
God-fearing Gentiles, it is to us that this message
of salvation has been sent. 27The people of Jerusalem and their rulers did not recognize Jesus, yet
in condemning him they fulfilled the words of the
prophets that are read every Sabbath. 28Though
they found no proper ground for a death sentence, they asked Pilate to have him executed.
29When they had carried out all that was written
about him, they took him down from the tree and
laid him in a tomb. 30But God raised him from
the dead, 31and for many days he was seen by
those who had traveled with him from Galilee to
Jerusalem. They are now his witnesses to our
people.

32"We tell you the good news: What God
promised our fathers 33he has fulfilled for us,
their children, by raising up Jesus. As it is written
in the second Psalm:

" 'You are my Son;
today I have become your Father.[b][c]

34The fact that God raised him from the dead,
never to decay, is stated in these words:

" 'I will give you the holy and sure blessings
promised to David.'[d]

35So it is stated elsewhere:

" 'You will not let your Holy One see
decay.'[e]

36"For when David had served God's purpose
in his own generation, he fell asleep; he was buried with his fathers and his body decayed. 37But
the one whom God raised from the dead did not
see decay.

38"Therefore, my brothers, I want you to know
that through Jesus the forgiveness of sins is proclaimed to you. 39Through him everyone who
believes is justified from everything you could
not be justified from by the law of Moses. 40Take
care that what the prophets have said does not
happen to you:

41" 'Look, you scoffers,
wonder and perish,
for I am going to do something in your days
that you would never believe,
even if someone told you.'[f]"

42As Paul and Barnabas were leaving the synagogue, the people invited them to speak further
about these things on the next Sabbath. 43When
the congregation was dismissed, many of the
Jews and devout converts to Judaism followed
Paul and Barnabas, who talked with them and
urged them to continue in the grace of God.

44On the next Sabbath almost the whole city
gathered to hear the word of the Lord. 45When
the Jews saw the crowds, they were filled with
jealousy and talked abusively against what Paul
was saying.

46Then Paul and Barnabas answered them
boldly: "We had to speak the word of God to you
first. Since you reject it and do not consider yourselves worthy of eternal life, we now turn to the
Gentiles. 47For this is what the Lord has commanded us:

" 'I have made you[g] a light for the Gentiles,
that you[g] may bring salvation to the ends
of the earth.'[h]"

48When the Gentiles heard this, they were

[a] 18 Some manuscripts *and cared for them* [b] 33 Or *have begotten you* [c] 33 Psalm 2:7 [d] 34 Isaiah 55:3
[e] 35 Psalm 16:10 [f] 41 Hab. 1:5 [g] 47 The Greek is singular. [h] 47 Isaiah 49:6

glad and honored the word of the Lord; and all
who were appointed for eternal life believed.
49The word of the Lord spread through the
whole region. 50But the Jews incited the God-
fearing women of high standing and the leading
men of the city. They stirred up persecution
against Paul and Barnabas, and expelled them
from their region. 51So they shook the dust from
their feet in protest against them and went to
Iconium. 52And the disciples were filled with joy
and with the Holy Spirit.

In Iconium

14 At Iconium Paul and Barnabas went as
usual into the Jewish synagogue. There
they spoke so effectively that a great number of
Jews and Gentiles believed. 2But the Jews who
refused to believe stirred up the Gentiles and
poisoned their minds against the brothers. 3So
Paul and Barnabas spent considerable time there,
speaking boldly for the Lord, who confirmed the
message of his grace by enabling them to do miraculous signs and wonders. 4The people of the
city were divided; some sided with the Jews, others with the apostles. 5There was a plot afoot
among the Gentiles and Jews, together with their
leaders, to mistreat them and stone them. 6But
they found out about it and fled to the Lycaonian
cities of Lystra and Derbe and to the surrounding
country, 7where they continued to preach the
good news.

In Lystra and Derbe

8In Lystra there sat a man crippled in his feet,
who was lame from birth and had never walked.
9He listened to Paul as he was speaking. Paul
looked directly at him, saw that he had faith to be
healed 10and called out, "Stand up on your feet!"
At that, the man jumped up and began to walk.
11When the crowd saw what Paul had done,
they shouted in the Lycaonian language, "The
gods have come down to us in human form!"
12Barnabas they called Zeus, and Paul they called
Hermes because he was the chief speaker. 13The
priest of Zeus, whose temple was just outside the
city, brought bulls and wreaths to the city gates
because he and the crowd wanted to offer sacrifices to them.
14But when the apostles Barnabas and Paul
heard of this, they tore their clothes and rushed
out into the crowd, shouting: 15"Men, why are
you doing this? We too are only men, human like
you. We are bringing you good news, telling you
to turn from these worthless things to the living
God, who made heaven and earth and sea and
everything in them. 16In the past, he let all nations go their own way. 17Yet he has not left
himself without testimony: He has shown kindness by giving you rain from heaven and crops in
their seasons; he provides you with plenty of food
and fills your hearts with joy." 18Even with these
words, they had difficulty keeping the crowd
from sacrificing to them.
19Then some Jews came from Antioch and Iconium and won the crowd over. They stoned Paul
and dragged him outside the city, thinking he
was dead. 20But after the disciples had gathered
around him, he got up and went back into the
city. The next day he and Barnabas left for Derbe.

The Return to Antioch in Syria

21They preached the good news in that city
and won a large number of disciples. Then
they returned to Lystra, Iconium and Antioch,
22strengthening the disciples and encouraging
them to remain true to the faith. "We must go
through many hardships to enter the kingdom of
God," they said. 23Paul and Barnabas appointed
elders[a] for them in each church and, with
prayer and fasting, committed them to the Lord,
in whom they had put their trust. 24After going
through Pisidia, they came into Pamphylia, 25and
when they had preached the word in Perga, they
went down to Attalia.
26From Attalia they sailed back to Antioch,
where they had been committed to the grace of
God for the work they had now completed. 27On
arriving there, they gathered the church together
and reported all that God had done through them
and how he had opened the door of faith to the
Gentiles. 28And they stayed there a long time
with the disciples.

The Council at Jerusalem

15 Some men came down from Judea to Antioch and were teaching the brothers:
"Unless you are circumcised, according to the
custom taught by Moses, you cannot be saved."
2This brought Paul and Barnabas into sharp dispute and debate with them. So Paul and Barnabas
were appointed, along with some other believers,
to go up to Jerusalem to see the apostles and
elders about this question. 3The church sent
them on their way, and as they traveled through
Phoenicia and Samaria, they told how the Gentiles had been converted. This news made all the
brothers very glad. 4When they came to Jerusalem, they were welcomed by the church and the
apostles and elders, to whom they reported everything God had done through them.
5Then some of the believers who belonged to
the party of the Pharisees stood up and said, "The
Gentiles must be circumcised and required to
obey the law of Moses."

a23 Or *Barnabas ordained elders*; or *Barnabas had elders elected*

6The apostles and elders met to consider this question. 7After much discussion, Peter got up and addressed them: "Brothers, you know that some time ago God made a choice among you that the Gentiles might hear from my lips the message of the gospel and believe. 8God, who knows the heart, showed that he accepted them by giving the Holy Spirit to them, just as he did to us. 9He made no distinction between us and them, for he purified their hearts by faith. 10Now then, why do you try to test God by putting on the necks of the disciples a yoke that neither we nor our fathers have been able to bear? 11No! We believe it is through the grace of our Lord Jesus that we are saved, just as they are."

12The whole assembly became silent as they listened to Barnabas and Paul telling about the miraculous signs and wonders God had done among the Gentiles through them. 13When they finished, James spoke up: "Brothers, listen to me. 14Simon[a] has described to us how God at first showed his concern by taking from the Gentiles a people for himself. 15The words of the prophets are in agreement with this, as it is written:

16" 'After this I will return
and rebuild David's fallen tent.
Its ruins I will rebuild,
and I will restore it,
17that the remnant of men may seek the Lord,
and all the Gentiles who bear my name,
says the Lord, who does these things'[b]
18 that have been known for ages.[c]

19"It is my judgment, therefore, that we should not make it difficult for the Gentiles who are turning to God. 20Instead we should write to them, telling them to abstain from food polluted by idols, from sexual immorality, from the meat of strangled animals and from blood. 21For Moses has been preached in every city from the earliest times and is read in the synagogues on every Sabbath."

The Council's Letter to Gentile Believers

22Then the apostles and elders, with the whole church, decided to choose some of their own men and send them to Antioch with Paul and Barnabas. They chose Judas (called Barsabbas) and Silas, two men who were leaders among the brothers. 23With them they sent the following letter:

The apostles and elders, your brothers,

To the Gentile believers in Antioch, Syria and Cilicia:

Greetings.

24We have heard that some went out from us without our authorization and disturbed you, troubling your minds by what they said. 25So we all agreed to choose some men and send them to you with our dear friends Barnabas and Paul— 26men who have risked their lives for the name of our Lord Jesus Christ. 27Therefore we are sending Judas and Silas to confirm by word of mouth what we are writing. 28It seemed good to the Holy Spirit and to us not to burden you with anything beyond the following requirements: 29You are to abstain from food sacrificed to idols, from blood, from the meat of strangled animals and from sexual immorality. You will do well to avoid these things.

Farewell.

30The men were sent off and went down to Antioch, where they gathered the church together and delivered the letter. 31The people read it and were glad for its encouraging message. 32Judas and Silas, who themselves were prophets, said much to encourage and strengthen the brothers. 33After spending some time there, they were sent off by the brothers with the blessing of peace to return to those who had sent them.[d] 35But Paul and Barnabas remained in Antioch, where they and many others taught and preached the word of the Lord.

Disagreement Between Paul and Barnabas

36Some time later Paul said to Barnabas, "Let us go back and visit the brothers in all the towns where we preached the word of the Lord and see

[a] *14* Greek *Simeon*, a variant of *Simon*; that is, Peter [b] *17* Amos 9:11,12 [c] *17,18* Some manuscripts *things'— / 18known to the Lord for ages is his work* [d] *33* Some manuscripts *them, 34but Silas decided to remain there*

15:36–37 Paul suggests visiting the areas where he and Barnabas had traveled previously (which would begin his second missionary journey—v. 41). ***John ... Mark.*** Barnabas' cousin (Col. 4:10) who accompanied Paul and Barnabas at the beginning of the first missionary journey, and later wrote the Gospel bearing his name. Mark left the missionary team at Perga in Pamphylia to return to Jerusalem (Acts 13:13). Luke does not say why Mark turned back, but Paul certainly viewed it as a serious deficit and was unwilling to let him try again.

15:39 ***a sharp disagreement.*** Barnabas' concern may have been motivated in part by the fact that Mark was his cousin, but it is characteristic of Barnabas. Years before, it was he who insisted that Paul be given a chance to prove himself to the apostles (Acts 9:27). On the other hand, Mark's earlier departure undoubtedly had placed increased demands on Paul and Barnabas, and Paul was unwilling to risk that again. ***they parted company.*** This irreconcilable difference led to an end to the joint ministry of Paul and Barnabas. However, in 1 Corinthians 9:6 Paul affirms the example of Barnabas; and Paul's letters clearly reveal that he and Mark were reconciled (Philem. 24; Col. 4:10). In fact, Paul respected Mark so much that he asked for him to come to him during his final days (2 Tim. 4:11).

15:40 ***commended by the brothers.*** This does not mean that Barnabas and Mark, who left Antioch on a missionary trip to Cyprus, were not likewise commended. It simply signals that Luke intends to concentrate on the efforts of Paul and Silas.

how they are doing." 37 Barnabas wanted to take
John, also called Mark, with them, 38 but Paul did
not think it wise to take him, because he had
deserted them in Pamphylia and had not continued with them in the work. 39 They had such a
sharp disagreement that they parted company.
Barnabas took Mark and sailed for Cyprus, 40 but
Paul chose Silas and left, commended by the
brothers to the grace of the Lord. 41 He went
through Syria and Cilicia, strengthening the
churches.

Acts 15:36–41

1. Who was your closest friend when you were 7 years old? Are you still friends?
2. Which is harder—breaking off a friendship or being dumped?
3. When you have a serious disagreement with a friend, do you generally "have it out" or give them the "silent treatment"?
4. What good can you see coming out of Paul and Barnabas parting ways in this story?
5. How should you deal with a broken relationship with someone in the Christian community?
6. What is the best way to save a friendship when you have a disagreement with a friend?
7. What relationship in your life needs prayer? How else can the group pray for you?

(Study notes on page 1014)

Timothy Joins Paul and Silas

16 He came to Derbe and then to Lystra,
where a disciple named Timothy lived,
whose mother was a Jewess and a believer, but
whose father was a Greek. 2 The brothers at Lystra and Iconium spoke well of him. 3 Paul wanted
to take him along on the journey, so he circumcised him because of the Jews who lived in that
area, for they all knew that his father was a
Greek. 4 As they traveled from town to town, they
delivered the decisions reached by the apostles
and elders in Jerusalem for the people to obey.
5 So the churches were strengthened in the faith
and grew daily in numbers.

Paul's Vision of the Man of Macedonia

6 Paul and his companions traveled throughout
the region of Phrygia and Galatia, having been
kept by the Holy Spirit from preaching the word
in the province of Asia. 7 When they came to the
border of Mysia, they tried to enter Bithynia, but
the Spirit of Jesus would not allow them to. 8 So

Acts 16:6–10

1. If you could visit any country in the world, where would you visit?
2. How do you go about making important decisions?
3. If God called you to be a missionary, like Paul, how would you respond? Where would you like to take the Gospel?
4. God gave Paul clear direction (v. 9). What has God said to you lately?
5. If you imagined someone asking you to share the Good News about Jesus with them, who would it be?
6. Where do you have an "open door" for sharing your faith now? How will you take advantage of it?
7. Where do you need God's direction in your life? How else can the group pray for you?

16:6–8 ***his companions.*** Silas and Timothy. ***Galatia / Asia / Bithynia.*** Roman provinces in modern western Turkey. ***Phrygia / Mysia.*** Smaller districts within these provinces. The travels in verses 6–8 represent a trip of some 250 miles, during which we are only told what Paul was *not* able to do. ***the Holy Spirit / the Spirit of Jesus.*** As these titles are used interchangeably, Luke clearly identifies the ongoing work of Jesus with the agency of the Holy Spirit in the lives of the apostles. ***would not allow them to.*** *Why* the Spirit would not allow the missionaries to preach in Asia and Bithynia is not given. Later on, the apostle Peter was in contact with churches in that area, so they were not left without the Gospel (1 Peter 1:1). *How* Jesus prevented them is also not explained. It may have been through circumstances, a vision or dream, or a gift of prophecy.

16:8 Troas was an important seaport on the Aegean Sea. It appears Paul did not do any evangelistic work there at this time, though he did so later on (2 Cor. 2:12). But while in Troas, Paul had a vision that finally gave him a positive sense of where the Lord wanted him to go next. ***Macedonia.*** This area of northern Greece had been the dominant power under Alexander the Great in the fourth century B.C., and became a Roman province in 148 B.C. ***Come over.*** By crossing the Aegean Sea.

16:10 ***we got ready.*** This is where the passages in Acts which were written in the first person begin, indicating that Luke himself was accompanying Paul at these points.

they passed by Mysia and went down to Troas.
[9]During the night Paul had a vision of a man of
Macedonia standing and begging him, "Come
over to Macedonia and help us." [10]After Paul had
seen the vision, we got ready at once to leave for
Macedonia, concluding that God had called us to
preach the gospel to them.

Lydia's Conversion in Philippi

[11]From Troas we put out to sea and sailed
straight for Samothrace, and the next day on to
Neapolis. [12]From there we traveled to Philippi, a
Roman colony and the leading city of that district
of Macedonia. And we stayed there several days.
[13]On the Sabbath we went outside the city
gate to the river, where we expected to find a
place of prayer. We sat down and began to speak
to the women who had gathered there. [14]One
of those listening was a woman named Lydia, a
dealer in purple cloth from the city of Thyatira,
who was a worshiper of God. The Lord opened
her heart to respond to Paul's message. [15]When
she and the members of her household were baptized, she invited us to her home. "If you consider me a believer in the Lord," she said, "come
and stay at my house." And she persuaded us.

Paul and Silas in Prison

[16]Once when we were going to the place of
prayer, we were met by a slave girl who had a
spirit by which she predicted the future. She
earned a great deal of money for her owners by
fortune-telling. [17]This girl followed Paul and the
rest of us, shouting, "These men are servants of
the Most High God, who are telling you the way
to be saved." [18]She kept this up for many days.
Finally Paul became so troubled that he turned
around and said to the spirit, "In the name of
Jesus Christ I command you to come out of her!"
At that moment the spirit left her.
[19]When the owners of the slave girl realized
that their hope of making money was gone,
they seized Paul and Silas and dragged them into
the marketplace to face the authorities. [20]They
brought them before the magistrates and said,
"These men are Jews, and are throwing our city
into an uproar [21]by advocating customs unlawful
for us Romans to accept or practice."
[22]The crowd joined in the attack against Paul
and Silas, and the magistrates ordered them to be
stripped and beaten. [23]After they had been severely flogged, they were thrown into prison, and
the jailer was commanded to guard them carefully. [24]Upon receiving such orders, he put them
in the inner cell and fastened their feet in the
stocks.
[25]About midnight Paul and Silas were praying
and singing hymns to God, and the other prisoners were listening to them. [26]Suddenly there was
such a violent earthquake that the foundations of
the prison were shaken. At once all the prison
doors flew open, and everybody's chains came
loose. [27]The jailer woke up, and when he saw the
prison doors open, he drew his sword and was

Acts 16:22–40

1. When you're down, what song or type of music lifts your spirits?
2. What do you do to get up when you're "down in the dumps"?
3. When was the last time you were threatened because you shared your faith?
4. Why did Paul and Silas stay when they could have left? What was the result?
5. If someone asked you "what must I do to be saved" (v. 30), what would you say?
6. How hard is it for you to pray and be thankful in the midst of hard times?
7. As a Christian, how can you be content even though your circumstances might be bad? Close by praying and singing together.

This story takes place in Philippi. Paul has just commanded an evil spirit to come out of a slave girl. This girl had made a lot of money for her owners by fortune-telling. Realizing their scheme of making money left with the evil spirit, they dragged Paul and Barnabas to the authorities (vv. 16–21).

16:22–25 The authorities should have put Paul and Silas in custody to be formally tried. But, pressured by the crowds, they beat them (with rods) without a trial. ***stocks.*** Used both for extra security and for torture.

16:25 The contrast between Paul and Silas' attitude and their situation is immense! In spite of their pain and humiliation they sang hymns and prayed to God, bearing witness to the other prisoners in the process.

16:27–34 ***about to kill himself.*** The punishment for a guard who allowed his prisoners to escape was that which the prisoner was to have received. ***what must I do to be saved?*** The jailer acknowledges that Paul and Silas indeed must be God's agents. Paul's response is summed up in a single phrase: deliverance from the power of evil and divine judgment is given to those who entrust themselves to Jesus as their Lord. This summary statement was followed by a late-night teaching session, resulting in a joyous conversion for the jailer's household.

16:35–40 Paul and Silas were not asking for the proper administration of justice or for an escort as a matter of self-vindication, as deserved as these things were. They wanted to establish their innocence publicly for the sake of the future of the church there.

about to kill himself because he thought the prisoners had escaped. 28But Paul shouted, "Don't
harm yourself! We are all here!"
29The jailer called for lights, rushed in and
fell trembling before Paul and Silas. 30He then
brought them out and asked, "Sirs, what must I
do to be saved?"
31They replied, "Believe in the Lord Jesus, and
you will be saved—you and your household."
32Then they spoke the word of the Lord to him
and to all the others in his house. 33At that hour
of the night the jailer took them and washed their
wounds; then immediately he and all his family
were baptized. 34The jailer brought them into his
house and set a meal before them; he was filled
with joy because he had come to believe in
God—he and his whole family.
35When it was daylight, the magistrates sent
their officers to the jailer with the order: "Release
those men." 36The jailer told Paul, "The magistrates have ordered that you and Silas be released. Now you can leave. Go in peace."
37But Paul said to the officers: "They beat us
publicly without a trial, even though we are Roman citizens, and threw us into prison. And now
do they want to get rid of us quietly? No! Let
them come themselves and escort us out."
38The officers reported this to the magistrates,
and when they heard that Paul and Silas were
Roman citizens, they were alarmed. 39They came
to appease them and escorted them from the prison, requesting them to leave the city. 40After Paul
and Silas came out of the prison, they went to
Lydia's house, where they met with the brothers
and encouraged them. Then they left.

In Thessalonica

17 When they had passed through Amphipo-
lis and Apollonia, they came to Thessalonica, where there was a Jewish synagogue. 2As
his custom was, Paul went into the synagogue,
and on three Sabbath days he reasoned with
them from the Scriptures, 3explaining and proving that the Christ[a] had to suffer and rise from
the dead. "This Jesus I am proclaiming to you is
the Christ,[a]" he said. 4Some of the Jews were
persuaded and joined Paul and Silas, as did a large
number of God-fearing Greeks and not a few
prominent women.
5But the Jews were jealous; so they rounded
up some bad characters from the marketplace,
formed a mob and started a riot in the city. They
rushed to Jason's house in search of Paul and Silas
in order to bring them out to the crowd.[b] 6But
when they did not find them, they dragged Jason
and some other brothers before the city officials,
shouting: "These men who have caused trouble
all over the world have now come here, 7and
Jason has welcomed them into his house. They
are all defying Caesar's decrees, saying that there
is another king, one called Jesus." 8When they
heard this, the crowd and the city officials were
thrown into turmoil. 9Then they made Jason and
the others post bond and let them go.

In Berea

10As soon as it was night, the brothers sent
Paul and Silas away to Berea. On arriving there,
they went to the Jewish synagogue. 11Now the
Bereans were of more noble character than the
Thessalonians, for they received the message
with great eagerness and examined the Scriptures every day to see if what Paul said was true.
12Many of the Jews believed, as did also a number of prominent Greek women and many Greek
men.
13When the Jews in Thessalonica learned that
Paul was preaching the word of God at Berea,
they went there too, agitating the crowds and
stirring them up. 14The brothers immediately
sent Paul to the coast, but Silas and Timothy
stayed at Berea. 15The men who escorted Paul
brought him to Athens and then left with instructions for Silas and Timothy to join him as soon as
possible.

In Athens

16While Paul was waiting for them in Athens,
he was greatly distressed to see that the city was
full of idols. 17So he reasoned in the synagogue
with the Jews and the God-fearing Greeks, as
well as in the marketplace day by day with those
who happened to be there. 18A group of Epicure-
an and Stoic philosophers began to dispute with
him. Some of them asked, "What is this babbler
trying to say?" Others remarked, "He seems to be
advocating foreign gods." They said this because
Paul was preaching the good news about Jesus
and the resurrection. 19Then they took him and
brought him to a meeting of the Areopagus,
where they said to him, "May we know what this
new teaching is that you are presenting? 20You
are bringing some strange ideas to our ears, and
we want to know what they mean." 21(All the
Athenians and the foreigners who lived there
spent their time doing nothing but talking about
and listening to the latest ideas.)
22Paul then stood up in the meeting of the
Areopagus and said: "Men of Athens! I see that

[a] 3 Or *Messiah* [b] 5 Or *the assembly of the people*

in every way you are very religious. 23For as I walked around and looked carefully at your objects of worship, I even found an altar with this inscription: TO AN UNKNOWN GOD. Now what you worship as something unknown I am going to proclaim to you.

24"The God who made the world and everything in it is the Lord of heaven and earth and does not live in temples built by hands. 25And he is not served by human hands, as if he needed anything, because he himself gives all men life and breath and everything else. 26From one man he made every nation of men, that they should inhabit the whole earth; and he determined the times set for them and the exact places where they should live. 27God did this so that men would seek him and perhaps reach out for him and find him, though he is not far from each one of us. 28'For in him we live and move and have our being.' As some of your own poets have said, 'We are his offspring.'

29"Therefore since we are God's offspring, we should not think that the divine being is like gold or silver or stone—an image made by man's design and skill. 30In the past God overlooked such ignorance, but now he commands all people everywhere to repent. 31For he has set a day when he will judge the world with justice by the man he has appointed. He has given proof of this to all men by raising him from the dead."

32When they heard about the resurrection of the dead, some of them sneered, but others said, "We want to hear you again on this subject." 33At that, Paul left the Council. 34A few men became followers of Paul and believed. Among them was Dionysius, a member of the Areopagus, also a woman named Damaris, and a number of others.

In Corinth

18 After this, Paul left Athens and went to Corinth. 2There he met a Jew named Aquila, a native of Pontus, who had recently come from Italy with his wife Priscilla, because Claudius had ordered all the Jews to leave Rome. Paul went to see them, 3and because he was a tentmaker as they were, he stayed and worked with them. 4Every Sabbath he reasoned in the synagogue, trying to persuade Jews and Greeks.

5When Silas and Timothy came from Macedonia, Paul devoted himself exclusively to preaching, testifying to the Jews that Jesus was the Christ.[a] 6But when the Jews opposed Paul and became abusive, he shook out his clothes in protest and said to them, "Your blood be on your own heads! I am clear of my responsibility. From now on I will go to the Gentiles."

7Then Paul left the synagogue and went next door to the house of Titius Justus, a worshiper of God. 8Crispus, the synagogue ruler, and his entire household believed in the Lord; and many of the Corinthians who heard him believed and were baptized.

9One night the Lord spoke to Paul in a vision: "Do not be afraid; keep on speaking, do not be silent. 10For I am with you, and no one is going to attack and harm you, because I have many people in this city." 11So Paul stayed for a year and a half, teaching them the word of God.

12While Gallio was proconsul of Achaia, the Jews made a united attack on Paul and brought him into court. 13"This man," they charged, "is persuading the people to worship God in ways contrary to the law."

14Just as Paul was about to speak, Gallio said to the Jews, "If you Jews were making a complaint about some misdemeanor or serious crime, it would be reasonable for me to listen to you. 15But since it involves questions about words and names and your own law—settle the matter yourselves. I will not be a judge of such things." 16So he had them ejected from the court. 17Then they all turned on Sosthenes the synagogue ruler and beat him in front of the court. But Gallio showed no concern whatever.

Priscilla, Aquila and Apollos

18Paul stayed on in Corinth for some time. Then he left the brothers and sailed for Syria, accompanied by Priscilla and Aquila. Before he sailed, he had his hair cut off at Cenchrea because of a vow he had taken. 19They arrived at Ephesus, where Paul left Priscilla and Aquila. He himself went into the synagogue and reasoned with the Jews. 20When they asked him to spend more time with them, he declined. 21But as he left, he promised, "I will come back if it is God's will." Then he set sail from Ephesus. 22When he landed at Caesarea, he went up and greeted the church and then went down to Antioch.

23After spending some time in Antioch, Paul set out from there and traveled from place to place throughout the region of Galatia and Phrygia, strengthening all the disciples.

24Meanwhile a Jew named Apollos, a native of Alexandria, came to Ephesus. He was a learned man, with a thorough knowledge of the Scriptures. 25He had been instructed in the way of the Lord, and he spoke with great fervor[b] and taught about Jesus accurately, though he knew only the baptism of John. 26He began to speak boldly in the synagogue. When Priscilla and Aquila heard him, they invited him to their home and explained to him the way of God more adequately.

[a] 5 Or *Messiah;* also in verse 28 [b] 25 Or *with fervor in the Spirit*

27When Apollos wanted to go to Achaia, the
brothers encouraged him and wrote to the disciples there to welcome him. On arriving, he was
a great help to those who by grace had believed.
28For he vigorously refuted the Jews in public
debate, proving from the Scriptures that Jesus
was the Christ.

Paul in Ephesus

19 While Apollos was at Corinth, Paul took
the road through the interior and arrived
at Ephesus. There he found some disciples 2and
asked them, "Did you receive the Holy Spirit
when[a] you believed?"

They answered, "No, we have not even heard
that there is a Holy Spirit."

3So Paul asked, "Then what baptism did you
receive?"

"John's baptism," they replied.

4Paul said, "John's baptism was a baptism of
repentance. He told the people to believe in the
one coming after him, that is, in Jesus." 5On
hearing this, they were baptized into[b] the name
of the Lord Jesus. 6When Paul placed his hands
on them, the Holy Spirit came on them, and they
spoke in tongues[c] and prophesied. 7There were
about twelve men in all.

8Paul entered the synagogue and spoke boldly there for three months, arguing persuasively
about the kingdom of God. 9But some of them
became obstinate; they refused to believe and
publicly maligned the Way. So Paul left them. He
took the disciples with him and had discussions
daily in the lecture hall of Tyrannus. 10This went
on for two years, so that all the Jews and Greeks
who lived in the province of Asia heard the word
of the Lord.

11God did extraordinary miracles through
Paul, 12so that even handkerchiefs and aprons
that had touched him were taken to the sick, and
their illnesses were cured and the evil spirits left
them.

13Some Jews who went around driving out evil
spirits tried to invoke the name of the Lord Jesus
over those who were demon-possessed. They
would say, "In the name of Jesus, whom Paul
preaches, I command you to come out." 14Seven
sons of Sceva, a Jewish chief priest, were doing
this. 15⌊One day⌋ the evil spirit answered them,
"Jesus I know, and I know about Paul, but who
are you?" 16Then the man who had the evil spirit
jumped on them and overpowered them all. He
gave them such a beating that they ran out of the
house naked and bleeding.

17When this became known to the Jews and
Greeks living in Ephesus, they were all seized
with fear, and the name of the Lord Jesus was
held in high honor. 18Many of those who believed now came and openly confessed their evil
deeds. 19A number who had practiced sorcery
brought their scrolls together and burned them
publicly. When they calculated the value of the
scrolls, the total came to fifty thousand drachmas.[d] 20In this way the word of the Lord spread
widely and grew in power.

21After all this had happened, Paul decided to
go to Jerusalem, passing through Macedonia and
Achaia. "After I have been there," he said, "I
must visit Rome also." 22He sent two of his helpers, Timothy and Erastus, to Macedonia, while he
stayed in the province of Asia a little longer.

The Riot in Ephesus

23About that time there arose a great disturbance about the Way. 24A silversmith named Demetrius, who made silver shrines of Artemis,
brought in no little business for the craftsmen.
25He called them together, along with the workmen in related trades, and said: "Men, you know
we receive a good income from this business.
26And you see and hear how this fellow Paul has
convinced and led astray large numbers of people
here in Ephesus and in practically the whole
province of Asia. He says that man-made gods
are no gods at all. 27There is danger not only that
our trade will lose its good name, but also that
the temple of the great goddess Artemis will be
discredited, and the goddess herself, who is
worshiped throughout the province of Asia
and the world, will be robbed of her divine
majesty."

28When they heard this, they were furious and
began shouting: "Great is Artemis of the Ephesians!" 29Soon the whole city was in an uproar.
The people seized Gaius and Aristarchus, Paul's
traveling companions from Macedonia, and
rushed as one man into the theater. 30Paul wanted to appear before the crowd, but the disciples
would not let him. 31Even some of the officials of
the province, friends of Paul, sent him a message
begging him not to venture into the theater.

32The assembly was in confusion: Some were
shouting one thing, some another. Most of the
people did not even know why they were there.
33The Jews pushed Alexander to the front, and
some of the crowd shouted instructions to him.
He motioned for silence in order to make a defense before the people. 34But when they realized
he was a Jew, they all shouted in unison for about
two hours: "Great is Artemis of the Ephesians!"

35The city clerk quieted the crowd and said:

[a]2 Or *after* [b]5 Or *in* [c]6 Or *other languages* [d]19 A drachma was a silver coin worth about a day's wages.

"Men of Ephesus, doesn't all the world know that
the city of Ephesus is the guardian of the temple
of the great Artemis and of her image, which fell
from heaven? 36Therefore, since these facts are
undeniable, you ought to be quiet and not do
anything rash. 37You have brought these men
here, though they have neither robbed temples
nor blasphemed our goddess. 38If, then, Demetrius and his fellow craftsmen have a grievance
against anybody, the courts are open and there
are proconsuls. They can press charges. 39If there
is anything further you want to bring up, it must
be settled in a legal assembly. 40As it is, we are in
danger of being charged with rioting because of
today's events. In that case we would not be able
to account for this commotion, since there is no
reason for it." 41After he had said this, he dismissed the assembly.

Acts 19:23–41

1. When you were 10 years old, what did you want to be? What do you want to be now?
2. In choosing a career, how much are you motivated by money? How much by personal fulfillment?
3. What are some jobs you won't consider because they conflict with your values?
4. How does Demetrius the idol-maker respond to Paul (v. 27)? What is his real concern?
5. In what ways is your relationship to Christ affecting your career choice?
6. What are you doing right now to prepare for the career you would like to pursue?
7. How can this group help you in prayer this week?

Through Macedonia and Greece

20 When the uproar had ended, Paul sent for
the disciples and, after encouraging them,
said good-by and set out for Macedonia. 2He traveled through that area, speaking many words of
encouragement to the people, and finally arrived
in Greece, 3where he stayed three months. Because the Jews made a plot against him just as he
was about to sail for Syria, he decided to go back
through Macedonia. 4He was accompanied by So-
pater son of Pyrrhus from Berea, Aristarchus and
Secundus from Thessalonica, Gaius from Derbe,
Timothy also, and Tychicus and Trophimus from
the province of Asia. 5These men went on ahead
and waited for us at Troas. 6But we sailed from
Philippi after the Feast of Unleavened Bread, and
five days later joined the others at Troas, where
we stayed seven days.

Eutychus Raised From the Dead at Troas

7On the first day of the week we came together to break bread. Paul spoke to the people and,
because he intended to leave the next day, kept
on talking until midnight. 8There were many
lamps in the upstairs room where we were meeting. 9Seated in a window was a young man
named Eutychus, who was sinking into a deep
sleep as Paul talked on and on. When he was
sound asleep, he fell to the ground from the third
story and was picked up dead. 10Paul went down,
threw himself on the young man and put his arms
around him. "Don't be alarmed," he said. "He's
alive!" 11Then he went upstairs again and broke
bread and ate. After talking until daylight, he left.
12The people took the young man home alive and
were greatly comforted.

Paul's Farewell to the Ephesian Elders

13We went on ahead to the ship and sailed for
Assos, where we were going to take Paul aboard.
He had made this arrangement because he was
going there on foot. 14When he met us at Assos,
we took him aboard and went on to Mitylene.
15The next day we set sail from there and arrived
off Kios. The day after that we crossed over to
Samos, and on the following day arrived at Mile-

19:23–24 *the Way.* Christianity. ***Artemis.*** A fertility goddess. The center for her worship was in Ephesus in a temple that was one of the seven wonders of the ancient world. Inside the temple was the many-breasted image of Artemis (perhaps a meteorite), which supposedly fell from heaven (v. 35).

19:25–27 Gathering together tradesmen involved in work that revolved around the worship of Artemis, Demetrius (probably a leader of their guild) identified the threat that Paul represented to them all: because of the popularity of his message which opposed idolatry, their income was in danger. People from near and far came to view the temple of Artemis, so selling shrines and images produced "a good income."

19:28–34 A mob scene resulted as the tradesmen poured out of their meeting and shouted to others about what Paul and his friends were doing. The mob simply takes up the shout for the honor of Artemis. The Jews, perhaps to disassociate themselves from the charges being made against Paul, tried to have one of their number make a statement. However, since the Jews were well known to be against idolatry as well, Alexander was shouted down by the crowd before he could even speak.

19:35–41 *city clerk.* The highest ranking official in the city accountable to the Roman provincial government for what happened in Ephesus. Not wanting to be charged with rioting which could lead to penalties for the city, he successfully worked to quiet down the crowd and dismiss them.

tus. 16Paul had decided to sail past Ephesus to
avoid spending time in the province of Asia, for
he was in a hurry to reach Jerusalem, if possible,
by the day of Pentecost.
17From Miletus, Paul sent to Ephesus for the
elders of the church. 18When they arrived, he
said to them: "You know how I lived the whole
time I was with you, from the first day I came
into the province of Asia. 19I served the Lord
with great humility and with tears, although I
was severely tested by the plots of the Jews.
20You know that I have not hesitated to preach
anything that would be helpful to you but have
taught you publicly and from house to house. 21I
have declared to both Jews and Greeks that they
must turn to God in repentance and have faith in
our Lord Jesus.
22"And now, compelled by the Spirit, I am going to Jerusalem, not knowing what will happen
to me there. 23I only know that in every city the
Holy Spirit warns me that prison and hardships
are facing me. 24However, I consider my life
worth nothing to me, if only I may finish the race
and complete the task the Lord Jesus has given
me—the task of testifying to the gospel of God's
grace.
25"Now I know that none of you among whom
I have gone about preaching the kingdom will
ever see me again. 26Therefore, I declare to you
today that I am innocent of the blood of all men.
27For I have not hesitated to proclaim to you the
whole will of God. 28Keep watch over yourselves
and all the flock of which the Holy Spirit has
made you overseers.[a] Be shepherds of the
church of God,[b] which he bought with his own
blood. 29I know that after I leave, savage wolves
will come in among you and will not spare the
flock. 30Even from your own number men will
arise and distort the truth in order to draw away
disciples after them. 31So be on your guard! Remember that for three years I never stopped
warning each of you night and day with tears.
32"Now I commit you to God and to the word
of his grace, which can build you up and give you
an inheritance among all those who are sanctified. 33I have not coveted anyone's silver or gold
or clothing. 34You yourselves know that these
hands of mine have supplied my own needs and
the needs of my companions. 35In everything I
did, I showed you that by this kind of hard work
we must help the weak, remembering the words
the Lord Jesus himself said: 'It is more blessed to
give than to receive.'"
36When he had said this, he knelt down with
all of them and prayed. 37They all wept as they
embraced him and kissed him. 38What grieved
them most was his statement that they would
never see his face again. Then they accompanied
him to the ship.

On to Jerusalem

21 After we had torn ourselves away from
them, we put out to sea and sailed
straight to Cos. The next day we went to Rhodes
and from there to Patara. 2We found a ship crossing over to Phoenicia, went on board and set sail.
3After sighting Cyprus and passing to the south
of it, we sailed on to Syria. We landed at Tyre,
where our ship was to unload its cargo. 4Finding
the disciples there, we stayed with them seven
days. Through the Spirit they urged Paul not to go
on to Jerusalem. 5But when our time was up, we
left and continued on our way. All the disciples
and their wives and children accompanied us out
of the city, and there on the beach we knelt to
pray. 6After saying good-by to each other, we
went aboard the ship, and they returned home.
7We continued our voyage from Tyre and landed at Ptolemais, where we greeted the brothers
and stayed with them for a day. 8Leaving the next
day, we reached Caesarea and stayed at the
house of Philip the evangelist, one of the Seven.
9He had four unmarried daughters who prophesied.
10After we had been there a number of days, a
prophet named Agabus came down from Judea.
11Coming over to us, he took Paul's belt, tied his
own hands and feet with it and said, "The Holy
Spirit says, 'In this way the Jews of Jerusalem will
bind the owner of this belt and will hand him
over to the Gentiles.'"
12When we heard this, we and the people
there pleaded with Paul not to go up to Jerusalem. 13Then Paul answered, "Why are you weeping and breaking my heart? I am ready not only
to be bound, but also to die in Jerusalem for the
name of the Lord Jesus." 14When he would not
be dissuaded, we gave up and said, "The Lord's
will be done."
15After this, we got ready and went up to Jerusalem. 16Some of the disciples from Caesarea accompanied us and brought us to the home of
Mnason, where we were to stay. He was a man
from Cyprus and one of the early disciples.

Paul's Arrival at Jerusalem

17When we arrived at Jerusalem, the brothers
received us warmly. 18The next day Paul and the
rest of us went to see James, and all the elders
were present. 19Paul greeted them and reported
in detail what God had done among the Gentiles
through his ministry.
20When they heard this, they praised God.
Then they said to Paul: "You see, brother, how

[a] 28 Traditionally *bishops* [b] 28 Many manuscripts *of the Lord*

many thousands of Jews have believed, and all of
them are zealous for the law. 21They have been
informed that you teach all the Jews who live
among the Gentiles to turn away from Moses,
telling them not to circumcise their children
or live according to our customs. 22What shall
we do? They will certainly hear that you have
come, 23so do what we tell you. There are four
men with us who have made a vow. 24Take
these men, join in their purification rites and pay
their expenses, so that they can have their heads
shaved. Then everybody will know there is no
truth in these reports about you, but that you
yourself are living in obedience to the law. 25As
for the Gentile believers, we have written to
them our decision that they should abstain from
food sacrificed to idols, from blood, from the
meat of strangled animals and from sexual immorality."
26The next day Paul took the men and purified
himself along with them. Then he went to the
temple to give notice of the date when the days
of purification would end and the offering would
be made for each of them.

Paul Arrested

27When the seven days were nearly over,
some Jews from the province of Asia saw Paul at
the temple. They stirred up the whole crowd and
seized him, 28shouting, "Men of Israel, help us!
This is the man who teaches all men everywhere
against our people and our law and this place.
And besides, he has brought Greeks into the temple area and defiled this holy place." 29(They had
previously seen Trophimus the Ephesian in the
city with Paul and assumed that Paul had brought
him into the temple area.)
30The whole city was aroused, and the people
came running from all directions. Seizing Paul,
they dragged him from the temple, and immediately the gates were shut. 31While they were trying to kill him, news reached the commander of
the Roman troops that the whole city of Jerusalem was in an uproar. 32He at once took some
officers and soldiers and ran down to the crowd.
When the rioters saw the commander and his
soldiers, they stopped beating Paul.
33The commander came up and arrested him
and ordered him to be bound with two chains.
Then he asked who he was and what he had
done. 34Some in the crowd shouted one thing
and some another, and since the commander
could not get at the truth because of the uproar,
he ordered that Paul be taken into the barracks.
35When Paul reached the steps, the violence of
the mob was so great he had to be carried by the
soldiers. 36The crowd that followed kept shouting, "Away with him!"

Paul Speaks to the Crowd

37As the soldiers were about to take Paul into
the barracks, he asked the commander, "May I
say something to you?"
"Do you speak Greek?" he replied. 38"Aren't
you the Egyptian who started a revolt and led four
thousand terrorists out into the desert some time
ago?"
39Paul answered, "I am a Jew, from Tarsus in
Cilicia, a citizen of no ordinary city. Please let me
speak to the people."
40Having received the commander's permission, Paul stood on the steps and motioned to the
crowd. When they were all silent, he said to
22 them in Aramaic[a]: 1"Brothers and fathers, listen now to my defense."
2When they heard him speak to them in Aramaic, they became very quiet.
Then Paul said: 3"I am a Jew, born in Tarsus of
Cilicia, but brought up in this city. Under Gamaliel I was thoroughly trained in the law of our
fathers and was just as zealous for God as any of
you are today. 4I persecuted the followers of this
Way to their death, arresting both men and wom-
en and throwing them into prison, 5as also the
high priest and all the Council can testify. I even
obtained letters from them to their brothers in
Damascus, and went there to bring these people
as prisoners to Jerusalem to be punished.
6"About noon as I came near Damascus, suddenly a bright light from heaven flashed around
me. 7I fell to the ground and heard a voice say to
me, 'Saul! Saul! Why do you persecute me?'
8" 'Who are you, Lord?' I asked.
" 'I am Jesus of Nazareth, whom you are persecuting,' he replied. 9My companions saw the
light, but they did not understand the voice of
him who was speaking to me.
10" 'What shall I do, Lord?' I asked.
" 'Get up,' the Lord said, 'and go into Damascus. There you will be told all that you have been
assigned to do.' 11My companions led me by the
hand into Damascus, because the brilliance of the
light had blinded me.
12"A man named Ananias came to see me. He
was a devout observer of the law and highly respected by all the Jews living there. 13He stood
beside me and said, 'Brother Saul, receive your
sight!' And at that very moment I was able to see
him.
14"Then he said: 'The God of our fathers has
chosen you to know his will and to see the Righteous One and to hear words from his mouth.
15You will be his witness to all men of what you

[a]40 Or possibly *Hebrew*; also in 22:2

have seen and heard. 16And now what are you
waiting for? Get up, be baptized and wash your
sins away, calling on his name.'
17"When I returned to Jerusalem and was
praying at the temple, I fell into a trance 18and
saw the Lord speaking. 'Quick!' he said to me.
'Leave Jerusalem immediately, because they will
not accept your testimony about me.'
19"'Lord,' I replied, 'these men know that I
went from one synagogue to another to imprison
and beat those who believe in you. 20And when
the blood of your martyr[a] Stephen was shed, I
stood there giving my approval and guarding the
clothes of those who were killing him.'
21"Then the Lord said to me, 'Go; I will send
you far away to the Gentiles.' "

Paul the Roman Citizen

22The crowd listened to Paul until he said this.
Then they raised their voices and shouted, "Rid
the earth of him! He's not fit to live!"
23As they were shouting and throwing off their
cloaks and flinging dust into the air, 24the commander ordered Paul to be taken into the barracks. He directed that he be flogged and questioned in order to find out why the people were
shouting at him like this. 25As they stretched him
out to flog him, Paul said to the centurion standing there, "Is it legal for you to flog a Roman
citizen who hasn't even been found guilty?"
26When the centurion heard this, he went to
the commander and reported it. "What are you
going to do?" he asked. "This man is a Roman
citizen."
27The commander went to Paul and asked,
"Tell me, are you a Roman citizen?"
"Yes, I am," he answered.
28Then the commander said, "I had to pay a
big price for my citizenship."
"But I was born a citizen," Paul replied.
29Those who were about to question him withdrew immediately. The commander himself was
alarmed when he realized that he had put Paul, a
Roman citizen, in chains.

Before the Sanhedrin

30The next day, since the commander wanted
to find out exactly why Paul was being accused by
the Jews, he released him and ordered the chief
priests and all the Sanhedrin to assemble. Then
he brought Paul and had him stand before them.
23 Paul looked straight at the Sanhedrin and
said, "My brothers, I have fulfilled my
duty to God in all good conscience to this day."
2At this the high priest Ananias ordered those
standing near Paul to strike him on the mouth.
3Then Paul said to him, "God will strike you, you
whitewashed wall! You sit there to judge me according to the law, yet you yourself violate the
law by commanding that I be struck!"
4Those who were standing near Paul said,
"You dare to insult God's high priest?"
5Paul replied, "Brothers, I did not realize that
he was the high priest; for it is written: 'Do not
speak evil about the ruler of your people.'[b]"
6Then Paul, knowing that some of them were
Sadducees and the others Pharisees, called out in
the Sanhedrin, "My brothers, I am a Pharisee,
the son of a Pharisee. I stand on trial because of
my hope in the resurrection of the dead." 7When
he said this, a dispute broke out between the
Pharisees and the Sadducees, and the assembly
was divided. 8(The Sadducees say that there is no
resurrection, and that there are neither angels
nor spirits, but the Pharisees acknowledge them
all.)
9There was a great uproar, and some of the
teachers of the law who were Pharisees stood up
and argued vigorously. "We find nothing wrong
with this man," they said. "What if a spirit or an
angel has spoken to him?" 10The dispute became
so violent that the commander was afraid Paul
would be torn to pieces by them. He ordered the
troops to go down and take him away from them
by force and bring him into the barracks.
11The following night the Lord stood near Paul
and said, "Take courage! As you have testified
about me in Jerusalem, so you must also testify in
Rome."

The Plot to Kill Paul

12The next morning the Jews formed a conspiracy and bound themselves with an oath not to
eat or drink until they had killed Paul. 13More
than forty men were involved in this plot. 14They
went to the chief priests and elders and said,
"We have taken a solemn oath not to eat anything until we have killed Paul. 15Now then, you
and the Sanhedrin petition the commander to
bring him before you on the pretext of wanting
more accurate information about his case. We are
ready to kill him before he gets here."
16But when the son of Paul's sister heard of
this plot, he went into the barracks and told Paul.
17Then Paul called one of the centurions and
said, "Take this young man to the commander;
he has something to tell him." 18So he took him
to the commander.
The centurion said, "Paul, the prisoner, sent
for me and asked me to bring this young man to
you because he has something to tell you."
19The commander took the young man by the

[a] *20* Or *witness* [b] *5* Exodus 22:28

hand, drew him aside and asked, "What is it you
want to tell me?"
20He said: "The Jews have agreed to ask you to
bring Paul before the Sanhedrin tomorrow on the
pretext of wanting more accurate information
about him. 21Don't give in to them, because more
than forty of them are waiting in ambush for him.
They have taken an oath not to eat or drink until
they have killed him. They are ready now, waiting for your consent to their request."
22The commander dismissed the young man
and cautioned him, "Don't tell anyone that you
have reported this to me."

Paul Transferred to Caesarea

23Then he called two of his centurions and
ordered them, "Get ready a detachment of two
hundred soldiers, seventy horsemen and two
hundred spearmen[a] to go to Caesarea at nine
tonight. 24Provide mounts for Paul so that he may
be taken safely to Governor Felix."
25He wrote a letter as follows:

26Claudius Lysias,

To His Excellency, Governor Felix:

Greetings.

27This man was seized by the Jews and
they were about to kill him, but I came with
my troops and rescued him, for I had
learned that he is a Roman citizen. 28I wanted to know why they were accusing him, so
I brought him to their Sanhedrin. 29I found
that the accusation had to do with questions
about their law, but there was no charge
against him that deserved death or imprisonment. 30When I was informed of a plot to
be carried out against the man, I sent him to
you at once. I also ordered his accusers
to present to you their case against him.

31So the soldiers, carrying out their orders,
took Paul with them during the night and
brought him as far as Antipatris. 32The next day
they let the cavalry go on with him, while they
returned to the barracks. 33When the cavalry arrived in Caesarea, they delivered the letter to the
governor and handed Paul over to him. 34The
governor read the letter and asked what province
he was from. Learning that he was from Cilicia,
35he said, "I will hear your case when your accusers get here." Then he ordered that Paul be kept
under guard in Herod's palace.

The Trial Before Felix

24 Five days later the high priest Ananias
went down to Caesarea with some of the
elders and a lawyer named Tertullus, and they
brought their charges against Paul before the governor. 2When Paul was called in, Tertullus presented his case before Felix: "We have enjoyed a
long period of peace under you, and your fore-
sight has brought about reforms in this nation.
3Everywhere and in every way, most excellent
Felix, we acknowledge this with profound gratitude. 4But in order not to weary you further, I
would request that you be kind enough to hear us
briefly.
5"We have found this man to be a troublemaker, stirring up riots among the Jews all over the
world. He is a ringleader of the Nazarene sect
6and even tried to desecrate the temple; so we
seized him. 8By[b] examining him yourself you
will be able to learn the truth about all these
charges we are bringing against him."
9The Jews joined in the accusation, asserting
that these things were true.
10When the governor motioned for him to
speak, Paul replied: "I know that for a number of
years you have been a judge over this nation; so
I gladly make my defense. 11You can easily verify
that no more than twelve days ago I went up to
Jerusalem to worship. 12My accusers did not find
me arguing with anyone at the temple, or stirring
up a crowd in the synagogues or anywhere else
in the city. 13And they cannot prove to you the
charges they are now making against me. 14How-
ever, I admit that I worship the God of our fathers
as a follower of the Way, which they call a sect.
I believe everything that agrees with the Law and
that is written in the Prophets, 15and I have the
same hope in God as these men, that there will
be a resurrection of both the righteous and the
wicked. 16So I strive always to keep my conscience clear before God and man.
17"After an absence of several years, I came to
Jerusalem to bring my people gifts for the poor
and to present offerings. 18I was ceremonially
clean when they found me in the temple courts
doing this. There was no crowd with me, nor was
I involved in any disturbance. 19But there are
some Jews from the province of Asia, who ought
to be here before you and bring charges if they
have anything against me. 20Or these who are
here should state what crime they found in me
when I stood before the Sanhedrin— 21unless it
was this one thing I shouted as I stood in their
presence: 'It is concerning the resurrection of the
dead that I am on trial before you today.' "

[a]23 The meaning of the Greek for this word is uncertain. [b]6-8 Some manuscripts *him and wanted to judge him according to our law. 7But the commander, Lysias, came and with the use of much force snatched him from our hands 8and ordered his accusers to come before you. By*

22Then Felix, who was well acquainted with
the Way, adjourned the proceedings. "When Lysias the commander comes," he said, "I will decide your case." 23He ordered the centurion to
keep Paul under guard but to give him some freedom and permit his friends to take care of his
needs.
24Several days later Felix came with his wife
Drusilla, who was a Jewess. He sent for Paul and
listened to him as he spoke about faith in Christ
Jesus. 25As Paul discoursed on righteousness,
self-control and the judgment to come, Felix was
afraid and said, "That's enough for now! You may
leave. When I find it convenient, I will send for
you." 26At the same time he was hoping that Paul
would offer him a bribe, so he sent for him frequently and talked with him.
27When two years had passed, Felix was succeeded by Porcius Festus, but because Felix
wanted to grant a favor to the Jews, he left Paul
in prison.

The Trial Before Festus

25 Three days after arriving in the province,
Festus went up from Caesarea to Jerusalem, 2where the chief priests and Jewish leaders
appeared before him and presented the charges
against Paul. 3They urgently requested Festus, as
a favor to them, to have Paul transferred to Jerusalem, for they were preparing an ambush to kill
him along the way. 4Festus answered, "Paul is
being held at Caesarea, and I myself am going
there soon. 5Let some of your leaders come with
me and press charges against the man there, if he
has done anything wrong."
6After spending eight or ten days with them,
he went down to Caesarea, and the next day he
convened the court and ordered that Paul be
brought before him. 7When Paul appeared, the
Jews who had come down from Jerusalem stood
around him, bringing many serious charges
against him, which they could not prove.
8Then Paul made his defense: "I have done
nothing wrong against the law of the Jews or
against the temple or against Caesar."
9Festus, wishing to do the Jews a favor, said to
Paul, "Are you willing to go up to Jerusalem and
stand trial before me there on these charges?"
10Paul answered: "I am now standing before
Caesar's court, where I ought to be tried. I have
not done any wrong to the Jews, as you yourself
know very well. 11If, however, I am guilty of doing anything deserving death, I do not refuse to
die. But if the charges brought against me by
these Jews are not true, no one has the right to
hand me over to them. I appeal to Caesar!"
12After Festus had conferred with his council,
he declared: "You have appealed to Caesar. To
Caesar you will go!"

Festus Consults King Agrippa

13A few days later King Agrippa and Bernice
arrived at Caesarea to pay their respects to Festus. 14Since they were spending many days there,
Festus discussed Paul's case with the king. He
said: "There is a man here whom Felix left as a
prisoner. 15When I went to Jerusalem, the chief
priests and elders of the Jews brought charges
against him and asked that he be condemned.
16"I told them that it is not the Roman custom
to hand over any man before he has faced his
accusers and has had an opportunity to defend
himself against their charges. 17When they came
here with me, I did not delay the case, but convened the court the next day and ordered the
man to be brought in. 18When his accusers got up
to speak, they did not charge him with any of the
crimes I had expected. 19Instead, they had some
points of dispute with him about their own religion and about a dead man named Jesus who Paul
claimed was alive. 20I was at a loss how to investigate such matters; so I asked if he would be willing to go to Jerusalem and stand trial there on
these charges. 21When Paul made his appeal to
be held over for the Emperor's decision, I ordered him held until I could send him to Caesar."
22Then Agrippa said to Festus, "I would like to
hear this man myself."
He replied, "Tomorrow you will hear him."

Paul Before Agrippa

23The next day Agrippa and Bernice came with
great pomp and entered the audience room with
the high ranking officers and the leading men of
the city. At the command of Festus, Paul was
brought in. 24Festus said: "King Agrippa, and all
who are present with us, you see this man! The
whole Jewish community has petitioned me
about him in Jerusalem and here in Caesarea,
shouting that he ought not to live any longer. 25I
found he had done nothing deserving of death,
but because he made his appeal to the Emperor
I decided to send him to Rome. 26But I have nothing definite to write to His Majesty about him.
Therefore I have brought him before all of you,
and especially before you, King Agrippa, so that
as a result of this investigation I may have something to write. 27For I think it is unreasonable to
send on a prisoner without specifying the charges
against him."

26 Then Agrippa said to Paul, "You have permission to speak for yourself."
So Paul motioned with his hand and began his
defense: 2"King Agrippa, I consider myself fortunate to stand before you today as I make my defense against all the accusations of the Jews, 3and
especially so because you are well acquainted

with all the Jewish customs and controversies.
Therefore, I beg you to listen to me patiently.
4"The Jews all know the way I have lived ever
since I was a child, from the beginning of my life
in my own country, and also in Jerusalem. 5They
have known me for a long time and can testify, if
they are willing, that according to the strictest
sect of our religion, I lived as a Pharisee. 6And
now it is because of my hope in what God has
promised our fathers that I am on trial today.
7This is the promise our twelve tribes are hoping
to see fulfilled as they earnestly serve God day
and night. O king, it is because of this hope that
the Jews are accusing me. 8Why should any of
you consider it incredible that God raises the
dead?
9"I too was convinced that I ought to do all
that was possible to oppose the name of Jesus of
Nazareth. 10And that is just what I did in Jerusalem. On the authority of the chief priests I put
many of the saints in prison, and when they were
put to death, I cast my vote against them. 11Many
a time I went from one synagogue to another to
have them punished, and I tried to force them to
blaspheme. In my obsession against them, I even
went to foreign cities to persecute them.
12"On one of these journeys I was going to
Damascus with the authority and commission of
the chief priests. 13About noon, O king, as I was
on the road, I saw a light from heaven, brighter
than the sun, blazing around me and my companions. 14We all fell to the ground, and I heard a
voice saying to me in Aramaic,[a] 'Saul, Saul, why
do you persecute me? It is hard for you to kick
against the goads.'
15"Then I asked, 'Who are you, Lord?'
" 'I am Jesus, whom you are persecuting,' the
Lord replied. 16'Now get up and stand on your
feet. I have appeared to you to appoint you as a
servant and as a witness of what you have seen of
me and what I will show you. 17I will rescue you
from your own people and from the Gentiles. I
am sending you to them 18to open their eyes and
turn them from darkness to light, and from the
power of Satan to God, so that they may receive
forgiveness of sins and a place among those who
are sanctified by faith in me.'
19"So then, King Agrippa, I was not disobedient to the vision from heaven. 20First to those in
Damascus, then to those in Jerusalem and in all
Judea, and to the Gentiles also, I preached that
they should repent and turn to God and prove
their repentance by their deeds. 21That is why
the Jews seized me in the temple courts and tried
to kill me. 22But I have had God's help to this
very day, and so I stand here and testify to small
and great alike. I am saying nothing beyond what
the prophets and Moses said would happen—
23that the Christ[b] would suffer and, as the first
to rise from the dead, would proclaim light to his
own people and to the Gentiles."
24At this point Festus interrupted Paul's defense. "You are out of your mind, Paul!" he shouted. "Your great learning is driving you insane."
25"I am not insane, most excellent Festus,"
Paul replied. "What I am saying is true and reasonable. 26The king is familiar with these things,
and I can speak freely to him. I am convinced that
none of this has escaped his notice, because it
was not done in a corner. 27King Agrippa, do you
believe the prophets? I know you do."
28Then Agrippa said to Paul, "Do you think
that in such a short time you can persuade me to
be a Christian?"
29Paul replied, "Short time or long—I pray
God that not only you but all who are listening
to me today may become what I am, except for
these chains."
30The king rose, and with him the governor
and Bernice and those sitting with them. 31They
left the room, and while talking with one another, they said, "This man is not doing anything
that deserves death or imprisonment."
32Agrippa said to Festus, "This man could have
been set free if he had not appealed to Caesar."

Paul Sails for Rome

27 When it was decided that we would sail
for Italy, Paul and some other prisoners
were handed over to a centurion named Julius,
who belonged to the Imperial Regiment. 2We
boarded a ship from Adramyttium about to sail
for ports along the coast of the province of Asia,
and we put out to sea. Aristarchus, a Macedonian
from Thessalonica, was with us.
3The next day we landed at Sidon; and Julius,
in kindness to Paul, allowed him to go to his
friends so they might provide for his needs.
4From there we put out to sea again and passed
to the lee of Cyprus because the winds were
against us. 5When we had sailed across the open
sea off the coast of Cilicia and Pamphylia, we
landed at Myra in Lycia. 6There the centurion
found an Alexandrian ship sailing for Italy and
put us on board. 7We made slow headway for
many days and had difficulty arriving off Cnidus.
When the wind did not allow us to hold our
course, we sailed to the lee of Crete, opposite
Salmone. 8We moved along the coast with difficulty and came to a place called Fair Havens, near
the town of Lasea.
9Much time had been lost, and sailing had already become dangerous because by now it was
after the Fast.[c] So Paul warned them, 10"Men, I

[a] 14 Or *Hebrew* [b] 23 Or *Messiah* [c] 9 That is, the Day of Atonement (Yom Kippur)

can see that our voyage is going to be disastrous and bring great loss to ship and cargo, and to our own lives also." 11 But the centurion, instead of listening to what Paul said, followed the advice of the pilot and of the owner of the ship. 12 Since the harbor was unsuitable to winter in, the majority decided that we should sail on, hoping to reach Phoenix and winter there. This was a harbor in Crete, facing both southwest and northwest.

The Storm

13 When a gentle south wind began to blow, they thought they had obtained what they wanted; so they weighed anchor and sailed along the shore of Crete. 14 Before very long, a wind of hurricane force, called the "northeaster," swept down from the island. 15 The ship was caught by the storm and could not head into the wind; so we gave way to it and were driven along. 16 As we passed to the lee of a small island called Cauda, we were hardly able to make the lifeboat secure. 17 When the men had hoisted it aboard, they passed ropes under the ship itself to hold it together. Fearing that they would run aground on the sandbars of Syrtis, they lowered the sea anchor and let the ship be driven along. 18 We took such a violent battering from the storm that the next day they began to throw the cargo overboard. 19 On the third day, they threw the ship's tackle overboard with their own hands. 20 When neither sun nor stars appeared for many days and the storm continued raging, we finally gave up all hope of being saved.

21 After the men had gone a long time without food, Paul stood up before them and said: "Men, you should have taken my advice not to sail from Crete; then you would have spared yourselves this damage and loss. 22 But now I urge you to keep up your courage, because not one of you will be lost; only the ship will be destroyed. 23 Last night an angel of the God whose I am and whom I serve stood beside me 24 and said, 'Do not be afraid, Paul. You must stand trial before Caesar; and God has graciously given you the lives of all who sail with you.' 25 So keep up your courage, men, for I have faith in God that it will happen just as he told me. 26 Nevertheless, we must run aground on some island."

The Shipwreck

27 On the fourteenth night we were still being driven across the Adriatic[a] Sea, when about midnight the sailors sensed they were approaching land. 28 They took soundings and found that the water was a hundred and twenty feet[b] deep. A short time later they took soundings again and found it was ninety feet[c] deep. 29 Fearing that we would be dashed against the rocks, they dropped four anchors from the stern and prayed for daylight. 30 In an attempt to escape from the ship, the sailors let the lifeboat down into the sea, pretending they were going to lower some anchors from the bow. 31 Then Paul said to the centurion and the soldiers, "Unless these men stay with the ship, you cannot be saved." 32 So the soldiers cut the ropes that held the lifeboat and let it fall away.

33 Just before dawn Paul urged them all to eat. "For the last fourteen days," he said, "you have been in constant suspense and have gone without food—you haven't eaten anything. 34 Now I urge you to take some food. You need it to survive. Not one of you will lose a single hair from his head." 35 After he said this, he took some bread and gave thanks to God in front of them all. Then he broke it and began to eat. 36 They were all encouraged and ate some food themselves. 37 Altogether there were 276 of us on board. 38 When they had eaten as much as they wanted, they lightened the ship by throwing the grain into the sea.

39 When daylight came, they did not recognize the land, but they saw a bay with a sandy beach, where they decided to run the ship aground if they could. 40 Cutting loose the anchors, they left them in the sea and at the same time untied the ropes that held the rudders. Then they hoisted the foresail to the wind and made for the beach. 41 But the ship struck a sandbar and ran aground. The bow stuck fast and would not move, and the stern was broken to pieces by the pounding of the surf.

42 The soldiers planned to kill the prisoners to prevent any of them from swimming away and escaping. 43 But the centurion wanted to spare Paul's life and kept them from carrying out their plan. He ordered those who could swim to jump overboard first and get to land. 44 The rest were to get there on planks or on pieces of the ship. In this way everyone reached land in safety.

Ashore on Malta

28 Once safely on shore, we found out that the island was called Malta. 2 The islanders showed us unusual kindness. They built a fire and welcomed us all because it was raining and cold. 3 Paul gathered a pile of brushwood and, as he put it on the fire, a viper, driven out by the heat, fastened itself on his hand. 4 When the islanders saw the snake hanging from his hand, they said to each other, "This man must be a murderer; for though he escaped from the sea,

a27 In ancient times the name referred to an area extending well south of Italy.
b28 Greek *twenty orguias* (about 37 meters)
c28 Greek *fifteen orguias* (about 27 meters)

Justice has not allowed him to live." 5But Paul
shook the snake off into the fire and suffered no
ill effects. 6The people expected him to swell up
or suddenly fall dead, but after waiting a long
time and seeing nothing unusual happen to him,
they changed their minds and said he was a god.
7There was an estate nearby that belonged to
Publius, the chief official of the island. He welcomed us to his home and for three days entertained us hospitably. 8His father was sick in bed,
suffering from fever and dysentery. Paul went in
to see him and, after prayer, placed his hands on
him and healed him. 9When this had happened,
the rest of the sick on the island came and were
cured. 10They honored us in many ways and
when we were ready to sail, they furnished us
with the supplies we needed.

Arrival at Rome

11After three months we put out to sea in a
ship that had wintered in the island. It was an
Alexandrian ship with the figurehead of the twin
gods Castor and Pollux. 12We put in at Syracuse
and stayed there three days. 13From there we set
sail and arrived at Rhegium. The next day the
south wind came up, and on the following day we
reached Puteoli. 14There we found some brothers
who invited us to spend a week with them. And
so we came to Rome. 15The brothers there had
heard that we were coming, and they traveled as
far as the Forum of Appius and the Three Taverns
to meet us. At the sight of these men Paul
thanked God and was encouraged. 16When we
got to Rome, Paul was allowed to live by himself,
with a soldier to guard him.

Paul Preaches at Rome Under Guard

17Three days later he called together the leaders of the Jews. When they had assembled, Paul
said to them: "My brothers, although I have done
nothing against our people or against the customs
of our ancestors, I was arrested in Jerusalem and
handed over to the Romans. 18They examined
me and wanted to release me, because I was not
guilty of any crime deserving death. 19But when
the Jews objected, I was compelled to appeal to
Caesar—not that I had any charge to bring
against my own people. 20For this reason I have
asked to see you and talk with you. It is because
of the hope of Israel that I am bound with this
chain."

21They replied, "We have not received any letters from Judea concerning you, and none of the
brothers who have come from there has reported
or said anything bad about you. 22But we want to
hear what your views are, for we know that people everywhere are talking against this sect."

23They arranged to meet Paul on a certain day,
and came in even larger numbers to the place
where he was staying. From morning till evening
he explained and declared to them the kingdom
of God and tried to convince them about Jesus
from the Law of Moses and from the Prophets.
24Some were convinced by what he said, but others would not believe. 25They disagreed among
themselves and began to leave after Paul had
made this final statement: "The Holy Spirit spoke
the truth to your forefathers when he said
through Isaiah the prophet:

26" 'Go to this people and say,
"You will be ever hearing but never
understanding;
you will be ever seeing but never
perceiving."
27For this people's heart has become calloused;
they hardly hear with their ears,
and they have closed their eyes.
Otherwise they might see with their eyes,
hear with their ears,
understand with their hearts
and turn, and I would heal them.'[a]

28"Therefore I want you to know that God's
salvation has been sent to the Gentiles, and they
will listen!"[b]

30For two whole years Paul stayed there in his
own rented house and welcomed all who came
to see him. 31Boldly and without hindrance he
preached the kingdom of God and taught about
the Lord Jesus Christ.

[a]27 Isaiah 6:9,10 [b]28 Some manuscripts *listen!" 29After he said this, the Jews left, arguing vigorously among themselves.*

Introduction to ROMANS

Personal Reading Plan

❒ Romans 1:1–32
❒ Romans 2:1–29
❒ Romans 3:1–31
❒ Romans 4:1–5:11
❒ Romans 5:12–6:23
❒ Romans 7:1–8:17
❒ Romans 8:18–9:29
❒ Romans 9:30–10:21
❒ Romans 11:1–36
❒ Romans 12:1–13:14
❒ Romans 14:1–15:13
❒ Romans 15:14–16:27

Author

The writer is the apostle Paul.

Date

Paul wrote his letter during a three-month period spent in Corinth at the home of his friend and convert Gaius (16:23). It was winter. The time was probably A.D. 56–57 (though it was certainly sometime between A.D. 54–59).

Theme

Being right with God through faith in Christ.

Historical Background

For nearly 10 years Paul had been at work evangelizing the Gentile territories ringing the Aegean Sea. Now that there were established churches throughout the region, he turns his eyes to fresh fields. He would go to Spain, the oldest Roman colony in the West. But first there was unfinished business: He had taken up a collection to aid the poor in Jerusalem—a fine gesture on the part of the newer churches—and now he had to take this to Jerusalem, though he did so with some misgiving (15:31).

After Jerusalem, he planned to travel to Spain, stopping enroute to fulfill a long-held dream. He would visit Rome—the capital of the world. In anticipation of that visit, he wrote the letter to the Romans by way of introduction (the Roman Christians did not know him, though—as chapter 16 reveals—he had friends there). He was also eager to assure the Roman Christians, contrary to false rumors they might have heard, that the Gospel he was preaching was, indeed, the gospel of Jesus Christ.

Paul's plan did not work as he intended. He would visit Rome, but not for three more years, and then he would come not as a tourist but as a prisoner. His misgivings about his Jerusalem trip proved accurate. Once there, he was quickly arrested and eventually sent to Rome for trial. Paul remained in Rome under house arrest for at least two years. Ultimately, according to reliable tradition, he was executed at a place just outside Rome. He never went to Spain.

It is not known how the Roman church began. It is not unlikely that some Roman Jews, converted on the Day of Pentecost (Acts 2:10), began the church. The Roman historian Suetonius writes that Jews were expelled from Rome about A.D. 50 for rioting, probably as a result of preaching Jesus in synagogues. As for the Gentile Christians in Rome, it is known that other Christian missionaries besides Paul were active in founding churches.

Characteristics

Romans is Paul's most complete theological statement—carefully written, precise and painstakingly logical. This is not to say, however, that Romans is boring and burdensome. Quite the contrary, it is alive and vibrant, colorful, compassionate, and sweeping in scope. In fact, the very magnitude of its themes makes Romans, at times, heavy going. Even the apostle Peter sometimes found Paul's writing hard to understand (2 Peter 3:16)!

The main issue Paul is addressing is the question of how God will judge each of us on the final day. Will it be on the basis of how "good" we were, that is, how well we kept the Law? If so, our life would be full of unending tension. Acutely aware of repeated failure, we would never have any assurance of acquittal.

But this is not how God intends life to be. Here the great theme of Romans emerges: We can have assurance of right standing before God and hence know we will be given a positive verdict on Judgment Day. Such confidence does not come because of what we have done. It comes because of what God does—thanks to Christ's death in our place, he freely offers us his grace.

Paul sets this theme against the teaching of certain Jewish Christians, legalists who would add circumcision to grace (thus nullifying grace). If we have to do anything to deserve it, salvation is not an unearned gift freely given by God. In the course of his argument, Paul sets up a series of opposites: faith versus works, Spirit versus flesh, and liberty versus bondage.

In answering the question of how we gain right standing before God, Paul argues first that both pagans and religious people stand condemned before God (1:18–3:20), that right standing comes only by God's grace shown in Christ's sacrificial death and accepted by faith (3:21–5:21), and that such righteousness leads to a whole new lifestyle (6:1–8:39). He then deals with the question of why Israel rejected Christ (9:1–11:36), ending with practical exhortations for a life of faith (12:1–15:13). The impact of Romans on the history of the church can hardly be overstated. From Augustine to Luther to Wesley, many lives were changed as the result of a fresh reading of this book.

Passages for Topical Group Study

1:18–32	SEXUALITY	God's Wrath Against Mankind
3:9–24	SIN	No One Is Righteous
	GUILT	
7:7–25	ADDICTION	Struggling With Sin
	TEMPTATION	
8:18–27	SHATTERED DREAMS	Future Glory
	CHRONIC ILLNESS / DISABILITY	
8:28–39	ABUSE	More Than Conquerors
	GRIEF AND LOSS	
12:1–8	ABILITIES	Living Sacrifices
	CHOOSING A CAREER	
	SPIRITUAL GIFTS	
12:9–21	GRUDGES	Sincere Love
	REJECTION	
13:1–7	RELATING TO AUTHORITY	Submission to the Authorities
13:8–14	RACISM	Love, for the Day Is Near

See the Lesson Plans in the front of this Bible.

Passages for General Group Study

1:1–7	Salutation
1:8–17	Paul's Longing to Visit Rome
2:1–16	God's Righteous Judgment
2:17–29	The Jews and the Law
4:1–25	Abraham Justified by Faith
5:1–11	Peace and Joy
5:12–21	Death Through Adam, Life Through Christ
6:1–14	Dead to Sin, Alive in Christ
6:15–23	Slaves to Righteousness
7:1–6	An Illustration From Marriage
8:1–17	Life Through the Spirit
9:1–29	God's Sovereign Choice
9:30–10:21	Israel's Unbelief
11:1–36	God's Dealings With Israel
14:1–15:13	The Weak and the Strong
15:14–33	Paul's Ministry and Plans
16:1–27	Personal Greetings

1 Paul, a servant of Christ Jesus, called to be an
apostle and set apart for the gospel of God—
2the gospel he promised beforehand through his
prophets in the Holy Scriptures 3regarding his
Son, who as to his human nature was a descendant of David, 4and who through the Spirit[a] of
holiness was declared with power to be the Son
of God[b] by his resurrection from the dead: Jesus
Christ our Lord. 5Through him and for his name's
sake, we received grace and apostleship to call
people from among all the Gentiles to the obedience that comes from faith. 6And you also are
among those who are called to belong to Jesus
Christ.

7To all in Rome who are loved by God and
called to be saints:

Grace and peace to you from God our Father
and from the Lord Jesus Christ.

Romans 1:1–7

1. What letters are you likely to save? Where do you put them?
2. What is the relationship of Paul to Jesus Christ? What is his life calling? For whom?
3. What facts do you learn about Jesus Christ in this passage?
4. How would you describe your relationship with Jesus Christ? Finish the sentence: "I am a ..." Seeker? Student? Beginner? Slave? Follower?
5. What is God saying to you in this passage?
6. How can this group help you in prayer this week?

Paul's Longing to Visit Rome

8First, I thank my God through Jesus Christ for
all of you, because your faith is being reported all
over the world. 9God, whom I serve with my
whole heart in preaching the gospel of his Son, is
my witness how constantly I remember you 10in
my prayers at all times; and I pray that now at last
by God's will the way may be opened for me to
come to you.
11I long to see you so that I may impart to you
some spiritual gift to make you strong— 12that is,
that you and I may be mutually encouraged by
each other's faith. 13I do not want you to be unaware, brothers, that I planned many times to
come to you (but have been prevented from doing so until now) in order that I might have a
harvest among you, just as I have had among the
other Gentiles.

Romans 1:8–17

1. What is one place you have never seen that you would like to visit?
2. What do you learn about Paul in this passage?
3. Reading between the lines, what is the problem in the church in Rome that Paul wants to address in this letter?
4. How would you compare your commitment to the Gospel to Paul's in verse 16?
5. What is God saying to you in this passage?
6. How can this group help you in prayer this week?

14I am obligated both to Greeks and non-
Greeks, both to the wise and the foolish. 15That
is why I am so eager to preach the gospel also to
you who are at Rome.
16I am not ashamed of the gospel, because it is
the power of God for the salvation of everyone
who believes: first for the Jew, then for the Gentile. 17For in the gospel a righteousness from God
is revealed, a righteousness that is by faith from
first to last,[c] just as it is written: "The righteous
will live by faith."[d]

God's Wrath Against Mankind

18The wrath of God is being revealed from
heaven against all the godlessness and wickedness of men who suppress the truth by their
wickedness, 19since what may be known about
God is plain to them, because God has made it
plain to them. 20For since the creation of the
world God's invisible qualities—his eternal power and divine nature—have been clearly seen,

[a]4 *Or who as to his spirit* [b]4 *Or was appointed to be the Son of God with power* [c]17 Or *is from faith to faith*
[d]17 Hab. 2:4

being understood from what has been made, so that men are without excuse.

21 For although they knew God, they neither glorified him as God nor gave thanks to him, but their thinking became futile and their foolish hearts were darkened. 22 Although they claimed to be wise, they became fools 23 and exchanged the glory of the immortal God for images made to look like mortal man and birds and animals and reptiles.

24 Therefore God gave them over in the sinful desires of their hearts to sexual impurity for the degrading of their bodies with one another. 25 They exchanged the truth of God for a lie, and worshiped and served created things rather than the Creator—who is forever praised. Amen.

26 Because of this, God gave them over to shameful lusts. Even their women exchanged natural relations for unnatural ones. 27 In the same way the men also abandoned natural relations with women and were inflamed with lust for one another. Men committed indecent acts with other men, and received in themselves the due penalty for their perversion.

28 Furthermore, since they did not think it worthwhile to retain the knowledge of God, he gave them over to a depraved mind, to do what ought not to be done. 29 They have become filled with every kind of wickedness, evil, greed and depravity. They are full of envy, murder, strife, deceit and malice. They are gossips, 30 slanderers, God-haters, insolent, arrogant and boastful; they invent ways of doing evil; they disobey their parents; 31 they are senseless, faithless, heartless, ruthless. 32 Although they know God's righteous decree that those who do such things deserve death, they not only continue to do these very things but also approve of those who practice them.

Romans 1:18–32

1. What are some things you have observed in nature that confirm to you that "there is a God"?
2. Do you think God unveils his wrath through the forces of nature? If so, when? Why?
3. Can you usually tell if someone is lying to you? How?
4. When did "the truth" about God become real in your life?
5. Do you think our society has changed for the better or the worse since Paul wrote this description?
6. Today, homosexuality is known as an "alternative lifestyle." How do you feel about that?
7. If Jesus was a student in your school, what would he do to clean up the moral standards?
8. How are things going between you and your Maker?

God's Righteous Judgment

2 You, therefore, have no excuse, you who pass judgment on someone else, for at whatever point you judge the other, you are condemning yourself, because you who pass judgment do the same things. 2 Now we know that God's judgment against those who do such things is based on truth. 3 So when you, a mere man, pass judgment on them and yet do the same things, do you think you will escape God's judgment? 4 Or do you show contempt for the riches of his kindness, tolerance and patience, not realizing that God's kindness leads you toward repentance?

5 But because of your stubbornness and your unrepentant heart, you are storing up wrath against yourself for the day of God's wrath, when his righteous judgment will be revealed. 6 God

---

Paul asserts that all people can know about God, because the essential facts are written into nature itself. He goes on to point out that knowing about God is not enough. Unless men and women honor him, their minds darken; they turn to various idolatries and become sinful beyond imagining.

1:18 ***wrath of God.*** Because God is God and therefore holy and loving, he cannot tolerate evil, injustice, cruelty, etc. Such wrath is not irrational rage or anger, but rather the inevitable response of a good God to evil. ***revealed.*** Unless individuals see the reality of wrath, they may never see their need for being counted as righteous.

1:19–20 Paul answers the unspoken objection: How can Gentiles be held accountable for their sins when they never heard the truth?

1:24–27 Not knowing who their Creator is, their own identity becomes confused and is expressed in a distorted sexuality. Greek and Roman writers support Paul's description: it was an age of unparalleled immorality.

1:29–31 Without a sense of self-identity, people do not know how to love their neighbor (Mark 12:31). Paul selects a few examples from hundreds of possible Greek words which define specific forms of sin.

1:32 ***they know.*** Sinful behavior was not due to complete ignorance of God's standards but to self-willed rebellion. ***approve.*** Sin seeks to encourage others to join with itself in defiance of the awareness that ultimately there will be a judgment.

"will give to each person according to what he has done."[a] 7To those who by persistence in doing good seek glory, honor and immortality, he will give eternal life. 8But for those who are self-seeking and who reject the truth and follow evil, there will be wrath and anger. 9There will be

Romans 2:1–16

1. When you were growing up, who often got you in trouble at home?
2. Reading between the lines, what is going on in the church in Rome between the Jewish and the Gentile factions? Who are the outsiders? Why?
3. What is the difference between "judging" and identifying sin when it is present? When are you most likely to become judgmental?
4. As you grow older in your own spiritual life, does your appreciation of God's grace grow stronger ... or more likely to be taken for granted?
5. What is God saying to you in this passage?
6. How can this group help you in prayer this week?

trouble and distress for every human being who does evil: first for the Jew, then for the Gentile; 10but glory, honor and peace for everyone who does good: first for the Jew, then for the Gentile. 11For God does not show favoritism.

12All who sin apart from the law will also perish apart from the law, and all who sin under the law will be judged by the law. 13For it is not those who hear the law who are righteous in God's sight, but it is those who obey the law who will be declared righteous. 14(Indeed, when Gentiles, who do not have the law, do by nature things required by the law, they are a law for themselves, even though they do not have the law, 15since they show that the requirements of the law are written on their hearts, their consciences also bearing witness, and their thoughts now accusing, now even defending them.) 16This will take place on the day when God will judge men's secrets through Jesus Christ, as my gospel declares.

The Jews and the Law

17Now you, if you call yourself a Jew; if you rely on the law and brag about your relationship to God; 18if you know his will and approve of what is superior because you are instructed by the law; 19if you are convinced that you are a guide for the blind, a light for those who are in the dark, 20an instructor of the foolish, a teacher of infants, because you have in the law the embodiment of knowledge and truth— 21you, then, who teach others, do you not teach yourself? You who preach against stealing, do you steal? 22You who say that people should not commit adultery, do you commit adultery? You who abhor idols, do you rob temples? 23You who brag about the law, do you dishonor God by breaking the law? 24As it is written: "God's name is blasphemed among the Gentiles because of you."[b]

Romans 2:17–29

1. In your family, who is more likely to observe the speed limit?
2. Why is Paul (a Jew) so vocal about Gentiles not having to be circumcised to come into the church?
3. How open are you to receiving someone into your group who is seeking God but struggling with a moral problem or an addiction?
4. What are you most likely to be hypocritical about regarding your spirituality: Bible knowledge? Wisdom? Maturity? Morality? Lack of hypocrisy?
5. What is God saying to you in this passage?
6. How can this group help you in prayer this week?

25Circumcision has value if you observe the law, but if you break the law, you have become as though you had not been circumcised. 26If those who are not circumcised keep the law's requirements, will they not be regarded as though they were circumcised? 27The one who is not circumcised physically and yet obeys the law will condemn you who, even though you have the[c] written code and circumcision, are a lawbreaker.

[a] *6* Psalm 62:12; Prov. 24:12 [b] *24* Isaiah 52:5; Ezek. 36:22 [c] *27* Or *who, by means of a*

28A man is not a Jew if he is only one outwardly, nor is circumcision merely outward and physical. 29No, a man is a Jew if he is one inwardly; and circumcision is circumcision of the heart, by the Spirit, not by the written code. Such a man's praise is not from men, but from God.

God's Faithfulness

3 What advantage, then, is there in being a Jew, or what value is there in circumcision? 2Much in every way! First of all, they have been entrusted with the very words of God.

3What if some did not have faith? Will their lack of faith nullify God's faithfulness? 4Not at all! Let God be true, and every man a liar. As it is written:

"So that you may be proved right when you
speak
and prevail when you judge."[a]

5But if our unrighteousness brings out God's righteousness more clearly, what shall we say? That God is unjust in bringing his wrath on us? (I am using a human argument.) 6Certainly not! If that were so, how could God judge the world? 7Someone might argue, "If my falsehood enhances God's truthfulness and so increases his glory, why am I still condemned as a sinner?" 8Why not say—as we are being slanderously reported as saying and as some claim that we say—"Let us do evil that good may result"? Their condemnation is deserved.

No One Is Righteous

9What shall we conclude then? Are we any better[b]? Not at all! We have already made the charge that Jews and Gentiles alike are all under sin. 10As it is written:

"There is no one righteous, not even one;
11 there is no one who understands,
no one who seeks God.
12All have turned away,
they have together become worthless;
there is no one who does good,
not even one."[c]
13"Their throats are open graves;
their tongues practice deceit."[d]
"The poison of vipers is on their lips."[e]
14 "Their mouths are full of cursing and
bitterness."[f]
15"Their feet are swift to shed blood;
16 ruin and misery mark their ways,
17and the way of peace they do not know."[g]
18 "There is no fear of God before their
eyes."[h]

ROMANS 3:9–24

1. What's something you did as a kid that got you in trouble?
2. Who is good at making you feel guilty: Family? Teachers? Friends? Yourself? How do you deal with guilt?
3. Do you think someone who grows up in a strong, religious home has a better chance of resisting sin?
4. If someone said to you, "Christians think having a good time is a sin," how would you respond?
5. When did you come to the place that you realized that you had "fallen short" of God's requirements? What did you do about it?
6. How do you deal with sin in your life right now?
7. Close in silent prayer. Confess your sin and receive the gift of God's forgiveness (1 John 1:9).

[a] *4* Psalm 51:4 [b] *9* Or *worse* [c] *12* Psalms 14:1-3; 53:1-3; Eccles. 7:20 [d] *13* Psalm 5:9 [e] *13* Psalm 140:3
[f] *14* Psalm 10:7 [g] *17* Isaiah 59:7,8 [h] *18* Psalm 36:1

Paul's opponent has pressed him for an admission that the Jew is superior to the Gentile. Paul responds by turning to the OT to demonstrate the universal fact of sin. There is no exception, no superiority. All are sinners. All are accountable before God. No one will be declared righteous.

3:9 ***under sin.*** Under the authority of sin. Paul is not thinking here about individual sins which a person commits, but rather about the way that sin controls people.

3:10–18 In Rabbinic fashion, Paul strings together (probably from memory) a more or less free rendering of various OT verses drawn mainly from the Psalms, all of which add up to a frightening description of human nature. The point of these verses is clear: all people, be they Jew or Gentile, are under sin's power. This is seen in the fact that no one seeks God and his ways (vv.10–12); their very words condemn them (vv.13–14), as do their violent and evil ways (vv. 15–18).

3:19 In having the "words of God" (3:2), the Jews, of all people, should know their sin (and hence their guilt) before God.

3:20 Once again Paul turns to the OT. Here he echoes (though does not directly quote) Psalm 143:2b. The function of the Law, rather than being a shield against God's wrath, is to make people aware of their sin. Once it has done that, its power is expended. It cannot hide a person from God's action on the Day of Judgment.

3:23 This is God's divine splendor which is reflected in the Law.

19Now we know that whatever the law says, it
says to those who are under the law, so that every
mouth may be silenced and the whole world held
accountable to God. 20Therefore no one will be
declared righteous in his sight by observing the
law; rather, through the law we become conscious of sin.

Righteousness Through Faith

21But now a righteousness from God, apart
from law, has been made known, to which the
Law and the Prophets testify. 22This righteousness from God comes through faith in Jesus
Christ to all who believe. There is no difference,
23for all have sinned and fall short of the glory
of God, 24and are justified freely by his grace
through the redemption that came by Christ
Jesus. 25God presented him as a sacrifice of
atonement,[a] through faith in his blood. He did
this to demonstrate his justice, because in his
forbearance he had left the sins committed beforehand unpunished— 26he did it to demonstrate his justice at the present time, so as to be
just and the one who justifies those who have
faith in Jesus.
27Where, then, is boasting? It is excluded. On
what principle? On that of observing the law?
No, but on that of faith. 28For we maintain that a
man is justified by faith apart from observing the
law. 29Is God the God of Jews only? Is he not the
God of Gentiles too? Yes, of Gentiles too, 30since
there is only one God, who will justify the circumcised by faith and the uncircumcised through
that same faith. 31Do we, then, nullify the law by
this faith? Not at all! Rather, we uphold the law.

Abraham Justified by Faith

4 What then shall we say that Abraham, our
forefather, discovered in this matter? 2If, in
fact, Abraham was justified by works, he had
something to boast about—but not before God.
3What does the Scripture say? "Abraham believed God, and it was credited to him as righteousness."[b]
4Now when a man works, his wages are not
credited to him as a gift, but as an obligation.
5However, to the man who does not work but
trusts God who justifies the wicked, his faith is
credited as righteousness. 6David says the same
thing when he speaks of the blessedness of the
man to whom God credits righteousness apart
from works:

7"Blessed are they
whose transgressions are forgiven,
whose sins are covered.
8Blessed is the man
whose sin the Lord will never count
against him."[c]

9Is this blessedness only for the circumcised,
or also for the uncircumcised? We have been saying that Abraham's faith was credited to him as
righteousness. 10Under what circumstances was
it credited? Was it after he was circumcised, or
before? It was not after, but before! 11And he
received the sign of circumcision, a seal of the
righteousness that he had by faith while he was
still uncircumcised. So then, he is the father of all
who believe but have not been circumcised, in
order that righteousness might be credited to
them. 12And he is also the father of the circumcised who not only are circumcised but who also
walk in the footsteps of the faith that our father
Abraham had before he was circumcised.

Romans 4:1–25

1. What was your first paying job outside of the house? How much did you make?
2. Why would the example of Abraham be so important to the Jewish people?
3. Would you be a more faithful and religious person if you had the judgment of God hanging over your head? What motivates you now to strive in your Christian life?
4. In what area of your life do you need to take a lesson from Abraham and focus not on "working" but on "believing"?
5. What is God saying to you in this passage?
6. How can this group help you in prayer this week?

13It was not through law that Abraham and his
offspring received the promise that he would be
heir of the world, but through the righteousness
that comes by faith. 14For if those who live by law
are heirs, faith has no value and the promise is
worthless, 15because law brings wrath. And
where there is no law there is no transgression.
16Therefore, the promise comes by faith, so
that it may be by grace and may be guaranteed to
all Abraham's offspring—not only to those who
are of the law but also to those who are of the
faith of Abraham. He is the father of us all. 17As
it is written: "I have made you a father of many

[a] 25 Or *as the one who would turn aside his wrath, taking away sin*
[b] 3 Gen. 15:6; also in verse 22
[c] 8 Psalm 32:1,2

nations."[a] He is our father in the sight of God,
in whom he believed—the God who gives life to
the dead and calls things that are not as though
they were.
18Against all hope, Abraham in hope believed
and so became the father of many nations, just as
it had been said to him, "So shall your offspring
be."[b] 19Without weakening in his faith, he faced
the fact that his body was as good as dead—since
he was about a hundred years old—and that Sarah's womb was also dead. 20Yet he did not waver
through unbelief regarding the promise of God,
but was strengthened in his faith and gave glory
to God, 21being fully persuaded that God had
power to do what he had promised. 22This is why
"it was credited to him as righteousness." 23The
words "it was credited to him" were written not
for him alone, 24but also for us, to whom God will
credit righteousness—for us who believe in him
who raised Jesus our Lord from the dead. 25He
was delivered over to death for our sins and was
raised to life for our justification.

Peace and Joy

5 Therefore, since we have been justified
through faith, we[c] have peace with God

> **ROMANS 5:1–11**
>
> 1. If you needed a kidney transplant to live, what family member would be willing to give you their kidney?
> 2. How does Paul describe mankind before Christ in verses 6, 8 and 10?
> 3. How does "justification" change things in our relationship with God?
> 4. How does this change the way a Christian is to look upon suffering and stress?
> 5. What is God saying to you in this passage?
> 6. How can this group help you in prayer this week?

through our Lord Jesus Christ, 2through whom
we have gained access by faith into this grace in
which we now stand. And we[c] rejoice in the
hope of the glory of God. 3Not only so, but we[c]
also rejoice in our sufferings, because we know
that suffering produces perseverance; 4persever-
ance, character; and character, hope. 5And hope
does not disappoint us, because God has poured
out his love into our hearts by the Holy Spirit,
whom he has given us.
6You see, at just the right time, when we
were still powerless, Christ died for the ungodly.
7Very rarely will anyone die for a righteous man,
though for a good man someone might possibly
dare to die. 8But God demonstrates his own love
for us in this: While we were still sinners, Christ
died for us.
9Since we have now been justified by his
blood, how much more shall we be saved from
God's wrath through him! 10For if, when we
were God's enemies, we were reconciled to him
through the death of his Son, how much more,
having been reconciled, shall we be saved
through his life! 11Not only is this so, but we also
rejoice in God through our Lord Jesus Christ,
through whom we have now received reconciliation.

Death Through Adam, Life Through Christ

12Therefore, just as sin entered the world
through one man, and death through sin, and
in this way death came to all men, because all

> **ROMANS 5:12–21**
>
> 1. Who do you take after in your temperament, your mother or your father? How about in your body build? Your musical ability?
> 2. What do you remember about the story in the Old Testament of Adam and his "fall"?
> 3. If you had to describe two types of individuals in parallel columns, how would you describe those "in Adam" and those "in Christ"?
> 4. When did you fully understand and appreciate all that God did for you in Jesus Christ?
> 5. What is God saying to you in this passage?
> 6. How can this group help you in prayer this week?

sinned— 13for before the law was given, sin was
in the world. But sin is not taken into account
when there is no law. 14Nevertheless, death

[a] *17* Gen. 17:5 [b] *18* Gen. 15:5 [c] *1,2,3* Or *let us*

reigned from the time of Adam to the time of Moses, even over those who did not sin by breaking a command, as did Adam, who was a pattern of the one to come.

[15]But the gift is not like the trespass. For if the many died by the trespass of the one man, how much more did God's grace and the gift that came by the grace of the one man, Jesus Christ, overflow to the many! [16]Again, the gift of God is not like the result of the one man's sin: The judgment followed one sin and brought condemnation, but the gift followed many trespasses and brought justification. [17]For if, by the trespass of the one man, death reigned through that one man, how much more will those who receive God's abundant provision of grace and of the gift of righteousness reign in life through the one man, Jesus Christ.

[18]Consequently, just as the result of one trespass was condemnation for all men, so also the result of one act of righteousness was justification that brings life for all men. [19]For just as through the disobedience of the one man the many were made sinners, so also through the obedience of the one man the many will be made righteous.

[20]The law was added so that the trespass might increase. But where sin increased, grace increased all the more, [21]so that, just as sin reigned in death, so also grace might reign through righteousness to bring eternal life through Jesus Christ our Lord.

Dead to Sin, Alive in Christ

6 What shall we say, then? Shall we go on sinning so that grace may increase? [2]By no means! We died to sin; how can we live in it any longer? [3]Or don't you know that all of us who were baptized into Christ Jesus were baptized into his death? [4]We were therefore buried with him through baptism into death in order that, just as Christ was raised from the dead through the glory of the Father, we too may live a new life.

[5]If we have been united with him like this in his death, we will certainly also be united with him in his resurrection. [6]For we know that our old self was crucified with him so that the body of sin might be done away with,[a] that we should no longer be slaves to sin— [7]because anyone who has died has been freed from sin.

[8]Now if we died with Christ, we believe that we will also live with him. [9]For we know that since Christ was raised from the dead, he cannot die again; death no longer has mastery over him. [10]The death he died, he died to sin once for all; but the life he lives, he lives to God.

[11]In the same way, count yourselves dead to sin but alive to God in Christ Jesus. [12]Therefore do not let sin reign in your mortal body so that you obey its evil desires. [13]Do not offer the parts of your body to sin, as instruments of wickedness, but rather offer yourselves to God, as those who have been brought from death to life; and offer the parts of your body to him as instruments of righteousness. [14]For sin shall not be your master, because you are not under law, but under grace.

ROMANS 6:1–14

1. What is the closest you have come to losing your life?
2. What is Paul's short answer to the addict who says he is a slave to his habit?
3. The idea of death and resurrection is mentioned repeatedly in this passage. What is Paul trying to say?
4. How does the knowledge of your death to sin affect your struggle with sin, or how can it? How can it affect your prayer life?
5. What is God saying to you in this passage?
6. How can this group help you in prayer this week?

Slaves to Righteousness

[15]What then? Shall we sin because we are not under law but under grace? By no means! [16]Don't you know that when you offer yourselves to someone to obey him as slaves, you are slaves to the one whom you obey—whether you are slaves to sin, which leads to death, or to obedience, which leads to righteousness? [17]But thanks be to God that, though you used to be slaves to sin, you wholeheartedly obeyed the form of teaching to which you were entrusted. [18]You have been set free from sin and have become slaves to righteousness.

[19]I put this in human terms because you are weak in your natural selves. Just as you used to offer the parts of your body in slavery to impurity and to ever-increasing wickedness, so now offer them in slavery to righteousness leading to holiness. [20]When you were slaves to sin, you were free from the control of righteousness. [21]What

[a]6 Or *be rendered powerless*

benefit did you reap at that time from the things
you are now ashamed of? Those things result in
death! 22But now that you have been set free
from sin and have become slaves to God, the
benefit you reap leads to holiness, and the result
is eternal life. 23For the wages of sin is death, but
the gift of God is eternal life in[a] Christ Jesus our
Lord.

Romans 6:15–23

1. Who was the first "boss" you worked for? Was this person easy to work for or a slave driver?
2. If Paul were around today, what would he say our society is enslaved to? What about the Christian community?
3. What is the difference between the pension plan that the old slave owner of your life offered ... and the new owner's plan?
4. If your body could talk, what would it say to you about the way you are using your "body" to the glory of God?
5. What is God saying to you in this passage?
6. How can this group help you in prayer this week?

An Illustration From Marriage

7 Do you not know, brothers—for I am speaking to men who know the law—that the law
has authority over a man only as long as he lives?
2For example, by law a married woman is bound
to her husband as long as he is alive, but if her
husband dies, she is released from the law of
marriage. 3So then, if she marries another man
while her husband is still alive, she is called an
adulteress. But if her husband dies, she is released from that law and is not an adulteress,
even though she marries another man.
4So, my brothers, you also died to the law
through the body of Christ, that you might belong
to another, to him who was raised from the dead,
in order that we might bear fruit to God. 5For
when we were controlled by the sinful nature,[b]
the sinful passions aroused by the law were at
work in our bodies, so that we bore fruit for
death. 6But now, by dying to what once bound
us, we have been released from the law so that
we serve in the new way of the Spirit, and not in
the old way of the written code.

Romans 7:1–6

1. What do you think is the ideal age to get married?
2. What were some of the "rules" that were laid on you in your religious upbringing?
3. When Paul says that you are "released" from the obligations of a religious life, is he discouraging spiritual discipline?
4. What motivates you now to live a godly life?
5. What is God saying to you in this passage?
6. How can this group help you in prayer this week?

Struggling With Sin

7What shall we say, then? Is the law sin? Certainly not! Indeed I would not have known what
sin was except through the law. For I would not
have known what coveting really was if the law
had not said, "Do not covet."[c] 8But sin, seizing
the opportunity afforded by the commandment,
produced in me every kind of covetous desire.
For apart from law, sin is dead. 9Once I was alive
apart from law; but when the commandment
came, sin sprang to life and I died. 10I found that
the very commandment that was intended to
bring life actually brought death. 11For sin, seizing the opportunity afforded by the commandment, deceived me, and through the commandment put me to death. 12So then, the law is holy,
and the commandment is holy, righteous and
good.
13Did that which is good, then, become death
to me? By no means! But in order that sin might
be recognized as sin, it produced death in me
through what was good, so that through the commandment sin might become utterly sinful.
14We know that the law is spiritual; but I am
unspiritual, sold as a slave to sin. 15I do not understand what I do. For what I want to do I do not
do, but what I hate I do. 16And if I do what I do
not want to do, I agree that the law is good. 17As
it is, it is no longer I myself who do it, but it is sin

[a] 23 Or *through* [b] 5 Or *the flesh*; also in verse 25 [c] 7 Exodus 20:17; Deut. 5:21

living in me. 18I know that nothing good lives in
me, that is, in my sinful nature.[a] For I have the
desire to do what is good, but I cannot carry it
out. 19For what I do is not the good I want to do;
no, the evil I do not want to do—this I keep on
doing. 20Now if I do what I do not want to do, it
is no longer I who do it, but it is sin living in me
that does it.
21So I find this law at work: When I want to do
good, evil is right there with me. 22For in my
inner being I delight in God's law; 23but I see
another law at work in the members of my body,
waging war against the law of my mind and making me a prisoner of the law of sin at work within
my members. 24What a wretched man I am! Who
will rescue me from this body of death? 25Thanks
be to God—through Jesus Christ our Lord!
So then, I myself in my mind am a slave to
God's law, but in the sinful nature a slave to the
law of sin.

ROMANS 7:7–25

1. What habit do you have that you can't seem to break: Cracking your knuckles? Smoking? Picking your nose? Swearing?
2. What New Year's resolution or other commitment have you started with good intentions only to have it fizzle out?
3. Have you ever known a person who was hooked on drugs? Alcohol? Were you able to help this person?
4. If you were a psychiatrist and Paul came to you and said what he wrote in this passage, what would your diagnosis be?
5. Do you think Paul is talking about his life before he became a Christian or after?
6. What's one good thing you know you need to do, you want to do, but just can't?
7. Who or what can rescue you (like Paul) from this?
8. How can this group pray and support you?

Life Through the Spirit

8 Therefore, there is now no condemnation for
those who are in Christ Jesus,[b] 2because
through Christ Jesus the law of the Spirit of life
set me free from the law of sin and death. 3For
what the law was powerless to do in that it was
weakened by the sinful nature,[c] God did by
sending his own Son in the likeness of sinful man
to be a sin offering.[d] And so he condemned sin
in sinful man,[e] 4in order that the righteous requirements of the law might be fully met in us,
who do not live according to the sinful nature but
according to the Spirit.
5Those who live according to the sinful nature
have their minds set on what that nature desires;
but those who live in accordance with the Spirit
have their minds set on what the Spirit desires.
6The mind of sinful man[f] is death, but the mind
controlled by the Spirit is life and peace; 7the
sinful mind[g] is hostile to God. It does not submit
to God's law, nor can it do so. 8Those controlled
by the sinful nature cannot please God.
9You, however, are controlled not by the sinful
nature but by the Spirit, if the Spirit of God lives
in you. And if anyone does not have the Spirit
of Christ, he does not belong to Christ. 10But if
Christ is in you, your body is dead because of sin,
yet your spirit is alive because of righteousness.
11And if the Spirit of him who raised Jesus from
the dead is living in you, he who raised Christ
from the dead will also give life to your mortal
bodies through his Spirit, who lives in you.
12Therefore, brothers, we have an obliga-

[a] *18* Or *my flesh* [b] *1* Some later manuscripts *Jesus, who do not live according to the sinful nature but according to the Spirit,* [c] *3* Or *the flesh*; also in verses 4, 5, 8, 9, 12 and 13 [d] *3* Or *man, for sin* [e] *3* Or *in the flesh* [f] *6* Or *mind set on the flesh* [g] *7* Or *the mind set on the flesh*

7:7 *Is the law sin?* It might seem that this is what Paul is saying (see 5:20; 6:14; 7:1–6). In fact, in verse 7 he shows that far from being evil or sinful, the Law serves, first, to reveal sin.

7:8 *produced in me.* The Law provokes sin (its second function), not simply by pointing out forbidden fruit, but by being misunderstood as setting an unreasonable limitation on one's personal freedom (thus inducing rebellion). ***sin is dead.*** Not that it is nonexistent, but that it is not totally perceived.

7:9 *I died.* Though living physically after the Law came, Paul fell under its judgment—under the sentence of death. This is the third function of the Law: it identifies the penalty for sin.

7:13 The Law offered life if it was obeyed, but it lacked the power to enable individuals to overcome sin.

7:17 *no longer I myself who do it, but it is sin living in me.* Not an excuse but a confession. The problem is not with the Law, but with Paul's sin.

7:22–23 Paul delights in God's Law in contrast to the law of sin, which is at work within him and at war against God's Law.

7:24 The nearer people come to God, the more aware they are of how short of perfection they fall.

7:25 Who indeed will rescue him? None other than the Lord Jesus Christ who met Paul on the Damascus Road, through whose death he at last found freedom from slavery to sin and bondage to the Law.

tion—but it is not to the sinful nature, to live
according to it. 13For if you live according to the
sinful nature, you will die; but if by the Spirit
you put to death the misdeeds of the body, you

ROMANS 8:1–17

1. Who is a powerful influence in your life right now for living a godly life?
2. In verses 5–11, what does Paul say about the option Christians have in living their life?
3. Where is the battle for the control of your life going to be fought ... and won or lost?
4. If there was a pollution control device on your thought life right now, what would it register: GREEN (no problem), ORANGE (warning signs) or RED (fire alert zone)?
5. What is God saying to you in this passage?
6. How can this group help you in prayer this week?

will live, 14because those who are led by the Spirit of God are sons of God. 15For you did not receive a spirit that makes you a slave again to fear,
but you received the Spirit of sonship.[a] And by
him we cry, *"Abba,*[b] Father." 16The Spirit himself testifies with our spirit that we are God's
children. 17Now if we are children, then we are
heirs—heirs of God and co-heirs with Christ, if
indeed we share in his sufferings in order that we
may also share in his glory.

Future Glory

18I consider that our present sufferings are not
worth comparing with the glory that will be revealed in us. 19The creation waits in eager expectation for the sons of God to be revealed. 20For
the creation was subjected to frustration, not by
its own choice, but by the will of the one who
subjected it, in hope 21that[c] the creation itself
will be liberated from its bondage to decay and
brought into the glorious freedom of the children
of God.

ROMANS 8:18–27

1. What is the sickest you have ever been?
2. When you were a kid, what did you want to be when you grew up?
3. When you are having a bad day, what's something that can lift your spirits?
4. Do you know of anyone that prays for you regularly? Who is someone you pray for?
5. What is the struggle you are facing at the moment that really gets you down?
6. What have you found helpful when you have to deal with pain and suffering?
7. What is your "expectation" of the future?
8. How would you like the group to pray for you this week?

22We know that the whole creation has been
groaning as in the pains of childbirth right up
to the present time. 23Not only so, but we ourselves, who have the firstfruits of the Spirit,
groan inwardly as we wait eagerly for our adoption as sons, the redemption of our bodies. 24For
in this hope we were saved. But hope that is seen
is no hope at all. Who hopes for what he already
has? 25But if we hope for what we do not yet
have, we wait for it patiently.

[a]15 Or *adoption* [b]15 Aramaic for *Father* [c]20,21 Or *subjected it in hope.* 21*For*

8:18 *present sufferings.* The persecutions that Christians face in the time between Jesus' first coming and his return. These are real—not pleasant, but slight in comparison with the glory ahead.

8:19–21 Paul has in view the second coming of Christ, at which time all that Christians now experience partially will be theirs completely (see Phil. 3:20–21 and 1 Cor. 15:51–52).

8:19 *for the sons of God to be revealed.* Christians are indeed sons and daughters of God here and now in this life. What Paul refers to here is the fact that they are, as it were, incognito. It will only be at the Second Coming that it is revealed for all to see who are, in fact, the children of God.

8:21 *bondage to decay.* All creation seems to be running down; deterioration and decomposition characterize the created order.

8:22 *pains of childbirth.* Such pain is very real, very intense, but also temporary (and the necessary prelude to new life). The image is not of the annihilation of the present universe, but of the emergence of a transformed order (see Rev. 21:1).

8:23 *groan inwardly as we wait eagerly.* In one sense a Christian is already an adopted child of God, but in another sense he or she has yet to experience fully his or her inheritance. Believers' bodies are subject to weakness, pain and death. The believer longs for the suffering to end and the redemption of the body to be complete.

26In the same way, the Spirit helps us in our
weakness. We do not know what we ought to
pray for, but the Spirit himself intercedes for us
with groans that words cannot express. 27And he
who searches our hearts knows the mind of the
Spirit, because the Spirit intercedes for the saints
in accordance with God's will.

More Than Conquerors

28And we know that in all things God works
for the good of those who love him,[a] who[b]
have been called according to his purpose. 29For
those God foreknew he also predestined to be
conformed to the likeness of his Son, that he
might be the firstborn among many brothers.
30And those he predestined, he also called; those
he called, he also justified; those he justified, he
also glorified.
31What, then, shall we say in response to this?
If God is for us, who can be against us? 32He who
did not spare his own Son, but gave him up for us
all—how will he not also, along with him, graciously give us all things? 33Who will bring any
charge against those whom God has chosen? It is
God who justifies. 34Who is he that condemns?
Christ Jesus, who died—more than that, who
was raised to life—is at the right hand of God and
is also interceding for us. 35Who shall separate us
from the love of Christ? Shall trouble or hardship
or persecution or famine or nakedness or danger
or sword? 36As it is written:

> "For your sake we face death all day long;
> we are considered as sheep to be
> slaughtered."[c]

37No, in all these things we are more than conquerors through him who loved us. 38For I am
convinced that neither death nor life, neither angels nor demons,[d] neither the present nor the
future, nor any powers, 39neither height nor
depth, nor anything else in all creation, will be
able to separate us from the love of God that is in
Christ Jesus our Lord.

God's Sovereign Choice

9 I speak the truth in Christ—I am not lying, my conscience confirms it in the Holy
Spirit— 2I have great sorrow and unceasing anguish in my heart. 3For I could wish that I myself
were cursed and cut off from Christ for the sake
of my brothers, those of my own race, 4the people of Israel. Theirs is the adoption as sons; theirs

ROMANS 8:28–39

1. Do you believe things generally turn out for the best? Why?
2. If you were in a fight, what person (real or fictional) would you want on your side?
3. How comfortable are you around someone who is dealing with grief?
4. If your close friend lost their parents in an accident, what could you share from your own experience that might be helpful?
5. On a scale of 1 (far away) to 10 (up close), how separated have you felt from God lately? How do you get closer?
6. What is the closest you have come to being persecuted because of your commitment to Jesus Christ?
7. How might you be able to share some hope with someone who is suffering, based on verses 31–39?
8. How can this group pray for you and help you feel closer to God?

[a]28 Some manuscripts *And we know that all things work together for good to those who love God those who love him to bring about what is good—with those who*
[b]28 Or *works together with*
[c]36 Psalm 44:22
[d]38 Or *nor heavenly rulers*

8:28 *in all things God works.* Some translations read "all things work together for good" almost as though for the Christian things will work out for the best on their own. In fact, it is God who takes that which is adverse and painful and brings profit out of it. ***for the good of those who love him.*** This does not mean that things work out so that believers preserve their comfort and convenience. Rather, such action on God's part enables these difficult experiences to assist in the process of salvation.

8:31–35 In one of his most eloquent passages, Paul hurls a challenge out to all who would oppose believers: Absolutely nothing can separate Christians from God's love.

8:31 Paul does not ask, "Who is against us?" In response, many enemies could be named: hostile society, Satan, sin, death. Rather, he prefaces the question with an assertion that "God is for us" and then asks, "Who can be against us?" Therefore, all potential enemies fade into insignificance.

8:38–39 *death / life.* For Paul, to die was no longer a threat—it was to "be with Christ" (Phil. 1:21–23). Life is used here in the sense of trials, distractions, and enticements that could easily lead one away from God. ***height / depth.*** These words were used in first-century astrology to signify spirits that ruled in the sky above or below the horizon. Or the reference could be to the influence of a star at the height or depth of its zenith. It may mean simply that neither heaven or hell can separate Christians from God's love.

the divine glory, the covenants, the receiving of
the law, the temple worship and the promises.
5Theirs are the patriarchs, and from them is
traced the human ancestry of Christ, who is God
over all, forever praised![a] Amen.
6It is not as though God's word had failed. For
not all who are descended from Israel are Israel.
7Nor because they are his descendants are they
all Abraham's children. On the contrary, "It is
through Isaac that your offspring will be reckoned."[b] 8In other words, it is not the natural
children who are God's children, but it is the
children of the promise who are regarded as
Abraham's offspring. 9For this was how the
promise was stated: "At the appointed time I will
return, and Sarah will have a son."[c]
10Not only that, but Rebekah's children had
one and the same father, our father Isaac. 11Yet,
before the twins were born or had done anything
good or bad—in order that God's purpose in election might stand: 12not by works but by him who
calls—she was told, "The older will serve the
younger."[d] 13Just as it is written: "Jacob I loved,
but Esau I hated."[e]
14What then shall we say? Is God unjust? Not
at all! 15For he says to Moses,

"I will have mercy on whom I have mercy,
and I will have compassion on whom I
have compassion."[f]

16It does not, therefore, depend on man's desire
or effort, but on God's mercy. 17For the Scripture
says to Pharaoh: "I raised you up for this very
purpose, that I might display my power in you
and that my name might be proclaimed in all the
earth."[g] 18Therefore God has mercy on whom
he wants to have mercy, and he hardens whom
he wants to harden.
19One of you will say to me: "Then why does
God still blame us? For who resists his will?"
20But who are you, O man, to talk back to God?
"Shall what is formed say to him who formed it,
'Why did you make me like this?'"[h] 21Does not
the potter have the right to make out of the same
lump of clay some pottery for noble purposes and
some for common use?
22What if God, choosing to show his wrath and
make his power known, bore with great patience
the objects of his wrath—prepared for destruction? 23What if he did this to make the riches
of his glory known to the objects of his mercy,
whom he prepared in advance for glory— 24even
us, whom he also called, not only from the Jews
but also from the Gentiles? 25As he says in Hosea:

"I will call them 'my people' who are not my
people;
and I will call her 'my loved one' who is
not my loved one,"[i]
26and,

"It will happen that in the very place where
it was said to them,
'You are not my people,'
they will be called 'sons of the living
God.'"[j]

27Isaiah cries out concerning Israel:

"Though the number of the Israelites be like
the sand by the sea,
only the remnant will be saved.
28For the Lord will carry out
his sentence on earth with speed and
finality."[k]

29It is just as Isaiah said previously:

"Unless the Lord Almighty
had left us descendants,
we would have become like Sodom,
we would have been like Gomorrah."[l]

Romans 9:1–29

1. When have you won something unexpected: A trip? Award of achievement? Class officer elections? The big game?
2. Is God fair? What does Paul say in verses 14–15?
3. How deeply do you hurt for unbelievers? As much as Paul?
4. Where are you growing in your understanding of God's will for your life? What questions would you like to ask God about this?
5. What is God saying to you in this passage?
6. How can this group help you in prayer this week?

Israel's Unbelief

30What then shall we say? That the Gentiles,

[a] 5 Or *Christ, who is over all. God be forever praised!* Or *Christ. God who is over all be forever praised!* [b] 7 Gen. 21:12 [c] 9 Gen. 18:10,14 [d] 12 Gen. 25:23 [e] 13 Mal. 1:2,3 [f] 15 Exodus 33:19 [g] 17 Exodus 9:16 [h] 20 Isaiah 29:16; 45:9 [i] 25 Hosea 2:23 [j] 26 Hosea 1:10 [k] 28 Isaiah 10:22,23 [l] 29 Isaiah 1:9

who did not pursue righteousness, have obtained it, a righteousness that is by faith; 31but Israel, who pursued a law of righteousness, has not attained it. 32Why not? Because they pursued it not by faith but as if it were by works. They stumbled over the "stumbling stone." 33As it is written:

"See, I lay in Zion a stone that causes men to
stumble
and a rock that makes them fall,
and the one who trusts in him will never be
put to shame."[a]

10 Brothers, my heart's desire and prayer to God for the Israelites is that they may be saved. 2For I can testify about them that they are zealous for God, but their zeal is not based on knowledge. 3Since they did not know the righteousness that comes from God and sought to establish their own, they did not submit to God's righteousness. 4Christ is the end of the law so that there may be righteousness for everyone who believes.

5Moses describes in this way the righteousness that is by the law: "The man who does these things will live by them."[b] 6But the righteousness that is by faith says: "Do not say in your heart, 'Who will ascend into heaven?'[c]" (that is, to bring Christ down) 7"or 'Who will descend into the deep?'[d]" (that is, to bring Christ up from the dead). 8But what does it say? "The word is near you; it is in your mouth and in your heart,"[e] that is, the word of faith we are proclaiming: 9That if you confess with your mouth, "Jesus is Lord," and believe in your heart that God raised him from the dead, you will be saved. 10For it is with your heart that you believe and are justified, and it is with your mouth that you confess and are saved. 11As the Scripture says, "Anyone who trusts in him will never be put to shame."[f] 12For there is no difference between Jew and Gentile—the same Lord is Lord of all and richly blesses all who call on him, 13for, "Everyone who calls on the name of the Lord will be saved."[g]

14How, then, can they call on the one they have not believed in? And how can they believe in the one of whom they have not heard? And how can they hear without someone preaching to them? 15And how can they preach unless they are sent? As it is written, "How beautiful are the feet of those who bring good news!"[h]

16But not all the Israelites accepted the good news. For Isaiah says, "Lord, who has believed our message?"[i] 17Consequently, faith comes from hearing the message, and the message is heard through the word of Christ. 18But I ask: Did they not hear? Of course they did:

"Their voice has gone out into all the earth,
their words to the ends of the world."[j]

19Again I ask: Did Israel not understand? First, Moses says,

"I will make you envious by those who are
not a nation;
I will make you angry by a nation that has
no understanding."[k]

20And Isaiah boldly says,

"I was found by those who did not seek me;
I revealed myself to those who did not ask
for me."[l]

21But concerning Israel he says,

"All day long I have held out my hands
to a disobedient and obstinate people."[m]

Romans 9:30–10:21

1. In elementary school, what was your hardest subject? What did you do to try to improve your grade?
2. What is the only way to be saved according to Paul in 10:9–10?
3. Are you more likely to want to fit into the group at any cost or to take a stand and be labeled different?
4. When did you first come to realize that it isn't so much what you do for God, but what he's done for you?
5. What is God saying to you in this passage?
6. How can this group help you in prayer this week?

The Remnant of Israel

11 I ask then: Did God reject his people? By no means! I am an Israelite myself, a descendant of Abraham, from the tribe of Benjamin. 2God did not reject his people, whom he foreknew. Don't you know what the Scripture says in the passage about Elijah—how he appealed to God against Israel: 3"Lord, they have

[a]33 Isaiah 8:14; 28:16 [b]5 Lev. 18:5 [c]6 Deut. 30:12 [d]7 Deut. 30:13 [e]8 Deut. 30:14 [f]11 Isaiah 28:16 [g]13 Joel 2:32 [h]15 Isaiah 52:7 [i]16 Isaiah 53:1 [j]18 Psalm 19:4 [k]19 Deut. 32:21 [l]20 Isaiah 65:1 [m]21 Isaiah 65:2

killed your prophets and torn down your altars; I
am the only one left, and they are trying to kill
me"[a]? 4 And what was God's answer to him? "I
have reserved for myself seven thousand who
have not bowed the knee to Baal."[b] 5 So too, at
the present time there is a remnant chosen by
grace. 6 And if by grace, then it is no longer by
works; if it were, grace would no longer be
grace.[c]

7 What then? What Israel sought so earnestly it
did not obtain, but the elect did. The others were
hardened, 8 as it is written:

"God gave them a spirit of stupor,
eyes so that they could not see
and ears so that they could not hear,
to this very day."[d]

9 And David says:

"May their table become a snare and a trap,
a stumbling block and a retribution for
them.
10 May their eyes be darkened so they cannot
see,
and their backs be bent forever."[e]

Ingrafted Branches

11 Again I ask: Did they stumble so as to fall
beyond recovery? Not at all! Rather, because of
their transgression, salvation has come to the
Gentiles to make Israel envious. 12 But if their
transgression means riches for the world, and
their loss means riches for the Gentiles, how
much greater riches will their fullness bring!

13 I am talking to you Gentiles. Inasmuch as I
am the apostle to the Gentiles, I make much of
my ministry 14 in the hope that I may somehow
arouse my own people to envy and save some of
them. 15 For if their rejection is the reconciliation
of the world, what will their acceptance be but
life from the dead? 16 If the part of the dough
offered as firstfruits is holy, then the whole batch
is holy; if the root is holy, so are the branches.

17 If some of the branches have been broken
off, and you, though a wild olive shoot, have been
grafted in among the others and now share in the
nourishing sap from the olive root, 18 do not boast
over those branches. If you do, consider this: You
do not support the root, but the root supports
you. 19 You will say then, "Branches were broken
off so that I could be grafted in." 20 Granted. But
they were broken off because of unbelief, and you
stand by faith. Do not be arrogant, but be afraid.
21 For if God did not spare the natural branches,
he will not spare you either.

22 Consider therefore the kindness and sternness of God: sternness to those who fell, but
kindness to you, provided that you continue in
his kindness. Otherwise, you also will be cut off.
23 And if they do not persist in unbelief, they will
be grafted in, for God is able to graft them in
again. 24 After all, if you were cut out of an olive
tree that is wild by nature, and contrary to nature
were grafted into a cultivated olive tree, how
much more readily will these, the natural
branches, be grafted into their own olive tree!

All Israel Will Be Saved

25 I do not want you to be ignorant of this mystery, brothers, so that you may not be conceited:
Israel has experienced a hardening in part until
the full number of the Gentiles has come in.
26 And so all Israel will be saved, as it is written:

"The deliverer will come from Zion;
he will turn godlessness away from Jacob.
27 And this is[f] my covenant with them
when I take away their sins."[g]

ROMANS 11:1–36

1. As a little kid, what item did a friend or sibling have that made you jealous?
2. Like the Jews in Paul's day, are churchgoers today relying more on performance of rituals than on God's grace? How so?
3. How does the church itself struggle with works versus grace? In what ways are works still important?
4. How has arrogance between groups of Christians hurt your church experience? When have you found yourself exhibiting this attitude too?
5. What is God saying to you in this passage?
6. How can this group help you in prayer this week?

28 As far as the gospel is concerned, they are
enemies on your account; but as far as election is
concerned, they are loved on account of the patriarchs, 29 for God's gifts and his call are irrevocable. 30 Just as you who were at one time disobedient to God have now received mercy as a result

[a] 3 1 Kings 19:10,14 [b] 4 1 Kings 19:18 [c] 6 Some manuscripts *by grace. But if by works, then it is no longer grace; if it were, work would no longer be work.* [d] 8 Deut. 29:4; Isaiah 29:10 [e] 10 Psalm 69:22,23 [f] 27 Or *will be*
[g] 27 Isaiah 59:20,21; 27:9; Jer. 31:33,34

of their disobedience, 31so they too have now
become disobedient in order that they too may
now[a] receive mercy as a result of God's mercy
to you. 32For God has bound all men over to
disobedience so that he may have mercy on them
all.

Doxology

33Oh, the depth of the riches of the wisdom
and[b] knowledge of God!
How unsearchable his judgments,
and his paths beyond tracing out!
34"Who has known the mind of the Lord?
Or who has been his counselor?"[c]
35"Who has ever given to God,
that God should repay him?"[d]
36For from him and through him and to him
are all things.
To him be the glory forever! Amen.

Living Sacrifices

12 Therefore, I urge you, brothers, in view
of God's mercy, to offer your bodies as
living sacrifices, holy and pleasing to God—this
is your spiritual[e] act of worship. 2Do not conform any longer to the pattern of this world, but
be transformed by the renewing of your mind.
Then you will be able to test and approve what
God's will is—his good, pleasing and perfect will.
3For by the grace given me I say to every one
of you: Do not think of yourself more highly than
you ought, but rather think of yourself with sober
judgment, in accordance with the measure of
faith God has given you. 4Just as each of us has
one body with many members, and these members do not all have the same function, 5so in
Christ we who are many form one body, and each
member belongs to all the others. 6We have different gifts, according to the grace given us. If a
man's gift is prophesying, let him use it in proportion to his[f] faith. 7If it is serving, let him
serve; if it is teaching, let him teach; 8if it is
encouraging, let him encourage; if it is contributing to the needs of others, let him give generously; if it is leadership, let him govern diligently; if
it is showing mercy, let him do it cheerfully.

ROMANS 12:1–8

1. What is your best subject in school?
2. What is the most memorable Christmas present you received as a child?
3. In your school, who do you admire because they march to a different drum?
4. How can you offer your "body" as a living sacrifice (see note on 12:1)?
5. Of the gifts listed in verses 6–8, which one is most evident in your life? How will that affect your choice of a career?
6. How do you use your gifts within the church (Christ's body)? What holds you back from using your gifts more fully?
7. This past week, did you feel more "conformed" or "transformed" (v. 2)?
8. If you knew you could not fail, what goal or dream would you like to set for next year?

Love

9Love must be sincere. Hate what is evil; cling
to what is good. 10Be devoted to one another in
brotherly love. Honor one another above yourselves. 11Never be lacking in zeal, but keep your
spiritual fervor, serving the Lord. 12Be joyful in
hope, patient in affliction, faithful in prayer.
13Share with God's people who are in need. Practice hospitality.
14Bless those who persecute you; bless and do

a31 Some manuscripts do not have *now.* b33 Or *riches and the wisdom and the* c34 Isaiah 40:13 d35 Job 41:11
e1 Or *reasonable* f6 Or *in agreement with the*

12:1 *in view of God's mercy.* A Christian's motivation to obedience is overwhelming gratitude for God's mercy. ***sacrifice.*** In the OT sacrificial system, the victim of the sacrifice becomes wholly the property of God. ***living sacrifices, holy and pleasing to God.*** God does not count "living sacrifices" the same as the slain animals in the old system, but rather wants Christians to live in fullness of life, in accord with his principles (i.e. sanctification), and hence to be the kind of sacrifice desired by God.

12:2 *be transformed.* The force of the verb is "continue to let yourself be transformed"; meaning a continuous action by the Holy Spirit which goes on for a lifetime. A Christian's responsibility is to stay open to this sanctification process. ***renewing of your mind.*** Develop a spiritual sensitivity and perception—learn to look at life on the basis of God's view of reality. Paul emphasizes the need to develop understanding of God's ways.

12:3–8 Paul now turns to the Christian community as a whole—understanding it to be composed of believers with different gifts.

12:4–5 Using a picture that could be understood in all cultures—the body—Paul defines the nature of the Christian community: diverse gifts, but all part of one body, the body of Christ.

12:6 *gifts.* Those endowments given by God to every believer are to be used in God's service. The gifts listed here (or elsewhere in the NT) are not meant to be exhaustive or absolute since no gift list overlaps completely.

not curse. 15Rejoice with those who rejoice;
mourn with those who mourn. 16Live in harmony with one another. Do not be proud, but be
willing to associate with people of low position.[a] Do not be conceited.

Romans 12:9–21

1. What is your favorite love song or romantic movie?
2. Who was your first true love? What happened to this relationship?
3. As a child, who was the troublemaker in your family? Who was the peacemaker?
4. When was the last time you were rejected by someone? How did it feel?
5. When you feel you've been wronged, what do you generally do: "Grin and bear it"? "Forgive and forget"? Get even? Or something else?
6. What can you do this week, in a practical way, to "live at peace" with someone who irritates you?
7. This past week, have you felt more "overcome with evil" or have you "overcome evil with good"?
8. How can this group pray for you?

17Do not repay anyone evil for evil. Be careful
to do what is right in the eyes of everybody. 18If
it is possible, as far as it depends on you, live at
peace with everyone. 19Do not take revenge, my
friends, but leave room for God's wrath, for it is
written: "It is mine to avenge; I will repay,"[b]
says the Lord. 20On the contrary:

"If your enemy is hungry, feed him;
if he is thirsty, give him something to drink.
In doing this, you will heap burning coals on his head."[c]

21Do not be overcome by evil, but overcome evil
with good.

Submission to the Authorities

13 Everyone must submit himself to the governing authorities, for there is no authority except that which God has established. The

Romans 13:1–7

1. What is the closest you have come to having a "run in" with the police?
2. On a scale of 1 (not at all) to 10 (extremely), how rebellious were you as a kid?
3. How do you feel about the taxes that are withheld from your paycheck?
4. Whose authority gives you the most problems (parents, teacher, boss, police, etc.)?
5. If submission to authority is expected of a Christian, what was Jesus doing when he "overturned the tables" of the money changers in the temple (see Mark 11:15)?
6. If you felt a law passed by Congress was contrary to God's law, what would you do?
7. How was your walk with the Lord this past week? Did you feel more submitted or rebellious in that relationship?
8. How can this group pray for you?

(Study notes on page 1047)

[a] *16* Or *willing to do menial work* [b] *19* Deut. 32:35 [c] *20* Prov. 25:21,22

Paul focuses first on relationships between Christians (vv. 9–13) and then on relationships with those outside the church (vv. 14–21).

12:9 ***Love.*** *Agape* love is self-giving action on behalf of others, made possible by God's Spirit. ***sincere.*** Genuine, not counterfeit or showy. It is possible to pretend (even to one's self) to love others.

12:10 ***brotherly love.*** A second word for love, *philadelphia,* denoting family affection.

12:12 What makes it possible to endure affliction is joyful hope in one's inheritance in the age to come, coupled with daily, continuous prayer.

12:13 To be "renewed" is not just a matter of mind and emotions, but involves concrete action such as giving to those in need.

12:17 ***Do not repay anyone evil for evil.*** A common Christian teaching (see 1 Thess. 5:15 and 1 Peter 3:4). Christians are called upon to do not just what the consensus calls "good," but those things that are inherently "good." These deeds will be recognized as such by those of good will.

12:20 ***heap burning coals on his head.*** Providing kindness of every sort to one's enemies may induce the kind of inner shame that leads to repentance, and hence to reconciliation and true friendship.

12:21 People who retaliate have allowed evil to overcome them. They have given in to their evil desires and have become like their enemy.

authorities that exist have been established by
God. 2Consequently, he who rebels against the
authority is rebelling against what God has instituted, and those who do so will bring judgment
on themselves. 3For rulers hold no terror for
those who do right, but for those who do wrong.
Do you want to be free from fear of the one in
authority? Then do what is right and he will commend you. 4For he is God's servant to do you
good. But if you do wrong, be afraid, for he does
not bear the sword for nothing. He is God's servant, an agent of wrath to bring punishment on
the wrongdoer. 5Therefore, it is necessary to
submit to the authorities, not only because of
possible punishment but also because of conscience.
6This is also why you pay taxes, for the authorities are God's servants, who give their full time
to governing. 7Give everyone what you owe him:
If you owe taxes, pay taxes; if revenue, then revenue; if respect, then respect; if honor, then
honor.

Love, for the Day Is Near

8Let no debt remain outstanding, except the
continuing debt to love one another, for he who
loves his fellowman has fulfilled the law. 9The
commandments, "Do not commit adultery," "Do
not murder," "Do not steal," "Do not covet,"[a]
and whatever other commandment there may be,
are summed up in this one rule: "Love your
neighbor as yourself."[b] 10Love does no harm to
its neighbor. Therefore love is the fulfillment of
the law.
11And do this, understanding the present time.
The hour has come for you to wake up from your
slumber, because our salvation is nearer now
than when we first believed. 12The night is nearly over; the day is almost here. So let us put aside
the deeds of darkness and put on the armor of
light. 13Let us behave decently, as in the daytime,
not in orgies and drunkenness, not in sexual immorality and debauchery, not in dissension and
jealousy. 14Rather, clothe yourselves with the
Lord Jesus Christ, and do not think about how to
gratify the desires of the sinful nature.[c]

ROMANS 13:8–14

1. Growing up, where did those of another ethnic race live in your community? Has this changed?
2. How do people of different races get along in your school or neighborhood?
3. Who is the closest friend you have that is of another race?
4. When have you seen racism? What does Paul recommend as the solution to this problem (vv. 8–10)?
5. How does love fulfill all of the other commandments (see note on 13:9)?
6. What grade would you give your church for breaking down walls and bringing races together?
7. How would a person from another background or race be accepted in this group?
8. How can the group pray for you and your ability to "Love your neighbor as yourself"?

(Study notes on page 1048)

The Weak and the Strong

14 Accept him whose faith is weak, without
passing judgment on disputable matters.
2One man's faith allows him to eat everything,
but another man, whose faith is weak, eats only
vegetables. 3The man who eats everything must

[a]9 Exodus 20:13-15,17; Deut. 5:17-19,21 [b]9 Lev. 19:18 [c]14 Or *the flesh*

Paul's concern is how Christians relate to those outside the church. The general principles in 12:17–21 (e.g., don't resort to violence to "get even") are now given specific focus in this discussion of the relationship of Christians to civil authorities.

13:1 ***Everyone.*** That is, every Christian in Rome; no one is exempt. ***submit.*** The word is sometimes mistranslated "obey" (there are three Greek words for obedience). Submission must be understood in light of 12:10 (honoring others above oneself) and Philippians 2:3–4 (counting others as better); Christians must recognize the claim that the authorities and civil government have upon them. But see also Acts 5:29: "Peter and the other apostles replied: 'We must obey God rather than men!' " See also Mark 12:13–17.

13:3–4 Paul is not discussing governments that are unjust and which punish good works and praise evil.

13:5 ***conscience.*** Since the Christian knows that the ruler has been appointed by God, to disobey would create a guilty conscience.

13:6–7 ***taxes.*** Local taxes such as duty, import/export taxes, taxes for the use of roads or for the right to drive a cart, etc. ***revenue.*** Any tribute, paid by members of a subject nation to Rome, consisting usually of three types: a general tax on agricultural produce, a 1% income tax and a poll tax paid by everyone between the ages of 14 and 65.

not look down on him who does not, and the
man who does not eat everything must not condemn the man who does, for God has accepted
him. 4Who are you to judge someone else's servant? To his own master he stands or falls. And
he will stand, for the Lord is able to make him
stand.
5One man considers one day more sacred than
another; another man considers every day alike.
Each one should be fully convinced in his own
mind. 6He who regards one day as special, does
so to the Lord. He who eats meat, eats to the
Lord, for he gives thanks to God; and he who
abstains, does so to the Lord and gives thanks to
God. 7For none of us lives to himself alone and
none of us dies to himself alone. 8If we live, we
live to the Lord; and if we die, we die to the Lord.
So, whether we live or die, we belong to the
Lord.
9For this very reason, Christ died and returned
to life so that he might be the Lord of both the
dead and the living. 10You, then, why do you
judge your brother? Or why do you look down on
your brother? For we will all stand before God's
judgment seat. 11It is written:

"'As surely as I live,' says the Lord,
'every knee will bow before me;
every tongue will confess to God.'"[a]

12So then, each of us will give an account of himself to God.
13Therefore let us stop passing judgment on
one another. Instead, make up your mind not to
put any stumbling block or obstacle in your brother's way. 14As one who is in the Lord Jesus, I am
fully convinced that no food[b] is unclean in itself.
But if anyone regards something as unclean, then
for him it is unclean. 15If your brother is distressed because of what you eat, you are no longer acting in love. Do not by your eating destroy
your brother for whom Christ died. 16Do not allow what you consider good to be spoken of as
evil. 17For the kingdom of God is not a matter of
eating and drinking, but of righteousness, peace
and joy in the Holy Spirit, 18because anyone who
serves Christ in this way is pleasing to God and
approved by men.
19Let us therefore make every effort to do what
leads to peace and to mutual edification. 20Do not
destroy the work of God for the sake of food. All
food is clean, but it is wrong for a man to eat
anything that causes someone else to stumble.
21It is better not to eat meat or drink wine or to
do anything else that will cause your brother to
fall.
22So whatever you believe about these things
keep between yourself and God. Blessed is the
man who does not condemn himself by what he
approves. 23But the man who has doubts is condemned if he eats, because his eating is not from
faith; and everything that does not come from
faith is sin.

15 We who are strong ought to bear with the
failings of the weak and not to please ourselves. 2Each of us should please his neighbor
for his good, to build him up. 3For even Christ
did not please himself but, as it is written: "The
insults of those who insult you have fallen on
me."[c] 4For everything that was written in the
past was written to teach us, so that through endurance and the encouragement of the Scriptures
we might have hope.
5May the God who gives endurance and encouragement give you a spirit of unity among
yourselves as you follow Christ Jesus, 6so that
with one heart and mouth you may glorify the
God and Father of our Lord Jesus Christ.
7Accept one another, then, just as Christ accepted you, in order to bring praise to God. 8For
I tell you that Christ has become a servant of the
Jews[d] on behalf of God's truth, to confirm the
promises made to the patriarchs 9so that the Gentiles may glorify God for his mercy, as it is written:

"Therefore I will praise you among the
Gentiles;
I will sing hymns to your name."[e]

[a] *11* Isaiah 45:23 [b] *14* Or *that nothing* [c] *3* Psalm 69:9 [d] *8* Greek *circumcision* [e] *9* 2 Samuel 22:50; Psalm 18:49

13:9 Paul points to the second half of the Ten Commandments and indicates that each law would be automatically fulfilled if people kept the more basic principle that underlies them—loving others in the same fashion in which they love themselves. If a person really loved his neighbor he wouldn't steal from him, etc. ***neighbor.*** In the OT, the neighbor is a fellow Jew; but the parable of the Good Samaritan (Luke 10:25–37) expands "neighbor" to include all people. One's neighbor is the person in need, regardless of race or nationality.

13:12 ***night.*** The present age. ***day.*** The coming age inaugurated by Christ's second coming. ***the day is almost here.*** The early church understood that the life, death and resurrection of Jesus had ushered in the last days—the end time. God, however, because of his patience, had provided an interval before the culmination of the "night," the purpose of which is to allow other men and women to come to faith. During this interval the call to the Christian is to remain alert, knowing that the Second Coming may occur at any time.

13:13 ***debauchery.*** The public display, without shame, of immoral acts. ***dissension.*** The desire for power and prestige; unwillingness to be in second place. ***jealousy.*** Envy which begrudges another's gifts.

13:14 ***clothe yourselves.*** To put on the armor of light (v. 12) is, in fact, to put on Christ. It means to follow him in discipleship and to strive to let our lives be shaped according to the pattern of the humility of his earthly life. It means trusting in him and relying on God's righteousness.

10Again, it says,

"Rejoice, O Gentiles, with his people."[a]

11And again,

"Praise the Lord, all you Gentiles,
and sing praises to him, all you
peoples."[b]

12And again, Isaiah says,

"The Root of Jesse will spring up,
one who will arise to rule over the
nations;
the Gentiles will hope in him."[c]

13May the God of hope fill you with all joy and
peace as you trust in him, so that you may overflow with hope by the power of the Holy Spirit.

ROMANS 14:1–15:13

1. What, if any, rules does your family have for what you can or can't do on Sunday?
2. By instructing the Romans not to judge each other, does Paul mean we are never to judge between right and wrong where others are concerned? Why or why not?
3. As time has passed, how has your sensitivity to the consciences of other Christians changed? Where do you draw the line on trying to please everyone?
4. Romans 15:7 states: "Accept one another, then, just as Christ accepted you, in order to bring praise to God." What individual or types of people, if you're honest, are stretching for you to accept? Can you commit that to the Lord?
5. What is God saying to you in this passage?
6. How can this group help you in prayer this week?

Paul the Minister to the Gentiles

14I myself am convinced, my brothers, that
you yourselves are full of goodness, complete in
knowledge and competent to instruct one another. 15I have written you quite boldly on some
points, as if to remind you of them again, because
of the grace God gave me 16to be a minister of
Christ Jesus to the Gentiles with the priestly duty
of proclaiming the gospel of God, so that the Gentiles might become an offering acceptable to God,
sanctified by the Holy Spirit.
17Therefore I glory in Christ Jesus in my service to God. 18I will not venture to speak of anything except what Christ has accomplished
through me in leading the Gentiles to obey God
by what I have said and done— 19by the power
of signs and miracles, through the power of the
Spirit. So from Jerusalem all the way around to
Illyricum, I have fully proclaimed the gospel of
Christ. 20It has always been my ambition to
preach the gospel where Christ was not known,
so that I would not be building on someone else's
foundation. 21Rather, as it is written:

"Those who were not told about him will
see,
and those who have not heard will
understand."[d]

22This is why I have often been hindered from
coming to you.

Paul's Plan to Visit Rome

23But now that there is no more place for me
to work in these regions, and since I have been
longing for many years to see you, 24I plan to do
so when I go to Spain. I hope to visit you while
passing through and to have you assist me on my
journey there, after I have enjoyed your company
for a while. 25Now, however, I am on my way to
Jerusalem in the service of the saints there. 26For
Macedonia and Achaia were pleased to make a

ROMANS 15:14–33

1. What subject in school is or was the most motivating to you?
2. What motivates and inspires Paul (see vv. 16–22)? What motivates and inspires you?
3. Who are you indebted to for your spiritual blessings?
4. How would you compare Paul's concerns with your own ambitions? Values? Worldview? Prayer life?
5. What is God saying to you in this passage?
6. How can this group help you in prayer this week?

[a] *10* Deut. 32:43 [b] *11* Psalm 117:1 [c] *12* Isaiah 11:10 [d] *21* Isaiah 52:15

contribution for the poor among the saints in Jerusalem.
27They were pleased to do it, and indeed they owe it to them. For if the Gentiles have shared in the Jews' spiritual blessings, they owe it to the Jews to share with them their material blessings.
28So after I have completed this task and have made sure that they have received this fruit, I will go to Spain and visit you on the way.
29I know that when I come to you, I will come in the full measure of the blessing of Christ.
30I urge you, brothers, by our Lord Jesus Christ and by the love of the Spirit, to join me in my struggle by praying to God for me.
31Pray that I may be rescued from the unbelievers in Judea and that my service in Jerusalem may be acceptable to the saints there,
32so that by God's will I may come to you with joy and together with you be refreshed.
33The God of peace be with you all. Amen.

Personal Greetings

16 I commend to you our sister Phoebe, a servant[a] of the church in Cenchrea.
2I ask you to receive her in the Lord in a way worthy of the saints and to give her any help she may need from you, for she has been a great help to many people, including me.

3Greet Priscilla[b] and Aquila, my fellow workers in Christ Jesus.
4They risked their lives for me. Not only I but all the churches of the Gentiles are grateful to them.
5Greet also the church that meets at their house.
Greet my dear friend Epenetus, who was the first convert to Christ in the province of Asia.
6Greet Mary, who worked very hard for you.
7Greet Andronicus and Junias, my relatives who have been in prison with me. They are outstanding among the apostles, and they were in Christ before I was.
8Greet Ampliatus, whom I love in the Lord.
9Greet Urbanus, our fellow worker in Christ, and my dear friend Stachys.
10Greet Apelles, tested and approved in Christ.
Greet those who belong to the household of Aristobulus.
11Greet Herodion, my relative.
Greet those in the household of Narcissus who are in the Lord.
12Greet Tryphena and Tryphosa, those women who work hard in the Lord.
Greet my dear friend Persis, another woman who has worked very hard in the Lord.
13Greet Rufus, chosen in the Lord, and his mother, who has been a mother to me, too.
14Greet Asyncritus, Phlegon, Hermes, Patrobas, Hermas and the brothers with them.
15Greet Philologus, Julia, Nereus and his sister, and Olympas and all the saints with them.

Romans 16:1–27

1. Is it harder for you to "say hello" (make friends) or to "say good-bye" (release friends)?
2. What kinds of things does Paul commend in the persons mentioned in 16:1–16? What does this say about how we ought to judge "success"?
3. In your opinion, how close did Paul let people get to him? How close do you let people get to you?
4. How do you handle individuals who cause strife and division (vv. 17–18): Avoid them? Talk about them? Confront them?
5. What is God saying to you in this passage?
6. How can this group help you in prayer this week?

16Greet one another with a holy kiss.
All the churches of Christ send greetings.
17I urge you, brothers, to watch out for those who cause divisions and put obstacles in your way that are contrary to the teaching you have learned. Keep away from them.
18For such people are not serving our Lord Christ, but their own appetites. By smooth talk and flattery they deceive the minds of naive people.
19Everyone has heard about your obedience, so I am full of joy over you; but I want you to be wise about what is good, and innocent about what is evil.
20The God of peace will soon crush Satan under your feet.
The grace of our Lord Jesus be with you.
21Timothy, my fellow worker, sends his greetings to you, as do Lucius, Jason and Sosipater, my relatives.
22I, Tertius, who wrote down this letter, greet you in the Lord.
23Gaius, whose hospitality I and the whole church here enjoy, sends you his greetings.
Erastus, who is the city's director of public

a *1* Or *deaconess* b *3* Greek *Prisca,* a variant of *Priscilla*

works, and our brother Quartus send you their
greetings.[a]
25 Now to him who is able to establish you by
my gospel and the proclamation of Jesus Christ,
according to the revelation of the mystery hidden
for long ages past, 26 but now revealed and made
known through the prophetic writings by the
command of the eternal God, so that all nations
might believe and obey him— 27 to the only wise
God be glory forever through Jesus Christ! Amen.

[a] *23* Some manuscripts *their greetings.* 24 *May the grace of our Lord Jesus Christ be with all of you. Amen.*

Introduction to
1 CORINTHIANS

Personal Reading Plan

❐ 1 Corinthians 1:1–2:5	❐ 1 Corinthians 7:1–40	❐ 1 Corinthians 12:1–13:13
❐ 1 Corinthians 2:6–3:23	❐ 1 Corinthians 8:1–9:27	❐ 1 Corinthians 14:1–40
❐ 1 Corinthians 4:1–5:13	❐ 1 Corinthians 10:1–11:1	❐ 1 Corinthians 15:1–58
❐ 1 Corinthians 6:1–20	❐ 1 Corinthians 11:2–34	❐ 1 Corinthians 16:1–24

Author

The writer is the apostle Paul.

Date

Paul wrote 1 Corinthians sometime between A.D. 53–55.

Theme

Christian lifestyle in a pagan society.

Purpose

First Corinthians is a practical, issue-oriented letter in which Paul tells his readers what they ought or ought not to do. Paul's typical pattern in other letters is to begin with a strong theological statement and then to follow up by applying this insight to daily life. But this is not the case in the letter which has come to be known as 1 Corinthians. Here we find little direct theological teaching. Rather Paul discusses, in turn, a number of behavioral issues.

The problem was that these proud, materialistic, independent ex-pagans were having a most difficult time learning how to live as Christians. It was at this level of lifestyle that paganism directed its attack on the newly emerging Christian faith. *Christian behavior* was the underlying issue. Where were the lines to be drawn? How much of one's culture had to be abandoned to become a Christian? Residual paganism was mounting a frontal attack on Christianity. If Christianity lost in Corinth, its existence would be threatened throughout the Roman Empire. So just as he did in Galatians, when residual Judaism attacked Christianity over the issue of whether or not one must keep the Law, here in 1 Corinthians Paul struck back decisively and directly.

Historical Background

Paul visited Corinth during his second missionary journey, probably in A.D. 50. Having been in some peril in Macedonia, he fled by ship to Athens (Acts 17:1–15). Not meeting with great success there (Acts 17:16–34), he then journeyed the short distance to Corinth where he met Priscilla and Aquila (Acts 18:1–3). At first he preached in the synagogue with some success (even the ruler of the synagogue was won to Christ). But then the Jews forced him to leave, so he moved next door into the home of a Gentile. Hoping to silence him, the Jews eventually hauled Paul before the governor Gallio, but Gallio threw the case out of court as having no merit. After some 18 months (his longest stay anywhere except Ephesus), Paul left and continued his missionary work in Syria.

Two events sparked the writing of 1 Corinthians some three or four years later. First, Paul heard that a divisive spirit was loose in the church (1 Cor. 1:11). Second, he received a letter in which the Corinthians asked him questions about marriage and other matters (1 Cor. 7:1). In addition, a delegation from Corinth completed his knowledge of the problems there (1 Cor. 16:15–17). Being unable to visit Corinth personally, Paul sought to deal with the issues by letter. Thus the Corinthian correspondence was begun.

The City of Corinth

Corinth was an unusual city. After its capture by the Roman legions in 146 B.C., the city was leveled. It lay in ruins for nearly 100 years until Julius Caesar rebuilt it in 44 B.C. Then it grew rapidly, thanks largely to its unique geographical location. Because it lay at the neck of a narrow isthmus connecting the Peloponnesus with central Greece, it controlled all north-south land traffic. To the east and the west of the city were two fine harbors. Both goods and ships were hauled across the four-mile-wide isthmus of Corinth. Thus Corinth also controlled most east-west sea routes. This strategic location commanded wealth and influence. By the time of Paul's visit some 100 years after its rebuilding, Corinth had become the capital of the province of Achaia and the third most important city in the Roman Empire, after Rome and Alexandria.

In this wealthy young city, excess seemed to be the norm. The city was stocked with art purchased from around the Roman Empire. It became a center of philosophy, though apparently few citizens were seriously interested in studying philosophy, preferring rather to listen to stirring orations on faddish topics delivered by the city's numerous itinerant philosophers. Even in religion, this excess was obvious. The Greek author Pausanias describes 26 pagan shrines and temples including the great temples of Apollo and Aphrodite. In Old Corinth, 1,000 temple prostitutes had served Aphrodite, the goddess of love, and New Corinth continued this tradition of sexual worship practices. The city developed a worldwide reputation for vice and debauchery.

Luxury was the hallmark of Corinth. Because storms in the Aegean Sea were frequent and treacherous, sailors preferred to put into one of the harbors and transport their ship overland to the other harbor, despite the exorbitant tolls charged by the Corinthians. Consequently, goods from around the world passed through Corinthian ports, and some 400,000 slaves were kept in the city to provide the labor for this arduous job.

Into Corinth flowed people from around the Roman Empire. There were "Greek adventurers and Roman bourgeois, with a tainting infusion of Phoenicians, a mass of Jews, ex-soldiers, philosophers, merchants, sailors, freed men, slaves, tradespeople, hucksters and agents of every form of vice" (Farrar, quoted by William Barclay, *The Letters to the Corinthians,* p. 4). Not surprisingly, it was in Corinth that Paul had to fight this battle to prevent Christianity from giving in to debilitating enticements offered by paganism.

Passages for Topical Group Study

1:10–17	CLIQUES POPULARITY	Divisions in the Church
1:18–2:5	DECISIONS	Christ the Wisdom of God
6:12–20	SEXUAL INTIMACY	Sexual Immorality
9:24–27	COMPETITION	The Rights of an Apostle
10:1–13	MEDIA / ENTERTAINMENT	Warnings From Israel's History
12:12–31	UNIQUENESS	One Body, Many Parts
13:1–13	TRUST LOVE	The "Love Chapter"
15:12–34	RESURRECTION	The Resurrection of the Dead
15:35–58	ETERNAL LIFE	The Resurrection of the Body

See the Lesson Plans in the front of this Bible.

Passages for General Group Study

2:6–16	Wisdom From the Spirit	10:14–11:1	The Believer's Freedom
3:1–23	On Divisions in the Church	11:2–16	Propriety in Worship
4:1–21	Apostles of Christ	11:17–34	The Lord's Supper
5:1–13	Expel the Immoral Brother!	14:1–25	Gifts of Prophecy and Tongues
6:1–11	Lawsuits Among Believers	14:26–40	Orderly Worship
7:1–40	Marriage	15:1–11	The Resurrection of Christ
8:1–13	Food Sacrificed to Idols	16:1–24	The Collection for God's People

1 Paul, called to be an apostle of Christ Jesus
by the will of God, and our brother Sosthenes,

2To the church of God in Corinth, to those
sanctified in Christ Jesus and called to be holy,
together with all those everywhere who call on
the name of our Lord Jesus Christ—their Lord
and ours:

3Grace and peace to you from God our Father
and the Lord Jesus Christ.

Thanksgiving

4I always thank God for you because of his
grace given you in Christ Jesus. 5For in him you
have been enriched in every way—in all your
speaking and in all your knowledge— 6because
our testimony about Christ was confirmed in you.
7Therefore you do not lack any spiritual gift as
you eagerly wait for our Lord Jesus Christ to be
revealed. 8He will keep you strong to the end, so
that you will be blameless on the day of our Lord
Jesus Christ. 9God, who has called you into fellowship with his Son Jesus Christ our Lord, is
faithful.

Divisions in the Church

10I appeal to you, brothers, in the name of our
Lord Jesus Christ, that all of you agree with one
another so that there may be no divisions among
you and that you may be perfectly united in mind
and thought. 11My brothers, some from Chloe's
household have informed me that there are quarrels among you. 12What I mean is this: One of
you says, "I follow Paul"; another, "I follow Apollos"; another, "I follow Cephas[a]"; still another,
"I follow Christ."

13Is Christ divided? Was Paul crucified for
you? Were you baptized into[b] the name of Paul?
14I am thankful that I did not baptize any of you
except Crispus and Gaius, 15so no one can say
that you were baptized into my name. 16(Yes, I
also baptized the household of Stephanas; beyond
that, I don't remember if I baptized anyone else.)
17For Christ did not send me to baptize, but to
preach the gospel—not with words of human
wisdom, lest the cross of Christ be emptied of its
power.

1 Corinthians 1:10–17

1. Who do you disagree with the most? Over what?
2. Where does the "in-crowd," the popular kids at your school, hang out? How interested are you in being a part of this group?
3. How "popular" is it to be a Christian at your school? How are Christians viewed by the other students?
4. Why are cliques and divisions, especially within the church, so damaging to the Christian community (see vv. 10,13,17)?
5. What issues cause the biggest division between people in your community? Your school? Your church? This group?
6. What's something you have in common with other Christians? How important is what you share versus what you don't?
7. How close do you feel to Jesus Christ right now? How unified with other Christians?
8. How can this group bring people together? Pray for unity.

Christ the Wisdom and Power of God

18For the message of the cross is foolishness to
those who are perishing, but to us who are being
saved it is the power of God. 19For it is written:

"I will destroy the wisdom of the wise;

[a]*12* That is, Peter [b]*13* Or *in*; also in verse 15

In Paul's letter to the Corinthians, he must first deal with divisions that have begun in the church. The Corinthians had begun to view Christianity as a new philosophy and the apostles were regarded (and judged) as if they were itinerant philosophers.

1:10 ***mind and thought.*** This disunity is rooted in differing ideas (doctrines). To be restored, to knit back together the church which is torn apart, requires a unity of understanding.

1:12 ***I follow Paul.*** Paul does not commend those "on his side." A faction in his name is no better than any other faction. In fact, these folks had probably exaggerated and falsified his actual viewpoints. (This was probably the Gentile party.) ***I follow Apollos.*** After he had been instructed in the Gospel by Priscilla and Aquilla, Apollos went to Corinth to assist the church there. A bright, articulate Jew from Alexandria with great skill in debate (see Acts 18:24–28) would be a natural leader for those who attempted to intellectualize Christianity. ***I follow Cephas.*** It is probable that Peter also visited Corinth. This faction probably would have been oriented toward a more Jewish Christianity. ***I follow Christ.*** These are possibly the people who profess allegiance to the Christ they know without following the teaching of anyone. This may even be a mystical or gnostic-like party, given to inner visions and revelations.

1:17 ***lest the cross of Christ be emptied.*** Paul is eager that people be persuaded by Christ crucified and not by mere eloquence.

the intelligence of the intelligent I will
frustrate."[a]

20Where is the wise man? Where is the scholar? Where is the philosopher of this age? Has not
God made foolish the wisdom of the world? 21For
since in the wisdom of God the world through
its wisdom did not know him, God was pleased
through the foolishness of what was preached to
save those who believe. 22Jews demand miraculous signs and Greeks look for wisdom, 23but we
preach Christ crucified: a stumbling block to Jews
and foolishness to Gentiles, 24but to those whom
God has called, both Jews and Greeks, Christ the
power of God and the wisdom of God. 25For the
foolishness of God is wiser than man's wisdom,
and the weakness of God is stronger than man's
strength.

26Brothers, think of what you were when you
were called. Not many of you were wise by human standards; not many were influential; not
many were of noble birth. 27But God chose the
foolish things of the world to shame the wise;
God chose the weak things of the world to shame
the strong. 28He chose the lowly things of this
world and the despised things—and the things
that are not—to nullify the things that are, 29so
that no one may boast before him. 30It is because
of him that you are in Christ Jesus, who has become for us wisdom from God—that is, our righteousness, holiness and redemption. 31Therefore,
as it is written: "Let him who boasts boast in the
Lord."[b]

2 When I came to you, brothers, I did not
come with eloquence or superior wisdom as
I proclaimed to you the testimony about God.[c]
2For I resolved to know nothing while I was with
you except Jesus Christ and him crucified. 3I
came to you in weakness and fear, and with
much trembling. 4My message and my preaching
were not with wise and persuasive words, but
with a demonstration of the Spirit's power, 5so
that your faith might not rest on men's wisdom,
but on God's power.

Wisdom From the Spirit

6We do, however, speak a message of wisdom
among the mature, but not the wisdom of this age
or of the rulers of this age, who are coming to
nothing. 7No, we speak of God's secret wisdom,
a wisdom that has been hidden and that God
destined for our glory before time began. 8None
of the rulers of this age understood it, for if they
had, they would not have crucified the Lord of
glory. 9However, as it is written:

"No eye has seen,

1 Corinthians 1:18–2:5

1. What did you want to be when you were 12 years old?
2. What do you want to be doing 10 years from now? What will it take to get there?
3. What do you feel are the most important decisions you will make in your life?
4. How much influence does your commitment to Christ have in choosing your career?
5. What's one of the best decisions you've made? What's one of the worst?
6. Looking back on the last big decision you made, did you listen more to the world's wisdom or to the wisdom of God?
7. Christ was "a stumbling block" and "foolishness" to some. What decision have you made about following Christ?
8. How can the group pray for you in making wise, Christ-centered decisions?

a19 Isaiah 29:14 *b31* Jer. 9:24 *c1* Some manuscripts *as I proclaimed to you God's mystery*

1:18 *the message of the cross.* Paul puts the issue in stark terms: the question of eternal destiny centers on the meaning of the cross. The Corinthians' misunderstanding and division is no slight matter. It strikes at the core of the Gospel. ***foolishness.*** It is absurd to think that God's redemptive activity involves death by crucifixion.

1:22 *Greeks look for wisdom.* Their delight was in clever logic delivered with soaring persuasiveness. That a Jewish peasant who died as a criminal could be the focus of God's redemptive plan was so silly to them as to be laughable.

1:23 To accept the cross is to accept that people cannot understand God on their own nor find ways to reach him by themselves. They must trust God, not human wisdom and power.

1:24 In fact, Christ is both the sign that is craved by the Jews (he is the power of God) and the ultimate truth desired by the Greeks (he is the wisdom of God).

1:30 *righteousness.* Christ is their righteousness in that he took upon himself the guilt of human sin. So on the Last Day when Christians stand before the Judge they are viewed as being "in Christ."

2:2 In Corinth, a city full of articulate philosophers, Paul's refusal to use persuasive speech was especially striking. Instead, he simply preached the crucified Christ. ***know nothing ... except Jesus.*** Paul resolved to make Christ the sole subject of his teaching and preaching while he was with them.

no ear has heard,
no mind has conceived
what God has prepared for those who love him"[a]—

10but God has revealed it to us by his Spirit.

The Spirit searches all things, even the deep things of God. 11For who among men knows the thoughts of a man except the man's spirit within him? In the same way no one knows the thoughts of God except the Spirit of God. 12We have not received the spirit of the world but the Spirit who is from God, that we may understand what God has freely given us. 13This is what we speak, not in words taught us by human wisdom but in words taught by the Spirit, expressing spiritual truths in spiritual words.[b] 14The man without the Spirit does not accept the things that come from the Spirit of God, for they are foolishness to him, and he cannot understand them, because they are spiritually discerned. 15The spiritual man makes judgments about all things, but he himself is not subject to any man's judgment:

16"For who has known the mind of the Lord
that he may instruct him?"[c]

But we have the mind of Christ.

1 Corinthians 2:6–16

1. How well did you keep secrets when you were a child? How about since then?
2. How do you feel about verse 9? How is your outlook on life affected by the promise in this verse?
3. Name one thing about the Christian life that a non-Christian would not understand.
4. What can you do to exercise "the mind of Christ" (v. 16) more fully in your life?
5. What is God saying to you in this passage?
6. How can this group help you in prayer this week?

On Divisions in the Church

3 Brothers, I could not address you as spiritual but as worldly—mere infants in Christ. 2I gave you milk, not solid food, for you were not yet ready for it. Indeed, you are still not ready. 3You are still worldly. For since there is jealousy and quarreling among you, are you not worldly? Are you not acting like mere men? 4For when one says, "I follow Paul," and another, "I follow Apollos," are you not mere men?

5What, after all, is Apollos? And what is Paul? Only servants, through whom you came to believe—as the Lord has assigned to each his task. 6I planted the seed, Apollos watered it, but God made it grow. 7So neither he who plants nor he who waters is anything, but only God, who makes things grow. 8The man who plants and the man who waters have one purpose, and each will be rewarded according to his own labor. 9For we are God's fellow workers; you are God's field, God's building.

1 Corinthians 3:1–23

1. If you could build a house, what would it look like? Describe your dream house.
2. Who did the planting in your spiritual life? Who did the watering?
3. What evidence do you have in your life that your "building materials" will pass the fire test of verse 13?
4. Name one thing you can do this week to build the foundation of your life with "gold, silver and costly stones."
5. What is God saying to you in this passage?
6. How can this group help you in prayer this week?

10By the grace God has given me, I laid a foundation as an expert builder, and someone else is building on it. But each one should be careful how he builds. 11For no one can lay any foundation other than the one already laid, which is Jesus Christ. 12If any man builds on this foundation using gold, silver, costly stones, wood, hay or straw, 13his work will be shown for what it is, because the Day will bring it to light. It will be revealed with fire, and the fire will test the quality of each man's work. 14If what he has built survives, he will receive his reward. 15If it is burned up, he will suffer loss; he himself will be saved, but only as one escaping through the flames.

16Don't you know that you yourselves are God's temple and that God's Spirit lives in you?

[a] 9 Isaiah 64:4 [b] 13 Or *Spirit, interpreting spiritual truths to spiritual men* [c] 16 Isaiah 40:13

17If anyone destroys God's temple, God will destroy him; for God's temple is sacred, and you are that temple.

18Do not deceive yourselves. If any one of you thinks he is wise by the standards of this age, he should become a "fool" so that he may become wise. 19For the wisdom of this world is foolishness in God's sight. As it is written: "He catches the wise in their craftiness"[a]; 20and again, "The Lord knows that the thoughts of the wise are futile."[b] 21So then, no more boasting about men! All things are yours, 22whether Paul or Apollos or Cephas[c] or the world or life or death or the present or the future—all are yours, 23and you are of Christ, and Christ is of God.

Apostles of Christ

4 So then, men ought to regard us as servants of Christ and as those entrusted with the secret things of God. 2Now it is required that those who have been given a trust must prove faithful. 3I care very little if I am judged by you or by any human court; indeed, I do not even judge myself. 4My conscience is clear, but that does not make me innocent. It is the Lord who judges me. 5Therefore judge nothing before the appointed time; wait till the Lord comes. He will bring to light what is hidden in darkness and will expose the motives of men's hearts. At that time each will receive his praise from God.

6Now, brothers, I have applied these things to myself and Apollos for your benefit, so that you may learn from us the meaning of the saying, "Do not go beyond what is written." Then you will not take pride in one man over against another. 7For who makes you different from anyone else? What do you have that you did not receive? And if you did receive it, why do you boast as though you did not?

8Already you have all you want! Already you have become rich! You have become kings—and that without us! How I wish that you really had become kings so that we might be kings with you! 9For it seems to me that God has put us apostles on display at the end of the procession, like men condemned to die in the arena. We have been made a spectacle to the whole universe, to angels as well as to men. 10We are fools for Christ, but you are so wise in Christ! We are weak, but you are strong! You are honored, we are dishonored! 11To this very hour we go hungry and thirsty, we are in rags, we are brutally treated, we are homeless. 12We work hard with our own hands. When we are cursed, we bless; when we are persecuted, we endure it; 13when we are slandered, we answer kindly. Up to this moment we have become the scum of the earth, the refuse of the world.

14I am not writing this to shame you, but to warn you, as my dear children. 15Even though you have ten thousand guardians in Christ, you do not have many fathers, for in Christ Jesus I became your father through the gospel. 16Therefore I urge you to imitate me. 17For this reason I am sending to you Timothy, my son whom I love, who is faithful in the Lord. He will remind you of my way of life in Christ Jesus, which agrees with what I teach everywhere in every church.

1 Corinthians 4:1–21

1. Who has been a father figure or mother figure in your life, outside of your parents?
2. Paul, when talking about judging himself, claims that even his conscience is not dependable (vv. 3–4). Has your conscience ever differed with God's will for you? What happened?
3. How do you feel about the Lord "bringing to light" what is hidden and exposing the motives of our hearts (v. 5)? How can we live so that what is revealed will be less surprising and embarrassing?
4. Reflecting honestly on verse 20, is your Christian life more a matter of talk or of power?
5. What is God saying to you in this passage?
6. How can this group help you in prayer this week?

18Some of you have become arrogant, as if I were not coming to you. 19But I will come to you very soon, if the Lord is willing, and then I will find out not only how these arrogant people are talking, but what power they have. 20For the kingdom of God is not a matter of talk but of power. 21What do you prefer? Shall I come to you with a whip, or in love and with a gentle spirit?

Expel the Immoral Brother!

5 It is actually reported that there is sexual immorality among you, and of a kind that does not occur even among pagans: A man has his father's wife. 2And you are proud! Shouldn't

[a] *19* Job 5:13 [b] *20* Psalm 94:11 [c] *22* That is, Peter

you rather have been filled with grief and have
put out of your fellowship the man who did this?
3Even though I am not physically present, I am
with you in spirit. And I have already passed judgment on the one who did this, just as if I were
present. 4When you are assembled in the name
of our Lord Jesus and I am with you in spirit, and
the power of our Lord Jesus is present, 5hand this
man over to Satan, so that the sinful nature[a]
may be destroyed and his spirit saved on the day
of the Lord.

1 Corinthians 5:1–13

1. Have your parents ever forbid you from associating with someone? How did you feel?
2. How can handing someone over to Satan result in their salvation on the Day of the Lord (v. 5)? In what ways does your sinful nature need to be destroyed?
3. Are you more lenient and tolerant of Christians or non-Christians? Why?
4. What happens when a church is more concerned with judging those outside the church than evaluating their own behavior and motives?
5. What is God saying to you in this passage?
6. How can this group help you in prayer this week?

6Your boasting is not good. Don't you know
that a little yeast works through the whole batch
of dough? 7Get rid of the old yeast that you may
be a new batch without yeast—as you really are.
For Christ, our Passover lamb, has been sacrificed. 8Therefore let us keep the Festival, not
with the old yeast, the yeast of malice and wickedness, but with bread without yeast, the bread
of sincerity and truth.
9I have written you in my letter not to associate with sexually immoral people— 10not at all
meaning the people of this world who are immoral, or the greedy and swindlers, or idolaters. In
that case you would have to leave this world.
11But now I am writing you that you must not
associate with anyone who calls himself a brother
but is sexually immoral or greedy, an idolater or
a slanderer, a drunkard or a swindler. With such
a man do not even eat.
12What business is it of mine to judge those
outside the church? Are you not to judge those
inside? 13God will judge those outside. "Expel
the wicked man from among you."[b]

Lawsuits Among Believers

6 If any of you has a dispute with another, dare
he take it before the ungodly for judgment
instead of before the saints? 2Do you not know
that the saints will judge the world? And if you
are to judge the world, are you not competent to
judge trivial cases? 3Do you not know that we
will judge angels? How much more the things of
this life! 4Therefore, if you have disputes about
such matters, appoint as judges even men of little
account in the church![c] 5I say this to shame you.
Is it possible that there is nobody among you wise
enough to judge a dispute between believers?
6But instead, one brother goes to law against
another—and this in front of unbelievers!

1 Corinthians 6:1–11

1. How do (did) your parents settle disputes among you and your siblings? How fair are (were) they?
2. Do you agree with Paul that it is better to be cheated than to go to court against a fellow believer? Why?
3. What attitudes in conflict situations do you see in yourself: An insistence on your rights? A desire for revenge? Peace at any cost? Apathy about your example to non-believers?
4. What "were you" before meeting Christ? What are you now?
5. What is God saying to you in this passage?
6. How can this group help you in prayer this week?

7The very fact that you have lawsuits among
you means you have been completely defeated
already. Why not rather be wronged? Why not
rather be cheated? 8Instead, you yourselves cheat
and do wrong, and you do this to your brothers.
9Do you not know that the wicked will not

[a] *5* Or *that his body*; or *that the flesh* [b] *13* Deut. 17:7; 19:19; 21:21; 22:21,24; 24:7 [c] *4* Or *matters, do you appoint as judges men of little account in the church?*

inherit the kingdom of God? Do not be deceived:
Neither the sexually immoral nor idolaters nor
adulterers nor male prostitutes nor homosexual
offenders 10nor thieves nor the greedy nor drunkards nor slanderers nor swindlers will inherit the
kingdom of God. 11And that is what some of you
were. But you were washed, you were sanctified,
you were justified in the name of the Lord Jesus
Christ and by the Spirit of our God.

Sexual Immorality

12"Everything is permissible for me"—but not
everything is beneficial. "Everything is permissible for me"—but I will not be mastered by anything. 13"Food for the stomach and the stomach
for food"—but God will destroy them both. The
body is not meant for sexual immorality, but for
the Lord, and the Lord for the body. 14By his
power God raised the Lord from the dead, and he
will raise us also. 15Do you not know that your
bodies are members of Christ himself? Shall I
then take the members of Christ and unite them
with a prostitute? Never! 16Do you not know that
he who unites himself with a prostitute is one
with her in body? For it is said, "The two will
become one flesh."[a] 17But he who unites himself with the Lord is one with him in spirit.
18Flee from sexual immorality. All other sins a
man commits are outside his body, but he who
sins sexually sins against his own body. 19Do you
not know that your body is a temple of the Holy
Spirit, who is in you, whom you have received
from God? You are not your own; 20you were
bought at a price. Therefore honor God with your
body.

1 Corinthians 6:12–20

1. What TV program would you give an Emmy to for presenting a healthy view of sexuality? What TV show would get last place?
2. How open are you about discussing sexuality: With your parents? With your friends?
3. Would you even consider being celibate for life? Why or why not?
4. How do you feel about the statement, "You are not your own; you were bought at a price" (vv. 19–20)?
5. Does God have "the right" to your body? Why or why not?
6. Where do you draw the line against sexual immorality?
7. What do you need to do to "flee sexual immorality" and "honor God with your body"?
8. How can the group pray for you?

Marriage

7 Now for the matters you wrote about: It is
good for a man not to marry.[b] 2But since
there is so much immorality, each man should
have his own wife, and each woman her own
husband. 3The husband should fulfill his marital
duty to his wife, and likewise the wife to her
husband. 4The wife's body does not belong to her
alone but also to her husband. In the same way,
the husband's body does not belong to him alone
but also to his wife. 5Do not deprive each other
except by mutual consent and for a time, so that
you may devote yourselves to prayer. Then come
together again so that Satan will not tempt you
because of your lack of self-control. 6I say this as
a concession, not as a command. 7I wish that all
men were as I am. But each man has his own gift
from God; one has this gift, another has that.
8Now to the unmarried and the widows I say:
It is good for them to stay unmarried, as I am.
9But if they cannot control themselves, they
should marry, for it is better to marry than to
burn with passion.

[a] *16* Gen. 2:24 [b] *1* Or "*It is good for a man not to have sexual relations with a woman.*"

6:12 *mastered.* To indulge one's appetites in unsuitable ways is to put oneself under the power of that appetite, and to open the possibility of slavery to a harmful habit. Such license is not really Christian liberty because it produces bondage!

6:13 *body.* The stomach is one thing (it will pass away in the natural course of things), but the body is something else (it will live on). "Body" means for Paul not just bones and tissues, but the whole person.

6:14 *raise us also.* In fact, the body will be resurrected, as was the Lord's body. (His was not a "spiritual" resurrection. Jesus' body was missing from the tomb.)

6:15 Since the body of the Christian belongs to the Lord and is for his use, it is inconceivable ("Never!") that it be handed over to a prostitute.

6:16 *unites.* Intercourse is not merely an inconsequential physical act. In fact, it is akin to the bonding between the believer and the Lord, as Paul shows in verse 17 (where he uses this same word).

6:19 *your body is a temple of the Holy Spirit.* Believers should respect their bodies as a special, holy place where the Holy Spirit lives, and realize that the indwelling power of the Spirit can bring victory over sins like sexual immorality (Rom. 8:9).

6:20 *bought at a price.* The image is that of ransoming slaves from their bondage. In the same way, Christ has paid the ransom price in order to free Christians from the bondage of sin. Out of sheer gratitude, a Christian ought to flee sin.

[10]To the married I give this command (not I,
but the Lord): A wife must not separate from her
husband. [11]But if she does, she must remain unmarried or else be reconciled to her husband.
And a husband must not divorce his wife.
[12]To the rest I say this (I, not the Lord): If any
brother has a wife who is not a believer and she
is willing to live with him, he must not divorce
her. [13]And if a woman has a husband who is not
a believer and he is willing to live with her, she
must not divorce him. [14]For the unbelieving husband has been sanctified through his wife, and
the unbelieving wife has been sanctified through
her believing husband. Otherwise your children
would be unclean, but as it is, they are holy.

1 Corinthians 7:1–40

1. What has been the best marriage you have ever seen? What has been that couple's "secret"?
2. What do verses 3–5 tell you about the role of sex in marriage?
3. How can being married hinder your Christian life? How can it contribute to your Christian life?
4. What obligation does a believing spouse have to their unbelieving mate? What limits to this obligation might you suggest?
5. What is God saying to you in this passage?
6. How can this group help you in prayer this week?

[15]But if the unbeliever leaves, let him do so. A
believing man or woman is not bound in such
circumstances; God has called us to live in peace.
[16]How do you know, wife, whether you will save
your husband? Or, how do you know, husband,
whether you will save your wife?
[17]Nevertheless, each one should retain the
place in life that the Lord assigned to him and to
which God has called him. This is the rule I lay
down in all the churches. [18]Was a man already
circumcised when he was called? He should not
become uncircumcised. Was a man uncircumcised when he was called? He should not be circumcised. [19]Circumcision is nothing and uncircumcision is nothing. Keeping God's commands
is what counts. [20]Each one should remain in the
situation which he was in when God called him.
[21]Were you a slave when you were called? Don't
let it trouble you—although if you can gain your
freedom, do so. [22]For he who was a slave when
he was called by the Lord is the Lord's freedman;
similarly, he who was a free man when he was
called is Christ's slave. [23]You were bought at a
price; do not become slaves of men. [24]Brothers,
each man, as responsible to God, should remain
in the situation God called him to.
[25]Now about virgins: I have no command from
the Lord, but I give a judgment as one who by the
Lord's mercy is trustworthy. [26]Because of the
present crisis, I think that it is good for you to
remain as you are. [27]Are you married? Do not
seek a divorce. Are you unmarried? Do not look
for a wife. [28]But if you do marry, you have not
sinned; and if a virgin marries, she has not
sinned. But those who marry will face many troubles in this life, and I want to spare you this.
[29]What I mean, brothers, is that the time is
short. From now on those who have wives should
live as if they had none; [30]those who mourn, as
if they did not; those who are happy, as if they
were not; those who buy something, as if it were
not theirs to keep; [31]those who use the things of
the world, as if not engrossed in them. For this
world in its present form is passing away.
[32]I would like you to be free from concern. An
unmarried man is concerned about the Lord's
affairs—how he can please the Lord. [33]But a married man is concerned about the affairs of this
world—how he can please his wife— [34]and his
interests are divided. An unmarried woman or
virgin is concerned about the Lord's affairs: Her
aim is to be devoted to the Lord in both body and
spirit. But a married woman is concerned about
the affairs of this world—how she can please her
husband. [35]I am saying this for your own good,
not to restrict you, but that you may live in a right
way in undivided devotion to the Lord.
[36]If anyone thinks he is acting improperly toward the virgin he is engaged to, and if she is
getting along in years and he feels he ought to
marry, he should do as he wants. He is not sinning. They should get married. [37]But the man
who has settled the matter in his own mind, who
is under no compulsion but has control over his
own will, and who has made up his mind not to
marry the virgin—this man also does the right thing.
[38]So then, he who marries the virgin does right,
but he who does not marry her does even better.[a]

[a] *36-38* Or *[36]If anyone thinks he is not treating his daughter properly, and if she is getting along in years, and he feels she ought to marry, he should do as he wants. He is not sinning. He should let her get married. [37]But the man who has settled the matter in his own mind, who is under no compulsion but has control over his own will, and who has made up his mind to keep the virgin unmarried—this man also does the right thing. [38]So then, he who gives his virgin in marriage does right, but he who does not give her in marriage does even better.*

39A woman is bound to her husband as long as
he lives. But if her husband dies, she is free to
marry anyone she wishes, but he must belong to
the Lord. 40In my judgment, she is happier if she
stays as she is—and I think that I too have the
Spirit of God.

Food Sacrificed to Idols

8 Now about food sacrificed to idols: We know
that we all possess knowledge.[a] Knowledge
puffs up, but love builds up. 2The man who
thinks he knows something does not yet know as
he ought to know. 3But the man who loves God
is known by God.

> **1 CORINTHIANS 8:1–13**
>
> 1. Have you ever been superstitious? In what ways?
> 2. What might hinder you from loving new Christians or those believers who do not know something you know? How can you love them more effectively?
> 3. Have you done anything lately to wound the conscience of a fellow believer (v. 12)? How is this sinning against Christ?
> 4. Name one thing you can do to show love to a brother or sister in your church.
> 5. What is God saying to you in this passage?
> 6. How can this group help you in prayer this week?

4So then, about eating food sacrificed to idols:
We know that an idol is nothing at all in the
world and that there is no God but one. 5For even
if there are so-called gods, whether in heaven or
on earth (as indeed there are many "gods" and
many "lords"), 6yet for us there is but one God,
the Father, from whom all things came and for
whom we live; and there is but one Lord,
Jesus Christ, through whom all things came
and through whom we live.
7But not everyone knows this. Some people
are still so accustomed to idols that when they eat
such food they think of it as having been sacrificed to an idol, and since their conscience is
weak, it is defiled. 8But food does not bring us
near to God; we are no worse if we do not eat,
and no better if we do.
9Be careful, however, that the exercise of your
freedom does not become a stumbling block to
the weak. 10For if anyone with a weak conscience
sees you who have this knowledge eating in an
idol's temple, won't he be emboldened to eat
what has been sacrificed to idols? 11So this weak
brother, for whom Christ died, is destroyed by
your knowledge. 12When you sin against your
brothers in this way and wound their weak conscience, you sin against Christ. 13Therefore, if
what I eat causes my brother to fall into sin, I will
never eat meat again, so that I will not cause him
to fall.

The Rights of an Apostle

9 Am I not free? Am I not an apostle? Have I
not seen Jesus our Lord? Are you not the
result of my work in the Lord? 2Even though I
may not be an apostle to others, surely I am to
you! For you are the seal of my apostleship in the
Lord.
3This is my defense to those who sit in judgment on me. 4Don't we have the right to food
and drink? 5Don't we have the right to take a
believing wife along with us, as do the other
apostles and the Lord's brothers and Cephas[b]?
6Or is it only I and Barnabas who must work for
a living?
7Who serves as a soldier at his own expense?
Who plants a vineyard and does not eat of its
grapes? Who tends a flock and does not drink of
the milk? 8Do I say this merely from a human
point of view? Doesn't the Law say the same
thing? 9For it is written in the Law of Moses: "Do
not muzzle an ox while it is treading out the
grain."[c] Is it about oxen that God is concerned?
10Surely he says this for us, doesn't he? Yes, this
was written for us, because when the plowman
plows and the thresher threshes, they ought to
do so in the hope of sharing in the harvest. 11If
we have sown spiritual seed among you, is it too
much if we reap a material harvest from you? 12If
others have this right of support from you,
shouldn't we have it all the more?
But we did not use this right. On the contrary,
we put up with anything rather than hinder the
gospel of Christ. 13Don't you know that those
who work in the temple get their food from the
temple, and those who serve at the altar share in
what is offered on the altar? 14In the same way,
the Lord has commanded that those who preach
the gospel should receive their living from the
gospel.
15But I have not used any of these rights. And
I am not writing this in the hope that you will do

[a] *1* Or *"We all possess knowledge," as you say* [b] *5* That is, Peter [c] *9* Deut. 25:4

such things for me. I would rather die than have
anyone deprive me of this boast. 16Yet when I
preach the gospel, I cannot boast, for I am compelled to preach. Woe to me if I do not preach the
gospel! 17If I preach voluntarily, I have a reward;
if not voluntarily, I am simply discharging the
trust committed to me. 18What then is my reward? Just this: that in preaching the gospel I
may offer it free of charge, and so not make use
of my rights in preaching it.

19Though I am free and belong to no man, I
make myself a slave to everyone, to win as many
as possible. 20To the Jews I became like a Jew, to
win the Jews. To those under the law I became
like one under the law (though I myself am not
under the law), so as to win those under the law.
21To those not having the law I became like one
not having the law (though I am not free from
God's law but am under Christ's law), so as to
win those not having the law. 22To the weak I
became weak, to win the weak. I have become all
things to all men so that by all possible means I
might save some. 23I do all this for the sake of the
gospel, that I may share in its blessings.

24Do you not know that in a race all the runners run, but only one gets the prize? Run in such
a way as to get the prize. 25Everyone who competes in the games goes into strict training. They
do it to get a crown that will not last; but we do
it to get a crown that will last forever. 26There-
fore I do not run like a man running aimlessly; I
do not fight like a man beating the air. 27No, I
beat my body and make it my slave so that after
I have preached to others, I myself will not be
disqualified for the prize.

Warnings From Israel's History

10 For I do not want you to be ignorant of
the fact, brothers, that our forefathers
were all under the cloud and that they all passed
through the sea. 2They were all baptized into
Moses in the cloud and in the sea. 3They all ate
the same spiritual food 4and drank the same spiritual drink; for they drank from the spiritual rock
that accompanied them, and that rock was

1 Corinthians 9:24–27

1. Who's your favorite athlete? What quality do you admire about that person?
2. Do you prefer watching, training or competing in sports? Why?
3. What is your best sport?
4. What goal have you set for yourself in your favorite sport?
5. How would you describe your passion for serving God on a scale of 1 (couch potato) to 10 (Olympic gold medalist)?
6. Are you more likely to keep to a training schedule for your physical fitness or your spiritual fitness?
7. What spiritual discipline do you need to practice in order to "get the prize"?
8. How can this group help hold each other accountable in their spiritual training?

Christ. 5Nevertheless, God was not pleased with
most of them; their bodies were scattered over
the desert.

6Now these things occurred as examples[a] to
keep us from setting our hearts on evil things as
they did. 7Do not be idolaters, as some of them
were; as it is written: "The people sat down to
eat and drink and got up to indulge in pagan
revelry."[b] 8We should not commit sexual immorality, as some of them did—and in one day
twenty-three thousand of them died. 9We should
not test the Lord, as some of them did—and were
killed by snakes. 10And do not grumble, as some
of them did—and were killed by the destroying
angel.

[a]6 Or *types*; also in verse 11 [b]7 Exodus 32:6

9:24–27 Paul turns to the concept of self-discipline. Discipline was exactly what the Corinthians had most need of. To make his point, Paul uses metaphors drawn from Greek games.

9:24 ***race ... runners.*** The Corinthians would be quite familiar with the competitive races in their own Isthmian games, which were second only to the Olympic games in prestige. ***prize.*** In the ancient games the prize was a perishable wreath (the temporary crown of v. 25).

9:25 The emphasis is on the self-control that is needed to win in the games. ***crown.*** In the Greek games, the winner received a crown made of pine boughs. The Christian's crown is eternal life.

9:26–27 Having first applied the metaphors to the Corinthians (vv. 24–25), Paul now applies them to himself. The body is not an enemy. It is simply that it responds readily to temptation and must be disciplined to be of service to God.

9:26 ***running aimlessly.*** A runner in a race cannot simply run in any direction he or she chooses. And no boxer swings wildly at the air, but concentrates on his opponent. Likewise, Paul's activities are not without a point. Everything he does is for the sake of the Gospel.

9:27 ***I beat my body.*** Like a boxer, Paul severely disciplines his own body in serving Christ. In his case, such beating of the body probably refers to hardships to which he voluntarily subjected himself in preaching to the Corinthians.

11 These things happened to them as examples
and were written down as warnings for us, on
whom the fulfillment of the ages has come. 12 So,
if you think you are standing firm, be careful that
you don't fall! 13 No temptation has seized you
except what is common to man. And God is faithful; he will not let you be tempted beyond what
you can bear. But when you are tempted, he will
also provide a way out so that you can stand up
under it.

1 Corinthians 10:1–13

1. How many hours did you spend watching TV last night? What did you watch?
2. If the TV was removed from your house, how many hours a week would you have to invest in better things?
3. How much do movies, TV, video games and other media influence your behavior or that of your friends?
4. What rules are you going to have on TV viewing when you raise your children?
5. What truths can you draw from verses 12 and 13 of this passage?
6. What standard will you set for yourself over the next month for TV viewing?
7. Would you allow this group to hold you accountable for this goal?
8. How can the group help you in prayer this week?

Idol Feasts and the Lord's Supper

14 Therefore, my dear friends, flee from idolatry. 15 I speak to sensible people; judge for yourselves what I say. 16 Is not the cup of thanksgiving
for which we give thanks a participation in the
blood of Christ? And is not the bread that we
break a participation in the body of Christ? 17 Because there is one loaf, we, who are many, are
one body, for we all partake of the one loaf.
18 Consider the people of Israel: Do not those
who eat the sacrifices participate in the altar?
19 Do I mean then that a sacrifice offered to an
idol is anything, or that an idol is anything? 20 No,
but the sacrifices of pagans are offered to demons, not to God, and I do not want you to be
participants with demons. 21 You cannot drink the
cup of the Lord and the cup of demons too; you
cannot have a part in both the Lord's table and
the table of demons. 22 Are we trying to arouse
the Lord's jealousy? Are we stronger than he?

1 Corinthians 10:14–11:1

1. What is the strangest food you have ever eaten?
2. When you participate in Communion, what does it mean to you?
3. In what ways is a Christian free (vv. 23–24)? How do you exercise your freedom in Christ?
4. Verses 27–33 describe what a believer should do in a relationship with an unbeliever. Do Paul's instructions sound hypocritical? Do you act differently around Christians and non-Christians?
5. Is there anything you do that does not bother your conscience but might bother the conscience of someone else? Explain.
6. What is God saying to you in this passage?
7. How can this group help you in prayer this week?

10:1 ***our forefathers.*** Though his readers are largely Gentiles, Paul considers them to be the spiritual heirs of Israel.

10:2–4 Paul notes that Israel had experiences which parallel the basic Christian rites: the passage through the Red Sea is analogous to baptism; the manna they ate (Ex. 16:4,13–18) and the water they drank (Ex. 17:6; Num. 20:6–13) were analogous to the bread and wine in Communion.

10:5–7 Israel also provides a warning, such as the incident with the golden calf.

10:8 ***sexual immorality.*** Paul explicitly condemns the sexual vice associated with pagan religion (6:12–20).

10:9 ***test the Lord.*** The Corinthians (as the Israelites before them) were testing God by these actions—they were seeing how much they could get away with.

10:10 ***grumble.*** They were also grumbling against Paul for telling them not to engage in temple feasts and ritual prostitution.

10:12 Israel felt it was secure, yet they lapsed into sin and destruction. So, too, the Corinthians were headed for the same fate.

10:13 Paul encourages the Corinthians to stand firm by reminding them that when Christians resist sin, they do so in the knowledge that they will be able to endure. ***temptation.*** To be tempted is to be tested. Facing the choice of deserting God's will or doing God's will, the person must either resist or yield. Temptation is not sin. Yielding is. ***a way out.*** Temptation is not unusual nor unexpected. Resisting it is not pleasant, but there will be a way out for those who seek it.

The Believer's Freedom

23 “Everything is permissible”—but not everything is beneficial. “Everything is permissible”—but not everything is constructive. 24 Nobody should seek his own good, but the good of others.

25 Eat anything sold in the meat market without raising questions of conscience, 26 for, “The earth is the Lord's, and everything in it.”[a]

27 If some unbeliever invites you to a meal and you want to go, eat whatever is put before you without raising questions of conscience. 28 But if anyone says to you, “This has been offered in sacrifice,” then do not eat it, both for the sake of the man who told you and for conscience' sake[b]— 29 the other man's conscience, I mean, not yours. For why should my freedom be judged by another's conscience? 30 If I take part in the meal with thankfulness, why am I denounced because of something I thank God for?

31 So whether you eat or drink or whatever you do, do it all for the glory of God. 32 Do not cause anyone to stumble, whether Jews, Greeks or the church of God— 33 even as I try to please everybody in every way. For I am not seeking my own good but the good of many, so that they may be

11 saved. 1 Follow my example, as I follow the example of Christ.

Propriety in Worship

2 I praise you for remembering me in everything and for holding to the teachings,[c] just as I passed them on to you.

3 Now I want you to realize that the head of every man is Christ, and the head of the woman is man, and the head of Christ is God. 4 Every man who prays or prophesies with his head covered dishonors his head. 5 And every woman who prays or prophesies with her head uncovered dishonors her head—it is just as though her head were shaved. 6 If a woman does not cover her head, she should have her hair cut off; and if it is a disgrace for a woman to have her hair cut or shaved off, she should cover her head. 7 A man ought not to cover his head,[d] since he is the image and glory of God; but the woman is the glory of man. 8 For man did not come from woman, but woman from man; 9 neither was man created for woman, but woman for man. 10 For this reason, and because of the angels, the woman ought to have a sign of authority on her head.

11 In the Lord, however, woman is not independent of man, nor is man independent of woman. 12 For as woman came from man, so also man is born of woman. But everything comes from God. 13 Judge for yourselves: Is it proper for a woman to pray to God with her head uncovered? 14 Does not the very nature of things teach you that if a man has long hair, it is a disgrace to him, 15 but that if a woman has long hair, it is her glory? For long hair is given to her as a covering. 16 If anyone wants to be contentious about this, we have no other practice—nor do the churches of God.

1 Corinthians 11:2–16

1. What was the worst “hair disaster” you ever had?
2. Why is Paul so concerned with the roles of men and women, showing glory to God in a proper way, and avoiding any similarity with pagan religious groups?
3. Does your church conduct worship services in a way that might confuse an unbeliever?
4. What changes do you need to make in your own worship life?
5. What is God saying to you in this passage?
6. How can this group help you in prayer this week?

The Lord's Supper

17 In the following directives I have no praise for you, for your meetings do more harm than good. 18 In the first place, I hear that when you come together as a church, there are divisions among you, and to some extent I believe it. 19 No doubt there have to be differences among you to show which of you have God's approval. 20 When you come together, it is not the Lord's Supper you eat, 21 for as you eat, each of you goes ahead without waiting for anybody else. One remains hungry, another gets drunk. 22 Don't you have homes to eat and drink in? Or do you despise the church of God and humiliate those who have nothing? What shall I say to you? Shall I praise you for this? Certainly not!

[a] *26* Psalm 24:1 [b] *28* Some manuscripts *conscience' sake, for “the earth is the Lord's and everything in it”* [c] *2* Or *traditions*
[d] *4-7* Or *4Every man who prays or prophesies with long hair dishonors his head. 5And every woman who prays or prophesies with no covering ⌞of hair⌟ on her head dishonors her head—she is just like one of the “shorn women.” 6If a woman has no covering, let her be for now with short hair, but since it is a disgrace for a woman to have her hair shorn or shaved, she should grow it again. 7A man ought not to have long hair*

23For I received from the Lord what I also
passed on to you: The Lord Jesus, on the night he
was betrayed, took bread, 24and when he had
given thanks, he broke it and said, "This is my
body, which is for you; do this in remembrance
of me." 25In the same way, after supper he took
the cup, saying, "This cup is the new covenant in
my blood; do this, whenever you drink it, in remembrance of me." 26For whenever you eat this
bread and drink this cup, you proclaim the Lord's
death until he comes.

27Therefore, whoever eats the bread or drinks
the cup of the Lord in an unworthy manner will
be guilty of sinning against the body and blood of
the Lord. 28A man ought to examine himself before he eats of the bread and drinks of the cup.

1 Corinthians 11:17–34

1. What is the biggest party you've ever given?
2. What changes would the Corinthians need to make to celebrate the Lord's Supper appropriately?
3. Can you think of a time when you approached a worship service or other Christian activity too lightly?
4. In verses 31 and 32, Paul discusses the inescapable aspect of judgment, either from ourselves or God. In what area of your life do you need to "judge yourself" right now so that God doesn't have to discipline you?
5. What is God saying to you in this passage?
6. How can this group help you in prayer this week?

29For anyone who eats and drinks without recognizing the body of the Lord eats and drinks judgment on himself. 30That is why many among
you are weak and sick, and a number of you
have fallen asleep. 31But if we judged ourselves,
we would not come under judgment. 32When
we are judged by the Lord, we are being disciplined so that we will not be condemned with
the world.

33So then, my brothers, when you come together to eat, wait for each other. 34If anyone is
hungry, he should eat at home, so that when you
meet together it may not result in judgment.

And when I come I will give further directions.

Spiritual Gifts

12 Now about spiritual gifts, brothers, I do
not want you to be ignorant. 2You know
that when you were pagans, somehow or other
you were influenced and led astray to mute idols.
3Therefore I tell you that no one who is speaking
by the Spirit of God says, "Jesus be cursed," and
no one can say, "Jesus is Lord," except by the
Holy Spirit.

4There are different kinds of gifts, but the
same Spirit. 5There are different kinds of service,
but the same Lord. 6There are different kinds of
working, but the same God works all of them in
all men.

7Now to each one the manifestation of the
Spirit is given for the common good. 8To one
there is given through the Spirit the message of
wisdom, to another the message of knowledge by
means of the same Spirit, 9to another faith by the
same Spirit, to another gifts of healing by that one
Spirit, 10to another miraculous powers, to another prophecy, to another distinguishing between
spirits, to another speaking in different kinds of
tongues,[a] and to still another the interpretation
of tongues.[a] 11All these are the work of one and
the same Spirit, and he gives them to each one,
just as he determines.

One Body, Many Parts

12The body is a unit, though it is made up of
many parts; and though all its parts are many,
they form one body. So it is with Christ. 13For we
were all baptized by[b] one Spirit into one body—
whether Jews or Greeks, slave or free—and we
were all given the one Spirit to drink.

14Now the body is not made up of one part but
of many. 15If the foot should say, "Because I am
not a hand, I do not belong to the body," it would
not for that reason cease to be part of the body.
16And if the ear should say, "Because I am not an
eye, I do not belong to the body," it would not for
that reason cease to be part of the body. 17If the
whole body were an eye, where would the sense
of hearing be? If the whole body were an ear,
where would the sense of smell be? 18But in fact
God has arranged the parts in the body, every one
of them, just as he wanted them to be. 19If they
were all one part, where would the body be? 20As
it is, there are many parts, but one body.

21The eye cannot say to the hand, "I don't
need you!" And the head cannot say to the feet,
"I don't need you!" 22On the contrary, those
parts of the body that seem to be weaker are

[a] 10 Or *languages*; also in verse 28 [b] 13 Or *with*; or *in*

indispensable, 23and the parts that we think are less honorable we treat with special honor. And the parts that are unpresentable are treated with special modesty, 24while our presentable parts

> ### 1 Corinthians 12:12–31
>
> 1. Have you ever broken a bone? If so, which one?
> 2. Which of the five senses is the most important?
> 3. What talent do you have that others in this group might not know about?
> 4. On a scale of 1 ("Whatever!") to 10 ("I care a lot"), how important is it to you to: Fit in? Be popular? Be unique?
> 5. Describe yourself as a "part" of the body of Christ (an eye, hand, etc.). Why did you select that part?
> 6. How connected are you to your church body? How can you help the "body" function better?
> 7. If you knew you could not fail, what would you like to do as a group to advance the cause of Christ in your school or in your community?
> 8. Close by praying for your church.

need no special treatment. But God has combined the members of the body and has given greater honor to the parts that lacked it, 25so that there should be no division in the body, but that its parts should have equal concern for each other. 26If one part suffers, every part suffers with it; if one part is honored, every part rejoices with it.

27Now you are the body of Christ, and each one of you is a part of it. 28And in the church God has appointed first of all apostles, second prophets, third teachers, then workers of miracles, also those having gifts of healing, those able to help others, those with gifts of administration, and those speaking in different kinds of tongues. 29Are all apostles? Are all prophets? Are all teachers? Do all work miracles? 30Do all have gifts of healing? Do all speak in tongues[a]? Do all interpret? 31But eagerly desire[b] the greater gifts.

Love

And now I will show you the most excellent way.

13 If I speak in the tongues[c] of men and of angels, but have not love, I am only a resounding gong or a clanging cymbal. 2If I have the gift of prophecy and can fathom all mysteries and all knowledge, and if I have a faith that can move mountains, but have not love, I am nothing. 3If I give all I possess to the poor and surrender my body to the flames,[d] but have not love, I gain nothing.

4Love is patient, love is kind. It does not envy, it does not boast, it is not proud. 5It is not rude, it is not self-seeking, it is not easily angered, it keeps no record of wrongs. 6Love does not delight in evil but rejoices with the truth. 7It always protects, always trusts, always hopes, always perseveres.

8Love never fails. But where there are prophecies, they will cease; where there are tongues, they will be stilled; where there is knowledge, it will pass away. 9For we know in part and we prophesy in part, 10but when perfection comes, the imperfect disappears. 11When I was a child, I talked like a child, I thought like a child, I reasoned like a child. When I became a man, I put childish ways behind me. 12Now we see but a poor reflection as in a mirror; then we shall see face to face. Now I know in part; then I shall know fully, even as I am fully known.

[a]30 Or *other languages* [b]31 Or *But you are eagerly desiring* [c]1 Or *languages* [d]3 Some early manuscripts *body that I may boast*

Once having established that Christians are all part of one body (vv. 12–13), Paul focuses on diversity, in which he not only points out the variety of gifts that exist, but the fact that none are inferior and all are necessary.

12:12 ***a unit ... made up of many parts.*** This is Paul's central point in verses 12–30: "diversity within unity." ***So it is with Christ.*** The church is the body of Christ (v. 27), and so indeed Christ can be understood to be made up of many parts. Yet he is also the Lord (v. 3), and thus head over that church.

12:13 Here Paul points to the unity side of the body of Christ. Unity exists because all were baptized into one Spirit, and all drink from one Spirit. His concern is not with how people become believers, but with how believers become one body.

12:15–26 Here Paul makes two points: There are a variety of gifts (vv. 15–20), and each gift is vital, regardless of its nature (vv. 21–26).

12:28 Paul offers a second list (see 12:8–10) of the types of gifts given by the Holy Spirit (see the parallel list in Eph. 4:11)—mixing together ministries (e.g., apostles) with charismatic gifts (e.g., the gift of healing). ***apostles.*** These individuals were responsible for founding new churches. They were pioneer church planters.

12:29–30 Paul is quite clear that no one has all the gifts. The implied answer to each question is "No."

12:31 Paul establishes the context within which all gifts should function: love, which is the more excellent way.

13 And now these three remain: faith, hope and love. But the greatest of these is love.

1 Corinthians 13:1–13

1. What is your favorite love story from a movie, book, TV show or fairy tale?
2. How easy is it for you to tell or show someone you love them?
3. When it comes to sacrificial and unconditional love, who would you nominate to be in the Hall of Fame?
4. On a scale of 1 (very little) to 10 (an abundance), how much love did you receive during the last week? How much did you give?
5. When in your life have you felt the most loved?
6. Why is love greater than the virtues of faith and hope?
7. Who is someone you need to show godly love to this week? How will you do this?
8. How can this group pray for you?

Gifts of Prophecy and Tongues

14 Follow the way of love and eagerly desire spiritual gifts, especially the gift of prophecy. 2 For anyone who speaks in a tongue[a] does not speak to men but to God. Indeed, no one understands him; he utters mysteries with his spirit.[b] 3 But everyone who prophesies speaks to men for their strengthening, encouragement and comfort. 4 He who speaks in a tongue edifies himself, but he who prophesies edifies the church. 5 I would like every one of you to speak in tongues,[c] but I would rather have you prophesy. He who prophesies is greater than one who speaks in tongues,[c] unless he interprets, so that the church may be edified.

6 Now, brothers, if I come to you and speak in tongues, what good will I be to you, unless I bring you some revelation or knowledge or prophecy or word of instruction? 7 Even in the case of lifeless things that make sounds, such as the flute or harp, how will anyone know what tune is being played unless there is a distinction in the notes? 8 Again, if the trumpet does not sound a clear call, who will get ready for battle? 9 So it is with you. Unless you speak intelligible words with your tongue, how will anyone know what you are saying? You will just be speaking into the air. 10 Undoubtedly there are all sorts of languages in the world, yet none of them is without meaning. 11 If then I do not grasp the meaning of what someone is saying, I am a foreigner to the speaker, and he is a foreigner to me. 12 So it is with you. Since you are eager to have spiritual gifts, try to excel in gifts that build up the church.

13 For this reason anyone who speaks in a tongue should pray that he may interpret what he says. 14 For if I pray in a tongue, my spirit prays, but my mind is unfruitful. 15 So what shall I do? I will pray with my spirit, but I will also pray with my mind; I will sing with my spirit, but I will also sing with my mind. 16 If you are praising God with your spirit, how can one who finds himself among those who do not understand[d] say "Amen" to your thanksgiving, since he does not know what you are saying? 17 You may be giving thanks well enough, but the other man is not edified.

18 I thank God that I speak in tongues more than all of you. 19 But in the church I would rather speak five intelligible words to instruct others than ten thousand words in a tongue.

20 Brothers, stop thinking like children. In regard to evil be infants, but in your thinking be adults. 21 In the Law it is written:

[a] 2 Or *another language*; also in verses 4, 13, 14, 19, 26 and 27 [b] 2 Or *by the Spirit* [c] 5 Or *other languages*; also in verses 6, 18, 22, 23 and 39 [d] 16 Or *among the inquirers*

13:1–3 If a person does not love, neither spiritual gifts, nor good deeds, nor martyrdom is of any ultimate value to that person. Love is the context within which these gifts and deeds become significant.

13:4 ***patient.*** Patience with people (not circumstances). ***not proud.*** Literally, not "puffed up." The loving person does not feel others to be inferior, nor looks down on people.

13:5 ***not self-seeking.*** Loving people not only do not insist on their rights, but will give up their due for the sake of others. ***keeps no record of wrongs.*** The verb is an accounting term, and the image is of a ledger sheet on which wrongs received are recorded. The loving person forgives and does not keep track of wrongs.

13:6 ***does not delight in evil.*** Loving people do not rejoice when others fail, nor enjoy pointing out wrong.

13:7 ***trusts.*** Literally, "believes all things"; that is, "never loses faith." ***hopes.*** Love does not lose hope. ***perseveres.*** Love keeps loving despite hardship.

13:8–12 Having described love, Paul once again contrasts love with spiritual gifts. He emphasizes the permanent quality of love over the transitory nature of the gifts.

13:13 ***remain.*** Charismatic gifts will cease, because they bring only partial knowledge of God; but three things always remain: faith, hope and love.

"Through men of strange tongues
and through the lips of foreigners
I will speak to this people,
but even then they will not listen to
me,"[a]
says the Lord.

[22]Tongues, then, are a sign, not for believers but for unbelievers; prophecy, however, is for believers, not for unbelievers. [23]So if the whole church comes together and everyone speaks in tongues, and some who do not understand[b] or some unbelievers come in, will they not say that you are out of your mind? [24]But if an unbeliever or someone who does not understand[c] comes in while everybody is prophesying, he will be convinced by all that he is a sinner and will be judged by all, [25]and the secrets of his heart will be laid bare. So he will fall down and worship God, exclaiming, "God is really among you!"

1 Corinthians 14:1–25

1. If you could play any musical instrument, what would it be? What songs would you like to play?
2. What is the difference between speaking in tongues and prophesying (vv. 2–4)?
3. What are Paul's corrective instructions to the "spiritually proud" Corinthians (v. 12)?
4. What have you done lately to build up others in your church?
5. What is God saying to you in this passage?
6. How can this group help you in prayer this week?

Orderly Worship

[26]What then shall we say, brothers? When you come together, everyone has a hymn, or a word of instruction, a revelation, a tongue or an interpretation. All of these must be done for the strengthening of the church. [27]If anyone speaks in a tongue, two—or at the most three—should speak, one at a time, and someone must interpret. [28]If there is no interpreter, the speaker should keep quiet in the church and speak to himself and God.

[29]Two or three prophets should speak, and the others should weigh carefully what is said. [30]And if a revelation comes to someone who is sitting down, the first speaker should stop. [31]For you can all prophesy in turn so that everyone may be instructed and encouraged. [32]The spirits of prophets are subject to the control of prophets. [33]For God is not a God of disorder but of peace.

As in all the congregations of the saints, [34]women should remain silent in the churches. They are not allowed to speak, but must be in submission, as the Law says. [35]If they want to inquire about something, they should ask their own husbands at home; for it is disgraceful for a woman to speak in the church.

1 Corinthians 14:26–40

1. What was your favorite song as a child? Can you remember a song from camp or Sunday School? Can you remember the hand motions?
2. In verse 26, Paul seems to describe a worship service where everyone has something to offer. What are the options? Which option would be most appealing to you?
3. How do you think your church could better include the contributions of more people in worship services?
4. What was the most inspiring part of the worship service you attended most recently: The sermon? A prayer? The music? A greeting from someone?
5. What is God saying to you in this passage?
6. How can this group help you in prayer this week?

[36]Did the word of God originate with you? Or are you the only people it has reached? [37]If anybody thinks he is a prophet or spiritually gifted, let him acknowledge that what I am writing to you is the Lord's command. [38]If he ignores this, he himself will be ignored.[d]

[39]Therefore, my brothers, be eager to prophesy, and do not forbid speaking in tongues. [40]But everything should be done in a fitting and orderly way.

[a]*21* Isaiah 28:11,12 [b]*23* Or *some inquirers* [c]*24* Or *or some inquirer* [d]*38* Some manuscripts *If he is ignorant of this, let him be ignorant*

The Resurrection of Christ

15 Now, brothers, I want to remind you of
the gospel I preached to you, which you
received and on which you have taken your
stand. 2 By this gospel you are saved, if you hold
firmly to the word I preached to you. Otherwise,
you have believed in vain.

1 CORINTHIANS 15:1–11

1. If you could interview someone who saw Jesus after he was resurrected, what would you ask him or her?
2. In verse 2, what do you think it means to "hold firmly to the word I preached to you"?
3. What does "Christ died for our sins" mean to you? How does the Gospel affect your life on a daily basis?
4. What evidence can you offer that Christ is alive in your life?
5. What is God saying to you in this passage?
6. How can this group help you in prayer this week?

3 For what I received I passed on to you as of
first importance[a]: that Christ died for our sins
according to the Scriptures, 4 that he was buried,
that he was raised on the third day according to
the Scriptures, 5 and that he appeared to Peter,[b]
and then to the Twelve. 6 After that, he appeared
to more than five hundred of the brothers at the
same time, most of whom are still living, though
some have fallen asleep. 7 Then he appeared to
James, then to all the apostles, 8 and last of all he
appeared to me also, as to one abnormally born.
9 For I am the least of the apostles and do not
even deserve to be called an apostle, because I
persecuted the church of God. 10 But by the grace
of God I am what I am, and his grace to me was
not without effect. No, I worked harder than all
of them—yet not I, but the grace of God that was
with me. 11 Whether, then, it was I or they, this
is what we preach, and this is what you believed.

The Resurrection of the Dead

12 But if it is preached that Christ has been
raised from the dead, how can some of you say
that there is no resurrection of the dead? 13 If

1 CORINTHIANS 15:12–34

1. How are you at saying "good-bye"?
2. What is your favorite memory of an Easter celebration?
3. Do you believe Christ rose from the dead? Why or why not?
4. How would you feel about following Christ if he hadn't risen from the dead?
5. How important is belief in Christ's resurrection to the Christian faith (see Rom. 10:9)?
6. How do you connect Christ's resurrection with your own hope of resurrection from death?
7. What do you say to someone who says there is no resurrection and the story of Christ's rising from the dead is a lie?
8. How can this group pray for you in the coming week?

[a] 3 Or *you at the first* [b] 5 Greek *Cephas*

15:12 Jesus' resurrection is a clear proof that there is such a thing as resurrection.

15:18–19 Relentlessly, Paul points out to the Corinthians the implications of no resurrection: (a) they are still lost and dead in sin, (b) those who have died are lost, (c) their "hope" is groundless, and (d) they are pitiable people. Without the resurrection of Christ, Christianity crumbles.

15:20 ***firstfruits.*** Those early-developing grains or fruits that demonstrate that the full harvest is not far behind. Similarly, the fact that Christ was raised from the dead is clear proof that the future resurrection of believers is assured.

15:22 ***all will be made alive.*** Though the wording has been made parallel to the previous clause (all die), the idea is that all who are in Christ will rise (as Paul says explicitly in 1 Thess. 4:16).

15:23–28 In order for the Corinthians to understand the future resurrection, Paul must place it in the context of the time when Christ returns.

15:26 The last of these enemies to be rendered inoperative is death itself. That Christ has won out is seen in the resurrection of believers.

15:29–34 Paul points out that both his actions and theirs demonstrate a belief in the resurrection.

15:29 ***if there is no resurrection.*** Here, Paul gives the first of three arguments which point out the absurdity of an action if there is no coming resurrection. In verse 29, the absurd action is baptism for the dead.

there is no resurrection of the dead, then not
even Christ has been raised. 14And if Christ has
not been raised, our preaching is useless and so
is your faith. 15More than that, we are then found
to be false witnesses about God, for we have testified about God that he raised Christ from the
dead. But he did not raise him if in fact the dead
are not raised. 16For if the dead are not raised,
then Christ has not been raised either. 17And if
Christ has not been raised, your faith is futile;
you are still in your sins. 18Then those also who
have fallen asleep in Christ are lost. 19If only for
this life we have hope in Christ, we are to be
pitied more than all men.

20But Christ has indeed been raised from the
dead, the firstfruits of those who have fallen
asleep. 21For since death came through a man,
the resurrection of the dead comes also through
a man. 22For as in Adam all die, so in Christ all
will be made alive. 23But each in his own turn:
Christ, the firstfruits; then, when he comes,
those who belong to him. 24Then the end will
come, when he hands over the kingdom to God
the Father after he has destroyed all dominion,
authority and power. 25For he must reign until he
has put all his enemies under his feet. 26The last
enemy to be destroyed is death. 27For he "has put
everything under his feet."[a] Now when it says
that "everything" has been put under him, it is
clear that this does not include God himself, who
put everything under Christ. 28When he has
done this, then the Son himself will be made
subject to him who put everything under him, so
that God may be all in all.

29Now if there is no resurrection, what will
those do who are baptized for the dead? If the
dead are not raised at all, why are people baptized for them? 30And as for us, why do we endanger ourselves every hour? 31I die every day—
I mean that, brothers—just as surely as I glory
over you in Christ Jesus our Lord. 32If I fought
wild beasts in Ephesus for merely human reasons, what have I gained? If the dead are not
raised,

"Let us eat and drink,
for tomorrow we die."[b]

33Do not be misled: "Bad company corrupts good
character." 34Come back to your senses as you
ought, and stop sinning; for there are some who
are ignorant of God—I say this to your shame.

The Resurrection Body

35But someone may ask, "How are the dead
raised? With what kind of body will they come?"
36How foolish! What you sow does not come to
life unless it dies. 37When you sow, you do not
plant the body that will be, but just a seed, perhaps of wheat or of something else. 38But God
gives it a body as he has determined, and to each
kind of seed he gives its own body. 39All flesh is

1 Corinthians 15:35–58

1. When have you been homesick? Where were you?
2. When you get to heaven, who is the first person you are going to look up?
3. Did you learn the verse John 3:16 as a child? Can you recite it now?
4. How do you feel about death? What do you think happens when a person dies?
5. How did Jesus win victory over death?
6. How can you share in this victory (see John 5:24)?
7. Who are you praying for that they would give their life to Christ: Family? Friends?
8. Pray together for the people you shared about in question #7.

[a]*27* Psalm 8:6 [b]*32* Isaiah 22:13

15:36–38 Death brings change, not extinction. Here, Paul probes the nature of the transformation; his point being that what one plants (or buries) is not what one gets in the end.

15:43 Paul now describes the nature of the changed body. The resurrection body is characterized by glory (brightness, radiance, splendor). This is a quality ascribed to God, in which believers will somehow share (Phil. 3:21). The resurrection body will also be filled with power—another word often used to describe Christ.

15:44 ***natural / spiritual.*** The natural body is that which is animated by the soul (that is, the natural life force), while the spiritual body has as its animating force the Holy Spirit.

15:45–49 Paul explains further the analogy of Adam and Christ (vv. 21–22), his point being that just as humans shared the likeness of Adam's mortal body, they will share the likeness of Christ's spiritual body (v. 48).

15:54–55 ***the saying that is written will come true.*** Paul cites two texts from the OT—Isaiah 25:8 and Hosea 13:14—which have yet to be fulfilled.

15:58 ***my dear brothers.*** Paul's letter is at an end; his chastening is finished, and so it is appropriate that he challenge them to allow this same Christ who has won victories for them to win victories through them. ***your labor ... is not in vain.*** Because the resurrection is real, the future is secure and magnificent.

not the same: Men have one kind of flesh, animals have another, birds another and fish another. 40There are also heavenly bodies and there
are earthly bodies; but the splendor of the heavenly bodies is one kind, and the splendor of the
earthly bodies is another. 41The sun has one kind
of splendor, the moon another and the stars another; and star differs from star in splendor.
42So will it be with the resurrection of the
dead. The body that is sown is perishable, it is
raised imperishable; 43it is sown in dishonor, it is
raised in glory; it is sown in weakness, it is raised
in power; 44it is sown a natural body, it is raised
a spiritual body.
If there is a natural body, there is also a spiritual body. 45So it is written: "The first man Adam
became a living being"[a]; the last Adam, a life-
giving spirit. 46The spiritual did not come first,
but the natural, and after that the spiritual. 47The
first man was of the dust of the earth, the second
man from heaven. 48As was the earthly man, so
are those who are of the earth; and as is the man
from heaven, so also are those who are of heaven.
49And just as we have borne the likeness of the
earthly man, so shall we[b] bear the likeness of
the man from heaven.
50I declare to you, brothers, that flesh and
blood cannot inherit the kingdom of God, nor
does the perishable inherit the imperishable.
51Listen, I tell you a mystery: We will not all
sleep, but we will all be changed— 52in a flash,
in the twinkling of an eye, at the last trumpet. For
the trumpet will sound, the dead will be raised
imperishable, and we will be changed. 53For the
perishable must clothe itself with the imperishable, and the mortal with immortality. 54When
the perishable has been clothed with the imperishable, and the mortal with immortality, then
the saying that is written will come true: "Death
has been swallowed up in victory."[c]

55"Where, O death, is your victory?
Where, O death, is your sting?"[d]

56The sting of death is sin, and the power of sin
is the law. 57But thanks be to God! He gives us
the victory through our Lord Jesus Christ.
58Therefore, my dear brothers, stand firm. Let
nothing move you. Always give yourselves fully
to the work of the Lord, because you know that
your labor in the Lord is not in vain.

The Collection for God's People

16 Now about the collection for God's people: Do what I told the Galatian churches
to do. 2On the first day of every week, each one
of you should set aside a sum of money in keeping with his income, saving it up, so that when I
come no collections will have to be made. 3Then,
when I arrive, I will give letters of introduction to
the men you approve and send them with your
gift to Jerusalem. 4If it seems advisable for me to
go also, they will accompany me.

Personal Requests

5After I go through Macedonia, I will come
to you—for I will be going through Macedonia.
6Perhaps I will stay with you awhile, or even
spend the winter, so that you can help me on my
journey, wherever I go. 7I do not want to see you
now and make only a passing visit; I hope to
spend some time with you, if the Lord permits.
8But I will stay on at Ephesus until Pentecost,
9because a great door for effective work has
opened to me, and there are many who oppose me.
10If Timothy comes, see to it that he has nothing to fear while he is with you, for he is carrying
on the work of the Lord, just as I am. 11No one,
then, should refuse to accept him. Send him on
his way in peace so that he may return to me. I
am expecting him along with the brothers.
12Now about our brother Apollos: I strongly
urged him to go to you with the brothers. He was
quite unwilling to go now, but he will go when
he has the opportunity.
13Be on your guard; stand firm in the faith; be
men of courage; be strong. 14Do everything in
love.
15You know that the household of Stephanas
were the first converts in Achaia, and they have

1 Corinthians 16:1–24

1. Who would you like to get together with that you haven't seen for a long time?
2. How do you feel about giving money to your church? What compels you to give?
3. What do you think Paul's reunion with the Corinthian church was like (vv. 5–7)?
4. What was the greatest "door for effective work" (v. 9) that ever opened for you? What happened?
5. What is God saying to you in this passage?
6. How can this group help you in prayer this week?

[a]*45* Gen. 2:7 [b]*49* Some early manuscripts *so let us* [c]*54* Isaiah 25:8 [d]*55* Hosea 13:14

devoted themselves to the service of the saints. I
urge you, brothers, 16to submit to such as these
and to everyone who joins in the work, and labors at it. 17I was glad when Stephanas, Fortuna-
tus and Achaicus arrived, because they have supplied what was lacking from you. 18For they
refreshed my spirit and yours also. Such men deserve recognition.

Final Greetings

19The churches in the province of Asia send
you greetings. Aquila and Priscilla[a] greet you
warmly in the Lord, and so does the church that
meets at their house. 20All the brothers here send
you greetings. Greet one another with a holy
kiss.

21I, Paul, write this greeting in my own hand.
22If anyone does not love the Lord—a curse be
on him. Come, O Lord[b]!
23The grace of the Lord Jesus be with you.
24My love to all of you in Christ Jesus.
Amen.[c]

[a]*19* Greek *Prisca*, a variant of *Priscilla* [b]*22* In Aramaic the expression *Come, O Lord* is *Marana tha.* [c]*24* Some manuscripts do not have *Amen*.

Introduction to
2 CORINTHIANS

Personal Reading Plan

❐ 2 Corinthians 1:1–2:4
❐ 2 Corinthians 2:5–3:18
❐ 2 Corinthians 4:1–18
❐ 2 Corinthians 5:1–6:2
❐ 2 Corinthians 6:3–7:1
❐ 2 Corinthians 7:2–16
❐ 2 Corinthians 8:1–9:5
❐ 2 Corinthians 9:6–15
❐ 2 Corinthians 10:1–18
❐ 2 Corinthians 11:1–15
❐ 2 Corinthians 11:16–12:10
❐ 2 Corinthians 12:11–13:14

Author

The apostle Paul was the writer of 2 Corinthians.

Date

Paul wrote this letter around A.D. 55–56.

Theme

The strength of weakness.

Historical Background

Paul's first visit to Corinth took place during his second missionary journey. It was then that he founded the Corinthian church. In 2 Corinthians 13:1, Paul proposes a third visit to the city. It seems that his second visit was the cause of much trouble and the reason he wrote 2 Corinthians.

This second visit had been promised in 1 Corinthians 16:1–9. Paul wrote that he would leave Ephesus, journey to Macedonia, and then come down to Corinth on his way to Jerusalem with the collection. As the time drew near to the trip, Paul changed to "Plan B," in which he went straight to Corinth, intending to go from there up to Macedonia and then back to Corinth once again. He thought this would bring the Christians in Corinth great pleasure, since he would be with them twice instead of just once (1:15–16). Instead, his unexpected visit proved so painful (because of a conflict with false apostles), he canceled his return trip from Macedonia. Instead he went back to Ephesus, then north again to Troas, and finally back once more to Macedonia. At Macedonia, he wrote 2 Corinthians to prepare them for a third visit.

Reconstructing the events surrounding the writing of 2 Corinthians is further complicated because Paul wrote at least two other letters to the Corinthians that have not been preserved (see 1 Cor. 5:9; 2 Cor. 2:3–4,9; 7:8–13). Paul wrote one of these letters prior to 1 Corinthians and another (the "sorrowful" letter) in between 1 and 2 Corinthians, probably to explain why he was not returning to Corinth from Macedonia (1:23; 2:4).

Some have suggested that 2 Corinthians may itself be not one but two letters: The fierce tone of chapters 10–13 stands in sharp contrast to the gentle, reconciling tone of chapters 1–9. According to this theory, the first nine chapters (Paul's fourth letter) seem to be based on the report of Titus (7:6–16) that the situation in Corinth had been rectified. But when Titus returned to Corinth with chapters 1–9, he found to his horror that the "super-apostles" were back in charge, so he beat a hasty retreat back to Macedonia. Reacting to the new situation, Paul penned chapters 10–13 (his fifth letter). The fourth and fifth letters were later copied together, since they were so closely related in subject matter, and they became what we know as 2 Corinthians.

Paul's New Opponents

Who then opposed Paul with such vigor during his second "painful" visit? The best guess (and it is only that) is that the troublemakers were not from the Corinthian church itself. Rather, they were a band of outside "apostles" (called cynically by Paul "super-apostles" in 11:5 and 12:11), probably

Jewish Christians from Palestine who sought to conform the Corinthian church to Jewish Law. In any case, they attacked Paul vigorously, calling him two-faced (10:1–11); they questioned his credentials as an apostle; and they criticized him for drawing no financial support from the Corinthians (the way a real apostle would). Apparently Paul's real pain came because the Corinthians did not rally to his support in this conflict. They remained on the sidelines, supporting neither party.

Paul's Pain

In many ways, 2 Corinthians is Paul's most personal letter. He reveals his pain and his joy, his outrage and his suffering, his love and his convictions. Second Corinthians is filled with profound feeling. As C. K. Barrett said: "Writing 2 Corinthians must have come near to breaking Paul, and ... a church that is prepared to read it with him and understand it, may find itself broken too" *(The Second Epistle to the Corinthians: Harper New Testament Commentaries).*

Not only is Paul's pain evident in this letter; but also his toughness. He was willing to fight tooth and nail to wrest the Corinthians from the corrupting influence of the false apostles. "It would have been natural for Paul simply to give up the ungrateful, unruly, unloving, unintelligent Corinthians and leave them to their destiny. There is no indication that this thought ever crossed his mind" (Barrett, *The Second Epistle to the Corinthians,* pp. 32–33). The reason for his tenacity is found in the strength of his calling. He was an apostle—called by God to bring men and women into the kingdom. No band of petty pretenders was going to defeat him in that God-given purpose. He was an apostle and so, of course, he had to write as he did.

Passages for Topical Group Study

1:3–11	SUICIDE TRAGEDY AND DISASTER	The God of All Comfort
4:1–18	SELF-CONFIDENCE DEPRESSION	Treasures in Jars of Clay
5:1–10	ASSISTED SUICIDE AIDS	Our Heavenly Dwelling
5:11–6:2	CONVERSION SHARING YOUR FAITH	The Ministry of Reconciliation
6:14–7:1	DATING—THE WRONG WAY FRIENDS	Do Not Be Yoked With Unbelievers
9:6–15	GIVING	Sowing Generously
11:16–33	WORKING ATTITUDES	Paul Boasts About His Sufferings

See the Lesson Plans in the front of this Bible.

Passages for General Group Study

1:12–2:11	Paul's Change of Plans
2:12–3:6	Ministers of the New Covenant
3:7–18	The Glory of the New Covenant
6:3–13	Paul's Hardships
7:2–16	Paul's Joy
8:1–15	Generosity Encouraged
8:16–9:5	Titus Sent to Corinth
10:1–18	Paul's Defense of His MInistry
11:1–15	Paul and the False Apostles
12:1–10	Paul's Vision and His Thorn
12:11–21	Paul's Concern for the Corinthians
13:1–14	Final Warnings

1 Paul, an apostle of Christ Jesus by the will of
God, and Timothy our brother,

To the church of God in Corinth, together
with all the saints throughout Achaia:

2 Grace and peace to you from God our Father
and the Lord Jesus Christ.

The God of All Comfort

3 Praise be to the God and Father of our Lord
Jesus Christ, the Father of compassion and the
God of all comfort, 4 who comforts us in all our
troubles, so that we can comfort those in any
trouble with the comfort we ourselves have received from God. 5 For just as the sufferings of
Christ flow over into our lives, so also through
Christ our comfort overflows. 6 If we are distressed, it is for your comfort and salvation; if we
are comforted, it is for your comfort, which produces in you patient endurance of the same sufferings we suffer. 7 And our hope for you is firm,
because we know that just as you share in our
sufferings, so also you share in our comfort.

8 We do not want you to be uninformed, brothers, about the hardships we suffered in the province of Asia. We were under great pressure, far
beyond our ability to endure, so that we de-
spaired even of life. 9 Indeed, in our hearts we felt
the sentence of death. But this happened that we
might not rely on ourselves but on God, who
raises the dead. 10 He has delivered us from such
a deadly peril, and he will deliver us. On him we
have set our hope that he will continue to deliver
us, 11 as you help us by your prayers. Then many
will give thanks on our[a] behalf for the gracious
favor granted us in answer to the prayers of
many.

Paul's Change of Plans

12 Now this is our boast: Our conscience testifies that we have conducted ourselves in the
world, and especially in our relations with you, in
the holiness and sincerity that are from God. We
have done so not according to worldly wisdom
but according to God's grace. 13 For we do not
write you anything you cannot read or understand. And I hope that, 14 as you have understood
us in part, you will come to understand fully that
you can boast of us just as we will boast of you in
the day of the Lord Jesus.

15 Because I was confident of this, I planned to
visit you first so that you might benefit twice. 16 I
planned to visit you on my way to Macedonia and
to come back to you from Macedonia, and then to
have you send me on my way to Judea. 17 When
I planned this, did I do it lightly? Or do I make my
plans in a worldly manner so that in the same
breath I say, "Yes, yes" and "No, no"?

2 CORINTHIANS 1:3–11

1. When you were a child, to whom did you go with a hurt finger? What would they do?
2. If you had a personal tragedy now, to whom would you turn?
3. When it comes to sharing pain, are you like Paul, able to tell others (vv. 8–11), or do you keep your pain to yourself?
4. Have you known of someone who committed suicide? What's the most recent tragedy at your school?
5. When have you experienced God's comfort in your life?
6. How has God's comfort enabled you to comfort others?
7. Who is someone you need to be there for this week?
8. Pray for the people you shared about in question #7.

a *11* Many manuscripts *your*

1:3 *comfort.* This word is used 29 times in one form or another in this letter. The word means to actively help, encourage and strengthen someone undergoing trial.

1:4 *our troubles.* This includes both the internal anguish and the physical hardships that Christians experience because of their choice to follow Jesus.

1:5 *our comfort overflows.* In the same way that the suffering of Christ led to benefits that overflow to his people, so the sufferings of Christians enable them to better help others who are afflicted.

1:6 *patient endurance.* This is not grim, bleak acceptance of difficulties, but a hopeful steadfastness in the midst of trial because of the confidence of the Lord's ultimate deliverance (see Col. 1:11).

1:8 *the hardships.* The book of Acts has no record of what was obviously an extremely difficult experience for Paul in Asia. Some commentators think it may refer to the imprisonment in Philippians 1:12–20 where Paul was not certain whether he would live or die. ***great pressure.*** This is to be weighed down like an overloaded ship.

1:9 Whatever the circumstances, Paul was in a situation that was beyond his control. His only hope was in God whom he knew had the power even to raise the dead.

1:11 *prayers.* Part of the value of intercessory prayer is that it leads to greater thanksgiving and glory to God.

18But as surely as God is faithful, our message
to you is not "Yes" and "No." 19For the Son of
God, Jesus Christ, who was preached among you
by me and Silas[a] and Timothy, was not "Yes"
and "No," but in him it has always been "Yes."
20For no matter how many promises God has
made, they are "Yes" in Christ. And so through
him the "Amen" is spoken by us to the glory of
God. 21Now it is God who makes both us and you
stand firm in Christ. He anointed us, 22set his
seal of ownership on us, and put his Spirit in our
hearts as a deposit, guaranteeing what is to come.

2 CORINTHIANS 1:12–2:11

1. From which parent can you bank on a "no" reply? A "yes" reply? Which one waffles? Why is that?
2. In what does Paul boast (1:12)? What is the basis for his integrity?
3. What does it mean that Jesus is the "Yes" of God's promise to us (1:20)?
4. Paraphrase the "business deal" of 1:22 in modern terms. How have you experienced this spiritual "new deal"?
5. What is God saying to you in this passage?
6. How can this group help you in prayer this week?

23I call God as my witness that it was in order
to spare you that I did not return to Corinth.
24Not that we lord it over your faith, but we work
with you for your joy, because it is by faith you
2 stand firm. 1So I made up my mind that I
would not make another painful visit to you.
2For if I grieve you, who is left to make me glad
but you whom I have grieved? 3I wrote as I did so
that when I came I should not be distressed by
those who ought to make me rejoice. I had confidence in all of you, that you would all share my
joy. 4For I wrote you out of great distress and
anguish of heart and with many tears, not to
grieve you but to let you know the depth of my
love for you.

Forgiveness for the Sinner

5If anyone has caused grief, he has not so
much grieved me as he has grieved all of you, to
some extent—not to put it too severely. 6The
punishment inflicted on him by the majority is
sufficient for him. 7Now instead, you ought to
forgive and comfort him, so that he will not be
overwhelmed by excessive sorrow. 8I urge you,
therefore, to reaffirm your love for him. 9The reason I wrote you was to see if you would stand the
test and be obedient in everything. 10If you forgive anyone, I also forgive him. And what I have
forgiven—if there was anything to forgive—I
have forgiven in the sight of Christ for your sake,
11in order that Satan might not outwit us. For we
are not unaware of his schemes.

Ministers of the New Covenant

12Now when I went to Troas to preach the
gospel of Christ and found that the Lord had
opened a door for me, 13I still had no peace of
mind, because I did not find my brother Titus
there. So I said good-by to them and went on to
Macedonia.

2 CORINTHIANS 2:12–3:6

1. What is the most memorable parade you've seen or taken part in?
2. Until Titus returns with "good news" (see 7:6–13), Paul has "no peace of mind" (2:13). What does that say about Paul's concern for this church?
3. How can the same Gospel be either the smell of death or the fragrance of life (2:16)?
4. How can you spread the aroma of Christ in the environment of your home? In your school?
5. What is God saying to you in this passage?
6. How can this group help you in prayer this week?

14But thanks be to God, who always leads us in
triumphal procession in Christ and through us
spreads everywhere the fragrance of the knowledge of him. 15For we are to God the aroma of
Christ among those who are being saved and
those who are perishing. 16To the one we are the
smell of death; to the other, the fragrance of life.
And who is equal to such a task? 17Unlike so
many, we do not peddle the word of God for

[a]19 Greek *Silvanus*, a variant of *Silas*

profit. On the contrary, in Christ we speak before
God with sincerity, like men sent from God.

3 Are we beginning to commend ourselves
again? Or do we need, like some people, letters of recommendation to you or from you? 2You
yourselves are our letter, written on our hearts,
known and read by everybody. 3You show that
you are a letter from Christ, the result of our
ministry, written not with ink but with the Spirit
of the living God, not on tablets of stone but on
tablets of human hearts.
4Such confidence as this is ours through Christ
before God. 5Not that we are competent in ourselves to claim anything for ourselves, but our
competence comes from God. 6He has made us
competent as ministers of a new covenant—not
of the letter but of the Spirit; for the letter kills,
but the Spirit gives life.

The Glory of the New Covenant

7Now if the ministry that brought death,
which was engraved in letters on stone, came
with glory, so that the Israelites could not look
steadily at the face of Moses because of its glory,
fading though it was, 8will not the ministry of the
Spirit be even more glorious? 9If the ministry that
condemns men is glorious, how much more glorious is the ministry that brings righteousness!
10For what was glorious has no glory now in comparison with the surpassing glory. 11And if what
was fading away came with glory, how much
greater is the glory of that which lasts!
12Therefore, since we have such a hope, we
are very bold. 13We are not like Moses, who
would put a veil over his face to keep the Israelites from gazing at it while the radiance was fading away. 14But their minds were made dull, for
to this day the same veil remains when the old
covenant is read. It has not been removed, because only in Christ is it taken away. 15Even to
this day when Moses is read, a veil covers their
hearts. 16But whenever anyone turns to the Lord,
the veil is taken away. 17Now the Lord is the
Spirit, and where the Spirit of the Lord is, there
is freedom. 18And we, who with unveiled faces
all reflect[a] the Lord's glory, are being transformed into his likeness with ever-increasing
glory, which comes from the Lord, who is the
Spirit.

2 CORINTHIANS 3:7–18

1. When did you last experience suddenly understanding something that once confused and puzzled you?
2. How does Paul here (also vv. 3,6) contrast the old and new covenants?
3. Why did that once-glorious covenant of Moses have to be replaced by the everlasting covenant of Christ?
4. What are the practical results of this new covenant (vv. 16–18)?
5. What is God saying to you in this passage?
6. How can this group help you in prayer this week?

Treasures in Jars of Clay

4 Therefore, since through God's mercy we
have this ministry, we do not lose heart.
2Rather, we have renounced secret and shameful
ways; we do not use deception, nor do we distort
the word of God. On the contrary, by setting
forth the truth plainly we commend ourselves to
every man's conscience in the sight of God. 3And
even if our gospel is veiled, it is veiled to those
who are perishing. 4The god of this age has blinded the minds of unbelievers, so that they cannot
see the light of the gospel of the glory of Christ,
who is the image of God. 5For we do not preach
ourselves, but Jesus Christ as Lord, and ourselves

[a]18 Or *contemplate*

4:2 *in the sight of God.* Whatever his critics might say, Paul stands with clear conscience before God, the only judge who really counts.

4:3–4 *veiled to those who are perishing.* The fact that all people do not respond to the Gospel is not because Paul hides it in some way. Rather, it is because they have a veil over their eyes, put there by Satan, so that they do not perceive God's glory demonstrated through the apparent weakness of Jesus.

4:5 *Jesus Christ as Lord.* This is the Gospel's central affirmation (Rom. 10:9–10; 1 Cor. 12:3; Phil. 2:10–11). It implies a commitment to shape one's life in accord with Jesus' character and teaching.

4:7 *jars of clay.* While the Gospel is a glorious treasure, its messengers are like fragile, common, earthenware vessels.

4:8–10 God's power is seen, not in that Paul rides above suffering, but that in the midst of suffering he is continually sustained by God.

4:15 *All this.* That is, Paul's sufferings. The apostles are willing to experience suffering as part of the process through which others (like the Corinthians) come to faith.

4:16–17 *outwardly / inwardly.* Although Paul experiences hardship, he is continually renewed by the hope of the glory that is to come (see also Rom. 8:18).

4:18 *seen / unseen.* Christians are not to shape their lives on the basis of visible standards of success, but in the light of Christ's kingdom.

as your servants for Jesus' sake. 6For God, who said, "Let light shine out of darkness,"[a] made his light shine in our hearts to give us the light of the knowledge of the glory of God in the face of Christ.

7But we have this treasure in jars of clay to show that this all-surpassing power is from God and not from us. 8We are hard pressed on every side, but not crushed; perplexed, but not in despair; 9persecuted, but not abandoned; struck down, but not destroyed. 10We always carry around in our body the death of Jesus, so that the life of Jesus may also be revealed in our body. 11For we who are alive are always being given over to death for Jesus' sake, so that his life may be revealed in our mortal body. 12So then, death is at work in us, but life is at work in you.

13It is written: "I believed; therefore I have spoken."[b] With that same spirit of faith we also believe and therefore speak, 14because we know that the one who raised the Lord Jesus from the dead will also raise us with Jesus and present us with you in his presence. 15All this is for your benefit, so that the grace that is reaching more and more people may cause thanksgiving to overflow to the glory of God.

16Therefore we do not lose heart. Though outwardly we are wasting away, yet inwardly we are being renewed day by day. 17For our light and momentary troubles are achieving for us an eternal glory that far outweighs them all. 18So we fix our eyes not on what is seen, but on what is unseen. For what is seen is temporary, but what is unseen is eternal.

Our Heavenly Dwelling

5 Now we know that if the earthly tent we live in is destroyed, we have a building from God, an eternal house in heaven, not built by human hands. 2Meanwhile we groan, longing to be clothed with our heavenly dwelling, 3because when we are clothed, we will not be found naked. 4For while we are in this tent, we groan and are burdened, because we do not wish to be unclothed but to be clothed with our heavenly dwelling, so that what is mortal may be swallowed up by life. 5Now it is God who has made us for this very purpose and has given us the Spirit as a deposit, guaranteeing what is to come.

6Therefore we are always confident and know that as long as we are at home in the body we are away from the Lord. 7We live by faith, not by sight. 8We are confident, I say, and would prefer

2 Corinthians 4:1–18

1. What's the most valuable thing in your wallet or purse right now?
2. What lifts your spirits when you are down: A song? Ice cream? A Bible verse? Words from a friend?
3. What coach or teacher would you nominate for the Hall of Fame for the way they motivated you in times of defeat?
4. How do you see yourself: As a crystal vase? An empty jar of clay? A jar of clay full of treasure? A paper bag full of last week's lunch?
5. Paul had steadfast confidence in the Lord and his work for the Lord (vv. 13–14). Where do you need more confidence in your life?
6. When tempted to "lose heart," what gives you the strength to go on?
7. Where are you needing help this week in overcoming trouble? How can this group help you?
8. Pray for one another.

(Study notes on page 1077)

[a]*6* Gen. 1:3 [b]*13* Psalm 116:10

5:1 This verse develops the theme of the unseen hope that energizes Paul (see 4:16–18). ***the earthly tent.*** The tent, as a temporary home, is a metaphor for the mortal body which is destroyed by suffering, weakness, and, finally, death. ***building / house.*** A heavenly building was a common image representing all the fullness of God's kingdom (Rev. 21:1–4).

5:5 God's promise for the future is guaranteed by the Holy Spirit. Whatever fears a person may have, the experience of the Holy Spirit guarantees that one day he/she will be with Christ and have a spiritual body.

5:6 ***as long as we are at home in the body we are away from the Lord.*** In this present life, Paul knows that the fullness of God's kingdom has not yet come, hence suffering will be part of the experience "in the body."

5:7 ***faith / sight.*** Christians' priorities are not to be determined by the appearance of things ("sight") but by their hope of God's kingdom ("faith").

5:8 ***would prefer to be away from the body and at home with the Lord.*** This statement is not a death wish but a way of stating that a Christian's orientation toward life is on pursuing God's future.

5:9 In light of believers' confidence and knowledge of the hope to come (v. 6), they desire to honor the Lord.

5:10 Paul underscores the importance of the Christian's goal (v. 9) through this reminder of the ultimate accountability each has before Christ (1 Cor. 3:12–15).

to be away from the body and at home with the
Lord. 9So we make it our goal to please him,
whether we are at home in the body or away
from it. 10For we must all appear before the judgment seat of Christ, that each one may receive
what is due him for the things done while in the
body, whether good or bad.

2 *Corinthians 5:1–10*

1. Where was home when you were a baby?
2. If you were to have a home built, what features would it have?
3. If your body could talk, what would it tell you to do about your lifestyle?
4. If you were a physician, what would you say if one of your patients asked you to end their life?
5. If Paul was alive today, what do you think he would say about assisted suicide?
6. If your friend got AIDS from homosexual contact, how would you deal with this friend?
7. How does knowing your life will be judged (v. 10) affect how you live?
8. How can the group help you in prayer this week?

(Study notes on page 1078)

The Ministry of Reconciliation

11Since, then, we know what it is to fear the
Lord, we try to persuade men. What we are is
plain to God, and I hope it is also plain to your
conscience. 12We are not trying to commend ourselves to you again, but are giving you an opportunity to take pride in us, so that you can answer
those who take pride in what is seen rather than
in what is in the heart. 13If we are out of our
mind, it is for the sake of God; if we are in our
right mind, it is for you. 14For Christ's love compels us, because we are convinced that one died
for all, and therefore all died. 15And he died for
all, that those who live should no longer live for
themselves but for him who died for them and
was raised again.

16So from now on we regard no one from a
worldly point of view. Though we once regarded
Christ in this way, we do so no longer. 17There-

2 *Corinthians 5:11–6:2*

1. If you were appointed to be an ambassador, in what country would you like to serve? Why?
2. When did you come to the place in your life when the "new creation" took the place of your old life?
3. What person was most influential in your spiritual conversion?
4. What does it mean to be reconciled (see note on 5:18)? How does God reconcile us to himself?
5. If the apostle Paul went to your school, how would he go about sharing his faith?
6. In your school, how can you tell the Christians from everyone else?
7. How are you at sharing the story of your spiritual journey of faith with others?
8. What can this group do to help you in the next step in your spiritual life?

a21 Or *be a sin offering* b2 Isaiah 49:8

5:14 ***Christ's love compels us.*** This is what lies behind all that Paul does. Here is his motivation. ***one died for all.*** Christ's love is demonstrated in his death, which was for the benefit of all people.

5:16 ***a worldly point of view.*** One consequence of this new life in Christ is that the believer no longer looks at other people in the light of superficial appearances or on the basis of selfish considerations ("What can I get?") but in terms of love ("What can I give?").

5:17 ***in Christ.*** A favorite phrase of Paul, signifying the union of the believer with Jesus Christ and hence with Jesus' death and resurrection; so that the believer enters into new life. ***a new creation.*** To be in Christ is to be new.

5:18 ***reconciliation.*** The image is of a state of war between two parties, now brought to an end so that peace prevails. Because Christ died, people can be forgiven their sins and therefore they can come back to God.

5:21 ***righteousness.*** This is a legal term meaning that before God believers are acquitted because their guilt has been borne by Jesus. It is because they are justified by Christ that reconciliation is possible.

6:1 ***in vain.*** Christ died for all but it is not true that all will therefore live for him.

6:2 Paul quotes Isaiah 49:8, indicating that this prophecy of a coming day of salvation is now fulfilled. All that remains is to accept the offer of reconciliation.

fore, if anyone is in Christ, he is a new creation;
the old has gone, the new has come! 18All this is
from God, who reconciled us to himself through
Christ and gave us the ministry of reconciliation:
19that God was reconciling the world to himself
in Christ, not counting men's sins against them.
And he has committed to us the message of reconciliation. 20We are therefore Christ's ambassadors, as though God were making his appeal
through us. We implore you on Christ's behalf:
Be reconciled to God. 21God made him who had
no sin to be sin[a] for us, so that in him we might
become the righteousness of God.

6 As God's fellow workers we urge you not to
receive God's grace in vain. 2For he says,

> "In the time of my favor I heard you,
> and in the day of salvation I helped
> you."[b]

I tell you, now is the time of God's favor, now is
the day of salvation.

Paul's Hardships

3We put no stumbling block in anyone's path,
so that our ministry will not be discredited.
4Rather, as servants of God we commend ourselves in every way: in great endurance; in troubles, hardships and distresses; 5in beatings, imprisonments and riots; in hard work, sleepless
nights and hunger; 6in purity, understanding, patience and kindness; in the Holy Spirit and in
sincere love; 7in truthful speech and in the power
of God; with weapons of righteousness in the
right hand and in the left; 8through glory and
dishonor, bad report and good report; genuine,
yet regarded as impostors; 9known, yet regarded
as unknown; dying, and yet we live on; beaten,
and yet not killed; 10sorrowful, yet always rejoicing; poor, yet making many rich; having nothing,
and yet possessing everything.

11We have spoken freely to you, Corinthians,
and opened wide our hearts to you. 12We are
not withholding our affection from you, but you
are withholding yours from us. 13As a fair
exchange—I speak as to my children—open
wide your hearts also.

Do Not Be Yoked With Unbelievers

14Do not be yoked together with unbelievers.
For what do righteousness and wickedness have
in common? Or what fellowship can light have
with darkness? 15What harmony is there between Christ and Belial[a]? What does a believer
have in common with an unbeliever? 16What
agreement is there between the temple of God
and idols? For we are the temple of the living
God. As God has said: "I will live with them and
walk among them, and I will be their God, and
they will be my people."[b]

2 Corinthians 6:3–13

1. What is the greatest physical hardship you've been through?
2. How does Paul defend the authenticity of his ministry here?
3. By appealing to these things instead of his supernatural conversion or miracles (Acts 9:3–5; 19:11–12), what is he saying the real test of faith is?
4. What is Paul asking the Corinthians (and us) to do in verses 11–13 (see 3:2–3)?
5. What is God saying to you in this passage?
6. How can this group pray for you?

2 Corinthians 6:14–7:1

1. When you were 12 years old, who was your TV heartthrob?
2. When has a "friend" gotten you into trouble? What happened?
3. In choosing a date, what do you look for? In choosing a mate, what will be important to you?
4. This past week, were you more yoked to the world or to Christ?
5. What standard have you set for yourself in choosing friends?
6. How can you be a friend to an unbeliever without becoming "yoked"?
7. In what area of your life do you need to "unyoke"—come out and separate?
8. How can the group pray for you and share your yoke?

(Study notes on page 1081)

a 15 Greek *Beliar*, a variant of *Belial*   b 16 Lev. 26:12; Jer. 32:38; Ezek. 37:27

17“Therefore come out from them
and be separate,
says the Lord.
Touch no unclean thing,
and I will receive you.”[a]
18“I will be a Father to you,
and you will be my sons and daughters,
says the Lord Almighty.”[b]

7 Since we have these promises, dear friends,
let us purify ourselves from everything that
contaminates body and spirit, perfecting holiness
out of reverence for God.

Paul's Joy

2Make room for us in your hearts. We have
wronged no one, we have corrupted no one, we
have exploited no one. 3I do not say this to condemn you; I have said before that you have such
a place in our hearts that we would live or die
with you. 4I have great confidence in you; I take
great pride in you. I am greatly encouraged; in all
our troubles my joy knows no bounds.
5For when we came into Macedonia, this body
of ours had no rest, but we were harassed at
every turn—conflicts on the outside, fears within. 6But God, who comforts the downcast, comforted us by the coming of Titus, 7and not only by
his coming but also by the comfort you had given
him. He told us about your longing for me, your
deep sorrow, your ardent concern for me, so that
my joy was greater than ever.
8Even if I caused you sorrow by my letter, I do
not regret it. Though I did regret it—I see that
my letter hurt you, but only for a little while—
9yet now I am happy, not because you were made
sorry, but because your sorrow led you to repentance. For you became sorrowful as God intended
and so were not harmed in any way by us. 10God-
ly sorrow brings repentance that leads to salvation and leaves no regret, but worldly sorrow
brings death. 11See what this godly sorrow has
produced in you: what earnestness, what eagerness to clear yourselves, what indignation, what
alarm, what longing, what concern, what readiness to see justice done. At every point you have
proved yourselves to be innocent in this matter.
12So even though I wrote to you, it was not on
account of the one who did the wrong or of the
injured party, but rather that before God you
could see for yourselves how devoted to us you
are. 13By all this we are encouraged.
In addition to our own encouragement, we
were especially delighted to see how happy Titus
was, because his spirit has been refreshed by all
of you. 14I had boasted to him about you, and you
have not embarrassed me. But just as everything
we said to you was true, so our boasting about
you to Titus has proved to be true as well. 15And
his affection for you is all the greater when he
remembers that you were all obedient, receiving
him with fear and trembling. 16I am glad I can
have complete confidence in you.

2 Corinthians 7:2–16

1. What finally gets your attention: Tough talk? Slammed door? Tears? Letter? Walkout? Give a recent example.
2. Why does Paul want this church to open up to him (vv. 2–4; see 6:11–13)?
3. What was the result of Paul's previous letter to them (vv. 8–13; see also 2:3–4)?
4. In light of his previous hurtful letter, why would he underscore his present joy and confidence (v. 16)? If you were the first to read this, how would you feel?
5. What is God saying to you in this passage?
6. How can this group help you in prayer this week?

[a] *17* Isaiah 52:11; Ezek. 20:34,41 [b] *18* 2 Samuel 7:14; 7:8

Having asked the Corinthians to open their hearts to him, Paul here points out that if they do so it will require a break with the false apostles who proclaim a different gospel.

6:14 ***yoked together.*** The idea of the double yoke has OT roots (Deut. 22:10) where it is forbidden to put an ox and a donkey in the same harness (Lev. 19:19). The point is that the fundamental incompatibility of ox and donkey would make it impossible to plow in a straight line. So too, Christians and pagans bound together would go astray. The nature of the forbidden bonding is not spelled out here but in 1 Corinthians Paul commands that a Christian widow not remarry an unbeliever (7:39); and he forbids eating meals with unbelievers at a pagan temple (10:21).

6:15 The point is that Christianity is exclusive. A person cannot be both a believer and an unbeliever. ***Belial.*** A synonym for Satan.

6:16 ***the temple of God.*** Paul uses this image to refer both to the church and to individual Christians (see 1 Cor. 3:16 and 6:19).

6:17 Having declared God's presence in the midst of the church, Paul points to what such presence demands, namely purity.

6:18 This sentence from 2 Samuel 7:14 was originally addressed to King Solomon. Paul makes it a promise that applies to all God's people (Isa. 43:6).

7:1 ***body and spirit.*** The outer and inner aspects of a person. In other words, keep your whole person pure. Paul calls for the Corinthians to keep their attitudes and actions pure.

Generosity Encouraged

8 And now, brothers, we want you to know
about the grace that God has given the Macedonian churches. 2Out of the most severe trial,
their overflowing joy and their extreme poverty
welled up in rich generosity. 3For I testify that
they gave as much as they were able, and even
beyond their ability. Entirely on their own, 4they
urgently pleaded with us for the privilege of sharing in this service to the saints. 5And they did
not do as we expected, but they gave themselves
first to the Lord and then to us in keeping with
God's will. 6So we urged Titus, since he had
earlier made a beginning, to bring also to completion this act of grace on your part. 7But just
as you excel in everything—in faith, in speech,
in knowledge, in complete earnestness and in your
love for us[a]—see that you also excel in this
grace of giving.

8I am not commanding you, but I want to test
the sincerity of your love by comparing it with
the earnestness of others. 9For you know the
grace of our Lord Jesus Christ, that though he was
rich, yet for your sakes he became poor, so that
you through his poverty might become rich.

2 Corinthians 8:1–15

1. With what are you generous: Your money? Time? Talents? Toys? With what are you stingy?
2. What do you learn about the Macedonians from their giving?
3. How can the equality principle (vv. 13–15) help you decide what cause needs your immediate attention?
4. What does this principle say about getting your own needs met?
5. What is God saying to you in this passage?
6. How can this group help you in prayer this week?

10And here is my advice about what is best for
you in this matter: Last year you were the first
not only to give but also to have the desire to do
so. 11Now finish the work, so that your eager
willingness to do it may be matched by your completion of it, according to your means. 12For if the
willingness is there, the gift is acceptable according to what one has, not according to what he
does not have.

13Our desire is not that others might be relieved while you are hard pressed, but that there
might be equality. 14At the present time your
plenty will supply what they need, so that in turn
their plenty will supply what you need. Then
there will be equality, 15as it is written: "He who
gathered much did not have too much, and he
who gathered little did not have too little."[b]

Titus Sent to Corinth

16I thank God, who put into the heart of Titus
the same concern I have for you. 17For Titus not
only welcomed our appeal, but he is coming to
you with much enthusiasm and on his own initiative. 18And we are sending along with him the
brother who is praised by all the churches for his
service to the gospel. 19What is more, he was
chosen by the churches to accompany us as we
carry the offering, which we administer in order
to honor the Lord himself and to show our eagerness to help. 20We want to avoid any criticism of
the way we administer this liberal gift. 21For we
are taking pains to do what is right, not only in
the eyes of the Lord but also in the eyes of men.

2 Corinthians 8:16–9:5

1. Do you like to save your money or spend it? Why?
2. What commends Titus for his role of ensuring this offering gets to Jerusalem and is used for mission relief work?
3. Why does Paul expect the Corinthians to be generous (9:1–5)? In what ways?
4. If Macedonians came to visit you, would they find your generosity lacking or overflowing? With what else besides money are you generous?
5. What is God saying to you in this passage?
6. How can this group help you in prayer this week?

22In addition, we are sending with them our
brother who has often proved to us in many ways
that he is zealous, and now even more so because

[a] 7 Some manuscripts *in our love for you* [b] 15 Exodus 16:18

of his great confidence in you. 23As for Titus, he
is my partner and fellow worker among you; as
for our brothers, they are representatives of the
churches and an honor to Christ. 24Therefore
show these men the proof of your love and the
reason for our pride in you, so that the churches
can see it.

9 There is no need for me to write to you about
this service to the saints. 2For I know your
eagerness to help, and I have been boasting about
it to the Macedonians, telling them that since last
year you in Achaia were ready to give; and your
enthusiasm has stirred most of them to action.
3But I am sending the brothers in order that our
boasting about you in this matter should not
prove hollow, but that you may be ready, as I said
you would be. 4For if any Macedonians come
with me and find you unprepared, we—not to
say anything about you—would be ashamed of
having been so confident. 5So I thought it necessary to urge the brothers to visit you in advance
and finish the arrangements for the generous gift
you had promised. Then it will be ready as a
generous gift, not as one grudgingly given.

Sowing Generously

6Remember this: Whoever sows sparingly will
also reap sparingly, and whoever sows generously will also reap generously. 7Each man should
give what he has decided in his heart to give, not
reluctantly or under compulsion, for God loves a
cheerful giver. 8And God is able to make all grace
abound to you, so that in all things at all times,
having all that you need, you will abound in every good work. 9As it is written:

> "He has scattered abroad his gifts to the poor;
> his righteousness endures forever."[a]

10Now he who supplies seed to the sower and
bread for food will also supply and increase your
store of seed and will enlarge the harvest of your
righteousness. 11You will be made rich in every
way so that you can be generous on every occasion, and through us your generosity will result
in thanksgiving to God.
12This service that you perform is not only sup-
plying the needs of God's people but is also overflowing in many expressions of thanks to God.

2 Corinthians 9:6–15

1. How much money do you have on you right now? Under what conditions would you give it all away?
2. What's your favorite charity?
3. Do you give money to your church? How regularly?
4. What does Paul mean in verse 6? If you give $100 you will get $1,000 back? Why or why not (see note on 9:6)?
5. Why do you think God cares about someone's attitude when they give?
6. In what ways, other than money, can you give to your church?
7. What is something you are willing to cheerfully give to God?
8. What can this group do in the coming week to give to someone in need?

13Because of the service by which you have
proved yourselves, men will praise God for the
obedience that accompanies your confession of
the gospel of Christ, and for your generosity in
sharing with them and with everyone else. 14And
in their prayers for you their hearts will go out to
you, because of the surpassing grace God has giv-
en you. 15Thanks be to God for his indescribable
gift!

[a]9 Psalm 112:9

9:6 Paul may be quoting a proverb as support for his encouragement for generous giving. It is not that a person can be assured of financial security by giving (and thus obligating God in some way), but that the exercise of the grace of giving leads to growth in grace.

9:7 ***God loves a cheerful giver.*** It is not that giving earns God's love, but that God "approves of" the character of a person who is generous, a common theme in Jewish wisdom literature (see v. 9).

9:8 ***having all that you need.*** This describes a person who is able to live on very little and therefore has few wants. Such a person is then able to give away a great deal to meet the needs of others (see also Phil. 4:11–12).

9:9 Paul quotes from Psalm 112:9 to show that it is important to give to the poor and that giving has an abiding moral quality to it.

9:10–11 Drawing upon Isaiah 55:10 and Hosea 10:12, Paul emphasizes that God supplies the basic needs of people and blesses our gifts when they are shared. ***you will be made rich.*** The purpose of such riches is to facilitate generosity, not to pamper personal indulgences. God could simply fulfill each person's needs directly, but instead works through the giving of others.

9:13–14 Paul explains how giving creates thanksgiving. People praise God because of the obedience they see in his people and because he has answered their prayers and met their needs. This leads them to warmth of fellowship. Giving is good for the health of the whole church!

Paul's Defense of His Ministry

10 By the meekness and gentleness of Christ, I appeal to you—I, Paul, who am "timid" when face to face with you, but "bold" when away! [2]I beg you that when I come I may not have to be as bold as I expect to be toward some people who think that we live by the standards of this world. [3]For though we live in the world, we do not wage war as the world does. [4]The weapons we fight with are not the weapons of the world. On the contrary, they have divine power to demolish strongholds. [5]We demolish arguments and every pretension that sets itself up against the knowledge of God, and we take captive every thought to make it obedient to Christ. [6]And we will be ready to punish every act of disobedience, once your obedience is complete.

2 CORINTHIANS 10:1–18

1. Is "authority" more of a positive or a negative word to you? Why is that?
2. How is Paul discredited (vv. 1–2,9–11)? How is Paul's gentleness and meekness being misunderstood?
3. How is Paul's exercise of authority (vv. 3–8) different than his usurpers, the so-called "super-apostles" (see 11:5,20)?
4. How do you feel about Paul's "reprimand" here in defense of himself? Do you see it as strength or weakness when a person admits his or her limitations? Why?
5. What is God saying to you in this passage?
6. How can this group help you in prayer this week?

[7]You are looking only on the surface of things.[a] If anyone is confident that he belongs to Christ, he should consider again that we belong to Christ just as much as he. [8]For even if I boast somewhat freely about the authority the Lord gave us for building you up rather than pulling you down, I will not be ashamed of it. [9]I do not want to seem to be trying to frighten you with my letters. [10]For some say, "His letters are weighty and forceful, but in person he is unimpressive and his speaking amounts to nothing." [11]Such people should realize that what we are in our letters when we are absent, we will be in our actions when we are present.

[12]We do not dare to classify or compare ourselves with some who commend themselves. When they measure themselves by themselves and compare themselves with themselves, they are not wise. [13]We, however, will not boast beyond proper limits, but will confine our boasting to the field God has assigned to us, a field that reaches even to you. [14]We are not going too far in our boasting, as would be the case if we had not come to you, for we did get as far as you with the gospel of Christ. [15]Neither do we go beyond our limits by boasting of work done by others.[b] Our hope is that, as your faith continues to grow, our area of activity among you will greatly expand, [16]so that we can preach the gospel in the regions beyond you. For we do not want to boast about work already done in another man's territory. [17]But, "Let him who boasts boast in the Lord."[c] [18]For it is not the one who commends himself who is approved, but the one whom the Lord commends.

Paul and the False Apostles

11 I hope you will put up with a little of my foolishness; but you are already doing that. [2]I am jealous for you with a godly jealousy. I promised you to one husband, to Christ, so that I might present you as a pure virgin to him. [3]But I am afraid that just as Eve was deceived by the serpent's cunning, your minds may somehow be led astray from your sincere and pure devotion to Christ. [4]For if someone comes to you and preaches a Jesus other than the Jesus we preached, or if you receive a different spirit from the one you received, or a different gospel from the one you accepted, you put up with it easily enough. [5]But I do not think I am in the least inferior to those "super-apostles." [6]I may not be a trained speaker, but I do have knowledge. We have made this perfectly clear to you in every way.

[7]Was it a sin for me to lower myself in order to elevate you by preaching the gospel of God to you free of charge? [8]I robbed other churches by receiving support from them so as to serve you. [9]And when I was with you and needed something, I was not a burden to anyone, for the brothers who came from Macedonia supplied what I needed. I have kept myself from being a burden to you in any way, and will continue to do so. [10]As surely as the truth of Christ is in me, nobody in the regions of Achaia will stop this

[a]*7* Or *Look at the obvious facts* [b]*13-15* Or *[13]We, however, will not boast about things that cannot be measured, but we will boast according to the standard of measurement that the God of measure has assigned us—a measurement that relates even to you. [14]. . . . [15]Neither do we boast about things that cannot be measured in regard to the work done by others.* [c]*17* Jer. 9:24

boasting of mine. [11]Why? Because I do not love
you? God knows I do! [12]And I will keep on doing
what I am doing in order to cut the ground from
under those who want an opportunity to be considered equal with us in the things they boast
about.
[13]For such men are false apostles, deceitful
workmen, masquerading as apostles of Christ.
[14]And no wonder, for Satan himself masquerades
as an angel of light. [15]It is not surprising, then, if
his servants masquerade as servants of righteousness. Their end will be what their actions deserve.

2 CORINTHIANS 11:1–15

1. What springs to mind when you hear the word "Satan"?
2. What upsets Paul about these "super-apostles"? How does this relate to 6:14?
3. What "different gospel" has at some point pulled you away from Jesus? How did you become aware of its deceitfulness?
4. Sin rarely approaches us as evil, but as "virtue in disguise." From verses 2–4, how can you guard yourself against this satanic strategy?
5. What is God saying to you in this passage?
6. How can this group help you in prayer this week?

Paul Boasts About His Sufferings

[16]I repeat: Let no one take me for a fool. But if
you do, then receive me just as you would a fool,
so that I may do a little boasting. [17]In this self-
confident boasting I am not talking as the Lord
would, but as a fool. [18]Since many are boasting in
the way the world does, I too will boast. [19]You
gladly put up with fools since you are so wise!
[20]In fact, you even put up with anyone who en-
slaves you or exploits you or takes advantage of
you or pushes himself forward or slaps you in the
face. [21]To my shame I admit that we were too
weak for that!
What anyone else dares to boast about—I am
speaking as a fool—I also dare to boast about.
[22]Are they Hebrews? So am I. Are they Israelites?
So am I. Are they Abraham's descendants? So am
I. [23]Are they servants of Christ? (I am out of my

2 CORINTHIANS 11:16–33

1. What is your idea of a dream job?
2. If you were putting together your resume, what would you list as your greatest accomplishment?
3. Do you have a job? What do you do? How many hours a week do you work?
4. What's the biggest hardship you face at work?
5. If you were a career counselor and reviewed Paul's work experience (vv. 23–28), how would you advise him?
6. On a scale from 1 (cool as a cucumber) to 10 (boiling over), what is the stress level in your life at the moment?
7. In what way does God provide relief from stress for you?
8. How can this group pray for you in the coming week?

mind to talk like this.) I am more. I have worked
much harder, been in prison more frequently,
been flogged more severely, and been exposed to
death again and again. [24]Five times I received

Paul's boasting was forced on him in order to show that in no way (heritage, calling, sacrifice for the Gospel) are the false apostles superior to him. Boasting reflects more of a worldly attitude than a Christlike character, and Paul was embarrassed by it.

11:21 ***we were too weak.*** In contrast to the assertive confidence of the false apostles stands Paul's own weakness: "weakness" that refuses to exploit others because that is not the Gospel way.

11:23–33 Having listed his Jewish credentials, Paul next turns to his qualifications as a Christian and how he has suffered greatly as the servant of Christ. As a pioneer missionary his life has been fraught with danger and toil. The accounts in Acts give but sketchy information about Paul, so it is not always possible to know specifically to what Paul refers in each incident.

11:28 Paul moves from physical to psychological discomfort. He felt a deep responsibility for the churches he started.

11:29 ***weak.*** All these pressures make Paul feel weaker than anyone at times. Paul's "boasting" has been about his unimpressive speech, his poor appearance, his poverty, his hardships and his inner turmoil. ***inwardly burn.*** In his concern for the churches, a constant source of anguish is over those who have been led astray from the faith.

11:30–33 To wrap up the stories of his weakness, Paul recounts an incident that was especially humiliating (Acts 9:23–25). The mighty apostle, far from being heralded with glory, was reduced to hiding in a basket.

from the Jews the forty lashes minus one.
25Three times I was beaten with rods, once I was
stoned, three times I was shipwrecked, I spent a
night and a day in the open sea, 26I have been
constantly on the move. I have been in danger
from rivers, in danger from bandits, in danger
from my own countrymen, in danger from Gentiles; in danger in the city, in danger in the country, in danger at sea; and in danger from false
brothers. 27I have labored and toiled and have
often gone without sleep; I have known hunger
and thirst and have often gone without food; I
have been cold and naked. 28Besides everything
else, I face daily the pressure of my concern for
all the churches. 29Who is weak, and I do not feel
weak? Who is led into sin, and I do not inwardly
burn?

30If I must boast, I will boast of the things that
show my weakness. 31The God and Father of the
Lord Jesus, who is to be praised forever, knows
that I am not lying. 32In Damascus the governor
under King Aretas had the city of the Dama-
scenes guarded in order to arrest me. 33But I was
lowered in a basket from a window in the wall
and slipped through his hands.

Paul's Vision and His Thorn

12 I must go on boasting. Although there is
nothing to be gained, I will go on to visions and revelations from the Lord. 2I know a
man in Christ who fourteen years ago was caught
up to the third heaven. Whether it was in the
body or out of the body I do not know—God
knows. 3And I know that this man—whether in
the body or apart from the body I do not know,
but God knows— 4was caught up to paradise. He
heard inexpressible things, things that man is not
permitted to tell. 5I will boast about a man like
that, but I will not boast about myself, except
about my weaknesses. 6Even if I should choose to
boast, I would not be a fool, because I would be
speaking the truth. But I refrain, so no one will
think more of me than is warranted by what I do
or say.

7To keep me from becoming conceited because of these surpassingly great revelations,
there was given me a thorn in my flesh, a messenger of Satan, to torment me. 8Three times I
pleaded with the Lord to take it away from me.
9But he said to me, "My grace is sufficient for
you, for my power is made perfect in weakness."
Therefore I will boast all the more gladly about
my weaknesses, so that Christ's power may rest
on me. 10That is why, for Christ's sake, I delight
in weaknesses, in insults, in hardships, in persecutions, in difficulties. For when I am weak, then
I am strong.

Paul's Concern for the Corinthians

11I have made a fool of myself, but you drove
me to it. I ought to have been commended by
you, for I am not in the least inferior to the
"super-apostles," even though I am nothing.
12The things that mark an apostle—signs, wonders and miracles—were done among you with
great perseverance. 13How were you inferior to
the other churches, except that I was never a
burden to you? Forgive me this wrong!

14Now I am ready to visit you for the third
time, and I will not be a burden to you, because
what I want is not your possessions but you. After
all, children should not have to save up for their
parents, but parents for their children. 15So I will
very gladly spend for you everything I have and
expend myself as well. If I love you more, will
you love me less? 16Be that as it may, I have not
been a burden to you. Yet, crafty fellow that I am,
I caught you by trickery! 17Did I exploit you
through any of the men I sent you? 18I urged
Titus to go to you and I sent our brother with
him. Titus did not exploit you, did he? Did we
not act in the same spirit and follow the same
course?

19Have you been thinking all along that we
have been defending ourselves to you? We have
been speaking in the sight of God as those in
Christ; and everything we do, dear friends, is for
your strengthening. 20For I am afraid that when

2 Corinthians 12:1–10

1. How often do you remember your dreams? What was your most recent or bizarre dream?
2. So far, how has Paul authenticated his apostleship (see 11:21–30; 6:3–10)? How would this sound if you read it on a minister's resume?
3. How has Paul's "thorn" affected his life?
4. How do you react when God appears to be silent in answer to your urgent request? How do you feel about God's promise in verse 9? Why doesn't God simply take the hurt away?
5. What is God saying to you in this passage?
6. How can this group help you in prayer this week?

I come I may not find you as I want you to be, and
you may not find me as you want me to be. I fear
that there may be quarreling, jealousy, outbursts
of anger, factions, slander, gossip, arrogance and
disorder. [21]I am afraid that when I come again my
God will humble me before you, and I will be
grieved over many who have sinned earlier and
have not repented of the impurity, sexual sin and
debauchery in which they have indulged.

2 *Corinthians 12:11–21*

1. What is one way your parents have sacrificed for you? How do you feel about that unselfish sacrifice?
2. What led Paul to write this letter (vv. 11–13)? How have the false "super-apostles" distorted his ministry (see also 2:17; 11:7)?
3. How would you feel about visiting a ministry you love which is behaving like verses 20–21? How persistent would you be in loving them?
4. To whom is God leading you to minister? How can you show the spirit of verses 14–15 to them?
5. What is God saying to you in this passage?
6. How can this group help you in prayer this week?

Final Warnings

13 This will be my third visit to you. "Every
matter must be established by the testimony of two or three witnesses."[a] [2]I already
gave you a warning when I was with you the
second time. I now repeat it while absent: On my
return I will not spare those who sinned earlier
or any of the others, [3]since you are demanding
proof that Christ is speaking through me. He is
not weak in dealing with you, but is powerful
among you. [4]For to be sure, he was crucified in
weakness, yet he lives by God's power. Likewise,
we are weak in him, yet by God's power we will
live with him to serve you.
[5]Examine yourselves to see whether you are in
the faith; test yourselves. Do you not realize that
Christ Jesus is in you—unless, of course, you fail
the test? [6]And I trust that you will discover that
we have not failed the test. [7]Now we pray to God
that you will not do anything wrong. Not that
people will see that we have stood the test but
that you will do what is right even though we
may seem to have failed. [8]For we cannot do anything against the truth, but only for the truth.
[9]We are glad whenever we are weak but you are
strong; and our prayer is for your perfection.
[10]This is why I write these things when I am
absent, that when I come I may not have to be
harsh in my use of authority—the authority the
Lord gave me for building you up, not for tearing
you down.

Final Greetings

[11]Finally, brothers, good-by. Aim for perfection, listen to my appeal, be of one mind, live in
peace. And the God of love and peace will be
with you.
[12]Greet one another with a holy kiss. [13]All the
saints send their greetings.
[14]May the grace of the Lord Jesus Christ, and
the love of God, and the fellowship of the Holy
Spirit be with you all.

2 *Corinthians 13:1–14*

1. What do you do to prepare yourself for big exams?
2. Paul prefers to come to them in "the gentleness and meekness of Christ" (10:1), and as a loving parent (12:14–15). How will he come, instead, if repentance has not occurred? How does this relate to the ministry of Jesus?
3. What does Paul hope for as he considers his upcoming visit (vv. 10–11)?
4. In which area of your spiritual life will you aim for "perfection" (13:9) this week? In which area will you be content with "weakness" (12:9–10)?
5. What is God saying to you in this passage?
6. How can this group help you in prayer this week?

[a]*1* Deut. 19:15

Introduction to
GALATIANS

Personal Reading Plan

- ❐ Galatians 1:1–24
- ❐ Galatians 2:1–21
- ❐ Galatians 3:1–25
- ❐ Galatians 3:26–4:20
- ❐ Galatians 4:21–5:15
- ❐ Galatians 5:16–6:18

Author
The apostle Paul was the author of Galatians.

Date
The date of Paul's epistle depends on whether he was writing to churches in North or South Galatia. If Paul had been writing to congregations in North Galatia, the letter could not have been written before his third missionary expedition after the journey mentioned in Acts 16:6 and 18:23, around A.D. 55. On the other hand, if Paul were writing to the churches in the southern region, the epistle to the Galatians is his earliest letter—written in A.D. 48 or 49, possibly while he was in Syrian Antioch just prior to the Council in Jerusalem (Acts 15:6–21).

Theme
Justification by faith alone.

Historical Background
Paul tells us he is writing "to the churches in Galatia" (1:2). But where are these churches located? This is a problem, because in 25 B.C. the Romans created a new imperial province that they named Galatia. This new province was made up of the original kingdom of Galatia plus a new region to the south forged out of territory originally belonging to six other regions. So when a first-century writer speaks of Galatia, it is not always clear whether he is referring to the original territory in the north or the new province extending southward—which included the cities of Pisidian Antioch, Iconium, Lystra and Derbe that Paul visited during his first missionary journey described in Acts 13–14.

Characteristics
Paul was furious and he didn't care who knew it. "You foolish Galatians!" he cried. "Who has bewitched you?" (3:1). He felt so strongly because the issue he was addressing in this letter was not a minor matter of church policy. It struck right to the heart of the Gospel.

Apparently some legalistic Jewish Christians (Judaizers) had been stirring up trouble. They had twisted the Gospel into something Jesus never intended, and then they had made false charges against Paul. "Who is that fellow, anyway. He wasn't one of the Twelve. He is a self-appointed apostle. No wonder he left out some crucial parts of the message. Let us set you straight ..." And the Galatians were taken in, so it seems. Paul wrote, "I am astonished that you are so quickly deserting the one who called you by the grace of Christ and are turning to a different gospel" (1:6).

What were the Judaizers saying? At first glance, they seemed to be adding only a little to the message. "Believe in Christ," they were saying (they were Christians), "but also be circumcised" (6:12). Now to be circumcised was not such a high requirement, but Paul saw the implications. If the Galatians let themselves be circumcised, it would be but the first step back to keeping the whole Law (5:3). This is slavery (4:9). This is bondage (5:1). This is not the Gospel. The Gospel is that salvation is a free gift, by grace. If you add anything else to grace, salvation is no longer free. It then becomes a matter of doing the "other thing."

The core issue in Galatians is justification. How does a person gain right standing before God? The Judaizers said that Christ (grace) plus circumcision (Law-keeping) equals right standing. Paul's equation was different. Christ (grace) plus *nothing else* equals right standing. Works are excluded from Paul's equation. "Know that a man is not justified by observing the law, but by faith in Jesus Christ. So we, too, have put our faith in Christ Jesus that we may be justified by faith in Christ and not by observing the law, because by observing the law no one will be justified" (2:16). This key verse sums up Paul's argument.

The Implications

To the modern reader, it may seem, at times, as if Paul is getting worked up over a relatively small issue. After all, the important thing is to believe in Jesus, and all the parties agreed to that. But in fact, as history demonstrated, this issue was profound. Paul's concerns were more than validated. Was Christianity for all people in all cultures (as Paul was arguing), or was it only a Jewish sect? To be a Christian, did you have to accept Jewish customs and submit to Jewish laws? If so, if the Judaizers had won, Christianity would probably have died out in the first century.

As we know, Christianity did not disappear along with all the Palestinian sects. Rather, the church was able to expand into the Graeco-Roman world because the Gospel was truly universal. It was not tied to temple sacrifice and the Law of Moses, about which most pagans neither knew nor cared. The Judaizers wanted a Christianity circumcised by Jewish exclusiveness, taboos and customs—in which Gentile believers would always be second-class citizens. Paul fought this with vehemence and passion, as had other believers from Stephen onward; so Christianity became the transcultural world religion Christ intended (Matt. 28:19–20).

The Relationship Between Galatians and Romans

It is obvious that there is a close thematic connection between Galatians and Romans. Galatians appears to be Paul's first attempt at wrestling with the issue of justification by faith alone. Paul does so in the context of having to deal with a local problem. Romans, on the other hand, is a more studied consideration of the same issue. It is an eloquent, carefully stated, logical argument, which stands as one of the finest pieces of theological writing ever penned.

Structure

After a terse greeting (1:1–5) and pronouncement of condemnation against the troublemakers (1:6–10), Paul launches into his first major theme: his *personal defense,* in which he deals with the charge that he is not a real apostle (1:11–2:21). This is followed by a *doctrinal defense,* in which he shows that Christianity lived under the Law is inferior to Christianity lived by faith (3:1–4:31). On the basis of these two arguments, he then shows what true Christian freedom is (5:1–6:10), ending with an unusual conclusion written in his own hand (6:11–18).

Passages for Topical Group Study

5:16–26	NO COMPROMISE DRUGS / ALCOHOL	Life By the Spirit
6:1–10	ACCOUNTABILITY TEEN PREGNANCY	Doing Good to All

See the Lesson Plans in the front of this Bible.

Passages for General Group Study

1:1–10	No Other Gospel	3:15–25	The Law and the Promise
1:11–24	Paul Called by God	3:26–4:7	Sons of God
2:1–10	Paul Accepted by the Apostles	4:8–20	Paul's Concern for the Galatians
2:11–21	Paul Opposes Peter	4:21–31	Hagar and Sarah
3:1–14	Faith or Observance of the Law	5:1–15	Freedom in Christ

1 Paul, an apostle—sent not from men nor by
man, but by Jesus Christ and God the Father,
who raised him from the dead— 2and all the
brothers with me,

To the churches in Galatia:

3Grace and peace to you from God our Father
and the Lord Jesus Christ, 4who gave himself for
our sins to rescue us from the present evil age,
according to the will of our God and Father, 5to
whom be glory for ever and ever. Amen.

No Other Gospel

6I am astonished that you are so quickly deserting the one who called you by the grace of
Christ and are turning to a different gospel—
7which is really no gospel at all. Evidently some
people are throwing you into confusion and are
trying to pervert the gospel of Christ. 8But even
if we or an angel from heaven should preach a
gospel other than the one we preached to you, let
him be eternally condemned! 9As we have already said, so now I say again: If anybody is
preaching to you a gospel other than what you
accepted, let him be eternally condemned!
10Am I now trying to win the approval of men,
or of God? Or am I trying to please men? If I were
still trying to please men, I would not be a servant of Christ.

GALATIANS 1:1–10

1. When you're upset with someone, do you usually give them a long lecture, a "piece of your mind," or the "silent treatment"?
2. What did Jesus voluntarily do for Paul and the Galatians ... and us (v. 4)?
3. What does Paul say will happen to anyone who promotes a "gospel" other than that which Paul preached—the good news of grace (vv. 8–9)?
4. Have you ever "deserted" God like some of the Galatians did?
5. What is God saying to you in this passage?
6. How can this group help you in prayer this week?

Paul Called by God

11I want you to know, brothers, that the gospel
I preached is not something that man made up.
12I did not receive it from any man, nor was I
taught it; rather, I received it by revelation from
Jesus Christ.
13For you have heard of my previous way of
life in Judaism, how intensely I persecuted the
church of God and tried to destroy it. 14I was
advancing in Judaism beyond many Jews of my
own age and was extremely zealous for the traditions of my fathers. 15But when God, who set me
apart from birth[a] and called me by his grace,
was pleased 16to reveal his Son in me so that I
might preach him among the Gentiles, I did not
consult any man, 17nor did I go up to Jerusalem
to see those who were apostles before I was, but
I went immediately into Arabia and later returned to Damascus.

GALATIANS 1:11–24

1. When you were in grade school, what did you want to be when you grew up?
2. How was Paul's life changed?
3. By whom (and what) was Paul called (v. 15)? What was he specifically called to do (v. 16)?
4. If you had to argue for the reality of the Gospel by giving one example of how you have changed as a result of your faith, what would you share?
5. What is God saying to you in this passage?
6. How can this group help you in prayer this week?

18Then after three years, I went up to Jerusalem to get acquainted with Peter[b] and stayed
with him fifteen days. 19I saw none of the
other apostles—only James, the Lord's brother.
20I assure you before God that what I am writing you is no lie. 21Later I went to Syria and Cilicia. 22I was personally unknown to the churches
of Judea that are in Christ. 23They only heard
the report: "The man who formerly persecuted
us is now preaching the faith he once tried
to destroy." 24And they praised God because
of me.

[a] *15* Or *from my mother's womb* [b] *18* Greek *Cephas*

Paul Accepted by the Apostles

2 Fourteen years later I went up again to Jerusalem, this time with Barnabas. I took Titus
along also. 2I went in response to a revelation and
set before them the gospel that I preach among
the Gentiles. But I did this privately to those who
seemed to be leaders, for fear that I was running
or had run my race in vain. 3Yet not even Titus,
who was with me, was compelled to be circumcised, even though he was a Greek. 4⌊This matter
arose⌋ because some false brothers had infiltrated
our ranks to spy on the freedom we have in
Christ Jesus and to make us slaves. 5We did not
give in to them for a moment, so that the truth of
the gospel might remain with you.

Galatians 2:1–10

1. Are you the type of person who usually "goes with the crowd" or "does your own thing"?
2. If Paul's converts had to become Jews to be Christians, what would that have done to Paul's ministry to the Gentiles (v. 2)? What would be different about the church today?
3. What did the spiritual "pillars" of the Jerusalem church recognize about Paul (v. 9)?
4. How does caring for the poor (v. 10) relate to proclaiming the Gospel of grace?
5. What is God saying to you in this passage?
6. How can this group help you in prayer this week?

6As for those who seemed to be important—
whatever they were makes no difference to me;
God does not judge by external appearance—
those men added nothing to my message. 7On
the contrary, they saw that I had been entrusted
with the task of preaching the gospel to the Gentiles,[a] just as Peter had been to the Jews.[b] 8For
God, who was at work in the ministry of Peter as
an apostle to the Jews, was also at work in my
ministry as an apostle to the Gentiles. 9James,
Peter[c] and John, those reputed to be pillars,
gave me and Barnabas the right hand of fellowship when they recognized the grace given to me.
They agreed that we should go to the Gentiles,
and they to the Jews. 10All they asked was that
we should continue to remember the poor, the
very thing I was eager to do.

Paul Opposes Peter

11When Peter came to Antioch, I opposed him
to his face, because he was clearly in the wrong.
12Before certain men came from James, he used
to eat with the Gentiles. But when they arrived,
he began to draw back and separate himself from
the Gentiles because he was afraid of those who
belonged to the circumcision group. 13The other
Jews joined him in his hypocrisy, so that by their
hypocrisy even Barnabas was led astray.
14When I saw that they were not acting in line
with the truth of the gospel, I said to Peter in
front of them all, "You are a Jew, yet you live like
a Gentile and not like a Jew. How is it, then, that
you force Gentiles to follow Jewish customs?
15"We who are Jews by birth and not 'Gentile
sinners' 16know that a man is not justified by
observing the law, but by faith in Jesus Christ. So
we, too, have put our faith in Christ Jesus that we
may be justified by faith in Christ and not by
observing the law, because by observing the law
no one will be justified.

Galatians 2:11–21

1. Have you ever "told off" your parents or other adult? What was the outcome?
2. What would it take for you to stand up at a dinner party and rebuke the recognized leader of the whole church (v. 14)?
3. In the Christian life, what dies and what gets resurrected (vv. 19–20)? How is that made possible?
4. Applying the spiritual concept of verse 20, who is "alive" in your life right now—"I," or "Christ in me"?
5. What is God saying to you in this passage?
6. How can this group help you in prayer this week?

17"If, while we seek to be justified in Christ, it
becomes evident that we ourselves are sinners,
does that mean that Christ promotes sin? Absolutely not! 18If I rebuild what I destroyed, I prove

[a]7 Greek *uncircumcised* [b]7 Greek *circumcised*; also in verses 8 and 9 [c]9 Greek *Cephas*; also in verses 11 and 14

that I am a lawbreaker. 19For through the law I died to the law so that I might live for God. 20I have been crucified with Christ and I no longer live, but Christ lives in me. The life I live in the body, I live by faith in the Son of God, who loved me and gave himself for me. 21I do not set aside the grace of God, for if righteousness could be gained through the law, Christ died for nothing!"[a]

Faith or Observance of the Law

3 You foolish Galatians! Who has bewitched you? Before your very eyes Jesus Christ was clearly portrayed as crucified. 2I would like to learn just one thing from you: Did you receive the Spirit by observing the law, or by believing what you heard? 3Are you so foolish? After beginning with the Spirit, are you now trying to attain your goal by human effort? 4Have you suffered so much for nothing—if it really was for nothing? 5Does God give you his Spirit and work miracles among you because you observe the law, or because you believe what you heard?

Galatians 3:1–14

1. What physical or personality traits have been passed on to you from your family?
2. Was Abraham considered righteous by God through his faith or through his works (vv. 5–9)?
3. What "additions" to faith might outsiders sense in your Christian circles regarding what they should do to be approved? How can you help break down these barriers?
4. How does Jesus solve this problem for us (vv. 13–14)?
5. What is God saying to you in this passage?
6. How can this group help you in prayer this week?

6Consider Abraham: "He believed God, and it was credited to him as righteousness."[b] 7Understand, then, that those who believe are children of Abraham. 8The Scripture foresaw that God would justify the Gentiles by faith, and announced the gospel in advance to Abraham: "All nations will be blessed through you."[c] 9So those who have faith are blessed along with Abraham, the man of faith.

10All who rely on observing the law are under a curse, for it is written: "Cursed is everyone who does not continue to do everything written in the Book of the Law."[d] 11Clearly no one is justified before God by the law, because, "The righteous will live by faith."[e] 12The law is not based on faith; on the contrary, "The man who does these things will live by them."[f] 13Christ redeemed us from the curse of the law by becoming a curse for us, for it is written: "Cursed is everyone who is hung on a tree."[g] 14He redeemed us in order that the blessing given to Abraham might come to the Gentiles through Christ Jesus, so that by faith we might receive the promise of the Spirit.

The Law and the Promise

15Brothers, let me take an example from everyday life. Just as no one can set aside or add to a human covenant that has been duly established, so it is in this case. 16The promises were spoken to Abraham and to his seed. The Scripture does not say "and to seeds," meaning many people, but "and to your seed,"[h] meaning one person, who is Christ. 17What I mean is this: The law, introduced 430 years later, does not set aside the covenant previously established by God and thus

Galatians 3:15–25

1. In your family, how far back can you trace your spiritual roots?
2. Can the Old Testament Law give "life" (v. 21)? Who can? How (v. 22)?
3. How would you share this passage with someone who thinks keeping the Ten Commandments or Golden Rule is enough to be right with God? Or to someone who was brought up believing that keeping rules wins approval?
4. How has, and is, your faith liberating you from this spiritual bondage?
5. What is God saying to you in this passage?
6. How can this group help you in prayer this week?

a21 Some interpreters end the quotation after verse 14. b6 Gen. 15:6 c8 Gen. 12:3; 18:18; 22:18 d10 Deut. 27:26
e11 Hab. 2:4 f12 Lev. 18:5 g13 Deut. 21:23 h16 Gen. 12:7; 13:15; 24:7

do away with the promise. [18]For if the inheritance depends on the law, then it no longer depends on a promise; but God in his grace gave it
to Abraham through a promise.
[19]What, then, was the purpose of the law? It
was added because of transgressions until the
Seed to whom the promise referred had come.
The law was put into effect through angels by a
mediator. [20]A mediator, however, does not represent just one party; but God is one.
[21]Is the law, therefore, opposed to the promises of God? Absolutely not! For if a law had been
given that could impart life, then righteousness
would certainly have come by the law. [22]But the
Scripture declares that the whole world is a prisoner of sin, so that what was promised, being
given through faith in Jesus Christ, might be giv-
en to those who believe.
[23]Before this faith came, we were held prisoners by the law, locked up until faith should be
revealed. [24]So the law was put in charge to lead
us to Christ[a] that we might be justified by faith.
[25]Now that faith has come, we are no longer under the supervision of the law.

Sons of God

[26]You are all sons of God through faith in
Christ Jesus, [27]for all of you who were baptized
into Christ have clothed yourselves with Christ.
[28]There is neither Jew nor Greek, slave nor free,
male nor female, for you are all one in Christ
Jesus. [29]If you belong to Christ, then you are
Abraham's seed, and heirs according to the promise.

GALATIANS 3:26–4:7

1. How affectionate is your relationship with your parents?
2. What does it take to become a child of God?
3. What effect does being "in Christ" have on relationships among believers (3:28)?
4. Do you feel more like a "slave" or a "son" (4:7)? Is your heart filled more with frustration or with the fellowship of God's Spirit?
5. What is God saying to you in this passage?
6. How can this group help you in prayer this week?

4 What I am saying is that as long as the heir
is a child, he is no different from a slave,
although he owns the whole estate. [2]He is subject to guardians and trustees until the time set
by his father. [3]So also, when we were children,
we were in slavery under the basic principles of
the world. [4]But when the time had fully come,
God sent his Son, born of a woman, born under
law, [5]to redeem those under law, that we might
receive the full rights of sons. [6]Because you are
sons, God sent the Spirit of his Son into our
hearts, the Spirit who calls out, *"Abba,*[b] Father." [7]So you are no longer a slave, but a son;
and since you are a son, God has made you also
an heir.

Paul's Concern for the Galatians

[8]Formerly, when you did not know God, you
were slaves to those who by nature are not gods.
[9]But now that you know God—or rather are
known by God—how is it that you are turning
back to those weak and miserable principles? Do
you wish to be enslaved by them all over again?
[10]You are observing special days and months and
seasons and years! [11]I fear for you, that somehow
I have wasted my efforts on you.

GALATIANS 4:8–20

1. What is one of your most compulsive habits? How are you trying to break it?
2. Overall, was Paul more concerned for himself or the Galatians?
3. How would you like for Paul to be your "apostle"?
4. Like the Galatians, have you slipped back into any bad habits or old ways, from which Christ once delivered you? Which ones? What can you do about it?
5. What is God saying to you in this passage?
6. How can this group help you in prayer this week?

[12]I plead with you, brothers, become like me,
for I became like you. You have done me no
wrong. [13]As you know, it was because of an illness that I first preached the gospel to you.
[14]Even though my illness was a trial to you, you

[a]24 Or *charge until Christ came* [b]6 Aramaic for *Father*

did not treat me with contempt or scorn. Instead,
you welcomed me as if I were an angel of God, as
if I were Christ Jesus himself. [15]What has happened to all your joy? I can testify that, if you
could have done so, you would have torn out
your eyes and given them to me. [16]Have I now
become your enemy by telling you the truth?
[17]Those people are zealous to win you over,
but for no good. What they want is to alienate
you ⌊from us⌋, so that you may be zealous for
them. [18]It is fine to be zealous, provided the purpose is good, and to be so always and not just
when I am with you. [19]My dear children, for
whom I am again in the pains of childbirth until
Christ is formed in you, [20]how I wish I could be
with you now and change my tone, because I am
perplexed about you!

Hagar and Sarah

[21]Tell me, you who want to be under the law,
are you not aware of what the law says? [22]For it
is written that Abraham had two sons, one by the
slave woman and the other by the free woman.

> ***Galatians 4:21–31***
>
> 1. What story do your parents tell about your birth?
> 2. What do you remember being extraordinary about Isaac's birth (Gen. 21:1–7)?
> 3. Why does Paul turn the tables on this story and indicate that the Jews are actually the ones in slavery with Hagar—their slave woman mother (v. 25)?
> 4. How can you live out your "freedom" in Christ, and still please him with your sacrificial obedience?
> 5. What is God saying to you in this passage?
> 6. How can this group help you in prayer this week?

[23]His son by the slave woman was born in the
ordinary way; but his son by the free woman was
born as the result of a promise.
[24]These things may be taken figuratively, for
the women represent two covenants. One covenant is from Mount Sinai and bears children
who are to be slaves: This is Hagar. [25]Now Hagar
stands for Mount Sinai in Arabia and corresponds
to the present city of Jerusalem, because she is in
slavery with her children. [26]But the Jerusalem
that is above is free, and she is our mother. [27]For
it is written:

"Be glad, O barren woman,
  who bears no children;
break forth and cry aloud,
  you who have no labor pains;
because more are the children of the desolate
  woman
  than of her who has a husband."[a]

[28]Now you, brothers, like Isaac, are children of
promise. [29]At that time the son born in the ordinary way persecuted the son born by the power
of the Spirit. It is the same now. [30]But what does
the Scripture say? "Get rid of the slave woman
and her son, for the slave woman's son will never
share in the inheritance with the free woman's
son."[b] [31]Therefore, brothers, we are not children of the slave woman, but of the free woman.

Freedom in Christ

5 It is for freedom that Christ has set us free.
Stand firm, then, and do not let yourselves
be burdened again by a yoke of slavery.

> ***Galatians 5:1–15***
>
> 1. How do you feel when others cut in front of you in line? What do you do?
> 2. What does Paul mean by a "yoke of slavery" (v. 1)?
> 3. Since our own efforts and achievements aren't the way to God, what is (vv. 5–6)?
> 4. Ironically, though we have been liberated from slavery, what kind of servants do we become (vv. 13–15)? How good of this kind of servant are you?
> 5. What is God saying to you in this passage?
> 6. How can this group help you in prayer this week?

[2]Mark my words! I, Paul, tell you that if you let
yourselves be circumcised, Christ will be of no
value to you at all. [3]Again I declare to every man
who lets himself be circumcised that he is obli-

[a]27 Isaiah 54:1 [b]30 Gen. 21:10

gated to obey the whole law. 4You who are trying
to be justified by law have been alienated from
Christ; you have fallen away from grace. 5But by
faith we eagerly await through the Spirit the righteousness for which we hope. 6For in Christ Jesus
neither circumcision nor uncircumcision has any
value. The only thing that counts is faith expressing itself through love.
7You were running a good race. Who cut in on
you and kept you from obeying the truth? 8That
kind of persuasion does not come from the one
who calls you. 9"A little yeast works through the
whole batch of dough." 10I am confident in the
Lord that you will take no other view. The one
who is throwing you into confusion will pay the
penalty, whoever he may be. 11Brothers, if I am
still preaching circumcision, why am I still being
persecuted? In that case the offense of the cross
has been abolished. 12As for those agitators, I
wish they would go the whole way and emascu-
late themselves!
13You, my brothers, were called to be free. But
do not use your freedom to indulge the sinful
nature[a]; rather, serve one another in love.
14The entire law is summed up in a single command: "Love your neighbor as yourself."[b] 15If
you keep on biting and devouring each other,
watch out or you will be destroyed by each other.

Life by the Spirit

16So I say, live by the Spirit, and you will not
gratify the desires of the sinful nature. 17For the
sinful nature desires what is contrary to the Spirit, and the Spirit what is contrary to the sinful
nature. They are in conflict with each other, so
that you do not do what you want. 18But if you
are led by the Spirit, you are not under law.
19The acts of the sinful nature are obvious:
sexual immorality, impurity and debauchery;
20idolatry and witchcraft; hatred, discord, jealousy, fits of rage, selfish ambition, dissensions, factions 21and envy; drunkenness, orgies, and the
like. I warn you, as I did before, that those who
live like this will not inherit the kingdom of God.
22But the fruit of the Spirit is love, joy, peace,
patience, kindness, goodness, faithfulness, 23gen-
tleness and self-control. Against such things
there is no law. 24Those who belong to Christ
Jesus have crucified the sinful nature with its
passions and desires. 25Since we live by the Spirit, let us keep in step with the Spirit. 26Let us not
become conceited, provoking and envying each
other.

Galatians 5:16–26

1. Are you more likely to get hooked on junk food, TV or computer games?
2. In your school, what's the general attitude towards drugs or alcohol? How big a problem are these?
3. If you were to go along with the in-crowd, would you have to compromise your values? In what ways?
4. How are the Spirit and the sinful nature in conflict (vv. 16–18)?
5. If you have kids, what are you going to say to them about drugs and alcohol?
6. Who do you admire for their stand against drugs and alcohol?
7. Where do you stand on the use of alcohol and drugs? Have you been tempted to compromise your position?
8. Based on the topic, how can this group help you? Close in prayer.

Doing Good to All

6 Brothers, if someone is caught in a sin, you
who are spiritual should restore him gently.

[a]13 Or *the flesh*; also in verses 16, 17, 19 and 24 [b]14 Lev. 19:18

5:16 Paul warns us about losing freedom by submitting to sinful desires. ***live by the Spirit.*** Let the way you live, your conduct, be directed by the Holy Spirit. It is the Holy Spirit, not the Law, who will bring about a moral lifestyle.

5:19 *acts of the sinful nature.* To illustrate the sort of lifestyle that emerges when the sinful nature is allowed its way, Paul produces a representative list of vices—touching upon the sins of immorality, idolatry, social strife and drunkenness.

5:21 *not inherit.* The issue here is not sins into which one falls, but sin as a lifestyle. These are evidence of a life not controlled by the Spirit, and therefore the implication is that such a person has not been born from above and become a child of God.

5:22–23 In contrast to the "acts of the sinful nature" is the "fruit of the Spirit"—those traits which characterize the child of God. ***there is no law.*** While it is possible to legislate certain forms of behavior, one cannot command love, joy, peace, etc. These are each gifts of God's grace. With this list of qualities one moves into a whole new realm of reality, well beyond the sphere of Law.

5:24 *have crucified the sinful nature.* It is by the cross that a person dies to the power of the Law (see 2:20). Paul indicates here that, in the same way, a person dies to the power of their sinful nature. The verb indicates that this is not something done *to* the Christian but *by* the Christian. The Christian actively and deliberately has repented of the old sinful patterns of life.

But watch yourself, or you also may be tempted.
2Carry each other's burdens, and in this way you
will fulfill the law of Christ. 3If anyone thinks he
is something when he is nothing, he deceives

GALATIANS 6:1–10

1. What's something heavy you've tried to lift? Did you need help to carry it? Who helped you?
2. Among your friends, who would accept you unconditionally if you were in big trouble?
3. If your friend was pregnant and came to you for help, what would you say to her? Would you also talk to the guy?
4. As "brothers" in Christ, what responsibilities for each other do we have as outlined in this passage?
5. Why are we also called to be accountable for ourselves: "Each one should carry his own load" (v. 5)?
6. If a girl who was pregnant came to this group, how would she be accepted?
7. What opportunity to do something good for another person will you take this week? Will you allow this group to hold you accountable for this?
8. How can this group pray for you and help you carry your burdens?

himself. 4Each one should test his own actions.
Then he can take pride in himself, without comparing himself to somebody else, 5for each one
should carry his own load.
6Anyone who receives instruction in the word
must share all good things with his instructor.
7Do not be deceived: God cannot be mocked.
A man reaps what he sows. 8The one who sows
to please his sinful nature, from that nature[a]
will reap destruction; the one who sows to please
the Spirit, from the Spirit will reap eternal life.
9Let us not become weary in doing good, for at
the proper time we will reap a harvest if we do
not give up. 10Therefore, as we have opportunity,
let us do good to all people, especially to those
who belong to the family of believers.

Not Circumcision but a New Creation

11See what large letters I use as I write to you
with my own hand!
12Those who want to make a good impression
outwardly are trying to compel you to be circumcised. The only reason they do this is to avoid
being persecuted for the cross of Christ. 13Not
even those who are circumcised obey the law,
yet they want you to be circumcised that they
may boast about your flesh. 14May I never boast
except in the cross of our Lord Jesus Christ,
through which[b] the world has been crucified to
me, and I to the world. 15Neither circumcision
nor uncircumcision means anything; what counts
is a new creation. 16Peace and mercy to all who
follow this rule, even to the Israel of God.
17Finally, let no one cause me trouble, for I
bear on my body the marks of Jesus.
18The grace of our Lord Jesus Christ be with
your spirit, brothers. Amen.

[a] 8 Or *his flesh, from the flesh* [b] 14 Or *whom*

6:1–2 Paul does not counsel harshness but rather burden-bearing love toward someone caught in sin. ***you who are spiritual.*** Those whose lives bear the mark of the Spirit. This is not a clique of "special" Christians but is a call to all Christians. ***gently.*** The temptation may be to display overt disapproval and judgment, but Paul counsels otherwise. ***watch yourself.*** No one is beyond temptation; all are vulnerable, so no one has any basis for self-righteousness. ***carry each other's burdens.*** Mutual burden-bearing lies at the heart of Christian fellowship. ***burdens.*** A heavy, crushing weight which a single individual cannot carry. ***law of Christ.*** The law of love (5:14), which stands in sharp contrast to the Law as practiced in first-century Israel. It involves submission to a *person* (Jesus), not to a *code* (the Law of Moses).

6:3 A warning against spiritual pride. A sense of self-importance would make it difficult for such a person to bear another's burden (much less to restore gently the person overtaken in sin).

6:5 ***load.*** This is not the same thing as the crushing burden in verse 2. Rather, the word is used to describe the small individual pack a hiker or soldier carries. This is the same word used by Jesus in Matthew 11:30 to describe the burden (load) of his yoke.

6:7–9 ***mocked.*** This is derived from the word for "snout," and means "to turn up one's nose" at somebody in contempt. ***give up.*** That is, lose heart. The idea is of fatigue, such as laborers in the field might feel under the blazing sun, yet they must keep working.

Introduction to

EPHESIANS

Personal Reading Plan

- ❐ Ephesians 1:1–23
- ❐ Ephesians 2:1–22
- ❐ Ephesians 3:1–21
- ❐ Ephesians 4:1–16
- ❐ Ephesians 4:17–5:21
- ❐ Ephesians 5:22–6:24

Author

The apostle Paul was the writer of Ephesians.

Date

Paul probably wrote this letter in the early A.D. 60s, some 30 years after Jesus' crucifixion and only a few years before Paul's death.

Theme

God's new society.

Historical Background

Paul is in prison once again, and Epaphras has come to visit him bearing disturbing news about the church at Colosse. Since Paul is about to send back the runaway slave Onesimus (now converted) to his owner Philemon, a member of the Colossian Church, he takes this opportunity to send along a letter in which he addresses the Colossian heresy. He also writes two more letters: one to Philemon and one to a neighboring area, the letter to the Ephesians. These three epistles form the core of what we now know as the Prison Epistles or the Captivity Letters. It is unclear which imprisonment produced these letters (see 2 Cor. 11:23), but most likely Paul was at Rome (Acts 28). The fourth Prison Epistle, Philippians, was written in prison on another occasion.

Ephesians and Colossians are more similar in language and content than any other two letters in the New Testament. Seventy-five of the 155 verses in Ephesians are found in parallel form in Colossians. It seems that Paul first developed those themes in Colossians while dealing with a local problem, and then expanded them, explained them and cast them into a universal setting in Ephesians.

Characteristics

In this letter, Paul takes us to the mountaintops of Christian truth and invites us to look at the breathtaking view! When we do so, we see that it is Jesus Christ who dominates that view. We see him breaking down the wall between God and humanity. We see him subduing the hostile cosmic powers. We see him creating the church, a new social order of love and unity that transcends the racial, ethnic and social distinctions between people. In conveying this vision, Paul reaches into eternity past and eternity future to demonstrate how God, out of his love and glory, calls people to be reconciled to himself and to one another through the cross of Christ. The cross provides forgiveness of sins, a new life and a new people. Between Paul's greeting (1:1–2) and salutation (6:21–24), the letter divides easily into two parts. Part one (chapters 1–3) focuses on *doctrine*, specifically, the new life and new society God has created through Jesus. Part two (chapters 4–6) focuses on *ethics*, specifically, the new standards and new relationships expected of believers.

The City of Ephesus

The city of Ephesus was the capital of the Roman province of Asia. It was a large, bustling, secular city situated on the west coast of Asia Minor (modern Turkey) on the Aegean Sea. Originally a Greek colony, by Roman times it had become a center for international trade, largely as a result of its fine, natural harbor.

Its key architectural feature was the temple of Artemis (of Diana), considered to be one of the seven wonders of the ancient world. The image of Artemis was thought to have descended from heaven (Acts 19:35). There was also a huge, outdoor Greek theatre, capable of holding 50,000 people as well as a stadium where fights, races and other athletic contests were held.

Paul's first visit to Ephesus was brief—little more than a reconnaissance trip (Acts 18:18–22). He later returned during his third missionary journey and spent over two years there. His ministry was both effective and controversial. After three months in the synagogue, he was forced out and took up residence in the lecture hall of Tyrannus (Acts 19:8–9). Paul probably worked as a tentmaker in the mornings and lecturer in the afternoons. News of his message spread throughout Asia Minor (Acts 19:10). Extraordinary things happened. Handkerchiefs touched by him were used to cure the sick (Acts 19:11–12). Demons were cast out in the name of Jesus, even by Jewish exorcists (Acts 19:13–17). Pagan converts burned their books of magic (Acts 19:18–20). Eventually, a riot broke out in Ephesus because of Paul. Demetrius, a silversmith, organized a citywide protest. He charged that Paul's success posed a threat to the economic well being of craftsmen who made their living from the worshipers of Artemis (Acts 19:23–41). As a result, Paul moved on to Macedonia. But by this time the church was firmly established.

Paul never visited Ephesus again. He did, however, stop at the nearby port of Miletus on his return to Jerusalem. He called the Ephesian elders to him there and gave a moving farewell address (Acts 20:13–38). Later on, Paul would write 1 and 2 Timothy in an attempt to deal with false teaching that had arisen in Ephesus—as he had warned in his farewell address might happen (Acts 20:28–31). His words and Timothy's ministry were apparently successful. The apostle John's book of Revelation records that the Ephesians resisted false teaching—though they had lost their first love (Rev. 2:1–7). Tradition has it that John spent the final years of his life in Ephesus—as the beloved bishop and last surviving apostle.

Passages for Topical Group Study

1:3–14	ADOPTED CHILDREN	Spiritual Blessings in Christ
2:1–10	GOD'S FORGIVENESS	Made Alive in Christ
2:11–22	STEPFAMILIES	One in Christ
4:1–16	THE CHURCH	Unity in the Body of Christ
4:17–32	HONESTY / INTEGRITY	Living as Children of Light
	ANGER	
5:1–21	FRIENDSHIPS	Imitators of God
	PEER PRESSURE	
5:22–33	DATING—THE RIGHT WAY	Wives and Husbands
6:1–4	PARENTAL DEMANDS	Children and Parents
	FAMILY INTERFERENCE	
6:10–20	SATAN / OCCULT	The Armor of God

See the Lesson Plans in the front of this Bible.

Passages for General Group Study

1:15–23	Thanksgiving and Prayer
3:1–21	Paul the Preacher to the Gentiles

1 Paul, an apostle of Christ Jesus by the will of
God,

To the saints in Ephesus,[a] the faithful[b] in
Christ Jesus:

2Grace and peace to you from God our Father
and the Lord Jesus Christ.

Spiritual Blessings in Christ

3Praise be to the God and Father of our Lord
Jesus Christ, who has blessed us in the heavenly
realms with every spiritual blessing in Christ.

> ### EPHESIANS 1:3–14
>
> 1. As a kid, when games were played and sides chosen, how soon were you generally picked?
> 2. Who do you know who has been adopted?
> 3. Would you ever choose to adopt children? Why?
> 4. How does knowing that you are or can be an adopted child of God affect your view of God? Yourself?
> 5. Who is the "agent" through which God adopts us (see v. 5)? Why (see v. 7)?
> 6. What would you say to an honest doubter in your school who has trouble believing in a personal God?
> 7. When did you come to appreciate what God has done for you through Jesus Christ?
> 8. How can the group remember you in prayer this week?

4For he chose us in him before the creation of the
world to be holy and blameless in his sight. In
love 5he[c] predestined us to be adopted as his
sons through Jesus Christ, in accordance with his
pleasure and will— 6to the praise of his glorious
grace, which he has freely given us in the One he
loves. 7In him we have redemption through his
blood, the forgiveness of sins, in accordance with
the riches of God's grace 8that he lavished on us
with all wisdom and understanding. 9And he[d]
made known to us the mystery of his will according to his good pleasure, which he purposed in
Christ, 10to be put into effect when the times
will have reached their fulfillment—to bring all
things in heaven and on earth together under one
head, even Christ.

11In him we were also chosen,[e] having been
predestined according to the plan of him who
works out everything in conformity with the purpose of his will, 12in order that we, who were the
first to hope in Christ, might be for the praise of
his glory. 13And you also were included in Christ
when you heard the word of truth, the gospel
of your salvation. Having believed, you were
marked in him with a seal, the promised Holy
Spirit, 14who is a deposit guaranteeing our inheritance until the redemption of those who are
God's possession—to the praise of his glory.

Thanksgiving and Prayer

15For this reason, ever since I heard about
your faith in the Lord Jesus and your love for all
the saints, 16I have not stopped giving thanks for
you, remembering you in my prayers. 17I keep
asking that the God of our Lord Jesus Christ, the
glorious Father, may give you the Spirit[f] of wisdom and revelation, so that you may know him
better. 18I pray also that the eyes of your heart
may be enlightened in order that you may know
the hope to which he has called you, the riches
of his glorious inheritance in the saints, 19and his
incomparably great power for us who believe.
That power is like the working of his mighty

[a] *1* Some early manuscripts do not have *in Ephesus.* [b] *1* Or *believers who are* [c] *4,5* Or *sight in love.* [5]*He* [d] *8,9* Or *us. With all wisdom and understanding,* [9]*he* [e] *11* Or *were made heirs* [f] *17* Or *a spirit*

1:3–14 In Greek, this is a single, complex sentence. So intent is Paul on praising the work of God in the lives of Christians that he simply heaps phrase upon phrase. In verses 3–6, his focus is on the past election by God the Father. In verses 7–12, he shifts to the present redemptive activity by Jesus Christ the Son, while in verses 13–14 his concern is with the future inheritance guaranteed by the Holy Spirit.

1:5 ***predestined.*** Literally, "marked out beforehand," a difficult but thoroughly biblical doctrine, characteristic of God's activity in the OT in choosing Israel (Ex. 19:4–6; Deut. 7:6–11; Isa. 42:1 and 43:1), and in the NT in choosing the church, which is the new Israel. ***adopted.*** This was a common Roman (but not Jewish) custom, in which a child was given all the rights of the adoptive family by grace, not by merit (or birth). ***his sons.*** The purpose of predestination is that people become the sons and daughters of God (the term "sons" is, of course, generic and intended to include both men and women).

1:9 ***mystery.*** What was once hidden is now revealed by God. In this case, the astonishing fact is that the final goal of history is for this hopelessly divided world (Jews against Gentiles, male against female, etc.) to be united under Christ.

1:13–14 ***seal.*** A mark placed by an owner on a package, a cow, or even a slave. For the Jews, circumcision was such a seal (Rom. 4:11); for Christians the Holy Spirit is his or her seal. ***deposit.*** A down payment which guarantees ownership by God.

strength, [20]which he exerted in Christ when he
raised him from the dead and seated him at his
right hand in the heavenly realms, [21]far above all
rule and authority, power and dominion, and every title that can be given, not only in the present
age but also in the one to come. [22]And God
placed all things under his feet and appointed
him to be head over everything for the church,
[23]which is his body, the fullness of him who fills
everything in every way.

Ephesians 1:15–23

1. What do you like best about Thanksgiving Day? Who keeps your family traditions alive now?
2. In your own words, what does Paul pray for the Ephesians?
3. In what way is the church Christ's "body" (vv. 22–23)?
4. How does Jesus give hope and power?
5. What is God saying to you in this passage?
6. How can this group help you in prayer this week?

Made Alive in Christ

2 As for you, you were dead in your transgressions and sins, [2]in which you used to live
when you followed the ways of this world and of
the ruler of the kingdom of the air, the spirit who
is now at work in those who are disobedient. [3]All
of us also lived among them at one time, gratify-
ing the cravings of our sinful nature[a] and following its desires and thoughts. Like the rest, we
were by nature objects of wrath. [4]But because of
his great love for us, God, who is rich in mercy,
[5]made us alive with Christ even when we were
dead in transgressions—it is by grace you have
been saved. [6]And God raised us up with Christ
and seated us with him in the heavenly realms in
Christ Jesus, [7]in order that in the coming ages he
might show the incomparable riches of his grace,
expressed in his kindness to us in Christ Jesus.
[8]For it is by grace you have been saved, through
faith—and this not from yourselves, it is the gift
of God— [9]not by works, so that no one can boast.
[10]For we are God's workmanship, created in
Christ Jesus to do good works, which God prepared in advance for us to do.

Ephesians 2:1–10

1. What's a really great gift you've received? What did you do to deserve it? How did you express thanks to the giver?
2. What's the unpardonable sin in your family? At your school?
3. Growing up, who was the disciplinarian in your family? What was the typical punishment?
4. If we are "dead" because of sin (v. 1), how are we made alive (see v. 5)?
5. What does the forgiveness of God mean to you?
6. How's your life different now than it was before you became a Christian?
7. What "good work" will you do this week as an expression of thanks to God for his forgiveness?
8. Close in prayer. Thank God for his forgiveness.

[a]3 Or *our flesh*

2:1–2 *dead.* Humanity in general is out of tune with God's ways and out of fellowship with God himself. ***ruler of the kingdom of the air***. This is the first of several references in Ephesians to Satan. Here we learn that he is reigning monarch over a real kingdom, and that his kingdom is located in "the air" or "atmosphere."

2:3–4 *our sinful nature.* The word here is literally the "flesh," and it refers to self-centered human nature which expresses itself in destructive activities of both body and mind. ***because of his great love for us.*** Love is the first of four words by which Paul explains God's motivation for reaching out and rescuing fallen humanity (the others are mercy, grace and kindness).

2:5 *made us alive.* Paul coins this word to describe exactly what happens to us when we are "in Christ"; namely, we share in Christ's resurrection, ascension and enthronement. ***by grace.*** This resurrection cannot be earned. It is simply given. Grace is God's unmerited favor or gift to us.

2:8–9 *through faith.* Salvation does not come about *because* of faith. Salvation comes by grace *through* faith. Faith is simply a person's grateful response by which he/she accepts the gift of grace which has been offered. ***not from yourselves ... not by works.*** Salvation is not a reward for what a person has done. It is not the result of being good or keeping the Law.

2:10 *good works.* Although good works do not save a person, they do flow from that person as a result of salvation.

One in Christ

11Therefore, remember that formerly you who
are Gentiles by birth and called "uncircumcised"
by those who call themselves "the circumcision"
(that done in the body by the hands of men)—
12remember that at that time you were separate
from Christ, excluded from citizenship in Israel
and foreigners to the covenants of the promise,
without hope and without God in the world.
13But now in Christ Jesus you who once were far
away have been brought near through the blood
of Christ.

Ephesians 2:11–22

1. What was your favorite wall, fence or playground equipment to climb over when you were little?
2. Who do you know who has a stepmother, stepfather, stepbrother or stepsister? Do they get along?
3. Who is the peacemaker in your family?
4. Where do you have a "dividing wall of hostility" (v. 14) in your life: Family tensions? Cliques at your school? Racial attitudes? Other?
5. Christ came to destroy hostility. How does he "put to death" hostility (see v. 16)?
6. If your friend was having family problems and came to you for advice, what would you say?
7. What relationship in your life still has walls to be knocked down?
8. Close in prayer. Pray specifically that the peace of Christ would be at work in your relationships.

14For he himself is our peace, who has made
the two one and has destroyed the barrier, the
dividing wall of hostility, 15by abolishing in his
flesh the law with its commandments and regulations.
His purpose was to create in himself one
new man out of the two, thus making peace,
16and in this one body to reconcile both of them
to God through the cross, by which he put to
death their hostility. 17He came and preached
peace to you who were far away and peace to
those who were near. 18For through him we both
have access to the Father by one Spirit.

19Consequently, you are no longer foreigners
and aliens, but fellow citizens with God's people
and members of God's household, 20built on
the foundation of the apostles and prophets,
with Christ Jesus himself as the chief cornerstone.
21In him the whole building is joined together
and rises to become a holy temple in the Lord.
22And in him you too are being built together to
become a dwelling in which God lives by his
Spirit.

Paul the Preacher to the Gentiles

3 For this reason I, Paul, the prisoner of Christ
Jesus for the sake of you Gentiles—
2Surely you have heard about the administration
of God's grace that was given to me for you,
3that is, the mystery made known to me by revelation,
as I have already written briefly. 4In reading
this, then, you will be able to understand my
insight into the mystery of Christ, 5which was
not made known to men in other generations as
it has now been revealed by the Spirit to God's
holy apostles and prophets. 6This mystery is that
through the gospel the Gentiles are heirs together
with Israel, members together of one body,
and sharers together in the promise in Christ
Jesus.

7I became a servant of this gospel by the gift of
God's grace given me through the working of his
power. 8Although I am less than the least of all
God's people, this grace was given me: to preach
to the Gentiles the unsearchable riches of Christ,
9and to make plain to everyone the administration
of this mystery, which for ages past was kept

Paul moves from the problem of human alienation from God (2:1–10) to the related problem of alienation between people themselves. In both cases, the problem is hostility and Christ is the one who, through his death, brings peace. The particular focus of this section is on the deep hostility between Jew and Gentile.

2:12–13 ***without hope.*** During this particular historical era, the Roman world experienced a profound loss of hope. The first century was inundated with mystery cults, all promising salvation from this despair. Living in fear of demons, people felt themselves to be mere playthings of the gods. ***through the blood of Christ.*** The Gentiles' union with Christ is made possible as a result of Jesus' death on the cross.

2:14–15 ***our peace.*** Jesus brings peace; that is, he creates harmony between human beings and God. ***the dividing wall of hostility.*** Paul has in mind an actual wall which existed in the temple in Jerusalem beyond which Gentiles could not go. They were cut off by a stone wall, bearing signs that warned in Greek and Latin that trespassing foreigners would be killed. ***one new man.*** In the place of divided humanity, Jesus creates a whole new quality of being—a new humanity, a "third race" (see also Gal. 3:28 and Col. 3:11).

2:21 ***temple.*** The new temple is not like the old one—beautiful, but forbidding and exclusive. Rather, it is alive all over the world, inclusive of all, and made up of the individuals in whom God dwells.

hidden in God, who created all things. 10His intent was that now, through the church, the manifold wisdom of God should be made known to the rulers and authorities in the heavenly realms, 11according to his eternal purpose which he accomplished in Christ Jesus our Lord. 12In him and through faith in him we may approach God with freedom and confidence. 13I ask you, therefore, not to be discouraged because of my sufferings for you, which are your glory.

A Prayer for the Ephesians

14For this reason I kneel before the Father, 15from whom his whole family[a] in heaven and on earth derives its name. 16I pray that out of his glorious riches he may strengthen you with power through his Spirit in your inner being, 17so that Christ may dwell in your hearts through faith. And I pray that you, being rooted and established in love, 18may have power, together with all the saints, to grasp how wide and long and high and deep is the love of Christ, 19and to know this love that surpasses knowledge—that you may be filled to the measure of all the fullness of God.

20Now to him who is able to do immeasurably more than all we ask or imagine, according to his power that is at work within us, 21to him be glory in the church and in Christ Jesus throughout all generations, for ever and ever! Amen.

EPHESIANS *3:1–21*

1. Who is your favorite mystery writer, or favorite mystery on TV or in the movies?
2. How much do you feel you understand and experience the "mystery" of unity with Christ and fellow believers (v.6)?
3. When have you felt overwhelmed by the love of God (see vv. 17–19)?
4. If a person knew only rejection and pain in their relationships, how can this person come to understand the love of God in a personal way?
5. What is God saying to you in this passage?
6. How can this group pray for you?

Unity in the Body of Christ

4 As a prisoner for the Lord, then, I urge you to live a life worthy of the calling you have received. 2Be completely humble and gentle; be patient, bearing with one another in love. 3Make every effort to keep the unity of the Spirit through the bond of peace. 4There is one body and one Spirit—just as you were called to one hope when you were called— 5one Lord, one faith, one baptism; 6one God and Father of all, who is over all and through all and in all.

7But to each one of us grace has been given as Christ apportioned it. 8This is why it[b] says:

"When he ascended on high,
he led captives in his train
and gave gifts to men."[c]

9(What does "he ascended" mean except that he also descended to the lower, earthly regions[d]? 10He who descended is the very one who ascended higher than all the heavens, in order to fill the whole universe.) 11It was he who gave some to be apostles, some to be prophets, some to be evangelists, and some to be pastors and teachers, 12to prepare God's people for works of service, so that the body of Christ may be built up 13until we all reach unity in the faith and in the knowledge of the Son of God and become mature, attaining to the whole measure of the fullness of Christ.

14Then we will no longer be infants, tossed back and forth by the waves, and blown here and there by every wind of teaching and by the cunning and craftiness of men in their deceitful scheming. 15Instead, speaking the truth in love, we will in all things grow up into him who is the

[a] *15* Or *whom all fatherhood* [b] *8* Or *God* [c] *8* Psalm 68:18 [d] *9* Or *the depths of the earth*

Paul begins by focusing on the attitudes and actions that foster unity in the body of Christ (vv. 1–6). Then he emphasizes the diversity of gifts within the one body (vv. 7–13), and the maturity produced by such diversity within unity (vv. 14–16).

4:4–6 The unity which Paul is urging is based upon the threefold work of the triune God. God the Holy Spirit creates the one body (v. 3). God the Son brings hope, faith and baptism to this body (vv. 4b–5), while God the Father fills the body (v. 6).

4:8–9 Paul quotes Psalm 68:18 (the triumphal procession of a conquering Jewish king up Mt. Zion and into Jerusalem). He uses this verse to describe Christ's ascension into heaven. The captives which follow along behind him are the powers which he has defeated (see 1:20–22; Col. 2:15). The gifts which he disperses are gifts of ministry given to his followers. ***descended.*** Paul is referring to Christ's coming from heaven to earth (see Phil. 2:5–11), or to Christ's death and subsequent invasion of hell (see 1 Peter 3:19; 4:6).

4:11–12 This is one of several lists of gifts (see 1 Cor. 12:8–10,28–30; Rom. 12:6–8). The emphasis in this list is on the teaching gifts. ***prepare.*** The prime task of the clergy is to train the laity to do ministry.

4:13–16 The aim of all these gifts is to produce maturity. Maturity is, in turn, vital to having unity. ***speaking the truth in love.*** Christians are to stand for both truth and love. Both are necessary. Truth without love becomes harsh. Love without having truth becomes weak.

Head, that is, Christ. 16From him the whole
body, joined and held together by every supporting ligament, grows and builds itself up in love,
as each part does its work.

Ephesians 4:1–16

1. Where do you and your friends like to go to hang out?
2. On a scale of 1 (low) to 10 (high), what rating would you give yourself on being humble? Gentle? Patient?
3. From your school, how many students attend church? What is the general attitude about church?
4. A healthy body "grows and builds itself up in love" (v. 16). How's your church doing in accomplishing this? Are you doing your part?
5. If you could change one thing about your church, what would it be?
6. Of all of the churches or groups you've been a part of, which came the closest to being a true Christian community?
7. What's keeping your group from modeling the church as it was meant to be?
8. Close in prayer. Pray for the needs of your church.

(Study notes on page 1102)

Living as Children of Light

17So I tell you this, and insist on it in the Lord,
that you must no longer live as the Gentiles do,
in the futility of their thinking. 18They are darkened in their understanding and separated from
the life of God because of the ignorance that is in
them due to the hardening of their hearts. 19Hav-
ing lost all sensitivity, they have given themselves over to sensuality so as to indulge in every
kind of impurity, with a continual lust for more.
20You, however, did not come to know Christ
that way. 21Surely you heard of him and were
taught in him in accordance with the truth that is
in Jesus. 22You were taught, with regard to your
former way of life, to put off your old self, which

Ephesians 4:17–32

1. When it comes to getting angry, do you tend to have a short or long fuse?
2. What percentage of the students in your school cheat? Lie? Steal?
3. How can someone tell when you are angry? How can they tell when you are lying?
4. What do verses 22 and 23 mean by "put off your old self" and "put on the new self"?
5. What's one thing that really makes you angry?
6. How do you usually deal with anger? What do you learn about anger from verses 26–27?
7. If you were hooked up to a "truth detector" and asked, "How are you doing, *really*?" what would you say?
8. Agree together to walk in truth this week. Pray for one another.

is being corrupted by its deceitful desires; 23to be
made new in the attitude of your minds; 24and to
put on the new self, created to be like God in true
righteousness and holiness.
25Therefore each of you must put off falsehood
and speak truthfully to his neighbor, for we are

4:17 ***as the Gentiles do.*** Paul begins this section on purity of life by describing the typical Gentile lifestyle from which Christians must flee. ***the futility of their thinking.*** Paul emphasizes the connection between thought and behavior—Gentiles live as they do because their thinking is amiss. Right thinking does matter.

4:22–24 ***put off ... put on.*** Paul develops a clothing metaphor here. At conversion, the Christian sheds (strips off) his/her old, ragged, filthy garment and puts on a fresh, new cloak. ***old self ... new self.*** At conversion, the Christian puts off his/her old, sinful nature and puts on the very life of Christ himself. ***be made new.*** The verb tense indicates the need for ongoing, continual renewal.

4:25–32 Paul now gives a few concrete examples of what this new lifestyle looks like. It is characterized by truth (v. 25), by proper control of anger (vv. 26–27), by honest labor (v. 28), by edifying talk (vv. 29–30), and by love (vv. 31–32).

4:25–26 ***speak truthfully.*** Lies destroy fellowship. Unity must be built on trust, and trust comes via truth. ***in your anger.*** Paul recognizes there is legitimate anger and identifies four ways to deal with it. First, do not act on your anger in a destructive way. Second, deal with it quickly. Do not nurse anger and let it grow. Third, do not let anger develop into resentment. Be reconciled if possible. Apologize if necessary. Fourth, do not let Satan exploit your anger, turning it into hostility (or using it to disrupt fellowship).

all members of one body. 26“In your anger do not
sin”[a]: Do not let the sun go down while you are
still angry, 27and do not give the devil a foothold.
28He who has been stealing must steal no longer,
but must work, doing something useful with his
own hands, that he may have something to share
with those in need.
29Do not let any unwholesome talk come out
of your mouths, but only what is helpful for building others up according to their needs, that it
may benefit those who listen. 30And do not
grieve the Holy Spirit of God, with whom you
were sealed for the day of redemption. 31Get rid
of all bitterness, rage and anger, brawling and
slander, along with every form of malice. 32Be
kind and compassionate to one another, forgiving
each other, just as in Christ God forgave you.

5 Be imitators of God, therefore, as dearly
loved children 2and live a life of love, just as
Christ loved us and gave himself up for us as a
fragrant offering and sacrifice to God.
3But among you there must not be even a hint
of sexual immorality, or of any kind of impurity,
or of greed, because these are improper for God’s
holy people. 4Nor should there be obscenity, foolish talk or coarse joking, which are out of place,
but rather thanksgiving. 5For of this you can be
sure: No immoral, impure or greedy person—
such a man is an idolater—has any inheritance in
the kingdom of Christ and of God.[b] 6Let no one
deceive you with empty words, for because of
such things God’s wrath comes on those who are
disobedient. 7Therefore do not be partners with
them.
8For you were once darkness, but now you are
light in the Lord. Live as children of light 9(for the
fruit of the light consists in all goodness, righteousness and truth) 10and find out what pleases
the Lord. 11Have nothing to do with the fruitless
deeds of darkness, but rather expose them. 12For
it is shameful even to mention what the disobedient do in secret. 13But everything exposed by the
light becomes visible, 14for it is light that makes
everything visible. This is why it is said:

“Wake up, O sleeper,
rise from the dead,
and Christ will shine on you.”

15Be very careful, then, how you live—not as
unwise but as wise, 16making the most of every
opportunity, because the days are evil. 17There-
fore do not be foolish, but understand what the
Lord’s will is. 18Do not get drunk on wine, which
leads to debauchery. Instead, be filled with the
Spirit. 19Speak to one another with psalms,

Ephesians 5:1–21

1. Who’s your best friend right now? What makes that person such a good friend?
2. What is the worst trouble a friend has ever gotten you into? Are you still friends?
3. What person has had the biggest influence on your life? What good advice did they give you?
4. What kind of people and what kind of advice should you avoid (vv. 5–7)?
5. When have you felt pressured to go along with the crowd even when you knew it was not right?
6. What have you found helpful in resisting pressure to do something you shouldn’t?
7. What can you do in the coming week to be a better friend to someone?
8. How can the group pray for you and your friendships?

[a] 26 Psalm 4:4 [b] 5 Or *kingdom of the Christ and God*

5:1–2 If the Ephesians want to know what the Christian lifestyle is all about, they simply have to look at how God lives. They can see this by looking at Jesus, who is God-come-in-the-flesh. In Jesus, they will see that the divine way is the way of self-giving love.

5:3 ***sexual immorality ... impurity.*** These two words cover all forms of promiscuous sexual behavior among married or unmarried people. Christians must not give in to sexual immorality.

5:4 Vulgar talk is out of place, because it demeans God’s good gift of sex (which is a subject for thanksgiving, not joking).

5:7 ***partners.*** Although Christians can have normal social relationships with others, as did the Lord Jesus (Luke 5:30–32; 15:1–2), they are not to participate in the sinful lifestyle of unbelievers.

5:8 ***darkness ... light.*** Darkness represents what is secret and evil, and is out of touch with God’s purposes. Light stands for goodness and truth, and for obedience to God, which issues in openness and transparency.

5:15–17 Another motivator to Christian living is wisdom. Paul assumes that wisdom will teach one how to live. In other words, wisdom is practical and not merely theoretical.

5:18 ***be filled with the Spirit.*** This is a command, not an option. It is issued to all Christians. The present tense of the verb signifies continuous action and since the command is in the passive voice, it means “let the Spirit fill you.”

hymns and spiritual songs. Sing and make music in your heart to the Lord, 20always giving thanks to God the Father for everything, in the name of our Lord Jesus Christ.

21Submit to one another out of reverence for Christ.

Wives and Husbands

22Wives, submit to your husbands as to the Lord. 23For the husband is the head of the wife as Christ is the head of the church, his body, of which he is the Savior. 24Now as the church submits to Christ, so also wives should submit to their husbands in everything.

> **EPHESIANS 5:22–33**
>
> 1. Who was your first "true love"?
> 2. How much thought have you given marriage? What age do you see yourself marrying at?
> 3. What couple do you know who have a really good marriage? What makes it work?
> 4. *Guys:* How do you feel about the standard for husbands in this passage (verses 25 and 28)? *Girls:* How about the standard for wives (verses 22 and 33)?
> 5. How would your dating practices change if you viewed every date as a potential marriage partner?
> 6. What's the best way to know if someone is right for you?
> 7. What is God saying to you about dating and marriage?
> 8. How can the group pray for you, specifically your relationships?

25Husbands, love your wives, just as Christ loved the church and gave himself up for her 26to make her holy, cleansing[a] her by the washing with water through the word, 27and to present her to himself as a radiant church, without stain or wrinkle or any other blemish, but holy and blameless. 28In this same way, husbands ought to love their wives as their own bodies. He who loves his wife loves himself. 29After all, no one ever hated his own body, but he feeds and cares for it, just as Christ does the church— 30for we are members of his body. 31"For this reason a man will leave his father and mother and be united to his wife, and the two will become one flesh."[b] 32This is a profound mystery—but I am talking about Christ and the church. 33However, each one of you also must love his wife as he loves himself, and the wife must respect her husband.

Children and Parents

6 Children, obey your parents in the Lord, for this is right. 2"Honor your father and mother"—which is the first commandment with a promise— 3"that it may go well with you and that you may enjoy long life on the earth."[c]

4Fathers, do not exasperate your children; instead, bring them up in the training and instruction of the Lord.

Slaves and Masters

5Slaves, obey your earthly masters with respect and fear, and with sincerity of heart, just as you would obey Christ. 6Obey them not only to win their favor when their eye is on you, but like slaves of Christ, doing the will of God from your heart. 7Serve wholeheartedly, as if you were serving the Lord, not men, 8because you know that the Lord will reward everyone for whatever good he does, whether he is slave or free.

9And masters, treat your slaves in the same way. Do not threaten them, since you know that he who is both their Master and yours is in heaven, and there is no favoritism with him.

[a]26 Or *having cleansed* [b]31 Gen. 2:24 [c]3 Deut. 5:16

5:22 *Wives.* In a radical departure from tradition, Paul addresses women in their own right as individuals, able to make their own choices. He does not address them through their husbands (as would have been common in the first century). He does not tell husbands: "Make your wives submit to you." ***submit.*** In both Jewish and Gentile cultures, a woman was a "thing" and had no legal rights. Against this, Paul proposes a radical, liberating view: (1) Submission was to be mutual, as stated in verse 21 (the man was no longer the absolute authority; (2) Wives are called to defer only to their husbands (not to every man); (3) Submission is defined and qualfied by Christ's headship of the church, for which he died. Therefore, what a wife is called to submit to is her husband's sacrificial love!

5:23 *as Christ is the head.* The metaphor of the relationship between Christ and the church is central to this passage. Wives are to respect their husbands' roles of spiritual leadership and caring provision. Christ earned, so to speak, this kind of relationship.

5:31–33 *one flesh.* Paul does not view marriage as some sort of spiritual covenant devoid of sexuality. His illustration here of how a husband is to love his wife revolves around their sexual union, as is made clear by his quotation of Genesis 2:24. Since husband and wife become "one flesh," for the man to love his wife is to love the person who has become part of himself. ***as he loves himself.*** The gauge by which husbands (and wives) will know if they are, indeed, loving their mates properly is self-love: "Is this how I want to be loved?"

Ephesians 6:1–4

1. What TV family best reflects your family?
2. Growing up, what chores did you have to do? Did you generally have to do more or less than your friends?
3. Among the students at your school, are they given too much or not enough freedom by their parents?
4. What does God ask of children (see note on 6:1)? What does God promise (6:3)? What does God ask of parents (6:4)?
5. When you are away from home, how often do your parents expect you to check in? Is this a reasonable expectation? Why?
6. If you have kids, are you going to be more or less strict than your parents? In what ways?
7. What is a way you can honor your parents this week? Will you do this?
8. How can this group pray for you regarding your family relationships?

The Armor of God

10Finally, be strong in the Lord and in his
mighty power. 11Put on the full armor of God so
that you can take your stand against the devil's
schemes. 12For our struggle is not against flesh
and blood, but against the rulers, against the authorities, against the powers of this dark world

Ephesians 6:10–20

1. What was the scariest movie you have ever seen?
2. Where do you see the devil's schemes being played out in today's society?
3. How common is it for students at your school to play around with tarot cards, Ouija boards, astrology or witchcraft?
4. What makes up the "armor of God" (see vv. 14–17)? How can this armor help you "stand your ground"?
5. What's the closest you've come to experiencing some of the things associated with the occult and satanism?
6. What would you say to a friend who is playing around with the occult and satanism?
7. This week, how do you need to arm yourself against the spiritual forces of evil?
8. Close in prayer. Put verse 18 into practice.

In these verses, Paul does not simply command obedience on the part of children. He gives reasons for it. In other words, Paul does not take obedience for granted.

6:1 ***children.*** That Paul even addresses children is remarkable. Normally, all such instructions would come from their parents. ***obey.*** Literally, "listen to." Paul uses a different word from the one he used in chapter 5 when speaking of the relationship between wives and husbands. Parents have authority over their children, but not husbands over their wives. Although "obey" is a stronger word than "submit," it is not without limits. ***in the Lord.*** There are two ways in which this phrase can be taken: Obey your parents because you are a Christian, and/or obey your parents in everything that is compatible with your commitment to Christ. ***for this is right.*** Obeying parents isn't just a pious obligation; it's the *right* thing to do.

6:2 ***"Honor your father and mother."*** God commands obedience in the fifth commandment (Deut. 5:16).

6:4 Just as children have a duty to obey, parents have the duty to instruct children with gentleness and restraint. ***Fathers.*** The model for a father is that of God, the "Father of all" (4:6). This view of fatherhood stands in sharp contrast to the harsh Roman father, who had the power of life and death over his children. ***exasperate.*** Parents are to be responsible for not provoking hostility in their children. By humiliating children, being cruel to them, overindulging them, or being unreasonable, parents crush rather than encourage children.

6:10 ***be strong ... in his mighty power.*** In order to wage successful warfare against Satan, the Christian must draw upon God's own power. This is a power outside him/herself, from beyond. This is not a natural power generated by the Christian.

6:11–12 Paul defines the Christian's opponent in this spiritual warfare. He is crafty ("the devil's schemes"), he is powerful ("the powers of this dark world"), and he is wicked ("the face of evil"). The devil is a real opponent, and his legions are not to be taken lightly. ***Put on.*** It is not enough simply to rely passively on God's power. The Christian must do something. Specifically, he or she must "put on" God's armor. ***the rulers ... the authorities ... the powers ... the spiritual forces.*** By these various titles, Paul names the spiritual forces which rage against humanity. These are intangible spiritual entities whose will is often worked out via historical, economic, political, social and institutional structures. Part of the call to Christians is to identify the places where these evil powers are at work.

6:13 ***stand your ground.*** This is the basic posture of the Christian in the face of evil: resistance. "Standing firm" is a military image. Paul may well have in mind the fighting position of the Roman legions. Fully-equipped soldiers were virtually impenetrable to enemy onslaught—unless they panicked and broke ranks.

6:14–17 Each piece of armor is used by Paul as a metaphor for what the Christian needs in order to stand against the dark forces.

and against the spiritual forces of evil in the heavenly realms. 13Therefore put on the full armor of
God, so that when the day of evil comes, you may
be able to stand your ground, and after you have
done everything, to stand. 14Stand firm then,
with the belt of truth buckled around your waist,
with the breastplate of righteousness in place,
15and with your feet fitted with the readiness that
comes from the gospel of peace. 16In addition to
all this, take up the shield of faith, with which
you can extinguish all the flaming arrows of the
evil one. 17Take the helmet of salvation and the
sword of the Spirit, which is the word of God.
18And pray in the Spirit on all occasions with all
kinds of prayers and requests. With this in mind,
be alert and always keep on praying for all the
saints.

19Pray also for me, that whenever I open my
mouth, words may be given me so that I will
fearlessly make known the mystery of the gospel,
20for which I am an ambassador in chains. Pray
that I may declare it fearlessly, as I should.

Final Greetings

21Tychicus, the dear brother and faithful servant in the Lord, will tell you everything, so that
you also may know how I am and what I am
doing. 22I am sending him to you for this very
purpose, that you may know how we are, and
that he may encourage you.

23Peace to the brothers, and love with faith
from God the Father and the Lord Jesus Christ.
24Grace to all who love our Lord Jesus Christ
with an undying love.

Introduction to
PHILIPPIANS

Personal Reading Plan

❐ Philippians 1:1–30
❐ Philippians 2:1–30
❐ Philippians 3:1–4:1
❐ Philippians 4:2–23

Author

The apostle Paul was the writer of Philippians.

Date

Philippians was probably written around A.D. 61–63, a dozen or so years after Paul had founded the church in Philippi (the first church in Europe; see Acts 16).

Theme

The joy of knowing Jesus.

Historical Background

Paul had founded the church around A.D. 50 as the result of a vision during the night in which a "man of Macedonia" beckoned him to "come over ... and help us" (Acts 16:9). He sailed immediately from Asia, thus launching Christianity in Europe. Paul's stay at Philippi was marked by joy and trial. On the positive side was the conversion of Lydia, the dealer in purple cloth, as well as the conversion of the jailer and his family after an earthquake unexpectedly released Paul from prison. On the negative side, in Philippi the first recorded conflict between Christians and Gentiles occurred, and Paul was thrown in jail for casting out a demon from a fortuneteller's slave girl.

Paul is in prison (probably in Rome) when Epaphroditus, an old friend from Philippi, arrives bearing yet another gift from the church. Unfortunately, Epaphroditus falls gravely ill. His home church hears about it and is grieved. In due course he recovers, and Paul is anxious for him to return home and relieve their fears. This affords Paul an opportunity to send along a letter.

So he writes these old friends in the warmest and most personal of his epistles. There is no need for him to assert his authority as an apostle, like he usually does when beginning a letter. There is no formality in his outline either. Paul puts down ideas as they occur to him, often with strong declarations of emotion.

Basically Philippians is a letter of thanksgiving (1:3–11 and 4:14–20) and a report on his imprisonment (1:12–26; 2:19–30; 4:10–13). In large part, it seems that Paul wrote Philippians as a thank-you for all that this, perhaps his favorite church, had done for him (particularly their gift, as seen in 4:10–19). Still, Paul has two concerns: a tendency in the church toward disunity (1:27–2:18 and 4:2–3) and potential dangers from Judaizers (3:2–16) and false teachers (3:17–21).

The City of Philippi

Located in the Roman province of Macedonia (a territory corresponding to northern Greece and parts of several other Balkan countries), Philippi was an historic city. Founded by Alexander the Great's father in 360 B.C. so he could mine its gold to pay for his army, Philippi eventually came to prominence as the result of two battles. In 42 B.C. on the plains of Philippi, the Caesarean forces of Anthony and Octavian defeated the Republican forces led by the assassins of Julius Caesar—Brutus and Cassius. Then in 31 B.C., Octavian (who later became the Emperor Caesar Augustus) became sole ruler by defeating his former colleague Anthony, who was in alliance with the Egyptian

Queen Cleopatra. Veterans from these conflicts were given land in Philippi, and Octavian declared it to be a Roman colony with all the accompanying rights, tax breaks and privileges. To be in Philippi was to be in a miniature Rome.

Characteristics

Philippians is the letter of joy. Joy permeates its pages from start to finish. And yet this is not joy forged out of privilege and abundance. It is not the joy of people who have no problems to face. This is joy in the midst of hard situations. Paul is writing from prison. He faces the very real possibility of execution. The Philippian church is confronted with internal dissension and with false teachers who would seduce it away from the Gospel. Furthermore, both Paul and the Philippians live with the sense that the world might end any day. The second coming of Jesus was a living reality for them.

How can you be joyful in that kind of world? How can you urge joy when you are in prison? How can you experience joy when your fellowship is pressed from within and without? How can you be joyful when the world is about to end? The average North American Christian does not know how to answer these questions. To him or her, joy is what comes with prosperity and success. Joy is the lack of pressure and hardship.

Since most of us are puzzled by the emphasis in this epistle, it is therefore most important to listen carefully to what Paul has to say. It is not that we do not want joy. We do. We go to incredible lengths to find satisfaction (which is how we often define joy). It is just that we do not want joy in the midst of hardship. We want the hardship to go away. Yet, the hardship would not go away for either Paul or the Philippians. This was the reality in which they lived and out of which this letter, brimming with joy, was written.

Structure

There is a question about whether the epistle to the Philippians is one letter or two. It opens in a traditional way. Paul talks about his imprisonment and about how the Gospel is advancing. He makes an appeal for harmony among the members of the Philippian church. He tells them that he will be sending both Epaphroditus and Timothy to see them. And in 3:1 he says, "Finally, my brothers ..." as if he is about to close the letter. But then he abruptly launches into a warning about dangerous men who will harm the church (3:2–21). This is followed by more exhortations (4:1–9) and by thanks for their gifts (4:10–20), after which he actually concludes his letter.

Most commentators regard Philippians as a single letter, but it is instructive to note the two sections that could be separate letters. First, there is the warning about troublemakers that begins in 3:2 and goes to at least 4:1 (and possibly to 4:9). Then, second, there is Paul's note of thanks in 4:10–20. Still, these parts do not have to stand alone.

Passages for Topical Group Study

1:12–30	FEARS AND HANG-UPS	Paul's Chains Advance the Gospel
2:1–11	A SERVANT'S HEART	Imitating Christ's Humility
3:1–11	SUCCESS / AMBITION	No Confidence in the Flesh
3:12–21	GOD'S CALL	Pressing Toward the Goal
4:2–9	WORRY AND ANXIETY	Rejoice in the Lord
4:10–20	INSECURITY CHANGE FINANCIAL PROBLEMS CONTENTMENT	The Secret of Being Content

See the Lesson Plans in the front of this Bible.

Passages for General Group Study

1:1–11	Thanksgiving and Prayer
2:12–18	Shining as Stars
2:19–30	Timothy and Epaphroditus

1 Paul and Timothy, servants of Christ Jesus,
To all the saints in Christ Jesus at Philippi,
together with the overseers[a] and deacons:

2Grace and peace to you from God our Father
and the Lord Jesus Christ.

Thanksgiving and Prayer

3I thank my God every time I remember you.
4In all my prayers for all of you, I always pray
with joy 5because of your partnership in the gospel from the first day until now, 6being confident
of this, that he who began a good work in you
will carry it on to completion until the day of
Christ Jesus.

PHILIPPIANS 1:1–11

1. When you care for someone, are you more likely to send a funny card or a touching one?
2. What are Paul's feelings for this church? What does that show about his leadership style?
3. How is God at work in a believer's life according to verses 6 and 9–11? How does this make you feel about uncertainties in your life?
4. Who was the "apostle Paul" in your spiritual life, who introduced you to Jesus Christ and cared about your spiritual growth?
5. What is God saying to you in this passage?
6. How can this group help you in prayer this week?

7It is right for me to feel this way about all of
you, since I have you in my heart; for whether I
am in chains or defending and confirming the
gospel, all of you share in God's grace with me.
8God can testify how I long for all of you with the
affection of Christ Jesus.
9And this is my prayer: that your love may
abound more and more in knowledge and depth
of insight, 10so that you may be able to discern
what is best and may be pure and blameless until
the day of Christ, 11filled with the fruit of righteousness that comes through Jesus Christ—to
the glory and praise of God.

Paul's Chains Advance the Gospel

12Now I want you to know, brothers, that
what has happened to me has really served to
advance the gospel. 13As a result, it has become
clear throughout the whole palace guard[b] and to
everyone else that I am in chains for Christ. 14Be-
cause of my chains, most of the brothers in the
Lord have been encouraged to speak the word of
God more courageously and fearlessly.

PHILIPPIANS 1:12–30

1. When you were little, what helped you get through the night: A flashlight? Teddy bear? Special blanket?
2. What gives you courage when you are afraid?
3. Paul was in prison but joyful. What trying circumstances are you dealing with? What's your attitude towards them?
4. What was Paul's attitude towards his future? Why? What's yours? Why?
5. Who is someone who opposes you? This group? Your church? Do they frighten you? Should they (see v. 28)?
6. What's the closest you've come to suffering for Christ? How does the possibility of future suffering for Christ's sake make you feel?
7. Give this group a "progress and joy in the faith" (v. 25) report. How's your spiritual journey going right now?
8. Pray for this group, that it will "stand firm in one spirit" (v. 27).

(Study notes on page 1111)

15It is true that some preach Christ out of envy
and rivalry, but others out of goodwill. 16The latter do so in love, knowing that I am put here for
the defense of the gospel. 17The former preach
Christ out of selfish ambition, not sincerely, supposing that they can stir up trouble for me while
I am in chains.[c] 18But what does it matter? The
important thing is that in every way, whether
from false motives or true, Christ is preached.
And because of this I rejoice.
Yes, and I will continue to rejoice, 19for I know

[a] *1* Traditionally *bishops* [b] *13* Or *whole palace* [c] *16,17* Some late manuscripts have verses 16 and 17 in reverse order.

that through your prayers and the help given by
the Spirit of Jesus Christ, what has happened to
me will turn out for my deliverance.[a] 20 I eagerly
expect and hope that I will in no way be
ashamed, but will have sufficient courage so that
now as always Christ will be exalted in my body,
whether by life or by death. 21 For to me, to live
is Christ and to die is gain. 22 If I am to go on
living in the body, this will mean fruitful labor for
me. Yet what shall I choose? I do not know! 23 I
am torn between the two: I desire to depart and
be with Christ, which is better by far; 24 but it is
more necessary for you that I remain in the body.
25 Convinced of this, I know that I will remain,
and I will continue with all of you for your progress and joy in the faith, 26 so that through my
being with you again your joy in Christ Jesus will
overflow on account of me.

27 Whatever happens, conduct yourselves in a
manner worthy of the gospel of Christ. Then,
whether I come and see you or only hear about
you in my absence, I will know that you stand
firm in one spirit, contending as one man for the
faith of the gospel 28 without being frightened in
any way by those who oppose you. This is a sign
to them that they will be destroyed, but that you
will be saved—and that by God. 29 For it has been
granted to you on behalf of Christ not only to
believe on him, but also to suffer for him, 30 since
you are going through the same struggle you saw
I had, and now hear that I still have.

Imitating Christ's Humility

2 If you have any encouragement from being
united with Christ, if any comfort from his
love, if any fellowship with the Spirit, if any tenderness and compassion, 2 then make my joy complete by being like-minded, having the same
love, being one in spirit and purpose. 3 Do nothing out of selfish ambition or vain conceit, but in
humility consider others better than yourselves.
4 Each of you should look not only to your own
interests, but also to the interests of others.

5 Your attitude should be the same as that of
Christ Jesus:

6 Who, being in very nature[b] God,
did not consider equality with God
something to be grasped,
7 but made himself nothing,
taking the very nature[c] of a servant,
being made in human likeness.
8 And being found in appearance as a man,
he humbled himself
and became obedient to death—
even death on a cross!
9 Therefore God exalted him to the highest
place

Philippians 2:1–11

1. Growing up, who was your role model—someone you looked up to? Why did you admire that person?
2. Who looks out for you? Who do you look out for?
3. Who do you know who consistently puts the interests of others before their own?
4. What does it mean to "consider others better than yourselves" (v. 3)?
5. Verse 5 says, "Your attitude should be the same as that of Christ." What is Christ's attitude? How does yours compare?
6. How would the relationships with your friends at school be different if you practiced the humility demonstrated by Jesus?
7. This week, what is one way you can demonstrate humility?
8. What is something this group can do to serve someone else? Close in prayer.

(Study notes on page 1112)

[a] 19 Or *salvation* [b] 6 Or *in the form of* [c] 7 Or *the form*

1:12 *I want you to know.* Paul assures the Philippians that good is coming out of his imprisonment and that it has had a positive effect on the spread of the Gospel. ***advance.*** A word used to describe an army that is marching forward despite obstacles.

1:18 *because of this I rejoice*. This is an unexpected conclusion to Paul's report on his imprisonment. One might have expected an appeal that they pray for him in his difficult circumstances or that they work to get him released. This exclamation of joy is not how most people would sum up the experience of being in prison. But Paul has learned to see his circumstances in the light of God's plan; and so what matters is not how comfortable he is but whether the Gospel is thriving—and since it is, Paul can rejoice!

1:19 *I know.* How he "knows" that all this will result in his deliverance is not certain. Probably what he is referring to is a deep inner conviction that God will make right this situation. His confidence is based on two factors: the prayers of his fellow Christians and the work of the Holy Spirit.

1:21 *to live is Christ.* For Paul, his whole existence revolves around Christ. He is inspired by Christ; he works for Christ; his sole focus in life is Christ. He is a man with a single, all-consuming passion. ***to die is gain.*** Death is the door into the presence of Christ. It is the path to reunion with the One with whom he is already in union. Death is not so much escape from hardship as it is an entrance into joy.

and gave him the name that is above every name,
[10]that at the name of Jesus every knee should bow,
in heaven and on earth and under the earth,
[11]and every tongue confess that Jesus Christ is Lord,
to the glory of God the Father.

Shining as Stars

[12]Therefore, my dear friends, as you have always obeyed—not only in my presence, but now much more in my absence—continue to work out your salvation with fear and trembling, [13]for it is God who works in you to will and to act according to his good purpose.

[14]Do everything without complaining or arguing, [15]so that you may become blameless and pure, children of God without fault in a crooked and depraved generation, in which you shine like stars in the universe [16]as you hold out[a] the word of life—in order that I may boast on the day of Christ that I did not run or labor for nothing. [17]But even if I am being poured out like a drink offering on the sacrifice and service coming from your faith, I am glad and rejoice with all of you. [18]So you too should be glad and rejoice with me.

Timothy and Epaphroditus

[19]I hope in the Lord Jesus to send Timothy to you soon, that I also may be cheered when I receive news about you. [20]I have no one else like him, who takes a genuine interest in your welfare. [21]For everyone looks out for his own interests, not those of Jesus Christ. [22]But you know

PHILIPPIANS 2:12–18

1. Which describes you best in the morning—a grouch or an angel?
2. Who does Paul sound like in this passage: Your dad? Army sergeant? Coach at halftime?
3. If Paul were around today, what would he think about the moral values in our society? About the moral standards in the Christian community?
4. How are you doing on allowing God to finish the job he started in your life?
5. What is God saying to you in this passage?
6. How can this group help you in prayer this week?

PHILIPPIANS 2:19–30

1. In what way are you most like your father (or mother, if you don't know your father)?
2. Consider verses 20–22 and 30. How true is verse 21 today? How rare are people like Timothy and Epaphroditus?
3. Who are the people in your life who have helped shape your self-image by their praise or lack of praise?
4. Do you give praise easily ... or do you find this hard to do? Where do you need to improve?
5. What is God saying to you in this passage?
6. How can this group help you in prayer this week?

[a]16 Or *hold on to*

2:1 By means of four "ifs," Paul urges the Philippians to say "Yes" to his request that they live together in harmony. They have a strong incentive to be united to one another because of their experience of the encouragement, love, fellowship, tenderness and compassion of God the Father, Son and Holy Spirit.

2:3 ***humility.*** Humility involves seeing others not on the basis of how clever, attractive or pious they are, but through the eyes of Christ (who died for them).

2:4 ***look not only to your own interests.*** Preoccupation with personal interests, along with selfish ambition and vain conceit, make unity impossible.

2:7 ***taking the very nature of a servant.*** Jesus gave up the glories of Godhood and took on slavehood. From being the ultimate master, he became the lowest servant. ***human likeness.*** The point is not that Jesus just seemed to be human. He assumed the identity of a person and was similar in all ways to other human beings.

2:8–9 ***he humbled himself.*** This is the central point that Paul wants to make. This is why he offered this illustration. Jesus is the ultimate model of one who lived a life of self-sacrifice, self-renunciation, and self-surrender. ***name.*** In the ancient world, a name revealed the inner nature of a person. Jesus is the name above all names.

2:11 ***Jesus Christ is Lord.*** The climax of this hymn (vv. 6–11). This is the earliest and most basic confession of faith by the church (see Acts 2:36; Rom. 10:9).

that Timothy has proved himself, because as a
son with his father he has served with me in the
work of the gospel. 23I hope, therefore, to send
him as soon as I see how things go with me.
24And I am confident in the Lord that I myself
will come soon.
25But I think it is necessary to send back to you
Epaphroditus, my brother, fellow worker and fellow soldier, who is also your messenger, whom
you sent to take care of my needs. 26For he longs
for all of you and is distressed because you heard
he was ill. 27Indeed he was ill, and almost died.
But God had mercy on him, and not on him only
but also on me, to spare me sorrow upon sorrow.
28Therefore I am all the more eager to send him,
so that when you see him again you may be glad
and I may have less anxiety. 29Welcome him in
the Lord with great joy, and honor men like him,
30because he almost died for the work of Christ,
risking his life to make up for the help you could
not give me.

No Confidence in the Flesh

3 Finally, my brothers, rejoice in the Lord! It is
no trouble for me to write the same things to
you again, and it is a safeguard for you.
2Watch out for those dogs, those men who do
evil, those mutilators of the flesh. 3For it is we
who are the circumcision, we who worship by
the Spirit of God, who glory in Christ Jesus, and
who put no confidence in the flesh— 4though I
myself have reasons for such confidence.
If anyone else thinks he has reasons to put
confidence in the flesh, I have more: 5circum-
cised on the eighth day, of the people of Israel, of
the tribe of Benjamin, a Hebrew of Hebrews; in
regard to the law, a Pharisee; 6as for zeal, persecuting the church; as for legalistic righteousness,
faultless.
7But whatever was to my profit I now consider
loss for the sake of Christ. 8What is more, I consider everything a loss compared to the surpassing greatness of knowing Christ Jesus my Lord,
for whose sake I have lost all things. I consider
them rubbish, that I may gain Christ 9and be
found in him, not having a righteousness of my
own that comes from the law, but that which is
through faith in Christ—the righteousness that
comes from God and is by faith. 10I want to know
Christ and the power of his resurrection and the
fellowship of sharing in his sufferings, becoming

PHILIPPIANS 3:1–11

1. What person in your school would you vote "most likely to succeed"? Why? What have they got going for them?
2. Would your parents say you have too much ambition or too little? Why?
3. What is it going to take for you to be a success in the eyes of your parents? Your friends? God?
4. According to Paul, what's the secret to success (see v. 8)?
5. Paul desires to know Christ better (v. 10). On a scale of 1 (none) to 10 (great), how does your desire in this area rank?
6. What "rubbish" do you need to give up to know Christ better?
7. How would you compare your life goals to the apostle Paul's goals in this passage?
8. How can the group help you in prayer this week?

like him in his death, 11and so, somehow, to attain to the resurrection from the dead.

Pressing on Toward the Goal

12Not that I have already obtained all this, or
have already been made perfect, but I press on to
take hold of that for which Christ Jesus took hold
of me. 13Brothers, I do not consider myself yet to
have taken hold of it. But one thing I do: Forgetting what is behind and straining toward what is

---

3:2 ***men who do evil.*** The Jews considered themselves to be the only people who did good in the eyes of God. But once again, Paul turns their self-image upside down and contends that, in fact, they are really evildoers (because they rely on their good works for their righteousness instead of on God's grace).

3:7 ***profit ... loss.*** Paul describes his change in outlook in terms of a balance sheet. What was once on the "profit" side of the ledger (when he was a Pharisee) has been shifted over to the "loss" side (now that he is a Christian). ***for the sake of Christ.*** When Paul met the resurrected Jesus, his whole way of looking at himself and God changed radically. He saw that his zeal had, in fact, driven him to kill people (so that he was guilty before God, and not righteous as he had assumed). He also saw that his view of what God wanted was wrong (God did not desire conformity to the Law, but rather trust in Christ).

3:8 ***compared to.*** He discovered that only one thing had any ultimate value—knowing Christ Jesus—and knowing Christ did not come as a result of personal accomplishment. ***rubbish.*** This is really quite a vulgar term, and refers to either "waste food bound for the garbage pit" or "human dung."

3:11 Although believers experience in the here-and-now the power of the resurrection, there also awaits them a future resurrection. ***somehow to attain.*** In humility, he expresses his sense that it is solely by God's grace that he would gain such a gift.

ahead, [14]I press on toward the goal to win the
prize for which God has called me heavenward in
Christ Jesus.
[15]All of us who are mature should take such a

PHILIPPIANS 3:12–21

1. If you could compete in the Olympics, what sport would you like to compete in?
2. What habits do you have in your school work? What about your spiritual study habits?
3. When it comes to moving on and letting go of the past, what grade would you give yourself?
4. What "prize" is Paul trying to win (v. 14)? What "prize" are you striving to win?
5. What kind of balance is there in your life between "earthly things" and spiritual things (vv. 19–20)?
6. Paul followed God's call on his life. What might God be calling you to do for him with your life?
7. If you compared your life with Christ right now to a track race, where would you be: Warming up? At the starting blocks? Giving it your all?
8. Share prayer requests and close by praying for one another.

view of things. And if on some point you think
differently, that too God will make clear to you.
[16]Only let us live up to what we have already
attained.
[17]Join with others in following my example,
brothers, and take note of those who live according to the pattern we gave you. [18]For, as I have
often told you before and now say again even
with tears, many live as enemies of the cross of
Christ. [19]Their destiny is destruction, their god is
their stomach, and their glory is in their shame.
Their mind is on earthly things. [20]But our citizenship is in heaven. And we eagerly await a Savior
from there, the Lord Jesus Christ, [21]who, by the
power that enables him to bring everything under his control, will transform our lowly bodies so
that they will be like his glorious body.

4 Therefore, my brothers, you whom I love
and long for, my joy and crown, that is how
you should stand firm in the Lord, dear friends!

Exhortations

[2]I plead with Euodia and I plead with Syntyche
to agree with each other in the Lord. [3]Yes, and I
ask you, loyal yokefellow,[a] help these women
who have contended at my side in the cause of
the gospel, along with Clement and the rest of
my fellow workers, whose names are in the book
of life.
[4]Rejoice in the Lord always. I will say it again:
Rejoice! [5]Let your gentleness be evident to all.
The Lord is near. [6]Do not be anxious about anything, but in everything, by prayer and petition,
with thanksgiving, present your requests to God.
[7]And the peace of God, which transcends all understanding, will guard your hearts and your
minds in Christ Jesus.
[8]Finally, brothers, whatever is true, whatever
is noble, whatever is right, whatever is pure,
whatever is lovely, whatever is admirable—if
anything is excellent or praiseworthy—think
about such things. [9]Whatever you have learned
or received or heard from me, or seen in me—
put it into practice. And the God of peace will be
with you.

Thanks for Their Gifts

[10]I rejoice greatly in the Lord that at last you
have renewed your concern for me. Indeed, you
have been concerned, but you had no opportuni-

[a]3 Or *loyal Syzygus*

3:12 *press on.* In this passage, Paul continues writing about his calling in life and his great desire to "know Christ" (v. 11) in a deeper way. His attitude is especially admirable in light of the fact he was in prison at the time.

3:13 *Forgetting what is behind.* In order to reach a successful conclusion to his spiritual pilgrimage, Paul must first cease looking at his past. He must forget past failures (such as persecuting the church). He must also forget past successes (such as reaching the pinnacle of Jewish spirituality).

3:14 *the prize.* What Paul has in mind is the moment when the winner of a race is called forward by the games master to receive the victory wreath. Likewise, on the day of resurrection, the Christian will be called forward by God to receive the prize, which is full knowledge of Christ Jesus.

3:17 *the pattern.* Paul has defined the pattern for the Christian life as forgetting what is behind and constantly forging ahead to grasp the fullness of Jesus Christ on all levels of one's being.

3:19–20 *their god is their stomach.* The Jews were obsessed with laws relating to what they could eat and drink and ritual preparation for eating. ***citizenship.*** In contrast to the Jewish teachers whose focus is on "earthly things" (v. 19), the focus of Christians is on heaven (where their true home lies). ***eagerly await.*** Paul captures the keen anticipation and happy expectation of the Christians who long for Christ's return, at which time they will be rescued from their trials and will experience new life in all its fullness.

ty to show it. 11I am not saying this because I am
in need, for I have learned to be content whatever the circumstances. 12I know what it is to be
in need, and I know what it is to have plenty. I

PHILIPPIANS 4:2–9

1. What makes you anxious: A trip to the dentist? A big test? A date?
2. How much time do you spend worrying about being accepted or popular at your school?
3. If you had two friends who weren't getting along, what would you say to them?
4. On a scale of 1 (not so good) to 10 (good), how are you at rejoicing in the Lord *always* (v. 4)?
5. What do you do to relieve stress from worry in your life? What does Paul say to do (see vv. 6 and 8)?
6. How does what you think about affect how you feel? How does it affect your relationship with God?
7. Look at verse 8. What are some things you can think about that fit these positive characteristics?
8. What's something you are anxious about right now? Present these requests to God in prayer.

have learned the secret of being content in any
and every situation, whether well fed or hungry,
whether living in plenty or in want. 13I can do
everything through him who gives me strength.
14Yet it was good of you to share in my troubles. 15Moreover, as you Philippians know, in the
early days of your acquaintance with the gospel,
when I set out from Macedonia, not one church
shared with me in the matter of giving and receiving, except you only; 16for even when I was
in Thessalonica, you sent me aid again and again

PHILIPPIANS 4:10–20

1. If you had to compare your life last week to a weather report, what was the "weather" in your life like last week?
2. If you gave a grade to your current financial condition, what grade would it get? How does this make you feel?
3. What would you say causes the most stress among students at your school?
4. What is your idea of a fulfilling life? A life without stress or a life of peace in the midst of storms?
5. What is the biggest change you've gone through recently?
6. What situations in your life are you feeling insecure about? How do verses 13 and 19 help you?
7. What is Paul's secret to contentment? What needs to change in your life for you to be content where you are?
8. How can this group share in your troubles this week? Pray together.

(Study notes on page 1116)

when I was in need. 17Not that I am looking for
a gift, but I am looking for what may be credited
to your account. 18I have received full payment
and even more; I am amply supplied, now that I

4:2 ***plead.*** This is a strong verb, meaning "to beg." This disunity issue is so serious that Paul is willing to go on "bended knee" to get it resolved. ***Euodia ... Syntyche.*** Unlike most Greek women who remained in the background and had little to do with public life, Macedonian women were in every way as active and involved as the men. These two women are, apparently, leaders in the Philippian church. ***in the Lord.*** The only hope for unity to return to this church and to these two women is to be found in the fact of their common commitment to Jesus.

4:4 ***Rejoice.*** This is the first of a series of attitudes that make it possible to cope successfully in a hard situation. If one is rejoicing, by definition, one cannot be despairing. Paul is not calling for people to rejoice because of the situation. Rather, it is the Lord, who is the source and cause of rejoicing. ***in the Lord.*** Faith in the Lord makes joyfulness both realistic and possible, despite persecution and trouble.

4:6–7 ***Do not be anxious.*** To worry is to display a lack of confidence in God's care and in God's control over the situation (see Matt. 6:25–34). ***the peace of God.*** This is the only time that this phrase is used in the NT. It is part of God's character, and also what he experiences. Amazingly, it is this peace which he offers to share with his children.

4:9 There is a style of life which goes beyond pagan goodness. Ultimately, the Philippians' behavior ought to reflect the commandments of God, which will at times be different from what popular culture commends.

have received from Epaphroditus the gifts you
sent. They are a fragrant offering, an acceptable
sacrifice, pleasing to God. 19And my God will
meet all your needs according to his glorious
riches in Christ Jesus.

20To our God and Father be glory for ever and
ever. Amen.

Final Greetings

21Greet all the saints in Christ Jesus. The
brothers who are with me send greetings. 22All
the saints send you greetings, especially those
who belong to Caesar's household.

23The grace of the Lord Jesus Christ be with
your spirit. Amen.[a]

[a] 23 Some manuscripts do not have *Amen*.

4:10 ***renewed.*** This is a rare Greek word which appears only at this place in the NT. It describes the flowering of a bush or tree and can be translated "blossomed." Paul is so grateful for the Philippians renewed care after this long silence that to him it is like seeing a shoot sprout out of the ground and burst into blossom.

4:11 ***content.*** This is another rare Greek word, found only at this place in the NT. Paul borrows it from the vocabulary of the Stoic philosophers, for whom it was a favorite word. It was used to describe the person who was self-sufficient and able to exist without anything or anyone. Paul's sufficiency is found in the Lord.

4:12 ***living in plenty or in want.*** It is by the experience of these extremes that Paul has come to know the secret of coping with all circumstances.

4:13 ***everything.*** A better translation of this word would be "all these things." ***through him who gives me strength.*** The source of Paul's ability to exist successfully in all circumstances is his union with Christ. This is his "secret." While it is true that by going through a variety of difficult circumstances he has learned the discipline necessary to cope with hardship and abundance, it is also true that this ability is not merely self-generated. It comes from Christ.

4:16 ***again and again.*** This is one of the few churches from which Paul has accepted multiple gifts—which is an indicator of the very special relationship he has with the Philippians.

Introduction to COLOSSIANS

Personal Reading Plan

- ❒ Colossians 1:1–23
- ❒ Colossians 1:24–2:23
- ❒ Colossians 3:1–4:1
- ❒ Colossians 4:2–18

Author

The apostle Paul was the writer of Colossians.

Date

Tradition has it that Paul wrote Colossians, Ephesians and Philemon during his imprisonment in Rome. This would mean these letters were written in the early A.D. 60s. However, other sites including Caesarea and Ephesus have been proposed as the place of Paul's confinement, so that neither date nor place is certain.

Theme

Fullness and freedom in Christ.

Historical Background

Paul did not found this church, at least not directly. It was probably established as a result of his ministry in Ephesus, since during Paul's two or three years in Ephesus the whole province of Asia was evangelized (Acts 19:10). Paul, however, evidently never visited the churches at Colosse or Laodicea (2:1).

Epaphras probably founded the Colossian church. A native of Colosse (4:12), he worked hard on behalf of the church there (4:13). In fact, in 1:6–7 Paul says: "All over the world this gospel is producing fruit and growing ... . You learned it from Epaphras ... ." Paul then commends Epaphras as his dear friend and a faithful minister of Christ. In fact, because of their friendship, Epaphras stayed with Paul during his imprisonment (Philem. 23) and so was unable to deliver the letter to the Colossians personally. We also meet the church at Colosse in Paul's letter to Philemon, where he requests that the runaway slave Onesimus (converted through Paul's ministry) be accepted back.

The church at Colosse was probably mainly Gentile in composition. In 1:21 Paul speaks of the Colossian Christians as having once been "alienated from God" and "enemies in your minds"—phrases he uses elsewhere to describe those who are not part of God's covenant with Israel. Then in 1:27, he talks about making the mystery of God clear to the Gentiles; the reference is obviously to the Colossians. Finally in 3:5–7, Paul lists their past sins, which are characteristic of Gentiles rather than Jews.

Religion in Colosse

A large number of Jews had lived in the region of Colosse, ever since the second century B.C. when Antiochus III brought 2,000 Jews from Mesopotamia and Babylon to settle there. By Paul's time there may have been as many as 50,000 Jews living in the region and practicing their religion. However, their synagogue had a "reputation for laxity and openness to speculation drifting in from the hellenistic world" (Ralph P. Martin, *Colossians and Philemon: New Century Bible Commentary,* p. 18).

But freethinking Judaism was not the major religious force in the Lycus Valley. The Greek religions also flourished there. The cult of Cybele, for example, was highly popular. This was a fertility cult characterized by ecstasy and excessive enthusiasm, though it also had an aspect of self-denial. Throughout the Roman Empire, the worship of Isis, Apollo, Dionysus, Asclepius and other gods was widespread. In particular, the cult of Mithras, a mystery religion based on astrology and sacrifice, abounded in Colosse. The church at Colosse, therefore, grew up in an atmosphere that blended a variety of religious traditions that may have been sources of heresy within the church.

Characteristics

As Paul does so often, he begins his letter with a strong doctrinal statement and concludes it by drawing out the behavioral implications of the doctrine. Here his doctrinal emphasis is on the cosmic nature of Jesus Christ. Jesus is the divine Lord of the universe who reconciles all things to himself through his death, not by rules and regulations. Paul sets this strong statement of Christ's deity (1:15–23) over against the mystical, ritualistic religion of the false teachers (2:8–23). (Apparently, these teachings had something to do with astrology. The "star-deities" could only be pleased by a life of abstinence and self-denial.) Once the truth about Christ is stated, Paul turns to the implications of Christ's lordship over all and describes how those in union with him ought to live (3:1–4:6).

The epistle to the Colossians begins, like most of Paul's letters, with a lengthy introduction (1:1–14). In the first major division on doctrine, Paul establishes the preeminence of Christ (1:15–2:23). He follows this with an exhortation to the Colossians to live in union with Christ (3:1–4:6). He concludes with personal greetings (4:7–18).

The City of Colosse

About 100 miles west of Ephesus in the Lycus River Valley lay the city of Colosse. In Paul's time, it was located in the Roman province of Asia (in what today is Turkey). It was one of three major population centers that had flourished in the region. Hierapolis and Laodicea (4:13) stood on opposite sides of the Lycus River, about six miles apart, while Colosse straddled the river some 12 miles upstream.

Since it was located on a major trade route from Ephesus, Colosse was considered a great city in the days of Xerxes, the Persian king (fifth century B.C.). One hundred years later, it had developed into a prosperous commercial center on account of its weaving industry. In fact, "Colossian" came to mean a certain color of dyed wool.

By the time of Paul, however, Colosse's prominence had diminished; though its sister cities, Laodicea and Hierapolis, were still prospering. Laodicea had become the seat of Roman government in the region, and Hierapolis was famous for its healing waters. But Colosse, when Paul wrote, was no longer even a city. In fact, Colosse was the least important town to which Paul ever wrote.

Passages for Topical Group Study

1:15–23	JESUS CHRIST	The Supremacy of Christ
3:1–25	PARENTAL EXPECTATIONS FORGIVENESS	Rules for Holy Living

See the Lesson Plans in the front of this Bible.

Passages for General Group Study

1:1–14	Thanksgiving and Prayer
1:24–2:5	Paul's Labor for the Church
2:6–23	Freedom From Human Regulations Through Life With Christ
4:1–18	Final Instructions and Greetings

1 Paul, an apostle of Christ Jesus by the will of
God, and Timothy our brother,

2To the holy and faithful[a] brothers in Christ
at Colosse:

Grace and peace to you from God our Father.[b]

Thanksgiving and Prayer

3We always thank God, the Father of our Lord
Jesus Christ, when we pray for you, 4because we
have heard of your faith in Christ Jesus and of the
love you have for all the saints— 5the faith and
love that spring from the hope that is stored up
for you in heaven and that you have already
heard about in the word of truth, the gospel 6that
has come to you. All over the world this gospel is
bearing fruit and growing, just as it has been doing among you since the day you heard it and
understood God's grace in all its truth. 7You
learned it from Epaphras, our dear fellow servant,
who is a faithful minister of Christ on our[c] behalf, 8and who also told us of your love in the
Spirit.

9For this reason, since the day we heard about
you, we have not stopped praying for you and
asking God to fill you with the knowledge of his
will through all spiritual wisdom and understanding. 10And we pray this in order that you may
live a life worthy of the Lord and may please
him in every way: bearing fruit in every good
work, growing in the knowledge of God, 11being
strengthened with all power according to his glorious might so that you may have great endurance and patience, and joyfully 12giving thanks to
the Father, who has qualified you[d] to share in
the inheritance of the saints in the kingdom of
light. 13For he has rescued us from the dominion
of darkness and brought us into the kingdom of
the Son he loves, 14in whom we have redemption,[e] the forgiveness of sins.

The Supremacy of Christ

15He is the image of the invisible God, the
firstborn over all creation. 16For by him all things
were created: things in heaven and on earth, visible and invisible, whether thrones or powers or
rulers or authorities; all things were created by
him and for him. 17He is before all things, and in
him all things hold together. 18And he is the head
of the body, the church; he is the beginning and
the firstborn from among the dead, so that in
everything he might have the supremacy. 19For
God was pleased to have all his fullness dwell in
him, 20and through him to reconcile to himself all
things, whether things on earth or things in heav-
en, by making peace through his blood, shed on
the cross.

21Once you were alienated from God and were
enemies in your minds because of[f] your evil
behavior. 22But now he has reconciled you by
Christ's physical body through death to present
you holy in his sight, without blemish and free
from accusation— 23if you continue in your faith,

Colossians 1:1–14

1. What were you the most thankful for when you got up this morning?
2. Why are faith and love the products of hope (v. 5)? Why must hope exist first?
3. When did you first come to know the hope offered through Christ in the Gospel?
4. How does what Paul prays for (vv. 9–11) compare with what he thanks God for (vv. 12–14)?
5. What is God saying to you in this passage?
6. How can this group help you in prayer this week?

[a]2 Or *believing* [b]2 Some manuscripts *Father and the Lord Jesus Christ* [c]7 Some manuscripts *your* [d]12 Some manuscripts *us* [e]14 A few late manuscripts *redemption through his blood* [f]21 Or *minds, as shown by*

1:15 *image of the invisible God.* All that God is, Jesus is (see John 1:18; 14:9; 2 Cor. 4:4–6; Heb. 1:3). One need not look anywhere else but to Christ in order to fully know God.

1:17–18 *He is before all things.* Christ's preeminence means he is Lord over all. ***the head of the body.*** This emphasizes the organic, living relationship between Christ and his people. ***firstborn.*** As Jesus is Lord over the original creation, so also he is Lord over the new creation.

1:21 *alienated from God.* Jews viewed Gentile idolatry and immorality as the chief evidence that humanity was in revolt against God. Paul utilizes that idea to contrast the Colossians' "before" and "after" status in Christ.

1:22 *holy / without blemish / free from accusation.* While the false teachers taught that the Colossians needed something more in order to be truly spiritual, Paul uses the language both of sacrifice and the law court to emphasize that believers are completely acceptable to God through Christ (see Rom. 8:1–4). ***in his sight.*** It is not in some distant future, but right now that believers are completely blameless.

1:23 *continue in your faith.* The work of Christ must be received with faith demonstrated by an ongoing loyalty and obedience to Christ. ***proclaimed to every creature.*** Paul reassures his readers that, in spite of what the false teachers have said, they have already received the complete Gospel as proclaimed everywhere else.

established and firm, not moved from the hope
held out in the gospel. This is the gospel that you
heard and that has been proclaimed to every
creature under heaven, and of which I, Paul,
have become a servant.

COLOSSIANS 1:15–23

1. As a kid, who was your favorite superhero? What special power did he or she have?
2. Do you tend to think of Jesus as a superhero? Why?
3. Name some of the things from verses 15–18 that Christ is "number 1" in.
4. How does the idea of "by him all things were created" (v. 16) compare to what is taught in your school?
5. How did Jesus reconcile us to God (v. 20)? Why was this necessary (v. 21)?
6. How does what Jesus did for you make you feel?
7. When did you make peace with God? If you haven't, what is keeping you from doing so?
8. How can the group help you in prayer this week?

(Study notes on page 1119)

Paul's Labor for the Church

24Now I rejoice in what was suffered for you,
and I fill up in my flesh what is still lacking in
regard to Christ's afflictions, for the sake of his
body, which is the church. 25I have become its
servant by the commission God gave me to
present to you the word of God in its fullness—
26the mystery that has been kept hidden for ages
and generations, but is now disclosed to the
saints. 27To them God has chosen to make
known among the Gentiles the glorious riches of
this mystery, which is Christ in you, the hope of
glory.
28We proclaim him, admonishing and teaching
everyone with all wisdom, so that we may
present everyone perfect in Christ. 29To this end
I labor, struggling with all his energy, which so
powerfully works in me.

2 I want you to know how much I am struggling for you and for those at Laodicea, and
for all who have not met me personally. 2My
purpose is that they may be encouraged in heart
and united in love, so that they may have the full
riches of complete understanding, in order that
they may know the mystery of God, namely,
Christ, 3in whom are hidden all the treasures of
wisdom and knowledge. 4I tell you this so that
no one may deceive you by fine-sounding arguments. 5For though I am absent from you in body,
I am present with you in spirit and delight to see
how orderly you are and how firm your faith in
Christ is.

COLOSSIANS 1:24–2:5

1. What memories do you have as a child hunting for "buried treasure" or Easter eggs?
2. In what sense are Paul's sufferings a continuation of Jesus' sufferings? Why would this lead him to rejoice (see 2 Cor. 12:9–10)?
3. Is Paul's stated purpose (1:28; 2:2) a reality in your life? Or are you still somewhere along the way?
4. What "fine-sounding arguments" hinder you in following Jesus? How does Paul speak to your concerns?
5. What is God saying to you in this passage?
6. How can this group help you in prayer this week?

Freedom From Human Regulations Through Life With Christ

6So then, just as you received Christ Jesus as
Lord, continue to live in him, 7rooted and built
up in him, strengthened in the faith as you were
taught, and overflowing with thankfulness.
8See to it that no one takes you captive
through hollow and deceptive philosophy, which
depends on human tradition and the basic principles of this world rather than on Christ.
9For in Christ all the fullness of the Deity lives
in bodily form, 10and you have been given fullness in Christ, who is the head over every power
and authority. 11In him you were also circumcised, in the putting off of the sinful nature,[a] not
with a circumcision done by the hands of men
but with the circumcision done by Christ, 12hav-

[a]11 Or *the flesh*

ing been buried with him in baptism and raised
with him through your faith in the power of God,
who raised him from the dead.
13When you were dead in your sins and in the
uncircumcision of your sinful nature,[a] God
made you[b] alive with Christ. He forgave us all
our sins, 14having canceled the written code,
with its regulations, that was against us and that
stood opposed to us; he took it away, nailing it to
the cross. 15And having disarmed the powers and
authorities, he made a public spectacle of them,
triumphing over them by the cross.[c]
16Therefore do not let anyone judge you by
what you eat or drink, or with regard to a religious festival, a New Moon celebration or a Sabbath day. 17These are a shadow of the things that
were to come; the reality, however, is found in
Christ. 18Do not let anyone who delights in false
humility and the worship of angels disqualify you
for the prize. Such a person goes into great detail
about what he has seen, and his unspiritual mind
puffs him up with idle notions. 19He has lost connection with the Head, from whom the whole
body, supported and held together by its liga-
ments and sinews, grows as God causes it to
grow.
20Since you died with Christ to the basic principles of this world, why, as though you still
belonged to it, do you submit to its rules: 21"Do
not handle! Do not taste! Do not touch!"? 22These
are all destined to perish with use, because they
are based on human commands and teachings.
23Such regulations indeed have an appearance of
wisdom, with their self-imposed worship, their
false humility and their harsh treatment of the
body, but they lack any value in restraining sensual indulgence.

Rules for Holy Living

3 Since, then, you have been raised with
Christ, set your hearts on things above,
where Christ is seated at the right hand of God.
2Set your minds on things above, not on earthly
things. 3For you died, and your life is now hidden
with Christ in God. 4When Christ, who is your[d]
life, appears, then you also will appear with him
in glory.
5Put to death, therefore, whatever belongs to
your earthly nature: sexual immorality, impurity,
lust, evil desires and greed, which is idolatry.
6Because of these, the wrath of God is coming.[e]
7You used to walk in these ways, in the life you
once lived. 8But now you must rid yourselves of
all such things as these: anger, rage, malice, slander, and filthy language from your lips. 9Do not
lie to each other, since you have taken off your
old self with its practices 10and have put on the
new self, which is being renewed in knowledge
in the image of its Creator. 11Here there is no
Greek or Jew, circumcised or uncircumcised, bar-
barian, Scythian, slave or free, but Christ is all,
and is in all.
12Therefore, as God's chosen people, holy and
dearly loved, clothe yourselves with compassion,
kindness, humility, gentleness and patience.
13Bear with each other and forgive whatever
grievances you may have against one another.
Forgive as the Lord forgave you. 14And over all
these virtues put on love, which binds them all
together in perfect unity.
15Let the peace of Christ rule in your hearts,
since as members of one body you were called to
peace. And be thankful. 16Let the word of Christ
dwell in you richly as you teach and admonish
one another with all wisdom, and as you sing
psalms, hymns and spiritual songs with gratitude
in your hearts to God. 17And whatever you do,
whether in word or deed, do it all in the name of
the Lord Jesus, giving thanks to God the Father
through him.

Rules for Christian Households

18Wives, submit to your husbands, as is fitting
in the Lord.

COLOSSIANS 2:6–23

1. Do you consider your parents "permissive" or "strict"?
2. What does "living in Christ" (v. 6) involve (see 1:10–12)? What does the phrase "rooted and built up" (v. 7) imply to you?
3. What are "the basic principles of this world" (vv. 8,20) and the "powers and authorities" (vv. 10,15)? How did Christ give the Colossians victory over these?
4. What is the result of trying to base one's relationship with God on rule keeping or on private visions, as the false teachers were doing?
5. What is God saying to you in this passage?
6. How can this group help you in prayer this week?

[a] 13 Or *your flesh* [b] 13 Some manuscripts *us* [c] 15 Or *them in him* [d] 4 Some manuscripts *our* [e] 6 Some early manuscripts *coming on those who are disobedient*

19Husbands, love your wives and do not be
harsh with them.
20Children, obey your parents in everything,
for this pleases the Lord.

COLOSSIANS 3:1–25

1. What's your favorite kind of clothes to wear?
2. What's something you've set your heart on? Do you tend to set your heart on things above or on earthly things?
3. How does God's forgiveness of you affect your willingness to forgive others?
4. Where are you feeling some pressure from your parents right now? Which virtue from verse 12 could help you in dealing with this?
5. What do you need to "put off" from verse 8? What could you replace this with from verse 12?
6. Verse 13 says, "forgive as the Lord forgave you." How good of a job are you doing at this?
7. How is your life different since "you have been raised with Christ" (v. 1)?
8. Close by forgiving "whatever grievances you may have against one another" (v. 13).

21Fathers, do not embitter your children, or
they will become discouraged.
22Slaves, obey your earthly masters in everything; and do it, not only when their eye is on
you and to win their favor, but with sincerity of
heart and reverence for the Lord. 23Whatever you
do, work at it with all your heart, as working for
the Lord, not for men, 24since you know that you
will receive an inheritance from the Lord as a
reward. It is the Lord Christ you are serving.
25Anyone who does wrong will be repaid for his
wrong, and there is no favoritism.

4 Masters, provide your slaves with what is
right and fair, because you know that you
also have a Master in heaven.

Further Instructions

2Devote yourselves to prayer, being watchful
and thankful. 3And pray for us, too, that God may

COLOSSIANS 4:1–18

1. In elementary school, who were two of your best friends? What was one quality about them that stands out to you?
2. In advancing the Gospel (vv. 2–6), what role is played by prayer?
3. Why is thankfulness such a key ingredient in a Christian's life (see 2:7; 3:15,17)?
4. What has helped you to grow the most in your prayer life?
5. What is God saying to you in this passage?
6. How can this group help you in prayer this week?

open a door for our message, so that we may
proclaim the mystery of Christ, for which I am in
chains. 4Pray that I may proclaim it clearly, as I
should. 5Be wise in the way you act toward outsiders; make the most of every opportunity. 6Let
your conversation be always full of grace, sea-
soned with salt, so that you may know how to
answer everyone.

Final Greetings

7Tychicus will tell you all the news about me.

3:1 ***raised with Christ.*** As the Christian's "death with Christ" cut the bonds to the old authorities (2:20), so one's life with Christ created new bonds with God and others.

3:3 ***hidden with Christ.*** Christian spirituality is not outwardly flashy like that of the false teachers. Its fullness comes when Christ appears (v. 4), not now. But, while the Christian's life is full of ups and downs, one who submits his life to Christ is in no danger of losing it.

3:5 ***sexual immorality ... greed.*** The list of sins proceeds from external actions to internal motives and attitudes.

3:9–10 ***taken off your old self.*** This phrase is used to describe the putting off of the sinful nature through Christ's death (2:11) and Christ's victory over the powers (2:15). ***put on the new self.*** The lifestyle of Christians is patterned after the attitudes and actions of Christ who is at work within them (1 Cor. 15:45; Gal. 3:27).

3:15 ***called to peace.*** While the reconciliation of people with God and one another is the major theme of Christian doctrine (1:20–22; 3:9–11), living out this reconciliation is the major emphasis of Christian ethics (3:12–14). ***be thankful.*** Thankfulness for God's grace is the central motive of Christian living (1:12; 3:16–17; 4:2).

3:16 ***the word of Christ.*** While the false teachers have "lost connection with the Head" (2:19), the message the Colossians teach one another must be centered on Jesus. ***dwell in you richly.*** Spiritual fullness is rooted in a commitment to Christ.

He is a dear brother, a faithful minister and fellow servant in the Lord. 8I am sending him to you
for the express purpose that you may know about
our[a] circumstances and that he may encourage
your hearts. 9He is coming with Onesimus, our
faithful and dear brother, who is one of you. They
will tell you everything that is happening here.
10My fellow prisoner Aristarchus sends you his
greetings, as does Mark, the cousin of Barnabas.
(You have received instructions about him; if he
comes to you, welcome him.) 11Jesus, who is
called Justus, also sends greetings. These are the
only Jews among my fellow workers for the kingdom of God, and they have proved a comfort to
me. 12Epaphras, who is one of you and a servant
of Christ Jesus, sends greetings. He is always
wrestling in prayer for you, that you may stand
firm in all the will of God, mature and fully assured. 13I vouch for him that he is working hard
for you and for those at Laodicea and Hierapolis.
14Our dear friend Luke, the doctor, and Demas
send greetings. 15Give my greetings to the brothers at Laodicea, and to Nympha and the church in
her house.

16After this letter has been read to you, see
that it is also read in the church of the Laodiceans
and that you in turn read the letter from Laodicea.

17Tell Archippus: "See to it that you complete
the work you have received in the Lord."

18I, Paul, write this greeting in my own hand.
Remember my chains. Grace be with you.

[a]8 Some manuscripts *that he may know about your*

Introduction to

1 THESSALONIANS

Personal Reading Plan

❒ 1 Thessalonians 1:1–2:16
❒ 1 Thessalonians 2:17–3:13
❒ 1 Thessalonians 4:1–12
❒ 1 Thessalonians 4:13–5:28

Author

The apostle Paul wrote 1 Thessalonians.

Date

First Thessalonians may well be the first document in what eventually became the New Testament. Many scholars believe that it is Paul's earliest letter, although a few say that Galatians has that honor. In any case, it is generally agreed that 1 Thessalonians was written about A.D. 50, during Paul's second missionary journey not long after the founding of the church in Thessalonica. Paul probably wrote from Corinth, where he went after he left Athens. Timothy had returned with news from Thessalonica, and this letter was Paul's response to his report.

Theme

Living in the light of the coming of Christ.

Historical Background

When Paul crossed over into Macedonia in A.D. 50, a new era began for Christianity. Now the Gospel had spread to Europe and only in a matter of time would it flow west, through Greece, into Italy, on to Spain and the limits of the Roman Empire. After the vision that sent Paul across the Aegean Sea to Philippi, in due course he came to Thessalonica, which turned out to be a key stop in his pioneering work in Europe.

His stay in Thessalonica was brief and stormy. After he had preached in the synagogue for three Sabbaths, the Jews were so jealous of his success that they organized a mob by rounding up "some bad characters from the marketplace" (Acts 17:5). The mob then rushed around looking for Paul and Silas. Failing to find them, they dragged Jason (at whose home Paul was staying) and a few other Christians before the city officials. They claimed that these men were associates of Paul who was preaching that Jesus, not Caesar, was king. That night after Jason and the others were released on bail, Paul and Silas slipped away to Berea.

Paul's Concerns About the Church at Thessalonica

Could three weeks of ministry produce a viable church at Thessalonica? Apparently this question troubled Paul. After ministering in Berea, Paul had gone on to Athens. He attempted to return to Thessalonica, but his efforts were frustrated (2:17–18). In his place he sent Timothy to see how they were doing and to give them what help he could (3:1–5).

What Timothy found was twofold. Generally the news was good. The converts were standing fast in their faith despite persecution and Paul's hasty departure from the city. In fact, they were even doing evangelistic work on their own. On the other hand, there were (not unexpectedly) some problems. Some of the converts had not fully understood the ethical implications of the Gospel. In particular, there was laxity in sexual matters (4:3–8). Some felt it unnecessary to work and had become a burden to the others (4:11–12; 5:14). There was also misunderstanding about the Second Coming. They knew Christ would return again and rescue them from the "coming wrath" (1:9–10; 5:9–10). But some worried about those Christians who died prior to the Lord's return (4:13–14). Quite possibly Paul and the others had departed from Thessalonica before their teaching on this subject was complete. So Paul assures them that the dead in Christ were at no disadvantage. In fact, the first event of the Second Coming would be the resurrection of the dead (4:16).

In his letter to them, Paul expresses his relief and joy at their good progress in the Gospel. They have become, he says, "a model to all the believers in Macedonia and Achaia" (1:7). Paul goes on to explain why he never returned to them. He ends his letter with further instruction about the life of holiness they ought to be leading and about the Second Coming.

The Converts

Who were these believers? Luke says (in Acts 17:1–4) that the church had its roots in the Jewish community. Some members of the synagogue where Paul preached, along with a large number of God-fearing Greeks—Gentiles who worshiped at the synagogue—and several prominent women, had become convinced that Jesus was the Messiah and so became Christians. These included Jason who opened his home to Paul and his companions, and Aristarchus who was later Paul's traveling companion and prison mate (Acts 19:29; 20:4; 27:2; Col. 4:10; Philem. 24).

In fact, throughout Paul's ministry in Macedonia many prominent women were converted. Lydia, the businesswoman, was his first convert in Philippi (Acts 16:14). Many "prominent Greek women" were converted in Berea (Acts 17:12). Unlike most other women in the first century, the women in Macedonia had been noted for their competence and for the active role they played in society. As it turns out, they were crucial to the growth of the church in Europe.

The greater part of the church, however, seems to have been made up of converted pagans, as Paul's comment in 1:9 indicates: "You turned to God from idols."

The City of Thessalonica

Thessalonica was a great city. Originally named Therme, its famous harbor became the base for the Persian fleet during Xerxes' invasion of Europe. In 315 B.C., Cassander, the Macedonian king, renamed the city Thessalonica after his wife, the half-sister of Alexander the Great. In 146 B.C. after Rome had taken over Greece, Thessalonica was made the capital of the Roman province of Macedonia. In 42 B.C., Rome granted it the status of a free city, which gave Thessalonica a high degree of autonomy.

The key to its importance was Thessalonica's location astride the famous *Via Egnatia*—the great Roman military road across northern Greece, which stretched from the Adriatic Sea on the west to Constantinople in the east. Hence trade between Rome and Asia Minor and points farther east flowed through Thessalonica, making it very wealthy. This was a crucial site for a church if Christianity were to spread throughout the world.

Characteristics

First Thessalonians stands out from the four books that precede it because, unlike them, this letter does not emphasize theology and doctrine. Rather, it reflects the concern, gratitude, disappointment and joy of a beloved missionary who can't stop thinking about the church he left behind. Certainly one reason for Paul's success focuses on his churches having made as big an impression on Paul as he made on them.

Passages for Topical Group Study

4:1–12	SEXUAL ABSTINENCE	Living to Please God
	DATE RAPE	
4:13–5:11	THE SECOND COMING	The Coming of the Lord

See the Lesson Plans in the front of this Bible.

Passages for General Group Study

1:1–10	Paul's Thanksgiving	2:17–3:13	Paul and Timothy
2:1–16	Paul's Ministry	5:12–28	Final Instructions

1

Paul, Silas[a] and Timothy,

To the church of the Thessalonians in God the
Father and the Lord Jesus Christ:

Grace and peace to you.[b]

Thanksgiving for the Thessalonians' Faith

2 We always thank God for all of you, mentioning you in our prayers. 3 We continually remember before our God and Father your work produced by faith, your labor prompted by love, and
your endurance inspired by hope in our Lord
Jesus Christ.

4 For we know, brothers loved by God, that he
has chosen you, 5 because our gospel came to you
not simply with words, but also with power, with
the Holy Spirit and with deep conviction. You
know how we lived among you for your sake.
6 You became imitators of us and of the Lord; in
spite of severe suffering, you welcomed the message with the joy given by the Holy Spirit. 7 And
so you became a model to all the believers in
Macedonia and Achaia. 8 The Lord's message rang
out from you not only in Macedonia and
Achaia—your faith in God has become known
everywhere. Therefore we do not need to say
anything about it, 9 for they themselves report
what kind of reception you gave us. They tell
how you turned to God from idols to serve the
living and true God, 10 and to wait for his Son
from heaven, whom he raised from the dead—
Jesus, who rescues us from the coming wrath.

1 Thessalonians 1:1–10

1. What teams have you belonged to? Of which team were you most proud?
2. What convinced Paul that the Thessalonians were indeed chosen by God?
3. How did they first become imitators of, and then models for, the faith (vv. 6–10)? What does this tell you about their growth in Christ?
4. In an age without mass media, how do you suppose their faith became so legendary?
5. What is God saying to you in this passage?
6. How can this group help you in prayer this week?

Paul's Ministry in Thessalonica

2

You know, brothers, that our visit to you was
not a failure. 2 We had previously suffered
and been insulted in Philippi, as you know, but
with the help of our God we dared to tell you his
gospel in spite of strong opposition. 3 For the appeal we make does not spring from error or impure motives, nor are we trying to trick you. 4 On
the contrary, we speak as men approved by God
to be entrusted with the gospel. We are not trying to please men but God, who tests our hearts.

1 Thessalonians 2:1–16

1. What was one of your most memorable failures in school?
2. What rumors about Paul have been spread by his opposition (vv. 1–6)? Does Paul sound reassuring to you?
3. What difficulties were the Thessalonians facing (vv. 14–15)? How would Paul's example of perseverance in the face of persecution encourage them?
4. List the characteristics of a faithful Christian worker given in this passage. Which do you possess? Which do you want to develop?
5. What is God saying to you in this passage?
6. How can this group help you in prayer this week?

5 You know we never used flattery, nor did we put
on a mask to cover up greed—God is our witness. 6 We were not looking for praise from men,
not from you or anyone else.

As apostles of Christ we could have been a
burden to you, 7 but we were gentle among you,
like a mother caring for her little children. 8 We
loved you so much that we were delighted to
share with you not only the gospel of God but our
lives as well, because you had become so dear to
us. 9 Surely you remember, brothers, our toil and
hardship; we worked night and day in order not
to be a burden to anyone while we preached the
gospel of God to you.

[a] 1 Greek *Silvanus*, a variant of *Silas* [b] 1 Some early manuscripts *you from God our Father and the Lord Jesus Christ*

10You are witnesses, and so is God, of how
holy, righteous and blameless we were among
you who believed. 11For you know that we dealt
with each of you as a father deals with his own
children, 12encouraging, comforting and urging
you to live lives worthy of God, who calls you
into his kingdom and glory.

13And we also thank God continually because,
when you received the word of God, which you
heard from us, you accepted it not as the word of
men, but as it actually is, the word of God, which
is at work in you who believe. 14For you, brothers, became imitators of God's churches in Judea,
which are in Christ Jesus: You suffered from your
own countrymen the same things those churches
suffered from the Jews, 15who killed the Lord
Jesus and the prophets and also drove us out.
They displease God and are hostile to all men 16in
their effort to keep us from speaking to the Gentiles so that they may be saved. In this way they
always heap up their sins to the limit. The wrath
of God has come upon them at last.[a]

Paul's Longing to See the Thessalonians

17But, brothers, when we were torn away
from you for a short time (in person, not in
thought), out of our intense longing we made
every effort to see you. 18For we wanted to come
to you—certainly I, Paul, did, again and again—
but Satan stopped us. 19For what is our hope, our
joy, or the crown in which we will glory in the
presence of our Lord Jesus when he comes? Is it
not you? 20Indeed, you are our glory and joy.

3 So when we could stand it no longer, we
thought it best to be left by ourselves in Athens. 2We sent Timothy, who is our brother and
God's fellow worker[b] in spreading the gospel of
Christ, to strengthen and encourage you in your
faith, 3so that no one would be unsettled by these
trials. You know quite well that we were destined
for them. 4In fact, when we were with you, we
kept telling you that we would be persecuted.
And it turned out that way, as you well know.
5For this reason, when I could stand it no longer,
I sent to find out about your faith. I was afraid
that in some way the tempter might have tempted you and our efforts might have been useless.

Timothy's Encouraging Report

6But Timothy has just now come to us from
you and has brought good news about your faith
and love. He has told us that you always have
pleasant memories of us and that you long to see
us, just as we also long to see you. 7Therefore,
brothers, in all our distress and persecution we
were encouraged about you because of your faith.
8For now we really live, since you are standing
firm in the Lord. 9How can we thank God enough
for you in return for all the joy we have in the
presence of our God because of you? 10Night and
day we pray most earnestly that we may see you
again and supply what is lacking in your faith.

1 Thessalonians 2:17–3:13

1. As a small child, when and where did homesickness strike hard? What did you do about it?
2. Why do you think Paul called the Thessalonian church his "hope," "joy" and "crown"?
3. What in Timothy's report particularly encourages Paul?
4. In what specific ways have you been encouraged by someone else's faith? Have you told them about it?
5. What is God saying to you in this passage?
6. How can this group help you in prayer this week?

11Now may our God and Father himself and
our Lord Jesus clear the way for us to come to
you. 12May the Lord make your love increase and
overflow for each other and for everyone else,
just as ours does for you. 13May he strengthen
your hearts so that you will be blameless and holy
in the presence of our God and Father when our
Lord Jesus comes with all his holy ones.

Living to Please God

4 Finally, brothers, we instructed you how to
live in order to please God, as in fact you are
living. Now we ask you and urge you in the Lord
Jesus to do this more and more. 2For you know
what instructions we gave you by the authority of
the Lord Jesus.

3It is God's will that you should be sanctified:
that you should avoid sexual immorality; 4that
each of you should learn to control his own
body[c] in a way that is holy and honorable, 5not
in passionate lust like the heathen, who do not
know God; 6and that in this matter no one should
wrong his brother or take advantage of him. The
Lord will punish men for all such sins, as we have

[a]16 Or *them fully* [b]2 Some manuscripts *brother and fellow worker*; other manuscripts *brother and God's servant* [c]4 Or *learn to live with his own wife*; or *learn to acquire a wife*

already told you and warned you. 7For God did
not call us to be impure, but to live a holy life.
8Therefore, he who rejects this instruction does
not reject man but God, who gives you his Holy
Spirit.

1 Thessalonians 4:1–12

1. What teacher, coach or other person really challenged you to live up to your best?
2. How big of a problem is date rape at your school?
3. What is "God's will" in regards to your sexual conduct (see v. 3)?
4. How can you "control your body in a way that is holy and honorable" (v. 4)? How "in control" are the students at your school?
5. What would you say to a Christian who tries to take advantage of you on a date?
6. What kind of life does God want us to live (see v. 7)? How are you doing at living a "holy life"?
7. What decisions have you made for yourself about sexual purity?
8. How can the group pray for you and support you in living a "holy and honorable" life?

9Now about brotherly love we do not need to
write to you, for you yourselves have been taught
by God to love each other. 10And in fact, you do
love all the brothers throughout Macedonia. Yet
we urge you, brothers, to do so more and more.
11Make it your ambition to lead a quiet life, to
mind your own business and to work with your
hands, just as we told you, 12so that your daily life
may win the respect of outsiders and so that you
will not be dependent on anybody.

The Coming of the Lord

13Brothers, we do not want you to be ignorant
about those who fall asleep, or to grieve like the
rest of men, who have no hope. 14We believe
that Jesus died and rose again and so we believe
that God will bring with Jesus those who have

1 Thessalonians 4:13–5:11

1. Who do you look forward to seeing in heaven someday?
2. What question would you like to ask God when you get to heaven?
3. If you announced to your school, "Jesus is coming again," what kind of responses would you get?
4. How can you have hope when it comes to death (4:13–14)?
5. On a scale of 1 (give me a minute) to 10 (I'm ready), how prepared are you for Christ's return?
6. What can you do to prepare yourself for his return (5:6–8)?
7. How can you be an encouragement to others in their Christian walk in the coming week?
8. How can the group help you in prayer this week?

(Study notes on page 1129)

fallen asleep in him. 15According to the Lord's
own word, we tell you that we who are still alive,
who are left till the coming of the Lord, will certainly not precede those who have fallen asleep.
16For the Lord himself will come down from

4:1 ***live in order to please God.*** Just as a spouse desires to please his or her mate, so the Christian's concern is how to please God. Neither is a matter of simply keeping legalistic rules, but rather involves a lifestyle that reflects an intimate awareness of the other person.

4:3 ***sanctified.*** This is to be set apart for God's use. The emphasis here is that Christians are not to passively wait for God to make them holy, but to pursue after it in dependence upon the Spirit (Rom. 8:13).

4:6 ***wrong his brother.*** Sexual sin hurts others besides those involved. In adultery, the spouse is always wronged. Premarital sex wrongs the future partner by robbing him or her of the virginity that is a gift to their spouse at marriage.

4:6–8 The three reasons for sexual purity are: (1) Jesus will punish those who continue in those practices; (2) God has called Christians to live a holy life which reflects his nature of faithfulness, integrity and purity; and (3) to reject this teaching is to reject God's Spirit in favor of an unholy way of life. The connection of the Holy Spirit with sexual purity is seen also in 1 Corinthians 6:17,19–20.

4:9–11 ***taught by God.*** Paul probably means the internal witness of the Holy Spirit in their lives which has encouraged them to actively pursue these commands. ***Make it your ambition to lead a quiet life.*** This means to strive hard to *not* strive with others! A Christian lifestyle grows out of a desire to please God and love others.

heaven, with a loud command, with the voice of
the archangel and with the trumpet call of God,
and the dead in Christ will rise first. 17After that,
we who are still alive and are left will be caught
up together with them in the clouds to meet the
Lord in the air. And so we will be with the Lord
forever. 18Therefore encourage each other with
these words.

5 Now, brothers, about times and dates we do
not need to write to you, 2for you know very
well that the day of the Lord will come like a thief
in the night. 3While people are saying, "Peace
and safety," destruction will come on them suddenly, as labor pains on a pregnant woman, and
they will not escape.

4But you, brothers, are not in darkness so that
this day should surprise you like a thief. 5You are
all sons of the light and sons of the day. We do
not belong to the night or to the darkness. 6So
then, let us not be like others, who are asleep,
but let us be alert and self-controlled. 7For those
who sleep, sleep at night, and those who get
drunk, get drunk at night. 8But since we belong
to the day, let us be self-controlled, putting on
faith and love as a breastplate, and the hope of
salvation as a helmet. 9For God did not appoint us
to suffer wrath but to receive salvation through
our Lord Jesus Christ. 10He died for us so that,
whether we are awake or asleep, we may live
together with him. 11Therefore encourage one
another and build each other up, just as in fact
you are doing.

Final Instructions

12Now we ask you, brothers, to respect those
who work hard among you, who are over you in
the Lord and who admonish you. 13Hold them in
the highest regard in love because of their work.
Live in peace with each other. 14And we urge
you, brothers, warn those who are idle, encourage the timid, help the weak, be patient with
everyone. 15Make sure that nobody pays back
wrong for wrong, but always try to be kind to
each other and to everyone else.

16Be joyful always; 17pray continually; 18give
thanks in all circumstances, for this is God's will
for you in Christ Jesus.

19Do not put out the Spirit's fire; 20do not treat
prophecies with contempt. 21Test everything.
Hold on to the good. 22Avoid every kind of evil.

23May God himself, the God of peace, sanctify
you through and through. May your whole spirit,
soul and body be kept blameless at the coming of
our Lord Jesus Christ. 24The one who calls you is
faithful and he will do it.

25Brothers, pray for us. 26Greet all the brothers
with a holy kiss. 27I charge you before the Lord to
have this letter read to all the brothers.

28The grace of our Lord Jesus Christ be with
you.

1 Thessalonians 5:12–28

1. What did you forget to do recently? Did someone remind you?
2. From this passage, what people make up the Christian community?
3. How would you summarize the goal and hope of the Christian life (vv. 23–24) in your own words?
4. Of the various commands, which one will you work on this week? How?
5. What is God saying to you in this passage?
6. How can this group help you in prayer this week?

4:13 ***fall asleep.*** This is simply a common metaphor for death and has no bearing on any doctrine of the intermediate state between the time of one's death and the resurrection of believers at Christ's return.

4:17 ***caught up.*** The only place in the NT where the "rapture" is clearly mentioned. Some interpret the rapture as being a secret event, but Paul is describing something open and public, with loud commands and trumpet blasts. He even uses words that describe a military advance.

5:3 ***While people are saying, "Peace and safety."*** As in Matthew 24:36ff, unbelievers, assuming that the Lord's coming is far off or not real, will take false comfort in the routines of daily life, missing the drama that is approaching its climax.

5:5–6 ***sons of the light and sons of the day.*** In Hebrew, to be a "son of" someone or something meant to share in the characteristics of that person or thing. Christians, who believe in the One who is the "light of the world" share in the characteristics of that light. Likewise, they share in the victory of the Day of the Lord. ***be alert and self-controlled.*** In contrast to the spiritual and moral grogginess of those who "sleep," Christians are to live temperate and balanced lives in full awareness of the coming of the Lord (see also Mark 13:34–37; Luke 12:37; 1 Peter 5:8; Rev. 3:2).

5:10 ***He died for us.*** The Christian's hope for life is rooted in Jesus' death on their behalf (Rom. 5:6–8; 2 Cor. 5:15; 1 Peter 2:21–24).

Introduction to

2 THESSALONIANS

Personal Reading Plan

❒ 2 Thessalonians 1:1–12
❒ 2 Thessalonians 2:1–17
❒ 2 Thessalonians 3:1–18

Author

The apostle Paul wrote 2 Thessalonians.

Date

Paul probably wrote 2 Thessalonians around A.D. 51; 1 and 2 Thessalonians or Galatians are the earliest letters of Paul.

Theme

Living in the light of the coming of Christ.

Historical Background

See the Introduction to 1 Thessalonians.

Characteristics

First and Second Thessalonians are very much alike. In fact 2 Thessalonians covers almost the same ground as 1 Thessalonians, although in a more routine fashion. There is thanksgiving for the faith and love of the Thessalonians, encouragement to them in the midst of their persecution, teaching about the Second Coming, and a warning against idleness. Second Thessalonians was probably written within months, if not weeks, of 1 Thessalonians. Why was it necessary?

The answer may well be that Paul's first letter to these young, untaught Christians produced a serious misunderstanding that necessitated a second, clarifying letter. Specifically, his teaching that "the day of the Lord will come like a thief in the night" (1 Thess. 5:2) may have encouraged people to abandon normal pursuits to prepare for the Second Coming. Thus, he wrote 2 Thessalonians 2:1–12, outlining the events that must take place *prior* to the return of Christ. "The Second Coming is imminent," he seems to be saying, "but not so imminent that you have to stop everything else." Then he goes on to reiterate what he said in his earlier letter: Stand firm and do not be idle.

In fact, 1 and 2 Thessalonians complement one another concerning the Second Coming. Paul's teaching in 1 Thessalonians is mainly on a personal level and it is given in response to questions about the lot of believers who have died before the Second Coming. In 2 Thessalonians believers are given further instructions on how they may be prepared for the great day. The ungodly will be taken by surprise, but believers will be awake and prepared for Christ's return.

Passage for Topical Group Study

3:6–15	TIME / LEISURE	Warning Against Idleness

See the Lesson Plans in the front of this Bible.

Passages for General Group Study

1:1–12	Thanksgiving and Prayer	2:1–17	The Man of Lawlessness

1 Paul, Silas[a] and Timothy,
To the church of the Thessalonians in God our
Father and the Lord Jesus Christ:

2Grace and peace to you from God the Father
and the Lord Jesus Christ.

Thanksgiving and Prayer

3We ought always to thank God for you, brothers, and rightly so, because your faith is growing
more and more, and the love every one of you has
for each other is increasing. 4Therefore, among
God's churches we boast about your perseverance and faith in all the persecutions and trials
you are enduring.

2 THESSALONIANS 1:1–12

1. What have your parents done right in raising you? What rewards and punishments worked best?
2. What has happened to this church since Paul wrote 1 Thessalonians (v. 4)? How has persecution affected them?
3. Why is God waiting until the Second Coming to punish these persecutors? Who benefits from this delayed justice? How so?
4. What quality do you think Paul admires most in these Christians?
5. What is God saying to you in this passage?
6. How can this group help you in prayer this week?

5All this is evidence that God's judgment is
right, and as a result you will be counted worthy
of the kingdom of God, for which you are suffering. 6God is just: He will pay back trouble to
those who trouble you 7and give relief to you
who are troubled, and to us as well. This will
happen when the Lord Jesus is revealed from
heaven in blazing fire with his powerful angels.
8He will punish those who do not know God and
do not obey the gospel of our Lord Jesus. 9They
will be punished with everlasting destruction and
shut out from the presence of the Lord and from
the majesty of his power 10on the day he comes
to be glorified in his holy people and to be marveled at among all those who have believed. This
includes you, because you believed our testimony
to you.
11With this in mind, we constantly pray for
you, that our God may count you worthy of his
calling, and that by his power he may fulfill every
good purpose of yours and every act prompted by
your faith. 12We pray this so that the name of our
Lord Jesus may be glorified in you, and you in
him, according to the grace of our God and the
Lord Jesus Christ.[b]

The Man of Lawlessness

2 Concerning the coming of our Lord Jesus
Christ and our being gathered to him, we ask
you, brothers, 2not to become easily unsettled or
alarmed by some prophecy, report or letter supposed to have come from us, saying that the day
of the Lord has already come. 3Don't let anyone
deceive you in any way, for ⌞that day will not
come⌟ until the rebellion occurs and the man of
lawlessness[c] is revealed, the man doomed to
destruction. 4He will oppose and will exalt himself over everything that is called God or is worshiped, so that he sets himself up in God's temple, proclaiming himself to be God.

2 THESSALONIANS 2:1–17

1. Who is the worst bad guy that you've seen on TV or in the movies?
2. What must have been happening in Thessalonica to lead Paul to write this?
3. What is God's ultimate purpose in allowing the "man of lawlessness" to deceive people? What signs mark his appearing?
4. How and why will God save his people (vv. 13–14)? In response to God's initiative and Paul's ministry, what are the people to do?
5. What is God saying to you in this passage?
6. How can this group help you in prayer this week?

5Don't you remember that when I was with
you I used to tell you these things? 6And now you
know what is holding him back, so that he may
be revealed at the proper time. 7For the secret
power of lawlessness is already at work; but the
one who now holds it back will continue to do so

[a] *1* Greek *Silvanus*, a variant of *Silas* [b] *12* Or *God and Lord, Jesus Christ* [c] *3* Some manuscripts *sin*

till he is taken out of the way. 8And then the
lawless one will be revealed, whom the Lord
Jesus will overthrow with the breath of his
mouth and destroy by the splendor of his coming.
9The coming of the lawless one will be in accordance with the work of Satan displayed in all
kinds of counterfeit miracles, signs and wonders,
10and in every sort of evil that deceives those
who are perishing. They perish because they refused to love the truth and so be saved. 11For this
reason God sends them a powerful delusion so
that they will believe the lie 12and so that all will
be condemned who have not believed the truth
but have delighted in wickedness.

Stand Firm

13But we ought always to thank God for you,
brothers loved by the Lord, because from the beginning God chose you[a] to be saved through the
sanctifying work of the Spirit and through belief
in the truth. 14He called you to this through our
gospel, that you might share in the glory of our
Lord Jesus Christ. 15So then, brothers, stand firm
and hold to the teachings[b] we passed on to you,
whether by word of mouth or by letter.
16May our Lord Jesus Christ himself and God
our Father, who loved us and by his grace gave us
eternal encouragement and good hope, 17encour-
age your hearts and strengthen you in every good
deed and word.

Request for Prayer

3 Finally, brothers, pray for us that the message of the Lord may spread rapidly and be
honored, just as it was with you. 2And pray that
we may be delivered from wicked and evil men,
for not everyone has faith. 3But the Lord is faithful, and he will strengthen and protect you from
the evil one. 4We have confidence in the Lord
that you are doing and will continue to do the
things we command. 5May the Lord direct your
hearts into God's love and Christ's perseverance.

Warning Against Idleness

6In the name of the Lord Jesus Christ, we command you, brothers, to keep away from every
brother who is idle and does not live according to
the teaching[c] you received from us. 7For you
yourselves know how you ought to follow our
example. We were not idle when we were with
you, 8nor did we eat anyone's food without paying for it. On the contrary, we worked night and
day, laboring and toiling so that we would not be
a burden to any of you. 9We did this, not because
we do not have the right to such help, but in
order to make ourselves a model for you to fol-

[a] 13 Some manuscripts *because God chose you as his firstfruits* [b] 15 Or *traditions* [c] 6 Or *tradition*

2 THESSALONIANS 3:6–15

1. What was your first paying job?
2. What is your most productive hour in the day? What is your least productive?
3. How do you typically spend your free time?
4. How do you feel about the "rule" in verse 10? What do you do to earn the bread you eat?
5. Where are you on the spectrum between a stressed-out workaholic and an unambitious slacker?
6. How well do you manage your time? Why is that important to God according to this passage?
7. In light of the command in verse 6, what changes, if any, do you need to make regarding who you hang out with?
8. What's one thing you would like this group to hold you accountable to in how you spend your time? Close in prayer.

Paul's words are directed toward those Thessalonians who have chosen not to work due to some false ideas about the coming Day of the Lord. They were content to live off of others until that day arrived.

3:6–7 ***keep away.*** While these people are not to be considered as enemies of the Gospel, they need to be disciplined so they will give up their mistaken practice. This "tough love" approach is to be carried out in a way that communicates that the "family ties" are still strong. ***you ought to follow our example.*** While Paul was in Thessalonica he worked to support himself so as not to be a financial burden to anyone else (see 1 Thess. 2:6–9).

3:11 ***They are not busy; they are busybodies.*** This is a good translation of the play on words Paul uses in Greek. These people are bothering others with their false notions, probably trying to convince them to wait for the Day of the Lord with them. Such action would also give a negative impression of the Christian community to outsiders, as it would appear they are lazy and content to live off the work of others.

3:12 ***settle down.*** Throughout church history there have been groups that have set the date for the return of the Lord, and responded by abandoning the normal pursuits of life in a feverish state of religious excitement. The end result is disenchantment and a discrediting of the Gospel. In contrast, Paul wants them to live in peace, providing themselves with their own needs (see 1 Thess. 4:11).

low. [10]For even when we were with you, we
gave you this rule: "If a man will not work, he
shall not eat."
[11]We hear that some among you are idle. They
are not busy; they are busybodies. [12]Such people
we command and urge in the Lord Jesus Christ to
settle down and earn the bread they eat. [13]And
as for you, brothers, never tire of doing what is
right.
[14]If anyone does not obey our instruction in
this letter, take special note of him. Do not associate with him, in order that he may feel ashamed.
[15]Yet do not regard him as an enemy, but warn
him as a brother.

Final Greetings

[16]Now may the Lord of peace himself give you
peace at all times and in every way. The Lord be
with all of you.
[17]I, Paul, write this greeting in my own hand,
which is the distinguishing mark in all my letters.
This is how I write.
[18]The grace of our Lord Jesus Christ be with
you all.

Introduction to
1 TIMOTHY

Personal Reading Plan

- ❒ 1 Timothy 1:1–2:15
- ❒ 1 Timothy 3:1–4:16
- ❒ 1 Timothy 5:1–6:2
- ❒ 1 Timothy 6:3–21

Author

The apostle Paul was most likely the author of 1 Timothy. However, based on considerations of vocabulary and style, the Pauline authorship of the Pastoral Epistles (1 and 2 Timothy, Titus) has been questioned by some scholars.

Date

First Timothy was written about A.D. 63–65.

Theme

A faithful ministry.

Historical Background

When Paul first met Timothy, he was living at Lystra in the Roman province of Galatia (modern Turkey). Timothy was the child of a mixed marriage. His father was a Gentile and his mother was Jewish (Acts 16:1). Timothy, along with his mother Eunice and his grandmother Lois, was probably converted during Paul's first missionary journey (Acts 14:8–25; compare 2 Tim. 3:10–11). By the time of Paul's second visit to the area a year or two later, Timothy had matured so much as a Christian that the local church recommended Timothy to Paul as a helpful traveling companion (Acts 16:2). However, Paul decided that Timothy must be circumcised first to legitimize him in the eyes of Paul's Jewish critics. Without circumcision, they would have considered him a Gentile (because of his Greek father), even though he had been brought up in his mother's religion.

From this point on, Timothy seems to be associated with Paul's ministry in one way or another. He was a coworker with Paul (Rom. 16:21; 1 Cor. 16:10; Phil. 2:22; 1 Thess. 3:2). He collaborated in the writing of six of Paul's letters (1 and 2 Thess., 2 Cor., Phil., Col. and Philem.). He was Paul's trusted representative on three missions before this one in Ephesus (to Thessalonica around A.D. 50; to Corinth between A.D. 53 and 54; and to Philippi around A.D. 60–62).

Timothy was not just a colleague of Paul's; he was a beloved friend. Paul called him "my son whom I love, who is faithful in the Lord" (1 Cor. 4:17). In Philippians 2:20–22, the aging apostle says: "I have no one else like him ... Timothy has proved himself, because as a son with his father he has served with me in the work of the gospel."

Audience

The three so-called Pastoral Epistles (plus Philemon) are set apart from the other letters written by Paul; they are addressed to persons, not churches. In the case of 1 Timothy, however, it seems that Paul intended to write his instructions directly to the church but was unable to do so, since the local leadership was itself the problem. Consequently, he wrote to the church through his representative, Timothy. There are few personal remarks in 1 Timothy, and all of these are directed toward Timothy's commission to restore proper order in the church (see 1:18–19; 4:6–16; 6:11–21).

Purpose

Paul tells us why he wrote 1 Timothy: "As I urged you when I went into Macedonia, stay there in Ephesus so that you may command certain men not to teach false doctrines any longer ... (1:3).

"Although I hope to come to you soon, I am writing you these instructions so that, if I am delayed, you will know how people ought to conduct themselves in God's household, which is the church of the living God, the pillar and foundation of the truth" (3:14–15).

Timothy had been left in Ephesus for one purpose: to prevent those who had "shipwrecked their [own] faith" (1:19) from corrupting the rest of the church (see 2 Tim. 2:17–18). He was Paul's apostolic delegate, taking temporary charge of the Ephesian church during the crises it was facing.

The False Teachers

Who were these false teachers who had so upset the Ephesian church? The best guess is that these troubling teachers were *elders* of that church! A careful reading of 1 Timothy seems to indicate this. First of all, it is clear that the teaching in Ephesians was done by the elders (3:2; 5:17). Furthermore, Paul devotes considerable space to outlining the qualifications for leaders in the church. These qualifications contrast sharply with what he says about the false teachers. For example, the false teachers "forbid people to marry" (4:3). Paul says that an overseer (elder), in contrast, "must be ... the husband of but one wife" and "must manage his own family well" (3:2,4–5; see also 3:12). The false teachers "think that godliness is a means to financial gain" (6:5); whereas an elder must "not [be] a lover of money" (3:3). In other words, Paul is saying: "Here is what true elders are like, in contrast to your erring elders." Finally in 5:17–25, he outlines the process of selection and discipline of elders "who sin" (v. 20).

Paul had a sense that this might happen in Ephesus. In his farewell address he said, "Even from your own number men will arise and distort the truth in order to draw away disciples after them" (Acts 20:30).

Two further notes: From various references (2:9–15; 5:11–15; 2 Tim. 3:6–7), it appears that these false teachers were listened to, supported and encouraged by some of the women in the church, especially younger widows. Second, it is likely that the church in Ephesus was not a single large body that met together on Sunday. Rather, it consisted of a number of house churches, some of which had been taken over by the false teachers.

The Nature of the False Teaching

As is often the case, since we have only Paul's response to the problem and not a clear explanation of it, we are forced to figure out the nature of the false teaching. From the text, it seems that the false teachers were involved in questionable speculation rather than the teaching of accepted Christian doctrine. Furthermore, the teachers were proud, arrogant, argumentative and greedy. They used religion to make money and gain power. Their false teaching was connected with the Old Testament, but it also had an aspect of self-denial and a strong Greek element. It appears to be much like the false teaching in the Lycus Valley churches (see the Introduction to Colossians).

Passages for Topical Group Study

1:12–20	FAILURE	The Lord's Grace to Paul
4:1–16	PHYSICAL FITNESS	Instructions to Timothy
	INDEPENDENCE	
	HEALTHY HABITS	
6:3–21	MONEY	Love of Money

See the Lesson Plans in the front of this Bible.

Passages for General Group Study

1:1–11	Warning Against False Teachers	3:1–16	Overseers and Deacons
2:1–15	Instructions on Worship	5:1–6:2	Widows, Elders and Slaves

1 Paul, an apostle of Christ Jesus by the command of God our Savior and of Christ Jesus
our hope,
2To Timothy my true son in the faith:
Grace, mercy and peace from God the Father
and Christ Jesus our Lord.

Warning Against False Teachers of the Law

3As I urged you when I went into Macedonia,
stay there in Ephesus so that you may command
certain men not to teach false doctrines any longer 4nor to devote themselves to myths and endless genealogies. These promote controversies

> **1 TIMOTHY 1:1–11**
>
> 1. What is your father's occupation? Your mother's?
> 2. What does Paul want Timothy to work toward (v. 5)? How does this differ from the work of the false teachers (v. 7)?
> 3. When did God become your "Savior" and Jesus Christ your "hope" (v. 1)? Has your understanding of God changed as you've come to know him? How?
> 4. Who would refer to you as their "son or daughter in the faith," as Paul addresses Timothy?
> 5. What is God saying to you in this passage?
> 6. How can this group help you in prayer this week?

rather than God's work—which is by faith. 5The
goal of this command is love, which comes from
a pure heart and a good conscience and a sincere
faith. 6Some have wandered away from these and
turned to meaningless talk. 7They want to be
teachers of the law, but they do not know what
they are talking about or what they so confidently
affirm.
8We know that the law is good if one uses it
properly. 9We also know that law[a] is made not
for the righteous but for lawbreakers and rebels,
the ungodly and sinful, the unholy and irreligious; for those who kill their fathers or mothers,
for murderers, 10for adulterers and perverts, for
slave traders and liars and perjurers—and for
whatever else is contrary to the sound doctrine
11that conforms to the glorious gospel of the
blessed God, which he entrusted to me.

The Lord's Grace to Paul

12I thank Christ Jesus our Lord, who has given
me strength, that he considered me faithful, appointing me to his service. 13Even though I was
once a blasphemer and a persecutor and a violent
man, I was shown mercy because I acted in ignorance and unbelief. 14The grace of our Lord was
poured out on me abundantly, along with the
faith and love that are in Christ Jesus.
15Here is a trustworthy saying that deserves
full acceptance: Christ Jesus came into the world
to save sinners—of whom I am the worst. 16But
for that very reason I was shown mercy so that in
me, the worst of sinners, Christ Jesus might display his unlimited patience as an example for
those who would believe on him and receive
eternal life. 17Now to the King eternal, immortal,
invisible, the only God, be honor and glory for
ever and ever. Amen.
18Timothy, my son, I give you this instruction
in keeping with the prophecies once made about
you, so that by following them you may fight the

> **1 TIMOTHY 1:12–20**
>
> 1. What's the worst grade you ever got on a report card? What did your parents say?
> 2. What is one thing you did last week that you wish you could do over again?
> 3. Who in your life has shown you the most patience when you fail?
> 4. Why did Jesus come to this world (see v. 15)? How does this make you feel?
> 5. In this passage, Paul tells how Jesus changed him. How has Jesus changed your life?
> 6. As a Christian, how can God use your failures (see v. 16)?
> 7. Where do you need Christ's unlimited patience and lifesaving mercy the most in your life right now?
> 8. How can the group help you in prayer this week?
>
> (Study notes on page 1137)

[a]9 Or *that the law*

good fight, 19holding on to faith and a good conscience. Some have rejected these and so have
shipwrecked their faith. 20Among them are Hymenaeus and Alexander, whom I have handed
over to Satan to be taught not to blaspheme.

Instructions on Worship

2 I urge, then, first of all, that requests,
prayers, intercession and thanksgiving be
made for everyone— 2for kings and all those in
authority, that we may live peaceful and quiet
lives in all godliness and holiness. 3This is good,
and pleases God our Savior, 4who wants all men
to be saved and to come to a knowledge of the
truth. 5For there is one God and one mediator
between God and men, the man Christ Jesus,
6who gave himself as a ransom for all men—
the testimony given in its proper time. 7And
for this purpose I was appointed a herald and an
apostle—I am telling the truth, I am not lying—
and a teacher of the true faith to the Gentiles.
8I want men everywhere to lift up holy hands
in prayer, without anger or disputing.
9I also want women to dress modestly, with
decency and propriety, not with braided hair or
gold or pearls or expensive clothes, 10but with
good deeds, appropriate for women who profess
to worship God.
11A woman should learn in quietness and full
submission. 12I do not permit a woman to teach
or to have authority over a man; she must be
silent. 13For Adam was formed first, then Eve.
14And Adam was not the one deceived; it was the
woman who was deceived and became a sinner.
15But women[a] will be saved[b] through childbearing—if they continue in faith, love and holiness with propriety.

1 TIMOTHY 2:1–15

1. How did you feel about church or Sunday School as a little kid?
2. For whom is Paul asking that prayers for salvation be made (vv. 1,4,6,7)? How do Paul's words make you feel about prayer?
3. Do you think verses 9–15 are meant to be applied at all times and places, or was Paul just dealing with a special problem at Ephesus (see also 1:3–4; 2 Tim. 3:6–7)?
4. What have you found in Christ that affirms your worth even when others put you down?
5. What is God saying to you in this passage?
6. How can this group help you in prayer this week?

Overseers and Deacons

3 Here is a trustworthy saying: If anyone sets
his heart on being an overseer,[c] he desires
a noble task. 2Now the overseer must be above
reproach, the husband of but one wife, temperate, self-controlled, respectable, hospitable, able
to teach, 3not given to drunkenness, not violent
but gentle, not quarrelsome, not a lover of money. 4He must manage his own family well and see
that his children obey him with proper respect.
5(If anyone does not know how to manage his
own family, how can he take care of God's
church?) 6He must not be a recent convert, or he
may become conceited and fall under the same
judgment as the devil. 7He must also have a good
reputation with outsiders, so that he will not fall
into disgrace and into the devil's trap.
8Deacons, likewise, are to be men worthy of
respect, sincere, not indulging in much wine,
and not pursuing dishonest gain. 9They must
keep hold of the deep truths of the faith with a
clear conscience. 10They must first be tested; and
then if there is nothing against them, let them
serve as deacons.
11In the same way, their wives[d] are to be

a *15* Greek *she* b *15* Or *restored* c *1* Traditionally *bishop*; also in verse 2 d *11* Or *way, deaconesses*

Paul gives his personal testimony and emphasizes the power of the Gospel to not only change sinners, but to make them into vibrant messengers of that Gospel.

1:15 *of whom I am the worst.* When Paul met Christ on the Damascus Road, he was overwhelmed both by the magnitude of his sin and by the expansiveness of God's grace. ***I am.*** Paul uses the present tense, because he is still flawed and fallen. However, he has been forgiven and redeemed, and he lives to serve his Savior.

1:16 *an example.* Paul is an illustration (or demonstration) of what can happen to anyone. ***believe on him.*** Conversion occurs when individuals accept Jesus by faith and place their trust in him. ***eternal life.*** People receive the gift of eternal life when they place their trust in Christ. The Greek phrase translated "eternal life" means not so much "life without end" (though it implies that) as it does the "life of the coming age." This life can be experienced in the here-and-now by those who are in Christ, but it will only be fully known when Christ returns again.

1:18 *fight the good fight.* It will be tough for Timothy as he comes up against the erring leadership of his church in Ephesus (v. 20). Paul encourages him to remember his divine call when the going gets rough, and so be inspired to carry on the battle.

1:20 *to be taught not to blaspheme.* The hope was that these two elders might be restored to faith by this form of discipline. Paul remembers that he too was once a "blasphemer" (v. 13), but by the grace of God he came to faith (v. 14).

women worthy of respect, not malicious talkers but temperate and trustworthy in everything.

[12]A deacon must be the husband of but one wife and must manage his children and his household well. [13]Those who have served well gain an excellent standing and great assurance in their faith in Christ Jesus.

[14]Although I hope to come to you soon, I am writing you these instructions so that, [15]if I am delayed, you will know how people ought to conduct themselves in God's household, which is the church of the living God, the pillar and foundation of the truth. [16]Beyond all question, the mystery of godliness is great:

He[a] appeared in a body,[b]
  was vindicated by the Spirit,
was seen by angels,
  was preached among the nations,
was believed on in the world,
  was taken up in glory.

1 Timothy 3:1–16

1. When have you served as a babysitter? How did you enjoy it?
2. Why is this list of qualifications for leadership focused on the *outward* as well as on the *inward?* Why would this be important considering the Ephesian church's problem with false teachers?
3. How do you interpret verse 4? What if a godly man who meets the other qualifications has a child who is rebellious and a troublemaker?
4. What central facts about Jesus are summed up in the hymn (v. 16)?
5. What is God saying to you in this passage?
6. How can this group help you in prayer this week?

Instructions to Timothy

4 The Spirit clearly says that in later times some will abandon the faith and follow deceiving spirits and things taught by demons. [2]Such teachings come through hypocritical liars, whose consciences have been seared as with a hot iron. [3]They forbid people to marry and order them to abstain from certain foods, which God created to be received with thanksgiving by those who believe and who know the truth. [4]For everything God created is good, and nothing is to be rejected if it is received with thanksgiving, [5]because it is consecrated by the word of God and prayer.

1 Timothy 4:1–16

1. What did you eat for breakfast today?
2. How often do you exercise? Are you in better physical or spiritual shape?
3. In your life, what's one habit you would like to break? What healthy habit would you like to start?
4. At what age did you start taking charge of your life—making your own decisions about clothes, school, goals and church?
5. When have you felt looked down on because you are young? How can you still influence others for Christ (v. 12) even though you may be younger than they are?
6. What part of your life do you tend to overemphasize: Physical? Mental? Relational? Spiritual? Which part do you tend to underemphasize?
7. In the next month, what would you like to work on in your life?
8. How can this group support you in prayer to achieve this goal?

(Study notes on page 1139)

[6]If you point these things out to the brothers, you will be a good minister of Christ Jesus, brought up in the truths of the faith and of the good teaching that you have followed. [7]Have nothing to do with godless myths and old wives' tales; rather, train yourself to be godly. [8]For physical training is of some value, but godliness has value for all things, holding promise for both the present life and the life to come.

[9]This is a trustworthy saying that deserves full acceptance [10](and for this we labor and strive), that we have put our hope in the living God, who is the Savior of all men, and especially of those who believe.

[a]16 Some manuscripts *God* [b]16 Or *in the flesh*

11Command and teach these things. 12Don't
let anyone look down on you because you are
young, but set an example for the believers in
speech, in life, in love, in faith and in purity.
13Until I come, devote yourself to the public reading of Scripture, to preaching and to teaching.
14Do not neglect your gift, which was given you
through a prophetic message when the body of
elders laid their hands on you.

15Be diligent in these matters; give yourself
wholly to them, so that everyone may see your
progress. 16Watch your life and doctrine closely.
Persevere in them, because if you do, you will
save both yourself and your hearers.

Advice About Widows, Elders and Slaves

5 Do not rebuke an older man harshly, but
exhort him as if he were your father. Treat
younger men as brothers, 2older women as mothers, and younger women as sisters, with absolute
purity.

3Give proper recognition to those widows who
are really in need. 4But if a widow has children or
grandchildren, these should learn first of all to
put their religion into practice by caring for their
own family and so repaying their parents and
grandparents, for this is pleasing to God. 5The
widow who is really in need and left all alone
puts her hope in God and continues night and
day to pray and to ask God for help. 6But the
widow who lives for pleasure is dead even while
she lives. 7Give the people these instructions,
too, so that no one may be open to blame. 8If
anyone does not provide for his relatives, and
especially for his immediate family, he has denied the faith and is worse than an unbeliever.

9No widow may be put on the list of widows
unless she is over sixty, has been faithful to her
husband,[a] 10and is well known for her good
deeds, such as bringing up children, showing
hospitality, washing the feet of the saints, helping
those in trouble and devoting herself to all kinds
of good deeds.

11As for younger widows, do not put them on
such a list. For when their sensual desires overcome their dedication to Christ, they want to
marry. 12Thus they bring judgment on themselves, because they have broken their first
pledge. 13Besides, they get into the habit of being
idle and going about from house to house. And
not only do they become idlers, but also gossips
and busybodies, saying things they ought not to.
14So I counsel younger widows to marry, to have
children, to manage their homes and to give the
enemy no opportunity for slander. 15Some have
in fact already turned away to follow Satan.

16If any woman who is a believer has widows
in her family, she should help them and not let
the church be burdened with them, so that the
church can help those widows who are really in
need.

17The elders who direct the affairs of the
church well are worthy of double honor, especially those whose work is preaching and teaching.
18For the Scripture says, "Do not muzzle the ox
while it is treading out the grain,"[b] and "The
worker deserves his wages."[c] 19Do not entertain an accusation against an elder unless it is
brought by two or three witnesses. 20Those who
sin are to be rebuked publicly, so that the others
may take warning.

21I charge you, in the sight of God and Christ
Jesus and the elect angels, to keep these instructions without partiality, and to do nothing out of
favoritism.

22Do not be hasty in the laying on of hands,
and do not share in the sins of others. Keep yourself pure.

23Stop drinking only water, and use a little
wine because of your stomach and your frequent
illnesses.

24The sins of some men are obvious, reaching
the place of judgment ahead of them; the sins
of others trail behind them. 25In the same way,
good deeds are obvious, and even those that are
not cannot be hidden.

6 All who are under the yoke of slavery should
consider their masters worthy of full respect,
so that God's name and our teaching may not be
slandered. 2Those who have believing masters

[a]9 Or *has had but one husband* [b]18 Deut. 25:4 [c]18 Luke 10:7

4:1 *deceiving spirits and ... demons.* Satan is behind the chaos in the Ephesian church as he has been in other churches (see 2 Cor. 2:11).

4:3 These false teachers were saying that the way to holiness was through self-denial.

4:6–16 Paul gives Timothy advice as to how he should deal with this heresy. He urges him to model genuine Christian faith by how he lives and what he teaches. It will be his positive example more than negative words that will defuse the power of the heretics.

4:8 Though physical training and discipline is affirmed, it pales in comparison to training for godliness.

4:10 *we have put our hope.* Paul elaborates on why Christians pursue godliness with such vigor. It is because they have placed their hope in God who is alive and the one who brings salvation (new life) to all. The verb tense indicates a continuous state of hope and not just a single act.

4:11–12 *command.* The first thing Paul says is that Timothy must speak with authority. The impression given is that Timothy was a somewhat timid person (1 Cor. 16:10–11; 2 Tim. 1:6–9;). Since this was a public letter, Paul is declaring to all who will read it that Timothy has been empowered by him to "command and teach." ***young.*** Timothy is probably only in his early 30s. However, he is living in a culture that respected age and he is being called upon to discipline elders. ***set an example.*** There is little he can do about his age, but Timothy can lead by example.

are not to show less respect for them because
they are brothers. Instead, they are to serve them
even better, because those who benefit from
their service are believers, and dear to them.
These are the things you are to teach and urge on
them.

1 *Timothy* 5:1–6:2

1. What is the best church or agency you know of that helps the needy?
2. What possible abuses of care for the needy does Paul imply in verses 4–8? Verses 9–10? Verses 11–15? Is a different response to each person in need appropriate in today's church as well?
3. Who in your church needs some help that you or your group can provide?
4. What should be the Christian's/church's response to the welfare issue?
5. What is God saying to you in this passage?
6. How can this group help you in prayer this week?

Love of Money

[3]If anyone teaches false doctrines and does not
agree to the sound instruction of our Lord Jesus
Christ and to godly teaching, [4]he is conceited and
understands nothing. He has an unhealthy interest in controversies and quarrels about words
that result in envy, strife, malicious talk, evil sus-
picions [5]and constant friction between men of
corrupt mind, who have been robbed of the truth
and who think that godliness is a means to financial gain.
[6]But godliness with contentment is great gain.
[7]For we brought nothing into the world, and we
can take nothing out of it. [8]But if we have food
and clothing, we will be content with that. [9]Peo-
ple who want to get rich fall into temptation and
a trap and into many foolish and harmful desires
that plunge men into ruin and destruction. [10]For
the love of money is a root of all kinds of evil.
Some people, eager for money, have wandered
from the faith and pierced themselves with many
griefs.

1 *Timothy* 6:3–21

1. What was your first job and how much money did you make?
2. What is something you're currently saving money for?
3. What effect has money had on the lifestyle of the "rich kids" in your school?
4. What's dangerous about wanting to be rich (see v. 9)? Why is this?
5. What is your biggest concern about money right now?
6. In the past week, have you been more focused on material things or spiritual things?
7. Verse 6 says, "Godliness with contentment is great gain." What do you need to do this week to gain this?
8. How can the group pray for you in the coming week?

Paul's Charge to Timothy

[11]But you, man of God, flee from all this, and
pursue righteousness, godliness, faith, love, endurance and gentleness. [12]Fight the good fight of
the faith. Take hold of the eternal life to which

6:5 ***godliness is a means to financial gain.*** Paul states that the bottom line motivation of these false teachers is the money they make from their teaching. Paul does not consider it wrong for a person to be paid for teaching (see 5:17–18), but he is incensed when greed is the main motivation for ministry.

6:6–10 Paul picks up on this problem of greed. First, godliness is to be much preferred to profit (vv. 6–8), and second, a love of money brings dire results (vv. 9–10).

6:10 ***For the love of money is a root of all kinds of evil.*** Paul is probably quoting a well-known proverb in order to support the assertion he makes in verse 9 that the desire for money leads to ruin. This verse is often misquoted as "money is the root of all evil." While Paul clearly sees the danger of money, he is not contending that *all* evil can be traced to greed.

6:11 ***flee from all this.*** Timothy is to move with haste from not only greed, but from the contentious doctrines of the false teachers.

6:17 ***not to be arrogant nor to put their hope in wealth.*** These are the twin dangers of wealth—causing people to think themselves better than others and to put their trust in their riches (and not in God). ***for our enjoyment.*** But Paul is no ascetic. That the wealthy should not place confidence in their wealth does not carry with it an attitude of total rejection. Enjoyment does not mean self-indulgent living. The enjoyment of wealth lies in the recognition that it is a gift from God, an expression of his generosity.

you were called when you made your good confession in the presence of many witnesses. [13]In
the sight of God, who gives life to everything, and
of Christ Jesus, who while testifying before Pontius Pilate made the good confession, I charge you
[14]to keep this command without spot or blame
until the appearing of our Lord Jesus Christ,
[15]which God will bring about in his own time—
God, the blessed and only Ruler, the King of
kings and Lord of lords, [16]who alone is immortal
and who lives in unapproachable light, whom no
one has seen or can see. To him be honor and
might forever. Amen.

[17]Command those who are rich in this present
world not to be arrogant nor to put their hope in
wealth, which is so uncertain, but to put their
hope in God, who richly provides us with everything for our enjoyment. [18]Command them to do
good, to be rich in good deeds, and to be generous and willing to share. [19]In this way they will
lay up treasure for themselves as a firm foundation for the coming age, so that they may take
hold of the life that is truly life.

[20]Timothy, guard what has been entrusted to
your care. Turn away from godless chatter and
the opposing ideas of what is falsely called knowledge, [21]which some have professed and in so doing have wandered from the faith.

Grace be with you.

Introduction to
2 TIMOTHY

Personal Reading Plan

- ❒ 2 Timothy 1:1–2:13
- ❒ 2 Timothy 2:14–3:9
- ❒ 2 Timothy 3:10–4:8
- ❒ 2 Timothy 4:9–22

Author

The apostle Paul was most likely the author of 2 Timothy. However, based on considerations of vocabulary and style, the Pauline authorship of the Pastoral Epistles (1 and 2 Timothy, Titus) has been questioned by some scholars.

Date

Second Timothy is probably the last epistle Paul ever wrote. The date is thought to be around A.D. 67–68. He is an old man now, in prison once again, deserted by most all of his friends, and facing the likely prospect of death. "For I am already being poured out like a drink offering, and the time has come for my departure. I have fought the good fight, I have finished the race, I have kept the faith. Now there is in store for me the crown of righteousness" (4:6–8).

Theme

Guard the Gospel.

Purpose

Second Timothy is deeply moving as Paul writes Timothy, imploring him to come and be with him in the waning days of his life. In 2 Timothy, the urgency of the problem in Ephesus is in the background. Paul's more pressing need is to have Timothy at his side once again. Even more than personal comfort, Paul wants to pass on the torch of his ministry to Timothy.

Timothy was the logical choice for this new responsibility. He had been Paul's trusted colleague for over 15 years, and he really cared for the welfare of the churches (Phil. 2:20–22). This was a crucial time for the churches in Europe and Asia. They seemed fragile in the face of the forces pressing against them. For one thing, Rome had turned against Christianity. Nero seemed bent on destroying the church. Furthermore, in the Roman province of Asia there had been widespread desertion (1:15). Only a generation after Christ's resurrection, Christianity appeared to be on the verge of annihilation. But Paul's ministry was over. No longer could he travel through the Roman Empire putting out fires, correcting errors, establishing order. Now it was up to Timothy and the others.

To lay this responsibility on Timothy was not easy. In many ways he was an unlikely leader. He was relatively young by Roman standards, in his mid-thirties (1 Tim. 4:12; 2 Tim. 2:22). He was prone to illness (1 Tim. 5:23). And he was, apparently, somewhat shy and in need of encouragement (1 Cor. 16:10; 2 Tim. 1:7–8; 2:1,3; 3:12–14); to his credit, Timothy overcame his natural inclination and tackled risky assignments for Paul (for example, in Corinth).

If Timothy did not make it to Rome in time, these instructions in 2 Timothy would have to suffice. Paul's last letter was a crucial one.

Historical Background

It is difficult to trace Paul's movements during the period when he wrote the Pastoral Epistles. The best guess is that after being released from the house arrest in Rome (described at the end of Acts),

Paul went on another preaching tour taking with him Timothy and Titus. In the course of their travels, they came to Crete. When it came time to move on, Paul left Titus behind to appoint proper leaders for the new church there. Paul and Timothy went to Macedonia via Ephesus. At Ephesus, Paul discovered that heresy was rotting away the church. So he excommunicated Hymenaeus and Alexander, two of the erring leaders (1 Tim. 1:19–20), and he left Timothy behind to help the church through its difficulties (1 Tim. 1:3–4). Paul himself went on to Macedonia. Once there he wrote 1 Timothy and Titus (hence the similarity between the two letters.)

Paul wintered in the Adriatic seacoast town of Nicopolis where he was (presumably) joined by Titus. In the spring, Paul started back to Ephesus, only to be arrested along the way—probably at Troas at the instigation of Alexander the metalworker (2 Tim. 4:14–15).

Paul was eventually taken back to Rome and thrown into prison. This time he was not allowed the relative comfort of a rented house with twenty-four-hour-a-day guards, as was the case during his first imprisonment. Instead he was chained and thrown into a dark, damp dungeon (1:16), "like a criminal" (2:9). Onesiphorus was able to find Paul only after a long search (1:17). Paul was cold ("bring the cloak," 4:13), bored ("bring ... my scrolls, especially the parchments," 4:13), and lonely ("only Luke is with me," 4:11). He had already had a preliminary hearing (4:16–17). His full trial was yet to come, and he did not expect to be acquitted. Nero's insane persecution of the Christians was at its height.

So Paul wrote Timothy to come to him in Rome. He sent this important letter (2 Timothy) via Tychicus, who was to replace Timothy in Ephesus.

Characteristics

Although 2 Timothy is similar in content and focus to both 1 Timothy and Titus, there are some marked differences. Second Timothy is far more personal than 1 Timothy. First Timothy has the feel of a business letter containing important instructions to be heeded by the local congregation. But in 2 Timothy, Paul is writing to Timothy and not to the church, and he reminisces about the work he and Timothy did together. His primary purpose is not combating heresy (although that is a background concern), but to call Timothy to join him in Rome.

In fact, it is Paul's altered situation that gives 2 Timothy its distinct flavor. There is an urgency to his writing. His ministry is over. He tells Timothy to "fan into flame the gift of God, which is in you" (1:6). Timothy must "not be ashamed to testify about our Lord" (1:8). He must "guard the good deposit that was entrusted" to him (1:14). "Preach the Word" (4:2), Paul says, "in season and out of season." So Paul instructs his heir apparent.

Second Timothy is also characterized, somewhat surprisingly, by a note of triumph. Paul knows that despite all the difficulties he is facing, despite the pressure on the church, the Gospel will prevail. It cannot be chained even if he is chained (2:9). Nor will the church ultimately be hampered. It, too, will prevail (2:11–13; 4:8). Therefore, Paul writes to Timothy to carry on the work of the Gospel despite persecution, despite Paul's death, because God's kingdom will prevail (3:10–4:8).

Passages for Topical Group Study

1:1–12	PERSONALITY	Encouragement to Be Faithful
3:10–4:8	THE BIBLE	Paul's Charge to Timothy
4:9–18	LONELINESS	Personal Remarks
	LOSING FRIENDS	

See the Lesson Plans in the front of this Bible.

Passages for General Group Study

2:14–26	A Workman Approved by God
3:1–9	Godlessness in the Last Days

1 Paul, an apostle of Christ Jesus by the will of
God, according to the promise of life that is
in Christ Jesus,

2To Timothy, my dear son:

Grace, mercy and peace from God the Father
and Christ Jesus our Lord.

Encouragement to Be Faithful

3I thank God, whom I serve, as my forefathers
did, with a clear conscience, as night and day I
constantly remember you in my prayers. 4Recall-
ing your tears, I long to see you, so that I may be
filled with joy. 5I have been reminded of your
sincere faith, which first lived in your grandmother Lois and in your mother Eunice and, I am
persuaded, now lives in you also. 6For this reason
I remind you to fan into flame the gift of God,
which is in you through the laying on of my
hands. 7For God did not give us a spirit of timidity, but a spirit of power, of love and of self-
discipline.

8So do not be ashamed to testify about our
Lord, or ashamed of me his prisoner. But join
with me in suffering for the gospel, by the power
of God, 9who has saved us and called us to a holy
life—not because of anything we have done but
because of his own purpose and grace. This grace
was given us in Christ Jesus before the beginning
of time, 10but it has now been revealed through
the appearing of our Savior, Christ Jesus, who has
destroyed death and has brought life and immortality to light through the gospel. 11And of this
gospel I was appointed a herald and an apostle
and a teacher. 12That is why I am suffering as I
am. Yet I am not ashamed, because I know whom
I have believed, and am convinced that he is able
to guard what I have entrusted to him for that
day.

13What you heard from me, keep as the pattern of sound teaching, with faith and love in
Christ Jesus. 14Guard the good deposit that was
entrusted to you—guard it with the help of the
Holy Spirit who lives in us.

15You know that everyone in the province of
Asia has deserted me, including Phygelus and
Hermogenes.

16May the Lord show mercy to the household
of Onesiphorus, because he often refreshed me
and was not ashamed of my chains. 17On the
contrary, when he was in Rome, he searched
hard for me until he found me. 18May the Lord
grant that he will find mercy from the Lord on
that day! You know very well in how many ways
he helped me in Ephesus.

2 You then, my son, be strong in the grace that
is in Christ Jesus. 2And the things you have
heard me say in the presence of many witnesses
entrust to reliable men who will also be qualified
to teach others. 3Endure hardship with us like a
good soldier of Christ Jesus. 4No one serving as a
soldier gets involved in civilian affairs—he wants
to please his commanding officer. 5Similarly, if

2 TIMOTHY 1:1–12

1. What physical traits (nose, smile, eyes, etc.) did you inherit from your father's side of the family? Your mother's?
2. What personality traits (temper, sense of humor, etc.) have you inherited?
3. Does your personality tend to be more reserved or outgoing?
4. Who are the people in your family who inspired you to faith?
5. Who has been your spiritual mentor?
6. Verse 7 says that God gave us a spirit of power, not timidity. Where do you need to experience the power of God in your life?
7. What are you doing to "fan into flame" the gift that God has given you?
8. Share prayer requests and pray for one another.

1:5–6 ***Eunice.*** Timothy's mother was a Jewish Christian (see Acts 16:1). His father was a Gentile, who probably was not a believer. ***the gift of God.*** Paul reminds Timothy not only of his spiritual roots (the faith of his mother and grandmother), but of the gift he has been given for ministry.

1:7 Paul makes this sort of appeal because Timothy is not a forceful person. ***timidity.*** The word for timidity, often appearing in battle contexts, actually suggests cowardice.

1:8 ***ashamed to testify about our Lord.*** The Gospel message about a dying Savior was not immediately popular in the first-century world. The Greeks laughed at the idea that the Messiah could be a convicted criminal, and that God was so weak that he would allow his own Son to die. And the Jews could not conceive of a Messiah (whom they knew to be all-powerful) dying on a cross (which they felt disqualified him from acceptance by God). It was not easy to preach the Gospel in the face of such scorn.

1:9–10 Paul reminds Timothy of the content of the Gospel. The glorious nature of the Gospel will bolster Timothy's confidence and will give him a strong reason not to be ashamed of it. ***has saved us.*** Timothy can face suffering because he has already experienced salvation. This is an accomplished fact. ***Savior.*** This was a common title in the first century. It was applied to the Roman emperor and to various redeemer-gods in the mystery religions. Christians came to see that Jesus was the one and only Savior.

anyone competes as an athlete, he does not receive the victor's crown unless he competes according to the rules. 6The hardworking farmer
should be the first to receive a share of the crops.
7Reflect on what I am saying, for the Lord will
give you insight into all this.

8Remember Jesus Christ, raised from the dead,
descended from David. This is my gospel, 9for
which I am suffering even to the point of being
chained like a criminal. But God's word is not
chained. 10Therefore I endure everything for the
sake of the elect, that they too may obtain the
salvation that is in Christ Jesus, with eternal
glory.

11Here is a trustworthy saying:

If we died with him,
  we will also live with him;
12if we endure,
  we will also reign with him.
If we disown him,
  he will also disown us;
13if we are faithless,
  he will remain faithful,
  for he cannot disown himself.

A Workman Approved by God

14Keep reminding them of these things. Warn
them before God against quarreling about words;
it is of no value, and only ruins those who listen.
15Do your best to present yourself to God as one
approved, a workman who does not need to be
ashamed and who correctly handles the word of
truth. 16Avoid godless chatter, because those
who indulge in it will become more and more
ungodly. 17Their teaching will spread like gan-
grene. Among them are Hymenaeus and Philetus,
18who have wandered away from the truth. They
say that the resurrection has already taken place,
and they destroy the faith of some. 19Neverthe-
less, God's solid foundation stands firm, sealed
with this inscription: "The Lord knows those
who are his,"[a] and, "Everyone who confesses
the name of the Lord must turn away from wickedness."

20In a large house there are articles not only of
gold and silver, but also of wood and clay; some
are for noble purposes and some for ignoble. 21If
a man cleanses himself from the latter, he will be
an instrument for noble purposes, made holy,
useful to the Master and prepared to do any good
work.

22Flee the evil desires of youth, and pursue
righteousness, faith, love and peace, along with
those who call on the Lord out of a pure heart.
23Don't have anything to do with foolish and stupid arguments, because you know they produce
quarrels. 24And the Lord's servant must not quarrel; instead, he must be kind to everyone, able to
teach, not resentful. 25Those who oppose him he
must gently instruct, in the hope that God will
grant them repentance leading them to a knowledge of the truth, 26and that they will come to
their senses and escape from the trap of the devil,
who has taken them captive to do his will.

2 Timothy 2:14–26

1. At the dinner table or in the car, what did you and your siblings quarrel about when you were little kids?
2. Looking over this passage, especially verses 15–16 and 22–24, what should you pursue (the "Do's") and what should you flee (the "Don'ts")?
3. When you hear the word "repentance," what do you think of? Since repentance means "changing directions," how does repentance (v. 25) relate to fleeing and pursuing (v. 22)?
4. Which of the positive qualities mentioned in verse 22 do you need to pursue: Righteousness? Faith? Love? Peace?
5. What is God saying to you in this passage?
6. How can this group help you in prayer this week?

Godlessness in the Last Days

3 But mark this: There will be terrible times in
the last days. 2People will be lovers of themselves, lovers of money, boastful, proud, abusive,
disobedient to their parents, ungrateful, unholy,
3without love, unforgiving, slanderous, without
self-control, brutal, not lovers of the good,
4treacherous, rash, conceited, lovers of pleasure
rather than lovers of God— 5having a form of
godliness but denying its power. Have nothing to
do with them.

6They are the kind who worm their way into
homes and gain control over weak-willed wom-
en, who are loaded down with sins and are
swayed by all kinds of evil desires, 7always learning but never able to acknowledge the truth. 8Just
as Jannes and Jambres opposed Moses, so also
these men oppose the truth—men of depraved

[a] *19* Num. 16:5 (see Septuagint)

minds, who, as far as the faith is concerned, are rejected. 9But they will not get very far because, as in the case of those men, their folly will be clear to everyone.

2 Timothy 3:1–9

1. What happens when you talk back to your parents?
2. How would you compare the sins of the first century to our culture today?
3. Jesus said we should have a pure love for God, other people and ourselves (Matt. 22:37,39). How are the sins listed in this passage a failure of that love?
4. According to verses 6–9, what is the character, danger and fate of false teachers?
5. What is God saying to you in this passage?
6. How can this group help you in prayer this week?

Paul's Charge to Timothy

10You, however, know all about my teaching, my way of life, my purpose, faith, patience, love, endurance, 11persecutions, sufferings—what kinds of things happened to me in Antioch, Iconium and Lystra, the persecutions I endured. Yet the Lord rescued me from all of them. 12In fact, everyone who wants to live a godly life in Christ Jesus will be persecuted, 13while evil men and impostors will go from bad to worse, deceiving and being deceived. 14But as for you, continue in what you have learned and have become convinced of, because you know those from whom you learned it, 15and how from infancy you have known the holy Scriptures, which are able to make you wise for salvation through faith in Christ Jesus. 16All Scripture is God-breathed and is useful for teaching, rebuking, correcting and training in righteousness, 17so that the man of God may be thoroughly equipped for every good work.

4 In the presence of God and of Christ Jesus, who will judge the living and the dead, and

2 Timothy 3:10–4:8

1. What's your all-time favorite book?
2. How old were you when you first started learning the Bible? Who taught you?
3. What type of literature would the average student in your school call the Bible: Fiction? History? Mystery? Nonfiction?
4. In what way has the Bible taught, rebuked, corrected or trained you?
5. How have you personally benefited from the study of the Bible?
6. Comparing your spiritual life to a race, are you: Just getting out of the blocks? Really hitting your stride? Tired out?
7. What would you like to accomplish for God in the future? How can the Word of God help?
8. How can the group pray for you this week?

in view of his appearing and his kingdom, I give you this charge: 2Preach the Word; be prepared in season and out of season; correct, rebuke and encourage—with great patience and careful instruction. 3For the time will come when men will not put up with sound doctrine. Instead, to suit their own desires, they will gather around them a great number of teachers to say what their itching ears want to hear. 4They will turn their ears away from the truth and turn aside to myths. 5But

---

3:14–15 ***continue in what you have learned.*** This is Paul's only command in verses 10–17, and as such defines his key point. ***you know those.*** Those who taught Timothy were reliable people whom he knew well, unlike the false teachers who seek to worm their way into one's confidence. ***wise for salvation through faith in Christ Jesus.*** The OT Scriptures lead one to an understanding of God's saving purpose. However, the Scriptures alone do not save. Salvation comes through Christ Jesus, the one to whom Scripture points.

3:16 ***All Scripture is God-breathed.*** Scripture has a divine origin. It comes from God. ***teaching.*** Scripture is the source of what Timothy teaches, in contrast to the speculative nature of the erring teachers' doctrine. ***rebuking.*** Not only does Scripture teach that which is true, it also reveals that which is in error. Thus Timothy can use Scripture to expose the fallacy of the false teachers. ***correcting.*** Scripture not only speaks about what is true, it also defines how to live. It is thus a measuring stick against which to assess behavior and change what is found wanting. ***training in righteousness.*** This is the positive side of "correcting." Scripture provides instructions in how one ought to live (and not just in how one ought *not* to live).

4:6–8 Paul now adds a few comments about his own situation. By understanding that Paul feels he is about to die, the urgency and energy of his appeal to Timothy makes real sense. What Paul is doing in this letter is passing on the torch of his ministry to Timothy.

you, keep your head in all situations, endure
hardship, do the work of an evangelist, discharge
all the duties of your ministry.
6 For I am already being poured out like a drink
offering, and the time has come for my departure.
7 I have fought the good fight, I have finished the
race, I have kept the faith. 8 Now there is in store
for me the crown of righteousness, which the
Lord, the righteous Judge, will award to me on
that day—and not only to me, but also to all who
have longed for his appearing.

Personal Remarks

9 Do your best to come to me quickly, 10 for
Demas, because he loved this world, has deserted
me and has gone to Thessalonica. Crescens has
gone to Galatia, and Titus to Dalmatia. 11 Only
Luke is with me. Get Mark and bring him with
you, because he is helpful to me in my ministry.
12 I sent Tychicus to Ephesus. 13 When you come,
bring the cloak that I left with Carpus at Troas,
and my scrolls, especially the parchments.
14 Alexander the metalworker did me a great
deal of harm. The Lord will repay him for what
he has done. 15 You too should be on your guard
against him, because he strongly opposed our
message.
16 At my first defense, no one came to my support, but everyone deserted me. May it not be
held against them. 17 But the Lord stood at my
side and gave me strength, so that through me
the message might be fully proclaimed and all the
Gentiles might hear it. And I was delivered from
the lion's mouth. 18 The Lord will rescue me from
every evil attack and will bring me safely to his
heavenly kingdom. To him be glory for ever and
ever. Amen.

Final Greetings

19 Greet Priscilla[a] and Aquila and the household of Onesiphorus. 20 Erastus stayed in Corinth,
and I left Trophimus sick in Miletus. 21 Do your
best to get here before winter. Eubulus greets
you, and so do Pudens, Linus, Claudia and all the
brothers.
22 The Lord be with your spirit. Grace be with
you.

2 Timothy 4:9–18

1. If you were in prison, who would come to visit you?
2. Do you change friends easily or with great pain?
3. When have you felt like nobody loved you but your mom? How did you deal with it?
4. When have you been deserted or stranded? Who *finally* came to your rescue?
5. How can Paul's words in verses 17–18 help you the next time you feel all alone?
6. Where in your life do you need God to rescue you?
7. In your friendship with Jesus last week, were you more like distant acquaintances or best friends?
8. On a scale from 1 (loose) to 10 (tight), how would you rank the closeness of this group? Close in prayer.

a 19 Greek *Prisca*, a variant of *Priscilla*

4:9 *come to me quickly.* It would not be an easy or quick journey for Timothy to take the 1,000 mile trip from Ephesus to Rome. Still, with the typical delays in the Roman judicial system, Paul anticipates that if Timothy hurries (and gets on a boat before the shipping closes down for winter—v. 21), there will be adequate time for him to reach Rome before his trial.

4:10 *Demas.* There is little information about Demas in the NT. He was, apparently, a coworker with Paul during Paul's earlier imprisonment. It must therefore have been particularly painful when Demas deserted. ***he loved this world.*** The "world" is that system which stands in opposition to God. To love it instead of God is to choose the temporal instead of the eternal.

4:11 *Get Mark and bring him with you.* It is a remarkable testimony to the power of the Gospel that after the argument over John Mark which had resulted in Paul and Barnabas parting company (because Mark had deserted them in Perga on their first missionary journey—see Acts 13:13; 15:36–41), reconciliation has taken place. Mark is now once again a valued coworker with Paul (Col. 4:10; Philem. 24).

4:17 *gave me strength.* The first thing the Lord did for Paul at his hearing was to enable him to proclaim the Gospel (as he had done during a previous arrest—see Acts 24:1–21). ***delivered.*** The second thing the Lord did for Paul was to delay his sentence. The judge was not able to render a verdict; therefore a full trial was required.

Introduction to

TITUS

Personal Reading Plan

❒ Titus 1:1–16
❒ Titus 2:1–15
❒ Titus 3:1–15

Author

The apostle Paul was most likely the writer of Titus. However, based on considerations of vocabulary and style, the Pauline authorship of the Pastoral Epistles (1 and 2 Timothy, Titus) has been questioned by some scholars.

Date

Titus was written about A.D. 63–65 (at the same time 1 Timothy was written).

Theme

Be devoted to what is good.

Historical Background

Paul and Titus, along with Timothy, went to Crete as part of a preaching tour following Paul's release from his first imprisonment in Rome. When Paul and Timothy left for Macedonia, Titus stayed behind to establish firmly the new church on Crete. When Paul reached Macedonia he wrote two letters—one to Timothy who had remained in Ephesus and the other to Titus.

In his letter to Titus, Paul reminds the younger man of his role: to appoint good leaders who will guide the church wisely. He also urges Titus to combat the false teachers found on the island. Finally, he tells him that either Artemas or Tychicus will come to relieve him (3:12), after which he is to join Paul for the winter. (See details of Paul's itinerary during this period in the Introduction to 2 Timothy.) Titus was a Greek (Gal. 2:3) who was probably converted through Paul's ministry. He was a trusted colleague of Paul's and was often sent on difficult assignments. For example, when the conflict between Paul and the Corinthian church had reached a breaking point, it was Titus who delivered Paul's "harsh" letter and restored order in that community (2 Cor. 7:5–7). At some point, Titus was sent to Dalmatia (modern Yugoslavia) for yet another mission.

Titus is strikingly similar to 1 Timothy. Apart from the greeting and two pieces of theological writing in 2:11–14 and 3:3–7 (which appear to be creeds), all the material is parallel to 1 Timothy. Still, the differences are notable. The main difference is found in the contrasting situation of Titus and Timothy. Timothy had been left to straighten out a mess in an already established church. Titus, on the other hand, had the job of appointing elders in a new church. As a result, there is less intensity in Titus. There are few imperatives ("Do this"); there is no mention of endurance (as one finds in 1 Timothy); and there are no appeals to "keep the faith." Establishing order in a new church was quite different from restoring order to an established church.

Passages for General Group Study

1:1–4	Salutation
1:5–16	Titus' Task on Crete
2:1–15	What Must Be Taught to Various Groups
3:1–15	Doing What Is Good

1 Paul, a servant of God and an apostle of Jesus Christ for the faith of God's elect and the knowledge of the truth that leads to godliness— 2 a faith and knowledge resting on the hope of eternal life, which God, who does not lie, promised before the beginning of time, 3 and at his appointed season he brought his word to light through the preaching entrusted to me by the command of God our Savior,

4 To Titus, my true son in our common faith:

Grace and peace from God the Father and Christ Jesus our Savior.

Titus 1:1–4

1. Who never forgets to send you a card or a gift for your birthday?
2. In verse 1, Paul explains that he has been called as an apostle to help people come to a "knowledge of the truth that leads to godliness." When did you come to a knowledge of the truth of Christ? What happened?
3. After coming to Christ, did your new knowledge lead to godliness? In what ways?
4. When have you ever questioned your own eternal life? How does verse 2 speak to someone questioning his or her salvation?
5. What is God saying to you in this passage?
6. How can this group help you in prayer this week?

Titus's Task on Crete

5 The reason I left you in Crete was that you might straighten out what was left unfinished and appoint[a] elders in every town, as I directed you. 6 An elder must be blameless, the husband of but one wife, a man whose children believe and are not open to the charge of being wild and disobedient. 7 Since an overseer[b] is entrusted with God's work, he must be blameless—not overbearing, not quick-tempered, not given to drunkenness, not violent, not pursuing dishonest gain. 8 Rather he must be hospitable, one who loves what is good, who is self-controlled, upright, holy and disciplined. 9 He must hold firmly to the trustworthy message as it has been taught, so that he can encourage others by sound doctrine and refute those who oppose it.

10 For there are many rebellious people, mere talkers and deceivers, especially those of the circumcision group. 11 They must be silenced, because they are ruining whole households by teaching things they ought not to teach—and that for the sake of dishonest gain. 12 Even one of their own prophets has said, "Cretans are always liars, evil brutes, lazy gluttons." 13 This testimony is true. Therefore, rebuke them sharply, so that they will be sound in the faith 14 and will pay no attention to Jewish myths or to the commands of those who reject the truth. 15 To the pure, all things are pure, but to those who are corrupted and do not believe, nothing is pure. In fact, both their minds and consciences are corrupted. 16 They claim to know God, but by their actions they deny him. They are detestable, disobedient and unfit for doing anything good.

Titus 1:5–16

1. Who in your family or group of friends is the most disciplined?
2. Why is Paul's list of leadership qualifications focused mostly on "being" and not on "doing" (vv. 6–9)?
3. Which of the qualities in verses 6–9 do you feel you need to develop in your own life?
4. How, in the past or present, have your actions not fit with your "claim to know God" (v. 16)?
5. What is God saying to you in this passage?
6. How can this group help you in prayer this week?

What Must Be Taught to Various Groups

2 You must teach what is in accord with sound doctrine. 2 Teach the older men to be temperate, worthy of respect, self-controlled, and sound in faith, in love and in endurance.

3 Likewise, teach the older women to be reverent in the way they live, not to be slanderers or addicted to much wine, but to teach what is good. 4 Then they can train the younger women

[a] *5* Or *ordain* [b] *7* Traditionally *bishop*

to love their husbands and children, 5to be self-controlled and pure, to be busy at home, to be kind, and to be subject to their husbands, so that no one will malign the word of God.

6Similarly, encourage the young men to be self-controlled. 7In everything set them an example by doing what is good. In your teaching show integrity, seriousness 8and soundness of speech that cannot be condemned, so that those who oppose you may be ashamed because they have nothing bad to say about us.

9Teach slaves to be subject to their masters in everything, to try to please them, not to talk back to them, 10and not to steal from them, but to show that they can be fully trusted, so that in every way they will make the teaching about God our Savior attractive.

TITUS 2:1–15

1. In what area do you need to exercise, or develop, the most self-control?
2. What one quality in each of the groups mentioned is most important for Christians in our society (look at older men, older women, younger women, young men)?
3. What is Paul implying about the importance of *mentors* (trusted guides or models)? How important have mentors been in your life?
4. What difference does our salvation make in our behavior in this "present age" (v. 12)? What is it hardest for you to say "No" to?
5. What is God saying to you in this passage?
6. How can this group help you in prayer this week?

11For the grace of God that brings salvation has appeared to all men. 12It teaches us to say "No" to ungodliness and worldly passions, and to live self-controlled, upright and godly lives in this present age, 13while we wait for the blessed hope—the glorious appearing of our great God and Savior, Jesus Christ, 14who gave himself for us to redeem us from all wickedness and to purify for himself a people that are his very own, eager to do what is good.

15These, then, are the things you should teach. Encourage and rebuke with all authority. Do not let anyone despise you.

Doing What Is Good

3 Remind the people to be subject to rulers and authorities, to be obedient, to be ready to do whatever is good, 2to slander no one, to be peaceable and considerate, and to show true humility toward all men.

3At one time we too were foolish, disobedient, deceived and enslaved by all kinds of passions and pleasures. We lived in malice and envy, being hated and hating one another. 4But when the kindness and love of God our Savior appeared, 5he saved us, not because of righteous things we had done, but because of his mercy. He saved us through the washing of rebirth and renewal by the Holy Spirit, 6whom he poured out on us generously through Jesus Christ our Savior, 7so that, having been justified by his grace, we might become heirs having the hope of eternal life. 8This is a trustworthy saying. And I want you to stress these things, so that those who have trusted in God may be careful to devote themselves to doing what is good. These things are excellent and profitable for everyone.

9But avoid foolish controversies and genealogies and arguments and quarrels about the law, because these are unprofitable and useless. 10Warn a divisive person once, and then warn him a second time. After that, have nothing to do with him. 11You may be sure that such a man is warped and sinful; he is self-condemned.

Final Remarks

12As soon as I send Artemas or Tychicus to you, do your best to come to me at Nicopolis,

TITUS 3:1–15

1. What memory comes to mind when you think of being disobedient as a child?
2. Why do you think Paul again stresses "doing good" (vv. 1,8,14)? What about human nature makes such reminders necessary (v. 3)?
3. What do verses 4–7 say about God's character? About his work in us?
4. Over the past year, where do you sense growth in leading a "productive" life for God (see v. 14)?
5. What is God saying to you in this passage?
6. How can this group help you in prayer this week?

because I have decided to winter there. 13Do everything you can to help Zenas the lawyer and
Apollos on their way and see that they have everything they need. 14Our people must learn to
devote themselves to doing what is good, in order
that they may provide for daily necessities and
not live unproductive lives.
15Everyone with me sends you greetings.
Greet those who love us in the faith.

Grace be with you all.

Introduction to

PHILEMON

Personal Reading Plan

❐ Philemon 1–25

Author

The apostle Paul wrote Philemon.

Date

Paul probably wrote Philemon in the early A.D. 60s.

Theme

Radical forgiveness.

Characteristics

Philemon is the shortest of Paul's New Testament letters and it is his only private letter preserved in Scripture. All his other letters, whether to churches or to coworkers, relate to Paul's ministry. But Philemon is a personal note written to a friend about a private matter—the fate of Onesimus, the runaway slave. As such, it gives us a valuable glimpse into Paul's personality. He is deeply sympathetic to the plight of Onesimus, so much so that he is willing to deprive himself of Onesimus' help and to pay Philemon for any loss Onesimus has caused him (vv. 18–19). This is certainly Christian compassion in action.

Historical Background

At this point in history, the 60 million slaves in the Roman Empire made up a critical component of Rome's social and economic structure. Runaways were considered criminals who were punishable by severe measures including death. Philemon, a member of the church at Colosse, was the owner of a slave (Onesimus) who had run away from him. Somehow Onesimus got to Rome, met Paul and became a Christian. We may wonder why Paul did not take this opportunity simply to condemn slavery. The reason is partially clear. For one thing, conditions were not yet right for such a massive social upheaval. The Romans would never have voluntarily freed their slaves. Any revolt would have been savagely crushed. For another thing, unlike the American experience, Roman slavery was not a permanent condition based on race. This meant that slaves could purchase their freedom and enter the mainstream of society. Still, Paul did strike the first note for emancipation by his teaching on how Christians, regardless of race or economic condition, are one "family" in Christ (v. 16; Col. 3:11). This letter is Paul's attempt to persuade Philemon to forgive the crime and receive Onesimus as he would receive Paul himself. Onesimus carried this letter (and possibly Colossians and Ephesians) back to his home (Col. 4:9). The outcome of this story is not recorded in Scripture, but about A.D. 110 Bishop Ignatius of Antioch wrote a letter to the bishop of Ephesus, who was a man named Onesimus. In it, he used the same word-play on his name as Paul does here in verses 10–11. Since many scholars think that the first collection of Paul's letters was made at Ephesus, Ignatius the bishop may have included this personal note as a vivid demonstration of how Christ can transform and use even a runaway slave.

Passage for General Group Study

1–25 Paul's Plea for Onesimus

1 Paul, a prisoner of Christ Jesus, and Timothy our brother,

To Philemon our dear friend and fellow worker, 2 to Apphia our sister, to Archippus our fellow soldier and to the church that meets in your home:

3 Grace to you and peace from God our Father and the Lord Jesus Christ.

Thanksgiving and Prayer

4 I always thank my God as I remember you in my prayers, 5 because I hear about your faith in the Lord Jesus and your love for all the saints. 6 I pray that you may be active in sharing your faith, so that you will have a full understanding of every good thing we have in Christ. 7 Your love has given me great joy and encouragement, because you, brother, have refreshed the hearts of the saints.

Paul's Plea for Onesimus

8 Therefore, although in Christ I could be bold and order you to do what you ought to do, 9 yet I appeal to you on the basis of love. I then, as Paul—an old man and now also a prisoner of Christ Jesus— 10 I appeal to you for my son Onesimus,[a] who became my son while I was in chains. 11 Formerly he was useless to you, but now he has become useful both to you and to me.

12 I am sending him—who is my very heart—back to you. 13 I would have liked to keep him with me so that he could take your place in helping me while I am in chains for the gospel. 14 But I did not want to do anything without your consent, so that any favor you do will be spontaneous and not forced. 15 Perhaps the reason he was separated from you for a little while was that you might have him back for good— 16 no longer as a slave, but better than a slave, as a dear brother. He is very dear to me but even dearer to you, both as a man and as a brother in the Lord.

17 So if you consider me a partner, welcome him as you would welcome me. 18 If he has done you any wrong or owes you anything, charge it to me. 19 I, Paul, am writing this with my own hand. I will pay it back—not to mention that you owe me your very self. 20 I do wish, brother, that I may have some benefit from you in the Lord; refresh my heart in Christ. 21 Confident of your obedience, I write to you, knowing that you will do even more than I ask.

22 And one thing more: Prepare a guest room for me, because I hope to be restored to you in answer to your prayers.

23 Epaphras, my fellow prisoner in Christ Jesus, sends you greetings. 24 And so do Mark, Aristarchus, Demas and Luke, my fellow workers.

25 The grace of the Lord Jesus Christ be with your spirit.

PHILEMON 1–25

1. What nicknames have you been given? What do they mean?
2. What qualities in Philemon does Paul commend (vv. 4–7)?
3. Does the fact that Onesimus has become a Christian lessen the seriousness of his crime? Why or why not?
4. Which of the qualities in Philemon (vv. 4–7) do you wish to develop for yourself? How could doing so cause you to grow in new areas?
5. What is God saying to you in this passage?
6. How can this group help you in prayer this week?

[a] 10 *Onesimus* means *useful.*

Introduction to
HEBREWS

Personal Reading Plan

- ❒ Hebrews 1:1–2:18
- ❒ Hebrews 3:1–19
- ❒ Hebrews 4:1–13
- ❒ Hebrews 4:14–6:12
- ❒ Hebrews 6:13–7:10
- ❒ Hebrews 7:11–28
- ❒ Hebrews 8:1–9:10
- ❒ Hebrews 9:11–28
- ❒ Hebrews 10:1–39
- ❒ Hebrews 11:1–40
- ❒ Hebrews 12:1–29
- ❒ Hebrews 13:1–25

Author

No one knows who wrote the epistle to the Hebrews. The author is nowhere named within it, nor is there any strong external evidence pointing to one particular person. These facts have not deterred speculation, however. At least eight good candidates for the role of author have been proposed.

A favorite choice has been Paul, probably because the King James version lists him as author, even though such a designation is found in none of the ancient manuscripts. It is unlikely that Paul wrote Hebrews. The style and language of this epistle is quite unlike Paul's, although this fact is more evident in the Greek original than in the English translation. The epistle to the Hebrews is a polished piece of writing. Its transitions are neatly in place and its argument carefully spelled out. This is in sharp contrast to Paul's more ragged style. He had the habit of losing the thread of his argument because he would become excited about some new piece of God's revelation before he had drawn to a logical conclusion the case he originally started to build.

Other suggested authors include Barnabas (Acts 4:36), Luke, Priscilla, Silas (1 Peter 5:12), Apollos (Acts 18:24) and Clement of Rome. Origen, a third-century Christian scholar, had the last word on this issue: He wrote that as to the identity of the author "only God knows certainly" (recorded in Eusebius, *Historia Ecclesiastica*).

Date

As with so much else about this epistle, it is difficult to be certain about its date of composition. If the persecution referred to is that of Nero, then Hebrews was written after A.D. 64. Some hold that it must have been written prior to the fall of Jerusalem and the destruction of the temple in A.D. 70, for such an unprecedented event would probably have been mentioned by the book's author as the sure sign of the end of the sacrificial system. Others argue for a later date. If the fall of Jerusalem were recent, they reason, it would be so gigantic and so fresh in the minds of the readers that it need not be mentioned. In that case, the book could have been written prior to the persecution by Emperor Domitian in A.D. 85, probably somewhere around A.D. 80.

Theme

The superiority of Jesus.

Historical Background

The title "To the Hebrews" can be traced back to manuscripts of the late second century. Even though it was not a part of the original document, it seems to be accurate given the very Jewish flavor of the epistle. This letter was probably written to a particular assembly of Jewish-Christian believers (perhaps a house church) that was part of a larger community, quite possibly in Rome.

Whoever these people were, it is clear that they had suffered great persecution (10:32–34) and that they were being tempted to abandon Christianity. What is less clear is the nature of the pressures weighing against them. Perhaps the constant injustices they suffered as Christians were beginning to take their toll. Or perhaps they were facing the prospect of severe persecution in the near future. Maybe they were being enticed away from Christ by false teaching that seemed to offer relief from their struggles. They might have been considering a return to a form of Judaism as one way to bring community acceptance and thus lessen tensions.

In any case, the temptation to give up their faith was severe enough that the letter to the Hebrews had to be written to encourage these beleaguered Christians to "hold on" (3:6), to "persevere" (10:36), and to "hold unswervingly to the hope we profess" (10:23) lest they compromise Christ and lose all the enormous blessings of the New Covenant.

Characteristics

To many modern readers, Hebrews is a strange book filled with references to ancient practices, with the traditions of a wholly different culture, and with images that evoke no recognition in today's society. It is true that to understand Hebrews, the reader must understand the Old Testament. Yet for all its strangeness, the book of Hebrews continues to fascinate readers because of its vivid images, its relentless argument that refuses to detour from the main point, its stirring remembrances of the heroes of the faith, and most of all its almost breathtaking portrait of Jesus—the ultimate priest who, for ourselves for a time, was made a little lower than the angels. This Jesus captivates the mind and imagination of people today—this Jesus who not only gave strength to those enduring persecution 2,000 years ago, but who still today gives strength to those facing the possibility of annihilation by modern weaponry.

This particular New Testament book has been called an epistle but in fact, it lacks several key features of a true letter. It has no introductory greeting, nor does it name either the sender or the recipients. Its ending is typical of a letter, however, with personal greetings and a standard conclusion.

If Hebrews is not a true letter, then what is it? Some have suggested that Hebrews is a written sermon. Its method of argument is sermonic in nature. Structurally, its closest New Testament parallel is 1 John, which also seems to be a sermon.

Purpose

How does one write to suffering Christians and tell them to stay faithful despite the price they are paying? The author wisely begins not by considering their difficult circumstances nor by simply telling them, "This is the right thing to do, so do it." Instead, he points them to Jesus, the only one who is worth such costly allegiance. As a result, in the book of Hebrews, we get a marvelous portrait of Christ—the prophet, priest and king whose New Covenant is so superior to the Old Covenant that to fall away from him should be unthinkable. The central theme of Hebrews, therefore, is the superiority of Christ. He is superior to the great religious leaders of the past such as Moses, Joshua and Aaron. He is superior to the great supernatural powers like angels. The New Covenant he established and the new order he inaugurated are superior to the old beliefs and practices of the Jewish religion.

Passages for Topical Group Study

1:1–14	ANGELS	The Son Superior to Angels
11:1–16	DREAMS AND DESIRES	By Faith
	FAITH	

See the Lesson Plans in the front of this Bible.

Passages for General Group Study

2:1–18	Jesus Made Like His Brothers	9:1–10	Worship in the Earthly Tabernacle
3:1–19	Jesus Greater Than Moses	9:11–28	The Blood of Christ
4:1–13	A Sabbath-Rest for the People of God	10:1–18	Christ's Sacrifice Once for All
4:14–5:10	Jesus the Great High Priest	10:19–39	A Call to Persevere
5:11–6:12	Warning Against Falling Away	12:1–13	God Disciplines His Sons
6:13–20	The Certainty of God's Promise	12:14–29	Warning Against Refusing God
7:1–28	Jesus Like Melchizedek	13:1–25	Concluding Exhortations
8:1–13	The High Priest of a New Covenant		

The Son Superior to Angels

1 In the past God spoke to our forefathers
through the prophets at many times and in
various ways, 2but in these last days he has spoken to us by his Son, whom he appointed heir of
all things, and through whom he made the universe. 3The Son is the radiance of God's glory and
the exact representation of his being, sustaining
all things by his powerful word. After he had
provided purification for sins, he sat down at the
right hand of the Majesty in heaven. 4So he became as much superior to the angels as the name
he has inherited is superior to theirs.

5For to which of the angels did God ever say,

"You are my Son;
today I have become your Father[a]"[b]?

Or again,

"I will be his Father,
and he will be my Son"[c]?

6And again, when God brings his firstborn into
the world, he says,

"Let all God's angels worship him."[d]

7In speaking of the angels he says,

"He makes his angels winds,
his servants flames of fire."[e]

8But about the Son he says,

"Your throne, O God, will last for ever and
ever,
and righteousness will be the scepter of
your kingdom.
9You have loved righteousness and hated
wickedness;
therefore God, your God, has set you
above your companions
by anointing you with the oil of joy."[f]

10He also says,

"In the beginning, O Lord, you laid the
foundations of the earth,
and the heavens are the work of your
hands.
11They will perish, but you remain;
they will all wear out like a garment.
12You will roll them up like a robe;
like a garment they will be changed.
But you remain the same,
and your years will never end."[g]

13To which of the angels did God ever say,

"Sit at my right hand

Hebrews 1:1–14

1. What is your favorite movie, TV show or story about an angel or angels?
2. When you were a kid, what were you told about angels?
3. Why might someone be tempted to worship angels instead of Jesus?
4. What does verse 14 say about the purpose of angels? How does that make you feel?
5. What is the difference between the biblical view of angels and modern ideas about angels?
6. How do you need an angel to minister to you right now?
7. A focus on angels can distract us from our devotion to Christ. What distracts you from focusing more on Christ in your life?
8. How has this group ministered to you? How can you minister to this group? Close in prayer.

[a]5 Or *have begotten you* [b]5 Psalm 2:7 [c]5 2 Samuel 7:14; 1 Chron. 17:13 [d]6 Deut. 32:43 (see Dead Sea Scrolls and Septuagint) [e]7 Psalm 104:4 [f]9 Psalm 45:6,7 [g]12 Psalm 102:25-27

1:2 ***but.*** In contrast to the limited revelation of the prophets, the Son fully reveals the Word of God to the world. ***he has spoken.*** The Word of God spoken through Jesus is superior to all forms of communication used in the past. This revelation of God to humanity is complete and final, needing nothing more to supplement it. ***made the universe.*** As in John 1:1–18, this author maintains that the divinity of Jesus stretches back to "the beginning" in which he played a part in the creation of the world.

1:3 This verse is based on the Song to Divine Wisdom in Proverbs 8:22ff. ***sustaining all things.*** The Son's role in creation is not limited to creation's origin or its future. It is his powerful word that keeps order and stability in creation (Col. 1:17). ***purification for sins.*** While popular thought held that people had to work for their own purification from sin, the author uses a term related to the Day of Atonement to show that the Son has dealt with sin. ***the right hand.*** The position of power and honor.

1:8–9 This quote (Ps. 45:6–7) directly attributes deity to the Son.

1:14 In contrast to the ruling authority of the Son, the function of the angels is to *serve* people at the Son's command. ***ministering.*** This word describes the priestly service at the tabernacle. In the New Testament angels perform tasks such as interceding for children (Matt. 18:10), protecting the apostles (Acts 12:7–10), revealing God's will (Luke 1:11ff), and carrying out God's judgment (Rev. 7:1).

until I make your enemies
a footstool for your feet"[a]?

14Are not all angels ministering spirits sent to
serve those who will inherit salvation?

Warning to Pay Attention

2 We must pay more careful attention, therefore, to what we have heard, so that we do
not drift away. 2For if the message spoken by
angels was binding, and every violation and disobedience received its just punishment, 3how
shall we escape if we ignore such a great salvation? This salvation, which was first announced
by the Lord, was confirmed to us by those who
heard him. 4God also testified to it by signs, wonders and various miracles, and gifts of the Holy
Spirit distributed according to his will.

Jesus Made Like His Brothers

5It is not to angels that he has subjected the
world to come, about which we are speaking.
6But there is a place where someone has testified:

"What is man that you are mindful of him,
the son of man that you care for him?
7You made him a little[b] lower than the
angels;
you crowned him with glory and honor
8 and put everything under his feet."[c]

In putting everything under him, God left nothing that is not subject to him. Yet at present we
do not see everything subject to him. 9But we see
Jesus, who was made a little lower than the angels, now crowned with glory and honor because
he suffered death, so that by the grace of God he
might taste death for everyone.
10In bringing many sons to glory, it was fitting
that God, for whom and through whom everything exists, should make the author of their salvation perfect through suffering. 11Both the one
who makes men holy and those who are made
holy are of the same family. So Jesus is not
ashamed to call them brothers. 12He says,

"I will declare your name to my brothers;
in the presence of the congregation I will
sing your praises."[d]

13And again,

"I will put my trust in him."[e]

And again he says,

"Here am I, and the children God has given
me."[f]

14Since the children have flesh and blood, he
too shared in their humanity so that by his death
he might destroy him who holds the power of
death—that is, the devil— 15and free those who
all their lives were held in slavery by their fear of
death. 16For surely it is not angels he helps, but
Abraham's descendants. 17For this reason he had
to be made like his brothers in every way, in
order that he might become a merciful and faithful high priest in service to God, and that he
might make atonement for[g] the sins of the people. 18Because he himself suffered when he was
tempted, he is able to help those who are being
tempted.

HEBREWS 2:1–18

1. When your parents went away, who were you "subject to" as a child? How did you look upon this person or the rules imposed on you?
2. What danger faces these people? What does it mean to "drift away" (v. 1)?
3. In what respects was Jesus "made lower than the angels" (v. 9)? What elevated him above them?
4. Why did we need someone with flesh and blood like us—not an angel—to die in our place (vv. 14–18)? What is the goal of our salvation (vv. 10–11)?
5. What is God saying to you in this passage?
6. How can this group help you in prayer this week?

Jesus Greater Than Moses

3 Therefore, holy brothers, who share in the heavenly calling, fix your thoughts on Jesus,
the apostle and high priest whom we confess.
2He was faithful to the one who appointed him,
just as Moses was faithful in all God's house.
3Jesus has been found worthy of greater honor
than Moses, just as the builder of a house has
greater honor than the house itself. 4For every
house is built by someone, but God is the builder
of everything. 5Moses was faithful as a servant in
all God's house, testifying to what would be said
in the future. 6But Christ is faithful as a son over

a13 Psalm 110:1 b7 Or *him for a little while*; also in verse 9 c8 Psalm 8:4-6 d12 Psalm 22:22 e13 Isaiah 8:17
f13 Isaiah 8:18 g17 Or *and that he might turn aside God's wrath, taking away*

God's house. And we are his house, if we hold on
to our courage and the hope of which we boast.

Warning Against Unbelief

7So, as the Holy Spirit says:

"Today, if you hear his voice,
8 do not harden your hearts
as you did in the rebellion,
during the time of testing in the desert,
9where your fathers tested and tried me
and for forty years saw what I did.
10That is why I was angry with that
generation,
and I said, 'Their hearts are always going
astray,
and they have not known my ways.'
11So I declared on oath in my anger,
'They shall never enter my rest.' "[a]

HEBREWS 3:1–19

1. Are you usually early or late getting to places? Why?
2. In what ways are Jesus and Moses similar? In what ways is Jesus greater? Why is that important?
3. What role does the Christian community play in keeping its fellow members true to God (v. 13)?
4. What does it mean to "enter God's rest" (vv. 11,18–19; 4:1–11; Matt. 11:28–30)?
5. What is God saying to you in this passage?
6. How can this group help you in prayer this week?

12See to it, brothers, that none of you has a
sinful, unbelieving heart that turns away from the
living God. 13But encourage one another daily, as
long as it is called Today, so that none of you may
be hardened by sin's deceitfulness. 14We have
come to share in Christ if we hold firmly till the
end the confidence we had at first. 15As has just
been said:

"Today, if you hear his voice,
do not harden your hearts
as you did in the rebellion."[b]

16Who were they who heard and rebelled?
Were they not all those Moses led out of Egypt?
17And with whom was he angry for forty years?
Was it not with those who sinned, whose bodies
fell in the desert? 18And to whom did God swear
that they would never enter his rest if not to
those who disobeyed[c]? 19So we see that they
were not able to enter, because of their unbelief.

A Sabbath-Rest for the People of God

4 Therefore, since the promise of entering his
rest still stands, let us be careful that none of
you be found to have fallen short of it. 2For we
also have had the gospel preached to us, just as
they did; but the message they heard was of no
value to them, because those who heard did not
combine it with faith.[d] 3Now we who have believed enter that rest, just as God has said,

"So I declared on oath in my anger,
'They shall never enter my rest.' "[e]

And yet his work has been finished since the
creation of the world. 4For somewhere he has
spoken about the seventh day in these words:
"And on the seventh day God rested from all his
work."[f] 5And again in the passage above he
says, "They shall never enter my rest."

HEBREWS 4:1–13

1. What is your favorite way to spend a Sunday afternoon?
2. How would you explain the "promised rest" to someone who is not a Christian?
3. What efforts (v. 11) can help you enter into God's rest (see Matt. 11:28–30 and John 6:27–29)?
4. What does it mean that God's Word is "living" (v. 12)? Active? That it penetrates?
5. What is God saying to you in this passage?
6. How can this group help you in prayer this week?

6It still remains that some will enter that rest,
and those who formerly had the gospel preached
to them did not go in, because of their disobedience. 7Therefore God again set a certain day, call-

[a] 11 Psalm 95:7-11 [b] 15 Psalm 95:7,8 [c] 18 Or *disbelieved* [d] 2 Many manuscripts *because they did not share in the faith of those who obeyed* [e] 3 Psalm 95:11; also in verse 5 [f] 4 Gen. 2:2

ing it Today, when a long time later he spoke
through David, as was said before:

"Today, if you hear his voice,
do not harden your hearts."[a]

8For if Joshua had given them rest, God would
not have spoken later about another day. 9There
remains, then, a Sabbath-rest for the people of
God; 10for anyone who enters God's rest also
rests from his own work, just as God did from his.
11Let us, therefore, make every effort to enter
that rest, so that no one will fall by following
their example of disobedience.
12For the word of God is living and active.
Sharper than any double-edged sword, it penetrates even to dividing soul and spirit, joints and
marrow; it judges the thoughts and attitudes of
the heart. 13Nothing in all creation is hidden
from God's sight. Everything is uncovered and
laid bare before the eyes of him to whom we
must give account.

Jesus the Great High Priest

14Therefore, since we have a great high priest
who has gone through the heavens,[b] Jesus the
Son of God, let us hold firmly to the faith we
profess. 15For we do not have a high priest who
is unable to sympathize with our weaknesses, but
we have one who has been tempted in every
way, just as we are—yet was without sin. 16Let
us then approach the throne of grace with confidence, so that we may receive mercy and find
grace to help us in our time of need.

5 Every high priest is selected from among
men and is appointed to represent them in
matters related to God, to offer gifts and sacrifices
for sins. 2He is able to deal gently with those who
are ignorant and are going astray, since he himself is subject to weakness. 3This is why he has to
offer sacrifices for his own sins, as well as for the
sins of the people.
4No one takes this honor upon himself; he
must be called by God, just as Aaron was. 5So
Christ also did not take upon himself the glory of
becoming a high priest. But God said to him,

"You are my Son;
today I have become your Father."[c][d]

6And he says in another place,

"You are a priest forever,
in the order of Melchizedek."[e]

7During the days of Jesus' life on earth, he
offered up prayers and petitions with loud cries
and tears to the one who could save him from
death, and he was heard because of his reverent
submission. 8Although he was a son, he learned
obedience from what he suffered 9and, once
made perfect, he became the source of eternal
salvation for all who obey him 10and was designated by God to be high priest in the order of
Melchizedek.

> **HEBREWS 4:14–5:10**
>
> 1. When you "blow it," how do you feel about the mistake? About yourself? About others involved?
> 2. What about Jesus' priesthood is most encouraging (4:14–15; see 2:17; 3:1)?
> 3. What two qualities of Jesus allows the comparison to Melchizedek (5:6,10; see chapter 7)?
> 4. What is the significance for our eternal salvation and current situation that Jesus was *fully human?* That Jesus was *without sin?*
> 5. What is God saying to you in this passage?
> 6. How can this group help you in prayer this week?

Warning Against Falling Away

11We have much to say about this, but it is
hard to explain because you are slow to learn.
12In fact, though by this time you ought to be
teachers, you need someone to teach you the elementary truths of God's word all over again. You
need milk, not solid food! 13Anyone who lives on
milk, being still an infant, is not acquainted with
the teaching about righteousness. 14But solid
food is for the mature, who by constant use have
trained themselves to distinguish good from evil.

6 Therefore let us leave the elementary teachings about Christ and go on to maturity, not
laying again the foundation of repentance from
acts that lead to death,[f] and of faith in God,
2instruction about baptisms, the laying on of
hands, the resurrection of the dead, and eternal
judgment. 3And God permitting, we will do so.
4It is impossible for those who have once been
enlightened, who have tasted the heavenly gift,
who have shared in the Holy Spirit, 5who have
tasted the goodness of the word of God and the
powers of the coming age, 6if they fall away, to be

[a] 7 Psalm 95:7,8 [b] 14 Or *gone into heaven* [c] 5 Or *have begotten you* [d] 5 Psalm 2:7 [e] 6 Psalm 110:4
[f] 1 Or *from useless rituals*

brought back to repentance, because[a] to their loss they are crucifying the Son of God all over again and subjecting him to public disgrace.

7Land that drinks in the rain often falling on it and that produces a crop useful to those for whom it is farmed receives the blessing of God. 8But land that produces thorns and thistles is worthless and is in danger of being cursed. In the end it will be burned.

9Even though we speak like this, dear friends, we are confident of better things in your case—things that accompany salvation. 10God is not unjust; he will not forget your work and the love you have shown him as you have helped his people and continue to help them. 11We want each of you to show this same diligence to the very end, in order to make your hope sure. 12We do not want you to become lazy, but to imitate those who through faith and patience inherit what has been promised.

Hebrews 5:11–6:12

1. What do you like hot out of the oven with a glass of cold milk: Chocolate chip cookies? Pound cake? Homemade bread? Apple pie?
2. How does "solid food" help one mature in Christ (5:14)?
3. What's wrong with this prolonged immaturity (6:4–6)?
4. How and why does the author encourage his readers to do "better" (6:9–12)?
5. What is God saying to you in this passage?
6. How can this group help you in prayer this week?

The Certainty of God's Promise

13When God made his promise to Abraham, since there was no one greater for him to swear by, he swore by himself, 14saying, "I will surely bless you and give you many descendants."[b] 15And so after waiting patiently, Abraham received what was promised.

16Men swear by someone greater than themselves, and the oath confirms what is said and puts an end to all argument. 17Because God wanted to make the unchanging nature of his purpose very clear to the heirs of what was promised, he confirmed it with an oath. 18God did this so that, by two unchangeable things in which it is impossible for God to lie, we who have fled to take hold of the hope offered to us may be greatly encouraged. 19We have this hope as an anchor for the soul, firm and secure. It enters the inner sanctuary behind the curtain, 20where Jesus, who went before us, has entered on our behalf. He has become a high priest forever, in the order of Melchizedek.

Hebrews 6:13–20

1. What tries your patience more: Slow elevators? Slow food service? Traffic jams?
2. How does Abraham's example help these people understand God's promise (see 3:12; 6:6)?
3. What effect did God's promise and oath have on Abraham's descendants? How does this affect Christians now?
4. Where in your life does trusting in God come hardest? Easiest? Why?
5. What is God saying to you in this passage?
6. How can this group help you in prayer this week?

Melchizedek the Priest

7 This Melchizedek was king of Salem and priest of God Most High. He met Abraham returning from the defeat of the kings and blessed him, 2and Abraham gave him a tenth of everything. First, his name means "king of righteousness"; then also, "king of Salem" means "king of peace." 3Without father or mother, without genealogy, without beginning of days or end of life, like the Son of God he remains a priest forever.

4Just think how great he was: Even the patriarch Abraham gave him a tenth of the plunder! 5Now the law requires the descendants of Levi who become priests to collect a tenth from the people—that is, their brothers—even though their brothers are descended from Abraham. 6This man, however, did not trace his descent from Levi, yet he collected a tenth from Abraham and blessed him who had the promises. 7And without doubt the lesser person is blessed by the

[a]6 Or *repentance while*   [b]14 Gen. 22:17

greater. 8In the one case, the tenth is collected by men who die; but in the other case, by him who is declared to be living. 9One might even say that Levi, who collects the tenth, paid the tenth through Abraham, 10because when Melchizedek met Abraham, Levi was still in the body of his ancestor.

Jesus Like Melchizedek

11If perfection could have been attained through the Levitical priesthood (for on the basis of it the law was given to the people), why was there still need for another priest to come—one in the order of Melchizedek, not in the order of Aaron? 12For when there is a change of the priesthood, there must also be a change of the law. 13He of whom these things are said belonged to a different tribe, and no one from that tribe has ever served at the altar. 14For it is clear that our Lord descended from Judah, and in regard to that tribe Moses said nothing about priests. 15And what we have said is even more clear if another priest like Melchizedek appears, 16one who has become a priest not on the basis of a regulation as to his ancestry but on the basis of the power of an indestructible life. 17For it is declared:

> "You are a priest forever,
> in the order of Melchizedek."[a]

18The former regulation is set aside because it was weak and useless 19(for the law made nothing perfect), and a better hope is introduced, by which we draw near to God.

20And it was not without an oath! Others became priests without any oath, 21but he became a priest with an oath when God said to him:

> "The Lord has sworn
> and will not change his mind:
> 'You are a priest forever.' "[a]

22Because of this oath, Jesus has become the guarantee of a better covenant.

23Now there have been many of those priests, since death prevented them from continuing in office; 24but because Jesus lives forever, he has a permanent priesthood. 25Therefore he is able to save completely[b] those who come to God through him, because he always lives to intercede for them.

26Such a high priest meets our need—one who is holy, blameless, pure, set apart from sinners, exalted above the heavens. 27Unlike the other high priests, he does not need to offer sacrifices day after day, first for his own sins, and then for the sins of the people. He sacrificed for their sins once for all when he offered himself. 28For the law appoints as high priests men who are weak; but the oath, which came after the law, appointed the Son, who has been made perfect forever.

The High Priest of a New Covenant

8 The point of what we are saying is this: We do have such a high priest, who sat down at the right hand of the throne of the Majesty in heaven, 2and who serves in the sanctuary, the true tabernacle set up by the Lord, not by man.

3Every high priest is appointed to offer both gifts and sacrifices, and so it was necessary for this one also to have something to offer. 4If he were on earth, he would not be a priest, for there are already men who offer the gifts prescribed by the law. 5They serve at a sanctuary that is a copy and shadow of what is in heaven. This is why Moses was warned when he was about to build the tabernacle: "See to it that you make everything according to the pattern shown you on the mountain."[c] 6But the ministry Jesus has received is as superior to theirs as the covenant of which he is mediator is superior to the old one, and it is founded on better promises.

7For if there had been nothing wrong with that first covenant, no place would have been sought for another. 8But God found fault with the people and said[d]:

> "The time is coming, declares the Lord,

Hebrews 7:1–28

1. If you could live to be 100, but could retain either the *body* or the *mind* of a 30-year-old, which would you choose? Why?
2. From verses 1–10, what do we know about Melchizedek? How did Abraham regard him?
3. In what ways is Jesus like the Melchizedek portrayed here (vv. 12–17)?
4. In what ways is Jesus a better priest than those under the Jewish system (see vv. 20–28)?
5. What is God saying to you in this passage?
6. How can this group help you in prayer this week?

[a] *17,21* Psalm 110:4 [b] *25* Or *forever* [c] *5* Exodus 25:40 [d] *8* Some manuscripts may be translated *fault and said to the people.*

when I will make a new covenant
with the house of Israel
and with the house of Judah.
9It will not be like the covenant
I made with their forefathers
when I took them by the hand
to lead them out of Egypt,
because they did not remain faithful to my covenant,
and I turned away from them,
declares the Lord.
10This is the covenant I will make with the house of Israel
after that time, declares the Lord.
I will put my laws in their minds
and write them on their hearts.
I will be their God,
and they will be my people.
11No longer will a man teach his neighbor,
or a man his brother, saying, 'Know the Lord,'
because they will all know me,
from the least of them to the greatest.
12For I will forgive their wickedness
and will remember their sins no more."[a]

13By calling this covenant "new," he has made
the first one obsolete; and what is obsolete and
aging will soon disappear.

HEBREWS 8:1–13

1. What are you best at forgetting: Names? Chores? Birthdays? Scripture references?
2. What is a covenant? What is the significance of the fact that God initiates and guarantees it?
3. What four promises does this new covenant involve (vv. 10–12)?
4. Which aspect of the new covenant do you wish to experience more? Why?
5. What is God saying to you in this passage?
6. How can this group help you in prayer this week?

Worship in the Earthly Tabernacle

9 Now the first covenant had regulations for
worship and also an earthly sanctuary. 2A
tabernacle was set up. In its first room were the
lampstand, the table and the consecrated bread;
this was called the Holy Place. 3Behind the second curtain was a room called the Most Holy
Place, 4which had the golden altar of incense and
the gold-covered ark of the covenant. This ark
contained the gold jar of manna, Aaron's staff that
had budded, and the stone tablets of the covenant. 5Above the ark were the cherubim of the
Glory, overshadowing the atonement cover.[b]
But we cannot discuss these things in detail now.
6When everything had been arranged like this,
the priests entered regularly into the outer room
to carry on their ministry. 7But only the high
priest entered the inner room, and that only once
a year, and never without blood, which he offered for himself and for the sins the people had
committed in ignorance. 8The Holy Spirit was
showing by this that the way into the Most Holy
Place had not yet been disclosed as long as the
first tabernacle was still standing. 9This is an illustration for the present time, indicating that the
gifts and sacrifices being offered were not able to
clear the conscience of the worshiper. 10They are
only a matter of food and drink and various ceremonial washings—external regulations applying
until the time of the new order.

HEBREWS 9:1–10

1. What thing were you told "Don't touch!" when you were a little kid?
2. How do you picture the earthly sanctuary described in verses 1–5?
3. Why were the gifts and sacrifices of the Old Testament worshipers not sufficient to clear their consciences (vv. 9–10)?
4. When you feel guilty, how do you try to clear your conscience?
5. What is God saying to you in this passage?
6. How can this group help you in prayer this week?

The Blood of Christ

11When Christ came as high priest of the good
things that are already here,[c] he went through
the greater and more perfect tabernacle that is
not man-made, that is to say, not a part of this
creation. 12He did not enter by means of the

[a] 12 Jer. 31:31-34 [b] 5 Traditionally *the mercy seat* [c] 11 Some early manuscripts *are to come*

blood of goats and calves; but he entered the
Most Holy Place once for all by his own blood,
having obtained eternal redemption. 13The blood
of goats and bulls and the ashes of a heifer sprinkled on those who are ceremonially unclean
sanctify them so that they are outwardly clean.
14How much more, then, will the blood of Christ,
who through the eternal Spirit offered himself
unblemished to God, cleanse our consciences
from acts that lead to death,[a] so that we may
serve the living God!
15For this reason Christ is the mediator of a
new covenant, that those who are called may
receive the promised eternal inheritance—now
that he has died as a ransom to set them free from
the sins committed under the first covenant.

Hebrews 9:11–28

1. Have you ever seen a blood and gore movie? Which one? How did you feel about watching it?
2. How is the priesthood of Christ distinguished from the old system (vv. 12–14)?
3. Why the emphasis on shed blood (vv. 19–22)? Whose blood? What for?
4. In verses 27–28, how is the once-and-for-all sacrifice of Christ's death illustrated?
5. What is God saying to you in this passage?
6. How can this group help you in prayer this week?

16In the case of a will,[b] it is necessary to
prove the death of the one who made it, 17be-
cause a will is in force only when somebody has
died; it never takes effect while the one who
made it is living. 18This is why even the first
covenant was not put into effect without blood.
19When Moses had proclaimed every commandment of the law to all the people, he took the
blood of calves, together with water, scarlet wool
and branches of hyssop, and sprinkled the scroll
and all the people. 20He said, "This is the blood
of the covenant, which God has commanded you
to keep."[c] 21In the same way, he sprinkled with
the blood both the tabernacle and everything
used in its ceremonies. 22In fact, the law requires
that nearly everything be cleansed with blood,
and without the shedding of blood there is no
forgiveness.
23It was necessary, then, for the copies of the
heavenly things to be purified with these sacrifices, but the heavenly things themselves with
better sacrifices than these. 24For Christ did not
enter a man-made sanctuary that was only a copy
of the true one; he entered heaven itself, now to
appear for us in God's presence. 25Nor did he
enter heaven to offer himself again and again, the
way the high priest enters the Most Holy Place
every year with blood that is not his own. 26Then
Christ would have had to suffer many times since
the creation of the world. But now he has appeared once for all at the end of the ages to do
away with sin by the sacrifice of himself. 27Just as
man is destined to die once, and after that to face
judgment, 28so Christ was sacrificed once to take
away the sins of many people; and he will appear
a second time, not to bear sin, but to bring salvation to those who are waiting for him.

Christ's Sacrifice Once for All

10 The law is only a shadow of the good
things that are coming—not the realities
themselves. For this reason it can never, by the
same sacrifices repeated endlessly year after year,
make perfect those who draw near to worship. 2If
it could, would they not have stopped being
offered? For the worshipers would have been
cleansed once for all, and would no longer have
felt guilty for their sins. 3But those sacrifices are
an annual reminder of sins, 4because it is impossible for the blood of bulls and goats to take away
sins.
5Therefore, when Christ came into the world,
he said:

"Sacrifice and offering you did not desire,
but a body you prepared for me;
6with burnt offerings and sin offerings
you were not pleased.
7Then I said, 'Here I am—it is written about
me in the scroll—
I have come to do your will, O God.' "[d]

8First he said, "Sacrifices and offerings, burnt offerings and sin offerings you did not desire, nor
were you pleased with them" (although the law
required them to be made). 9Then he said, "Here
I am, I have come to do your will." He sets aside
the first to establish the second. 10And by that
will, we have been made holy through the sacrifice of the body of Jesus Christ once for all.
11Day after day every priest stands and performs his religious duties; again and again he offers the same sacrifices, which can never take

[a] 14 Or *from useless rituals* (see Septuagint)
[b] 16 Same Greek word as *covenant*; also in verse 17
[c] 20 Exodus 24:8
[d] 7 Psalm 40:6-8

away sins. 12But when this priest had offered for
all time one sacrifice for sins, he sat down at the
right hand of God. 13Since that time he waits for
his enemies to be made his footstool, 14because
by one sacrifice he has made perfect forever
those who are being made holy.
15The Holy Spirit also testifies to us about this.
First he says:

16"This is the covenant I will make with them
after that time, says the Lord.
I will put my laws in their hearts,
and I will write them on their minds."[a]

17Then he adds:

"Their sins and lawless acts
I will remember no more."[b]

18And where these have been forgiven, there is
no longer any sacrifice for sin.

HEBREWS 10:1–18

1. What part of your daily routine do you enjoy the most? The least?
2. In what ways does Christ replace the inadequate sacrifices of the Law?
3. How does Jesus' obedience relate to our holiness (vv. 9–10)?
4. Do you live your life as if you were being made holy (v. 14)? In what way is God calling you to practice greater holiness?
5. What is God saying to you in this passage?
6. How can this group help you in prayer this week?

A Call to Persevere

19Therefore, brothers, since we have confidence to enter the Most Holy Place by the blood
of Jesus, 20by a new and living way opened for us
through the curtain, that is, his body, 21and since
we have a great priest over the house of God,
22let us draw near to God with a sincere heart in
full assurance of faith, having our hearts sprinkled to cleanse us from a guilty conscience and
having our bodies washed with pure water. 23Let
us hold unswervingly to the hope we profess, for
he who promised is faithful. 24And let us consider
how we may spur one another on toward love
and good deeds. 25Let us not give up meeting
together, as some are in the habit of doing, but let
us encourage one another—and all the more as
you see the Day approaching.
26If we deliberately keep on sinning after we
have received the knowledge of the truth, no
sacrifice for sins is left, 27but only a fearful expectation of judgment and of raging fire that will
consume the enemies of God. 28Anyone who rejected the law of Moses died without mercy on
the testimony of two or three witnesses. 29How
much more severely do you think a man deserves
to be punished who has trampled the Son of God
under foot, who has treated as an unholy thing
the blood of the covenant that sanctified him, and
who has insulted the Spirit of grace? 30For we
know him who said, "It is mine to avenge; I will
repay,"[c] and again, "The Lord will judge his
people."[d] 31It is a dreadful thing to fall into the
hands of the living God.
32Remember those earlier days after you had
received the light, when you stood your ground

HEBREWS 10:19–39

1. What is your favorite part of the church service you attend?
2. Note the four "let us" statements in verses 22–25. What does each one mean? What incentives are given?
3. In rejecting Christ, of what three grievous sins would a person be guilty (v. 29)? With what consequence (v. 31)?
4. After such a dire warning, how does the author encourage the people he was writing to (vv. 32–39)? Which appeal do you find persuasive?
5. What is God saying to you in this passage?
6. How can this group help you in prayer this week?

in a great contest in the face of suffering. 33Some-
times you were publicly exposed to insult and
persecution; at other times you stood side by side
with those who were so treated. 34You sympa-
thized with those in prison and joyfully accepted
the confiscation of your property, because you
knew that you yourselves had better and lasting
possessions.

[a] *16* Jer. 31:33 [b] *17* Jer. 31:34 [c] *30* Deut. 32:35 [d] *30* Deut. 32:36; Psalm 135:14

35 So do not throw away your confidence; it
will be richly rewarded. 36 You need to persevere
so that when you have done the will of God, you
will receive what he has promised. 37 For in just
a very little while,

"He who is coming will come and will not
delay.
38 But my righteous one[a] will live by faith.
And if he shrinks back,
I will not be pleased with him."[b]

39 But we are not of those who shrink back and
are destroyed, but of those who believe and are
saved.

By Faith

11 Now faith is being sure of what we hope
for and certain of what we do not see.
2 This is what the ancients were commended for.
3 By faith we understand that the universe was
formed at God's command, so that what is seen
was not made out of what was visible.
4 By faith Abel offered God a better sacrifice
than Cain did. By faith he was commended as a
righteous man, when God spoke well of his offerings. And by faith he still speaks, even though he
is dead.
5 By faith Enoch was taken from this life, so
that he did not experience death; he could not be
found, because God had taken him away. For before he was taken, he was commended as one
who pleased God. 6 And without faith it is impossible to please God, because anyone who comes
to him must believe that he exists and that he
rewards those who earnestly seek him.
7 By faith Noah, when warned about things not
yet seen, in holy fear built an ark to save his
family. By his faith he condemned the world and
became heir of the righteousness that comes by
faith.
8 By faith Abraham, when called to go to a
place he would later receive as his inheritance,
obeyed and went, even though he did not know
where he was going. 9 By faith he made his home
in the promised land like a stranger in a foreign
country; he lived in tents, as did Isaac and Jacob,
who were heirs with him of the same promise.
10 For he was looking forward to the city with
foundations, whose architect and builder is God.

HEBREWS 11:1–16

1. What is the riskiest thing you have done recently?
2. Who has inspired you the most by their example of faith?
3. How do you define faith? How does your answer compare with verse 1?
4. What is the essential ingredient in a life that is pleasing to God (see v. 6)?
5. If you knew you could not fail, what big dream would you like to pursue? What is keeping you from this?
6. Read verse 13. On a scale of 1 (totally comfy) to 10 ("Take me to your leader!"), how much does your faith make you feel like "an alien and stranger on earth"?
7. Where is God asking you to step out in faith right now?
8. How can the group help you in prayer this week?

11 By faith Abraham, even though he was past
age—and Sarah herself was barren—was enabled to become a father because he[c] considered him faithful who had made the promise.
12 And so from this one man, and he as good as
dead, came descendants as numerous as the stars

[a] 38 One early manuscript *But the righteous* *bear children because she*
[b] 38 Hab. 2:3,4
[c] 11 Or *By faith even Sarah, who was past age, was enabled to*

11:1 *being sure.* Faith is driven by hope (Rom. 8:24–25). Faith also brings into view the unseen, heavenly realities of which the Law is only a shadow (10:1). The examples that follow reflect how through faith the OT saints were able to lay hold of invisible realities that shaped their lives.

11:2 *were commended for.* Genesis 15:6 states that Abraham's faith was credited to him as righteousness. The author asserts this as the general principle that applies to all the saints in the OT.

11:3–4 The stories of faith begin with creation, which dramatically exemplifies how God brings into being things that are unseen. ***Abel.*** Abel's faith is not mentioned in Genesis, but the reason God accepted his sacrifice and not Cain's had to do with a matter of attitude (Gen. 4:7).

11:6 *without faith it is impossible to please God.* That Enoch pleased God is proof of his faith. ***he exists.*** The faith called for is faith in the invisible God, confident that God rewards those who pursue him.

11:7 *not yet seen.* Acting upon that which God promises (or warns), even when unseen, is the essence of faith (v. 1). ***in holy fear.*** Faith lives in recognition of the awesome power of God. ***righteousness that comes by faith.*** In contrast to the Jewish emphasis on law-keeping, a right relationship with God was based upon one's faith and trust in God even from the earliest times.

11:8–16 These examples reflect the obedience, patience, power and vision of faith.

in the sky and as countless as the sand on the
seashore.
13All these people were still living by faith
when they died. They did not receive the things
promised; they only saw them and welcomed
them from a distance. And they admitted that
they were aliens and strangers on earth. 14People
who say such things show that they are looking
for a country of their own. 15If they had been
thinking of the country they had left, they would
have had opportunity to return. 16Instead, they
were longing for a better country—a heavenly
one. Therefore God is not ashamed to be called
their God, for he has prepared a city for them.
17By faith Abraham, when God tested him, offered Isaac as a sacrifice. He who had received
the promises was about to sacrifice his one and
only son, 18even though God had said to him, "It
is through Isaac that your offspring[a] will be
reckoned."[b] 19Abraham reasoned that God
could raise the dead, and figuratively speaking,
he did receive Isaac back from death.
20By faith Isaac blessed Jacob and Esau in regard to their future.
21By faith Jacob, when he was dying, blessed
each of Joseph's sons, and worshiped as he
leaned on the top of his staff.
22By faith Joseph, when his end was near,
spoke about the exodus of the Israelites from
Egypt and gave instructions about his bones.
23By faith Moses' parents hid him for three
months after he was born, because they saw he
was no ordinary child, and they were not afraid of
the king's edict.
24By faith Moses, when he had grown up, refused to be known as the son of Pharaoh's daughter. 25He chose to be mistreated along with the
people of God rather than to enjoy the pleasures
of sin for a short time. 26He regarded disgrace for
the sake of Christ as of greater value than the
treasures of Egypt, because he was looking ahead
to his reward. 27By faith he left Egypt, not fearing
the king's anger; he persevered because he saw
him who is invisible. 28By faith he kept the Passover and the sprinkling of blood, so that the destroyer of the firstborn would not touch the firstborn of Israel.
29By faith the people passed through the Red
Sea[c] as on dry land; but when the Egyptians
tried to do so, they were drowned.
30By faith the walls of Jericho fell, after the
people had marched around them for seven days.
31By faith the prostitute Rahab, because she
welcomed the spies, was not killed with those
who were disobedient.[d]
32And what more shall I say? I do not have
time to tell about Gideon, Barak, Samson, Jephthah, David, Samuel and the prophets, 33who
through faith conquered kingdoms, administered
justice, and gained what was promised; who
shut the mouths of lions, 34quenched the fury
of the flames, and escaped the edge of the sword;
whose weakness was turned to strength; and
who became powerful in battle and routed foreign armies. 35Women received back their dead,
raised to life again. Others were tortured and refused to be released, so that they might gain a
better resurrection. 36Some faced jeers and flogging, while still others were chained and put in
prison. 37They were stoned[e]; they were sawed
in two; they were put to death by the sword.
They went about in sheepskins and goatskins,
destitute, persecuted and mistreated— 38the
world was not worthy of them. They wandered in
deserts and mountains, and in caves and holes in
the ground.
39These were all commended for their faith,
yet none of them received what had been promised. 40God had planned something better for us
so that only together with us would they be made
perfect.

God Disciplines His Sons

12 Therefore, since we are surrounded by
such a great cloud of witnesses, let us
throw off everything that hinders and the sin that
so easily entangles, and let us run with perseverance the race marked out for us. 2Let us fix our
eyes on Jesus, the author and perfecter of our
faith, who for the joy set before him endured the
cross, scorning its shame, and sat down at the
right hand of the throne of God. 3Consider him
who endured such opposition from sinful men, so
that you will not grow weary and lose heart.
4In your struggle against sin, you have not yet
resisted to the point of shedding your blood.
5And you have forgotten that word of encouragement that addresses you as sons:

"My son, do not make light of the Lord's
discipline,
and do not lose heart when he rebukes
you,
6because the Lord disciplines those he loves,
and he punishes everyone he accepts as a
son."[f]

7Endure hardship as discipline; God is treating
you as sons. For what son is not disciplined by his
father? 8If you are not disciplined (and everyone
undergoes discipline), then you are illegitimate
children and not true sons. 9Moreover, we have
all had human fathers who disciplined us and we

[a]18 Greek *seed* [b]18 Gen. 21:12 [c]29 That is, Sea of Reeds [d]31 Or *unbelieving* [e]37 Some early manuscripts *stoned; they were put to the test;* [f]6 Prov. 3:11,12

respected them for it. How much more should we submit to the Father of our spirits and live! [10]Our fathers disciplined us for a little while as they thought best; but God disciplines us for our good, that we may share in his holiness. [11]No discipline seems pleasant at the time, but painful. Later on, however, it produces a harvest of righteousness and peace for those who have been trained by it.

[12]Therefore, strengthen your feeble arms and weak knees. [13]"Make level paths for your feet,"[a] so that the lame may not be disabled, but rather healed.

HEBREWS 12:1–13

1. What discipline did you sometimes resent as a child that you appreciate now: Practicing piano? Submitting work on time? Not overspending your allowance?
2. How should Christians "run the race"? What does it mean to you to "fix your eyes on Jesus"?
3. How does Christ's discipline differ from human discipline? What benefits does discipline bring?
4. What's the hardest thing you're going through right now? How is God using this in your life?
5. What is God saying to you in this passage?
6. How can this group help you in prayer this week?

Warning Against Refusing God

[14]Make every effort to live in peace with all men and to be holy; without holiness no one will see the Lord. [15]See to it that no one misses the grace of God and that no bitter root grows up to cause trouble and defile many. [16]See that no one is sexually immoral, or is godless like Esau, who for a single meal sold his inheritance rights as the oldest son. [17]Afterward, as you know, when he wanted to inherit this blessing, he was rejected. He could bring about no change of mind, though he sought the blessing with tears.

[18]You have not come to a mountain that can be touched and that is burning with fire; to darkness, gloom and storm; [19]to a trumpet blast or to such a voice speaking words that those who heard it begged that no further word be spoken to them, [20]because they could not bear what was commanded: "If even an animal touches the mountain, it must be stoned."[b] [21]The sight was so terrifying that Moses said, "I am trembling with fear."[c]

[22]But you have come to Mount Zion, to the heavenly Jerusalem, the city of the living God. You have come to thousands upon thousands of angels in joyful assembly, [23]to the church of the firstborn, whose names are written in heaven. You have come to God, the judge of all men, to the spirits of righteous men made perfect, [24]to Jesus the mediator of a new covenant, and to the sprinkled blood that speaks a better word than the blood of Abel.

[25]See to it that you do not refuse him who speaks. If they did not escape when they refused him who warned them on earth, how much less will we, if we turn away from him who warns us from heaven? [26]At that time his voice shook the earth, but now he has promised, "Once more I will shake not only the earth but also the heavens."[d] [27]The words "once more" indicate the removing of what can be shaken—that is, created things—so that what cannot be shaken may remain.

[28]Therefore, since we are receiving a kingdom that cannot be shaken, let us be thankful, and so

HEBREWS 12:14–29

1. If you could choose any city to move to with the right job, by what criteria would you choose: Friends or family? Climate? Housing? Cultural or athletic pursuits?
2. What is the point of the comparison between Mt. Sinai (vv. 18–21) and Mt. Zion (vv. 22–24)?
3. What happens to any who *refuse* to hear God's voice (vv. 18–21,25–29)? To those who *heed* his call?
4. What efforts have you made to "live in peace with all" (v. 14)?
5. What is God saying to you in this passage?
6. How can this group help you in prayer this week?

[a]*13* Prov. 4:26 [b]*20* Exodus 19:12,13 [c]*21* Deut. 9:19 [d]*26* Haggai 2:6

worship God acceptably with reverence and awe,
29for our "God is a consuming fire."[a]

Concluding Exhortations

13 Keep on loving each other as brothers.
2Do not forget to entertain strangers, for
by so doing some people have entertained angels
without knowing it. 3Remember those in prison
as if you were their fellow prisoners, and those
who are mistreated as if you yourselves were suffering.

4Marriage should be honored by all, and the
marriage bed kept pure, for God will judge the
adulterer and all the sexually immoral. 5Keep
your lives free from the love of money and be
content with what you have, because God has
said,

"Never will I leave you;
never will I forsake you."[b]

6So we say with confidence,

"The Lord is my helper; I will not be afraid.
What can man do to me?"[c]

7Remember your leaders, who spoke the word
of God to you. Consider the outcome of their way
of life and imitate their faith. 8Jesus Christ is the
same yesterday and today and forever.

9Do not be carried away by all kinds of strange
teachings. It is good for our hearts to be strengthened by grace, not by ceremonial foods, which
are of no value to those who eat them. 10We have
an altar from which those who minister at the
tabernacle have no right to eat.

11The high priest carries the blood of animals
into the Most Holy Place as a sin offering, but the
bodies are burned outside the camp. 12And so
Jesus also suffered outside the city gate to make
the people holy through his own blood. 13Let us,
then, go to him outside the camp, bearing the
disgrace he bore. 14For here we do not have an
enduring city, but we are looking for the city that
is to come.

15Through Jesus, therefore, let us continually
offer to God a sacrifice of praise—the fruit of lips
that confess his name. 16And do not forget to do
good and to share with others, for with such sacrifices God is pleased.

17Obey your leaders and submit to their authority. They keep watch over you as men who
must give an account. Obey them so that their
work will be a joy, not a burden, for that would
be of no advantage to you.

18Pray for us. We are sure that we have a clear
conscience and desire to live honorably in every
way. 19I particularly urge you to pray so that I
may be restored to you soon.

20May the God of peace, who through the
blood of the eternal covenant brought back from
the dead our Lord Jesus, that great Shepherd of
the sheep, 21equip you with everything good for
doing his will, and may he work in us what is
pleasing to him, through Jesus Christ, to whom
be glory for ever and ever. Amen.

HEBREWS 13:1–25

1. In one or two words, how would you describe the relationship you have with your brothers and sisters?
2. In what areas should "brotherly love" define Christians (vv. 1–7)?
3. What "strange teaching" was a particular temptation to the Hebrew Christians (vv. 9–10)? What rituals, mores and other forms of legalism tempt believers of any age?
4. From verses 1–19, how would you sum up the Christian lifestyle?
5. What is God saying to you in this passage?
6. How can this group help you in prayer this week?

22Brothers, I urge you to bear with my word of
exhortation, for I have written you only a short
letter.

23I want you to know that our brother Timothy
has been released. If he arrives soon, I will come
with him to see you.

24Greet all your leaders and all God's people.
Those from Italy send you their greetings.

25Grace be with you all.

[a]29 Deut. 4:24 [b]5 Deut. 31:6 [c]6 Psalm 118:6,7

Introduction to
JAMES

Personal Reading Plan

- ❐ James 1:1–27
- ❐ James 2:1–26
- ❐ James 3:1–4:12
- ❐ James 4:13–5:20

Author

In the New Testament there are apparently five men by the name of James, but only two who might conceivably have written this epistle—either James the apostle, or James the brother of Jesus. Since it is almost certain that the apostle James (the son of Zebedee) was killed by Herod in A.D. 44 (before the epistle could have been written), traditionally the author has been assumed to be James, the leader of the church in Jerusalem and the brother of Jesus (Mark 6:3).

The pilgrimage of James to faith is fascinating. At first Jesus' family was hostile to his ministry (John 7:5) and, in fact, tried to stop it at one point (Mark 3:21). Yet after Jesus' ascension, Jesus' mother and brothers are listed among the early believers (Acts 1:14). For James, this coming to faith may have resulted from Jesus' postresurrection appearance to him (1 Cor. 15:7).

James eventually emerged as a leader of the church in Jerusalem. It was to James that Peter reported after his miraculous escape from Herod's prison (Acts 12:17). James presided over the first Jerusalem Council which decided the important question of whether to admit Gentiles to the church (Acts 15, especially vv. 13–21). James was consulted by Paul during his first trip to Jerusalem after his conversion (Gal. 1:19), and then James joined in the official recognition of Paul's call as apostle to the Gentiles (Gal. 2:8–10). It is to James that Paul later brought the collection for the poor in Jerusalem (Acts 21:17–25).

We also know that James was a strict Jew who adhered to the Mosaic Law (Gal. 2:12), yet unlike the Judaizers, he supported Paul's ministry to the Gentiles (Acts 21:17–26). Later accounts indicate that James was martyred in A.D. 62.

The question of who wrote the book of James is, however, still somewhat of a puzzle primarily because Jesus and his saving work is mentioned so little—a curious omission if the author was Jesus' brother. This question baffled even the ancient church. Both the Latin Father Jerome and the church historian Eusebius (as well as others) observe that not all accept James as having been written by our Lord's brother.

Date

It is difficult to date the book of James. Some place it very early, around A.D. 45, making it the first New Testament book. Others date it quite late.

Theme

Christianity in action.

Audience

James is one of the General Epistles (along with 1 and 2 Peter, John's epistles and Jude), so called because it has no single destination. Thus, it is not clear to whom James is addressing his comments. At first glance, it appears that he is writing to Jewish Christians dispersed around the Greek world: "to the twelve tribes scattered among the nations" (1:1). But since Peter uses the same sort of inscription (1 Peter 1:1–2) when he is clearly addressing Gentile Christians who consider themselves the New Israel, James' destination remains unclear. In fact, a strong case can be made that James was writing to a community of God-fearers, that is, Gentiles who had been deeply attracted to Judaism. That such folk were then drawn to Christianity is clear from examples in Acts, such as Cornelius (Acts 10:2,22), Lydia (Acts 16:14), Titius Justus (Acts 18:7) and others. This would help to explain the convergence of Jewish, Greek and Christian elements in the book of James.

Purpose

While James clearly stands in the tradition of other Christian writers, he has some special concerns. The relationship between rich and poor crops up at various points (1:9–11; 5:1–6)—an issue of special significance to the modern affluent West. He is concerned about the use and abuse of speech (1:19,26; 2:12; 3:3–12; 5:12). He gives instruction on prayer (1:5–8; 4:2–3; 5:13–18). Above all, he is concerned with ethical behavior. How believers act, he says, has significance for the Day of Judgment; future reward or punishment depends on it. In this regard, James bemoans the inconsistency of human behavior (1:6–8,22–24; 2:14–17; 4:1,3). Human beings are "double-minded" (1:8; 4:8) in sharp contrast to God who is one (2:19) and does not change (1:17).

James has been incorrectly understood by some to be contradicting Paul's doctrine of justification of faith (2:14–26). In fact if James had Paul in mind at all, he was addressing himself to those who had perverted Paul's message—insisting that it doesn't matter what you do, as long as you have faith. James responded by asserting that works are the outward evidence of inner faith. Works make faith visible to others. In contrast, Paul was concerned with our standing before God. As is evident from Romans 12–15, Paul certainly agreed with James that faith in Christ has direct implications for how believers live.

Characteristics

Among the New Testament books, James is an oddity. It is written in quite a different style from the others, more like the book of Proverbs than Paul's epistles. But even more than its style, its contents set James apart. It does not treat many of those themes we have come to expect in the New Testament. Although Jesus is seldom referred to or quoted, his teachings on the Sermon on the Mount underlie much of this letter (compare 2:5 with Matt. 5:3; 3:10–12 with Matt. 7:15–20; 3:18 with Matt. 5:9; 5:2–3 with Matt. 6:19–20; 5:12 with Matt. 5:33–37).

Its Omissions

There is no mention of the Holy Spirit and no reference to the redemptive work or resurrection of Christ. In fact, it contains only two references to the name Jesus Christ (1:1 and 2:1). Furthermore, when examples are given, they are drawn from the lives of Old Testament prophets, not from the experiences of Jesus. Although the title *Lord* appears 11 times, it generally refers to the name of God (in Old Testament fashion) and not to the kingly authority of Jesus. Indeed, it is God the Father who is the focus of the book of James.

Thus, Martin Luther wrote in his preface to the New Testament that "St. John's Gospel and his first epistle, St. Paul's epistles, especially Romans, Galatians and Ephesians and St. Peter's first epistle are the books that show you Christ and teach you all that is necessary and salvatory for you to know, even if you were never to see or hear any other book or doctrine. Therefore, St. James' epistle is really an epistle of straw, compared to these others, for it has nothing of the nature of the gospel about it."

Its Contributions

Luther notwithstanding, James is clearly a Christian piece of writing. Full of wisdom, it is based solidly on the teaching of Jesus and is a genuine product of first-century Christianity. To be sure, it is not as directly theological as many other New Testament epistles, but then James' concern is not doctrinal (which he seems to assume) but rather ethical—how the Christian faith is to be lived on a day-by-day basis.

Historical Background

James draws his language, images and ideas from three worlds: Judaism, Greek culture and early Christianity. From Christianity, he uses language referring to the Second Coming (5:7–9), common patterns of Christian ethical instruction, which parallel those in 1 Peter (1:2–4,21; 4:7–10), and especially the teachings of Jesus (1:5,17; 2:5,8,19; 4:3; 5:12). From Judaism, he draws his insistence on the unity of God, concern for keeping the Law and quotations from Jewish Scriptures (2:8,11,21–25; 4:6; 5:11,17–18) along with his use of Jewish terms (e.g., the word translated "hell" in 3:6 is the Hebrew word *gehenna*). Christianity and Judaism shared his concern for the poor and oppressed. From the Greek-speaking world he takes the language (which he uses with skill), the source of his Old Testament quotations (he uses the Greek Old Testament, not the Hebrew version), Greek forms of composition and metaphors drawn from Greek and Latin sources (e.g., the horse and the ship in 3:3–4).

Structure

Written in epistle (letter) form, James is loosely structured and rambling in style. It seems to jump from one idea to another without any overall plan, apart from that of providing a manual of Christian conduct. In fact, the book of James shares many characteristics of the sermonic style of both Greek philosophers and Jewish rabbis. As in Greek sermons, James carries on a conversation with a hypothetical opponent (2:18–26; 5:13–16), switches subjects by means of a question (2:14; 4:1), uses many commands (60 of the 108 verses in James are imperatives), relies on vivid images from everyday life (3:3–6; 5:7), illustrates points by reference to famous people (2:21–23,25; 5:11,17), uses vivid opposites in which the right way is set alongside the wrong way (2:13,26), begins the sermon with a striking paradox that captures the hearers' attention (1:2—"Consider it pure joy ... whenever you face trials"), is quite stern (2:20; 4:4), and clinches a point by means of a quotation in 4:6 (James Hardy Ropes, *The International Critical Commentary;* William Barclay, *The Letters of James and Peter*). It should be noted, as William Barclay writes:

> The main aim of these ancient preachers, it must be remembered, was not to investigate new truth; it was to awaken sinners to the error of their ways, and to compel them to see truths which they knew but deliberately neglected or had forgotten (pp. 33–34).

Jewish sermons had many of the same characteristics. But rabbis also had the habit, as did James, of constructing sermons that were deliberately disconnected—a series of moral truths and commands strung together like beads.

Passages for Topical Group Study

1:2–18	SCHOOL / GRADES	Trials and Temptations
1:19–27	FAMILY CONFLICTS	Listening and Doing
2:1–13	APPEARANCE	Favoritism Forbidden
	ACCEPTANCE	
3:1–18	SIBLING RIVALRY	Taming the Tongue
4:1–12	JEALOUSY	Submit Yourselves to God
4:13–17	FUTURE PLANS	Boasting About Tomorrow
5:7–20	PATIENCE AND WAITING	Patience in Suffering

See the Lesson Plans in the front of this Bible.

Passages for General Group Study

2:14–26	Faith and Deeds
5:1–6	Warning to Rich Oppressors

1

James, a servant of God and of the Lord Jesus
Christ,

To the twelve tribes scattered among the nations:

Greetings.

Trials and Temptations

2Consider it pure joy, my brothers, whenever
you face trials of many kinds, 3because you know
that the testing of your faith develops perseverance. 4Perseverance must finish its work so that
you may be mature and complete, not lacking
anything. 5If any of you lacks wisdom, he should
ask God, who gives generously to all without
finding fault, and it will be given to him. 6But
when he asks, he must believe and not doubt,
because he who doubts is like a wave of the sea,
blown and tossed by the wind. 7That man should
not think he will receive anything from the Lord;
8he is a double-minded man, unstable in all he
does.

9The brother in humble circumstances ought
to take pride in his high position. 10But the one
who is rich should take pride in his low position,
because he will pass away like a wild flower.
11For the sun rises with scorching heat and withers the plant; its blossom falls and its beauty is
destroyed. In the same way, the rich man will
fade away even while he goes about his business.
12Blessed is the man who perseveres under
trial, because when he has stood the test, he will
receive the crown of life that God has promised
to those who love him.

13When tempted, no one should say, "God is
tempting me." For God cannot be tempted by
evil, nor does he tempt anyone; 14but each one
is tempted when, by his own evil desire, he is
dragged away and enticed. 15Then, after desire
has conceived, it gives birth to sin; and sin, when
it is full-grown, gives birth to death.

16Don't be deceived, my dear brothers. 17Ev-
ery good and perfect gift is from above, coming
down from the Father of the heavenly lights, who
does not change like shifting shadows. 18He
chose to give us birth through the word of truth,
that we might be a kind of firstfruits of all he
created.

Listening and Doing

19My dear brothers, take note of this: Everyone should be quick to listen, slow to speak and
slow to become angry, 20for man's anger does not
bring about the righteous life that God desires.
21Therefore, get rid of all moral filth and the evil
that is so prevalent and humbly accept the word
planted in you, which can save you.

22Do not merely listen to the word, and so
deceive yourselves. Do what it says. 23Anyone
who listens to the word but does not do what it

JAMES 1:2–18

1. What's your G.P.A.?
2. What's your usual approach to a test: Fear? Joy? Prayer? Study all night?
3. How satisfied are you with your grades? How satisfied are your parents?
4. Why is perseverance important (see v. 4)? What reward comes with persevering in the faith (see v. 12)?
5. On a scale from 1 (not very) to 10 (very), how serious are you about your school work?
6. When have you been tempted to cheat on a test or assignment? What's your response to temptation?
7. If God were handing out crowns today according to how well you have persevered over the last week, would you get one? Why?
8. Where do you need wisdom? Pray, asking God for this.

1:2 ***Consider it pure joy.*** Christians ought to view the difficulties of life with enthusiasm, because the outcome of trials will be beneficial. ***trials of many kinds.*** The word "trials" has a dual meaning of adversity (difficulties that come from the outside) and temptations (inner moral trials).

1:4 ***finish its work.*** Perfection is not automatic—it takes time and effort. ***mature and complete.*** James is thinking of the integrated life, in contrast to the divided person of verses 6–8.

1:5 ***wisdom.*** This is not just abstract knowledge, but God-given insight which leads to right living. It is the ability to make right decisions, especially about moral issues (as one must do during trials).

1:6 Both here and in 4:3, unanswered prayer is connected to the quality of the asking, not to the unwillingness of God to give. ***believe.*** To be in *one mind* about God's ability to answer prayer, to be sure that God will hear and will act in accord with his superior wisdom.

1:12 ***blessed.*** Happy is he or she who has withstood all the trials to the end (see also Matt. 5:3–12). ***perseveres.*** In verse 3, James says that testing produces perseverance. Here he points out that such perseverance brings the reward of blessedness. ***stood the test.*** Such a person is like metal which has been purged by fire and is purified of all foreign substances. ***crown of life.*** As with Paul (Rom. 5:1–5) and Peter (1 Peter 1:6–7), James now focuses on the final result of endurance under trial: eternal life (see also 2 Tim. 4:8; Rev. 2:10).

says is like a man who looks at his face in a mirror
[24]and, after looking at himself, goes away and
immediately forgets what he looks like. [25]But the
man who looks intently into the perfect law that
gives freedom, and continues to do this, not forgetting what he has heard, but doing it—he will
be blessed in what he does.
[26]If anyone considers himself religious and yet
does not keep a tight rein on his tongue, he deceives himself and his religion is worthless. [27]Re-
ligion that God our Father accepts as pure and
faultless is this: to look after orphans and widows
in their distress and to keep oneself from being
polluted by the world.

JAMES 1:19–27

1. What family on TV reminds you most of your own family?
2. On long family trips, how did your parents resolve conflicts in the car?
3. Who is the peacemaker in your family—the one who stays calm, cool and collected?
4. How quick are you to: Listen? Speak? Get angry? How about your parents?
5. How does your family resolve conflict when it happens? What would James recommend (see v. 19)?
6. What do you need to "get rid of" (v. 21) in your life?
7. What's one way this group can practice pure religion (see v. 27) this week?
8. How can the group pray for you this week?

Favoritism Forbidden

2 My brothers, as believers in our glorious
Lord Jesus Christ, don't show favoritism.
[2]Suppose a man comes into your meeting wearing a gold ring and fine clothes, and a poor man
in shabby clothes also comes in. [3]If you show
special attention to the man wearing fine clothes
and say, "Here's a good seat for you," but say to
the poor man, "You stand there" or "Sit on the
floor by my feet," [4]have you not discriminated
among yourselves and become judges with evil
thoughts?
[5]Listen, my dear brothers: Has not God chosen
those who are poor in the eyes of the world to be
rich in faith and to inherit the kingdom he promised those who love him? [6]But you have insulted
the poor. Is it not the rich who are exploiting
you? Are they not the ones who are dragging you
into court? [7]Are they not the ones who are slan-
dering the noble name of him to whom you belong?
[8]If you really keep the royal law found in Scripture, "Love your neighbor as yourself,"[a] you are
doing right. [9]But if you show favoritism, you sin

[a]8 Lev. 19:18

1:19 ***slow to speak.*** One needs to consider carefully what is to be said, rather than impulsively and carelessly launching into words that are not wise. ***slow to become angry.*** James does not forbid anger. However, James does caution against responding in anger at every opportunity.

1:20 This verse is reminiscent of what Jesus said in the Sermon on the Mount (Matt. 5:21–22). ***the righteous life.*** Human anger does not produce the kind of life that God wants.

1:21 Repentance and faith are the key to living out the Christian life. ***the word.*** This is the same "word of truth" mentioned in verse 18. In contrast to the quick and angry words of people (words which hurt and destroy), there is the word of God which saves.

1:22 ***merely listen.*** The Christian must not just hear the word of God. A response is required. ***deceive yourselves.*** It does not matter how well a person may know the teaching of the apostles or how much Scripture he or she has memorized. To make mere knowledge of God's will the sole criterion for the religious life is dangerous and self-deceptive.

1:25 ***the perfect law.*** The reference is probably to the teachings of Jesus which set one free, in contrast to the Jewish Law which brought bondage (see Rom. 8:2). ***continues.*** Such people make obedience to the Gospel a continuing part of their lives.

1:27 ***world.*** Not the world of nature but the world of people in their rebellion against and alienation from God (see 1 John 2:15).

James emphasizes that Christians are to have a different ethic than that of the world. They are not to favor the wealthy simply because they are wealthy, nor are they to despise the poor simply because they are poor. The poor are to be welcomed and aided. In fact, one's faith is shown by acts of generosity to the poor.

2:1–2 ***glorious.*** In Jesus one sees a manifestation of God's presence. ***favoritism.*** This is the act of paying special attention to someone because he or she is rich, important, famous or powerful. ***poor man.*** The word used here denotes a beggar, a person from the lowest level of society. Had this been a low-paid worker, a different Greek word would have been used.

2:4–5 All social distinctions are null and void in the church. Partiality is clearly out of place. Both rich and poor are to be received equally. Notice that the rich are not condemned here. They are welcome in the church. What is condemned is the insult to the poor person (v. 6).

2:6–8 ***exploiting you.*** In a day of abject poverty the poor were often forced to borrow money at exorbitant rates of interest just to survive. ***the royal law.*** The law of love is the central moral principle by which Christians are to order their lives (see Mark 12:28–33).

2:10–13 Christians are not bound by rigid laws by which they will one day be judged, as Judaism taught. So the fear of future punishment is not a deterrent to behavior. Rather, it is the inner compulsion of love that motivates the Christian to right action.

and are convicted by the law as lawbreakers.
10For whoever keeps the whole law and yet stumbles at just one point is guilty of breaking all of it.
11For he who said, "Do not commit adultery,"[a]
also said, "Do not murder."[b] If you do not commit adultery but do commit murder, you have
become a lawbreaker.
12Speak and act as those who are going to be
judged by the law that gives freedom, 13because
judgment without mercy will be shown to anyone who has not been merciful. Mercy triumphs
over judgment!

JAMES 2:1–13

1. Where do you sit in church? Where do you like to sit at a concert? At a ball game? In class?
2. Who are the kids at your school you have the hardest time accepting?
3. When have you either misjudged someone or been misjudged yourself based on appearance?
4. How does God look upon favoritism (v. 9)? When has favoritism hurt you? Are you guilty of showing favoritism?
5. How accepted do you feel at home? School? Church? In this group?
6. How well are you loving your neighbor as yourself?
7. What grade would you give this group on accepting others? What can the group do to be more accepting?
8. Share prayer requests and close by praying together.

(Study notes on page 1173)

Faith and Deeds

14What good is it, my brothers, if a man claims
to have faith but has no deeds? Can such faith
save him? 15Suppose a brother or sister is without
clothes and daily food. 16If one of you says to him,
"Go, I wish you well; keep warm and well fed,"
but does nothing about his physical needs, what
good is it? 17In the same way, faith by itself, if it
is not accompanied by action, is dead.
18But someone will say, "You have faith; I have
deeds."
Show me your faith without deeds, and I will
show you my faith by what I do. 19You believe

JAMES 2:14–26

1. Are you a doer or a thinker? Are you more likely to act without thinking or think without acting?
2. Is James saying that faith or belief doesn't really matter? Why *does* it matter?
3. When have you been challenged to put your faith to the test in a major way?
4. What is the significance of verse 22? In what way does your faith need to be more complete?
5. What is God saying to you in this passage?
6. How can this group help you in prayer this week?

that there is one God. Good! Even the demons
believe that—and shudder.
20You foolish man, do you want evidence that
faith without deeds is useless[c]? 21Was not our
ancestor Abraham considered righteous for what
he did when he offered his son Isaac on the altar?
22You see that his faith and his actions were
working together, and his faith was made complete by what he did. 23And the scripture was
fulfilled that says, "Abraham believed God, and it
was credited to him as righteousness,"[d] and he
was called God's friend. 24You see that a person
is justified by what he does and not by faith
alone.
25In the same way, was not even Rahab the
prostitute considered righteous for what she did
when she gave lodging to the spies and sent them
off in a different direction? 26As the body without
the spirit is dead, so faith without deeds is dead.

Taming the Tongue

3 Not many of you should presume to be teachers, my brothers, because you know that we
who teach will be judged more strictly. 2We all
stumble in many ways. If anyone is never at fault
in what he says, he is a perfect man, able to keep
his whole body in check.
3When we put bits into the mouths of horses

[a]11 Exodus 20:14; Deut. 5:18 [b]11 Exodus 20:13; Deut. 5:17 [c]20 Some early manuscripts *dead* [d]23 Gen. 15:6

to make them obey us, we can turn the whole
animal. 4Or take ships as an example. Although
they are so large and are driven by strong winds,
they are steered by a very small rudder wherever
the pilot wants to go. 5Likewise the tongue is a
small part of the body, but it makes great boasts.
Consider what a great forest is set on fire by a
small spark. 6The tongue also is a fire, a world of
evil among the parts of the body. It corrupts the
whole person, sets the whole course of his life on
fire, and is itself set on fire by hell.
7All kinds of animals, birds, reptiles and creatures of the sea are being tamed and have been
tamed by man, 8but no man can tame the tongue.
It is a restless evil, full of deadly poison.
9With the tongue we praise our Lord and Father, and with it we curse men, who have been
made in God's likeness. 10Out of the same mouth
come praise and cursing. My brothers, this
should not be. 11Can both fresh water and salt[a]
water flow from the same spring? 12My brothers,
can a fig tree bear olives, or a grapevine bear figs?
Neither can a salt spring produce fresh water.

Two Kinds of Wisdom

13Who is wise and understanding among you?
Let him show it by his good life, by deeds done
in the humility that comes from wisdom. 14But if
you harbor bitter envy and selfish ambition in
your hearts, do not boast about it or deny the
truth. 15Such "wisdom" does not come down
from heaven but is earthly, unspiritual, of the
devil. 16For where you have envy and selfish ambition, there you find disorder and every evil
practice.
17But the wisdom that comes from heaven is
first of all pure; then peace-loving, considerate,
submissive, full of mercy and good fruit, impartial
and sincere. 18Peacemakers who sow in peace
raise a harvest of righteousness.

Submit Yourselves to God

4 What causes fights and quarrels among you?
Don't they come from your desires that battle within you? 2You want something but don't
get it. You kill and covet, but you cannot have
what you want. You quarrel and fight. You do not
have, because you do not ask God. 3When you
ask, you do not receive, because you ask with
wrong motives, that you may spend what you get
on your pleasures.
4You adulterous people, don't you know that
friendship with the world is hatred toward God?
Anyone who chooses to be a friend of the world

JAMES 3:1–18

1. What was your bedtime at age 7? What time did your brother(s) or sister(s) have to go to bed? When did your parents let you set your own bedtime?
2. In your family, are you more likely to tease or be teased? Who do you tease or who teases you?
3. Who deserves the Nobel Peace Prize for knowing how to settle disputes between you and your sibling(s)?
4. In your everyday conversation, how seriously do you take verses 9–10?
5. When has your mouth gotten you into trouble?
6. Where in your life do you feel the pressure to measure up to someone else?
7. What have you found helpful in relating to your brother(s) or sister(s) in a positive way?
8. Make it a point to speak "blessings" to those in your family this week. Close in prayer.

[a] *11* Greek *bitter* (see also verse 14)

James now examines the connection between speech and wisdom. Words can be wise but they can also be deadly. The tongue is so small, yet it has great power. It can control the very direction of one's life.

3:9 ***With the tongue we praise.*** The tongue is vital to all worship: praying, singing, praising and thanking. ***we curse men.*** It is by means of words that people bring real harm to others. ***in God's likeness.*** Since people are made in the image of God, when they are cursed, God too is being cursed. The same tongue that praises God is also used to curse him, a point James makes explicit in verse 10.

3:13 ***by his good life, by deeds.*** Understanding, like faith, is shown by *how one lives.* Specifically, understanding is demonstrated by a good life and by good deeds. This is also what Jesus taught (see Matt. 7:15–23).

3:14 ***in your hearts.*** The question to be answered is—What lies at the core of the person's being? Is it true wisdom from God or is it ambition? True wisdom will show itself by a good life filled with loving deeds done in a humble spirit. But envy and ambition will display itself by quite a different sort of life (see v. 16).

3:17 ***wisdom.*** Wisdom is looked at in terms of moral virtue and practical goodness. ***peace-loving.*** This is the opposite of envy and ambition. True wisdom produces right relationships between people, which is the root idea behind the word "peace" when it is used in the New Testament.

becomes an enemy of God. 5Or do you think
Scripture says without reason that the spirit he
caused to live in us envies intensely?[a] 6But he
gives us more grace. That is why Scripture says:

"God opposes the proud
but gives grace to the humble."[b]

7Submit yourselves, then, to God. Resist the
devil, and he will flee from you. 8Come near
to God and he will come near to you. Wash
your hands, you sinners, and purify your hearts,
you double-minded. 9Grieve, mourn and wail.
Change your laughter to mourning and your joy
to gloom. 10Humble yourselves before the Lord,
and he will lift you up.

11Brothers, do not slander one another. Anyone who speaks against his brother or judges him
speaks against the law and judges it. When you
judge the law, you are not keeping it, but sitting
in judgment on it. 12There is only one Lawgiver
and Judge, the one who is able to save and destroy. But you—who are you to judge your neighbor?

JAMES 4:1–12

1. What's something you would really like to have?
2. Who do you quarrel with the most? Over what?
3. How do you usually react when you don't get something you want?
4. What are two reasons we don't get what we want (see verses 2 and 3)?
5. When have you been envious of one of your friends or of something they had? How did that affect your relationship?
6. On a scale of 1 (far) to 10 (near), how close do you feel to God right now? How does that compare to 6 months ago?
7. Where do you need to submit yourself to God and resist the devil this week?
8. Share prayer requests and pray for one another now and during the coming week.

Boasting About Tomorrow

13Now listen, you who say, "Today or tomorrow we will go to this or that city, spend a year
there, carry on business and make money."
14Why, you do not even know what will happen
tomorrow. What is your life? You are a mist that
appears for a little while and then vanishes. 15In-
stead, you ought to say, "If it is the Lord's will,
we will live and do this or that." 16As it is, you
boast and brag. All such boasting is evil. 17Any-
one, then, who knows the good he ought to do
and doesn't do it, sins.

[a]5 Or *that God jealously longs for the spirit that he made to live in us*; or *that the Spirit he caused to live in us longs jealously*
[b]6 Prov. 3:34

4:1 ***desires.*** James is not saying that personal pleasure is inherently wrong. However, there is a certain desire for gratification that springs from the wrong source and possesses a person in the pursuit of its fulfillment. ***within you.*** The struggle is within a person—between the part of him or her which is controlled by the Holy Spirit and that which is controlled by the world.

4:2 ***You want something.*** This is desire at work (see 1:14). ***but don't get it.*** This is desire frustrated. ***kill and covet.*** This is how frustrated desire responds. It lashes out at others in anger and abuse. (This is "killing" in a metaphorical sense—see Matt. 5:21–22.) It responds in jealousy to those who have what it wants.

4:6 But all is not hopeless. God does give grace. Repentance is possible. They can turn from their misbehavior. ***grace.*** To receive grace, a person must *ask* for it. To be able to ask, one must see the need to do so. The proud person can't and doesn't see such a need. Only the humble do.

4:7–10 James tells how to repent. ***Resist the devil.*** Submission to God begins with resistance to Satan. ***he will flee from you.*** Since Satan has no ultimate power over a Christian, when resisted he withdraws. ***Wash your hands.*** Originally this was a ritual requirement whereby one became ceremonially clean in preparation for the worship of God (Ex. 30:19–21). Now it is a symbol of the sort of inner purity God desires. ***sinners.*** Those whose lives have become more characteristic of the enemy than of God—lapsed or "worldly" Christians.

4:13 ***"Today or tomorrow we will go ..."*** James lets us listen in on the plans of a group of businessmen. They are planning for the future and are concerned with where they will go and how much profit they will make. But "there is absolutely nothing about their desires for the future, their uses of money, or their way of doing business that is any different from the rest of the world. Their worship may be exemplary, their personal morality, impeccable; but when it comes to business they think entirely on a worldly plane" (Davids).

4:14 ***tomorrow.*** All such planning presupposes that tomorrow will unfold like any other day, when in fact, the future is anything but secure (Prov. 27:1). ***What is your life?*** These businessmen are like the rich fool of Jesus' parable, who had made a large honest profit through farming. Feeling secure, he makes plans for a comfortable retirement. "But God said to him, 'You fool! This very night your life will be demanded from you' " (Luke 12:16–21). By thinking on a worldly plane, James' Christian businessmen have gained a false sense of security.

4:16 ***boast.*** Boasting about what will happen tomorrow is in the same category as judging one another (vv. 11–12). Judgment is arrogant because God is the only legitimate judge. Boasting about the future is arrogant because God is the only one who knows what will happen in the future. ***brag.*** Claiming to be able to do something you could not do.

4:17 ***who knows the good.*** Christians can sin by doing what they ought not to do (lawbreaking); or by not doing what they know they should do (failure).

JAMES 4:13–17

1. What are your plans for this weekend?
2. How do you go about deciding what to do for the weekend?
3. How far into the future have you planned your life?
4. What attitude should you have towards planning (see v. 15)?
5. Who do you admire for the way they live one day at a time—making every day count for God?
6. On a scale from 1 (little) to 10 (much), how much influence does your commitment to Jesus Christ affect your life goals?
7. Where do you need God's guidance in your plans for the future?
8. How can the group pray for you and support you?

(Study notes on page 1176)

Warning to Rich Oppressors

5 Now listen, you rich people, weep and wail
because of the misery that is coming upon
you. 2Your wealth has rotted, and moths have
eaten your clothes. 3Your gold and silver are cor-
roded. Their corrosion will testify against you and
eat your flesh like fire. You have hoarded wealth
in the last days. 4Look! The wages you failed to
pay the workmen who mowed your fields are
crying out against you. The cries of the harvesters
have reached the ears of the Lord Almighty. 5You
have lived on earth in luxury and self-indulgence.
You have fattened yourselves in the day of slaughter.[a] 6You have condemned and murdered innocent men, who were not opposing you.

JAMES 5:1–6

1. If you won the lottery, how would you spend your first $100,000?
2. To whom is this passage addressed?
3. What are the abuses the rich committed (vv. 4–6)? How do these injustices happen in the world today? How should Christians respond and be involved?
4. What do you think James would say about the concerns most people have for saving money, preparing for retirement, estate planning, etc.?
5. What is God saying to you in this passage?
6. How can this group help you in prayer this week?

Patience in Suffering

7Be patient, then, brothers, until the Lord's
coming. See how the farmer waits for the land to
yield its valuable crop and how patient he is for
the autumn and spring rains. 8You too, be patient
and stand firm, because the Lord's coming is
near. 9Don't grumble against each other, brothers, or you will be judged. The Judge is standing
at the door!
10Brothers, as an example of patience in the
face of suffering, take the prophets who spoke in
the name of the Lord. 11As you know, we consider blessed those who have persevered. You have
heard of Job's perseverance and have seen what
the Lord finally brought about. The Lord is full of
compassion and mercy.

[a]5 Or *yourselves as in a day of feasting*

5:7–8 ***patient.*** The basic idea is that of *patient waiting.* It is related to the endurance that James commended in 1:3 ("perseverance"), though patience connotes a more passive holding on than the active endurance of chapter 1. ***until.*** Such patient waiting on the part of the Christians, suffering from poverty and persecution, is possible because they know that an event is coming that will radically change their situation, namely the Lord's return. ***stand firm.*** The longer they wait, the stronger the temptation to doubt the Second Coming, and even to doubt the Christian faith itself. They must resist these temptations. ***near.*** The common feeling in the New Testament days was that the Lord's return was imminent—any day now (see Rom. 13:11–12).

5:11 ***persevered.*** Endurance of suffering, a concept which describes Job's experience. ***finally brought about.*** In the end, God blessed Job with far more than he had at the beginning of his trials (Job 42:10–17). The implications of this are clear: if they will stand firm, their reward too will be great.

5:16 ***confess your sins.*** Confessing your sins to one another removes barriers between people and promotes honesty in the Christian community.

5:19–20 James concludes his letter by summarizing its purpose. ***wander.*** Christian truth captivates not only the mind, but one's whole life, including how one lives. Hence James can speak about wandering from Christian truth, into other styles of living. It is not primarily doctrinal deviation that has concerned James. It is how one lives.

12Above all, my brothers, do not swear—not
by heaven or by earth or by anything else. Let
your "Yes" be yes, and your "No," no, or you will
be condemned.

The Prayer of Faith

13Is any one of you in trouble? He should pray.
Is anyone happy? Let him sing songs of praise.
14Is any one of you sick? He should call the elders
of the church to pray over him and anoint him
with oil in the name of the Lord. 15And the
prayer offered in faith will make the sick person
well; the Lord will raise him up. If he has sinned,
he will be forgiven. 16Therefore confess your sins
to each other and pray for each other so that you
may be healed. The prayer of a righteous man is
powerful and effective.
17Elijah was a man just like us. He prayed earnestly that it would not rain, and it did not rain
on the land for three and a half years. 18Again he
prayed, and the heavens gave rain, and the earth
produced its crops.
19My brothers, if one of you should wander
from the truth and someone should bring him
back, 20remember this: Whoever turns a sinner
from the error of his way will save him from
death and cover over a multitude of sins.

JAMES 5:7–20

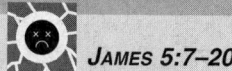

1. What do you hate waiting for?
2. Who is the most patient person you know?
3. Rank yourself on the patience meter from 1 (none) to 10 (plenty).
4. As Christians, what are we waiting for (see verses 7–8)?
5. How are you at keeping your word—letting your "Yes" be yes, and "No," no?
6. What's something in your life for which you've been waiting a long time?
7. How do you feel about sharing the needs in your life with this group?
8. "Confess your sins to each other and pray for each other so that you may be healed" (v. 16).

(Study notes on page 1177)

Introduction to
1 PETER

Personal Reading Plan

❒ 1 Peter 1:1–2:3
❒ 1 Peter 2:4–3:7
❒ 1 Peter 3:8–4:11
❒ 1 Peter 4:12–5:14

Author

Traditionally, the apostle Peter is credited with writing this letter. Peter was one of the first disciples called by Jesus. From Galilee, he was by trade a fisherman. His father was Jonah. His brother was Andrew the apostle. He was married, and his wife accompanied him on some of his preaching tours. Peter quickly became one of the leaders among the 12 apostles; later, he was a leader of the church in Jerusalem. He was the apostle to the Jews, yet because of his response to a vision, the first Gentile convert, Cornelius, was admitted to the church (Acts 10). Tradition says that Peter was martyred in Rome, around A.D. 68, by crucifixion upside down.

Date

First Peter was written sometime between the fire in Rome (A.D. 64) and Peter's death (A.D. 68).

Theme

Hope in the midst of suffering.

Audience

First Peter is a circular letter to Christians living in the northwest section of Asia Minor (in what is now modern Turkey). Pontus, Galatia, Cappadocia, Asia and Bithynia (1:1) are all Roman provinces. This area had a large population and the fact that Christians were living throughout the region testifies to the success of early Christian missionaries.

That these Christians were mainly Gentiles is clear from the way Peter describes their preconversion life; he uses categories and phrases typically applied to pagans but not to Jews (1:14; 2:9–10; 4:3–4). Peter also uses the Greek form of his name, Cephas, in this letter, and not Simon, his Jewish name.

Historical Background

One hot July night in A.D. 64, Rome caught fire. For three days and three nights the fire blazed out of control. Ancient temples and landmarks were swept away. Homes were destroyed. Ten of the 14 city sections suffered damage; three sections were reduced to rubble. The people of Rome were distraught and angry, especially because it was widely believed that if Emperor Nero had not actually set the fire, he certainly had done nothing to contain it. In fact, certain of Nero's officers were caught with firebrands trying to rekindle the waning fire. Many felt that Nero's passion for building caused him to want the city destroyed so he might rebuild it. No matter what Nero did to refute this rumor—and he aided the homeless extensively—nothing reduced the suspicion that the fire was his doing. Clearly he needed a scapegoat on which to blame the fire.

The Christians were nominated for this dubious honor. Up to this time, they were thought to be simply a Jewish sect and were hardly noticed by Roman authorities. In fact, the Roman courts protected Christians against the wrath of the synagogue and others. But now all this changed. Nero introduced the church to martyrdom. What began in Rome would soon wash across the Roman Empire.

Under Roman law there were two types of religious systems: those that were legal, such as Judaism, and those that were forbidden. Anyone who practiced a forbidden religion was considered a criminal and was subject to harsh penalties. After the great fire, Christianity was judged to be distinct from Judaism, and it was quickly prohibited. This meant that throughout the Roman Empire, Christians were now technically outlaws and thus subject to persecution. Just such persecution was taking place in Asia Minor among the Christians to whom Peter writes (4:12).

Purpose

In the midst of the "painful trial" (4:12) they are suffering, Peter writes to comfort and encourage. "Rejoice that you participate in the sufferings of Christ" (4:13), he says. How can they rejoice at such a difficult time? Because of the great *hope* they have as Christians. Hope is the theme of Peter's letter to these suffering believers.

Characteristics

When reading 1 Peter, one keeps hearing echoes from other parts of the Bible. Certainly the Old Testament is present. Peter quotes a number of passages, particularly from Isaiah. For example in 1:24–25, he quotes Isaiah 40:6–8; in 2:6, Isaiah 28:16; in 2:8, Isaiah 8:14; and in 2:22, Isaiah 53:9. Furthermore, he frequently alludes to Old Testament ideas and stories.

Peter is also familiar with Paul's writings. This letter contains parallels to Romans and, in particular, Ephesians. For example, compare 1:3 with Ephesians 1:3 and 1:20 with Ephesians 1:4. Note also the similarity between Peter and Paul in their instructions to family members and slaves (2:18–3:7; Eph. 5:21–6:9; Col. 3:18–25). In addition, there are parallels to Hebrews, James and, not surprisingly, to Peter's own sermons in Acts.

Of course, this does not necessarily mean that Peter was consciously quoting from New Testament documents. It may simply be that there was a common pattern of teaching in the early church and that Peter is tapping into this as did other New Testament writers.

First Peter is written in excellent Greek, so much so that some have questioned whether a Galilean fisherman like Peter could have had such a sophisticated command of the language. First Peter contains some of the best Greek in the New Testament. Its style is smoother even than Paul's with his years of training; its rhythmic structure is not unlike that of the Greek masters.

The answer to this question is found in 5:12: "With the help of Silas ... I have written to you." The Greek here indicates that Silas was more than just a stenographer. In fact, he could well be the source of the excellent style as he helped Peter draft the letter and polish up the language.

Passages for Topical Group Study

1:3–12	SPIRITUAL STRUGGLES	Praise to God for a Living Hope
2:4–12	SELF-IMAGE	The Living Stone and a Chosen People
4:1–11	PRIORITIES	Living for God
5:1–11	WEATHERING LIFE'S STORMS	To Elders and Young Men

See the Lesson Plans in the front of this Bible.

Passages for General Group Study

1:13–2:3	Be Holy
2:13–25	Submission to Rulers and Masters
3:1–7	Wives and Husbands
3:8–22	Suffering for Doing Good
4:12–19	Suffering for Being a Christian

1 Peter, an apostle of Jesus Christ,
To God's elect, strangers in the world, scattered throughout Pontus, Galatia, Cappadocia,
Asia and Bithynia, 2who have been chosen according to the foreknowledge of God the Father,
through the sanctifying work of the Spirit, for
obedience to Jesus Christ and sprinkling by his
blood:

Grace and peace be yours in abundance.

Praise to God for a Living Hope

3Praise be to the God and Father of our Lord
Jesus Christ! In his great mercy he has given us
new birth into a living hope through the resurrection of Jesus Christ from the dead, 4and into
an inheritance that can never perish, spoil or
fade—kept in heaven for you, 5who through faith
are shielded by God's power until the coming
of the salvation that is ready to be revealed in
the last time. 6In this you greatly rejoice, though
now for a little while you may have had to suffer
grief in all kinds of trials. 7These have come so
that your faith—of greater worth than gold,
which perishes even though refined by fire—may
be proved genuine and may result in praise,
glory and honor when Jesus Christ is revealed.
8Though you have not seen him, you love him;
and even though you do not see him now, you
believe in him and are filled with an inexpressible and glorious joy, 9for you are receiving the
goal of your faith, the salvation of your souls.
10Concerning this salvation, the prophets,
who spoke of the grace that was to come to you,
searched intently and with the greatest care,
11trying to find out the time and circumstances to
which the Spirit of Christ in them was pointing
when he predicted the sufferings of Christ and
the glories that would follow. 12It was revealed to
them that they were not serving themselves but
you, when they spoke of the things that have
now been told you by those who have preached
the gospel to you by the Holy Spirit sent from
heaven. Even angels long to look into these
things.

Be Holy

13Therefore, prepare your minds for action; be
self-controlled; set your hope fully on the grace to
be given you when Jesus Christ is revealed. 14As
obedient children, do not conform to the evil desires you had when you lived in ignorance. 15But
just as he who called you is holy, so be holy in all
you do; 16for it is written: "Be holy, because I am
holy."[a]
17Since you call on a Father who judges each
man's work impartially, live your lives as strangers here in reverent fear. 18For you know that it
was not with perishable things such as silver or
gold that you were redeemed from the empty

1 PETER 1:3–12

1. In this group, who has had the most broken bones?
2. If you were to chart your spiritual life on a graph, what would be the high point? The low point?
3. What has this past week in your spiritual life been like—up or down?
4. What purpose do life's trials serve (v. 7)?
5. In what can you "greatly rejoice" despite the trials you face (see vv. 3–5)?
6. What spiritual struggle are you going through right now?
7. What have you found helpful when you are dealing with struggles?
8. How can the group lift you up in prayer and share in your spiritual struggles?

[a] *16* Lev. 11:44,45; 19:2; 20:7

1:3 *new birth.* When people encounter Jesus, something so radical happens that they can be said to be reborn into a whole new life. This is no mere metaphor, but an accurate description of the transformation whereby a person becomes a part of the family of God and aware of spiritual reality.

1:5 *salvation.* This is the object of the believers' hope and the content of their inheritance. The reference here is not to individual salvation, but to that moment in history when Christ will return again and all believers will come into the full enjoyment of eternity.

1:6 The experience of rebirth and the anticipation of an inheritance (both fruits of salvation) enable Christians to "greatly rejoice" despite trials and adversities. ***for a little while you may have had to suffer.*** Trials are temporary in comparison with eternity, and certain circumstances make them inevitable. However, such trials do not fall outside God's providence. ***grief.*** This stands in contrast to "rejoice." Within the trials there is both real grief and authentic rejoicing.

1:7 *gold.* Gold was the most precious of metals in the first century. Their faith is worth even more. ***fire.*** Fire was used to burn away the impurities and so reveal the pure gold. In the same way, trials reveal the inner quality of faith. ***proved genuine.*** This will make evident the actual quality and strength of the faith that is possessed. Such trials do not create faith; they reveal what is already there.

way of life handed down to you from your forefathers, 19but with the precious blood of Christ, a
lamb without blemish or defect. 20He was chosen
before the creation of the world, but was revealed in these last times for your sake.
21Through him you believe in God, who raised
him from the dead and glorified him, and so your
faith and hope are in God.
22Now that you have purified yourselves by
obeying the truth so that you have sincere love
for your brothers, love one another deeply, from

1 Peter 1:13–2:3

1. What do you do to keep in shape physically? Mentally?
2. According to Peter, what does it mean to be holy (vv. 13–16)? Which of these characteristics is the greatest challenge for you?
3. What is a good test to see if a Christian has really had a change of heart (v. 22)?
4. What makes loving others deeply and actively possible (vv. 22–23)?
5. What is God saying to you in this passage?
6. How can this group help you in prayer this week?

the heart.[a] 23For you have been born again, not
of perishable seed, but of imperishable, through
the living and enduring word of God. 24For,

"All men are like grass,
and all their glory is like the flowers of the field;
the grass withers and the flowers fall,
25 but the word of the Lord stands
forever."[b]

And this is the word that was preached to you.

2 Therefore, rid yourselves of all malice and all
deceit, hypocrisy, envy, and slander of every
kind. 2Like newborn babies, crave pure spiritual
milk, so that by it you may grow up in your salvation, 3now that you have tasted that the Lord is
good.

The Living Stone and a Chosen People

4As you come to him, the living Stone—
rejected by men but chosen by God and precious
to him— 5you also, like living stones, are being
built into a spiritual house to be a holy priesthood, offering spiritual sacrifices acceptable to

1 Peter 2:4–12

1. What's something you've made or built recently?
2. How have you been feeling about yourself lately?
3. How does it make you feel to know you are chosen by God—that you belong to him?
4. What process is God undertaking in your life (see v. 5)?
5. On a scale of 1 (no way) to 10 (no problem), how easy is it for you to feel chosen by God and special?
6. What has your "spiritual house" been like lately: A safe castle? A leaky hut? A new house under construction?
7. Peter talks about things "which war against your soul" (v. 11). What are you fighting against right now?
8. Close by saying something to encourage or affirm someone else in the group.

(Study notes on page 1183)

God through Jesus Christ. 6For in Scripture it
says:

"See, I lay a stone in Zion,
a chosen and precious cornerstone,
and the one who trusts in him
will never be put to shame."[c]

7Now to you who believe, this stone is precious.
But to those who do not believe,

"The stone the builders rejected
has become the capstone,[d]"[e]

8and,

"A stone that causes men to stumble
and a rock that makes them fall."[f]

They stumble because they disobey the message—which is also what they were destined
for.

[a] 22 Some early manuscripts *from a pure heart* [b] 25 Isaiah 40:6-8 [c] 6 Isaiah 28:16 [d] 7 Or *cornerstone*
[e] 7 Psalm 118:22 [f] 8 Isaiah 8:14

9But you are a chosen people, a royal priesthood, a holy nation, a people belonging to God, that you may declare the praises of him who called you out of darkness into his wonderful
light. 10Once you were not a people, but now you are the people of God; once you had not received mercy, but now you have received mercy.

11Dear friends, I urge you, as aliens and strangers in the world, to abstain from sinful desires,
which war against your soul. 12Live such good lives among the pagans that, though they accuse you of doing wrong, they may see your good deeds and glorify God on the day he visits us.

Submission to Rulers and Masters

13Submit yourselves for the Lord's sake to every authority instituted among men: whether to
the king, as the supreme authority, 14or to governors, who are sent by him to punish those who do wrong and to commend those who do right.
15For it is God's will that by doing good you should silence the ignorant talk of foolish men.
16Live as free men, but do not use your freedom as a cover-up for evil; live as servants of God.
17Show proper respect to everyone: Love the brotherhood of believers, fear God, honor the king.

18Slaves, submit yourselves to your masters with all respect, not only to those who are good and considerate, but also to those who are harsh.
19For it is commendable if a man bears up under the pain of unjust suffering because he is con-
scious of God. 20But how is it to your credit if you receive a beating for doing wrong and endure it? But if you suffer for doing good and you endure it,
this is commendable before God. 21To this you were called, because Christ suffered for you, leaving you an example, that you should follow in his steps.

22"He committed no sin,
and no deceit was found in his mouth."[a]

23When they hurled their insults at him, he did not retaliate; when he suffered, he made no threats. Instead, he entrusted himself to him who judges justly. 24He himself bore our sins in his body on the tree, so that we might die to sins and live for righteousness; by his wounds you have
been healed. 25For you were like sheep going astray, but now you have returned to the Shepherd and Overseer of your souls.

[a]22 Isaiah 53:9

1 PETER 2:13–25

1. In what job or task have you ever felt like a slave?
2. How are Christians to act toward governmental authority? Why?
3. How can Jesus' example help you when you face hardships you cannot change?
4. How does Peter say that Christ's death has both an ending and a beginning effect on our lives (v. 24)?
5. What is God saying to you in this passage?
6. How can this group help you in prayer this week?

Wives and Husbands

3 Wives, in the same way be submissive to your husbands so that, if any of them do not believe the word, they may be won over without words by the behavior of their wives, 2when they
see the purity and reverence of your lives. 3Your
beauty should not come from outward adornment, such as braided hair and the wearing of
gold jewelry and fine clothes. 4Instead, it should be that of your inner self, the unfading beauty of a gentle and quiet spirit, which is of great worth
in God's sight. 5For this is the way the holy women of the past who put their hope in God used to make themselves beautiful. They were submis-

2:4 *the living Stone.* Peter gets this metaphor from Isaiah 28:16 (v. 6) and Psalm 118:22 (v. 7). Despite his rejection by the world, Christ is the chosen one of God who is alive and able to give his resurrection life to those who come to him.

2:5 *you also, like living stones.* So close is the relationship between Christians and Christ that Peter uses the same metaphor to describe both. ***a spiritual house.*** The church is the temple of God, made up of a close-knit community. ***a holy priesthood.*** Not only are they a "spiritual house," they are the priests who serve in it! ***offering spiritual sacrifices.*** Christ's great sacrifice of himself for the sins of the world was the ultimate and final blood sacrifice (1:18–19). Rather than offering animal sacrifices, the sacrifices of Christians are spiritual—such as declaring the praises of God (v. 9).

2:8 *destined for.* Those who have obeyed the Gospel are chosen and destined for a glorious inheritance. Those who have stumbled over Christ have a different destiny.

2:9–10 In contrast to their persecutors, they have a great destiny. Peter lists a series of titles drawn from the OT which once were applied to Israel, but now belong to them as Christians. Just as Jesus is "chosen by God" (v. 4), so too they are God's "chosen people." ***a holy nation.*** The church is the true Israel, heirs of God's promises and privileges.

2:11 *aliens and strangers.* They may be a chosen nation and a royal priesthood, but they are also outsiders in terms of the world, and need to be on their guard.

sive to their own husbands, [6]like Sarah, who
obeyed Abraham and called him her master. You
are her daughters if you do what is right and do
not give way to fear.
[7]Husbands, in the same way be considerate as
you live with your wives, and treat them with
respect as the weaker partner and as heirs with
you of the gracious gift of life, so that nothing will
hinder your prayers.

1 Peter 3:1–7

1. How would you rate your parents on their husband/wife relationship?
2. How does Peter define beauty? When appreciating or striving for beauty, which kind do you tend to focus on—that in verses 3 or 4?
3. What does the fact that husband and wife together are "heirs of the gift of life" say about their equality in the eyes of God? Whose marriage do you respect as a model in carrying out this passage?
4. In a society somewhat changed from that of the first century, how should men and women today follow the spirit of Peter's teaching on submission in this passage and 2:13–15?
5. What is God saying to you in this passage?
6. How can this group help you in prayer this week?

Suffering for Doing Good

[8]Finally, all of you, live in harmony with one
another; be sympathetic, love as brothers, be
compassionate and humble. [9]Do not repay evil
with evil or insult with insult, but with blessing,
because to this you were called so that you may
inherit a blessing. [10]For,

"Whoever would love life
    and see good days
must keep his tongue from evil
    and his lips from deceitful speech.
[11]He must turn from evil and do good;
    he must seek peace and pursue it.
[12]For the eyes of the Lord are on the righteous
    and his ears are attentive to their prayer,
but the face of the Lord is against those who
    do evil."[a]

[13]Who is going to harm you if you are eager to
do good? [14]But even if you should suffer for what

1 Peter 3:8–22

1. Who is the "goody two shoes" in your family? Who is the troublemaker?
2. How is it really possible to live like verses 8–12: Prayer? Effort? Obedience no matter what? A deepening relationship with Christ?
3. How can suffering for what is right be a means of blessing (v. 14)?
4. How does *hope* change your everyday behavior (v. 15)? What situation seemed hopeless to you until God brought hope?
5. What is God saying to you in this passage?
6. How can this group help you in prayer this week?

is right, you are blessed. "Do not fear what they
fear[b]; do not be frightened."[c] [15]But in your
hearts set apart Christ as Lord. Always be prepared to give an answer to everyone who asks
you to give the reason for the hope that you have.
But do this with gentleness and respect, [16]keep-
ing a clear conscience, so that those who speak
maliciously against your good behavior in Christ
may be ashamed of their slander. [17]It is better, if
it is God's will, to suffer for doing good than for
doing evil. [18]For Christ died for sins once for all,
the righteous for the unrighteous, to bring you to
God. He was put to death in the body but made
alive by the Spirit, [19]through whom[d] also he
went and preached to the spirits in prison [20]who
disobeyed long ago when God waited patiently in
the days of Noah while the ark was being built. In
it only a few people, eight in all, were saved
through water, [21]and this water symbolizes baptism that now saves you also—not the removal of
dirt from the body but the pledge[e] of a good
conscience toward God. It saves you by the resurrection of Jesus Christ, [22]who has gone into heav-

[a] *12* Psalm 34:12-16 [b] *14* Or *not fear their threats* [c] *14* Isaiah 8:12 [d] *18,19* Or *alive in the spirit,* [19]*through which*
[e] *21* Or *response*

en and is at God's right hand—with angels, authorities and powers in submission to him.

Living for God

4 Therefore, since Christ suffered in his body,
arm yourselves also with the same attitude,
because he who has suffered in his body is done
with sin. 2As a result, he does not live the rest of
his earthly life for evil human desires, but rather
for the will of God. 3For you have spent enough
time in the past doing what pagans choose to
do—living in debauchery, lust, drunkenness, orgies, carousing and detestable idolatry. 4They
think it strange that you do not plunge with them
into the same flood of dissipation, and they heap
abuse on you. 5But they will have to give account
to him who is ready to judge the living and the
dead. 6For this is the reason the gospel was
preached even to those who are now dead, so
that they might be judged according to men in
regard to the body, but live according to God in
regard to the spirit.
7The end of all things is near. Therefore be
clear minded and self-controlled so that you can
pray. 8Above all, love each other deeply, because
love covers over a multitude of sins. 9Offer hospitality to one another without grumbling. 10Each
one should use whatever gift he has received to
serve others, faithfully administering God's grace
in its various forms. 11If anyone speaks, he should
do it as one speaking the very words of God. If
anyone serves, he should do it with the strength
God provides, so that in all things God may be
praised through Jesus Christ. To him be the glory
and the power for ever and ever. Amen.

1 Peter 4:1–11

1. What are the top three priorities in your life?
2. Where do the party kids in your school go after a ball game and what do they do? Have they ever gotten in trouble?
3. When has someone "heaped abuse on you" (v. 4) because you didn't join them in something you considered wrong?
4. What are some priorities that a Christian should have in their life (see vv. 7–10)?
5. How have your priorities changed since becoming a Christian or since you got serious about your faith?
6. Right now, are you living more for yourself or for God?
7. What gift that God has given you can you use this week in service to someone else? Give a specific example.
8. How can the group pray for you and support you in using your gifts?

Suffering for Being a Christian

12Dear friends, do not be surprised at the painful trial you are suffering, as though something
strange were happening to you. 13But rejoice that
you participate in the sufferings of Christ, so that
you may be overjoyed when his glory is revealed.
14If you are insulted because of the name of
Christ, you are blessed, for the Spirit of glory and
of God rests on you. 15If you suffer, it should not
be as a murderer or thief or any other kind of
criminal, or even as a meddler. 16However, if you
suffer as a Christian, do not be ashamed, but
praise God that you bear that name. 17For it is
time for judgment to begin with the family of
God; and if it begins with us, what will the outcome be for those who do not obey the gospel of
God? 18And,

"If it is hard for the righteous to be saved,
what will become of the ungodly and the
sinner?"[a]

[a] *18* Prov. 11:31

4:1–6 A difficult passage to interpret correctly. However, it is clear that Peter is reassuring these Asian Christians that despite the suffering they face, they will prevail because of their identification in baptism with Jesus' death and resurrection.

4:4–5 Their pagan friends are astonished that they no longer lead this out-of-control lifestyle, but then their amazement turns into reaction and abuse. This attitude will bring its own reward. These abusive pagans will face judgment for their actions.

4:7–11 Peter gives yet another reason for forsaking their old, self-indulgent lifestyle: history is about to end. This is the time, he says, for self-discipline, prayer, and active love. In particular they must care for each other. Mutuality is the key: mutual love (v. 8), mutual hospitality (v. 9), and mutual ministry (vv. 10–11).

4:7 ***the end of all things.*** The second coming of Jesus will mark the close of history when this world as it is now known passes away. ***be clear minded and self-controlled.*** As history draws to a close, their temptation might be to let their excitement get out of hand. ***so that you can pray.*** When people are not thinking clearly or when their lives are out of control, they cannot pray properly.

4:8 Love is the key to a lifestyle of the last days. ***love covers over a multitude of sins***. A paraphrase of Proverbs 10:12. People tend to forgive those whom they love. Love also forgives again and again (Matt. 18:21–22;1 Cor. 13:5; Eph. 4:32).

[19]So then, those who suffer according to God's
will should commit themselves to their faithful
Creator and continue to do good.

1 PETER 4:12–19

1. What kind of pain affects you the most: physical or emotional?
2. What false assumption does Peter set straight in verse 12? How often are you surprised at the trials of life?
3. Christians in our society are not physically persecuted. What form, then, does your suffering for Christ take?
4. What is the first and most important course of action amidst suffering (v. 19)? How will this lift some of the burden of suffering?
5. What is God saying to you in this passage?
6. How can this group help you in prayer this week?

To Elders and Young Men

5 To the elders among you, I appeal as a fellow
elder, a witness of Christ's sufferings and
one who also will share in the glory to be revealed: [2]Be shepherds of God's flock that is under
your care, serving as overseers—not because you
must, but because you are willing, as God wants
you to be; not greedy for money, but eager to
serve; [3]not lording it over those entrusted to you,
but being examples to the flock. [4]And when the
Chief Shepherd appears, you will receive the
crown of glory that will never fade away.
[5]Young men, in the same way be submissive to
those who are older. All of you, clothe yourselves
with humility toward one another, because,

"God opposes the proud
but gives grace to the humble."[a]

[6]Humble yourselves, therefore, under God's
mighty hand, that he may lift you up in due time.
[7]Cast all your anxiety on him because he cares
for you.

1 PETER 5:1–11

1. Where do you keep the equipment (flashlight, fire extinguisher, first aid kit, etc.) in your house in case of an emergency?
2. What do you do when you are anxious or stressed out: Bite your nails? Eat? Stop eating? Withdraw?
3. What teacher do you respect the most? Why?
4. During storms in your life, what are some good things to do (see vv. 6–9)?
5. Among your Christian friends, what is the greatest cause for spiritual collapse?
6. What anxiety in your life right now do you need to turn over to God?
7. Spiritually, how has the battle gone during this last week?
8. What prayer requests do you have for the group this week?

[8]Be self-controlled and alert. Your enemy the
devil prowls around like a roaring lion looking for
someone to devour. [9]Resist him, standing firm in
the faith, because you know that your brothers
throughout the world are undergoing the same
kind of sufferings.

[a]*5* Prov. 3:34

5:1–4 Peter has specific instructions for the leaders of the fellowship. It will not be easy for them to lead a church that is under fire. ***Chief Shepherd.*** Peter has already described Jesus as the "Shepherd" (2:25).

5:6 *Humble yourselves.* The same humility which is owed one another is owed God as well. ***that he may lift you up in due time.*** This will happen when Christ returns and they experience his glory.

5:8 *Be self-controlled and alert.* That they are not to be passive in the face of trouble is seen in this command. Coupled with reliance on God, there must also be diligent effort on their part. ***the devil.*** Behind all their trials stands the devil. In the OT he is known by the Hebrew name Satan. In the NT he is seen as the one who tempts (as he did with Jesus), as the prince of evil who rebelled against God, and as the one who seeks to undo God's purposes.

5:9 *Resist him.* Peter's advice is plain: do not run away, stand your ground and face him, refuse to give in to his purposes, trust in God (see also Eph. 6:10–13; James 4:7; Rev. 12:9–11). ***your brothers throughout the world are undergoing the same kind of sufferings.*** Solidarity with Christian brothers and sisters around the world is a strong motivation for standing firm.

5:10–11 Satan may be their enemy and he is indeed powerful and vicious ("like a roaring lion looking for someone to devour"), but he is no match for God. Assurance of strength and victory is another motivation for continuing to resist evil.

10 And the God of all grace, who called you to
his eternal glory in Christ, after you have suffered
a little while, will himself restore you and make
you strong, firm and steadfast. 11 To him be the
power for ever and ever. Amen.

Final Greetings

12 With the help of Silas,[a] whom I regard as a
faithful brother, I have written to you briefly,
encouraging you and testifying that this is the
true grace of God. Stand fast in it.

13 She who is in Babylon, chosen together with
you, sends you her greetings, and so does my son
Mark. 14 Greet one another with a kiss of love.

Peace to all of you who are in Christ.

[a] *12* Greek *Silvanus*, a variant of *Silas*

Introduction to
2 PETER

Personal Reading Plan

❒ 2 Peter 1:1–21
❒ 2 Peter 2:1–22
❒ 2 Peter 3:1–18

Author

Traditionally, the apostle Peter is thought to have authored this letter. However, questions about his authorship have existed since the earliest times. It was not uncommon in the first century to attribute pieces of writing to famous people. In fact, Peter's name is attached to several other books that clearly were not written by him (e.g., the Gospel of Peter, the Preaching of Peter and the Apocalypse of Peter).

So questions arise when the language and thought of 1 and 2 Peter are compared. In their original Greek form, these two books are strikingly different. Could the same man have written both? This difference in style, of course, may simply be the result of Peter's use of several different secretaries. Peter indicates in his first letter that Silas helped him write it (1 Peter 5:12), and it is known that Peter had other secretaries (e.g., Mark and Glaucias). In any case, 2 Peter is a part of the New Testament, and it has a valuable message for our modern society which is important to hear.

Date

Second Peter was probably written near the time of Peter's death in A.D. 68 (see 1:12–15).

Theme

Be eager and on your guard.

Audience

On the basis of 1:1, it appears that there were no specific recipients of the letter. It seems to be for all Christians everywhere (hence its description as a General Epistle). However, in the body of the letter it becomes clear that 2 Peter was sent to a church or group of churches that had previously received 1 Peter (3:1). This would make the recipients Gentile Christians in Asia Minor. Furthermore, the tone of the letter makes it clear that a specific problem and specific false teachers are in view. All of this indicates that this is a letter to a particular people living in a particular area.

Purpose

Second Peter is a very important book for today because it deals with the very issues confronting the modern church: a lax lifestyle based on weak theology. Some church members in Peter's time were arguing that the doctrine of the Second Coming had to be reconsidered. "The plain fact is that Christ has not returned yet," they said, "and he probably won't" (see 3:4,9). In fact, they suggested that this doctrine may have been invented by the apostles rather than revealed by God (1:16), perhaps to keep Christians in line. The doctrine of the Second Coming was sort of a moral club used to inhibit one's lifestyle. In contrast, the false teachers were saying that behavior does not matter. "Freedom" was their catchword, and evidently they felt free to indulge in sexual immorality, drunkenness and the like.

"Not so!" exclaims Peter in this letter. And it is his "not so" that we need to hear in this day of "New Age" thought and self-centered lifestyles. We, too, need to remain firmly established within the truth we received from the prophets and from our Lord (chapter 1). We, too, need to be warned against those who would lead people away from that truth (chapter 2). And we, too, need to be reminded (in a passage that is chillingly real in this day of nuclear weapons), that the world will one day end when the Lord returns (chapter 3).

Characteristics

Chapter 1 is an exhortation to grow in the Christian virtues. Chapter 2 is very similar to the epistle of Jude (see the Introduction to Jude). A marked contrast is drawn there between the character and teaching of true apostles (like Peter and Paul) and that of the false teachers whose lives are marked by their denial of Jesus, immorality, rejection of authority, enslavement to sin and misuse of Scripture. Chapter 3 addresses the Second Coming of Christ.

Structure

Second Peter is a letter like other New Testament letters. It calls itself a letter (3:1). It begins like a typical first-century letter (1:1–2) by identifying sender and recipients and offering a Christian greeting. And then, in typical fashion, it announces its theme (1:3–11) and tells the occasion of writing (1:12–15). The only thing 2 Peter lacks is personal greetings at the end, but these were not characteristic of all first-century letters.

Second Peter is also a farewell speech or a testament. It sounds like the last words of a great leader. There are many examples of this form of literature in the first century. In the New Testament, Paul's farewell speech to the Ephesian elders had this character (Acts 20:17–35), as does the book of 2 Timothy.

In 1:12–15, Peter says that his death is soon to take place, and the way he writes his letter is typical of testament literature in general. The letter contains ethical instructions in which the author summarizes his view, and then he makes predictions about the future.

The Early Church

Controversies abounded in the early church. One group denied Jesus was God, and then another declared him God but not fully man. The apostles denounced obtaining salvation by works, only to encounter those who took it to the extreme and assumed "anything goes." Members of one church quit working and gathered together to await Jesus' return; while those of another gave up on his coming again at all.

Second Peter was written in response to a young church's questioning and doubting tendencies. Where 1 Peter centered on dangers from outside the church, this letter speaks to dangers from within. False teachers were stirring up problems, casting doubt on doctrine, and leading Christians into immoral behavior.

Passage for Topical Group Study

1:1–11 MUSIC, MOVIES, ETC. Making One's Calling and Election Sure

See the Lesson Plans in the front of this Bible.

Passages for General Group Study

1:12–21	Prophecy of Scripture
2:1–22	False Teachers and Their Destruction
3:1–18	The Day of the Lord

1 Simon Peter, a servant and apostle of Jesus
Christ,

To those who through the righteousness of our
God and Savior Jesus Christ have received a faith
as precious as ours:

[2]Grace and peace be yours in abundance
through the knowledge of God and of Jesus our
Lord.

2 Peter 1:1–11

1. What is your all-time favorite movie? What's your favorite radio station?
2. How would you compare your taste in music and movies to your parents?
3. What is the worst movie you've seen? What made it so bad?
4. How much influence does music have on the lifestyle of kids in your school?
5. How much of today's music, movies and entertainment emphasizes the qualities listed in verses 5–7?
6. What qualities from verses 5–7 are you adding to your faith? How? Which quality do you need to work on?
7. How does your commitment to Christ affect your choice of movies and music?
8. How can this group help hold each other accountable in making good entertainment choices? Close in prayer.

Making One's Calling and Election Sure

[3]His divine power has given us everything we
need for life and godliness through our knowledge of him who called us by his own glory and
goodness. [4]Through these he has given us his
very great and precious promises, so that through
them you may participate in the divine nature
and escape the corruption in the world caused by
evil desires.

[5]For this very reason, make every effort to add
to your faith goodness; and to goodness, knowledge; [6]and to knowledge, self-control; and to self-
control, perseverance; and to perseverance, godliness; [7]and to godliness, brotherly kindness; and
to brotherly kindness, love. [8]For if you possess
these qualities in increasing measure, they will
keep you from being ineffective and unproductive in your knowledge of our Lord Jesus Christ.
[9]But if anyone does not have them, he is nearsighted and blind, and has forgotten that he has
been cleansed from his past sins.

[10]Therefore, my brothers, be all the more eager to make your calling and election sure. For if
you do these things, you will never fall, [11]and you
will receive a rich welcome into the eternal kingdom of our Lord and Savior Jesus Christ.

Prophecy of Scripture

[12]So I will always remind you of these things,
even though you know them and are firmly established in the truth you now have. [13]I think it is
right to refresh your memory as long as I live in
the tent of this body, [14]because I know that I will
soon put it aside, as our Lord Jesus Christ has
made clear to me. [15]And I will make every effort
to see that after my departure you will always be
able to remember these things.

[16]We did not follow cleverly invented stories
when we told you about the power and coming of
our Lord Jesus Christ, but we were eyewitnesses
of his majesty. [17]For he received honor and glory
from God the Father when the voice came to him
from the Majestic Glory, saying, "This is my Son,
whom I love; with him I am well pleased."[a]
[18]We ourselves heard this voice that came from
heaven when we were with him on the sacred
mountain.

[19]And we have the word of the prophets made

[a] *17* Matt. 17:5; Mark 9:7; Luke 9:35

1:3 *everything we need for life and godliness.* God has made available to us all that we need spiritually through our knowledge of him. Second Peter may have been written to combat Gnosticism—a belief that salvation is a product of knowledge and matter is entirely evil, thereby the breaking of the Law is of no moral consequence. Peter is emphasizing that no secret, esoteric knowledge is necessary for salvation.

1:4 *participate in the divine nature.* This does not indicate that Christians become divine in any sense, but are indwelt by God through his Holy Spirit (see John 14:16–17). The human personality and the divine remain distinct and separate.

1:5–7 *faith.* The cornerstone of the Christian life. ***knowledge.*** The best antidote for false teaching. ***self-control.*** Many of the false teachers taught that knowledge made self-control unnecessary. However, Peter stresses that Christian knowledge leads to self-control. ***perseverance.*** This is steadiness and faithfulness in the face of suffering and trials. ***godliness.*** A true reverence toward God that governs one's attitude toward every aspect of life. ***brotherly kindness.*** Warm-hearted feelings toward all in the family of faith. ***love.*** The kind of selfless attitude that leads one to sacrifice for the good of others.

1:10 *make your calling and election sure.* By cultivating the qualities listed in verses 5–7, they can be assured that God has chosen and called them (see Matt. 7:20). When God calls and elects, it is to obedience and holiness (see 1 Peter 1:2; Eph. 1:3–6).

more certain, and you will do well to pay attention to it, as to a light shining in a dark place,
until the day dawns and the morning star rises in
your hearts. 20 Above all, you must understand

2 PETER 1:12–21

1. What event in your life this past year was the most memorable?
2. What event of Jesus' life does Peter recall (vv. 16–18)?
3. If so much prophecy has already been fulfilled in Christ's first coming, how then are we to regard prophecy yet to be fulfilled?
4. If you could have been with Jesus at one event in his life, which would you choose? Why?
5. What is God saying to you in this passage?
6. How can this group help you in prayer this week?

that no prophecy of Scripture came about by the
prophet's own interpretation. 21 For prophecy
never had its origin in the will of man, but men
spoke from God as they were carried along by the
Holy Spirit.

False Teachers and Their Destruction

2 But there were also false prophets among the
people, just as there will be false teachers
among you. They will secretly introduce destructive heresies, even denying the sovereign Lord
who bought them—bringing swift destruction on
themselves. 2 Many will follow their shameful
ways and will bring the way of truth into disre-
pute. 3 In their greed these teachers will exploit
you with stories they have made up. Their condemnation has long been hanging over them, and
their destruction has not been sleeping.
4 For if God did not spare angels when they
sinned, but sent them to hell,[a] putting them
into gloomy dungeons[b] to be held for judgment;
5 if he did not spare the ancient world when he
brought the flood on its ungodly people, but protected Noah, a preacher of righteousness, and
seven others; 6 if he condemned the cities of Sodom and Gomorrah by burning them to ashes, and
made them an example of what is going to happen to the ungodly; 7 and if he rescued Lot, a
righteous man, who was distressed by the filthy
lives of lawless men 8 (for that righteous man,
living among them day after day, was tormented
in his righteous soul by the lawless deeds he saw
and heard)— 9 if this is so, then the Lord knows
how to rescue godly men from trials and to hold
the unrighteous for the day of judgment, while
continuing their punishment.[c] 10 This is especially true of those who follow the corrupt desire
of the sinful nature[d] and despise authority.
Bold and arrogant, these men are not afraid to
slander celestial beings; 11 yet even angels, although they are stronger and more powerful, do
not bring slanderous accusations against such beings in the presence of the Lord. 12 But these men
blaspheme in matters they do not understand.
They are like brute beasts, creatures of instinct,
born only to be caught and destroyed, and like
beasts they too will perish.

2 PETER 2:1–22

1. If people have pets that are like them in some way, what does your choice of pet say about you?
2. If it is so plain that judgment awaits these false teachers, why does anyone follow them (vv. 2–3,14,18–19)?
3. Who are the gross sinners in verses 13–16? What are they like? On what basis is Peter assured they will be paid back for what they've done?
4. What do verses 20–22 imply about a person's salvation? Can one lose it? Or were these people never converted? Why do you think so?
5. What is God saying to you in this passage?
6. How can this group help you in prayer this week?

13 They will be paid back with harm for the
harm they have done. Their idea of pleasure is
to carouse in broad daylight. They are blots and
blemishes, reveling in their pleasures while they
feast with you.[e] 14 With eyes full of adultery,
they never stop sinning; they seduce the unstable; they are experts in greed—an accursed

[a] 4 Greek *Tartarus* [b] 4 Some manuscripts *into chains of darkness* [c] 9 Or *unrighteous for punishment until the day of judgment* [d] 10 Or *the flesh* [e] 13 Some manuscripts *in their love feasts*

brood! 15They have left the straight way and wandered off to follow the way of Balaam son of Beor, who loved the wages of wickedness. 16But he was rebuked for his wrongdoing by a donkey—a beast without speech—who spoke with a man's voice and restrained the prophet's madness.

17These men are springs without water and mists driven by a storm. Blackest darkness is reserved for them. 18For they mouth empty, boastful words and, by appealing to the lustful desires of sinful human nature, they entice people who are just escaping from those who live in error. 19They promise them freedom, while they themselves are slaves of depravity—for a man is a slave to whatever has mastered him. 20If they have escaped the corruption of the world by knowing our Lord and Savior Jesus Christ and are again entangled in it and overcome, they are worse off at the end than they were at the beginning. 21It would have been better for them not to have known the way of righteousness, than to have known it and then to turn their backs on the sacred command that was passed on to them. 22Of them the proverbs are true: "A dog returns to its vomit,"[a] and, "A sow that is washed goes back to her wallowing in the mud."

The Day of the Lord

3 Dear friends, this is now my second letter to you. I have written both of them as reminders to stimulate you to wholesome thinking. 2I want you to recall the words spoken in the past by the holy prophets and the command given by our Lord and Savior through your apostles.

3First of all, you must understand that in the last days scoffers will come, scoffing and following their own evil desires. 4They will say, "Where is this 'coming' he promised? Ever since our fathers died, everything goes on as it has since the beginning of creation." 5But they deliberately forget that long ago by God's word the heavens existed and the earth was formed out of water and by water. 6By these waters also the world of that time was deluged and destroyed. 7By the same word the present heavens and earth are reserved for fire, being kept for the day of judgment and destruction of ungodly men.

8But do not forget this one thing, dear friends: With the Lord a day is like a thousand years, and a thousand years are like a day. 9The Lord is not slow in keeping his promise, as some understand slowness. He is patient with you, not wanting anyone to perish, but everyone to come to repentance.

10But the day of the Lord will come like a thief. The heavens will disappear with a roar; the elements will be destroyed by fire, and the earth and everything in it will be laid bare.[b]

11Since everything will be destroyed in this way, what kind of people ought you to be? You ought to live holy and godly lives 12as you look forward to the day of God and speed its coming.[c] That day will bring about the destruction of the heavens by fire, and the elements will melt in the heat. 13But in keeping with his promise we are looking forward to a new heaven and a new earth, the home of righteousness.

14So then, dear friends, since you are looking forward to this, make every effort to be found spotless, blameless and at peace with him. 15Bear in mind that our Lord's patience means salvation, just as our dear brother Paul also wrote you with the wisdom that God gave him. 16He writes the same way in all his letters, speaking in them of these matters. His letters contain some things that are hard to understand, which ignorant and unstable people distort, as they do the other Scriptures, to their own destruction.

17Therefore, dear friends, since you already know this, be on your guard so that you may not be carried away by the error of lawless men and fall from your secure position. 18But grow in the grace and knowledge of our Lord and Savior Jesus Christ. To him be glory both now and forever! Amen.

2 Peter 3:1–18

1. When did your dad promise a fishing trip, a ball game or a graduation present and then fail to deliver? How did that make you feel?
2. What frustrations are produced by God's patience in coming again? How is God's patience beneficial (vv. 9,15)?
3. In verses 10–16, is Peter addressing the certainty, the timing or the manner of Christ's coming?
4. What is Peter's final antidote to the false teachers of his day (vv. 17–18)?
5. What is God saying to you in this passage?
6. How can this group help you in prayer this week?

[a] *22* Prov. 26:11 [b] *10* Some manuscripts *be burned up* [c] *12* Or *as you wait eagerly for the day of God to come*

Introduction to
1 JOHN

Personal Reading Plan

- ❐ 1 John 1:1–2:17
- ❐ 1 John 2:18–3:24
- ❐ 1 John 4:1–21
- ❐ 1 John 5:1–21

Author

Despite the fact that the author is nowhere named in the epistle, it is highly probable that he is none other than the beloved apostle John, now an old man living in Asia Minor and pastoring the churches in and around Ephesus. There are a number of reasons for attributing this anonymous epistle to John, including the following:

1. A strong tradition dating back to the early days of the church holds that John is the author.
2. There are many similarities in style and content between the Gospel of John and this epistle. The same sharp contrasts appear in both—light and darkness, truth and falsehood, love and hate. The differences between them can be traced to differences in purpose and to the length of time that elapsed between the composition of each.
3. The internal information in the epistle points to John. For example, the author tells us that he was one of the original eyewitnesses of Jesus (1:1–2). Also, the author writes with the air of authority that would be expected of an apostle (4:6).

Date

There is little clear evidence by which to date this letter accurately. Although it can be dated as early as A.D. 60, it was probably written toward the end of the New Testament era (A.D. 90–95), by which time many false teachings had flourished.

Theme

Walking in the light.

The Problem of False Teachers

Apparently a group of Christians got involved in false teaching, split off from the church (2:19), and were now hassling their former friends, probably trying to convince them to accept their new and "advanced" views (2:26). This deeply troubled the church and thus John, as pastor, wrote to assure the Christians in and around Ephesus that they were, indeed, true Christians with the assurance of eternal life.

The nature of the false teaching is not completely clear. John does not describe it. The recipients of his letter knew well enough what was being taught. Still, by the nature of John's defense of orthodox Christianity, certain features of the incorrect doctrine emerge.

In particular, the false teachers had a low view of Jesus. They did not believe he was the Messiah (2:22; 5:1). They did not believe he was the Son of God (5:5). They denied that Jesus had come in the flesh (4:2). They apparently claimed they did not need Jesus because they already knew God (2:4) and had fellowship with him (1:6). They did not believe that sin separated a person from God (1:6,8,10), and thus they had no need of Jesus' atoning death (5:6) to provide forgiveness and a way back to God. It is not by accident that John calls them "antichrists" (2:22).

Spiritual "Superiority"

This group had come to think of themselves as some sort of spiritual elite, claiming that they had a "deeper" understanding of Christianity, probably by direct revelation (4:1–6). As an antidote to such spiritual pride, John reminded his readers over and over that Christians are called to love one another, not to look down on their brothers and sisters who do not measure up to their own supposed, superior insight.

It is not clear what labels to affix to this group of false teachers. They were probably related to what later became Gnosticism—a philosophy in which matter (including the body) was impure and spirit was all that counted. Therefore, these false teachers denied that Christ was fully human. They kept his deity, but at the expense of his humanity. To them, salvation came by illumination. Thus, secret "knowledge" was eagerly sought, often at the expense of apostolic doctrine.

Purpose

John's central concerns are quite clear. He wants to define the marks of a true Christian against the claims of the false teachers. He wants his congregation to have assurance that they have eternal life (5:13). He wants them to know the characteristics of a true Christian: right belief (the doctrinal test), righteousness (the moral test) and love (the social test).

Characteristics

First John is written in the simplest Greek of all the New Testament. (It is usually the first book seminary students learn to translate.) Although 5,437 different Greek words appear in the New Testament, only 303 are used in the three letters of John—less than six percent of the total. This is not to say, however, that 1 John is a superficial book. On the contrary, here the apostle John, now an old man, is writing a summary of all he has learned. "This is what Christianity is all about," he is saying. "This is what it all boils down to: God is light (1:5); God is love (4:16); Jesus is the Messiah (2:22), the Son of God (4:15), who has come in the flesh (4:2). We are to be God's children (3:1); as such we have eternal life (2:25). We do not continue in sin (2:1), but we love one another (3:11). I repeat, we are to love one another (4:7–12)."

Structure

First John is not a letter like 2 and 3 John or most of Paul's writings. It lacks identification of writer and recipients, a salutation and a final greeting. Still, it is not a generalized document written to all Christians. John has a specific audience in mind, probably the churches in his charge in Asia Minor. Despite the lack of usual greetings, he writes in personal terms. Many see 1 John as a tract, perhaps intended to be read as a sermon, in which John deals with a specific problem.

Passages for Topical Group Study

1:5–2:6	MORAL FAILURE BLOWING IT	Walking in the Light
3:11–24	REACHING OUT COMPASSION	Love One Another
4:1–6	CULTS	Test the Spirits
4:7–21	GANGS / VIOLENCE GOD'S LOVE	God's Love and Ours
5:1–15	DOUBTS	Faith in the Son of God

See the Lesson Plans in the front of this Bible.

Passages for General Group Study

1:1–4	The Word of LIfe	2:15–27	Warnings About the World and Antichrists
2:7–14	A New Command	2:28–3:10	Children of God

The Word of Life

1 That which was from the beginning, which
we have heard, which we have seen with
our eyes, which we have looked at and our hands
have touched—this we proclaim concerning the
Word of life. 2The life appeared; we have seen it
and testify to it, and we proclaim to you the eternal life, which was with the Father and has appeared to us. 3We proclaim to you what we have
seen and heard, so that you also may have fellowship with us. And our fellowship is with the Father and with his Son, Jesus Christ. 4We write
this to make our[a] joy complete.

1 JOHN 1:1–4

1. What was your house like at age 7? What do you remember about your room?
2. John makes a point of saying that he has heard, seen and touched Jesus. What were your "beginnings" with Jesus like? In what ways have you "seen," "heard" and "touched" him?
3. What could not be proclaimed if Jesus hadn't died (v. 2)? Have you ever come close to losing your faith in Christ? What happened?
4. Who has been like the apostle John in your life—a person who has convinced you of Jesus' love and cared about your spiritual growth?
5. What is God saying to you in this passage?
6. How can this group help you in prayer this week?

Walking in the Light

5This is the message we have heard from him
and declare to you: God is light; in him there is
no darkness at all. 6If we claim to have fellowship
with him yet walk in the darkness, we lie and do
not live by the truth. 7But if we walk in the light,
as he is in the light, we have fellowship with one
another, and the blood of Jesus, his Son, purifies
us from all[b] sin.
8If we claim to be without sin, we deceive
ourselves and the truth is not in us. 9If we confess
our sins, he is faithful and just and will forgive us
our sins and purify us from all unrighteousness.
10If we claim we have not sinned, we make him
out to be a liar and his word has no place in our
lives.

2 My dear children, I write this to you so that
you will not sin. But if anybody does sin,
we have one who speaks to the Father in our
defense—Jesus Christ, the Righteous One. 2He is
the atoning sacrifice for our sins, and not only for
ours but also for[c] the sins of the whole world.

1 JOHN 1:5–2:6

1. When was the last time the lights went out in your house and you were plunged into darkness?
2. How do you get someone to "see the light" when they've been messing up their life?
3. When you've blown it, what should you do to "clean up" (see 1:9)?
4. How does it make you feel to know Jesus speaks to God "in our defense" (2:1)?
5. What are two ways you can tell if you are walking in the light (see 1:7 and 2:3)?
6. Where have you been walking lately—in the light or in the darkness?
7. How can you shine your "light" (Jesus in you) this week?
8. What would you like the group to remember in prayer for you this week?

(Study notes on page 1196)

3We know that we have come to know him if
we obey his commands. 4The man who says, "I
know him," but does not do what he commands
is a liar, and the truth is not in him. 5But if anyone obeys his word, God's love[d] is truly made
complete in him. This is how we know we are in
him: 6Whoever claims to live in him must walk as
Jesus did.
7Dear friends, I am not writing you a new command but an old one, which you have had since
the beginning. This old command is the message
you have heard. 8Yet I am writing you a new
command; its truth is seen in him and you, because the darkness is passing and the true light is
already shining.

[a]4 Some manuscripts *your* [b]7 Or *every* [c]2 Or *He is the one who turns aside God's wrath, taking away our sins, and not only ours but also* [d]5 Or *word, love for God*

9Anyone who claims to be in the light but
hates his brother is still in the darkness. 10Who-
ever loves his brother lives in the light, and there
is nothing in him[a] to make him stumble. 11But
whoever hates his brother is in the darkness and
walks around in the darkness; he does not know
where he is going, because the darkness has
blinded him.

1 John 2:7–14

1. What game did you play as a child where you were blindfolded? What was the experience like?
2. What characteristics of light reflect who God is? Has God brought light to your life? In what way? Or do you more often feel like you're "in the dark"?
3. How can the command to love God and others (v. 7) be new and old at the same time? How is its truth seen in Jesus (think of examples from the Gospels)? Whom have you known as someone who models this behavior?
4. What three things does John stress again in verses 12–13? Which one of these do you most need to hear this week?
5. What is God saying to you in this passage?
6. How can this group help you in prayer this week?

12I write to you, dear children,
because your sins have been forgiven on account of his name.
13I write to you, fathers,
because you have known him who is from the beginning.
I write to you, young men,
because you have overcome the evil one.
I write to you, dear children,
because you have known the Father.
14I write to you, fathers,
because you have known him who is from the beginning.
I write to you, young men,
because you are strong,
and the word of God lives in you,
and you have overcome the evil one.

Do Not Love the World

15Do not love the world or anything in the
world. If anyone loves the world, the love of
the Father is not in him. 16For everything in the
world—the cravings of sinful man, the lust of his
eyes and the boasting of what he has and does—
comes not from the Father but from the world.
17The world and its desires pass away, but the
man who does the will of God lives forever.

Warning Against Antichrists

18Dear children, this is the last hour; and as
you have heard that the antichrist is coming,
even now many antichrists have come. This is
how we know it is the last hour. 19They went out
from us, but they did not really belong to us. For
if they had belonged to us, they would have remained with us; but their going showed that
none of them belonged to us.

20But you have an anointing from the Holy
One, and all of you know the truth.[b] 21I do not
write to you because you do not know the truth,
but because you do know it and because no lie
comes from the truth. 22Who is the liar? It is the
man who denies that Jesus is the Christ. Such a
man is the antichrist—he denies the Father and
the Son. 23No one who denies the Son has the
Father; whoever acknowledges the Son has the
Father also.

24See that what you have heard from the beginning remains in you. If it does, you also will

[a] 10 Or *it* [b] 20 Some manuscripts *and you know all things*

1:5–6 *God is light.* In the Bible, "light" was connected on the intellectual level with truth, and on the moral level with purity. ***to have fellowship ... yet walk in the darkness.*** It is claimed by the false teachers that it is possible to be in union with God and yet habitually sin. But if God is *light,* then those who walk in *darkness* cannot be part of him. This was a common error. It was felt that since the body was insignificant, it did not matter what a person did. The true essence of the person—the "spirit"—remained untouched and thus uncontaminated by sin.

1:7 *walk in the light.* The image here is of a person confidently striding forth, illuminated by the light of God's truth, in contrast to the person who stumbles around in darkness.

2:1–2 *if anybody does sin.* While urging sinlessness as a goal to strive for, John knows that in this present life this cannot be achieved. So the issue then is how to deal with sin. The answer is found in the triple role of Jesus as the advocate, the righteous one, and the atoning sacrifice. ***one who speaks ... in our defense.*** Since people have no basis on which to ask for forgiveness, Jesus does so on their behalf. ***the atoning sacrifice.*** Jesus, the advocate, bases his plea (that their sin should be forgiven) on the fact of his death to pay for their sin. Such a sacrifice is effective because he himself was without sin, and so could take the place of another.

2:6 John introduces the idea of the "imitation of Christ." Christians are habitually to live the way Jesus lived. He is their model. As he walked, so should they walk.

remain in the Son and in the Father. 25And this
is what he promised us—even eternal life.
26I am writing these things to you about those
who are trying to lead you astray. 27As for you,

1 John 2:15–27

1. What kind of disobedience do you remember as being the most tempting for you as a little kid: Lying? Hitting? Saying bad words?
2. What does John mean by "the world" (vv. 15–16)? Is it wrong to love the outdoors, or your pet? Are all human desires contrary to God's will? Why?
3. In what areas of your life does love for the world compete with love for God: In your use of money? Time? Priorities? Relationships? Ambitions?
4. What criteria can you use to distinguish between: (a) new insights into Christian truths that the Holy Spirit brings to light, and (b) false teachings that undermine the Christian faith?
5. What is God saying to you in this passage?
6. How can this group help you in prayer this week?

the anointing you received from him remains in
you, and you do not need anyone to teach you.
But as his anointing teaches you about all things
and as that anointing is real, not counterfeit—
just as it has taught you, remain in him.

Children of God

28And now, dear children, continue in him, so
that when he appears we may be confident and
unashamed before him at his coming.
29If you know that he is righteous, you know
that everyone who does what is right has been
born of him.

3 How great is the love the Father has lavished
on us, that we should be called children of
God! And that is what we are! The reason the
world does not know us is that it did not know
him. 2Dear friends, now we are children of God,
and what we will be has not yet been made
known. But we know that when he appears,[a]
we shall be like him, for we shall see him as he
is. 3Everyone who has this hope in him purifies
himself, just as he is pure.
4Everyone who sins breaks the law; in fact, sin
is lawlessness. 5But you know that he appeared
so that he might take away our sins. And in him
is no sin. 6No one who lives in him keeps on
sinning. No one who continues to sin has either
seen him or known him.
7Dear children, do not let anyone lead you
astray. He who does what is right is righteous,
just as he is righteous. 8He who does what is
sinful is of the devil, because the devil has been
sinning from the beginning. The reason the Son
of God appeared was to destroy the devil's work.
9No one who is born of God will continue to sin,
because God's seed remains in him; he cannot go
on sinning, because he has been born of God.
10This is how we know who the children of
God are and who the children of the devil are:
Anyone who does not do what is right is not a
child of God; nor is anyone who does not love
his brother.

1 John 2:28–3:10

1. Do people say you look more like your father or mother? What do you think?
2. How would you feel if Jesus returned right now: Excited? Relieved? Ashamed?
3. How easy is it for you to see God as your loving Father (3:1–2)? How can these verses help you when your self-image is low?
4. How can you know you are a child of God (3:10)? When has it recently been difficult for you to love?
5. What is God saying to you in this passage?
6. How can this group help you in prayer this week?

Love One Another

11This is the message you heard from the beginning:
We should love one another. 12Do not
be like Cain, who belonged to the evil one and
murdered his brother. And why did he murder
him? Because his own actions were evil and his
brother's were righteous. 13Do not be surprised,

[a]2 Or *when it is made known*

my brothers, if the world hates you. 14We know
that we have passed from death to life, because
we love our brothers. Anyone who does not love
remains in death. 15Anyone who hates his brother is a murderer, and you know that no murderer
has eternal life in him.
16This is how we know what love is: Jesus
Christ laid down his life for us. And we ought to

1 John 3:11–24

1. Who is someone you *really* love?
2. How do you know when someone *really* loves you?
3. Who is the most compassionate person you know? What do they do to show compassion?
4. What is the definition of love in this passage (see vv. 16–18)? How does this compare with the definition of love at your school?
5. If Jesus was a student at your school, who would he reach out to and how would he do it?
6. What is the closest you've come to going on a mission trip to reach out and serve others in the name of Christ?
7. Who is someone you know who is in need that you can help this week?
8. What prayer needs would you like to share?

lay down our lives for our brothers. 17If anyone
has material possessions and sees his brother in
need but has no pity on him, how can the love of
God be in him? 18Dear children, let us not love
with words or tongue but with actions and in
truth. 19This then is how we know that we belong to the truth, and how we set our hearts at
rest in his presence 20whenever our hearts condemn us. For God is greater than our hearts, and
he knows everything.
21Dear friends, if our hearts do not condemn
us, we have confidence before God 22and receive
from him anything we ask, because we obey his
commands and do what pleases him. 23And this
is his command: to believe in the name of his
Son, Jesus Christ, and to love one another as he
commanded us. 24Those who obey his commands
live in him, and he in them. And this is how we
know that he lives in us: We know it by the Spirit
he gave us.

Test the Spirits

4 Dear friends, do not believe every spirit, but
test the spirits to see whether they are from
God, because many false prophets have gone out
into the world. 2This is how you can recognize
the Spirit of God: Every spirit that acknowledges
that Jesus Christ has come in the flesh is from
God, 3but every spirit that does not acknowledge
Jesus is not from God. This is the spirit of the
antichrist, which you have heard is coming and
even now is already in the world.
4You, dear children, are from God and have
overcome them, because the one who is in you is
greater than the one who is in the world. 5They
are from the world and therefore speak from
the viewpoint of the world, and the world listens to them. 6We are from God, and whoever
knows God listens to us; but whoever is not
from God does not listen to us. This is how we
recognize the Spirit[a] of truth and the spirit of
falsehood.

God's Love and Ours

7Dear friends, let us love one another, for love
comes from God. Everyone who loves has been
born of God and knows God. 8Whoever does not

[a]6 Or *spirit*

3:12 ***Cain.*** Cain was a farmer, the firstborn son of Adam and Eve. God was pleased with his brother Abel's offering, but not with his (Gen. 4:3–5). ***why did he murder him?*** Cain knew that, unlike Abel's gift, his offering did not arise from the desire to do right. Therefore, because of his anger, Cain slew Abel (Gen. 4:6–8).

3:14 ***We know ... because we love.*** Love is evidence that one possesses eternal life.

3:16–17 John offers a positive example of love: Jesus' sacrificial love for the human race. Cain's act sprang from hatred and he took the life of another, while Jesus' act sprang from love and he gave his own life for others. ***brother.*** John asks his readers to consider the needs of a particular individual ("brother" is singular). "Loving everyone in general may be an excuse for loving nobody in particular" (Lewis). ***pity.*** Such self-giving love is not without emotion, even though it is primarily an action. John calls for genuine concern in the face of the plight of others.

3:20 ***whenever.*** It is not an unusual experience for the conscience of a Christian to be troubled. ***he knows everything.*** The human conscience is not infallible, but God is. The implication is that God—who knows a person's innermost secrets—will be more merciful than the heart of that person.

3:23 ***to believe ... and to love.*** John clarifies that Christianity is not just a set of theological truths (though it is that). It is also a life of active self-giving to others. Neither belief nor love is sufficient without the other. These two themes dominate the rest of his letter.

love does not know God, because God is love.
9This is how God showed his love among us: He
sent his one and only Son[a] into the world that
we might live through him. 10This is love: not
that we loved God, but that he loved us and sent
his Son as an atoning sacrifice for[b] our sins.

1 John 4:1–6

1. What is the strangest religious group you have heard of?
2. When you are unsure, how do you determine if someone is telling you the truth?
3. How do you feel when you hear of strange cult happenings, such as a mass suicide?
4. What power equips you to overcome false prophets (see v. 4)?
5. What is it about cults that seems to attract students?
6. What have you found is the best strategy in resisting cults?
7. How has God been working in your life this last week?
8. Share prayer requests and pray for one another.

11Dear friends, since God so loved us, we also
ought to love one another. 12No one has ever
seen God; but if we love one another, God lives
in us and his love is made complete in us.
13We know that we live in him and he in us,
because he has given us of his Spirit. 14And we
have seen and testify that the Father has sent his
Son to be the Savior of the world. 15If anyone
acknowledges that Jesus is the Son of God, God
lives in him and he in God. 16And so we know
and rely on the love God has for us.
God is love. Whoever lives in love lives in
God, and God in him. 17In this way, love is made
complete among us so that we will have confidence on the day of judgment, because in this
world we are like him. 18There is no fear in love.
But perfect love drives out fear, because fear has
to do with punishment. The one who fears is not
made perfect in love.

1 John 4:7–21

1. When have you written a "love letter"? Who did you write it to? What did it say?
2. When you were a kid, who were the members of your gang? What was your dress code? Secret password?
3. Who are the gangs in your community? Where do they hang out? What's their dress code?
4. What is it about gangs that attracts kids?
5. What do you offer in this Christian community that cannot be found in a gang?
6. How has God demonstrated that he is love (see verses 9–10)? How can a person know God and experience his love (see verses 15–17)?
7. What can you do this week that will clearly reflect God's love in your life?
8. Express your love to this group in some way. Then close in prayer.

(Study notes on page 1200)

[a] 9 Or *his only begotten Son* [b] 10 Or *as the one who would turn aside his wrath, taking away*

4:1 ***do not believe every spirit.*** Not everything a person says is automatically of God. In fact, it is dangerous to accept uncritically everything that is said "in the name of God." Not everyone claiming inner revelation is hearing God's voice! ***test.*** The test by which to distinguish between spirits has to do with who Jesus is. False spirits will not acknowledge Jesus as the incarnate Christ. Notice that the focus of this test is upon the *spirit* who is the source of the prophecy—not upon what is said. ***spirits.*** The issue is not whether supernatural spirits exist and actually inspire prophecy. This was assumed to be the case by almost everyone in the first century (see Mark 1:21–28, 32–34). ***false prophets.*** Prophets are those men and women who claim to speak on God's behalf. They allow the Holy Spirit—or another spirit—to speak through them. John does not deny the reality or the value of prophecy. He simply warns against false prophets, much as Jesus did (see Matt. 7:15; Mark 13:22–23).

4:2 To deny that Jesus, the Messiah, was truly human is incompatible with divine inspiration. Prophets who will not affirm this confession of faith are not of God. ***acknowledges.*** What John has in mind is not mere recognition of who Jesus is—since even the demons know him (Mark 1:24). Rather, what is called for is an open, positive, public declaration of faith in Jesus.

4:4 ***the one who is in you.*** It is not by means of their own unaided strength that they are able to resist these false prophets. The source of their power is the Spirit of God who resides in them.

[19]We love because he first loved us. [20]If anyone says, "I love God," yet hates his brother, he
is a liar. For anyone who does not love his brother, whom he has seen, cannot love God, whom
he has not seen. [21]And he has given us this command: Whoever loves God must also love his
brother.

Faith in the Son of God

5 Everyone who believes that Jesus is the
Christ is born of God, and everyone who
loves the father loves his child as well. [2]This is
how we know that we love the children of God:
by loving God and carrying out his commands.
[3]This is love for God: to obey his commands. And
his commands are not burdensome, [4]for everyone born of God overcomes the world. This is
the victory that has overcome the world, even
our faith. [5]Who is it that overcomes the world?
Only he who believes that Jesus is the Son of
God.

[6]This is the one who came by water and
blood—Jesus Christ. He did not come by water
only, but by water and blood. And it is the Spirit
who testifies, because the Spirit is the truth. [7]For
there are three that testify: [8]the[a] Spirit, the water and the blood; and the three are in agreement. [9]We accept man's testimony, but God's
testimony is greater because it is the testimony of
God, which he has given about his Son. [10]Anyone
who believes in the Son of God has this testimony in his heart. Anyone who does not believe
God has made him out to be a liar, because he has
not believed the testimony God has given about
his Son. [11]And this is the testimony: God has
given us eternal life, and this life is in his Son.
[12]He who has the Son has life; he who does not
have the Son of God does not have life.

Concluding Remarks

[13]I write these things to you who believe in
the name of the Son of God so that you may know
that you have eternal life. [14]This is the confidence we have in approaching God: that if we ask
anything according to his will, he hears us. [15]And
if we know that he hears us—whatever we ask—
we know that we have what we asked of him.
[16]If anyone sees his brother commit a sin that
does not lead to death, he should pray and God
will give him life. I refer to those whose sin does
not lead to death. There is a sin that leads to
death. I am not saying that he should pray about
that. [17]All wrongdoing is sin, and there is sin that
does not lead to death.
[18]We know that anyone born of God does not

1 John 5:1–15

1. What's one thing that you take for granted?
2. What part of a worship service helps to strengthen your faith the most?
3. In your school, who casts doubts about the Christian faith, especially about the birth, life and death of Jesus Christ?
4. When did you come to the place where you personally believed in the Gospel of Jesus Christ?
5. When have you doubted whether your faith in God was real or not?
6. What would you say to a friend who has doubts that they are really a Christian (see vv. 11–12)?
7. With how much confidence can you say that you "*know* that you have eternal life" (v. 13)?
8. How can the group help you in prayer this week?

(Study notes on page 1201)

[a]*7,8* Late manuscripts of the Vulgate *testify in heaven: the Father, the Word and the Holy Spirit, and these three are one. [8]And there are three that testify on earth: the* (not found in any Greek manuscript before the sixteenth century)

4:7 *love one another.* John will use this phrase three times in the next five verses (vv. 7,11,12). Each time, however, he uses it in a slightly different way. Here he urges his readers to love others because love originates in God. ***Everyone who loves.*** Since "love comes from God," all acts of love are reflections of God's nature.

4:10 *an atoning sacrifice for our sins.* The idea of atonement is tied up with the OT concept of substitution and sacrifice. In the OT, sin was dealt with when a person symbolically placed his sins on an animal that he had brought to the temple. This animal had to be without spot or blemish. It was then sacrificed in place of the sinful person. Such substitutionary sacrifices were a picture of what Jesus would one day do for all men and women.

4:11 *love one another.* Jesus' sacrificial death on behalf of the human race assures people that God loves them, and thus releases in them the ability to love others. Because they are loved they can love.

4:12 *love one another.* In the third use of this phrase, John states that although God cannot be seen directly, his life can be experienced by people as they love one another. Since God is love, they know him when they love.

4:18 *no fear in love.* People cannot love and fear at the same time. The love casts out the fear.

4:20 Love for God is not merely warm, inner feelings. Love is not love unless it finds expression via active caring for others.

continue to sin; the one who was born of God keeps him safe, and the evil one cannot harm
him. 19We know that we are children of God, and that the whole world is under the control of the
evil one. 20We know also that the Son of God has come and has given us understanding, so that we may know him who is true. And we are in him who is true—even in his Son Jesus Christ. He is the true God and eternal life.
21Dear children, keep yourselves from idols.

5:6–9 How is it that one comes to faith in Jesus? By means of reliable witnesses, John answers. He names three such witnesses: the water, the blood and the Holy Spirit. ***by water and blood.*** John is referring to Jesus' baptism and death. These events are crucial in understanding who Jesus is. At his baptism, Jesus publicly identified himself with the sins of the people (even though he was without sin). At his death, Jesus died to take away those sins. Water and blood would also remind John's readers of the ordinances of baptism and Communion. ***it is the Spirit who testifies.*** John has already stated the fact that there is an inner witness given by the Holy Spirit as to the truth of who Jesus is (see 3:24; 4:13; 1 Cor. 12:3). ***the Spirit is the truth.*** The Holy Spirit is the third witness, and is qualified to be such because the Spirit is truth itself.

5:11 ***eternal life.*** In receiving the testimony and thus receiving the Son, one also receives eternal life. The Greek word which is here translated "eternal" means "that which belongs to the coming age." But since that age has broken into the present age, eternal life can be enjoyed even now.

5:14 ***confidence.*** By this word John refers to the bold assurance Christians have—that they can approach God in prayer and freely speak their minds. ***according to his will.*** In 3:22, John says that the condition for answered prayer is obedient behavior. Here John adds another condition: what we ask must be in accord with God's plans and purposes (see also Matt. 26:39,42).

Introduction to
2 JOHN / 3 JOHN

Personal Reading Plan

❐ 2 John 1–13
❐ 3 John 1–14

Author

There is much similarity of style and content between 2 and 3 John. For example, compare 2 John 1 with 3 John 1, 2 John 4 with 3 John 4; 2 John 12 with 3 John 13–14. Undoubtedly both were written by the same person. There is also a close connection between 1 John and these two shorter letters (compare, for example, 1 John 4:3 with 2 John 7). All three epistles seem to deal with the same situation. Therefore, it seems very likely that the "elder" who wrote 2 and 3 John is, indeed, the apostle John.

Date

The dates are uncertain, but both letters were probably written in the late A.D. 80s or early 90s, when the false doctrine which they rebuke began to flourish.

Theme

Hospitality for traveling missionaries.

Purpose

The issue addressed by 2 and 3 John is that of wandering missionaries. In a time when Roman inns were notorious for being dirty and flea-infested, visiting Christian teachers would turn to the local church for hospitality. The problem was that some of the people seeking room and board were false teachers, expounding erroneous doctrines; others were phony, pretending to be true prophets to get free hospitality. Even a pagan Greek author like Lucian noticed this sort of abuse. In his satirical work *Peregrinus,* he wrote about a religious charlatan who lived off the generosity of the church simply as a way to avoid working. In an attempt to cope with this problem, the *Didache,* an early church manual, laid down a series of regulations guiding the reception of itinerant ministers. It said, for example, that true prophets were indeed to be entertained—for a day or two. But if a prophet stayed three days, this was a sign that he was false. Likewise, if a prophet under the inspiration of the Spirit asked for money, he was a false prophet.

These concerns are found in 2 and 3 John. In 2 John, the author worries about false prophets who are teaching erroneous doctrine, such as Gnosticism (salvation is a product of special knowledge). "Do not welcome such," he says (2 John 10). But in 3 John, he addresses the opposite problem: Christians who failed to provide hospitality for genuine teachers.

Passages for General Group Study

2 John 1–13	To the Chosen Lady and Her Children
3 John 1–14	To John's Dear Friend Gaius

1The elder,

To the chosen lady and her children, whom I
love in the truth—and not I only, but also all who
know the truth— 2because of the truth, which
lives in us and will be with us forever:

3Grace, mercy and peace from God the Father
and from Jesus Christ, the Father's Son, will be
with us in truth and love.

4It has given me great joy to find some of your
children walking in the truth, just as the Father
commanded us. 5And now, dear lady, I am not
writing you a new command but one we have
had from the beginning. I ask that we love one
another. 6And this is love: that we walk in obedience to his commands. As you have heard from
the beginning, his command is that you walk in
love.

7Many deceivers, who do not acknowledge
Jesus Christ as coming in the flesh, have gone out
into the world. Any such person is the deceiver
and the antichrist. 8Watch out that you do not
lose what you have worked for, but that you may
be rewarded fully. 9Anyone who runs ahead and
does not continue in the teaching of Christ does
not have God; whoever continues in the teaching
has both the Father and the Son. 10If anyone
comes to you and does not bring this teaching, do
not take him into your house or welcome him.
11Anyone who welcomes him shares in his wicked work.

12I have much to write to you, but I do not
want to use paper and ink. Instead, I hope to visit
you and talk with you face to face, so that our joy
may be complete.

13The children of your chosen sister send their
greetings.

2 John 1–13

1. Whose home could you drop in on unexpectedly and know that you would be welcome?
2. How do John's exhortations to true believers (vv. 4–6) help them resist the deception and wickedness of the religious frauds (vv. 7–11)?
3. Have you ever been involved in a deep relationship that had to be ended because of an overriding issue involving your faith? What happened?
4. When was the last time you spent time with someone who was really hurting, lonely or needing help (no names)? Should you do this more often? What's stopping you?
5. What is God saying to you in this passage?
6. How can this group help you in prayer this week?

1The elder,

To my dear friend Gaius, whom I love in the
truth.

2Dear friend, I pray that you may enjoy good
health and that all may go well with you, even as
your soul is getting along well. 3It gave me great
joy to have some brothers come and tell about
your faithfulness to the truth and how you continue to walk in the truth. 4I have no greater joy
than to hear that my children are walking in the
truth.
5Dear friend, you are faithful in what you are
doing for the brothers, even though they are
strangers to you. 6They have told the church
about your love. You will do well to send them on
their way in a manner worthy of God. 7It was for
the sake of the Name that they went out, receiving no help from the pagans. 8We ought therefore
to show hospitality to such men so that we may
work together for the truth.
9I wrote to the church, but Diotrephes, who
loves to be first, will have nothing to do with us.
10So if I come, I will call attention to what he is
doing, gossiping maliciously about us. Not satisfied with that, he refuses to welcome the brothers. He also stops those who want to do so and
puts them out of the church.
11Dear friend, do not imitate what is evil but
what is good. Anyone who does what is good is
from God. Anyone who does what is evil has
not seen God. 12Demetrius is well spoken of by
everyone—and even by the truth itself. We also
speak well of him, and you know that our testimony is true.
13I have much to write you, but I do not want
to do so with pen and ink. 14I hope to see you
soon, and we will talk face to face.

Peace to you. The friends here send their greetings. Greet the friends there by name.

3 John 1–14

1. Did you ever run out of money when you were away from home?
2. Why is John urging that these teachers be cared for in their travels? Why would this be so important at this time?
3. Do you find opening up to new people easy or difficult? Why is that?
4. In picking close friends (like Gaius was to John), what do you look for? How can you be that kind of friend to others?
5. What is God saying to you in this passage?
6. How can this group help you in prayer this week?

Introduction to
JUDE

Personal Reading Plan

❐ Jude 1–25

Author

Traditionally Jude, the brother of Jesus, is considered the author of Jude (see Matt. 13:55, Jude is a form of the name "Judas"). In the New Testament there are five people by the name of Jude or Judas (Mark 6:3; Luke 6:16; John 14:22; Acts 9:11; 15:22,27,32) but only the brother of Jesus is a serious candidate as author. Little is known about Jude. He was one of four brothers (Mark 6:3). He was probably not a follower of Jesus during the years of his brother's ministry (Mark 3:21,31–35; John 7:5). It was only after the Resurrection that Jude became a believer (Acts 1:14). The brothers of Jesus eventually became itinerant missionaries (1 Cor. 9:5). Tradition has it that they spread the Gospel throughout Palestine. Jude's brother, James the Just, was leader of the church in Jerusalem. So in the book of Jude, a reader comes in touch with the early church in which Jesus' own blood relatives were leaders.

Date

The date of Jude is hard to determine. If the author of 2 Peter made use of it, then it would be dated around A.D. 65; otherwise it could be dated as late as A.D. 80.

Theme

Contend for the faith.

Purpose

Jude gives an overview of his book in verses 3–4. He makes two points: First, Christians are "to contend for the faith"; second, they are to do so against false Christians who "have secretly slipped in among [them]." The rest of the book develops these two points. In verses 5–19, the nature of the false teachers is explained. Jude makes it exceedingly clear that this is not a new problem and, furthermore, their condemnation is sure. In verses 20–23, Jude gets to his main point: He appeals to the Christians to hold on to the Christian faith despite false teachers.

The False Teachers

Jude's opponents are a band of smooth-talking teachers who go from church to church, receiving hospitality in return for their instruction. Such itinerant teachers were often a source of trouble in the early church (Matt. 7:15; 2 Cor. 10–11; 1 John 4:1; 2 John 10). In this case, the teachers were antinomians, that is, they rejected all moral standards (since they misunderstood grace) and indulged in all manner of immoral behavior, particularly of a sexual sort. Their teaching was derived largely from individual emotional experiences ("God told me"), and they considered themselves the sole judge of their own actions.

Characteristics

Most people know Jude only because of its benediction (vv. 24–25):

> To him who is able to keep you from falling and to present you before his glorious presence without fault and with great joy—to the only God our Savior be glory, majesty, power and authority, through Jesus Christ our Lord, before all ages, now and forevermore! Amen.

Today, Jude is less frequently read than the other NT letters. To its first readers, however, Jude was anything but obscure. It was heard as a fiery call to defend the faith against the heretics who had wormed their way into the church (v. 4).

This is a sermon, and in true sermonic fashion, Jude quotes (or alludes to) various texts and then explains them. What sets Jude's sermon apart from contemporary Christian sermons is his choice of texts. His first references are to Old Testament stories (vv. 5–7,11), and his concluding reference is to "what the apostles of our Lord Jesus Christ foretold" (v. 17). This is familiar material. But in between, Jude quotes 1 Enoch (vv. 14–15), a Jewish apocryphal book, and alludes to the Assumption of Moses (v. 9), probably to the Testament of Naphtali (v. 7) and to the Testament of Asher (v. 8).

The Apocryphal books Jude quotes were written during the time between the Old and New Testament. They were not accepted as orthodox and so never became part of the Bible itself.

Certain of the church fathers concluded (wrongly) that any book that used apocryphal literature such as Jude did could not be genuine. But this view says more about the presuppositions of those theologians than it does about what can and cannot be included within Scripture.

Certainly, other New Testament authors used nonbiblical Jewish writing (such as 2 Tim. 3:8). Paul quotes the heathen poets in Acts 17:28; 1 Corinthians 15:32–33; and Titus 1:12. The author of Hebrews echoes the works of Philo; James makes reference to nonbiblical sources. The issue is not where the specific words came from but how the New Testament writer used these words to reveal God's truth.

Relationship to Second Peter

It is clear that Jude and 2 Peter are somehow related. Of the 25 verses in Jude, 15 of them appear in whole or in part in 2 Peter. The question is: What is the nature of the relationship between Jude and 2 Peter? Did Jude quote from 2 Peter? Or was the reverse true? Or did they both quote from the same outside source? The answer to this question is by no means certain.

Old Testament Links in Jude

1. The way of Cain (v. 11)—Adam and Eve's first son, Cain, consumed with jealousy and anger, murdered his brother, Abel (Gen. 4:3–8).
2. Balaam's error (v. 11)—Balaam was an ancient pagan sorcerer hired to curse God's people. Though God compelled him to bless Israel instead, his greed apparently motivated him to give advice that proved destructive to the Israelites (Num. 22–24; 31:16).
3. Korah's rebellion (v. 11)—Korah was a Levite who led a rebellion against the authority God had given to Moses and Aaron (Num. 16:1–3,11).

Structure

Jude is a genuine letter. It has a standard opening (vv. 1–2), and in verses 3–4 the theme and occasion of the epistle are defined—again typical of a letter. But Jude is also a short sermon. The bulk of the book (vv. 5–25) consists of an exposition of certain texts as related to a particular problem facing the church. Thus, Jude is a sermon sent by mail to be read before the congregation(s).

The book of Jude is a painstakingly crafted document. Jude packs a lot of content into a few words by carefully choosing his words and images. Verses 11–13 are particularly vivid in imagery, evoking a wide range of thought in remarkably few words.

Passage for General Group Study

1–25 The Sin and Doom of Godless Men; A Call to Persevere

1Jude, a servant of Jesus Christ and a brother
of James,

To those who have been called, who are loved
by God the Father and kept by[a] Jesus Christ:

2Mercy, peace and love be yours in abundance.

The Sin and Doom of Godless Men

3Dear friends, although I was very eager to
write to you about the salvation we share, I felt
I had to write and urge you to contend for the
faith that was once for all entrusted to the saints.
4For certain men whose condemnation was written about[b] long ago have secretly slipped in
among you. They are godless men, who change
the grace of our God into a license for immorality
and deny Jesus Christ our only Sovereign and
Lord.

5Though you already know all this, I want to
remind you that the Lord[c] delivered his people out of Egypt, but later destroyed those who
did not believe. 6And the angels who did not
keep their positions of authority but abandoned
their own home—these he has kept in darkness,
bound with everlasting chains for judgment on
the great Day. 7In a similar way, Sodom and Gomorrah and the surrounding towns gave themselves up to sexual immorality and perversion.
They serve as an example of those who suffer the
punishment of eternal fire.

8In the very same way, these dreamers pollute
their own bodies, reject authority and slander
celestial beings. 9But even the archangel Michael, when he was disputing with the devil about
the body of Moses, did not dare to bring a slanderous accusation against him, but said, "The
Lord rebuke you!" 10Yet these men speak abusively against whatever they do not understand;
and what things they do understand by instinct,
like unreasoning animals—these are the very
things that destroy them.

11Woe to them! They have taken the way of
Cain; they have rushed for profit into Balaam's
error; they have been destroyed in Korah's rebellion.

12These men are blemishes at your love feasts,
eating with you without the slightest qualm—
shepherds who feed only themselves. They are
clouds without rain, blown along by the wind;
autumn trees, without fruit and uprooted—twice
dead. 13They are wild waves of the sea, foaming
up their shame; wandering stars, for whom blackest darkness has been reserved forever.

14Enoch, the seventh from Adam, prophesied
about these men: "See, the Lord is coming with
thousands upon thousands of his holy ones 15to
judge everyone, and to convict all the ungodly of
all the ungodly acts they have done in the ungodly way, and of all the harsh words ungodly sinners have spoken against him." 16These men are
grumblers and faultfinders; they follow their own
evil desires; they boast about themselves and flatter others for their own advantage.

A Call to Persevere

17But, dear friends, remember what the apostles of our Lord Jesus Christ foretold. 18They said
to you, "In the last times there will be scoffers
who will follow their own ungodly desires."
19These are the men who divide you, who follow mere natural instincts and do not have the
Spirit.

JUDE 1–25

1. What scary experience with fire have you had?
2. How does Jude describe himself and his fellow Christians (vv. 3–5)? From this description, what does it mean to be a Christian?
3. What goes on daily at your school, in your community or even in your church, which would fall within the range of Jude's indicting sermon?
4. In light of the warnings in Jude, what hope do you find in verses 24–25? How does that help as you struggle?
5. What is God saying to you in this passage?
6. How can this group help you in prayer this week?

20But you, dear friends, build yourselves up in
your most holy faith and pray in the Holy Spirit.
21Keep yourselves in God's love as you wait for
the mercy of our Lord Jesus Christ to bring you to
eternal life.

22Be merciful to those who doubt; 23snatch
others from the fire and save them; to others

[a] *1* Or *for*; or *in* [b] *4* Or *men who were marked out for condemnation* [c] *5* Some early manuscripts *Jesus*

show mercy, mixed with fear—hating even the clothing stained by corrupted flesh.

Doxology

24To him who is able to keep you from falling and to present you before his glorious presence without fault and with great joy— 25to the only God our Savior be glory, majesty, power and authority, through Jesus Christ our Lord, before all ages, now and forevermore! Amen.

Introduction to REVELATION

Personal Reading Plan

❐ Revelation 1:1–20	❐ Revelation 8:1–9:21	❐ Revelation 17:1–18
❐ Revelation 2:1–29	❐ Revelation 10:1–11:19	❐ Revelation 18:1–24
❐ Revelation 3:1–22	❐ Revelation 12:1–13:1a	❐ Revelation 19:1–21
❐ Revelation 4:1–5:14	❐ Revelation 13:1b–18	❐ Revelation 20:1–15
❐ Revelation 6:1–17	❐ Revelation 14:1–20	❐ Revelation 21:1–27
❐ Revelation 7:1–17	❐ Revelation 15:1–16:21	❐ Revelation 22:1–21

Author

Although the author only refers to himself as "John" (1:4), it has traditionally been assumed that he was none other than John the apostle. In fact, this simple designation "John" is strong proof in itself that the apostle was the writer. Typically, apocalyptic literature claimed to be authored by famous heroes of the past (e.g., Abraham, Ezra, Enoch and Baruch). But John writes in his own name, and only a person of the stature of an apostle could expect to have such a work received as authoritative. Furthermore, when Revelation is compared to the Gospel of John and the three letters of John, there are striking similarities in ideas, theology and language.

John wrote from the island of Patmos, a rocky, barren island in the Aegean Sea (10 miles long and five miles wide), where he had been exiled because of his Christian witness. Tradition says that he was eventually released from Patmos and spent the remaining years of his long life in Ephesus.

Date

Most scholars feel that the book of Revelation was written toward the end of the reign of Domitian, that is, around A.D. 90–95. This is what Irenaeus, a second-century bishop, claimed. Still, this dating is not conclusive. Evidence has been offered that it might have been written during the last years of Nero's reign (between A.D. 65 and 68) or when Vespasian was emperor (A.D. 69–79).

Theme

Christ shall overcome!

Audience

The book of Revelation was addressed to seven churches in the western part of the Roman province of Asia. The order in which these churches are addressed is the order in which a messenger from Patmos would come to each church if he followed the great circular Roman road connecting the cities.

Historical Background

Rome is a central and consistently negative image in the book of Revelation. This view of the Roman government stands in sharp contrast to most of the rest of the New Testament, where Rome is seen as the protector of Christianity. In the early days of missionary activity, Roman judges protected Christians from Jewish mobs (Acts 18:1–17; 19:13–41). It was Roman justice to which Paul turned in his time of need (Acts 23:12–35; 25:10–11). As a result, the apostles urged submission to Rome (Rom. 13:1–7; 1 Peter 2:13–17). But in Revelation, the attitude is quite different. Rome is seen as a whore, drunk with the blood of Christians (17:5–6), deserving nothing but destruction.

This shift in attitude is due to one thing—Caesar worship. Although Roman rulers were long considered divine, their centrality in Roman civil religion was not enforced until the end of the first century. Then it became obligatory for citizens all across the Roman Empire to appear once a year before a magistrate to burn a pinch of incense and declare, "Caesar is Lord." This was more an act of loyalty to Rome than a religious statement, but Christians simply could not bring themselves to declare that anyone except Jesus was Lord. As a result, they were hounded mercilessly by civil authorities. This is the situation to which Revelation speaks. It attempts to encourage Christians by giving them the long view. They may suffer now while Caesar pretends to be Lord, but ahead lies unimaginable glory when Jesus, the true Lord, comes in power. This kind of vision would give harassed Christians the strength to endure.

Apocalyptic Literature

The book of Revelation is unique. It is the only apocalyptic book in the New Testament. What makes this so unusual is that while the New Testament books were being written, apocalyptic literature flourished. In fact, during the period between the Old and New Testaments, apocalyptic literature was the most common type of Jewish religious writing.

At the heart of apocalyptic literature was *hope*—hope that God would right wrongs and rescue the righteous. The Jews knew that they were God's chosen people, yet they had been subject to ungodly rules for so long. As a result, they longed for that great day when God would intervene in history and bring about what he promised. They gave shape to these longings in the so-called apocalyptic writings (*apocalypse* is a Greek word meaning an "unveiling" or "uncovering" of future events or hidden realms, like heaven).

Apocalyptic literature dealt with the details of God's return: how he would burst into history, whom he would destroy, how he would set up his kingdom. These books were, of necessity, the products of dreams and visions. Consequently, they were filled with swirling images and vivid pictures of death, supernatural places and creatures, destruction and redemption, and so on. Since the events described were unlike anything that had ever happened, they could only be alluded to, often in cryptic language. The resulting mystery surrounding such writing was further compounded by the need for secrecy. Were these books to fall into the hands of the rulers (the ones singled out for destruction), they would be considered traitorous and would land their authors in jail or worse. So the books were written in code. They could be understood only by those on the writer's side who had the key to the code. Outsiders, such as the police, would find them unintelligible. Of course, this is why we have a problem today in deciphering apocalyptic literature. In many cases, we have lost the key.

The Apocalyptic World View

Underlying both Jewish and Christian apocalyptic literature was the view that history is divided into two ages. The present age is evil and corrupt and it will be destroyed. The age to come is characterized by goodness and by God's presence and power. The central turning point in history, on which apocalyptic writers often focused, is the Day of the Lord, when the present age will give way to the new age.

Christian writers understood this to be the day of Christ's return—the Second Coming. He had come once, as a baby in Bethlehem, and by his first coming had set in motion the events that would draw the present age to a close. When he came again, it would not be as an infant but as a king before whom the whole creation would bow. For the moment, however, Christians live in the in-between time. Christ's ultimate victory was secured at the Cross; Satan was defeated. But the victory had yet to be claimed in its fullness. Satan still pretended that he was in charge and would do so until the Second Coming.

What is striking is how similar the pattern is in Christian and Jewish apocalyptic literature. Beyond the obvious difference over the role of Christ, the same outline is found in Jewish literature as in Revelation. Specifically:

1. The Messiah will be the central figure in the Day of the Lord.

2. The coming of the new age will be preceded by a terrible time in history filled with war, famine and calamity of all sorts. In fact, the elements themselves will disintegrate, and hatred and anger will prevail in human affairs.

3. The Day of the Lord will be the time when judgment is rendered.
4. Following judgment, there will be a time of great peace and joy. The New Jerusalem will descend. The dead will rise and the Messiah will reign.

Characteristics

Not only is Revelation strange; it is also difficult. The world of the book of Revelation is so remote from the modern world that one hardly knows where to begin in trying to understand it. It is a world filled with weird beasts who have 10 horns and seven heads; a world of seals and trumpets and bowls that bring disaster; a world populated with angels and demons, with lions and lambs, with horses and dragons. Who can make sense out of all this?

The book of Revelation is well worth reading, but it must be approached with humility and caution. To pin one's whole theology on details in the book of Revelation is dangerous indeed. With prayer and patience, the reader needs to work at understanding the text.

Revelation is written in the worst Greek of any book of the New Testament. There are mistakes in grammar and stylistic errors such as a schoolboy would make. Experts on apocalyptic literature consider the bad grammar deliberate. It is felt that John wrote this way for emphasis. His clumsy Greek style reflects his attempt to translate Old Testament passages—the author was thinking in Hebrew but writing in Greek. Furthermore, a vision such as John had can never be adequately captured by mere words. John had to push language to its limits even to approximate what he had seen. The poor Greek may also have resulted from John's imprisonment on Patmos, where he probably had no secretary to smooth out his style.

Structure

John begins with a description of the vision from which the book of Revelation came (chapter 1). Chapters 2 and 3 contain specific messages to seven churches in Asia Minor. Chapters 4 and 5 describe a vision of God and of Christ. Then in chapters 6–19 various plagues of judgment are described. The book is concluded (chapters 20–22) by a description of the coming kingdom. While the overall structure is clear, how it all fits together varies with the reader's interpretation.

Interpretation

There are widely varying ways to interpret Revelation. Some limit its meaning to the first-century struggle between the church and Rome. Others see Revelation as a collection of symbols that predict future events (e.g., the locusts from the bottomless pit represents the invasion of Europe by Islam). In fact, the book of Revelation probably speaks both to the immediate first-century struggle of Christians and to the future when the Lord will return.

Passage for Topical Group Study

20:11–21:8 HEAVEN AND HELL The Dead Are Judged

See the Lesson Plans in the front of this Bible.

Passages for General Group Study

1:1–20	One Like a Son of Man	14:1–15:8	The Lamb and the Harvest
2:1–3:22	Jesus' Words to the Churches	16:1–17:18	The Seven Bowls of God's Wrath
4:1–5:14	The Throne in Heaven	18:1–19:10	The Fall of Babylon
6:1–7:17	The Seals	19:11–20:10	The Rider on the White Horse
8:1–9:21	The Trumpets	21:9–22:6	The New Jerusalem
10:1–11:19	The Two Witnesses	22:7–21	Jesus Is Coming
12:1–13:18	The Woman and the Dragon		

Prologue

1 The revelation of Jesus Christ, which God
gave him to show his servants what must
soon take place. He made it known by sending
his angel to his servant John, 2who testifies to
everything he saw—that is, the word of God and
the testimony of Jesus Christ. 3Blessed is the one
who reads the words of this prophecy, and
blessed are those who hear it and take to heart
what is written in it, because the time is near.

Greetings and Doxology

4John,

To the seven churches in the province of Asia:

Grace and peace to you from him who is, and
who was, and who is to come, and from the sev-
en spirits[a] before his throne, 5and from Jesus
Christ, who is the faithful witness, the firstborn
from the dead, and the ruler of the kings of the
earth.

To him who loves us and has freed us from our
sins by his blood, 6and has made us to be a kingdom and priests to serve his God and Father—to
him be glory and power for ever and ever! Amen.

7Look, he is coming with the clouds,
and every eye will see him,
even those who pierced him;
and all the peoples of the earth will mourn
because of him.
So shall it be! Amen.

8"I am the Alpha and the Omega," says the
Lord God, "who is, and who was, and who is to
come, the Almighty."

One Like a Son of Man

9I, John, your brother and companion in the
suffering and kingdom and patient endurance
that are ours in Jesus, was on the island of Patmos
because of the word of God and the testimony of
Jesus. 10On the Lord's Day I was in the Spirit, and
I heard behind me a loud voice like a trumpet,
11which said: "Write on a scroll what you see and
send it to the seven churches: to Ephesus, Smyrna, Pergamum, Thyatira, Sardis, Philadelphia and
Laodicea."

12I turned around to see the voice that was
speaking to me. And when I turned I saw seven
golden lampstands, 13and among the lampstands
was someone "like a son of man,"[b] dressed in a
robe reaching down to his feet and with a golden
sash around his chest. 14His head and hair were
white like wool, as white as snow, and his eyes
were like blazing fire. 15His feet were like bronze
glowing in a furnace, and his voice was like the
sound of rushing waters. 16In his right hand he
held seven stars, and out of his mouth came a
sharp double-edged sword. His face was like the
sun shining in all its brilliance.

REVELATION 1:1–20

1. How often do you remember your dreams? Do you dream in color?
2. If the book of Revelation were dropped from the Bible, what would be missing from the story of God's saving work in history?
3. To John, Jesus is the reigning King. How could this view of Jesus affect your day-to-day dealings with sin? With discouragement? With peer pressure? With apathy?
4. Close your eyes and have someone read verses 12–18 slowly. What do the images suggest about Christ? How does this make you feel?
5. What is God saying to you in this passage?
6. How can this group help you in prayer this week?

17When I saw him, I fell at his feet as though
dead. Then he placed his right hand on me and
said: "Do not be afraid. I am the First and the
Last. 18I am the Living One; I was dead, and
behold I am alive for ever and ever! And I hold
the keys of death and Hades.

19"Write, therefore, what you have seen, what
is now and what will take place later. 20The mystery of the seven stars that you saw in my right
hand and of the seven golden lampstands is this:
The seven stars are the angels[c] of the seven
churches, and the seven lampstands are the sev-
en churches.

To the Church in Ephesus

2 "To the angel[d] of the church in Ephesus
write:

These are the words of him who holds
the seven stars in his right hand and walks
among the seven golden lampstands: 2I
know your deeds, your hard work and your
perseverance. I know that you cannot tolerate wicked men, that you have tested those

[a] 4 Or *the sevenfold Spirit* [b] 13 Daniel 7:13 [c] 20 Or *messengers* [d] 1 Or *messenger*; also in verses 8, 12 and 18

who claim to be apostles but are not, and
have found them false. 3You have persevered and have endured hardships for my
name, and have not grown weary.
4Yet I hold this against you: You have
forsaken your first love. 5Remember the
height from which you have fallen! Repent
and do the things you did at first. If you do
not repent, I will come to you and remove
your lampstand from its place. 6But you
have this in your favor: You hate the practices of the Nicolaitans, which I also hate.
7He who has an ear, let him hear what
the Spirit says to the churches. To him who
overcomes, I will give the right to eat from
the tree of life, which is in the paradise of
God.

To the Church in Smyrna

8"To the angel of the church in Smyrna write:

These are the words of him who is the
First and the Last, who died and came to life
again. 9I know your afflictions and your
poverty—yet you are rich! I know the slander of those who say they are Jews and are
not, but are a synagogue of Satan. 10Do not
be afraid of what you are about to suffer. I
tell you, the devil will put some of you in
prison to test you, and you will suffer persecution for ten days. Be faithful, even to the
point of death, and I will give you the crown
of life.
11He who has an ear, let him hear what
the Spirit says to the churches. He who
overcomes will not be hurt at all by the
second death.

To the Church in Pergamum

12"To the angel of the church in Pergamum
write:

These are the words of him who has the
sharp, double-edged sword. 13I know
where you live—where Satan has his
throne. Yet you remain true to my name.
You did not renounce your faith in me, even
in the days of Antipas, my faithful witness,
who was put to death in your city—where
Satan lives.
14Nevertheless, I have a few things
against you: You have people there who
hold to the teaching of Balaam, who taught
Balak to entice the Israelites to sin by eating
food sacrificed to idols and by committing
sexual immorality. 15Likewise you also have
those who hold to the teaching of the Nicolaitans. 16Repent therefore! Otherwise, I
will soon come to you and will fight against
them with the sword of my mouth.
17He who has an ear, let him hear what
the Spirit says to the churches. To him who
overcomes, I will give some of the hidden
manna. I will also give him a white stone
with a new name written on it, known only
to him who receives it.

To the Church in Thyatira

18"To the angel of the church in Thyatira write:

These are the words of the Son of God,
whose eyes are like blazing fire and whose
feet are like burnished bronze. 19I know
your deeds, your love and faith, your service
and perseverance, and that you are now doing more than you did at first.
20Nevertheless, I have this against you:
You tolerate that woman Jezebel, who calls
herself a prophetess. By her teaching she
misleads my servants into sexual immorality and the eating of food sacrificed to idols.
21I have given her time to repent of her
immorality, but she is unwilling. 22So I will
cast her on a bed of suffering, and I will
make those who commit adultery with her
suffer intensely, unless they repent of her
ways. 23I will strike her children dead. Then
all the churches will know that I am he who
searches hearts and minds, and I will repay
each of you according to your deeds. 24Now
I say to the rest of you in Thyatira, to you
who do not hold to her teaching and have
not learned Satan's so-called deep secrets (I
will not impose any other burden on you):
25Only hold on to what you have until I
come.
26To him who overcomes and does my
will to the end, I will give authority over the
nations—

27'He will rule them with an iron scepter;
he will dash them to pieces like
pottery'[a]—

just as I have received authority from my
Father. 28I will also give him the morning
star. 29He who has an ear, let him hear what
the Spirit says to the churches.

To the Church in Sardis

3 "To the angel[b] of the church in Sardis
write:

These are the words of him who holds
the seven spirits[c] of God and the seven
stars. I know your deeds; you have a reputation of being alive, but you are dead. 2Wake

[a] 27 Psalm 2:9 [b] 1 Or *messenger*; also in verses 7 and 14 [c] 1 Or *the sevenfold Spirit*

up! Strengthen what remains and is about to die, for I have not found your deeds complete in the sight of my God. 3Remember, therefore, what you have received and heard; obey it, and repent. But if you do not wake up, I will come like a thief, and you will not know at what time I will come to you.

Revelation 2:1–3:22

1. When were you on a losing team that worked itself up and tried again?
2. Which of the qualities in 2:19 apply to you this week? Why?
3. If Jesus addressed the "wake-up call" in 3:2 to you, what would he want you to strengthen?
4. What is Jesus waiting for at the door of your life right now (3:20)? What room in your life is not open to Jesus?
5. What is God saying to you in this passage?
6. How can this group help you in prayer this week?

4Yet you have a few people in Sardis who have not soiled their clothes. They will walk with me, dressed in white, for they are worthy. 5He who overcomes will, like them, be dressed in white. I will never blot out his name from the book of life, but will acknowledge his name before my Father and his angels. 6He who has an ear, let him hear what the Spirit says to the churches.

To the Church in Philadelphia

7"To the angel of the church in Philadelphia write:

These are the words of him who is holy and true, who holds the key of David. What he opens no one can shut, and what he shuts no one can open. 8I know your deeds. See, I have placed before you an open door that no one can shut. I know that you have little strength, yet you have kept my word and have not denied my name. 9I will make those who are of the synagogue of Satan, who claim to be Jews though they are not, but are liars—I will make them come and fall down at your feet and acknowledge that I have loved you. 10Since you have kept my command to endure patiently, I will also keep you from the hour of trial that is going to come upon the whole world to test those who live on the earth.

11I am coming soon. Hold on to what you have, so that no one will take your crown. 12Him who overcomes I will make a pillar in the temple of my God. Never again will he leave it. I will write on him the name of my God and the name of the city of my God, the new Jerusalem, which is coming down out of heaven from my God; and I will also write on him my new name. 13He who has an ear, let him hear what the Spirit says to the churches.

To the Church in Laodicea

14"To the angel of the church in Laodicea write:

These are the words of the Amen, the faithful and true witness, the ruler of God's creation. 15I know your deeds, that you are neither cold nor hot. I wish you were either one or the other! 16So, because you are lukewarm—neither hot nor cold—I am about to spit you out of my mouth. 17You say, 'I am rich; I have acquired wealth and do not need a thing.' But you do not realize that you are wretched, pitiful, poor, blind and naked. 18I counsel you to buy from me gold refined in the fire, so you can become rich; and white clothes to wear, so you can cover your shameful nakedness; and salve to put on your eyes, so you can see.

19Those whom I love I rebuke and discipline. So be earnest, and repent. 20Here I am! I stand at the door and knock. If anyone hears my voice and opens the door, I will come in and eat with him, and he with me.

21To him who overcomes, I will give the right to sit with me on my throne, just as I overcame and sat down with my Father on his throne. 22He who has an ear, let him hear what the Spirit says to the churches."

The Throne in Heaven

4 After this I looked, and there before me was a door standing open in heaven. And the voice I had first heard speaking to me like a trumpet said, "Come up here, and I will show you what must take place after this." 2At once I was in the Spirit, and there before me was a throne in heaven with someone sitting on it. 3And the one who sat there had the appearance of jasper and carnelian. A rainbow, resembling an emerald, encircled the throne. 4Surrounding the throne were

twenty-four other thrones, and seated on them
were twenty-four elders. They were dressed in
white and had crowns of gold on their heads.
5From the throne came flashes of lightning, rumblings and peals of thunder. Before the throne,
seven lamps were blazing. These are the seven
spirits[a] of God. 6Also before the throne there
was what looked like a sea of glass, clear as crystal.

In the center, around the throne, were four
living creatures, and they were covered with
eyes, in front and in back. 7The first living creature was like a lion, the second was like an ox,
the third had a face like a man, the fourth was
like a flying eagle. 8Each of the four living creatures had six wings and was covered with eyes all
around, even under his wings. Day and night
they never stop saying:

"Holy, holy, holy
is the Lord God Almighty,
who was, and is, and is to come."

9Whenever the living creatures give glory, honor
and thanks to him who sits on the throne and
who lives for ever and ever, 10the twenty-four
elders fall down before him who sits on the
throne, and worship him who lives for ever and

REVELATION 4:1–5:14

1. What is the biggest church, palace or castle you've ever been in? How did you feel while inside?
2. Imagine yourself in this incredible scene before God's throne. What impresses you about God?
3. How do you feel about the way you worship God? How can this vision of God enhance your worship life? Your everyday life?
4. Why is Christ the only one worthy enough to open the scroll (5:4–9; see John 1:29)? What does it mean that he is both a Lion and a Lamb? What does this mean to you?
5. What is God saying to you in this passage?
6. How can this group help you in prayer this week?

ever. They lay their crowns before the throne and
say:

11"You are worthy, our Lord and God,
to receive glory and honor and power,
for you created all things,
and by your will they were created
and have their being."

The Scroll and the Lamb

5 Then I saw in the right hand of him who sat
on the throne a scroll with writing on both
sides and sealed with seven seals. 2And I saw a
mighty angel proclaiming in a loud voice, "Who
is worthy to break the seals and open the scroll?"
3But no one in heaven or on earth or under the
earth could open the scroll or even look inside it.
4I wept and wept because no one was found who
was worthy to open the scroll or look inside.
5Then one of the elders said to me, "Do not
weep! See, the Lion of the tribe of Judah, the Root
of David, has triumphed. He is able to open the
scroll and its seven seals."

6Then I saw a Lamb, looking as if it had been
slain, standing in the center of the throne, encircled by the four living creatures and the elders.
He had seven horns and seven eyes, which are
the seven spirits[a] of God sent out into all the
earth. 7He came and took the scroll from the
right hand of him who sat on the throne. 8And
when he had taken it, the four living creatures
and the twenty-four elders fell down before the
Lamb. Each one had a harp and they were holding golden bowls full of incense, which are the
prayers of the saints. 9And they sang a new song:

"You are worthy to take the scroll
and to open its seals,
because you were slain,
and with your blood you purchased men
for God
from every tribe and language and people
and nation.
10You have made them to be a kingdom and
priests to serve our God,
and they will reign on the earth."

11Then I looked and heard the voice of many
angels, numbering thousands upon thousands,
and ten thousand times ten thousand. They encircled the throne and the living creatures and
the elders. 12In a loud voice they sang:

"Worthy is the Lamb, who was slain,
to receive power and wealth and wisdom and
strength
and honor and glory and praise!"

13Then I heard every creature in heaven and

[a] 5,6 Or *the sevenfold Spirit*

on earth and under the earth and on the sea, and
all that is in them, singing:

"To him who sits on the throne and to the
Lamb
be praise and honor and glory and power,
for ever and ever!"

[14]The four living creatures said, "Amen," and the
elders fell down and worshiped.

The Seals

6 I watched as the Lamb opened the first of the
seven seals. Then I heard one of the four
living creatures say in a voice like thunder,
"Come!" [2]I looked, and there before me was a
white horse! Its rider held a bow, and he was
given a crown, and he rode out as a conqueror
bent on conquest.
[3]When the Lamb opened the second seal, I
heard the second living creature say, "Come!"
[4]Then another horse came out, a fiery red one. Its
rider was given power to take peace from the
earth and to make men slay each other. To him
was given a large sword.
[5]When the Lamb opened the third seal, I
heard the third living creature say, "Come!" I
looked, and there before me was a black horse!
Its rider was holding a pair of scales in his hand.
[6]Then I heard what sounded like a voice among
the four living creatures, saying, "A quart[a] of
wheat for a day's wages,[b] and three quarts of
barley for a day's wages,[b] and do not damage the
oil and the wine!"
[7]When the Lamb opened the fourth seal, I
heard the voice of the fourth living creature say,
"Come!" [8]I looked, and there before me was a
pale horse! Its rider was named Death, and Hades
was following close behind him. They were given
power over a fourth of the earth to kill by sword,
famine and plague, and by the wild beasts of the
earth.
[9]When he opened the fifth seal, I saw under
the altar the souls of those who had been slain
because of the word of God and the testimony
they had maintained. [10]They called out in a loud
voice, "How long, Sovereign Lord, holy and true,
until you judge the inhabitants of the earth and
avenge our blood?" [11]Then each of them was giv-
en a white robe, and they were told to wait a
little longer, until the number of their fellow servants and brothers who were to be killed as they
had been was completed.
[12]I watched as he opened the sixth seal. There
was a great earthquake. The sun turned black like
sackcloth made of goat hair, the whole moon
turned blood red, [13]and the stars in the sky fell to
earth, as late figs drop from a fig tree when shak-
en by a strong wind. [14]The sky receded like a
scroll, rolling up, and every mountain and island
was removed from its place.
[15]Then the kings of the earth, the princes, the
generals, the rich, the mighty, and every slave
and every free man hid in caves and among the
rocks of the mountains. [16]They called to the
mountains and the rocks, "Fall on us and hide us
from the face of him who sits on the throne and
from the wrath of the Lamb! [17]For the great day
of their wrath has come, and who can stand?"

REVELATION 6:1–7:17

1. Have you ever wanted a horse? What experience have you had riding horses?
2. How have each of the forces in 6:1–17 operated throughout history? How do they prevail today? What do you think this means for the interpretation of the vision?
3. What sort of seal has God placed on your life (7:3)? How is this seal evident to other Christians? To non-Christians? Why?
4. What is your greatest tribulation or persecution? How difficult does it seem next to the majesty of God seen in 17:9–17? Why? How will you incorporate this into your life?
5. What is God saying to you in this passage?
6. How can this group help you in prayer this week?

144,000 Sealed

7 After this I saw four angels standing at the
four corners of the earth, holding back the
four winds of the earth to prevent any wind from
blowing on the land or on the sea or on any tree.
[2]Then I saw another angel coming up from the
east, having the seal of the living God. He called
out in a loud voice to the four angels who had
been given power to harm the land and the sea:
[3]"Do not harm the land or the sea or the trees
until we put a seal on the foreheads of the servants of our God." [4]Then I heard the number of
those who were sealed: 144,000 from all the
tribes of Israel.

[5]From the tribe of Judah 12,000 were
sealed,

[a]6 Greek *a choinix* (probably about a liter) [b]6 Greek *a denarius*

from the tribe of Reuben 12,000,
from the tribe of Gad 12,000,
6from the tribe of Asher 12,000,
from the tribe of Naphtali 12,000,
from the tribe of Manasseh 12,000,
7from the tribe of Simeon 12,000,
from the tribe of Levi 12,000,
from the tribe of Issachar 12,000,
8from the tribe of Zebulun 12,000,
from the tribe of Joseph 12,000,
from the tribe of Benjamin 12,000.

The Great Multitude in White Robes

9After this I looked and there before me was a
great multitude that no one could count, from
every nation, tribe, people and language, standing before the throne and in front of the Lamb.
They were wearing white robes and were holding palm branches in their hands. 10And they
cried out in a loud voice:

"Salvation belongs to our God,
who sits on the throne,
and to the Lamb."

11All the angels were standing around the throne
and around the elders and the four living creatures. They fell down on their faces before the
throne and worshiped God, 12saying:

"Amen!
Praise and glory
and wisdom and thanks and honor
and power and strength
be to our God for ever and ever.
Amen!"

13Then one of the elders asked me, "These in
white robes—who are they, and where did they
come from?"
14I answered, "Sir, you know."
And he said, "These are they who have come
out of the great tribulation; they have washed
their robes and made them white in the blood of
the Lamb. 15Therefore,

"they are before the throne of God
and serve him day and night in his
temple;
and he who sits on the throne will spread his
tent over them.
16Never again will they hunger;
never again will they thirst.
The sun will not beat upon them,
nor any scorching heat.
17For the Lamb at the center of the throne will
be their shepherd;
he will lead them to springs of living
water.
And God will wipe away every tear from
their eyes."

The Seventh Seal and the Golden Censer

8 When he opened the seventh seal, there was
silence in heaven for about half an hour.
2And I saw the seven angels who stand before
God, and to them were given seven trumpets.
3Another angel, who had a golden censer,
came and stood at the altar. He was given much
incense to offer, with the prayers of all the saints,
on the golden altar before the throne. 4The
smoke of the incense, together with the prayers
of the saints, went up before God from the angel's hand. 5Then the angel took the censer, filled
it with fire from the altar, and hurled it on the
earth; and there came peals of thunder, rumblings, flashes of lightning and an earthquake.

The Trumpets

6Then the seven angels who had the seven
trumpets prepared to sound them.
7The first angel sounded his trumpet, and
there came hail and fire mixed with blood, and
it was hurled down upon the earth. A third of
the earth was burned up, a third of the trees
were burned up, and all the green grass was
burned up.
8The second angel sounded his trumpet, and
something like a huge mountain, all ablaze, was
thrown into the sea. A third of the sea turned
into blood, 9a third of the living creatures in the
sea died, and a third of the ships were destroyed.
10The third angel sounded his trumpet, and a
great star, blazing like a torch, fell from the sky
on a third of the rivers and on the springs of
water— 11the name of the star is Wormwood.[a]
A third of the waters turned bitter, and many
people died from the waters that had become
bitter.
12The fourth angel sounded his trumpet, and a
third of the sun was struck, a third of the moon,
and a third of the stars, so that a third of them
turned dark. A third of the day was without light,
and also a third of the night.
13As I watched, I heard an eagle that was flying
in midair call out in a loud voice: "Woe! Woe!
Woe to the inhabitants of the earth, because of
the trumpet blasts about to be sounded by the
other three angels!"

9 The fifth angel sounded his trumpet, and I
saw a star that had fallen from the sky to the
earth. The star was given the key to the shaft of
the Abyss. 2When he opened the Abyss, smoke
rose from it like the smoke from a gigantic furnace. The sun and sky were darkened by the
smoke from the Abyss. 3And out of the smoke

[a] 11 That is, Bitterness

locusts came down upon the earth and were given power like that of scorpions of the earth. [4]They were told not to harm the grass of the earth or any plant or tree, but only those people who did not have the seal of God on their foreheads. [5]They were not given power to kill them, but only to torture them for five months. And the agony they suffered was like that of the sting of a scorpion when it strikes a man. [6]During those days men will seek death, but will not find it; they will long to die, but death will elude them.

Revelation 8:1–9:21

1. What is one of the most excruciating pains you've ever experienced? What happened?
2. What do altars and incense teach about prayer (8:3–5)? When was the last time you cried for justice or mercy?
3. What events are begun by the sixth trumpet? What response should this woe elicit from the unbelieving world? Why? Why did this woe fail to bring the majority to repentance as originally intended?
4. What do you see in our society that fits with the actions listed in 9:20–21? Which of these actions do you see in your own life? In what way? What can you do about this in the coming week?
5. What is God saying to you in this passage?
6. How can this group help you in prayer this week?

[7]The locusts looked like horses prepared for battle. On their heads they wore something like crowns of gold, and their faces resembled human faces. [8]Their hair was like women's hair, and their teeth were like lions' teeth. [9]They had breastplates like breastplates of iron, and the sound of their wings was like the thundering of many horses and chariots rushing into battle. [10]They had tails and stings like scorpions, and in their tails they had power to torment people for five months. [11]They had as king over them the angel of the Abyss, whose name in Hebrew is Abaddon, and in Greek, Apollyon.[a]

[12]The first woe is past; two other woes are yet to come.

[13]The sixth angel sounded his trumpet, and I heard a voice coming from the horns[b] of the golden altar that is before God. [14]It said to the sixth angel who had the trumpet, "Release the four angels who are bound at the great river Euphrates." [15]And the four angels who had been kept ready for this very hour and day and month and year were released to kill a third of mankind. [16]The number of the mounted troops was two hundred million. I heard their number.

[17]The horses and riders I saw in my vision looked like this: Their breastplates were fiery red, dark blue, and yellow as sulfur. The heads of the horses resembled the heads of lions, and out of their mouths came fire, smoke and sulfur. [18]A third of mankind was killed by the three plagues of fire, smoke and sulfur that came out of their mouths. [19]The power of the horses was in their mouths and in their tails; for their tails were like snakes, having heads with which they inflict injury.

[20]The rest of mankind that were not killed by these plagues still did not repent of the work of their hands; they did not stop worshiping demons, and idols of gold, silver, bronze, stone and wood—idols that cannot see or hear or walk. [21]Nor did they repent of their murders, their magic arts, their sexual immorality or their thefts.

The Angel and the Little Scroll

10 Then I saw another mighty angel coming down from heaven. He was robed in a cloud, with a rainbow above his head; his face was like the sun, and his legs were like fiery pillars. [2]He was holding a little scroll, which lay open in his hand. He planted his right foot on the sea and his left foot on the land, [3]and he gave a loud shout like the roar of a lion. When he shouted, the voices of the seven thunders spoke. [4]And when the seven thunders spoke, I was about to write; but I heard a voice from heaven say, "Seal up what the seven thunders have said and do not write it down."

[5]Then the angel I had seen standing on the sea and on the land raised his right hand to heaven. [6]And he swore by him who lives for ever and ever, who created the heavens and all that is in them, the earth and all that is in it, and the sea and all that is in it, and said, "There will be no more delay! [7]But in the days when the seventh angel is about to sound his trumpet, the mystery of God will be accomplished, just as he announced to his servants the prophets."

[8]Then the voice that I had heard from heaven

[a] *11 Abaddon* and *Apollyon* mean *Destroyer.*
[b] *13* That is, projections

spoke to me once more: "Go, take the scroll that lies open in the hand of the angel who is standing on the sea and on the land."

9So I went to the angel and asked him to give me the little scroll. He said to me, "Take it and eat it. It will turn your stomach sour, but in your mouth it will be as sweet as honey." 10I took the little scroll from the angel's hand and ate it. It tasted as sweet as honey in my mouth, but when I had eaten it, my stomach turned sour. 11Then I was told, "You must prophesy again about many peoples, nations, languages and kings."

Revelation 10:1–11:19

1. Where would you least like to live: An area prone to earthquakes? Hurricanes? Floods?
2. What happens to the small scroll in 10:9–10? What has been an experience you once savored for a moment, but later turned sour? How has God's Word been both sweet and sour to you?
3. Who is the prophecy directed toward (10:11)? How open are you right now to receiving God's instruction for your own life?
4. What do you learn in 11:1–14 about what it means to be a witness? What has been toughest about living out your faith at school, home or work? Why is there such difficulty?
5. What is God saying to you in this passage?
6. How can this group help you in prayer this week?

The Two Witnesses

11 I was given a reed like a measuring rod and was told, "Go and measure the temple of God and the altar, and count the worshipers there. 2But exclude the outer court; do not measure it, because it has been given to the Gentiles. They will trample on the holy city for 42 months. 3And I will give power to my two witnesses, and they will prophesy for 1,260 days, clothed in sackcloth." 4These are the two olive trees and the two lampstands that stand before the Lord of the earth. 5If anyone tries to harm them, fire comes from their mouths and devours their enemies. This is how anyone who wants to harm them must die. 6These men have power to shut up the sky so that it will not rain during the time they are prophesying; and they have power to turn the waters into blood and to strike the earth with every kind of plague as often as they want.

7Now when they have finished their testimony, the beast that comes up from the Abyss will attack them, and overpower and kill them. 8Their bodies will lie in the street of the great city, which is figuratively called Sodom and Egypt, where also their Lord was crucified. 9For three and a half days men from every people, tribe, language and nation will gaze on their bodies and refuse them burial. 10The inhabitants of the earth will gloat over them and will celebrate by sending each other gifts, because these two prophets had tormented those who live on the earth.

11But after the three and a half days a breath of life from God entered them, and they stood on their feet, and terror struck those who saw them. 12Then they heard a loud voice from heaven saying to them, "Come up here." And they went up to heaven in a cloud, while their enemies looked on.

13At that very hour there was a severe earthquake and a tenth of the city collapsed. Seven thousand people were killed in the earthquake, and the survivors were terrified and gave glory to the God of heaven.

14The second woe has passed; the third woe is coming soon.

The Seventh Trumpet

15The seventh angel sounded his trumpet, and there were loud voices in heaven, which said:

"The kingdom of the world has become the
 kingdom of our Lord and of his
 Christ,
 and he will reign for ever and ever."

16And the twenty-four elders, who were seated on their thrones before God, fell on their faces and worshiped God, 17saying:

"We give thanks to you, Lord God Almighty,
 the One who is and who was,
because you have taken your great power
 and have begun to reign.
18The nations were angry;
 and your wrath has come.
The time has come for judging the dead,
 and for rewarding your servants the
 prophets
and your saints and those who reverence
 your name,
 both small and great—

and for destroying those who destroy the
earth."

19Then God's temple in heaven was opened,
and within his temple was seen the ark of his
covenant. And there came flashes of lightning,
rumblings, peals of thunder, an earthquake and a
great hailstorm.

The Woman and the Dragon

12 A great and wondrous sign appeared in
heaven: a woman clothed with the sun,
with the moon under her feet and a crown of
twelve stars on her head. 2She was pregnant and
cried out in pain as she was about to give birth.
3Then another sign appeared in heaven: an enormous red dragon with seven heads and ten horns
and seven crowns on his heads. 4His tail swept a
third of the stars out of the sky and flung them to
the earth. The dragon stood in front of the woman who was about to give birth, so that he might
devour her child the moment it was born. 5She
gave birth to a son, a male child, who will rule all
the nations with an iron scepter. And her child
was snatched up to God and to his throne. 6The
woman fled into the desert to a place prepared for
her by God, where she might be taken care of
for 1,260 days.

7And there was war in heaven. Michael and
his angels fought against the dragon, and the
dragon and his angels fought back. 8But he was
not strong enough, and they lost their place in
heaven. 9The great dragon was hurled down—
that ancient serpent called the devil, or Satan,
who leads the whole world astray. He was hurled
to the earth, and his angels with him.

10Then I heard a loud voice in heaven say:

"Now have come the salvation and the
power and the kingdom of our God,
and the authority of his Christ.
For the accuser of our brothers,
who accuses them before our God day and
night,
has been hurled down.
11They overcame him
by the blood of the Lamb
and by the word of their testimony;
they did not love their lives so much
as to shrink from death.
12Therefore rejoice, you heavens
and you who dwell in them!
But woe to the earth and the sea,
because the devil has gone down to you!
He is filled with fury,
because he knows that his time is short."

13When the dragon saw that he had been
hurled to the earth, he pursued the woman who
had given birth to the male child. 14The woman
was given the two wings of a great eagle, so that
she might fly to the place prepared for her in the
desert, where she would be taken care of for a
time, times and half a time, out of the serpent's
reach. 15Then from his mouth the serpent
spewed water like a river, to overtake the woman
and sweep her away with the torrent. 16But the
earth helped the woman by opening its mouth
and swallowing the river that the dragon had
spewed out of his mouth. 17Then the dragon was
enraged at the woman and went off to make war
against the rest of her offspring—those who obey
God's commandments and hold to the testimony
13 of Jesus. 1And the dragon[a] stood on the
shore of the sea.

The Beast out of the Sea

And I saw a beast coming out of the sea. He
had ten horns and seven heads, with ten crowns
on his horns, and on each head a blasphemous
name. 2The beast I saw resembled a leopard, but
had feet like those of a bear and a mouth like that
of a lion. The dragon gave the beast his power
and his throne and great authority. 3One of the
heads of the beast seemed to have had a fatal

Revelation 12:1–13:18

1. Who do you think is one of the most dynamic leaders living today? How has charisma helped him or her to lead?
2. When has Satan seemed very real to you? How do you overcome Satan (see 12:11)? How could you apply these tactics in your own life?
3. Who are some of the "beasts" or "idols" in your life (people, things, entertainment, etc.) that test your allegiance to Christ? How is God helping you to deal with that?
4. Is your name written in the Book of Life (13:8)? How do you know?
5. What is God saying to you in this passage?
6. How can this group help you in prayer this week?

a 1 Some late manuscripts *And I*

wound, but the fatal wound had been healed.
The whole world was astonished and followed
the beast. 4Men worshiped the dragon because
he had given authority to the beast, and they also
worshiped the beast and asked, "Who is like the
beast? Who can make war against him?"
5The beast was given a mouth to utter proud
words and blasphemies and to exercise his authority for forty-two months. 6He opened his
mouth to blaspheme God, and to slander his
name and his dwelling place and those who live
in heaven. 7He was given power to make war
against the saints and to conquer them. And he
was given authority over every tribe, people, language and nation. 8All inhabitants of the earth
will worship the beast—all whose names have
not been written in the book of life belonging to
the Lamb that was slain from the creation of the
world.[a]

9He who has an ear, let him hear.

10If anyone is to go into captivity,
  into captivity he will go.
If anyone is to be killed[b] with the sword,
  with the sword he will be killed.

This calls for patient endurance and faithfulness
on the part of the saints.

The Beast out of the Earth

11Then I saw another beast, coming out of the
earth. He had two horns like a lamb, but he spoke
like a dragon. 12He exercised all the authority of
the first beast on his behalf, and made the earth
and its inhabitants worship the first beast, whose
fatal wound had been healed. 13And he performed great and miraculous signs, even causing
fire to come down from heaven to earth in full
view of men. 14Because of the signs he was given
power to do on behalf of the first beast, he deceived the inhabitants of the earth. He ordered
them to set up an image in honor of the beast
who was wounded by the sword and yet lived.
15He was given power to give breath to the image
of the first beast, so that it could speak and cause
all who refused to worship the image to be killed.
16He also forced everyone, small and great, rich
and poor, free and slave, to receive a mark on his
right hand or on his forehead, 17so that no one
could buy or sell unless he had the mark, which
is the name of the beast or the number of his
name.
18This calls for wisdom. If anyone has insight,
let him calculate the number of the beast, for it is
man's number. His number is 666.

The Lamb and the 144,000

14 Then I looked, and there before me was
the Lamb, standing on Mount Zion, and
with him 144,000 who had his name and his
Father's name written on their foreheads. 2And I
heard a sound from heaven like the roar of rushing waters and like a loud peal of thunder. The
sound I heard was like that of harpists playing
their harps. 3And they sang a new song before
the throne and before the four living creatures
and the elders. No one could learn the song except the 144,000 who had been redeemed from
the earth. 4These are those who did not defile
themselves with women, for they kept themselves pure. They follow the Lamb wherever he
goes. They were purchased from among men and
offered as firstfruits to God and the Lamb. 5No lie
was found in their mouths; they are blameless.

The Three Angels

6Then I saw another angel flying in midair,
and he had the eternal gospel to proclaim to
those who live on the earth—to every nation,
tribe, language and people. 7He said in a loud
voice, "Fear God and give him glory, because the
hour of his judgment has come. Worship him
who made the heavens, the earth, the sea and the
springs of water."
8A second angel followed and said, "Fallen!
Fallen is Babylon the Great, which made all the
nations drink the maddening wine of her adulteries."
9A third angel followed them and said in a loud
voice: "If anyone worships the beast and his image and receives his mark on the forehead or on
the hand, 10he, too, will drink of the wine of
God's fury, which has been poured full strength
into the cup of his wrath. He will be tormented
with burning sulfur in the presence of the holy
angels and of the Lamb. 11And the smoke of their
torment rises for ever and ever. There is no rest
day or night for those who worship the beast and
his image, or for anyone who receives the mark
of his name." 12This calls for patient endurance
on the part of the saints who obey God's commandments and remain faithful to Jesus.
13Then I heard a voice from heaven say,
"Write: Blessed are the dead who die in the Lord
from now on."
"Yes," says the Spirit, "they will rest from
their labor, for their deeds will follow them."

The Harvest of the Earth

14I looked, and there before me was a white
cloud, and seated on the cloud was one "like a
son of man"[c] with a crown of gold on his head

[a] 8 Or *written from the creation of the world in the book of life belonging to the Lamb that was slain* [b] 10 Some manuscripts *anyone kills* [c] 14 Daniel 7:13

and a sharp sickle in his hand. 15Then another
angel came out of the temple and called in a loud
voice to him who was sitting on the cloud, "Take
your sickle and reap, because the time to reap has
come, for the harvest of the earth is ripe." 16So
he who was seated on the cloud swung his sickle
over the earth, and the earth was harvested.

Revelation 14:1–15:8

1. When did you take a vacation to a lake, river or the ocean? What did you like best about it?
2. Who is the Lamb? What has he done? Why are the people following him?
3. Regarding the harvest of the earth, how ripe do you think the world is now? Do you feel that the end of the world is close at hand? Why? How does this affect your life?
4. What great and mighty deeds has God done in your life for which you will praise him today? How appropriate is the song in 15:3–4 to your experience with God? Why?
5. What is God saying to you in this passage?
6. How can this group help you in prayer this week?

17Another angel came out of the temple in
heaven, and he too had a sharp sickle. 18Still another angel, who had charge of the fire, came
from the altar and called in a loud voice to him
who had the sharp sickle, "Take your sharp sickle
and gather the clusters of grapes from the earth's
vine, because its grapes are ripe." 19The angel
swung his sickle on the earth, gathered its grapes
and threw them into the great winepress of God's
wrath. 20They were trampled in the winepress
outside the city, and blood flowed out of the
press, rising as high as the horses' bridles for a
distance of 1,600 stadia.[a]

Seven Angels With Seven Plagues

15 I saw in heaven another great and marvelous sign: seven angels with the seven last
plagues—last, because with them God's wrath is
completed. 2And I saw what looked like a sea of
glass mixed with fire and, standing beside the
sea, those who had been victorious over the beast
and his image and over the number of his name.
They held harps given them by God 3and sang the
song of Moses the servant of God and the song of
the Lamb:

"Great and marvelous are your deeds,
  Lord God Almighty.
Just and true are your ways,
  King of the ages.
4Who will not fear you, O Lord,
  and bring glory to your name?
For you alone are holy.
All nations will come
  and worship before you,
for your righteous acts have been revealed."

5After this I looked and in heaven the temple,
that is, the tabernacle of the Testimony, was
opened. 6Out of the temple came the seven angels with the seven plagues. They were dressed
in clean, shining linen and wore golden sashes
around their chests. 7Then one of the four living
creatures gave to the seven angels seven golden
bowls filled with the wrath of God, who lives for
ever and ever. 8And the temple was filled with
smoke from the glory of God and from his power,
and no one could enter the temple until the sev-
en plagues of the seven angels were completed.

The Seven Bowls of God's Wrath

16 Then I heard a loud voice from the temple saying to the seven angels, "Go, pour
out the seven bowls of God's wrath on the
earth."

2The first angel went and poured out his bowl
on the land, and ugly and painful sores broke out
on the people who had the mark of the beast and
worshiped his image.

3The second angel poured out his bowl on the
sea, and it turned into blood like that of a dead
man, and every living thing in the sea died.

4The third angel poured out his bowl on the
rivers and springs of water, and they became
blood. 5Then I heard the angel in charge of the
waters say:

"You are just in these judgments,
  you who are and who were, the Holy One,
  because you have so judged;
6for they have shed the blood of your saints
    and prophets,
  and you have given them blood to drink as
    they deserve."

7And I heard the altar respond:

[a]20 That is, about 180 miles (about 300 kilometers)

"Yes, Lord God Almighty,
true and just are your judgments."

8The fourth angel poured out his bowl on the
sun, and the sun was given power to scorch people with fire. 9They were seared by the intense
heat and they cursed the name of God, who had
control over these plagues, but they refused to
repent and glorify him.
10The fifth angel poured out his bowl on the
throne of the beast, and his kingdom was plunged
into darkness. Men gnawed their tongues in agony 11and cursed the God of heaven because of
their pains and their sores, but they refused to
repent of what they had done.
12The sixth angel poured out his bowl on the
great river Euphrates, and its water was dried up
to prepare the way for the kings from the East.
13Then I saw three evil[a] spirits that looked like
frogs; they came out of the mouth of the dragon,
out of the mouth of the beast and out of the
mouth of the false prophet. 14They are spirits of
demons performing miraculous signs, and they
go out to the kings of the whole world, to gather
them for the battle on the great day of God Almighty.
15"Behold, I come like a thief! Blessed is he
who stays awake and keeps his clothes with him,
so that he may not go naked and be shamefully
exposed."
16Then they gathered the kings together to the
place that in Hebrew is called Armageddon.
17The seventh angel poured out his bowl into
the air, and out of the temple came a loud voice
from the throne, saying, "It is done!" 18Then
there came flashes of lightning, rumblings, peals
of thunder and a severe earthquake. No earthquake like it has ever occurred since man has
been on earth, so tremendous was the quake.
19The great city split into three parts, and the
cities of the nations collapsed. God remembered
Babylon the Great and gave her the cup filled
with the wine of the fury of his wrath. 20Every
island fled away and the mountains could not be
found. 21From the sky huge hailstones of about a
hundred pounds each fell upon men. And they
cursed God on account of the plague of hail, because the plague was so terrible.

The Woman on the Beast

17 One of the seven angels who had the sev-
en bowls came and said to me, "Come, I
will show you the punishment of the great prostitute, who sits on many waters. 2With her the
kings of the earth committed adultery and the
inhabitants of the earth were intoxicated with
the wine of her adulteries."
3Then the angel carried me away in the Spirit
into a desert. There I saw a woman sitting on a
scarlet beast that was covered with blasphemous
names and had seven heads and ten horns. 4The
woman was dressed in purple and scarlet, and
was glittering with gold, precious stones and
pearls. She held a golden cup in her hand, filled
with abominable things and the filth of her adulteries. 5This title was written on her forehead:

MYSTERY
BABYLON THE GREAT
THE MOTHER OF PROSTITUTES
AND OF THE ABOMINATIONS OF THE EARTH.

6I saw that the woman was drunk with the blood
of the saints, the blood of those who bore testimony to Jesus.
When I saw her, I was greatly astonished.

Revelation 16:1–17:18

1. What would be the worst plague for you to experience: Sores all over your body? Intense heat without air conditioning? Total darkness? Or great thirst with very little water? Why?
2. What has God done in your life to help you repent? How receptive are you to admitting your guilt and repenting when you sin?
3. If "war is hell," could John's vision be that "hell is war"? What does this passage tell you about God's judgment?
4. As you study Revelation, how frightened are you by the power of evil? How will you translate that fear into action or hope?
5. What is God saying to you in this passage?
6. How can this group help you in prayer this week?

7Then the angel said to me: "Why are you astonished? I will explain to you the mystery of the
woman and of the beast she rides, which has the
seven heads and ten horns. 8The beast, which
you saw, once was, now is not, and will come up
out of the Abyss and go to his destruction. The
inhabitants of the earth whose names have not
been written in the book of life from the creation
of the world will be astonished when they see the

[a]13 Greek *unclean*

beast, because he once was, now is not, and yet
will come.
9“This calls for a mind with wisdom. The sev-
en heads are seven hills on which the woman
sits. 10They are also seven kings. Five have fallen,
one is, the other has not yet come; but when he
does come, he must remain for a little while.
11The beast who once was, and now is not, is an
eighth king. He belongs to the seven and is going
to his destruction.
12“The ten horns you saw are ten kings who
have not yet received a kingdom, but who for one
hour will receive authority as kings along with
the beast. 13They have one purpose and will give
their power and authority to the beast. 14They
will make war against the Lamb, but the Lamb
will overcome them because he is Lord of lords
and King of kings—and with him will be his
called, chosen and faithful followers.”
15Then the angel said to me, “The waters you
saw, where the prostitute sits, are peoples, multitudes, nations and languages. 16The beast and the
ten horns you saw will hate the prostitute. They
will bring her to ruin and leave her naked; they
will eat her flesh and burn her with fire. 17For
God has put it into their hearts to accomplish his
purpose by agreeing to give the beast their power
to rule, until God’s words are fulfilled. 18The
woman you saw is the great city that rules over
the kings of the earth.”

The Fall of Babylon

18 After this I saw another angel coming
down from heaven. He had great authority, and the earth was illuminated by his splendor.
2With a mighty voice he shouted:

“Fallen! Fallen is Babylon the Great!
She has become a home for demons
and a haunt for every evil[a] spirit,
a haunt for every unclean and detestable bird.
3For all the nations have drunk
the maddening wine of her adulteries.
The kings of the earth committed adultery with her,
and the merchants of the earth grew rich from her excessive luxuries.”

4Then I heard another voice from heaven say:

“Come out of her, my people,
so that you will not share in her sins,
so that you will not receive any of her plagues;
5for her sins are piled up to heaven,
and God has remembered her crimes.
6Give back to her as she has given;
pay her back double for what she has done.
Mix her a double portion from her own cup.
7Give her as much torture and grief
as the glory and luxury she gave herself.
In her heart she boasts,
‘I sit as queen; I am not a widow,
and I will never mourn.’
8Therefore in one day her plagues will overtake her:
death, mourning and famine.
She will be consumed by fire,
for mighty is the Lord God who judges her.

9“When the kings of the earth who committed
adultery with her and shared her luxury see the
smoke of her burning, they will weep and mourn
over her. 10Terrified at her torment, they will
stand far off and cry:

“ ‘Woe! Woe, O great city,
O Babylon, city of power!
In one hour your doom has come!’

11“The merchants of the earth will weep and
mourn over her because no one buys their cargoes any more— 12cargoes of gold, silver, precious stones and pearls; fine linen, purple, silk
and scarlet cloth; every sort of citron wood, and
articles of every kind made of ivory, costly wood,
bronze, iron and marble; 13cargoes of cinnamon
and spice, of incense, myrrh and frankincense, of
wine and olive oil, of fine flour and wheat; cattle
and sheep; horses and carriages; and bodies and
souls of men.
14“They will say, ‘The fruit you longed for is
gone from you. All your riches and splendor have
vanished, never to be recovered.’ 15The merchants who sold these things and gained their
wealth from her will stand far off, terrified at her
torment. They will weep and mourn 16and cry
out:

“ ‘Woe! Woe, O great city,
dressed in fine linen, purple and scarlet,
and glittering with gold, precious stones and pearls!
17In one hour such great wealth has been brought to ruin!’

“Every sea captain, and all who travel by ship,
the sailors, and all who earn their living from the
sea, will stand far off. 18When they see the smoke
of her burning, they will exclaim, ‘Was there
ever a city like this great city?’ 19They will throw
dust on their heads, and with weeping and
mourning cry out:

[a]2 Greek *unclean*

"'Woe! Woe, O great city,
where all who had ships on the sea
became rich through her wealth!
In one hour she has been brought to ruin!
20Rejoice over her, O heaven!
Rejoice, saints and apostles and prophets!
God has judged her for the way she treated
you.'"

21Then a mighty angel picked up a boulder the
size of a large millstone and threw it into the sea,
and said:

"With such violence
the great city of Babylon will be thrown
down,
never to be found again.
22The music of harpists and musicians, flute
players and trumpeters,
will never be heard in you again.
No workman of any trade
will ever be found in you again.
The sound of a millstone
will never be heard in you again.
23The light of a lamp
will never shine in you again.
The voice of bridegroom and bride
will never be heard in you again.
Your merchants were the world's great men.
By your magic spell all the nations were
led astray.
24In her was found the blood of prophets and
of the saints,
and of all who have been killed on the
earth."

Hallelujah!

19 After this I heard what sounded like the roar of a great multitude in heaven shouting:

"Hallelujah!
Salvation and glory and power belong to our
God,
2 for true and just are his judgments.
He has condemned the great prostitute
who corrupted the earth by her adulteries.
He has avenged on her the blood of his
servants."

3And again they shouted:

"Hallelujah!
The smoke from her goes up for ever and
ever."

4The twenty-four elders and the four living creatures fell down and worshiped God, who was seated on the throne. And they cried:

"Amen, Hallelujah!"

5Then a voice came from the throne, saying:

"Praise our God,
all you his servants,
you who fear him,
both small and great!"

Revelation 18:1–19:10

1. What is the greatest "win" you've seen your favorite ball team pull off? How did you celebrate?
2. When has an important part of your life collapsed? What did other individuals say about this situation? What perspective did God bring to your struggle?
3. What are three things for which you are extremely grateful to God? Be specific. How do you usually express your gratitude to him about these things?
4. How is John (and how might we be) tempted to worship the angel or messenger of the good news (19:10)?
5. What is God saying to you in this passage?
6. How can this group help you in prayer this week?

6Then I heard what sounded like a great multitude, like the roar of rushing waters and like loud peals of thunder, shouting:

"Hallelujah!
For our Lord God Almighty reigns.
7Let us rejoice and be glad
and give him glory!
For the wedding of the Lamb has come,
and his bride has made herself ready.
8Fine linen, bright and clean,
was given her to wear."
(Fine linen stands for the righteous acts of the saints.)

9Then the angel said to me, "Write: 'Blessed are those who are invited to the wedding supper of the Lamb!'" And he added, "These are the true words of God."
10At this I fell at his feet to worship him. But he said to me, "Do not do it! I am a fellow servant with you and with your brothers who hold to the testimony of Jesus. Worship God! For the testimony of Jesus is the spirit of prophecy."

The Rider on the White Horse

11I saw heaven standing open and there before me was a white horse, whose rider is called Faithful and True. With justice he judges and makes war. 12His eyes are like blazing fire, and on his head are many crowns. He has a name written on him that no one knows but he himself. 13He is dressed in a robe dipped in blood, and his name is the Word of God. 14The armies of heaven were following him, riding on white horses and dressed in fine linen, white and clean. 15Out of his mouth comes a sharp sword with which to strike down the nations. "He will rule them with an iron scepter."[a] He treads the winepress of the fury of the wrath of God Almighty. 16On his robe and on his thigh he has this name written:

KING OF KINGS AND LORD OF LORDS.

17And I saw an angel standing in the sun, who cried in a loud voice to all the birds flying in midair, "Come, gather together for the great supper of God, 18so that you may eat the flesh of kings, generals, and mighty men, of horses and their riders, and the flesh of all people, free and slave, small and great."

19Then I saw the beast and the kings of the earth and their armies gathered together to make war against the rider on the horse and his army. 20But the beast was captured, and with him the false prophet who had performed the miraculous signs on his behalf. With these signs he had deluded those who had received the mark of the beast and worshiped his image. The two of them were thrown alive into the fiery lake of burning sulfur. 21The rest of them were killed with the sword that came out of the mouth of the rider on the horse, and all the birds gorged themselves on their flesh.

The Thousand Years

20 And I saw an angel coming down out of heaven, having the key to the Abyss and holding in his hand a great chain. 2He seized the dragon, that ancient serpent, who is the devil, or Satan, and bound him for a thousand years. 3He threw him into the Abyss, and locked and sealed it over him, to keep him from deceiving the nations anymore until the thousand years were ended. After that, he must be set free for a short time.

4I saw thrones on which were seated those who had been given authority to judge. And I saw the souls of those who had been beheaded because of their testimony for Jesus and because of the word of God. They had not worshiped the beast or his image and had not received his mark on their foreheads or their hands. They came to life and reigned with Christ a thousand years. 5(The rest of the dead did not come to life until the thousand years were ended.) This is the first resurrection. 6Blessed and holy are those who have part in the first resurrection. The second death has no power over them, but they will be priests of God and of Christ and will reign with him for a thousand years.

REVELATION 19:11–20:10

1. What has been your scariest moment with an animal?
2. Why do you think it is fitting that Christ has a name "that no one knows but he himself" (19:12)? What mystery about Christ are you looking forward to understanding in heaven?
3. What hopes and fears does this triumphant picture of chapter 19 bring out in you? Why? How has Jesus been your deliverer this year?
4. What will life be like without Satan deceiving people (20:3,10)? To what extent is that already the reality of your life?
5. What is God saying to you in this passage?
6. How can this group help you in prayer this week?

Satan's Doom

7When the thousand years are over, Satan will be released from his prison 8and will go out to deceive the nations in the four corners of the earth—Gog and Magog—to gather them for battle. In number they are like the sand on the seashore. 9They marched across the breadth of the earth and surrounded the camp of God's people, the city he loves. But fire came down from heaven and devoured them. 10And the devil, who deceived them, was thrown into the lake of burning sulfur, where the beast and the false prophet had been thrown. They will be tormented day and night for ever and ever.

The Dead Are Judged

11Then I saw a great white throne and him who was seated on it. Earth and sky fled from his

[a] *15* Psalm 2:9

presence, and there was no place for them. 12And I saw the dead, great and small, standing before the throne, and books were opened. Another book was opened, which is the book of life. The dead were judged according to what they had done as recorded in the books. 13The sea gave up the dead that were in it, and death and Hades gave up the dead that were in them, and each person was judged according to what he had done. 14Then death and Hades were thrown into the lake of fire. The lake of fire is the second death. 15If anyone's name was not found written in the book of life, he was thrown into the lake of fire.

Revelation 20:11–21:8

1. What's one of the most beautiful places you have ever been? What impressed you about it?
2. Imagine a book made of your life, with everything you've done recorded, then read by all. How would you feel?
3. What do you find comforting in this passage? What do you find disturbing?
4. What won't there be in heaven (see 21:4)?
5. Who is heaven reserved for (see 21:7)? Who is hell reserved for (see 21:8)?
6. What must one do to overcome and share in God's eternal inheritance (see 1 John 5:5,11–12)?
7. What do you say when your non-Christian friends ask you about the existence of another life after death?
8. Who is someone you would like to share the Good News of Christ and hope of heaven with this week? Close in prayer.

The New Jerusalem

21 Then I saw a new heaven and a new earth, for the first heaven and the first earth had passed away, and there was no longer any sea. 2I saw the Holy City, the new Jerusalem, coming down out of heaven from God, prepared as a bride beautifully dressed for her husband. 3And I heard a loud voice from the throne saying, "Now the dwelling of God is with men, and he will live with them. They will be his people, and God himself will be with them and be their God. 4He will wipe every tear from their eyes. There will be no more death or mourning or crying or pain, for the old order of things has passed away."

5He who was seated on the throne said, "I am making everything new!" Then he said, "Write this down, for these words are trustworthy and true."

6He said to me: "It is done. I am the Alpha and the Omega, the Beginning and the End. To him who is thirsty I will give to drink without cost from the spring of the water of life. 7He who overcomes will inherit all this, and I will be his God and he will be my son. 8But the cowardly, the unbelieving, the vile, the murderers, the sexually immoral, those who practice magic arts, the idolaters and all liars—their place will be in the fiery lake of burning sulfur. This is the second death."

9One of the seven angels who had the seven bowls full of the seven last plagues came and said to me, "Come, I will show you the bride, the wife of the Lamb." 10And he carried me away in the Spirit to a mountain great and high, and showed me the Holy City, Jerusalem, coming down out of heaven from God. 11It shone with the glory of God, and its brilliance was like that of a very precious jewel, like a jasper, clear as crystal. 12It had a great, high wall with twelve gates, and with twelve angels at the gates. On the gates were written the names of the twelve tribes of Israel. 13There were three gates on the east, three on the north, three on the south and three on the west. 14The wall of the city had twelve founda-

---

20:12 *according to what they had done.* The idea of judgment on the basis of one's works is found in the OT and NT (Ps. 62:12; Jer. 17:10; Rom. 2:6; 1 Peter 1:17). The issue is not salvation by works but works as the evidence of a person's actual relationship with God. ***the book of life.*** Another book is opened. In it are recorded the names of those who belong to Christ (Ex. 32:32–33; Dan. 12:1; Luke 10:20; Phil. 4:3; Rev. 3:5; 13:8; 21:27).

20:13 *Hades.* This is not the same as hell. It is the place where departed souls go. It was thought of as an intermediate state (Luke 16:23).

21:1 *there was no longer any sea.* In ancient times the sea was often pictured as dark and mysterious; it was an enemy not a friend. The lack of any seas in the new earth indicates how radically different the new will be.

21:2 *the new Jerusalem.* The new Jerusalem will be described in detail in 21:9–22:5 (see Gal. 4:26; Heb. 12:22). ***prepared as a bride.*** The church has already been pictured as the bride of Christ (19:7; see also Eph. 5:25–27).

21:4 *He will wipe every tear from their eyes.* The suffering is over; it is finished. No longer will there need to be a call to hold on and endure. ***There will be no more death or mourning or crying or pain.*** All the old enemies of humanity are gone. Death itself is vanquished, so there will be no need anymore for mourning. Crying too is a thing of the past. Pain will be unknown.

tions, and on them were the names of the twelve apostles of the Lamb.

[15]The angel who talked with me had a measuring rod of gold to measure the city, its gates and its walls. [16]The city was laid out like a square, as long as it was wide. He measured the city with the rod and found it to be 12,000 stadia[a] in length, and as wide and high as it is long. [17]He measured its wall and it was 144 cubits[b] thick,[c] by man's measurement, which the angel was using. [18]The wall was made of jasper, and the city of pure gold, as pure as glass. [19]The foundations of the city walls were decorated with every kind of precious stone. The first foundation was jasper, the second sapphire, the third chalcedony, the fourth emerald, [20]the fifth sardonyx, the sixth carnelian, the seventh chrysolite, the eighth beryl, the ninth topaz, the tenth chrysoprase, the eleventh jacinth, and the twelfth amethyst.[d] [21]The twelve gates were twelve pearls, each gate made of a single pearl. The great street of the city was of pure gold, like transparent glass.

[22]I did not see a temple in the city, because the Lord God Almighty and the Lamb are its temple. [23]The city does not need the sun or the moon to shine on it, for the glory of God gives it light, and the Lamb is its lamp. [24]The nations will walk by its light, and the kings of the earth will bring their splendor into it. [25]On no day will its gates ever be shut, for there will be no night there. [26]The glory and honor of the nations will be brought into it. [27]Nothing impure will ever enter it, nor will anyone who does what is shameful or deceitful, but only those whose names are written in the Lamb's book of life.

Revelation 21:9–22:6

1. What is the biggest city you've been in? Would you like to live there?
2. What impresses you most about the New Jerusalem and its central figure? Why?
3. How do you feel about the fact that the Holy City will be your hometown—that this is what Jesus has prepared for you?
4. When in the recent past have you needed a vision of the Holy City—the joyous place that awaits you?
5. What is God saying to you in this passage?
6. How can this group help you in prayer this week?

The River of Life

22 Then the angel showed me the river of the water of life, as clear as crystal, flowing from the throne of God and of the Lamb [2]down the middle of the great street of the city. On each side of the river stood the tree of life, bearing twelve crops of fruit, yielding its fruit every month. And the leaves of the tree are for the healing of the nations. [3]No longer will there be any curse. The throne of God and of the Lamb will be in the city, and his servants will serve him. [4]They will see his face, and his name will be on their foreheads. [5]There will be no more night. They will not need the light of a lamp or the light of the sun, for the Lord God will give them light. And they will reign for ever and ever.

[6]The angel said to me, "These words are trustworthy and true. The Lord, the God of the spirits

Revelation 22:7–21

1. If you could choose a few words to represent who you are, what would they be?
2. Regarding Jesus' claims in verses 12–17, how is the final state of humanity determined: By some arbitrary reward system, fixed from eternity? By what we have done in this present life? Or by our response to his *universal* and *undeserved* invitation to simply "come"?
3. Is it ever too late for people to change their ways and come to Christ? Why?
4. How have you prepared yourself for Christ's second coming? In what way has this study of Revelation helped to prepare you? How is your lifestyle in keeping with verse 7?
5. What is God saying to you in this passage?
6. How can this group help you in prayer this week?

[a]*16* That is, about 1,400 miles (about 2,200 kilometers) [b]*17* That is, about 200 feet (about 65 meters) [c]*17* Or *high*
[d]*20* The precise identification of some of these precious stones is uncertain.

of the prophets, sent his angel to show his servants the things that must soon take place."

Jesus Is Coming

7"Behold, I am coming soon! Blessed is he
who keeps the words of the prophecy in this
book."

8I, John, am the one who heard and saw these
things. And when I had heard and seen them, I
fell down to worship at the feet of the angel who
had been showing them to me. 9But he said to
me, "Do not do it! I am a fellow servant with you
and with your brothers the prophets and of all
who keep the words of this book. Worship God!"
10Then he told me, "Do not seal up the words
of the prophecy of this book, because the time is
near. 11Let him who does wrong continue to do
wrong; let him who is vile continue to be vile; let
him who does right continue to do right; and let
him who is holy continue to be holy."

12"Behold, I am coming soon! My reward is
with me, and I will give to everyone according to
what he has done. 13I am the Alpha and the Omega, the First and the Last, the Beginning and the
End.

14"Blessed are those who wash their robes,
that they may have the right to the tree of life and
may go through the gates into the city. 15Outside
are the dogs, those who practice magic arts, the
sexually immoral, the murderers, the idolaters
and everyone who loves and practices falsehood.
16"I, Jesus, have sent my angel to give you[a]
this testimony for the churches. I am the Root
and the Offspring of David, and the bright Morning Star."

17The Spirit and the bride say, "Come!" And
let him who hears say, "Come!" Whoever is
thirsty, let him come; and whoever wishes, let
him take the free gift of the water of life.

18I warn everyone who hears the words of the
prophecy of this book: If anyone adds anything to
them, God will add to him the plagues described
in this book. 19And if anyone takes words away
from this book of prophecy, God will take away
from him his share in the tree of life and in the
holy city, which are described in this book.
20He who testifies to these things says, "Yes, I
am coming soon."
Amen. Come, Lord Jesus.
21The grace of the Lord Jesus be with God's
people. Amen.

[a] *16* The Greek is plural.

Table of Weights and Measures

BIBLICAL UNIT		APPROXIMATE AMERICAN EQUIVALENT	APPROXIMATE METRIC EQUIVALENT
WEIGHTS			
talent	(60 minas)	75 pounds	34 kilograms
mina	(50 shekels)	1 1/4 pounds	0.6 kilogram
shekel	(2 bekas)	2/5 ounce	11.5 grams
pim	(2/3 shekel)	1/3 ounce	7.6 grams
beka	(10 gerahs)	1/5 ounce	5.5 grams
gerah		1/50 ounce	0.6 gram
LENGTH			
cubit		18 inches	0.5 meter
span		9 inches	23 centimeters
handbreadth		3 inches	8 centimeters
CAPACITY			
Dry Measure			
cor (homer)	(10 ephahs)	6 bushels	220 liters
lethek	(5 ephahs)	3 bushels	110 liters
ephah	(10 omers)	3/5 bushel	22 liters
seah	(1/3 ephah)	7 quarts	7.3 liters
omer	(1/10 ephah)	2 quarts	2 liters
cab	(1/18 ephah)	1 quart	1 liter
Liquid Measure			
bath	(1 ephah)	6 gallons	22 liters
hin	(1/6 bath)	4 quarts	4 liters
log	(1/72 bath)	1/3 quart	0.3 liter

The figures of the table are calculated on the basis of a shekel equaling 11.5 grams, a cubit equaling 18 inches and an ephah equaling 22 liters. The quart referred to is either a dry quart (slightly larger than a liter) or a liquid quart (slightly smaller than a liter), whichever is applicable. The ton referred to in the footnotes is the American ton of 2,000 pounds.

This table is based upon the best available information, but it is not intended to be mathematically precise; like the measurement equivalents in the footnotes, it merely gives approximate amounts and distances. Weights and measures differed somewhat at various times and places in the ancient world. There is uncertainty particularly about the ephah and the bath; further discoveries may give more light on these units of capacity.

SUBJECT INDEX

Subject Index

The numbers in heavy type are the page numbers.
The verses containing the reference are given after the page numbers.

B

D

T

U

Dictionary Concordance

Dictionary-Concordance

A

Aaron—the brother of Moses; he served as Moses' spokesman before Pharaoh (Ex 4:14-16,27-31; 7:1-2); he was Israel's first high priest (Ex 28:1; Nu 17; Heb 5:1-4).

abandon—to desert or forsake with no intention to return or reclaim.

Abba—the word for *father* in Aramaic, one of the three languages Jesus spoke.
Ro 8:15 And by him we cry "*A,* Father."
Gal 4:6 the Spirit who calls out, "*A,* Father."

Abel—the second son of Adam (Ge 4:2); he offered the proper sacrifice to God (Ge 4:4; Heb 11:4), but was murdered by his brother Cain (Ge 4:8; Mt 23:35; 1Jn 3:12).

abhor—to hate or to turn away from.

Abigail—the wife of Nabal; she helped save David's life (1Sa 25:14-35) and later became his wife (1Sa 25:36-42).

abolish—to destroy completely; to put an end to.

abomination—a thing to be hated.

abound—to be more than enough; to overflow.
Ex 34:6 slow to anger, *a* in love
Php 1:9 that your love may *a* more

Abraham—the father of the Jewish nation and of all believers. God promised that he would make a mighty nation of Abraham's children and would give them the land of Canaan (Ge 15; 17; 22; Ro 4; Heb 6:13-15). As a test, God told him to offer his son Isaac as a sacrifice (Ge 22; Heb 11:17-19) but withdrew this command when Abraham showed that he would trust the Lord even in this matter.

Absalom—a son of David (2Sa 3:3); he plotted to take David's throne. He met death when his long hair became entangled in an oak tree and Joab, David's commander, thrust javelins into his heart (2Sa 14–18).

abstain—to keep from doing something.

abundance, abundant—having plenty, more than enough.
Jude 2 Mercy, peace and love be yours in *a.*

Abyss—the place of the dead; the place where evil spirits live.

Achan—an Israelite who kept spoil from the conquest of Jericho for himself; as a result of Achan's stealing what belonged to God, the Israelites were defeated at Ai and he and his family were stoned to death (Jos 7; 22:20).

acknowledge—to know and to say that something is true; to recognize.
Mt 10:32 *a* him before my Father in heaven.
2Ti 3:7 but never able to *a* the truth.

acts—deeds.
Ps 150:2 Praise him for his *a* of power
Isa 64:6 all our righteous *a* are like filthy

Adam—the first man God created (Ge 1:26–2:25); he sinned by disobeying God (Ge 3) thereby bringing all people under the curse of sin (Ro 5:12-21).

admonish—to give warning or advice in a caring way.

adorn—to make more beautiful.

adultery—having sexual relations with someone other than one's husband or wife. Spiritual adultery means being unfaithful to God (Jer 3).
Ex 20:14 You shall not commit *a.*
Mt 5:28 lustfully has already committed *a*

adversary—enemy; opponent.

advice—an opinion given regarding a decision to be made.
1Ki 12:14 he followed the *a* of the young men
Pr 20:18 Make plans by seeking *a;*

advocate—1. *(v.)* to speak in favor of; 2. *(n.)* someone who speaks in another person's defense. Jesus is our advocate.

affliction—trouble or pain that lasts a long time.
Ro 12:12 patient in *a,* faithful in prayer.

agony—extreme pain of mind or body.

Ahab—a wicked king of Israel; the husband of Jezebel (1Ki 16:31). He caused Israel to worship Baal rather than God (1Ki 16:31-33) and was opposed by God's prophet Elijah (1Ki 17:1; 18; 21).

alabaster—a hard marblelike material that can be made into jars, vases or sculptures.

alien—a foreigner or stranger.
Ex 22:21 "Do not mistreat an *a*
Eph 2:19 no longer foreigners and *a,* but fellow citizens
1Pe 2:11 as *a* and strangers in the world,

alienate—to make unfriendly; to turn a person's interest or affection away from another person or thing.

allot—to divide and give away in parts. In Old Testament times the land of Canaan was allotted to the twelve tribes of Israel.

Almighty—a name used to show how strong and powerful God is.
Ge 17:1 "I am God *A;* walk before me
Isa 6:3 "Holy, holy, holy is the LORD *A;*

altar—a raised platform, made of stones, metal, dirt or wood, on which sacrifices were made.

ambush—a trap in which hidden persons lie in wait to attack by surprise.

Amen—Hebrew word that means "so be it" or "let it become true."

Amos—a prophet of Israel who ministered about the same time as Hosea and Jonah; he spoke about God's justice and righteousness.

Ananias—1. the husband of Sapphira; he was struck dead for lying to God (Ac 5:1-11); 2. the disciple who baptized Saul (Ac 9:10-19); 3. the high priest before whom Paul was tried in Jerusalem (Ac 22:30–24:1).

ancient—very old; in existence for many years.

Andrew—one of the twelve apostles; the brother of Peter (Mt 4:18; 10:2; Ac 1:13).

angel—a heavenly being.
Ps 34:7 The *a* of the LORD encamps
Heb 1:14 Are not all *a* ministering spirits
Heb 2:7 made him a little lower than the *a*;
1Pe 1:12 Even *a* long to look

anger—a strong feeling of displeasure; rage; fury.
Ps 103:8 slow to *a,* abounding in love.
Jas 1:20 for a man's *a* does not bring

anguish—extreme pain or distress of mind or body.
Jer 49:24 *a* and pain have seized her,

annihilate—to destroy completely.

anoint—to pour oil on a person's head, either for a physical benefit (Jas 5:14) or in order to set apart someone for service to God (Ex 28:41).

antichrist—a person who is against Christ.
1Jn 2:18 have heard that the *a* is coming,
1Jn 2:22 a man is the *a*—he denies

anxiety—worry.
1Pe 5:7 Cast all your *a* on him

Apollos—a Christian from Alexandria who knew the Scriptures well (Ac 18:24-28) and helped Paul to minister in Corinth (Ac 19:1; 1Co 1:12).

apostle—1. any of the twelve men Jesus chose to work with him during his earthly ministry; after being equipped by the Holy Spirit, they were sent out to preach about Jesus; 2. later, someone who had been with Jesus, had seen his miracles and then taught others about him.
Mk 3:14 twelve—designating them *a*—
1Co 12:28 God has appointed first of all *a,*
1Co 15:9 For I am the least of the *a*

appalled—overcome with shock or dismay.

appeal—to make an earnest request.
Phm 9 I *a* to you on the basis of love.

appoint—to assign someone officially to a job or position.

Aquila—the husband of Priscilla; Aquila and Priscilla were co-workers with Paul in Corinth (Ac 18; Ro 16:3).

Aramaic—the language that was commonly spoken in the countries east of the Mediterranean Sea during Jesus' earthly ministry.

ark of the Testimony—also called the ark of the covenant; a large gold-covered box, which contained the Ten Commandments (Tablets of Testimony), a jar of manna and Aaron's staff, and was kept inside the Most Holy Place in the tabernacle (Tent of Meeting). It was a reminder to the Israelites of God's presence with them.

armor—protective clothing worn in battle, usually made of metal.
Eph 6:11 Put on the full *a* of God

aroma—an odor or smell, usually pleasant.

arouse—to excite; to stir to action.

arrest—to officially or lawfully make a prisoner of someone.

arrogant—proud; conceited.

arrow—See bow.

ascend—to go up. Jesus ascended to heaven to return to God the Father.

ascribe—to think of as caused by, coming from or belonging to.
1Ch 16:28 *a* to the LORD glory and strength,

assemble—to bring a group of people together; to meet together.

Assyria—one of the powerful nations of Biblical times; it often attacked the Israelites; its capital was Nineveh.

astray—mistaken; not on the right path; lost.
Isa 53:6 We all, like sheep, have gone *a,*

atone—to make right, by paying the penalty, the relationship between God and humans that was broken through sin. In the Old Testament people atoned symbolically for their sins by offering sacrifices to God. In the New Testament Jesus corrected the relationship between God and people once and for all by dying to take away sins.

atonement—the payment that corrects the relationship between God and humans that was broken through sin.
Lev 17:11 it is the blood that makes *a*
Lev 23:27 this seventh month is the Day of *A.*
Ro 3:25 presented him as a sacrifice of *a,*
Heb 2:17 that he might make *a* for the sins

attack—to set upon with force, as in a battle.

authority—the right and power to give orders.
Mt 9:6 the Son of Man has *a* on earth
Mt 28:18 "All *a* in heaven and on earth has
Ro 13:1 for there is no *a* except that which
Heb 13:17 your leaders and submit to their *a.*

avenge—to get back at or punish someone who has done wrong.
Dt 32:35 It is mine to *a;* I will repay.

avoid—to keep away from.
1Th 5:22 *A* every kind of evil.

awe—respect and wonder; a holy fear of God because of his great power.
Ecc 5:7 Therefore stand in *a* of God.

B

Baal—the name of many false gods in Canaan.
1Ki 18:25 Elijah said to the prophets of *B,*

Babel—a tower built soon after the flood; the builders were attempting to reach up to God, but God confused their language so that the building was discontinued.

Babylon—the beautiful capital of Babylonia; it was a powerful and influential city in the Near East from the eighteenth to the sixth centuries B.C. In the New Testament, Babylon represents the godless city.
Ps 137:1 By the rivers of *B* we sat and wept
Rev 14:8 Fallen is *B* the Great,

Balaam—a seer who tried to curse Israel during their journey to the promised land, but God would not allow it (Nu 22–24).

balm—a skin cream used to heal sores and relieve pain.
Jer 8:22 Is there no *b* in Gilead?

banish—to force a person away from a place.

banquet—a formal meal, usually for a large group of people.

baptize—a religious ceremony in which water is used as a symbol of cleansing from sin. Churches today baptize by sprinkling or pouring or immersing in water. Baptism is a sign that sin is washed away.
Mk 1:9 and was *b* by John in the Jordan.
Mk 16:16 believes and is *b* will be saved,
Ac 1:5 but in a few days you will be *b*
Ac 2:38 "Repent and be *b,* every one of you,

Barabbas—the Jews chose this criminal, rather than Jesus, to be released by Pilate (Mt 27:26).

Barnabas—an apostle; he was a co-worker with Paul on his first missionary journey (Ac 9:27; Ac 13–15).

barren—1. unable to have children; 2. unable to produce crops.

Bartholomew—one of the twelve apostles (Mt 10:3; Ac 1:13). He was also probably known as Nathanael (Jn 1:45-49; 21:2).

Bathsheba—the wife of Uriah; she committed adultery with David and later became his wife (2Sa 11); she was the mother of Solomon (2Sa 12:24).

Beelzebub—the prince of demons; Satan.
Lk 11:15 "By *B,* the prince of demons,

Beersheba—an important town that marked the southern boundary of Judah.

believe—to accept as true; to trust; to have faith.
Mk 1:15 Repent and *b* the good news!"
Mk 9:24 "I do *b;* help me overcome my
Jn 1:7 that through him all men might *b.*
Jn 3:18 does not *b* stands condemned
Jn 20:27 Stop doubting and *b.*"
Ac 16:31 They replied, "*B* in the Lord Jesus,
Ro 3:22 faith in Jesus Christ to all who *b.*
1Th 4:14 We *b* that Jesus died and rose again

Benjamin—the twelfth son of Jacob. Rachel was his mother and he was the younger brother of Joseph (Ge 35:16-24; Ge 42–45).

besiege—to surround a city or town completely with an army, so that nothing can go in or out.

bestow—to give.

Bethlehem—the city in Judea where Jesus was born (Mt 2:1).

betray—to turn a friend over to his or her enemies; to be unfaithful to.
Mt 27:3 When Judas, who had *b* him,
1Co 11:23 on the night he was *b,* took bread,

betroth—to promise to marry.

bewildered—confused; puzzled.

bind—1. to tie with a rope or string; 2. to make tight or firm.
Dt 6:8 and *b* them on your foreheads.
Mt 16:19 whatever you *b* on earth will be

birthright—the special rights of the firstborn son. In the Old Testament, after the father died the oldest son received the father's power and right to make decisions for the entire family. He also got twice as much money and property as each of his brothers.

bitter—having harsh or hateful feelings.
Eph 4:31 Get rid of all *b,* rage
Heb 12:15 and that no *b* root grows up

blameless—without fault.
Ge 17:1 walk before me and be *b.*
1Co 1:8 so that you will be *b* on the day

blaspheme—to speak carelessly, falsely or insultingly about God or holy things.
Mk 3:29 whoever *b* against the Holy Spirit

blemish—a spot or mark that makes something imperfect.
1Pe 1:19 a lamb without *b* or defect.

bless—1. to make holy; 2. to show favor to; 3. to ask God to show favor to.
Ge 2:3 And God *b* the seventh day
Ge 12:3 I will *b* those who *b* you,
Mt 5:3 "*B* are the poor in spirit
Ro 12:14 *b* those who persecute you; *b*

blight—a disease in plants that makes them shrivel up and die.

blind—unable to see. Spiritual blindness is an inability to understand the things of God.
Mt 11:5 The *b* receive sight, the lame walk,
Jn 9:25 I was *b* but now I see!"

blood—as the life-giving fluid in the body, it represents life itself. In the Old Testament the blood of sacrifices symbolized the giving of life for life. Through the blood of Jesus on the cross, believers are saved from death for their sins.
Ex 12:13 and when I see the *b,* I will pass
Lev 17:11 For the life of a creature is in the *b,*
Mt 26:28 This is my *b* of the covenant,
Eph 1:7 we have redemption through his *b,*
Heb 9:12 once for all by his own *b,*

blot—to erase or get rid of.
Ex 32:32 then *b* me out of the book you have
Ps 51:1 *b* out my transgressions.

boast—to brag; to call attention to.
Ps 34:2 My soul will *b* in the LORD;
Gal 6:14 May I never *b* except in the cross

Boaz—a wealthy man who lived in Bethlehem in the days of the judges; he married Ruth (Ru 2; 4).

body—1. physical part of a person; 2. a group working as a unit.
Ro 6:13 Do not offer the parts of your *b*
Ro 12:1 to offer your *b* as living sacrifices,
1Co 6:19 not know that your *b* is a temple
Eph 5:30 for we are members of his *b.*

bondage—slavery.
Ezr 9:9 God has not deserted us in our *b.*

born again—refers to the experience of salvation; entering God's family through faith in Christ.
Jn 3:3 no one can see the kingdom of God unless he is *b*
1Pe 1:23 For you have been *b*

bow—a weapon made of a strip of flexible material with a cord connecting the two ends and holding the strip bent; used to propel arrows.

branch—an extension of another body or system.
Jer 33:15 I will make a righteous *B* sprout
Jn 15:5 "I am the vine; you are the *b.*

bread—in Bible times the most important food in the diet.
Dt 8:3 that man does not live on *b* alone
Mt 6:11 Give us today our daily *b.*
Jn 6:35 Jesus declared, "I am the *b* of life.

breastpiece—a decorated square of linen cloth worn by the high priest when he entered the Holy Place.

breastplate—a chest-covering made of metal or leather, worn by soldiers for protection.

bribe—money or favor given to influence judgment or conduct.
Ex 23:8 "Do not accept a *b,*

bride—a woman who is about to get married. The church is called Jesus' bride.

bridegroom—a man who is about to get married. Christ is called the church's bridegroom.

bronze—a metal, the combination of copper and tin, used to make tools, weapons and ornamental articles.

brother—a male member of the same family.
Ge 4:9 "Am I my *b* keeper?"
Ps 133:1 is when *b* live together in unity!
Mt 18:15 "If your *b* sins against you,

burden—a heavy load.
Mt 11:30 my yoke is easy and my *b* is light.
Gal 6:2 Carry each other's *b,*

burnt offering—in the Old Testament a sacrifice to the Lord that expressed devotion and complete surrender (Ge 8:20; Ex 29:18).

C

Caesar—the title of many Roman emperors.
Lk 2:1 In those days *C* Augustus
Mt 22:21 "Give to *C* what is *C*

Cain—Adam and Eve's firstborn son; he murdered his brother Abel (Ge 4:1-16).

calamity—a disaster, usually causing great loss and suffering.

Caleb—one of the twelve men who spied out Canaan. He came back with a positive report and encouraged the Israelites to take possession of Canaan (Nu 13:6–14:38; Dt 1:36).

call—1. (*v.*) to ask to come; 2. to give a name to; 3. (*n.*) a summons for a particular purpose or job.
2Ch 7:14 if my people, who are *c*
Ps 145:18 near to all who *c* on him,
Mt 9:13 come to *c* the righteous,
Ro 8:30 And those he predestined, he also *c,*
Ro 11:29 gifts and his *c* are irrevocable.
1Pe 2:9 of him who *c* you out of darkness

camel—a large animal, able to travel long distances and used for transportation of people and goods.

Canaan—1. the land God promised to the nation of Israel; 2. the promised land.

capstone—the stone that holds two walls together; the stone that finishes a wall.
1Pe 2:7 has become the *c,*"

care—to show concern for.
Ps 8:4 the son of man that you *c* for him?
1Pe 5:7 on him because he *c* for you.

cavalry—a group of soldiers riding horses.

censer—a bowl or dish used for carrying hot coals or for burning incense.

census—a count of the population of a group of people.

centurion—a Roman army officer in charge of one hundred soldiers.

chaff—the seed covering of a grain such as wheat. In Bible times the grain and chaff were separated by tossing the grain into the air so the wind could blow the chaff away.
Ps 1:4 They are like *c*
Mt 3:12 up the *c* with unquenchable fire."

chariot—a two-wheeled vehicle pulled by horses.
2Ki 6:17 and *c* of fire all around Elisha.

cheerful—full of joy; pleasant.
Pr 15:13 A happy heart makes the face *c,*
2Co 9:7 for God loves a *c* giver.

cherub (pl. **cherubim**)—an angel, with an appearance something like a human being.

children—sons and daughters.
Mt 19:14 "Let the little *c* come to me,
Eph 6:1 *C,* obey your parents in the Lord,
1Jn 3:1 that we should be called *c* of God!

choose (chosen)—to select.
Jos 24:15 then *c* for yourselves this day
Mt 22:14 "For many are invited, but few are *c.*"
Jn 15:16 You did not *c* me,
Eph 1:4 he *c* us in him before the creation
1Pe 2:9 But you are a *c* people, a royal

Christ—the official title of Jesus, meaning "the Anointed One." It is a Greek word, and it means the same as the Hebrew word *Messiah.*
Mt 1:16 was born Jesus, who is called *C.*
Jn 20:31 you may believe that Jesus is the *C,*
Ro 5:8 While we were still sinners, *C* died
Eph 5:23 as *C* is the head of the church,
Php 1:21 to live is *C* and to die is gain.

Christian—a believer in or follower of Christ.
Ac 11:26 The disciples were called *C* first
1Pe 4:16 as a *C,* do not be ashamed,

chronicles—a history of events in the order in which they took place.

church—the entire group of people who believe in Christ.
Mt 16:18 and on this rock I will build my *c,*
Eph 5:23 as Christ is the head of the *c,*
Col 1:24 the sake of his body, which is the *c.*

circumcision—the cutting off of the loose fold of skin at the end of the penis; it symbolized the agreement God made with the Israelites, and they came to be known as "the circumcision" (Eph 2:11).

Ge 17:10 Every male among you shall be *c.*

cistern—a pit dug into the ground for storing rainwater.

citadel—a tower or building, especially in a city, equipped for war.

city of refuge—one of six cities set aside by Moses and Joshua for those who had accidentally killed someone. Such people would be safe there until a fair trial could be held (Nu 35:9-15).

clan—a group of people belonging to the same extended family.

Ge 24:38 to my father's family and to my own *c,*
Zec 12:12 The land will mourn, each *c* by itself,

clean animals—animals God allowed the Israelites to sacrifice and eat.

cleanse—to make clean; to wash.

cloak—a loose-fitting coat without sleeves.

comfort—to relieve from distress; to console.

Ps 23:4 rod and your staff, they *c* me.
2Co 1:4 so that we can *c* those

commandment—an order given by God. God gave the Ten Commandments to the Israelites while they were encamped in the area of Mount Sinai.

Ex 20:6 who love me and keep my *c.*
Mt 22:38 This is the first and greatest *c.*
Jn 13:34 "A new *c* I give you: Love one

commend—1. to praise; 2. to hand over to someone for safekeeping.

Ps 145:4 One generation will *c* your works

companion—one who is a friend or associate or helper.

compassion (compassionate)—sympathy; pity.

Ne 9:17 gracious and *c,* slow to anger
Ps 103:4 and crowns you with love and *c,*
Mt 9:36 When he saw the crowds, he had *c*
Ro 9:15 and I will have *c* on whom I have *c.*"
Col 3:12 clothe yourselves with *c,* kindness,

conceive—1. to become pregnant; 2. to think up or imagine.

Mt 1:20 what is *c* in her is from the Holy
1Co 2:9 no mind has *c*

concubine—in Bible times, a woman who belonged to a man but did not have the rights of a wife. She was often one of the spoils of war, and her primary purpose was to bear children for the man.

condemn (condemnation)—to give out punishment to; to pronounce guilty.

Jn 3:17 Son into the world to *c* the world,
Ro 8:1 there is now no *c* for those who are

confess—1. to say what you believe; 2. to tell your sins to someone.

Ro 10:9 That if you *c* with your mouth,
Php 2:11 every tongue *c* that Jesus Christ is
1Jn 1:9 If we *c* our sins, he is faithful

conform—to agree with and try to be like someone; to do what others say to do.

Ro 8:29 predestined to be *c* to the likeness
1Pe 1:14 do not *c* to the evil desires you had

conscience—the sense of knowing if something is good or bad; a sense of right and wrong.

Ro 2:15 their *c* also bearing witness,
Tit 1:15 their minds and *c* are corrupted.
Heb 9:14 cleanse our *c* from acts that lead

consecrate—to set aside or dedicate for God's use.

Ex 13:2 "*C* to me every firstborn male.
Lev 20:7 "*C* yourselves and be holy,

consider—to think about carefully.

Jdg 19:30 Think about it! *C* it!

console—to comfort.

conspire—to plan together to do evil.

consult—to ask the advice or opinion of someone.

consume—1. to use up or eat up; 2. to destroy completely.

Jn 2:17 "Zeal for your house will *c* me."
Heb 12:29 for our "God is a *c* fire."

contempt—lack of respect; looking down on someone or something as being worthless.

Pr 14:31 He who oppresses the poor shows *c*
1Th 5:20 do not treat prophecies with *c.*

contend—to struggle, as in a contest or against difficulties.

content—satisfied.

Php 4:11 to be *c* whatever the circumstances.
Heb 13:5 and be *c* with what you have,

contrite—to feel sorry for one's sins; to feel repentant.

Ps 51:17 a broken and *c* heart,
Isa 66:2 he who is humble and *c* in spirit,

convert—a person who has changed from one belief to another.

1Ti 3:6 He must not be a recent *c*

convict—1. to prove one wrong; 2. to make a person feel sorrow.

Jn 16:8 he will *c* the world of guilt in regard

copper—a common metal, easy to work with; often used to make coins.

Cornelius—a Roman to whom Peter preached the gospel; he became the first Gentile Christian (Ac 10).

cornerstone—the first or most important stone laid when constructing a building.

Eph 2:20 with Christ Jesus himself as the chief *c.*

corrupt—1. (*v.*) to change from good to bad; 2. (*adj.*) wicked.

Ge 6:11 Now the earth was *c* in God's sight
1Co 15:33 "Bad company *c* good character."

counsel—to give advice to.

Pr 15:22 Plans fail for lack of *c,*

Counselor—another name for the Holy Spirit.

Jn 14:26 But the *C,* the Holy Spirit,
Jn 15:26 "When the *C* comes, whom I will

covenant—1. an agreement between two people or two groups of people, in which both usually make specific promises; 2. the promises of God for salvation.

Ge 9:9 "I now establish my *c* with you

Ex 19:5 if you obey me fully and keep my *c*,
Jer 31:31 "when I will make a new *c*
1Co 11:25 "This cup is the new *c* in my blood;
Heb 9:15 Christ is the mediator of a new *c*,

covet—to want for oneself something that belongs to another person.
Ex 20:17 "You shall not *c* your neighbor's

crafty—sly, clever.
Pr 12:2 but the LORD condemns a *c* man.

crave—to desire strongly; to feel a deep need for.
1Pe 2:2 newborn babies, *c* pure spiritual

create—to make; to bring into being.
Ge 1:1 In the beginning God *c* the heavens
Ps 51:10 *C* in me a pure heart, O God,
Col 1:16 For by him all things were *c*:
Rev 10:6 who *c* the heavens and all that is

crime—an unlawful act.

criminal—someone who commits an unlawful act.
Lk 23:32 Two other men, both *c*,

cripple—a disabled person or animal.

cross—a tall beam with a crossbar on which a criminal was hung or tied to die.
Mt 10:38 and anyone who does not take his *c*
Gal 6:14 in the *c* of our Lord Jesus Christ,
Php 2:8 even death on a *c*!
Col 2:14 he took it away, nailing it to the *c*.
Heb 12:2 set before him endured the *c*,

crown—a headpiece worn to symbolize glory, honor and victory.
1Co 9:25 it to get a *c* that will last forever.
2Ti 4:8 store for me the *c* of righteousness,
Rev 2:10 and I will give you the *c* of life.

crucify—to put to death by nailing or tying a person's body to a cross.
Mt 27:22 They all answered, "*C* him!"
1Co 1:23 but we preach Christ *c*: a stumbling
Gal 2:20 I have been *c* with Christ

cruel—causing envy, grief or pain.

cubit—a measure of length in Bible times; about 18 inches.

cupbearer—an officer of considerable responsibility who tasted the king's food and wine before serving them to him (Ne 1:11).

curse—1. (*v.*) to ask God to bring evil or injury to; 2. (*n.*) a prayer or desire that evil or injury come upon someone.
Lev 20:9 "If anyone *c* his father or mother,
Lk 6:28 bless those who *c* you, pray
Gal 3:13 "*C* is everyone who is hung on a tree."

custom—a practice common to a particular place or group of people.
Mk 15:6 Now it was the *c* at the Feast
Ac 17:2 As his *c* was, Paul went into the synagogue

cymbals—a musical instrument; round metal disks either struck with a stick or struck together to produce a clanging sound.

cypress—an evergreen tree of the pine family.

D

Daniel—a young Jewish exile; he lived in Babylon during the reign of several kings, including Nebuchadnezzar. He prayed to God rather than obey an order to pray only to the king and was thrown into a lion's den (Da 1-6).

daughter—a female descendant.

David—the son of Jesse; anointed by Samuel to become king of Israel (1Sa 16:1-13); killed the giant Goliath (1Sa 17); during his reign Israel's place in the land of Canaan was made secure.

day—1. the period of time between dawn and darkness; 2. a specified time.
Ge 1:5 God called the light "*d*,"
Ps 118:24 This is the *d* the Lord has made;
Ecc 12:1 Creator in the *d* of your youth,
Joel 2:31 and dreadful *d* of the LORD.
Mic 4:1 In the last *d*
Lk 11:3 Give us each *d* our daily bread.
Heb 1:2 in these last *d* he has spoken to us
2Pe 3:8 With the Lord a *d* is like

deacon—a church officer whose qualifications are given in 1 Ti 3:8-13.

death—the end of physical life; also the penalty for sin (Ro 6:23).
Ps 23:4 the valley of the shadow of *d*,
Ecc 7:2 for *d* is the destiny of every man;
Isa 25:8 he will swallow up *d* forever.
1Co 15:21 For since *d* came through a man,
1Co 15:55 "Where, O *d*, is your sting?"
Rev 21:4 There will be no more *d*

debauchery—living an immoral life or a life without religion; living to please only oneself.

Deborah—a prophetess who led Israel to victory over the Canaanites (Jdg 4–5).

debt—something that one person owes another.
Mt 6:12 Forgive us our *d*,

deceive—(*v.*) to fool or trick; to lie.
Ge 3:13 "The serpent *d* me, and I ate."
Gal 6:7 Do not be *d*: God cannot be
1Jn 1:8 we *d* ourselves and the truth is not

declare—to make known formally; to state forcefully.
Ps 19:1 The heavens *d* the glory of God;
Eph 6:20 Pray that I may *d* it fearlessly,

decree—1. (*v.*) to order or command; 2. (*n.*) an order or law given by someone with power and authority.

dedicate—to set apart for a special purpose, often for God's use.

defect—imperfection; fault.

defile—to make something that is good and pure into something impure or unclean.

defraud—to cheat someone by trickery.

Deity—God.
Col 2:9 of the *D* lives in bodily form,

delight— something that gives great pleasure.
Ps 119:47 for I *d* in your commands
Mt 12:18 the one I love, in whom I *d*;

deliver—to rescue; to set free.

demon—evil spirit. A demon-possessed person is one who is controlled by evil spirits.
Mk 5:15 possessed by the legion of *d*,
Jas 2:19 Good! Even the *d* believe that

denarius—a small Roman coin made of silver. During Jesus' earthly ministry, one denarius was the payment for about one day's work.

denounce—to say a person or thing is evil.

deposit—something pledged or given as part of the payment.
Eph 1:14 who is a *d* guaranteeing our

depraved (depravity)—evil or sinful.
Php 2:15 fault in a crooked and *d* generation,
2Pe 2:19 they themselves are slaves of *d*

deprive—to take something away from.
Am 5:12 *d* the poor of justice

depths—the deepest part of a thing.
Ps 130:1 Out of the *d* I cry
La 3:55 from the *d* of the pit.

descendant—a member of a particular family line.

desecrate—to treat without respect or reverence.

desolate—not lived in; lonely; deserted.

despise—to look down on with contempt.
Pr 1:7 but fools *d* wisdom
Tit 2:15 Do not let anyone *d* you.

destiny—(*n.*) a predetermined course of events.
Php 3:19 Their *d* is destruction,

destitute—not having necessary things such as money and food.

destroy—to ruin completely.

detest—to hate.

devastate—to bring to ruin by violent action.
Jer 19:8 I will *d* this city

devil—the great enemy of God and tempter of people.
Lk 4:2 forty days he was tempted by the *d*.
Eph 6:11 stand against the *d* schemes.
2Ti 2:26 and escape from the trap of the *d*,
Jas 4:7 Resist the *d*, and he will flee
1Pe 5:8 Your enemy the *d* prowls

devote—to set apart for a special person or for a special reason; to set apart for God's use.

devour—1. to eat up greedily; 2. to destroy.
1Pe 5:8 looking for someone to *d*.

devout—religious; giving much time to prayer and worship.

die—1. to become lifeless; 2. to become insensitive to, as to die to, the law (Gal 2:19).
Ge 2:17 when you eat of it you will surely *d*."
Ecc 3:2 a time to be born and a time to *d*.
Eze 18:4 soul who sins is the one who will *d*.
Jn 11:26 and believes in me will never *d*.
1Co 15:22 in Adam all *d*, so in Christ all will
Php 1:21 to live is Christ and to *d* is gain.

diligence (diligent)—characterized by hard work or earnest effort.

disaster—a sudden event bringing great damage, loss or destruction.
Dt 31:29 *d* will fall upon you

discern—to understand; to come to know the difference between two or more things.
Php 1:10 you may be able to *d* what is best

disciple—a follower or student, especially one who believes what the leader teaches. Anyone who believes in Jesus is his disciple.
Lk 14:27 and follow me cannot be my *d*.
Jn 13:35 men will know that you are my *d*,

discipline—1. (*v.*) to correct; to teach what is right; 2. (*n.*) training that corrects, molds or perfects moral character.
Pr 29:17 *D* your son, and he will give you
Heb 12:6 the Lord *d* those he loves,
Rev 3:19 Those whom I love I rebuke and *d*.

disgrace—to bring shame to.

disobey (disobedient)—to fail to obey.
1Pe 2:8 because they *d* the message

disown—to reject someone or something so completely that it no longer belongs to you.
Mt 26:34 you will *d* me three times."
2Ti 2:12 If we *d* him,

disperse—to scatter; to spread around.

dispute—to argue irritably.

dissension—disagreement; quarreling.

distress— suffering, misery, agony.
Ps 57:6 I was bowed down in *d*.
Ro 2:9 There will be trouble and *d*

divination—seeing into the future by magic.
Lev 19:26 "Do not practice *d* or sorcery.

divine—given by God; belonging to God.
Ro 1:20 his eternal power and *d* nature

divorce—to legally dissolve a marriage.
Mal 2:16 "I hate *d*," says the LORD God
Mt 19:3 for a man to *d* his wife for any
1Co 7:11 And a husband must not *d* his wife.

doctrine—teachings or beliefs about God.
1Ti 4:16 Watch your life and *d* closely.
Tit 2:1 is in accord with sound *d*.

dominion—power; rule.
Ps 22:28 for *d* belongs to the LORD
Eph 1:21 far above all rule and authority, power and *d*,

doom—1. (*v.*) to make certain something will fail or be destroyed; 2. (*n.*) fate; condemnation; ruin.

door—a barrier that can be opened and closed; Christians open the doors of their hearts to Jesus.
Mt 7:7 and the *d* will be opened to you.
Rev 3:20 I stand at the *d* and knock.

doubt—uncertainty.
Mt 21:21 if you have faith and do not *d*,
Mk 11:23 and does not *d* in his heart
Jas 1:6 he must believe and not *d*,

dread—great fear.

dream—thoughts, images or emotion occurring during sleep; God sometimes spoke to his people through dreams.
Da 2:4 Tell your servants the *d*,

dross—the impure scum that floats on the surface of molten metals; sometimes used as a picture of the wicked.

drought—a long period of time without rain.

dwelling—place in which people live; house; in Scripture usually refers to the place where God lives.
1Ki 8:30 Hear from heaven, your *d* place,
Ps 84:1 How lovely is your *d* place,

E

earth—the place that God created for human beings to live.
Ge 1:1 God created the heavens and the *e*.
Ps 24:1 *e* is the LORD's and everything
Mt 6:10 done on *e* as it is in heaven.
Mt 24:35 Heaven and *e* will pass away,
Lk 2:14 on *e* peace to men
Php 2:10 in heaven and on *e* and under the *e*,
2Pe 3:13 to a new heaven and a new *e*,

Eden—the location of the beautiful garden God planted for Adam and Eve.

edict—an order or law made by a person who has the power to enforce it.

edify—to teach someone to live a godly life, or to help someone to live in such a way.
1Co 14:4 but he who prophesies *e* the church.

Egypt—one of the most powerful nations of ancient times, located in the northeast corner of Africa; the Israelites were captives in Egypt at the beginning of the book of Exodus.

elders—1. the older men of a town or nation; they were the leaders of their community and made all the important decisions; 2. the leaders of the church.
1Ti 5:17 The *e* who direct the affairs
Tit 1:5 and appoint *e* in every town,

election—the choosing of Christians by God, as people who belong to him. Christians are called "the elect" (2Ti 2:10).
Ro 9:11 God's purpose in *e* might stand:
2Pe 1:10 to make your calling and *e* sure.

Eli—the high priest with whom Samuel spent the early years of his life (1Sa 2:11-26).

Elijah—a prophet of the Lord who predicted a famine in Israel (1Ki 17:1) and defeated the prophets of Baal in the test of whose God would set fire to the altar (1Ki 18:16-46).

Elisha—the prophet who succeeded Elijah. He was present when God took Elijah to heaven, and he took his place as prophet to Israel (2Ki 2:1-18).

Elizabeth—the mother of John the Baptist. Mary went to visit her when she found out she, too, was pregnant (Lk 1:5-58).

enchanter—a magician or snake charmer.

encourage—to inspire with courage or hope.
2Sa 19:7 Now go out and *e* your men.
1Th 4:18 Therefore *e* each other with these words.

endure—to continue; to keep on going; to bear something that is difficult or painful.
Ps 136:1 His love *e* forever.
Mal 3:2 who can *e* the day of his coming?
2Ti 2:3 *E* hardship with us like a good

enemy—a person who opposes another person or a cause.
Mt 5:44 Love your *e* and pray
Php 3:18 many live as *e* of the cross of Christ.

enjoy—to take pleasure in.
Jdg 19:9 Stay and *e* yourself.
Jer 33:6 and will let them *e* abundant peace
3Jn 2 I pray that you may *e* good health

Enoch—a man who "walked with God." Later in life, God "took him away" (Ge 5:18-24).

entice—to tempt or lure.

envoy—a person who represents one government in its dealings with another.

envy—to want for oneself something that belongs to another person.
1Co 13:4 It does not *e*, it does not boast,

ephod—a linen apron worn by a priest over his robe. It was decorated with gold, blue, purple and scarlet yarns.

Ephraim—1. one of Joseph's sons; 2. the tribe of Israel whose members were descendants of Ephraim; 3. a name for the northern kingdom of Israel after the ten tribes of Israel and the two tribes of Judah separated from each other.

Esau—the firstborn son of Isaac and twin of Jacob (Ge 25:21-26). He sold his birthright to Jacob for a pot of stew (Ge 25:29-34) and was tricked out of his blessing by this same brother (Ge 27).

esteem—1. (*v.*) to value; to consider important; 2. (*n.*) high regard or respect.
Pr 22:1 to be *e* is better than silver or gold.
Isa 53:3 he was despised, and we *e* him not.

Esther—a Jewish woman who lived in Persia (Est 2:7) and became queen (Est 2:8-18). Upon being told of a plot to kill the Jews, she went to the king and pleaded for the Jewish people and thus saved them (Est 3–4; 7–9).

eternal—without beginning or end; forever; timeless.
Dt 33:27 The *e* God is your refuge,
Jn 3:16 him shall not perish but have *e* life.
Ro 6:23 but the gift of God is *e* life
1Jn 5:13 you may know that you have *e* life.

eunuch—a man whose sex organs have been removed so that he cannot produce children. Often in Bible times these men were important officials in royal palaces.

Eve—the first woman God created (Ge 2:20-24). Her name means "mother of all the living" (Ge 3:20).

everlasting—forever; without end.
Ps 90:2 from *e* to *e* you are God.
Isa 9:6 *E* Father, Prince of Peace.
Isa 55:3 I will make an *e* covenant with you,
Jn 6:47 the truth, he who believes has *e* life.

evil—wicked; doing things against God's will.
Ge 2:9 of the knowledge of good and *e*.
Ps 23:4 I will fear no *e*.
Mt 6:13 but deliver us from the *e* one."
Ro 12:9 Hate what is *e;* cling
Ro 12:17 Do not repay anyone *e* for *e*.
Eph 6:16 all the flaming arrows of the *e* one.

exalt—to praise; to raise to an important position.

Ps 118:28 you are my God, and I will *e* you.
Ps 148:13 for his name alone is *e*;
Pr 14:34 Righteousness *e* a nation,
Mt 23:12 For whoever *e* himself will be

examine—to look over carefully; to test.
1Co 11:28 A man ought to *e* himself

exclaim—to cry out or speak in sudden or strong emotion.
Lk 1:42 In a loud voice she *e*: "Blessed

exclude—to leave out.

execute—to put to death, especially as punishment for an illegal act.
Lk 23:32 were also led out with him to be *e*.

exile—1. (*v.*) to force someone to leave his or her country or home; 2. (*n.*) forced removal from one's country or home.

exodus—the departure of a large group of people from one place to go to another. The book of Exodus is the story of the Israelites' journey from Egypt to Canaan.

expanse—the atmosphere or sky as seen from the earth.
Ge 1:8 God called the *e* "sky."

exploit—to take unfair advantage of.

extol—to praise.
Ps 34:1 I will *e* the LORD at all times;
Ps 95:2 and *e* him with music and song.

extortion—something gotten from a person by force or by using other illegal means.

Ezekiel—a priest who was called to be a prophet to the Jewish people when they were in exile in Babylon (Eze 1–3). He had many visions from the Lord (Eze 37; 40).

Ezra—a priest and teacher of the Law; he led a group of Jewish exiles back to Israel and helped them reestablish the temple of God and restore proper worship (Ezr 7–8).

F

fail—to be unsuccessful.
Ecc 6:6 but *f* to enjoy his prosperity
1Co 13:8 Love never *f*.

faint—1. (*adj.*) lacking courage; 2. (*v.*) to lose courage.
Ps 142:3 When my spirit grows *f* within me;
Lk 21:26 Men will *f* from terror,

faith—belief and trust in God; knowing that God is real, even though one can't see him.
Hab 2:4 but the righteous will live by his *f*
Mt 17:20 if you have *f* as small as a mustard
Lk 7:9 I have not found such great *f*
Ro 1:17 "The righteous will live by *f*."
Ro 3:22 comes through *f* in Jesus Christ
1Co 13:2 and if I have a *f* that can move
2Co 5:7 We live by *f*, not by sight.
Eph 6:16 to all this, take up the shield of *f*,
1Ti 6:12 Fight the good fight of the *f*.
Heb 11:1 *f* is being sure of what we hope for
Heb 11:8 By *f* Abraham, when called to go
Heb 12:2 the author and perfecter of our *f*
Jas 2:26 so *f* without deeds is dead.

faithful (faithfulness)—trustworthy; loyal.
Ps 145:13 The LORD is *f* to all his promises
La 3:23 great is your *f*.
Mt 25:21 "Well done, good and *f* servant!
Ro 12:12 patient in affliction, *f* in prayer.
1Co 10:13 And God is *f*; he will not let you
1Jn 1:9 he is *f* and just and will forgive us
Rev 1:5 who is the *f* witness, the firstborn

false (falsehood)—a lie.
Ex 20:16 "You shall not give *f* testimony

family—a group of people who are related to each other.
Ps 68:6 God sets the lonely in *f*,
Lk 9:61 go back and say good-by to my *f*."
1Ti 3:4 He must manage his own *f* well

famine—1. a time when there is not enough food; 2. any severe shortage.
Am 8:11 but a *f* of hearing the words
Mt 24:7 There will be *f* and earthquakes

fast—1. (*adj.*) firmly fixed; not movable; 2. (*v.*) to go without food for a period of time.
Ps 139:10 your right hand will hold me *f*.
Mt 6:16 "When you *f*, do not look somber

father—a male parent; God is also known as one's father.
Ge 2:24 this reason a man will leave his *f*
Ge 17:4 You will be the *f* of many nations.
Ex 20:12 "Honor your *f* and your mother,
Mt 6:9 "Our *F* in heaven,
Lk 11:11 "Which of you *f*, if your son asks
Jn 10:30 I and the *F* are one."
Jn 14:6 No one comes to the *F*

favor—goodwill; a positive attitude toward another person.
1Sa 20:3 I have found *f* in your eyes,

fear—(*v.*) 1. to respect highly; to feel reverence and awe for; 2. to be afraid of; (*n.*) 1. profound reverence toward God; 2. anticipation or awareness of danger.
Dt 6:13 *F* the LORD your God, serve him
Ps 91:5 You will not *f* the terror of night
Ps 111:10 *f* of the LORD is the beginning
Isa 41:10 So do not *f*, for I am with you
Php 2:12 to work out your salvation with *f*

feast—a special celebration that was part of the Jewish religion.
Ezr 6:22 with joy the *F* of Unleavened Bread,
Jn 4:45 in Jerusalem at the Passover *F*,

fellowship—companionship or friendship.
1Jn 1:6 claim to have *f* with him yet walk
1Jn 1:7 we have *f* with one another,

fertile—producing fruit in great quantities; productive.

festival—a religious celebration.
Nu 29:12 Celebrate a *f* to the LORD

fig—1. a brownish pear-shaped fruit that grows in countries near the Mediterranean Sea; 2. the tree that grows this fruit.

firstborn—a family's first child. The firstborn son in an Israelite family became the head of the family when his father died, and he received twice as much money and property as each of his brothers.
Ex 11:5 Every *f* son in Egypt will die,

firstfruits—the first vegetables, fruits and grains harvested from the field.
Ex 23:19 "Bring the best of the *f* of your soil

flesh—1. the soft parts of the bodies of humans and animals; 2. the believer's sinful nature.
Job 6:12 Is my *f* bronze?
Php 3:3 put no confidence in the *f*

flock—a collection of sheep under the care of a shepherd.
Ps 65:13 The meadows are covered with *f*
Isa 40:11 He tends his *f* like a shepherd:

flog—to beat with a stick or a whip.

flood—a large amount of water that covers the ground, as in the time of Noah (Ge 6–8).

foe—an enemy.
Ps 61:3 a strong tower against the *f.*

folly—foolishness; the lack of wisdom.
Pr 26:5 Answer a fool according to his *f,*
2Ti 3:9 their *f* will be clear to everyone.

fool—a person who is not wise.
Ps 14:1 The *f* says in his heart,
Lk 12:20 "But God said to him, 'You *f*!

forefather—a male ancestor.

forever—for a limitless time.
Dt 32:40 As surely as I live *f,*
Ps 136:1 His love endures *f.*

forgive—to pardon or excuse; to no longer blame or be angry with someone who has done you wrong.
Mt 6:14 For if you *f* men when they sin
Lk 23:34 Jesus said, "Father, *f* them,
Col 3:13 *F* as the Lord forgave you.
1Jn 1:9 and just and will *f* us our sins

forsake—to leave another completely alone, with no hope that you will ever return.
Jos 1:5 I will never leave you nor *f* you.
Isa 55:7 Let the wicked *f* his way
Mt 27:46 my God, why have you *f* me?"

fortified—to make strong, such as a town with a wall.

fortress—a city that is fortified.

fragrance (fragrant)—a sweet or pleasant odor.
SS 4:10 the *f* of your perfume
Php 4:18 They are a *f* offering,

free (freedom)—not bound; liberated.
Jn 8:32 and the truth will set you *f.*"
Ro 6:18 You have been set *f* from sin
2Co 3:17 the Spirit of the Lord is, there is *f.*

friend—a person who loves and respects another person.
Pr 18:24 there is a *f* who sticks closer
Jn 15:13 that he lay down his life for his *f.*
Jas 4:4 Anyone who chooses to be a *f*

fruitful—productive; yielding much fruit.
Ge 1:22 "Be *f* and increase in number
Jn 15:2 cleans so that it will be even more *f.*

fulfill (fulfillment)—to complete a promise or project.
Ps 116:14 I will *f* my vows to the LORD
Mk 14:49 But the Scriptures must be *f.*"
Ro 13:10 Therefore love is the *f* of the law.

fury—intense anger.
Ge 34:7 They were filled with grief and *f,*

G

Gabriel—the angel who announced the births of John the Baptist and Jesus (Lk 1:11-20, 26-38).

Galilee—the northern part of Palestine. Jesus grew up, preached and did most of his miracles there. Today this area is in northern Israel.

gall—1. a plant with an extremely bitter-tasting fruit; 2. the liquid made by the liver.
Mt 27:34 mixed with *g;* but after tasting it,

genealogy—a list of a person's ancestors or descendants; a family tree.

generation—the entire number of people born and living at about the same time. Grandparents, parents and children are three different generations.
Ps 102:12 your renown endures through all *g.*
Lk 1:48 now on all *g* will call me blessed,

Gentile—anyone who is not a Jew.
Ro 3:9 and *G* alike are all under sin.
Ro 11:13 as I am the apostle to the *G,*

Gideon—a judge who freed Israel from the rule and terror of the Midianites (Jdg 6–8). He asked for a sign from God, and God showed him his will by means of dew and a fleece (Jdg 6:36-40).

gift—1. a present; 2. a talent or ability.
Ro 6:23 but the *g* of God is eternal life
1Co 12:4 There are different kinds of *g,*
2Co 9:15 be to God for his indescribable *g*!

glean—to pick up the grain or fruit left behind after harvesting; usually a way for the poor to get food.

glorify—to praise and honor in worship.
Ps 34:3 *G* the LORD with me;
Jn 17:1 *G* your Son, that your Son may

glory—1. honor; praise; 2. a source of pride or worthiness.
Ps 8:5 and crowned him with *g* and honor.
Ps 19:1 The heavens declare the *g* of God;
Lk 2:14 "*G* to God in the highest,
Jn 1:14 We have seen his *g,* the *g* of the One
1Co 10:31 whatever you do, do it all for the *g*
Rev 4:11 to receive *g* and honor and power

glutton—a person who eats too much.

gnash—to grind (one's teeth) together.
Mt 8:12 there will be weeping and *g* of teeth."

goat—an animal raised for its meat and milk; sometimes used in religious sacrifices.

God—the supreme creator and the powerful force of the universe; the one who is to be worshiped.
Ge 1:1 In the beginning *G* created
Ex 20:5 the LORD your *G,* am a jealous *G,*
Nu 23:19 *G* is not a man, that he should lie,
Dt 6:4 LORD our *G,* the LORD is one.
Dt 6:5 Love the LORD your *G*
Ps 46:1 *G* is our refuge and strength,
Jn 1:18 ever seen *G,* but *G* the One
Jn 3:16 "For *G* so loved the world that he
Jn 4:24 *G* is spirit, and his worshipers must
1Jn 4:16 *G* is love.

Rev 4:8 holy is the Lord *G* Almighty,

godly—to be devoted and loving toward God, wanting to do his will.

1Ti 4:7 train yourself to be *g.*

2Pe 3:11 live holy and *g* lives

Golgotha—the hill outside Jerusalem where Jesus was hung on a cross.

Goliath—the Philistine giant who was killed by David (1Sa 17; 21:9).

gospel—1. the good news that Jesus died for sins and rose again; 2. any of the first four books of the New Testament.

Ro 1:16 I am not ashamed of the *g,*

1Co 9:16 Woe to me if I do not preach the *g*!

1Co 15:2 By this *g* you are saved,

gossip—to talk too much about others, especially in a way that is hurtful.

2Co 12:20 slander, *g,* arrogance and disorder.

grace—an undeserved favor or gift; the undeserved forgiveness, kindness and mercy that God gives us.

Ro 3:24 and are justified freely by his *g*

Ro 5:20 where sin increased, *g* increased all

2Co 12:9 "My *g* is sufficient for you,

Eph 2:5 it is by *g* you have been saved.

Tit 3:7 having been justified by his *g,*

greed—selfish desire for more money or possessions than one needs.

Lk 12:15 on your guard against all kinds of *g;*

Col 3:5 evil desires and *g,* which is idolatry.

grieve—to cause someone pain or sorrow.

Jn 16:20 You will *g,* but your grief will turn

Eph 4:30 do not *g* the Holy Spirit of God,

guarantee—a pledge that something will take place.

Eph 1:14 who is a deposit *g* our inheritance

guide—to direct or point out the way.

Ps 23:3 He *g* me in paths of righteousness

guilty—deserving punishment for having broken a law or commandment.

Ex 34:7 does not leave the *g* unpunished;

Heb 10:22 to cleanse us from a *g* conscience

Jas 2:10 at just one point is *g* of breaking all

H

Hades—hell; the place where the spirits of the dead live.

Mt 16:18 the gates of *H* will not overcome it.

Hagar—a servant of Sarah and one of Abraham's wives; the mother of Ishmael (Ge 16:1-6; 25:12).

Haggai—a prophet who encouraged the Israelites returning from exile in Babylon to rebuild the temple (Ezr 5:1; Hag 1-2).

hallelujah—praise the Lord; a song of praise.

Rev 19:1 "*H!* Salvation and glory and power

hallowed—holy; sacred.

Mt 6:9 *h* be your name,

Ham—the youngest of Noah's three sons (Ge 5:32).

Hannah—she prayed for a son and God gave her Samuel. She dedicated him to God and he lived in the temple as a boy and became a prophet and judge (1Sa 1–2).

harp—a musical instrument with twelve strings for strumming; frequently used in religious ceremonies.

harvest—the season for gathering in crops.

Ge 8:22 "As long as the earth endures, seedtime and *h,*

hate—to detest, to have extreme dislike for.

Ps 5:5 you *h* all who do wrong.

Mk 13:13 All men will *h* you because of me,

haughty—proud.

Pr 16:18 a *h* spirit before a fall.

heal—to make well again.

Lk 8:43 but no one could *h* her.

Ac 28:27 I would *h* them.'

heart—the center of a person's life, including the mind, the will and the emotions.

Dt 6:5 LORD your God with all your *h*

1Sa 16:7 but the LORD looks at the *h.*"

Ps 51:10 Create in me a pure *h,* O God,

Ps 119:11 I have hidden your word in my *h*

Ps 139:23 Search me, O God, and know my *h;*

Eze 36:26 I will give you a new *h*

Mt 5:8 Blessed are the pure in *h,*

heaven—1. the place where God lives; 2. the sky.

Ge 14:19 Creator of *h* and earth.

Mt 19:23 man to enter the kingdom of *h.*

Mk 16:19 he was taken up into *h*

Php 3:20 But our citizenship is in *h.*

Rev 21:1 Then I saw a new *h* and a new earth,

Hebrew—1. another name for an Israelite; a descendant of Abraham; 2. the language spoken by the Jews. The Old Testament was written in Hebrew.

heir—someone who receives the property or blessings of a person who has died.

Ro 8:17 then we are *h*—*h* of God

Eph 3:6 gospel the Gentiles are *h* together

herd—a large number of animals of one kind kept together in a group.

Herod—the family name of five kings who ruled Palestine under the Roman emperor: Herod the Great (Mt 2:16); Herod Antipas (Mk 6:14-29); Herod Philip (Mt 14:3; Mk 6:17); Herod Agrippa I (Ac 12:1-4,19-23); Herod Agrippa II (Ac 23:35; 25:13–26:32).

Herodias—the wife of Herod Antipas; she persuaded her daughter to ask Antipas for the head of John the Baptist (Mk 6:17).

Hezekiah—a king of Judah; he restored the temple, reinstituted proper worship and sought the Lord's help against the Assyrians.

high priest—the chief religious official in the Jewish religion. In the Old Testament he offered the most important sacrifices to God in behalf of the people.

Heb 4:14 have a great *h* who has gone

Heb 7:26 Such a *h* meets our need

hinder—to hold back; to prevent; to delay.

Mt 19:14 come to me, and do not *h* them,

holy—set apart for God; belonging to God; pure; godly.
Ex 20:8 the Sabbath day by keeping it *h.*
Lev 11:44 and be *h,* because I am *h.*
Isa 6:3 "*H, h, h* is the LORD Almighty;
Ro 12:1 as living sacrifices, *h* and pleasing
Rev 4:8 "*H, h, h* is the Lord God Almighty,

Holy Spirit—the third person of the Trinity; he lives and works in the hearts and minds of believers; he came at Pentecost in a powerful way (Ac 2). Other names are: the Spirit, Counselor and Comforter.
Ps 51:11 or take your *H* from me.
Jn 14:26 But the Counselor, the *H*
Jn 20:22 and said, "Receive the *H*
Ac 2:4 of them were filled with the *H*
Gal 5:22 But the fruit of the *H* is love, joy,

honor—to show respect to; to give credit to.
Ex 20:12 "*H* your father and your mother,
Ps 8:5 and crowned him with glory and *h.*

hope—the anticipation of something good.
Ps 42:5 Put your *h* in God,
Isa 40:31 but those who *h* in the LORD
Ro 8:24 But *h* that is seen is no *h* at all.
1Co 15:19 for this life we have *h* in Christ,
Heb 11:1 faith is being sure of what we *h* for

hordes—a loosely organized or disorderly crowd of people; usually committing harmful acts.

horror—strong and painful fear or dread.
Jer 8:21 I mourn, and *h* grips me.

hosanna—a Hebrew word of praise meaning "save."
Mt 21:9 "*H* in the highest!"

hospitality—welcoming people into one's home; sharing one's home and food with others.
Ro 12:13 Practice *h.*
1Pe 4:9 Offer *h* to one another

hostile—like an enemy; unfriendly.

human—like people rather than animals, in actions or thoughts or appearance.

humble—1. (*v.*) to make lower; 2. (*adj.*) not proud; not pretending to be important.
Ps 147:6 The LORD sustains the *h*
Mt 23:12 whoever exalts himself will be *h,*
Jas 4:10 *H* yourselves before the Lord,

humiliate—to make humble; to reduce to a lower position; to make ashamed.
1Co 11:22 and *h* those who have nothing?

humility—the absence of pride.
Php 2:3 but in *h* consider others better
1Pe 5:5 clothe yourselves with *h*

hymn—a song of praise to God.
Eph 5:19 to one another with psalms, *h*

hypocrite—a person who pretends to be better than he or she is.
Mt 6:5 when you pray, do not be like the *h,*
Mt 7:5 You *h,* first take the plank out

hyssop—a plant used to sprinkle water or blood for religious cleansing.
Ps 51:7 with *h,* and I will be clean;

I

idle—1. lacking worth or basis; 2. lazy.
Dt 32:47 They are not just *i* words
1Th 5:14 warn those who are *i,*

idol—a statue made by people and worshiped as if it had the power of a god; anything that takes the place of God in a person's life. Worshiping idols is called idolatry.
1Co 8:4 We know that an *i* is nothing at all
Col 3:5 evil desires and greed, which is *i.*

image—likeness.
Ge 1:27 So God created man in his own *i,*
Da 3:12 nor worship the *i* of gold you have set up."

Immanuel—a name for Jesus meaning "God with us."
Mt 1:23 and they will call him *I*"

immoral (immorality)—wicked; not living by right standards.
1Co 6:18 Flee from sexual *i.*
Eph 5:5 No *i,* impure or greedy person

immortal (immortality)—free from death; not able to die.
1Co 15:53 and the mortal with *i.*
1Ti 1:17 Now to the King eternal, *i,*

imperishable—not able to die or to be destroyed.
1Pe 1:23 not of perishable seed, but of *i,*

impure—not pure; not clean.
Ac 10:15 not call anything *i* that God has
1Th 4:7 For God did not call us to be *i,*

incense—1. spices burned to make a sweet-smelling smoke, as a way of worshiping God; 2. the sweet smell or the smoke of burning spices.
Ps 141:2 my prayer be set before you like *i;*
Mt 2:11 him with gifts of gold and of *i*

indignation—anger.

infirmity—physical weakness; disease.
Isa 53:4 Surely he took up our *i*

inflict—to cause to be endured.
Eze 5:8 I will *i* punishment on you
2Co 2:6 The punishment *i* on him by

inhabitant—one who lives in a particular place.
Rev 6:10 the *i* of the earth and avenge

inherit—to receive money, property or keepsakes from a person after his or her death.
Mt 5:5 for they will *i* the earth.
Mk 10:17 "what must I do to *i* eternal life?"

inheritance—money, property or keepsakes received from a person after his or her death.
Dt 4:20 to be the people of his *i,*
1Pe 1:4 and into an *i* that can never perish,

iniquity—sin; wickedness.
Ps 51:2 Wash away all my *i*
Ps 103:10 or repay us according to our *i.*
Isa 53:6 the *i* of us all.

injustice—unfairness.

inscription—1. the writing on a coin; 2. a written title or message.

instruct—to give knowledge or information; to teach.
Pr 9:9 *I* a wise man and he will be wiser
1Th 4:1 we *i* you how to live

instruction—the action of a teacher; a lesson.

Ac 1:2 after giving *i* through the Holy Spirit
2Ti 4:2 with great patience and careful *i*

insult—1. (*v.*) to treat with contempt by word or action; to offend; 2. (*n.*) an act or speech of contempt.
Ro 15:3 "The *i* of those who *i* you have fallen

insurrection—revolt or rebellion against a government.

integrity—complete honesty.

intercede—to beg or plead for another person.
Ro 8:26 but the Spirit himself *i* for us

intercession—the plea made on behalf of another person.
Isa 53:12 and made *i* for the transgressors.

intermarry—to marry someone from a different race or religion.
Dt 7:3 Do not *i* with them.

interpret—to explain the meaning of.
Mt 16:3 you cannot *i* the signs of the times.
1Co 12:30 Do all *i*? But eagerly desire

invoke—to call for help or support.
Ac 19:13 to *i* the name of the Lord Jesus

Isaac—the promised son of Abraham and Sarah (Ge 17:19; 21:1-7); offered as a sacrifice by Abraham (Ge 22); married Rebekah (Ge 24) and was the father of Esau and Jacob (Ge 25).

Isaiah—prophet called by God (Isa 6) to prophesy to Judah (Isa 1:1). Some of his prophecies are about the coming Messiah (Isa 53).

Ishmael—the son of Abraham and Hagar (Ge 16); he was not to be the son of the covenant (Ge 17:18-21).

Israel—1. the new name God gave to Jacob (Ge 32:28); 2. the nation made up of descendants of the twelve sons of Jacob; 3. the northern ten tribes after they separated from Judah and Benjamin.
Dt 6:4 Hear, O *I*: The LORD our God,
Lk 22:30 judging the twelve tribes of *I*.
Eph 3:6 Gentiles are heirs together with *I*,

Israelites—the people of Israel.
Ex 14:22 and the *I* went through the sea
Ro 9:27 the number of the *I* be like the sand

J

Jacob—the son of Isaac and Rebekah; he was the twin brother of Esau (Ge 25:21-26); he bought Esau's birthright for a pot of stew (Ge 25:29-34); he wrestled with God, and his name was changed to Israel (Ge 32:22-32); the descendants of his twelve sons became the nation of Israel.

James—1. one of the twelve apostles; the brother of John (Mt 4:21-22); 2. one of the twelve apostles; the son of Alphaeus (Mt 10:3); 3. the brother of Jesus (Mk 6:30); the author of the letter of James (Jas 1:1).

Japheth—one of the sons of Noah (Ge 5:32); he was blessed because he covered his father's nakedness (Ge 9:18-28).

jealous (jealousy)—1. afraid of losing someone's love or affection; 2. angry or unhappy because of what someone else has; 3. careful to guard or keep what one has.
Joel 2:18 the LORD will be *j* for his land
2Co 11:2 I am *j* for you with a godly *j*.
Gal 5:20 hatred, discord, *j*, fits of rage,

Jeremiah—a prophet called by God to prophesy to Judah (Jer 1:1-3). He is often referred to as the prophet of gloom, because he prophesied about the destruction of Judah.

Jericho—the ancient city destroyed by Joshua as the Hebrews entered Canaan (Jos 6).

Jeroboam—an official in Solomon's court; he rebelled and became the first king of the northern ten tribes of Israel (1Ki 11:26-40; 12:1-20).

Jerusalem—the political and religious center of the Jews; it was the site of many important events in the Biblical accounts; also called "Zion" and "the City of David."
2Ki 23:27 and I will reject *J*, the city I chose,
Ne 2:17 Come, let us rebuild the wall of *J*,
Ps 137:5 If I forget you, O *J*,
Jn 4:20 where we must worship is in *J*."
Rev 21:2 I saw the Holy City, the new *J*,

Jesse—the father of David, king of Israel (1Sa 16:10-13).

Jesus—The Son of God; the Savior of the world; the Messiah, through whom people can be saved.
Mt 1:21 you are to give him the name *J*,
Php 2:10 name of *J* every knee should bow,

Jew—an Israelite; one of the chosen people of God; a descendant of Abraham through Jacob.
Mt 2:2 who has been born king of the *J*?
Ro 3:29 Is God the God of *J* only?
Gal 3:28 There is neither *J* nor Greek,

Jezebel—the wife of King Ahab (1Ki 16:31). She promoted Baal worship in Israel (1Ki 16:32-33), had many prophets of God killed (1Ki 18:4,13) and opposed the prophet Elijah (1Ki 19:1-2).

Joab—the commander of the armies of King David.

Joash—the boy-king of Judah; he repaired the temple (2Ki 12).

Job—a wealthy man from the land of Uz who feared God (Job 1:1-5). His righteousness was tested by disaster (Job 1:6-22) and personal affliction (Job 2), but in the end God restored wealth and honor to him (Job 42).

John—1. the Baptist (Mk 1:2-8); the son of Zechariah and Elizabeth (Lk 1). He preached in the desert, preparing the people for Jesus (Mt 3:11-12); baptized Jesus in the Jordan River (Mt 3:13-17); executed by Herod (Mk 6:14-29); 2. one of the twelve apostles; brother of the apostle James (Lk 5:1-10); wrote the Gospel of John, the letters of John (2Jn 1; 3Jn 1) and the book of Revelation (Rev 1:1; 22:8).

John Mark—See Mark, John.

Jonah—a prophet who was called to preach to Nineveh but instead fled to Tarshish (Jnh 1:1-3). While at sea a great storm arose because of his disobedience; he was thrown into the sea and was swallowed by a large fish (Jnh 1:4-17). He then repented and went to Nineveh and preached, telling the people to repent (Jnh 3).

Jonathan—a son of King Saul (1Sa 13:16) who had a special friendship with David (1Sa 18:1-4; 19–20; 23:16-18). When he was killed (1Sa 31) David mourned greatly for him (2Sa 1).

Joppa—an ancient walled town on the coast of Palestine.

Jordan—a river in Palestine that flows between the Sea of Galilee and the Dead Sea.
Jos 4:22 "Israel crossed the *J* on dry ground."
Mt 3:6 baptized by him in the *J* River.

Joseph—1. the son of Jacob and Rachel (Ge 30:24), who was favored by his father but hated by his brothers (Ge 37:3-4). He was sold into slavery (Ge 37:12-36), taken to Egypt and eventually given a high position under Pharaoh (Ge 41:41-57); 2. the husband of Mary and childhood father of Jesus (Mt 1:16-24; 2:13-19); 3. a disciple of Jesus from Arimathea; he gave his tomb for Jesus' burial (Mt 27:57-61); 4. the original name of Barnabas (Ac 4:36).

Joshua—1. the son of Nun (Nu 13:8); Moses' aide and later his successor (Dt 31:1-18); he led the Israelites across the Jordan River into Canaan (Jos 3–4); was the commander in the conquest of Jericho (Jos 6), Ai (Jos 7–8), and a large part of Canaan (Jos 10–12); oversaw the dividing up of the promised land among the twelve tribes of Israel (Jos 13–22); 2. the high priest in Israel during the rebuilding of both the temple (Hag 1–2) and the altar (Ezr 3:2,8); also called Jeshua.

Josiah—godly king of Judah for thirty-one years shortly before the destruction of Jerusalem.

Judah—1. Jacob's fourth son; 2. the tribe of Israel whose members were descendants of Judah; 3. a name for the southern kingdom after Judah and Benjamin separated from the northern ten tribes.
Zec 10:4 From *J* will come the cornerstone,
Mt 2:6 Bethlehem, in the land of *J*,
Rev 5:5 See, the Lion of the tribe of *J*,

Judaism—the teachings of the Jewish religion.

Judas—1. one of the twelve apostles (Lk 6:16; Ac 1:13); was probably also called Thaddaeus (Mt 10:3); 2. one of the brothers of Jesus (Mt 13:55); author of the last letter in the New Testament (Jude 1); 3. one of the twelve apostles, also called Iscariot; he betrayed Jesus (Mk 3:19; 14:10-50) and then hung himself (Mt 27:3-5).

Judea—the area of Palestine where the tribe of Judah lived after the exile.
Mk 10:1 into the region of *J* and across the Jordan.
Gal 1:22 to the churches of *J* that are in Christ.

judge—to decide if something is good or bad; to condemn.
Ps 9:8 He will *j* the world in righteousness;
Mt 7:1 "Do not *j*, or you too will be judged.
2Ti 4:1 who will *j* the living and the dead,

judgment—1. a decision or opinion; 2. a decision of guilt or innocence made by a judge in a court of law; punishment decided on by a court; 3. a decision from God, especially the final judgment when God will reward those who believe in him and condemn all others to hell.
Dt 1:17 of any man, for *j* belongs to God.
Ps 119:66 Teach me knowledge and good *j*,
Isa 66:16 the LORD will execute *j*
Mt 5:21 who murders will be subject to *j*.'
Mt 12:36 have to give account on the day of *j*
Jn 5:22 but has entrusted all *j* to the Son,
Ro 14:10 stand before God's *j* seat.
2Co 5:10 appear before the *j* seat of Christ,

just—righteous, legally correct.
Ps 111:7 The works of his hands are faithful and *j*;
Rev 16:7 true and *j* are your judgments."

justice—fairness.
Isa 30:18 For the LORD is a God of *j*.
Isa 61:8 "For I, the LORD, love *j*;
Zec 7:9 'Administer true *j*; show mercy
Lk 11:42 you neglect *j* and the love of God.

justify (justification)—to erase someone's sins; to declare righteous.
Ac 13:39 him everyone who believes is *j*
Ro 3:24 and are *j* freely by his grace
Ro 4:25 and was raised to life for our *j*.
Ro 5:1 since we have been *j* through faith,
Gal 3:24 to Christ that we might be *j* by faith.

KL

kind—considerate, loving.
Eph 4:32 Be *k* and compassionate

king—ruler over a country or kingdom; Christ is often referred to as the King of kings.
1Ki 22:3 The *k* of Israel had said
Rev 19:16 he has this name written: *K* OF *k*

kingdom—an area or group of people headed by a king; God's kingdom, or the kingdom of heaven, is made up of all believers.
Ex 19:6 you will be for me a *k* of priests
Mt 3:2 "Repent, for the *k* of heaven is near."
Mt 5:3 for theirs is the *k* of heaven.
Mt 6:33 But seek first his *k* and his
Mt 16:19 the keys of the *k* of heaven;
Jn 18:36 "My *k* is not of this world.
1Co 15:24 hands over the *k* to God the Father
Rev 11:15 of the world has become the *k*

kinsman-redeemer—in Old Testament times a close male relative who had the responsibility to marry a widow and buy ("redeem") her husband's property (Dt 25:5-6).
Ruth 3:9 over me, since you are a *k*."

Kish—the father of King Saul, the first king of Israel.

knowledge—possessing the facts, understanding.
Pr 1:7 of the LORD is the beginning of *k*,
Hos 4:6 are destroyed from lack of *k*.
1Co 8:1 *K* puffs up, but love builds up.

Laban—the brother of Rebekah (Ge 24:29-51) and father of Rachel and Leah (Ge 29-31).

labor—1. (*v.*) to work; 2. (*n.*) a task; 3. (*n.*) the time just before giving birth.

Ge 5:29 the *l* and painful toil of our hands
Ex 20:9 Six days you shall *l* and do all your work,
Jer 13:21 like that of a woman in *l*?

lack—1. (*v.*) to stand in need of; 2. (*n.*) the state of being in need of something.

lamb—a principal sacrificial animal in the Old Testament; since Jesus is the supreme sacrifice of God, he is called the "Lamb of God."
Isa 53:7 he was led like a *l* to the slaughter,
Jn 1:29 *L* of God, who takes away the sin
1Co 5:7 our Passover *l*, has been sacrificed.
Rev 5:6 Then I saw a *L*, looking

lament, lamentation—a cry of grief.

law—1. God's rules, which help his people know what is right and wrong (the Ten Commandments are part of God's law); 2. (cap.) the first five books of the Bible, written by Moses.
Ps 1:2 and on his *l* he meditates day
Ps 19:7 The *l* of the LORD is perfect,
Ps 119:97 Oh, how I love your *l*!
Mt 22:40 All the *L* and the Prophets hang
Ro 8:3 For what the *l* was powerless to do
Ro 13:10 love is the fulfillment of the *l*.
Gal 3:24 So the *l* was put in charge to lead us

Lazarus—1. the poor man in one of Jesus' parables (Lk 16:19-31); 2. the brother of Mary and Martha; Jesus raised him from the dead (Jn 11:1–12:19).

Leah—the wife of Jacob; she had six sons and one daughter (Ge 29:16–30:21).

leprosy—a word used in the Bible for many different skin diseases and infections.

Levite—a member of the tribe of Levi. The Levites took care of the temple. Only Levites could become priests, but not all Levites were priests.

lewd—indecent; wicked.

life—the total substance of a person's existence; can refer to both physical and spiritual existence.
Ge 2:7 into his nostrils the breath of *l*,
Jn 3:16 shall not perish but have eternal *l*.
Jn 11:25 "I am the resurrection and the *l*.
Jn 14:6 am the way and the truth and the *l*.
Ro 6:23 but the gift of God is eternal *l*

light—the form of energy that allows a person to see; in the Old Testament it symbolized life and blessing.
Ge 1:3 "Let there be *l*," and there was *l*.
Ps 27:1 LORD is my *l* and my salvation
Ps 119:105 and a *l* for my path.
Isa 9:2 have seen a great *l*;
Mt 5:16 let your *l* shine before men,
Jn 8:12 he said, "I am the *l* of the world.
1Jn 1:5 God is *l*; in him there is no

linen—cloth made from the fiber of flax plants.

live—to be alive; may refer to both physical and spiritual existence.
Ex 20:12 so that you may *l* long
Ro 1:17 "The righteous will *l* by faith."
2Co 5:7 We *l* by faith, not by sight.
Php 1:21 to *l* is Christ and to die is gain.

locusts—a type of grasshopper. When they settle in a grain field, orchard or other cultivated area, they can devastate the crop.

Lord—refers to God as the master. (See also LORD.)
Mt 3:3 'Prepare the way for the *L*,
Lk 2:9 glory of the *L* shone around them,
Ac 16:31 replied, "Believe in the *L* Jesus,
Ro 10:13 on the name of the *L* will be saved."
Php 2:11 confess that Jesus Christ is *L*,
2Pe 1:16 and coming of our *L* Jesus Christ,
Rev 17:14 he is *L* of lords and King of kings
Rev 22:20 Come, *L* Jesus.

LORD (Yahweh)—the intimate and personal name of God; it emphasizes his role as Israel's Redeemer and covenant Lord. (See also Lord.)
Ge 2:4 When the *L* God made the earth
Ex 20:2 "I am the *L* your God, who
Ps 23:1 The *L* is my shepherd, I shall not
Ps 103:1 Praise the *L*, O my soul
Pr 1:7 The fear of the *L* is the beginning
Isa 6:3 "Holy, holy, holy is the *L* Almighty;
Isa 55:6 Seek the *L* while he may be found;

Lot—the nephew of Abraham (Ge 12:5). He chose to live in Sodom (Ge 13); Abraham pleaded with God for Lot's life when God was about to destroy Sodom (Ge 19:1-29).

lot—one of the ways used in Bible times to find out God's will about a matter. It is something like drawing straws.
Mt 27:35 divided up his clothes by casting *l*.
Ac 1:26 Then they cast *l*, and the *l* fell

love—wanting good to come to another person; being concerned and willing to work for another person's benefit.
Ex 20:6 showing *l* to thousands of those who *l* me
Ps 23:6 Surely goodness and *l* will follow
Ps 136:1-26 His *l* endures forever.
Mt 3:17 "This is my Son, whom I *l*;
Mt 5:44 *L* your enemies and pray
Mt 19:19 and " '*L* your neighbor as yourself.' "
Jn 13:34 I give you: *L* one another.
Jn 15:13 Greater *l* has no one than this,
Ro 13:10 Therefore *l* is the fulfillment
Gal 5:22 But the fruit of the Spirit is *l*, joy,
Eph 1:4 In *l* he predestined us
1Jn 3:10 anyone who does not *l* his brother.
1Jn 3:16 This is how we know what *l* is:
1Jn 4:7 for *l* comes from God.
1Jn 4:10 This is *l*: not that we loved God,
1Jn 4:16 God is *l*.

Luke—a co-worker with Paul; he wrote the books of Luke and Acts (Col 4:14).

lust—a strong desire for something wrong.
Pr 6:25 Do not *l* in your heart
Ro 1:26 God gave them over to shameful *l*.

lyre—a small lap harp with three to twelve strings.

M

Macedonia—a Roman province; the first part of Europe to receive Christianity.

Magi—men of Arabia and Persia who studied the stars. People thought they had the power to tell the meaning of dreams.
Mt 2:1 *M* from the east came to Jerusalem

maimed—crippled; having lost a part of one's body, such as an arm or leg.

majestic (majesty)—great and powerful.
Ex 15:6 was *m* in power.
Ps 8:1 how *m* is your name in all the earth!
Ps 111:3 Glorious and *m* are his deeds,

malice—hatred; wishing harm on someone else.
1Pe 2:1 rid yourselves of all *m*

Manasseh—1. the older son of Joseph and the tribe descended from him (Ge 41:51; Nu 1:34); 2. one of the kings of Judah (2Ki 21:1).

manger—a feed box for cows or other animals.
Lk 2:7 placed him in a *m,* because there

manna—the special food God gave daily to the Israelites until they reached the promised land.
Ex 16:31 people of Israel called the bread *m.*
Jn 6:49 Your forefathers ate the *m*

Mark, John—the cousin of Barnabas (Col 4:10); a helper to Paul and Barnabas (Ac 13:5); later a co-worker with Barnabas (Ac 15:39) and then Paul (Phm 24); author of the second Gospel, according to early church tradition.

marriage—the joining together before God and other people of a man and a woman to form a new family.
Mt 22:30 neither marry nor be given in *m;*
Ro 7:2 she is released from the law of *m.*
Heb 13:4 by all, and the *m* bed kept pure,

Martha—the sister of Mary and Lazarus, the man whom Jesus raised from the dead (Jn 11; 12:2).

marvelous—something that surprises, that fills one with wonder.
Ps 118:23 and it is *m* in our eyes.
Lk 2:33 mother *m* at what was said

Mary—1. the mother of Jesus (Mt 1:16-25); 2. Mary Magdalene—a woman whom Jesus freed from demons (Lk 8:2), who was present at the cross (Mk 15:40) and who came on Easter morning to the tomb (Mt 27:61); 3. the sister of Martha and Lazarus; she washed Jesus' feet with expensive perfume (Jn 12:1-8).

master—one who rules over others.
Mt 6:24 "No one can serve two *m.*
Jn 13:16 no servant is greater than his *m,*

Matthew—a tax collector who became one of the twelve apostles (Mt 9:9-13); also called Levi (Mk 2:14-17).

mediator—one who makes peace between two people or two groups who are displeased and/or angry with each other. Jesus is the mediator between us and God.1Ti 2:5 and one *m* between God and men,
Heb 9:15 For this reason Christ is the *m*

meditate—to think seriously and carefully.
Ps 1:2 and on his law he *m* day and night.
Ps 119:15 I *m* on your precepts

medium—a person who can supposedly talk with the spirits of people who have died.

meek—patient; mild; gentle.
Mt 5:5 Blessed are the *m,*

Melchizedek—a priest and king of early Salem (Jerusalem); Jesus was said to be a priest like Melchizedek (Heb 5:6).

Mephibosheth—son of Jonathan and grandson of Saul; he lived out his life under King David's protection (2Sa 9:11).

mercy—kindness and forgiveness, especially when given to a person who doesn't deserve it.
Mic 6:8 To act justly and to love *m*
Ro 9:15 "I will have *m* on whom I have *m,*
1Pe 1:3 In his great *m* he has given us new

Messiah—the "Anointed One"; Christ; the one the Jews expected to come and be their king.
Jn 1:41 "We have found the *M*"

Methuselah—a man in early Bible times who lived 969 years (Ge 5:27).

Michal—daughter of Saul, wife of David, both of whom were kings of Israel.

midwife—a woman who helps with the birth of a baby.

millstone—one of a pair of stones used to crush grain for flour.
Lk 17:2 sea with a *m* tied around his neck

minister—1. (*v.*) to serve; to give care or attention to; 2. (*n.*) one who serves others as God directs.
2Co 3:6 as *m* of a new covenant
1Ti 4:6 you will be a good *m*

miracle—an unusual happening, one that goes against the normal laws of nature. Miracles are done by the power of God.
Ps 77:14 You are the God who performs *m;*
Jn 14:11 the evidence of the *m* themselves.
Ac 2:22 accredited by God to you by *m,*
Heb 2:4 it by signs, wonders and various *m,*

Miriam—the sister of Moses and Aaron (Nu 26:59); led the Israelites in praising God in dance and song after he had parted the waters of the Red Sea (Ex 15:20-21); later temporarily struck with leprosy because she criticized Moses (Nu 12).

Moab—1. a son of Lot whose descendants became bitter enemies of the Israelites; 2. the land occupied by the Moabites, to the east of the Dead Sea.

money—a medium of exchange.
Ecc 5:10 Whoever loves *m* never has *m*
Mt 6:24 You cannot serve both God and *M.*
1Co 16:2 set aside a sum of *m* in keeping
1Ti 6:10 For the love of *m* is a root

Mordecai—cousin of Esther, queen of Persia; he and Esther saved the Jews from a plot to put them all to death.

mortal—human; able to die.
1Co 15:53 and the *m* with immortality,

Moses—the leader of Israel in the exodus out of Egypt, culminating in their passing through the Red Sea (Ex 12–14). He received the law of God at Sinai (Ex 19–23) and gave it to the people of Israel. Moses was allowed to view the land of

Canaan from the top of Mount Nebo, but died without entering it (Nu 20:1-13; Dt 34:5-12).

mother—the female parent.
Ge 2:24 and *m* and be united to his wife,
Dt 5:16 "Honor your father and your *m*,

mourn—to feel deep sorrow; to grieve.
Mt 5:4 Blessed are those who *m*,

murder—to kill someone illegally.
Ex 20:13 "You shall not *m*.

muster—to gather together, especially to gather soldiers for war.

mute—unable to speak.

myrrh—the sweet-smelling sap of the myrrh bush. It was used to make the sacred anointing oil.
Mt 2:11 of gold and of incense and of *m*.

N

Nabal—a rich sheepherder in Judah who insulted David; when David planned to take revenge, Nabal's wife Abigail brought gifts to calm David; Nabal died shortly thereafter and Abigail married David (1Sa 25:1-42).

Naboth—owner of a vineyard that King Ahab wanted and gained by having Naboth accused of blasphemy and stoned (1Ki 21:1-29).

Naomi—the mother-in-law of Ruth (Ru 1); she advised Ruth to seek marriage with Boaz (Ru 2-4).

Naphtali—a son of Jacob and father of the tribe of Naphtali (Nu 1:42-43).

nard—an expensive, pleasant-smelling oil from the spikenard, a plant that grew in India.

Nathan—the prophet of God who exposed David's sin with Bathsheba, causing David to repent (2Sa 12:1-25).

Nathanael—one of the twelve apostles (Jn 1:45-49); was probably also called Bartholomew (Mt 10:3).

Nazarene—a person who lived in or came from the town of Nazareth in Galilee.
Mk 16:6 looking for Jesus the *N*,

Nazirite—a person who separated himself or herself by taking a vow to do special work for God. This included a promise not to cut one's hair and not to drink wine.

Nebuchadnezzar—king of Babylon who took Judah into captivity.

Negev—the desert region south of Judea.
Ge 24:62 for he was living in the *N*.

Nehemiah—the Jewish "cupbearer" of King Artaxerxes of Persia (Ne 2:1); while in Jerusalem rebuilt the walls of the city (Ne 2–6) and with Ezra reestablished the worship of God there after the Babylonian exile (Ne 8).

neighbor—1. someone who lives nearby; 2. any fellow human being.
Lev 19:18 but love your *n* as yourself.
Lk 10:36 of these three do you think was a *n*

Nicodemus—a Pharisee who visited Jesus at night (Jn 3) and learned about being born again.

Nile—the primary river in Egypt.

Nineveh—the city to which Jonah was sent to preach (Jnh 1:2); the ancient capital of Assyria.

Noah—"a righteous man" in early Bible times; he built an ark, as God commanded him (Ge 6–8). God made a covenant with him never again to cover the entire earth with a flood (Ge 9).

nullify—to make of no value; to make unimportant.
Mk 7:13 Thus you *n* the word of God

O

oath—a promise in which one asks God to witness that something is true.

obey (obedience)—to do as asked; to yield to someone's commands or wishes.
Dt 6:3 careful to *o* so that it may go well
1Sa 15:22 To *o* is better than sacrifice,
Jn 14:23 loves me, he will *o* my teaching.
Ac 5:29 "We must *o* God rather than men!
Eph 6:1 *o* your parents in the Lord,

offense—an act that makes someone angry by what was done.

offering—1. something given to God as an act of worship; 2. the sacrifice of an animal to make the relationship between God and man right again. In the Old Testament, animals and grains were regularly used as offerings in an attempt to bring the people closer to God.
Ge 22:8 provide the lamb for the burnt *o*,
Isa 53:10 the LORD makes his life a guilt *o*,
Mk 12:33 is more important than all burnt *o*
Eph 5:2 as a fragrant *o* and sacrifice to God.

offspring—children.
Ge 3:15 and between your *o* and hers;
Ge 12:7 "To your *o* I will give this land."

oil—almost always refers to olive oil; used to anoint someone for a physical benefit or to set someone apart for service.
2Ki 9:6 the prophet poured *o* on Jehu's head
Lk 7:46 You did not pour *o* on my head

olive—a tree whose fruit gives olive oil, which was used for varied purposes.

oppress—to control people unfairly and cruelly by the use of one's power.
Isa 53:7 He was *o* and afflicted,
Zec 7:10 Do not *o* the widow

oracle—1. a saying or answer; 2. the word of the Lord.

ordain—1. to set apart for a specific office or duty; 2. to order or command.

ordinance—1. an official law; 2. a law made or commanded by God.

overseer—one of the terms used for leaders in the early church.
Ac 20:28 the Holy Spirit has made you *o*.
1Ti 3:2 Now the *o* must be above reproach,

oxen—strong animals that were used in various ways in farming communities.

P

pagan—a person who does not worship God, especially someone who worships idols.

1Pe 2:12 such good lives among the *p* that,

papyrus—1. a large water plant, similar to the reed, which grows in marshes and lakes. Moses' mother put him in a basket made from papyrus (Ex 2:3); 2. a paper made from this plant.

parable—a story that tells a special lesson or truth. Jesus told many parables.

paralytic—a person who is unable to move certain parts of his or her body.

Mk 2:3 bringing to him a *p,* carried by four

parents—fathers and mothers.

Pr 17:6 and *p* are the pride of their children.
Eph 6:1 Children, obey your *p* in the Lord,
Col 3:20 obey your *p* in everything,

Passover—an annual Jewish holiday that yet today reminds the Jewish people of how God freed them from slavery in Egypt. The Lord "passed over" the homes marked with the blood of a lamb on their doorframes, but he killed all the other firstborn in Egypt.

Ex 12:11 Eat it in haste; it is the LORD's *P.*

Passover lamb—the lamb killed on the Passover as a sacrifice. Jesus is our Passover lamb, because he was sacrificed for our deliverance from sin, in the same way a lamb was sacrificed when the Israelites were delivered from Egypt.

1Co 5:7 our *P* lamb, has been sacrificed.

pasture—a plot or section of grassy land used for grazing cattle.

patient (patience)—able to put up with problems or pain without complaining or becoming angry.

Ro 12:12 Be joyful in hope, *p* in affliction,
1Co 13:4 Love is *p,* love is kind.
Gal 5:22 joy, peace, *p,* kindness, goodness

patriarch—the father and ruler of a family; the head of a tribe.

Paul—a Pharisee from Tarsus (Ac 9:11); named Saul at birth (Ac 13:9). Jesus appeared to him on the road to Damascus (Ac 9:4-9), and he became a powerful apostle (Gal 1). His writings make up a significant portion of the New Testament, ranging from intricate theology to passionate letters to struggling churches.

peace—freedom from disturbance; calm.

Isa 9:6 Everlasting Father, Prince of *P.*
Lk 2:14 on earth *p* to men on whom his
Jn 14:27 *P* I leave with you; my *p*
Ro 5:1 we have *p* with God
Gal 5:22 joy, *p,* patience, kindness,

Pentecost—a Jewish feast celebrated fifty days after the Passover. Today the Christian church celebrates Pentecost because it was the day the Holy Spirit came to dwell with Christ's followers (Ac 2:1-4).

people—a collective group.

2Ch 7:14 if my *p,* who are called by my name,
1Pe 2:9 you are a chosen *p,*

perfect—flawless; without defect.

Col 1:28 we may present everyone *p* in Christ.

perish—to spoil; to be destroyed.

Ps 102:26 They will *p,* but you remain;

persecute (persecution)—to continually treat someone cruelly and unfairly, even though that person has done nothing wrong. The early Christians were persecuted for believing in Jesus as the Son of God.

Jn 15:20 they *p* me, they will *p* you
Ac 26:14 'Saul, Saul, why do you *p* me?
Ro 12:14 Bless those who *p* you; bless

persevere (perseverance)—to refuse to give up; to keep on trying; to continue in one's actions or beliefs in spite of problems.

Ro 5:3 we know that suffering produces *p;*
Heb 10:36 You need to *p* so that

Persia—ancient geographical area and kingdom located north of the Persian Gulf.

pervert—to use wrongly; to turn from what is right.

pestilence—a plague; a disease that spreads quickly and kills many people.

Peter—one of the twelve apostles; the brother of Andrew; also called Simon (Lk 6:14) and Cephas (Jn 1:42); he denied Jesus three times (Mk 14:66-72) but became a bold evangelist. He wrote the books of 1 and 2 Peter.

petition—to make a formal request.

pharaoh—the title given to the ruler of Egypt.

Pharisees—a group of Jews who obeyed very strictly both God's laws and all their own rules about God's laws.

Mt 5:20 surpasses that of the *P*

Philip—1. one of the twelve apostles (Mt 10:3); 2. a deacon (Ac 6:1-7) and evangelist in Samaria; he witnessed to an Ethiopian (Ac 8:4-40).

Philistines—enemies of the Israelites throughout much of Old Testament history; they were especially powerful during the reigns of Saul and David.

Pilate—the governor of Judea who questioned Jesus (Lk 22:66–23:25) and then sent him to Herod (Lk 23:6-12). Pilate finally consented to Jesus' crucifixion when the crowds chose Barabbas rather than Jesus to be released (Lk 23:13-25).

pity—a sympathy or sorrow for the suffering of another.

Mk 9:22 take *p* on us and help us."

plague—1. a disease that kills many people, such as the plague of boils; 2. an event that causes much suffering or loss, especially a trouble in which there is a great number of offending agents, such as the plague of locusts.

plead—to appeal earnestly; to beg.

pledge—a binding promise or agreement.

plot—to plan, usually secretly; to scheme.

Ps 83:5 With one mind they *p* together;

plowshare—the pointed part of the plow; it cuts into the soil to make rows.

plunder—1. (*v.*) to loot or rob during a war; 2. (*n.*) property taken by plundering.

pomegranate—a reddish fruit about the size of an orange. It has many seeds and a juicy pulp.

poor—those who have little money.

Dt 15:4 there should be no *p* among you,
Isa 61:1 me to preach good news to the *p*.
Mt 26:11 The *p* you will always have
1Co 13:3 If I give all I possess to the *p*
2Co 8:9 yet for your sakes he became *p*,

portico—a porch, usually at the front of a building.
2Ch 3:4 The *p* at the front of the temple

praise—1. (*v.*) to glorify; to say good things about someone or something; 2. (*n.*) approval; worship.
Ex 15:2 He is my God, and I will *p* him,
Ps 119:175 Let me live that I may *p* you,
Eph 1:12 might be for the *p* of his glory.

pray—to talk with God.
2Ch 7:14 will humble themselves and *p*
Mt 6:5 "And when you *p*, do not be like
Ro 8:26 do not know what we ought to *p*
1Th 5:16-17 Be joyful always; *p* continually;

preach—to tell the message of the gospel in public; to deliver a sermon.
Isa 61:1 me to *p* good news to the poor.
Ro 10:15 how can they *p* unless they are sent?

precept—command; law; rule.
Ps 19:8 The *p* of the LORD are right,
Ps 119:69 I keep your *p* with all my heart.

precious—valuable; of great worth.
Ps 139:17 How *p* to me are your thoughts,

predestine—to decide or decree ahead of time.
Ro 8:30 And those he *p*, he also called;
Eph 1:5 he *p* us to be adopted

pregnant—carrying an unborn child within a woman's body.

prevail—to triumph or succeed.

pride—1. (negative) the attitude that one is better than others; 2. (positive) a healthy self-respect or sense of satisfaction.
Pr 16:18 *P* goes before destruction,
Gal 6:4 Then he can take *p* in himself,

priest (priesthood)—a Levite who offered sacrifices and prayers to God for the people.
1Pe 2:9 you are a chosen people, a royal *p*,

prince—a male member of a royal family.

prison—a building where people are held, usually for committing a crime.

proclaim—to announce or declare.
1Ch 16:23 *p* his salvation day after day.
Ps 19:1 the skies *p* the work of his hands.
1Co 11:26 you *p* the Lord's death

profane—to make a holy thing impure by treating it with disrespect or irreverence.
Lev 22:32 Do not *p* my holy name.

prophecy—a message from God that a prophet brings to the people.
1Co 13:8 where there are *p*, they will cease;
2Pe 1:20 you must understand that no *p*

prophesy—to give the message of God to the people.
Joel 2:28 Your sons and daughters will *p*,
1Co 14:39 my brothers, be eager to *p*,

prophet—a person who receives messages from God to tell to his people. A prophet is called by God to speak for him.
Dt 18:18 up for them a *p* like you
Lk 24:25 believe all that the *p* have spoken!
Ac 10:43 All the *p* testify about him that
2Pe 1:19 word of the *p* made more certain,

prosper—to succeed; to achieve economic success.
Pr 11:25 A generous man will *p*;

prostitute—a person who lets someone use his or her body for sexual relations in exchange for money.
1Co 6:9 male *p* nor homosexual offenders

prostrate—lying facedown on the ground.

proud—to have pride.
Ro 12:16 Do not be *p*, but be willing
Jas 4:6 "God opposes the *p*

proverbs—1. wise sayings; 2. (cap.) a book of the Bible that contains many wise sayings.

provoke—to make angry; to cause trouble.

prudent—wise.
Pr 19:14 a *p* wife is from the LORD.

psalms—1. poetry written to praise God; 2. (cap.) a book of the Bible that contains many psalms.
Eph 5:19 Speak to one another with *p*,

punish (punishment)—to cause someone to suffer for doing wrong.
Ge 4:13 "My *p* is more than I can bear.
Ex 20:5 jealous God, *p* the children for the sin

pure—perfectly free from fault or blemish.
Ps 51:10 Create in me a *p* heart, O God,

purify—to make pure or clean.
1Jn 1:7 of Jesus, his Son, *p* us from all sin.
1Jn 1:9 and *p* us from all unrighteousness.

Purim—an annual Jewish holiday celebrating Queen Esther's rescue of the Jews when Haman plotted to destroy them.

pursue—1. to follow in order to overtake; to chase; 2. to seek a goal.
Lev 26:7 You will *p* your enemies,
1Ti 6:11 and *p* righteousness,

QR

queen—1. the female ruler of a country; 2. the wife of a king.

Rabbi—a teacher of Jewish law.

Rachel—the daughter of Laban (Ge 29:16); she became Jacob's wife (Ge 29:28) and bore him two sons, Joseph and Benjamin (Ge 30:22-24; 35:16-24).

rage—a fit of anger.
Eph 4:31 Get rid of all bitterness, *r*

ram—a male sheep.

ransom—the price paid to get back a person who is held as a slave. Because people are slaves of sin, a ransom has to be paid, which is the death of the sinless one, Jesus.
Mt 20:28 and to give his life as a *r* for many."
Heb 9:15 as a *r* to set them free

reap—1. to cut down grain at harvest time; to gather a crop together; 2. to get as a result or reward.
Gal 6:7 A man *r* what he sows.

Rebekah—Isaac's wife (Ge 24); the mother of Esau and Jacob (Ge 25:19-26). With her encouragement Jacob tricked his father into giving him the blessing that belonged to Esau (Ge 27:1-17).

rebel—1. (*v.*) to disobey and turn against those in authority; 2. (*n.*) a person who disobeys and flaunts authority.

rebuke—to scold sharply.
2Ti 4:2 correct, *r* and encourage
Rev 3:19 Those whom I love I *r*

reconcile (reconciliation)—to return to friendship after a quarrel; human beings are 'reconciled' to God through Christ.
Mt 5:24 First go and be *r* to your brother;
Ro 5:10 we were *r* to him through the death
2Co 5:18 and gave us the ministry of *r*:

redeem (redemption)—1. to free from evil by paying a price (Gal 3:13); 2. to buy back.
Gal 3:13 Christ *r* us from the curse
Eph 1:7 In him we have *r* through his blood,
Col 1:14 in whom we have *r*, the forgiveness

Red Sea—the body of water the Israelites crossed in a miraculous way when they were running from slavery in Egypt.

refuge—a place of shelter and safety.
Ps 46:1 God is our *r* and strength,

regard—to pay attention to.
Ps 41:1 Blessed is he who has *r* for the weak

regulations—rules dealing with procedure or ceremony.

Rehoboam—the son of Solomon; he became king after his father's death (1Ki 11:43). Because of his harsh treatment of the people, Israel was divided into two kingdoms (1Ki 12:1-24; 14:21-31).

reign—the time during which a king or other official rules.

rejoice—to express joy or gladness.
Ps 118:24 let us *r* and be glad in it.
Lk 1:47 and my spirit *r* in God my Savior,
Php 4:4 *R* in the Lord always.

remnant—a small part remaining; a small surviving group.

repent (repentance)—to turn away from sin; to be sorry for what one has done and to promise not to do it again.
Mt 4:17 "*R*, for the kingdom of heaven is
Lk 3:8 Produce fruit in keeping with *r*.
Ac 2:38 Peter replied, "*R* and be baptized,

reproach—1. (*v.*) to blame or accuse; 2. (*n.*) something for which one can be blamed or criticized.

require (requirement)—to demand as necessary
1Ki 8:31 is *r* to take an oath
Zec 3:7 walk in my ways and keep my *r*,

rescue—to save or deliver.
Ps 140:1 *R* me, O LORD from evil men;

respect—to look up to or hold in high esteem.

restore—to bring back; to return something to its former condition.
Ps 23:3 he *r* my soul.
Ps 51:12 *R* to me the joy of your salvation

resurrection—the act of coming back to life after being dead.
Jn 11:25 Jesus said to her, "I am the *r*
Ro 1:4 Son of God by his *r* from the dead:
1Co 15:12 some of you say that there is no *r*

retribution—punishment for doing wrong.
Jer 51:56 For the LORD is a God of *r*;

Reuben—oldest son of Jacob and founder of the tribe of the same name.

revelation—the act of making known or telling about.
Gal 1:12 I received it by *r* from Jesus Christ.
Rev 1:1 *r* of Jesus Christ, which God gave

revenge—to hurt or punish a person who has wronged you; to get back at someone who has hurt you.
Lev 19:18 " 'Do not seek *r* or bear a grudge
Ro 12:19 Do not take *r*, my friends,

reverence (revere)—a deep respect, honor and awe.
Ps 5:7 in *r* will I bow down
Col 3:22 of heart and *r* for the Lord.

reward—1. (*v.*) to repay with good for something someone has done; 2. (*n.*) the gift one receives for good behavior or character.
Ps 127:3 children a *r* from him.
Jer 17:10 to *r* a man according to his conduct,
Mt 5:12 because great is your *r* in heaven,
Mt 6:5 they have received their *r* in full.

righteous (righteousness)—being "in the right" in relation to God; "not guilty" before God.
Isa 64:6 and all our *r* acts are like filthy rags;
Ro 3:10 "There is no one *r*, not even one;

Rome—1. the empire that controlled much of the known world at the time of Christ; 2. the capital city of the Roman Empire, located in Italy.

royal—of or belonging to the ruler of a country and his family.

Ruth—a Moabite widow who went with her mother-in-law Naomi to Bethlehem (Ru 1). There she gathered the gleanings from the field of Boaz (Ru 2), whom she later married (Ru 3–4:12). She was an ancestor of David (Ru 4:13-22) and of Jesus (Mt 1:5).

ruthless—merciless; cruel.
Hab 1:6 that *r* and impetuous people,
Ro 1:31 they are senseless, faithless,
heartless, *r*

S

Sabbath—the seventh day of the week; the Jewish day of rest and worship. It extended from Friday sunset until Saturday sunset.
Ex 20:8 "Remember the *S* day

sackcloth—a rough cloth, usually woven from goats' hair. Clothing made of sackcloth was worn as a sign of mourning for the dead or as a sign that a person was sorry for his or her sins.

sacred—holy; set apart for God in a special way.

sacrifice—1. (*v.*) to offer something as a gift to God; 2. (*n.*) an offering given to God. In the Old Testament God commanded the people to pay for their sins by sacrificing the blood of cattle, lambs, goats, doves or pigeons. These sacrifices were pictures of Jesus' coming as a once-for-all sacrifice for sinners.

Ex 12:27 'It is the Passover *s* to the LORD,
1Sa 15:22 To obey is better than *s*,
Ro 12:1 to offer your bodies as living *s*,
Heb 9:28 so Christ was *s* once
1Jn 2:2 He is the atoning *s* for our sins,

Sadducees—a group of Jewish leaders, many of them priests. Unlike the Pharisees, the Sadducees did not believe in a resurrection of the dead, but they agreed with the Pharisees in their hatred of Jesus.

Mk 12:18 *S*, who say there is no resurrection,

saints—Christians; people whom God has made holy. A saint can be either a Christian who is alive on earth or one who is already in heaven.

Ro 8:27 intercedes for the *s* in accordance
Eph 1:1 To the *s* in Ephesus,

salvation—deliverance from the guilt and power of sin. By his death and resurrection, Jesus brings salvation to people who believe in him.

Ps 27:1 The LORD is my light and my *s*
Lk 2:30 For my eyes have seen your *s*,
Ac 4:12 *S* is found in no one else,
2Co 7:10 brings repentance that leads to *s*
Php 2:12 to work out your *s* with fear
Heb 2:3 escape if we ignore such a great *s*?

Samaritan—a person who lived in or came from Samaria. Because the Samaritans were only partly Jewish and worshiped God differently from the Jews, Jews from Judea and Galilee hated the Samaritans. They would go out of their way to travel around Samaria (Lk 10:30-37).

Samson—an Israelite judge who was known for his great strength. He was betrayed by Delilah but in the end was used by God to punish the Philistines (Jdg 16).

Samuel—often called the last of Israel's judges and the first of her prophets (see also Heb 11:32). His birth was earnestly prayed for by his mother Hannah (1Sa 1:10-18), and when he was old enough she brought him to the temple and he was dedicated to the Lord (1Sa 1:21-28). There he was raised by Eli (1Sa 2:11; 18–26) and was called to be a prophet (1Sa 3).

sanctify (sanctification)—to make holy; sanctification is the ongoing work of the Holy Spirit in the hearts of believers.

Ro 15:16 to God, *s* by the Holy Spirit.
1Th 5:23 *s* you through and through.
2Th 2:13 through the *s* work of the Spirit

sanctuary—a place where God is worshiped; a holy place.

Sanhedrin—the ruling council of the Jews in Jesus' time. It was made up of seventy men, and the leader was the high priest. The Sanhedrin could decide whether someone was innocent or guilty of breaking a Jewish law, but it could not put anyone to death without the permission of the Roman governor.

Mk 14:55 the whole *S* were looking for evidence

Sarah—the wife of Abraham and mother of Isaac; first called Sarai (Ge 11:29-31). God promised her that, though she had been barren throughout her life, she would give birth to a son in her old age (Ge 17:15-21; 18:10-15).

Satan—the devil; the leader of the fallen spirits; the most powerful enemy of God and humans.

Mk 4:15 *S* comes and takes away the word
2Co 11:14 for *S* himself masquerades
Rev 12:9 serpent called the devil, or *S*,

satisfy—1. to please, to make happy; 2. to fulfill a condition.

Ps 103:5 who *s* your desires with good things

satrap—the governor of a province in ancient Persia.

Saul—1. the first king of Israel (1Sa 9–10). He was anointed by Samuel but was later rejected by God because of disobedience; David was chosen to be his successor; 2. see Paul.

saved—1. (*v.*) rescued from danger; 2. (*n.*) people who acknowledge that by Jesus' death they have been rescued from the punishment of death that their sins deserve.

Ro 10:13 on the name of the Lord will be *s*."
Eph 2:8 For it is by grace you have been *s*,

Savior—a name for Jesus that means he saves his people from sin.

Lk 1:47 and my spirit rejoices in God my *S*,
1Ti 4:10 who is the *S* of all men,
1Jn 4:14 Son to be the *S* of the world.

scarlet—the color bright red.

scepter—a rod or stick held by a king or queen as a sign of royal power and authority.

Ge 49:10 The *s* will not depart from Judah,

scoff—to mock or sneer at.

scorn—to despise, to reject with anger or contempt.

scorpion—a spider-like animal with a poisonous stinger at the end of its tail.

scoundrel—a mean, worthless person; a villain.

scourge—to whip.

2Ch 10:11 My father *s* you with whips;

scribe—a person with the important task of copying letters, books and legal papers.

Scripture—all or part of the Bible. When the Bible uses this word it means the Old Testament, since the New Testament had not yet been written. Today we call the Old and New Testaments the Bible or Scripture.

Jn 10:35 and the *S* cannot be broken
2Ti 3:16 All *S* is God-breathed
2Pe 1:20 that no prophecy of *S* came about

scroll—a book made of a long piece of leather or paper that was rolled around a stick at both ends.
Eze 3:1 eat what is before you, eat this *s;*

seal—1. a tool with a design raised on it or cut into it; 2. the mark made by pressing this tool onto wax, paper or other soft material. A seal was used to close a letter or legal paper or to prove the authority of the paper.
2Co 1:22 set his *s* of ownership on us,
Rev 5:2 "Who is worthy to break the *s*

sect—a group of people who hold one or more beliefs in common; especially, a small religious group that has separated from a larger group.

seer—a prophet; a person who, with God's help, can see what will happen in the future.

self-control—the ability to control one's own actions and feelings.
Gal 5:23 gentleness and *s.*
2Pe 1:6 and to knowledge, *s;* and to *s,*

selfish—centered on oneself; not interested in others.
Php 2:3 Do nothing out of *s* ambition

Sennacherib—an Assyrian king who raided Judah during the time of Hezekiah.

sexual immorality—using sex in ways God says are wrong.
1Co 6:13 body is not meant for *s*
1Th 4:3 that you should avoid *s*

shame—a painful emotion caused by an awareness of guilt or shortcoming.
Pr 19:26 a son who brings *s* and disgrace.
1Co 15:34 I say this to your *s.*

sheep—the animal most often mentioned in Scripture, probably because it was the animal most often raised in Bible times; used for meat, for cloth, and for religious sacrifice.

shekel—a specific weight of silver, used as money.

Shem—one of the three sons of Noah (Ge 5:32). He, along with his brother Japheth, covered his father when he was naked (Ge 9:21-31). Abraham was one of his descendants (Ge 11:10-32).

shepherd—someone who takes care of a flock of sheep. It is often used in the Bible as a figure of speech for anyone who cares for a group of people.
Ps 23:1 LORD is my *s,* I shall not be in want.
Jer 31:10 will watch over his flock like a *s.*'
Jn 10:11 The good *s* lays down his life
Ac 20:28 Be *s* of the church of God,

shield—a defensive weapon, usually carried on the arm; often a figure of speech in the Bible used to describe God's protection of his people.
Ps 7:10 My *s* is God Most High,

shrine—a dwelling for a god.

sickle—a tool with a long, curved blade and a short handle, used for cutting grain.

siege—See besiege.

signet—a ring with a design on it. The design was stamped in wax to seal a letter or legal paper. Signet rings were usually worn by people in authority.

Silas—a member of the church in Jerusalem; he traveled with Paul.

Simon—1. see Peter; 2. one of the twelve apostles; also called the Zealot (Mt 10:4; Ac 1:13); 3. a sorcerer in Samaria who had great influence on the Samaritan people during the early days of the church; he was severely rebuked by Peter (Ac 8:9-24) for attempting to buy the power of the Holy Spirit.

sin—1. (*v.*) to break the law of God; 2. (*n.*) the act of not doing what God wants.
Nu 32:23 be sure that your *s* will find you
Ps 51:2 and cleanse me from my *s.*
Ps 119:11 that I might not *s* against you.
Isa 1:18 "Though your *s* are like scarlet,
Mt 1:21 he will save his people from their *s.*"
Lk 11:4 Forgive us our *s,*
Jn 1:29 who takes away the *s* of the world!
Ro 3:23 for all have *s* and fall short
Ro 6:23 For the wages of *s* is death,
2Co 5:21 God made him who had no *s* to be *s*
1Jn 1:9 If we confess our *s,* he is faithful

Sinai, Mount—the mountain where Moses received the Ten Commandments (Ex 19–20).

sinner—a person who breaks the law of God.
Ps 1:1 or stand in the way of *s*
Mt 9:13 come to call the righteous, but *s.*"
Lk 15:7 in heaven over one *s* who repents
Lk 18:13 'God, have mercy on me, a *s.*'
Ro 5:8 While we were still *s,* Christ died

slander—1. (*v.*) saying untrue things about another person in order to hurt him or her; 2. (*n.*) false charges or misrepresentations about another person.
Lev 19:16 "'Do not go about spreading *s*
Tit 3:2 to *s* no one, to be peaceable

slaughter—1. the butchering of livestock for food; 2. the killing of great numbers of human beings, as in a battle.

slave—1. a person who is owned by another; 2. a person who is dominated or controlled by an outside force.
Ro 7:14 I am unspiritual, sold as a *s* to sin.
Gal 3:28 *s* nor free, male nor female,

slay, slain—to kill violently or in great numbers.

sluggard—a lazy person.

slumber—to sleep.

snare—a trap; something risky that tempts or endangers a person.

snatch—to grab suddenly, often without permission or right.

Sodom and Gomorrah—the two cities destroyed by God because the people were so wicked.
Ge 19:24 rained down burning sulfur on *S*

Solomon—the son of David and Bathsheba (2Sa 12:24). He became king of Israel after David died (1Ki 1). He asked God for wisdom and was given it (1Ki 3), and he built the temple (1Ki 5–7). His many foreign wives turned his heart away from God (1Ki 11:1-13).

son—a male descendant.
Pr 10:1 A wise *s* brings joy to his father,

Joel 2:28 Your *s* and daughters will prophesy,
Jn 12:36 so that you may become *s* of light."
Ro 8:14 by the Spirit of God are *s* of God.
1Jn 4:9 only *S* into the world that we might

Son of Man—a title Jesus used for himself to show his humanity as distinct from his divinity. It was also a reference to the Messiah prophesied about in Daniel 7:13.
Mt 20:18 and the *S* will be betrayed
Mk 14:62 you will see the *S* sitting
Lk 19:10 For the *S* came to seek
Jn 3:14 so the *S* must be lifted up,

sorcery—the use of magic and supernatural powers that are evil; witchcraft.
Lev 19:26 'Do not practice divination or *s*.

soul—the spiritual part of a person; the part of a person that does not die.
Dt 6:5 with all your *s* and with all your
Ps 23:3 he restores my *s*.
Mt 10:28 kill the body but cannot kill the *s*.
Mt 11:29 and you will find rest for your *s*.
Mt 16:26 yet forfeits his *s*? Or what can
Mt 22:37 with all your *s* and with all your

sovereign—having authority over everything; often used in Scripture as a descriptive title for God, "Sovereign LORD."

sow—to plant seeds. In Jesus' time seeds were sown by scattering them by hand over the ground.
Job 4:8 and those who *s* trouble reap it.
Mk 4:3 A farmer went out to *s* his seed.
Gal 6:7 A man reaps what he *s*.

spear—a weapon with a long handle and a sharp head, usually thrown.

spirit—1. the part of a person that is not the body; the soul; 2. a being who does not have a body; 3. (cap.) see Holy Spirit.
Ps 31:5 Into your hands I commit my *s*;
Eze 36:26 you a new heart and put a new *s*
Mt 5:3 "Blessed are the poor in *s*,
Mt 26:41 *s* is willing, but the body is weak."
1Jn 4:1 Dear friends, do not believe every *s*,

splendor—something magnificent or splendid.

spoils—booty or plunder taken from an enemy in war.

springs—a source of water coming up from the ground.
Dt 8:7 with *s* flowing in the valleys
Rev 7:17 lead them to *s* of living water.

staff—a stick used to lean on; a rod used by a shepherd.
Ps 23:4 your rod and your *s*,

statutes—established rules or laws.
Ps 19:7 *s* of the LORD are trustworthy,

steadfast—settled; not changing or wavering.
Ps 51:10 and renew a *s* spirit within me.

steal—to rob; to take what belongs to someone else.
Ex 20:15 "You shall not *s*.
Mk 10:19 do not *s*, do not give false

stench—a terrible smell.

Stephen—one of the first seven men to serve the Jerusalem church (Ac 6:5); he became the first Christian martyr (Ac 7:60).

stiff-necked—stubborn.

stone—to kill or to try to kill someone by throwing rocks or stones.

strength—power; forcefulness.
Ex 15:2 The LORD is my *s* and my song;
Dt 6:5 all your soul and with all your *s*.
Ps 46:1 God is our refuge and *s*,
Isa 40:31 will renew their *s*.
Php 4:13 through him who gives me *s*.

strife—bitter and sometimes violent conflict.
Pr 30:33 stirring up anger produces *s*."

stronghold—a fortified place; a place of security.
1Sa 24:22 David and his men went up to the *s*.
Ps 27:1 The LORD is the *s* of my life—

subdue—to bring under control; to conquer.

submission—humbleness; obedience.
1Co 14:34 but must be in *s*, as the Law says.
1Ti 2:11 learn in quietness and full *s*.

submit—to willingly yield to another.
Ro 13:1 Everyone must *s* himself
Eph 5:21 *S* to one another out of reverence
Col 3:18 Wives, *s* to your husbands,
Jas 4:7 *S* yourselves, then, to God.

succeed—1. to turn out well; 2. to follow another as heir or successor of a title or rank.

suffer—to bear or endure something painful.
Mk 8:31 the Son of Man must *s* many things
Lk 24:26 the Christ have to *s* these things
1Co 12:26 If one part *s*, every part *s* with it;

suffering—the experience of enduring pain.
Isa 53:3 of sorrows, and familiar with *s*.
Ac 5:41 worthy of *s* disgrace for the Name.
Ro 8:17 share in his *s* in order that we may
2Ti 1:8 But join with me in *s* for the gospel,

summon—to issue a call to come together; to send for.
Isa 43:1 I have *s* you by name; you are mine.

sustain—to give support; to help; to comfort.
Ps 18:35 and your right hand *s* me;
Ps 146:9 and *s* the fatherless and the widow,

swear—to promise forcefully or earnestly.
1Sa 30:15 "*S* to me before God that you will

sword—a weapon with a long blade for cutting or thrusting.

symbol—an object or action that stands for or suggests something else. The cross is a symbol of Jesus' death.

synagogue—the Jewish place of worship and religious teaching.
Lk 4:16 the Sabbath day he went into the *s*,
Ac 17:2 custom was, Paul went into the *s*,

T

tabernacle—the tent used by the Israelites for meeting with God; the place where God chose to show his presence. The tabernacle was made by God's command and according to his plans. It is

described in detail in Exodus 26. Also called the Tent of Meeting.
Ex 40:34 the glory of the LORD filled the *t.*

talent—a large amount of silver or gold, worth very much money.
Mt 25:15 to another one *t,* each according

tax—money a government requires its citizens to pay.

teach—to instruct; to help someone learn.
Ex 33:13 *t* me your ways so I may know you
Ps 90:12 *T* us to number our days aright,
Lk 11:1 said to him, "Lord, *t* us to pray,
Jn 14:26 will *t* you all things and will remind

tempest—a violent storm.

temple—1. the place where the Jewish people worshiped and sacrificed in Jerusalem; the first temple was built by King Solomon as a house for God; 2. any place of worship. In this sense, the human body is referred to as a temple (1Co 6:19).
1Ki 8:27 How much less this *t* I have built!
Ac 17:24 does not live in *t* built by hands.
2Co 6:16 For we are the *t* of the living God.

temptation—trying to get someone to do wrong.
Mt 4:1 into the desert to be *t* by the devil.
1Co 10:13 No *t* has seized you except what

tenant—one who rents land or a house from a landlord.

Tent of Meeting—See tabernacle.

testimony—a statement made by a witness to prove that something is true.
Lk 18:20 not give false *t,* honor your father

tetrarch—a ruler over one-fourth of a kingdom.

Thaddaeus—one of the twelve apostles (Mk 3:18); son of James and probably also known as Judas (Lk 6:16; Ac 1:13).

thanks—the expression of gratitude.
1Ch 16:8 Give *t* to the LORD, call
Ps 100:4 give *t* to him and praise his name.
1Co 15:57 *t* be to God! He gives us the victory
2Co 9:15 *T* be to God for his indescribable
1Th 5:18 give *t* in all circumstances,

thanksgiving—recognizing and thanking the one who has provided a gift.
Ps 100:4 Enter his gates with *t*
Php 4:6 by prayer and petition, with *t,*

Thomas—one of the twelve apostles (Lk 6:15; Ac 1:13); he doubted Jesus' resurrection but, upon seeing Jesus, he believed (Jn 20:24-28).

thrive—to grow vigorously.

Thummim—See Urim.

threshing floor—the place where grain was trampled by oxen or beaten with a stick to separate it from the stalk.

Timothy—fellow-traveler and official representative of the apostle Paul. He joined Paul on his second missionary journey (Ac 16–20), and at one point in this journey Paul sent him to minister to the church at Corinth (1Co 4:17; 16:10). He was the leader of the church at Ephesus (1Ti 1:3) and a co-writer with Paul (1Th 1:1; 2Th 1:1; Phm 1).

tithe—the giving to God of one-tenth of what one earns.
Lev 27:30 " 'A *t* of everything from the land,
Mal 3:10 the whole *t* into the storehouse,

Titus—a Gentile co-worker with Paul (Gal 2:1-3; 2Ti 4:10). Paul sent him to Corinth to aid in solving some of the problems there (2Co 2:13; 7–8; 12:18).

toil—1. (*n.*) strenuous and tiring work; 2. (*v.*) to work long and hard.

tomb—a burial place. In Bible times, a tomb was often either a cave or a cavity dug into a stone cliff, with a large stone rolled in front to close it.
Mt 27:65 make the *t* as secure as you know
Lk 24:2 the stone rolled away from the *t,*

tongue—1. the organ of speech in the mouth; 2. a language.
Ps 39:1 and keep my *t* from sin;
Ac 2:4 and began to speak in other *t*
Php 2:11 every *t* confess that Jesus Christ
Jas 1:26 does not keep a tight rein on his *t,*

torment—extreme pain or anguish; agony.
2Co 12:7 a messenger of Satan, to *t* me.

tradition—the handing down of information and beliefs from one generation to another.
Mt 15:2 break the *t* of the elders?

trample—to walk heavily causing injury or damage.
Ps 60:12 he will *t* down our enemies.

transfigure—to change the appearance of; to make bright and glorious.
Mt 17:2 There he was *t* before them.

transgression—sin; disobeying the law of God.
Ps 32:1 whose *t* are forgiven,
Isa 53:5 But he was pierced for our *t,*
Eph 2:1 you were dead in your *t* and sins,

treacherous—untrustworthy, unreliable, faithless.

tread—to step or walk on or over.
Job 24:11 they *t* the winepresses,

treasure—1. (*n.*) wealth that is stored up or hidden away; 2. (*v.*) to hold or keep something precious, something of value; to cherish.
Mt 6:21 your *t* is, there your heart will be also.

treaty—an agreement between two people or groups or nations.

trespass—sin; wrongdoing.
Ro 5:17 For if, by the *t* of the one man,

tribe—a social group made up of a particular branch of a family.

tribute—payment by one ruler or nation to another as an act of submission or in order to guarantee protection.

triumph—a victory; a notable success.
Pr 28:12 the righteous *t,* there is great elation;

true—certain; exactly right.
Ps 119:160 All your words are *t;*
Jn 17:3 the only *t* God, and Jesus Christ,
Ro 3:4 Let God be *t,* and every man a liar.
Php 4:8 whatever is *t,* whatever is noble,

trust—firm belief or faith in another.
Ps 37:3 *T* in the LORD and do good;

Pr 3:5 *T* in the LORD with all your heart
Isa 30:15 in quietness and *t* is your strength,
Jn 14:1 *T* in God; *t* also in me.
1Co 4:2 been given a *t* must prove faithful.

trustworthy—deserving of trust; reliable.
Ps 19:7 The statutes of the LORD are *t*,
1Ti 1:15 Here is a *t* saying that deserves full

truth—that which conforms to the facts.
Ps 51:6 Surely you desire *t*
Zec 8:16 are to do: Speak the *t* to each other,
Jn 8:32 know the *t* and the *t*
Jn 14:6 I am the way and the *t* and the life.
Ro 1:25 They exchanged the *t* of God
1Co 13:6 in evil but rejoices with the *t*.
Eph 4:15 Instead, speaking the *t* in love,
Heb 10:26 received the knowledge of the *t*,
1Jn 1:6 we lie and do not live by the *t*.
1Jn 1:8 deceive ourselves and the *t* is not

tunic—a long shirt worn by men in Bible times.
Lk 6:29 do not stop him from taking your *t*.

turban—a head-covering made by winding a cloth around the head.

UV

unbelief—doubt.
Mk 9:24 help me overcome my *u*!"

unbeliever—one who does not believe in Jesus.
2Co 6:14 Do not be yoked together with *u*.

unclean—morally or spiritually impure; unclean animals were those which the Israelites were not allowed to sacrifice or to eat.

unity—being one.
Ps 133:1 when brothers live together in *u*!
Col 3:14 them all together in perfect *u*.

unleavened bread—bread made without yeast. It is usually flat, like a pancake or cracker.
Ex 12:17 "Celebrate the Feast of *U*

uphold—to give support to.
Ps 37:17 the LORD *u* the righteous.

upright—honest; doing what is right and good.

Urim and Thummim—objects that were placed on the vest of the high priest; used to determine God's will for the nation of Israel.

usury—very high and unfair interest charged on a loan.
Ne 5:10 But let the exacting of *u* stop!

utter—to pronounce, to speak.
Ps 78:2 I will *u* hidden things,
Jer 15:19 if you *u* worthy, not worthless, words,

utterly—completely, totally.

vain—worthless; unsuccessful; foolish. "In vain" means without success or result.

valiant—courageous.

vast—very great in size or amount; huge.

vengeance—hurt or punishment done to another person who has done something wrong against another.
Isa 34:8 For the LORD has a day of *v*,

vigor—strength and health in the body and its growth.
Job 20:11 The youthful *v* that fills his bones

vile—disgusting, evil.

vindicate—to defend; to provide justice for; to set free.

violate—1. to rape; 2. to make something unholy; 3. to fail to obey.

viper—1. a venomous snake; 2. a treacherous or vicious person.

virgin—a woman or girl who has never had sexual intercourse.
Isa 7:14 The *v* will be with child
Mt 1:23 "The *v* will be with child

vision—a dream from God.
Nu 12:6 I reveal myself to him in *v*,
Joel 2:28 your young men will see *v*.
Ac 26:19 disobedient to the *v* from heaven.

vow—a solemn promise made before God or to God.
Jdg 11:30 Jephthah made a *v* to the LORD:
Ps 116:14 I will fulfill my *v* to the LORD

W

wages—payment received for work completed.

wail—to cry loudly.

walk—to follow a certain course.
Ps 1:1 who does not *w* in the counsel
Isa 2:5 let us *w* in the light of the LORD.
Mic 6:8 and to *w* humbly with your God.
2Jn 6 his command is that you *w* in love.

wander—to move about without a fixed course.
Nu 32:13 he made them *w* in the desert forty years,
Jas 5:19 if one of you should *w* from the truth

warn—to give notice beforehand of danger or evil.

warrior—a soldier.

wash—to clean.
Ps 51:7 *w* me, and I will be whiter
Ac 22:16 be baptized and *w* your sins away,

watch—to be on the lookout for someone or something.
Jer 31:10 will *w* over his flock like a shepherd.'
Mt 26:41 "*W* and pray so that you will not fall

way—the means of getting somewhere; the path.
2Sa 22:31 "As for God, his *w* is perfect;
Ps 1:1 or stand in the *w* of sinners
Ps 37:5 Commit your *w* to the LORD;
Isa 53:6 each of us has turned to his own *w*;
Jn 14:6 "I am the *w* and the truth
1Co 12:31 will show you the most excellent *w*.

wean—to help a child or animal begin to eat solid food rather than his or her mother's milk.

weapon—an object used for fighting.

weary—1. tired; 2. having one's patience or tolerance exhausted.
Dt 25:18 When you were *w* and worn out,
Zec 11:8 and I grew *w* of them

weep, wept—to cry.

welcome—1. to greet a person pleasantly; 2. to make a person feel at home.
Jdg 19:20 "You are *w* at my house,"

wholehearted—sincere; devoted without holding anything back.

wicked—sinful.
Ps 1:1 walk in the counsel of the *w*
Isa 55:7 Let the *w* forsake his way

widow—a woman whose husband has died.

will—desire; seeking God's will means looking for what God wants to be done.
Ps 143:10 Teach me to do your *w*,
Isa 53:10 Yet it was the LORD's *w*
Mt 6:10 your *w* be done
Mt 26:39 Yet not as I *w*, but as you *w*."
Ro 12:2 and approve what God's *w* is
Eph 5:17 understand what the Lord's *w* is.
1Jn 5:14 we ask anything according to his *w*,
Rev 4:11 and by your *w* they were created

winepress—a vat or tub in which the juice of grapes is pressed out. Used in the Bible as a symbol for the anger of God against wickedness.
Rev 14:19 into the great *w* of God's wrath.

wisdom—the understanding that comes from God.
Lk 2:52 And Jesus grew in *w* and stature,
Jas 1:5 of you lacks *w*, he should ask God,

wither—to dry or shrivel up, usually from a lack of moisture.

witness—one who personally sees an event take place.
Ac 22:15 You will be his *w* to all men

woe—great misery; distress.
Isa 6:5 "*W* to me!" I cried.
Lk 11:42 "*W* to you Pharisees, because you

womb—the organ within a woman's body where a child grows before birth.

word—1. the means of expressing oneself through language; 2. the Bible, as God's written message to people; 3. (cap.) Jesus is the Word sent from God because his life on earth told the message of God.
Jn 1:14 The *W* became flesh and made his
Heb 4:12 For the *w* of God is living

work—1. (*n.*) employment; duty; 2. (*v.*) to bring about; to try to achieve a goal.
Ex 23:12 "Six days do your *w*,
Jn 9:4 we must do the *w* of him who sent
Php 2:12 continue to *w* out your salvation
2Ti 3:17 equipped for every good *w*.

world—1. the earth and those who live in it; 2. the secular, as opposed to the spiritual or religious.
Mt 5:14 "You are the light of the *w*.
Mk 16:15 into all the *w* and preach the good
Jn 1:29 who takes away the sin of the *w*!
Jn 3:16 so loved the *w* that he gave his one
Jn 8:12 he said, "I am the light of the *w*.
1Jn 2:15 not love the *w* or anything in the *w*.

worldly—loving the things of the world more than the things of God.
Tit 2:12 to ungodliness and *w* passions,

worry—to feel anxious and uneasy.
Mt 6:25 I tell you, do not *w* about your life,

worship—1. (*v.*) to give praise, honor and respect to God; 2. (*n.*) reverence given to God.
Ps 95:6 Come, let us bow down in *w*,
Jn 4:24 and his worshipers must *w* in spirit

worthy—having value; honorable; deserving.
1Ch 16:25 For great is the LORD and most *w*
Eph 4:1 to live a life *w* of the calling you
Rev 5:2 "Who is *w* to break the seals

wrath—great anger; the strong anger of God.
Pr 15:1 A gentle answer turns away *w*,
Ro 5:9 saved from God's *w* through him!

XYZ

Xerxes—king of Persia; he made Esther, a young Jewess, his queen (Est 2:15-18).

yearn—to long for; to want very much.

yeast—the ingredient that makes dough rise; sometimes a figure of speech for the influence someone has over others.
Mt 16:6 guard against the *y* of the Pharisees
Gal 5:9 little *y* works through the whole

yield—1. to submit; 2. to grow or produce fruit.
Ps 67:6 Then the land will *y* its harvest,
Isa 48:11 I will not *y* my glory to another.

yoke—1. (*v.*) to join together; 2. (*n.*) a wooden bar that goes over the necks of two animals, usually oxen. The yoke holds the animals together as they pull an object, such as a plow or a cart.
Mt 11:29 Take my *y* upon you and learn
2Co 6:14 Do not be *y* together

youth—the time when a person is young.
Ecc 12:1 Creator in the days of your *y*,

Zacchaeus—a tax collector who climbed a tree in order to see Jesus.

zeal—eagerness; strong desire.
Ro 12:11 Never be lacking in *z*,

Zealot—a member of the Jewish group that wanted to fight against and overthrow the Roman government.

Zechariah—a prophet and priest who returned to Jerusalem from the Babylonian captivity; he encouraged the Jews to rebuild the temple (Ezr 5:1; 6:14; Zec 1:1).

Zerubbabel—a descendant of David (1Ch 3:19); he led the return of the Jews from the Babylonian captivity (Ezr 1–3; Ne 7:7; Hag 1–2; Zec 4).

Zion—1. the hill on which the city of Jerusalem first stood; David's royal palace and the temple were both built on Mount Zion; 2. the entire city of Jerusalem.
Jer 50:5 They will ask the way to *Z*
Ro 11:26 "The deliverer will come
from *Z*;